Who Was Who in America®

Who Was Who in America®
with world notables

2008-2009
Volume XX

MARQUIS
Who's Who®

890 Mountain Avenue, Suite 300
New Providence, NJ 07974 U.S.A.
www.marquiswhoswho.com

Who Was Who in America®
Marquis Who's Who

Chairman	James A. Finkelstein
Chief Executive Officer	Jeanne Goffred
Chief Financial Officer	Vincent Papa
Chief Technology Officer	Ariel Spivakovsky
Chief Operating Officer	Fred Marks
Senior Director, Marketing & Business Development	Michael Noerr

EDITORIAL

Managing Editors	Patricia Delli Santi
	Alison Perruso
Content Manager	Todd Kineavy
Content Editors	Shawn Erickson
	Laura Franklin
	Sara J. Gamble
	Ian O'Blenis
	Bill Schoener
	Kate Spirito
	Jessica Wisniewski
Customer Service Content Editor	Christine Fisher

International Standard Book Number	978-0-8379-0278-4	(22-Volume Set)
	978-0-8379-0275-3	(Volume XX)
	978-0-8379-0276-0	(Index Volume)
	978-0-8379-0277-7	(Volume XX & Index Volume)
International Standard Serial Number	0146-8081	

Manufactured in the United States of America.

Table of Contents

Preface

Marquis Who's Who is proud to present the 2008-2009 Edition of *Who Was Who in America*. This 20th edition features over 3,800 profiles of individuals who had previously been profiled in *Who's Who in America* and other Marquis Who's Who publications, whose deaths have been brought to our attention since the publication of the last edition of *Who Was Who in America*.

Among the notable Americans profiled in this volume are individuals as influential and diverse as Michael Jackson, Patrick Swayze, Farrah Fawcett, Walter Cronkite, Robert McNamara, Ted Kennedy, John Updike, Steve LaTreal McNair, and Robert H. Rines. The impact of these individuals during their lifetimes was enormous and their influence is certain to live on.

Of course, not every person profiled in this volume is a household name. These pages include the profiles of doctors, lawyers, entrepreneurs, researchers, inventors, and other prominent achievers.

The biographical information included in the profiles that follow was gathered in a variety of manners. In most cases, those listed had submitted their personal biographical details during their lifetime.

In many cases, though, the information was collected independently by our research and editorial staffs, which use a wide assortment of tools to gather complete, accurate, and up-to-date information.

Who Was Who in America is an important component of the Marquis Who's Who family of publications. Along with *Who's Who in America* and *Who's Who in the World*, Marquis Who's Who also publishes a number of specialized and regionalized volumes. These include *Who's Who of American Women*, *Who's Who in American Law*, *Who's Who in Medicine and Healthcare*, and *Who's Who in the East*, to name a few.

It has been an honor to compile this edition of *Who Was Who in America*. It is our hope that the biographical profiles will do justice to the individuals memorialized on the pages that follow.

Key to Information

[1] **LINDELL, JAMES ELLIOT,** [2] literature educator; [3] b. Jacksonville, Fla., Sept. 27, 1947; [4] s. Elliot Walter and Tamara Lindell; [5] m. Colleen Marie, Apr. 28, 1969; [6] children: Richard, Matthew, Lucas, Samantha. [7] BA in English, Temple Univ., 1970, MA in English, 1972; PhD in English Lit., Univ. Chgo., 1976. [8] Cert. ESL 1972. [9] Assoc. prof. English Univ. Chgo., 197580, prof. 1980-1988, English dept. head 1989-2007; [10] mem. ESL Coalition, Teach for Tomorrow; bd. dir, Chgo. HS Scholarship Assn. [11] Contbr. articles to profl. jours. [12] vol. Red Cross, 1980-90. [13] Served to USMC, 1972-74. [14] Recipient Outstanding Tchr. award Univ. Chgo., 1990; grantee Teach for Tomorrow, 2000. [15] Fellow Assn. Tchrs. for ESL; mem. MADD, Am. Soc. ESL Tchrs. [16] Democrat. [17] Roman Catholic. [18] Achievements include the expansion of teaching English as a second language to European countries. [19] Avocations: swimming, reading, traveling. [20] Home: 1919 Greenridge Ln Chicago, IL 90921 [21] Office: Univ Chicago English Dept 707 Batsman Hall Chicago IL 90735 [22] Died Sept. 19, 2007.

KEY

[1]	Name
[2]	Occupation
[3]	Vital statistics
[4]	Parents
[5]	Marriage
[6]	Children
[7]	Education
[8]	Professional certifications
[9]	Career
[10]	Career-related
[11]	Writings and creative works
[12]	Civic and political activities
[13]	Military
[14]	Awards and fellowships
[15]	Professional and association memberships, clubs and lodges
[16]	Political affiliation
[17]	Religion
[18]	Achievements
[19]	Avocations
[20]	Home address
[21]	Office address
[22]	Death

Table of Abbreviations

The following is a list of some of the most frequently used Marquis abbreviations:

A

A Associate (used with academic degrees)
AA Associate in Arts
AAAL American Academy of Arts and Letters
AAAS American Association for the Advancement of Science
AACD American Association for Counseling and Development
AACN American Association of Critical Care Nurses
AAHA American Academy of Health Administrators
AAHP American Association of Hospital Planners
AAHPERD American Alliance for Health, Physical Education, Recreation, and Dance
AAS Associate of Applied Science
AASL American Association of School Librarians
AASPA American Association of School Personnel Administrators
AAU Amateur Athletic Union
AAUP American Association of University Professors
AAUW American Association of University Women
AB Arts, Bachelor of
AB Alberta
ABA American Bar Association
AC Air Corps
acad. academy
acct. accountant
acctg. accounting
ACDA Arms Control and Disarmament Agency
ACHA American College of Hospital Administrators
ACLS Advanced Cardiac Life Support
ACLU American Civil Liberties Union
ACOG American College of Ob-Gyn
ACP American College of Physicians
ACS American College of Surgeons
ADA American Dental Association
adj. adjunct, adjutant
adm. admiral
adminstr. administrator
adminstrn. administration
adminstrv. administrative

ADN Associate's Degree in Nursing
ADP Automatic Data Processing
adv. advocate, advisory
advt. advertising
AE Agricultural Engineer
AEC Atomic Energy Commission
aero. aeronautical, aeronautic
aerodyn. aerodynamic
AFB Air Force Base
AFTRA American Federation of Television and Radio Artists
agr. agriculture
agrl. agricultural
agt. agent
AGVA American Guild of Variety Artists
agy. agency
A&I Agricultural and Industrial
AIA American Institute of Architects
AIAA American Institute of Aeronautics and Astronautics
AIChE American Institute of Chemical Engineers
AICPA American Institute of Certified Public Accountants
AID Agency for International Development
AIDS Acquired Immune Deficiency Syndrome
AIEE American Institute of Electrical Engineers
AIME American Institute of Mining, Metallurgy, and Petroleum Engineers
AK Alaska
AL Alabama
ALA American Library Association
Ala. Alabama
alt. alternate
Alta. Alberta
A&M Agricultural and Mechanical
AM Arts, Master of
Am. American, America
AMA American Medical Association
amb. ambassador
AME African Methodist Episcopal
Amtrak National Railroad Passenger Corporation
AMVETS American Veterans
ANA American Nurses Association
anat. anatomical
ANCC American Nurses Credentialing Center

ann. annual
anthrop. anthropological
AP Associated Press
APA American Psychological Association
APHA American Public Health Association
APO Army Post Office
apptd. appointed
Apr. April
apt. apartment
AR Arkansas
ARC American Red Cross
arch. architect
archeol. archeological
archtl. architectural
Ariz. Arizona
Ark. Arkansas
ArtsD Arts, Doctor of
arty. artillery
AS Associate in Science, American Samoa
ASCAP American Society of Composers, Authors and Publishers
ASCD Association for Supervision and Curriculum Development
ASCE American Society of Civil Engineers
ASME American Society of Mechanical Engineers
ASPA American Society for Public Administration
ASPCA American Society for the Prevention of Cruelty to Animals
assn. association
assoc. associate
asst. assistant
ASTD American Society for Training and Development
ASTM American Society for Testing and Materials
astron. astronomical
astrophys. astrophysical
ATLA Association of Trial Lawyers of America
ATSC Air Technical Service Command
atty. attorney
Aug. August
aux. auxiliary
Ave. Avenue
AVMA American Veterinary Medical Association
AZ Arizona

B

B Bachelor
b. born
BA Bachelor of Arts
BAgr Bachelor of Agriculture
Balt. Baltimore
Bapt. Baptist
BArch Bachelor of Architecture
BAS Bachelor of Agricultural Science
BBA Bachelor of Business Administration
BBB Better Business Bureau
BC British Columbia
BCE Bachelor of Civil Engineering
BChir Bachelor of Surgery
BCL Bachelor of Civil Law
BCS Bachelor of Commercial Science
BD Bachelor of Divinity
bd. board
BE Bachelor of Education
BEE Bachelor of Electrical Engineering
BFA Bachelor of Fine Arts
bibl. biblical
bibliog. bibliographical
biog. biographical
biol. biological
BJ Bachelor of Journalism
Bklyn. Brooklyn
BL Bachelor of Letters
bldg. building
BLS Bachelor of Library Science
Blvd. Boulevard
BMI Broadcast Music, Inc.
bn. battalion
bot. botanical
BPE Bachelor of Physical Education
BPhil Bachelor of Philosophy
br. branch
BRE Bachelor of Religious Education
brig. gen. brigadier general
Brit. British
Bros. Brothers
BS Bachelor of Science
BSA Bachelor of Agricultural Science
BSBA Bachelor of Science in Business Administration
BSChemE Bachelor of Science in Chemical Engineering
BSD Bachelor of Didactic Science
BSEE Bachelor of Science in Electrical Engineering
BSN Bachelor of Science in Nursing
BST Bachelor of Sacred Theology
BTh Bachelor of Theology
bull. bulletin

bur. bureau
bus. business
BWI British West Indies

C

CA California
CAD-CAM Computer Aided Design–Computer Aided Model
Calif. California
Can. Canada, Canadian
CAP Civil Air Patrol
capt. captain
cardiol. cardiological
cardiovasc. cardiovascular
Cath. Catholic
cav. cavalry
CBI China, Burma, India Theatre of Operations
CC Community College
CCC Commodity Credit Corporation
CCNY City College of New York
CCRN Critical Care Registered Nurse
CCU Cardiac Care Unit
CD Civil Defense
CE Corps of Engineers, Civil Engineer
CEN Certified Emergency Nurse
CENTO Central Treaty Organization
CEO Chief Executive Officer
CERN European Organization of Nuclear Research
cert. certificate, certification, certified
CETA Comprehensive Employment Training Act
CFA Chartered Financial Analyst
CFL Canadian Football League
CFO Chief Financial Officer
CFP Certified Financial Planner
ch. church
ChD Doctor of Chemistry
chem. chemical
ChemE Chemical Engineer
ChFC Chartered Financial Consultant
Chgo. Chicago
chirurg., der surgeon
chmn. chairman
chpt. chapter
CIA Central Intelligence Agency
Cin. Cincinnati
cir. circle, circuit
CLE Continuing Legal Education
Cleve. Cleveland
climatol. climatological
clin. clinical
clk. clerk
CLU Chartered Life Underwriter
CM Master in Surgery
cmty. community

CO Colorado
Co. Company
COF Catholic Order of Foresters
C. of C. Chamber of Commerce
col. colonel
coll. college
Colo. Colorado
com. committee
comd. commanded
comdg. commanding
comdr. commander
comdt. commandant
comm. communications
commd. commissioned
comml. commercial
commn. commission
commr. commissioner
compt. comptroller
condr. conductor
conf. Conference
Congl. Congregational, Congressional
Conglist. Congregationalist
Conn. Connecticut
cons. consultant, consulting
consol. consolidated
constl. constitutional
constn. constitution
constrn. construction
contbd. contributed
contbg. contributing
contbn. contribution
contbr. contributor
contr. controller
Conv. Convention
COO Chief Operating Officer
coop. cooperative
coord. coordinator
corp. corporation, corporate
corr. correspondent, corresponding, correspondence
coun. council
CPA Certified Public Accountant
CPCU Chartered Property and Casualty Underwriter
CPH Certificate of Public Health
cpl. corporal
CPR Cardio-Pulmonary Resuscitation
CS Christian Science
CSB Bachelor of Christian Science
CT Connecticut
ct. court
ctr. center
ctrl. central

D

D Doctor
d. daughter of
DAgr Doctor of Agriculture
DAR Daughters of the American Revolution
dau. daughter

DAV   Disabled American Veterans
DC   District of Columbia
DCL   Doctor of Civil Law
DCS   Doctor of Commercial
   Science
DD   Doctor of Divinity
DDS   Doctor of Dental Surgery
DE   Delaware
Dec.   December
dec.   deceased
def.   defense
Del.   Delaware
del.   delegate, delegation
Dem.   Democrat, Democratic
DEng   Doctor of Engineering
denom.   denomination,
   denominational
dep.   deputy
dept.   department
dermatol.   dermatological
desc.   descendant
devel.   development, developmental
DFA   Doctor of Fine Arts
DHL   Doctor of Hebrew
   Literature
dir.   director
dist.   district
distbg.   distributing
distbn.   distribution
distbr.   distributor
disting.   distinguished
div.   division, divinity, divorce
divsn.   division
DLitt   Doctor of Literature
DMD   Doctor of Dental Medicine
DMS   Doctor of Medical Science
DO   Doctor of Osteopathy
docs.   documents
DON   Director of Nursing
DPH   Diploma in Public Health
DPhil   Doctor of Philosophy
DR   Daughters of the Revolution
Dr.   Drive, Doctor
DRE   Doctor of Religious
   Education
DrPH   Doctor of Public Health
DSc   Doctor of Science
DSChemE   Doctor of Science in
   Chemical Engineering
DSM   Distinguished Service
   Medal
DST   Doctor of Sacred Theology
DTM   Doctor of Tropical
   Medicine
DVM   Doctor of Veterinary
   Medicine
DVS   Doctor of Veterinary
   Surgery

E

E   East
ea.   eastern
Eccles.   Ecclesiastical

ecol.   ecological
econ.   economic
ECOSOC   United Nations
   Economic and Social Council
ED   Doctor of Engineering
ed.   educated
EdB   Bachelor of Education
EdD   Doctor of Education
edit.   edition
editl.   editorial
EdM   Master of Education
edn.   education
ednl.   educational
EDP   Electronic Data Processing
EdS   Specialist in Education
EE   Electrical Engineer
EEC   European Economic
   Community
EEG   Electroencephalogram
EEO   Equal Employment
   Opportunity
EEOC   Equal Employment
   Opportunity Commission
EKG   electrocardiogram
elec.   electrical
electrochem.   electrochemical
electrophys.   electrophysical
elem.   elementary
EM   Engineer of Mines
EMT   Emergency Medical
   Technician
ency.   encyclopedia
Eng.   England
engr.   engineer
engring.   engineering
entomol.   entomological
environ.   environmental
EPA   Environmental Protection
   Agency
epidemiol.   epidemiological
Episc.   Episcopalian
ERA   Equal Rights Amendment
ERDA   Energy Research and
   Development Administration
ESEA   Elementary and Secondary
   Education Act
ESL   English as Second
   Language
ESSA   Environmental Science
   Services Administration
ethnol.   ethnological
ETO   European Theatre of
   Operations
EU   European Union
Evang.   Evangelical
exam.   examination, examining
Exch.   Exchange
exec.   executive
exhbn.   exhibition
expdn.   expedition
expn.   exposition
expt.   experiment
exptl.   experimental

Expy.   Expressway
Ext.   Extension

F

FAA   Federal Aviation
   Administration
FAO   UN Food and Agriculture
   Organization
FBA   Federal Bar Association
FBI   Federal Bureau of
   Investigation
FCA   Farm Credit Administration
FCC   Federal Communications
   Commission
FCDA   Federal Civil Defense
   Administration
FDA   Food and Drug
   Administration
FDIA   Federal Deposit Insurance
   Administration
FDIC   Federal Deposit Insurance
   Corporation
FEA   Federal Energy
   Administration
Feb.   February
fed.   federal
fedn.   federation
FERC   Federal Energy Regulatory
   Commission
fgn.   foreign
FHA   Federal Housing
   Administration
fin.   financial, finance
FL   Florida
Fl.   Floor
Fla.   Florida
FMC   Federal Maritime
   Commission
FNP   Family Nurse Practitioner
FOA   Foreign Operations
   Administration
found.   foundation
FPC   Federal Power Commission
FPO   Fleet Post Office
frat.   fraternity
FRS   Federal Reserve System
FSA   Federal Security Agency
Ft.   Fort
FTC   Federal Trade Commission
Fwy.   Freeway

G

GA, Ga.   Georgia
GAO   General Accounting Office
gastroent.   gastroenterological
GATT   General Agreement on
   Tariffs and Trade
GE   General Electric Company
gen.   general
geneal.   genealogical
geog.   geographic, geographical
geol.   geological
geophys.   geophysical

geriat. geriatrics
gerontol. gerontological
GHQ General Headquarters
gov. governor
govt. government
govtl. governmental
GPO Government Printing Office
grad. graduate, graduated
GSA General Services
Administration
Gt. Great
GU Guam
gynecol. gynecological

H

hdqs. headquarters
HEW Department of Health,
Education and Welfare
HHD Doctor of Humanities
HHFA Housing and Home Finance
Agency
HHS Department of Health and
Human Services
HI Hawaii
hist. historical, historic
HM Master of Humanities
homeo. homeopathic
hon. honorary, honorable
House of Dels. House of
Delegates
House of Reps. House of
Representatives
hort. horticultural
hosp. hospital
HS High School
HUD Department of Housing and
Urban Development
Hwy. Highway
hydrog. hydrographic

I

IA Iowa
IAEA International Atomic Energy
Agency
IBRD International Bank for
Reconstruction and
Development
ICA International Cooperation
Administration
ICC Interstate Commerce
Commission
ICCE International Council for
Computers in Education
ICU Intensive Care Unit
ID Idaho
IEEE Institute of Electrical and
Electronics Engineers
IFC International Finance
Corporation
IL, Ill. Illinois
illus. illustrated
ILO International Labor
Organization

IMF International Monetary Fund
IN Indiana
Inc. Incorporated
Ind. Indiana
ind. independent
Indpls. Indianapolis
indsl. industrial
inf. infantry
info. information
ins. insurance
insp. inspector
inst. institute
instl. institutional
instn. institution
instr. instructor
instrn. instruction
instrnl. instructional
internat. international
intro. introduction
IRE Institute of Radio Engineers
IRS Internal Revenue Service

J

JAG Judge Advocate General
JAGC Judge Advocate General
Corps
Jan. January
Jaycees Junior Chamber of
Commerce
JB Jurum Baccalaureus
JCB Juris Canoni Baccalaureus
JCD Juris Canonici Doctor, Juris
Civilis Doctor
JCL Juris Canonici Licentiatus
JD Juris Doctor
jg. junior grade
jour. journal
jr. junior
JSD Juris Scientiae Doctor
JUD Juris Utriusque Doctor
jud. judicial

K

Kans. Kansas
KC Knights of Columbus
KS Kansas
KY, Ky. Kentucky

L

LA, La. Louisiana
LA Los Angeles
lab. laboratory
L.Am. Latin America
lang. language
laryngol. laryngological
LB Labrador
LDS Latter Day Saints
lectr. lecturer
legis. legislation, legislative
LHD Doctor of Humane Letters
LI Long Island
libr. librarian, library
lic. licensed, license

lit. literature
litig. litigation
LittB Bachelor of Letters
LittD Doctor of Letters
LLB Bachelor of Laws
LLD Doctor of Laws
LLM Master of Laws
Ln. Lane
LPGA Ladies Professional Golf
Association
LPN Licensed Practical Nurse
lt. lieutenant
Ltd. Limited
Luth. Lutheran
LWV League of Women Voters

M

M Master
m. married
MA Master of Arts
MA Massachusetts
MADD Mothers Against Drunk
Driving
mag. magazine
MAgr Master of Agriculture
maj. major
Man. Manitoba
Mar. March
MArch Master in Architecture
Mass. Massachusetts
math. mathematics, mathematical
MB Bachelor of Medicine,
Manitoba
MBA Master of Business
Administration
MC Medical Corps
MCE Master of Civil Engineering
mcht. merchant
mcpl. municipal
MCS Master of Commercial
Science
MD Doctor of Medicine
MD, Md. Maryland
MDiv Master of Divinity
MDip Master in Diplomacy
mdse. merchandise
MDV Doctor of Veterinary
Medicine
ME Mechanical Engineer
ME Maine
M.E.Ch. Methodist Episcopal
Church
mech. mechanical
MEd. Master of Education
med. medical
MEE Master of Electrical
Engineering
mem. member
meml. memorial
merc. mercantile
met. metropolitan
metall. metallurgical
MetE Metallurgical Engineer

meteorol. meteorological
Meth. Methodist
Mex. Mexico
MF Master of Forestry
MFA Master of Fine Arts
mfg. manufacturing
mfr. manufacturer
mgmt. management
mgr. manager
MHA Master of Hospital
  Administration
MI Military Intelligence, Michigan
Mich. Michigan
micros. microscopic
mid. middle
mil. military
Milw. Milwaukee
Min. Minister
mineral. mineralogical
Minn. Minnesota
MIS Management Information
  Systems
Miss. Mississippi
MIT Massachusetts Institute of
  Technology
mktg. marketing
ML Master of Laws
MLA Modern Language
  Association
MLitt Master of Literature,
  Master of Letters
MLS Master of Library Science
MME Master of Mechanical
  Engineering
MN Minnesota
mng. managing
MO, Mo. Missouri
moblzn. mobilization
Mont. Montana
MP Member of Parliament
MPA Master of Public
  Administration
MPE Master of Physical Education
MPH Master of Public Health
MPhil Master of Philosophy
MPL Master of Patent Law
Mpls. Minneapolis
MRE Master of Religious
  Education
MRI Magnetic Resonance
  Imaging
MS Master of Science
MSc Master of Science
MSChemE Master of Science in
  Chemical Engineering
MSEE Master of Science in
  Electrical Engineering
MSF Master of Science of
  Forestry
MSN Master of Science in Nursing
MST Master of Sacred Theology
MSW Master of Social Work
MT Montana

Mt. Mount
mus. museum, musical
MusB Bachelor of Music
MusD Doctor of Music
MusM Master of Music
mut. mutual
MVP Most Valuable Player
mycol. mycological

N

N North
NAACOG Nurses Association of
  the American College of
  Obstetricians and Gynecologists
NAACP National Association for the
  Advancement of Colored People
NACA National Advisory
  Committee for Aeronautics
NACDL National Association of
  Criminal Defense Lawyers
NACU National Association of
  Colleges and Universities
NAD National Academy of Design
NAE National Academy of
  Engineering, National Association
  of Educators
NAESP National Association of
  Elementary School Principals
NAFE National Association of
  Female Executives
N.Am. North America
NAM National Association of
  Manufacturers
NAMH National Association for
  Mental Health
NAPA National Association of
  Performing Artists
NARAS National Academy of
  Recording Arts and Sciences
NAREB National Association of
  Real Estate Boards
NARS National Archives and
  Record Service
NAS National Academy of
  Sciences
NASA National Aeronautics and
  Space Administration
NASP National Association of
  School Psychologists
NASW National Association of
  Social Workers
nat. national
NATAS National Academy of
  Television Arts and Sciences
NATO North Atlantic Treaty
  Organization
NB New Brunswick
NBA National Basketball
  Association
NC North Carolina
NCAA National College Athletic
  Association

NCCJ National Conference of
  Christians and Jews
ND North Dakota
NDEA National Defense
  Education Act
NE Nebraska
NE Northeast
NEA National Education
  Association
Nebr. Nebraska
NEH National Endowment for
  Humanities
neurol. neurological
Nev. Nevada
NF Newfoundland
NFL National Football League
Nfld. Newfoundland
NG National Guard
NH New Hampshire
NHL National Hockey League
NIH National Institutes of Health
NIMH National Institute of
  Mental Health
NJ New Jersey
NLRB National Labor Relations
  Board
NM, N.Mex. New Mexico
No. Northern
NOAA National Oceanographic
  and Atmospheric Administration
NORAD North America Air
  Defense
Nov. November
NOW National Organization for
  Women
nr. near
NRA National Rifle Association
NRC National Research Council
NS Nova Scotia
NSC National Security Council
NSF National Science Foundation
NSTA National Science Teachers
  Association
NSW New South Wales
nuc. nuclear
numis. numismatic
NV Nevada
NW Northwest
NWT Northwest Territories
NY New York
NYC New York City
NYU New York University
NZ New Zealand

O

ob-gyn obstetrics-gynecology
obs. observatory
obstet. obstetrical
occupl. occupational
oceanog. oceanographic
Oct. October
OD Doctor of Optometry

OECD Organization for Economic Cooperation and Development
OEEC Organization of European Economic Cooperation
OEO Office of Economic Opportunity
ofcl. official
OH Ohio
OK, Okla. Oklahoma
ON, Ont. Ontario
oper. operating
ophthal. ophthalmological
ops. operations
OR Oregon
orch. orchestra
Oreg. Oregon
orgn. organization
orgnl. organizational
ornithol. ornithological
orthop. orthopedic
OSHA Occupational Safety and Health Administration
OSRD Office of Scientific Research and Development
OSS Office of Strategic Services
osteo. osteopathic
otol. otological
otolaryn. otolaryngological

P

PA, Pa. Pennsylvania
paleontol. paleontological
path. pathological
pediat. pediatrics
PEI Prince Edward Island
PEN Poets, Playwrights, Editors, Essayists and Novelists
penol. penological
pers. personnel
PGA Professional Golfers' Association of America
PHA Public Housing Administration
pharm. pharmaceutical
PharmD Doctor of Pharmacy
PharmM Master of Pharmacy
PhB Bachelor of Philosophy
PhD Doctor of Philosophy
PhDChemE Doctor of Science in Chemical Engineering
PhM Master of Philosophy
Phila. Philadelphia
philharm. philharmonic
philol. philological
philos. philosophical
photog. photographic
phys physical
physiol. physiological
Pitts. Pittsburgh
Pk. Park
Pky. Parkway
Pl. Place
Plz. Plaza

PO Post Office
polit. political
poly. polytechnic, polytechnical
PQ Province of Quebec
PR Puerto Rico
prep. preparatory
pres. president
Presbyn. Presbyterian
presdl. presidential
prin. principal
procs. proceedings
prod. produced
prodn. production
prodr. producer
prof. professor
profl. professional
prog. progressive
propr. proprietor
pros. prosecuting
pro tem. pro tempore
psychiat. psychiatric
psychol. psychological
PTA Parent-Teachers Association
ptnr. partner
PTO Pacific Theatre of Operations, Parent Teacher Organization
pub. publisher, publishing, published, public
publ. publication
pvt. private

Q

quar. quarterly
qm. quartermaster
Que. Quebec

R

radiol. radiological
RAF Royal Air Force
RCA Radio Corporation of America
RCAF Royal Canadian Air Force
Rd. Road
R&D Research & Development
REA Rural Electrification Administration
rec. recording
ref. reformed
regt. regiment
regtl. regimental
rehab. rehabilitation
rels. relations
Rep. Republican
rep. representative
Res. Reserve
ret. retired
Rev. Reverend
rev. review, revised
RFC Reconstruction Finance Corporation
RI Rhode Island
Rlwy. Railway

Rm. Room
RN Registered Nurse
roentgenol. roentgenological
ROTC Reserve Officers Training Corps
RR rural route, railroad
rsch. research
rschr. researcher
Rt. Route

S

S South
s. son
SAC Strategic Air Command
SAG Screen Actors Guild
S.Am. South America
san. sanitary
SAR Sons of the American Revolution
Sask. Saskatchewan
savs. savings
SB Bachelor of Science
SBA Small Business Administration
SC South Carolina
ScB Bachelor of Science
SCD Doctor of Commercial Science
ScD Doctor of Science
sch. school
sci. science, scientific
SCV Sons of Confederate Veterans
SD South Dakota
SE Southeast
SEC Securities and Exchange Commission
sec. secretary
sect. section
seismol. seismological
sem. seminary
Sept. September
s.g. senior grade
sgt. sergeant
SI Staten Island
SJ Society of Jesus
SJD Scientiae Juridicae Doctor
SK Saskatchewan
SM Master of Science
SNP Society of Nursing Professionals
So. Southern
soc. society
sociol. sociological
spkr. speaker
spl. special
splty. specialty
Sq. Square
SR Sons of the Revolution
sr. senior
SS Steamship
St. Saint, Street
sta. station

stats. statistics
statis. statistical
STB Bachelor of Sacred Theology
stblzn. stabilization
STD Doctor of Sacred Theology
std. standard
Ste. Suite
subs. subsidiary
SUNY State University of New York
supr. supervisor
supt. superintendent
surg. surgical
svc. service
SW Southwest
sys. system

T

Tb. tuberculosis
tchg. teaching
tchr. teacher
tech. technical, technology
technol. technological
tel. telephone
telecom. telecommunications
temp. temporary
Tenn. Tennessee
TESOL Teachers of English to Speakers of Other Languages
Tex. Texas
ThD Doctor of Theology
theol. theological
ThM Master of Theology
TN Tennessee
tng. training
topog. topographical
trans. transaction, transferred
transl. translation, translated
transp. transportation
treas. treasurer
TV television
twp. township
TX Texas
typog. typographical

U

U. University
UAW United Auto Workers
UCLA University of California at Los Angeles
UK United Kingdom
UN United Nations
UNESCO United Nations Educational, Scientific and Cultural Organization
UNICEF United Nations International Children's Emergency Fund
univ. university
UNRRA United Nations Relief and Rehabilitation Administration
UPI United Press International
urol. urological
US, USA United States of America
USAAF United States Army Air Force
USAF United States Air Force
USAFR United States Air Force Reserve
USAR United States Army Reserve
USCG United States Coast Guard
USCGR United States Coast Guard Reserve
USES United States Employment Service
USIA United States Information Agency
USMC United States Marine Corps
USMCR United States Marine Corps Reserve
USN United States Navy
USNG United States National Guard
USNR United States Naval Reserve
USO United Service Organizations
USPHS United States Public Health Service
USS United States Ship
USSR Union of the Soviet Socialist Republics
USTA United States Tennis Association
UT Utah

V

VA Veterans Administration
VA, Va. Virginia
vet. veteran, veterinary
VFW Veterans of Foreign Wars
VI Virgin Islands
vis. visiting
VISTA Volunteers in Service to America
vocat. vocational
vol. volunteer, volume
v.p. vice president
vs. versus
VT, Vt. Vermont

W

W West
WA, Wash. Washington (state)
WAC Women's Army Corps
WAVES Women's Reserve, US Naval Reserve
WCTU Women's Christian Temperance Union
we. western
WHO World Health Organization
WI Wisconsin, West Indies
Wis. Wisconsin
WV, W.Va. West Virginia
WY, Wyo. Wyoming

X, Y, Z

YK Yukon Territory
YMCA Young Men's Christian Association
YMHA Young Men's Hebrew Association
YM & YWHA Young Men's and Young Women's Hebrew Association
yr. year
YT Yukon Territory
YWCA Young Women's Christian Association

Alphabetical Practices

Names are arranged alphabetically according to the surnames, and under identical surnames according to the first given name. If both surname and first given name are identical, names are arranged alphabetically according to the second given name.

Surnames beginning with De, Des, Du, however capitalized or spaced, are recorded with the prefix preceding the surname and arranged alphabetically under the letter D.

Surnames beginning with Mac and Mc are arranged alphabetically under M.

Surnames beginning with Saint or St. appear after names that begin Sains, and are arranged according to the second part of the name, e.g., St. Clair before Saint Dennis.

Surnames beginning with Van, Von, or von are arranged alphabetically under the letter V.

Compound surnames are arranged according to the first member of the compound.

Many hyphenated Arabic names begin Al-, El-, or al-. These names are alphabetized according to each biographee's designation of last name. Thus Al-Bahar, Neta may be listed either under Al- or under Bahar, depending on the preference of the listee.

Also, Arabic names have a variety of possible spellings when transposed to English. Spelling of these names is always based on the practice of the biographee. Some biographees use a Western form of word order, while others prefer the Arabic word sequence.

Similarly, Asian names may have no comma between family and given names, but some biographees have chosen to add the comma. In each case, punctuation follows the preference of the biographee.

Parentheses used in connection with a name indicate which part of the full name is usually omitted in common usage. Hence, Chambers, E(lizabeth) Anne indicates that the first name, Elizabeth, is generally recorded as an initial. In such a case, the parentheses are ignored in alphabetizing and the name would be arranged as Chambers, Elizabeth Anne.

However, if the entire first name appears in parentheses, for example, Chambers, (Elizabeth) Anne, the first name is not commonly used, and the alphabetizing is therefore arranged as though the name were Chambers, Anne.

If the entire middle name is in parentheses, it is still used in alphabetical sorting. Hence, Belamy, Katherine (Lucille) would sort as Belamy, Katherine Lucille. The same occurs if the entire last name is in parentheses, e.g., (Brandenberg), Howard Keith would sort as Brandenberg, Howard Keith.

For visual clarification:

Smith, H(enry) George: Sorts as Smith, Henry George
Smith, (Henry) George: Sorts as Smith, George
Smith, Henry (George): Sorts as Smith, Henry George
(Smith), Henry George: Sorts as Smith, Henry George

Who Was Who in America®

AAGAARD, CARL MUNK JEASEN, forensic pathologist; b. San Francisco, Mar. 18, 1922; s. Viktor M.J. and N. Fay (Shepard) A.; m. Earla Gardner; children: Carla, Earl, Victor, Lola. BA, Pacific Union Co., 1942; MD, Loma Linda U., 1945. Diplomate Am. Bd. Pathology. Intern Los Angeles County Gen. Hosp., 1945-46; general practice medicine San Mateo and Ukiah, Calif., 1948-51; with pathology tng. dept. Stanford U., San Francisco, 1951-53, Mt. Zion Hosp., San Francisco, 1953-55; practice medicine specializing in pathology Ukiah, from 1955. Coroner's surgeon San Francisco Coroner's Office, 1953-55. Corp. bd. dirs. Am. Cancer Soc., San Francisco, 1960-80. Served to capt. Med. Service Corp, AUS, 1946-48. Fellow Coll. Am. Pathology, Am. Soc. Clin. Pathology; mem. AMA, Mendo Lakes Med. Soc. (pres. 1958), Calif. Soc. Pathology, Calif. Med. Assn. Lodges: Rotary. Libertarian. Avocation: pilot. Home: Morehead, Ky. Died May 11, 2008.

AARONS, JULES, physicist; b. NYC, Oct. 3, 1921; s. Joseph and Sadie (Gold) A.; m. Jeanette Lampert, 1944 (dec.); children: Herbert Gene, Philip Ellis. BS in Edn., CCNY, 1942; MA in Sci., Boston U., 1949; Doctorate, U. Paris, 1954. Scientist Air Force Cambridge Research Lab., 1946-55; chief radio astronomy br. Air Force Geophysics Lab., Hanscom AFB, Mass., 1955-81; research prof. astronomy & space sci. Boston U., 1981—2008. Chmn. Commn. Ionospheric Radio Propagation-Internat. Union Radio Sci., 1980-83 Editor Radio Astronomical Studies of the Atmosphere; contbr.articles to profl. jours. Served with USAAF, 1942-45. Recipient Disting. Civilian Service award USAF, 1969 Fellow IEEE (Harry Diamond award 1982 former chmn. Agard Panel Electromagnetic Propagation); mem. Am. Geophys. Union Home: Auburndale, Mass. Died Nov. 21, 2008.

ABBOT, WILLIAM WRIGHT, history professor; b. Louisville, Ga., May 20, 1922; s. William Wright and Lillian (Carswell) A.; m. Eleanor Pearre, Mar. 31, 1958; children—William Wright, John Pearre. Student, Davidson Coll., NC, 1939-41; AB, U. Ga., 1943; MA, Duke U., 1949, PhD, 1953; LHD, Coll. William and Mary, 1998. Tchr. Louisville Acad., 1946-47, McCallie Sch., 1951-52; from asst. prof. to prof. history Coll. William and Mary, 1953—61, 1963—66; assoc. prof. Northwestern U., 1958-59, Rice U., 1961-63; James Madison prof. history U. Va., 1966-92, prof. emeritus, 1992—2009, chmn. history dept., 1972—74. Author: The Royal Governors of Georgia, 1754-1775, 1957, The Colonial Origins of the United States, 1607-1763, 1975, In Search of George Washington, 2006; editor in chief: The Papers of George Washington, 1977-92, Colonial Series, Vols. I-X, Revolutionary War Series, Vols. I-VI, Confederation, Vols. I-VI, 1992-97, Presidential, Vols. I-V, Retirement Series, Vols. I-IV, 1998; editor Jour. So. History, 1961-63; book rev. editor William and Mary Quar., 1955-61, editor, 1963-66; bd. editors Va. Quarterly Rev., 1971-90. Served to lt. USNR, 1943-46. Mem. Inst. Early Am. History and Culture (coun. 1976-79), So. Hist. Assn. (exec. coun. 1978-81), Mass. Hist. Soc., Am. Antiquarian Soc., Va. Hist. Soc. (hon.), Gridiron Club (U. Ga.), Raven Soc. (U. Va.), Phi Beta Kappa (pres. Alpha chpt. 1984-87). Home: Charlottesville, Va. Died Aug. 31, 2009.

ABE, MASAO, religion educator; b. Osaka, Japan, Feb. 9, 1915; came to U.S., 1980; d. Yoshio and Risa Tomomatsu; m. Ikuko Abe, Oct. 20, 1979. Shogakushi, Osaka U., 1936; Bungakushi, Kyoto U., 1944, LLD, 1985. Vis. prof. dept. philosophy Purdue U., West Lafayette, Ind., from 1991. Bd. dirs. Buddhist-Christian Theol. Encounter Meeting, 1982—. Author: Zen and Western Thought, 1985 (Am. Acad. Religion award); editor: A Zen Life: D.T. Suzuki, 1986; translator: An Inquiry into the Good (Kitaro Nishida), 1990; contbr. to The Emptying God. A Buddhist-Jewish-Christian Conversation, 1990; mem. editorial bd. Ea. Buddhist, 1970—. Rockefeller Found. fellow, 1955-57; recipient Rising Sun decoration Govt. of Japan, 1987. Fellow Soc. Arts, Religion and Contemporary Culture; mem. Internat. Assn. History of Religion (v.p. 1975-80), Soc. Buddhist Christian Studies (bd. dirs. 1989—), Am. Acad. Religion, FAS Soc. (bd. dirs.), Japanese Assn. Religious Studies (trustee), Theta Chi Beta. Home: West Lafayette, Ind. Died Sept. 10, 2006.

ABERCROMBIE, JOYCE REHBURG, trade association director; b. Sewickley, Pa., Feb. 13, 1939; d. William Max and Agnes Marion (Rumsey) Rehburg; m. Donald H. Abercrombie, Aug. 18, 1962 (dec. July 10, 1993). BS, Ind. State Coll., 1961; postgrad., Pa. State U., 1963-65, Carnegie-Mellon U., 1963-65; MEd, Ind. U. of Pa., 1974. Home service rep. Peoples Natural Gas Co., Pitts., 1961-62; tchr. home econs. Avalon Sch. Dist., Pitts., 1962-71; grad. asst. Ind. U. Pa., 1971-72; tchr. home econs. Blairsville (Pa.)-Saltsburg Sch. Dist., 1972-73; program dir. Dairy and Nutrition Council-Mid-East, Pitts., 1973-80, area dir., 1980-88; nutrition edn. mgr. Dairy & Nutrition Coun.-Mid East, Pitts., from 1989. Adj. staff Health Edn. Ctr., Pitts., 1978-83; mem. curriculum devel. team Nat. Dairy Coun., Chgo., 1976-77. Mem. exec. com. United Mental Health, Inc., Pitts., 1980-86, bd. dirs., 1978-86; participant Big Bros./Big Sisters, Pitts., 1986—. Presch. Nutrition Edn. grantee Pa. Dept. Edn., 1980-81; named Big Sister of Yr., 1988. Mem. Am. Home Econs. Assn. (v.p. profl. devel. 1992—), Pa. Home Econs. Assn. (chmn. subject matter 1987-89, v.p. western area 1989-92, named Outstanding Home Economist), Pa. Nutrition Coun. (chmn. pub. relations 1986-88, pres.-elect 1988-89, pres. 1989-90), Soc. for Nutrition Edn., Nutrition Coun. Southwestern Pa. (steering com. 1978-84), Soc. Pub. Health Educators (sec. 1976-77). Avocations: cross country skiing, rowing, bicycling, community theatre. Home: Pittsburgh, Pa. Died Mar. 6, 2008.

ABLE, JAMES AUGUSTUS, JR., writer; b. Decatur, Ill., Dec. 30, 1928; s. James Augustus and Florence Elizabeth (Gerhardt) A.; m. Martha Frances Collins, Feb. 10, 1952 (div. Apr. 1972); children: James B., Cynthia L. Able Singh, Robert G., Cheryl A. Able Moulton; m. Mary Louise Mathews, Apr. 26, 1972; children: Stephanie Ann, Victoria Ann. Student, James Millikin U., 1946, 49-50, USAF Inst., 1946-49; LLB, Atlanta Law Sch., 1953, LLM, 1954. Bar: Ga. 1955. Reporter Decatur Herald-Rev., 1943-46, 49-50; regional legal counsel Assocs. Investment Co., Atlanta, 1955-61; pvt. practice law Atlanta, 1961-70; security supr. State of Ga., Atlanta, 1970-72; pvt. investigator Advance Indsl. Security, Atlanta, 1972-75; freelance writer Tampa, Fla., from 1975. Spkr., advisor on writing and careers Hillsborough County Sch. Sys., Tampa, 1993—. Author: (novel) Victims, 1979; (nonfiction) Inside Swing, 1987, Writing Nostalgia, 1988; contbr. columns, numerous features, articles and short stories to lit. publs. and mags. Campaign aide various polit. campaigns, 1960s and 70s. Sgt. U.S. Army, 1946-49, 50-51. Mem. Tampa Writers Alliance (pres. 1986-89, publicity/pub. rels. dir. 1992—, workshop instr./coord. 1990—, 10-yr. Meritorious Svc. plaque 1996). Methodist. Avocations: listening, collecting, and chronicling jazz and swing music. Home: Tampa, Fla. Died Oct. 28, 2007.

ABRAHAM, EUGENE V., engineering executive; Chmn., CEO Sargent and Lundy Engrs., Chgo. Recipient James N. Lardis medal ASME, 1995. Died 2009.

ABRAMS, RUTH, hospital administrator; b. Haverhill, Mass., Apr. 22, 1924; d. Harry M. and Anne (Simons) Abrams; m. Albert R. Mezoff (div. 1974); children:Robert Abrams, Bette Abrams-Esche, Jane Mezoff; m. Hyman B. Finkelstein, Mar. 1976. BFA in Photography, Ohio U., 1945. Owner, operator Me Jane and Miss Rue, 1945-70; vol./amenities dir. New Eng. Bapt. Hosp., Boston, 1971-94. Presenter at workshops, meetings and confs. in field; support staff Age Wave Summer Inst., 1992. Contbr. articles to profl. jours. Rep. Mass. at presdl. confs. Mass. Commn. on Status of Women, 1965-68; past pres. LWV; dir. of the Brookline Access TV Bd., 1994; hospitality chmn. internat. conf. Alliance for Cmty. Media, 1995; adv. bd. Brookline Coun. on Aging, 1995; vol. prodr. Eldervision on Brookline Access TV, 1989—. Recipient Nat. Disting. Alumnus of the Yr. award Ohio U., 1994, Nat. Media Owl Award for Best Cmty. Produced Video, MacArthur Found., 1995. Avocations: swimming, crafts, sewing, creative writing. Home: Brookline, Mass. Died May 1, 2008.

ACKOFF, RUSSELL LINCOLN, social systems designer, educator; b. Phila., Feb. 12, 1919; s. Jack and Fannie (Weitz) A.; m. Alexandra Makar, July 17, 1949 (dec. Feb. 1987); children: Alan W., Karen B., Karla S.; m. Helen Wald, Dec. 20, 1987. BArch, U. Pa., 1941, PhD in Philosophy, 1947; DSc, U. Lancaster, 1967; DSc (hon.), Washington U., St. Louis, 1993, U. Lincolnshire and Humberside, UK, 1999, Fla. Internat. U., 2001, U. Hull, Eng., 2007; DL (hon.), U. New Haven, 1997; Dr. (hon.), Pontificia U. Cath. del Peru, Lima, 1999. Asst. instr. philosophy U. Pa., Phila., 1941-42, 46-47; asst. prof. philosophy and math. Wayne U., Detroit, 1947-51; assoc. prof., prof. ops. rsch. Case Inst. Tech., Cleve., 1951-64, Silberberg prof. systems scis. U. Pa., 1964-86, chmn. dept. stats. and ops. rsch., 1964-66, chmn. grad. faculty ops. rsch., 1964-69, dir. Mgmt. Sci. Ctr., 1964-67, 69-70, chmn. Busch Ctr., 1970-74, 76-79, chmn. social systems sci. unit, 1974-78, 86—, Anheuser-Busch prof. emeritus of mgmt. scis., from 1986. Chmn. INTERACT: The Inst. Interactive Mgmt., 1986—; methodological cons. U.S. Bur. Census, 1950-51; cons. Eastern Airlines, Emerson Electric Co., Gen. Foods Co., Mobil Oil Co., Nat. Acad. Scis., Nat. U. Mex., Sci. and Tech. Rsch. Coun., Turkey, Western Electric Co.; bd. dirs. Mantua Indsl. Devel. Corp.; August A. Busch Jr. vis. prof. mktg. Washington U., St. Louis, 1989-95; mem. core faculty Union Inst., Cin., 1989-91, Ackoff Ctr. Advanced Sys. Approaches Univ. Penn., 2000—; vis. prof. U. Hull, U.K., 2005—. Author: (with C.W. Churchman) Psychologistics, 1946, Methods of Inquiry, 1950, (with C.W. Churchman and M. Wax) Measurement of Consumer Interest, 1947, The Design of Social Research, 1953, (with C.W. Churchman and E.L. Arnoff) Introduction to Operations Research, 1957, Progress in Operations Research, I, 1961, Scientific Method, 1962, (with P. Rivett) A Manager's Guide to Operations Research, 1963, (with M. Sasieni) Fundamentals of Operations Research, 1968, A Concept of Corporate Planning, 1970, (with F.E. Emery) On Purposeful Systems, 1972, Redesigning The Future, 1974, (with T.A. Cowan et al) Designing a National Scientific and Technological Communication System, 1976, The Art of Problem Solving, 1978, Creating the Corporate Future, 1981, (with E. V. Finnel, J. Gharajedaghi) A Guide to Controlling Your Corporation's Future, 1984, (with P. Broholm and R. Snow) Revitalizing Western Economics, 1984, Management in Small Doses, 1986, Ackoff's Fables, 1991, The Democratic Corporation, 1994, Exploring Personality: An Intellectual Odyssey, 1998, Ackoff's Best, 1999, Re-Creating the Corporation, 1999, (with Sheldon Rovin) Redesigning Society, 2003, Beating the System, 2004; (with Jason Magidson and Herbert Addison) Idealized Design, 2006, (with Herbert J. Addison and Sally Bibb) Management f-laws, 2007; (with Herbert J. addison and Sally Bibb) Management f-Laws, 2007, Turning Learning Right Side Up, 2008 Philosophy of Science, 1947-53; mem. abstracting staff: Biological Abstracts, 1950-51; adv. editor mgmt. sci. John Wiley & Sons, 1964-86; adv. bd. Math. Spectrum, 1968-86; mem. editl. bd. Management Decision, 1968-86, Reflections, 2001-03, European Jour. Operational Rsch.; contbr. articles to profl. jours. Bd. dirs. Tallberg Found., Sweden, 1997—2000, Ctr. for Quality Mgmt., Cambridge, Mass., 1996—2004; mem. UN Devel. Adv. Coun., 1996—. Recipient award ASTD, 1993, award for outstanding achievement in sys. thinking and practice U.K. Sys. Soc., 1999, The Tallberg Found. and SupdBank Leadership award, 2005. Fellow Am. Statis. Assn., Ops. Rsch. Soc. Am. (v.p., pres. 1956-57), Internat. Acad. Mgmt., Inst. Mgmt. Cons.; mem. Internat. Acad. Mgmt., Russian Acad. Natural Scis. (fgn. mem.), Inst. Mgmt. Scis. (v.p. 1965), Operational Rsch. Soc. (U.K.) (Silver medal 1971), Soc. Gen. Systems Rsch. (pres. 1987-88), Oprational Rsch. Soc. India, Peace Rsch. Soc., Sigma Xi, Tau Sigma Delta. Achievements include Ackoff Ctr. for Advancement of Sys. Approaches (2000) the Russell L. Ackoff Endowment (2001) established at U. Pa. Home: Bryn Mawr, Pa. Died Oct. 29, 2009.

ACTON, WILLIAM JOHN, real estate appraiser and consultant; b. Jackson, Mich., Apr. 17, 1958; s. Richard David and Patricia Jean (Rifenberg) A. BA in Econs./Mgmt. and Polit. Sci., Albion Coll., Mich., 1980. Cert. gen. real estate appraiser, Ariz. Sr. appraiser cons. Greenberg Chin Cons., Tucson, 1984-87; chief appraiser Pima County Govt., Tucson, 1987-92; pres. Acton Valuation Group, Inc., Tucson, from 1992. Pima County rep. Govt. Chief Appraisers Inter-Agy. Coalition, Phoenix, 1988-93. Benefactor Boys and Girls Club, Tucson, 1993—, bd. dirs., 1996; benefactor Jacobs YMCA, Tucson, 1994—; precinct committeeman Pima County Rep. Party, 1995—. Paul Harris fellow Rotary Internat. Mem. Internat. Right of Way Assn., MAI Appraisal Inst., Rotary Club of Tucson, Encanto Canyon Homeowners Assn. (bd. dirs). Home: Las Vegas, Nev. Died Sept. 10, 2007.

ADAMCIK, JOE ALFRED, retired chemistry professor, lawyer; b. Taylor, Tex., June 28, 1930; s. Joseph John Adamcik and Pearle Mae Offield. BS, U. Tex., Austin, 1951, MA, 1954; PhD, U. Ill., 1958; JD, Tex. Tech. U., 1991. Bar: Tex. 1991. Asst. prof. chemistry Tex. Tech. U., Lubbock, 1957-61, assoc. prof. chemistry, 1961-88; ret., 1988; practiced in Lubbock, 1991-95; ret., 1995. Mediator Dispute Resolution Ctr., Lubbock, 1991—2004. Contbr. articles to profl. chemistry jours. Fellow AAAS, Tex. Acad. Sci. (v.p.); mem. Am. Chem. Soc. (dir. 1981-88), Am. Geophys. Union, Royal Soc. Chemistry. Avocation: computers. Home: Lubbock, Tex. Died Aug. 20, 2008.

ADAMS, LINDA RUTH, elementary school educator; b. Canton, Ill., Feb. 21, 1948; d. Robert Linn and Annalee (Post) Haggerty; m. Gary Lee Adams, Mar. 11, 1967; children: Colin, Heather, Dawn. BA in Music, So. Ill. U., 1971; MS in Elem. Edn., Western Ill. U., 1992. Cert. elem. tchr., Ill. Music tchr., Bunker Hill, Ill., 1969-73, Dunfermline (Ill.) Sch. Dist., 1992-93; elem. tchr. Canton Christian Sch., from 1991, adminstr., from 1998. Project facilitator Project Wild, Ill., 1991-97, Project Wild/Aquatics, Ill., 1991-97. Dir. Christian edn. Covenant Comty. Fellowship Ch., Canton, 1992—; bd. dirs. Comty. Concert Assn., Canton, 1982—; sec. Canton Christian Sch. Bd., 1992-95. Mem. Nat. Coun. Tchrs. Math., Ill. Sci. Tchrs. Assn.,

Lamoine Emergency Amateur Radio Club, Fulton County Amateur Radio Club, Phi Kappa Phi. Avocations: gardening, photography, quilting, world travel, poetry. Home: Canton, Ill. Died June 8, 2008.

ADAMS, MARIAN L., gerontology nurse, educator; b. La Harpe, Ill., Feb. 5, 1954; d. Marion L. and Rosie I. (Bundy) Shaver; children: Ronald J. Burgess, Robert J. Burgess. Remotivation cert., Galesburg Mental Health Ctr., 1984; AA in Nursing, Carl Sandburg Coll., Galesburg, Ill., 1985. RN, La., Ill. Nurse West Calcasieu Cameron Hosp., Sulphur, La.; nurse, charge nurse Galesburg Nursing and Rehab. Ctr., La Harpe Hosp.; nurse, clin. tchr. nurses aides La Harpe Davier Healthcare Ctr.; surg. staff nurse Carthage Meml. Hosp. Home: Sunrise, Fla. Deceased.

ADAMS, MARY LOUISE, education educator, archivist; b. Troy, Mo., Oct. 15, 1919; d. Robert Andrews and Mary Louise (Harbaugh) A. AB, Harris Coll., 1941; MA, St. Louis U., 1951, PhD, 1960; BA, Maryville U., 1980; M of Liberal Arts, Washington U., St. Louis., 1989. Tchr. St. Louis Pub. Schs., 1941-43; asst. prof. edn. St. Louis U., 1960-67; assoc. prof. edn. Maryville Coll., St. Louis, 1967-72, prof., 1972-89, prof. emeritus, from 1989. Resident scholar Radcliffe Coll.-Harvard U., Cambridge, Mass., 1980-82; hon. trustee St. Louis U. Arts and Sci. Alumni Bd. Dirs., 1989—. Bd. dirs. UNICEF, St. Louis, 1980-85; historian Gateway Waves, St. Louis, 1980—. Lt. comdr. USNR, 1943-73. Scholar Bleweit scholar, 1959—60. Mem. NEA, AAUP (local chpt. pres.), UN Assn., St. Louis Area Archivists Assn. (bd. dirs. 1986—), Enfant de Marie (prefect 1983-87), Mo. Hist. Assn., Assn. Alumnae Sacred Heart Acad., Cardinal Newman Assn., Friends St. Louis Art Mus., Res. Officers Assn., Landmarks Club, DuBourg Soc. St. Louis U., Alpha Sigma Nu, Gamma Phi Epsilon. Roman Catholic. Died Apr. 12, 2008.

ADAMS, PETER, operations and technical support administrator; b. Cumberland, Md., July 5, 1945; s. George H. Adams and Dorene E. Patton. BA, Cath. U. Am., 1968. Exec. dir. Integrated Resources, NYC, 1970-84; cons. NYC, 1984-89; mgr. of ops. and tech. svcs. Insteel Industries, Inc., Mt. Airy, N.C., from 1989. Home: Pinnacle, NC. Died June 7, 2008.

ADAMS, THURMAN G., state legislator; b. Bridgeville, Del., July 25, 1928; s. Thurman and Bessie Adams; m. Hilda Adams (dec.); children: Brent(dec.), Polly, Lynn. BS in Agr., U. Del., Newark, 1950. Pres. T.G. Adams & Sons, Inc., from 1961; mem. Dist. 19 Del. State Senate, Dover, 1972—2009, majority leader, 1999—2002, pres. pro tempore, 2003—09. Mem. Hwy. Commn., Del., 1961—70; chmn. Gov. Safety Com., Del., 1966—69. Dir. Milford State Fair. Recipient Medal of Distinction, U. Del., Liberty Bell award, Del. State Bar Assn.; named to U. Del. Wall of Fame. Mem.: U. Del. Agr. Alumni Assn., Lions Club. Democrat. Methodist. Home: Bridgeville, Del. Died June 23, 2009.

ADAMSON, MALCOLM MONROE, healthcare facility administrator; b. Goodwater, Ala., July 25, 1921; s. Walter marion and Theresa Viola (Parker) A.; ptnr. George Fodel Hankins, Jan. 12, 1948; children: Michael Monroe, Marion Jerome. BS, Ala. State U., Athens, 1944; BD, Duke U., 1947, MDiv, 1949. Ordained to ministry, United Meth. Ch., 1948. Dean Holston Home, Greeneville, Tenn., 1947-50; headmaster The Bonny Oaks Sch., Chattanooga, 1950-81; exec. dir. Big Bros./Big Sisters, Chattanooga, 1981-86; adminstrv. rep. to patients Erlangen Medical Ctr., Chattanooga; protestant chaplain Meml North Park Hosp. Sec.-treas. Bonny Oaks Found., Chattanooga, 1981—; registrar Tenn. Election Commn., Chattanooga, 2000. Avocation: coin collecting/numismatics. Home: Chattanooga, Tenn. Died Apr. 8, 2008.

ADELMAN, WILLIAM JOHN, retired academic administrator, industrial relations specialist; b. Chgo., July 26, 1932; s. William Sidney and Annie Teresa (Goan) A.; m. Nora Jill Walters, June 26, 1952; children: Michelle, Marguerite, Marc, Michael, Jessica. Student, Lafayette Coll., 1952; BA, Elmhurst Coll., 1956; MA, U. Chgo., 1964. Tchr. Whitecross Sch., Hereford, Eng., 1956-57, Jefferson Sch., Berwyn, Ill., 1957-60, Morton High Sch., Berwyn, 1960-66; mem. faculty dept. labor and indsl. relations U. Ill., Chgo., 1966-91, prof., 1978-91, prof. emeritus, 1991—2009; coordinator Chgo. Labor Edn. Program, 1981-87. Lectr. Road Scholar Program, Ill. Humanities Coun., 1997. Author: Touring Pullman, 1972, Haymarket Revisited, 1976, Pilsen and the West Side, 1981; writer: film Packingtown U.S.A., 1968; narrator: Palace Cars and Paradise: Pullman's Model Town, 1983' appeared on PBS Am. Experience, City of the Century, 2003, PBS History Detective, 2007. Bd. dirs. Chgo. Regional Blood Program, 1977-80; mem. Ill. State Employment Security Adv. Bd., 1974-75; Democratic candidate U.S. Ho. of Reps. from 14th dist. Ill., 1970; organizer Haymarket Centennial Events, 1986; chmn. adv. bd. Jane Addams' Hull House, 1991-99; mem. adv. bd. Maxwell St. Mus., 2001—; mem. Haymarket Monument Adv. Panel, 2002-04; dir. Maxwell St. Found., 2008-. Ill. Humanities Council grantee, 1977; German Marshall Fund U.S. grantee, 1977; recipient Tradition of Excellence award Oak Park/River Forest H.S., 1993, Eugene V. Debs award Midwest Labor Press assn., 1995. Mem. Ill. Labor History Soc. (founding mem., v.p., Union Hall of Honor 1993), Am. Fedn. Tchrs., Doris Humphrey Soc. (v.p. 1990—). Unitarian Universalist. Died Sept. 15, 2009.

ADLER, HOWARD, JR., lawyer; b. Chgo., Jan. 25, 1925; s. Howard and Martha (Grossman) A.; m. Mary E. Williamson, Oct. 30, 1955; children: Martine, Karla, Elizabeth. MA in Econs., U. Chgo., 1951, JD, 1951. Bar: Ill. 1952. Atty. U.S. Dept. Justice, Washington, 1952—54, law clk., 1954—55; ptnr. Bergson, Borkland, Margolis & Adler, Washington, 1956—85, Davis, Graham & Stubbs, Washington, 1986—96; of counsel Baker & McKenzie, Washington, 1996—2001, Ridberg Sherbill & Arenson, LLP, Bethesda, Md., from 2002. 1st lt. USAAF, 1946, PTO. Fellow Am. Bar Found.; mem. ABA (vice chmn. coun. 1978-79, sect. on antitrust law 1973-77). Home: Bethesda, Md. Died 2006.

ADLER, POSY (ROSLYN ADLER), artist, educator; b. Chgo., Feb. 6, 1916; d. Leon and Julia (Sonnenschein) Woolf; m. Leon Adler, Nov. 1, 1937 (dec.); children: Larry, Janet. BE, Nat. Coll. Edn., Evanston, Ill., 1975; MFA in Sculpture, Goddard Coll., Plainfield, Vt., 1975; studied with Roger Armstrong, Eliot O'Hara, Barbara Neijna, Robert Stoetzer. Art tchr. Miami (Fla.)-Dade Coll., Miami, Fla., 1964-84; sculpture tchr. Saddleback Coll., Mission Viejo, Calif., from 1984. Art tchr. Newport Harbor Mus., Irvine Fine Arts Ctr., Met. Art Ctr., Dade County C.C., New Sch. Fine Arts. Exhibited at Art Angles, Calif., Artist's Unlimited, Fla., Bacardi Art Gallery, Fla., Blunt Gallery, Ctr. for the Arts, Boca Raton, Fla., Design Ctr. South, Calif., Grove House Gallery, Fla., Jockey Club Art Gallery, Fla., U. Fla. Lowe Art Gallery, Fla., Met. Art Ctr., Fla., Mus. Science, Miami, Neiman Marcus Art Gallery, Rauchbach Galleries, Tolley Gallery, Turnberry Gallery; commissions include: Sherman Gardens, Calif., Sports Clinic, Laguna Hills, Calif., Temple Or Olom, Miami; represented in permenant collections Clubhouse 3 Leisure World, Laguna Woods, Calif. Ind. state v.p. Mental Health Soc., Frankfort, 1954-55, bd. dirs., Miami, Fla., 1957-62; hospice vol., Laguna Hills, Calif., 1990-99; vol. Adult Day Care Ctr., Laguna Hills, 1999. Mem. Am. Crafts Coun., Orange Co. Fine Arts, Ceramic League Miami, Creative Arts Guild, Dana Point Coastal Arts Coun., Florida Craftsman, Laguna Arts Assn., Miami Cultural Arts Alliance, Nat. League Am. Penwomen (pres. Laguna Beach br.), Nat. Mus. Women in the Arts, Niguel Art Assn., Sculptors of Fla., Women's Caucus for Art. Democrat. Jewish. Avocations: travel, sculpting, painting, craft work. Home: Bethesda, Md. Deceased.

ADLER, SIDNEY W., lawyer; b. Steubenville, Ohio, June 22, 1952; AB in Geography, Clark U., 1976; JD summa cum laude, Syracuse U., 1979. Bar: Mass. 1979, U.S. Dist. Ct. Mass. 1980. Ptnr. Morrison, Mahoney & Miller, Boston, 1979-85, Taylor, Anderson & Travers, Boston, 1985-95, Adler, Cohen, Harvey, Wakeman & Guekguezian, LLP, Boston, from 1995. Home: Brighton, Mass. Died Nov. 2, 2007.

ADOLF, RAMOND ROMER, marketing executive; b. American Falls, Idaho, June 9, 1932; s. Eric Frederick and Frances Clara (Wuebbenhorst) A.; m. Imogene Love, Aug. 23, 1953; 1 child, Derek S. BSChemE, Oreg. State U., 1961. With GE, Oakland, Calif., 1961, Dow Chem. Co., from 1963, mgr. product sales Walnut Creek, Calif., 1966-70, mgr. dist. sales, 1970-75, mgr. group mktg. Midland, Mich., 1975-79, mgr. mktg. resources, 1980-85, mgr. comml. resources, 1985-87, mgr. human resources, 1987-90, case adminstr. legal dept., 1990-91; ret., 1992. Active Little League Football and Baseball, Midland; chmn. Music Parent Assn., Midland, 1980-84. 1st lt. U.S. Army, 1962-63. Mem. Am. Mgmt. Assn., Masons (Shriner). Republican. Lutheran. Avocations: skiing, scuba diving, gardening. Home: Pinckney, Mich. Died Nov. 19, 2007.

ADRINE, HERBERT A., lawyer; b. Rockmart, Ga., Sept. 1, 1915; s. Wister and Carrie (Russell) A.; m. Laura R. Nellems, Sept. 10, 1947 (div. May 1955); children: Carol A., Parker A.; m. Ethel M. Spencer, Oct. 26, 1956. BBA, Wilberforce U., 1938; LLD, Cleve. State U., 1952. Bar: Ohio 1952, U.S. Dist. Ct. (no. dist.) Ohio 1952, U.S. Supreme Ct. 1971. Legal advisor Tried Stone Baptist Ch.; mem. Ctrl. Area Cmty., Cleve. Sgt. USAF, 1942-46. Recipient Meritorious award Cleve. Bar Assn., 1971, award Cuyahoga County Bar, 1972. Republican. Avocations: bowling, bridge. Died Apr. 3, 2008.

AHRENS, ROLLAND WILLIAM, chemist, consultant; b. Clarkson, Nebr., Sept. 28, 1933; s. William John and Josephine (Swoboda) A.; m. Rosalind Zucker, Feb. 23, 1963; children: Scott Rolland, Todd Michael. BS, U. Nebr., 1954, MS, 1955; PhD, U. Wis., 1959. With E.I. duPont de Nemours & Co., 1959-93, rsch. supr. fibers dept. Seaford, Del., 1968-77, sr. rsch. chemist fiber surfaces rsch. Kinston, N.C., 1987-93; pres. Physiochem. Cons., Inc., from 1993. Wis. Alumni Rsch. Found. fellow, 1955-57. Mem. Am. Chem. Soc., North Augusta (S.C.) Jr. C. of C., Rotary, Phi Beta Kappa, Phi Lambda Upsilon, Sigma Xi, Pi Mu Epsilon. Republican. Presbyterian. Avocations: golf, sports cars. Home: Greenville, NC. Died Feb. 23, 2008.

AIGES, HARVEY WAYNE, pediatrician, medical educator; b. NYC, Jan. 13, 1947; s. Louis and Estelle (Rubin) A.; m. Judith Ann Moel, Mar. 20, 1982; 1 child, Laura. BA, Bklyn. Coll., 1967; MD, NYU, 1971. Diplomate Am. Bd. Pediats., Am. Bd. Pediat. Gastroenterology. Resident Bronx Mcpl. Hosp. Ctr., 1971-74; chief resident in pediatrics Albert Einstein Coll. of Medicine, Bronx, 1974-75; pediatric fellow in gastroenterologist Med. Coll. Cornell U., Manhasset, N.Y., 1977-79; pediatric gastroenterologist North Shore Univ. Hosp., Manhasset, from 1979, chief clin. svcs., from 1984, vice chmn., from 1989. Chmn. grad. med. edn. North Shore Health Sys. Author: Cystic Fibrosis, 1990, Pediatric Gastoenterologist, 1990; contbr. articles to profl. jours. Maj. U.S. Army, 1975-77. Fellow Am. Gastroenterologic Assn., Am. Assn. for Study of Liver Disease, Alpha Omega Alpha. Jewish. Home: Prt Washingtn, NY. Died Feb. 1, 2008.

AIGNER, EMILY BURKE, Christian lay minister; b. Henrico, Va., Oct. 28, 1920; d. William Lyne and Susie Emily (Willson) Burke; m. Louis Cottrell Aigner, Nov. 27, 1936; children: Lyne, Betty, D. Muriel (dec.), Willson, Norman, William, Randolph, Dorothy. Cert. in Bible, U. Richmond, 1969; postgrad., So. Bapt. Sem. Extension, Nashville, 1987, Va. Commonwealth U., 1981; diploma in Bible, Liberty Home Bible Inst., 1992, masterlife grad., 1994. Deacon Four Mile Creek Bapt. Ch., Richmond, Va., from 1972, trustee, 1991, dir. Woman's Missionary Union, 1986-94, treas., 1984-89, dir. Sunday sch., 1969-78, 84-85, 1989-93. Spl. edn. tchr., 1993-99; acctg. tech., 1959-80; farm owner. Prodr. Dial-A-Devotion for pub. by telephone, 1978-85, 2003—. Solicitor ARC, Henrico County, 1947-49, induction ctr. vol., 1994-97; solicitor, United Givers' Fund, Henrico County, 1945-48; sec.-treas. soliciting funds Bible Edn. in Varina Sch., 1946-49; singer Bellwood Choir, Chesterfield County, Va., 1965-70; telephone counselor Richmond Contact, 1980-82, Am. Cancer Soc., Richmond, 1980-82; program chmn. Varina (Va.) Home Demonstration Club, 1950-53; worker Vol. Visitor Program Westport Convalescent Home, 1983-2000; vol. patient rep. Richmond Meml. Hosp., 1994-98, chaplain, 1996-97; jail min. Richmond City Jail, 1973—; lay minister to sr. adults Four Mile Creek Bapt. Ch., 2002—, chairperson bd. deacons, 2004—. Named Woman of Yr., Henrico Farm Bur., 1996. Mem. UDC, Am. Assn. Christian Counselors, Gideons Internat. (sec. Va. aux. 1977-80, 82-84, new mem. plan rep. 1981, 85, 91, 94, zone leader 1988-91, state cabinet rep. 1989-90, pres. Richmond N.E. Camp 1976-78, sec.-treas. 1980-82, 93, scripture sec. 1973-75, 87-89, v.p., 1997-98, chmn. Va. state widows com. 1993-97, pres. Richmond East Camp, 2000-02, 2005—), State Aux. (tng. leader, 2004), Henrico Farm Bur. (women's com. 1994—), Alpha Phi Sigma. Died Feb. 16, 2008.

AIKEN, DAVID VOLLMAR, recording industry executive, educator; b. East Cleveland, Ohio, July 31, 1943; s. William James and Amelia (Vollmar) A.; m. Nancy Ellen Bryan, July 3, 1965; children: Jessica Nicole, Marianne Jefferson. BBA in Mgmt., Ohio U., 1965, MEd in Higher Edn., 1981. Gen. supr. quality control Delco-Remy div. GM, Anderson, Ind., 1965-76; owner, operator Lost Nation Sound Recording Studio, Guysville, Ohio, from 1976. Audio recording instr. Ohio U., Athens, 1979—; instr. bus. Hocking Coll., Nelsonville, Ohio, 1979—; engr. (albums) Strings Alone by Grey Eagle Band, 1990, Federal Hocking Jazz Band, 1990; producer (album) Powers That Be, 1990; producer, engr. (album) All The Way Home by The Believers, 1989, Exit, 1995, Venus Pflox, 1996. With USNG, 1966-72. Mem. Pi Kappa Alpha (chpt. advisor Ohio U. 1985—), Delta Epsilon Chi (chpt. advisor Hocking Tech. Coll. 1987-89), Alpha Beta Gamma (chpt. advisor HC 1993—). Avocations: sports, trains and train travel, music. Home: Guysville, Ohio. Died July 1, 2008.

AINSLEY, LUCY ELIZABETH, retired educational administrator; b. Bad Axe, Mich., June 29, 1942; d. Kenneth Sylvester and Mildred (Grekowicz) Smith; m. Alan Kent Ainsley, Sept. 9, 1967 (div. 1977). BS in Edn., Cen. Mich. U., 1964; MA, Mich. State U., 1969; MLS, Wayne State U., 1975, EdD, 1987. Speech tchr. MacArthur High Sch., Saginaw, Mich., 1964-66, librarian, 1966-67; media cons. Saginaw Intermediate Schs., 1967-68; media dir. Waterford (Mich.) Mott High Sch., 1968-73; coordinator media services Birmingham (Mich.) Pub. Schs., 1973-85, dir. instructional tech., from 1985. Lectr. in field; cons. Lenawee Intermediate Schs., Adrian, Mich., 1985. Editor Media Mgmt. Jour., 1986; author: Sch. Library Media Annual, 1985; contbr. articles to profl. jours. Mem. adv. bd. Children's Com. for TV, Detroit, 1984—; ad hoc advisor Birmingham Cablecasting Bd., 1980—; chmn. Bloomfield Cable Access Com., 1985. Mem. Nat. Assn. for Edn. Comm. and Tech. (bd. dirs. 1983-86, pres.-elect 1989, Edgar Dale award 1978), Mich. Assn. for Media in Edn. (chpt. pres. 1974), LWV (cable coord. 1987—), Phi Delta Kappa (newsletter editor). Avocations: photography, reading, hiking, canoeing, skiing, sailing. Home: Phoenix, Ariz. Died Sept. 1, 2007.

AINSWORTH, DAVID A., company executive; b. Bury, Lancashire, Eng., Feb. 28, 1950; m. Joanne Ainsworth. BSC, U. Manchester Inst. Sci./Tech., Eng., 1971. Research chemist MacPherson Coatings, Bury, 1971-72; sales exec. Sutcliffe Speakman Co., Leigh, Eng., 1972-75, sales mgr., 1975-77; N. Am. mgr. Sutcliffe Speakman Inc., Balt., 1978-87; pres. Cameron Carbon Inc., Balt., from 1987. Contbr. articles to profl. jours. Mem. ASTM, Am. Water Works Assn. Home: Baltimore, Md. Died Nov. 10, 2007.

AKE, JEFFREY JAMES, management consultant; b. Raleigh, NC, Feb. 28, 1958; s. James Wrigley and Elizabeth (Rowbottom) A. BA in History, U. Ill., 1981, BS in Psychology magna cum laude, 1981. Mktg. rep. Armstrong World Industries, Inc., Sacramento, Calif., 1981-83; regional sales mgr. Electronic Liquid Fillers, La Porte, Ind., 1984-85, nat. sales, mktg. mgr., 1986-88; founder Electronic Liquid Fillers, UK Ltd., Leicester, Eng., 1989; internat. sales mgr. Electronic Liquid Fillers, La Porte, 1990-91, v.p. mktg., 1992-95; founder, pres. Internat. Vision, Inc., Ind., from 1995; pres. Equipment Express, Inc., from 1998. Bd. dirs. Small Bus. Devel. Ctr., N.W. Ind. Entrepreneurship Acad.; chmn. LaPort Small Bus. Devel. Ctr. Bd., 1994; mem. adv. bd. Regional Export Adv. Team Com., NWI Entrepreneurship Conf.; mem. Cato Inst. Author: Aggressive Exporting: How to Make Your Company an International Tiger, Channing: Paradigm Transition Figure, Youthful Musings. Active Big Brothers/Big Sisters Program, M2 Prison Sponsor Program, Jr. Achievement, Jaycees. Recipient Export Achievement award Packaging Machinery Mfrs. Inst. Mem. Aircraft Owners and Pilots Assn., Young Entrepreneurs Assn. Nat. Spkrs. Assn. (profl. mem.), Nat. Assn. Parliamentarians (cert. parliamentarian), Packaging Machinery Mfrs. Inst. (bd. dirs. 1991—, chmn. global mktg. com. 1993-95, Export Achievement award), Sacramento Assn. Entrepreneurs (pres. 1982-83), World Trade Coun. (pres. 1995-96), Golden Key, Phi Alpha Theta, Rho Epsilon. Avocations: flying, comparative religion, comparative economics, scuba diving, triathlons. Died Dec. 1, 2005.

AKSYONOV, VASSILY PAVLOVICH, author; b. Kazan, Russia, Aug. 20, 1932; came to U.S., 1980; s. Pavel Vassilievich and Eugenia Solomonovna (Ginzburg) A.; m. Maya Zmeul, May 30, 1980; 1 child, Alex. MD, Leningrad Med. Inst., 1956; LHD, Goucher Coll., 1988. Intern Inst. for Tb Study, 1957-60; Clarence Robinson prof. George Mason U., Fairfax, Va., from 1988. Author: (fiction) Kollegi, 1961 (pub. as Colleagues, 1961), Zvezdnyi bilet, 1961 (pub. as A Starry Ticket, 1962, A Ticket to the Stars, 1963), Na polputi k lune, 1962 (pub. as Halfway to the Moon, 1964), Apel'siny iz Marokko, 1963, Katapul'ta, 1964, Tovarishch Krasivii Furazhkin, 1964, Pora, moi drug, pora, 1965 (pub. as It's Time, My Friend, It's Time, 1969, It's Time, My Love, It's Time, 1970), Malen'kii kit-lakirovshchik deistvitel'nosti, 1965, Mestnyi "khuligan" Abramashvili, 1966, Zatovarennaia bochkotara, 1968 (pub. as Surplussed Barrelware, 1985), Zhal', chto vas ne bylo s nami, 1969, Liubov'k elektrichestvu, 1971, Dzhin Grin-neprikasaemii, 1972, Samson and Samsoness, 1972, Kruglye sutki non-stop, 1976, Poiski zhanra, 1977, Stal'naia ptitsa, 1977 (pub. as The Steel Bird, and Other Stories, 1979), Zolotaia nasha Zhelezka, 1980 (pub. as Our Golden Ironburg, 1988), Ozhog, 1980 (pub. as The Burn, 1984), Ostrov Krym, 1981 (pub. as The Island of Crimea, 1983), Pravo na ostrov: rasskazy, 1983 (pub. as Quest for an Island, 1987), Bumazhnyi peizazh, 1983, Skazhi izium: roman v moskovskikh traditsiiakh, 1985 (pub. as Say Cheese!, 1989), Sobranie sochinenii, 1987, Den' pervogo snegopada, 1990, Kapital'noe peremeshchenie, 1990, Rai devu, 1991, Zheltok iaitsa, 1991, Moskovskaia saga, 1991, Ran-devu, 1991, The Winters Hero, 1996, Voltairian Men and Women, 2004, Moskva-kva-kva', 2006; (plays) Kollegi, 1962, Vsegda v prodazhe, 1965, Vash ubiytsa, 1977, Chetyre temperamenta, 1979, Aristofaniana s liagushkami, 1981, Tsaplya, 1984; (screenplay) Bliuz s russkim aksentom, 1986; (children's) Moi dedushka pamiatnik, 1969, Sunduchok v kotorom chto-to stuchit, 1976; (non-fiction) Geografia liubovi: dialog v 2 chasti, 1975, Progulka v Kalashnyi riad, 1984, Afisha glasila: k 125-letiiu Chekhova, 1985, V poiskakh grustnogo bebi: knigi ob Amerike, 1987 (pub. as In Search of Melancholy Baby, 1987). Kennan Inst. Advanced Russian Study fellow, 1981; Wilson Center fellow, 1982; recipient Golden prize Internat. Competition of Satirical Authors, 1967. Mem. French P.E.N., Sweden P.E.N., Denmark P.E.N. Christian Orthodox. Home: Moscow, Russia. Died July 6, 2009.

ALBIN, CHRISTIAN (HITSCH ALBIN), chef; b. Graubünden, Switzerland, Sept. 21, 1947; m. Johanna Albin; children: Stephanie, Christopher. Chef de cuisine Swiss Pavilion; chef Forum of the 12 Ceasars, The Four Seasons, NYC, 1973—90, exec. chef, 1990—2009. Recipient Best Food award, Where Mag., 1999. Died June 13, 2009.

ALBRIGHT, CARL WAYNE, JR., banker; b. Birmingham, Ala., Apr. 27, 1944; s. Carl Wayne Sr. and Grace Charlotte (Teas) A.; m. Sally Rainer Lamar, Sept. 7, 1968; children: Sally, Carl W. III. BS in Aerospace Engring., U. Ala., 1967, JD, 1970. Bar: Ala. 1970, U.S. Dist. Ct. (no. dist.) Ala. 1973, U.S. Dist. Ct. (so. dist) Ala. 1978, U.S. Ct. Appeals (11th cir.) 1981. Ptnr. Rosen, Wright, Harwood, Albright & Cook P.A., Tuscaloosa, Ala., 1970-80; sr. v.p., gen. counsel 1st Nat. Bank Tuscaloosa, 1981-83, exec. v.p., 1984-88; pres., CEO AmSouth Bank of Tuscaloosa, 1988. Judge Northport Mcpl. Ct., Ala., 1975-80 V.p., treas., bd. dirs. Family Counseling Service; coord. regional campaign Am. Heart Fund, Ala.; active United Way, YMCA, Boy Scouts Am., DCH Found.; chmn. Tuscaloosa Port Authority, 1985—, Tuscaloosa County Indsl. Devel. Authority, 1989—; pres. Stillman Found., 1985—; exec. com., bd. dirs. Indsl. Devel. Authority; trustee Stillman Coll., 1984—; bd. dirs. Indian Rivers Community Mental Health Ctr.; pres. West Ala. Chamber Found., Inc., 1987. 150th Anniversary Disting. Engring. fellow U. Ala. Coll. Engring., 1988. Mem. Tuscaloosa County Bar Assn. (pres. 1981-82), U. Ala. Law Sch. Alumni Assn. (pres. 1985), West Ala. C. of C. (chmn. 1986, vice chmn. 1985). Clubs: NorthRiver Yacht, Indian Hills Country (Tuscaloosa). Presbyterian. Avocations: golf, hunting. Home: Tuscaloosa, Ala. Died Dec. 11, 1997.

ALBRIGHT, JOSEPH P., state supreme court justice; b. Parkersburg, W.Va., Nov. 8, 1938; s. M.P. and Catherine (Rathbone) A.; m. Patricia Ann Deem, 1958 (dec. 1993); children: Terri Albright Cavi, Lettie Albright Muckley, Joseph P. Jr., John Patrick (dec.); m. Nancie Gensert Divvens, 1995; stepchildren: Susan Divvens Bowman, Debbic Divvens Rake, Sandy Divvens Fox. BBA cum laude, U. Notre Dame, JD, 1962. Bar: W.Va. 1962, U.S. Dist. Ct. W.Va. 1962. Pvt. practice, Parkersburg, 1964-95; asst. prosecuting atty. Wood County, 1965-68; city atty. City of Parkersburg, W.Va., 1968; pvt. practice Parkersburg and Charleston, 1997—2000; justice W.Va. Supreme Ct. Appeals, Charleston, W.Va., 1995—96, 2001—09, chief justice, 2005. Bd. dirs. Albrights of Belpre (Ohio), Inc. Mem. W.Va. Ho. of Dels., 1970-72, 74-86, mem. jud. com., chmn. com. on edn., 1977-78, chmn. com. on judiciary, 1979-84, 52d spkr., 1985-86; mem., former chmn. Blennerhassett Hist. Park Commn.; former co-chmn. Blennerhassett Hist. Commn.; mem. St. Francis Xavier Ch., Parkersburg, past pres. parish adv. coun. Named Freshman Legislator of Yr., Charleston Gazette, 1971. Democrat. Roman Catholic. Died Mar. 20, 2009.

ALBRIGHT, LOVELIA FRIED, art import company executive; b. NYC, Dec. 13, 1934; d. George and Hilda (Lazanov) Fried; m. Lee Albright, Nov. 30, 1958; children: Gregre Scott, Glenn Keith, Todd Cameron. Student, Bennington Coll., 1952-55, Grad. Sch. Internat. Studies, Geneva, 1955-56. Publicist Doubleday & Co., NYC, 1960-63; owner Foley & Robinson, Inc., NYC, from 1988; pres., owner Lovelia Enterprises, Inc., NYC, from 1972. Monthly columnist home furnishings N.Y. Antique Guide, 1972. Avocations: swimming, collecting antiques, designing miniature home furnishings. Home: New York, NY. Died Sept. 5, 2007.

ALDWINCKLE, JOSEPH GEORGE, retired electronic engineer; b. Leicester, Eng., Oct. 14, 1927; came to U.S., 1959; s. Walter George and Hilda Jennie (Smith) A. BS, U. London, 1947. Jr. engr. Elec. and Musical Industries, Feltham, United Kingdom, 1952-56; engr. Can. Westinghouse, Hamilton, Ont., 1956-59, Westinghouse Corp., Balt., 1959-64; sr. engr. RCA, Burlington, Mass., 1964-71, Raytheon, West Andover, Mass., 1972-76; project engr. Computer Scis. Corp., Bedford, Mass., 1976-80, Analytical Sys. Engring. Corp., Burlington, 1980-96. Bd. dirs. Acton (Mass.) Cmty. Ctr. Inc., 1968-82. Sgt. Armed Forces United Kingdom, 1947-49. Recipient Exch. Student scholarship Fulbright, Ohio State U., 1950-51. Mem. AIAA, Air Force Assn. Avocations: amateur dramatics, hiking, chess. Home: Acton, Mass. Died Nov. 13, 2007.

ALEXANDER, ALONZO, III, music educator, composer; b. Cin., Sept. 4, 1956; s. Alonzo Alexander Jr. and Mamie (Comer) Alexander. MusB, U. Cin., Coll. Conservatory of Music, 1978, MusM, 1982, MusD, 1997. Music dir. St. Mark Cath. Ch., Cin., 1980—84, 1990—99; instr. Pasadena Conservatory of Music, Pasadena, Calif., 1985—90; adj. instr. Coll. Conservatory of Music, Cin., 1996—99, Antioch U., Yellow Springs, Ohio, 1996—97; asst. prof. music Morris Brown Coll., Atlanta, 1999—2003, Spelman Coll., Atlanta, 2004—05. Accompanist Americolor Opera Alliance, Atlanta, from 2000. Recipient Cert. of Honor award, Pi Kappa Lambda (Pi Chpt.), 1977, Recognition award, Phi Mu Alpha Sinfonia, 2004. Mem.: Phi Mu Alpha Sinfonia (faculty adv. 2001—04). Democrat. Cath. Avocations: poetry, singing, Greek mythology. Home: Atlanta, Ga. Died July 12, 2008.

ALEXANDER, DOLORES ANNE, retired journalist, advocate; b. Newark, Aug. 10, 1931; d. Dominick DeCarlo and Cecelia Irene Osekavage; m. Aaron J. Alexander, Mar. 1, 1957 (div. May 1, 1961). BA, CCNY, 1961. Stringer N.Y. Times, NYC, 1959—60; reporter Newark Evening News, 1961—64, Newsday, Garden City, NY, 1964—69; exec. dir. Nat. NOW, NYC, 1969—70; co-owner Mother Courage Restaurant, NYC, 1971—77; copy editor Time Inc., NYC, 1974—94; co-founder, spokeswoman Women Against Pornography, NYC, 1979—83; freelance writer nat. women's mags., NYC. Spkr. on feminist issues numerous colls. nationwide, 1970—94; organizer 1st Congress to Unite Women. Co-founder NOW, NYC, 1966; del. Nat. Women's Conf., Houston, 1977; Pres. Carter appointee Nat. Adv. Com. for Women, Washington, 1978—79; officer North Fork Women for Women Fund, Greenport, NY, 1996—2002. Finalist, Catherine L. O'Brian award, 1967, Wonder Woman award, 1983. Mem.: Vet. Feminists Am. (medal of honor 1996, Feminist Authors award 2002). Achievements include pioneering work as leader of second wave women's movement. Avocations: gardening, sailing, bicycling, travel. Home: Southold, NY. Died May 13, 2008.

ALEXANDER, DONALD CRICHTON, lawyer; b. Pine Bluff, Ark., May 22, 1921; s. William Crichton and Ella Temple (Fox) A.; m. Margaret Louise Savage, Oct. 9, 1946; children: Robert C. (dec.), James M. BA with honors, Yale U., 1942; LLB magna cum laude, Harvard U., 1948; LLD (hon.), St. Thomas Inst., 1975, Capital U., 1989. Bar: D.C. 1949, Ohio 1954, N.Y. 1978. Assoc. Covington & Burling, Washington, 1948-54, Taft, Stettinius & Hollister, Cin., 1954-56, ptnr., 1956-66, Dinsmore, Shohl, Coates & Deupree, Cin., 1966-73; commr. IRS, US Dept. Treasury, 1973-77; mem. Commn. on Fed. Paperwork, 1975-77; ptnr. Olwine, Connelly, Chase, O'Donnell & Weyher, NYC, Washington, 1977-79, Morgan, Lewis & Bockius, NYC and Washington, 1979-85, Cadwalader, Wickersham & Taft, Washington, 1985-93; ptnr., tax. practice group Akin, Gump, Strauss, Hauer & Feld, Washington, 1993—2009. Mem. adv. bd. NYU Tax Inst., 1969-73, 77-87, Tax Mgmt., Inc., 1968-73, 77-2009; mem. adv. US Dept. Treasury, 1970-72; mem. adv. group to commr. IRS, 1969-70, chmn. exempt orgns. adv. group, 1987-89; mem. adv. bd. Mertens, 1986-2002, Maxwell Macmillan fed. Taxes 2d, 1989-92; commr. Martin Luther King, Jr. Fed. Holiday Commn., 1993-96; mem. Harvard Bd. Overseers' vis. com. to law sch., 1999-2005; mem. com. on univ. resources Harvard U., 2002-09; mem. interior dept. commn. on coal leasing, 1983-84. Author: The Arkansas Plantation, 1943; editor Harvard Law Rev., 1947-48; contbr. more than 50 articles on fed. taxation. Co-chmn. bd. advisors NYU/IRS Continuing Profl. Edn. Program, 1982-85; dir. Treasury Hist. Assn., 1996-2006; Served to maj. AUS, 1942-45. Decorated Silver Star, Bronze Star; re. Mem. ABA (vice chmn. taxation sect. 1967-68), Am. Law Inst. (tax adv. group), U.S. C. of C. (taxation com. 1981-91, bd. dirs. 1984-89, health and employee benefit com. 1989-94, regulatory affairs com. 1993-98), Chevy Chase Club (Md.), Met. Club, Nantucket Yacht Club (Mass.), Mill Reef Club (Antigua, B.W.I.), Yale Club N.Y. Home: Washington, DC. Died Feb. 2, 2009.

ALEXANDER, JAMES KENNETH, financial consultant; b. Peoria, Ill., Oct. 13, 1953; s. Albert Lee and Betty Louise (Thomas) A.; m. Lee Ann Legner, Feb. 16, 1974; children: Matthew James, Jason Michael. AA in Mktg., Ill. Cen. Coll., 1975; BABA, Sangamon State U., 1978; grad. fin. courses, Investment Tng. Inst., Atlanta, 1984, 85, 86; cert. in personal fin. planning, Am. Coll., Bryn Mawr, Pa., 1987. CLU; ChFC; cert. fin. planning, broker; lic. agt. health, life, variable life and variable annuity ins., Ga., Tenn., Ala.; lic. securities dealer series 6, 7, 22 and 63, Nat. Assn. Securities Dealers. Owner A & A Food Stores, Peoria, 1975-80; cert. bus. broker V.R. Bus. Brokers, Atlanta, 1980-83; fin. cons. State Mut. Life Ins. Co., Atlanta, 1983-86, Mut. of N.Y. Ins. Co., Atlanta, from 1986; owner 5th Ave. Cleaners, Inc., Atlanta, from 1993. Bd. dirs. Chryslis, Atlanta, 1993; foster parent Dept. Family and Children's Svcs., Cobb County, Marietta, Ga., 1983-88; discipleship leader Meth. Ch., Kennesaw, Ga., 1991-93. Republican. Avocations: swimming, tennis, investment. Home: Kennesaw, Ga. Died June 26, 2008.

ALEXIS, MARCUS, economics professor; b. NYC, Feb. 26, 1932; 3 children. BA, Bklyn. Coll., 1953; MA, Mich. State U., 1954; PhD, U. Minn., 1959; DHL, Bklyn. Coll., 1986. Instr. economics U. Minn., 1954-57; asst. prof. economics & mktg. Macalester Coll., 1957-60; assoc. prof. mktg. DePaul U., 1960-62; assoc. prof. to prof. bus. adminstrn. U. Rochester, 1962-70; prof. economics Northwestern U., Evanston, Ill., 1970-85, chmn., 1976-79, 82-85; dean Coll Bus. Adminstrn. U Ill., Chgo., 1985-90; prof. economics, prof. mgmt. & strategy Northwestern U., 1991—2005. Ford Found. vis. scholar Harvard U. and MIT, Cambridge, Mass., 1961-62; vis. assoc. prof. U. Minn., 1962; vis. prof. U. Calif., Berkeley, 1969-71; vis. assoc. prof. U. Minn., 1962, 65; bd. dirs. Fed. Res. Bank Chgo., dep. chmn. 1986-89, chmn., 1990, Ctrl. Ill. Light Co. Bd. dirs. Operation Push (People United to Save Humanity), 1971-73; dir. summer program in econs. for minority students, 1974-79; commr. Interstate Commerce Commn., 1979-80, vice chmn., 1981, acting chmn., 1981; trustee Macalster Coll, 1984-87. Recipient Outstanding Achievement award U. Minn., 1981; Mich. State U. scholar; Hinman fellow, U. Minn. fellow, Harvard Grad. Sch. Bus. fellow, 1961-62. Mem. Am. Econ. Assn. (mem. com. to increase supply of minority economists, chmn. 1974-84, mem. com. on honors and awards 1972-78, mem. nominating com. 1981-82), Am. Mktg. Assn. (bd. dirs. 1968-70), Caucus Black Economists (chmn. 1969-71, steering com. 1969-73, 75-76), Nat. Econ. Assn. (steering com., Samuel Z. Westerfield award 1979), Tchr. Ins. and Annuity Assn. (bd. dirs., trustee, dep. chmn.). Died May 27, 2009.

ALIPRANTIS, CHARALAMBOS DIONISIOS, mathematician, economist, educator; b. Cephalonia, Greece, May 12, 1946; came to US, 1969; s. Dionisios Elias and Sofronia Aliprantis; m. Bernadette Aliprantis, Aug. 31, 1974; children: Claire, Dionissi. Diploma in Math., U. Athens, 1968; MS in Math., Calif. Inst. Tech., Pasadena, 1971, PhD in Math., 1973. Tchg. asst. U. Athens, 1969; grad. tchg. asst. Calif. Inst. Tech., Pasadena, 1969—73; instr. Occidental Coll., 1973—74, asst. prof. math., 1974—75, Ind. U.-Purdue U., Indpls., 1975—78, assoc. prof. math., 1978—81, prof. math., from 1981, prof. math. and econs., 1994—97, acting chmn. depts. math. and computer sci., 1988—89; prof. econs. and math. Purdue U., West Lafayette, Ind., 1998—2003, disting. prof. econs. and prof. math., 2003—09. Rsch. scientist STD Rsch. Corp., Arcadia, Calif., 1973-74; vis. prof. math. Calif. Inst. Tech., spring 1982, vis. prof. math. and econs., 1989-90, vis. prof. econs., 1996; vis. assoc. prof. math. U. So. Calif., 1981; sr. rsch. fellow Inst. for Math. and its Applications U. Minn., 1983; vis. prof. econs. Cornell U., Ithaca, NY, 1996; spkr. in field. Author: Problems in Equilibrium Theory, 1996; author: (with O. Burkinshaw) Locally Solid Riesz Spaces, 1978, Principles of Real Analysis, 1981, 1998, Positive Operators, 1985, Problems in Real Analysis, 1990, 1998; author: (with D.J. Brown and O. Burkinshaw) Existence and Optimality of Competitive Equilibria, 1989; author: (with K.C. Border) Infinite Dimensional Analysis, 1994, 2006; author: (with S.K. Chakrabarti) Games and Decision Making, 2000; author: (with Y.A. Abramovich) Problems in Operator Theory, 2002, An Invitation to Operator Theory, 2002; co-editor: Advances in Equilibrium Theory, 1985, Positive Operators, Riesz Spaces and Economics, 1991; editor-in-chief Positivity, Econ. Theory, Annals of Finance, mem. editl. bd. Panam. Math. Jour., editor series Studies in Economic Theory; contbr. over 90 articles to profl. publs. Rsch. grantee NSF, 1981-83, 83-84, 84-86, 2001—, NATO, 1995-97, Fulbright travel grantee, 1969, Purdue U. summer faculty grantee, 1979; Ind. U. summer faculty fellow, 1977;

scholar Ford Found., 1970-72, Calif. Inst. Tech., 1969-73, Greek State, 1964-68. Mem.: Math. Assn. America, Soc. Advancement of Econ. Theory, Am. Math. Soc. Died Feb. 27, 2009.

ALLEN, BETTY (MRS. RITTEN EDWARD LEE III), mezzo-soprano; b. Campbell, Ohio, Mar. 17, 1927; d. James Corr and Dora Catherine (Mitchell) Allen; m. Ritten Edward Lee, III, Oct. 17, 1953; children: Anthony Edward, Juliana Catherine. Student, Wilberforce U., 1944-46; certificate, Hartford Sch. Music, 1953; pupil voice, Sarah Peck More, Zinka Milanov, Paul Ulanowsky, Carolina Segrera Holden; LHD (hon.), Wittenberg U., 1971; MusD (hon.), Union Coll., 1981; DFA (hon.), Adelphi U., 1990, Bklyn. Coll., 1991; LittD (hon.), Clark U., 1993; MusD (hon.), New Sch. Social Rsch., 1994. Mem. voice faculty Manhattan Sch. Music, from 1969; mem. faculty NC Sch. Arts, 1978-87, Phila. Mus. Acad., 1979, Curtis Inst. Music; exec. dir. Harlem Sch. Arts, 1979—92. Tchr. master classes Inst. Teatro Colon, 1985-86, Curtis Inst. Music; vis. faculty Sibelius Akademie, Helsinki, Finland, 1976; mem. adv. bd. music panel Amherst Coll.; mem. music panel NY State Coun. of the Arts, Dept. State Office Cultural Presentations, Nat. Endowment Arts.; bd. dirs. Arts Alliance, Karl Weigl Found., Diller-Quaile Sch. Music, US Com. for UNICEF, Manhattan Sch. Music, Theatre Devel. Fund, Children's Storefront; mem. adv. bd. Bloomingdale House of Music; bd. vis. artists Boston U.; bd. dirs., mem. exec. com. Carnegie Hall, Nat. Found. for Advancement in the Arts; bd. dirs. Chamber Music Soc. of Lincoln Ctr., NYC Housing Authority Orch., Ind. Sch. Orch., NYC Opera Co., Joy in Singing, Arts & Bus. Coun.; mem. Mayor's adv. commn. Cultural Affairs. Appeared as soloist: Leonard Bernstein's Jeremiah Symphony, Tanglewood, 1951, Virgil Thomson's Four Saints in Three Acts, NYC and Paris, 1952, NYC Light Opera Co., 1954; recitalist, also soloist with major symphonies on tours including ANTA-State Dept. tours, Europe, North Africa, Caribbean, Can., US, S.Am., Far East, S.Am. tour, 1968, Bellas Artes Opera, Mexico City, 1970; recital debut, Town Hall, NYC, 1958, ofcl. debuts, London, Berlin, 1958, formal opera debut, Teatro Colon, Buenos Aires, Argentina, 1964; US opera debut San Francisco Opera, 1966; NYC opera debut, 1973, Mini-Met. debut, 1973; Broadway debut in Treemonisha, 1975; opened new civic theaters in San Jose, Calif., and Regina, Sask., Can., concert hall, Lyndon Baines Johnson Libr., Austin, Tex., 1971; artist-in-residence, Phila. Opera Co.; appeared with Caramoor Music Festival, summer 1965, 71, Cin. May Festival, 1972, Santa Fe Opera, 1972, 75, Can. Opera Co., Winnipeg, Man., 1972, 77, Washington Opera Co., 1971, Tanglewood Festival, 1951, 52, 53, 67, 74, Oslo, The Hague, Montreal, Kansas City, Houston and Santa Fe operas, 1975, Saratoga Festival, 1975, Casals Festival, 1967, 68, 69, 76, Helsinki Festival, 1976, Marlboro Festival, 1967-74, numerous radio and TV performances, US, Can., Mex., Eng., Germany, Scandinavia; rec. artist, London, Vox, Capitol, Odeon-Pathe, Decca, Deutsche Grammophon, Columbia Records, RCA Victor records; represented US in Cultural Olympics, Mexico City, 1968. Recipient Marian Anderson award, 1953-54, Nat. Music League Mgmt. award, 1953, 52 St Am. Festival Duke Ellington Meml. award, 1989, Bowery award Bowery Bank, 1989, Harlem Sch. Arts award Harlem Sch. and Isaac Stern, 1990, Womans Day Celebration award St. Thomas Episcopal Ch., 1990, St. Thomas Ch. award St. Thomas Cath. Ch., 1990, Men's Day Celebration award St. Paul's Ch., 1990, Martell House of Segram award Avery Fisher Hall, 1990; named Best Singer of Season Critics' Circle, Argentina and Chile, 1959, Best Singer of Season Critics' Circle, Uruguay, 1961; Martha Baird Rockefeller Aid to Music grantee, 1953, 58; John Hay Whitney fellow, 1953-54; Ford Found. concert soloist grantee, 1963-64 Mem. NAACP, Urban League, Hartford Mus. Club (life), Am. Guild Mus. Artists, Actors Equity, AFTRA, Silvermine Guild Artists, Jeunesses Musicales, Gioventu Musicale, Student Sangverein Trondheim, Unitarian-Universalist Women's Fedn., Nat. Negro Musicians Assn. (life), Concert Artists Guild, Met. Opera Guild, Amherst Glee Club (hon. life), Union Coll. Glee Club (hon. life), Met. Mus. Art, Mus. Modern Art, Am. Mus. Natural Hist., Century Assn., Sigma Alpha Iota (hon.) Unitarian-Universalist. Clubs: Cosmopolitan, Second. Died June 22, 2009.

ALLEN, DAVID JAMES, lawyer; b. East Chicago, Ind. BS, Ind. U., 1957, MA, 1959, JD, 1965. Bar: Ind. 1965, U.S. Dist. Ct. (so. dist.) Ind. 1965, U.S. Ct. Appeals 1965, U.S. Tax Ct. 1965, U.S. Supreme Ct. 1965, U.S. Ct. Appeals (fed. and 7th cirs.) 1983. Of counsel Hagemier, Allen and Smith, Indpls., from 1975. Adminstrv. asst. Gov. of Ind. Mathew E. Welsh, 1961—65; counsel Ind. Gov. Roger D. Branigin, 1965—69; asst. to Gov. Edgar D. Whitcomb, 1969; univ. counsel Ind. State U., Terre Haute, 1969—70; legis. counsel Ind. Gov. Evan Bayh, 1989—90; spl. counsel Gov. Frank O'Bannon State of Ind., 1999—2002; mem. Spl. Commn. on Ind. Exec. Reorgn., 1967—69; commr. Ind. Utility Regulatory Commn., 1970—75; mem. Ind. Law Enforcement Acad. Bd. and Adv. Coun., 1968—85, Ind. State Police Bd., 1968—2008; commr. for revision Ind. Commn. Recommend Changes Ind. Legis. Process, 1990—2002; commr. Ind. Criminal Code Revision Study Commn., 1998—2002; nat. judge adv. Acacia Frat., 1980—86, 1992—2002, internat. pres., from 2002; chief counsel Ind. Ho. Reps., 1975—76, spl. counsel, 1979—89, Ind. Senate, 1990—97; adj. prof. pub. law Sch. Pub. and Environ. Affairs, Ind. U., Bloomington, from 1976. Author: (book) New Governor in Indiana: Transition of Executive Power, 1965. Mem.: ABA, Indpls. Bar Assn., Ind. State Bar Assn. (criminal justice law exec. com. 1966—72, mem. adminstrv. law com. 1968—77, chmn. adminstrv. law com. 1973—76, mem. law sch. liaison com. 1977—78). Home: Munster, Ind. Died Oct. 2, 2009.

ALLEN, GERALD STUART, civil engineer; b. Benton, Ark., Sept. 15, 1938; s. Clarence J. and Geneva S. (Coburn) A.; m. Joyce E. Thomas, June 1, 1959; 1 child, Anthony S. BSCE, U. Ark., 1962. Registered profl. engr. Ark., Fla., Mo., Pa., Ohio, Mo., Mich., India; diplomate Am. Acad. of Envrion. Engrs. Mgr., engr. Little Rock (Ark.) Mcpl. Water Works, 1983-86; sr. v.p. engring. and water resources Pa. Water and Gas, Wilkes Barre, 1986-88; v.p. engring. Avatar Utilities Inc., Coral Gables, Fla., 1988-90, exec. v.p., 1990-91, exec. v.p., COO Sarasota and Coral Gables, Fla., 1991-96, pres., CEO Sarasota, from 1996. Asst. mgr. engr. Little Rock Mcpl. Water Works, 1979-83, chief engr., 1971-77; v.p., ptnr. Hodges, Vines, Fox, Allen and Assn., Little Rock, 1977-79; regional engr. Ductile Iron Pipe Rsch. Assn., Oak Brook, Ill., 1970-71. Mem. Ark. State Bd. of Health, Little Rock, 1986. Col. U.S. Army Res., 1963-86. Recipient Outstanding Engr. of Yr. Ark. Soc. of Profl. Engrs., 1974, 85, Water Mgr. of Yr. Ark. Water Works and Pollution Control Assn., 1985. Mem. NSPE, Water Environ. Fedn., Fla. Engring. Soc., Am. Water Works Assn. (hon., bd. dirs. 1993—, other offices). Home: Bradenton, Fla. Died Apr. 26, 2008.

ALLES, RODNEY NEAL, SR., information management executive; b. Orleans, Nebr., Aug. 24, 1950; s. Neal Stanley and Evelyn Dorothy (Zelske) A.; m. Diana Kay Koenig, Nov. 25, 1978; children: Rodney Neal Jr., Jennifer E., Victoria E. BS in Indsl. Engring., U. Okla., 1973, MBA, 1977, PhD in Info. Systems, 1998. Asst. to the pres. Skytop Brewster Co., Inc., Houston, 1978-79, mgr. planning and mfg., 1979-83; v.p. adminstrn. Internat. Meter Co. Inc., Arkansas City, Kans., 1983-84, v.p., 1984-85; dir. info. mgmt. McAlester (Okla.) Army Ammunition Plant, 1987-96; chief info. sys. divsn. S.E. Regional Civilian Pers. Ops. Ctr., Ft. Benning, Ga., from 1996. Lt. USN, 1973-76. Mem. Am. Inst. Indsl. Engrs., Fed. Info. Processing Coun., Fed. Mgrs. Assn., U.S. Golf Assn., Okla. Golf Assn., Loyal Knight of Old Trusty, U. Okla. Alumni Assn. (alumni coun. Coll. Bus. Adminstrn.), Rotary Internat., McAlester Country Club, Omicron Delta Kappa, Tau Beta Pi, Sigma Tau, Alpha Pi Mu. Democrat. Lutheran. Avocation: golf. Home: Phenix City, Ala. Died July 18, 2007.

ALLISON, IRA SHIMMIN, geologist, educator; b. Gardner, Ill. s. John William and Eva Catherine (Shimmin) Allison; children: Margaret Allison Clauss, David Elmer, Frances Allison Sunderland. AB, Hanover Coll., 1917; postgrad., U. Chgo., 1920; PhD, U. Minn., 1924. From instr. to asst. prof. U. Minn., Mpls., 1920—28; instr. U. Chgo., summers, 1922, 1923; prof. geologi Oreg. State U., Corvallis, 1928—65, chmn. dept. geology, 1950—60. Author: Geology: The Science of a Changing Earth, 7th edit., 1980; contbr. numerous articles on geology of Pacific N.W. to profl. jours. Sgt. med. dept. US Army, 1917—19. Fellow: AAAS, Geol. Soc. Am.; mem.: AAUP, AIME, Sigma Gamma Epsilon, Phi Kappa Phi, Sigma Xi. Republican. Presbyterian. Home: Gresham, Oreg. Died May 31, 1990.

ALLISON, LYNN DEE, university program administrator, consultant; b. Long Beach, Calif., July 22, 1948; d. Herbert Jesse and Jean Mavis (Ellis) Neff; m. Michael Joseph Allison, Dec. 16, 1967 (div. Oct. 1978); children: Leland Michael, William Joseph. AA, Long Beach City Coll., Calif., 1976; BA, Calif. State U., Long Beach, 1986, MPA, 1992. Adminstrv. asst. to gen. ptnr. Little & Gray, Inc., Irvine, Calif., 1978-82; bookkeeping cons. Trafalgar Tours West, Inc., Irvine, Calif., 1982-83; adminstrv. asst. Ctr. Multicultural/Multilingual Rsch. U. So. Calif., LA, 1986; adminstrv. coord. for grad. nursing Calif. State U., Long Beach, 1985-87, adminstrv. asst. to the dean Sch. Bus. Adminstrn., 1987-89, acting faculty and staff coord. Sch. Bus. Adminstrn., 1989-92, fiscal officer Ocean Studies Inst., from 1992. Mem. ASPA, Golden Key Honor Soc., Phi Kappa Phi. Avocations: reading, cooking, film. Home: Long Beach, Calif. Died Apr. 4, 2008.

ALLUMS, RONALD L., environmental consulting executive; b. Leakesville, Miss., Dec. 24, 1960; s. Donald L. and Jamie H. Allums; m. Robbin Lowery, Sept. 24, 1983; children: Clare, Carmen. BS in Biol. Engring., Miss. State U., 1982. Engr.-in-tng. Quality control lab. mgr. Rainbo Foods, Inc., 1982-83; field engr., project mgr. Environ. Protection Sys., Jackson, Miss., 1983-85, v.p., br. mgr. Nashville, 1986-88; sr. v.p. Kaselaan & D'Angelo Assocs., Haddon Heights, N.J., 1988-92; pres. CRC Environ., Inc., Metairie, La., 1992, CRC Environ. Risk Mgmt., Inc., Ft. Worth, from 1992. Contbr. articles to profl. jours. and convs. Mem. City Club, Mira Vista Country Club. Baptist. Avocations: racquetball, golf, reading, music, travel. Home: Arlington, Tex. Died Apr. 8, 2008.

ALTER, JOANNE HAMMERMAN, retired city commissioner; b. Chgo., July 3, 1927; d. Sol and Celia (Kagen) Hammerman; m. James M. Alter, May 17, 1952; children: Jennifer Alter Warden, Jonathan, Elizabeth, Harrison. BA in Polit. Sci. & Economics cum laude, Mt. Holyoke Coll., 1949. Mem. Met. Water Reclamation Dist., Chgo., 1972—90; founder, chmn. Working in the Schools, 1993—2003. Mem. adv. coun. Ill. Dept. Local Govtl. Affairs, Chgo., 1973-76; mem. Internat. Joint Commn. on Lake Levels, 1977-81; bd. dirs. Coun. Govs. Cook County, Chgo., 1978-80; mem. Northeastern Ill. Planning Commn., Chgo. Mem. woman's bd. Art Inst. Chgo.; bd. trustees Mt. Holyoke Coll., 1980-85; former trustee YWCA Met. Chgo., Augustana Luth. Gen. Hosp., Jane Addams Ctr., Hull House Assn., Internat. Visitors Ctr.; former mem. women's bd. Children's Meml. Hosp.; committeewoman Dem. Nat. Com., 1980-89; del. Dem. Nat. Conv., 1984, 88; founder, co-convenor Ill. Dem. Women's Caucus; mem. Friends Chicago River, Friends of Park, Operation Lakewatch, also other local and nat. environ. groups. Recipient Leadership award YWCA Met. Chgo., 1975, award Operation Lakewatch, 1982, Thomas Jefferson award for Outstanding Cmty. Svc., Amistad award, Nat. Women's Leadership Coun. award; named Protedtor of Environment, Audobon Soc., 1979; named to Chgo. Women Hall of Fame, City of Chgo., 1988. Mem. Water Pollution Control Fedn., Am. Pub. Works Assn., Am. Met. Sewerage Assn., Audubon Soc. (Protector of Environ. award 1979), LWV, ACLU, NAACP, Sierra Club, Lake Michigan Fedn., Midwest Women's Ctr., Arts Club. Democrat. Jewish. Home: Chicago, Ill. Died Nov. 9, 2008.

ALTHEIMER, EDITH L., social worker; b. Crossett, AR, Dec. 5, 1942; d. Leon and Daisy (Sims) Lowe; m. Milton Green, Aug. 30, 1968 (div. Aug. 1982); 1 child, Karen G. Irving; m. Berton Corbin Altheimer, May 19, 1983. BA, Lincoln U., 1962; MSW, Washington U., St. Louis, 1964; PhD, Century U., Albuquerque, 1996. Lic. cert. social worker. Psychiatric social worker St. Louis State Hosp., 1964-1969; instr. Washington U., St. Louis, 1969-70; asst. prof. State Cmty. Coll., E. St. Louis, IL, 1970-77; program mgr. Sr. Health Day Care, Sacramento, 1978-81; coord. adult day health VA Med. Ctr., Little Rock, from 1984, supr. cmty. svc. assoc. chap., from 1984, chief, social work svc., from 1984. Pres., mem. adv. bd. 2nd Genesis, 1992-97, Divsn. Mental Health, Little Rock, 1994-97; mem. adv. bd. CareLinks, Little Rock, 1994—. Contbr. article to profl. jour. Grantee Levi Strauss Found., Little Rock, Ark., 1993, Dept. Veteran Affairs, Washington, DC, 1992, 93, Ark. Dept. Health, 1991, 95, 96, Divsn. Substance Abuse, Little Rock, Ark., 1994. Co-chair Ark. Dept. Health Cmty. Planning (certificate, 1996); mem. Nat. Assn. Social Workers (nominee Social Worker of Yr., 1994), Women's Missionary Soc. (com. chair, 1995—, recipient 2d Mile Plaque, 1999), Little Rock, Ark. Chamber of Commerce women/minorities bus. coun., Delta Sigma Theta Sorority (social action com. chair, coord. 1996—). African Methodist Episcopalian. Avocations: music, writing and directing original works. Home: Little Rock, Ark. Died Mar. 17, 2008.

AMENDOLA, JOSEPH, retired academic administrator, hotel and recreational facility consultant; b. New Haven, Conn., Oct. 19, 1920; s. Joseph and Caroline (Lucibello) A.; m. Marjorie Doreen Meatyard, Dec. 29, 1945; children: Joseph Brian, Jeanette Marjorie. AA, U. Mass., 1970; BS, U. New Haven, 1972. Cert. pastry chef, cert. educator. Apprentice Lucibellos Pastry Shop, New Haven, 1929-39; bakery supr. Gilberts Bakery, New Haven, 1939-42; instr. Conn. Bd. Edn., New Haven, 1946-47; baking instr. Culinary Inst. Am., New Haven, 1947-62, dean students, 1962-65, v.p. student affairs, 1965-72, v.p. ops. Hyde Park, N.Y., 1972-78, sr. v.p. acting pres., 1978-87, ret., 1987; v.p. Fessell Internat., Orlando, Fla., from 1987. Internat. bakery cons., 1965-91; dir. devel. Culinary Inst. Am., Hyde Park, 1980-87; dir. Diamond Foods, San Mateo, Calif., 1986—; founder Chef and Child, Hyde Park, 1987. Author: Bakers Manual, 1960, Understanding Baking, 1961, Ice Carving Made Easy, 1962, Professional Baking, 1965; contbr. articles to profl. jours. Evaluator mil. food svcs. world wide, 1975-83. Sgt. USAF, 1942-46. Named to the Am. Culinary Fedn. Hall of Fame, 1992. Mem. Am. Culinary Fedn. (scholarsip chmn. 1978-88, Educator of Yr. 1978), Am. Soc. Bakery Engring., Cen. Fla. Chefs Assn., Mid Hudson Chefs Assn. (scholarship chmn. 1972-86), Golden Toque (dir. 1982-86), Chaine De Rottisseure (Balli pres. 1980—), Escoffier Soc. (chpt. pres. 1968-70, Careme medal 1986). Roman Catholic. Avocations: golf, bowling, swimming. Home: Orlando, Fla. Died Jan. 23, 2008.

AMES, WILLIAM FRANCIS, mathematician, educator; b. Brandon, Man., Can., Dec. 8, 1926; s. Paul Main and Della Johanna (Hebel) A.; m. Theresa Danielson, May 29, 1951; children: Karen Anne, Susan Lynn, Pamela Margaret. MS, U. Wis., 1950. Instr. U. Wis., Racine, 1953-55; sr. engr. DuPont Co., Wilmington, Del., 1955-59; prof. U. Del., Newark, 1959-67, U. Iowa, Iowa City, 1967-75, Ga. Inst. Tech., Atlanta, from 1975, Regents prof., 1980-91, prof. emeritus, from 1991, dir., 1981-87; research prof. U. Ga., Athens, 1977-79. Cons. in field. Author: Nonlinear Partial Differential Equations in Engineering, Vol. I, 1965, Vol. II, 1972, Nonlinear Ordinary Differential Equations in Transport Processes, 1968, Numerical Methods for Partial Differential Equations, 1970, 77, 92, Nonlinear Boundary Value Problems in Science and Engineering, 1989; book and jour. editor for Academic Press; editor 9 books.; contbr. articles to profl. jours. Served with USNR, 1944-46, 51-52. NSF faculty fellow, 1963-64, NATO sr. fellow, 1972-73; grantee, 1964-67, 76-79, 79-81, 83-85, 89-91, 92-95, NBS grantee, 1967-71, USPHS grantee, 1961-63, EPA grantee, 1978-81, U.S. Army grantee, 1968-75, 81-87; Humboldt sr. scientist, 1974-75. Mem.: Sigma Xi, Tau Beta Pi, Phi Beta Kappa. Home: Atlanta, Ga. Died Aug. 9, 2009.

AMMAR, RAYMOND GEORGE, physicist, researcher; b. Kingston, Jamaica, July 15, 1932; arrived in US, 1950, naturalized, 1965; s. Elias George and Nellie (Khaleel) A.; m. Carroll Ikerd, June 17, 1961 (dec. 2004); children: Elizabeth, Robert (dec.), David. AB, Harvard U., 1953;

PhD, U. Chgo., 1959. Rsch. assoc. Enrico Fermi Inst., U. Chgo., 1959-60; asst. prof. physics Northwestern U., Evanston, Ill., 1960-64, assoc. prof., 1964-69; prof. physics U. Kans., Lawrence, from 1969, chmn. dept. physics and astronomy, 1989—2003; (on sabbatical leave Fermilab and Deutsches Elektronen Synchrotron, 1984-85). Cons. Argonne (Ill.) Nat. Lab., 1965-69, vis. scientist, 1971-72; vis. scientist Fermilab, Batavia, Ill., summers 1976-81, Deutsches Elektronen Synchroton, Hamburg, Germany, summers 1982-88, lab. of nuclear studies Cornell U., summers 1989-98; project dir. NSF grant for rsch. in high energy physics, 1962-2001. Contbr. articles to sci. jours. Fellow Am. Phys. Soc.; mem. AAUP. Home: Lawrence, Kans. Died June 21, 2009.

AMMERMAN, DAN SHERIDAN, communications executive; b. Tyrone, Pa., June 10, 1932; s. Eugene Harry and Helen L. (Morrow) Ammerman; m. Mary T. Graca, Jan. 10, 1953; children: Terri L., Mark Alan. Broadcast journalist Sta. WVAM, Altoona, Pa., 1953—59, Sta. KGNC-AM-TV, Amarillo, Tex., 1959—66, Sta. KTRH, Houston, 1966—67; contbg. corr. CBS Radio Network, 1967—68; anchorman KTRK-TV, Houston, 1968—72; with ABC Radio Network, 1972—73; founder, CEO The Ammerman Experience, Houston, 1973, Ammerman Broadcasting. Nat. speaker in field. Actor: (TV appearances) Dallas (4 episodes), 1978—89; (TV films) Red Alert, 1977, The Sky's No Limit, 1984, The Jesse Owens Story, 1984, Guilty of Innocence: The Lenell Geter Story, 1987, Pancho Barnes, 1988, The Fulfillment of Mary Gray, 1989, Margaret Bourke-White, 1989, A Taste for Killing, 1992. Served to 2d lt. US Army, 1947—51, Korea. Named Big Bro. of Yr., Amarillo, 1965. Mem.: Internat. Platform Speakers Assn., Pub. Rels.s Soc. Am., Sugar Creek Country (Houston), Press. Republican. Roman Catholic. Home: Stafford, Tex. Died May 11, 2009.

AMTHOR, CARL BURLEIGH, business company executive; b. Port Washington, NY, May 16, 1934; s. Franklin Ryder and Alma Loretta (Byerly) A.; m. Gara Virginia Grosse, Aug. 12, 1961 (div. Apr. 1986); children: Lindsay Gara, Geoffrey Ryder; m. Jacqueline Coy Hamilton, Nov. 14, 1986. BS, Yale U., 1955; MBA, Harvard U., 1963. With IBM Corp., Poughkeepsie and White Plains, N.Y., 1958-65; corp. contr. Cummins Engine Co., Columbus, Ind., 1965-67; v.p., treas. Ctr. for Naval Analyses, Arlington, Va., 1967-72; v.p. mktg. Louis Harris & Assocs., NYC, 1972-74; v.p. adminstrn., contr., treas. Associated Universities, Inc., Washington, 1974-85; pres. The Pace Group, Inc., McLean, Va., 1985-87; CFO AAAS, Washington, 1987—97. Sr. warden St. Francis Episcopal Ch., Great Falls, Va., 1985-87. Served with U.S. Army, 1956-58. Baker scholar Harvard Bus. Sch., Cambridge, Mass., 1962. Republican. Avocations: tennis, skiing, jogging, sailing, woodworking. Home: Great Falls, Va. Died Feb. 22, 2009.

AMUNDSON, JUDITH LOUISE ALLISON, psychologist; b. Wagoner, Okla., Dec. 12, 1921; d. William Mosby and Alberta Alma (Abbott) Allison; m. Paul E. Potts, June 1942 (div. July 1959); 1 child, Alberta Gay Potts; m. Theodore Arden Amundson, June 11, 1960. BS, Pittsburg State Coll., 1959; MEd, Prairie View A&M U., 1974; PhD, Tex. A&M U., 1982. Tchr., Kans., 1940s-50s, Colo., 1959-60, N.Mex., 1967-68; grad. asst. Tex. A&M U., College Station, 1975-76; psychology instr., counselor Winona (Minn.) State U., 1977-79; asst. prof. psychology St. Augustine's Coll., Raleigh, N.C., 1984-90; pvt. practice psychologist Raleigh, from 1984. Vol. Rep. Party, Denver, 1962-67, Dorothea Dix State Hosp., Raleigh, 1983-85, Raleigh Women's Ctr., 1983—. Mem. APA, Psi Chi, Kappa Delta Pi. Avocations: poetry, camping, hiking, golf. Died Dec. 21, 2007.

ANDERSON, CHARLES ARTHUR, retired science administrator; b. Columbus, Ohio, Nov. 14, 1917; s. Arthur E. and Huldah (Peterson) A.; m. Elizabeth Rushforth, Oct. 27, 1942; children: Peter C., Stephen E., Julia E. AB, U. Calif., Berkeley, 1938; MBA, Grad. Sch. Bus. Adminstrn., Harvard U., 1940; LHD, Colby Coll., 1975. Asst. prof. Grad. Sch. Bus. Adminstrn., Harvard U., Boston, 1945-48; v.p. Magna Power Tool Corp., Menlo Park, Calif., 1948-58; prof., asso. dean Stanford Grad. Sch. Bus., 1959-61; v.p. Kern County Land Co., San Francisco, 1961-64; pres. Walker Mfg. Co., Racine, Wis., 1964-66, J.I. Case Co., Racine, 1966-68; pres., chief exec. officer SRI Internat., Menlo Park, 1968-79. Bd. dirs. KRI Internat., Japan, Eaton Corp., Conoco, Owens-Corning Fiberglas, NCR, Boise Cascade, Saga; mem. adv. council Bus. Sch., Stanford, 1966-72, 74-79; mem. industry adv. council Dept. Def., 1971-73 Author (with Anthony) The New Corporate Director. Mem. Menlo Park Planning Commn. and City Coun., 1955-61, Govs. Commn. on Reorgn. Wis. State Govt., 1965-67; bd. dirs. Calif. State C. of C., 1972-77, Internat. House, U. Calif., Berkeley, 1979-90; bd. dirs. Lucile Salter Packard Children's Hosp., Stanford, 1979-95, chmn., 1992-94. With USNR, 1941-45. Recipient Exceptional Service award USAF, 1965 Mem. Palo Alto Club, Pacific-Union Club, Menlo Country Club. Presbyterian. Died Apr. 17, 2009.

ANDERSON, EDGAR WILLIAM, music educator; b. Galveston, Tex., Aug. 1, 1931; s. Edgar William Sr. and Genevieve George (Golden) A.; m. Connie Sones, Feb. 19, 1960; children: Kirk, April, Lynlee. BS, Sam Houston State U., 1953, MA, 1958. Dir. bands Blinn Coll., Brenham, Tex., 1959-61, St. Thomas High Sch., Houston, 1961-70; instr. music Houston Ind. Sch. Dist., 1970-73; chmn. music Alvin (Tex.) C.C., 1973-86, instr. music, 1986—2009. Co-leader The Andersons Entertainment Groups, Houston, 1960-2009 Composer jazz ensemble, 1980, 90, TV show theme, 1990. With U.S. Army, 1953-55. Mem. Tex. Music Educators Assn., Tex. Faculty Assn., Houston Profl. Musicians Assn. Roman Catholic. Avocations: boating, gardening, chess. Home: Seabrook, Tex. Died Apr. 1, 2009.

ANDERSON, FRANCES, critical care nurse; b. Lancaster, SC, Nov. 25, 1946; d. Frank J. and Annie Rae (Rollins) Taylor; m. Robert Wayne Anderson, June 21, 1968; children: Jennifer Renee, Cynthia Diann. Diploma, Spartanburg Hosp. Sch. Nursing, Spartanburg, SC, 1969. Cert. critical care nurse, advanced cardiac life support instr. Staff nurse Ononee Meml. Hosp., Seneca, S.C.; pvt. duty nruse in home Maxton, N.C.; staff nurse Scotland Meml. Hosp., Laurinbang, N.C.; sr. staff nurse, transport nurse Allen Bennett Meml. Hosp., Greer, S.C. Mem. AACN. Home: Auburn, Ala. Died Jan. 27, 2008.

ANDERSON, GAIL MARIE, retired librarian; b. St. Cloud, Minn., Apr. 26, 1945; d. George Elroy Carpenter and Blanche Doris (Flam) Carpenter Neel; m. Gordon Alexander Anderson, Aug. 24, 1971. BS, St. Cloud State U., 1969. Cert. libr. Minn., cert. elem. tchr. Minn. Libr. Cloquet Pub. Sch., Minn., 1969—70; jr. high media ctr. dir. Roseville Pub. Sch., Minn., 1970—78; asst. program dir., group dir. Afton Alps Ski Sch., 1973—82; libr. asst. U. Minn. Sch. Dentistry, Mpls., 1979—86; sch. libr. Desert Valley Sch., Bullhead City, Ariz., 1986—2006. Sec. Minn. Christian Youth Coun., Mpls., 1960—63; mem. Minn. Ednl. Media Orgn. Methodist. Mem.: Pheasants Forever, Jobs Daus., Bullhead City Tchrs. Union. Home: Bullhead City, Ariz. Deceased.

ANDERSON, GERALDINE LOUISE, medical researcher; d. George M. and Viola Julia-Mary (Abel) Havrilla; m. Henry Clifford Anderson, May 21, 1966; children: Bruce Henry, Julie Lynne. BS in Med. Tech., U. Minn., Mpls., 1963. Cert. med. technologist Am. Soc. Clin. Pathology, 1963, clin. lab. scientist Nat. Cert. Assn., 1965, clin. rsch. assoc. Assn. Clin. Rsch. Profls., 1998. Med. technologist Swedish Hosp., Mpls., 1963-68; hematology supr. lab. Glenwood Hills Hosp., Golden Valley, Minn., 1968-70; assoc. scientist pediats. U. Minn. Hosps., Mpls., 1970-74; instr. health occupations, med. lab. asst. Suburban Hennepin County Area Vocat. Tech. Ctr., Brooklyn Park, Minn., 1974-81, 92-95, St. Paul Tech. Vocat. Inst., Brooklyn Park, 1978-81; rsch. med. technologist Miller Hosp., St. Paul, 1975-78; rsch. assoc. Children's and United Hosps., St. Paul, 1979-88; sr. lab. analyst Cascade Med. Inc., Eden Prairie, Minn., 1989-90; lab. mgr. VAMC, Mpls., 1990; tech. support scientist INCSTAR Corp., Stillwater, Minn., 1990-94; mem. network staff Clin. Design Group, Chgo., 1992-98; regulatory affairs product analysis coord. Medtronic Neurol., Mpls., 1995; quality assurance documentation coord. Lectec Corp., Minnetonka, Minn., 1995; clin. rsch. monitor Eli Lilly Rsch. Labs., Indpls., 1995-98; sr. clin. rsch. assoc. Covance, Inc., Princeton, NJ, 1998-99. Sr. clin. rsch. assoc. Parexel Internat., Inc., Chgo., 1999—2000; clin. rsch. assoc. AAI Internat., Boston, 2000—01; regional clin. rsch. assoc. Wyeth, Collegeville, Pa., 2001—02; health occupations adv. com. Hennepin Tech. Ctrs., 1975—90, chairperson, 1978—79; mem. hematology slide edn. rev. bd. Am. Soc. Hematology, 1977—96; mem. flow cytometry and clin. chemistry quality controll subcoms. Nat. Com. for Clin. Lab. Stds., 1988—92; cons. FCM Specialists, 1989—99, from 2002, Clin. Design Group, 1992—98; mem. rev. bd. Clin. Lab. Sci., 1990—91, The Learning Laboratorian Series, 1991; presenter in field. Contbr. articles to profl. jours. Charter orgns. rep. Viking coun. Boy Scouts Am., 1988—90; resource person lab. careers Robbinsdale (Minn.) Sch. Dist., 1970—79; active Women Scientists Spkrs. Bur., 1989—92, Helping Hands, 2002—06, Med. Lab. Tech. Polit. Action Com., 1978—99; observer UN 4th World Conf. on Women, Beijing, 1995; del. Crest View Home Assn., 1981—2009; sci. and math. subcom. Minn. High Tech. Coun., 1983—88; bd. dirs. Big Pine Lake Property Owners, 1996—2009. Recipient Svc. awards and honors, Omicron Sigma. Mem.: NAFE, AAUW, AAAS, Grad. Women in Sci., Inc., Great Lakes Internat. Flow Cytometry Assn. (charter mem. 1992), Internat. Soc. Analytical Cytology, Am. Soc. Hematology, Minn. Med. Tech. Alumni, World Future Soc., Assn. Women in Sci., Twin Cities Hosp. Assn. (spkrs. bur. 1968—70), Am. Soc. Clin. Lab. Sci. (del. to ann. meetings from 1972, chmn. hematology sci. assembly 1977—79, nomination com. 1979—81, bd. dirs. 1986—88), Am. Soc. Profl. and Exec. Women, Minn. Soc. Med. Tech. (sec. 1969—71), Minn. Emerging Med. Orgns., Nat. Assn. Women Cons., Inc., Soc. Tech. Comm., Assn. Clin. Rsch. Profls. (cert. clin. rsch. assoc. from 1998), Women in Comm., Inc., Am. Med. Writers Assn., Nat. Ch. Libr. Assn., Alpha Mu Tau, Sigma Delta Epsilon (corr. sec. XI chpt. 1980—82, pres. 1982—84, nat. membership com. 1990—92, nat. nominations chair 1991—92, nat. v.p. 1992—93, nat. pres.-elect 1993—94, nat. pres. 1994—95, bd. dirs. 1996—2001, chmn. bd. dirs. 2000—01). Avocations: photography, travel, reading. Died Sept. 23, 2009.

ANDERSON, LUISE GRACE, geriatrics nurse; b. Banes, Cuba, Oct. 26, 1921; d. Theophilus and Adeline (Hutchins) Hibbert; m. Kearne Anderson, Jan. 25, 1964. Diploma, Lambeth and Miller Gen. Hosps., London, 1956; student in midwifery, Lewisham Gen. Hosp., London, 1957; diploma, Queens Inst. Dist. Nursing, London; BS, St. Joseph's Coll., Bklyn., 1981. Cert. in community health, health adminstrn. Staff nurse Kew Gardens (N.Y.) Gen. Hosp., 1972-74, Coler Meml. Hosp., NYC, 1974-77, head nurse, from 1977. Staff nurse per diem, Bronx, N.Y., 1981—. Mem. N.Y. State Nurses Assn. Died June 24, 2008.

ANDERSON, RICHARD ROY, insurance company executive; b. Salt Lake City, May 17, 1941; s. Roy Lewis and Gwen (Price) A.; m. Heather Graff, Mar. 16, 1964; children: Shannon, Elizabeth, Andy, David, Ginny, Robert. BS, U. Utah, 1966. CLU, ChFC. Agt. Continental Life & Accident Ins. Co., Boise, Idaho, 1966-68; field underwriter Mutual of N.Y. Ins. Co., Boise, 1968-72; field adminstr. The Life Underwriting Tng. Coun., Washington, 1972-73; agy. mgr. Mutual of N.Y. Ins. Co., Santa Barbara, Calif., 1973-80; gen. agt. Mutual Trust Life Ins. Co., Provo, Utah, 1981-83; agy. dir. Beneficial Life Ins. Co., Salt Lake City, 1983-87, agy. mgr., from 1987. Mem. Maud May Babcock Reading Arts Soc. (pres. 1990-93), Salt Lake City Life Underwriters Assn. Mem. Ch. of Jesus Christ of LDS. Home: Orem, Utah. Died Jan. 19, 2008.

ANDERSON, ROBERT ARTHUR, renal technologist; b. Waterloo, Iowa, Sept. 2, 1945; s. Albert and Willia Marie (Sallis) A. AAS, City Colls. Chgo., 1974. Dialysis tech. U. Ill. Hosp., Chgo., 1970-74, Cathedral Shelter Dialysis, Chgo., 1974-76, Doctors Dialysis, LA, 1977-78, Mobile Dialysis Svc., Compton, Calif., 1978-81; Dialysis tech. Cedars Sinai Hosp., LA, 1981-86, Home Intensive Care, Carson, Calif., from 1987; dialysis tech. Mobile Dialysis Svc., Compton, from 1986. Chief technician Home Intensive Care, Burbank, Calif., 1987—. Mem. Am. Assn. Nephrologist Nurses and Technicians. Democrat. Methodist. Avocations: photography, reading, tennis. Home: Los Angeles, Calif. Died Feb. 20, 2008.

ANDERSON, ROBERT LYTLE, retired chemist; b. Mayfield, Ky., Feb. 13, 1927; s. Elmer A. and Hylah (Stokes) A. BS in Indsl. Chemistry, U. Ky., 1948. Chemist R&D Dept., Union Carbide Corp., South Charleston, W.Va., 1948-65, group leader, 1966-83, specification specialist, 1983-85, ret., 1985, cons., 1989-91. Author: Practical Statistics for Analytical Chemists, 1987. Instr. Am. Assn. Ret. Persons 55 Alive/Mature Driving Program, Washington, 1987—. Mem. ASTM (chmn. E-15 com. 1976-79, membership sec. 1992—, Award of Merit and Hon. fellow 1976, Award of Appreciation 1979, Award for Outstanding Svc. 1990). Avocations: photography, travel, music, computers. Home: Saint Albans, W.Va. Died June 19, 2008.

ANDERSON, ROBERT WOODRUFF, playwright, novelist, screenwriter; b. NYC, Apr. 28, 1917; s. James Hewston and Myra Esther (Grigg) A.; m. Phyllis Stohl, June 24, 1940 (dec. 1956); m. Teresa Wright, Dec. 11, 1959 (div. 1978). AB magna cum laude, Harvard U., 1939, MA, 1940. Tchr. playwriting Am. Theatre Wing, 1946-50; writer for radio and TV, 1947-53; ind. playwright, author, screenwriter, 1951—2009; mem. Playwrights Co., 1953-60; faculty Salzburg Seminar in Am. Studies, 1968, Iowa Writers Workshop, 1976. Writer: (plays) Come Marching Home, 1946, Love Revisited, 1951, Tea and Sympathy, 1953, All Summer Long, 1955, Silent Night, Lonely Night, 1959, You Know I Can't Hear You When the Water's Running, 1967, I Never Sang for My Father, 1968, Solitaire/Double Solitaire, 1971, Absolute Strangers, 1991, The Last Act Is A Solo (Ace award 1991), 1991; screenwriter: (films) Tea and Sympathy, 1956, Until They Sail, 1957, The Nun's Story, 1959, The Days Between, 1965, The Sand Pebbles, 1966, I Never Sang for My Father, 1970 (Writers Guild Am. award for best screenplay), Free and Clear, 1983, The Kissing Was Always the Best, 1985; (TV drama) The Patricia Neal Story, 1979, Absolute Strangers, 1991;(novels) After, 1973, Getting Up and Going Home, 1978; co-editor: (six vol. set) Elements of Literature, 1988. Served to lt. USNR, 1942-46. Recipient 1st prize for Come Marching Home Army-Navy Playwriting Contest for servicemen overseas, 1945, William Inge Lifetime Achievement award 1985; named to Theater Hall of Fame, 1980; honoree Conn. Commn. on the Arts, 1992. Mem. Dramatists Guild Coun. (past pres.), New Dramatists Com. (past pres.), Harvard Club (N.Y.C.). Died Feb. 9, 2009.

ANDREWS, ERIC EDWIN, construction inspector; b. Windsor, Colo., June 27, 1936; s. Nathan Edwin and Ellen Margaret (Samson) A.; m. Lura May Robertson, July 19, 1969. Distbn. engr. assoc. Los Angeles County Engrs., 1961-78; sr. constrn. inspector Theodore Barry and Assocs., Los Angeles, 1979-84, Dennis Lykins and Assocs., Los Angeles, 1984-85; quality control engr. Crown Contracting Inc., Lemon Grove, Calif., from 1985. Tchr. uniform bldg. codes IUSD, Ingelwood, Calif., 1975-77. Served with USAF, 1953-57. Mem. Internat. Conf. Bldg. Officials (cert.), Nat. Rifle Assn., Am. Legion, VFW. Republican. Avocations: shooting, fishing, leatherwork. Home: Lancaster, Calif. Died Feb. 25, 2008.

ANDREWS, GLENN C., pharmaceutical company executive; b. Lebanon, Tenn., Sept. 5, 1950; s. Claude A. and Alma Lee (Qualls) A.; m. Charlotte Suzanne White, Dec. 2, 1970; children: Jonathan, Kathleen. BS, U. Tenn., 1974, MBA, 1977. Chartered fin. analyst. Fin. analyst Huyck Corp., Wake Forest, N.C., 1978-79, supr. budget and forecasting, 1979-80, corp. planning analyst, 1980-81; internat. fin. analyst Cooper Industries, inc., Houston, 1981-82, mgr. budget and performance reporting, 1982-84; mgr. fin. planning Burroughs Wellcome Co., Raleigh, N.C., 1984-87, asst. to v.p. fin., chief fin. officer, 1987-88, dir. bus. analysis, 1988-90, dir. bus. analysis and planning, 1990-92; treas., from 1992. Bd. dirs. Wake County Ednl. Advancement

Com., 1992—; bd. dirs. mem. exec. com. Jr. Achievement of N.C. Mem. Inst. Chartered Fin. Analysts, N.C. Soc. Fin. Analysts (v.p., bd. dirs. 1990-92, pres. 1992—), Planning Forum. Methodist. Home: Raleigh, NC. Died Nov. 11, 2007.

ANDREWS, ROBERT PARKER, aerospace executive; b. Camden, Ala., June 25, 1923; s. Leon Parker and Reba (Hart) A.; m. Selma Louise Reese, Jan. 26, 1946; children: Rebecca Allyn, Reese Parker, Jennifer Dianne. BS in Aero. Engring., Auburn U., 1947. Registered profl. engr., Tex.; cert. mgr. Engring. draftsman Consolidated-Vultee Aircraft, Ft. Worth, 1947, aerodynamicist; flight test engr. Convair, Ft. Worth, asst. project engr., project engr., mgr. flight test; engring. program mgr. Gen. Dynamics, Ft. Worth. Mem. CAP, Ft. Worth. 2d lt. field arty. U.S. Army, 1942-43; sr. Army Aviator; col. Res. Decorated Silver Star. Mem. AIAA (chmn. flight test tech. com. 1979-80), Soc. Flight Test Engrs., Nat. Mgmt. Assn. (pres. Ft. Worth chpt. 1981-82, chmn. bd. 1986-87), Nat. Asns. Uniformed Svcs., Auburn Alumni Assn. (life.). Republican. Methodist. Avocations: photography, mechanics, gardening, aviation. Home: Weatherford, Tex. Died Dec. 18, 2007.

ANDREWS, THOMAS PATRICK, city planner; b. Detroit, Aug. 30, 1939; s. Harry Clarence and Sophie Irene (Jankowski) A.; m. Jo Ann Ferrario, Nov. 25, 1966; children: Marilyn, David. BA, Wayne State U., 1961, M.Urban Planning, 1970. Registered profl. community planner, Mich. Social economist Detroit City Plan Commn., 1964-67; sr. city planner Detroit Mayor's Com. for Community Renewal, 1967-69, Detroit City Plan Commn., 1969-75, Detroit Planning Dept., 1975-82, prin. city planner, from 1982. Cons. in field. Author: Introduction to Historic Preservation in Detroit, 1979. Mem. Cath. Archdiocesan Pastoral Council, Detroit, 1985-88; pres. Hyde Park Housing Coop., Detroit, 1983-84; vice chmn. St. Joseph Cath. Ch. Parish Council, Detroit, 1986—. Mem. Am. Inst. Cert. Planners, Am. Planning Assn., Mich. Community Devel. Dirs. Assn., Wabash Investment Club. Roman Catholic. Avocations: travel, photography. Home: Clarkston, Mich. Died July 8, 2008.

ANDRUS, JOHN STEBBINS, military and political affairs consultant; b. Ft. Riley, Kans., Jan. 18, 1927; s. Burton Curtis and Katharine Elizabeth (Stebbins) A.; m. Jane Braham, Apr. 3, 1954; children: Priscilla Hinchey, Marcella Lewis, Drucilla Haugh. BS, U.S. Mil. Acad., 1949; disting. grad., Squadron Officer Sch., Maxwell AFB, Ala., 1955; grad., Air Command and Staff Coll., Maxwell AFB, Ala., 1963; MPA, George Washington U., 1963. USAF internat. politico-mil. affairs officer, command pilot, parachutist. Commd. 2d lt. USAF, 1949, advanced through grades to lt col., 1968, airlift pilot Mil. Air Transport Westover AFB, Mass., 1951-52, combat control team leader Tactical Air Command Ft. Bragg, N.C., 1953, instr. Squadron Officer Sch. Air U. Command Maxwell AFB, 1955-58, comdr. nuclear weapon site Italy, 1960, action officer spl. air warfare policy hdqrs. The Pentagon Washington, 1963-65, air ops. officer 606 Air Commando Wing Nakom Phanom, Thailand, 1966-67, polit./mil. liaison Hdqrs. 13th Air Force, Clark Air Base Phila., 1967-70; chief Okinawa area field office U.S. Forces, Japan, Zukiran, Okinawa, 1972-74; dir. mgmt. seminar Dale Carnegie, Honolulu, 1978-79; cons. mil./polit. affairs Andrus Enterprises Internat., Prides Crossing, Mass., from 1980. Lectr. polit./mil. subjects, various colls., 1975-91; pres. Andrus Enterprises Internat., Prides Crossing, 1986—. Author: Air Force Military Doctrine (Air Power award 1955); author essay, My Vote--Freedom's Privilege (Freedom Found. award 1960); author various stories and poems; inventor hand calculators. Vice chmn. (facilities) N.J. Spl. Olumpics, McGuire AFB, 1975; adult friend Big Bro. Program, East Providence, R.I., 1984; charter mem. Rep. Presdl. Task Force, Washington, 1980-92; sponsor NAt. Rep. Congl. Com., Washington, 1980-91, chmn. 8th congl. dist. Citizens for Am., Rehoboth, Mass., 1982-85; mem. speakers bur. High Frontier, 1975-85; active in the 300th anniversary re-enactment of Waldensians Glorious Return, 1989; chmn. 6th congl. dist. Mass. United We Stand Am., 1992-93. Decorated Bronze Star, Meritorious Svc. medal Mem. Am. Security Coun., Internat. Platform Assn., Air Force Assn., West Point Soc. New Eng., Friends of West Point Libr., Mil. Order of World Wars (life companion), Acad. Am. Poets, Boston Computer Soc., Lions, Alpine Club of Italy (Torre Pellice). Avocations: travel, hiking, swimming, photography, music. Died Apr. 27, 2008.

ANKROM, CHARLES FRANKLIN, landscape architect, consultant; b. Parkersburg, W.Va., Nov. 7, 1936; s. Donsel and Elva Dale (Cale) A.; m. Alice Lynell Glass, Aug. 24, 1968; children: Steven Charles, Cheryl Lyn, Jan Ellen Lambert, Beverly Lyn Webster. Student, W.Va. U., 1955, Eli Frank Sch. Design Arts, Tampa, Fla., 1956, Indian River C.C., Stuart, Fla., 1993—94, student, from 2007. Exec. dir. golf, corp. golf course arch. Gen. Devel. Corp., Miami, Fla., 1964-70; exec. dir. golf, golf course arch. Boise Cascade Recreation Communities Group, Palo Alto, Calif., 1970-73; pres. Charles F. Ankrom, Inc., Internat. Golf Course Archs., Cons. & Planners, Stuart, Fla., from 1973. Founder Ankrom and Miartus Internat., Fla., Venezuela; cons. in field. Prin. works include Panther Woods Country Club, Ft. Pierce, Fla., Sabal Trace C.C., Port Charlotte, Fla., Sun 'N Lake Country Club, Turtle Run Golf Course, Sebring, Fla., Cocoa Beach Mcpl. Golf Course, Cocoa Beach City, Fla., Ft. Lauderdale (Fla.) Country Club, Boca Raton (Fla.) Mcpl. Golf Course, The Cypress Golf Course at Woodmont Country Club, Tamarac, Fla., The Club at Emerald Hills, Hollywood, Fla., The Habitat Golf Course, Brevard County, Fla., Aquarina Beach & Country Club, Melbourne, Fla., Crane Creek C.C., Palm City, Fla., Indian River Plantation Resort, Hutchinson Island Marriott Beach Resort and Marina, Jensen Beach, Fla., Metro Country Club Resort, Dominican Republic, Osprey Creek Golf Course, Palm City, Fla., San Miguel Country Club, Venezuela, others; over 60 planned cmtys. including Indian River Plantation Marriott Resort, Hutchinson Island, Fla., Joe's Point, Hutchinson Island, Stuart West, Martin County, Fla., Pinecrest Lakes, Jensen Beach, Crystal Lakes, Okeechobee, Fla., Panther Woods, Ft. Pierce, Crane Creek, Palm City, Fla., River Ridge, Tequesta, Fla., River Landing, Palm City. Donated design & adminstrv. svcs. for Bulldog Sportsturf Complex, Martin County (Fla.) Schs. Recipient Outstanding Achievement by Ind. in Bus. or Industry award State of Fla. Coun. on Vocat. Edn., 1992, Bus. Ptnr. award Martin County Sch. Dist., 1991. Home: Palm City, Fla. Died July 2009.

ANNAKIN, KENNETH COOPER, film director, writer; b. Beverly, Yorkshire, Eng., Aug. 10, 1914; came to US, 1979; s. Edward C. and Hannah J. (Gains) A.; m. Pauline Mary Carter, 1960; children: Jane, Deborah. DLitt (hon.), Hull U., 1935. Writer, dir. 14 documentaries, 1941-46; movie dir. Holiday Camp, 1946, Miranda, 1948, Quartette, 1948, Trio, 1950, Hotel Sahara, 1951, Planter's Wife, 1952, Robin Hood and Hist Merry Men, 1952, Sword and the Rose, 1953, Loser Takes All, 1956, Three Men in a Boat, 1956, Across the Bridge, 1957, Third Man on the Mountain, 1959, The Swiss Family Robinson, 1960, A Very Important Person, 1961, The Hellions, 1961, Crooks Anonymous, 1962, The Fast Lady, 1962, The Longest Day, 1962, Those Magnificent Men in Their Flying Machines, 1965, The Battle of the Bulge, 1965, The Biggest Bundle of Them All, 1967, Those Daring Young Men in Their Jaunty Jalopies, 1969, The Call of the Wild, 1972, Paper Tiger, 1974, The Fifth Musketeer, 1977, The Pirate Movie, 1982, Pippi Longstocking, 1986, 99; rev. screenwriter Coco Chanel, 2007, Chiffon, 2007, Fair Play, 2006, Lady With the Redwing, 2007; author (autobiography): So You Wanna Be A Director?, 2001. Named an Officer of the Most Excellent Order of the British Empire, Her Majesty Queen Elizabeth II, 2003. Home: Beverly Hills, Calif. Died Apr. 22, 2009.

ANNENBERG, LEONORE, foundation administrator; b. NYC, Feb. 20, 1918; d. Maxwell & Clara Cohn; m. Belden Katleman (div.); 1 child, Diane; m. Lewis S. Rosentiel, 1946 (div.); 1 child, Elizabeth; m. Walter Hubert Annenberg, 1951 (dec. Oct. 1, 2002); 1 stepchild, Wallis BA, Stanford U., 1940; PhD (hon.), Pine Manor Coll., LaSalle U., U. Pa., Brown U.; DHL (hon.), U. So. Calif., 1998. Chief of protocol US Dept. State, 1981—82; pres., chair Annenberg Found., 2002—09. Founding mem. governing bd. Annenberg sch. comm. U. Pa., Annenberg sch. comm. U. So. Calif.; founder Am. Friends Covent Garden; past chmn., hon. chmn. Friends Art and Preservation Embassies; mem. trustee's coun. Nat. Gallery Art; mem. Com. Preservation White House; mng. dir. Met. Opera; mem. Acad. Music Com.; past pres., hon. trustee Palm Springs Desert Mus.; hon. trustee performing arts coun. LA Music Ctr.; trustee emeritus U. Pa.; former bd. dirs. Pa. Acad. Fine Arts, Phila. Orch. Assn.; bd. dirs. Met. Mus. Art, Phila. Mus. Art. Decorated Cavaliere Dell'Ordine Al Merito Della Republica Italiana, Grand Officio Order of Orange-Nassau (Netherlands); recipient Wagner medal Robert F. Wagner grad. sch. pub. svc. NYU, Colonial Williamsburg Churchill Bell award, Nat. Medal of Arts, NEA, 1993; named an Hon. Comdr. of the British Empire, Queen Elizabeth II, 2004 named one of The 400 Richest Americans Forbes mag., 2006. Fellow Am. Acad. Arts and Scis.; mem. Disting. Daus. Pa. Died Mar. 12, 2009.

ANSLEY, DARLENE H., marketing and communications executive; b. Anderson, Ind., Aug. 21, 1942; d. Byron J. and Edith O. (Earlywine) Howell; children: David, Bradley, Lisa. Student, Anderson U., 1960-61; BS in Communications, Fla. State U., 1978. Asst. project Boydston Advt. & Creative Svcs., Tallahassee, 1978; asst. dir. Pub. Broadcasting Svc., Alexandria, Va., 1982-85, assoc. dir., 1985-87, advt. mgr., nat. programming & promotion svcs., 1987-93; prin. Ansley Comms., Inc., 1993-97; dir. mktg. and comms. Divsn. of continuing edn. George Washington U., Washington, 1997; dir. mktg. and publs. Nat. Office Orthotics and Prosthetics, Alexandria, Va., 1997-98; creative dir., mktg. promotions Bur. Nat. Affairs, Washington, 1999—2000; dir. mktg. comms. i2, Inc., Springfield, Va., 2000—01; brand mgr. U.S. Internat. Broadcasting Bur., Washington, 2002—03. Home: Burke, Va. Died Jan. 10, 2008.

ANTHONY, JACK MALCOLM, lawyer; b. Abilene, Tex., June 17, 1943; s. Jack Malcolm and Marguerite (Barrow) A.; m. Judy Locy Wright, Aug. 2, 1966 (div. 1974); 1 child, Ellen Barrow; m. Rebecca Lynn Westbrook, June 2, 1981; 1 child, Jillian Ann. Student, Tex. Tech U., 1961-65; JD, Baylor U., 1967. Bar: Tex. 1967, U.S. Dist. Ct. (no., ea. dists.) Tex. 1974, U.S. Ct. Appeals (5th cir.), U.S. Supreme Ct. 1990; cert. in personal injury trial law and civil trial law Tex. Bd. Legal Specialization. House counsel Garvon Inc., Garland, Tex., 1967-69; assoc. Hirsch & Reese, Garland, 1969-71; ptnr. Hirsch, Reese & Anthony, Garland, 1971-80; pvt. practice Dallas, 1980-85; ptnr. Anthony & Vereeke, Dallas, from 1970. Lt. USNR, 1971-78. Mem. ABA, State Bar Tex., Dallas Bar Assn., Tex. Trial Lawyers Assn. (bd. dirs.), Dallas Trial Lawyers Assn. (bd. dirs.), Assn. Trial Lawyers Am. (sustaining), So. Trial Lawyers Assn., Phi Delta Theta, Phi Alpha Delta. Died July 17, 2008.

ANTON, WILLIAM R. (BILL ANTON), retired school system administrator; b. El Paso, Tex., July 22, 1924; s. Roque and Luisa Anton; m. Anna Harlow; children: Brian, Lin, Willie. BA, Calif. State U., L.A., 1952, MA, 1954. Tchr. Rowan Elementary Sch., 1952—90; supt. of schools City of L.A., 1990—92. Served in US Army. Died July 28, 2009.

ANTONSON, NEWMAN NEIL, minister; b. Waco, Tex., Aug. 8, 1926; s. Toby and Iva Myrtle (McNiel) A.; m. Dorothy Lee Cox, Mar. 4, 1948; children: Deborah Lee Mai, Roberta Lynn Jenkins, Peggy Sue Burns. BA, Baylor U., 1949; BD, Southwestern Bapt. Theol. Sem., 1953. Ordained to ministry So. Bapt. Conv., 1947. Pastor First Bapt. Ch., Davis, Okla., 1955-60, Carnegie, Okla., 1960-61, Dumas Ave. Bapt. Ch., Oklahoma City, 1961-63, Trinity Bapt. Ch., Lawton, Okla., 1963-78, Tyler Rd. So. Bapt. Ch., Wichita, Kans., from 1978. Mem. Brotherhood Commn., So. Bapt. Ch., Memphis, 1965-71; v.p. KNCSB, Topeka, 1990—; pres. KNCSB Found., 1983-84, others. With USN, 1944-46. Democrat. Home: Wichita, Kans. Died Jan. 25, 2008.

APEL, CAROLYN RUTH, singer, aerospace company system administrator; b. Detroit, Aug. 13, 1943; BS, Wayne State U., 1969; postgrad. in engring., U. Wash., 1975-77, Seattle U., 1977-79. Chemist Reichhold/Sherwin Williams, Detroit and Oakland, Calif., 1969-71; psychol. counselor Youth Work Tng. Program, Seattle, 1977-79; system adminstr. Boeing-BCS-Renton (Wash.), 1980-91. Singer fgn. music, Seattle, 1980—; author: (poems) Never, 1990 (World of Poetry award), (fiction) Dr. Jones and Carolyn, 1989. Active NOW, MADD, gun control issues, Seattle; vol. Communist Chinese exch. program. ARCO scholar, 1975. Mem. Single Book Friends (v.p. 1989-90). Avocations: foreign languages, music, culture. Home: Seattle, Wash. Died Feb. 24, 2008.

APGOOD, ROBERT D., financial consultant; b. Idaho Falls, Idaho, Feb. 20, 1941; s. Dale Marvin and Esther (Palmer) A.; m. Marsha Foreman; children: Allyson, Anthony, Richard. BA, Brigham Young U., 1965, U. Utah, 1980, MBA, 1967, PhD, 1985. Cert. pub. acct. CPA Peat Marwick, LA, 1965-67; asst. prof. Weber State U., Ogden, Utah, 1970-75; v.p. KUTV, Salt Lake City, 1975-77; pvt. practice Utah, from 1977; prof. San Francisco State U., 1985-86. Home: Salt Lake City, Utah. Died Aug. 1, 2008.

APONTE DE LA TORRE, JOSE, former Mayor, Carolina, PR; b. Barrio Beatriz Cayey, PR, PR, Dec. 5, 1941; s. Ernesto Aponte Mendoza and Justine de la Torre; m. Carmen Idalia Dalmay Ferrer; children: Jose, Ernesto, Javier. BA, U. PR, 1963; MA, NYU, 1967. Dir. Carols F Daniels Tech. Sch., Carolina, PR, 1974—78, 1981—84; mayor City of Carolina, PR, 1984—2007; v.p. Popular Dem. Party, 1993, pres., 1997. Mem.: America Vocat. Assn., Teachers Assn. PR, Mayors Assn. PR (v.p. 1993—95), Nat. Edn. Assn., Lions Club (former pres.). Died 2007.

APPEL, ALFRED, JR., retired literature educator; b. NYC, Jan. 31, 1934; s. Alfred and Beatrice (Hoffman) A.; m. Nina Schick, Sept. 1, 1957; children: Karen Appel Oshman, Richard James. Student, Cornell U., 1952-54; BA, Columbia U., 1959, MA, 1960, PhD in English, 1963. Lectr. English Columbia U., 1961-62, perceptor in English, 1962-63; asst. prof. Stanford U., 1963-68, Northwestern U., Evanston, Ill., 1968-69, assoc. prof., 1969-74, prof., 1974—2000, prof. emeritus, 2000—09. Author: A Season of Dreams, 1965, Nabokov's Dark Cinema, 1974, Signs of Life, 1983, The Art of Celebration: The Expression of Joy in 20th Century Art, Literature, Photography and Music, 1992, Jazz Modernism: From Ellington and Armstrong to Matisse and Joyce, 2004; author, editor: The Annotated Lolita, 1970; editor: John DeForest's Witching Times, 1967, (with Charles Newman) Nabokov: Criticism, Reminiscences, Translations, Tributs, 1970, (with Simon Karlinsky) The Bitter Air of Exile: Russian Writers in the West 1922-72, 1977; contbg. author: Nabokov: The Man and his Work, 1967, The Single Voice, 1969, A Book of Things About Vladimir Nabokov, 1974, Vladimir Nabokov: A Tribute, 1979, Nabokov's Fifth Arc, 1982. Served with U.S. Army, 1955-57. Guggenheim fellow, 1972; Rockefeller fellow, 1976; recipient Best Creative Essay award Arts Council Ill., 1974 Home: Wilmette, Ill. Died May 2, 2009.

APPLEBERRY, WALTER THOMAS, aerospace engineering project executive; b. Wilmington, NC, Mar. 8, 1926; s. William Pembroke and Carroll Ernesteen (Shingleton) A.; m. Mae Magdalene Bozeman, Feb. 21, 1953; children: Thomas Kent, Robert William, Rebecca Jean. BS in Mech. Engring., Calif. State U., Long Beach, 1974. Facilities engr. Douglas Aircraft, Long Beach, 1942-50; missionary Mormon Ch., Salt Lake City, 1950-53; supr. engring. test McDonnell Douglas, Huntington Beach, Calif., 1953-74; adv. engring. project mgr. Rockwell Internat., Downey, Calif., 1974-94. Patentee in field. Mem. Pi Tau Sigma. Republican. Mem. Lds Ch. Avocations: music, violin, piano, choir. Home: Long Beach, Calif. Died June 11, 2008.

ARAKKAL, ANTONY LONA, engineering executive, researcher; b. Kattoor, Kerala, India, Dec. 15, 1937; came to U.S., 1969; s. Lona Joseph and Catherine N. A.; m. Bridget F. Fernandez, Feb. 4, 1967; 1 child, Antony, Jr. BS in Mech.

Engring., U. Kerala, 1964; MS, Ill. Inst. Tech., Chgo., 1972. Mgr. mfg. engring. Black & Decker, Tarboro, N.C., 1977-86; pres. Arakkal Enterprises, Inc., Carlisle, Pa., 1986-93, from 2002; v.p. advanced engring. Airtex Products, Inc., Fairfield, Ill., 1993—2002. Cons. Fasco, Ozark, Mo., 1986-87, Ametek, Gram, N.C., 1990-91, Penn Ventilator, Phila., 1991, Fawn Industries, Middlesex, N.C., 1992. Mem.: Inst. Indsl. Engrs. (pres. Tri-state chpt.), Soc. Mfg. Engrs. (N.C. chmn. 1985—86), Soc. Auto Engrs. (chmn. St. Louis chpt.), Lions Club (v.p. 1985), Internat. Rotary. Roman Catholic. Achievements include patent for Unipole Motor. Home: Fairfield, Ill. Died June 18, 2008.

ARCHER, JAMES ELSON, engineering educator; b. Hedley, Tex., Dec. 1, 1922; s. James M. and Mary Minerva (Bolles) A.; m. Reta Faye Turner, Nov. 8, 1942; 1 son, James Elson. BS, Tex. Tech. U., 1947; PhD, Mass. Inst. Tech., 1950. Instr. Mass. Inst. Tech., 1950-52, Sloan fellow in indsl. mgmt., 1963-64; researcher Pitts. Plate Glass Co., Pitts., 1952-53, asst. dir., 1953-54, asso. dir., 1954-56, dir. research, 1956-62; mng. partner Archer Assos., Dallas, 1962-64; corporate dir. mgmt. systems Tex. Instruments, Dallas, 1964-68; prof. Tex. Tech U., Lubbock, 1968-95, prof. emeritus, 1995—2009. With USAAF, 1943—46. Home: Portola Valley, Calif. Died June 1, 2009.

ARCHERD, ARMY (ARMAND A. ARCHERD), columnist, retired commentator; b. Bronx, NY, Jan. 13, 1922; m. Selma Archerd. Grad., UCLA, 1941, U.S. Naval Acad. Postgrad. Sch., 1943. With Hollywood bur. AP, 1945—2005; columnist Herald-Express, Daily Variety, 1953—2005. Master of ceremonies numerous Hollywood premieres, Acad. Awards shows; co-host People's Choice Awards shows. Served to lt. USN. Recipient awards Masquers, L.A. Press Club, Hollywood Fgn. Press Club, Newsman of Yr. award Publicists Guild, 1970. Mem. Hollywood Press Club (founder). Died Sept. 8, 2009.

ARESKOG, DONALD CLINTON, retired chiropractor; b. Bklyn., Aug. 6, 1926; s. Andrew Albert and Jennie Margaret (Dickson) A.; m. Julia Catherine Koskela, May 15, 1954. D Chiropractic, Logan Coll., St. Louis, 1950; Philosopher of Chiropractic, Atlantic States Chiropractic Coll. Ret., 1989; pvt. practice Bklyn., 1952-56, Wappingers Falls, N.Y., 1956-61, Poughkeepsie, N.Y., 1961-89; retired, 1989. Bd. govs. Atlantic States Chiropractic Coll., Bklyn., 1954; research in field. Developer technique for removal of mental aberrations. Mem. Am. Chiropractic Assn. (speakers bur. 1964), Ednl. Rsch. Soc., Internat. Basic Rsch. Inst., Internat. Platform Assn., Wappingers Falls C. of C. (treas. 1959), Toastmasters. Achievements include developing a technique to create peak experiences known as "the flow", 1995, technology for pure being, 1999, technology to create whole brain thinking, 2000, removal of all energy breaks, 2003. Home: Deerfield Beach, Fla. Died July 10, 2008.

ARMOUR, GORDON CHARLES, technology and contract manager; b. Denver, June 1, 1929; s. Gordon Thomas and Doris Hilda (Stoker) A.; m. Margaret Christine Graney, Sept. 22, 1951; children: Doris C., Thomas S. BS, UCLA, 1953, MBA, 1957, PhD, 1961. Registered profl. engr., Calif. Sr. indsl. engr., Calif. mfg. engr. Johns-Manville Co., Long Beach, Calif., 1957-59; asst. prof. Grad. Sch. Bus., Ind. U., Bloomington, 1961-64; mgmt. systems specialist N.Am. Aviation Co., Anaheim, Calif., 1964-68; chief mgmt. systems and planning N.Am. Rockwell, Anaheim, Calif., 1968-69, exec. advisor, 1969-73; indsl. planning specialist Rockwell Internat., Anaheim, 1973-79, exec. advisor for computers, 1979-81, mgr. telecommunications and computer tech., 1981-83, specialist for emerging tech., 1983-92, mgr. emerging tech. and contract adminstrn., 1992-95. Vis. prof. UCLA, 1963; cons. Gen. Water Heater Co., Burbank, Calif., 1960. Contbr. articles to profl. publs. Mem. selection panel for data procesing mgr. City of Anaheim, 1980. With USMC, 1953-55. Jo Downing scholar, 1953; Ford Found. fellow, 1959-61, 63-64, Ind. U. rsch. fellow, 1962. Avocations: scuba diving, tennis. Home: Santa Ana, Calif. Died Mar. 29, 2008.

ARNETT, JANICE E., secondary school educator; b. Kenton, Ohio, May 15, 1942; d. Lewis S. and Lucille M. (Oates) A. BS in Edn., Bowling Green State U., 1964. Tchr. Pinelas County, St. Petersburg, Fla., 1964-65, Fairview Pk., Ohio, 1965-70; social sci. sch. cons. Ednl. Research Council, Cleve., 1970-71; tchr. Fairview Pk., 1971-94. Mem. NEA, Ohio Edn. Assn., Fairview Pk. Edn. Assn., Internat. Reading Assn., Westshore Reading Assn., Kappa Delta Alumnae Assn., Kappa Delta Found. (chmn. 1989-91). Methodist. Home: Rocky River, Ohio. Died Nov. 27, 2007.

ARNOLD, DAVID BROWN, educator; b. Hackensack, NJ, Oct. 24, 1940; s. Robert Brown and Virginia Louise (Bunn) A.; m. Georgia Louise Carss, Dec. 28, 1963 (div. 1971); 1 child, Christopher Carss; m. Mary Helen Tryson, Dec. 23, 1971 (div. Dec. 1985); children: Phoebe Lynn, Jennifer Suzanne; m. Lauretta D'Orazio, Dec. 27, 1992. BSc in Chemistry, U. Pa., 1963; PhD in Chemistry, Bryn Mawr Coll., 1970. Asst. prof. Widener U. (formerly Widener Coll., then PMC Colls.), Chester, Pa., 1968-75; assoc. prof. Widener U., Chester, Pa., from 1975. Vis. prof. U. Del., Newark, 1982-83; part-time vis. prof. Bryn Mawr (Pa.) Coll., 1981; head judge Del. County Sci. Fair, 1976—. Mem. Am. Chem. Soc., Royal Soc. Chemistry, Nat. Sci. Tchrs. Assn., Penn. Sci. Tchrs. Assn. (bd. dirs. 1976—), Del. County Sci. Tchrs. Assn. (bd. dirs. 1970—, past pres.), Catalysis Club of Phila. Avocations: trains, skiing, camping. Home: Media, Pa. Died June 9, 2008.

ARNOLD, DAVID PAUL, sales professional; b. Pitts., May 11, 1942; s. Arthur and Elizabeth (Novak) A.; m. Patricia Arda Graham, Sept. 3, 1966; children: Nichelle, Bret, Janelle. BA in Bus., Ohio No. U., 1964; grad., Ohio State Inst. Fin., 1971. Sales engr. Reliance Electric, various cities, 1964-70; sales dir. Columbia Nat., Columbus, Ohio, 1970-73; owner Mint Lake Valley Lumber, Ashtabula, Ohio, 1973-76; v.p. sales Preformed Line Products, Cleve., from 1976. Founder, BOGSAT. Named to Hon. Order Ky. Cols. Mem. Am. Mgmt. Assn. Republican. Methodist. Avocations: farming, architecture, private pilot. Home: Ashtabula, Ohio. Died Feb. 16, 2008.

ARNOLD, ERIC ANDERSON, JR., history professor; b. Dec. 4, 1939; AB, Oberlin Coll., 1967; MA, Columbia Coll., 1963, PhD, 1969. Assoc. prof. History U. Denver, Colo., from 1969. Home: Denver, Colo. Died Aug. 6, 2008.

ARNOLD, WALTER MARTIN, retired vocational education educator; b. Steelton, Pa., June 14, 1906; s. Philip and Ella (Sullenberger) A.; m. Evelyn Reeser, June 5, 1931; children: Jean Elizabeth Arnold Rudolph, Philip Elbert, Marilyn Ethel (Mrs. James A. Miller). BS, Pa. State U., 1929, M.Ed., 1935; Ed.D., Okla. State U., 1957. Instr. Lancaster (Pa.) Boys High Sch., 1929-37; supt. Stevens Trade Sch., Lancaster, 1937-41; spl. rep. trade and indsl. edn. U.S. Office Edn., 1941-43; dir. vocat. edn. Allentown (Pa.) city schs., 1943-45; personnel mgr. Mack Mfg. Corp., 1945-49; assoc. H.W. Beyer Assos., pension cons. Allentown, 1949-50; supr. trade and indsl. edn. Okla., 1950-54; dir., exec. officer vocat. edn. Kans., 1954-59; dir. area vocat. edn. br., div. vocational and tech. edn. U.S. Office Edn., 1959-61, asst. commnr. vocat. and tech. edn., 1961-67; cons. vocat. and tech edn., also dir. of Pa. Study of Vocational Edn., 1967-69; pres. Am. Vocat. Research Corp., 1969-71; Walter M. Arnold Assocs., Inc. Arlington, Va., 1971-75; adj. prof. Fla. Internat. U., 1976-78. Pres. Kans. Adult Edn. Assn., 1958-59; mem. Gov. Kans. Com. Mental Retardation, 1958, Gov. Kans. Inter-Deptl. Com. Aging, 1956-59, Kans. Adv. Council Edn., 1954-59; chmn. planning com. Four State Conf., 1957; tng. dir. Kans. Survival Plan Project, 1956-59; mem. north area Broward County Sch. Dist. Adv. Exec. Bd. and Com., 1979-83; chmn. adv. com. Atlantic Area Vocat. Tech. Center, 1976-83; mem. Curriculum task force Supts. Commn. on Public Edn., chmn. task force on vocat. edn., 1980-81; council mem. Coconut Creek City Council (Fla.), 1983-85; cons. Fla. Commn. Vocat. Edn., 1985-86; v.p. Fla. Life Care Residents Assn., 1990. Recipient Outstanding Alumnus citation Pa. State U. Sch. Edn., 1986. Mem. Am. Soc. Engring. Edn., Am. Tech. Edn. Assn., Council Local Admistrs. Vocat. Edn. and Practical Arts, Am. Vocat. Assn., NEA, Pa. State U. Alumni Assn., Okla. State U. Alumni Assn., Nat. Assn. State Directors Vocational Edn., Alpha Chi Rho, Kappa Phi Kappa, Kappa Delta Pi, Phi Delta Kappa, Iota Lambda Sigma. Died Jan. 12, 2009.

ARNOLD, WYNN EDMUND, utilities executive, lawyer; b. Ludlow, Mass., Sept. 27, 1947; s. William Edmund and Barbara Eileen (Smith) A.; m. Helen Janice Falkson, Aug. 27, 1978; children: Sara Lesley, Merrin Falkson. Student, Glasgow U., Scotland, 1968-69; BA, U. N.H., 1970; JD, Suffolk U., 1981. Bar: N.H. 1981, Mass. 1982, U.S. Dist. Ct. N.H. 1981. Vol. U.S. Peace Corps, Ecuador, 1970-73; specialist office for civil rights HEW, Boston, 1974-78; specialist equal opportunity Office fed. Contract Compliance Programs, Boston, 1978-81; assoc. Tetler & Holmes, Hampton, N.H., 1981-83; exec. dir., sec. N.H. Pub. Utilities Commn., Concord, from 1984. Co-author, dir. (film) Despertad, 1972. Chmn. N.H. Episcopal Diosecan Stewardship Commn., Concord, 1986-88. Mem. Nat. Assn. Regulatory Utility Commrs. (chair, exec. dirs. com. 1990-93), N.H. Bar Assn. (long-range planning com.), Mass. Bar Assn., Phi Delta Phi. Episcopalian. Avocations: guitar, piano, folk music, water sports. Home: Manchester, NH. Died Jan. 28, 2008.

ARORA, SARDARI LAL, chemistry educator; b. Lahore, Pakistan, June 4, 1929; came to U.S., 1964; s. Uttam Chand and Kushal Devi Arora; m. Sunita Chawla, May 9, 1960; children: Nita, Nalini. MSc, Luchnow U., India, 1953, PhD, 1959. Chief chemist, dir. R & D, Internat. Liquid Crystal Co., Cleve., 1971-74; rsch. assoc. Liquid Crystal Inst., Kent (Ohio) State U., 1966-71, researcher, from 1983, casual asst. prof. chemistry, 1975-77, vis. asst. prof., 1977-80, asst. prof., 1980-86, assoc. prof., from 1986. Cons. Crystaloid Electronic Corp., 1976-78, Timex Corp., 1976-78, Liquid Crystal Application, Inc., 1983; presenter in field. Contbr. articles to sci. jours.; inventor, patentee in field. Fellow Coun. Sci. Indsl. Rsch, Govt. of India, 1957; fellow Aerospace Med. Rsch Lab., 1966, NASA, 1968; grantee NSF, 1983, indsl. grantee, 1986. Fellow Am. Inst. Chemists; mem. AAAS, Am. Chem. Soc., Internat. Union Pure and Applied Chemistry, Sigma Xi. Achievements include patents for Field Effect Light Shutter Employing Low Temperature Nematic Liquid Crystals; for Liquid Crystal Materials; research in development of polymer and other new liquid crystal materials, their characterization and technical applications. Home: Munroe Falls, Ohio. Died Nov. 3, 2007.

ARTHUR, BEA, actress; b. NYC, May 13, 1923; d. Philip and Rebecca Frankel; m. Gene Saks, May 28, 1950 (div. 1978); children: Matthew, Daniel. Student, Blackstone Coll., also Franklin Inst. Sci. and Arts; student acting with, Erwin Piscator, Dramatic Workshop, New Sch. Social Research. Theatrical appearances include: Lysistrata, 1947, Dog Beneath the Skin, 1947, Gas, 1947, Yerma, 1947, No Exit, 1948, The Taming of the Shrew, 1948, Six Characters in Search of An Author, 1948, The Owl and the Pussycat, 1948, Le Bourgeois Gentilhomme, 1949, Yes Is for a Very Young Man, 1949, Creditors, 1949, Heartbreak House, 1949, Three Penny Opera, 1954, 55, Shoestring Revue, 1955, Seventh Heaven, 1955, The Ziegfield Follies, 1956, What's The Rush?, summer 1956, Mistress of the Inn, 1957, Nature's Way, 1957, Ulysses in Nightown, 1958, Chic, 1959, Gay Divorcee, 1960, A Matter of Position, 1962, Mame, 1966 (Tony award for Best Supporting Actress in a Musical), Fiddler on the Roof, 1964, Bermuda Avenue Triangle, 1996, For Better or Worse, 1996; one woman shows, ...And Then There's Bea, San Francisco, 2001, An Evening With Bea Arthur, L.A., 2001, Bea Arthur on Broadway: Just Between Friends, 2002; stock appearances with Fiddler on the Roof, Circle Theatre, Atlantic City, summer 1951, State Fair Music Hall, Dallas, 1953, Music Circus, Lambertville, NJ, 1953, resident commedienne, Tamiment (Pa.) Theatre, 1953; actress: (films) That Kind of Woman, 1959; Lovers and Other Strangers, 1970, Mame, 1974, History of the World: Part I, 1981, For Better or Worse, 1995, Enemies of Laughter, 2000; (TV movies) Max Lieberman Present: Kaleidoscope, 1955, THe Gift of the Magi, 1958, P.O.P., 1984, My First Love, 1988; (TV series) Maude, 1972-78 (Emmy award for Best Actress in a Comedy Series 1977), Amanda's, 1983, The Golden Girls, 1985-92 (Emmy award for Best Actress in a Comedy Series 1988); (TV guest appearances) Kraft Television Theatre (8 episodes), 1951-58, One Upon a Tune, 1951, Studio One (3 episodes), 1951-53, Caesar's Hour, 1956-57, Washington Square, 1956, Omnibus, 1958, The Seven Lively Arts, 1958, The Sid Caesar Show, 1963, All in the Family (2 episodes), 1971-72, Laugh-In, 1977, The Star Wars Holiday Special 1978, The Mary Tyler Moore Hour, 1979, Soap, 1980, a.k.a Pablo, 1984, Empty Nest, 1989, The Golden Palace (2 episodes), 1992, Dave's World (3 episodes), 1997, Malcolm in the Middle, 2000, Futurama, 2001, Curb Your Enthusiasm, 2005. Vol. med. tech. USMC, WWII. Recipient Award of Achievement, Emerson College's Musical Theater Soc., 2000. Mem. Artists Equity Assn., SAG, AFTRA. Died Apr. 25, 2009.

ARZT, DONNA ELAINE, law educator; b. Phila., Dec. 9, 1954; d. Alvin H. and Lois (Silver) A.; m. Stephen J. Whitfield, Aug. 21, 1977 (div. Sept. 1982). BA, Brandeis U., 1976; JD, Harvard U., 1979; LLM, Columbia U., 1988. Bar: Mass. 1979, N.Y. 1988. Assoc. Rosenfeld, Botsford & Krokidas, Boston, 1980-82; asst. atty. gen. Commonwealth of Mass., Boston, 1982-85; cons. Assn. for Civil Rights, Jerusalem, 1986; from asst. prof. to assoc. prof. Syracuse U., NY, 1988-96, prof. NY, 1996—2008; assoc. dir. Ctr. for Global Law and Practice, 1996—2008. Adj. prof. Touro Law Ctr., Huntington, NY, 1987-88; gen. coun. Soviet Jewry Legal Adv. Ctr., Waltham, Mass., 1979-88; Eng. editor Israel Yearbook on Human Rights, Tel Aviv, 1986-87; cons. Human Rights Watch, Helsinki, 1996-97, Dean's Disting. Rsch. Scholar Syracuse U. Author: Refugees into Citizens, 1997; co-author: Religious Human Rights, 1995, Beyond Confrontation, 1995, Der Einflus deutscher Emigranten 1993, Refugees Into Citizens: Palestinians and the End of the Arab-Israeli Conflict, 1997 Bd. adv., mem. Refugee Resettlement Com., Ithaca, NY; exec. com. Program on Analysis & Resolution of Conflicts, 1993-97; project dir. Coun. Fgn. Rels., 1994-96; exec. com. Union of Couns. for Soviet Jews, 1980-87, dir. Lockerbie Trial Families Project, co-dir. Sierra Leone Project. Recipient Michael J.Tyson award for Excellence in Human Rights Advocacy Union of Coun. for. Soviet Jews, 1990; travel grant Internat. Com. of Red Cross, Geneva, Switzerland, 1993; rsch. grant. Jacob Blaustein Inst. for Human Rights, 1987-88. Mem. ABA, Am. Soc. Internat. Law, Assn. of Am. Law Sch. Democrat. Jewish. Avocation: photography. Home: Ithaca, NY. Died Nov. 15, 2008.

ASH, WALTER BRINKER, lawyer; b. Wichita, Kans., June 8, 1932; s. Walter Bonsall and Gladys Elvira (Brinker) A.; m. Fern Ostrom, Sept. 16, 1986; children: Paul B., Allison L., Carolyn A. BA, U. Kans., 1955, BL, 1957. Bar: Kans. 1957, Colo. 1959. Personal asst. to Solicitor Gen. U.S. Dept. Justice, Washington, 1957-58, trial atty., 1958-59; assoc. Davis, Graham & Stubbs, Denver, 1959-63, ptnr., 1964-82, Wade Ash Woods Hill & Guthery P.C., Denver, 1982-91, Wade Ash Woods & Hill P.C., Denver, 1991-93, Wade Ash Woods Hill & Farley, P.C., Denver, from 1993. Fellow Am. Coll. Trust and Estate Counsel; mem. ABA, Colo. Bar Assn., Denver Bar Assn., Internat. Acad. Estate and Trust Law. Home: Aurora, Colo. Died Apr. 29, 2008.

ASHBY, CHARLES FERG, physician; b. Fairmont, Nebr., Feb. 9, 1920; s. Albert A. and Gertrude (Ferg) Ashby; m. Jean Fricke, Nov. 9, 1943; children: Sara Sawtell, James R. BS, U. Nebr., 1939, AB, 1940; MD, U. Nebr., Omaha, 1942. Diplomate Am. Bd. Family Practice. Family practice physician, Geneva, Nebr. Home: Geneva, Nebr. Died May 15, 2008.

ASHBY, EDWARD HOWARD, publisher; b. Harrisburg, Pa., Mar. 24, 1935; s. William Mack Ashby and Jane Elizabeth (Coomer) Pue; m. Susan T. Koyama, Jan. 29, 1991; children: Joann Linda, Michael Richard, Charles Wesley, Paul Fitzgerald. BA, U. Md., 1965; MS, U. So. Calif., LA, 1971. State editor Meridian Star, Miss., 1971-74; pub. Rifle Citizen-Telegram, Colo., 1974-77; reporter Gazette-Telegraph, Colorado Springs, 1977-79; editor and pub. Military Times, Colorado Springs, 1979-84; dir. publs. Assn. Operating Room Nurses, Denver, 1984-85; pub. Sr.

Spotlite, Denver, from 1986. Contbr. articles to profl. jours. Recipient Essay award Freedoms Found., Valley Forge, Pa., 1964, 72, Feature Writing award Colo. Press Assn., Denver, 1978. Mem. Toastmasters (area gov. 1968-94). Home: Arvada, Colo. Died July 3, 2008.

ASHLEY, ELEANOR TIDABACK, retired elementary educator; b. Yonkers, NY, May 29, 1910; d. Frederick Victor and Bessie (Van Tassel) Tidaback; m. Kenneth Miller Ashley, June 25, 1938; 1 child, Robert Bruce. Grad., New Paltz Tchrs. Coll., 1931; BS in Edn., NYU, 1936. Tchr. 3d grade, Spring Valley, N.Y., 1931-36; tchr. jr. high sch. English, 1936-38; tchr. 5th and 6th grades Elementary Sch., New City, N.Y., 1938-44, tchr. 2d grade Ossining, N.Y., 1941-67. Introduced moral values program Ossining (N.Y.) Pub. Schs. Mem. AAUW, Sr. Citizens Club of Niantic (Conn.), Am. Assn. Ret. Persons. Home: Niantic, Conn. Died Nov. 13, 2007.

ASHTON, THOMAS WALSH, investment banker; b. Rochester, NY, May 11, 1929; s. Charles Edward and Marie Margaret (Walsh) A.; m. Frances E. Hickey, May 16, 1953 (div. 1977); children: Lucy M. Van Atta, Mary B. Ashton Anders, Monica H., William T; m. Mary K Joy, Dec. 20, 1978 (dec. 1997); m. Carolyn B. Richardson, Jan. 26, 2002. BS, U.S. Mil. Acad., 1952; MBA, Harvard U., 1957. Assoc. corp. fin. Eastman Dillon Union Securities, NYC, 1957-61, gen. ptnr., 1967-69; asst. v.p. Harris Upham & Co., NYC, 1961-67; v.p. duPont Glore Forgan, Inc., NYC, 1971-73; sr. v.p. ABD Securities Corp., NYC, 1973-75; fin. cons. Am. Cancer Soc. of N.Y.C., East West Group Inc. Chmn. Peninsular Investments, Treasure Island, Fla., 1977-87; cons. Dept. Commerce, 1971; chmn. Ashton Investments, Inc., 1987—. Chmn. parents's coun. Smith Coll., 1974-76. With AUS, 1946-48, 52-55. Mem. Soc. Harvard Engrs. and Scientists (gov. 1974-75), West Point Soc. N.Y. (dir. 1971-75), Army and Navy Club (Washington), Ponte Vedra Inn and Club. Republican. Home: Jacksonville Beach, Fla. Died June 24, 2008.

ASMAR, CHARLES EDMOND, structural engineer, consultant; b. Beirut, Oct. 6, 1958; came to U.S., 1984; s. Edmond Eid and Constantina (Canarelli) A.; m. Suad Omer Mohamud; children: Karina, Camil. BSCE, U. Toledo, 1986; MBA, U. Bridgeport, 1995. Registered profl. engr., N.Y. Inspector Paul Zein Cons., Jounieh, 1976-82; structural engr. Parsons Brinckerhoff, Hartford, Conn., 1987-89, N. Massand P.C., Bayside, N.Y., 1989-91, Goodkind & O'Dea, Inc., Rutherford, N.J., 1991-93; cons. pvt. practice, Stamford, Conn., from 1993. Mem. ASCE. Home: Frederick, Md. Died May 5, 2008.

ASTRACHAN, BORIS MORTON, psychiatry educator, consultant; b. NYC, Dec. 1, 1931; s. Isaac and Ethel (Kahn) A.; m. Batja Sanders, June 17, 1956; children: David Isaac, Joseph Henry, Michael Sanders, Ellen Beth Astrachan-Fletcher. BA cum laude, Alfred U., NY, 1952; MD, Albany Med. Coll., 1956. Lic. Ill.; bd. cert. in psychiatry. Intern, resident USN Hosp., St. Albans and Phila., N.Y., 1956-57, 57-58; asst. depot psychiatrist recruitment tng. depot USMC, Parris Island, S.C., 1958-61; resident in psychiatry dept. psychiatry Yale U., New Haven, 1961-63, from asst. prof. to assoc. prof. dept. psychiatry, 1963-71; dir. Conn. Mental Health Ctr., New Haven, 1971-87; prof. dept. psychiatry Yale U., New Haven, 1971-90; prof., head dept. psychiatry U. Ill., Chgo., 1990-98, disting. prof. psychiatry, 1998—2001, disting. prof. emeritus psychiatry, from 2001. Mem. NIMH Initial Rev. Group, Rockville, Md., 1987-90, chmn., 1989-91; mem. IBM Mental Health Adv. Bd., White Plains, N.Y., 1990—; mem. adv. bd. Alcohol, Drug Addiction, Mental Health Adminstrn., Washington, 1985-86; mem. rsch. task force Pres. Commn. on Mental Health and Illness, Washington, 1977-78; vis. prof. U. Rotterdam, Amsterdam, 1986, Boston U., 1996. Co-author: (with Tischler) Quality Assurance in Mental Health, 1983; contbr. articles to profl. jours. (Citation classic 1986). Mem. State Health Clin. Coordinating Com., Hartford, Conn., 1980s; mem. clin. adv. com. Ill. Dept. Mental Health and Devel. Disabilities, Chgo., 1995-97; chair mental health task force Ill. Dept. Children and Family Svcs., Chgo., 1993-97; chair Mental Health Svc. Sys. Adv. Coun., Springfield and Chgo., Ill., 1992-95. Lt. comdr. USN, 1955-61. Recipient Disting. Faculty award U. Ill., Chgo., 1997; named Alumnus of Yr., Albany Med. Coll., 1999. Fellow Am. Coll. Psychiatrists, Am. Psychiat. Assn. (life, trustee-at-large, Adminstrv. Psychiatry award 1995), Am. Assn. Psychiat. Adminstrs. (Past. Pres. award 1992); mem. AMA. Jewish. Avocations: time with family, listening to music, reading. Home: Chicago, Ill. Deceased.

ATOYNATAN, TANASH, child psychiatrist; b. Istanbul, Turkey, Aug. 23, 1920; came to U.S., 1948; s. Harry and Agatha (Pokias) A.; m. Dorothy Atoynatan, Mar. 31, 1964. MD, U. Istanbul, Turkey, 1944. Resident in psychiatry Duke U. Hosp., Durham, N.C., 1952; resident in neurology Louisville U. Hosp., 1953; resident in child psychiatry Univ. Hosp., Balt., 1957; exec. and clin. dir. Community Child Guidance Ctr., Manchester, Conn., from 1962. Asst. clin. prof. U. Conn. Sch. Medicine, Farmington, 1984—. Contbr. articles to med. jours. Served to lt. USAF, 1945-48. Fellow Am. Psychiat. Assn. (life), Am. Orthopsychiat. Assn. (life), Am. Assn. Psychiat. Svcs. for Children (life). Democrat. Greek Orthodox. Avocations: tennis, golf, bridge, chess. Home: Naples, Fla. Died Dec. 17, 2007.

AUSTRIA, JOSE LAZARO, retired construction company executive; b. Philippines, Mar. 28, 1921; s. Ricardo Austria and Marciana Lazaro; m. Josefina Cruz Concepcion, Jan. 23, 1947; eight children. A in Chem. Engring., Manila Inst. Technology, 1941, A in Civil Engring., 1950. Lic. registered master plumber, plumbing engr., Mapua Inst. Tech. Mgr. Gregorio Lazaro Constrn., Manila, The Philippines, 1938-41; constrn. supervisor Yukim Teng Constrn., Okinawa, Japan, 1947-49; sanitary and plumbing contractor Jose L. Austria Plumbing, Quezon, Philippines, 1961-72; cons., mgr. constrn. work Anta Constrn. Corp., Quezon, 1978-93. Mem. Nat. Master Plumber Assn. Philippines, Philippine Contractor Assn. Roman Catholic. Avocation: writing. Home: Northlake, Ill. Died Dec. 19, 2007.

AUSUBEL, DAVID PAUL, retired psychiatrist, author; b. Bklyn., Oct. 25, 1918; s. Herman and Lillian (Leff) A.; m. Pearl Leibowitz, Nov. 23, 1943 (div. 1979); m. Gloria Grace George, Sept. 24, 1983; children: Frederick Michael, Laura Ruth. BA, U. Pa., Phila., 1939; MA, Columbia U., 1940, PhD, 1950; MD, Middlesex U., Waltham, Mass., 1943. Intern Gov. Hosp., NYC, 1943-44; resident USPHS Hosp., Lexington, Ky., 1946-47, Buffalo (N.Y.) Psychiat. Ctr., 1947-48; profl. ednl. psychology U. Ill., Urbana, 1950-66; prof. med. edn. rsch. U. Toronto Grad. Sch., 1966-68; prof. ednl. psychology, program head CUNY, NYC, 1968-73; resident Albert Einstein Coll. Medicine/Bronx Psychiat. Ctr., 1976-77; psychiatrist N.Y. State Divsn. Youth, Highland, 1986-94. Vis. prof. psychology Salesian U., Rome, 1964-65, Hochschule der Bundeswehr, Munich, Germany, 1980; cons. U.S. Office Edn., Washington, 1968-70; mem. internat. adv. bd. Psychologie in Erziehung und Untervicht, 1981-85. Author: Ego Development and the Personality Disorders, 1952, Theory and Problems of Adolescent Development, 1954, Theory and Problems of Child Development, 1957, Ego Development and Psychopathology, 1996; mem. editl. bd. Child Devel. Monograph Social Rsch. Child Devel., 1963-65, Internat. Jour. Addictions, 1963—. Capt. USPHS, 1945-47. Recipient Fulbright award to New Zealand, 1957. Fellow APA (Thorndike award 1976); mem. Am. Psychiat. Assn., Am. Psychol. Soc., Am. Ednl. Rsch. Assn. Democrat. Roman Catholic. Avocations: gardening, music (cd's), hiking, boating. Home: Port Ewen, NY. Died July 9, 2008.

AVERY, WILLIAM HENRY, former Governor of Kansas, former United States Representative from Kansas; b. Wakefield, Kans., Aug. 11, 1911; s. Herman W. and Hattie M. (Coffman) A.; m. Hazel Bowles, June 16, 1940; children: Bill, Barbara Ann, Bradley Eugene, Martha Sue. AB, U. Kans., 1934. Farmer, stockman, nr. Wakefield, Kans., 1935-55; mem. US Congress from 2nd Kans. Dist., 1955—65; gov. State of Kans., Topeka, 1965-67; with Garvey Enterprises, 1967-68; asst. to pres. Clinton Oil Co., 1969; pres. Real Petroleum (merged with Clinton Oil Co. 1971), 1969-71; congressional liaison to asst. sec. US Dept. Interior, Washington, 1973-77; chmn. bd. Farmers and Merchants Bank, Wakefield, Kans., 1977-80. Mem. Kans. Legislature, 1951-55, Legis. Council Kans., 1953-55; dir. bd. edn. Wakefield High Sch. Mem. Kans. Farm Bur., Delta Upsilon. Clubs: Masons (Wakefield), Lions (Wakefield). Republican. Methodist. Died Nov. 4, 2009.

BAARS, DONALD LEE, petroleum geologist, researcher; b. Oregon City, Oreg., May 27, 1928; s. George William and Happy Lela (Wallace) B.; m. Neva Jane Weaver, Aug. 30, 1948; children: Karla Denise Baars English, Jodie Megan Baars Neil, Cayli Dawn. BS in Geology, U. Utah, 1952; PhD in Geology, U. Colo., 1965. Petroleum geologist Shell Oil Co., Durango, Colo., 1952-61; rsch. geologist Conoco Ponca City, Okla., 1961-62; assoc. prof. Washington State U., Pullman, 1965-68; prof. geology Ft. Lewis Coll., Durango, 1968-80; cons. various petroleum cos., Evergreen, Colo., 1980-88; sr. scientist Kans. Geol. Survey, Lawrence, from 1988. Cons. numerous oil cos., Durango, Evergreen, 1968—; pub. Canon Pubs. Ltd., 1985—. Author: Red Rock Country, 1972, The Colorado Plateau, 1982, Canyonlands Country, 1990, The American Alps: The San Juan Mountains, Colorado, 1992; contbr. articles to profl. jours. With U.S. Army, 1952-54. Fellow Geol. Soc. of Am. (various coms.); mem. Am. Assn. Petroleum Geologists (cert. profl. petroleum geologist, various coms.), Soc. Econ. Paleontologists, Mineralogists, Four Corners Geol. Soc. (hon. life mem., past pres.), Kans. Geol. Soc. Avocations: photography, river rafting, mountain climbing, skiing. Home: Lawrence, Kans. Died July 7, 2008.

BABCOCK, DOROTHY ELLEN, nursing educator, author; b. Phila., July 10, 1931; d. Peter Joseph and Dorothy Ambrosia (Muldowney) Kreinbihl; m. Clarence Otis Babcock, June 28, 1958; children: Donna Miller, Phyllis Pennington, Karen Nern. Diploma, Misericordia Hosp. Sch. Nursing, 1952; BSNEd, U. Pa., 1956; MSN, Cath. U. of Am., 1958. RN, Colo. Clin. specialist Denver Health & Hosps., 1968-81; educator Metro State Coll. of Denver, Denver, 1981-97. Author: Introduction to Growth Development and Family Life, 3d edit., 1972; co-author: Raising Kids OK, 1986, Client Education Theory and Practice, 1995, Critical Thinking Applied to Nursing, 1996. Mem. Am. Assn. Marriage and Family Therapists, Colo. Nurses Assn., Nat. League for Nursing, Sigma Theta Tau. Home: Lakewood, Colo. Died Oct. 17, 2007.

BABINSKY, ANDREW DANIEL, manufacturing executive; b. South River, NJ, July 13, 1930; s. Andrew and Julia (Kayati) B.; m. Frances Olivia Stem, Aug. 20, 1953; 1 child, Jane Ellen. BS in Physics, Heidelberg Coll., 1952; MS in Physics, Case Western Res. U., 1962. Aeronautical research scientist Lewis Lab NASA, Cleve., 1952-55, nuclear propulsion engr., 1958-59; mgr. aircraft systems TRW, Cleve., 1959-71; dir. materials and chem. res. Diamond Shamrock, Concord, Ohio, 1971-83; pres. Mitech Corp., Willoughby, Ohio, 1983-86, chmn., from 1986. Patentee in field; contbr. articles to profl. jours. Served to lt. USNR, 1955-58. Republican. Avocations: videography, golf, woodworking, photography. Home: Chagrin Falls, Ohio. Died Jan. 22, 2008.

BACON, KENNETH HOGATE, relief organization executive, former federal agency administrator; b. Bronxville, NY, Nov. 21, 1944; s. Theodore S. and Sarah (Hogate) B.; m. Darcy; children: Katharine, Sarah. BA in English, Amherst Coll., 1966; MS in Journalism, MBA, Columbia U., 1968. Legis. asst. to Senator Thomas J. McIntyre US Senate, 1968-69; various editl. position The Wall Street Jour., 1969-94, Pentagon correspondent, 1976—80; asst. to sec. for pub. affairs US Dept. Def., 1994-96, asst. sec. for pub. affairs, 1996—2001; pres. Refugess Internat., 2001—09. Co-chmn. Partnership for Effective Peacekeeping (PEP); bd. mem. Am. U., Cairo, Population Action Internat., InterAction. Served in USAR, 1968—74. Died Aug. 15, 2009.

BADTKE, SANDRA ANN, retired psychotherapist; b. Cedarburg, Wis., Jan. 23, 1938; d. Eldred Herman and Rose Mary (Jensterle) B. BS in Edn., U. Wis., Milw., 1960. LCSW MSW U. Wis./Milwaukee, Wis., 1995. Tchr. Appleton Schs., Wis., 1960-67, Franklin Schs., Wis., 1960—67, Oconomowoc Schs., Wis., 1960—67; exec. dir. Cambridge House, Inc., Milw., 1967-79; prodn. mgr. Anderson Graphics, 1979-80; alcohol/drug abuse counselor, coord. DePaul Hosp., Inc., 1980-89, dir. outpatient clinic, 1989-91, dir. outpatient ops. for elderly programming, 1992—2001, ret., 2001. Programming cons. DePaul Hosp., Inc.; alcohol and drug counselor for SE Wis., Med. and Soc. Svcs.; psychotherapist for Aurora Health Care, Milwaukee, Wis. Author: videotape Substance Abuse and the Elderly, 1985. Recipient Faye McBeath Found. grant for rsch. in elderly substance abuse, 1982. Mem. NAFE, NASCO Avocations: music, fine arts, gourmet cooking, crafts, creative writing, profl. writing. Home: West Allis, Wis. Died Sept. 14, 2007.

BAEUMEL, MARY LOU, nurse, administrator; b. Mifflintown, Pa., Dec. 20, 1934; d. Guy Joseph and Violet Mae (Mefferd) Hower; m. William J. Beaumel, Nov. 9, 1963; 1 child, Joseph William. Diploma, Polyclinic Med. Ctr., Harrisburg, Pa., 1955; student, U. Colo., Denver. Head nurse Jewish Hosp., Denver; staff nurse Wyckoff (N.J.) Sanatorium; nurse Polyclinic Med. Ctr.; dir. nursing Med. Staff Svcs. Inc., Virginia Beach, Va. Mem. Va. Beach Task Force on Aging. Lt. col. USAF, 1957-79. Decorated Air Force Commendation medal with oak leaf cluster. Mem. ANA, Va. Nurses Assn., Ret. Nat. Officers Assn., Soc. Ret. Air Force Nurses. Home: Virginia Bch, Va. Died Oct. 24, 2007.

BAILEY, BETTY LOU, retired environmental engineer; b. Chgo., Apr. 25, 1929; d. Otterbein Andrew and Mable Mann (Young) B. BSME, U. Ill., 1950; M of Engring., Pa. State U., 1967. Registered profl. engr., Ohio, N.Y. Test engr. GE, various locations, 1950-51; design engr. GE-Jet Engine dept., Cin., 1951-60; engr. GE-Knolls Atomic Power Lab., Schenectady, N.Y., 1960-61; system engr. GE-Space Div., King of Prussia, Pa., 1961-69; sr. engr. GE-Gas Turbine Div., Schenectady, 1969-86; sr. environ. engr. GE-Power Plant Systems Dept., Schenectady, 1986-94; ret., 1994. Patentee in field. Conservation chair Schenectady (N.Y.) chpt., Adirondack Mountain Club, 1981—. Recipient Disting. Alumnus award mech. engring. dept. Univ. Ill., Urbana, 1988. Fellow Soc. Women Engrs. (counselor student sect. 1978—, Pioneer award 1994); mem. ASME, AIAA, NSPE, Am. Soc. for Engring. Edn., Air and Waste Mgmt. Assn., Tau Beta Pi. Methodist. Avocations: whitewater canoeing, hiking, bicycling, showshoeing, choral singing. Home: Schenectady, NY. Died Nov. 13, 2007.

BAILEY, JOHN ARTHUR, management consultant; b. Bryan, Tex., July 6, 1918; s. Arthur Chester and Laura Elizabeth (Brogdon) B.; m. Barbara Jane Elliott, Jan. 6, 1946; children: Louise B. Duback, John Elliott. BS in Mech. Engring., Tex. A & M U., 1939; M in Govt. Adminstrn. cum laude, U. Pa., 1949, PhD in Polit. Sci., 1966. Registered profl. engr., Pa. Engr. Pepsi-Cola Co., LI, N.Y., 1946-48; mgr. Edgeworth (Pa.) Borough, 1949-53; dep. mng. dir. City of Phila., Pa., 1953-61; exec. dir. Passenger Svc. Improvement Corp., Phila., 1961-64; dep. gen. mgr. S.E. Pa. Transp. Authority, Phila., 1964-67; dir., prof. Transp. Ctr., Northwestern U., Evanston, Ill., 1967-75; v.p. Murphy Engring., Chgo., 1975-76; ptnr. L. T. Klauder & Assoc., Phila., 1976-81; pres. Transp. Sys. Associates, Inc., Santa Fe, 1983—92. Pres., chmn. Soc. for Advancement of Mgmt., Phila., 1953-55, Met. Planning Coun., Chgo., 1969-73; mem. rapid transit com. Transp. Rsch. Bd., Washington, 1984-90. Mem., chmn. Santa Fe County Transp. Devel. Dist., 1993-98; mem., pres. Park Plazas Cmty. Svcs. Assn., Santa Fe, 1995-98; mem. N.Mex. First; mem. com. on rail transit sys. Transp. Rsch. Bd., Washington, 1992-98. Fels scholar, Phila., 1948-49. Mem. Am. Pub. Works Assn. (life), Am. Soc. for Polit. & Social Scis., Santa Fe Coun. on Internat. Rels. (treas. 1995-97), Cosmos Club (Washington), Tau Beta Pi. Democrat. Unitarian Universalist. Home: Mendham, NJ. Died Apr. 1, 2009.

BAIR, EDWARD JAY, chemistry professor; b. Ft. Collins, Colo., June 30, 1922; s. Jay Albert and Edith Hectos (Pegg) B.; m. Dorothy Helen Bimson, June 29, 1958. BS, Colo. State U., 1943; PhD, Brown U., 1949. Chemist Tenn. Eastman Corp., Oak Ridge, 1943-46; research assoc. U. Wash., 1949-54; mem. faculty Ind. U., 1954-90, prof. chemistry, 1965-90, prof. chemistry emeritus, from 1990. Mem. Am. Chem. Soc. Home: Bloomington, Ind. Died Nov. 11, 2008.

BAIRD, PHILLIP ALLAN, trial judge; b. Elyria, Ohio, Mar. 1, 1923; s. Dow Abram and Florence Madge (Barnes) B.; m. Claire Louise Duvall, Aug. 5, 1950 (dec. Feb. 22, 1976); children: Christine, Phillip Jr., Ellen, Margaret, Nancy, David, Barbara; m. Barbara Ann Lucia, May 14, 1978; stepchildren: Jeffrey, Cari, Susan, Gregory. BA in Econs., Hiram Coll., 1948; JD, Akron U. Coll. of Law, 1959. Naval officer, lt. comdr. USN, 1942-45; claims adjuster Liberty Mut. Ins. Co., Pitts., 1948-50; teller Old Phoenix Bank, Medina, Ohio, 1950-51; naval officer USN, 1952-54; claims adjuster Ohio Farmers Ins. Co., Westfield County, Ohio, 1954-63; atty. pvt. practice Medina, 1963-75; judge Medina County, from 1975. Chmn. Am. Cancer Soc., Medina, 1978. Mem. Medina County Bar Assn., Ohio State Bar Assn., Common Pleas Assn. Republican. Episcopalian. Avocations: fishing, camping, model ship bldg., reading. Home: Medina, Ohio. Died Sept. 16, 2007.

BAJEK, FRANK MICHAEL, retired military officer, financial consultant; b. Chgo., July 4, 1950; s. Edward Joseph and Anna J. (Banik) Bajek; m. Renee Ann Kaspar, Aug. 1, 1981; children: David, Amanda, Erica. BBA, Loyola U., Chgo., 1972; MBA, Keller Grad. Sch. Mgmt., 1981. CPA Ill. Asst. mgr. svc. auditing Aldens, Inc., Chgo., 1976—78, indsl. engr., 1978—79, internal auditor, 1979—80; field auditor Stewart-Warner Corp., Chgo., 1980—81; commd. 2d lt. USAR, 1972, advanced through grades to lt. col., 1992, ret., 1996; tax, fin. cons. Ill., from 1989; contr. Overland Bond and Investment Corp., 2000—06. Adj. instr. acctg. Nat.-Louis U., 1994, Northwestern Bus. Coll., 1997—99, from 2001, Robert Morris Coll., 1998—99. Mem.: AICPA, Assn. Profls. Bus. Mgmt. (cert. bus. mgr.), Assn. Govt. Accts. (cert. govt. fin. mgr.), Ill. CPA Soc., Am. Soc. Mil. Comptrs. Roman Catholic. Home: Plainfield, Ill. Died Jan. 19, 2008.

BAJOR, JAMES HENRY, musician, jazz pianist; b. Detroit, May 7, 1953; s. Henry Stanley and Irene (Hetmanski) B. Student, Wayne State U., 1976. Rec. artist Sugo Music, Half Moon Bay, Calif. Produced albums of own piano compositions: Awakening, 1987 (nominated for New Age solo acoustic Grammy award 1987), Gentle Images, 1988; appears regularly on radio and TV programs. Mem. ASCAP, NARAS. Died Dec. 21, 2006.

BAKER, CARL GWIN, retired science administrator, educator; b. Louisville, Nov. 27, 1920; s. Edward Forrest and Naomi (Taylor) B.; m. Lois Eleane Oxsen, Mar. 24, 1949 (div. May 1975); children: Cathryn, Jeannette; m. Catherine Valerie Smith, May 23, 1975. AB in Zoology, U. Louisville, 1942, MD, 1944, DSc (hon.), 1980; MA in Biochemistry, U. Calif., Berkeley, 1949. Lic. med. practice, Ky., Calif. Rsch. investigator Biochemistry Lab. Nat. Cancer Inst., NIH, Bethesda, Md., 1949-52, 53-55, staff grants and fellowships br., 1952-53, asst. to NIH assoc. dir., 1956-57, asst. dir., acting sci. dir., 1958-61, assoc. dir. program, 1961-67, sci. dir. etiology, 1967-69; dir. Nat. Cancer Inst., Bethesda, 1969-72; dir. program policy staff Health & Human Svcs. Adminstr., Rockville, Md., 1975-76; med. dir. Ludwig Inst. Cancer Rsch., Zurich, Switzerland, 1977-85, ret., 1985; adj. instr. U. Md., College Park, 1989. Mem. gov. coun. Internat. Agy. for Cancer Rsch., Lyon, France, 1969-72. Assoc. editor Jour. of the Nat. Cancer Inst., 1954-55; mem. editl. adv. bd. Cancer Jour., 1965-73; contbr. articles to jours. Biochemistry, Oncology, Mgmt. Sci. Del. State Bd. Edn., Annapolis, Md., 1957; mem. exec. com. adv. panel on health Am. Revolution Bicentenial Commn., Washington, 1970-72; v.p. 10th Internat. Cancer Congress, Houston, 1970. Asst. surgeon gen. (RAd rank) USPHS, 1970—. Decorated PHS Meritorious Svc. medal; Jane Coffin Childs Fund fellow, 1946-48, Spl. fellow Nat. Cancer Inst., NIH, 1949. Mem. Am. Assn. Cancer Rsch. (bd. dirs. 1972-76), Am. Chem. Soc. (divsn. biol. chemistry, sec. 1955-57, councillor 1958-61), Am. Soc. Biochemistry and Molecular Biology, Soc. Exptl. Biology and Medicine, Cosmos Club, Sigma Xi, Alpha Omega Alpha, Phi Kappa Phi. Achievements include research in application of systems analysis and planning to strategic planning in medical research and laying the foundations for development of national cancer plan. Died Feb. 11, 2009.

BAKER, DAVID EARLE, retired military officer; b. West Stewartstown, NH, 1946; m. Carol Ann Baker; children: David Jr., Christopher. BBA, Hofstra U., 1968; student, Squadron Officer Sch.; MBA in Human Resources Mgmt., U. Hawaii, 1974; student, Air Command and Staff Coll., 1978, Armed Forces and Staff Coll., 1983, Air War Coll., 1987, Nat. Defense Coll. Can., 1992, Capstone Nat. Defense U., 1994. Pilot USAF, 1970, advanced through grades to brigadier gen., ret., 1997; vice dir. operational plans & interoperability The Joint Staff US Dept. Def., 1994—97. Decorated Disting. Svc. medal, Air medal with four oak leaf clusters, Prisoner of War Medal, Republic of Vietnam Gallantry Cross with bronze star, Legion of Merit, Purple Heart, Bronze Star Medal with V device and oak leaf cluster, Disting. Flying Cross with oak leaf cluster, others. Died Jan. 29, 2009.

BAKER, DAVID LLOYD, university administrator; b. Louisville, Nov. 23, 1940; s. David L. Baker and Evelyn Diana (Beville) Woods; m. Mary Anne King, Sept. 7, 1961 (div. Aug. 1984); m. Sara Marie Martin, May 25, 1985; children: David III, Margaret Anne, Simon. BA, U. Louisville, 1963, JD, 1969. Bar: Ky. 1970, U.S. Supreme Ct. 1980, Wyo. 1987. Dir. pub. rels. U. Louisville, 1968-76, univ. counsel, 1976-86; spl. asst. to pres. U. Wyo., Laramie, from 1986. Home: Owensboro, Ky. Died July 26, 2008.

BAKER, HARRISON SCOTT, application developer, consultant; b. Marion, Ohio, Mar. 12, 1950; s. Stanley Wallace and Starling (Dixon) Baker. BA, BS, Fla. State U., 1972-80; MBA, Embry-Riddle Aeronaut. U., 1986. MCSE, cert. computing tech. Computing Tech. Industry Assn., network assoc. Cisco Sys., Inc., 2003, A+, Network+, Security +, Server +, iNet + Comptia, Microsoft cert. database adminstr., Microsoft cert. sys. adminstr.; lic. radio-telephone with radar endorsement FCC. Mgr. Vincent Auto Parts, Inc., Marathon, Fla., 1972-78; maintenance supr. Eastern Air Lines, Inc., Miami, 1980-92; computer cons. Upper Sandusky, Ohio, from 1992. Author: Index to the Muster Rolls of PA in War of 1812, 1995, Early Settlers of Wyandot County, 1995, 1890 Veterans Census For Wyandot County, Ohio, 2004; indexer Obituaries in Upper Sandusky newspapers 1868-1911, 1994, Obituaries in Upper Sandusky newspapers 1912-1937, 1996, Obituaries in Upper Sandusky newspapers 1938-1958, 1997, Obituaries in Upper Sandusky newspapers 1959-1979, 1997, Journal of William Kennedy Beall, 1999, Civil War Soldiers Buried in Wyandot County, Ohio, 2000, Civil War Veterans Buried at the Ohio Veterans Home, 2001, American Prisoners of War Held at Halifax During the War of 1812, 2004, Marriage License and Records 1845-1868 Wyandot County, Ohio, 2006, others. Trustee Wyandot County Geneal. Soc., 1995—2001. Mem.: SAR (pres. Hancock chpt. 1995—96), Assn. Computing Machinery, IEEE Computer Soc., Sons of Vets. Res. (capt., pub. info. officer 2000—03), Sons of Union Vets. (camp sec. 1994—98, Dept. of Ohio signals officer 1999—2000, nat. chief of staff 2002—03), Soc. War of 1812 (Ohio pres. 1996—99). Avocations: electronics, genealogy. Home: Upper Sandusky, Ohio. Died June 29, 2008.

BALASSONI, LUIGI PAULINO ALFREDO FRANCESCO ANTONIO See BELLSON, LOUIS

BALCOM, ORVILLE, engineer; b. Inglewood, Calif., Apr. 20, 1937; s. Orville R. and Rose Mae (Argo) B.; children: Cynthia, Steven. BS in Math., Calif. State U., Long Beach, 1958, postgrad., 1958-59, UCLA, 1959-62. Engr. AiResearch Mfg. Co., 1959-62, 64-65; chief engr. Meditron, El Monte, Calif., 1962-64, Astro Metrics, Burbank, Calif., 1965-67; chief engr., gen. mgr. Varadyne Power Systems, Van Nuys, Calif., 1968-71; owner, chief engr. Brown Dog Engring., Lomita, Calif., from 1971. Patentee in field. Mem. IEEE Computer Group, Independent Computer Cons. Assn., Torrance Athletic Club. Home: Lomita, Calif. Died Feb. 14, 2008.

BALDINO, MICHAEL EDWARD, communications electronics specialist; b. New Haven, Sept. 2, 1963; s. Domenic Frank and Kathleen Mary (Ranney) B. Diploma in electronic tech., Conn. Sch. Electronics, New Haven, 1985; diploma in broadcasting, Conn. Sch. Broadcasting, Stratford, 1985. Radio announcer WELI, WPLR, Hamden, Conn., 1985-88; field svc. technician Associated Graphics, Hamden, Conn., 1986-88; freelance electronics specialist Hamden, Conn., 1988-97; prodn. technician Evax Systems, Milford, Conn., from 1997. TV prodr. Citizens TV, New Haven, 1997; projectionist State of Conn., 1996. Author: How to Make Money on Your Knowledge of Cars, 1995. Avocations: amateur radio, computers. Died Dec. 5, 2007.

BALL, CLYDE CURTIS, journalist, public information officer, public relations executive; b. Jeffrey Boone County, W.Va., June 25, 1921; BS in Journalism, Marshall U., Huntington, W.Va., 1943. Reporter Assoc. Press, Huntington, 1945—59; pub. rels. exec. Philco Ford Corp., Washington, 1963—70; pub. rels. officer US Govt. Commerce Dept., Dept., Energy, Dept. Trans., Maritime Adminstrn., Washington, 1970—86; et. Speech writer, science writer Philco Ford, Phila., 1963—70; speech writer US Govt. Spiro Agnew Maritime Adminstrn., Washington, 1970—86. Ghost writer (speeches for Spiro Agnew), 1972—73. 1st lt. USN, 1943—45, South Pacific. Recipient Poetry Works award, Va. Poetry Soc., Charolottesille, 1998. Mem.: Nat. Press Club. Avocations: walking, poetry. Home: Potomac Falls, Va. Died Jan. 28, 2008.

BALMUTH, BERNARD ALLEN, retired film editor; b. Youngstown, Ohio, May 19, 1918; s. Joseph and Sadie (Stein) B.; m. Rosa June Bergman, Mar. 2, 1952; children: Mary Susan, Sharon Nancy. BA in English, UCLA, 1942. Postal clk. U.S. Postal Svc., LA, 1946-53, asst. and apprentice film editor, film editor LA, 1955-90; ret., 1990. Instr. film editing dept. of the arts UCLA Ext., 1979-99 (cert. of appreciation); film editing cons. Am. Film Inst., LA, 1982-92. Author: The Language of the Cutting Room, 1979, Introduction to Film Editing, 1989. Initiator petition STOP Save TV Original Programming and Stop Excessive Reruns, 1971-75. Adminstrn. non-commd. officer U.S. Army, 1942-45. Recipient Honor Cert. for Contbn. Acad. TV Arts and Scis., 1974, Emmy nomination Best Editing, 1982, Mimes award for acting Youngstown Coll., 1937. Mem. Am. Cinema Editors (life, bd. dirs. 1982-85, 97-99, sec. 1985-87, v.p. 1987-91, chmn. spl. awards com. 1988-99, hon. historian 1993-, Ace Heritage award, 2003), Hollywood Entertainment Labor Coun. (rep. for Editors Guild 1972-2002), Stage Soc. (bd. dirs., sec. 1949-54), TV Acad. Motion Picture Editors (mem. exec. com. peer group 1988-). Democrat. Jewish. Avocations: cinema, theater, dance, cinema books. Died Dec. 6, 2007.

BANDEL, BETTY, retired English educator; b. Washington, July 28, 1912; d. George Edwin and Emma Louise (Frederick) B. MusB, U. Ariz., 1933; MA, Columbia U., 1947, PhD, 1951; DLitt (hon.), U. Vt., 1983. Reporter Ariz. Daily Star, Tucson, 1935-42; from instr. to prof. U. Vt., Burlington, from 1947. Author: (book) Sing the Lord's Song in a Strange Land, 1981, also history articles. Mem. Chittenden County Hist. Soc., Burlington, 1965. Lt. col. USAF, 1942-45. Decorated Legion of Merit. Avocations: genealogy, historical research. Home: S Burlington, Vt. Died July 2, 2008.

BANKS, DOUGLAS O'NEAL, gerontology nurse, educator; b. Tuscaloosa, Ala., Dec. 7, 1943; s. Floyd and Clister A. (Parham) B. ASN, Jefferson State Jr. Coll., Birmingham, Ala., 1973; BA, U. Ala., 1969; MA, U. of South Fla., 1977, BSN, 1980. RN, Fla., Ala.; cert. in continuing edn./staff devel. and gerontology. Staff nurse psychiat. unit VA of Lexington, Ky.; staff nurse med. ICU/CCU VA Hosp., Birmingham; with hemodialysis dept. J.A. Haley VA, Tampa, Fla., nurse educator, from 1979. Mem. Fla. Nurse's Assn., Sigma Theta Tau. Home: Tampa, Fla. Died Nov. 13, 2007.

BANNON, JOSEPH KEVIN, brokerage house executive; b. Waterbury, Conn., Oct. 31, 1949; s. Tobias Francis and Arlene (Keefe) B.; m. Barbara McNellis, June 4, 1971; children: Joseph, Tiffany, Tobias, Shaun. BS in Bus. Adminstrn., Boston U., 1971, MBA, 1972. CPA, Conn. Investment cons. Merrill Lynch, Hartford, Conn., 1981-83, Paine Webber, Hartford, 1983-89; pres. Bannon & Whitney, Inc., West Hartford, Conn., from 1989, Bannon & Whitney Investment Advisors, Inc., 1990. Mem. AICPA, Nat. Assn. Accts., Internat. Assn. Fin. Planners, Conn. Soc. CPAs, Conn. Fin. Officers Assn. (assoc.), Elks. Avocation: jogging. Home: Southington, Conn. Died Dec. 31, 2007.

BANOFF, HARRY, ophthalmology educator; b. Chgo., Mar. 31, 1915; s. Benjamin and Rose (Goldsmith) B.; m. Alice Young, Dec. 4, 1943 (dec. Aug. 1991); children: Barbara Ann, David Alan; m. Helen Kroboth, May 22, 1993. BA, U. Ill., 1935; MA, NYU, 1939; MD, U. So. Calif., LA, 1947. Diplomate Am. Bd. Ophthalmology. Resident ophthalmology L.A. County Gen. Hosp., LA, 1948-50; pvt. practice ophthalmology Los Gatos, Calif., 1954-80; clin. instr. Sch. Medicine Stanford U., Palo Alto, Calif., 1954-84, clin. assoc. prof. ophthalmology Sch. Medicine, 1985-95; ret., 1995. Pres. Pacific Coast Unitarian Coun., Berkeley, Calif., 1959-62; v.p. Am. Unitarian Assn., Boston, 1961-62; treas. Los Gatos Homeowner's Assn., 1980-92. Capt. Med. Corps, U.S. Army, 1948-54. Fellow Am. Acad. Ophthalmology; mem. AMA, Santa Clara County Med. Soc., Calif. Med. Assn., Los Gatos Rotary Club (hon.), Phi Beta Kappa, Sigma Xi. Democrat. Avocations: music, reading. Home: Tulsa, Okla. Died Jan. 17, 2008.

BARBIER, MARCEL MARIE, engineer, physicist; b. Warsaw, Dec. 20, 1924; s. Jean Baptiste and Antoinette Georgine (Feyerick) B.; m. Nicole Claude Roos; children: Frederique, Anne, Helene, Cyrille, Patrick. Diploma elec. engring., Eidgenoessishe Technische Hochschule, Zurich, Switzerland, 1946; PhDEE, Eidgenoessishe Technische Hochschule, 1950; PhD in Physics, U. Paris, 1954. Rsch. Eidgenoessishe Technische Hochschule, Zurich, 1947-50; engr. Compagnie Generale de Telegraphie Sans Fil, Paris, 1950-54; engr./physicist Conseil Europeen Pour la Recherche Nucleaire, Geneva, 1954-73; scientist Sci. Applications Internat. Corp., McLean, Va., 1973-75, Mitre Corp., McLean, 1975-79, Marcel M. Barbier, Inc., Herndon, Va., from 1980. Author: Induced Radioactivity, 1969. Died Feb. 7, 2008.

BARDGETT, JOHN E. (JACK BARDGETT), lawyer, former state supreme court justice; b. St. Louis, Apr. 28, 1927; s. Alfred L. and Catherine C. (Heverin) Bardgett; m. Mary Jean Branch, Aug. 1, 1953; children: John E., Suzanne, Bruce, Beth. LLB, St. Louis U., 1951. Bar: Mo. 1951, Ill. 1963, US Dist. Ct. (ea. dist.)/ Mo. 1954, US Supreme Ct. 1957. Sole practice, St. Louis, 1955—68; city atty. Normandy, Mo.; judge St. Louis County Cir., 1968—70; justice Supreme Ct. Mo., Jefferson City, Mo., 1970—82, chief justice, 1979—81; ptnr. Guilfoil, Petzall, Shoemake, St. Louis; gen. counsel Ctrl. States Southeast & Southwest Health Welfare & Pension Funds, 1984—87. Served in USN. Died Nov. 29, 2008.

BARKLEY, LINDA DOROTHY, engineer; b. San Diego, Dec. 12, 1931; d. James Falls and Helen Patricia (Yoo) B. BA, U. San Diego, 1974; MS, Loyola Marymount U., 1980. Project mgr. Hughes Aircraft Co., LA, from 1978. Recipient Bausch and Lomb Sci. award, 1970, Achievement award YWCA, Los Angeles, 1986. Mem. Soc. Women Engrs., Am. Math. Soc., Assn. Women in Math., Mat./Sci. Interchange of L.A. (v.p. 1980—). Died Aug. 15, 2009.

BARNES, CLIVE ALEXANDER, drama and dance critic; b. London, Eng., May 13, 1927; arrived in US, 1965; s. Arthur Lionel and Freda Marguerite (Garratt) Barnes; m. Joyce Elizabeth Tolman (div.); m. Patricia Amy Evelyn Winckley (div.); children: Christopher John Clive, Joanna

Rosemary Maya; m. Amy Pagnozzi (div.); m. Valerie Margetson Taylor, July 24, 2004. BA, U. Oxford, Eng., 1951; LittD (hon.), Adelphi U., 1976, Albright Coll., 1982. Co-editor dance mag. Arabesque, 1950; asst. editor Dance and Dancers, 1950-58, assoc. editor, 1958-61, exec. editor, 1961-65, editor NYC, from 1965; writer music, dance, drama, films Daily Express, London, 1956-65; dance critic The Spectator, London, 1959-65, The Times, London, 1962-65, NY Times, NYC, 1965—67, chief drama and dance critic, 1967—77; assoc. editor, drama and dance critic NY Post, 1977, dance, opera and sr. theater critic, 2002—08; NY corr. The Evening Standard, London, 1988—91; sr. consulting editor, adv. editor Dance Mag.; contbr. Dance mag., 1956—2008, reviewer & author, monthly column Attitudes. Adj. prof. dept. journalism NYU, 1968—75. Author: Ballet in Britain Since the War, 1953, Frederick Ashton and His Ballets, 1961, NY Times Directory of the Theatre, 1973, Nureyev, 1982; co-author: Ballet Here and Now, 1961, Dance Scene, USA, 1967, Inside American Ballet Theatre, 1977; co-author: (with Elizabeth Kaye) American Ballet Theatre: A 25 Year Retrospective, 1999; co-author: (with Rose Eichenbaum) Masters of Movement: Portraits of America's Great Choreographers, 2004; co-editor: Best American Plays. With RAF, 1946—48. Decorated Knight Order of Dannebrog Denmark, Comdr. Order Brit. Empire; recipient Dance Mag. award, 2005. Mem.: NY Drama Critics Cir. (pres. 1973—75), Critics Cir. London (past. sec., chmn. ballet sect.), Century Assn. (NY). Died Nov. 19, 2008.

BARNETT, MARY LORENE, real estate manager; b. Saline County, Mo., Nov. 29, 1927; d. Grover Cleveland Renno and Emma Zue Rennison; m. Eugene Earl Boone, Aug. 24, 1946 (div. Aug. 1961); 1 child, Priscilla Sue Boone; m. Charles Owen Barnett, Nov. 11, 1961; 1 child, Robert E. BA in Psychology magna cum laude, Washburn U., 1979. Asst. contr. 1st State Savs., Sedalia, Mo., 1960-61; bookkeeper New Empire Ins., Sedalia, 1961-63; office mgr. Klassic Mfg., Sedalia, 1963-66; real estate mgr. Topeka, Kans., from 1970. Author: Charles Renno Family Record, 1996, Charles Renno Family, 1997. Bd. dirs. Shawnee County Coun. on Aging, Topeka. Recipient cert. of appreciation Bd. of County Commrs., Topeka, 1995. Mem. DAR, AAUW, LWV, Topeka Women's Club (1st v.p.), Ea. Star, Phi Kappa Phi, Psi Chi. Republican. Avocations: genealogy, poetry. Home: Topeka, Kans. Died Mar. 30, 2008.

BARNETT, STEPHEN ROGER, retired law educator; b. Bklyn., Dec. 25, 1935; BA, Harvard U., 1957; post grad, St. Anthony's Coll., Oxford U., 1958—59; LLB, Harvard U., 1962. Bar: NY 1963, DC 1966, Calif. 1977. Law clk. to judge US Cir. Ct. Appeals, 1962—63; law clk. to Justice Brennan US Supreme Ct., 1963—64; sole practice NYC, 1965—67; pvt. law practice Washington, 1965—67; spl asst. to asst. sec. for internat. affairs US Dept. Def., 1967; dep. solicitor gen. US Dept. Justice, 1975—76; prof. law U. Calif Berkeley, 1979—2003. Mem.: Am. Law Inst., Sta. KQED (Bd. dir. 1976—77), Com. on Acad. Freedom (chmn. 1976—77). Died Oct. 13, 2009.

BARNETTE, HENRY WESLEY (PETE BARNETTE), higher education public relations professional; b. Ila, Ga., May 2, 1934; s. Perry Sexton Barnett and Hattie Clara Mae (Draper) Bostian; m. Jo Gayle Sides, June 12, 1953 (div. May 1960); m. Delores Atkinson, June 25, 1960 (div. Aug. 1978); children: Joseph Wesley, Ian Kevin Drew, Derek Scott, Welinda Leigh Barnette Randall; m. Sharon Yolanda Blake, May 5, 1990. Student, U. Md., Guam, Marianas Islands, Territorial Coll. Guam, Catawba Coll., Salisbury, NC; MA in Psychology, Ind. State U., 1970. Br. mgr. 1st Citizens Bank and Trust Co., Charlotte, N.C., 1960-61, Provident Fin. Co., Charlotte, 1961-62; credit-pers. mgr. Nat. Mfg. Stores Corp., Kannapolis and Salisbury, N.C., 1962-65; co-owner, gen. mgr. Structural Steel Engring. and Drafting Firm, Bildo Co., Chattanooga and Ooletewah, Tenn., 1965-66; asst. mktg. mgr. field ops. Cen.-Soya, Chattanooga and Ft. Wayne, Ind., 1966-69; fund raising counsel, sr. dir. Ketchum, Inc., Pitts., 1969-74; devel. exec. fin. div. nat. coun. Boy Scouts Am., North Brunswick, N.J., 1974-78; pres. Circle B & Assocs., Inc. Fund-Raising Counsel, China Grove, N.C., 1978-81; assoc. Worrell Assocs., Inc. Fund-Raising Counsel, Sweetwater, Tenn., 1981-86; pub. rels. and mktg. dir. The Brunswick Hosp. (HCA), Supply, N.C., 1986-87; exec. v.p. Total Devel. Group-Fund Raising Counsel, Tenn., 1987-90; cartographer, tax appraiser Brunswick Co., N.C., 1990-91; exec. dir. Vol. and Info. Ctr., N.C., from 1991. With USN, 1952-57, Korea, USAF, 1958-60. Republican. Mem. Pentecostal Ch. Avocations: golf, tennis, dance, karati, reading. Home: Leland, NC. Died Feb. 18, 2008.

BARON, FREDERICK MARTIN, lawyer; b. Cedar Rapids, Iowa, June 20, 1947; m. Lisa Blue; children: Andrew, Courtney. BA, U. Tex., 1968, JD, 1971. Assoc. editor Tex. Law Rev., 1969—71; founder, ptnr. Baron & Budd P.C., Dallas, 1977—2002. Author: Honoring Occupational Disease Cases; Edit. Board. BNA Class Action Reporter, BNA Toxic Tort Reporter. Trustee U. Tex. Law Sch., 2002—08. Named one of 100 Most Influential Lawyers, Nat. Law Jour., 2000, 2006, Dallas' top lawyers, D Mag., 2001—07. Mem.: ABA, D.C. Bar Assn., Am. Law Inst., Trial Lawyers for Pub. Justice (founder, pres. 1997), Dallas Trial Lawyers Assn. (pres. 1980), Tex. Trial Lawyers Assn., Assn. Trial Lawyers of Am. (pres. 2000—01), Am. Bd. Trial Advocates, State Bar of Tex., Dallas Bar Assn. Democrat. Died Oct. 30, 2008.

BARON, LEORA, education educator; b. Tel-Aviv, Sept. 8, 1943; d. Klement and Valentina (Vitkind) Brainin; m. Shilo True Nixon; 1 child, Gil Alexander. AA, Grayson Cmty. Jr. Coll., 1968; BA, U. Mass., 1970, MA, 1971, EdD, 1973. Cert. psychotech. tester, interviewer. Asst. prof. U. Mass., Amherst, 1971-76; sch. prin. Tex. and Calif., 1976-92; career devel. cons. Princeton/Masters, Irvine, Calif., 1992-95; dir. edn. Nat. Edn. Ctr. for Women in Bus., Greensburg, Pa., 1995-97; assoc. v.p. bus. and cmty. learning, dir. bus. partnerships William Penn Coll., Oskaloosa, Iowa, 1997-98; dir. Acad. for the Art of Tchg., Fla. Internat. U., Miami, from 1998. Author, presenter in field. Dir. Ocwn, Irvine, Calif., 1987-95. Mem. ASTD, NAFE (adv. bd. 1995-97, regional network coord. 1993-95), Soc. for Human Resource Mgmt., Internat. Assn. Innovation in Higher Edn., Orgnl. Devel. Network. Avocations: writing, tennis, travel. Home: Las Vegas, Nev. Died July 29, 2008.

BARRASS, STANLEY RUSSELL, electrical contractor; b. Bishop, Calif., Dec. 17, 1926; s. Russell Onslow and Iris Eula (Ayres) B.; m. Katherine Anne Spanyers, Feb. 14, 1954; children: Nancy Kathleen, Janet Gayle Garcia, Donna Elizabeth Hecker, Laurie Anne Adams. Tech. Deg., Calif. Poly., 1949; BSEE, Heald Engring., San Francisco, 1953. Elec. estimator ETS Hokin & Galvin, San Francisco, 1953-54, Coopman Elec., San Francisco, 1954-62; elec. contr. Northgate Elec., San Rafael, Calif., 1962-85, NBC Ventures, San Rafael, Calif., 1985-90; elec. cons. San Rafael, Calif., from 1990. Dir. Marin Bldrs. Exch., San Rafael, Calif., 1973-79, State of Calif. Apprenticeship Coun., Santa Rosa, 1964-73; elder, deacon Christ Presbyn. Ch., 1959—. Recipient Cert. of Meritorious Svc., State of Calif. Apprentice Coun., 1973. Mem. Terra Linda Rotary (pres. 1987-88, Rotarian of Yr. 1982-83, 85-86). Avocations: golf, bowling, travel. Home: San Rafael, Calif. Died Sept. 21, 2007.

BARRETT, MARY HELEN, editor, writer; b. Ozark, Mo., June 8, 1926; d. Paul Watson and Dorothy M. (Bingham) B. AB, Drury Coll., 1948; MA, U. Mo., 1950. Reporter, feature writer Globe-Democrat, St. Louis, 1951-60; book editor Albert Whitman Co., Chgo., 1961-63; encylopedia editor Compton's, Chgo., 1963-67; publs. editor Drury Coll., Springfield, Mo., 1967-70; alumnae quarterly editor Mills Coll., Oakland, Calif., from 1972. Free-lance writer, 1970—. Contbr. short stories to Ellery Queen Mag., Alfred Hitchcock Mag. Mem. Mystery Writers Am. Republican. Died Jan. 26, 2008.

BARRON, INGE FALK, state official; b. Berlin, Oct. 26, 1927; came to U.S., 1941; d. Gustav Peter and Bettina (Schuller) Falk; widow; children: Diana, Alexander, Eleanor (dec.). BA, Barnard Coll., 1949; MA, Columbia U., 1951; cert., N.Y. Inst. Fin., 1953, Coll. Fin. Planning, Denver, 1987. Economist, researcher Nat. Bur. Econ. Rsch., Riverdale, N.Y., 1949-51; securities analyst A.G. Becker, A.M. Kidder, Smith Barney, NYC, 1951-56; social worker Balt. Dept. Welfare, 1959-61; tchr. Balt. Sch. System, 1963-66; prof. econs. Morgan State U., Balt., 1966-67; chief rsch. Dept. Pub. Welfare State of Md., Balt., 1967-71, adminstr. dept. human resources, 1971-73, chief rsch. analyst for quality control, 1973-85, adminstr. Juvenile Svcs. Agy., from 1985. Fin. cons. Barron Travel, Balt., 1985—. Fundraiser Assoc. Jewish Charities, Balt., Balt. United Way, Am. Israel Pub. Affairs Com., Washington. Mem. Am. Assn. Cert. Fin. Planners, N.Y. Soc. Securities Analysts, Balt. Fgn. Affairs Coun., Na'amat Hadassah, Zionist Orgn. Am. Avocations: gardening, travel, music, swimming, art. Home: Baltimore, Md. Died June 22, 2008.

BARROW, LIONEL CEON, JR., communications and marketing consultant; b. NYC, Dec. 17, 1926; s. Lionel Ceon and Wilhelmina Barrow; m. Frederica Harrison; children: Lia, Kirsten Erin; stepchildren: Brenda Marie Feliciano, Aurea Nellie (dec.), Rhonda Patricia (dec.), Emily Harrison Smith, Laura Harrison. BA in English, Morehouse Coll., 1948; MA in Journalism, U. Wis., 1958, PhD in Mass Communications, 1960. Reporter Spring Field Star, Mass., 1948—49, Richmond Afro-Am., Va., 1953-54; teaching and research asst. U. Wis., Madison, 1954-60; asst. prof. dept. communication Mich. State U., Lansing, 1960-61; research project dir. Bur. Advt., NYC, 1961-63; research project supr. Kenyon & Eckhardt Advt. Agy., NYC, 1963-64; research group head Foote Cone & Belding, NYC, 1964-68, assoc. research dir., v.p., 1968-71; chmn. dept. Afro-Am. studies U. Wis., Milw., 1971-72, 74-75, prof. mass comms. and Afro-Am. studies, 1971-75; dean Sch. Communication Howard U., Washington, 1975—85, prof. communications, 1975-86; pres. The Barrow Info. Group, Columbia, Md., 1986—2009. Vis. prof. Stanford U., 1971, Ohio State U., 1986; pres. Journalism Coun. Inc., 1971-79; sec. elected advs. Md. Conf. on Small Bus., 1987-89. Contbr. articles to profl. jours. Active Higher Edn. Group Washington, 1985-92. Served with AUS, 1945-47, 50-53. Recipient media citation Journalism Edn. Assn., 1974; recipient radio pioneer award Medgar Evers Coll., 1979 Mem. Assn. for Edn. in Journalism and Mass Comms. (founder, first head minorities and comm. divsn. 2003, chair commn. on the status of minorities 2003-05), Nat. Assn. Black Journalists, Soc. Profl. Journalists, Capitol Press Club, NAACP (life), 24th Inf. Regimental Combat Team Assn. (life, Combat Inf. badge). Home: Tampa, Fla. Died Jan. 23, 2009.

BARROWS, RICHARD ANTHONY, music educator, musician; b. Passaic, NJ, May 16, 1928; s. Richard Thornton and Loretta Helena (Conroy) B.; m. Dorothy Mildred Auletta, June 29, 1958; children: Steven David, Mark Anthony. BA, N.J. State Coll., 1950; MA, Columbia Univ., 1954, EDD, 1965. Cert. tchr., N.J.; supervisor cert. N.J. Music tchr. pub. schs., E. Rutherford, N.J., 1950-57; music. tchr., supr. Riverdell Schs., Oradell, N.J., 1957-84; dir. music Assumption Roman Catholic Parish, Bayonne, N.J., 1984-86, St. Thomas The Apostle Parish, Bloomfield, N.J., 1986-91, St. Gabriel The Archangel Parish, Saddle River, N.J., from 1990; dir. edn. African Art Museum, Tenafly, N.J., from 1990. Dir. music The Reformed Ch., Oradell, 1966-84; organist Temple Beth-El, Stamford, Conn., 1981-88, Temple Beth-El, Closter, N.J., 1976-81. Author: Robert Schumann's Use of Musical Codes, 1986, 88. Sgt. U.S. Army, 1950-52. Recipient N.J. State Tchr. of Yr., 1975, Princeton Prize Princeton Univ., 1965; organ recitalist Notre-Dame Cathedral, Paris, 1975. Mem. NEA, N.J. Edn. Assn., Nat. Assn. Parish Musicians, Am. Guild Organists (dean). Democrat. Roman Catholic. Avocations: travel, astrology, numerology, computer music applications, organ recitalist. Home: Paramus, NJ. Died Oct. 20, 2007.

BARRY, BRIAN, philosophy professor; b. London, Aug. 7, 1936; came to U.S., 1976; s. James Frederick and Doris Rose (Manners) B.; m. Joanna Hill, Aug. 27, 1960 (div. 1988); 1 child, Austin K.; m. Anni Parker, 1991 MA, Oxford U., Eng., 1958, D in Philosophy, 1964; D (hon.), U. York, 2006. Asst. lectr. Keele U., 1962—63; lectr. U. Southhampton, 1963—65; tutorial fellow U. Coll., 1965—66; fellow Nuffield Coll., Oxford U., 1966-69, 1972-75; prof. polit. sci. U. Essex, Colchester, England, 1969-72, dean social studies, 1971—72; prof. polit. sci. U. B.C., Vancouver, Canada, 1975-77, U. Chgo., 1977-82, Calif. Inst. Tech., Pasadena, 1982—86, European U. Inst., Florence, Italy, 1986—87, London Sch. Economics, 1987—98, prof. emeritus, 1998—2009; Lieber prof. polit. philosophy Columbia U., 1998—2005, prof. emeritus, 2005—09. Author: Political Argument, 1965, Sociologists, Economists & Democracy, 1970, The Liberal Theory of Justice, 1973, Democracy, Power, and Justice: Essays in Political Theory, 1989, Theories of Justice (WJM Mackenzie prize, Polit. Studies Assn.), 1989, Justice as Impartiality (WJM Mackenzie Prize, Polit. Studies Assn.) 1995, Culture & Equality: An Egalitarian Critique of Multiculturalism (WJM Mackenzie Prize, Polit. Studies Assn.) 2001, Culture & Equality: An Egalitarian Critique of Multiculturalism, 2005, Game Theory and the Classics, 2007, The Politics of Doom: Collected Essays, 2007; co-editor: (with Russel Hardin) Rational Man and Irrational Society?, 1982; founding editor: Brit. Jour. Polit. Sci., 1970-72; editor: Ethics, 1979-82. Fellow, U. Birmingham, 1960-61, Rockefeller fellow in legal & polit. philosophy, 1961-62; fellow, Center for Advanced Study in Behavioral Sciences, 1975-77, Am. Council Learned Societies., 1979-80; Guggenheim fellow, awardee, 1979-80; recipient Lifetime Achievement in Polit. Studies, Polit. Studies Assn., 2000, Johan Skytte Prize in Polit. Sci., 2001 Fellow Am. Acad. Arts and Scis.; mem. Am. Philos. Assn., Am. Econ. Assn., Am. Polit. Sci. Assn., Polit. Studies Assn. (U.K.), Am. Soc. for Legal and Polit. Philosophy Clubs: Athenaeum (London). Home: San Marino, Calif. Died Mar. 10, 2009.

BARRY, KEVIN JEROME, retired military officer; b. NYC, 1942; s. Francis J. and Margaret (O'Donnell) B.; m. Roslyn Larkin, Dec. 3, 1966; 3 children: Michael Francis, Daniel Kevin, Melissa Rose BA in Philosophy, Cathedral Coll., Bklyn., 1964; JD, Coll. William and Mary, 1975; grad. level course work, DeSales Sch. Theology, Washington, 1988-93. Bar: Va. 1975, U.S. Ct. Mil. Appeals 1983, U.S. Supreme Ct. 1986, D.C. 1990, U.S. Ct. Appeals (D.C. cir.) 1992, U.S. Ct. Claims 1992, U.S. Ct. Vets. Appeals, 1992. Ensign USCG, 1966, advanced through grades to capt., 1990, ops. officer, 1966-67, 71-72; instr. USCG Officer Candidate Sch., 1967-71; asst. legal officer 8th Coast Guard Dist., New Orleans, 1975-78; dist. legal officer 2d Coast Guard Dist., St. Louis, 1978-81, marine safety staff officer, 1981-82, 84-85, gen. ct.-martial mil judge, 1982-84; asst. chief gen. law divsn. USCG, Washington, 1985-87, chief legis. divsn., 1987-90; judge USCG Ct. Mil. Rev., Washington, 1987-90, ret., 1990; pvt. practice law and mediation Chantilly, Va., 1990—2005. Mng. editor William & Mary Law Rev., 1974-75; contbr. articles to profl. jours. Recipient Judicial award for Pub. Svc., US Ct. Appeals Armed Forces, 2001, Disting. Svc. award, US Ct. Appeals Veterans Claims, 2002, Judge Advocates Assn. Lifetime Achievement award, 2004, Lawyer of the Yr. award, DC Bar Assn., 2007. Mem. ABA, Fed. Bar Assn. (pres. Pentagon chpt. 1987), Judge Advs. Assn. (pres. 1989-90). Died Apr. 24, 2009.

BARTON, JOHN HAYS, law educator; b. Chgo., Oct. 27, 1936; s. Jay and Agnes (Heisler) B.; m. Julianne Marie Gunnis, June 13, 1959; children: John II, Robert, Anne, Thomas, David. BS, Marquette U., Milw., 1958; JD, Stanford U., Calif., 1968. Bar: DC 1969. Engr. Sylvania Electronic Def. Labs., Mountain View, Calif., 1961-68; assoc. Wilmer, Cutler and Pickering, Washington, 1968-69; George E. Osborne prof. Stanford U. Law Sch., Calif., 1969—2002, prof. emeritus Calif., 2002—09. Vis. prof. U. Mich. Law Sch., 1981, Harvard Law Sch., 1988; vis. scholar dept. clin. bioethics, NIH, 2004-05. Author: Politics of Peace, 1981; co-author: Law in Radically Different Cultures, 1983 (Am. Soc. Internat. Law award 1984), International Trade and Investment, 1986, The Evolution of the Trade Regime: Politics, Law and Economics of the GATT and the WTO, 2006; co-editor Words over War, 2000. Past chair Nat. Genetic Resources Adv. Coun.; past mem. NAFTA Dispute Settlement Panel; former mem. NRC Com.

Intellectual Property Rights in Knowledge Based Econ., 2000-03; chair Commn. Intellectual Property Rights UK Dept. Internat. Devel., 2001-02. Lt. (j.g.) USN, 1958-61. Rockefeller Found. fellow, 1976-77; recipient Jenny Lanjouw Meml. Prize U. Calif. Berkeley, 2007. Fellow Am. Assn. Advancement Sci.; mem. Am. Soc. Internat. Law. Home: Los Altos, Calif. Died Aug. 3, 2009.

BASS, JAMES EDWIN, minister; b. Merced, Calif., Feb. 7, 1953; s. J.E. and Nellie Grace (Rudy) B.; m. Leah Gayle Surface, May 27, 1977; children: Rachel Amanda Arwen, Jonathan Jared Elrond. BS in Forestry, Stephen F. Austin State U., Nacogdoches, Tex., 1975. Ordained to ministry Assemblies of God Ch., 1981. Campus minister XA Ministries, Nacogdoches, 1977-82; pastor Woodland Park Assembly of God Ch., Conroe, Tex., from 1983. Com. person N. Tex. dist. Assemblies of God, Hurst, 1980, S. Tex. Dist., Houston, 1983; assoc. chaplain Woodlands Community Hosp., 1988—, Conroe (Tex.) Med. Ctr., 1990—. Author newspaper column in Conroe Courier, 1988—; contbr. articles to profl. jours. Pres. Fox Run Homeowners Assn., Spring, Tex., 1989—, bd. dirs., 1988. Mem. Quill and Scroll. Home: Burleson, Tex. Died July 21, 2008.

BASS, KENNETH CARRINGTON, III, lawyer; b. Richmond, Va., Feb. 11, 1944; s. Kenneth Carrington Jr. and Mary Bennett (Owen) B.; m. Shirley Ann Pierce, June 18, 1966; children: Timothy, Christopher. AB summa cum laude, Duke U., 1965; LLB, Yale U., 1969. Bar: Va. 1970, U.S. Dist. Ct. (D.C. dist.) 1971, U.S. Supreme Ct. 1973. Law clk. to Justice Hugo Black Supreme Ct., Washington, 1969-70; legis. asst. to E.Q. Daddario US House Reps., Washington, 1970-71; assoc. Paul, Weiss, Rifkind, Washington, 1970—74, Reasoner, Davis & Vinson, Washington, 1974-77; counsel for intelligence policy US Dept. Justice, Washington, 1979—81; ptnr. Reasoner, Davis & Fox, Washington, 1981-85, Venable, Baetjer, Howard & Civiletti, Washington, 1985—2002, Sterne, Kessler, Goldstein & Fox, Washington, 2002—09. Contbg. author editorials N.Y. Times, Washington Post; contbr. articles to profl. jours. Mem. Am. Acad. Appellate Lawyers. Democrat. Baptist. Avocations: hiking, amateur radio, astronomy. Home: Great Falls, Va. Died Apr. 27, 2009.

BASSETT, ROBERT ROSS, JR., retired architect; b. Akron, Ohio, June 11, 1920; s. Robert Ross and Lavina (Eberts) B.; m. Marion Carrol Blumer, Nov. 24, 1948; children: Harlan Wray, Robert Ross III, David Carl. BArch, Carnegie Mellon U., 1951. Registered architect, Miss. Office mgr. Real Estate Maintenance, Inc., Pitts., 1940-42; draftsman, designer Ben Hoffman, Architect, Pitts., 1948-51; draftsman Malvaney, Naef & Overstreet, Architects, Jackson, Miss., 1951-52; draftsman, designer Raymond Birchett, Architect, Jackson, 1952-54; v.p., designer, architect Godfrey & Bassett, Architects, Jackson, 1954-55; bus. mgr., v.p. Godfrey, Bassett & Pitts, Architects, Jackson, Vicksburg, Miss., 1955-60, Godfrey, Bassett, Pitts & Tuminello, Jackson, Vicksburg, 1960-65, Godfrey, Bassett, Maisel & Tuminello, Jackson, Vicksburg, 1965-75, Godfrey, Bassett & Kuykendall, Architects, Jackson, 1985-90; semi-ret. architect Godfrey, Bassett, Kuykendall & Campbell, Architects, Jackson, from 1990. Participant Agribusiness Sem., Khaborovsk, Siberia, Citizens Network for Fgn. Affairs, 1994. Prin. works include Gunboat Cairo Exhibit, Vicksburg Mil. Pk., Miss. Interstate Hwy. Welcome Stas., designer numerous poultry and catfish processing plants in U.S., Nigeria, Iran. Sec. Hinds County Planning Commn., Jackson, 1956-60; bd. dirs. West Point Plz., Inc., Jackson, 1984—, Helm Inc., Jackson, 1991-93; past pres. Leavel Woods Exchange Club, 1970, Lake Mimosa Park Assn., 1989, sec.-treas., 1989-91. Fellow Jackson North Lions Club. Presbyterian. Home: Brandon, Miss. Died Oct. 5, 2007.

BASSO, MELODY LEA, accountant, auditor; b. Chgo., Sept. 11, 1963; d. John Nicholas and Christine Anita (Letto) B.; m. Matthew Christian Ove, Apr. 19, 1991. BS in Commerce, DePaul U., 1985, M of Accountancy, 1987. CPA, Ill. Sr. assoc. Coopers & Lybrand, Chgo., from 1987. Mem. AICPA, Ill. Cert. Pub. Accts. Soc. Home: Chicago, Ill. Died Jan. 27, 2008.

BATEMAN, ROBERT EDWIN, aeronautical engineer; b. Butte, Mont., Apr. 11, 1923; s. Edwin Joseph and Katherine (Bronner) B.; m. Sarah Elizabeth Hayes, Mar. 2, 1947; children: Robert Eugene, Lucy Annette, Paul William. BS in Aero. Engring., Purdue U., 1946; ED (hon.), Purdue, 1992. Aero. staff Boeing Co., Seattle, 1946-59; devel. program mgr. Boeing Aerospace, Seattle, 1959-65, gen. mgr. turbine div., 1965-67, 747 program exec., 1967-71, v.p., mgr. Washington D.C. ops., 1971-75, v.p. gen. mgr. marine systems, 1975-85; v.p. govt. and internat. affairs Boeing Co., Seattle, 1985-88. Chmn., bd. dirs. Mus. Flight, Seattle, 1989—. Bd. dirs. Naval War Coll., Newport, R.I., 1976—, Naval Meml. Found., 1983-88; pres. World Affairs Coun., Seattle, 1988—. Lt. comdr. USNR, 1946-66. Sec. Navy Meritorius Pub. Svc. award, 1968, Disting. Pub. Svc. award, 1972; named Disting. Engring. Alumnus Purdue U., 1974, Old Master award, 1988. Fellow (assoc.) AIAA; mem. Navy League U.S. (exec. com., nat. dir. 1965—, Disting. Svc. award 1986, Hall of Fame 1991). Home: Seattle, Wash. Died Mar. 23, 2008.

BATES, CLYDE THOMAS, retired economics professor; b. Sadieville, Ky., June 6, 1933; s. Thomas Marion and Carrie Josephine Bates; m. Frances Ruth Phillips, July 10, 1956; children: Bobby Gene, Calvin Thomas. BS, U. Ky., Lexington, 1960, MS, 1962, PhD, 1969. Asst. prof. Western Ky. U., Bowling Green, Ky., 1961—63; prof. Georgetown Coll., 1964—95; ret., 1995. Quality control statistician Allied Signal, Frankfort, Ky., 1980—89. Pres. Royal Springs Credit Union. With intelligence US Army, 1954—56, Germany. Named Tchr. of Yr., Georgetown Coll., 1969. Mem.: Ky. Econ. Assn. (pres. 1984), Optimist Club. Democrat. Avocations: reading, gardening. Home: Georgetown, Ky. Died May 27, 2008.

BATES, DENNIS JAMES, telecommunications engineer; b. Cin., Nov. 27, 1958; s. James L. and Sylvia S. (Smith) B.; m. Cheryl Diane Woodward, Mar. 18, 1977; children: Eric Hayden, Ryan James. BS in Acctg., Ball State U., 1979; BS in Engring., Purdue U., 1983; BS in Bus., Ind. U. East, Richmond, 1985. Asst. engr. GTE, Pendleton, Ind., 1978-81, engr. Valparaiso, Ind., 1982-85, sr. engr. Terre Haute, Ind., 1986-91, supr. engr., 1991-96. Dir. Clay Youth League, Brazil, Ind., 1989-94, Clay County Park Bd., Brazil, 1997—. Mem. Home Builders Assn. (state dir. 1991-97), Elks, Internat. Engring. Assn. (bd. dirs. 1991-93). Avocations: golf, fishing, indy car racing. Home: Wausau, Wis. Died Nov. 20, 2007.

BATTAGLIA, ROSEMARIE ANGELA, English language educator; b. Wilmington, Del., Dec. 17, 1936; d. Martin Fortunate and Norma Agnes (Ciaramella) B. BA, U. Del., 1958; MA, Temple U., 1973; PhD, SUNY, Binghamton, 1985. Cert. secondary English and French tchr., Del. Tchr. Dover (Del.) High Sch., 1961-62; grad. asst. U. Del., Newark, 1963-64, SUNY, 1978-81; instr. Rider Coll., Lawrenceville, N.J., 1964-65, Cheyney (Pa.) U., 1965-66, Lincoln U., Lincoln University, Pa., 1974-76; vis. instr. Temple U., Phila., 1982-84; asst. prof. Kutztown (Pa.) U., 1984-86; asst. prof. English Mich. State U., East Lansing, 1987-92, Morehead (Ky.) State U., 1992-98; instr. U. Del., Newark, 1998—2001, West Chester U., Pa., from 2001. Test cons. Am. Coll. Testing, Iowa City, 1976, Ednl. Testing Svc., Princeton, N.J., 1976; editorial cons. Yeats Eliot Rev., Little Rock, 1987—; adj. prof. U. Del., Newark, 1998-2001, Drexel U., Wilmington, Del., 2000; referee-reader Cornell U. Press, Ithaca, N.Y., 1990—; presenter in field. Contbr. articles to profl. jours. Recipient prize Acad. Am. Poets, 1958; Woodrow Wilson fellow, 1958; grantee Princeton U., 1986, NEH, 1986, 89, Sch. Critics Theory, Portmouth Coll., 1987. Mem. Internat. James Joyce Found., Phi Beta Kappa, Phi Kappa Phi. Avocations: music, walking, theater. Home: Wilmington, Del. Died May 8, 2008.

BATTEN, FRANK, retired broadcast executive; b. Norfolk, Va., Feb. 11, 1927; s. Frank and Dorothy (Martin) B.; m. Jane Neal Parke; children: Frank, Mary, Dorothy. Grad., Culver Mil. Acad., 1945; AB, U. Va., 1950; MBA, Harvard U., 1952; LittD (hon.), Washington and Lee U., 1996. Reporter The Norfolk Ledger-Star; with advt. and circulation depts. The Virginian-Pilot and Norfolk Ledger-Star newspapers; v.p. The Norfolk Virginian-Pilot and Norfolk Ledger-Star newspapers, 1953, pub., from 1954; chmn. bd. Landmark Comm., Norfolk, 1967-97, chmn. exec. com., 1998—2008; 2d vice chmn. AP, 1977-79, 1st vice chmn., 1979-81, chmn. bd., 1982-87; founder The Weather Channel, 1982. Formerly chmn. AP Pension, Tech., Fgn. ops. coms.; past chmn. AP Nominating Com., Va. AP Members; former dir. So. Newspapers Pubs. Assn.; former chmn. bd. Newspaper Advt. Bur. Trustee Culver Ednl. Found., U.S. Naval Acad. Found., So. Newspaper Pubs. Found., U. Va. Grad. Bus. Sch. Sponsors, Hollins Coll.; past chmn. bd. Old Dominion U.; past vice chmn. State Coun. Higher Edn. for Va.; past pres. and campaign chmn. Norfolk Area United Fund; chmn. com. for Internat. Naval Rev., 1957; mem. bd. visitors Coll. William and Mary. With U.S. Merchant Marine, World War II, also USNR. Recipient Norfolk's First Citizen award, 1966, Alumni Achievement award Harvard Bus. Sch., 1998, Va. Press Assn. Lifetime Achievement award, 2009 Mem. Newspaper Assn. of Am. (dir., Katherine Graham Lifetime Achievement award), Delta Kappa Epsilon. Episcopalian. Died Sept. 10, 2009.

BATTISTA, CATHERINE P., hypnotherapist; b. New Haven, Jan. 28, 1932; d. Peter J. and Alice (Piscopo) Landolfi; m. Alfred Battista, Nov. 15, 1952. Diploma, Hosp. St. Raphael, 1952; BS, So. Conn. U.; postgrad., U. Conn., Hartford, U. New Haven. Cert. clin. hypnotherapist. Exec. dir. Alcohol Coun. Greater New Haven; pub. affairs dir. Health Systems Agy., Woodbridge, Conn.; asst. exec. dir. Conn. Nurses Assn., Meriden; dir., founder Ctr. for Integrative Hypnosis, Ft. Myers, Fla. Lectr., cons. in field. Freelance writer. Named Woman of Yr. Am. Bus. Women's Assn., 1982. Mem. Am. Assn. Profl. Hypnotherapists, Fla. Soc. Profl. Hypnotherapists, Am. Bd. Hypnotherapy, Nat. Bd. Hypnotic Anaesthesiology, Nat. Soc. Hypnotherapists, Assn. for Past Life Rsch. and Therapy, Nurse Healers, Profl. Assocs., Am. Coun. fo Hypnotist Examiners. Home: Fort Myers, Fla. Died June 11, 2008.

BATTISTICH, VICTOR ANTHONY, psychology professor, researcher; b. Sacramento, Sept. 9, 1952; s. Carl Anthony Battistich and Marian Rita Hansen; m. Martha Susan Montgomery, Jan. 17, 1976; children: Sarah Montgomery, Caitlin Montgomery. BA, Calif. State U., Sacramento, 1974; MA, Mich. State U., East Lansing, 1976, PhD, 1979. Sr. rsch. assoc. ctr. evaluation and assessment Mich. State U., 1978—79; asst. prof. Cleve. State U. and First Coll., 1979—80; dep. dir. rsch. Devel. Studies Ctr., Oakland, Calif., 1981—2003; assoc. prof. U. Mo., St. Louis, from 2003. Recipient Spl. award Disting. Rsch., Am. Assn. Sch. Adminstrs., 1987. Mem.: APA, Assn. Moral Edn., Am. Ednl. Rsch. Assn. Home: Creve Coeur, Mo. Died July 2, 2008.

BAUER, RANDALL RICHARD, science teacher; b. Long Prairie, Minn., Aug. 15, 1949; s. Byron Louis and Phyllis Emily Ann (Thomas) B. BS in Wildlife Biology, U. Minn., 1971; BS in Biology Edn., St. Cloud State U., 1979, postgrad., 1979-82. Cert. life scis. tchr., Minn. Lectr. Triology Enterprises, Coon Rapids, Minn., 1976-78; dir. various positions area YMCAs, Minn., 1979-82; tchr. sci. Belle Plaine (Minn.) High Sch., 1982-83; dir. post secondary preparation program Cook County High Sch., Grand Marais, Minn., from 1984. Ranger Nat. Park Svc., Grand Portage, Minn., 1982-87, Voyageurs Nat. Park, 1991. Photographer Northshore Scenics postcard series, 1987. Mem. Minn. Environ. Edn. Bd., St. Cloud, 1978-81, chmn., 1981; mem. St. Cloud Area Environ. Council, 1977-82, chmn., 1981; emergency med. technician Grand Portage (Minn.) Ambulance, 1984-88. With U.S. Army, 1971-73. Recipient Vol. in Park award Nat. Park Svc., Grand Portage, 1986, award Grand Portage Ambulance, 1986, 87, Fulbright scholarship, 1990; named Eagle Scout, 1965; holder world record in long-distance canoeing Guinness Book of Records, 1978-82. Mem. Minn. Indian Edn. Assn., N.E. Region Emergency Med. Technicians Assn., Phi Kappa Phi Honor Soc., Northshore Camera Club. Democrat. Roman Catholic. Avocations: photography, kayaking, distance running. Home: Minneapolis, Minn. Died Aug. 29, 2007.

BAUERSFELD, CARL FREDERICK, lawyer; b. Balt., June 9, 1916; s. Emil George and Irene Marie (Hulse) B.; m. Ann Yancey, Mar. 3, 1944 (div.); children: Elizabeth Bauersfeld Garnett, Carl F. Student, George Washington U., 1937-42; LLB, Am. U., 1937. Bar: D.C. 1937, U.S. Dist. Ct. D.C. 1937, U.S. Ct. Appeals (D.C. cir.) 1937, U.S. Supreme Ct. 1941, U.S. Ct. Claims 1946, U.S. Tax Ct. 1946, Md. Ct. Appeals 1957, U.S. Ct. Appeals (5th cir.) 1947, (9th cir.) 1956, (3d cir.) 1958, (8th cir.) 1960, (4th cir.) 1966, (2d cir.) 1970. Ptnr. Bauersfeld, Burton, Hendricks & Vanderhoof, L.L.C., 1956—2009. Lectr. on fed. taxation at various univs. Lt. comdr. USNR, 1942-46. Mem. ABA, Md. Bar Assn., Bar Assn. D.C., Congl. Country Club, Burning Tree Club, Sigma Nu Phi, Phi Sigma Kappa. Lutheran. Died Sept. 13, 2009.

BAUGH, SAMMY (SAMUEL ADRIAN BAUGH), retired professional football player; b. Temple, Tex., Mar. 17, 1914; m. Edmonia Smith, 1938 (dec. 1990); children: Bruce(dec.), Tod, David, Stephen, Frances. Attended, Tex. Christian U., Fort Worth, 1934—36. Quarterback Washington Redskins, 1937—52; head football coach Hardin-Simmons U., 1955—60, NY Titans, 1960—61, Houston Oilers, 1964. Actor: King of the Texas Rangers, 1941. Named First Team All-Pro, 1937, 1940, 1942, 1943; named to NFL Pro Bowl, 1938—42, 1951, Coll. Football Hall of Fame, 1951, Pro Football Hall of Fame, 1963, The NFL 75th Anniversary All-Time Team, 1994. Achievements include leading the NFL in: pass attempts, 1937, 43, 47, 48; pass completions, 1937, 43, 45, 47, 48; passing yards, 1937, 40, 47, 48; passing touchdowns, 1940, 47; interceptions, punts, punting yards, 1943; member of the NFL Championship winning Washington Redskins, 1937, 1942. Died Dec. 17, 2008; Rotan, Tex.

BAUMAN, JON WARD, retired music educator; b. Big Rapids, Mich., June 7, 1939; s. Alvin Henry and Hilda (Nordberg) Bauman; m. Carole Diane Folk, June 21, 1980. MusB, U. Colo., 1961; MusM, U. Ill., 1963, Doctor in Musical Arts, 1972. Instr. Chgo. (Ill.) Pub. Schs., 1969—70; prof. music Frostburg (Md.) State U., 1970—2003; prof. compositon Conservatorio Statale di Musica, Adria, Italy, 2002, 2004, 2005; conductor Western Md. Symphony, Penn. Alps Chamber Orch., Potomac Highlands Symphony. Bd. dirs. Young Audiences of Md., Balt., 1998. Composer (arranger): over 100 compositions and arrangements; seven CDs produced. Founder Music at Penn. Alps, Grantsville, Md. Named Outstanding Mentor, Frostburg State U., 1992, Sr. Citizens Hall Fame, Md., 2007; Fulbright scholar, U.S. Gov., 1965. Mem.: ASCAP, Am. Composers Forum, Rotary Club Frostburg (Paul Harris fellow 1999). Democrat. Roman Catholic. Home: Frostburg, Md. Died May 31, 2009.

BAUMGARTEN, RONALD JOSEPH, chemistry educator; b. NYC, May 7, 1935; s. Albert B. and Lillian (Klein) B. BS, Bklyn. Coll., 1952; MA, Johns Hopkins U., 1958, PhD, 1962. Postdoctoral fellow Ind. U., Bloomington, 1961-62; rsch. assoc. U.S. Govt., Natick, Mass., 1962-64; postdoctoral fellow Brandeis U., Waltham, Mass., 1964-65; prof. chemistry U. Ill., Chgo., from 1965. Cons. U.S. Congress, Chgo., 1991-92; vis. prof. U. Ill., Champagne/Urbana, 1966-67; vis. rsch. assoc. U. Leiden, Holland, 1971-72; vis. lectr. U. Christchurch, N.Z., 1981. Contbr. 20 scholarly rsch. publs., 2 revs. to profl. jours. Vol., officer Nuclear Energy Info. Soc., Evanston, Ill., 1980—. Recipient Tchg. awards U. Ill., Chgo., 1975, 77, 83, 86, 89, 92, 95. Mem. Sigma Xi, Phi beta Kappa. Avocations: music, nature study. Home: Chicago, Ill. Died Jan. 28, 2008.

BAUMSTEIN, PASCHAL M., priest; b. Coffee County, Tenn., Sept. 16, 1950; s. Josef ben-Abram and Mae (Winton) Baumstein. AA, Aquinas Coll., Nashville, 1972; AB, Holy Apostles Coll., Cromwell, Conn., 1973; MDiv, St. Meinrad Coll., Ind., 1979; AM, Ind. U., 1979. Monk Benedictine Order, 1974, ordained priest Roman Cath. Ch., 1979. Faculty Belmont Abbey Coll., Belmont, NC,

1977—80; archivist-historian Belmont Abbey/Belmont Abbey Coll., 1979—96, archivist-historian emeritus, from 1996; editor CRESCAT, Belmont, 1977—87; book editor Cistercian Studies Quar., Gethsemani, Ky., 1997—98. Chaplain Abbey Players of Belmont Abbey Coll., from 1977; calligrapher Cath. Worker, from 1999; expert, cons. on work and life of Anselm of Canterbury and Robert Hugh Benson. Author: My Lord of Belmont, 1985, Blessing the Years to Come, 1997; contbr. over 100 revs. to scholarly and profl. jours., numerous articles to scholarly and profl. jours. Mem. Pax Christi, Cath. Peace Fellowship; mem. archivists exec. bd. Cath. Libr. Assn., 1982—96; bd. trustees Belmont Abbey Coll., 1986—94. Mem.: Am. Cath. Philos. Soc., Acad. Cert. Archivists (cert. archivist), Internat. Arthurian Soc. (life), Am. Cath. Hist. Assn. (life), Phi Sigma Tau (sec. 1979—84), Delta Epsilon Sigma, Alpha Phi Gamma. Died Oct. 4, 2007.

BAXTER, JOAN, writer; b. Rochester, NY, Dec. 7, 1927; d. Ernest Loring and Evelyn (Sheldon) B. BA, Oberlin Coll., 1948; MA, Webster U., Bermuda, 1982. Occupational analyst Bur. Naval Pers., Washington, 1948-51, job classifier, 1951-53; pers. specialist, job classifier Walter Reed Army Med. Ctr., Washington, 1954-74; job classifier FCC, Washington, 1974-79; pers. specialist U.S. Naval Air Sta., Bermuda, 1979-83; writer, Chapel Hill, N.C., from 1983. Contbr. nonfiction articles to Cobblestone, various career guidance publs., Song Sheet, Remember That Song, Sheet Music Exch., also other mags. and newspapers; author: Television Musicals, 1997. Mem. Nat. Sheet Music Soc., N.Y. Sheet Music Soc., Soc. for Comml. Archeology, Wilson Ctr. (assoc.). Avocations: piano, painting, drawing. Home: Chapel Hill, NC. Died May 8, 2008.

BAYAR, JULIA BERYL, interior designer; b. Washington, June 12, 1949; BA, Vassar Coll., 1971; MS, Boston U., 1972. Press aide Dem. Nat. Com., Washington, 1972-73, U.S. Ho. Reps., Washington, 1973-76, U.S. Senate, Washington, 1976-77; speechwriter U.S. Dept. Justice, Washington, 1977-79; cons. Jules Kroll Assocs., NYC, 1980-81; interior designer, owner Interiors by Julia Bayar, Scarsdale, N.Y., from 1984. Home: Scarsdale, NY. Died Jan. 14, 2008.

BEACH, DANIEL MAGEE, IV, record producer; b. Boston, Feb. 21, 1962; s. Daniel M. Beach III and Judith (Cann) Berkes. Chmn. Concert Prodn., Pueblo, Colo., 1981-83; engr. asst. Starfleet Studios, Boston, 1978-80; prodn. clk. EPCOT Ctr. Walt Disney World, Orlando, FLa., 1983-86; engr., programmer Starke Lake Studios, Orlando, 1986-89; owner, engr. Pinebark Studios, Orlando, from 1989. Dir. music Orlando Magic-NBA Basketball, 1989—; cons. Orlando Sun-Rays AAA Baseball, 1990—, Orlando Entertains, 1990—; system designer Gettings Prodns., Ocoee, Fla., 1986—; sound designer Universal Studios, Orlando, 1989. Producer recordings The Minimalists, 1989, Big Sky, 1989-90, Sportsmoods, 1989, Abstract as Nature, 1990. Mem. Greenpeace, The Wilderness Soc., People for the Ethical Treatment of Animals. Avocations: skiing, hiking, explorign, tennis. Home: Orlando, Fla. Died Apr. 19, 2008.

BEALL, BETTY MCCULLAR, accountant; b. El Paso, Tex., Nov. 23, 1928; d. Blount and Jane Elizabeth (Kirby) McCullar; m. Jerry Presley Beall, June 15, 1955 (dec. 1973); children: Julie, Jerrie, Kirby. BS magna cum laude, Calif. State U., Northridge, 1966. CPA, Calif. Staff acct. Seideman & Seideman, Beverly Hills, Calif., 1966-68; v.p. Internat. Bus. Mgmt., Century City, Calif., 1969-80; prin. Betty M. Beall, CPA, Culver City, Calif., from 1980. Mem. AICPA, Calif. Soc. CPAs (entertainment and sports industry com. 1988-90). Republican. Episcopalian. Avocation: competitive ballroom dancing. Home: Los Angeles, Calif. Died June 12, 2008.

BEAR, HENRY LOUIS, lawyer; b. Kansas City, Kans. s. Max and Mary (Kagon) B.; m. Betty Jean Isenhart, Jan. 4, 1951; 1 child, Dinah. JD, U. Mo., 1939. Bar: Mo. 1939, Calif. 1949, U.S. Dist. Ct. (so. dist.) Calif. 1949, U.S. Supreme Ct. 1959. Assoc. O'Hern & O'Hern, Kansas City, Mo., 1939-42; ptnr. Bear, Kotob, Ruby & Gross, and predecessors, Downey, Calif., from 1949. Sec., dir. Pyrotronics Corp.; dir. Bank of Irvine. Author: California Law of Corporations, Partnerships and Associations, 1970. Chmn. Midland dist. coun. Boy Scouts Am., 1954; active Cmty. Chest, Lynwood, Calif. Served to lt. USAF, 1942-46. Named Lynwood Man of Yr., 1952. Fellow Am. Coll. Probate Counsel; mem. ABA, Mo. Bar Assn., Calif. Bar Assn., Calif. Trial Lawyers Assn., L.A. County Bar Assn., Exec. Dinner Club (pres.), Rotary, Elks. Deceased.

BEAR, HERBERT STANLEY, JR., mathematics professor; b. Phila., Mar. 13, 1929; s. Herbert Stanley and Katharine (Schaeffer) B.; m. Jean I. Munro, May 30, 1951 (div. 1982); children: Katharine, John; m. Ruth E. Murashige Wong, June 30, 1984. BA, U. Calif.-Berkeley, 1950, PhD, 1957. Instr. U. Oreg., Eugene, 1955-56; vis. asst. prof. Princeton U., 1959-60; instr. to asst. prof. U. Wash., Seattle, 1957-59, 60-62; assoc. prof. math. U. Calif.-Santa Barbara, 1962-67; prof. math. N.Mex. State U., Las Cruces, 1967-69; vis. prof. math. U. Erlangen-Nurnberg, 1969, dept. chmn. math., 1969-74, grad. chmn., 1980-83; prof. math. U. Hawaii, Honolulu, 1969-74, prof. emeritus, from 1974. Contbr. articles to profl. jours. Trustee Math. Scis. Rsch. Inst., Berkeley, 1981-91. Home: Honolulu, Hawaii. Died Dec. 22, 2007.

BEARD, LEO ROY, retired civil engineer; b. West Baden, Ind., Apr. 6, 1917; s. Leonard Roy and Barbara Katherine (Frederick) B.; m. Marian Janet Wagar, Oct. 21, 1939 (dec.); children: Patricia Beard Huntzicker, Thomas Edward, James Robert; m. Marjorie Elizabeth Pierce Wood, Aug. 30, 1974. AA, Pasadena City Coll., 1937; BS, Calif. Inst. Tech., 1939. Engr. U.S. Army C.E., Los Angeles, 1939-49; engr. Office Chief of Engrs., Washington, 1949-52; chief of Reservoir Regulation, Sacramento, 1952-64; dir. Hydrologic Engring. Center, Davis, Calif., 1964-72; prof. civil engring. U. Tex., Austin, 1972-87, prof. emeritus, 1987—2009. Cons. Espey, Huston & Assos., Austin, 1980-92; v.p. Internat. Commn. of Water Resource Sys.; water sci. and tech. bd. NRC. Editor-in-chief: Water International; Editor: Jour. of Hydrology. Served with USNR, 1945-46. Recipient Meritorious Civilian Service award U.S. Army C.E., 1972. Fellow AAAS,. Internat. Water Resources Assn. (exec. bd.), ASCE (water resources exec. com., Julian Hinds award 1981, hon. mem. 1987, Hunter Rouse award 1993, Lifetime Achievement award 2001); mem. Am. Water Resources Assn. (hon.), Am. Geophys. Union (pres. hydrology sect.), Nat. Soc. Profl. Engrs., Internat. Assn. Hydrol. Scis., World Meteorol. Orgn. (chmn. com. on hydrol. design data), U.S. Com. on Irrigation, Drainage and Flood Control, Univs. Council on Water Resources (exec. bd.), Nat. Acad. Engring. Home: Austin, Tex. Died Mar. 21, 2009.

BEARDEN, FRED B(URNETTE), JR., marketing executive; b. McKinney, Tex., July 25, 1923; s. Fred Burnette and Gladys (Chaddick) B.; m. Elizabeth Emery Jackman, Dec. 6, 1947 (div. Nov. 21, 1994); children: Devon Elizabeth Bearden Stiles, Fred Burnette III. BBA, So. Meth. U., 1946. Cert. practitioner Neuro Linguistic Programming NLP Ctr. for Counseling and Tng. Bus. mgr. Tom Galligan Prodns., Dallas, 1943-47; mfrs. rep. F.B. Bearden Co., Dallas, 1948-53; regional mgr. Waste-King Corp., Dallas, 1955-61; pres. Fred Bearden Co., Dallas, from 1961. Founder, chmn. Inst. for Human Achievement/Self Realization; cons., speaker in field. Patentee; contbr. articles to profl. publs. Mem. Mktg. Agts. Food Svc. Industry (dir., pres. 1976-81), Richardson Jaycees (co-founder, pres. 1951), Mensa. Avocations: photography, writing, hiking. Home: Abingdon, Md. Died Jan. 7, 2008.

BEARN, ALEXANDER GORDON, physician, researcher, retired pharmaceutical executive; b. Surrey, Eng., Mar. 29, 1923; arrived in U.S., 1951; s. Edward Gordon Bearn; m. Margaret Slocum, Dec. 20, 1952; children: Helen B. Pennoyer, Gordon Clarence Frederic. Student, Epsom Coll.; MB, BS, Guy's Hosp., U. London, Eng., 1945, MD, 1951; MD (hon.), U. René Descartes, Paris, 1974, Cath. U., Korea, 1968. Assoc. Rockefeller Inst., Rockefeller U., NYC, 1951—57; assoc. prof., physician Rockefeller U., NYC, 1957—64, prof., sr. physician, 1964—66, adj. prof., vis. physician, from 1966; prof. medicine Cornell U., 1966—77, Stanton Griffis Disting. med. prof., 1977—79, chmn. dept., 1966—77, prof. medicine emeritus; physician-in-chief N.Y. Hosp., 1966—77; sr. v.p. for med. and sci. affairs Merck, Sharp & Dohme Internat., Rahway, NJ, 1979—88; v.p. Am. Philos. Soc., 1990—96, exec. officer, 1997—2002, exec. officer emeritus, 2002—09; Disting. vis. fellow Christ's Coll., Cambridge, England, 1996—97, fellow commoner, 1997—2009. Mem. commn. human resources NAS, 1974—77; chmn. divsn. med. scis. Assembly Life Scis., 1978—79; bd. sci. counselors Nat. Inst. Arthritis, Metabolism and Digestive Diseases, 1976—80; mem. Space Sci. Bd., 1978—79; cons. genetics tng. com., divsn. gen. med. scis. USPHS, 1961—65, cons. genetics study sect., 1966—70; cons. Fogarty Ctr. NIH, 1991—94; pres. Royal Soc. Medicine Found., Inc., 1976—78; bd. sci. overseers Jackson Lab., Bar Harbor, 1969—82. Author: Archibald Garrod and the Individuality of Man, 1993, Sir Clifford Allbutt: Scholar and Physician, 2007, Sir Francis Richard Fraser: A Canny Scot Shapes British Medicine, 2008; editor: Am. Jour Medicine, 1971—77; editor-in-chief:, 1977—79; co-editor: Progress in Medical Genetics, 1962—87; assoc. editor: Cecil-Loeb Textbook of Medicine; contbr. articles to profl. jours. Trustee Rockefeller U., 1971—98, trustee emeritus, 1998—2009; trustee Helen Hay Whitney Found., 1970—97, Macy Found., 1981—98, Howard Hughes Med. Inst., 1987—2009. Med. officer RAF, 1947—49. Recipient Alfred Benzon prize, Denmark, 1979, Benjamin Franklin medal, 2001, David Rockefeller award, 2002; fellow, Fulbright Found., 1951—52. Fellow: AAAS, Royal Coll. Physicians (London), Royal Coll. Physicians (Edinburgh, Scotland); mem.: Norwegian Acad. Sci. and Letters (fgn. assoc.), Med. Soc. London, Med. Rsch. Soc. Great Britain, Assn. Physicians Great Britain and Ireland, Harveian Soc. London (coun. 1959), Harvey Soc. (pres. 1972—73, Harvey lectr. 1975), Soc. Exptl. Biology and Medicine, Am. Soc. Biol. Chemists, Genetics Soc. Am., Am. Soc. Human Genetics (pres. 1971), Am. Soc. Clin. Investigation, Assn. Am. Physicians, Am. Philos. Soc. (exec. officer 1997—2002, v.p. 1990—96), Inst. Medicine NAS, Century Assn., Misquamicut Club (Watch Hill, R.I.), Knickerbocker Club, Phila. Club, Crail Golf Club (Scotland), Sigma Xi (pres. Rockefeller chpt. 1962—63). Presbyterian. Died May 15, 2009.

BEAVERS, BILLY CHARLES, vocational education educator; b. Morton, Miss., Sept. 30, 1937; s. Byron Mondell and Nellie Mae (Baker) B.; m. Mittie Pearl Lum, June 27, 1959; 1 child, Charles Calvin. BS, Miss. State U., 1980, MEd, 1982, EdD in Spl. Edn., 1985. With Talon Inc., Morton, 1957-60; machinist Vickers, Inc., Jackson, Miss., 1960-68; tool and die maker Sunbeam Corp., Forest, Miss., 1968-73; tchr. metal trades Forest Scott Vocat. Tech. Ctr., Forest, Miss., from 1973. Performance examiner Nat. Occupational Competency Testing Inst. With Miss. Army N.G., 1959-64. Mem. Miss. Cert. Commn. (com. mem. 1987-93), Vocat. Indsl. Clubs of Am. (advisor). Baptist. Avocations: hunting, fishing, football, basketball, baseball. Home: Morton, Miss. Died Sept. 12, 2007.

BECKER, MURIEL ROGOW, English language educator; b. NYC, Feb. 17, 1924; d. Harry and Helen Rogow; m. Hyman Becker (dec.); children: Joanellen Blakeley, Gail Anne. BA in English, Hunter Coll., 1958; MA in English, Montclair State Coll., 1964; MLS, Rutgers U., 1971. Cert. tchr. English, N.J. English tchr. Lincoln Jr. High Sch., West Orange, N.J., 1958-66; English demonstrator Coll. High, Upper Montclair, N.J., 1966-72; English prof., coord. English tchr. program Montclair State U., Upper Montclair, 1966-93, prof. emeritus, from 1994. Author, compiler: Clifford D. Simak, 1980; author: (with others) Anatomy of Wonder, 1987; cons. editor Sci. Fiction Rsch. Assn. Rev., 1991—; also reviews. Mem. AAUW, Nat. Coun. Tchrs. English (folio rev., cons. reader, judge), N.J. Coun. Tchrs. English (past pres., past treas., awards com., judge, parliamentarian, exec. bd. 1976—), Sci. Fiction Rsch. Assn. (v.p. 1990—). Avocations: reading sci. fiction and fantasy, travel, groundskeeping, home maintenance, film viewing. Home: Caldwell, NJ. Died Feb. 15, 2008.

BECKNELL, WILLIAM EDWARD, SR., general practitioner; b. Booneville, Ky., May 1, 1911; s. Thomas Andy and Grace (Campbell) B.; m. Nancy Asher, July 10, 1943; children: William Edward Jr., John Thomas, Nancy Hopkins. BS, Ea. State U., Richmond, Ky., 1935; MD, U. Louisville, 1940. Pvt. practice, Booneville, 1940-49, Beattyville, Ky., 1949, Manchester, Ky., from 1949. Recipient Russell E. Teague award, Ky. Pub. Health Assn., Louisville, 1992. Mem. Ky. Acad. Family Physicians (past pres.), Clay County Med. Soc. (sec., treas.), Ky. Med. Assn. (del.), Masons (warden). Republican. Protestant. Home: Manchester, Ky. Died Sept. 29, 2007.

BECKSON, KARL, English language educator, author; b. NYC, Feb. 4, 1926; m. Estelle Zimmerman, Feb. 9, 1957; children: Mace, Eric. BA, U. Ariz., 1949; MA, Columbia U., 1952, PhD, 1959. Lectr. Columbia U., NYC, 1956-59; instr. Bronx Community Coll., NYC, 1959-60, Fairleigh-Dickinson U., Rutherford, N.J., 1960-61, CUNY Bklyn. Coll., 1961-65, asst. prof., 1965-70, assoc. prof., 1970-75, prof., from 1976. Lectr. Cornell U. Med. Coll., N.Y.C., 1981-95. Author: (with Arthur Ganz) A Reader's Guide to Literary Terms, 1961, 2d edit., pub. as Literary Terms: A Dictionary, 1975, 3d edit., 1990, Henry Harland: His Life and Work, 1978, Arthur Symons: A Life, 1987 (with Ian Fletcher, John Stokes, Lawrence Markert) Arthur Symons: A Bibliography, 1990, London in the 1890s: A Cultural History, 1993; editor: (with M. Lago) Great Theories in Literary Criticism, 1963, Aesthetes and Decadents of the 1890s: An Anthology of British Poetry and Prose, 1966, 2d edit., 1981, Oscar Wilde: The Critical Heritage, 1970, Max and Will: Max Beerbohm and William Rothenstein: Their Friendship and Letters, 1893-1945, 1975, The Memoirs of Arthur Symons: Life and Art in the 1890s, 1977, (with J. Monro) Arthur Symons: Selected Letters, 1880-1935, 1989. Served to yeoman 2d class U.S. Navy, 1943-46, Southwest Pacific. Mellon fellow 1978, NEH fellow 1989-90. Mem. MLA. Home: Flushing, NY. Died Apr. 29, 2008.

BEHRENS, HILDEGARD, soprano; b. Oldenburg, Germany, Feb. 9, 1937; m. Seth Scheidman. Student, Music Conservatory, Freiburg, Fed. Republic of Germany. Opera debut in Freiburg, 1971; resident mem. Deutsche Opera Am Rhein, Dusseldorf, Fed. Republic of Germany; debut Covent Garden, 1976, as Leonore in Fidelio, in Salzburg, 1977, as Salome; appeared in Tosca, N.Y. Met., 1985, as Brünnhilde in Siegfried, N.Y. Met., 1988, title role in Elektra, N.Y. Met., 1994; appeared in new Production of The Ring, Bayreuth, 1988; appeared with Frankfurt (Fed. Republic of Germany) Opera, Teatro Nacional de San Carlo, Lisbon, Portugal, Vienna Staatsoper, Met. Opera, N.Y.C., Orchestre Nat. de Paris, 1990; soloist Chgo. Symphony Orch., 1984. Recipient Leonie Sonning Music prize, Govt. of Denmark, 1998. Died Aug. 18, 2009.

BEHRENS, ROBERT KARL, sculptor, architectural designer, urban planner; b. Teaneck, NJ, May 12, 1939; s. George Henry and Gaetanina (Idarolla) B.; m. Elizabeth Carroll Jackson, Apr. 22, 1966 (div. 1976); 1 child, Francis Gaeta. BFA, Kans. City Art Inst., 1965; postgrad., U. Wis.; MA in Sculptor, U. Denver, 1972. Instr. design Denver U., 1969-72; project architect G. Cabell Childress Architects, Denver, 1968-75; prin. Behrens/Friberg Site Specific Art/Design, Sonoma, Calif., from 1985. Vis. lectr. U. Colo. Grad. Sch. Archtecture, Denver, 1979-83. Prin. works include pub. site sculptures, Cambridge, Mass., Boston, New Orleans, Denver, Fairbanks, Alaska, Oxnard, Calif., Stanford U., U. Colo., Beaver Creek, Colo., Vancouver, B.C., Can., U. So. Colo., Davis, Calif., Sonoma, Calif. Coord. Green Belt Alliance, Santa Rosa, Calif., 1995; chmn. Broadway Landscape Improvement Com., Sonoma, 1989; pres. Mountain Area Planning Coun., Evergreen, Colo., 1965; mem. adv. bd. Wright Ingram Inst., 1967-79; pres. North Mission Assn., 1997-98; bd. dirs. Sonoma Citizen Coalition, 1998; mem. adv. bd. Am. Sculpture Soc., 1985-87; mem. Sonoma Town Design Task Force, 1998. Recipient citation AIA, 1973, award of excellence Calif. Coun. Landscape Architects, 1987, Yolo County Bd. Realtors,

1987, Am. Planning Assn. Edn. award, 1992, Sonoma League Hist. Preservation award of Excellence, 1995; 1993 NEA grantee, 1975-95. Died Feb. 16, 2008.

BEILMAN, TERESA MARIE, artist, poet; d. Carl Joseph Buchholz and Marie Theresa Sigg; m. Lavern Joseph Beilman, Aug. 23, 1958; children: Gregory, Douglas, Elizabeth, Rose Marie, James, Jane. BA Kans. Newman U., Wichita, 1958. Portrait painter, sculpture, Wichita, 1958—2004; ret., 2004. Sculpture, St. Peter, Marie de Mattias, Gaspar de Bufalo, one-man shows include Kansas Newman U., 1978, Ursaline Coll., Louisville, 2004, mag., Birds and Blooms, 2004, Best of Birds and Blooms, 2005. Vol. Habitat for Humanity, Wichita. Mem.: Amnesty Internat. Avocations: reading, gardening. Died Feb. 3, 2008.

BEJSOVEC, EMIL THEOPHILUS, transportation executive, accountant; b. Mineola, NY, Mar. 15, 1926; s. Emil Joseph and Amelia Mary (Kubik) B.; m. Virginia Elaine Mangan, June 25, 1950 (div. Nov. 1976); children: Todd, Glenn, Patricia, Brook; m. Sarah Etta Jones, Dec. 4, 1976; 1 child, Eric David. BS, Hofstra U., 1948; MBA, NYU, 1950. CPA, Fla., N.Y. Acct. Emil J. Bejsovec, CPA, Hempstead, N.Y., 1948-53; ptnr. Bejsovec & Sumner, CPA's, Hempstead, 1953-67, Main Lafrentz & Co., CPA's, NYC, 1967-73; pres. Bejsovec & Garone, P.C., CPA's, Woodbury, N.Y., 1973-78; mgr. Coopers & Lybrand, CPA's, Ft. Lauderdale, Fla., 1978-80; v.p. fin. Gray Line, Yellow Cab Cos. and subs., Ft. Lauderdale, Miami, Orlando and Tampa, Fla., 1980-87; owner, mgr. Emil T. Bejsovec, CPA, Davie, Fla., from 1988. Trustee, treas. Nassau County Hist. Soc., L.I., N.Y., 1965-76; elder, treas. Brookville (N.Y.) Reformed Ch., 1970-75; bd. dirs., treas. Brookville Taxpayers Assn., 1974-76. Served with USAAF, 1944-45. Recipient Alumnus of Yr. award Hofstra U., Hempstead, 1963-64. Mem. Am. Inst. CPA's, Fla. Inst. CPA's, Hofstra Alumni Assn. (chmn. bd. 1960, G.M. Estabrook Service award 1961), Am. Legion. Clubs: L.I. Athletic (Old Westbury, N.Y.) (bd. dirs. 1975-77). Lodges: Kiwanis (lt. gov. N.Y. dist. 1963), Masons (line officer 1964-68). Republican. Died Jan. 29, 2008.

BEKOFF, OSCAR, psychotherapist; b. Bklyn., Aug. 27, 1917; s. Irving and Eva (Horowitz) B.; m. Beatrice Mendelow, June 9, 1940; children: Roberta, Marc, Marjorie. BA, City U. L.A., 1979, MS in Psychology, 1981, Litt.D (hon.), 1984, PhD in Psychology, 1986. Fellow and Diplomate Am. Bd. Med. Psychotherapists and Diagnosticians; fellow and diplomate Internat. Acad. Behavioral Medicine Counseling and Psychotherapy. Pvt. practice psychotherapy & behavioral medicine, Tamarac, Fla., from 1982; exec. v.p. Clinton Oil Co., 1961-67; asst. to the chmn. of the bd. Real Petroleum Co., 1968-71; pres. Nantod Corp., Brookville, N.Y., 1963-77. Bd. govs. Behavioral Sci. Ctr., Nova U., Ft. Lauderdale, 1985-88; instr. continuing edn. Broward Community Coll., Coconut Creek, Fla., 1985, L.I. U., Greenvale, N.Y., 1984-88; prof. psychology dept. L.I. U. Developed Intra-Persona Therapy. Author: It's Yours for the Asking, 1988. Dist. commr. Boy Scouts Am., 1938-42; commr. City of N.Y., 1948; adv. bd. Fla. State Crime Commn., 1985—; cons., advisor Fla. Pepper Commn. on Aging, Tallahassee, 1990—. Recipient Cert. of Merit Nat. Coun. ARC, 1985, 50-Yr. Svc. award, 1990, Letter of Honor for pro bono work with the elderly from Pres. Ronald Reagan, 1988. Fellow Internat. Acad. Behavioral Medicine Counseling and Psychotherapy; mem. APA (Am. Psychol. Soc.), Am. Assn. Counseling and Devel., Am. Assn. Family Counseling and Mediators (supr. 1986), Nat. Ski Patrol (life), Amateur Ski Instrs. Assn. (life, cert. ski instr. 1946—), Oddfellows, Masons (32 deg.). Jewish. Home: Tamarac, Fla. Died Sept. 12, 2007.

BELCHER, DOROTHY S., state correctional department administrator; b. Macon, Ga., Sept. 3, 1954; d. Lawyer B. Stanley and Lena Mae Montgomery; divorced; children: Ayotunde Ronke Ware, Aziza Asha Belcher. BA, U. Wis., Madison, 1976. Cert. correctional probation officer, correctional officer inspector, Fla. Probation and parole officer I State of Fla. Dept. of Corrections, Miami, 1978-80, probation and parole officer II, 1980-83, pub. svc. officer, 1983-87, gold program coord., 1987-89, probation and parole supr., 1989-90, correctional probation sr. supr., 1990-91, correctional officer, sr. inspector, 1991-97, correctional probation sr. supr. Ft. Lauderdale, 1997-98, correctional probation dep. adminstr. Miami, 1998-99, correctional probation sr. cir. adminstr., from 1999. Fellow Eta Phi Beta; mem. 100 Black Women, Fla. Coun. on Crime and Delinquency, Criminal Justice Inst. (hon.). Democrat. Pentecostal. Avocations: reading, writing, singing, playing piano, gardening. Home: Opa Locka, Fla. Died Apr. 27, 2008.

BELINGER, HARRY ROBERT, retired business executive; b. Phila., Sept. 16, 1927; s. Harry and Florence (McGovern) B.; m. Jean Marie O'Neill, Nov. 30, 1957 (dec. Aug. 1998); 1 child, Lizanne. BS, Temple U., 1957. Reporter UPI, Phila., 1957-62, Phila. Daily News, 1962-63, asst. city editor, 1963-66, city editor, 1966-68, 70-71, Phila. Inquirer, 1968-70; city rep., dir. commerce City of Phila., 1972-76; v.p. pub. affairs ARAMARK Inc., Phila., 1976-95; ret., 1995. Pres. Great Flag Gateway, Inc., 2002. Former ex-officio mem. City Planning Commn.; former v.p. Phila. Indsl. Devel. Corp.; past dir., mem. exec. com. Phila. Port Corp.; former mem. sch. bd. Archdiocese of Phila.; past bd. dirs., mem. exec. com. Conv. and Tourist Bur., Phila.; past bd. dirs. Phila. Civic Ctr., Mercy Fitzgerald Hosp. With inf., AUS, 1950-52. Mem. Phila. Press Assn. (bd. dirs. 1964-66). Home: Bryn Mawr, Pa. Died Sept. 23, 2009.

BELK, SAMUEL ELLISON, III, cultural activist, former government foreign policy officer; b. Monroe, NC, June 9, 1920; s. James Patrick and Sarah (Nisbet) B.; m. Joanne Hebb, Sept. 8, 1949 (div. 1964); 1 child, Samuel Ellison IV. BA, U. N.C., 1949; MA, U. Calif., 1952; postgrad., U. London, 1949-50, London Sch. of Econs., 1949-50. Fgn. policy officer U.S. Govt., Washington, 1952-59, Nat. Security Council, The White House, Washington, 1959-65; UN affairs officer U.S. Dept. of State, Washington, 1965-67, asst. dir. internat. edn. program, 1967-79; patron, founder The Canterbury Cathedral Trust In Am., Washington, from 1987. Mem. Council of Friends, Folger Shakespeare Library, Washington, 1977-80; trustee Am. U. of Rome, Washington, 1979-80; founding trustee Friends of English Heritage, Washington, 1987; officer Order of St. John of Jerusalem, 1987—. Served as capt. U.S. Army, 1942-46, ETO. Decorated Bronze Star; recipient Presdl. Commendation, 1965. Mem.: F Street. Avocations: anglophile studies and pursuits, music, swimming, travel. Home: Washington, DC. Died Dec. 23, 2007.

BELL, CHARLES A., hotel development and management executive; b. New Brighton, Pa., Aug. 30, 1925; s. Charles and Elizabeth (Pollock) B.; m. Claire Naughton, Oct. 1, 1949; children: Charles A. (dec.), Jane Bell Cammarata. BS, Cornell U.; student, U. Grenoble, France. Purchasing agt., cost contr. Hilton Internat./Caribe Hilton Hotel, P.R., 1949-51; chief steward Hotel Plaza Hilton, NYC, 1952; analyst Pannell Kerr Forster, 1953-54; restaurant mgr. Hotel Roosevelt-Hilton, NYC, 1955; food and beverage mgr. Hotel New Yorker-Hilton, NYC, 1956; asst. dir. food and beverage Hilton Hotels Corp., NYC, 1960; v.p. food and beverage Hilton Hotels Internat., NYC, 1965, sr. v.p. adminstrn., 1975, exec. v.p., COO, 1985; pres. internat. hotel mgmt. consulting and devel. Charles A. Bell, Ltd., NYC, from 1986. Contbr. articles to profl. jours. Bd. dirs. Washington Sq. Assn., 1982-92; mem. Washington Sq. Coalition, 1986—. With USAF, 1943-46. Mem. Internat. Soc. Hospitality Consultants, Quaker Hill Country Club, Marco Polo Club, World Trade Club, Confrerie des Chevaliers du Tastevin (comdr.), Angler's Club N.Y., Alpha Sigma Phi, Phi Kappa Phi. Republican. Home: Scarsdale, NY. Died Dec. 2, 2007.

BELL, GRIFFIN BOYETTE, lawyer, former United States attorney general; b. Americus, Ga., Oct. 31, 1918; s. A. C. and Thelma (Pilcher) Bell; m. Mary Foy Powell, Feb. 20, 1943 (dec. 2000); 1 child, Griffin; m. Nancy Duckworth Kinnebrew, June 8, 2001. Student, Ga. Southwestern Coll.; LL.B. cum laude, Mercer U., 1948, LL.D., 1967; HHD (hon.), Ga. Southwestern Coll., 2008. Bar: Ga. 1947. Pvt. practice law, Savannah, Rome, Ga., 1947-53; ptnr. firm King & Spalding, Atlanta, 1953—58, mng. ptnr., 1959-61, sr. ptnr., 1976—77, 1979—2004, sr. counsel, 2004—09; chief of staff to Gov. Ernest Vandiver State of Ga., Atlanta, 1959-61; judge US Ct. Appeals (5th Cir.), 1961-76; atty. gen. US Dept. Justice, Washington, 1977-79. Mem. vis. com. Vanderbilt U. Law Sch.; head Am. del. Madrid Conf. Security and Coop. Europe, 1980. Co-author (with Ronald J. Ostrow): Taking Care of the Law, 1982; author: Footnotes to History: A Primer on the American Political Character, 2008. Co-chmn. Nat. Task Force Violent Crime, 1981, Pres. Bush's Com. Fed. Ethics Law Reform, 1989; mem. Sec. of State's Adv. Com. South Africa; mem. rev. panel U.S. Office Mil. Commn. for Mil. Tribunals at Guantanamo Bay, Cuba, 2003—07; chmn. Atlanta Commn. Crime Delinquency, 1965—66; bd. dirs. Fed. Jud. Ctr., 1974—76; trustee Mercer U., Ga. Served to maj. US Army, 1941—46. Recipient Thomas Jefferson Meml. Found. award for Excellence in Law, 1984. Mem.: ABA (chmn. divsn. jud. adminstrn. 1975—76), Am. Law Inst., Am. Coll. Trial Lawyers (pres. 1985—86), Order of Coif. Democrat. Baptist. Died Jan. 5, 2009.

BELL, GUS KAISER, clinical psychologist, consultant; b. Knoxville, Tenn., June 27, 1927; s. Fred E. and Jean (Kaiser) B.; m. Norma Jean Maddox, Aug. 24, 1952; children: Ellen (dec.), Jeffrey, Linda. BA in Psychology with honors, Rhodes Coll., 1951; PhD in Clin. Psychology, U. Tenn., 1956. Psychometrist Oak Ridge (Tenn.) Sch. Adminstrn., 1953; psychology trainee VA Mental Hygiene Clinic, Knoxville, 1953-54, Kennedy VA Med. Teaching Group, Memphis, 1954-55; asst. clin. psychologist Psychol. Svc. Ctr., U. Tenn., Knoxville, 1955-56; clin. psychologist Knoxville Mental Health Ctr., 1955-56, Nashville Mental Health Ctr., 1956-58; sr. clin. psychologist, dir. tng. Dede Wallace Mental Health Ctr., Nashville, 1958-64, chief clin. psychologist, 1965-67; pvt. practice clin. and cons. psychology, Nashville, from 1967. Cons. children and youth divsn. Mid. Tenn. Mental Health Inst., Nashville, 1964-95, YWCA TryAngle House, Nashville, 1978-91, Respite Coordination Svcs., Nashville, 1989-91. Mem. APA, Tenn. Psychol. Assn. (sec.-treas. 1963-64, pres. 1969-70), Southeastern Psychol. Assn., Nashville Area Psychol. Assn., Am. Soc. Clin. Hypnosis, Soc. for Clin. and Exptl. Hypnosis. Home: Nashville, Tenn. Died Jan. 19, 2008.

BELL, HOLLEY MACK, retired foreign service officer, writer; b. Windsor, NC, May 9, 1922; s. John Cartwright and Minnie Turner (Bond) B.; m. Clara Murphy Bond, Apr. 11, 1953; children: Elisabeth Turner Bell Loncella, Clara Bond Bell Guess, Mack III. AB in Journalism, U. N.C., 1943; diploma, Grad. Inst. Internat. Studies, Geneva, 1948; MA, Fletcher Sch. Law & Diplomacy, 1970. Historian U.S. War Dept., Bad Nauheim, Germany, 1947-48; reporter Charlotte (N.C.) News, 1948-52; editor-mgr. Bertie Ledger-Advance, Windsor, 1952-55; editl. writer Greensboro (N.C.) Daily News, 1956-61; press attaché, info. officer U.S. Embassy, Santiago, Chile, 1961-66, Bogotá, Colombia, 1966-69, pub. affairs officer Quito, Ecuador, 1972-77, Santo Domingo, Dominican Republic, 1977-80; desk officer U.S. Info. Agy., Washington, 1970-72, chief media reaction staff, 1980-87; ret., 1987. Mem. Episcopal Found., Kinston, N.C., 1990-93; mem. N.C. Task Force on Cultural Resources, Raleigh, 1991—, Historic Murfreesboro (N.C.) Commn., 1995—; chmn. pub. affairs com. Hist. Hope Plantation, Windsor, 1980—; historiographer Episcopal Diocese of East Carolina, Kinston, N.C., 1992—. 1st lt. U.S. Army, 1943-46, ETO. Recipient Nat. Order Al Mérito, Govt. of Ecuador, 1977. Mem. Nat. Episcopal Historians and Archivists, Coun. of Fgn. Rels., N.C. Art Soc. (chmn. outreach com. 1991-95, co-chmn. 50th anniversary com. 1995—), Rotary. Democrat. Avocations: historical and genealogical research, historic preservation. Home: Windsor, NC. Died May 11, 2008.

BELL, J(AMES) MILTON, religious society official; b. Orillia, Ont., Can., Nov. 12, 1925; s. Harold James and Margaret Olive (Deck) B.; m. Ellen Virginia Gibb, Nov. 14, 1953. BA, Queens U., 1946; BD, Queens Theol. Sem., 1950; ThM, Princeton Theol. Sem., 1951; STD, Temple U., 1955. Asst. pastor St. Paul Presbyn. Ch., Phila., 1950-52; pastor Christ-West Hope Presbyn. Ch., Phila., 1952-60; sr. pastor Cen. Brick Presbyn. Ch., East Orange, N.J., 1960-70; dir. planned giving Am. Bible Soc., NYC, 1970-93; sr. cons. Robert F. Sharpe and Co., Inc., from 1993. Vis. evangelist Ranchmens' Camp Meetings, Tex., 1967-68, N.Mex., 1967-68; pvt. charitable trust cons. numerous charitable, religious and ednl. instns., 1974—; pvt. fiduciary, trust adminstr., 1969—; specialist creation in pubs., developing charitable gift annuities, charitable remainder trusts and charitable bequests; planning giving lectr. Internat. Fund Raising Workshop, Amsterdam, The Netherlands, 1991, European Fund Raisers' Meeting, 1992. Author: The Churchman's Almanac, 1959, The Minister As Investor, 1961. Mem. Presbytery of Newark. Republican. Home: Verona, NJ. Died Jan. 14, 2008.

BELL, WHITFIELD JENKS, JR., historian; b. Newburgh, NY, Dec. 3, 1914; s. Whitfield Jenks and Lillian Victoria (Hengstler) B. AB, Dickinson Coll., 1935, LL.D., 1964; A.M., U. Pa., 1938, PhD, 1947; Litt.D., Franklin Coll., 1960; LL.D., Washington Coll., 1981. Instr. history Dickinson Coll., 1937, 38-39, 41-43, asso. prof. 1945-50, prof. 1950-54; vis. prof. Coll. William and Mary, 1953-54; asst. editor Papers of Benjamin Franklin, 1954-55, assoc. editor, 1955-61; assoc. librarian Am. Philos. Soc., 1961-66, librarian, 1966-80, exec. officer, 1977-83. Adminstrv. bd. Papers of Benjamin Franklin, 1969-91; mem. Nat. Hist. Publs. Commn., 1965-73, Nat. Portrait Gallery Commn., 1969-73; mem. Inst. Early Am. History, Williamsburg, 1956-59, 62-65, chmn. 1964-65; mem. com. sponsors Joseph Henry Papers, 1965-91. Author: Needs and Opportunities for Research in the History of Early American Science, 1955, John Morgan, 1965, Continental Physician, 1975, The College of Physicians of Philadelphia, 1987, Patriot - Improvers: Biographical Sketches of Members of the American Philosophical Society, 1998; editor: Bibliography of the History of Medicine in the U.S. and Canada, 1948-53; vis. editor: William and Mary Quar., 1953-54; editor: (with L.W. Labaree) Mr. Franklin, 1956, Cumberland County (Pa.) History, 1995-2003. Trustee Rosenbach Found., 1968-79, Henry F. Du Pont Winterthur Mus., 1971-79; vol. Am. Field Service, Italy, Germany, 1943-45. Hon. fellow Coll. Physicians, Phila.; recipient Lifetime Achievement award, Am. Assn. History of Medicine, 1996 Mem. Am. Antiquarian Soc., Mass. Hist. Soc., Am. Assn. Med. History (pres. 1970-72), Colonial Soc. Mass., Phi Beta Kappa. Clubs: Cosmos (Washington). Died Jan. 2, 2009.

BELLER, FRITZ K., gynecologist and obstetrician, educator; b. Munich, Fed. Republic Germany, May 17, 1924; came to U.S., 1961, naturalized, 1966; s. Carl Friedrich and Antonie (Woerz) B.; m. Marlis Duhl, Nov. 27, 1948; children: Verena, Christoph. Student, U. Berlin, 1942, U. Prague, Czechoslavakia, 1944-45; MD, U. Marburg, Fed. Republic Germany, 1949; DMS (hon.), Akita U., Japan, 1988. Intern Med. Klink Giessen, Fed. Republic Germany, 1948-49; resident in obstetrics and gynecology Staedtisch, Krankenhaus Karlsruhe, Fed. Republic Germany, 1949-52; resident and asst. prof. in obstetrics and gynecology U. Giessen Med. Sch., 1952-56; assoc. prof. U. Tuebingen Med. Sch., Fed. Republic Germany, 1956-61; assoc. prof., then prof. NYU Med. Sch., NYC, 1961-72; prof. ob-gyn., chmn. dept. Franuenklinik Westfâelische Wilhelms U., Munster, Fed. Republic Germany, 1972-88. Author 20 books, over 300 scientific articles and papers. Recipient Career Scientist award N.Y.C. Health Rsch. Coun., 1961. Fellow Royal Soc. Medicine, Am. Coll. Ob-gyn.; mem. N.Y. Acad. Scis., Am. Soc. Exptl. Pathology, Soc. for Gynecol. Investigation, Harvey Soc., European Soc. Hematology, Am. Gyn. Soc., Deutsche Gesellschaft Geb. Gynecologists, Am. Coll. Surgery. Died Mar. 12, 2008.

BELLMON, HENRY LOUIS, former Governor of Oklahoma; b. Tonkawa, Okla., Sept. 3, 1921; s. George D. and Edith Eleanor (Caskey) B.; m. Shirley Osborn, 1947 (dec. 2001); children: Patricia, Gail, Ann; m. Eloise Bollenbach, 2002 BS, Okla. State U., 1942. Mem. Okla. House Reps., 1947-49; chmn. Rep. State Com., 1960-62; gov. State of Okla., 1963-67, 87-91; US Senator from Okla., 1969—81; dir. US Dept. Human Services, 1983-84. Farmer; rancher; co-founder, co-owner Rush Metal, Billings, 1968-; co-founder, co-chmn. Com. for Responsible Fed. Budget;

former prof., lectr. Oklahoma City U., Cen. State U., U. Okla., Okla. State U.; fomerly TV commentator. Served to 1st lt. USMC, 1942-46, PTO. Decorated Legion of Merit, Silver Star. Mem. Okla. Health Sci. Found., Okla. Med. Research Found. Presbyterian. Home: Red Rock, Okla. Died Sept. 29, 2009.

BELLSON, LOUIS PAUL (LUIGI PAULINO ALFREDO FRANCESCO ANTONIO BALASSONI), drummer; b. Rock Falls, Ill., July 6, 1924; s. Louis and Carmen (Bartolucci) B.; m. Pearl Bailey, Nov. 19, 1952 (dec. 1990); children: Tony, Dee Dee; m. Francine Student, Augustana Coll., Rock Island, Ill., 1942; PhD (hon.), No. Ill. U., DeKalb, 1985, Denison U., Granville, Ohio, 1995, Augustana Coll., Rock Island, Ill., 1996, DePaul U., Chgo., 2001. With Ted Fio Rito, 1942, Benny Goodman, 1943, 46, Tommy Dorsey, 1947-50, Duke Ellington, 1951-54, Jazz at Philharm., 1954; concert artist, 1955—2009; mem. Big Band Now. Albums include Louis Bellson at the Flamingo, Big Band at the Summit, Louis Bellson's Septet Recorded Live at the 1976 Concord Jazz Festival, Louis Bellson and His Jazz Orch., 1989, Peaceful Thunder, 1992, Big Band Explosion, 1994, Louie Bellson and His Big Band Live from New York, 1994, Cool, Cool blue, 1995, Live at the Concord Summer Festival, 1995, Their Time was the Greatest, 1996, The Art of the Chart, 1998, Soul On Top, 2004, The Sacred Music of Louie Bellson & the Jazz Ballet, 2006, Louie & Clark Expedition 2, 2008 and others; composer: Skin Deep, Halk Talks, Ting-a-Ling, Drumology, ballet The Marriage Vows (Las Vegas Jazz Festival), Symphony in Jazz Americana, Composition for Piano and Orch., London Ste. Served with AUS, 1943-46. Recipient Am. Jazz Masters award, Nat. Endowment for the Arts, 1994, Jazz Living Legend award, Kennedy Ctr. for the Performing Arts, Washington, DC, 2007; named one of Living Legends of Music-Am. Drummers Achievement award, Zildjian Co., 1998; named to Hall of Fame, Modern Drummer mag., Percussive Arts Soc., Jazz Wall of Fame-Living Legend, Am. Soc. of Composers, Authors and Publishers. Lincoln Ctr., NYC, 2007; Duke Ellington fellow, Yale U., 1977. Mem. Musicians Union Died Feb. 14, 2009.

BELNAP, DAVID F., journalist; b. Ogden, Utah, July 27, 1922; s. Hyrum Adolphus and Lois Ellen B.; m. Barbara Virginia Carlberg, Jan. 17, 1947. Student, Weber Coll., Ogden, 1940. Asst. city editor Seattle Star, 1945-47; bur. chief UP Assns., Helena, Mont., 1947-50, Honolulu, 1950-52; regional exec. Pacific N.W., 1952-55, dir. Latin Am. services, 1955-67; Latin Am. corr. L.A. Times, 1967-80, asst. fgn. news editor, 1980-93. Recipient Overseas Press Club Am. award for best article on Latin Am., 1970, Maria Moors Cabot prize, 1973 Mem. Overseas Press Club Am., LA Press Club, Am. Club of Buenos Aires, Phoenix Club of Lima (Peru). Died Nov. 8, 2009.

BENDER, BURWYN BOYNE, truck manufacturer; b. Columbus, Ohio, Oct. 2, 1929; s. Alfred Carl and Ethel May (Ryan) B.; m. Evelyn Juanita Roden, May 14, 1955; children: Kathy, Michael, Gregory. BSME, Case Inst. Tech., 1951; MS in Automotive Engring., Chrysler Inst. Tech., 1953; grad. advanced mgmt. program, Harvard U., 1978. Registered profl. engr., Mich. Mgr. advance prodn. planning missile div. Chrysler Corp., Sterling Heights, Mich., 1960-62, mgr., mfg. engr. space div. New Orleans, 1962-68, ops. mgr. missile div. Sterling Heights, 1968-70; v.p., gen. mgr. Cooper Bessemer div. Cooper Industries, Mt. Vernon, Ohio, 1970-80; group v.p. Gulf & Western Mfg. Co., Southfield, Mich., 1980-83; owner, chief exec. officer Ottawa (Kans.) Truck Corp., from 1983. Served with U.S. Army, 1954-56. Mem. Soc. Automotive Engrs. (New Orleans sect. chmn. 1963-65), Computer-Aided Systems Assn. of Soc. Automotive Engrs. (bd. dirs. 1978-80), Machine and Allied Products Inst. (mem. mktg. council 1986—), Soc. Mfg. Engrs. (bd. dirs. 1978-80). Lodges: Masons. Republican. Home: Lawrence, Kans. Died July 27, 2008.

BENDICK, ROBERT LOUIS, producer, director, consultant; b. NYC, Feb. 8, 1917; s. Louis George and Ruth (Feis) B.; m. Jeanne L. Garfunkel, Nov. 24, 1940; children: Robert Louis Jr., Karen Watson Holton. Student, NYU, 1935; grad., C.H. White Sch. Photography, 1937. TV cameraman CBS, NYC, 1941-43, dir. news, sports, spl. events, 1946-75; pres. Bendick Assocs., 1975-77; program cons. various cos. including Warner Cable, Times-Mirror Cable, EPCOT, ABC and IBM-TV, 1977-82; freelance producer various documentary projects Guildford, Conn., from 1983. Lectr. TV prodn. NYU Grad. Sch. Film, U. Okla. Sch. Communications, U. Maine; producer Today. Author: (with Jeanne Brudick) Markets: From Barter ro Bar Codes, (with Jeanne Bendick) 5 books on TV, film; editor: Filmstrips, Monsters and Other Science Mysteries (Internat. Film Festival Gold medal 1977), Dreams and Other Science Mysteriesproducer: (TV spls.) Opening of the 1968 World's Fair, 1968 Olympics, NET, The Great American Dream Machine, 1971-72 (Emmy award 1971, 72), Feeling Good, 1975 (exec. producer with Dick Cavett), Fight for Food, 1978, Twenty-Five Years of Life, Merrily We Roll Along, The Today Show (Albert Lasker award, TV Guide award, Critics' award) The First Look (Ohio State Sci. award), Cinerama Holiday (Swiss Govt. Directorial award) This is Cinerama (Christopher award) The American West (Emmy award nomination), others; freelance photographer various mags.; free lance producer documentary PBS/Sta. WQED Fight for Food. Bd. dirs. Urban League Westchester, White Plains, N.Y., 1960-63; pres. Rye (N.Y.) Council for Human Rights, 1960-64. Served to capt. USAC, 1943-46, CBI. Recipient Gold medal Internat. Film Festival, 1978. Mem. Nat. Acad. TV Arts and Scis. (gov., mem. awards com.), Dirs. Guild Am., TV Acad.-Silver Cir., Guilford Boat Owners Assn. (pres. 1985-86). Democrat. Avocations: boating, fishing, photography. Died June 22, 2008.

BENEDICT, PAUL, actor; b. Silver City, N.Mex., Sept. 17, 1938; s. Mitchell M. and Alma Marie (Loring) B. AB in English, Suffolk U., Boston, 1960. Actor: (films) The Double-Barrelled Detective Story, 1965, The Virgin President, 1968, Cold Turkey, 1971, Taking Off, 1971, They Might Be Giants, 1971, The Gang That Couldn't Shoot Straight, 1971, Deadhead Miles, 1972, Jeremiah Johnson, 1972, Up the Sandbox, 1972, The Front Page, 1974, Mandingo, 1975, Smile, 1975, The Goodbye Girl, 1977, Billy in the Lowlands, 1979, The Man with Two Brains, 1983, This Is Spinal Tap, 1984, The Chair, 1988, Arthur 2: On the Rocks, 1988, Cocktail, 1988, The Freshman, 1990, Sibling Rivalry, 1990, The Addams Family, 1991, Guns and Lipstick, 1995, Waiting for Guffman, 1996, The Devil's Advocate, 1997, Who Was That Man, 1998, A Fish in the Bathtub, 1999, Isn't She Great, 2000, A Mighty Wind, 2003, After the Sunset, 2004; (TV series) Sesame Street, 1969—76, The Jeffersons, 1975—85; (TV films) Hustling, 1975, The Electric Grandmother, 1982, Babycakes, 1989, Attack of the 50 Ft. Woman, 1993; (Broadway plays) Richard III, 1979, The White House Murder Case, Hughie, 1996, The Music Man, 2000. Mem. Actors Equity Assn., AFTRA, Screen Actors Guild, Greater LA Zool. Assn. Died Dec. 2008.

BENEWITZ, MAURICE CHARLES, labor arbitrator, educator; b. Hartford, Conn., Nov. 16, 1923; d. Doris L. Benewitz; m. Lesley Frank Alan Benewitz. AB in Econs., Harvard U., 1947; PhD in Econs., U. Minn., 1954. From asst. prof. to prof., dept. chair Baruch Coll., NYC, 1955-75; arbitrator Manhasset, NY, from 1958. Dir. Nat. Ctr. for the Study of Collective Bargaining in Higher Edn., N.Y.C., 1970-73. Author: Higher Education Arbitration, 1988. Mem. Am. Arbitration Assn. (panel mem.), Fed. Mediation and Conciliation Svc. (panel mem.), N.Y. State Pub. Employee Rels. Bd. (panel mem.), N.Y.C. Office Collective Bargaining (panel mem.), N.J. State Med. Bd., Nat. Acad. Arbitrators, Phi Beta Kappa. Died Aug. 9, 2008.

BENNETT, EDWARD HENRY, reinsurance executive; b. Glens Falls, NY, July 22, 1917; s. Harry and Elizabeth Chandler (Clark) B.; m. Louise Faris, Aug. 3, 1946; children: Faris Elizabeth Ramseur, Anne Louise Petronis. AB, Princeton U., 1940. With Guy Carpenter & Co., Inc., NYC, 1940-51, asst. v.p., 1951-54, v.p., dir., 1954-76, vice chmn., chief adminstrv. officer, 1976-82; dir. Mitsui Sumitomo Ins. USA Inc. (formerly Mitsui Marine & Fire Ins. Co. of Am.), NYC, from 1987. Bd. dirs. Bartlett Carry Club, Inc., Tupper Lake, N.Y., 1988—, Mitsui Sumitomo Ins. Co. Am., N.Y.C., 2002—. Maj. USAAF, 1942-46, lt. col. USAFR. Decorated Legion of Merit. Mem. SAR, Res. Officers Assn., Princeton Club of N.Y., Nassau Club of Princeton, The Down Town Assn. N.Y. Republican. Episcopalian. Died May 23, 2008.

BENSCHNEIDER, DONALD CARL, interior designer, educator; b. Downey, Calif., May 7, 1946; s. Carl F. and Lucile (Bettinger) B. AA, Cerritos Coll., Norwalk, Calif., 1971; BA, Brigham Young U., 1973; MA, Calif. State U., Long Beach, 1986. Designer Looking Glass Design, Long Beach, Efrati Internat., LA, Ray O'Donnell Interiors, Lake Park, Fla.; owner Don C. Benschneider Designs, West Palm Beach, Fla.; interior designer Baer's Furniture & Design, West Palm Beach. Interior design dir. Palm Beach Community Coll.; instr. N.D. State U., Rancho Santiago Coll., Santa Ana, Calif., Calif. State U. Long Beach. Active AIDS movement. Sgt. USMC, 1969-75. Mem. Am. Soc. Interior Designers. Avocations: singing, dance. Died Aug. 20, 2007.

BENSON, ALISON COLTON, university official; b. Boston, Apr. 13, 1951; d. David Marshall and Mary Jean Allerton (Dunsmore) Cox; married; children: James Scott, Robert Stuart. BA, U. Nev., 1975, MA, 1981. With U. Nev., Reno, from 1976, dir. student fin. svcs., from 1985. Bd. dirs. No. Nev. Reading Ctr., 1986—. Recipient Most Watchable Woman award Reno Toastmaster's Club, 1987. Mem. NCAA (advisement bd.), Nev. Assn. Fin. Aid Adminstrs. (pres. 1982-83), Western Assn. Student Fin. Aid Adminstrs. (sec. 1986-87, conf. chair 1989, state membership chair), Nat. Assn. Student Fin. Aid Adminstrs. (state membership chair), Nat. Assn. Vets. Programs (adminstr.), Nat. Assn. Student Employment Adminstrs., Ducks Unltd., Nev. Club (charter, bd. dirs.), Skyline Assn. (bd. dirs.). Avocations: jogging, skiing, sailing, travel. Home: Reno, Nev. Died Sept. 30, 2007.

BENSON, JESSE THOMAS, obstetrics and gynecology educator; b. Kokomo, Ind., Apr. 23, 1934; BS, U. Toledo, 1954; MD, U. Cin., 1959. Diplomate Am. Bd. Ob-Gyn., Am. Bd. Electrodiagnostic Medicine. Intern Orange Meml. Hosp., Orlando, Fla., 1959-60; ob-gyn resident Meth. Hosp. of Ind., Inc., Indpls., 1962-65; pvt. practice Indpls., from 1965; chmn. ob-gyn dept. Meth. Hosp. of Ind., Inc., Indpls., 1979-88, dir. ob-gyn residency, from 1979, dir. urogynecology fellowship program, from 1988; assoc. clin. prof. Ind. U. Med. Ctr. Sch. Medicine, Indpls., 1983-88, clin. prof., from 1988; EMG fellow Mayo Clinic, 1995. Vis. prof. ob-gyn. Rush Med. Coll., Chgo., 1991—. Contbr. chpts. and articles to various profl. publs. Bd. dirs. United Meth. Children's Home, 1980-89, Indpls. Westside YMCA, 1978-80. Recipient Ross C. Griffith Disting. Tchr. award, 1972, 83, numerous rsch. grants. Fellow ACS, Am. Coll. of Ob-Gyn (risk mgmt. com. 1991—, quality assurance com. 1983—, edn. com. 1968-78, 82—, surg. policy com. 1981—, svc. chmn. 1976-78, 83-89, med. coun. 1976-78, 82-89, tissue com. chmn. 1979-81, med. records com. 1966-68); mem. Assn. for Hosp. Med. Edn., Am. Uro-Gyn Soc. (bd. dirs., pres. 1993), Am. Fertility Soc., Marion County Med. Soc., Ind. State Med. Soc., Assn. Profs. Ob-Gyn, Gyn Laser Soc., Assn. Ind. Dirs. Med. Edn., Internat. Uro-Gyn Soc., Soc. Gyn Surgeons, Urodynamics Soc. Home: Indianapolis, Ind. Died June 28, 2008.

BENSON, MARIE CHAPMAN, insurance agent; b. Geneva, Ala., June 1, 1909; d. Charles Daniel and Lollie (Pilley) Chapman; m. Wilfred Tyner Benson, June 28, 1933 (wid. Mar. 1984); children: Laurie Lynn Benson Morris, Beverly Ree Benson, Joseph Daniel Benson; 1 foster child: Juan Manuel Hernandez. BS in Piano, Huntingdon Coll., 1930, Cert. in Pub. Sch. Music, 1930; postgrad., U. Va. Lic. ins. agt.; cert. music instr., Ala. Instr. of piano, Geneva, 1930-32; organizer/instr. music Geneva Elem. Sch., 1930-32; attendance officer Geneva County Schs., 1932-33; v.p. Benson Wholesale Co., Geneva, 1956-74, v.p. of leasing co., 1964-74; v.p., dir. Dixieland Foodstores, Geneva, 1956-74, Brundidge (Ala.) Mfg. Co., 1961; ins. agt. Security Ins., Geneva, from 1963. Pianist/organist Meth. Ch., Geneva, 1919-79; ptnr. C.D. Chapman Co., Geneva, 1930—. Vice-pres. PTA, Geneva, 1947-48, pres. Geneva Garden Club, 1954-56; bd. dirs. Geneva Recreation Ctr.; pres. United Meth. Women, Dothan (Ala.) Dist., 1956-60, organizer dist. prayer groups; sec. Christian Personhood/Ala.-W. Flor. Meth. Conf., Montgomery, 1962-64; mem. Rep. Presdl. Club, Washington; endowed chmn. Christian faith and philosophy Huntingdon Coll., Montgomery, 1991; elected del. to 4th Assembly, Dothan Dist. Soc. Christian Svc., Milw., 1960; others. Hon. Mother of Yr., Am. Mothers Com., State of Ala., Birmingham, 1971; Paul Harris fellow Geneva Rotary Club, 1979. Mem. Athenaeum Federated Club (pres. 1955-57, pres. 1968-70, Merit Mother award 1968), 6th Dist. Federated Club of ALA (treas.). Avocations: growing roses, gardening, reading, travel, writing. Died Oct. 26, 2007.

BERA, MICHAEL JOHN, secondary school educator; b. Fremont, Nebr., Apr. 30, 1943; s. Michael Joseph Bera and Edith Hermine Asche; m. Cynthia K. Ellis Hofer, June 16, 1973 (div. Aug. 1981); children: Melanie, Kim. Cert. in radiol. tech., St. Louis County Hosp., 1964; BA, U. Mo., St. Louis, 1973. Radiology technician St. Louis County Hosp., 1962-68, Deaconess Hosp., St. Louis, 1971-74, St. John's Mercy Med. Ctr., St. Louis, 1976-78, John Cochran VA Hosp., St. Louis, 1978-79, Cardinal Glennon Hosp., St. Louis, 1980, DePaul Med. Ctr., St. Louis, 1983-86; tchr. St. Thomas Aquinas H.S., St. Louis, 1974-76, Belfontaine Neighbors Sch. Dist., St. Louis, 1979-81; substitute tchr. Topeka Unified Sch. Dist., from 1990. Pvt. tutor English, Latin, anatomy, physics, St. Louis, 1982, Topeka, 1993, 94, 95; tutor Topeka Unified Sch. Dist., 1993, 94. Bldg. rep. Safe Streets. Topeka, 1996-97; vol. St. Francis Hosp., Topeka, 1996—. With USMC, 1968-71. Mem. Internat. Soc. Poets. Roman Catholic. Avocations: writing, painting, wood refinishing, gourmet cooking. Home: Topeka, Kans. Died June 22, 2008.

BERD, MORRIS, artist; b. Phila., Mar. 12, 1914; s. Benjiman and Ida (Solatsky) B.; m. DeEtta Nelson, Oct. 12, 1943; children: Jared, Caleb. Diploma, Phila. Coll. Art, 1936; studied and painted, U. Stranieri de Perugia, Europe, Mex., North Africa, 1956. Prof. Phila. Coll. of Art, 1936-86. Represented by Ross-Constantin Gallery, N.Y.C.; represented in many pvt. and pub. collections. Recipient mural award Gimbel Bros., 1952. Mem. Phila. Artists Equity (pres. 1955-56). Home: Media, Pa. Died Sept. 26, 2007.

BERDENSEY, HAROLD KENNETH, real estate broker; b. Deep River, Conn., Feb. 10, 1924; s. Arthur and Effie (Dickerson) B.; m. Charlotte Belle Smith, May 30, 1946. Student bus. adminstrn., Coll. William and Mary; student adult edn. sys., Warwick H.S., Newport News, Va.; student real estate bus., Christopher Newport Coll.; grad. Am. Inst. Real Estate Appraisers, U. N.C. Commd. U.S. Army, 1945, advanced through grades to lt. col., ret., 1972, sr. amphibious adv. Trans. Sch. Ft. Eustis, Va., 1954, tng. adminstr. dept. aviation trades Trans. Sch.; owner, founder Realty World-H.K. Berdensey Realty, Newport News, Va., from 1957; commn. lt. col. U.S Army, 1969. Trustee Menchville (Va.) Bapt. Ch., Sunday sch. dir., chmn. personnel com., chmn. deacon. Mem. Va. Rental Assn. Realtors (chmn. grievance com., mem. profl. stds. com.), Masons, Shriners. Baptist. Avocation: hunting. Home: Newport News, Va. Died July 10, 2008.

BERG, CAROLYN NOURSE, research analyst; b. Des Moines, July 17, 1938; d. Archie B. and Katie Matilda (Taylor) Nourse; divorced; children: Christina Carole, Anna Lorraine. BA in History, U. Idaho, 1971; MBA, Ariz. State U., 1983. Sr. sec. U. Idaho, Moscow, 1972-74; owner, mgr. Something Different, Moscow, 1974-79, Inner Space, Moscow, 1979-81; coord. Moscow Downtown Assn., 1981-82; rsch. asst. Ariz. State U., Tempe, 1982-84; mgr. Door Store, Mesa, Ariz., 1984-86; rsch. analyst O'Neil Assocs., Tempe, 1986-89; faculty rsch. assoc. Ariz. State U., Tempe, 1989-90; adminstrv. coord. Maricopa County Dept. Pub. Health, Phoenix, from 1990. Home: Pinetop, Ariz. Died Aug. 8, 2008.

BERGER, ELLEN TESSMAN, psychologist; b. Berlin, Feb. 3, 1922; came to U.S., 1938; d. Arthur and Regina (Schainthal) Philipsborn; m. Jack Robert Tessman, June 20, 1951 (div. 1961); m. Arthur Victor Berger, Dec. 8, 1967 (dec. Oct. 2003). BA, U. Calif., Berkeley, 1944; PhD, Pa. State U., 1955. Lic. psychologist, Mass. Pre-doctoral intern U. Calif. Psychiat. Inst., San Francisco, 1947-48; postdoctoral intern Judge Baker Child Ctr., Boston, 1956-57, staff psychologist, 1957-93, cons., 1993—95; instr. Med. Sch. Harvard U., Cambridge, Mass., 1969—92, postdoctoral rsch. fellow sch. edn., 1970—71, ret., 1992. Assoc. The Tavistock Clinic, London, 1975-76; cons. in field. Contbr. articles to profl. jours. Fellow Mass. Psychol. Assn.; mem. APA, N.Y. Acad. Sci., Sigma Xi. Avocations: visual arts, art collector. Home: Cambridge, Mass. Died Aug. 21, 2007.

BERGER, PHILIP RAYMOND, seismological consulting company executive; b. Richmondville, NY, Aug. 11, 1924; s. Lester Dow and Edith Harding (Jones) B.; m. Eleanor Madeline De Pauw, June 25, 1949; children: Leslie A. Berger Ehrmann, Philip Raymond Jr. AB cum laude, Harvard U., 1949, AM, 1954. Asst. to dir. Harvard (Mass.) Seismol. Obs., 1949-54; field engr. Leet Assocs., Harvard, 1950-55; v.p. Vibra-Tech. Engrs., Inc., Pitts., 1955-69, chmn. bd., sr. seismologist, 1969-71; pres., CEO Philip R. Berger & Assoc., Inc. (now GeoSonics Inc.), Warrendale, Pa., 1971-86, now chmn. bd. dirs. and sr. seismological cons. Contbr. chpt. to The Aggregate Handbook (publ. of Nat. Stone Assn.), 1992. Bd. dirs. North Allegheny Sch. Dist., Pitts., 1961-71, Northland Pub. Libr. Found., Pitts., 1992; vol. area libr.; sch. class corr. Sgt. U.S. Army, 1944-46; ETO. Mem. Am. Inst. Profl. Geologists, Internat. Soc. Explosives Engrs., Nat. Stone ASsn. (life), Seismol. Soc. Am. Home: Bradfordwoods, Pa. Died May 12, 2008.

BERGER, PHILMORE, rabbi; b. Cleve., Apr. 10, 1927; s. Harry W. and Rose (Reich) B.; m. Anita Silberstein, Nov. 21, 1951; children: Debra, Daniel, David, Diane. BA, U. Cin., 1950; M Hebrew Lit., Hebrew Union Coll., 1953; diploma in pastoral counseling, Postgrad. Ctr. Mental Health, NYC, 1967. Ordained rabbi, 1953. Rabbi Temple Avodah, Oceanside, N.Y., from 1963, now life tenure. Pres. N.Y. Assn. Reform Rabbis, 1976-78; rabinnic dir., counselor N.Y. Fedn. Reform Synagogues, 1970—; chmn. family life com. Cen. Conf. Am. Rabbis, 1973-75; chaplain South Nassau Communities Hosp., L.I., 1972—. Mem. B'nai B'rith. Home: Oceanside, NY. Died Nov. 1, 2007.

BERGER, RICK, graphic design consultant; b. Bethlehem, Pa., Sept. 30, 1958; s. Elbert Edward and Gloria Ethel (Person) B.; m. Mary Kovacevich, June 22, 1991. Student, Bucknell U., Lewisburg, Pa., 1975; BFA, Kutztown U., 1980. Graphic design dir. JG Furniture Systems, Quakertown, Pa., 1982-85; cons. graphic design Caterpillar Inc., Peoria, Ill., from 1986. Contbr. book Office Systems: Designs, 1986. Judge Raddy awards, 1992. Recipient Gold medal Art Dirs. Club, 1980, Calif., 1983, Design Ann. award Arts Mag., 1983, Pre-Miere award, 1989, honorable mention, 1992, PIA Graphic Arts Award Ann., 1989; named one of Top 10 in Issue Archtl. Record Mag. Mem. Am. Ctr. for Design, Am. Inst. Graphic Arts. Avocations: skiing, bicycling, tennis. Home: East Peoria, Ill. Died Feb. 7, 2008.

BERGMAN, ROBERT CLAYTON, singer, master of ceremonies; b. Mpls., May 23, 1935; s. Parker Cyrus and Pearl (Hiltenon) B.; m. Sandy Joann Tangen, April 11, 1962; children: Jon E., Gretchen A., Kristine A., Barbara L., James R. Cert. Broadcasting, Brown Inst., 1958; student, U. Minn., 1965. Cartured roles St. Paul Civic Opera, 1963-64; featured roles Minn. Opera, Mpls., 1964-65; lead roles Fargo (N.D.) Moorhead Opera, 1966-78, 89, 90; featured roles Chgo. Oprea Theatre, 1975, Florentine Opera, Milw., 1976; lead role Opera St. Paul, 1982; performer Medora (N.D.) Mus., 1981-93. Entertainer Associated Club Dinner Clubs, nat. tour, 1981—, Cruise Lines, Azure Seas, 1982; entertainer, tchr. Nat. Sch. Assembly, nat. tours, 1985-91. Served with U.S. Army, 1954-57. Avocations: golf, touch football, big bands, old movies. Home: Glenwood, Minn. Died Feb. 25, 2008.

BERGNA, HORACIO ENRIQUE, research consultant; b. La Plata, Argentina, Feb. 11, 1924; s. Luis B. and Nelida Elena Lagos Guarte; m. Susana Cieza Rodriguez, May 5, 1951; children: Jose Enrique, Cieza. D of Chemistry, U. La Plata, Argentina, 1950. Chemist LEMIT, La Plata, Argentina, 1944-51; rsch. assoc. MIT, 1951-56; rsch. chemist Du Pont Exptl. Sta., Wilmington, Del., 1956-59, sr. rsch. chemist, 1959-82, staff mem., 1959-93, cons., 1993-99. Adj. rsch. assoc. U. La Plata, 1950-51; rsch. cons. IMPSA, Mendoza, Argentina, 1999—. Editor, author: The Colloid Chemistry of Silica, 1992. Avocations: music, art, sports. Died Nov. 10, 2007.

BERKELMAN, KARL, retired physics professor; b. Lewiston, Maine, June 7, 1933; s. Robert George and Yvonne (Langlois) Berkelman; m. Mary Bowen Hobbie, Oct. 10, 1959; children: Thomas, James, Peter. BS, U. Rochester, NY, 1955; PhD, Cornell U., 1959. From asst. prof. to prof. physics Cornell U., Ithaca, NY, 1961—2006, dir. lab. nuclear studies, 1985-2000; prof. emeritus, 2006; sci. assoc. DESY, Hamburg, Germany, 1974-75, CERN, Geneva, 1967-68, 81-82, 91-92, 2000-2001. Home: Ithaca, NY. Deceased.

BERLINER, HENRY ADLER, JR., banker, lawyer; b. Washington, Feb. 9, 1934; s. Henry Adler and Josephine (Mitchell) B.; m. Bodil Iversen, Sept. 16, 1961 (div. Aug. 1984); children: Marie Christine, John Mitchell, George Iversen; m. Margaret Rouse, Sept. 22, 1985; children: Meghan Mitchell, Michael Hardt. BA, U. Mich., 1956; JD, George Washington U., 1964. Bar: DC 1965, US Supreme Ct. 1968. Assoc. Craighill, Aiello, Gasch & Craighill, Washington, 1964-66; asst. US atty. Dept. Justice, Washington, 1966-67; ptnr. Berliner & Maloney (now Berliner, Corcoran & Rowe), Washington, 1969-84; pres., CEO Second Nat. Fed. Savs. Bank, Salisbury, Md.; founder Nat. Mortgage Corp, 1993; corp. sec., mktg. dir. Balt. Contractors, 1999; exec. Balt. Air Balance Co., Tamiami Air Balancing and Commissioning; mem., treas. Md. Econ. Devel. Corp., 2005; spl. asst. to mayor City of Annapolis, Md. Chmn. Pennsylvania Avenue Devel. Corp., Washington, 1984-89, Region One, 1990—; mem. nat. adv. bd. Resolution Trust Corp., 1990—. Contbr. articles to profl. jours. Chmn. D.C. del. Nat. Republican Conv., 1972, 76; mem., chmn. DC Commn. on Jud. Disabilities and Tenure, 1973-78; chmn. corp. adv. bd. Second Genesis, Inc., Bethesda, Md., 1985—. Lt USNR, 1956-59. Mem. Met. Club, Chevy Chase Club, Annapolis Yacht Club, Phi Delta Phi (internat. pres.), Sigma Chi. Episcopalian. Avocations: fishing, tennis, running, piano. Died Sept. 8, 2009.

BERLINSKI, EDWARD GERARD, writing educator, writer; b. Spokane, Wash., Apr. 18, 1961; s. Edward Joseph and Dorothy Florence (Chojnowski) B.; m. Lucretia Watkins, 2001 BA in History, Cath. U., Washington, 1984; MFA in Creative Writing, Am. U., Washington, 1990; PhD in Rhetoric and Composition, Cath. U., 1997. Writer/editor Naval Surface Warfare Ctr., Silver Spring, Md., 1984-90; writing instr. Cath. U., 1990-96; adj. prof. humanities Strayer U., Takoma Park, Md., 1993-97; adj. profl. writing program U. Md., College Park, Md., 1996—2009; adj. profl. comm. program Johns Hopkins U., 2002—06; pvt. practice cons. Cheverly, Md., 2006—09. Specialities include: medical, bus., tech., and creative writing (poetry). Recipient Top Paper award, Kenneth Burke Soc., 1999; Ctr. for Tchg. Excellence grant, U. Md., 2003—07. Avocation: poetry. Died May 6, 2009.

BERNAT, JOHN PAUL, lawyer, healthcare administrator; b. Chgo., Jan. 16, 1952; s. Jack and Isabelle Ann (Liberacki) B.; m. Lynette C. Wolf, July 4, 1981; children: Michael John, Alicia Jayne. BS, Ill. Inst. Tech., 1973, MBA, 1975; JD, Chgo.-Kent Coll. Law, 1979. Bar: Ill. 1979, U.S. Dist. Ct. (no. dist.) Ill. 1979. Instr. Ill. Inst. Tech., Chgo., 1975-80; labor rels. specialist Rush-Presbyn. St. Luke's Med. Ctr., Chgo., 1980-83, dir. employment svcs., 1984-86, dir. pers., 1986-89; mgr. employee rels. Little Company of Mary Hosp., Evergreen Park, Ill., 1983-84; dir. human resources Ravenswood Healthcare Corp., Chgo., 1989-90; v.p. human resources DePaul Med. Ctr., Norfolk, Va., 1990-93, Bapt./St. Vincent Health System, Jacksonville, Fla., from 1993. Contbr. chpt. to textbook. Bd. dirs. Neighborhood Justice of Chgo., 1985-90, Leadership Coun. for Met. Open Communities, Oak Lawn, Ill., 1983-90. Mem. Triangle Frat. (pres. 1972-73). Avocation: model railroads. Home: Kingsport, Tenn. Died July 30, 2008.

BERNHARD, HERBERT ASHLEY, lawyer; b. Jersey City, Sept. 24, 1927; s. Richard C. and Amalie (Lobl) B.; m. Nancy Ellen Hirschaut, Aug. 8. 1954; children: Linda, Alison, Jordan, Melissa. Student, Mexico City Coll., 1948; BEE, N.J. Inst. Tech., 1949; MA in Math., Columbia U., 1950; JD cum laude, U. Mich., 1957. Bar: Calif. 1958, U.S. Dist. Ct. (cen. dist.) Calif. 1958, U.S. Dist. Ct. (no., ea. and so. dists.) Calif. 1963, U.S. Ct. Claims 1966, U.S. Dist. Ct. (ea. dist.) Wis. 1982, U.S. Dist. Ct. (ea. and we. dists.) Ark. 1982, U.S. Dist. Ct. Nebr. 1982, U.S. Ct. Internat. Trade 1979, U.S. Tax Ct. 1969, U.S. Ct. Appeals (2d, 3d, 4th, 5th, 7th, 8th, 9th, 10th, 11th and D.C. cirs.) 1969, U.S. Supreme Ct. 1965. Research engr. Curtis-Wright Co., Caldwell, NJ, 1950-52, Boeing Aircraft Co., Cape Canaveral, Fla., 1952-55; assoc. O'Melveny & Myers, Los Angeles, 1957-62; ptnr. Greenberg, Bernhard, et al, Los Angeles, 1962-85, Jeffer, Mangels, Butler & Marmaro, Los Angeles, from 1985. Instr. math. U. Fla., Cape Canaveral, 1952-55; instr. elec. engring. U. Mich., Ann Arbor, 1955-57; referee L.A. Superior Ct., 1985—, arbitrator, 1988—, judge pro tem, 1988—; judge pro tem L.A. Mcpl. Ct., 1985—, Beverly Hills Mcpl. Ct., 1989—, Malibu Mcpl. Ct., 1994—. Contbr. articles to profl. jours. Chmn. adv. com. Skirball Mus., 1976-98; bd. overseers Hebrew Union Coll., 1976-98. With USAF, 1946-47. Recipient Disting. Achievement award N.J. Inst. Tech., 1998. Mem. Jewish Publ. Soc. (trustee 1986-96). Deceased.

BERNKOPF, MICHAEL, retired college educator; b. Boston, Jan. 11, 1927; s. Harold E. and Elizabeth (Rintels) B.; m. Jeanne Frank, Sept. 5, 1965 (dec. Feb. 1992); 3 children; m. Sarah Rosen, Sept. 22, 1992; 1 child, Ariella. BA, Dartmouth Coll., 1949; MA, Columbia U., 1956; PhD, N.Y.U., 1965. Prof. Pace U., NYC, 1967-95, ret., 1995. Author: Mathematics: An Appreciation, 1970, Galileo: A Scientific Biography, 1986. With U.S. Army, 1944-46. Avocations: ship models, fishing, wood sculpture. Died July 30, 2008.

BERRY, ANDREW T., lawyer; b. 1940; s. Philip and Ann Berry; m. Gita Rothschild, 1995. BA cum laude, Princeton U., 1962; LLB, Harvard U., 1965. Bar: NJ 1965, NY 1981, U.S. Dist. Ct. (ea. dist. NY), U.S. Dist. Ct. (Tex.), U.S. Dist. Ct. (Colo.), U.S. Ct. Appeals (2d, 3rd, 5th, and 11th cir.), U.S. Supreme Ct. Assoc. McCarter & English LLP, Newark, 1965—72, ptnr., 1972—2009, chmn., 1997—2009. Arbitrator U.S. Dist. Ct. (Dist. NJ), 1987—2009; spkr. in field. Contbr. articles to profl. jours. Bd. dirs. NJ Performing Arts Ctr., Newark Alliance. Fellow: Am. Coll. Trial Lawyers, Am. Acad. Appellate Lawyers, Am. Bar Found.; mem.: ABA, London Ct. Internat. Arbitration, Am. Arbitration Assn. (arbitrator, mem. comml. adv. coun. NJ), Am. Law Inst. (cons. various projects and coms.), Internat. Bar Assn., NJ State Bar Assn., Essex County Bar Assn., Assn. Bar City NY. Died July 24, 2009.

BERRY, HENRY NEWHALL, III, lawyer; b. Boston, Sept. 25, 1930; s. Henry Newhall Jr. and Mary Antoinette Berry; m. Elizabeth Lee Kononen, Mar. 31, 1956 (div. June 1983); children: Henry, Wendy, Bethany, Melissa; m. Susan Jane Deitchman, Oct. 6, 1990. BA, U. Maine, Orono, 1955; LLB, U. Maine, Portland, 1964. Bar: Maine 1964, U.S. Dist. Ct. Maine, 1964, U.S. Ct. Appeals (1st cir.) 1969, U.S. Supreme Ct. 1967. Title atty. Maine Dept. Transp., Augusta, 1964-65; law clk. U.S. Bankruptcy Ct., Portland, 1965-66; pvt. practice Portland, 1966-72; legal aid atty. Pine Tree Legal Assistance, Portland, 1967; county atty. Cumberland County, Portland, 1973-74, dist. atty., 1975-83; pvt. practice South Portland, 1984-99, Portland, from 1999. Fed. hearing examiner U.S. Govt., Portland, 1969-70. Town councilor Cape Elizabeth (Maine) Coun., 1967-71, 97—; mem. budget com. Cumberland County, Portland, 1997—. Cpl. U.S. Army, 1952-54. Mem. Cumberland Bar Assn. Republican. Roman Catholic. Home: Cape Elizabeth, Maine. Died Mar. 30, 2008.

BERRY, KATHLEEN A., English language educator; b. LA, Calif., June 22, 1958; d. Raymond Albert and Robin Lee Berry. BA in Linguistics, U. Calif., Berkeley, 1981, MA in Edn., 1981, credential in single subject tchg./English, 1982. Instr. English U. Calif. Ext., Berkeley, 1992—2004, tchr. trainer, 1992—2004; instr. English U. Calif., Berkeley, 1994, Contra Costa C.C., San Pablo, Calif., from 1996, Laney C.C., Oakland, Calif., from 2001; instr. Las Positas C.C., Livermore, Calif., from 2004. Cons. grammar Am. Med. Writers Assn., San Francisco, from 1999. HS program coord. Albany Adult Sch., Calif., 1984. Mem.: Tchrs. of English to Spkrs. of Other Langs. Avocations: yoga, quilting. Home: Oakland, Calif. Died June 27, 2008.

BERRY, PATRICK LOWELL, chemical engineer; b. Hillsboro, Ohio, Mar. 24, 1951; s. Russell Luther and Phyllis Louise Berry; m. Verna Ann McMullen, Sept. 11, 1971; children: Sean Patrick, Brenna Kathleen. BS in Chem. Engring., Ohio State U., 1973; MS in Ops. Rsch., George Washington U., 1986. Cert. Army Acquisition Corps - Level III U.S. Army, 1992. Chem. officer US Army, Aberdeen Proving Ground, Md., 1974—78, chem. engr., 1978—86, supervisory chem. engr., 1986—2006; ret. federal svc., 2006; pvt. biol. defense cons., 2006. Comdr. 2d lt. USAR, 1973, 2d lt. US Army, 1974—76, 1st lt. US Army, 1976—78, resigned capt. USAR, 1983. Recipient US Army R&D Achievement Award, 1994, 1998, 2000, US Army Meritorious Civilian Svc. Award, 2000, US Army Achievement Medal Civilian Svc., 2004. Mem.: AIChE, Internat. Soc. for the Systems Scis., Am. Assn. for Aerosol Rsch., Inst. for Ops. Rsch. and the Mgmt. Scis., Hon. Order of the Dragon, Omega Rho. Democrat. Achievements include designing and developing the first fielded US Army Biological Detection Systems, M31, M31A1 and M31E2. Avocations: birdwatching, travel, history. Home: Hereford, Ariz. Died Oct. 1, 2007.

BERRY, RICHARD CAMERON, engineer, educator; b. Wichita Falls, Tex., Sept. 3, 1927; s. Robert McNeil and Velda Ruth (Morris) B.; m. Betty Jean Cooper, June 4, 1949; children: Richard A., Suzanne Berry Antley. BSChemE, La. State U., 1949; MDiv, New Orleans Bapt. Theol. Sem., 1955; MS in Engring. Sci., U. Ark., 1967. Registered profl. engr., Tex.; ordained minister Bapt. Ch., 1952. Control chemist Armour Fertilizer Works, New Orleans, 1949; indsl. engr. Lane Cotton Mills, New Orleans, 1950; chem. engr. Coastwise Petroleum Co., Good Hope, La., 1950-52; mech. engr. Johnson Controls, New Orleans, 1952-55; pastor Goodman (Miss.) Baptist Ch., 1955-57, Woodworth (La.) Bapt. Ch., 1958-59; engring. prof. Bluefield (Va.) Coll., 1959-68; prof., acad. v.p., pres. LeTourneau Coll., Longview, Tex., 1968-85, chmn. engring. dept., v.p. emeritus, adj. prof. engring., from 1989. Bd. mem. Gregg County Child Welfare Bd., East Tex. Alliance for Minorities in Engring.; cons. in field. Mem. ASME (sect. chmn. 1974-75, Outstanding Engring. Educator 1983), Am. Soc. Engring. Edn. Republican. Avocations: tennis, gardening, walking, camping. Home: Longview, Tex. Died Jan. 9, 2008.

BERTALAN, FRANK JOSEPH, retired academic administrator; b. Edwardsville, Ill., Sept. 18, 1914; s. Frank Joseph and Ida (Barthi) B.; m. Helen G. Scheck, Apr. 6, 1942; children: Edward, Mary, Patricia, Frank, Elaine, John, Joan. BEd, Ill. State U., 1938; BS in Libr. Sci., U. Ill., 1939, MS, 1945; PhD, Cath. U. Am., 1962. Head reference and bibliog. svcs. U.S. Office Edn. Libr., Washington, 1946-50, chief libr. svcs. div. Legis. LIbr. Svc. Libr. of Congress, Washington, 1950-55; head engring. info. br. Navy Bur. Aeros., Washington, 1955-58; exec. asst. for sci. info. Office Naval Rsch., Washington, 1958-62; chief emergency measures div. Office Emergency Planning Exec. Office of Pres., Washington, 1963-65; dir. U. Okla. Sch. Libr. Sci., Norman, 1965-74; dir. Sch. Libr. Sci. Tex. Women's U., Denton, 1974-80; ret., 1980. Cons. Goddard Space Flight Ctr. Libr., NASA Hdqrs. Libr., comdt. USCG, U.S. Senate Fin. Com.; spl. rep. U.S. Book Exch., 1962-65. Author: Books for Junior Colleges, 1954, Provision of Federal Benefits for Veterans, 1955, Proposed Scope and Coverage of the Goddard Space

Flight Center Library, 1963, The Junior College Library Collection, 1968, rev. 1970. Comdr. USNR, 1942-46, ETO. Mem. ALA (nat. chmn. libr. orgn. and mgmt. sect. 1968—), Assn. Am. Libr. Schs. (chmn. recruiting and pers. com. 1967—), Spl. Librs. Assn., Okla. Libr. Assn., Kappa Delta Pi, Kappa Mu Epsilon, Kappa Phi Kappa. Home: Arvada, Colo. Died Nov. 28, 2007.

BEST, CHARLES WILLIAM, JR., lawyer; b. Atlanta, Aug. 18, 1936; s. Charles William and Virginia C. (Clark) B.; m. Kate Livingstone Ewing, Aug. 23, 1958 (div. Feb. 1976); children: Charles William III, Karen L. Habighorst, Thomas Ewing; m. Mary Ewing Fears, Apr. 12, 1980; 1 child, Michael Allen. BSEE, Va. Mil. Inst., Lexington, 1958; JD, U. Va., 1971. Bar: Va. 1971. Ptnr. Kaufman & Canoles, Norfolk, Va., 1971-90, Wilks, Best & Alper, Norfolk, Va., 1990-95, Best & Best, PLC, Norfolk, Va., 1995-98; sole practitioner Norfolk, from 1998. Capt., USAF, 1958-63. Mem. ABA, Va. State Bar ASsn., Norfolk Portsmouth Bar Assn., Order of Coif. Presbyterian. Avocation: offshore fishing. Home: Virginia Beach, Va. Died Aug. 20, 2008.

BETANCOURT, RALPH ERNEST, mayor; b. NYC, May 17, 1924; s. Raoul and Jacinta (Fernandez) B.; m. Carol Jean Betancourt, Aug. 27, 1955; children: Jean Ellen, Ralph Andrew. BS, Wagner Coll., 1949; MA, NYU, 1953; PhD, U. Madrid, 1964. Cert. tchr. N.Y. Tchr. St. Luke's Sch., NYC, 1951—53, Massapequa (N.Y.) Pub. Schs., 1953—83; ind. photographer Daytona Beach Shores, Fla., 1983—89. Songwriter, music pub., Daytona Beach Shores, 1984—. Composer: (song) We Salute the United Nations; author (songs): Fla. Great Survivors, Peli Peli, Caretta the Turtle, Natalie the Manatee, Ralphin the Dolphin. Mayor Daytona Beach Shores, 1997-01; exec. bd., ednl. adv. bd. for sch. dist., Massapequa, 1970s; bd. dirs. UNA-USA Assn. of Volusia Co., Fla., 1999; deacon, elder, 1st Presbyn. Ch., Babylon, N.Y., Westminster By the Sea Presbyn. Ch., Daytona Beach Shores. With U.S. Army Signal Corp, 1943-45. Decorated medal Battle of the Bulge, WWII. Mem. ASCAP, Massepequa Tchrs. Assn. (v.p. 1960s), Casements Songwriters (pres. 1980s), Fla. Motion Picture and TV Assn. Achievements include patents for multi-foreign language kit. Avocations: tennis, swimming, performing arts, travel. Died Nov. 23, 2007.

BETTERLY, JOHN ANDREW, history educator; b. Scranton, Pa., June 20, 1935; s. John Austin and Margaret (Palmer) B.; m. Mary Louise Grenizenberg, Aug. 3, 1957 (div.); children: Margaret Louise Betterly Robinson, John DeCamp, Jessica Diane; m. Nancy Cushman, July 30, 1982; 1 child, Jillian Lund Barkley. BA, Yale U., 1955; MA, Harvard U., 1964. Cert. secondary social studies tchr., N.Y. History tchr. Wyoming Sem., Kingston, Pa., 1958-62, St. Mary's Hall, San Antonio, 1962-66, Emma Willard Sch., Troy, N.Y., from 1966. Cmty. leader, tutor Acad. Assistance Ctr., Am. Online, 1996-67. Sgt. U.S. Army, 1955-58. Fulbright grantee, India, 1964, Travel/Study grantee Japan Soc., 1970, Regents grantee N.Y. State Regents, 1971. Mem. World History Assn. Democrat. Buddhist. Died Mar. 7, 2008.

BEUCHLER, LINDA GRAY, special education educator; b. Alexandria, La., Jan. 13, 1942; d. James Nicholas and Ethel (Pittman) Gray; m. John David Beuchler, Feb., 1968 (div. Feb. 1975); children: Nicole Leigh, Katrina Ann, Michael John. BA, U. Southwestern La., 1964; BS, Northwestern State Coll., 1981; MEd, U. New Orleans, 1985. Cert. elem. edn. tchr., tchr. blind/partially sighted, supr. student tchrs., computer literacy, La. Exec. sec. Humble Oil & Refinery, New Orleans, 1963-65; home svc. rep. Cen. La. Electric Co., Alexandria, 1966-68; itinerant tchr. Rapides Parish Sch. Bd., Alexandria, from 1981. Mem. AAUP, AAUW, Coun. for Exceptional Children, Phi Delta Kappa, Kappa Delta Pi. Baptist. Home: Alexandria, La. Died Dec. 31, 2007.

BEVARD, LINDA SONNICHSEN, community health nurse, musician; b. Phila., Apr. 15, 1950; d. Thomas Henry and Gertrude Elaine (Hogg) Sonnichsen; m. Charles W. Bevard Jr., Dec. 30, 1972. Student, Giuseppe Verdi Conservatory, Milan, Italy, 1964; cert. in German, U. Salzburg, Austria, 1969; BA, Mt. Holyoke Coll., 1972; postgrad. in musicology, U. Pa., 1974—77, BSN magna cum laude, 1984. RN, N.J., Pa.; cert. cmty. health nurse, ANCC. Staff Regional EEO Office/Dept. Health and Human Svcs., Phila., 1980-81; staff nurse oncology unit Pa. Hosp., Phila., 1985; health educator Clover Fork Clinic, Evarts, Ky., 1987; staff nurse IV chemotherapy Roxbury Med. Group, Succasunna, N.J., 1988; case mgr. Spl. Child Health Svcs., Passaic County, NJ, 1989-90; pvt. practice health edn./advocacy/support, from 1991. Composer, chair, dir., performer (piano, voice, organ), Phila. and Heidelberg, Germany, from 1973. Contbr. articles to health pubs. Mem. agency rels. team United Way of Morris County, 1993—98, cmty. ptnr. com., from 1996; hotline counselor Contact of Burlington County, 1976—77; support group leader Office of Chaplain, Ft. Leavenworth, Kans., 1977—78; ESL tutor Literacy Vols. Am., from 1995; facilitator, co-founder, newsletter editor (Northern Lights) North N.J. Support Group Nat. Orgn. Rare Disorders, from 1996; mem. adminstrv. coun. Boonton United Meth. Ch., from 1990, chair health and welfare ministries, missions coord., nominating com., from 1990; missions chair, nominating com., church rep. Bishop's Initiative on Children and Poverty; mem. exec. bd. United Meth. Women; bd. dirs. Morris County Hotline, 1989—95, coord. insvc. tng., newsletter editor, v.p. tng.; bd. dirs. Mental Health Assn. Morris County, 1989—93, cmty. outreach com., 1996—98; founder, dir. Woodland Consort (early music ensemble), 1980—86; dir. Jubilate (youth choir), 1983—86. Recipient letter of commendation, DHHS, 1981, Oncology Nursing Externship, Am. Cancer Soc., 1983, Spl. Mission Recognition award, United Meth. Women, 1996, 1st place photography award, Morris County All-Media Art Show, 2000, 1st place mixed media award, 2000. Mem.: ANA, N.J. State Nurses Assn., Disability Advocates Working in N.W. N.J., Families USA, Ctrl. Jersey Parish Nursing Network, Christian Cmty. Health Fellowship, Religious Coalition for Reproductive Choice, So. Poverty Law Ctr., Amnesty Internat. Freedom Writers, Nat. Multiple Sclerosis Soc., Am. Autoimmune and Related Disorders Assn., Nat. Sjogren's Syndrome Assn., Assn. for Spl. Children and Families, Immune Deficiency Found., Assn. Birth Defect Children, Nat. Orgn. Rare Disorders. Avocations: languages, reading, gardening, computers. Home: Parsippany, NJ. Died July 6, 2008.

BEVERLEY, JOHN GRAY, JR., investment banker; b. Winchester, Va., Mar. 10, 1935; s. John Gray and Julia Potter (Smith) B.; m. Rosa Noel Roth, June 3, 1967; children: John Gray III, Caroline Noel. BA, U. Va., 1958. Advt. exec. Dancer-Fitzgerald-Sample, NYC, 1961-63, BBDO, NYC, 1964-66, Wells, Rich, Greene, NYC, 1966-70; investment banker NYC, from 1970; founder, pres. Blandfield Securities, Inc., NYC, from 1982. Capt. USAR, 1958-63. Democrat. Episcopalian. Home: New York, NY. Died Aug. 5, 2008.

BEVERLY, ROBERT GRAHAM, retired state legislator; b. Belmont, Mass., July 1, 1925; s. William James and Helen Lucille (Graham) B.; m. Elizabeth Louise Weisel, May 17, 1946; children: Barbara, William, Robert Jr., Brian. Student, UCLA, 1948; LLB, Loyola U., LA, 1951. Ptnr. Richards, Watson & Gershon, L.A., 1954—2009; mem. Calif. State Assembly, Sacramento, 1967-76, Calif. State Senate, Sacramento, 1976—96. City atty. various Calif. cities, 1954-67. Mem. Manhattan Beach (Calif.) City Coun., 1958-67; mem. Manhattan Beach Planning Com., 1956-58; mem. Rep. State Cen. Com., 1967—. Cpl. USMC, 1943-46. Recipient Pub. Svc. award UCLA Alumni Assn., Outstanding Alumnus award Loyola U., L.A., 1990, Esteemed Alumnus award Loyola U. Sch. of Lw, 1974. Mem. Calif. State Bar Assn., L.A. County Bar Assn., So. Bay Bar Assn., Am. Legion. Republican. Avocations: tennis, walking, spectator sports. Home: Manhattan Beach, Calif. Died Oct. 14, 2009.

BEYER, BARBARA LYNN, transportation executive, consultant; b. Miami, Fla., Feb. 16, 1947; d. Morten Sternoff and Jane (Hartman) Beyer. BA, George Washington U., 1978. Supr. printing office Saudi Arabian Airlines, 1966-67; ops. coord. Modern Air Transport, Miami, 1968-70, acct. Berlin, 1970-72; rep. Johnson Internat. Airlines, Washington, 1974-75; v.p., bd. dirs. Avmark, Inc., Washington, from 1975, pres., 1989—2009; chmn., bd. dirs. Avmark Internat., London, 1985—2009; mng. dir. Avmark Asia Ltd., Singapore, 1988-89, chmn. bd. dirs. Hong Kong, 1989—2009; pub. Avmark Aviation Economist, London, 1986—2009. Mem. adv. bd. aviation bus. dept. Embry-Riddle Aero. U. Mem.: Nat. Bus. Aircraft Assn., Aviation Space Writers (internat. bd. dirs. 1986—88, award 1978), Am. C. of C., Nat. Press Club, Internat. Aviation Club, Aero Club, Fgn. Corr. Club. Avocations: reading, horseback riding, home improvement. Home: Daytona Beach, Fla. Died Oct. 23, 2009.

BIANCO, BARBARA JUNE, mental health nurse; b. Glen Cove, NY, Dec. 17, 1953; d. George M. and Dorothy J. (Luhmann) DeLalio; m. Jerry P. Bianco, June 15, 1974; children: Benjamin, Beth Ann. Diploma, Pilgrim State Sch. Nursing, 1975; student, Adelphi U.; BA in Humanities, New Sch. for Social Rsch., 1990, MPS in Health Care Adminstrn., 1990. Cert. in gerontology, venipuncture, CPR; cert. Lamaze childbirth instr., PRI assessor, cosmetic dermatologist. Sch. nurse AHRC, Bohemia, N.Y., 1984-89; staff nurse State of N.Y., Pilgrim Psychiat. Ctr., 1984-93; nurse adminstr. Cen. Islip Psychiat., also Kings Park Psychiat. Ctr., 1990-91; cmty. nurse N.Y. State LIDDSO, from 1993. Part-time BOCES instr., 1992-93. Home: North Babylon, NY. Died Aug. 9, 2008.

BICE, EDNA JEWEL, artist, educator; b. Bridge Port, Ala., Dec. 27, 1927; d. Edward Jack and Suzanne Reeves; m. Ronald H. Bice, June 27, 1954; children: Ronald H. Jr., Randy Reeves. Grad., Bridge Port Schs., 1945. Mothers patrol officer Charra Police Dept., Tenn., 1963—70; merchandiser Chattanooga, 1973—78; ceramics tchr. Soddy Daisy, Tenn., 1978—2004. Recipient Leadership award, Chattanooga Schs., 1965, award for commitment and svc. to elderly, City of Chattanooga, 1980. Mem.: NAACP, Nat. Hist. Soc. (life). Democrat. Presbyterian. Avocations: ceramics, arts and crafts, knitting, gardening, cross stitch. Home: Soddy Daisy, Tenn. Died July 2, 2008.

BICK, RODGER LEE, hematologist, researcher, oncologist, educator; b. San Francisco, May 21, 1942; s. Jack Arthur and Pauline (Jensen) B.; m. Marcella Bick, Mar. 3, 1980 (dec. Feb. 1995); children: Shauna Nicole, Michelle Leanne. MD, U. Calif., Irvine, 1970; PhD, Acad. Medicine, Bialystok, Poland, 1995. Diplomate Am. Bd. Quality Assessment, Am. Bd. Forensic Medicine in Oncology, Hematology, Thrombosis, Hemostasis and Product Liability, Internat. Bd. Thrombosis, Hemostasis & Vascular Medicine, Am. Bd. Pain Mgmt. Med. intern Kern County Gen. Hosp., UCLA, Bakersfield, Calif., 1970-71, internal medicine resident, 1971-72; fellow in hematology-med. oncology UCLA/Bay Area Hematology Oncology Med. Group, West Los Angeles, Calif., 1974-76; med. staff various hosps., Calif., 1974-77, med. staff, extensive adminstrv. and com. work Bakersfield, Calif., 1977-92; med. dir. oncology hematology Presbyn. Comprehensive Cancer Ctr., Presbyn. Hosp., Dallas, 1992-95. Staff hematologist/oncologist Bay Area Hematology Oncology Med. Group, Santa Monica, Calif., 1976-77, med. dir. Calif. Coagulation Labs., Inc., Bakersfield, 1977-92, San Joaquin Hematology Oncology Med. Group, 1977-92, Regional Cancer and Blood Disease Ctr. Kern, Bakersfield, 1986-92; asst. clin. prof. to clin. prof. medicine UCLA Ctr. Health Scis., 1976-94, assoc. prof. to prof. allied health profns. Calif. State U., Bakersfield, 1980-92, clin. prof. nursing and health scis., 1982-92; adj. assoc. prof. medicine/physiology, Wayne State U., Detroit; adj. clin. faculty Wesley Med. Ctr. and U. Kans. Med. Sch., Wichita, 1984-86; clin. prof. medicine U. Tex. Southwestern Med. Ctr., 1993—, clin. prof. pathology, 1993—; prof. hematology U. Tasmania Sch. Medicine, 1996; hematology cons. NASA; med. dir. UCLA/Kern Cancer Program, 1991-92, Ctrl. Calif. Heart Inst., 1990-92; invited spkr. and presenter in field, numerous internat. symposia and confs.; dir. numerous workshops in field. Author: Disseminated Intravascular Coagulation and Related Syndromes, 1983, Disorders of Hemostasis and Thrombosis: Principles of Clinical Practice, 1985, 2d. edit., 1992, 3d edit., 1997, Disorders of Thrombosis and Hemostasis, 2002; guest editor, contbr.: Thrombohemorrhagic Disorders Perplexing to the Hematologist Oncologist, 1992; guest editor: Laboratory Diagnosis of Hemostasis Problems, I, 1994, II, 1995, (monograph) Seminars in Thrombosis and Hemostasis, 1994, Common Bleeding and Clotting Problems for the Internist, 1994; editor-in-chief: Hematology: Principles of Clinical and Laboratory Practice, 2 vols., 1993, Paraneoplastic Syndromes, Hematology Oncology Clinics of North America, 1996, Hematological Complications of Obstetrics, Pregnancy and Gynecology, 2006; editor: Current Concepts of Thrombosis, 1998; contbr. numerous chpts. to books; author monographs and lab. manuals; contbr. over 250 articles and papers and numerous revs. to profl. jours. and conf. procs.; patentee in field; editor-in-chief Jour. Clin. and Applied Thrombosis/Hemostasis & Vascular Medicine, Thrombosis and Thrombophilia, 2003; mem. editl. bd. Am. Jour. Clin. Pathology, Internat. Jour. Haematology. Bd. dirs., exec. com. Bakersfield Symphony Orch., 1988-92. Fellow ACP, Am. Soc. Clin. Pathologists, Assn. Clin. Scientists, Am. Soc. Coagulationists, Internat. Soc. Hematology, Am. Coll. Angiology, Internat. Coll. Angiology, Nat. Acad. Clin. Biochemistry, Am. Heart Assn. (coun. on thrombosis, circulation and atherosclerosis; rsch. and grant peer rev. com. 1980-86), Am. Geriat. Soc. (founding fellow, Am. Stroke Assn., Am. Soc. Angiology; mem. AMA, AAAS, Am. Assn. Blood Banks, Am. Soc. Internal Medicine, Am. Soc. Hematology, Internat. Soc. Thrombosis and Haemostasis, Am. Assn. Study of Neoplastic Disease, Am. Assn. Clin. Rsch., Am. Cancer Soc., Internat. Assn. Study of Lung Cancer (founding mem.), Fedn. Am. Scientists, N.Y. Acad. Scis., Calif. Soc. Internal Medicine, Calif. Med. Assn., Calif. Thoracic Soc., Haematology Soc. Australia, Internat. Consensus Com. on Autithrombotic Therapy, numerous others. Lutheran. Avocations: ocean sailing, classical piano, brass musical instruments, photography, target archery, astronomy and astrophotography. Died 2008.

BIENSTOCK, FREDDY, music publishing company executive; b. Vienna, Apr. 24, 1928; came to U.S., 1939; s. Max and Bertha (Aberbach) B.; m. Miriam Kahan, July 9, 1957; children: Robert, Caroline. Student, NYU, 1942-43. Stockroom clk., promotional mgr. Chappell & Co., 1943-44, promotional mgr., 1945-53; v.p. Hill & Range, 1953-66; pres., owner Carlin Music, 1967, Hudson Bay, 1969, Starday-King, N.Y. Times Music. Pres., co-owner E.B. Marks; pres., chief exec. Chappell & Co., 1984-88. Mem.: Nat. Music Publishers' Assn. (bd. dirs.), Regency Whist, Cavendish Bridge. Home: New York, NY. Died Sept. 20, 2009.

BIERENBAUM, MARVIN LEONARD, cardiology educator, consultant; b. Phila., Aug. 30, 1926; s. Bernhard and Anna (Eckert) B.; m. Nettie Bella Eiser, July 1, 1951; children: Michele Bierenbaum Reichstein, Robert. BS in Biology, Rutgers U., 1947; MD, Hahnemann Med. Coll., 1953; postgrad. in Epidemiology, The London Hosp., 1965. Diplomate Am. Bd. Internal Medicine. Intern Beth Israel Hosp., Newark, 1953-54; resident VA Hosp., Bklyn., 1954-57; cons. Montclair, N.J., from 1957; coord. and sr. pub. health physician heart disease control program N.J. State Dept. Health, Montclair, 1957-81; dir. Kenneth L. Jordan Cardiac Rsch. Group, Montclair, from 1959; clin. assoc. prof. medicine U. Medicine and Dentistry N.J., from 1965; dir. dept. medicine St. Vincent's Hosp., Montclair, 1969-82; med. dir. Disability Determination Svc., 1985-88; prof. community medicine Seton Hall U., South Orange, N.J., from 1988. Resident cons. Netherlands Heart Assn., 1976-77, cons. N.J. Commn. for the Blind, 1981-85; regional med. adv. Social Security Adminstrn., 1973-85; hon. prof. medicine Chongqing Med. Sch., People's Republic China, 1987. Contbr. over 150 articles to profl. jours. Fellow coun. epidemiology Am. Heart Assn., fellow coun. atherosclerosis. With U.S. Army, 1945-46. Milbank Fund fellow, 1965. Fellow ACP, Am. Coll. Cardiology, Am. Soc. Clin. Nutrition, Am. Coll. Nutrion; mem. Am. Fedn. Clin. Rsch., Am. Inst. Nutrition, Am. Pub. Health Assn., Essex County (N.J.) Med. Soc. Home: West Orange, NJ. Died Jan. 28, 2008.

BIGLOW, ROBERT ROY, lawyer; b. Ashland, Wis., June 14, 1922; s. Craque Chester and Mildred Maria (Byrne) B.; m. Genevieve Johanna Jaeger, Sept. 3, 1953; children: Michael J., Mark W., Crague C., John B., Jennifer A., Laura A., Mary, Eileen. BS, Duluth (Minn.) State U., 1942; BSL, LLB, JD, U. Minn, 1948. Bar: Minn. 1949, U.S. Dist. Ct. 1949, U.S. Ct. Appeals 1949, U.S. Supreme Ct. 1949. Pvt. practice, Mpls., from 1949. With USAAF, 1942—45, with USAAF, 1951—52, with USAAF, 1961. Avocations: music, sports, hunting, fishing. Home: Saint Louis Park, Minn. Died July 21, 2008.

BIJOU, SIDNEY WILLIAM, retired psychology educator; b. Arlington, Md., Nov. 12, 1908; s. Leon and Leah (Barbert) B.; m. Janet R. Tobias, Aug. 31, 1934 (dec. 2000); children: Robert Kenneth, Judith Ann. Student, Lehigh U., 1929-31; BA in Bus., U. Fla., 1933; MA, Columbia U., 1936; PhD, U. Iowa, 1941. Diplomate Am. Bd. Examiners in Profl. Psychology; cert. psychologist, Wash.; cert. Acad. Clin. Psychology. Psychologist Del. State Hosp. and Mental Hygiene Clinic, 1937-39; research child psychologist Wayne County Tng. Sch., 1941-42, 46-47; asst. prof. Ind. U., 1946-48; assoc. prof., prof., dir. Inst. Child Devel., U. Wash., 1948-65. Dir. (Child Behavior Lab.); mem. Inst. Research in Exceptional Children, U. Ill., Champaign, 1965-75; adj. prof. psychology and spl. edn. and rehab. U. Ariz., Tucson, 1975-93, prof. psychology U. Nev., Reno, 1993-2001; assoc. (Ctr. for Advanced Study), 1972; cons. NIMH, 1959-63, Nat. Inst. Child Health and Human Devel., 1964-67, Bur. Edn. for Handicapped, U.S. Office Edn., 1975-88; hon. prof. psychology U. Peruana Cayetano Heredia, Lima, Peru; mem. rsch. adv. bd. Nat. Assn. for Retarded Children, 1965-90; chmn. task force rsch. on parent tng.; mem. nat. adv. bd. Ill. Inst. Developmental Disabilities, 1972-75; mem. nat. sci. adv. bd. nat. program on early childhood edn. Ctrl. Midwest Regional Ednl. Lab., 1969-74; nat. adv. bd. Kans. Mental Retardation Rsch. Ctr., U. Kans.; adv. panel on behavior modification therapy NAS, NRC, Assembly Life Scis. Divsn. Med. Scis.; profl. adv. com. Johnny Cake Child Study Ctr. Found.; cons. rsch. Portage Project on Parent Tng.; chmn. com. organizers Symposia on Behavior Modification in Latin-Am. Countries; mem. human rels. and ethics com. Ariz. Tng. Program at Tucson, 1977-84; trustee Assn. for Advancement Psychology, 1973-76; bd. dirs. Intermountain Ctrs. for Human Devel., Santa Fe, Desert Survivors, 1982-91; cons. Internat. Portage Assn.; mem. nat. adv. com. on mental retardation, U. Kans. Author: (with D.M. Baer) Behavior Analysis of Child Development, 1978, Child Development: The Universal Stage of Infancy, 1965, Child Development: Readings in Experimental Analysis of Behavior, 1967, (with E. Ribes-Inesta) Behavior Modification: Issues and Extensions, 1972, Child Development: The Basic Stage of Early Childhood, 1978, (with E. Rayek-Zaga) Analisis de la Conducta Appicado a Ensenanza, 1978; editor: Behavior Modification: Contributions to Education, 1980, Behavior Analysis of Child Development, 1993, (with P.M. Ghezzi) Outline of J.R. Kantor's Psychological Linguistics, 1994; founding editor Jour. Exptl. Child Psychology, 1964-71, mem. editorial bd. 1971-76; assoc. editor Internat. Rev. of Research in Mental Retardation, 1965-75, Jour. Behavior Therapy and Exptl. Psychiatry; mem. editorial bd., Jour. Abnormal Child Psychology, 1972-84, Jour. Applied Behavior Analysis, 1975-77, The Psychol. Record, Quar. Rev. of Devel, 1980-85, Behavior Analyst, 1980-85, Edn. and Treatment of Children, 1986-90; mem. bd. advisors The Interbehaviorist Bd. dirs. Washoe Assn. for Retarded Citizens. Capt. USAAF, 1942-46. Recipient research award Am. Assn. Mental Deficiency, 1974; cert. of merit U. Veracruz, Mexico, 1974; Career Research Scientist award Am. Acad. Mental Retardation, 1980; Disting. Scientist award Nat. Assn. Retarded Citizens, 1980; NIMH Sr. fellow Harvard U., 1961-62; Japan Soc. for Promotion of Sci. fellow, 1978; Fullbright-Hays fellow, 1976 Fellow Am. Psychol. Assn. (chmn. commn. on behavior modification, past div. devel. psychology pres. bd. social and ethical responsibility for psychology 1976-78, recipient G. Stanley Hall award in devel. psychology 1980, Egar A. Boll award in mental retardation 1984, Don Hake award in basic and applied psychology 1992, ABA Internat. award 1994), Am. Psychol. Soc. (charter); mem. Psychonomic Soc., Soc. Rsch. in Child Devel., Interam. Soc. Psychology, Assn. Behavior Analysis (pres. 1978), Behavior Therapy and Exptl. Psychiatry, AAUP, Midwestern (coun. 1975-78), Rocky Mountain Psychol. Assn., Southwestern Psychol. Assn., Am. Assn. Applied and Preventive Psychology, Sigma Xi. Died June 11, 2009.

BILDERBACK, CAROLYN, choreographer, performer, dance educator; b. Portland, Oreg., May 11, 1915; d. Joseph Brown and Carolyn (Leete) B. BA, Reed Coll., 1938; postgrad., San Francisco State Coll., 1939-41. Performing mem. Katherine Litz Dance Co., NYC, 1950-53; dir. Carolyn Bilderback Dance Theaater, NYC, from 1967. Mem. faculty Manhattan Sch. Music, N.Y.C., 1965-82; workshop leader Am. Dance Festival, Duke U., Durham, N.C., 1974, Internat. Women's Writing Guild, N.Y.C., 1987; resident The Strong Dance Fund, Emma Willard Sch., Troy, N.Y., 1978; resident centennial edn. program U. Nebr., Lincoln, winter 1979; co-designer, tchr. workshop Hollyhock Holistic Learning Ctr., Cortes Island, B.C., Can., 1994; adj. prof. movement and dance Union Theol. Sem., N.Y.C., 1960—, guest instr. fantasy and religious experience, 1988; choreographer operas Aspen (Colo.) Music Festival, summers 1956-58; choreographer, dancer Cauldron Prodns., N.Y.C., 1992. Author: Gatherings from a Dancer's Journal, 1992; choreographer Fragments and Observaations, 1969; choreographer, prodr. solo dance concert, 1990, 95; dir., prodr. film From the Inside Out, 1969. Grantee Mary Reynolds Babcock Found., 1969. Fellow Am. Dance Guild; mem. NOW. Avocation: hiking in oregon. Home: New York, NY. Died Feb. 2, 2008.

BILENAS, JONAS, mechanical engineer, educator; b. Kaunas, Lithuania, Dec. 2, 1928; came to U.S., 1949; s. Pranas and Jadvyga (Ambraziejus) B.; m. Dana Melynis, Apr. 17, 1955; children: Jonas V., Andrius R., Laura R. B in Mech. Engring., CCNY, 1955; diploma, Oak Ridge (Tenn.) Sch. Reactor Tech., 1957; PhD, CUNY, 1969. Registered profl. engr., N.Y. Engr. Babcock & Wilcox Co., NYC, 1955-56, Oak Ridge (Tenn.) Nat. Lab., 1956-57; group head Am. Machine & Foundry Co., Greenwich, Conn., 1957-64, Grumman Aerospace Corp., Bethpage, N.Y., 1964-72, specialist infrared countermeasures (IRCM) tech., 1972-83, projects mgr. IRCM, 1983-93; retired, 1993; prof. CCNY and CUNY Grad. Ctr., NYC, from 1969. Part-time prof. mech. engring. SUNY, Stony Brook, 1988—; mem. program com. Nat. Infrared Countermeasures Symposia, 1990-93. Assoc. editor feature sect. The Engring. Word Jour., 1971—; reviewer of various publs. in field; contbr. articles to profl. jours. Chmn. bd. dirs. Lithuanian Cultural Ctr., Inc., Bklyn., 1995—; mem. platform planning com., del.-at-large Nat. Rep. Senatorial Com., Washington, 1993—. Nuc. scholar U.S. Atomic Energy Commn., 1956-57; recipient citation for infrared suppression advancement Army Sci. Adv. Panel, Carlisle Barracks, Pa., 1972, citation for OV-1 aircraft infrared program, Army Aviation Sys. Command, St. Louis, 1978; recipient best paper award 25th Ann. Infrared Countermeasures Conf., 1987. Mem. ASME (tech. com. on aero. and aerospace heat transfer 1974-80), NSPE, AIAA, Tau Beta Pi, Pi Tau Sigma. Achievements include patents and pioneering work in and devel. of infrared (IR) suppressors and IR countersurveillance equipment for U.S. Army OV-1D Mohawk aircraft, M1 Abrams battle tank, M2 Bradley fighting vehicle, mil. ground installations, and for the USAF Joint-STARS aircraft. Home: Melville, NY. Died June 25, 2008.

BILLINGS, RICHARD WHITTEN, professional society administrator; b. Bar Harbor, Maine, Jan. 5, 1924; s. John Theodore and Evelyn (Ritchie) B.; m. Norma Julia Taraldsen, Apr. 19, 1947; children: Cynthia, Marilyn, John, Amy. BA, Colby Coll., 1948; MEd, Springfield Coll., 1951; PhD, LaSalle U., 1995. Program exec. YMCA, Watertown, N.Y., 1948-50, youth work exec. Schenectady, N.Y., 1951-56, dist. dir. Hudson Valley, N.Y., 1956-60; exec. dir. Assn. Island, YMCA, Henderson Harbor, N.Y., 1960-67; exec. dir. ea. region FCA, Canton, Conn., 1967-70; exec. dir. Assn. Island REcreat. Corp., Henderson Harbor, 1970-74; bur. dir. Maine Land Use Regulation Commn., Augusta, 1974-76; ins. agt. John Hancock Mut. Life Ins., Augusta, 1976-86; exec. dir. Maine Assn. Life Underwriters, Augusta, 1987-93; owner Maine Assn. Mgmt. Svcs., Augusta, from 1992; exec. dir. Informed Notaries of Maine, Augusta, 1993-98; pub. Day Mountain Publs., Augusta, from 1998. Fellow Life Underwriters Tng. Coun.; mem. Chartered Life Underwriters, Chartered Fin. Cons., VFW, Golden Key Soc., Am. Soc. Assn. Execs. Republican. Congregationalist. Avocations: boating, fishing, writing, painting. Died Nov. 15, 2007.

BINGHAM, JUNE, playwright; b. White Plains, NY, June 20, 1919; d. Max J.H. and Mabel (Limburg) Rossbach; m. Jonathan B. Bingham, Sept. 20, 1939 (dec. July 1986); children: Sherry B. Downes, Micki B. Esselstyn (dec. 1999), Timothy, Claudia B. Meyers; m. Robert B. Birge, Mar. 28, 1987; 1 stepchild, Robert R. Student, Vassar Coll., 1936-38; BA, Barnard Coll., 1940; LittD (hon.), Lehman Coll., 2002. Writer, editor U.S. Treasury, Washington, 1943-45; editorial asst. Washington Post, 1945-46; writer Tarrytown (N.Y.) Daily News, 1946. Author: Do Cows Have Neuroses?, Do Babies Have Worries?, Do Teenagers Have Wisdom?, Courage to Change: An Introduction to Life and Thought of Reinhold Niebuhr, 1961, Courage to Change: An Introduction to Life and Thought of Reinhold Niebuhr, paperback edit., 1992, U Thant: The Search for Peace, 1970, (plays) Triangles, 1986, Eleanor and Alice, 1996, You and the I.C.U., 1990; author: (with others) The Inside Story: Psychiatry and Everyday Life, 1953, The Pursuit of Health, 1985; author: (mus.) Squanto and Love, 1992, Young Roosevelts, 1993, The Other Lincoln, 1995, The Strange Case of Mary Lincoln, 2001; contbr. articles to nat. mags., newspapers and profl. jours. Bd. dirs. Riverdale Mental Health Assn., 1983-2005, Woodrow Wilson Found., Princeton, NJ, 1959-64, 83-89, Lehman Coll. Found., 1983-90, Ittleson Ctr. for Childhood Rsch., 1958-90, Franklin and Eleanor Roosevelt Inst., 1992-2002; founder T.L.C.; trained liaison comforter Vol. Program of Presbyn. Hosp., NYC, hosp. ethics com., 2003-06. Named Alumna of the Yr., Rosemary Hall, 1976. Mem. Authors Guild (nominating com. 1987-90), Dramatists Guild, PEN, Cosmopolitan Club. Democrat. Avocations: theater, movies, reading. Died Aug. 21, 2007.

BIRDWELL, CAROLYN CAMPBELL, public relations executive; b. Nashville, July 8, 1947; d. Harvcll Hitc and Martha (Pentecost) Campbell. Exec. sec. RCA Records, Nashville; receptionist WKDA Radio, Nashville; sec. Country Music Assn., Nashville; adminstr. Chet Atkins, Nashville. Notary public. V.p. Music City B&PW, 1980-88; chmn. celebrity auction Tenn. Heart Assn., Cerebral Palsey Fundraising, 1987. Mem. nat. Acad. Recording Arts and Sci., Beta Sigma Phi. Democrat. Baptist. Avocation: coordinating and catering weddings. Died Dec. 4, 2007.

BIRK, ROBERT EUGENE, retired internist; b. Buffalo, Jan. 7, 1926; s. Reginald H. and Florence (Diebolt) B.; m. Janet L. Davidson, June 24, 1950; children— David Eugene, James Michael, Patricia Jean, Thomas Spencer, Susan Margaret AB, Colgate U., Hamilton, NY, 1948; MD, U. Rochester, NY, 1952. Diplomate Am. Bd. Internal Medicine. Intern, resident Henry Ford Hosp., Detroit, 1952-57, chief 2d med. div., 1961-66, asst. to chmn. dept. medicine, 1965-66; practice medicine specializing in internal medicine Grosse Pointe, Mich., 1966-89; sr. active staff St. John Hosp., 1966-89, chief dept. medicine, 1967-70, dir. health edn., dir. grad. med. edn., 1975-86, exec. dir. continuing med. edn., 1975-86; dir. med. affairs St John Ambulatory Care Corp., St. John Home Care Svcs., 1980-89; v.p. clin. affairs St. John Health Corp., 1985-89. Assoc. prof. medicine Wayne State U., 1969-89 Contbr. articles to profl. jours. Mem. trustee's coun. U. Rochester, 1973-75, Med. Ctr. alumni coun., 1974-75; bd. trustees St. John Hosp., Macomb Ctr., 1986-89; corp. mem. bd. Boys Clubs Met. Detroit, 1973-89; trustee Mich. Cancer Found., 1980-89, bd. dirs., 1982-85. With US Army, 1943-46. Fellow ACP, Detroit Acad. Medicine; mem. AMA, Assn. Hosp. Med. Edn. (trustee region IV 1986-87), Mich. Assn. Med. Edn. (trustee 1985-86), Am. Soc. Internal Medicine, Am. Acad. Med. Dirs., Alpha Tau Omega. Republican. Episcopalian. Home: Hilton Head Island, SC. Died June 7, 2009.

BIRMAN, RONNIE RATHKOPF, retired elementary school educator; b. NYC, Dec. 24, 1947; d. Julius and May (Levy) Rathkopf. BS in Edn., CCNY, 1969; MA in Sociology, MS in Social Rsch., CUNY, 1977, MS in Sci. Edn., 1990; cert. in Adminstrn., Bklyn. Coll., 1992; PD in Reading, Fordham U., 2000. Cert. tchr., NYS, image cons., color specialist, FIT, 2004, 2005, life coach, business coach, NYU, 2005, corp. training, mgmt., career coaching, NYU 2006. Elem. sch. tchr. P.S. 316, Bklyn., 1969-84, elem. sch. sci. tchr., 1984-91; bldg. sci. mentor, 1991-92; freelance curriculum writer NYC, from 1989; impact II intern, coord. tchr. workshops Impact II Grants, NYC, 1991; sci. magnet tchr. P.S. 64, NYC, 1992—93; Chpt. 1 reading tchr., 1993—94; tchr. 1st and 2d grades P.S. 19, NYC, 1995—2003, reading tchr., 1997—99; ret., 2003. Curriculum disseminator, facilitator workshops Impact II Office, Bklyn. Coll., several sch. dists. in NY, from 1990; grant writer for PIP Bklyn. Coll., 1992, adj. prof. literacy, 95; seminar leader Whole Lang. Inst. for Ctrl. Bd. at Dist. 8, 1992; image cons., color specialist, from 2004; career/life coach, bus. coach, from 2004; corporate trainer image and mgmt. skills, 2006; profl. makeup artist Christine Valmay, 2005. Author oral comms. curriculum "Can We Talk?"; writer for CIMS Sci. K Level Dist. 8 and Learning-Link Curriculum. Active parent workshops in communication/experimentation in sci. P.S. 316, Dist. 17, Bklyn., 1991-92. Recipient Impact II grant, 1991, NIC Sci. award; grantee N.Y.C., 1992, Int'l Reading Assoc. grant, 2002. Mem. United Fedn. Tchrs., Kappa Delta Pi. Avocations: poetry, creative writing, reading, acting, drawing, Scenery design, Costume design. Home: New York, NY. Died July 16, 2008.

BIROSIK, PJ, music company executive; b. NYC, Sept. 2, 1956; BA, U. Redlands, 1977; MA, Columbia Coll., LA, 1979. 3d class radiotelephone lic., FCC. Disc jockey, music dir. Sta. KUOR-FM, Redlands, Calif., 1973-76; music dir. Sta. KFXM-FM, San Bernadino, Calif., 1976-77; owner, mgr. Musik Internat. Corp., Hollywood, Calif., 1977-95, Boulder, Colo., from 1995. Author: How to Manage Talent, 1985, The New Age Music Guide, 1988, The Burrito Book, 1990, Salsa, 1992, Cilanto, 1994; editor, reviewer Body Mind Spirit, Billboard, L.A. Resources, New Frontier, BAM, Life Times, EarthStar, New Age Retailer, Nexus, Monthly Aspectarian, Conscious Connection, Healthy & Natural, Yoga Jour., Planetary Connections, Sedona Red Rock News, Boulder Weekly, New Tex., New Age Voice, AudioGliphix, Lotus, CDNOW, Crossroads, also others. Fundraiser Children of the Night, Hollywood, 1987. Recipient 2 Gold Record awards Mem. NARAS, Assn. for Ind. Music, Coalition Visionary Retailers, Los Angeles Women in Music (founder, v.p. 1986-88), Ind. Music Assn., Am. Booksellers Assn. Avocations: martial arts, music industry public speaking. Died Jan. 7, 2006.

BISGAARD, EDWARD LAWRENCE, JR., financial services executive, accountant; b. El Cento, Calif., July 26, 1946; s. Edward Lawrence Sr. and Gail (Chambers) B.; m. Kathleen Susan Borenitsch; 1 child, Jackie. BS, Calif. Polytech. Coll., Pomona, 1971. CPA, Calif. Sr. auditor Arthur Young & Co., LA, 1971-74; v.p. King Internat. Corp., Beverly Hills, Calif., 1975-78; v.p., mgr. fund ops. Capital Rsch. & Mgmt. Co., LA, 1979-86; chief fin. officer Dunham & Greer, San Diego, 1987-89; v.p., treas. Atlas Securities, Atlas Assets, Oakland, Calif., from 1989. Mem. AICPA, Calif. Soc. CPAs. Republican. Died Nov. 29, 2007.

BISHOP, GERALD IVESON, pharmaceutical executive; b. Madras, India, Apr. 19, 1935; came to U.S., 1961; s. James Alfred and Muriel Madeleine (Waller) B.; m. Bridget Carey, June 30, 1960; children: Elizabeth, James, Frances, Catherine. BSME, Durham U., Newcastle Upon Tyne, Eng., 1960; MS in Indsl. Engring., MBA, SUNY, Buffalo, 1971. Bus. cons. Associated Indsl. Cons., London, 1964-67; mgr. indsl. engring. Bell Aerospace, Buffalo, 1967-70; exec. asst. to CEO Ayerst Labs. Inc., Rouses Point, N.Y., 1971-76; mgr. I.E. E.R. Squibb & Sons, North Brunswick, N.J., 1977-78; mgr. internat. tech. ops. Johnson & Johnson, New Brunswick, N.J., 1978-92. Mayor Champlain (N.Y.) Cmty., 1975-77. Fellow IEE, Mech. Engrs. (U.K.); mem. Profl.

Engrs. Ont., Freemasons (Barger lodge #325). Republican. Avocations: gourmet cooking, shooting, computer technology, travel, reading non-fiction. Died July 29, 2008.

BISHOP, HARRY CRADEN, surgeon; b. NYC, Apr. 1, 1921; m. Katherine Thayer (dec.); children: Robert, Thomas, Katharine; m. Deborah Dilworth, 1984; stepchildren: William, Daisy, Noel. AB, Dartmouth Coll., 1943; MD, Harvard U., 1945; MA (hon.), U. Pa., 1971. Diplomate Nat. Bd. Med. Examiners, Am. Bd. Surgery. Intern in surgery N.Y. Hosp., 1945-46; asst. resident in surgery, then chief resident Mary Imogene Bassett Hosp., Cooperstown, N.Y., 1948-50; surg. pathologist Presbyn. Med. Center, NYC, 1950; asst. resident in surgery Children's Med. Center, Boston, 1950-51, sr. asst. resident, then chief surg. resident, 1952-54; sr. asst. resident Peter Bent Brigham Hosp., Boston, 1951-52; instr. Harvard U. Med. Sch., 1954; mem. faculty U. Pa. Med. Sch., from 1955, prof. pediatric surgery, 1979-87, prof. emeritus, 1987—2009; mem. staff Children's Hosp., Phila., 1954—91, sr. surgeon, 1960—91, pres. staff, 1971-73. Med. staff Hosp. U. Pa.; adv. bd. Pa. Blue Shield, 1976-91, mem. corp., 1986-91. Editorial bd. Clin. Pediatrics, 1970-80. Served to capt. M.C. AUS, 1946-48. Fellow ACS (chmn. adv. council pediatric surgery 1980—91), Am. Acad. Pediatrics; mem. Am. Pediatric Surg. Assn. (gov. 1979-82), AMA, Phila. County Med. Soc., Phila. Pediatric Soc., Brit. Assn. Pediatric Surgeons, Phila. Acad. Surgery, Coll. Physicians Phila., Lilliputian Surg. Soc. Avocations: sailing, gardening. Home: Haverford, Pa. Died May 4, 2009.

BISHOP, PATRICIA D., geriatrics nurse, administrator; b. Natrona Heights, Pa., Apr. 2, 1948; d. Steven Jr. and Vinca (Kuco) Pochiber; m. Jay T. Bishop, July 11, 1970; 1 child, Tracey. Diploma, Montefiore Hosp. sch. nursing, 1970. Head nurse Curtis Home, Meriden, Conn., infection control nurse, DNS. Home: Meriden, Conn. Died July 12, 2008.

BIVINS, MILES TEEL (TEEL BIVINS), former ambassador, retired state legislator; b. Nov. 22, 1947; s. Lee T. and Betty Bivins; m. Cornelia Wadsworth Ritchie (div.); children: Andrew, William, Catherine; m. Patricia Frances Hamilton, Apr. 6, 2002; 1 child, Carolyn. BA, Tulane U., 1970; JD, So. Meth. U., 1974. Mem. Tex. State Senate Dist. 31, 1989—2004, pres. pro tempore, 1999; US amb. to Sweden US Dept. State, Stockholm, 2004—06. Recipient Legislative Leadership award, Tex. C. of C., 1992, Golden Nail award, Amarillo C. of C. Arts Com., 1992; named Ten Best Legislators, Tex. Monthly, 1999, 2003. Republican. Died Oct. 26, 2009.

BJORKLUND, NANCY MARGARETTE WATTS, music educator; b. Maryville, Tenn., Aug. 14, 1942; d. Charles Burdett and Alma Pauline (Calhoun) Watts; m. Ralph Edward Bjorklund, June 14, 1963; children: James Andrew, Deborah Elisabeth, John Carl. AA, Manatee C.C., Bradenton, Fla., 1962; BA, MusB, Stetson U., 1964. Founder, dir. music, pianist First Bapt. Ch., Freeport, Grand Bahama Is., 1964—70; dir. Cmty. Chorus Choir, Freeport, Grand Bahama Island, 1964—70. Recipient Crystal Heart award, Girl Scouts Am., 1995. Mem.: Musical Manatee Club (treas. from 2006), Fla. State Music Tchr. Assn. (exec. bd. 1993—95, 1993—2006, pres. dist. 8 2001—06), Manatee County Music Tchr. Assn. (exec. bd. from 1978, chmn. Pianorama 1980, exec. bd. from 1983, pres. 1993—95, chmn. music spectacular 2001, 2004, 2006, pres. from 2006), Nat. Assn. Music Clubs (chmn. Fedn. Festival Manatee County from 1980), Manatee County Assn. Retarded Citizens, Fla. State Assn. Retarded Citizens. Republican. Bapt. Avocations: reading, crewel, swimming, cooking. Died Sept. 11, 2007.

BLACK, LAVONNE PATRICIA, special education educator; b. West Palm Beach, Fla., Sept. 28, 1924; d. Harvey Francis Paul and Elsie Marguerite (Theegarten) B. Diploma, Palm Beach Jr. Coll., 1945; BA in Edn., Fla. State Coll. for Women, 1947; MA in Edn., George Peabody Coll. Tchrs., 1964. Cert. tchr. elem. edn. reading, hearing disabilities, motor disabilities, Fla.; cert. tchr. social studies, elem. edn., Kans.; cert. elem. edn. spl. hard of hearing-orthopedic, Ky. Tchr. physically handicapped Bd. Pub. Instr., West Palm Beach, 1947-58; tchr. deaf and hard of hearing Royal Palm Sch., West Palm Beach, 1952-58; tchr. physically handicapped/learning disorders Bd. Pub. Instrn. Exceptional Child Ctr., Ft. Lauderdale, Fla., 1958-69; dir., tchr. Sceniland Sch., Chattanooga, 1969-70; occupational edn. tchr. John Gorrie Jr. H.S., Jacksonville, Fla., 1970-71; substitute tchr. Iliff Pre-Sch., Denver, 1972, University Park Coop., Denver, 1973, Austin Presch., 1973; house mother Sigma Alpha Epsilon Fraternity, U. Denver, from 1971. Organizer, mgr. Sigma Alpha Epsilon Summer Rental Program, 1976—. Inventor portable sound chart for Lang., reading, speech, 1964. Active Jr. Welfare League, Inc., Palm Beach and Ft. Lauderdale.; secret spl. messenger Morrison Field, West Palm Beach, World War II, summer 1942. Recipient Thomas G. Goodale award for disting. svc. U. Denver, 1991. Mem. Coun. Exceptional Children, PEO, Palm Beach Jr. Coll. Alumni Assn., Kappa Alpha Theta. Democrat. Methodist. Avocations: swimming, dance, backgammon, walking, travel. Died Nov. 28, 2007.

BLACK, MARY LEE, writer, educator; b. Brookings, SD, Dec. 2, 1935; d. Robert Emmet and Kathryn Bonesteel Coffey; children: Katherine, Theodore, Douglas, Thomas. Student (hon.), U. Heidelberg Dolmetcher Inst., Germany, 1964; BA, Mary Hardin-Baylor U., 1976; MA, U. Tex., 1983. Tchr. Belton (Tex.) Ind. Sch. Dist., 1980—2000, Salado (Tex.) Ind. Sch. Dist., 1976—80; music tchr. Salado, 1972—76; organist 2d Armored Divsn., Ft. Hood, Tex., 1967—72; sec. Collins Radio, Seattle, 1959—60, USAF, 1958—59, Turner Constrn. Co., Chgo., 1957—58; adj. prof. ESL Ctrl. Tex. Coll., 2004. Stringer Belton Jour., 1973—76. Author, dir., prodr.: mus. play Jack in the Bean Stalk, 1983, Christmas in a Bus Station, 1985; prodr., dir.: (maj. prodns.) Many Moons, 1991; Ransom of Red Chief, 1992; Charlotte's Web, 1993; Aladdin, 1994; Once Upon a Clothesline, 1995; editor, prodr. (puppet plays), 1995; dir.: (plays) The Lesson, 1977; The Importance of Being Earnest, 1978; Mrs. McWilliams and the Lightening, 1979; Comedy of Errors, 1980; actor: Of Thee I Sing, 1988, Annie Get Your Gun, 1990. Leader 4H, Salado, 1972—76. Mem.: Daus. of the U.S. Army (pres. 1964—65), Soc. Children's Book Writers and Illustrators, Ft. Hood Officers' Wives Club (program chmn. 1970—71, reporter, editor newsletter 1970—71). Republican. Christian Scientist. Avocations: horseback riding, golf, reading, crossword puzzles. Home: Salado, Tex. Died Dec. 22, 2007.

BLACKBURN, JOHN LESLIE, retired academic administrator; b. Malta Bend, Mo., Dec. 21, 1924; s. Clarence Oliver and Vivian (Mitchener) B.; m. Gloria Bullington, June 10, 1950; 1 child, Holly. BS, Mo. Valley Coll., 1950; MEd, U. Colo., 1952; PhD, Fla. State U., 1969. Counselor to men Fla. State U., Tallahassee, 1952-56; from asst. dean of men to dean student devel. U. Ala., Tuscaloosa, 1956-69, v.p. devel., 1978-90; vice chancellor student affairs U. Denver, 1969-74, vice chancellor univ. resources, 1974-78; pres. Blackburn Ednl. Techs., Tuscaloosa, 1990—2008; gen. sec. Am. Assn. of U. Administrators, Tuscaloosa, Ala., 1993-97; interim dir. Challenge 21, Tuscaloosa, 1998-99. Mem. Model City Mayor's Adv., Denver, 1970-73, Nat. Adv. Coun. on Extension and Continuing Edn., Washington, 1976-78; cons. to sec. US Dept. Health Edn. & Welfare, Washington, 1976; mem. Ala. Commn. on Aging, 2000-09; mem. Gov.'s Task Force on Devel. of Economically Distressed Counties, 2000-01. Contbr.: Pieces of Eight, 1978. Sgt. AUS, 1943-46, CBI. The Blackburn Inst. was created in his honor by U. Ala., 1995, John L. Blackburn Exemplary award in his honor by AAUA, 1991. Mem. AAUA (pres. 1977-79), Am. Coun. on Edn. (acad. affairs commn. 1970-73), Nat. Assn. Student Pers. Adminstrn. (pres. 1973-74), Nat. Inst. Rsch. and Devel. (founder 1974). Home: Tuscaloosa, Ala. Died July 3, 2009.

BLACKBURN, JOY MARTIN, retired librarian; b. Marietta, Ohio, Oct. 28, 1925; d. Jonathan George and Helen Joy (Smith) Martin; m. Paul Edward Blackburn, Dec. 18, 1948 (dec. Dec. 1996); children: Paul Conrow, Amy Joy. BA, Ohio Wesleyan U., 1947; MA, U. Minn, 1948. Student counselor Ohio State U., Columbus, 1948—54; editor/libr. Jones & Laughlin Steel Co., Pitts., 1955—57; rsch. libr. Tech. Mktg. Assn., Concord, Mass., 1964—66; mgr. corp. libr. Washington Nat. Ins., Evanston, Ill., 1966—85; systems libr. Luth. Gen. Hosp., Park Ridge, Ill., 1986—88; info. specialist C. Berger & Co., Carol Stream, Ill., 1989—93; ret., 1993. Rschr./editor U. Pitts. Med. Sch., 1959. Author: J&L Rsch. Bull., 1955—57. Vol. Chgo. Bot. Garden Libr., Glencoe, Ill., 1997—99, U. Va. Health Sys. Mktg. and Cmty. Outreach, from 2002, U. Va. Alderman Libr., from 2002, Va. Found. Humanities, from 2004. Mem.: U. Va. Libr. Assocs. (bd. dirs. from 2001, from 2004), Cook County Hort. Soc. (hon.), Phi Beta Kappa. Avocations: history, photography, Arctic travel, art. Home: Keswick, Va. Died Jan. 29, 2008.

BLACKSTOCK, JERRY B., lawyer; b. Monticello, Ga., Mar. 9, 1945; s. J.B. and Eugenia (Jones) B.; m. Margaret Owen, June 10, 1967; children: Towner Anson, Michael Owen, Kendrick. BA, Davidson Coll., 1966; JD, U. Ga., 1969. Bar: Ga. 1969, U.S. Ct. Appeals (5th cir.) 1970, U.S. Supreme Ct. 1978, U.S. Ct. Appeals (11th cir.) 1981, U.S. Ct. Appeals (fed. cir.) 1984. With Powell, Goldstein, Frazer & Murphy, Atlanta, 1969—2002; chair Atlanta litigation team Hunton & Williams, LLP, from 2002. Adj. prof. law Emory U., Atlanta, 1975-81; mem. adv. bd. Jour. Intellectual Property Law, U. Ga. Sch. Law, 1992-2005; chair Ga. Jud. Qualifications Commn., 1994-2002. Author: Georgia Appellate Practice Handbook, 1977, Preparation of a Lawsuit for Trial, Pre-Trial Practice, Appellate Practice, 1980; (with others) Georgia Lawyers Basic Practice Handbook, 2d edit. Pres. parents coun. Trinity Sch. Inc., 1981-82; pres. parents club Woodward Acad. Lower Sch., 1986-88, bd. dirs., treas., Woodward Acad. Upper Sch., 1988-91, v.p., 1991-92, pres., 1992-94; chmn. Ga. Athlete Agt. Regulatory Commn., 1989-2000; chmn. bd. dirs. Pastoral Counseling Svc. Atlanta; chmn. bd. visitors U. Ga. Sch. Law, 2001-04; bd. trustees Ga. Legal History Found., 1990-93; mem. Leadership Ga., 1980; mem. Leadership Atlanta, 1990, exec. com., 1991-92; chair bd. trustees Riverside Mil. Acad., 1996—. Recipient Tradition of Excellence award for Def. Lawyer of Yr., State Bar Ga., 2002. Fellow Am. Bar Found., Am. Coll. Trial Lawyers, Internat. Acad. Trial Lawyers, Ga. Bar Assn. (editor-in-chief jour. 1984-85, bd. govs. 1982-98, exec. com. 1990-95, intellectual property law, tech. law and gen. practice and trial sects.), Ga. Bar Found.; mem. ATLA (intellectual property litig. com.), ABA (intellectual property, sci. and tech., tort and ins. practice and litig. sects.), So. Trial Lawyers Assn., Ga. Trial Lawyers Assn., Atlanta Bar Assn. (editor-in-chief Atlanta Lawyer 1972-73), Am. Law Inst., Atlanta Legal Aid Soc. (adv. bd. 1979-86), Atlanta Lawyers Club, Ga. Def. Lawyers Assn. (bd. dirs. 1989-91, dir. Trial Acad. 1987), Am. Bd. Trial Advs. (diplomate, bd. dirs. 1990—, state exec. com. 1985—), Am. Arbitration Assn. (arbitrator, comml. and constrn. panels, Ga.-Ala. adv. com. for large complex cases), Licensing Execs. Soc., Internat., Am. Intellectual Property Law Assn., Computer Law Assn., Davidson Coll. Atlanta Alumni Assn. (pres. 1982-83), Bleckley Am. Inn of Ct. (master of the bench), Commerce Club, Old War Horse Lawyers Club, Cherokee Town and Country Club, 191 Club. Methodist. Avocation: running. Home: Atlanta, Ga. Died Apr. 1, 2006.

BLACKWELL, DALE BASCOM, physicist; b. Toledo, Ohio, Nov. 1, 1930; s. Clyde Bascom and Minnie Velma (Myers) B.; m. Elizabeth Nell Dawson (div.); children: Marka Blackwell Barbour, Victoria Blackwell Bush; m. Nina Marie Gover, Sept. 10, 1967 (dec. Oct. 2004). BS, Ind. U., 1956. Acoustic engr. Electro-Voice, Inc., Buchanan, Mich., 1956-58; R&D engr. Kawneer, Co., Niles, Mich., 1958-61; acoustic engr. Empire Scientific, Garden City, N.Y., 1961-63; sr. engr. Fairchild Camera and Instrument Corp., Hauppage, N.Y., 1963-73; chief engr. Comml. Radio Sound Corp., NYC, 1973-78, Dumont Instrumentation, Inc., Hauppage, N.Y., 1978-84; R&D engr. Northrop-Grumman Corp. assignment, Star Wars Sys. Los Alamos (N.Mex,) Nat. Lab., 1984—91; owner Design Group Ltd., Brazil, Ind., from 1991. Cons. Fairchild Graphics Corp., Plainview, N.Y., 1964-66, 3M Corp., Woodbury, Minn., 1995, Japan Electronics Mfg. Agy., Wilmette, Ill., 1996—, Protech Comms., Fort Pierce, Fla., 1993—. Contbr. articles to profl. jours. including Electrical Design News, Radio Electronics mag., Electronics Now mag. With USAF, 1951-52. Mem.: Wabash Valley Amateur Radio Assn. Achievements include inventor Cockpit Voice Recorder (Black Box) used in all commercial airline planes, high speed, rotational magnetic detent with accuracy of 2 seconds of arc, transistorized version of the Color Film Analyzer that allows printing movie film with proper color balance, movie film projection system with an electronically driven mirror tracking film rather than a CAM-driven claw movement of film. Home: Brazil, Ind. Died Mar. 12, 2008.

BLADE, ROBERT ERIC, minister; b. Phila., Oct. 31, 1923; s. John Emil and Henrietta Evelyn (Nessen) B.; m. Alice Elizabeth Ott, Feb. 18, 1956. BA, Temple U., 1951; BD, Princeton Sem., 1954; MA, Temple U., 1959. Ordained to ministry Presbyn. Ch., 1954. Student pastor Bd. Nat. Missions Presbyn. Ch. (U.S.A.)., Alaska, 1952-53; pastor James Evans Mem. Presbyn. Ch., Phila., 1954-59, Hamptonburgh Presbyn. Ch., Campbell Hall, N.Y., 1969-82; chaplain Otterkill Engine Co., Campbell Hall, N.Y., 1969-82; historian Presbyn. Hist. Soc., Phila., from 1982. Editorial asst. Am. Presbyns., Phila., 1990—. Author: Pioneer Presbyterian Congs., 1989, Hudson River Presbyterian History, 1980; contbr. articles to profl. jours. Mem. South Phila. Planning Commn., 1955-59. With U.S. Army, 1942-45, Lt comdr. USN, 1959-68. Mem. Mil. Chaplains Assn., Canterbury Cleric, Presbyn. Hist. Soc., Hamptonburgh Hist. Soc. (founder). Home: Philadelphia, Pa. Died Apr. 8, 2008.

BLAIR, WILLIAM RICHARDSON, state legislator, lawyer; b. Phila., Dec. 31, 1908; s. William Richardson and Ethel (Ashton) B.; m. Evelyn Flower Morris, June 18, 1937 (dec. 1957); children: Frances Ellen, Thomas Ashton, Deborah Hollingsworth, William Richardson; m. Mary Patricia Grier, May 24, 1958; stepchildren: Helen Patricia, George Washington III, Thomas Lee. B.A., Haverford Coll., 1930; LL.B., Harvard U., 1933. Bar: Pa. 1934. Ptnr. Ballard, Spahr, Andrews & Ingersoll, 1947-77, ret., 1977; mem. N.H. Ho. of Reps., 1982-88. Mem. Baronial Order Magna Charta, Mtl. Order of Crusades, Soc. Colonial Wars, Colonial Soc., S.R., Soc. War 1812, Scotch-Irish Soc. Republican. Episcopalian. Clubs: Harvard (Boston); Rittenhouse (Phila.). Home: Quakertown, Pa. Died July 1997.

BLASE, ANTHONY IDOMENEUS, retired electronics executive, writer, poet; b. Chgo., July 30, 1929; s. Nicholas George and Tousa Marie Blase; m. Aspacia Mary Manos, Aug. 31, 1952; children: Mary Kadie Burgner, Nicolette Stephane Young. BSBA, Loyola U., Chgo., 1955. Lic. gen. ins. broker Ill.; real estate broker Ill. Contr. Universal Wire and Cable Co., Chgo., 1958—64; v.p., contr. Rockola Mfg. Corp., Chgo., 1964—78; exec. v.p., treas., CFO, Wells-Gardner Electronics, Chgo., 1978—88, also bd. dirs. Author: In Search of Alexander, 1990, Contemplating Forms, 1989, Thus the Gods Taught Man, 1991, On Moral Purpose, 1992, Byzantium, 1992, Religious Paradigm?, 1993, Vessels Without Dimension, 1994, The Ultimate Comprehension, 1995, The History of Western Philosophy, 1996, The Universal Will, 1997, Historical Essays, 1998, Embracing the Universe, 1998, But Grain of Sand, 1999, The Etaireia, 1999, Uncompromising Nature, 2000, As I Understand Aristotle, 2000, Hellenism in the Post Classical World, 2001, Idomenian Ethics, 2002, From Acorn to Oak--Princip to Ground Zero, 2003, The Unlosable Wager, 2003, Unscripted Shadows, 2004, The Ideal Concept, 2004, Eternal Recurrence, 2004, Of Cardinal Virtues, 2004, Criterion of Truth, 2005, Analogous to Man, 2005, The Glow of Words in all their Prism, 2005, Philosophic Edicts, 2005, Of Laurels Bright, 2005;: Of Wreaths and Thorns, 2005, A Nation Keens, 2005, Unjeweled Crown, 2005, Twilight's Smold'ring Embers, 2005, A Lightning's Bolt, 2005, A Leapt Relief, 2005, A Depth Unknown, 2005, A Harvest's Glean, 2005, Ontology's Demand, 2005, Time in Space, 2005, Orphaned World, 2005, Affectation's Decept, 2005, Credulity in Crept, 2005, Surgical Precision, 2005, A Mind Distilled, 2005, A Heart Fulfilled, 2005, To Fate's Unknow, 2005, A Meadow Lark, 2005, A Sonrous Hark, 2006, A Book to Mark, 2006, Climactic Clime, 2006, Sieving Mind, 2006, Pandemics Rise, 2006, Charting the Theogonies, 2006;: The Whirlwind Creeps, 2006, Kinder, Gentler

Thoughts, 2006, Realities Apprise, 2006, A Promise Bid, 2006, In Darkness Hid, 2006, A Horror's Rid, 2006, A Future's Hid, 2006, Of Ages Tolled, 2006, Beauty Compromised, 2006, Silver Lining Blurred, 2006, Confounded World, 2007, A Martyr's Crown, 2007, A Mount to Climb, 2007, A Sights Behold, 2007, Collective Consciousness, 2007, Warfare's Scourge, 2007, Avoiding the Apocalypse, 2007, Our Daily Bread, 2007, Historical Behold, 2007, Universal Greet, 2007, Awesome Arsenals, 2007, Horizon's Blanched, 2007, Idealistic Renderings, 2007, Where Stray the Gods?, 2007, Humanity to Rise, 2007. Cpl. US Army, 1948—50. Avocation: world travel. Home: Glenview, Ill. Died Aug. 19, 2008.

BLATZ, PAUL EUGENE, chemistry educator, researcher; b. Pitts., Aug. 29, 1923; s. William John and Clara (Metzger) B.; m. Nancy McGraw, Jan., 1952 (dec. Feb. 1964); m. Eleanor Arlene Hoffman; children: Francene, Roger, John, Bonnic, Paul. BS, So. Meth. U., 1951; PhD, U. Tex., 1955. Rsch. chemist Dow Chem. Co., Freeport, Tex., 1955-59; sr. rsch. chemist Mobil Oil Co., Dallas, 1959-63; assoc. prof. VFW Mex. Highlands U., Las Vegas, N.Mex., 1963-64; prof. U. Wyo., Laramie, 1964-71; prof., chair U. Mo., Kansas City, 1971-76, prof., from 1976. Vis. prof. Inst. Molecular Biophysics, Fla. State U., 1979, March NIH, Pan-Am. U., 1980. Contbr. articles Biochemistry, Jour. Am. Chem. Soc., Jour. Phys. Chemistry, Photochemistry Photobiology. 1st lt. USAF, 1943-45, ETO. NIH grantee Eye Inst., 1982-90. Mem. Am. Chem. Soc. (chmn. local sect. 1988), Am. Soc. Photobiology, Biophys. Soc., Sigma Xi. Episcopalian. Achievements include establishment of relationship between electrosonic charge and wavelength in visual pigments. Home: Linn Creek, Mo. Died July 3, 2008.

BLAUROCK, ALLEN EDWARD, biophysicist, food scientist, educator; b. Detroit, Aug. 28, 1940; s. Edward Emil Blaurock and Irma Florence (Allen) MacArthur; m. Teresa Noel Urban, May 1964 (div. Jan. 1988); children: Madeleine Cecile Blaurock Gutow, Rosalind Noel, Carl Allen; m. Bernadette Guzzy, Apr. 2, 1988; children: Walter Edward, Linnea Bertina. BS in Physics magna cum laude, U. Mich., 1963, MS in Physics, 1963, PhD in Physics, 1967; MA in Tchg., Nat. Louis U., 2000. NSF predoctoral fellow in physics U. Mich., Ann Arbor, 1964-66; NIH/PHS fellow in biophysics King's Coll., London, Eng., 1967-69; rsch. biophysicist Cardiovasc. Rsch. Inst. U. Calif., San Francisco, 1969-71; European molecular biology orgn. sr. fellow in biophysics King's Coll., London, 1971-72, NIH/PHS sr. fellow in biophysics, 1972-75; rsch. chemist Calif. Inst. Tech., Pasadena, 1975-79; assoc. prof. in anatomy and biochemistry U. N.C., Chapel Hill, 1979-85; sr. rsch. scientist Kraft Foods Rsch. Ctr., Glenview, Ill., 1986-99; tchr. math., physics and chemistry local hs, from 2000. Vis. assoc. prof. in physiology Duke U., Durham, N.C., 1985-86; adj. supr. grad. rsch. Ill. Inst. Tech., Chgo., 1995-99; cons. on neurol. rsch. Synchrotron Radiation Lab., Daresbury, Eng., 1996—; co-founder BioCAT at Advanced Photon Source, Argonne (Ill.) Nat. Lab.; sci. reviewer Biochimica et Biophysica Acta, 1982, Methods of Enzymology, 1982, Jour. Neurosci. Rsch., 1995; spkr. 3d Internat. Biophysics Congress, Boston, 1969, Neurosci. Rsch. Program Work Session on Myelin, Brookline, Mass., 1970, Klausur in Schwartzwald, Titisee, Germany, 1971, Rank Prize Funds Symposium on Vertebrate Photoreception Royal Soc., London, 1976, Am. Phys. Soc., Washington, 1976, 36th Annual Pitts. Diffraction Conf., 1978, 4th Taniguchi Symposium in Biophysics, Osaka, Japan, 1978, Synchrotron X-Rays in Medicine, Daresbury, Eng., 1996, others; presenter in field. Author: (with others) Vertebrate Photoreception, 1977, Progress in Lipid-Protein Interactions, 1986, Applications of NMR in Agriculture and Biochemistry, 1990, Myelin: Biology and Chemistry, 1992, Food Processing: Recent Developments, 1995; contbr. over 60 articles to profl. jours. including Biochemistry, Jour. Food Engring., Brain Rsch., Chemistry and Physics of Lipids, Jour. Molecular Biology, Jour. Neurochemistry, Neurochem. Rsch., Neuropathology and Applied Neurobiology, others. Grantee NIH, 1979-82, Kroc Found., 1983-85. Mem. Am. Oil Chemists Soc. (immediate past pres. North Ctrl. sect. 1996-97, chair Bailey award com. 1996-97, pres. North Ctrl. sect. 1995-96, sec. 1993-95, phys. methods com. 1988-99), Am. Soc. for Neurochemistry, Internat. Soc. for Neurochemistry, Sigma Xi, Phi Beta Kappa. Achievements include demonstration of lipid bilayer structure generally in biol. membranes; with various collaborators demonstrated bilayer and protein orgn. in nerve myelin; co-discoverer crystalline structure of purple membrane from H. halobium and demonstrated periplasmic space within its cell wall; co-discoverer crystalline structure of all-protein gas-vesicle membrane in blue-green algae; discovered non-spherical supra-molecular structure of human serum low-density lipoprotein; pioneered measurements of fat crystallization kinetics in foods/food ingredients using scanning calorimetric x-ray diffraction and video methods. Home: Evanston, Ill. Died Dec. 27, 2007.

BLAZY, DIANE EDITH, photographer; b. Kingston, NY, Dec. 27, 1952; d. Nicholas George and Albert (Youngs) Blazy. BA, U. Ky., 1976; MFA, Rochester Inst. Tech., 1991. Tchr. photograhpy Living Art and Sci. Ctr., Lexington, Ky., 1975-78; tchr. art Fayette County Schs., Lexington, 1978-79; art dir. Lexington Pub. Libr., 1979-80; photographer U. Ky., Lexington, 1981-82; freelance photographic asst. Rochester, 1984-85; freelance photographer NYC, from 1985, Fla., from 1985. Photography instr. Barry U., Miami, 1989, Palm Beach Photographic Workshops; instr. Art Inst., Ft. Lauderdale, from 1989; asst. prof. photography New World Sch. Arts, Miami, Fla.; cons. in field; condr. photographic workshops; lectr. in field; gallery rep. 1st St. Gallery, Boca Raton, Fla., 2005; creative cons. Polaroid Corp., 2002—04; freelance photographer Miami Herald Pub. Co., 1991—98. Exhibitions include Norton Mus., West Palm Beach, Miami Art Mus., Samuel Ham Mus. Fine Art, Gainesville, Mus. Fine Arts, St. Petersburg, Fla. State U. Art Mus., Tallahassee; contbr. articles to profl. jours. Mem.: Internat. Ctr. Photography, Soc. Photographic Edn., Am. Soc. Mag. Photographers. Home: Davie, Fla. Died Oct. 5, 2007.

BLEDSOE, PAULA LA JUAN, nurse practitioner, nursing supervisor; b. Murfreesboro, Ark., Oct. 24, 1960; d. Paul Val and Mildred Louise (Parker) Pennington; m. Billy Don Bledsoe, Aug. 1, 1977; children: Nikki, Bobi Jo. ADN, El Reno Jr. Coll., Okla., 1984; BSN, U. Ark., 1990. RN, Ark.; registered nurse practitioner; cert. BCLS instr., ACLS, pediatric advanced life support, CPR instr., hearing and vision screening, scoliosis screening instr. Nursing asst. Parkview Hosp., El Reno, Okla., 1980-82; nurse technician Bapt. Med. Ctr., Oklahoma City, Okla., 1983-84; RN, team leader, charge nurse neonatal ICU, Level III Okla. Children's Meml. Hosp., Okla. City, 1984-86; charge nurse neurol. Unit St. Joseph's Regional Health Ctr., Hot Springs, Ark., 1986-90; registered nurse practitioner Hot Springs Neurosurgery, Hot Springs, Ark., 1990-93; nursing house supr., charge nurse intensive care DeQueen (Ark.) Med. Ctr., 1993-94; nurse practitioner Family Med. Clinic of Dierks, Ark., 1994-95, Delight (Ark.) Rural Health Clinic, from 1995, Med. Park Hosp., Hope, Ark., from 1995. Preceptor U. Ark. Med. Sch. nursing students. Mem. ANA (policy and procedure com. 1989), Nat. Nurse Practitioner Assn., Nat. Stroke Assn., Ark.-Mo. Nurse Practitioners Assn., NAFE, NOW, Sigma Theta Tau. Avocations: reading, basketball, horseback riding, kick boxing, crafts. Home: Hot Springs National Park, Ark. Died May 20, 2008.

BLOCH, BERNARD JEROME, architect; b. Chgo., Jan. 12, 1927; s. Harry Aaron and Charlotte (Frank) B.; m. Janice May Stern, Apr. 5, 1952; children: Wendy Ann, Lauren Jaye, Deanne Lynn. AA, UCLA, 1948; BA, U. Calif., Berkeley, 1952. Registered architect, Calif. Project job capt. John Carl Warnecke Architects, San Francisco, 1957-59; architect Blanchard & Maher Architects, San Francisco, 1959-65; pvt. practice architecture San Francisco, 1965-70; project mgr. Robert B. Liles Inc. Architects, Corte Madera, Calif., 1970-81; dir. quality assurance, sr. assoc. Whisler-Patri Architects, San Francisco, from 1981. Mem. AIA (chmn. code com. 1984-88), Constrn. Specifications Inst. (chpt. sec. 1986-87), Nat. Fire Protective Assn. Democrat. Jewish. Avocations: painting, photography. Home: Napa, Calif. Died Sept. 12, 2007.

BLOCH, JOSEPH MEYER, musician, educator; b. Indpls., Nov. 6, 1917; s. Joseph Meyer and Rosyln Sommers (Liepold) B.; m. Dana Pauline Kendrick, Jan. 14, 1944 (dec. 2008); children: Leslie E., John D., Andrew L. MusB, Chgo. Mus. Coll., 1939; MA, Harvard U., 1946; D (hon.), The Juilliard Sch., 2004. Mem. faculty Denver U., 1946-48; prof. piano lit. The Juilliard Sch., NYC, 1948—83, 1990—96; concert pianist, 1950—2009. Vis. artist, instr. Indiana U., Bloomington, 1958, Boston U., 1965-69, Miyagi Jogakuin, Sendai, Japan, 1971, U. Auckland (New Zealand), 1972, Peabody Conservatory, Balt., 1983-85, Cen. Conservatory, Beijing, 1984-85, Shanghai Conservatory, Repblic of China, 1984-85, 88, Johannesen Sch. of Arts, Victoria, B.C., Can., 1979-86, U. Hawaii, Honolulu, 1983, 85, 87; mem. editorial staff The Piano Quarterly, Wilmington, Vt., 1978-87. Recs. include Piano Music of Moevs, DeMenasce and Seeger; author: Debussy Preludes, 1987, Thematic Guide Piano Music of Liszt, 1987; contbr. articles profl. jours. and mags. Served to capt. USAAF, 1941-46, PTO. Recipient Chevalier De l'Ordre des Palmes Académiques, govt. of France, 1985. Mem. Musicians Found. (bd. dirs.); Clubs: Musicians of N.Y. (bd. dirs.), Bohemians, Harvard (N.Y.C.). Avocation: collecting prints. Home: Larchmont, NY. Died Mar. 4, 2009.

BLOCH, PETER, historian, writer; b. Frankfurt-Main, Fed. Republic Germany, Oct. 19, 1921; came to U.S., 1949; s. Arthur and Else (Israel) B. Student, U. Brussels, 1939-40, U. Geneva, 1943-45. Corres. European publs., radio stas., from 1949; U.S. del. League of Belgian and Allied Patriots, Brussels, 1949-70; founder, pres. Assn. for Puerto Rican-Hispanic Culture, Inc., NYC, from 1965; U.S. del. Acad. Soc. Arts-Scis.-Letters of France, Paris, from 1976. Author: La-Le-Lo-Lai Peurto Rican Music, 1973, Painting and Sculpture of the Puerto Ricans, 1978, James Israel 1848-1936, 1983, De Van Eyck a Chagall-Once Grandes Pintores, 1987; culture editor mag. Canales, 1976-92; author numerous essays and articles, 3 plays. Recipient Key to the city, Mayor of San Juan, P.r., 1964; named Knight of the Order of Isabel la Católica, Spain, 1969. Home: New York, NY. Died July 31, 2008.

BLOCK, ELAINE CARLIN, history educator; b. NYC, Dec. 18, 1925; d. Philip and Flora (Kramer) Cohen; children: Randall, Laurie Spigel, Linda. BA, Cornell U., 1946; postgrad., U. Paris, 1948; MA, Hunter Coll., 1951; PhD, U. Wis., 1965. Prof. history Hunter Coll./CUNY, 1965-90, prof. emerita, from 1990. Cons. Monument Historignes, Bescancon, France, 1994, U. Toulouse, France, 1993-94. Contbr. articles to profl. jours.; prodr., writer (film): Misericords: Hidden Mirrors of Medieval Life, 1993. Recipient III award U.S. Office of Edn., 1969-72. Mem. Medieval Acad., Misericordia Internat. (pres.). Home: New York, NY. Died Mar. 7, 2008.

BLOOM, HYMAN (CHAIM MELAMED), artist; b. Brunoviski, Latvia, Mar. 29, 1913; came to U.S., 1920; s. Joseph Melamed and Anna Soloman; m. Nina Bohlen, 1954 (div. 1961); m. Stella Caralis, 1978. Student, West End Community Center, Boston; studied under, Harold K. Zimmerman, Danman Waldo Ross. Instr. Wellesley (Mass.) Coll., 1949-51, Harvard U., Cambridge, Mass., 1951-53. One-man shows, Stuart Gallery, Boston, 1945, Inst. Contemporary Art, Boston, Whitney Mus. Art, N.Y.C., 1945, 54, 68, Albright Knox Art Gallery, Buffalo, 1954, Wadsworth Atheneum, 1957, U. Conn. Mus. Art, 1969, Terry Dintenfass Gallery, 1972, 75, Fogg Mus. Harvard, 1933, Dintenfass Gallery, 1983, retrospective, Paul Mus., U. N.H., 1992, U. N.H. Mus., 1992, Bateo Coll. Mus., 2001, Kennedy Galleries, 1986, St. Botolph Club Boston, 1989, Hyman Bloom Painting, Martin Summer Graphics, 1989, Fuller Mus., 1996, The Sprits of Hyman Bloom, Brockton Mass., Bloom Baskin, Nat. Acad. Design, 2002, others; exhbns. include Butler Inst. Am. Art, 1972, Esther Robles Gallery, Brentwood Park, 1976, Ind. U. Mus., Bloomington, 1977, Ind. Mus. Art, 1977-78, Inst. Contemporary Art, Boston, 1979, others; represented in permanent collections, Hirshorn Mus., Washington, Mus. Modern Art, NYC, 1942, Whitney Mus. Art, Harvard U., Kalamazoo Inst. Arts, Mich., Minn. Mus. Art, St. Paul, Mus. Fine Arts, Boston, Jewish Mus., N.Y.C., Bloom Found., The Pan Orient Arts Mus., Mus. Modern Art. NYC, 1942 Fellow, Ford Found.; Guggenheim fellow. Mem.: Nat. Acad. Design, Am. Acad. Arts and Letters. Died Aug. 26, 2009.

BLOUGH, DOUGLAS DUANE, art director; b. Johnstown, Pa., July 23, 1949; s. S. Duane Blough and Marjorie Romaine (Seese) O'Dell; m. Linda Gay Goldsby, Mar. 1, 1986; children: Justin Lee, Amanda Leigh. AA, Lorain County Community Coll., 1969; BFA, Bowling Green State U., 1971, postgrad. Graphic designer Walbridge & Bellg Prodns., Toledo, 1971-73; art dir. Sta. WBGU-TV, Bowling Green, Ohio, 1974-75; ptnr., art dir. Barnstorm Studios, Colorado Springs, Colo., 1975-86; owner Barnstorm Design Creative, Colorado Springs, Colo., from 1986. Advisor Pikes Peak Community Coll., Colorado Springs, 1980—. Co-producer (multi-image presentation) Where the Rivers Begin, 1980; writer/producer/dir. (video) Fairfield Pagosa, 1983; writer-co-producer (multi-image presentation) Cuchara Resort, 1984, (multi-image video) An Investment in Fun, 1986. Mem. Pikes Peak Advt. Fedn. (bd. dirs., Best of Show 1987, AAF Silver award 1990), Colorado Springs Exec. Assn. (pres., bd. dirs.), Ducks Unltd., Rocky Mountain Elk Found. Republican. Mem. United Ch. of Christ. Avocations: hunting, fishing, racquetball, backpacking. Home: Woodland Park, Colo. Died Mar. 22, 2008.

BLUE, E(MANUEL) MORSE, consulting chemical engineer; b. Spokane, Wash., June 27, 1912; s. Louis and Amelia (Dias) B.; m. Harriet Tieburg, Sept. 2, 1938 (dec. Feb. 1980); children; William A., Bonnie A., Thomas C.; m. Mary Heath Nelson, Aug. 8, 1981. BS, U. Calif., Berkeley, 1935; MS, MIT, 1937. Registered chem. engr., Calif. Sr. engr. assoc. Chevron Research, Richmond, Calif., 1938-66, mgr. invention devel. San Francisco, 1964-77; cons. chem. engring. Walnut Creek, Calif., 1977-79; pres. E.M. Blue and Assocs., Inc., Walnut Creek, from 1979; lectr. in chem. engring. U. Calif., Berkeley, from 1959. Contbr. articles to profl. jours.; patentee in field. Served to capt. USN, 1941-46. Fellow Am. Inst. Chem. Engring. (held various offices); mem. Am. Chem. Soc., Licensing Execs. Soc. Clubs: San Francisco Engring., Faculty (Berkeley). Avocation: golf. Died Feb. 15, 2008.

BLUM, JOHN CURTIS, agricultural economist; b. Terryville, Conn., July 5, 1915; s. John A. and Marion D. (Curtis) B.; m. Mable L. Brooks, Oct. 21, 1939 (dec. 2001); children: Joanne M. Blum Kraft, John Curtis, Nancy J. BS, U. Conn., Storrs, 1937, MS, 1939; postgrad., U. Wis., Madison, 1941, US Dept. Agr. Grad. Sch., Washington, 1946, Indsl. Coll. Armed Forces, 1965—66. With USDA, 1939-75, asst. dir. dairy div., 1960-61, dir. div., 1961-63, economist, 1963-64, asst. dept. adminstr., 1964-67, dep. adminstr., 1967-74, assoc. adminstr., 1974-75; economist E.A. Jaenke & Assos., Inc., Washington, 1975-83. Violinist Fairfax Symphony Orch., Va., 1957-95, bd. dirs., 1957-70, pres., 1959-61, treas., 1965-67; violinist McLean Symphony, Va., 1995-2009, Reston Cmty. Orch., Va., 1998-2009; dist. dir. North Va. dist. PTA, 1961-63; treas. Va. Congress Parents and Tchrs., 1963-65, regional v.p., 1965-67, chmn. extension com. 1967-69, budget chmn., 1969-71, bd. mgrs., 1961-71. Lt. (j.g.) USNR, 1944-46, PTO. Mem. Am. Agr. Econ. Assn., Grange. Home: Sterling, Va. Died Jan. 27, 2009.

BLUMBERG, LEROY NORMAN, physicist; b. Atlantic City, June 22, 1929; s. Abraham and Elizabeth (Cohen) B.; m. Sydel Barkin, Mar. 2, 1957; children: Manya Helman, Deborah, Julia Haykin. BS, MIT, 1951; MA, Columbia U., 1955, PhD, 1962. Physicist Los Alamos (N.Mex.) Nat. Lab., 1955-60, Oak Ridge (Tenn.) Nat. Lab., 1962-65; rsch. fellow Harvard U., Cambridge (Mass.) Electron Accelerator, 1965-66; physicist alternating gradient synchrotron Brookhaven Nat. Lab., Upton, N.Y., 1966-78, sr. physicist Nat. Synchrotron Light Source, from 1978. Vis. prof. Nat. Lab. High Energy Physics, Tsukuba, Ibaraki, Japan, 1975-76; vis. scholar Stanford (Calif.) U., Stanford Synchrotron Radiation Lab., 1982-83; vis. physicist div. high energy physics U.S. Dept. Energy, Germantown, Md., 1985-88. Contbr. articles to Phys. Rev., Physics Rev. Letters, Nuclear Physics, Nuclear Instruments and Methods, IEEE Proc. Nuclear Sci. Fulbright fellow Technische Hogeschool, Delft, The Netherlands, 1951. Fellow Am. Phys. Soc. Achievements include discovery of target spin effect in neutron-induced fission;proposal for strong focusing of neutrons and Monte-Carlo multiple integration; design calculations for extraction systems of Alternating Gradient Synchrotron External Beams (BNL), for synchrotron radiation X-ray source for coronary angiography, for BNL VUV storage ring, for BNL x-ray lithography (computer chip) source. Home: Portland, Oreg. Died Oct. 12, 2007.

BLYTHE, CATHERINE L., writer, consultant; b. Bklyn., Apr. 2, 1958; d. Alexander Frett and Pearl Blythe; m. Muhammed Hasan (div.). MS in Bus. Mgmt., Northwestern Internat. U., Cyprus, Denmark. Rschr., panelist, mgr., cons. Comm. Worldwide Fund, Long Island City, NY, 1995—2003, mktg. analyst, from 1995. Vol. UNICEF, NYC, 1995—2003. Democrat. Home: Long Island City, NY. Died June 11, 2008.

BOBBITT, JOHN MAXWELL, surgeon, medical educator; b. Jan. 20, 1927; MD, U. Mich., Ann Arbor, 1952. Intern, then resident in surgery U. Mich., Ann Arbor, 1952-57; clin. assoc. prof. surgery Med. Sch. Marshall U., Huntington, W.Va., 1972-80. Contbr. numerous articles on nautical rsch. to popular publs., 1985—. Elected to W.Va. Ho. Dels., 1966, 68. Home: Newport News, Va. Died Jan. 5, 2008.

BODENHEIMER, BERT ARNO, mechanical engineer, consultant; b. Loerrach, Germany, May 22, 1928; came to U.S., 1939; s. Alfred and Martha (Model) B.; m. Ellen Schleicher, Aug. 15, 1954 (dec. Jan. 1981); children: Brenda, Carol, Andrew; m. Bertha Allen, Oct. 9, 1953. BS in Mech. Engring., CUNY, 1950; MS in Mgmt., Columbia U., 1955. Registered profl. engr., N.Y., Conn. Chief engr. Slater Elec., NYC, 1950-54; sr. engr. Am. Machine and Foundry, Greenwich, Conn., 1956-64, CBS Labs., Stamford, Conn., 1964-68; dir. R&D Sea Land Svc., Newark, N.J., 1968-76; consulting engr. B.A. Bodenheimer and Co., Stamford, from 1976. Dir. Almoros Realty, N.Y.C., 1985—. Patentee in field. With U.S. Army, 1950-52. Avocation: theater. Died Mar. 8, 2008.

BODEY, BELA, immunologist, pathologist, oncologist; b. Sofia, Bulgaria, Jan. 18, 1949; arrived in US, 1985, naturalized, 1994; s. Joseph and Rossitza (Derebeeva) B.; m. Victoria Psenko, Aug. 29, 1979; children: Bela Jr., Vivian. MD, Med. Acad., Sofia, 1973; PhD in Immuno-Biology, Inst. Morphology, Bulgarian Acad. Sci., Sofia, 1977. Lic. physician, exptl. pathologist, embryologist, immunomorphologist, thymologist, exptl. oncologist. Asst. prof. Semmelweis Med. U., Budapest, 1977-80; prof. Inst. Hematology, Budapest, 1980-83; rsch. assoc. Tufts U., Boston, 1985; rsch. fellow immuno-pathology Mass. Gen. Hosp./Harvard U., Boston, 1986; rsch. fellow Childrens Hosp. L.A., 1987-90, rsch. scientist, 1991-92; asst. prof. rsch. pathology, Sch. of Medicine Univ. Southern Calif., from 1992, prof. pathology Sch. Medicine, from 1995. Vis. prof. Alexander von Humboldt Found., Ulm, Fed. Republic Germany, 1984. Mem. Am. Assn. Cancer Rsch., Am. and Can. Acad. Pathology, French Soc. Cell Biology, French Soc. Electronmicroscopy, Internat. Soc. Exptl. Hematology, Internat. Soc. Comparative Oncology, N.Y. Acad. Scis., Free Masons. Roman Catholic. Avocations: travel, swimming, dance. Home: Canoga Park, Calif. Died Aug. 25, 2008.

BODINGTON, CHARLES E., chemical engineer; b. Alameda, Calif., Aug. 23, 1930; s. Harold Pierce and Mercedes Veronica (Jackson) B.; m. Helen Champlin Lohman, June 28, 1952; children: Jeffrey, Celia. BS, Stanford U., 1952; MS, MIT, 1954. With Chevron Rsch. Co., Richmond, Calif., 1954-86, sr. engring. assoc., 1968-86; ind. cons. San Anselmo, Calif., from 1986. Contbr. articles on gasoline mfg. and petroleum industry to profl. jours.; author: Planning, Scheduling and Control Integration in the Process Industries, 1995. Mem. Am. Inst. Chem. Engrs. (session chair 1989, 90, 91, 93). Achievements include patents on chem. recovery and dewaxing process. Home: San Rafael, Calif. Died Aug. 9, 2008.

BODKIN, RUBY PATE, retired real estate broker, educator; b. Frostproof, Fla., Mar. 11, 1926; d. James Henry and Lucy Beatrice (Latham) P.; m. Lawrence Edward Bodkin Sr., Jan. 15, 1949; children: Karen Bodkin Snead, Cinda, Lawrence Jr. BA, Fla. State U., 1948; MA, U. Fla., 1972. Lic. real estate broker Fla. Banker Barnett Bank, Avon Park, Fla., 1943-44, Lewis State Bank, Tallahassee, 1944-49; ins. underwriter Hunt Ins. Agy., Tallahassee, 1949-51; tchr. Duval County Sch. Bd., Jacksonville, Fla., 1952-77; pvt. practice realty Jacksonville, 1976—2007; ret., 2007. Tchr. Nassau County Sch. Bd., Jacksonville, 1978—83; sec., treas., v.p. Bodkin Corp., R&D/Inventions, Jacksonville, 1983—2007. Author: 100 Teacher Chosen Recipes, 1976, Bodkin Bridge Course for Beginners, 1996, (autobiography) Grandma Bodkin, 2000, Essay on Death, 2003; author numerous poems. Mem. Jacksonville Symphony Guild, from 1985, Southside Bapt. Ch. Recipient 25 Yr. Svc. award Duval County Sch. Bd., 1976, Tchr. of Yr. award Bryceville Sch., 1981, 30 Yr. Svc. award State of Fla. Dept. Edn. Mem. Am. Contract Bridge League, Nat. Realtors Assn., Southside Jr. Woman's Club, Garden Club Sweetbriar (bd. dirs.), Oak St. Woman's Club Jacksonville (fin. dir. 1991-92, 3rd v.p. social dir. WCOJ, 1992-99), UDC (Martha Reid chpt.

#19), Fla. Edn. Assn. (pers. problems com. 1958), Duval County Classrooms Tchrs. (v.p. membership 1957), Woman's Club Jacksonville Bridge Group, Fla. Ret. Tchrs. Assn., Fla. Realtors Assn., N.E. Fla. Realtors Assn., Jacksonville Geneal. Soc. (practicing genealogist, family historian 1986—), Friday Musicale of Jacksonville, San Jose Golf Country Club, Jacksonville Sch. Bridge. Baptist. Avocations: reading, writing, genealogy, photography, bridge. Home: Jacksonville, Fla. Died July 29, 2008.

BOGLE, BOB, musician; b. Okla., Jan. 16, 1934; m. Yumi Bogle. Co-founder, bassist, guitarist The Ventures, 1958—2009. Musician albums, The Ventures, 1960, Another Smash, 1960, The Colorful Ventures, 1960, Twist with the Ventures, 1960, Mashed Potatoes & Gravy, 1961, Going to the Ventures' Dance Party, 1961, The Ventures Play Telstar & Lonely Bull, 1962, Bobby Vee Meets the Ventures, 1962, Surfing, 1963, The Ventures Play the Country Classics, 1963, Let's Go!, 1963, Ventures in Space, 1963, The Fabulous Ventures, 1964, Knock Me Out!, 1965, On Stage, 1964, A Go-Go, 1964, Christmas Album, 1965, Adventures in Paradise, 1965, Where the Action Is, 1965, The Ventures Play the Batman Theme, 1966, Go with the Ventures, 1966, Runnin' Strong, 1966, Wild Thing!, 1967, Guitar Freakout, 1967, Super Psychedelics, 1967, $1,000,000 Weekend, 1967, Flights of Fantasy, 1968, The Horse, 1968, Underground Fire, 1969, Hawaii Five-O, 1969, Swamp Rock, 1969, The Ventures' 10th Anniversary Album, 1970, New Testament, 1971, Theme from Shaft, 1971, Joy!, 1972, Rock & Roll Forever, 1972, The Jim Croce Songbook, 1974, Now Playing, 1974, Hollywood, 1975, Sunflower '76, 1976, Rocky Road, 1976, TV Themes, 1977, Latin Album, 1979, Chameleon, 1980, St. Louis Memory, 1982, The Last Album on Liberty, 1982, NASA 25th Anniversary Commemorative Album, 1983, Wild Again, 1997, New Depths, 1998, 60's Rocking Christmas, 2001, Christmas Joy, 2002, Ventures Forever, 2004, Summer & Winter, 2004, Space 2001, 2005, Play Seaside Story, 2006. Named to The Rock & Roll Hall of Fame (as mem. of The Ventures), 2008. Died June 14, 2009.

BOGNER, DARLENE RUTH, retired social worker; b. Elgin, Ill., Nov. 19, 1932; d. Carroll Benjamin and Ruth Clara (Bruns) Bennorth; m. Dennis Dean Bogner, June 15, 1963; children: Sharon Marie, Barbara Jean. BS, Hamline U., 1955; MSW, U. Louisville, 1959. Cert. clin. social worker, S.D. Social worker Yankton (S.D.) State Hosp., 1955-57, 58, psychiat. social worker, 1963-72, Butler Count Mental Health Ctr., Hamilton, Ohio, 1959-63, Lewis & Clark Mental Health Ctr., Yankton, 1972-99; ret., 1999. Mem. Drug Prevention Coun. S.E. S.D., Drug Prevention Coun, Crofton, Nebr., 1991; sec. Sr. Citizens, Crofton, 1990—92; vol. Crofton Sr. Citizens, from 1997, Yankton (S.D.) Hospice Program, 1999—2000; mem. Vo. Corps of Discovery Welcome Ctr., Crofton, 2001—04. Democrat. Avocations: walking, sewing, knitting, music, reading, bridge. Home: Crofton, Nebr. Died Mar. 19, 2008.

BOLOOKI, HOOSHANG, cardiac surgeon; b. Langeh, Iran, Mar. 28, 1937; came to U.S., 1960, naturalized, 1976; s. Hossein and Fatima (Arjomand) B.; m. C. Joanne McDonald, Aug. 30, 1975; children: Hooshang Michael, Cyrus William, Andrew John. BS cum laude, Alborz Coll., Tehran, 1954; MD, Tehran U., 1960. Intern, resident in surgery Kings County Hosp.; asst. instr. SUNY Med. Center, Bklyn., 1961-67; resident in thoracic and cardiovascular surgery Jackson Meml. Hosp. and U. Miami Sch. Medicine, 1967-69; faculty U. Miami (Fla.) Med. Sch., 1969-77, prof. surgery, from 1977; attending surgeon, dir. adult cardiac surgery Jackson Meml. Hosp., from 1969; dir. cardiopulmonary transplant program U. Miami Jackson Meml. Hosp., 1986-98. Cons. VA Hosp., Miami, 1977-90; mem. adv. panel cardiovascular surgery Ethicon Inc., Davis & Geck Co., Inc., 1974-1995; hon. prof. U. Marón Sch. Medicine, Argentina. Author: Clinical Application of Intra-Aortic Balloon Pump, 1976, 3d edit., 1998, Medical Examination Review, Thoracic Surgery, 2d edit., 1972, 3d edit. Vol. 18, 1981, Cardiovascular Surgery, Vol. 38, 1981; contbr. articles to profl. jours. Recipient Rsch. Career Devel. award NIH, 1972-77, grantee, 1972-75; recipient Grand award U. Tex. Med. Br., 1968, Masterpiece award Transplant Found. South Fla., 1996, Achievement award Iranian-Am. Med. Assn., 1999, award for outstanding svc. 2000, award for contbn. to cardiovasc. surgery Onassis Cardiac Surgery Ctr., 2000, Achievement award Onassis Surg. Found., 2000. Fellow ACS, Royal Coll. Surgeons Can., Am. Coll. Cardiology, Am. Coll. Chest Physicians; mem. AMA (cert. merit), Am. Surg. Assn., Am. Assn. Thoracic Surgery, Soc. Univ. Surgeons, Am. Heart Assn., Fla. Heart Assn. (cert. of merit), Fla. Thoracic Soc., Soc. for Thoracic Surgeons (membership com. 1983-85), So. Thoracic Surg. Assn. (membership com. 1985-87, chmn. 1989, v.p. 1991), Soc. Internat. de Chirugie, Internat. Cardiovascular Soc., Soc. Vascular Surgery, Internat. Soc. Heart and Lung Transplantation, Soc. Acad. Surgeons, David Park Racquet Club, Ski Club. Republican. Muslim. Home: Hollywood, Fla. Died Dec. 15, 2008.

BOLTON, KATHLEEN C., case management and legal nurse consultant; b. Stoneham, Mass., Jan. 14, 1958; Cert., New England Deaconess Hosp., 1979; BSN, Sonoma State U., 1988. RN, Calif.; cert. pub. health nurse. Case mgmt., legal cons. pvt. practice, San Francisco, from 1988. Author: Model Policy and Procedure Manual for Residential Care Facilities. Mem. Sigma Theta Tau. Home: San Francisco, Calif. Died Apr. 14, 2008.

BOMBERGER, RUSSELL BRANSON, lawyer, writer; b. Lebanon, Pa., May 1, 1934; s. John Mark and Viola (Aurentz) B.; divorced; children— Ann Elizabeth, Jane Carmel. BS, Temple U., 1955; MA, U. Iowa, 1956, MA, 1961, PhD, 1962; MS, U. So. Calif., 1960; LLB, JD, LaSalle U.; grad., U.S. Marine Corps Command and Staff Coll., 1987, U.S. Naval War Coll., 1991. Bar: Calif. 1970, U.S. Supreme Ct. 1975. Mem. editorial staff Phila. Inquirer, 1952-54; lectr. U. Iowa, 1955-57, U. So. Calif., 1957-58; asst. prof. U.S. Naval Postgrad. Sch., Monterey, Calif., 1958-62, assoc. prof., 1963-75, prof., 1975-89, prof. emeritus, from 1989; practice law, from 1970. Freelance writer, 1952—, communications cons., 1963—; safety cons. internat. program U. So. Calif. Inst. Safety and Systems Mgmt., 1983—; cons. Internat. Ctr. for Aviation Safety, Lisbon, 1984—; vis. fellow Oxford U. Author: (novel) The Alternate Candidate, (broadcast series) The World of Ideas, (motion picture) Strokes and Stamps, (stage play) Closely Held; abstracter-editor: Internat. Transactional Analysis Assn. Capt. USNR, 1966-94. Decorated Meritorious Civilian Svc. medal, 1989; Am. Psychol. Found. fellow Columbia U., 1954-55, CBS fellow U. So. Calif., 1957-58, Keith fellow, 2004, Oxford U., 2004 Home: Monterey, Calif. Died Apr. 19, 2009.

BONAR, ROBERT ADDISON, biochemist, educator; b. Kalamazoo, Aug. 23, 1925; s. Lee and Margaret Scot (Pengelly) B.; m. Joy Lee Walker, May 13, 1951; children: Susan Elizabeth, Bruce Robert, David Lee, Nancy Jean. AB, U. Calif., Berkeley, 1949, PhD, 1953. Rsch. fellow med. sch. UCLA, 1953-55; rsch. assoc. med. sch. Duke U., Durham, N.C., 1955-57, from asst. to assoc. prof. med. sch., 1957-87, prof. emeritus med. sch., from 1987; rsch. chemist VA Hosp., Durham, 1972-87. Adj. faculty Rappahannock C.C., Warsaw, Va., 1989—. Chmn. Orange County Planning Bd., N.C., 1972-80. Sgt. U.S. Army, 1943-46, ETO. Home: Jamul, Calif. Died Jan. 30, 2008.

BOND, JAMES MAX, JR., architect; b. Louisville, July 17, 1935; s. James Max and Ruth (Clement) B.; m. Jean Davis Carey, Oct. 11, 1961; children: Carey Julian, Ruth Marion. BA magna cum laude, Harvard U., 1955, MArch., 1958; DHL (hon.), N.J. Inst. Tech., 1993. Registered architect, N.Y., 1963. Archtl. apprentice various offices, Paris, NYC, 1959-64; arch. Ghana Nat. Constrn. Corp., Accra, Ghana, 1964-65; instr. U. Sci. and Tech., Kumasi, Ghana, 1965-67; exec. dir. Architect's Renewal Commn., NYC, 1967-68; asst. prof. to prof., chmn. Grad. Sch. Architecture and Planning Columbia U., NYC, 1970-85, chmn. Grad. Sch. Architecture & Planning, 1980—84; prof., dean Sch. Architecture and Environ. Studies CCNY, 1985-92; ptnr. Bond, Ryder & Associates, NYC, 1969-90, Davis Brody Bond, LLP, NYC, 1990—2009. Favrot chair Tulane U. Sch. Arch., 1999; Charles Moore vis. prof. Taubman Sch. Arch. U. Mich., 2003. Prin. works include Bolgatanga Libr. bldg., Ghana, Schomburg Ctr., N.Y., Studio Mus., Harlem, N.Y.C., Martin Luther King Jr. Ctr. and Tomb, Atlanta, Birmingham Civil Rights Museum; firm selected assoc. arch., World Trade Ctr. Memorial site. Commr. City Planning Commn., N.Y.C., 1980-87; bd. dirs. Mcpl. Arts Soc., N.Y.C., 1986; mem. N.Y. Bldg. Congress, 2002-09; bd. dirs. Regional Plan Assn., 2003-09 Fulbright grantee, 1958. Fellow AIA (Harry B. Rutkins Meml. award for svc. to profession 1983, Whitney M. Young Jr. Citation award 1987); mem. Am. Acad. Arts and Scis., Nat. Orgn. Minority Architects, Phi Beta Kappa. Democrat. Home: New York, NY. Died Feb. 18, 2009.

BONHAM, CLIFFORD VERNON, retired social work educator; b. Paradise, Calif., July 11, 1921; s. Leon C. and Mary M. (Horn) B.; m. Vesta H. Williamson, May 4, 1956; children: William Robert Rohde (stepson), Larry Dean, Tami Marie. Student, San Francisco State U., 1948-49; BA, U. Calif., Berkeley, 1951, MSW, 1953. Lic. clin. social worker, marriage and family counselor, Acad. Cert. Social Workers. Parole agt. Calif. State Dept. Youth Authority, 1953-59, rsch. interviewer, supervising parole agt., 1959-64; field instr. Grad. Sch. Social Work, Calif. State U., Fresno, 1964-67, assoc. prof., 1967-74, prof., 1974-91, prof. emeritus social work, from 1991, field sequence coord., 1971-80. Assoc. coord. field program Grad. Sch. Social Work, 1967-71, coord. field program, Fresno, 1971-80; counselor Suicide Prevention Program, Fresno, Calif., 1964-70; cons. Fresno County Domestic Rels., 1967-70, Fresno County Pub. Defenders' Office, 1986-88; commr. Fresno County Juvenile Justice Commn., 1971-81; mem. state legis. com. on housing felons, 1980; social work cons. various hosps., Fresno, 1971-89; mem. Dept. Youth Authority Youth Justice Task Force, 1986-88. Bd. dirs. Piedmont Pines Assn., Oakland, Calif., 1960-64; mem. Fresno County Emergency Housing Bd., 1970-72; mem. adv. com. on Correctional Edn., 1989-90; mem. Correctional Bd. Edn., 1991-92; mem. Madera County Mental Health Bd., 1991-93. With USN, 1940-46. Mem. NASW, Calif. Probation and Parole Assn. (regional v.p. 1973-74), Soc. Clin. Social Workers, Assn. Advancement of Social Work with Groups. Democrat. Unitarian Universalist. Home: Sunnyvale, Calif. Died Apr. 25, 2009.

BOOTH, GEORGE EDWIN, facilities engineering manager; b. Visalia, Calif., Jan. 4, 1951; s. Carl Eugene and Mary Elizabeth Booth; m. Lisa Ann Booth, Jan. 5, 1986; children: James Joseph, George Gerst, Courtney Marie. AS, Coll. Sequoia, 1979; BS, Calif. Poly., 1982. Facilities engr. Trilogy Sys., Cupertino, Calif., 1982-84; facilities engring. supr. VLSI Tech., San Jose, Calif., 1984-93; facilities engr. mgr. Linear Tech. Corp., Milpitas, Calif., from 1993. Com.

mem. ednl. task force Silicon Valley (Calif.) Mfg. Group, 1997-98. Contbr. articles to tech. jours. Cubmaster, asst. scoutmaster Boy Scouts Am., 1995—; Sgt. U.S. Army, 1971-73. Recipient Cubmaster award, Scouter of Yr. award Boy Scouts Am., 1997. Mem. NRA, Internat. Assn. Scientologists (vol. 1986—, Patron with Honors). Avocations: camping, fishing, mechanics, shooting, scientology. Home: San Jose, Calif. Died Apr. 30, 2008.

BOOTH, WILLIAM BOLAND, JR., retired military officer, retired elementary school educator; b. Belleville, Ill., Mar. 19, 1921; s. William Boland Booth Sr. and Grace Van Eizinga; m. JoAnn Wiest, July 7, 1946; children: Cynthia Ann Booth James, William Bennett. B in Mil. Sci., U. Md., 1961; M in Edn., So. Ill. U., 1974. With USAF, 1939—41, sgt., 1941—43, warrant officer (j.g.), 1943—51, weather officer, meteorologist weather bur. forecast ctr. Washington, 1948—60, chief warrant officer, 1951—66, payroll officer, ret., 1966; tchr. Jr. HS, Mascoutah, Ill., 1968—86. Songwriter: songs Open Up Your Heart and Let Me In, poet: poems An Event or Happening, Life Gets Tedious-Doesn't It?, Survival (Hon. mention, 1990), Fishing or Golf, Take your Pick, 1997, The Candle is Burnt Out, At Least at One End, 1999, Steer Your Own Course, 1998, Affairs of The Heart, 2000, Beauty All Around You, 2000, Babe Didrikson, Zaharias, Female Athlete of the year 6 times, 2002, Leslie Townes Hope, 2003. Decorated Good Conduct Medal, Cluster, Air Force Longivity with 1 Silver Cluster, Legion of Merit, Cold War Recognition, Am. Campaign Medal, Air Force Outstanding Unit award, European Mid. East Ribbon Battle Stars for Egypt-Libya and Tunisia, Air Force Commendation Medal, WWII Victory Medal; named to, Internat. Poetry Hall of Fame, 1998. Mem.: DAV, Internat. Poetry Soc., Grand Lodge Ancient Free Accepted Masons (50 Yr. Pin 1995). Independent. Protestant-Methodist. Avocations: music, dance. Home: North Las Vegas, Nev. Died Apr. 25, 2008.

BOREK, MARY BURNS, retired psychologist; b. Pitts., Sept. 6, 1916; d. Joseph Anthony and Myral (Anderson) Burns; m. Theodore Borek, Mar. 3, 1943; 1 child: Theodore B. AB, West Liberty Coll., 1942; MA, Columbia U., 1953; EdD, Ariz. State U., 1970. Lic. psychologist Ariz. Instr. chemistry West Liberty Coll., W.Va., 1945—48; counselor Phoenix Union HS Dist., 1953—75, psychologist, 1975—82; pvt. practice psychology Phoenix, from 1982. Co-dir. human rels. workshops. Author: Problem Solving, 1977. Mem.: Ariz. Psychol. Assn., Am. Psychol. Assn. United Ch. Of Christ. Died June 13, 2008.

BORK, ALFRED, information and computer science educator; b. Jacksonville, Fla., Sept. 18, 1926; BS, Ga. Inst. Tech., 1947; MS, Brown U., 1950, PhD, 1953. Scholar Dublin Inst. for Advanced Studies, 1952-53; asst. to assoc. to prof. physics U. Alaska, 1953-62; staff physicist Commn. on Coll. Physics, 1963; cons. Harvard Project Physics, Harvard U., 1966-68; prof. physics Reed Coll., 1963-68; vice chair undergrad. studies, physics dept. U. Calif., Irvine, 1973-80, prof. info. and computer sci., from 1968. Mem. internat. adv. bd. Internat. Conf. Series on Computer-Assisted Learning in Post-Secondary Edn. Author: FORTAN for Physics, 1967, Using the IBM 1130, 1968, Programmierund und Benutzung des Computersystems IBM 1130, 1970, Notions About Motion, 1970, 71, Computer Assisted Learning in Physics Education, 1980, Learning with Computers, 1981, Personal Computers for Education, 1985, (in Spanish) 1986, Learning With Personal Computers, 1986; (with A. Arons) Science and Ideas, 1964; editor: Science and Language, 1966, and others; contbg. editor Technol. Horizons in Edn. Jour., AEDS Monitor, Ednl. Computer Mag.; mem. editorial bd. Interactive Learning Internat., Jour. Ednl. Computing Rsch., Teaching Thinking & Problem Solving, Computer Grpahics '84 Daily, Jour. Interactive Instrn. Devel., Jour. Artificial Intelligence in Edn.; chair tech. com. on computers in edn. TCCE Newsletter; fgn. advisor Informatica Educativa; contbr. numerous articles to profl. jours. Rsch. fellow, Harvard U.; faculty fellow NSF, fellow Assn. for the Devel. of Computer Based Instructional Systems, 1986; recipient Millikan award Am. Assn. of Physics Tchrs., Rsch. award AEDS Outstanding Computer Educator, 1985. Home: Irvine, Calif. Died Dec. 18, 2007.

BORLAUG, NORMAN ERNEST, agricultural scientist; b. Cresco, Iowa, Mar. 25, 1914; s. Henry O. and Clara (Vaala) Borlaug; m. Margaret G. Gibson, Sept. 24, 1937 (dec. Mar. 7, 2007); children: Norma Jean, William Gibson. BS in Forestry, U. Minn., Minneapolis, 1937, MS in Plant Pathology, 1940, PhD in Plant Pathology, 1942; ScD (honoris causa), Punjab Agrl. U., India, 1969, Royal Norwegian Agrl. Coll., Norway, 1970, Luther Coll., 1971, Kanpur U., India, 1972, Uttar Pradesh Agrl. U., 1971, Mich. State U., 1971, U. de la Plata, Argentina, 1971, U. Ariz., 1972, U. Fla., 1973, U. Católica de Chile, Chile, 1974, U. Hohenheim Germany 1976, Punjab Agrl. U., Pakistan, 1978, Columbia U., 1980, Ohio State U., 1981, U. Minn., 1982, U. Notre Dame, 1987, Oregon State U., 1988, U. Tulsa, 1991, Washington State U., 1995, Andhra Pradesh Agrl. U., India, 1996, Indian Agrl. Rsch. Inst., 1996, De Montfort U., UK, 1997, Emory U., 1999, U. Philippines, 1999; LHD, Gustavus Adolphus Coll., 1971, Iowa State U., 1992; LLD (hon.), New Mexico State U., 1973; D. of Agr. (hon.), Tufts U., 1982; D. of Agrl. Scis. (hon.), U. Agrl. Scis., Godollo, Hungary, 1980, Tokyo U. Agriculture, 1981, U. Nacional Pedro Henríquez Turena, Dominican Republic, U. Cen. del Estes, Dominican Republic, 1983; D. Honoris Causa, U. Mayor de San Simón, Bolivia, U. de Buenos Aires, 1983, U. de Cordoba, Spain, U. Politécnica de Catalunya, Barcelona, Spain, 1986, Colegio Postgraduados, Montecillo, Mexico, 1990; PhD (hon.), U. degli Studi di Bologna, Italy, 1991, Warsaw Agrl. U., Poland, 1993, Bangladesh Agrl. U., 1998, U. LaSalle-Noroeste, Mex., 1999, U. Politécnica de Madrid, Spain, 2000, U. Américas Puebla, Mex., 2000; D. Honoris Causa, U. Autónoma Nuevo León, 2001; PhD (hon.), U. Autónoma de Chapingo, 2001, Rector U. Dubuque, 1992-93; PhD (hon.), U. Studi de Bologna, Italy, 1991, Warsaw Agrl. U., Poland, 1993; ScD (hon.), Dartmouth Coll., 2005. With U.S. Forest Service, 1935—38; instr. U. Minn., 1941; microbiologist E.I. Du-Pont de Nemours, 1942—44; rsch. scientist in charge wheat improvement Coop. Mexican Agrl. Program, Mexican Ministry Agr. Rockefeller Found., Mexico, 1944—60, assoc. dir. assigned to Inter-Am. Food Crop Program, 1960—63; assoc. dir. CIMMYT, 1964-82; dir. wheat research and prodn. program Internat. Maize and Wheat Improvement Ctr., Mexico City, 1964—79, acting dir., 1981, cons., 1980—2009; disting. prof. internat. agr. dept. soil & crop scis. Texas A&M U., College Station, Tex., 1984—2009. Cons., collaborator nst. Nacional de Investigationes Agricolas, Mexican Ministry Agr, 1960—64; cons. FAO, North Africa and Asia, 1960; ex-officio cons. wheat research and prodn. problems to govts. in Latin Am., Africa, Asia, from 1960; mem. Citizen's Commn. on Sci. Law and Food Supply, 1973; mem. Commn. Critical Choices for Am, 1973, Council Agr. Sci. and Tech., from 1973, Presdl. Commn. on World Hunger U.S.A., 1978—79, Presdl. Coun. Advisers Sci and Tech., 1990—93; dir. Population Crisis Com., 1971—92; asesor especial Fundacion para Estudios de la Poblacion A.C., Mexico, 1971—80; mem. adv. council Renewable Natural Resources Found., 1973; A.D. White Disting. prof.-at-large Cornell U., 1983—85; Disting. prof. Internat. Agr., Dept. Soil & Crop Scis. Tex. A&M U., from 1984; adj. prof. dept. biology Emory U., Atlanta, 1991—92; advisor The Population Inst., U.S.A., 1971—78; bd. trustees Winrock Internat. U.S.A.; life fellow Rockefeller Found., from 1983; sr. cons. CIMMYT, from 1979; hon. vis. prof. U. Minn., 1980; adj. prof. dept. biology Emory U., Atlanta, 1991—92. Recipient Disting. Service awards, Wheat Producers Assns., and state govts. Mexican States of Guanajuato, Queretaro, Sonora, Tlaxcala and Zacatecas, 1955—60, Recognition award, Agrl. Inst. Can., 1966, Instituto Nacional de Tecnologia Agropecuaria de Marcos Juarez, Argentina, 1968, Sci. Service award, El Colegio de Ingenieros Agronomos de Mexico, 1970, Outstanding Achievement award, U. Minn., 1959, Elvin Charles Stakman award, 1961, Disting. Citizen award, Cresco Centennial Com., 1966, Nat. Disting. Service award, Am. Agrl. Editors Assn., 1967, Genetics and Plant Breeding award, Nat. Council Comml. Plant Breeders, 1968, Star of Distinction, Govt. of Pakistan, 1968, citation and street named in honor, Citizens of Sonora and Rotary Club, 1968, Internat. Agronomy award, Am. Soc. Agronomy, 1968, Distinguished Service award, Wheat Farmers of Punjab, Haryana and Himachal Pradesh, 1969, Nobel Peace prize, 1970, Diploma de Merito, El Instituto Tecnologico y de Estudios Superiores de Monterrey, Mexico, 1971, medalla y Diploma de Merito, Antonio Narro Escuela Superior de Agricultura de la U. de Coahuila, Mexico, 1971, Diploma de Merito, Escuela Superior de Agricultura Hermanos Escobar, Mexico, 1973, award for service to agr., Am. Farm Bur. Fedn., 1971, Outstanding Agrl. Achievement award, World Farm Found., 1971, Medal of Merit, Italian Wheat Scientists, 1971, outstanding Achievement award, Minn. Athletic Club, 1971, Service award for outstanding contbn. to alleviation of world hunger, 8th Latin Am. Food Prodn. Conf., 1972, Nat. award for Agrl. Excellence in Sci., Agri-Mktg. Assn., 1982, Disting. Achievement award, Council for Agrl. Scis. and Tech., 1982, inaugural lectr., medal, Dr. S.B. Hendrick's Meml. Lectureship., 1981, Henry G. Bennett Disting. Svc. award, 1984, dedicated in his name, Norman E. Borlaug Centro de Capitación y Formación de Agrs., Santa Cruz, Bolivia, 1983, Borlaug Hall U. Minn., 1985, Borlaug Bldg. Internat. Maize and Wheat Improvement Ctr., 1986, Nat. Medal Sci. in Biol. Sciences, 2004, Congl. Gold medal, 2007, numerous other honors and awards from govts., ednl. instns., citizens groups, other honored lectureships; named Uncle of Paul Bunyan, 1969; named to Hall of Fame, Oreg. State U. Agrl., 1981, Agrl. Nat. Ctr., Bonner Springs, Kans., 1984, Scandinavian-Am., U.S.A., 1986, Nat. Wrestling, 1992. Fellow: Indian Soc. Genetics and Plant Breeding; mem.: NAS, Acad. Nat. Agronomía and Veterinaria Argentina, Chinese Acad. Agrl. Sci., Royal Soc. Eng., Internat. Food Policy Research Inst. (trustee 1976—82), Am. Council on Sci. and Health (trustee from 1978), N.I. Vavilov Acad. Agrl. Scis. Lenin Order (USSR.), Adv. Coun. Renewable Natural Resources Acad. Found. (mem. adv. coun. 1973), Coun. Agrl. Sci. and Tech., Soil Sci. Soc. Am. (hon.), Sociedad de Agronomia do Rio Grande do Sul Brazil (hon.), Royal Agrl. Soc. Eng. (hon.), Royal Soc. Edinburgh (hon.), Hungarian Acad. Sci. (hon.), Indian Nat. Sci. Acad. (hon.), Am. Acad. Arts and Scis. (hon.), Hungarian Acad. Scis. (hon.), Mexican Acad. Scis. (hon.), Am. Assn. Cereal Chemists (hon.; life, Meritorious Service award 1969), Crop Sci. Soc. Am. (hon.), Population Crisis Com., Chinese Acad. Agrl. Scis. (hon. prof. 1994), Sasakawa Africa Assn. (pres. 1986), Academia Nat. de Agronomia y Veterinaria (Argentina), Royal Swedish Acad. Agr. and Forestry (fgn. 1971), India Nat. Sci. Acad., Am. Soc. Agronomy (1st Internat. Svc. award 1960, 1st hon. life), Sigma Xi, Xi Sigma Pi, Alpha Zeta. Home: Mexico City, Mexico. Died Sept. 12, 2009.

BORODKIN, CLARICE, administrative assistant to federal judges; b. Bklyn., Nov. 26, 1924; d. Joseph and Rebecca (Blumenfeld) Haberman; m. Joshua Borodkin Feb. 22, 1948 (dec. Dec., 1968). Student, St. John's U., 1945-48. Sec. to ptnr. Davis, Polk & Wardell, NYC, 1968-73; confidential asst. Justice State Supreme Ct., NYC, 1974-75; sec., adminstrv. asst. U.S. Dist. Judges, NYC, 1975-87. Adj. lectr. NYU, 1974-85; archivist Jewish Archives of Fedn. of Jewish Philantrophies, Milw., 1992—. Reviewer (book) Volkell Legal Terminology, 1978; co-author: (with Douglas Finney) (student work manual) Legal Word Processing, 1984. Mem. Hadassah (group pres. N.Y. 1966-68, Presdl. award 1968, region recording sec. Milw. 1994-97, chapter co-v.p. membership Milw. 1995-97, group pres. Milw. 1995, Woman of Yr. Milw. 1994). Mem. NOW, Nat. Assn. Retired Fed. Employees, Planned Parenthood, U. Wis. Guild for Learning in Retirement. Jewish. Avocations: opera, theater, classical music. Home: Milwaukee, Wis. Died Apr. 22, 2008.

BORYSKO, EMIL, biologist; b. Scranton, Pa., Sept. 24, 1918; s. Damyan and Katherine (Podgorno) B.; m. Gladys Lucille Roberts, May 30, 1955 (div. 1986); children: Katherine Z., Steven D. (twins), Robert A. BA in Biology, Bklyn. Coll., 1940; MA in Biology, George Washington U., 1951; PhD, Johns Hopkins U., Balt., 1955. Fibr technologist Nat. Bur. Stds., Washington, 1947-51; rsch. fellow, instr. Johns Hopkins U., Balt., 1951-56; rsch. assoc. NYU Dental Coll., NYC, 1956-58; prin. rsch. scientist Ethicon, Inc., Bridgewater, N.J., 1958-91, ret., 1991. Recipient Disting. Analytical Chemist award, Johnson & Johnson, 1988, Phil B. Hoffman Rsch. award, 1985; Damien Runyon W. Winchell Cancer Soc. rsch. fellow, 1951-54. Fellow AAAS; mem. Electron Microscopy Soc. Am., N.Y. Acad. Sci., Am. Inst. Biol. Sci., Sigma Xi. Achievements include patents related to surgical sutures, needles and polymers; research in the development of methods for embedding and sectioning tissues for electron microscopy. Home: Bridgewater, NJ. Died Nov. 29, 2007.

BOSTON, HOLLIS BUFORD, JR., retired military officer; b. Athens, Ala., Sept. 29, 1930; s. Hollis Buford Sr. and Opie (Hargrove) B.; m. Nancy Thomas Delbridge, Dec. 27, 1955; children: Elizabeth Lynn Boston Chesnutt, James Warren, John David. BBA, Baylor U., 1958; M Polit. Sci., Auburn U., 1972. Commd. 2d lt. USAF, 1953, advanced through grades to col., 1972, ret., 1975; sr. assoc. Program Control Corp., Van Nuys, Calif., 1977-89. Author: Estate Papers of Jones Boston, 1995. Chmn. planning com. City of Montgomery, Ala., 1983; pres. Capital City Kiwanis Club, Montgomery, 1987. Mem. Natchez Trace Geneal. Soc., Smith County Tenn. Hist. Assn., Sons of the Republic of Tex., First Families Ala., Sigma Alpha Epsilon. Republican. Episcopalian. Avocation: historical research and writing. Home: Montgomery, Ala. Died Mar. 4, 2008.

BOSWELL, FRED C., retired soil science educator, researcher; b. Monterey, Tenn., Aug. 20, 1930; s. Ferdando Cortez and Julia Ann (Speck) B.; m. Marjorie Sue Brown, Sept. 3, 1954; children: Elaine Joy Boswell King, Julia Alma Boswell Merry. BS, Tenn. Tech., 1954; MS, U. Tenn., 1956; PhD, Pa. State U., 1960. Asst. agron U. Tenn., Knoxville, 1955-56; asst. soil chemist Ga. Agrl. Experimental Sta., Experimental, Ga., 1956-57; asst. prof. U. Ga., Athens, 1960-82, prof., head agronomy dept., 1982-89, prof. Griffin, 1989-91, prof. emeritus, from 1991; adj. prof. U. Tenn., from 1993. Contbr. chpts. to numerous books and sci. jours. on agrl. concerns; mem. editorial com. Fertilizer Technology and Use, 1985. Mem. com. State of Ga. Goals for Ga., 1971; chmn. subcom. Griffin Spalding Co., Ga., 1988. With U.S. Army, 1951-53. Fellow Am. Soc. Agronomy, Soil Sci. Soc. Am. (bd. dirs. 1978-80, so. branch pres. 1983-84), Toastmasters (v.p. 1972). Achievements include research related to certain micronutrients nitrification transformation and nitrogen movement and nitrification inhibitors; published/researched in environmental science, emphasis on land treatment waste materials. Home: Cookeville, Tenn. Died Mar. 1, 2008.

BOTHMER, DIETRICH FELIX VON, curator, archaeologist; b. Eisenach, Thuringia, Oct. 26, 1918; arrived in US, 1939, naturalized, 1944; s. Wilhelm Friedrich Franz Carl and Marie Julie Auguste Karoline (Freiin von und zu Egloffstein) von B.; m. Joyce de la Bégassière, May 28, 1966; children: Bernard Nicholas, Maria Elizabeth Villalba. Student, Friedrich Wilhelms U., Berlin, 1937-38, Wadham Coll., Oxford, 1938-39; diploma classical archaeology, Oxford U., 1939; PhD in Classical Archaeology, U. Calif., Berkeley, 1944; DPhil (hon.), U. Trier, 1997. Asst. curator Greek and Roman art Met. Mus. Art, 1946-51, assoc. curator, 1951-59, curator, 1959-73, chmn., 1973-90, Disting. rsch. curator, 1990—2009. Adj. prof. NYU, 1966— Book rev. editor: Am. Jour. Archaeology, 1950-57; assoc. editor, 1970-76; author: Amazons in Greek Art, 1957, Ancient Art from New York Private Collections, 1961, An Inquiry into the Forgery of the Etruscan Terracotta Warriors, 1961, Corpus Vasorum Antiquorum, USA fasc. 12, 1963, Greek Vase Painting: An Introduction, 1972, Corpus Vasorum Antiquorum, USA fasc. 16, 1976, Greek Art of the Aegean Islands, 1979, A Greek and Roman Treasury, 1984, The Amasis Painter and His World, 1985, Greek Vase Painting, 1987, Glories of the Past, Ancient Art from the Shelby White and Leon Levy Collection, 1990, Euphronios, Peintre á Athènes au VI siècle avant Jesus Christ, 1990. Mem. Chancellor's Ct. of Benefactors, Oxford U. With AUS, 1943-45. Decorated Bronze Star, Purple Heart; Rhodes scholar Wadham Coll., 1938-39; Internat. House fellow U. Calif., Berkeley, 1940, Alfred B. Jordan fellow, 1940-41, Univ. fellow, 1941-42; Martin Ryerson fellow U. Chgo., 1942-43; Guggenheim Meml. Found. fellow, 1966, hon. fellow Wadham Coll.; Chevalier Légion d'Honneur, 1997. Mem. Archaeol. Inst. Am. (benefactor), Soc. Promotion Hellenic Studies (hon.), Deutsches Archaeol. Inst., Vereinigung der Freunde Antiker Kunst (Basle, Switzerland), Archaeologische Gesellschaft zu Berlin, Institut de France, Académie des Inscriptions et Belles-Lettres (fgn. assoc.), Piping Rock Club. Home: Oyster Bay, NY. Died Oct. 12, 2009.

BOTTOMS, SAM, actor; b. Santa Barbara, Calif., Oct. 17, 1955; s. James and Elizabeth (Chapman) Bottoms; m. Susan Arnold, Apr. 27, 1980 (div.); children: Clara, Io; m. Laura Condé, Sept. 21, 2002. Actor: (films) The Last Picture Show, 1971, Class of '44, 1973, Zandy's Bride, 1974, The Outlaw Josey Wales, 1976, Apocalypse Now, 1979, Up from the Depths, 1979, Bronco Billy, 1980, Prime Risk, 1985, Gringo mojado, 1986, Hunter's Blood, 1987, Gardens of Stone, 1987, After School, 1989, Ragin' Cajun, 1991, North of Chiang Mai, 1992, Dolly Dearest, 1992, The Trust, 1993, Sugar Hill, 1994, Project Shadowchaser III, 1995, Sticky Fingers, 1997, Snide and Prejudice, 1997, Joseph's Gift, 1997, My Neighbor's Daughter, 1998, The Unsaid, 2001, Shadow Fury, 2001, True Files, 2002, Looking Through Lillian, 2002, Seabiscuit, 2003, Havoc, 2005, Shopgirl, 2005, Winter Passing, 2005, SherryBaby, 2006, Finishing the Game: The Search for a New Bruce Lee, 2007; (TV films) Savages, 1974, Cage Without a Key, 1975, Desperate Lives, 1982, No Earthly Reason, 1984, The Witching of Ben Wagner, 1987, Island Sons, 1987, Zooman, 1995, Mercenary II: Thick & Thin, 1997; (TV mini-series) East of Eden, 1981, Return to Eden, 1983; (TV appearances) Doc Elliot, 1974, Lucas Tanner, 1974, Marcus Welby, M.D., 1976, Greatest Heroes of the Bible, 1978, The Eddie Capra Mysteries, 1978, 21 Jump Street, 1990, Murder, She Wrote, 1989, 1991, The X-Files, 1995, NYPD Blue, 2004; prodr.: (documentaries) Picture This: The Times of Peter Bogdanovich in Archer City, Texas, 1991 Died Dec. 16, 2008.

BOULANGER, LINDA RENÉ, occupational health nurse; b. Manchester, NH, Dec. 23, 1949; d. Aimé W. and Genevieve A. (Tomaszewska) René; m. Leonard J. Boulanger, May 27, 1972; children: Gregory, Nicole, Danielle. Diploma, Elliot Hosp. Sch. Nursing, 1972. Nurse ICU, Valley Regional Hosp., Claremont, N.H., 1972-74, head nurse surg. floor, 1974-81; occupational health nurse Joy Mfg., Claremont, N.H., 1981-84, Sullivan Machinery, Claremont, N.H., 1984-86, Sturm, Ruger & Co., Inc., Newport, N.H., from 1986. Mem. N.H. Assn. Occupational Health Nurses. Home: Claremont, NH. Died Jan. 17, 2008.

BOURET, PIERRE GEORGE, brokerage house executive; b. Feb. 15, 1924; m. Marie Elizabeth O'Halloran; children: Gregory Pierre, Marc Patrick, Colleen Marie. AB, Stanford U., 1948, MBA, 1949. V.p. major accounts, Dictaphone Corp. Divsn. Pitney Bowes, Rye, N.Y., 1952-89; sr. v.p. Whitehall-Parker Securities, San Francisco, from 1995. 1st lt. mil. intelligence USAR, 1943—54. Mem.: Phi Beta Kappa. Home: Alamo, Calif. Died Dec. 16, 2007.

BOVERINI, WALTER JOHN, retired state senator; b. 1925; s. Attilio Boverini and Luisa B. Francia; m. Christine M. Kirvan, 1968; 1 child, Luisa. Mem. house of reps. 9th Essex Dist., Mass., 1971—73; state senate 1st Essex Dist., 1973—94; majority leader, 1985—94; chmn. Redistricting, Com, Joint Com. Post Audit & Oversight & Govt. Rels.; mem. Mass. Commn. Arts & Humanities & Commn. Interstate Coop., Commn. Study Future U. Mass, Edn. Commn. States; head football coach St. Mary's HS, Lynn, Mass., 1950—54, Lynn English HS, 1955—65; dir. Phys. Edn., 1955—70. Mem.: Boy Scouts (exec. coun.), Sons of Italy, Amvets, KofC, Mass. Assn. Legis, Mass. Assn. Phys. Edn (dirs.). Democrat. Catholic. Died Nov. 29, 2008.

BOWEN, GEORGIA L., educational coordinator; b. Berwick, Pa., Apr. 30, 1949; d. George Sylvester and Elizabeth Josephine (Moharter) Hunter; m. Douglas Jon Bowen, Oct. 30, 1971; children: G. Braxton, Zachary T. BS in Bus. Edn., Bloomsburg U., 1971. Bus. tchr. Bethlehem (Pa.) Area Sch. Dist., 1974-81; ednl. coord. Guardian Life Ins. Co., Bethlehem, from 1994. Vol. tng. specialist Aid Assn. for Luths., Appleton, Wis., 1998—. Fin. coord. Morning for Mothers, Nazareth, Pa., 1983. Mem. ASTD. Lutheran. Died Mar. 16, 2008.

BOWEN, WILLIAM RAY, retired biology professor; b. Iowa City, Oct. 15, 1936; m. Jan Bowen. BS in Biology, Grinnell Coll., 1960; MS, PhD, U. Iowa, 1964. Prof. U. Ark., Little Rock, 1975-90; prof. biology, dept. head Jacksonville (Ala.) State U., 1990—2001, prof. emeritus, 2001—09. Home: Maumelle, Ark. Died Jan. 19, 2009.

BOWER, JOHN, retired fluid mechanics engineer, commissioner; b. Somerset, Mass., Sept. 16, 1920; s. Matthew H. and Alice (Winterbom) Bower; m. Marion Louise Cadorette, Aug. 2, 1948; children: John C., Jeffrey J., Douglas J. BS, Brown Univ., Providence, RI, 1938—41. Cert. WPI, Water Works Op. & Mgmt., Worcester, Mass., 1962. Sales & engr. WW Grainger, Chgo., 1949—86; commr. Somerset Indsl. Fin. Authority, from 1980. Commr. Town of Somerset, Somerset, Mass.; chmn. Bd. of Sewer and Water Commissioners, Somerset, Mass. Warrant officer USAAF, 1942—45. Recipient State Award, Mass Consulting Engr./ Mass., 1999, Nat. Award, Nat. Assoc. Cons. Engr./ Seattle, Wash., 1999. Mem.: NY Acad. of Sci., New Eng. Water Works (life mem. for 40 yrs. svc.), Am. Water Works (life mem. for 30 yrs. svc.), RI Shriners Club (Legion of Honor), Pioneer Lodge (Master 1955). Republican. Episcopalian. Avocation: ski patrol. Home: Somerset, Mass. Died Apr. 4, 2008.

BOYD, CARL RITTER, radiologist; b. Paoli, Ind., July 14, 1943; s. Carl McKinley and Rosemary (Ritter) B.; m. Cherylynn Anne Morazewski, July 11, 1970; children: Michael, James. BS in Aeronautical Engring., Purdue U., 1965; MD, Ind. U., 1969. Diplomate Am. Bd. Radiology. Intern Wilford Hall USAF Med. Ctr., San Antonio, 1969-70, resident, 1972-75; staff radiologist Scott USAF Med. Ctr., Scott AFB, Ill., 1975-76; ptnr. Assoc. Radiologists, Inc., Logansport, Ind., from 1976. Served to lt. col. USAF, 1969-76, res. 1976—. Mem. AMA, Am. Coll. Radiology, Radiologic Soc. N. Am., Soc. Nuclear Medicine, Tau Beta Pi. Lodges: Elks. Presbyterian. Home: Culver, Ind. Died Aug. 25, 2008.

BOYD, JOHN ENOS, educational administrator; b. Lebanon, Pa., Apr. 26, 1933; s. John Enos and Anne (Quinn) B.; m. Miriam Elaine Close, Dec. 26, 1953 (div. Feb. 1979); children: Penelope Anne, Candace Marie, Therese Diane, John Enos, Carl Jude; m. Constance D. Novinski, Feb. 23, 1980. BS, Pa. State U., 1955; MEd, Temple U., 1966. Tchr. Kimberton (Pa.) Farms Sch., 1955-57, Springfield Cen. Sch., East Springfield, N.Y., 1957-59; reading specialist Pottstown (Pa.) Sch. Dist., 1959-69; curriculum writer Rsch. for Better Schs., Inc., Phila., 1969-72; reading coord. Owen J. Roberts Sch. Dist., Pottstown, 1972-86; dir. learning ctr. Manor Jr. Coll., Jenkintown, Pa., 1986—95, reading & testing specialist, Office Admission, 1996—2005. Adj. instr. Pa. State U., Malvern; book reviewer Children's Book Rev. Svc., Inc., Bklyn., Kliatt Paperback Books, Newton, Mass.; pvt. tutor, King of Prussia, Pa.; presenter in field. Author conf. proc. in field; mem. editorial adv. bd. Jr. Reading; contbr. articles to profl. jours. Recipient Appreciation award Keystone State Rading Assn., 1986, Manor's teaching Excellence award, 1995 Mem. Tri-County Reading Assn. (co-founder, past pres., Svc. awrd 1990), Internat. Reading Assn., Pa. Assn. Devel. Edn. (bd. dirs. 1992-97), Readibility Spl. Interest Group (treas., Svc. award 1990). Republican. Roman Catholic. Home: Kng Of Prussa, Pa. Died Aug. 15, 2009.

BOYEA, RUTHE W., retired education educator; b. Waltham, Mass., Sept. 22, 1918; d. George Walter and Ethel Maude Wright; m. Douglas Paul Boyea, 1944; children: Ruthe Priscilla Boyea-Boiczyk, Douglas Paul. B Social Sci., Boston U., 1940; MEd, Ctrl. Conn. State U., 1960; cert. in polit. sci., Trinity Coll., 1970. Cert. elem. tchr., Conn. Dir. religious edn., Springfield, Mass., 1945; tchr. New Britain, Conn., 1945-51; prof. edn. Ctrl. Conn. State U., New Britain, 1951-65, dir., founder Women's Ctr. (now Ruthe Boyea Women's Ctr.), 1965-85, prof. emeritus, 1985, lectr. on women's issues; ret. Adj. prof. Tunxis C.C., Mattatuck C.C., 1960-70. Commr. Human Rights and Opportunity, City of New Britain; vol., chair bd. dirs. ARC, New Britain; elected mem. Vets. Commn., City of New Britain, 1999. Lt. (j.g.) USN, 1942-45. Named Women's Educator of Yr., YWCA, 1975, Vol. of Yr. United Way, 1999; recipient Women Helping Women award Soroptimist Internat., 1982, Disting. Alumni award Boston U. Sch. Theology, 2002, Cmty. Svc. award, NAACP. Mem. AAUW (officer), LWV (bd. dirs.), Nat. Women's Mil. Meml. (founder), Nat. Women's Art Mus., Nat. Women's Hall of Fame. Mem. United Ch. of Christ. Died Dec. 7, 2007.

BOYLE, BRADLEY CHARLES, civil engineer; b. St. Paul, Dec. 18, 1959; s. Fosten Annett and Beverly Ann (Rehbein) B.; m. Dana Satenick Ramezzano, Aug. 20, 1983. BSCE, U. Minn., 1984, MBA, 1995. Rsch. asst., environ. engring. dept. U. Minn., Mpls., 1984—85; project mgr. Ramsey Engring. Co., St. Paul, 1985—87, N.W. Airlines, Inc., St. Paul, 1987—91; mktg. dir. M.A. Mortenson Co., Mpls., 1991—93; internat. sales mgr. Continental Hydraulics, Mpls., 1995—2002; v.p. sales and mktg. AgMotion, Inc., St. Paul, 2002—04, JetChoice LLC, from 2004. Mem. ASCE, U. Minn. Alumni Assn., Minn. Surveyors and Engrs. Soc., Chi Epsilon, Beta Gamma Sigma. Republican. Episcopalian. Achievements include patent pertaining to load cell technology. Home: Woodbury, Minn. Died Aug. 21, 2008.

BRACE, WILLIAM, information science educator; b. Cortez, Colo., Aug. 20, 1929; s. James and Katherine (Weaver) B.; m. Phyllis Mayer, Feb. 19, 1957. BA, Brigham Young U., 1951; MA, U. Chgo., 1956; PhD, Case Western Res. U., 1975. Instr. libr. sci. Brigham Young U., Provo, 1954-57; asst. prof., libr. Chgo. Tchrs. Coll., 1957-60; asst. prof. sch. library sci. Fla. State U., Tallahassee, 1960-61, Rosary Coll., River Forest, Ill., 1961-68, assoc. prof., from 1968, assoc. dean Grad. Sch. Library and Info. Sci., from 1992. Asst. prof. Northeastern Ill. U., Chgo. 1963-69. Mem. ALA, Am. Soc. Info. Sci., Rotary (pres. Oak Park, Ill. chpt. 1992-93), University club. Home: Oak Park, Ill. Died Oct. 1, 2008.

BRACHFELD, ROSALIND ROTH, retired clinical social worker; b. Hartford, Conn., Feb. 4, 1930; d. Bernard and Etta (Finklestein) Roth; m. Jonas Brachfeld, Apr. 3, 1955; children: Claude, Renee, Eric. BA, Smith Coll., 1951, MSS, 1953. Diplomate in clin. social work Acad. Cert. Social Workers. Psychiat. social worker Hosp. of Univ. Pa., Phila., 1953-57; psychiat. social worker, supr., clin. instr. Hahnemann Med. Coll., Phila., 1969-74; dir. dept. social svc. Jewish Geriatric Home, Cherry Hill, N.J., 1974-86. Lectr. various ednl. orgns., civic orgns., and self-help groups, Phila., Camden County, N.J., Burlington, N.J., 1974—. Past mem. bd. dirs., sec. Drenk Meml. Guidance Ctr., Mt. Holly, N.J.; founding mem. Family Svc. Burlington County; bd. dirs., v.p., chair Interfaith Caregivers, Morrestown, 1985—, Vis. Nurse Assn., Morrestown, 1989-93. Jewish. Avocations: jogging, hiking, art museums, study foreign languages. Home: Philadelphia, Pa. Died Mar. 4, 2008.

BRACKEN, RICHARD H., osteopath, vascular surgeon; b. Ashland, Ohio, June 5, 1940; s. Stanley and Elizabeth Katherine (Shag) B.; m. Beverly Ann Walker, Dec. 19, 1965 (div. Feb. 1981); children: Christopher, Kathleen, Todd; m. Sheila Ann Moloney, Sept. 9, 1983. BS, Kent State U., 1962; DO, Kirksville Coll. Osteo. Medicine, Mo., 1968. Intern Doctor's Hosp., Columbus, Ohio, 1968-69, resident in surgery, 1969-73; practice medicine specializing in vascular surgery Columbus, from 1973. Dir. resident program Doctor's Hosp., 1980-84, chmn. dept. surgery, 1982-84, pres. staff, 1987—. Fellow Am. Coll. Osteo. Surgeons; mem. Am. Osteo. Assn., Ohio Osteo. Assn. Clubs: Worthington Hills Country (Worthington, Ohio). Republican. Lutheran. Avocation: surgery. Home: Powell, Ohio. Died Mar. 8, 2008.

BRADEN, TOM (THOMAS WARDELL BRADEN II), news correspondent; b. Greene, Iowa, Feb. 22, 1917; s. Thomas Wardell and Louise (Garl) Braden; m. Joan E. Ridley, Dec. 18, 1948 (dec. 1999); children: David, Mary, Joan, Susan, Nancy, Elizabeth, Thomas Wardell III(dec.), Nicholas. BA, Dartmouth Coll., 1940, MA, 1964; LittD, Franklin Coll. Ind., 1979. Newspaperman, instr. English Dartmouth, 1946, asst. to pres. and asst. prof., 1947—48; exec. sec. Mus. Modern Art, NYC, 1949; dir. Am. Com. on United Europe, 1950; editor, pub. Blade Tribune, Oceanside, Calif., 1954—68; columnist Los Angeles Times Syndicate, 1968—86; commentator CNN, CBS, NBC, 1978—89; creator, host Crossfire, 1982—91. Co-author (with Stewart Alsop): Sub Rosa: the OSS and American Espionage, 1946; author: Eight is Enough, 1975. Mem. Calif. Bd. Edn., 1959—67; past pres. Trustee Calif. State Coll., 1961—64, Dartmouth, 1964—74, Carnegie Endowment, 1970—82. With King's Royal Rifle Corps Brit. Army, 1941—44, Africa and Italy, trans. to inf. AUS, 1944, served as a parachutist office of Strategic Svc. Died Apr. 3, 2009.

BRADFORD, LORENE LEWIS, retired secondary school educator; b. Eva, Ala., Feb. 23, 1925; d. William Thomas and Susie Anna (Oden) Lewis; m. A. B. Bradford, June 22, 1952; children: Susan, Michael. BS, U. North Ala., 1949; MS, U. Ala., 1967. Cert. tchr. Ala. Bus. edn. tchr. Falkville (Ala.) HS, 1945-52, Hanceville (Ala.) HS, 1952-54, Kate Duncan Smith DAR HS, Grant, Ala., 1963-96; mem. treas. office U. North Ala., Florence, 1954-55; city engr. Macon County Ct. House, Decatur, Ill., 1955-57; ret., 1996. Rec. sec. Marshall County Dem. Club, 1991—93; Sunday sch. tchr. ladies adult class 1st Bapt. Ch., Grant, 1967—96. Named Advisor of the Yr., Ala. Future Bus. Leaders Am., Inc., 1994. Mem.: NEA, Marshall County Ret. Tchrs. Assn. (pres. 2000—02), Marshall County Vocat. Assn., Ala. Bus. Edn. Assn. (pres. 1986—87), Ala. Vocat. Assn., Ala. Edn. Assn., Am. Vocat. Assn., Nat. Bus. Edn. Assn., Delta Kappa Gamma (pres. Alpha Mu chpt. 1974—76, v.p. Alpha Mu chpt. 2000—02). Democrat. Avocations: travel, reading, gardening, needlecrafts. Home: Grant, Ala. Died Jan. 2, 2008.

BRADSHAW, DENNIS ERIC, philosophy educator; b. Estherville, Iowa, Apr. 5, 1960; s. Ivan Earl and Annie Sarah Bradshaw. BA, Mankato State U., 1982; PhD, U. Iowa, 1988. Vis. asst. prof. Memphis State U., 1988-91, U. Ky., Lexington, 1991-92; asst. prof. U. Tex., Arlington, from 1992. Asst. editor So. Jour. of Philosophy, 1988-91; contbr. articles to profl. jours. Grad. fellow U. Iowa, 1983-84. Mem. Am. Philos. Assn., Cen. States Philos. Assn., So. Soc. Philosophy and Psychology, Phi Kappa Phi. Home: Arlington, Tex. Died Apr. 22, 2008.

BRADY, ALICE M., critical care and surgical nurse; b. Sandusky, Ohio, Dec. 1, 1943; d. William and Ethel (Obergefell) Chamberlain; m. Patrick W. Brady, Oct. 28, 1967; children: Lisa, Shana. Diploma, Mercy Hosp. Sch. Nursing, Toledo, 1964. RN, Ga., Calif., Fla.; cert. nurse adminstr. Shift relief supr. Phoebe Putney Meml. Hosp., Albany, Ga., Clairmont Community Hosp., San Diego; relief supr. Fla. Keys Meml. Hosp., Key West, clin. nurse leader operating room. Mem. Assn. Operating Room Nurses, Fla. Nurses Assn. Home: Key West, Fla. Died Mar. 7, 2008.

BRADY, GEORGE MOORE, real estate company executive; b. Balt., Aug. 6, 1922; s. George Moore and Ellen Latimer (Atkinson) Brady; m. Maria Nomita von Barby, Dec. 3, 1971; 1 stepchild, William L. Amoroso III;children from previous marriage: Elizabeth Grant Brady Andrews, Frances Relyea Brady Siegler, Ellen Atkinson, George Moore III, Madeleine Vaughn Brady Cohen, Richard Grant. BA, Johns Hopkins U, 1947; JD, U. Md., 1949. Sr. v.p. The Rouse Co., Columbia, Md., 1950—70; chmn. bd. Rouse-Wates, Columbia, 1970—72; pres., chmn. bd. Nat. Corp. for Housing Partnerships, Washington, 1972—88, ret., 1988. Bd. dirs. The Rouse Co., First Am. Bank, NA, Washington, Enterprise Social Investment Corp. Former chair Ptrns. for Liveable Cmtys.; mem. exec. com Mem. Md. State Planning Commn., Md. Adv. Commn. on Industrialized Bldg. and

Mobile Homes, 1989—95; exec. com. Nat. Housing Conf., life bd. dirs.; bd. overseers Corcoran Sch. Art; bd. dirs Jubilee Enterprise Greater Washington, Washington Area Housing Partnership. With U.S. Army US Army, POW. Decorated Purple Heart; named Man of Yr. Nat. Housing Conf., 1986. Mem.: Sovereign Mil. Order of Malta So. Assn., Chevy Chase Club (Md.)., Met. Club (Washington). Home: Bethesda, Md. Died Aug. 10, 2009.

BRADY, JAMES WINSTON, commentator, writer, editor; b. NYC, Nov. 15, 1928; s. James Thomas and Marguerite Claire (Winston) B.; m. Florence Kelly, Apr. 12, 1958; children: Fiona, Susan. BA, Manhattan Coll., 1950. Pub. Women's Wear Daily, NYC, 1964-71; editor, pub. Harper's Bazaar, NYC, 1971-72; editor N.Y. Mag., NYC, 1977; syndicated columnist N.Y. Post, NYC, 1980-83; news commentator WCBS-TV, NYC, 1981-87; editor-at-large Advt. Age, NYC, 1977—2005; weekly columnist Parade mag., 1986—2009, Forbes.com, 2006. Author: Superchic, 1974, Paris One, 1976, Nielsen's Children, 1978, The Press Lord, 1981, Holy Wars, 1983, Designs, 1986, The Coldest War, 1990, Fashion Show, 1992, The House That Ate the Hamptons, 2000, Warning of War: A Novel of the North China Marines, 2002, The Marines of Autumn: A Novel of the Korean War, 2000, The Marine: A Novel of War from Guadalcanal to Korea, 2003, The Scariest Place in the World: A Marine Returns to North Korea, 2005 Served to 1st lt. USMC, 1951-52. Recipient Emmy award N.Y. TV Acad., 1975 Mem.: University (N.Y.C.). Democrat. Roman Catholic. Home: East Hampton, NY. Died Jan. 26, 2009.

BRAND, MALCOLM LEIGH, lawyer; b. Inglewood, Calif., Mar. 5, 1935; s. Robert L. and Jeannette E. (Schureman) B.; m. Myra Jean Friesen, Sept. 19, 1958; children: Martin L., Janice E. BA in Econs., Willamette U., 1957, JD, 1964. Bar: Oreg. 1964. Atty. examiner Salem (Oreg.) Title Co., 1964-68; asst. city atty. City of Salem (Oreg.), 1968-69; ptnr. Rhoten, Rhoten et al, Salem, 1969-84; sole practice Salem, from 1984. Served with USAF, 1960-61. Mem. ABA, Oreg. Bar Assn., Marion County Bar Assn. (pres. 1976), Assn. Trial Lawyers Am., Oreg. Trial Lawyers Assn., Oreg. Assn. Def. Counsel. Republican. Presbyterian. Avocations: woodworking, golf, tennis. Home: Salem, Oreg. Died Apr. 9, 2008.

BRAND, MYLES, sports association and former academic administrator; b. NYC, May 17, 1942; s. Irving Philip and Shirley (Berger) B.; m. Wendy Hoffman (div. 1976); 1 child: Joshua; m. Margaret Zeglin, 1978. BS in Philosophy, Rensselaer Poly. Inst., Troy, NY, 1964; PhD, U. Rochester, 1967; PhD (hon.), Rensselaer Poly. Inst., Troy, NY, 1991. Asst. prof. philos. U. Pitts., 1967—72; assoc. prof. to prof., dept. chmn. U. Ill., Chgo., 1972—81; prof., dept. head U. Ariz., Tucson, 1981—83, dir. cognitive sci. prog., 1982—85, dean social & behavioral scis. Tucson, 1983—86; provost, v.p. acad. affairs Ohio State U., Columbus, 1986—89; pres. U. Oreg., Eugene, 1989—94, Ind. U., Bloomington, 1994—2002, NCAA (Nat. Collegiate Athletic Assn.), Indpls., 2003—09. Author: Intending and Acting, 1984; editor: The Nature of Human Action, 1970, The Nature of Causation, 1976, Action Theory, 1976. Bd. dirs. Ariz. Humanities Coun., 1984-85, Am. Coun. Edn., Washington, 1992-97. Named one of Most Influential People in the World of Sports, Bus. Week, 2007, 2008. Mem. Clarion Hosps. Assn. of Am. Phi, Assn. Am. Univs. (pres. 1999). Home: Indianapolis, Ind. Died Sept. 16, 2009.

BRANDAU, EUGENE CLINTON, real estate executive; b. Balt., Sept. 20, 1934; s. John Raymond and Elizabeth (Cassidy) B.; m. Bertha A. Densmore, Nov. 1955 (div. 1975); children: Daniel Eugene, Nancy Carol, Susan Elizabeth. AS, Southwestern Coll., Chula Vista, Calif., 1966; BA, San Diego State Coll., 1969; MBA, Nat. U., San Diego, 1977; PhD, Columbia Pacific U., 1985; LLB (hon.), La Salle Ext. U., Chgo., 1975. Commd. ensign USCGR, 1961, advanced through grades to lt. comdr., 1988; claims mgr. Century Nat. Ins., San Diego; port capt., mgr. U. So. Calif., LA; ships mgr. U.S. Mcht. Marine, Oakland, Calif.; corp. pres. Bano Corp., Reno, from 1980. Instr. Chapman Coll Acad. Ctr., Reno, Nev., 1989. Author ADP and the Administrator, 1969, Corporate Tax Advantages, 1985. With USCGR. Recipient USCG Achievement Medal for Outstanding and Sustained Leadership and Tng., 1981, Disting. Toastmaster award, 1989. Mem. Res. Officers Assn., Toastmasters (Internat. Speakers Bur., pres., dist. treas., Outstanding Club Pres. award 1987), Masons. Avocation: calligraphy. Home: Reno, Nev. Died Dec. 2, 2007.

BRANDSMA, JEFFREY MELVIN, psychiatry educator; b. Chgo., Dec. 14, 1943; m. Anne Fortiun, June 25, 1963; children: Michael, Jamie, Anneke. BA magna cum laude in Psychology, Cen. Coll., Pella, Iowa, 1965; MS, Pa. State U., 1967, PhD, 1971. Lic. psychologist, Ky., Ga. Intern Mendota State Hosp., Madison, Wis., 1969-70; instr. psychiatry U. Ky. Med. Coll., Lexington, 1970-72, asst. prof. psychiatry and psychology, 1972-75, assoc. prof., 1975-81; prof. psychology, dir. psychology residency tng. program Med. Coll. Ga., Augusta, from 1981; prof. social work U. Ga., Athens, from 1987; assoc. chmn. dept. psychiatry and health behavior Med. Coll. Ga., Augusta, 1989-90, interim chmn. dept., 1990-91; assoc. fellow Inst. for Advanced Study in Rational Psychotherapy, NYC, 1974. Cons. to several VA hosps. and med. facilities including Eisenhower Army Med. Ctr., Ft. Gordon, Ga.; organizer workshops in field; mem. numerous coms. and subcoms., faculty chmn. Med. Coll. Ga., 1993 (Dist. Faculty award 1994); mem. Ga. State Bd. Examiners of Psychologists, Atlanta, 1986—, v.p., 1987, pres., 1988-89; author, co-adminstr. Vietnam Era Readjustment Counseling Program, VA Med. Ctr., Augusta, 1986—; examiner Ky. Bd. Psychology, Frankfurt, 1978-81; speaker in field. Referee, contbr. articles and revs. to profl. jours.; assoc. editor: The Ga. Psychologist Jour., 1985-91. Bd. dirs. 1st Presbyn. Day Care Ctr., Lexington, Ky., 1973-75; mem. Collegium Musicum, Lexington, 1973-76. Nat. Inst. Alcohol and Alcohol Abuse grantee U. Ky. Sch. Medicine, 1972-77; recipient Roy M. Dorcas award Soc. Clin. and Exptl. Hypnosis, 1972. Fellow APA, Ga. Psychol. Assn., Am. Assn. State and Provincial Psychology Bds.; mem. Ky. Psychol. Assn. (parliamentarian, profl. and pub. affairs com. 1979-81), Internat. Soc. Study of Multiple Personality (charter, steering com. 1983-86, treas. 1984-86, rep.-at-large 1987-88). Home: Trenton, SC. Died Feb. 19, 2008.

BRANDT, ELSA LUND ERICKSON, music educator; b. Bklyn., Oct. 3, 1932; d. Ernst Ansgar Erickson and Astrid Osestad; m. Carl David Brandt, Apr. 25, 1964; children: Karen, Erik. BMus, Manhattan Sch. Music, NYC, 1953; MMus, Manhattan Sch. Music, 1963; BMusE, Hartt Coll. Music, Hartford, Conn., 1957. Violinist Hartford Symphony Orch., 1954—57; instrumental instr. pub. schs., New Rochelle, NY, 1958—60; violinist New Orleans Symphony Orch., 1960—61; violin tchr., prep. dept. Manhattan Sch. Music, NYC, 1961—63; freelance musician Washington, 1967—89; asst. prof. music Howard U., Washington, 1968—90; pvt. studio Silver Spring, Md., from 1985. Founder Maggini String Quartet, Silver Spring; past adjudicator string festivals Md. State Tchrs. Assn.; tape audition com. Johansen Internat. String Competition, 1997, 2000, 03; v.p. Norwegian Soc. Washington. Performer: (violin solo recital) Carnegie Recital Hall, 1966. Mem.: Friday Morning Music Club (soloist, violin and viola from 1967), Am. String Tchrs. Assn. (curriculum com. Am. String Tchrs. Assn. Md.-DC chpt., pres. Md. DC chpt., Outstanding Tchr. of Yr. Am. String Tchrs. Assn. Md.-DC chpt. 2000), Coll. Music Soc. (life), Photographic Soc. Am. Avocation: photography. Died Jan. 15, 2009.

BRANDT, FREDERICK ROBERT, art curator; b. Paterson, NJ, June 7, 1936; s. Carl Louis and Fredericka Mary Brandt; m. Carol Johnson, Sept. 7, 1962; children: Frederick R. Jr., Karen Lynn. BA, Pa. State U., 1960, MA, 1963. Assoc. curator Va. Mus. Fine Arts, Richmond, 1976-79; curator Sydney and Frances Lewis Coll., Richmond, from 1973; curator 20th century art Va. Mus. Fine Arts, Richmond, from 1983. Bd. dirs. fine arts adv. com. Longwood Coll., Farmville, Va.; lectr. in field. Author: Late 19th and Early 20th Century Decorative Arts, 1985, German Expressionist Art, 1987, Designed to Sell: American Turn-of-the-Century Posters, 1994.; mem. editorial bd. advs. Bard Grad. Ctr. for Studies in Decorative Arts, 1992—; contbr. articles to profl. jours. Bd. dirs. Monument Ave. Commn., City of Richmond, 1993—. Recipient Disting. Alumni award Pa. State U., 1989. Avocations: collecting american arts and crafts, 20th century design. Home: Richmond, Va. Died Dec. 12, 2007.

BRANN, EDWARD R(OMMEL), editor; b. Rostock, Germany, May 20, 1920; came to U.S., 1938, naturalized, 1966; s. Guenther O.R. and Lilli (Appel) B.; m. Helen Louise Sweet, Dec. 9, 1948; children: Johannes Weidler, Paul George. BA, Berea Coll., 1945; MA, U. Chgo., 1946; postgrad., U. Wis., 1948-56. Asst. membership sec. ctrl. YMCA, Chgo., 1946-48; asst. editor Credit Union Mag., Madison, Wis., 1955-65; dir. hist. projects, asst. dir. publs. CUNA Internat., Inc., Madison, 1965-70, staff historian, 1958-65; asst. dir. publs. Credit Union Nat. Assn., Inc., Madison, 1970-72, 83-84, asst. dir. comm., 1973-83; sr. editor Credit Union mag., 1973-84; coord. Innovative Ideas Ctr., 1980-84. Contbg. editor Credit Union Exec. mag., 1982-84; dir. hist. projects World Coun. of Credit Unions, Inc., 1970-79, dir. European rels., 1972-83; vol. cons. ARC, Madison, Wis. Contbr. articles to profl. jours. Active ARC, various coms. Dane County chpt., vol. cons., 1984-96, vol. cons. Badger chpt., 1997-2002. Recipient Christo et Ecclesiae award Concordia Coll., Milw., 1968, Disting. Alumnus award Berea Coll., 1977, Risser award Dane County chpt. ARC, 1983; named Ky. col. Mem. NEA, Am. Hist. Assn. Lutheran. Died July 28, 2006.

BRANNIGAN, WILLIAM ANTHONY, retired public affairs officer; b. Mineola, NY, Jan. 12, 1936; s. James William and Viola Agnes (Perkins) b.; m. Rosalind Beth Prophet, Feb. 12, 1972 (dec. 2005); children: Beth Marie, Brigid Ann. BA, Tufts U., 1957. Reporter/trainee N.Y. World Telegram & Sun, 1962-63; reporter UPI Newsfilm, NYC, 1963-65; newswriter ABC News, NYC, 1965-66, corr. worldwide, 1966-73, bur. chief, corr., 1973-78; press rels. officer Bank of America Corp., San Francisco, 1978-82; sr. pub. info. officer The World Bank, Washington, 1982—97. Served to lt. USNR, 1957-62, PTO. Coun. Fgn. Rels. fellow, 1969-70. Mem. Soc. Profl. Journalists, Overseas Press Club. Home: Arlington, Va. Died May 20, 2009.

BRANSON, EUGENE HALE, retailer; b. Tecumseh, Okla., Oct. 8, 1934; s. Ferron Van and Emma Amanda (Rader) B.; m. Margaret Hooley (div. 1963); children: Robert Eugene, Reesa Ann Branson Heilaman; m. Judith L. Fuxa. Grad. high sch., Okla. Mgr. Safeway Store, Shawnee, 1953-56, 58-63, 64-76, Goodyear Foods, Norman, Okla., 1963-64, Pratt Foods, Shawnee, from 1976. Served with U.S. Army, 1956-58. Democrat. Baptist. Avocation: restoration of old automobiles. Home: Tecumseh, Okla. Died Feb. 23, 2008.

BRANTON, LEROY J., chemical company manager; b. Wake County, NC, Dec. 9, 1935; s. Dwight A. and Pauline (Carpenter) B.; m. Marjorie C. Stephens, Dec. 25, 1958; children: Angela D., Belinda C., Julie A. Cert. firefighter, safety profl. Enlisted USAF, 1954, advanced through rank to sr. master sgt., 1972, retired, 1975; marine terminal mgr. UNOCAL Chems., Wilmington, N.C., 1975-76, regional supply mgr. Atlanta, from 1976. Home: Neptune Beach, Fla. Died Mar. 30, 2008.

BRATTON, WILLIAM EDWARD, electronics executive, management consultant; b. Dallas, Oct. 25, 1919; s. William E. and Edna (Walker) B.; m. Betty Thume, May 30, 1942; children: Dale, Janet, Donna. AB in Econs., Stanford U., 1940; MBA, Harvard U., 1945. From v.p. to pres. Librascope, Glendale, Calif., 1947-63; v.p., gen. mgr. Ampex, Culver City, Calif., 1963-66; pres. Guidance Tech., Santa Monica, Calif., 1967-68; v.p. electronics div. Gen. Dynamics, San Diego, 1969-72; pres. Theta Cable T.V., Santa Monica, 1974-82; pres., chief exec. officer Stagecoach Properties, Salado, Tex., 1959-99, ret., 1999. Served to lt. (j.g.) USNR, 1944-46. Mem.: El Niguel Country (Laguna, Calif.) (pres. 1978-79). Republican. Episcopalian. Avocations: golf, skindiving. Home: Monarch Beach, Calif. Died Jan. 6, 2008.

BRAULT, JAMES WILLIAM, physicist; b. New London, Wis., Feb. 10, 1932; s. Lucian Joseph and Alvina Lucy (Boville) B.; m. Margueritte Elaine Bryan, June 29, 1952 (div. May 1986); children: Stephen Michael, Lisa Lynn, Jennifer Elaine; m. Lynda Margaret Harris Faires, July 5, 1992. BS in Physics, U. Wis., 1953; student, Cornell U., 1953-55; PhD in Physics, Princeton U., 1962. Research staff member project Matterhorn Princeton U., NJ, 1955-57, instr. NJ, 1961-64; asst. physicist Kitt Peak Nat. Obs., Tucson, 1964-68, assoc. physicist, 1969-70; physicist Nat. Solar Obs., Tucson, 1971-94; rsch. assoc. U. Colo., Boulder, Colo., from 1994. Contbr. articles to profl. jours. Recipient Alexander von Humboldt award (Rep. of Germany), 1986-87. Fellow Optical Soc. Am.; mem. Am. Phys. Soc., Am. Geophysical Union. Democrat. Died Nov. 1, 2008.

BREAK, GEORGE FARRINGTON, economics professor; b. London, Ont., Can., June 10, 1920; came to U.S., 1945, naturalized, 1951; s. Thomas Howard and Florence (Farrington) B.; m. Helen Dean Schnacke, July 31, 1948. B. Commerce, U. Toronto, 1942; PhD, U. Calif., Berkeley, 1951; Litt.D. (hon.), Hamilton Coll., 1974. Instr. Pomona Coll., Claremont, Calif., 1949-51; mem. faculty U. Calif., Berkeley, 1951-90, prof. economics, 1963-90, chmn. economics dept., 1969-73, prof. emeritus, 1990—2009. Mem. Gov. Deukmejian's Tax Reform Adv. Commn., 1984-85. Author: Intergovernmental Fiscal Relations in the United States, 1967, The Economic Impact of Federal Loan Insurance, 1961, (with E.R. Rolph) Public Finance, 1961, Federal Lending and Economic Stability, 1965, Agenda for Local Tax Reform, 1970, (with A.S. Blinder, R.M. Solow, P.O. Steiner, Dick Netzer) The Economics of Public Finance, 1974, (with J.A. Pechman) Federal Tax Reform: The Impossible Dream?, 1975, Financing Government in a Federal System, 1980; contbg. author: The Promise of Tax Reform, 1985, Forging New Relationships Among Business, Labor and Government, 1986, Proposition 13: A Ten-Year Retrospective, 1991, The Jamaican Tax Reform, 1991. Served with RCAF, 1942-45. Home: Berkeley, Calif. Died Mar. 13, 2009.

BREGEN, LOUIS, music professional; b. Nov. 9, 1915; Grad. high sch., Phila. Free-lance writer, from 1956; vocalist, mgr. Wilkinsen Dance Band, Northridge, from 11979; prodr. Cafe Rosse Cabaret, Northridge, Calif., from 1992. Sec., treas. Club Comedy (formerly Hollywood Comedy Club), 1985—. Author: Grasshopper's Journey, Golden Legacy. Home: Northridge, Calif. Died May 2, 2008.

BRENNAN, JOSEPH THOMAS, retired auto parts distribution company executive; b. Shamokin, Pa., Mar. 30, 1931; s. Edward William and Julia E. (Wychulis) B.; m. Margaret C. Brennan, Sept. 1953; children: Margaret Kathleen, Robert Joseph, Matthew Edward. BS in Econs., U. Pa., Phila., 1951. Commd. 2d lt. USAF, 1952, advanced through grades to lt. col., 1969; fighter pilot, flight commdr. various bases, 1958-66; chief Tactical Air Control Ctr., Osan Air Base, Korea, 1969-70; exec. officer exec. office, Dover, Del., 1966-69, Loring, Maine, 1970-72; ret., 1972; sr. v.p. Quaker City Motor Parts, Middletown, Del., 1972-97; ret., 1997. Recipient Meritorious Achievement award DAV, 1975. Died Dec. 20, 2007.

BREUER, WERNER ALFRED, retired plastics company executive; b. Sinn, Hessia, Germany, Jan. 30, 1930; came to U.S., 1959; s. Christian and Hedwig (Cunz) B.; m. Gertrud Ackermann, June 21, 1950 (dec. 1998); children: Patricia, Julia, Eva-Maria. LLB, La Salle Ext. U., 1970; BS in Human Rels. and Orgnl. Behavior, U. San Francisco, 1983; MS in Bus. Mgmt., U. La Verne, 1985, DPA, 1988. Lab. supr. Dayco Corp. (Am. latex divsn.), Hawthorne, Calif., 1959-65; tech. ops. mgr. Olin Corp., Stamford and New Haven, Conn., 1965-69; gen. mgr., exec. v.p. Expanded Rubber and Plastics Corp., Gardena, Calif., 1969-96; ret., 1996; gen. mgr. Schlobohm Co. Inc., Dominguez Hills, Calif., 1989-96; ret. Cons. human resources Stabond Corp., Gardena, 1988-95. Author/composer various recordings, 1970s; contbr. articles to jours. Founder Worlds Peace and Diplomacy Forum, Cambridge, England; founding mem. Nat. Campaign for Tolerance in Am. Recipient Portfolio award, USF, Calif., 1984, Lifetime Achievement award,

IBC, 2001, Am. Medal of Honor award, 2002. Mem. ASTM, ASCAP, Am. Soc. for Metals, Soc. for Plastics Engrs., N.Y. Acad. Scis., Nat. Space Soc., Planetary Soc., U. La Verne Alumni Assn. Republican. Achievements include pioneering use of plastics especcially polyurethanes in defence missiles and space and communication aviation industry; defense projects from DEW Line N.A. radar to stealth bomber, B-2 project. Home: Longmont, Colo. Died Apr. 30, 2008.

BREUNIG, ROBERT HENRY, foundation executive; b. Phila., May 12, 1926; s. Robert Henry and Gertrude Florence (Burke) B.; m. Ruth Carolyn Cole, Aug. 30, 1947; children: Lynn Carol, Mark Robert, Christopher John, Eric Martin. BA, Ind. U., 1950; MA, Goddard Coll., 1979; PhD, Union Inst., 1981. Dir. pub. affairs Calif. State U., Long Beach, 1974-85; co-founder, exec. dir. Found. for the 21st Century, San Diego, 1985-87; sec. Found. for Pvt. Sector, San Diego, from 1987; dep. chmn. Sammis Co., San Diego, 1987-90. Cons. Pres.'s Coun. on Phys. Fitness and Sports, 985, Am. for the Reagan Agenda, 1985-87; U.S. exec. dir. Pacific Intercultural Exch.-Japan, World Intercultural Network. With U.S. Army, 1943-46. Decorated Bronze star, Belgian Fourragere, Presdl. Citation. Episcopalian. Died Dec. 30, 2007.

BREW, RICHARD DOUGLAS, lawyer, consultant; b. LA, Jan. 1, 1947; s. Albert Kaylor and Elizabeth Jane (Warfel) B.; m. Cathleen Ellen Coyle, Sept. 8, 1973; children: Francoise Sandahl Elizabeth Coyle. BA, U. Calif., 1968; JD, Loyola U., 1971; MBA, Pepperdine U., 1977; LLM, Cambridge U., 1979. Bar: Calif., D.C., U.S. Dist. Ct. Calif., U.S. Dist. Ct. D.C., U.S. Ct. Appeals (9th and D.C. cirs.), U.S. Supreme Ct. Ptnr. Rose, Klein & Marias, LA, 1972-77; practitioner Europe, NY, Calif., 1978-82; owner Gianelli Brew, Modesto, Calif., 1982-94, Richard Douglas Brew, PLC, Modesto, from 1994. Bd. dirs., officer Les Etoiles Group, L.A., 1972-94; cons. Calif. Bus. Law Practitioner; lectr. in bus. law Troy State U., 1979. Pro bono svcs. for numerous organizations. Recipient Cert. Appreciation Stanislaus County, 1995. Republican. Presbyterian. Home: Modesto, Calif. Died Aug. 28, 2007.

BREWER, LEROY EARL, physicist; b. Hagerstown, Md., June 1, 1936; s. LeRoy Earl and Odessa Marie (Green) B.; m. Sue Strother Yancey, Dec. 29, 1956; children: Jennifer Olivia. BS, U. Fla., 1960; MS, U. Tenn., 1965; PhD, U. Brussels, 1975. Research physicist ARO, Inc., Tullahoma, Tenn., 1960-66; staff physicist GE, Valley Forge, Pa., 1966-69; sr. physicist ARO, Inc., Tullahoma, 1969-81; mgr., exec. scientist Calspan Corp., Tullahoma, 1981-85; sr. infrared phenomenologist GE, Valley Forge, from 1985. Adj. faculty mem. Motlow Community Coll., Tullahoma, 1976-80. Contbr. articles to profl. jours. Mem. Charlestown Civic Assn., Chester County, Pa., 1986—. Fellow AIAA (assoc.), mem. Am. Physical Soc., Sigma Pi Sigma, Sigma Xi. Republican. Methodist. Avocations: sailing, reading, skiing, model railroading. Died May 20, 2008.

BRIDGES, MARY JO, music educator; b. Russellville, Ark., Apr. 16, 1946; d. Ernest Christopher Graves and Mary Glynn Overbey-Graves; m. David Merrill Bridges, Dec. 22, 1967; children: David Christopher, Jolyn. BA in Music Edn., Northeastern State Coll., Tahlequah, Okla., 1968. Tchr. music and drama Andrew Jackson Elem. Sch., Tulsa, Okla., 1968—71; tchr. music, choir accompanist Tulsa Jr. Coll., Okla., 1980—83; tchr. music, drama, Spanish, Robert E. Peary Elem. Sch., Tulsa, Okla., from 1990. Ch. choir accompanist Ch. of the Shepherd United Meth.Ch., Tulsa, Okla., from 1977. Recipient Tulsa Tchr. award, Tulsa Pub. Schs., 2006. Avocations: camping, playing the piano, crossword puzzles. Died July 29, 2008.

BRIDGES, WILLIAM LLOYD, radiologist; b. Knightstown, Ind., Aug. 31, 1921; MD, Ind. U., 1944. Diplomate Am. Bd. Radiology. Intern Meml. Hosp., South Bend, Ind., 1945; pvt. practice Markleville, Ind., 1947-50; resident in Radiology Ind. U. Med. Ctr., Indpls., 1950-53; mem. staff Parkview Hosp., Ft. Wayne, Ind., 1953-95. Fellow Am. Col. Radiology; mem. AMA, Radiology Soc. North Am. Home: Fort Wayne, Ind. Died Oct. 28, 2007.

BRIDWELL, NAIDYNE BROWN, classical languages educator; b. Owensboro, Ky., Jan. 6, 1924; d. Edward Mitchell and Nina (Nelson) Brown; m. Wilburn Fowler Bridwell, June 21, 1958; children: Marion Mitchell, Laura Naidyne. BA summa cum laude, Georgetown Coll., Ky., 1945; MA, U. Mich., 1950; postgrad. Am. Sch. Classical Studies, Athens, Greece, 1970, Northwestern U., 1972-75. Cert. all grade supr., Ill. Tchr. Latin, Washburn High Sch., Mpls., 1956-62, Forest View High Sch., Arlington Heights, Ill., 1965-68, John Hersey High Sch., Arlington Heights, 1968-84; prof. classical langs. Regis U., Denver, from 1985. Coord. host program for internat. students Colo. Sch. Mines, Golden. Mem. Vergilian Soc. (trustee 1979-82), Classical Assn. Mid. West and South (v.p. 1980-84, merit com. 1990—, Semple fellow 1970, V.P.'s award 1984), Am. Classical League, Colo. Classics Assn. (sec. 1991—), Nat. Com. for Promotion Latin and Greek (state liaison chmn. 1988-92), Archaeol. Inst. Am. Home: Reno, Nev. Died Sept. 24, 2007.

BRIGHAM, HENRY DAY, JR., retired lawyer; b. Pittsfield, Mass., Dec. 12, 1926; s. Henry Day and Gladys M. (Allen) B.; m. Catherine T. Van't Hul, Dec. 16, 1961; children: Henry Day, Johan Van't Hul, Alexander Frederick. BA, Yale U., 1947, JD, 1950. Bar: N.Y. 1951, Mass. 1966. Assoc. Milbank, Tweed, Hope & Hadley, NYC, 1951-52, 54-56, Simpson Thacher & Bartlett, NYC, 1956-66; v.p., gen. counsel, dir. Eaton & Howard, Inc., Boston, 1966-73, pres., 1973-79; v.p., chmn. exec. com. Eaton & Howard, Vance Sanders, Inc., Boston, 1979-81, Eaton Vance Corp., Boston, 1981—96; ret., 1996. Former trustee Eaton Vance Cash Mgmt. Fund, Boston; former v.p., trustee Eaton Vance Tax Free Reserves, Boston; former sec., clk., dir. Investors Bank & Trust Co., Boston; v.p., sec., trustee Wright Managed Income Trust, Boston, Wright Managed Equity Trust, Boston. Pres. Trustees of Donations of Episc. Diocese Mass., 1984-89; sr. warden Ch. of the Redeemer, Chestnut Hill, 1975-79; sec., bd. dirs. Chestnut Hill Assn. (Mass.), 1969—. Lt. USNR, 1952-54. Mem.: Soc. of the Cin., Assn. Yale Alumni (bd. govs.), Investment Counsel Assn. Am. (bd. govs.), Somerset Club, Longwood Cricket Club, Downtown Club, The Country Club, Tennis & Racquet Club, Harvard Club, Tarratine Club, Soc. Colonial Wars, Phi Delta Phi, Phi Beta Kappa. Episcopalian. Home: Chestnut Hill, Mass. Died Aug. 12, 2008.

BRINKER, NORMAN E., retired restaurant chain executive; b. Denver, June 3, 1931; s. Eugene and Katherine Brinker; m. Maureen Catherine Connolly, 1955 (dec. June 21, 1969); children: Cindy, Brenda; m. Nancy Goodman (div.); 1 child, Eric. BS, San Diego State U., 1957. Gen. ptnr. Jack in the Box, 1962—66; chmn., CEO Steak & Ale Restaurants, 1966-72; restaurant group pres. Pillsbury, 1976—82; chmn., CEO Burger King S&A Restaurant Group, Chili's Inc., Dallas, 1983-91; chmn. Brinker Internat. Inc., Dallas, 1991—2000. Avocation: horseback riding. Died June 9, 2009.

BRINKLEY, WILLIAM ANTHONY, army officer, operations research analyst; b. Lafayette, Ky., Sept. 6, 1942; s. James William and Pauline (Daughtery) B.; m. Priscilla Ann Pittman; children: William Anthony Jr., Christopher M., Joshua P. BS in Indsl. Engring., Tenn. Technol. U., 1964; MS in Ops. Rsch., Tex. Tech U., 1976. Commd. 2d lt. U.S. Army, 1965, advanced through grades to col., 1985; chief scheduling and analysis U.S. Army Arctic Test Ctr., Ft. Greely, Alaska, 1972-74; chief ops. rsch. br. U.S. Army Armor Ctr., Ft. Knox, Ky., 1977-80; comdr. lst squadron 2d U.S. Cavalry, Bindlach, Fed. Republic Germany, 1981-84; dir. Studies and Analysis Activity, Ft. Monroe, Va., 1985-87, Tradoc Analysis Command, Ft. Monroe, 1987-90; asst. dep. chief of staff Tng. and Doctrine Command, from 1990. Decorated Silver Star. Mem. Mil. Ops. Rsch. Soc., U.S. Army Armor Assn., Assn. U.S. Army, Alpha Pi Mu. Baptist. Avocations: photography, reading. Home: Huntsville, Ala. Died Sept. 14, 2007.

BRINSON, CORA KATHERINE, principal; b. Palatka, Fla., Mar. 18, 1951; d. Walter Horne Jr. and Katherine Blossom; m. Milton Adams, Dec. 20, 1986 (div. June 1989); m. Rupert Glenn Brinson, May 11, 1991; 1 child, William Milton. BS in Edn., Ga. So. U., 1974, MEd, 1978; EdD, Nova Southeastern U., 1995. Coord. Liberty County Bd. Edn., Hinesville, Ga., 1974-86; coord. project success Fulton County Bd. Edn., Atlanta, 1986-88, Rockdale County Bd. Edn., Conyers, Ga., 1988-89, Lee County Bd. Edn., Leesburg, Ga., 1989-91, Bulloch County Bd. Edn., Statesboro, Ga., 1991-96; prin. Glynn County Bd. Edn., Brunswick, Ga., from 1996. Com. mem. Ga. Dept. Edn., Atlanta, 1997-98, Govs. Com. Drop Outs Ga., Atlanta, 1986. Bd. dirs. Boys & Girls Club Glynn, 1997. Mem. Ga. Vocat. Assn., Ga. Assn. Spl. Needs Personnel (pres. 1982-96), Ga. Assn. Mid. Sch. Prins., Ga. Assn. Secondary Sch. Prins., Ga. Assn. Ednl. Leaders, Profl. Assn. Ga. Educators. Methodist. Avocations: golf, fishing, reading, needlepoint. Home: Statesboro, Ga. Died Jan. 5, 2008.

BRITTAN, MARTIN R., biologist, educator; b. San Jose, Calif., Jan. 28, 1922; s. Ralph Hinton Brittan and Addie Belle Martin; m. Ruth Marie Luebke, Aug. 10, 1947; children: Penelope, Pamela(dec.). AB, San Jose State U., 1946; PhD, Stanford U., 1951. Cert. fishery scientist Am. Fisheries Soc., 1968. Tchg. asst. Stanford U., Calif., 1946—49; asst. prof. biol. scis. S.D. Sch. Mines and Tech., Rapid City, 1949—50, San Diego State U., 1950—53; from asst. prof. to prof. biol. scis. Calif. State U., Sacramento, 1953—93. Ranger-naturalist U.S. Nat. Pk. Svc., Yosemite, Calif., 1949—52, ranger, naturalist, Glacier, Mont., 1954; environ. cons., Brazil, US, 1964, 73, 93-96; mem. numerous adv. bd. Author: Rasbora, 1954, 1998; contbr. articles to profl. jours. With US Army, 1942—46. Recipient award for outstanding ichthyological work, Internat. Fedn. Aquarium Societies, 1958. Mem.: Am. Fisheries Soc. (Svc. award 2002), Am. Soc.Ichthyologists and Herpetologists (v.p. Pacific divsn. 1946). Democrat. Avocations: photography, fishing, history, travel. Home: Folsom, Calif. Died May 24, 2008.

BRITTELL, FRANK LEE, service executive; b. Gresham, Nebr., Aug. 1, 1928; s. Clarence and Vada B. (McGinley) B.; m. Norma Shearles Lutz, May 28, 1948; 1 child, Nancy Kay. AA, East Los Angeles Jr. Coll., 1975. Comdr. Los Angeles Police Dept., 1953-77; owner Frank Brittell & Assocs., Hacienda Heights, Calif., 1977-82; owner, dir. Brittell & Hoy, Inc., Newport Beach, Calif., 1982-85; v.p. Bus. Risks Internat., Inc., Newport Beach, Calif., from 1985. Cons. for two studies in nuclear industry security U.S. Nuclear Regulatory Commn., 1980, 81. Mem. Am. Nuclear Soc., Am. Soc. for Indsl. Security (law enforcement liaison Los Angeles chpt. 1977—), Inst. Nuclear Materials Mgmt., Internat. Assn. Chiefs of Police, Newport Beach C. of C. Republican. Avocation: horseback riding. Home: Yorba Linda, Calif. Died May 20, 2008.

BRITTON, DANE BLACKMOUR, investment banker; b. Kansas City, Kans., Mar. 13, 1952; s. Roy Porter and Margaret Jean (Baker) B.; m. Julie Ann Sawer, Jan. 30, 1982 (div. Sept. 1991); 1 child, Mackenzie Baker. Student, Stephen F. Austin State U., 1973, U. Houston, 1977, U. Wis., 1985. Investigator Houston Police Dept., 1973-80; pres., CEO, Citizens State Bank & Trust Co., Ellsworth, Kans., 1980-88, 89-93; dir. security and drug enforcement U.S. Dept. Interior, Washington, 1988-89. V.p. Coronado Area Coun. Boy Scouts Am., Salina, Kans., 1983—; mem. Ellsworth City Coun., 1985—; chmn. Smoky Hills Pub. TV, Bunker Hill, Kans., 1985-88, Gov's. Task Force on Rural Communities, Topeka, Kans., 1986. Recipient Merit award Am. Bankers Assn., Washington, 1987, Disting. Svc. award, Pub. TV System, Bunker Hill, 1989; named Kans. Indsl. Developer of Yr. 1986, Kans. Indsl. Developers Assn., Topeka, Eisenhower Fellow, Eisenhower Fellowships, Phila.-Budapest, Hungary, 1992. Mem. Kans. Bankers Assn. (bd. dirs.), Kans. C. of C. (bd. dirs., Citizen of Yr. 1988), Ellsworth County Indsl. Devel. (chmn. 1985-88), Kiwanis Club (Mem. of Yr. 1988). Republican. Presbyterian. Avocations: travel, gardening, politics, flying. Home: Abilene, Kans. Died Mar. 17, 2008.

BRITTON, LEONARD, retired school system administrator; b. Tarentum, Pa., Nov. 16, 1930; s. Charles Mellon Britton and Margaret McFall; m. June Kness (div.); children: Jane, Laura; m. Sherill Wood, 1985; stepchildren: Douglas, Adam. BA, U. Pitts.; EdD, U. Pitts, 1962. Supt. schools Dade County, Fla., 1980—87; supt. L.A. Unified Sch. Dist., 1987—90. Died Aug. 9, 2009.

BROBECK, JOHN RAYMOND, physiology educator; b. Steamboat Springs, Colo., Apr. 12, 1914; s. James Alexander and Ella (Johnson) B.; m. Dorothy Winifred Kellogg, Aug. 24, 1940; children: Stephen James, Priscilla Kimball, Elizabeth Martha, John Thomas. BS, Wheaton Coll., 1936, LL.D., 1960; MS, Northwestern U., 1937, PhD, 1939; MD, Yale U., 1943. Instr. physiology Yale U., 1943-45, asst. prof., 1945-48, assoc. prof. physiology, 1948-52; prof. physiology, chmn. dept. U. Pa., Phila., 1952-70, Herbert C. Rorer prof. med. scis., 1970-82, prof. emeritus, 1982—2009. Editor: Yale Jour. Biology and Medicine, 1949-52; chmn. editorial bd.: Physiol. Revs, 1963-72. Fellow Am. Acad. Arts and Scis.; mem. Am. Physiol. Soc. (pres. 1971-72), Am. Inst. Nutrition, Nat. Acad. Scis., Am. Soc. Clin. Investigation, Halsted Soc., Phila. Coll. Physicians, Sigma Xi, Alpha Omega Alpha. Home: Media, Pa. Died Mar. 6, 2009.

BRODHURST, ALBERT EDWARD, business executive, lawyer; b. St. Petersburg, Fla., Sept. 26, 1934; s. George Henry and Olive Agnes (Padget) B. BS in Civil Engring., Tri-State Coll., 1960; LLB, John Marshall Law Sch., 1965; BS in Logistics Engring., Army-Navy Sch., Washington, 1969. Bar: Ill. 1966. Cadastrial surveyor U.S. Coast and Geodetic Survey, Menlo Park, Calif., 1956-59; design engr. Boeing Corp., New Orleans, 1965-67; pres. The Brodhurst Corp., from 1974. Alderman Chgo., 1963. Served to comdr. U.S. Army, 1952-92. Mem. ABA, Am. Preparedness Assn., Soc. Logistics Engrs. Lodges: Elks. Democrat. Roman Catholic. Died Aug. 22, 2008.

BRODIE, BRUCE ORR, veterinarian, educator; b. Allegan, Mich., Apr. 19, 1924; s. Robert Nelson and Viona Joyce (Smith) B.; m. Alma Routsong, June 1947 (div. 1962); children: Natalie, Joyce, Charlotte, Louise; m. Wanda Colleen Wells, June 8, 1963; children: Julie, Robert. DVM, Mich. State U., 1951; MS, U. Ill., 1958. Lic. veterinarian, Ill., Minn., Mich. Veterinarian Gehrman Clinic, Maple Plain, Minn., 1951-52; pvt. practice Delton, Mich., 1952-54; instr. U. Ill., Urbana, 1954-58, asst. prof., 1959-62, assoc. prof., 1963-69, prof. vet. clin. medicine, from 1969. Prof. U.S. AID, Nairobi, Kenya, Africa, 1974-76, U. Alexandria, Egypt, 1983-84; Fullbright prof. Zimbabwe, Africa, 1992-93. Contbr. chpts. to textbooks, articles to profl. jours. Cpl. U.S. Army, 1943-46, ETO. Mem. Am. Vet. Med. Assn., Ill. Vet. Med. Assn., Ea. Ill. Vet. Med. Assn., Am. Assn. Bovine Practitioners, Soc. Theriogenology, Am. Assn. Vet. Clinicians, Phi Zeta. Avocations: travel, sports. Home: Champaign, Ill. Died Dec. 13, 2007.

BROIN, THAYNE LEO, geologist; b. Kenyon, Minn., Sept. 18, 1922; s. Oscar Arthur and Ella (Hoff) B.; m. Beverly Ruth Johnson, Dec. 21, 1949; children: Martin, Dana, Valerie. BS, St. Cloud U., 1943; MA, U. Colo., 1952, PhD, 1957. Instr. Colo. State U., Fort Collins, Colo., 1950-54, asst. prof., 1956-57; rsch. geologist Cities Svc. R & D Co., Tulsa, 1957-58, tech. group leader, 1958-60, head geol. rsch., 1960-65; rsch. coord. Cities Svc. Oil Co., Bartlesville, Okla., 1965-72, chief computer geologist Tulsa, 1972-75, computer technology mgr., 1975-83; cons. Broin and Assocs., Colorado Springs, Tulsa, from 1983. Capt. USAF, 1943-48, South Pacific. Recipient Regents fellowship U. Colo., 1954, 55. Mem. Geol. Soc. Am., Tulsa Geol. Soc. (pres. 1971, 72), Sons of Norway (pres. 1991, 92). Avocations: norwegian ethnology, sailing. Died Oct. 12, 2007.

BROLLEY, JOHN EDWARD, JR., freelance/self-employed physicist; b. Chgo., Jan. 15, 1919; s. John Edward and Marie Josephine (Schaeffer) B.; m. Barbara Bowen, July 14, 1946 (div. 1965); m. Joyce Hicks, Mar. 20, 1965.

BS, U. Chgo., 1940; MS, Ind. U., 1948, PhD, 1949. Physicist U. Chgo. Metall. Lab., 1941-43, Oak Ridge (Tenn.), 1943-44, Los Alamos (N.Mex.) Nat. Lab., 1949-83, Los Alamos, from 1983. Contbr. numerous articles on nuclear physics, deconvolution and info. processing to profl. jours. Master mission pilot CAP, Los Alamos, 1967-87. Fellow AAAS, Am. Phys. Soc.; mem. Am. Astron. Soc., Astron. Soc. Pacific, Sigma Xi. Home: Los Alamos, N.Mex. Died Jan. 28, 2008.

BROMBERGER, FREDERICK SIGMUND, English language educator; b. El Paso, Tex., Mar. 5, 1918; s. Frederick Sigmund and Agnes Ardena (Landstrom) B.; m. Corrine Aldridge, Oct. 21, 1944; children: Eric, Troy, Corinth, Matthew, Thrace. AB, Knox Coll., 1940; BA, U. Cin., 1941; PhD., U. So. Calif., 1964; postgrad., Harvard U., 1947, Stanford U., 1977. Tchr. Kemper Mil. Sch., Boonville, Mo., 1941-42; instr. English, U. Mo., Columbia, 1946-47; prof. U. Redlands, Calif., 1948-84, part-time prof. Calif., from 1984, instr. lit. and music Elderhostel programs Calif., from 1981. Spl. instr. U. Calif., Riverside, 1965. Author: (manual) Leadership in the U.S. Air Force, 1954; contbr. numerous articles to profl. jours. Chmn. citizen's adv. com. Redlands Unified Sch. Dist., 1964-66; mem. Redlands Cultural Arts Commn., 1987—; founding mem. Redlands Symphony Orch. Maj. USAAF, 1942-46, CBI. Recipient Directive Tchr. award Danforth Found., 1959; Top Tchr. award Alumni Assn. U. Redlands, 1983, Alumni Svc. award, 1992; grantee Lilly Found., 1977. Mem. Riverside-San Bernardino Orchid Soc. (pres. 1982-83), Redlands Hort. Soc. (pres. 1981-82), Redlands Fortnightly Club (pres. 1990). Republican. Congregationalist. Avocations: gardening, music, foreign travel, american philately. Home: Redlands, Calif. Died Mar. 17, 2008.

BRONSWICK, LEONARD, electrical engineer; b. Chgo., Mar. 9, 1933; s. Louis and Rose (Kenzer) B.; m. Estelle Pearl Katz, Dec. 20, 1959; children: David, Debra. BS in Elect. Engring., U. Ill., 1958. Engr. Admiral Corp., Chgo., 1958-64; project engr. Dynascan Corp., Chgo., 1964-65, Stewart-Warner Electronics, Chgo., from 1965. Served with U.S. Army, 1953-55. Mem. IEEE, Am. Def. Prepardness Assn. Avocations: bonds, stocks, investments. Home: Skokie, Ill. Died Dec. 11, 2007.

BROOKS, MARVIN ALAN, chemist, researcher; b. Trenton, NJ, Jan. 28, 1945; s. Hyman and Miriam (Lipschutz) B.; m. Susan Pristoop, June 16, 1968; children: Paul, Cheryl. BS, Lafayette Coll., 1966; PhD, U. Md., 1971. Chemist Hoffmann-LaRoche, Nutley, N.J., 1971-85, Merck Sharp & Dohme Rsch. Labs., West Point, Pa., from 1985. Author monographs on pharm. analysis. Mem. Am. Chem. Soc., Am. Assn. Pharm. Scientists. Avocation: stamp collecting/philately. Home: Ambler, Pa. Died Dec. 6, 2007.

BROOKSBY, GERALD ARMOND, ophthalmologist; b. Provo, Utah, Dec. 12, 1937; s. Wilford Armond and Myrna Mae (Thorson) B.; m. Linda Lee Larson, June 21, 1961; children: Scott, Alisa, Emily, Rachel, Craig, Anne, Ben. BS, Brigham Young U., 1960; PhD, U. Minn., 1971, MD, 1972. Diplomate Am. Bd. Ophthalmology. Rsch. scientist NASA, 1962-67; fellow Mayo Clinic, Rochester, Minn., 1967-71; instr. in physiology U. Minn. Med. Sch., Mpls., 1971-72; NIH fellow U. Oreg. Med. Sch., Portland, 1972-76, ophthalmology fellow, 1972-76, clin. asst. prof., from 1976; pvt. practice Portland, from 1976. Cons. Alcon Rsch. Coun., Dallas, 1980-86; clin. asst. prof. U. Oreg. Med. Sch., Portland, 1983—. Contbr. articles to profl. jours. Rsch. grant U. Oreg. Med. Sch., 1972-76, spl. fellow, 1972-76. Fellow Am. Acad. Ophthalmology; mem. Oreg. Acad. Ophthalmology, Oreg. Med. Assn., Multnomah County Med. Soc., Oreg. Acad. Ophthalmology, Am. Physiol. Soc. Republican. Mem. Ch. LDS. Home: Portland, Oreg. Died Nov. 23, 2007.

BROOKS SHOEMAKER, VIRGINIA LEE, librarian; b. Oklahoma City, Sept. 16, 1944; d. Leo B. and Eloise Gilreath; m. Phil Ashley Brooks, Aug. 10, 1972 (dec. Oct. 1982); 1 child, Philip Brooks; m. Gene Darrel Shoemaker, Feb. 16, 1986; children: Rob Shoemaker, Julie Shoemaker, Donna Shoemaker, Gary Shoemaker. Student, Oklahoma City C.C., 1980; BS, U. Ctrl. Okla., 1988, M in Sch. Media, 1991, postgrad., from 2000; attended, Okla. State U. With Dept. Human Svcs., Oklahoma City, 1970-75, State Dept. Librs., Oklahoma City, 1980-87; substitute tchr. Oklahoma City Schs., 1989-91, 1995; vol. libr. Children's Libr., Children's Hosp., Oklahoma City, from 1992; libr. vol. Corpus Christi Sch. Libr., from 1998; vol. children's sect. First Bapt. Libr.; vol. Libr. for Blind. Sponsor World Vision, Seattle, from 1994; active cub scouts Boy Scouts Am.; vol. Habitat for Humanity, Vista Care Hospice; dir. project transformation summer reading program First Bapt. Good Shepherd Children's Dental Clinic; vol. Vista Care Hospice, from 2002; project transformation reading program Wesley Meth.; reading sch. libr. tutor First Bapt. Good Shepherd Children's Dental Clinic; active, life mem. Meth. Ch. of the Servant; women mission groups Wesley Meth., First Bapt. Ch.; vol. children's sect. First Bapt. Libr. Recipient Adopt-a-Park award, 1985, 1986, 1987, Oklahoma City Beautiful award, 1985—88, Omniplex Sci. Mus., Oklahoma City, 1986—89. Mem.: Omniplex Sci. Mus. (Adpot-a-Park award 1986—89), Internat. Reading Assn. (reading tutor city schs.), Coun. Exceptional Children, Zool. Soc., Classen Alumni Assn., U. Ctrl. Okla. Alumni Assn. Baptist. Avocations: piano, reading, creative writing, making greeting cards. Home: Oklahoma City, Okla. Deceased.

BROUGH, H. O., business administrator, consultant; b. Bucklin, Mo., May 2, 1929; s. Henry Otto and Floy Alice (Williams) B.; married (div. Aug. 1979); children: Sherri Wagner, Rick, Brett; m. Penelope Raye Miller, Sept. 22, 1989. BS, Mo. State U., 1956, MA, 1959; EdS, U. Wyo., 1964. Supr. Davenport Community Schs., Iowa, 1956-59; coord. U. Wyo., Laramie, 1959-63; asst. dir. U. Iowa, Iowa City, 1963-68; asst. dean U. Colo., Boulder, 1968-89; v.p. Pacific Luth. Theol. Sem., Berkeley, Calif., from 1989. Con. Mo. State U., Kirksville, 1959, U. Wyo., 1961, Nat. C. of C., Washington, 1968-79. Contbr. article to profl. jour. Fundraiser senatorial campaign, Boulder, 1979. With USN, 1949-53, Korea. Mem. Nat. Savings and Loan Assn. (edn. cons. 1977), Nat. U. Continuing Edn. Assn. (chmn. 1961-63, Key ward 1989), Colo. Assessors Assn. (edn. cons. 1979), Boulder C. of C. (bd. dirs. 1975-79). Lutheran. Avocations: fishing, restoring classic vehicles. Home: Broomfield, Colo. Died Apr. 13, 2008.

BROWDER, WILLIAM BAYARD, lawyer; b. Urbana, Ill., Sept. 6, 1916; s. Olin Lorraine and Nellie Sheldon (Taylor) B.; m. Mary Bain Lehmann, Sept. 6, 1942 (dec. Feb. 1984); children: David Sheldon, Wendy Elisabeth, Amy Spence (dec.); m. Betty M. Kennedy, Jan. 5, 1985 AB, U. Ill., 1938, JD, 1941; LLD, MacMurray Coll., Jacksonville, Ill., 1979, Ill. Coll., 1990. Bar: Ill. 1941. Atty. I.C.R.R., 1941-47, Union Tank Car Co., Chgo., 1948-81, sec., 1952-77, dir., 1954-81, gen. counsel, 1956-79, v.p., 1965-74, sr. v.p., 1974-81; v.p., dir. Trans Union Corp., 1969-81, gen. counsel, 1969-79, sr. v.p., 1974-79, sr. v.p. law, 1979-81; v.p., dir. Ecodyne Corp., 1972-81. Dir. Procor, Ltd., 1952-81 Mem. Citizens Com. To Study Police-Community Relations in Chgo., 1966-67; chmn. Com. To Study Financing Community Colls. in Ill., 1974-75; pres. Chgo. Crime Commn., 1965-67; mem. adv. com. U. Ill. Coll. Commerce and Bus. Adminstrn., Champaign-Urbana, 1969-73; mem. Ill. Racing Bd., 1973-74; mem. Ill. Bd. Higher Edn., 1975-91, chmn., 1979-91; pres. Wilmette United Fund, 1962; life trustee YMCA-U Ill., 1966—, chmn., 1967-79; bd. dirs. Mid Am. chpt. ARC, 1963-65, Wilmette Pub. Libr., 1964-67, Northwestern Meml. Hosp., 1970-75; mem. U. Ill. Found., 1969—, bd. dirs., 1973-79, mem. pres.'s coun., 1974—; mem. Ill. Gov.'s Task Force on Pvt. Sector Initiatives, 1983-86, Ill. Gov.'s Commn. on Sci. and Tech., 1983-87; mem. Ill. Gaming Bd., 1993-99; bd. dirs. organized crime com. Chgo. Crime Commn.; trustee Trinity United Meth. Ch., chmn. bd. trustee, 1973-85. Mem. Am., Ill. bar assns., U. Ill. Law Alumni Assn. (pres. 1968-71), Chgo. Legal Club, Order of Coif, Union League Club (Chgo.) (dir. 1974-76), Westmoreland Country Club (Wilmette, Ill.) (sec., dir. 1979), Phi Beta Kappa, Phi Eta Sigma, Beta Theta Pi, Phi Alpha Delta. Methodist. Home: Sierra Madre, Calif. Died Feb. 3, 2009.

BROWN, BARBARA MAHONE, communications educator, poet, consultant; b. Chgo., Feb. 27, 1944; d. Loniel Atticus and Anne (Savage) Mahone. BA, Wash. State U., 1968; MBA, U. Chgo., 1975; PhD, Stanford U., 1988. Dir. corp. comm. NBC, NYC, 1975-77; assoc. prof. dept. bus. adminstrn. and econs. Clark Coll., Atlanta, 1978-84; assoc. prof. depts. journalism and advt. U. Tex., Austin, 1988-91; assoc. prof. dept. mktg. San Jose (Calif.) State U., from 1990. Pres. Elbow Room Cons., 1994—; cons. The Fielding Inst., Santa Barbara, Calif., 1995—; evaluator Western Assn. Schs. and Colls., Oakland, Calif., 1993—; cons. KQED-TV (PBS), San Francisco, 1991; OBAC Poet, Orgn. Black Am. Culture, Chgo., 1970-75; mentor Ctr. for Devel. Women Entrepreneurs, 1995-97; founding faculty Fielding Inst. ODE Program, 1996. Author: (vol. poetry) Sugarfields, 1970; writer-rschr. pub. affairs documentary, WMAQ-TV (NBC Chgo.) 1973, WNET-TV (PBS N.Y.C.) 1971; contbr. articles to profl. acad. jours. Bd. dirs. Kids in Common, San Jose, 1997-98; trustee Hillbrook Sch., Los Gatos, Calif., 1995-98; vestry St. Edward's Episcopal Ch., San Jose, 1994-96; steering com. UN Mid-Decade of Women, Southeast Regional Conf., 1980. Regents fellow in comm., U. Tex. at Austin, 1989; tchr.-scholar San Jose State U., 1993. Mem. Delta Sigma Pi, Beta Gamma Sigma. Episcopalian. Avocations: art, literature, orchids, photography. Home: Santa Cruz, Calif. Died Aug. 5, 2007.

BROWN, DONALD RICHARD, capacitor engineer; b. Milw., Sept. 25, 1925; s. Edwin Frances and Loretta Ethlyn (Howard) B.; m. Dorothy Jane (Carey), Sept. 5, 1947; children: Donald R. Jr., Kenneth Allen. BS in Physics and Math., Monmouth Coll., Ill., 1950. Dept. chief engring. Western Electric, Cicero, Ill., 1951-85; pres. D.R.B. Tech. Svcs. Ltd., Downers Grove, Ill., 1985—90. Patentee in field. Pres. Bruce Lake Home Owners Assn., 1960, Downer's Grove PTA, 1962. Served with USAF, 1944-45. Named one of top 100 technologists in western world by Tech. Mag., 1981. Avocations: fishing, personal computers, gardening, tennis, sports. Died Apr. 12, 2008.

BROWN, GARY ALLEN, defense analysis company executive; b. Lincoln, Nebr., Aug. 31, 1938; s. Kenneth Wesley and Erma Bethine (Barker) B.; m. Anita Katharine Jacobsen, May 8, 1959; children: Allen Ernst, Brian Kenneth. BS in Systems Sci., U. West Fla., 1971. Enlisted man USAF, 1956, advanced through grades to master sgt., 1974; ret., 1977; math tchr. Meigs Middle Sch., Shalimar, Fla., 1977-78; sr. programmer ASI Systems Internat., Ft. Walton Beach, Fla., 1977-88, v.p., dir., from 1988. Councilman Niceville (Fla.) City Coun., 1981—; dir. Okaloosa County Gas Dist., Valparaiso, Fla., 1983—. Mem. Niceville-Valparaiso C. of C. Avocations: hunting, computers, reading, travel. Home: Niceville, Fla. Died Oct. 22, 2007.

BROWN, GERALD SONNY, musician; b. Cin., Apr. 20, 1936; Student, Cin. Conservatory Mus. Army, 1953-56. Drummer with various artists including Eddie Vinson, Amos Milburn, Dinah Washington, Cin., Chgo., Detroit, 1956-60, Frank Foster, Randy Weston, Ray Bryant, Sonny Rollins, Zoot Sims, NYC, 1961-68; drummer N.Y. Bass Choir, 1968-70; drummer with Joe Henderson, Ron Carter, Scandinavia, 1970-75, Rahsaan Roland Kirk, from 1975. Lectr. Mark Twain Jr. High Sch., Aug. 1968; tchr. Jazzmobile Workshop, 1972, Jazz Interactions Workshop, 1973. Drummer critics symposium, Smithsonian Inst., Washington, 1974; TV appearances Today, Tonight, Soul. Mem.: Hiram Grand. Died Sept. 3, 2007.

BROWN, HARLEY PROCTER, JR., zoology educator, entomologist, researcher; b. Uniontown, Ala., Jan. 13, 1921; s. Harley Procter Brown and Martha Ida (McGinniss) Brown Coleman; m. Laura Clifford Williams, June 1, 1942 (dec. 1989); 1 child, Mary Hamilton Brown Catron; m. Marie Magdalen Jenkins, Dec. 20, 1989 (dec. 1997); m. Dorothy Ellis McGregor, Oct. 26, 1997. AB, AM, Miami U., Oxford, Ohio, 1942; PhD, Ohio State U., 1945. Grad. asst. in zoology Ohio State U., Columbus, 1942-45; instr. zoology U. Idaho, Moscow, 1945-47, Oreg. Inst. Marine Biology, Charleston, 1946; instr. biology Queens Coll., Flushing, N.Y., 1947-48; asst. prof., then assoc. prof. U. Okla., Norman, 1948-62, prof. zoology, 1962-84, prof. emeritus, from 1984; curator of invertebrates Stovall Mus. Sci. & History (now S.N. Okla. Mus. Natural History), Norman, from 1962. Rsch. prof. Franz Theodore Stone Inst., Put-In-Bay, Ohio, 1949. Author: Aquatic Dryopoid Beetles of the U.S.A., 1972; editor: Highlights and Lowlights, 1981; contbr. chpts. to Immature Insects, vol. 2, 1991; contbr. over 100 articles to biol. jours. Instl. rep., mem. dist. com., counselor Norman area Boy Scouts Am., 1949-70. NSF fellow, 1964, 70. Fellow AAAS (life); mem. Am. Inst. Biol. Scis. (governing bd.), Am. Microscopical Soc. (pres. 1975-76), N.Am. Benthological Soc., Sigma Xi, Phi Eta Sigma, Phi Sigma (nat. v.p. 1980—). Democrat. Presbyterian. Achievements include discovery of new genera and species of wasps (Pteromalidae, Eulophidae, Diapriidae) and water beetles (Elmidae, Dryopidae, Psephenidae, Lutrochidae, Limnichidae); research in life histories of various aquatic insects and their insect parasites (Sisyrids, Psephenids). Home: Edmond, Okla. Died June 6, 2008.

BROWN, JANE DELANO, journalism and mass communication educator; b. West Chester, Pa., Aug. 22, 1950; d. Clarence Wherry and Florence (Delano) B.; m. James A. Protzman, Dec. 19, 1987; 1 child, Lillian Delano Brown. BA, U. Ky., 1972; MA, U. Wis., 1974, PhD, 1978. Prof. journalism and mass communication U. N.C., Chapel Hill, from 1977, dir. grad. studies, 1991-94, chmn. faculty, 1994-97. Vis. lectr. U. Mich., Ann Arbor, 1977; vis. prof. U. Wis., Madison, 1987; fellow Gannett Ctr. for Media Studies, N.Y.C., 1987-88. Co-author: Media, Sex and the Adolescent, 1991; co-editor: Social Science, the Media and Policy for Children, 1981; also numerous articles. Mem. Non-Violence Project, N.Y., Women's Ctr., Chapel Hill, N.C., Media Task Force, Nat. Coaliton to Prevent Teen Pregnancy. Mem. Assn. for Edn. in Journalism and Mass Communication (exec. com. 1988-89, Hillier Kreighbaum award 1988), Internat. Assn. for Mass Communication Rsch., Internat. Communication Assn. Democrat. Unitarian Universalist. Avocations: travel, gardening. Home: Chapel Hill, NC. Died Oct. 8, 2007.

BROWN, LAWRENCE CLIFTON, JR., foundation administrator; b. Wakefield, Mass., July 9, 1950; s. Lawrence Clifton and Marguerite Anne (MacLellan) B.; m. Rosemary Dixon, Aug. 21, 1976. BA, Boston Coll., 1972; JD, Suffolk U., 1979. Bar: Mass. 1979. Dir. planning and devel. 735, Inc., Melrose, Mass., 1972-73; regional supr. Mass. Office for Children, Toppsfield, 1973-75; exec. dir. Youth and Family Resources Inc., Melrose, 1975-78; pres. Wave, Inc., Washington, 1978—2009. Bd. dirs. Jobs for the Future, Boston, Nat. Youth Employment Coalition, N.Y.C., Nat. Ctr. for Appropriate Tech., Washington. Mem. ABA, Mass. Bar Assn. Avocation: golf. Home: Burke, Va. Died Aug. 18, 2009.

BROWN, MARY LOUISE, nursing educator; b. Phila., Jan. 5, 1939; d. Harold E. and Beatrice Louise (Welch) Dunn. Diploma, Chestnut Hill Hosp., 1960; BS summa cum laude, U. Md., 1977; MSN in Forensic Psychiat. Nursing, Cath. U. Am., 1983; PhD, U. Pitts. Sch. Nursing, 1990. RN, Pa., Va., Ill., W.Va. Staff nurse, psychiatric unit Washington Hosp. Ctr., 1974-75; clin. instr. Shenandoah Coll. & Conservatory Music, Winchester, Va., 1979-80; asst. prof. St. Francis Coll., Loretto, Pa., 1983-90; asst. prof., coord. coop. nursing program Glenville State Coll./W.Va. U., 1990-91; dean acad. affairs St. Joseph Coll. Nursing, Joliet, Ill, from 1991. Instr. Va. Alcohol Safety Action Program; participant in numerous profl. workshops. Contbr. articles to profl. jours. Grantee NIMH. Mem. Nat. League for Nursing. Home: Gettysburg, Pa. Died June 4, 2007.

BROWN, MURIEL WINDHAM, librarian, writer; b. Dallas, Nov. 19, 1926; d. Charles Wyatt and Gladys Mae (Patman) Windham; m. George W. Brown, II, Jan. 28, 1951; children— Laurence Windham, David Mitchum, Leslie Ann. B.A., So. Meth. U., 1949, M.A., 1950; M.L.S., North Tex. State U., 1974, postgrad., 1974—. Library assoc. Dallas Pub. Library, 1964-66, librarian lit. and history, 1966-66 children's librarian, 1966-72, head children's dept., 1967-69, children's selection new brs., 1972-77, children's lit. specialist, 1977—; cons. in field. Author: Books for You,

1981; co-author: Notable Children's Books 1976-1980, 1986; compiler bibliographies for Behind the Covers, 1984, Behind the Covers II, 1988; contbr. chpt. to School Library Media Annual, 1987. Mem. presch. edn. com. Am. Heart Assn., Dallas, 1982-83. Jesse Jones fellow, 1949. Mem. ALA (children's Notable books re-evaluation com. 1983—, Newberry award com. 1984-85), Tex. Library Assn. (chmn. children's roundtable, Siddie Joe Johnson Children's Librarian award 1988), So. Meth. U. Alumni Assn. (sec. 1972-73), Alpha Theta Phi, Beta Phi Mu, Alpha Lambda Sigma. Democrat. Unitarian. Deceased.

BROWN, NEIL W., religious organization administrator; b. Columbus, Ohio, Jan. 15, 1938; s. William Dent and Grace (Wood) B.; m. Margaret Hawthorne, Aug. 20, 1960; children: Bethel Nagy, C. Todd. BA, Westminster Coll., 1959; MDiv, Pitts. Theol. Sem., 1962. Ordained to ministry Presbyn. Ch. (U.S.A.), 1962. Pastor Community Presbyn. Ch., Oakland, Oreg., 1962-66, Covenant Presbyn. Ch., Gresham, Oreg., 1966-77; assoc. exec. Synod of the Covenant, Columbus, 1977-88; exec. presbyter Presbytery San Diego, from 1988. Bd. drs. San Diego Ecumenical Conf., 1988—. Precinct committeeman Douglas County, Oreg. Dem. Com., Roseburg, 1965-66, Multnomah County, Oreg. Dem. Com., Portland, 1970-74. Mem. Lions (pres. Oakland chpt. 1965-66, Portland chpt. 1966-71). Home: Waterloo, Iowa. Died Mar. 13, 2008.

BROWN, ROBERT CECIL, lawyer; b. Portland, Oreg., Dec. 29, 1928; s. Cecil Doak and Louise Elizabeth (Leaming) B.; m. Virginia Lea Egge, Feb. 6, 1954 (div. May 1972); children: Jay M., Randall C., Kevin B.; m. Karen Virginia Baer, June 12, 1972. BA, Reed Coll., 1951; JD, U. So. Calif., 1959. Bar: U.S. Patent Office, 1954, Calif. 1959, U.S. Dist. Ct. (so. dist.) Calif. 1959, U.S. Ct. Customs & Patent Appeals 1959, U.S. Supreme Ct. 1963, N.Y. 1969, U.S. Ct. Appeals (2d cir.) 1969, U.S. Ct. Appeals (Fed. cir.) 1982, Conn. 1989. Examiner U.S. Patent Office, Washington, 1951-53; patent counsel Aerojet Gen. Corp., Azusa, Calif., 1953-62, asst. v.p., 1962-65; v.p., sec. Aerojet Delft Corp., Melville, N.Y., 1965-68; patent atty. Union Carbide Corp., NYC, 1969-78, group patent counsel, 1978-86, mng. patent counsel Danbury, Conn., 1986-93, assoc. chief patent counsel, 1993-94, ret., 1994. Spl. patent counsel Kelley Drye & Warren, 1994-96; of counsel DOrsey & Witney, 1996—. 1st lt. U.S. Army, 1947-53, Korea. Mem. ABA, Am. Intellectual Property Law Assn., Calif. Bar, N.Y. Bar, Conn. Bar. Died Aug. 2, 2008.

BROWN, ROBERT W., insurance company executive; b. Chariton, Iowa, Aug. 25, 1950; s. James Robert and Ermyne Olivia (Hatch) B.; children from a previous marriage: Christopher James, Jeffrey Joseph; m. Allison Gene Kracht, Oct. 24, 1986; 1 child, Timothy Robert. BA, Iowa State U., Ames, 1972; JD, U. Mich., 1974; LLM, NYU, 1979. CLU Am. Coll., 1978; CHFC, Am. Coll., 1984; cert. fin. planner, 1994; accredited estate planner, 1996. Sr. underwriting cons. HomeLife Ins. Co. N.Y., NYC, 1975-79; prin., shareholder Moneta Group, Inc., Clayton, Mo., 1979-96; founder R.W. Brown & Assocs., Ladue, Mo., from 1997. Chmn. adv. com. Phoenix Home Life Nat. Field, Hartford, Conn., 1992. Coach Clayton (Mo.) Parks and Recreation, 1994—. Home: Clayton, Mo. Died Feb. 13, 2008.

BROWN, RONALD E., chemical engineer, researcher; b. Hammond, Ind., July 18, 1954; s. Berton E. and Jeanne S. (Leiffers) B.; m. Dawn Erickson, May 14, 1977; children: Grete Dawn, Ethan William. BA in Chemistry, Hope Coll., Holland, Mich., 1976; BSChemE, Purdue U., 1978; MSChemE, Okla. State U., 1995. Registered profl. engr., Okla. Staff engr. Phillips Petroleum, Bartlesville, Okla., 1978-84, rsch. engr., 1984-86, rsch. process engr., 1986-91, sr. rsch. engr., from 1991. Contbr. articles to profl. jours. Mem. AIChE. Presbyterian. Achievements include numerous patents; inventor processes for synthetic lubricants, cyclohexane separation, ethylene furnace additive technology, and heavy oil upgrading. Home: Bartlesville, Okla. Died Dec. 8, 2007.

BROWN, RONALD LAMING, lawyer; b. Springfield, Mass., Aug. 26, 1944; s. Douglas Seaton and Elizabeth Ruth (Stover) B.; m. Barbara Jo Roesler Moher, June 13, 1967 (div. Mar., 1987); children: Kimberly Lynn, Kathryn Jo, Karen Elizabeth, Kristine Ann, John Paul; m. Susan Janet Toth, Jan. 2, 1988; 1 child, Megan Christina., Chapman Col., 1968-70; JD, Creighton U., 1972. Bar: Nebr. 1973, U.S. Dist. Ct. Nebr. 1973, U.S. Ct. Appeals (8th cir.) 1974, U.S. Dist. Ct. Wyo. 1974, U.S. Ct. Appeals (10th cir.) 1976, Colo. 1987, U.S. Dist. Ct. Colo. 1987. 2d v.p., comml. loan counsel Omaha Nat. Bank, Omaha, 1973-74; prosecuting atty. Natrona County Atty., Casper, Wyo., 1974-75; partner Brown, Drew, Apostolos, Massey & Sullivan, Casper, Wyo., 1975-83; shareholder Burke & Brown, Casper, Wyo., 1983-86; pvt. practice Casper, Wyo., 1986-88, Ft. Collins, Colo., from 1987. Lectr. Casper (Wyo.) Coll., 1980. Mem. sch. bd. St. Anthony's Sch., Casper, Wyo., 1979-82, Ft. Collins (Colo.) Connections, 1995—. Sgt. USMC, 1964-68. Mem. Neb. Bar Assn., Wyo. Bar Assn., Colo. Bar Assn., Marine Corps League. Republican. Avocations: golf, motor cycling, auto restoration, reading, home repair. Home: Fort Collins, Colo. Died Dec. 30, 2007.

BROWN, THOMAS J., fiber optic specialist; b. NYC, Jan. 18, 1960; s. Joseph J. and Catherine S. (Arcidiacono) B.; m. Lisa Ann Marchesano, Sept. 2, 1984; children: Casey James, Victoria Michael. Svc. technician Suffolk Cable, Central Islip, N.Y., 1979-84; chief technician Huntington (N.Y.) Cable, 1984-85; engr. Cablevision, Woodbury, N.Y., 1985-86; chief engr. S.I. (N.Y.) Cable, 1986-94; fiber optic specialist Antec, Middletown, N.J., from 1994. Mem. Soc. Cable Telecomms. Engrs. (Field Ops. award 1991). Home: Middletown, NJ. Died May 14, 2008.

BROWNE, ALPH H., insurance company executive; b. Vero Beach, Fla., Aug. 16, 1940; s. Alph H. and Ruth (Knowles) B.; m. Diana Elizabeth Dillard, Aug. 27, 1977; children: Daniel William, Elizabeth Jansen. BS, Erskine Coll., Due West, SC, 1963. Field underwriter Travelers Ins. Co., Jacksonville, Fla., 1963-65; v.p. Frank B. Hall & Co., Jacksonville and Miami, Fla., 1965-74; mgr., bd. dirs. CTH Reinsurance, Memphis, 1975-78; corp. v.p. mktg. Duncanson & Holt Inc., Atlanta and NYC, 1978-82; founder, chmn., pres. Associated Reinsurance Mgmt. Corp., Atlanta, from 1982. Contbr. articles to U.S. Reinsurance Report. Founding mem. Rep. Task Force, Washington, 1985—; sustaining mem. Rep. Nat. Com., Washington, 1985—; elder N.W. Presbyn. Ch., Atlanta. Mem. Nat. Assn. Reinsurance Brokers (sec.-treas. 1986—, bd. dirs., mem. exec. com.), Atlanta Area C. of C., Omicron Delta Kappa. Clubs: Assocs. (Atlanta); Univ. Yacht (Flowery Branch, Ga.) (bd. govs. 1986, sec. 1987, treas. 1988), The Buckhead. Lodges: Kiwanis. Avocations: boating, swimming, mountain recreation. Home: Flowery Branch, Ga. Died Feb. 21, 2008.

BROWNE, RAY BROADUS, popular culture educator; b. Millport, Ala., Jan. 15, 1922; s. Garfield and Annie Nola (Trull) Browne; m. Olwyn Orde, Aug. 21, 1952 (dec. 1964); children: Glenn, Kevin; m. Alice Pat Matthews, Aug. 25, 1965; 1 child, Alicia. AB, U. Ala., 1943; A.M., Columbia U., 1947; PhD, UCLA, 1956. Instr. U. Nebr., Lincoln, 1947-50; instr. U. Md., College Park, 1956-60; asst. prof., assoc. prof. Purdue U., Lafayette, Ind., 1960-67; prof. popular culture Bowling Green (Ohio) State U., 1967—75, Univ. disting. prof., 1975—92. Author, editor: Melville's Drive to Humanism, 1971, Popular Culture and the Expanding Consciousness, 1973, The Constitution and Popular Culture, 1975, Dominant Symbols in Popular Culture, 1990, The Many Tongues of Literacy, 1992, Continuities in Popular Cultures, 1993, The Cultures of Celebrations, 1994, Popular Culture Studies in the Future, 1996, Lincoln-Lore: Lincoln in Contemporary Popular Culture, 1996, Pioneers in Popular Culture Studies, 1998, The Defining Guide to United States Popular Culture, 2000, The Detective as Historian, 2000, vol. II, 2007, Preview, 2001, Mission Underway: The History of the Popular Culture Association/American Culture Association and Popular Culture Movement, 2002, Popular Culture of the Civil War and Reconstruction, 2003, Murder on the Reservation: American Indian Crime Fiction, 2004, Popular Culture Studies Across the Curriculum, 2005, Profiles of Popular Culture, 2005, The Detective as Historian: History and Art in Historical Crime Fiction, vol. II, 2007, creator, editor: Jour. Popular Culture, 1967—82, Jour. Am. Culture, 1977—82, Values and Popular Culture, 2008. With US Army, 1942—46. Mem.: Am. Culture Assn. (sec.-treas. from 1977), Popular Culture Assn. (sec. 1970—2002, treas. 1970—2009, founder). Democrat. Avocation: scholarly research. Home: Bowling Green, Ohio. Died Oct. 22, 2009.

BROWNELL, GORDON LEE, physicist, researcher; b. Duncan, Okla., Apr. 8, 1922; s. Roscoe David and Mabel (Gourley) B.; m. Anna-Liisa Kairento; children: Wendy Silverman, Peter G., David L., James K., Piia Kairento, Janne Kairento. BS, Bucknell U., Lewisburg, Pa., 1944; PhD, Mass. Inst. Tech., 1950. Mem. faculty MIT, 1950—2008, prof., 1970-91, prof. emeritus, 1991—2008. Bd. dirs. Neuroresearch Fund. Served to lt. (j.g.) USNR, 1944-46. Fellow Am. Phys. Soc., Am. Nuclear Soc., Am. Coll. Radiology (hon.); mem. Am. Assn. Physicists in Medicine (Coolidge award 1987), Soc. Nuclear Medicine (Paul C. Aebersold award 1975), European Soc. Nuclear Medicine (de Hevesy medal 1979, 2003), Inst. Med. Nat. Acad. Clubs: Union Boat (Boston). Home: Salem, Mass. Died Nov. 11, 2008.

BROWNING, ROBERTA FULLERTON, university administrator; b. Swedesboro, NJ, Aug. 23, 1937; d. John Sr. and Josephine Cecil (Broome) Fullerton; m. 1 child, John Jarvis Browning; m. Lee Arthur Broadbent, May 6, 1977. BS in Psychology, Bucknell U., 1959; MS in Counseling, Calif. State U., Fullerton, 1974. Elem. tchr. Elem. Sch. Dist., Salem, N.J., 1960-61; statistician Rsch. Inst. of Am., NYC, 1961-64; coord. testing Calif. State U., Fullerton, 1970-82, acting asst. v.p. student affairs, 1982-84, dir. career devel. ctr., from 1984. Co-founder women's ctr. Calif. State U., Fullerton, 1972; mem. women's coun. Calif. State U. Bd. dirs. YWCA, Fullerton, 1986-92. Mem. AACD, Am. Coll. Pers. Assn., Western Coll. Placement Assn., Calif. State U. Dirs. of Career Ctrs. (chair 1991-93). Home: Fullerton, Calif. Died Aug. 7, 2008.

BROWNING, SCOTT DAVID, minister; b. Columbus, Ohio, Jan. 16, 1931; s. Dallas Lynn and Ella Mae (West) B.; m. Ruth Anna Wright, June 8, 1953; children: Donald Wayne, Douglas William. BA, Earlham Coll., 1953; BD, Garrott Theol. Sem., 1956, MDiv, 1972; DMin, Drew Theol. Sem., 1980. Ordained to ministry United Meth. Ch. Exec. sec. Goodwill Industries, St. Paul, 1957-60, chaplain Pitts., 1961; pastor Mars United Meth. Ch., Pa., 1962-66, Homer City United Meth. Ch., Pa., 1966-75, Herminie United Meth. Ch., Pa., 1975-82, Ford Meml. United Meth. Ch., Ford City, Pa., 1982-90, Clymer United Meth. Ch., Pa., from 1990. Dist. sec. Bd. of Missions, 1982-84; conf. sec. Global Missions, 1984-90. Bd. dirs. Keystone Tall Trees Girl Scout, 1983-89. Mem. Kiwanis (Disting. lt. gov. div. 10 1973, Disting. pres. 1979, sec.-treas. 1983-90, Internat. Found. fellow 1988), Masons. Democrat. Avocations: photography, travel. Home: Indiana, Pa. Died Mar. 15, 2008.

BRUENING, JAMES THEODORE, mathematician, educator; b. Cape Girardeau, Mo., Feb. 27, 1949; s. Paul Henry and Thekla Elizabeth Bruening; m. Fayleen M. Wessel, Aug. 3, 1973; children: Aaron, Sarah. BS in Applied Math., U. Mo., 1971, MS in Applied Math., 1972, PhD in Math., 1977. Instr. math. Westmar Coll., LeMars, Iowa, 1976—77; asst. prof. Baker U., Baldwin City, Kans., 1977—82, assoc. prof., 1982—85; from asst. prof. to prof. Southeast Mo. State U., Cape Girardeau, Mo., 1985—2005, prof., from 2005. Editor: Math. Informatics Qua., from 2002; co-editor: Coll. Math. Jour., 2003; contbr. articles to profl. jours. Mem.: Math. Assn. Am. (newsletter editor Mo. sect. 1999—2005). Avocations: music, gardening. Home: Cape Girardeau, Mo. Died Sept. 9, 2007.

BRUNDIN, BRIAN JON, lawyer; b. St. Paul, Oct. 11, 1939; s. Milton E. Brundin and LuVerne (Johnson) Roddan; m. Carolyn Bagley, June 30, 1961; children: Iana L. Sayer, Ian S., Dane E. BBA in Acctg. cum laude, U. Alaska, 1961; JD, Harvard U., 1964. Bar: Alaska 1966, U.S. Ct. Appeals (9th cir.) 1966, U.S. Supreme Ct. 1986; CPA, Alaska. Assoc. Hughes, Thorsness, Gantz, Powell & Brundin, Anchorage, 1966-70, ptnr., 1970-96, prin. ptnr., 1975-96, chair comml. div. and corp. sect., 1970-96, from vice-chmn. to chmn., 1972-82, mgmt. group, 1994-96; disting. exec. in residence, vis. asst. prof. acctg. Sch. Bus. and Pub. Policy, U. Alaska, Anchorage, 1996-97. Instr. acctg. and law U. Alaska, 1965-69; bd. dirs., pres. Brundin, Inc., 1979—, Kyak Oil, Inc., 1985-90; bd. dirs., sec. Far North Fishermen, Inc., 1981-85; trustee Humana Hosp. Alaska, 1982-83; adv. bd. World Trade Ctr. Alaska, 1992-97; bd. dirs. World Trade Ctr. Alaska, Inc., 1997-98. Chmn. subcom. on sales taxes Operation Breakthrough, Anchorage, 1968; mem. U. Alaska Bd. Regents, 1969-77, chmn. fin. com., 1970-75, v.p. 1973-75, pres., 1975-77; mem. Alaska Postsecondary Commn., 1973-75; founder, trustee U. Alaska Found., 1974-95, trustee emeritus, 1995—, pres., 1974-77, mem. exec. com., 1987—, chmn. Bullock prize for execellence com., 1989—; Alaska chmn. Harvard U. Law Sch. Fund, 1975-78; mem. adv. bd. alaska Ctr. for Internat. Bus., 1986-88; trustee AnchorAGE Sr. Ctr., Inc. Endowment Fund, 1996—, pres., 1997—. Capt. U.S. Army, 1964-66. Mem. ABA, AICPA, Anchorage Bar Assn. (legis com.), Alaska Bar Assn. (ethics and client security, corp. banking, bus. law and taxation WICHE, higher edn.), Am. Acad. Hosp. Attys., Am. Soc. Atty./CPAs, Alaska Soc. CPAs, U. Alaska Alumni Assn, (pres. Anchorage chpt. 1968-69), Sons of Norway, Pioneers of Alaska Igloo 15, Am. Legion, Amvets, Lions, Rotary, Ancient Teachings of Masters (bd. dirs., treas.). Avocation: metaphysics. Died Feb. 26, 2008.

BRUNER, JOHN MARTIN RUTHERFORD, anesthesiologist; b. Phila., Nov. 3, 1925; s. Martin Daniel and Ethel Blanche (Dent) B.; m. Barbara Temple, July 24, 1950; children: Temple, John Curtis, Bradford Calvin. MD, Harvard U., 1949. Practice gen. medicine, Groton, Mass., 1954-62; resident Peter Bent Brigham Hosp., Boston, 1963-64; practice medicine specializing in anesthesiology Mount Auburn Assocs., Cambridge, Mass., 1965-67, Mass. Gen. Hosp., Boston, from 1967. Author: Handbook of Blood Pressure Monitoring, 1978, (with P.F. Leonard) Electricity, Safety, and the Patient, 1989; contbr. several articles to profl. jours. Served to lt. USNR, PTO. Mem. AMA, Am. Soc. Anesthesiologists (del. to Nat. Fire Protection Assn. 1970—), Mass. Med. Soc., IEEE, Alpha Omega Alpha. Avocations: aviation, photography, music, nature. Home: Groton, Mass. Died May 28, 2008.

BRUNETTI, MELVIN T., federal judge; b. Reno, Nov. 11, 1933; m. Gail Dian Buchanan; children: Nancy, Bradley, Melvin Jr. Attended, U. Nev., 1951-53, 1956-57, 1960; JD, U. Calif., San Francisco, 1964. Mem. firm Vargas, Bartlett & Dixon, 1964-69, Laxalt, Bell, Allison & Lebaron, 1970-78, Allison, Brunetti, MacKenzie, Hartman, Soumbeniotis & Russell, 1978-85; judge US Ct. Appeals (9th cir.), Reno, 1985-99, sr. judge, 1999—2009. Mem. Council of Legal Advisors, Rep. Nat. Com., 1982-85. Served with US Army N.G., 1954-56. Mem. State Bar of Nev. (pres. 1984-85, bd. govs. 1975-84). Died Oct. 30, 2009.

BRUNNER, RONALD GENE, trade association administrator; b. Carthage, Mo., Oct. 10, 1947; s. Otis John and Alice Maxine (Richardson) B.; m. Diana Louise Davis, Aug. 11, 1967; children: Di Rhronda, Amber. BS in Mech. Engring., U. Mo., 1970. Reg. profl. engr., Okla. Project engr. Cities Svc. Oil & Gas, Tulsa, Okla., 1970-76, project mgr., 1976-82; measurement mgr. Occidental Oil & Gas, Tulsa, 1982-89; sr. project mgr. Edeco Engrs., Tulsa, 1989-94; dir. tech. svcs., corp. sec. Gas Processors Assn., Tulsa, from 1994. Contbr. articles to profl. jours. With U.S. Army, 1970. Mem. Am. Petroleum Inst. (Citation for Svc. 1989, 90). Avocations: fishing, boating, hunting, computers. Home: Tulsa, Okla. Died July 6, 2008.

BRUNT, MICHAEL, automotive executive; b. Springfield, Mass., July 24, 1940; s. Edmond Brunt and Louise (Kleinkauf) Brunt Sansone; m. Carol Jean Thompson, Nov. 5, 1966; children: Michael, Jim, John. Owner Mike's Motors, New Haven, 1967-70; v.p., then pres. Autocraft Corp., Branford, Conn., from 1971. Co-chmn. Inter-Industry Conf. on Auto Collision Repair, 1979-81; v.p., then pres. Autobody Concepts, Inc., Branford, 1984—; sec.-

treas. C.A.R.S. Software, Inc., Branford, 1984—. Mem. Autobody Assn. Conn. (pres. 1979-81), Autobody Assn. Greater New Haven (pres. 1979-81, 87—). Lodges: Masons (past officer), Rotary. Democrat. Home: Branford, Conn. Died May 29, 2008.

BRYAN-BROWN, PETER, psychiatrist; b. Ta Tung, China, Dec. 2, 1924; s. Douglas Stephen and Edith Emily (Loverock) B.; m. Evelyn Mary Smith, Feb. 12, 1949; children: Diana Jane, Nicholas Stephen, Susan Rose, Michael James. BA, Cambridge U., Eng., 1946; MD, $, 1949. Rsch. fellow Harvard Med. Sch., Cambridge, Mass., 1965-67; asst. prof. Hahnemann Med. Sch., Phila., 1978-93; psychiatrist Carrier Clinic, Belle Mead, N.J., 1978-93, G. Pierce Wood Meml. Hosp., Arcadia, Fla., from 1994. Mem. Am. Psychiat. Assn. (life). Avocations: sailing, gardening. Died Jan. 6, 2008.

BRYANT, JAMES CECIL, JR., academic administrator; b. Lake Wales, Fla., Oct. 21, 1931; s. James Cecil and Mary Lou (McCranie) B.; m. Marion Lois Carnett, June 19, 1955; children: David Mixon, Albert Carnett. BA, Stetson U., 1954; BD/MDiv, So. Bapt. Theol. Sem., 1958; MA, U. Miami, 1961; PhD, U. Ky., 1967. Asst. prof. English Fla. State U., Tallahassee, 1967-73; prof. English Mercer U., Atlanta, 1973-92, historian, spl. asst. to pres. Macon, Ga., from 1992. Author 13 books; contbr. articles to profl. jours., mags. and newspapers. Chaplain, editor Yaarab Shrine Temple, 1975—. Mem. Soc. Profl. Journalists, Scottish Rite, Masons, York Rite, Kiwanis (com. mem. 1986—), Atlanta Press Club. Avocations: historical research, freelance writing, walking, cooking, concerts. Died Feb. 11, 2008.

BUCHER, FRANÇOIS, art history educator; b. Lausanne, Switzerland, June 11, 1927; came to U.S., 1952; s. Alois J. and Gabrielle (Zundel) B.; divorced; 2 children. PhD, Bern U., Switzerland, 1955. With U. Minn., 1952-53, Yale U., 1954-60, Brown U., 1960-62, Princeton U., 1963-69, SUNY, Binghamton, 1970-77; prof. medieval art and architecture Fla. State U., Tallahassee; ret., 1997. Dir. Soc. Arch. Historians, 1964-67; mem. Exec. Coun. of Arts, State of N.J., 1965-70; pres. Internat. Ctr. Medieval Art, 1966-70; vis. prof. Ctr. d'Etudes Supérieures Mediévales, Poitiers, 1968; co-dir. Ctr. Medieval and Early Renaissance Studies, SUNY, Binghamton, 1973-77, sr. fellow, 1975—; mem. exec. coun. Southeastern Medieval Assn., 1983-86; pres. Nautilus Found., Lloyd, Fla., 1989—, mem. exec. coun.; mem. Archtl. Rsch. Ctr., 1993—; active numerous coms. Fla. State U., Tallahassee. Author: Notre-Dame de Bonmont und die ersten Zisterzienserabteien der Schweiz, 1957, Josef Albers, Trotz der Geraden, 1961, Josef Albers, Despite Straight Lines, 1969, 2d edit., 1977, paperback edit., 1978, Japanese edit., 1987, The Pamplona Bibles, 1970, Architector, The Lodge and Sketch-Books of Medieval Architects, 1979, The Traveler's Key to Medieval France, 1986, A Blazing End, 1984, paperback edit., 1986; founder, editor Gesta jour., 1961-70; contbr. articles to profl. jours. Chmn. Planning Bd., Millstone, N.J., 1964-70; trustee Interfuture, 1968—. With Swiss Armed Forces, 1948-51. Guggenheim fellow, 1956, 66, Inst. for Advanced Study fellow, 1962-63, Southeastern Inst. for Medieval and Renaissance Studies fellow, 1967; life fellow Internat. Ctr. Medieval Art, 1975—; Disting. scholar S.C. Coll., 1968-69, Faculty Exch. scholar SUNY, 1976-77. Democrat. Avocation: writing. Home: Tallahassee, Fla. Deceased.

BUCHMEYER, JERRY, retired federal judge; b. Overton, Tex., Sept. 5, 1933; Student, Kilgore Jr. Coll., 1953; BA, U. Tex., 1955, LL.B., 1957. Bar: Tex. 1957. Assoc. Thompson, Knight, Simmons & Bullion, Dallas, 1958-63, ptnr., 1963-66, sr. ptnr., 1968-79; judge U.S. Dist. Ct. (no. dist.) Tex., Dallas, 1979—2003, chief judge, 1995—2001, sr. judge, 2003—08. Mem. ABA, Dallas Bar Assn. (pres. 1979), State Bar Tex. (chmn. com. 1978-79, dir. 1982-84, 94-95). Died Sept. 21, 2009.

BUCK, PAUL, botany educator; b. Highland Park, Mich., Sept. 9, 1927; s. Paul and Ruth Virginia (Sharp) B.; m. Lou Ann Clark, 1950; children: Dana Lou, Paul BS, U. Tulsa, 1958, MS, 1959; PhD, U. Okla., 1962. Prof. botany U. Tulsa, 1962-87, prof. emeritus, from 1991. Instr. Rocky Mountain Biology Lab., Gothic, Colo., 1979—. Author: Winter Botany, Oklahoma, 1983, 2d edit., 1992; contbr. articles to profl. publs. With USN, 1945-52. Fellow Okla. Acad. Sci. (all offices, exec. sec.-treas. 1988-91). Home: Tulsa, Okla. Died Jan. 16, 2008.

BUCK, RICHARD EDWIN, lawyer; b. Boston, June 6, 1934; s. Robert Somerville and Alliette Greta (Valliere) B.; m. Anne Elizabeth Wivel, Dec. 29, 1956; children: Patricia A., Richard E., Jr., Steven D., David B., Lesley A., Karin E. A.B., Brown U., 1956; J.D., Villanova U., 1972. Bar: Pa. 1972. Vice pres. Cabot, Cabot & Forbes, Boston, 1965-67; assoc. Waters, Fleer, Cooper & Gallager, Norristown, Pa., 1972-75; sole practice, Flourtown, Pa., 1975-81; pres Richard E. Buck, Profl. Corp., Erdenheim, Pa., 1981-2009; dir. several corps. Township commr. Springfield Twp., Wyndmoor, Pa., 1983-92, pres. 1986-92 Recipient Disting. Achievement in Art and Sci. of Advocacy award Internat. Acad. Trial Lawyers, 1972. Mem. ABA, Pa. Bar Assn., Third Circuit Court Appeals. Republican. Lutheran. Club: Phila. Cricket (treas. 1971-77, v.p. 1977-78, former pres. 1988). Home: Philadelphia, Pa. Died June 14, 2009.

BUCKLEY, JOHN LEO, retired environmental biologist; b. Binghamton, NY, Sept. 22, 1920; s. Leo J. and Anna (Rounds) B.; m. Claire Bennett, May 24, 1947; children: Susan, John, James, David. BS, SUNY, 1942, MS, 1948, PhD, 1951. Instr. U. Alaska, Fairbanks, 1950-51, adj. prof., 1958; leader coop. wildlife rsch. unit U.S. Fish and Wildlife Svc., Fairbanks, 1951-58, dir. Patuxent Wildlife Rsch. Ctr. Laurel, Md., 1959-64; staff mem. office of sci. and tech. Office of the Pres., Washington, 1962-65, 68-71; environ. quality advisor sci. advisors office Dept. Interior, Washington, 1965-68; dep. dir. rsch. EPA, Washington, 1971-75, ret., 1975, mem. sci. adv. bd., 1975-81; cons. Nat. Inst. Environ. Health & Sci., Rsch. Triangle Park, N.C., 1975-76. Cons. Broome County Health Dept., Binghamton, 1981-91; mem. U.S. delegations on environ. pollution to Sweden, Japan, Fed. Republic Germany, USSR, Egypt, 1962-76. Author: (Nat. Acad. Press publ.) Ecological Knowledge and Environmental Problem Solving, 1986. City councilman Laurel, 1970-72; mem. Broome County Environ. Mgmt. Coun., 1978-95, Broome County Resource Recovery Aty., 1984-88. Capt. USMC, 1942-46, PTO. Fellow AAAS; mem. The Wildlife Soc., Sigma Xi. Democrat. Home: Fort Myers, Fla. Died Nov. 19, 2007.

BUGOS, JOSEPH VINCENT, retired food products company executive; b. Aug. 27, 1935; m. Gerry Bugos; children: Kevin, Joseph, Janine, Amy(dec.), Robert, Karen, Laurie. Grad., Loyola U., 1956; MBA, U. Chgo. Pres. Jewel Food Stores subs. Am. Stores Co., Melrose Park, Ill. Died June 11, 2009.

BUGOSH, JOHN, chemical company executive; b. Cleve., July 1, 1924; s. Andrew and Mary Veronica (Forgach) B.; m. Nancy Ann Perron, May 31, 1952; children: Nancy Jane, Pamela Marie, John Andrew. Student, Heidelberg Coll., Tiffin, Ohio, 1942; BS, Case Western Res. U., 1945, MS, 1947, PhD, 1949; dipl., Escuela Interam. De Verano, Saltillo, Mexico, 1948. Physics instr. Western Res. U., Cleve., 1950-51; rsch. assoc. E.I. DuPont de Nemours & Co., Inc., Wilmington, Del., 1949-63, devel. supr., 1963-66, planning specialist, 1966-70, mgr. environ. venture, 1970-78, mgr. distbr. programs, 1978-89; pres., chief exec. officer Trakon, Inc., West Chester, Pa., from 1989. Pres., chief exec. officer Trakon Inc., West Chester, Pa., 1989—. Contbr. over 25 articles to profl. jours.; author or co-author of 31 patents in colloidal alumina/silica/zirconia. Named Man of the Yr. Nat. Assn. Chem. Distbrs., 1979. Mem. Am. Chem. Soc. (Best Tech. paper of the Yr. 1961), Scientific Rsch. Soc. Am., Plantation Golf and Country Club, Radley Run Country Club, Dupont Country Club, Sigma Xi, Lambda Chi Alpha, Delta Phi Alpha. Avocations: gardening, golf, genealogy, european history, photography. Home: Venice, Fla. Died June 12, 2008.

BUITER, JEANNE, alumni association director; b. Chgo., Mar. 2, 1946; d. John and Anna (Vroom) B. BA, Calvin Coll., 1969; MFA, Art Inst. Chgo., 1977; MBA, U. Chgo., 1986. Tchr. Oakdale Christian Sch., Grand Rapids, 1969-73, Lab. Schs., U. Chgo., Ill., 1976-86; broker Marvene Fischer Sales, Chgo., 1986-88; exec. dir. alumni assn. U. Chgo., Ill., from 1988. Home: Oak Park, Ill. Died Feb. 23, 2008.

BULKELEY, CHRISTY CLAIRE, retired foundation administrator; b. Galesburg, Ill., Feb. 10, 1942; d. Geraldand Clough and Patricia Ann (Pettingell) Bulkeley; m. Perry David Finks, Sept. 6, 1975. BJ, U. Mo., 1964; MA in Theological Studies, Wesley Theological Seminary, 1994. Reporter The Times-Union, Rochester, NY, 1964—72, editl. page editor, 1973—74; pres., pub., editor Saratogian, Saratoga Springs, NY, 1974—76, 1984, Comml. News, Danville, Ill., 1976—84; v.p. cen. region newspaper div. Gannett Co. Inc., 1981—84, v.p. spl. corp. projects, 1984; v.p. Gannett Found., 1985—92. Contbr. New Guardians of the Press, 1983. Bd. dirs. Danville Area Econ. Devel. Corp., Cmty. Coll. Found., Danville, Vermilion County OIC, Danville, Travers Com., Saratoga, NY; leadership giving capt., nominating com Greater Rochester United Way, 1986—89; adv. bd. U. Mo. Sch. Journalism, 1986; v.p. Rochester Grantmakers Forum, 1986—88; mem. steering com. Rochester Womens Fund, 1986—88. Recipient awards Gannett Co. Inc., 1984, Outstanding Contbns. Ill., Mcpl. Human Rels. Assn., 1981, Young Achiever Nat. Coun. Women, 1976. Mem.: Danville Area C. of C. (bd. dirs. 1980—84), Soc. Profl. Journalists, Inland Daily Press Assn. (bd. dirs. 1983—84), Am. Soc. Newspaper Editors (bd. dirs. 1983—84), Women in Comm. Inc. (pres. 1975—76, headliner 1978), Women and Found/Corp. Philanthropy (program com. 1988—89), AP (nominating com. 1979—84), Carolina Trace Club. Home: Sanford, NC. Died Sept. 13, 2009.

BULL, THOMAS EYVIND, physical chemist; b. Richmond, Va., Aug. 5, 1945; s. Storm and Ellen Elizabeth (Cross) B.; m. Carin Margaretha Elisabeth Bertilsson, Sept. 18, 1981. BS, U. Calif., Berkeley, 1967; PhD, U. Ill., 1970. Postdoctoral fellow in phys. chemistry Lund (Sweden) Inst. Tech., 1970-74, docent, 1975-78; project dir. Office of Tech. Assessment, Washington, 1978-85, sr. assoc., 1985-87; rsch. chemist CBER/FDA, Bethesda, Md., 1985-92 and from 99; dep. dir. Divsn. Allergenic Products/Parasitology, CBER/FDA, Bethesda, 1992-99. Participant U.S.-China Sci. Policy Conf., Washington, 1983; leader of panel to evaluate performance of U.S. Agy. for Internat. Devel. "Bioenergy Sys. and Tech." project, Washington, 1982; U.S. del. to UN Food and Agr. Orgn. expert consultation, Rome, 1980; others. Contbr. over 50 articles to profl. jours. Mem. reg. parliament Swedish tenant's Union, Lund, 1975-78. Mem. AAAS, Am. Phys. Soc., Phi Beta Kappa, Phi Lambda Upsilon. Died July 22, 2008.

BUNDY, FRANCIS PETTIT, physicist; b. Columbus, Ohio, Sept. 1, 1910; s. Lyman Edmund and Edith Claire (Scott) B.; m. Hazel Victoria Forwood, Oct. 24, 1936; children: John F., Suzanne V., Freda M., David S. BS, Otterbein Coll., 1931; MS, Ohio State U., 1932, PhD, 1937, DSc (hon.), 1959. From instr. to assoc. prof. physics Ohio U., Athens, 1937-42; rsch. assoc. Harvard Underwater Sound Lab., Cambridge, Mass., 1942-45; rsch. physicist USN Underwater Sound Lab., New London, Conn., 1945; rsch. assoc. GE Rsch. Lab., Schenectady, N.Y., 1946-87. Co-author, co-editor: Progress in Very High Pressure Research, 1961; contbr. articles to profl. jours. Mem. sch. bd. Niskayuna (N.Y.) Sch. Dist., 1962-70. Recipient Roozeboom Gold medal Netherlands Acad. Arts & Sci., 1969, Bridgman Gold medal Internat. Soc. High Pressure Sci. and Tech., 1987. Fellow Am. Phys. Soc.; mem. AAAS, Internat. Assn. Advancement High Pressure Sci. and Technology, Sigma Xi. Methodist. Achievements include 23 U.S. patents relating to sonar transducers, vacuum thermal insultation, ultra-high pressure apparatus, diamond synthesis. Home: Lebanon, Ohio. Died Feb. 23, 2008.

BURCHFIELD, JERRY LEE, artist, educator, author; b. Chgo., July 28, 1947; s. Darrell and Margaret (Reames) B.; m. Barbara Jane Blaha, Aug. 24, 1968; 1 child, Brian. BA, Calif. State U.-Fullerton, 1971, MA in Art, 1976; MFA, Calif. State U., Fullerton, 1990. One-man shows include Laguna Beach (Calif.) Mus. Art, 1974, Arco Ctr. Visual Art, L.A., 1976, Tyler Sch. Art, Phila., Laguna Beach Sch. Art, 1977, Eastern Wash. U., 1978, Foto Gallery, N.Y.C., L.A. Mcpl. Art Gallery, Barnsdall Park, Hollywood, 1979, Susan Spiritus Gallery, Newport Beach, Calif., Yuen Lui Gallery, Seattle, Ufficio Dell Arte, Paris, France, 1980, No. Ill. U., Colo. Coll., 1981, George Eastman House, Rochester, N.Y., Orange Coast Coll., Gallery Graphics, San Diego, 1982, Golden West Coll., 1983, Irvine (Calif.) Fine Arts Ctr., 1985, Amarillo (Tex.) Coll., 1985, Andover (Mass.) Gallery, 1984, Osaka Contemporary Art Ctr., Japan Min Gallery, Tokyo, 1988, Long Beach Mus. of Art, Calif., 1989, Calif. State U., Fullerton, La., 1990, Newport Harbor Art Mus., Calif., 1993, Orange County Ctr. Contemporary Art, 1993, Irvine Valley Coll., Calif., 1998, Laguna Art Mus., Ga., 2000, UCR/Calif. Mus. Photography, 2003, Scape Gallery, Corona DelMar, Calif., 2004, Fahey/Klein, LA, 2005, Scape Gallery, Corona Del Mar, 2007; group exhbns. include Rochester Inst. Tech., Chgo. Art Inst., Bowers Mus., Santa Ana, Calif., Sioux City (Iowa) Art Ctr., L.A. Ctr. for Photog. Studies, Franklin Inst., Phila., L.A. County Mus. Art, George Eastman House, Rochester, Am. House, Berlin, Fed. Republic Germany, Columbia Coll., Chgo., Orange County Mus. Art, Ufficio Dell Arte, Harvard U., Kicken Gallery, Koln, Fed. Republic Germany, Fla. State U., Tallahassee, 1984, Pavillion Des Arts de La Ville de Paris, 1984, New Photo Montage, Chgo. Art Inst., 1984, Calif. State U. Long Beach Art Mus., 1985, John Michael Kohler Arts Ctr., Sheboygan, Wis., 1985, Clarence Kennedy Gallery, Cambridge, Mass., 1985, Gallery Min, Tokyo, 1986, La Ctr. for Photo Studies, L.A., 1986, Laguna Beach (Calif.) Mus., 1986, Photo Resource Ctr., Boston, 1986, U. So. Calif., L.A., 1986, Photokina, Germany, 1986, La Joua Mus. Contempart, L.A., 1987, L.A. County Mus., 1989, Pomona Coll., 1990, Calif. Mus. Photoge, Riverside, 1992, Laguna Art Mus., Calif., 1993, UCLA Armand Hammer Mus., 1995, Mus. Fine Arts, Fla. State U., 1997, Orange County Mus. Art, Calif., 1997, Biola U., L.A., 1997, Mt. St. Mary's Coll., L.A., 1997, Mus. Photographic Art, San Diego, 2003, Yuma Art Symposium, Ariz., 2006, Laguna Art Mus., Laguna Beach, Calif., 2006, Art Ctr. Coll. of Design, Pasadena, Calif, 2007; represented in permanent collections in L.A. County Mus. Art, Oakland, Mus., George Eastman House, Long Beach State U., Bibliotheque Nationale, Paris, Bellevue (Wash.) Art Mus., Denver Art Mus., Security Pacific Bank, Chase Manhattan Bank, Ea. Wash. U., St. Louis Mus. Art, Newport Harbor Art Mus., U. Calif.-Riverside Mus., Photography, Mus. Photog. Arts, San Diego, Laguna Beach Mus. and So. Coast Plz., Mountain Bell, Gould Corp., Chgo., Ctr. Creative Photography, Tuscon; cons. KOCE-TV, Huntington Beach, Calif., 1983, Laguna Beach Mus., 1982—; author: Darkroom Art, 1981, Photography in Focus, 1996, Light as Substance, 1998, Habitat, 2000, In Transition, 2003, Primanl Image Amazonas, 2004, Edge of Air, 2005; editor: No Mo Po Mo Mag., 1995-98; illus., contbr.: The Basic Darkroom Book, 1978; contbr. articles to photog. mags. Recipient Excellence award Nat. Inst. Staff and Orgnl. Devel., Faculty Devel. award Cypress Coll., 1996, Out of Box Thinkers award Calif. C.C. League, 1999, Outstanding Individual Artist award Orange County, 2001, Outstanding Contrbn. to Arts award Cypress Cultural Arts Commn., 2001, Art in Pub. Places award, AIA, Orange County Arch. Found., 2006; fellow Nat. Endowment Arts, 1981. Mem. Soc. Photog. Edn., Laguna Beach Arts Alliance (dir. 1980), Laguna Wilderness Press (co-founder, 2002), Found. for Innovation and Sustainability (adv. bd.), The Legacy Project (pres.). Home: Irvine, Calif. Died Sept. 11, 2009.

BUREAU, ANGELA MARY, publishing executive; b. Rochester, Minn., Dec. 3, 1939; d. Frank Theodore and Angela Maria (Stachowiak) Kubista; m. John Frederick Bureau, Dec. 26, 1964; children: Angela Mary, John Frederick, Julie Ann, David Joseph, Ann Louise, Theresa Marie. BA, Coll. St. Catherine, 1960; postgrad., Cath. U. Am., 1962, U. Minn., 1964. Pres. Theo's Books, St. Paul, from 1982; gen. comdr. God's Army, St. Paul, from 1981. Guest nat. cable TV, Birmingham, Ala., 1987-88; instr. seminars on holiness Minn., Wis., Mo. Author: Nine Keys to Sanctity, 1976; editor God's Army News, 1981—. Avocations: drama, music, sports. Died Oct. 7, 2007.

BURG, WALTER A., retired airport terminal executive; b. Detroit, 1942; m. Sue Burg. B in Bus., U. Ariz. Airport firefighter Tucson Airport Authority, 1966, gen. manager (title later changed to CEO) Ariz., 1966-79, pres., CEO Ariz., 1979—2003. Chmn. Metropolitan Tucson Convention & Visitors Bur., Carondelet Health Network, Tucson Metropolitan C. of C. Served Ariz. Air Nat. Guard. Recipient William E. Downes Jr. Memorial award, Airports Coun. Internat.- N.Am. (ACI-NA), 2008. Mem.: Airports Coun. Insternat. (chmn.), Ariz. Airport Assn. (founding mem.), Tucson Conquistadores, Tucson Centurions (chmn.). Achievements include being the second-longest serving commercial airport chief executive in the US and only the third chief executive the authority had since its formation in 1948 upon retirement in 2002. Died Nov. 9, 2005.

BURGELIN, JOHN GEORGE, chemical company executive, consultant; b. Phila., Aug. 29, 1944; s. John George and Mary Elizabeth (Little) B.; m. Joanna Faye DuBois, Dec. 28, 1965; children: Jeffrey Todd, Michael Alan, Christopher Scott. Student, Palm Beach Jr. Coll., 1962-64, U. Va., 1968-69. Supr. field Am.-DuBois, Lake Worth, Fla., 1969-72; mgr. territory Winston Industries, Noel, Mo., 1972-74; tech. rep. Nat. Chemsearch, Dallas, 1974-79; owner, operator Tech-Reps, Joplin, Mo., from 1979. Pres. com. for Better Schs., Carl Junction, Mo., 1980. Served as staff sgt. USMC, 1965-69, Vietnam. Mem.: Rotary. Republican. Presbyterian. Avocations: tennis, golf. Home: Joplin, Mo. Died Nov. 3, 2007.

BURGER, JOSEPH VICTOR, education educator; b. NYC, June 29, 1946; s. Alfred Benedict and Bertha (Glanzman) B.; m. Carol Ann Ungarten, Feb. 15, 1947 (div. Apr. 1991); children: Robert, Jordan, Daniel; m. Marsha Joyce Keller, Sept. 5, 1993; children: Jaime, Cheryl. BA in Psychology, Queens Coll., NYC, 1968; MA in Ednl. Psychology, NYU, 1971; PhD in Human Rels., Ind. No. U., 1973. Tchr. spl. edn. jr. high sch., high sch. and elem. sch. N.Y.C. Bd. Edn., 1969-71; tchr. spl. edn. Comsewogue Schs., Port Jefferson Station, N.Y., 1971-75; supervising counselor Narcotics Guidance, Riverhead, N.Y., 1971-75; cons. Bd. Coop. Ednl. Svcs. III Intercultural Rels., NYC, 1972-74; assoc. prof. edn. Dowling Coll., Oakdale, N.Y., from 1975; pvt. practice marriage, family, child counselor LI, N.Y., from 1975. Bd. dirs. Commn. Resources, Cons. in Quality Performance, N.Y.C., Common Visions; adj. prof. Suffolk C.C./Adelphi U., L.I., 1972-76; cons. Spl. Edn. Tng. and Resource Ctr., Bd. Coop. Ednl. Svcs. II, Patchogue, N.Y., 1984—, N.E. Regional Ctr./Drug-Free Schs., Sayville, N.Y., 1989—; evaluator Drug Abuse Resistance Edn.-Suffolk County Police, Yaphank, N.Y., 1992. Contbr. articles to profl. jours. Mem. NEA, Coun. Exceptional Children, Nat. Acad. Counselors and Family Therapists, N.Y. State United Tchrs., Assn. N.Y. State Educators of Emotionally Disturbed, Phi Delta Kappa, Kappa Delta Pi. Jewish. Avocations: music, athletics, paraplaning, travel. Home: Setauket, NY. Died Nov. 12, 2007.

BURGESS, RICHARD HENRY, securities firm executive; b. Geneva, Ill., Apr. 26, 1934; s. M. Henry and Gladys (Newton) B.; m. Charlotte S. Crumbaugh, Aug. 8, 1959; 1 child, Mary Katherine. BA, DePauw U., 1956. Salesman Procter & Gamble, Chgo., 1959-62; sales mgr. IDS, Chgo., 1962-80; v.p. Dreher & Assocs., Oakbrook Terrace, Ill., from 1980. With U.S. Army, 1957-59, Korea. Mem. Villa Park Hist. Soc. (life), Ill. Prairie Path, Villa Park Rotary (pres. 1985-86, Paul Harris fellow). Avocations: tennis, gardening, antiques. Home: Sycamore, Ill. Died Aug. 15, 2008.

BURI, CAROLYN, management consultant; BS in Music Edn., Ohio State U., 1964; M in Consulting, Hubbard Coll. Adminstrn. Internat., 2000. Lic. master cons. World Inst. Scientology Enterprises. Tchr. music Ohio Schs., New Philadelphia, Ohio, 1964—69, Dept. of Def. Overseas Tchg. Sys., Clark Air Base, Philippines, 1969—72; mem. staff Scientology, Hollywood, Calif., 1972—96; exec. mgr. Manago Chiropractic Inc., Mission Viejo, Calif., 1997—98, Wiseman & Burke, Glendale, Calif., 1998—99; pvt. practice as cons. in pers. efficiency and bus. expansion LA, from 1999. Spkr. in field, presenter seminars, workshops. Mem.: C. of C., World Inst. Scientology, Bus. Expansion Club (bd. dirs., Commendation award 2002). Avocations: swimming, movies, reading, poetry, writing. Home: Tujunga, Calif. Died Nov. 24, 2007.

BURKETT, EUGENE JOHN, chemical engineer; b. Cin., Nov. 15, 1937; s. James E. and Amelia (Kues) B.; married, Apr. 15, 1977; 1 child, Matthew. BSChemE, U. Cin., 1962. Mgr. chem. plants engring. Goodyear Tire and Rubber Co., Akron, Ohio, 1973-75, mgr. corp. environ. engring., 1975-84, engring. mgr., 1985-88; tech. supt. Shell Chem. Co. (formerly Goodyear Tire and Rubber Co.), Apple Grove, W.Va., from 1988. Mem. AICE (sect. pres. 1978). Home: Scott Depot, W.Va. Died Aug. 6, 2008.

BURNETT, BOBBY J., minister; b. Alexander City, Ala., Jan. 28, 1932; s. Rueben J. and Mollie (Newman) B.; m. Nobie Ruth O'Neal, Sept. 8, 1963; children: Tracy Ann Burnett Taylor, Bobby J. Jr. MusB, La. State U., 1956; DD (hon.), Bapt. Christian U., 1982. Ordained to ministry Bapt. Ch. Pastor Temple Bapt. Ch., Baton Rouge, La., from 1956. Evangelist; tchr. music Stamps Quartet Sch. Music, Dallas, 1954-58, Gospel Singers of Am. Sch. Gospel Music, Pass Christian, Miss., 1956—; song writer Stamps Quartet Music Co., Dallas; bd. dirs. Gospel Singers Am., Inc., Pass Christian, 1956—; prin. Temple Christian Ch., Baton Rouge, 1973—. Composer various gospel songs. Mem. La. Bapt. Bible Fellowship (chmn. 1980-81). Home: Baton Rouge, La. Died Mar. 13, 2008.

BURNS, JAMES MILTON, retired music educator; b. Coal City, Ind., Feb. 22, 1922; s. Ray L. and N. Eugenie (Pickett) B.; m. Thomasina Ciofalo, Aug. 22, 1970. MusB, Manhattan Sch. Music, 1949, MusM, 1953; EdD, Fairleigh Dickinson U., 1984. Tchr. music Atlantic City Bd. Edn., 1968-92. Researcher acoustics of band instruments. Home: Woodbine, NJ. Died Feb. 17, 2008.

BURNS, JAY, III, retired science educator, research scientist; b. Lake Wales, Fla., Mar. 22, 1924; s. Jay Burns, Jr. and Harlan Sheafe Burns; m. Dulcie Evans Burns, Oct. 14, 1948; children: Jay IV, Wendy Waggoner, William Scott. BSChemE, Northwestern U., Evanston, Ill., 1947; MS in Physics, U. Chgo., 1951, PhD, 1959. Rsch. scientist U. Chgo. Midway Labs., 1951—61; assoc. prof. astronomy and astrophysics Northwestern U., Evanston, 1965—72; CEO Lakeside Labs., Highland Park, Ill., 1972—75; prof., head, dept. physics and space sci. Fla. Inst. Tech., Melbourne, Fla., 1975—88, prof., 1988—93, prof. emeritus, physics & space sci., from 1993; dir. U. of Chgo. Lab. Applied Sci., Ill., 1961—65. Cons. rsch. scientist US Naval Rsch. Lab, Orlando, 1988—93. Contbr. over 40 articles to profl. jours. With USN, 1942—45. Avocations: flying, sailing, cruising, tennis. Home: Wellington, Fla. Died Apr. 11, 2008.

BURNS, JOSEPHINE DORA, artist; b. Llandudno, Wales, July 2, 1917; came to U.S., 1926; d. Vincent Leo and Harriet Matilda (Williams) Lazzaro; m. Jerome Burns, Nov. 17, 1943. Cert., Cooper Union Art Sch., NYC, 1939; BFA, Cooper Union Art Sch., 1976. Draftsman George Sharp, Marine Architect, NYC, 1941-45; co-dir. Hicks St. Gallery, Bklyn., 1958-63; assoc. dir. Brownstone Gallery, Bklyn., 1969-76. Exhibited in group shows at C.W. Post Coll. Mus., Bklyn. Mus., Nat. Arts Club, Nat. Acad., Audubon Artists Exhibit, Alonzo Gallery, N.Y.C., Okla. Mus. Art, Salena Gallery L.I. U., 1984, Thompson's Gallery, London, 1999, 2000; solo exhibit Auld Alliance Gallery, Nashville, 1994; exhibit of 32-page color catalogue for exhibit Gallery Ynys Môn, Anglesey, North Wales, 1998. Fellow MacDowell Colony, 1960, 62, 64, 65, 68, Yaddo, 1961. Died June 20, 2008.

BURNS, MARY MITCHELL, special education educator; b. LA, Oct. 22, 1928; d. William Henry Flynn and Fern Ruth Cummins; m. John David Mitchell, Aug. 2, 1962 (dec. Mar. 1972); children: Nancy Lynne Thomas, John William Thomas II; m. Robert Berry Burns, June 19, 1982; 1 child, Tobias. MA, Calif. State U., Chico, 1978; EdD, Calif. State U., Santa Ana, 1980, PhD, 1995. Tchg. credentials. Tchr. Calif. pub. schs., Redding and Sacramento, 1972-87; substitute tchr. Calif. pub. schs. Redding, from 1987. Avocation: travel agent. Home: Redding, Calif. Died Nov. 20, 2007.

BURNS, WILLIAM EDGAR, chemical engineer; b. Altus, Okla., Oct. 23, 1924; s. Edgar Willimer and Thelma Mollie (Kelly) B.; m. Geraldine Era McCarty, Aug. 30, 1946; children: David W, Edgar M., Molly I., Patricia Gail, James H. BS in Chem. Engring., U. Okla., 1945. Engring. mgr. Phillips Petroleum Co., Bartlesville, Okla., 1946-69; group v.p. Iowa Beef Processors, Dakota City, Nebr., 1969-75; mgr. process engring. Crest Engring., Tulsa, 1976-85; cons. William E. Burns, Inc., Tulsa, 1985-89; mgr. process and tech. John Brown E&C, Tulsa, 1989-94; cons. Tulsa, from 1994. Lt. (j.g.) USN, 1943-46, PTO. Mem. Am. Inst. Chem. Engrs. Republican. Mem. Ch. of Christ. Achievements include 3 patents in petrochems. Home: Tulsa, Okla. Died Nov. 12, 2007.

BURSON-DYER, LORRAINE, library executive; b. Omaha, Dec. 20, 1925; d. Elmer Ivan and Marie Eleanor (Benedict) Eastman; m. Francis Mark Burson, Apr. 25, 1948 (wid.); children: Melanie Burson Daniel, Brent Donald, Brian Lee; m. Eldon A. Dyer, July 11, 2004. BA with honors, Portland State U., 1975. Cons. Congregational Libr., Portland, from 1975; libr. Peace Ch. of Brethren, Portland, 1948—55, Burlingame Bapt. Ch., Portland, 1961—88, Village Bapt. Ch., Beaverton, Oreg., 1987—93; exec. dir. Ch. and Synagogue Libr. Assn., Portland, 1987—2006; ret. Author: Recruiting and Training Volunteers for Church/Synagogue Libraries, 1986; contbr. articles to numerous mags. Named Outstanding Scholar, Portland State U., 1974. Mem. Pacific N.W. Assn. Ch. Librs. (pres. 1988-89), N.W. Assn. Christian Librs., Assn. Christian Librs., Nat. Ch. Libr. Coun., Congregational Librs. Assn. of B.C., Luth. Ch. Libr. Assn., Evangel. Ch. Libr. Assn. Baptist. Home: Beaverton, Oreg. Died June 30, 2008.

BURT, JOHN HARRIS, retired bishop; b. Marquette, Mich., Apr. 11, 1918; s. Bates G. and Emily May (Bailey) B.; m. Martha M. Miller, Feb. 16, 1946; children: Susan, Emily, Sarah, Mary. BA, Amherst Coll., 1940, D.D. (hon.), 1960; BA, Va. Theol. Sem., 1943, B.D., 1967; D.D., Youngstown U., 1958, Kenyon Coll., 1967. Boys worker Christodora House, NYC, 1940-41; ordained to ministry Episcopal Ch., 1943; canon Christ Ch. Cathedral; rector St. Paul's Ch., St. Louis, 1943-44; chaplain to Episc. students U. Mich., 1946-50; rector St. John's Ch., Youngstown, Ohio, 1950-57, All Saints Ch., Pasadena, Calif., 1957-67; bishop coadjutor Ohio, 1967-68; Episc. bishop of Ohio, 1968-84. Pres. So. Calif. Council Chs., 1962-65; mem. bd. Ch. Soc. Coll. Work, 1964-71; chmn. clergy deployment bd. Episc. Ch., 1971-73 Co-author: World Religions and World Peace, 1969, Joy in the Struggle - Memoirs of Ecumenical Dialogue, 1993; author: Economic Justice and the Christian Conscience, 1987. Pres. Youngstown Coordinating Coun., 1953-56, Pasadena Cmty. Coun., 1964-66; trustee Pomona Coll., 1963-66, Va. Theol. Sem., 1967-72, Colgate-Rochester Div. Sch., 1968-84, Kenyon Coll., 1967-84; bd. dirs. United Way L.A., 1964-67, Cleve. Urban Coalition, 1968-70, Ams. for Energy Independence, 1975-85; bd. dirs. Nat. Com. Against Censorship, 1974—; chmn. bd. dirs. St. John's Home for Girls, Painesville, Ohio, 1968-84; governing bd. Nat. Coun. Chs., 1970-81; mem. Com. on Ch. Order, Consultation of Ch. Union, 1980-88; chmn. com. on theology Episc. Ch. House Bishops, 1973-80; chmn. Urban Bishops Coalition, 1977-93, Faith and Order Commn. Ohio Coun. Chs., 1970-74; bd. dirs. Episcopal Ch. Pub. Co., 1985-92, pres., 1990-92; chmn. commn. ecumenical rels. Episc. Ch., 1973-79, also chmn. commn. mid. judicatories, cons. on ch. union, 1975-79; chmn. com. human affairs and health Episc. Ch., 1982-85; chmn. Bishops Com. Nat. and Internat. Affairs, 1982-85; chmn. Ecumenical Gt. Lakes Project on Econ. Crisis, 1983-89; chmn. Presiding Bishop's Com. Christian-Jewish Rels., 1986-91; pres. Nat. Christian Leadership Conf. on Israel, 1988-99; mem. ch. rels. com. U.S. Holocaust Meml. Coun., 1989-96; mem. Ecumenical Consultation on New Religions Movements, 1985-87; bd. dirs. Ams. for Med. Progress, Inc., 1992-95. Chaplain USNR, 1943-46. Recipient Arvona Lynch Human Relations award Youngstown, 1956; Rissica Human Relations award Jewish War Vets., 1966; Pasadena Community Relations award, 1967; Cleve.'s Simon Bolivar award, 1972; Pitts.'s Thomas Merton award, 1978; Human Rights award Ohio br. ACLU, 1980; Ecumenical Leadership award Christian Ch. (Disciples of Christ), 1986, Am. Jewish Com. award, 1991. Mem. Phi Gamma Delta. Episcopalian. Home: Marquette, Mich. Died Oct. 20, 2009.

BURTON, ROBERT CLYDE, science educator; b. Borger, Tex., Feb. 27, 1929; s. Earl and Edith Belle Burton; m. Betty Jean Hill, Oct. 6, 1951; children: Randall L., Roger E., Jana S. Cornett, Jill E. Brown. BA, Tex. Tech U., 1957, MA, 1959; PhD, U. N.Mex, 1965. From asst. prof. to assoc. prof. W. Tex. State U., Canyon, 1959—63, prof., dept. head, 1966—76, prof. geology, 1976—89; prof. Temple U., Tokyo, 1989—91; prof. emeritus W. Tex. A&M U., Canyon, from 1991. Owner Geomag Surveys, Canyon, from 1970. Contbr. articles to profl. jours. Sgt. USAF, 1948—52. Recipient Favorite Prof. award, W. Tex. State Coll., Canyon, 1960. Democrat. Presbyterian. Avocation: golf. Home: Canyon, Tex. Died Feb. 26, 2008.

BUSBY, JHERYL, record company executive; b. L.A., May 5, 1949; Attended, Long Beach State Coll. Nat. promotions dir. Casablanca Records; pres., black music divsn. MCA Records, 1984-88; pres., CEO Motown Records, 1988-95; head urban divsn. DreamWorks Records, 1998—2001; CEO Def Soul Classics, 2004—08. Bd. dirs. Founders Nat. Bank, 2001—08. Recipient Path of Excellence award, Hutson-Tillotson Coll., 2001. Died Nov. 4, 2008.

BUSCH, DANIEL ADOLPH, geologist, educator; b. St. Paul, May 31, 1912; s. Karl George Adolph and Lulu Elizabeth Busch; m. Emilie Louise Finch; children: Daniel Andrew(dec.), David Arthur. BSc, Capital U., Columbus, Ohio, 1934, DSc (hon.), 1960; MA, Ohio State U., Columbus, 1936, PhD, 1939. Instr. U. Pitts., 1938—42; with Pa. Geol. Survey, Pitts., 1943—44, Huntley & Huntley Petroleum Cons., Pitts., 1944—46; sr. rsch. geologist Carter Rsch. Lab., Tulsa, 1946—51; chief geologist Zephyr Petroleum Co., Tulsa, 1951—54; petroleum geology cons. Tulsa, 1955—89; ret., 1989. Vis. prof. geology U. Okla., Norman, 1964—74; lectr. Oil & Gas Cons., Internat., Tulsa, 1967—89; lectr. in field; cons. in field. Author: Stratigraphic Traps in Sandstones - Exploration Techniques, 1974 (Robert Dott Best Publ. award, 1975), Exploration Methods for Sandstone Reservoirs, 1985. Fellow: Geol. Soc. Am. (sr.); mem.: Am. Assn. Petroleum Geologists (hon.; v.p. 1966—67, pres. 1973—74, Matson award 1959, Leverson award 1971, Sidney Powers medal 1982, Monroe Cheney award 2003, Am. Registry of Outstanding Profls. from 2003), Sigma Xi. Avocations: travel, gardening, investments. Died Nov. 7, 2007.

BUSSE, KATHERINE CHAPIN, social worker, public administrator; b. Chgo., June 10, 1911; d. Ira J. and Lillian (Holznogel) Chapin; widowed; children: Katha Busse Martin, Barbara, Susan Busse Terzuoli, James, Martha Busse Cavanagh, Peter. BS, De Pauw U., 1932; MS in Retailing, NYU, 1933; MA, U. Chgo., 1964. Cert. social worker, Ill., real estate broker. Buyer girls wear Emporium, San Francisco, 1934-36; buyer Fair Store, Chgo., 1936-39; real estate broker Piersen Realty, Deerfield, Ill., 1952-59; social worker Ill. Dept. Pub. Aid, Waukegan, 1960-64, family welfare cons., 1964-65, dir. edn., asst. to downstate mgr., supr. self support, 1965-74; asst. to downstate mgr. Ill. Dept. Pub. aid. Founder Friends of Pauma Valley, Calif., 1988; vol patient care Elizabeth Hospice. Recipient Big Apple award Pauma Valley Sch., 1990, JC Penney Golden Rule award 1993, Unity award Palomar Pomerado Health Systems, 1996. Mem. Acad. Certified Social Workers. Republican. Methodist. Avocation: collecting bing grondahl plates and music boxes. Died July 4, 2008.

BUTERO, LAURA LEE, education association professional; b. Berkeley, Calif., Nov. 25, 1946; d. Percy Dorval and Gertrude (Brown) Barchard. BS in Journalism, U. Oreg., 1984. Sr. tester quality control Owens Corning

Fiberglas, Santa Clara, Calif., 1965-67, 70-72; serviceperson Pacific Gas & Electric Co., San Jose, Calif., 1975-77; pipeperson, gas serviceperson N.W. Natural Gas Co., Eugene, Oreg., 1979-81; field rep. Oreg. Edn. Assn. Choice Trust, Tigard, from 1985. Served with USN, 1967-70. Democrat. Avocations: sports, politics, reading. Died Nov. 14, 2007.

BUTHERUS, MARJORIE ELAINE, retired bank officer; b. Burlington Junction, Mo., Aug. 21, 1927; d. William Achilles and Florence Elizabeth (Wallace) Thornhill; m. Paul Francis Butherus, Feb. 15, 1947; children: Ted Francis, Mark Franklin, Paula Elaine, Thomas David, Pamela Ann, Martin Albert. Grad. high sch., Maryville, Mo. Sec. Nodaway Valley Bank, Maryville, Mo., 1945-49; utility stenographer City Nat. Bank, Kansas City, Mo., 1952-53; consumer banking officer Commerce Bank of Kansas City, Lexington, Mo., 1972-94; ret., 1994. Treas., Lafayette County chpt. ARC, 1974—, county chmn., 1989—, also bd. dirs.; treas. Lexington Cmty. Betterment, 1985—, Lexington Literacy Coun., 1991, Lead 200 Leadership Coun., 1990—. Mem. Bus. and Profl. Women (1st v.p. Lexington 1991-92, bd. dirs., Woman of Yr. award 1991), Lexington Bus. and Profl. Women's Club (pres.), Gen. Federated Women's Club (treas. Lexington chpt., v.p.), Lexington Hist. Soc., Woman's Club Lexington, Optimists (charter Lexington, sec.-treas. 1989—). Roman Catholic. Home: Lexington, Mo. Died Apr. 20, 2008.

BUTLER, EULOUS SONNY, small business owner; b. Eastman, Ga., Feb. 18, 1939; s. Eulous S. Butler and Johnnie Lois (Youngblood) Hanson; m. Sondra Arnold; children: Lindy Renee Butler, Tracy Leigh. BS, U Nebr., 1969; MS, George Washington U., 1972. Commd. 2d lt. U.S. Army, 1963, advanced through grades to lt. col., 1978, assigned to Europe, Vietnam, CONUS, 1963-83; dir. med. mktg. Martin Marietta Data Systems Co., Greenbelt, Md., 1983-85; gen. mgr. govt. ops. Baxter Travenol Corp., Washington, 1985-86; owner, pres. SYSA, Inc., San Antonio, from 1986. Instr. U. Md., Roosevelt U., San Antonio Coll., Cen. Tex. Coll., 1972-83; asst. chair dept. computer sci. U. North Tex.; cons. Travenol Labs., U.S. Office Pers. Mgmt., Identity Rsch. Inst., Inc., 1983—, CIS (Computer Info. Scis.), Inc., Nat. Video Inc. Contbr. chpts. to books, articles to profl. jours. Decorated Bronze Star. Avocations: scuba, tennis, golf, sailing. Home: Lexington, Ky. Died Dec. 15, 2007.

BUTTERWORTH, ROBERT ROMAN, psychologist, researcher, media therapist; b. Pittsfield, Mass., June 24, 1946; s. John Leon and Martha Helen (Roman) B. BA, SUNY, 1972; MA, Marist Coll., 1975; PhD in Clin. Psychology, Calif. Grad. Inst., 1983. Asst. clin. psychologist N.Y. State Dept. Mental Hygiene, Wassaic, 1972-75; pres. Internat. Trauma Assocs., L.A. and Downey, Calif., from 1976. Cons. L.a. County Dept. Health Svc.; staff clinician San Bernardino County Dept. Mental Health, 1983-85; staff psychologist State of Calif. Dept. Mental Health, 1985—; media interviews include PA, L.A. Times, N.Y. Times, USA Today, Wall St Jour., Washington Post, Redbook mag., London Daily Mail and many others; TV and radio interviews include Larry King Live, CBA, NBA and ABC networks, Oprah Winfrey Show, CNN Newsnight, Can. Radio Network, Mut. Radio Network and many others. Served with USAF, 1965-69. Mem. Am. Psychol. Assn. for Media Psychology, Calif. Psychol. Assn., Nat. Accreditation Assn. Psychoanalysis. Home: Los Angeles, Calif. Died Jan. 14, 2008.

BUTTLER, FRANCIS A. (FRANK BUTTLER), public relations executive; b. Columbus, Ohio, Dec. 26, 1927; s. Herman J. and Eleanor M. (Theado) B.; m. Jewell A. Moranda, July 28, 1973; 1 child, Frances E, Buttler Saavedra. BS in Journalism, Ohio State U., 1950. Polit. reporter UPI, Columbus, 1950-51; pub. info. officer Ohio Dept. Indsl. Relations, Columbus, 1951; asst. news mgr. Columbia Gas System, Columbus, 1952-53; asst. news editor Chesapeake & Ohio Ry., Cleve., 1953-54; pub. relations mgr. Am. Motors Corp., Detroit, 1955-67; dir. devel. Detroit Inst. Tech., 1967-68; dir. communications Greater Detroit C. of C., 1968-70; pres. Buttler Pub. Relations Counsel, Troy, Mich., from 1970. Contbr. articles to newspapers and mags. Chmn. dist. pub. relations Vols. for Romney, 1961; cons. Warren mayoral campaign, 1970, Ellie Peterson for U.S. Senate, 1964. Mem. Pub. Relations Soc. Am. (accredited mem.), Soc. Profl. Journalists, Am. Arbitration Assn., Am. Legion, Adcraft Club Detroit, Detroit Press Club, Elks. Avocations: art, music, travel. Died Feb. 13, 2008.

BUTTON, DANIEL EVAN, consultant, editor, former United States Representative from New York; b. Dunkirk, NY, Nov. 1, 1917; m. Rebecca B. Pool; children: Nancy, Sarah, Daniel, Jefferson (dec. 1986), Mary; m. Rena P. Posner, 1969. AB, U. Del., 1938; MS, Columbia U., 1939. Reporter, editor News-Jour. Papers, Wilmington, Del., also; AP, NYC, 1939-46; dir. pub. rels. U. Del., 1947-51; asst. to pres. SUNY, Albany, 1952-58; mem. staff Rensselaer Poly. Inst., 1959; editorial page editor Times-Union, Albany, 1959-60, exec. editor, 1960-66; mem. US Congress from 29th NY Dist., 1967-70; exec. dir., pres. Arthritis Found., 1971-75; exec. asst. to pres. NY State Commn. on Independent Colleges and Universities, 1994—2003. Editor-in-chief Sci. Digest, N.Y.C., 1976-80; editor Health Protection mag., N.Y.C., 1981-82; cons. Button and Button, pub. affairs com. Author: Lindsay: A Man for Tomorrow, 1965, Take City Hall!: Mayor Tom Whalen and the Transformation of New York's Capital to an All-American City, 2002. Democrat. Died Mar. 7, 2009.

BUTTON, ROBERT EASTON, communications executive; b. Englewood, NJ, July 25, 1915; s. John Conyers and Olive Lyle (Demarest) B.; m. Decima Knight, July 2, 1945; children: Phyllis Ann, Marilyn, Allyson. BA, Dartmouth Coll., 1936; LLB, Bklyn. Law Sch., 1939. Clk. Guaranty Trust Co., NYC, 1936-39; program mgr. NBC, NYC, 1939-41; col. U.S. Army, 1941-46; sales exec. NBC, NYC, 1946-54; cons. Sec. Def., Washington, 1954-55; dir. Voice of Am., Washington, 1955-58; counselor of embassy U.S. Govt., Paris, 1958-64; exec. asst. to chmn. Comsat, Washington, 1964-73; dir. satellite ops. Teleprompter, NYC, 1973-75; pres. Am. TransCom, Greenwich, Conn., from 1975. Instr. in field. Contbr. articles to local publs. Mem. Res. Officers Assn., 1991—, Broadcast Pioneers, N.Y.C., 1991—; dir. Orch., Greenwich, N.Y., 1991—, Mens Chorus, 1991—. With U.S. Army, 1944-45. Recipient 2 Bronze Stars. Mem. High Arctic Explorers Club, Lions, Acadia Lodge F&AM, Univ. Club D.C., Ret. Men's Assn. Republican. Avocations: music, performing and composing. Home: Old Greenwich, Conn. Died Aug. 9, 2008.

BYERRUM, RICHARD UGLOW, college dean; b. Aurora, Ill., Sept. 22, 1920; s. Earl Edward and Florence (Uglow) B.; m. Claire Somers, Apr. 3, 1945; children: Elizabeth, Mary, Carey. AB, Wabash Coll., 1942, D.Sc. (hon.), 1967; PhD, U. Ill., 1947. Teaching asst. U. Ill., 1942-44; research asso. U.S. Chem. Corps, toxicity dept. U. Chgo., 1944-47; faculty Mich. State U., East Lansing, from 1947, prof. biochemistry, 1957-91, prof. emeritus, from 1991; acting dir. Mich. State U. (Inst. Biology and Medicine), 1961-62; dean Mich. State U. (Coll. Natural Sci.), 1962-86. Author: (with others) Experimental Biochemistry, 1956; Editorial bd.: (with others) Phytochemistry, 1961-81; Contbr. (with others) numerous articles to profl. jours. Mem. Project Hope, 1961—; Trustee Mich. Health Council, 1961—, pres., 1966. Travel grantee Internat. Congress Biochemistry, Vienna, 1958; Travel grantee Internat. Congress Biochemistry, Montreal, 1959 Mem. Am. Chem. Soc. (lectr. vis. scientist program, awards com., visitor for com. profl. tng.), N. Central Assn. Colls. and Secondary Schs., A.A.A.S., Am. Soc. Plant Physiologists (trustee, exec. com.), Am. Soc. Biol. Chemists, Soc. Exptl. Biology and Medicine, Mich. Acad. Arts, Sci. and Letters, Phi Beta Kappa (pres. local chpt. 1962), Sigma Xi (awards com., Jr. Research award Mich. State U. chpt. 1958), Phi Kappa Phi (pres. 1968-69), Phi Lambda Upsilon, Alpha Chi Sigma, Beta Theta Pi. Achievements include patent in cancer tumor inhibiting material. Home: East Lansing, Mich. Died Sept. 28, 2009.

BYLINSKY, GENE MICHAEL, magazine editor; b. Belgrade, Yugoslavia, Dec. 30, 1930; s. Michael Ivan and Dora (Shadan) B.; m. Gwen Gallegos, Aug. 14, 1955; children: Tanya, Gregory. BA in Journalism, La. State U., 1955. Staff reporter Wall St. Jour., Dallas, 1957-59, San Francisco, 1959-61, NYC, 1961; sci. writer Nat. Observer, Washington, 1961-62, Newhouse Newspapers, Washington, 1962-66; bd. editors Fortune Mag., NYC, 1966—2001, contbg. writer, from 2002. Author: The Innovation Millionaires, 1976, Mood Control, 1978, Life in Darwin's Universe, 1981, Silicon Valley, High Tech Window on the Future, 1985. Served with AUS, 1956. Recipient 21st Ann. Albert Lasker Med. Journalism award, 1970, Deadline award Sigma Delta Chi, 1970, 72, 79, spl. commendation AMA, 1967, 68, 72, Journalism award, 1974, Claude Bernard Sci. Journalism award Nat. Soc. Med. Rsch., 1973, 74, James T. Grady award for interpreting chemistry to pub. Am. Chem. Soc., 1976, Am. Space Writers Assn. award, 1976-79, Bus. Journalism award U. Mo.-Columbia, 1984, Journalism award Am. Assn. Engring. Socs./Engring. Found., 1995, hon. mention award, 1970, 71, hon. mention award AAAS-Westinghouse Corp., 1975, 76, 77, hon. mention award Overseas Press Club, 1988. Mem. Nat. Assn. Sci. Writers, N.Y. Acad. Scis. Mem. Russian Orthodox Ch. Home: Fort Collins, Colo. Died Sept. 18, 2008.

BYRNE, ALLAN DEAN, minister; b. Pontiac, Ill., Oct. 3, 1930; s. Ira Council and Vera Ruth (Rittenhouse) B.; m. Louise Marie Wichmann, Aug. 12, 1951 (div. Mar. 1983); children: Allan Mark, Wesley Charles, Rae Marie; m. Mary Elizabeth Gottula, Apr. 27, 1985. B. Philosophy, Ill. Wesleyan U., 1952; MDiv, Garrett Theol. Sem., Evanston, Ill., 1955; DMin, Christian Theol. Sem., Indpls., 1980. Ordained minister in Meth. Ch., 1955. Pastor Dyer (Ind.) Meth. Ch., 1954-59; assoc. pastor City Meth. Ch., Gary, Ind., 1959-64; pastor Grace Meth. Ch., Rochester, Ind., 1964-68; sr. pastor First United Meth. Ch., Hobart, Ind., 1968-73, Waynedale United Meth. Ch., Ft. Wayne, Ind., 1973-77, College Ave. United Meth. Ch., Muncie, Ind., 1977-83, Woodmar United Meth. Ch., Hammond, Ind., 1983-86, First United Meth. Ch., South Bend, Ind., from 1986. Commn. mem. Commn. on Christian Unity and Interreligious Concerns, Ind., 1987-91; chairperson South Bend Cluster of United Meth. Ministers, 1987-91; mem. exec. com. South Bend Dist. Coun. on Ministries, 1987-91. Bd. dirs. Madison Ctr., South Bend 1989-91, Bashor Children's Home, Goshen, Ind., 1989-91. Mem. Rotary. Home: Whitewater, Wis. Died Sept. 23, 2007.

CAILLIET, MARCEL EMILE, artist, educator; b. Dijon, France, Sept. 8, 1914; came to U.S., 1926; s. Lucien and Valentine Margarite (Thome) C.; m. Helene Amoy, May 20, 1940 (dec. Feb. 1986); m. Dorothy Kirk Frederick, Nov. 30, 1986; children: Jon, Michelle, Lorella. BS, Villanova U., 1938; BA, U. So. Calif., 1940, MFA, 1941. Cert. tchr. fine arts. V.p. Far East ops. Grolier, Inc., NYC, 1948-62; tchr./lectr. pvt. studio/sch., Honolulu, 1962-70; sales mgr., v.p. United Realty, Inc., Honolulu, 1970-80; painter, lectr. pvt. studio, Honolulu, from 1980. Executed 8 murals in Ct. of the Flowers, San Francisco Exposition, 1930; exhibited in one-man shows and travelling exhbns.; numerous paintings in pvt. collections worldwide. Lt. USN, 1941-46, PTO. Mem. Windward Artists Guild (Hawaii), Cercle Francais (Hawaii). Roman Catholic. Avocations: photography, jogging. Died Dec. 20, 2007.

CAIN, ROSA MARIE, nurse, educator; b. Balt., Aug. 29, 1942; d. Milton Allen and Viola (Clinton) Blow; m. Alonzo Cain Jr., Feb. 18, 1967; children: Deborah Lachelle, Michael Terrell. Diploma, Provident Hosp., Balt., 1968; BSN, Coppin State Coll., Balt., 1980; MSN, U. Md., Balt., 1984. RN, Md.; cert. CPR instr./trainer. Nurse Provident Hosp., Balt., 1968-70, supr. ICCU, 1970-71, cardiac care coord., 1971-72, adult nurse practitioner, from 1973; instr. nursing Watterson Skills Ctr., Balt., 1985-89; asst. prof. div. nursing Coppin State Coll., from 1989. Coord. nursing asst. program Edmondson-Westside Adult Ctr., 1992, instr., 1992—. Contbr. articles to profl. jours. Tchr. diabetes and CPR Shiloh Bapt. Ch., Turner Station, Md., 1984-88; mem. Gov.'s Commn. on High Blood Pressure, 1983-89. Mem. ANA, Md. Nurses Assn., Coun. Nurse Practitioners, Sigma Theta Tau, Chi Eta Phi. Avocations: travel, shopping. Home: Baltimore, Md. Died Jan. 12, 2008.

CALAMITA, KATHRYN ELIZABETH, nursing administrator; b. Portland, Maine, Oct. 12, 1943; d. Maurice Daniel and Eleanor Elizabeth (Sullivan) Casey; m. John Joseph Calamita, Jan. 9, 1965; children: Angela Marie, Carla Anne, Daniel John. RN, Mercy Hosp. Sch. Nursing, Springfield, Mass., 1964; student, Midwestern State U., Wichita Falls, Tex., 1979-86, Vernon Regional Coll., 1987; BS, St. Joseph's Coll., Windham, Maine, 1992; BSN, Fla. State U., 2001. Cert. ACLS, PALS. Staff nurse Mercy Hosp., Springfield, 1964; med/surg. nurse Wichita Gen. Hosp., Wichita Falls, Tex., 1976-77, nurse ICU, 1977-79, supr. dept. nursing, 1979-86, assoc. adminstr. nursing dept., 1986-92; health facility adminstr. Wichita Falls Rehab. Hosp., 1992; rehab. nurse Bay Convalescent and Rehab. Ctr., Panama City, Fla., 1993-94; asst. DON L.A. Wagner Nursing and Rehab. Ctr., Panama City, Fla., 1994-99; nursing supr. Gulf Coast Cmty. Hosp., Panama City, Fla., from 1999. Mem. ANA (cert. in mgmt., 1995, cert. gerontology 1997), Fla. Nursing Assn., NACN. Democrat. Roman Catholic. Avocations: travel, music, swimming, boating, sewing. Home: Panama City, Fla. Died July 14, 2008.

CALDEIRO, FERNANDO (FRANK CALDEIRO), astronaut; b. Buenos Aires, June 12, 1958; m. Donna Marie Emero; 2 children. AAS in Aerospace Tech., SUNY, Farmingdale, 1978; BSME, U. Ariz., 1984; MS in Engring. Mgmt., U. Ctrl. Fla., 1995. Test dir. B-1B bomber Rockwell/USAF, 1985—88; sys. specialist space shuttle main propulsion, Kennedy Space Ctr. Rockwell, Fla., 1988—91; cryogenics and propulsion sys. expert NASA, Kennedy Space Ctr., 1991—96; astronaut NASA, Johnson Space Ctr., Houston, 1996—2009. Mem. Presdl. Commn. for Ednl. Excellence for Hispanic Americans, 2002. Mem.: Aircraft Owners and Pilots Assn., Exptl. Aircraft Assn. Avocations: experimental aircraft, snorkeling, amateur radio, metalworking. Died Oct. 3, 2009.

CALDERONE, MARLENE ELIZABETH, toxicology technician; b. DuBois, Pa., Apr. 10, 1940; d. James Joseph and Elizabeth Madge (Marando) C. Student, Canisius Coll., 1960. Rsch. chemist SUNY, Buffalo, 1960-64, UCLA, 1965-67; toxicology technician Damon Reference Labs., Newbury Park, Calif., from 1967. Lectr. in toxicology Calif. Luth. U., Thousand Oaks, 1985-86. Contbr. abstracts to profl. jours., presenter papers to sci. meetings. Mem. Am. Assn. Clin. Chemistry, Calif. Assn. Toxicologists. Home: Canyon Cntry, Calif. Died Aug. 5, 2008.

CALDWELL, WILLARD E., psychologist, educator; b. Flushing, LI, NY, July 10, 1920; s. Howard Eugene and Lillian (Warner) Caldwell. AB in Psychology, U. Fla., Gainesville, 1940, MA in Psychology, 1941; PhD in Psychology, Cornell U., Ithaca, NY, 1946; postgrad., Washington Sch. Psychiatry, 1948-53. Lic. psychologist DC, diplomate clin. psychology Am. Bd. Forensic Examiners, cert. diplomate psychotherapy Am. Psychotherapy Assn., diplomate neuropsychology Am. Bd. Psychological Specialties. Grad. asst. psychology U. Fla., Gainesville, 1940-41; teaching asst. Psychology Dept. Cornell U., 1943-46; prof. psychology, dept. chmn. Mary Baldwin Coll., Staunton, Va., 1947-48; asst. prof., assoc. prof., prof. psychology George Washington U., Washington, 1948-85, prof. emeritus, 1985—2008. Psychotherapist. Editor, contbg. author: Principles of Comparative Psychology, 1960; contbr. over 50 articles to profl. jours. Pvt. US Army, 1941-42. Mem. APA, Am. Coll. Forensic Examiners, Am. Psychol. Soc. (diplomate), DC Psychology Assn., Internat. Soc. Biometerology. Republican. Episcopalian. Avocations: swimming, gardening, travel. Home: Washington, DC. Died Dec. 14, 2008.

CALISHER, HORTENSE (MRS. CURTIS HARNACK), writer; b. NYC, Dec. 20, 1911; d. Joseph Henry and Hedvig (Lichtstern) Calisher; m. Curtis Harnack, Mar. 23, 1959; children from previous marriage: Bennet, Peter. AB, Barnard Coll., NY, 1932; LittD (hon.), Skidmore Coll., 1980, Grinnell Coll., 1986; LittD, Adelphi U., 1988. Adj. prof. English Barnard Coll., 1956—57; vis. lectr. U. Iowa,

1957, 1959-1960, Stanford U., Calif., 1958, Sarah Lawrence Coll., 1962, 1967, Bronxville, NY; adj. prof. Columbia U., NYC, 1968—70, CCNY, 1969; vis. prof. lit. SUNY, Purchase, 1971—72, Brandeis U., 1963—64, U. Pa., 1965, Bennington Coll., 1978, Washington U., St. Louis, 1979, Brown U., 1986; Regent's prof. U. Calif., 1976; guest lectr. US/China Arts Exch., China, 1986. Author: (fiction) In the Absence of Angels, 1951, False Entry, 1961, Tales for the Mirror, 1962, Textures of Life, 1963, Extreme Magic, 1964, Journey from Ellipsia, 1966, The Railway Police, and The Last Trolley Ride, 1966, The New Yorkers, 1970, Standard Dreaming, 1972, Eagle Eye, 1973, Queenie, 1973, The Collected Stories of Hortense Calisher, 1975, On Keeping Women, 1977, Mysteries of Motion, 1983, Saratoga Hot, 1985, The Bobby-Soxer, 1986 (Janet Heidinger Kafka prize, U. Rochester, 1987), Age, 1987, Kissing Cousins: A Memory, 1988, The Small Bang (under the pseudonym of Jack Fenno), 1992, In the Palace of the Movie King, 1993, In the Slammer with Carol Smith, 1997, The Novellas of Hortense Calisher, 1997, Sunday Jews, 2003, (autobiography) Herself, 1972, (memoir) Tattoo for a Slave, 2004; contbr. numerous short stories to mags. and periodicals. Recipient Nat. Coun. Arts award, 1967, Lifetime Achievement award, Nat. Endowment for Arts, 1989; grantee Guggenheim fellowship, 1952, 1955. Mem.: AAAL (pres. 1987—90), Authors Guild, PEN Am. Ctr. (pres. 1986—87). Home: New York, NY. Died Jan. 15, 2009.

CALKINS, HAROLD LEROY, minister; b. Ruthren, Iowa, Mar. 8, 1920; s. Ernest Alva and Daisy (Zielstra) C.; m. Fern Louise Wagner, Sept. 17, 1944; children: Kent LeRoy, Ross Calvin. BA, Andrews U., 1943, MA, 1958, MDiv, 1966. Ordained to ministry Seventh-day Adventist, 1947. Pastor Seventh-day Adventist, Temple City, Calif., 1956-66; pres. So. Calif. Seventh-day Adventist Conf., Glendale, Calif., 1972-81, British Union Seventh-day Adventist, Watford, Herts, Eng., 1981-86, ret., 1986. Pres. So. Calif. Assn. Seventh-day Adventists, Glendale, 1972-81. Author: Master Preachers, 1960; contbr. articles to mags. Vice-chmn. bd. White Meml. Med. Ctr., L.A., 1972-81, Glendale Adventist Med. CTr., 1972-81; bd. dirs. Loma Linda (Calif.) U., 1972-81. Home: Loma Linda, Calif. Died Jan. 4, 2008.

CALKINS, KENNETH ELBERT, lawyer; b. Oklahoma City, Okla., Oct. 12, 1931; s. Kenneth Elbert and Sarah Jane (Robison) C.; m. Pamela Vee Redding, Aug. 28, 1979; children: Michael, Deborah, Sandra, Karen, Benjamin. BME, U. Tex., El Paso, 1953; cert. composer, Berklee Sch. Music, Boston, 1959; BS in Law, Glendale U., 1976, JD, 1979. Bar: Calif. 1982. Social ins. rep. HHS, 1961-87; pvt. practice Glendale, Calif., from 1982. With U.S. Army, 1954-56. Avocation: music. Home: Alamogordo, N.Mex. Died Nov. 26, 2007.

CALLAWAY, JOHN DOUGLAS, broadcasting executive; b. Spencer, W.Va., Aug. 22, 1936; s. Charles E. and Dorothy (Garwood) C.; m. Shirley A. Andersen, Aug. 16, 1957 (div. Oct. 1978); children: Ann Hampton, Elizabeth Garwood; m. Patrice Fletcher, 1983. Student, Ohio Wesleyan U., 1954-56, U. Chgo., 1958-59. Gen. assignment reporter WBBM Radio & TV CBS, Chgo., 1957-64, pub. affairs dir., 1964-66, news dir., 1966-68; v.p. program services CBS Radio, NYC, 1968-70, nat. group corr., 1971-73; reporter WBBM-TV, Chgo., 1973-74; dir. news WTTW-TV, Chgo., 1974-83; host Chgo. Tonight, 1984—99; contbg. editor WLS-TV, ABC, 1981-83. Guest lectr. Notre Dame U., Northwestern U., Columbia Coll., Manchester Coll., Loyola U., Chgo., U. Chgo. Div. Sch.; Welles disting. vis. scholar George Williams Coll., 1980-81; bd. dirs. William Benton Fellowships in Broadcast Journalism, U. Chgo. Author: (with others) Action on the Streets; contbr. (with others) numerous articles to mags. Mem. adv. com. Am. Refugee Commn.; mem. vis. com. student programs and facilities U. Chgo.; bd. dirs. Chgo. Theol. Sem.; mem. Chgo. com. Chgo. Council Fgn. Relations. Recipient Assoc. Press award, NCCJ award, Ohio State Broadcast award, Chgo. Emmy award, 1978, Peabody award, 1980, Emmy award, 1981, 83 Mem. Radio-TV News Dirs. Assn., Soc. Midland Authors, Sigma Delta Chi. Mem. United Ch. Christ. Died June 23, 2009.

CALVERT, JAMES FRANCIS, manufacturing company executive, retired military officer; b. Cleve., Sept. 8, 1920; s. Charles Spence and Grace (Gholson) C.; m. Nancy Ridgeway King, Aug. 9, 1942 (dec. Dec. 1965); children: James, Margaret (dec. 1994), Charles; m. Margaretta Sergeant Harrison, Apr. 8, 1968. Student, Oberlin Coll., 1937-39, D.Sc. (hon.), 1960; BS in Elec. Engring., U.S. Naval Acad., 1942. Commnd. ensign U.S. Navy, 1942, advanced through grades to vice-adm., 1970; served on 9 war patrols in submarines PTO, World War II; comdr. diesel submarine U.S.S. Trigger, 1952-55; comdr. nuclear power submarine U.S.S. Skate, 1957—60, engaged in polar ops., 1958, 59; (1st submarine to break through ice and surface in Arctic Ocean), 1958; (1st ship to surface at North Pole), 1959; dir. politico-mil. policy Navy Dept., 1965-67; comdr. Cruiser-Destroyer Flotilla Eight, 1967-68; supt. U.S. Naval Acad., Annapolis, Md., 1968-72; comdr. U.S. First Fleet, 1972-73; ret., 1973; asst. to chmn. bd. Texaco Inc., NYC, 1973-74; v.p. Combustion Engring., Inc., Stamford, Conn., 1974-75, v.p. ops., 1975-84, dir., 1975-84; chmn. bd. Aqua-Chem. Inc., Milw., 1989-93. Corp. mem. Woods Hole Oceanographic Inst. Author: Surface at the Pole: The Extraordinary Voyages of the U.S.S. Skate, 1960 (paperback edit. 1996), A Promise to Your Country, 1961, The Naval Profession, 1965, Silent Running, 1995. Decorated D.S.M. (2), Silver Star (2), Bronze Star (2), Legion of Merit (4), Navy Commendation ribbon, Dept. Def. Commendation medal; French Govt. Merite Maritime; recipient Presdl. Unit citation. Mem. U.S. Naval Acad. Alumni Assn. (Disting. Graduate award, 2004), U.S. Naval Inst., Univ. Club (N.Y.C.), N.Y. Yacht Club, Chesapeake Bay Yacht Club (Easton, Md.). Home: Bryn Mawr, Pa. Died June 3, 2009.

CAMBON, ELISE MURRAY, music educator, musician; b. New Orleans, Feb. 27, 1917; d. Maurice Cornelius Cambon and Marie Camilia Murray. BA, Tulane U., 1939, PhD, 1975; postgrad., Benedictine Abbey of Solesmes, France, 1955; MusM, U. Mich., 1947. Organist, music dir. St. Louis Cathedral, New Orleans, from 1941; instr. music Ursuline Coll., New Orleans, 1949—51, Ursuline Acad., New Orleans, 1942—49, McGhee Sch., New Orleans, 1951—61; prof. music Loyola U., New Orleans, 1959—82, founding chmn. dept. liturgical music Coll. Music. Condr. St. Louis Cathedral Choir in Europe, England and Ireland. Coord. choirs and brass choir One Shell Sq. La. Philharm. Orch., New Orleans, from 1989. Recipient 1st prize musicol. rsch., Mu Phi Epsilon, 1975—76, Order of Chevalier des Arts et Lettres, French Govt., 1983; grantee, Schlieder Found., 1959, for concert tours, Archdiocese of New Orleans and St. Louis Cathedral, 1987—98; Fulbright scholar, Hochschule Musik in Frankfurt-am-Main, Germany, 1951—53. Mem.: Bach Oratorio Soc. (founding mem.), Am. Guild Organists (founding mem., dean). Roman Catholic. Home: Spring, Tex. Died Dec. 30, 2007.

CAMERON, ELEANOR CRANSTON FOWLE, writer; b. Palo Alto, Calif., Nov. 22, 1909; d. William McGregor and Carol Edith (Dixon) Cranston; m. John Miller Fowle, June 19, 1929 (dec. Apr. 1983); children: Michael, Linda Fowle Burke; m. Donald Churchill Cameron, Aug. 25, 1984 (dec. Nov. 1996). Student, Stanford U., 1928-31. Author: Cranston, The Senator from California, 1980. Chmn. Dem. State Women, Calif., 1966-80; officer Dem. State Ctrl. Com., 1966-80; pres. Foothill-De Anza C.C. Found., 1980-90, bd. dirs., 1996-98; bd. dirs. Stanford U. Founding Grant Soc., 1980—; trustee Hidden Villa, Los Altos Hills, Calif., 1996—. Congregationalist. Avocations: travel, politics, community activist. Home: Portola Valley, Calif. Died May 21, 2008.

CAMPBELL, ARLINGTON FICHTNER, retired military officer; b. Steubenville, Ohio, Mar. 11, 1939; s. John Arlington and Ruth Elinor (Fichtner) C.; m. Bonnie Lee Jackson, Sept. 14, 1963; children: William, Caroline. BEE, U.S. Naval Acad., 1961; MS in Fin. Mgmt., U.S. Naval Postgrad. Sch., 1970. Commd. ensign USN, 1961, advanced through grades to rear admiral, 1985, various assignments, 1961-77, commanded, 1977-80, 1st commanding officer, 1980-81, comdg. officer Trident submarine Gold, 1981-83, comdr. submarine squadron 18, 1983-84, dep. dir. attack submarine div., 1984-86, comdr. naval telecommunications command, 1986-88, comdr. submarine group 6, 1988—89, comdr. submarine group 10, 1989—93; v.p. Decision Systems Tech., Rockville, Md., 1994—96. Deocrated 4 Legion of Merits, Commendation medals, Meritorious Unit Commendation medal, Battle Efficiency E Ribbon, Navy Expeditionary medal, Nat. Def. Svc. medal, Sea Svc. Deployment Ribbons. Mem. U.S. Naval Acad. Alumni Assn., U.S. Naval Inst., Armed Forces Communications and Electronics Assn. (assoc. dir. 1987), Rotary, Am. Legion. Republican. Mem. Christian Ch. Avocations: reading, golf, photography, personal computing, music appreciation. Died Jan. 27, 2009.

CAMPBELL, CAROL ANN, former city councilwoman; d. Edgar Campbell. City councilwoman, Dist. 4, Phila., 2006—07; chair Com. Transport & Pub. Utilities; mem. Com. Appropriations, Commerce & Econ. Devel., Ethics, Law & Gov., Legis. Oversight, Streets & Svcs. Died Nov. 19, 2008.

CAMPBELL, JAMES ROSS, chemistry professor, secondary school educator; b. Hamilton AFB, Calif., June 23, 1952; s. David Anderson Campbell and Shirley Jean Zivney; m. Kathrine Anne Edwards, Oct. 18, 1991; children: Sarah Sabina, David Colin. BS, MacMurray Coll., Jacksonville, Ill., 1974; MA, Ea. Ill. U., Charleston, 1992. Cert. in phys. sci. educator Ill., 1979. Math tchr. Talbot County Schs., Talbotton, Ga., 1975—79; sci. and math. tchr. Putnam County CUSD 535, Granville, Ill., 1979—87, Westmer CUSD 203, 1987—2001; chemistry instr. Scott Cmty. Coll., Bettendorf, Iowa, from 2000; chemistry and physics instr. Riverdale CUSD 100, Port Byron, Ill., from 2001. Scholastic bowl Putnam County HS, 1981—86, girls basketball coach, 1981—87, golf coach, 1986—87; girls basketball coach Westmer HS, 1987—97, volleyball coach, 1987—2001, scholastic bowl coach, 1995—2001, Riverdale HS, from 2001, volleyball coach, 2003—07. Contbr. articles to profl. jours. Mem.: Riverdale Tchr.s' Assn. (pres. 2005). Avocations: politics, movies, reading, travel. Home: Joy, Ill. Died Oct. 25, 2007.

CAMPBELL, JOAN, insurance company executive; b. Chgo., July 1, 1929; d. Patrick Henry and Ida Josephine (Miller) C. BA, Loretto Heights Coll., Denver, 1950; MA, Cath. U. Am., 1963; PhD, U. Iowa, 1970. CLU, 1984. Agt. N.Y. Life Ins. Co., New Orleans, from 1976; reg. rep. N.Y. Life Securities Corp., New Orleans, from 1982. Mem. Nat. Assn. Securities Dealers, Nat. Assn. Life Underwriters, Am. Soc. CLU and ChFC. Home: Harvey, La. Died Dec. 31, 2007.

CAMPBELL, JOHN CARL, retired engineering educator; b. Wilsey, Kans., Apr. 20, 1920; s. Alfred Wray and Zoa May (Henderson) C.; m. Eula Marie Hagan, Aug. 31, 1941 (div. 1978); children: Frederick J., Chris J., Victor C., Terry D.; m. Roberta Louise DeVoe, Feb. 14, 1980. BS in Agrl. Engring., Kans. State U., 1947; MS in Agrl. Engring., Oreg. State U., 1949. Registered profl. engr., Oreg., cert. safety profl. of the Ams. Ext. specialist agrl. engring. U. Ill., Champaign, 1954—55, Oreg. State U., Corvallis, 1948—54, assoc. prof. gen. engring., 1955—66, head dept. gen. engring., 1966—77, dir. safety, 1978—85, prof. emeritus, from 1985. Safety engring. cons. Rust Engring. Co., Albany, Oreg., 1978—79, Daniels Atty. at Law, Albany, 1980—81; civil engr. Bur. Reclamation, Salem, Oreg., 1960—61. Author: (novels) The New Blend, 1972, History of Wilsey and Morris County, Kansas, 1990, History of the Campbell Family, 1991, Historic Happenings in Morris County, Kansas, 1820 to 1993, 1993, Living on the Edge on Planet Earth, 1994, Living on the Edge on the Early Kansas Prairie, 1998; contbr. articles to sci. jours. Capt. arty. US Army, 1942—46, Philippines. Democrat. Avocations: travel, birdwatching. Home: Apache Junction, Ariz. Died May 3, 2008.

CAMPION, NARDI REEDER, writer; b. Honolulu, June 27, 1917; d. Russell P. and Narcissa (Martin) Reeder; m. Thomas Baird Campion, July 5, 1941; children: Thomas, Jr., Edward, Frederick, Narcissa, Russell. AB, Wellesley Coll., 1938. Tchr. of English Newport News (Va.) High Sch., 1940-42; freelance writer. Contbr. articles to numerous jours. including The New Yorker, American Heritage, Reader's Digest, Family Circle, Life, others; co-author: (with Sgt. Marty Maher) Bring Up The Brass, 1951, (with Col. Red Reeder) The West Point Story, 1956, (with Rosamond W. Stanton) Look To This Day! The Lively Education of a Great Woman Doctor, Connie Guion, M.D., 1965; author: Patrick Henry, Firebrand of the Revolution, 1961, Kit Carson, Pathfinder of the West, 1963, Casa Means Homes, 1970, Ann the Word, The Story of Mother Ann Lee, 1996, Bringing up the Brass, 2002, Mother Ann Lee, Morning Star of the Shakers, 1990, Everyday Matters, A Love Story, 2004, Over the Hill You Pick Up Speed: Reflections on Aging (For Anyone Who Happens To), 2006, others. Founder annual book and author luncheon, Friends of Hopkins Ctr., Dartmouth Coll., Hanover, N.H., 1979—. Died Nov. 29, 2007.

CAMPLIN, MARK EUGENE, small business owner; b. Anderson, Ind., July 25, 1954; s. Eugene and Martha E. (Markle) C.; m. Kimberleigh A. LaPierre, June 28, 1986; children: Laura A., Lindsay Michelle. Student, Ball State U., 1973-76. Owner Mark Camplin Ins. and Rentals, Anderson, from 1979. Sponsor Little League teams, 1981—. Named one of Outstanding Young Men of Am., 1983. Mem. Kiwanis (chmn. local club 1985), Sertoma (chmn. 1984). Democrat. Avocations: golf, travel, family. Died Oct. 11, 2007.

CAMPOS, JOAQUIN PAUL, III, chemical physicist, regulatory affairs analyst; b. LA, Feb. 16, 1962; s. Joaquin Reyna and Maria Luz (Chavez) C.; m. Barbara Ann Esquivel, Oct. 31, 1987; children: Courtney Luz, Nathaniel Alexander. Student, U. Calif., Santa Cruz, 1980-85, UCLA, 1985-86. Tutor U. Calif., Santa Cruz, 1980-82, admissions liaison, 1982-84; chem. teaching assoc. L.A. Unified Sch. Dist., 1985-87; pvt. tutor Santa Clara, L.A., 1987-89; tech. specialist Alpha Therapeutics Corp., LA, 1989-95; regulatory affairs specialist III Gensia Labs., Ltd., Irvine, Calif., 1995-96; sr. assoc. Genentech, Inc., South San Francisco, from 1996. Cons. L.A. Unified Sch. Dist., 1985-87. Docent in tng. L.A. Mus. of Sci. and Industry, 1989. Scholar, grantee So. Calif. Gas Co., L.A., 1980-84, Sloan Rsch. fellow, 1981-82. Mem. Am. Chem. Soc., N.Y. Acad. Sci., Am. Inst. Chemists, Am. Assn. Physics Tchrs., AAAS, Fed. Am. Scientists, Pharm. Rsch. Mfrs. Am., Internat. Union of Pure and Applied Chemistry, Drug Info. Assn., Math. Assn. Am., Soc. Hispanic Profl. Engrs., IEEE. Avocations: reading, playing chess, computer programming, family. Home: San Diego, Calif. Died Oct. 30, 2007.

CAMRAS, CARL BRUCE, ophthalmologist, educator; b. Chgo, Nov. 23, 1953; s. Marvin and Isabelle Lillian (Pollack) C.; m. Nancy Louise Ross, June 3, 1979; children: Melanie, Lucinda. BA, Yale U., 1975; MD, Columbia U., 1979. Diplomate Am. Bd. Ophthalmology. Med. intern LA County Harbor-UCLA Med. Ctr., Torrance, Calif.; resident in ophthalomogy Jules Stein Eye Inst., UCLA Med. Ctr.; asst. prof. ophthalmology Mt. Sinai Med. Ctr., NYC, 1983-87, assoc. prof., 1988-91; prof., vice-chmn. dept. ophthalmology U. Nebr. Med. Ctr., Omaha, 1991—2000, chmn., 2000—09. Contbr. articles to Investigative Ophthalmology and Visual Sci., Exptl. Eye Rsch., Current Eye Rsch., Ophthalmology, Am. Jour. Ophthalmology, Archives of Ophthalmology, Ophthalmic Surgery. NIH grantee, 1988-2009; Heed Ophthalmic Found. fellow, 1983; recipient Travel Fellowship award Assn. for Rsch. in Vision, 1977, Sandoz award, 1979, Alvin Behrens Meml. Fund award, 1979. Fellow ACS, Am. Glaucoma Soc., Am. Acad. Ophthalmology, NY Acad. Medicine, Assn. for Rsch. in Vision and Ophthalmology. Achievements include discovery that prostaglandins reduce intraocular pressure when applied topically to eye. Home: Omaha, Nebr. Died Apr. 14, 2009.

CANNING, FRED FRANCIS, retired drug store chain executive; b. Chgo., Apr. 1, 1924; s. Fred and Lillian (Popiolek) C.; m. Margaret Luby, Nov. 23, 1944; children: Jeanette, Laura, Debbie, Terry, Patrick, Marggie, Timothy,

Kathleen. Registered Pharmacist, Hynes Sch. Pharmacy, 1950. With Walgreen Co., Deerfield, Ill., 1946—90, v.p., 1972-76, sr. v.p., 1976-78, exec. v.p., 1978, pres., COO, 1978—90. Served with USCG, 1942-45. Mem. Am. Pharm. Assn., Am. Mktg. Assn. Roman Catholic. Home: Lake Forest, Ill. Died June 27, 2009.

CANSLER, PHILIP TRENT, music educator; b. Kansas City, Mo., Nov. 3, 1953; s. Loman Doyle and Laura June (McElwain) C.; m. Jeannine Ann Zielke, May 24, 1975. MusB in Edn., Washburn U., 1976; MusM, U. Oreg., 1977, D in Mus. Arts, 1984. Asst. dir. marching band U. Oreg., Eugene, 1977-78; asst. prof. music Buena Vista Coll., Storm Lake, Iowa, 1978, 80; assoc. prof. U. Portland, Oreg., from 1980. Condr. trumpet workshops; adjudicator mus. ensembles, N.W. U.S. Author: Twentieth-Century Music for Trumpet and Organ, 1984, Cansler's Proven Routine for Trumpet, 1986; trumpet performances on tours to Europe, Japan, Sri Lanka, Africa; performer CDs Thine is the Glory, 1997, Bravo! Baroque!, 1998. Min. of music 1st Bapt. Ch., 1995-99; dir. music, choir and orchestra cond. Moreland Presbyn. Ch. Recipient Cmty. Svc. award Music Dept., Topeka, 1976, Contbn. to Arts award City of Gresham, Oreg., 1991; grantee Portland Musicians Union, 1992, Albert J. Dennis Fund, Portland, 1993. Mem. Coll. Band Dirs. Assn., Internat. Trumpet Guild (news corr. 1991—), Toastmsters Internat. (pres. 1996-98, numerous Disting. awards). Avocations: carving, hiking, bird watching. Home: Hillsboro, Oreg. Died June 2, 2008.

CANTONE, VIC, political cartoonist; b. NYC, Aug. 7, 1933; Grad., Sch. Art and Design, NYC, 1952, Art Instrn. Schs., Inc., Mpls., 1978; AA cum laude, Nassau Coll., Garden City, NY, 1978; BA, Hofstra U., 1979, postgrad., from 1985. Cartoonist, courtroom artist Newsday, Garden City, NY, 1954—59; polit. cartoonist/caricaturist N.Y. Daily News, 1959—91, Editor & Pub. mag., 1973—78; syndicated polit. cartoonist/caricaturist Rothco Cartoon Syndicate, 1980—91, King Features/N.Am. Syndicate, 1991—2002, ArtistMarket.com Syndicate, 2002—05; corp. cartoonist/caricaturist Sta. WPIX-TV, Wall St. Jour. Report Nat. Broadcast Syndicate Report, 1982—83. Bd. dirs., curator Hofstra U. Internat. Environ. Polit. Cartoon Exhibit, 1990; lectr. on media, terrorism; courtroom artist WPIX-TV, CableVision News 12, 1991-2000, polit. cartoonist/caricaturist O'Dwyer's PR Mag., 1987-2003, Bklyn. Papers Pub, 1996-2001. Permanent collections include 3 U.S. Presdl. librs.; author books and articles; curator, exhibitor Smithsonian Instn., U.S.A. Tour, Internat. Polit. Cartoons on the Environment, 1992-96; polit. cartoonist/caracturist Travel Weekly newspaper, 1974-91; creator comic strips Topo the Mouse, 1969, Dianna, 1975-77, Sea Circus, 1969. Recipient Bicentennial Trophy award, Aux. Am. Legion, 1976, Golden Press award, 1979, Fourth Estate award, Am. Legion, 1976, Valley Forge Honor cert., Freedoms Found., 1976, George Washington Honor medal, 1978, cert. of recognition, NCCJ, 1977, Patriotic Svc. award, U.S. Dept. Treasury, 1978, Honor Legion award, N.Y.C. Police Dept., 1994, 1996, The Deadline Club award, 1999, Reuben award, 2003; Fulbright scholar, 1987. Mem.: Nat. Cartoonists Soc., N.Y.C. Deadline Club (exec. coun. from 1999), Soc. Profl. Journalists (spkrs. bur. from 1999), N.Y. Press Club (bd. govs. 1995—99), Assn. Am. Editl. Cartoonists. Died Apr. 2005.

CANTWELL, WILLIAM FREDERICK, electrical engineer, real estate broker; b. Kenosha, Wis., June 10, 1924; s. John Henry and Ella Marie (Tanck) C.; m. Beverly Ann Danner, May 25, 1963; children: William Joseph, Paul John, Laura Marie, Kevin Ronald, David Alexander. BEE, Marquette U., 1949. Registered profl. engr., Wis.; lic. real estate broker, Wis. Asst. to welding engr. Simmons Co., Kenosha, 1949-51; engr. plant engring. dept. Am. Motors Corp., Kenosha, 1951-56; elec. engr. electric drives div. Eaton Corp., Kenosha, 1957-91. Pres. Boston T. Corp., Kenosha, 1981—. Contbr. articles to profl. jours. Mem., vice chmn. Somers (Wis.) Plan Commn., 1971-81; supr. #2 Somers Town Bd., 1991—; mem., pres. St. Joseph High Sch. Home and Sch. Assn., Kenosha, 1977-87; mem. Kenosha County Rep. Com., 1981—, mem. exec. bd., 1985-87; active Holiday Folk Fair, Milw., 1980—; Rep. candidate 64th Assembly Dist., Wis. State Legislature, 1993. With AUS, 1943-46, ETO. Mem. Kenosha Bd. Realtors, Marquette U. Engring. Alumni Assn. (bd. dirs. 1965-68), VFW (life), Am. Mensa Ltd., Serra Internat. (v.p. 1984-85, pres. 1992-93, 93—), KC (4th degree, grand knight 1951-52, faithful navigator 1956-58). Roman Catholic. Home: Kenosha, Wis. Died Feb. 8, 2008.

CAPLAN, SHELDON M., family practitioner; b. Balt., May 15, 1918; children: Paul B., William E. BA, U. Pa., 1939; MD, Middlesex U., 1943. Diplomate Am. Bd. Family Practice. Pvt. practice, New Bedford, Mass., from 1946. Lt. (s.g.) USN, 1944-46. Fellow Am. Acad. Family Practice; mem. Am. Bd. Family Practice (charter), Mass. Med. Soc., Masons. Avocations: golf, travel. Home: New Bedford, Mass. Died Sept. 22, 2007.

CAPORALE, ROCCO, sociology educator, writer; b. St. Catherine Ionio, Italy, Aug. 21, 1927; came to U.S., 1960; s. Francesco and Francesca (Badolato) C.; m. Taina E. Elg, May 2, 1982; children: Raoul, Francesca. PhD in Sociology, Columbia U., 1965. Asst. prof. Manhattanville Coll., Purchase, N.Y., 1963-65; rsch. assoc. U. Calif., Berkeley, 1966-68; rsch. dir. The Claremont (Calif.) Colls., 1968-72; prof. St. John's Univ., Jamaica, N.Y., from 1972. Pres. Inst. for Italian-Am. Studies, Inc., N.Y.C., 1982—, Internat. Assn. Magna Grecia, Rome, 1989—, Internat. Com. Mezzogiorno, Naples, Italy, 1986—. Author: Vatican II, Last of the Councils, 1964; author, editor: The Culture of Unbelief, 1972; editor: The Italian Americans through the Generations, 1985; editor-in-chief series Mezzogiorno Revisited, 1989—. Mem. Am. Sociol. Assn., Italian-Am. Hist. Assn. Roman Catholic. Home: New York, NY. Died June 30, 2008.

CAPPELLETTI, MARIETTA, management consultant; b. Elkhart, Ind., Sept. 28, 1940; d. Anthony James and Helen (Ciavarelli Minelli. BS Psychology, Ind. U., South Bend, 1980; student, Rutgers U., New Brunswick, NJ, 1981; MS in Counseling & Guid, Ind. U., South Bend, 1984; MS in Mgmt., Lesley Coll., Cambridge, Mass., 1986. Placement coord. Goodwill Industries, Inc., South Bend, 1980-81; cons. Michiana EAP, South Bend, 1981-86; clin. coord. Pathways Chem. Dependency Program, South Bend, 1986-87; cons. Employee Assistance Plus, South Bend, 1987-89; program mgr. workwell EAP Welborn Bapt. Hosp., Evansville, Ind., from 1989. Focus group mem. chem. dependency United Way of St. Joseph County, Inc. S. Bend Ind. 1988. Bd. Mem. YMCA S. Bend Ind., 1986--, Ind. U. Adv. Bd. Counseling & GUidance S. Bend Ind., 1988-. Recipient Honorary Tribute to Women award Young Women's Christian Assn., Mem. Employee Assistance Soc. N. Am., No. Ind. Assn. Counseling. Avocations: physical fitness, cooking, reading. Home: Evansville, Ind. Died Apr. 21, 2008.

CAPPO, LOUIS CESARE, priest; b. Baltic, Mich., Dec. 16, 1919; s. Caesar and Jennie (Marie) C. BA in Theology, St. Francis Sem., Milw., 1943. Ordained priest Roman Cath. Ch., 1946. Min. Diocese of Marquette, Mich., 1946-52; adminstr. Christ the King Parish, Ramsay, Mich., 1952-58, pastor, 1956-65, St. Cecilia Parish, Hubbell, Mich., 1965-68, Sacred Heart Parish, L'Anse, 1969, St. Ann's Parish, Escanaba, 1969-72; rector St. Peter's Cathedral, Marquette, from 1975; exec. dir. Dept. Community Svcs. and Family Life, Marquette, 1972-85. Chaplain Mich. State Police, 1966—; diocesan rep. to Social Action Bd., Mich. Cath. Conf., 1963; past pres. Bishop Baraga Assn.; bd. dirs. Bishop Noa Home; health coord. Diocese of Marquette, diocesan dir. of cemeteries, exec. dir. Tower of History.; v.p. bd. dirs. Cath. Social Svcs. Bd. dirs. Marquette Gen. Hosp., 1973—, United Way; mem. bd. of control Lake Superior State Coll.; co-founder, chairperson Lake Superior Jobs Coalition; chairperson Mich. Tourist Coun.; mem. Internat. Trade Commn., adv. coun. SBA, Planning Commn. Houghton County, Water Commn. of Adams Township and Village of South Range, Ancillary Manpower Planning Bd., Vol. Commn.; vice chmn. Tri-State Interfaith Devel. Enterprise; adv. com. Inst. Wood Rsch., Mich. Tech. U., Houghton; chmn. Action Non-Profit Housing Corp. Recipient Pres.'s award No. Mich. U., 1974. Died Dec. 10, 2007.

CAPPY, RALPH JOSEPH, lawyer, retired state supreme court justice; b. Pitts., Aug. 25, 1943; s. Joseph R. and Catherine (Miljus) C.; m. Janet Fry, Apr. 19, 1985; 1 child, Erik. BS in Psychology, U. Pitts., 1965, JD, 1968; LLD (hon.), Widener U. Bar: Pa. 1968, U.S. Dist. Ct. (we. dist.) Pa. 1968, U.S. Supreme Ct. 1975. Law clk. to president judge Ct. of Common Pleas of Allegheny County, 1968—70; atty. civil & family court litigation pvt. practice, 1968—78; trial defender, first asst. homicide atty., dep. dir. Allegheny County, 1970—75, pub. defender, 1975—78; judge Family and Juvenile Ct. Ct. of Common Pleas, Allegheny County, 1978—89, judge criminal divsn., 1979—85, judge civil div., 1985—86, presiding admin. judge civil div., 1986—90; justice Pa. Supreme Ct., 1989—2008, chief justice, 2003—08; ptnr., mem. litig. section Buchanan Ingersoll & Rooney LLP, Pitts., 2008—09. Lectr. constl. law U. Pitts., 1970-72; instr. criminal law and trial tactics City of Pitts. Police Acad., Allegheny County Police Acad., 1970-74; liaison justice to Supreme Ct. Appellate Procedural Rules Com., 1990-94, Minor Judiciary of Pa., 1990-94, Pa. Bd. of Law Examiners, 1990-94, First Jud. Dist., 1990-94, Supreme Ct. Civil, Domestic Relations & Orphans' Ct. Procedural Rules Com., 1994-96, Pa. Bd. of Law Examiners, 1994-96, Civil Procedural Rules Com., Pa. Bd. of Law Examiners, Pa. Continuing Legal Education Bd., 1996-2009 Mem. Pitts. Health and Welfare Planning Agy., 1984-2009; mem. jud. ethics com. Pa. Law Jour., 1980-82; trustee U. Pitts., 1992-2009, bd. visitors, 1992-2009 Recipient Acad. of Trial Lawyers award, Citation of Merit, Mothers Against Drunk Driving, Disting. Laureate Alumni award, U. Pitts., Disting. Alumnus award, U. Pitts. Law Sch., Gold medal for Disting. Svc., Order Sons of Italy, Grand Judge of Pa., Phila. Bar Assn. Bar medal, Pa. Bar Assn. Bar medal, Harry Carrico award, Nat. Ctr. State Courts, 2007; named Man of Yr., Pa. State Police, Pa. Fraternal Order of Police, Sons of Italy, Italian Am. Heritage Found. Fellow Am. Bar Found.; mem. ABA, Pa. Bar Assn. (Jud. award 1997), Allegheny Bar Assn., Pa. Conf. State Trial Judges (legis. and planning com. 1978-83, legis. com., zone rep. 1984-2000, chmn. adm. com. 1986-88), Pa. Coll. Judiciary (lectr., treas., sec.), NACCP (life), Pitts. Athletic Assn. Died May 1, 2009.

CARBONE, ROBERT FRANK, retired educator; b. Plentywood, Mont., July 27, 1929; s. Charles and Antoinette (Sack) C.; m. Suzanne M. Wirth, Mar. 23, 1968; children: Angela Michelle, Christopher Wirth. BS, Eastern Mont. Coll., 1953; M.Ed., Emory U., 1958; PhD, U. Chgo., 1961. Instr. U. Chgo., 1960-61; asso. Dr. James B. Conant (A Study of Edn. of Am. Tchrs.), 1961-62; asst. prof. Emory U., 1962-65; asst. to pres. U. Wis., 1965-70; dean Coll. Edn., U. Md., College Park, 1970-74, prof. higher & adult edn., 1974—93, prof. emeritus, 1993—2009. Mem. Danforth Conf. on Liberal Arts Edn., summer 1964 Author: (with others) The Nongraded School, 1967, Resident or Nonresident, 1970, Students and State Borders, 1973, Alternative Tuition Systems, 1974, Presidential Passages, 1981, Agenda for Research on Fund Raising, 1986, Fund Raisers of Academe, 1987. Contbr. articles to profl. jours. Served with U.S. Army, 1953-55. Home: Silver Spring, Md. Died July 29, 2009.

CARDOZO, BENJAMIN SAMUEL, lawyer; b. Bklyn., Nov. 9, 1942; s. Morris and Sylvia (Willer) C.; m. Andrea Kathleen King, Aug. 16, 1973; 1 child, Nathan. BA in History, U. Calif., Riverside, 1964; JD, U. So. Calif., 1978. Bar: Calif. 1979, U.S. Dist. Ct. (ctrl. dist.) Calif. 1979, U.S. Dist. Ct. (so. dist.) Calif. 1983, U.S. Dist. Ct. (ea. dist.) Calif. 1985, U.S. Dist. Ct. (no. dist.) 1993, U.S. Ct. Appeals (9th cir.) 1979, U.S. Supreme Ct. 1994. Data processing mgr. L.A. (Calif.) County, 1964-76; lawyer L.A. (Calif.) City Atty., 1979-81, Lord, Bissell & Brook, LA, 1981-86, Kurlander & Hix, San Marino, Calif., 1986-88, Fireman Fund, Glendale, Calif., 1988-91, Fuchs & Marshall, LA, 1991-93, Stone & Hiles, Beverly Hills, Calif., 1993-98, Jackson, Lewis Schnitzler & Krupman, Los Angeles, from 1998. Mem. ATLA, Calif. State Bar, L.A. County Bar. Home: Marina Dl Rey, Calif. Died May 28, 2008.

CAREY, ELIZABETH BORGMANN, organization executive; b. Pitts., Jan. 13, 1938; d. Carl Williams and Mable Dorothy (Gaiser) Borgmann; children: Marc, Jeff, Ann, Julie. BA, U. Colo., 1959; postgrad., U. Denver, 1986-87. Dir. Cmty. Resources Inc., Denver, 1979-81; cmty. cons. Denver Pub. Schs., 1982-83; bookseller Tattered Cover Bookstore, 1983-84; pub. Woman Source, A Guide to Women's Resources, 1982-85; owner, pub. Metro Source Publs., 1985-88; devel. dir. Am. Heart Assn., 1988-90; exec. dir. Colo. Tennis Assn., 1990-94; dir. capital campaign Colo.'s Ocean Journey, 1994-95; devel. dir. Denver Victims Svc. Ctr., from 1995. Pub. Solo in the City, 1986, Having a Baby in Denver, 1986, Learning in the Mile High City, 1987. Bd. dirs., publicity chmn. Denver Women's Career Ctr., 1979-83; bd. dirs., mem. exec. com. Colo. Outward Bound, 1985-92; bd. dirs. Friends of Big Sisers, 1987-88, Citizens Appreciate Police, 1995-96, Parenting After Divorce, Denver, 1995-96; bd. dirs., chmn. award sect. Women's Found., 1988-90; mem. Martin Luther King Jr. Commn., Cmty. Edn. Coun.; founder, 1st chmn. Montclair Cmty. Assn., Denver. Avocations: golf, tennis, skiing, theater, reading. Died May 6, 2008.

CAREY, RONALD ROBERT, former labor union administrator; b. NYC, Mar. 22, 1936; s. Joseph and Loretta Carey; m. Barbara Murphy; children: Ronald, Sandra, Daniel, Pamela, Barbara Driver United Parcel Svc., 1956—58; shop steward Teamsters Local 804, 1958—65, sec., 1965—67, pres. Long Island City, NY, 1967—91, Internat. Brotherhood of Teamsters, Washington, 1992-99. Served in USMC, 1953—55. Avocations: swimming, diving, fishing. Home: Sardinia, NY. Died Dec. 11, 2008.

CARIDES, GEORGE WARREN, health economic statistics director; s. Peter and Constance Carides; m. Alexandra Doina Carides, Aug. 18, 1993; 1 child, Aliona Maria. BS in Econs., Coll. NJ, Ewing, 1983; AM in Econs., U. Chgo., 1985; PhD in Stats., Temple U., Phila., 1998. Cons. Merck & Co., Blue Bell, Pa., 1994—98, health econ. stats. North Wales, Pa., from 1998. Mem.: Am. Statis. Assn. (assoc. Student Paper award 1997). Achievements include research in estimation of mean treatment cost in the presence of right-censoring. Died Mar. 16, 2008.

CARLSON, DORIS STEWART, entrepreneur; b. Moorcroft, Wyo., Jan. 3, 1930; d. Frank Royal and Della Maud (Torbert) Stewart; m. Roy W. Carlson, Sept. 10, 1949 (dec. 1974); children: Ronald Roy, Michael Alan, Nikki Carlson Niemen, Christine Carlson Brannan. Student, Sheridan Coll., 1968-69. Owner, operator Stewart #5 Ranch, Sheridan, Wyo., from 1974, Carlson's Unltd. Clothing & Sporting Goods Store, Gillette, Wyo., 1975-85, D. Stewart Subdiv., Moorcroft, from 1979. Sec.-treas. Community Theatre, Gillette, 1974. Recipient Congl. award Wyo. State Art Conv., Laramie, 1973. Mem. Am. Quarter Horse Assn. (participation in races and shows), Wyo. Artist Assn., Wyo. Racing Assn., Wyo. Writers Assn., Sheridan C. of C., Beta Sigma Phi. Republican. Avocations: art, writing, golf, showing horses. Died Oct. 27, 2007.

CARMEAN, JERRY RICHARD, broadcast engineer; b. Greenfield, Ohio, Apr. 2, 1938; s. Cloyde B. and Mary F. (Hedges) C.; m. Patricia H. Carmean; 1 child, Steven. BS in Edn., Ohio U., 1965, BS in Elec. Engring., 1984. Lic. FCC gen. class radiotelephone operator. Tchr. New Philadelphia (Ohio) High Sch., 1965-66; broadcast engr. Ohio U. Telecommunications Ctr., Athens, 1966-81, dir. engring., 1981-92; pvt. broadcast engring. cons., from 1992. Cons. Sta. WLGN, Logan, Ohio, 1964-2000; tech. cons. Sta. 4VEH, Cap Hatien, Haiti. Served with U.S. Army, 1961-64. Mem. Antique Wireless Assn., Men for Missions Internat., Planetary Soc., Rotary. Avocations: astronomy, photography, amateur radio, antiques. Home: Logan, Ohio. Died Dec. 2008.

CARMICHAEL, DONALD CHARLES, research center administrator; b. Cin., May 22, 1933; s. Howard Russell and Alma Anna (Lucken) C.; m. Marilyn Jean Dyson, Dec. 1, 1956; children: John Charles, Eric Andrew. BS with distinction, Purdue U., 1955, MS, 1957. Metall. engr. Allison div.

Gen. Motors, Indpls., 1955; research scientist Battelle Meml. Inst., Columbus, Ohio, 1956-62, div. chief, 1962-73, program mgr., 1973-83, sect. mgr., from 1983. Contbr. numerous articles to profl. jours.; patentee in field. Mem. Am. Vacuum Soc. (trustee 1989—), Nat. Vacuum Symposium (div. chmn. 1985—), Vacuum Metallurgy div. Am. Vacuum Soc. (treas. 1976—), Internat. Conf. Metall. Coatings (exec. com. 1974—, Disting. Service award 1984), Internat. Vacuum Metllurgy Conf. (exec. com. 1979, 88). Republican. Presbyterian. Home: Farragut, Tenn. Died Sept. 21, 2007.

CARMICHAEL, DONALD SCOTT, retired lawyer, corporate financial executive; b. Toledo, Feb. 19, 1912; s. Grey Thornton and Edna Earle (Jaite) C.; m. Mary Glenn Dickinson, May 28, 1940; children: Mary Brooke McMurray, Pamela Hastings Keenan. AB, Harvard U., 1935, student Sch. Law, 1935-37; LLB, U. Mich., 1942. Bar: Ohio 1942. Staff dept. law City of Cleve., 1938-40; chief renegotiation br. Cleve. Ordnance Dist., War Dept., 1942-46; practiced in Cleve., 1946; asst. sec. Diamond Alkali Co., 1946-48, sec., 1948-57, gen. counsel, 1957-58; v.p.-gen. counsel Stouffer Corp., 1959-60, exec. v.p., 1960-64; practiced in Cleve., 1964-71; pres. Schrafft's divsn. Pet, Inc., NYC, 1971-75, Sportsvc. Corp., Buffalo, 1975-80, Del. North Cos., Inc., Buffalo, 1980-89, vice chmn., 1989; officer, dir. various corps.; dir., cons. Editor: F.D.R; Columnist, 1947; Contbr. to law revs. Mem. Cuyahoga County Charter Commn., 1959; chmn.; mem. Cleve. Met. Services Commn., 1957-59, President's Task Force on War Against Poverty, 1964; Del. Democratic Nat. Conv., 1960, 64; mem. Cuyahoga County Dem. Exec. Com.; Chmn. bd. trustees Cuyahoga County Hosps., 1958-64, Urban League, Karamu House. Mem. ABA, Ohio Bar Assn., Cleve. Bar Assn., Union Club Cleve., Chagrin Valley Hunt Club, Harvard Club N.Y.C., River Club N.Y.C., Buffalo Club, Phi Gamma Delta. Home: Lyme, NH. Deceased.

CARMODY, ROBERT EDWARD, human resource information systems professional; b. NYC, Dec. 13, 1942; s. Henry Adrian and Lucille Dorothy (Dorsey) C.; m. Sara Jane Morris, Oct. 4, 1969; children: Jon Andrew, Heather Brooke. BA in Psychology, U. Va., 1964. CLU. Pers. sys. supt. State Farm Ins. Co., Bloomington, Ill., 1966-78; exec. project dir. Info. Sci. Inc., Chgo., 1978-79; dir. human resources sys. CIGNA Corp., Phila., 1979-88, asst. v.p., human resources info. svcs., 1988-91; CEO INTECON Assocs., from 1991; product mgr. and bus. intelligence cons. ERP Sys., Info. Builders Inc., NYC, from 1996. Founding mem. Ins. Personnel Systems Group, 1987—. Contbr. articles to profl. jours.; spkr. at Human Resources Info. Svcs. workshops, confs. With Va. and Ill. N.G., 1964-70. Mem. Am. Mgmt. Assn., Internat. Assn. Human Resource Info. Mgmt., Conf. Bd., Info. Industry Assn., Ins. Personnel Syss. Group (founding mem. 1987), Optimists Internat., PeopleSoft Software Alliance, SAP Complementary Software Ptnr., BAAN Ptnrs.), Data Warehouse Inst. Avocations: quantum physics, history, music, literature, medicine. Home: Haddonfield, NJ. Died May 14, 2008.

CARNER, BRADFORD ALLEN, real estate broker; b. Anderson, Ind., June 17, 1947; s. Herbert Allen and Hilda (Simpson) C.; m. Kaye Wood, Sept. 25, 1977; children: Fearon, Tyler, Ned. Student, Ind. State U., Terre Haute, 1966-68; BS, Ind. U., 1970-72. Comml. brokerage Coldwell Banker, Denver, 1973-83; dir. mktg. Stan Miles Properties, Denver, 1983-85, Wright Runstad & Co., Seattle, 1985-88; comml. brokerage Grubb & Ellis, Seattle, from 1987. Mem. Valley Area Transp. Authority, Seattle, 1986-88, Seattle Zoning Com., 1985-86; chmn. Downtown Devel., Boulder, 1973-74, Arapahoe Corridor Devel., Denver, 1983-85. With U.S. Army, 1969-70. Mem. VADA, CCIM, Wing Point Athletic, Toastmasters, Elephant Club. Republican. Methodist. Avocations: climbing, running, sailing, swimming. Home: Bainbridge Is, Wash. Died Apr. 15, 2008.

CARNEVALE, JAMES LEE, retail executive; b. Trenton, NJ, Nov. 25, 1954; s. Vincent P. and Bessie I. (Iman) C.; m. Leslie A. Otier, June 13, 1981; children: Savanna, Luke, Tara. BA, Trenton State Coll., 1974. With . Channel Home Ctrs., Inc., Hamilton Twp., N.J., 1970-81; store mgr. Super X Drugs, Inc., Staten Island, N.J., 1981-92, Revco Drugs, Inc., Staten Island, from 1992. Liason to labor bd., N.Y.C., 1990-92. Chmn. Roosvelt (N.J.) Environ. Commn., 1991-95. Various awards for achievement in Drug Industry Retailing. Mem. Assn. N.J. Environ. Commns. Roman Catholic. Home: Roosevelt, NJ. Died Jan. 31, 2008.

CARNEY, PAUL M., small business owner; b. Youngstown, Ohio, Aug. 10, 1939; s. Paul and Katherine C.; m. Frances Mulholland (div. 1970); children: Paul M., Colleen, Sean Patrick; m. Norma Jean Rorick, Nov. 22, 1974. Student, Youngstown State U., 1984-85. Pres., co-owner Concept 2000, Inc., Youngstown, 1978-80; gen. mgr. Baker Plastics, Inc., Youngstown, 1980-86; pres., owner Carney Plastics, Inc., Girard, Ohio, from 1986. With U.S. Army, 1955-58. Avocations: sailing, writing. Home: Columbiana, Ohio. Died Sept. 28, 2007.

CAROTHERS, CHARLES GRAHAM, lawyer; b. Tampa, Oct. 15, 1934; s. Milton Washington and Julia Holiday (Stover) C.; m. Nancy Anne Browne, Feb. 3, 1964; children: Allison, Graham Jr., Melissa. BS, Fla. State U., 1956; JD, Stetson Coll. Law, 1963. Bar: U.S. Supreme Ct. 1970, U.S. Ct. Appeals (11th cir.) 1981. Asst. atty. gen. Atty. Gen., Tallahassee, 1963-64; pvt. practice law Tallahassee, from 1964. 1st lt. U.S. Army, 1956-58. Mem. FBA, Tallahassee Bar Assn., Fla. Sch. Bd. Attys. Assn. (pres. 1972). Democrat. Presbyterian. Died May 14, 2008.

CARPENTER, BRUCE H., retired academic administrator; b. Rapid City, SD, Feb. 5, 1932; s. Ralph A. Carpenter and Anna F. (Davis) Langworthy; m. Olivia J. clark, Nov. 23, 1953 (div. 1974); children: Lynne A., Ralph D.; m. Kathryn A. West, June 7, 1975. BA, Calif. State U., Long Beach, 1957, MA, 1958; PhD, UCLA, 1962. Prof. Calif. State U., Long Beach, 1962-72, assoc. acad. v.p., 1972-75; provost, acad. v.p. Western Ill. U., Macomb, 1975-82; pres. Eastern Mont. Coll., Billings, 1982—94. Bd. dirs. Norwest Bank Billings. Contbr. articles to profl. jours. Chmn. Macomb United Way, 1982; mem. exec. bd. Billings United Way, 1983, pres. 1986; bd. dirs. Billings YMCA, 1985-91, Deaconess Hosp. Found., 1988—. Cpl. U.S. Army, 1952-54. NSF research grantee, 1963-70 Mem. AAAS, Am. Soc. Plant Physiologists, N.Y. Acad. Scis., Am. Assn. State Coll. and Univs. (bd. dirs.), Rotary (bd. dirs. Billings Club, pres. 1992). Home: Folsom, Calif. Died Jan. 28, 2009.

CARPENTER, CHARLES CURTISS, media producer; b. Pinehurst, NC, Nov. 25, 1961; s. Virgil Lee and Mildred Louis (Gray) C. Radio producer Pierside Entertainment, Pinebluff, N.C., from 1980; record producer Studio East/Pierside, Charlotte, N.C., from 1984. Club cons. Thru Pierside Entertainment, Pinebluff, 1977—, music dir. Muirfield Broadcasting, Southern Pines, N.C., 1978—; producer WEBOP radio show, 1985—; music dir. Sta. WRDX-FM, Salisbury, 1990—; pres. Weekend Radio Network, 1991—. Democrat. Methodist. Died July 20, 2008.

CARPENTER, EDMUND NELSON, II, retired lawyer; b. Phila., Jan. 27, 1921; s. Walter S. and Mary (Wootten) C.; m. Carroll Morgan, July 18, 1970; children: Mary W., Edmund Nelson III, Katherine R.R., Elizabeth Lea; stepchildren: John D. Gates, Ashley du Pont Gates. AB, Princeton U., 1943; LLB, Harvard U., 1948; LLD (hon.), Widener U., 1985, U. Del., 1999. Bar: Del. 1949, U.S. Supreme Ct. 1957. Assoc. Richards, Layton & Finger, Wilmington, Del., 1949-53, ptnr., 1953-78, dir., 1978-91, pres., 1982-85; ret., 1991. Dep. atty. gen. State of Del., 1953-54, spl. dep. atty., 1960-62; chmn. Del. Superior Ct. Jury Study Com., 1963-66, Del. Supreme Ct. Cts. Consol. Com., 1985-87; mem. Del. Gov.'s Commn. Law Enforcement and Adminstrn. Justice, 1969; chmn. Del. Supreme Ct. Adv. Com. on Profl. Fin. Accountability, 1974-75, Del. Jud. Nominating Commn., 1977-83, Del. Superior Ct. Study Com., 1991-92; mem. Long Range Cts. Planning Com., 1976-89, Del. Ct. Common Pleas Study Com., 1992, Del. Supreme Ct. Com. on Judicial Code of Conduct, 1991-93; co-chmn. Del. Justice Ctr. Com., 1994-97; mem. lawyers adv. com. U.S. Ct. Appeals (3d cir.) 1975-80, chmn., 1975-77; chmn. local rules com. U.S. Dist. Ct. Del., 1978-83, Del. Ct. on the Judiciary Rules Com., 1996-98; bd. dirs. Bank of Del., Barclay's Bank. Trustee Wilmington Med. Ctr., 1965—, U. Del., 1971-77, Princeton U., 1974-85, 86-91, Winterthur Mus., 1991-99, World Affairs Coun. Wilmington, 1968-80, Woodrow Wilson Found., 1985—, Lawrenceville Sch., 1953-74, trustee emeritus, 1974—; trustee Nat. Humanities Ctr., 1995-98, U.S. Supreme Ct. Hist. Soc., 2004—, U. Del. Libr. Assocs., 2006—; bd. dirs. Good Samaritan Inc., 1973—, pres., 1998—; mem. Del. Health Care Injury Ins. Study Commn., 1976-80. With U.S. Army, 1942-46, 50-52 Decorated Bronze Star, Soldier's medal, Chinese Order of the Flying Cloud with four battle stars; recipient 1st State Disting. Svc. award, Del. State Bar Assn., 1984, Josiah Marvel Cup award Del. State C. of C., 1990, Benjamin Franklin Disting. Pub. Svc. award Am. Philos. Soc., 1996, Am. Inns of Ct. Professionalism award U.S. Ct. Appeals, 3d cir., 2003, Sister Eva Fink award Ministry of Caring, 2003, Ellis Island medal of honor Nat. Ethnic Coalition Orgns., 2006. Fellow Am. Coll. Trial Lawyers, Am. Bar Found.; mem. ABA (ho. of dels. 1979-86), Del. State Bar Assn. (pres. 1971-72, Presdl. citation 1987), ATLA, Am. Judicature Soc. (bd. dirs. 1974-83, exec. com. 1978-80, v.p. 1980-81, pres. 1981-83, Justice award 1991). Died Dec. 19, 2008.

CARPENTER, PAUL B., state legislator; b. Iowa, Feb. 24, 1928; m. Doris Morrow; 2 children. Senator 37th Dist. State of Calif., Sacramento. Democrat. Died Jan. 24, 2002.

CARPENTER, R(OBERTA) LYNN, cosmetic industry executive; b. Fall River, Mass., July 23, 1948; d. Robert Leonard Carpenter and Alice E. (Raphael) Carpenter Zais. BA, Southeastern Mass. U., 1970. Cosmetic rep. Cherry & Webb, Newport, R.I., 1970-71, Jordan Marsh, Boston, 1971-73; account mgr. Etherea/Norell div. Revlon-N.Y., Atlanta & Ft. Lauderdale, Ga. & Fla., 1973-77, Vidal Sassoon, Inc., Ft. Lauderdale, 1977-78; mfr.'s rep. Renauld Sunglasses, Ft. Lauderdale, 1978-79; account mgr., regional mgr. Alfin Fragrances, Ft. Lauderdale, 1980-87; regional mgr. Parfumes Pierre Cardin, Chgo., 1987-89, Trina, Inc., Chgo., from 1990; ptnr. Mystery Mail. Ptnr. Mystery Mail. Mem. NAFE, Fla. Cosmetic Assn. Roman Catholic. Avocations: workouts, movies, theater. Died Nov. 25, 2007.

CARR, PETER EMILE, publisher; b. La Habana, Cuba, Oct. 16, 1950; came to U.S., 1962; s. Pedro Emilio Carr and Carmen Emelina Luaces; m. Sheryl A. Strayer, Nov. 18, 1995. BA in Anthropology, Calif. State U., Long Beach, 1986. Asst. mgr. Hides & Skins Unltd., LA, 1976-85; archaeol. cons. Archaeol. Enterprises, LA, 1985-91; pres. The Cuban Index, San Luis Obispo, Calif., from 1991. Cons. Soc. for Hispanic Hist. and Ancestral Rsch., Westminster, Calif., 1992—, Calif. Geneal. Alliance, San Francisco, 1992—. Author: Guide to Cuban Genealogical Research, 1991 (reference book series) San Francisco Passenger Departure Lists, Vols. I-V, 1992, 93, 94, Censos, Padrones y Matriculas de la Poblacion de Cuba, 1993, Genealogical Resources of Hispanic Central and South America, 1996; author, editor jours. Caribbean Hist. and Geneal. Jour., 1993-94. Recipient Spl. Honor award Anthropology Students Assn., 1985, Gold Poet award Internat. Poetry, 1988. Mem. Nat. Geneal. Soc., Coun. for Genealogy Columnists, Inc. (co-editor newsletter 1992-95), Manchester and Lancashire Family History Soc., Cercle Genealogique de la Brie, Mortar Bd. Honor Soc. Mem. Humanist Party. Roman Catholic. Avocations: swimming, golf, hiking, fishing, old books. Died Jan. 9, 2008.

CARRADINE, DAVID, actor; b. Hollywood, Calif., Dec. 8, 1936; s. John Arthur Carradine & Ardanelle Abigail McCool; m. Donna Lee Becht, Dec. 29, 1960 (div. 1968); 1 child, Calista Miranda; m. Linda Gilbert Feb. 2, 1977 (div. 1983); 1 child, Kansas; m. Gail Jensen, Dec. 4, 1988 (div. 1997); m. Marina Anderson, Feb. 20, 1998 (div. Dec. 12, 2001); m. Annie Bierman, Dec. 26, 2004; 1 child, (with Barbara Hershey), Tom Carradine Attended, Oakland Jr. Coll., San Francisco State Coll. Actor: (Broadway plays) The Deputy, 1963, The Royal Hunt of the Sun, 1965; Off-Broadway The Transgressor Rides Again, 1969, The Ballad of Johnnny Pot, 1970; (TV series) Shane, 1966, Kung Fu, 1972-75, Kung Fu, The Legend Continues, 1993-97; (TV films) Maybe I'll Come Home in the Spring, 1971, Mr. Horn, 1978, Gaugin the Savage, 1980, High Noon, Part II: The Return of Will Kane, 1980, A Distant Scream, 1983, Jealousy, 1984, North and South, 1985, The Bad Seed, 1985, Oceans of Fire, 1986, North and South II, 1986, Kung Fu the Movie, 1986, Six Against the Rock, 1987, I Saw What You Did, 1987, The Cover Girl and the Cop, 1988, Deadly Surveillance, 1991, Luck of the Draw: The Gambler Returns, 1991, Brotherhood of the Gun, 1991, Last Stand at Saber River, 1997, Lost Treasure of Dos Santos, 1997, Martian Law, 1998, Nosferatu: The First Vampire, 1998, By Dawn's Early Light, 2000, Largo Winch: The Heir, 2001, Warden of Red Rock, 2001, The Defectors, 2001, Out of the Wilderness, 2001, The Outsider, 2002, Kung Fu Killer, 2008; (films) Taggart, 1965, Bus Riley's Back In Town, 1965, Too Many Thieves, The Violent Ones, 1967, Heaven With A Gun, 1969, Young Billy Young, 1969, The Good Guys and the Bad Guys, 1969, The McMasters, 1970, Macho Callahan, 1970, Boxcar Bertha, 1972, Mean Streets, 1973, The Long Goodbye, 1973, Death Race 2000, 1975, Cannonball, 1976, Bound for Glory, 1976, Thunder and Lightning, 1977, The Serpent's Egg, 1977, Fast Charlie - The Moonbeam Rider, 1978, Gray Lady Down, 1978, Deathsport, 1978, The Silent Flute, 1978, Circle of Iron, 1979, Cloud Dancer, 1980, The Long Riders, 1980, Safari 3000, 1981, "Q", 1981, Trick or Treat, 1982, Lone Wolf McQuade, 1983; The Warrior and the Sorceress, 1984, Rio Abajo, 1984, POW: The Escape, 1986, Armed Response, 1986, Tropical Snow, 1986, The Misfit Brigade, 1986, Marathon, 1987, Project Eliminator, 1989, Crime Zone, 1989, Nowhere to Run, 1989, Night Children, 1989, Wizards of the Lost Kingdom II, 1989, Sundown, 1989, Sauf votre respect, 1989, Fatal Secret, 1990, Midnight Fear, 1990, Sonny Boy, 1990, Think Big, 1990, Bird on a Wire, 1990, Martial Law, 1990, Dune Warriors, 1991, Future Zone, 1991, Future Force, 1992, Evil Toons, 1992, Night Rhythms, 1992, Roadside Prophets, 1992, Double Trouble, 1992, Animal Instincts, 1992, Distant Justice, 1992, Field of Fire, 1992, Waxwork II: Lost in Time, 1992, Omega Cop II: The Challenge, 1993, Kill Zone, 1993, Dead Center, 1994, Macon County Jail, 1997, Full Blast, 1997, The New Swiss Family Robinson, 1998, The Effects of Magic, 1998, Sublet, 1998, Lovers and Liars, 1998, Light Speed, 1998, Knocking on Death's Door, 1999, Zoo, 1999, Sherpherd, 1999, Dangerous Curves, 2000, Natural Selection, 2000, Down 'n Dirty, 2000, The Donor, 2000, G.O.D., 2001, Wheatfield with Crows, 2002, Bala perdida, 2002, Kill Bill: Vol. 1, 2003, American Reel, 2003, Kill Bill: Vol. 2, 2004, (voice only) Hair High, 2004, Last Goodbye, 2004, Max Havoc: Curse of the Dragon, 2004, Brothers in Arms, 2005, Miracle at Sage Creek, 2005, Last Hour, 2006, The Last Sect, 2006, Final Move, 2006, Homo Erectus, 2007, Epic Movie, 2007, Fall Down Dead, 2007, Camille, 2007, Treasure Raiders, 2007, How to Rob a Bank, 2007, The Trident, 2007, Permant Vacation, 2007, Fuego, 2007, Big Stan, 2007, The Golden Boys, 2008, Kandisha, 2008, Richard III, 2008, Hell Ride, 2008, (voice only) Death Race, 2008, My Suicide, 2008, Road of No Return, 2009, Absolute Evil, 2009, Bad Cop, 2009, Crank: High Voltage, 2009, Break, 2009, Autumn, 2009; dir.: (films) You & Me, 1975, Americana, 1981; Author: Spirit of Shaolin: A Kung Fu Philosophy, 1993, David Carradine's Tai Chi Workout, Endless Highway, 1995. Died June 3, 2009.

CARRAHER, JOHN BERNARD, retired lawyer; b. Denver, Feb. 13, 1934; s. Thomas Peter and Mary Agnes (Carroll) C.; m. Carol J. Steffens Carraher, June 28, 1958 (dec. Apr. 1999); children: Steven, Constance, Lee Anne, Patti. BS, Regis Coll., Denver, 1956; JD, Denver U., 1958. Bar: Colo., U.S. Dist. Ct. 1959. Pvt. practice, Denver, 1958—80; lawyer, shareholder, dir. Feder, Morris, Tamblyn & Goldstein, Denver, 1980-96; of counsel Bryant and Van Nest LLC, Denver, 1997-99, Van Nest LLC, Englewood, 1999-2000; ret., 2000. Lectr. advanced estate planning symposium U. Denver, 1993, Guardianship Symposium, 1997; presiding judge Mcpl. Ct., Greenwood Village, 1978-2002. Contbr. articles to profl. jours. Coord. Risen Christ Parish Edn. Program, Denver, 1968-71; mem. jud. adv. coun. Colo. Supreme Ct., 1987-93; lectr. Nat. Bus. Inst., Eau

Claire, Wis., 1992, 94; named to comty. adv. bd. Wildlife Experience Art Mus., 2004. Named Presidency Colo. Mcpl. Judges Assn., 1984-85; mem. Nat. Hon. Soc., 1992. Fellow Am. Acad. Forensic Scis. (lectr. Cin. 1990, L.A. 1991, New Orleans 1992, Boston 1993, Seattle 1995, Reno, Nev., 2000, co-chair edn. jurisprudence sect. 1996, 97); mem. Denver Probate Ct. Vis. program, Greenwood Village Ct. Mediation Program, Greenwood Village Ct. Jud. Intern Program Colo. Bar Assn. (bd. govs. 1984-85), Colo. Trial Lawyers Assn. (lectr. 1989), Am. Colo. Denver Arapahoe Bar Assn., Elder Law Adv. Coun. U. Denver Inst. for Advanced Legal Studies (coun. co-chair 1995-97). Avocations: skiing, reading. Home: Lone Tree, Colo. Died May 27, 2008.

CARROLL, JIM (JAMES DENNIS CARROLL), poet; b. NYC, Aug. 1, 1951; s. Thomas Joseph and Agnes (Coyle) C.; m. Rosemary Klemfuss, 1978 (div.) Writer, poet, spoken word performer, writing instr. The Naropa Inst., Calif. Author: (poetry) Organic Trains, 1967, Living at the Movies, 1973, The Book of Nods, 1986, Fear of Dreaming, 1993; (autobiographies) The Basketball Diaries, 1978, Forced Entries: The Downtown Diaries: 1971-73, 1987; singer: (albums)Praying Mantis, 1992; (albums with the Jim Carroll Band) Catholic Boy, 1980, Dry Dreams, 1982, I Write Your Name, 1984, The Best of the Jim Carroll Band, 1993; (soundtracks) Tuff Turf, 1985 Recipient young writer's award Random House Books, 1970. Died Sept. 11, 2009.

CARROLL, SIBYL, writer; b. Cuervo, N.Mex., Aug. 5, 1918; d. Joe Abbot and Lela Eugenia (Bell) Callaway; m. Jack Richard Carroll, Oct. 11, 1942 (wid. Jan. 1965); children: Robert Wayne, Jesse Richard, Clifford G., Tamara E. Diploma/Montessori Primary Edn., St. Nicholas Sch., London, 1975. Operator Sunshine Montessory Sch., Yuma, Ariz., 1951-89. Advisor in child devel. Ariz. Western Coll., Yuma, 1965-80, Ariz. Welfare Dept., Phoenix, 1963-66. Author: (books) Lela and joe, 1996, Complete Montessori for Home and School, 1997, From theMouth of Babes, 1997. Mem. Yuma Writers Club, Phi Theta Kappa. Republican. Mem. Ch. of Christ. Avocations: drawing, painting. Home: Yuma, Ariz. Died Mar. 14, 2008.

CARROW, ROBERT DUANE, lawyer, barrister; b. Marshall, Minn., Feb. 5, 1934; s. Meddie Joseph and Estelle Marie (Kough) C.; m. Jacqueline Mary Givens, Sept. 3, 1960; children: Leslie, Tamara, Amelia, Vanessa, Creighton, Jessica, Ramsey. Student, U. Colo., 1952; BA, U. Minn., 1956; JD, Stanford U., 1958. Bar: Calif. 1959, U.S. Supreme Ct. 1978, Eng., 1981, N.Y. 1983. Pvt. practice, Calif., from 1959; barrister London, from 1981. Judge pro tem Superior Ct. of Calif., San Francisco, 1992—. Bd. editors Minn. Law Rev., 1956-57. Mayor City of Novato, Calif., 1964-66. Fellow Ctr. Internat. Legal Studies, Soc. Advanced Legal Studies (assoc.); mem. ABA (accredited mediator), N.Y. Bar Assn., L.A. Bar Assn., San Francisco Bar Assn., Internat. Bar Assn., Chartered Inst. Arbitrators, Assn. Conflict Resolution, Honourable Soc. Mid. Inn of Ct. Died May 11, 2008.

CARSELLO, CARMEN JOSEPH, psychologist, educator; b. Chgo., July 16, 1915; s. Joseph and Mary Domenica (Tomasone) C.; m. Nicoletta Dalesio, June 18, 1939; children: Camille (dec.), Frank, Robert. BPE, DePaul U., 1938, MA, 1953; PhD, U. Sarasota, 1971; degree in gerontology, U. Ill., 1983. Registered psychologist, Ill. Tchr. parochial schs., Chgo., 1939—42, pub. schs., Cicero, Ill., 1942—43, Chgo., 1950—57; reading specialist Bur. Child Study Pub. Schs., Chgo., 1957—63; counselor, reading specialist U. Ill., Chgo., 1963—85, prof. emeritus, from 1985, Nat.-Louis U., Evanston, Ill., from 1986; prof. emeritus psychology Triton Coll., River Grove, Ill., 1986—88. Cons. in field. Contbr. articles to profl. jours. Vol. Loyola U., Chgo., 1960—; northwest rep. Mont-Clare Leyden Srs., Chgo., St. Williams Srs., 1985—; mem. career com. Joint Civic Com. Italian Ams., Chgo., 1985; pres. Mont Clare Leyden Srs., Chgo., 1989-91, St. Williams Srs., Chgo., 1989-91. Served with USN, 1943-45, PTO. Recipient Service award Loyola U., Chgo., WWII Victory medal, Asian Pacific Campaign medal, Philippine Liberation ribbon, Cook County Sheriff's Sr. Medal of Honor award, 1999, Chgo. Sr. Citizens Hall of Fame Cert. of Honor, 2000; named to Illinoisans Hall of Fame, 2001. Mem. Internat. Reading Assn., Chgo. Psychol. Assn., Asian-Am. Literacy Assn. of Internat. Reading Assn., U. Ill. Retirement Assn., U. Ill. Scholarship Assn., Chgo. Area Reading Assn., Gregroians Tchrs. Assn. (various offices Chgo. chpt.). Roman Catholic. Avocations: reading, swimming, dance, travel, photography. Died Mar. 21, 2008.

CARSON, STEVEN LEE, editor, writer, historian; b. NYC, Mar. 23, 1943; s. Harold and Mathilde (Seidel) C.; m. Yvonne DeDrozizhki, Aug. 8, 1971 (dec. Feb. 1980). BA, NYU, 1964, MA, 1965. Archivist, conf. dir. Nat. Archives, Washington, 1967—73; chmn. White House Conf. Pres. & Children, Washington, 1974; conf. dir. The Manuscript Soc., 1974—80; editor, writer Manuscript Soc. News, Washington, 1987—2003, The Lincoln Forum Bull., from 2004. Dir. history pavilion Hall of Fame Great Am., NYC, 1964; editor US Pres. Commn. Civil Disorders, Washington, 1968; mem. (charter) Hildene Robert Todd Lincoln estate; TV commentator; spkr. in field. Author: Maximilien Robespierre, 1988; (plays) The Last Lincoln, Princess Alice; contbr. articles to profl. jours. Speechwriter The White House, US Congress, Md. Ho. Dels., 1974—; historian Rock Creek Cemetery, Washington, 1997—; presdl. historian Woodrow Wilson House, Washington, DC, 2006-. Recipient NYU Heights Daily News Alumni award, 1964, medal, NY Civil War Roundtable, 1969, Archival medal, Republic of Korea, 1972, Internat. Psychohistory Assn. award, 1983, Lincoln Group of NY award, 1988, 1992, Man of the Month award, Washington Bus. Jour., 1989, Surratt Soc. award, 1993, award, Rowfant Club, 1996, Smithsonian lectr., from 1999; grantee, Md. Commn. Humanities, 1986, 1987, US Dept. Interior, 1985; Ford Found. fellow, 1964, Johns Hopkins U. Chas Carroll Fulton fellow, 1965. Fellow: The Manuscript Soc.; mem.: Washington Ind. Writers, Nat. Writers Union, Nat. Press Club (chmn. White Ho. panel 2006), Walt Whitman Leaves of Grass Sesquicentennial Comn., US Abraham Lincoln Bicentennial Com. (trustee from 2003), Abraham Lincoln Inst. (trustee from 1997), Lincoln Group D.C. (pres. 1985—88, Lincoln Recognition award 2003), Lincoln Forum (trustee from 1997), Lincoln Group III (trustee 1986—91), NYU Soc. of the Torch, NYU Perstare et Praestare, NYU Hon. Soc. Achievements include delivered official Lincoln Day Address, Ford's Theatre, Washington, 1996, 2005, National Defense University, 2006, Army-Navy Club, Washington, 2007; delivered Bicentennial Lincoln Address to University of Maryland Medical Center, 2007. Avocation: collecting historic manuscripts & letters. Died Mar. 27, 2009.

CARSON, WILLIAM MORRIS, manpower planning and development advisor; s. Edward Belmont and Frances Lucretia (Powell) C.; children: Lincoln Bruce Carson, Adrien Lee Allen, Anthony Lunt Carson, Karen Tracy Carson. BS, Columbia U., 1949; MA, Johns Hopkins U., 1951; postgrad., U. Chgo., 1955, London Sch. Econs., 1956; diploma in Arabic, Middle East Ctr. Arab Studies, 1969. Cairo corr. MBS, 1951-53; asst. prof. Mid. East Studies, SAIS, 1955-56; tng. officer U.S. AID, 1958-64; indsl. rels. staff analyst ARAMCO, Dhahran, Saudi Arabia, 1964-70; mgr. mgmt. deve. and tng. Saudi Arabian Airlines, Jeddah, 1970-72; chief tng. sect. UN Devel. Programme, NYC, 1973-75; mgr. mgmt. devel. and tng. Sulvania Tng. Ops., Waltham, Mass., 1975-76; dir. tng. Ingersoll-Rand Constrn. Svcs., Winston-Salem, N.C., 1977-79; sr. advisor manpower planning and devel. Internat. Human Resources Devel. Corp., Boston, 1979-83; gen. mgr. ITECO divsn. Saudi Tng. Svcs., Riyadh, Saudi Arabia, 1983-84; mng. dir. Arab Resources Devel. Corp., Mass., 1984-87; mgr. Turkish tech. projects GE Internat. Svc. Corp., 1987-92; prin. Carson & Assocs., Balt., 1992-96, Nat. Manpower Strategies, from 1997. Cons. UN; Middle East Inst. fellow; Ford Found. area fellow. Co-author: International Manpower Planning: The Developing World, 1982; also articles. Recipient Outstanding Performance award AID. Fellow Royal Anthrop. Inst. Gt. Britain and No. Ireland, Inst. Comml. Mgmt.; mem. Ineamus Meloria Honor Soc. Deceased.

CARSTENS, HAROLD HENRY, publisher; b. Ft. Lee, NJ, June 20, 1925; s. Henry G. and Johanna L. (Wolf) C.; m. Phyllis M. Merkle, Apr. 25, 1959; children: Rebecca, Heidi, Henry, Harold. Student, Wagner Coll., 1946-48; BS, Fairleigh Dickinson U., 1951. Asso. editor Model Craftsman Pub. Corps., Penn Publs., Inc. (became Carstens Publs., Inc., 1973), Fredon, N.J., 1951-54, mng. editor, 1954-57, v.p., 1957-63, pres., pub., 1963—2009; editor Railroad Model Craftsman mag., Carstens Hobby Books, 1952—2009; staff photographer N.Y. Lumber Trade Jour., 1954; mng. editor Toy Trains mag., 1954; pub. Flying Models mag., 1969—2009, Creative Crafts mag., Railfan and R.R. mag., 1974—2009, The Miniature mag., 1977. Chmn. Fredon Bicentennial Com., 1975-77; mem. Sussex County Overall Econ. Devel. Planning Comm., 1977-79; trustee Wagner Coll., 1977-88; mem. exec. com. Wagner Coll., 1981-88, sec. bd. trustees, 1985-88. Served with AUS, 1943-46. Recipient Alumni Achievement award Wagner Coll., 1976; Paul Harris fellow. Mem. Soc. Profl. Journalists, Acad. Model Aeros., Train Collectors Assn. (pres. 1964-65), Photg. Soc. Am. (assoc. editor jour. 1960-62), Hobby Industry Assn. America (bd. dirs. 1965-68, 70-76, 77-80, pres. 1971-72, Big Wheel award 1987), Nat. Model R.R. Assn. (bd. dirs. 1975-83, pres. 1977-79, Disting. Svc. award 1962, Man of Yr. award 1989, inductee Model Railroad Industry Hall of Fame 1996, Pioneer in Model Railroading award 2003), Friends of N.J. R.R. and Transp. Mus. (pres. 1989-93), Mag. Pubs. Assn., VFW, Rotary, Phi Sigma Kappa. Lutheran. Home: Newton, NJ. Died June 23, 2009.

CARTER, ASHLEY HALE, physicist, educator; m. Eva Horvath Carter; children: Deborah Anne, Sarah Judith, Ashley Hale, Jr. AB, Harvard Coll., 1946; PhD, Brown U., 1963. Rsch. assoc. Woods Hole Oceanographic Instn., Mass., 1946—47; dept. head AT&T Bell Labs., Whippany, NJ, 1953—90; adj. prof. physics Drew U., Madison, NJ, from 1975, dir. Charles A. Dana Rsch. Inst. for Scientists Emeriti, from 1999. Author: (book) Classical and Statistical Thermodynamics, 2001. Lt. (j.g.) USN, 1943—46. Mem.: Acoustical Soc. Am., Am. Assn. Physics Tchrs., Am. Phys. Soc. Democrat. Avocations: literature, art, music, essay writing. Home: Madison, NJ. Died Apr. 6, 2008.

CARTER, RALPH C., state agency official; b. Genera, Ala., June 25, 1932; s. Ralph Clarence and Annie Cronin Carter; m. Joyce Howard (dec. Feb. 1997); children: Ralph Jr., Angelo Marie, Nancy Inez. Student, Chipola Jr. Coll., U. Fla. Owner, operator Carter Cattle Farm, from 1951; dist. vegetation specialist Fla. Dept. Transp.; supr. Evergreen Constrn. Co., Inc., 1964-85. Mem. Fla. Ho. of Reps., 1961-66, mem. select com. for vocat. edn., select com. on natural resources; vice chmn. agr. com., vice chmn. rds. and hwys. com., chmn. forestry com., chmn. commerce com., mem. edn. com., appropriations com., joint house/senate com. on reapportionment; presenter programs on wildflowers; cons. in field. County pres. Fla. Farm bur., Washington, 1953-60; officer First presbyn. Ch., Chipley; pres. Washington County chpt. Fla. Farm Bur., mem. state policy and resolutions com.; officer local, dist. and state 4-H and FFA. Recipient award for excellent workmanship USN, 1975, Pres.' Citation Fla. Fedn. Garden Clubs, 1994, Soil Conservation award Woodmen of the World. Mem. Nat. Roadside Vegetative Mgmt. Assn. Democrat. Presbyterian. Avocation: boating. Home: Chipley, Fla. Died Sept. 4, 2007.

CARTER, WILLIAM HAROLD, SR., physicist, researcher, electrical engineer; b. Houston, Nov. 17, 1938; s. William Henry and Fannie Augusta (Simpson) Carter; children: William Harold Jr., Elizabeth Lee. BSEE, U. Tex., 1962, MSEE, 1963, PhD, 1966. Rsch. asst. U. Tex., Austin, 1962-66; program dir. Office of R&D, CIA, Washington, 1966—69; rsch. assoc. U. Rochester, NY, 1969-70; rsch. physicist Naval Rsch. Lab., Washington, 1971-93; prof. U. Nebr., Lincoln, 1981-82; instr. Johns Hopkin's U., Balt., 1989-93; program dir. NSF, Arlington, Va., 1993—95. Vis. rsch. fellow U. Reading, Eng., 1976-77; vis. scientist applied physics lab. Johns Hopkin's U., Columbia, Md., 1991-92. Contbr. articles to profl. jours. Cellist Alexandria (Va.) Symphony, 1979-88, Georgetown Symphony, 1981-2003. Capt. U.S. Army, 1967-69. Fellow Optical Soc. Am. (topical editor jour. 2000-03), Internat. Soc. for Optical Engrng. (chmn. tech. coun. 1980-82, chmn. pub. com. 1981-83, chmn. fellows com. 1986); mem. IEEE (sr., conf. chmn. 1988), Am. Phys. Soc., Cosmos Club, Sigma Xi, Tau Beta Pi, Eta Kappa Nu. Achievements include co-discovery of the quasi-homogeneous source model; research in optical coherence, in applications of speckle phenomena, and in processing images and data from optical sensors. Home: Alexandria, Va. Died Mar. 20, 2009.

CASADABAN, MALCOLM JOHN, molecular biologist; b. New Orleans, Aug. 12, 1949; s. John Adrian and Delores Anna (Poche) Casadaban; m. Joany Chou, June 17, 1977; children: Brooke Lori, Leigh Chou. SB, MIT, 1971; PhD, Harvard U., 1976; postgrad., Stanford U., 1976—79. Rch. fellow Stanford U., Palo Alto, Calif., 1976—79; asst. prof. molecular genetics & cell biology U. Chgo., 1980—85, assoc. prof., 1985—2009; cons., advisor Thermogen, Inc., Chgo.; reviewer NIH Biomedical Scis., Study Sec., Bethesda, Md., 1986—90. Contbr. articles to profl. jours. Recipient NIH Rsch. Career Devel. award, HEW, 1981—86. Mem.: AAAS, Genetics Soc. Am., Am. Soc. Microbiology, Midwest Prokaryotic Biology Club. Home: Chicago, Ill. Died Sept. 20, 2009.

CASAZZA, JO ANN, neonatal nurse; b. Middletown, Ohio, May 3, 1952; d. Erastus and Betty Jo (Perdykes) Simmons; m. Robert J. Casazza, Dec. 15, 1973; children: Holly, Asher, Logan, Courtney. ADN, Indian River Community Coll., 1985; BSN, Barry U., 1991. RNC, Fla.; NALS; cert. low risk neonatal nursing, perinatal nursing, profl. childbirth educator. Staff nurse newborn nursery Lawnwood Med. Ctr., Ft. Pierce, Fla., 1989-92; coord. Healthy Start Program of St. Lucie County, Fla., from 1992. Adj. faculty Indian River Community Coll., Ft. Pierce, Fla., 1992—. Mem. ANA, Fla. Nurses Assn., Nat. Assn. Neonatal Nurses, Internat. Childbirth Edn. Assn. Home: Pine Beach, NJ. Died Jan. 24, 2008.

CASE, REGINALD, artist; b. Watertown, NY, Dec. 23, 1937; s. Reginald Case and Madalyn Belcher; m. Bonnie Case, Aug. 15, 1961; children: Jennifer Case Ralls, Stephen T., Sarah Case Wright. BS, SUNY, Buffalo, 1959; BFA, Boston U., MFA, 1968. Vis. artist Munson Williams Proctor Inst., Utica, NY; instr. Phillips Exeter Acad., Exeter, NH, 1966—68; prof. Norfolk State Coll., Va., 1968—73, nat. tchg. fellow. Represented permanent collection Boston Mus. Fine Art, Princeton U. Art Mus., NJ, Smithsonia Mus. Art, Washington, Victoria & Albert Mus., London, Brit. Mus., London, Bklyn. Mus., Fogg Art Mus., Harvard U., Cambridge, Mass., Solomon R. Guggenheim Mus., NYC, Jewish Mus., NYC, Jewish Mus. Belgium, Brussels, Jewish Mus. Westfalen, Dorsten, Germany, Mus. Am. Folk Art, NYC. Exhibitions include Reginald Case, Paintings (Boston U. Skowhegan award, 1967), Reginald Case, Hollywood Without Politics, Art Design & Barbie, Valerie Steele, Elvis & Marilyn 2 x Immortal, Wendy McDaris, Collage Assemblage, Louis Zona, Reginald Case, Hollywood Without Politics, Reginald Case, Marilyn Monroe. Home: Miami Beach, Fla. Died Apr. 24, 2009.

CASHEL, WILLIAM S., JR., retired food products company executive; b. 1920; m. Marie Cashel; children: William III, Robert, Peter, Christine. BA, Dartmouth Coll., 1941. With Bell Telephone Co., Phila., 1946-60, 63-76, pres., 1970—77; vice chmn., CFO AT&T, 1976-83; chmn. bd. Campbell Soup Co., Camden, NJ, 1984—88; ret., 1990. Maj. USMC, 1942—46. Died Aug. 22, 2000.

CASHIN, RICHARD MARSHALL, international aid official; b. Boston, Apr. 3, 1924; s. William David and Anna Genevieve (Keefe) C.; m. Mary Catherine Walsh, Nov. 25, 1950; children: Anne Jordan, Richard Marshall, Jane Kevill, Stephen Douglas. AB, Harvard U., 1946; AM, Boston U., 1949; postgrad., Sch. Advanced Internat. Studies, Johns Hopkins, 1959. Mgmt. staff Dept. State, 1949-52; staff U.S. Escapee Program, 1952-56; program officer USOM, Libya, 1956-59, Ethiopia, 1959-62; dir. Office Central African Affairs, AID, Washington, 1962-66; assigned Sr. Seminar Fgn. Policy, Fgn. Service Inst., Washington, 1966-67; dep. dir. AID mission, Ghana, 1967-68, dir., 1968-70, AID mission to Indonesia, Jakarta, 1970-75; assoc. asst. adminstr. Office Legis. Affairs AID, Washington, 1975-77; dir. AID mission, Pakistan, 1977-78; dir. project mgmt. div. UN/FAO World Food Programme, Rome, 1978-86; sr. dir. Office of Policy and Planning Cath. Relief Svcs.-U.S. Cath. Conf., 1986-89, sr. advisor, 1989-90; cons. Interfaith Hunger Appeal, NYC, 1990-92, Cath. Near East Welfare Assn., NYC, 1991—97. Home: New York, NY. Died Feb. 13, 1997.

CASPERSEN, FINN MICHAEL WESTBY, diversified financial services company executive; b. NYC, Oct. 27, 1941; s. Olaus Westby and Freda Caspersen; m. Barbara Caspersen, June 17, 1967. BA in Econs. with honors, Brown U., 1963; LLB cum laude, Harvard U., 1966; DHL (hon.), Johns Hopkins U., 1999; various hon. degrees. Assoc. Dewey, Ballantine, Bushby, Palmer & Wood, NYC, 1969-72; chmn., CEO, mem. exec. com. Beneficial Corp., Wilmington, Del., 1976-98; chmn., CEO Knickerbocker LLC; chmn. Hodson Trust, from 1976; chmn., CEO Westby Corp., 1976—2009. Past bd. dirs., mem. exec. com. Beneficial Nat. Bank; chmn. bd. dirs. Beneficial Bank, Plc; bd. advisors Inst. Law and Econs., U. Pa.; past chmn. Coalition for Better Transp.; past co-chair Prosperity NJ; commr., dir. Hosp. for Spl. Surgery. Emeritus trustee Brown U.; former chmn. Save Ellis Island; moderator, bd. dirs. Shelter Harbor Fire Dist., 1993-2007, commr., Jupiter Island; pres. O.W. Caspersen Found.; chmn. bd. trustees Peddie Sch., Hightstown, NJ; former chmn. bd. trust Gladstone Equestrian Assn. Inc.; past bd. dirs. Drumthwacket Found.; charter mem. Partnership for NJ, New Brunswick; mem. Martin County Econ Devel. Coun., Treasure Coast, Regional Planning Council; bd. dirs. Coalition of Svc. Industries, Inc., Washington, 1982-95, vice chair, 1995; chmn. World Pair Driving Championship, 1993, pres., Keep Martin County Green, chmn. Princeton World Cup Regatta, 2000; dir. chmn. emeritus Princeton Nat. Rowing Assn.; dir. Nat. Rowing Found.; mem. corp. Cardigan Mountain Sch.; mem. exec. com. Harvard Resources Com.; former trustee John Carter Libr.; chmn. dean's adv. bd. Harvard Law Sch., Harvard Law Sch. Campaign; past dir. Clay Math. Inst. Lt. USCG, 1966-69; commr. Jupiter Island, chmn. South Martin County Regional Utilities(SMRU). Recipient Pres.'s medal, Johns Hopkins U., 1981, Jack Keilly award, Rowing, 2008, Ethics in Bus. award, BBB, 1992, Gov.'s award, Alexander Hamilton Econ. Devel., 1997, President's medal Brown U., 1997, Brightest Star award, Boys and Girls Clubs Newark, Inc., 1997, Humanities Citizen of Yr. award, NJ Coun. for Humanities, 1999; named Civic Leader of Yr., YMCA, 1982, Citizen of Yr., Morristown Meml. Hosp., 1993, Outstanding Alumnus, Harvard Law Sch., 2008, Peddie Sch., 2009. Mem. Am. Fin. Svcs. Assn. (bd. dirs., chmn. govt. affairs com., chmn. membership com., adminstrn. com., past chmn.), Fla. Bar Assn., NY Bar Assn., Harvard Club, Knickerbocker Club, Univ. Club, Wilmington Club, Shelter Harbor Golf Club (founder, chmn.), Weekapaug Found. Conservation (chmn.). Died Sept. 7, 2009.

CASSIDY, MAUREEN SMITH, gerontology advocate; b. NYC, June 14, 1935; d. Adelbert Ward and Cathleen Veronica (Ryan) Smith; m. Harold E. Cassidy, July 14, 1954; children: Bruce Edward, Cynthia Maureen, Craig Smith. Student, SUNY, Albany, 1952-53; AAS with honors, Dutchess Community Coll., Poughkeepsie, NY, 1983; grad., Nat. Acad. Paralegal Studies, Middletown, NY, 1991-92; B in Profl. Studies, Empire State Coll., Saratoga Springs, NY, 1994; postgrad., Empire State Coll., from 1996. Pvt. duty RN Unique Nursing Svc., Poughkeepsie; patient care coord. Hudson Valley Home Care, Poughkeepsie; case mgr. Dutchess Manor Home for Adults, Poughkeepsie; sr. advocacy coord. Dutchess County Assn. for Sr. Citizens, Poughkeepsie; freelance writer. Mem. AARP, Dutchess County Mental Health Assn., Older Womens League, Dutchess C.C. Alumni Assn., Empire State Coll. Alumni Assn., Ossining Med. Soc., DAR. Home: Hyde Park, NY. Died May 18, 2008.

CASTAÑEDA, JAMES AGUSTÍN, language educator, golf coach; b. Bklyn., Apr. 2, 1933; s. Ciro Castañeda and Edna May Sincock; m. Terrill Lynn McCauley, Sept. 14, 1957; 1 child, Christopher James; m. Clara Luz Gutiérrez, Dec. 9, 1991. BA summa cum laude, Drew U., 1954; MA, Yale U., 1955, PhD, 1958; Certificat d'Aptitude à l'Enseignement du Français à l'Etranger, Université Paris, 1957; postgrad., Universidad de Madrid, from 1957; student summer inst. tchrs. fgn. langs., Purdue U., 1959. Asst. to assoc. prof. Spanish and French Hanover (Ind.) Coll., 1958-61; asst. prof. Spanish Rice U., Houston, 1961-63, assoc. prof. Spanish, 1963-67, prof. Spanish, 1967—2008. Vis. prof. Spanish U. So. Calif., 1959, U. N.C., 1962, 68, Western N.Mex. U., 1970; Florence Purington vis. prof. Mt. Holyoke Coll., 1976-77; prof. summer program Hispanic studies in Spain Rice U., 1979, 82, 83-90, head freshman baseball coach, 1962-67, asst. varsity coach, 1962-83, chmn. dept. Classics, Italian, Portuguese, Russian and Spanish, 1964-72, moderator television series, 1964-67, 68-69, head golf coach, 1983-98; lectr., dir., adviser and sponsor numerous acad. and other coms. in field. Author: A Critical Edition of Lope de Vega's Las paces de los reyes, y Judía de Toledo, 1962, introducción, edición, 1971, Agustín Moreto, 1974, Mira de Amescua, 1977, El esclavo del demonio, 1980; contbr. numerous articles to profl. jours. Chmn. interview team in Europe Kent Fellowship Program, 1968; active Internat. Good Neighbor Coun. Rose Meml. scholar Drew U., 1950-54, Varsity Club scholar, Alumni Assn. Meml. scholar, Fulbright scholar Université de Paris, 1956-57, scholar Instituto de Cultura Hispánica, 1971; Danforth fellow Yale U., 1954-58, teaching fellow 1958—; named Miembro Titular, Instituto de Cultura Hispánica de Madrid, 1972, Hon. Master Will Rice Coll., 1976, Spanish Tchr. of Yr. and Fgn. Lang. Tchr. of Yr., Tex. Fgn. Lang. Tchrs.' Assn., 1982; recipient Drew U. Alumni Achievement award in Humanities, 1973, Will Rice Coll. James St. Fulton Svc. award 1973, Bklyn. Cadets Alumni Assn. Achievement award, 1976, Spanish Heritage award 1982, Disting. Svc. award Assn. Rice Alumni, 2000; named to Drew U. Athletics Hall of Fame, 1997. Mem. Am. Assn. Spanish and Portugese (numerous coms. and offices), Am. Assn. Tchrs. French, Am. Coun. Tchrs. Fgn. Langs. (del. affiliate assembly, 1970-75), S. Ctrl. Modern Lang. Assn. (various coms. and offices), Houston Area Tchrs. Fgn. Langs. (various coms. and offices), Modern Lang. Assn. (various coms. and offices), Inst. Hispanic Culture Houston (founding mem. 1966, numerous other coms. and offices), Hispanic Soc. Am. (hon.), Sigma Delta Pi (hon. pres. 1998). Home: Houston, Tex. Died Nov. 1, 2008.

CASTETTER, WILLIAM BENJAMIN, retired education educator, educational director; b. Shamokin, Pa., Aug. 31, 1914; s. Edward Franklin and Stella (Zimmerman) C.; m. Roberta Vera Breitmeyer, Aug. 6, 1947 (dec. 2003) BS, U. N.Mex., Albuquerque, 1936, MA, 1937; PhD, U. Pa., Phila., 1948. Cert. tchr. sci. and fgn. langs., Pa. Tchr., prin. Melrose Sch. Dist., N.Mex., 1937-40; prof. Lebanon Valley Coll., Annville, Pa., 1947-49; prof. edn. U. Pa., Phila., 1949—81, dir. edn. svc. bur., 1970-81, interim dean. Author: (textbook) The Human Resources Function in Educational Administration, others; contbr. articles to profl. jours. Capt. US Infantry, 1942-45, WWII., mem. Waverly Heights Cmty. Recipient Tchg. and Svc. award Phi Delta Kappa, U. Pa. Chpt., Phila., 1980, Bronze Star medal, Food Conduct medal, Am. Campaign medal, European-African-MiddleE astern Campaign medal, Worm War II Victory medal, Army of Occupation medal, Combat Infantryman Badge 1st award, Honorable Service Lapel Button WWII, French Croix Guerre. Republican. Episcopalian. Avocations: wood working, gardening. Home: Bryn Mawr, Pa. Died Feb. 23, 2009.

CASTLE, DONALD ROBERT, industrial engineer, consultant; b. Phila., June 1, 1936; s. John Cleveland and Elsie (Wilson) C.; m. Martha Ann Smith, Aug. 24, 1957 (div. Dec. 1975); children: Judith Ellen, Susan Louise; m. Andrea Faye Harin, July 3, 1976. AB, Coll. of Wooster, 1958; postgrad., Western Res. U., 1958-59. Cert. mfg. engr. Time study observer Fisher Body-GMC, Cleve., 1958-59; indsl. engr. TRW, Cleve., 1959-60; cost control mgr. Speer Resistor, Bradford, Pa., 1960-62; chief indsl. engr. Bliss-Gamewell, Newton Upper Falls, Mass., 1963-66; asst. gen. mgr. Singer Knitting Machinery, NYC, 1966-69; v.p., gen. mgr. Lightolier, LA, 1969-75; plant mgr. Sarama Lighting, Nesquehoning, Pa., 1976-78; v.p. H.B. Maynard & Co., Inc., Pitts., from 1978; v.p. mfg. Mueller Steam Splty. divsn. Core Industries, St. Pauls, N.C.; pres. Quality Resource Assocs., Charlotte, from 1994. Prof. Def. System Mgmt. Coll., Ft. Belvoir, Va., 1986-89; ind. distbr. ednl. and environ. products. Contbr. articles to mags. Mem. IEEE (sr.), Soc. Mfg. Engrs. (sr.). Republican. Presbyterian. Avocations: golf, reading. Home: Murrells Inlt, SC. Died Mar. 18, 2008.

CASTRO, LORETTA FAITH, singer, pianist; b. Whitesville, W.Va., Mar. 23, 1930; d. Joseph and Amelia (Gossen) Haddad; m. Joseph Armand Castro, Oct. 21, 1966; children: John Joseph, James Ernest. BA, Marshall U., 1953. Singer, pianist Greenbrier Hotel, White Sulphur Springs, W.Va., 1957-64, Outrigger Canoe Club, Honolulu, 1966, Sorrentino's, Toluca Lake, Calif., 1968, Flamingo Hotel, Las Vegas, Nev., 1971, Desert Inn Hotel, Las Vegas, 1977, Tropicana Hotel, Las Vegas, 1981-87, Joe Castro Orch. Tropicana Hotel Spl. Events, Las Vegas, from 1987. Record album Loretta Sings with Joe Castro Trio, 1991. Republican. Died June 10, 2008.

CATALANO, RICHARD, retired educational association administrator; b. Pitts., Apr. 19, 1934; s. Michael Joseph and Roma Agnes Catalano. BA, Bowdoin Coll., Brunswick, 1955; MA, Fletcher Sch., Medford, Mass., 1958; LLB, JD, George Washington Univ., Washington, 1963. Sec. bd. trustees City Univ. of N.Y., NYC, 1976—78, vice chancellor, 1976—84; assoc. v.p. employee & labor rels. Office of Pres., Oakland, Calif., 1984—90; deputy dir. San Francisco Mus. Modern Art, San Francisco, 1990—92; ret. Cons. labor rels., San Francisco, 1992—96. Mem.: San Francisco Zen Ctr. (bd. dir.). Avocations: music, tennis, history, travel. Home: San Francisco, Calif. Died Nov. 15, 2007.

CAVARRA, ROBERT N, music educator, musician; b. Denver, Colo., Feb. 23, 1934; s. Alfonso and Mary M. (Bianco) C.; m. Barbara Sedlmayr, Aug. 9, 1941; children: Karla Marie Cavarra Britton, R. Christopher, Stephan Gian, Matthew Nicholas. BA, St. Thomas Sem., Denver, 1956; MusB summa cum laude, U. Colo., 1961, MusM cum laude, 1963. Organist St. Joseph Ch., Denver, 1946-52, St. Thomas Sem., Denver, 1952-57, Pontifcal N. Am. Coll., Rome, 1957-58, First U. Meth. Ch., Ft. Collins, 1986-97; prof. music Colo. State U., Ft. Collins, from 1961; organist, producer Mus. Heritage Soc., from 1968. Co-founder Pro Organo Pleno XXI Found., Ft. Collins, Colo., 1994—. Composer: Suite for Organ, 1974, Two Pieces for Organ and Trumpet, 1983; organist, producer: recordings for Musical Heritage Soc., 1968—. Fellow Danforth Found., 1979. Mem. Am. Guild Organists (dean), Iota Kappa Lambda. Avocations: photography, salt-water acquaria, model railroading. Home: Fort Collins, Colo. Died Feb. 8, 2008.

CAVETT, DORCAS C., elementary school educator; b. Alliance, Nebr., July 1, 1916; d. Theodore Ray and Bertha Barrett Crawford; m. Alva Bayard Cavett, Dec. 27, 1947 (dec. Jan. 1994); 1 stepchild, Dick. BSc, U. Nebr., Lincoln, 1937; MA, U. Nebr., 1949. Elem. tchr. pub. schs., Snyder, Nebr., 1937-38, Mitchell, Nebr., 1938-39, Des Moines, 1939-43, Lincoln, Nebr., from 1949. TV tchr. pub. schs. and U. Nebr., Lincoln, 1953; assoc. prof. U. Nebr., 1958-84. Author: My First 81 Years, 1998. Com. mem. Cooper Found., Woods Bros. Found.; mem. Bereuter Mil. Selections, Lincoln. Capt. USMC, 1943-46. Cavett Elem. Sch. named in her (and husbands) honor; recipient Amoco award for disting. tchg. U. Nebr., 1976, Alumni Achievement and Svc. award. Mem. PEO, Am. Legion, Faculty Women's Club, TTT Soc., U. Nebr. Alumni Assn. (life), Delta Kappa Gamma, Phi Delta Kappa (hon. mem.). Congregationalist. Home: Lincoln, Nebr. Died Sept. 8, 2007.

CAWEIN, KATHRIN (MRS. SEABURY CONE MASTICK), artist; b. New London, Conn., May 9, 1895; d. Henry and Barbara (Franz) Cawein; M.A. (hon.), Oberlin Coll., 1966; D.F.A. (hon.), Pacific U., 1980, Forest Grove, Oreg.; student Art Students League; m. Seabury Cone Mastick, Apr. 3, 1964. Music roll editor, music interpreter with various musicians, 1911-32; tchr. County Center Work Shop, 1935-36; owner studio for children, 1950-55; one man shows; County Center, White Plains, N.Y., 1935, Village Art Center, N.Y.C., 1945, Town Hall, N.Y.C., 1950, 8th St. Playhouse, N.Y.C., 1953, Sarasota, Fla., 1973, U. Tampa (Fla.), 1973, Oberlin (Ohio) Coll., 1975, St. John's Ch., Pleasantville, N.Y., 1976, Berea (Ky.) Coll., 1977, Pacific U., Forest Grove, Oreg., 1979, 80, 81, 83, 85, 90, Mt. Kisco (Ky.) Libr., 1991, Internat. Kisco Libr., 1991; exhibited group shows U.S., Eng., France, Italy, Ecuador, including Century of Progress, 1934, Tex. Centennial, 1937, World's Fair, 1939; represented in permanent collections at Met. Mus., Nat. Mus., Washington, Pa. State U., Tampa U., Oberlin Coll.; illuminated books St. Marks Ch., Van Nuys, Calif.; illuminated manuscripts Pacific U., The Life of Christ Congl. Ch., Portland. Oreg., 1991, The 13 Steps of Christ, 1991 now in permanent collection Cmty. Ch., Portland. Recipient Frank Talcott Non-Mem. prize Soc. Am. Etchers, 1936, prize for lithography Village Art Center, 1944, prize for etching Nat. Assn. Women Artists, 1947, prize for dry point Pleasantville Woman's Club, 1950, prize for etching, 1952, prize for dry point Westchester Fedn. Women's Clubs, 1951, others; Kathrin Cawein Gallery of Art named in her honor Pacific U., 1985. Mem. Nat. Assn. Women Artists, Art Students League (life), Chgo. Soc. Etchers, Soc. Graphic Artists. Died 1996.

CEGLAREK, JOHN PETER, physician; b. Bay City, Mich., Apr. 10, 1947; s. Wallace John and Jeanette Agnes (Piotrowski) C.; divorced; children: Katherine Joan, John Alexander; divorced; 1 child, Jozsef Andrew. BA with high distinction, Wayne State U., 1974, MD, 1983; MPH, U. Mich., 1975. Diplomate Nat. Bd. Med. Examiners. Resident in family practice Providence Hosp., Southfield, Mich., 1987; staff physician emergency medicine North Detroit Gen. Hosp., 1987, med. dir. emergency medicine, 1987-88; staff physician MED STOP, Sterling Heights, Mich., 1988-89; med. dir., Eleven Oaks Med. Ctr., Madison Heights, Mich., 1988-89; staff physician Madison Cmty. Hosp., Madison Heights, Mich., 1989; pvt. practice Madison Heights, Mich., 1989-91, Midland, Mich., 1991, Warren, Mich., from 1992. Cons. epidemiologist Oaklnad County Dept. Health, Pontiac, Mich., 1977. Maj. M.C., USAR, 1985—. Mem. AMA, Am. Acad. Family Practice, Mich. State Med. Soc., Macomb County Med. Soc., Assn. Mil. Surgeons U.S., Res. Officers Assn., Wayne State U. Alumni Assn., U. Mich. Alumni Assn., Detroit Zool. Soc.,Cranbrook Inst. Sci., Phi Beta Kappa. Home: Royal Oak, Mich. Died Aug. 1, 2008.

CENTOLA, STEVEN RONALD, English language educator; b. Phila., Aug. 1, 1952; s. Mario Thomas and Gloria Florence (D'Alessio) C.; m. Susan Joy Smith, Aug. 17, 1974; children: Tamara, Paul, Devon. BS in English, West Chester U., 1974; MA in English, U. R.I., 1977, PhD in English, 1981. Asst. prof. English Va. Tech. Coll., Blacksburg, 1981-85; prof. English Millersville (Pa.) U., from 1985. Author: Arthur Miller in Conversation, 1993; editor: The Achievement of Arthur Miller, 1995. Coord. intramural Soccer U-10 program Hempfield Soccer Club, Lancaster, Pa., 1992-94. Mem. MLA, Pa. Writing Across the Curriculum Assn. (bd. dirs. 1987—), Eugene O'Neill Soc., Nat. Coun. Tchrs. English, Arthur Miller Soc. (pres.), Phi Kappa Phi. Democrat. Roman Catholic. Avocations: coaching children's soccer, fishing, playing guitar, reading. Home: Lancaster, Pa. Died Jan. 9, 2008.

CERNY, MARY ANN, administrator; b. Kendalia, Tex., Nov. 8, 1948; d. Frank Joseph and Stella (Piper) Lombardino; m. Owen Edward Cerny, Oct. 20, 1968; children: Kelly Marie, Allen Shane. Student, U. Houston, 1966-67, Del Mar Coll., from 1980. Gen. mgr. Corpus Christi (tex.) Creditors Assn., Check Stop, Inc., 1979-95; exec. v.p. Check Stop, Inc., San Antonio, from 1992; pres. San Antonio Creditors Assn., from 1992. Mem. Credit Women Internat./Credit Profls., Corpus Christi, 1987-88. Pres. bd. trustees Calallen Independent Sch. Dist., Corpus Christi,

1992, sec. bd. dirs., 1990-91. Mem. Am. Collectors Assn. Roman CAtholic. Avocations: reading, crocheting, fishing, computers. Home: Robstown, Tex. Died July 11, 2008.

CESNIK, JAMES MICHAEL, retired labor union administrator, printing company executive; b. Marshfield, Wis., Oct. 6, 1935; s. Ignatius Anthony and Mary Catherine (Bayuk) C.; m. Elizabeth Louise Havlik, Aug. 1, 1959 (div. 1987); children: Margaret Mary, Sarah Elizabeth, Michael Ignatius; m. Barbara E. Nelson, Jan. 1, 1990. BA, St. John's U., Collegeville, Minn., 1958. Reporter, Rice Lake (Wis.) Chronotype, 1958; reporter, copy, makeup and layout editor Mpls. Star & Tribune, 1958-64; internat. rep., asso. dir. rsch. and info., dir. rsch. and info. Newspaper Guild, CWA,AFL-CIO/CLC, Washington, 1965-75; editor Guild Reporter, 1973-93; v.p. Internat. Labor Press Assn., Washington, 1973-79, pres., 1980-82; sec.-treas. Internat. Labor Comm. Assn., Washington, 1984-87; editor Internat. Labor Comm. Assn. Reporter, Washington, 1983-84; sec.-treas. JBTM Enterprises Inc., Winchester, Va., 1989-91, 2002, pres., 1991—2001, Signet Screen Printing and Embroidery, Winchester, Va., 1993—2007; ptnr. TJC LLC, Winchester, Va., 1999—2009. Elijah P. Lovejoy lectr. So. Ill. U., Carbondale, 1970; cons. in field. Mem. Falls Church (Va.) Democratic Com., 1970-84; founding mem. Falls Church Com. on Status of Women, 1975-76; pres. Montessori Sch. No. Va., 1970. Mem. Slovenian Heritage Com. Washington, Slovenian Choral Soc. Washington, Am. Slovenian Cath. Union, Soc. for Slovene Studies. Roman Catholic. Died Feb. 27, 2009.

CHABEK, DANIEL JAMES, journalist, writer, public relations professional; b. Cleve., Apr. 8, 1915; s. Daniel James Sr. and Hattie (McLkovsky) C.; m. Margaret Pangrace, Oct. 28, 1939; children: Cynthia, Christopher. BS in Journalism, Ohio State U., 1936. Reporter Cleve. Press., 1936-52; pub. rels. rep. Ford Motor Co., Dearborn, Mich., 1952-58, Cleve., 1958-80; newspaper columnist North Ridgeville (Ohio) Light, 1980-88, Lakewood Sun Post, North Olmsted, Ohio, from 1988. Adv. bd. Lakewood Sun Post, 1989—. Author: (stories) Lakewood Lore, 1998; contbr. articles to newspapers. Bd. trustees Lakewood Hist. Soc., 1989-2000; jury voter, mem. selection commn. City of Lakewood, 1993. Lt. (j.g.) USN, 1944-46, PTO. Mem. Soc. Profl. Journalists, Cleve. Press Club, Kiwanis (editor Kiwanigram 1982-89, Best Newsletter 14th divsn. award 1984). Avocations: running, calisthenics. Died Jan. 29, 2008.

CHAIKIN, DONALD JOEL, lawyer; b. Jersey City, Aug. 12, 1933; s. Arthur and Ruth (Steinberg) C.; m. Mimi Abitbol, Feb. 6, 1965 (dec. 2002); children: Marney, Stephen. BA, U. Md., 1960; LLB, Am. U., 1963. Bar: DC 1964, Md. 1964. Sr. ptnr. Chalkin & Karp, Washington, 1963—2000. Baseball commr. D.C. City Coun., Washington. Mem. Ass. Trial Lawyers D.C. (Trial Lawyer of Yr. award 1986), Assn. Trial Attys. (past pres.). Died Oct. 26, 2009.

CHALMERS, FRANKLIN STEVENS, JR., engineering consultant; b. Atlanta, Mar. 21, 1928; s. Franklin Stevens Sr. and Martha (Bratton) C.; m. Anne Upshaw, June 11, 1955; children: Franklin Steven III, Martha Chalmers Hamilton, James MacAllen, S. Elizabeth Chalmers Smith. BChemE, Ga. Inst. Tech., 1949; postgrad., Harvard U., 1987. With plant ops. Stauffer Chem. Co., Houston and Baytown, Tex., 1952-56, Chemical Products Corp., Cartersville, Ga., 1949-50; with project engring. and mgmt. CF Braun & Co., Alhambra, Calif., 1956-67; with bus. devel. Jacobs Engring. Co., Pasadena, Calif., 1967-70; asst. dir. alt. fuels devel. and cons. devel. Arthur G. McKee & Co., Cleve., 1970-76; dir. govt. rels. Davy McKee Corp., Washington, 1976-83; cons. Chalmers & Co., Washington, 1983—86, 1989—2001; dir. policy OSHA/US Dept. Labor, Washington, 1986-89. Presenter seminars in People's Republic of China. Contbr. articles to profl. jours.; patentee tar sands oil recovery, apparatus for oil recovery, fluegas desulfurization, elemental sulfur recovery. Deacon San Marino (Calif.) Community Ch., 1969; pres. YMCA-YMen's Club, South Pasadena, Calif., 1967; trustee Plymouth Ch. of Shaker Heights, Ohio, 1973-76. With Chem. Corps, U.S. Army, 1950-52. Mem. Am. Inst. Chem. Engrs., Nat. Constructors Assn. (chair govt. affairs com. 1979), Nat. Bldg. Mus. (docent), Congl. Country Club, Cosmos Club, Rotary, Scottish Rite (32d degree), Knight Templar York Rite Freemasonry. Presbyterian. Achievements include engineering, design and construction of many process plants to produce chemical, petroleum and fertilizer products, research and reports on technical, economic and political feasibility of methods for utilization of indigenous resources and/or generation of electric power at remote locations; hosting of delegations from People's Republic of China to U.S. and seminars in China regarding recovery of sulfur for industrial use by flue gas desulfurization. E-mail: frankschalmer@com. Died July 18, 2009.

CHAMBERS, CHARLES MACKAY, academic administrator, lawyer, consultant; b. Hampton, Va., June 22, 1941; s. Charles McKay and Ruth Ellanora (Wallach) C.; m. Barbara Mae Fromm, June 9, 1962; children: Charles M., Catherine M., Christina M., Carleton M. BS, U. Ala., 1962, MS, 1963, PhD, 1964; JD, George Washington U., 1976; DSc (hon.), Lawrence Tech. U., Southfield, Mich., 2006. Bar: Va. 1977, DC 1978, US Patent & Trademark Office, 1978, US Supreme Ct. 1980, US Dist. Ct. DC 1985, US Ct. Appeals (DC cir.) 1987, US Dist. Ct. (ea. dist.) Va. 1988, US Ct. Appeals DC, 1987, US Ct. Appeals (4th cir.) 1990, Mich. 1994; cert. comml. pilot, multiengine, land and instrument. Aerospace engr. NASA, Huntsville, Ala., 1962-63; rsch., teaching asst. U. Ala. Rsch. Inst., Huntsville, Ala., 1963-64; research fellow NASA, Cambridge, Mass., 1964-65; assoc. prof. U. Ala., Tuscaloosa, 1965-69; mng. dir. Univ. Assocs., Washington, 1969-72; prof., assoc. dean George Washington U., Washington, 1972-77; v.p., gen. counsel Council on Postsecondary Accreditation, Washington, 1977-83; exec. dir. Am. Inst. Biol. Sci., Washington, 1983-87; pres. Am. Found. Biol. Scis., Washington, 1987-93, Lawrence Tech. U., 1993—2006, chancellor, 2006—09. Cons., evaluator, accreditation rev. coun. commn. on instns. of higher edn. Noth Ctrl. Assn. Colls. and Schs., Chgo.; bd. dirs. Automation Alley, Mich. Sci. and Math. Alliance, Mich. Small Aircraft Transp. Sys. Author: (with others) Understanding Accreditation, 1983; pub. BioScience; contbr. chpts. to books. Mem. Diocesan Adv. Coun., Arlington, Va., 1978-84, Fairfax County Dem. Com., Va., 1979-95; judge No. Va. Sci. Fair, 1976-2009; trustee, sec. Southeastern U., Washington, 1983-87; trustee BIOSIS, Inc., Phila. and London, 1991-93; mem. Oakland County Workforce Devel. Bd., Mich., 1996-2009; bd. dirs. Automation Alley, 1999-2009, Detroit area coun. Boy Scouts Am., 2003-09. Recipient Citizenship award Am. Legion, 1959, Olive Branch award Editors and Writers Com., NYC, 1986, Horace H. Rackham award Engring. Soc. Detroit, 2004; fellow NSF, 1964. Fellow AAAS; mem. ABA, AAUP, Am. Assn. Univ. Adminstrs. (pres. 1984-85), Engring. and Sci. Devel. Found. (bd. dirs., pres. 1996-2000, fellow Engring. Soc. 1997), Am. Coun. Edn. (bus. and higher edn. forum), Soc. Automotive Engrs., Nat. Soc. Black Engrs. (hon.), The Engring. Soc. Detroit (bd. dirs. 1999—), Assn. Ind. Colls. and Univs. Mich., Mich. Small Aircraft Transp. Program, Detroit Regional C. of C. (bd. dirs.), Circumnavigators Club, Detroit Econ. Club (bd. dirs.), Detroit Athletic Club, Cosmos Club, Capitol Hill Club, Phi Beta Kappa, Sigma Xi, Tau Beta Pi. Roman Catholic. Avocations: flying, history, sailing. Home: Alexandria, Va. Died May 20, 2009.

CHANCE, KENNETH DONALD, engineer; b. Denver, July 27, 1948; s. John Jefferson and Evelyn Pauline (Jacobs) C. AA, Red Rocks Coll., Golden, Colo., 1982. Stationery operating engr. EG&G Rocky Flats, Golden, from 1980. Home: Englewood, Colo. Died Sept. 27, 2007.

CHANDLER, JULIE LIGHT, secondary school educator; b. Indpls., Dec. 8, 1949; d. Edward Carl and Genneve Elder Light; m. Felix Chandler Jr. (dec. Dec. 30, 1991); 1 child, Scott Andrew. BS in Edn., Ind. U., Bloomington/Indpls., 1984, MS, 1984. Tchr. Cathedral HS, Indpls., 1981—84; h.s. tchr. Indpls. Pub. Schs., from 1984. Recipient Scholastic Achievement award, Sigma Pi Alpha, 1981. Home: Westfield, Ind. Died Aug. 22, 2008.

CHANDLER, NETTIE JOHNSON, artist; b. Christian County, Ky., Nov. 15, 1912; d. Sol James and Georgia Bell (Davis) Johnson; m. Percy Scott Chandler, Oct. 14, 1944. Student, Watkins Inst., Nashville, 1937—45, Watkins Inst., 1953—56, Harris Sch. Art, Nashville, 1937, Oklahoma City U., 1952, Coll. William and Mary, 1957—58; AS cum laude, Thomas Nelson C.C., 1983. Bookkeeper Keach Furniture Co., Hopkinsville, Ky., 1929—32; office sec., bookkeeper Baus Mfg. Co., Hopkinsville, 1933—35; bookkeeper Castner Knott Co., Nashville, 1936—39; sec., artist, editor Young South page' Baptist & Reflector, Nashville, 1939—45; real estate saleswoman Grinnell Realty, Nashville, 1950—51; typist Griffiss AFB, Rome, NY, 1952—53; sec., artist Tenn. State Libr., Nashville, 1953—56; tech. illustrator NASA, Hampton, 1956—72. Comml. artist to 1972, fine arts painter, from 1973. Represented in permanent collections Va. Air and Space Mus., Bapt. and Reflector, Nashville. Vol. ARC, Nashville, 1985—86. Recipient awards for art including 2d pl. Watkins Inst., 1955, 1st place Parthenon, Nashville, 1956, 1st place Watkins Inst., 1956, 1st place (3 times) Tenn. State Fair, 1985-96, Best of Show, Watkins Inst., 1986, 3d pl. Watkins Inst., 1987, 2d pl. for miniatures Tenn. Art League (3 times), 1988-92, 3d pl. Tenn. Art League, 1989, Best of Show, 1990, 2d pl. for graphics, 1996, 2d pl. oils, 2005, Best of Show, Gallery Eight WDCN TV, 1997, Daily Press Newport News, Va. Snapshot award, 1983. Mem.: Tenn. Art League (leader Monday Painters 1984—98). Republican. Baptist. Avocations: writing, reading, painting, computer designing and printing, knitting. Died Jan. 22, 2009.

CHANEY, ALBION HENRY, pastor; b. King City, Calif., Nov. 12, 1921; s. Leonardo Eldridge and Marie Bertha (Menke) D.; m. Mary Jacqueline Mooney, Apr. 1, 1945; children: Kathleen, James, Steven, Terri Eileen, David, Colleen. Student, U. Calif., Davis, 1941; naval officer, USN U. of Air, Corpus Christi, Tex., 1943; student, Moody Bible Inst., Chgo., 1950, Missionary Training Inst., Seattle, 1961. Lic. C.B.A. Ch., 1954; ordained to ministry Am. Evang. Christ Chs., 1956. Pastor various chs., Calif. and Iowa, 1954-1985, First Bapt., Healdsburg, Calif., 1986. Pres. San Joaquin Conservative Bapt. Assn., Mariposa, Calif., 1966-67. Lt. USNR, 1942-45. Recipient Presdl. Citation USN, 1944. Republican. Home: Healdsburg, Calif. Died Mar. 23, 2008.

CHANEY, ETHEL SCOTLAND, English language educator; b. Cleve., Mar. 16, 1914; d. Bayard Scott and Beatrice Louise (Homan) Scotland; m. William Stanton Chaney, Oct. 8, 1939 (div. Mar. 1988), remarried Jan. 10, 2001; children: Scott Clay, Karen Marie Kauffman, Norma Chaney Shear, Ruth Margot Walker. BS, U. Ill., 1935; MA, Roosevelt U., 1966. Tchr. English Rutledge Jr. Coll., Raleigh, N.C., 1987, Huntington Learning Ctr., Raleigh, 1988; substitute tchr. Wake County Sch., Raleigh, 1988-98; tchr. Joliet (Ill.) H.S., 1936—75, Gulf H.S., Fla., 1975—81. Docent N.C. Mus. Art, Dickens Soc., Jane Austen Soc., Crime Writers Soc. Mem. Univ. Women (life), U. Ill. Alumni (life), Roosevelt U. Alumni (life), Pi Beta Phi (life). Democrat. Unitarian-Universalist. Home: Raleigh, NC. Died Oct. 30, 2007.

CHANG, CLIFFORD W.J., chemistry educator, researcher, consultant; b. Honolulu, July 25, 1938; BS, U. So. Calif., 1960; PhD, U. Hawaii, 1964. Rsch. assoc. U. Hawaii, Honolulu, 1964, U. Ga., Athens, 1964-68; asst. prof. U. West Fla., Pensacola, 1968-73, assoc. prof., 1973-79, prof., from 1979. Cons. Monsanto, Pensacola, 1987-90; mem. adv. review panel NSF, Washington, 1990-91. Contbr. articles to profl. jours. and chpts. to books. Mem. Am. Chem. Soc. Am. Soc. Pharmacology, Chem. Soc. London, N.Y. Acad. Scis., Sigma Xi. Achievements include research in marine natural products including rare marine isonitriles, work on antistaining and antisoiling agents for carpets. Died Oct. 15, 2007.

CHANG, KWAI SING, retired educator; b. Honolulu, Aug. 22, 1921; s. Jan and Agnes (Lee) C.; m. Miyoko Hokama, July 10, 1951; children: Forsythia, Jasmine. BA, U. Hawaii, 1944; BD, Princeton Theol. Sem., 1947, ThM, 1948; PhD, U. Edinburgh, Scotland, 1952. Ordained to ministry, United Ch. of Christ, 1948. Min. Lanai Union Ch., Lanai City, Hawaii, 1948-50, Kalahikiola Congl. Ch., Kohala, Hawaii, 1952-56; prof. Bible and religion Agnes Scott Coll., Decatur, Ga., 1956-86. Mem. Am. Acad. Religion. Home: Decatur, Ga. Died Apr. 12, 2008.

CHANG, SHENG-YEN, Buddhist monk, educator; b. Nan T'ung, People's Republic China, Dec. 4, 1931; arrived in US, 1975; s. Hsuan Ts'ai and Chin Chang. MA, Rissho U., Tokyo, 1971, LittD, 1975. Wireless telegraph operator, telecom. officer & warrant officer Nationalist Army, China, 1949—59; solitary retreat Chao Yuan Monastery, Taiwan, 1961—68; received formal transmission from Ch'an Master Dong Chu of the Cao Dong tradition of Ch'an, 1975; received formal transmission from Ch'an Master Ling Yuan of the Lin Ji tradition, 1978; abbot The Temple of Enlightenment, NY, 1977; prof., dir. Chinese Culture U., Taipei, China, 1978-87; abbot Nung Ch'an Monastery, Taiwan, 1979; founder Ch'an Meditation Ctr., 1980; pres. Chung-Hwa Inst. Buddhist Culture, Taipei and Elmhurst, NY, from 1980; dir. Chung-Hwa Inst. Buddhist Studies, Taipei, from 1985. Pub. Tungchu Pub. Co., Taipei, from 1980, Humanity Monthly, Taipei, from 1982, Dharma Drum Publs., NYC, from 1982; prof. Tung-Wu U., Taipei, from 1986, Fu-Jen U., Taipei, from 1989. Author: The Life and Practice of Ou-Yi Chih-Hsu, 1975, Getting the Buddha Mind, 1982, Poetry of Enlightenment, 1987, Faith in Mind, 1988, Zen: Tradition and Transition, 1988, Ox Herding at Morgan's Bay, 1989, The Infinite Mirror, 1990, The Sword of Wisdom, 1990, Illuminating Silence, 2002, numerous books in Chinese. Founder Internat. Cultural & Ednl. Found. Dharma Drum Mountain, 1989. Mem.: Internat. Assn. Buddhist Studies, Japanese Assn. Indian Buddhist Studies. Died Jan. 27, 2009.

CHANON, BERNARD L., lawyer, mediator; b. Houston, Sept. 15, 1934; s. Sam and Lena Chanon; m. Pat Chanon, June 21, 1953; children: Gregory, Richard, Todd, Caren. BS, U. Houston, 1957; JD, U. Houston Bates Coll. Law, 1959. Bar: U.S. Supreme Ct., U.S. Dist. Ct. (so. dist.) Tex., U.S. Ct. Appeals (5th cir.), U.S. Dist. Ct. Iowa, Tex., cert.: mediator, collaborative lawyer, family law specialist. Counsel Lee, Duroff (later Duroff & Chanon), Houston, from 1959. Home: Houston, Tex. Died May 19, 2008.

CHAPDELAINE, LORRAINE ELDER, gerontology nurse; b. Yonkers, NY, Sept. 29, 1939; d. Alexander Lindsay Elder and Evelyn Emma Flower Bellini; m. Bernard Grant Dostal, May 15, 1960 (div. Nov. 1972); children: Dana Arthur Dostal, Jeffrey Alexander Dostal. Diploma, Mass. Genl. Hosp. Sch. Nursing, Boston, 1961; BS cum laude, Elms Coll., Chicopee, Mass., 1990; MS, U. Mass., 1992. RN, Mass.; cert. gerontol. clin. specialist. Staff nurse Cooley Dickinson Hosp., Northampton, Mass., 1961-67, Holyoke (Mass.) Hosp., 1967-74; health svc. supr. Mountain View Nursing Home, Montgomery, Mass., 1979-85; staff nurse, supr. Port Charlotte (Fla.) Care Ctr., 1985-87; staff nurse Holyoke Geriatric Authority, 1987-89; temporary staff O'Connell Profl. Svc., Holyoke, 1987-90; asst. prof. clin. nursing U. Mass. Sch. Nursing, Amherst, 1992-93; clin. specialist/wound cons. Hampshire County Vis. Nurse Assn., Northampton, 1992-96; clin. specialist, vis. staff Vis. Nurse Svcs Western Mass., Holyoke, Mass., from 1989; grant writer, adminstr. Innovative Nurse-Managed Well Elderly Foot Clinics, from 1993; pvt. practice in nursing foot care, 1987—2005; cons. and lectr. in field. Lectr. in field; initiator, adminstr. grant-funded nurse-managed foot clinics for elderly poor.; prin. The Foot Care Nurse, Holyoke, 1997—. Mem.: Nat. Assn. Clin. Nurse Specialists, Nat. Gerontol. Nurses Assn., Order Eastern Star (Worthy Matron 1981, 1984), Advanced Practice Gerontol. Nurses Interest Group, Sigma Theta Tau. Episcopalian. Avocations: music, gardening. Died Jan. 1, 2008.

CHAPIN, RICHARD EARL, retired librarian; b. Danville, Ill., Apr. 29, 1925; s. Harry W. and Lula May (Briggs) C.; m. Eleanor Jane Lang, Aug. 15, 1949; children: Robert Lang, David Brian, Rebecca Anne. AB, Wabash Coll., 1948; MS, U. Ill., 1949, PhD, 1954; LHD (hon.), Wabash Coll., 1991. Reference asst. Fla. State U., 1949-50; libr. asst. U. Ill., 1950-53, vis. prof., 1957; asst. dir., asst. prof. Sch. Libr.

Sci., U. Okla., 1953-55; assoc. libr., assoc. prof. Mich. State U., East Lansing, 1955-59, dir. librs., prof. journalism, 1959-89, dir. librs. emeritus, prof. emeritus, from 1989; libr. advisor United Arab Emirates U., 1989-92. Dir. Mich. State U. Press, 1986-90; cons. to govts., founds., colls., and univs.; bd. dirs. Ctr. for Rsch. Librs., 1978-83; bd. dirs. OCLC Users' Coun., 1980-83, pres., 1983. Contbr. articles to libr. periodicals and encys. Mem. East Lansing Human Relations Commn., 1966-69, chmn., 1969; mem. East Lansing Bd. Edn., 1970-74, 75, pres., 1973-74; bd. dirs. W.B. and Candace Thoman Found., 1991—. Served to lt. (j.g.) USNR, 1943-46. Mem. ALA, Mich. Library Assn. (pres. 1967), Assn. Research Libraries (bd. dirs. 1984-87), Blue Key, Sigma Chi, Phi Kappa Phi Home: East Lansing, Mich. Died July 29, 2009.

CHAPIN, SCHUYLER GARRISON, retired cultural organization administrator, retired dean; b. NYC, Feb. 13, 1923; s. L.H. Paul and Leila Howard (Burden) C.; m. Elizabeth Steinway, Mar. 15, 1947 (dec. 1993); children: Henry Burden, Theodore Steinway, Samuel Garrison, Miles Whitworth; m. Catia Zoullas Mortimer, Sept. 15, 1995. Student, Longy Sch. Music, 1940-41; LHD (hon.), NYU, 1974, Hobart/William Smith Coll., 1974, Hofstra Coll., 1999; DLitt (hon.), Emerson Coll., 1976; MusD (hon.), Mannes Coll., New Sch., 1990, Curtis Inst. Music, 2000. Spot salesman NBC-TV, NYC, 1947-51; gen. mgr. Tex and Jinx McCrary Enterprises, NYC, 1951-53; booking dir. Judson, O'Neill & Judd divsn. Columbia Artists Mgmt., 1953-59; dir. masterworks to v.p. creative svcs. Columbia Records divsn. CBS, 1959-63; v.p. programming Lincoln Center for the Performing Arts, 1964-69; exec. producer Amberson Enterprises, NYC, 1969-71; acting gen. mgr. Met. Opera, NYC, 1972-73, gen. mgr., 1973-75; dean faculty arts Columbia U., 1976-87, dean emeritus, from 1987; v.p. worldwide concert and artist activities Steinway & Sons, NYC, 1990-92; commr. of cultural affairs City of N.Y., 1994—2002; ret., 2002. Cons. Carnegie Hall Corp., 1979-87. Author: (autobiography) Musical Chairs, 1977, Leonard Bernstein: Notes from a Friend, 1992, Sopranos, Mezzos, Tenors, Bassos and Other Friends, 1995. Past chmn. Bagby Music Lovers Found.; past chmn., trustee Am. Symphony Orch. League, 1985-92; trustee Naumburg Found., 1949, Richard Tucker Found., 1975-92, Am. Inst. for Verdi Studies, 1975, Bklyn. Philharm., 1978-92, Lenox Music Theatre Group, 1984, Lincoln Ctr. Theatre, 1985-94, 2001—, Carnegie Hall Soc., 1987-94, 2001—, Curtis Inst. Music, 1986-92, Pres.'s Com. on Arts and Humanities, 1982-90, Redwood Libr. and Athenaeum, 1990-96; chmn., exec. com. Franklin and Eleanor Roosevelt Inst., 1982-2004, co-chair bd. govs., 2004—. 1st lt. Air Corps US Army, 1942—46, China, Burma, India. Decorated chevalier Legion of Honor (France); recipient N.Y. State Conspicuous service cross, 1951, Christopher award, 1971, Emmy awards 1972, 76, 80, Gold Medal Nat. Arts Club, 1983. Fellow Am. Acad. Arts & Scis. Clubs: Century Assn. (N.Y.C.), Knickerbocker. Home: New York, NY. Died Mar. 7, 2009.

CHAPMAN, ALVAH HERMAN, JR., retired newspaper executive; b. Columbus, Ga., Mar. 21, 1921; s. Alvah Herman and Wyline (Page) Chapman; m. Betty Bateman, Mar. 22, 1943; children: Dale Page Chapman Webb, Chris Ann Chapman Hilton. BS, The Citadel, 1942, degree (hon.), 1971, Barry U., 1985, Fla. Internat. U., 1988, U. Miami, Coral Gables, Fla., 1989, U. Notre Dame, 1991. Bus. mgr. Columbus Ledger, 1945-53; exec. v.p., gen. mgr. St. Petersburg (Fla.) Times, 1953-57; pres., pub. Morning News and Evening Press, Savannah, Ga., 1957-60; exec. Knight-Ridder Newspapers, Inc., Miami, Fla., 1960-89, exec. com., 1960-2000, exec. v.p., 1967-73, pres., 1973-82, CEO, 1976-88, chmn., 1982-89, dir., chmn. exec. com., 1984-95; v.p., gen. mgr. Miami Herald, 1962-70, pres., 1970-82. Bd. dirs. Knight-Ridder Newspapers, Inc., 1962-2000; lectr. Am. Press Insts., Columbia; vice chmn., exec. com. Miami Coalition for Safe & Drug-Free Cmty.; mem. Pres.'s Drug Adv. Coun., 1989-92; chmn. emeritus Fla. Internat. U. Found.; bd. trustees Fla. Internat. U., 2001-2002; trustee John S. and James L. Knight Found., 1971-2002. Founder, chmn. emeritus Cmty. Anti-Drug Coalitions Am.; chmn. We Will Rebuild, 1992—93, Gov.'s Commn. on Homeless, 1992—94; founding chmn. Cmty. Partnership for Homeless, Inc., from 1993; mem. State's Commn. on the Homeless, 2000; bd. dirs. ARC Greater Miami and the Keys, 2001—04. Maj. USAAF, World War II. Decorated Croix de Guerre, D.F.C. with 2 oak leaf clusters, Air medal with 5 clusters U.S.; recipient Citadel Palmetto award, 1985, Isaiah Thomas award, Rochester Inst. Tech., 1986, Joseph Wharton Statesman award, 1988, United Negro Coll. Fund's Disting. Svc. award, 1988, The Miami Herald Spirit of Excellence Lifetime Achievement award, 1989, Anne Ackerman Disting. Floridian award, 1991, LeRoy Collins Lifetime Achievement award, Leadership Fla., 1992, United Way Dorothy Shula award for Volunteerism, 1994, Salvation Army Red Shield award, 1994, ARC Humanitarian of Yr. award, 1994, Health Found. of South Fla. Concern award, 1995, Drum Maj. of Justice award, Miami-Dade C. C., 1996, Spirit of Martin Luther King Jr. Parade & Festivities Dinner Com. award, 1996, Citizen of Yr. award, Gray Panthers North Dade, 1996, Resolution State Fla., 1996, Lifetime Achievement award, Cmty. Anti-Drug Coalitions Am., 1999, Ellis Island medals of honor, 2000, Pontifical medal Benemerenti, 2000, Fla. Meml. Coll. Cmty. Leadership award, 2001, Pillar award, Fla. Internat. U., 2001, 1st recipient Cmty. Partnership for Homeless's Alvah H. Chapman, Jr. Humanitarian award, 2002, Corp. Citizenship award, Nat. Coalition for Homeless, 2002, Disting. Svc. award, Cmty. Anti-Drug Coalitions Am., 2004, Mayor's Lifetime Achievement award, 2004, Advocacy award, Homeless/Formerly Homeless Forum Inc., 2004, Peace and Unity award, St. Martin de Porres Assn., 2005, Cornerstone award, Broward Partnership Homeless, 2007, Lifetime Achievement award, Miami Coalition Christian and Jews, 2007, Citadel 1842 Soc., 2007, Assn. of Fundraising Professionals, Greater Miami Chapter Nat. Philanthropy Day Com., 2007; named Outstanding Young Man, Columbus Jr. C. of C., 1952, Dade County's Outstanding Citizen of 1968-69, Brigham Young U. Internat. Businessman of Yr., 1984, Hon. Dir., Fla. C. of C., 1997, Grad. Sch. Bus. Fla. Internat. U. in honor of Alvah H. Chapman, Jr., 2001, Alvah H. Chapman, Jr. and Betty B. Chapman Ctr. in honor of Betty and Alvah Chapman, Cmty. Partnership Homeless, 2002; named one of 22 Who Make a City Magic, Jr. League, 2003, Legends South Fla., South Fla. CEO mag., 2004; named to South Fla. Bus. Hall of Fame, 2000, Arland D. Williams Soc. at The Citadel, 2002, Builders Assn. South Fla. Housing Hall of Fame, 2003, Fla. Newspaper Hall of Fame, 2004. Mem. Newspaper Assn. Am., Am. Newspaper Pub. Assn. (chmn., pres. 1986-87), So. Newspapers Pubs. Assn. (pres. 1976). Methodist. Home: Miami, Fla. Died Dec. 25, 2008.

CHARLES, HOWARD CLIFTON, JR., public warehousing executive; b. Winston-Salem, NC, Mar. 31, 1918; s. Howard Clifton Sr. and Jessie Mae (Idol) C.; m. Rachel Louise Charles, June 14, 1941; children: Rachel Diana Phillips, Janie Leah McKnight. AA, Mars Hill Coll., NC, 1939. Mgr. Firestone Home & Auto Store, Reidsville, N.C., 1946-48, Ctrl. Carolina Warehouses, Inc., Greensboro, N.C., 1949-55, CEO, pres., 1955-80, chmn. bd., from 1980. Trustee Mars Hill Coll., 1987—; bd. dirs. Chapels for the Retarded Ctrs. in N.C., 1976-88; deacon First Bapt. Ch., Greensboro, 1980-84, Sunday Sch. tchr., 1956—. Served to maj. USAAC, 1941-45, to lt. col. Res. ret. Named Alumnus of Yr., Mars Hill Coll., 1996. Mem. Ret. Officers Assn. (pres. 1990), N.C. Warehousemen's Assn. (pres. 1975), Toastmasters (pres. 1957), Kiwanis. Republican. Avocations: golf, flying, woodworking, gardening, travel. Home: Greensboro, NC. Died Jan. 18, 2008.

CHARRY, STEPHEN WALTER, historian, educator; b. Trenton, NJ, Nov. 4, 1958; s. Michael Ronald and Jane Charry; m. Karin Tunis, June 22, 1965; children: Kaylyn Jane Tunis, Benjamin Michael, Genevieve Cecielle. MA, Wash. State U., Pullman, Washington, 1990; PhD, Wash. State U., 1997. Adj. prof. of history Ctrl. Wash. U., Ellensburg, 1993—99; prof. history Ill. Valley C.C., Oglesby, from 1999. Contbr. articles to profl. jours. Mem.: Ill. Fedn. of Teachers (pres. Local 1810 from 2003), Orgn. of Am. Historians, Am. Hist. Assn., Phi Alpha Theta. Home: Princeton, Ill. Died Mar. 18, 2008.

CHARVAT, REGINA (REGI KLEIN), artist; b. Chgo., Apr. 1, 1931; d. Ernest L. and Emma (Holstein) Klein; m. Leo M. Charvat (dec.); children: Stephanie Kathryn, Rebecca Leonore. Student, Bennington Coll., Art Inst. Chgo. Exhbns. include 1020 Art Ctr., Chgo., Ann Ross Gallery, White Plains, N.Y., U. Miami, Fla., Morris Gallery, N.Y.C., Waverly Gallery, N.Y.C., Gallery 3, Greenwivh, Conn., Rye (N.Y.) Free Reading Rm., Katonah (N.Y) Gallery, U. Notre Dame, South Bend, Ind., Schoolhouse Gallery, Sanibel Island, Fla., Byways Gallery, Irvington, N.Y., Ward-Nasse Gallery, N.Y.C., Wakefield Gallery, Scotts Corners, N.Y., Cos Cob Gallery, Greenwich, Conn., Pelham (N.Y.) Art Ctr., Wainwright House, Rye, N.Y., among others; represented in permanent collections Arrowood Conf. Ctr., Rye Brook, N.Y., Westchester Conty Courthouse Bldg., White Plains, N.Y., Red Lion Inn, Stockbridge, Mass., Westchester Country Club, Rye, N.Y. Bot. Garden, Bronx. Recipient awards Emily Lowe Competition, 1956, 18th Annual Joseph P. Mayer prize, Audubon Artists Exhbn., 1960, 11th Annual Treadway award, Silvermine Guild Artists, 1960, Purchase prize Dulin Art Gallery, grand prize Watercolor USA. Home: Chandler, Ariz. Died Sept. 10, 2007.

CHASAN, ALEXANDER ANSCHEL, paint chemist, researcher; b. Berne, Switzerland, Apr. 17, 1926; came to U.S., 1947; s. Boris and Liuba (Gorsky) C.; m. Betty Chasan, June 1, 1952; children: Alan Bryan, Elise Gail. MS, Fed. Inst. Tech., Zurich, 1947. Chemist Publicker, Inc., Phila., 1947-49; chief chemist Balt. Paint & Chem. Corp., 1950-66; chief paint chemist J.M. Huber Corp., Havre de Grace, Md., 1966-70; cons. Balt., 1970-71; spec. mgr. Fed. Supply Svc. Gen. Svc. Adminstrn., Washington, 1971-81; coatings specialist Carderock div. Naval Surface Warfare Ctr., Annapolis, Md., from 1981. Chartered orgn. rep. Boy Scouts Am. Troop 97, Balt., 1979—; bd. dirs. Brotherhood Temple Oheb Shalom, Balt., 1980—. Recipient Superior Performance award, Boy Scouts Am. Troop 97, Balt., 1985. Fellow Am. Inst. Chemists; mem. Washington Paint Tech. Group (pres. 1974, bd. dirs. 1990—, Man of Yr. 1976), Balt. Soc. for Coatings Tech. (pres. 1971). Democrat. Jewish. Home: Baltimore, Md. Died June 22, 2008.

CHASE, GARY ANDREW, statistician, educator; b. NYC, Jan. 5, 1945; s. Allen Leonard and Janet Elaine (Rubensohn) C.; m. Carol S. Weisman, Nov. 21, 1980; 2 children. AB magna cum laude, Harvard U., 1966; PhD, Johns Hopkins U., 1970. Rsch. fellow Johns Hopkins U., Balt., 1970-71, asst. prof., 1971-78, assoc. prof., 1978-85, prof., 1985-94; prof. medicine, dir. consulting biostat. Georgetown U., Washington, from 1994. Cons. Armed Forces Inst. Pathology, Washington, 1984-85, NIMH, Rockville, Md., 1986-90, NIH, 1992—. Co-author: Principles of Genetic Counseling, 1975; contbr. articles to profl. jours. Mem. Am. Statis. Assn. (bd. dirs. 1981-84), Soc. for Epidemiol. Rsch., Internat. Genetic Epidemiol. Soc. Jewish. Avocation: american and british history. Home: Ann Arbor, Mich. Died Oct. 22, 2007.

CHASZEYKA, MICHAEL ANDREW, mechanical engineer, consultant; b. Youngstown, Ohio, July 28, 1920; s. Michael and Anastasia (Klim) C.; m. Libuse Panosh, Nov. 30, 1946 (dec. May 1993). BME, Ohio State U., 1943; MS in Mech. Engring., Ill. Inst. Tech., 1959; postgrad., U. Chgo., 1959-63. Jr. engr. Republic Steel Corp., Youngstown, 1947; engr. Gen. Motors Corp., McCook, Ill., 1947-51; rsch. engr. Armour Rsch. Found., Chgo., 1953-61; phys. sci. coord. Office of Naval Rsch., Chgo., 1961-81; owner, cons. M.A. Chaszeyka Assocs., Western Springs, Ill., 1981-93. Contbr. articles to profl. jours. Lt. USN, 1944-46, World War II, lt. comdr., 1951-53, Korea. Recipient Outstanding Service award Office of Naval Rsch., 1981. Mem. ASME (life, award for pub. policy devel. 1986), VFW (life), Naval Res. Assn. (life), Am. Mensa. Avocations: photography, foreign travel, writing, travel lectures, skiing. Home: Western Springs, Ill. Died July 27, 2008.

CHAU, BENJAMIN J., ophthalmologist; b. Hong Kong, Aug. 18, 1940; came to U.S., 1942; s. Sham Tai and Kitty (Chan) C.; m. Anita Leong, June 25, 1975; children: Melissa, Kimberly. BME, CCNY, 1963; MD, SUNY, Buffalo, 1969. Diplomate Am. Bd. Ophthalmology. Resident in ophthalmology White Med. Hosp., LA, 1970-73; pvt. practice Torrance, Calif., from 1973; clin. instr. ophthalmology U. So. Calif./White Meml. Hosp.-Loma Linda, LA, 1973-78. Fellow ACS, Am. Acad. Ophthalmology. Home: Rolling Hills, Calif. Died Sept. 18, 2007.

CHEN, GEORGE CHI-MING, energy company executive; b. Shanghai, Sept. 21, 1923; s. Harvey Kun-Fan and Margaret Wen-Yao (Sang) C.; m. Nora Tzu-Ling Pan, Oct. 15, 1953; children: Priscilla Hsu-Lu, Peter Hsu-Ling. BS, Harvard U., 1946. Mgr. Kian Gwan Co., Shanghai, 1947-49, Hong Kong, 1949-50, mng. dir. Taipei, 1950-51; chmn. George Chen & Co., Taipei, 1951-87, Lien Chen Ltd., Taipei, 1951-87; mng. dir. Shing Nung Group, Tai Chung, 1961-87; chmn. Shell Pacific Devel., Singapore, 1970-87. Trustee Northfield Mt. Hermon Sch., Mass., 1988-98, Libr. Found. of San Francisco, 1996—; mem. bd. overseers Harvard U., 1998—. Lt. Col. Chinese Army. Mem. China Petroleum Soc. (life). Republican. Roman Catholic. Home: San Francisco, Calif. Died Sept. 7, 2007.

CHENEY, LOIS SWEET, infection control nurse; b. Clifton Springs, NY, Oct. 26, 1933; d. Merton E. Sr. (dec.) and Jennie M. (Smith) S. (dec.); divorced; children: Linda Cheney Thorpe, Susan Cheney Post Kehler, Douglas A. Cheney. Diploma in nursing, Rochester Hosp., NY, 1954; BS in Edn. with high honors, Mansfield U., Pa., 1973; MS, Columbia Pacific U., Mill Valley, Calif., 1982. RN N.Y., Pa. With Meml. Hosp., Towanda, Pa., 1974—82; coord. infection control and employee health Clifton Springs Hosp. and Clinic, 1982—87; infection control officer Monroe Cmty. Hosp., Rochester, 1987—2000. Spkr. on mgmt. AIDS in long term care, 1987, 88, 89, 92; spkr. and cons. in infection control. Contbr. articles to profl. jours. Mem. Assn. Profls. in Infection Control and Epidemiology (cert., Rochester-Finger Lakes chpt.), Bus. and Profls. Women's Club, Toastmasters Internat., N.Y. State Pub. Health Assn. Home: Towanda, Pa. Died May 7, 2008.

CHENG, WU C., retired patent examiner; b. Shanghai, Aug. 11, 1922; came to US, 1948; s. Ting-yih and Wei-chi (Kiang) C.; married 1963; 1 child, Robert C. BS, St. John's U., Shanghai, 1944; MS, Kans. State Coll., 1949; PhD, Ga. Inst. Tech., Atlanta, 1954. Asst. prof. to prof., head chemistry dept. Union U., Jackson, Tenn., 1955-66; assoc. prof. chemistry George Peabody Coll., Nashville, 1966-72; tchr. with rank I Lyman HS, Longwood, Fla., 1972-75; asst. prof. chemistry to assoc. prof. physics Paine Coll., Augusta, Ga., 1975-89; patent examiner US Dept. Commerce, Washington, 1990—99. Vis. instr. chemistry Ga. Inst. Tech., Atlanta, summer 1956; chemist No. Regional Rsch. Ctr., Peoria, Ill., summer 1976, 88; faculty rsch. participant Savannah River Lab., Aiken, SC, summer 1977, Argonne Nat. Lab., Chgo., summer 1982, Oak Ridge Nat. Lab., Tenn., summer 1984; mem. faculty Rockwell Hanford Ops., Wash., summer 1979; faculty rsch. fellow USAF Acad., Colorado Springs, Colo., summer 1986. Contbr. articles to profl. jours. Mem.: Ga. Acad. Sci., Am. Chem. Soc., Sigma Xi. Achievements include patents in field. Home: Martinez, Ga. Died Jan. 5, 2008.

CHERNAK, JOHN ANDREW, food equipment manufacturing company executive; b. Bridgeport, Conn., Feb. 26, 1929; s. John and Elizabeth (Mosko) C.; m. Arlene B. Rasile, Nov. 1, 1974; children: Linda Beth, Christie Anne, Paula Jo, Michelle Marie. BA, Brown U., 1951; JD, Northwestern U., Chgo., 1956. Bar: Ohio 1956. Assoc. Baker & Hosteler, Cleve., 1956-57; with Tomlinson Industries, Cleve., from 1957, pres., 1966-95; chmn., from 1995. Contbr. articles on food svc. to profl. publs. Capt. USMCR, 1951-53. Mem. Nat. Assn. Food Equipment Mfrs. (bd. dirs., officer 1985—, v.p. 1992, pres. 1993). Home: Sparks, Nev. Died Jan. 22, 2008.

CHERNISH, LELIA MARGARET, retired not-for-profit fundraiser; b. Collins, Mo., Mar. 19, 1921; d. Aubra F. and Velta Lelia (Nance) Higgins; m. Stanley M. Chernish, June 19, 1949; 1 child, Dwight Landers. Student, U. Md.,

1947—48. Tchr. kindergarten, Silver Springs Bethesda, Md., 1945-51; apptd. del. White House Conf. on Aging, 1971, Ind. Health Careers, 1974-84; mem. Ind. Impaired Physicians Com., 1976-79; appointee Ind. Mus. Art, 1976-84; apptd. bd. trustees Ind. Med. Distbn. Loan Fund, 1977-92, Ind. Med. & Nursing Distbn. Loan Fund, 1981-85; mem. Marion County Impaired Physicians Com., 1983-84. Liaison to med. student wives, rec. sec., program, publicity and fin. chmn., historian and by-laws chmn. Ind. State Med. Aux.; pres. Marion County Med. Aux., 1965-66, med. student liaison, historian, United Fund chmn., by-laws com., parliamentarian, chmn. cookbook prodn.; mem., fin. chmn., parliamentarian Boys Club Aux. Mem. Winona Meml. Hosp. Aux.; founder Vol. Observer Program, Ind., 1970—71; mem., yearbook chmn. Alliance of Indpls. Mus. of Art; active Women United Against Rape, 1975, Sch. Drop Out Program, Diabetes Detection Dr.; drug and internat. health activities; regular ct. watcher Indpls. Anti-Crime Crusade; vol. Ronald McDonald House, 1982—2007; trustee, chmn. needle art project; facilities com.; chmn. 10th anniversary calendar fund raising project, 1992; bd. dirs., 2003—06; sec. to bd. dirs., 1992—99. Recipient Theta Sigma Phi award, 1969, Sagamores of the Wabash award for disting. pub. svc. Gov. Otis R. Bowen, 1977, by Gov. Robert D. Orr, 1981, Ind. Jefferson award, 1982, Lori Kleiman award for svcs. over and above call of duty Ronald McDonald House, 1992, Indpls. Mayors Vol. Partnership award, 1999; named Ind. Mother of Yr., 1981. Mem.: Crossroads Guild (pres. 1969, parlimatarian 2002—06, Heart of Gold award 2002), Women in Neighborhood Svc., Indpls. chpt. Embroiderers Guild Am. (chmn. nat. embroiderers guild exhibit 1989, dean of faculty seminar 1990, co-chmn. nat. seminar 1992, pres. 1997—98), Hillcrest Garden Club (treas., chmn. flower show), Faculty Women's Club of Ind. U. Sch. Medicine. Home: Indianapolis, Ind. Died June 14, 2008.

CHETON, CHARLES WILLIAM, furniture company executive; b. Canton, Ohio, Nov. 23, 1924; s. Simeon and Theodora (Morar) C.; m. Carolyn Popa, July 1, 1945 (div. Apr. 1972); children: Anna, Barbara and Charles (twins), Debra, Michelle, Charles II; m. Catherine Condos Gaston, July 14, 1973. Student, U. Tenn., 1944; exec. mgmt. degree, Northwestern U., 1954. Office mgr. Worshill Auto Parts, Canton, Ohio, 1946-47; gen. mgr. Home Furniture Co., Canton, 1947-52; pres. Cheton Furniture Co., Canton, from 1952. Pres. Beachcomber Corp., Fla., 1968-81. Pres. Internat. Festival, Canton, 1980-82; pres. bd. St. George Cath. Ch., Canton, 1968-82; exec. v.p. Save Palace Theater Com., 1981-82, pres. 1988—. C pl. USAF, 1943-46. Recipient Mayor's Award, Canton, 1981. Mem.: Cath. Order Foresters (pres. local chpt. 1958-70, 1981—), Traian and Iliu Maniu Soc., K.C. Republican. Home: Canton, Ohio. Died Jan. 7, 2008.

CHIAPPONE, ROBERT CARL, orthodontist; b. Fresno, Calif., May 4, 1938; s. Carlo Paul and Clotilda Elena (Gaiato) C.; children: Tracy, Christopher, Cary, Craig. BA, U. Calif., Berkeley, 1960; DDS, U. Calif., San Francisco, 1966. Pvt. practice, Concord, Calif., from 1966. Contbr. articles to profl. jours. Republican. Avocations: scuba diving, pilot, tennis. Home: Lafayette, Calif. Died July 14, 2007.

CHILCOTE, THOMAS FRANKLIN, retired college president, clergyman; b. Dayton, Pa., May 25, 1918; s. Thomas Franklin and Emma Jane (Peters) C.; m. Margaret Virginia Mossor, Sept. 18, 1943; children— Wayne Leslie, Deborah Jean. Student, Taylor U., 1936-38; B.A., U. Pitts., 1940; postgrad. Western Theol. Sem., 1940-41; M.Div., Boston U., 1943; D.D. (hon.), U. Chattanooga, 1955; postgrad. Harvard Inst. Ednl. Mgmt., 1973. Ordained elder Methodist Ch., 1943. Pastor, McCandless Ave Meth. Ch., Pitts., 1939-41, Walnut Ave. Meth. Ch., Roxbury, Mass., 1942-43, Cresson (Pa.) Meth. Ch., 1943; news editor The Christian Advocate, Chgo., 1943-45; mng. editor New Life Mag., Nashville, 1945-48; pastor First Meth. Ch., Chattanooga, 1948-55; supt. Abingdon (Va.) dist. Meth. Ch., 1955-58; pastor First Meth. Ch., Maryville, Tenn., 1958-62; sr. minister Fountain City United Meth. Ch., Knoxville, Tenn., 1962-68, First United Meth. Ch., Oak Ridge, 1968-70, First Broad St. United Meth. Ch., Kingsport, Tenn., 1970-73; pres. Emory and Henry Coll., Emory, Va., 1973-84; del. World Meth. Conf., Oxford and Oslo, 1951-61, Pacific Rim Higher Edn. Seminar in Far East, 1980; mem. Theol. Study Commn. on Doctrine and Doctrinal Standards, United Meth. Ch., 1968-72, mem. uniting conf., 1970. Mem. Alpha Pi Omega. Republican. Methodist. Author: Quest for Meaning, God's Twenty-Two, 1982. Home: Woodlyn, Pa. Died Jan. 20, 2009.

CHIN, JANET JUE, nurse, secretary; b. Portland, Oreg., Feb. 25, 1930; d. Herbert Sue and Margaret Mai (Lum) Jue; m. George Wai Chin, Mar. 1, 1952; children: Martin, David, Daniel, Cathryn, Cheri, Nancy. BS in Liberal Arts and Nursing, U. Oreg., 1952. RN, Oreg. Sec. Sam Wong & Son, Klamath Falls, Oreg., from 1952; office nurse Dr. J. Robertson, M.D., Merrill, Oreg., 1958-80; charge nurse Oreg. Health Sci. U. Hosp., Portland, 1951-52; staff nurse Merle West Med. Ctr., Klamath Falls, 1988; pub. health nurse Klamath County Health Dept., 1952-53; sch. nurse Klamath County Sch. Dist., Klamath Falls, from 1990. Vol. nurse ARC, 1952—; vol. Klamath County Mental Health Ctr., Klamath Falls, 1979-90; organist 1st Presbyn. Ch., Merrill, 1959-81; bd. dirs. Mental Health Adv. Bd., Klamath Falls, 1979-85, Local Alcohol & Drug Adv. Bd., Klamath Falls, 1984-90, Health Bd., 1993—. Mem. Oreg. Nurses Assn., AAUW, Lost River Garden Club (pres. 1958-60), Zuleima Temple 13, Dau. of the Nile. Republican. Avocations: violinist, choir. Home: Klamath Falls, Oreg. Died Apr. 30, 2008.

CHISHOLM, FRANK ANDERSON, investment banker; b. Savannah, Ga., Aug. 24, 1910; s. Frank Miller and Elsie (Barnard) C.; m. Katherine Crutcher, Mar. 3, 1956; children: Frank A. Jr., Elsie Robinson. AB, Yale U. Pres. Varnedoe Chisholm & Co., Savannah, 1956-69; chmn. Varnedoe Chisholm & Skinner, Savannah, 1969-73; v.p., fin. cons. Robinson-Humphrey Co., Inc., from 1973. Home: Savannah, Ga. Died June 9, 2008.

CHRISTENSON, ALLEN CECIL, retired mathematics educator; b. Montrose, Calif., Aug. 25, 1931; s. Clarence and Cecil Edna (Wells) Christenson; children: Gary Allen, Teresa Ann Thompson. Student, Glendale Coll., Calif., 1949—52; BA in Secondary Edn., Ariz. State Coll., Tempe, 1956; MA in Secondary Edn., San Fernando Valley State Coll., Northridge, Calif., 1966. Gen. secondary life diploma credential. Engring. analyst Rockedyne, Canoga Park, Calif., 1956—62; math. tchr. LA Unified Sch. Dist., 1962—97; ret., 1997. Sgt. US Army, 1953—55. Mem.: Am. Mensa. Republican. Avocations: sports, camping, fishing, hiking. Died June 19, 2008.

CHRISTIAN, RICHARD CARLTON, dean, former advertising agency executive; b. Dayton, Ohio, Nov. 29, 1924; s. Raymond A. and Louise (Gamber) C.; m. Audrey Bongartz, Sept. 10, 1949; children: Ann Christian Carra, Richard Carlton Jr. BS in Bus. Adminstrn, Miami U., Oxford, Ohio, 1948; MBA, Northwestern U., 1949; LLD (hon.), Nat.-Louis U., 1986; postgrad., Denison U., The Citadel, Biarritz Am. U. Mktg. analyst Rockwell Mfg. Co., Pitts., 1949-50; exec. v.p. Marsteller Inc., Chgo., 1951-60, pres., 1960-75; bd. dirs., exec. com. Young and Rubicam, Inc., 1979-84; chmn. bd. Marsteller Inc., 1975-84, chmn. emeritus, from 1984; assoc. dean Kellogg Grad. Sch. Mgmt. Northwestern U., 1984-91, assoc. dean Medill Sch. Journalism, 1991-99. Dir., chmn. Bus. Publs. Audit Circulation, Inc., 1969-75; spkr. in field. Trustee Northwestern U., 1970-74, Nat.-Louis U., Evanston, Ill., 1970-92, James Webb Young Fund for Edn., U. Ill., 1962-95; pres. Nat. Advt. Rev. Coun., 1976-77; bd. adv. coun. mem. Miami U.; mem. adv. coun. J.L. Kellogg Grad. Sch. Mgmt., Northwestern U.; v.p., dir. Mus. Broadcast Comm.; dir. Can. U.S. Ednl. Exch. (Fulbright Found.), 1988-92. With inf. AUS, 1942-46, ETO. Decorated Purple Heart, 1945; recipient Ohio Gov.'s award 1977, Alumni medal, Alumni, Merit and Svc. awards Northwestern U.; named to the Advt. Hall of Fame, 1991. Mem. Am. Mktg. assn., Indsl. Mktg. Assn. (founder, chmn. 1951), Bus. Profl. Advt. Assn. (life mem. Chgo., pres. Chgo. 1954-55, nat. v.p. 1955-58, G. D. Crain award 1977), U. Ill. Found., Northwestern U. Bus. Sch. Alumni Assn. (founder, pres.), Am. Assn. Advt. Agys. (dir., chmn. 1976-77), Am. Acad. Advt. (1st disting. svc. award 1978), Northwestern U. Alumni Assn. (nat. pres. 1968-70), Mid-Am. Club, Comml. Club, Econ. Club Chgo., Kenilworth Club, Westmoreland Country Club, Alpha Delta Sigma, Beta Gamma Sigma, Delta Sigma Pi, Phi Gamma Delta. Baptist. Home: Evanston, Ill. Died Oct. 3, 2009.

CHRISTIANSEN, PAUL ARTHUR, botanist, consultant; b. Mitchell County, Iowa, June 7, 1932; s. Carl H. and Myrtle Christiansen; m. Barbara Lindley, June 25, 1955; children: Dana, Scot. BA, U. Iowa, 1959; MS, U. Oreg., 1964; PhD, Iowa State U., 1967. Instr. biology Humboldt (Iowa) Community Schs., 1959-64; prof. biology Cornell Coll., Mt. Vernon, Iowa, from 1967, now prof. emeritus. Mem., chair Iowa State Preserves Bd., Des Moines, 1984-91; bd. dirs. Iowa chpt. The Nature Conservancy, Des Moines, 1984—. Author: (chpt. in book) Prairies/Iowa's Natural Heritage, 1982, Prairies Past & Prairies Present/Take This Exit, 1989, Illus. Guide to Iowa Prairie Plants, 1999. Mem. Mt. Vernon Community Sch. Bd., 1971-83. With USN, 1950-54. Recipient Roadside Vegetation Mgmt. grant Iowa Dept. Transp., Linn County, 1971-73, Soil Structure Under Prairie Grass grant Leopold Ctr. for Sustainable Agr., Ames, Iowa, 1990-92. Fellow Iowa Acad. Sci. (pres. 1988-89), Sigma Xi; mem. AAAS. Democrat. Achievements include research in methods of establishing and managing prairies. Home: Cedar Rapids, Iowa. Died Oct. 2, 2007.

CHRISTO, THOMAS KENNETH, management consultant, data processing executive; b. Southbridge, Mass., Feb. 12, 1948; s. Christi Thomas and Dorothy (Lapery) C.; m. Marjorie T. Ugo, Mar. 29, 1970 (div. Oct. 1978); children: Courtney, Thomas K. Jr.; m. Deirdre Jane O'Leary. Student, U. Miami, 1966-67; BS, Suffolk U., 1969; JD, Boston U., 1972. Bar: Mass. 1972, Fed. Dist. Mass., 1973, Fed. Dist. Ct. R.I., 1976, Fed. Dist. Ct. Puerto Rico, 1976, U.S. Ct. Appeals (1st cir.) 1976, U.S. Supreme Ct. 1977, U.S. Ct. Appeals (2d. cir.) 1978. Owner, operator Christo and Co., Boston, 1968-72; assoc. Fanger and Birnbaum, Boston, 1972-73; with Suffolk County Dist. Attys., Boston, 1973-75; sole practice Boston, 1974-79; sr. ptnr. Christo and Watson, Boston, 1976-79; pvt. practice North Hampton, N.H., from 1980. Bd. dirs. Chgo./Pacific Railway, 1987; editor contract and tort Computer Law Reporter, 1984-86; pres., chief ops. officer MDS Qantel, 1986, bd. dirs., 1985-86; mem. bd. editors Computer Law Strategist, 1978-79; lectr. numerous data processing and legal trade orgns.; cons. in field. Contbr. articles to profl. jours. Dir. northeast area Haig for Pres., N.H., 1987-88; Rep. candidate U.S. Senate from N.H., 1990. Republican. Albanian Orthodox. Avocations: reading, sailing, skiing, tennis. Died Feb. 9, 2008.

CHURCH, FRANK FORRESTER, minister, writer; b. Boise, Idaho, Sept. 23, 1948; s. Frank Forrester and Bethine (Clark) C.; m. Amy Furth, May 30, 1970 (div. 1991); children: Frank Forrester, Nina Wynne; m. Carolyn Buck Luce, July 25, 1992. AB, Stanford U., 1970; MDiv, Harvard U., 1974, PhD, 1978. Min. All Souls Unitarian Ch., NYC, 1978—2009. Columnist The Chicago Tribune, 1987-88, The New York Post, 1989; vis. prof. Dartmouth Coll., Hanover, N.H., 1989. Author: Father and Son: A Personal Biography of Senator Frank Church of Idaho, 1985, The Devil and Dr. Church, 1985, Entertaining Angels, 1987, The Seven Deadly Virtues, 1988, Everyday Miracles, 1988, Our Chosen Faith: An Introduction to Unitarian Universalism, 1989, God and Other Famous Liberals, 1991, Life Lines, 1996, A Chosen Faith, 1998, Lifecraft, 2000, Bringing God Home, 2002, The American Creed, 2002, Freedom from Fear, 2004, So Help Me God, 2007, Love and Death, 2008; translator: Greek Word-Building (Matthias Stehle), 1976; editor: Continuity and Discontinuity in Church History, 1978, The Essential Tillich, 1987, 2d edit., 1999, The Macmillan Book of Earliest Christian Prayers, 1988, The Macmillan Book of Earliest Christian Hymns, 1988, The Macmillan Book of Earliest Christian Meditations, 1989, One Prayer at a Time: A 12 Step Anthology, 1989, The Jefferson Bible, 1989, Without Apology: The Liberal Faith of A. Powell Davies, 1998, Restoring Faith: America's Religious Leaders Answer Terror With Hope, 2001, The Separation of Church and State: Writings on Religious Freedom by America's Founders, 2004; contbr. chapters to books; contbr. (articles) Harvard Theol. Rev., (speeches) Rep. Am. Speeches, 1983—84, 1986—87, 1987—88, 1989—90, 1992—93, 1995—96, 1997—98. Bd. dir. Union Theol. Sem., NYC, 1992-98, 2007—, Internat. Bridges Toward Justice, 2002; mem. exec. com. Franklin and Eleanor Roosevelt Inst., NYC, 1990—; chmn. Coun. on Environment NYC, 1995-2006. Montgomery fellow Dartmouth Coll., 1989, FDR Four Freedoms award 2008, UUA Disting. Svc. award, 2008. Mem. Unitarian Universalist Mins. Assn. Democrat. Home: New York, NY. Died Sept. 24, 2009.

CIAMPA, GEORGE RICHARD, lawyer; b. Boston, Apr. 27, 1945; s. George and Josephine (Gangi) C.; m. Suzanne C. Seitz, Sept. 18, 1971 (div. 1981); m. Patricia L. Hughes, Apr. 21, 1985. BS, Tufts U., 1968; JD, Boston U., 1971. Bar: Conn. 1989, Mass. 1971, U.S. Dist. Ct. Mass. 1971, U.S. Dist. Ct. Vt. 1972, U.S. Supreme Ct. 1980, U.S. Dist. Ct. Conn. 1989. Asst. regional counsel U.S. EPA, Boston, 1971-88; ptnr. Tarlow, Levy, Harding & Droney, Farmington, Conn., 1988-89; pvt. practice Burlington, Conn., 1989-91. Active Inland Wetlands Commn., Burlington, 1988-91, Conservation Commn., Winchester, Mass., 1978-83. Avocations: softball, photography, auto racing. Died Nov. 23, 2007.

CICCHINO, ANGELO ANTHONY, insurance company executive; b. Chgo., Aug. 10, 1950; s. Vincent and Jean (Cox) C.; m. Susan Mae Sherry, Dec. 27, 1974; children: Carri Ann, Michael Angelo. AA, Western Ill. U., 1972. Ins. agt. Home Life of N.Y., Chgo., 1973-76; ins. broker A.S.C. Fin. Services, Berwyn, Ill., 1977-83; asst. regional mgr. Jackson Nat. Life Ins., Park Ridge, Ill., 1982-88, regional mgr. Metairie, La., from 1988. Mem. Nat. Assn. Life Underwriters. Avocations: boating, exercising. Died June 24, 2008.

CIONGOLI, ALFRED KENNETH, neurologist; b. Phila., Jan. 11, 1943; s. Alfred Anthony and Antoinette Marie (Ragano) C.; m. Barbara, Nov. 22, 1966; children: Adam, Happy, Gregory, Alessandra, Antonio. AB, U. Pa., 1964; DO, Phila. Coll. Osteopathic Med., 1968. Diplomate Am. Bd. Psychiatry & Neurology. Resident in neurology, chief resident neurology unit U. Vt. Coll. Medicine, 1968-73; attending neurologist U. Pa. Med. Sch., Phila., 1974-75; rsch. fellow in neuroimmunology Danish Muscular Sclerosis Soc., Copenhagen, 1973-74, Hosp. U. Pa., Phila., 1975-77; pres. Neurol. Assocs. Vt., Burlington, 1977—2008. Attending neurologist Hosp. U. Pa. Med. Sch., 1975-77; clin. asst. prof. neurology U. Vt. Coll. Medicine, Burlington, 1977-87, clin. assoc. prof., 1987-2008, dir. Multiple Sclerosis clinic, 1975; pres. Bd. Alumni Dirs. Phila. Coll. Osteopathic Med., 1994-2008, chmn. internat. fellowship com., 1990-2008; chmn. com. NIH, 1990-2008. Author, editor: Beyond The Godfather, 1995, Passage To Liberty, 2002. Apptd. boxing commr. State of Vt., 1982; sr. med. officer U.S. Olympics team, 1986. Recipient Ellis Island Medal of Honor, 1998, Grand Officiale Order Merit Republic Italy, Italian Pres. Scalfero, 1998. Mem. AMA, Am. Assn. Neurology, Phila. Neurol. Soc., Ethan Allan Club (bd. govs.), Nat. Italian-Am. Found. (sr. v.p. 1992-95, pres. 1996-2000, vice chmn. 2000 05, chmn., 2005 08). Home: Burlington, Vt. Died Oct. 28, 2008.

CLAFLIN, JEFFREY LAIRD, pianist, singer; b. Phila., Aug. 29, 1953; s. Leander Chapin Jr. and June Lorraine (Stallings) C. Student, Phila. Mus. Acad., 1972-76. Pianist, singer Tomo Devel. Corp., NYC, 1983-90. Mus. dir. Duplex Summer Cabaret Festival, N.Y.C., 1982—; pianist annually at Le Sirenuse, Positano, Italy. Pianist various parties, 1970—; concert performances include North Am. premier William Timmings Symphony No. 2, 1976, narrator U.S. Commn. Small Bus. film, 1978; accompanist Pa. Opera Co., 1974-76, Pa. Ballet, 1976-78. Named to 1st chair Upper

Southeastern Dist. Choir, Phila., 1971, recipient Keyboard award Drexel Inst. Tech., Phila., 1971. Avocations: travel, books, bicycling, theater. Died Nov. 29, 2007.

CLAPP, KENT W., insurance company executive; b. Montpelier, Ohio; BS in Acctg., Tri-State Univ., Angola, Ind.; graduate Advanced Mgmt. Program, Harvard Sch. Bus.Adminstrn., 1989. CPA 1972. Corp. controller Blue Cross, NW Ohio (merged into Medical Mutual), 1976—89; sr. v.p. Medical Mutual of Ohio, Cleve., 1989—92, COO, 1992—97, pres., 1992—2008, CEO, 1997—2008, chmn., 1997—2008. Graduate Leadership Cleve., 1992; bd. dir. Harvard Bus. Club, Cleve., United Way Greater Cleve. Recipient Franklin Delano Roosevelt Humanitarian award, March of Dimes, 2000; named Bus. Exec. Yr., Sales & Mktg. Execs, Cleveland, 2002; named an honoree at NE Ohio Multiple Sclerosis Soc. Dinner of Champions, 2002. Died Dec. 4, 2008.

CLARK, BURKE FARIS, manufacturing executive; b. Parkersburg, W.Va., Apr. 28, 1946; s. Bruce Lloyd and Janet (Strachen) c.; m. Dara Lynne Franklin, Dec. 27, 1972; children: Jamie Lynne, John Wetzel. BSBA, East Carolina U., 1969. Sales rep. Millhiser, Inc., Richmond, Va., 1972-74; acct. mgr. IBM, Augusta, Ga., 1974-80; dist. mgr. Word Power, Inc., Kernersville, N.C., 1980-81; nat. account mgr. Nat. Cash Register, Richmond, from 1981. Sponsor Jr. Achievement, Augusta, 1978-80; bd. dirs. Augusta's Hope, 1975-78. Mem. Theta Chi. Republican. Unitarian Universalist. Avocations: tennis, fishing, collecting old cars. Home: Greenville, NC. Died Aug. 1, 2008.

CLARK, DONALD JUDSON, academic trainer; b. North Adams, Mass., Oct. 27, 1932; s. Judson Elmer and Mildred (Swan) C.; m. Ruth Pruyn, July 18, 1956 (div. 1970); children: Craig, Geoffrey, Bradford; m. Christina Welty, June 28, 1970 (div. 1983); 1 child, Matthew; m. Suemi Tanaka, Aug. 27, 1983. BA, Williams Coll., Williamstown, Mass., 1954; M in Divinity, Union Seminary, NYC, 1957. Assoc. minister Mathewson St. Meth. Ch., Providence, 1957-60; minister First Meth. Ch., Pawtucket, R.I., 1960-64; dean, dir. Rolling Ridge Conf. Ctr., North Andover, Mass., 1964-67; nat. program dir. Inst. Cultural Affairs, Sydney, Australia, 1967-70; regional dir. Singapore, 1970-72, Miami, 1972-73; area dir. southeastern U.S. Houston, 1973-78; area dir. Tokyo, 1978-83; research dir. Hong Kong, 1982-83; lectr. Sagami Women's U., Sagamihara City, Japan, 1983-86, Sangyo Bus. U., Isehara City, Japan, 1983-86; dir. dept. continuing edn. for bus. U. So. Maine, Portland, 1986-92; ptnr. The COS Group Internat., Portland, from 1990; corp. trainer quality mgmt. U. So. Maine, Portland, 1992-94, ret., 1994. Bd. dirs. Maine Quality Ctr. Mem. Am. Soc. for Quality Control. Home: Scarborough, Maine. Died Nov. 30, 2007.

CLARK, FRANK JAMES, writer; b. Bklyn., Aug. 4, 1922; s. James Franklin and Anna Marie (Koch) C.; m. Betty Schulti Hoyt, Nov. 8, 1946 (div. July 1964); children: John R., Donald J.; m. Sara Ann Gulisano, May 26, 1979. BS, NYU, 1953; MA, Columbia U., 1961. Asst. prof. data processing Dutchess C.C., Poughkeepsie, N.Y., 1965-68; dir. data processing Genesee C.C., Batavia, N.Y., 1968-78, assoc. prof. data processing, 1968-72; adj. assoc. prof. computer sci. Rochester (N.Y.) Inst. Tech., 1978-80; mgr. tech. pubs. Radio Shack, Ft. Worth, Tex., 1980-81; documentation specialist various firms NYC, 1982-83, AT&T, Lincroft, N.J., 1983-86, Bell Labs., Piscataway, N.J., 1988-89; free-lance writer Depew, N.Y., from 1989. Trumpet player Boston Pops Orch., 1952, Band of Am., 1962-65. Author: Computers, 1961, Science and Music, 1961, Contemporary Math, 1964, Contemporary Math for Parents, 1966, Speed Math, 1968, Information Processing, 1970, Accounting Programs (Assembler) and Business Case Studies, 1971, Introduction to PL/I Programming, 1971, Business Systems and EDP Procedutes, 1972, Mathematics for Data Processing, 1974, RPG I and RPG II, 1974, The Data Recorder, 1974, The Accountant and the Personal Computer, 1986, Mathematics for Programming Computers, 1987, (books of compositions) Instrumental Arrangements for Edition Musicus, 1955-61, Music for the Trumpet, 1960; co-author: (text by Melvin Berger, Music by Frank James Clark) Music in Perspective, Sam Fox, 1962. Committeeman United Fund, Poughkeepsie, 1966-68, Rep. Party, Batavia, 1972-78. With USN, 1942-45; PTO. Mem. Buffalo IBM Users Group, Sinfonia. Assemblies of God. Avocation: music. Home: Buffalo, NY. Died Oct. 4, 2007.

CLARK, HAROLD WILLIAM, JR., biomedical engineer; b. Painesville, Ohio, Dec. 15, 1922; s. Harold W. and Elizabeth A. (Fox) C.; m. Bonnie J. Greer, May 7, 1946; children: Stewart W., Linda J., Marjorie A., John D., Janet G., Laurie E. Student, Rochester Inst. Tech., 1940-41; AB, Coll. of Wooster, Ohio, 1947; PhD, U. Rochester, NYC, 1952. Lab instr. biochemistry U. Rochester, 1948-50, USPH fellow, 1950-52; assoc. in biochemistry George Washington U., Washington, 1952-63, rsch. biochemist, 1958-63, asst. rsch. prof. medicine, 1963-65, assoc. rsch. prof., 1965-70, dir. rehab. rsch., 1965-70; dir. rsch. Arthritis Inst. Nat. Hosp., Arlington, Va., 1970-87; dir. Mycoplasma Rsch. Inst., Beverly Hills, Fla., from 1987. Co-author: Centennial Symposium on Science and Research, 1974, The Comparative Pathology of Zoo Animals, 1980, Medical Management of the Elephant, 1994; author: Why Arthritis? Searching for the Cause and the Cure, 1997. Deacon Falls Church (Va.) Presbyn. Ch., 1960-70. With USNR, 1942-46, PTO. Rsch. grantee John A. Hartford Found., 1965-71, NIH, 1958-70. Mem. AAAS, Am. Soc. for Microbiology, Internat. Orgn. for Mycoplasmology. Achievements include research in a safe and effective control of rheumatoid arthritis and its probable mycoplasma cause. Home: Beverly Hills, Fla. Died Aug. 30, 2007.

CLARK, JAMES EDWARD, retired nephrologist; b. Elkins, W.Va., Nov. 19, 1926; s. Orda and Fannie May C.; m. Virginia Arvold, Aug. 19, 1977; children: David William, Stephen Edward, Anne Woodburn; stepchildren: Kristen Oberdiek, Anne, Heidi, John F. K. AB, W. Va. U., 1948; MD, Jefferson Med. Coll., 1952. Diplomate: Am. Bd. Internal Medicine. Intern Jefferson Med. Coll. Hosp., Phila., 1952-53; resident in medicine Jefferson Me. Coll. Hosp., Phila., 1953-55; chief resident in medicine Jefferson Med. Coll. Hosp., Phila., 1955-56; asst. in medicine Jefferson Med. Coll., Phila., 1956-58, instr. medicine, 1958-62, assoc. medicine, 1962-64, asst. prof., 1964-67, assoc. prof., 1968-69; prof. medicine Hahnemann Med. Coll., Phila., 1969—2005; chmn. dept. medicine, dir. med. edn. Crozer-Chester Med. Ctr.; cons. nephrology Riddle Meml. Hosp.; cons. Taylor Hosp., Sacred Heart Hosp., Chester County Hosp., Brandywine Hosp., Paoli Meml. Hosp., 1968—2005; cons. internal medicine Elwyn Inst., 1971—2005; dir. health services Swarthmore Coll. Contbr. articles to profl. jours. Trustee Thomas Jefferson U., 1979-85; bd. govs. Southeastern Pa. chpt. Am. Heart Assn., 1981-85. Served with USN, 1944-46. Recipient Citizen of Yr. award HEW, 1974 Mem. AMA, AAAS, ACP (gov. Ea. Pa. region 1980-84, Laureate award 1985), Internat. Soc. Artificial Organs, Internat. Soc. Nephrology, Am. Fedn. Clin. Research, Am. Heart Assn., Am. Soc. Artificial Internal Organs, Am. Soc. Nephrology, Assn. Hosp. Med. Edn., European Dialysis and Transplant Assn., Nat. Kidney Found., Royal Soc. Medicine, Delaware County Med. Soc., Coll. Physicians Phila., Indsl. Med. Soc. Phila., Inc., Pa. State Med. Soc., Physiol. Soc. Phila., Bernard J. Alpers Silver Stick Soc. Nephrology, Katahdin Med. and Philos. Soc., J. Aitken Meigs Med. Assn., Sigma Xi, Alpha Omega Alpha. Clubs: Union League; Corinthian Yacht (Phila.). Home: Swarthmore, Pa. Died Nov. 24, 2008.

CLARK, LEONOR ANDRACA, social worker; b. Habanai, Cuba, Jan. 26, 1943; came to U.S., 1961; d. Jose and Esther (Lamadriz) Andraca; m. Jose B. Clark, June 27, 1961; children: Leonor, Ana, Jose Jr., Eddie. B Social Work, Fla. Internat. U., 1987, MSW, 1991. Lic. clin. social worker, 1997. Student advisor MDCC, Miami, Fla.; social worker, clinic asst. Epilepsy Found., Miami, 1988; clin. social worker Coral Gables Hosp., Miami, 1993, South Miami Hosp., from 1996. William McKnight scholar. Mem. Nat. Assn. Social Workers. Home: Miami, Fla. Died Aug. 13, 2008.

CLARK, MARGARET MORRISON, registrar; b. Stuart, Va., Sept. 19, 1942; d. Hubert Lee and Vera (Foley) Morrison; m. Tobe Martin Clark, Dec. 20, 1963; 1 child, Christopher. Diploma, Nat. Bus. Coll., 1963; AA, Ferrum Coll., 1981, BS, 1985. Sec. Ferrum (Va.) Coll., 1963-65, asst. registrar, 1965-82, registrar, from 1982. Treas. Patrick County Rep. Party, Stuart, 1978—; election official Patrick County, Critz, Va., 1980—; bd. dirs. Am. Heart Assn., Stuart, 1989-91. Mem. Am. Assn. Collegiate Registrars and Admissions Dirs., Va. Assn. Collegiate Registrars and Admissions Dirs. Methodist. Avocations: sewing, cross-stitch, crafts. Home: Stuart, Va. Died June 3, 2008.

CLARK, MARY MACHEN, community health nurse; b. LeCompte, La., Jan. 13, 1940; d. Isaac and Louella (Snowden) Machen; m. Johnnie L. Clark, Nov. 5, 1961; 1 child, Roxane M. ADN, La. State U., 1969; BS in Nursing, Northwestern State U., 1985. Cert. med-surg. nurse, ACLS and CPR instr. Staff nurse VA Med. Ctr., Alexandria, La., 1973-90; staff nurse ob-gyn. ICU Rapids Gen. Hosp., Alexandria, 1969-73; med. nurse VA Med. Ctr., Alexandria, from 1990, community health nursing coord., from 1990. Reporter Monitor Alexandria VA Med. Ctr. Newsletter, 1988-90. Mem. Rapides Parish Libr. Bd. of Control, 1989-94. Recipient Svc. award Girl Scouts U.S., 1982, Spl. Advancement for Performance award Alexandria VA Med. Ctr., 1982, 86, 91, Cert. of Appreciation Profl. Image award Dept. Veterans Affairs, 1993, Performance award, 1996, 97, James MacGregor Burns Leadership award from Senator Bill Bradley, 1998. Mem. ANA, La. State Nurses Assn., Alexandria Dist. Nurses Assn. (bd. dirs. 1997-98), Nurses Orgn. Vets. Affairs, Am. Heart Assn., Sigma Theta Tau (Nu Tau chpt.). Home: Lecompte, La. Died Jan. 28, 2008.

CLARK, PAUL ALAN, accountant; b. Ft. Wayne, Ind., Nov. 15, 1943; s. Harold L. and C. Ruth (Kantzer) C.; m. Patricia L. Martin, Sept. 13, 1980. BS, Ind. U., 1967, postgrad., 1967-68. CPA, Ohio, Ind. Staff acct. Arthur Young & Co., Toledo, 1969-74; ptnr. Chastain, Due & Thomas, CPA's, Anderson, Ind., 1974-81; prin. Paul A. Clark, CPA, Anderson, from 1981. Bd. dirs. March of Dimes, 1975-76; treas. House of Hope, 1986-87. Mem. Am. Inst. CPA's, Ind. CPA Soc., Ohio Soc. CPA's, Ind. U. Alumni Assn. (life), Ind. Tax Practioners Assn., Evans Scholars Alumni, Nat. Rifle Assn. (life, cert. instr.), Alpha Kappa Psi. Lodges: Lions (local pres. 1985-86, dep. dist. gov. 1988-89), Elks. Avocations: golf, hunting, community service. Home: Anderson, Ind. Died Jan. 1, 2008.

CLARK, ROSS TOWNSEND, lawyer; b. Jacksonville, Fla., Nov. 21, 1956; s. William George and Isabel (Blanc) C. BA, U. Fla., 1977, JD, 1981. Bar: Fla. 1981, U.S. Dist. Ct. (no. and mid. dists.) Fla. 1981, U.S. Ct. Appeals (5th and 11th cirs.) 1981. Assoc. Boyer, Tanzler, Blackburn, Boyer & Nichols P.A., Jacksonville, 1981-83, Fowler & Clark P.A., Jacksonville, 1983-88, Bateh & Clark, Jacksonville, from 1988. Mem. Jacksonville Bar Assn., Assn. Trial Lawyer Am., Acad. Fla. Trial Lawyers. Republican. Home: Jacksonville, Fla. Died May 30, 2008.

CLARK, WILLIAM ADAMS, JR., biochemist, research facility administrator; b. Macon, Ga., May 3, 1943; s. William Adams and Jean Elizabeth (Smith) C.; m. Sandra Gene Hasenoehrl, Sept. 2, 1967; children: Jennifer Ann, Carolyn Renee, Robyn Elizabeth. BS, Seattle U., 1965; PhD, U. Wash., 1973. Rsch. assoc., asst. prof. U. Chgo., 1977-83; asst. prof. medicine Michael Reese Hosp.-U. Chgo., 1983-88; assoc. prof. medicine Northwestern U. Med. Sch., Chgo., 1988-94; rsch. dir. Cardiovascular Inst., Michael Reese Hosp., Chgo., 1994-97, Michael Reese Hosp., Chgo., from 1997. Mem. Rsch. Coun., Am. Heart Assn. Met. Chgo., 1987-91. Grantee NIH, 1983-85, Am. Heart Assn., 1977-96. Mem. Am. Soc. Biochemistry and Molecular Biology, Am. Soc. Cell Biology, Internat. Soc. Heart Rsch. Achievements include development of advanced methods for culture and analysis of protein metabolism in cultured adult heart cells, of new methodology to assess protein turnover in heart cells; first to prepare monoclonal antibody to cardia myosin; research in myocardial cell biology and biochemistry. Home: Oak Park, Ill. Died Mar. 30, 2008.

CLARKE, EVELYN WOODMAN, volunteer; b. National City, Calif., May 24, 1917; d. William Irving and Lena Edah (Crouse) Woodman; m. George Samuel Clarke, May 25, 1935 (dec. Nov. 1974); children: Peter Brian, August William, George Woodman. Grad., Herbert Hoover H.S., San Diego, 1935; student, San Diego State Coll., 1935. Clk. U.S. Post Office, Grossmont, Calif., 1943-70. Del. 49th Congl. Dist. Calif. White House Conf. on Aging, 1995-96; mem. San Diego County Dem. Cen. Com., 1978-83; chair 78th Assembly Dist., 1985-86; alt. del. Dem. Nat. Conv., N.Y., 1980; commr. San Diego City Pub. Utilities Adv. Commn., 1992-2000, San Diego County Commn. on Status of Women, 1980-83; mem. program/budget rev. panel United Way, 1980-83; observer U.S. Nat. Conf. for Women, Houston, 1977, UN Internat. Women's Yr. Tribunal, Mexico City, 1975; mem. U.S. Dem. Congl. Campaign Com., U.S. Dem. Senatorial Campaign Com., Clinton/Gore '96 Campaign. Recipient Vol.'s commendation United Way, San Diego, 1983, Susan B. Anthony cert. NOW, San Diego, 1982; named Hon. Life Mem. Calif. Congress Parents and Tchrs., 1948. Mem. YWCA, Uptown Dem. Club, Emily's List, Nat. Women's Polit. Caucus (Spl. Recognition award 1993, Alice Paul award 1985), Older Women's League (Wonderful Older Woman's award 1985), San Diego Hist. Soc., San Diego Opera, San Diego Zool. Soc., UN Assn. Avocations: current events, photography. Home: San Diego, Calif. Died July 16, 2008.

CLARKE, GEORGE ARTHUR, lawyer; b. Sioux City, Iowa, Apr. 8, 1918; s. George William and Ora Mae (Bronson) C.; m. Della Mae Jordan, Apr. 17, 1940; 1 child, Sharron K. JD, U. Wyo., 1967. Bar: Wyo. 1967, Nebr. 1967, U.S. Dist. Ct. Wyo. 1967, U.S. Ct. Appeals (10th and 8th cirs.) 1967, U.S. Supreme Ct. 1970, U.S. Tax Ct. 1982. Pvt. practice, Lusk, Wyo., from 1967. Mem. Wyo. Bar Assn., Nebr. Bar Assn. (mcpl. judge 1986-89). Republican. Congregationalist. Avocations: golf, fishing, hunting. Home: Lusk, Wyo. Died Jan. 29, 2008.

CLARKE, LEO CREUSOT, retired meteorologist; b. Concordia, Kans., Jan. 9, 1920; s. Charles Clarke and Gabrielle (Creusot) Prime; m. Vivian, May 11, 1946 (dec. Aug. 1995); children: Julie, Anne, Jacqueline, Elizabeth, Leo, Vivian, Patricia. BS, U. Miami, 1941; MS, USN Postgrad. Sch., Monterey, Calif., 1962. Comdr. USN, 1942-62; meteorologist, head models dept. Fleet Numerical METOC Ctr., Monterey, 1962-97, cons., from 1997. Fellow Am. Meteorol. Soc. (Charles L. Mitchell award 1987). Home: Carmel, Calif. Died Nov. 20, 2007.

CLARKE, MCKINLEY A., secondary school educator; b. Greensboro, Ala., Oct. 27, 1937; s. Nathaniel and Rebecca (White) C.; m. Cassandra L. Redwood. BA, Miles Coll., 1961; MAT in Teaching, U. Montevallo, 1973; BTh, Bapt. Bible Coll., 1974; AA cert., U. Montevallo, 1984. Ret. tchr. Bessemer (Ala.) Bd. Edn.; English tchr. Jackson S. Abrams High sch., Bessemer; tchr. English and Speech Drake High sch., Thomaston, Ga.; tchr. English and History George W. Carver High Sch., Bessemer. Recipient Cert. of Merit Booker T. Washington Bus. Coll., Award of Recognition State of Ga. Dept. Edn. Mem. NCTE, Ala. Coun. Tchrs. of Compositions, Zeta Phi Lambda. Home: Bessemer, Ala. Died Jan. 29, 2008.

CLARKSON, CAROLE LAWRENCE, insurance company professional; b. Fredericksburg, Va., Dec. 18, 1942; d. Jerry Allen and Gladys Mae (Eubank) Lawrence; m. David Wendell Morris, Aug. 14, 1965 (div. 1977); 1 child, Peyton Lawrence; m. Lawrence Herbert Clarkson, Aug. 14, 1982. BA, Purdue U., 1965; postgrad., Ind. U., Indpls., 1970, U. Ill., 1971-73, U. Louisville Sch. of Bus., 1980-82. Pub. sch. tchr. various, Ind., Okla., Ill., N.C., Italy, 1965-75; librarian documentation U. Louisville Computing Ctr., 1980-82, IBM Corp., Austin, Tex., 1983-85; ins. mgr. Ohio State Life Ins. Co., Columbus, 1985-88, Community Life Ins. Co., Columbus, 1988-90; hosp. audit/stop loss coord. Health Adminstrn. Svcs., Houston, from 1991. Supervisory mgr. Ins. Inst.

of Am., 1987—. Mem. Internat. Claims Assn. (assoc. life and health claims 1987), Nat. Assn. Female Execs., Purdue U. Alumni Assn. Home: Florence, SC. Died Feb. 18, 2008.

CLAUSE, HARRY PAUL, thoracic surgeon; b. Lynchburg, Va., May 2, 1930; s. Harry Paul and Mayme Ruth (Slaughter) C.; m. Mary Anne Harris, Mar. 14, 1992; children: H. Paul III, Sandra Lee, William Carey. AA, Mars Hill Coll., NC, 1949; BS, Wake Forest U., 1951; MD, Johns Hopkins U., 1955. Diplomate Am. Bd. Thoracic Surgery, Am. Bd. Surgery. Intern Jefferson Davis Hosp., Houston, 1955-56; surg. resident Baylor Coll. Medicine, Houston, 1956-57, 59-61; chief thoracic surg. resident Charlotte (N.C.) Meml. Hosp., 1961-63; pvt. practice thoracic surgery Roanoke, Va., 1963-94; med. dir. Alliant Techsystems, Radford, Va., from 1994. Founding mem. Bapt. Med.-Dental Fellowship, Memphis; vol. missionary surgeon So. Bapt. Hosps., Gaza, 1974, 80, Yemen Arab Republic, 1976; mem. ch. choir, deacon Bapt. Ch. With USPHS, 1957-59; capt. U.S. Navy, 1985-94. Fellow ACS; mem. Am. Coll. Occupl. and Environ. Medicine, So. Thoracic Surg. Assn., Johns Hopkins Med.-Surg. Assn., Michael E. DeBakey Internat. Cardiovascular Soc., Elks, Phi Beta Kappa. Home: Bedford, Va. Died July 31, 2008.

CLAUSER, DONALD ROBERDEAU, retired musician; b. Ft. Worth, Tex., Mar. 2, 1941; s. Donald Milton and Selina Almira (Sizer) C. B.F.A., U. N.M., 1962; Mus.M., Boston U., 1964; diploma, Curtis Inst. Music, 1967. Mem. viola sect., Phila. Orch., 1966—04, ret., 2004. Home: Cherry Hill, NJ. Died Dec. 7, 2008.

CLAUS-WALKER, JACQUELINE LUCY, rehabilitation and physiology educator; b. Paris, Dec. 13, 1915; came to U.S., 1947; d. Gaston and Suzanne Rosalie (Alexandre) Claus; widowed. PhB, U. Paris, 1935; MS, Sorbonne U., France, 1946; BS in Pharmacy, Union Coll., 1951; MS in Pharmacy, U. Houston, 1955; PhD in Physiology, Baylor U., 1966. Asst. dept. clin. pathology Hosp. Necker-Enfants Malades, Paris, 1936-40; lab. technician Robert Packer Hosp., Sayre, Pa., 1947-48; chief pharmacist James Walker Meml. Hosp., Wilmington, N.C., 1951-53; rsch. asst. dept. exptl. medicine M.D. Anderson Hosp. and Tumor Inst., Houston, 1955-58; rsch. asst. endocrine lab. Baylor U., Houston, 1961-66, instr. depts. rehab. and biochemistry, 1966-69, asst. prof. depts. reahb. and biochemistry, 1969-72, assoc. prof. depst. rehab. and physiology, 1972-83, prof. dept. rehab. and physiology, 1983-86. Dir. neuroendocrine lab. Inst. for Rehab. and Rsch., 1986-86; cons. in field. Mem. edtl. bd. Arch. Phys. Med. Rehab, 1984-90, Paraplegia, 1985-91; contbr. articles to profl. jours. 2d lt. M.C., French Mil., 1944-46. Mem. AAAS, Am. Pharm. Assn., Am. Soc. Hosp. Pharmacists, Endocrine Soc. Am., Am. Congress Rehab. Medicine, Am. Physiol. Soc., Am. Soc. for Bone and Mineral Rsch., N.Y. Acad. Scis., Soc. Francaise de Pharmacodynamie et Therapeutique, Houston Rsch. Club, Sigma Xi. Avocation: oil and water color painting. Home: Houston, Tex. Died Dec. 27, 2007.

CLAY, RYBURN GLOVER, JR., resort executive; b. Atlanta, Oct. 15, 1928; s. Ryburn Glover and Catherine (Sanders) S.; m. Patricia Markwell, Nov. 10, 1951; children: Ryburn Clover III, Thomas Markwell, Zaida Sanders. BS, U.S. Mil. Acad., 1951. Commd. 2d lt. U.S. Army, 1951, advanced through grades to capt., 1955, resigned, 1955; pres. St. Simons Co., St. Simons Island, Ga., 1971-73, Sea Gate Inn, Inc., St. Simons Island, from 1973. Pres. ARC, Glynn County, Ga., 1974; vestryman Christ Ch. Frederica, St. Simons Island, 1987, sr. warden, 1988— Decorated Silver Star, Purple Heart. Mem. St. Simons C. of C. (pres. 1972). Clubs: Piedmont Driving (Atlanta), Sea Island Club. Episcopalian. Home: Saint Simons Island, Ga. Died Apr. 23, 2008.

CLEGHORN, REESE, journalism educator, retired dean; b. Lyerly, Ga., Apr. 9, 1930; s. John Storey and Nona (Reese) C.; m. Cheree Briggs, 1975; children by previous marriage: Nona Elizabeth Cleghorn Gibbs, John Michael. BA, Emory U., 1950; MA in Pub. Law & Govt., Columbia U., 1956. Gen. assignments reporter Atlanta Jour., 1950-51, 52-54; reporter editor AP, 1954-58; editor, co-pub. Calif. Courier, Fresno, 1958-60; asst. city editor, state news editor Atlanta Jour., 1960-63, editorial writer, 1963- 64, assoc. editor, 1964-69; dir. Leadership Project, So. Regional Council, editor South Today, 1969-71; editor, editorial pages Charlotte (N.C.) Observer, 1971-76; assoc. editor Detroit Free Press, 1976-81; dean Philip Merrill Coll. Journalism U. Md., College Park, 1981—2000, acting. v.p. instnl. advancement, 1989-90. Tchr. journalism Ga. State U., 1963-65; mem. exec. bd. Nat. Conf. Editorial Writers, 1974-81, sec., 1977, treas., 1978, v.p., 1979, pres., 1980, life mem., 1990; trustee Nat. Conf. Editorial Writers Found., 1981-85, v.p., 1982, pres., 1985, sec. 1992-93; mem. steering com. Journalism Awards Program William Randolph Hearst Found.; mem. scholarships com. Gannett Found., 1984-89; mem. Com. for Freedom Forum Publ. Program for Journalists in Edn., 1987-96; Knight Ct. adv. bd. Author: (with Pat Watters) Climbing Jacob's Ladder: The Arrival of Negroes in Southern Politics, 1967 Trustee Christian Century Found.; mem. Md. Humanities Coun., 1991-95. With USAF, 1951-52. Named Journalism Adminstr. of Yr., Freedom Forum, 1995; named to N.C. Journalism Hall of Fame, 1996. Mem. Assn. Edn. in Journalism and Mass Communication, Assn. Schs. of Journalism and Mass Communication, Soc. Profl. Journalists (pres. Atlanta 1966), Am. News Women's Found. (adv. bd. 1991-94), Cosmos Club (adv. bd. Cosmos jour. 1993-95), Nat. Press Club, Omicron Delta Kappa, Chi Phi. Presbyterian. Died Mar. 16, 2009.

CLEMONS, ROBERT EARL, non-profit organization administrator; b. Wagoner, Okla., Aug. 25, 1932; s. Ernest and Exzee (Smith) C. BFA, Calif. Coll. Arts and Crafts, 1971. Pres., dir. Ctrl. East Oakland (Calif.) Neighborhood Housing, from 1979, Ctrl. East Oakland (Calif.) Local Devel. Corp., from 1979. With USAF, 1951-55, Korea. Democrat. Baptist. Avocations: pen and ink drawing, watercolor painting, wood sculpture. Died Nov. 23, 2007.

CLETSOWAY, RICHARD WILLIAM, urologist; b. Las Vegas, June 3, 1924; s. Eric and Ruth Hemans (Schlott) C.; m. Emily Gertrude Coons, Dec. 19, 1949; children: Deborah Ruth, Eric Lloyd. MD, Southwestern Med. Coll., 1948. Intern Kans. City (Mo.) Gen. Hosp., 1948-49, resident in urology, 1949-53; pvt. practice San Luis Obispo, Calif., 1956-95; ret., 1995. Mem. urol. surg. staff Sierra Vista Hosp., San Luis Obispo, 1956-96, French Hosp., San Luis Obispo, 1956-90, San Luis Obispo Gen. Hosp., 1956-90, chief of staff, 1968, French Hosp., 1971. Capt. U.S. Army, 1953-56. Avocations: flying, skiing, bicycling, computers, photography. Home: San Luis Obispo, Calif. Died Sept. 26, 2007.

CLEVELAND, JOHN TRUMAN, graphic designer; b. Long Beach, Calif., June 3, 1939; s. Truman Weston and Verna Grace (Jones) C.; divorced; children: Tracy Allison, Christopher John. BA, Art Ctr. Coll. of Design, 1963. Design dir. J. Chris Smith Inc., Los Angeles, 1963-68; ptnr. The Co., Los Angeles, 1969-76; prin. John Cleveland Inc., Los Angeles, from 1976; exec. v.p., creative dir. Bright & Assocs. Recipient Gold medal Art Dir.'s Club of N.Y., 1981. Mem. Art Dirs. Club of Los Angeles (pres. adv. com. 1979-80, Gold medal 1969, 78, Hugo Hammer medal 1969), Am. Inst. Graphic Arts, Soc. Typographic Arts, Univ. and Coll. Designers Assn. (hon.). Clubs: Riviera Tennis (Gov. 1977-79), Pacific Mariners Yacht (Los Angeles). Republican. Died May 19, 2008.

CLIFFORD, DEBORAH PICKMAN, historian; b. Boston, Mar. 22, 1933; d. Edward Motley and Hester Marion (Chanler) Pickman; m. Nicholas Rowland Clifford, June 22, 1957; children: Mary Tittmann, Sarah Laughlin, Susannah Blachly, Rebecca. BA cum laude, Radcliffe Coll., Cambridge, Mass., 1957; MA in History, U. Vt., 1974. Assoc. editor Historic Roots: A Mag. of Vt. History, Middlebury, 1995—2000. Author: (book) Mine Eyes Have Seen the Glory, 1979, Crusader for Freedom, 1992, The Passion of Abby Hemenway, 2001. Pres. Vt. Hist. Soc., Barre, 1981—84, Henry Sheldon Mus. of Vt. History, Middlebury, 1981—84. Recipient Stephen Greene award, Vt. Hist. Soc., 1975, Gov.'s award in Vt. history, 1995, Ben Lane award, Vt. Hist. Soc., 1996. Home: New Haven, Vt. Died July 25, 2008.

CLIFFORD, THOMAS JOHN, retired academic administrator; b. Langdon, ND, Mar. 16, 1921; s. Thomas Joseph and Elizabeth (Howitz) C.; m. Florence Marie Schmidt, Jan. 25, 1943 (dec. 1984); children: Thomas John, Stephen Michael; m. Gayle A Kielty, May 17, 1986. BCS, U. ND, 1942, JD, 1948; MBA, Stanford U., 1957, Stanford exec. fellow, 1958; LLD (hon.), Jamestown Coll., ND, 1973. Bar: N.D. 1949; CPA, N.D. Instr. accounting U. N.D., 1946-47, counselor men, 1947-49, head acctg. dept., 1948-49, dean sch. commerce, 1950-71, pres., 1971-92; chancellor N.D. Univ. System, 1990-91. Bd. dirs. Red River Nat. Bank, Grand Forks, N.D., Ottertail Power Co., Fergus Falls, Western States Life Ins. Co., Rough Rider Equity Corp., Biodigestive Devel. Tech.; pres., bd. dirs. Nodak Trust; pres. Orbis Corp., 1988-92; chmn. bd. U. N.D. Aerospace Found.; chmn. bd. Meridian Environ. Technology, Inc., Aerospace Internat., Ltd. Bd. dirs. Greater N.D. Assn., Fargo, Bush Found., St. Paul, N.D. Futures Fund; pres. No. Lights coun., Boy Scouts Am., 1981-82. Maj. USMC, 1942-45. Decorated Purple Heart, Bronze Star medal, Silver Star. Mem. AIM, N.D. Soc. CPAs (pres. 1953-54), Am. Inst. Accountants, Am. Bar Assn., Beta Gamma Sigma, Beta Alpha Psi, Phi Eta Sigma, Kappa Sigma, Blue Key, Order Coif. Clubs: K.C. Home: Grand Forks, ND. Died Feb. 4, 2009.

CLINE, ROBERT ALEXANDER, JR., banker; b. Cin., June 8, 1935; s. Robert Alexander Sr. and Martha (Kunkel) C.; m. Rosalen Ehemann, Sept. 30, 1978; children: John Emery, Christopher Raymond. BA, Williams Coll., 1957; MBA, Xavier U., 1965. Staff asst. Procter & Gamble Co., Cin., 1960-63; mktg. rep. IBM, Cin., 1963-66; sr. v.p. Fifth Third Bank, Cin., 1966-80; pres. Harley's Inc., Charleston, S.C., 1980-84; v.p. First Nat. Bank Commerce, New Orleans, 1984-85; group v.p. Fifth Third Bank, Cin., 1985-89; pres. Performance Unltd. Corp., 1990-93. Lt. USAF, 1957-58. Mem. Cin. Country Club, Commonwealth Club, Charleston Country Club, Sailfish Point Yacht and Country Club. Home: Stuart, Fla. Died June 6, 2008.

CLOSE, DONALD PEMBROKE, management consultant; b. Orange, NJ, July 11, 1920; s. Charles Mollison and Simah Close; m. L. Carolyn Reck, Apr. 22, 1950 (dec. Mar. 1983); children: Geoffrey Stuart, Cynthia Leigh, Sara Carolyn; m. Diane M. Wisdo Kendzor, Dec. 31, 1996. BS in Econs., U. Pa., 1942. Sales rep. IBM, Newark, 1946-47; asst. budget dir. L. Bamberger & Co., Newark, 1947-53; staff exec. Am. Express, NYC, 1953; contr., sec. Ciba Co., Inc., NYC, 1953-59; dir. fin. and control Avon Products Inc., NYC, 1960-72; pres. Corp. Fin. Assocs., Inc., NYC, 1973-76; v.p. Nelson Walker Assocs., NYC, 1973-76, Internat. Mgmt. Advisors, Inc., NYC, 1976-86; prin. Deven Assocs. Internat. Inc., NYC, 1986-91, The Pembroke Close Mgmt. Group, NYC, from 1991. Mem. Pvt. Sector Study on Cost Control in Fed. Govt., 1982. Trustee Morristown Beard Sch., NJ, 1974-77; pres. Jr. Essex Troop Calvary, 1964-68 With 102nd div. US Army, 1942—45. Decorated Bronze Star with oak leaf cluster, Letter of Commendation, NJ Disting. Svc. medal with oak leaf cluster. Mem. Fin. Execs. Inst., Am. Soc. Corp. Secs., Systems and Procedures Assn., Internat. Assn. Accts., Human Resources Planning Soc., Group for Strategic Organizational Effectiveness, St. Andrews Soc. NY, St. George's Soc. NY, Navy League US, 102d Inf. Divsn. Assn., U.S. Naval Inst., Campbell Soc., Internat. Assn. Corp. and Profl. Recruiters, Human Resources Exch. Assn., Univ. Club (NYC), Morristown Club, Wharton Club, Essex Hunt Club, Burnt Mills Polo Club, Phi Sigma Kappa (past sec.). Republican. Episcopalian. Home: Gladstone, NJ. Died Sept. 21, 2008.

CLOTHIAUX, EUGENE EDMUND, climate research scientist, meteorology educator; b. Las Cruces, N.Mex., Oct. 13, 1961; s. Eugene John and Clara Ann Clothiaux; m. Jessica Rhoda Staley, Aug. 11, 1990; children: Daniel Blair, Joshua David. BS, Auburn U., Ala., 1983; ScM, Brown U., 1986, PhD, 1990. Tchg. asst. Brown U., Providence, 1984-85, rsch. asst., 1985-90; postdoctoral fellow Pa. State U., University Park, 1991-93, rsch. assoc., 1993-99, asst. prof. meteorology, from 1999. Sci. field expts. to study clouds and their impact on climate -- Fire Cirrus II, Coffeyville, Kans., 1991, ASTEX, Santa Maria, Azores, 1992, MCTEX, Darwin, Australia, 1995, U.S. Dept. Energy, Lamont, Okla., 1995—. Contbr. articles to profl. jours. Univ. scholar, 1983; U.S. Dept. Energy Global Change Disting. Postdoctoral fellow, 1991-93. Mem. Am. Geophys. Union, Am. Meteorol. Soc. Home: State College, Pa. Died May 10, 2007; unknown.

CLUTTER, RODERICK WILLIAM, mayor; b. Boonville, Ind., Feb. 16, 1933; s. Robert Gaines and Ada Carie (Pittman) C.; m. Mary Del Gudgel, Jan. 24, 1953; children: Roderick W., Lisa L. Miller. BA, U. Evansville, Ind., 1955; postgrad., Ind. U., 1982-84. Commd. 2d lt. USAF, 1955, advanced through grades to lt. col., 1972, Soviet specialist air intelligence, 1966-76, ret., 1976; councilman-at-large City of Boonville, 1984-88, mayor, from 1988. Lectr. Soviet strategic, polit. and mil. affairs; dir. alumni affairs U. Evansville, 1976-81. Del. State Dem. Conv., 1984-86. Mem. Com. on the Present Danger, Am. Security Coun., Freedom House, Amnesty Internat., Accuracy-in-Media, U. Evansville Nat. Alumni Assn., Warrick County C. of C., Booneville Am. Legion, VFW, Elks. Methodist. Home: Boonville, Ind. Died July 27, 2008.

COBE, SANDY, film company executive; b. NYC, Nov. 30, 1928; s. Mark H. and Alma (Moxley) C.; m. Marianne Findler, Feb. 1950 (div. 1966); children: Lori, Donna; m. Sharyon Reis, Oct. 26, 1968. Theater mgr. Loews Theater Corp., NYC, 1948; photographer N.Y. Daily News, 1949-50; cinephotographer Sta. WPIX-TV, 1951-52; producer Artmart Pictures, from 1955; v.p. Pepco Spl. Events N.Y. World's Fair Pepsico, 1964-65; exec. v.p. distbn. Gen. Studios, 1966-68; pres. First Cinema Releasing Corp., Atlanta, 1969-70, Intercontinental Releasing, Los Angeles, from 1974. Exec. producer (movies): Terror on Tour, 1980, Access Code, 1984, Terminal Entry, 1986; producer: Open House, 1986. Served with the U.S. Army, ETO, 1944, 45; also Korean war, 1952-53. Recipient Outstanding Contribution award City of Los Angeles, 1978, County of Los Angles, 1978, Resolutions award Calif. State Senate, Calif. State Assembly, 1978, honors Los Angeles Mayor Tom Bradley, Lt. Gov. Mervyn Dymally, 1978, Gov. George Deukmejian, 1984. Mem. Am. Film Assn. (founder), Am. Film Mkt. (bd. drs. 1980—), Acad. TV Arts and Scis., Masons, Shriners. Clubs: Variety Internat. Home: Los Angeles, Calif. Died Feb. 20, 2008.

COBERLEY, KATHY, critical care nurse, educator; b. Ada, Okla., Apr. 1, 1961; d. Bobby Ray and Wanda Jean (Gallemore) Malloy; m. Carl Stephen Coberley, Aug. 15, 1981; children: Eric Ray, Ryan Houston. BSN, East Cen. U., Ada, 1983; postgrad., Cen. State U., Edmond, Okla. Charge nurse med. and surg. floor Ardmore (Okla.) Adventist Hosp.; nurse ICU Meml. Hosp. of So. Okla., Ardmore, surg. nurse Ada; instr., dir. practical nursing Pontotoc County Area Vocat. Tech. Sch., Ada; nursing instr. Seminole (Okla.) Jr. Coll. Mem. Am. Vocat. Assn., Okla. Vocat. Assn., Okla. Health Occupation Edn. Tchrs. Assn., Pontotoc County Am. Diabetes Assn. (bd. dirs.). Died Oct. 9, 2007.

COBEY, RALPH, industrialist; b. Sycamore, Ohio, Aug. 15, 1909; m. Hortense Kohn, Feb. 27, 1944; children: Minnie, Susanne. ME, Carnegie Inst. Tech., 1932; DSc (hon.), Findlay Coll., 1958. Pres. Perfection Steel Body Co., Galion, Ohio, 1945-70, Perfection-Cobey, Co., Galion, Ohio, 1949-70, Eagle Crusher Co., 1954-90, chmn. bd., from 1990; pres. Philips-Davies Co., 1965-70, Cobey Co., 1946-70, Diamond Iron Works, 1972-90, Austin-Western Crusher Co., 1974-90, Scoopmobile Co., 1978-90, Madsen Co., 1979-90, World Wide Investment Co., from 1950. Aide in preparation of prodn. and design of Army tanks OPM, 1939-42. Mem. contbg. com. NCCJ, 1951-55, now area chmn. spl. gifts com.; founder, pres. Harry Cobey Found.; area chmn. U.S. Savs. Bonds; mem. pres.'s adv. coun. for devel. Ashland Coll., Ohio, mem. Ohio Gov.'s Citizens' Task Force on Environ. Protection, 1971-72, Pres.'s Tax Com., 1962-66; pioneer chaplain svcs. in indsl. plants;

mem. Ohio Expns. Commn., 1964, Radio Free Europe Com.; chmn. Cmty. Heart Fund Campaign, 1971-72; pres., spl. gifts chmn. Crawford County Heart Fund, 1972-78; mem. Ohio fin. bd. Heart Fund, 1973—; mem. Ohio Rep. Fin. Com.; mounted dep. sheriff, Morrow County (Ohio), 1974-84; bd. dirs., chmn. long range planning com. Johnny Appleseed Area coun. Boy Scouts of Am.; hon. life mem. Galion Cmty. Ctr.; trustee Galion City Hosp. Found. Bd.; mem. pres.'s coun. Ohio State U.; chmn., founder Minnie Cobey Meml. Libr.; founder, chmn. bd. trustees Louis Bromfield Malabar Farm Found.; bd. dirs. Morrow County United Appeals; State of Ohio amb. of natural resources; numerous other civic activities. Capt. USAAF, 1942-46, 51, Korea. Baden-Powel World fellow King Carl Gustaf of Sweden, 1992; recipient Disting. Citizen of Yr. award Heart of Ohio Coun., Boy Scouts Am., 1995, Lifetime Commitment to Humanitarianism award from Rep. Joan Lawrence, Ohio Ho. Reps., 1996, award Louis Bromfield Soc., 2001, resolution from Ohio Dist. 5 Agy. on Aging, Cert. of Appreciation USDA, 2003; inductee Ohio State Fair Hall of Fame, 1992, Ohio Agrl. Hall of Fame, 1999, Ohio Natural Resources Hall of Fame, 2001, Ohio Sr. Citizens Hall of Fame, 2002, N. Ctrl. Ohio Entreprenureal Hall of Fame, 2003; Ralph Cobey Day in City of Galion, 1995, City of Bucyrus, 1999. Mem. NAM, Nat. Assn. 4-H Clubs, Future Farmers Am., U.S. C. of C. (mem. taxation, fgn. affairs, labor rels. coms.), Masons (32 degree, awarded 75 yr. pin 2007), Shriners (sec.-treas.). Home: Galion, Ohio. Died Jan. 16, 2009.

COBURN, JOHN BOWEN, retired bishop; b. Danbury, Conn., Sept. 27, 1914; s. Aaron Cutler and Eugenia Bowen (Woolfolk) C.; m. Ruth Alvord Barnum, May 26, 1941; children: Thomas, Judith, Michael, Sarah. AB with high honors, Princeton U., 1936, DD, 1960; BD cum laude, Union Theol. Sem., 1942; DD, Amherst Coll., 1955, Harvard U., 1964, Huron Coll., 1964, Middlebury Coll., 1970, Bucknell U., 1971, Trinity Coll., 1980, Hamilton Coll., 1982, Williams Coll., 1982; STD, Berkeley Div. Sch., 1958; DD, Hobart Coll., William Smith Colls., 1967; D of Canon Law, Kenyon Coll., 1968; DST, Gen. Theol. Sem., 1968; DCL, U. Kent, Canterbury, Eng., 1978. Ordained to ministry Protestant Episcopal Ch., as deacon, 1943, as priest, 1943. Tchr. English and biology Robert Coll., Istanbul, Turkey, 1936-39; asst. minister Grace Ch., NYC, 1942-44, rector Amherst, Mass.; chaplain Amherst Coll., 1946-53; dean Trinity Cathedral, Newark, 1953-57, Episcopal Theol. Sch., Cambridge, Mass., 1957-68; tchr. St. Acad., Urban League, Harlem, NYC, 1968-69; rector St. James' Ch., NYC, 1969-75; Episcopal bishop of Mass., 1976-86. Dir. Corning Glass Works.; del. Epsicopal Gen. Conv., 1955, 61, 64, 67, 69, 70, 73, pres. house deps., 1967-76 Author: Prayer and Personal Religion, 1957, One Family in Christ, 1958, Minister, Man in the Middle, 1963, Anne and the Sand Dobbies: A Story About Death for Children and Their Parents, 1964, Twentieth Century Spiritual Letters, 1967, A Life to Live: A Way to Pray, 1973, A Diary of Prayers: Personal and Private, 1975, The Hope of Glory, 1976, Christ's Life: Our Life, 1978, Feeding Fire, 1980; editor: (with Norman Pittenger) Viewpoints, 1959. Trustee Princeton, Wooster Sch., Union Theol. Sem. Lt. (s.g.), Chaplains Corps USNR, 1944-46. Home: Bedford, Mass. Died Aug. 8, 2009.

COCKBURN, ROBERT MILROY, physician, surgeon; b. Walla Walla, Wash., Feb. 4, 1928; s. George Samuel and Mildred Ione (Nettleship) C.; m. Gloria Fae Douma, June 12, 1955; children: Timothy Ryan, Dan Kinman, Brigitte Andrea. BA, U. Oreg., 1950, MS in Biochemistry, MD, 1955. Diplomate Am. Bd. Family Practice. Intern Multnomah County Hosp., Portland, Oreg., 1955-56; gen. practice medicine Portland, from 1958. Contbr. articles to profl. jours. Served to capt. USAR, 1956-58. Mem. AMA, Oreg. Med. Assn., Multnomah County Med. Soc., Am. Acad. Family Physicians (edn. commn. 1978-84), Oreg. Acad. Family Physicians (pres. 1983-84),, Sigma Xi. Republican. Episcopalian. Avocations: woodworking, stained glass, collections. Home: Portland, Oreg. Died Aug. 9, 2008.

COCKRELL, MICHAEL KEVIN, film and video production company executive; b. Grafton, W.Va., Aug. 19, 1957; s. William Michael and Loretta Jewell (Carpenter) C. AA, Community Coll. Allegheny County, 1978; BA, Duquesne U., 1982. Prodn. asst. Dynamic Cablevision, Pitts., 1971-75; asst. tutorial supr. Community Coll. Allegheny County, West Mifflin, Pa., 1975-78; prodn. asst. Warner Cable Corp., Pitts., 1980-81; studio ops. mgr., head tech. Duquesne U., Pitts., 1982-86; pres., dir. Prodn. Consulting Svcs., Pitts., 1986-91, Digimedia Tng. & Prodn. Svcs., Pitts., from 1991. Audio-visual chmn. Pitts. L-5 Soc., 1982—; cons. Ketchum Pub. Rels., Pitts., 1986, South Arts, Pitts., 1986-87; location asst. CBS News 60 Minutes, Pitts., 1984; mgr. audio-visual Ketchum Advt. Temporary, 1989—. Writer, producer (prodn. proposal) Die Wintereise, 1989-90; supr., producer (video) Computers and the College Student, 1982; spl. effects supr. (video) The Armageddon Affair, 1977 (festival award 1977); producer, dir., scriptwriter (patient orientation video) Laser Surgery-The Bright Alternative, 1987, (series) The DNA Detectives, 1990, Science Teacup, 1990. Mem. staff Duquesne U. Scholastic Press Assn., Pitts., 1979-82, Baldwin Boro Crime Watch, Pitts., 1986-87; spkr. Religion in Media Seminar, Pitts., 1986. Recipient Outstanding Achievement in TV Prodn. award Producer/Videographer, 1978, Mark of Excellence award Soc. Profl. Journalists, 1980, 82; named one of Outstanding Young Man in Am., 1986. Mem. Am. Film Inst., Film Soc. Lincoln Ctr., Internat. TV Assn. (edn. com. 1984—), Soc. Profl. Journalists, Soc. Broadcasting Engrs., Duquesne U. Journalism Alumni Assn. (edn. and tech. com. 1994). Republican. Roman Catholic. Avocations: laser research, tennis, swimming, reading, photography. Died Jan. 30, 2008.

CODE, ARTHUR DODD, retired astrophysics professor; b. Bklyn., Aug. 13, 1923; 4 children. MS, U. Chgo., 1947, PhD in Astronomy & Astrophysics, 1950. Asst. Yerkes Obs. U. Chgo., 1946-49; instr. U. Va., Charlottesville, 1950; instr. then asst. prof. astronomy U. Wis., Madison, 1951-56, prof., 1969-92, prof. emeritus, 1992—2009; mem. staff Mt. Wilson and Palomar Obs. Calif. Inst. Tech., Pasadena, 1956-58, prof., 1958-69; adj. prof. U. Ariz., Tucson, 1992—2009. Hilldale prof., dir. Space Astronomy Lab. U. Wis. Recipient Disting. Pub. Svc. medal & Pub. Svc. award, NASA, 1992, Profl. Achievement award, U. Chgo. Mem. NAS, Am. Acad. Arts and Scis., Internat. Acad. Astronautics, Assn. Universities for Rsch. in Astronomy (chmn. bd. dirs. 1977-80.), Am. Astonomical Soc. (pres. 1982-84). Died Mar. 11, 2009.

COE, LINDA MARLENE WOLFE, retired marketing professional, freelance photographer; b. Logan, Ohio, Apr. 5, 1941; d. Kenneth William and Mary Martha (Eddy) Wolfe; m. Frederic Morrow Coe, Sept. 15, 1962; children: Christopher, Jennifer, Peter, Michael. BFA, Columbus Coll. of Art and Design, 1978. Freelance photographer, Columbus, from 1978; sec., receptionist Plaza Dental, Columbus, 1983; sec. Worthington (Ohio) Dental Group, 1983-85; mktg. and devel. adminstr. Custom Corp. Gift Svc., Worthington, 1985-92, Grandparents Living Theatre, 1993, Premiums & Promotions, Inc., 1995-96; ret., 1996. Trustees Met. Women's Ctr., Columbus, 1986-87. Docent trainee Columbus Mus. Art, 1982-83; mem. Worthington Arts Coun., 1982, 83, 85, 87, 89-93, 94. Mem. Zephrus League, Phoenix Soc. (mem. exec. bd.), Nat. Soc. Fund Raising Execs., Women's Bus. Bd., Columbus Bus. and Profl. Women, Columbus C. of C., Columbus Coll. Art and Design Alumni Assn. Republican. Roman Catholic. Avocations: photography, reading, gardening, sailing. Home: Worthington, Ohio. Deceased.

COE, MARVIN PARNICK, real estate broker; b. Benton, Tenn., Sept. 14, 1931; s. John Denton and Viola (Pettit) C.; m. Annie Ruth Compton, Apr. 8, 1950 (dec. Feb. 1987); children: Deloris Stephenson, Mariah Evelyn. Graduate of Theology, Tenn. Temple U., 1962; BA, Belmont U., 1970; MA, Scarritt Coll., 1978. Constrn. carpenter, Ga., Tenn., 1951-69; constrn. supt. Culbert Constrn. Co., Nashville, 1971-79; salesman Owen Reese Realty & Auction, Franklin, Tenn., 1977-78, Realty and Assocs., Franklin, 1978-79, Inman Realtors, Franklin, 1980-82; owner Coe Realty & Auction Co., Franklin, from 1983. Mission pastor 23 St. Baptist Ch., Chattanooga, Tenn., 1961-62; assoc. pastor 1st Baptist Cohutta, Ga., 1962-65; pastor Hillsboro Baptist Ch., Franklin, 1965-76, Hillview Baptist Ch., Franklin, 1984-92. Past mem. new ch. com. Nashville Bapt. Assn., student com., 1986, chmn. network com. Mem. Williamson County Bd. Realtors (Realtors Polit. Action Com. and Benevolence com.), Nashville Bd. Realtors, Tenn. Bd. Realtors, Nat. Bd. Realtors, Tenn. Auctioneers Assn. Died Aug. 9, 1995.

COE, RALPH ELI, advertising executive; b. Boonville, NY, Dec. 26, 1927; s. Milton Dean and Mary Elizabeth (Nugent) C.; m. Ethel Jane Keitsch, June 12, 1949; children: Mark Edward, Deborah Lynn, Cherie Lee, Jeffrey Dean. Student, Syracuse U., 1947-48, Ringling Sch. Art, 1948-50, Utica Coll., 1950-52. Registered comml. artist. Comml. artist, prodn. mgr. Advertiser's Svc. & Jones-Stephenson Printing Co., Inc., Utica, N.Y., 1950-53; window decorator Ballantine Beer, Utica, 1953-54; creative sales dir. Utica-Mohawk Engraving Co., Utica, 1954-55; pres. Coe Advt. Corp., Utica, 1955-87, Coe Ad Outdoor Divsn., Barneveld, N.Y., 1957-87; freelance appraisal and cons., from 1987. Instr. advt. design Mohawk Valley Community Coll., 1960-63; dir. Small Bus. Service Bur., Worcester, Mass., 1979—. Editor: Pan-O-Rama, 1975-85; represented in permanent collection Holland Patent Cen. Sch., 1968. Allstate comdr. VFW, N.Y., 1986-87, charter comdr. VFW, Holland Patent, N.Y., 1986-87; mem. Trenton Vol. Fire Co., 1955-75; cons. Trenton Planning Bd., 1987—. With U.S. Army, 1946-47. Recipient 1st place award archtl. rendering for Sarasota Mcpl. Auditorium, 1948; citation VFW (Post 8259), Holland Patent, 1986-87. Mem. Cen. Adirondack Assn., Mohawk Valley Advt. Club. Clubs: Trenton Fish & Game (pres. 1957-59), 1958-64. Republican. Avocation: restoring antique paintings and frames. Home: Daytona Beach, Fla. Died May 14, 2008.

COE, TUCKER See WESTLAKE, DONALD

COFFEY, CHARLES MOORE, communication research professional, writer; b. Chgo., July 8, 1941; s. Charles Adams and Helen Marie (Moore) C. BA in Econs., Beloit Coll., 1963; postgrad., Purdue U., 1980. WDBJ radio and TV reporter Times-World Corp., Roanoke, Va., 1964-65; reporter, anchor, prodr. WHAS AM FM TV, Louisville, 1967-72; asst. to chancellor Ind. U. S.E., New Albany, 1972-77; dir. spl. events Ind. U., Bloomington, 1977-82; dir. alumni affairs Ind. U.-Purdue U., Indpls., 1982-88; comm. advisor Bayh-O'Bannon Campaign, Indpls., 1988; comm. asst. Lt. Gov. of Ind., Indpls., 1989-97; dir. comm. rsch. Ind. Dept. Adminstrn., Indpls., 1997—2005. Lt. gov.'s rep. Intelenet Commn., Indpls., 1990-97, gov.'s rep., 1997-2004; gov.'s rep. Enhanced Data Access Rev. Com., Indpls., 1997-2005 Contbr. articles to profl. jours. Pres. Coun. for Retarded Children, Clark County, Ind., 1975—76, Bloomington Restorations; chmn. Clark-Floyd Conv. Bur., Jeffersonville, Ind., 1977; bd. dirs. YMCA Greater Indpls., 1989—95, 1997—98, 2000—03, 2004—05, sec. bd., 1998—2000, trustee, 1999—2004. With USAF, 1963. Recipient AP award for comprehensive reporting Va. AP Broadcasters, 1964-65. Mem. Internat. Assn. Protocol Cons., Soc. Profl. Journalists. Democrat. Home: Indianapolis, Ind. Died June 24, 2008.

COGHLAN, FRANK EDWARD, JR., actor; b. New Haven, Mar. 15, 1916; s. Frank Edward and Katherine Veronica (Coyle) C.; m. Betty Corrigan, Dec. 22, 1945 (dec. Feb. 1974); children: Michael, Patrick, Libbey, Cathy, Judy; m. Letha Monette Justice (dec. 2001); stepchildren: Gary, Ronald, Kenneth. Student, UCLA, 1935-37, U. So. Calif., 1942; degree in naval aviation, NAS, Pensacola, Fla., 1944. Commd. ensign USN, 1944, advance through grades to lt. comdr., 1956, naval aviator, 1944-65, retired, 1965. Appeared in comedies including Our Gang; films include The Poverty of Riches, 1921, The Spanish Dancer, 1923, A Woman of Paris: A Dream of Fate, 1923, The Darling of New York, 1923, The Road to Yesterday, 1925, The Yankee Clipper, 1927, Slide, Kelly, Slide, 1927, Let 'Er Go Gallegher, 1928, River's End, 1930, Penrod and Sam, 1931, The Public Enemy, 1931, The Last of the Mohicans, 1932, Racetrack, 1933, Charlie Chan at the Race Track, 1936, Henry Aldrich for President, 1941, Adventures of Captain Marvel (series), 1941, The Sand Pebbles, 1966; author: They Still Call Me Junior, 1992 Coord. spl. events Port of L.A., San Pedro, Calif., 1971-74, dir. pub. and community rels., 1977-81; dir. pub. rels. L.A. Zoo, 1974-77. Mem. Assn. Naval Aviation. Republican. Roman Catholic. Home: Los Alamitos, Calif. Died Sept. 7, 2009.

COHEN, GENE DAVID, psychiatrist; b. Brockton, Mass., Sept. 28, 1944; s. Benjamin and Lillian S. (Strashun) Cohen; m. Joyce Tenneson, June 25, 1967 (div.); 1 child, Alexander Tenneson. AB cum laude, Harvard U., 1966; MD, Georgetown U., 1970; PhD in Geriatric Health and Mental Health, Union Experimenting Colls. and Univs., 1981. Diplomate Am. Bd. Psychiatry and Neurology. Intern to resident psychiatry Georgetown U. Hosp., 1971—73; capt. USPHS, from 1973; staff psychiatrist div. mental health svcs. programs NIMH, Rockville, Md., 1973—75; 1st chief Studies Mental Health Aging, NIMH, 1975—83, dir. program aging, 1983—88; dep. dir. Nat. Inst. Aging, Bethesda, Md., 1988—91, acting dir., 1991—93; clin. prof. psychiatry Georgetown U., 1983—2009; dir. Ctr. on Aging. Health & Humanities George Washington U., 1994—2009. Author: The Brain in Human Aging, 1988, The Creative Age: Awakening Human Potential in the Second Half of Life, 2000, The Mature Mind: The Positive Power of the Aging Brain, 2005; contbr. articles to profl. jours. Recipient Plaque award, USPHS, 1977, Disting. Svc. medal, 1984, cert. of appreciation, Surgeon Gen., 1988. Fellow: Gerontol. Soc. (chmn. clin. medicine sect. 1987—88); mem.: Internat. Psychogeriatic Assn., Am. Geriatrics Soc., Group Advancement Psychiatry, Am. Psychiat. Assn. (chmn. coun. aging 1985—89), Am. Assn. Geriatric Psychiatry (bd. dirs. 1978—80). Home: Kensington, Md. Died Nov. 7, 2009.

COHEN, ROBERT, mental health facility administrator; b. Bklyn., Aug. 16, 1932; s. Julius and Anna Cohen; m. Pearl Eimbinder, Dec. 19, 1952 (div. 1981); 1 child, Meryle; m. Beatrice Schwartz, Nov. 15, 1982. BA, NYU, 1953, JD, 1956; MSW, Fordham U., 1970. Cert. social worker. Assoc. Dreyer & Traub, Bklyn., 1954-58; parole officer N.Y. State, NYC, 1958-71; social worker SE Nassau Guidance Ctr., Seaford, N.Y., 1971-80; adminstr. Sunrise Psychiat. Clinic, Inc., Amityville, N.Y., from 1980. Pres. Suffolk Coalition Mental Health, 1985—; chmn. SE Regional Coun. Mental Health, Nassau County, 1987; sec., bd. dirs. N.Y. State Assn. Comty Mental Health Ctrs., 1995—. Mem. agy. coun. United Way, Nassau/Suffolk, 1987, bd. dirs., 1988-89. Mem. NASW (diplomate), N.Y. State Assn. Cmty. Mental Health Ctrs. (sec. 1995), Lions (v.p. Amityville Club 1987). Avocations: hi-fi, fishing, boating, computers. Home: Massapequa, NY. Died Dec. 26, 2007.

COHEN, ROBERT ABRAHAM, retired physician; b. Chgo., Nov. 13, 1909; s. Ezra Harry and Catherine (Kurzon) C.; m. Mabel Jean Blake, Mar. 21, 1933 (dec. Oct. 1972); children: Donald Edward, Margery Jean; m. Alice L. Muth, Mar. 31, 1974. BS, U. Chgo., 1930, PhD, MD, 1935. Intern Michael Reese Hosp., Chgo., 1936-37; resident Henry Phipps Psychiat. Clinic Johns Hopkins U., 1937-38; resident Sheppard-Pratt Hosp., Towson, Md., 1938-39, 40-41; sr. fellow Inst. Juvenile Research, Chgo, 1939-40; pvt. practice psychiatry Washington, 1946-48; clin. dir. Chestnut Lodge, Rockville, Md., 1948-53, dir. psychotherapy, 1981-91; dir. clin. investigations NIMH, Bethesda, Md., 1953-69, dir. div. clin. and behavioral research, 1969-81, dep. dir. intramural research program, 1969-81; dir. pyschiat. Chestnut Lodge Hosp., 1981; ret., 1991. Pres. Washington Sch. Psychiatry, 1973-82; bd. dirs. Founds. Fund for Rsch. in Psychiatry, 1960-63, chmn. bd., 1962-63; trustee William Alanson White Psychiat. Found. Served from lt. (j.g.) to comdr. M.C. USNR, 1941-46. Recipient HEW Disting. Svc. award, 1970, Salmon medal N.Y. Acad. Scis., 1978, Fromm-Reichmann award Am. Acad. Psychoanylsis, 1979, Woodley House award, 1982. Fellow Am. Psychiat. Assn. (disting. life); mem. Am. Psychoanalytical Assn., Am. Psychopathol. Assn., Assn. Rsch. in Nervous and Mental Disease, Washington Psychoanalytic Soc. (pres. 1951-53),

Washington Psychiat. Soc. (pres. 1958-59), Washington Psychoanalytic Inst. (chmn. edn. com. 1955-59), Washington Acad. Medicine, Cosmos Club. Home: Bethesda, Md. Died Oct. 9, 2009.

COHEN, ROBERT SELDON, chemical executive, consultant; b. Rochester, NY, Sept. 23, 1923; s. Samuel J. and Jean Eleanor (Goldstein) C.; m. Roberta Joan Klar, May 4, 1958; children: Matthew Stuart, Mardah Beatrice. BS in Chem. Engring., U. Mich., 1944, MS in Physics, 1947. Registered profl. engr., Pa., Ohio. Founder, pres. Dover (Ohio) Chem. Corp., 1949-74; founder Power Grip Co., 1960; v.p. ICC Industries (merger The Ansul Co. and Dover Chem. Corp.), 1975-77; founder Enterprise Chem. Corp., Ltd., from 1977; pvt. cons. to chem. industry Dover, from 1984. Chmn. bd. dirs. Cripple Creek Trout Farm, Inc., Rural Retreat, Va., 1985-95; pres. J-C Tech, Inc., Dover, Ohio, 1987—; mem. Nat. Adv. Coun. Consumer Products Safety Commn., 1975-77. Patentee in chlor hydrocarbons field. Pres. bd. dirs. Jr. Achievement, Inc., Tuscarawas County, Ohio; trustee Wilderness Ctr., Wilmot, Ohio. With U.S. Army, 1944-46, Manhattan Project. Fellow Am. Inst. Chem. Engrs.; mem. Fire Retardant Chems. Assn. (founding mem.), Ohio Soc. Profl. Engrs., Am. Chem. Soc., Chem. Specialties Mgmt. Coun. (founding mem.). Avocations: tennis, fishing, boating. Home: Dover, Ohio. Died Oct. 17, 2007.

COHN, J. GUNTHER, retired research executive; b. Berlin, Mar. 6, 1911; came to U.S., 1941; s. Hermann and Gertrud (Stiasny) C.; m. Catherine Wolf, Feb. 25, 1940; 1 child, Miriam Viveka. PhD in Chemistry, U. Berlin, Germany, 1934. Rsch. fellow Nobel Inst. for Chemistry, Stockholm, 1934-36; instr. Chalmers Tech. U., Gothenburg, Sweden, 1936-41; Carnegie-M.W. Welch fellow U. Minn., Mpls., 1941-43; with Engelhard Divsn. of Engelhard Minerals and Chems. Corp., Iselin, N.J., 1943-76; dir. rsch. Engelhard Minerals and Chems. Corp., Iselin, N.J., 1955-72; v.p. Engelhard Minerals and Chems. Corp., now Engelhard Corp., Iselin, 1963-72, v.p. for rsch., 1972-76, sci. and tech. cons., from 1976. Lectr. at univs. Contbr. articles to rsch. publs.; patentee in field. Recipient Disting. Achievement award Internat. Precious Metal Inst., 1987. Mem. Am. Chem. Soc. (emeritus), Electrochem. Soc. Home: West Orange, NJ. Died Mar. 24, 2008.

COHN, MILDRED, retired biochemist, educator; b. NYC, July 12, 1913; d. Isidore M. and Bertha (Klein) Cohn; m. Henry Primakoff, May 30, 1938 (dec. 1983); children: Nina, Paul, Laura. BA, Hunter Coll., 1931, DSc (hon.), 1984; MA, Columbia U., 1932, PhD, 1937; DSc (hon.), Women's Med. Coll., 1975, Radcliffe Coll., 1978, Washington U., St. Louis, 1981, Brandeis U., 1984, U. Pa., Phila., 1984, U. N.C., 1985; PhD (hon.), Weizmann Inst. Sci., 1988; DSc (hon.), U. Miami, 1990. Rsch. asst. biochemistry George Washington U. Sch. Medicine, 1937—38; rsch. assoc. Cornell Med. Coll., 1938—46, Washington U. Sch. Medicine, 1946—58, assoc. prof. biol. chemistry, 1958—60; assoc. prof. biophysics and phys. biochemistry U. Pa. Med. Sch., 1960—61, prof., 1961—71, prof. biochemistry and biophysics, 1971—82, Benjamin Rush prof. physiol. chemistry, 1978—82, prof. emerita, 1982—2009; sr. mem. Inst. Cancer Rsch., Phila., 1982—85; chancellor's vis. prof. biophysics U. Calif., Berkeley, 1982; vis. prof. biol. chemistry Johns Hopkins U. Med. Sch., 1985—91. Rsch. assoc. Harvard U. Med. Sch., 1950—51; established investigator Am. Heart Assn., 1953—59; career investigator, 1964—78; vis. prof. chemistry Yale U., 1973. Mem. editl. bd. Jour. Biol. Chemistry, 1958—63, 1967—72. Recipient Hall of Fame award, Hunter Coll., 1973, Disting. Alumni award, 1975, Cresson medal, Franklin Inst., award, Internat. Assn. Women Biochemists, 1979, Humboldt award, Germany, 1980, 1982, Nat. Medal Sci., 1983, award, Am. Acad. Achievement, 1984, Mack award, Ohio State U., 1985, Chandler medal, Columbia U., 1986, Women in Sci. award, N.Y. Acad. Sci., 1992, Gov.'s award for excellence in sci., Pa., 1993, Founders medal, Magnetic Resonance in Biology, 1994, Stein-Moore award, Protein Soc., 1997. Mem.: NAS (Named to Nat. Womens Hall of Fame), ISMAR, Coll. Physicians of Phila. (Disting. Svc. award 1987), Am. Biophys. Soc., Am. Soc. Biochemistry and Molecular Biology (pres. 1978—79), Harvey Soc., Am. Chem. Soc. (chmn. divsn. biol. chemistry 1975—76, Garvan medal 1963, Remsen award Md. sect. 1988, Cinn. sect. Oesper award 2000), Am. Philos. Soc. (v.p. 1994—2000, sec. 2005—09), Am. Acad. Arts and Scis., Iota Sigma Pi (hon. nat. mem. 1988), Sigma Xi, Phi Beta Kappa. Home: Philadelphia, Pa. Died Oct. 12, 2009.

COHN, SAM (SAM CHARLES COHN), retired motion picture and theatrical agent; b. Altoona, Pa., May 11, 1929; s. Charles C.; m. Julia Miles (div.); m. Jane Gelfman; children: Marya, Peter BA in English & German Literature, Princeton U.; JD, Yale Law Sch., 1956. With legal dept., bus. affairs dept. CBS, Inc., until 1959; TV prodr., 1959-61; counsel Goodson-Todman Prodns., 1961; assoc. ptnr. Marshall, Bratter, Greene, Allison & Tucker, NYC, 1961—65; counsel Gen. Artists Corp., 1965—68; co-mgr. Creative Mgmt. Assn., NYC, 1968-74; agt. Internat. Creative Mgmt. (ICM), NYC, 1974—2009. Bd. dirs. Josephson Internat. Served with U.S. Army. Died May 6, 2009.

COLBURN, RICHARD BUELL, manufacturing/retail executive; b. Buffalo, Dec. 21, 1938; s. Harry S. and Kathleen (Keeler) C.; m. Nancy L. Gaudet, Apr. 12, 1958; children: Kevin, Colleen, Jeffrey, Elizabeth, Christopher, Kathleen. BS in Acctg., Canisius Coll., 1961. CPA, N.Y. Supr. Ernst and Whinney, Buffalo, 1961-69; mgr. AVCO Corp., Greenwich, Conn., 1969-73; controller Transway Internat., White Plains, N.Y., 1973-82; v.p., controller Nat. Med. Care, Waltham, Mass., 1982-84; exec. v.p. First Consumer Life Ins. Co., Framingham, Mass., 1984-86; v.p. fin. Yield House, Merrimack, N.H., from 1986. Mem. Fin. Execs. Inst., Am. Inst. CPA's, N.Y. State Soc. CPA's. Republican. Roman Catholic. Avocations: golf, swimming, gardening. Home: Cohasset, Mass. Died Aug. 28, 2007.

COLCORD, ELMER DANFORTH, minister; b. Canton, Mass., Nov. 4, 1895; s. Frederick Elmer and Sadie Holway (Hill) C.; m. Evelyn Ruth Huntsinger, May 6, 1930; children: Robin Hill, Carol Ann. AB, Tufts U., 1917, STB, 1919; HM, Springfield Coll., 1923, EdM, 1928. Minister 2d Universalist Ch., Springfield, Mass., 1919-26, Unitarian Ch., Trenton, N.J., 1926-30, Mt. Vernon (N.Y.) Unitarian-Universalist Ch., 1930-39, Universalist Ch., Provincetown, Mass., 1939-42, Gardiner, Maine, 1942-50, Unitarian Universalist Ch., Somerville, Mass., 1950-87. Minister Universalist Ch., Greene, Maine, summers 1943-90; prof. psychology Springfield Coll., 1925-26; tchr. Boston Ctr. for Adult Edn., 1966-72; lectr. on poet Edwin Arlington Robinson. Author: Cultural History of a Small Town, (poetry) The Smiling of the Mind, The Progressive Vertical, others. Sec., dir. Nat. Universalist Summer Meetings, Ferry Beach, Maine, 1922-44; pres. City Somerville Council Chs., 1972-79. Named Poet of Yr., World Poetry Assn., 1987. Mem. Odd Fellows, Lions, KP, Rotary, Phi Delta Kappa. Avocations: stamp collecting/philately, coin collecting/numismatics, collecting old books. Home: Somerville, Mass. Died Aug. 12, 1994.

COLEMAN, GEORGE WILLIAM, company executive; b. Eckman, W.Va., June 13, 1928; s. William Cleveland and Roxie Lee (Taylor) C.; m. Abbie Allen Coleman, July 5, 1950 (dec. 1982); children: George W., Joseph, David, Kathy, Karen; m. Pearlie McGhee, Feb. 26, 1983. Student, Alexander Hamilton Corres. Sch. Lic. real estate broker, Va. Plant foreman Fontaine Cond. Wks., Martinsville, Va., 1946-58; credit mgr. Continental Homes, Boones Mill, Va., 1958-59; br. mgr. to sr. v.p. Nationwide Homes, Martinsville, 1959-86; v.p. Plymouth Capital Mortgage, Martinsville, 1983-86; pres. Graves Supply Co., Inc., Martinsville, 1987-90; ret. Republican. Pentecostal Holiness Ch. Avocation: gardening. Home: Martinsville, Va. Died Oct. 8, 2007.

COLESCOTT, ROBERT HUTTON, artist, educator; b. Oakland, Calif., Aug. 26, 1925; s. Warrington Wickham and Lydia Kenner (Hutton) C.; m. Zdenka Falarova, 1950 (div. 1962); children: Alexander, Nicholas; m. Sally Dennett, 1962 (div. 1972); 1 son, Dennett; m. Susan Ables, 1979 (div. 1983); 1 son, Daniel; m. Jandava Cattron AB, U. Calif.-Berkeley, 1949, MA, 1952; postgrad., Atelier F. Leger, Paris, 1949-50. Assoc. prof. art Portland State Coll, Oreg., 1957-66; vis. prof. art Am. U., Cairo, 1966-67; prof. art Calif. State Coll., Stanislaus, 1970-74; vis. lectr. painting and drawing U. Calif.-Berkeley, 1974-79; prof. painting and drawing San Francisco Art Inst., 1976—2009; vis. artist U. Ariz., Tucson, 1983-84. Exhibited numerous one-man shows, N.Y.C., 1973, 75, 77, 79-82, Albright Coll., Reading, Pa., 1983, group shows, Palm Springs Desert Mus., Calif., 1982, Orgn. Ind. Artists, N.Y.C., 1982, Indpls. Mus. Art, 1982, Corcoran Mus. Art, Washington, 1983, Whitney Mus. Am. Art, N.Y.C., 1983, Fla. Internat. U., 1983, Bucknell Coll., Pa., 1983, Hamilton Coll., N.Y., 1983, Contemporary Arts Mus., Houston, 1983, others; represented permanent collections, Seattle Art Mus., San Francisco Mus. Modern Art, Oakland Mus., Calif., Met. Mus. Art, Portland Art Mus., U. Mass., Amherst, U. S. Steel Corp., Pitts, Reed Coll., Oreg., U. Oreg., Columbia Coll., Oreg., pvt. collections; panelist painting selection, Nat. Endowment for Arts, Washington, 1982. Am. Research Center fellow, Egypt, 1965-66; grantee NEA, 1971, 80, 83. Died June 4, 2009.

COLLING, CATHARINE MARY, nurse, hospital administrator; b. Broomfield, Colo., Jan. 15, 1909; d. Patrick and Margaret Mary (Ryan) Kirby; m. Anthony Joseph Colling; 1 child, Mary Helen Colling Nightingale. BA, Ursuline Coll., 1934. RN, Calif. Supr. Mary's Help Hosp., 1945-50; adminstrv. indsl. nurse Standard Oil Co. of Calif., San Francisco, 1951-62; ward conservator Bank of Am. Trust Dept., 1964-67; instr. indsl. nursing Univ. San Francisco, 1954-69; adminstr. White Sands Convalescent Hosp., Pleasant Hill, Calif., 1967-70, Hillhaven Lawton Convalescent Hosp., San Francisco, 1970-91; dir. Hillhaven, San Francisco, 1991-95; ret., 1994. Founder, chmn. Vols. Aux. for Hillhaven, San Francisco, 1994—. Recipient numerous nursing awards. Mem. Am. Coll. Nursing Home Adminstr., No. Calif. Assn. Indsl. Nurses, Western Indsl. Nurses, Calif. Nurses Assn., Mary's Help Hosp. Alumni Assn., Calif. Assn. Hosp. Facilities. Republican. Roman Catholic. Home: San Bruno, Calif. Died Aug. 13, 2007.

COLLING, JOAN JOYCE, farmer; b. Wessington, SD, Oct. 26, 1934; d. Lloyd Franklin and Mabel Maude (McNeely) Cavenee; m. Darrel Edmund Dean, Feb. 8, 1953 (div. July 1972); children: Vickie Joan, Debbie Ann; m. David Carl Colling, Feb. 10, 1979. BS in Elem. Edn., No. State U., 1972. Cert. tchrs., S.D., Nebr. Tchr. Tri-County Sch., Emery, S.D., 1969, Mobridge (S.D.) Sch., 1969-70, Harrold (S.D.) Sch., 1972-73, Ridgeview (S.D.) Sch., 1973-74, East Charles Mix Sch., Wagner, S.D., 1974-75, Wood (S.D.) Sch. #30, 1975-77, White River (S.D.) Sch., 1977-78, Irwin Sch. #78, Gordon, Nebr., 1981-82; farmer Hartington, Nebr., from 1979. Mem. VFW, Gen. Fedn. Women Club. Presbyterian. Avocations: walking, reading. Home: Hartington, Nebr. Died Oct. 19, 2007.

COLLINS, GEORGE J., JR., surgeon; b. Nov. 19, 1939; BS, Tex. A&M U., 1961, MS, 1963; MD, U. Tex. Med. Br., 1966. Chief vascular surgery svc. Brooke Army Med. Ctr., 1982-83, Walter Reed Army Med. Ctr., 1983-86, chief dept. of surgery, 1984-86; chief cardiovascular/thoracic surgery Madigan Army Med. Ctr., from 1997. Home: La Grange, Tex. Died Dec. 5, 2007.

COLLINS, GERALD CHESTER, banking and money management executive; b. LA, July 28, 1946; s. Chester Walter and Harriet Iva (Hart) C.; m. Midge A. Bigham, May 31, 1968; children: Julie L., Bart C. BA, Calif. State U., Northridge, 1970. V.p., regional mgr. Calif. Fed., LA, 1970-85; v.p., loan mgr. no. Calif. Gibraltar Savs., San Francisco, 1985-87, sr. v.p. residential lending Simi Valley, Calif., 1987-88; with Wells Fargo Bank, Tulare, from 1988. Bd. dirs. The King's Strategist, Inc., Visalia, Calif.; tchr. Coll. Sequoias, Visalia, 1988-89; pres., CEO Visalians Interested in Affordable Housing, 1982-84. Past pres. Calif. Polit. Action Com., L.A. With U.S. Army, 1966-69, Korea. Recipient Cert. of Merit, HUD, Visalia, 1984. Mem. Christian Bus. Men's Com. Republican. Methodist. Avocations: reading, walking. Home: Visalia, Calif. Died Apr. 18, 2008.

COLLINS, JAMES TROY, JR., academic administrator; b. Savannah, Ga., Oct. 31, 1940; s. James Troy and Bertis (Bland) C.; m. Elizabeth Wylly, Sept. 14, 1963; children: James T. III, Wylly Habersham, Susan Lachlan Collins Ivy. BS, U. Ga., 1961, JD, 1964. Pvt. tax practice, Ga., Mo., 1964-77; dir. fin. divsn. Miller Brewing Co., Milw., 1977-96; dir. Deloitte and Touche Multistate Tax Ctr., U. Wis., Milw., from 1996. V.p. bd. dirs. U. Wis., Milw., 1992—; pres. bd. dirs. St. Michael Hosp., Milw., 1992-93. Editor: Jour. of State Taxation, 1982—, Jour. of Property Tax Mgmt., 1982—. Treas. Joint Orgn. for Better Sewers, Milw., 1983—; pres. Blue Ridge Fund-S.S.W., Milw., 1994—. Recipient Philip Morris Chmn.'s award, 1981, Philip Morris Silver Ring award, 1988; named Wis. Outstanding Tax Profl., 1994. Republican. Presbyterian. Home: Beaufort, SC. Died Aug. 10, 2008.

COLLINS, ROY DALE, illustrator, writer; b. Kilgore, Tex., Mar. 13, 1934; s. Roy Garland and Verna Anna Collins; m. Dortha Jean Roberson, June 19, 1959; 1 child, Michael Sean. AA, Kilgore Coll., 1954; BBA, U. Tex., 1957. Sales John Young, Inc., Kilgore, 1960—61; tax auditor Tex. Employment Commn., Austin, 1963—67; statistician, budget mgr. Tex. Dept. Health, Austin, 1967—76; freelance photographer Collins Comments, Las Cruces, N.Mex., 1976—79, writer, graphic artist Dublin, Tex., from 1995; tech. writer, illustrator FDA, Pine Bluff, Ark., 1979—95. Capt. US Army, 1961—63. Mem.: Am. Legion. Avocations: history, photography, painting. Died Oct. 10, 2007.

COMEAU, PEGGY, professional association executive; b. Los Angeles, May 10, 1943; d. Nicholas Thomas and Catherine Mary (Fink) Sagalewicz; m. Robert F. Comeau, Aug. 31, 1968 (div. Sept. 1985); 1 child, Michelle. BA in Econs., Santa Clara U., Calif., 1965; MA in Econs., Am. U., 1969. Tchr. Peace Corps, Turkey, 1965-67; econometrician J.M.T. Assocs., Philippines, 1969-70; sr. economist Ops. Research Inc., Washington, 1970-72; assoc. Messer Assocs., Washington, 1972-74; economist Dept. Labor, State of Hawaii, Honolulu, 1975-76; analyst Dept. Finance, State of Hawaii, Honolulu, 1976-81; dir. office of info. and complaints, exec. asst. to mayor City and County of Honolulu, 1981-85; exec. v.p. Honolulu Bd. Realtors, from 1985. Co-author: Area Handbook on Turkey, 1968. Mem. Lanikai Community Assn., Kailua, Hawaii, 1975-85, Eileen Anderson Campaign Com., Honolulu, 1980, 84, Hawaii chpt. ARC, Honolulu, 1983-84; mem. bd. Girl Scout Council of the Pacific, Honolulu, 1987-88; 1st v.p. Girl Scouts Council of the Pacific, Honolulu, 1988-89. State of Calif. scholar, 1961-65. Mem. Am. Soc. Assn. Execs. (bd. dirs. Aloha chpt. 1989-90), Nat. Assn. Realtors (various coms.), Orgn. Women Leaders (bd. dirs. 1989-90), Honolulu C. of C. (legis. com.), Kaimuki Bus. Assn., Employers' Coun., Better Bus. Bur., Honolulu Club. Democrat. Roman Catholic. Avocations: golf, reading, travel, biking, theater. Home: Honolulu, Hawaii. Died Nov. 17, 2007.

COMPRATT, ROBERT ARTHUR, technology management consultant; b. Chicago Heights, Ill., Feb. 26, 1942; s. Arthur Robert and Virginia Catherine (Reynolds) C.; m. Lucinda Lee Lobdell, Aug. 15, 1964 (div. Sept. 1982); children: Sarah Elizabeth, Andrew Robert; m. Sue Ann Schierholtz, Feb. 14, 1987 (div. Sept. 2001). Student, U. Ill., 1960-63, 65-67. Contr. Robeson's Inc., Champaign, Ill., 1967-68; acct. U. Ill., Urbana, Ill., 1969-79, contract negotiator, 1982-83, policy specialist Urbana and Chgo., 1983-88; cons. Techknowledge, Champaign and Chgo., from 1988. Attended advanced seminars Chgo. Ctr. for Religion and Sci. Author: (essays) Creating Tomorrow, Sacred Patterns, G.F. Handel's The Messiah: A Musical Time Machine, The High Costs of Wretched Excess. Mem. Assn. U. Tech. Mgrs., Licensing Execs. Soc., Japan-Am. Soc.-Chgo., MIT Enterprise Forum, U. Ill. Pres.'s Coun. Died Apr. 8, 2008.

CONANT, JEFFREY SCOTT, marketing educator; b. Buffalo, Apr. 5, 1955; s. Howard Somers Conant; m. Carol Susan Conant; children, Danielle Christine, Scottie, Trevor

BA in Polit. Sci., NYU, 1977; MBA, U. Ariz., 1979; PhD in Mktg., Ariz. State U., 1986. Fin. analyst Ford Aerospace and Communications Corp., Newport Beach, Calif., 1979-80; grad. programs advisor U. Ariz., Tucson, 1980-81; asst. prof. mktg. Tex. A&M U., College Station, 1986—2009, chmn. mktg. dept., 2006—09. Ad hoc mem. editorial rev. bd. Jour. Health Care Mktg.; contbr. articles to profl. jours. Recipient Outstanding Article of the Yr. award (3), Jour. Mktg. Edn., Best Article award, Mktg. Edn. Review, Piper Prof. award, Great Teachers in Mktg. award, Disting. Achievement award, U. Assn. Former Students. Mem. Am. Mktg. Assn., Western Mktg. Educators Assn., Acad. Mktg. Sci., Am. Acad. Mgmt., Alpha Mu Alpha. Home: Bryan, Tex. Died June 30, 2009.

CONDELLO, DANA JOSEPH, photographic services executive; b. Canton, Ohio, Feb. 18, 1948; s. Anthony Joseph and Betty (Yeagy) C.; m. Sandra Kay Osborne, Feb. 14, 1970; children: Tiffany, Anthony. BS, Kent State U., 1973. Sales rep. Am. Greeting Corp., Cleve., 1971-75; mktg. mgr. Progressive Industries, Dayton, Ohio, 1975-77; gen. mgr. Phototron Corp., Rialto, Calif., 1977-79; v.p. sales Berkey Film Processing, White Plains, N.Y., 1979-83, Qualex/Am. Photo Group Inc., San Clemente, Calif., from 1983. Cons. Miller-Heiman, Berkeley, Calif., 1986—. Asst. coach Saddleback Valley (Calif.) Soccer League, 1987-88. Served to cpl. USMC, 1967-68. Mem. Photo Mktg. Assn. Internat. (territorial v.p.). Democrat. Methodist. Avocations: golf, travel, reading. Home: San Clemente, Calif. Died Feb. 6, 2008.

CONDON, MARIA DEL CARMEN, retired elementary school educator; b. Laredo, Tex., Aug. 31, 1929; d. Florencio and Carmen (Diaz) Briseno; m. James Robert Condon, July 24, 1967 (dec. Apr. 1978). BA, Tex. Woman's U., 1962. Tchr. Laredo Ind. Sch. Dist., 1963-9. Supervising tchr. Laredo State U., 1984—. Mem. Tex. ASCD, Tex. Ret. Tchrs. Assn., Tex. Classroom Tchrs. Assn., Nat. Alumnae Assn. of Tex. Woman's U. Democrat. Roman Catholic. Avocations: stamp collecting/philately, classical records, walking, travel. Home: Laredo, Tex. Died June 17, 2008.

CONE, LAWRENCE ARTHUR, medical educator; b. NYC, Mar. 23, 1928; s. Max N. and Ruth (Weber) C.; m. Julia Haldy, June 6, 1947 (dec. 1956); m. Mary Elisabeth Osborne, Aug. 20, 1960; children: Lionel Alfred. AB, NYU, 1948; MD, U. Berne, Switzerland, 1954; DSc (hon.), Rocky Mountain Coll., 1993. Diplomate Am. Bd. Internal Medicine, Am. Bd. Infectious Diseases, Am. Bd. Allergy and Immunology, Am. Bd. Med. Oncology. Intern Dallas Meth. Hosp., 1954-55, resident internal medicine, 1955; resident Flower 5th Hosp., NYC, 1957-59, Met. Hosp., NYC, 1959-60; rsch. fellow infectious diseases and immunology NYU Med. Sch., NYC, 1960-62; from asst. prof. to assoc. prof. NY Med. Coll., NYC, 1962-72, chief sect immunology and infectious diseases, 1962-72; assoc. clin. prof. medicine Harbor UCLA Med. Sch., 1984—2004; clin. prof. internal medicine U. Calif., Riverside, from 1998; clin. prof. medicine UCLA, 2004—07. Career scientist Health Rsch. Coun. N.Y.C., 1962-68; chief sect. immunology and infectious diseases Eisenhower Med. Ctr., Rancho Mirage, Calif., 1973-2002, chmn. dept. medicine, 1976-78, pres. elect, pres., past pres. med. staff, 1984-90; cons. infectious disease Desert Hosp., Palm Springs, Calif., 1980-85; lectr. basic sci. U. Calif., Riverside Biomed. Scis.; mem. mycosis study group NIAID, 1993—, co-investigator Coccidiodomycosis study group, 1993—, eastern coop. oncology group affil. Stanford U., 1994, 2003-. Contbr. articles to profl. jours. Bd. dirs., trustee Desert Bighorn Rsch. Inst., Palm Desert, Calif., pres., bd. dirs., 1995-99; nat. adv. coun., trustee Rocky Mountain Coll., Billings, Mont., 2001—; mem. med. adv. staff Coll. of Desert, Palm Desert; Pres. Cir. Desert Mus., Palm Springs, Calif., Idaho Conservation League, Gilcrease Mus., Tulsa, Sun Valley Ctr. for Arts and Humanities. L.A. County Mus., Smithsonian Inst., Buffalo Bill Historic Mus., Cody, Wyo.; mem. Nat. Mus. Wildlife Art, Yellowstone Art Mus., Billings, Mont.; life mem. The Living Desert, Palm Desert, L.A. County Mus.; mem. cmty. adv. coun. Jr. League; CEO Genetic Rsch. Inst. of Desert; sustaining mem. Rep. Nat. Com. Recipient Outstanding Contbn. to Medicine award Riverside County Med. Assn., 1998, Disting. Achievement award AMC Cancer Rsch. Ctr., 1998, Steven Chase award, 2000, Eisenhower Med. Ctr. award. Fellow ACP, Royal Soc. Medicine, Interam. Soc. Chemotherapy, Am. Coll. Allergy, Am. Acad. Allergy and Immunology, Infectious Diseases Soc. Am., Am. Geriatric Soc. (founding fellow we. divsn.); mem. AAAS, Internat. AIDS Soc., Am. Fedn. Clin. Rsch., Am. Soc. Microbiology, Reticulocudothelial Soc., Am. Fedn. for Clin. Rsch., Faculty Soc. UCLA, Surg. Soc. N.Y. Med. Coll. (hon.), Woodstock Artists Assn., Harvey Soc., N.Y. Acad. Scis., European Soc. Clinical Microbiology and Infectious Disease, Internat. Soc. Infectious Disease, NYU Alumni Assn., Berne Alumni Assn., Hoover Found., Yellowstone Art Mus., Autry Mus. Western Heritage, Nat. Mus. Am. Indian, Palm Springs Art Mus., Lotos Club, Tamarisk Country Club, Faculty Soc. UCLA Harbor Med. Ctr., O'Donnell Golf Club, Sigma Xi. Republican. Avocations: golf, fishing, hunting, skiing. Home: Palm Springs, Calif. Deceased.

CONGDON, THOMAS BOSS, JR., editor, author; b. New London, Conn., Mar. 17, 1931; s. Thomas B. and Lula Hanes (Caffey) C.; m. Constance Michele Bossard, Sept. 20, 1958; children: Pamela Lemle, Elizabeth Caffey. Student, St. George's Sch., 1946-49; BA, Yale U., 1953; MS in Journalism, Columbia U., 1956. Editor Saturday Evening Post, Phila., 1956-64, NYC, sr. editor, 1964-68; editor Harper & Row, NYC, 1968-71; sr. editor Doubleday & Co., NYC, 1971-74; editor-in-chief E.P. Dutton & Co., NYC, 1974-75; editorial dir. Thomas Congdon Books, Inc., NYC, 1976-79, pres., 1984—2008; pres., pub. Congdon & Weed Inc., NYC, 1979-84. Collaborator: Learned Optimism (Martin Seligman), 1991; author: Having Babies: Nine Months Inside an Obstetrical Practice, 1994. Served to lt. (j.g.) USNR, 1950-55. Died Dec. 23, 2008.

CONINE, MERLAND JUNIOR, realtor; b. Howell, Mich., Apr. 18, 1936; s. Milton Albert and Margaret Louise (Hazelman) C.; m. Anabel Brister, July 28, 1973. AA, Paso-Hernando Community Coll., New Port Richey, Fla., 1977, BS in Bus. Ins., 1986. Enlisted U.S. Army, 1959; served to staff sgt.; various adminstrv. positions U.S. Army, Fed. Republic Germany, 1959-66, asst. historian Korea, 1967-68, various adminstrv. Vietnam, Korea, 1968-70, leasing supr. Saigon, Vietnam, 1970-72, resigned, 1972; real estate cons. St. Robert, Mo., 1973-74, New Port Richey, Fla., from 1975. Pres. Gulfside Town and Country Real Estate, Port Richey, 1980—, Tri-County Machine, 1978-87, GULFCO, Port Richey, 1985—, WOLVERINE, Port Richey, 1985—, Port Richey Fin. Services Inc. Chmn. Pasco County Rep. Exec. Com., New Port Richey, 1983; fin. chmn. West. Pasco Rep. Club, New Port Richey, 1981-83; active Pasco County Planning and Zoning Com., 1980-83, Pasco Zoning Adjustment Bd., 1989—; steering com. local Dole for U.S. Pres. campaign; sr. warden Anglican Episc. Ch., Port Richey; hon. chmn. Grassroots Ideas for Tomorrow, 1988—. Mem. West Pasco Bd. Realtors, Port Richey United C. of C. (pres. 1985-86), Bayonet Point C. of C., United C. of C. (pres. 1985—), Kiwanis (local pres. 1984-85, Outstanding Citizen 1985). Lodges: Kiwanis (local pres. 1984-85, Outstanding Citizen 1985). Episcopalian. Avocation: genealogy. Home: Port Richey, Fla. Died July 2, 2008.

CONINO, JOSEPH ALOYSIUS, lawyer; b. Hammond, La., Aug. 17, 1920; s. Dominic and Catherine (Tamborella) C.; m. Mae Evelyn Moragas, Feb. 27, 1943; children: Joseph Aloysius Jr., Robert Carl. BBA, Tulane U., 1950; MBA, U. Pa., 1951; JD, Loyola U., 1961. Bar: La. 1961, U.S. Dist. Ct. (ea. dist.) La. 1961, U.S. Ct. Appeals (5th cir.) 1972, U.S. Supreme Ct. 1989. Pvt. practice, Jefferson, La., from 1961. County judge State of La. Parish, Jefferson, 1970; del. State of La. Constl. Conv., Baton Rouge, 1973-74; asst. atty. Parish of Jefferson, 1977-2006. With USN, 1942—45. Mem. La. Bar Assn. (ho. of dels. 1963-92, bd. dirs. 1981-83, 96-99, 2005—), Jefferson Bar Assn. (pres.), New Orleans C. of C. (bd. dirs. 1974-77), Kiwanis (pres. Metairie, La. chpt.). Avocations: golf, swimming, tennis. Home: Metairie, La. Died Oct. 10, 2008.

CONNELLY, DIANE CECILE, communications executive; b. Mpls., Sept. 27, 1945; d. Howard R. Bloomquist and Ingrid (Brostrom) Bloomquist Pope; m. William Mowry Connelly, Aug. 19, 1967; children: Karin Ingrid, Susan Anne, Heather Mowry. BA in English, Smith Coll., 1967. Assoc. rsch. editor Readers Digest, NYC, 1967-70; freelance writer, editor, rschr. Readers Digest, Time, Bus. Week, Nation, others, 1970-86; mgr. strategic comm. Rockwell Automation, Cleve., 1986-95, Eaton Corp., Cleve., from 1996. V.p. bd. trustees Ruffing Montessori Sch., Cleveland Heights, 1980-84; pub. rels. rep. parent bd. Shaker Heights (Ohio) H.S., 1986. Mem. Internat. Assn. Bus. Communicators (v.p. 1994, pres. 1995, sr. del. 1996). Mem. United Ch. of Christ. Home: Shaker Hts, Ohio. Died Jan. 6, 2008.

CONNELLY, MICHAEL JOSEPH, communications executive; b. NYC, Mar. 29, 1929; s. Michael Joseph and Sarah Gertrude (Kuczinski) C.; m. Jo Anne Sarazan, Mar. 24, 1956; children: Michael David, Michelle Louise. BS, U. Ill., 1950. Asst. city editor City News Svc., LA, 1953-56; reporter The Chronicle, San Francisco, 1956-58; real estae salesman Wm. A. Colley & Co., Ft. Worth, 1958-60; pub. affairs officer U.S. AID, Washington, 1961-62; writer Ill. Bell Tel. Co., Chgo., 1968-70; mng. editor Odyssey Mag., Chgo., 1971-76; editl. dir. Signature Pubs., Evanston, Ill., 1976-80; editor Consumers Digest, Chgo., 1981-83; editor-in-chief Interpress 77, Washington, 1988-90; pres. WorldCom, Inc., Annapolis, Md., from 1990. Writer, co-prodr. (TV documentary) Seven Days That Stunned the Navy, 1993. Advance man Dem. Nat. Com., Washington, 1960. 2d lt. USAF, 1950-53. Mem. Soc. Profl. Journalists, Washington Ind. Writers. Democrat. Roman Catholic. Home: Severna Park, Md. Died Mar. 12, 2008.

CONNER, WILLIAM CURTIS, federal judge; b. Wichita Falls, Tex., Mar. 27, 1920; s. D.H. and Mae (Weeks) C.; m. Janice Files, Mar. 22, 1944; children: William Curtis, Stephen, Christopher, Molly. BBA, U. Tex., 1941, LLB, 1942; student, Harvard, 1942-43, MIT, 1943. Bar: Tex. bar 1942, N.Y. State bar 1949. Atty. Curtis, Morris & Safford (and predecessor firm), NYC, 1946-73; judge US Dist. Ct. (so. dist.) NY, White Plains, 1973—87, sr. judge, 1987—2009. Editor Tex. Law Rev. Served to lt. USNR, 1942-45, PTO. Recipient Jefferson medal N.J. Patent Law Assn., Outstanding Pub. Svc. award N.Y Intellectual Property Law Assn. Mem. NY Patent Law Assn. (pres. 1972-73), St. Andrews Golf Club. Presbyterian (elder). Home: Dobbs Ferry, NY. Died July 9, 2009.

CONOVER, MONA LEE, retired adult education educator; b. Lincoln, Nebr., Nov. 9, 1929; d. William Cyril and Susan Ferne (Floyd) C.; m. Elmer Kenneth Johnson, June 14, 1953 (div. 1975); children: Michael David, Susan Amy, Sharon Ann, Jennifer Lynne. AB, Nebr. Wesleyan U., 1952; student, Ariz. State U., 1973-75; MA in Edn., No. Ariz. U., 1985. Cert. tchr., Colo., Ariz. Tchr. Jefferson County R-1 Sch., Wheat Ridge, Colo., 1952-56, Glendale (Ariz.) Elem. Sch. 40, 1972-92; dir. Glendale Adult Edn., 1987-92; ret., 1992. Author: ABC's of Naturalization, 1989. Mem. FOGG, Garden of Gods volunterr Information Ctr.,, NIA (Nat. Assn for Interpretation), NEA Ret. Life, Heard Mus., Cheyenne Mountain Zoo, Order of Ea. Star. Republican. Methodist. Avocations: music, travel, photography, history. Home: Colorado Springs, Colo. Died Sept. 11, 2008.

CONROY, SARAH BOOTH, retired columnist; b. Valdosta, Ga., Feb. 16, 1927; d. Weston Anthony and Ruth (Proctor) Booth; m. Richard Timothy Conroy, Dec. 31, 1949; children: Camille Booth, Sarah Claire. BS, U. Tenn., 1950. Continuity writer Sta. WNOX, 1945-48; commentator, writer Sta. WATO, 1948-49; reporter, architecture columnist Knoxville News Sentinel, 1949-56; assoc. editor The Diplomat mag., 1956-58; columnist The Washington Post, 1957-58, design editor, columnist, editor in chief Living in Style, 1970-82, feature writer, columnist, 1982-94, "Chronicles" columnist, 1986—2001; reporter, art critic The Washington Daily News, 1968-70; regular contbr. The NY Times, 1968-70. Mem. adv. bd. Horizon mag., 1978-85 Author: Refinements of Love A Novel about Clover and Henry Adams, 1993. Recipient Raven award Mystery Writers Am., 1990, U. Tenn. Disting. Alumni award, 1995, Mortar Bd. award, 1997. Mem.: AIA (hon. first recipient Glenn Brown award 2000). Died Jan. 12, 2009.

CONSTANTINE, MILDRED, art historian, consultant; b. Bklyn., June 28, 1913; d. Joseph and Eva Bernard; m. Ralph W. Bettelheim, 1942 (dec. 1993); children: Judith Bettelheim, Vicki McDaniel. BA, NYU, 1936, MA in Fine Arts, 1939; postgrad., Nat. Autonomous U., Mex., 1938. Asst. to dir., sec. traveling exhbns. Coll. Art Assn., 1930—37; rschr. Office Coord. Inter-Am. Affairs-U.S. Govt., 1940—41; asst. to keeper of archive Archive of Hispanic Culture, Libr. of Congress, 1941—42; asst. curator dept. architecture and design Mus. Modern Art, 1948—53, assoc. curator, 1953—70, spl. asst. to dir. of mus., cons., 1971; cons. in art arch. and design to museums, univs. and industry including Amon Carter Mus., Ft. Worth, 1972—2008, U.S. Geol. Survey, Reston, Va., Smithsonian Inst., Washington, Getty Conservation Inst., Marina del Rey, Calif. Vis. critic, lectr. Banff Ctr., Sch. Fine Arts, Alta., Canada, 1975; vis. lectr. U. São Paulo, São Paulo, 1987; juror various art shows. Author (with J.L. Larsen): Beyond Craft: The Art Fabric, 1973; author: Tina Modotti: A Fragile Life, 1975; author: (with J.L. Larsen) The Art Fabric: Mainstream, 1981, with J.L. Larsen: 2d edit., 1986;; editor: Jack Lenor Larsen, Musee des Arts Decoratifs, 1981, Whole Cloth, 1988. Grantee, Asian Art Coun., 1984, ISE Cultural Coun., 1986, NEA, 1988, Tides Found., 1993. Mem.: Coll. Art Assn. Home: Nyack, NY. Died Dec. 10, 2008.

COOK, ANGELA DENISE, business analyst; b. Chgo., Oct. 31, 1963; d. Mary Grey; m. Joseph Clinton Cook, Jan. 1, 1989; 1 child, Meaghan Mary. BS in Computer Sci., Northeastern U., Chgo., 1984; MBA, Northwestern U., Evanston, Ill., 1986. Quality assurance mgr. Quality Assurance Inst., Orlando, Fla., from 1985. Guest speaker Harold Washington Womens Affairs com., Chgo., 1987. Counselor Rape Victim Adv., Chgo., 1984-88; bd. dirs. Rape Trauma Victim Assistance, Chgo., 1989; adv. at large Chgo. Com. on Homeless, 1988; dir. ministries homeless coun. United Meth. Ch., 1995-96. Democrat. Home: Richmond, Va. Died Mar. 22, 2008.

COOK, CARL LABORDE, radio announcer, producer, photojournalist; b. San Francisco, Mar. 8, 1945; Student, Acad. Art Coll., 1969-70; BA in Communications, Evergreen State Coll., 1976. Announcer, producer Sta. KGY Radio, Olympia, Wash., 1977-86, Sta. KQEU Radio, Olympia, from 1986; freelance photojournalist Olympia, from 1971. Mem. communications bd. Evergreen State Coll., 1981-82. Photographer The Wolves At Your Door, 1986, numerous other projects. Drug counsellor Tacoma/Pierce County Narcotics Ctr., 1972; cons. St. Peter Hosp. Aux. Guild, Olympia, 1981-83, Girl Scouts U.S.A., Olympia, 1983; fund raiser Thurston County Food Bank. Olympia, 1981-82; events producer Spinal Cord Soc., Olympia pub. schs., 1984-86; bd. dirs. Wolf Haven, Tenino, Wash., 1984-87. Served to sgt. USAF, 1965-69. Avocations: world history, natural sciences, working with children. Home: Olympia, Wash. Died Nov. 6, 2007.

COOK, HOWARD LAWRENCE, trade association executive; b. NYC, July 27, 1925; s. Howard Alfonse and Agnes Veronica (Honohan) C.; m. Ann Hathaway, Apr. 18, 1964. BSChemE, Columbia U., 1950. Sr. design engr. RCA, Harrison, N.J., 1950-66; tech. and mktg. cons. Robertson & Assocs., Summit, N.J., 1966-68; asst. to the pres. Aluminum Assn., NYC (now Washington), 1968-76; exec. sec. Transp. Safety Equipment Inst., Englewood Cliffs, from 1976; group adminstr. Motor & Equipment Mfrs. Assn., Englewood Cliffs, from 1976, Automotive Chem. Mfrs. Coun., Englewood Cliffs, from 1985. Lt. USNR, 1951-54. Avocation: fine woodworking. Home: Cedar Grove, NJ. Died Mar. 25, 2007.

COOK, JAMES HARRISON, construction company executive, retired; b. Red Wing, Minn., Sept. 6, 1920; s. Harry Cleveland and Alvida Caroline (Lillyblad) C.; m. Elizabeth Hamilton Hull, Dec. 28, 1946; children: James H. Jr., Edward H., Caroline E. BME, U. Minn., 1942; postgrad.,

Ohio State U., 1947; student, United Theol. Sem., New Brighton, Minn., 1975-77. Registered profl. engr., Minn., Wis. Jr. engr. Red Wing Potteries, 1940-42; plant layout engr. N. Am. Aviation, Inc., Kansas City, 1942-43; research engr. Battelle Inst., Columbus, Ohio, 1946-74; owner, mgr. Red Wing Iron Works, 1954-83; pres. N. Star Mech. Contractors, Red Wing, 1965-83, also bd. dirs. Engring. cons. S.B. Foot Tanning Co., Red Wing, 1967-80; ind. cons. engr., Red Wing, 1983—. Mem. Bd. Pub. Works, Red Wing, 1955-61, Red Wing Libr. Bd., 1964-69; pres. Goodhue County Alliance for Mentally Ill., Red Wing, 1984—; nonstipendiary priest Episcopal Ch., 1977—; mem. adv. com. mental health Goodhue County, 1988—, Coalition for Transitional Housing, 1990—. With USN, 1944-46, PTO. Mem. Nat. Assn. Self Supporting Active Ministry. Lodges: Masons. Republican. Home: Red Wing, Minn. Died Dec. 22, 2007.

COOLEY, JOHN WAYNE, lawyer, former federal judge; b. St. Louis, Oct. 28, 1943; s. Clyde W. and Mary Angela (Brewer) Cooley; m. Maria L. Kenefick, Sept. 3, 1966 (dec. 2002); children: John Christopher, Christina Marie. BS, US Mil. Acad., 1965; JD, U. Norte Dame, 1973. Bar: Ill. 1973, Mo. 1973, US Dist. Ct. (no. dist.)/Ill. 1973, US Ct. Appeals (7th cir.) 1974, US Supreme Ct. 1982. Law clk. US Ct. Appeals (7th cir.), 1973—74, sr. staff atty., 1977—79; asst. US atty. (no. dist.) Ill. US Dept. Justice, Chgo., 1974—77; US magistrate US Dist. Ct. (no. dist.) Ill., Chgo., 1979—81; ptnr. Stone, McGuire & Benjamin, Chgo., 1981—2009; lectr. law Loyola U., Chgo. Contbr. articles legal jour. Capt. arty. US Army, 1965—70. Decorated Air medal, Bronze Star medal, Army Commendation medal with oak leaf cluster, Spl. Achievement award Dept. Justice. Mem.: North Suburban Bar Assn., Chgo. Bar Assn., Ill. Bar Assn., ABA, Alt. to Present Fed. Ct. System (chmn. subcom.), 7th Cir. Ad Hoc Com. to Study High Cost of Litig. Home: Evanston, Ill. Died July 21, 2009.

COOPER, CHARLES GRAFTON, retired military officer; b. Clarksdale, Miss., Dec. 24, 1927; s. Charles Grafton and Anna (Gaston) C.; m. Carol Edgerton, Sept. 23, 1950; children: Charles Grafton III, Linda C. Thompson BS in Elec. Engring., U.S. Naval Acad., 1950; postgrad, U.S. Army War Coll., 1968-69. Commd. 2d lt. U.S. Marine Corps, 1950; advanced through grades to lt. gen., 1982; rifle platoon comdr. 1st bn., 5th Marines, 1st Marine Div., Korea, 1951; casual co. comdr. Marine Barracks, Camp Lejeune, N.C., 1952-53; insp. instr. Marine Corps Res. Rifle Co., Columbia, S.C., 1953-56; rifle co. comdr., weapons co. comdr., anti-tank co. comdr., regimental asst. ops. officer 4th Marines/1st Marine Brigade, Kaneohe Bay, Hawaii, 1956-58; platoon comdr., instr., co. comdr. Basic Sch., Quantico, Va., 1958; div. tng. officer 3d Marine Div., Okinawa, 1962-63; Marine aide Chief Naval Ops., Washington, 1963-66; comdr. 2d Bn., 8th Marines, 2d Marine Div., Camp Lejeune, 1966, regimental exec. officer, div. ops. officer, 1967-68; sec. to gen. staff III Marine Amphibious Force, Vietnam, 1969; comdg. officer 1st Bn., 7th Marines, 1st Marine Div., 1970; col. Logistics Directorate J-4, Office Joint Chiefs of Staff, Washington, 1970-73; comdr. Marine Barracks, Washington, 1973-75, legis. asst. to commandant, 1975-77; comdg. gen. 1st Marine Div., Camp Pendleton, 1977-79; comdr. Marine Corps Recruit Depot, San Diego, 1979-81; comdg. gen. Marine Corps Base, Camp Lejeune, 1981-82; dep. chief staff for manpower Hdqrs. Marine Corps, Washington, 1982-83; comdg. gen. Fleet Marine Force Pacific, Camp H.M. Smith, Hawaii, 1983-85; comdr. Marine Corps Bases, Camp H.M. Smith, Hawaii, 1983-85, ret., 1985. Author: Cheers and Tears: A Marine's Story of Combat in Peace and War, 2002. Decorated D.S.M., Silver Star, Purple Heart (2), Legion of Merit with Combat V (2), Vietnamese Cross of Gallantry; named a Disting. Graduate, US Naval Acad., 2004 Mem. U. Miss. Alumni Assn., U.S. Naval Acad. Alumni Assn., Phi Delta Theta. Clubs: M Club U. Miss.; N Club U.S. Naval Acad. Home: Falls Church, Va. Died Apr. 26, 2009.

COOPER, JOHN IRELAND, pharmaceutical company executive; b. Pikeville, Ky., Oct. 30, 1955; s. John Allan and Frances Lyvonne (Elkins) C.; m. Cathy Jean Hammon, Apr. 18, 1981; children: Joshua Ireland, Joseph Richard, Nicholas Mitchell. BS in Chem. Engring., U. Ky., 1979; MSBA, Ind. U., 1983; diploma energy mgmt., Va. Polytechnic Inst., 1984. Project engr. Miles Labs., Elkhart, Ind., 1979-82, sr. environ./energy engr., 1982-83, mgr. wastewater treatment plant, 1983-84, mgr. corp. energy, 1984-85, mgr. utility ops., 1985-87, mgr. corp. pharm. engring., 1987-90; dir. Site Engring., Clayton, N.C., 1990; dir. engr. and mfg. Glaxo Inc., Zebulon, N.C., from 1990. Contbr. articles to profl. jours. Chmn. Elkhart Energy Conservation Commn., 1985. Mem. Am. Inst. Chem. Engrs., Assn. Energy Engrs., Internat. Assn. Energy Economists, Ind. Indsl. Energy Consumers (past vice chmn., chmn., founder 1983). Avocation: basketball. Home: Wake Forest, NC. Died Nov. 28, 2007.

COOPER, MARILYN, actress; b. Bronx, NY, Dec. 14, 1939; Actress: (plays) Woman of the Year (Tony award for Best Actress, 1981, Drama Desk award), female version of The Odd Couple, Broadway Bound, West Side Story, Gypsy, Two by Two, I Can Get It for You Wholesale, The Perfect Party; (films) The Survivors, 1983, Brighton Beach Memoirs, 1986, Penn & Teller Get Killed, 1989, Family Business, 1989, Keeping the Faith, 2000; (TV movies) Woman of the Year, 1984, Sam Found Out: A Triple Play, 1988, Broadway Bound, 1992 (TV series) The Thorns, 1988; (TV appearances) Alice, 1982, Kate & Allie, 1989, Cheers, 1992, Law & Order, 1994, The Nanny, 1996, Caroline in the City, 1997, Welcome to New York, 2000 Died Apr. 22, 2009.

COOPER, THOMAS JOSHUA, lawyer; b. Cambridge, Mass., Dec. 8, 1943; BA, George Washington U., 1966, MA in Internat. Affairs, 1971; JD, Tulane U., 1974. Bar: DC 1975, admitted to practice: US Ct. Appeals (DC Cir.). Minority counsel US House Adminstrn. Com., 1976—77; adminstrv. asst. to Congressman Matthew J. Rinaldo, 1979—82; exec. asst. to asst. sec. for trade adminstrn. US Dept. Commerce, 1983, asst. to dep. asst. for export adminstrn., 1983—86; ptnr., Internat. Trade Dept. Venable LLP, Washington, 1986—2009. Lectr. in field. Mem.: Phi Delta Phi. Died Feb. 27, 2009.

COOVER, DORIS DIMOCK, artist; b. Beaverdam, Wis., Aug. 8, 1917; d. Almon Crowe and Alma Josephine (Johnson) Dimock; m. Francis Merle Coover, Apr. 11, 1945; children: Cheryl, Danelle. Student in Fashion and Design, Woodbury U., 1937. One-woman shows include Chappqua (N.Y.) Pub. Libr., 1964-79, Katonah (N.Y.) Gallery, 1967-72, Briarcliff (N.Y.) Coll., 1969, Silvermine (Conn.) Guild of Artists, 1965-81, Am. Can Corp., Greenwich, Conn., 1971—, Village Gallery at Gallmofry, Croton, N.Y., 1974-81, Manhattan Savs. Bank N.Y.C.-White Plains, 1963-68; gallery artist Virginia Barrett, Chappqua, 1964-98; exhibited in groups shows at Okla. Art Ctr., Oklahoma City, 1959, Tex. Oil Industry, Dallas, 1958, Delgado Mus., New Orleans, 1958, Dallas Mus. art, 1958-59, Westchester Art Soc., White Plaine, N.Y., 1962-74, Silvermine Guild Artists, 1970-81, Crocker Art Mus. Art Auction, 1981-98, Neuberger Mus., Purchase, N.Y., 1985, Sacramento Fine Arts, 1985 and many others; cover artist Sci. and Tech. Mag., 1966; work included in Am. Refs., 1978, Who's Who in Am. Art, 1996-97, Rockport Pubs.-Painting Color, 1997, 98, Sketching and Drawing, 1998. Mem., historian Officers Club, L.A., 1940-45; artist judge No. Westchester chpt. Cancreare, Bedford Village, N.J., 1958. Recipient numerous awards for art, including Helbein award Western Colo. Watercolor Soc. Mem. Nat. Watercolor Soc. (assoc.), Am. Watercolor Soc. (assoc.), Nat. Mus. Woman in Arts (charter), Crocker Art Mem. Republican. Avocations: visiting galleries with friends, reading mysteries, experimenting with art. Home: Cameron Park, Calif. Died Aug. 31, 2007.

COPPOLA, AUGUST, retired dean; b. Hartford, Conn., Feb. 16, 1934; s. Carmine and Italia (Pennino) C.; m. Joy Vogelsang(div.); children: Marc Andre, Christopher Remy, Nicolas. BA, UCLA, 1955; MA, Hofstra U., 1956; PhD, Occidental Coll., 1960. Prof. comparative lit. Calif. State U., Long Beach, 1962-73; program designer Media Mktg., L.A., Washington, 1975-77; exec. dir. Technimedia, L.A., Washington, 1978; creative dir. spl. projects US Dept. Health Edn. & Welfare (HEW), Washington, 1979-80; exec. Zoetrope Studios, L.A., 1980-84; dean Sch. Creative Arts San Francisco State U., 1984-92; chmn., CEO Edn. First, L.A., 1992—2009. Bd. dirs. Audiovision, San Francisco; artistic dir. Disting. Artists Forum Author: The Intimacy, 1978; creator: Tactile Dome, 1971, World's Largest Puzzle, 1975. Trustee Calif. State U. System, Long Beach., 1981-84; chmn. San Francisco Film and Video Commn.; bd. dirs. Nueva Learning Ctr.; mem. adv. bd. The Lab, San Francisco Toy Mus., Young Audiences; premier Edn. Advocacy. Recipient Scholar of Yr. award Occidental Coll., 1964, Disting. Industry Tchr. award Calif. State U. System, 1967, Outstanding Faculty award Phi Beta Kappa, 1969; Ford Found. fellow, 1957-60. Mem. San Francisco Internat. Film Festival (bd. dirs. 1984—). Avocation: cuisine. Died Oct. 27, 2009.

CORBETT, ROBERT EUGENE, electrical engineer, engineering executive; b. Phila., May 9, 1941; s. Eugene C. and Dolores M. (Hoffmann) C.; m. Kimiko M.J. Yi, Mar. 22, 1969; 1 child, Stephen. BS in Math., St. Joseph's U., Phila., 1968; MSEE, Santa Clara U., 1976. Rschr. Honeywell, Montgomeryville, Pa., 1965-67; mgr., power engr. Lockheed M&S Co., Sunnyvale, Calif., 1967-88; dir. engring. Sanders Assoc., Nashua, N.H., 1988-90, Motorola Lighting, Buffalo Grove, Ill., 1990-91; dir. govt. programs Ferranti-Sciaky, Chgo., 1991-92; v.p. engring. Magnetek, Huntington, Ind., 1992-96; dir. lighting strategy Internat. Rectifier, El Segundo, Calif., from 1996. Mem. NASA Space Tech. Advisory Group, Washington, 1984-86, USAF Space Tech. Advisory Comm, El Segundo, 1980-86; adj. faculty Joliet Jr. Coll, Joliet, Ill., 1990-91, Moraine Valley Coll., Chgo., 1990-91. Mem. IEEE (gov. 1980-86, chair 1981-83, v.p. adminstr. 1986-88). Home: Gilroy, Calif. Died July 20, 2008.

CORDELL, ALFRED ROBERT, cardiothoracic surgeon, educator; b. Union, SC, Oct. 16, 1924; s. Carl Eugene and Ann Louise (Elsmore) C.; m. Dewitt Cromer, June 4, 1956 (dec. Feb. 1984); children: Alfred Robert Jr., Carl Dewitt, Mark Bynum. BS, U. N.C., 1945; MD, Johns Hopkins U., 1947. Diplomate Am. Bd. Surgery, Am. Bd. Thoracic Surgery. Intern Johns Hopkins U. Hosp., Balt., 1947—48; asst. resident in surgery Yale VA Surg. Svc., Newington, Conn., 1948—50; med. corps, surgeon USNR (1st M.A.S.H.), Korea and Va., 1950—52; asst. resident gen. and thoracic surgery N.C. Bapt. Hosp., Winston-Salem, 1952—55, resident gen. and thoracic surgery, 1955—56; asst. prof. surgery, assoc. prof. Wake Forest U.-Bapt. Med. Ctr., Winston-Salem, 1957—70, prof. surgery, 1970—79, Howard Holt Bradshaw Prof. Surgery, dept. chmn., 1979—91, emeritus prof., from 1995; vis. asst. prof. surgery U. Buffalo, 1956—57. Contbr. chpts. to books, articles to profl. jours. Bd. dirs. Piedmont Opera Theatre Inc., Winston-Salem, Centenary Meth. Ch., Winston-Salem, Winston-Salem Piedmont Triad Symphony; active United Way Forsyth County, Arts Coun. Winston Salem. Recipient Gold Heart Forsyth-Stokes-Davie County (N.C.) Heart Assn., 1997, Dean's Divsn. Disting. Sc. award, 2004. Fellow Assn. Physician Assts. in Cardiovasc. Surgery (hon.); mem. ACS (bd. govs. 1983-89, pres.-elect 1999-00, pres. N.C. chpt. 2000-01, Surgeon of Yr. N.C. chpt. 1997), N.C. Stroke Assn. (bd. dirs., pres. 2000-02), Soc. Thoracic Surgeons, Am. Heart Assn. (chmn. mid-Atlantic region 1970-71, bd. dirs. 1966-67), Am. Assn. Thoracic Surgery, So. Thoracic Surg. Assn. (pres. 1971-72), N.C. Heart Assn. (pres. 1966-67, bd. dirs. 1956-75), So. Assn. Vascular Surgery (pres. 1984), Thoracic Surgery Found. (bd. dirs. 1994-2001). Methodist. Avocations: bonsai, opera, symphony. Home: Winston Salem, NC. Died Apr. 9, 2008.

COREY, RAYMOND CANFIELD, organist; b. Poughkeepsie, NY, Mar. 10, 1918; s. Herbert Edgar and Alida Matilda Corey; m. Heather Alicia Harrison, May 19, 1957; children: Cheryl Corey Hoffman, Raymond Kier. BS, Juilliard Sch. Music, 1955, MS, 1957. Ch. organist St. Margaret's Episc. Ch., Staatsburg, 1938—42; chaplain's asst. Baton Rouge, 1942—45, Malden, Mo., 1942—45; organist various local chs., 1946—54; organist St. James Meth. Ch., Kingston, NY, from 1954, 1st Luth. Ch., Poughkeepsie, 1970—94, Ch. of Messiah, Rhinebeck, NY, from 1994. Organ cons. for redesign instruments St. James Meth. Ch., Kingston, Washington St. Meth. Ch., Poughkeepsie, 1st Luth. Ch., Poughkeepsie, 1968—93. Sgt. USAF, 1943—45. Mem.: Am. Guild Organists (life; sgt.-at-arms local 238/291). Home: Poughkeepsie, NY. Died Aug. 6, 2008.

CORMIER, ROMAE J(OSEPH), mathematics educator; b. NYC, May 17, 1928; s. Arthur J(oseph) and Marie Anna (Richard) C.; m. Sue Lee Stacks, May 16, 1954; children: Ivan, Richard, Landall, Darrin. BS, U. Chattanooga, 1951; AM, U. Tenn., 1956; MA, U. Mo., 1963. Garbage man Longueuil (Que., Can.) Sanitation, 1947-48; penman Hooven Letters Inc., NYC, summers 1949-51; pairing master AAU Wrestling, Indpls., 1978-88, USA Wrestling, Tulsa, 1978-88; math. prof. No. Ill. U., De Kalb, from 1956; owner, operator Mandarin Restaurant, De Kalb, 1971-72; realtor Nat. Assn. Realtors, De Kalb, from 1971; police, fire commr. City of De Kalb, 1978-81; ind. ins. agt., from 1982. Assoc. mathematician Vitro Corp. Am., Eglin AFB, Fla., 1955; cons. GE, De Kalb, 1965, Commonwealth Edison, Braidwood, Ill., 1982. Violinist Chattanooga Civic Opera, 1948-51, Chattanooga Symphony, 1948-51, Knoxville (Tenn.) Symphony, 1954-56; editor solutions Jour. Recreational Math., 1978-84; contbr. articles to profl. jours. Pres. German Am. Nat. Congress, De Kalb, 1980-81, fin. sec., 1984—; candidate alderman city of De Kalb, 1978. With U.S. Army, 1952-54. Recipient S.P.O.K.E. award Jr. C. of C., Dekalb, 1959. Fellow Royal Numismatic Soc. (London); mem. Am. Math. Soc., Math. Assn. Am. Mem. Free Apostolic Ch. Avocations: music, art, linguistics, orchids, greco-roman and freestyle wrestling. Home: De Kalb, Ill. Died July 24, 2008.

CORNELIUS, WALTER FELIX, lawyer; b. Homewood, Ala., Apr. 20, 1922; s. William Felix and Nancy Ann (Cross) C.; m. Virginia Holliman, Jan. 30, 1942, (div. Feb. 1973); children: Nancy Carol, Susan Elaine; m. Lenora Black, May 4, 1974; 1 stepchild, Kristy Ann Wells. AB, Birmingham So. U., 1949; JD, U. Ala., 1953. Bar: Ala. 1953, U.S. Dist. Ct. (no. dist.) Ala. 1953, U.S. Tax Ct. 1954. Sole practice, Birmingham, Ala., from 1953. Bd. dirs. numerous corps., Birmingham. Elder, teacher Presbyn. Ch., Birmingham, 1963—; chmn. bd. dirs. Brother Bryan Mission, Birmingham, 1981—; pres. bd. trustees Cahaba Valley Fire and Medical Res. Dist., Shelby County, Ala., 1984—; mem. Horizon 280 Assn., Birmingham, 1985—. Served to cpl. USAAF, 1943-46, PTO. Recipient Pacific Theater Victory Med. award, Army Air Corps, Saipan and Iwo Jima, 1946. Mem. ABA, Ala. Bar Assn., Birmingham Bar Assn., Farrah Order Jurisprudence. Avocations: guitar, hunting, hiking, fishing, bird watching. Died Sept. 16, 2007.

CORNELL, EDGAR, plastic manufacturing executive; b. Vienna, Dec. 27, 1918; came to U.S., 1947; s. Max and Camilla (Spitzer) C.; m. Luna Ghedalia, July 19, 1947. BA in Engring., U. Zurich, Switzerland, 1943. Pres. Prepac, Inc., Bronx, N.Y., from 1947. Chmn. Regional Aid For Interim Needs, Inc., 1985—. Chmn. council Einstein Coll. of Medicine, 1981-84; v.p. N.Y. Boys Club, 1982-87. Recipient Compassion award USO, 1983; named Hon. Gov., State of Kans., 1978. Mem.: Rotary (pres. 1985-86, dist. gov. rep. 1987). Avocations: tennis, chess, bridge, travel. Home: Bronx, NY. Died Oct. 9, 2007.

CORNELL, ROBERT JOHN, Former United States Representative from Wisconsin; b. Gladstone, Mich., Dec. 16, 1919; s. Ralph Florman and Veronica Sullivan Cornell. BA, St. Norbert Coll., 1941; MA, Catholic U. America, 1945, Ph.D, 1957. Tchr. Southeast Cath. HS, Phila., 1941—47; chmn. Dist. 8 Wis. Dem. Party, 1969—74; mem. Dist. 8 US Congress, Wis., 1975—78; prof. St. Norbert Coll., De Pere, Wis., 1947—74, 1979—2009. Author: The Anthracite Coal Strike of 1902, 1971. Mem.: Orgn. Am. Hist., Labor Hist., Am. Hist. Assn. (founding mem.). Democrat. Roman Catholic. Died May 10, 2009.

CORPENING, GENE SURLES, publishing executive; b. Granite Falls, NC, Nov. 10, 1928; s. Oscar J. and Alice (Surles) C. BA in Radio and TV, U. N.C., 1971. Pub. Alice Pub., Granite Falls, from 1993. Author: I Love To Hear The Cold Wind Howl, 1993, Harlequin Hitler, 1994; inventor of bd. game. With U.S. Army, 1950-52, Korea. Avocations: tennis, dance. Home: Granite Falls, NC. Died Apr. 30, 2008.

CORRALES, FRANK CAMPA, composer, writer, guitarist; b. San Antonio, Dec. 30, 1931; s. Candelario Chavez and Benigna (Campa) C.; m. Yolanda Oyervides, May 30, 1959; children: Frank Jr., Cecilia, Nancy, Jackie, Steven. Student, Tex. Vocat. Coll., Amistad Sch. Mem. adv. com. KLRN-PBS TV Prodns., San Antonio, 1996—; toured with Air Force shows, 1954-56, Tejano bands in U.S., 1957-67; clk., salesperson So. Music Co. Book Dept., 1968-76; recording artist for Talking Taco Records, 1979—. Author: Easy Guide to Conjunto, 1987, Mariachi Guitar for Beginners, 1995, Tex-Mex Music for Guitar, 1998. With USAF, 1952-56. Avocations: scrapbook collection, cartooning, composing, recording, old photographs. Home: San Antonio, Tex. Died Sept. 13, 2007.

CORRIGAN, JOHN EDWARD, JR., retired banker, lawyer; b. Chgo., Sept. 26, 1922; s. John Edward and Veronica (Mulvey) C.; m. Eileen Williams, Nov. 4, 1950 (div. 1979); m. Sylvia Dennison McElin, Sept. 24, 1983. BA, Harvard U., 1943, JD, 1949. Bar: Ill. 1950. With First Nat. Bank Chgo., 1949-79, asst. atty., 1954—59, asst. v.p., 1960-61, v.p., 1961-72, sr. v.p., 1972-79; prin. Hedberg, Tobin, Flaherty & Whalen P.C., Chgo., 1980-87; of counsel Hedberg, Tobin, Flaherty & Whalen Inc., Chgo., 1988-92. With AUS, 1943-46, 51-52. Home: Kenilworth, Ill. Died Aug. 2009.

CORRIGAN, WILLIAM THOMAS, retired broadcast news executive; b. Bridgeport, Conn., Sept. 18, 1921; s. Thomas F. and Anna M. (Callan) C.; m. Harriett Bell, Sept. 1, 1951; children: Kevin, Brian. BS, Am. U., 1948. Reporter Bridgeport Herald, sports broadcaster sta. WUST, Washington, 1947; writer, reporter, prodr. NBC News, 1948-51; prodr., editor NBC-TV (newsreel), 1951-52; assignment editor NBC-TV News, 1952-53; Washington mgr. CBS Newsfilm, Washington bur. chief, 1953-59; dir. news and pub. affairs Sta. KNXT-TV, West Coast bur. chief CBS TV News, 1959-61; Am. Networks prodr./editor Eichmann Trial, Jerusalem, Israel, 1961; mgr. Washington bur. NBC News, 1962; prodr. Huntley Brinkley Report, Wash., 1963-65; dir. news ops. NBC, NYC, 1965-68; gen. mgr. ops. NBC News, NYC, 1968-73, gen. mgr., 1973-79, dir. broadcast svc., 1979-81. Staff sgt. USAAF, 1943—45, WWII. Decorated D.F.C., Air medal. Mem.: Soc. Profl. Journalists, Nat. Press Club, Radio-TV Corrs. Assn., White House Photographers Assn., Radio-TV News Dirs. Assn., Bath Club (Nokomis), Phi Sigma Kappa. Achievements include flying 35 combat missions over Japan as a B29 Tail Gunner. Home: Sarasota, Fla. Died Jan. 25, 2009.

CORTS, THOMAS EDWARD, retired academic administrator; b. Terre Haute, Ind., Oct. 7, 1941; s. Charles Harold and Hazel Louise (Vernon) C.; m. Marla Ruth Haas, Feb. 15, 1964; children: Jennifer Ruth Corts Fuller, Rachel Anne Corts Wachter, Christian Haas BA, Georgetown Coll., Ky., 1963; MA, Ind. U., 1968, PhD, 1972; DLitt (hon.), Georgetown Coll., Ky., 1991; DHL (hon.), Campbell U., 1995, U. Ala., 2002; DD (hon.), Judson Coll., 2006. Asst. to pres. Georgetown Coll., 1963-64, 67-69, asst. prof., 1967-69, exec. dean, 1969-73, exec. v.p. Ky., 1973; coord. Higher Edn. Consortium, Lexington, Ky., 1973-74; pres. Wingate Coll., NC, 1974-83, Samford U., Birmingham, Ala., 1983—2006, pres. emeritus, 2006—09. Bd. dirs. Samford U. Found., 1990-2006, Found. Ind. Higher Edn., 1988-92; chmn. Ala. Commn. on Sch. Performance and Accountability, 1993-94. Contbr. articles to profl. jours. Bd. dirs. Birmingham chpt. ARC, 1983-89, Ala. Citizens for Constl. Reform, 2000-05; mem. adv. bd. Salvation Army, 1987-97; mem. exec. coun. Boy Scouts Am., Birmingham, 1984-2005; bd. dirs. Leadership Birmingham, 1984-95; mem. exec. com. Birmingham Better Bus. Bur., 1996-2006, Birmingham Summerfest, 1984-95, Birmingham Area Consortium on Higher Edn., Ala. Poverty Project, Inc.; mem. gen. coun. Baptist World Alliance, 1996-; mem. Pub. Affairs Rsch. Coun. Ala. Recipient Outstanding Alumnus award Georgetown Coll., 1987, Jefferson award Downtown Action Com., Birmingham, 1988, Outstanding Educator award Ala. Assn. Coll. and Univs.-Ala. Assn. Women, Birmingham, 1989, Good Shepherd award Assn. Bapt. for Scouting, 1990, Citizen of Yr., 1990, Most Supportive Pres. award Am. Assn. Colls. for Tchr. Edn., 1991, Charles D. Johnson Disting. Sc. award Internat. Assn. Bapt. Colls. and Univs., 2006; named to Birmingham Bus. Hall of Fame, 2005, U. Ala. Comms. Hall of Fame, 2005. Mem. Am. Assn. Pres. of Ind. Colls. and Univs. (v.p. 1990-92, pres. 1992-95, bd. dirs. 1989-2002, 2004-06), Coun. for Advancement of Pvt. Colls. in Ala. (past pres.), Ala. Assn. Ind. Colls., Nat. Fellowship Bapt. Educators (pres. 1988-89), Assn. So. Bapt. Colls. and Schs. (v.p. 1988-89, pres. 1990-91, bd. dirs. 2004-09), So. Assn. Colls. and Schs. (trustee 1991-98, mem. commn. on colls., vice chmn. 1991, chmn. exec. coun. 1992-94, pres. 1996, Disting. Leadership award 2001), Coun. Higher Edn. Accreditation (bd. dirs. 1995-97), Assn. Governing Bds. (pres.'s commn., chmn. 2003-04), Birmingham Area C. of C. (bd. dirs. 2000-04), Ala. Acad. Honor. Democrat. Home: Birmingham, Ala. Died Feb. 4, 2009.

CORWEN, LEONARD, business owner, consultant; b. Phila., Oct. 17, 1921; s. Herman and Ann (Richstone) C.; m. Bernice Roth, Sept. 3, 1958; 1 child, CArol. Student, TEmple U., 1948, NYU, 1950. Editor Am. Traveler, Inc., NYC, 1950-58; pres. CRS Assocs., NYC, from 1958. Adj. prof. N.Y.C. Community Coll., Bayside, 1986—. Author: The Job Hunters Handbook, 1972, Your Future in Publishing, 1975, Your Job-Where to Find It, 1982, Fifty and Fired, 1986, Your Resume-Key to a Better Job, 1987. 1st lt. USAF, 1942-46. Mem. Am. Soc. Journalists and Authors, Writers Guild, Bus. Press Editors Assn. Avocation: sculpting. Home: Brooklyn, NY. Died Feb. 4, 2008.

COSSETTE, PIERRE, agent, producer; b. Valleyfield, Que., Can., Dec. 15, 1923; m. Mary Cossette; children: John, Andrew; 5 stepchildren. BA in Journalism, U. So. Calif., 1949. Agt. Music Corp. America, head dept. art; owner Pierre Cossette Prodns., L.A., Dunhill Records. Producer: (TV) Johnny's Man's Stand Up and Cheer, The Andy Williams Show, The Glen Campbell Show, Sammy & Company, Salute, Sha Na Na, Down to Earth, Grammy Awards, Alcatraz, Promise of Love, Too Young the Hero, The New Adventures of Heidi, Fire and Rain; (musical) The Will Rogers Follies; author: (autobiography) Another Day in Showbiz: One Producer's Journey, 2003 Fundraiser Concern Found. for Cancer Rsch. Recipient ShowMan of the Yr. award Publicists Guild of America Mem. Hollywood Radio & TV Soc. (past pres.). Died Sept. 11, 2009.

COSTA, THOMAS PETER, clergyman, writer, lecturer; b. Mt. Pleasant, Pa., June 21, 1922; s. Louis A. and Carmela (Rega) C. BA in Psychology and Sociology, UCLA, 1955; Doctorate, Religious Sci. Internat., Spokane, Wash., 1984. Ordained to ministry Ch. of Relieioug Sci., 1974. Founder Ch. of Religious Sci., Palm Desert, Calif., 1973, min., from 1973. Author: Excuse Me While I Call God, 1984, Life, Wanna Make Something of It, 1988. Mem. adv. bd. Desert AIDS Project, Palm Springs, 1995—; bd. dirs. Religious Sci. Int., Spokane, 1982-94. Avocations: theater, golf, walking, piano. Home: Palm Desert, Calif. Died June 6, 2008.

COSTELLO, GARY EWING, brokerage agency executive; b. San Francisco, Feb. 2, 1940; s. Charles Louis Costello and Ruth Hamilton (Ewing) McKenna; divorced; 1 child, Brett Gregory. Student, Coll. San Mateo, 1957-59. Agy. mgr. Travelers Ins. Co., San Jose, Calif., 1973-82; brokerage rep. Paul Revere Ins. Co., San Jose, 1983-86; brokerage mgr. Prin. Fin. Group, San Jose, from 1987. With U.S. Army, 1958-62. Life Underwriters Tng. Coun. fellow Nat. Assn. Life Unerwriters. Mem. Nat. Assn. Health Underwriters (rep. 1989—), San Jose Life Underwriters, Greater Bay Area Assn. Health Underwriters. Republican. Avocation: active with san francisco 49ers booster club. Died Sept. 30, 2007.

COTTLE, HAROLD RANSON, pathologist, laboratory executive; b. Bklyn., Dec. 7, 1925; s. Kenneth Raymond and Katharine Habershon (Blelloch) C.; m. Betty Lowell, July 15, 1950; children: David Lowell, Andrew Geoffrey, Susan Elizabeth. Student, Bard Coll., 1942-43, Dartmouth Coll., 1943-44; MD, N.Y. Med. Coll., 1948. Diplomate Nat. Bd. Med. Examiners; cert. Am. Bd. Pathology. Intern Meth. Hosp., Bklyn., 1948-49, resident in pathology, 1949-50, Kings County Hosp., Bklyn., 1952-54; asst. pathologist Kings County Hosp., SUNY, 1954-55, asst. to dir. of labs., 1955-56, chief autopsy svc., 1956-60, chief surg. pathology, 1960-62, vis. pathologist, 1962-70; clin. assoc. prof. SUNY, Downstate Med. Ctr., Bklyn., 1970-85; dir. Harold R. Cottle, M.D. Lab., from 1975. Asst. instr. SUNY, 1953-54, instr., 1954-56, asst. prof., 1956-62, prof., 1956-62, clin. asst. prof., 1962-70; assoc. dir. labs. Maimonides Hosp., Bklyn., 1962-66; dir. anatomic pathology Bklyn.-Cumberland Med. Ctr., 1966-70; pathologist Altoona (Pa.) Hosp., 1970-72, dir. lab. svcs., 1972-74, mem. exec. com., 1972-74; dir. lab. medicine Indiana (Pa.) Hosp., 1974-84; cons. pathologist VA Hosp., Altoona, 1973-89; coroner's pathologist various counties, Pa.; cons. staff Mercy Hosp., Altoona; mem. staff Conemaugh Valley Meml. Hosp. Contbr. articles to profl. jours. Chair Bklyn. chpt., bd. N.Y. State ACLU, 1956-70; various offices Sheepshead Bay Meth. Ch., 1950-70, 1st United Meth. Ch., Altoona, 1971-80; mem. Human Rights Commn., 1971-74. Lt. USNR, 1944-45, 50-52. Fellow Coll. Am. Pathologists, Am. Soc. Clin. Pathologists; mem. AMA, AAAS, AAUP, Pa. Med. Soc., Blair County Med. Soc., N.Y. Path. Soc., N.Y. State Soc. Pathologists, N.Y. State Assn. Pub. Health Labs., Pitts. Pathology Soc., Pitts. Comparative Pathology Soc., Ctrl. Pa. Regional Soc. Pathologists, Pa. Assn. Pathologists, Internat. Assn. Coroners and Med. Examiners, Pa. Assn. Coroners and Med. Examiners. Avocations: outdoor sports, firearms, books. Died Apr. 5, 2008.

COTTNER, DONALD, pathologist; b. Wichita, Mar. 26, 1937; s. Edward Floyd and Augusta Mae Cottner; m. Joreen Smith, Sept. 6, 1974 (div. June 1994); children: Dereck, Regina, John; m. Karolynne Kelly Cottner, June 12, 1996; stepchildren: Greg, Michael, Laquinta, Clifford. BA, Wichita State U., 1961; M of Religious Edn., Midwestern Sem., 1966; PhD, Southeastern U., 1982; D of Min., Evangel. Bible Sem.; DDiv, U. Ctrl. Am., 1984. Janitor Dunbar Elem. Sch., Wichita, 1958—61; lawn cutter Ctrl. Bapt. Theol. Sem., 1961—62; agt. Western So. Life Ins., 1962—63; ins. cons. MEt. Life Ins., 1964—66; counselor Todd Phillips Home for Boys, Detroit, 1967; instr. Wolverine Bapt. Assn., 1967—68; counselor Neighborhood Youth Corps, Kansas City, 1968—69, exec. dir., 1969—70; with Operation Mainstream, 1970—72; tng. officer, counselor Neighborhood Youth Corp.s, 1972—73; dir. bus. inst. Black Econ. Union, 1973—78; psychotherapist pvt. practice, Kansas City, 1978—85; ret. Grant writer Eastside Ctr., St. Joseph, Mo., 1973—74; adj. prof. Penn Valley C.C., Kansas City, 1974. Mem.: Charles F. Menninger Soc. Republican. Baptist. Avocations: reading, writing. Home: Fort Worth, Tex. Died May 6, 2008.

COULTER, JAMES BENNETT, state official; b. Vinita, Okla., Aug. 2, 1920; s. Robert Leslie and Louise (Robinson) C.; m. Norma R. Brink, June 1, 1942; children: Linda Coulter Prandoni, James Bennett. BS in Civil Engring, U. Kans., 1950; MS, Harvard U., 1954; DSc (hon.), Washington Coll., 1979. Registered profl. engr., Md., Kans. Commd. officer USPHS, 1950-66; asst. commr. environ. health Md. Dept. Health, Balt., 1966-69; sec. Md. Dept. Natural Resources, Annapolis, 1969-82. Mem. vis. com. Sch. Engring. and Applied Physics, Harvard U.; mem. adv. com. Sch. Engring., U. Kan., Civitan. Bd. dirs. Blue Shield Md.; trustee Chesapeake Research Consortium; mem. exec. bd. Md. Save Our Streams. Served with C.E. AUS, 1940-45. Decorated Bronze Star Mem. APHA, NAE, Am. Acad. Environ. Engrs. (Gordon M. Fair award 1971, pres. 1978), Am. Water Works Assn. (Fuller award 1987), Water Pollution Control Fedn., Tau Beta Pi, Sigma Tau. Died Sept. 9, 2005.

COUNTER, JAMES NICHOLAS, III, trade association executive, lawyer; b. Phoenix, Mar. 21, 1940; s. James Nicholas and Margaret (Plettner) C.; m. Jacqueline Dee Tompkins, July 25, 1982; children: Samantha, Nicholas. BSEE, U. Colo., 1963; JD, Stanford U., 1966. Assoc. ptnr. Rutan & Tucker, Santa Ana, Calif., 1966-72; ptnr. Mitchell, Silberberg & Knupp, LA, 1972-82; pres. Alliances of Motion Picture & Television Producers, Sherman Oaks, Calif., 1982—2009. Bd. dirs. Motion Pictur & Television Fund, Woodland Hills, Calif., 1982-2009, Permanent Charities Com., Studio City, Calif., 1982-2009, Nat. Film Preservation Bd., Washington, 1989-2009, Internat. Found. Employee Benefits, Brookfield, Wis., 1990-2009. Bd. dirs. L.A. C. of C., 1985-2009 Mem. Tau Beta Pi. Died Nov. 6, 2009.

COURTNEY, ELLA VIRGINIA, retired elementary school educator; b. Florence, Miss., Aug. 5, 1930; d. John Webster Courtney and Mary Ellen Jackson. BA in Religion and Social Studies, Millages Coll., 1952; MA in Religion and Social Studies, Scarsitte Coll., 1953; MEd, U. Ga., 1971; student, Emory U. Tchr. Elem. Sch. Floyd County Bd. Edn., Rome, Ga., 1956—91, ret., 1991; pastor United Meth. Ch., Yorkville, Ga., 1982—83, Rome, 1984—99. Cmty. worker Bd. Missions Meth. Ch., Carrollton, Ga., 1953—54, Rome, 1954—56; vol. Rome (Ga.) Urban Ministries, 1999. Named Clergy Vol. of Yr., Rome (Ga.) Urban Ministries, 1999. Mem.: Floyd County Ret. Tchrs., Dist. Ret. Preachers. Methodist. Avocations: reading, piano. Home: Rome, Ga. Deceased.

COUSINS, WILLIAM JOSEPH, lawyer, litigation consultant; b. New Haven, Conn., Sept. 28, 1917; s. Salvatore Colombieri and Mary (Arpaia) C.; m. Betty Jean Collins, June 25, 1954; children: Mimi Causey, Anna Maria, William J. Jr. BA, Yale U., 1940, LLB, 1943. Bar: Conn., U.S. Dist. Ct. Conn., U.S. Ct. Appeals (2d cir.) 1946. Law clk. New Haven (Conn.) Superior Ct., 1946-48; pvt. practice New Haven, 1946-52; ptnr. Arpaia & Cousins, New Haven, 1952-56; sr. ptnr. Cousins, Dooley & Barnston, Conn., 1956-68, Cousins, Ritter & Silverstone, New Haven, 1968-81, Carmody & Torrance, New Haven, 1981-87; dir. William J. Cousins & Assoc., Woodbridge, Conn., 1987; ret., 1987. Apptd. spl. master and parajud. officer U.S. Dist. Ct. Conn.; sr. ptnr. conflict resolution svc. Cousins and Cooper; prosecutor Woodbridge Town Ct., 1948-60, town counsel Town of Woodbridge, 1948-76, chmn. Citizens Action Commn., 1952-55. Chmn. New Haven County Reps., 1960-64; chmn. Cath. Interracial Council, 1952-56. Served as sgt. USAAF 1943-46, PTO. Mem. ABA (lawyers conf. of jud. adminstrn. divsn.), Fed. Bar Assn., Am. Judicature Soc., Soc. Profl. Dispute Resolution, Nat. Inst. for Dispute Resolution (assoc.), Law and Soc. Assn. Clubs: Yale, Mory's, The Graduate. Republican. Roman Catholic. Died Aug. 14, 2007.

COWLES, WALTER CURTIS, naval architect; b. Chgo., Aug. 25, 1919; s. Harry Samuel and Blanche Lee (Gates) C.; m. Betty Ann McDuff, July 28, 1945; children: Mark Allan, Garry Stephen, Kent Edward, Joy Elizabeth. BS in Engring., U. Mich., 1942. Draftsman Am. Ship Bldg. Co., Cleve., 1942-51, chief hull draftsman, 1951-57, naval architect, 1957—63; marine designer Esso/Exxon, NYC and Morristown, N.J., 1963-84; ret., 1984. Contbr. paper to Transactions of Soc. Naval Architects and Marine Engrs., 1980; coord. publ. of centennial hist. vol., 1993; pub. Antrim Steamers A Brief History of Steam Navigation on the Inland Lakes of Antrim County Michigan, 1997. Mem. Soc. Naval Architects (life), U.S. Naval Inst. (life), Am. Soc. Naval Engrs. Home: Bellaire, Mich. Died July 28, 2008.

COX, BERRY GORDON, rancher; b. Garden City, Tex., Mar. 6, 1923; s. Sam W. and Thelma (Berry) C.; m. Edna Earle Jonas, Dec. 21, 1941; children: Karen, Berry S. Grad. high sch., Martin County, Tex. Rancher, Andrews, Tex. Pres. Andrews Livestock Show, West Tex. Livestock Show; bd. dirs. Commerce State Bank, Andrews, Soil and Water Dist., Andrews; chmn. USDA Agr. Stablzn. Conservation Svcs. Com., Andrews, Andrews Tax Revue; life career counselor

Andrews Sch. System. Bd. dirs. Permian Gen. Hosp. Mem. West Tex. Cattle Raisers Assn. (pres.), Goldenspread Charolais Cattle Raisers Asns. (bd. dirs.), Andrews C. of C. (life; bd. dirs.), Masons, Chambership Gold Coats. Baptist. Avocation: quarter horse racing. Died Apr. 12, 2008.

COX, DAVID M., theater educator, set designer; s. Harold E. Cox; m. Joan R. Ritz, May 14, 1989; 1 child, Sean. MFA in Theatre, U. Utah, Salt Lake City, 1978. Chair theatre and speech Mesa State Coll., Grand Junction, Colo., 1999—2003, head theatre arts, 2004—06. Mem.: United Scenic Artists NY, U.S.I.T.T (assoc.). Avocation: scenography. Home: Grand Junction, Colo. Died July 9, 2006.

COX, DOUGLAS CHARLES, museum executive; b. Pocatello, Idaho, July 24, 1944; s. Edwin Charles and Mary LaVerel (Sorensen) C.; m. Anne Bischoff, June 28, 1969; children: Robert Douglas, Kenneth Edwin, Jonathan Charles, Melissa Jane, Jenny Johanna, Trevor Dean. A, So. Utah State, 1967; BS, Brigham Young U., 1968, PhD, 1976. Cert. secondary tchr. Utah, 1976. Secondary math. tchr. Dixon Sch. Provo Sch. Dist., 1976-77; mus. exec. Monte L. Bean Life Sci. Mus., Provo, from 1978. Scoutmaster local chpt. Boy Scouts of Am., 1985-89, chairperson scout com. 1989—. With U.S. Army, 1968-71. Mem. Mus. Edn. Round Table, Am. Assn. Mus. (edn. com.). Republican. Mem. Lds Ch. Home: Orem, Utah. Died Nov. 8, 2007.

COX, FRANK D. (BUDDY COX), oil industry executive; b. Shreveport, La., Dec. 20, 1932; s. Ohmer M. and Beulah O. (Scott) Cox; m. Betty Jean Hand, June 19, 1956; children: Cynthia Cox Sanford, Carolyn Cox Patton, Frank D. Jr. BS in Bus. Adminstrn., La. Tech. U., 1956; postgrad., Centenary Coll., 1958-59. Cert. profl. landman; lic. real estate, Fla. Various positions Exxon Corp., Houston, 1955-86, chief landman, v.p. coal resources, 1980-86; pvt. practice Houston, 1986-89; sr. v.p. Energy Exploration Mgmt. Co., Houston, 1989-94; v.p., mgr. T-Bar-X Ltd. Co., Houston, 1994-2000; v.p., dir. Power Exploration Internat., Houston, 1994-2000; ptnr. East Tex. Reef Fund, Ltd., from 1994; land mgr. Thomson-Barrow Corp., 1994-2000, Tecolotita, Inc., 1994-2000; exploration cons. Houston, from 2000. Active Second Bapt. Ch., Houston. Capt. USAF, 1956-58. Named disting. mil. grad. La. Tech. U., Ruston, 1955. Mem. Am. Assn. Profl. Landmen, Houston Assn. Profl. Landmen, W. Houston Assn. Profl. Landmen, W. Houston Exxon Annuitant Club, 100 Club of Greater Houston, La. Tech. U. Found., Crimestoppers Inc., Pi Kappa Alpha Ednl. Found., Omicron Delta Kappa Found., Delta Sigma Pi. Republican. Avocations: golf, tennis, amateur radio. Died Sept. 22, 2007.

COX, JOHN J., construction executive; b. NYC, Sept. 16, 1946; s. John J. and Catherine (Hughes) C.; children: John, Chris, James. BSBA, Xavier Coll., 1968. Fin. analyst NCR, Dayton, Ohio, 1968-69; salesman Nationwide Devel., Columbus, Ohio, 1969-70; v.p. devel. Deffet Co., Columbus, Ohio, 1970-74, exec. v.p., from 1974; chmn. Bill Halfacre, Inc., Sarasota, Fla.; pres. CDS, Inc. Mem. adv. bd. S.E. Bank N.A., Sarasota, 1986-87; chmn. Masonry Contractors, Inc.; pres. Gulf Coast Flooring, Inc. Bd. dirs. Com. of 100, Sarasota, Fla.; mem. exec. bd. Sunny Land Council Boy Scouts Am. Mem. Sarasota C. of C. (trustee 1984—). Home: Sarasota, Fla. Died Feb. 10, 2008.

COX, MARGARET, pediatrics nurse; b. Keyser, W.Va., Dec. 27, 1948; d. James and Doris G. (McMahon) Wildesen; m. Kenneth J. Cox, Apr. 5, 1969; children: Lynette, Jason, James. Diploma, Cumberland Meml. Sch. Nursing, 1970; BS, U. Md., 1990. RN, D.C. Charge nurse, asst. dir. nursing Children's Nat. Med. Ctr., Washington; staff nurse Children's Home Health Svcs., Washington; referral coord., assoc. dir. for discharge planning Children's Home Health Care Svcs., Washington; mgr. infectious disease/cystic fibrosis unit Children's Hosp., Washington. Mem. Assn. Care of Children's Health (cert. continuity of care). Home: Glenn Dale, Md. Died Aug. 6, 2008.

COX, MERVYN KAY, orthodontist; b. St. George, Utah, Sept. 24, 1936; s. Rulon B. and Ida Mae (Iverson) C.; m. Martha Sue Stout, Nov. 2, 1984; children: Daniel Mervyn, Jeffrey Boots, Kimberly D., Joseph Ballard, Kyla Dawn, Katrina Marie, Damon Michael, Jamison Stout, Kiarah Sue, Joshua Kay, Katosha Lyn, Dallin Mervyn. AS, Dixie Coll., 1956; BS, Brigham Young U., 1962; DDS, U. Calif., San Francisco, 1964. Pvt. practice, ptnr. Orthodontic Specialists, St. George, from 1964. Bd. dirs. Skywest Airlines, St. George, Tritek Corp., St. George; owner Pinestead Subdivs., St. George, 1974—; owner, mgr. Sunburst Investments-Shopping Ctr., St. George, 1986—. Patentee removable orthopedics cast, 1972. Sgt. USNG. Mervyn K. Cox Performing Arts Bldg. named in his honor. Mem. Am. Dental Assn., Am. Assn. Orthodontists, Utah State Dental Assn., Rocky Mountain Soc. Orthodontists, St. George C. of C., Colonels Club Dixie Coll. (bd. dirs. 1990), Blue Key, Omicron Kappa Upsilon. Mem. Lds Ch. Avocations: sports, water-skiing, tennis. Home: Saint George, Utah. Died Dec. 15, 2007.

CRAFT, KATIE ANN, health facility administrator; b. Southbridge, Mass., Dec. 18, 1979; d. David Roy and Cheryl Ann Craft. A in Veterinay Sci. Tech., and Liberal Arts, NH Tech; BA in Holistic Life Counseling and Ministerial, U. Sedona; PhD in Metaphysics and DD, Monastary U.; PhD in Naturopathy, Avicenna Inst. Natural Healing, Iowa. Cert. tchr. Internat. Inst. Reiki Profl. and Ethereal Energies, in reflexologist, aromatherapist Avicenna Inst. Natural Healing, 2008, in holistic health practitioner Nat. Accredation and Certification Bd., 2008, in lightarian reiki tchr. Lightarian Inst. For Global Transformation, 2008, shamballa tchr. Divine Light Acadamy Healing, karuna tchr. Healing Art Forms Acadamy; in spl. minister to animals, and ordained chaplain pets Chaplain of Pets Interfaith Ministry, 2008; in angel healing practitioner Divine Healing, 2007. Medicine technician Vet. Hosp. Throughout NH, 2000—07; founder and practitioner providing holistic care Halo Integrated Healing, Derry, NH, from 2006. Reiki treatment vol. Animal Shelters and Hosp., VA Ctr. Clin., NH. Prodr.: (television host) Manifest A Miracle. Reiki treatment pub., educator Internat. Assn. Reiki Professionals, NH. Mem.: Internat. Assn. Reiki Profls., Order New Compassionate Animal Ministry (spl. min. to animals), Internat. Natural Healers Assn. (registered healer), Am. Holistic Health Assn. Home: Derry, NH. Died Apr. 24, 2009.

CRAGNOLINO, GUSTAVO ADOLFO, research scientist; b. Marcos Juarez, Cordoba, Argentina, July 23, 1940; arrived in US, 1976; s. Roberto Clemente and Maria Antonia (Ferrer) Cragnolino; m. Aida Apter, Aug. 16, 1966; children: Ana, Ernesto. Licenciado in Chem. Scis., U. Buenos Aires, 1966, D in Chem. Scis., 1975. Rsch. assoc. Atomic Energy Commn., Buenos Aires, 1968—76; rsch. scientist Ohio State U., Columbus, 1976—86; assoc. scientist Brookhaven Nat. Lab., Upton, NY, 1986—88; sr. rsch. scientist Atomic Energy Commn., Buenos Aires, 1988—90; prin. scientist S.W. Rsch. Inst., San Antonio, 1990—95, staff scientist, 1995—2003, inst. scientist, 2003—05, tech. advisor, from 2005. Lectr., adv. Internat. Atomic Energy Agy., Vienna, 1994; presenter in field. Co-editor: Accelerated Corrosion Tests for Service Life Prediction of Materials, 1994, Scientific Basis for Nuclear Waste Management XXV, 2002, Corrosion Resistant Materials in Extreme Environments, 2005; co-author: ASME Handbook on Water Technology for Thermal Power Systems, 1998; contbr. articles to profl. jours. Fellow: Nat. Assn. Corrosion Engrs. Internat. (chmn. tech. com. 1996—98); mem.: Rsch. Com, ASTM Internat., Am. Nuc. Soc., Electrochem. Soc. Home: San Antonio, Tex. Died May 14, 2009.

CRAIG, MARY LAURI, accountant; b. Helena, Mont., Jan. 19, 1936; d. Henry and Hilma (Newman) Lauri; m. William Craig (div. 1982); children: Nona Marie, Lauri Sue. BS cum laude, Rocky Mtn. Coll., 1973. CPA. Acct. various firms, Billings, Mont.; sole practice CPA Billings, 1973-78; dir. Mont. Dept. Revenue, Helena, 1979-81; sole practice CPA Helena, from 1982. Commr.'s adv. group IRS, Washington, 1994-96; exec. com. Multi-State Tax Commn., Denver. Co-author: Adventure Bound in Montana. Mem. Am. Soc. Women Accts. (pres. chpt. 100 1976), Mont. Soc. CPAs. Avocations: fly fishing, gold mining, woodworking, watercolors, music. Died Oct. 9, 2007.

CRAIG, RAYMOND CORCORAN, English language educator; b. Independence, Mo., July 20, 1928; s. Raymond Luther and Edna Amelia (Forsha) C.; m. Mary Francis Shura, Dec. 4, 1960 (div. Aug. 1982); children: Alice, Mary; m. Faye Dene Wolfe, Dec. 17, 1988. BA, William Jewel Coll., 1950; MA, Vanderbilt U., 1952; PhD, U. Ill., 1982. Regional mgr. U.S. Refugee Relief Team, Bremen, Germany, 1955-60, CBS Pub. Co., Chgo., 1960-80; vis. assoc. prof. U. Ill., Champaign, 1981-82; assoc. prof. Marian Coll., Indpls., from 1982, chmn. dept. English, from 1987. Cons. LBM Pub. Co., Chgo., 1989-90, Fla. U. Press, Gainesville, 1978-80. Author: The Humor of H.E. Taliaferro, 1988; contbr. articles to profl. jours. Sgt. U.S. Army, 1952-55. Mem. MLA, Ind. Assn. Tchrs. of English (chmn. 1990-91). Republican. Avocations: aviation, cooking. Home: Indianapolis, Ind. Died Jan. 24, 2008.

CRAIGHEAD, OWEN LINDSAY, writer; b. Cross River, NY, Aug. 30, 1934; s. Robert Feuchter Craighead and Alice Wilson; m. Janice Lee Rankin, Jan. 23, 1954; children: Carol Lee Yugovich, Thomas Wilson, Lauren Lindsay Maxwell, William Owen. Owner Craighead Kennels, Cross River, NY; radio talk show host WGHQ, Kingston, NY; author and owner Crunk Publishing, Lubbock, Tex.; editor and founder Tom's E-zine for Am. Awareness. Author: (book) Skydivers Flying with their Pants, 1999, The Way It Is, Is, 2002, One of God's Salesmen, 2003, (advisory pamphlet) Home Buyer, Be Aware, 2003; prodr.(and dir.): (video) Skydiving, The New Frontier, 2003; author: (book) The Lethal Liberal Society in America, 2004. Vol. fireman South Salem Fire Dept., 1952—89, chmn., bd. fire commn., 1984—89; founder Lewisboro Vol. Ambulance Corp., 1977, pres., 1977—79, Lewisboro Lions Club, 1975—76; zone chmn. Saugerities Lions Club, 1992—93; sec. South Plains Lions Club, 2000—01; bulletin editor Lubbock Habitat for Humanity, 1999—2004; rep. candidate Lewisboro Town Bd., 1972; committeeman Lewisboro Rep. Com., 1977—85. Recipient Citizen of the Yr., Lewisboro C. of C., 1984, Lion of the Yr., Lewisboro Lions Club, 1984, Appreciation award, US Army Parachute Team Golden Knights, 1999. Mem.: Lewisboro Vol. Ambulance Corp. (life), South Salem Fire Dept. (life), Lions Internat. (life). Home: Lubbock, Tex. Died Mar. 28, 2008.

CRAIN, MARY TOM, volunteer; b. Vernon, Tex., Aug. 27, 1918; d. Samuel Asa Leland and Mary Verna (Johnson) Morgan; m. David Rasco, Dec. 24, 1941 (dec. Apr. 1955); children: Sarah M. Rasco Thomas, Mary Prudence Rasco Courtney; m. Sam H. Crain, Sept. 17, 1975 (dec. June 1980). Student, Stephens Coll., 1936-38, U. Tex., 1938-39; BS, U. Wis., 1941. Tchr. Williams Bay (Wis.) Schs., 1941; reporter Amarillo (Tex.) Globe News, 1957-65; exec. sec. Potter-Randall County Med. Soc., Amarillo, 1960-69; ret., 1969. Mem. lay adv. bd. St. Anthony's Hosp., Amarillo, 1957; mem. devel. bd. High Plains Hosp., 1995; coun. pres. Girl Scouts U.S., Amarillo, 1953-55; pres. Jr. League, Amarillo, 1956; bd. dirs. Amarillo Symphony, Art Mus., Panhandle Plains Hist. Soc., Amarillo Area Found., 1945—, Llano Cemetary; mem. City of Amarillo Park and Recreation Commn.; bd. dirs. Amarillo Coll. Found., Amarillo Pub. Libr., Art Force. Named Amarillo's Woman of yr., Beta Sigma Phi, 1955; named to Amarillo H.S. Hall of Fame, 1971. Methodist. Home: Amarillo, Tex. Deceased.

CRAMP, JOHN FRANKLIN, retired lawyer; b. Ridley Park, Pa., Mar. 14, 1923; s. Alfred Charles and Mildred Frances (Cummins) C.; m. Suzanne Surrick, Sept. 15, 1951 (div.); children: John F., Catherine T., David B., Andrew H., Daniel E.; m. Gloria C. Maddox, Jan. 29, 1972. BS, Pa. Mil. Coll. (now Widener U.), 1943; LLB, Dickinson Sch. Law, 1948. Bar: Pa. 1949, US Dist. Ct. (ea. dist.) Pa. 1951, US Ct. Appeals (3d cir.) 1951. Assoc. Hodge, Hodge & Balderston, Chester, Pa., 1949-53; ptnr. Hodge, Hodge & Cramp, Media, Pa., 1953—56; sr. ptnr. Cramp & D'Iorio, 1956—70; pres. Cramp, D'Iorio, McConchie & Forbes, P.C., 1970—90; founding counsel Beatty, Cramp, Kauffman & Lincke, 1996—2003; ret., 2003. Gen. counsel, bd. dirs. Bryn Mawr Group (name now Dixon Ticonderoga Inc.), 1965-79, pres. 1973-74; gen. counsel Widener U., 1968-91; bd. dirs. Phila. Subtransp. Co. Trustee Williamson Sch., 1968-91; bd. dirs., chmn. Crozer Chester Med. Ctr., Elwyn Inst., Jerusalem Elwyn; bd. dirs. Chester Hosp., Crozer-Keystone Health System; chmn. bd. dirs. Am. Inst. Mental Studies, Can. Friends of Elwyn; Rep. county chmn., 1957-61; del. Rep. Nat. Conv., 1960; state chmn. Citizens for Scranton, 1962. Mem. ABA, Del. County Bar Assn., Pa. Bar Assn., Internat. Soc. Barristers, Nat. Assn. Coll. and Univ. Attys., Def. Rsch. Inst., Vasari Country Club, Masons. Episcopalian. Home: Naples, Fla. Died Apr. 25, 2009.

CRANSTON, JOHN WELCH, historian, educator; b. Utica, NY, Dec. 21, 1931; s. Earl and Mildred (Welch) C. BA, Pomona Coll., 1953; MA, Columbia U., 1964; PhD, U. Wis., 1970. Asst. prof. history West Tex. State U., 1970-74, U. Mo., Kansas City, 1970, Rust Coll., Holly Springs, Miss., 1974-80, assoc. prof., 1980-83; historian U.S. Army Armor Ctr., Ft. Knox, Ky., 1983-95; ret., 1995. Adj. prof. history and govt. Elizabethtown C.C., Ft. Knox, 1988-2002. Contbr. history articles to profl. lit. With U.S. Army, 1953-55. NEH fellow, summers 1976, 81. Mem. Am. Hist. Assn., Orgn. Am. Historians. Democrat. Episcopalian. Home: Upper Lake, Calif. Died Oct. 12, 2008.

CRAVER, DONALD H., retired English language educator; b. Winston-Salem, NC, Dec. 22, 1935; s. Roy Howard and Fairy (Carter) C. BS, Wake Forest U., 1956; MA, Duke U., 1959; MPh, George Washington U., 1969, PhD, 1972. Instr. in English U. Cin., 1959-62; prof. English Towson U., Md., 1962-93, co-chmn. English dept., 1974-92, prof. emeitus, from 1994. Contbr. articles and reviews to profl. jours. Mem. theater panel Md. State Arts Coun., Balt., 1982-85. Recipient NDEA fellowship, George Washington U., 1969. Mem. Modern Lang. Assn., Nat. Coun. Tchrs. of English, Phi Beta Kappa, Omicron Delta Kappa, Alpha Sigma Lambda, Theta Chi. Home: Lutherville Timonium, Md. Died Dec. 10, 2007.

CRAWFORD, LARRY S., county official; b. Newport, Oreg., Apr. 16, 1944; s. Thomas D. and Ruth P. (Nix) Graham; children: Kerry D. Crawford, Amy M. Crawford. AAS, Odessa Coll., Tex., 1978. Cert. hypnotherapist; cert. forensic investigative hypnotist. Res. police officer and spl. dep. Carlsbad (N.Mex.) Police Dept., 1965-67, Eddy County Sheriff's Dept., Carlsbad, 1965-67; quality control lab. technician Internat. Minerals and Chem. Corp., Carlsbad, 1962-67; identification technician Odessa Police Dept., 1967-71; asst. chief Ector County Juvenile Probation Dept., Odessa, 1971-73; br. mgr. Electrolux div. Consolidated Foods, Odessa, 1974-82; instr. Odessa Coll./Odessa Coll. Police Acad., from 1982; owner, hypnotherapist Inst. Hypnotherapy and Behavior Modification, Odessa, from 1983; capt. ID bur. Ector County Sheriff Dept., Odessa, from 1977. Chmn. bd. Ector County Employees Credit Union, 1980-89; law enforcement liaison Ector County React, 1984—; bd. dirs. adv. com. Law Enforcement Acad.; staff mem. Ector County Sheriff Dept. Police and Corrections Acad.; forensic expert in fingerprints, photography, hypnosis and trace metal detection. Author various slide programs on law enforcement; producer hypnotherapy and subliminal tapes on behavior modification; inventor hynosis-brain wave synchronizer "The Dream Machine", 1985. Mem. Nat. Rep. Congl. Com., 1984—, Rep. nat. Com., 1984—, Reps. of Tex., 1985—, Rep. Presdl. Task Force, 1985—; mem. State Dept. Pub. Safety Adv. Com. for Uniform Crime Reports. Mem. Tex. Corrections Assn. (bd. dirs. 1973-74), Internat. Soc. Profl. Hypnotists, Tex. Assn. for Investigative Hypnosis, Internat. Soc. Investigative and Forensic Hypnosis, Internat. Assn. for Identification, Nat. Guild of Hypnotists, Masons (32nd deg.). Baptist. Avocations: flying, photography. Home: Sioux Falls, SD. Died Apr. 25, 2008.

CRAWFORD, LAWRENCE ROBERT, aviation and aerospace consultant; b. Ft. Lewis, Wash., May 4, 1936; s. Richard G. and Olive O. (Ericksen) C.; m. Yvonne G. Thompson, Nov. 8, 1957; children: Scott D., Robin L., Crawford Lafrankie. BS in Indsl. Engring., Ga. Inst. Tech., 1959; MS in Mgmt. with honors, Rensselaer Poly. Inst., 1965. Lic. comml. pilot. Commd. ensign USN, 1959, command pilot anti sub, advanced through grades to lt.

comdr., hon. discharge, 1968; airline pilot Pan Am, San Francisco, 1968-70, dir. corp. budgets NYC, 1970-73; dir. methods and standards Am. Airlines, NYC, 1973-75, sr. dir. reservations, 1975-79; v.p. mktg. Ransome Airlines, Phila., 1979-83; sr. v.p. mktg. and planning Empire Airlines, Utica, N.Y., 1983-85; founder, pres., CEO Avitas, Inc., Reston, Va., 1985-98; founder, chmn., CEO Avitas Engrng., Inc., Miami, Fla., 1991-98; founder, pres., CEO Spectrum Aviation Svcs. Inc., Reston, 1998—2006. Exec. adv. bd. EDS Fin. Corp., Dallas, 1987-90; v.p. Det Norske Veritas, Oslo, 1992-98; frequest spkr. at aircraft fin. confs. Contbr. articles to profl. jours. Bd. dirs. Internat. Aviation Found. Mem. AIAA, Exptl. Aircraft Assn. (builder 1987), U.S. Ultralight Flying Assn., Am. Aero. Soc., Internat. Soc. Transport Aircraft Trading, Nat. Aeronautics Assn., Royal Aeronautics Soc., Sr. Aerospace Execs. Assn., Stearman Restorers Assn., Wings Club, Washington Aero Club, Culpeper Aero Squadron (founder). Republican. Methodist. Achievements include devel. of the comml. aviation industry's first aircraft tech. monitoring product to ensure condition and value of leased aircraft; founded and devel. Avitas into world's largest appraiser and inspector of comml. aircraft. Home: Aldie, Va. Died Mar. 21, 2009.

CRAWFORD, LORETTA, social worker supervisor; b. Greenwood, SC, Feb. 19, 1944; d. Joseph and Mable (Starks) C. BS in Psychology and Sociology cum laude, Johnson C. Smith U., 1965; postgrad., Temple U., 1966, U. Ga., 1972, Erskine Coll., 1973. Floating case worker Dept. Pub. Assistance, Phila., 1966-70; dep. dir. CETA project GLEAMS Human Resources Commn., Greenwood, S.C., 1970-76; site supr. MAAC Project Employment and Tng. Svcs., National City, Calif., 1977-85; benefits analyst Dept. Social Svcs., San Diego, 1985-86, protective svcs. worker, 1986-89, protective svcs. social worker supr., from 1989. Assessor Mgmt. Acad., San Diego, 1991—; mem. Cross Cultural Concerns Com., San Diego, 1988—. Dir. children's plays, 1965 (Cup); author: Our Child Foster Placement Publs., 1991; contbr. articles to newspapers. Chair tng. com. Affirmative Action Com., Dept. Social Svcs., San Diego, 1990—. Named scholar United Negro Coll. Fund, 1961-65, Little River Bapt. Assn., 1961-65, Alpha Kappa Alpha, 1961-65, Nat. Merit Assn., 1961-65, Delta Sigma Theta, 1961-65; named Outstanding Young Woman of Am., 1973. Mem. Nat. Assn. Black Social Workers, Black Women's Issues Com., Alpha Kappa Mu. Democrat. Baptist. Avocation: gospel music. Home: San Diego, Calif. Died Jan. 23, 2008.

CREAMER, BRUCE CUNNINGHAM, retired safety educator, property manager; b. Champaign, Ill., Oct. 27, 1941; s. Carl Moore and Eunice (Cunningham) C.; m. Judith Ann Pride, June, 1968 (div. Apr. 1972). BS in Indsl. Edn., U. Ill., Urbana, 1964, MS in Libr. Sci., 1972, CAS in Libr. Sci., 1975. Auditorium mgmt. U. Ill. Assembly Hall, Urbana, Ill., 1968-70; documents libr. U. Ill. Library, Urbana, Ill., 1972-74; property mgr. Creamer Interests, Champaign, Ill., 1975-97; instr. motorcycle rider program U. Ill., Urbana, Ill., 1977-81, project coord. motorcycle rider program, 1982-93. Chmn. Curriculum Com., Ill. Cycle Rider Training Program, Springfield, Ill., 1982-86. Co-author: Motorcycle Rider Program, 1982. Bd. dirs. Orpheum Children's Sci. Mus., 1996-2006; bd. govs. Ill. Heritage Assn., 2004—; mem. mus. adv. com. Early Am. Mus, 2002—; Champaign city historian, 2005—. 1st lt. USAF, 1964-67. Mem. Pres. Coun. U. Ill., U. Ill. Alumni Assn., Air Force Assn., Am. Motorcyclist Assn., Civil Air Patrol, Loyal Order of Moose, Res. Officers Assn. Avocations: military history, local history, family history, historic preservation. Home: Champaign, Ill. Died Dec. 15, 2007.

CREAN, HUGH, art educator; BA, Nat. U. Ireland, 1974; MA, U. Calif., Davis, 1978; PhD, CUNY, 1990. Lectr. N.Y. Sch. Interior Design, NYC, from 1976, Met. Mus. Art, NYC, from 1976; chair restoration dept. Fashion Inst. Tech., NYC, from 1986. Cons. in field. Prodr.(dir.): (films, documentary) Area of Glory, 2000. Mem.: Decorating Arts Soc., Coll. Art Assn., Nat. Arts Club. Home: New York, NY. Died Nov. 3, 2008.

CREED, SUSAN LYNN, business educator; b. Lincoln Park, Mich., Nov. 22, 1950; d. Charles Olen and Betty Jane (Bauser) Mohr; m. Charles Douglas Creed III, Aug. 11, 1973; children: Joanna, Katie, Chip. BS, Ea. Mich. U., 1972; M in Bus. Edn., Cen. Mich. U., 1989. Office mgr. career placement office Ea. Mich. U., Ypsilanti, 1972-75; instr. Harrisburg Area Community Coll., Harrisburg, Pa., 1978-79; mktg. support rep. Lanier Bus. Products, Saginaw, Mich., 1980-81; assoc. prof. Delta Coll., Univ. Ctr., Mich., from 1981. Troop leader Girl Scouts U.S., Saginaw, 1981-84; vol. fund raiser Swan Valley Athletic Assn., Saginaw, 1989--. Mem. AAUP, Mich. Bus. Edn. Assn., Beta Gamma Sigma. Roman Catholic. Avocations: skiing, snowmobiling, fishing, golf, needlecrafts. Home: Saginaw, Mich. Died Mar. 27, 2008.

CRENSHAW, H(ENRY) C(ARLTON), minister; b. Quitman, Miss., Apr. 1, 1929; s. Henry Grady and Eunice (Hudson) C.; m. Bertha Elzine Mangum, Aug. 16, 1949; children: Kareen Crenshaw Brantley, David B., Terry C. Student, Meridian Jr. Coll., Miss., 1952-53, U. Tenn. ext., 1974-75; diploma, So. Sem., Nashville, 1979. Ordained to ministry So. Bapt. Conv., 1969; cert. in pastoral ministries, counseling to deaf. Min. to deaf 1st Bapt. Ch., Meridian, 1969-83; pastor Emmanual Bapt. Ch., Meridian, 1973-83, Grandview Bapt. Mission, Meridian, 1983-85, Cen. Grove Bapt. Ch., Meridian, 1985-90; missionary to deaf, pastor Corinth Bapt. Ch., Kemper County, Miss., 1990-94. Vol. missionary to deaf So. Bapt. Conv., Neshoba County, 1968-94; tchr. sign lang. Choctaw Indian H.S., Neshoba, Choctaw Cen. H.S., 1968, 82. Mem. Ind. Gov.'s Com. on Rehab. of Handicapped, Meridian, 1982-86. Sgt. USMC, 1950-52. Recipient Talking Hand award 1st Bapt. Ch., Meridian, 1973. Mem. Lauderdale Mins. Assn., Kemper County Min. Assn. Home: Meridian, Miss. Died Mar. 3, 2008.

CREUTZ, EDWARD CHESTER, physicist, museum director; b. Beaver Dam, Wis., Jan. 23, 1913; s. Lester Raymond and Grace (Smith) C.; m. Lela Rollefson, Sept. 13, 1937 (dec. Feb. 1972); children: Michael John, Carl Eugene, Ann Jo Carmel Creutz Cosgrove; m. Elisabeth B. Cordle, Oct. 5, 1974. BS, U. Wis., 1936, PhD, 1939. From rsch. assoc. to instr. physics Princeton U., 1939-41; physicist NDRC, 1941-42; physicist metall. lab. U. Chgo., 1942-44; physicist Manhattan Project, Los Alamos, 1944-46; assoc. prof. Carnegie Inst. Tech., Pitts., 1946—48, prof., head dept. physics, dir. Nuc. Rsch. Ctr., 1948—55; dir. John Jay Hopkins Lab. for Pure and Applied Sci., 1955-59; dir. rsch. Gen. Atomic Divsn. Gen. Dynamics Corp., San Diego, 1955-59, v.p. R&D, 1959-67, Gulf Gen. Atomic, San Diego, 1967-70; asst. dir. NSF, Washington, 1970-77, acting dep. dir., 1976-77; dir. Bernice Pauahi Bishop Mus., Honolulu, 1977-84, cons., from 1984. Mem. sea water conversion com. Water resources Ctr., U. Calif.-Berkeley, 1958-68; adv. com. office Sci. Pers. NRC, 1960-63; mem. exec. coun. Argonne Nat. Lab. (1946-51); cons. NSF, 1950-68; scientist-at-large Project Sherwood divsn. rsch. AEC, 1955-56; mem. com. sr. reviewers Dept. Energy, 1972-79, fusion power coordinating com., 1971-79; cons. Oak Ridge Nat. Lab., 1946-58; adv. panel gen. scis. Dept. Def., 1959-63; rsch. adv. com. electrophysics NASA, 1964-71, tech. adv. com., 1971-77; adj. prof. physics and astronomy U. Hawaii, 1977-87; adj. prof. physics U. Calif., San Diego, 1987-1990 Co-editor: Handbuch der Physik, vols. 14, 15; mem. editl. bd. Ann. Rev. Nuclear Sci., 1961-66, 72-75, Handbook of Chemistry and Physics, 1961-71; mem. editorial bd.: Interdisciplinary Science Reviews, London, 1976—1999; editl. adv. com. ann. revs.: Nuclear Sci. and Engrng., 1959-72. Bd. dirs. San Diego Hall Sci. and Planetarium, v.p., 1956-70; v.p. San Diego Industry-Edn. Coun., 1956-65; mem. adv. coun. Dept. Edn. San Diego County. Fellow AAAS, Am. Phys. Soc. (NRC rep. 1956-57), Am. Nuclear Soc.; mem. NAS, Am. Assn. Physics Tchrs., Phys. Soc. Pitts. (pres. 1949), Am. Inst. Physics (dir.-at-large bd. govs. 1965-68) Home: Rancho Santa Fe, Calif. Died June 27, 2009.

CREVELING, CYRUS ROBBINS, chemist, neuroscientist; b. Washington, May 30, 1930; s. Cyrus Robbins and Edith Lois (Hill) C.; m. Cornelia Mills Rector, Sept. 3, 1954; children: Victoria Anne Mariano, Diana Rector Mears. BS, George Washington U., 1954, MS, 1955, PhD, 1962. Chemist Naval Ordinance Lab., Washington, 1953-54; med. tech. Sibley Meml. Hosp., Washington, 1955-57; chemist Nat. Heart Inst., Bethesda, Md., 1957-62; rsch. assoc. Harvard U., Boston, 1963-64; chemist NIH, Bethesda, 1964-98; adj. prof. pharmacology Howard U. Sch. Medicine, Washington, 1967-86; coord. technology dept. NIH, Bethesda, 1989-95; dir. office tech. devel. Nat. Inst. Diabetes and Digestive and Kidney Diseases, 1995-98; prof. pharmacology and toxicology Med. Coll. Va., Richmond, 1985-98. Mem. divsn. rsch. grants NIH, 1966-70; lectr. in field; mem. task force on environ. cancer and heart and lung diseases, Project Group on standardization, measurements and tests, EPA, 1979-82; project adv. bd. screening food additives, FDA, 1979-83; organizer 8th Internat. Catecholamine Symposium, 1995, 9th, 2001; pres.-elect Washington Acad. Sci., 1997-99; counselor Chem. Soc. Washington, 1998—. Contbr. numerous articles to profl. jours., chpts. to books; editor: Transmethylation Series I, 1979, II, 1982, III, 1986; reviewer Analytical Biochemistry, Archives of Biochemistry and Biophysics, Biochem. Jour., Biochem. Pharmacology, Brain Rsch., Drug Metabolism and Disposition, Endocrinology, European Jour. Pharmacology, Life Scis., Jour.Neurosci., Jour. Neurochemistry, Jour. Molecular Pharmacology, Jour. Medicinal Chemistry, Jour. Biol. Chemistry, Jour. Am. Chem. Soc., others. Chmn. adv. bd. Montgomery Libr., Kensington, 1984-86; mem. Bethesda HELP, 1987—; mem. BB Telecasts, Channel 7, Washington, 1982-91. Fellow Am. Diabetes Found., 1955, Mass. Gen. Hosp., 1963-64; recipient Disting. Sci. award Soc. Exptl. Biology and Medicine, 1979, Pub. Health Svc. award NIH, 1991; rsch. grantee Eli Lilly, 1984, E.I. duPont de Nemours & Co., 1985. Fellow World Acad. Arts and Scis.; mem. Am. Fedn. Scientists, Am. Chem. Soc., Am. Soc. Pharmacology and Exptl. Therapeutics, Soc. Exptl. Biology and Medicine (pres. D.C. chpt. 1977-78, councilor 1975—), Washington Acad. Scis. (fellow, bd. mgrs. 1979-80, chmn. biol. scis. panel 1980—, v.p. membership affairs 1991-98, pres. 1998), Found. Advanced Edn. in Scis. (chair scholarship com. 1989—), Catecholamine Club (pres. 1980-81), Soc. Neurosci., Gordon Conf. on Cyclic Nucleotides, Chem. Soc. Washington, Internat. Soc. Study Xenobiotics, Internat. Union Physiol. Scis., Internat. Union Pure and Applied Chemistry (affiliate), Internat. Narcotics Rsch. Conf. 1989—, Internat. Union Physiol. Sci., Assn. Fed. Tech. Transfer Execs., many others. Republican. Methodist. Achievements include discovery and synthesis of 6-hydroxydopamine; discovery and characterization of "synaptoneurosomes"; measurement of sodium channels with batrachotoxin, catechol-O-methyl transferase in prevention of estrogen induced carcinogenesis. Home: Bethesda, Md. Died July 22, 2008.

CRIBBET, JOHN EDWARD, law educator, former university chancellor; b. Findlay, Ill., Feb. 21, 1918; s. Howard H. and Ruth (Wright) C.; m. Betty Jane Smith, Dec. 24, 1941; children: Carol Ann, Pamela Lee. BA, Ill. Wesleyan U., 1940, LLD, 1971; JD, U. Ill., 1947. Bar: Ill. 1947. Pvt. practice in law, Bloomington, Ill., from 1947; prof. law U. Ill. Coll. Law, Urbana, 1947-67, dean., 1967-79, Corman prof. law, 1984-88, prof. emeritus, 1988—2009; chancellor U. Ill., Urbana-Champaign, 1979-84. Author: Cases and Materials on Judicial Remedies, 1954, Cases on Property, 8th edit., 2002; (with others) Principles of the Law of Property, 1975; (with Corwin Johnson), 3d edit., 1989; editor: U. Ill. Law Forum, 1947-55; contbr. articles to profl. jours. Chmn. com. on jud. ethics Il. Supreme Ct.; pres. United Fund Champaign County, (Ill.), 1962-63; trustee Ill. Wesleyan U.; mem. exec. com. Assn. Am. Law Schs., 1973-75, pres., 1979. Served to maj. AUS, 1941-45. Decorated Bronze Star; decorated Croix de Guerre Mem. ABA, Ill. State Bar Assn., Champaign County Bar Assn., Order of Coif Lodges: Rotary. Home: Urbana, Ill. Died May 23, 2009.

CRICHTON, MICHAEL (JOHN MICHAEL CRICHTON), writer, film director; b. Chgo., Oct. 23, 1942; m. Joan Radam, 1965 (div. 1967); m. Kathy St. Johns, Dec. 31, 1978 (div. 1980); m. Suzanne Childs, Oct. 22, 1981 (div.); m. Ann-Marie Martin, 1987 (div. 2002); m. Sherri Alexander, 2005; 1 child, Taylor. AB summa cum laude, Harvard U., 1964, MD, 1969. Postdoctoral fellow Salk Inst., La Jolla, Calif., 1969-70. Vis. writer MIT, Cambridge, 1988; vis. lectr. Cambridge U., 1965; creator, co-exec. prodr. TV show ER, 1994. Author: The Andromeda Strain, 1969, Five Patients, 1970 (Writer of the Year award Assn. American Medical Writers 1970), The Terminal Man, 1972, The Great Train Robbery, 1975 (Edgar award Mystery Writers of America 1979), Eaters of the Dead, 1976, Jasper Johns, 1977, Congo, 1980, Electronic Life, 1983, Sphere, 1987, Travels, 1988, Jurassic Park, 1990, Rising Sun, 1992, Disclosure, 1994, The Lost World, 1995, Airframe, 1996, Timeline, 1999, Prey, 2002, State of Fear, 2004 (Publishers Weekly bestseller list), Next, 2006; (as Jeffrey Hudson) A Case of Need, 1968 (Edgar award Mystery Writers of America 1968); (as John Lange) Odds On, 1966, Scratch One, 1967, Easy Go, 1968, Venom Business, 1969, Zero Cool, 1969, Grave Descend, 1970, Drug of Choice, 1970, Binary, 1972; co-author (with Douglas Crichton) Dealing: Or, The Berkeley to Boston Forty-Brick Lost-Bag Blues, 1971; dir.: (films) Pursuit, 1972, Physical Evidence, 1989: screenwriter, dir. (films) Westworld, 1973, Coma, 1978, The Great Train Robbery, 1979, Looker, 1981, Runaway, 1984; co-screenwriter: (films) Jurassic Park, 1993, Rising Sun, 1993; co-screenwriter, co-writer (films) Twister, 1996; co-prodr. (films) Disclosure, 1994, Sphere, 1998, 13th Warrior, 1999, Timeline, 2003; creator, co-exec., prodr. (TV series) ER, 1994-2008 Mem. bd. overseers Harvard U. Recipient George Foster Peabody award ER, 1995, Emmy Best Dramatic series ER, 1996, Best Long Form Television Script for ER, Writer's Guild Am., 1995, Acad. Motion Pictures Arts and Scis. Tech. Achievement award for pioneering computerized motion picture budgeting and scheduling, 1995, Journalism award, Am. Assn. Petroleum Geologists, 2006; named one of Top 200 Collectors, ARTnews, 2006-08; Henry Russell Shaw traveling fellow, 1964-65. New ankylosaur named in honor Crichtonsaurus bohlini, 2003. Mem. Authors Guild (coun. 1995-2008), Writers Guild Am. West, Dirs. Guild Am., PEN Am. Ctr., Acad. Motion Picture Arts and Scis.; bd. dirs. Internat. Design Conf. at Aspen, 1985-91, Western Behavioral Scis. Inst., La Jolla, 1986-91; Phi Beta Kappa. Avocations: computer games, collecting modern art. Died Nov. 4, 2008.

CRILLEY, JOSEPH JAMES, artist; b. Phila., Jan. 8, 1920; s. James John and Anna (Spoerl) C.; m. Marion Gertrude Haly, Jan. 31, 1948 (div.); children: Pamela, Geraldine, Candace, Joseph; m. Suzanne Corlette, Aug. 16, 1982. Student, Phila. Coll. Art, 1937—41. Art tchr. New Hope (Pa.)-Solebury High Sch., 1955-61; photographer William J. Keller, Inc., Buffalo, 1960-71. Photographer: New York, Island of Islands, 1965; one-man exhibn. Lambertville (N.J., 1976-80, 82-85, Coryell Gallery, Lambertville, 1981, Kiski Sch., Saltsburg, Pa., 1985, Genest Gallery, Lambertville, 1986-90, Phila. Sketch Club, 1990, Gratz Gallery, New Hope; exhibited in group shows at Nat. Acad. of Design, N.Y.C., Phila., Art and Alliance, Phila. Mus. of Art, Michener Art Mus., Doylestown, Pa., Mystic, Conn., others; represented in permanent collections at Kiski Sch., Atlantic Salmon Mus., Cape Breton, N.S., Can., Australia, France, others. Capt. AUS, 1942-45, ETO. Recipient 64 awards including Best of Show, 1983, New Hope Borough Seal, 1984, New Hope Arts Commn. Competition, 3 Gold medals, 1980-95, DaVinci Art Alliance Phila., Award of Excellence, 1991, 29th Mystic Internat., Conn., Anthony Cirino award 1992, Grumbacher Gold medal, 1996, Audubon Artists, N.Y., 15 awards 1962-95 Salmagundi Club, N.Y., 3 awards 1985-95, Phila. Sketch Club, Pa. Mem.: Salmagundi Club, DaVinci Art Alliance., Phila. Sketch Club, Audubon Artists. Avocations: fly fishing, skiing. Died Dec. 4, 2008.

CRIMMINS, CATHY ELIZABETH, writer; b. East Orange, NJ, Aug. 22, 1955; d. David Joseph Crimmins and Elizabeth Ann (Kelly) Lancaster; m. David Ledger, Oct. 5, 1973 (div. 1978); m. Alan Steven Forman, May 31, 1982; 1 child, Kelly Crimmins. BA in English, Rutgers U., 1976; MA in English, U. Pa., 1978. Author: Curse of the Mommy, 1993, When My Parents Were My Age, They Were Old, 1995, The Seven Habits of Highly Defective People, 1996,

Where Is the Mango Princess?, 2000, How the Homosexuals Saved Civilization: The True and Heroic Story of How Gay Men Shaped the Modern World, 2004, A Mother's Nightmare: A Heartrending Journal into Near Fatal Childhood Illness, 2009; co-author: (with Tom Maeder) Newt Gingrich's Bedtime Stories for Orphans, 1995, Tamagotchi Egg: The Unofficial Guide to the Care of Your Egg, 1997, (with Rain Pryor) Jokes My Father Never Taught Me, 2007 Lit. fellow Pa. Coun. on the Arts, 1989. Mem. Am. Soc. Journalists and Authors. Avocations: gardening, singing. Home: Philadelphia, Pa. Died Sept. 4, 2009.

CRIPPS, DEREK J., dermatologist, educator; b. Sept. 17, 1928; s. Edmund James and Susan Ann (Mayell) C.; m. Eileen Wright, Dec. 21, 1963; children: Andrew, Alasdair, Annabelle, Amanda. MB BS, U. London, 1953, MD, 1965; MS, U. Mich., 1961. Diplomate Am. Bd. Dermatology. Resident in dermatology U. Mich., 1959-62; asst. prof. medicine U. Wis., Madison, 1965-68, assoc. prof. medicine, 1968-72, prof., head dermatology, 1972-2000, emeritus prof. medicine, from 2001; pvt. practice Advanced Dermatology, Inc., Madison, from 2006. Cons. for sunscreens FDA, 1974-85; lectr. in field. Author: Royal Navy Ships, Captains, and Stations Vol. I 1773-1972, 2003, Vol. II 1793-1800, 2003, Steel's List of the Royal Navy Ships Commanders and Stations: 1793-1805, 2004; conbr. over 100 articles to profl. jours. Mem. Great Brit. Nat. Swimming Team, 1950-51; surgeon lt. Royal Navy, 1954-58. Recipient Merit award AMA, 1968; grantee EPA, Porphyria in Turkey, 1979-84, NIH, 1965-84, Action spectra and Biochemistry of Photodermatoses. Fellow ACP; mem. Am. Acad. Dermatology (photobiology com., pres. 1976, Exhibit Gold award 1975), Brit. Dermatologic Assn., Ctrl. Soc. for Clin. Rsch., Soc. for Investigative Dermatology, Royal Soc. of Medicine, Wis. Dermatological Soc. (pres. 1976). Avocations: swimming, travel. Home: Madison, Wis. Died Jan. 23, 2009.

CRISP, ROSEMARY BERKEL, community health nurse; b. Chgo., Feb. 22, 1937; d. Albert James and Roslea Catherine (Bayles) Berkel; m. Harry Lee Crisp II, Jan. 16, 1960; children: Cynthia, Catherine, Cheryl, Carole, Harry Lee III, Cara. Diploma, St. Mary's Hosp. Sch. Nursing, 1958; student, John Robert Powers Fashion & Finishing Sch., St. Louis. RN, Ill. Night supr. Marion (Ill.) Meml. Hosp., staff nurse med./surg. unit. Chair So. Ill. Women's Health Conf. Rosemary Berkel Crisp Bldg. named in her honor S.E. Mo. State U.; recipient Quality Svc. award Health Care in So. Ill., 1990. Mem. Nat. League Nursing (bd. govs. N.Y.C. chpt. 1987—). Home: Marion, Ill. Died Dec. 1, 2007.

CRISS, DARLENE JUNE, English language educator; b. Potwin, Kans., Feb. 4, 1931; d. Leroy Eckard and Sarah Caroline (Weber) Edwards; m. James Harold Criss, July 18, 1948; children: Melissa Colleen, Melinda Collette, James Anthony, Michael Jordan, Troy Mitchell, Shayne Lee. BA, Wichita State U., 1976, MEd., 1979. Cert. tchr., Kans. Tchr. English Unit Sch. Dist. 265, Goddard (Kans.) High Sch., from 1976, chmn. dept. lang. arts, from 1979. Lectr. on creativity, 1977—; adviser yearbook, 1976-91, Prism, 1976—. Editor (newsletter) Sunflower Seeds, 1974-84; contbr. poetry to English Jour. Leader Camp Fire Girls, Wichita, dist. program leader, Wichita 1960-65; area chair Am. Heart Assn., Wichita 1958-73; pres. South High PTA, Wichita, 1969-71. Recipient Wakan award Camp Fire Girls, Wichita, 1968; named one of 5 state finalists Tchrs. in Space Program, 1985, Outstanding Young Tchr., Goddard Sch. Dist., 1985. Mem. NEA, Kans. Edn. Assn., Goddard Edn. Assn. (chief negotiator 1981-84), Nat. Assn. Tchrs. English, Kans. Assn. Tchrs. English, Mensa (life, nat. rep. internat. bd. dirs. 1987-95, nat. sec. 1988-91, nat. 1st vice chmn. 1991-95, chmn. 1995, bd. dirs. 1995—, editor nat. bull. 1982-84, editor Isolated M newsletter 1984-95, pub. agt. Internat. Mensa Jour. 1985-91, Disting. Svc. award 1986). Democrat. Presbyterian. Avocations: travel, writing, photography, editing. Home: Wichita, Kans. Died Apr. 23, 2008.

CRISWELL, JOHN, business executive; b. Canton, Ohio, Sept. 5, 1929; Ptnr. Pro-Machine, Canton, Ohio, 1976-85; pres. Gewell Machine & Comco Inc., Canton, Ohio, from 1985. Mem. Canton C. of C., Elks. Avocation: fishing. Died Aug. 7, 2008.

CROCKER, ALBERT RUDOLPH, emergency management consultant; b. Higganum, Conn., May 28, 1914; s. Albert Nathan and Laura (Gundlach) C.; m. Gertrude Elizabeth Jewell Crocker; children: Jewell Ann, James Albert, Jonathan Alan, Jane Alice. BS, NYU, 1936, MS, 1937; postgrad., Inst. Nuclear Studies, 1949-53. Registered profl. engr., Calif. Exptl. test engr. Pratt & Whitney Aircraft Co., East Hartford, Conn., 1938-40; asst. chief engr. Propeller div. Engr. and Research Co., Riverdale, Md., 1941-48; chief exptl. engring, nuclear engring. propulsion aircraft Fairchild, Oak Ridge, Tenn., 1949-51; mgr. mech. devel. aircraft nuclear propulsion Gen. Electric Co., Cin., 1951-53, mgr. test ops. Idaho Falls, 1953-61, program mgr. radiation effects ops. Syracuse, N.Y., 1961-64, mgr. advanced systems engring. Bay St. Louis, Miss., 1964-72, program mgr. internat. NYC, 1972-74. Emergency mgmt. cons.; cons. N.Y. State Atomic Research and Devel. Authority, 1964. Contbr. articles to profl. jours. Vol. cons. disaster Ea. N.Y. Territory ARC, Albany, 1983—; exec. bd. Teton Peaks Council Boy Scouts Am., Idaho Falls, 1954-61; v.p. N.Y. State Assn. Conservation com., Syracuse, 1980-83; exec. com. Onondaga Co. Environ. Mgmt. Council, Syracuse, 1980-82; mem. tng. team N.Y. State Emergency Mgmt. Office, Albany, 1983-87. Recipient Silver Beaver award, Boy Scouts Am., 1961. Fellow AIAA (assoc.) (chmn. instrumentation and communications com. 1960-61); mem. Tau Beta Pi, Sigma Pi Sigma. Avocations: amateur radio, genealogy. Home: Memphis, NY. Died Apr. 14, 2008.

CROCKETT, DAVID GIDEON, lawyer; b. Columbus, Ga., Sept. 29, 1943; s. G.P. and Mable (Brookins) C.; m. Amelia Ann Rood, Apr. 2, 1977; children: Elisabeth Ann, Carolyn Rood, David Gideon Jr. BA in History, Yale U., 1966; JD, NYU, 1969. Bar: Ga., US Dist Ct. (no. and mid. dists.) Ga. 1969, US Ct. Appeals (5th cir.) 1970, US Ct. Appeals (11th cir.), US Supreme Ct. 1977. Assoc. counsel Atlanta Legal Aid Soc., 1969-72; assoc. Nall, Miller & Cadenhead, Atlanta, 1973-77; sole practice Atlanta, from 1978. Contbr. articles to profl. jours. Bd. dirs. Southside Day Care Assn., Atlanta, 1970-84; pres. Neighborhood Justice Ctr. Atlanta, Inc., 1972-92, chmn., 1997, chmn. emeritus, 1997—; mem. Northwest Presbyn. Ch., Atlanta, 1981, elder, 1987-90, 02-05. Recipient Cmty. Svc. award WXIA-TV, 1981, Nat. Jefferson award Am. Inst. Pub. Svc., 1981, Jefferson Lifetime Achievement award Am. Inst. Pub. Svc., 1997. Mem. Ga. Bar Assn., Atlanta Bar Assn. (chmn. indigent program com. 1975-78, chmn. spl. projects com. 1986-87), Am. Judicature Soc., Am. Bankruptcy Inst., Coun. of Personal Fin. Law, Comml. Law League Am., Atlanta Lawyer's Club, Ansley Golf Club, 191 Club, Yale Club Ga., Yale Club NY. Independent. Home: Atlanta, Ga. Died Jan. 21, 2008.

CROCKETT, GEORGE EPHRIAM, secondary school educator; b. Chgo., July 5, 1940; s. Edmund and Ethel Teva (Cowan) C.; m. Ethelene Standifer, Nov. 25, 1968; children: Patricia Johnson, Ronald O'Neal, Michael O'Neal. BS, Ill. State U., 1964; MA in History, Northeastern Ill. U., 1981; postgrad., U. Ill., Champaign. Cert. tchr., Ill. History tchr. John Marshall Metro High Sch., Chgo., from 1964, chmn. social studies dept., from 1992. Tng. specialist John Marshall Metro Evening High Sch., 1966-69, counselor, 1980-83; cons. curriculum guide Chgo. Bd. Edn., 1970. Active Cen. Meml. Bapt. Ch., Chgo., 1957—; mem. com. explorer scouts Boy Scouts Am., 1977-79; mem. Citi-Educators Team Project, DePaul U., 1989. Recipient Tchr. of Yr. award Chgo. Bd. Edn., 1974, Black Educator award Push Found., 1977, Blum-Kovler Ednl. Found. award, 1984, merit award N. Eastern Ill. Alumni, 1985, Midwest Community award, 1990—. Mem. Ill. Coun. Social Studies, Chgo. Social Studies, Chgo. Afro-Am. Tchrs. Assn., Chgo. Area Alliance Black Sch. Educators, NAACP, Nat. Urban League, Midwest Community Coun., Operation Push, So. Christian Leadership Conf. Avocations: reading, sports, public speaking, gardening. Died Aug. 15, 2008.

CROMWELL, JUDY KAY, social studies educator; b. Hoisington, Kans., Apr. 26, 1944; d. Myrl and Lucy (Miller) C. BS, Emporia State U., 1966, MS, 1968. Cert. secondary tchr. social studies and lang. arts, Kans. Tchr. social studies Dist. 501, Topeka, from 1966. Author: T.H.S. Scrapbook; co-author: (state history) Kansas History 7-8, 1994; contbr. articles to hist. jours. Schedule coord. John Carlin Congress Campaign, Topeka, 1994. Named Outstanding Kans. Tchr. of Am. History, DAR, 1987. Mem. Nat. Coun. for Social Studies, Kans. Coun. for Social Studies (bd. dirs. 1980-94), Silver Dollar Club (bd. dirs. 1992-94), PDK. Avocations: local history, writing, organizing tour groups for state history locations. Home: Topeka, Kans. Died Oct. 6, 2007.

CRONE, ANNA LISA, Russian literature educator; b. Bklyn., June 9, 1946; d. James Clarence Jr. and Ethel Margaret (Donnelly) C.; m. Vladimir Donchik, July 12, 1982; 1 child, Liliana Donchik. BA in Russian Lit., Goucher Coll., 1967; MA in Russian Lang. and Lit., Harvard U., 1969, PhD in Russian Lang. and Lit., 1975; LHD (hon.), Goucher Coll., 1988, DHC (hon.), 1998. From instr. to asst. prof. Russian and Russian lit. Goucher Coll. Johns Hopkins U., Balt., 1971—74; tchr., translator Associated Jewish Charities, Balt., 1974—75; rschr. Radcliffe Inst., Harvard U., Cambridge, Mass., 1975—76; from asst. prof. to prof. Slavic languages & literature U. Chgo., 1977—2009. Hon. vis. fellow Slavonic Inst. U. London, 1998-2009; internat. lectr. on Russian topics. Author: (scholarly study) Rozanov and the End of Literature, 1978; author: The Daring of Derzhavin, 2001, My Petersburg/Myself, 2004, Christianizing Freud: Eros, Sublimination and Creativity in Modern Russian Religious Thought, 2008; editor, contbr.: New Studies in Russian Language and Literature, 1986; mem. editl. bd. Russian Lang. Jour., Ency. of Russian Literature, Ency. of the Essay; contbr. articles to profl. jours. Mem. Univ. Senate U. Chgo., 1992-95. Nat. Def. Fgn. Lang. fellow, 1967-71, Woodrow Wilson fellow, 1967: recipient Quantrell Tchr. of Yr. award, U. Chgo., 1985, Best Grad. Tchr.award, 2000, Barbara Heldt prize for scholarship and mentoring in Slavic studies, 2004, Main Nat. Lifetime Achiev. award for woman in the Slavic field. Mem. Am. Assn. Tchrs. of Slavic and East European Langs. (Best Grad. Prof. award 2000), Am. Assn. Advancement of Slavic Studies, Stochastic Soc. (pres. 1991-92, 96-97), Phi Beta Kappa. Democrat. Avocations: music, travel, intellectual history, history of culture, amateur acting. Home: Chicago, Ill. Died June 19, 2009.

CRONER, JOHN ALTON, journalist; b. Soldier, Idaho, Feb. 10, 1916; s. Frank and Louella Croner; m. Jennie Frederickson, May 20, 1939 (div. June 1977); children: Dennis, Charles, John, Carol, Kerry; m. June Pitkin Bates, Mar. 4, 1978. Columnist, feature writer Ontario (Oreg.) Argus Observer, from 1973. Author: The Basque and the Boy, 1975; contbr. 20 Years in the Making, 1976. With USN, 1934-38. Democrat. Nazarene. Avocations: photography, fly tying, gunsmithing. Home: Fruitland, Idaho. Died Aug. 31, 2007.

CRONKITE, WALTER (WALTER LELAND CRONKITE JR.), retired broadcast journalist; b. St. Joseph, Mo., Nov. 4, 1916; s. Walter Leland and Helen Lena (Fritsche) Cronkite; m. Mary Elizabeth Maxwell, Mar. 30, 1940 (dec. Mar. 15, 2005); children: Nancy Elizabeth, Mary Kathleen, Walter Leland III. Student, U. Tex., Austin; LLD (hon.), Rollins Coll., 1966, Bucknell U., Syracuse U.; LHD (hon.), Ohio State U.; degree (hon.), Am. Internat. Coll., Harvard U. News writer, editor Scripps-Howard, also UP, Houston, Kansas City, Dallas, Austin, El Paso; UP war corr., 1942—45; fgn. corr., reopening burs. in Amsterdam, Brussels, chief corr. Nuremberg war crimes trials, bur. mgr., Moscow, 1946—48; lectr., mag. contbr., 1948—49; CBS-News corr., 1950—81; spl. corr. CBS, CNN, NPR, from 1981; mng. editor CBS Evening News with Walter Cronkite, 1962—81. Chmn. The Cronkite Ward Co., from 1993; host spl. Universe, CBS, The Holocaust: In Memory of Millions, The Discovery Channel, 1993; anchor for TV news spls. Vietnam: A War That is Finished, 1975, In Celebration of US, 1976, Our Happiest Birthday, 1977, The President in China, 1975, Solzhenitsyn: 1984 Revisited. Author: Eye on the World, 1971, The Challenges of Change, 1971, A Reporter's Life, 1996, Around America, 2002; co-author: South by Southeast, North by Northeast, Westwind; prodr.(host): The e Reports (12 episode series for Discovery Channel), 1994—96, Cronkite Remembers (8 part series for CBS and Discovery Channel), 1996. Recipient Cable Ace award for best program interviewer, 1993, Peabody award, 1962, 1981, Emmy awards, William A. White award for journalistic merit, 1969, George Polke Journalism award, 1971, Gold medal, Internat. Radio and TV Soc., 1974, Alfred I. DuPont-Columbia U. award in broadcast journalism, 1978, 1981, Presdl. medal of Freedom, 1981. Mem.: Assn. Radio News Analysts, Acad. Arts and Scis. (pres. nat. acad. N.Y. chpt. 1959, Gov.'s award 1979), Bohemian Club, N.Y. Yacht Club, Nat. Press Club, Overseas Press Club, Explorers Club, Chi Phi. Avocation: sailing. Died July 17, 2009.

CROOK, WENDY P., management consultant, educator; b. Trenton, NJ, May 28, 1952; B. Psychology, Trenton State Coll., 1979; MSW, Rutgers U., 1986, PhD, 1996. Rsch. asst. Princeton (N.J.) U., 1977-79; shelter mgr. Womanspace, Inc., Trenton, 1980-82; asst. exec. dir. Mercer unit N.J. Assn. Retarded Citizens, Inc., Trenton, 1982-87; acting exec. dir. United Cerebral Palsy Assns. of N.J., Inc., Trenton, 1988; exec. dir. United Cerebral Palsy of Mercer County, Inc., Hamilton, N.J., 1987-93; mgmt. cons. DWC Enterprises, from 1993. Adj. prof. Columbia U., N.Y.C., 1993-96, Temple U., Phila., 1993-96, Rutgers U., 1993-96, Monmouth Coll., 1993-96, Ocean County Coll., 1993-96; field cons. Sch. Social Work, Rutgers U., 1993-96, rsch. asst., 1993-96; asst. prof. Fla. State U., Tallahassee, 1996—. Author: (manual) Accessary and ECHO Housing, 1994. Team leader Stand Down for Homeless Vets., 1994; chmn. Mercer County Disabilities Coalition, 1991-93; peer mentor UCPA Regional Adminstrs. Coun., chmn. N.E. region, 1988-93; mem. contracting task force N.J. Dept. Human Svcs., 1992-93; mem. steering com., vice chmn. Mercer County Human Svcs. Coalition, 1986-89; mem. N.J. Ctrl. Region Human Rights Com., 1986-88; mem. United Way Spkrs. Bur., mem. allocations com., Princeton area, Ocean County, Delaware Valley, 1985-93; mem. Mayor Holland's Task Force on Emergency Housing, Trenton, 1981; steering com. Mercer County Food Coalition, 1980-81; pres. bd. dirs., chmn. pers. com. Womanspace, Inc., 1983-84; bd. pres. Tallahassee Coalition for the Homeless, 1998-99. Mem. NASW (conf. chmn., co-chair Ctr. for Social Policy Campaign), N.J. Assn. Cmty. Providers (bd. trustees 1983-93, past v.p.). Avocations: sailing, scuba diving, travel. Home: Tallahassee, Fla. Died Oct. 21, 2007.

CROSSEN, REV. JOHN F., writer, researcher; b. South Laguna, Calif., Feb. 17, 1960; PhD, Ind. U., Bloomington, Indiana, 2003; MDiv, St. Thomas Seminary, Denver, Colorado, 1990; BA, Ariz. State U., Tempe, Arizona, 1982. Exec. dir. Force Internat., Inc., Scottsdale, Ariz., from 1980; chaplain Ft. Logan Mental Health Ctr., Denver, 1985—88; educator Yavapai Coll., Prescott, Ariz., 1991—92, Ind. U., Bloomington, Ind., 1992—97, Mansfield U., Mansfield, Pa., 1999—2001, Regis U., Denver, 2001—02. Contbr. articles to profl. jours. Fellow Mellon Fellowship, St. Louis U., 1998; scholar Sigma Delta Pi, Ariz. State U., 1982, Alpha Mu Gamma, 1982. Mem.: Ibero-American Soc. for 18th Century Studies, MLA. Avocations: music, autograph collecting. Died Sept. 12, 2006.

CROW, TRAMMELL, retired real estate company executive; b. Dallas, June 11, 1914; m. Margaret Doggett, 1942; children: Robert, Howard, Harlen, Trammell, Lucy. Attended, So. Methodist U. Chmn. bd. Trammell Crow Co., Dallas. Bd. dirs. Jones-Blair Co., Inc.; founder The Trammell & Margaret Crow Collection of Asian Art Served in USN. Named to The Woodrow Wilson High School Hall of Fame, 1978, The US Bus. Hall of Fame, 1987. Died Jan. 14, 2009.

CROWE, BRUCE ALAN, art educator; b. Montgomery, Ala., Nov. 3, 1947; s. Patrick Oscar and Marian Jane (Greatorex) C.; m. Karen Sue Ward, May 20, 1977; 1 child, Allyson Elizabeth. BS in Edn., U. Ala., 1971, MA, 1972,

MFA, 1974; EdD, Miss. State U., 1989. Cert. tchr., Ala. Asst. prof. U. Ala., Tuscaloosa, 1972-89; art dept. head N.W. Ala. Community Coll., Phil Campbell, Ala., from 1990. Workshop dir. Arts Coun. of Tuscaloosa, 1990; exec. bd. mem. Ala. Art Edn. Assn., Ala., 1976-87. Contbr. articles to profl. jours. Art coord. Very Spl. Arts Festival, Starkville, Miss., 1988; juror Scholastic Art Competition, Tuscaloosa, 1990; assoc. counselor Kappa Delta Pi, U. Ala., 1980-87. Named Outstanding Art Educator, Art Edn. Assn., 1991, grant dir. U.S.A./Japan Student Art Exch., 1987, 93. Mem. Nat. Art Edn. Assn., S.E. Coll. Art Conf., Watercolor Soc. of Ala. (pres. 1991-92, catalog editor 1988), Seminar for Rsch. in Art Edn., Mid-South Ednl. Rsch. Assn. Home: Russellville, Ala. Died June 22, 2008.

CROWE, CLIFFORD HENRY, JR., health facility administrator; b. Chgo., Mar. 12, 1921; s. Clifford Henry and Norine (Wohlenberg) C.; m. Ina Bryson, June 11, 1965; 1 child, Clifford Henry III. BS in Commerce, Iowa State U., 1942; MBA, Harvard U., 1947. Trainee Gen. Electric Co., 1947-49; with J.C. Penney Co., from 1949, store mgr. Akron, Ohio, 1957-61, Valley Stream, N.Y., 1961-64, Kokomo, Ind., 1964-84; corp. coord. Howard Community Hosp., Kokomo, from 1991. Pres. Grisson AFB Community Coun., Peru, Ind., 1974, Howard County Conv. and Visitors Commn., 1982—; mem. Mayor's Community Com. on Drug Abuse, 1974; chmn. adv. bd. Kokomo Ctr. Distbv. Edn. Com.; bd. dirs. Kokomo YMCA, Credit Bur. Kokomo Ind. Retail coun., Howard Community Hosp. Found., 1975—, pres. 1978; mem. program adv. com. Ind. U., Kokomo. Lt. col. USAAF, 1942-45. Decorated Bronze Star; Croix de Guerre (France). Mem. Ind. C. of C., Kokomo Area C. of C. (pres. 1971), Elks, Rotary (pres. 1976, dir. 1974-76), Kokomo Country Club (bd. dirs.). Home: Kokomo, Ind. Died Dec. 22, 2007.

CROWLEY, RICHARD SUMNER, science writer; b. Madison, Wis., Aug. 11, 1952; s. James William and Katharine Elizabeth Crowley; m. Linda Page, Jan. 10, 1987; children: Elissa Kathleen, Lucas James. BS, U. Wis., Madison, 1974. Sr. sci. writer Covance, Madison, Wis., from 1986. Editor: (periodical) Evolutions, Covance Food Science Newsletter; contbr. columns in newspapers featured columns, chapters to books, articles to profl. jours. Mem.: Soc. for Tech. Comm., Nat. Assn. of Sci. Writers. Home: Madison, Wis. Died Aug. 22, 2008.

CROZIER, JOHN HUNTINGTON, patent attorney; b. Waukegan, Ill., Nov. 10, 1935; s. Ronald Gilpin and Ruth Minerva (Huntington) C.; m. Eleanor Jean Wood, Aug. 20, 1967; 1 child, Julia Lynn; children from previous marriage: Susan Ruth, Jean Louise, Jacqueline Ann, Anne Huntington. BS in Chem. Engring., Northwestern U., 1959; JD, U. Akron, 1974. Bar: Conn. 1975, U.S. Dist. Ct. Conn. 1981, U.S. Patent Office 1981; registered profl. engr., Ohio. Project engr. Union Carbide Corp., Charleston, W.Va., 1959-66; engring. supr. Mobay Chem Co., New Martinsville, W.Va., 1966-68; project mgr., engr. Gen. Tire and Rubber Co., Akron, Ohio, 1968-74; corp. counsel Crawford and Russell, Stamford, Conn., 1974-80; gen. counsel, sec. The Superior Electric Co., Bristol, Conn., 1980-87; pvt. practice Trumbull, from 1987. Active various community orgs. Mem. ABA, Conn. Bar Assn., Am. Arbitration Assn. (comml. arbitrator). Avocations: sailing, skiing. Died Feb. 12, 2008.

CRYOR, JEAN B., retired state legislator; b. Landsdowne, Pa., Dec. 13, 1938; 3 children. Grad., U. Pa.; MBA, Loyola Coll., 1979. Mem. Dist. 15 Md. House of Delgates, 1995—2007; mem. Md. House Ways & Mean Com., 1995—2005, Md. House Rules & Nominations Com., 2004—07, Md. House Legis. Policy Com., 2005—07, Md. House Spl. Com. on State Employees Rights & Protections, 2005—07, Md. House House Facilities Com., 2005—07. Co-founder TACKLE, 1996; mem. steering com. Md. House Republican Caucus, 1997—2007; delegate Republican Party Nat. Convention, 2000; mem. Montgomery County Planning Bd., 2007—09. Recipient Prize for Investigative Journalism, Md. Soc. Profl. Journalists, 1993, Award for Building the Bridge to Ednl. Excellence, Md. State Bd. Edn., 2002, Thornton Commn. award, 2002, Woman of Achievement award, Suburban Md. Bus. & Profl. Women Assn., 2005, Lifetime Svc. award, Potomac C. of C., 2006; named Legislator of the Yr., Md. Retailers Assn., 2000, Childhood Brain Tumor Found., 2002, Citizen of the Yr., Almanac Newspapers, Businessperson of the Yr., Md. Bus. for Responsive Govt., Hero of the Taxpayer, Md. Taxpayers Assn.; named one of Maryland's Top 100 Women, The Daily Record, 2003, 2006. Mem.: Woman Legislators Md. (mem. exec. bd. 2006—07, pres. elect 2003—04, pres. 2004—05). Republican. Home: Potomac, Md. Died Nov. 3, 2009.

CUBEÑAS, JOSÉ ANTONIO, social worker, consultant; b. Manzanillo, Oriente, Cuba, Sept. 27, 1925; came to U.S., 1961; s. José Amador Cubeñas and Maximina Peluzzo; m. Elsie Mujica, Sept. 22, 1979. LLD, U. Havana, 1950; MA in Spanish, St. John's U., 1975. Practice law, Cuba, 1950-60; co-founder Fundación Cultura Hispánica, NYC, from 1980. Author: Rubén Darío: Restaurador de la conciencia de armonía del mundo, 1975, Spanish and Hispanic Presence in Florida - The Oliveros House, 1979, Pandemocracia: La solución política de Iberoamérica?, 1991; contbr. articles to profl. and polit. jours. Cand. N.Y. State Assembly, 1994; mayor City of Manzanillo, Cuba 1959; co-founder Hispanic sect. of N.Y. State Rep. Party, 1980. Mem. Acad. Norteamericana de la Lengua Expañola, Círculo de Escritores y Poetas Iberoamericanos de N.Y. Republican. Roman Catholic. Avocations: soccer, history, literature. Home: New York, NY. Died Feb. 14, 2008.

CULLITAN, REGINALD KENNETH, lawyer; b. El Paso, Tex., Oct. 3, 1943; s. Kenneth Robert and Evelyn Emily (Boyd) Cullitan; m. Emelita Grajo. AA, Spokane Falls Community Coll., Spokane, Wash., 1965, Assoc. in Applied Sci., 1979; BA, Eastern Wash. State U., Cheney, 1967; JD, Gonzaga U., 1982. Bar: Wash. 1982. Staff atty. U.S. Dist. Ct. (ea. dist.) Wash., Spokane, from 1982. Exec. editor Gonzaga Law Rev., 1981-82. Dem. precinct committeman, Spokane, 1966-67; polit. advisor Grass Roots Citizens Com., Spokane, 1964-70. Mem. ABA, Spokane County Bar Assn., Phi Delta Phi. Home: Spokane, Wash. Died Dec. 11, 2007.

CULP, PAULA NEWELL, symphony musician; b. Ft. Smith, Ark., Apr. 9, 1941; MusB, Oberlin Coll., 1963; MusM, Ind. U., 1965. Tympanist Met. Opera Nat. Co., NYC, 1965-67; prin. percussionist Indpls. Symphony, 1967-68; percussion Minn. Orch., Mpls., from 1968. Staff U. Minn., 1969—. Author: (poetry) A Thousand Portholes, 1973. Mem. Percussive Arts Soc. Home: Minneapolis, Minn. Died Sept. 18, 2007.

CUMMINGS, PATRICK HENRY, retired manufacturing executive; b. Cleve., May 3, 1941; s. Henry Patrick and Ruth (Farrell) C.; m. Sharon Lynn Slama; children: Dawn, Kelly, Patrick. BS in Indsl. Engring., Kettering U., 1964. Prodn. analyst Euclid (Ohio) Divsn. Gen. Motors Corp., 1964-65, methods engr. Euclid Divsn. Hudson, Ohio, 1965-68, supr. parts, methods and warehouse Terex divsn., 1968-71, gen. supr., prodn. planning Terex divsn., 1972; parts mgr. Lorain divsn. Koehring Co., Chattanooga, 1973-74, material control mgr. Lorain divsn., 1974-77; materials mgr. Robbins divsn. Joy Mfg. Co., Birmingham, Ala., 1977-80; materials mgr. Unit Rig and Equipment Co., Tulsa, 1980-85; data processing mgr. Kendavis Holding Co., Ft. Worth, 1985-87; info. svcs. mgr. Parker Hannifin, Ft. Worth, 1987-89, materials mgr. Stratoflex Aerospace & Mil. Connectors divsn., 1990-99; ret., 1999. Republican. Roman Catholic. Died Sept. 29, 2008.

CUNNINGHAM, ANTHONY WILLARD, lawyer; b. Lakeland, Fla., Nov. 10, 1931; s. Elmo and Anna Catherine Cunningham; m. Kathleen, 1960 (div. 1974); children: Matthew, Tracy, Melisse, Megan, Joshua, Alexandra; m. Robin Richards, Nov. 22, 1980 (div. 2006). LLB, U. Fla., 1962. Bar: Fla. 1963, U.S. Dist. Ct. (mid. dist.) Fla. 1964, U.S. Ct. Appeals (5th cir.) 1964, U.S. Supreme Ct. 1975. Assoc. Fishback, Davis, Dominick & Troutman, Orlando, Fla., 1962-64, Nichols, Gaither, Beckham, Colson, Spence & Hicks, Miami, Fla., 1964-65, Orlando and Tampa, Fla., 1965-67; prin. Wagner, Cunningham, Vaughan & McLaughlin, P.A., Tampa, 1967-92, Cunningham Law Group, P.A., Tampa, from 1992. 1st lt. fighter pilot USAF, 1951—56. Mem. ATLA (bd. govs. 1979—, 90, 95), Trial Lawyers Pub. Justice (bd. dirs. 1986—, pres. elect 1990-91, pres. 1991-92), Acad. Fla. Trial Lawyers (bd. dirs., past pres. 1971—). Democrat. Avocations: boating, fishing, skiing. Home: Tampa, Fla. Deceased.

CUNNINGHAM, MERCE PHILIP, performing company artistic director, dancer; b. Centralia, Wash., Apr. 16, 1919; Student, Cornish Sch.; PhD (hon.), U. Ill.; DFA (hon.), Wesleyan U., 1995. Tchr. Sch. Am. Ballet, 1948—51; own dance co., 1953—2009; propr. own dance sch. NYC, 1959—2009. Dancer with company on world tour, 1964, S.Am. tour, 1968, numerous tours including US, Europe, Far East, Australia, South Am., others, choreographer The Seasons, 1947, Sixteen Dances for Soloist and Company of Three, 1951, Septet, 1953, Minutiae, 1954, Suite for Five, 1956, Nocturnes, 1956, Rune, 1959, Crises, 1960, Aeon, 1961, Story, 1963, Winterbranch, 1964, Variations V, 1965, How to Pass, Kick, Fall and Run, 1965, Place, 1966, Canfield, 1969, Tread, 1970, Second Hand, 1970, Signals, 1970, Landrover, 1972, Changing Steps, 1975, Solo, 1975, Un Jour ou Deux, 1973, Sounddance, 1975, Rebus, 1975, Torse, 1976, Squaregame, 1976, Travelogue, 1977, Inlets, 1977, Fractions, 1977, Exchange, 1978, Locale, 1979, Duets, 1980, Channels/Inserts, 1981, Trails, 1982, Quartet, 1982, Coast Zone, 1983, Roaratorio, 1983, Pictures, 1984, Doubles, 1984, Phrases, 1984, Native Green, 1985, Arcade, 1985, Points in Space, 1986, Fabrications, 1987, Shards, 1987, Five Stone Wind, 1988, Cargo X, 1989, August Pace, 1989, Polarity, 1990, Neighbors, 1991, Trackers, 1991, Beach Birds, 1991, Loosestrife, 1991, Change of Address, 1992, Touchbase, 1992, Enter, 1992, Doubletoss, 1993, CRWDSPCR, 1993, Ocean, 1994, Ground Level Overlay, 1995, Windows, 1995, Rondo, 1996, Installations, 1996, Scenario, 1997, Pond Way, 1998, BIPED, 1999, Interscape, 2000, Way Station, 2001, Loose Time, 2002, Fluid Canvas, 2002, Split Sides, 2003, Views on Stage, 2004, eyespace, 2006—07, Xover, 2007. Decorated comdr. Order of Arts and Letters Legion of Honor (France); recipient Gold medal, Internat. Festival Dance, 1966, Grand prix, Belgrade Internat. Theatre Festival, 1972, Creative Arts award, Brandeis U., 1973, Capezio award, 1977, Samuel H. Scripps/Am. Dance Festival award, 1982, Mayor's award of honor for arts and culture, NYC, 1983, Kennedy Ctr. honors, 1985, Laurence Olivier award, 1985, Meadows award for Excellence in Arts, So. Meth. U., 1987, Nat. Medal of Arts, 1990, Digital Dance Premier award, 1990, Wexner prize, Wexner Ctr. for Arts, Columbus, Ohio, 1993, Golden Lion award, Venice Biennale, 1995, Nellie Cornish Arts Achievement award, Cornish Coll. of Arts, Seattle, 1996, Medal of Distinction, Barnard Coll., 1997, Grand Prix, SACD, France, 1997, Belknap award in Humanities, Princeton U., 1998, Key to City, Montpellier, France, 1999, Established Artists award, Bagley Wright Fund, Seattle, 1998, Isadora Duncan award for Lifetime Achievement in Dance, Nat. Dance Week, San Francisco, 1999, Premio Tani, Rome, 1999, Handel Medallion, NYC, 1999, Nijinsky Spl. prize, Monaco, 2000, Dorothy and Lillian Gish prize, 2000, Praemium Imperiale award (Theatre/Film), Japan Art Assn., 2005, Nelson A. Rockefeller award, 2007, Skowhegan Medal for Performance, Skowhegan Sch Painting & Sculpture, 2009; MacArthur Found. fellow, 1985. Mem.: Am. Acad. and Inst. Arts and Letters (hon.). Died July 26, 2009.

CURRY, EDWARD THOMAS, JR., tire dealership executive; b. Phila., May 23, 1926; s. Edward Thomas and Ethel Vincent (Reeve) C.; m. Kathleen Wiegand, June 1950 (div. July 1971); children: Reeve, Michael; m. Violet O'Daniel, July 16, 1971; children: Rosalind, Ann, Edgar, Richard. BSBA, Rutgers U., 1950. With mktg. Standard Oil Indiana, Madison, Wis., 1951-52, Sun Oil Co., Camden, N.J., 1952-55, Atlantic Richfield, Charlotte, N.C., 1956-64; pres. Hub City Oil Co., Inc., Hickory, N.C., 1964-69, Ind. Enterprises, Inc., Greensboro, N.C., from 1970. Arbitrator Am. Arbitration Assn., Greensboro, 1990—, Ford Consumers Appeal Bd., 1987-90; bd. arbitrators Nat. Assn. Security Dealers, 1991—; panel arbitrators N.Y. Stock Exch., 1991—. Bd. dirs. Adult Ctr. for Enrichment, 1994—. Mem. BBB Cen. N.C. (Arbitrator of Yr. 1991), Mediation Svc. of Guilford County (bd. chmn. 1986-89, 94—, cert. N.C. mediator mediated settlement conf. pilot program 1994), Forest Oaks Country Club. Republican. Presbyterian. Home: Greensboro, NC. Died June 16, 2008.

CURTIN, PHILIP DE ARMOND, retired history professor; b. Phila., May 22, 1922; s. Ellsworth F. and Margaretta (Cope) C.; m. Anne Gilbert, 1957; children: Steven D., Charles G., Christopher C. BA, Swarthmore Coll., 1948; MA, Harvard U., 1949, PhD, 1953; LHD (hon.), Swarthmore Coll., 1987. Instr. then asst. prof. Swarthmore Coll., 1953-56; mem. faculty U. Wis., Madison, 1956-75, prof. history, from 1961, M.J. Herskovits prof. history and African studies, 1970-75, chmn. program comparative tropical history, 1959-75, chmn. African studies program, 1961-64, chmn. dept. African langs. and lit., 1963-66; prof. history Johns Hopkins U., Balt., 1975—98, Herbert Baxter Adams prof., 1982—98. Author: Two Jamaicas, 1955, The Image of Africa: British Ideas and Actions, 1780-1850, 1964, (with Michael B. Petrovich) The Human Achievement, 1967, Africa Remembered, 1967, The Atlantic Slave Trade: A Census, 1969, (with Paul Bohannan) Africa and the Africans, 4th edit., 1995, Imperialism, 1971, Africa and the West, 1972, Economic Change in Pre-Colonial Africa, 1975, (with S. Feierman, J. Vansina and L. Thompson) African History, 2d edit., 1995, Cross-Cultural Trade in World History, 1984, Death by Migration: Europe's Encounter With the Tropical World in the 19th Century, 1989, The Rise and Fall of the Plantation Complex: Essays in Atlantic History, 1990, On the Fringes of History, 2005 Served with U.S. Mcht. Marine, 1943-46. Ford fellow, 1958-59, Guggenheim fellow, 1966, 80, MacArthur fellow, 1983-88. Mem. Am. Philsophical Soc., African Studies Assn. (pres. 1960, past dir.), Am. Hist. Assn. (council 1967-70, pres. 1983), Social Sci. Research Council (dir. 1967-73), Internat. Congress Africanists (v.p. 1969-73), Phi Beta Kappa. Home: Kennett Square, Pa. Died June 4, 2009.

CURTIS, RONALD SANGER, research scientist, computer science educator; b. Claremont, NH, Nov. 1, 1950; s. Harding Sanger and Dorothy May (Therrian) C. BA, Keene State Coll., NH, 1972; MS, U. N.H., Durham, 1974; PhD, SUNY, Buffalo, 1995. Sci. tchr. Windsor (Vt.) H.S., 1974-76; rsch./teaching asst. SUNY Buffalo, 1976-79; program dir. Computer Sci. Canisius Coll., Buffalo, N.Y., 1979-80; chair Computer Sci., 1980-83; rsch. asst. Stony Brook, N.Y., 1983-84; faculty Computer Sci. Canisius Coll., Buffalo, N.Y., 1984-89; vis. faculty Computer Sci. SUNY Buffalo, 1989-91; rsch. scientist, project mgr. CEDAR/SUNY Buffalo, 1991-95; mem. faculty computer sci. William Paterson U., Wayne, N.J., from 1995. Author: Multicomputers and Applications, 1982; contbr. papers in field to profl. jours. Mem. IEEE, Assn. Computing Machinery, Kappa Delta Phi. Home: Claremont, NH. Died Oct. 15, 2007.

CURTRIGHT, GLADYS STEELE, real estate broker; b. Evansville, Wis., May 13, 1904; Robert L. and Mamie L. (Haley) Steele; m. Walter L. Curtright, Dec. 22, 1923; children— Lois Rae Curtright Henderson, Jay B. Student, Rockford (Ill.) Coll., Beloit (Wis.) Coll. Cosmotologist, Cin., 1922—28; agt. Prudential Ins. Co., Beloit, Wis., 1930—33, various acctg. positions, 1942—50; owner retail gift shop and real estate office Beloit, Wis., 1950—64; broker, salesman J.R. Schuster Agy., Beloit, Wis., 1964—72, Exec. Services, Sanibel, Fla., 1974—78; v.p., broker Bluebill Properties, Inc., Sanibel Island, from 1978. Past pres. Beloit Bd. Realtors. Mem. Nat. Assn. Relators, Fla. Assn. Realtors, Ft. Myers Bd. Realtors, Naples Area Bd. Realtors. Methodist. Home: Sanibel, Fla. Died Apr. 2, 1989.

CUTLER, CHARLES RUSSELL, lawyer; b. Macomb, Ill., July 15, 1924; s. Russell Lowell and Amy (Short) Cutler; m. Margaret Hughes, Dec. 3, 1949; children: Thomas, Alan, Patricia, Roger. BEE, Calif. Inst. Tech., 1945; JD (hon.), George Washington U., 1949. Bar: DC 1949, US Ct. Appeals (DC cir.) 1949, Md. 1955, US Supreme Ct. 1955,

US Ct. Appeals (4th cir.) 1975, US Ct. Appeals (2d cir.) 1977. Assoc. editor George Washington U. Law Review, 1949; assoc. Kirkland & Ellis LLP, Washington, 1949—57, ptnr., 1957—87, counsel, 1988—92. Lectr. on develop. computer comm. law, 1965—80; bd. dir. Unitarian-Universalist Housing Found., 1978—86. Contbr. articles papers ato profl. lit. Fellow Fellow Am. Bar Found. Mem.: George Washington U. Law Alumni Assn., Calif. Tech. Inst. Alumni Assn., Am. Arbitration Assn., Fed. Comm. Bar Assn., Computer Law Assn., DC Bar (gen. counsel to bd. governors 1981—83), Bar Assn. DC, Md. State Bar Assn., ABA, Cosmos (Washington). Home: Bethesda, Md. Died July 1, 2009.

CUTTLER, CHARLES DAVID, art historian, educator; b. Cleve., Ohio, Apr. 8, 1913; s. Morris Joseph and Nettie (Wolff) Cuttler; m. Betty Iverson Monroe, Jan. 4, 1989; 1 child, Judith Ann. BFA, Ohio State, 1935, MA, 1937; PhD, NYU, 1952. Asst. instr. Ohio State U., Columbus, Ohio, 1935—37; tchr. art hist. U. Colo., Boulder, Colo., 1938; asst. prof. Mich. State U., E. Lansing, Mich., 1947—57; assoc. to prof. U. Iowa, Iowa City, 1957—83; ret., 1983. Eng., designer Allen Kauderer Engring., Detroit, 1940—47. Mem.: Midwest Art History Soc. (co-founder, first pres.). Home: Iowa City, Iowa. Died Jan. 16, 2008.

CYGAN, ROBERT ADAM, medical products company executive, consultant; b. Chgo., June 5, 1932; s. Adam S. and Estelle D. (Ryan) C.; m. Helen Mae Hall, June 5, 1971. BS in Bus., U. Ill., 1953. Regional mgr. Internat. Register Co., Chgo., 1957-68; v.p. Amalgamated Brush Co., Chgo., 1968-72; dir. sales Portion Pac Corp., Chgo., 1972-77; pres. Reliance Med., Inc., Palatine, Ill., from 1977, also bd. dirs. Cons. Wheaton (Ill.) Brace Co., 1989—, Tropai Condominiums, Palatine, 1979—. Contbr. articles to profl. jours. Lt. comdr. USN, 1953-56, Korea. Recipient Best Speaker award Am. Health Congress, 1975, Mgmt. Contbns. award Cen. Internat. Hosp. Biennial, 1973. Mem. Am. Mktg. Assn., Am. Mgmt. Assn., Ill. Businessmen's Assn., Assn. for Practioners in Infection Control. Avocations: antique watches, clocks, fishing, running. Home: Palatine, Ill. Died Mar. 5, 2008.

CZYZAK, STANLEY JOACHIM, astronomy educator, researcher; b. Cleve., Aug. 21, 1916; s. John J. and Sophia Jane (Jezierski) Czyzak; m. Ruth Louise Long, Sept. 10, 1942; children: Stanley Robert, James William, Patricia Ann, David Martin. BS in Chem. Engring., Cleve. State U., 1935, BS in Civil Engring., 1936; MS in Chemistry, John Carroll U., 1939; DSc in Physics and Math., U. Cin., 1948. Registered profl. engr., Ohio. Asst. to chief metallurgist Forest City Foundry, Cleve., 1935-36; asst. rsch. metallurgist Aluminum Co. of Am., Cleve., 1936-37; rsch. engr. Una Welding, Inc., Cleve., 1937-41; commd. 1st lt. USAF, 1941, advanced through grades to brig. gen., 1966, ret., 1976; Stephen H. Wilder fellow U. Cin., 1945-48; assoc. rsch. physicist Argonne (Ill.) Nat. Lab., 1948-49; rsch. physicist Batelle Meml. Inst., Columbus, Ohio, 1949-50; asst. prof. physics U. Detroit, 1950-51, assoc. prof. physics, vice chmn. dept., 1953-59, prof. of physics, 1959-60; prof. astronomy Ohio State Univ., Columbus, 1966-85. Contbr. approximately 160 articles to profl. jours. including: Am. Jour. Physics, Phys. Review, Jour. Optical Soc. Am., Jour. of Mechanics and Physics of Solids, Jour. of Chem. Physics, Astrophys. Jour. Supplement, Monthly Notices of the Royal Astron. Soc., Astron. Soc. of the Pacific, Astrophys. Jour., Jour. of Applied Physics, Memoirs of Royal Astron. Soc., Proceedings of Phys. Soc., Internat. Astron. Union Symposia. Recipient Disting. Svc. award Fenn Coll., (now Cleve. State U.), 1965. Fellow Royal Astron. Soc.; mem. Internat. Astron. Union, Am. Astron. Soc., Sigma Xi, Tau Beta Pi. Roman Catholic. Achievements include two U.S. patents: on a method for growing single crystals of Cds and Zns & an apparatus for growing single crystals of Cds and Zns. Avocation: flying. Died June 10, 2008.

DAANSEN, JUDITH ANN, clinical therapist, medical social worker; b. San Francisco, Sept. 8, 1959; d. Adrian John and Patricia Margaret (Linney) D. AA in Liberal Arts, Coll. of San Mateo, 1979; BS in Therapeutic Recreation, Calif. State U., Fresno, 1983, MSW, 1990. Lic. clin. social worker, Calif. Rehab. therapist Atascadero (Calif.) State Hosp., 1983-87, Fresno County Mental Health, 1987-90; clin. therapist, coord. sexual abuse team Tulare (Calif.) Youth Svc. Bur., from 1990; med. social woker Valley Children's Hosp., Fresno, from 1994. Presenter, spkr. Child Abuse Conf., Visalia, Calif., 1991—. Vol. Planned Parenthood, Fresno, 1994—, Fresno County Juvenile Hall, Big Bros. and Big Sisters, Fresno, 1996; pres. N.W. region Parents United, sexual abuse prevention and treatment, 1994—. Scholar Penisnula Hosp. Aux., Burlingame, Calif., 1978-79. Mem. NASW, NOW. Unitarian Universalist. Avocations: white water rafting, reading, mountains, beach, movies. Home: Monterey, Calif. Died May 15, 2008.

DAHL, EVERETT E., lawyer; b. Sandy, Utah, June 21, 1923; m. Ann Kosovich, June 21, 1947; children: Annette, EvAnn BS, U. Utah, 1947, JD, 1949. Bar: Utah 1949, U.S. Dist. Ct. Utah 1949, U.S. Ct. Mil. Appeals 1959, U.S. Supreme Ct., U.S. Ct. Appeals (10th cir.). Commd. 2d lt. U.S. Army, 1943, advanced through grades to col., ret., 1975; pvt. practice Midvale, Utah, from 1949. Bd. dirs. Trans Jordan Landfill. Mayor City of Midvale, 1986-94; exec. sec. Midvale C. of C., 1950-60; bd. dirs. Rsch. Inst.; pres. Palo Verde Park, Inc., Safford, Ariz., 1970's; chmn. Salt Lake County Coun. Govts., South Valley Emergency Ctr Mem. Res. Officers Assn. (life, dept. comdr. nat. exec. com.), Amvets (dept. pres. nat. exec. com. 1993—), VFW, Phi Kappa Phi Avocations: fishing, golf. Home: Midvale, Utah. Died Nov. 2, 2007.

DAHLBERG, CARL FREDRICK, JR., entrepreneur; b. New Orleans, Aug. 20, 1936; s. Carl Fredrick and Nancey Erwin (Jones) D.; m. Constance Weston, Dec. 30, 1961; children: Kirsten Erwin Dahlberg Turner, Catherine Morgan Dahlberg Stokes BSCE, Tulane U., 1958; MBA, Harvard U., 1964. Regional mgr. bond dept. E.F. Hutton & Co., Inc., New Orleans, 1965—67; chmn. exec. com. Dahlberg, Kelly & Wisdom, Inc., New Orleans, 1967—71; pres. St. Mary Galvanizing Co., Inc., New Orleans, 1971—2000, chmn., from 2000; pres. The South Coast Co., LLC, from 2004. Co-organizer, dir. Charter Med. Corp., 1969-72; adv. dir. Rathborne Cos., 1985-91; with Internat. Trade Mart, 1974-89, exec. com., 1981-84, treas., 1983-84; consul gen. of Monaco, New Orleans, 1981-98; treas. Consul Corps of New Orleans, 1990-94 Co-author: Hydrochloric Acid Pickling, 1979 Trustee Metairie Park Country Day Sch., New Orleans, 1976-85, treas., 1980-82, chmn., 1982-84; trustee Eye, Ear, Nose and Throat Hosp., New Orleans, 1980-96, exec. com., 1980-83; trustee Eye, Ear, Nose and Throat Found., 1980-83, U. South, Sewanee, Tenn., 1984-90; bd. dirs. New Orleans Tech. Coun., 1993-98, Mus. Arts Soc. New Orleans, 2000-06, Metro. Crime Comm. New Orleans, 2006—; vis. com. Monroe libr. Loyola U., New Orleans, 2002-06; vestryman Christ Ch. Cathedral, New Orleans, 1981-85. With U.S. Army, 1958-59 Mem. ASCE, Nat. Assn. Mfrs. (bd. dirs. 1997-2003), Venerable Order Hosp. of St. John of Jerusalem, Mil. and Hospitaller Order St. Lazarus, Order of Merit of Italian Republic, Order of Grimaldi (Monaco), New Orleans Country Club, Pickwick Club, Army and Navy Club Washington, The Brook Club NYC Republican. Episcopalian. Home: New Orleans, La. Died Aug. 12, 2008.

DAHLQUIST, BRUCE LEE, government official; b. Worcester, Mass., June 7, 1949; s. Howard Leonard and Dorothy Helen (Mallquist) D.; 1 child, Johanthan Tait. BS, Clark U., 1977; MBA, Anna Maria Coll., 1979. Pres. Bruce L. Dahlquist Graphic Arts, Worcester, 1975-79; asst. personnel dir. City of Worcester, 1979-91, acting personnel dir., 1991-92; acting exec. dir. Regl. Employment Bd., 1992-93, assoc. dir., from 1993. Advisor Clark U. Human Resources Adv. Bd., Mcpl. Mgmt. Inst., Ctr. for Human Resource Devel. Editorial bd. HR Mag., Persoonnel Joour., The Supervisor's Newsletter, Personnel Practices Newsletter. Chmn. Big Bros./Big Sisters of Worcester County, Inc., First Call Adv. Bd., United Way of Cen. Mass., Greater Worcester Com. for Employment of Individuals with dis-Abilities; official Spl. Olympics. Ssgt. USAF, 1968-72. Named to Outstanding Young Men of Am.; recipient Vol. awards United Way, Nat. Multiple Sclerosis Soc., Greater Worcester Com. for Employment of People with disAbilities; recipient citations: Thomas S. Green Pub. Svc. award Worcester Mcpl. Rsch. Bur., Worcester Pub. Schs., State Senate, others. Mem. Nat. Ctr. for Health Edn. (charter), Nat. Edn.-for-Health Issues Panel, Personnel Mgmt. Assn. of Cen. Mass. (bd. dirs.), Mass. Mcpl. Personnel Assn., Mass. Assn. Labor Svc. Dirs., ASTD, Cen. Mass. Chpt. ASTD, Soc. for Human Resource Mgmt. Avocations: profl. piano, synthesizer and organ, golf, racquetball. Home: Worcester, Mass. Died Oct. 25, 2007.

DALE, DEBRA EILEEN, elementary school educator; b. Schurz, Nev., Dec. 1, 1953; d. William Winston and Marlene Coffey; m. Kee Dale Jr., Oct. 11, 1970; 1 child, Eileen Frances. AA, Truckee Meadows C.C., 1980; BS in Elem. Edn., U. Nev., 1982; M in Curriculum Instrn., Lesley Coll., Cambridge, Mass., 1992. Cert. tchr. K-8, Nev. Tchr. aide Reno/Sparks Headstart Program, Reno, 1972-73; tchr. aide summer sch. Washoe County Sch. Dist., Reno, 1972-81; community rels. tchr. aide Libby Booth Elem. Sch., Reno, 1973-78; tutor Reno/Sparks Colony, Reno, 1979-82; tchr. summer sch. Washoe County Sch. Dist., 1982; community rels. counselor Wooster/Reed High Schs., Reno, 1982-83; tchr. Roger Corbett Elem. Sch., Reno, 1983—97, Esther Bennett Elem. Sch., Sun Valley, Nev., 1997—2000, Natchez Elem. Sch., Wadsworth, Nev., from 2000. Mem. multi-cultural com. Washoe County Sch. Dist., 1992-93, mentor and lead tchr.; tchr. rep. Title V Indian Edn. Program, 1991—. Co-author: Celebrating Nevada Indians, 1992. Res. police officer Reno/Sparks Indian Colony Tribal Police, Reno, 1989-94. Recipient Outstanding Student Tchr. award U. Nev., 1982. Mem. NEA, Nev. State Edn. Assn., Nev. Native Am. Edn. Assn., Nev. Indian Rodeo Assn., Washoe Edn. Assn., Delta Kappa Gamma (nat. and internat.), Nev. Literacy Coalition, Nev. State Libr. Archives. Avocations: sewing, arts and crafts, drawing and painting. Home: Reno, Nev. Died July 19, 2008.

DALKE, WAYNE L., management consultant; b. Marion, SD, June 4, 1920; s. Gust and Esther (Graber) D.; m. Joanne J. Waltner, Sept. 2, 1949; children: Marie, Gwenn, Lisa. BS in Met. Engr., S.D. Sch. Mines, Rapid City, 1951. Gen. foreman Minntac Plant, Mt. Iron, Minn., 1963-67; gen. foreman Minn. Ore Ops., Mt. Iron, Minn., 1967-70, supt. crusher conct., 1970-76; gen. mgr. Can. Met. Chem., Kudremukh, India, 1976-81; div. supt. taconite Minn. Ore Ops., Mt. Iron, 1981-82; gen. mgr. engr. U.S.S. Domestic Ore & Stone, Minn., 1982-83; gen. mgr. U.S.S. Engrs. & Cons., Linden, Guyana, S.A., 1983-85, Minn. Ore Ops., Mt. Iron, 1984-87; mgmt. and devel. cons. Chisholm, Minn., from 1987. Dir. Zuari Chem. Corp., Goa India 1979-81, Northeastern Minn. Devel. Assn. Duluth 1984-87, Lake Superior Indsl. Bur., Duluth Minn. 1984-87, United Way, Chisholm Minn., 1986. Chmn. Headwaters Boy Scout Coun., Hibbing, Minn., 1971; treas. First Bapt. Ch., Chisholm, 1975, deacon, 1985—. Mem. Am. Inst. Mining Engrs., Engrs. Club Northeastern Minn. Republican. Baptist. Home: Chisholm, Minn. Died Dec. 7, 2007.

DALTON, MATT, retired foundry executive; b. Chgo., June 27, 1922; s. Donald J. and Jessie (Shrimplim) D.; children: D. J., J. B., Katherine A.; m. Frances Walter, Jan. 1, 1994. Student, Pomona Coll., Claremont, Calif., Butler U.; grad. advanced mgmt. program, Harvard U., 1956. Pres. Dalton Foundries, Inc., Warsaw, Ind., 1959-68, chmn. bd., 1968-91, chmn. emeritus, 1992-94. Founder Warsaw Jr. Achievement, 1953; charter mem. bd. dirs. Warsaw Devel. Corp., 1973; mem. Warsaw Cmty. Sch. Bd., 1962-68, Kosciusko County Coun., 1981-84—; trustee Ind. Vocat. Tech. Coll., 1964-70; chmn. Gov. of Ind. Com. on Youth Employment, 1979-82; pres. Lake Tippecanoe Property Owners Assn., 1979-82; founder, chmn. Kosciusko Econ. Devel. Corp., 1984, Kosciusko Leadership Acad., 1981; mem. Ind. Econ. Devel. Coun., 1984-88, Ind. Commn. on Vocat. and Tech. Edn., 1988-89; del. Ind. Gov.'s Far East Tour, 1987. With AUS, 1943-45. Mem. Ind. State C. of C. (chmn. 1982-84) Died Apr. 2, 2009.

DALY, DONALD FRANCIS, retired consultant, investment counsel; b. Bridgeport, Conn., Aug. 6, 1928; s. Christopher M. and Anne F. (Kelleher) D.; m. Magdalene Johnston, July 10, 1953 (div. 1975); children: Candace, Jacqueline, Elizabeth, Patrick; m. Susan S. Coyle, Mar. 21, 1976 (div. 1984); 1 child, Jennifer (dec.); m. Sandra R. Godfrey, Apr. 19, 1985; 1 child, Samuel. AB, Yale U., 1950. Account exec. Hemphill Noyes, NYC, 1957-63; v.p. Scudder Stevens & Clark, NYC, 1963-78; ptnr. Brundage Story & Rose, NYC, 1978-95; sr. v.p. Mellon Bank Pvt. Asset Mgmt., Phila., 1995-96; dir. acquisitions Mellon Pvt. Asset Mgmt., 1996-98; cons. Mellow Pvt. Asset Mgmt., 1998-2000. Pres. Brundage Story & Rose Mut. Funds, 1990-95; adv. bd. Charles Schwab & Co., 1993-94; cons. in field. Mem. Korean Meml. Commn., 1989-91; pres. Diocesan Trust, Episc. Diocese of NY, 1990-94; trustee PLAN of Penn. Capt. U.S. Army, 1950-57. Decorated Disting. Svc. Cross, Bronze Star medals (2), Purple Heart (2), Gold Medal of Valor, Greece, Chung Mu Disting. Svc. Cross, Korea. Fellow Phila. Soc. Security Analysts; mem. Am. Inst. Investment Mgrs., Investment Counsel Assn. (former gov.), Phila. Estate Planning Coun., Order of St. John of Jerusalem, Yale Club N.Y., Church Club Phila., Point O'Woods Club, The Pilgrims. Republican. Died Dec. 5, 2007.

DALY, JOHN, film producer; b. London, July 16, 1937; children: Michael, Julian, Timothy, Jenny. Co-founder Hemdale Co., 1966; chmn. Hemdale Group Ltd., 1971; chmn., pres., CEO Film and Music Entertainment, Inc., 2003—08. Exec. prodr.: (films) The Border, 1979, The Passage, 1979, Race for the Yankee Zephyr, 1981, Going Ape!, 1981, Cattle Annie and Little Britches, 1981, Strange Behavior, 1981, Turkey Shoot, 1982, Yellowbeard, 1983, The Terminator, 1984, The Falcon and the Snowman, 1985, The Return of the Living Dead, 1985, Salvador, 1986, At Close Range, 1986, River's Edge, 1986, Hoosiers, 1986, Platoon, 1986, Scenes from the Goldmine, 1987, Best Seller, 1987, The Last Emperor, 1987, Love at Stake, 1988, Criminal Law, 1988, Buster, 1988, The Boost, 1988, Out Cold, 1989, Shag, 1989, Blood Red, 1989, Staying Together, 1989, Chattahoochee, 1989, Hidden Agenda, 1990, Don't Tell Her It's Me, 1990, Bright Angel, 1991, The Petersburg-Cannes Express, 2003, Moonpie, 2006, Played, 2006, Drifter, 2007, Killer Weekend, 2007, The Heavy, 2008; prodr.: Sunburn, 1979, A Breed Apart, 1984; exec. prodr., prodr.: (films) Miracle Mile, 1988, War Party, 1988, Vampire's Kiss, 1989, Alec to the Rescue, 1999, The Aryan Couple, 2004 (Best Dir., Beverly Hills Film Festival, 2005), Waking Up Dead, 2005, Tournament of Dreams, 2007. Died Oct. 31, 2008.

DALY, MARY C., dean, law educator; BA, Thomas More Coll., 1969; JD cum laude, Fordham U. Sch. Law, 1972; LLM in Comparative Law, NYU Sch. Law, 1975—78. Assoc. Rogers & Wells, 1973—75; asst. U.S. Atty. Civil Div., 1975—80; chief of civil div. U.S. Atty. Office, So. Dist. N.Y., 1981—83; prof. Fordham Law Sch., 1983—2004, co-dir. Louis Stein Ctr. for Law and Ethics, dir. Grad. Prog., James H. Quinn Prof. Legal Ethics; dean, John V. Brennan Chair Law and Ethics St. John's U. Sch. Law, 2004—08. Grantee Zichkla Fellow, Université de Paris, Faculté de Droit, 1973. Mem.: ABA (reporter Commn. Multidisciplinary Practice 1998—2000, mem. Out-of-the Box Com.), Fed. Bar Coun. (trustee 1997—2004), Assn. Bar N.Y.C. (chair Com. Profl. and Judicial Ethics 1996—99, mem. Delegation to Chile, Rwanda and Brazil 2002—03). Died Nov. 2009.

DANIEL, J. REESE, lawyer; b. Sanford, NC, Dec. 24, 1924; AB, U. S.C., 1949, JD cum laude, 1956. Bar: S.C. 1955, U.S. Dist. Ct. S.C. 1956, U.S. Tax Ct. 1959, U.S. Cr. Appeals (4th cir.) 1959. Sr. ptnr. Daniel & Daniel, Litchfield, S.C. Mem. S.C. Supreme Ct. Bd. Commrs. on Grievances and Discipline, 1970-73, Columbia Zoning Bd. of Adjustment, 1970-79. Contbg. author 7 South Carolina Law Quarterly; contbr. articles to profl. jours. With USNR, 1943-46. Mem. ABA, S.C. Bar Assn. (assoc. editor S.C. Bar Assn. News Bull. 1957, editor 1958-59), Phi Delta Phi. Home: Pawleys Island, SC. Died May 9, 2008.

DANIELS, BARBARA GAYLE, state official, real estate broker; b. St. Paul, July 15, 1950; d. Edwin W. and Hedwig D. (Wiereke) Grossman; m. James R. Daniels, July 10, 1971 (div. 1983); 1 child, Robyn. Attended, U. Minn., 1968-70; BA in Social Work and Psychology, Avila, 1973. Caseworker Kansas City Divsn. Family Svcs., 1971-74, supr., 1974-76, agt. rep. hearing, 1976-77, staff devel. specialist, 1977-83, program devel. specialist, from 1983. Mem. NASW, NAFE, Women in Energy. Home: Blue Springs, Mo. Died Oct. 16, 2007.

DANIELS, HOWARD See ZIMMERMAN, HOWARD IRWIN

DANNENBERG, KONRAD K., aeronautical engineer; b. Weissenfels, Germany, Aug. 5, 1912; came to U.S. 1945. s. Hermann and Klara (Kittler) D.; m. Ingeborg M. Kamke, Apr. 8, 1944 (dec.); 1 child, Klaus Dieter; m. Jacquelyn E. Staiger, Mar. 31, 1990. MS Engring., Techn. U., Hannover, Ger., 1938. Asst. Tech. U., Hannover, 1938, engr. Frankfurt, Germany, 1939; rschr. HAP-Peenemuende, Germany, 1940-45; mgr. U.S. Army Ordnance, Ft. Bliss, Tex., 1945-50, ABMA, Huntsville, Ala., 1950-60, NASA/MSFC, Huntsville, 1960-73; assoc. prof. UTSI-U. Tenn., Tullahoma, 1973-78; cons. The Space & Rocket Ctr., Huntsville, 1978—2009. Author: In Memory of H. Oberth, 1990, Vahrenwald to Dresden, 1990; (with E. Stuhlinger) Rocket Center Peenemünde, 1993, Albert Püllenberg and the Gesellschaft für Raketenforschung, 1995, (with Donald Tarter) Mitchell R. Sharpe-Aerospace Historian, 1997. Lt. German Army, 1939—40. Recipient Meritorious Svc. award U.S. Army, 1960, Exceptional Svc. award NASA, 1969, Konrad K. Dannenberg scholarship, 1992, Gov. of Ala. Commendation, 2002, Genesis award Ala. Info. Tech. Assn., 2004. Fellow AIAA (chpt. chmn. 1967, Durand lectr. pub. svc. 1990), Holger N. Toftoy award, Hermann Oberth award 1996); mem. Hermann Oberth Soc. (hon., Golden Hermann Oberth medal 1994), Nat. Space Soc. (charter), Am. Rocket Soc. (chmn. 1962). Lutheran. Achievements include patents in rocket engine design. Died Feb. 16, 2009.

D'ANTONIO, NICHOLAS, retired bishop; b. Rochester, NY, July 10, 1916; s. Pasquale and Josephine (Salza) D'Antonio. Attended, St. Francis Seraphic Sem., Andover, Mass., 1931, St. Anthony Friary, Catskill, NY, 1939. Professed Order of Friars Minor; ordained priest, 1942; pastor Trail, Canada, 1943-45; provincial del. USA Friars working in Guatemala, Honduras and El Salvador, 1953-63; named prelate of Olancho, Honduras, 1966; bishop Diocese Olancho, 1966-76; vicar gen. Archdiocese of New Orleans, 1977-91, also vicar of Hispanics; pastor Annunciation Ch., New Orleans, 1979-91, pastor emeritus, 1991—2009. Liaison Family Life in La.; observer Nat. Conf. of Cath. Bishops. Mem. KC (2d, 3d and 4th degree), Equestrian Order of the Holy Sepulchre. Roman Catholic. Died Aug. 1, 2009.

DARLINGTON, FRANK, industrial engraving company executive; b. Manchester, Eng., Mar. 2, 1928; came to U.S., 1955; s. Harry and Louisa Ann (Aikin) D.; m. Ivy Waite, Jan. 28, 1950; children: Peter Barrie, Pamela Darlington Duval. Student in Photo Engraving Processes, Manchester Coll. of Tech., 1946-50. Apprentice engraver Lockett Crossland Co., Manchester, 1943-49; sketch maker Std. Engraving, Eccles, Eng., 1950-53; artist, photo engraver Roll Phot Engravers, Manchester, 1953-55; head sketch making dept. Consolidated Engravers, Charlotte, N.C., 1955-59, plant prodn. control, 1959-63, v.p. sales and prodn., 1963-67, dir., part owner, 1967-70, pres., 1970-89; CEO Consolidated Group, Charlotte, N.C., 1989-91; ret., 1991. Founding dir. First Charlotte Bank and Trust, 1983-93; chmn. graphic arts bd. Clemson (S.C.) U., 1985-94; city bd. dirs. Centura Bank, Charlotte. Mem. adv. bd. Boy Scouts of Am., Charlotte, 1991—. Mem. Lds Ch. Died Oct. 21, 2007.

DARNELL, WILLIAM HEADEN, chemical engineer, medical/surgical nurse, educator; b. Roanoke, Va., May 14, 1925; s. William Lee and Edythe Headen (Scott) Darnell; m. Kathryn Jane McManaway, June 3, 1950; 1 child, William Jamison. BS, Va. Poly. Inst. and State U., 1950; MS, U. Wis., 1951, PhD, 1953; ASN, Tri-County Tech. Coll., 1989. Registered profl. engr., Va., 1950, Del., 1954; RN SC 1989. Prodn. asst. Merck Pharm. Co., Elkton, Va., 1946; rsch. engr., supr. E.I. du Pont de Nemours Co., Wilmington, Del., 1953—60, nylon tech. supt. Victoria, Tex., 1960—63, devel. mgr. Wilmington, 1963—68, rsch. mgr., 1968—72, lab. adminstr., 1972—77, environ. mgr., 1977—85; RN Oconee Meml. Hosp. Inc., Seneca, SC, 1989—2001; pvt. practice RN educator Salem, SC, 2001—04. Contbr. editor: (handbook) Processing Thermoplastics, 1959; contbr. articles to profl. jours. Chpt. pres. Rotary Internat., Wilmington, 1970—71, dist. sec., NJ and Del., 1971—72; affiliate faculty Am. Heart Assn., Del., Pa., 1974—83; election judge Kennett Twp., Kennett Sq., Pa., 1976—78; bd. dir. Am. Cancer Soc., Del., 1968—70; bd. dirs., pres. Advanced Life Support, Inc., West Grove, Pa., 1982—85; exec. dir., treas., v.p., bd. dirs., pres. Hospice of the Foothills, Inc., Seneca, SC, 1987—98; v.p., vice-chmn., bd. dirs. Hospice Found., 1998—2005. 2d Lt. US Army, 1943—53, ATO, ETO, PTO. Recipient Best Tech. Paper award, AIChE, 1959, Silver Dove award, Hospice Found., 2004, Patriot award, SAR, 1994. Fellow: Nat. Sci. Found., Tau Beta Pi; mem.: SAR (pres. SC state soc. 1995—97, trustee nat. soc. 1997—98). Republican. Presbyterian. Avocations: music, furniture reproductions, swimming. Home: Salem, SC. Died Feb. 17, 2009.

DARON, HARLOW H., biochemist; b. Chgo., Oct. 25, 1930; s. Garman H. and Gulah V. (Hoover) D.; m. Carol Fields, Aug. 8, 1969; children: Barbara P., Charles E.; children: Ruth A., Leslie S. BS, U. Okla., 1956; PhD, U. Ill., 1961. NSF postdoctoral fellow Calif. Inst. Technology, Pasadena, 1961-63; asst. prof. Tex. A&M U., College Station, Tex., 1963-67, Auburn (Ala.) U., 1967-72, assoc. prof., 1972-80, prof., from 1980. Mem. Am. Soc. Biochemistry and Molecular Biology, AAAS, Am. Chem. Soc., Sigma Xi. Home: Auburn, Ala. Died June 3, 2008.

DASKAL, JAY LEONARD, obstetrician-gynecologist; b. Chgo., Apr. 14, 1938; s. Nathan and Gertrude (Brooks) D.; m. Lee Francis Mason, Sept. 3, 1961; children: Meryl, Ellyn, Sharyn. BS, U. Ill., Urbana, 1959; MD, U. Ill., Chgo., 1963. Cert. Am. Bd. Ob-Gyn. Clin. asst. prof. ob-gyn. U. Ill., Chgo., from 1969, clin. assoc. prof. ob-gyn., from 1987; asst. chief ob-gyn dept. Ill. Masonic Med. Ctr., Chgo., from 1975. Bd. dirs. United Way, Northfield, Ill., 1986. Served to capt. U.S. Army, 1965-66, Vietnam. Decorated Bronze Star. Mem. AMA, Am. Coll. Ob-Gyn (treas. Ill. sect. 1985—), Am. Fertility Soc., Inst. of Medicine of Chgo. Jewish. Home: Winnetka, Ill. Died Sept. 27, 2007.

DAUGHERTY, ANN ELOISE, health facility director; b. Russell Springs, Ky., June 15, 1936; d. Clifford D. and Rectie (Whittle) Leach; m. Charles A. Daugherty, Sept. 1959 (div. Mar. 1981); children: Theresa, David, Diana; m. Jimmy James, Nov. 22, 1982 (div. July 1994). AA, Ind. U., Indpls., 1967, BS in Nursing, 1972, MS in Nursing, 1981; M in Psychiat. Nursing, Ind. U.-Purdue U., 1981. Lic. nursing home adminstr., Ind. Nurse ob-gyn Johnson County Meml. Hosp., Franklin, Ind., 1969-71, acting head nurse, 1972-75; adminstr., dir. nursing Franklin Nursing Home, 1971-72; nurse psychiatry drug detoxification unit VA Med. Ctr., Indpls., 1979-81; asst. supr. Ind. Masonic Home Hosp., Franklin, 1981; with in-patient unit Quinco, Columbus, Ind., 1982, with outpatient unit, 1982-85; exec. dir. Tara Treatment Ctr., Inc., Franklin, from 1985. Named to Hon. Order Ky. Cols. Mem. Nat. and State Assn. Alcoholism and Drug Abuse Counselors (bd. dirs.), Johnson County Mental Health Assn. (pres.), Johnson Mental Health Clinic (pres., bd. dirs.), Franklin C. of C. Baptist. Died Aug. 25, 2008.

DAUGHERTY, BEN P., real estate professional; b. Cleve., Mar. 31, 1918; s. Ben B. and Rose Ann (Krevo) D.; m. Dorothy Hay, June 25, 1946; 1 child, Sharon L. Student in bus./acctg., Cleve. Coll./Western Res. U.; student, Computer Mgmt. Sch., NYC and San Jose, Calif., 1950-53. V.p. opers. Equifax, Inc., Atlanta, 1938-81; pres. ESP Properties, Inc., Seminole, Fla., from 1981. Author/editor: (pamphlet) Make It Happen, 1976. With USN, 1941-45, PTO. Avocation: travel. Died Jan. 11, 2008.

DAUNS, JOHN, mathematician, educator; b. Riga, Latvia, June 11, 1937; BS, MIT, 1960; PhD, Harvard U., 1964. Asst. prof. Tulane U., New Orleans, 1964—68, assoc. prof., 1968—81, prof., 1981—2009. Vis. prof. U. Natal, Durban, South Africa, 1984. Author: A Concrete Approach to Division Rings, 1982, Modules and Rings, 1994; co-author (with K.H. Hofmann): Representations of Rings by Sections, 1968; co-author: (with Yiqiang Zhou) Classes of Modules, 2006; contbr. 67 articles to profl. jours. Fellow Woodrow Wilson, Harvard U., 1960, Humboldt Rsch. fellow, Tübingen U., 1972—73. Mem.: Am. Math. Soc. Avocation: swimming. Died June 4, 2009.

D'AVANZO, VICTOR NUNZIO, human resources professional; b. NYC, Mar. 31, 1935; s. John Victor and Mary Antoinette (De Falco) D'A.; m. Patricia Anne Mescal, Nov. 19, 1933; children: Anne Patricia, John James, Christine Marie, Mary Katherine, Joseph Victor. BS, NYU, 1957, MBA, 1963. Personnel mgr. Latin Am. Chase Manhattan Bank, N.Am., NYC, 1959-66; dir. tng. Rutgers U., New Brunswick, N.J., 1966-68; corp. human resources mgr. J.M. Huber Corp., Edison, N.J., 1968-90; pres. Davan Assocs., Atlanta, from 1988. Charter mem. Personnel Dirs. Roundtable, Ga. State U., Atlanta, 1987-88. With U.S. Army, 1957-59. Mem. Am. Soc. Human Resource Mgmt., Am. Compensation Assn., Am. Mgmt. Soc. Republican. Roman Catholic. Avocations: computers, carpentry, reading. Home: Tucker, Ga. Died Dec. 16, 2007.

DAVENEL, GEORGE FRANCIS, educational consulting association executive; b. Woodhaven, NY, June 18, 1914; s. Edward Alfred and Elizabeth (Johanna) D.; m. Viola Ferraino, Aug. 22, 1940; children: George F., Ann Marie. BS cum laude, CCNY, 1935; MA in Guidance and Pers., Columbia U., 1943. Dean's asst. Queens Coll. NYC, 1937-45, dir. career counseling and placement ctr., 1945-76, instr. student pers., 1952-57, asst. prof. student pers., 1958-64, assoc. prof. student pers., 1965-71, prof. student pers., 1972-76, prof. emeritus, from 1977; v.p. Nat. Ctr. Career Life Planning, NYC, 1977-80; pres. George Davenel & Assocs., NYC, from 1981. Examiner N.Y. State Civil Svc.; asst. examiner N.Y.C. Bd. Examiners; vocat. expert Social Security Adminstrn. Author: Help Your Child Develop Career Talents, 1957, Make Your Life More Interesting, 1958, Learn to Succeed, 1961; author, editor: Merit Students' Encyclopedia, 1961-74; contbr. articles to profl. jours. Recipient Citation of Merit, Kiwanis, 1969, Honor Scroll, Placement Assn. CUNY, 1976, Citation for Retirement Counseling, CUNY, 1978; fellow Found. Econ. Edn., 1954-55, N.Y. Life Co., 1955-56. Mem. Career Devel. Assn., Nat. Vocat. Guidance Assn. (chairperson nat. place-ment sect. 1955-57), Career Counseling and Placement Assn. (chairperson 1972-75), N.Y. Pers. Assn. (dir. 1960-62), Coll. Fed. Agy. Coun. (bd. dirs. 1956-58). Roman Catholic. Died Jan. 9, 2008.

DAVIDSON, ALAN CHARLES, insurance executive; b. LA, Nov. 8, 1937; s. Charles Evans and Anna Louise (Wilson) D.; m. Gail Louise Ziebarth, June 17, 1961 (dec.); children: Karen Ashley, Douglas McPhail. BA, Whittier Coll., 1962. CLU, ChFC. Pres. Davidson & Pierson Ins., Whittier, Calif., 1967-71, Davidson, Pierson & Roth Inc., Whittier, 1971-81; ptnr. Davidson & Poyner, Whittier, 1978-79; pres. Davidson Co., Whittier, 1961-67 and from 79. Producer, host Cable TV show Financial Sense, 1990—. Bd. dirs. Whittier Hist. Soc., 1989-91, Oralingua Sch. for Hearing Impaired, Whittier, 1991—. Recipient numerous awards Provident Mut., Will G. Farrell award, 1995. Mem. Am. Soc. CLU, Am. Soc. Pension Actuaries, Nat. Assn. Life Underwriters, Calif. Assn. Life Underwriters, Million Dollar Round Table, Life Leaders Round Table (pres.), Life Underwriters of L.A. (pres.), Life Underwriters of Whittier (pres.), Whittier Area C. of C. Republican. Mem. Soc. Of Friends. Avocation: gourmet cooking. Home: Whittier, Calif. Died Aug. 2, 2008.

DAVIDSON, WILLIAM MORSE, manufacturing executive, professional sports team owner; b. Dec. 5, 1922; m. Karen Davidson; children from previous marriage: Ethan, Maria. BBA, U. Mich., 1947; JD, Wayne State U., 1949; LHD (hon.), Jewish Theol. Sem. Am., 1996, U. Mich., 2001. Pres., CEO Guardian Glass Co., Northville, Mich., 1957-68, Guardian Industries Corp., 1968—2009; mng. ptnr., part owner Detroit Pistons, 1974—2009; owner Detroit Shock, 1998—2009, Tampa Bay Lightning, 1999—2008; majority owner Palace Sports and Entertainment. Donated to the establishment of William Davidson Inst., U. Mich. Sch. Bus. Adminstrn., 1992, William Davidson Grad. Sch. of Jewish Edn. at Jewish Theological Seminary of Am., NY, Davidson Inst. of Science Edn. at Weizmann Inst. of Sci., Rehovot, Israel, 1999; founder Pistons/Palace Found. Served in USN. Recipient Honors for Lifelong Philanthropy, Coun. Mich. Foundations, 1997; named one of America's Most Generous Donors, The NY Times, 1997, Forbes' Richest Americans, 1999—2009, World's Richest People, Forbes mag., 2001—09; named to Naismith Meml. Basketball Hall of Fame, 2008. Died Mar. 13, 2009.

DAVIS, ADA ROMAINE, retired nursing educator; b. Cumberland, Md., June 7, 1929; d. Louis Berge and Ethel Lucy (Johnson) Romaine; m. John Francis Davis, Aug. 1, 1953 (dec. 1999); children: Kevin Murray, Karen Evans-Romaine, William Romaine. Diploma in nursing, Kings County Hosp., Bklyn., 1949; BSN, U. Md., Balt., 1973, MS, 1974; PhD, U. Md., 1979, postdoctoral student, 1985—89. Cert. editor in life scis. Asst. prof. grad. program U. Md., Balt., 1974-79; chmn. dept. nursing Coll. Notre Dame, Balt., 1979-82; assoc. dean grad. program Georgetown U. Sch. Nursing, Washington, 1982-87; nurse cons. Health Resources & Services Adminstrn., Rockville, Md., 1987-93, US Dept. Health & Human Services, US Pub. Health Svc., Bur. Health Professionals, Rockville, 1987-93; assoc. prof., dir. undergraduate program Johns Hopkins U. Sch. Nursing, Balt., 1993-98, prof. emeritus, 1998—2009. Reviewer Choice, ALA; evaluator methodology and findings for rsch. studies; hist./med. biographer; prof., editor Johns Hopkins U. Sch. Nursing, 2003-09 Author: John Gibbon and His Heart-Lung Machine, 1992, Advanced Practice Nurses: Education, Roles and Trends, 1997; editor: Ency. of Home Care for the Elderly, 1995; contbr. articles to nursing jours.; assoc. editor Hopkins InteliHealth, Johns Hopkins Family Health Guide, 1999, Johns Hopkins Insider, 1998; sr. editor: Am. Nurses Certification Ctr., 2000-01. Recipient excellent performance award HRSA; rsch. grantee U. Md. Grad. Sch. Mem. AAAS, ANA (cert. adult nurse practitioner), Soc. for Neoplatonic Studies, Nat. Orgn. Nurse Practitioner Faculties, Am. Acad. Nurse Practitioners, APHA, Gerontol. Soc. Am., Nat. Trust for Hist. Preservation, Am. Geriat. Soc., Md. History of Medicine Soc., Soc. for the Social History of Medicine (Oxford U.), N.Y. Acad. Scis., Coun. Sci. Editors, Sigma Theta Tau. Home: Bethesda, Md. Died Apr. 6, 2009.

DAVIS, BRITTON ANTHONY, retired lawyer; b. Highland Park, Ill., Jan. 2, 1936; s. James Archie and Anita (Blanke) D.; m. Lynn Marriott Wegner, 1958 (dec. 1975); children: Hilary, Shepard; m. Peggy M. Swint, 1986; children: Stephen Swint, Thomas Swint. Student, Denison U., 1954-57; BS in Law, Northwestern U., 1959, LLB, 1960. Bar: Ill. 1960. Assoc. Haight & Hofeldt, Chgo., 1959-89; pvt. practice Winnetka, Ill., 1989—96; ret., 1996. Vol. Children's Spl. Edn. Programs, Winnetka. Mem.: ABA, Patent Law Assn. Chgo., Bar Assn. 7th Fed. Cir., Chgo. Curling Club, Indian Hill Club (Winnetka). Home: Long Grove, Ill. Died Dec. 11, 2008.

DAVIS, DONALD DEAN, surgeon; b. Pitts., Mar. 15, 1927; s. Walter Scott and Eileen H. (Port) D.; m. Jeanne Dorothy Goohs; children: Clifford, Gary, Keith. AB, Washington & Jefferson Coll., 1950; MD, Yale U., 1954. cert. Am. Bd. Gen. Surgery. Intern Phila. Gen. Hosp., 1954-55; resident in surgery Pa. Hosp., Phila., 1955-59; surgeon VA Hosp., Pitts., 1959-61, Allegheny Gen. Hosp., Pitts., from 1961, Suburban Gen. Hosp., Pitts., from 1961, North Hills Passavant Hosp., Pitts., 1982-88. Trustee North Hills Passavant Hosp. Mem. Franklin Park (Pa.) Planning Commn., 1971—, chmn. 1986—; bd. dirs. North Hills Art Ctr., Pitts., 1986-89. With USNR, 1945-47. Fellow Am. Coll. of Surgeons; mem. AMA, Pa. Med. Assn., Pitts. Surg. Soc. Republican. Methodist. Avocations: skiing, sailing, choral singing. Home: Pittsburgh, Pa. Died May 8, 2008.

DAVIS, GLORIA (KING), association administrator; b. Grand Saline, Tex., Aug. 22, 1940; d. Needom Leroy and Roxie Belle (Stevens) King; m. Perry N. Davis, Sept. 9, 1961; children: Steven P., Kenneth P., S. Suzanne. AA magna cum laude, Tyler Jr. Coll., Tex., 1978; BA, U. Tex., Tyler, 1979, MA, 1982. Sales coord. Dearborn Brass, Tyler, 1979-81; tchr. English T.K. Gorman High Sch., Tyler, 1981-82; membership devel. dir. Tejas Girl Scout Coun., Dallas, from 1982. Instr. part-time Tyler Jr. Coll., 1982—; mem. steering com. DOVIA of Tyler, 1987-88; mem. Tyler Human Svc. Providers, 1985-91. Mem. Assn. Girl Scout Exec. Staff (sec. VI sec. 1990-93, 94—), AAUW, U. Tex. at Tyler Alumni Assn. (sec. 1984-85, v.p. 1985-86, pres. 1986-87), Zonta bd. dirs. Tyler 1989-90). Republican. Baptist. Avocation: attending and participating in musical performances. Home: Tyler, Tex. Died Apr. 7, 2008.

DAVIS, GWENDOLYN LOUISE, military officer, literature educator; b. Toledo, Dec. 8, 1951; d. Robert Louis and Marietta Beatrice (Sautter) Davis; m. Barry Dennis Fayne, Jan. 6, 1979 (div. Feb. 2001); children: Ashleigh Elizabeth, Zachary Alexandur-John. BFA, So. Meth. U., 1972; MEd, U. North Tex., 1978; MA, U. Denver, 1987. Cert. tchr., Tex., Ala.; cert. secondary tchg. Am. Montessori Soc. Substitute tchr., Toledo and Dallas, 1972-73; film dir. Channel 39 Christian Broadcasting Network, Dallas, 1973-75; engr., air oper. Channel 40 Trinity Broadcasting Network, Tustin, Calif., 1978; commd. 2d lt. USAF, 1978, advanced through grades to maj., 1989, ret., 1995; mgr. western area Hdqrs. USAFR Officers Tng. Corp., Norton AFB, Calif., 1979-81; chief tng. systems support Hdqrs. Air Force Manpower Pers. Pentagon, Washington, 1981-84; pers. policies officer J1, Orgn. of Joint Chiefs of Staff Pentagon, Washington, 1984-85; asst. prof. English, dir. forensics USAF Acad., Colorado Springs, Colo., 1987-92; adj. faculty mem. dept. English Auburn U., Montgomery, Ala., 1994-95; adj. faculty mem. dept. arts and scis. Troy State U., Montgomery, 1994-96; dir. Bullock County HS Learning Ctr., Union Springs, Ala., 1995-96; tech. and acad. tchr. Ctr. for Advanced Tech. Booker T. Washington Magnet H.S., Montgomery, 1996; tchr. speech and English Mountain Brook H.S., Birmingham, Ala., 1997-98; tchr. humanities Joseph Bruno Montessori Acad., Birmingham, 1998-2000; upper-school dir. Sacred Heart Ch. Sch., 2000—01, ednl. cons., from 2001; founder, dir. Shiloh Village Montessori H.S., 2002—04; tchr. Spring Valley Sch., 2004—07; writer, journalist, from 2007. Assoc. editor Airpower Jour., Maxwell AFB, Ala., 1992-94, mil. doctrine analyst, 1994-95; chmn. mil. affairs Jr. Officer's Coun., Norton AFB, 1981; invited spkr. in field; chmn. program devel. com. for nat. orgn. Cross Exam. Debate Assn., 1990-91. Contbr. articles to profl. jours. Tchr., mem. choir, soloist various chs., 1973; chair publicity com. Birthright, Inc., Woodbridge, Va., 1983. Named Command Jr. Officer of Yr., Hdqrs. USAFR Officers Tng. Corps, 1979. Mem. Nat. Parliamentary Debate Assn. (co-founder, editor Parliamentary Debate jour. 1992-95), Am. Montessori Soc., Phi Upsilon Omicron. Avocations: reading, antiques, sight-seeing. Died Mar. 19, 2008.

DAVIS, HOWARD TED, engineering educator; b. Hendersonville, NC, Aug. 2, 1937; s. William Howard and Gladys Isabel (Rhodes) D.; m. Eugenia Asimakopoulos, Sept. 15, 1960 (dec. July 1996); children: William Howard II, Maria Katherine; m. Catherine Asimkopoulos, Mar. 9, 2000. BS in Chemistry, Furman U., 1959; PhD in Chem. Physics, U. Chgo., 1962. Postdoctoral fellow Free U. of Brussels, 1962-63; asst. prof. U. Minn., Mpls., 1963-66, assoc. prof., 1966-69, prof., 1969-80, prof., head chem. engring. and materials sci., 1980-95, dean Inst. Tech., 1995—2004, Regent's prof., 1997—2009; Humboldt rschr. Cologne U., Germany, 2005; dir. Biotechnology Inst., 2008. Editor: Springs of Creativity, 1981; author: Statistical Mechanics of Phases, Interfaces and Thin Films, 1995, (with K. Thomson) Linear Algebra and Linear Operators in Engineering, 2000; contbr. over 500 articles to sci. and engring. jours. Fellow Sloan Found., 1967-69, Guggenheim Found., 1969-70. Mem. AAAS, AIChE (Walker award for excellence in publs. 1990), NAE, Am. Chem. Soc., Soc. Petroleum Engrs., Minn. Fedn. Engring. Socs. (Disting. Engr. 1998). Democrat. Avocations: tennis, golf, reading, movies. Home: Golden Valley, Minn. Died May 17, 2009.

DAVIS, JAMES CARL, retired government official, government consultant; b. St. Louis, Jan. 13, 1945; m. Linda L. Coston, Dec. 22, 1976. AA, St. Leo, Fla., 1977; BS, U. State of N.Y., Albany, 1989. Cert. pilot. Commd. 2d. lt. U.S. Army, 1963, advanced through grades to maj., 1980, ret., 1984; pres. Knights of Malta Found., New Orleans, 1984-86; adminstrn. cons. McTernan, Parr & Rumage, New Orleans, 1986-87; spl. asst. to the comdg. gen. Hdqrs. D.C. N.G., Washington, 1987-90; cons. local and U.S. govt., 1990-95; cons. internat. ops., bus. mgr. Alton F. Doody Co., 1995-96. Author: Where's My Award, 1982. Decorated two Bronze stars, two Purple Hearts. Mem. NRA, Res. Officers Assn., The Ret. Officers Assn. Avocations: coin and currency collecting, flying, travel. Home: Brandon, Miss. Died Aug. 21, 2008.

DAVIS, KENT R., finance executive; b. Elmhurst, Ill., Jan. 23, 1933; s. William S. and Helen R. (Raymond) D.; m. Donna L. Farrar, May 30, 1980; children: Stephan, Gregory, Scott, Elizabeth, Francene, Rodney. BS in Mktg., U. Ill., 1954. Owner K. Davis and Assocs., Lombard, Ill., 1954-66; chief fin. officer Furnival Machinery, Phila., 1966-70; v.p. fin. and securities Rivinius Inc., Eureka, Ill., 1970-76; v.p. fin., adminstrn. Relco Equipment, Joliet, Ill., 1976-80; exec. v.p. and chief operating officer Utilities and Industry, Neponset, Ill., 1980-84; chief fin. officer Resource Tech. Inc. (name changed to PAL Health Techs. 1989), Peoria, Ill., from 1985. Trustee Village of Lombard, 1964-66, mem. planning commn., 1963. Mem.: Kiwanis (v.p. 1961-66). Republican. Protestant. Avocations: gliding, golf, water-skiing, gardening. Died Oct. 24, 2007.

DAVIS, MARGARET THACKER, retired critical care, medical and surgical nurse; b. Greensboro, NC, June 7, 1925; d. Tiller Foltz and Lucy Wright (Spencer) Thacker; m. Joe Southard Davis, Feb. 4, 1961; 1 child, Dana Lee. Diploma in nursing, Baylor U., Dallas, 1947; student, Ea. N.Mex. U., Roswell, 1978. RN, N.Mex., Tex., Fla. Office nurse Drs. Britt & Cafaro, St. Augustine, Fla., 1947-50, Dr. Robert J. Rowe, Dallas, 1950-61, Dr. F.A. English, Roswell, 1964-74; charge nurse post anesthesia care unit Ea. N.Mex. Med. Ctr., Roswell, 1990-91, ret., 1991. Named Employee of Month, Ea. N.Mex. Med. Ctr., 1985; recipient N.Mex. Nursing Legends award, 2005. Mem. ANA, Am. Soc. Post Anesthesia Nurses (charter), Post Anesthesia Nurses Assn. N.Mex. (bd. dirs. 1980-86, sec. 1986-87, legis. com. 1989-90), N.Mex. Nurses Assn. (dist. 5 sec. 1983-85, 91-93, pres. 1986-88, bd. dirs. 1988-90, 92-94, 96-98, membership chmn. 1988-90, chmn. nominating com. 1990, Nurse of Yr. award 1989, search for excellence award 1990, dist. 5 honored nurse 1995,N.Mex. Nursing Legends award 2005), Baylor U. Sch. Nursing Alumni Assn. Home: Albuquerque, N.Mex. Died July 4, 2009.

DAVIS, MARIE CAROLYN, nurse, artist; b. Ridgway, Pa., Aug. 25, 1908; d. Fred W. and Ada A. (Nelson) Loncoske; m. Arthur W. Davis, Mar. 3, 1933. RN, Orange Meml. Hosp., NJ, 1930; BS, Temple U., 1957, MS, 1959. RN, N.J. Charge nurse Orange (N.J.) Meml. Hosp., 1930, supr., 1930-37; indsl. nurse Western Electronic Co., Kearny, N.J., 1937, Elliot Co.; founder Cmty. Nurse Ctr., Ridgway, Pa., 1945-46; sch. nurse Ctrl. Bucks Sch. Doylestown (Pa.) Sch. Dist., 1947-73. Mem. NOW, Greenpeace, Feminist Majority, Sierra, Young Women's Club Ridgway, Planned Parenthood, Village Improvement Assn., Gen. Fedn. Women's Clubs. Democrat. Lutheran. Avocations: painting, collecting, gardening, cartooning. Home: Ridgway, Pa. Died Dec. 9, 2007.

DAVIS, MARY ELIZABETH, medical office administrator; b. Schenectady, May 17, 1957; d. William McColl and Phyllis Ann (Longo) Hope; m. Mark Hudson Davis, Oct. 25, 1986; 1 child, Scarlett Eileen. Student, Idaho State U., Pocatello, 1975-80. Reg. pharmacy tech. Children's reference librarian Pocatello Pub. Libr., 1978-80; pharmacy tech. South Coast Med. Ctr., South Laguna, Calif., 1980-82; operating rm. pharmacy tech. Mission Hosp., Mission Viejo, Calif., 1982-86; office mgr. Mark H. Davis, MD, Mission Viejo, 1987-91. Author various pharmacy procedure manuals. Active various charitable orgns. Mem. Women's Hosp. Aux. (v.p. 1988-89, co-chmn. fundraiser 1988). Republican. Roman Catholic. Avocations: ballet, swimming, skiing, reading, floral arranging, writing, decorating. Home: New Iberia, La. Died June 29, 2008.

DAVIS, MARY ELIZABETH, speech pathologist, educator, counselor; b. Larned, Kans., July 1, 1930; d. LeRoy D. and Katheryn (Herndon) Harris; m. W.G. Davis, Apr. 3, 1969; children: Pamela Koch, Michelle Dalton; 1 stepchild, Wendy Garton. BA, Calif. State U., Fresno, 1959, MA, 1982. Cert. resource specialist, speech pathologist tchr., deaf tchr., counselor, Calif. Dir. recreation and occupl. therapy Wyo. State Hosp., Evanston, 1956-58; tchr. Fresno Unified Sch. Dist., 1960-80, Barton County C.C., Great Bend, Kans., 1990-98. Bd. dirs. Larned Historical Soc., Santa Fe Trail Ctr., Larned, Kans., 2001—04. Mem. Am. Counseling Assn., Nat. Bd. Cert. Counselors. Home: Hutchinson, Kans. Died Aug. 17, 2008.

DAVIS, ROBERT WILLIAM (BOB DAVIS), lobbyist, former United States Representative from Michigan; b. Marquette, Mich., July 31, 1932; s. George Walter and Darlene Hazel (Hagen) D.; m. Brook Davis; children: Robert, Lisa, George, Alexandra. Student, No. Mich. U., 1950-52, Hillsdale Coll., 1951-52; BS in Mortuary Sci, Wayne State U., 1954. Funeral dir. Davis Funeral Home, St. Ignace, Mich., 1954-66; city councilman St. Ignace, 1964-66; mem. 106th Dist. Mich. House of Reps., 1966-70; mem. Dist. 37 Mich. State Senate, 1970-78, majority whip, 1970—74, Senate Republican leader, 1974-78; mem. US Congress from 11th Mich. Dist., 1979—93. Named Outstanding State legislator Nat. Council Sr. Citizens, 1973 Mem. Mich. Funeral Dirs. Assn., North-east Midwest Econ. Advancement Coalition, Mich. Cystic Fibrosis Assn., Young Ams. for Freedom. Clubs: Lions, Elks, Eagles. Republican. Episcopalian. Home: Gaylord, Mich. Died Oct. 16, 2009.

DAVIS, STEPHEN K., engineering and management consultant; b. Irving, Tex., Dec. 6, 1966; s. J. Lee and Mary Ann (Yarborough) Davis; m. Susan M. Stephens, Apr. 14, 1990; children: Garrett, Jeremy, Lindsay, Jennifer. Sr. sys. officer Citicorp, NYC, 1990—95; pres. Park Ave. Tech., Inc., Bedford, Tex., from 1990. Cons. merger, acquisition & divesture info. tech. Park Ave. Tech., Inc., from 1990. Pilot Angel Flight, Addison, Tex., from 2000. Served with aviation, USCG Aux., 2002—04, Grapevine, Tex. Christian. Avocations: networks, travel, aviation. Died Feb. 14, 2008.

DAVIS, SUZY, information center owner; b. Duncan, Okla., July 19, 1936; d. Elmer Arvin and Reba Dorril (Johnson) Gilstrap; m. Francis Jerome Dillard, Jan. 22, 1955 (div. May 1975); children: Jeri S., Lawrance A., Joe P., Marie E.; m. William Thomas Davis, Dec. 20, 1984 (dec.). Grad. high sch., Newman, Calif., 1954. Guest lectr. Calif. State U., Long Beach, 1986, 89, model Riverside, 1988-90, San Bernardino, 1988—90, Cmty. Coll., San Bernardino, 1988—90, Robert E. Wood Watercolor Workshop, Palm Springs, Calif., 1990, U. Nev., Las Vegas, 1993-95, Cheyenne C.C., North Las Vegas, 1993-95, Las Vegas Art Mus. Studio, 1994-95; owner, operator Nudist Info. Ctr., North Las Vegas, Nev., 1984-92; prodn. coord. Heritage Video, Las Vegas, 1992; bd. dirs. Beachfront USA, Moreno Valley. Bd. dirs. Callen-Davis Meml. Fund, Moreno Valley, Calif., 1988—, Western Sunbathing Assn., Studio City, Calif., 1989-92; active adopt-a-hwy. Western Sunbathing Assn., Victorville, Calif., 1990-92, Earth Week (city clean-up), Daggett, 1990. Named as part of Family of Yr., Western Sunbathing Assn., 1986, for Membership Increase by Percentage, Am. Sunbathing Assn., 1986, Woman of the Yr., Am. Sunbathing Assn., 1992; recipient Glen Eden award Am. Sunbathing Assn., 1986. Mem. Am. Assn. Nude Recreation (life), Western Sunbathing Assn. (life). Avocations: dance, reading, coin collecting/numismatics, stamp collecting/philately. Home: Pahrump, Nev. Died Mar. 9, 2008.

DAVIS, THOMAS EUGENE, automotive supplier executive; b. Ann Arbor, Mich., Nov. 23, 1937; s. Frank Guy and Bertha Marie (Warner) D.; m. Joan Louis Pollack, May 16, 1959 (div. 1977); children: Timothy, Tina, Melissa, Edward; m. Marcia Suzanne Wysocki, June 18, 1988. BS, Ea. Mich. U., 1964; MBA, Wayne State U., 1969. Research tech. Am. Metal Research, Ann Arbor, Mich., 1958-63; tech. supr. Hoover chem. Products, Whitmore Lake, Mich., 1963-64; devel. engr. Ford Motor Co., Utica, Mich., 1965-69; pres. Foamcraft, Inc., Roseville, Mich., 1970-81, Cerline Ceramic Corp., Anderson, Ind., 1982-87; dir. product devel. Dunnage Engring., Brighton, Mich., from 1987. Patentee in field. Pres. Huron High Sch. Music Assn., 1988. Mem. Soc. Mfg. Engrs., Soc. Plastics Engrs., Am. Ceramic Soc. Republican. Roman Catholic. Avocations: golf, woodworking, antique gunsmithing. Home: Bay City, Mich. Died Jan. 30, 2008.

DAVIS, WILLIAM LIPSCOMB, III, furniture company executive; b. Nashville, Aug. 5, 1957; s. William Lipscomb Jr. and Florence (Stumb) D.; m. Kimberly Ann Miller, May 30, 1980; children: William Lipscomb IV, Elizabeth Haley. BA, Vanderbilt U., 1979. Asst. engr. Davis Cabinet Co., Nashville, 1979-81, purchasing agt., 1981-83; mktg. rep., then sales rep. Jacques-Miller, Inc., Nashville, 1983-86; pres. Davis Furniture Co., Inc., Nashville, 1987-90, Davis Cabinet Co., Nashville, from 1990. Bd. dirs. Buddies of Nashville, 1983-90, Downtown YMCA, 1985-90, Martha O'Bryan Community Ctr., Nashville, 1990; mem. Mayoral Ctr. City Com., Nashville, 1989—; deacon 1st Presbyn. Ch., Nashville. Recipient Disting. Svc. award Nashville YMCA, 1988. Mem. Downtown Rotary Club, Belle Meade Country Club, Dominion Bank Young Exec. Com. Republican. Avocations: tennis, racquetball, golf. Home: Nashville, Tenn. Died Aug. 12, 2007.

DAVISON, ELIZABETH JANE LINTON, education educator; b. Las Cruces, N.Mex., Mar. 9, 1931; d. Melvy Edgar Linton and Clara Virginia Hale; m. Curwood Lyman Davison, Jan. 29, 1954; 1 child, Lawrence. BS, N.Mex. State U., 1957; postgrad., U. N.Mex.; Grad., Norris Sch. Real Estate, Albuquerque, 1984. Cert. tchr., N.Mex., Oreg.; cert. real estate agt., N.Mex., appraiser. Sec., treas. C.L. Davison, Md., Pa., 1975—88, Clovis, N.Mex., 1975—88; ind. real estate contractor Century 21, Las Cruces, 1984—85; ret. Albuquerque Pub. Schs., 1957—60, 1964—68; pres. Sun Dial Enterprises, 1984—95; tchr. Beaverton Pub. Schs., 1960—64. Mem. NEA, Legis. Coun., N.Mex. Albuquerque Classroom Tchrs. Inter-City Coun. (v.p.), AAUW, Phi Delta Kappa (Svc. key). Died May 21, 2008.

DAVISON, JOHN SAMUEL, retired ambassador; b. Detroit, May 21, 1933; m. Judith Kapp Davison (div.); children: Alice, Juliet; m. Therese Davison; 2 stepchildren: Gwenaelle, Jean-Francois BA, Harvard U.; MA, Oxford U., Eng., 1957; JD, Harvard U., 1961. With Fgn. Svc., Brussels, 1963-65; polit. officer US Dept. State, Leopoldville, 1963-65, rsch. analyst for Africa, 1972-74, desk officer Nigeria, 1969-70, staff asst. bur. African affairs, 1972-74, politico-mil. affairs officer, 1974-75, dep. chief mission Antananarivo, Madagascar, 1980-81, Khartoum, Sudan, 1981-83, charge d'affaires Cotonou, Benin, 1978-80, Maseru, Lesotho, 1983-84; dep. polit. adviser US Mission to NATO, Brussels, 1984-87; dir. East African Affairs US Dept. State, 1987-91, US amb. to Niger, 1993—96, dir. West African affairs, 1996—98; sr. examiner Bd. Fgn. Svc. Examiners, 1991-93. Mem. Am. Fgn. Svc. Assn., Am. Assn. Rhodes Scholars, D.C. Bar Assn. Died June 16, 2009.

DAY, EMERSON, physician; b. Hanover, NH, May 2, 1913; s. Edmund Ezra and Emily Sophia (Emerson) D.; m. Ruth Fairfield, Aug. 7, 1937 (dec. Oct. 1994); children: Edmund Perry, Robert Fairfield, Nancy, Bonnie, Sheryl; m. Germaine Scherman, Sept. 24, 1999. BA, Dartmouth Coll., 1934; MD, Harvard U., 1938. Intern Presbyn. Hosp., NYC, 1938- 40; fellow in cardiology Johns Hopkins U., 1940-42; asst. resident medicine NY Hosp., 1942; med. dir. internat. divsn. Trans World Airline, NYC, 1945-47; asst. prof. preventive medicine and pub. health Cornell U. Med. Coll.,

1947-50, assoc. prof. clin. preventive medicine and pub. health, 1950-54, prof. preventive medicine Sloan Kettering divsn., 1954-64; chmn. dept. preventive medicine Meml. Hosp., NYC, 1954-63; dir. Strang Cancer Prevention Clinic, 1950-63; mem., chief divsn. preventive medicine Sloan-Kettering Inst., NYC, 1954-64; cons. in geriat. Cold Spring Inst., Cold Spring-on-Hudson, NY, 1952-57; dir. NYC Dept. Health Cancer Detection Ctr., 1947-50, Strang Clinic/Meml. Sloan Kettering Cancer Ctr., 1950-63, PMI-Strang Clinic, 1963-69; pres. Preventive Medicine Inst., Strang Cancer Prevention Ctr., from 1969; hon. pres., mem. bd. trustees Preventive Medicine Inst., from 1969; v.p., med. dir. Medequip Corp., 1969-76, sr. med. cons., 1976-82; med. v.p. Health Mgmt. Internat., Inc., 1982-84; med. dir. Physicians for Med. Cost Containment, Inc., 1984-94; prof. medicine Northwestern U. Med. Sch., 1976-81, prof. emeritus, from 1981; assoc. dir. Northwestern U. Cancer Ctr., 1976-81; med. dir. Portes Cancer Prevention Ctr., 1978-79; attending physician Northwestern Meml. Hosp., 1976-81, vis. physician, 1981-99. Lectr. Cook County Grad. Sch. Med., 1977-90; mem. Northwestern U. Med. Assocs., 1980-81; med. dir., chmn. dept. internal medicine Chgo. Splty. Hosp. and Med. Ctr., 1981-84; hon. staff physician Evanston, Glenbrook hosps., 1976-99; attending physician, mem. med. bd. James Ewing Hosp., Meml. Hosp., NYC, 1950-64; founder, sr. mem. PMX Med. Group, NYC, 1956— 70; adj. prof. biology NYU, 1965-70; mem. cancer detection com. Internat. Union Against Cancer, 1954-70; pres. NYC div. Am. Cancer Soc., 1963-64; med. cons. Medidata Health Svcs., Inc., 1985-90; mem. Dean's Coun. for Future of Dartmouth Med. Sch. Contbr. numerous articles to profl. jours. Dir. Am. Found. for Children and Youth. Served as flight surgeon ATC USAAF, 1942-45. Recipient Bronze medal Am. Cancer Soc., 1956, professorship in early detection Ill. divsn., 1976-79, Lifetime Achievement award Strang Cancer Prevention Ctr., 2003. Fellow ACP, NY Acad. Medicine, NY Acad. Scis. (pres. 1965), APHA, Am. Occupl. Med. Assn., Am. Geriat. Soc., Internat. Acad. Cytology (hon.); mem. AMA, Am. Soc. Cytopathology (founder, pres. 1958, hon., Papanicolaou award 1978), Am. Soc. Preventive Oncology, Internat. Health Evaluation Assn., Soc. for Advanced Med. Sys. (founding dir. 1969-81), Am. Assn. Med. Sys. and Informatics (founding dir. 1981-84), Harvey Soc., Chgo. Clin. Ethics Program (charter), Century Assn., Ill. Med. Soc., Chgo. Med. Soc., Med. Cons. Svcs. Assn., Dartmouth Club (mem. dean's coun., award 1955), Phi Beta Kappa, Alpha Omega Alpha, Zeta Psi. Home: Wilmette, Ill. Died Oct. 21, 2008.

DEACIUC, ION VICTOR, molecular biologist, researcher; b. Sacel, Maramures, Romania, June 17, 1938; arrived in U.S., 1983; s. Victor Deaciuc and Agripina Danci; m. Kyoko Okumura, Jan. 21, 1958; children: Victor, Simona. MS, Babes-Bolyai U., Cluj-Napoca, Romania, 1960; PhD, Inst. Biochemistry, Kiev, Ukraine, 1967. Rschr. Acad. Scis., Cluj-Napoca, Romania, 1967—73; lectr. Babes-Bolyai U., 1974—78, assoc. prof., 1979—82; vis. scientist Boehringer GmbH, Mannheim, Germany, 1982—83; assoc. prof. La. State U., New Orleans, 1984—96; prof. molecular biology U. Ky., Lexington, 1996—2003, Ohio State U., Columbus, from 2005. Author: Cellular Regulation of Glucose and Fatty Acid Metabolism, 1973; contbr. articles to profl. jours. Mem.: Fedn. Am. Socs. Exptl. Biology, Rsch. Soc. on Alcoholism, Am. Assn. Study of Liver Diseases, Internat. Soc. Biomed. Rsch. on Alcoholism. Avocations: travel, folkloric music, reading. Home: Louisville, Ky. Deceased.

DEAN, ROBERT LIONEL, chemist; b. Phila., June 25, 1948; s. Everett Eugene and Roberta Lee (Conklin) D.; m. Inge S.R. Dean, Aug. 29, 1970; children: Renee K., Rebeccah M., Robert L. Jr., Ryan E. BA in Chemistry, Calif. State U., Sacramento, 1978. Rsch. assoc. dept. elec. engring. U. Ariz., Tucson, 1981-84; engr. Perkin Elmer EBT, Hayward, Calif., 1984; sr. staff engr. Etec Systems (formerly Perkin Elmer EBT), Hayward, from 1985. Contbr. articles to profl. jours. Mem. Am. Chem. Soc., SPIE, Bay Area Chrome Users. Republican. Presbyterian. Achievements include development of puddle process for photomart manufacture; patentee in field. Home: Castro Valley, Calif. Died Apr. 7, 2008.

DEANE, L(YTTLETON) NICHOLAS, restaurant and night club owner, publishing consultant; b. Kilgore, Tex., Nov. 1, 1954; s. L. and Dorothy (DeSesso) D.; m. Claire Dowling, Sept. 6, 1986. AB, Boston Coll., 1976; JD, Loyola U., New Orleans, 1979. Bar: N.Y. 1980. Editor Prentice-Hall, Englewood Cliffs, N.J., 1981-82; tax acct. Oppenheimer Appel, NYC, 1982-83; editor Warren Gorham & Lamont, NYC, 1983-86, Rsch. Inst. Am., NYC, 1986-87; sr. v.p., group pub. Faulkner & Gray, NYC, 1987-98; restaurant and night club owner, from 1998. Tax editor Physicians Mgmt., 1984-98; contbr. articles to profl. jours. Judge Lit. Mag., N.Y.C., 1993, 94. Democrat. Roman Catholic. Avocations: scuba, reading, travel, caribbean travel, music. Home: Montauk, NY. Died Aug. 10, 2008.

DEARDORFF, JOHN MILTON, JR., camera manufacturing executive, product designer; b. Villa Park, Ill., Sept. 17, 1935; s. John Milton and Dorothy Izella Anna (Witt) D.; m. Clare Lillian Greenwood, June 10, 1961 (div. Dec. 1989); children: Stephen John, Therese Marie. Student, Elmhurst Coll., 1963-64, Coll. of DuPage, 1977-85. From machinist to pres. L. F. Deardorff & Sons Inc., Chgo., 1948-88; pres. D.P.P.I., Valparaiso, Ind., from 1989. Engr., designer specialized photog. equipment for Chgo. Police Dept., NASA, Met. Mus. Art, USDA, also aerial mapping projectors for Sidwell Studios, Army Map Svc. Active Boy Scouts Am., 1972-85. With U.S. Army, 1958-60. Recipient numerous certs. from camera clubs and assns. Mem. Mid-states Indsl. Photographers Assn. (membership chmn. 1959—, citation 1984). Republican. Methodist. Avocations: stamps, photography, crafts. Died Nov. 7, 2007.

DECARAVA, ROY RUDOLPH, photographer, educator; b. NYC, Dec. 9, 1919; m. Sherry Turner, June 16, 1947; children: Susan, Wendy, Laura. Student, Cooper Union Art Sch., NYC, 1938-40; PhD (hon.), R.I. Sch. Design, 1985. Sign painter and display artist, N.Y., 1936-37; tech. draftsman, 1939-42; comml. artist and illustrator, 1944-58; freelance photographer for various advt. agys., rec. and TV cos., mags. including Scientific American, Fortune, McCall's, Look, Newsweek, Time, Life, 1959-68 and from 75; contract photographer Sports Illustrated mag., NYC, 1968-75; prof. art Hunter Coll., 1978, disting. prof. art, 1989—2009. Founder, dir. A Photographers Gallery, N.Y.C., 1954-56, Kamolinge Workshop for Black Photographers, N.Y.C., 1963-66; adj. prof. photography Cooper Union Inst., 1969-72, assoc. prof., 1975-78; mem. curatorial council Studio Mus., Harlem, N.Y., 1976. One-man shows include 44th Street Gallery, N.Y.C., 1950; Countee Cullen Br. N.Y. Pub. Library, 1951; Little Gallery N.Y. Pub. Library, 1954; A Photographers Gallery, N.Y.C., 1955; Studio Mus., Harlem, N.Y., 1969; Sheldon Meml. Art Ctr. U. Nebr., Lincoln, 1970; U. Mass., Amherst, 1974; Mus. Fine Arts, Houston, 1975; Corcoran Gallery, Washington, 1976; Benin Gallery, N.Y.C., 1976; Witkin Gallery, N.Y.C., 1977; Light Work Gallery, Syracuse, N.Y., 1977; Port Washington Pub. Library, N.Y.C., 1978; Friends of Photography, Carmel, Calif., 1980; Akron Art Inst. (Ohio), 1980; group exhbns. include Mus. Modern Art, N.Y.C., 1953, 55, 78, Met. Mus. Art, N.Y.C., 1964, Nat. Gallery of Can., Ottowa (toured Can. and U.S.), 1967, Ctr. Creative Photography, U. Ariz., Tucson, 1980, Tampa (Fla.) Mus., 1983, Barbican Art Gallery, London (toured Eng.), 1985, Fotografiska Museet, Stockholm, 1986; represented in permanent collections Mus. Modern Art, N.Y.C., Met. Mus. Art, N.Y.C., Harlem Art Collections, N.Y. State Office Bldg., N.Y.C., Andover Art Gallery Phillips Acad. (Mass.), Corcoran Gallery; Atlanta U., Sheldon Meml. Art Gallery U. Nebr., Mus. Fine Arts, Houston, Ctr. for Creative Photography U. Ariz., Tucson; photographer books: The Sweet Flypaper of Life (text by Langston Hughes), 1955, 2d edit., 1984; Photographs/DeCarava, (text by Sherry Turner) 1981; The Sound I Saw, 1983 (exhibited throughout Japan and Near East 1986). Served with U.S. Army, 1943. Recipient Art Svc. award Mt. Morris United Presbyn. Ch., N.Y.C., 1969; Nat. Medal Arts Nat. Endowment Arts, 2006; named hon. citizen of Houston, 1975; Guggenheim fellow. Mem. Am. Soc. Mag. Photographers. Home: Brooklyn, NY. Died Oct. 27, 2009.

DECKER, ELIZABETH ANNE, secondary school educator; b. Hilo, Hawaii, Feb. 16, 1952; d. Floyd Edward Jr. and Dorothy (Wilson) D. BA in English, U. Hawaii, 1974, BA in Polit. Sci., 1989. Cert. secondary tchr., Hawaii. Feature writer Coalfield Progress newspaper, Norton, Va., 1974-75; tchr. St. Joseph High Sch., Hilo, 1975-78, Hilo High Sch., 1979-80, 81-82, Mountain View (Hawaii) Elem.-Intermediate Sch., 1980-81, Waiakea Intermediate Sch., Hilo, from 1982. Tchr.-coord. econs. program Project Bus., Hilo, 1984—; student tchr. trainer U. Hawaii-Hilo, Chaminade, U. No. Colo., 1985-89; tchr. Upward Bound Summer Program, Hilo, 1989. Layreader Holy Apostles Ch., Hilo, 1986—. Mem. NEA, ASCD, Nat. Coun. Tchrs. English, Internat. Reading Assn. (v.p. 1983-84, pres. 1984-85, exec. bd. 1985-86), Hawaii Tchrs. Assn., Delta Kappa Gamma. Republican. Episcopalian. Avocations: reading, sewing, cooking, crafts, swimming. Died Dec. 19, 2007.

DECKER, THEODORE GEORGE, artist; b. Birmingham, Ala., Sept. 10, 1948; s. Francis Decker and Mary Isabell; m. Vaunda Jean Hills, May 22, 1970; children: Melissa Ann, Michelle Lynn. Co-author Morrison-Decker Act, 1983. With US Army, 1968. Democrat. Roman Catholic. Avocations: reading, photography. Home: Everett, Wash. Died Mar. 25, 2008.

DEERING, THOMAS PHILLIPS, retired lawyer; b. Winfield, Kans., Feb. 15, 1929; s. Frederick Arthur and Lucile (Phillips) D.; m. Marilyn Marie Anderson, Sept. 6, 1952; children: Thomas P. Jr., Robert E., Paul A. BS, U. Colo., 1951, LLB, 1956. Bar: Oreg. 1956, Colo. 1956, U.S. Dist. Ct. Oreg. 1956. Assoc. Hart Spencer McCulloch Rockwood & Davies (now Stoel Rives), Portland, Oreg., 1956-62; ptnr. Stoel Rives LLP, Portland, 1962—99; ret., 1999. Mem. We. Pension and Benefits Conf., 1989-2002; mem. faculty Am. Law Inst.-ABA, 1985-96. Co-author: Tax Reform Act of 1986, 1987. Bd. dirs. Girl Scouts Columbia River Coun., Portland, 1961-70; trustee, moderator First Unitarian Ch., Portland, 1967-70; trustee, pres. Catlin Gabel Sch., Portland, 1970-76; bd. dirs., v.p. ACLU, Portland, 1966-71, 73-80; chmn. Multnomah County Task Force on Edgefield Manor, Portland, 1972-75; bd. dirs., treas. Portland Art Mus., Contemporary Arts Coun., 1986-88; mem. City County Task Fore on Svc. Evaluation, Portland, 1982-85, Citizen's Adv. Com. West Side Corridor Project, Portland, 1988-93; bd. govs. Pacific N.W. Coll. Art, 1991-2000, 2002-, chair, 1996-2000, chair presdl. search com. 2002-2003; mem. collections com. Portland Art Mus., 1992-96; trustee Oreg. Coll. Art and Craft Endowment, Portland, 1991-97. With U.S. Army, 1952-54. Recipient Disting. Mem. award We. Pension and Benefits Conf., 1999. Fellow Am. Coll. Benefits Counsel (emeritus); mem. ABA (tax sect., EB com. 1989-2000), City Club of Portland (bd. govs. 1968-70, 2000-03, rsch bd. 2003—). Democrat. Avocations: hiking, skiing, sailing, reading. Home: Portland, Oreg. Deceased.

DEES, BOWEN CAUSEY, retired institute executive; b. Batesville, Miss., July 20, 1917; s. John Simeon and Ida Lea (Causey) D.; m. Sarah Edna Sanders, Aug. 25, 1937 (dec. 1999); 1 child, Sarah Edna; m. Dorothea Regina Simoneau, Sept. 24, 2001. AB, Miss. Coll., Clinton, 1937, DSc (hon.), 1963; PhD, NYU, NYC, 1942; LLD, Lehigh U., 1976, Phila. Coll. Textiles and Sci., 1979; DSc (hon.), Temple U., 1981. Prof. physics Miss. Coll., 1943-44; instr. elec comms. Radar Sch., MIT, 1944-45; asst. prof. physics Rensselaer Poly. Inst., 1945-47; physicist, then div. chief sci. and tech. div., gen. hdqrs. SCAP, Tokyo, 1947-51; program dir. fellowships NSF, 1951-56, dep. asst. dir. sci. personnel and edn., 1956-59, asst. dir., 1959-63, assoc. dir. for edn., 1963-64, assoc. dir. planning, 1963-66; v.p. U. Ariz., 1966-68, provost acad. affairs, 1968-70; pres. Franklin Inst., Phila., 1970-82, pres. emeritus, 1982—2009. Adv. com. U.S. Army Command and Gen. Staff Coll., 1967-69; sci. info. coun. NSF, 1970-74; mem. Sci. Manpower Commn., Washington, 1976-79; U.S. co-chmn. U.S.-Japan Com. on Sci. Cooperation, 1981-87. Author: Fundamentals of Physics, 1945, The Allied Occupation and Japan's Economic Miracle: Building the Foundations of Japanese Science and Technology 1945-52, 1997; contbr. articles to profl. jours. Mem. Cosmos (Washington). Home: Escondido, Calif. Died June 15, 2009.

DEFORD, PAUL STEVEN, lawyer; b. Kansas City, Mo., Aug. 26, 1956; s. Lee R. and Kathleen P. (Flynn) DeF.; m. Threasa F. Benezette, Aug. 12, 1978; children: Alexander, Kyle, Kathleen. BS, SW Mo. State U., 1978; JD, Drake U., 1981. Bar: Iowa 1981, Mo. 1981, U.S. Dist. Ct. (so. and we. dists.) Iowa 1981. Hearing examiner Mo. Pub. Svc. Commn., Jefferson City, 1981-84, dep. chief hearing examiner, 1984-87; assoc. Lathrop, Norquist & Miller, Kansas City, Mo., from 1987. Mem. ABA, Iowa Bar Assn., Mo. Bar Assn., Kansas City Bar Assn. Home: Lees Summit, Mo. Died May 31, 2008.

DE GASPER, EDGAR EUGENE, food services consultant; b. Buffalo, Oct. 16, 1922; s. James Joseph and Marie-Theresa (Vidan) De G.; married, 1951, divorced, 1972; m. Beatrice Louise Herskin, Dec. 22, 1976; children: Michael, Kathleen, Lisa, Mary Jo, Colleen, Rosemary. BS, Cornell U., 1948; MS, Canisius Coll., Buffalo, 1949; Doctorate (hon.), Nat. Assn. Food Equipment Mfr., 1972. Cert. Food Exec., Internat. Food Svc. Execs. Assn., Fla., 1973. Owner, mgr. Riviera Restaurant, Niagara Falls, N.Y., 1948-51; mgr. Brookfield Country Club, Clarence, N.Y., 1951-53, Bethlehem Steel Suprs. Club, Lackawanna, N.Y., 1953-54, Howard Johnson's Restaurants, Buffalo, 1955-56; dir. food svcs. City of Buffalo Bd. Edn., 1957-90; ret., 1990. Food svc. cons., Western N.Y., 1991—. Capt., USMC, 1942-47, U.S. and Pacific. Named Hon. Rear Admiral, USN, Washington, 1986, Hon. Brigadier Gen., U.S. Army, Ft. Lee, Va., 1991, Hon. Brigadier Gen., USMC, Washington, 1992. Mem. Internat. Food Svc. Execs. Assn. (internat. pres. 1972-74, 86), N.Y. State Sch. Food Svc. Assn. (pres. 1968), Cornell Soc. Hotelmen (pres. 1971-72), Can. Food Svc. Execs. Assn. (dir. 1988—). Roman Catholic. Avocation: recreational flying. Died Jan. 17, 2008.

DE GEORGE, LAWRENCE JOSEPH, diversified financial services company executive; b. NYC, May 6, 1916; s. Frank Phillip and Frances (Cavallo) DeG.; m. Florence A. Efel, Dec. 18, 1943; children: Lawrence F., Peter R. BSEE, Princeton U., 1936; MS, MIT, 1938; PhD in Advanced Math., Columbia U., 1939. Assoc. prof. elec. engring. Columbia U., 1938-39; field engr. Radio Engring. Lab., NYC, 1939-41; pres. Times Wire and Cable Co., Inc., div. Internat. Silver Co., Wallingford, Conn., 1946; also v.p., dir. Times Wire and Cable div., 1958-64, pres., 1964-68; v.p., dir. Insilco Corp., Meridan, Conn., 1968-72, exec. v.p., 1972-77, vice chmn., 1976-77; chmn., pres. Times Fiber Communications, Inc., Meriden, 1977-84, chmn., chief exec. officer, 1985-92, LPL Techs. Inc., Wallingford, Conn., 1985-97, Amphenol Corp., Wallingford, Conn., 1987-97; chmn., CEO DeG Capital Ptnrs. Ltd., Wallingford. Dir. Travelers Equities Fund, Inc., Hartford, Conn. Lt. comdr. USNR, 1941-46. Mem.: Club Collette, Admirals Cove Yacht Club, City Club, Palm Beach Yacht Club. Republican. Home: Jupiter, Fla. Died Apr. 13, 2009.

DEIMEN, JAMES MALSCH, lawyer; b. Detroit, Mar. 14, 1938; s. Albert David and Margarethe (Malsch) D. BS in Engring., U. Mich., 1960, MS in Engring., 1962, PhD, 1965, JD, 1967. Bar: Mich. 1968, U.S. Patent Office 1970, U.S. Ct. Appeals (6th cir.) 1975, U.S. Dist. Ct. (ea. dist.) Mich. 1976, U.S. Supreme Ct. 1977, U.S. Ct. Appeals (fed. cir.) 1978,; registered profl. engr., Mich. Assoc. Farley, Forster & Farley, Detroit, 1968-74; pvt. practice Ann Arbor, Mich., 1974-83 and from 1988; of counsel Conner, Harbour & Green, Ann Arbor, 1983-88. Cons. EPA Motor Vehicle Emissions Lab., Ann Arbor 1975-77. Co-author rsch. reports in field, 1965-77. Pres. Portage and Base Lakes Property Owners Assn., Pinckney 1975-77; chmn. Putnam Twp. Planning Commn., 1981-93. Mem. AAAS, NSPE, Am. Intellectual Property Law Assn., Mich. Patent Law Assn., State Bar Mich., Washtenaw County Bar Assn., Livingston County Bar Assn., Fed. Cir. Bar Assn. Avocations: sailing, swimming. Home: Pinckney, Mich. Died Nov. 6, 2007.

DE LA CRUZ, ANTONIO, otolaryngologist; b. San Jose, Costa Rica, June 13, 1944; children: Anthony, Jeanette. MD, U. Costa Rica, 1967. Diplomate Am. Bd. Otolaryngology, 1973. Otolaryngology House Ear Clinic, L.A., 1974—2009. Bd. trustees House Ear Inst., 1984—2009. Mem.: Am. Acad. Otolaryngology Head & Neck Surgery (pres. 1997—98, Presdl. Citation 2004, Disting. Svc. award 2007). Home: Marina Del Rey, Calif. Died July 31, 2009.

DELAMARTER, THELDA JEAN HARVEY, secondary school educator; b. Stafford, Kans., June 15, 1924; d. Guy Wright and Versa Jane (Reece) Harvey; m. Floyd Lourain Delamarter, Dec. 13, 1944 (dec. May 1996); children: Linda Lee, Donna Harris, Janie Stelljes. BA, Friends U., Wichita, Kans., 1945; teaching cert., Northwestern State Tchrs. Coll., 1958; MA in English, Wichita State U., 1965, postgrad., 1965-92. Cert. tchr. speech, theatre arts, English, psychology, music, social studies, Kans. Tchr. music Jet (Okla.) Pub. Schs., 1951-54, 57-59; tchr. lang. arts Unified Sch. Dist. 260, Derby, Kans., 1959-95, chmn. dept., 1972-84, ret., 1995. Pvt. tchr. piano and organ; lectr. Weight Watchers, 1972—. Organist Woodlawn United Meth. Ch., Derby, 1959-98. Nominated Kans. Tchr. of Yr. 1990. Mem. Derby Edn. Assn. (sec. 1962-63, various comms. 1963-70, Derby's Master Tchr. 1994-95). Home: Derby, Kans. Died Apr. 7, 2008.

DELANEY, MARK STEVEN, chemistry educator; b. Milw., Nov. 29, 1952; s. George W. and Ruth Marie (Schwartz) D.; m. Valerie Jean Conchis, July 12, 1980; children: Bridget, Briana. BS in Chemistry, Calif. State U., Fullerton, 1975; PhD, UCLA, 1980. Sr. rsch. chemist, project leader M.E. Pruitt Rsch. Ctr. (Cen. Rsch.), Dow Chem. Co., Midland, Mich., 1980-87; assoc. prof. McNeese State U., Lake Charles, La., from 1987. Contbr. articles Jour. Am. Chem. Soc.; inventor, patentee in field. Shearman rsch. fellow McNeese State U., 1988, 89, 92. Mem. La. Acad. Sci., Am. Chem. Soc. (polymer div. 1981—, inorganic div. 1981—, chmn. southwest La. sect. 1990). Lutheran. Avocations: fishing, bicycling. Home: Lake Charles, La. Died Apr. 4, 2008.

DELANEY, MARTIN EDWARD, health advocate; b. Boston, Dec. 9, 1945; Founding dir. Project Inform, San Francisco, 1985—2009. Spkr. on AIDS treatment and rsch.; mem. AIDS Rsch. Advisory Com. Nat. Inst. Allergy and Infectious Diseases, NIH, 1991—95; mem. bd. adv. Inst. Human Virology, U. Md., Baltimore. Co-author: Strategies for Survival: A Gay Men's Health Manual for the Age of AIDS, 1987; editor: Project Inform's HIV Drug Book, 1995; contbr. writings to med. pubs. and nat. mags. Recipient Stonewall award, Anderson Prize Found., 1991, Award of Courage, Found. AIDS Rsch., 2001, Director's Spl. Recognition award, Nat. Inst. Allergy & Infectious Diseases, 2009. Mem.: Am. Assn. Med. Coll. (mem. task force on fin. conflicts of interest in clin. rsch. 2001—09). Died Jan. 23, 2009.

DE LARROCHA, ALICIA, concert pianist; b. Barcelona, May 23, 1923; d. Eduardo and Teresa (De La Calle) de L.; m. Juan Torra, June 21, 1950; children: Juan, Alicia. Grad. (prize extraordinary, Gold medal), Acad. Marshall, Barcelona; MusD (hon.), U. Ann Arbor, 1979, Middlebury Coll., 1981, Carnegie-Mellon, 1985. Debut, Barcelona, 1929, solo recitalist, concert pianist maj. orchs. in, Europe, U.S., Can., Cen. and S.Am., South Africa, New Zealand, Australia, Japan; dir. Acad. Marshall, 1959—; rec. artist: Hispavox, CBS, Decca, London; records; (Grammy awards 1974, 75, 88, 91, nominations 1967, 75, 77, 82, 84, 90, 91, 92, 93, 1st Gold medal Merito a la Vocacion 1973), Spanish Encores, Spanish Fireworks, Spanish Music (I-IV). Recipient Harriet Cohen Internat. Music award, 1956, Franz Liszt award, 1989, Principe de Asturias award 1994, UNESCO award 1995; Paderewski Meml. medal, 1961; Grand prix du Disque Acad. Charles Cros, 1960, 74; Edison award, 1968, 78, 89, Ondas award, Spain, 1992, 2000; decorated Civil Merit Order, 1962, Isabel la Catolica, Spain, 1972; hon. academician Bayerische Akademie der Schönen Künste, Munich; Real Academia Bellas Artes San Fernando, Madrid, Real Academia de Bellas Artes, Granada, R.A.B-B.AA Sant Jordi, Barcelona; comdr. dans l'Ordre des Arts et des lettres, Paris, Fundación Guerrero Spanish Music award, 1999, Spanish Arts Tchr. nat. award, 2000. Mem. Musica en Compostela (dir.), Hispanic Soc. Am. (corr.), Internat. Piano Archives (hon. pres.) Died Sept. 25, 2009.

DE LEON, RUBEN L., lawyer; b. Habana, Cuba, Jan. 26, 1955; came to U.S., 1960; s. Ruben and Maria C. (Grau) deL.; m. Juana Maria de Leon. BA in Politics & Pub. Affairs, U. Miami, 1977; JD, Nova U., 1980. Bar: Fla. 1980, U.S. Dist. Ct. (so. dist.) Fla. 1980. Assoc. Law Offices of Gaston R. Alvarez, Miami, 1980-82; pvt. practice Miami, from 1982. Cons. Ram-Mart Investments, Inc., Miami, 1982-85, Edclamer Corp., Miami, 1985-87; mem. nominating com. Fla. Bar, 1995. Campaign worker Rep. Party Nat. Conv., Miami, 1972. Recipient Cert. of Appreciation, Pres. of the U.S., Washington, 1972. Mem. ABA, Assn. Trial Lawyers Am., Cuban-Am. Bar Assn., Nova Univ. Internat. Law Soc., Nova Univ. Alumni Assn. Roman Catholic. Died May 27, 2008.

DE LUISE, DOM, actor; b. Bklyn., Aug. 1, 1933; s. John and Jennie (DeStefano) De L.; m. Carol Arata, Nov. 23, 1965; children: Peter John, Michael Robert, David Dominick. Student, Tufts Coll. Actor: (off-Broadway play) Half Past Wednesday, (Broadway plays) The Student Gypsy, 1963, Luv; (TV series) Kraft Music Hall Presents: The Des O'Connor Show, 1970, Lotsa Luck, 1973, The Dom De Luise Show, 1987-88, Wake, Rattle & Roll, 1990, Candid Camera, 1991-92, All Dogs Go To Heaven: The Series, (voice only), 1996-98, Holllywood Squares, 1999-2004; (films): Diary of a Bachelor, 1964, Fail Safe, 1964, The Glass Bottom Boat, 1966, The Busy Body, 1967, What's So Bad About Feeling Good?, 1968, The Twelve Chairs, 1970, Norwood, 1970, Who is Harry Kellerman and Why Is He Saying Those Terrible Things About Me?, 1971, Every Little Crook and Nanny, 1972, Blazing Saddles, 1974, The Adventure of Sherlock Holmes' Smarter Brother, 1975, Silent Movie, 1976, The World's Greatest Love, 1977, Sextette, 1978, The End, 1978, The Cheap Detective, 1978, The Muppet Movie, 1979, Fatso, 1980, The Last Married Couple in America, 1980, Wholly Moses!, 1980, Smokey and the Bandit II, 1980, History of the World Part I, 1981, Cannonball Run, 1981, Pelle Svanslos, 1981, The Secret of NIMH (voice only), 1982, The Best Little Whorehouse in Texas, 1982, Cannonball Run II, 1984, Johnny Dangerously, 1984, Haunted Honeymoon, 1986, An American Tail (voice only), 1986, A Taxi Driver in New York, 1987, Space Balls (voice only), 1987, Going Bananas, 1987, Oliver & Company (voice only), 1988, The Princess and the Dwarf, 1989, All Dogs Go to Heaven, 1989, Loose Cannons, 1990, Driving Me Crazy, 1991, An American Tail II: Fievel Goes West (voice only), 1991, The Magic Voyage, 1992, Munchie, 1992, Almost Pregnant, 1992, The Skateboard Kid (voice only), 1993, Happily Ever After (voice only), 1993, Robin Hood: Men in Tights, 1993, The Silence of the Hams, 1994, A Troll in Central Park (voice only), 1994, All Dogs Go to Heaven II (voice only), 1996, Red Line, 1996, Toonstruck, 1996, Killer per Caso, 1997, The Secret of NIMH 2: Timmy to the Rescue (voice only), 1998, An American Tail: The Treasure of Manhattan Island (voice only), 1998, An All Dogs Christmas Carol, 1998, The Godson, 1998, My X-Girlfriend's Wedding Reception, 1999, Baby Geniuses, 1999, An American Tail: The Mystery of the Night Monster (voice only), 1999, Lion of Oz, (voice only), 2000, The Braniacs.com, 2000, Always Greener, 2001, It's All About you, 2002, Remembering Mario (voice only), 2003, Girl Play, 2004, Breaking the Fifth, 2004, Bongee Bear and the Kingdom of Rhythm (voice only), 2006, You Don't Mess with the Zohan, 2008; (TV films): Evil Roy Slade, 1972, Only With Married Men, 1974, Diary of a Young Comic, 1977, The Muppets Go Hollywood, 1979, Happy, 1983, Timmy's Gift: Precious Christmas Moments, 1991, Don't Drink the Water, 1994, The Tin Soldier, 1995, Shari's Passover Surprise, 1996, Boys Will Be Boys, 1997; (TV appearances) Tinker's Workshop, 1954, The Shari Lewis Show, 1963, The Entertainers, 1964, The Munsters, 1966, Please Don't Eat the Daisies, 1966, The Girl from U.N.C.L.E., 1966, The Dean Martin Summer Show, 1966, The Hollywood Palace, 1967, The Smothers Brothers Comedy Hour, 1967, The Jackie Gleason Show (2 episodes), 1967-68, The Merv Griffin Show (2 episodes), 1967-70, The Dean Martin Show (8 episodes), 1967-73, The Ghost & Mrs. Muir, 1969, Dinah's Place, 1970, The Carol Burnett Show, 1971, The Flip Wilson Show (4 episodes), 1971-73, The Roman Holidays, 1972 Rown & Martin's Laugh-In, 1973, Medical Center, 1974, The Muppet Show, 1977, Mike Hammer, 1984, Amazing Stories, 1985, 21 Jump Street, 1989, B.L. Stryker, 1989, All My Children, 1991, Fievel's American Tales (13 episodes), 1992, Diagnosis Murder, 1993, Marrier with Children, 1993, SeaQuest DSV, 1994, The Magic School Bus, 1994, Murphy Brown, 1995, The Ren & Stimpy Show, 1995, Burke's Law (4 episodes), 1995, Cybil, 1996, Duckman: Private Dick/Family Man, 1997, Beverly Hills, 90210, 1997, I Am Weasel, 1997, Cow and Chicken (2 episodes), 1997, Dexter's Laboratory (2 episodes), 1997, 3rd Rock from the Sun, 1998, Hercules, 1998, Sabrina, the Teenage Witch, 1998, The Wild Thornberrys, 1998, Stargate SG-1, 2000, Duck Dodgers, 2005; dir.: (films) Hot Stuff, 1979; (plays) Same Time Next Year, 1980, Butterflies Are Free, 1980, Brighton Beach Memoirs, 1986; author: Eat This ... It Will Make You Feel Better: Mama's Italian Home Cooking and Other Favorites of Family and Friends, 1987, Eat This Too!: It'll Also Make You Feel Better, 1997; (children's books) Charlie the Caterpillar, 1990, Goldilocks, 1992, Hansel & Gretel, 1997, The Nightingale, 1998, King Bob's New Clothes, 1999, The Pouch Potato, 2001. Died May 4, 2009.

DE MATTIA, MARLENE J., psychotherapist; b. Rochester, NY, July 1, 1932; d. Arthur Horace De Mattia and Corinne Grace Simonetti-De Mattia; m. Almerino Pappano, Feb. 2, 1957 (div. Dec. 1993); children: John A. Pappano, Maria Mykins. BA in Sociology and Psychology, Mercyhurst Coll., 1954; student, Rochester Inst. Tech., 1969; specialization in alcoholism and chem. dependency counseling, SUNY, Brockport, 1987, postrad. in liberal studies, 1989; MA in Addiction Counseling, St. Regis Univ., Wash., DC, 2001, PhD Psychol., 2002. Nat. accredited substance abuse counselor Credentialled Alcohol Substance Abuse Counselors, cert. addictions counselor N.Y., nat. cert. addictions counselor. Dir. U.S. escapee program Cath. Relief Svcs. for Italy, 1954—56; social worker Cath. Charities, Rochester, 1956—58; outpatient therapist Park Ridge Chem. Dependency, Rochester, 1988—99; ret., 1999; pvt. practice Rochester, from 2000; min. Prison Ministry, Monroe County Prison Sys., 2000—01. Spkr. in field; trainer cultural diversity awareness Park Ridge Hosp., Rochester, 1997—99; implementor women's track outpatient program Park Ridge Chem. Dependency, Rochester, 1993—99; oral examiner Office Alcoholism and Substance Abuse Svcs., N.Y. State, 1993. Sec., v.p. Park Ridge Aux., Rochester, from 1986, bd. dirs., exec. com., ann. ball com.; active St. John's Parish, Greece, NY; bd. dirs. Western Monroe Mental Health Ctr., Rochester, 1985, profl. adv. com., adv. coun. single parent project; women's guild bd. dirs. Cardinal Mooney H.S., program dir., coord. ann. play; bd. dirs. Prison Ministry Inc., Rochester, 2001. Mem.: Greece C. of C., Ridgemont Country Club (social chairperson), Rotary. Republican. Roman Catholic. Avocations: interior decorating, painting, calligraphy, travel, theater arts. Home: Rochester, NY. Died Sept. 28, 2007.

DEMING, FRANK STOUT, lawyer; b. Oswego, Kans., Aug. 12, 1927; s. Robert Orin Jr. and Helen Josephine (Stout) D.; m. Carolyn Ruth Kauffman, June 24, 1950; children: Frank S. Jr., Christiana Deming Jacobsen, David M., Robert W. BS in Econs., U. Pa., 1949, LLB, 1952. Bar: Pa. 1953, U.S. Dist. Ct. (ea. dist.) Pa. 1953, U.S. Ct. Appeals (3d cir.) 1953, U.S. Ct. Appeals (9th cir.) 1965. Assoc., then ptnr., now of counsel Montgomery, McCracken, Walker & Rhoads, Phila., 1952—2009. Bd. dirs. New Covenant Trust co. Contbr. articles to profl. jours. Trustee Bricker Found., Phila., Presbyn. Ch. (U.S.A.) Found., Jeffersonville, Ind., 1989-94, chmn., 1993, mem. gen. assembly coun., Louisville, 1990-91; dir. Presbyn. Children's Village, 1992-94. Sgt. U.S. Army, 1946-47. Fellow Am. Coll. Trust and Estate Counsel; mem. ABA, Pa. Bar Assn., Phila. Bar Assn., Mil. Figure Collectors Am., Phi Delta Theta, Beta Alpha Psi, Beta Gamma Sigma. Republican. Avocation: travel. Home: Media, Pa. Died June 18, 2009.

DENISON, JEANETTE, medical/surgical nurse; b. Fargo, ND, Jan. 26, 1931; d. Alfred J. and Agnes J. (Lahlum) Anderson; m. James J. Denison, Mar. 30, 1954; children: Gary J., Debra J. Denison Allen. Diploma, Sisters of St. Joseph Sch., 1952. Staff nurse Teton Meml. Hosp. (name changed to Teton Med. Ctr.), Choteau; office nurse Dr. D.E. Bosshardt, Whitefish, Mont., Dr. M.A. Johnson, Great Falls, Mont.; staff nurse Teton Nursing Home, Choteau. Recipient Community Svc. awards. Home: Choteau, Mont. Died Aug. 2, 2008.

DENNEHY, JOHN JOSEPH, internist; b. Phila., Jan. 30, 1930; s. John and Winifred (Byrne) D.; children: Michael, John, Patrick, Kathleen, Mary, Thomas. BA, La Salle Coll., Phila., 1952; MD, Hahnemann U., 1956. Diplomate Am. Bd. Internal Medicine, Am. Bd. Infectious Disease. Intern St. Agnes Hosp., Phila., 1956-57, resident in family practice, 1957-58; resident in internal medicine Hahnemann Hosp., Phila., 1958-61; dir. dept. infectious disease Geisinger Med. Ctr., Danville, Pa., 1964-88, sr. cons., 1988—96. Drug reviewer U.S. Pharmacopeial Conv., Washington, 1980-96. Contbr. articles to med. jours. Exec. bd. Columbia-Montour coun. Boy Scouts Am., 1970—, pres., 1984-85, scoutmaster, Riverside, Pa., 1972-74; pres. St. Joseph Parish coun., Danville, 1987-89. Capt. Med. Corp., U.S. Army, 1961-64. Recipient Silver Beaver award Boy Scouts Am., 1980. Fellow ACP; mem. AMA, Infectious Disease Soc. Am., Am. Soc. Tropical Medicine and Hygiene, Am. Venereal Disease Assn., Am. Fedn. for Clin. Rsch., Am. Soc. for Microbiology, Pa. Med. Soc. (mem. DUR com., mem. coun. on edn. and sci.), Montour County Med. Soc. (pres. 1976), Kiwanis, Elks. Republican. Roman Catholic. Home: Danville, Pa. Died Aug. 23, 2007.

DENNETT, JAMES ARTHUR, production manager, producer, director; b. NYC, Mar. 3, 1934; s. James Burns and Florence (McNally) D.; m. Nancy Barbara Schreiber, Jan. 19, 1957 (dec. Oct. 1984); children: James II, Mark, Steven, Victoria, Preston, Valerie. Student, Loyola U., Chgo., 1952-57, Columbia U., 1957. Film and TV unit prodn. mgr., 1st asst. dir., line producer. Film and TV credits include: American Revolution 2, 1969, The Murder of Fred Hampton, 1971, China Syndrome, 1977, Final Terror, 1980, Who am I This Time?, 1982, Wavelength, 1981, The Killing Floor, 1983, Beat Street, 1983, Code of Silence, 1984, Starman, 1987, Above the Law, 1987, The Package, 1989, Newsdogs, 1989, But He Loves Me, Matters of the Heart, 1990, Bad Attitudes, 1991, Dead in the Water, 1991, Wild Card, The Last Hit, 1992, The Fugitive, 1993, The Munsters, Shattered Mind, 1995, The Three Lives of Karen, 1996, L.A. Firefighters, Fire Company 132, The Barbara Mandrell Story, 1997. Mem. Dirs. Guild Am., Producers Guild Am., Soc. Oper. Cameramen. Died Aug. 11, 2009.

DENNIS, CHARLES ERWIN, JR., professional association executive; b. Newport, RI, Dec. 25, 1925; s. Charles Erwin Dennis and Catherine Helena (Pingley) Clelland; m. Marion Irene Kistler, Jan. 1, 1947; children: Kathleen I, Mary Ellen, Elizabeth Ann, Charles Erwin III. Student, George Washington U., 1947-48. Pres. Dennis Detective Agy., Inc., Severna Park, Md., 1955-87; exec. dir. World Assn. Detectives, Inc., Severna Park, from 1987. Pres. Nat. Coun. Investigators and Security Svcs., Inc., 1980-82, treas., 1982—; pvt. security adv. coun. Law Enforcement Assistance Adminstrs., Washington, 1976-77; com. mem. tng. curriculum Model Security Guard Tng., 1977. Bd. dirs. Severna Park Health Ctr., 1964-68, Anne Arundel Trade Coun., 1976-78. With USN, 1943-46, 50-54. Recipient Wayne Wunder award Nat. Coun. Investigators and Security Svcs., Inc., 1989, John J. Duffy award, 1990, Norman J. Sloan award World Assn. Detectives, 1991. Mem. DAV, SAR, World Assn. Detectives (pres. 1980-81, Investigator of Yr.), Severna Park C. of C. (past pres.) Kiwanis Club Severna Park (past pres.), Masons, Scottish Rite, Am. French Genealogical Soc., Newport (R.I.) Hist. Soc., R.I. Genealogical Soc., Annapolitan Club, Chartwell Golf and Country Club. Avocations: photography, camping, fishing. Home: Severna Park, Md. Died Sept. 13, 2007.

DEPEW, NANCY S.C., gifted education educator; b. Richmond, Va., Mar. 3, 1933; d. Elmer Lewis and Hattie Virginia (Shaw) Stanley; m. Hunter Gates Cockrell, June 21, 1956 (div. Aug. 1982); children: Charles Hunter, Elizabeth Hughes, Ann Wren, Thomas Stanley; m. Frederick Gerald DePew, Aug. 30, 1986. BA, Westhampton Coll., 1956; MEd, Va. Comty. U., 1977. Cert. elem. and secondary math., supervision; elem. and mid. sch. adminstrn., gifted edn. Tchr. math. Manchester N.S., Richmond, 1956-57, Stony Point Sch., Bon Air, Va., 1967-69, 71-72; tchr. math., dept. chair St. Edwards, Bon Air, 1974-78, Robicus Mid. Sch., Midlothian, Va., 1978-86, tchr. highly gifted math. mid. sch., from 1986. Mem. adv. bd. Stony Point Sch., Bon Air, 1977-79; mem. parents adv. com. gifted edn. Chesterfield County, 1988—. Chmn. ann. giving fund Westhampton Coll., Richmond, 1979. Mem. Nat. Coun. Tchrs. Math., Va. Coun. Tchrs. Math., Greater Richmond Coun. Tchrs. Math., Va. Assn. for Edn. of Gifted, Phi Beta Kappa, Pi Mu Epsilon, Phi Alpha Theta. Episcopalian. Home: Midlothian, Va. Died Jan. 5, 2008.

DEPINTO, RONALD DUNCAN, business owner; b. Chgo., Aug. 28, 1932; s. Angus Jacque and Margaret (Bensema) DeP.; m. Nancy West, Aug. 21, 1954 (div. 1972); children: Debora, Steven, Christopher. BS in Radio/TV, Northwestern U., 1954. Promotion mgr. KPHO-TV, Phoenix, 1955-57; owner, mgr. Hi-Fidelity House, Phoenix, 1958-60; v.p. Recording Ctr., San Diego, 1960-63; sales tng. specialist Ampex Corp., Sunnyvale, Calif., 1963-66; nat. sales mgr. TV Rsch. Internat., Palo Alto, Calif., 1967-69, Convergence Corp., Irvine, Calif., 1970-73; mktg. cons. Interquest, Fountain Valley, Calif., 1974-79; bus. owner New Video Exch., Fountain Valley, Calif., from 1980. Owner Electrotek: R & D & Mktg. Cons., Fountain Valley, 1985—. Author: Short Stories, 1954 (Schuman award 1954), (manual) Professional Salesmanship, 1965, (radio script) CBS Radio Network, 1957. Recipient Best In-House Publication award, 1956. Mem. Tiger Moth Club of Great Britain, Acad. Model Aeronautics, Soc. Motion Picture & TV Engrs., Soc. Broadcast Engrs., Phi Kappa Sigma Frat. Episcopalian. Avocations: photography, radio controlled aircraft-builder/flyer, cooking, electric powered aircraft specialist. Died July 1, 2008.

DERR, WILLIAM JAMES, retired non-commissioned officer; b. Catawissa, Pa., Oct. 24, 1934; s. Cyrus Sylvester and Dorothy Mae Derr; m. Marie Louise Parise, Oct. 27, 1956; children: Tina Marie, Theresa Ann. Grad. with GED, 1957. Enlisted U.S. Army, 1951, served in Korea, Japan, Germany, Vietnam, Alaska, 1951—72, ret., 1972; warehouse supt. Pa. Liquor Control Bd., Harrisburg, Pa., 1972—94, ret., 1994. Author: Righteousness or Iniquity, 2001. Mem. retiree coun. U.S. Army, Carlisle Barracks, Pa., from 1984; vol. ombudsman Dept. of Aging, Carlisle, Pa., 1999—2000. Decorated Army meritorious Unit Commendation, Vietnam Gallantry Cross with bronze palm., Vietnam Civil Action medal, Army Commendation Medal with Oak Leaf Cluster, Nat. Defense Svc. Medal with Bronze Star, Korean Svc. Medal, Vietnam Service Medal with Silver Star, UN Svc. Medal (Korea), Republic of Vietnam Campaign Medal, Korean Def. Svc. medal. Mem.: AARP, VFW (life), Disabled Am. Vet. (life), Nat. Assn. for Uniformed Svc. (life), Mechanicsburg Lions Club (pres. 2000—01, 2005—06, Lion of Yr. 2001—02), Am. Legion (life). Avocations: world travel, hunting, fishing, reading, gardening. Home: Mechanicsburg, Pa. Died June 26, 2008.

DESCH, CHRISTOPHER E., oncologist; MD, Ohio State Univ., 1981. Resident Strong Meml. Hosp., Rochester, NY, 1981—84; fellow in hematology & oncology Univ. Wash., 1985—88; assoc. dir. Massey Cancer Ctr., Va. Commonwealth Univ.; rsch. dir. Va. Cancer Inst.; nat. med. dir. Nat. Comprehensive Cancer Network, Jenkintown, Pa., from 2006. Contbr. chapters to books, articles to profl. jours. Fellow: Am. Coll. Physicians; mem.: Soc. for Med. Decision Making, Va. Soc. Hematology/Oncology, Am. Soc. Hematology, Am. Soc. Clinical Oncology (chmn. health svc. com.). Died Dec. 10, 2006.

DESPRES, LEON MATHIS, lawyer, former city official; b. Chgo., Feb. 2, 1908; s. Samuel and Henrietta (Rubovits) D.; m. Marian Alschuler, Sept. 10, 1931 (dec. Jan. 2007); children: Linda Baskin, Robert Leon. PhB, U. Chgo., 1927, JD, 1929; DLitt (hon.), Columbia Coll., Chgo., 1990, U. Ill., 2000. Bar: Ill. 1929. Ptnr. Despres, Schwartz and Geoghegan, Chgo.; alderman 5th Ward Chgo. City Council, 1955-75, parliamentarian, 1979-87. Co-author (with Kenan Heise): Challenging the Daley Machine: A Chicago Alerman's Memoir, 2005. Mem. Chgo. Plan Commn., 1979-89. Recipient Benton medal, U. Chgo., 2005. Mem.: Phi Beta Kappa, Order of Coif. Home: Chicago, Ill. Died May 6, 2009.

DETRICH, KALMAN, piano rebuilder, museum administrator; b. Budapest, Hungary, June 1, 1936; came to U.S., 1956; s. Ferenc and Gertrude (Benedek) D.; m. Anna Palinkas, July 4, 1957 (div. Nov. 1976); children: Tamas, Dora. BS in Mech. Engring., N.Y. Inst. Tech., 1967. Pres. Detrich Pianos, NYC, from 58; founder, exec. dir. Mus. of the Am. Piano, NYC, from 1984. Mem. Piano Tech. Guild, Master Piano Technicians, Airplane Owners and Pilots Assn. Avocations: flying, sailing, travel. Died June 8, 2008.

DETWEILER, DAVID KENNETH, veterinary physiologist, educator; b. Phila., Oct. 23, 1919; s. David Rieser and Pearl Irene (Overholt) Detweiler; children: Ellen, Diane, Judith, Inge, Kenneth, David. VMD, U. Pa., 1942, MS, 1949; ScD (hon.), Ohio State U., 1966; MVD (hon.), U. Vienna, Austria, 1968; DMV (hon.), U. Turin, Italy, 1969. Asst. instr. physiology and pharmacology Sch. Vet. Medicine, U. Pa., Phila., 1942—43, instr., 1943—45, assoc. in physiology, pharmacology, 1945—47, asst. prof., 1947—51, assoc. prof., 1951—62, assoc. prof. Grad. Sch. Arts and Scis., chmn. dept. vet. med. scis. Grad. Sch. Medicine, 1956—68, dir. comparative cardiovasc. studies unit, 1960—90, prof., head lab. physiology and pharmacology, 1962—68, prof., head lab. physiology, 1968—90, prof. faculty arts & sciences, 1968—90, chmn. grad. group comparative med. scis., 1971—87, prof. emeritus, 1990—2009. Mem. Inst. Medicine of NAS, 1974—2009; guest USSR Acad. Sci.; cons. cardiovasc. toxicology, 1950—2009. Contbr. articles to profl. jours. Recipient Disting. Veterinarian award, Pa. Vet. Med. Assn., 1989, Disting. Practitioner award, Nat. Acads. of Practice in Vet. Medicine, 1989, D.K. Detweiler prize in cardiology established in his honor, German Group of World Vet. Med. Assn., 1982, David K. Detweiler Conf. Rm. named in honor, Veterinary Sch. U. Pa., 1993, Centennial medal, Sch. Vet. Medicine, U. Pa., 1994, cert. appreciation, FDA, 1998; named Father of Vet. Cardiology, Veterinary Sch. U. Pa., 1994; fellow Guggenheim Found. Fellow: AAAS; mem.: Vet. Med. Alumni Soc. (Merit award U. Pa. 1981), Am. Coll. Vet. Internal Medicine (diplomate, cardiology group), Acad. Vet. Cardiology (pres.), Am. Heart Assn., Coun. Basic Scis., Am. Vet. Med. Assn. (Gaines award and medal 1960, Honor Roll award 1990), N.Y. Acad. Scis., Am. Assn. Vet. Physiology and Pharmacology (pres.), Am. Physiol. Soc., Phi Zeta, Sigma Xi. Died Feb. 15, 2009.

DEUFEL, ROBERT DAVID, management consultant, microbiologist; b. Chgo., Mar. 22, 1928; s. Robert Marian and June Pearl (Larsen) D.; m. Geraldine Ruth Kappe, June 14, 1952; children: David, Susan, Ruth, Karen, Andrew. BS in Biology with honors, Elmhurst Coll., Ill., 1950; MS, U. Ill., 1951, PhD in Bacteriology/Biochemistry, 1957. Head microbiol. testing/devel. Eli Lilly, Indpls., 1957-63; chmn. dept. biology U. Indpls., 1963-69, Centenary Coll. of La., Shreveport, 1969-75; head rsch. and devel. McDonnell Douglas Diagnostic Products, St. Louis, 1975-78; mgr. quality assurance Vitek Systems, Inc., Hazelwood, Mo., 1978-80; mgr. quality control Rexall Corp., St. Louis, 1980-84; pres. Deufel & Assocs., Chesterfield, Mo., from 1984. Author lab. manuals and tng. workbook. Dist. tng. chmn. Boy Scouts Am., Indpls., 1958; pres. Rockwood Citizens and Execs. Assn., Chesterfield, 1976; chmn. adv. bd. St. Louis Community Coll., 1985. With U.S. Army Chem. Corps, 1951-53. NSF grantee, 1968, 69-70, 74; NASA grantee, 1971-72. Mem. Am. Soc. for Quality Control (chmn. St. Louis chpt. 1985-87, editor newsletter 1986—), West. St. Louis C. of C. (bd. dirs.), Rotary Club (bd. dirs. 1990), Sigma Xi. Presbyterian. Avocations: writing, painting, furniture refinishing, sailing, canoeing, tennis, scuba diving. Died Aug. 4, 2008.

DEUTSCHMAN, LOUISE TOLLIVER, curator; b. Taylorville, Ill., Sept. 6, 1921; m. Paul Eugene Deutschman, Dec. 20, 1941 (div. 1966); 1 child, Deborah Elliott. BA, MacMurray Coll., 1937; postgrad., Northwestern U., Sorbonne, Paris, 1950—66; PhD (hon.), 2008. Assoc. dir. Waddell Gallery, NYC, 1966—74, Sidney Janis Gallery, NYC, 1975—78; dir. Alex Rosenberg Gallery, NYC, 1978—80; assoc. Sidney Janis Gallery, NYC, 1980—2000; curator PaceWildenstein, NYC, from 2000. Guest curator Nasher Sculpture Ctr., Dallas, 2004—06. Home: New York, NY. Died May 10, 2009.

DEVANEY, JOSEPH JAMES, physicist, researcher; b. Boston, Mass., Apr. 29, 1924; s. Joseph Patrick and Madeline Elinor (Darragh) D.; m. Marjorie Ann Jones, Sept. 9, 1954; 1 child, Kathleen. Student, Tex. Tech U., 1943-44, USCG Acad., 1944-45; SB, MIT, 1947, PhD, 1950. Research asst. MIT, Cambridge, 1942, 46-48; staff physicist Los Alamos Nat. Lab., from 1950. Adj. prof. math. U. N.Mex., Los Alamos, 1956-59, adj. prof. physics, 1959-79. Contbr. articles to profl. jours. Adv. Gov.'s policy bd. on pollution, State of N.Mex., 1969-70; mem. County and State Cen. Com., Los Alamos and Santa Fe, 1953-71; co-founder Anti-Smog Fedn. N.Mex., 1967, patrolman Nat. Ski Patrol, 1953-82, water safety and first aid instr. ARC, Los Alamos, 1952-79. Served with AUS, 1942-44; served with USCG, 1944-45. MIT scholar, 1941, 42, 45, 46, 47; AEC fellow, 1947-50. Mem. AAAS, Am. Phys. Soc., Am. Nuclear Soc., Los Alamos Ski Club (ski patrol leader 1962-63Z), Sigma Xi. Home: Los Alamos, N.Mex. Died Sept. 23, 2007.

DEVEREAUX, EVELYN JANINE, librarian, civilian military employee; b. Hamilton Field, Calif., Apr. 4, 1947; d. Ray Wilson and Evelyn Louise (Olin) D.; 1 child, Kenneth Devereaux Black. BS with honors, U. So. Miss., 1976, MLS with honors, 1978. Adminstrv. asst. to dean Sch. Libr. Sci., U. So. Miss., Hattiesburg, 1974-78; mktg. specialist AT&T, 1978-79; aircrew instr. USAFR, Keesler AFB, Miss., 1979-86; base libr. Lajes Field, Azores, Portugal, 1986-89, Rhein-Main Air Base, Fed. Republic of Germany, 1989-91; chief libr. svcs. Charleston AFB, SC, 1991—95; supervisory libr. Air Force Info. Welfare Ctr., San Antonio, 1995—98. Vol. literacy tutor. Decorated Air Res. Forces meritorious svc. medal, Air Force Achievement medal, Combat Readiness medal, Air Force Longevity Svc. award, Small Arms Expert Marksmanship ribbon; named Fed. Civilian Woman of Yr., USAF, 1987, Meritorius Libr., USAF, 1994. Mem. ALA, Spl. Librs. Assn., Fed. Librs. Assn., Internat. Assn. Aquatic and Marine Sci. Librs. and Info. Ctrs., Southeastern Affiliate Internat. Assn. Aquatic and Marine Sci. Librs. and Info. Ctrs., Air Force Assn. Died Nov. 24, 2007.

DEVIVO, ANGE, retired small business owner; b. Bay Shore, NY, Oct. 20, 1925; d. Romeo Zanetti and Karolina (Hodapp) King; m. John Michael DeVivo, Dec. 30, 1950; 1 child, Michael. Student, Washington Sch. for Secs., NYC, 1945-46. Sec. Am. Airlines, NYC, 1946-51; exec. sec. W.C. Holzhauer, NYC, 1951-52; dist. sales mgr. Emmons Jewelers, Inc., Bound Brook, NJ, 1952-53; exec. sec. NJ Rep. State Com., 1960—64; dist. office supr. 19th Decenniel census US Dept. Commerce, Charlotte, NC, 1970; NC rep. chair, 5 state and dist., Columbia leadership conf., 1971; Meck county precinct chair, 1971—73; Meck county rep., precinct chair, 1971—73; mem., NAD rep. Women Conv. Credentials Com., Washington, 1972; mem., NC rep. exec. com., 1972—77; adminstrv. sec. Mercy Hosp., Charlotte, NC, 1973—81; pres. Secs., Plus, Convs., Plus, Charlotte, 1983—91; prin. Ange DeVivo & Assocs., Inc., Charlotte, 1991—92; ret., 1992. Editor: The North Carolina Republican Woman, 2d edit., 1994, 3d edit., 1995; author Precinct Training Manual, 1971.(Pres. Cert., 1975) First woman chair Mecklenburg County Rep. Party, 1976; adminstrv. sec. Nat. Broadcast Assn. for Cmty. Affairs, 1987-90; active in local politics, NJ, 1956-64, Conn., 1964-68, NC, 1968-96; conducted polit. seminars, 1973, 74, 76; panelist Seminar for Tchrs., Robert A. Taft Inst. Govt., 1977; small bus. action coun. Greater Charlotte C. of C., 1983-89, mem. transpotation com., 1984, Govt. action coun., 1985, discount com., 1985, co-chair minority and women owned bus. directory, 1988, chair Bus. Opportunity Network and Mixer Exhibit, 1987, chair Carolina Bus. Fair, 1989; active Human Svcs. Coun., Charlotte, 1984-88; conf. mgr., 8th Nat. Recycling Congress, 1989; active Emergency Med. Svc. Adv. Coun., Charlotte, 1981-92, chmn., 1988-90; active Charlotte Women's Polit. Caucus, 1972-96; chair Mecklenburg County Rep. Party, 1976-77, NC Plan reveiw com., 1973,1977; alt. del. at large, nute rep. women, 1972; mem. Mech. county rep. exec. com., 1968-78, 1981-87, 1993-94; mem. Mecklenburg Evening Rep. Women's Club, Charlotte, 1968-2006, pres., 1973-74, 93-94; mem. Mecklenburg County Women's Commn., 1990-96, newsletter editor, 1979-83, 86, 93, 94, repulican task froce hon. mem., 2000, Women's Roundtable, 1994-95; citizens adv. com. Conv. and Visitors Bur., 1986-90; coord. Women's Equality Day celebration Mecklenburg County Women's Commn., 1990, coord., fin. chair, 1991-92, co-chmn., fin. chair, 1993-96, adv. bd. 1993-96, vice-chair bd., 1995; fundraiser March of Dimes and Leukemia, Ala., 1999, 2002, 2006, 2008; active Rep. Women Today Ala., 1997-2001, tel. com., 2001; pres. Cardinal Bus. and Profl. Women's Club, 1979-81, chair southern reg. BPW political action conf., chair cardinal pol. health conf., 1981-82, newsletter editor, 1979-83, vol habitat for humanity, 1993; site insp. for spl. events in Jamaica, 1987. Recipient Seal of City of Stamford, Conn., 1968, Order of Long Leaf Pine award Gov. of NC, 1974, nominee WBT Woman of Yr, Charlotte chpt. Nat. Sec. Assn., 1977, Cert. Appreciation Cardinal Bus. and Profl. Womens' Club, 1978, Woman of Yr. award Cardinal Bus. and Profl. Womens' Club, 1982, Entrepreneur of Yr. award Women Bus. Owners, 1987, Cert. Appreciation outstanding leadership and dedicated svc. Charlotte Women's Bus. Owners Assn., 1990-91, Award of Honor in recognition of outstanding svc. Mecklenburg County Women's Com., 1991, Spl. Recognition award for devotion, dedication and untiring efforts Mecklenburg County Women's Commn., 1996, Seal of Mecklenberg County, NC, 1996; honoree NC Fedn. Rep. Women, 1987; nominee Cmty. Svc. award Mecklenburg County Women's Commn., 1994, Hall Fame, NC Rep. Party, 1995. Mem.: Rep. Women of the South (telephone com. 2004—08, mem., achievement com. 2005—08, bd. dirs. 2006, membership com. 2008). Roman Catholic. Avocations: politics, community service. Home: Hoover, Ala. Died Sept. 6, 2006.

DEVOE, DOROTHY S., retired elementary school educator; d. Hadley and Rachael Sirmans; m. Allen A. Devoe Jr., Jan. 4, 1965; children: Tonya L., Wrenettia K. BS, Albany State U., Ga., 1966; MEd, U. No. Fla., 1988; student, Jacksonville U., 1969, Fla. A&M U., 1977-78. Cert. tchr. Fla. Classroom tchr., computer lead tchr. Duval County Pub. Schs., 1986—88, reading recovery tchr., 1998—2005, ret., 2005. Presenter in field. Mem. Duval County Reading Coun. Recipient various awards and certs. Mem. Fla. Reading Assn., Fla. Edn. Assn., Nat. Reading Recovery Coun. N.Am., Nat. Coun. Negro Women, Zeta Phi Beta. Home: Jacksonville, Fla. Died June 5, 2008.

DEVON, WESLEY SCOTT, food company executive; b. Van Dyke, Mich., Apr. 25, 1939; s. Branko and Sophie (Devonovich) D.; children: Kimber Lynn Patane, Wesley Scott Jr. Student, Ferris State U., 1957, U. Detroit, 1959. Retail sales mgr. Awrey Bakeries, Inc., Detroit, 1963-69; mktg. cons. Buttercup Bakeries, Grand Rapids, Mich., 1969-71, Cole's Bakeries, Inc., Muskegon, Mich., 1969-71, v.p. mktg., 1971-73, pres. frozen div., 1975-79, exec. v.p., 1975-79, pres., gen. mgr., 1979-83; pres., chief exec. officer, chmn. bd. dirs. Cole's Quality Foods, Inc., Muskegon, Mich., from 1983. Pres., chmn. bd. dirs. Lakeshore Yacht Harbour, Inc., Muskegon, 1982—. Active Bus. for Blanchard Com., Lansing, Mich., 1987, Pres. Task Force, Washington, 1987. Mem. Am. Mgmt. Assn., Mich. C. of C., Muskegon C. of C. Died Aug. 15, 2007.

DEVORE, PAUL CAMERON, lawyer; b. Great Falls, Mont., Apr. 25, 1932; s. Paul Theodore and Maxine (Cameron) DeV.; m. Roberta Humphrey, Feb. 3, 1962; children: Jennifer Ross, Andrew Cameron, Christopher Humphrey. BA, Yale U., 1954; MA, Cambridge U., 1956; JD, Harvard U., 1961. Bar: Wash. 1961. Assoc. Wright, Innis, Simon & Todd, Seattle, 1961-66; ptnr. Davis Wright Tremaine, Seattle, 1967—2002, chmn. exec. com., 1983-95. Mem. adv. bd. BNA Media Law Reporter, 1978-2008 Chmn. Seattle C.C., 1967-68, Bush Sch., Seattle, 1976-79, Virginia Mason Med. Found., 1984-85, Virginia Mason Rsch. Ctr., 1983-84, Seattle Found., 1985-87, Children's Hosp. Found., 1993—; trustee Lakeside Sch., 1995-2004, Lopez Cmty. Land Trust; chmn. bd. visitors U. Wash. Sch. Comm., 1989-98; pres. A Contemporary Theatre, Seattle, 1972-74; sec. Seattle Art Mus., 1973-2000. Mem. ABA (chmn. forum on comm. law 1981-84), Wash. State Bar Assn. (chmn. sect. corp. bus. and banking law 1981-82, bench, bar, press com. 1984-90), Seattle-King County Bar Assn. (trustee 1975-76), Seattle Tennis Club, Phi Beta Kappa, Beta Theta Phi. Home: Seattle, Wash. Died Oct. 26, 2008.

DEWITT, EDWARD FRANCIS, artist; b. Jersey City, Aug. 1, 1938; s. Elmer and Linda (Kroll) DeW.; m. Cora Finn, Nov. 11, 1959 (separated 1970); children: April, Lenneice, Edward, Linda; m. Mary Golazizian, Sept. 17, 1972. Artist cons. Bronx Zoo, 1968-70, Aquarius Art Ltd., Fairview, N.J., 1971-73; artist, sculptor, v.p. Artistic Classics, Rutherford, N.J., 1974-77; artist, sculptor, Browns Mills, N.J., 1977-97. Artist 5-yr. silverplate series Anheuser Busch; commemorative works for Pub. Svc., Babe Ruth, Gen. Doolittle, Jim Thorpe PA; sculptures Ford Motor Co., GM Corp., Bicentennial Soc., Boy Scouts Am., Thomas Edison, NATO, Chesapeake Reproductions, Mappsville, Va.; award programs for Progresso Foods, Kentucky Fried Chicken; medallions John F. Kennedy, Dwight D. Eisenhower, Winston Churchill, Bobby Kennedy, Charles A. Lindbergh, Gerald Ford: President; artist prints-sculptures models and collector plates Abundant Ocean Treasures, Saddlebrook, N.J., Double Eagle Sculpture (ofcl. symbol for New Millenium chosen by U.S. Hist. Soc.); series of prints chosen for Zallies Shop-Rite chain; commd. to sculpt profiles of Am. Presidents Medallion Series, Chesapeake Reprodns., Mappsville, Va., 2003, Louis and Clark 200th anniversary sculpture, 2003; represented in numerous pvt. collections in U.S. and Europe; patentee on door striker plate. Double eagle sculpture chosen as official symbol by U.S. Hist. Soc., 2000. Avocations: the arts, music, guitar, fishing. Home: Browns Mills, NJ. Died June 6, 2008.

DIAL, WILLIAM ALLEN, writer, television producer; b. Columbia, SC, June 17, 1943; s. Fred William and Ruth Allen (Faris) D.; m. Pamela Jean Biles, Dec. 16, 1967 (div. 1971); m. Joy Dewitt Malone, June 18, 1973; stepchildren: Barbara, Daniel Manning, David Manning, Margaret, Melanie. Student, Ga. State U., 1961-65. Writer MTM Enterprises, North Hollywood, Calif., 1978-79; writer, producer Universal City (Calif.) Studios, 1979-86, Walt Disney Studios, Burbank, Calif., 1986-89; freelance writer, producer Paramount, MGM, Lorimar, LA, from 1986. Writer (TV) Tony Randall Show, 1978; writer, producer (TV) WKRP in Cincinatti, 1978-79, House Calls, 1980, Lobo, 1981, Simon and Simon, 1982-86, Legman, 1983, Codename: Foxfire, 1984, Sidekicks, 1986-87, Absent-Minded Professor, 1988, E.A.R.T.H. Force, 1989-90. Mem. AFTRA, SAG, Writer's Guild of Am. Democrat. Avocations: classical music, Am. history, baseball fan. Died June 2, 2008.

DIAMOND, ELAYNE FERN, interior designer, small business owner; b. Newark, July 1, 1945; d. Charles Ronald and Louise Pearl (Fern) Newman; m. Stanley Diamond, Nov. 20, 1965; children: Garrett L., Robin Fern. Student, N.Y. Sch. Interior Design, 1963-67. Pres. Elayne Diamond Interiors, Union, N.J., from 1964; owner, pres. Novelty Express, Union, Springfield, Totowa, N.J., 1975-80, Personalitees, Beach Haven, N.J., 1978-84, Put Togethers, Surf City, N.J., 1979-81, Designer's View Inc., Greenbrook, N.J., from 1988. Cons. in field; designer, owner Yellow Brick Rd., Inc., Springfield, Beach Haven, 1975-79; cons. to constrn. cos., window mfgs., N.J., 1969—; distbr. Energy Controls, Springfield, 1985-86; pres. Advantage Point, Woodbridge, N.J., 1990. Publisher, editor Trade Secrets Interior Design Directory; contbr. designs to trade and comml. mags., various home tours, newspaper articles, 1964—. Fund raiser Ctr. Sch. for the Learning Disabled, N.J., Am. Cancer Soc., others. Mem. Allied Bd. Trade. Avocations: painting, antique collecting, spending time with family. Died July 13, 2008.

DIAMOND, NANCY ABBOTT, small business owner; b. Winchester, Va., Nov. 15, 1937; d. Reverdy Estil and Nancy Hundley (Boyd) Winfree; m. Richard Henry Abbott III, Sept. 4, 1964 (div. 1974); children: Robert M., Louisa E.; m. Howard Diamond, Aug. 19, 1984. Student, Longwood Coll., 1956-58; BS in Sec. Edn., Old Dominion U., 1961. Social worker Dept. Pub. Welfare, Norfolk, Va., 1963-64; art tchr. Norfolk Pub. Schs., Norfolk, Va., 1961-63, 64-66; graphic artist Audio Visual Edn. Dept. U. Mich., Ann Arbor, 1966-68, P.R.I.D.E. Project, Wayne, Mich., 1973-74, Yesterday's Printing, Ypsilanti, Mich., 1974-79; tchr.art, English Ypsilanti, 1979-85; mgr., owner Ad Hoc Advt., Ann Arbor, 1987-91. Exhibits include galleries and art fairs in Va., Mich., Ill., Ohio, Fla., and Ind.; group shows include Ann Arbor (Mich.) Art Assn., 1980, Windmore Found., Culpeper, Va., 2000-05, Orange Art Ctr., 2002, 03, Fredericksburg (Va.), 2005 (hon. mention award); contbr. articles to profl. jours; creator Cat Gems, 1987. Active Windmore Found. Artists Group, 2000—; chmn. study group Hadassah, 1985-87; designer, Ann Arbor Ethnic Fair, Mich., 1988. Recipient Tech. Manual Design award Soc. Tech. Writers, 1979. Jewish. Avocation: travel. Home: Locust Grove, Va. Died Aug. 14, 2008.

DIAMOND, THOMAS DIXON, retired computer software company executive; b. Phila., Oct. 6, 1925; s. Gilbert and Elinor (Dixon) D.; m. Joanne Lyon (div. Feb. 1992); children: T. David, Douglas L. BS in Economics, Lafayette Coll., Easton, Pa., 1950. Salesman Remington Rand, Phila., 1950-56; mgmt. cons. Arthur Andersen & Co., Phila., 1956-59; founder, pres. Diamond Mgmt. Systems, Rydal and Jenkintown, Pa., 1969-93, chmn. Jenkintown, 1994—99. Mem. ch. coun. Gloria Dei Luth. Ch., Huntingdon Valley, Pa., 1961-89; bd. dirs. Frankford Hosp., Phila., 1989-92 Recipient Assn. Systems Mgmt. Achievement award, 1974; named Pres. Keystone chpt. Assn. Systems Mgmt., 1969. Mem. Nat. Assn. Accts., Hosp. Fin. Mgmt. Assn., Assn. for Sys. Mgmt. (Achievment award 1974, pres. 1969-70), Data Processing Mgmt. Assn. (cert. 1963), Nat. Club Assn. (assoc.). Home: Philadelphia, Pa. Died Oct. 29, 2009.

DIAMOND, WILLIAM, retired bank executive; b. Balt., Dec. 20, 1917; s. Isidor and Yetta (Mirtenbaum) D.; m. Lois Wilhelm, Oct. 28, 1946 (dec. 2004) AB, Johns Hopkins U., 1937, PhD, 1942. Loan officer World Bank, 1947-55, div. chief, 1958-59; mem. staff Econ. Devel. Inst., 1955-58; adviser Indsl. Credit and Invesment Corp. India, Bombay, 1959-60; asst. dir. dept. ops. Western Hemisphere, 1960-62; dir. devel. fin. cos. dept. Internat. Fin. Corp., 1962-68, World Bank, 1968-72, dir. South Asia dept., 1972-75, advisor to v.p. fin., 1975-77; sr. fellow Econ. Devel. Inst., 1977-78. Cons. in field; bd. dirs. DFC Ltd., London, DFC SA, Paris; advisor FRIDA, Amsterdam; cons. BPI, Porto Author: The Economic Thought of Woodrow Wilson, 1943, Czechoslovakia between East and West, 1947, Development Banks, 1957; editor: Development Finance Companies: Aspects of Policy and Operation, 1968, (with V.S. Raghavan) Aspects of Development Bank Management, 1982; contbr. numerous articles to profl. jours. Died May 16, 2009.

DIBNER, DAVID ROBERT, architect, writer; b. NYC, May 29, 1926; s. Harry Jesse and Masha Leah (Goldberg) D.; m. Dorothy Joyce Siegel, June 22, 1947; children: Mark Douglas, Amy Lauren. B.Arch., U. Pa., 1949. Registered architect, N.Y., Md., Va., D.C. Ptnr. Fordyce & Hamby Assocs., NYC, 1956-66, The Grad Ptnrship., Newark, 1966-77; pres. Grad-Hoffman, Inc., 1971-75; v.p. Walker-Grad, NYC, 1972-77; exec. v.p. Grad Associates P.A., Newark, 1975-77; asst. commr. design & constrn. Gen. Services Adminstrn., Washington, 1977-82; sr. v.p. Bernard Johnson Inc., Bethesda, Md., 1982-89; v.p. and prin. architect Sverdrup Corp., Arlington, Va., 1989-92. Adj. prof. Seton Hall U., South Orange, N.J., 1972-77; mem. Bldg. Rsch. Bd. of Nat. Acad. Sci., com. chmn., 1984-92. Author: Joint Ventures for Architects and Engineers, 1972, You and Your Architect, 1973, (with Amy Dibner-Dunlap) Building Additions Design, 1985; editor (with Andrew Lemer) The Role of Public Agencies in Fostering New Technology and Innovation in Building, 1992, Dreams and Schemes: Stories of People and Architecture, 2001; chmn. editorial bd. Architecture/N.J., 1968-71; contbr. articles to profl. jours. Mem. West Orange Bd. of Adjustment, N.J., 1970-77, Nat. Trust for Historic Preservation. Served with USN, 1944-46, PTO. Fellow AIA (Washington chpt.). Home: Mc Lean, Va. Died May 30, 2009.

DICKES, ROBERT, psychiatrist; b. NYC, Apr. 15, 1912; s. Benjamin and Anna (Adler) D.; m. Bernice Livingston, June 12, 1938; children: Richard A., Susan R. Dickes Hubbard. BS, CCNY, 1933; MS, Emory U., 1934, MD, 1938. Diplomate: Am. Bd. Internal Medicine, Am. Bd. Psychiatry and Neurology. Intern L.I. Coll. Hosp., Bklyn., 1938-39, asst. resident in internal medicine, 1938-39, resident in medicine, 1939-41, dir. med. clinics, 1946-50; asso. in medicine L.I. Coll. Medicine, 1946, asst. prof. psychiatry, 1949; fellow in medicine Western Res. U.-Lakeside Hosp., 1941-42; fellow in psychiatry Kings County Hosp. Center-SUNY Bklyn., 1950-52, mem. staff, from 1952, pres. med. br., 1977-78. Clin. assoc. prof. psychiatry Downstate Med. Center SUNY, Bklyn., 1950-54, assoc. prof., 1954-56, clin. assoc. prof., 1956-61, assoc. prof., 1961-63, prof., 1963, 78-82, prof. emeritus, 1982—, tng. and supervising analyst, 1965—, acting chmn. dept. psychiatry, 1965-66, 71-72, dir. infant behavior study lab., 1973, dir. center human sexuality, 1973—, chmn. dept. psychiatry, 1975-78; clin. prof. psychiatry NYU Coll. Medicine, 1982—; cons. VA hosps., Bklyn., Northport, N.Y.; v.p. Am. Bd. Sexology, 1989—. Contbr. articles to profl. publs. Bd. govs., mem. acquisitions com. Bklyn. Museum. Maj. M.C. U.S. Army, 1942-46. Commonwealth fellow, 1941-42, 48-49 Fellow A.C.P., Am. Psychiat. Assn., Am. Coll. Psychiatry; mem. Am. Psychoanalytic Assn., Psychoanalytic Assn. N.Y. (treas. 1962-64), Bklyn. Psychiat. Soc. (pres. 1967), Kings County Med. Soc., Kings County Psychiat. Soc. (pres. 1967-68), Soc. Sex Therapy and Research (pres. 1979-81), Am. Bd. Sexology (v.p. 1989—). Home: Morristown, NJ. Died Apr. 26, 2009.

DICKEY, WILLIAM KENNEDY, lawyer, state legislator; b. Phila., Sept. 12, 1920; s. William Kennedy and Catherine (Meiklejohn) D.; m. Irene Catherine Campbell, Apr. 12, 1980; 4 stepchildren BA, U. Pa.; JD, Rutgers U., 1945. Bar: N.J. 1946. Pvt. law practice, 1950—2007. Mem. NJ State Assembly, Trenton, 1963-74, majority leader, 1968-69, spkr., 1970; commr. Del. River Port Authority, Camden, N.J., 1983-94, chmn., 1985-87, vice chmn., 1988-91; chmn. Camden County epublican Com., 1980-81; delegate to RNC, 1976, 1984, 1988, 1992 Mem. ABA (Traffic Ct. award for Outstanding Judicial Standards, 1960), N.J. Bar Assn., Camden County Bar Assn. Clubs: Greater Camden Jaycees (pres., 1950), NJ Jaycees (pres., 1954), Collingswood Republican Club (pres. 1961-77), Collingswood Lions Club (pres., 1976) Tavistock Country (Haddonfield, N.J.), Salvation Army Republican. Presbyterian. Home: Haddonfield, NJ. Died Nov. 3, 2008.

DICKS, JOYCE CAROLEE, adult education administrator; b. Centerville, Iowa, Mar. 21, 1936; d. Max Arlee and Laura Jean (Oehler) Martin; m. Donald Dean Dicks, May 5, 1955; children: Stephanie Lynn Dicks Hall, Dawn Michelle. AA in Social Sci., Ohlone Coll., Fremont, Calif., 1978; BA in History, Calif. State U., Hayward, 1980, MA, 1984; Adminstrv. credential, San Jose State U., 1987. Instrnl. aide GATE program Fremont Unified Schs., 1972-77; instr. social scis. Fremont Adult Edn., 1980-88; instr. history Ohlone Coll., from 1982, DeAnza Coll., Cupertino, Calif., 1986-88; asst. dir. East Side Adult Edn. Program, San Jose, Calif., from 1988. Lectr. Ottawa (Kans.) U., 1979-80; cons. Calif. Adult Schs. Assessment System Task Force, Sacramento, 1987—; reviewer Pacific Historian mag., Stockton, Calif., 1984-90. Author, narrator several video study programs. Active Fremont PTA, 1970-76; founding pres. Parents of Gifted Children, Fremont, 1975; charter mem. Ohlone Coll. Mus. Com., 1978—. Mem. Assn. Calif. Sch. Adminstrs., Calif. Council for Adult Edn., Orgn. Am. Historians, Inst. Hist. Study, Washington Twp. (Calif.) Hist. Soc. Home: Plano, Iowa. Died Jan. 3, 2008.

DICKSON, HELEN, principal; b. Florence, SC, Sept. 27, 1941; d. John Wesley and Helen (Oates) D. BA, Winthrop Coll., 1963; MA in Teaching, Converse Coll., 1967; doctoral studies, U. Va. Dept. chmn. Greenville County Sch. Dist., 1967-70, supr., 1970-76; instr. U. S.C., 1972-74; grad. instr. U. Va., Charlottesville, 1977-78; supr. Sch. Dist. Greenville County, 1978-87, adult edn. supr., 1979-87, asst. prin., 1986-88; adminstrv. asst. Bamberg Dist. II, Denmark, S.C., 1988-89, prin., from 1989. Commr. Edn. Commn. of the States, S.C., 1979-85; bd. advisors Edn. Svc. Corps; Action 2000, S.C., 1991—; bd. edn. Diocese of Charleston, S.C., 1986-89; assessor S.C. Assessment Ctr., 1991—; cons. and speaker in field. Adv. bd. Baby PATS, Bambert County, 1991—; adv. com. Voorhees Coll, Denmark, 1992—; synod preparation Diocese of Charleston, S.C., 1991-92. Rsch. fellow ednl. Testing Svcs., 1985; Fulbright fellow U. New Delhi, 1975, U. Georgetown/Sophia, Tokyo, Japan, 1968; grantee Ford Found., S.E. Regional Tng. Ctr., U. Colo., NSF, U. Hawaii, NDEA. Mem. NEA, Nat. Coun. for Social Studies, Social Studies Suprs. Assn., Va. Consortium for Social Studies Suprs. and Coll. Educators, S.C. Coun. for Social Studies, Greenville County Coun. for Social Studies, S.C. Edn. Assn., Greenville County Edn. Assn., Phi Delta Kappa, Alpha Delta Kappa. Roman Catholic. Avocations: reading mysteries, good conversation, trek lore. Died Aug. 12, 2008.

DIETRICH, DONNA JEAN, mental health nurse; b. Springfield, Ill., Apr. 7, 1952; d. James and JoAnn D. BS in Edn. and Psychology, Western Ill. U., 1974; AAS in Nursing, Lincoln Land Community Coll., 1983; postgrad., Western Carolina U. RN, Ga. Counselor supr. McCambridge House, Springfield, Ill., dir.; staff nurse St. John's Hosp., Springfield, Ill.; DON Woodridge Hosp., Clayton, Ga. Mem. ANA, Ga. Nurses Assn. Home: Franklin, NC. Died May 25, 2008.

DIETZ, ROWLAND ERNEST, real estate manager; b. Cin., Oct. 26, 1920; s. William C.F. and Bertha (Stephens) D.; divorced; children: Christopher P., Brian Luther. BA, Swarthmore Coll.; MA, Columbia U., 1946, PhD, 1962. Instr. polit. sci. CCNY, NYC, 1945-47, U. Cin., 1948-49; asst. prof. govt. Western Coll., Oxford, Ohio, 1963-68; pres. RE Dietz & Co. REal Estate Mgmt., Cin., from 1952. Sec., trustee Ft. Washington Trust, Cin., 1970-88; trustee Better Housing League, Cin., 1953-64; dir., pres. Inst. Real Estate Mgmt., Cin., 1955-57. V.p. Cin. Coun. World Affairs, 1957; trustee, dir. City Charter Com., Cin., 1952-65; trustee Human Rels. Com., Cin., 1955-57; v.p., trustee Friends of CCM, Cin., 1995-96; mem. Cincinnatus Assn., Cin., 1975-95. Mem. Univ. Club., Master Gardner Assn. Gr. Cin. (dir. exec. com. 1994-96). Home: Cincinnati, Ohio. Died Jan. 24, 2008.

DIGBY, JAMES FOSTER, research engineer; b. Farmerville, La., Aug. 11, 1921; s. Sebe Lee and Maud Eloise (McLees) D.; m. Mary Jane Bruck, Dec. 5, 1959; children: Ward McLees, Drew James, Leslie Jane. BS, La. Tech., 1941; MA, Stanford U., Calif., 1942. Editor Watson Labs., USAF, Eatontown, N.J., 1946-47, def. planner, 1947-49; rsch. engr. The Rand Corp., Santa Monica, Calif., 1949-55, dept. head, 1956-58, program mgr. internat. studies, project leader, 1959-86, cons., from 1986. Exec. dir. Calif. Seminar, Santa Monica, 1976-90; cons. Pres.'s Sci. Adv. Com., Washington, 1959-73, Commn. on Long Term Strategy, Washington, 1986-88; vice dir. Pan Heuristics, Marina del Rey, Calif., 1986-88; v.p. Am. Inst. for Strategic Coop., L.A., 1986-90; bd. dirs. European Am. Inst. for Security Rsch., L.A., 1976-95. Author: (monograph) Precision-Guided Weapons, 1976. 1st lt. USAF, 1942-46, ETO. Mem. Internat. Inst. for Strategic Studies. Democrat. Home: Durham, NC. Died Oct. 10, 2007.

DIGGINS, JOHN PATRICK, history professor; b. San Francisco, Apr. 1, 1935; s. James Joseph and Anne (Naugton) D.; m. Jacy Battles (div. Sept. 1976); children: Sean, Nicole. AB, U. Calif., Berkeley, 1957; MA, San Francisco State U., 1959; PhD, U. So. Calif., LA, 1964. Asst. prof. history San Francisco State U., 1966-69; prof. history U. Calif., Irvine, 1969-90; disting. prof. history Grad. Ctr. CUNY, NYC, 1990—2009, acting dir. Ctr. for Humanities, Grad. Ctr., 1996-97. Vis. fellow U. Cambridge, 1976-77; vis. prof. Princeton U., 1977-78; chair Am. civilization L'Ecole des Hautes Etudes en Scis. Sociales, Paris, 1988-89; Commonwealth lectr. U. London, 1991; spkr. Lionel Trilling seminar, Columbia U., 1992; lectr. and cons. in field. Author: Mussolini and Fascism: The View From America, 1972, The American Left in the Twentieth Century, 1973, Up From Communism: Conservative Odysseys in American Intellectual History, 1975, The Bard of Savagery: Thorstein Veblen and Modern Social Theory, 1978, The Lost Soul of American Politics: Virtue, Self-Interest and the Foundations of Liberalism, 1984, The Proud Decades: America in War and in Peace, 1941-1960, 1988, The Rise and Fall of the American Left, 1992, The Promises of Pragmatism: Modernism and the Crisis of Knowledge and Authority, 1994, Max Weber: Politics and the Spirit of Tragedy, 1996, The Liberal Persuasion: Arthur Schlesinger, Jr., and the Challenge of the American Past, 1997, On Hallowed Ground: Abraham Lincoln and the Foundations of American History, 2000, Eugene O'Neil's America: Desire Under Democracy, 2007, Ronald Reagan: Fate, Freedom and the Making of History, 2007; co-editor: (with M. Kann) The Problem of Authority in America, 1982; contbr. articles to profl. jours. and newspapers. Recipient prizes Soc. for Italian Hist. Studies, 1965, Am. Studies Assn., 1966, John Dunning award Am. Hist. Assn., 1972; fellow Am. Philos. Soc., Social Sci. Rsch. Coun., Am. Coun. Learned Socs., NEH, John Simon Guggenheim Found., 1978; residence scholar Rockefeller Found., 1989; conf. grantee Rockefeller Found. Democrat. Died Jan. 28, 2009.

DIGGS, EDWARD JACKSON, III, engineer, engineering executive; b. Detroit, Apr. 1, 1931; s. Edward J. Jr. and Margaret A. (Noll) D.; m. Lucia Joana de Oliveira, Dec. 26, 1970; children: Paul, Matthew. B in Indsl. Engring., Kettering U., Flint, Mich., 1958; MBA, U. Detroit, 1960. Plant mgr. Rockwell-Tilbury, Tilbury, Ont., Can., 1973-75; chief engr. Rockwell-Ashtabula, Ashtabula, Ohio, 1975-76, Rockwell-Bremsen, Hanau, Germany, 1976-77; quality control dir. Rockwell-Europe, Maudslay, Worcester, England, 1977; plant mgr. Rockwell-HWT, Bonneiul-sur-Marne, France, 1977-78; tech dir. Rockwell-Europe, Llay, Wales, 1978-88; pres. Maintenance Free Brakes, Inc., McMurray, Pa., 1990—2002, Hope Tech. Sales and Svcs., Inc., 1998—2007. Mgr. dir. USA Worldwise Industries, 2002—07; pres. Jack Diggs LLC, from 2007. Patentee in field. With U.S. Army, 1953-55, Korea. Fellow Am. Soc. Quality (bd. dirs. 1971-73); mem. Sigma Alpha Epsilon. Republican. Episcopalian. Avocations: golf, tennis. Home: Venice, Fla. Died Jan. 2009.

DILLABAUGH, ROY GRANT, insurance agent; b. Gary, Ind., June 14, 1940; s. Grant Earl and Lena Mae (Blackman) D.; m. Audrey Jean Johnson, June 15, 1962 (div. May 1974); children: Lorne, Julie, Ralph; m. Alice Jane Weddle Wilson, Oct. 23, 1974; children: Scott, Stacia. BA, Phillips U., 1962; MDiv, Christian Theol. Sem., Indpls., 1970. Sales rep. John Hancock Mut. Life Ins. Co., Boston, from 1970. Treas., bd. dirs., vis. vol. Man to Man, Woman to Woman/New Life Connections, Dayton, Ohio, 1985-90. Mem. Rotary (Centerville, Ohio club, editor Beacon 1990-91, Paul Harris fellow 1991). Republican. Methodist. Avocation: water-skiing. Home: Dayton, Ohio. Died Nov. 27, 2007.

DILLARD, REBECCA MARIE, nursing educator; b. Middlesboro, Ky., Jan. 5, 1951; d. Andy and Anna Lee (Mayes) Leabow; m. Clarence Dillard III; children: Tressa, Julie, Erin. ADN, Coll. of the Sequoias, 1976. RN, Calif. EMT II Tulare County/Woodlake (Calif.) Ambulance; instr. in emergency med. care Coll. of the Sequoias, Visalia, Calif.; patient care mgr. Kaweah Delta Dist. Hosp., Visalia. Mem. Am. Soc. Post-Anesthesia Nurses, Cert. Post-Anesthesia Nurse Assn. Calif. Home: Visalia, Calif. Died Sept. 11, 2007.

DILLON, GREGORY RUSSELL, retired hotel executive; b. Chgo., Aug. 26, 1922; s. Gregory Thomas and Margaret Moore (Russell) D.; m. Nancy Jane Huntsberger, Nov. 8, 1969; children: Michael Gregory, Patricia Jean, Margaret Esther, Richard Thomas, Daniel Russell. Student, Elmhurst Coll., Ill., 1941-43, 45-46; JD, DePaul U., Chgo., 1948. Bar: Ill. Sole practice, Chgo.; ptnr. Friedman Mulligan Dillon & Urist, Chgo., 1950-63; asst. to pres. Hilton Hotels Corp., Beverly Hills, Calif., 1963-65, v.p., asst. sec., 1965-71, sr. v.p., asst. sec., 1971-80, exec. v.p., 1980-90, vice chmn., 1990-93, vice chmn. emeritus, 1993—2009; pres. Conrad Internat. Hotels, 1986-90, vice chmn., 1990-93, vice chmn. emeritus, 1993—2009. Bd. dirs. Hilton Hotels Corp., 1977-96, Conrad Internat. Hotels, 1980-96, Jupiters Ltd., Surfer's Paradise, Queensland, Australia. Served to 1st lt. USAAF, 1943-46, ETO. Mem. Urban Land Inst. (trustee 1980), ABA, Ill. Bar Assn., Chgo. Bar Assn., Am. Hotel and Motel Assn. Clubs: Chicago Athletic (Chgo.); Bel-Air Country (Los Angeles); Marco Polo (N.Y.C.). Republican. Roman Catholic. Home: Los Angeles, Calif. Died Feb. 18, 2009.

DILLON, JOSEPH FRANCIS, lawyer; b. Bklyn., Oct. 15, 1938; s. Joseph and Elizabeth (Sullivan) D.; m. Pamela Margaret Higbee, May 15, 1966 (div. Feb. 1972); children: Elizabeth Margaret, J. Alexander; m. Diane K. Long, Mar. 17, 1978. BBA, St. John's U., 1960; LLB, U. Va., 1963. Bar: Va. 1963, N.Y. 1964, U.S. Tax Ct. 1965, Mich. 1968, Ohio 1975, Fla. 1983. Tax trial atty. IRS, Washington and Detroit, 1963-68; mem. Raymond & Dillon, P.C., Detroit, 1969-93, Dykema Gossett PLC, Detroit, 1993-97, Giarmarco, Mullins & Horton, P.C., Detroit, 1997—2008, Joseph & Dillon & Assoc., from 2009. Adj. prof. taxation U. Detroit Law Sch., 1977-87; spkr., planning chmn. Inst. CLE Programs; mem. magistrates merit selection panel and profl. assistance com. U.S. Dist. Ct. for Ea. Dist. Mich.; mem. U.S. Ct. Internat. Trade. Bd. dirs., exec. com. Met. Ctr. for High Tech., Detroit, 1993-96. Cpl. USAR, 1958-64. Fellow Mich. State Bar Found.; mem. ABA (taxation and internat. sects. 1963—), FBA (officer, pres. Detroit chpt. 1978-82), Mich. Bar Assn. 1988—, (taxation counsel 1979-82, internat. sec. 1990—), Detroit Bar Assn. (taxation com. 1973—), Ohio Bar Assn., Fla. Bar Assn., Am. Judicature Soc., Am. C. of C. in Japan, London Ct. of Internat. Arbitration, Inter-Pacific Bar Assn., Internat. Bar Assn., Greater Detroit-Windsor Japan Am. Soc. (bd. dirs. 1992—, exec. com. 1999—), Japanese Bus. Soc. Detroit Found. (v.p. 1992—), Detroit Regional Chamber (nominating com. for dirs.), French-Am. C. of C. of Detroit (bd. dirs. 1997-2000), Detroit Athletic Club, Lochmoor Club, Vineyards Country Club, World Trade Club, Econ. Club (Detroit). Republican. Roman Catholic. Avocations: golf, squash, skiing. Deceased.

DILLON, PAUL LEE, electrical engineer, consultant, real estate manager; b. Walla Walla, Wash., Aug. 21, 1914; s. William Louis and Dema Ellen (Thomas) D.; m. Esther Melissa Pickett, June 4, 1939; children: Paul Lee Jr., Ferman Lewis, Wilson Kent, Eileen Ruth, Warren Michael. BSEE summa cum laude, Wash. State U., 1937. Engr. Gen. Electric Co., Schenectady, NY, San Francisco, Los Angeles, Portland, Oreg., 1937-49; owner, operator farm, Spokane, Wash., 1949-56; elec. engr. Indsl. Electric Co., Roseburg, Oreg. and Everett, Wash., 1956-64; sr. elec. engr. Hughes Helicopters, Culver City, Calif., 1968-74, Hallanger Engrs., Bellingham, Wash., 1974-81; elec. engr. cons. Profl. Engr. and Cons. Service, Bellingham, Wash., 1981-89; ret. Mem. Am. Inst. Plant Engrs. (cert., pres. Los Angeles chpt. 1973-74). Republican. Methodist. Avocations: boating, fishing, travel. Home: Bellingham, Wash. Died June 23, 2008.

DILLON, THOMAS E., retired academic administrator; b. Daly City, Calif., Apr. 18, 1946; m. Teri Dillon; children: Thomas, Daniel, Christine, Maria. BA, St. Mary's Coll.; MA in Philosophy, U. Notre Dame; Ph.D in Philosophy, U. Notre Dame. Asst. dean for student affairs Thomas Aquinas Coll., Santa Paula, Calif., academic dean, pres., 1991—2009. Founder Am. Acad. for Liberal Edn. Died Apr. 15, 2009.

DILLON, VALERIE VANCE, church executive, author, magazine columnist; b. Chgo., Oct. 19, 1930; d. James Robert and Rose Matilda (Beauchamp) Vance; m. Raydon Thomas Dillon, Sept. 26, 1953; children: Karen, Patricia, Valerie, Donna. BS in Journalism, U. Ill., 1952; MA in Religion, Butler U., 1979; MA in Family Studies, Regis Coll., Denver, 1990. Radio newswriter UPI, Chgo., 1952-53; reporter Austin News and Garfieldian, Chgo., 1953-54; researcher, writer N.J. Cath. Conf., Trenton, 1966-73; family life educator Cath. Diocese of Trenton, 1968-73; dir. communications Ind. Cath. Conf., Indpls., 1973-79; news editor Criterion newspaper, Indpls., 1979-82; dir. family life Archdiocese of Indpls., 1982-91. Advisor U.S. Bishops' Com. on Family, Washington, 1987—. Author: Your Child's Sex Life, 1966, Life in Our Hands, 1973, Becoming a Woman, 1990, (sch. curriculum) Choose Life, 1976; monthly columnist Columbia mag., 1981-92. Trustee St. Meinrad (Ind.) Sem. and Coll., 1987—, vice chair bd. overseers, 1987—; bd. dirs. Cath. Youth Orgn., 1992—. Recipient various writing awards Cath. Press Assn., 1981, 83, Women's Press Club, Indpls., 1984, 86, Nat. Leadership award Nat. Family Life Dirs. Assn., 1991, Respect Life award Archdiocese Indpls., 1991; Lady of Equestrian Order of Holy Sepulchre of Jerusalem, 1993. Mem. Nat. Assn. Cath. Family Life Ministers (pres. 1987-89). Avocations: painting, golf, grandparenting. Home: Indianapolis, Ind. Died Nov. 6, 2007.

DINWOODIE, ROXAN EMMERT, marketing consultant; b. Lancaster, Pa., Feb. 15, 1955; d. Joseph Wellington Emmert and Mary Ann Sherrard; m. Winston Olivier Dinwoodie, Apr. 24, 1983. BA with honors, Eckerd Coll., 1976; MS in Mktg., Ga. State U., 1985. Prin. Via Nova Consulting, Atlanta, from 1982; planning dir. Ga. Rehab. Svcs., Atlanta, 1987-91; asst. staff mgr. Privatization Task Force Gov's. Commn. on Effectiveness & Economy in Govt., Atlanta, 1991-92. Vol. Citizen's Democracy Corps, Czech Rep., 1993, 94; active Jefferson Park Neighbor Assn.; bd. dirs. Advs. for Self Govt., Inc. Recipient Dimensions of Excellence Leadership award, 1988. Mem. Am. Mktg. Assn., Inst. Mgmt. Cons., Alpha Mu Alpha. Libertarian. Episcopalian. Avocations: creative writing, gourmet cooking, antiques, music, languages. Died Mar. 17, 2008.

DIPPEL, CHESTER HORN, painter, sculptor; b. Wilkinsburg, Pa., Mar. 12, 1919; s. Cameron Leonard and Jean Murray (McLaren) D.; m. Constance Joella Waller, Juen 2, 1946; children: Martha Constance, Conrad Christopher. Student, Chouinard Art Inst., LA. Lettering designer Allied Advt., LA, 1938-42; owner, layout, sales Waller & Dippel Art, LA, 1944-58; owner Chet Dippel Advt., Fullerton, Calif., 1957-69, Bull 'n Brush Retail Art Store, La Habra, Calif., 1965-69, Right Angle Gallery Fine Art, Mountain View, Calif., 1971-74; painter, from 1972. Exhibited paintings at John Bolles Gallery, 1971; exhibited paintings and sculpture at Virginia Brier Gallery, 1982-89, Banaker Gallery, L.A., 1977-80, Calif. Folk Art Gallery, 1980, Yankee Doodle Gallery of Folk Art, 1989-91, Kati Gingrass, Santa Fe, 1986, The Heights Gallery, Little Rock, Southside Gallery, Oxford, Miss., others. Sgt. U.S. Army, 1942-45, PTO. Avocation: tennis. Home: Hot Springs National Park, Ark. Died Aug. 30, 2007.

DIRKS, KENNETH RAY, medical educator, army officer; b. Newton, Kans., Feb. 11, 1925; s. Jacob Kenneth and Ruth Viola (Penner) Dirks; m. Betty Jean Worsham, June 9, 1946; children: Susan Jan, Jeffrey Mark, Deborah Anne, Timothy David, Melissa Jane. MD, Washington U., St. Louis, 1947. Diplomate Am. Bd. Pathology. Rotating intern St. Louis City Hosp., 1948, asst. resident in gen. surgery, 1948-49; resident in pathology VA Hosp., Jefferson Barracks, Mo., 1951-53, resident in pathology, asst. chief lab. service Indpls., 1953-54; resident in pathology Letterman Army Hosp., San Francisco, 1956-57; fellow in tropical medicine and parasitology La. State U., Central Am., 1958; asst. in pathology Washington U. Sch. Medicine, 1952-53; asst. chief lab. service VA Hosp., Jefferson Barracks, 1953; instr. pathology U. Ind. Med. Center, Indpls., 1953-54; commd. capt. M.C. U.S. Army, 1954, advanced through grades to maj. gen., 1976; dir. research Med. Research and Devel. Command, Washington, 1968-69, dep. comdr., 1969-71, comdr., 1973-76; asst. surgeon gen., research and devel. U.S. Army, 1973-76; dep. comdr., comdr. Med. Research Inst. Infectious Diseases, Ft. Detrick, Frederick, Md., 1972-73; comdr. Fitzsimons Army Med. Center, Denver, 1976-77; supt. Acad. Health Scis., Ft. Sam Houston, Tex., 1977-80; assoc. prof. to prof. pathology and lab. medicine Coll. Med. Tex. A&M U., College Station, 1980-95; interim head dept. Coll. Medicine, Tex. A&M U., College Station, 1990-91; prof. emeritus pathology, from 1995; asst. dean coll. Coll. Medicine, Tex. A&M U., College Station, 1985-88; dir. dept. student health svcs. and A.P. Beutel Health Ctr. Tex. A&M U., College Station, 1989-95; dir. student health svcs. emeritus, from 1995. Contbr. articles to profl. jours. Decorated DSM, Legion of Merit with oak leaf cluster, Meritorious Svc. medal, Army Commendation medal with oak leaf cluster. Fellow: Am. Soc. Clin. Pathology (emeritus), Internat. Acad. Pathology, Coll. Am. Pathologists. Republican. Baptist. Died 2009.

DISERENS, HELEN BARNETT, research chemist; b. Huntington, W.Va., Feb. 16, 1919; d. Arthur Leroy and Leah (Gilmore) Barnett; m. Robert Carver Diserens, Jr., Apr. 5, 1947 (dec. July 1989); children: Deborah Fairbanks, Robert Carver III. BS in Chemistry, U. Mich., 1941. Coll. bd. editor Mademoiselle Mag., NYC, 1940; with pub. rels. mktg. dept. Elizabeth Arden, NYC, 1941—42; analytical rschr. Hoffman LaRoche, Nutley, NJ, 1942—43; head new product R & D Bristol Myers Co., Hillside, NJ, 1943—50; bus. mgr. Rippowam Cisqua Sch., Bedford, NY, 1962—92; prin. Moneyminder Svc., Mt. Kisco, NY, from 1981. Chmn. bus. affairs com. Nat. Assn. Ind. Schs., Boston, 1978-81, N.Y. State Assn. Ind. Schs., Albany, 1980; mem. fin. com. Rippowam Cisqua Sch., 1993—. Inventor Ban Deodorant, 1948; co-prodr. (book) Accounting for Independent Schools, 1977; contbr. articles to profl. jours. Trustee Dublin (N.H.) Sch., 1974-87; bd. dirs. Adoption Svc. West, White Plains, N.Y., 1953-63, Mt. Kisco Cmty. Concerts, 1970-73; mem. adv. com. St. Matthews Ch., 1993; rep. St. Matthews N.Y. Samuel Diocese Conv. Republican. Episcopalian. Avocations: reading, tennis, walking, travel. Home: Rye, NY. Died Apr. 15, 2008.

DIZARD, WILSON PAUL, JR., international affairs consultant, educator; b. NYC, Mar. 6, 1922; s. Wilson Paul and Helen Marie (Oliver) D.; m. Lynn Margaret Wood, Mar. 11, 1944; children: John William, Stephen Wood, Wilson Paul III, Mark Christopher. BS, Fordham Coll., 1947; postgrad., Columbia U., 1947—49. Writer, editor Time Inc., NYC, 1947—51; with US Dept. State, 1951—80; vice consul US Embassy, Istanbul, Turkey, 1951—53; chief Greece-Turkey-Iran br., 1953—55; info. officer US Embassy, Athens, Greece, 1955—60; pub. affairs officer consulate-gen. Dacca, Pakistan, 1960—62; spl. asst. dep. dir. Am. Embassy, 1964—65; asst. dep. dir. US Embassy, 1966—67, 1st sec. Warsaw, 1968—70; asst. dir. Pub. Affairs Office, Saigon, Vietnam, 1970; spl. adviser polit. sect. U.S. Embassy, Saigon, 1971; comm. adviser to dir. US Agy. for Internat. Devel. (USAID), Washington, 1971—73, chief plans and program policy, 1973—77; vice-chmn. U.S. del. to 1979 World Adminstrv. Radio Conf. US Dept. State, Washington, 1978—79; v.p. Kalba-Bowen Assocs., Cambridge, Mass., 1980—86; adj. prof. internat. affairs Georgetown U., 1975—95, sr. fellow, 1983—89; sr. assoc. Ctr. for Strategic and Internat. Studies, 1989—2001; cons. comm. policy US Dept. State, 1984—88. Mem. U.S. del. and exec. asst. to conf. dir. Internat. Telecom. Satellite Conf., Washington, 1968-69; rsch. assoc. Ctr. Internat. Studies, MIT, 1962-63; lectr. Nat. War Coll., 1978-79; vis. lectr. polit. sci. dept. MIT, 1981. Author: The Strategy of Truth, 1961, Television-A World View, 1966, The Coming Information Age, 1981, Mikhail Gorvachev's Information Revolution, 1987, Old Media, New Media, 1994, Meganet: Building the Global Information Highway, 1997, Digital Diplomacy, 2001, Inventing Public Diplomacy, 2004; contbr. articles to profl. jours. Cons. Carnegie Found. Commn. on Endl. TV;

bd. dirs. Pub. Diplomacy Found., 2000-04. With AUS, 1943-46. Rsch. fellow Assn. Diplomatic Studies and Tng., 1997—. Mem.: Washington Inst. Fgn. Affairs, Am. Fgn. Svc. Assn., Soc. Historians Am. Fgn. Rels., Assn. Diplomatic Studies and Tng., Am. Polit. Sci. Assn., Cosmos Club (Wash.), Diplomatic and Consular Officers Ret. Club. Home: Washington, DC. Died Aug. 31, 2009.

DJERMAKOYE, MOUMOUNI ADAMOU, Nigerian government official, former ambassador; b. Dosso, Niger, Niger Republic, May 22, 1939; s. Moumouni Aouta and Mariama (Mayaki) D.; m. Fati Lagare; children: Abdul'Aziz, Zaratou, Kadidjiatou, Karim. Officer cert., Efortom of Frejus, France, 1964; staff coll. cert. in polit. scis. studies, Mil. Sch. Staff-Office, Paris, 1973. Minister fgn. affairs Niger Govt., 1974-79, minister youth, sports and culture, 1979-82, minister health and social affairs, 1982-83, pres. nat. coun. of devel., 1983, gov. dept. of Zinder, 1983-88, amb. to the U.S. Washington, 1988-93; permanent rep. UN, NYC, from 1988; pres. Nat. Assembly, Republic of Niger, 1993—94, High Ct. of Justice, 2005—09. Speaker UN Gen. Assembly, 1974-79, pres. social devel. com., 1980-83; pres., initiator, organizer first African-Am. Summit, Ivory Coast, 1990; pres. Nigerien Alliance for Democracy & Progress Col. Niger Army, present. Decorated comdr. Nat. Order from Niger, Germany, Burkina Faso, Korea, Guinea Mali, Saudi Arabia, Togo, 1974-83, comdr. Nat. Order of Legion of Honour, France, 1983; recipient Africa Leadership award, 1990. Mem. Internat. Assn. Permanent Reps. to the UN., Fgn. Soc. Members of Legion of Honour, Coun. Mil. Supreme, Superior Coun. Nat. Orientation. Avocations: photography, music, sports, reading, bicycling, languages (french, english, german). Home: Washington, DC. Died June 14, 2009.

DJORDJEVIC, DIMITRIJE, historian, educator; b. Belgrad, Yugoslavia, Feb. 27, 1922; came to U.S., 1970, naturalized, 1977; s. Vladimir and Jelena (Rasic) D.; m. Nan Fletcher, June 1981; 1 child, Jelena Grad., U. Beograd, 1954, PhD, 1962. Sr. staff mem. Inst. History, Serbian Acad. Scis. and Arts, 1958-69, Inst. Balkan Studies, 1969-70; prof. U. Calif., Santa Barbara, 1970-91, prof. emeritus, from 1991, chmn. Russian area studies, 1976-82. Mem. Nat. Com. to Promote History of Habsburg Monarchy, 1973-79 Author: Austro-Serbian Customs War 1906-1911, in Serbian, 1962, Revolutions nationales des peuples balkaniques, 1804-1914, 1965, Scars and Memory, 1997; co-author: The Balkan Revolutionary Tradition, 1981, also papers, essays, revs.; editor: The Creation of Yugoslavia, 1914-1918, 1980; editorial bd. profl. jours. Mem. Am. Hist. Assn., Am. Assn. Advancement Slavic Studies, Conf. Slavic and East European History (pres. 1984), Serbian Acad. Scis., N. Am. Assn. Serbian Studies (pres. 1986-88). Serbian Orthodox. Home: Santa Barbara, Calif. Died Mar. 5, 2009.

D'LUGOFF, ARTHUR JOSHUA, producer, director; b. NYC, Aug. 2, 1924; s. Raphael and Rachel (Mandelbaum) D'L.; m. Avital Achai, Apr. 7, 1957; children: Raphael, Sharon, Dahlia, Rashi. Student, NYU; BA, Washington Square Coll., 1949. Owner Village Gate, 1958—94. Producer: (plays) One Mo' Time, 1980-83, The Golden Land, 1984-85. Active Community Bd. Number Two, N.Y.C. Served with U.S. Army Air Force, WWII. Mem. Actors Studio, Nat. Trustees and Advisors Group. Clubs: Friar's. Democrat. Jewish. Died Nov. 4, 2009.

DOAN, KAREN L. W., medical center maternity unit coordinator; b. Ft. Worth, Mar. 29, 1951; d. Perry Vernon and Myra Owaisa (Pierce) Ware; m. Jerry Paul Doan, June 6, 1970; children: Steven Michael, Scott Adam. BS in Nursing, U. Tex., Arlington, 1975. R.N.C. in low-risk neonatal nursing NAACOG. Staff nurse Ft. Worth Children's Hosp.; unit coord. Dallas/Ft. Worth Med. Ctr., Grand Prairie, Tex. Mem. Greater Dallas Area Perinatal Mgrs. Home: Arlington, Tex. Died Aug. 17, 2007.

DOBESH, ERNEST LEONARD, farmer, mayor; b. Spring Ranch, Nebr., July 31, 1921; s. John Frank and Mary Lucille (Barta) D.; m. Wilma Jane Bangert, Sept. 15, 1946; children: Cletis, Gregory, Michael. Attended, Internat. Detective Sch., Washington. Foreman Hamilton County Farms, Aurora, Nebr., 1940-46; mgr. seed corn prodn. Cornhusker Hybrid Co., Kearney, Nebr., 1946-52; farmer Wood River, Nebr., 1952-63; corp. farmer, chmn. bd. dirs. Dobesh Farms Inc., Wood River, Grand Island, Nebr., 1963-90, chmn. bd. dirs., from 1990. Served on Dist. 76 Sch. Bd., Wood River; city councilman Grand Island, 1988, 89, mayor, 1990-94; former mem. Draft Bd., Agrl. Stabilization & Conservation Svc.; panel mem. Doane Agrl. Svc.; bd. dirs. Farmers Home Adminstrn. With U.S. Army, 1942-45. Recipient Award of Honor Top Farmers of Am. Assn., U.S. Govt., 1968, Award of Appreciation President of U.S., 1973, 1976. Mem. Grand Island C. of C., Grand Island Indsl. Found., Am. Legion, Rotary, Eagles. Republican. Lutheran. Avocation: fishing. Home: Grand Island, Nebr. Died Apr. 21, 2008.

DODD, ROBERT DENNIS, cinematographer; b. China Lake, Calif., Dec. 8, 1955; s. Luther William and Janice Mae (Lambie) D.; m Jerri Lynn Newkirk, Sept. 21, 1985; 1 child, Molly Jane. Cert., Navy Photography Sch., Pensacola, Fla., 1975, Navy Cinema Sch., 1983, U. So. Calif., 1987. Operator Columbia Studios, La Crosse, Wis., 1978-80, USN, Corpus Christie, Tex., 1975-78, producer combat camera team aboard USS Nassau, 1980-83, dir. photography motion picture unit Washington, 1983-86, dir. documentary photography combat camera team Norfolk, Va., 1987-91; cameraman documenting the Presidency White House Staff, Washington, from 1991. Cons. Organized Crime Unit, Corpus Christi, 1976-78. Operator (film) Tomb of the Unknown, 1985 (Commendation award 1985); dir. photography (film) Waiting Man, 1986 (Silver Eagle award 1986); video news dir. Ernest Will, Persian Gulf Crisis, 1988, Desert Shield, 1990. Leader Boy Scouts Am., Corpus Christi, 1978 (Leadership award 1978). Serving with USN, 1973—. Mem. Soc. Motion Picture and TV Engrs., Internat. Combat Cameraman's Assn. United Methodist. Home: Virginia Beach, Va. Died Oct. 4, 2007.

DODD, WILLIAM FERRALL, educator; b. Louisville, Miss., Mar. 31, 1942; s. William S. and Elsie Rae (Chappell) D.; m. Kaysie Dawn Deaton, Aug. 24, 1968; children: Kaysie, Patton. BA, Colo. Christian U., 1989; MA, U. No. Colo., 1991. Pastor So. Bapt. Ch., Medina, Tenn., 1969-70; v.p., bus. adminstr. Ea. European Bible Mission, Colorado Springs, Colo., 1985-89; educator Colo. Christian Univ., Colorado Springs, from 1989; prof. Pikes Peak Community Coll., Colorado Springs, from 1991. Deacon First So. Bapt. Ch., Colorado Springs, 1989—. Sec. Exchange Club, Jackson, Tenn., 1974, Christian Ministries Assn., Colorado Springs, 1989. With USNG, 1959-68. Mem. Colo. Speech Communication Assn. (chair interest group 1991—). Home: Broken Arrow, Okla. Died Dec. 11, 2007.

D'OENCH, ELLEN GATES, curator; b. NYC, Oct. 2, 1930; d. John Monteith Gates and Ellen (Crenshaw) Houghton; m. Russell Grace D'Oench; children: Peter, Ellen D'Oench Ruimerman, Russell III. BA, Wesleyan U., 1973; MA, Yale U., 1976, PhD, 1979. Asst. curator Yale Ctr. for British Art, New Haven, Conn., 1977-79; curator Davison Art Ctr., Middletown, Conn., from 1979. Adj. assoc. prof. art dept., Wesleyan U., Middletown, 1979—; bd. dirs. Farmers and Mechanics Bank, Middletown. Author: Robert Sheehan: Color Photographs 1948-58, 1987; co-author: Sylvia Plimack Mangold Works on Paper 1968-91, 1992, Jime Dine Prints 1977-85, 1986; contbr. articles to profl. jours. Bd. dirs. Miss Porter's Sch., Farmington, Conn., 1986—, Middlesex County NAACP, 1989-90. Recipient exhibiton grant, New Eng. Found. Art, Boston, 1986, Nat. Endowment Arts, Washington, 1984, cataloguing grant, Nat. Endowment Arts, 1984. Mem. Print Council Am., The Conn. Acad. Arts and Scis. Episcopalian. Home: Middletown, Conn. Died May 22, 2009.

DOERSCHUK, JEANCLAIRE OAKES, business owner; b. Allentown, Pa., Mar. 11, 1925; d. Charles Ernest and Anna M. (Buckley) Oakes; m. Albert Peter Doerschuk, Oct. 15, 1949; children: Claire Margarete, Peter Charles, David Oakes, John Albert. Student, Mass. Wellesley Coll., 1942-45; BA, U. Pa., 1946; MA, Columbia U., 1949. Pres., chief exec. officer JCD Press dba Minuteman Press, Boston, 1978-85, Hermes Printing, Inc., San Clemente, Calif., from 1988. Home: Shaker Hts, Ohio. Died Apr. 20, 2008.

DOHERTY, DENNIS CARL, county official; b. Mpls., July 24, 1940; s. Lawrence Anthony Anna Marie (Billstein) D.; m. Olivia Ann Herzan, Dec. 26, 1964; children: Stephen, Mark, Timothy. BS, U.S. Naval Acad., 1963; postgrad., Bryant Coll., 1970-71; MBA, Coll. St. Thomas, St. Paul, 1982. Cert. safety profl. Commd. USN, 1963, advanced through grades to comdr., 1979, resigned, 1971; sr. engring. rep. Travelers Ins., Mpls., 1971-76; asst. risk mgr. Dayton Hudson Corp., Mpls., 1976-79; risk mgr. Hennepin County, Mpls., from 1980. Adj. faculty Coll. of St. Thomas, 1982—. Contbg. editor: (textbook) Risk Management and Insurance, 1985. Cub master Boy Scouts Am., Minnetonka, Minn., 1972-77; bd. dirs. IHM Dayschool,, Minnetonka, 1976-77; function chmn. IHM Ch. Festival, Minnetonka. Decorated Bronze Star with V. Mem. Nat. Safety Council, Minne. Safety Council, Risk and Ins. Mgmt. Soc. (bd. dirs. 1978-80, legis. chmn. 1984—), Pub. Risk and Ins. Mgmt. Assn. (legis. chmn. 1982—), Minn. Self Insurers Assn., U.S. Naval Acad. Alumni Assn. (pres. 1979-80), Workers Compensation Reins. Assn. (bd. dirs., mgmt. and self insurers coms.). Clubs: Northwest Raquet and Swim (Golden Valley, Minn.). Roman Catholic. Avocations: auto restoration, reading, swimming. Home: Austin, Tex. Died Apr. 9, 2008.

DONADIO, BEVERLY ROSE, writer; b. Winston-Salem, NC, Dec. 28, 1930; d. Lawson Francis and Katherine Lucille (Thrift) Ivester; m. Karl G. Smith (div.); children: Vickie Lee, Karl Gregor, Theodore Francis; m. Joseph Donadio, Dec. 21, 1968 (dec. May 1987); 1 child, Joseph Christopher. Student, Greensboro Coll., NC, Ringling Sch. of Art, Sarasota, Fla. Interior designer, N.C., Fla.; writer, illustrator Rosebrier Pub. Co., Laurel Pub. Co., Inc., Charleston, S.C., from 1996. Author: (children's books) The Rabbit Family, 1989 (Best Illustrated Book 1989). Home: Boone, NC. Died Aug. 21, 2007.

DONALD, DAVID HERBERT, writer, history professor; b. Goodman, Miss., Oct. 1, 1920; s. Ira Unger and Sue Ella (Belford) D.; m. Aida DiPace, 1933; 1 son, Bruce Randall. Student, Holmes Jr. Coll., 1937-39; AB, Millsaps Coll., 1941, LHD, 1976; AM, U. Ill., 1942, PhD, 1946, LHD (hon.), 1992; MA (hon.), U. Oxford, 1959, Harvard U., 1973; LittD (hon.), Coll. Charleston, 1985; D in History, Lincoln U., 1996; LHD, U. Calgary, 2000; LLD, Ill. Coll., 2002; LittD, Middlebury Coll., 2003. Teaching fellow U. N.C., 1942; research asst. history U. Ill., 1943-45, research assoc., 1946-47; fellow Social Sci. Research Council, 1945-46; instr. history Columbia U., 1947-49; assoc. prof. history Smith Coll., 1949-51; asst. prof. history Columbia U. Grad. Faculty, 1951-52, assoc. prof., 1952-57, prof. history, 1957-59, Princeton U., 1959-62; prof. Am. history Johns Hopkins U., Balt., 1962-73, Harry C. Black prof., 1963-73, dir. Inst. So. History, 1966-72; Charles Warren prof. Am. history and prof. Am. civilization Harvard U., 1973-91, prof. emeritus, 1991—2009, chmn. grad. program in Am. civilization, 1979-85. Vis. assoc. prof. Amherst Coll., 1950; Fulbright lectr. Am. history U. Coll. North Wales, 1953-54; mem. Inst. Advanced Study, 1957-58; Harmsworth prof. Am. history Oxford U., 1959-60; John P. Young lectr. Memphis State U., 1963; Walter Lynwood Fleming lectr. La. State U., 1965; Benjamin Rush lectr. Am. Psychiat. Assn., 1972; Commonwealth lectr. Univ. Coll., London, 1975; Samuel Paley lectr. Hebrew Univ. of Jerusalem, 1991; mem. U.S. del. to UNESCO, 2003. Author: Lincoln's Herndon, 1948, Divided We Fought, A Pictorial History of the War, 1861-65, 1952, Inside Lincoln's Cabinet: The Civil War Diaries of Salmon P. Chase, 1954, Lincoln Reconsidered: Essays on the Civil War Era, 1956, rev. 3d edit., 2001, A Rebel's Recollections, (G.C. Eggleston), 1959, Charles Sumner and the Coming of the Civil War, 1960 (Pulitzer prize for Biography, 1961), Why the North Won the Civil War, 1960, rev. edit., 1996, (with J.G. Randall) The Civil War and Reconstruction, 2d edit., 1961, rev., enlarged edit., 1969, (with Jean H. Baker and Michael F. Holt) rev. edit., 2001, The Divided Union, 1961, The Politics of Reconstruction, 1863-67, 1965, The Nation in Crisis, 1861-1877, 1969, Charles Sumner and the Rights of Man, 1970, (with Sidney Andrews) The South Since the War, 1970, Gone for a Soldier, 1975, (with others) The Great Republic, 1977, rev. edit., 1981, 3rd edit., 1985, 4th edit., 1992, Liberty and Union, 1978, Look Homeward: A Life of Thomas Wolfe, 1987 (Pulitzer prize for Biography, 1988), Lincoln, 1995 rev. edit., 1996, Charles Sumner, 1997, Lincoln at Home: Two Glimpses of Abraham Lincoln's Domestic Life, 1999, We Are Lincoln Men: Abraham Lincoln and His Friends, 2003; editor: War Diary and Letters of Stephen Minot Weld, 1979; gen. editor: Documentary History of American Life, The Making of America Series, 6 vols.; co-editor: (with wife) Diary of Charles Francis Adams, 2 vols., 1964, (with Harold Holzer) Lincoln in the Times: The Life of Abraham Lincoln as Originally Reported in The New York Times, 2004; contbr. articles to periodicals. Recipient Abraham Lincoln Lit. award Union League Club N.Y.C., 1977, C. Hugh Holman prize MLA, 1988, Joseph R. Levenson award Harvard U. 1993, Benjamin L.C. Wailes award Miss. Hist. Soc., 1994, Barondess-Lincoln prize, 1996, Award of Achievement, Lincoln Group N.Y.C., 1995, 03 Christopher award, 1996, Lincoln prize Gettysburg Coll., 1996, Jefferson Davis award Mus. of Confederacy, 1996, Nevins/Freeman award Chgo. Civil War Round Table, 1999, Life-time Achievement award Abraham Lincoln Presdl. Mus., Springfield, 2005, Bruce Catton Lifetime Achievement award Soc. Am. Historians, 2006, Lincoln medal Ford's Theatre, 2007; Guggenheim fellow, 1964-65, 85-86, fellow Am. Coun. Learned Socs., 1969-70, Ctr. for Advanced Study Behavioral Scis., 1969-70, George A. and Eliza G. Howard fellow, 1957-58, sr. fellow NEH, 1971-72. Fellow Am. Acad. Arts and Scis.; mem. Orgn. Am. Historians, Am. Hist. Assn., So. Hist. Assn. (v.p. 1968, pres. 1969), Soc. Am. Historians, Mass. Hist. Soc., Am. Antiquarian Soc., Phi Beta Kappa, Phi Kappa Phi, Pi Kappa Delta, Pi Kappa Alpha, Omicron Delta Kappa. Clubs: Harvard (N.Y.C.); Cosmos, Signet, Fox. Episcopalian. Home: Lincoln, Mass. Died May 17, 2009.

DONALDSON, COLEMAN DUPONT, retired aeronautical and aerospace engineer, consultant; b. Phila., Sept. 22, 1922; s. John W. and Renee (duPont) Donaldson; m. Barbara Goldsmith, Jan. 17, 1945; children: B. Beirne, Coleman duPont, Evan F., Alexander M., William M. BS in Aero. Engring., Rensselaer Poly. Inst., 1943; MA, Princeton U., 1954, PhD, 1957. Staff, NACA, Langley Field, Va., 1943-44, head aerophysics sect., 1946-52; gen. aerodynamics USAC, Wright Field, Ohio, 1945-46; aerodynamic evaluation Bell Aircraft, Niagara Falls, NY, 1946; sr. cons., pres. Aero Research Assos. of Princeton, NJ, 1954-79, chmn. bd. NJ, 1979-86; group gen. mgr. Aero Research Assocs. Princeton Inc., 1986-87; v.p. Titan Systems, Inc., 1986-87; ret., 1987. Cons. missile guidance and control Gen. Precision Equipment Corp., 1957—68; cons. magnetohydro-dynamics Thompson Ramo Woolridge, Inc., 1958—61; cons. aerodynamic heating, gen. aerodynamics Martin Marietta Corp., 1955—72, adv. devel. and tech. ops., 1989—96; gen. editor Princeton series on high speed aerodynamics and jet propulsion, 1955—64; cons. boundary layer stability, aerodynamic heating, missile and ordnance sys. dept. GE, 1956—72; cons. Grumman Aerospace Corp., 1959—72; Robert H. Goddard vis. lectr. with rank of prof. Princeton (N.J.) U., 1970—71, chmn. adv. coun. dept. aerospace and mech. scis., 1973—78; mem. rsch. tech. adv. coun. panel rsch. NASA, 1969—76, hypersonic tech. com., 1986—90; indsl. profl. adv. com. Pa. State U.; mem. Pres.' Air Quality Adv. Bd., 1973—74; chmn. lab. adv. bd. for air warfare Naval Rsch. Adv. Com., 1986—89, DARPA Tech. Adv. Panel on Hydrodynamics and Acoustics, 1991—94; cons. Ctr. Naval Analysis, 1990—98; adv. panel NASA Ctr. Turbulence Rsch., 1993—95. Contbr. articles to profl. jours. Recipient Meritorious Pub. Svc. award, Chief Naval Rsch., 1990. Fellow: AIAA (gen. chmn. 13th aerospace scis. meeting 1975, Dryden Rsch. lectr. award 1971); mem.: NAE, Am. Phys. Soc., Delta Phi, Sigma Xi. Home: Newport News, Va. Died Aug. 7, 2009.

DONDERO, GRACE MARIE, education educator; b. Bklyn., Feb. 28, 1949; d. Henry Angelo and Grace Veronica (Lagomarsino) D. BS, St. John's Univ., 1970, MS, 1971, Pace Univ., 1975; EdD, Fordham Univ., 1993. Tchr. day elem. sch. Pub. Sch. 58 N.Y.C. Pub. Schs., 1970-91; asst. prof. St. John's Univ., SI, N.Y., from 1991. Mem. ASCD, Doctorate Assn. of N.Y. (Laurel Wreath award), N.Y. Acad.

of Pub. Edn., Phi Delta Kappa (Dissertation award 1992). Roman Catholic. Home: Greenacres, Fla. Died May 23, 2008.

DONLEVIE, RITA DELORES, critical care nurse; b. Chester, Pa., Jan. 19, 1948; d. James E. and Rita (Doherty) D. Diploma, Fitzgerald Mercy Hosp., Darby Pa., 1968; BS in Profl. Arts, St. Joseph's Coll., Windham, Maine, 1990; postgrad., St. Joseph's U., Phila. Staff nurse coronary care unit Fitzgerald Mercy Hosp., Darby, 1968-78, head nurse, 1978-88, nurse mgr. coronary care-IV therapy and stepdown unit, 1988-90, nurse mgr. coronary care stepdown and cardiac rehab., 1990-93, nurse mgr. coronary care, stepdown cardiac rehab., and catheter lab, 1993-95, case mgr. cardiology, from 1995. Mem. Am. Assn. Critical Care Nurses, Tri-state Cardiopulmonary Rehab. Assn. Home: Chester, Pa. Died Aug. 18, 2008.

DONNELL, WILLIAM RAY, small business owner, communications executive; b. Lewiston, Maine, Oct. 3, 1931; s. William Thomas and Gladys Mae (Spinney) Donnell; m. Mayra Cintia Colon, June 16, 1962 (div. Jan. 1996); children: William Thomas, Jose Ismael, Ariadne Elizabeth. BA, U. Maine, 1959. Comml. capt. lic. Comml. fisherman, Maine, 1948-52, 55-60; tchr. Bath (Maine) Jr. HS, 1962, substitute tchr., 1963; tchr. Deer Isle (Maine) HS, 1965, 71, tchr. adult edn., 1976; tchr. St. Jude Integrated HS, St. Fintons, Nfld., Canada, 1972, Stonington (Maine) Elem. Sch., 1973; v.p., bd. dirs. Fisheries Comm., Inc., from 1977; owner, operator Donnell's Clapboard Mill, Sedgwick, Maine, from 1983. Recreational dir. City of Bath, 1963; capt. prin. comml. passenger schooner, 1965—71; remedial instr. Harpwell Islands Sch., Maine, 1965; farmer, Deer Isle, 1968—71, Deer Isle, 1972—78, Highlands, Nfld., 1971—72, Sedgwick, from 1978; lectr. in field; guest spkr. TV Can.-U.S. offshore boundary issue. Contbg. editor: Comml. Fisheries News, 1981—83; editor: Maine Comml. Fisheries, 1979—80, Fisheries Fed. Register Rev., 1981—82; author: numerous poems. Active Gov.'s Lobster Adv. Coun., Maine, 1980—85, Downeast Resource Conservation & Devel. Coun., from 1994, Sedgwick Budget Com., from 1995; co-chmn. Hancock County 4-H Citizenship Com., 1987—88; exec. com. Hancock County Extension, from 1988; moderator Sedgwick Town Meeting, 1993—94, from 2002; v.p. Brooklin Sedgwick Hist. Soc., 2000—02, 2004—05, hon. trustee, from 2005; candidate state legis. from Bath area Sagadahoc County, Maine, 1969; charter mem., bd. dirs. Maine Fishermen's Forum, Inc., 1985; lectr. discussion team Thelme's, Laguna Beach, Calif., 1985. Sgt. US Army, 1952—54, Korea. Decorated Bronze Star, Korean Svc. medal with 2 bronze stars, Combat Infantryman's Badge; recipient Poetry award, Nfld. and Labrador Arts and Letters Contest, 1972. Mem.: Sigma Chi (pres.). Avocations: antique vehicles, vessels and machinery. Died Jan. 31, 2009.

DONNELLY, PETER F., retired art association administrator; s. Peter Francis Donnelly and Marjorie Isobel Gale/Donnelly. BFA, Boston U., 1960. Asst. to prodr. Barter Theatre, Abingdon, Va., 1960—61; gen. mgr. Seattle Repertory Theatre, 1964—69, producing dir., 1969—85; exec. mng. dir. Dallas Theatre Ctr., 1986—89; pres., CEO Arts-Fund (formerly Corp. Coun. Arts), Seattle, 1989—2005. Chair Theatre Comm. Group, NYC, 1966—2002; former vice chair Americans for Arts, Washington; bd. dirs. Nat. Coalition United Arts Funds, Washington, past pres. Contbr. articles to profl. jours. Com. mem. Governor's Task Force Arts, Olympia, Wash. With US Army, 1961—62. Recipient President's award Individual Achievement Theatre, Wash. Assn. Theatre Artists, 1980, Sch. Fine Arts Outstanding Alumni award, Boston U., 1988, Michael Newton award Excellence Outstanding Leadership, Nat. Coalition United Arts Fund, 1995, Howard S. Wright award Outstanding Support Arts, Seattle Arts Commn., 1996, Seattle Mayor's Arts award, 1995; fellow, The Ford Found., 1963. Mem.: The Rainier Club (bd. dirs. 1999—2002). Achievements include development of Creation of statewide capital building fund for arts related buildings. Over $40 milllion of state money given to arts organizations during the last decade. Home: Seattle, Wash. Died Mar. 28, 2009.

DONNER, PAUL CHRISTOPHER, baby products manufacturing company executive; b. Chgo., Sept. 24, 1959; s. Frank Donald and Dorothy (Kanabay) D.; m. Christy Lynn Irwin, Feb. 28, 1980 (div. June 1988); children: Jason Christopher, Sean Michael; m. Tamsen Elizabeth Strong, Sept. 10, 1988. Asst. mgr. Wild West Clothing Stores, Northridge, Calif., 1977-79; svc. coord. Ladds Trucking Co., Northridge, 1979-82; prodn. mgr. Reddi Brake, Canoga Park, Calif., 1982-83; svc. mgr. Guy Martin Oldsmobile, Woodland Hills, Calif., 1983-87, Nesen Motor Car Inc., Thousand Oaks, Calif., 1987-88; sr. v.p. Degree Baby Products, Thousand Oaks, from 1988-. Democrat. Unitarian Universalist. Avocations: horseback riding, water-skiing, reading, weight training, bicycling. Home: Alhambra, Calif. Died Feb. 19, 2008.

DONNEWALD, JAMES HENRY, former state treasurer; b. Carlyle, Ill., Jan. 25, 1925; s. Henry and Cecelia (Luepke) Donnewald; m. Ruth E. Holtgrave, June 24, 1953; children: Eric J., Craig J., Jill Y. Student, St. Louis U., 1944; LLB, Lincoln Coll. Law, 1949. Bar: Ill. 1951. Mem. Ill. House Reps., 1960—64, Ill. Senate, 1964—66, 1970—76, Ill. State Senate, 1978, asst. majority leader, asst. minority leader; treas. State of Ill., Springfield, Ill., 1983—87. Gen. practice law, Breese, Ill., 1951—2009. With US Army, 1950—51. Mem.: Am. Legion, Ill. Bar Assn., KC. Democrat. Roman Catholic. Home: Breese, Ill. Died Sept. 18, 2009.

DONOVAN, PAUL F., electronics executive; b. Boston, Dec. 31, 1932; s. John Anthony and Marie Pelletier. BS in Chemistry, Northea. U., Boston, 1955, DSc (hon.), 1974; PhD in Nuclear Chemistry, U. Calif., Berkeley, 1958. Rsch. chemist Frederick S. Bacon Labs., Watertown, Mass., 1955; tchg. asst. U. Calif., Berkeley, 1955-56; mem. tech. staff Bell Tel. Labs., Murray Hill, N.J., 1958-67; acting dir. elem. particles phys. facilities/nuclear physics NSF, Washington, 1967-68, program dir. intermediate and high energy physics, 1968-70, head physics sect., 1970-71, dir. divsn. advanced tech. applications, 1971-73, dir. office energy R & D policy, 1973-76; pres. Donovan, Hamester & Rattien, Inc., Washington, 1976-79; Regents prof. U. Calif., Santa Cruz, 1980, adj. prof., 1981; chmn. R & C Enterprises, Ltd., Santa Cruz, from 1981; chmn., mktg. dir. ANADYNE, Inc., Santa Cruz, from 1986. Cons. Lawrence Radiation Lab., 1958-60, rsch. collaborator, guest scientist Brookhaven Nat. Lab., 1960-71; grad. faculty assoc. Rutgers U., 1964-71; cons. to pres. Electric Power Rsch. Inst., 1974; presenter/lectr. ednl. and rsch. instns. and profl. confs. Contbr. over 50 articles to sci. and tech. publs. NSF predoctoral fellow U. Calif., Berkeley, 1956-58. Fellow Am. Phys. Soc.; mem. Am. Inst. Chemists (medal), AAAS, Sigma Xi, Phi Kappa Phi. Home: Santa Cruz, Calif. Died Mar. 28, 2008.

DONOVAN, RICHARD P., lawyer; b. NYC, Aug. 14, 1921; s. Gerald and Louise (Priddie) D.; m. Edythe Walden Thurber, Aug. 12, 1943 (dec.); children: Edythe Donovan Oakley (dec.), Patrick, Nena Donovan Levine, Caroline, Margaret Donovan Donovan, William. AB, Brown U., 1942; JD, Cornell U., 1948. Bar: N.Y. 1948. Staff atty. SEC, Washington, 1948-50; asst. U.S. atty. So. Dist. N.Y., NYC, 1950-53; from assoc. to sr. ptnr. Sullivan & Donovan (formerly Sullivan, Donovan, Heenehan & Hanrahan and successor firms), NYC, 1953—2003. Asst. prof. Fordham U. Law Sch., N.Y.C., 1958-69; lectr. Cornell U. Law Sch., Ithaca, N.Y., 1957. Bd. govs. Sound Shore Med. Ctr. of Westchester, New Rochelle, N.Y., 1974—, N.Y. Soc. for Prevention of Cruelty to Children, N.Y.C., 1969—. Lt. USNR, 1941-45, ETO, PTO. Mem. N.Y. State Bar Assn., Assn. of Bar of City of N.Y., Yale Club N.Y.C., Dunes Club, Order of Coif, Phi Beta Kappa, Delta Kappa Epsilon. Democrat. Roman Catholic. Home: Essex, Conn. Died Oct. 7, 2007.

DOOLEY, THOMAS JOSEPH, organic chemist; b. NYC, Jan. 12, 1940; s. John P. and Anna (Ferrari) D. BS, Queens Coll./CUNY, 1961; MA, U. Oreg., 1964; PhD, U. R.I., 1967. Rsch. assoc. NIH-U. Wis., Madison, 1967; chemist Dexter-Midland, Waukegan, Ill., 1968-69; cons. Elmhurst, N.Y., 1969-72; rsch. chemist White Chem. Corp., Bayonne, N.J., 1972-81; sr. devel. assoc./chemist Polychrome Corp., Carlstadt, N.J., from 1981. Am. Hoechst fellow, 1966. Mem. AAAS, N.Y. Acad. Sci., Am. Chem. Soc., Sigma Xi, Beta Delta Chi. Achievements include 5 patents in field. Home: Teaneck, NJ. Died Oct. 23, 2007.

DORMUTH, CAROL KEENAN, secondary school mathematics educator; b. Phila., May 24, 1950; d. John Joseph and Merrill Theresa (Trimbur) Keenan; m. Bruce Lawrence Dormuth, July 15, 1978; 1 child, Kristin Victoria. BS, Chestnut Hill Coll., 1972; MEd, Pa. State U., 1974. Math. tchr. Colonial Sch., Plymouth Meeting, Pa., from 1972. Bd. dirs., co-treas. William Jeanes Friends of Libr., Lafayette Hill, Pa., 1988-90; leader Girl Scout U.S.A., Lafayette, 1989-93. Mem. Assn. Tchrs. Math., Nat. Coun. Tchrs. Math., Pa. Coun. Tchrs. Math. Avocations: reading, sewing, needlecrafts. Home: Lafayette Hill, Pa. Died Nov. 13, 2007.

DOUGLAS, ROBERT OWEN, writer; b. Aberdeen, SD, Feb. 18, 1940; s. James Garrison and Lorene Augusta (Soper) D. BA, Claremont McKenna Coll., 1962. Maritime editor San Pedro (Calif.) News Pilot, 1968-70; freelance photographer Nat. Geog. Mag., Washington, 1969; pvt. practice writer Tacoma, from 1977. Lyricist Bravo, You're High Voltage, 1996, The Vacation Song, 1996, Writer The Seven Seals, 1999, Heart of Gold, 1999, Secret Pandemonium, 1999, Holy Smokes!, 1999; inventor Douglas Tower Turbine, 1996. Lt. USN, 1963-68. Recipient Song of the Month award Chapel Rec. Co., Wollaston, Mass., 1996. Mem. The Camelot Soc. (dir.). Avocations: photography, music. Home: Tacoma, Wash. Died May 7, 2008.

DOUGLASS, FRANK RUSSELL, lawyer; b. Dallas, May 29, 1933; s. Claire Allen and Caroline (Score) D.; m. Carita Calkins, Feb. 5, 1955 (div. 1983); children: Russell, Tom, Andrew, Cathy; m. Betty Elwanda Richards, Dec. 31, 1983. BBA, Southwestern U., 1953; LLB, U. Tex., 1958. Bar: Tex. 1957, U.S. Dist. Ct. (we. dist.) Tex. 1960, U.S. Dist. Ct. (so. dist.) Tex. 1981, U.S. Dist. Ct. (no. dist.) Tex. 1985, U.S. Dist. Ct. (ea. dist.) Tex. 1987, U.S. Supreme Ct. 1964, U.S. Ct. Appeals (5th cir.) 1985; cert. in civil trial law, and oil, gas and energy law. Various positions to ptnr. McGinnis, Lochridge & Kilgore, Austin, Tex., 1957-76; sr. ptnr. Scott, Douglass & McConnico, Austin, from 1976. Contbr. articles to profl. jours. City atty., Westlake Hills, Tex., 1968. Served as airman USAF, 1953-55. Named Dist. Alumus Southwestern U., 1999. Fellow Am. Coll. Trial Lawyers; mem. ABA (natural resources law sect., coun. 1987-90), Am. Bar Found., Am. Inns of Ct., State Bar of Tex., Tex. Bar Found., The Tex. Ctr. for Legal Ethics and Professionalism (founding), Dallas Bar Assn., The Littlefield Soc. U. Tex. (charter). Died Nov. 23, 2007.

DOWLING, JAMES ANTHONY, physicist; b. Washington, Jan. 23, 1939; s. James Aloysius and Thelma Gertrude (Ellicott) D.; m. Carol Ann Smith, Sept. 14, 1963 (div. Sept. 1986); children: Brigid Dowling-Kenney, Stephen J., Kevin V.; m. Patricia Lee Coil, Jan. 30, 1993. BA in Physics, Cath. U. Am., 1961, PhD in Physics, 1967. Grad. rsch. asst. Cath. U. Am., Washington, 1961-67; staff scientist Avco Corp., Wilmington, Mass., 1967-69; rsch. physicist, supr. rsch. physicist U.S. Naval Rsch. Lab., Washington, 1969-80; sr. scientist Optimetrics, Inc., Las Cruces, N.Mex., 1980-85; v.p. for R&D, pres. Muffoletto Optical Co., Balt., 1985-87; pres., CEO Nu-Tek Precision Optical Corp., Belcamp, Md., 1987-92; sr. scientist Applied Tech. Assocs., Albuquerque, from 1992. Co-author: Atmospheric Water Vapor, 1979; contbr. articles to SPIE, Applied Optics, Jour. Optical Soc. Am., Optical Letters, Applied Phys. Letters. Mem. Soc. Photographic and Instrumentation Engring., Optical Soc. Am. Democrat. Avocations: grape growing and wine making, model ships and planes, household remodeling. Home: Albuquerque, N.Mex. Died July 7, 2008.

DRAUGHON, WALTER D., JR., retired dean; b. Newton, Ala., Mar. 6, 1925; s. Walter D. Sr. and Addie B. (Davis) D.; m. Jacqueline Louise Perry, Dec. 19, 1948; children: Gwendalyn Louise, Walter D. III, Perry Kenyon. BBA, Tulane U., 1946; MDiv, New Orleans Bapt. Theol. Sem., 1952, MRE, 1953; EdD, Southwestern Bapt. Theol. Sem., 1960. Instr. in bus. edn. Houston County High Sch., Columbia, Ala., 1948-50, Connors State Agrl. Coll., Warner, Okla., 1954-58; pastor Main St. Bapt. Ch., Stigler, Okla., 1954-58; prof. religious edn. Bapt. Bible Inst., Graceville, Fla., 1958-61; pastor Malvern (Ala.) Bapt. Ch., 1959-63; acad. dean, prof. counseling Bapt. Bible Inst. (now Fla. Bapt. Theol. Coll.), 1961-91, dean emeritus, 1991—2008; coord. theol. edn. Fla. Bapt. Conv., Graceville, 1991—2008. Dir. Graceville, Fla. Ctr. to New Orleans Bapt. Theol. Sem. Dir. Graceville Ctr.-New Orleans Bapt. Theol. Sem. M.Div. program. Mem. Conf. Acad. Deans of the So. Assn. Colls. and Schs. (sec. membership com. 1967-70), So. Bapt. Adult Edn. Assn. (pres. 1978), Kiwanis (bd. dirs. Graceville chpt.). Avocations: reading, computers, fishing. Died Nov. 3, 2008.

DRAZNIN, JULIUS NATHAN, arbitrator, mediator; b. Chgo., Sept. 14, 1920; s. Max and Ida (Kramen) D.; m. Yaffa Bernstein, Dec. 29, 1942; children: Anne Louise, Michael Ernest. Student, Wright Jr. Coll., 1938-39, U. Chgo., 1942-44. Field examiner Region 18, NLRB, Mpls., 1944-47, Region 19, NLRB, Seattle, 1947-54, Region 13, NLRB, Chgo., 1954-60, supervisory examiner, 1960-65; asst. regional dir. Region 31, NLRB, LA, 1960-65; pvt. practice LA, 1965-75. Commr. employee rels. bd., FMCS, NMB, L.A., 1976—; master U.S. Dist. Ct. (cen. dist.) Calif. Contbg. editor Personnel Jour., 1978-88; contbr. articles to profl. jours., labor rels. and newspapers. Mem. Inst. Indsl. Rels. Assn. (pres. 1987-88), Indsl. Rels. Rsch. Assn., Am. Arbitration Assn. Jewish. Home: Chicago, Ill. Died Nov. 23, 2007.

DREIKAUSEN, MARGRET, artist, educator; b. Cologne, Germany, Jan. 9, 1937; came to U.S., 1961; AAS, Fashion Inst. Tech., 1968; BA, CUNY, 1975, MA, 1978. Asst. prof. U. Conn., Storrs, 1978-79; instr. Fashion Inst. Tech., NYC, 1980, Parsons Sch. Design, NYC, from 1979. Dir. LIC Artists, Inc., 1987-95, founder, bd. dirs., pres., 1990—; fashion designer IGS, Istanbul, Turkey, 1970, various mfrs., N.Y.C., 1963-78. Artist numerous group and one-person exhibitions, U.S., Germany; author: Aerial Perception, 1985; contbg. author: Essays on Creativity & Science, 1986. Mem. Coll. Art Assn. Avocation: travel. Home: Long Beach, NY. Died Dec. 13, 2007.

DRISKELL, CLAUDE EVANS, college director, educator, dentist; b. Chgo., Jan. 13, 1926; s. James Ernest and Helen Elizabeth (Perry) D., Sr.; m. Naomi Roberts, Sept. 30, 1953; 1 child, Yvette Michele; stepchildren: Isaiah, Ruth, Reginald, Elaine. BS, Roosevelt U., 1950; BS in Dentistry, U. Ill., 1952, DDS, 1954. Practice dentistry, Chgo., from 1954; adj. prof. Chgo. State U., from 1971; dean's aide, adviser black students Coll. Dentistry U. Ill., from 1972. Dental cons., supervising dentist, dental hygienists supportive health services Bd. Edn., Chgo., 1974. Author: The Influence of the Halogen Elements Upon the Hydrocarbon, and their Effect on General Anesthesia, 1962; History of Chicago's Black Dental Professionals, 1850-1983; co-author (with Claude Driskell) Essays on Professor Dr. Earl Renfroe-A Man of Firsts, 2001; author, editor and publisher: Original Forty Club's 75th Anniversary Book (1920-1995); author, editor, archivist, historian Forty Club, 1993-2000; mem. editl. bd. Nat. Dental Assn. Quar. Jour., 1977—; contbr. articles to profl. jours. Vice pres. bd. dirs. Jackson Park Highlands Assn., 1971-73. Served with AUS, 1944-46; ETO. Fellow Internat. Biog. Assn., Royal Soc. Health (Gt. Britain), Acad. Gen. Dentistry; mem. Lincoln Dental Soc. (editor), Chgo. Dental Soc., ADA, Nat. Dental Assn. (editor pres.'s newsletter; dir. pub. relations, publicity; recipient pres.'s spl. achievement award 1969) dental assns., Am. Assn. Dental Editors, Acad. Gen. Dentistry, Soc. Med. Writers, Soc. Advancement Anesthesia in Dentistry, Omega Psi Phi. Home: Chicago, Ill. Died May 23, 2009.

DROKE, EDNA FAYE, retired elementary school educator; b. Sylvester, Tex., Dec. 4, 1932; d. Ira Selle and Faye Emily (Seckinger) Tucker; m. Louis Albert Droke, June 2, 1951 (dec.); children: Sherman Ray, Lyndon Allen, Lona Faye Droke Cheairs. BEd, Tarleton State U., Stephenville, Tex., 1983. Cert. ESL and 3d-8th lang. arts tchr., Tex. Tchr. ESL and lang. arts Wingate Ind. Sch. Dist., Tex., 1983-86;

tchr. 2d grade and ESL Collidge Ind. Sch. Dist., Tex., 1986-88; tchr. 4th grade and ESL Peaster Ind. Sch. Dist., Tex., 1988-89, tchr. Chpt. I in 1st-6th grades, ESL in K-12th grades Tex., 1989-96; tchr. ESL 3d grade, reading recovery tchr. Ranger Ind. Sch. Dist., Tex., 1996-98, ret. Tex., 1998; substitute tchr. Blanket Ind. Sch. Dist., Tex., 1998—2004; ESL tchr. 220th CSCD, Comanche, Tex., 1998—2004, Gustine Ind. Sch. Dist., Tex., 2004—07, ret., 2007. Tutor Hispanic probationers in English for 220th Dist. Ct., Comanche, Tex., Gustine Ind. Sch. Dist. Reading Improvement, 2000-03; tchr. reading improvement Gustine Ind. Sch. Dist., 2004-05, tchr. ESL, 2004-07. Mem. ASCD, Kappa Delta Pi, Alpha Chi. Baptist. Avocations: reading, quilting, knitting, playing piano, painting. Home: Comanche, Tex. Died Feb. 3, 2009.

DROPKIN, ALLEN HODES, lawyer; b. Chgo., Oct. 26, 1930; s. Nathan I. and Zelda (Hodes) D.; m. Corrine S. Rose, Aug. 22, 1954; children: Ruth, David, Zachary, Noah. AB, U. Chgo., 1948, JD, 1951. Bar: Ill. 1951, D.C. 1956. Assoc. Arvey, Hodes & Mantynband, Chgo., 1951-54, 57-61; asst. states atty. Cook County, Ill., 1954-56; spl. counsel subcom. on housing, banking/currency com. U.S. Ho. of Reps., Washington, 1956; ptnr. Arvey, Hodes, Costello & Burman, Chgo., 1961-91, Fishman & Merrick PC, Chgo., 1992-98; pvt. practice Chgo., from 1998. Pres. Bd. Jewish Edn., Chgo., 1975-78, Midwest Region United Synagogue Am., 1981-84; dir. Jewish Cmty. Ctrs., Chgo., 1972-76. Avocation: community svc. Died Nov. 2, 2007.

DRYDEN, JAMES DALE, real estate company executive; b. North Platte, Nebr., Aug. 11, 1937; s. J. Dale and Evelyn Theodora (From) D.; divorced; children: Angela Rene, Julianne Marie; m. Adela Guerrero, Dec. 16, 1978; children: Amanda Lynne, Lisa Lauren. BS in Pharmacy, U. Nebr., 1959. Registered real estate broker, Tex.; registered pharmacist, Nebr., Tex. Prin. Dryden Pharmacies, North Platte, Nebr., 1959-73, Dryden Fin. Corp., Corpus Christi, Tex., from 1973, Dryden Real Estate, Corpus Christi, from 1978; pres. So. Med. Recruiters, Inc., Corpus Christi, from 1978. Avocation: trans-oceanic sailing. Home: Silt, Colo. Died June 2, 2008.

DUBIEL, MARK BALDWIN, psychiatrist; b. LA, Sept. 12, 1956; s. Joseph Michael and Catherine (Arthur) D. BA in Biochemistry magna cum laude, Occidental Coll., 1978; MD, UCLA, 1982. Intern San Francisco Sch. Medicine, Fresno VA, Fresno, 1982-83; resident in psychiatry Sleep Rsch. Lab. U. Calif., Fresno, 1983-86; chief resident in psychiatry San Francisco Sch. Medicine, Fresno VA, 1985-86. Mem. Corp. for the Advancement of Psychiatry, 1989-90. Regents scholar U. Calif., 1978-82. Mem. AMA, N.Y. Acad. Scis., Phi Beta Kappa, Avocations: bicycle riding, swimming, weightlifting, laminating plaques. Home: Mesa, Ariz. Died Sept. 2, 2007.

DU BOIS, JON DAVID, computer company owner, graphic artist; b. Lindsborg, Kans., Sept. 15, 1959; s. Ronald Perry and Thora A. du Bois. BS in Chemistry, U. Okla., 1988; BS in Computer Sci., U. Ctrl. Okla., 1991. Rsch. assoc. UCLA Sch. Pub. Health, 1988-89; animation checker Mattel Toys, Inc., Hawthorne, Calif., 1989; rsch. assoc. Okla. U. Health Sci. Ctr., Oklahoma City, 1989-90; graphic artist KFOR-TV, Oklahoma City, from 1990; pres. du Bois Animation, Edmond, Okla., from 1991. Author: (software) Animatrix Modeler, 1991, Animatrix 3-Digitizer, 1992. Died Apr. 3, 2008.

DUBOSE, ELIZABETH (BETTYE DUBOSE), community health nurse; b. Ozark, Ala., Nov. 11, 1930; d. Samuel D. and Mattie Victoria (Harrell) Preston; m. Charles Raymond Hudson, July 31, 1949; 1 child, Julianne Schenker Adams; m. Frederick William Schenker, Jr., Dec. 15, 1962; m. John Calvin DuBose, July 15, 1978. ADN, Columbus State U., 1973, BSN, 1977. Lab tech. II Ala. Bureau of Labs., Dothan, Ala., 1951-62; student nurse CCU St. Francis Hosp., Columbus, Ga., 1972-73; charge nurse The Med. Ctr., Columbus, 1973-75, infection control nurse, 1975-78; charge nurse The Bradley Ctr., Columbus, Ga., 1974-78; clin. instr. nursing Columbus State U., 1977-78; dir. nursing Oakview Manor Nursing Home, Ozark, Ala., 1979-84; patient care coord. Wiregrass Home Health Agy., 13 Counties in SE Ala., 1984-86; home health coord. Ala. Pub. Health Dept., Abbeville, Ala., 1986-90; home health nurse Dale Co. Health Dept., Ozark, Ala., 1990—2002. Libr. com. mem. The Medical Ctr., Columbus, Ga., 1974-77; chmn. adv bd. Oakview Manor, Ozark, 1980-84. Mem. adv. bd. Henry Co. Health Dept., Abbeville, 1986-88, chmn. adv. bd., 1988-90. Republican. Protestant. Avocations: music, theater, chess. Home: Ariton, Ala. Died Sept. 24, 2007.

DUCKWORTH, RUTH, sculptor; b. Hamburg, Germany, Apr. 10, 1919; arrived in US, 1964; d. Edgar Windmüller and Ellen Elise Strack. Student, Liverpool U., Eng., 1936—40, Hammersmith Sch. of Art, 1955, Ctrl. Sch. Arts & Crafts, London, 1956—58; D (hon.), DePaul U., 1982; D, Detroit Inst. Art, 2007. Tchr. Ctrl. Sch. Arts & Crafts, London, 1959—64, U. Chgo., 1964—66, 1968—77; vis. artist Corsham Sch. of Art, England, 1965. Tchr. various workshops and seminars, 1972—93; lectr. in field, from 1994. One-woman shows include Appolinaire Gallery, London, 1953, Primavera, 1960, 1962, 1967, Arnolfini, Bristol, Eng., 1964, U. Chgo., 1965, Craftsmen's Gallery, Chgo., 1965, Agra Gallery, Washington, 1965, The Chgo. Pub. Libr., 1966, Gallery Mid-North, Chgo., 1966, Matsuya Dept. Store, Tokyo, 1967, Jacques Barach Gallery, Chgo., 1972, Kunstkammer Ludger Koster, Monchen-Gladbach, Germany, 1973, Calvary Sch. of Art, Alta., Can., 1974, Mus. fur Kunst und Gewerbe, Hamburg, 1976, Exhibit A, Evanston, Ill., 1977, Chgo., 1980, 1982, 1984, Hadler Gallery, N.Y.C., 1978, Mus. Boymans-Van Beuningen, Rotterdam, The Netherlands, 1979, Lake Forest (Ill.) Coll., 1984, Helen Drutt Gallery, Phila., 1986, Contemporary Art Ctr., London, 1986, Soc. of Art in Crafts, Pitts., 1987, Dorothy Weiss Gallery, San Francisco, 1989, 1992, 1994, Garth Clark Gallery, N.Y.C., 1990, 1996, 1999, 2002, L.A., 1991, Bellas Artes Gallery, Santa Fe, 1991, 1993, 1996, 2000, Pewabic Gallery, Detroit, 1992, Keramik-Galerie Bowig, Hannover, Germany, 1993, Schleswig-Holsteinische Landesmuseum, Rendsburg, Germany, 1994, galerie b15, Munich, 2000, exhibited in group shows at Art Inst. Chgo., 1969, Victoria and Albert Mus., London, 1972, Mus. Contemporary Art, Chgo., 1976, 1984, 1996, Milw. Art Mus., 1984, Am. Craft Mus., N.Y.C., 1987, Internat. Acad. Ceramics, Saga, Japan, 1996, Met. Mus. of Art, N.Y.C., 1999, L.A. County Mus. of Art, 2000, numerous others, prin. works include St. Joseph's Ch., New Malden, Eng., 1959—60, Solel Synagogue, Highland Park, Ill., 1965, Lab. for Geophys. Sci. Bldg., U. Chgo., 1967—68, Purdue U., Lafayette, Ind., 1972, Dresdner Bank, Bd. of Trade (moved to Options Exch. Bldg.), Chgo., 1976, Hodag Chem. Co. (transferred to Lewis & Clark Coll., Godfrey, Ill.), Skokie, Ill., 1978, Rozansky & Kay Co., Bethesda, Md., 1981, Sonnenschein, Carlin, North and Rosenthal Offices, Chgo., 1981, Main Bank of Chgo., 1982, Perkins & Will Arch. Offices, Chgo., 1982, Congregation Beth Israel, Hammond, Ind., 1982—83, Amcore Bank, Rockford, Ill., 1983, Teradyne Ctrl., Deerfield, Ill., 1984, Dr. R. Lee Animal Care Ctr. (commd. by Chgo. Coun. on Fine Arts 1/2% for the Arts Program), 1984, State of Ill. Bldg., Capitol Devel. Bd., Springfield, 1984—85, Unisys Offices, N.Y.C., 1986, St. Mary's Ch., Walsingham, Eng., 1987, Stowell, Cook, Frolichstein, Inc., Clearwater, Fla., 1988, Palm Beach (Fla.) Airport Terminal, 1990, State of Ill. Bldg., State Commn., Rockford, 1992, Chgo. Children's Mus., 1995, State of Ill. Commn., Lewis and Clark Coll., Godfrey, Ill., 1997—98, City of Chgo., Dept. Cultural Affairs, 1999, First Nat. Bank Collection, Columbia, Mo., 1999, Represented in permanent collections Windsor Castle, Eng., Nat. Mus. Modern Art, Japan, Smithsonian Instn., Washington, Mus. Contemporary Art, Chgo., St. Louis Art Mus., Boston Mus. Fine Arts, Art Inst. of Chgo., Phila. Mus. of Art, Fine Arts Mus. of San Francisco, Am. Craft Mus., N.Y.C., L.A. County Art Mus., Nat. Mus. Scotland, Edinburgh, Met. Mus. of Art, N.Y.C., numerous others. Recipient Gold medal, Ceramic Art of the World, Calgary, Can., 1973, Gold medal in craft arts category, Ill. Acad. Fine Arts, 1992, Lifetime Achievement in the Craft Arts Gold medal, Nat. Mus. of Women in the Arts, Washington, 1993, Gold medal, Nat. Soc. Arts and Letters, Washington, 1996, The Madigan prize for best sculpture in State of Ill., Springfield, 1999, Master of the Medium Gold medal, Renwick Alliance, Renwick Gallery, Washington, 2001, 3 Art award, Disting. Artist of Yr., 2003, Arts in Edn. award, 2003, 3 Arts award, 3Arts Club Chgo., 2003, Visionary award, Mus. Arts and Design, NY, 2003, Beaux Arts Celebration award, Union League Club Chgo., 2003, Internat. Lifetime Achievement award, U. Wales, 2007. Fellow: Am. Craft Coun. (award 1993, Gold medal 1997); mem.: Internat. Acad. Ceramics, Arts Club. Died Oct. 18, 2009.

DUDDEN, ARTHUR POWER, historian, educator; b. Cleve., Oct. 26, 1921; s. Arthur Clifford and Kathleen (Bray) D.; m. Adrianne Churchill Onderdonk, June 5, 1965 (dec. Oct. 15, 2005); 1 child, Alexis Dudden; children by previous marriage: Kathleen Dudden Rowlands, Candace L. Dudden (Schweitzer). AB, Wayne State U., 1942; A.M., U. Mich., 1947, PhD, 1950. Faculty Bryn Mawr Coll., from 1950, prof. history, 1965-92, Fairbank prof. humanities, 1989-92, Katharine E. McBride prof. history, 1992-95, 98-99, prof. emeritus history and Fairbank prof. emeritus humanities, 1992—2009. Instr. CCNY, 1950; vis. asst. prof. Am. civilization U. Pa., 1953-54, ednl. coord. spl. program Am. civilization, 1956, faculty Inst. Humanistic Studies for Execs., 1953-59, vis. assoc. prof. history, 1958, 62-65, vis. prof. history, 1965-68; vis. assoc. prof. Princeton U., NJ, 1958-59, Haverford Coll., 1962-63; vis. prof. Trinity Coll., 1965; cons. Peace Corps, 1962-66; mem. Bicentennial Com. on Internat. Confs. of Americanists, 1973-76; founding pres. Fulbright Assn. of Alumni, 1976-2009, exec. dir., 1980-84; cons. Nat. Archives, 1993-95; adj. prof. history Lehigh U., 1993-95. Author: Teachers Manual to the American Republic, vols. I and II, 1959, 60, 70, Understanding the American Republic, vols. I and II, 1961, 70, Objective Tests, The American Republic, 1962, The Assault of Laughter, 1962, The United States of America: A Syllabus of American Studies, 2 vols, 1963, The Instructor's Guide to the United States, 3d edit, 1972, The Student's Guide to the United States, 2d edit, 1967, Joseph Fels and the Single Tax Movement, 1971, Pardon Us, Mr. President!, 1975, The Fulbright Experience, 1946-1986, 1987, American Humor, 1987, paperback edit., 1989, The American Pacific, 1992, paperback edit., 1993; editor: Woodrow Wilson and the World of Today, 1957, The Logbook of the Captain's Clerk, 1995; compiler: International Directory of Specialists in American Studies, 1975; contbr. Ency. Am. Social History, 1993, Ency. U.S. Fgn. Rels., 1997, American Empire in the Pacific, 2004. Served with USNR, 1942-45. Sr. Fulbright scholar Denmark, 1959-60 and West Europe, 1992. Mem. Fellows Am. Studies (sec.-treas. 1957-59, pres. 1960-61), Am. Studies Assn. (treas. 1968, 72, exec. sec. 1969-72, Bode-Pearson prize 1991), Am. Hist. Assn., Orgn. Am. Historians (local arrangements chmn. Phila. 1969), Harriton Assn. (bd. dirs. 1962-2007), Hist. Soc. of Pa. (trustee 1993-99). Died Oct. 14, 2009.

DUFFY, DENNIS ANTHONY, transportation personnel leasing executive; b. Chgo., July 26, 1940; s. John Daniel and Margaret L. (Hayden) D.; m. Carol Ann Steves, Aug. 19, 1957 (div. 1963); m. Terry Ann Steward, July 16, 1966; children: Debra Jane, Margaret Lucille. Grad. high sch., Prairie du Chien, Wis. Sales dist. mgr. Canada Dry Corp., Maywood, Ill., 1963-70; driver Transpersonnel, Inc., Chgo., 1971-78; ops. mgr. Transport Drivers, Inc., Bensenville, Ill., 1978-82, v.p. ops., 1982-93, prin., from 1988, exec. v.p., from 1993. Bd. dirs. Computer Insights, Inc., Arlington Heights, Ill., 1987—, Optimum Staffing, Inc., Bensenville, 1992—; prin. Pinnacle Transport Svcs., Inc., Bensenville, 1989—. Precinct capt. Cook County Rep. Orgn., Mt. Prospect, Ill., 1980; communications officer Elk Grove Civil Def., Elk Grove Village, Ill., 1980—. With USN, 1957-62. Mem. Nat. Pvt. Truck Coun. (safety com.), Nat. Trucking Indsl. Rels. Assn., Driver Leasing Coun. Am., Am. Legion. Avocations: amateur radio, golf. Home: Elk Grove Village, Ill. Died Feb. 3, 2008.

DUFFY, HARRY ARTHUR, violin expert and dealer; b. Eureka, Calif., Nov. 29, 1915; s. Harry Arthur and Caroline Mary (Reason) D.; m. Clara Nell Cromwell, Oct. 15, 1941 (div. 1971); children: Duane Arthur, Glenn Ellis; m. Olga Romanov, Oct. 28, 1989. AB, BS, U. Calif., Berkeley, 1939; postgrad., San Jose State U., 1939—40. Archivist, appraiser Rembert Wurlitzer, NYC, 1946-70; pres. Harry A. Duffy Violins, Inc., Miami, Fla., 1970-86. 1st lt. U. S. Army, 1941-46. Mem. Westshore Music Club (L.A.). Episcopalian. Avocations: tennis, coin collecting/numismatics. Died Nov. 2, 2005.

DULANEY, LUTHER CARROLL, retired postmaster; b. Doucette, Tex., Jan. 10, 1925; s. James David and Ida Jeanette (Wise) D.; m. Juanita M. Lester, Aug. 2, 1950; children: Arlan Glenn, Andria Joette. Grad. high sch., Spurger, Tex. Chem. lab analyst Neches Butane Products Co., Port Neches, Tex., 1946-47; chem. lab. leaderman Jefferson Chem. Co., Port Neches, 1947-48; with U.S. Postal Svc., Port Neches, 1948-89, asst. postmaster, 1965-71, postmaster, 1971-89; ret., 1989. Legis. chmn. Postal Clk. Union, Port Neches, 1953-57. With USN, 1943-46, mem. USNR ret. Mem. Lions (sec. 1970-71, 1st v.p. 1987-89, bd. dirs. 1989—). Democrat. Avocations: stamp and coin collecting, photography, restoration of old furniture. Home: Port Neches, Tex. Died Jan. 29, 2008.

DULIN, MAURINE STUART, volunteer; b. Lonerock, Iowa, Feb. 16, 1919; d. Frank Meagher and Fern Adrienne (Wetzel) Stuart; m. William Carter Dulin, Oct. 5, 1940; children: Jacquelyn Dulin Wilson, Patricia F., Stuart M. AB in Polit. Sci./Econs., Coll. of William and Mary, 1939. Coll. cons. Woodward and Lothrop, Washington, 1939-40; adminstv. asst. Sightler and Cox, Washington, 1942-43; acctg. dept. asst. Am. U., Washington, 1964-69; corp. sec. Bittinger and Dulin, Arlington, Va., 1949-73; ptnr. 41 Ltd. Partnership, Bethesda, Md., from 1979, Montrose-270 Ltd. Partnership, Bethesda, from 1979. Mem. Rock Creek Womens Rep. Club, Bethesda, 1951-57; sgt.-at-arms Montgomery County Fed. of Rep. Women, Bethesda, 1952-53, State Fedn. of Womens Rep. Club, 1953-54; charter mem., com. chmn. Nat. Mus. of Women in the Arts; women's bd. Cathedral Choral Soc. 1975—, com. chmn., 1988-90; women's bd. George Washington U. Hosp., 1970—, Save Our Seminary at Forest Glen, Md., 1989—. Mem. The Town Club (pres. 1958-59), Pi Beta Phi (nat. com. chmn. 1971-75, province officer 1967-71). Episcopalian. Home: Bethesda, Md. Died Jan. 24, 2008.

DULL, R. JEAN SEYMOUR, office nurse; b. NYC, Apr. 20, 1919; d. Aubrey and Pearl C. (Smith) Moore; m. Roy M. Dull, Mar. 19, 1973; children: Larry Seymour, Peggy Jo Haas, Jon R. Seymour, Bonnie J. Seymour. RN degree, Crouse-Irving Hops., Syracuse, NY, 1937. Night supr. Annie Warner Hosp., Gettysburg, Pa.; night supr., emergency rm. head nurse Carroll County Gen. Hosp., Westminster, Md.; gen. duty and evening supr. Onodaga Gen. Hosp., Syracuse; office nurse Dr. Marilyn Miller, Westminster, Md. Home: Westminster, Md. Died Oct. 7, 2007.

DULLES, AVERY, cardinal, theologian; b. Auburn, NY, Aug. 24, 1918; s. John Foster and Janet Pomeroy (Avery) D. AB, Harvard U., 1940, attended, 1940—41; PhL, Woodstock Coll., 1951, STL, 1957; STD, Pontifical Gregorian U., Rome, 1960; LLD (hon.), St. Joseph's Coll., Phila., 1969; LHD (hon.), Georgetown U., 1977; ThD (hon.), U. Detroit, 1978; LLD (hon.), Iona Coll., New Rochelle, NY, 1980; DD (hon.), St. Anselm Coll., Manchester, NH, 1981; LHD (hon.), Creighton U., 1983; DD (hon.), Jesuit Sch. Theology, Berkeley, Calif., 1984, Protestant Episcopal Theol. Sem., Alexandria, Va., 1986; LHD (hon.), Seton Hall U., 1989, Stonehill Coll., 1990, Loyola U., Chgo., 1990; STD (hon.), Providence Coll., 1991; DD (hon.), Carthage Coll., Kenosha, Wis., 1991; ThD (hon.), U. Dayton, 1992; LHD (hon.), Christ the King Seminary, East Aurora, NY, 1994; DD (hon.), Nashotah House, Wis., 1996; LittD (hon.), Fordham U., 1996; DD (hon.), John Carroll U., Cleveland, Ohio, 1997; LLD (hon.), U. Mass., Boston, 1998; LHD (hon.), St. Francis Coll., Bklyn., 1999; ThD (hon.), Theol. Faculty Paderborn, Germany, 2000; LLD (hon.), U. Notre Dame, 2001; LHD (hon.), LeMoyne Coll., Syracuse, NY, 2001, Univ. St Thomas, Miami, 2001, Seminary St. Charles Borromeo, Overbrook, Pa., 2002, Univ. St. Thomas, St. Paul, Minn., 2002; DD (hon.), Univ. Scranton, Pa., 2002; STD (hon.), Franciscan Univ., Steubenville, Ohio, 2002; LHD (hon.), St. Joseph's Coll., Renssalear, Ind., 2003, Christendom Coll. Front Royal, Va., 2003, Coll. of the Holy

Cross, Worcester, Mass., 2003; STD (hon.), Siena Coll., Londonville, NY, 2003, Coll. New Rochelle, 2003, Bobolanum, Warsaw, Poland, 2003; DD (hon.), Heythrop Coll., London, 2003; LHD (hon.), Ohio State U., 2004; DHL (hon.), Wheeling Jesuit U., W.Va., 2006, Ave Maria U., Naples, Fla., 2006; DRE (hon.), Marquette U., Milw., 2006. Joined S.J., 1946; ordained priest, 1956; instr. philosophy Fordham U., 1951-53, vis. lectr., 1970; mem. faculty Woodstock Coll., NYC, 1960-74, prof. theology, 1969-74, Cath. U. America, Washington, 1974-88, prof. emeritus, 1988—2008; Gasson prof. theology Boston Coll., Boston, 1981-82; Laurence J. McGinley prof. religion and society Fordham U., 1988—2008; elevated to cardinal, 2001; cardinal-deacon SS. Nome di Gesu e Maria in Via Lata, 2001—08. Mem. Commn. on Christian Unity, Archdiocese of Balt., 1962—70; consultor to Papal Secretariat Dialogue with Non-Believers, 1966—73; mem. Cath. Bishops' Adv. Coun., 1969—75, USA Luth.-Cath. Dialogue, 1972—92, Internat. Theol. Com., 1992—97, Luth.-Roman Cath. Co-ord. Com., 1994—96; vis. lectr. Weston Coll., 1971, Union Theol. Sem., 1971—74, Princeton Theol. Sem., 1972, Pontifical Gregorian U., 1973, 90, 93, Episcopal Theol. Sem., 1975, Luth. Sem. Pa., 1978; fellow Woodrow Wilson Internat. Ctr. for Scholars, 1977; Martin C. D'Arcy lectr. Campion Hall, Oxford U., England, 1983; vis. John A. O'Brien prof. theology Notre Dame U., 1985; vis. prof. theology Cath. U. of Leuven, 1992; cons. to doctrine com. Nat. Conf. Cath. Bishops, 1991—2008; vis. prof. religious studies Yale U., New Haven, 1996; scholar-in-residence St. Joseph's Sem., Dunwoodie, NY, 1996. Author: Princeps Concordiae, 1941, A Testimonial to Grace, 1946, (with others) Introductory Metaphysics, 1955, Apologetics and the Biblical Christ, 1963, The Dimensions of the Church, 1967, Revelation and the Quest for Unity, 1968, Revelation Theology: A History, 1969, (with others) Spirit, Faith and Church, 1970, The Survival of Dogma, 1971 (Christopher award 1972), A History of Apologetics, 1971, 2d edit., 2005, Models of the Church, 1974, 3d rev. edit., 2002, Church Membership as a Catholic and Ecumenical Problem, 1974, The Resilient Church, 1977, A Church to Believe In, 1982, Models of Revelation, 1983, 2d rev. edit., 1992, (with Patrick Granfield) The Church: A Bibliography, 1985, The Reshaping of Catholicism, 1988, The Craft of Theology, 1992, expanded edit., 1995 (Best Book in Theology Cath. Press Assn. 1993), The Assurance of Things Hoped For, 1994, A Testimonial to Grace and Reflections on a Theological Journey, 1996, The Priestly Office, 1997, (with Patrick Granfield) The Theology of the Church: A Bibliography, 1999, The Splendor of Faith: The Theological Vision of Pope John Paul II, 1999, rev. edit., 2003, The New World of Faith, 2000, Newman, 2002, Magisterium: Teacher and Guardian of The Faith, 2007; assoc. editor: Ecumenism Concilium, 1963-70, adv. editl. bd., 1970-92; adv. editl. bd.: Midstream: An Ecumenical Jour., 1974-2008; mem. editl. bd.: Logos: A Jour. of Cath. Thought and Culture, 1997-2008; contbr. column to Theology for Today, America, 1967-68; contbg. editor New Oxford Rev., 1990-2001; cons. Theology Digest, 1985-2008; mem. adv. coun. Pro Ecclesia, 1991-2008; contbr. articles to theol. publ. Bd. dirs. Georgetown U., 1966-68, Woodstock Theol. Ctr., 1974-79; trustee Fordham U., 1969-72, St. Mary's Sem. and Univ., Balt., 1992-98; acad. coun. Irish Sch. Ecumenics, 1971-78. Served to lt. USNR, 1942-46. Decorated Croix de Guerre with silver star (France); recipient Cardinal Spellman award for disting. achievement in theology, 1970, Religious Edn. Forum award, Nat. Cath. Edn. Assn., 1988, Campion award, Cath. Book Club, NY, 1989, F. Sadlier Dinger award, 1994, Choate Alumni Seal prize, Choate Rosemary Hall, 1995, Christus Magister medal, U. Portland, 2001, James Cardinal Gibbons medal, Cath. U. Am., Washington, 2001, Gold Medal award, Nat. Inst. Social Sci., NYC, 2001, John Henry Newman award, Cardinal Newman Soc., 2001, John Carroll Soc. medal, Washington, 2002, John Paul II award, Inst. for Social Sci., Arlington, Va., 2002, Jerome award, Cath. Libr. Assn., 2002, Newman medal, Loyola Coll., Md., 2004, Marianist award, U. Dayton, Ohio, 2004, Saint Thomas Aquinas medallion, Saint Thomas Aquinas Coll., Santa Paula, Calif., 2005, St. Joseph's Sem. 7th Ann. Dinner award, 2005, Pres. medal, Canisius Coll., Buffalo, 2005, Loyola medal, Seattle U., 2006, Veritas medal, Aquinas Ctr. for Theol. Renewal, Ave Maria U., 2007, Cath. Chaplaincy award, Harvard U., 2007, Bene Merenti medal, Fordham U., 2007; named to Hall of Fame, NY Mil. ROTC, 2004, Order of St. Thomas, U. St. Thomas, Houston, 2006. Mem. Cath. Theol. Soc. Am. (bd. dir. 1970-72, 74-77, v.p. 1974-75, pres. 1975-76), Am. Theol. Soc. (v.p. 1977-78, pres. 1978-79), Cath. Commn. on Intellectual and Cultural Affairs (exec. com. 1991-94), Phi Beta Kappa. Roman Catholic. Died Dec. 12, 2008.

DUMINUCO, VINCENT JOSEPH, academic administrator, educator; b. Bronx, NY, Jan. 13, 1934; s. Joseph S. Duminuco and Mary Dora Morreale. BA, Fordham U., 1957; degree in Sacred Theology, Woodstock Coll., 1965; MA, Stanford U., 1966, PhD, 1969. Headmaster Xavier H.S., NYC, 1969—74; dir. rsch. U.S. Jesuit Conf., Washington, 1974—77; pres. Jesuit Secondary Edn. Assn., Washington, 1977—86; sec. edn. Soc. Jesus, Rome, 1987—97; rector Jesuit Cmty. Fordham U., Bronx, 2001—07. Bd. adv. H.K. Internat. Inst. Ednl. Leadership, Hong Kong, 1998—2007; dir. worldwide Internat. Jesuit Leadership Program, Rome, from 1996; dir. Joseph O'Hare Jesuit Tchr. Leadership Program, NYC, from 2003; bd. dirs. St. Barnabus Hosp., Bronx; bd. trustees Fordham U., Loyola U., New Orleans, 1976—92; mem. pontifical coun. interreligious dialogue, Rome, 1990—96; bd. trustees St. Peters Coll., LeMoyne Coll. Author: Ignatian Pedagogy: A Practical Approach, 1993; editor: The Jesuit Ratio Studiorum, 2000;

co-author: Catholic Education: Inside Out, Outside In, 1999. Recipient The Guerra award, Nat. Cath. Edn. Assn., 2003; fellow, Stanford U., 1967—69, 1969. Mem.: Nat. Cath. Ednl. Assn. (pres. secondary sch. dept. 1983—86), N.Y. Botanical Gardens. Independent. Roman Catholic. Avocations: bonsai, fishing, gardening, swimming. Deceased.

DUNCAN, REGINALD WALLACE, clergyman, former municipal judge and educator; b. Wichita Falls, Tex., May 20, 1925; s. Howell Cobb and Eva Lois (Kelley) D.; m. Patsy Jean Gunnell, Nov. 1, 1946; children: Ralph, Barbara, Reginald, Lydia, Beth, Clydene. BS with honors, Ea. N.Mex. U., 1976; MA in Rels., Pepperdine U., 1979. Cert. tchr. N.Mex. Enlisted man USN, 1943, advanced through grades to chief electronic technician, 1956; assigned to Yokosuka, Japan, 1955-57; instr. U.S. Naval Electronic Sch., Treasure Island, Calif., 1957-62; ret., USN, 1962; tchr. Pacific Christian Acad., Graton, Calif., 1962-63; svc. tech. and mgr. Sears Roebuck, various cities Calif., N.Mex., 1963-72; tchr. electronics Clovis (N.Mex.) High Sch., 1972-76; asst. supr. trades and indsl. edn. Santa Fe, N.Mex., 1976-78; dir. indsl. edn. Lubbock (Tex.) Christian Coll., 1978-80; min. Church of Christ, Appleton, Wis., 1980-84; tchr. indsl. arts Gadsden H.S., Anthony, N.Mex., 1984-90; mcpl. judge Town of Anthony, Tex., 1991-93. Mem. N.Mex. State Vica Adv. Com., 1985-90; mem. adv. com. vocat. elec. Dona Ana C.C., Las Cruces, 1988-90. Mem. Fleet Reserve Assn., Am. Radio Relay League, Am. Vocat. Assn. (life mem.). Avocations: amateur radio, wood working, painting, wood carving, recreational vehicles. Home: Cloudcroft, N.Mex. Died July 4, 2008.

DUNN, BERNARD JOSEPH, retired defense contracting company executive; b. NYC, May 26, 1924; s. Bernard Joseph and Katheryn Christine (Gray) D.; m. Anne Marie McNiff, June 21, 1952; children: Bernard, William, Anne Marie, Robert. BS, Fordham U., 1947, PhD, 1958; MA, Columbia U., 1949. Asst. prof. physics Fordham U., NYC, 1949-60; prin. BDM Inc., McLean, Va., 1960-86, cons., 1986—2009. Served as 2d lt. USAAF, 1943-45, PTO. Mem. Assn. of U.S. Army, Sigma Xi. Home: Middleburg, Va. Died Mar. 14, 2009.

DUNNE, DOMINICK, writer; b. Hartford, Conn., Oct. 29, 1925; s. Richard and Dorothy B. D.; m. Ellen Griffin, Apr. 24, 1954 (dec. 1997); children: Griffin, Alexander, Dominique (dec. Nov. 4, 1982). BA, Williams Coll., 1949. Stage mgr. Howdy Doody Show, NBC-TV; prodr. CBS Studio One, Dunne-Didion-Dunne, from 1970s; exec. prodr. 20th Century Fox; v.p. Four Star Co.; contributing editor Vanity Fair Mag., 1982—93, spl. corr., 1993—2009. Prodr.: (films) The Boys in the Band, 1970, Panic in Needle Park, 1971, Play It As It Lays, 1972, Ash Wednesday, 1973, (TV series) Adventures in Paradise, ABC-TV, 1959-62, (TV movies) The Users, ABC-TV, 1978; author (novels): The Winners: Part II of Joyce Haber's The Users, 1982, The Two Mrs. Grenvilles, 1985, People Like Us, 1988, An Inconvenient Woman, 1990, The Mansions of Limbo, 1991, A Season in Purgatory, 1993, Sins of the Sons, 1995, Another City Not My Own, 1997, (non-fiction) Fatal Charms and Other Tales of Today, 1986, The Way We Lived Then: Recollections of a Well-Known Name Dropper, 1999, Justice: Crimes, Trials, and Punishments, 2001; adaptations: The Two Mrs. Grenvilles, 1987, People Like Us, 1990; host (TV), Power Privilege & Justice, Court TV, 2003-09. Served in US Army. Decorated Bronze Star, Battle of Bulge. Democrat. Roman Catholic. Died Aug. 26, 2009.

DUPPSTADT, J. ROBERT, mechanical engineer; b. Somerset, Pa., Mar. 11, 1918; s. Clarence William and Laura Sarah (Zufall) D.; m. Lois Naoma Parish, April 29, 1957; children: Jay Robert Jr., Debi Kay. BSME, Pa. State U., 1942. Registered profl. engr., N.Y., Tex. Stress analyst Curtiss Wright Corp., Buffalo, N.Y., 1942-45; from helicopter engr. to dir. engring. Bell Helicopter, Niagra Falls, N.Y., 1945-88, dir. engring. Ft. Worth, Tex., 1985-1988, retired 1988; prin., owner Duppstadt Cons., Bedford, Tex., from 1989. Contbr. articles to profl. jours. Chmn. Zoning Bd. of Adjustment, Hurst, Tex., 1968-71. Recipient Lawrence D. Bell Meml. award Helicopter Assn. Internat., 1996. Mem. Am. Helicopter Soc. (v.p. 1966-68). Republican. Methodist. Achievements include being involved in the engineering and development of nearly all of the Bell Helicopter models from 1946 until 1988; holder of numerous patents related to helicopters. Died Aug. 5, 2008.

DUPUIS, PATRICIA LARAMIE, elementary and middle school educator; b. Exeter, NH, Nov. 20, 1948; d. Eugene and Eleanor Maude (Cammett) Laramie; m. Ivan Dupuis. Aug. 23, 1969; 1 child, David Ivan. BEd, Keene State Coll., 1970; MEd, U. N.H., 1980. Cert. in elem. edn., early childhood edn., spl. edn. Cooperating tchr., intern coord. U. N.H., Durham, 1986-89; tchr. primary Pollard Elem. Sch., Plaistow, N.H., 1969-70; tchr. grades 1-4 Maple Wood Sch., Somersworth, N.H., 1970-93; tchr. grade 5 Somersworth Mid. Sch., from 1993, coord. after sch. homework lab., 1994-95. Mem. NEA, N.H. Edn. Assn., Somersworth Assn. Educators, Keene State Coll., Alumni Assn., U. N.H. Alumni Assn. Home: Barrington, NH. Died May 15, 2008.

DUPUY, PAMELA MARIE, elementary school educator; b. Inglewood, Calif., Jan. 9, 1957; d. Glen Olan and Pauline Marie (King) DuP. AA, L.A. Community Coll., 1977; BA, Calif. State U., LA, 1979. Tchr. L.A. Unified Sch. Dist., from 1981. Democrat. Methodist. Home: North Hollywood, Calif. Died Mar. 6, 2008.

DURHAM, MARY SHERRILL, psychologist, writer; b. Covington, Tenn., Nov. 22, 1924; d. Lewis Joseph and Helen (Hardwicke) Sherrill; m. Hugh Durham; children: Thomas, John, Sherry. Grad., George Washington U., 1950, MS in Clinical Psychology, 1951; PhD in Human Devel., U. Md., 1978. Clin. psychologist Va. hosp., 1950—60, DC orgn., 1960—80; pvt. practice Arlington, Va., 1955—2007. Author: The Therapist's Encounters with Revenge and Foregivenss, 2000, It's All Right to Write: How Famous Authors Overcame the Same Roadblock You Face, 2006. Mem.: New Directions. Democrat. Presbyterian. Avocation: writing. Home: Mc Lean, Va. Died Apr. 11, 2009.

DURNELL, NOLAND REED, construction engineer; b. Mt. Grove, Mo., Nov. 27, 1939; s. Amo Reed and LaVern Fannie (Crapenhoft) D.; m. Melba Darlene Rakestraw, June 5, 1959; children: Terry L., A. Jenell. BSCE with highest honors, Mo Sch. Mines & Metallurgy, 1965. Registered profl. engr., Ariz., Colo., Kans., Mo. Engring. technician Mo. Highway Dept., 1958-63; owner, operator Durnell Mobile Home Insurance & Svc., Rolla, Mo., 1961-65; constrn. engr. Ill. Highway Dept., Effingham, 1963-67; supervisory engr. U.S. Forest Svc., Colo., Wyo. and S.C., 1967-78; owner Chrysler dealership, Willow Springs, Mo., 1978-82; ptnr., cons. engr. Siedler & Moore Engring., Pittsburg, Kans., 1981-82; county engr. Crawford County, Girard, Kans., 1982-85; resident engr. Ariz. Dept. Transp., Safford, from 1985. V.p., bd. dirs., loan officer, Montrose Federal Credit Union, Delta, Colo., 1968-69; v.p. Double-Sqs. Dance Club, Durango, Colo., 1971-72, Fla. Mesa PTA, Durango, 1972; sponsor NSPE model bridge bldg., Sheridan, Wyo., 1973-76; v.p., dance chmn. Mt. Graham Skirts and Flirts, Safford, 1989-91; pres., treas. S.E. Ariz. Sq. and Round Dance Assn., 1989-93. Mem. NSPE, ASCE, Ariz. Soc. Profl. Engrs. Avocations: photography, hiking, travel. Home: Safford, Ariz. Died Nov. 1, 2007.

DURRETT, GEORGE MANN, corporate executive; b. Balt., Oct. 11, 1917; m. Ethel M. Durrett; children: Douglass, Roger W., Gary W., Kyle D., Balt. City Coll., 1936-39, Johns Hopkins U., 1940-41, 46-47; grad. comml. artist, Md. Inst. Art, 1933-38. V.p. William G. Wetherall Inc., 1945-63; pres. Ea. Shore Steel Co. Inc., 1957-62, Wetherall Machine Sales Co., 1958-62, Durrett Sheppard Steel Co., Inc., Balt., from 1963, gen. ptnr., from 1984; v.p. S-D Realty Co., from 1964, D-S Pipe & Supply co. Inc., 1979-88, Grinding Svcs. Inc., from 1983, Durrett Galleries Ltd., from 1983; pres. Durrett-Sheppard Steel Co. Inc., Balt., from 1963, Ridgely Leasing, Inc., Balt., from 1983; ptnr. Durrett Sheppard Assoc., from 1984. Bd. govs. Wesley Theol. Sem.; trustee, mem. adminstrv. bd. and fin. commn. Towson United Meth. Ch. With U.S. Army, 1941-45. Mem. Am. Numis. Assn., Steel Club Balt., Balt. Country Club, Masons. Avocations: antiques, art, coin collecting/numismatics, golf. Home: Glyndon, Md. Died Nov. 10, 2007.

DURST, ALAN R., mechanical engineer; b. Warren, Ohio, Jan. 25, 1952; s. Robert Wayne and Donna Jean (Irwin) D. A in Mech. Engring., ATES Tech. Sch., 1974. Draftsman engring. United Telephone Sys., Warren, 1975-80; checker engring. dept. Kennametal Inc., Cleve., from 1980. Presbyterian. Avocations: bicycling, basketball. Died Aug. 1, 2008.

DUVEEN, ANNETA, artist; b. Bklyn., May 21, 1924; d. Julius and Shirley (Klugman) Applebaum; m. Charles J. Duveen Jr., Dec. 21, 1942 (div. 1954); children: Wendy, Charles III, Peter; m. Benjamin Duveen Nov. 24, 1976. Student, U. Iowa, 1941, Adelphi Acad., 1941, Columbia U., 1941, 42, 56; HHD, St. Francis Coll., 1986. Founder, pres. Duveen Internat. Ltd., Port Chester, N.Y., from 1987. Lectr. Westchester Arts Coun., White Plains, N.Y., 1993-94. Prin. works exhibited in group and retrospective and one-woman shows including Pacem in Terris Gallery, N.Y.C., 1970, The Signs of God in the World, Santa Croce Basilica Grand Cloister, Florence, Italy, 1985, Marymount Manhattan Coll., 1986, Artiste 86, Rome, 1986; commd. sculptures include heroic meml. busts of Ella T. Grasso, Robert F. Kennedy, St. Maximilian Kolbe and the Papal Family, The Child: Moments in Bronze, Our Lady of the Eucharist, Tabernacle: Our Lady of the Eucharist, many others; also 49 stained glass window designs of St. Anthony; also collage Alas, She Died in Childbirth; co-author, illustrator: Essentials of Astronomy, 1976. Mem. exec. com. Franciscans Internat., Bklyn., 1989-99; internat. rep. for justice, peace and ecology Secular Franciscan Order, Rome, 1990-92; tchr., dir., ednl. specialist, proposal designer, rschr., cons. Fellow Royal Astron. Soc.; mem. AAAS, AAUW, Sede di Dante, N.Y. Acad. Scis., Inst. for Theol. Encounter with Sci. and Tech., Nat. Fedn. Press Women, Portchester Coun. for Arts, Westchester Arts Coun. Home: Salem, NY. Died Oct. 28, 2007.

DUVO, MECHELLE LOUISE, oil company executive, consultant; b. East Stroudsburg, Pa., Apr. 25, 1962; d. Nicholas and Arlene Birdie (Mack) D. AS, Lehigh County C.C., 1982. Rehab. counselor Phoenix Project, Bakersfield, Calif., 1982-84; nat. sales mgr. Olympia Advt., LA, 1984-85; oil exploration cons. Cimmaron Mgmt., Nashville, 1985-86; exec. sec. Pueblo Resources Corp., Bowling Green, Ky., 1986-87; nat. oil cons. El Toro, Inc., Bowling Green, 1986-87; founder, pres. and CEO Majestic Mgmt. Corp., Glasgow, Ky., from 1987; nat. oil cons. Impact Oil, Inc., Glasgow, from 1987. Lease procurator El Toro, Inc., 1986-87; spkr. Nat. Investment Seminars, 1994—. Editor, pub.: (newsletter) The Majestic Field Copy, 1994—. Fundraiser Am. Cancer Soc., LA, 1984-85; vol. Humane Soc.,

Nashville, 1985-86, Humane Soc., Bowling Green, 1986-87, Boy Scouts Am., 2001-02; counselor Salvation Army, Bakersfield, 1982-84, vol. Kettle and Angel Tree programs, 2001—; vol. mgr. Food Pantry Outreach Program, 1999-2001, Strut Your Mutt, 1999—, Relay for Life, 2001—, Am. Cancer Soc. fundraiser, 2001—, Glasgow chpt. Ky. Assn. for Gifted Edn., 2004—; fundraiser Ky. Assn. for Gifted Edn. Mem. NAFE (exec. program), Internat. Platform Assn. Avocations: house plants, gardening, music, gourmet cooking. Deceased.

DWINELL, JAMES FISHER, JR., bank executive; b. Winchester, Mass., Feb. 26, 1909; s. James F. Sr. and Florence (Smith) D.; children: Jean D. Ferguson, James F. III. AB, Harvard U., 1931. Chmn. Winchester (Mass.) Savs. Bank, from 1940. Chmn. Bd. Selectmen, Winchester, 1948. Home: York, Maine. Died Oct. 3, 2007.

DYKEMA, DOROTHY ETHEL, retired counselor; b. Chgo., Jan. 26, 1923; d. Herbert H. and Ethel (Erikson) D. BA, Am. Conservatory of Music, 1946; MS in Rehab., So. Ill. U., 1964, MA in Music, 1985. Tchr., counselor Ill. Div. Rehab. Svcs., Chgo. and Peoria, Ill., 1946-66; mental health counselor Ill. Dept. Mental Health, Anna, 1967-80; ret. Author: They Shall Have Music, 1986. Vol. Crisis Line, Carbondale, Ill., 1980-85; bd. dirs. Jackson County Mental Health, Carbondale, 1982-88, Radio Reading Svc., Carbondale, 1985—. Mem. Morning Etude Club (pres. 1989—). Presbyterian. Avocation: music. Died Dec. 17, 2007.

DYSON, LOWELL KEITH, historian; b. Adel, Iowa, Mar. 17, 1929; s. Harvey Bryan and Sylvia May (Chilson) D.; m. B. Patricia Parish, Sept. 9, 1961. BS, Iowa State U., 1952; MA, Columbia U., 1959, PhD, 1968. Civil engr., SPirit Lake, Iowa, 1954-63; lectr. U. Md., College Park, 1964-67; prof. Va. Tech. Inst., Blacksburg, 1967-80; writer, TV cons. Alexandria, Va., 1980-84; historian Ctr. Mil. History, Washington, 1984-87, USDA, Washington, from 1987. Vis. prof. U. Iowa, Iowa City, 1963-64, Nankai U., Tianjin, China, 1983, Jilin U., Changchun, China, 1989; pres. Historians Am. Communism, Washington, 1987-89. Author: Red Harvest: The Communist Party and American Farmers, 1982, Farmers ORganizations, 1986; contbr. articles to profl. jours. Chair Dem. Presdl. Campaign, Southwest Va., 1976, Dem. Gubernatorial Campaign, Southwest Va., 1977. With U.S. Army, 1952-54, Korea. Humanities fellow Duke U., 1969-70, Am. Coun. Learned Socs. fellow, 1977. Mem. Nat. Press Club, U.S. Commn. Mil. History, Agrl. History Soc. (exec. sec.-treas. 1993—), Mil. Order of Loyal Legion, Masons, Royal Order of Scotland. Avocations: reading, travel. Home: Alexandria, Va. Died Jan. 11, 2008.

DZIK, RICHARD ANTHONY, school principal; b. Chgo., Nov. 23, 1942; s. Joseph Vincent and Marie Frances (Majzrczak) D.; m. Diane Josephine Feliks, June 25, 1966. BS, U. Detroit, 1965; MA, Wayne State U., 1969, EdD, 1977. Cert. secondary and elem. adminstr., Mich. Tchr. Detroit Pub. Schs., Detroit, 1965-68; adminstr. fed. programs Archdiocese of Detroit, Detroit, 1968-71; adminstr. Fla. Schs., various cities, 1971-78; prin. H.S. Mich. Schs., Pontiac, Troy, Mich., 1971-78; dep. commr. City of Phila., Phila., 1978-83; prin. Muskegon Heights (Mich.) Pub. Schs., from 1990. Adj. prof. Western. Mich. U., Grand Valley State Coll., Mich., St. Leo Coll., Fla. Creator: (edn. bd. game) Consequence of Choice, 1988, Dynamics of Communications, 1989. Planning commr. City of Muskegon Heights, 1994—. Mem. ASCD, Muskegon Area Prins. Assn. (pres. 1990-92), Muskegon Heights Adminstrs. Union (pres. 1994-95). Roman Catholic. Avocations: tennis, basketball, glass beads, teaching college. Home: Muskegon Hts, Mich. Died July 14, 2008.

EARLOUGHER, ROBERT CHARLES, SR., petroleum engineer; b. Kans., May 6, 1914; s. Harry Walter and Annetta (Partridge) E.; m. Jeanne D. Storer, Oct. 6, 1937; children: Robert Charles, Jr., Janet Earlougher Craven, Anne Earlougher O'Connell. Grad., Colo. Sch. Mines, 1936. Registered profl. engr., Calif., Okla., Tex., Kans. Supr. core lab. The Sloan and Zook Co., Bradford, Pa., 1936-38; co-owner, cons. Geologic Standards Co., Tulsa, 1938-45; owner, cons. Earlougher Engring., Tulsa, 1945-73; chmn., cons. Godsey-Earlougher, Inc., Tulsa, 1973-76, Petroleum Cons. div. Williams Bros. Engring. Co., Tulsa, 1976-88, Reactivated Earlougher Engring., Inc., Tulsa, 1988. Patentee in field Mem. AIME (hon., Anthony F. Lucas Gold medal 1980), Am. Petroleum Inst. (chmn. mid-continent dist. 1961-62, citation for service 1964), Ind. Petroleum Assn. Am. (bd. dirs. 9 yrs.), Interstate Oil Compact Commn. (oil recovery com. 1947-96), Soc. Petroleum Engrs. (disting. svc. award 1973, disting. mem. award 1983, hon. mem. 1985, enhanced oil recovery pioneer 1992), Soc. Petroleum Evaluation Engrs. (hon. life award 1993), Summit Club, Petroleum Club, Southern Hills Country Club (Tulsa), Masons, Tau Beta Pi. Republican. Episcopalian. Died Jan. 17, 2007.

EATON, WILLIAM LAWRENCE, lawyer; b. Boston, Mar. 12, 1946; s. Lawrence V. and Jeanne K. Eaton; m. Sally Ackerman, 1986. AB, Stanford U., 1969; JD, Boston Coll., 1972; LLM in Taxation, Boston U., 1980. Bar: Mass. 1972. Law clk. to presiding justice Mass. Superior Ct., Boston, 1972-73; trial atty. U.S. Dept. Justice, Washington, 1973-75; with Parker, Coulter, Daley & White, Boston, 1975-77, Snyder, Tepper & Comen, Boston, 1977-82; ptnr. Woodman & Eaton, P.C., Concord, Mass., from 1982. Assoc. editor Boston Coll. Indsl. and Comml. Law Rev., 1972. Mem. ABA, Mass. Bar Assn., Order of Coif. Home: Concord, Mass. Died Oct. 1, 2007.

EBEL, HENRY, communications consultant; b. Berlin, July 5, 1938; came to U.S., 1939; s. Richard and Anna (Salomon) Ebel; m. Sheila Krinsky (div. May 1986); 1 child, Adam. AB summa cum laude, Columbia Coll., 1959; MA, Cambridge U., Eng., 1964; PhD, Columbia U., 1965. Asst. prof. Wesleyan U., Middletown, Conn., 1964-68; assoc. prof. Richmond Coll., SI, N.Y., 1969-76; editor-in-chief Behavior Today, NYC, 1976-80; assoc. v.p. U. Hartford, West Hartford, Conn., 1981-88; internal cons. George Washington U., Washington, from 1989. Author: After Dionysus: An Essay on Where We Are Now, 1972; co-editor: Jimmy Carter and American Fantasy, 1978. Home: West Hartfrd, Conn. Died Apr. 4, 2008.

ECKEL, THOMAS WARNE, counseling administrator, musician; b. Phillipsburg, NJ, Nov. 5, 1962; s. Henry W. Jr. and Marie L. (Curry) E.; m. Nicole A. Frumerie, May 28, 1988 (div. Jan. 1991). Cert., Tech. Career Inst., NYC, 1985; MusB, Berklee Coll. Music, 1991; MA in Counseling Psychology, NYU, 1996; EdD in Counseling Psychology, Argosy U., 2002. Cert. guidance counselor, N.Y., N.J., Pa., N.Y.C.; cert. music educator Mass., N.Y., Pa., N.J., N.Y.C. Electrician Renaissance Elec., Stewartsville, N.J., 1986-91; tchr. music Morris H.S., Bronx, N.Y., 1992-94; psychotherapist Cath. Charities, Phillipsburg, 1995-97; tchr. music Frederick Douglass Acad., NYC, from 1997; sch. counselor Yonkers Pub. Schs., 1999—2004; pvt. practice lic. mental health counselor. Pres. Eckelworks Pub./BMI, N.Y.C., 1990—, Eckelworks Inc., N.Y.C., 1996—. Pianist, singer, songwriter: Thomas Eckel, 1994; artist: (music videos) Alone, 1995, When Will We See, (original music CDs) Thomas Eckel, The Story, (double CD) Reflections and Inside Out; composer over 90 popular/rock songs, 1989-96. Mem. Am. Fedn. Musicians, United Fedn. Tchrs. Avocations: hiking, swimming, camping, performing arts, in-line skating. Home: Easton, Pa. Died Aug. 29, 2007.

EDDY, JOHN ALLEN (JACK EDDY), research astrophysicist, geophysicist; b. Pawnee, Nebr., Mar. 25, 1931; children from previous marriage: Alexandra, Amy, Jack Jr., Elisabeth; m. Barbara Eddy, 1992 BS, US Naval Acad., 1953; PhD in Astrogeophysics, U. Colo., 1962. Sr. scientist High Altitude Observatory Nat. Ctr. Atmospheric Rsch., Boulder, Colo., 1978—85, sr. scientist advances studies program, 1985—86, dir. interdisciplinary earth studies, 1986—2009. Adj. prof. U. Colo.; rsch. assoc. Harvard-Smithsonian Ctr. Astrophysicst, 1967-70, 77-79. Recipient Boulder (Colo.) Scientist award Sci. Rsch. Soc. Am., 1965, Arctowski medal NAS, 1987. Fellow AAAS, Am. Geophys. Union, Sigma Xi; mem. Am. Astronom. Soc. Achievements include research in infrared astronomy, history of astronomy, archaeo-astronomy. Died June 10, 2009; Tucson, Ariz.

EDDY, LOWELL PERRY, retired research chemistry educator; b. Portland, Oreg., Nov. 25, 1920; s. Delmar and Anna Belle (Weisenborn) E.; m. M. Caroline Wall, Jan. 13, 1946; children: Candice M., Kati J., Lowell Stacy. BS, Oreg. State U., 1942, MS, 1947; PhD, Purdue U., 1952. Instr. chemistry U. Wyo., Laramie, 1950-51; research assoc. Reed Coll., Portland, 1951, instr., 1951-53; research chemist Puget Sound Pulp and Timber Co., Bellingham, Wash., 1953-57; from instr. to assoc. prof. chemistry Western Wash. U., Bellingham, 1957-85, ret., 1986. Vis. assoc. prof. U. New South Wales, Sydney, Austrialia, 1975; hon. research asst. U. Coll. London, 1964. Contbr. articles to profl. jours. Served to 1st lt. inf. U.S. Army, 1942-46. Mem. Am. Chem. Soc., Sigma Xi. Republican. Mem. Christian Ch. Lodge: Kiwanis (pres. Bellingham club 1980-81). Died Sept. 10, 2007.

EDELSTEIN, JEAN, purchasing professional; b. Chgo., Mar. 6, 1929; d. Sam and Sadie (Cutler) Klein; divorced; children: David Allen, Raymond Lewis. Sec. various firms, Milw., 1947-64; purchasing agt. Milw. Pub. Schs., 1964-66, sec., 1966-68; dir. corp. services/purchasing agt. Career Acad., Milw., 1968-74; buyer Kenosha (Wis.) Unified Sch. Dist. 1, 1974-81, purchasing agt., from 1981. Bd. dirs. Willow Creek Condominiums, Milw., 1979-80, pres., 1980-81; mem. citizen panel United Way, Kenosha, 1984—; mem. citizen adv. bd. social services Kenosha County, 1985-86; mem. hon. bd. Girl Scouts U.S., Kenosha County, 1985—. Mem. Nat. Assn. Pub. Purchasing, Nat. Assn. Purchasing Mgmt., Bus. Forms Mgmt. Assn. (charter mem. Milw. chpt.), Word Processing Assn. (charter mem. Milw. chpt.) Wis. Assn. Pub. Purchasing, Milw. Assn. Purchasing Mgmt. (chmn. attendance com. 1976-78, local dir. 1979-80, v.p. 1980-83, award 1984), Nat. Inst. Govtl. Purchasers. Democrat. Jewish. Avocations: knitting, sewing, gardening. Home: Kenosha, Wis. Died Sept. 1, 2007.

EDENS, BETTY JOYCE, reading recovery educator; b. Hillsboro, Tex., Oct. 20, 1944; d. Edward Alton and Mary Alma (Pendley) Harbin; m. Eugene Cliett Edens, May 29, 1964; children: Michael Eugene, Anne-Marie DeWitt, Kristen Babovec. BEd, Ind. U., 1985; MS, Tex. A&M of Commerce, 1995. Cert. elem. tchr., reading tchr., Tex. 1st grade tchr. Monday Primary, Kaufman, Tex., 1986-93, Franklin Elem., Hillsboro, Tex., 1993-96, reading recovery tchr., 1994-98, 99-00, 2nd grade tchr., 1998-99; reading recovery tchr. Hillsboro Elem. Sch., 1999—2005, reading specialist 2d and 3d grades, from 2005. Mem. early literacy com. TSRA, 1998, Susan G. Komen Found. Mem. Reading Recovery Coun. of N.Am., Internat. Reading Assn., Tex. Reading Assn., Heritage League hillsboro. Republican. Mem. Ch. of Christ. Avocations: recreational reading, walking, computers. Home: Hillsboro, Tex. Died June 26, 2008.

EDINGER, CHARLES B., retired physician; b. NYC, Mar. 8, 1934; s. Isidore and Augusta (Yigdoll) E.; m. Bridgid Hilda Kerr-Baulch, Aug. 26, 1956; children: Valerie Jean, Jacqueline Gail, Paul Douglas. BA, Columbia U., 1954; MD, U. de Geneve, Switzerland, 1959. Diplomate Am. Bd. Ob-Gyn. Pvt. practice, Westbury and Plainview, N.Y., 1967-76; v.p. M&E Obstetrics & Gynecology, P.C., Plainview, 1976-88, pres., from 1988; pres. med. staff Cen. Gen. Hosp., 1979. Capt. USAF, 1961-63. Fellow Am. Coll. Surgeons, Am. Coll. Ob-Gyn.; mem. AMA, Nassau Surg. Soc. Republican. Jewish. Avocations: boating, sport fishing. Home: New York, NY. Died Oct. 13, 2007.

EDIRISOORIYA, GUNAPALA, finance educator; s. Sadiris A. P. Edirisooriya and Abanchihamy K. Hennedige; m. Ariyamala W. Edirisooriya, Sept. 13, 1948; children: Milinda C. P., Sithari P. BCom, U. of Ceylon, Peradeniya, Sri Lanka, 1967; MLitt, U. of Glasgow, 1974; MA, U. Del., Newark, 1988, PhD, 1990. Asst. lectr., dept. of economics U. of Colombo, Colombo, Western, Sri Lanka, 1968—77, lectr., dept. of econs., 1977—80, sr. lectr., dept. of econs., 1980—81; inaugural chair, dept. of econs. and commerce Ruhuna U., Matara, Sri Lanka, 1978—79; grade one lectr. U. of Nigeria, Enugu, Anambra, Nigeria, 1981—84; rsch. asst. / temp. lectr. / merit grad. fellow / tchg. asst. U. of Del., Newark, 1984—90; rsch. and evaluation specialist Balt. City Pub. Schools, 1990—94; prof. East Tenn. State U., Johnson City, 1995—2002, assoc. dean, coll. of edn., 1998—2002; prof. Youngstown State U., Youngstown, Ohio, from 2002. Cons. ednl. restructuring project Ministry of Edn., Govt. of Sri Lanka, Colombo, Sri Lanka, 1999; del. Oxford Round Table, England, 2006. Cons. reviewer (manuscript reviewer) Ednl. Rschr. jour., mem. editl. bd. Edn. Policy Analysis Archives, from 2006. Maj. benefactor / founding chair Edirisooriya Found., Tangalle, Sri Lanka, 2001—05. Recipient British Coun. Overseas Students award, U. Glasgow, 1973—74; scholar, U. Colombo, 1970—73. Mem.: Am. Ednl. Rsch. Assn. (co-chair, best paper award comm.; judge, nominating comm. 1992—2005, web mgr. SIG-SRE chair 1997—2002, chair SIG on survey rsch. in edn. 1999—2002, web mgr. SIG-SRE chair 2004—05), Phi Kappa Phi. Achievements include research in evolution of the American higher education sector; doctoral research that laid the groundwork for Delaware Cost Study (estimation of institutional cost in higher education); complexity of state-university relationship; Attitude formation as the basis for attitude measurement: A new approach; development of SAS programming for graphical presentation of survey data. Avocations: jogging, travel. Home: Canfield, Ohio. Died June 2009.

EDMONDSON, FRANK KELLEY, retired astronomer; b. Milw., Aug. 1, 1912; s. Clarence Edward and Marie (Kelley) E.; m. Margaret Russell, Nov. 24, 1934 (dec. Jan. 1999); children: Margaret Jean Olson, Frank K. Jr. AB, Ind. U., 1933, A.M., 1934; PhD, Harvard U., 1937. Lawrence fellow Lowell Obs., 1933-34, research asst., 1934-35; Agassiz fellow Harvard Obs., 1935-36, asst., 1936-37; instr. astronomy Ind. U., Bloomington, 1937-4O, asst. prof., 1940-45, assoc. prof., 1945-48, prof., 1949-83, prof. emeritus, from 1983, dir. Kirkwood Obs., 1945-78; dir. Goethe Link Obs., 1948-78, chmn. astronomy dept., 1944-78; research asso. McDonald Obs., 1944-83. Observations of asteroids in cooperation with Internat. Astron. Union's Minor Planet Ctr.; statistical adviser to Prof. Alfred Kinsey for gall wasp and human sex behaviour rsch., 1939-56; program dir. for astronomy NSF, 1956-57; acting dir. Cerro Tololo Inter-Am. Obs., 1966; lectr. astron. socs.; mem. adv. bd. Lowell Obs., 1988-2000. Author: AURA and its US National Observatories, 1997; contbr. numerous papers to Am., Brit., German astron. jours. Decorated Order of Merit Chile, 1964; recipient Meritorious Pub. Svc. award NSF, 1983, Disting. Alumni Svc. award Ind. U., 1997; honored with Daniel Kirkwood (1814-95) in Ho. Resolution No. 58 adopted by Ind. 109th Gen. Assembly, First Session, 1995. Fellow AAAS (chmn. sect. D, v.p. 1962); mem. Assn. Univs. Rsch. in Astronomy (v.p. 1957-61, pres. 1962-65, dir. 1957-83, cons./historian 1983—2003, historian emeritus 2003—), Can. Astron. Soc., Am. Astron. Soc. (treas. 1954-75, 70 yr. attendence award 2001), Astron. Soc. Pacific, Internat. Astron. Union (chmn. U.S. nat. com. 1963-64, v.p. commn. minor planets, comets and satellites 1967-70, pres. 1970-73), Ind. Acad. Sci. (named Disting. Scholar 2004), Am. Mus. Natural History (corr. mem.), Friends of Ctr. for History of Physics (exec. com. 2001—), Explorers Club, Phi Beta Kappa, Sigma Xi. Home: Bloomington, Ind. Died Dec. 0, 2000.

EDWARDS, BENJAMIN FRANKLIN, III, retired investment banker; b. St. Louis, Oct. 26, 1931; s. Presley William and Virginia (Barker) E.; m. Joan Moberly, June 13, 1953; children: Scott P., Benjamin Franklin IV, Pamela M. Edwards Bunn, Susan B. BA, Princeton U., 1953. With A.G. Edwards & Sons, Inc., St. Louis, 1956—2001, pres., 1967—2001, chmn., 1983—2001. Bd. dirs. Jefferson Bank and Trust Co., Psychol. Assocs., Helig-Meyers, Inc., N.Y. Stock Exch., Washington U., St. Louis Art Mus., Barnes Hosp. Mem. U. Mo., St. Louis, Civic Progress, Arts and Edn. Coun. With USNR, 1953-56. Mem. Investment Bankers Assn. (gov. 1968—), Securities Industry Assn. (gov. 1974-81, chmn. 1980—). Clubs: Old Warson Country (St. Louis); Bogey. Presbyterian. Home: Saint Louis, Mo. Died Apr. 20, 2009.

EDWARDS, DAVID NESBIT, JR., university administrator; b. Winston Salem, NC, May 26, 1939; s. David Nesbit and Sadye Victoria (Ripple) E.; m. Marcia Jene Baldwin, Dec. 30, 1972; children: Lisa Lynn, Holly Ann. BA, Davidson Coll., 1961; JD, Duke U., 1964. Bar: N.C. Law clk. Womble, Carlyle, Sandridge & Rice, Winston Salem, 1966-67; assoc. atty. Surratt & Early, Winston Salem, N.C., 1967-68; dir. field experience Elmira (N.Y.) Coll., 1968-71; assoc. dir. N.C. Internship Office, Raleigh, N.C., 1971-73; spl. asst. to pres. U. N.C., Chapel Hill, N.C., from 1973. Negotiation team mem. ACE-NACUBO Music Licensing, Washington, 1980—. Author: (with others) Legal Deskbook for Adminstrators of Independent Colleges and Universities, 1982; contbr. articles to profl. jours. Pres. Gideons Internat. Durham South Camp., 1996—; elder Presbyn. Ch., Durham. Mem. N.C. Bar Assn., State Bar N.C., Am. Canal Soc. (life.). Avocation: choral and trumpet music. Home: Durham, NC. Died Mar. 24, 2008.

EDWARDS, DEBORAH HORTON, pediatrics nurse; b. Spartanburg, SC, Nov. 9, 1957; d. Benjamin Jones and Louise (Williams) Horton; m. Randall F. Edwards, Jan. 17, 1981; 1 child, Brian. ASN, U. S.C., 1978, BSN, 1993. RN, S.C.; PALS, ABLS. Clin. staff nurse pediatrics and operating rm. Spartanburg Regional Med. Ctr., nurse mgr. pediatrics unit. PALS and BLS instr. and provider. Mem. ETV, S.C. Orgn. Nurse Execs., Assn. for the Care of Children's Health, ARC. Home: Chesnee, SC. Died June 24, 2008.

EDWARDS, DONNA HOHMANN, psychologist; b. Denver, Colo., Sept. 1, 1934; d. Lee Kerwith and Irene Hohmann; m. John Edwards, Aug. 15, 1989; children: Marguerite, Suzanne, Rodger, Lee. BA, U. Colo., 1956; EdD, U. No. Colo. Tchr. San Francisco Pub. Sch. Dist., 1959—65; mem. faculty Lamaze Internat., Washington, from 1970; dir. youth svcs. YWCA, Boulder, Colo., 1980—83; teen pregnancy counselor Boulder Pub. Schs., 1980—87; dir. perinatal edn. U. Colo. Health Svcs., Denver, 1983—92; psychologist Colo. Ctr. Biobehavior, Boulder, 2005; family specialist, from 1990. Cons. in field. Author: 113 books on perinatal education, translated into German, Japanese and Spanish. Bd. dirs. Lamaze Internat., Boulder Pub. Schs. Named Outstanding Citizen, Boulder YWCA, 1980, Outstanding Contbr., Lamaze Internat. Home: Boulder, Colo. Died May 14, 2008.

EDWARDS, MARIE BABARE, psychologist; b. Tacoma; d. Nick and Mary (Mardesich) Babare; B.A., Stanford, 1948, M.A., 1949; m. Tilden Hampton Edwards (div.); 1 son, Tilden Hampton Edwards Jr. Counselor guidance center U. So. Calif., Los Angeles, 1950-52; project coordinator So. Calif. Soc. Mental Hygiene, 1952-54; pub. speaker Welfare Fedn. Los Angeles, 1953-57; field rep. Los Angeles County Assn. Mental Health, 1957-58; intern psychologist UCLA, 1958-60; pvt. practice, human rels. tng., counselor tng. Mem. Calif., Am., Western, Los Angeles psychol. assns., AAAS, So. Calif. Soc. Clin. Hypnosis. Author: (with Eleanor Hoover) The Challenge of Being Single, 1974, paperback edit., 1975. Died Dec. 31, 2008.

EGAN, RICHARD JOHN, retired information technology executive, former ambassador; b. Boston, Feb. 28, 1936; s. Kenneth Joseph and Constance Bianca E.; m. Maureen E. Fitzgerald; children: John R., Michael J., Maureen E. Petracca, Christopher, Catherine. BEE, Northeastern U., 1961; postgrad., MIT, 1963-64; LLD (hon.), Northeastern U., 1995; DSc (hon.), New England Inst. Tech., 1999. V.p. mktg. Cambridge Memories (now Cambex Corp.), Waltham, Mass., 1968-75; gen. mgr. comml. systems div. Intel Corp., Santa Clara, Calif., 1975-77; co-founder, dir. EMC Corp., Hopkinton, Mass., from 1979, pres., CEO, 1979-88, chmn., CEO, 1988—92, founder, chmn. emeritus, 2001—09; US amb. to Ireland US Dept. State, Dublin, 2001—02. Bd. dirs. Tech. Fin. Svcs., Westford, Mass.; steering com. chair George W. Bush Info. Tech. Nat. Steering Coun.; mem. Transition Adv. Group, US Dept. Commerce; dir. Mass. High Tech. Coun., Cognition Corp. and NetScout Sys. Inc. Supporter Boston Symphony Orch; dir., founder Hopkinton Tech. for Edn. Found.; trustee Cath. Schs. Found., Northeastern U., Inner City Scholarship Fund. Named one of Forbes Richest Americans, 2006. Mem.: Mass. Bus. Roundtable, Semper Fidelis Soc. Republican. Roman Catholic. Avocations: fishing, reading, music. Home: Westborough, Mass. Died Aug. 28, 2009.

EHRLICH, LOUIS WILLIAM, mathematician; b. Balt., Oct. 4, 1927; s. Isaac and Rae Ehrlich; m. Barbara Joyce Belkin, Feb. 8, 1959; children: Tami, Kim, Todd. BS, U. Md., 1951, MS, 1956; PhD, U. Tex., 1963. Chem. engr. Allegany Ball Lab. Hercules Powder Co., Cumberland, Md., 1951-54; mathematician Rams Wooldrige Space Tech. Lab., LA, 1956-59; programmer, analyst U. Tex., Austin, 1959-62; mathematician Applied Physics Lab. Johns Hopkins U., Laurel, Md., from 1962. Contbr. over 50 articles to profl. jours. With U.S. Army, 1946-47. Mem. Am. Math. Soc., Assn. for Computing Machinery (bd. dirs. spl. interest group numerical analysis 1977-80), Soc. for Indsl. and Applied Math., Sigma Xi, Phi Kappa Phi, Tau Beta Pi. Home: Owings Mills, Md. Died Oct. 1, 2007.

EIKERENKOETTER, FREDERICK JOSEPH, II, (REVEREND IKE), evangelist, educator; b. Ridgeland, SC, June 1, 1935; s. Frederick Joseph and Rema Estelle (Matthews) Eikerenkoetter; m. Eula Mae Dent, Feb. 17, 1964; 1 child, Xavier Frederick III. BTh, Am. Bible Coll., 1956; DS of Living, Sci. of Living Inst., 1971. Founder, pres. United Christian Evangelist Assn., 1962—2009, United Ch. Sci. of Living Inst., 1969—2009, Rev. Ike Found., 1973—2009; vis. lectr. dept. psychiatry Harvard Med. Sch., 1973, U. Ala., 1975, Atlanta U. Ctr., 1975; vis. lectr. dept. sociology Rice U., Houston, 1977. Chaplain USAF, 1956—58. Recipient World Svc. award Outstanding Contbns. to Mankind, Prince Hall Masons, 1975. Achievements include founder of the Science of Living philosophy, church and inst. Died July 28, 2009.

EILERS, ROBERT FREDERICK, general contractor; b. Far Rockaway, NY, May 1, 1931; s. Anton F. and Margaret (Munch) E.; m. Anita I. Pinzaronni, Apr. 15, 1932; children: Robert F. Jr., Kenneth J., Craig A., Teresa M. BS in civil engring., Va. Polytech. Inst., 1953. Corp. officer Anderson & Fairoaks Const. Co., Hartford, Conn., 1956-80; owner Eilers Estimating Svc., West Hartford, Conn., from 1980. Sec. Contractors Against Inflation, Hartford, 1974; pres. Conn. Utility Contractors, 1971-72; treas. Nat. Utility Contractors, Washington, 1973. 1st lt. U.S. Army, 1954-56. Mem. Am. Arbitration. Avocations: golf, skiing, landscape architect, cooking. Home: Bonita Spgs, Fla. Died May 1, 2008.

EISENBERG, LEON, psychiatrist, educator; b. Phila., Aug. 8, 1922; s. Morris and and Elizabeth (Sabreen) E.; m. Ruth Harriet Bleier, June 11, 1948 (div. 1967); children: Mark Philip, Kathy Bleier; m. Carola Blitzman Guttmacher, Aug. 31, 1967; children: Laurence, Alan. AB, U. Pa., 1944, MD, 1946; MA (hon.), Harvard U., 1967; DSc (hon.), U. Manchester, Eng., 1973, U. Mass., 1991. Diplomate: in child psychiatry and psychiatry Am. Bd. Psychiatry and Neurology. Intern Mt. Sinai Hosp., NYC, 1946—47; instr. physiology U. Pa., 1947-48; resident psychiatry Sheppard-Pratt Hosp., Towson, Md., 1950-52; with Johns Hopkins, 1952-67, prof. child psychiatry Med. Sch., 1961-67; psychiatrist-in-charge children's psychiat. service Harriet Lane Home, 1958-67; prof. psychiatry Harvard U. Med. Sch., Boston, 1967—93, prof. psychiatry emeritus, 1993—2009, prof. of social medicine emeritus, from 1993, Maude and Lillian Presley prof. psychiatry, 1975-80, Maude and Lillian Presley prof. social medicine, 1980-93, chmn. exec. com. dept. psychiatry, 1973-80, chmn. dept., 1980-91; psychiatrist-in-chief Mass. Gen. Hosp., 1967-74, mem. bd. consultation, 1974—2009; sr. assoc. in psychiatry Children's Hosp., Boston, 1974—2009. Paley lectr. Cornell U., 1983; Schilder lectr. NYU, 1984; Eli Robins lectr. Washington U., St. Louis, 1985; plenary session lectr. Internat. Pediat. Assn., Amsterdam, 1998; lectr. Italian Psychiat. Soc., Bologna, 1998; Alpha Omega Alpha lectr. U. Rochester, 1999; plenary lectr. World Psychiat. Assn., Athens, 1999; vis. lectr. Yale U., 1987, John Peters lectr., 2002; R.W. Johnson vis. prof. U. Rochester, 1987; Carolyn Voorsanger lectr. Stanford U. Med. Sch., 1989; Willard Sears Simpkins lectr. Johns Hopkins U., 1989; William Potter lectr. Thomas Jefferson U., 1992; vis. prof. McMaster U., Canada, 1991, Charles U., Prague; psychiat. cons. Crownsville (Md.) State Hosp., 1954—58, Rosewood State Tng. Sch., Owings Mills, Md., 1957—60, Balt. City Hosp., 1959—62, Children's Guild, Balt., 1954—61; cons. Sinai Hosp., Balt., 1963—67; Mapother-Lewis ann. lectr. Maudsley Hosp., London, 1977; Baan Meml. lectr. Netherlands Psychiat. Soc., Amsterdam, 1978; Royal Soc. Medicine vis. prof., London, 83; mem. subcom. psychiat. nomenclature com. vital stats. USPHS; chmn. WHO Conf. Devel. Regulation, 1964—67; mem. Joint Commn. Mental Health of Children; cons. divsn. mental health WHO, from 1974, chmn. sci. group on evaluation of psychiat. treatment, 1989; mem. adv. com. to dir. NIH, 1977—80; lectr. Can. Royal Coll. Psychiatry, 1993, Italian Soc. for Biol. Psychiatry, Cagliari, Sardinia, 1994; Richard Goldbloom lectr. Dalhousie U., Halifax, N.S., Canada, 1995; Wolfe Adler lectr. Sheppard-Pratt Hosp. Sys., Balt., 1995; spl. lectr. Health of the Child of the Eve of the Yr. 2000, Bologna, Italy, 1995; plenary lectr. Royal Australian & New Zealand Coll. Psychiatry, 1999, World Congress of Psychiatry, Hamburg, 1999, XII World Congress of Psychiatry, Yokohama, Japan, 2002. Editor Am. Jour. Orthopsychiatry, 1963-73; mem. editl. bd.: Culture, Medicine and Psychiatry, Am. Jour. Psychiatry, 2004—, Psychol. Medicine, Jour. Psychiat. Research, 2005. Capt. M.C., U.S. Army, 1948-50. Recipient Theobald Smith award Albany Med. Coll., 1979, Orton award Orton Soc., 1980, Disting. Alumnus award U. Pa., 1992, Presdl. Commendation Am. Psychiat. Assn., 1992, Agnes Purchell McGavin award, 1994, Camille Cosby World of Children award Judge Baker Children's Ctr., 1994, Salmon medal N.Y. Acad. Medicine, 1995, Mumford award and lecture, 1996, Walshe McDermott Medal, Inst. of Medicine, 2003, Ruane prize for child and adolescent psychiatry rsch. Nat. Alliance for Rsch. on Schizophrenic and Affecive Disorder, 2003, Child Psychiatry Rsch. award, Nat. Assn. Rsch. in Schizophrenia and Affective Disorder, 2005, Harold Amos Divsn. award, Harvard Med. Sch., 2007, Joss Lopez Ibor award, World Psychiat. Assn., 2008 Fellow: AAAS, Royal Soc. Medicine, Soc. Rsch. Child Devel. (Pub. Policy award 2003), Am. Orthopsychiat. Assn. (Ittleson Meml. award 1996), Am. Psychiat. Assn. (life; trustee 1973—76, Disting. Svc. award 2003, Human Rights award 2005), Royal Coll. Psychiatrists (hon.; Eli Lilly lectr. 1986); mem.: I.O.M. (chair com. on planned childbearing 1993—95, chair com. bridging the brain, behavioral and clin. scis. 1999—2000), AAUP (past pres. Johns Hopkins chpt.), Mass. Med. Soc., Soc. Neurosci., Psychiat. Rsch. Soc. (past pres.), Am. Acad. Arts and Scis. (comm. sec. 1995—2002), Md. Psychiat. Soc. (past pres.), Greek Soc. Neurology and Psychiatry (hon.), Ecuadorean Soc. Neurosci. (hon.), Am. Psychopath. Assn., Assn. Rsch. Nervous and Mental Disease, Can. Pediat. Soc. (Queen Elizabeth II lectr. 1986), Am. Pediat. Soc., Am. Acad. Pediat. (Dale Richmond lectr. 1989, Aldrich award 1980), Inst. Medicine NAS (coun. 1975—77, program and membership coms. 1979—82, bd. on health sci. policy 1989—91, Rhoda and Bernard Samat prize in mental health 1996), Johns Hopkins Soc. Scholars, Alpha Omega Alpha (lectr. Jefferson Med. Coll. 1994), Sigma Xi, Phi Beta Kappa (chpt. pres. 1958, vis. scholar 1994—95). Home: Cambridge, Mass. Died Sept. 15, 2009.

EISENHUT, RICHARD JEAN, pharmacist, owner pharmacy; b. Indpls., Dec. 8, 1929; s. George Robert and Dorothy Mae (Weber) E.; m. Donna Lee Kinney, May 5, 1956; children: Richard Jr., Timothy, Robert, Theresa. BA, Butler U., 1950; PhD (hon.), Ind. Pharm. Assn., 1980. Pharmacist, owner Eisenhut Drugs, Indpls., 1950-86; with Peoples Pharmacy, Indpls., from 1987. Served as cpl. U.S. Army, 1952-54. Mem. Ind. Pharm. Assn. Home: Indianapolis, Ind. Died Nov. 1, 2007.

EITNER, LORENZ EDWIN ALFRED, art historian, educator; b. Brunn, Czechoslovakia, Aug. 27, 1919; came to U.S., 1935, naturalized, 1943; s. Wilhelm and Katherina (Thonet) E.; m. Trudi von Kathrein, Oct. 26, 1946; children: Christy, Kathy, Claudia. AB, Duke U., 1940; MFA, Princeton U., 1948, PhD, 1952. Research unit head Nuremberg War Crimes Trial, 1946-47; from instr. to prof. art U. Minn., Mpls., 1949-63; chmn. dept. art, dir. mus. Stanford U., Calif., 1963-89. Organizer exhbn. works of Gericault for museums of Los Angeles, Detroit and Phila., 1971-72 Author: The Flabellum of Tournus, 1944, Gericault Sketchbooks in the Chicago Art Institute, 1960, Introduction to Art, 1951, Neo-Classicism and Romanticism, 1969, Gericault's Raft of the Medusa, 1972, Gericault, His Life and Work, 1983 (Mitchell prize 1984, C.R. Morey award 1985), An Outline of 19th Century European Painting from David through Cezanne, 1987, Nat. Gallery, Washington, French Nineteenth Century Paintings, 2000; (with others) The Arts in Higher Education, 1963, Stanford Mus. Art, The Drawing Collection, 1993; contbr. articles to profl. jours. Mem. Regional Area Arts Coun. San Francisco Bay Area. Officer OSS, AUS, 1943-46; sect. head ministries divsn. Nuremberg War Crimes Trial, 1946-47. Fulbright grantee, Belgium, 1952-53; Guggenheim fellow, Munich, Federal Republic Germany, 1956-57; recipient Gold Medal for Meritorious Service to Austrian Republic, 1990. Mem. AAAS, Am. Acad. Arts and Scis., Coll. Art Assn. Am. (bd. dirs., past v.p.), Phi Beta Kappa Home: Stanford, Calif. Died Mar. 11, 2009.

ELAM, LLOYD CHARLES, retired psychiatrist, educator; b. Little Rock, Oct. 27, 1928; s. Harry and Ruth (Davis) Elam; m. Clara Carpenter, Feb. 16, 1957; children: Gloria, Laurie. BS, Roosevelt U., 1950, LHD (hon.), 1974; MD, U. Wash., 1957; postgrad., U. Ill., 1957-58, U. Chgo., 1957-61; LLD (hon.), Harvard U., 1973. Staff psychiatrist Billings Hosp., Chgo., 1961, Hubbard Hosp., Nashville, 1961, asst. prof., chmn. dept. psychiatry, 1961-63, prof., chmn. dept. psychiatry, 1963; interim dean Meharry Med. Coll., Nashville, 1966, 6th pres., 1968-81, chancellor, 1981-82, Disting. Svc. prof. psychiatry, 1983-95, prof. emeritus, chmn. emeritus dept. psychiatry and behavioral scis., 1996—2000, ret., from 2001. Mem. Frontiers of Am., Nashville. Recipient Eleanor Roosevelt Key award Roosevelt U., 1972, Bus. and Profl. Leader of Yr. award Heritage of Am., 1974. Mem. AMA, Am. Psychiat. Assn., Nat. Med. Assn., Inst. Medicine, Nashville Acad. Medicine, R.F. Boyd Med. Soc. Home: Nashville, Tenn. Died Oct. 4, 2008.

ELBIN-SCHELL, CAROL GETRUDE, television promotion manager; b. Sept. 30, 1937; d. Harry C. and Gertrude I. (Simms) Elbin; 1 child, Karen Denise Schell. BFA, Cin. Coll.-Conservatory, 1959; student, Foley Modeling Sch., 1961; postgrad., Tidewater C.C., 1976-77. Promotion mgr. Sta. WAVY-TV, Norfolk, Va., 1975-76; promotion pub. svc. mgr. Sta. WNYS-TV (now WIXT), Syracyse, N.Y., 1962-71; asst. promotion dept. Sta. KRCA (now KNBC-TV), Hollywood, Calif., 1959; asst. promotion-pub. svc. mgr. Sta. WCPO-TV, Cin., 1956-59, 60-61; promotion-pub. svc. mgr. Sta. KUSK-TV, Prescott, Ariz., 1982-83; promotion mgr. Sta. KMIR-TV, Palm Springs, 1984; sta. mgr., promotion mgr. Gt. S.W. Broadcasting, Bakersfield, Calif., 1987-88; freelance writer Prescott, from 1983. Writer Videoview Mag., Phoenix, 1985; gen. mgr. Prescott Cmty. Access Channel, 1988-91; supr. personal appearances: Mike Douglas, Jack LaLanne, Vic Morrow, others, 1961-83; personal appearance coord., publicist to Elizabeth Taylor-Warner, 1977-78; exec. prodr., writer, editor TV series, spls., 1962-91. Author: Great Hospital Connection, 1976, Self Signs, 1976. Campaign coord. Sen. John W. Warner of Va., 1977-78; campaign worker Sen. Barry Goldwater of Ariz., 1980. Recipient Gabriel award Office of Cath. Dioceses, Washington, 1971. Mem. Women in Comms., Am. Women in Radio and TV, Broadcast Promotion Assn., Am. Film Inst., Delta Omicron. Republican. Methodist. Home: Bethel, Ohio. Died Nov. 11, 2005.

ELDRIDGE, MARIE DELANEY, statistician, education researcher; b. Balt., June 1, 1926; d. James Howard and Mathilda (Belz) Delaney; m. Paul Eldridge, Apr. 3, 1961; children: Julia Delaney, Dan Pattengill, Susan. AB in Math., Coll. Notre Dame Md., 1948; MSc in Biostats., Johns

Hopkins U., 1953. Statistician, indsl. quality control Revere Copper and Brass, Balt., 1948—49; statistician Ralph Parsons & Co., Frederick, Md., 1953—54, US Govt., 1954—60; instr. U. Balt., 1958—60; supr. statistician US Dept. Health Edn. & Welfare, Washington, 1960—65; with Office Statis. Programs and Stds., US Postal Svc., Washington, 1965—72, dep. dir., 1968—70, dir., 1970—72; dir. math. analysis divsn. Nat. Hwy. Traffic Safety Adminstrn., US Dept. Transp., 1972—73, dir. office stats. & analysis, 1973—75; adminstr. Nat. Ctr. Edn. Stats., US Dept. Edn., Washington, 1976—84; mem. Edn. Commn. of States, 1976—84; mem. tech. adv. com. Calif. Assessment Program, from 1978; dir., Ctr. Ednl. Sudies Rsch. Triangle Inst., Rsch. Triangle Pk., NC, 1984—88; chair Durham Math. Collaborative NC Sch. Scis. and Math., 1987—88; cons. stats., 1988. Mem. nat. accident sample adv. com. Dept. Transp.; profl. lectr. George Washington U., 1981—84; adj. faculty Fed. Exec. Inst., 1982—84. Recipient Superior Accomplishment award, US Postal Svc., 1970, Outstanding Performance award, US Dept. Transp., 1975, Cert. Recognition, HEW, 1976, 1980, Presdl. Rank award, 1981. Fellow: Am. Statis. Assn. (exec. coun. 1975—79, co-chmn. subcom. tng. statisticians govt. 1979—81, com. fellows 1978—80, cons. com. govt. stats. 1985—88); mem.: Durham Math. Coun. (bd. dirs. from 1985, chmn. bd. 1987—88), Washington Statis. Soc. (pres. 1976—77), Fed. Exec. Inst. (dir. 1982—85), Internat. Statis. Inst., Internat. Assn. Survey Statisticians, Am. Edn. Rsch. Assn., Phi Delta Kappa. Democrat. Episcopalian. Died June 13, 2009.

ELFVIN, JOHN THOMAS, federal judge; b. Montour Falls, NY, June 30, 1917; s. John Arthur and Lillian Ruth (Dorning) E.; m. Peggy Pierce, Oct. 1, 1949. B.E.E., Cornell U., 1942; JD, Georgetown U., 1947. Bar: D.C. 1948, N.Y. 1949. Confidential clk. to Hon. E. Barrett Prettyman US Ct. Appeals (DC Cir.), 1947-48; asst. US atty. (we. dist.) NY US Dept. Justice, Buffalo, 1955-58, US atty., 1972-75; ptnr. Cravath, Swaine & Moore, NYC, 1948-51, Dudley, Stowe & Sawyer, Buffalo, 1951-55, Lansdowne, Horning & Elfvin, Buffalo, 1958-69, 70-72; justice NY Supreme Ct., 1969; judge US Dist. Ct. (we. dist.) NY, Buffalo, 1975—87, sr. judge, 1987—2009. Mem. bd. suprs. Erie County, N.Y., 1962-65, mem. bd. ethics, 1971-74, chmn., 1971-72; mem., minority leader Buffalo Common Council Delaware Dist., 1966-69. Served in USN, 1943—46. Mem.: Tech. Socs. Niagara Frontier (pres. 1960—61), Engring. Soc. Buffalo (pres. 1958—59), Erie County Bar Assn., Am. Judicature Soc., Saturn Club, Cornell Club (pres. 1957—58), Phi Kappa Tau. Republican. Home: Buffalo, NY. Died Jan. 6, 2009.

ELIEL, ERNEST LUDWIG, chemist, educator; b. Cologne, Germany, Dec. 28, 1921; came to US, 1946, naturalized, 1951; s. Oskar and Luise (Tietz) E.; m. Eva Schwarz, Dec. 23, 1949; children: Ruth Louise, Carol Susan. Student, U. Edinburgh, Scotland, 1939-40; degree in phys.-chem. sci., U. Havana, Cuba, 1946; PhD, U. Ill., 1948; DSc (hon.), Duke U., 1983, U. Notre Dame, 1990, Babes-Bolyai U., Cluj, Romania, 1993, U. Havana, Cuba, 2004. Mem. faculty U. Notre Dame, South Bend, Ind., 1948-72, prof. chemistry, 1960-72, head dept., 1964-66; W.R. Kenan Jr. prof. chemistry U. NC, Chapel Hill, 1972—93; prof. emeritus U. N.C., from 1993. Le Bel Centennial lectr., Paris, 1974, Geoffrey Coates lectr. U. Wyo., 1989, Smith, Kline and French lectr. U. Ill., 1990, Richard and Doris Arnold lectr. U. So. Ill., 1997, Fry lectr. U. Ark., 2005; Sir C.V. Raman vis. prof. U. Madras, India, 1981. Author: Stereochemistry of Carbon Compounds, 1962, Elements of Stereochemistry, 1969, From Cologne to Chapel Hill, 1990; co-author: Conformational Analysis, 1965, Stereochemistry of Organic Compounds, 1994, Basic Organic Stereochemistry, 2001; co-editor: Topics in Stereochemistry, vols. I-XXI, 1967-94. Pres. Internat. Rels. Coun., St. Joseph Valley, Ind., 1961-63; chmn. bd. U.S.-Mex. Found. for Sci., 1994-96. Recipient Coll. Chem. Tchrs. award Mfg. Chemists Assn., 1965, Laurent Lavoisier medal French Chem. Soc., 1968, Amoco Teaching award U. N.C., 1975, Thomas Jefferson award U. N.C., 1991, N.C. award in Sci., 1986, Chirality medal Internat. Symposium on Chiral Discrimination, 1996; NSF sr. rsch. fellow Harvard U., 1958, Calif. Inst. Tech., 1958-59, E.T.H. Zurich, Switzerland, 1967-68, Guggenheim fellow Stanford U., Princeton U., 1975-76, Duke U., 1983-84; named One of Top 75 Disting. Contbrs. to Chem. Enterprise, Chem. and Engring. News, 1998. Fellow AAAS (chmn. chemistry sect. 1991-92), Royal Soc. Chems.; mem. NAS (award for chemistry in svc. to society 1997), AAUP (chpt. pres. 1971-72, 78-79), Am. Acad. Arts and Scis., Am. Chem. Soc. (chmn. St. Joseph Valley sect. 1960, councillor 1965-73, 75—, chmn. com. publs. 1972, 76-78, dir. 1985-93, chmn. bd. dirs. 1987-89, pres. 1992, Morley medal Cleve. sect. 1965, Harry and Carol Mosher award Santa Clara Valley sect. 1982, Herty medal Ga. sect. 1991, So. Chemist award Memphis sect. 1991, Madison Marshall award North Ala. sect. 1993, George C. Pimentel award in Chem. Edn. 1995, Priestley medal 1996), Coun. Sci. Soc. Pres.'s (pres. 1996), Royal Spanish Chem. Soc. (hon.), Argentine Chem. Assn. (hon.), Peruvian Chem. Soc. (corr.), Mex. Chem. Soc. (hon.), Mex. Acad. Scis. (corr.), Chilean Chem. Soc. (hon.), Cuban Chem. Soc. (hon.), Sigma Xi (pres. U. Notre Dame chpt. 1968-69), Phi Lambda Upsilon, Phi Kappa Phi. Home: Chapel Hill, NC. Died Sept. 18, 2008.

ELKINS, THOMAS RICHARD, consultant, freelance writer; b. Davenport, Iowa, Apr. 25, 1931; s. Richard M. and Nadienne C. (Blemker) E.; m. Joan E. Winters, Aug. 28, 1955 (div. Mar. 1972); children: Richard H., Geoffrey A., Wendy J., Marjorie N.; m. Prentice Brannan, Apr. 10, 1972 (dec. Apr. 1985); m. Patricia Jensen, Nov. 10, 1989. AB cum laude, Wabash Coll., 1953. Lic. FCC. Announcer, reporter Sta. WKJG, Ft. Wayne, Ind., 1953-56; announcer Sta. WOC, Davenport, 1956-58; disc jockey Sta. KSTT, Davenport, 1958-59; owner, mgr. Sta. KBUS, Mexia, Tex., 1959-63, Sta. KKJO, Saint Joseph, Mo., 1963-71, Stas. KNUI and KHUI, Kahului, Hawaii, 1973-90; cons., freelance writer, from 1990. Bd. dirs. 1st Amendment Congress; commentator Voice of Am., 1982-83. Over 240 broadcast editorials per yr., 1961-90. Pres. Maui chpt. Hawaii Heart Assn., 1978. Mem. Nat. Broadcast Editorial Assn. (bd. dirs. 1981-88, pres. 1986-87, nat. excellence award 1981, regional excellence award 1981, 84, Mgmt. award 1989), Nat. Assn. Broadcasters (1st Amendment com.), Nat. Conf. Editorial Writers (bd. dirs. 1986-87), Soc. Profl. Journalists (bd. dirs. 1986-87), Radio-TV News Dirs. Assn. (bd. dirs. 1986-87), Hawaiin Assn. Broadcasters (bd. dirs. 1978-82, pres. 1980-81), Maui C. of C. (bd. dirs. 1987—). Home: Montgomery, Tex. Died Apr. 29, 2008.

ELLION, M. EDMUND, engineering executive; b. Boston, Jan. 20, 1923; s. Michael N. and Beatrice Elizabeth (Patterson) E.; m. Dolores Diana Rolph, July 3, 1954; children: Laurie Ann, Thomas Michael. BS, Northeastern U., 1943, Tufts U., 1944; MS in Mech. Engring., MIT, Harvard U., 1947; PhD in Engring. and Physics, Calif. Inst. Tech., 1953. Exec. dir., v.p. Nat. Engring. Sci. Corp., Pasadena, Calif., 1955-60; pres. Dynamic Sci. Corp., Pasadena, 1960-64; dir. tech. GM Hughes Electronics, LA, 1964-88; pres., CEO, chmn. bd. Sci. Industries Inc., Santa Ynez, Calif., from 1988. Lectr. Stanford U., Calif. Inst. Technology, UCLA, 1957-87. Contbr. articles to profl. jours. Served to lt. USNR, 1943-46, PTO. Calif. Inst. Tech. scholar. Fellow Am. Inst. Aeros. (assoc.), IEEE (assoc.). Republican. Achievements include 38 patents. Home: Santa Ynez, Calif. Died Dec. 23, 2007.

ELLIOTT, EMORY BERNARD, language educator, school system administrator; b. Balt., Oct. 30, 1942; s. Emory Bernard and Virginia L. (Ulbrick) E.; m. Georgia Ann Carroll, May 14, 1966; children: Scott, Mark, Matthew, Laura, Constance. AB, Loyola Coll., Balt., 1964; MA, Bowling Green State U., 1966; PhD, U. Ill., 1972. Instr. Cameron Coll., Lawton, Okla., 1966-67, US Mil Acad., West Point, NY, 1967-69; from asst. prof. to prof. English, Princeton U., NJ, 1972-89, chmn. Am. studies program NJ, 1976-82, master Lee D. Butler Coll. NJ, 1982-86, chmn. English dept. NJ, 1987-89; Pres.'s chair English U. Calif., Riverside, 1989-91, disting. prof., from 1992, univ. prof., 2001—09; dir. Ctr. for Ideas and Soc., 1996—2009. Writing cons. Bell Labs., Holmdel, NJ, 1975-79, RCA, Princeton, 1980-81; edn. cons. Western Electric Corp. Edn. Ctr., Hopewell, NJ, 1974-79; internat. adv. bd. Kennedy Inst. Am. Studies Free U. Berlin; pres., Am. Studies Assn., 2006-07. Author: Power and the Pulpit in Puritan New England, 1975, Puritan Influences in American Literature, 1979, Revolutionary Writers: Literature and Authority in the New Republic, 1982, The Literature of Puritan New England in The Cambridge History of American Literature, Vol. 1, 1994, The Cambridge Introduction to Early American Literature, 2002, New Directions in American Literary Scholarship, 1980-2002, 2004; editor: Dictionary of Literary Biography, 3 Vols., 1606-1810, 1983-84; Columbia Literary History of the United States, 1988 (Am. Book award), American Literature: A Prentice Hall Anthology 3 Vols., 1990, Columbia History of The American Novel, 1991, The Jungle, 1991, Wieland, 1994, Huckleberry Finn, 1998, Aesthetics in a Multicultural Age, 2002, Global Migration, Social Change and Cultural Transformation, 2007; series editor Am. Novel Series, 1985-2009, Critical Studies in Contemporary Am. Fiction, 1987—; mem. editl. bd. Am. Quar., 1976-80, PMLA, 1990-92, Am. Lit., 1995—98, Modern Fiction Studies, 1993-2009, Ill. Studies Lang. Lit., 1993—, Studies in Am. Puritan Spirituality, 1991-2009; mem. adv. com. Gale Bibliography of Am. Lit., 1981-2009; editor-at-large Am. Studies Internat., 1993-2009. Served to capt. U.S. Army, 1966-69. Recipient Disting. Tchr. award U. Calif., Riverside, 1993, Outstanding Advisor/Mentor award, 2004, Rosemary Schaer Humanitarian award, 1997; fellow Woodrow Wilson Found., 1971-72, Am. Coun. Learned Socs., 1973, Guggenheim Found., 1976, Nat. Humanities Ctr. 1979-80, NEH, 1986-87, Inst. for Rsch. in the Humanities, 1991-92, Ford Found., 1998—2005, Rockefeller Found., 2000-03; Richard Stockton preceptor Princeton U., 1975-78; named to Acad. Disting. Tchrs., 2006. Mem. MLA (chmn. Early Am. lit. div., Am. lit. div. 1991, regional del.), Am. Studies Assn. (pres. 2006-07). Home: Riverside, Calif. Died Mar. 31, 2009.

ELLIOTT, OWEN BASIL, corporate professional; b. Danville, Va., Oct. 3, 1922; s. Jesse McCay and Dora (Hart) E.; m. Alicia Louise Stauf, July 9, 1946; children: Alicia, Kristin, Louise, Leslie. Student, U. Richmond, 1943-44; BA in History and English, Coll. of William and Mary, 1947. Asst. dir., data ctrs. NCR Corp., Dayton, Ohio, 1947-78; asst. to pres. Pergamon Press, Elmsford, N.Y., 1978-84; v.p. Pafford Acctg., Jupiter, Fla., 1986-87; owner Basil Owen Assocs., Juno Beach, Fla., from 1987. Mem. Colonial Williamsburg (Va.) Found. Lt. (j.g.) USN, 1943-46. Mem. Nat. Assn. of Self-Employed, Nat. Wildlife Fedn. Avocations: photography, reading, swimming, community theatre. Home: Juno Beach, Fla. Died Jan. 19, 2008.

ELLIOTT, WILLIAM PAUL, climatologist; b. Geneva, Ill., June 16, 1928; s. William and Freda Emert (Umbreit) E.; m. Marie Gross, June 21, 1952; children: Erica, Paul. BA, St. John's Coll., Annapolis, Md., 1947; MS, U. Chgo., 1952; PhD, Tex. A&M U., 1958. From instr. to asst. prof. dept. oceanography Tex. A&M U., College Station, 1955-57; rsch. physicist Air Force Cambridge Rsch. Lab., Bedford, Mass., 1957-68; assoc. prof. rsch. sch. oceanography Oreg. State U., Corvallis, 1968-74; rsch. meteorologist Nat. Oceanic and Atmospheric Adminstrn., Silver Spring, Md., 1974-90, supervisory meteorologist, from 1990. Chmn. rapporteurs on CO2 World Meterol. Orgn., Geneva, 1983-87. Contbr. articles to profl. jours. Mem. AAAS, Am. Meteorol. Soc. (mem. radiation com. 1962-64, editor 1983-87), Am. Geophys. Union (editor 1984-89), Audubon Soc. Corvallis (pres. 1973-74). Achievements include first theoretical calculation of internal boundary layer in atmosphere, first demonstration that vertical diffusion does not lead to Gaussian profile, demonstration of shore line effect in precipitation; development of methods for assessing changes in water vapor in the lower atmosphere. Home: Gaithersburg, Md. Died Jan. 29, 2008.

ELLIS, BURLEN WILLIAM, retired fire department chief; b. Huntington, W.Va., Sept. 27, 1922; s. James Burlen and Nellie (Carven) E.; m. Betty Jane Ellis, Dec. 7, 1945; children: Jane D. Hutchinson, William R. Ellis. Grad. h.s., Huntington, 1943. Firefighter Huntington Fire Dept., 1948-53, lt., 1953-58, capt., 1958-66, dep. chief, 1966-85, ret., 1985. Mem. Huntington City Coun., 1990—; mem. cmty. adv. panel BASF Corp., 1995—. Mem. Kyoua Planning Commn., 1994—; mem. Highland Neighborhood Assn., 1996—. With U.S. Army, 1943. Mem. Internat. Assn. Fire Fighters, Am. Legion. Democrat. Baptist. Home: Huntington, W.Va. Died Jan. 14, 2008.

ELLIS, HAROLD ROGER, mental health services professional; b. NYC, July 10, 1915; s. Abraham Havelock and Berta Frances (Rohtman) Eisenstadt; m. Estelle nancy Tabachnick; children: Norman, Jonathan. BS in Psychology, City Coll. N.Y., 1974; MEd, Columbia U., 1984; PhD in Counseling Psychology with honors, Union Inst., 1990. Cert. rehab. counselor Commn. Rehab. Counselor Cert. Tech. editorRadio Retailing Mag. Caldwell-Clements, Inc., NYC, 1951-55; pres. The Ellis-Haber Corp., NYC, 1955-78; employment coord. CETA outreach program Fedn. Employment and Guidance Svc., NYC, 1978-79; coord. disabled computer programmer tng. Human Resources Ctr., Albertson, N.Y., 1979-83; counselor, tchr. various schs., ctrs., NYC, 1983-89; disabled worker counselor U.S. Dept. Labor, NYC, 1989-93; network organizer Cmty. Dreamsharing Network, NYC, from 1995. Cons. Goodwill Industries, Mfrs. Hanover Bank; instr. continuing edn. Nassau C. C., Garden City, N.Y., Counselor disabled students svcs., substitute dir., 1983; substitute vocat. rehab. counselor Rosemary Kennedy Ctr., Wantagh, N.Y., 1984; vocat., ednl. counselor Aurora Concept, Queens, N.Y., 1984-85; adj. prof. psychology Coll. New Resources, Bronx, N.Y., 1986-87; psychotherapist externship Family Ctr. Mental Health, Bkly., 1985-86; counselor to visual disabled Social Svc. Fedn., Englewood, N.J.; dir., therapist tng. inst. Ctr. Dream Drama; lectr., presenter expressive arts therapies program Pratt Inst., Assn. Humanistic Psychology, Assn. Study of Dreams. Vol. participant The Games Club, Synanon, N.Y., The Bridge Manhattan State Hosp., N.Y.C. With U.S. Army Signal Corps, U.S. Army Air Corps., Rome. Mem. Am. Group Psychotherapy Assn., Am. Soc. Group Psychotherapy and Psychodrama, Nassau County Mental Health assn., Nat. Assn. Drama Therapy, Nat. Coalition of Arts Therapy Assns. Avocation: amateur radio. Home: Levittown, NY. Died Feb. 15, 2008.

ELLIS, JAMES LEONARD, broadcast marketing executive; b. Cin., Mar. 3, 1947; s. William H. and Kathryn (Ravenscroft) E. BS in Graphic Design and Advt., U. Cin., 1970. Creative dir. James A. Jacobs Advt., Cin., 1970-75; promotion mgr. WKRC-TV, Cin., 1976-79; v.p. mktg. and advt. Frank N. Magid Rsch., Marion, Iowa, 1980-82; v.p. creative svcs. Tribune Broadcasting Co., Chgo., from 1982. Mktg. dir. numerous TV prodns. including Charles in Charge, 1987, Geraldo, 1988, Soul Train, 1988, Monsters, 1988 (Gold Medallion award, 1989), Joan Rivers Show, 1989, Remote Control, 1989 (Gold Medallion award, 1989). Recipient three Addy awards Am. Advt. Fedn., 1975. Mem. NATAS (two Emmy awards, 1975), Broadcasting Promotion and Mktg. Execs. Assn. (bd. dirs. 1985-87, Gold medallions 1972, 88-89). Republican. Presbyterian. Avocations: writing, poetry, antiques. Home: Boca Raton, Fla. Died July 7, 2008.

ELLIS, JOHN HUBERT, retired history professor; b. Memphis, Sept. 29, 1931; s. John Hubert Ellis and Esther Verlin Sides, m. Wanda Ann Roper, July 1, 1949, children: Elaine Tucci, John, Suzanne Panick. BA, Memphis State Coll., 1955; MA, Memphis State U., 1958; PhD, Tulane U., 1962. Asst. prof. Memphis State U., 1960—64, Ga. State Coll., Atlanta, 1964—65; post-doctoral fellow Nat. Inst. of Gen. Med. Scis., New Orleans, 1965—67; assoc. prof. Georgetown Coll., Ky., 1967—71; prof. Lehigh U., Bethlehem, Pa., 1971—93; ret. Dir. Ctr. for Health Scis., Lehigh U., Bethlehem, 1971—77. Bd. of editors Chiropractic Hist. Jour., Davenport, Iowa, 1987—92; author: Medicine in Kentucky, 1977, Yellow Fever & Public Health in New South, 1992 (Book of Yr., 1992). Sgt. USAF, 1948—51. Danforth fellow, Danforth Found., 1980—86, Penrose Summer fellow, Am. Philos. Soc., 1975. Mem.: Nat. Assn. of Scholars, So. Hist. Assn. Avocations: reading, gardening. Home: Bethlehem, Pa. Died July 29, 2008.

ELOWSON, DAVID EINAR, broker, marketing consultant; b. Chgo., May 6, 1938; s. Einar Rudolph and Marguerite Anita Elowson; m. Marilyn F. Elowson, Dec. 23, 1967; children: Anne-Marie, James F., Suzanne E. BS in Mgmt., U. Ill., 1961; MBA in Mktg., U. Chgo., 1964. Dir. mail mgr. McMaster Carr Supply Co., Chgo., 1961-65; salesman McBee Systems Litton Inc., Chgo., 1965-66; mktg. rschr. Enerpac divsn. Applied Powder Ind., Brookfield, Wis., 1966-67, Hosp. Svc. Corp., Chgo., 1967-70; pres. David E. Elowson Mktg., Kenosha, Wis., 1970-72; mktg. dir., CEO Franks Poultry Co., Racine, Wis., 1972-93; CEO, pres. Entrepreneurs Ltd., Racine, from 1993. Author/editor: Pages at a Time Tropical Fish, 1969. Cpl. U.S. Army, 1956-64. Mem. Alpha Kappa Psi. Republican. Roman Catholic. Avocations: reading, fishing, researching various topics. Died Oct. 17, 2007.

ELSON, MIRIAM, retired social work educator; b. Chgo., July 21, 1909; d. David and Elizabeth (Elson) Almond; m. Alex Elson, July 6, 1933 (dec. 2008); children: Jacova Miller (dec.), Karen O'Neil. BA, Northwestern U.; AM in Social Svc. Adminstrn., U. Chgo. Researcher Jewish Children's Bur., Chgo., 1939-42; supr. adoptions Ill. Children's Home and Aid Soc., Chgo., 1945-53; chief psychiat. social worker student mental health unit U. Chgo., 1956-79, lectr. Sch. Social Svc. Adminstrn., 1979-94, emeritus lectr., 1994—2009. Author: Self Psychology in Clinical Social Work, 1986; editor: Vulnerable Youth, Adolescent Psychiatry, 1980, Kohut Seminars: On Self Psychology and Psychotherapy with Late Adolescents and Young Adults, 1987. Fellow Am. Orthopsychiat. Assn.; mem. NASW (life, cert.). Home: Chicago, Ill. Died May 6, 2009.

ELSTER, J. ROBERT, lawyer; b. Mar. 10, 1938; m. Suzan Douglas, July 9, 1960; children: John Robert Jr., Mary Douglas Peters. BA in History, Rice U., 1959; JD, Duke U., 1964. Bar: N.C. 1964, N.C. Supreme Ct., U.S. Dist. Ct. N.C. 1964, U.S. Ct. Appeals (4th cir.) 1964, U.S. Tax Ct., U.S. Supreme Ct. 1972. Assoc. Petree & Stockton, Winston-Salem, N.C., 1964-70; ptnr., litig. practice Kilpatrick Stockton LLP (formerly Petree & Stockton), from 1970. Adj. prof. law Wake Forest U., 1995-96. Contbr. articles to profl. publs. Bd. dirs. NC Stroke Assn., YMCA, 1978-80, Summit Sch., Winston-Salem, 1978-81, Forsyth Country Day Sch., Winston-Salem, 1981-83; bd. trustees Centenary United Meth. Ch., 1988-91; mem. ethics com. Wake Forest U. Baptist Med. Ctr.; Capt. USMC, 1959-61. Fellow Am. Coll. Trial Lawyers (trial comp. com. 1987-92, trial advocacy com. 1992—); barrister Joseph Branch Inn of Ct.; mem. N.C. Assn. Def. Attys. (pres. 1978-79), Forsyth County Bar Assn. (sec. 1966-67), N.C. Bar Assn. (bd. govs. 1987-90, mem. ethics and grievance com. 1986-89, endowment com. 1990-2000, chair professionalism com. 1996-99, v.p. 2001--), Rotary (bd. dirs. 1984-89, pres. 1987-88). Republican. Home: Winston Salem, NC. Died May 2007.

ELTRINGHAM, THOMAS JAMES GYGER, telecommunications professional; b. Riverside, Calif., Nov. 4, 1943; s. Thomas Lamar and May Katharyn (Gyger) E.; m. Hana Libuse Strachen, Jan. 21, 1966 (Feb. 1978); m. Lydia Rose Boss, Oct. 4, 1980; children: Glenn Alexander, Eric Douglas. HSST, Hubbard Coll., Copenhagen, 1969. Ordained to ministry. Minister Ch. of Scientology, L.A. and Clearwater, Fla., 1961-83; installations mgrs. Am. Sun, Inc., Commerce, Calif., 1984-86; v.p. ops. Power Ins. Inc., Santa Fe Springs, Calif., 1986-90; dir. L.D. Svcs., Inc., Santa Fe Springs, Calif., 1990-98; CEO GCC Telecomm. Inc., 1991-98; v.p. quality control Airespring Inc. Telecom, Van Nuys, Calif., from 2004. Contbr. articles to profl. jours.; developer drug rehab. program, L.A., 1966. Chmn. bd. trustees Eltringham Family Found. Mem. Internat. Assn. Scientologists. Republican. Avocations: tennis, skiing, reading, computers, golf. Home: Tujunga, Calif. Died Aug. 5, 2007.

EMBRY, GEORGANN, music educator; b. Kansas City, MO, Aug. 24, 1935; d. Charles Calvin and Frances Dinah Embry. BFA, U. Nebr., 1957; BA in Music, Nebr. Wesleyan Coll., 1981; MMus, U. Nebr., 1985. Tchr. Miller Sch. of Piano, Lincoln, Nebr., 1965—82; tchr. piano music theory/composition Lincoln, from 1982. Home: Lincoln, Nebr. Died June 12, 2008.

EMERSON, DENLEY WILLIS, realtor; b. Boston, Apr. 9, 1918; s. Bispham Homer and Marian Dudley (Richards) E.; m. Harriet Rathbun, May 13, 1939 (div. Dec. 1945); children: Gail Denley, Jill Beverly, Pamela Arnold. Student, Northeastern U. Prin. Denley W. Emerson, Realtor, Center Sandwich, N.H., from 1939, Denley W. Emerson Ins. Agy., Center Sandwich, N.H., 1939-87, Emerson's Garage, Center Sandwich, 1947-53, The Village Inn, Center Sandwich, 1952-67. Bd. dirs. Meredith (N.H.) Bank & Trust. Mem. Sandwich Planning Bd. Mem. Lakes Region Bd. of Realtors (local pres. 1967, 68). Clubs: Town (Sandwich). Lodges: Masons. Republican. Avocation: tree farming. Home: Sandwich, NH. Died Mar. 1, 2008.

EMERY, WESTON LEWIS, retired diplomat; b. Gardiner, Maine, Jan. 7, 1924; s. Theodore Evans and Eleanor Weston Lewis Emery; m. Brigitte Jacqueline LeMaire, Aug. 21, 1954; children: Christine Vientiane, Caroline Carthage, Eric Weston. Student, Tex. A&M, 1943-44; BA, Rollins Coll., 1948; postgrad., Boston U., 1948-50, U. Grenoble, France, 1950. Treas. Fla. Audubon Soc., Winter Park, 1950, 51; sales mgr., supr. Coffman Iron Works, Orlando, Fla., 1951-56; procurement advisor Howell & Co., Vientiane, Laos, 1956-58; fgn. svc. officer US Agy. for Internat. Devel. (USAID), Washington, 1959-86, Office Fgn. Disaster Assistance, Washington, 1974-82. Author: C-66: A World War II Chronicle of an Armored Infantry Company, 1992. Skipper, leader Sea Scouts, Winter Park and Orlando, 1950-56. Pvt. first class U.S. Army, 1943-45, ETO. Decorated Bronze Star medal with oak leaf cluster U.S. Army, 1945, Combat Infantry Badge. Mem. VFW (life), Diplomatic and Consular Officers Ret. (life), 12th Armored Divsn. Assn. (life), Roots Users Group (charter), French Croix de Guerre (life), Am. Fgn. Svc. Assn. Democrat. Episcopalian. Avocations: genealogy, tennis, swimming, jogging, gardening. Home: Mc Lean, Va. Died Sept. 13, 2009.

ENDICOTT, WAYNE ALLEN, writer, photographer; b. Chgo., Dec. 6, 1939; s. John Girard and Edith Margaret (Wolf) E.; m. Holly Evelyn Skreko, Sept. 2, 1961; children: Mark Allen, Karen Denise. Student, U. Wis., 1957-59. Mng. editor Profl. Builder, Chgo., 1966-68; editor-in-chief Automation in Housing, Chgo., 1968-74; exec. editor Constrn. Equipment, Chgo., 1974-81; editor-in-chief Brick & Clay Record, Chgo., 1981-86; owner, operator Comm Con, Palatine, Ill., from 1986. Deacon St. John United Ch. Christ, Arlington Heights, Ill., 1976-78, elder, 1988—. Mem. Soc. Profl. Journalists, Am. Bus. Press (Jesse H. Neal award 1970), Athletic Ofcls. Am. (pres. 1980-82), Nat. Assn. Athletic Ofcls., Ill. High Sch. Assn., Jaycees (pres. Arlington Heights 1975). Avocations: racquetball, golf, reading. Home: Palatine, Ill. Died June 28, 2008.

ENGEL, JAN MARCIN, research physicist; b. Gdansk, Poland, May 1, 1924; came to U.S., 1946, naturalized 1951; s. Adam and Jola Rosa (Frenkel) E.; m. Janet Zelda Greenky, June 11, 1955 (dec. Sept. 1962); children: Karen Y., Stephen A. BSc, U. London, 1946; student, U. Pa., 1946-48, Temple U., 1949-50, UCLA, 1956-57. Diamond polisher Owen & Kuropatwa Ltd., London, 1941-43; engr. E. Shipton & Co. Ltd., Northwood Hills, Eng., 1943-46; research physicist Socony-Vacuum Oil Co., Paulsboro, N.J., 1950-51, Gen. Electric Co., Syracuse, N.Y., 1951-53; sr. project engr. Motorola Inc., Phoenix, 1953-54; research physicist Pacific Semicondrs. Inc., Culver City, Calif., 1954-57; adv. physicist IBM Corp., Poughkeepsie, NY, San Jose, Calif., 1958-84; pres. Geneal. Data Systems, San Jose, Calif., from 1980. Cons. Electro-Optical Systems, Inc., Pasadena, Calif., 1957-58; lectr. liberal arts U. Calif., Los Angeles and Berkeley, 1956-60. Contbr. articles to profl. jours. Co-founder Santa Clara Valley Assn. Widows and Widowers, 1964-65, chmn. Fellow Inst. Physics London; mem. IEEE (sr. mem., founder, 1st editor IEEE Electron Devices newsletter 1966-70), Am. Phys. Soc., Am. Inst. Physics, Soc. Info. Display, Sigma Xi (founder, 1st pres. Poughkeepsie br. 1961-63). Lodges: B'nai Brith (co-founder, treas. Thomas Jefferson Lodge, Syracuse N.Y. 1952-53). Home: San Jose, Calif. Died July 9, 2008.

ENGELKE, PAUL HENRY, retail executive; b. Platteville, Wis., May 18, 1925; s. Henry Nickolas and Fern Olive (Robinson) E.; m. Mary Lydia Hass, Feb. 14, 1954. Grad. high sch., Platteville. Owner, operator Farm, Platteville, 1948-59, Engelke Feed Store, Chadwick, Ill., 1959-71, Mary's Shoppe, Stockton, Ill., from 1971. With USMC, 1946-48. Republican. Lutheran. Home: Stockton, Ill. Died May 13, 2008.

ENGELS, PATRICIA LOUISE, lawyer; b. Joliet, Ill., July 2, 1926; d. Fred Bridges and Loretta Mae (Fisk) B.; m. Henry William Engels, Feb. 1, 1947; children: Patrick Henry, Michael Bruce, Timothy William. BS in Edn., Olivet Nazarene Coll., 1970, MEd, 1971; JD, John Marshall Law Sch., 1979. Bar: Ill. 1979, Ind. 1979; cert. elem. and high sch. tchr., edn. adminstrn., Ill. Tchr. Bourbonnais (Ill.) and Momence (Ill.) Unit Schs., 1970-76; instr. Kankakee (Ill.) Community Coll., 1975; sole practice Ind. and Ill., from 1979. Qualified divorce mediator, 1991—. Active Lake Village (Ind.) Civic Assn., 1980—; edn. coord. St. Augusta Ch., Lake Village, 1985-89. Avocations: exercise, swimming, sewing, country dancing, reading. Mem. ABA, Ind. Bar Assn., Ill. Bar Assn., Pub. Defender Bar Assn., Theta Chi Sigma, Kappa Delta Pi. Roman Catholic. Avocations: exercise, swimming, sewing, dance, reading. Died Nov. 26, 2007.

ENGER, EDWARD HENRY, JR., retired editor, writer; b. Mpls., Mar. 16, 1930; s. Edward Henry Sr. and Anastasia (Barber) E.; m. Carolyn Sue Bush, June 1, 1964. BS in Edn., U. Minn., 1952. Cert. tchr., Calif. Tchr. Downers Grove (Ill.) Pub. Sch., 1956-58; editor Harper & Row, Evanston, Ill., 1958-62, author NYC, 1975—78; editor Silver Burdett Co., Morristown, N.J., 1962-68, Dell Pub. Co., NYC, 1968-75; author Nat. Textbook Co., Chgo., 1979-81; editl. dir. Amsco Sch. Publs., NYC, 1982-97; ret., 1997. Author: Writing by Doing, 1981, (textbook series) Language Basics, 1975-78. Served to cpl. U.S. Army, 1954-56, Korea. Mem. Nat. Council Tchrs. English. Democrat. Avocations: gardening, cooking, hiking, jogging. Died Oct. 11, 2007.

ENGLE, BARBARA JOANNE, nurse; b. Waukegan, Ill., Nov. 27, 1933; d. Clarence Dwight and Ethel Viola (Reed) Russell; m. Robert Edward Engle, Oct. 11, 1932; children: Robert Edward Jr., Robbin Elizabeth Neher, Tina Marie Gabriel, Mary Beth Russell. Diploma in nursing, Bklyn. Hosp. Sch. Nursing, 1955; BS, St. Joseph's Coll., 1983. RN, Md.; cert. post-anesthesia nurse, ACLS, PALS. Staff nurse The Bklyn. Hosp., 1955-59, VA Hosp., Bklyn., 1955-60; asst. head nurse Anne Arundel Med. Ctr., Annapolis, Md., 1960-79, staff nurse, from 1979, post anesthesia care unit nurse, 1979-91, mem. nurse retention task force, 1983-85, mem. profl. nursing coun., 1987-89, mem. profl. peer rev. com., from 1990, patient care coord. Annapolis, Md., from 1991. JCAHO task force clin. nurse II program mgr. Career Tract, Boulder, Colo, 1987-93. Trustee Ballet Theatre of Annapolis, 1981-92, mem adv. bd. 1987-89, gen. mgr., v.p. 1987-91. Mem. NAFE, Am. Soc. Post Anesthesia Nurses, Va. Soc. Post Anesthesia Nurses, Md./D.C. Soc. Post Anesthesia Nurses, Nurse Practice Coun., Friendship Sqs. (Linthicum, Md., pres. 1981-82). Republican. Methodist. Home: Pasadena, Md. Died Apr. 15, 2008.

ENGLE, HOWARD AARON, retired pediatrician; b. Wis., Sept. 11, 1919; married; three children. BS, U. Wis., 1939, MS, 1941, MD, 1943. Diplomate Am. Bd. Pediatrics. Intern Michael Reese Hosp., Chgo., 1943, resident in pediatrics, 1943-44; pvt. practice Miami Beach, Fla., from 1947; assoc. clin. prof. U. Miami Sch. of Medicine, assoc. prof. pediatrics emeritus. Sr. cons., past chmn. dept. pediatrics, Mount Sinai Med. Ctr., Miami Beach; com. mem., operation newborn U. Miami Sch. of Medicine; instr. dept. pediatrics U. Fla. Sch. of Nursing; pediatric preceptor Fla. Internat. U. Sch. Nursing; sr. cons. pediatrics Mount Sinai Med. Ctr.; courtesy staff Miami Childrens Hosp.; sr. attending pediatrics Jackson Mem. Hosp.; cons. Fla. Atlantic U. Dept. Spl. Edn., neuropediatrics, Childrens Home Soc. of Fla.; cons., lectr. Dupont de Nemours Found., State Miss.; cons. pediatric neurology Hope Sch.; dir. Symposium Cerebral Palsy, Miami; med. rep. Symposia Cerebral Palsy, State of Tex.; lectr. in field. Contbr. articles to profl. jours. Com. mem. Edn. and Therapy for the Handicapped, Dade County Sch. Bd.; past med. dir. United Cerebral Palsy of Miami; cons. neuropediatrics United Cerebral Palsy of Fla.; past. mem. clin. adv. bd. United Cerebral Palsy; nat. del. World Commn. on Cerebral Palsy, Copenhagen, 1963; med. cons. divsn. exceptional student edn. Miami-Dade County Sch. Bd. Recipient Ralph Hawley award for 50 yrs. svc. to medicine and the cmty. U. Wis., 1993. Mem. Am. Acad. Pediat., Child Neurology Soc., Am. Acad. Cerebral Palsy (exec. com.), Am. Acad. Neurology, Am. Assn. on Mental Retardation, Am. Population and Reproduction Assn. (pres., founder), Fla. Rehab. Assn., Internat. Soc. for Rehab. of Crippled and Disabled, Am. Acad. Phys. Medicine and Rehab., Internat. Soc. for Cerebral Palsy, Internat. Child Neurology Assn. (assoc.), Japanese Soc. Child Neurology, Dade County Med. Assn., Fla. Med. Assn., Fla. Pediatric Soc., Miami Pediatric Soc. (past pres.), Southeastern Med. Assn., European Paediatric Neurology Soc., World Med. Assn., Internat. Population and Reproduction Com. (chmn. edn. programs, bd. dirs., past pres. 1981-82), Alpha Omega Alpha, Sigma Sigma. Home: Miami Beach, Fla. Died July 22, 2009.

ENGLUND, GAGE BUSH, dancer, educator; b. Birmingham, Ala., Sept. 7, 1931; d. Morris Williams and Margaret Wallace (Gage) Bush; m. Richard Bernard Englund, Dec. 1, 1959 (dec. 1991); children: Alixandra Gage, Rachel Rutherford. Student, Sch. Am. Ballet, 1960. Founder Birmingham Civic Ballet, 1952; mem. Robert Joffrey Ballet, NYC, 1957-60, soloist, 1959-60; mem. Am. Ballet Theatre, NYC, 1960-63, Huntington Dance Ensemble, LI, N.Y., 1968-69; soloist Dance Repertory Co., 1969-72; tchr. ballet, assoc. chmn. Friends of Am. Ballet Theatre, NYC, 1972—2009. Dir. Ala. By-Products Corp., 1971—77; rehearsal coach Am. Ballet Theatre II, 1973—85; mem. scholarship com. Am. Ballet Theatre Sch., NYC, 1974—2009; rehearsal coach Joffrey Ballet II, 1985—95, Am. Ballet Theatre Studio Co., 1995—2009. Trustee Ballet Theatre Found., 1974—87, v.p., 1980—81; trustee Chapin Sch., 1982—2003, Animal Med. Ctr., NYC, 1982—2009, Cancer Rsch. Inst., 1984—2009, Episcpoal Sch. N.Y., 1979—83; bd. dirs. Children's Hosp. Clinic, Birmingham, 1955—57, Spoleto Festival, U.S.A., 1980—83, Ala. State Ballet, from 1967, Birmingham Civic Ballet, 1952—67. Recipient Silver Bowl award, Birmingham Festival Arts, 1957, Lucia Chase award for svcs. to Am. Ballet Theatre, Soc. Fine Arts U. Ala., 2001, Patron of the Arts award, 2002; named Queen, Birmingham Festival Arts, 1957; Ford Found. scholar, 1960. Mem.: Am. Guild Mus. Artists, Jr. League N.Y.C., Colonial Dames Ala., Colony Club, Lakewood Country Club. Episcopalian. Home: Point Clear, Ala. Died Jan. 12, 2009.

ENNS, ANN WILSON, retired mathematics educator; b. Salem, NJ, Dec. 9, 1928; d. Merritt Bingham and Jennie (Flanegan) Wilson; m. John Frank Enns, June 25, 1983 (dec. June 1995); stepchildren: Susan Kristine, Stephen John. BS, Rutgers U., 1950; MEd, U. Del., 1955. Cert. tchr., supr., prin., N.J. Tchr. Salem City Bd. Edn., 1950-92, chmn. dept. math., 1955-92; ret., 1992. Moderator 1st Bapt. Ch., Salem, 1976-77, 2000-03, clk., 1984-89, pres. Women's Fellowship, 1988-99; pres. Am. Bapt. women's ministries West N.J. Bapt. Assn., 1996-2002. Grantee NSF, 1959-69. Mem. AAUW (pres. Salem County br. 1957-59), NEA, N.J. Edn. Assn., Salem City Tchrs. Assn. (pres. 1973-74), Assn. Math. Tchrs. N.J. (exec. coun. 1984-87), Nat. Coun. Tchrs. Math., Salem Women's Club (3d v.p., chmn. edn. and membership 1992-2002), Delta Kappa Gamma (pres. Beta chpt. 1986-88). Republican. Avocations: travel, stamp collecting/philately, photography, piano, organ. Home: Salem, NJ. Died Apr. 9, 2008.

ENSIGN, RUTH SINGLEY, artist; b. Tokyo, Apr. 22, 1923; parents Am. citizens; d. Dewees Franklin and Ada (Schlichter) S.; m. John Edward Ensign, Sept. 13, 1947; children: Jacqueline, Martha, Stephen, Josephine. BS in

Edn. with honors, BFA with honors, Temple U., 1946, MFA, 1947. Adj. prof. Presbyn. Sch. Christian Edn., Richmond, 1967-70, Va. Commonwealth U., Richmond, 1987-88, Va. State U., Petersburg, Va., 1988-89; artist in residence Henrico Pub. Schs., Highland Springs, Va., 1985-88. Numerous one-woman shows including Denler Gallery of Northwestern Coll., St. Paul, Minn., 1999; group exhbns. include Phila. Print Club, Libr. Congress Print Exhbn., Smithsonian Inst., Va. Mus. Fine Arts, Women's Contemporary Art Winston-Salem, N.C., Hunterdon Nat. Print Anns.,Clinton, N.J., Montgomery (Ala.), Mus. Fine Arts (purchase prizes) Mus. Fine Arts, Richmond, Traveling Exhbns., Valentine Mus., Richmond, Somerhill Gallery, Chapel Hill, N.C., Schoolhouse Gallery, Sanibel, Fla., Duck Blind Ltd., Kitty Hawk, N.C., Greenleaf Gallery Mother-Dau. Printmaking, Nag's Head, N.C., 1996, Eight Fine Art Printmakers, 2004, Addison Gallery, Bonita Springs, Fl., 2005, others; exhbns. Greenleaf Gallery, Duck, N.C., Sanibel Gallery, Fla., Little Art Gallery, Raleigh, N.C., Addison Gallery, Bonita Springs, Fla.; represented in permanent collections including Philip Morris Corp., Federal Reserve Bank, NIH, Colonial Williamsburg Motor Lodge; author: Camping Together as Christians, 1958, Make that Story Live, 1964; subject of film: Nature's Poet of Vision, 1989 Elder Presbyn. Ch. BLAI fellow Temple U., 1945. Mem. Richmond Artists Assn. (pres. 1966). Deceased.

EPSTEIN, FRANKLIN HAROLD, internist, educator; b. Bklyn., May 5, 1924; s. Max and Fannie (Geduld) E.; m. Sherrie Spivack, Aug. 12, 1951; children: Mark, Ann, Sara, Jonathan. BA, Bklyn. Coll., 1944; MD, Yale U., 1947; Doctor Honoris Causa, Med. Acad., Gdansk, 1992. Diplomate: Am. Bd. Internal Medicine (chmn. subsplty. bd. in nephrology 1969-72). Asst. prof. medicine Yale U., 1954-59, assoc. prof., 1959-66, prof. medicine, 1966-72, chief, divsn. metabolism, 1965-72; prof. medicine Harvard U., from 1972, H.L. Blumgart prof. medicine, W. Applebaum prof. medicine; dir. Thorndike Meml. Lab., Boston City Hosp., 1972; physician-in-chief Beth Israel Hosp., 1973-80, dir. renal divsn., 1980-93; Macy Found. fellow and vis. scientist Oxford (Eng.) U., 1980-81. Cons. to surgeon gen. U.S. Army, 1964-80; mem. metabolism study sect. USPHS, 1962-66; pres. Mt. Desert Island Biol.Lab., 1986-95. Editor: Yearbook of Medicine, 1967-96; assoc. editor: Jour. Clin. Investigation, 1957-62, New Eng. Jour. Medicine, 1982-2001, Quar. Jour. Medicine, 1984-93; contbr. papers, book chpts. on renal physiology, disease of kidneys. Capt. M.C., U.S. Army, 1950-53. Recipient Rsch. Career award, USPHS, 1964, John P. Peters award, Am. Soc. Nephrology, 1985, Bywaters award, Internat. Soc. Nephrology, 1999, David Hume award, Nat. Kidney Found., 2003, Gibbs award, NY Acad. Medicine, 2007. Fellow AAAS, Assn. Physicians Gt. Britain and Ireland, Royal Coll. Physicians; mem. Am. Soc. Clin. Investigation (v.p. 1970), Assn. Am. Physicians, Interurban Clin. Club, Sigma Xi, Alpha Omega Alpha. Jewish. Home: Brookline, Mass. Died Nov. 5, 2008.

ERB, JOHN EDWARD, lawyer; b. Marietta, Ohio, Aug. 4, 1944; s. Ernest Edward and Edith Lucille (Hall) E.; m. Dorothy Jean Caulkins, June 11, 1977; children: Cynthia, Eric, Andrea, Jared. BSBA, Ohio State U., 1966, JD, 1968. Ptnr. Theisen, Brock, Frye, Erb and Leeper Co. LPA, Marietta, Ohio, from 1972. Mem. Marietta Civil Svc. Com., Marietta, 1986—, chmn., 1999—; mem. Washington County Childrens Svcs. Bd., Marietta, 1986—, pres., 1999. Mem. ABA, Washington County Bar Assn., Ohio Bar Assn. Avocations: golf, gardening. Home: Marietta, Ohio. Died Apr. 29, 2008.

ERICKSON, DAVID JAMES, steel distributor executive; b. Eau Claire, Wis., Dec. 14, 1949; s. Harold Jerome and Gladys Eileen (Gynnild) E.; m. Jennifer Jo Blodgett, Jan. 20, 1972; children: Tracy John, Mark Owen, Jonathan David. BS in Sociology, BS in Bus., U. Wis., 1977, postgrad., 1978. Pres. Sagittario Imports, Aspen, Colo., 1972-75; v.p., gen. mgr. Wausau (Wis.) Steel Corp., 1978-90; pres., chief exec. officer Badger Steel Products Inc., Edgerton, Wis., from 1990; pres., chief exec.officer Badger Coated Products, Inc., Waunakee, Wis., from 1991. Organizer, mgr. United Way of Marathon County, Wausau, 1985-89; bd. dirs. Boy Scouts Am., Wausau, 1981-83. Mem. Assn. Steel Distrs., Cen. Wis. Purchasing Assn. Avocations: skiing, golf, curling, sailing, travel. Died July 19, 2008.

ERIKSON, G(EORGE) E(MIL) (ERIK ERIKSON), information specialist, anatomist, archivist, science historian; b. Palmer, Mass., May 3, 1920; s. Emil and Sofia (Gustafson) Erikson; m. Suzanne J. Henderson, Apr. 23, 1950; children: Ann, David, John, Thomas. BS, U. Mass., 1941; MA in Biology, Harvard U., 1946, PhD in Biology, 1948. Reader in history of sci. and learning Harvard U., 1943—45, asst. prof. gen. edn. in biology, 1949—52, lectr. anthropology, 1965; instr. anatomy Harvard Med. Sch., 1947—49, rsch. fellow anatomy, 1949—52, assoc. in anatomy, 1952—55, asst. prof. anatomy, 1955—65, assoc. curator Warren Anat. Mus., 1961—65; prof. med. sci. Brown U., Providence, 1965—90, chmn. sect. morphology, 1968—85, co-chmn. sect. population biology, morphology & genetics and chmn. for anatomy, 1985—90, prof. emeritus, from 1990; vis. prof., Dept. Anatomy and Cellular Biology Harvard U. Med. Sch., 1990—91; vis. lectr. in surgery Med. Sch. Harvard U., 1990—99; anatomist dept. surgery Mass. Gen. Hosp., Boston, 1990—2004; pres. Erikson Biog. Inst., Inc., Providence, from 1990. Adv. bd. Reed Elsevier, 1990; anatomist various Boston Hosps., 1952—82, Mass. Gen. Hosp. Sch. Med. Illus., 1947—60, Mass. Gen. Hosp., from 1990, Lahey Clinic, Boston, 1947—60; anatomist depts. surgery, orthopedics, rehab. and neurosurgery R.I. Hosp., from 1967; cons. anatomist Surg. Techniques Illus., 1976—80; cons. Dorlands Illus. Med. Dictionary, Rockefeller Found. med. and pub. health, S. Am., 1949; specialist State Dept., Brazil, 1962; adj. mem. faculty R.I. Sch. Design, from 1970; Kate Hurd Mead lectr. Coll. Physicians Phila., 1977; Raymond C. Truex lectr. Hahnemann U. Sch. Med., 1985. Fellow Sheldon Traveling, Harvard Ctrl. Am., 1946, Guggenheim, S. Am., 1949, Fulbright, Brazil, 1962. Mem.: Assn. of Anatomy Chairmen (emeritus), Oral History Medicine, Am. Assn. History Medicine (coun. 1972—74), Am. Assn. Anatomists (historian and archivist 1972—86, archivist 1986—90, historian and archivist from 1990), Am. Assn. Phys. Anthropologists (archivist and co-historian from 1981), History Sci. Soc. (life), Alpha Omega Alpha Honor Med. Soc. (faculty election 1957). Achievements include research in new world primates and gen. intellectual history, especially biology and medicine; development of of database foundation of Erikson Biographical Institute, 1990, with database of 450,000 individuals. Home: Norton, Mass. Died Jan. 15, 2009.

ESKOWITZ, LEONARD IRVING, English and American literature educator; b. Boston, June 28, 1948; s. William and Bertha (Lipkind) E.; m. Evelyn Josephine Dorosz, June 2, 1978; 1 child, Michael Morris. MA, U. Wis., 1973, ABD, 1973-75. Cert. secondary English, history and social studies tchr., Mass., Maine. Tchr. mid. sch. Westbrook (Mass.) Pub. Schs., 1979-80; coord. exch. student program E.F. Inst., Portland, Maine, 1980; tchr. high sch. Somerville (Mass.) Pub. Schs., 1980-81; survey processor, editor ABT Assocs., Cambridge, Mass., 1985-90; acad. support tutor Middlesex Community Coll., Lowell, Mass., 1990-91; instr. Mt. Wachusetts Community Coll., Gardner, Mass., from 1992. Participant Seeing New Eng. Conf., U. So. Maine, Portland, 1980; vol. tchr. Eastern Mass. Literacy Coun., Lexington, 1990-93. Author: (monograph) The Shaping of Typee, 1986; author poetry. Travelli fellow Clark U., 1968-71. Mem. MLA, Am. Acad. Poetry, Worcester (Mass.) County Poetry Assn. (awards 1984, 90), Ind. Scholars in Lang. and Lit., New Eng. Poetry Club. Avocations: painting, photography, architecture, basketball, baseball. Home: Boston, Mass. Died May 3, 2008.

ESPOSITO, JOSEPH ANTHONY, lawyer; b. Spokane, Wash., Oct. 4, 1941; s. Charles Esposito and Angela (Migliuri) E.; m. Joyce A. Chastek, July 7, 1966; children: Kate, Molly, Jill, Sara, Amy. BBA, Gonzaga U., Spokane, Wash., 1963, JD, 1969. Bar: Wash., U.S. Dist. Ct. Wash., U.S. Ct. Appeals (9th cir.). Law clk. to presiding justice Wash. State Ct. Appeals, Spokane, 1969-70; lawyer in prin. Dellwo, Rudolph and Grant, Spokane, 1970-73; ptnr. Trezona Lorenz and Esposito, Spokane, 1973-85; prin. Esposito, Tombari and George, Spokane, from 1985. Trustee St. Joseph's Children's Home, Spokane, 1970-85, Gonzaga Preparatory Sch., 1982-88; legal counsel, bd. dirs. Spokane Jr. C. of C., 1969-75; bd. dirs. Spokane Legal Svcs. Bd., 1970-75. Recipient svc. award Spokane Jr. C. of C., 1973. Mem.: Wash. Bar Assn., Rotary, Manito Golf and Country Club. Roman Catholic. Avocations: golf, fly fishing, hunting. Home: Spokane, Wash. Died May 30, 2008.

ESTAVILLO, WILLIAM, mineralogist, museum official, exhibits consultant; b. Paris, Jan. 9, 1946; (parents Am. citizens); s. Robert and Paulette B. (LeMarchand) E.; m. Victoria E. Larriva, Nov. 14, 1987. AA, Grossmont Coll., El Cajon, Calif., 1966; BS in Geology, San Diego state U., 1972; cert. audio engr., Del Mar Communications Ctr., 1985; grad., La Jolla Acad. Advt. and Art, 1987. Data analyst Naval Undersea R & D Ctr., San Diego, 1968-70; chmn. mineralogy dept. Calif. Acad. Scis., San Francisco, 1974-79; sci. edn. cons., San Diego, 1979-86; producer community TV Sta., Del Mar, Calif., 1983-86; chmn. dept. mineralogy San Diego Natural History Mus., from 1986, co-editor Trans., from 1986. Lectr. in field, 1975—, co-pi NSF, Interactive Sci. Exhibits, 1987-91; earth sci. capt. San Diego County Sci. Olympiad, 1990; freelance photographer, 1964—; teaching asst. San Diego State U., 1963-72; rsch. participant NSF, Baja California, Mex., 1969; columnist Nature Trails, photographer Star News, Chula Vista, Calif., 1972; tchr. earth sci. Elem. Inst. Sci., San Diego, 1973, San Diego Outdoor Edn. Dept., 1983; mem. mineral mus. adv. coun. 1976—. Author: Gems and Minerals of California, 1992; contbr. articles to profl. jours. Bd. dirs., corr. sec. So. Calif. sect. Friends of Mineralogy. Mem. Mineral. Soc. Am., Geol. Soc. Am., Internat. Platform Assn., San Diego Mineral and Gem Soc. (hon.). Home: Prescott, Ariz. Died Nov. 16, 2007.

ESTEP, SARAH VIRGINIA, association executive; b. Altoona, Pa., Mar. 1, 1926; d. Benner Marshal and Helen Rebecca (Sellers) Wilson; m. Charles Sheldon Estep, Apr. 12, 1952; children: Cynthia Jane, Rebecca Anne, Robert Wilson. BA, Mary Washington U., Fredericksburg, Va., 1947. Social worker Blair County Childrens's Aid Soc., Altoona, Pa., 1947-52; tchr. Anne Arundel Bd. Edn., Annapolis, Md., 1952-75; pvt. camp dir. Hartford County, Md., summer 1963; camp dir. Girl Scouts of Cen. Md., Balt., summer 1964; dir. camping Camp Fire Girls Md., Balt., 1966-67; founder, dir. Am. Assn. Electronic Voice Phenomena, Severna Park, Md., 1982-2000. Cons. in field; lectr. in field; conductor workshops in field. Author: Voices of Eternity, 1988; editor/pub. quar. newsletter, AA-EVP News, 1982; contbr. articles to profl. jours. Recipient Dr. A. Hedri prize for Epipsychology, 1996, Epipsychology award Swiss Found. for Parapsychology, 1996, Berne. Avocations: reading, music, electronics, travel. Died Jan. 3, 2008.

ESTES, EDWARD RICHARD, JR., engineer, consultant, retired educator; b. Richmond, Va., Mar. 2, 1925; s. Edward Richard Sr. and Mamie Cleveland (Bugg) E.; m. Elizabeth Hood Lee, Oct. 28, 1950; children: Virginia Lee Zimmerman, Susan Page, Edward Richard III, Elizabeth Anne, William Thomas. B in Engring., Tulane U., 1945; MS, Va. Polytech. Inst., 1948. Structural engr. Baskerville & Son, Richmond, 1947-48; asst. prof. Sch. Engring. U. Va., Charlottesville, 1948-55; rsch. engr. Am. Inst. Steel Constrn., NYC, 1955-60; dir. engring. Fla. Steel Corp., Tampa, 1960-66; dir. engring. dept. Montague-Betts Co., Lynchburg, Va., 1966-68; chief rsch. engr. Am. Iron & Steel Inst., NYC, 1968-69; engring. mgr. Rep. Steel Corp., Youngstown, Ohio, 1969-72; cons. engr. Estes & Assocs., Youngstown, 1972-78, Norfolk, Va., from 1978; prof. Old Dominion U., Norfolk, 1978-94, prof. emeritus, 1994, chmn. civil engring. tech. dept., 1978-84, assoc. dean coll. engring. and tech., 1984-88. Tech. cons. Nat. Assn. Archtl. Metal Mfrs., from 1991. Contbr. articles to profl. jours. With USNR, 1943—46. Fellow ASTM (award of merit 2000), ASCE (pres. Norfolk chpt. 1983-84); mem. Am. Welding Soc. (disting., sect. chmn. 1986-87, A.F. Davis Silver medal 1964), Am. Iron and Steel Inst. (specification com.), Rsch. Coun. on Structural Connections (chmn. 1974-79), Norfolk Yacht and Country Club, Rotary. Republican. Methodist. Avocations: golf, tennis. Died Mar. 30, 2008.

ESTILETTE, FELIX FRANCIS, retired designer, consultant; b. New Iberia, La., Apr. 14, 1928; s. Grady Francis and Eula Mary (Vincent) E.; m. Barbara Lee Thurmond, June 19, 1948; children: Barbara Ann, Felix Jr., Darrell, Stacey, Dayne. Attended, South La. Inst., 1944-46. Drill stem dresser Am. Iron Works, New Iberia, 1948-50; flagman Seaboard Rlwy., Abbeville, S.C., 1950-51; wireline helper Tuboscope, Inc., Houma, Harvey, New Iberia, La., 1951-53; wireline operator Camco, Inc., Lafayette, Buras, La., 1953-63; owner Lower Coast Wireline, Buras, 1963-73; dist. mgr. Camco Internat., 1973-92. Seaman 1st class USN, 1946-48. Democrat. Roman Catholic. Achievements include patent for wireline tension jar. Died Sept. 6, 2007.

EVANS, EMORY GIBBONS, history professor; b. Richmond, Va., Jan. 21, 1928; s. Wallace R. and Margaret (Strickl) E.; m. Winifred Burton, Dec. 19, 1953; children— Jeffrey, Christopher, Philip. BA, Randolph-Macon Coll., 1950; MA, U. Va., 1954; PhD, 1957. Instr. Darlington Sch., Rome, Ga., 1950-52, U. Pitts., 1958-60, asst. prof. history, 1960-64; instr. U. Md., College Park, 1956-58, prof., 1976—96, chmn. dept. history, 1976-86; assoc. prof. No. Ill. U., DeKalb, 1964-68, prof., 1968—76, chmn. history dept., 1964-74, acting v.p., provost, 1975-76. Vis. prof. U. Va., Charlottesville, 1969-70 Author: Thomas Nelson of Yorktown: Revolutionary Virginian, 1975, A Topping People: The Rise and Decline of Virginia's Old Political Elite, 1680-1790, 2009 Served with AUS, 1946. Recipient grants-in-aid, summers; Am. Philos. Soc., 1959, 64; Colonial Williamsburg, Inc., 1959, 60, 61, 62, 64 Mem. AAUP, Am. Hist. Soc., Orgn. Am. Historians, So. Hist. Assn., Va., Md. Hist. Socs., Inst. Early Am. History and Culture (coun. 1991—). Home: Beltsville, Md. Died Sept. 20, 2009.

EVANS, GEORGE LEONARD, microbiologist; b. Wilkes-Barre, Pa., Aug. 3, 1931; s. George Leonard and Anna M. (Check) E.; m. Joan Marie Snyder, Feb. 8, 1958; children: Paula Jean, Gregory Allen, Christopher Thomas. BS, King's Coll., 1954; MS, Fordham U., 1957; PhD, Temple U., 1962. Specialist microbiologist Am. Acad. Microbiology. Sr. scientist Warner-Lambert Pharm. Co., Morris Plains, N.J., 1961-64; rsch. virologist Univ. Labs., Inc., Highland Park, N.J., 1964-65; group chief Hoffmann-La Roche, Inc., Nutley, N.J., 1965-70; dir. diagnostic rsch. Schering Corp., Bloomfield, N.J., 1970-75; rsch. fellow Becton Dickinson & Co., Hunt Valley, Md., from 1975. Chmn., advisor subcom. Nat. Com. Clin. Lab. Standards, Wayne, Pa., 1980—. Contbr. articles to Jour. Immunology, Jour. Reticuloendothelial Soc., Jour. Bacteriology, Am. Jour. Med. Tech., Jour. Clin. Microbiology. Mem. Am. Soc. Microbiology, Am. Assn. Clin. Chemistry. Achievements include 10 patents for Process for Preparation of a Soluble Bacterial Extract, Diagnostic Preparation and Process for Detection of Acetylmethylcarbinol, Paper Strip Test for Citrate Utilization, Colorimetric Method for Determining Iron in Blood, Growth Inhibition of Selected Mycoplasmas, Polyanionic Compounds in Culture Media, Novel Diagnostic System for Differentiation of Enterobacteriaceae, Diagnostic Test for Determination of Sickling Hemoglobinopathies, Serologic Test for Systemic Candidiasis, Selective Medium for Growth of Neisseria. Died Feb. 11, 2008.

EVANS, HERBERT DAVID, evangelist; b. Stockton, Calif., Apr. 27, 1944; s. Audie and Grace Mozell (Lewis) E.; m. Janis Elaine Bush, Nov. 7, 1964; children: Tina Elaine Evans Cook, Fredrick Douglas. Student, Preston Rd. Sch. Preaching, Dallas, 1977. Preacher Ch. of Christ, Elkhart, Tex., 1977-79, Diboll, Tex., from 1979. Instr. South Meadows Nursing Home, Diboll, 1979—, Ron Willinham Courses, Diboll, 1978—. With U.S. Army. 1961-64. Mem. Rotary (treas. 1990—). Home: Waco, Tex. Died Feb. 1, 2008.

EVANS, JAMES WILLIAM, lawyer; b. Taylor, Pa., Mar. 27, 1926; s. Alvin R. and Irene C. (Vonderhey) E.; m. Pamela Burr, Aug. 25, 1951 (dec. Mar. 1988); children: James W. Jr., Jeffrey B., Beth Evans Davis., Andrew T. BA, Dickinson Coll., 1951, JD, 1953. Bar: Pa. 1954, U.S. Dist. Ct. (mid. dist.) Pa., U.S. Ct. Appeals (3d cir.), U.S. Supreme Ct. Sr. ptnr. Goldberg, Evans & Katzman, Harrisburg, Pa., 1960-85; ptnr. Mette, Evans & Woodside, Harrisburg, from 1985. Mem. adv. com. U.S. Dist. Ct. (mid. dist.) Pa.; chief counsel Pa. Pub. Sch. Bldg. Authority. Pres. Harrisburg Sch. Dist., 1964-67; chmn. Greater Harrisburg Movement, 1971-76; founding trustee, chmn. bd. trustees Harrisburg Area Community Coll., 1964-90, mem. adv. com. Capitol Campus, Pa. State U.; 1st pres. Harristown Devel. Corp.; elder Presbyn. Ch., Harrisburg. With USMCR, 1942-46. Recipient award Gov. of Pa., 1978, Humanitarian award Am. Cancer Soc., 1983. Mem. ABA, Pa. Bar Assn. (civil litigation council, chmn. med.-legal com. 1982-84), Dauphin County Bar Assn. (chmn. interprofl. relations com., pres. 1978), Am. Coll. Trial Lawyers, Pa. Trial Lawyers Assn., Fedn. Ins. Counsel, Am. Soc. Law and Medicine, Marine Corps League, West Shore Country Club, Masons. Home: Harrisburg, Pa. Died July 28, 2008.

EVANS, MARY ANN, county administrator; b. Marion, Va., Feb. 22, 1942; d. Joseph Emory and Ruth Hazel (Burnop) Cress; m. Robert C. Evans, Feb. 29, 1970; children: Michael, Steven, Jill. AS, Marion Coll., 1962. Cashier Roses, Marion, 1960-62; sec. Dr. Pepper Bottling Co., Marion, 1962-71; sec. then asst. county adminstr. County of Smyth, from 1971. Mem. Profl. Secs. Internat. Avocation: reading. Home: Atkins, Va. Died Oct. 28, 2007.

EVANS, MICHAEL DAVID, mechanical engineer; b. Middlesboro, Ky., Oct. 18, 1957; s. Claude Gerald and Betty Jo (Welch) E.; m. Rhonda Renee Evans, Aug. 28, 1982; children: Michael D. Jr., Dustin Dwight. AA, N.W. Miss. Community Coll., 1976; postgrad., Miss. State U., 1976-78; BS in Engring. Mgmt., Calif. Coast U., 1991. Designer Econ Labs., Memphis, Tenn., 1978-79; designer elevator div. Dover Corp., Horn Lake, Miss., 1979-80; engring. tech. Azo Inc., Memphis, 1980-83, design supr., 1983-85, project engr., 1985-88, sales engring. mgr., from 1988. Mem. Soc. Mfg. Engrs., Soc. Plastic Engrs., Internat. Soc. Pharm. Engrs. Home: Olive Branch, Miss. Died May 23, 2008.

EVDOKIMOVA, EVA, prima ballerina assoluta, director, producer, consultant, actress; b. Geneva, Dec. 1, 1948; parents Am. citizens; m. Michael S. Gregori, 1982. Student, Munich State Opera Ballet Sch., Royal Ballet Sch., London; studied privately with Maria Fay (London), Vera Volkova (Copenhagen), Natalia Dudinskaya (Leningrad), 1964-66; student in Music Studies, Guild Hall Sch. Music, London, 1964—66; student in Drama Studies, H.B. Studio, NYC, 1997—2000. Pres. of jury Rudolf Nureyev Internat. Ballet Competition, Budapest, 1994, 96, 98; chm. Jury Varna Internat. Ballet Competition, Bulgaria, 1996; ballet mistress Boston Ballet, 2002-03; ballet coach; drama performances 5 off offBroadway drama prodns., 1997-2002; contemporary dance performances created for her by Igal Perry, Henning Rübsam, Angela Jones; simultaneous translation and interpretation between English, French, German, Russian, Italian, Danish. Latin Studies. Debut Royal Danish Ballet, Copenhagen, 1966; Prima Ballerina Assoluta, Deutsche Oper Berlin, 1969-90; frequent guest artist with numerous major ballet cos. worldwide including London Festival Ballet, English Nat. Ballet, Am. Ballet Theatre, Paris Opera Ballet, La Scala, Kirov Ballet, Tokyo Ballet, Teatro Colon, Nat. Ballet of Can., Stuttgart Ballet, Royal Danish Ballet, and all other major nat. ballet cos.; premiered roles in Rudolf Nureyev's classical ballet prodns., ptnr., 1971-86; appeared in over 16 classical and modern ballets with Rudolf Nureyev across the world; repertoire of more than 130 roles includes Swan Lake, Giselle, La Sylphide, Sleeping Beauty, Romeo and Juliet, Don Quixote, La Bayadere, Onegin, Raymonda; created roles in many contemporary ballets for stage, film and TV; film appearances include The Nutcracker, La Sylphide, Cinderella, A Family Portrait, The Romantic Era, Invitation to the Dance, Portrait of Eva Evdokimova, and others. Recipient Diploma, Internat. Ballet Competition, Moscow, 1969; winner Gold medal Varna Internat. Ballet competition, 1970; awarded title Prima Ballerina Assoluta, Berlin Senate, 1973, Berlin Critic's Prize, 1974; first fgn. mem. Royal Danish Ballet, first Am. and Westerner to win any internat. ballet competition, first Am. to perform with Kirov Ballet, 1976, first Am. to perform in Peking after the Cultural Revolution, 1978, first and only Am. dancer with portrait in permanent collection, Mus. Drama and Dance, Leningrad, St. Petersburg, Russia, only Am. performer ever to be honored in a German opera house, Grand Défilé ceremony, 1990 Deutsche Oper Berlin; recipient letter for meritorious svc. from Pres. Bush, 1990, numerous other awards; holder world record for 67 curtain calls with 40 minute standing ovation, Berlin, 1990. Achievements include world record performing in two different Giselles, two full length Prokofiev Ballets and eight other works with three companies; at Lincoln Center, New York, in three debuts with three different companies within a three month period. Home: New York, NY. Died Apr. 3, 2009.

EVERETT, ROBINSON OSCAR, federal judge, educator; b. Durham, NC, Mar. 18, 1928; s. Reuben Oscar and Kathrine McDiarmid (Robinson) E.; m. Linda Moore McGregor, Aug. 27, 1966; children: Robinson Oscar Jr., James Douglas McGregor, Lewis Moore AB magna cum laude, Harvard U., 1947, JD magna cum laude, 1950; LL.M., Duke U., 1959. Bar: N.C. 1950, D.C. 1954. Prof. law Duke U. Law Sch., Durham, NC, 1950—51, 1956—2009, founder, Ctr. on Law, Ethics and Nat. Security, 1993—2009; commr. U.S. Ct. Mil. Appeals, Washington, 1953-55; chief judge US Ct. Appeals for the Armed Forces, Washington, 1980-90, judge, 1990—92, sr. judge, 1992—2009; practice law Durham, 1955-80. Councilor N.C. State Bar Council, 1978-83; pres., dir. Triangle Telecasters, Durham, 1966-77. Author: Military Justice, 1956; assoc. editor Law and Contemporary Problems, 1950-51, 56-66; contbr. articles to legal jours. Chair, Durham Redevel. Commn., 1959-75. Served as 1st lt. USAF, 1951-53; to col. Res. (ret.) Recipient Judge John J. Parker award, NC Bar Assn., 2004; named to Assn. Gen. Practice Hall of Fame, 2006. Mem. Am. Law Inst. (life), Conf. Commrs. Uniform State Laws (life), Durham Bar Assn. (pres. 1976-77). Democrat. Presbyterian. Died June 12, 2009.

EVERHART, LEON EUGENE, retired career officer; b. Abilene, Kans., Jan. 14, 1928; s. Charles Francis and Florence Etta (Amess) E. BS with distinction, Ariz. State U., 1957; postgrad., U. Tenn., 1965. Commd. 2d lt. USAF, 1952, advanced through grades to col., 1970, ops. officer Berlin Air Safety Ctr., 1961-63, project officer Missile Devel. Ctr. Holloman AFB, N.Mex., 1963-65, chief spl. projects div. Missile Devel. Ctr., 1965-66, tactical fighter pilot, flight commander South Vietnam, 1967-68, system program dir. Aero. Systems Div. Wright Patterson AFB, Ohio, 1968-72, dir. test engring. Devel. and Test Ctr. Eglin AFB, Fla., 1973-78, comdr. Air Force Western Test Range Vandenberg AFB, Calif., 1978-82, ret., 1982. Cons. in field. Speaker on big-game hunting in Africa and wildlife conservation for various civic and ednl. orgns. Mem. Amateur Trapshooting Assn. Ohio, NRA. Avocations: golf, trapshooting, big-game hunting, deep-sea fishing. Home: Santa Maria, Calif. Died June 21, 2008.

EVERT, JOHN ANDREW, JR., surgeon; b. Brainerd, Minn., Oct. 31, 1917; s. John A. and Pearl Alma (Nash) E.; m. Nora Staael, May 10, 1980. BS, Haverford Coll., Pa., 1938; MD, Harvard U., 1942; MS in Surgery, U. Minn., 1946. Diplomate Am. Bd. Surgery. Pvt. practice surgery, St. Paul, 1947-53, Missoula, Mont., from 1955. Dir. Health Svc. Assn., St. Paul, 1975-90. Chmn. Montpac, Mont., 1962-64.Capt. U.S. Army 1953-55. Fellow in Surgery Mayo Found., Rochester, N.Y., 1943-46. Fellow ACS; mem. Am. Soc. Colon and Rectal Surgeons (assoc. fellow), Western Mont. Med. Soc. Avocations: sports, nature, skiing. Home: Missoula, Mont. Died Mar. 2, 2008.

EWING, BLAIR GORDON, retired federal official; b. Kans. City, Mo., Dec. 3, 1933; s. Lynn Moore and Margaret (Blair) E.; m. Barbara F. Thompson, Jan. 3, 1959 (div. Nov. 1991); children: Blair Gordon, Chatham Boyd; m. Martha L. Brockway, Apr. 30, 1994. AB, U. Mo., 1954; postgrad., U. Bonn, Germany, 1957—58; AM, U. Chgo., 1960. Reporter Chgo. City News Bur., 1958-59, UPI, 1959-60, Traffic World Mag., 1960-61; instr. polit. sci. Chgo. City Jr. Coll., 1961-62, SUNY, Binghamton, 1962-67; planning and mgmt. cons. Harold Wise and Assocs., Washington, 1967-69; program analyst Office of Asst. Sec. US Dept. Health Edn. & Welfare, Washington, 1969-70; dir. criminal justice planning DC Govt., 1970-72; dir. dept. pub. safety Met. Washington Coun. Govts., 1972-74; dir. planning & evaluation divsn. US Dept. Justice, Washington, 1974—76, dep. dir. Nat. Inst. Law Enforcement & Criminal Justice, 1976—77, acting dir., 1977—79. U.S. Office Pers. Mgmt., asst. dir., 1979-81, dep. dir., 1981-83; sr. exec. U.S. Office Mgmt. and Budget, 1983-86; dir. Mgmt. Improvement, Dept. Def., 1986-98; adj. prof. Law Ctr., Georgetown U., 1971-74; coll tchr. Montgomery Coll., Md., 2003-09. Author: Peace Through Negotiation: The Austrian State Treaty, 1966; contbr. articles to profl. jours. Active Montgomery County Human Rels. Commn., Md., 1975-76, Montgomery County Bd. Edn., 1976-98, pres., 1982-83, 90-91; coun. mem. Montgomery County, 1998-2002 pres., 2000-01; mem. Md. State Bd. Edn., 2007-09, v.p., 2008-09, With US Army, 1954-56. Recipient Disting. Svc. award Office Pers. Mgmt., 1981, U.S. Dept. Def. Disting. Civil Svc. award, 1990, Presdl. Rank award Meritorious Sr. Exec., 1990; Rotary Found. fellow U. Bonn, 1957-58; Woodrow Wilson fellow, 1956-57. Mem. Phi Beta Kappa. Democrat. Died June 29, 2009.

EXLER, SAMUEL, retired advertising executive, writer; b. Bklyn., July 7, 1922; s. Harry and Regina Exler; m. Florence Schoenbaum, June 20, 1948 (div. 1976); children: Judith Nora, Harriet Elizabeth. BA, Bklyn. Coll., 1943. With advt. agencies, NYC. Author: (children's book) Growing and Changing, 1957, (poetry book) Ambition, Fertility, Loneliness, 1982; contbr. poems to lit. mags. and anthologies. Pvt. 1st class infantry US Army, 1942—45, ETO. Decorated Bronze Star U.S. Army, ETO Ribbon with 3 battle stars. Home: Philadelphia, Pa. Died Apr. 20, 2008.

EYE, WILLIAM GLENN, industrial executive; b. Clarkfield, Minn., Oct. 4, 1944; s. Alvin Theodore and Agness (Carlson) E.; m. Marilyn Jane Strecker, Nov. 28, 1965; children: Mike, James, Kris. AA, Brainerd (Minn.) State Coll., 1974. Surveyor Cons. Engring. Diversified, Osseo, Minn., 1965-66, office mgr. constrn. div., 1966-72, chief insp., 1972-73; mgr. trainee fishing tackle div. Ray-O-Vac, Isle, Minn., 1973-75, plant mgr., 1975-76, dir. mfg., 1976-78; owner, pres. Merit Enterprises, Inc., Isle, from 1978; v.p. Minn. Precision Plastics, Wyoming, from 1990. Treas. Metro, Inc., Cross Lake, Minn., 1987—; bd. dirs. Community Devel. Corp., Onamia, Minn. Scoutmaster Boy Scouts Am., Isle, 1975; treas. Isle Civic Assn., 1982. With U.S. Army, 1963-64. Recipient Disting. Service award Ducks Unltd., 1982. Mem. Am. Electroplaters Soc., Sportsmans Club, Lions (bd. dirs. Isle chpt. 1986—) Lutheran. Avocations: fishing, hunting, photography. Home: Wahkon, Minn. Died July 13, 2008.

EZEIKE, GABRIEL O.I., agricultural engineering educator; b. Nanka, Anambra, Nigeria, Mar. 3, 1944; came to U.S., 1995; permanent resident; s. Ezekiel Nwankwo and Adeline Nwama (Ezechigbo) E.; m. Sandra Kodilichukwu Ugokwe, Mar. 29, 1975; children: Richard, Brian, Darlene, Audrey, David. BS in Agrl. Engring., U. Nigeria, 1973; MS in Agrl. Engring., U. Guelph, Ont., Can., 1976; PhD in Agrl. Engring., U. Guelph, 1978. Profl. engr., Coun. for the Regulation of Engring. in Nigeria. Jr. rsch. fellow U. Nigeria, Nsukka, 1973-74, lectr. II, 1978-80, lectr. I, 1980-82, sr. lectr., 1982-85, reader, 1985-88, prof., from 1988; tchg./rsch. asst. U. Guelph, 1976-78; vis. rsch. scientist U. Ga., Athens, from 1995. Mem. editl. bd. Internat. Agrophysics, Budapest, Hungary, 1988-92; editor Jour. Agrl. Engring. and Tech., NCAM, Ilorin, Nigeria, 1992—; assoc. dean engring. U. Nigeria, 1989-90; head agrl. engring. dept. U. Nigeria, 1990-93; chmn. consultancy mgmt. U. Nigeria, 1992-95; co-dir. CIDA-TUNS-UNN Linkage Project U. Nigeria, 1990-93; chmn. NUC accreditation Ahmadu Bello U., Zaria, Nigeria, 1992; internat. accreditation team Kaduna (Nigeria) Poly. U., 1982; Nigerian counterpart to FAO on strategic grain reserve project Fed. Govt.; external examiner Fed. U. Tech., Owerri, Nigeria, 1993-95, Rivers State U. Sci. & Tech., Port Harcourt, 1990-93, Amadu Bello U., Zaria, Nigeria, 1990-92, Anambra Polytech., Oko, Anambra State, Nigeria, 1988-90, Coll. Tech., Owerri, 1984-87. Editor: (book) Book of Inventions and Creative Works, 1986; editor Univ. Nigeria Press; invented triple-pass solar collector, 1986; designer software on crop drying, storage design and heat and mass transfer. Recipient Gold medal West African Univs. Games, Silver medal Nigerian Univs. Games, Nat. Victor Ludorum trophy. Fellow Nigerian Soc. Agrl. Engrs. (nat. sec. 1980-82), Am. Soc. Agrl. Engrs. (editl. reviewer 1996), Internat. Soc. Tropical Root Crops, Can. Soc. Agrl. Engrs., Nigerian Soc. Engrs., Inst. Food Technologists (profl.), Sigma Xi. Mem. Anglican Ch. Avocation: triple jump. Home: Griffin, Ga. Died May 16, 2008.

FABRIS, HUBERT JAKOB, chemist, consultant; b. Vienna, Sept. 16, 1926; came to U.S., 1958; s. Jakob and Stefanie (Muellner) F.; m. Elisabeth M. Eska, July 3, 1957; children: Martin H., Eric W. PhD in Organic Chemistry, U. Vienna, 1956. Rsch. chemist Bundesanstalt für Lebensmittel Untersuchung, Vienna, 1956-58; sr. rsch. chemist Gen. Tire & Rubber Co., Akron, Ohio, 1958-60, group leader, 1960-61, sect. head, 1961-72; mgr. Gencorp, Inc., Akron, Ohio, 1972-85, assoc. dir., 1985-92, cons., from 1992. Contbr. articles to profl. jours.; patentee in field. Died Aug. 16, 2008.

FACKLER, NANCY GRAY, nursing administrator, military officer; b. Norfolk, Va., Jan. 24, 1941; d. Albert Edward and Rita Marie (Murray) Gray; m. Martin L. Fackler, Sept. 29, 1964. BSN, Fla. State U., 1962; postgrad., San Francisco State U., 1988, Golden Gate U., 1989-91, M of Adminstrn. and Health Svcs. Mgmt., 1991; postgrad., U. Fla., 1993-94. RN, Fla.; cert. gerontology; lic. pvt. and comml. pilot. Commd. ensign USNR, 1962, advanced through grades to rear adm. Nurses Corps, 1994; nurse Chelsea Naval Hosp., Boston, Yokosuka (Japan) Naval Hosp.; with N.W. Region, mem. navy med. command NW region policy bd. USNR, Oakland, Calif., 1986-89, readiness command nurse San Francisco, 1989-91; DON Univ. Nursing Care Ctr., Gainesville, Fla.; dep. dir. Navy Nurse Corps, from 1995. Originator res. same day surgery program Naval Hosp. Jacksonville and Naval Hosp. Oakland. Mem. Sec. of Navy Nat. Navy Res. Policy Bd.; active Alachua County Health Coalition. Mem. ANA, Nat. Naval Res. (policy bd.), Nat. Gerontol. Nursing Assn., Naval Res. Assn., Am. Tennis Assn., Fla. Tennis Assn. Avocations: tennis, skiing, photography, languages. Died Apr. 29, 2008.

FADAOL, ROBERT FREDERICK, lawyer; b. Opelousas, La., Oct. 3, 1939; s. Joseph Charles and Marie (Nassar) F.; m. Carolyn Ann Chapman, Jan. 1, 1970; children: Charles, Tracy, Robert. BS in Pharmacy, Auburn U., 1962; JD, Loyola U., New Orleans, 1970. Bar: La. 1971, U.S. Dist. Ct. (ea. and mid. dists.) La. 1971, U.S. Ct. Appeals (5th cir.) 1971, U.S. Dist. Ct. (we. dist.) La. 1975, U.S. Ct. Appeals (11th cir.) 1980, U.S. Tax Ct. 1984, U.S. Ct. Appeals (fed. cir.) 1994, U.S. Supreme Ct. 1976. Sole practice, New Orleans, from 1971. Judge ad hoc Parish Ct., 1986. Served to 2nd lt. U.S. Army, 1962-67. Mem. ABA, La. Bar Assn., Assn. Trial Lawyers Am., La. Trial Lawyers Assn. Republican. Roman Catholic. Died July 12, 2008.

FAGAN, CHRISTOPHER BRENDAN, lawyer; b. South Bend, Ind., Sept. 1, 1937; s. Christopher J. and Clara A. (Poirier) F.;m. Mary K. O'Neill, Feb. 11, 1961 (div. July 1977); children: Kathleen, Patricia, Colleen, Matthew, Timothy, Daniel; m. Janyce R. Brock, Sept. 1, 1978 (div. May 1997); m. Barbara A. Vargo, Apr. 10, 1999. BSME, U. Notre Dame, 1959; JD, Georgetown U., 1965. Bar: Ohio 1965, U.S. Dist. Ct. (no. dist.) Ohio 1967. Patent examiner U.S. Patent Office, Washington, 1963-65; patent atty. Eaton Corp., Cleve., 1965-67; assoc. Fay, Sharpe, Fagan, Minnich & McKee, Cleve., 1967-70, ptnr., from 1970. Lt. USN,

1959-63. Mem. Ohio State Bar Assn., Cleve. Bar Assn., Am. Patent Law Assn., Cleve. Patent Law Assn. Republican. Roman Catholic. Died Aug. 2006.

FAIR, JEAN EVERHARD, retired education educator; b. Evanston, Ill., July 21, 1917; d. Drury Hampton and Bess Marion (Everhard) F. BA, U. Ill., 1938; MA, U. Chgo., 1939, PhD, 1953. Tchr. Evanston (Ill.) Twp. High Sch., 1940-48, 1954-58; tchr. U. Minn. High Sch., 1948-49, U. Ill. High Sch., 1951-53; prof. edn. Wayne State U., Detroit, 1958-82, now prof. emeritus. Cons. in edn.; cons. Mich. Ednl. Goals, Objectives and Assessment in Social Studies; reviewer of position statements for teaching and learning, standards, assessment and other manuscripts for Nat. Coun. Social Studies. Contbr. articles to profl. jours. Mem. AAUW, Nat. Council for Social Studies (pres. 1972, dir. 1958-61, 73-75), Assn. for Supervision and Curriculum Devel., Social Sci. Edn. Consortium, LWV, Phi Beta Kappa. Mem. United Ch. Christ. Home: Grosse Pointe, Mich. Deceased.

FAIRCLOTH, WAYNE REYNOLDS, botany educator; b. Whigham, Ga., Jan. 15, 1932; s. G. Henry and Ruby M. (Sanders) F.; m. Juanita Jane Norsworthy, Sept. 5, 1966; children: Anna Marjorie, Amy Claire, Wilson Henry. BS, Valdosta State Coll., 1955; MEd, U. N.C., 1959; PhD, U. Ga., 1971. Sci. instr. Whigham High Sch., 1951-54, biology instr., chair sci. dept., 1956-60, prin., 1960-61; asst. prof. biology Valdosta (Ga.) State Coll., 1961-67, assoc. prof. biology, 1967-71, prof. biology, curator herbarium, 1971-85, prof. biology, head biology dept., 1985-94, prof. emeritus, from 1994. Author: Common Trees of Central South Georgia, 1979; contbr. articles on bot. rsch. to profl. jours. Chmn. Valdosta Tree Commn., 1984—. Named Environ. Educator of Yr., Soil Conservation Svc. Am., 1986. Fellow Ga. Acad. Sci. (pres. 1975-76). Baptist. Avocation: local history research. Home: Whigham, Ga. Died Mar. 4, 2008.

FALK, JAMES ROBERT, marketing executive, consultant; b. Rensselaer, Ind., Feb. 13, 1953; s. Robert J. and Ruth Ann (LeGrand) F.; m. Mary Margaret DePrey, May 31, 1975; children: Adam J., Ashley M. BA in Mktg., U. Wis., 1982; MS in Bus., Ball State U., Muncie, Ind., 1977. Purchasing agt. Van Camp Hardware & Iron, Indpls., 1975-78; chief exec. officer, pres. LeGrande Communications, Neenhah, Wis., 1978-85; pres. Summit Communications Radio, Rensselaer, 1978-85; chief exec. officer, pres. Universal Wire & Stamping, Two Rivers, Wis., 1985-89; pres. J.R. Falk & Assocs. Mktg., Two Rivers, from 1987; chief exec. officer J.R. Falk, Inc., Two Rivers, from 1987. Mktg. cons. plastic injection design metals engring. rsch. J.R. Falk & Assoc., 1990—. Inventor mobile and speaker phones, bio degradeable wire tree baskets; author: High Resolution Plastic's Aerospace, 1989. Mem. Young Reps., Ind., 1975—. U.S. Govt. Rsch. grantee, 1988. Republican. Lutheran. Avocation: water sports. Home: Oshkosh, Wis. Died Oct. 20, 2007.

FARAHMAND, JANET M., retired medical/surgical nurse; b. Hershey, Pa., Aug. 16, 1935; d. William and Ruth N. (Lemke) Hatter; m. Alex Farahmand, Jan 8, 1963. Diploma, Lankenau Hosp., 1956; BSN, Villanova U., 1960; MSN, U. Pa., 1965, EdD, 1984. RN, Pa.; cert. gerontol. nursing. Clin. supr. Hosp. U. Pa., coord. quality assurance Phila., faculty mem.; asst. prof. nursing Widener U., Chester; assoc. prof. Neumann Coll., Aston, Pa., ret. Rsch. grantee Widener U. Mem. ANA, Nat. League Nursing, Am. Diabetic Assn., Coalition Rights for Info. and Edn, Assn. Rehab. Nurses, Am. Assn. Rep. Persons, Sigma Theta Tau. Home: Glen Mills, Pa. Died Apr. 11, 2008.

FARBER, EVAN IRA, librarian; b. NYC, June 30, 1922; s. Meyer M. and Estelle H. (Shapiro) F.; m. Hope Wells Nagle, June 13, 1966; children: Cynthia, Amy, Jo Anna, May Beth; stepchildren: David Nagle, Jeffrey Nagle, Lisa Nagle. AB, U. N.C., 1944, MA, BLS, U. N.C., 1953; DHL (hon.), St. Lawrence U., 1980, Susquehanna U., 1989, Ind. U., 1996. Instr. polit. sci. U. Mass., Amherst, 1948-49; librarian State Tchrs. Coll., Livingston, Ala., 1953-55; chief serials and binding div. Emory U. Library, Ga., 1955-62; head librarian Earlham Coll., Richmond, Ind., 1962-94, coll. libr. emeritus, from 1994. Cons. Bates Coll., Eckerd Coll., Colo. Coll., Hartwick Coll., Macalester Coll., Maryville Coll., Knox Coll., Ill. Coll., Messiah Coll., Hiram Coll., Centenary Coll., Colby Coll., Ga. State U., Ripon Coll., Hampshire Coll., Reed Coll., Williams Coll., NEH, Lilly Endowment, North Ctrl. Assn., Assn. Am. Colls., Pew Meml. Trust. Author: (with Andreano and Reynolds) Student Economists Handbook, 1967, Classified List of Periodicals for the College Library, 5th edit., 1972; assoc. editor: Southeastern Librarian, 1959-62; asst. editor: Explorations in Entrepreneurial History, 1964-66; co-editor: Earlham Rev., 1965-72; editor: Combined Retrospective Index to Book Revs. in Scholarly Jours., 1886-1974, 1979-83, Combined Retrospective Index to Revs. in Humanities Jours., 1802-1974, 1983-85 (with Ruth Walling) Essays in Honor of Guy R. Lyle; columnist: Choice Mag., 1974-80, Library Issues, 1982-88; mem. editl. bd. Coll. and Undergrad Librs., Internet and Higher Edn. Recipient Acad./Rsch. Libr. of the Yr., 1980, B.I. Libr. of Yr. award, 1987. Mem. Assn. Coll. and Rsch. Librs. (pres. 1978-79, bd. dirs. 1989-93), ALA (council 1969-71, 79-83). Home: Richmond, Ind. Died Feb. 12, 2009.

FARIAN, BABETTE SOMMERICH, artist; b. NYC, June 6, 1916; d. Hugo Joseph and Clara Julia (Hart) Somerich; m. Robert Alan Farian, Sept. 27, 1944 (dec.); 1 child, Robert Alan. Student, N.Y. Sch. Fine and Applied Art, 1933-35, Cooper Union Sch. Art, 1939-42, Modern Mus. Art Sch., 1965-68; pvt. student, Morris Kantor, 1941, Joseph Margulies, 1947-49, Donald Stacy, 1969-89. Instr. color and design Cooper Union, NYC, 1941-42; designer Hanscom Fabrics, Kransom Co., NYC, 1955-57; free lance textile and greeting card designer, 1958-59; asst. head of studio Manhattan Shirt Co., 1960-64. One women shows include Serial Fed. Savs. Bank, N.Y.C., 1976, Walter Reade Theatres, N.Y.C., 1977, 81; exhibited in group shows at Atelier Gallery of Contemporary Art, N.Y.C., 1967, 68, Am. Artist Profl. League, N.Y.C., 1958-59, Impulse Gallery, Martha's Vineyard, 1968, U.S. Fine Arts Registry, 1968, Fine Artists Ctr., Taos, N.Mex., Nat. Arts Club, 1987-97, Audubon Artists Assn., 1988-89, 90, Nat. Soc. Painters in Casein & Acrylic, 1989, 90, Morin-Miller Galleries, 1989, Met. Mus., St. John's U., 1990, Villanova U., 1991, Queens Coll., 1991, 97, Corner Gallery, 1991, Fed. Pla., 1991, and numerous others; represented in permanent collections Bklyn. Botanic Garden Collection, Women's Inter.-Art Mus., N.Y.C., Sloan-Kettering Hosp., Tammassee D.A.R. Sch. Gallery, Unitarian-Universalist Ch. Gallery, also pvt. collections. Recipient Internat. Women's Yr. award, 1976, Grumbacher award Nat. Art League, 1984-87, 1st prize Jackson Hts. Art Club, 1989, Spl. award Jackson Hts. Art Club, 1991, Honorable Mention, Queens Coll., 1991, 97. Mem. Burr Artists (meml. chair), Composers, Authors and Artists Am. (watercolor prize 1980, 83, 1st prize short story 1981), Nat. Arts Club, Artist's Equity Assn., N.Y. Nat. League Am. Pen Women (bd. dirs., Merit award 1979, achievement award 1997), Eleanor Gay Lee Found., Internat. Soc. Artists Internat., Cath. Artists of the 1990's, Orgn. Internat. Artists, Orgn. Ind. Artists, Queens Coun. on Culture of Arts, Eleanor Gay Gallery Found. (bd. dirs.). Died Oct. 29, 2007.

FARLEY, FRANK DONALD, mathematician; b. Flat Top, W.Va., Mar. 8, 1928; s. Frank Dewey and Goldie Marie (Richmond) F.; m. Renate Johanna Schweizer, Aug. 18, 1953. BS, Concord Coll., 1948; MS, W.Va. U., 1956; postgrad., U. Mich., 1956-59. Rsch. assoc. U. Mich., Ann Arbor, 1958-67; engring. specialist Chrysler Corp., Centerlime, Mich., 1967-82, Gen. Dynamics, Troy, Mich., 1982-92, ret., 1992. Mem. Founders Soc., Detroit Inst. Arts, 1970. Sgt. U.S. Army, 1951-53. Mem. Am. Math. Soc., N.Y. Acad. Sci., Sigma Xi. Home: Beckley, W.Va. Died Aug. 28, 2007.

FARMER, JAMES LEE, genetics educator; b. South Gate, Calif., Aug. 8, 1938; s. James Ira and Ellen Eliza (Sheeks) F.; m. Gladys Clark, Jan. 27, 1967; children: Sarah, Clark, Rachel, Jared, Deborah. BS in Chemistry, Calif. Inst. Tech., 1960; PhD in Biology, Brown U., 1966. Instr. biophysics U. Colo. Med. Ctr., Denver, 1966-68; from asst. prof. to prof. zoology Brigham Young U., Provo, Utah, from 1969. Contbr. articles to profl. jours. Mem. AAAS. Home: Provo, Utah. Died Aug. 17, 2008.

FARMER, PHILIP JOSÉ, writer; b. North Terre Haute, Ind., Jan. 26, 1918; s. George and Lucile Theodora (Jackson) F.; m. Bette V. Andre, May 10, 1941; children: Philip Laird, Kristan. BA, Bradley U., 1950. Laborer, steel mill, Peoria, 1941-52; tech. writer, various cos., 1956-69. Author: 75 books including The Lovers, 1951, Strange Relations, 1960, The Alley God, 1962, Riders of the Purple Wage, 1967, Riverworld Series: To Your Scattered Bodies Go, 1971, The Fabulous Riverboat, 1971, Venus on the Half Shell, 1975, The Dark Design, 1977, The Magic Labyrinth, 1980, Riverworld and other Stories, 1979, Tarzan Alive, 1972, The Adventure of the Peerless Peer by John H. Watson, M.D., 1974, The Cache, 1981, A Barnstormer in Oz, 1982, Dayworld, 1983, The Unreasoning Mask, 1983, River of Eternity, 1983, Two Hawks from Earth, 1985, Traitor to the Living, 1985, Fantastic Voyage II, 1985, Dayworld Rebel, 1987, The Grand Adventure, 1987, Venus on the Half-Shell, 1988, Dayworld Breakup, 1990, The World of Tiers, 1993, Naked Came the Farmer, 1998, Nothing Burns in Hell, 1999, The Green Odyssey, 2004, The Best of Philip Jose Farmer, 2005, Tarzan Alive: A Definitive Biography of Lord Greystoke, 2006; short stories Riverworld, 1980. Recipient Hugo award, 1953, 68, 72, Nebula award, 2000, Damon Knight Meml. Grand Master Lifetime Achievement award, 2000, World Fantasy award for Lifetime Achievement, 2001. Died Feb. 25, 2009.

FARNSWORTH, MARJORIE ANNE WHYTE, retired genetics educator; b. Detroit, Nov. 18, 1921; d. Thomas Callan and Anna Irene (Carter) Whyte; m. Wells Eugene Farnsworth, Sept. 15, 1945; children: Samuel B., Marjorie W. BA, Mt. Holyoke Coll., 1944; MS, Cornell U., 1946; PhD, U. Mo., 1951. Lectr. zoology U. Mo., Columbia, 1946-49, AEC predoctoral fellow zoology, 1949-50, asst. prof. zoology, 1950-52; cancer cytologist Roswell Park Meml. Inst., Buffalo, 1952-53; lectr., rsch. assoc. U. Buffalo, 1953-64; assoc. prof. SUNY, Buffalo, 1964-78. Adj. prof. SUNY, Buffalo, 1978-81. Author: Young Woman's Guide to Academic Career, 1974, Genetics, 1978, 2d edit., 1988; contbr. articles on devel./biochem. genetics of drosophila to profl. jours. Rsch. grantee U. Buffalo, 1954-60, NIH rsch. grantee SUNY, Buffalo, 1960-75. Home: Schaumburg, Ill. Died Aug. 21, 2008.

FARR, JOHN WESLEY, retired principal; b. Birmingham, Ala., Aug. 4, 1920; s. Johnny Walter and Neva Love (Monor) F.; m. Dorothy Jane Berre, Apr. 11, 1947; children: Jane Leslie,, John Wesley Jr., Carole Anne, Janice Lynne. BS in Aero. Engring., Aero. U. Chgo., 1942; MA, Cen. Mich. U., 1972; MEd, Ga. State U., 1977. Commd. 2d lt. USAF, 1943, advanced through grades to col., ret., 1973; asst. air attache Ct. of Saint James, U.S. Embassy, London, 1960-64; aircraft analyst, chief tech. evaluation br. aerospace Office of Asst. Chief of Staff Intelligence, Pentagon, Va., 1964-68, chmn sci. intelligence com. USIB aircraft working group, 1964-68; asst. DCS intelligence Hdqrs. Air Force Systems Command, Silver Springs, Md., 1969-70, vice comdr. fgn. tech. div. Dayton, Ohio, 1970-73; instr. Forest Park (Ga.) High Sch., 1973-77, prin., 1977-82; ret., 1982. Head master Meadowcreek Acad., 1987; speaker in fields. Author numerous papers in field. Mem. adv. com. Greater Atlanta Christian Schs., Meadowcreek Acad.; vol. Am. Heart Assn., Forest Park, 1973—. Decorated Legion of Merit with oak leaf cluster. Fellow AIAA (assoc.); mem. Jaycees (hon.), Masons, Shriners. Baptist. Avocations: family, golf. Home: Atlanta, Ga. Died Apr. 11, 2008.

FARRELL, DUNCAN GRAHAM STUART, professional society administrator; b. Evanston, Ill., Apr. 29, 1935; s. Lawrence Stewart and Katherine Ellen (Wiggins) F.; m. Emily Moore Mahan, Aug. 3, 1957 (div. 1970); children: Laura Emily, Grace Moore III, Anne Stuart; m. June Martinick, July 31, 1971. BA in Econs., Wesleyan U., 1957; MBA in Econs., U. Chgo., 1959. Cert. meeting profl. Assoc. McKinsey and Co., Chgo., 1962; mgr. Interstate Vending Co., Chgo., 1962-64, Lippincott and Margulies, NYC, 1964-67, Batten, Barton, Durstine and Osborn, NYC, 1967-69, Ea. Airlines, Miami, Fla., 1969-74; v.p. Travel Industry Assn. Am., Washington, 1974-80; sr. v.p. Nat. Tour Assn., Lexington, Ky., 1980-82; pres. Am. Mgmt. Svcs., Inc., Chevy Chase, Md., from 1982; gen. mgr. Soc. Travel Agts. in Govt., Washington, from 1984. Mem. Meeting Planners Internat., Am. Soc. Assn. Execs. Republican. Episcopalian., Home: Bethesda, Md. Died Dec. 29, 2007.

FARRELL, JOHN DENNIS, screenwriter; b. Downey, Calif., May 29, 1951; s. John Edward and Phyllis Bernice (Summerbell) F.; m. Susan Marie Warren, Oct. 25, 1980 (div. 1985). BA in Radio-TV-Film, Calif. State U., Northridge, 1975. Researcher various ind. producers, LA, from 1983, screenwriter, from 1985; founding ptnr. Sullivan Farrell Prodns., Montrose, Calif., from 1990. Playwright Regional/Equity Waiver, L.A., 1989—. Co-author screenplays Street Legal, 1990, Asia, 1988, The Darby House, 1986, Shotgun Jack Dylan, 1985, Letters, 1991; stories The Big Beat, 1990, Bits and Pieces, 1989, play Pursue the Story, 1990. Mem. Isshinryu World Karate Assn. Avocations: jazz guitar, composing, Karate. Died Apr. 29, 2008.

FARRELL, THOMAS F., accountant; b. Bronxville, NY, Apr. 14, 1945; s. John T. and Anna Marie (Kreig) F.; m. Melissa Ann DeFriese, Apr. 20, 1968 (div. Nov. 1982); 1 child, Thomas D. BS in Indsl. Mgmt., Ga. Inst. Tech., 1971; M of Bus. Info. Systems, Ga. State U., 1975. CPA, Ga. Supr., gen. acctg. City of Atlanta, 1973-76; mgr. staff Coopers & Lybrand, Atlanta, 1976-84, ptnr., 1984-91, Litigation Support Svcs., Stone Mountain, Ga., from 1991; pres. The Telluride Controls Co., Littleton, Colo., from 1994, also bd. dirs., from 1994. Bd. dirs. Videomatrix Tech., Inc., Molena, Ga. Co-author: Business Controls for Computerized Systems, 1992; contbg. editor: Handbook of EDP Auditing, 1985; contbr. articles to profl. jours. Bd. dirs. Yes! Atlanta, 1991—; chmn. Dem. Party of Dekalb, Ga., 1974-75; mem. exec. com. Greater Dem. Party, Atlanta, 1974-75; campaign chmn. various campaigns, 1972-90. Sgt. U.S. Army, 1968-69, Germany. Decorated Legion of Dragoons, U.S. Army. Mem. Atlanta Internat. Golf and Country Club, AICPA, Ga. Soc. CPAs, Internat. Inst. Internal Auditors (vice-chmn. profl. issues com. 1988—), Am. Acctg. Assn. (vice-chmn. info-sys. sect. 1985-88). Roman Catholic. Avocations: golf, skiing, bicycling. Home: Castle Rock, Colo. Died Apr. 17, 2008.

FARROW, MARILYNN LOUISE, consulting nutritionist; b. Chgo., July 5, 1950; d. William John and Gertrude Rita (Dahm) Buchmiller; m. David Russell Farrow, Jan. 3, 1987; children: Curtis Wayne Berry, Brian Christopher. BS, So. Ill. U., 1972; MS, Ga. State U., 1985. Cert. tchr., Ga.; lic. dietitian, Ga. Pvt. practice nutritionist, Woodstock, Ga., from 1984. Nutritionist USDA, Atlanta, 1984, Atlanta March of Dimes, 1985, Nutri-Sport, Inc., Snellville, Ga., 1986, Southwind Health Resort, Cartersville, Ga., 1987-88, Nutrition Edn. and Tng. Co., Cordele, Ga., 1987—, Carrollton, Ga., 1988; frequent TV guest. Contbr. articles and book revs. to profl. jours and mags.; contbr. to Whole Foods for the Whole Family cookbook, 1978. Chair Chapman Elem. PTA Nutrition Edn. Project, Woodstock, 1988. Mem. Soc. for Nutrition Edn., Ctr. for Sci. in the Pub. Interest, Ga. Nutrition Council. Died May 14, 2008.

FASSER, PAUL JAMES, JR., labor arbitrator; b. Gary, Ind., June 15, 1926; s. Paul James and Julia (Thomas) F.; m. Mae Ann Carino, July 31, 1954; children: Paula, Michael (dec. 2005), Thomas. BS, Cornell U., 1951; student, Grove City Coll., 1946-48, U. Pitts., 1948-49. Nat. staff rep. United Steelworkers of America, 1951-70; dep. asst. sec. for manpower US Dept. Labor, Washington, 1970-73, asst. sec. for labor mgmt. services, 1973-76; panelist Nat. Mediation Service, Fed. Mediation and Conciliation Service, Pa. Gov.'s Office, Pa. Mediation Service, coal industry and various United Mine Workers Am. dists. Arbitrator various steel and other heavy industry, light mfg., mining, also state, local and fed. agys.; Spl. Master Weirton Steel/ISU Consent Decree/impartial umpire for Weirton Steel/ISU; panelist Thompson Steel, Madison Hotel, FAA, NATCA. With inf. U.S. Army, World War II. Recipient Judge William B. Groat

Alumni award; Pres.'s award for Employment of Handicapped. Mem. Nat. Acad. Arbitrators, Am. Arbitation Assn. Home: Vienna, Va. Died Nov. 22, 2008.

FAST, JULIUS, writer, editor; b. NYC, Apr. 17, 1919; s. Barnett Arthur and Ida (Miller) F.; m. Barbara Hewitt Sher, June 8, 1946; children: Jennifer, Melissa, Timothy Hewitt. BA, NYU, 1941. Sr. writer Smith, Kline & French Pharms., Phila., 1955-57; chief dept. med. communications Purdue Fredericks, NYC, 1957-62; feature editor Med. News, 1962-63; sr. editor Med. World News, 1963-64; editor Ob-Gyn Observer, NYC, 1965-75. Author: (mystery novels) Watchful at Night, 1945, Bright Face of Danger, 1946, Walk in Shadow, 1948, Model for Murder, 1956, Street of Fear, 1959, A Trunkfull of Trouble, 2002, (fiction) What Should We Do About Davey?, 1987, (sci. fiction) League of Grey-Eyed Women, 1970, (nonfiction) Blueprint for Life, 1963, Beatles: The Real Story, 1968, What You Should Know About Sexual Response, 1966, Body Language, 1970, Incompatibility of Men and Women, 1971, You and Your Feet, 1971, The New Sexual Fulfillment, 1972, Bisexual Living, 1974, The Pleasure Book, 1975, Creative Coping, 1976, The Body Language of Sex Power and Aggression, 1977, Psyching Up, 1978, Weather Language, 1979, Talking Between the Lines: How We Mean More Than We Say, 1979, Body Politics, 1980, The Body Book, 1981, Sexual Chemistry, 1983, Ladies Man, 1983, The Omega-3 Breakthrough, 1987, Subtext, 1990, Legal Atlas of the United States, 1996, Courtroom Communication Skills, 1994. Served with AUS, 1942-46. Recipient Edgar, Mystery Writers America award, 1945 Home: Shady, NY. Died Dec. 16, 2008.

FAUSKIN, GARY NEALE, pediatrician; b. Fargo, ND, Dec. 11, 1931; s. Arthur Oliver and Laurette Aretta (Kruger) F.; m. Elizabeth Nevelo (div.); children: Michael, James, Laura, Jean Eric; m. Lana Lea Halstead; 1 child, Jeffrey Jon. BS in Chemistry, N.D. State Coll., 1952; BS in Medicine, U. N.D., 1958; MD, U. Tex., 1960. Control chemist Montrose Chem. Corp., Torrance, Calif., 1953-54; intern Rotating Gen. Cedars Lebanon Hosp., LA, 1960-61; pediatric resident Cedars of Lebanon Hosp., LA, 1961-63; pvt. practice pediatrics El Cajon, Calif., from 1963. Chmn. infection control com. Valley Med. Ctr., El Cajon; mem. dept. pediatrics, spkrs. bur. Grossmont Dist. Hosp., La Mesa, Calif.; mem. dept. pediatrics, pharmacy and therapeutics com. Alvarado Hosp. Med. Ctr., San Diego; clin. asst. prof. internal medicine and pediatrics Coll. Osteo. Medicine of the Pacific, Pomona, Calif.; asst. clin. prof. dept. pediatrics Harbor UCLA Med. Ctr., Torrance, 1966-85, U. Calif. San Diego; presenter and cons. in field; others. Contbr. articles to profl. jours. With USAF, 1954-56. Mem. Am. Acad. Pediatrics (chairperson com. on hosp. care dist. 9 Calif. chpt. 3), Soc. for Ear, Nose and Throat Advances in Children, Calif. Med. Soc., L.A. Pediatric Soc., San Diego County Med. Soc., German Am. Soc. San Diego (2d v.p. 1994-96). Avocations: cooking, music. Home: El Cajon, Calif. Died Feb. 27, 2008.

FAUST, JOHN JOSEPH, JR., performing arts educator, theater director; b. St. Louis, Feb. 16, 1939; s. John J. and Elinor (Cafferata) F.; m. Deborah Doyle, Aug. 18, 1969; children: John Charles, Mark Doyle. AB in Speech, St. Louis U., 1961; MA in Speech and Dramatic Arts, State U. Iowa, 1964. Tchr. speech/theatre Columbus High Sch., Waterloo, Iowa, 1963-64; chair English dept., dir. theatre Augustinian Acad., St. Louis, 1964-70; chair fine arts dept., dir. activities De Smet Jesuit High Sch., St. Louis, 1970-79; dir. theatre John Burroughs Sch., St. Louis, 1979-88, Barrington (Ill.) High Sch., 1988-94. Dir. nat. high sch. inst. theatre Northwestern U., Evanston, Ill., 1963-72, 89, Webster U. High Sch. Inst., St. Louis, 1978-80, creative drama workshop Barrington Area Arts Coun., 1990-93; adjudicator, panel mem. arts recognition and talent search Nat. Found. Advancement Arts, Miami, Fla., 1978-88; tchr. Mark Twain Summer Inst., St. Louis, 1985-88; founder, exec. dir. Theatre Whatever A Prodn. Co. For, By and With Young Adults, 1996. Assoc. editor: Theatre Technology & Design, 1984; contbg. editor: Model/Theatre Curriculum. Americorps vol. in HIV/AIDS awareness in teenagers ARC, 1994-95. Mem. Am. Alliance Theatre and Edn. (John Barner award 1992, Secondary Theatre Tchr. of Yr.), Ednl. Theatre Assn. Deceased.

FAVIN, DAVID LEONARD, electrical engineer; b. Phila., Feb. 14, 1926; s. Louis and Jennie (Green) F.; m. Marion Favin; children: Carol S., Jean L. BSEE, U. Pa., 1950; MSEE, MIT, 1952. Disting. mem. tech. staff AT&T Bell Labs., Holmdel, N.J., from 1952. Chmn. Tech. Oriented/Telephone Pioneers, Holmdel, 1968—. 25 patents in field. With USAAF, 1944-45. Mem. IEEE. Avocations: piano, woodworking, tennis, swimming, computers. Home: Little Silver, NJ. Died Apr. 15, 2008.

FAWCETT, DON WAYNE, retired anatomist; b. Springdale, Iowa, Mar. 14, 1917; s. Carlos J. and Mabel (Kennedy) F.; m. Dorothy Marie Secrest, 1941; children: Robert S., Mary Elaine, Donna, Joseph. AB cum laude, Harvard, 1938, MD, 1942; DSc (hon.), U. Siena, Italy, 1974, NY Med. Coll., 1975, U. Chgo., 1977, U. Cordoba, Argentina, 1978; MD (hon.), U. Heidelberg, Germany, 1977; DVM (hon.), Justus Liebig U., Giessen-Lahn, Germany, 1977; DSc (hon.), Georgetown U., 1987, U. Rome, 1997. Intern surgery Mass. Gen Hosp., Boston, 1942-43; instr. anatomy Harvard Med. Sch., 1946-48, asso. anatomy, 1948-51, asst. prof. anatomy, 1951-55, Hersey prof. anatomy, 1958-80, James Stillman prof. comparative anatomy, 1962-80, sr. asso. dean preclin. affairs, 1975-77; prof. anatomy Cornell Med. Coll., 1955-58; scientist Internat. Lab. Research on Animal Diseases, Nairobi, Kenya, 1980-85. Author: The Cell, 1966, 2d edit., 1981, Textbook of Histology, 1968, 10th edit., 1975, 11th edit., 1986, 12th edit., 1993. Served as capt. M.C. AUS, 1943-46; bn. surgeon A.A.A. John and Mary Markle scholar med. sci., 1949-54; recipient Lederle Med. Faculty award, 1954 Fellow Am. Acad. Arts and Sci., Nat. Acad. Sci. US, Royal Microscopical Soc. (hon.); mem. AAAS, NY Acad. Sci., Am. Assn. Anatomists (pres. 1964-65, Henry Gray award 1983, Centennial medal 1987), NY Soc. Electron Microscopists (pres. 1957-58), Histochem. Soc., Tissue Culture Assn. (v.p. 1954-55), Soc. Exptl. Biology and Medicine, Assn. Anatomy Chairmen (pres. 1973-74), Am. Soc. Zoologists, Am. Soc. Mammalogists, Electron Microscope Soc. Am. (Disting. Scientist award in Life Scis. 1989), Soc. Study Devel. and Growth, Harvey Soc., Am. Soc. Cell Biology (pres. 1961-62), Argentine Nat. Acad. Sci., Anat. Soc. So. Africa (hon.), Japanese Anat. Soc. (hon.), Anat. Soc. Australia and N.Z. (hon.), Japanese Electron Microscope Soc., Internat. Fedn. Soc. Electron Microscopy (pres. 1976-78), Am. Soc. Andrology (pres. 1977-78), Soc. Study Reprodn. (Carl Hartman award 1985), Mexican (hon.), Canadian (hon.) Assn. Anatomists. Home: Missoula, Mont. Died May 7, 2009.

FAWCETT, FARRAH LENI, actress, model; b. Corpus Christi, Tex., Feb. 2, 1947; d. James William and Pauline Alice (Evans) Fawcett; m. Lee Majors, July 28, 1973 (div. 1982); 1 child (with Ryan O'Neal), Redmond James O'Neal. Attended, U. Tex., Austin, 1966—67. Actress (TV films) Three's a Crowd, 1969, The Feminist and the Fuzz, 1971, Inside O.U.T., 1971, The Great American Beauty Contest, 1973, Of Men and Women, 1973, The Girl Who Came Gift-Wrapped, 1974, Murder on Flight 502, 1975, Murder in Texas, 1981, The Red-Light Sting, 1984, The Burning Bed, 1984, Between Two Women, 1986, Nazi Hunter: The Beate Klarsfeld Story, 1986, Poor Little Rich Girl: The Barbara Hutton Story, 1987, Margaret Bourke-White, 1989, Small Sacrifices, 1989, Criminal Behavior, 1992, The Substitute Wife, 1994, Children of the Dust, 1995, Dalva, 1996, Silk Hope, 1999, Baby, 2000, Jewel, 2001, Hollywood Wives: The New Generation, 2003, (films) Myra Breckinridge, 1970, Logan's Run, 1976, Somebody Killed Her Husband, 1978, Sunburn, 1979, Saturn 3, 1980, The Cannonball Run, 1981, Extremities, 1986, See You in the Morning, 1989, Man of the House, 1995, The Apostle, 1997, The Lovemaster, 1997, (voice) The Brave Little Toaster Goes to Mars, 1998, Dr T and the Women, 2000, The Cookout, 2004, (TV series) Harry O, 1975—76, The Six Million Dollar Man, 1974, 1976, Charlie's Angels, 1976—77, actress (guest appearances) I Dream of Jeannie, 1969, The Flying Nun, 1969, 1970, The Partridge Family, 1970, The Young Rebels, 1970, Owen Marshall: Counselor at Law, 1971, McCloud, 1974, Marcus Welby, M.D., 1974, Apple's Way, 1974, S.W.A.T., 1975, Johnny Bravo, 1997, Ally McBeal, 1999, Spin City, 2001, The Guardian, 2002, 2003, featured in (documentaries) Farrah's Story, 2009. Recipient People's Choice award for Favorite Female Performer in New TV Program, 1977; named to Tex. Film Hall of Fame, 2003. Died June 25, 2009.

FEAREY, WILMA GWEN, nurse; b. Can., Oct. 21, 1935; d. Thomas and Helena (Kuleski) Taylor; children: Robert, Thomas, Donna, John. AA, Clackamas Community Coll., 1980; student, Portland State U., 1981. RN. Nurse mgr. East Moreland Hosp., Portland. Mem. Emergency Dept. Nurses Assn. Home: Manzanita, Oreg. Died Dec. 11, 2007.

FECK, ASMUS WILHELM, retired mechanical engineer; b. Hamburg, Germany, July 11, 1920; arrived in US, 1965; s. Wilhelm A. and Frieda (Hafel) Feck; m. Elisabeth M. Feck-Unruh, Nov. 5, 1947 (dec. Mar. 2007); children: Axel, Jens. BS in Internat. Bus. Adminstrn., Comml. Coll., Hamburg, Germany, 1939; grad., Technische U., Hannover, Germany, 1951; MS in Mech. Engring., Engring. Coll., Hamburg, 1952. Lic. mech. and marine engr., Germany, UK. Engring. apprentice AERO airplane mfg. co., 1936—39; marine design, application and patent engr. Kort Propulsion Co., 1947—51; mgr. marine engring. sales Worthington Corp., Germany, 1951, mkgr. engineered products, 1953, gen. sales dir., 1957—59, European mgr. marine and nuc. energy Paris, 1960—65, mgr. internat. marine divsn. NJ, 1965—70; mgr. internat. marine and govt. dept. Studebaker-Worthington, Harrison, NJ, 1970—72; mem. staff internat. tanker design dept. ESSO/EXXON Co., NYC and Florham Park, NJ, 1972—87; ret., 1987. Instr. in field. Lt. German Air Force, 1942—45, prisoner of war, 1945—47, US, UK. Recipient Internat. Marine Engring. Merit award, Worthington Corp., 1967. Mem.: Soc. Naval Archs. and Marine Engrs., Soc. Naval Archs. and Marine Engrs. Germany, Soc. Mech. Engrs. Germany, Inst. Marine Engrs. London, NY Br. (past chmn., vice chmn.,), Propeller Club Port NY. Home: Myrtle Beach, SC. Died Feb. 17, 2009.

FEDERMAN, RAYMOND, writer, literature and language educator; b. Paris, May 15, 1928; s. Simon and Marguerite (Epstein) Federman; m. Erica Hubscher Federman, Sept. 19, 1960; 1 child, Simone Juliette. BA, Columbia U., 1957; MA, UCLA, 1958, PhD, 1963. Asst. prof. U. Calif.-Santa Barbara, 1959—64; assoc. prof. SUNY, Buffalo, 1964—68, prof. English & comparative lit., from 1968, Disting. prof., 1990—99, Melodia E. Jones prof., 1994—99; vis. prof. U. Montreal, Que., Canada, 1969—70, Hebrew U. Jerusalem, 1982—83. Author: Journey to Chaos: Samuel Beckett's Early Fiction, 1965, Double Or Nothing, 1971, Take It or Leave It: An Exaggerated Second-Hand Tale to Be Read Aloud Either Standing or Sitting, 1976, The Voice in the Closet, 1979, The Twofold Vibration, 1982, Smiles on Washington Square: A Love Story of Sorts, 1985, To Whom It May Concern, 1990, Now Then, 1991, Critifiction, 1993, The Supreme Indecision of The Writer, 1999, The Precipice and Other Catastrophes, 1999, Shhh: A Story of Childhood, 2009; co-author (with John Fletcher): Samuel Beckett: His Works and His Critics, 1970. Served with US Army, 1951—54, Republic of Korea. Guggenheim fellow, 1966—67, Camargo Found. fellow, Cassis, France, 1977, Fulbright fellow, Israel, 1982—83, Nat. Endowment Arts fellow, 1985. Mem.: Fiction Collective (co.-dir. 1978—81), PEN Am. Ctr., Samuel Beckett Soc. (life; hon. trustee), Bernardo Heights Country Club (San Diego), Phi Beta Kappa. Democrat. Jewish. Avocations: golf, tennis, jazz. Home: San Diego, Calif. Died Oct. 6, 2009.

FEDORUK, JOAN DIANE, accountant; b. Youngstown, Ohio, Feb. 20, 1956; d. Nicholas David and Elaine Francis (Kucher) F. BSBA, Youngstown State U., 1995. LPN, Ohio. Staff nurse South Side Hosp., Youngstown, 1980-83; pvt. duty nurse LPN Ofcl. Registry, Youngstown, 1983-90; staff nurse, counselor Physician's Weight Loss Ctr., Liberty, Ohio, 1990-93; acctg. intern Delphi Packard Electric Sys., Warren, Ohio, 1994-95; plant acct. U.S. Can Co., Columbiana, Ohio, from 1995. Bus. owner, acct. Profl. Bus. Svcs., Austitown, Ohio, 1996. Univ. Found. scholar Youngstown State U., 1992-95, Dist. Dir.'s Tax Inst. scholar, 1995. Mem. Ohio Soc. CPAs, Inst. Mgmt. Accts., Phi Kappa Alpha, Alpha Tau Gamma. Republican. Roman Catholic. Avocations: running, tennis, gardening, softball, reading. Home: Youngstown, Ohio. Died July 12, 2008.

FELDER, RICHARD EMERSON, physician; b. Fulton, Ind., July 30, 1918; s. Ernest Emerson and Ruth Anna (Adamson) F.; m. Blanche Taylor McCall; children: Marion Ruth, Virginia, William Richard, Sara Ann. AB, Emory U., 1940, MD, 1944. Asst. anatomy Emory U., Atlanta, 1941-42, instr. internal medicine, psychiatry, 1949-50, resident, 1950-53; psychiatrist Atlanta Psychiat. Clinic, 1953-95, pvt. practice, Atlanta, from 1995. Co-author: Experiential Psychotherapy: A Symphony of Selves, 1991. Capt. U.S. Army, 1942-47. Avocations: music, boating. Home: Gainesville, Ga. Died May 2, 2008.

FELDMAN, FRANCES LOMAS, social sciences educator; b. Phila., Dec. 3, 1912; d. Harry and Dora (Hoffman) Lomas; m. Albert George Feldman, Mar. 16, 1935 (dec. Dec. 1975); 1 child, Dona Feldman Munker. BA, U. So. Calif., 1934, MSW, 1940; post-masters cert., U. Chgo., 1953. Social work supr. State Relief Adminstrn., LA, 1934-39; dir. slum clearance, tenant selection Housing Authority, LA, 1940-41; dir. Family Svc. L.A., 1941-43; dep. dir. L.A. County Bur. Pub. Assistance, LA, 1943-50; dir. Jewish Family & Cmty. Svc., Chgo., 1950-53; prof. U. So. Calif. Sch. Social Work, LA, 1954-82. Pres. Calif. Social Welfare Archives U. So. Calif. Author: Family in Money World, 1957, Family Social Welfare: Helping Troubled Families, 1967, Work and Cancer, 1976, 78, 82, Rural Alaska Services, 1973 Evolution of Professional Social Work, 1996, Human Services in the City of Angels: 1850-2000, 2004 Founder, pres. Calif. Social Welfare Archives, USC. Honors include Calif. Kochland award; designated Disting. Prof. Emerita, U. So. Calif., Dart award for Disting. Tchg., Los Amigos award for Outstanding Cmty. Svc., others. Mem. NASW, Phi Kappa Phi. Avocations: travel, music, writing. Home: Pasadena, Calif. Died Sept. 30, 2008.

FELDT, DAVID A., community health administrator; b. Cleve., Apr. 1, 1958; s. Edwain A. and Betty J. Feldt. ADN, C.C. Morris, Randolph, NJ, 1982. RN, Ohio. Staff nurse burn unit St. Barnabas Med. Ctr., Livingston, N.J., 1980-84; staff nurse ICU Mercy Hosp., Toledo, Ohio, 1984-85; asst. clin. mgr. Toledo Hosp., 1985-86; dir. br. office Kimberly Home Care, Toledo, 1986-87; asst. nurse mgr. infectious diseases Cleve. Clinic Found., 1987-91; mgr. AIDS program and spl. projects Vis. Nurses Assn., Cleve., from 1991. Featured spkr. 5th Ann. Ohio Nurses Assn. AIDS Conf., Columbus, 1993; mem. North Coast AIDS Coalition, Cleve.; author, presenter workshop Developing an HIV Sensativity Tng. Program, 1992—. Grantee, 1993. Mem. ANA, APHA, Assn. Nurses in AIDS Care, Ohio League Nursing, Ohio Nurses Assn. (co-chair AIDS Task Force 1992—, co-chair candidate selection Toledo dist. 1985-86), Amnesty Internat. Democrat. Unitarian Universalist. Avocations: foreign films, historical biographies. Home: Cleveland Hts, Ohio. Died July 4, 2008.

FELDT, ROBERT JUNIOR, retired conservationist; b. St. Ansgar, Iowa, Feb. 17, 1929; s. Robert Ferdinand and Laura Emma Louise (Schroeder) F.; m. Catherine Christina Dworshak. Farm ops., Iowa State U., 1950. Soil conservationist U.S. Soil Conservation Svc., Waterloo, Iowa, 1951-52, Waseca, Minn., 1952-53, work unit conservationist Redwood Falls, Minn., 1953-67, dist. conservationist Crookston, Minn., 1967-77, resource conservation and devel. coord. Eau Claire, Wis., 1977-88. Organizer Shiitake Growers Assn. Wis., Eau Claire; instr. U. Minn., Crookston, 1968-70, USAR, Fort McCoy, Wis., 1968-77. Prodn. asst. 20-minute film. Mem. Nat. Assn. Ret. Fed. Employees (life; chpt. pres. 1994-98), Ret. Officers Assn. (life; chpt. pres.), Soil and Water Conservation Soc. Am. (bd. dirs. 1986-87), Shiitake Growers Assn. Wis. (life; charter), Minn. Wheat Growers Assn. (charter), Minn. Inventors Congress (charter;

pres. 1963-65, presdl. award 1964), Eau Claire Rod and Gun Club, Ruffed Grouse Soc., Nat. Wild Turkey Fedn., Elks, Beta Sigma Psi. Avocations: hunting, golf, photography, reading, travel. Died May 27, 2008.

FELKNOR, BRUCE LESTER, publishing executive, consultant, writer; b. Oak Park, Ill., Aug. 18, 1921; s. Audley Rhea and Harriet (Lester) F.; m. Joanne Sweeney, Feb. 8, 1942 (div. Jan. 1952); 1 child, Susan Harriet Felknor Pickard; m. Edith G. Johnson, Mar. 1, 1952; children: Sarah Anne Felknor Ragland, Bruce Lester II. Student, U. Wis., 1939—41. Reporter Dunn County News, Menomonie, Wis., 1937—39; freight brakeman Pa. R.R., NYC, 1941, asst. yardmaster, 1942; prodn. coord. Hwy. Trailer Co., Edgerton, Wis., 1943; radio officer U.S. Maritime Svc., 1944—45; flight radio officer Air Transport Command, 1945; mem. pub. rels. dept. Am. Airlines, 1945; writer pub. rels. dept. ITT, 1946; Southeast regional pub. rels. dir. Ford Motor Co., Chester, Pa., 1946—48; free lance pub. res. NYC, 1948—49; pub. rels. exec. Foote, Cone & Belding, Inc., NYC, 1950—53; v.p. Market Rels. Network, NYC, 1954—55; exec. dir. Fair Campaign Practices Com., Inc., NYC, 1956—66; asst. to chmn. and pub. William Benton Encyclopedia Britannica, 1966—70, dir. mktg. info. internat. divsn., 1970—73, dir. advt. and promotion, 1973, dir. pub. info., 1974—76, exec. editor, 1977—83, dir. yearbooks, 1983—85; editl. cons., 1985—2008. Vis. lectr. Hamilton Coll., 1966, 75, 82; history editor Mcht. Marine internet web site www.usmm.org, 1999-2008 Author: Fair Play in Politics, 1960, State-by-State Smear Study, 1956, You Are They, 1964, (with C.P. Taft) Prejudice & Politics, 1960, Dirty Politics, 1966, reprinted, 1975, 2001, (with Frank Jonas et al) Political Dynamiting, 1970, How to Look Things Up and Find Things Out, 1988, Political Mischief: Smear, Sabotage, and Reform in U.S. Elections, 1992, The Highland Park Presbyterian Church: A History 1871-1996, 1996 (Robert Lee Stowe award 1997), The U.S. Merchant Marine at War 1775-1945, 1998, The Great Witch Hunt of the Presbyterian Left, 2001, Of Clubbable Nature: Chicago's Tavern Club at 75, 2005; editor: The U.S. Government: How and Why it Works, 1978; also various newspaper, jour. and yearbook articles on politics; contbg. editor (with Clifton Fadiman) The Treasury of the Encyclopaedia Britannica, 1992; contbr. Encyclopedia of the American Presidency, 1993. Chmn. Citizens Com. for Sch. Centralization in Armonk, N.Y., 1957-61; ruling elder, chmn. com. religion and race Presbytery Hudson River, 1963-67, mem. nat. coun. on ch. and soc., 1966-72; bd. dirs., mem. exec. com. Fair Campaign Practices Com.; mem. nat. adv. bd. Amigos de las Americas, 1982-89, Am. U., Washington, 1982-2008. Ill. Literacy Coun., 1984-86; mem. bd. advisors, acad. adv. coun. Nat. Strategy Forum, 1987-2008; mem. bd. edn. Lake Forest (Ill.) H.S. Dist., 1989-93. Republican. Presbyterian. Home: Evanston, Ill. Died Sept. 27, 2008.

FELLHAUER, FELIX HAMILTON, retired letter shop operator, newsletter editor; b. Dunn County, ND, Sept. 5, 1919; s. Frank Leo and Lee (Brandenburg) F.; m. Ruth Anna Bedford (div. 1982); 1 child, Anna Kathryn Fellhauer Hamilton; m. Jane Jennings, Jan. 7, 1989. AA, Orange Coast Coll., Costa Mesa, Calif., 1967-68; student, Calif. State U., Long Beach, 1969. Operator Letter Shop, Bellflower, Calif., 1948-55, Costa Mesa, 1955-80, Santa Rosa, Calif., 1980-88; writer, newsletter editor, Kansas City, Mo., from 1989. Home: Lees Summit, Mo. Died Mar. 25, 2008.

FELLNER, MORRIS JOSEPH, lawyer; b. NYC, May 29, 1913; s. Harry and Dora (Ravin) F.; children: Lenore Heckler, Narissa Treu. BS, City Colls. N.Y., 1934; LLB, St. Lawrence U., 1937. Bar: N.Y. 1938, U.S. Dist. Ct. (so. and ea. dists.) N.Y., U.S. Ct. Appeals N.Y., U.S. Supreme Ct. Ptnr. Fellner, Rovins & Gallay, NYC, 1955-80, Burns, Summit, Rovins, NYC, 1980-86; of counsel Summit, Rovins & Feldesman, NYC, 1987. With U.S. Army, 1943-45. Mem. ABA, N.Y. State Bar Assn., N.Y. County Lawyers Assn. Died Feb. 29, 2008.

FENNESSEE, WILLIAM, rehabilitation services education educator; b. Mt. Pleasant, Tenn., Apr. 9, 1951; BS, Austin Peau State U., 1974; MS, U. Tenn., 1976; RhD, So. Ill. U., 1987. Cert. rehab. counselor, nat. cert. counselor. Counselor intern Tex. Commn. for the Blind, Houston, 1975-76; program mgr. Tenn. Rehab. Ctr., Smyrna, 1977-82; program developer Community Human Svc. Ctr., Carbondale, Ill., 1986; asst. prof., coord. rehab. counseling program R.I. Coll., Providence, 1987-88; asst. prof., coord. rehab. svcs. edn. Murray (Ky.) State U., from 1989. Chair R.I. Ind. Living Coun., Providence, 1988-89, panelist Fifth Ave. Conf. region I, Worchester, Mass., 1989. Grad. Deans fellow So. Ill. U., 1982-83, Patricia Roberts Harris fellow, 1984-85. Mem. Rho Chi Sima (pres. Nu chpt. 1984-85), Chi Sigma Iota. Home: Mount Pleasant, Tenn. Died July 16, 2008.

FERGUSON, MARILYN, writer, lecturer, consultant; b. Grand Junction, Colo., Apr. 5, 1938; d. Luke Michael and Helen Olinda (Bauer) Grasso; m. Ray Gottlieb, July 24, 1984 (div. 1992); children: Eric, Ann Kristin, Lynn. AA, Mesa Coll.; LLD (hon.), John F. Kennedy U., 1989. Pub. Brain/Mind Bull., LA, 1975—96. Mem. adv. bd. Inst. Noctic Sousale Scis., Calif., 1982-84. Author: The Brain Revolution: The Frontiers of Mind Research, 1973, The Aquarian Conspiracy, 1980, Aquarius Now, 2005; co-author: (with Michael Ferguson) Champagne Living on a Beer Budget, 1968 Recipient Elmer and Allyce award for career achievement Inst. for Study of Subtle Energy Medicine, 1997. Mem. ASTD (Brain/Trainer of Yr. 1994). Home: Los Angeles, Calif. Died Oct. 19, 2008.

FERGUSON, MARK DOUGLAS, educational broadcasting administrator; b. Kingsport, Tenn., Jan. 21, 1967; s. Leonard Douglas and Janice Earlene Ferguson; m. Katina Faye Fields, June 24, 1995. BS in Mass Comm., East Tenn. Stat U., Johnson City, 1989; MA in Bibl. Studies, Victory Bible Inst., Roan Mountain, Tenn., 1994. Disc jockey J.T. Parker Broadcasting, Kingsport, 1986-90, gen. mgr., 1990-92; program mgr. Appalachian Ednl., Bristol, Tenn., from 1992. Campaign mgr. Friends for Brian Addington, Bristol, 1996; assoc. mem. Rep. Women, 1992—; referee, umpire Tenn. Secondary Schs, 1985. Methodist. Avocations: golf, bowling, directing music, putt-putt. Home: Kingsport, Tenn. Died July 4, 2008.

FERGUSON, THOMAS MARSHALL, photography company owner; b. Pitts., Aug. 30, 1936; s. John Boyd and Ruth Naomi (Willis) F.; m. Patricia Catherine Hammock, July 10, 1970; children: Stephanie Patricia, Joshua Thomas. Owner, mgr. Sta. KADI-FM Radio, St. Louis, 1966-68; talk show host Sta. WKIS-AM, Orlando, Fla., 1968-74, Sta. WDBO-AM, Orlando, 1972-74; owner Tom Marshall Photography, Orlando, from 1974. Tchr. adult computers Seminole Community Coll., Sanford, Fla., 1983-84; dir. Serendity Workshop, Maitland, Fla., 1984-85. Author: (computer software program) Escape to Equatus; pub., editor Mediad, 1975-76, Racquet Mag., 1975-76. Chmn. Vietnam POW/MIA Campaign, Cen. Fla., 1972-73; pres. Sanford Youth Soccer Club, 1980-81, Southside Elem. PTA, Sanford, 1980-81, mem. Cousteau Soc., Common Cause, So. Poverty Law Ctr. Named Hon. Ex-Convict Internat. Assn. Ex-Convicts, 1972. Mem. Amnesty Internat. (freedom writer), ACLU. Avocations: reading, travel, philosophy, world affairs. Home: Winter Park, Fla. Died July 9, 2008.

FERNEA, ELIZABETH WARNOCK, retired literature professor; b. Milw., Oct. 21, 1927; m. Robert A. Fernea; children: Laura Ann, David, Laila. B.A., Reed Coll., 1949; postgrad. in English, Mt. Holyoke Coll., 1949-50, U. Chgo., 1954-56, Ph.D (hon.), SUNY, Plattsburg, 1994; Lectr. dept. English and Ctr. Middle Eastern Studies U. Tex., Austin, 1975—99, prof. emeritus, 1999-2008; cons. Nat. Pub. Radio, 1982—2008, Ind. Broadcasting Assoc., Concord, Mass., Mellon Found. Project on Women and Social Change, Smith Coll.; lectr. Smithsonian Study Tour Morocco, 1982, 84; contributing editor Texas Books in Review, Dallas; bd. dirs. Am. Near East Refugee Aid, Washington, Am.-Mideast Ednl. and Tng. Services, Washington; speaker Tex. Union Ideas and Issues Com., 1977, 82, Liberal Arts Coll. Forum, 1979. Author: (with Robert A. Fernea) The Arab World, 1985; A Street in Marrakech, 1975; A View of the Nile, 1970; Guests of the Sheik, 1965. Editor: Women and the Family in the Middle East: New Voices of Change, 1984; (with Marilyn Duncan) Texas Women in Politics, 1977. Co-editor and translater: (with Basima Qattan Bezirgan) Middle Eastern Muslim Women Speak, 1977. Writer, producer films on Middle East; contbr. articles to profl. jours.; translater short stories, poems from Arabic; book reviewer; presenter of lectures, forums and film showings to confs. and symposia, U.S. and abroad. Grantee Ford Found., 1983, NEH, 1978, 80; named Outstanding Woman in Lit., Tex. AAUW, 1978. Mem. Tex. Inst. Letters, Middle East Studies Assn. N.Am. (pres. elect 1984). Died Dec. 2, 2008.

FERRAND, EDWARD FRANCIS, science administrator; b. NYC, Aug. 26, 1921; s. Edward and Irene Carmen (Jordan) F.; m. Irene Rosemary Benschine, Feb. 17, 1945; children: Linda, Edward, Valeria. BS in Chemistry, St. John's U., 1942; PhD in Chemistry, Pa. State U., 1965. Chemist Amer. Cyanamid, Bound Brook, N.Y., 1941-43; mem. faculty The Cooper Union Sch. Engring., NYC, 1946-67; asst. commr. sci. and tech. N.Y.C. Dept. Environ. Protection, 1967-86; cons. EPA, NYC, 1986-88; program dir. NSF, Washington, from 1989. Co-author: National Academy Press, 1977, Carbon Monoxide; author: Encyclopedia of Environmental Science and Engineering, Effects of Air Pollutants, Hazardous Wastes, 1992. Bd. dirs. N.Y. Lung Assn., 1980-91, Coun. on the Environment of N.Y.C., 1989—; mem. sci. adv. bd. EPA, 1976-86. Recipient special merit award, EPA, 1977, special environment award, N.Y.C., 1977, 1979, outstanding profl. achievement award, Boricua Coll., 1979, Alfred T. White Ecology award, Bklyn. Engrs. Club, 1980. Mem. Am. Chem. Soc., N.Y. Acad. Scis., N.Y. Acad. Medicine (working group chair 1980—). Home: Huntington, NY. Died June 30, 2008.

FERREIRA, ARMANDO THOMAS, sculptor, educator; b. Charleston, W.Va., Jan. 8, 1932; s. Maximiliano and Placeres (Sanchez) F.; children: Lisa, Teresa. Student, Chouinard Art Inst., 1949—50, Long Beach City Coll., 1950—53; BA, UCLA, 1954, MA, 1956. Asst. prof. art Mt. St. Mary's Coll., 1956-57, mem. faculty dept. art Calif. State U., Long Beach, from 1957, prof., from 1967, chmn. dept. art, 1971-77, assoc. dean Sch. Fine Arts, acting dean Coll. Arts. Lectr., cons. on art adminstrn. to art schs. and univs., Brazilian Ministry Edn. One-man shows include, Pasadena Mus., 1959, Long Beach Mus., 1959, 69, Eccles Mus., 1967, Clay and Fiber Gallery, Taos, 1972; exhibited in group shows at L.A. County Art Mus., 1958, 66, Wichita Art Mus., 1959, Everson Mus., 1960, 66, San Diego Mus. Fine Arts, 1969, 73, Fairtree Gallery, N.Y.C., 1971, 74, L.A. Inst. Contemporary Art, 1977, Utah Art Mus., 1978, Bowers Mus., Santa Ana, Calif., 1980, No. Ill. U., 1986, Beckstrand Gallery, Palos Verdes (Calif.) Art Ctr., 1987, U. Madrid, 1993; permanent collections include Utah Mus. Art, Wichita Art Mus., Long Beach (Calif.) Mus. Art, State of Calif. Collection, Fred Jones Jr. Mus. Art U. Okla., U. Okla. Art Mus.; vis. artist, U. N.D., 1974. Fulbright lectr. Brazil, 1981. Fellow: Nat. Assn. Schs. Art and Design (bd. dirs.). Home: Los Angeles, Calif. Died 2009.

FERRELL, MILTON MORGAN, JR., lawyer; b. Coral Gables, Fla., Nov. 6, 1951; s. Milton M. and Annie (Blanche) Bradley; m. Lori R. Sanders, May 22, 1982; children: Milton Morgan III, Whitney Connolly. BA, Mercer U., 1973, JD, 1975. Bar: Fla. 1975, Ga. 1975, NY 2005, DC 2005, US Dist. Ct. (mid. dist. Ga.), US Dist. Ct. (mid. and so. dists. Fla.), US Dist. Ct. (so. and ea. dists. NY), US Supreme Ct., US Ct. Fed. Claims, US Ct. Appeals (2nd, 3rd, 5th, 9th and 11th cirs.), US Ct. Appeals (dist. DC). Asst. state's atty. State's Atty.'s Office, Miami, 1975—77; ptnr. Ferrell & Ferrell, 1977—84, Ferrell Williams, P.A., 1987—90; pvt. practice Ferrell Law, P.A., 1990—2006, CEO. Bd. dirs. Authentix, Inc., 2000—05, Stone Technologies, 2000—01. Trustee Mus. Sci. and Space Transit Planetarium, 1977—82; trustee, mem. legal. com., chair com. Project to Cure Paralysis U. Miami, 1985—94; mem. Ambs. of Mercy, Mercy Hosp. Found., Inc., 1985—94; trustee Greater Miami and the Keys chpt. ARC, mem., from 2001, bd. dirs., from 2001, Robinson Charitable Found., from 1993, Performing Arts Ctr. Found., from 1998, Jackson Meml. Found., 1999—2004; bd. trustees Eaglebrook Sch., 1995—98, Mercer U., from 2004; trustee United Way of Miami-Dade, from 2000; bd. dirs. The Founders Mount Sinai Med. Ctr. Found., from 2002; chmn. Jackson Meml. Found., from 2004. Named one of Top 100 Attys., Worth mag., 2006. Mem. ABA (grantee 1975), Am. Bd. Criminal Lawyers (bd. dirs. 1982-83, sec. 1983-85, v.p. 1985-86, pres. 1986-87), Nat. Assn. Criminal Def. Lawyers, Am. Bar Found., Fla. Bar Assn. (jury instrns. com. 1987-89, chmn. grievance com. L 1987-90), Dade County Bar Assn. (bd. dir. 1977-80), Assn. Trial Lawyers Am., Bath Club (bd. gov. 1992-95), Miami City Club, Univ. Club, Banker's Club, Indian Creek Country Club, LaGorce Country Club, Fisher Island Club, GlenArbor Golf Club. Home: Miami, Fla. Deceased.

FERRIER, MICHAEL GLEN, data processing executive; b. Greenville, SC, Aug. 7, 1944; s. Jack G. and Barbara (Himes) F.; m. Carol A. Simione, Jan. 20, 1968; children: Christine, Michael A. BA, Kent State U., Ohio, 1966; JD, American U., 1982. Programmer/analyst Official Airline Guide, Oak Brook, Ill., 1972, programming group leader, 1972-74, tariff mgr., 1974-79; dir. computer services Airline Tariff Pub. Co., Washington, 1979-80, v.p. computer services, 1980-87, sr. v.p. computer services, from 1987. Mem. electronic tariff filing adv. com. U.S. Dept. Transp., Washington, 1987—; mem. industry fares and rules exchange standards group Internat. Air Transport Assn., Geneva, Switzerland, 1987—. Served to capt. USAF, 1967-72. Mem. Va. State Bar. Roman Catholic. Home: Fairfax Station, Va. Died Nov. 15, 2007.

FERRIS, GEORGE MALLETTE, JR., investment banker; b. Washington, Mar. 11, 1927; s. George Mallette and Charlotte (Hamilton) F.; m. Nancy Strouce, Jan. 25, 1964; children: George Mallette III, Willard Bradley, Kimberly Anne, David Hamilton. BS in Engring. magna cum laude, Princeton U., 1948; MBA, Harvard U., 1950. Chmn. Ferris, Baker Watts, Inc., Washington, from 1971. Commr. Md. Aviation Commn.; past bd. govs. NY Stock Exch.; past chmn. Pres.'s Commn. on Mgmt. Aid Programs; past pres. Washington Soc. Investment Analysts. Past gen. campaign chmn. United Givers Fund, 1966; past gen. chmn. sustaining fund drive Nat. Symphony Orch.; past mem. Pres.'s Task Force Internat. Pvt. Enterprise; past chmn. investment adv. bd. AID. Recipient Princeton in Nation's Svc. award, Washingtonian award Jaycees, Order Red Triangel award YMCA Greater Washington, Silver Beaver award Boy Scouts Am. Mem. Harvard Bus. Sch. Club Washington (past pres.), Met. Club, Chevy Chase Club (Md.), Burning Tree Club (Md.), The Ctr. Club (Balt.), Phi Beta Kappa, Tau Beta Phi. Home: Bethesda, Md. Died Oct. 20, 2008.

FERRY, ARTHUR GEORGE, JR., minister; b. Brazil, Ind., Aug. 13, 1938; s. Arthur George and Helen Irene (Howard) F.; m. Anna Louise Ashby, May 28, 1959; children: Scott Alan, Lori Ann Garcia. BTh, Trinity Coll. of the Bible, 1987; M of Ministry, Trinity Theol., 1990. Assoc. pastor Woodville Bapt. Ch., Mitchell, Ind., 1982-85; pastor First Bapt. Ch., Williams, Ind., 1985-87, New Winchester Bapt. Ch., Danville, Ind., 1987-90; sr. pastor First Bapt. Ch., Garrett, Ind., from 1991. Chaplain in field; treas., dir. Concerned Citizens for Abused Adults, Plainfield, Ind., 1987-91; moderator White Lick Bapt. Assn., Amo, Ind., 1989-91. Town chmn. Rep. Party, Staunton, Ind., 1965-72, precinct com., 1964-66; rep. Town Bd., Staunton, 1969-72. Mem. Am. Bapt. Chs., Internat. Conf. Police Chaplains, Garrett Police, Garrett Minister's Coun., Northeastern Minister's Coun., Lions (v.p. 1988-90), Masonic #264 (chair 1960-70), Eastern Star. Republican. Home: Garrett, Ind. Died July 16, 2008.

FIALA, ROBERT HENRY, electrical engineer; b. Ft. Dodge, Iowa, Oct. 31, 1939; s. Henry A. and Julia (Urban) F.; m. Janet Elizabeth Durke, June 12, 1971 (div. Sept. 1987); m. In Jin Yi, Dec. 5, 1987; 1 child, Sarah T. Yi. AAS, Devry Tech. Inst., Chgo., 1959; BSEE, Northrop Inst., Inglewood, Calif., 1969; MSEE, Loyola U., Westchester, Calif., 1975. Tech. supr. Hughes Aircraft Co., Fullerton,

Calif., 1976-84; project engr. Raytheon Sys. Co., El Segundo, Calif., from 1984. With USN, 1962-66, Vietnam. Avocation: computers. Home: Corona, Calif. Died Feb. 18, 2008.

FIEDLER, DONALD B., lawyer; b. Omaha, Feb. 2, 1943; BA, U. Ariz., 1965; JD, Creighton U., 1969. Bar: Nebr., U.S. Dist. Ct. Nebr., U.S. Ct. Appeals (7th, 8th and 9th cirs.), U.S. Supreme Ct. Pvt. practice, Omaha, from 1970. Mem. faculty Nat. Criminal Def. Coll., 1988—. Author: NE Forms, 1986. With USCGR, 1967-72. Recipient Fonda award Playhouse, 1981, Critics awards Playhouse, 1981, Teal award, 1995. Mem. Nat. Criminal Def. Lawyers Assn. (bd. dirs. 1986-91), State Criminal Def. Atty. Assn. (bd. dirs., pres.). Democrat. Avocation: acting. Died May 15, 2008.

FIELDS, ARMOND, writer, artist; b. Chgo., Nov. 22, 1930; s. Louis Max and Esther Fields; m. Rona Marcia Fields, June 26, 1953 (div. 1966); children: Marc, Sean, Miriam; m. Sara Lee Fields, June 29, 1969; children: Jason, Seth. BS, U. Wis., 1953; MA, U. Ill., 1955; PhD, U. Chgo., 1956. Mktg. and rsch. v.p. Interpublic Co., LA, 1960-69; self-employed mktg. cons. and artist, from 1969; self-employed author, from 1985; self-employed tchr., 1990-95. Corp. officer Audio-Video Entertainment, Inc., Laguna Niguel, Calif., 2000—. Author: (art history) Henri Riviere, 1983, George Auriol, 1985, (theater biographies) From the Bowery to Broadway, 1993 (Kurt Weill award 1995), Lillian Russell, 1999, Eddie Foy, 2000, James J. Corbett, 2001. Art vol., ESL planner, site coun. chair Culver City (Calif.) Unified Sch. Dist., 1983-90. Democrat. Jewish. Avocations: travel, art collecting and curating, writing. Home: Culver City, Calif. Died Aug. 17, 2008.

FIELDS, DENNIS FRANKLIN, SR., educator, clergyman; b. Abingdon, Va., Jan. 29, 1947; s. Joe Frank and Mabel (Overbay) F.; m. Barbara Glenna Roberts, July 6, 1965; children: Dennis Franklin II, Miriam Ruth. BS, Liberty Bapt. Coll., 1979; MA, Liberty Bapt. Theol. Sem., 1982; D Ministry, Trinity Evang. Div. Sch., 1986; DD (hon.), No. Fla. Bapt. Theol. Sem., 1990. Ordained to ministry Bapt. Ch., 1982. Dir. ch. planting Liberty U., Lynchburg, Va., 1978-91, dir. Christian and community svc., 1979-91. Assoc. pastor Thomas Rd. Bapt. Ch., Lynchburg, Va., 1977-91; interim pastor several chs.; chmn. bd. dirs. Mainland China Mission Internat., Forest, Va., 1989—; bd. dirs. Unevangelized Field Missions Internat., Inc., Bala-Cynwyd, Pa.; founding mem., exec. sec. Internat. Asian Mission Inc., Lynchburg, 1981-90; founding bd. dirs. Reynard Faber Found., Dulce, N.Mex., 1991. Contbr. articles to religious jours. Died June 27, 2008.

FIELDS, WILLIAM COFFIELD, III, artist; b. Fayetteville, NC, Sept. 27, 1917; s. William Coffield Jr. and Elizabeth Mitchell (Gibson) F. BFA, U. N.C., 1938; postgrad., Sch. of Mus. of Fine Arts, Boston, 1942-44; DHL (hon.), Dowling Coll., Oakdale, NY, 1975; Dr. Humanities (hon.), Meth. Coll., Fayetteville, 1984. Dir. Fed. Art Project Ctr., Sanford, N.C., 1938-39, Fed. Art Project Ctr. and N.C. State Art Soc. Gallery, Raleigh, 1939-40; asst. state dir. N.C. Fed. Art Project, 1940-42. Editor: (books) Cumberland County, N.C. Court Minutes, 1755-1791, Vol. I, 1978 Vol. II, 1981, A Guide to Historic Sites in Fayetteville and Cumberland County, N.C., 1993, Cumberland County, N.C., Deeds, 1754-70, Vol. I, 1994. Artist painting portraits including the late Pope Pius XII, Prince Enrico Barberini, Prince Urbano Barberini, Princess Maria Barberini, Prince Ludovico Chigi-della Rovere-Albani, Grand Master of Sovereign Mil. Order of Malta, Prince Raimondo Orsini, Princess Maria Silvia Boncompagni-Ludovisi, Princess Maria Elena Pignatelli, Vittorio Orlando, Prime Minister of Italy during World War I, others; numerous one-man shows in Rome, N.Y., N.C. and numerous group shows in eastern galleries. Vice pres. N.C. Symphony Soc., also exec. and fin. coms.; mem. Carolina Charter Tercentenary Commn., 1962, mem. com. on arts and chmn. dance-drama com.; adv. com. N.C. Recreation Commn., 1964; mem. N.C. Arts Coun.; bd. dirs. Carolina Charter Corp., Raleigh, 1963—, Friends of Archives, Raleigh, 1990—; pres. N.C. Ballet Co., 1967-69. Recipient N.C. Award in Fine Arts, 1974. Fellow Royal Soc. Arts (London, life); mem. Assoc. Artists of N.C. (pres. 1961-64). Democrat. Died Dec. 5, 2007.

FIGGIE, HARRY E., JR., retired consumer products company executive; b. 1923; married; 3 children. BS, Case Inst. Tech., 1947, MS in Indsl. Engring, 1951; MBA, Harvard U., 1949; LLB, Cleve. Marshall Law Sch., 1953. Formerly with Western Automatic Screw Machine Co., Parker-Hannifin Corp. and, Booz, Allen & Hamiliton; group v.p. indsl. products A. O. Smith Corp., 1962-64; chmn., CEO Figgie Internat. (formerly A-T-O Inc.), 1960—94; chmn. Clark Reliance Corp. Author: Bankruptcy 1995. Mem. World Bus. Council. Died July 14, 2009.

FINCH, JIMMY LESLIE, marine engineer; b. Oak Ridge, Tenn., June 21, 1950; s. Frank Ira and Marcella Justine (Williams) F.; m. Melody Ellen Beach, June 21, 1980; children: Jonathon, Jody. BS in Marine Engring., U.S. Mcht. Marine Acad., Kings Point, NY, 1973. Chief engr. Exxon Shipping Co., Houston, from 1973. Serving as lt. comdr. USNR, 1987—. Named to Eagle Scouts Boy Scouts Am., 1964, Order of Arrow, 1964. Avocations: golf, woodworking. Home: Montgomery, Ala. Died Oct. 2, 2007.

FINE, SIDNEY, retired history professor; b. Cleve., Oct. 11, 1920; s. Morris Louis and Gussie (Redalia) F.; m. Jean Schechter, Dec. 5, 1942; children: Gail Judith, Deborah Ann. BA summa cum laude, Western Res. U., 1942; MA, U. Mich., 1944, PhD, 1948; LittD, Wittenberg U., 1984. Mem. faculty U. Mich., 1948—2001, prof. history, 1959—2001, prof. emeritus, 2001—09, Andrew Dickson White disting. prof. history, from 1974, Henry Russel lectr., 1984-85, chmn. dept., 1969-71. Mem. faculty Salzburg Seminar Am. Studies, 1959; Mem. Nat. Archives Adv. Council, 1968-71 Author: Laissez Faire and the General Welfare State, 1956, The Automobile Under the Blue Eagle, 1963 (U. Mich. Press Book award 1965), (with G.S. Brown) The American Past, 2 vols, 1961, Recent America, 1962, Sit-Down: The General Motors Strike of 1936-1937, 1969 (U. Mich. Press Book award 1971), Frank Murphy: The Detroit Years, 1975, Frank Murphy: The New Deal Years, 1979, Frank Murphy: The Washington Years, 1984 (U. Mich. Press book award 1985), Violence in the Model City, 1989 (Outstanding Book award 1990, U. Mich. Press book award 1991), The Mark of a Civilized Society, 2001; also articles; bd editors: Jour. Am. History, 1964-67, Revs. in American History, 1973-80; bd. editors: Labor History, chmn. editorial bd.; bd. editors: Mich. Hist. Review Rackham predoctoral fellow U. Mich., 1946-48, Guggenheim fellow, 1957-58; named Prof. of Yr. State of Mich., 1986; recipient Golden Apple award Students Honoring Outstanding Univ. Teaching, 1993. Mem. Am. Hist. Assn., Orgn. Am. Historians, Labor Historians (pres. 1969-71), U. Mich. Research Club (pres. 1983-84), U. Mich. Sci. Club, Phi Beta Kappa (chpt. pres. 1975-76), Phi Kappa Phi. Home: Ann Arbor, Mich. Died Mar. 31, 2009.

FINGER, BERNARD L., financial services consultant, expert witness; b. NYC, Aug. 21, 1927; s. Morris and Anna (Weinberg) F.; m. Naomi Wesler, Feb. 1, 1948; children: Stephanie, Eric. BA, CCNY, 1949; MA, Columbia U., 1950. Securities investigator Securities and Exch. Commn., NYC, 1957-61; dir. fl. procedures and allocations Am. Stock Exch., NYC, 1961-67; compliance dir. Purcell Graham & Co., NYC, 1967-69, Bruns, Nordeman, Rea & Co., NYC, 1969-81, Securities Settlement Corp., NYC, 1981-91; pvt. practice West Palm Beach, Fla., from 1992. Arbitrator N.Y. Stock Exch., N.Y.C., 1987—, Nat. Assn. Securities Dealers, N.Y.C., 1987—, Am. Stock Exch., 1996—. With U.S. Army, 1944-46. Mem. Phi Beta Kappa (Gamma chpt. of N.Y.). Avocations: golf, classical music, avid hockey fan. Died Sept. 5, 2008.

FINKEL, DONALD ALEXANDER, poet; b. NYC, Oct. 21, 1929; s. Saul A. and Meta (Rosenthal) F.; m. Constance Urdang, Aug. 14, 1956 (dec. 1996); children: Elizabeth Antonia, Thomas Noah, Amy Mariah. BS in Philosophy, Columbia U., 1952, MA in English, 1953. Poet-in-residence Washington U., St. Louis, 1965-91, Poet-in-residence emeritus, 1991—2008; cons. prosody Random House Dictionary. Author: The Clothing's New Emperor, 1959, Simeon, 1964, A Joyful Noise, 1966, Answer Back, 1968, The Garbage Wars, 1970, Adequate Earth, 1972, A Mote in Heaven's Eye, 1975, Endurance: An Antarctic Idyll, 1978, Going Under, 1978, What Manner of Beast, 1981, The Detachable Man, 1984, The Wake of the Electron, 1987, Selected Shorter Poems, 1987, A Splintered Mirror: Chinese Poetry from the Democracy Movement, 1991, Beyond Despair, 1994, A Question of Seeing, 1998, Not So the Chairs: Selected and New Poems, 2003 Recipient Theodore Roethke Meml. award, 1974, Morton Dauwen Zabel award, 1980, Dictionary of Literary Biography award, 1994; Guggenheim fellow, 1966; grantee Ingram Merrill Found., 1972; grantee Nat. Endowment for Arts, 1973. Mem. Cave Rsch. Found., Phi Beta Kappa. Died Nov. 15, 2008.

FINKELSTEIN, JACOB, chemist; b. NYC, Oct. 27, 1910; BS, CCNY, 1933; MA, Columbia U., 1934, PhD, 1939. Organic chemist The Rsch. Corp., NYC, 1935; rsch. chemist Merck & Co., Rahway, N.J., 1935-43, Hoffmann-LaRoche, Inc., Nutley, N.J., 1943-75; prof. organic chemistry St. Peter's Coll., Jersey City, N.J., 1976-77; chem. cons. Teaneck, N.J., from 1977. Patentee in field; contbr. articles to profl. publs. Fellow Am. Inst. of Chemists; mem. Am. Chem. Soc. (Eminent Chemist of N.J., 1981, exec. com. North Jersey sect., chmn. organic chemistry discussion group), Sci. Rsch. Soc. of Am., Phi Lambda Upsilon, Sigma Xi. Avocations: gardening, photography. Died Jan. 19, 2008.

FINNEGAN, WILLIAM ROBINSON (WILLIAM ROBINSON FINNEGAN), film producer; b. June 29, 1928; m. Patricia Marie Quinn, Jan. 27, 1953; children: William, Kevin, Colleen, Michael. Prodr.: (films) Support Your Local Sheriff, 1969, Support Your Local Gunfighter, 1971, Night of the Creeps, 1986, North Shore, 1987, Going to the Chapel, 1988, The Fabulous Baker Boys, 1989, White Palace, 1990, The Babe, 1992, CrissCross, 1992, Reality Bites, 1994, Tis the Season, 1994, Ed, 1996, The Axe in the Attic, 2007; (TV films) Hec Ramsey, 1972, Chelsea D.H.O., 1973, Dea Man on the Run, 1975, Danger in Paradise, 1977, Maneaters Are Loose!, 1978, Stranger In Our House, 1979, The Ordeal of Patty Hearst, 1979, A Vacation in Hell, 1979, The $5.20 an Hour Dream, 1980, Valentine Magic on Love Island, 1980, Father Figure, 1980, The Choice, 1981, Inmates: A Love Story, 1982, Callahan, 1982, World War III, 1982, Between Two Brothers, 1983, Your Place...or Mine, 1983, Summer Place, 1983, Flight 90: Disaster on the Potomac, 1984, The Dollmaker, 1984, Generation, 1985, This Child Is Mine, 1985, News at Eleven, 1986, Circle of Violence: A Family Drama, 1986, Louis L'Amour's Down the Long Hills, 1986, Babes in Toyland, 1986, American Harvest, 1987, The Alamo: Thirteen Days to Glory, 1987, Lincoln, 1988, She Knows Too Much, 1989, Dark Holiday, 1989, Murder By Night, 1989, Laker Girls, 1990, Hell Hath No Fury, 1990, Hope, 1997; (TV mini-series) King, 1978, The Atlanta Child Murders, 1985; (TV series) Hawaii Five-O, 1971-75, The Days and Nights of Molly Dodd, 1987, She-Wolf of London, 1990, Northern Exposure, 1990-91, Any Day Now, 1998 Home: New York, NY. Died Nov. 28, 2008.

FINO, PAUL ALBERT, Former United States Representative from New York; b. NYC, Dec. 15, 1913; s. Isidoro and Lucia Patane Fino; m. Esther Fino; children: Paul Jr., Lucille. JD, St. John's U., 1937. Asst. atty. gen. State of NY, Albany, 1943—44; mem. 27th Dist. NY State Senate, Albany, 1945—50; mem. NYC Civil Svc. Commn., 1950—52, US Congress from 25th NY Dist., 1953—63, US Congress from 24th NY Dist., 1963—68; delegate Rep. State Conv., 1940—66, Rep. Nat. Conv., 1960, 1964, 1968; justice NY State Supreme Ct., 1969—72; atty. White, Fleischner & Fino. Author: My Life in Politics and Public Service., 1986. Republican. Died June 16, 2009; North Woodmere, NY.

FINTA, FRANCES MICKNA, secondary school educator; b. Stafford Springs, Conn., June 17, 1927; d. John Joseph Mickna and Mary Frances Breslin; m. Quinn Finta, Aug. 21, 1951; children: John Wright, Susan Frances Finta Phillips. BA in Math., Boston U., 1949; postgrad., U. Va., 1963—69, Prince George's C.C., Largo, Md., 1982, No. Va. C.C., Alexandria, 1982—84, postgrad., 1994, U. Va., Fairfax, 1988—89; MEd in Guidance and Counseling, George Mason U., 1975. Cert. tchr. Va. Food prodn. mgr., dining rm. mgr., waitress, field ops. rep., liaison to airlines Marriott Corp., Marriott In-Flight Svcs., Inc., Washington, 1950—62; tchr. math, Arlington Pub. Schs., Va., 1963—72, from 1963. Substitute tchr. Fairfax (Va.) Pub. Schs., 1972—73; 'substitute tchr. Arlington (Va.) County Pub. Schs., from 1972. Mem. Arlington County Scholarship Fund for Tchrs., Inc., from 1990, sec., 1994—2002, treas., from 2002; mem. Friends of Arlington Parks, from 1995, Maywood Cmty. Assn., from 1966; treas. Washington-Lee H.S. Band Booster Club, 1979—81, Evelyn Staples for County Bd., 1991; vol. coord. David Foster for Sch. Bd., 1994, 2003; mem. Arlingtonians for a Better County, 1999—2003, Arlington County Rep. Com., from 1994, chmn. hdqrs., from 2000, mem. fin. com., 1994—95, canvass chmn., 2000, 2000, 2002, 2004, 2006, 2008, chmn. nominations com., 2000—01, chmn. credentials com., 2006—08, mem. credentials com., 2008; mem. steering com. John Hager for Gov., 2000; del. to state conv. Rep. Party Va., 1996, 1998, 2000, 2008, Va. Fedn. Rep. Women, from 1996, co-chair credential com., 2007, 2008; mem. credential com. Va. 8th Dist. Rep. Conv., 1998, 2008; sec.'s adv. com. Commonwealth of Va., 1998—2002; mem. Organized Women Voters of Arlington, from 1997, mem. nominating com., 2000, treas., 2000—04; rep. Va. Fed. Rep. Women's 8th Dist., 2008. Recipient Hon. Guardian of Srs.' Rights award, 60 Plus Assn., 1999, Vol. Svc. award, Arlington County Rep. Com., 1995—99, Hilda Griffith Lifetime Achievement award, 1999, Leon Delyannis Cmty. Involvement award, 1997, award of Excellence, 2004, Cert. of Appreciation, Arlington County Civic Fedn., 1988, 1997, Jour. Newspapers trophy, 2001, Parent Vol. award, Washington-Lee H.S. Band Boosters Club, 1979, Appreciation award, 1981, Parent Vol. award, Woodmont Elem. Sch., 1975, Patrick Henry award, Commonwealth of Va., 2001, Disting. Meritorious Svc. award, Arlington County Civic Fedn., 2003, Vol. Svc. award, Arlington County Rep. Com., 2003, Cert. of Appreciation, Arlington County Voters in Partnership Program, 2001. Mem.: AAUW (del. to Arlington County Civic Fedn. from 1994, co-1st v.p. programs 2001—03, exec. com. from 2001, 1st v.p. programs 2002—03, policy chair 2003—05, co-policy chair from 2005), NEA, Arlington County Civic Assn. (pres. from 2008), Arlington Co. Civic Fed., Arlington Ret. Tchrs. Assn. (v.p. programs 2003—06, 1st v.p. programs from 2004, exec. com. from 2004, pres. from 2006), Arlington Edn. Assn., Va. Edn. Assn., Va. Ret. Tchrs. Assn. (life), Arlington County Civic Fedn. (mem. numerous coms. from 1985, treas. 1998—2006, v.p. from 2006, co. chair 2007—08, Chair Awards Com. 2008, chair, award com. chair 2008), Arlington County Taxpayers' Assn., Maywood Cmty. Assn. (del. Arlington Civic Fedn. from 1982, nominating com. 2006), Arlington Rep. Women's Club (auditor 1996, asst. treas. 1997, pres. 1998—99, newsletter editor 1998—99, exec. bd. from 1998, chmn. achievement awards 2000, chmn. bylaws com. 2000, chmn. Barbara Bush literacy com. 2000, dir. 2000—01, auditor 2002—03, chair fin. com. from 2002). Republican. Roman Catholic. Avocations: civic and political activities, reading. Died June 19, 2008.

FISCHER, DAVID JOHN, chemist; b. Jefferson City, Mo., Apr. 30, 1928; s. Leonard Emmanuel and Clara Lily (Beck) F.; m. Jean Charlotte Tiemann, June 19, 1954; children: Kristin Gail, Charlotte Claire. BA, U. Mo., 1950, MS, 1952, PhD, 1954. Supr. Dow Corning Corp., Midland, Mich., 1956-62; sr. chemist Midwest Rsch. Inst., Kansas City, Mo., 1962-65; mgr. Corning (N.Y.) Glass Works, 1965-75; dir. ophthalmic R & D, Milton Roy, Sarasota, Fla., 1975-79; pres. Universal R & D, Sarasota, 1979-81; sr. rsch. advisor Gulf South R & D, New Orleans, 1981-82; mgr. advanced quality tech. and labs. Manned Space Systems divsn. Martin Marietta Co., New Orleans, 1982-93; ret., 1993. Contbr. articles to profl. jours., chpts. to books. Vice pres. Redeemer Luth. Ch., Corning, N.Y., 1968-72, pres., 1972; v.p. Bethany Luth. Ch., Slidell, La., 1981-84. 1st lt. USAF, 1954-56. Mem. AIAA, Am. Chem. Soc., Sigma Xi, Phi Beta Kappa.

Achievements include patents on contact lens and elastomers; research on radiation resistant elastomer and fluid, toric contact lenses, laser marking of contact lenses, anoerobic digester design, stabilized enzymes, methane generation, hyper pure silicon, restoration of flood-damage museum library archival items. Home: Slidell, La. Died Jan. 16, 2008.

FISHER, DONALD G., retail executive; b. 1928; m. Doris Fisher; 3 children. BS, U. Calif., 1950. With M. Fisher & Son, 1950-57; former ptnr. Fisher Property Investment Co.; co-founder Gap Stores, San Bruno, Calif., 1969; chmn. Gap Inc., San Bruno, Calif., 1969—2004, chmn. emeritus, 2004—09, pres., 1969—83. Bd. dirs. Gap, Inc., 1969—2009, Schwab Charles Corp., 1988—2009; mem. adv. coun. Office of US Trade Rep., 1987—98. Trustee Presidio Trust, 1997—2009; bd. mem. Calif. State Bd. Ed. Named one of Top 200 Collectors, ARTnews Mag., 2004—08, Forbes Richest Americans, 2006. Avocation: art collector. Died Sept. 27, 2009.

FISHER, EDWIN R., pathologist; b. Pitts., Sept. 2, 1923; s. Reuben and Anna (Miller) F.; m. Carole Levy; chlildren: Marjorie, Abbe Dava. BS, U. Pitts., 1945, MD, 1947. Staff pathology Cleve. Clin., 1953-54; prof. pathology U. Pitts., 1954; chief pathology VA Hosp., Pitts., 1954-70, Shadyside Hosp., Pitts., 1970-95. Mem. editorial bd. Breast Cancer Research and Treatment, European Cancer; chief pathologist Nat. Surg. Adj. Breast Project. Contbr. articles to profl. jours. Sr. surgeon USPHS, 1951-53. Recipient Parke-Davis award Soc. Exptl. Pathology, 1963. Mem. Am. Assn. Cancer Research, Am. Soc. Clin. Pathologists, Internat. Acad. Pathologists, Am. Thoracic Soc., Coll. Am. Pathology. Republican. Jewish. Avocations: golf, landscaping. Died Mar. 13, 2008.

FISHER, JOHN WESLEY, retired manufacturing executive; b. Walland, Tenn., July 15, 1915; s. Arthur Justin and Rachel (Malott) F.; m. Janice Kelsey Ball, Aug. 10, 1940; children: Joan Fisher Woods, Michael J., James A., Jeffrey E., Judith Fisher Oetinger, John Wesley III, Jerrold M. BS, U. Tenn., 1938; MBA, Harvard U., 1942; LLD (hon.), Ball State U., 1972, Butler U., 1977, DePauw U., 1981, Ind. U., 1985. Field sec. Delta Tau Delta Frat., Indpls., 1938-40; trainee, various mfg., sales and adminstrv. positions Ball Corp., Muncie, Ind., 1941-70, pres., CEO, 1970-78, chmn. bd., CEO, 1978-81, chmn. bd., 1981-86, chmn. emeritus, 1986—2009. Bd. dirs. Kindel Furniture Co., Grand Rapids, Mich.; ptnr. Blackwood & Nichols Corp., Oklahoma City; chmn. CID Equity Ptnrs., Indpls., Old Nat. Trust Co., Muncie; pres. Nature's Catch, Inc., Clarksdale, Miss., Fisher Properties of Ind., Inc. State del. Rep. Party, Ind., 1950-70; mem. Rep. State Fin. Com., 1952-56, del. nat. conv., 1952, 54, 64, 68; chmn. Cardinal Health Sys.; chmn., pres. Ball Bros. Found. Mem. NAM (chmn. 1979-80, bd. dirs.), Glass Packaging Inst. (trustee 1962-68, pres. 1965-67), Grocery Mfrs. Assn. (bd. dirs.), Ind. C. of C. (dir. 1959—, pres. 1966-68), Muncie C. of C. (past pres.), Conf. Bd., Ind. Acad., Delaware Country Club, Columbia Club (Indpls.), Royal Poinciana Country Club, Naples (Fla.) Yacht Club, Rotary, Naples Nat. Golf Club, Delta Tau Delta. Republican. United Methodist. Home: Muncie, Ind. Died June 28, 2009.

FISHER, JOY DEBORAH, lawyer; b. Chgo., Mar. 15, 1952; d. J. Barry and Rochelle Barbara (Levin) F.; m. Arthur Walter Stawinski, Nov. 2, 1979; 1 child, Steven Lee Fisher-Stawinski; step children: Kathryn, Elizabeth Kline. BA, U. Ill., Champaign, 1973, JD, 1976. Bar: Ill. Supreme Ct. 1976, Fed. Dist. Ct. (no. dist.) Ill. 1976. With Fisher & Sherman, Chgo., 1976-78; ptnr. J.B. Fisher & J.D. Fisher, Chgo., 1978-87; pvt. practice Chgo., 1987—99, Buffalo Grove, Ill., 1987—99, Long Grove, Ill., from 1999. Contract atty. Ill. Sec. State, Chgo., 1981-83; mem. real estate panel Am. Arbitration Assn., Chgo., 1982-92; v.p. for legal counsel Discovery Sci. Edn. Found.; spkr. in field. Contbr. articles to profl. jours., poems to profl. jour. Vol. atty. Free Women's Legal Clinic, Chgo., 1976-79; mem. steering com. Com. for ERA, Chgo., 1976-78; pro bono legal counsel for misc. non-profit orgns. and abused women, Cook County, Ill., 1976—; v.p. for legal counsel Discovery Learning Found., 1990-94; elected mem., sec. Bd. Edn. Wheeling (Ill.) Dist. 21, 1985-93; family sponsor JCC Family to Family, Cook County, 1990; elected mem. Wheeling Twp. Bd. Trustees, 2001-05; pres. Power Net Networking Group, 2005; mem. Lake County Women's Dem. Orgns. Recipient Cert. of Appreciation, Decalogue Soc. Lawyers, Chgo., 1980, Indian Trail Pub. Lib. Dist., Lavisso Sch. Mem. Ill. Real Estate Lawyer's Assn., Ill. State Bar Assn., Northwest Suburban Bar Assn. (chair estate planning com. 1999-2001), Internat. Alliance of Holistic Lawyers. Avocations: politics, reading, travel, crocheting, writing. Home: Buffalo Grove, Ill. Died Dec. 17, 2007.

FISHER, WILLIAM HALDER, retired economist; b. Richmond, Va., Mar. 4, 1914; s. William James and Marguerite (Halder) F.; m. Regina Elmore Bowles, May 15, 1937 (dec. 2007); children: Marguerite Halder, Nell Beard, William Halder Jr. BS in Chemistry, Richmond Coll., 1934; MA in Econs., U. Va., 1943, PhD in Econs., 1945. Supr. WPA and NYA of Va., Richmond, 1939-41; fellow Bur. Bus. Rsch., Charlottesville, Va., 1941-43; economist Fed. Res. Bank, Richmond, 1943-46; asst. prof. U. Del., Newark, 1946-52; economist FTC, Washington, 1952-54, Robert R. Nathan Assoc., Washington, 1954-56; prin. Fisher & Associates, Washington, 1956-60; rsch. economist C. of C., U.S.A., Washington, 1960-63, Battelle Meml. Inst., Columbus, Ohio, 1963—2002. Author numerous books, monographs and articles in field. Avocation: fly fishing. Home: Dublin, Ohio. Died May 18, 2009.

FITE, LEA, state legislator; m. Judy Fite; children: Laurie, Wes, Trae, Jerrod. Attended, Jacksonville State U., Ala. Supermarket owner; mem. Dist. 40 Ala. House of Reps, Montgomery, 2002—09. Democrat. Died Oct. 26, 2009.

FITZGERALD, JOHN MOONAN, judge; b. Rochester, Minn., Jan. 20, 1923; s. William Alphonse and Rosemary Kathleen (Moonan) F.; m. Mary Alice Mach, May 5, 1951; children: Maureen, Erin, Brigid, Sheila, Megan, John. BS in Law, U. Minn., 1946, LLB, 1948. Bar: Minn. 1948, U.S. Dist. Ct. Minn. 1948. State rep. Minn. Legis., 1957-62; dist. ct. judge State of Minn., 1963-93, ret., 1993. Mem. Minn. State Bar Assn. (trustee 1980-81), Minn. Dist. Judges Assn. (pres. 1981-82). Roman Catholic. Avocation: fishing. Home: New Prague, Minn. Died June 16, 2008.

FLAGELLO, EZIO DOMENICO, basso; b. NYC, Jan. 28, 1931; s. Dionisio and Genoveffa (Casiello) F.; m. Anna Mione (div.); children: Genoveffa, Dante, Josine, Christine; m. Myra Bianco, 2008 Student, Manhattan Sch. Music, U. Perugia, Italy. Lectr. master classes numerous univs. Debut in Boris Godunov, Carnegie Hall, 1952; leading roles as basso at Met. Opera, N.Y.C.; appeared major opera houses throughout world, including La Scala, Milan, Italy, Vienna State Opera, Berlin Opera; performed at opening night inaugural opera, Met. Opera, inaugural performance, Philharmonic Hall, Lincoln Center, N.Y.C.; rec. artist, RCA Victor, Columbia, Deutsche Grammophon, Decca/London, Delhi, Scope, Internos, Musical Heritage Series; appeared in film Godfather II, 1974. Served with U.S. Army, 1952-54. Recipient Grammy award Alumni award Evander Childs High Sch., N.Y.C., Grand Prix du Disque award, award Manhattan Sch. Music, Albanese/Puccini award, 1997; Fulbright fellow. Roman Catholic. Home: Palm Bay, Fla. Died Mar. 19, 2009.

FLANSBURGH, EARL ROBERT, architect; b. Ithaca, NY, Apr. 28, 1931; s. Earl Alvah and Elizabeth (Evans) F.; m. Louise Hospital, Aug. 27, 1955; children: Earl Schuyler, John Conant. BArch, Cornell U., 1954; MArch, MIT, 1957; S.C.M.P., Harvard U. Sch. Bus., 1982. Job capt., designer The Architects Collaborative, Cambridge, Mass., 1958-62; partner Freeman, Flansburgh & Assos., Cambridge, 1961-63; prin. Earl R. Flansburgh & Assocs., Cambridge, 1963-69, pres., dir. design, from 1969. Bd. dirs. daka, Inc.; exec. v.p. Environment Systems Internat., Inc.; vis. prof. archtl. design Mass. Inst. Tech., 1965-66; instr. art Wellesley Coll., 1962-65, lectr. art, 1965-69; cons. Arthur D. Little, Inc., Cambridge, 1964-70. Archtl. works include Weston (Mass.) High Sch. Addition, 1965-67, Cornell U. Campus Store, 1967-70, Cumnock Hall, Harvard U. Bus. Sch, 1973-75, Acton (Mass.) Elementary schs, 1966-68, 69-71, Wilton (Conn.) High Sch, 1968-71, 14 Story St. Bldg, 1970, Boston Design Ctr., 1985-86, Glenwood Sch., Dallas, 1985-88, New Univ. No. B.C., Prince George, Can., 1991-2009, Boston Coll. Law Sch., 1992-2009; exhibited works Light Machine I, IBM Gallery, N.Y.C., 1958, Light Machine II, Carpenter Center, Harvard, 1965, 5 Cambridge Architects, Wellesley Coll., 1969, Work of Earl R. Flansburgh and Assos, Wellesley Coll., 1969, New Architecture in New Eng, DeCordova Mus., 1974-75, Residential Architecture, Mead Art Gallery, Amherst Coll., 1976, works represented in, 50 Ville del Nostro Tempo, 1970, Nuove Ville, New Villas, 1970, Vacation Houses, 1970, Vacation Houses, 2d edit., 1977, Interior Design, 1970, Drawings by American Architects, 1973, Interior Spaces Designed by Architects, 1974, New Architecture in New England, 1974, Great Houses, 1976, Architecture Boston, 1976, Presentation Drawings by American Architects, 1977, Architecture, 1970-1980, A Decade of Change, 1980, Old and New Architecture, A Design Relationship, 1980, 25 Years of Record Houses, 1981, School Ways: The Planning and Design of American Schools, 1992, Elem. and Secondary Schs., 2001; Author: (with others) Techniques of Successful Practice, 1975. Chmn. architecture com. Boston Arts Festival, 1964, Downtown Boston Design adv. com.; bd. dirs. Cambridge Ctr. Adult Edn.; pres. Downtown North Boston, 1994-2009; trustee Cornell U., 1972-2009; chmn. bldgs. and properties com., 1976-87; mem. exec. com. acad. affairs com.; class sec. SCMP VII Harvard Bus. Sch., 1982-89. 1st lt. USAF, 1954-56. Recipient design awards Progressive Architecture, design awards Record Houses, design awards AIA, design awards City of Boston, design awards Mass. Masonry Inst., spl. design citations Am. Assn. Sch. Adminstrs., spl. 1st prize Buffalo-Western N.Y. chpt. AIA Competition., Walter Taylor award Am. Assn. Sch. Adminstrs., 1986, William Candill award Am. Coll. & Univ. Mag., 1993, Award of Honor, Boston Soc. Archs., 1999; Fulbright Rsch. grantee Bldg. Rsch. Sta., Eng., 1957-58. Fellow AIA, Nat. Acad. Design; mem. Royal Inst. Brit. Architects, Boston Soc. Architects (chmn. program com., 1969-71, commr. pub. affairs 1971-73, commr. design 1973-74, dir. 1971-74, pres. 1980-81), Boston Found. Architecture (treas. 1984-89), Cornell U. Coun., Quill and Dagger Soc., St. Botolph Club, Tau Beta Pi. Home: Lincoln, Mass. Died Feb. 3, 2009.

FLATO, JUD B., business owner; b. Bklyn., Feb. 21, 1940; s. Harry and Edith (Kleinman) F.; m. Anne Carol Horowitz, Aug. 21, 1963; children: Lauren P., Gillian B. BS in Chemistry, Poly. Inst. Bklyn., 1961; MS, NYU, 1963, PhD, 1968. Sr. research chemist Technicon Instruments, Ardsley, N.Y., 1966; various positions to sr. v.p. EG&G Princeton Applied Research, Princeton, N.J., 1967-83; pres., chief exec. officer Spex Industries, Inc., Edison, N.J., 1983-88; pres. Tetragon Co., Lawrenceville, N.J., from 1988; mng. ptnr. J.B. Flato & Assocs., Lawrenceville, from 1988, Internat. Mktg. Venture M&A Ops., Greenbelt, Md., from 1988; pres., mng. ptnr. Upton, Flato & Co., from 1990; mng. ptnr. Lab. Venture Partners, Lawrenceville, N.J., from 1991; exec. v.p. Strategic Directions Internat., Inc., LA, from 1992. Bd. dirs. Analytical Instrument Assn., Washington. Contbr. articles to profl. jours. Mem. Am. Chem. Soc., Instrument Soc. Am., Scientific Apparatus Makers Assn. (del., adv. bd. mem.). Avocations: band music, orchestra music, arranging. Died May 9, 2008.

FLEMING, HORACE WELDON, JR., retired academic administrator; b. Elberton, Ga., Jan. 14, 1944; s. Horace Weldon Sr and Alma G (Dove) Fleming; m. Orene Stephens Greene, Feb. 8, 1970; children: Susan Renee, Patrick Weldon. BA, U. Ga., 1965, MA, 1966; PhD, Vanderbilt U., 1973. Mem. faculty Clemson (S.C.) U., 1971-87; chief economist U.S. Senate Judiciary Com., 1981; staff dir. Office of Pres. Pro Tem U.S. Senate, 1981-82; founding dir. Strom Thurmond Inst. Govt. and Pub. Affairs, Clemson, 1982-90; exec. v.p. U. of the Pacific, Stockton, Calif., 1990-92; exec. v.p., provost Mercer U., Macon, Ga., 1992-96; pres. U. So. Miss., Hattiesburg, 1997—2001. Consult to fed, state and local govt agys on fin, orgn and mgt, energy and water policy; frequent media columnist and speaker; bd dirs Miss Technology Inc, Inst Technology Develop. Charter trustee Dropout Prevention Fund, 1986—90, Palmetto Project, 1987—90; vpres Hill Found, 1982—96; mem SC Reorganization Commn., 1987—90, Stockton-San Joaquin Conv and Visitors Bur, Calif., 1990—92; mem Vision 2000 task force Stockton Bus Coun, 1990—92; bd visitors Air Univ, from 1998; mem Pres's Nat Vol Adv coun, 1986—89, Assembly Future SC, 1988, Gov's Transition Task Force Govt Reform, 1986—87. Capt US Army, 1969—71, Vietnam. Recipient Order Palmetto, SC, 1990, Award of Merit, SC Water Resources Comn, 1990, Palmetto Pride Award, Palmetto Project, 1990; fellow Faculty, Leadership Hilton Head Island, 1989. Mem.: Tiger Brotherhood, Blue Key, Scabbard and Blade, Phi Kappa Phi, Omicron Delta Kappa, Sigma Phi Epsilon, Pi Sigma Alpha, Phi Mu Alpha. Home: Macon, Ga. Died May 1, 2009.

FLEMING, JOHN C., lawyer; b. Mar. 18, 1942; BA, St. John's U., Jamaica, NY, 1963; JD cum laude, Harvard U., 1966. Bar: N.Y. 1967, U.S. Supreme Ct. 1970, N.J. 1982. Assoc. Willkie, Farr & Gallagher, NYC, 1969-74, Rosenman, Colin, Freund, Lewis & Cohen, NYC, 1974-76; mem. faculty sch. law Rutgers U., Camden, N.J., 1976-81; sr. atty. Am. Homes Products Corp., NYC, from 1981. Mem. editorial bd. Harvard U. Law Rev., 1964-66. Mem. ABA, N.Y. State Bar Assn. Died Dec. 10, 2007.

FLEMING, PETER EMMET, JR., lawyer; b. Atlantic Highlands, NJ, Aug. 18, 1929; s. Peter Emmet and Anna (Sullivan) F.; m. Jane Breed, June 2, 1956 (dec. 1990); children: Peter Emmet III, James M., William B., David W., Jane H. AB, Princeton U., 1951; LL.B., Yale U., 1958. Bar: N.Y. 1959, U.S. Dist. Ct. (so. and ea. dists.) N.Y. 1960, U.S. Ct. Appeals (2d cir.) 1963, U.S. Ct. Appeals (4th cir.) 1979, U.S. Supreme Ct. 1985. Assoc. Davis, Polk & Wardwell, NYC, 1958-61; asst. US atty. (so. dist.) NY US Dept. Justice, NYC, 1961-70; ptnr. Curtis, Mallet-Prevost Colt & Mosle LLP, NYC, 1970—2009. Temporary spl. ind. counsel to Senators Bob Dole and George Mitchell US Senate Investigation of the dissemination of confidential information during Clarence Thomas nomination hearings, 1992. Mem.: NY State Assn. on Criminal Def. Lawyers, Fed. Bar Coun., NY State Bar Assn., NY County Lawyers Assn., Assn. Bar of the City of NY, Am. Coll. Trial Lawyers, Supreme Ct. Historical Soc. Home: Cos Cob, Conn. Died Jan. 14, 2009.

FLETCHER, DOUGLAS CHARLES, lawyer; b. Rockford, Ill., Mar. 5, 1943; s. Fred Leland and Dorothy Edwards Fletcher; children: Adrian, Lauren, Robin. BA in Econs. and Engring., U. Nev., Reno, 1969, MBA in Fin. cum laude, 1972; JD, U. of Pacific, 1975; postgrad., Colo. State U., 1976. Bar: Nev. 1975, U.S. Ct. Appeals (9th cir.) 1976. Exec. v.p. PanWorld Engring., 1967-68; design engr. Nev. Bell, 1968-70; economist Sierra Pacific Power Co., 1970-72, gen. counsel, 1975-78; operating trustee William Lear Motors Co., 1978-79; ptnr. Leslie Gray & Assocs., 1979-81; oper. trustee Horseshoe Club Casinos, 1981-82, Mapes Hotel and Money Tree Casinos, 1982-85; owner, ptnr. Douglas C. Fletcher, Ltd., from 1985; operating receiver Echo Summit Tahoe Ski Resort, 1989-92. Advisor U. Nev. Grad. Bus. Sch., Reno, 1976-85; mem. U.S. Trustee Panel, 1978-95; judge pro tem Reno Mcpl. Ct., 1980-82. Author: Bond Reverse Yield Gaps of Public Utilities, 1972. Mem. ctrl. planning com. Republican Party of Washoe County, 1978-82; bd. dirs. Washoe County Youth Found., Reno, 1983-92, Eagles Nest Assn., Reno, 1998; founder, bd. dirs. Sierra League, Reno, 1989-99; bd. dirs., pres. ski team advisors U. Nev., Reno, 1982—. Mem. No. Nev. Bankruptcy Bar Assn. (founding mem.), Washoe County Bar Assn., State Bar Nev. (environ. law com. 1975—), Reno Tennis Club (pres., bd. dirs.), U.S. Ski Coaches Assn. (cert.), Reno Ski and Recreation Club (bd. dirs., pres. 1982—), Prospectors Club (bd. dirs.), Prof. Ski Instr. of Am. (cert.), Sigma Nu, Phi Kappa Phi, Beta Gamma Sigma. Died Apr. 11, 2008.

FLETCHER, LEE (DEWEY LEE FLETCHER), legislative staff member; b. Monroe, La., Apr. 29, 1966; BS in Agrl. Edn., La. Tech. U., 1989; MBA, La. State U., 2000. Chief of staff to Rep. John Cooksey US House of Reps., Washington, 1997—2003, chief of staff to Rep. John Fleming, 2009; founder The Fletcher Group, Web Completors; owner Sta. 92.7 FM, La., from 2008, radio host., Town Hall with Lee Fletcher, 2008—09. Republican. Baptist. Died Sept. 30, 2009.

FLINDT, FLEMMING, ballet master; b. Copenhagen, Sept. 30, 1936; s. Charles and Elly F.; m. Vivi Gelker, Jan. 28, 1967; children— Tina, Bernadette, Vanessa Student, Royal Danish Ballet, 1945-46. Prin. dancer London Festival Ballet, London, 1955-58; danseur etoile Paris Opera Ballet, 1960-65; balletmaster, artistic dir. Royal Danish Ballet, Copenhagen, 1966-78; artistic dir. Dallas Ballet, 1981—89. Choreographer/stage dir. (ballets) The Lesson, 1963 (Prex Italia 1963), The Young Man Must Marry, 1964, The Three Musketeers, 1966, Triumph of Death, 1971, Salome, 1977, The Toreador, 1978, Marriage in Hardanger, 1981, Texas on Point, 1982, Quartet for Two, 1983, Tarantelle Classique, 1985, Cinderella, 1985, Children's Songs, 1986, Swan Lake, 1986, Phaedra, 1987, La Sylphide, 1987, Il Capotto, 1989, Caroline Mathhilde, 1991, Legs of Fire, 1998 Decorated Chevalier Ordre Des Artes of Des Lettres, Knight 1st Degree of Danneborg, Knight Swedish Order Vasa Home: Austin, Tex. Died Mar. 3, 2009.

FLINT, RANDELL SHERMAN, computer software executive; b. Lynwood, Calif., Sept. 17, 1955; s. Harold James and Elenor Gamble (Bornemann) F.; m. Martin Carla Hanzlik, Sept. 2, 1978. BS, U. Calif., Irvine, 1976, MS, 1979, PhD, 1984. Asst. prof. computer sci. Calif. State U., Fullerton, 1979-82; dir. software devel. Ordain Inc., Torrance, Calif., 1982-84; v.p. Dahlia Assocs. Inc., Seal Beach, Calif., 1985-88; pres. Sundial Systems Corp., Seal Beach, from 1988. Book reviewer Addison-Wesley Pub., Reading, Mass., 1980—; cons. Jet Propulsion Lab., Pasadena, Calif., 1985-89. Contbr. articles to profl. jours. Mem. IEEE Computer Soc., Assn. for Computing Machinery. Avocations: railroading, gardening. Home: Seal Beach, Calif. Died Oct. 5, 2007.

FLOCK, ROBERT ASHBY, retired entomologist; b. Kellogg, Idaho, July 16, 1914; s. Abraham Lincoln and Florence Louise (Ashby) F.; m. Elsie Marie Ronken, Apr. 8, 1950; children: Karen Marie, Anne Louise Checkai. BS, U. Ariz., 1938, MS, 1941; PhD, U. Calif., Berkeley, 1951. Inspector Ariz. Commn. Agriculture and Horticulture, Phoenix, 1938-41, asst. entomologist, 1941-46; lab. tech. U. Calif., Riverside, 1947-52, asst. entomologist, 1952-63; entomologist Imperial County Dept. Agriculture, El Centro, Calif., 1963-85, part-time entomologist, from 1985. Contbr. articles to profl. jours. Mem. Entomol. Soc. Am., Am. Phytopathol. Soc., Pan-Pacific Entomol. Soc., AAAS, Ctr. for Process Studies, Kiwanis (pres. Imperial Valley chpt. 1984-86, Man of Yr. 1986), Sigma Xi. Republican. Methodist. Avocations: taxonomy and biology of homoptera, desert ecology, science, religion. Home: El Centro, Calif. Died Oct. 1, 2007.

FLOR, LOY LORENZ, retired chemist, corrosion engineer, consultant; b. Luther, Okla., Apr. 25, 1919; s. Alfred Charles and Nellie M. (Wilkinson) F.; m. Virginia Louise Pace, Oct. 1, 1946; children: Charles R., Scott R., Gerald C., Donna Jeanne, Cynthia Gail. BA in Chemistry, San Diego State Coll., 1941. Registered profl. engr., Calif. With Helix Water Dist., La Mesa, Calif., 1947-84, chief chemist, 1963-2001, supr. water quality, 1963-2001, supr. corrosion control dept., 1956-2001; ret. 1st lt. USAAF, 1941-45. Mem. Am. Chem. Soc. (chmn. San Diego sect. 1965—), Am. Water Works Assn. (chmn. water quality divsn. Calif. sect. 1965—), Nat. Assn. Corrision Engrs. (chmn. western region 1970), Masons. Republican. Home: Lakeside, Calif. Died Aug. 2, 2007.

FLORES, IVAN, computer science consultant; b. NYC, Jan. 3, 1923; s. Angel and Ruth (Blumuner) F.; m. Helen Rosenberg, 1955 (div. 1966); children: Pamm, Glenn. BA in Math., Bklyn. Coll., 1948; MA in Math., Columbia U., 1949; PhD, NYU, 1955. Project engr. Nuclear Devel. Co., White Plains, N.Y., 1955-57; project supr. Univac Rsch., South Norwalk, Conn., 1957-58; computer cons. Dunlap Assocs., Darien, Conn., 1958-60; pres., prin. Flores Assocs., Bklyn., South Orange, N.Y., N.J., from 1960. Adj. prof. elec. engring. Polytech. Inst. Bklyn., 1958-62, assoc. prof. 1961-63; adj. prof. elec. engring NYU, 1963-64, computer sci., N.J. Inst. Tech., Newark, 1994-96; adj. prof. computer sci., Pace U., 1997—; assoc. prof. elec. engring. Stevens Inst. Tech., Hoboken, N.J., 1965-67; prof. statistics and computer sci. Baruch Coll. CUNY, 1967-90; cons. U.S. Army Sci. Adv. Panel, 1968-69, UN Devel. Program, 1973, 78, Tech. Hogesch. Twente, Netherlands, 1978; vis. prof. U. Waikato, New Zealand, Hefei Polytech. U., China, others. Author: 20 books in the field of computers including many translated into fgn. langs. including Logic of Computer Arithmetic, 1963, Computer Programming, 1966, The Professional Microcomputer Handbook, 1986; contbr. numerous articles to profl. jours.; past editor Jour. of Assn. of Computing Machinery; contbg. editor Modern Data, 1968-74; editor Jour. of Computer Langs., 1973—; reviewer for APIPS Confs., IEEE Computer, Jour. of Franklin Inst., ACM Computing Reviews; also contbr. to encyclopedias. Fellow British Computer Soc.; mem. IEEE, Assn. for Computing Machinery, Sigma Xi. Died Feb. 15, 2008.

FLOWERS, HAROLD LEE, aerospace engineer, consultant; b. Hickory, NC, June 25, 1917; s. Edgar Lee and Olive K. Flowers; m. Doris Louis Hexamer, Apr. 18, 1941; children: Josselyn, Harold Jr. BSEE, Duke U., 1938; MS in Engring., U. Cin., 1941; DSc (hon.), Lenoir Rhyne Coll., Hickory, NC, 1993. Rsch. scientist Naval Rsch. Lab., Washington, 1942-50; mgr. electronic programs Goodyear Aerospace, Akron, Ohio, 1950-61; dir. engring. div. AVCO Electronics, Cin., 1961-63; from dir. to chief engr. of missiles div. McDonnell Douglas Astronautics Co., St. Louis, 1963-87; engring. cons. CP Assocs., Washington, from 1987. Mem. adv. bd. Mark Twain Bank, Chesterfield, Mo. Contbr. articles to profl. jours. and mags. Mem. bd. visitors Duke U., Durham, N.C. Recipient Disting. Alumni awards U. Cin., Duke U. Fellow IEEE; assoc. fellow AIAA; mem. Phi Beta Kappa, Tau Beta Pi. Presbyterian. Achievements include patents for Radar Receiver Design, Atran Dead Reckoning Navigation System. Home: Chesterfield, Mo. Died Mar. 27, 2008.

FLYNN, KEVIN FRANCIS, nuclear chemist, consultant; b. Chgo., Oct. 28, 1927; s. Edward Joseph and Anna Marie (McDonnell) F.; m. Norma Jean Williams, May 20, 1950; children: Karen M., Nance J., James M., Mary T. BSChemE, Ill. Inst. Tech., 1950, MSChemE, 1952, MS in Chemistry, 1953. Nuclear chemsit Argonne (Ill.) Nat. Lab., from 1951. Cons. NAS/NRC, Washington. Contbr. over 100 articles to profl. jours. Active Human Rels. Coun., Chgo., 1991—, SCOPE, Chgo., 1991—. With USN, 1945-47. Mem. Am. Nuclear Soc., Am. Chem. Soc., M.P. Soc., DAV, Sigma Xi. Democrat. Roman Catholic. Home: Chicago, Ill. Died Jan. 3, 2008.

FOCH, NINA, actress, creative consultant, film director, educator; b. Leyden, The Netherlands, Apr. 20, 1924; arrived in US, 1927; d. Dirk and Consuelo (Flowerton) Foch; m. James Lipton, June 6, 1954; m. Dennis de Brito, Nov. 27, 1959; 1 child, Dirk de Brito; m. Michael Dewell, Oct. 31, 1967 (div.). Grad., Lincoln Sch., 1939; studies with Stella Adler. Adj. prof. drama U. So. Calif., Grad. Sch. Cinema & TV, LA, 1966—68, 1978—80, adj. prof. film, from 1987; creative cons. to dirs., writers, prodrs. of all media. Founder, actress LA Theatre Group, 1960—65; artist-in-residence U. NC, 1966, Ohio State U., 1967, Calif. Inst. Tech., 1969—70; mem. sr. faculty Am. Film Inst., 1974—77; founder, tchr. Nina Foch Studio, Hollywood, Calif., from 1973. Actor: (films) Nine Girls, 1944, Return of the Vampire, 1944, Shadows in the Night, 1944, Cry of the Werewolf, 1944, Escape in the Fog, 1945, A Song to Remember, 1945, My Name is Julia Ross, 1945, I Love a Mystery, 1945, Johnny O'Clock, 1947, The Guilt of Janet ames, 1947, The Dark Past, 1948, The Undercover Man, 1949, Johnny Allegro, 1949, An American in Paris, 1951, Scaramouche, 1952, Young Man with Ideas, 1952, Sombrero, 1953, Fast Company, 1953, Executive Suite, 1954 (Oscar award nominee), Four guns to the Border, 1954, You're Never Too Young, 1955, Illegal, 1955, The Ten Commandments, 1956, Three Brave Men, 1957, Cash McCall, 1959, Spartacus, 1960, Such Good Friends, 1971, Salty, 1973, Mahogany, 1976, Jennifer, 1978, Rich and Famous, 1981, Skin Deep, 1988, Silver, 1993, Morning Glory, 1993, 'Til There Was You, 1996, Hush, 1998, Shadow of Doubt, 1998, How to Deal, 2003; (Broadway plays) John Loves Mary, 1947, Twelfth Night, 1949, A Phoenix Too Frequent, 1950, King Lear, 1950, Second String, 1960; (plays) Am. Shakespeare Festival in Taming of the Shrew, Measure for Measure, 1956, San Francisco Ballet and Opera in the Seven Deadly Sins, 1966, Seattle Repertory Theatre, TV from 1947; (TV series) Playhouse 90, Studio One, Pulitzer Playhouse, Playwrights 56, Producers Showcase, Lou Grant (Emmy nominee, 1980), Mike Hammer, Shadow Chasers, 1985, War and Remembrance, 1988, LA Law, 1990, Hunter, 1990, Dear John, 1990, 1991, Tales of the City, 1993, Dharma and Greg, 1999, Just Shoot Me, 2000, Bull, 2000—01, State of Grace, 2003, When We Were Grown-ups, 2004, NCIs, 2005, 2006, The Closer, 2007, numerous other series, network spls. and TV films; panelist, guest (TV series) The Dinah Shore Show, Merv Griffin Show, The Today Show, Dick Cavett, The Tonight Show, moderator Let's Take Sides, 1957—59; dir.: (films) The Diary of Anne Frank, 1959; (plays) Tonight at 8:30, 1966—67, Family Blessings, 1997; assoc. prodr.: Ford's Theatre, 1968. Bd. dirs. Nat. Repertory Theatre, 1967—75; hon. chmn. LA chpt. Am. Cancer Soc., LA, 1970. Recipient Film Daily award, 1949, 1953. Mem.: AAUP, Hollywood Acad. TV Arts and Scis. (bd. govs. 1976—77), Acad. Motion Picture Arts and Scis. (co-chair exec. com. fgn. film award, mem. membership com., chair fgn. lang. award com. 1998—99). Avocation: work. Died Dec. 5, 2008.

FODSTAD, HARALD, neurosurgeon; b. Mo-i-rana, Norway, Sept. 4, 1940; came to the U.S., 1991; s. Reidar and Agathe Ursula (Jorfald) F.; m. Michiko Okayasu, Apr. 6, 1965; children: Tor, Henrik. MD, U. Berne, 1967; PhD, U. Umea, 1980. Intern Bodens Ctrl. Hosp., Sweden, 1968-71; resident Umea U. Hosp., Sweden, 1971-76; cons. neurosurgeon Umea Univ. Hosp., Sweden, 1976-88, Tawam Univ. Hosp., Alain, United Arab Emirates, 1988-90; chief surgeon Dobelle Inst., Glen Cove, N.Y., 1991-92; cons. neurosurgeon Health Ins. Plan Greater N.Y., NYC, 1992-94; acting chief of neurosurgery Bklyn. Hosp. Ctr., from 1995; clin. asst. prof. neurosurgery NYU Sch. Medicine, from 1995; chief of neurosurgery N.Y. Meth. Hosp., from 1996. Expert witness Supreme Ct. South Australia, Adelaide, 1992; assoc. prof. U. Umea, 1981. Author: Untersuchung Zur Frage der Alkoholparanoia, 1968, Tranexamic Acid in Subarachnoid Hemorrhage, 1980, Antifibrinolytics in Subarachnoid Hem-

orrhage, 1990, Epidemiology of Aneurysmal SAH, 1990; cons. editor: Emirates Med. Jour., 1990' author, co-author 160 scientific publs. Lt. Norwegian Navy, 1970-71. Scholar Swedish-Japanese Found., 1981. Mem. World Confedn. Neuroscis. (pres. 1979-87), Study Group for Microphysiology in Stereotaxy, European Neurosurg. Standards Com. EANS. Lutheran. Achievements include development of phrenic nerve stimulators for respiratory paralysis of central nervous origin. Home: New York, NY. Died Mar. 8, 2008.

FOGARTY, THOMAS NILAN, electronic materials engineer; b. Easton, Pa., July 5, 1936; s. Francis Joseph and Catherine Nilan (Noonan) F.; m. Margaret Ann Easterly, Oct. 11, 1958; children: Michael, Mary Beth, Kathleen, Kevin, Patricia. BS in ME, U. Notre Dame, Ind., 1958; MS in Metallurgy, Lehigh U., Bethlehem, Pa., 1962; PhD in Matl. Sci., Lehigh U., 1967. Registered prof. engr., Tex. Devel. engr. We. Elec. Co., Allentown, Pa., 1958-62; mem. tech. staff Bell Labs., Allentown, 1961-89; AT&T Bell Labs. prof. Prairie View (Tex.) A & M U., 1979-87 and from 92; dir. lab. for radiation studies Prairie View A & M U., from 1992; cons. AT&T, Hampton U., 1990; advisor Consortium of Space Radiation Effects, NASA/JSC; prof. engring. Tex. A&I, 1990-92; AT&T Disting. prof. elec. engring. Prairie View A&M U., Prairie View, Tex., from 1992; dir. ctr. materials, microdesign, microfabrication Ctr. for Applied Radiation Rsch., Prairie View A&M U., from 1992; prof. engring. Tex. A&I Univ., Prairie View, 1990-92. Patentee in field; contbr. articles to profl. jours. Named Disting. Mem. Tech. Staff, AT&T Bell Labs., 1984. Mem. IEEE (sr.), Am. Vacuum Soc., Electrochem. Soc. Democrat. Roman Catholic. Avocations: sailing, water sports. Home: Houston, Tex. Died July 7, 2008.

FOLEY, BRIANA, music educator, consultant; b. Jersey City, Sept. 23, 1958; d. Daniel Joseph and Jane Catherine Moriarty; m. Gregory Howard Foley, Oct. 12, 1980; 1 child, Elizabeth Ann. Student, Fla. State U., 1978; B of Music Edn., Westminster Choir Coll., Princeton, NJ, 1981. Cert. music edn.K-12 Fla. Voice and piano instr. pvt. home studio, Clearwater, Fla., 1981—83; choral dir. N.W. Presbyn. Ch., St. Petersburg, Fla., 1981—94; music specialist Mildred Helms Elem. Sch., Largo, Fla., 1982—90, Garrison-Jones Elem. Sch., Dunedin, Fla., from 1990. Cons. profl. edn. music dept. Pinellas County Schs., Largo, 1986—2003; mem. Pinellas County Student Achievement Grant. Author: (study guide) The Florida Orchestra Youth Concert Series Guide, 1986—2003. Vol. Clearwater Jazz Holiday, 1984—87; coord. Adopt-a-Grandparent Program, Largo, 1985—89. Recipient grantee, Fla. Dept. Edn., 1989. Mem.: Music Educators Nat. Conf., Pinellas Classroom Tchrs. Assn. Achievements include development of first music inclusion program in Pinellas County School District. Avocations: yoga, walking, playwriting, reading, travel. Home: Palm Harbor, Fla. Died June 18, 2008.

FOLEY, JOHN FRANCIS, retired judge, lawyer; b. Detroit, Feb. 10, 1928; s. Henry Michael and Rosemary (O'Neill) F.; m. Joan Marlow, Aug. 17, 1957; children: Sean, Patrick, Rosemary, Joan, Margaret, Ella. BS, Georgetown U., 1948; JD, U. Mich., 1957. Bar: Mich. 1957, U.S. Dist. Ct. (ea. dist.) Mich. 1961, U.S. Dist. Ct. (we. dist.) Mich. 1969, U.S. Ct. Appeals (6th cir.) 1983. Assoc. firm Wilson, Ingraham and Kavanagh, Birmingham, Mich., 1957-59; atty. NLRB, Detroit, 1959-61; ptnr. firm Swartz, O'Hare, Sharples & Foley, Detroit, 1961-66, Gergely & Foley, P.C., Vicksburg, Mich., 1969-85; judge Kalamazoo County Cir. Ct., Mich., 1985-98; ret. Commr. Mich. Ct. Appeals, Lansing, 1966-68. Mem. Dem. Exec. Com., Oakland City, Mich., 1961-64, Kalamazoo, 1980; bd. dirs. Kalamazoo ACLU, 1971-83. Lt. (j.g.) USN, 1951-55. Mem. ABA, Mich. Bar Assn., Kalamazoo County Bar Assn. Home: Schoolcraft, Mich. Died Aug. 29, 2007.

FONDAHL, JOHN WALKER, civil engineering educator; b. Washington, Nov. 4, 1924; s. John Edmund and Mary (DeCourcy) F.; m. Doris Jane Plishker, Mar. 2, 1946; children: Lauren Valerie, Gail Andrea, Meredith Victoria, Dorian Beth. BS, Thayer Sch. Engring., Dartmouth, 1947, MSCE, 1948. Instr., then asst. prof. U. Hawaii, 1948-51; constrn. engr. Winston Bros. Co., Mpls., 1951-52; project engr. Nimbus Dam and Powerplant project, Sacramento, 1952-55; mem. faculty Stanford U., 1955—90, prof. civil engring., 1966-90, Charles H. Leavell prof. civil engring., 1977-90, prof. emeritus, 1990—2008. Author reports in field. Served with USMCR, 1943-46. Recipient Golden Beaver award Heavy Constrn. Industry, 1976. Fellow ASCE (Constrn. Mgmt. award 1977, Peurifoy Constrn. Rsch. award 1990), Project Mgmt. Inst. (hon. life, Fellow award 1981, Jim O'Brien Lifetime Achievement award 2007); mem. Nat. Acad. Engring., Nat. Acad. Constrn., Phi Beta Kappa. Achievements include patent in field. Died Sept. 13, 2008.

FOOTE, HORTON (ALBERT HORTON FOOTE JR.), playwright, scriptwriter; b. Wharton, Tex., Mar. 14, 1916; s. Albert Horton and Hallie (Brooks) Foote; m. Lillian Vallish, June 4, 1945 (dec. 1992); children: Barbara Hallie, Albert Horton, Walter Vallish, Daisy Brooks. Student, Pasadena Playhouse Sch. Theatre, Calif., 1933-35, Tamara Daykarhanova Sch. Theatre, NYC, 1937-39. Actor, NYC, 1939-42; mgr. prodn. co. Productions Inc., Washington, 1942-45; vis. disting. dramatist Baylor U., 2002—09. Tchr. playwriting. Author: (screenplays) Storm Fear, 1956, To Kill a Mockingbird, 1962 (Academy Award for Best Screenplay, 1962, Writers Guild America award, 1962), Baby, the Rain Must Fall, 1965, Hurry Sundown, 1966, Tomorrow, 1971, Tender

Mercies, 1983 (Academy Award for Best Screenplay, 1983), 1918, 1984, On Valentine's Day, 1985, The Trip to Bountiful, 1985, Spring Moon, 1987, Convicts, 1991, Of Mice and Men, 1992, (plays) Texas Town, 1941, Out of My House, 1942, Only The Heart, 1944, Celebration, 1948, The Chase, 1952, The Trip to Bountiful, The Midnight Caller, 1953, A Young Lady of Property, 1954, The Traveling Lady, The Roads to Home, 1955, Harrison, Texas: Eight Television Plays, 1959, The Chase, 1956, Tomorrow, 1960, Three Plays, Roots in a Parched Ground, 1962, The Road to the Graveyard, 1985, Blind Date, 1986, Selected One Act Plays of Horton Foote, Habitation of Dragons, 1988, Dividing the Estate, 1989 (Obie award for Playwriting, Village Voice, 2008), Talking Pictures, 1990, Horton Foote: Four New Plays, 1994, The Young Man From Atlanta, 1994 (Pulitzer Prize for Drama, 1995), Night Seasons, Laura Dennis, Talking Pictures, 1994, The Carpetbagger's Children, also (play series) The Orphans' Home Cycle, 2001, The Last of the Thorntons, 2002; author, dir. (plays) When They Speak of Rita, 2000; author: (plays) (musical adaption) Gone with the Wind, 1971, (TV films) Only The Heart, 1947, Ludie Brooks, 1951, The Travelers, 1952, The Old Beginning, The Trip to Bountiful, Midnight Caller, John Turner Davis, Young Lady of Property, The Oil Well, Rocking Chair, Expectant Relations, Death of the Old Man, Tears of My Sister, 1953, The Shadow of Wilie Greer, The Dancers, 1954, The Roads to Home, 1955, Flight, 1956, Drugstore: Sunday Noon, 1956, Member of the Family, Traveling Lady, 1957, Old Man, 1959, Tomorrow, 1960, 1971, The Shape of the River, 1960, The Night of the Storm, 1961, Gambling Heart, 1964, The Displaced Person, 1977, Barn Burning, 1980, Keeping On, 1983, The Habitation of Dragons, 1992, Mr. and Mrs. Loving, 1996. Recipient Evelyn Burkey award Writer's Guild, 1989, Nat. Medal of Arts, Nat. Endowment Arts (NEA), 2000. Died Mar. 4, 2009.

FOOTE, ROBERT HUTCHINSON, medical educator; b. Gilead, Conn., Aug. 20, 1922; s. Robert E. and Annie (Hutchinson) F.; m. Ruth E. Parcells, Jan. 12, 1946 (dec. Jan. 1992); children: Robert W., Dale H.; m. Barbara J. Johnson, Sept. 25, 1993. BS, U. Conn., 1943; MS, Cornell U., 1947, PhD Animal Physiology/Biochem. Genetics, 1950. Grad. asst. Cornell U., Ithaca, NY, 1946-50, asst. prof. animal physiology, 1950-56, assoc. prof., 1956-63, prof., 1963-93, Jacob Gould Schurman chair, 1980-93, prof. emeritus, 1993—2008. Mem. study sect. NIH, 1974-78; cons. Shell Oil, 1985-89, EPA, 1988-96; program mgr. USDA competitive grants, 1986-87. Author: Animal Reproduction, 1954, AI to Cloning, 1998; mem. editl. bds. 5 jours., 1958-96, Cloning, 1999-2002, Reproductive Physiology, 1992-99, Cryobiology, 1991-94; contbr. some 500 articles to profl. jours., chpts. to books. Chmn. trustees Congregation Ch., Ithaca, 1955-60. Served to capt. inf. US Army 1943-46, ETO. Recipient Sci. medal NY Farmers, 1969, Nat. Physiology and Endocrinology award Am. Soc. Animal Sci., 1970, SUNY Chancellor award, 1980, Superior Svc. award USDA, 1988, Alumni Merit award U. Conn., 1996, Casida Physiology Reprodn. award, 1991, JSPS award, 1996, CALS Alumni Outstanding Faculty award, 2003, Outstanding Alumnus award U. Conn., 2005; named hon. prof. Beijing Agrl. U., 1995. Fellow: AAAS; mem.: Internat. Embryo Transfer Soc. (Pioneer Biotech. award 2002), Am. Soc. Theriogenology (editl. bd. 1976—89, Robert H. Foote Symposium in his honor 1992), Am. Soc. Andrology (editl. bd. 1982—88, Outstanding Andrologist 1984, Upjohn physiology award 1985), Nat. Assn. Animal Breeders (Physiology award 1970), Soc. Study Reprodn. (bd. dirs. 1976—78, pres. 1985, Hartman Lifetime Rsch. award 2000, Pioneer award 2007, 2008), Am. Dairy Sci. Assn. (spkr.), Gamma Sigma Delta, Phi Kappa Phi, Sigma Xi. Republican. Home: Ithaca, NY. Died Oct. 27, 2008.

FOOTMAN, GORDON ELLIOTT, educational administrator; b. LA, Oct. 10, 1927; s. Arthur Leland and Meta Fay (Neal) F.; m. Virginia Rose Footman, Aug. 7, 1954; children: Virginia, Patricia, John. BA, Occidental Coll., 1951, MA, 1954; EdD, U. So. Calif., 1972. Tchr., Arcadia, Calif., 1952, Glendale, Calif., 1956; psychologist Burbank (Calif.) Schs., 1956-64, supr., 1964-70, dir. pupil pers. svcs., 1970-72; dir. divsn. ednl. support svcs. L.A. County Office Edn., Downey, Calif., 1972-91; cons. ednl. adminstrn., counseling and psychol. svcs., from 1991. Pres. Calif. Assn. Adult Devel. and Aging, 1994-95; lectr. ednl. psychology U. So. Calif., 1972-75, asst. prof. ednl. psychology, 1976-85. Pres. Coun. for Exceptional Children, 1969-70; pres. Burbank Coordinating Coun., 1969-70; mem. Burbank Family Svc. Bd., 1972-72. Served with AUS, 1945-47. Mem. ACA (senator 1983-86, gov. coun. 1989-93, exec. com. 1990-93, parliamentarian 1991-92, western region br. assembly publs. editor 1985-87, chair 1988-89, chair bylaws com. 1995-97), Am. Ednl. Rsch. Assn., Am. Assn. Humanistic Edn. and Devel. (bd. dirs., treas. 1996—), Calif. Assn. for Counseling & Devel. (pres. 1981-82, exec. coun. 1996—. bylaws chair 2000), Calif. Assn. for Counseling and Devel. Found., Nat. Assn. Pupil Pers. Adminstrs., Calif. Assn. Pupil Pers. Adminstrs. (monograph editor 1977-80), Calif. Assn. Counselor Educators and Suprs. (trustee), Calif. Soc. Ednl. Program Auditors and Evaluators (sec. 1975-76, v.p. 1976-77, pres.), Calif. Assn. Measurement and Evaluation in Counseling and Devel. (sec. 1976, pres. 1979-80, 96-97, pres. 1997-98, cons. ednl. and pupil svcs. adminstrn. 1991—), Calif. Inst. Tech. Assocs., Assn. Humanistic Edn. and Devel. (bd. dirs. 1996-99, treas. 1996—, pres. 2000-2001. conv. coord. 1999--), Huntington Libr. Soc. Fellows, Phi Delta Kappa, Phi Beta Kappa, Phi Alpha Theta, Psi Chi. Republican. Presbyterian. Died Jan. 21, 2009.

FORBES, ALVIS R., orthopaedic surgeon; b. Yakima, Wash., Nov. 29, 1950; s. Carl Earl and Pearl Evelyn (Carter) F.; m. Barbara Ann Norris, Sept. 8, 1973; children: Amy, Colleen, Michelle, Ryan. BS in Food Sci. and Tech., Wash. State U., 1974; MD, U. Wash., 1978. Diplomate Am. Bd. Orthop. Surgery. Intern William Beumont Army Med. Ctr., El Paso, Tex., 1978-79; orthop. on-job-trainee U.S. Army, Frankfurt, Germany, 1979-81; orthop. resident Madigan Army Med. Ctr., Tacoma, 1981-85; chief orthop. surgery U.S. Army, Ft. Leavenworth, Kans., 1985-87; orthop. surgeon Lakeport, Calif., 1987-89, Orthopaedics of Jackson Hole, Wyo., 1989—2004, Orthop. Assocs., Jackson Hole, from 2004. Sports medicine fellow Jackson Orthopaedics, 1985. Lt. col. USAR, 1991, lt. col. Nat. Guard US Army, from 1991. Fellow Am. Acad. Orthop. Surgeons. Avocations: water-skiing, skiing, softball. Home: Jackson, Wyo. Died Oct. 1, 2007.

FORD, AMASA BROOKS, physician, medical educator; b. Cleve., July 13, 1922; s. David Knight and Elizabeth (Brooks) F.; m. Mary Elizabeth Simmons, July 7, 1951; children: Edward Clark, Charles Keith, Donald Brooks. BA, Yale U., 1944; MD cum laude, Harvard, 1950. Lic. physician, Ohio; diplomate Am. Bd. Internal Medicine. Intern, then asst. resident Mass. Gen. Hosp., Boston, 1952-53; sr. asst. resident, tchg. fellow U. Hosp. Cleve., 1953-54; instr. in medicine, tchg. fellow Case Western Res. Sch. Medicine, Cleve., 1954-58, from asst. prof. to prof. medicine, 1960-93; prof. epidemiology and biostats., family medicine Case Western Reserve Sch. of Medicine, 1975-93; assoc. dean geriatric medicine Case Western Res. Sch. Medicine, Cleve., 1980-95, prof. emeritus epidemiology and biostats., from 1993. Asst. assoc. physician U. Hosp. Cleve., 1954-71; asst. physician, med. dir. Benjamin Rose Hosp., Cleve., 1960-80; mem. review com. NIH,th, 1965-89. Author: Urban Health in America, 1976; co-editor: The Practice of Geriatrics, 1986, 2d edit., 1992-; contbr. articles to JAMA, New Eng. Jour. Medicine, others; contbr. chpts. to med. books. Trustee, pres. Cleve. Neighborhood Health Svcs., 1972-79, Eliza Bryant Ctr., Cleve., 1973-; trustee Long-Term Care Ombudsman, Cleve., 1981-1994, Fairhill Ctr. for Aging, Cleve., 1995. 2d lt. U.S. Army, 1943-46. Recipient Burroughs Welcome Vis. Professorship, Royal Soc. Medicine, Eng., 1982, Heller Meml. Award for Excellence in Geriatrics, Menorah Park, Cleve., 1985. Fellow APHA Am. Geriatrics Soc. (Nascher/Manning Meml. award 1989), mem. Am. Epidemiological Soc. Democrat. Acheivements include establishing Dept. of Family Medicine and Geriatric Medicine at Case Western Reserve Medical School and Univ. Hosps. of Cleveland; helping to introduce Index of Activities of Daily Living with Sidney Katz. Home: Cleveland, Ohio. Died Oct. 8, 2007.

FORD, GEORGE BURT, retired lawyer; b. South Bend, Ind., Oct. 1, 1923; s. George W. and Florence (Burt) Ford; m. Charlotte Ann Kupferer, June 12, 1948; children: John, Victoria, George, Charlotte. BS in Enging. Law, Purdue U., 1946; LLB, Ind. U., 1949. Bar: Ind. 1949, US Dist. Ct. (no. dist.) Ind. 1949. Assoc. Jones, Obenchain & Butler, South Bend, 1949-52; ptnr. Jones, Obenchain, Ford, Pankow & Lewis, South Bend, 1953-93, of counsel, 1994—2003; ret., 2003. Co-author: (book) Forms for Indiana Corporations, 1967, 2d edit., 1977. With US Army, 1943—45, ETO. Fellow: Am. Coll. Trust and Estate Counsel; mem.: ABA, St. Joseph County Bar Assn. (pres. 1976—77), Ind. Bar Assn., Phi Delta Phi, Phi Gamma Delta. Home: Notre Dame, Ind. Died Nov. 19, 2008.

FORD, JOHN CHETLEY, physicist; b. Richmond, Va., July 18, 1958; s. Melvin Lee and Mary Janet (Miller) F.; 1 child, Karmen Elizabeth; m. Eleanor Kassab, July 7, 1990; children: Melanie Jane, Diana Marie. BS in Physics, Va. Commonwealth U., 1981; MS in Physics, U. Conn., 1983, PhD of Physics, 1988. NIH postdoctoral fellow U. Pa., Phila., 1988-90; physicist magnetic resonance imaging VA Med. Ctr., Phila., 1990-91; rsch. asst. prof. U. Pa., Phila., from 1991. Dep. editor: Magnetic Resonance in Medicine, 1994—; presenter confs. in field; patentee in field; contbr. articles to profl. jours. Grantee Whitaker Found., 1994-96, NIH, 1997. Mem. AAAS, Am. Phys. Soc., Internat. Soc. Magnetic Resonance in Medicine. Achievements include application of MRI to experimental models of disease; development of novel MR imaging hardware and techniques. Home: Lexington, Mass. Died May 19, 2008.

FORD, RUTH, actress; b. Brookhaven, Miss., July 7, 1911; d. Charles and Gertrude (Cato) F.; m. Peter van Eyck (div.); 1 child, Shelley; m. Zachary Scott, July 6, 1952 (dec. Oct. 3, 1965); 1 child BA, MA, U. Miss. Actress: (plays) Ivoryton Playhouse, Conn., 1937, Ways and Means, Ivoryton Playhouse, Conn., 1937; Orson Welles' Mercury Theatre Co., 1938, Cyrano de Bergerac, 1946, No Exit, 1947, Hamlet, 1949, Macbeth, The Failures, A Phoenix Too Frequent, Six Characters in Search of an Author, Requiem for a Nun, Royal Ct., London, 1957, Lovey, 1965, Dinner at Eight, 1966, The Ninety-Day Mistress, 1967, The Grass Harp, 1971, Madame de Sade, 1972, A Breeze from the Gulf, 1973, The Charlatan, 1974, The Seagull, 1977, The Aspern Papers, 1978, Harold and Maude, 1980, The Visit, 1983; (films) Too Much Johnson, 1938, Roaring Frontiers, 1941, Secrets of the Lone Wolf, 1941, The Man Who Returned to Life, 1942, The Lady is Willing, 1942, Lady Gangster, 1942, Murder in the Big House, 1942, In This Our Life, 1942, The Devil's Trail, 1942, Escape from Crime, 1942, Men of the Sky, 1942, Secret Enemies, 1942, Divide and Conquer, 1942, Across the Pcific, 1942, The Hidden Hand, 1942, The Gorilla Man, 1943, Truck Busters, 1943, Air Force, 1943, Murder on the Waterfront, 1943, Adventure in Iraq, 1943, Princess O'Rourke, 1943, Wilson, 1944, The Keys of the Kingdom, 1944, Circumstantial Evidence, 1945, The Woman Who Came Back, 1945, Strange Impersonation, 1946, Dragonwyk, 1946, Act One, 1963, The Tree, 1969, 7254, 1971, Play It As It Lays, 1972, The Eyes of the Amaryllis, 1982, Too Scared to Scream, 1985; (TV movies) Sorry, Wrong Number, 1946; (TV appearances) Studio One (5 episodes), 1949-53, Cameo Theatre, 1950, The Adventure of Ellery Queen, 1951, Musical Comedy Time, 1951, Suspense, 1951, Hallmark Hall of Fame, 1952, Armstrong Circle Theatre (2 episodes), 1950-53, Campbell Playhouse, 1954, Star Tonight, 1955, The Chevy Mystery Show, 1960, Play of the Week, 1960, The United States Steel Hour (3 episodes), 1954-61, Naked City, 1962, The Nurses, 1964, The Defenders, 1965, Camera Three, 1977 Mem. AFTRA, Screen Actors Guild, Actors Equity. Democrat. Died Aug. 12, 2009.

FOREMAN, JOSEPH EDWARD, lawyer; b. Wadsworth, Ohio, Nov. 23, 1936; s. Cecil Edward and Nina Marie (O'Meara) F.; divorced; children: Susannah, Andrew. BA, Ohio Wesleyan U., 1958; JD, Ohio State U., 1964. Bar: Ohio 1965. Ptnr. Palacek McIlvaine Foreman & Paul, Wadsworth, 1967-89; pvt. practice Wadsworth, from 1989. Ptnr., officer various corps. and partnerships in field of realty, Wadsworth, 1989—. City atty. City of Wadsworth, 1967-73; candidate for mcpl. judgeship, 1977. Lt. USNR, 1958-62. Mem. Ohio Bar Assn., Medina County Bar Assn. (pres. 1975), Ohio Acad. of Trial Lawyers. Republican. Roman Catholic. Died Mar. 2, 2008.

FORYS, KAREN ANN, superintendent; b. Rochester, NY, Sept. 3, 1944; d. Harold Thornton and Dolores Marian (Fremming) Olson; m. Edward Forys, Aug. 14, 1971. BA in English Lit., U. Calif., Davis, 1966; MA in Counseling & Guidance, Calif. State U., 1971; PhD in Ednl. Adminstrn., U. Ariz., 1977. Counselor, tchr. San Juan Sch. Dist., Sacramento, 1966-75; asst. prof. U. Ariz., Tucson, 1977-79; adminstrv. intern San Juan Sch. Dist., 1974-75; asst. prin. Tucson Dist. # 1, 1975-76; asst. dean, grad. coll. U. Ariz., 1977-79; adminstr. for instruction Clover Park Sch. Dist., Tacoma, 1979-85; supt. Riverview Sch. Dist., Carnation, Wash., 1985-90, Clover Park Sch. Dist., Tacoma, from 1991. Adj. prof. U. Puget Sound, Tacoma, 1984-88, 83-91. Bd. dirs. Tacoma Youth Symphony, 1990-91; edn. chmn. United Way, Pierce County, Wash., 1991.; bd. dirs. Lakewood C. of C., Tacoma, 1990-91. Mem. Am. Assn. Sch. Adminstrs., Wash. Assn. Sch. Adminstrs., Rotary (Clover Park youth exch. program 1991). Avocations: theater, sports, travel. Home: Woodinville, Wash. Died Sept. 17, 2007.

FOSS, LUKAS, composer, conductor, pianist; b. Berlin, Aug. 15, 1922; came to US from Paris, 1937, naturalized, 1942; s. Martin and Hilde (Schindler) F.; m. Cornelia Brendel, Sept. 1951; children: Christopher, Eliza Student, Paris Lycée Pasteur, 1932-37; grad., Curtis Inst. Music, 1940; independent study, Yale U., 1940-41; studied with Paul Hindemith, studied with Julius Herford, studied with Serge Koussevitzky, studied with Fritz Reiner, studied with Isabelle Vengerova; doctorate (hon.), Yale U., 1991. Pianist Boston Symphony Orch., Boston, 1944—50; prof. composition U. Calif., Los Angeles, 1953—62; music dir. Buffalo Philharmonic, 1963—71, Brooklyn Philharmonic, 1971—90; musical adviser Jerusalem Symphony, 1972—75; music dir. Milwaukee Symphony, 1982—86, conductor laureate, 1986—2009. Founder & conductor Improvisation Chamber Ensemble, 1957—62; composer-in-residence Harvard, Manhattan Sch. of Music, Carnegie Mellon U., Yale U.; guest conductor Boston Symphony, Chicago Symphony, Cleveland Orch., Los Angeles Philharmonic, NY Philharmonic, Phila. Symphony Orch., San Francisco Symphony, Berlin Philharmonic, Leningrad Symphony, London Symphony Orch., Santa Cecilia Orch., Tokyo Philharmonic. Former conductor, music dir., Buffalo Philharmonic; music dir., conductor, Bklyn. Philharmonic, 1971-90, conductor laureate, 1990-2009; music dir., conductor Milw. Symphony Orch., 1981-86, conductor laureate, 1986-2009; orchestral compositions performed by many major orch.; best known works include (opera) Griffelkin, Baroque Variations (orch.), Echoi (4 instruments), Time Cycle (songs with orch.), Renaissance concerto (flute and orch.); orch., chamber music, ballets, works commd. by, League of Composers, Nat. Endowment for Arts, NY Arts Coun., NBC opera on TV, Am. Choral Condrs. Assn., Ind. U., 1979 Olympics, Boston Symphony, Chgo. Symphony; (recipient NY Critic Circle citation for Prairie 1944, Soc. for Pub. Am. Music award for String Quartet in G 1948, Rome prize 1950, Horblit award for Piano concerto #2 1951, Naumburg Rec. award for Song of Songs 1957, Creative Music grant Inst. Arts and Letters 1957, NY Music Critics Circle award for Time-Cycle orch. songs 1961, for Echoi 1963, Ditson award for condr. who has done the most for Am. music 1973, NYC award for spl. contbn. to arts 1976, ASCAP award for adventurous programming 1979, CRI rec. award for Thirteen Ways of Looking at a Blackbird 1979). Guggenheim fellow, 1945; Creative arts award Brandeis U., 1983; Laurel leaf award Am. Composers Alliance, 1983; elected to Am. Acad. & Inst. of Arts & Letters, 1983; inductee Am. Classical Music Hall of Fame, 2002. Mem. Am. Acad. of Arts and Letters (Gold medal 2000). Died Feb. 1, 2009.

FOSTER, MARIETTA ALLEN, rehabilitation specialist; b. Greensboro, NC, Feb. 10, 1934; d. Joseph Thomas and Marietta (Sowel) Allen; children: Thomas Allen, Michelle

Jeanette. BS, U. N.C., Greensboro, 1956; MS, U. N.C., 1962; postgrad., N.C. State U., Raleigh, 1965-69, Macon Coll., Ga., 1982-83. Cert. ins. rehab. specialist, case mgr.; lic. profl. counselor, Ga. rehab. supplier. Home economist Duke Power Co., Greensboro, 1955-59, Wise Prefab Homes, Greensboro, 1961; rsch. spr. N.C. State U., Raleigh, 1962; social worker Woman's Prison, Raleigh, 1963-65, Alcoha Rehab. Clinic, Macon, Ga., 1979; caseworker DFCS Welfare Dept., Macon, 1980; cons. counselor Mid-Ga. Counseling Ctr., Macon, 1975-79; counselor Foster Clinic, Macon, 1973-82; logistics specialist Robins AFB, Ga., 1983-84; profl. counselor Macon, from 1982; rehab. counselor, supr. Gen. Rehab. Svcs., 1991-96; office owner, counselor Allen Women's Counseling Svcs., Macon, from 1996. Rehab. specialist Intracorp, Macon, 1985-88; rschr. Dept. Health Human Svcs., 1999—. Contbr. articles to profl. jours. Recipient numerous scholarships. Mem. Nat. Rehab. Assn. (steering com. 1987-90), Ga. Rehab. Assn., Ga. Marriage and Family Therapists, Am. Legion. Methodist. Home: Macon, Ga. Died July 6, 2008.

FOSTER, ROBERT JOE, retired biochemist; b. Glendale, Calif., June 6, 1924; s. Joel Pierce and Lorena (Garner) F.; m. Helen Dorothy Hemestray, July 7, 1951; children: Robin Ann, Robert Louis. BS, Calif. Inst. Tech., 1948, PhD in Chemistry, 1952. Biochemist Wash. State U., Pullman, 1955-88, biochemist emeritus, from 1988. Contbr. articles to profl. jours. Served to 1st lt. USAAF, 1943-46. European Molecular Biology Orgn. fellow, 1970-71. Mem. AAAS, Am. Soc. Biol. Chemists. Democrat. Avocations: skiing, personal computing, travel. Home: Pullman, Wash. Died Mar. 16, 2008.

FOUNTOUKIDIS, NOIMON, naval architect, mathematician; b. Komotini, Greece, Jan. 9, 1929; came to U.S., 1965; s. Kostantine and Magdalini (Kitsatoglou) F.; m. Dona Lee McAninch, Dec. 26, 1966; 1 child, Kimon. BS in Naval Architect & Marine Engring., U. Mich., 1968; MS in Ocean Engring., Stevens Inst. Tech., 1973. From 2dto chief officer Hellenic LInes Ltd.i, Piraeus, Greece, 1959-63, master, 1963-65; from surveyer to prin. engr. in charge Am. Bur. Shipping, NYC, 1968-91; ret., 1991. Adj. prof. math. William Paterson Coll., Wayne, N.J., 1992—; mem. Safety of Life at Sea/Stability Loadline Fishing Vessels group USCG, Washington, 1980-89; subcom. load lines and stability Govt. Liberia, London, 1984-89. Loadlines and stability group Internat. Assn. Classific Soc., London, 1986-89; referee U.S. Soccer Fedn., Chgo., 1983-95. Lt. Greek Royal Navy, 1952-54. Mem. Portas Karate Acad., No. N.J. Police Revolver League (co-capt., Most Improved award 1989). Avocations: Karate (black belt), target shooting, chess, computers. Home: Chapel Hill, NC. Died Jan. 16, 2008.

FOURNIER, DONALD CHARLES, allergist, immunologist; b. Lewiston, Maine, Apr. 16, 1949; s. Charles A. and Doris L. (Lessard) F.; m. Linda Faye Dix, Feb. 10, 1977; children: Dana, Alyson, Ashley. AA, Blinn Coll., Brenham, Tex., 1966-68; BA, Trinity U., 1970; MD, U. Tex. Med. Br., Galveston, 1974. Diplomate Am. Bd. Allergy and Immunology, Am. Bd. Internal Medicine. Commd. med. officer USAF, 1970, advanced through grades to chief allergy immunology, 1983; intern Wilford Hall USAF Med. Ctr., 1974-75, resident, 1975-77, fellow, 1977-79, mem. staff Lackland AFB, 1979-80; chief internal medicine svc. USAF Med. Ctr., Scot AFB, Ill., 1981-83, chief allergy immunology, 1980-83; lt. col. USAFR, from 1983; allergist, immunologist Collom and Carney Clinic, Texarkann, Tex., 1983-85; pvt. practice Texarkana, Tex., from 1985. Courtesy faculty St. Louis U., 1980-83; clin. asst. prof. allergy immunology La. State U., Shreveport, 1986—, assoc. dir. allergy tng. program; asst. clin. prof. Area Health Edn. Ctr., S.W., U. Ark. Med. Sci., 1987—; cons. in field. Contbr. articles to profl. jours. State bd. dirs. Am. Lung Assn., Little Rock, 1986-92; mem. AIDS adv. com. Tri State chpt. ARC, Texarkana, Tex., 1988—. Recipient Baylor award Assn. Mil. Allergists; decorated Air Force Commendation medal. Fellow ACP, Am. Acad. Allergy Asthma Immunology, Am. Coll. Chest Physicians, Am. Assn. Cert. Allergists, Am. Coll. Allergy Asthma Immunology; mem. AMA, Tex. Allergy & Immunology Soc. (bd. dirs. 1994-98, chair practice standards com. 1994-98, pres.-elect 1998—). Home: Hooks, Tex. Died Feb. 9, 2008.

FOWLER, DAVID G., secondary school educator; b. Chester, SC, Sept. 8, 1944; s. William Randall and Lucille J. (Duncan) F. BS in Physics, Emory U., 1966, MS in Physics, 1967. Cert. secondary tchr., Md. Tchr. Balt. City Pub. Schs., from 1978, head math. dept., from 1984. Mem. adv. bd. maths. Md. Sci. Ctr., Balt., 1994—. V.p. Balt. Tchrs. Union, 1982-86. U.S. Dept. of Energy scholar, 1991; Martin Marietta fellow, 1993. Mem. Nat. Counsel Math. Tchrs., Phi Delta Kappa. Democrat. Avocations: chess, computers. Home: Baltimore, Md. Died June 5, 2008.

FOX, GERALD JULIAN, psychologist; b. NYC, June 10, 1927; s. Max Winter and Leah (Lieberman) F.; m. Roberta Churgin, July 11, 1934; children: Ellen Gene, Theresa Hope, Florence Ruth. BA, NYU, 1949; MA, Fordham U., 1951; postgrad., New Sch. for Social Rsch., NYC, 1953-57; PhD in Exptl. Psychology, SUNY, Stony Brook, 1995. Rsch. asst. psychology dept. Princeton U., NJ, 1952; assoc. scientist rsch. div. Coll. Engring, NYU, Bronx, 1952-56; flight trainers branch head human engring. dept. U.S. Naval Tng. Device Ctr., Port Washington, N.Y., 1956-58; asst. human factors group head Grumman Aircraft Engring. Corp., Bethpage, N.Y., 1958-69; human factors group head Grumman Aerospace Corp., 1969-87; prin. engr. Grumman Corp. Aircraft Systems Div., 1987-90. V.p. Seitz Assocs., Huntington, N.Y., 1960-72; adj. asst. prof. psychology dept. SUNY, Stony Brook, 1996. With USAAF, 1945-47. Mem. APA, Ea. Psychol. Assn., Human Factors Soc. (v.p. 1970-71, pres. 1972 met. chpt.), Kiwanis (v.p. Grumman Bethpage chpt. 1987-90). Home: Stony Brook, NY. Died Dec. 30, 2007.

FOX, MAUREEN ANN, oncology nurse, administrator; b. Phila., June 11, 1956; d. Leonard R. and Clarice M. (Strain) Brady; m. Robert H. Fox Jr., July 16, 1977; children: Eric Robert, Gregory Leonard. BSN, Thomas Jefferson U., 1990; MS, U. South Fla., Tampa, 1993. Dir. edn., tng. and rsch. Hospice of Hillsborough, Inc., Tampa, from 1994. Commonwealth Exec. Nurse fellow, 1991; Joseph C. Connolly scholar, Clara M. Melville-Adele Lewis scholar, Carolyn B. Brown awardee. Mem. West Ctrl. Fla. Hospice Nurses Assn. (pres.), Oncology Nursing Soc., Sigma Theta Tau. Home: Lansdale, Pa. Died Sept. 18, 2007.

FOY, EDWARD JOSEPH, sociologist, educator, social worker; b. Passaic, NJ, Oct. 22, 1931; s. William and Alice Ellen Foy. MSS, Fordham U., 1958; PhD, St. John's U., 1965; MPH, Harvard U., 1975. Cert. social worker N.Y. State Edn. Dept. Edn. specialist U.S. Army Hdqs., Antilles, San Juan, PR, 1953—56; assoc. study dir. N.Y.C. Dept. Correction, 1963—65; rsch. assoc. Child Welfare League Am., NYC, 1965—67; dir. rsch. N.Y. Office Probation, 1967—68; sr. ptnr. Foy, Falcier Assocs., 1968—73; dir. rsch. ICIS/The Door, NYC, 1975—77; asst. prof. U. Miami, Fla., 1976—78; pvt. practice clin. social work, NYC, 1978—94; semi-ret., from 1996. Dir. rsch. Renaissance House, Newark, 1994—96; dir. Counseling Ctr. U.S. Army, Pusan, Republic of Korea, 1987—88; condr. insvc. tng. Contbr. articles to profl. jours. Grant writer Meml. Sloan-Kettering Cancer Ctr., NYC, 1980—81. Fellow, NIMH, Harvard U., 1974. Avocations: photography, writing. Home: Jersey City, NJ. Died Oct. 1, 2007.

FRAENKEL, GEORGE KESSLER, chemistry professor; b. Deal, NJ, July 27, 1921; s. Osmond Kessler and Helene (Esberg) F.; m. Johanna-Maria Herzog, June 30, 1951 (div. Aug. 1965); m. Elizabeth R. Rosen, Nov. 11, 1967 (div. Jan. 1990); m. Eva S. Cantwell, Feb. 3, 1990. BA, Harvard U., 1942; PhD, Cornell U., 1949. Research group leader National Def. Research Com., 1943-46; instr. chemistry Columbia U., NYC, 1949-53, asst. prof., 1953-57, assoc. prof., 1957-61, prof., 1961-91, Eugene Higgins prof. Grad. Sch. Arts and Scis., 1986-91, prof. emeritus, 1992—2009, chmn. dept. chemistry, 1966-68, dean grad. sch. arts and scis., 1968-83, dean emeritus, 1983—2009, v.p. spl. projects, 1983-86. Mem. postdoctoral fellowship com. Nat. Acad. Sci.-NSF, 1964-65; chmn. Gordon Research Conf. Magnetic Resonance, 1967; mem. Arts Coll. adv. council Cornell U., 1964-74; mem., bd. dirs. Atran Found., N.Y.C., 1968—2005, com. on budget and fin., 1986—2005; treas. Atran Found., 1988—2005. Assoc. editor: Jour. Chem. Physics, 1962-64; Mem. adv. editorial bd.: Chemical Physics Letters, 1966-71; editorial bd.: Jour. Magnetic Resonance, 1969-70. Trustee Columbia U. Press, 1968-71, Walden Sch., N.Y.C., 1964-66. Recipient Army-Navy certificate of appreciation, 1948; Harold C. Urey award Phi Lambda Upsilon, 1972; decorated officer Ordre des Palmes Académiques. Fellow AAAS, Am. Phys. Soc., Am. Chem. Soc., Internat. Electron Spin Resonance Soc.; mem. Assn. Grad. Schs. (exec. com. 1976-80, v.p. 1977-78, pres. 1978-79, chmn. com. policies on grad. edn. 1969-71), Phi Beta Kappa, Sigma Xi, Phi Kappa Phi. Achievements include research in field of electron spin resonance with particular emphasis on the electron spin resonance of organic free radicals. Home: New York, NY. Died June 10, 2009.

FRAME, JOHN DAVIDSON, public health physician; b. Resht, Iran, Feb. 16, 1917; (parents Am. citizens); s. John Davidson and Grace Jennette (Murray) F.; m. Dorothy V. Anderson, Sept. 26, 1943 (div. 1959); children: Sarah Frame Kasacks, J. Davidson, Deborah Frame Middleton; m. Veronica Foldes, July 12, 1962. BA, BS, Wheaton Coll., Ill., 1938; MD, Northwestern U., Chgo., 1943. Internship Cook County Hosp., Chicago, 1942-43; med. officer, supt. Am. Christian Hosp., Hamadan, Iran, 1947-51; pvt. practice, N.Y.C., 1952-87; med. dir. The Interch. Ctr., 1989-91. Med. cons. Interdenominational Fgn. Mission Assn., N.Y.C., 1953-87; adj. asst. prof. Columbia U. Sch. Pub. Health, N.Y.C., 1966-74, adj. assoc. prof., 1974-90, clin. prof. pub. health (tropical medicine), 1990—. Contbg. author: Infectious Diarrheal Diseases, 1985; contbr. articles to med. jours. Maj. M.C., U.S. Army, 1943-46, ETO. Named Alumnus of Yr., Wheaton Coll., 1990. Mem. AMA, Am. Soc. Tropical Medicine and Hygiene (bus. adv. coun. 1988-91), Royal Soc. Tropical Medicine and Hygiene, N.Y. Soc. Tropical Medicine (pres. 1973-74), Nat. Coun. Internat. Health (governing bd. 1975-85), Sigma Xi (assoc.), Alpha Omega Alpha. Presbyterian. Achievements include discovery of Lassa virus and fever which infects between one-quarter and one-half million people in west and central Africa; research on illnesses afflicting missionaries in parts of the world where the state of local facilities does not allow accurate investigation on the indigenous population. Home: Forest Hills, NY. Died Jan. 16, 2008.

FRANCHINI, GENE EDWARD, retired state supreme court justice; b. Albuquerque, May 19, 1935; s. Mario and Lena (Vaio) F.; m. Glynn Hatchell, Mar. 22, 1969; children: Pamela, Lori (dec.), Gina, Joseph James, Nancy. BBA, Loyola U., 1955; degree in adminstrn., U. N.Mex., 1957; JD, Georgetown U., 1960; LLM, U. Va., 1995. Bar: N.Mex. 1960, U.S. Dist. Ct. N.Mex. 1961, U.S. Ct. Appeals (10th cir.) 1970, U.S. Supreme Ct. 1973. Ptnr. Matteucci, Gutierrez & Franchini, Albuquerque, 1960-70, Matteucci, Franchini & Calkins, Albuquerque, 1970-75; judge State of N.Mex. 2d Jud. Dist., Albuquerque, 1975-81; atty.-at-large Franchini, Wagner, Oliver, Franchini & Curtis, Albuquerque, 1982-90; chief justice N.Mex. Supreme Ct., Santa Fe, 1990-99, justice, 1999—2003. V.p. bd. dirs. Conf. Chief Justices, 1997-98. Chmn. Albuquerque Pers. Bd., 1972, Albuquerque Labor Rels. Bd., 1972, Albuquerque Interim Bd. Ethics, 1972. Capt. USAF, 1960-66. Recipient Highest award Albuquerque Human Rights Bd., 1999. Mem. Am. Bd. Trial Advocates, N.Mex. Trial Lawyers (pres. 1967-68), N.Mex. Bar Assn. (bd. dirs. 1976-78), Albuquerque Bar Assn. (bd. dirs. 1976-78, Outstanding Judge award 1997). Democrat. Roman Catholic. Avocations: fishing, hunting, golf, mushroom hunting. Home: Albuquerque, N.Mex. Died Nov. 4, 2009.

FRANCIOSI, RALPH ANTHONY, pathologist, educator; b. Montclair, NJ, July 3, 1937; MD, N.J. Coll. Medicine-Dentistry, Newark, 1962. Diplomate Am. Bd. Pathology; anatomic and clin. bd. cert. pediat. pathology. Pediat. intern Seton hall U. Coll. Medicine, Jersey City, 1962-63; pathology resident Columbia Presbyn. Med. Ctr./Babies Hosp., NYC, 1963-67; asst. dir. pathology Children's Hosp. Denver, 1969-72; chief pathology Children's Hosp. Mpls., 1972-88, Children's Hosp. Wis., Milw., from 1988; prof. pathology and pediatrics Med. Coll. Wis., Milw., from 1988. Med. dir. Minn. Suddent Infant Death Ctr., Mpls., 1976-88, Wis. Sudden Infant Death Ctr., Milw., 1990— Contbr. articles to med. jours. Lt comdr. M.C., USN, 1967-69. Fellow Am. Acad. Pediatrics. Home: Mequon, Wis. Died Feb. 5, 2008.

FRANCK, THOMAS MARTIN, law educator; b. Berlin, July 14, 1931; naturalized, 1977; s. Hugo and Ilse (Rosenthal) F. BA, U. B.C., 1952, LLB, 1953, LLD (hon.), 1995; LLM, Harvard U., 1954, SJD, 1956; DHL (hon.), Monterey Inst. Internat. Studies, 2003; LLD (hon.), U. Glasgow, 2004. Asst. prof. law U. Nebr., 1954-56; from assoc. prof. to prof. law NYU, 1960—2002, prof. law emeritus, 2002—09, dir. Ctr. Internat. Studies, 1965—2002; judge ad hoc Internat. Ct. Justice, 2001—02. Acting dir. internat. law Carnegie Endowment Internat. Peace, 1973-75, dir., 1975-79; vis. prof. Stanford U., 1963, U. East Africa, 1964, 65, York U., 1972-73, 74-76, U. Calif., San Francisco, 2004, Georgetown U. Law Ctr., 2006, Am. U. Wash. Coll. Law, 2008; dir. rsch. UN Inst. Tng. and Rsch., 1980-82; cons. US Agy. for Internat. Devel. (USAID), 1970-72, 85; constl. adviser govts. Tanganyika, 1963, Zanzibar, 1963, 64, Mauritius, 1965; mem. Sierra Leone Govt. Commn. Legal Edn., 1964, Nat. Liberal Adv. Coun. Can., 1952-53; lectr.in field; vis. fellow Trinity Coll., Cambridge, Eng., 1996-97. Author: Race and Nationalism, 1960, The United Nations in the Congo, 1963, East African Unity Through Law, 1965, Comparative Constitutional Process, 1968, The Structure of Impartiality, 1968, Why Federations Fail, 1968, A Free Trade Association, 1968, Word Politics, 1971, Secrecy and Foreign Policy, 1973, Resignation in Protest, 1975, Control of Sea Resources by Semi-Autonomous States, 1978, Foreign Policy by Congress, 1979, The Tethered Presidency, 1981, Human Rights in Third World Perspective, 1982, Nation Against Nation: What Happened to the U.N. Dream and What the U.S. Can Do About It, 1985, Judging the World Court, 1986, Foreign Relations and National Security Law, 1987, The Power of Legitimacy Among Nations, 1990, Political Questions/Judicial Answers, 1992, Fairness in the International Legal and Institutional System, 1993, Fairness In International Law and Institutions, 1995, The Empowered Self: Law and Society in the Age of Individualism, 1999, Recourse to Force: State Action Against Threats and Armed Attacks, 2002; co-author: U.S. Foreign Relations Law, vols. I-III, 1980-81, vols. IV & V, 1984, Foreign Relations and National Security Law, 2d edit., 1993, Law and Practice of the United Nations, 2008, Foreign Relations and National Security Law, 3rd edit, 2008; editor-in-chief Am. Jour. Internat. Law, 1984-93; editor: Delegating State Powers: The Effect of Treaty Regimes on Democracy and Sovereignty, 2000; co-editor: Internat. Law Decisions in Nat. Cts., 1996. Lt. Can. Army, 1953. Guggenheim fellow, 1973-74, 82-83. Mem. Inst. de Droit Internat., State Dept. Adv. Com. on Internat. Law, Can. Coun. Internat. Law, Assn. Am. Law Schs., Am. Soc. Internat. Law (pres. 1998-2000), Am. Acad. Arts and Scis., Internat. Law Assn. (v.p. U.S. br.), Coun. on Fgn. Rels. Home: New York, NY. Died May 27, 2009.

FRANKLIN, JOHN HOPE, historian, writer; b. Rentiesville, Okla., Jan. 2, 1915; s. Buck Colbert and Mollie (Parker) Franklin; m. Aurelia E. Whittington, June 11, 1940 (dec. 1999); 1 child, John Whittington. AB, Fisk U., 1935; AM, Harvard, 1936, PhD, 1941; degree (hon.), Morgan State Coll., Va. State Coll., Lincoln U., Pa., Cambridge U., Drake U., Mich. State U., U. Ill., Carnegie-Mellon U., Columbia U., Columbia Coll., Chgo., Loyola U., Bklyn. Coll., Bard Coll., Boston Coll., Brown U., Tuskegee Inst., Grand Valley Coll., Marquette U., Lincoln Coll., Ill., Princeton U., Hamline U., Fisk U., RI Coll., Dickinson Coll., Howard U., U. Md., U. Notre Dame, Tulsa U., Morehouse Coll., Miami U., Johnson C. Smith U., Lake Forest Coll., Tougaloo Coll., Union Coll., Northwestern U., Whittier Coll., U. Mass., U. Mich., Seattle U., U. Toledo, Yale U., LI U., Catholic U. Am., Tulane U., Temple U., Kalamazoo Coll., Washington U., St. Louis, Trinity Coll., Conn., Ariz. State U., SUNY, Albany, No. Mich. U., U. Utah, Coll. New Rochelle, George Washington U., Governors State U.,

Harvard U., U. Pa., Ripon Coll., Atlanta U., Wayne State U., U. NC, Dillard U., Manhattan Coll., Roosevelt U., NC Central U., Ind. State U., St. Olaf Coll., Emory U., U. Miami, U. Conn., U. NC, Brandeis U., Wake Forest U., Wilkes Coll., Queen's Coll., NY, Wilmington Coll., U. NC, Greensboro, Queens Coll., Charlotte, NC, Ill. State U., Bates Coll., Williams Coll., U. South, U. NC, Am. U., Furman U., Georgetown U., Tufts U., Elizabeth City State U., Shaw U., San Francisco U., Washington Lee U., Columbia Coll., Chgo., Lincoln Meml. U., Elmira Coll., Lane Coll., Bethune-Cookman Coll., Amherst Coll., U. Cin., Dartmouth Coll., U. Ky., Duke U., San Francisco State U., York Coll., Northeastern U., Occidental Coll., U. Akron, U. Vermont, Bennett Coll., San Diego U., Pa. State U., Tex. A&M U., Pomona Coll., U. San Diego, U. Vt., U. Akron, U. NC, Pembroke, SC State U., U. DC, Wesleyan U., 2006, Lafayette Coll., 2006. Prof. hist. St. Augustine's Coll., 1939—43, NC Coll., Durham, 1943—47, Howard U., 1947—56; chmn. dept. hist. Bklyn. Coll., 1956—64; prof. Am. hist. U. Chgo., 1964—82, chmn. dept. hist., 1967—70, John Matthews Manly Disting. Svc. prof., 1969—82; James B. Duke prof. hist. Duke U., 1982—85, prof. emeritus, 1985—2008; prof. legal hist. Duke U. Law Sch., 1985—92. Pitt. prof. Am. hist. and instns. Cambridge U., 1962—63; vis. prof. Harvard U., U. Wis., Cornell U., Salzburg Seminar, U. Hawaii, U. Calif.; chmn. bd. fgn. scholarships Nat. Coun. Humanities, 1966—69, 1976—79; trustee Nat. Humanities Ctr., 1980—91, chmn. adv. bd. to pres.'s initiative on race, 1997—98; Fulbright prof., Australia, 1960; lectr. in field; chmn. adv. bd. Nat. Pk. Svc. Author: The Free Negro in North Carolina, 1790-1860, 1943, The Militant South, 1800-1861, 1956, Reconstruction: After the Civil War, 1961, The Emancipation Proclamation, 1963, A Southern Odyssey: Travelers in the Antebellum North, 1976, Racial Equality in America, 1976, George Washington Williams, A Biography, 1985, Race and History: Selected Essays, 1938-1988, 1990, The Color Line: Legacy for the 21st Century, 1993, Mirror to America: The Autobiography of John Hope Franklin, 2005; co-author (with Alfred A. Moss): From Slavery to Freedom: A History of African Americans, 1947, 9th edit., 2007; co-author: (with John W. Caughey & Ernest R. May) Land of the Free: A History of the United States, 1966; co-author: (with Loren Schweninger) Runaway Slaves: Rebels on the Plantation, 1999, In Search of the Promised Land: A Slave Family in the Old South, 2005; editor: Civil War Diary of James T. Ayers, 1947, A Fool's Errand by Albion Tourgee, 1961, Army Life in a Black Regiment by Thomas Higginson, 1962, Color and Race, 1968, Reminiscences of an Active Life by John R. Lynch, 1970; co-editor (with others): Illustrated History of Black Americans, 1970; co-editor: (with August Meier) Black Leaders in the Twentieth Century, 1982; co-editor: (with Abraham Eisenstadt) Harlan Davidson's American History Series; co-editor: (with Genna Rae McNeil) African Americans and the Living Constitution, 1995; co-editor: (with John Whittington Franklin) My Life and An Era: The Autobiography of Buck Colbert Franklin, 1997; mem. editl. bd.: Am. Scholar, 1972—76, from 1994; subject of (documentaries) First Person Singular: John Hope Franklin, PBS, 1997. Trustee Chgo. Symphony, 1976—80, Fisk U., 1947—80; bd. dirs. Salzburg Seminar, Mus. Sci. and Industry, 1968—80, DuSable Mus., 1970—2009. Recipient Cleanth Brooks medal, Fellowship So. Writers, 1989, Gold medal, Ency. Britannica, 1990, Caldwell medal, NC Coun. on Humanities, 1992—93, Charles Frankel medal, 1993, Bruce Catton award, Soc. Am. Historians, 1994, Cosmos Club award, 1994, Spingarn medal, NAACP, 1995, Presdl. Medal of Freedom, The White House, 1995, Peggy V. Helmerich Disting. Author award, 1997, Smithson Bicentennial medal, 1997, Lincoln prize, 2000, Harold Washington Lit. award, 2000, Gold medal award, Am. Acad. Arts and Letters, 2002, Disting. Author award, Bergen County, 2002, Arthur Schlesinger Jr. Lifetime Hist. award, 2002, John F. Kennedy award, Mass. Hist. Soc., 2005, Benjamin Franklin medal, 2006, Robert F. Kennedy award, 2006, Lifetime Achievement award, Indigo Found., 2006, John W. Kluge prize for Study of Humanity, 2006; named one of The 100 Most Influential Black Americans, Ebony mag., 2006; named to Okla. Hall of Fame, 1978, Okla. Historians Hall of Fame, 1996, The Power 150, Ebony mag., 2007, 2008; fellow Edward Austin fellow, 1937—39, Guggenheim fellow, 1950—51, 1973—74, Pres.'s fellow, Brown U., 1952—53, Ctr. Advanced Study in Behavioral Sci., 1973—74, Sr. Mellon fellow. Fellow: Am. Acad. Arts and Scis.; mem.: AAUP, Am. Philos. Soc. (Jefferson medal 1993, Benjamin Franklin medal 2006), Am. Studies Assn. (past pres.), Assn. for Study Negro Life and Hist., Orgn. Am. Historians (pres. 1974—75), So. Hist. Assn. (pres. 1970—71), Am. Hist. Assn. (pres. 1978—79), Phi Alpha Theta, Phi Beta Kappa (senate 1966—82, pres. 1973—76, Sidney Hook award 1994). Democrat. Home: Durham, NC. Died Mar. 25, 2009.

FRANZ, F(LOYD) PERRY, plastic surgeon; b. Liberty, Tex., Aug. 16, 1958; s. Floyd Lyntor Franz and Audrey Marie (Perry) Cooper. BS, Okla. State U., 1979; MD, U. Okla., 1983. Diplomate Am. Bd. Plastic Surgery. Microsurgery fellow Chang Gung Med. Coll., Taipei, Taiwan, 1988-89; dir. Plastic Surgery Ctr. Holt-Krock Clinic, Fort Smith, Ark., 1989-95; dir. Found. for Advanced Reconstructive Surgery, Austin, Tex., from 1994; dir. microsurg. svcs. Personique Personal Surgery Ctr., Austin, Tex., 1997-99. Contbr. articles to profl. jours. Fellow ACS; mem. AMA, Am. Soc. Reconstructive Microsurgery, Am. Soc. Plastic and Reconstructive Surgeons, Am. Soc. Aesthetic Plastic Surgery, Lipoplasty Soc. N.Am., Plastic Surgery Ednl. Found., Aesthetic Surgery Edn. & Rsch. Found. (charter), Tex. Med. Soc., Ark. Med. Soc., Midwestern Assn. Plastic Surgeons, Southeastern Soc. Plastic and Reconstructive Surgeons (candidate), Ark. Found. Med. Care (specialist reviewer), Found. Advanced Reconstructive Surgery (pres.), Travis County Med. Soc., Alpha Omega Alpha. Died Aug. 29, 2007.

FRAZIER, WILLIAM TUCKER, insurance company official; b. St. Louis, Aug. 14, 1928; s. William Fowler and Gladys Elizabeth (Tucker) F.; m. Carol Doris Jacobs, Aug. 19, 1950 (div. July 1970); children: John Timothy, Bradley Jacobs; m. Beverly Ann Jung, Apr. 17, 1984. BS in Psychology, U. Ill., 1950. CLU; CPCU; LUTCF. Salesman Jacobs-Lane Co. Inc., jewelers, West Frankfort, Ill., 1950-51, 53-61; agt. State Farm Ins. Cos., West Frankfort, 1961-65, asst. agy. mgr. Belleville, Ill., 1965-68, agy. mgr., 1968-75, agt. Granite City, Ill., from 1976. Participant Life Underwriters Polit. Action Com., Belleville and Alton, Ill., 1965-91. Participant Ill. Legis. Action Network, Bloomington, 1989—. Sgt. C.E. U.S. Army, 1951-53, capt. U.S. Army Nat. Guard, 1956-65. Mem. Soc. CLU's and ChFC, Soc. CPCU's, So. Ill. Gen. Agts. and Mfrs. Assn. (pres. 1974), Estate Planning Coun. St. Louis, East Side Life Underwriters (pres. 1973), Lewis and Clark Life Underwriters Assn. (bd. dirs. 1987—, v.p. 1990-92, pres. elect 1991-92, pres. 1992-93). Avocations: boating, flying, photography, golf, travel. Died Aug. 6, 2008.

FREDNER, ROLF MORTEN, small business owner; b. Oslo, July 7, 1913; came to U.S., 1945; s. Morien Johannes and Sigrid E. (Frölich) Fredriksen; m. Astrid Hardis Knobel Fredner, Dec. 10, 1948 (dec. Dec. 1983); children: Nemi Vivian, Robin, Randolph. BA, Otto Treider, Oslo, 1932; cert. in archtl. drafting, Mechs. Inst., 1960. Owner Rolf Fredner, Inc., New Rochelle, N.Y., from 1946. Bd. dirs., co-owner Norsk Labrador & Granitindustri, Larvik, Norway, 1954—. Decorated Knight First Class (Norway). Mem. Am. Scandinavian Found., Norwegian-Am. C. of C., Inc. (former pres., bd. dirs.), Norwegian Club Inc. of N.Y.C., Bonnie Briar Country Club. Lutheran. Avocations: music, golf, skiing. Died June 14, 2008.

FREEBORN, JOHN B., lawyer; b. Chgo., Feb. 12, 1925; s. John and Margaret (Rendall) Freeborn; m. Marguerite Mueller Freeborn; children: John Frederick, Alison, Catherine. BS, Ga. Tech., Atlanta, 1946; MS, U. Ill., Champaign, 1947; JD, Stetson U., St. Petersburg, Fla., 1957. Bar: Fla. 1957, US Supreme Ct. Constrn. estimator J.T. Ryerson, Chgo.; trust officer First Nat. Bank, Dunedin, Fla.; atty. Reebles, Robertson, Cracy & Freeborn, Dunedin, Freeborn, Venninos & Ruggles, Dunedin, Freeborn & Freeborn, PA, Dunedin; of counsel Son & Dau. Ptnrs., Dunedin. Trustee Morton Hosps. Found., Clearwater, Fla., 1999—2005; bd. mem. Dunedin Fine Art Ctr., 1999—2005. Lt. USNR, 1943—46, Okinawa. Fellow: Am. Coll. & Trust Estate Counsel; mem.: Mensa Internat. Republican. Episcopalian. Home: Dunedin, Fla. Died Aug. 7, 2008.

FREEDBERG, A. STONE, physician; b. Salem, Mass., May 30, 1908; s. Hyman and Rachel Leah (Freedberg) F.; m. Beatrice Gordon, Aug. 29, 1935; children: Richard Gordon, Leonard Earl. AB, Harvard U., 1929; MD, U. Chgo., Rush, 1935. Diplomate: Am. Bd. Internal Medicine (cardiology). Intern Mt. Sinai Hosp., Chgo., 1934-35, Mass. Meml. Hosp., Boston, summer 1935; resident Cook County Hosp., Chgo., 1935-36; house officer pathology R.I. Hosp., 1936-37; practice medicine, specializing in internal medicine Boston, 1946—2009. Asst. in medicine Beth Israel Hosp., 1938-40, jr. vis. physician, 1940-46, assoc. in med. research, 1940-50, assoc. vis. physician, 1946-48, vis. physician, 1949-63, assoc. dir. med. research, 1950-63, sr. Ziskind fellow, 1956, physician, 1964-84, acting physician-in-chief dept. medicine, 1973, dir. cardiology unit, 1964-69, bd. consultation, 1984-87, hon. bd. consultation, 1988-2009; research fellow medicine Med. Sch., Harvard U., 1941-42, asst. in medicine, 1942-46, instr. medicine, 1946-47, assoc. in medicine, 1947-50, asst. prof., 1950-57, assoc. prof., 1958-69, prof., 1969-74, prof. emeritus, 1974-2009, adminstrv. bd. faculty medicine, 1958-62; physician Harvard U. Health Svcs., 1974-2004, hon. physician emeritus, 2004-09; cons., com. mem. med. div. Oak Ridge Inst. Nuclear Studies, 1955-56; spl. cons. metabolism study sect. USPHS, 1956-60; mem. sr. cons. staff Nuclear Medicine Inst., 1966-67 Mem. editorial bd.: Circulation, 1956-60, 62-67; contbr. articles profl. jours. Guggenheim fellow Oxford U., 1967-68 Fellow Am. Heart Assn. (bd. dirs.; mem. council clin. cardiology); mem. Mass. Heart Assn. (dir., past pres., com. chmn.), Am. Thyroid Assn. (v.p.), Mass., Charles River Dist. med. socs., Am. Soc. Clin. Investigation, Am. Physiol. Soc., Assn. Am. Physicians, New Eng. Cardiovascular Soc. (pres. 1971-72), Assn. Profs. Medicine. Home: Boston, Mass. Died Aug. 18, 2009.

FREEDMAN, DAVID AMIEL, statistics educator, consultant; B.Sc., McGill U., Montreal, 1958; MA, Princeton U., 1959, PhD, 1960. Prof. stats. U. Calif.-Berkeley, 1961—2008, Miller prof., 1991, chmn. dept. stats., 1981-86. Cons. Bank of Can., Ottawa, 1971-72, WHO, 1973, Carnegie Commn., 1976, US Dept. Energy, 1978-87, Bur. Census, 1983, 98, US Dept. Justice, 1984, 89-92, 96, 2002-05, Brobeck, Phleger & Harrison, 1985-89, Skadden Arps, 1986, 2002, 2005-08, County of Los Angeles, 1989, Fed. Jud. Ctr., 1993. Author: Markov Chains, 1971, Brownian Motion and Diffusion, 1971, Approximating Countable Markov Chains, 1972, Mathematical Methods in Statistics, 1977, Statistics, 1978, 4th edit., 2007, Statistical Models, 2005; contbr. numerous articles to profl. publs. Recipient John J. Carty award for Advancement of Sci., NAS, 2003; fellow, Can. Coun., 1960, Sloan Found., 1964. Mem.: Am. Acad. Scis. Home: Berkeley, Calif. Died Oct. 17, 2008.

FREEMAN, ISADORE, pianist, educator; b. Paterson, NJ, Sept. 5, 1912; s. Abram and Anna (Katch) F.; m. Sara Freeman, July 10, 1947 (dec. 1986); m. Anne Freeman, Mar. 1, 1987. MusB, Perfield Music Sch., NYC, 1958. Dir. Summer Music Festival, Fair Lawn, N.J., 1960-97. Pvt. piano instr.; prof. Kean Coll., N.J.; chamber music performer N.Y. Philharmonic. Named Man of Yr. Knights of Pythias, Fair Lawn, 1981, Fair Lawn C. of C., 1990; Star over Paterson honoree, 1990. Mem. Bohemians N.Y. Musicians Club, Am. Fedn. Musicians (pres. emeritus Local 248), Rotary Club (pres. Fair Lawn unit 1952). Avocations: travel, organizational work. Home: Hackensack, NJ. Died Sept. 3, 2007.

FRENCH, MARILYN, writer, critic, historian; b. NYC, Nov. 21, 1929; d. E. Charles and Isabel (Hazz) Edwards; m. Robert M. French, Jr., June 4, 1950 (div. 1967); children: Jamie, Robert. BA, Hofstra Coll., 1951, MA, 1964; PhD, Harvard U., 1972. Secretarial, clerical worker, 1946-53; lectr. Hofstra Coll., 1964-68; asst. prof. English Holy Cross Coll., Worcester, Mass., 1972-76; Mellon fellow Harvard U., 1976-77; writer, lectr., 1967—2009. Author: (criticism) The Book as World: James Joyce's Ulysses, 1976, Shakespeare's Division of Experience, 1981, The Women's Room, 1977, The Bleeding Heart, 1980, Beyond Power: On Women, Men and Morals, 1986, Her Mother's Daughter, 1987, The War Against Women, 1992, Our Father: A Novel, 1994, My Summer with George, 1996, A Season in Hell: A Memoir, 1998, From Eve To Dawn: A History of Women, Vol. I-III, 2002—03, The Love Children, 2005, In the Name of Friendship, 2007, (introductions) Summer and The House of Mirth, 1981, Her Mothers, 1985, A Weave of Women, 1985. Mem. Phi Beta Kappa. Home: New York City, NY. Died May 2, 2009.

FREUND, PHILIP HERBERT, writer, educator; b. Vancouver, BC, Canada, Feb. 5, 1909; s. Henry and Augusta (Robinson) Freund. BA, Cornell U., 1929, MA, 1932. Lectr. Inst. Film Techniques CCNY, NYC, 1945—65; lectr. Hunter Coll., NYC, 1946—78, Cornell U., NYC, 1948; lectr. U. B.C., 1949—51; prof. Fordham U., NYC, 1960—79, prof. emeritus, from 1979. Author: The Volcano God, 1959, The Zoltans, a Trilogy, The Dark Shore, The Evening Heron, Dreams of Youth, 1938, Easter Island, Searching, 1972, (plays) Black Velvet, 1931, Simon Simon, 1932, Mario's Well, 1934, Prince Hamlet, 1953, numerous short stories, criticisms in collections, Myths of Creation, 1963, The Art of Reading the Novel, 1965, Stage by Stage: Birth of the Theatre, 2004, Stage by Stage: Oriental Drama, 2005, Stage by Stage: Dramatis Personae, 2006, Stage by Stage: Laughter and Grandeur, 2007. Head scenario bd. rev. Signal Corp Photographic Ctr., NYC, 1943—45; pres. Herbert Robinson Philanthropic Fund, from 1960. Fellow, Bur. New Plays, 1941. Mem.: Sigma Delta Chi. Home: New York, NY. Died Dec. 20, 2007.

FREVERT, JAMES WILMOT, retired financial planner, investment advisor; b. Richland Twp., Iowa, Dec. 19, 1922; s. Wesley Clarence and Grace Lotta (Maw) F.; m. Jean Emily Sunderlin, Feb. 12, 1949; children: Douglas James, Thomas Jeffrey, Kimberly Ann. BS in Gen. Engring., MIT, 1948. Prodn. mgr. Air Reduction Chem. Co., Calvert City, Ky., 1955-61; plant mgr. Air Products & Chems., West Palm Beach, Fla., 1961-62; pres. Young World HWD, Ft. Lauderdale, Fla., 1962-66; v.p. Shareholders Mgmt. Co., LA, 1966-73, Thomson McKinnon Secs., North Palm Beach, Fla., 1973-89, Raymond James & Assoc., West Palm Beach, Fla., 1989-91; ret. Founder, past pres. MIT Club Palm Beach County, dir., 1976—; ednl. council mem. 1977-81. Served to 1st lt. USAF, 1943-46. Mem. Palm Beach Pundits. Republican. Presbyterian. Died Feb. 13, 2009.

FRIEDEL, HELEN BRANGENBERG, counselor, therapist; b. Kampsville, Ill., May 16, 1938; d. Carl Morris and Martha Marie (Zipprich) Brangenberg; m. John Laverne Friedel; children: Vincent Joseph, John Francis. BS, So. Ill. U., 1969, MS, 1973. Lic. profl. counselor, Mo. Educator Archdiocese of St. Louis, 1956-87; counselor Diocese of Belleville, Waterloo, Ill., 1988-89, Christian Bros. H.S., St. Louis, from 1989; pvt. practice Florissant, Mo., from 1987. Mem. parents adv. bd. St. Louis Prep. Sem., Florissant, 1973-79; youth moderator Sacred Heart Parish, Florissant, 1967-71, lector and eucharistic min. Named Disting. Lasallion Educator, Midwest Dist. of the Christian Bros., 1998. Mem. ACA, Mo. Counseling Assn. (bd. dirs. 1986-88, 90-93, sec. 1990, pres. 1992, legis. chair 1992-93, Kitty Cole Human Rights award 1993), St. Louis Counseling Assn., Mo. Multicultural Counselors, Mid Rivers Counseling Assn. (pres. 1986), Am. Sch. Counselors Assn., Mo. Sch. Counselors Assn., St. Louis Learning Disabilities Assn. (bd. dirs. 1994), Kappa Delta Pi. Roman Catholic. Avocations: music, drama, history writing. Home: Kampsville, Ill. Died Feb. 5, 2008.

FRIEDLANDER, GERHART, nuclear chemist; b. Munich, July 28, 1916; came to U.S., 1936, naturalized, 1943; s. Max O. and Bella (Forchheimer) F.; m. Gertrude Maas, Feb. 6, 1941 (dec. 1966); children: Ruth Ann F. Huart, Joan Claire F. Hurley; m. Barbara Strongin, 1983. BS, U. Calif., Berkeley, 1939, PhD, 1942; D (hon.), Clark U., 1991, U. Mainz, Germany, 1992. Instr. U. Idaho, Moscow, 1942-43; staff Los Alamos Sci. Lab., 1943-46; research assoc. Gen. Electric Co. Research Lab., Schenectady, 1946-48; vis.

lectr. Washington U., St. Louis, 1948; chemist Brookhaven Nat. Lab., Upton, N.Y., 1948-52, sr. chemist, 1952-81, 89-91, cons., 1981-89, 91-93, chmn. chemistry dept., 1968-77. Chmn. Gordon Rsch. Conf. on Nuclear Chemistry, 1954. Author: (with J.W. Kennedy) Introduction to Radiochemistry, 1949, Nuclear and Radiochemistry, 1955, (with J.M. Miller), 1964, (with E.S. Macias), 1981; editor-in-chief Sci. Spectra, 1993-2000; editor Radiochimica Acta, 1972-73; assoc. editor Ann. Rev. Nuc. Sci., 1958-67; contbr. articles to profl. jours. Recipient Alexander von Humboldt award Institut für Kernchemie, Mainz, Fed. Republic of Germany, 1978-79, 87, 92, 93. Fellow AAAS; mem. Hungarian Acad. Scis. (hon.), Nat. Acad. Sci., Am. Acad. Arts and Scis., Am. Chem. Soc. (chmn. divsn. nuclear chemistry and tech. 1967, award for nuclear applications in chemistry 1967). Achievements include research in chemical effects of nuclear transformations, properties of radioactive isotopes, mechanisms of nuclear reactions, especially those induced by protons of very high energies; solar neutrino detection; cluster impact phenomena. Home: South Setauket, NY. Died Sept. 6, 2009.

FRIEDLANDER, RALPH, thoracic and vascular surgeon; b. NYC, Oct. 2, 1913; s. Samuel and Mollie (Drimmer) F.; m. Sybil Rainsbury, Apr. 10, 1950; children: Andrea Lynn, Beth Caryn. BA, Columbia Coll., 1934; MD, U. Chgo., 1938. Diplomate Am. Bd. Surgery, Am. Bd. Thoracic Surgery. Intern Bellevue Hosp., NYC, 1938; intern surg. Michael Reese Hosp., Chgo., 1939, resident in surgery, 1940, Mt. Sinai Hosp., NYC, 1941; sr. resident in surgery Michael Reese Hosp., Chgo., 1942; adj. surgeon Mt. Sinai Hosp., NYC, 1946-50; chief surgery and thoracic surgery VA Hosp., Castle Point, N.Y., 1947-50, Ft. Hamilton, N.Y., 1950-53; dir. surgery Bronx-Lebanon Hosp. Ctr., NYC, 1953-64, attending surgeon, cons. thoracic, vascular, gen. surgery, from 1964. Attending surgeon, cons. thoracic, vascular and gen. surgery Union Hosp., N.Y.C., 1976—; attending surgeon thoracic and vascular surgery Beth Israel Hosp. North, N.Y.C., 1977—; cons. gen. and thoracic surgery Dept. of Health N.Y. State, 1963—; cons. thoracic and cardiovascular surgery Hebrew Hosp. for the Chronic Sick, N.Y.C., 1955-89, Hebrew Home for the Aged, Riverdale, N.Y., 1956—, Health Ins. Plan, N.Y.C., 1954—, Bur. Disability Determinations, State of N.Y., 1960—, City of N.Y. Med. Assistance Program, 1966—, Bronx County Supreme Ct., 1958-91; instr. anatomy Sch. Medicine NYU, 1946-49; assoc. clin. prof. surgery Albert Einstein Coll. Medicine, 1959-90. Contbr. articles to Diseases of the Chest, Tuberculosis, N.Y. State Jour. Medicine, Am. Jour. Gastroenterology, Clin. Rsch. Mem. med. bd. Bronx-Lebanon Hosp. Ctr., sec., v.p., pres., 1975-78. Major Med. Corps, U.S. Army, 1942-46, ETO. Alfred Moritz Michaelis fellow in physics Columbia U., 1934; grantee USPHS, 1960. Fellow ACS, N.Y. Acad. Scis., N.Y. Acad. Medicine; mem. AMA, Am. Heart Assn. (coun. on cardiovascular surgery), N.Y. Heart Assn., N.Y. County Med. Soc., N.Y. State Med. Soc., N.Y. Soc. for Thoracic Surgery, Am. Assn. for Thoracic Surgery, Harvey Soc., N.Y. Gastroent. Assn., Phi Beta Kappa, Alpha Omega Alpha. Died Nov. 14, 2007.

FRIEDMAN, BARTON ROBERT, language educator; b. Bklyn., Feb. 5, 1935; s. Abraham Isaac and Mazie Diana (Cooper) F.; m. Sheila Lynn Siegel, June 22, 1958; children— Arnold, Jonathan, Daniel, Esther. BA, Cornell U., 1956, PhD (univ. dissertation fellow), 1964; MA, U. Conn., 1958. Instr. Bowdoin Coll., Brunswick, Maine, 1961-63; from instr. to prof. English lit. U. Wis., Madison, 1963-78; prof. English lit. Cleve. State U., 1978-97, chmn. dept. English, 1978-87, prof. emeritus, from 1997. Visitor Psychoanalytic Inst. Cleve. Author: Adventures in the Deeps of the Mind: The Cuchulain Cycle of W.B. Yeats, 1977, You Can't Tell the Players, 1979, Fabricating History: English Writers on the French Revolution, 1988 (Nancy Dasher award for best scholarly book by mem. Coll. English Assn. Ohio 1989); mem. editl. bd. Irish Renaissance Ann., 1980-84, Lit. Monographs, 1970-76. Recipient William Kiekhofer Teaching Excellence award U. Wis., 1967, Disting. Scholar award Cleve. State U., 1990. Mem. MLA, Am. Com. Irish Studies, Coll. English Assn. Ohio (bd. govs. 1980-81), Soc. Lit. and Sci. (bibliographer Bibliography of Lit. and Sci. in Configurations 1996-98), Phi Kappa Phi. Jewish. Home: Cleveland, Ohio. Died May 5, 2009.

FRIEND, DAVID BRUCE, physics and astronomy educator; b. San Diego, Jan. 29, 1954; s. William D. and Lynn D. (Rogers) F.; m. Diane S. Lakey, June 7, 1975; 1 child, Scott. BS in Physics, San Diego State U., 1976; PhD in Astrophys., U. Colo., 1982. Teaching asst. San Diego State U., 1977; rsch. asst. U. Colo., Boulder, 1977, 79-82, teaching asst., 1977-79; rsch. assoc. U. Wis., Madison, 1984-87; asst. prof., assoc. prof. U. Mont., Missoula, from 1990. Vis. asst. prof. Williams Coll., Williamstown, Mass., 1987-89, Weber State Coll. Ogden, Utah, 1989-90. Columnist Missoulian, 1993—; contbr. articles to profl. jours. Rsch. grantee Fund Astrophys. Rsch., Missoula, 1990, NASA, Missoula, 1991-93; postdoctoral fellow High Altitude Obs., Boulder, 1982-84. Mem. Am. Astron. Soc. (rsch. grantee 1992-93), Astron. Soc. Pacific, The Planetary Soc., Sigma Xi. Avocations: science fiction, skiing, mountain biking, tennis. Home: Missoula, Mont. Died May 22, 2008.

FRITSCH, RICHARD ELVIN, trust company executive; b. Lancaster, Pa., Feb. 3, 1955; s. Elvin Richard and Dolores Audrey (Deppeller) F.; m. Jennifer Lynn Rhodes, June 29, 1996. BS, Elizabethtown Coll., 1977; BA, Lebanon Valley Coll., 1981. Asst. v.p., trust officer First Union Nat. Bank, Lancaster, from 1983. Bd. dirs. Hershey Symphony. Mem. Am. Guild Organists (dean, sub-dean, sec., bd. dirs.), Assn. Luth. Ch. Musicians. Home: Millersville, Pa. Died June 5, 2007.

FRITSCHLER, LAWRENCE JOHN, industrial engineer, plant engineer; b. Wisconsin Rapids, Wis., Nov. 29, 1950; s. LeRoy Henry and Loretta Marie (Jaworski) F.; m. Gail Elenore Goska, Feb. 3, 1973; children: Jeffrey Lawrence, Timothy John. BS in Indsl. Tech., U. Wis., Menomenee, 1972. Asst. plant engr. Preway Inc., Wisconsin Rapids, 1972-74, prodn. engr., 1974-77, process engr., 1977-80, plant engr., from 1980. Bd. dirs. Preway Credit Union, Wisconsin Rapids, 1973-74. Chmn. United Way, Wisconsin Rapids, 1974. Mem. Am. Water-ski Assn. Republican. Roman Catholic. Home: Eau Claire, Wis. Died June 12, 2008.

FRITZ, THOMAS VINCENT, business executive; b. Pitts., July 6, 1934; s. Zeno and Mary M. (Briley) F.; m. Barbara L. Jacob, Jan. 31, 1959; children: William T., James Z., Juliann W. BBA in Acctg. cum laude, U. Pitts., 1960; JD, Duquesne U., 1964; LLM, NYU, 1966; Advanced Mgmt. Program, Harvard Bus. Sch., 1975. Bar: Pa. 1964, U.S. Supreme Ct. 1969; CPA, Pa. 1962. Ptnr. Ernst & Young (formerly Arthur Young & Co.), Pitts., NYC, Washington, 1970, regional mng. ptnr., vice chmn., 1977-89, vice chmn., 1989-92; pres., CEO, bd. dirs. Pvt. Sector Coun., Inc., Washington, 1992-2000; pres. Thomas V. Fritz & Assocs., Washington, from 2000. Adj. prof. Sch. Law Duquesne U., Pitts., 1966-79; adv. dirs. Pvt. Sector Coun., Washington, 1983-2004; bd. dirs. Innovative Sys., Inc.; chmn. Alliance for Free Enterprise, Washington, 1987-89. Editor Duquesne U. Law Rev., 1963-64. Active Century Club, Duquesne U.; bd. dirs. Evermay Comty. Assn., pres., 1994-96; bd. dirs. McLean Citizens Assn., 1994-97; co-chmn. U. Pitts. Katz Campaign 3d Century, 1988-91. With US Army, 1955—57, with USAR, 1957—63. Recipient Gorley award, 1964, Disting. Alumni award U. Pitts., 1981, Advancement Info. Tech. award, 1988, Federal 100 Info. Tech. award, 1997. Mem. AICPA, ACBA, Pa. Inst. CPAs, Duquesne Club, Met. Club, Rolling Rock Club, Avenel Club, Beta Gamma Sigma, Beta Alpha Psi. Died Jan. 25, 2009.

FROST, CHARLES ESTES, JR., lawyer; b. Houston, Aug. 17, 1950; s. Charles Estes and Lucille Fourmey (DeGravelles) F. BS, U.S. Mil. Acad., 1972; MBA, Armstrong State Coll., 1979; JD, U. Tex., 1981. Bar: Tex. 1982, U.S. Dist. Ct. (no., ea. and so. dists.) Tex., 5th circuit ct. appeals. Commd. 2d lt. U.S. Army, 1972, advanced through grades to capt., 1979; resigned from active duty, 1979; assoc. Strasburger & Price, Dallas, 1982-84, Chamberlain, Hrdlicka et al, Houston, 1985-88; shareholder Chamberlain Hrdlicka et al, Houston, from 1989. Mem. bd. advocates U. Tex. Law Sch. Note editor: Tex. Law Rev., U. Tex. Law Sch.1981-82. Mem. ethics com. Haris County Rep. Party, 2000. Lt. col. USAR, 1979-98. Mem. Am. Arbitration Assn. (comml. arbitrator, comml. panel 2003—), Houston Bar Assn. (dir. litigation sect. 2000-02). Avocations: running, church. Died Feb. 21, 2008.

FROST, LOUIS O'MELVILLE, JR., public defender; b. NYC, Sept. 19, 1931; s. Louis O'Melville and Emma Marie (Lemké) F.; m. Shirley Clyde Bush, Oct. 22, 1960; children: Louis O., Deborah Allison. BSBA, U. Fla., 1953, JD, 1958. Bar: Fla. 1958, U.S. Supreme Ct. 1966, U.S. Ct. Appeals (11th cir.) 1971, U.S. Dist. Ct. (mid. dist.) Fla. 1981. Assoc. Smith Axtell & Howell, Jacksonville, 1958-59; asst. state atty. State Atty.'s Office, Jacksonville, 1959-63; ptnr. Durrance & Frost, Jacksonville, 1960-69; chief asst. pub. defender Pub. Defender's Office, Jacksonville, 1963-68, pub. defender, from 1968; gen. counsel Fla. State Bd. Health, Jacksonville, 1965-67. 1st lt. U.S. Army, 1954-56. Mem. William B. Barnett Lodge #187 (master mason 1964—), Fla. Blue Key, Arlington Rotary Club (pres. 1981-82, Paul Harris fellow 1982), Scottish Rite (master of Kadosh, 33 deg., insp. gen. hon. 1995), Morocco Temple Shrine N.Am. (potentate 1987). Democrat. Episcopalian. Avocations: fishing, golf, camping. Home: Jacksonville, Fla. Died Jan. 16, 2008.

FRUMKIN, SIMON, political organization worker, writer; b. Kaunas, Lithuania, Nov. 5, 1930; came to U.S., 1949; s. Nicholas and Zila (Oster) F.; m. Rhoda Hirsch, June 1953 (div. 1978); children: Michael Alan, Larry Martin; m. Kathy Elizabeth Hoopes, June 22, 1981 (dec. 1994); m. Ella Zousman, Dec. 11, 1995. BA, NYU, 1953; MA in History, Calif. State U., Northridge, 1964. Pres., CEO Universal Drapery Fabrics, Inc., Los Angeles, 1953-87; chmn. So. Calif. Coun. for Soviet Jews, Studio City, 1969—2009. Lectr. Simon Wiesenthal Ctr. for Holocaust Studies, Los Angeles, 1980-2009; chmn. Union of Councils for Soviet Jews, 1972-73. Columnist Heritage, numerous other So. Calif. newspapers; corr. to columnist Panorama, U.S.A. Russian Lang.; contbr. articles to newspapers. Pres. Media Analysis Found., Los Angeles, 1988; chmn. Americans for Peace and Justice, 1972-74; mem. Pres.' Senatorial Inner Circle, U.S. Senatorial Club. Honored by Calif. Govt., Los Angeles City Council, Los Angeles Office of City Atty., numerous Jewish orgns. Mem. Assn. Soviet Jewish Emigre's (pres.), Zionist Orgn. Am., Am. Israel Polit. Action Com., Russian Republican Club, Mensa. Jewish. Avocations: writing, photography, skiing, exercise. Died May 15, 2009.

FRY, JUDY ARLINE, hypnotherapist; b. Great Falls, Mont., July 25, 1938; d. Ernest Leroy and Leota M. (Lyon) Workman; m. Kenneth J. Fry, Nov. 11, 1956 (div. 1974); children; Kenneth J., Kathy K. Studied with, Glen Meyers, 1956—65, Vista Robbins, 1965—69, studied with, from 1974; student, Calif. State U., Northridge, 1978. Cert. clin. hypnotherapist. Co-owner, dir. Artistic Designs in Iron, Huntington Beach, Calif., 1974—75; ops. mgr., sales coord., purchasing agt. Komfort Industries Inc., Santa Ana, Calif., 1975—81; corp. adminstr. OEM accounts Greer Hydraulics, Inc., City of Commerce, Calif., 1978; office svc. supr. Pacific Pumps/Dresser Industries, Inc., Huntington Park, Calif., 1981-83, aftermarket order entry mgr., 1982; ops. dir., dir. pub. rels. Calif. Assn. Real Estate Investors, Laguna Niguel, 1986-87; founder, co-owner Advance Resource Ctr., Garden Grove, Calif., 1987-94; ops. dir., dir. pub. rels. Robinson Prod., Ltd., Calif. Assn. Real Estate Investors, Laguna Niguel, Calif., 1987—94; founder, co-owner Advance Resource Ctr., North Las Vegas, from 1994. Co-author two books, sub-feature articles, newspaper, radio talk shows, TV; represented pvt. collections Ariz., Calif., Ind., Nev., Oreg., Wis. including Fine Arts Gallerie, Carnegie Inst., Pa. Past v.p. NW Arts League. Recipient 1st pl. Nat. Scholastic mag. art award, 1953, 1954, 1955, 1st pl. nat. scholastic mag. art award, 1956. Mem. Nat. Mgmt. Assn., United Hypnotherapists Calif., Internat. Assn. Clin. Hypnotherapists (past pres. Orange County chpt.), Artistic Equity Assn., Wabash Valley Art Guild, Hoosier Salon Patrons Assn., Arts Illiana, Inland Empire Art Assn., Oregon Crafted. Home: Eugene, Oreg. Died Dec. 15, 2007.

FRYE, JOHN WILLIAM, mechanical engineer; b. Kansas City, Mo., Aug. 27, 1939; s. George and Maud Genevieve (Cashman) F.; m. Roslyn Ramer, May 7, 1966; children: Darlene, Steven. BSME, Kans. U., 1960; MSE, UCLA, 1966; student, NYU, 1967-68. Mech. engr. Naval Weapoins Ctr., China Lake, Calif., 1960-69; loads engr. Sykorsky Aircraft, Stratford, Conn., 1969; mech. engr. Naval Underwater Systems Ctr., New London, Conn., 1969-80; systems engr. TRW, Redondo Beach, Calif., from 1980. Contbr. articles to IEEE Jour., Fourth Nastran Colloquium, confs. Mem. AIAA. Democrat. Unitarian Universalist. Home: Fountain Vly, Calif. Died July 7, 2008.

FRYE, PATRICK KEITH, television producer, director, writer; b. Harrisburg, Pa., Sept. 26, 1947; s. David Albert and Margureite Elizabeth (Cooney) F.; m. Therese Ellen Ronald, Oct. 2, 1972; children: Catherine Amy-Collen, Erin Lindsay-Dawn. AA, Middle Ga. Coll., 1971; AB, U. Ga., 1974, MA, 1981. Disc jockey, program mgr. Sta. WUOG-FM, U. Ga., Athens, 1972-74; TV crew worker Instrnl. Resouces Ctr., U. Ga., 1980-81, prodn. asst., 1981-82, TV dir., 1982-83, producer, dir., 1983-85, prodn. mgr., from 1985. Mem. Sertoma, Athens, 1985—. Served with U.S. Army, 1968-70, Vietnam. Mem. Internat. TV Assn. (newsletter editor 1985-86). Methodist. Avocation: all sports and outdoor activities. Home: Danielsville, Ga. Died Mar. 13, 2008.

FUGATE, JACK MILLARD, optometrist; b. Columbus, Ohio, Mar. 27, 1927; s. Millard Perl and Helen (McKinley) F.; m. Cassie Adkins (div. 1972); children: Deborah, Sandra, Sue Ann, Steven; m. Glenn Workman, July 1977 (div. June 1991); m. Carolee Houchard, July 6, 1996. BS in Optometry, Ohio State U., 1951, MS in Phisiol. Optics, 1954, OD, 1966. Cert. optometry. Asst. prof. emeritus optometry and physiol. optics Ohio State U. Coll. Optometry and Grad. Sch., Columbus, from 1953; pvt. practice optometry Columbus, from 1954. Mem. med. staff Columbus Cmty. Hosp.; lectr. in field. Contbr. articles on physiol. optics and optometry to profl. jours. Former trustee Ohio Lions Eye Rsch. Found.; chmn. Visual Med. Adv. Com.; former mem. bd. trustees, former pres. Vision Ctr. Cen. Ohio; former bd. dirs. Ohio Soc. for the Prevention of Blindness; trustee Vision Svc. Plan Ohio, 1974—, chmn. bd. dirs., 1980-83, mem. vision svc. plan nat., 1984—; past mem. adv. com. Bur. Vocat. Rehab. With USN, 1945-46. Fellow Am. Acad. Optometry (diplomate low vision); mem. Am. Optometric Assn., Ohio Optometric Assn., Lions. Avocations: travel, tennis, theater. Home: Columbus, Ohio. Died Apr. 2, 2008.

FULLER, ANGELA M., secondary school educator, assistant principal; b. Rochester, NY, Jan. 17, 1956; d. Mary K.; 1 child, Shannon Mary. AA, Finger Lakes C.C., 1992, AS, 1998; BA, St. John Fisher U., 1994, MS in Edn., 2003. Tchr. chemistry Victor (N.Y.) H.S., Greece Arcadia H.S., Rochester, NY; asst. prin. Greece Athena H.S., Rochester. Tchr. Johns Hopkins C.C., Albany, NY. Recipient Presdl. Leadership award, St. John Fisher Sch., 2003. Home: Fairport, NY. Died Nov. 20, 2007.

FULLER, E. LOREN, JR., chemist; b. Alliance, Nebr., Sept. 9, 1930; s. Elmer Loren and Beulah Veta Mae (League) F.; m. D. Elaine Smithberger, June 18, 1960; children: Dorothy, Glenn. BS, Nebr. State U., 1957; PhD, U. Nebr., 1962. Mem. sr. rsch. staff Oak Ridge (Tenn.) Nat. Lab., from 1962. Conf. chmn. Colloid & Surface Sci., Knoxville, Tenn., 1968. Editor: Advances in Analyses of Coal, 1982; contbr. over 100 articles to profl. jours. With U.S. Army, 1952-54. Mem. Am. Chem. Soc., AAAS (exec. com. 1987—), N.Y. Acad. Scis., ASTM (com. chmn. 1989—), Am. Chem. Soc. (div. colloid and surface chemistry exec. com. 1987—), Sigma Xi. Methodist. Home: Stanton, Nebr. Died Dec. 17, 2007.

FULLER, MILLARD DEAN, foundation administrator, lawyer; b. Lanett, Ala., Jan. 3, 1935; s. Render and Estin (Cook) F.; m. Linda Caldwell; children: Christopher, Kimberly, Faith, Georgia. BS in Econs., Auburn U., 1957; LLB, U. Ala., 1960; LHD (hon.), Ea. Coll., Pa., 1985, Ottawa U., 1987, Susquehanna U., 1989; D Pub. Svcs. (hon.), DePauw U., 1988; HHD (hon.), Coll. of Wooster, 1989, Wake Forest U., 1990, Mercer U., 1990, Westminster Coll., 1990, Whitworth Coll., 1990, Dallas Bapt. U., 1994, Lynchburg Coll., 1992, North Park Coll., 1992, Tech. U. Nova Scotia, 1992, U. North Ala., 1994, Providence Coll., 1994, Presbyn. Coll., Clinton, SC, 1995, Bluffton Coll., 1995, Elon Coll., 1995, Nova Southeastern U., 1996; HHD (hon.), U. Ala., 2004. Bar: Ala. 1960, Ga. 1972. Co-founder Fuller and Dees Mktg. Group, Inc., Montgomery, Ala., 1960, pres., 1960-65; ptnr. Fuller and Dees (law firm), Montgomery, 1960-65; devel. dir. Tougaloo (Miss.) Coll., 1966-68; dir. Koinonia Ptnrs., Inc. (developer various bus. ops. for Koinonia Christian community), Americus, Ga., 1968-72; dir. devel. Ch. of Christ, Zaire, Equator region Africa, 1973-76, initiator housing project for low-income families, Mbandaka, Zaire Equator region Africa; founder, CEO Habitat Humanity Internat., Inc., Americus, 1976—2005; founder, pres. The Fuller Ctr. Housing, Inc., 2005—09. Author: Bokotola, 1977, Love in the Mortar Joints, 1980, No More Shacks!, 1986, The Excitement is Building, 1990, Theology of the Hammer, 1994, A Simple, Decent Place to Live, 1995, More than Houses, 2000, Building Materials for Life, vol. I, 2002, vol. II, 2004, vol. III, 2007. Adv. com. Albert Schweitzer Fellowship of Am., 1992. Lt. U.S. Army, 1960. Recipient Outstanding Achievement award Coun. State Housing Agys., 1986, Clarence Jordan Exemplary Chistiran Svc. award So. Bapt. Theol. Sem., 1986, Dr. Marting Luther King, Jr. Humanitarian award, 1987, Disting. chrisitan Svc. in Social Welfare award N.Am. Assn. christians in Social Work, 1988, Internat. Humanity Svc. award Am. Overseas Assn. ARC, 1989, Pub. Svc. Achievement award Common Cause, 1989, M. Justin Herman Meml. award Nat. Assn. Housing and Devel. Ofcls., 1989, The Temple award for Creative Altruism, 1990, Joseph C. Wilson award Rochester Assn. for the UN, 1990, Amicus Certus award Luth. Social Svcs. Ill., Martin Luther Jr. Humanitarian award Ga. State Holiday Commn., 1992, Profl. Achievement award Partnership Affordable Housing, 1993, Harry S. Truman Pub. Svc. award City of Independence, 1994, The McConnell award Truett-McConnell Coll., Ga., 1995, Faithful Servant award Nat. Assn. of Evangelicals, 1996, Spirit of Ga. award, 1996; named Builder of Yr. Profl. Bldr. mag., 1995, Nat. Housing Hall of Fame, 1996, Presdl. Medal of Freedom, 1996, Jefferson award 1999. Mem. Ala. Bar Assn., Ga. Bar Assn. Baptist. Avocations: reading, walking. Home: Americus, Ga. Died Feb. 3, 2009.

FUNK, WARREN KEITH, retired military officer, consultant; b. Minneapolis, Kans., Apr. 8, 1943; s. Leslie Ivan and Charlotte Aline (Rogers) F.; m. Linda Joan Dickerson, Aug. 15, 1965 (div. Sept. 1976); children: Ryan Adam, Rachel Regan; m. Lesley Jean Bartman, Feb. 4, 1979. BA in Tech. Journalism, Kans. State U., 1966; MS in Human Resource Mgmt., Gonzaga U., 1978. Commd. 2d lt. USAF, 1966, advanced through grades to maj., 1977; squadron section comdr 21st Supply Squadron, Elmendorf AFB, Alaska, 1973-75; chief of protocol Alaskan Air Command Hdqrs., Elmendorf AFB, Alaska, 1975-76; dir. adminstrn USAF Survival Sch., Fairchild AFB, Wash., 1976-78; chief base adminstr 2nd Combat Support Group, Barksdale AFB, La., 1979-84, 60th Air Base Group, Travis AFB, Calif., 1984-86, cons., 1984-86; ret., 1986; cons. Fairfield, Calif., 1986-87; support services mgr. City of Monterey Park, Calif., from 1987. Counselor Rape Crisis Network Luth. Family and Child Service, Spokane, Wash., 1977-79, counselor and trainer Rape Crisis Ctr., YWCA, Shreveport, La., 1980-84. Mem. Am. Mgmt. Assn., Air Force Assn., Assn. of Info. Systems Profls. (v.p. Shreveport chpt. 1978-79). Clubs: Officers (Travis AFB). Republican. Presbyterian. Avocations: fishing, canoeing, chess, reading, coin collecting/numismatics. Died Dec. 10, 2007.

FURCHGOTT, ROBERT FRANCIS, pharmacologist, educator; b. Charleston, SC, June 4, 1916; married, 1941; 3 children. BS, U. N.C., 1937; PhD in Biochemistry, Northwestern U., 1940; DM (hon.), Autonomous U. Madrid, 1984, U. Lund, 1984; DSc (hon.), U. N.C., 1989, U. Ghent, 1995; degree (hon.), Mt. Sinai Med. Sch., 1995, Ohio State U., 1996, Med. U. S.C., 1997, Med. Coll. Ohio, 1997, Northwestern U., 1998, U. Coll., London, 1998, Washington U., 2001, Charles U., Prague, 2003. Rsch. fellow medicine Med. Coll. Cornell U., 1940—43, rsch. assoc., 1943—47, instr. physiology, 1943—48, asst. prof. med. biochemistry, 1947—49; from asst. prof. to assoc. prof. pharmacology Med. Sch. Wash. U., 1949—56; chmn. dept. pharmacology SUNY Coll. Med. (now SUNY Health Sci. Ctr.), Bklyn., 1956—82; prof. dept. pharmacology SUNY Health Sci. Ctr., Bklyn., 1956—88, Disting. prof., 1988—89, Disting. emeritus prof. pharmacology, 1990—2009. Mem. pharmacol. tng. com. USPHS, 1961—64, mem. pharmacotoxicol. rev. com., 1965—68, Commonwealth fellow, 1962—63; vis. prof. U. Geneva, 1962—63, U. Calif., San Diego, 1971—72, Med. U. S.C., 1980, UCLA, 1980; adj. prof. pharmacology, Sch. Medicine U. Miami, 1988—2001; disting. vis. prof. Med. Univ. South Carolina, 2001. Recipient rsch. achievement award, Am. Heart Assn., 1990, Bristol-Myers Squibb award for achievement in cardiovasc. rsch., 1991, Gairdner Found. Internat. award, 1991, medal, N.Y. Acad. Medicine, 1992, Roussel Uclaf prize for rsch. in cell communication and signalling, 1993, Wellcome Gold medal, Brit. Pharmacology Soc., 1995, ASPET award for exptl. therapeutics, 1996, Gregory Pincus award for rsch., 1996, Albert Lasker award for Basic Med. Rsch., Lasker Found., 1996, Lucian award, 1997, Nobel prize for Medicine, 1998. Mem.: NAS, AAAS, Harvey Soc., Am. Soc. Pharmacology and Exptl. Therapeutics (pres. 1971—72, Goodman and Gilman award 1984), Am. Soc. Biochemistry, Am. Chem. Soc., Am. Acad. Arts and Scis., Polish Physiol. Soc. (hon.), Sigma Xi. Home: Seattle, Wash. Died May 19, 2009.

FURMAN, ROBERT RALPH, real estate developer; b. Trenton, NJ, Aug. 21, 1915; s. William Amies and Lelia Ficht F.; m. Mary Eddy, Dec. 21, 1951; children: Martha, Julia, David, Serena. BSE, Princeton U., 1937; D in Pub. Svc. (hon.), Carroll C.C., 1999. Prin., owner Furman Bldrs., Inc., Rockville, Md., 1946-83, Greentree Assocs., Inc., Rockville, Md., from 1983. Chmn. bldg. adv. bd. Prince George's C.C., 1988-98; exec. office for construction The Pentagon Bldg. U.S. Army Engrs., 1942-43; spl. asst. to Lt. Gen. Leslie R. Groves Manhattan Dist. U.S. Army Engrs., 1943-45. Lt. Col. U.S. Army, 1940-46. Mem. United Way (pres. 1970), Bethesda Chevy Chase Rotary (pres. 1960), Bethesda Chevy Chase C. of C. (pres. 1955), Edgemoor Tennis Club (pres. 1966). Republican. Episcopalian. Home: Adamstown, Md. Died Oct. 14, 2008.

GABEL, ELI, disability analyst; b. Bklyn., Aug. 12, 1939; s. Israel and Bertha (Orenbuch) G.; m. Leslie Ellin Heit, Mar. 22, 1964; children: Marc Matthew, Melissa Rachel. BA, Hunter Coll., 1962; M of Profl. Studies, NYU, 1984. Sales and ops. coord. Global Tours, Inc., NYC, 1965-69; staff mgr. Japan Air Lines, NYC, 1969-74; pub. rels. cons. Internat. Tourism and Commerce, NYC, 1974-77; disability analyst N.Y. State Office of Disability Determinations, NYC, from 1977. Rep. Gov.'s Com. on Paperwork and Forms Reduction, Albany, N.Y., 1984-86; travel mktg. instr. Adelphi U., Garden City, N.Y., 1973, Sobelsohn Sch., N.Y.C., 1970-73. Exec. v.p. New Springville Jewish Ctr., S.I., 1990, 91; mem. parent adv. bd. On Your Mark, S.I., 1990. Mem. Nat. Assn. Disability Analysis (nat. conf. publicist 1981-83, mem. svcs. chmn. 1981-82). Jewish. Avocation: advocate for non-stereotypcial portrayal of disabled in the media. Home: Staten Island, NY. Died Aug. 14, 2008.

GABRIA, JOANNE BAKAITIS, health and education volunteer; b. Washington, Pa., Jan. 16, 1945; d. Vincent William and Mary Jo (Cario) Bakaitis. BA in English, U. Dayton, 1965, MA in Mktg. Comm., 1973, MBA, 1979. Advt. writer Dancer-Fitzgerald-Sample, Dayton, Ohio, 1969-72; advt. coord. Monarch Marking Sys., Dayton, 1972-73; product tech. editor Frigidaire divsn. GM, Dayton, 1973-77; dir. tech. comm. Mead Tech. Lab., Dayton, 1977-79; publs. mgr. NCR Corp., Dayton, 1979-81, internat. product mgr., 1981-86, mgr. internat. market analysis, 1986-87, mgr. internat. market rsch., 1987-93, mgr. European info. resources, 1993-94. Patient adv. coun. rep. Renal Network, Inc., from 2002. Author: Microwave Cooking in 3 Speeds, 1976, Communications Standards, 1978, Retail Operations, 1982; editor Ivy Jour., 1980-82; editor (newsletter) Miami Valley Hosp., 2001—. Chair numerous coms. St. Leonard Cmty., Centreville, Ohio, 1978-88; tel. vol. Contact-Dayton Crisis Intervention, 1982-86; big sister Big Bros./Big Sisters, Dayton, 1985-86; bd. dirs. Miami Valley chpt. Nat. Kidney Found. Ohio, 1987-91, spkrs. bur., 1995—; Ohio patient adv. com. Renal Network, Inc., 1989-91, Patient Leadership Com., Renal Network, 1997-99; bd. dirs. Contact-Dayton, 1984-85; local coord. Friends of Polycystic Kidney Rsch. Found., 1994-99; leadership com. PKD Found., Dayton-Cin. chpt., 2002—; tutor Miami Valley Literacy Coun., Proliteracy Worldwide, 1997—; liaison Nat. Kidney Found., Patient and Family Coun., 2000—; moderator Osher Lifelong Learning Inst. U. Dayton, 2001—. Recipient Disting. Achievement award Contact-Dayton, 1985, Outstanding Svc. award Miami Valley chpt. Nat. Kidney Found. Ohio, 1988, Edn. award, 1990. Mem. Marianist Affiliates (co-chmn. 1981-86), Leo Meyer Soc. Democrat. Roman Catholic. Avocations: nature, classical music. Died June 9, 2005.

GABRIELSON, WALTER OSCAR, artist; b. Eveleth, Minn., July 25, 1935; s. Walter Oscar and Marie Hope (Harris) G.; m. Nancy Heather Goldberg, Mar. 24, 1983. BS, UCLA, 1958; BFA, MFA, Otis Art Inst., LA, 1965. Printer Tamarind Lithography Workshop, LA, 1964-66; prof. art Calif. State U., Northridge, 1966-81. Exhibited at Arco Ctr. for Visual Arts, 1976, others. Author: 41 Airplanes, 1970, Persistence, 1993. Bd. dirs. Santa Barbara (Calif.) Contemporary Arts. Forum, 1991-95. 1st lt. USAF, 1958-61 Ford Found. Tamarind grantee, 1964-66. Avocations: aviation, jazz, reading. Home: Santa Barbara, Calif. Died Nov. 12, 2008.

GAJDUSEK, DANIEL CARLETON, pediatrician, research virologist; b. Yonkers, NY, Sept. 9, 1923; s. Karl A. and Ottilia D. (Dobroczki) G.; children: Ivan Mbagintao, Josede Figirilyong, Jesus Raglmar, Jesus Mororui, Mathias Maradol, Jesus Tamel, Jesus Salalu, John Paul Runman, Yavine Borima, Arthur Yolwa, Joe Yongorimah Kintoki, Thomas Youmog, Toni Wanevi, Toname Ikabala, Magame Prima, Senavayo Anua, Igitava Yoviga, Luwi Ikavara, Iram'bin'ai Undae'mai, Susanna Undapmaina, Steven Malrui, John Fasug Raglmar, Launako Wate, Louise Buwana, Regina Etangthaw Raglmar, Vincent Ayin, Daniel Sumal, Iyo Fanechigiy Raglmar, John Clayton Harongsemal, Peter Paul Ffiran, Jason Sohorang, Edwina Wes Mugunbey, Brenda Gillippin, Carleton Kalikaipapadaua Mbagintao, Basil Talonu, Gideon Waiwaime, Okovi Yarao, Sesario Sigam Salalu. BS, U. Rochester, 1943; MD, Harvard U., 1946, DSc (hon.), 1987; NRC fellow, Calif. Inst. Tech., 1948-49; DSc (hon.), U. Rochester, 1977, Med. Coll. Ohio, 1977, Washington & Jefferson Coll., 1980, Hahneman Med. Coll., 1983, Med. and Dental Coll. of N.J., 1987; DHL (hon.), Hamilton Coll., 1977, U. Hawaii, 1986; LLD (hon.), U. Aberdeen, Scotland, 1980; PhD (hon.), U. Aix-Marseille, France, 1977, U. Lisbon, Portugal, 1991, U. Milan, Italy, 1992, U. Lodz, Poland, 1995, U. Las Palmas, Spain, 1995, U. Komenius, Bratislava, Slovakia, 1996. Diplomate Am. Bd. Pediatrics. Intern, resident Babies Hosp., Columbia Presbyn. Med. Center, NYC, 1946-47; resident pediat. Children's Hosp., Cin., 1947-48; pediat. med. mission Germany, 1948; resident, clin. and rsch. fellow Childrens Hosp., Boston, 1949-51; rsch. fellow pediat. and infectious diseases Harvard U., 1949-52; rsch. virologist Walter Reed AMSGS, Washington, 1952-53; with Institut Pasteur, Teheran, Iran, 1954-55; vis. investigator Nat. Found. Infantile Paralysis, Walter and Eliza Hall Inst. Med. Research, Melbourne, Australia, 1955-57; dir. program for study child growth and devel. and disease patterns in primitive cultures and lab. slow, latent and temperate virus infections NINDS, NIH, Bethesda, Md., 1958—97; chief Lab. Ctrl. Nervous System Studies, 1970—97. Chief scientist rsch. vessel Alpha Helix expdn. to Banks and Torres Islands, New Hebrides, South Solomon Islands, 1971; hon. prof. virology Hupei Med. Coll., Wuhan, China, 1986; hon. prof. neurology Beijing Med. U., 1987, Las Palmas de Gran Canaria, Spain, 1993; hon. faculty Med. Sch. U. of Papua New Guinea, 1980; vis. prof. Royal Soc. Medicine, London, 1987; Schulz lectr. Stanford U., 1995. Author: Hemorrhagic Fevers and Mycotoxicoses in the USSR, 1951; contbr. over 45 articles to profl. jours. Recipient E. Meade Johnson award Am. Acad. Pediatrics, 1963, Superior Svc. award NIH, HEW, 1970, Disting. Svc. award HEW, 1975, Prof. Lucian Dautrebande prize in Pathophysiology Belgium, 1976, Nobel prize in Physiology and Medicine, 1976, Cotzias prize Am. Neurol. Assn., 1978, Huxley medal Royal Anthrop. Inst. Gt. Britain and Ireland, 1989, Gold medal Czechoslovak Med. Soc., 1989, Mudd award Internat. Union Microbiol. Socs., 1990, Gold medal, prize 3d. Internat. Congress on Alzheimers Disease, 1992, 2nd Pacific Rim Biotech. award, 1992, Gold medal Basque Acad. Med., 1993, Disting. Lectr. award Internat. Human Retrovirlogy, 1994, Disting. Scientist award Montefiore Hosp. Albert Einstein Sch. Medicine, 1995, Gold Medal Slovak Acad. Sci., Bratislava, 1996—; Dyer lectr. NIH, 1974, Heath Clark lectr. U. London, 1974, B.K. Rachford lectr. Children's Hosp. Research Found., Cin., 1975, Langmuir lectr. CDC, Atlanta, 1975, Withering lectr. U. Birmingham, Eng., 1976, Cannon Elie lectr. Boston Children's Med. Center, 1976, Zale lectr. U. Tex., Dallas, 1976, Bayne-Jones lectr. Johns Hopkins Med. Sch., Balt., 1976, Harvey lectr. N.Y. Acad. Medicine, 1977, J.E. Smadel lectr. Infectious Disease Soc. Am., 1977, Burnet lectr. Australasian Soc. Infectious Disease, 1978, Mapother lectr. U. London, 1978, Disting. lectr. in medicine Mayo Clinic, 1978, Kaiser Meml. lectr. U. Hawaii, 1979, Eli Lilly lectr. U. Toronto, 1979, Payne lectr. Children's Hosp. D.C., 1981, Ray C. Moon lectr. Angelo State U., Tex., 1981, Silliman lectr. Yale U., 1981, Blackfan lectr. Children's Hosp. Med. Ctr., Boston, 1981, Hitchcock Meml. lectr. U. Calif.-Berkeley, 1982, Nelson lectr. U. Calif.-Davis, 1982, Derick-MacKerres lectr. Queensland Inst. Med. Research, 1982, Bicentennial lectr. Harvard U. Sch. Medicine, 1982, Cartwright lectr. Columbia U., 1982, lectr. Chinese Acad. Med. Sci., 1983, Michelson lectr., prof., U. Tenn., Memphis, 1986, plenary lectr., Chinese Assn. Med. Virology, Yentai, 1986, returned Nobel Laureate, Karolinska Inst., Stockholm and U. Tromsö, Norway, 1986, Nobel Jubilee lectr. Karolinska U., Uppsala U., U. Trondheim, Norway, 1991, Rubbo Orator Australian Soc. Microbiology, 1992, Ashton Graybiel lectr. Naval Aerospace Med. Rsch. Lab, 1994. Mem. NAS, Am. Acad. Arts and Scis., Am. Philos. Soc., Deutsche Akad., Naturförscher Leopoldina, Russian Acad. Med. Sci., Australian Acad. Sci., Acad. Sci. Sakha Republic, Russian Acad. Sci., World Acad. Art and Sci., Acads. Nacionales de Medicina Mexico, Colombia and Argentina, Czechoslovak Acad. Scis., Third World Acad. Scis., Internat. Acad. Scis., Royal Coll. Physicians (Edinburgh), Royal Anthrop. Inst. Gt. Britain and Ireland, Soc. Pediat. Rsch., Am. Pediat. Soc., Am. Soc. Human Genetics, Am. Acad. Neurology (Cotzias prize 1979), Soc. Neurosci., Am. Epidemiol. Soc., Infectious Diseases Soc. Am., Soc. des Oceanistes, Paris, Papua and New Guinea Sci. Soc., Phi Beta Kappa, Sigma Xi. Home: Frederick, Md. Died Dec. 2008.

GAJEC, JOHN JOSEPH, music educator, musician; b. Caro, Mich., Feb. 20, 1918; s. John Joseph Gajec and Anna Stephanie (Gurgul) Jaroszewski; m. Stephanie Sylvia Schneikart, July 1, 1961. MusB, U. Mich., 1942, MusM, 1951. Music dir., orch. leader pub. schs., Mich., 1946-79; founder, music dir. Redford Twp. (Mich.) Civic Symphony Orch., from 1956. Asst. condr. U. Mich. Extension Symphony Orch., Detroit, 1946-67. Oboeist Leonard Smith Belle Isle Band, numerous orchs.; performer (various instruments) shows, musicals, operettas, concerts. Sponsor Redford Township Music Soc. Served to sgt. USAAF, 1942-46. Mem. Am. Symphony Orch. League, Am. String Tchrs. Assn., Music Educators Nat. Conf., NEA, Detroit Fedn. Musicians, Mich. Band and Orch. Assn. Democrat. Roman Catholic. Avocations: photography, cabinet-making, golf, crafting musical instruments. Died Nov. 17, 2007.

GALANIC, ELIZABETH ANN, nursing administrator; b. Lorain, Ohio, Oct. 9, 1935; d. Daniel and Magdalene (Kitlitz) Rottari; m. Peter P. Galanic, Oct. 18, 1958; children: Sandra Jean Zawalski, Peter P. Galanic II. Diploma,

M.B. Johnson, Elyria, Ohio, 1956; BS in Health Care, St. Joseph Coll., Windham, Maine, 1986. With Shields Nursing Home, Lorain, Ohio, 1966-71; asst. adminstr., dir. nursing Weber's Nursing Home, Wellington, Ohio, 1971-75; dir. nursing Ohio Extended Care Ctr., Lorain, 1976-94; asst. adminstr., dir. nursing The Renaissance, Olmsted Twp., Ohio, from 1994. Instr. St. Joseph Sch. Nursing, Lorain County Community Coll.; mem. pro care adv. bd. Nurse Aide Competency Test, 1989; item writer Edn. Tsting System, Princeton, N.J., 1988. Preceptor Med. Coll. Ohio, Toledo. Named Outstanding Alumni, St. Joseph Coll., 1986. Mem. Am. Bus. Women's Assn. (v.p. 1986-88), Ohio Health Care Assn. (nurse shortage task force 1988, dir. nursing of yr. 1988, sec. dist. V 1982—). Home: Lorain, Ohio. Died Jan. 24, 2008.

GALAZKA, HELEN GORDON MACROBERT, minister, psychotherapist; b. Paisley, Scotland, June 8, 1915; came to U.S., 1953; d. John and Helen (Cunningham) MacRobert; m. Michal Galazka, Sept. 9, 1941 (dec. 1972); 1 child, Michal J. M. MA, Glasgow U., Scotland, 1935; BD, Trinity Coll., Scotland, 1938; D. Ministry, Andover Newton, 1974. Ordained to ministry Presbyn. Ch., 1940. Pastor Montrose and Kilmarnock U.F. Chs., Scotland, 1940-53, Conant Meml. Ch., Dudley, Mass., 1953-60, 1st Ch., Glenwood, Iowa, 1960-61; exec. Mpls. Coun. of Chs., 1961-69; pastor First Ch., Ludlow, Mass., 1969-81; interim pastor Three Rivers, Mass.; psychotherapist dept. psychiatry Baystate Med. Ctr., Springfield, Mass., from 1974. Mem. pastoral care dept., mem. grief com. Baystate Med. Ctr., Springfield, 1978. Contbr. articles to profl. jours. Named Woman of Achievement Women's Profl. Club, 1980, Outstanding Citizen Channel 22, 1984. Mem. Mass. Psychology Assn., Am. Assn. Marriage & Family Therapy (clin.), Beta Sigma Phi. Died June 28, 2008.

GALEA'I, FAI'IVAE APELU, state legislator; b. Leone, Pago Pago, Am. Semoa, Dec. 13, 1930; s. Apelu Galea'i and Linea Schmidt; m. Julia Leituala, Jan. 30, 1960 (div. 1981); children: Apelu, Fitiuta, Rosa Mana. BA, U. Hawaii, 1972, MA, 1980. Vice prin. Leone (Am. Samoa) HS, 1954—55; pres., cons. Samoa Tours and Travel, 1956—72; freelance cons., 1964—2007; dir. Office Tourism Am. Samoa Govt., 1973—73; pres., cons. Samoa Tours and Travel, 1977—80; mem. Am. Samoa Senate, 1981—2007. Chmn. scholarship bd. Edn. Dept., Pago Pago, 1982—2007; coord. constl. conv. Am. Semoa Govt., 1984—2007. Chmn. exec. com. Gov. P.T. Coleman Re-election Com., 1982. Mem.: Am. Samoa Tchrs. Assn., Individual Travel Assn., Internat. East West Ctr. Alumni, Lions. Democrat. Conglist. Died June 2007.

GALLAGHER, JOHN PATRICK, priest, historian, educator; b. Scranton, Pa., July 10, 1924; s. Michael J. and Beatrice (Peyton) G. AA, St. Charles Coll., Catonsville, Md., 1944; BA, U. Western Ont., London, Can., 1946; MA, Cath. U. Am., 1961, PhD in History, 1964. Ordained priest Roman Cath. Ch., 1951. Pastor St. David's Parish, Scranton, 1970-73, Holy Rosary Parish, Scranton, 1973-86, Christ the King Parish, Dunmore, Pa., 1986-97, pastor emeritus, from 1997; prof. history St. Pius X Sem., Dalton, Pa., 1962-73; historian Diocese of Scranton, 1964-97. Professorial lectr. U. Scranton, 1967-73, lectr. history Marywood Coll., Scranton, 1968-70; bd. edn. Diocese of Scranton, 1976-79, pres., 1978-79; pres., exec. bd. Bishops Hannan and Klonowski H.S., 1973-83; pres., bd. pastors West Cath. H.S., Scranton, 1971-73, Bishop Hannan H.S., Scranton, 1975-77. Author: Scranton, Labor and Politics, 1961, Scranton, Industry and Politics, 1964, A Century of History: The Diocese of Scranton, 1968, Saint John Neponucene and the Diocese of Scranton, 1977, The Polish National Catholic Church: Its Roman Catholic Origins, 1990, A Second Century Begins: The Diocese of Scranton Begins, 1968-93; assoc. editor The Cath. Light, 1967-84; contbr. articles to profl. jours. Bd. dirs. Scranton Pub. Libr., 1976-84, pres. bd., 1982-84. Named Reverend Monsignor Pope Paul VI, 1976. Mem. Am. Hist. Assn., Am. Ch. History Assn., Am. Cath. Hist. Assn., Am. Cath. Hist. Soc. Phila. (contbr. Dimension: A Jour. of Pastoral Concern), Lackawanna Hist. Soc., St. Peter's Alumni Assn. of London (Can.). Home: Scranton, Pa. Died Dec. 9, 2007.

GALLOWAY, DON, actor; b. Brooksville, Ky., July 27, 1937; s. Paul Smith and Malee (Poe) G.; m. Linda Robinson, Sept. 27, 1963; children: Tracy Dale, Jennifer Malee. BA, U. Ky., 1961. Actor: (TV series) The Secret Storm, 1962-63, Ironside, 1967-75, Hizzonner, 1979, General Hospital, 1985-87; (TV appearances) The Alfred Hitchcock Hour, 1963, Arrest and Trial (3 episodes), 1963-64, Tom, Dick and Mary, 1964, Wagon Train, 1965, Convoy, 1965, 12 O'Clock High, 1966, Run for Your Life, 1966, The Virginian (2 episodes), 1963-66, The Bold Ones: The New Doctors, 1972, The ABC Afternoon Playbreak, 1972, Love, American Style (2 episodes), 1971-73, Get Christie Love!, 1975, Medical Story, 1975, Marcus Welby, M.D. (2 episodes), 1970-75, Medical Center, 1976, Gemini Man, 1976, The Life and Times of Grizzly Adams, 1977, Police Woman (2 episodes), 1975-78, Vega$, 1978, Charlie's Angels, 1978, Mork & Mindy, 1979, Hart to Hart, 1979, CHiPs (2 episodes), 1980, Fantasy Island (4 episodes), 1980-84, Automan, 1983, Knight Rider (2 episodes), 1983-85, Hotel, 1984, E/R, 1984, The Fall Guy, 1985, Scarecrow and Mrs. King, 1985, Crazy Like a Fox, 1985, Matlock, 1989, Hunter, 1989, Murder, She Wrote (2 episodes), 1989-91, MacGyver (2 episodes), 1989-91, Dallas (4 episodes), 1990, In the Heat of the Night, 1990; (films) The Rare Breed, 1966, Gunfight in Abilene, 1967, Ride to Hangman's Tree, 1967, Rough Night in Jericho, 1967, The Vendors, 1969, Satan's Mistress, 1982, The Big Chill, 1983, Two Moon Junction, 1988, Listen to Me, 1989, Original Intent, 1992, Clifford, 1994, The Doom Generation, 1995; (TV movies) The Priest Killer, 1971, Lieutenant Schuster's Wife, 1972, Portrait: A Man Whose Name Was John, 1973, You Lie So Deep, My Love, 1975, Riding with Death, 1976, Cover Girls, 1977, Ski Lift to Death, 1978, One Upon a Starry Night, 1978, Condominium, 1980, Rearview Mirror, 1984, Perry Mason: The Case of the Avenging Ace, 1988, Rock Hudson, 1990, Perry Mason: The Case of the Defiant Daughter, 1990, The Return of Ironside, 1993 Active March of Dimes, Spl. Olympics, Am. Heart Assn., Actors and Others for Animals. Served with U.S. Army, 1955-57. Home: Sherman Oaks, Calif. Died Jan. 8, 2009.

GALLOWAY, EILENE MARIE, space and astronautics consultant; b. Kansas City, Mo., May 4, 1906; d. Joseph Locke Slack and Lottie Rose (Harris) Slack; m. George Barnes Galloway, Dec. 23, 1924; children: David Barnes, Jonathan Fuller. Student, Washington U., St. Louis, 1923—25; AB, Swarthmore Coll., 1928, LLD (hon.), 1992; postgrad., Am. U., 1937—38, postgrad., 1943; LLD (hon.), Lake Forest Coll., 1990. Tchr. polit. sci. Swarthmore Coll., 1928-30; editor Student Svc., Washington, 1931; staff mem. edn. div. Fed. Emergency Relief Adminstrn., 1934-35; asst. chief info. sect. div. spl. info Library of Congress, 1941-43; editor abstracts Legis. Reference Svc., 1943-51, nat. def. analyst, 1951-57, specialist in nat. def., 1957-66; sr. specialist internat. rels. (nat. security) Congl. Rsch. Svc., 1966-75, cons. internat. space activities, 1975—2006; ret.; hon. dir. Internat. Inst. Space Law, from 2006. Staff mem. US Senate Fgn. Rels. Com., 1947; profl. staff mem. U.S. group Interparliamentary Union, 1958-66; cons. Senate Armed Svcs. Com., 1953-74, Ford Found., 1958; spl. cons. Spl. Senate Com. on Space and Astronautics, 1958; spl. cons. to Senate Com. on Aero. and Space Sci., 1958-77; cons. to Senate Com. on Commerce, Sci. and Transp., 1977-82; chmn. com. edn. and recreation Washington, 1937-38; forum leader, 1976-79; guest Soviet Acad. Sci., 1982, adult edn. U.S. Office Edn., 1938; mem. Internat. Inst. Space Law of Internat. Astronautical Fedn., 1958—, U.S. bd. dirs., v.p., 1967-79, hon. dir., 1979—, Fedn. ofcl. observer at sessions UN Com. on Peaceful Uses Outer Space and legal sub-com., 1970-94, com. for rels. with internat. orgns., 1979—; space law and sociology com. Am. Rocket Soc., 1959-62; adv. panel Office Gen. Counsel, NASA, 1971; adviser outer space del. U.S. Mission to UN Working Group on Direct Broadcast Satellites, 1973-75; observer UN Conf. Exploration and Peaceful Uses of Outer Space, Vienna, 1982; lectr. NAS, 1972, U.S. CSC, Exec. Seminar Ctr., Oak Ridge, 1973-78; ednl. counselor Purdue U., 1974; lectr. Inst. Air and Space Law McGill U., 1975, Inter Am. Def. Coll., 1977-78, U. Akron, 1984, 91; mem. panel on solar power for satellites and U.S. space policy Office Tech. Assessment, 1979-80, 82-86, cons., 1982; cons. COMSAT, 1983, FCC Commn. on U.S. Telecomm. Policy, 1983-87; spkr. internat. space law UN, N.Y.C., 1995; mem. NASA Nat. Adv. Com. on Internat. Space Sta., 1996-99, NASA Spaceflight Adv. com., 2000-03, UN seminar Space Futures and Human Security, Alpbach, Austria, 1997, chmn. Session in Internat. Astronautical Fed. Congress Concepts of Space Law, 1997; active European Space Agy. Internat. Lunar Workshop, 1994, 97; chair UN Workshop UNISPACE III Space Treaties: Strengths and Needs, Vienna, Austria, 1999; invited spkr. UN Com. Peaceful Uses of Outer Space and Internat. Astronautical Fedn., Paris, 2007. Author: Atomic Power: Issues Before Congress, 1946; author: (with Bernard Brodie) The Atomic Bomb and the Armed Services, 1947; author: History of United States Military Policy on Reserve Forces, 1775-1957, 1957, The Community of Law and Science, 1958, United Nations Ad hoc Committee on Peaceful Uses of Outer Space, 1959, Space Policy Guidelines, 2003, Space Law for the Moon-Mars Program, 2004; contbr. articles to profl. jours. Pres. Theodore Von Karman Meml. Found., 1973-84; mem. alumni council Swarthmore Coll., 1976-79; mem. organizing com., author symposium on Conditions Essential For Maintaining Outer Space for Peaceful Uses, Peace Palace, Netherlands, 1984; bd. advisers Student for Exploration and Devel. of Space, 1984-2009. Rockefeller Found. scholar-in-residence, Bellagio, Italy, 1976; elected to Coun. of Advanced Internat. Studies, Argentina, 1985, Uruguyan Centro de Investigacion y Difusion Aeronautica-Expacial, 1985; recipient Andrew G. Haley gold medal Internat. Inst. Space Law, 1968, Disting. Svc. award Libr. Congress, 1975, NASA Gold Medal for Pub. Svc., 1984, USAF Space Command plaque, 1984, Internat. Acad. Astronautics' Theodore Von. Karman award, 1986, Women in Aerospace Lifetime Achievment award Internat. Inst. Space Law, 1989, Leadership award NASA Johnson Space Ctr., 1997, NASA award for contbns. to internat. space sta., 1999, Cologne U. Inst. Air and Space Law and German Aerospace Ctr. award, 2003, Contbns. to Preserve Outer Space award UN Office Outer Space Affairs, NASA, Inst. Air and Space Law, Germany, Can. Space Agy., McGill U., 2006; Wilton Park fellow, Eng., 1968; Eilene M. Galloway award established by Internat. Inst. Space Law, 2000; honored Annals Vol. award Galloway NASA Adv. Com. on Internat. Space Sta., Internat. Inst. Space Laws, The Netherlands, 2006, UN Offices for Outer Space Affairs, NASA, Inst. Air and Space Law, U.S. Congress, Can. Space Agy., McGill U. Inst. Air and Space Law, 2006; dedication Informational Workshops on Policy and Law on Moon, Mars and Celestial Bodies, Montreal, 2006, Proceedings Internat. Space Law, Valencia, Spain, 2006; 3rd. Eilene M. Galloway Symposium on Space Law, Washington, 2008. Fellow: AIAA (hon.; tech. com. on legal aspects of aeros. and astronautics 1980—84, internat. activities com. from 1985, European space agy. internat. lunar workshop 1994, Pub. Policy award 2002, Pub. Svc. award and medal 2003), Internat. Acad. Astronautics (trustee emeritus, Social Scis. award 1999, Moot Ct. Best Brief award 2002), Am. Astronautical Soc. (John F. Kennedy Astronautics award 1999); mem.: Internat. Inst. Space Law, Nat. Aeronautic Assn. (Katharine Wright award 2003, 2003), Internat. Law Assn., LWV (chmn. study groups housing, welfare in DC 1937—38, mem. tech. com. on law and sociology task force on legal aspects from 1979), World Peace Through Law Ctr., Lamar Soc. Internat. Law, Am. Soc. Internat. Law, Kappa Alpha Theta, Phi Beta Kappa. Died May 2, 2009.

GANSZ, FRANK, college football coach; b. Altoona, Pa., Nov. 22, 1938; m. Barbara Gansz; children: Frank Jr., Jennifer. Grad., U.S. Naval Acad. Comd. 2d lt. USN, 1961, advanced through grades to capt., resigned, 1966; asst. football coach USAF Acad., Colorado Springs, Colo., 1964-66, Colgate U., Hamilton, N.Y., 1968, US Naval Acad., Annapolis, Md., 1969-72, Okla. State U., Stillwater, 1973, 75, US Mil. Acad., West Point, NY, 1974, UCLA, 1976-77, San Francisco 49ers, 1978, Cin. Bengals, 1979-80; asst. coach Kansas City Chiefs, 1981-82, 86, head football coach, 1987-88; asst. coach Phila. Eagles, 1983-85; spl. teams coach Detroit Lions, 1989—93, St. Louis Rams, 1997—2000, Jacksonville Jaguars, 2000—01, So. Methodist U., 2008—09; asst. head coach, spl. teams coach Atlanta Falcons, 1994—96. Died Apr. 27, 2009.

GANZARAIN, RAMON CAJIAO, psychoanalyst; b. Iquique, Chile, Apr. 18, 1923; s. Eusebio Ganzarain and Maria Cajiao; m. Matilde Vidal Soto, Oct. 10, 1953; children: Ramon, Mirentxu, Alejandro. BS, St. Ignacio Coll., Santiago, Chile, 1939; MD, U. Chile, Santiago, 1947; postgrad., Chilean Psychoanalytic Inst., 1947—50, cert. tng. analyst, 1953. Assoc. prof. psychiatry U. Chile, Santiago, 1955—68, dir. dept. med. edn., 1962—68; prof. depth psychology, sch. psychology Cath. U., Santiago, 1962—68; dir. Chilean Psychoanalytic Inst., Santiago, 1967—68; tng. analyst Topeka Inst. Psychoanalysis, 1968—87; dir. group psychotherapy svcs. Menninger Found., Topeka, 1978—87; geog. tng. analyst Columbia U. Ctr. for Psychoanalytic Tng. and Rsch., Atlanta, 1987; assoc. prof. psychiatry Emory U., Atlanta, from 1988; tng. analyst Emory U. Psychoanalytic Inst., from 1988; geog. tng. analyst Fla. Psychoanalytic Inst., from 2000. Interviewed by CNN on numerous topics concerning trauma and/or the Middle East conflict; lectr. on incest www.thecjc.org. Author: Fugitives of Incest, 1988, Object Relations Group Psychotherapy, 1989; contbr. articles to profl. jours., chapters to books. Fellow: Am. Group Psychotherapy Assn. (bd. dirs. 1984—87, 1993—96, disting. fellow from 2005); mem.: AMA, Topeka Psychoanalytic Soc. (pres. 1985—87), Atlanta Psychoanalytic Soc., Kans. Med. Soc., Am. Psychoanalytic Assn., Internat. Psychoanalytic Assn., Internat. Assn. Group Therapy (bd. dirs., exec. counselor 1986). Roman Catholic. Avocations: music, swimming, photography, writing, collecting antarctic stamps. Home: Decatur, Ga. Died Mar. 7, 2008.

GARCIA, ROSENDO LUIS, secondary school educator; b. Laredo, Tex., Aug. 12, 1961; s. Tomas and Julieta (Guerra) G. BA in Biology, U. Tex., 1984; MEdn in Counseling and Guidance, S.W. Tex. State U., 1992. Admin. counselor N.Mex. State U., Las Cruces, 1985; adminstrv. asst. U. Tex., Austin, 1986; sci. tchr. 5th, 6th, 7th grades United Day Sch., Laredo, Tex., 1987-88; tchr. mid.-sch. Laredo Ind. Sch. Dist., 1986-87, sci. tchr. H.S., from 1988. Active Mi Laredo, 1998, Border Olympics baseball, 1995; bd. dirs. Tex. Alliance Minorities in Engring., Austin, 1995—; co-chmn. Webb County Alliance Minorities in Engring., 1997—. Mem. Sci. Tchrs. Assn. Tex., Assn. Chemistry Tchr. Tex. (newsletter editor 1997—), Tex. Counseling Assn. Democrat. Roman Catholic. Avocations: reading, movies, bowling. Home: Laredo, Tex. Died July 23, 2008.

GARDINER, RITA M., medical, surgical nurse, administrator; b. Waltham, Mass., May 23, 1946; d. Charles F. and Cecilia T. (Castanino) Clifford; m. Robert P. Gardiner, Nov. 18, 1967; children: Charlotte M., Wayne R. Diploma, Mt. Auburn Hosp., Cambridge, Mass., 1967. RN, Mass. Staff nurse Mt. Auburn Hosp., Cambridge, Morton Hosp., Taunton, Mass.; substitute sch. nurse Town of Belmont (Mass.); nurse Waverley Family Practice, Belmont. Mem. Nat. Assn. Physicians Nurses, Am. Assn. Office Nurses. Home: Belmont, Mass. Died Nov. 2, 2007.

GARDNER, ALAN MARTIN, anesthesiologist; b. Battle Creek, Mich., Apr. 23, 1953; s. Walter Lawrence and Maxine Laverne (Willacker) G.; m. Susan Margead Horacz, Aug. 4, 1972 (div. 1976); children: Emily, Dominic; m. Gayle Alison Stanton, Feb. 28, 1986; children: Anthony, Alison. BS, Mich. State U., 1975; MD, U. Mich., 1980. MD, Mich., Calif., Ind. Staff physician Redicare Ctr., Fremont, Calif., 1984-85; anesthesiology resident Med. Coll. of Ohio, Toledo, 1985-87; emergency room physician Mercy-Meml. Hosp., Monroe, Mich.; clin. instr. U. Mich., 1987-91; asst. prof. U. Ky., from 1991. Family support services instr. cons., U.S. Navy Mountain View, Calif., 1982-84; red cross basic life support Mountain View Calif., 1983-84. With USN 1980-84, Calif., Japan. Recipient Nat. Merit Scholarship Nat. Merit Corp., 1971, Evans Scholarship 1972, Armed Forces Health Professions Scholarship U.S.Navy 1975. Mem. Am. Soc. Anesthesiologists, Assn. Mil. Surgeons of the U.S., Wash. County & Mich. State Med. Soc., Toledo & Ohio Med. Assn., Internat. Anesthesia Rsch. Soc.,

Aerospace Med. Assn., Phi Kappa Phi. Democratic. Roman Catholic. Avocations: golf, video, flying, stained glass work, swimming. Died Dec. 29, 2007.

GAREY, DONALD LEE, oil industry executive; b. Ft. Worth, Sept. 9, 1931; s. Leo James and Jessie (McNatt) G.; m. Elizabeth Patricia Martin, Aug. 1, 1953; children: Deborah Anne, Elizabeth Laird. BS in Geol. Engring., Tex. A&M U., College Station, 1953. Registered profl. engr., Tex. Sr. geologist Gulf Oil Corp., 1956-65; v.p., mng. dir. Indsl. Devel. Corp. Lea County, Hobbs, N.Mex., 1965-72, dir., 1972-86, pres., 1978-86; v.p., dir. Minerals, Inc., Hobbs, N.Mex., 1966-72, pres., dir., 1972-86, CEO, 1978-82; mng. dir. Hobbs Indsl. Found. Corp., 1965-72, dir., 1965-76; v.p. Llano, Inc., 1972-74, exec. v.p., COO, 1974-75, pres., 1975-86, CEO, also dir., 1978-82; pres., CEO Pollution Control, Inc., 1969-81. Pres. NMESCO Fuels, Inc., 1982-86; chmn., pres., CEO Estacado, Inc., 1986—, Natgas Inc., 1987—; pres. Llano Co2, Inc., 1984-86; cons. geologist, geol. engr., Hobbs, 1965-72. Chmn. Hobbs Manpower Devel. Tng. Adv. Com., 1965-72; mem. Hobbs Adv. Com. for Mental Health, 1965-67; chmn. N.Mex. Mapping Adv. Com., 1968-69; mem. Hobbs adv. bd. Salvation Army, 1967-78, chmn., 1970-72; mem. exec. bd. Conquistador coun. Boy Scouts Am., Hobbs, 1965-75; vice chmn. N.Mex. Gov's Com. for Econ. Devel., 1968-70; bd. regents Coll. Southwest, 1982-85. Capt. USAF, 1954-56. Mem. AIPG, AAPG, SPE of AIME. Home: Hobbs, N.Mex. Died Nov. 2008.

GARNER, ESTHER RUTH, state agency director; b. Rochester, NY, July 27, 1936; d. William G. and Minnie (Sorge) Jaster; m. Wilbur T. Garner, April 22, 1956; children: Marlene, Treva, Jody. BS in Pub. Adminstrn., City U., Bellevue, Wash., 1977, MPA, 1985. Office mgr. M&S Maintenance Co., Orange, Calif., 1960-65; ct. clk. Thurston County Superior Ct., Olympia, Wash., 1967-70; adminstrv. asst. State Adminstr. for Cts., Olympia, 1971-80; program auditor Dept. Social and Health Services, Olympia, 1980-81; exec. dir. State Jud. Qualifications Commn., Olympia, from 1981. Author: Agency Annual Report, 1981; contbr. articles to profl. jours. Fellow Ctr. for Jud. Conduct Orgns., Inst. Ct. Mgmt. (cert.); mem. Nib n' Ink Club. Seventh-day Adventist. Clubs: Altrusa (Olympia) (1st v.p. 1986—, pres. 1987-88). Avocations: music, sewing, calligraphy, travel, tennis. Home: Myrtle Creek, Oreg. Died Mar. 27, 2008.

GARNER, JEANETTE M., mental health nurse; b. Chgo., Mar. 7, 1943; d. Martin Cermacek and ARanka Krajcovic; m. James R. Garner, Dec. 26, 1964; 1 child, Kimberly A. BS in Psychology, St. Joseph's Coll., North Windham, Maine, 1982; MS in Counseling, Mercer U., Macon, Ga., 1986; RN, Gordon Keller Hosp., Tampa, Fla., 1963; BSN, Graceland Coll., 1995. ACLS provider, BLS instr. Head nurse Tampa (Fla.) Gen. Hosp., St. Elizabeth's Hosp., Washington; supr. Coll. St. Hosp., Macon, Ga.; staff nurse VA Med. Ctr., Salem, Va. Vol. Crisis Line, Citizen Advocate, EMT Rescue Squad; active Am. Cancer Soc. Mem. Va. Nurses Assn. Home: Roanoke, Va. Died July 5, 2008.

GARRISON, ANN MCBRAYER, retired gift and antique shop owner; b. Lawrenceburg, Ky., Aug. 19, 1925; d. Wesley and Emma Lee (Van Arsdell) McBrayer; m. Rumsey Elliott Garrison, Mar. 8, 1947 (div. Feb. 1964); 1 child, Elliott Wesley Student, U. Ky., 1943—45. Tchr. music, piano, voice, dance, Lawrenceburg, 1745—1975; continuity writer Sta. WVLK, Lexington, Ky., 1964—65; labor market analyst Ky. State Govt., Frankfort, 1965—82; antique dealer Annie's Gifts and Antiques, Lawrenceburg, from 1977. Author: Going Home, Come In, Mrs. Murphy, When Dandelions Were Mother's Roses, (cook book) A Taste of Mama's Cooking, (verse) Silhouettes Mem. Ky. Fedn. Music Clubs, 1945-75, Ky. Hist. Soc., Frankfort, 1965—, Harrison Fisher Soc., 1965—, Kate Greenway Soc., 1965— Mem. DAR, Tenure Club, Lawrenceburg Mchts'. Assn., Phi Beta, Kappa Delta, Anderson Humane Soc Democrat. Methodist. Home: Lawrenceburg, Ky. Died Oct. 17, 2007.

GARRISON, MAURICE ALLEN MARTIN, missionary, minister; b. Margie, Minn., Sept. 4, 1924; s. Edward Richard and Malvina Anna (Brown) G.; 1 foster child, Simeon Ben. BS(med.), U. Minn., 1946, BA cum laude, 1947; STB, Gen. Theol. Sem., NYC, 1952, STM, 1954; grad., Macalester Coll., St. Paul, 1943. Ordained priest, Episc. Ch., 1953. Lectr. St. Andrew's Sem., Manila, The Philippines, 1953-57; founder St. Mary's Sem., Odibo, Namibia, 1962-66; lectr. St. John's Sem., Lusaka, Zambia, 1967; prin. Codrington Coll., Barbados, 1969-70; lectr. Trinity Coll., Legon, Ghana, 1979-85, St. Paul's Theol. Coll., Limuru, Kenya, 1985-87, St. Mark's Theol. Coll., Dar es Salaam, Tanzania, 1987-89, 92-94; apptd. missionary Episc. Ch. U.S.A., 1953 57, 80 90, ret., 1990. Curate Trinity Ch., N.Y.C., 1957-61, 72-73; parish priest Resurrection Ch., N.Y.C., 1970-71, Church House, Khartoum, Sudan, 1981, St. Matthew Ch., Addis Ababa, Ethiopia, 1985; chaplain Bklyn. House of Detention, 1968-75; asst. priest Transfiguration Ch., N.Y.C., 1990, 99-2002, St. Mary the Virgin Ch., N.Y.C., 1998-2002. V.p. Am. Indian Cmty. House, N.Y.C., 1975; bd. edn. Sch. Dist. 9, N.Y.C., 1975; asst. priest St. Mary the Virgin, 1993-2001, Ch. of the Transfiguration, 1995—. With U.S. Army, 1943-46. Canonry award Diocese of Kumasi, 1979; named Sr. Episc. Missionary, World Mission Com. Episcopal Ch. Ctr., 1990. Home: Rye Brook, NY. Died Apr. 14, 2008.

GARVEY, EVELYN JEWEL, retired mental health nurse; b. Carrizozo, N.Mex., Aug. 23, 1931; d. Everett E. and Jewel A. (Bullard) Bragg; m. Robert J. Garvey, July 10, 1949; children: Nancy, Annie, Catherine, Robert, Michael, Betty. AD, Ea. N.Mex. Coll., 1972. RN, N.Mex.; cert. EMT., N.Mex. Staff nurse N.Mex. Rehab. Ctr., Roswell, 1972, Villa Solano State Sch., Roswell, 1972-79, DON, 1979-81; staff nurse Ft. Stanton (N.Mex.) Hosp., 1981-95, Sunset Villa Nursing Home, Roswell, N.Mex., 1995-96; ret., 1996; sch. nurse Roswell Pub. Schs., 1999-2000; ret. Home: Roswell, N.Mex. Died Oct. 23, 2007.

GASKIN, MARY, educational administrator; b. Mobile, Ala., June 16, 1925; d. Andrew and Hattie (Fornis) Burroughs; m. Leonard O. Gaskin, Dec. 10, 1951; children: Leonard Jr., Poppy. BA magna cum laude, Bklyn. Coll., 1971; MA, Columbia Ul, 1973; profl. diploma, St. John's U., Queens, NY, 1975. Tchr. blind N.Y.C. Pub. Schs., Bklyn., 1970-76, asst. dir., 1976-79, dir., from 1979. Cons. New Orleans Pub. Schs., 1987, Anti-Defamation League B'nai B'rith, N.Y.C., 1989, Ctr. for Vocat. Edn., Akron, Ohio, 1980; adj. prof. NYU, 1984—. Editor curriculum documents: Occupational Education, 1991. Columbia U. scholar, 1988. Mem. Am. Vocat. Assn., Adminstrv. Women in Edn. Avocations: tailoring, swimming, poetry writing. Home: Jamaica, NY. Died Dec. 1, 2007.

GASS, GERTRUDE ZEMON, psychologist, researcher; b. Detroit; d. David Solomon and Mary (Goldman) Zemon; m. H. Harvey Gass, June 19, 1938; children: Susan, Roger. BA, U. Mich., 1937, MSW, 1943, PhD, 1957. Lic. clin. psychologist Mich. Mem. faculty Merrill-Palmer Inst., Detroit, 1958-69, lectr., 1967; mem. faculty Advanced Behavioral Sci. Ctr., Grosse Pointe, Mich., 1969-72; pvt. practice clin. psychology Birmingham, Mich., from 1972. Adj. prof. psychology U. Detroit, 1969-75; cons. Continuum Ctr. Oakland U., Rochester, Mich., 1961-77, Traveler's Aid, Detroit, 1959-75; pres. Shapero Sch. Nursing, Detroit, 1967-72, cons. 1958-78; psychol. cons. Physician's Ins. Co. of Mich., 1988—, mgmt. Mich. Bell Telephone, 1979-82. Mem. Adv. Com Sch. Needs, 1954-56; trustee Sinai Hosp. Detroit, 1972-99; bd. dirs. Tribute Fund United Cmty. Svcs., 1955-67. Fellow Am. Assn. Marriage-Family, Am. Orthopsychiatric Assn. (v.p. 1975-76), Mich. Psychol. Assn.; mem. Am. Psychol. Assn., Psychologists Task Force (v.p. 1977-84), Mich. Inter-Profl. Assn. (pres. 1976-78), Mich. Assn. Marriage Counselors (1979-80, pres. 1979-80), Mental Health Adv. Svc., Blue Cross and Blue Shield of Mich., Phi Kappa Phi, Pi Lambda Theta. Died Aug. 1, 2008.

GASSTROM, EVALD HERMAN, social services agency administrator; b. Bronx, NY, Dec. 29, 1912; s. Matts. Herman and Helmi Johanna (Noppa) G.; m. Valma J. Nylund, Sept. 12, 1942; children: John, Lisa. AB, Columbia U., 1934, BS in Engring., 1935, MS in Indsl. Engring., 1936. Pres., owner Eagle Rule Mfg. Corp., 1947-70; dir. sales Durall-Eagle Tools, Yonkers, N.Y., 1970-75; exec. asst. to pres. Allway Tools, Inc., 1975-76; dir. mental retardation svcs. Massive Econ. Neighborhood Devel., 1976; co-bus. mgr. Westchester Assn. for Retarded Citizens, 1977-85; founder, prin. Gasstrom Mktg. Co. (now Gasstrom Mktg. and Packaging Co.), from 1986. Lt. USNR, 1943-46. Died June 26, 2008.

GATES, CLIFTON W., real estate company executive; b. Pine Bluff, Ark., Aug. 13, 1923; s. Lance and Mattie (Berry) G.; m. Harriet C. Craddock, June 14, 1947; children:Mark, Lisa. Pres. Gates Realty, St. Louis, from 1959; v.p. Mid Ctrl. Mortgage, St. Louis, 1969-74; pres. Gates Investments, St. Louis, from 1992. Chmn. Gateway Nat. Bank, St. Louis, 1966—; pres. Lismark Distbg. Co., St. Louis,1975-92. Commr., St. Louis Police Dept., 1967-74; dir. Boy Scouts Am., St. Louis, 1992—, dir. Airport Commn., St. Louis, 1992—, St. Louis Zoo Commn., 1992—, Mcpl. Opera,St. Louis, 1992—. Recipient Mgmt. award, City of Hope, St. Louis, Calif., 1972. Mem. Mo. Athletic Club, Stadium Club, Media Club, Clayton Club, Vagabond Club, Press Club. Democrat. Roman Catholic. Avocation: golf. Home: Saint Louis, Mo. Died Dec. 12, 2007.

GATES, MAHLON EUGENE, retired research and development company executive, military officer; b. Tyrone, Pa., Aug. 21, 1919; s. Samuel Clayton and Elsie (Nieweg) G.; m. Esther Boone Campbell, July 4, 1972; children by previous marriage: Pamela Townley, Lawrence Alan. BS, US Mil. Acad., 1942; MS, U. Ill., 1948; postgrad., Command and Gen. Staff Coll., 1957, Army War Coll., 1962, Harvard U., Cambridge, Mass., 1965. Commd. 2d lt. U.S. Army, 1942, advanced through grades to brig. gen., 1966; area engr. Iran, Gulf Dist., 1960-61; chief, engr. br., officer Personnel Directorate, Dept. Army, 1963-64; gen. staff Dept. Army, 1964 66; comdg. gen. Cam Ranh Bay, Vietnam, 1966-67; dir. constrn. Vietnam, 1967; dir. research, devel. and engring. Army Materiel Command, Washington, 1971; ret., 1972; mgr. Nev. ops. office AEC now Dept. Energy, Las Vegas, 1972-82; sr. v.p. S.W. Rsch. Inst., San Antonio, 1982-89, ret., 1989. Leader US sci. team to N.W. Territories during recovery ops. for crashed nuclear-powered Russian satellite, 1978. Past pres. Boulder Dam Area council Boy Scouts Am.; past chmn. adv. bd. Clark County C.C. Decorated D.S.M., Legion of Merit, Bronze Star, Air medal; Army Distinguished Service Order 1st class Govt. Vietnam; Meritorious Service award; named Meritorious Exec. ERDA. Home: San Antonio, Tex. Deceased.

GATES, VIOLA R., writer; b. St. Joseph, Mo., Oct. 13, 1931; d. Howard and Elsie (Lynch) Bennett; m. James E. Gates, May 7, 1949; children: Barbara Gates Bauguess, Nancy Gates Davis. Student, U. Denver, 1959—60; AA, U. Chgo., 1968; student, U. Colo., 1981—83. Tchr. piano pvt. practice, 1961—85, Brico Studios, Denver, 1970—82, Hamilton Mid. Sch., 1983—85, Englewood Christian, 1983—85. Author: Snow Storm, Journey to Center Place, 1996, Amanda's Gone; co-author: Winning Works, 1992. Ch. pianist, choral dir. Mem.: Denver Area Music Tchrs., Colo. State Music Tchrs. Assn., West Wind Writers, Nat. Writers Assn. (2d pl. award 1991), Brico Symphony Guild (sec.). Avocation: exploring ancient Pueblos. Home: Montrose, Colo. Died Oct. 21, 2007.

GATRIA, AMERICA I, retired writer; b. Havana, Cuba, Mar. 6, 1943; US, 1968; d. Jose F Gatria and Pilar T Varela. B, Havana's Inst., 1962. Clk. Citibank, NYC, 1969—70, asst. mgr., 1970—72, mgr., 1972—80, asst. v.p., 1980—90, v.p., 1990—95, sr. v.p., 1995—98; exec. dir. Dime Savings Bank, NYC, 1998—2002. Author: (book) Kristaluaght, 2004. Named Woman of the Yr., Hispanic Assn. Human Civil Rights, 1979, Hispanic Bus. Person of the Yr., State of NY, 1991. Republican. Avocations: writing, antiques, photography. Home: Canovanas, PR. Died Jan. 23, 2008.

GATTI, ARTURO, retired boxer; b. Calabria, Italy, Apr. 15, 1972; m. Amanda Rodrigues; 1 child. Profl. boxer, 1991—2007. Super featherweight champion US Boxing Assn., 1994, Internat. Boxing Fedn., 1995—98; light welterweight champion World Boxing Commn., 2004—05. Named Fight of Yr. & Knockout of Yr., A. Gatti vs. G. Ruelas, Ring Mag., 1997, Fight of Yr. & Upset of Yr., A. Gatti vs. I. Robinson, 1998, Comeback of Yr., 2002, Fight of Yr., A. Gatti vs. M. Ward, 2002, 2003. Achievements include professional boxing record of: 40 wins (31 by knockout) and 9 losses. Died July 11, 2009; Porto de Galinhas, Brazil.

GAVIN, MARY C., rehabilitation services professional; b. Chgo., Mar. 5, 1934; d. Percy A. and Eileen (Rooney) Reed; divorced; children: John, Michael, Loretta, Peter, Margaret Anne. BS in Occupational Therapy, Mount Mary Coll., 1955; MS in Counseling, U. Wis., 1981. Occupational therapist Sherwood Nursing Home, Williams Bay, Wis., 1974-76, Lakeland Counseling Ctr., Elkorn, Wis., 1977-82; instr. occupational therapy dept. Univ. Wis., Milw., 1981-82; instr. occupational therapist dept. Elizabethtown (Pa.) Coll., 1982-85; mgr. psychiat. rehab. Swedish Am. Hosp., Rockford, Ill., from 1985; counselor M.K.G. Counseling Svc., Fontana, Wis., to date. Interviewer League of Women Voters, Rockford, 1988. Mem. Am. Occupational Therapy Assn., Ill. Occupational Therapy Assn., Wis. Occupational Therapy Assn., Assn. Guidance and Counseling, Internat. Psycho Geriatric Assn., Am. Soc. on Aging. Died Apr. 8, 2008.

GAW, LLOYD EDWARD, SR., stockbroker; b. Gainesboro, Tenn., Mar. 23, 1930; s. Cleveland C. and Hallie Pearl (Wisdom) G.; m. Jeannette Cecile Arnold, June 10, 1958; children: Ed, Richard, Susan. BS, David Lipscomb U., 1951; MS, Peabody Coll., 1954. Tchr. Davidson City Bd. Edn., Nashville, 1960; stockbroker, ptnr. Tenn. Securities, Inc., Nashville, 1960-81; asst. mgr., assoc. v.p. Dean Witter Reynolds, Nashville, from 1981. Avocations: farming purebred duroc hogs, angus cattle. Home: Nashville, Tenn. Died Feb. 21, 2008.

GAYNOR, HAROLD M., dentist, educator; b. Phila., Apr. 25, 1930; s. David Jay and Ida (Kremens) G.; m. Sandra Lee Woodoff, June 25, 1955; 1 child, Eric Reid. BSc in Pharmacy cum laude, Phila. Coll. Pharmacy & Scis., 1953; DDS, DMD, Temple U., 1957; postgrad., Yale Sch. Pub. Health, 1973-75. Registered pharmacist. Dir. Univ. Conn. Sch. Dental Medicine, Farmington, 1975-76, asst. dean, 1976-77, assoc. dean, 1977-82, univ. dir., 1982-83; pvt. practice dentistry Branford, Conn., from 1983. Cons. Bowman Gray Med. Sch., Winston-Salem, N.C., 1982—, ADA Coun. on Dental Therapeutics, Chgo, 1983—. Contbr. chpt. to Accepted Dental Therapeutics, 1991. Dir. Bd. Health Branford, 1974-76; bd. dirs. East Shore Health Dist., Branford, 1974-76. Capt. U.S. Army Dental Corps., 1957-59. Recipient fellowship Am. Coll. of Dentists, 1979, Internat. Coll. of Dentistry, 1986. Fellow Am. Coll. Dentistry, Acad. Gen. Dentistry (mastership 1982, Dentist of Yr. 1980); mem. Conn. State Dental Assn. (sec., treas. 1992-98, pres.-elect 1999—), Pierre Fauchard Acad., New Eng. Dental Soc., Cosmopolitan Club (marshall 1960-61). Died Feb. 27, 2008.

GEARIN, LOUVAN ANITA, retired school librarian; b. St. Louis, July 5, 1917; d. William Sherman and Ira Mae (Haskell) Brabham. BA, Fisk U., 1937; BSLS, Atlanta U., 1949; MSLS, U. Mich., 1955. Cert. tchr., Mo. Libr. Lincoln Inst., Ky., 1950-53; reference libr. Tuskegee (Ala.) Inst., summers 1951-54; jr. high and sr. high libr. Webster Groves (Mo.) Schs., 1954-82; ret., 1982. Cons. selection of titles M. W. Wilson Libr. Catalog, N.Y.C., 1974-82; cons. book bait, reference and subscription books, rev. com. for young adults ALA, Chgo., 1980-82. Vol. Eldercare Ctr., U. Mo., St. Louis, 1985—, County Older Resident Program, St. Louis County, 1987—, Meals on Wheels, Creve Couer, Mo., 1982—. Recipient award Mo. Assn. Sch. Librs., 1984, Vol. award U. Mo., St. Louis, 1985. Mem. AAUW (sec. 1970-82). Avocations: reading, music, discussion, exercise, dance. Home: Saint Louis, Mo. Died Jan. 25, 2008.

GEDDES, LESLIE ALEXANDER, forensic engineer, educator, physiologist; b. Scotland, May 24, 1921; s. Alexander and Helen (Humphrey) G.; m. Irene P. Bloomer; 1 child, James Alexander; m. La Nelle E. Nerger, Aug. 3, 1962. BEE, MEngring., ScD (hon.), McGill U.; PhD in Physiology, Baylor U. Med. Coll. Demonstrator in elec. engring. McGill U., 1945, research asst. dept. neurology, 1945-52; cons. elec. engring. to various indsl. firms Que., Can.; biophysicist dept. physiology Baylor Med. Coll., Houston, asst. prof. physiology, 1956-61, assoc. prof., 1961-65, prof., 1965-74; dir. Lab. of Biophysics, Tex. Inst. Rehab. and Research, Houston, 1961-65; prof. physiology Coll. Vet. Medicine, Tex. A. and M. U., College Station, 1965-74, prof. biomed. engring., 1969-74; Showalter Disting. prof. bioengring. and elec. engring. Purdue U., West Lafayette, Ind., 1974-91, Showalter Disting. prof. emeritus, 1991—2009. Cons. NASA Manned Spacecraft Center, Houston, 1962-64, USAF, Sch. Aerospace Medicine, Brooks AFB, 1958-65; expert witness, 1981-2009. Author: 22 books; cons. editor: Med. and Biol. Engring., 1969-2009, Med. Research Engring., 1964-74, Med. Electronics and Data, 1969-2009, Jour. Cardiovasc. Engring., 2004-09; mem. editl. bd. Jour. Electrocardiology, 1968-2009, med. instr., 1974-2009; contbr. over 800 articles to bioengring. Mem. Soc. Free Space Floaters, 1961. With Can. Army OTC. Recipient Ctrl. Ind. Corp. award for Commercialization, 2003—04, Corp. Vitae award, Am. Heart Assn., 2005; named 2006 Nat. Medal Tech. Laureate. Fellow: IEEE (Lee De Forest award 2001, Leadership award, Edison gold medal, IEEE 3d Millennium award, World of Difference award), AAAS (Am. Heart Vital award 2005, Nat. Tech. medal 2006), Biomed. Engring. Soc., Royal Soc. Medicine, Australasian Coll. Physicists in Biology and Medicine, Am. Inst. Med. and Biol. Engring., Am. Coll. Cardiology, Nat. Acad. Forensic Engrs.; mem.: NAE, NSPE, Am. Physiol. Soc., Assn. Advancement Med. Instrumentation (Health Care Hero award 2007, Leadership award), Tex. Soc. Profl. Engrs., Radio Club Am., Phi Zeta, Tau Beta Pi, Sigma Xi. Achievements include holder 33 US patents. Home: West Lafayette, Ind. Died Oct. 25, 2009.

GEESLIN, GENE SMITH, artist, filmmaker; b. Bay City, Tex., Apr. 11, 1927; d. Weldon Bailey and Elizabeth (Kilbride) Smith; m. Lee Gaddis Geeslin, Aug. 17, 1947; 1 child, Anne Elizabeth Lee Student, Sophie Newcomb Coll., Tulane U., 1945, Southwestern U., 1946—48; BA Art, Sam Houston State U., 1960. Asst. prof. art Field Sch. Sam Houston U., Puebla, Mexico, 1950; illustrator Ednl. Filmstrips, Huntsville, Tex., 1953—56; owner, pub. Visual Aids Studio, Huntsville, 1956—81; exhibiting artist various locations, from 1948. Editor, pub. Paint Rag Mag., Huntsville, 1952-53 One-person shows include Hayden Calhoun Gallery, Dallas, 1961, Helen Coffee Gallery, Houston, 1962, Prudhomme Gallery, Texarkana, Tex., 1964, Sam Houston State U. Gallery, 1985, Happening, "The Rise of the Great Pumpkin", 1976, Village Art Gallery, Houston, 1988; exhibited in group shows at Tex. Fine Arts Assn., Austin, 1956, Studio Seven, Huntsville, 1955, Tex. Watercolor Soc., San Antonio, 1963, Hayden Calhoun Galleries, Dallas, 1959-64, Prudhomme Gallery, Tex., Ark., La., Calif., 1964; film maker 42 films including the Louvre, Beaubourg, The Jeu de Paume, 1956-81 Bd. dirs., Tex. Fine Arts Assn., 1948; organizer, Walker County Art Assn Mem. Delta Delta Delta Home: Houston, Tex. Died 2008; unknown.

GEFSKY, HAROLD LEON, cultural organization executive; b. Youngstown, Ohio, Sept. 16, 1917; s. David M. and Jennie (Goldstein) G. BSEd., Miami U., Oxford, Ohio, 1940; postgrad., Youngstown Coll., 1944, UCLA. Agt. Helen Singworth, Beverly Hills, Calif., 1947-48, Maureen Oliver Agy., LA, 1946-47, Mitchell Gertz Agy., Beverly Hills, 1948-50; pres. Harold L. Gefsky Agy., LA, 1950-62; v.p. Agy. for Performing Arts, L.A. and NYC, from 1962. Maj. U.S. Army, World War II, ETO. Mem. Actors Guild, Amvets, Am. Legion, Jewish War Vets., DAV. Democrat. Home: West Hollywood, Calif. Died June 25, 2008.

GEHRING, GEORGE JOSEPH, JR., dentist; b. Kenosha, Wis., May 24, 1931; s. George J. and Lucille (Martin) G.; m. Ann D. Carrigan, Aug. 2, 1982; children: Michael, Scott. DDS, Marquette U., 1955. Pvt. practice dentistry, Long Beach, Calif., from 1958. Author: The Happy Flosser. Chmn. bd. Long Beach affiliate Calif. Heart Assn.; mem. Long Beach Grand Prix com. of 300; ind. candidate for pres. of the U.S., 1988, 92, 2000. Served with USNR, 1955-58. Fellow Internat. Coll. of Dentists, Am. Coll. Dentists; mem. Harbor Dental Soc. (dir.), Pierre Fauchard Acad., Delta Sigma Delta, Rotary (Long Beach pres. 1981-82). Home: Long Beach, Calif. Deceased.

GEHRING, RICHARD WEBSTER, structural engineer; b. Rockford, Ill., Mar. 16, 1927; s. John Gottlieb and Lucia Mae (Webster) G.; m. Ellen Elizabeth Hansen, Sept. 4, 1948; children: Katherine Louise, John Webster, Richard Mentor. BS in Aerospace Engr., Tri-State Coll., 1949; postgrad., Pa. State U., 1965-66. Structural test engr. Glenn L. Martin Co., Balt., 1950-52; structures engr. N.Am. Aviation Inc., Columbus, Ohio, 1952-68; sr. engr. specialist Rockwell Internat., Columbus, 1968-89; cons. Snow Aviation Internat., Columbus, from 1990, Paragon Aviation, from 1995. Mem. MIL-HOBK-5 com. Rep. from N.Am. Aviation, Columbus, 1964-68; reviewer USAF Design Guide for Advanced Composites, USAF/Rockwell Internat., Dayton and Columbus, 1971; guest lectr. airframe design Ohio State U., Columbus, 1982, 84. With USCG, 1944-46. Recipient Letter of Appreciation, U.S. Naval Air Engring. Ctr., Phila., 1967. Mem. AIAA (vice-chmn. local chpt. 1954), U.S. Naval Inst., Lions Internat. (dir. local chpt. 1970-72). Republican. Lutheran. Achievements include development of structural analysis method for inelastic structural joints with temperature and mixed materials, methods for defining elevated temperature strength of airframes using room temperature tests. Home: Columbus, Ohio. Died Dec. 3, 2007.

GEIMER, ROGER ANTHONY, English language educator; b. Evanston, Ill., Oct. 6, 1932; s. Nicholas Charles and Violet Hazel (Rundgren) G.; children: Joan C., Carol T., Gregory A., James A., Georgiana M. BA, St. Mary's Coll., Winona, Minn., 1954; MA, Marquette U., Milw., 1956; PhD, Northwestern U., Evanston, Ill., 1965. Instr. St. Mary's Coll., Winona, 1958-59, Wis. State U., Superior, 1959-60; instr., asst. prof. Loyola U., Chgo., 1962-66; asst. prof., assoc. prof. English Purdue U., Hammond, Ind., from 1966. Contbg. author: Magill's Literary Annual, 1977-85, Magil's Survey of Cinema, 1980, Great Events From History, 1980, English Literature: Shakespeare, 1980, Shakespeare and the Triple Play, 1988. With U.S. Army, 1956-58. Mem. Nat. Coun. Tchrs. English, Coll. English Assn., Midwest Modern Lang. Assn., English Renaissance Text Soc. Roman Catholic. Home: Venice, Fla. Died June 15, 2008.

GEIST, ERNEST EDWARD, minister; b. Zanesville, Ohio, Dec. 8, 1938; s. Ernest Walter and Erma Carmen (Shrake) G.; m. Ruth Elaine Keppel, July 2, 1960 (div. Feb. 1980); m. Nancy Sue Simpson, Mar. 27, 1981; children: Ernest Edwin, Douglas Alan, Daniel Jay. B Bible Philosophy, Am. Bible Inst., 1967, M Bible Philosophy, 1969, DD, 1972; BBA, Stanton U., 1969. Ordained to ministry Meth. Ch., 1965. Assoc. pastor Christ Meth. Ch., Tampa, Fla., 1963-64; pastor Hernando (Fla.) Meth. Ch., 1964-65, Hartford (Ohio) Community Ch., 1966-70, Olive Chapel United Ch. Christ, New Carlisle, Ind., 1970-71; sr. pastor Community Christian Ch, New Carlisle, 1970-75; pastor Sherman (N.Y.) Community Ch., 1975-90; sr. pastor Evendale Community Ch., Cin., from 1990. Chaplain Ind. Guard Res., 1970, N.Y. Guard Res., 1970-90; pres. United Religious Community, South Bend, Ind., 1972-74. Juvenile officer New Carlisle Police Dept., 1972, chief of police, 1974; mem. adv. bd. St. Joseph County Planned Parenthood, South Bend, 1975. Capt. USNG, 1970—. Recipient Oustanding Clergy award Hill and Dale Men's Club, New Carlisle, 1987. Mem. Acad. Parish Clergy, Police Clergy Team, Sycamore Clergy Assn., Am. Legion (Chaplains award 1975), Hamilton County Police Assn. Died Nov. 22, 2007.

GELBART, LARRY, scriptwriter, television and theater producer; b. Chgo., Feb. 25, 1928; s. Harry and Frieda (Sturner) G.; m. Pat Marshall, Nov. 25, 1956; children: Gary, Paul, Adam, Becky. LittD (hon.), Union Coll., Schnectady, NY, 1986; LHD (hon.), Hofstra U., 1999. Writer: (radio series) The Eddie Cantor Show, 1946, Maxwell House Coffee Time with Danny Thomas, 1946, Duffy's Tavern, 1946, Command Performance, 1946-47, Jack Carson, 1947-48, The Jack Paar Show, 1949, The Joan Davis Show, 1949, The Bob Hope Show, 1949-52; (ballet) Peter and the Wolf, 1992; (plays) My L.A., 1950, The Conquering Hero, 1960, A Funny Thing Happened on the Way to the Forum, 1962 (Tony award with Burt Shevelove best musical play 1963), Sly Fox, 1976, One, Two, Three, Four, Five, 1988, City of Angels, 1989 (Drama Desk award best book of musical 1989, Tony award best musical, best book of musical 1990, Best New Musical citation NY Drama Critics Circle 1990, Outer Critics Circle award outstanding Broadway musical, contbn. to comedy award 1990, Edgar Allan Poe award best mystery play 1990), Mastergate, 1989 (Outer Critics Circle award contbn. to comedy 1990), (co-author) Jerome Robbins' Broadway, 1989; (films) The Notorious Landlady, 1962, The Thrill of It All, 1963, (also co-producer) The Wrong Box, 1966, Not With My Wife You Don't, 1966, The Chastity Belt, 1968, A Fine Pair, 1969, Oh, God, 1977 (Acad. award nomination best screenplay material from another medium 1977, Edgar Allan Poe award, Mystery Writers Am. award, Writers Guild award), Movie, Movie, 1978 (Writers Guild award, Christopher award), Neighbors, 1981, Tootsie, 1982 (Acad. Award nomination best screenplay written directly for screen 1982, LA Film Critics award, NY Film Critics award, Nat. Soc. Film Critics award), (also exec. producer) Blame It on Rio, 1984, Bedazzled, 2000; writer, prodr., co-prodr.: (TV series) M*A*S*H, 1972-76 (Emmy award nomination outstanding writing comedy 1972, 75, Writers Guild Am. award 1972, 74, Emmy award outstanding comedy series 1973, Emmy award nominations outstanding comedy series 1974, 75, George Foster Peabody award 1975, Humanitas award), Roll Out!, 1973-74, Karen, 1975, United States, 1980, After M*A*S*H, 1983-84 (Emmy award nomination outstanding directing comedy series 1983); TV adaptation Mastergate, 1992; writer, exec. prodr.: (TV films) Barbarians at the Gate, 1993 (Outstanding Made-for-TV-Movie Emmy award, Best Made-for-TV-Motion Picture award The Am. TV Awards, Program of Yr., The TV Critics Assn., Cable Ace award, Writing in a Movie or Miniseries), Weapons of Mass Distraction, 1997; Best Teleplay awd., PEN Ctr. USA West, writer TV shows The All-Star Revue, 1950-53, The Red Buttons Show, 1952-55, Honestly, Celeste!, 1954, The Patrice Munsel Show, 1954-62, Caesar's Hour, 1955-57 (Emmy award nominations best comedy writing 1955, 56, 57), The Pat Boone Chevy Showroom, 1957-60, The Danny Kaye Show, 1963 (Emmy award nomination outstanding writing comedy or variety show 1963), The Marty Feldman Comedy Machine, 1972, (TV movie) And Starring Pancho Villa as Himself, 2003, Like Jazz, A New Kind of Musical, 2003; author: Laughing Matters, 1998. Served with AUS, 1945-46. Recipient Lee Strasberg Lifetime Achievement in Arts and Sci. award, 1990, William S. Paley award for excellence in TV, Anti-Defamation League, 2001, citation for disting. svc., AMA, 2001, Valentine Davies award, Writers Guild Am., West, 2007. Mem. Dramatists Guild, Writers Guild America (award 1972, 74), ASCAP, Dir. Guild America Died Sept. 11, 2009.

GELFAND, ISRAIL MOISEEVICH (IZRAIL), mathematician, biologist; b. Krasnye Okny, Odessa, Ukraine, Sept. 2, 1913; arrived in US, 1990; s. Moshe and Perl G.; m. Tanya Alexeevskaya, 1979; children: Sergey, Vladimir, Tanya. DSc, Moscow State U., 1935; degree (hon.)., U. Oxford, Eng., 1973, Harvard U., 1976, U. Paris VI-VII, 1974, U. Uppsala, 1977, Scuola Norm. Sup., Pisa, 1985, Kyoto U., 1989, NYU, 1992, U. Pa., 1990. Tchr. USSR Acad. Sci., 1935—41; prof. Moscow State U., 1941, Harvard., 1989—90, MIT, 1990; prof. math. Rutgers U., New Brunswick, NJ, 1990—2009. Co-founder Inst. Biol. Physics, USSR Acad. Sci., 1960. Contbr. more than 600 books and papers in math., biology, and math. edn. MacArthur fellowship John T. and Catherine D. MacArthur Found., 1994; recipient Wolf prize in math. Wolf Found., Israel, 1978, Wigner medal, 1979, Kyoto prize Inamory Found., 1989. Mem. NAS (life), Am. Acad. Arts and Sci., Royal Soc. Sweden, Royal Soc. (Eng.), Japan Acad. Sci., Acad. Sci. (Paris), Royal Irish Acad., Accademia dei Lincei, Am. Math. Soc.(Lifetime Achievement award, 2005), London Math. Soc., Moscow Math. Soc. (pres. 1968-70). Achievements include development of theory of commutative normed rings; research in fields of biology and medicine, including development of general principles of organization of control in complex systems; research in C*-algebras, representations theory, integral geometry, inverse problems, nonlinear differential equations, modern theory of hypergeometric functions, and noncommutative algebra. Died Oct. 5, 2009.

GELLERSTEDT, LAWRENCE L., JR., construction executive; Pres. Beers Inc., Atlanta, 1960, owner, 1969, chmn. bd. dirs. Bd. dirs. Cousins Properties Inc., from 2009. Bd. dirs. Ga. Tech. Found., pres., 1973—75. Recipient Ga. Tech. Exceptional Achievement award. Mem.: Ga. Tech. Alumni Assn. (pres. 1968—69, Disting. Svc. medal 1981). Died Apr. 12, 2003.

GELSTHORPE, EDWARD, retired marketing executive; b. Phila., June 14, 1921; m. Mary Ann McLaughlin, Feb. 1943; children: Cynthia, Seth, Ted, Tom. Student, Hamilton Coll., 1942. With Gelsthrope assocs., 1945-48; v.p., dir. mktg. Bristol Myers, 1948-60; v.p. Colgate Palmolive Co., 1960-62; pres., CEO Ocean Spray Cranberries, 1962-68; pres. Hunt Wesson Foods, 1968-72, Gillett Co., 1972-74; exec. v.p. United Brands Co., 1975-77; pres., CEO H.P. Hood Inc., 1975—86. Served in USN. Died Sept. 12, 2009.

GENDRON, MARY W., retired educator; b. Columbia, Miss., Oct. 9, 1926; d. Henry W. and Mary Elizabeth (Pace) Williamson; m. Robert Louis Gendron, Aug. 18, 1960; children: Gina, Robert John. BA, Southeastern U., Hammond, Ind., 1950; M of Edn., La. State U., 1953; postgrad., U. Fla., 1957—61. Tchr. Calcasieu Parish, Lake Charles, La., East Baton Rouge Parish, Baton Rouge; assoc. prof. U. Fla., Gainesville; tchr. Brevard County, Melbourne, Palm Bay. Sec./treas. Palm Bay H.S. Music Dept. Contbr. poetry to anthologies. Sec. La. Dept. Classroom Tchrs., treas.; deacon Meth. Ch., Palm Bay. Mem.: AAUW, NEA (life; regional dir., bd. regents Rep. La. 6th Congl. Dist.), Nat. Women's History Mus. (charter mem.), Fla. Edn. Assn. (life). Avocations: reading, swimming. Died Jan. 5, 2008.

GENDUSA, CHARLES JOSEPH, accounting educator; b. New Orleans, July 11, 1934; s. Anthony Joseph and Lena (Russo) G.; m. Marilyn Misuraca, Feb. 5, 1956 (dec.); 1 child, MarilynEve; m. Deborah Marie Boasso, Apr. 19, 1971; children: Christy Marie, Michele Marie. BBA, Tulane U., 1956, MBA, 1960; postgrad., La. State U., 1967-68. CPA, La. Staff accountant J. Earl Pedelahore & Co. CPAs, New Orleans, 1956-59; asst. prof. Loyola U., New Orleans, 1960-68; assoc. prof. Delgado C.C., New Orleans, 1968-89; prof. C.C. of So. Nev., Las Vegas, from 1989. Cons. C.J. Gendusa CPA, New Orleans, 1960-86. Adv. bd. Carrollton Sr. Citizens Ctr., New Orleans, 1972-89. Capt. USAR, 1956-64. Mem. AAUP, Am. Fedn. Tchrs., Nev. Faculty Alliance, La. Retired Tchrs. Assn., La. Soc. CPAs. Roman Catholic. Home: Arabi, La. Died Oct. 10, 2007.

GENENSKY, SAMUEL MILTON, retired visual rehabilitation center administrator; b. New Bedford, Mass., July 26, 1927; s. Maurice and Jessie Marion (Kaufman) G.; m. Marion Malis, Nov. 26, 1953 (dec. Apr. 1989); children: Marsha Lynn, Judy Mara. BS in Physics magna cum laude, Brown U., 1949, PhD in Applied Math., 1958; MA in Math., Harvard U., 1951; LHD (hon.), Ill. Coll. Optometry, 1979. Mathematician Nat. Bur. Standards, Washington, 1951-54; sr. mathematician Rand Corp., Santa Monica, Calif., 1958-76; exec. dir. Ctr. for Partially Sighted, Santa Monica, 1976-91, chmn. exec. com. bd. dirs., 1991—2009. Mem. adv. com. on services to blind and partially sighted Calif. Dept. Rehab., 1972-81, mem. study group on services to blind and partially sighted, 1981; mem. adv. com. low vision services Am. Found. for Blind, 1975-77, 80-81; cons. Rand Corp.; mem. nat. implementation adv. com. White House Conf. on Handicapped Individuals, 1979; mem. ad hoc com. on standards for low vision clinics Nat. Accreditation Council, 1980; mem. long term care planning group

Calif. Health and Welfare Agy., 1981; lectr. dept. ophthalmology Sch. Medicine, UCLA, Coll. Optometry U. So. Calif.; mem. NRC Commn. Aging Workers and Visual Impairment, 1985-86; task force Low Vision Am. Found. Blind. Contbr. articles on visual research and rehab. to profl. jours; patentee underground boring equipment. Bd. dirs., past pres. Council Citizens with low vision; trustee So. Calif. Coll. Optometry, Fullerton, 1972-86; founder The Ctr. for the Partially Sighted. Recipient Meritorious Service award South Bay Mayor's Com. on Employment for Handicapped, 1972, Paul Yarwood award Calif. Optometric Assn., 1972, Disting. Services award NCCJ, 1979, Mainstream Milestones award Los Angeles Jaycees, 1980, Pub. Affairs award Coro Found., 1986, Low Vision Disting. Achievement award Am. Optometric Assn., 1985, Access award Am. Found. for Blind, 1991; named to Gov.'s Hall of Fame for People with Disabilities, Calif., 1988; fellow Brown U., 1954-55; Francis Wayland scholar Brown U., 1946. Fellow Am. Acad. Optometry (Carel C. Koch Meml. award 1988); mem. AAAS, Am. Math. Soc., Sigma Xi. Achievements include design and development of a closed circuit TV systems for use by the partially sighted; design of more efficient signage system for use by the partially sighted and functionally blind. Home: Santa Monica, Calif. Died June 26, 2009.

GERLOVICH, KAREN J., historian, musicologist; b. Duluth, Minn., Apr. 28, 1944; m. Edward Gerlovich, Apr. 27, 1974. Grad. high sch., Duluth. Freelance accordian historian. Composer polkas; author: Happy Gals USA & Their Wonderful Music USA. Home: Las Vegas, Nev. Died Oct. 30, 2007.

GERSHENFELD, MATTI KIBRICK, psychologist; b. Phila. d. Hyman and Esther Kibrick; m. Marvin A. Gershenfeld, 1946 (dec. 1989); children: Robert, Howard, Richard, Kenneth. BA, U. Pa., 1947, M in Govt. Adminstrn., 1951; EdD, Temple U., 1967. Lic. psychologist, Pa.; cert. marriage and family therapist. Pres. MKG Associates, Elkins Park, Pa., 1975—2008, Couples Learning Ctr., Jenkintown, Pa., 1975—2008. Mem. organizing com., co-chair 1st Internat. Interdisciplinary Conf. on Women, Haifa, Israel, 1982. Author: Groups: Theory and Experience, 1973, 7th edit., 2004, Making Groups Work, 1983, How to Find Love, Sex and Intimacy after 50: A Woman's Guide, 1991; contbr. chpts. to Contemporary Marriage, 1986, Adult Development, 1984, conservation of Marriage and the Family Studies, 1986. Chair bd. dirs. Gratz Coll., Elkins Park, 2001-04; pres. Hillel Greater Phila., 1996-99; mem. pres.' coun. Gwynedd (Pa.) Mercy Coll., 1981-84; past pres. Am. Diabetes Assn., Phila., 1987-90, affiliate, past pres. Pa. affiliate, 1990-93. Fellow APA, Am. Assn. Marriage and Family Therapists; mem. Nat. Coun. on Family Rels., Pa. Coun. Family Rels. (past pres.), Assn. State Couns. Nat. Coun. Family Rels. (past pres.), Internat. Coun. Psychologists (past pres., sec.-gen.). Jewish. Avocations: travel, theater. Home: Philadelphia, Pa. Died Nov. 11, 2008.

GERSON, RICHARD F., management and marketing consultant; b. Bklyn., Dec. 27, 1951; s. Mark S. Gerson and Faith (Schuster) Laudia; m. Robbie G. Goodson, Dec. 20, 1981; children: Michael, Mitchell. BS, Bklyn. Coll., 1972; MS, Brockport State Coll., 1974; PhD, Fla. State U., 1978. Cert. Mgmt. Cons. Pres. Gerson Goodson Inc., Safety Harbor, Fla., from 1979. Author: The Right Vitamins, 1984, Vitamins and Minerals for a Healthy Pregnancy, 1987, Marketing Health Fitness Services Workbook, 1987, Marketing Health/Fitness Services, 1989, Physician, Market Thyself, 1990, Writing and Implementing a Marketing Plan, 1991, Beyond Customer Service, 1992, The Fitness Director's Guide to Marketing Strategies and Tactics, 1992, Measuring Customer Satisfaction, 1993, Marketing Strategies for Small Businesses, 1994; contbr. over 250 articles to profl. jours. Mem. ASTD (sr. advisor 1992-94), Am. Mktg. Assn. Avocations: exercise, reading, meditation, mentoring. Died June 9, 2008.

GETKER, SUSAN J., gerontology nurse, administrator; b. Astoria, NY, June 16, 1947; d. Carl Wilhelm and Elizabeth Mary (Conibear) Nystrom; m. John P. Getker, Nov. 15, 1969; children: Marie-Chantal, Karl. AAS, Delaware County Community Coll, Media, Pa., 1975; BSN, Felician Coll., Lodi, NJ, 1988; MSN, Sacred Heart U., Fairfield, Conn., 1992. Head rehab. nurse, Rehab. Unit Bridgeport (Conn.) Hosp.; asst. dir. nursing Mediplex of Westport (Conn.). Mem. ANA, Assn. Rehab. Nurses, Tres Dignitas Honor Soc., Sigma Theta Tau. Home: Homosassa, Fla. Died Apr. 11, 2008.

GHENT, KENNETH SMITH, retired mathematician; b. Hamilton, Ontario, Can., June 29, 1911; came to U.S., 1932; s. Harry James and Ruby (Smith) G.; m. Helen Marjorie Tillman, Nov. 1, 1942; children: Robert Charles, Dorothy Claire Turchi, Margaret Morgan. BA, McMaster U., 1932; SM, U. Chgo., 1933, PhD, 1935. From instr. to prof. U. Oreg., Eugene, 1935-76; retired, 1976. Fulbright lectr. U. Dacca, Bangladesh, 1962-63, U. Western Australia, Perth, (summer) 1974. Home: Eugene, Oreg. Died Jan. 12, 2008.

GHOLSON, HUNTER MAURICE, lawyer; b. Columbus, Miss., Feb. 19, 1933; s. Leonidas Carter and Hunter Marie (McDonell) G.; m. Hortense Jones, June 3, 1961; children: Roberts, William Webster. BA, U. Miss., 1954, LLB, JD, U. Miss., 1955. Bar: Miss. 1955, U.S. Ct. Appeals (5th and 11th cirs.) 1955, D.C. 1975, U.S. Supreme Ct. 1975. Ptnr. Gholson, Hicks & Nichols, Columbus, Miss., 1959—2007; lawyer pvt. practice. Sec., dir. Columbus Marble Works, Inc., 1970—, Cadence Fin. Corp., Starkville, Miss., 1984—; dir. Gulf States Mfr., Starkville, 1968-94. Sr. warden St. Paul's Ch., Columbus, 1990-93. Lt. USNR, 1955-59. Episcopalian. Home: Columbus, Miss. Died Aug. 12, 2008.

GIBBON, EDMUND MULFORD, chemical company executive; b. NYC, Oct. 11, 1929; s. Charles O. and Helene F. (Fry) G.; m. Valerie A. Dessert, Apr. 7, 1957 (div. Nov. 1972); children: Valerie A., Melanie F.; m. Patricia A. Edgley, Oct. 19, 1974; 1 child, Matthew E. BS in Polit. Sci., U Mich., 1952. Salesman Alcoa, Memphis, 1955-59, Nat. Starch & Chem. Corp., Atlanta, 1959-63, Am. Cyanamid Corp., Atlanta, and Bound Brook, N.J., 1963-65; nat. sales mgr. Valchem U.M. & M. Inc., Langley, S.C., 1965-69; mgr. textile chem. dept. Geigy (name now Ciba-Geigy), Atlanta, 1969-72; group bus. mgr. M&T (name now Elf Atochem), Woodbridge, N.J., 1972-90; v.p. Amspec Chem. Corp., Gloucester City, N.J., 1990-96. Ptnr., cons. C.O. Fry Co., Iselin, N.J., 1970-94; pres., cons. Catalytic Chem. Corp., Iselin, 1981-94, Petchem Corp., Iselin, 1984-94. Bd. dirs. ctrl. N.J. chpt. U. Mich. Club, Princeton, 1993-94. Lt. USN, 1952-55, Korea. Patentee in field. Mem. Am. Assn. Textile Chemists and Colorists, Am. Chem. Soc., Catalyst Soc. Episcopalian. Avocations: flying, hunting, fishing. Home: Henderson, Nev. Died June 12, 2008.

GIBBONS, LEROY, developer, fundraiser; b. Holbrook, Ariz., May 3, 1937; s. Lee Roy and Amy (Patterson) G.; m. Lorine Donna Porter, Dec. 18, 1956; children: Donna Lee, Donald LeRoy, Barry Alan, Felicia Anne Sorensen, Joseph Richey, Tricia Dawn Reynolds, Sara Denae. BS in Music, Brigham Young U., 1959, MA in Music, 1965, EdD, 1992. Tchr. pub. schs., Mesa, Phoenix, Ariz., 1969-73; prof. Brigham Young U., Provo, Utah, 1975-77, admissions officer, 1973-75, devel. adminstr., from 1977. Del. Exec. Leadership Inst., Ctr. on Philanthropy, Ind. U., Indpls., 1991; mem. Mormon Tabernacle Choir, 1965—. Author: Philanthropy in Utah Higher Education, 1992, Comparative Methods of Teaching Music Reading, 1965; composer/arranger (casette) Sing Unto the Lord Nov., 1988. State del. Rep. Conv., Salt Lake City, 1990; music dir. The Miss Utah Pageant, Salt Lake City; bd. dirs. Acad. Square Sci. Found., Provo, 1989-92. Named Outstanding Band Musician KSL Radio, Salt Lake City, 1959. Mem. Rotary (chpt. Man of the Yr. 1966), Phi Kappa Phi. Republican. Mem. Lds Ch. Home: Snowflake, Ariz. Died Mar. 30, 2008.

GIBBS, LEONARD EARL, social work educator; b. Wilmington, NC, Sept. 3, 1943; s. Albert J. and Odelia I. (Paulson) G.; m. Mary E. McDougall, July 9, 1988; children: Martin, Jeffrey. BS in Sociology, U. Wis., 1966, MSW, 1968, PhD, 1977. Cert. Acad. Cert. Social Workers. Psychiat. social worker USAF, San Antonio, 1968-69, dir. mental health clinic Lajes, Azores, 1969-72; lectr. U. Wis., Madison, 1976-77, prof., from 1977. Rep. NASW Legal Def. Svc., 1982-86; abstractor social work rsch. and abstracts, 1984-87. Author: (book) Scientific Reasoning for Social Workers, 1991; reviewer Jour. Social Svc. Rsch., 1983-87. Capt. USAF, 1968-72. Recipient Comparative Evaluation Patient-Treatment Interaction award Minn. Dept. Pub. Welfare, 1983-86, Replication of Typology of Alcoholics award Nat. Inst. Alcohol Abuse, 1978-80 Avocations: flint knapping, long distance skiing. Home: Eau Claire, Wis. Died June 13, 2008.

GIBLETT, ELOISE ROSALIE, retired hematologist; b. Tacoma, Jan. 17, 1921; d. William Richard and Rose (Godfrey) Giblett. BS, U. Wash., 1942, MS, 1947, MD with honors, 1951. Mem. faculty U. Wash. Sch. Medicine, 1957—2009, research prof., 1967—87, emeritus research prof., 1987—2009. Assoc. dir., head immunogenetics Puget Sound Blood Ctr., 1957—79, exec. dir., 1979—87, emeritus exec. dir., 1987—2009. Author: Genetic Markers in Human Blood, 1969; mem. editl. bd. numerous jours. including: Blood, Am. Jour. Human Genetics, Transfusion, Vox Sanguinis; contbr. over 200 articles to profl. jours. Recipient fellowships, grants Emily Cooley, Karl Landsteiner, Philip Levine and Alexander Wiener immunohematology awards, disting. alumna award, U. Wash. Sch. Medicine, 1987. Fellow: AAAS; mem.: NAS, Assn. Am. Physicians, Western Assn. Physicians, Am. Fedn. Clin. Rsch., Internat. Soc. Hematologists, Brit. Soc. Immunology, Am. Assn. Immunologists, Am. Soc. Hematology, Am. Soc. Human Genetics (pres. 1973), Alpha Omega Alpha, Sigma Xi. Home: Seattle, Wash. Died Sept. 16, 2009.

GIBSON, GORDON DAVIS, retired anthropologist; b. Vancouver, BC, Can., June 22, 1915; came to U.S., 1922; s. Ross Clark and Rebecca (Davis) G.; m. Bethune Millen, 1938 (div. 1973); children: Linda Caroline, Roger Eliot; m. Mary Horgan, Mar. 31, 1978. Student, Calif. Inst. Tech., 1933-35; BA, U. Chgo., 1937, MA, 1950, PhD, 1952. Asst. prof. anthropology U. Utah, Salt Lake City, 1955-58, curator Smithsonian Instn., Washington, 1958-82, emeritus curator, from 1982. Film review editor: American Anthropologist, 1965-69; author, editor: The Kavango Peoples, 1981; translator: The Ethnography of Southwestern Angola, 1976-81; creator numerous mus. displays on the cultures of Africa, 1961-80; producer numerous documentaries, 1969-82; contbr. articles and reviews to profl. jours. Social Sci. Res. Council grantee, 1952, NSF grantee, 1961, NIH grantee, 1972, Smithsonian Instn. grantee, 1960, 71. Fellow Am. Anthrop. Assn. Avocations: photography, cacti and succulent gardening. Home: Escondido, Calif. Died Sept. 18, 2007.

GIBSON, ROBERT H., public relations executive; b. Los Angeles, Nov. 28, 1939; s. William Gibson and Suzanne (Hazard) Johns; m. Collette Campbell (div. 1979); 1 child, Courtney; m. Pearl Guttman, Jan. 1982; children: Christian, Robert. Ptnr. Gibson and Stromberg Pub. Relations, Los Angeles, 1969-75; v.p. ABC/Dunhill Records, Los Angeles, 1975-77; pres. The Gibson Group Pub. Relations, Los Angeles, 1977-80, The Group Pub. Relations, Los Angeles, from 1980. Mem.: Balboa Bay (Newport, Calif.). Home: Los Angeles, Calif. Died Nov. 16, 2007.

GIBSON, SHARYN DELAINE, medical educator; b. Bluefield, W.Va., Apr. 9, 1947; d. Clayton Monroe and Josephine (Havens) G. Cert., Roanoke Meml. Hosp. Radiologic Tech. Sch., Va., 1967; AA, Armstrong State Coll., 1981, M of Health Scis., 1986; BS, St. Joseph's Coll., North Windham, Maine, 1983, ABD, 1997. Staff technologist Martinsville (Va.) Gen. Hosp., 1967-69, Meml. Med. Ctr., Savannah, Ga., 1969-71, neuroradiographer, angiographer, 1971-73, instr., clin. coordinator, 1973-80, dir. radiologic techs., 1980-83; instr., clin. coordinator Armstrong State Coll., Savannah, 1983-87, asst. prof., 1987-87, dir. radiologic techs., head dept. rad scis., from 1987. Vol. Historic Savannah, 1982, Nat. Ballet Council Savannah, 1987, Sav-A-Life Animal Welfare, 1986—; mem. adv. bd. Spl. Olympics; pres. Sacred Heart Parish Coun. Mem. AAUP (pres. chpt. 1994-95, 95-96), ASCD, Am. Soc. Radiologic Technologists, Ga. Soc. Radiologic Technologists (sec. 1976-77, pres. 1978-80, chmn. bd. dirs. 1983-84, site visitor at Chgo. for joint rev. com. 1984—), Alpha Eta. Democrat. Roman Catholic. Home: Savannah, Ga. Died Mar. 28, 2008.

GIBSON, WALKER, retired language educator, poet, writer; b. Jacksonville, Fla., Jan. 19, 1919; s. William Walker Sr. and Helen (Jones) G.; m. Nancy Close, 1942; children: David R., Susan M., William Walker. III, John S. BA, Yale U., 1940; MA, U. Iowa, 1946. Rsch. asst. writers workshop U. Iowa, 1945-46; instr. English Amherst (Mass.) Coll., 1946-48, asst. prof., 1948-54, assoc. prof., 1954-57; assoc. prof., dir. freshman English Washington Square Coll. NYU, NYC, 1957-61, prof., 1961-67; prof. English U. Mass., Amherst, 1967-87, dir. freshman English, 1967-70, dir. rhetoric program, 1970-72, dir. undergrad. studies in English, 1974-76, prof. emeritus, 1984. Lectr. Yale Summer Music Sch., 1948-56; dir. NYU Summer Inst. for Secondary Tchrs. English, 1962, NDEA Summer Inst. for Secondary Tchrs. English, NYU, 1965, Summer Seminars for Coll Tchrs, NEH, 1973-75; prof. summer intern teaching program Smith Coll., 1963-64, 66-67; vis. prof. Swarthmore Coll., 1965-66; prof. NDEA Summer Inst. at Mass., 1968, Bread Loaf Sch. English, Middlebury Coll., 1976, 77. Author: (verse) The Reckless Spenders, 1954 Come As You Are, 1957, (texts) Seeing and Writing: Fifteen Exercises in Composing Experience, 1959, Tough Sweet & Stuffy, 1966, Persona: A Style Study for Readers and Writers, 1969, (antholgy text) Poems in Progress, 1963; co-author: The Macmillan Handbook of English, 1960, 2nd edit, 1965; contbg. author: Traditions of Inquiry, 1985, The Legacy of Language, 1987, others; editor: Limits of Language, 1962, New Students in Two-Year Colleges, 1979; co-editor: The Play of Language, 1971; contbr. articles to profl. jours.; contbns. to TV and film include Sunrise Semester, CBS-TV, full-year course Modern Literature: British and American, 1962-63, semester course Studies in Style, 1966-67, film The Speaking Voice and the Teaching of Composition, 1963, videotapes on dramatic role-playing in student writing, 1971, 84; author numerous poems in publs. including The New Yorker, Harpers, Atlantic Poetry, others. 1st lt. U.S. Army Air Corps, 1941-45. Ford Found. fellow 1955-56; John Simon Guggenheim Found. fellow, 1963-64; grantee NEH, 1973-77. Mem. MLA (selection com. for scholar's libr. 1968-71, del. assembly 1976-77, exec. com. divsn. on tchg. of writing 1976-80, chmn. divsn. 1979), Nat. coun. Tchrs. English (commn. on curriculum 1962-65, chmn. coll. sect. 1969-71, pres. elect and pres. coun. 1971-73, com. pub. doublespeak 1972-90, chmn. emeritus assembly 1986-87, Disting. Lectr. award 1969, Disting. Svc. award 1988), CCCC (exec. com. 1966-69), 5 Coll. Learning in Retirement (pres. 1990-91). Avocations: reading, writing. Home: Amherst, Mass. Died Feb. 15, 2009.

GIBSON, WILLIAM, author; b. NYC, Nov. 13, 1914; s. George Irving and Florence (Doré) G.; m. Margaret Brenman, Sept. 6, 1940 (dec. 2004); children: Thomas, Daniel. Student, Coll. City N.Y. Author: (plays) I Lay in Zion, 1943, A Cry of Players, 1948, The Ruby, 1955, The Miracle Worker, 1957 (TV play 1957 Sylvania award 1957, stageplay 1959 Tony award for best dramatic author 1960, screenplay 1962), Two for the Seesaw, 1958, Dinny and The Witches: A Frolic on Grave Matters, 1959, John and Abigail, 1969 (published as American Primitive, 1972), The Body and The Wheel, 1971, The Butterfingers Angel, Mary and Joseph, Herod the Nut, and The Slaughter of 12 Hit Carols In A Pear Tree, 1974, Golda, 1977, Goodly Creatures, 1980, Monday After The Miracle, 1982, Handy Dandy, 1987, Golda's Balcony, 2003, Jonah's Dream, 2005; (poetry) Winter Crook, 1948; (novels) The Cobweb, 1954; (chronicles) The Seesaw Log: A Chronicle of the Stage Production with the Text of Two for the Seesaw, 1959, A Mass for the Dead, 1968, A Season in Heaven, 1974; (criticism) Shakespeare's Game, 1978; (musicals) (with Clifford Odets) Golden Boy, 1964, Raggedy Ann, 1984. Recipient Harriet Monroe Meml. prize, 1945; named to Theater Hall of Fame, 2005. Died Nov. 25, 2008.

GIEDT, WALVIN ROLAND, epidemiologist, educator; b. Eureka, SD, Aug. 17, 1905; s. Theodore John Peter and Augusta Elizabeth (Pritzkau) G.; m. Lois Della Hosking, Nov. 4, 1932; children: Carol Augusta, Barbara Ellen. BS in Medicine, U. S.D., 1933; MD, U. Chgo., 1937; MPH, Johns Hopkin's U., 1941. Lab. instr. Sch. of Medicine U. S.D., Vermillion, 1933-36, asst. prof. microbiology Sch. of Medicine, 1938-40; chief epidemiologist div. S.D. Dept. Health, Pierre, 1941-43, Wash. State Dept. Health, Seattle, 1943-71, ret., 1971. Contbr. articles to profl. jours. With USPHS, 1941-66. Mem. Wash. State Pub. Health Assn. (past pres). Democrat. Avocations: travel, photography, reading, politics and foreign affairs, antiwar activist and supporter united nations. Died Sept. 30, 1999; unknown.

GIFFORD, JOHN F. (JACK GIFFORD), retired electronics executive; b. 1941; BA in Electrical Engring., UCLA, 1963. With Fairchild Semiconductor, Intersil, 1971—83; founder Advance Micro Devices, Sunnyvale, Calif., 1969—71, Maxim Integrated Products, Sunnyvale, Calif., 1983—2007, chmn., pres., CEO, 1992—2007, strategic adv., 2007—09. Died Jan. 11, 2009.

GILBERT, EDITH HARMON, medical, surgical and occupational health nurse; b. Fla., May 4, 1917; d. Edwin and Blanche Pansy (Howe) Harmon; m. Chas. J. Gilbert, July 27, 1952; 1 child, Karen LaReau Hale. Diploma, S.I. Hosp. Sch. Nursing, 1940; student, Wagner Coll., SI, 1940. Head nurse Charter Internat. Oil, Houston, A.O. Smith Pipe Mill, Houston, Reed Roller Bit Co., Houston; ret., 1981. Mem. ANA, Tex. Nursing Assn., Occupl. Health Nurses, Occupl. Nurses Assn. Home: Bryan, Tex. Died Oct. 25, 2007.

GILBERTSON, EVA L., radiologist, retired; b. Maddock, ND, Dec. 23, 1916; d. Henry A. and Anna (Brandrud) G. BA, U. N.D., 1938, BS in Medicine, 1939; MD, Temple U., 1941; MS in Radiology, U. Minn., 1947. Diplomate Am. Bd. Radiology. Fellow in radiology Mayo Clin., Rochester, Minn., 1942-46; radiologist Portland (Oreg.) Clinic, 1946-49; instr. U. Oreg. Med. Sch., Portland, 1946-49; pvt. practice radiology Seattle, 1949-75. Staff radiologist U. Wash. Med. Sch., Seattle, 1950-80, Children's Med. Ctr., Seattle, 1955-85, Pacific Med. Ctr., 1981-93, retired. Fellow Am. Coll. Radiology; mem. AMA, Am. Roentgen Ray Soc., Radiol. Soc. N.Am., Pacific N.W. Radiol. Soc., Wash. State Radiol. Soc., Mayo Clinic Alumni Assn. Lutheran. Avocations: photography, travel. Home: Seattle, Wash. Died Nov. 16, 2007.

GILBRETH, EDWARD S., retired editor; b. Chgo., Feb. 19, 1933; s. Robert Aquilla and Bessie (Sanderson) G. Student, U. Ill., 1951-54. Reporter The Hammond (Ind.) Times, 1955-60, Chgo. Daily News, 1960-73, polit. editor, columnist, 1973-78; dir. pub. rels. to sec. state State of Ill., Springfield, 1981-83; dep. editor editorial pages Chgo. Sun-Times, 1983—94. Co-author: Quest for a Constitution: A Man Who Wouldn't Quit, 1984; contbr. articles to Nation mag. Mem. Am. Newpaper Guild (internat. v.p. 1973-75), Nat. Assn. Editorial Writers, City Club Chgo. (bd. dirs. 1983—, v.p. 1983-86) Home: Chicago, Ill. Died June 17, 2009.

GILCHRIST, DON KARL, orthopaedic surgeon; b. Iowa Falls, Iowa, Dec. 21, 1928; s. Leo Karl and Fae Ailene (Mossman) G.; m. Barbara Jean Patterson, Aug. 21, 1954; children: Richard, Ann, Patti, John. BA, Ill. Coll., 1951; BS, U. Ill., Chgo., 1953, MD, 1955. Diplomate Am. Bd. Orthopaedic Surgery. Intern St. Francis Hosp., Peoria, Ill., 1955-56; resident U.S. Naval Hosp., Portsmouth, Va., 1957-60, Orange Meml. Hosp., Orlando, Fla., 1961-62; orthopaedic surgeon U.S. Naval Hosp., Jacksonville, Fla., 1962-67, The Quincy (Ill.) Clinic, from 1967. Clin. assoc. in family practice and surgery So. Ill. U. Med. Sch., Springfield and Quincy, Ill., 1981—; staff Blessing Hosp., St. Mary Hosp. Served to commdr. USN, 1956-67. Fellow Am. Acad. Orthopaedic Surgeons; mem. Ill. Orthopaedic Soc., Cen. Ill. Orthopaedic Club. Home: Quincy, Ill. Died July 12, 2008.

GILL, CHARLES BURROUGHS, engineering educator; b. Sudbury, Ont., Can., Apr. 8, 1921; came to U.S., 1957; s. James Richard and Marion Pearl (Burroughs) G.; m. Mary Carolyn Somervill, Oct. 29, 1955; children: Catherine, Joseph. BSc, U. Toronto, Can., 1945; MSc, U. Mo., 1947, PhD, 1952. Smelter engr. Falcon Bridge (Ont., Can.) Nickel Mines Ltd., 1945-46; rsch. scientist U. Mo., Rolla, 1952-55; tech. supt. DeLoro (Ont., Can.) Smelting & Refining, 1955-57; prof. metall. engring. Lafayette Coll., Easton, Pa., 1957-89, prof. emeritus, from 1989. Author: Nonferrous Extrative Metallurgy, 1980, Material Beneficiation, 1991; contbr. article on extractive metallurgy to Ency Brit.; co-inventor titanium plating. Mem. Assn. Profl. Engrs., Metals Soc. of AIME, Sigma Xi. Episcopalian. Home: Easton, Pa. Died Nov. 7, 2007.

GILL, THOMAS PONCE, lawyer, former United States Representative from Hawaii; b. Honolulu, Apr. 21, 1922; s. Thomas and Lorin Tarr G.; m. Lois Angelina Hanawalt, Aug. 25, 1947; children: Thomas A., Andrea T., Eric W., Ivan P., Timothy M., Gary L. Attended, U. Hawaii, 1940—41; BA, U. Calif., Berkeley, 1948, JD, 1951. Bar: Hawaii. Mem. Hawaii Legis., 1958-61, majority floor leader, 1959—62; mem. US Congress from Hawaii, 1963—65; lt. gov. State of Hawaii, 1966-70. Mem. ACLU of No. Calif., 1948-51, chmn., Oahu County Democratic Com., 1954-58; dir. State of Hawaii Office Econ. Opportunity, 1964-66. Hawaii Territorial Guard, 1941-42; Tech. sgt. U.S. Army, 1942-45. Decorated Bronze Star, Purple Heart. Democrat. Home: Honolulu, Hawaii. Died June 3, 2009.

GILLIAM, RUSSELL TURNER, chemist; b. Spartanburg, SC, Jan. 12, 1938; s. James Olin and Inza (Turner) G.; m. Aurora Kalbfleisch, June 15, 1968; children: Russell, Jr., Steven D., Ashlee D. BS in Chemistry, Wofford Coll., 1959; MS in Textile Chemistry, Clemson U., 1963. Rsch. and devel. scientist United Merchants and Mfrs., Langley, S.C., 1963-68, Statesville, S.C., 1968-88; rsch. and devel. mgr. Clark-Schwebel Tech.-FAB, Anderson, S.C., from 1988. Mem. Am. Assn. Textile Chemists and Colorists. Methodist. Achievements include patent for research and development of foam finishing; development of several finishes for non-woven applications, such as sails, roofing and reinforcement. Home: Iva, SC. Died Mar. 11, 2008.

GILLIOM, JUDITH CARR, federal official; b. Indpls., May 19, 1943; d. Elbert Raymond and Marjorie Lucille (Carr) G. BA, Northwestern U., 1964; MA, U. Pa., 1966. Feature writer, asst. women's editor Indpls. News, summers 1961-63; rsch. asst. cultural anthropology Northwestern U., 1963-64, asst. instr. freshman English, 1964; editorial asst. to dir. div. cardiology Phila. Gen. Hosp., 1965-67; asst. to ophthalmologist-in-chief Wills Eye Hosp., Phila., 1967-69; editor, writer Nat. Assn. Hearing and Speech Agencies, Washington, 1969-70; free-lance speech writer White House Conf. Children and Youth, 1969-70; free-lance editor, writer, abstractor, 1971-78; free-lance speechwriter President's Com. Mental Retardation, 1971-78; from dir. publs. to dir. comm. Nat. Assn. Hearing and Speech Action, Silver Spring, Md., 1972-77; editor Hearing & Speech Action mag., 1969-70, 72-77; program mgr. Interagy. Com. on Handicapped Employees, 1978, dep. exec. sec., 1979-83; mgr. disability program Dept. Def., from 1983. Cons. U.S. Archtl. and Transp. Barriers Compliance Bd., 1976-77, Office Ind. Living for Disabled, HUD, 1977-78, Office for Handicapped Individuals, HEW, 1978, Women's com. Pres.'s Com. Employment Handicapped, 1985-86. Mem. Nat. Spinal Cord Injury Assn., 1970-90, editor, pub. conv. jour., 1974-82, bd. dirs. D.C. chpt., 1975-81, 89-90, nat. trustee, 1975-81, nat. bd. dirs., 1978-79; bd. dirs. Nat. Ctr. for a Barrier-Free Environment, 1979-84, v.p., 1980-81, pres., 1981-82; nat. bd. dirs., treas. League Disabled Voters, 1980-85; local bd. dirs. Easter Seal Soc. Disabled Children and Adults, 1985-90; active Montgomery County Commn. on People with Disabilities, 1989-95; mem. Taxicab Svcs. Adv. Com., 1995-99. Recipient Smittkamp award Nat. Paraplegia Found., 1976, Outstanding Svc. award Fed. Asian Pacific Am. Coun., 1990, Geico Pub. Svc. award, 1996, Civilian Career Svc. award Office of Sec. of Def., 1997, Outstanding Leadership award Fed. Asian Pacific Am. Coun., 2002; Woodrow Wilson fellow, 1965. Mem. Phi Beta Kappa, Delta Delta Delta. Home: Silver Spring, Md. Died Oct. 15, 2008.

GILLMAN, LEONARD, mathematician, educator; b. Cleve., Jan. 8, 1917; s. Joseph Moses and Etta Judith (Cohen) G.; m. Reba Parks Marcus, Dec. 24, 1938; children: Jonathan Webb, Michal Judith. Diploma (fellow in piano 1933-38), Juilliard Grad. Sch. Music, 1938; BS, Columbia U., 1941, MA (Carnegie fellow math. statistics 1942-43), 1945, PhD, 1953. Asst. in math. dept. Columbia U., 1941-42, lectr., 1942-43; ops. analyst Tufts Coll., MIT, 1943-51; from instr. to assoc. prof. math. Purdue U., 1952-60; prof. math., chmn. dept. U. Rochester, 1960-69; prof. math. U. Tex., Austin, 1969-87, prof. emeritus, 1987, chmn. dept., 1969-73. Mem. Inst. Advanced Study, Princeton, 1958-60; cons. editor W.W. Norton Co., Inc., 1967-80. Author: (with Meyer Jerison) Rings of Continuous Functions, 1960, 76, You'll Need Math, 1967, (with Robert H. McDowell) Calculus, 1973, 78, Writing Mathematics Well, 1987; mem. editorial bd. Topology and Its Applications, 1971-94. Guggenheim fellow, 1958-59; NSF sr. post-doctoral fellow, 1959-60. Mem. Am. Math. Soc. (assoc. sec. 1969-71, mem. com. to monitor problems in commn. 1972-77), Nat. Coun. Tchrs. Math., Math. Assn. Am. (bd. govs. 1973-95, treas. 1973-86, pres.-elect 1986-87, pres. 1987-89, past pres. 1989-90, Lester R. Ford award for expository writing 1994, 2003, Yueh-Gin Gung and Dr. Charles Y. Hu award for disting. svc. to math. 1999). Died Apr. 7, 2009.

GINSBERG, HARVEY SLOM, retired editor; b. Bangor, Maine, June 23, 1930; s. George Snow and Lena (Slom) G. BA, Harvard U., 1952. Asst. editor Book of Knowledge Ann., NYC, 1953-54; reader Bobbs Merril, NYC, 1956-57; editor Doubleday, NYC, 1957-59, Thomas Y. Crowell, NYC, 1959-60; sr. editor G.P. Putnam's Sons, NYC, 1961-76, Harper & Row, NYC, 1976-81, William Morrow & Co., NYC, 1981-90, v.p., 1984-89, sr. v.p., 1989—93. With U.S. Army, 1954-56. Mem. Century Assn. Jewish. Home: New York, NY. Died Dec. 30, 2008.

GINTY, ROBERT WINTHROP, actor; b. NYC, Nov. 14, 1948; s. Michael J. and Elsie (O'Hara) Ginty; m. Francine Tacker, May 23, 1980 (div. Oct. 1983); 1 child, James; m. Lorna Patterson, Nov. 23, 1983 (div. Mar. 1988); children: James, Marissa. Student, CCNY, 1966-68, Neighborhood Playhouse, NYC, 1968-69, Yale U., 1970-72. Ind. actor, from 1972; chmn., CEO Ginty Films Ireland, Ginty Films Can., Sligo Entertainment, Inc. Lectr. Trinity Coll. Actor: (films) Bound for Glory, 1976, Coming Home, 1978, The Exterminator, 1980, Gold Raiders, 1981, The Alchemist, 1982, Scarab, 1983, The Act, 1983, Warrior of the Lost World, 1984, White Fire, 1984, Exterminator II, 1985, Three Kinds of Heat, 1986, Mania, 1987, Out on Bail, 1988, Loverboy, 1988, The Prophet's Game, 1999; actor, dir.: Bounty Hunter, 1988; actor: (TV series) Baa Baa Blacksheep, Paper Chase, Hawaiian Heat, (Broadway prodns.) The Great God Brown, Don Juan, The Government Inspector, (off-Broadway prodns.) Indian Wants the Bronx, Silent Partner, Bring It All Back Home; screenwriter, actor Mission Kill, 1985, Retaliator, 1986, Code Name Vengeance, 1987, exec. prodr., scriptwriter, actor (TV pilot) Hardesty House, 1986; dir.: Early Edition, 1997, Nash Bridges, 1996, Charmed, 1998, Tracker, 2002. Founder, artistic dir. Irish Theater Arts Ctr., LA. Fellow Branford Coll., Yale U. Mem.: Irish Soc. Contemporary Art, Royal Soc. Arts London, Soc. Irish Playwrights, Can. Film Ctr., PEN Ireland, Internat. Writers' Orgn., Royal Dublin Soc., Oxford Univ. Soc., Harrow Assn. (assoc.), Irish Georgian Soc., Knickerbocker Club, Antheneum Club London, Univ. Club, Kildare St. Club, English Parliamentary Rugby Club. Democrat. Roman Catholic. Avocations: baseball, tennis, skiing. Home: Malibu, Calif. Died Sept. 21, 2009.

GITECK, EVELYN B., poet, educator, artist; b. Bklyn., Mar. 9, 1920; d. Max and Sophie Berman; m. Jack Bernard Giteck, Sept. 21, 1940; children: Anita Drujon Prager, Janice Susan, Sharon Phyllis Drujon. AA magna cum laude, L.A. City Coll., 1979; BA magna cum laude, Immaculate Heart Coll., 1980; MA in Humanities magna cum laude, Calif. State U., Dominiguez Hills, 1984. Office mgr. nursing dept. Cedars Sinai Hosp., LA, 1968—70; office mgr. acad. dean's office L.A. City Coll., 1970—81; dir. program for women reentering the job market Assabet H.S., Marlboro, Mass., 1981—85; dir. lit. Friends of the Marlboro Libr., 1981—85; prodr. programs Santa Barbara (Calif.) Writers' Consortium, 1985—87, The Unquiet Woman; tchr. poetry continuing edn. Lexington, Mass., from 1989; tchr. poetry Bedford (Mass.) Pub. Libr., from 2003. Founder, dir. automobile resource conservation L.A. City Coll. Dist., 1973; founder, pres., program chair L.A. City Coll. chpt. Assn. for Women's Active Return to Edn., 1974—77; responsible for creation of women's and day care ctr. L.A. City Coll., 1974—78, coord. 50th anniversary celebration, 1979. Editor, contbr.: book of poetry Woven Word (Friends of the Libr. award, 1985); author: Everywhere There are Gardens, Everlasting Spirit, (poetry art) Santa Barbara's Writers' Consortium Anthology, The Writing Finger Moves, 1985, 1986. Vol. Santa Barbara Housing for the Needy, 1985—87; pres. Brandeis U. Women, Santa Barbara, 1987. Recipient Minerva award, AWARE Assn., 1975—76, Cmty. Svc. to Lexington award for poetry film prodns., Comcast Cable Co., 2003. Mem.: Longfellow Poetry Soc. (life), Internat. Women's Writers' Guild (life). Avocations: writing, travel, swimming, reading, helping family. Home: Lexington, Mass. Died Mar. 7, 2008.

GIVAN, RICHARD MARTIN, retired state supreme court justice; b. Indpls., June 7, 1921; s. Clinton Hodel and Glee (Bowen) G.; m. Pauline Marie Haggart, Feb. 28, 1945; children: Madalyn Givan Hesson, Sandra Givan Chenoweth, Patricia Givan Smith, Elizabeth Givan Whipple. LL.B., Ind. U., 1951. Bar: Ind. 1952. Ptnr. with Clinton H. Givan, 1952-59, Bowen, Myers, Northam & Givan, 1960-69; dep. pub. defender City of Indpls., Ind., 1952-53; dep. atty. gen. State of Ind., Indpls., 1953—64; dep. pros. atty. Marion County, 1965-66; assoc. justice Ind. Supreme Ct., 1969-74, 1987-95, chief justice, 1974-87. Mem. Ind. Ho. Reps., 1967-68 Served to 2d lt. USAAF, 1942-45. Mem. Ind. Bar Assn., Indpls. Bar Assn., Ind. Soc. Chgo., Newcomen Soc. N.Am., Internat. Arabian Horse Assn. (past dir., chmn. ethical practices rev. bd.), Ind. Arabian Horse Club (pres. 1971-72), Indpls. 500 Oldtimers Club, Lions, Sigma Delta Kappa. Mem. Soc. Of Friends. Home: Indianapolis, Ind. Died July 22, 2009.

GLADSTONE, ARTHUR ABRAHAM, judge, educator; b. NYC, Nov. 15, 1911; s. Phillip L. and Rena (Kaplan) G.; m. Beatrice Thatch, Oct. 3, 1978 (dec. Oct. 1991); children: Kenneth M., Donald E. AB, Columbia Coll., 1932; JD, Columbia U., 1934. Bar: N.Y. 1934, D.C. 1948, U.S. Supreme Ct. 1942. Pvt. practice, NYC, 1934-39; atty. U.S. Govt., Washington, 1939-60, adminstrv. law judge, 1960-75; Indian tribal judge Reno, 1992—2002; settlement judge Supreme Ct. Nev., Reno, from 1997. Mem. faculty Nat. Jud. Coll., Reno, 1974-2002; cons. adminstrv. law, Washington, 1975-92; chmn. bd. Inst. for Study of Regulation, Washington, 1978-87; fellow Coun. on Econ. Regulation, Washington, 1987-91; chmn. Conf. of Adminstrv. Law Judges, ABA, Washington, 1973-74. Contbr. articles to law jours. 2d lt. U.S. Army, 1940-42. Avocations: fishing, amateur radio. Home: Reno, Nev. Died May 8, 2009.

GLADSTONE, BERNARD, columnist; b. NYC, Nov. 26, 1921; m. Olga Glasser (div.); 1 child, Robin; m. Sandra Zalbowitz; 1 child, Carol stepchildren: Amy, Laurie, David, Daniel. Attended, CCNY, 1941—42. Contbr. expert Motor Boating mag.; Home Improvement editor NY Times, 1956—86, Leisure editor, 1972—83, syndicated columnist, 1987—91. Author: (books include) Hints & Tips for the Handyman, 1960, The Complete Manual of Home Repair, 1969; co-author: Boatkeeper: The Boatowner's Guide to Maintenance, Repair & Improvement, 1984. Served in US Army Air Corps, 1942—46. Recipient Lawrence Tiefer award. Died Jan. 29, 2009.

GLAESSNER, PHILIP JACOB WALK, retired economist; b. Lausanne, Switzerland, June 29, 1919; came to U.S., 1942; s. Charles Louis and Suzanne (Walk) G.; m. Elisabeth Schnabel, June 27, 1953; children: Thomas, Philip, Barbara, Katheryn. BA, Cambridge U., 1940; MA,

Columbia U., 1946. Economist Fed. Reserve Bank, NYC, 1946-57; chief economist Brazil-U.S. Joint Commn., Rio De Janeiro, 1951-53, Klein-Saks Mission, Santiago, Chile, 1955-58; deputy dir. Pan-Am. Union Econ. Dept., Washington, 1959-60; div. chief Inter-Am. Devel. Bank, Washington, 1960-62; asst. adminstr. Alliance For Progress, U.S. Aid, Washington, 1962-68; div. chief World Bank, Washington, 1969-70, asst. dir., 1970-84; econ. cons. United Nats. Devel., NYC, Washington, from 1984. Lectr. US Dept. State & Fgn. Svc. Inst., Washington, 1985-88; cons. Planning Secretariat, Brasilia, 1985-89; mem. UN Devel. Program, Guatemala City, 1989, Kingston, Jamaica, 1987; cons. World Bank; cons. Mexico City transport air quality mgmt. project GTZ (Germany), 1990-91. Co-author: (2 vols.) Report of Brazil, U.S. Joint Commision, 1954. Treas. Housing Counseling Svcs., Washington, 1987-89. Mem. Am. Econ. Assn., 1818 Soc. of Retirees World Bank. Democrat. Avocations: hiking, jogging, poetry, history. Home: Bethesda, Md. Died June 23, 2009.

GLASER, VERA ROMANS, journalist; b. St. Louis, Apr. 21, 1916; d. Aaron L. and Mollie (Romans); m. Herbert R. Glaser, Apr. 16, 1939 (dec. 1992); 1 dau., Carol Jane Barriger. Student, Washington U., St. Louis, George Washington U., Am. U., 1937-40. Reporter-writer Nat. Aero. mag., 1943-44; reporter Washington Times Herald, 1944-46; pub. relations specialist Great Lakes-St. Lawrence Assn., 1950-51; promotion specialist, writer Congl. Quar. News Features, 1951-54; writer-commentator radio sta. WGMS, Washington, 1954-55; mem. Washington bur. N.Y. Herald Tribune, 1955-56; press officer U.S. Senator Charles E. Potter, 1956-59; dir. pub. relations, women's div. Rep. Nat. Com., 1959-62; press officer U.S. Senator Kenneth B. Keating, 1962-63; Washington corr. N.Am. Newspaper Alliance, 1963-69, bur. chief, 1965-69; columnist, nat. corr. Knight-Ridder Newspapers, Inc., 1969-81; assoc. editor Washingtonian Mag., 1981-88, contbg. editor, 1988—2008; columnist Maturity News Svc., 1988-94. Mem. Pres.'s Commn. on White House Fellows, 1969, Pres.'s Task Force on Women's Rights and Responsibilities, 1970; judge 1981 Robert Kennedy Journalism Awards. Free-lance writer nat publs., radio and TV appearances Stas. WTOP-TV, ABC, PBS, C-SPAN. Mem. nat. bd. Med. Coll. Pa., 1977-88; bd. dirs. Washington Press Club Found., 1986-88; bd. dirs. Internat. Women's Media Found., 1990-98. Mem. White House Corrs. Assn., Nat. Press Club (bd. govs. 1988, 89), Washington Press Club (pres. 1971-72), Cosmos Club. Unitarian Universalist. Died Nov. 26, 2008.

GLASSELL, ALFRED CURRY, JR., investor; b. Cuba Plantation, La., Mar. 31, 1913; s. Alfred Curry and Frances (Lane) G.; m. Clare Attwell; children: Jean Curry, Alfred Curry III. BA, La. State U., 1934. Cons. Glassell Producing Co., 1938—2008. Past bd. dirs. Transco Cos., El Paso Nat. Gas, First City Bancorp. Trustee Houston Mus. Natural Sci., Internat. Oceanographic Found.; truste, chmn. emeritus Houston Mus. Fine Arts; former trustee Kinkaid Sch., Tex. Children's Hosp., Smithsonian Nat. Bd. Recipient Marine Sci. ann. award Internat. Oceanographic Found., 1971, Soc. Grand Founders medallion U. Miami, 1984, James Smithson award, 1991. Mem. Am. Geog. Soc., Am. Mus. Natural History, Tex. Angus Assn., Can. Chianini Assn., Houston Horse Show Assn., Tex. Cattle Breeders Assn., Am. Nat. Cattlemen's Assn., Tex. and Southwestern Cattle Raisers Assn., Mil. and Hospitaller Order St. Lazarus of Jerusalem. Clubs: Atlantic Tuna (Providence), Boston (New Orleans), Cabo Blanco Fishing (Peru), Tex. Game Fishing (Dallas), Tex. Corinthian Yacht (Kemah), Bay of Islands Swordfish and Mako Shark (New Zealand), Anglers of N.Y., Houston, Petroleum, Ramada, Bayou, Houston Country, River Oaks Country. Achievements include being a holder of the record of world's largest fish, former holder of numerous world record salt water game fish. Died Oct. 29, 2008.

GLAVIN, KEVIN CHARLES, lawyer, educator; b. Providence, Aug. 1, 1949; s. Charles Francis and Lola Glavin; m. Donna Bettencourt, Aug. 23, 1980. AB, Providence Coll., 1971; JD, Suffolk Law Sch., 1974. Bar: R.I. 1975, Mass. 1984, U.S. Dist. Ct. R.I. 1975, U.S. Supreme Ct. 1979, 1st cir. ct. appeals, 2007, 2nd cir. ct. appeals. Spl. asst. atty. gen. R.I. Dept. Atty. Gen., Providence, 1975-79; mng. atty. Kemper Ins. Co., Providence, 1979-94; arbitrator R.I. Superior Ct., Providence, from 1989; ptnr. Murray, Cutcliffe & Glavin, Providence, 1994-2001, Cutcliffe, Glavin & Archetto, Providence, from 2001. Adj. faculty Roger Williams U., Bristol, R.I., 1986—. V.P. Kent Heights PTA, East Providence, 1989; treas. Colt Andrews PTA, Bristol, 1993; judge Acad. Decathlon R.I., 1999-00. Recipient Order of the Gavel, Newport Ski Club, 1982. Mem. R.I. Superior Ct. (bench bar com. 1992—), Pawtucket Bar Assn. (exec. com. 2001, pres. 2007). Avocations: tennis, skiing, sailing, golf. Home: Bristol, RI. Died May 10, 2008.

GLEN, WILLIAM B., chemical plastics industry executive; b. Providence, Aug. 13, 1932; s. William F. and Rosanna (Boulay) G.; m. Joan B. Ellis, Apr. 11, 1964; children: Douglas S., Laura J. BA in Chemistry, Brown U., 1958. Chemist CPL Corp., East Providence, R.I., 1958-66; plant mgr., purchasing mgr. Engineered Yarns Inc., Coventry, R.I., 1966-75; gen. mgr. Oxford Mills, Compton, Calif., 1975-77; dir. purchasing United Foam Corp., Compton, 1970-85; mgr. purchasing and traffic Petrolite Corp., from 1985. Cons. in polyvinlyn chloride and polyurethane, 1975—. Chmn. bldg. com. Calvin Presbyn. Ch., Cumberland, R.I., 1971-74, also elder/trustee; decon 1st. Presbyn. Ch. Fullerton, 1981-83, elder, 1984—. Served with C.E., U.S. Army, 1952-54. Mem. Am. Chem. Soc., Soc. Plastics Engrs., Nat. Assn. Purchasing Mgrs. Home: Goffstown, NH. Died Oct. 1, 2007.

GLENDON, WILLIAM RICHARD, lawyer, former mayor; b. Medford, Mass., May 1, 1919; s. Henry Richard and Ellen L. (Harrigan) G.; m. Susan Webb, Apr. 1, 1945 (dec. 1999); children: W. Richard, John B. Lisa A. AB, Holy Cross Coll., 1941; postgrad., Harvard U. Bus. Sch., 1941; LL.B., Georgetown U., 1948. Bar: D.C. 1948, N.Y. 1958. Law clk. to judge US Dist. Ct. D.C., 1948-49; asst. US atty. US Dept. Justice, Washington, 1950-53; from assoc. to sr. ptnr. Rogers & Wells, and predecessors, NYC and Washington, 1953—2008. Mem. 2d Circuit Jud. Nominating Panel, 1980-81 Trustee Village of Scarsdale, N.Y., 1982-85; bd. regents Georgetown U.; Served to lt. (s.g.) USN, 1942-46. Recipient John Carroll medal of honor Georgetown U., 1973 Mem. ABA, Assn. Bar City N.Y., D.C. Bar, Fed. Bar Council Clubs: Fishers Island Yacht (N.Y.) (commodore 1977-79); Scarsdale Town (pres. 1979-80), Scarsdale Golf. Democrat. Roman Catholic. Home: Scarsdale, NY. Died Dec. 25, 2008.

GLICK, EDWARD MAURICE, newspaper columnist, writer; b. Cleve., May 23, 1920; s. Phillip and Lillian (Levin) G.; m. Florence Goldman, Sept. 22, 1946; children: Linda Ruth, Ellen Adrienne. BA cum laude, Ohio State U., 1943; MA in Polit. Sci., Western Res., 1947; PhD in Polit. Sci., Ohio State U., 1960. Presdl. and cabinet-level speechwriter, 1951-53; spl. corr. The Times of London, 1960-62; prof. George Wash. U., Am. U., Washington, 1961-66; cons. U.S. Senate Judiciary Com., Washington, 1963-64; pres., mng. dir. Am. Inst. Polit. Communication., Washington, 1965-76; cons. various govts. and orgns., 1977-82; daily syndicated newspaper columnist Daily News-Record, Harrisonburg, Va., 1984-97. Author: Federal Government and Daily Press Relationship, 1966, New Methodology: Study of Political Strategy & Tactics, 1967, Anatomy of a Crucial Election, 1970, Media Monopoly & Politics, 1973, The 1974 Campaign Etc., 1975, American Politics in Complex World, 1988; co-author: TV Station Ownership, 1971. Polit. adv. U.S. Senator Thomas J. Dodd's 1964 reelection campaign, Conn., 1963-64; polit. adv. and adminstrv. asst. U.S. Senator Matthew Neely, W.Va., 1953-54. Sgt. U.S. Army, 1943-45. Decorated Purple Heart; recipient rsch. grant Cudahy Found. Wis., 1970-75, US News & World Report, 1971, Nat. Assn. Broadcasters, 1972, Milw. Jour., 1970, Rutland Herald, 1970, Gen. Svcs. Found., 1973-74. Mem. Nat. Press Club, Phi Beta Kappa. Avocations: reading, pub. speaking, writing poetry, amateur astronomy. Died July 22, 2008.

GLICKMAN, ELAINE JEANNE, retired artist; b. Des Moines, Jan. 21, 1922; d. Isaac Davidson and Rae (Miller) Ginsberg; m. Eugene David Glickman, Mar. 15, 1942; children: Richard Lorin, James Allan. Student, Northwestern U., 1939-41, Am. Acad. Art Chgo., 1941—43. Columnist, illustrator Register Tribune, Des Moines, 1943—44. Art tchr. One-woman shows include Bernard Heights Country Club, 1994-95, Remington, 1996; group shows include La Jolla Art Assn., Poway Ctr. Performing Arts, 1994-95, San Diego Med. Soc., 1995. Bd. dirs., past pres. Davenport Mus. of Art (first woman pres. of the bd. dirs.); vol. nurse's aide Camp Dodge Iowa, Des Moines, Cook County Hosp., Chgo., Broadlawn County Hosp., Des Moines, 1943-44. Mem.: LWV. Democrat. Avocations: museums, art, painting, drawing. Home: Sturbridge, Mass. Died Apr. 17, 2008.

GLUCKSTERN, ROBERT LEONARD, physics professor; b. Atlantic City, July 31, 1924; BEE, CCNY, 1944; PhD, MIT, 1948. Asst. prof. physics Yale U., New Haven, 1950-57, assoc. prof., 1957-64; prof. physics U. Mass., Amherst, 1964-75, head dept., 1964-69, asso. provost, 1969-70, provost, vice chancellor for acad. affairs, 1970-75; prof. physics U. Md., College Park, 1975-97, chancellor, 1975-82, sr. rsch. scientist, 1997—2005; ret., 2005. Vis. prof. U. Tokyo, Japan, 1969; cons. on theory of high energy particle accelerators Brookhaven Nat. Lab., Fermi Nat. Accelerator Lab., Lawrence Berkeley Nat. Lab., Los Alamos Nat. Lab., Stanford Linear Accelerator Ctr. With USN, 1944-46. AEC fellow U. Calif., Berkeley, 1948-49, Cornell U., Ithaca, N.Y., 1949-50, Yale fellow, 1961-62. Fellow AAAS, Am. Phys. Soc.; mem. SSC (bd. overseers 1990-93), SURA (trustee 1982-98, chmn. bd. trustees 1994-96, high energy physics adv. panel 1990-93), Fedn. Am. Scientists, Am. Assn. Physics Tchrs. Home: Baltimore, Md. Died Dec. 17, 2008.

GMUCA, JACQUELINE LAURA, English language educator; b. Johnstown, Pa., Nov. 12, 1950; d. Andrew Paul Jr. and Mary (Kucharyk) G. BS in Edn., Clarion State U., 1972; MA, Kent State U., 1973, PhD, 1980. Instr. U. N.C., Charlotte, 1978-80, asst. prof., 1980-84, U. S.C. Coastal Carolina Coll., Conway, 1984-90; assoc. prof. Coastal Carolina U., Conway, 1990—99; asst. prof. U. Tex., El Paso, 1999—2009. Dir. Coastal Area Writing Project, Conway, 1986-91; higher edn. rep. Project Reach, Conway, 1987-91. Contbr. articles to profl. jours. Historian, choral mem. Cmty. Choral Soc., Myrtle Beach, S.C., 1985-91; vol. Tallahassee (Fla.) Mus. of Natural History and Sci., 1994. Mem. MLA, Nat. Coun. Tchrs. English (conf. sponsorship 1984), Carolinas Symposium on Brit. Studies (v.p. 1994-95), Philol. Assn. of The Carolinas (local arrangements co-chair 1989-90), Children's Lit. Assn. Avocations: travel, bird-watching. Home: El Paso, Tex. Died Oct. 17, 2009.

GOBEL, JOHN HENRY, lawyer; b. Oak Park, Ill., Oct. 21, 1926; s. Henry Andrew and Mary Ann (Coughlan) G.; m. Carol Zvara, Mar. 8, 1969; children: Kristina, Gregory. BA cum laude, DePaul U., 1950, JD cum laude, 1952. Bar: Ill. 1951, Md. 1975, Ohio 1976. Various positions law dept. Chgo. and North Western R.R. Co., Chgo., 1952-60, Balt. and Ohio R.R. Co., Balt., 1960-75; asst. gen. counsel Chesapeake and Ohio Ry. Co., Cleve., 1975-77, gen. solicitor, 1977-80, gen. counsel, 1980-82; v.p. govt. relations CSX Corp., Cleve., 1982-86; v.p., regional trial counsel CSX Transp., 1987. Served with U.S. Army, 1945-46. Fellow Internat. Soc. Barristers; mem. ABA (spl. com. on rules 1967-71), Ill. Bar Assn. (chmn. profl. ethics com., mem. assembly 1973-74), Nat. Assn. R.R. Trial Counsel (nat. sec. 1971-75), Soc. Trial Lawyers Ill. (dir. 1968-70), Ohio C. of C. (bd. dirs.), Ohio Pub. Expenditures Council (v.p. 1979-88), Ohio R.R. Assn. (chmn. 1979-87), W.Va. R.R. Assn. (chmn. 1975-87). Clubs: Union League (Chgo.), Law (Chgo.). Home: Cleveland, Ohio. Died Oct. 2008.

GODDARD, EDWARD DEAN, stockbroker, accountant; b. Danville, Ill., Oct. 13, 1929; s. Oscar E. and Dorothea Goddard; m. Mary Lenny, Jan. 29, 1955; children: James, Daniel, Steven, Mark. BS in Acctg., U. Ill., 1955. CPA, Ill. Auditor Ernst & Ernst, Chgo., 1955-58; comptr., treas. various small/large corps., Chgo./Grand Rapids, Mich., 1958-69; stockbroker Kenower McArthur/The Ohio Co., Grand Rapids, 1969-80, Morgan Stanley Dean Witter, Orlando, Fla., from 1980. Writer, prodr. host TV shows: Relax It's Income Tax 13 Weeks, 1981, 89, Corporate Profile Weekly, 1982-87, Ballroom Dance Class, 13 weeks series, 1989. Candidate U.S. Congreess, Dist. 7, 1994. With U.S. Army, 1946-48, Korea. Mem. Maitland Toastmasters Club (pres. 1997-98, gov. area 49 1998-99, Disting. Toastmaster 1999). Democrat. Episcopalian. Avocations: ballroom dance instructing, stamp collecting/philately. Home: Longwood, Fla. Died 2008.

GODRIDGE, JOSEPH EDWARD, JR., financial consultant; b. Flushing, NY, Oct. 29, 1926; s. Joseph Edward Godridge and Dorothy Louise (Anderson) McLeod; m. Barbara Lillian Krauss, June 19, 1948; children: Joseph Edward III (dec.), Victoria Anne. BS in Commerce, U. Va., 1949. Salesman Burroughs Corp., Detroit, 1949-55; broker, sales mgr., sr. v.p., bd. dirs. Ferris & Co., Washington, 1955-76; v.p. Quick & Reilly, Inc., NYC, 1976-78; fin. cons., asst. v.p. Merrill Lynch, Pierce, Fenner & Smith, NYC, from 1979. Pres. Exchange Club Washington, 1975. Served with USNR, 1945-46. Fellow Fin. Analysts Fed.; mem. Washington Soc. Investment Analysts, Nat. Economists Club. Clubs: Columbia Country (Chevy Chase, Md.). Republican. Avocations: golf, gardening, photography, electronics. Home: Bethesda, Md. Died Apr. 26, 2008.

GOING, WILLIAM THORNBURY, retired language educator; b. Birmingham, Ala., June 3, 1915; s. Clarence Johnston and Louise (Thornbury) G.; m. Margaret Moorer, Dec. 15, 1951. AB with honors, U. Ala., 1936; MA (scholar, fellow English), Duke U., 1938; Ed.D., U. Mich., 1954; LHD (hon.), So. Ill. U., 2000. Tchr. English West End High Sch., Birmingham, 1938-39; asst. prof. edn. Samford U., Birmingham, summer 1939; instr. to asso. prof. English U. Ala., 1939-57; teaching fellow U. Mich., 1952-53; prof. English So. Ill. U., Edwardsville, 1957-80, prof. emeritus, from 1980, dean instruction, 1958-63, dean acad. affairs, 1963-65, dean emeritus, from 2004. Mem. faculty com. Ill. Bd. Higher Edn.; mem. Ill. Fulbright com. Author: Wilfrid Scawen Blunt and the Tradition of the English Sonnet Sequence in the 19th Century, 1953; editor: 99 Fables by William March, 1960, Regional Perspective: Essays on Alabama Literature, 1975, Scanty Plot of Ground: Studies in the Victorian Sonnet, 1976; contbg. author: (casebook) A Rose for Emily, 1970, Victorian Britain: An Encyclopedia, 1987, Scribner Novel Guide: To Kill a Mockingbird, 1990, Gale Contemporary Literary Criticism, 1990, World Literature Criticism, 1500 to the Present, 1992, DISCovering Authors—British, 1994, Modern American Literature, Vol. II, 5th edit., 1998, Bloom's Guide: To Kill a Mockingbird, 2004; On Harper Lee: Essays and Reflections, 2007; contbr. articles on lang. and lit. to profl. jours. including Victorian Poetry, Ga. Rev., Ala. Rev., Jour. Modern Lit., Jour. Pre-Raphaelite Studies, Papers on Lang. and Lit. Organist 2d Presbyn. Ch., Birmingham, Ala., 1939-42, 1st Meth. Ch., Tuscaloosa, Ala., 1943-50; mem. adv. bd. Alton Meml. Hosp. Nursing Sch. Recipient Pres'. award of Merit So. Ill. Univ., 1992; named Outstanding Educator of Am., 1973; Rhodes scholar-elect from Ala., 1938. Mem. NEA, Midwest MLA., Nat. Coun. Tchrs. English, MLA Am. Ill. Edn. Assn., Phi Beta Kappa, Phi Delta Kappa, Phi Kappa Phi, Phi Eta Sigma, Sigma Alpha Epsilon. Democrat. Presbyterian. Home: Edwardsville, Ill. Died Sept. 6, 2008.

GOLD, MARVIN HAROLD, chemist, consultant; b. Buffalo, June 23, 1915; s. Max and Jennie (Frankel) G.; m. Sophye Mendelson, Aug. 31, 1940; children: Judith May Bloom, Norman Charles. BA, UCLA, 1937; PhD, U. Ill., 1940. Rsch. assoc. Northwestern U., Evanston, Ill., 1940-42; rsch. group leader The Visking Corp., Chgo., 1942-48; sr. scientist Aerojet Gen. Corp., Sacramento and Azusa, Calif., 1948-72; tech. cons./chemist Sacramento, from 1972. Contbr. articles to profl. jours.; inventor/patentee (more than 85) in chems., plastics, coatings, insulations, lubricants. Pres. People to People of Sacramento, 1962-65. Recipient Civilian Meritorious Svc. Citation USN, 1962; Anna Fuller Fund Cancer Rsch. fellow Nat. Cancer Inst., 1940-42. Mem.

Am. Chem. Soc. (sec. councilor 1967-68), Sigma Xi (chpt. pres. 1966), Phi Lambda Upsilon. Jewish. Avocations: painting, photography, reading, music. Home: Sacramento, Calif. Died Oct. 21, 2007.

GOLDBERG, WILLIAM B., composer, musician; b. NYC, Jan. 24, 1917; s. Harry B. and Frances B. Goldberg; 1 child, Mark. BSS, CCNY; postgrad. studies, Julliard Sch. of Music, NYC. Composer; tchr. of music, 1937—87; publisher, 1980—95. Home: Hallewell, Maine. Died June 7, 2008.

GOLDBERGER, MELVIN TOBIAS, bank executive; b. Knoxville, Tenn., June 6, 1919; s. Harry and Grace (Reich) G.; m. Betty Knox, June 4, 1944; children: Diane, Susan, Margy. BSBA, Ohio State U., 1940; postgrad., U. Tenn., 1940—41. Pres. Sq. Supply Co., Knoxville, 1946-64; chmn. Vector Co., 1965-72; pres. Seventh Investment Bancing Corp., Boca Raton, Fla., from 1973, Regency Highland Corp., Boca Raton, 1973—81. Treas. Fla. Philharm. Orch., Ft. Lauderdale, Fla., 1985-94, life bd. dirs., hon. life treas. emeritus, 1992-. Shrine mem. Kerbela Temple, 1947—; vice chmn. bd. dirs. Mae Volen Sr. Ctr., Boca Raton, 1989-2000, chmn. bd. dirs., 2001-02. Capt. Med. Adminstrn. Corps, U.S. Army, 1943-46. Mem. Elks Club. Avocations: golf, tennis, sports. Home: Dayton, Ohio. Died Nov. 2008.

GOLDEN, ELLIOTT, judge; b. Bklyn., June 28, 1926; s. Barnet David and Rose (Fistel) G.; m. Ana Valbuena, July 8, 1990; children: Jeffrey Stephen, Marjorie Ruth, Peter Michael (dec.); stepchildren: Robert, Elizabeth, William, John. Student, Maritime Acad., 1944-46, NYU, 1947-48; LLB, Bklyn. Law Sch., 1951. Bar: N.Y. 1952, U.S. Dist. Ct. (ea. dist.) N.Y. 1953, U.S. Tax Ct., U.S. Dist. Ct. (so. dist.) N.Y. 1953, U.S. Supreme Ct. 1961. Assoc. Golden & Golden, 1952-64; asst. dist. atty. Kings County, 1956-64, chief asst. dist. atty., 1964-76, acting dist. atty., 1968; judge Civil Ct. of City of N.Y., 1977-78; justice Supreme Ct. State of N.Y., 1979-98, jud. hearing officer, 1998-2000. Adj. assoc. prof. N.Y.C. Tech. Coll., 1987-93; arbitrator, mediator Nat. Arbitration & Mediation, 1998—; cons. in field. Contbr. articles to profl. jours. Bd. trustees Greater N.Y. coun. Boy Scouts Am.; hon. vice chmn. March of Dimes; bd. dirs. Bklyn. Philharmonia; mem. adv. bd. Bklyn. PAL; chmn. Bklyn. Lawyers div. Fedn. Jewish Philanthropies; co-chmn. Bklyn. Lawyers div. State of Israel Bonds; assoc. trustee Temple Beth Emeth of Flatbush; mem. exec. com. Lawyers div. United Jewish Appeal; past pres. counsel Hosp. Relief Assn.; bd. dirs. Kings Bay YM-YMHA of Bklyn.; bd. dirs. Bklyn. ARC, Archway Sch. for Spl. Children, Bklyn. Sch. for Spl. Children. Recipient Cert. of Merit, Hosp. Relief Assn., numerous plaques, awards and certs. of appreciation various civic orgns. Mem. Nat. Dist. Attys. Assn. (dir. 1976-77, Disting. Svc. award), Combined Coun. Law Enforcement Ofcls. State N.Y., N.Y. State Dist. Attys. Assn. (sec. 1965-77), K.P. (supreme coun.). Avocations: golf, fishing, computers. Died July 25, 2008.

GOLDFARB, RUTH, poet, educator; b. Bklyn., Aug. 13, 1936; d. Nathan Alter and Florence Goldfarb. BA in Psychology, L.I. Univ., 1980; MA in Edn., NYU, 1984. Tchr. kindergarten N.Y.C. Bd. Edn., 1963-64, early childhood tchr., 1993-94, NYC, Bklyn., 1970-84; tchr. common br. Bklyn. Bd. Edn., 1986-93; clk. Primary Health Care Ctr. North Broward Med. Ctr., Pompano Beach, Fla., from 1998. Author (poetry) Whispers and Chants, 1997, Poems That Elevate the Soul, 2006; CD recs. include Christmas Memories, 1999, The Miracle of Christmas, 2000, Songs of Praise, 2000. Mem.: AARP, Gold Coast Poetry Group, Acad. Am. Poets, Internat. Soc. Poets. Avocations: poetry, music, sculpture, writing stories. Home: Deerfield Beach, Fla. Died July 2, 2008.

GOLDGAR, BERTRAND ALVIN, literary historian; b. Macon, Ga., Nov. 17, 1927; s. Benjamin Meyer and Annie (Shapiro) G.; m. Corinne Cohn Hartman, Apr. 6, 1950; children: Arnold Benjamin, Anne Hartman. BA, Vanderbilt U., 1948, MA, 1949, Princeton U., 1957, PhD, 1958. Instr. in English Clemson (S.C.) U., 1948-50, asst. prof., 1951-52; instr. English Lawrence U., Appleton, Wis., 1957-61, asst. prof., 1961-65, assoc. prof., 1965-71, prof. English, 1971—2009, John N. Bergstrom prof. humanities, 1980—2009. Mem. fellowship panel NEH, 1979 Author: The Curse of Party: Swift's Relations with Addison and Steele, 1961, Walpole and the Wits: The Relation of Politics to Literature, 1722-1742, 1976; editor: The Literary Criticism of Alexander Pope, 1965, Henry Fielding's The Covent-Garden Jour., 1988, Henry Fielding's Miscellanies, Vol. 2, 1993, Jonathan Wild, 1997, The Grub Street Jour. 1730-1733, 2002, Jonathan Swift's English Political Writings 1711-1714, Cambridge Editor of the Works of Swift, vol. 8, 2008; adv. editor: 18th Century Studies, 1977-82; contbr. essays to books. With AUS, 1952-54. Fellow, Am. Coun. Learned Socs, 1973-74, NEH, 1980-81. Mem. Am. Soc. 18th Century Studies, Johnson Soc. Cen. Region. Home: Appleton, Wis. Died Oct. 14, 2009.

GOLDIN, LEON, artist; b. Chgo., Jan. 16, 1923; s. Joseph P. and Bertha (Metz) G.; m. Meta Solotaroff, July 30, 1949; children: Joshua, Daniel. BFA, Art Inst. Chgo., 1948; MFA, U. Iowa, 1950. From instr. to assoc. prof. Columbia U., NYC, 1964-82, prof., 1982-92, prof. emeritus, from 1992. Former tchr. Calif. Coll. Arts and Crafts, Phila. Coll. Art, Queen's Coll., Cooper Union; vis. prof. painting Stanford, summer 1973 One-man shows Oakland Art Mus., 1955, Felix Landau Gallery, LA, 1956, 57, 59, Galleria L'Attico, Rome, 1958, Kraushaar Galleries, NYC, 1960, 64, 68, 72, 84, 88, 90, 93, 96, 98, 2001, 04 U. Houston, 1981, Binghamton U. Art Mus., 2000, Ctr. for Maine Contemporary Art, 2000; represented in permanent collections Bklyn. Mus., City Mus. St. Louis, Worcester Mus., Addison Gallery Am. Art, Pa. Acad. Fine Arts, LA County Mus., Santa Barbara Mus., Oakland Art Mus., Munson Proctor Inst., Va. Mus. Fine Arts, Portland Mus., Maine, Everson Mus., U. Ark., Okla. Art Ctr., Cleve. Mus. Fine Art, Work on Paper Guston Gallery, Stoningta, 2008. Served with AUS, 1943-46, ETO. Fulbright scholar to France, 1952, Prix de Rome Am. Acad. Rome, 1955-58, Jennie Sesnan Gold medal Pa. Acad. Fine Arts, 1966; Tiffany grantee, 1951; Guggenheim fellow, 1959, Nat. Endowment for Arts grantee, 1967, 80; Nat. Inst. Arts and Letters grantee, 1968, NY Caps grantee, 1981, Ranger Fund Purchase award, 2005. Mem. NAD (Benjamin Altman Landscape prize 1993, 1999, Adolph and Clara Obrig prize, 2003). Home: New York, NY. Died Jan. 30, 2009.

GOLDMAN, DORIS TORAN, not-for-profit developer; b. Phila., Feb. 5, 1932; d. Samuel Joshua and Bella Adler Nimoityn; m. Jule Goldman, Oct. 16, 1978 (dec. Mar. 1, 1980); m. Alan L. Toran, Mar. 15, 1953 (div. Nov. 1972); children: Nancy Duitch, Jack Steven Toran(dec.), Sharon Turner Turner(dec.). Student, Temple Univ., Phila., 1950—53. Admin. asst. Del. County Commr., Media, Pa., 1972—80; office ops. supr. 1980 U.S. Census, Media, Pa., 1980; area dir. Am. Jewish Com., Phila., 1986—90; nat. dir. Cardiac Arrhyhimias Rsch. and Edn. Found., Irvine, Calif., 1996—2009. Co-founder C.A.R.E. Found. Inc., Irvine, Calif., 1995—2009; bd. dirs. Orange County Interfaith Coun., Newport Beach, Calif., 1990—95, Am. Jewish Com., Irvine, Calif., 1996—99. Campaign coord. Del. County Dem. Comm., Media, Pa., 1972; chair Young Citizens for Johnson, Phila., 1965; coord. Citizens for Hart, Montgomery County, Pa., 1984. Recipient Nat. Human Rels. award, Am. Jewish Assn., 1996, Heart of A Child award, C.A.R.E. Found., 1997. Mem.: Operation Heartbeat (steering com. from 2000), Pub. Interest Orgn. NHLBI. Democrat. Jewish. Avocations: reading, bridge, walking, public speaking. Home: Laguna Woods, Calif. Died July 29, 2009.

GOLDSMITH, LUDWIG MICHAEL, architect; b. New Brunswick, NJ, Oct. 17, 1950; s. Karl Kappel and Marianne Hilde (Michaelis) G.; m. Linda Engelhardt, Apr. 8, 1979; children: Marla, Gary, Wendy. BArch, Cornell U., 1973; M in Urban Planning, CCNY/CUNY, 1985. Lic. architect, N.Y., N.J., NCARB. Draftsman Russo and Sonder, NYC, 1977-78; designer I.M. Pei & Ptnrs., NYC, 1978-80; assoc. John Carl Warnecke & Assocs., NYC, 1980-84; v.p. Stephen Leigh & Assocs., NYC, 1984-91; prin. Ludwig Michael Goldsmith, AIA, NYC, from 1991. Guest lectr. NYU, 1993, 94, 97. Subject of jour. articles. V.p. bd. dirs. Congregation Shomrei Emunah, Montclair, N.J., 1992—; active Cub Scouts. Lt. USN, 1973-77. Recipient award of excellence Archtl. Woodwork Inst., 1995. Mem. AIA. Jewish. Avocations: skiing, photography, swimming. Died July 23, 2008.

GOLDSMITH, MAUREEN P., English as second language educator; b. Washington, Feb. 28, 1931; d. William and Sarah (Morris) Pomerantz; m. Harold S. Goldsmith, Dec. 10, 1950 (div. 1965); chldren: Andy R., Adam D. BS in Elem. Edn., U. Md., 1966; MA in Edn. and Human Devel., George Washington U., 1979. Cert. in elem. edn., spl. edn., Md. Tchr. elem. grades D.C. Pub. Schs., Washington, 1965-80; pvt. practice cons. Educaid, Silver Spring, Md., 1981-98; isntr. reading and writing Prince Georges C.C., Largo, Md., 1976-92; learning disability specialist Fairfax (Va.) Pub. Schs., 1989-90; adj. prof. ESL and English, Montgomery Coll., Rockville, Md., from 1980; cons. English and ESL, Educaid, from 1981. Contbr. chpt. to book. Mem. adv. bd. Md. State Senator Ida Mae Garrott, 1978-88; radio reader Washington Ear, 1981-86; bd. dirs. Jewish Found. for Group Homes, 1997-98; mem. edn. staff Temple Sinai, 1963—. Union Am. Hebrew Congregations fellow, 1970. Mem. TESOL. Avocations: gourmet cooking, choir, literary group, writing. Home: Silver Spring, Md. Died Aug. 12, 2008.

GOLDSTEIN, MANFRED, retired management consultant; b. Vienna, Jan. 30, 1927; arrived in US, 1939, naturalized, 1945; s. Isidore and Anna (Hahn) G.; m. Shirley Marie Lavine, Aug. 27, 1950 (dec. Feb. 2001); children: Cindy Marie, Lynn Alyse; m. Rhonda J. Demarsh, Mar. 23, 2005 Student, Manhattan Trade Ctr., 1947; E.E., Capitol Radio Engring. Inst., 1963; student, L.I. U., 1961, Indsl. Coll. Armed Forces, 1967-68; postgrad., SUNY at Delhi, 2003. Sr. technician Bklyn. Radio, 1953-55, Budd Stanley, Inc., Long Island City, N.Y., 1955; lead engr. telephone equipment Precision Indsl. Design Newark, 1955-57; project engr., contract adminstr., sales mgr. Leico, Inc., Syossett, NY, 1957-65, v.p., 1964-65; mgmt. and engring. cons., 1965-91; ret. Pres. Positive Cons. Inc., Bellmore, N.Y., 1967-86, Lake Luzerne, N.Y., 1986-91, 95—; owner Lake Luzerne Seaplane Base, 1969-2005; tchr. intermediate computer courses Hadley-Luzerne Pub. Libr., Lake Luzerne, 2003—. Mem. small bus. adv. com. to Congressman Thomas J. Downey, 1977-91; mem. small bus. adv. council L.I. Assn. Commerce; founder NCMA L.I. Scholarship Fund; pilot Civil Air Patrol, 1968-74; mem. Town of Lake Luzerne Zoning Bd. of Appeals, 2002-07. Served with AUS. Fellow Nat. Contract Mgmt. Assn. (bd. dirs. L.I. chpt., v.p. 1983-85); mem. IEEE (sr.), Soc. Plastics Engrs., Am. Indsl. Preparedness Assn. (exec. bd. mgmt. div.), ABA (assoc.), Air Force Assn., Capitol Radio Engring. Inst. Alumni (sr.), Nat. Pilots Assn., Aircraft Owners and Pilots Assn., Internat. Platform Assn., Am. Legion, VFW. Inventor torpedo fire control cable and connector for Polaris, high pressure seals for Polaris submarine antennae. Home: Lake Luzerne, NY. Died Sept. 16, 2009.

GOLDSTEIN, WALTER CARL, retired physician; b. NYC, Jan. 23, 1927; s. Charles and Sadie (Fink) G.; m. Eleanore Monica Bugler, May 16, 1959; 1 child, Charles. BS, George Washington U., 1951; MD, U. Chgo., 1955. Diplomate Am. Bd. Internal Medicine, Nat. Bd. Med. Examiners. Intern Phila. Gen. Hosp., 1955-56; resident in internal medicine Cook County Hosp., 1956-58; sr. resident in internal medicine Bklyn. VA Med. Ctr., 1958-59; resident in internal medicine Cook County Hosp., 1956-58; sr. resident Bklyn. VA Hosp., 1958-59; resident in pathology Univ. Hosp., Balt., 1959-60; staff internist Lebanon VA Hosp., Pa., 1967-75; chief med. svc., clin. asst. prof. Wilkes-Barre VA Hosp., Hahnemann Med. Sch., Pa., 1976-87; internist Medigroup Ctr., Trenton, NJ, 1987-90; physician, med. dir. Interstate Blood and Plasma Ctr., Phila., from 1991. Fellow: ACP. Home: Yardley, Pa. Died Feb. 28, 2008.

GOLLOBIN, IRA, lawyer; b. Newark, July 18, 1911; s. Harry and Clara (Abeles) G.; m. Esther Adler, Jan. 16, 1943 (dec. Dec. 1981); children: Ruth Basta, Jeana Beker; m. Ruth Baharas, June 16, 1994. LLB, Fordham U., 1933. Bar: N.Y. 1935, U.S. Ct. Appeals (2d, 3d, 5th cirs.). Pvt. practice Law Offices of Ira Gollobin, NYC, from 1935; atty probono Amer. Com. for Protection Fgn. Born, NYC, 1936-82, League of Amer. Writers, NYC, 1937-40, Nat. Coun. Chs., NYC, 1973-85. Contbr. articles to profl. jours., 1975, 88, 91. Host radio program on immigration policy issues WLIB, N.Y.C., 1976-79; Chair legal com. Nat. Coalition for Haitian Refugees, 1983—. Staff sgt. U.S. Army, 1942-46, New Guinea, Philippines. Recipient Jack Wasserman Meml. award Amer. Immigration Lawyers Assn., Phila., 1987, Rudy Lozano Meml. award Nat. Network for Immigrant and Refugee Rights, Chgo., 1988. Home: New York, NY. Died Apr. 4, 2008.

GONZALES, JOHN EDMOND, history professor; b. New Orleans, Sept. 17, 1924; s. Joseph Edmond and Sadie Julia (Albritton) G. BS, La. State U., 1943, MA, 1945; PhD, U. N.C., 1957. Mem. faculty U. So. Miss., Hattiesburg, 1945-95, William D. McCain prof. history, 1968-95, Disting. Univ. prof., 1973-95, prof. emeritus Hattiesburg, from 1995. Editor: Jour. of Miss. History, 1963-92, A Mississippi Reader, Hattiesburg: A Pictorial History; asso. editor: A History of Mississippi, 1973; contbr. to: Readers Ency. of the Am. West; contbr. articles to profl. jours. Bd. dirs. Univ. Press of Miss., 1970-89. Named Outstanding Faculty Mem. Kappa Sigma, 1968 Mem. So., La. hist. assns., Miss. Hist. Soc. (pres. 1975-76), Omicron Delta Kappa, Phi Kappa Phi (pres. chpt.), Kappa Phi Kappa, Kappa Delta Pi, Pi Gamma Mu, Phi Alpha Theta, Mu Phi Epsilon, Alpha Psi Omega Democrat. Baptist. Died Aug. 27, 2005.

GONZALEZ, CECILIA H., lawyer; b. Caracas, Venezuela, Sept. 18, 1955; d. Rene Gonzalez and Cecilia (Horwitz); m. Stephen M. Foster. BA, McGill U., 1976; JD, Georgetown U., 1979. Bar: DC 1980. Ptnr. Plaia & Schaumberg, Howrey LLP, Washington, 1986—2009, co-chair intellectual property practice grp., mem. exec. bd., co-chair intellectual property group, mem. intellectual property practice group mgmt. team, co-chair bus. affairs com., mng. ptnr. practice devel. Named one of 15 of DC Area's Top IP Attorneys, Legal Times, 2003, The 50 Most Influential Women Lawyers in America, Nat. Law Jour., 2007, 2008, The 50 Most Influential Minority Lawyers in America, 2008. Mem.: US Internat. Trade Commn. Trial Lawyers Assn., Minority Corp. Counsel Assn., Hispanic Bar Assn., Am. Intellectual Property Law Assn., ABA, DC Bar Assn. Died May 4, 2009.

GOOD, ESTELLE M., minister; b. Charleston, SC, Oct. 5, 1927; d. John Wesley and Minnie Estelle Hilton; divorced; children: Raymond L., Lee Good Sanders. BTh, Clarksville Sch. Theology, 1972, ThM, 1975, ThD, 1976, ThD, 1978, B in Sacred Music, 1980; PhD of Christian Psychology, Cornerstone U., 1992. Ordained to preach 1955; cert. hypnotherapist Internat. Assn. Counselors and Therapists, 1994. Organizer, pastor Covenant Life Cathedral, Macon, Ga., from 1962. Pres. Lighthouse Bible Tng. Ctr., 1976—88. Fellow: Nat. Christian Counselors Assn. (diplomate 1993, lic. temperament therapist 1991, Christian counselor and therapist 1992); mem.: Women Preachers Coun. Am., Full Gospel Fellowship of Churches and Ministers Internat. Home: Macon, Ga. Died Nov. 2008.

GOOD, IRVING JOHN, statistician, philosopher, educator; b. London, Dec. 9, 1916; arrived in US, 1967; s. Morris Edward and Sophia (Polikoff) Good. ScD, Cambridge U., Eng., 1963; DSc, Oxford U., Eng., 1964. Sci. officer Fgn. Office, Bletchley, England, 1941—45; lectr. math. and electronic computing Manchester (Eng.) U., 1945—48; sr. prin. sci. officer Govt. Comm. Hdqrs., Cheltenham, England, 1948—59; spl. merit dep. chief sci. officer Admiralty Rsch. Lab., Teddington, England, 1959—62; sr. rsch. fellow Trinity Coll., Oxford U. and Atlas Computer Lab., Didcot, England, 1964—67; Univ. disting. prof. stats, adj. prof. philosophy Va. Poly. Inst. and State U., Blacksburg, 1967—2009. Adj. prof. Ctr. Study of Sci. in Society; mem. comm. theory com. Ministry Supply, London, 1953-56; mem. comm. com. electronics rsch. com. Ministry Aviation, London, 1960-62; mem. rsch. sect. com. Royal Statis. Soc., London, 1965-67. Author: Probability and the Weighing of Evidence, 1950, The Estimation of Probabilities, 1965,

Good Thinking, 1983; co-author (with Donald Michie and Geoffrey Timms): General Report on Tunny with Emphasis on Statistical Methods, 1945; co-author: (with David B. Osteyee) Information, Weight of Evidence, the Singularity between Probability Measures and Signal Detection, 1974; gen. editor: The Scientist Speculates, 1962, (also French and German translations); contbr. chapters to books, over one thousand articles to profl. jours. Recipient Smith's prize, Cambridge, Eng., 1940, Internat. Order of Merit, 1993, Congl. medal of excellence, 2004; grantee NIH, 1970—89. Fellow Royal Stats. Soc. (hon.), Am. Acad. Arts and Scis., Va. Acad. Scis., Inst. Math. Stats., Am. Statis. Assn.; mem. IEEE Computer Soc. (Pioneer award 1998), Internat. Statis. Inst. (hon.). Home: Blacksburg, Va. Died Apr. 5, 2009.

GOOD, STEVEN LOREN, real estate consultant; b. Tokyo, Nov. 16, 1956; came to U.S., 1957; s. Sheldon F. and Lois (Kroll) G. Student, Oxford U., 1975; BS in Fin., Syracuse U., 1978; JD, DePaul U., 1981; LHD (hon.), Robert Morris Coll., Chgo., 1998. Bar: Ill. 1981, U.S. Dist. Ct. (no. dist.) Ill. 1982, Fla. 1983, U.S. Ct. Appeals (7th cir.) 1983, U.S. Supreme Ct. 2006. Assoc. Sheldon Good & Co., Internat., Chgo., 1978-82; v.p., gen. counsel Sheldon Good & Co., Chgo., 1982-87, pres., 1987—2000, chmn., CEO, 2001—09. Instr. FDIC, Washington, 1985, Mo. Auction Sch., Kansas City, 1981-97, Reppert's Sch. Auctioneering, 1998-; bd. dirs. Real Estate Ctr., Kelly Sch. Bus., Ind. U., Sch. Bus. Adminstrn, Citadel Mil. Coll., Ohn Marshall Law Sch.; lectr., spkr. in field. Author: Churches, Jails, and Gold Mines: Mega-Deals from a Real Estate Maverick, 2003; columnist: Auction World mag., from 2004; contbr. articles. Mem. men's coun. Mus. Contemporary Art, Chgo., 1985-91; vice chmn. real estate divsn. Jewish United Fund, Chgo., 1986, 88, 91; bd. dirs. United Cerebral Palsy, Chgo., 1987-97, chmn. Chgo. telethone, 1996; trustee Robert Morris Coll., Chgo., 1991-96; assoc. trustee U. Chgo. Cancer Rsch. Found., 1989-93, chmn. dean's coun., 1997-2000. Recipient Alumni Service Award for Outstanding Service to the Business Community, DePaul U. Coll. Law, 2001, Infinitec Corporate Leadership award, United Cerebral Palsy Assn., Community Svc. award, Easter Seals, 2003. Mem. ABA, Ill. Bar Assn., Fla. Bar Assn., Chgo. Bar Assn., Nat. Assn. Realtors (dir., chmn. Real Estate Auction Forum, 2004), Ill. Assn. of Realtors (dir. from 2000), Chgo. Assn. Realtors (pres. 2003-2004, instr. from 1981, Realtor of Yr. 2005), Young Pres. Orgn., Standard Club, Lamda Alpha. Avocations: tennis, skiing, shooting skeet, music, theater. Died Jan. 5, 2009.

GOODSTEIN, SANDERS ABRAHAM, scrap iron company executive; b. NYC, Oct. 3, 1918; s. Samuel G. and Katie (Lipson) G.; m. Rose Laro, June 28, 1942; children: Peter, Esther, Jack, Rachel. Student, Wayne State U., 1934-36; AB, U. Mich., 1938, MBA, 1939, JD, 1946; postgrad., Harvard, 1943. Bar: Mich., 1946. Sec. Laro Coal & Iron Co., Flint, Mich., 1946-60, pres., from 1960; owner, operator Paterson Mfg. Co., Flint, 1953-94. Gen. ptnr. Indianhead Co., Pontiac, Mich., 1955-70, pres., 1965-70; sec. Amatac Corp., Erie, Pa., unitl 1969; chmn. bd. Gen. Foundry & Mfg. Co., Flint, 1968—, pres., 1970-92; pres. Lacron Steel Co., Providence, 1975-80, ETL Corp., Flint, 1983-91, Can. Blending and Processing, Windsor, 1988-97; mem. corp. body Mich. Blue Shield, 1970-76. Served to lt. comdr. USNR, 1942-46. Mem. ABA, Fed. Bar Assn., Bar Mich., Am. Pub. Works Assn., Am. Foundrymen's Soc., Order of Coif, Beta Gamma Sigma, Phi Kappa Phi. Jewish. Home: Flint, Mich. Died Aug. 28, 2007.

GORDON, ALBERT HAMILTON, retired investment banker; b. Scituate, Mass., July 21, 1901; s. Albert Franklin and Sarah V. (Flanagan) G.; m. Mary F. Rousmaniere, Oct. 5, 1935 (dec. 1980); children: Albert F., Mary Gordon Roberts, Sarah F., John R., Daniel F. AB, Harvard U., 1923, MBA, 1925, LLD (hon.), 1977, St. Anselm Coll., 1974; grad. hon., Winchester Coll., Eng. Statistician Goldman Sachs & Co., 1925-31; ptnr. Kidder, Peabody & Co., Inc., NYC, 1931-86, also chmn.; hon. chmn. Kidder, Peabody Group Inc., 1986-95; adv. dir. Paine Webber Inc., NYC, from 1995. Bd. dirs. Allen Group, Inc., Deltec Internat. S.A. Trustee, chmn. Roxbury Latin Sch., Chapin Sch.; bd. overseers, bd. mgrs. Meml. Sloan-Kettering Cancer Ctr.; bd. dirs. Richard Nixon Libr. and Birthplace. Mem. Coun. on Fgn. Rels., Americas Soc. (bd. dirs.), The Trollope Soc. (chmn.). Clubs: Links (N.Y.C.), N.Y. Road Runners (bd. dirs.), Harvard (N.Y.C.); Somerset (Boston); Piping Rock (Locust Valley, N.Y.). Republican. Home: New York, NY. Died May 1, 2009.

GORDON, EZRA, architect, educator; b. Detroit, Apr. 5, 1921; s. Abraham and Rebecca (Reimer) G.; m. Jeanette Greenberg, Oct. 8, 1942 (dec. 2008); children: Cheryl P. Gordon Van Ausdal, Rana Gordon Oremland, Judith Gordon Eichhorn. Student, Roosevelt Coll., Chgo., 1946-48; BS in Architecture, U. Ill., Champaign-Urbana, 1951. Draftsman Pace Assos. Architects, 1951-53, sr. planner Chgo. Plan Commn., 1953-54; project architect Harry Weese & Assos., 1954-61; ptnr. Gordon-Levin & Assocs., Chgo., 1961-84, Gordon & Levin, Inc., Chgo., 1984-95; cons. Dept. Urban Renewal City Chgo., Council for Jewish Elderly, Chgo. Jewish Fedn. Prof. emeritus U. Ill.-Chgo. Sch. Architecture; former mem. Mayor's Adv. Coun. on Bldg. Code Amendments; master juror Nat. Coun. Archtl. Registration Bds. Works include Long-Kogan Office Bldg., 1957, 5401 Hyde Park Apt. Bldg., Chgo., 1962, South Commons, Chgo., 1968, The Commons Townhouse Devel., Chgo., 1968, Hyde Park West Apts., Chgo., 1969, IBM Office bldgs., Kalamazoo, 1969, Moline, Ill. 1970, Jefferson City, Mo., Omaha, 1971, Eastwood Tower Apts., Chgo., 1970, Wexler Pavilion and Siegel Inst., Hearing & Speech Clinic, Michael Reese Hosp., Chgo., 1992, U. Chgo. Stats. Lab.-Design & Constrn., 1970, Cardiac Intensive Care Unit and Tumor Clinic, 1971, Michael Reese Hosp., Chgo., 1971, Arbor Trails Apts. and Townhouses, Park Forest, Ill., 1972, Kenmore Plaza Apts. Sr. Housing, Chgo., 1972, Kennaly Sq. Warehouse Apts., Chgo., 1972-74, Pontiac Office Bldg., Mich., 1972, Concourse Office Towers, Skokie, 1972, Belle Plaine Apts., Chgo., 1972, Stats. Lab, U. Chgo., 1972, Newberry Plaza Apts., Chgo., 1973, Greenwood Park Apts., Chgo., 1974, River Plaza Apts., Chgo., 1976, Elm St. Plaza Apts., Chgo., 1976, Dearborn Park, Twin Tower Apts., Chgo., 1979, Huron Plaza Apt., Chgo., 1981, 400 E. Ohio Condominiums, Streeterville, Chgo., 1983, East Bank Club, Chgo., 1983, U. (Champaign) Ill. Speech and Hearing Clinic, 1985, Dearborn-Elm Apts., Chgo., 1986-87; designer World Trade Ctr. Apts., Chgo., 1989, Lachman Montisorri Sch. for Hearing Impaired Children, Deerfield, Ill., 1990, Elm Street Apts., 1990, restoration of 1130 S. Michigan Ave., 1991, Chgo. Montessori Sch. for the Hearing Impaired, 1991, Love residence addition, Glencoe, Ill., 1991, Periodontist offices, Skokie, Ill., 1991, Oral Rehab. Ctr., Skokie, 1992, residence addition, Glencoe, 1998. Former bd. dirs. Hyde Park-Kenwood Cmty. Conf., Chgo., Astor St.-Lake Shore Dr. Assocs., Chgo.; former v.p. Harper Ct. Found., Chgo.; mem. Art Inst. Chgo., Mus. Sci. and Industry, Spertus Mus., Mus. Contemporary Art, Chgo. Hist. Soc.; mem. Landmarks Preservation Coun., Chgo. Archtl. Found.; former v.p. bd. dirs. 1300 Lake Shore Drive Condo Assn., Chgo. Decorated Croix de Guerre with palm; recipient Honor award Dept. Housing and Urban Devel., 1967, Honor award AIA-Chgo. C. of C., 1967, award AIA-House & Home Mag., 1967, Distinguished Bldg. award AIA, 1957, 63, 69, 71, 73, 75, award City of Chgo. Beautification, 1969, 75, award of excellence Concrete Post Tensioning Inst., 1984, Silver Circle award for excellence in teaching U. Ill., Chgo., 1985. Fellow AIA (former mem. bd. dirs Chgo. chpt.); mem. AIA, Peace Now, Am. Jewish Congress, Chgo. Archtl. Found., Lambda Alpha. Clubs: Cliff Dwellers. Jewish. Home: Chicago, Ill. Died June 28, 2009.

GORDON, MICHAEL MACKIN, lawyer; b. Boston, Apr. 15, 1950; s. Lawrence H. and Gladys (Mackin) G.; m. Linda Lowry, June 8, 1991; children: Alexandra, Harrison. AB, Vassar Coll., 1972; JD, Columbia U., 1976. Bar: N.Y. 1977, U.S. Dist. Ct. (so. and ea. dists. N.Y. 1977), D.C. 1980, U.S. Ct. Appeals (2d cir.) 1985, U.S. Supreme Ct. 1985, U.S. Claims Ct. 1991, U.S. Ct. Appeals (3d cir.), 1992, U.S. Dist. Ct. (no. dist.), Tex. 1993, U.S. Ct. Appeals (5th cir.) 1995, U.S. Dist. Ct. (ea. dist.) Tex. 1996, U.S. Dist. Ct. (no. dist. N.Y.) 1999, U.S. Ct. Appeals (8th cir.) 2008. Assoc. Seward & Kissel, NYC, 1977-79, Cadwalader, Wickersham & Taft, NYC, 1979-85, ptnr., 1985—2005, King & Spalding, LLP, NYC, 2005—07, McKee Nelson LLP, NYC, 2007—09. Mem.: ABA, N.Y. State Bar Assn., N.Y. County Lawyers Assn., Vassar (N.Y.C.). Home: New York, NY. Died Mar. 5, 2009.

GORDON, PAUL GENE, consulting chemist; b. Denver, Oct. 2, 1928; s. Morris Charles and Anna (Katz) G.; m. Beverly Olken, June 12, 1951; children: Bradley Malcolm, Shana Mendel. BS, U. Denver, 1950; MS, U. Ill., 1951, PhD, 1954. Chief chemist Chem. Sales Co., Denver, 1954-55, mgr. customer service, 1955-59, mgr. purchasing, 1959-61, mgr. chem. div., 1961-67, gen. mgr., 1967-78, pres., chief exec. officer, 1978-84; pres. Chem. Cons. Inc., Englewood, Colo., from 1985. Mem. Am. Chem. Soc. (employment chmn. 1984-87), Colo. Chem. Club (pres.), The Expert Witness Network, Sigma Xi, Phi Lambda Upsilon, Phi Sigma Delta (chpt. pres. 1948-49). Avocations: photography, war memorabilia, stamps, coins, walking. Died Aug. 2, 2008.

GORDON, PAUL JOHN, management educator; b. NYC, Oct. 14, 1921; s. Arthur L. and Georgiana (McDonough) G.; m. Mary Brigid Keany, Jan. 28, 1950; children: Brian Joseph, Peter Christopher, Martha Ann, Hugh John, Paul John. BBA, CCNY, 1945; MBA, Cornell U., 1949; PhD, Syracuse U., 1958. With Brooks Bros., NYC, 1941-43, Lago Oil & Transp. Co., Ltd., Netherlands W. Indies, also Bayway Refinery, Linden, N.J. and Standard Oil Co. N.J., 1943-48; asst. prof. Cornell U., Ithaca, NY, 1949-54; prof., chmn. dept. mgmt. Sch. Bus. Duquesne U., Pitts., 1954-55; rsch. cons. Sloan-Kettering Meml. Ctr. for Cancer, NYC, 1955-56; assoc. prof. bus. adminstrn., planning dir. grad. program hosp. adminstrn. Sch. Bus. Adminstrn. Emory U., Atlanta, 1956—59; assoc. prof. Grad. Sch. Bus. Ind. U., 1959-63, prof., chmn. dept. mgmt. adminstrv. studies Grad. Sch. Bus., 1963-67, prof. mgmt. Grad. Sch. Bus., 1963-89, chmn. adminstrv. and behavioral studies Grad. Sch. Bus., 1980-83, prof. emeritus mgmt. Grad. Sch. Bus., 1989—2009; disting. prof. mgmt. St. John's U., NYC, 1990-93. Fulbright/FLAD chair in strategic mgmt. Tech. U. Lisbon, Portugal, 1997, chief U.S. Dept. State-Ford Found. party Ljubljana U., Yugoslavia, 1967; vis. prof. Trinity Coll., Dublin, 1967; vis. prof., Fulbright lectr. Instituto Post-Universitario Per Lo Studio Dell Organizzazione Aziendale, Turin, Italy, 1963; Fulbright lectr., cons. Nat. U. Republic Uruguay, 1970; disting. guest Systems Rsch. Inst., Polish Acad. Scis., 1980; vis. Fulbright prof. Helsinki Sch. Econs. and Bus. Adminstrn., Finland, 1990; mem. U.S. AID Mgmt. Edn. Reconnaissance Survey, India, also Pakistan, 1971; cons. IRS, 1956-63, Am. Coll. Hosp. Adminstrs., 1957—; with Inst. Higher Studies of Adminstrn., Caracas, Venezuela, 1973-79. Editor Acad. Mgmt. Jour, 1964-66, mem. editorial bd., 1961-75; editorial cons. adv. bd.: Bus. Horizons, Hosp. Adminstrn, W.B. Saunders Co.; contbr. articles to profl. jours. Mem. Cath. Commn. on Intellectual and Cultural Affairs, 1973-2009, chmn., 1980-81; chmn. UNESCO multi-nat. bus. conf. Ind. U., 1972; chmn. adv. screening com. in bus. mgmt. Coun. for Internat. Exch. of Scholars, Fulbright-Hays Program, 1979-80, 90-93, chmn., 1991-93; bd. dirs. Ind. Newman Found., 1971-82; mem. adv. bd. Abbey Press, St. Meinrad, Ind., 1991-95. Grantee, Ford Found., 1963, 1966, 1970; fellow, IBM, 1964. Fellow Acad. Mgmt. (v.p. program 1967, pres. 1969, Disting. Svc. award 1992), Internat. Acad. Mgmt., Am. Acad. Med. Adminstrs. (hon.); mem. Fulbright Assn. (life). Home: Bloomington, Ind. Died Jan. 5, 2009.

GORELICK, KENNETH PAUL, psychiatrist; b. Paterson, NJ, Apr. 16, 1942; s. Irving and Sylvia (Glassman) Gorelick; m. Linda Eisenberg (div.); m. Cheryl Opacinch. BA, Rutgers U., 1962; MD, Harvard U., 1967. Diplomate Am. Bd. Psychiatry and Neurology. Intern Mt. Zion Hosp. and Med. Ctr., San Francisco, 1967-68; resident in psychiatry Mass. Mental Health Ctr., Boston, 1968-71; asst. surgeon USPHS St. Elizabeth's Hosp., Washington, 1971-73, tng. officer, psychiatry, 1973-79, chief continuing med. edn., 1979-87, DC Commn. on Mental Health Svcs., Washington, 1987-99. Assoc. clin. prof. psychiatry, behavioral sci. George Washington U., Washington, 1987—2009; tchr. poetry therapy Cath. U. of America, Lesley Coll., Cambridge, Mass.; co-dir. Wordsworth Ctr. for Poetry Therapy, Nat. Assn. for Poetry, 1994—2007. Contbg. editor Jour. Poetry Therapy, 1987; mem. editorial bd. Jour. Arts in Psychotherapy, 1987-2009. Fellow Am. Psychiat. Assn.; mem. Washington Psychiat. Soc. (coun. mem. D.C. chpt. 1985-86), Nat. Assn. for Poetry Therapy (pres. 1987-89, 89-91). Died June 9, 2009.

GORMAN, STEVEN, health insurance executive; b. LA, Sept. 9, 1945; 1 child, Brian. Student, Beverly Coll., Woodbury Coll. Pres., ceo Alt. Health Ins. Svcs., Inc., Thousand Oaks, Calif., from 1985. Pres., ceo Alliance for Alternatives in Healthcare, Inc., Thousand Oaks, 1990—. Died Feb. 2, 2008.

GORTON, CYNTHIA RUTH, counselor; b. Williston, ND, Oct. 5, 1951; d. George Frank and Ruth (Gilbert) Hapip; m. James Sheldon Gorton, Aug. 19, 1972; children: Victoria Kathryn, Deborah Elizabeth. BEd, U. No. Colo., 1972, BA in EArly Childhood Edn.; M in Counseling, Ariz. State U., 1988, PhD, 1992. Campus min. Campus Crusade for Christ, San Bernadino, Calif., 1972-78; pvt. music tchr. Rowley, Mass., 1980-83; substitute tchr. Pine Grove Elem. Sch., Rowley, 1983-84, Scottsdale (Ariz.) Sch. Dist., 1985-87; counselor, cons. Ctr. for Counseling and Cons., Scottsdale, from 1988. Program dir. Ariz. State U., Tempe, 1987-90, adj. prof., 1990—, grant coord. residence life, 1988-89. Host family Lang. Exch. Inst., Belmont, Mass., 1990; active Scottsdale Bible Ch. Counseling Task Force, 1990—. Ariz. Dept. Health Svcs. grantee, 1988-89; named one of Outstanding Young Women Am., 1988, 90. Mem. Am. Assn. for Counseling and Devel., Am. Psychol. Assn., Am. Coll. Personnel Assn., Ariz. Coll. Personnel Assn. (bd. dirs. 1990—), Ariz. Rsch. Counsel. Republican. Mem. Christian Ch. Avocations: cross country skiing, alpine skiing. Home: Scottsdale, Ariz. Died June 29, 2008.

GOSSARD, EARL EVERETT, physicist; b. Eureka, Calif., Jan. 8, 1923; s. Ralph Dawson and Winifred (Hill) G.; m. Sophia Poignand, Nov. 21, 1948; children: Linda Margaret, Kenneth Earl, Diane Winifred. BA, UCLA, 1948; MS, U. Calif., San Diego, 1951; PhD in Phys. Oceanography, Scripps Instn. Oceanography, 1956. Meteorologist Navy Electronics Lab., San Diego, 1949-55, head radio meteorol. sect., 1955-61; head radio physics div. Navy Electronics Lab. (name now Naval Ocean Systems Ctr.), San Diego, 1961-71; chief geoacoustics program Wave Propagation Lab., NOAA, Boulder, Colo., 1971-73, chief meteorol. radar program, 1973-82; sr. rsch. assoc. Coop. Inst. for Rsch. in Environ. Scis. U. Colo., Boulder, 1982-98; sr. rsch. assoc. Sci. and Tech. Corp., Colorado Springs, Colo., 1998-99; emeritus sr. scientist Environment Rsch. Lab. of NOAA. Co-author: (with Hooke) Waves in the Atmosphere (Disting. Authorship award Dept. Commerce 1975), 1973; (with Strauch) Radar Observation of Clear Air and Clouds (Disting. Authorship award Dept. Commerce 1985); editor: Radar Observation of the Clear Air, 1980; contbr. over 74 articles to profl. jours. 1st lt. USAAF, 1943-46, CBI. Recipient Silver medal Dept. Commerce, 1976, Citation Am. Geophys. Union, 1986. Fellow Am. Meteorol. Soc.; mem. Nat. Acad. Engrs., Internat. Union Radio Sci. (past chmn. U.S. Commn. F.). Republican. Presbyterian. Home: Fortuna, Calif. Deceased.

GOSSICK, LEE VAN, rental company executive, consultant, retired military officer; b. Meadville, Mo., Jan. 23, 1920; s. Clark and Myrtle (Staats) G.; m. Ruth Matter, Apr. 25, 1942; children: Roger V., Cynthia L. BS in Aero. Engring, Ohio State U., 1951, MS, 1951; grad., Air War Coll., 1959, Advanced Mgmt. Program, Harvard, 1961. Aviation cadet, 1941-42; commd. 2d lt. USAAF, 1942; advanced through grades to maj. gen. USAF, 1968; fighter pilot (87th Fighter Squadron), North Africa, 1942- 43; various R & D posts, 1951-64; comdr. Arnold Engring. Devel. Center, 1964-67; dep. for F-111 Aero. Systems div., Wright-Patterson AFB, Ohio, 1967-68; vice comdr. Aero. Systems Div., 1968-69, comdr., 1969-70; dep. chief staff systems Hdqrs. Air Force Systems Command, Andrews AFB, Md., 1970-71, chief of staff, 1971-73, ret., 1973; asst. dir. regulation AEC, Washington, 1973-74; exec. dir. ops.

Nuclear Regulatory Commn., Washington, 1975-79; v.p., dep. gen. mgr. Sverdrup Tech. Inc., Tullahoma, Tenn., 1980-89. Decorated D.S.M. with oak leaf cluster; Legion of Merit with oak leaf cluster; D.F.C.; Air medal with 9 oak leaf clusters; named Distinguished Alumnus Ohio State U., 1960, Centennial Achievement award, 1970; recipient Vandenberg trophy Arnold Air Soc., 1967, Distinguished Service award AEC, 1974; named to Tenn. Aviation Hall of Fame, 2004. Fellow AIAA, Arnold Engring. Devel. Ctr. Died Apr. 12, 2005.

GOSTIN, IRWIN, retired lawyer; b. NYC, July 22, 1927; s. Herman and Vera (Ostrinsky) G.; m. Ruth Koenig (div. 1963); children: Theodore David, Leslie Ann Gostin Sikes, Deborah Lynn Gostin; m. Margit Nellaway (div. 1984); m. Mary L. Dekker, Jan. 27, 1990. AB, UCLA, 1948; LLB, Harvard U., 1951, JD, 1967. Bar: Calif. 1952, U.S. Dist. Ct. (cen. dist.) Calif. 1952, U.S. Ct. Appeals (9th cir.) 1952, U.S. Dist. Ct. (so. dist.) Calif. 1957. Pvt. practice, LA, 1952-56; ptnr. Gostin & Katz, San Diego, 1957-70; pres. Gostin & Katz Inc., San Diego, 1971-78, Irwin Gostin, APL, San Diego, 1979-94; admin. sec. Nat. Lawyer's Guild, LA, 1953—56. Mem. legal panel, chmn. ACLU, San Diego, 1958-67, pres., 1968, San Diego Children's Home Soc., 1967; sec.-treas. Breeden-Schmidt Found., 1991—2007. With US Army, 1945—46. Mem. San Diego County Bar Assn., Assn. Trial Lawyers Am., Calf. Trial Lawyers Assn., San Diego Trial Lawyers Assn. (pres. 1969). Avocation: thoroughbred horse racing. Home: Las Vegas, Nev. Died Mar. 20, 2008.

GOTTLIEB, DAVID, mathematics professor; BSc, MSc, Tel-Aviv U., PhD in Applied Math., 1972. Instr., lectr. dept. applied math. MIT, Cambridge, 1972—75; assoc. mem. ICASE NASA Langley Rsch. Ctr., Hampton, Va., 1974—98, rsch. scientist ICASE, 1975—76; sr. lectr. dept. applied math. Tel-Aviv U., 1976—77, assoc. prof., 1978—82, prof., 1982—86, chmn., 1983—85; prof. divsn. applied math. Brown U., Providence, 1985—2008, Ford Found. prof., 1993—2008, chair, 1996—99. Contbr. articles to sci. jours.; co-author (with S. Orszag): Numerical Analysis of Spectral Methods/Theory and Applications, 1977; co-author: (with J. Hesthaven and S. Gottlieb) Spectral Methods for Time Dependent Problems, 2006. Fellow: Am. Acad. Arts and Sciences; mem.: NAS, Am. Math. Soc., Math. Assn. America. Died Dec. 6, 2008.

GOTTLIEB, JULIUS JUDAH, retired podiatrist; b. Jersey City, May 27, 1919; s. Joseph Uziel and Gussie (Farber) G.; m. Charlotte Papernik, Oct. 18, 1942; children: Sheldon, Cynthia, Lorinda, David, Jonathan. Student, NYU, 1938-39, Ill. Coll. Podiatric Medicine, 1940-42; DPM, Ohio Coll. Podiatric Medicine, 1943. Diplomate Am. Podiatric Med. Specialties Bd. Pvt. practice podiatric medicine, Washington, 1943—92; pres. Chevy Chase Profl. Cons., 1993—96; ret., 1996. Past cons. Army Footwear Clinic. Co-inventor fiberglass foot prosthetics and plastic shoe lasts. Podiatry dir. Greater Washington Hebrew Home for the Aged, 1963; pres. Franklin Knolls Citizens Assn., 1963, Ridgefield Citizens Inc., 1994-96, 97-2003; chmn. com. Nat. Capital Area coun. Boy Scouts Am., 1969-73; pres. Active Retirees of Kehilat Shalom, 1996-98. Recipient Shofar award Boy Scouts Am. Fellow Acad. Ambulatory Foot Surgeons (region 8 sci. chmn. 1987-88); mem. Am. Podiatric Med. Assn. (life), Am. Pub. Health Assn., Am. Podiatric Circulatory Soc., Am. Bd. Foot Surgeons (founding diplomate), D.C. Podiatric Med. Soc. (past pres.), Am. Assn. Foot Specialists (past pres., Foot Specialist of the Yr. 1973), Am. Assn. Individual Investors, Am. Physicians Fellowship Inc. for Medicine in Israel, Columbia Heights Bus. Men's Assn. (past pres., Man of Yr. 1964), Parents Assn. U. Md. (co v.p. parents fund 1980-81, co-recipient Outstanding Svc. Award), B'nai B'rith. Republican. Jewish. Home: Darnestown, Md. Died Dec. 15, 2008.

GOTTLIEB, MORTON EDGAR, theatrical and film producer; b. Bklyn., May 2, 1921; s. Joseph William and Hilda (Newman) G. BA, Yale U., 1941. Asst. press rep. Theatre Inc., NYC, 1945, bus. mgr., 1946; gen. mgr. Cape Playhouse, Dennis, Mass., 1947-48, New Stages, NYC, 1947-48; mgr. to Robert Morley during Australian prodn., Theatre Royal, Sydney, 1949; gen. mgr. Gilbert Miller Prodns. and Henry Miller's Theatre, NYC, 1948-53. Guest lectr. Emerson Coll., Yale U., Columbia U., Northwestern U., Queens Coll., Harvard U., Wesleyan U. Singer charity show: Go Home and Tell Your Mother, Bklyn. Acad. Music, 1928; producer, Broadway, London shows, 1954-62; gen. mgr.: Sail Away, 1961, The Affair, 1962, The Hollow Crown, 1963; co-producer: (with Helen Bonfils) Enter Laughing, 1963, Chips With Everything, 1963, The White House, 1964, The Killing of Sister George, 1966, The Promise, 1967, Lovers, 1968, We Bombed in New Haven, 1968, The Mundy Scheme, 1969, Sleuth, 1970; producer: (films) Sleuth, 1972, Same Time Next Year, 1978, Romantic Comedy, 1982, (plays) Veronica's Room, 1973, Same Time Next Year, 1975, Tribute, 1978, Faith Healer, 1979, Romantic Comedy, 1979, Special Occasions, 1982, Dancing in the End Zone, 1985, Of Thee I Sing-Let 'Em Eat Cake, 1987, Bklyn. Acad. Music; contbr. articles to popular mags. Mem. League N.Y. Theatres. Clubs: Yale; Players. (N.Y.C.). Died June 25, 2009.

GOTTSCHALK, ALFRED, retired academic and museum administrator; b. Oberwesel, Germany, Mar. 7, 1930; came to U.S., 1939, naturalized, 1945; s. Max and Erna (Trum-Gerson) G.; m. Deanna Zeff, 1977; children by previous marriage: Marc Hillel, Rachel Lisa. AB, Bklyn. Coll., 1952; MA with honors, Hebrew Union Coll.-Jewish Inst. Religion, 1957; PhD, U. So. Calif., 1965, STD (hon.), 1968, LLD (hon.), 1976, U. Cin., 1976, Xavier U., 1981, Mt. St. Joseph Coll., 1995, No. Ky. U., 1996; DHL (hon.), U. Judaism, 1971, Jewish Theol. Sem., 1986, Bklyn. Coll., 1991, Trinity Coll., 1996; LittD (hon.), Dropsie U., 1974, St. Thomas Inst., 1982; D Religious Edn. (hon.), Loyola-Marymount U., 1977; DD (hon.), NYU, 1985. Ordained rabbi, 1957. Dir. Hebrew Union Coll., Jewish Inst. Religion, LA, 1957-59, dean, 1959-71, prof. Bible and Jewish intellectual history, from 1965, pres., 1971-95, chancellor, 1996—2000, chancellor emeritus, 2000—09, disting. prof. emeritus of Jewish Intellectual History, 1995—2009; pres. Mus. of Jewish Heritage, NYC, 1999—2001; sr. fellow Mus. Jewish Heritage, 2001—09. Hon. fellow Hebrew U., Jerusalem, 1972, Oxford Ctr. for Hebrew and Jewish Studies, 1994. Author: Your Future as a Rabbi-A Calling that Counts, 1967, (translator) Hesed in the Bible, 1967, The Man Must be the Message, 1968, Jewish Ecumenism and Jewish Survival, 1968, Ahad Ha-Am, Maimonides and Spinoza, 1969, Ahad Ha-Am as Bible Critic, 1971, A Jubilee of the Spirit, 1972, Israel and the Diaspora: A New Look, 1974, Limits of Ecumenicity, 1979, Israel and Reform Judaism: A Zionist Perspective, 1979, Ahad Ha-Am and Leopold Zunz: Two Perspectives on the Wissenschaft Des Judentums, 1980, Hebrew Union College and Its Impact on World Progressive Judaism, 1980, Diaspora Zionism: Achievements and Problems, 1980, What Ecumenism Means to a Jew, 1981, Introduction: Religion in a Post-Holocaust World, 1982, Problematics in the Future of American Jewish Community, 1982, Introduction to the American Synagogue in the Nineteenth Century, 1982, A Strategy for Non-Orthodox Judaism in Israel, 1982, (in Chinese) Ahad Ha-Am and the Jewish National Spirit, 1982, Our problems and Our Future: Jews and America, 1983, From the Kingdom of Night to the Kingdom of God: Jewish Christian Relations and the Search for Religious Authenticity after the Holocaust, 1983, The Making of a Contemporary Reform Rabbi, 1984, Is Yom Kippur Obsolete?, 1985, Ahad Ha-am: Confronting the Plight of Judaism, 1987, To Learn and To Teach, Your Future as a Rabbi, 1988, Preface to Gezer V: The Field I Caves, 1988, The American Reform Rabbinate Retrospect and Prospect, A Personal View, 1988, The German Pogrom of November 1938 and the Reaction of American Jewry, 1988, Building Unity in Diversity 1989, Ahad Ha'am and the Jewish National Spirit (Hebrew), 1992; contbr. to Studies in Jewish Bibliography, History, and Literature, 1971, The Yom Kippur War: Israel and the Jewish People, 1974, The Image of Man in Genesis and the Ancient Near East, 1976, The Public Function of the Jewish Scholar, 1978, The Reform Movement and Israel: A New Perspective, 1978, The Use of Reason in Maimonides--An Evaluation by Ahad Ha-Am, 1993, Reform Judaism of the New Millenium: A Challenge, 2001, Israel and America: Beyond Survival and Philanthropy, 2000, Life of Reason, Ahad Ha-Am and His Work, 2003; also numerous articles to profl. jours. Mem. Pres. Johnson's Com. on EEO, 1964-66, Gov.'s Poverty Support Corps Program, Calif., 1964-66, Pres.'s Commn. on Holocaust, 1979, U.S. Holocaust Meml. Coun., 1980-92, 96-01 (exec. com., 1980-87, 96-2009, chmn. edn. com., 1986-88, chmn. acad. com., 1988-96, com. on conscience, 1996-2009); chmn. N.Am. Assoc. Internat. Ctr. Univ. Teaching of Jewish Civilization, 1982-93, North Am. Assn. Oxford Ctr. Jewish Studies, 2004-09; bd. trustees Am. Sch. Oriental Rsch., Albright Inst. Archaeol. Rsch., 1972-95; sr. fellow Mus. of Jewish Heritage, N.Y.C., 2001-09; bd. govs. Oxford Ctr. for Hebrew and Jewish Studies, 1995—; bd. trustees Mus. Jewish Heritage, N.Y.C., 2001-09; exec. com. Nat. Underground Railroad Freedom Ctr., 1997-2000, Nat. Adv. Bd., Nat. Underground Freedom Ctr., 1996-2009; mem. coun. World Union Jewish Studies, 1997. Recipient award for contbns. to edn. L.A. City Coun., 1971, Human Relations award Am. Jewish Com., 1971, Tower of David award for cultural contbn. to Israel and Am., 1972, Gold medallion Jewish Nat. Fund, 1972, Alumnus of Yr. award Bklyn. Coll., 1972, Myrtle Wreath award Hadassah, 1977, Brandeis award Z.O.A., 1977, Nat. Brotherhood award NCCJ, 1979, Alfred Gottschalk Chair in Communal Svc. HUC, 1979, Jerusalem City of Peace award 1988, Defender of Jerusalem award honoree, 1990, Isaac M. Wise award, 1991, Heritage award Jewish Club of 1933, 1991, Nat. award NCCJ, 1994, Shanghai Acad. Social Scis. award, 1994, others, Xavier Medallion, Xavier U., 1996, Elie Wiesel Holocaust Rememerance award, State of Israel bonds, 2001; grantee State Dept./Smithsonian Instn., 1963, 67.; honoree Assn. Hebrew Union Coll., 1996; recipient Award Svc. to City, Cin. City Council, 2001. Mem. AAUP, NEA, Union Am. Hebrew Congregations and Ctrl. Conf. Am. Rabbis (exec. com., bd. govs. Hebrew Union Coll.), Soc. Study Religion, Am. Acad. Religion, Soc. Bibl. Lit. and Exegesis, Internat. Conf. Jewish Communal Svc., Israel Exploration Soc., So. Calif. Assn. Liberal Rabbis (past pres.), So. Calif. Jewish Hist. Soc. (hon. pres.), World Union Jewish Studies (internat. coun.), World Union Progressive Judaism (hon. life, gov. bd.), Coun. for Initiatives in Jewish Edn. (bd. dirs.), Phi Beta Kappa. Died Sept. 12, 2009.

GOTTSCHALK, LEONARD, actor, musician; b. NYC, Apr. 17, 1924; s. Milton and Rose (Greenberg) G.; m. Hilda Weiner; children: Michele, Melinda, Stacee. Student, Juilliard Sch. Music, 1947. Trumpetist Tommy Tucker Orch., NYC, 1946-47, George Towne Orch., NYC, 1948-50, Blue Barron Orch., NYC, 1950-52, Ted Huston Orch., NYC, 1952-53; salesman Leonard Hardware, Inc., Fair Lawn, N.J., 1954-59; builder, developer Arlen Constrn., Inc., Neptune, N.J., 1959-71; actor, mem. Prather Prodns., Inc., Lancaster, Pa., 1973-91. Served as cpl. U.S. Army, 1943-46, PTO. Avocations: collecting pre-1950 jazz and pop records, reading, movies. Home: Hazleton, Pa. Died Aug. 9, 2008.

GOUGH, EUGENE V., vocational education educator; b. Salt Lake City, Apr. 3, 1931; s. Frank and Veneda Carrie (Stewart) G.; m. Penny Diane Fry, Dec. 28, 1956; children: Liane, Loren Jay, Noel Dion. BA, San Jose State U., 1959; M of Indsl. Edn., Brigham Young U., 1979; postgrad., U. Utah, 1962-80. Cert. secondary edn. tchr., vocat. edn./drafting and carpentry, Utah, Calif. Tchr., dept. chmn. Mapusaga High Sch., Tutuila, Am. Samoa, 1959-62, Butte Valley High Sch., Dorris, Calif., 1962-64; tchr. Skyline High Sch., Salt Lake City, 1966-67, Bonneville Jr. High Sch., Salt Lake City, 1967-70; tchr., co-op edn. coord. Cottonwood High Sch., Salt Lake City, 1970-81; tchr., dept. chmn. Taylorsville High Sch., Salt Lake City, 1981-91. Dist. Boy Scout exec., Snake River Coun., Boy Scouts Am., Twin Falls, Idaho, 1962-64. Sgt. U.S. Army, 1953-55. Named Vocat. Tchr. of Yr., Granite Sch. Dist., Salt Lake City, 1987. Mem. NEA, Am. Vocat. Assn., Utah Edn. Assn., Granite Edn. Assn., Vocat. Indsl. Clubs of Am. (advisor 1970-91). Republican. Mem. Lds Ch. Avocations: woodworking, landscaping, gardening, fly fishing. Home: Salt Lake City, Utah. Died May 7, 2008.

GOULD, PHILLIP, engineer; b. NYC, Feb. 19, 1940; s. Isaac and Blanche Gould; m. Elizabeth West Ratigan, Nov. 29, 1980; children: David Elliot, Jessica Ann. BSME, CCNY, 1961; MS, MIT, 1963, ScD, 1965. Asst. prof. mech. engring. MIT, Cambridge, 1965-67; mem. staff Inst. Def. Analyses, Alexandria, Va., 1967—2008, sr. fellow, 2008—09. Dir. Def. Sci. Study Group, 1998—2009. Fellow, Ford Found., 1965. Fellow: AAAS; mem.: N.Y. Acad. Scis., Internat. Inst. Secular Humanistic Judaism (bd. mem.), Soc. for Humanistic Judaism (past pres.), Washington Congregation for Secular Humanistic Judaism (past pres.), Sigma Xi. Home: Washington, DC. Died Sept. 19, 2009.

GOUVERNET, GERARD RAOUL, language educator; b. Aigues Vives, Gard, Sept. 19, 1939; s. Raoul Marius Gouvernet and Andrée Rose Pinol; m. Suzanne d'Autremont Gouvernet, Mar. 30, 1968; 1 child, Philippe. PhD, Harvard U., 1978. Prof. dept. fgn. lang. SUNY, Geneseo, from 1982. Author: (book) Le Valet chez Molière et ses successeurs, 1985; co-author: Homage to Paul Benichou, 1994, Dictionnaire Analytique du Théâtre, 1998. Avocations: reading, tennis, Pétanque. Home: Rochester, NY. Died July 18, 2008.

GOVAN, GLADYS VERNITA MOSLEY, retired critical care nurse, medical/surgical nurse; b. Tyler, Tex., July 24, 1918; d. Stacy Thomas and Lucy Victoria (Whitmill) Mosley; m. Osby David Govan, July 20, 1938; children Orbrenett K. (Govan) Carter, Diana Lynn (Govan) Gray. Student, East Los Angeles Coll., Montebello, Calif., 1951; lic. vocat. nurse, Calif. Hosp. Med. Ctr., LA, 1953; cert., Western States IV Assn., LA, 1978. Lic. vocat. nurse, Calif.; cert. in EKG. Intravenous therapist Calif. Hosp. Med. Ctr., cardiac monitor, nurse; ret. Past pres. PTA, also hon. mem., 1963-2000; charter mem. Nat. Rep. Presdl. Task Force. Died Mar. 23, 2008.

GRABSTALD, HARRY, urologist, oncologist; b. Hope, Ark., Feb. 17, 1922; s. Meier and Bessie Grabstald; m. Herta Grabstald, July 14, 1979 (div.). BS, So. Meth. U., Dallas, 1942; MD, U. Tex. Southwestern Med. Coll., Dallas, 1945. Diplomate Am. Bd. Urology. Attending surgeon Meml. Hosp. Sloan- Kettering Cancer Ctr., NYC, 1958—80; prof. urology Coll. Medicine Cornell U., 1960—80. Author: History of Urology at Memorial Hospital, 1997; contbr. more than 175 papers to sci. jours. Comdr. USPHS, 1947—53. Fellow: ACS. Home: New York, NY. Died Sept. 30, 2007.

GRAF, ERVIN DONALD, municipal official; b. Crow Rock, Mont., Mar. 9, 1930; s. Emanuel and Lydia (Bitz) G.; m. Carolyn Sue Robinson, Mar. 15, 1956 (div. 1958); m. Eleanor Mahlein, Apr. 13, 1959 (dec. Oct. 1990); children: Debra, Belinda, Corrina, Melanie (dec.), Ervin Jr. (dec.). Enlisted U.S. Army, 1948; served two tours of duty in Vietnam; ret. U.S. Army, 1972; with office and maintenance staff Greenfields Irrigation Dist., Fairfield, Mont., 1972-77, sec. to Bd. Commrs., 1977-95; ret., 1995. Decorated Bronze star with oak leaf cluster. Mem. Am. Legion (all offices Post #80 and Dist. 8 incl. dist. comdr.). Democrat. Lutheran. Avocations: bowling, coin collecting/numismatics, fishing, camping. Home: Fairfield, Mont. Died Sept. 16, 2007.

GRAFMAN, DAYTON FOWLER, musical instrument executive, pianist; b. Chgo., Jan. 25, 1923; m. Laura Ruth Samuels, June 4, 1950; 1 child, Lynn. MusB, Lawrence U., 1944, MusM, 1948. Admissions counselor Lawrence U., Appleton, Wis., 1944-53; dir. admissions Nat. Coll. Edn., Evanston, Ill., 1953-58, asst. to pres., 1958-64, v.p., 1964-76; pres. Friends of Our Little Bros., Phoenix, 1976-78; v.p. devel. Phoenix Symphony Orch., 1978-82; sr. devel. officer Ariz. State U., Tempe, 1983-89; v.p. Steinway div. Allen Piano Co., Scottsdale, Ariz., from 1989. Chmn. bd. dirs. Phoenix Symphony Assn., 1990-92, vice chmn., 1992—; Steinway artist, Steinway and Sons, 1989. Performer for recs. Wouldn't It Be Loverly, 1989, Hello Young Lovers, 1989. Home: Phoenix, Ariz. Died June 27, 2008.

GRAHAM, ROBERT, sculptor; b. Mex. City, Aug. 19, 1938; s. Roberto Pena and Adeline Graham; m. Anjelica Huston, May 23, 1992; 1 child from previous marriage,

Steven. Study, San Jose Coll., Calif., 1961-63, San Francisco Art Inst., 1963-64. Prin. works include Whitney Mus. Am. Art & Mus. Modern Art, NY, Hirshhorn Mus. & Sculpture Garden, LA County Mus., Dallas Mus. Fine Art, Kunstmus., Cologne, Germany; commd. Fed. Res. Bank San Francisco, 1983, San Jose Fed. Bldg., 1984, LA Olympic Organizing Com., 1984, Joe Louis Meml., Detroit, Duke Ellington Meml., Central Park, NY, 1992, and others; exhbited in group shows at Galerie Neuendorf, Hamburg, Germany, 1979; one-man shows include Walker Art Ctr., 1981, LA County Mus. Art, 1988, Dorothy Rosenthal Gallery, 1981, Sch. Visual Arts, NY, 1981; Robert Miller Gallery, NY, 1982, 89, 90, 92, Whitney Mus. Am. Art, 1983, 84, 86, 88, 89, Mus. Fine Arts, Houston, 1987-89, Contemporary Arts Ctr., New Orleans, 1990; author: (bibliography) Maurice Tuchman, The Duke Ellington Meml. In Progress, LA County Mus. Art, 1989, John McEwen, Robert Graham Statues, Frankfurt, Galerie Neuendorf, Twenty-one Figures, NY, Robert Miller Gallery. Named to Calif. Hall of Fame, 2008. Died Dec. 27, 2008.

GRAHAM, VERNON LEE, corporate executive; b. Oquaka, Ill., Dec. 2, 1930; s. Grover Cleveland and Pearl (Fisher) G.; m. July 27, 1952; children: Steven, Dione, Rhonda. BA, San Jose U., 1954; MS, San Diego State U., 1962. CLU, Chartered Fin. Cons. Commd. USAF, 1954, advanced through ranks to capt., 1954, resigned, 1965; exec. v.p. Kennedy Sinclaire Inc., N. Haledon, N.J., 1967-81, pres., 1981-84; sr. v.p. Am. Fin. Svcs. Inc., Honolulu, 1984-87; pres. Fund All Svcs. Inc., Wilton, Calif., from 1988. Newspaper columnist Downtown Planet, Honolulu, 1986-88; contbr. articles to mags. Fund raising cons. ARC, Am. Heart Assn., Am. Cancer Soc., Honolulu, 1984-87. Sgt. U.S. Army 1946-47. Recipient Upson Meml. award U.S. Jaycees, Tulsa, 1962, Dunagan Meml award, 1964, Anela award Am. Cancer Soc., Honolulu, 1986-87. Mem. Nat. Soc. Fund Raising Execs. (cert., charter pres. Hawaii 1985-86), Elks. Republican. Avocations: flying, fishing, gardening, golf. Home: Wilton, Calif. Died Sept. 2, 2007.

GRAMM, WARREN STANLEY, economics educator; b. Seattle, Sept. 23, 1920; s. Paul Francis and Genevieve Hazel (Barnecut) G.; m. Marilyn Lorraine Post, June 25, 1949; children: Karen, Christie, Randolph. BA, U. Wash., 1944, MA, 1948; PhD, U. Calif., Berkeley, 1955. Asst. prof. Econs. U. Calif., Davis, 1955-63; assoc. prof. Econs. Alaska Meth. U., Anchorage, 1963-65; prof. Econs. Wash. State U., Pullman, 1965-91, prof. emeritus, from 1991. Contbr. articles profl. jours. Mem. Am. Econs. Assn., Assn. for Evolutionary Econs., History of Econs. Soc. Home: Pullman, Wash. Died Dec. 3, 2007.

GRANGER, SIR CLIVE WILLIAM JOHN (SIR CLIVE GRANGER), retired economist; b. Swansea, Wales, Sept. 4, 1934; arrived in U.S., 1974; s. Edward John and Evelyn Agnes (Hessey) G.; m. Patricia Anne Loveland, May 14, 1960; children: Mark, Claire. BA, U. Nottingham, Eng., 1955, PhD in Stats., 1959, DSc, 1992; DSc (hon.), Carlos III, Madrid, 1997; D in Econs. (hon.), Stockholm Sch. Econs., 1998; DSc (hon.), Loughborough U., 2002. Lectr. in math. U. Nottingham, 1956—64, prof. stats., 1964—74; prof. econs. U. Calif., San Diego, 1976—2002, chancellor's assoc. chair, 1994—2002; ret., 2003. Author: Forecasting Stock Markets, 1970; editor: Commodity Markets, 1973. Decorated knight bachelor Royal Order Queen Elizabeth of Britain, 2005; fellow Harkness Fund, 1959-60, Econometric Soc., 1973, Guggenheim Found., 1988, recipient Nobel Prize in Economics, 2003. Fellow: Am. Econ. Soc. (Disting.), Am. Acad. Arts and Scis., Brit. Acad. (corr.); mem.: We. Econ. Assn. (pres. 2002—03), Econometric Soc. Avocations: hiking, swimming, travel, reading. Home: La Jolla, Calif. Died May 27, 2009.

GRANT, DOROTHY ALICE, medical/surgical nurse, administrator; b. Dumas, Tex., July 23, 1943; d. Lawrence and Alta Jean (Arnold) Hendrickson; m. Winford Grant, June 26, 1964; children: Mark Dwayne, Michael Wayne. Diploma, St. Anthony's Hosp., Amarillo, Tex., 1964; BSN, West Tex. State U., 1984. Cert. operating room nurse. Head nurse, operating room High Plains Bapt. Hosp., Amarillo. Mem. Assn. Operating Room Nurses. Died Mar. 22, 2008.

GRANT, SHIRLEY MAE, retired business affairs director; b. Barberton, Ohio, Feb. 4, 1936; d. Chester Claude and Virginia Hutchison (Crispin) Culp; m. Stewart K. Grant, June 19, 1960 (dec. 1975); children: Michelle C. Grant Fontes, Sabrina K. Fox, Michael S. AA in Liberal Arts, Graceland Coll., 1956; BS in Edn. magna cum laude, Calif. State Ul., Long Beach, 1965, MS in Counseling/Student Affairs, 1974; AA in Real Estate, Fullerton Coll., 1979. Lic. real estate broker; life cert. community coll. instr. Asst. registrar Graceland Coll., Lamoni, Iowa, 1956-58; adminstrv. asst., dean of students Calif. State U., Long Beach, 1958-61, tchr. Vista Unified/Rossmoor, Los Alamitos, Calif., 1965-70; asst. dean admissions and records Calif. State U., Long Beach, 1970-74, dir. sch. and coll. rels. Fullerton, 1974-77, dir. sch. and coll. res. Dominguez Hills, Carson, Calif., 1978-80; coord. tour and travel Knotts Berry Farm, Buena Park, Calif., 1980-85; chief info. officer Pro Value, Cerritos, Calif., 1985-89, Gen./Vascular Surg. Assocs., Long Beach, 1989-93; dir. bus. affairs Unyeway, Ramona, Calif., 1993-95; ret., 1995. Steering com. Calif. Women in Higher Edn., Sacramento, 1977. Danforth scholar, 1954, Univ. scholar, 1974. Mem. Nat. Honor Soc. (pres. 1954). Avocations: travel, music, breeding hybrids. Died July 2, 2008.

GRANT, SYDNEY R., education educator, consultant; b. NYC, Feb. 3, 1926; s. Herman S. and Ethel H. G.; m. Margarita Henderson, Sept. 4, 1951. BS in Edn. cum laude, CCNY, 1950; MA in Spanish Letters, Nat. U. Mex., Mexico City, 1951; EdD, Columbia U. Tchrs. Coll., 1961. Program asst. Sch. Gen. Studies CCNY, 1951-52, instr. Spanish Sch. Gen. Studies evening program, 1952-64; tchr. Spanish and common brs., cons. The P.R. study N.Y.C. Bd. Edn., 1952-60; dir. of instrn. K-12 Verona (N.J.) Pub. Schs., 1961-64; assoc. chief of party, assoc. prof. Columbia U. Tchrs. Coll., US./AID contract team, Lima, Peru, 1964-68; assoc. supt. for curriculum Bellevue (Wash.) Pub. Schs., 1968-69; dir. office internat. edn. Coll. Edn. Fla. State U., Tallahassee, 1969-72, assoc. prof., dir. Ctr. for Ednl. Tech., 1972-75, assoc. dean for grad. studies Coll. Edn., 1975-78, prof. Coll. Edn., from 1972, prof., head dept. ednl. founds. and policy studies, 1986-89, prof. internat.-intercultural devel. edn., 1979-85, prof. emeritus, from 1994. Cons. U.S./AID, UN Devel. Program, UNESCO, Fundacion Natura, Fla. State U., Latin Am., S.E. Asia, Africa, 1969-90; sr. resident tech. adv. Min. Edn. and Culture for Fla. State U. in Windhoek, Namibia, 1991-93. With U.S. Army, 1944-46, ETO. Recipient Esso award Esso Standard Oil Co., 1960, Palmas Magisteriales Peruvian Ministry of Edn., 1967, Pres.'s Teaching award Fla. State U., 1978; Downer scholar CCNY, 1950. Mem. Nat. Soc. for Study Edn., Comparative and Internat. Edn. Soc., Common Cause, Amnesty Internat. Avocations: short wave radio, reading. Home: Tallahassee, Fla. Died 2009.

GRASS, ALEXANDER, retail executive; b. Scranton, Pa., Aug. 3, 1927; s. Louis and Rose (Breman) G.; m. Lois Lehrman, July 30, 1950; children: Linda Jane, Martin L., Roger L., Elizabeth Ann; m. Louise B. Gurkoff, Apr. 26, 1974. LLB, U. Fla., Gainesville, 1949; D (hon.), Hebrew U., 2000, Doctorate (hon.) of Philosphy, 2000. Bar: Fla. 1949, Pa. 1953. Pvt. practice, Miami Beach, Fla., 1949-51; v.p. Rite Aid Corp., Shiremanstown, Pa., 1952—62, pres., 1966-69, 77-89, chmn., chief exec. officer, 1969-95, chmn. exec. com., 1995-99; chmn., CEO Super Rite Foods, Inc., 1983-95. Chmn. bd. govs. Hebrew U. of Jerusalem, 1996-99, exec. com. mem., 1999-2009. Nat. exec. com. United Jewish Appeal, 1968-79, nat. vice chmn., 1970-79, gen. chmn., 1984-86, chmn. bd. trustees, 1986-88, bd. trustees, 1988-99; pres. Harrisburg Jewish Fedn., Pa., 1970-72; chmn. Israel Edn. Fund, 1975-78; bd. dirs. Pa. Right to Work Found., 1972-74, Harrisburg Hosp., 1977-81, Nat. Mus. Am. Jewish History, 2007; vice chmn. Harrisburg Hosp., 1988-95; bd. dirs. Pinnacle Health Sys., 1995-2001; active Pa. Coun. Arts, 1982; bd. dirs. Keystone State Games, 1982-92, Israel Ctr. Social and Econ. Studies, 1983; trustee Jerusalem Inst. Mgmt., 1983; exec. com. Jewish Agy. for Israel, 1984-88, bd. govs. 1984-90, chmn. bd. govs., 1999-2003, exec. com., 2003-09; treas. United Israel Appeal, 1986-90. With USNR, 1945-46. Recipient Disting. Alumnus award U. Fla., 1992, Nat. Scopus award Hebrew U., 1993, Americanism award Anti Defamation League, 1995. Mem. Nat. Am. Wholesale Grocers Assn. (bd. dirs. 1971-73), Nat. Assn. Chain Drug Stores (bd. dirs. 1972-95, chmn. 1985-86, Nat. Achievement award 1995). Jewish (dir. temple). Home: Harrisburg, Pa. Died Aug. 27, 2009; Harrisburg, Pa.

GRAY, DORIS MACK, information specialist; b. Balt., Feb. 1, 1950; d. Silas James and Lelia Elizabeth (Coleman) M.; divorced; children: Jonathan Derrell, Donita Montré. AA, Community Coll. Balt., 1974; BS in Econs., Towson U., Md., 1976. Lic. real estate agt., Md. Instr. Bay Coll. Md., Balt., 1977-79; tech. writer Sci. Mgmt. Corp-Data Tech. Industries, Inc., Lanham, Md., 1979-80; sr. tech. writer L.R. Davis & Co., Silver Spring, Md., 1980-81, Maxima Corp., Bethesda, Md., 1981-83, Bus. Methods and Systems Inc., Lanham, 1983-84; specialist documentaton Montgomery County Sch. System, Rockville, Md., 1984-85; info. specialist Citicorp Fin., Inc., Lutherville, Md., 1985-91, Tri-Cor Industries, Washington, 1991-96, AAI-SMI (Aerotek), Hunt Valley, Md., from 1996. Real estate aft. Preston T. Johnson & Co., Balt., 1978—; cons. writing numerous contractors, Balt., 1979-82. Contbr. articles to profl. jours.; dir. community theater group, 1986 (award 1986). Bd. dirs. Student Day Care Ctr., Towson, 1974-77; organizer various polit. campaigns, Balt., 1978-82; organist, choir dir. Caroline St. Meth. Ch., Balt., 1981-86, backup organist Howard Park and St. Mark United Meth. Chs., Morgan State U. Christian Ctr.; lobbyist Lida Lee Tall PTA, Towson, 1982; arbitrator Better Bus. Bur., Balt., 1987. Mem. NAFE, C.C. Balt. Student Govt. Assn. (treas. reunion alumni com. 1987—). Democrat. Avocations: computers, tennis, music. Home: Baltimore, Md. Died May 9, 2008.

GREEN, DOROTHY SELMA, environmental volunteer; b. Detroit, Mar. 16, 1929; d. David M. and Helen (Beckwitt) Cohen; m. Jacob (Jack) Isak Green, Aug. 26, 1951; children: Avrom, Hershel, Joshua. BA, U. Calif., Berkeley, 1951. Mem. Environ. Water Leadership Coun.; mem. exec. com., treas. Pub. Ofls. for Water and Environ. Reform; commr. L.A. Bd. Water and Power Commrs.; founder, pres. Heal the Bay, L.A., 1985-91; bd. dirs. Planning and Conservation League, Westside Urban Forum, Calif. League of Conservation Voters, 1975-89, Calif. for Nuclear Safeguards, 1975-76; mem. steering com. Women For, 1972-84; active state and nat. gov. bds. Common Cause, 1973-84, others. Recipient Citation Exceptional Children's Found., 1973, First Annual award Calif. League of Conservation Voters, 1983, Sierra Club L.A. chpt. spl. award, 1987, Superhealer award, Heal the Bay, 1987, Mount Gay Coll. award, 1990; Mayor's Cert. Appreciation, L.A., 1990, Cert. of Tribute, L.A. City Coun., 1991, Citation, County of L.A., 1991, LULU award L.A. Advt. Women, 1992. Democrat. Jewish. Avocations: music, hiking, reading. Home: Los Angeles, Calif. Died Oct. 13, 2008.

GREEN, ROBERT CHARLES, film company executive; b. Charlotte, NC, Jan. 28, 1956; s. Ladson Leroy and Dorothy June (Feindt) G.; m. Barbara Gail Gordon, July 26, 1987. AS, Wingate Coll., 1976; student, U. N.C., 1976-78. Prodn. specialist Sta. WCCB-TV, Charlotte, 1972-76, Sta. WUNC-TV, Chapel Hill, N.C., 1976-78; news photographer Sta. WFMY-TV, Greensboro, N.C., 1979; studio supr. Sta. WBTV-TV, Charlotte, 1979-81; asst. dir. Jefferson Prodns., Charlotte, 1981-85; sales mgr. Patete Taylor Films, Charlotte, from 1985. Home: Charlotte, NC. Died Jan. 25, 2008.

GREEN, WILLIAM S., lawyer; b. Presque Isle, Maine, Dec. 21, 1917; s. Saul Guy and Julia (Segal) G.; m. Joan Jacobson, June 27, 1942; children: William Scott, Nancy Green Fleming, Richard Steven. AB, Dartmouth Coll., 1939; LLB, Harvard U., 1947; LLD (hon.), New Hampshire Coll., 1976, St. Anselm Coll., Goffstown, NH, 1979, Franklin Pierce Coll., 1988, Notre Dame Coll., Manchester, NH, 1991. Bar: N.H., U.S. Dist. Ct. N.H., U.S. Ct. Appeals (1st cir.). Now pres. emeritus Sheehan, Phinney, Bass & Green, Manchester, N.H.; dep. atty. gen. Office of Atty. Gen., Concord, N.H., 1950-51, asst. atty. gen., 1949-50; assoc. Orr & Reno, Concord, 1947-49. Bd. dirs. Waterville Co., Waterville Valley, N.H., 1965—, New England Cir., Boston, 1977—, Numerica Fin. Corp., 1983-91. Trustee Elliot Hosp., N.H. Coll., Manchester Hist. Assn. Maj. USMC, 1942-46. Republican. Jewish. Avocation: tennis. Died Oct. 22, 2007.

GREENBERG, MICHAEL HOWARD, lawyer; b. Bklyn., Aug. 3, 1933; s. Joseph and Lillian (Newman) G.; m. Eulalia Virgili Elias, June 11, 1960; children: Peter E., Edward L. BS magna cum laude, Cornell U., 1955; JD magna cum laude, Harvard U., 1958; student, Institut de Droit Comparé, Luxembourg, 1959. Clk. to Hon. Charles M. Metzner U.S. Dist. Ct. (So. Dist.) N.Y., 1959-60; from assoc. to ptnr. Graubard Moskovitz et al, NYC, 1960-88; of counsel Sharretts Paley Carter & Blauvelt, P.C., NYC, 1989-92. Chair Bi-national Art 19 Panel, U.S.-Can. Free Trade Agreement, 1992; corp. sec. Spain-U.S. C. of C. Editor Harvard Law Rev., 1956-58; contbr. articles to profl. jours. Committeeman, Democratic Party, Nassau County, N.Y., 1973-92. Mem. ABA, N.Y. County Lawyers Assn. Died Mar. 10, 2008.

GREENE, ALBERT LAWRENCE, healthcare executive; b. NYC, Dec. 10, 1949; s. Leonard and Anne (Birnbaum) G.; m. Jo Linda Anderson, Sept. 3, 1972; children: Stacy, Jeremy. BA, Ithaca Coll., 1971; MHA, U. Mich., 1973. Adminstrv. asst. Harper Hosp., Detroit, 1973-74, asst. adminstr., 1974-77, assoc. adminstr., 1977-80; adminstr. Grace Hosp., Detroit, 1980-84, Harper Hosp., Detroit, 1984-87; pres., CEO Sinai Samaritan Med. Ctr., Milw., 1988-90, Alta Bates Med. Ctr., Berkeley, Calif., 1990-98; CEO Sutter Health East Bay Svc. Area, Berkeley, Calif., 1998-99, HealthCtrl., Emeryville, Calif., 1999—2001, Hollywood Presbyn. Med. Ctr., L.A., 2002—06, Valley Presbyn. Hosp., 2006—09. Bd. dirs. Sierra Health Svcs.; chmn. Calif. Assn. Hosps. and Health Sys., 1998. Trustee Huron Valley Hosp., Milford, Mich., 1984-87. Fellow: Am. Coll. Healthcare Execs.; mem.: World Pres. Orgn., Calabasas Country Club. Avocations: tennis, golf. Home: Calabasas, Calif. Died Apr. 16, 2009.

GREENE, HERBERT BRUCE, lawyer, investor, entrepreneur; b. NYC, Apr. 13, 1934; s. Joseph Lester and Shirley (Kasen) G.; m. Judith Jean Metricks, Dec. 31, 1958; children: Pamela S., Scott L. AB, Harvard U., 1955; JD, Columbia U., 1958. Bar: N.Y. 1959, Conn. 1975. Asst. U.S. atty So. Dist. N.Y., Dept. Justice, NYC, 1958-61; assoc. Kaye, Scholer, Fierman, Hays & Handler, NYC, 1961-66; asst. to gen. counsel CIT Fin. Corp., NYC, 1966-67; group gen. counsel Xerox Corp., Rochester, NY, 1967-68, v.p. adminstrn., 1968-71; sr. v.p. Xerox Edn. Group, Stamford, Conn., 1971-75; v.p., gen. counsel, sec. Lone Star Industries, Inc., Greenwich, Conn., 1976-79, sr. v.p., asst. to chmn., 1979-82; chmn., CEO Earle and Greene & Co., Westport, 1982-96, Portland, Oreg., from 1997. Mem. Phi Delta Phi. Republican. Died Apr. 20, 2009.

GREENE, MARÍA CRISTINA, educational counselor; b. Rosario, Santa Fe, Argentina, Mar. 16, 1941; arrived in U.S., 1973; d. Norberto Ramón and Carmen (Ortega) Oroño; m. Homer Edwin Greene, July 24, 1967; children: Sharon Cristina, Brian David. BA in Lit., U. Nat. Rosario, 1966; MS in Edn., Western Ill. U., 1988. Cert. tchr. adult and secondary edn., Ill. Tchr. secondary edn. Academia Estudios Paralelos, Rosario, 1966-73; tchr. adult edn. Black Hawk Coll., Moline, Ill., 1979-83, career counselor, 1983-88, coord. pub. assistance program, 1989-90, counselor, assoc. prof., from 1990, dept. chair counseling, from 1995. Mem. Ill. Quad Cities Higher Edn. Com., Moline, 1991—; mem. Comm. U. Bd. Dirs., Davenport, Iowa, 1992—; project advisor Hispanic Program for Ednl. Advancement of Western Ill. U., Moline, 1990—; mem. Regional Adv. Coun. for Hispanic Affairs, 1991—. Bilingual editor The Healing Journey, 1992—. V.p. Coun. Community Svcs., Moline, 1987-92; adminstr. Ch. Women United Ednl. Support Program, Moline, 1991—; mem. Ill. Migrant Coun. Regional Adv. Bd., East Moline, Ill., 1989-95. Mem. ACA, Am. Coll.

Counseling Assn., Assn. for Multicultural Counseling and Devel., Ill. Counseling Assn. (Black Hawk chpt.), Nat. Acad. Advising Assn. Home: East Moline, Ill. Died Jan. 1, 2008.

GREENE, ROBERT WARREN, education educator, real estate broker; b. Boston, Apr. 17, 1928; s. Benjamin Martin and Mary (Wilson) G.; m. Elizabeth Ann Army, Sept. 11, 1956; 1 child, Mary Elizabeth. BS, Worcester State Coll., 1954; MEd, Northea. U., 1956; PhD, U. Conn., 1965. Notary public, Mass. Tchr. math. Shrewsbury (Mass.) High Sch., 1954-60; supr. sci. edn. Campus Sch., Fitchburg (Mass.) State Coll., 1960-65, asst. to acad. dean, 1965-67, dir. placement, registrar, 1967-74, chmn. grad. program in sch. adminstrn., 1968-76, prof. edn. and sch. adminstrn., from 1976; pres. Greene & Greene Properties, Worcester and Hyannis, Mass., from 1978. Bd. dirs., incorporator United Educators Life Ins. Corp., Framingham, Mass., 1974-86. Chmn. bd. trustees Shrewsbury Pub. Libr., 1968-76; pres. Shrewsbury Fed. Credit Union, 1968-74, also past pres., incorporator; mem. personnel bd. edn. Roman Cath. Diocese of Worester, 1978-84; chmn. bd. dirs. Worcester Area Mental Retardation Bd., 1987—. With USN, 1951-53. Mem. Assn. for Supervision and Curriculum Devel., Mass. State Coll. Placement Dirs. (chmn. 1974-75), Mass. Tchrs. Assn. (bd. dirs. 1964-76), Fitchburg State Coll. Faculty Assn. (pres. 1971-75), Holy Cross Coll. Cath. Alumni Assn., Econ. Club (Worcester), Kappa Delta Pi (faculty advisor 1979—). Democrat. Avocation: golf. Home: Shrewsbury, Mass. Died Nov. 12, 2007.

GREENLAW, ROBERT HIRAM, radiation oncologist; b. Norway, Maine, Dec. 14, 1927; s. Norman U. and Bernice H. (Hood) G.; m. Louise A. Zurovski, Feb. 19, 1955; children: Ann, Mary, Sarah, Paul N. BS, Tufts Coll., 1948; MD, U. Rochester, 1952. Diplomate Am. Bd. Radiology. Prof. radiation medicine U. Ky., Lexington, 1961-70; instr. U. Rochester, N.Y., 1968-70; radiation oncologist Marshfield (Wis.) Clinic, from 1970. Mem. Am. Cancer Soc. Served to capt. USAF, 1955-57. Fellow Am. Coll. Radiology; mem. AMA, Am. Soc. Therapeutic Radiology and Oncology. Home: Marshfield, Wis. Died July 25, 2008.

GREENSTONE, REYNOLD, meteorologist; b. NYC, Sept. 30, 1924; s. Joseph and Ethel Lena (Bishoff) G.;m. Carolyn Louise Guinn, Dec. 20, 1952; children: Todd, Holly, Jay, Jon, Heather. BS, NYU, 1947; MS, U. Md., 1958. Physicist Nat. Bur. Standards, Washington, 1949-55, Tech. Ops. Inc., Washington, 1955-60, ORI Inc., Silver Spring, Md., 1960-88, McDonnell Douglas, Seabrook, Md., 1988-90, ST Systems Corp., Lanham, Md., from 1990. Mem. AAAS, Am. Meteorol. Soc., Am. Geophys. Union. Home: Brookeville, Md. Died Feb. 7, 2008.

GREENWALD, EDWARD SAMUEL, physician; b. New Rochelle, NY, May 13, 1928; s. Irving and Belle Elizabeth (Jacobson) G.; m. Edith Deborah Aaronson, Dec. 4, 1949; children: David, Daniel, Joel, Joshua. BA, Amherst Coll., 1948; MD, NYU, 1952. Intern Kings County Hosp., Bklyn., 1952-53; resident in internal medicine Montefiore Med. Ctr., Bronx, N.Y., 1955-56, Bronx Mcpl. Hosp. Ctr., 1956-57; Am. Cancer Soc. fellow Montefiore Hosp., Bronx, 1957-58; attending physician dept. oncology Montefiore Med. Ctr., from 1978; prof. dept. medicine (Oncology) Albert Einstein Coll. Medicine, Bronx, from 1982. Prin. investigator Ea. Coop. Oncology grant Montefiore Med. Ctr., Bronx, N.Y., 1978-92. Capt. USAF, 1953-55. Fellow ACP; mem. Am. Soc. Clin. Oncology, Am. Assn. for Cancer Rsch., Phi Beta Kappa. Democrat. Jewish. Home: New Rochelle, NY. Died June 27, 2008.

GREENWICH, ELLIE (ELEANOR LOUISE GREENWICH), songwriter, producer, singer; b. BKlyn., NY, Oct. 23, 1940; d. William and Rose Greenwich; m. Jeff Barry, 1962 (div. 1965). BA, Hofstra U., 1962. Adv. bd. MIRI Prodns., B.M.I. Found. Song writer: Be My Baby, Da Doo Ron Ron, Why Do Lover's Break Each Others Hearts, Today I Met The Boy I'm Gonna Marry, Do Wah Diddy Diddy, Leader of The Pack, hanky Panky, Maybe I Know, And Then He Kissed Me, Look of Love, River Deep/Mountain High; prodr.: Cherry Cherry, Thank The Lord For The Night, Shilo, Kentucky Woman and many others; written and produced songs for films and TV; performed background and lead for many albums, singles and commercials. Recipient 19 B.M.I. awards for great nat. popularity attained for broadcast performance, B.M.I. spl. award for long and outstanding contbns. to popular music, 1984, spl. award for River Deep, Mountain High, The Songwriters Hall of Fame and The Nat. Acad. of Popular Music, 1984, 2 Clio award nominations for excellence in the writing of radio and tv. commercial jingles, George M. Esterbrook award Hofstra U.; named to The Songwriters Hall of Fame, 1991 Mem. Songwriters Guild (coun.). Died Aug. 26, 2009.

GREER, THOMAS VERNON, agribusiness educator; b. Lincoln, Nebr., Sept. 17, 1944; s. Vernon Francis and Lucille Elizabeth (Laune) G.; m. Patricia Ann Libbey, Apr. 19, 1975; 1 child, Vernon Charles. BA in Econs. and Polit. Sci., U. Nebr., 1966, MS in Agrl. Econs., 1969; PhD in Agrl. Econs., Purdue U., 1992. Commodity/industry analyst U.S. Internat. Trade Commn., Washington, 1972-82; dir. sugar analysis Connell Commodities, INc., Westfield, N.J., 1982-87; rsch. asst. Purdue U., West Lafayette, Ind., 1988-92; asst. prof. agribusiness U. Tenn., Martin, from 1993. Chmn. faculty equipment com. Dept. Agr. and Natural Resources, U. Tenn., Martin, 1993-94; presenter in field. Chmn. Nebr. Internat. Assn., Lincoln, 1964-66; student senator Assn. Students U. Nebr., Lincoln, 1966-68; active Church Choir. With U.S. Army, 1968-69, Vietnam. Mem. Am. Legion. Methodist. Home: Martin, Tenn. Died Apr. 2, 2008.

GREGORY, JAMES ALEXANDER, retired editor, film producer; b. Marshall, Mich., Apr. 11, 1930; s. Alexander and Chrissoula (Shoupilla) Gregory; life ptnr. Zachariah Brown; children: Ben Tea, Robert Nuñez, Jim Davidson, Daniel G., Chris Montalban. B of English with honors, U. Mich., 1951, MA in English, 1952. Publicist Columbia Pictures, NYC, 1956; press book editor-in-chief RKO Radio Pictures, NYC, 1956—57; editor-in-chief Movieland and TV Time, NYC, 1958—61; West Coast editor, writer Silver Screen, Screenland, Movieland and TV Time, LA, 1960—69; staff reporter Nat. Enquirer, 1974—76, freelance writer, 1976—80; editor, writer Larry Flynt Publ., LA, 1980—83; editor Landscape and Irrigation, Van Nuys, Calif.; sr. editor Arbor Age, 1984—91, ret., 1992. Author: David David David, 1972, The Soul of the Jackson 5, 1973, Donny!, 1973, Donny and the Osmond Family, 1974, The Lucille Ball Story, 1974; co-author: The Wallaces of Alabama with George Wallace, Jr., 1975; author, editor: The Elvis Presley Story, 1960; prodr.: (films) Flaco and the Wizard of Hugs, Lucy Luvs Flaco. Lt. (j.g.) USNR, 1953-55. Democrat. Died June 24, 2008.

GREIFER, AARON P., retired chemistry educator; b. Passaic, NJ, Sept. 29, 1919; s. Morris and Mamie (Margolis) G.; m. Rita Weiss, Mar. 14, 1943; children: Roberta, Margaret. BA, Ohio State U., 1942; MA, Columbia U., 1948. Chemist Elwood Ordnance Plant, Joliet, Ill., 1942-43; rsch. assoc. Ohio State U., Columbus, 1944; chemist Kellex Corp., NYC, Jersey City, 1948-49; supervising chemist Fed. Telephone & Radio Corp., Clifton, N.J., 1951; scientist GE Co., Syracuse, N.Y., 1951-56; sr. mem. tech. staff RCA, Needham, Mass., 1956-60; project leader Clevite Corp., Cleve., 1961-64; staff scientist Sperry Rand Corp., Blue Bell, Pa., 1964-81; instr. Del. County Community Coll., Media, Pa., 1983-84; lectr. Villanova (Pa.) U., 1984-88. Co-author (with others): Magnetism and Magnetic Materials, 1967; contbr. articles on magnetic materials to profl. jours.; contbr. to Landolt-Bornstein III/46, 1970. Sgt. U.S. Army, 1945-46. Recipient Cert. of Appreciation, U.S. Sec. War, 1945. Fellow Am. Inst. Chemists; mem. Am. Chem. Soc., Am. Phys. Soc., Toastmasters Internat. (Club Pres. of Yr. dist. 38 1980). Achievements include research on glass gapped recording heads, square loop ferrites, low loss ferrites, magnetostrictive ferrites, single crystal growth, and thin garnet films. Home: Ardmore, Pa. Died Sept. 5, 2007.

GRESKOVICH, CHARLES D., retired materials engineer; BS in Ceramic Tech., Pa. State U., 1964, MS in Ceramic Sci., 1966, PhD, 1968. NSF post-doctoral fellow Clausthal Tech. U., Germany, 1968; ceramist R&D Ctr. Ceramics Lab, GE Corp. R&D, Schenectady, NY, 1969—2002. Contbr. numerous articles to profl. jours. Recipient Real Advances in Materials award Nat. Assn. Sci., Tech., and Soc., Charles L. Hoslar Alumni Scholar medal Pa. State U. Coll. Earth and Sci.; named Centennial fellow Pa. State U. Coll. Earth and Sci., 1997, 98. Fellow Am. Ceramic Soc. (Ross Coffin Purdy award 1978, Richard M. Fulrath award 1983); mem. NAE, Nat. Inst. Ceramic Engrs., Electrochemical Soc. Achievements include research in polycrystalline ceramics, useful as scintillators in advanced medical x-ray detectors, arc tube envelopes for high intensity discharge lamps, and as possible ceramic lasers and optical windows; co-contributor to first efficient ceramic scintillator, composed of multicomponent rare-earth oxides; more than 50 U.S. patents in field. Home: Schenectady, NY. Died July 7, 2007.

GRIESS, GARY ALLEN, biophysicist; b. Omaha, Mar. 8, 1940; s. Herbert Charles and Alice Mae (Butherus) G.; m. Evelyn Elfrida Jaeger, July 1, 1967 (div. 1984); children: Kristine Elizabeth, David Carl. BS in Physics, MIT, 1962; PhD, U. Mass., 1970. Rsch. asst. Mass. Gen. Hosp., Boston, 1962-64; instr. Sch. Medicine U. Rochester, N.Y., 1970-76; prin. investigator Tech., Inc., San Antonio, 1977-83; rsch. faculty Health Sci. Ctr. U. Tex., San Antonio, from 1983. Cons. Marine Colloids div. FMC, Rockland, Maine, 1991—. Contbr. articles to profl. jours. Bd. dirs. S.E. Area Coalition, Rochester, 1976, Terra-Genesis, San Antonio, 1984—; campaign com. State and Congrl. Rep., San Antonio, 1988, 90. Grantee Fight for Sight Found., 1973—, NSF, 1987—. Mem. Am. Chem. Soc., Biophys. Soc. Democrat. Lutheran. Achievements include patent for Electrophoresis Apparatus and Method of Varying Pore Size of Agarose Gels; discovery of actinic ocular effects of laser radiation. Home: San Antonio, Tex. Died Apr. 25, 2008.

GRIFFIN, CHARLES KEVIN, financial executive; b. Boston, May 24, 1943; s. Gerald Francis and Phyllis Marie (Jenkins) G.; m. Carolyn Boland, Apr. 1968 (div. 1982); children: Grace, Charles K. Jr., Sean R.; m. Joan Rosley, Oct. 5, 1989. BSBA, U. Albuquerque, 1975, BS in Aerospace Sci., 1976; MS in Systems Mgmt., U. So. Calif., 1978; LLD (hon.), U. Tex., 1982. Cert. leasing profl. Commd. 1st lt. U.S. Army, 1960, advanced through grades to maj., ret., 1980; pres. Albuquerque Fin. Svcs., 1981-83; exec. v.p. Albuquerque Leasing Corp., 1983-89, Griffin & Assoc. Leasing Inc., from 1990. Bd. dirs. Albuquerque Conv. and Visitors Bur., 1989—. Mem. Western Assn. Equipment Lessors (bd. dirs. 1988-92), Civitan Club (pres. 1989-90, dist. lt. gov. 1990-91, dist. gov.-elect 1993-94). Home: Albuquerque, N.Mex. Died Sept. 5, 2007.

GRIFFIN, SALLIE T., artist, photographer, retired technologist; b. Whiteville, NC, Sept. 2, 1940; d. Benjamin Oliver and Virginia Alma (Ponton) Thompson; m. C.H. Griffin, Dec. 26, 1964; children: A.F. Griffin, M.A. Griffin. Grad., St, Mary's High Sch. and Jr. Coll., Duke U. Med. Ctr., Sch. Radiological Tech. and Nuclear Medicine; student, Anson Tech. Coll., Ctrl. Piedmont C.C., 1976-80, Wingate U., 1976-91, 97; studied with Sally B. Miller. With Stanley Meml. Hosp., Albermark, N.C.; technician, tchr. Moses Cine Hosp. Founding mem. Union Co. Art Coun., Monroe, N.C., 1980-84., found. first libr. gallery Union Co. Libr., Marshville, NC, 1998. One woman shows include: Union County Pub. Libr., Monroe, N.C., 1980, 82, Wingate Coll., 1980, United Carolina Bank, 1981, Ivey's Southpark, Charlotte, 1985, Dove Pottery and Gallery, Monroe, 1990, Stanley County Libr., Albemarle, 1992, Artisan Ctr., Kannapolis, 1992, St. Mary's Coll., 1992, Union County Arts Coun., 1995, 50 piece show, 2000; Group shows include: Blooming Arts Festival (named Union County's Finest, 1981, 1st place winner, 1994), N.C. State U. Show, 1988, Dove Pottery and Gallery, 1991, Watercolor Soc. N.C., 1995, U. N.C. 1996, Myrtle Beach Convention Ctr., 1996, 22nd Nat. Show, Shelby, 1996, Greensboro Cultural Ctr., 1997, Mus. of York County, 1997, Shelby Nat. Show #23, 1997, Greenhill Gallery of N.C. Art, 1998, Taladega Mus., Ala., 1998, Wingate U., 1998, Union County Libr., 1998, Weatherspoon Gallery, 1999, Fayetteville Mus. Art, 1999, 25th Ann. Art Show of N.W., Fla., 1999, Burroughs and Chapin Art Mus., Myrtle Beach, S.C., 1999, MOMA, N.Y.C., 2000; Fe-Mail E-Mail 2000. Bd. dirs. Wingate Coll. Libr., Wingate, NC, 1985-89, Union County Arts Coun., Monroe; founder Union County Arts Coun. NE N.C. Mem. The Marshville Rsch. Club, The Union Co. Art League (pres. 1986-87, 2000-01), The Watercolor Soc. N.C., Ariz., Ala., Conn., The Guild of Charlotte Artists, The Charlotte Art League, The Jaycettes (founder, bd. mem. 1965-75, pres. 1965-67). Democrat. Baptist. Died Mar. 20, 2008.

GRIFFITH, CHARLES EDWARD, electrical engineer; b. Washington, Oct. 20, 1923; s. Ward Willson and Alice Margaret (Nickels) G.; m. Elizabeth Zane Morrison, July 14, 1951; children: Maureen, James Willison, Roxana, Elizabeth Zane, Tracy, David Morrison, John Nickels. BSEE, U. Md., 1950. Registered profl. engr., D.C. Engr.-in-tng. Potomac Elec. Power Co., Washington, 1950-51, engr. sys. protection, 1951-54, engr. sys. planning, 1954-58, engr. transmission and distbn. engring., 1958-62, engr. transmission and distbn. stds., 1962-75, sr. engr. transmission and distbn. stds., 1975-98. Engr. liaison Potomac Elec. Power and Edison Elec. Inst., Washington, 1976—; cons. in power distbrn., 1998—. With USN, 1943-46. Mem. IEEE/PES (sr.), Southeastern Elec. Assn. (chmn. underground distbn. com. 1969-79), Am. Inst. Elec. Engrs., Power Engrs. Soc. Republican. Episcopalian. Achievements include major contribution to design of the PEPCO LVAC network and foure wire distribution systems; patentee on fused short circuit and grounding switch, single phase T-connectors for a pair of tap cables; lockable assembly for engaging and disengaging a motor operator with an overhead distribution gauge switch. Home: Silver Spring, Md. Died Mar. 28, 2008.

GRIFFITH, MELVIN EUGENE, entomologist, public health service officer; b. Lawrence, Kans., Mar. 24, 1912; s. George Thomas and Estella (Shaw) G.; m. Pauline Sophia Bogart, June 23, 1941. AB, U. Kans., 1934, AM, 1935, PhD, 1938; postgrad., U. Mich., summers 1937-40. Instr. zoology N.D. Agrl. Coll., Fargo, 1938—39, asst. prof., 1939—41, assoc. prof., 1941—42; commd. officer USPHS, 1943—71; entomologist malaria control in war areas State Dept. Health, Oklahoma City, 1943—46; assoc. prof. zool. scis. U. Okla., Norman, 1945—52, prof., 1952—56; extended malaria control program, 1946—51; chief malaria advisor ICA, Bangkok, 1951—60; assoc. dir. Malaria Eradication Tng. Ctr., Kingston, Jamaica, 1960; regional malaria advisor SE Asia, AID, New Delhi, 1960—62, Near East and South Asia, AID, 1962—64; dep. chief malaria eradication br. AID, Washington, 1964—67, chief, 1967—71; ret. as capt. USPHS, 1971. Rapporteur founding conf. SE Asia antimalaria coord. bd., Saigon, 1956; cons. Office of Health, AID, Washington, 1971—75; mem. rev. team ind. status assessment of advanced nat. malaria eradication programs WHO, Iran, 1962, Philippines, 73; chmn. first all-Asia malarai eradication conf., Bangkok, 53. Contbr. articles and monographs on entomology, malaria control and pub. health. Recipient citation for disting. svc. U. Kans., 1962. Mem. APHA, Am. Soc. Tropical Medicine and Hygiene, Am. Soc. Limnology and Oceanography, Entomol. Soc. Am., Explorers Club, N.Y. Acad. Scis., Siam Soc., Phi Beta Kappa, Sigma Xi. Deceased.

GRIFFITH, WILLIAM ALEXANDER, former mining company executive; b. Sioux Falls, SD, Mar. 28, 1922; s. James William and Adeline Mae (Reid) G.; m. Gratia Frances Hannan, Jan. 27, 1949; children— Georgeanne Reid, James William, Wade Andrew. BS in Metall. Engring., S.D. Sch. Mines and Tech., 1947; MS in Metallurgy, M.I.T., 1950; Mineral Dressing Engr. (hon.), Mont. Coll. Mineral Sci. and Tech., 1971; D in Bus. Adminstrn. (hon.), S.D. Sch. Mines & Tech., 1986; D in Sci. (hon.), U. Idaho, 1990. With N.J. Zinc Co., 1949-57, chief milling and maintenance Bertha minerals divsn., 1956-57; metallurgist Rare Metals Corp. Am., Tuba City, Ariz., 1957-58; dir. rsch. Phelps Dodge Corp., Morenci, Ariz., 1958-68; with Hecla Mining Co., Coeur d'Alene, Idaho, 1968-87, exec. v.p., 1978, pres., chief exec. officer, 1979-86, chmn., chief exec. officer, 1986-87; pres. Granduc Mines Ltd., 1987-88; chmn. Inland

N.W. Bancorp., Inc., 1989-96. Bd. dirs. The Coeur d'Alenes Co. With USNR, 1943-46. Mem. AIME (Gaudin award 1977, Richards award 1981, Disting. mem. 1977, Hon. 1987), NAE, Am. Mining Congress (past dir.), Idaho Mining Assn. (past pres.), Idaho Assn. Commerce and Industry (past bd. dirs.), Western Regional Coun. (chmn. 1986-87), Nat. Strategic Materials and Minerals Adv. Com. to Sec. Interior, Silver Inst. (past pres., past chmn.), Nat. Acad. of Engring., Sigma Tau, Theta Tau. Lodges: Rotary. Republican. Home: Hayden, Idaho. Died Apr. 30, 2009.

GRIGORIAN, MARCOS, artist, art gallery director; b. Krapotkin, Krasnadar, Russia, Dec. 25, 1924; came to U.S., 1962; d. Bagrat and Shoushanik (Aloyan) G. BA, Acad. Fine Arts, Rome, 1954. Founder, executor Iranian First Biennial, Tehran, Iran, 1957; del. Iranian Pavilion to Venice (Italy) Biennial, 1958; dir. Universal Gallery, Mpls., 1963-64; prof. arts Minnetonka Ctr. of Arts, Wayzata, Minn., 1963-64; guest prof. arts Tehran U., 1970-78; dir. Gorky Gallery, NYC, 1980-98. Lectr. Iranian Folk Art, Tehran, 1958-78; founder Near East Mus. Nat. Instn., Yerevan, Armenia, 1993. One-man shows in N.Y.C., rome, Paris, Tehran, Iran, Mpls., Yerevan, Bochum; exhibited in group shows at Walker Art Ctr., 1963, Johnson Mus., Ithaca, N.Y., 1981, Near East Mus., Tehran, Gorky Gallery, N.Y.C., 1988, Mus. Modern Art N.Y., others. Recipient Hon. Citizen award Mayor of Yerevan, 1994. Dem. Died Aug. 27, 2007.

GRIMME, A. JEANNETTE, retired elementary school educator, small business owner, volunteer; b. Eaton, Ohio, Jan. 13, 1921; d. Charles H. and Nelle L. (Scott) G. BA, Ohio Wesleyan U., 1943; MA, Oberlin Sch. Theology, 1953. Tchr. Eaton Pub. Sch., 1943-47, Zanesville (Ohio) Religious Edn. Coun., 1947-49; dir., tchr. Findlay (Ohio) Religious Edn. Coun., 1949-64; tchr. Findlay Pub. Schs., 1964-65, Consol. Dist. 2, Mo., 1965-83; dir. Christian edn. Unity of Independence, 1983-85. Co-owner Bess's Tea Room, Independence, 1996-98. Author: What is the Church, 1953; editor: Mutant Message Downunder (by Marlo Morgan), 1991; contbr. chpt. to books and articles to profl. jours. Program coord. Shepherd's Ctr. of Independence, 1987—, pres., 2000—. Mem. AAUW, Mission Work Area, Edn. Work Area, Raytown Ret. Tchrs. (pres. 1989-90), Delta Kappa Gamma. Meth. Avocations: travel, clown ministry. Home: Independence, Mo. Deceased.

GRINBERG, GEDALIO, retired watch manufacturing company executive; b. Quivican, Cuba, Sept. 26, 1931; arrived in US, 1960; m. Sonia Crugliac; children: Efraim, Alex, Miriam. Founder Movado Group, Inc., 1961, CEO, 1961—2001, chmn., 1961—2008. Recipient Lifetime Achievement Award, Jewelry Industry Coun., 2003. Died Jan. 4, 2009.

GRINSTEIN, ALEXANDER, psychoanalyst; b. Russia, Aug. 21, 1918; came to U.S., 1923; s. Mark L. and Esther (Alpert) G.; m. Adele Brotslaw, Sept. 27, 1941; children: David, Richard. BA, U. Buffalo, 1938, MD, 1942. Cert. psychoanalyst, Mich. Pvt. practice, Detroit, 1944-74, Beverly Hills, Mich., from 1974; professorial lectr. Sch. Social Work Wayne State U., Detroit, 1948-52, from instr. to asst. prof. Sch. Medicine, 1948-69, clin. assoc. prof., 1969-73, clin. prof. psychiatry, from 1973; professorial lectr. Mich. State U., Detroit, 1949-50; lectr. Detroit Psychoanalytic Inst., 1955-56; analyst tng., supervising Mich. Psychoanalytic Inst., Southfield, from 1960; clin. prof. psychiatry Detroit Psychiatric Inst., from 1973. Bd. dirs. Sigmund Freud Archives, Inc., N.Y.C., 1982-85, pres. bd. trustees, 1985—. Author: The Index of Psychoanalytic Writings, 14 vols., 1956-75, On Sigmund Freud's Dreams, 1968, Freud's Rules of Dream Interpretation, 1983, Freud at the Crossroads, 1990, Conrad Ferdinand Meyer and Freud: The Beginnings of Applied Psychoanalysis, 1991; The Remarkable Beatrix Potter, 1995; (with Editha Sterba) Understanding Your Family, 1957; editor: Sigmund Freud: A Comprehensive Bibliography, 1978; contbr. articles to profl. jours. Grantee Found. for Rsch. in Psychoanalysis, N.Y.C., 1959-73, McGregor Found., Detroit, 1964, NIMH, Washington, 1968-73. Fellow Am. Psychoanalytic Assn. (life), Am. Psychiatric Assn. (life); mem. Am. Psychoanalytic Assn. (life, bd. profl. standards 1966-72), Internat. Psychoanalytical Assn., Mich. Psychiat. Soc. (life), Mich. Psychoanalytic Soc. (life), Mich. Psychoanalytic Inst. (pres. 1977-79, 85-87), Oakland Country med. Soc. (life), Mich. State Med. Soc. (life), Mich. Assn. for Psychoanalysis (pres. 1972-74). Avocations: photography, playing violin, horseback riding. Home: Beverly Hills, Mich. Died Dec. 11, 2007.

GRISWOLD, GARRY MARTIN, optometrist; b. Cortland, NY, July 30, 1957; s. Hubert C. and Virginia F. (Martin) G.; m. Rebecca R. Gebert, Aug. 9, 1980; children: Sara, Jason, Christopher, Kyle. MusB, U Cin, 1979; OD, Ohio State U., 1993. Store mgr. sales Oakdale Music Ctrs., Rochester, N.Y., 1979-88; salesman Coyle Music Ctrs., Columbus, Ohio, 1989-93; optometrist Ada-Boise (Idaho) Vision Clinic, from 1993. Writer several mus. compositions. Umpire, bd. dirs. Little League Baseball, Boise, 1993—; choir dir. LDS Ch., 1984—. Recipient J. Harold Bailey Rsch. award Am. Optometric Found., Ohio State U. Coll. Optometry, 1993. Mem. Am. Optometric Assn. (contact lens sect.), Idaho Optometric Assn. Avocations: music, sports, reading. Home: Boise, Idaho. Died Mar. 8, 2008.

GRODER, MARTIN GARY, psychiatrist; b. NYC, Nov. 15, 1939; s. William Victor and Frances (Sturm) G.; m. Raquel Strauss, May 4, 1961 (div. Dec. 1984); children: Andrea Mia, Eric Bennett, Marc Alexander. BA, Columbia U., 1960, MD, 1964. Diplomate Am. Bd. Psychiatry and Neurology. Intern Maimonides Hosp., Bklyn., 1964-65; resident in psychiatry, Langley Porter Neuropsychiat. Inst. U. Calif., San Francisco, 1965-68; psychiatrist U.S. Bur. Prisons, 1968-72; warden-designate Fed. Corrections Inst., Butner, N.C., 1972-75; asst. clin. prof. Duke U., Durham, N.C., from 1973; practice medicine specializing in psychiatry Chapel Hill, N.C., from 1975. Vis. prof. So. Ill. U., Carbondale, 1969-75 Author: Business Games, 1981. Served to lt. commdr. USPHS, 1968-70. Mem. Internat. Transactional Analysis Assn. (teaching mem.). Libertarian. Avocations: art, photography, gardening. Home: Chapel Hill, NC. Died Oct. 12, 2007.

GROGAN, MICHAEL WAYNE, columnist, editor-in-chief, poet; b. Mabelvale, Ark., Feb. 15, 1940; s. Horace Milton and Charmel Elaine Grogan. BA in Art, Henderson Coll., Arkadelphia, Ark., 1963. Freelance work Ark. Gazette, 1961—91; newspaper columnist Southern Standard, Arkadelphia, Ark., 1979—87, Daily Siftings Herald, 1987—94; editor and publisher Heroes from Hackland mag., from 1995. Contbg. editor: The Best of Grogan Essay Collection, 1987. Democrat. Methodist. Avocations: comic book collecting, juvenile book series collecting. Home: Arkadelphia, Ark. Died Feb. 4, 2008.

GRONER, SAMUEL BRIAN, retired federal judge; b. Buffalo, Dec. 27, 1916; s. Louis and Lena (Blinkoff) G.; m. Beverly Anne Groner (dec. 2003); children: Jonathan B. (dec. 1962), Morri Lou Morell, Lewis A. Davis, Laurence M., Andrew G. Davis. AB, Cornell U., 1937, JD, 1939; MA in Econs., Am. U., 1950. Bar: N.Y. 1939, D.C. 1952, Md. 1953, U.S. Supreme Ct. 1944. Pvt. practice law, Buffalo, 1939-40; atty. U.S. Dept. War and Office Price Adminstrn., 1940-43; atty.-adviser U.S. Dept. Justice, Washington, 1946-53; pvt. practice law Md. and Washington, 1953-63; ptnr. Groner, Stone & Greiger, Washington, 1955-57, Groner & Groner, Silver Spring and Bethesda, Md., 1962-98. Asst. counsel Naval Ship Systems Command, Washington, 1963-73; trial atty. Office Gen. Counsel, Dept. Navy, Washington, 1973-74, assoc. chief trial atty., 1974-79; adminstrv. law judge and mem. Bd. Contract Appeals US Dept. Labor, Washington, 1979-95, acting chmn., 1987, mem. Bd. Alien Labor Certification Appeals, acting adminstrv. appeals judge Benefits Rev. Bd., 1988-89; instr. Terrell Law Sch., Washington, 1948; mem. faculty USDA Grad. Sch.; reporter Md. Gov.'s Commn. on Domestic Rels. Laws, 1977-87; participant in continuing legal and jud. edn. Author: Modern Business Law, 1983, (with others) The Improvement of the Administration of Justice, 6th edit., 1981; assoc. editor Fed. Bar Jour., 1948-55; contbr. articles to profl. jours. Active PTA, civic assns., Jewish Community Coun., Community Chest; mem. Montgomery County Commn. on Handicapped Individuals, 1977-85, vice chmn., 1980-81. 1st lt. inf. and M.I.S., U.S. Army, 1943-46, ETO. Recipient Navy Superior Civilian Service award, 1979. Mem. ABA (liaison commn. on professionalism, advisor to standing com. on lawyer competence 1986—, family law sect., jud. adminstrn. div., vice chmn. pub. contract law sect., com. on adminstrv. claims and remedies 1976-79, chmn. 1979-80), Fed. Bar Assn., Montgomery County Bar Assn. and Bar Found., Bar Assn. of D.C., Bar Assn. Met. St. Louis, Cornell Law Assn. (pres. D.C. chpt. 1947-54), Am. Law Inst., Inst. for Jud. Adminstrn., Am. Judicature Soc.,. Supreme Ct. Hist. Soc., Govt. Adminstrv. Trial Lawyers Assn., Nat. Lawyers Club, Cosmos Club, Cornell Club N.Y.C., Officers and Faculty Club (U.S. Naval Acad., Annapolis), Phi Beta Kappa. Home: Chevy Chase, Md. Died May 16, 2009.

GRONLUND, ROBERT B., art collector, fund raising consultant; b. Duluth, Minn., May 2, 1926; s. Bernard S. and Lena J. (Manske) G.; m. Dorothy M. Dahlstrom, June 2, 1951; children: Gaye, Robin, Gregg, Jamie. BA, Wartburg Coll., Waverly, Iowa, 1949; MDiv, Wartburg Sem., Dubuque, 1953; LittD, Thiel Coll., Greenville, Pa., 1973. Ordained Luth. Ch., 1953. Pastor Newport Harbor Luth. Ch., Newport Beach, Calif., 1953-56; exec. dir. Inter Ch. Fellowship, LA, 1956-59; asst. to pres. Calif. Luth. U., Thousand Oaks, Calif., 1959-62; exec. dir. Am. Luth. Ch. Found., Mpls., 1962-63; v.p. devel. Capital U., Columbus, Ohio, 1963-69, U. Tampa, Fla., 1969-76; founding ptnr. Gronlund Sayther Brunkow, West Palm Beach, Fla., from 1976; pres. Fla. campus Northwood U., West Palm Beach, 1981-83. Mem. works of art com. Norton Mus., West Palm Beach, 1993-96; chair PBCC Art Gallery, Palm Beach Gardens, Fla., 1995-96; chair Tampa Bay Art Ctr., Tampa, 1973-74; chair Vision for Mission Com., Evang. Luth. Ch. Am., Chgo., 1995-99. Exhibited collection at Norton Mus., Pensacola Mus., Tampa Mus., Wartburg Coll., Lighthouse Gallery, Tequesta, Fla., Ctr. for Arts, Vero Beach, Fla., others. Chair Fla. Repertory Theater, West Palm Beach, 1990—92; founding pres. Planned Giving Coun., West Palm Beach, 1982—84; sr. warden Bethesda By Sea Episcopal Ch., 1995; founding chair S.E. Diocese Episcopal Found., 1999—2002. Cpl. US Army, 1943—46, ETO. Mem.: Men of Bethesda (chair from 2002). Republican. Episcopalian. Avocations: golf, travel, grandchildren. Home: West Palm Beach, Fla. Died Sept. 9, 2007.

GROSS, GEORGE CLAYBURN, English language educator; b. Wilmington, Calif., May 14, 1922; s. Henry and Rebecca Ada (Bachman) G.; m. Marlo Vane Mumma, Apr. 30, 1941; children: George Timothy, John Henry. BA in English, San Diego State Coll., 1948, MA in English, 1950; PhD in English, U. So. Calif., LA, 1963. Cert. gen. secondary tchr., Calif. Tchr. English Grossmont H.S., El Cajon, Calif., 1948-49; instr. English San Diego State Coll., 1949-51; head English dept. Grossmont H.S., El Cajon, 1951-61; grad. teaching asst. U. So. Calif., L.A., 1958-59; from asst. to assoc. to full prof. San Diego State U., 1961-85, assoc. dean faculty pers., 1970-72, dean faculty affairs, 1972-81, prof. English, 1981-85, prof. English emeritus, 1985—2009. Cons. Sweetwater Sch. Dist., Chula Vista, Calif., 1967-68, Calif. State Com. on Pub. Edn., Berkeley, 1967; lectr. in field. Contbr. articles to scholarly jours. 2d lt. U.S. Army, 1943-45, ETO, com. 2nd lt. 1945. Mem. AAUP (officer 1969-70, chpt. v.p.), MLA, Keats-Shelley Assn., Mortar Board (svc. award 1995), Phi Beta Kappa (chpt. sec. 1977-80, pres. chpt. 1987-88, spl. award 1985), Phi Delta Kappa, Phi Kappa Phi (chpt. pres. 1969-70, svc. award 1985, honors coun.). Avocations: travel, reading, boxing, hiking, writing. Home: Spring Valley, Calif. Died Feb. 1, 2009.

GROSS, SHELLY (SHELDON HARVEY GROSS), theatrical producer, author; b. Phila., May 20, 1921; s. Samuel W. and Anna (Rosenblum) G.; m. Joan Seidel, May 1, 1946; children: Byron, Frederick, Daniel. AB, U. Pa., 1942; MS in Journalism, Northwestern U., 1947. Local news dir. and commentator Sta. WFPG, Atlantic City, 1948-49; spl. events dir. and announcer Sta. WFIL-AM and TV, Phila., 1949-58; CEO Music Fair Group Inc., Devon, Pa., 1955—2009. Author: The Crusher, 1970, Havana X, 1978, Stardust, 1985, Roots of Honor, 1987; co-producer Broadway and off Broadway shows include Catch Me If You Can, Lorelei, The King and I, Inquest, Bring Back Birdie, Camelot. Served to lt. USNR, 1942-46, PTO. Named Outstanding Comml. Announcer TV Guide, 1954; recipient Super Achiever award Juvenile Diabetes Found., 1976; Benjamin Franklin medal Poor Richard Club, 1985; named to Hall of Fame, Central High Sch. Mem. League of N.Y. Theatres and Producers, Phi Beta Kappa, Phi Gamma Mu, Sigma Delta Chi Died June 19, 2009.

GROSSBERG, JOHN MORRIS, psychologist, educator; b. Bklyn., Oct. 11, 1927; s. Percy and Edith (Garcee) G.; m. Carolyn Waldkoetter, July 2, 1955; children: Paul, Michael, Andrew. AB, Bklyn. Coll., 1950; MA, Ind. U., 1955, PhD, 1956. Asst. prof. psychology U. Calif., Riverside, 1955-58; chief psychologist Mound Bldrs. Guidance Ctr., Newark, Ohio, 1958-62; lectr. in psychology Denison U., Granville, Ohio, 1958-62; asst. prof. San Diego State U., 1962-68, prof. psychology, from 1969, chmn. dept. psychology, 1976-81, co-founder joint PhD program, 1978-80. Vis. prof. psychology Stanford U., 1968-69; cons. energy usage Navy Ocean Systems Ctr., San Diego, 1977-78; co-prin. investigator U.S. Dept. HEW, Vocat. Rehab. Adminstrn., San Diego, 1963-64; prin. investigator NIMH, San Diego, 1966-68; faculty participant NSF Undergrad. Rsch. Participant Program, 1964-65. Co-author: Eccentric and Bizarre Behaviors, 1995; contbr. numerous articles to profl. jorus. With USN, 1945-46; PTO. Mem. AAAS (Pacific div. v.p. 1981-82, pres. 1982-83), APA, Am. Psychol. Soc., Western Psychol. Assn. (co-mgr. ann. conv. 1979, bd. dirs. 1978-80), Sigma Xi, Phi Beta Kappa. Home: San Diego, Calif. Died June 18, 2008.

GROSSI, EDWARD JAMES, entertainment industry executive; b. Elizabeth, NJ, Mar. 16, 1949; s. August Cosmo and Anita Martha (Wilding) G.; m. Merry Louann Griffith, Nov. 30, 1974 (div. Dec. 1977); m. Leslie Ann Hayter, Dec. 25, 1981; 1 child, Tess Elizabeth. BA in Econs., Wesleyan U., Middletown, Conn., 1971; postgrad., U. Conn., 1972. V.p. JEM Records Group of Co.'s, South Plainfield, N.J., 1972-88; chmn. Pacific Records PLC, United Kingdom, 1984-88; pres. JEM/Eagle Multimedia, Somerset, N.J., 1988-89; chief exec. officer REC Track (USA) Inc., from 1989. Bd. dirs. The Phonomatic Music Group A.G., JEM Communications Inc., 1986-88, Passport Records Inc., South Plainfield, 1974-88; pres. JEM Records West Inc., Reseda, Calif., 1973-88. Mem. Recs. Internat. Trade Com. (pres. 1987). Clubs: Roxiticus Golf (Mendham, N.J.), Tupper Lake Country (N.Y.). Republican. Avocations: golf, white-water rafting, skiing, weightlifting. Home: Mendham, NJ. Died Mar. 31, 2008.

GROTH, CHARLES DONALD, actuary; b. Sheffield, Iowa, Nov. 4, 1932; s. George Henry and Jennie Tonnettie (Peterson) G.; m. Irene Theresa Schommer, June 9, 1954; children: Andrew Thomas, Patricia Ann. Student, Luther Coll., 1950-52; BA, Stetson U., 1954. Actuarial student Provident Life & Accident Ins. Co., Chattanooga, Tenn., 1954-62; group actuary Gulf Life Ins. Co., Jacksonville, Fla., 1962-85; cons. Wakely and Assocs., Clearwater, Fla., 1985-87; sr. v.p., chief actuary Am. Gen. Group Ins. Co., Dallas, 1987-90; v.p., chief actuary Anthem Life Ins. Cos., Dallas, from 1990. Bd. dirs. Anthem Life Ins. Co., Dallas, Anthem Life Ins. Co. of Calif., Sacramento, Anthem Life Ins. Co. of Ind., Inpls. Mem. Am. Acad. Actuaries, Soc. Actuaries (assoc.), Actuaries Club of the S.W., Southeastern Actuaries Club (exec. com. 1972-74). Methodist. Avocations: choral music, travel, photography. Home: Clearwater, Fla. Died Jan. 19, 2008.

GRUGER, EDWARD HART, JR., retired chemist; b. Murfreesboro, Tenn., Jan. 21, 1928; s. Edward Hart and Edith (Sundin) G.; m. Audrey Ruth Lindgren, June 27, 1952; children: Sherri Jeanette, Lawrence Hart, Linda Gay. BS, U. Wash., 1953, MS, 1956; PhD, U. Calif., Davis, 1968. Chemist U.S. Bur. Comml. Fisheries, Seattle, 1953-54, organic chemist, 1955-59, supervisory chemist, 1959-65, rsch. chemist, 1965-70; rsch. assoc. Agrl. Exptl. Sta. U. Calif., Davis, 1965-68; supervisory rsch. chemist NOAA,

Seattle, 1970-83; ret., 1983. Rsch. prof. Seattle U., 1977-82; coord., rsch. advisor NRC resident rsch. associateship postdoctoral program NOAA, Seattle, 1977-83. Contbr. papers to profl. publs., chpts. to books. Mem. adv. com. Planned Parenthood of Seattle-Puget Sound, 1983-87; precinct com. officer Legis. Dist., Seattle, 1984-94. With USN, 1946-48. Mem. AAAS (emeritus), Am. Oil Chemists' Soc. (emeritus), Am. Chem. Soc. (ret.), Elks (Wash. State Emerald award 1992), Sigma Xi. Democrat. Achievements include research to support vitamin E and similar molecules as biological antioxidants; polychlorinated biphenyls in fish activating enzymic systems for biotransformations of petroleum hydrocarbons; analysis of fish fatty acids. Home: Seattle, Wash. Died Jan. 13, 2008.

GRUNEWALD, RAYMOND BERNHARD, lawyer; b. NYC, Feb. 10, 1928; s. Ivan Oscar and Verna Allesandria (Lindgren) G.; m. Irma Geiser; children: Peter Bernhard, Iris Elizabeth. BS, Fordham U., 1949, JD, 1952. Bar: NY 1952, US Ct. Mil. Appeals 1956, US Dist. Ct. (so. and ea. dists.) NY 1957, US Ct. Appeals (2d cir.) 1962, US Supreme Ct. 1963, US Tax Ct. 1970, US Ct. Appeals (fed. cir.) 1986, US Ct. Appeals (3d cir.) 2000. Sole practice law, NYC, 1956-60 and from 70; asst. U.S. Atty., chief criminal and civil divsns. Dept. Justice, NYC, 1961-70. Candidate for Nassau County Comptroller, 1985, Nassau County Exec., 1987, Nassau County Ct., 1990, NY Supreme Ct., 1991, 92; dep. chmn. Nassau County Dem. Com., Mineola, NY. Served to Col. JAGC, US Army, 1952-56, Korea, with Res. 1957-83. Decorated Legion of Merit, Meritous Svc. medal, Oak Leaf Cluster, Combat Infantry Badge. Mem. ABA, Nassau County Bar Assn., Fed. Bar Council, Assn. Bar City N.Y., N.Y. County Lawyers Assn. Clubs: Squadron "A". Lutheran. Avocations: politics, reading, art collecting. Home: Greenvale, NY. Died Dec. 12, 1998.

GRYC, GEORGE, geologist; b. St. Paul, Minn., July 27, 1919; s. Anthony Stanley and Lillian (Teply) G.; m. Jean L. Funk, Feb. 4, 1942; children: James, Stephen, Christina, Paula, Georgina. BA, U. Minn., 1940, MS, 1942; postgrad., Johns Hopkins U., 1946-49. Geologist Alaskan Br. U.S. Geol. Survey, Washington, 1943-63; chief Alaskan br. U.S. Geol. Survey, Menlo Park, Calif., 1963-76, regional geologist, 1976, chief Office of Nat. Petroleum Resource in Alaska Anchorage, 1976-82, dirs. rep. Western region Menlo Park, 1982-95, gen. chmn. Circum-Pacific Map Project, from 1982. Recipient Meritorious Svc. award Dept. of Interior, Washington, 1974, Disting. Svc. award, 1978; named Hon. Mem., Alaska Geol. Soc., 1987. Fellow Geol. Assn. Am., Sigma Xi; mem. Am. Assn. Petroleum Geologists (editor), Paleontological Soc., Cosmos Club Washington. Home: Sunnyvale, Calif. Died Apr. 27, 2008.

GRZYBOWSKI, JAMES, manufacturing executive; b. Detroit, Feb. 4, 1949; s. Gregory Joseph and Rita (Andjewski) G.; m. Voula Katherine Armyros, Apr. 12, 1980. Student, Pacific Western U., 1980-86. Engring. mgr. Martin Engring., Detroit, 1975-79; maintenance engr. ITT, Brighton, Mich., 1979-81; engring. mgr. United Techs., Alma, Mich., 1982-86; mgr. engring. Dott Mfg., Deckerville, Mich., 1986-87, Baylock Mfg. ITT, Leonard, Mich., from 1987. Inventor in field. Served with USMC, 1969-75. Mem. Soc. Plastic Engrs. Orthodox. Lodge: Elks. Avocations: golf, tennis. Home: Etiwanda, Calif. Died May 11, 2008.

GUEST, BARBARA LEE, clothing store owner; b. Orange, NJ, June 17, 1938; d. Harry Sr. and Lula Iona (Gordon) Schwarz; m. Donald G. Guest, May 3, 1958; children: Susan Carole, Paul Jeffrey, Margaret Doris, David Allen. Grad. high sch., Middletown, NJ. Salesperson Kislin's Dept. Store, Red Bank, N.J., 1955-56, Grand Union, Keansburg, N.J., 1957-58; sec. Les Stewart Lincoln-Mercury, Mt. Holly, N.J., 1959-60; salesperson W.T. Grant, Mt. Holly, 1970-71; traffic sec. radio sta., Mt. Holly, 1971-72; salesperson, independent rep. Avon Products Inc., Newark, Del., 1973-81; mgr. SHE, Burlington, N.J., 1981-84; mgr., salesperson Leroy's, Lawrenceville, N.J., 1984; mgr., buyer Fashion Corner, Mt. Laurel, N.J., 1984-87; owner A Lady's Choice, Inc., Marlton, N.J., from 1987. Sec. N.J. Foster Parents Assn., Mt. Holly, 1962, Easthampton Helping Hand, Mt. Holly, 1975; mem. Easthampton Neighborhood Watch, Mt. Holly, 1982. Mem. Nat. Assn. Female Execs. Democrat. Methodist. Avocations: reading, sewing, painting, gardening, bowling. Home: Whiting, NJ. Died May 25, 2008.

GUGGENHEIM, RICHARD BENDER, hotel chain company executive; b. Chgo., Apr. 22, 1923; s. Milton S. and Sylvia (Bender) G.; m. Gail Porges; children: Paul, Jenny, Michael, Robert. BA, U. N.C., 1945. With Julius Bender, Inc., 1945-53; mgr. Midwest Terr. Design, Inc., St. Louis, 1953-57; v.p. mktg. Americana Congress Hotels, Chgo., 1957-87; pres., chief operating officer Comfort Inns of Elmhurst, Ill., from 1987. Regional adv. bd. Quality Internat. Bd. dirs. Am. Lung Assn. DuPage and McHenry Counties; mem. Econ. Devel. Commn., Highland Park, Ill.; active exec. com. Anti-Defamation League. Served with USMCR, 1943-45. Mem. Am. Hotel and Motel Assn. (pub. relations com.), Hotel Sales Mgmt. Assn. Home: Highland Park, Ill. Died Jan. 30, 2008.

GUIDERA, JOHN VICTOR, insurance loss prevention consultant, engineer; b. LA, Feb. 17, 1950; s. George and Shirley Ann (Gottlieb) G. BS in Civil Engring., Calif. Poly. U., 1982. Asst. engr. Indsl. Risk Insurers, Anaheim, Calif., 1973-74, engr., 1974-76, resident engr. Phoenix, 1976-78, dist. supr. engr. Anaheim, 1978-85, account cons. San Francisco, 1985-91, sr. account cons., 1991-94, divsn. loss prevention mgr., from 1994. Mem. Am. Inst. Avionics & Astronautics (assoc.), Soc. of Fire Protection Engrs. Avocation: corvette afficiando. Home: Concord, Calif. Died Nov. 16, 2007.

GULLICKSON, JOANNE LOIS, writer; b. Mpls., May 18, 1931; d. Leslie Robert and Alice Maratanna (Schnabel) Johnson; m. R. Burton (div.); children: Bonnie Mae, Debra Ann, Katheryn Alice; m. Leslie Marshall Gullickson, Dec. 6, 1969. Student, Augsburg Luth. Coll., Mpls., 1949—50. Cert. lic. real estate Minn., 1975, Ariz., 1978, reservations cert., airline tng. 1962. Mgr. Radelle Products, Mpls., 1954—57; reservationist United Airlines, Mpls., 1962—69; realtor News Realty, Mpls., 1975—78, Osselear Realty, Phoenix, 1979—85; metaphysical counselor, 1986—99; writer, guest numerous radio and TV shows, from 1989. Mem. Ariz. Assocs. Astrologers, Scottsdale, 1985—2000. Author: (book) On Angels' Wings, 1998 (Cert. of Merit, 1998), A 5 Step Guide: For the Woman Just Diagnosed With Breast Cancer, 2002, (newsletter) With Light and Love, JoAnne, 1992—94; exhibitions include Bob Duncan Ctr., Arlington, Tex., 2006, Arlington Visual Arts Assn., 2006. Mem. Luther League, sec./treas., 1946, pres., 1947; mem. Scottsdale Soroptamists, 1990—93; founder, chairperson Cancer Support Group, Scottsdale, Ariz., 2001—03; choir mem. Mpls. & St. Louis Pk., 1945—70. Recipient St. Louis Park award, City of St. Louis Park, Minn., 1949. Mem.: The Authors Guild, Inc. Independent. Lutheran. Avocations: writing, oil painting, travel, music. Died Oct. 18, 2006.

GUMBINER, ROBERT, health services executive; b. St. Louis, Jan. 31, 1923; s. Benjamin and Anna (Bleiweiss) G.; m. Josephine Schlenck, Dec. 23, 1948 (div. July 1990); children: Burke, Jay, Lee, Alis. BS, Ind. U., 1944, MD, 1948. Internship Ind. City Hosp., Bloomington, Ind., 1949; pvt. practice Indiana, 1948-49, Long Beach, Calif., 1949-61; pres., chief exec. officer FHP, Inc., Fountain Valley, Calif., 1961-90, chmn., cons., from 1990. Author: HMO-Putting It All Together, 1975. Chmn. FHP Found.; 1985—, Hippodrome Gallery, 1985—; bd. govs. Calif. State U., Long Beach, 1990—, mem. U. Calif. CEO Roundtable, Irvine, 1990—,, 1991—; Dem. Nat. Com., Washington, 1991, Dem. Senatorial Campaign Com., Washington, 1991. 1st lt. USAF, 1951-52. Recipient Disting. Alumni award Ind. U., Bloomington, 1991. Mem. Long Beach Yacht Club, Old Ranch Tennis Club. Avocations: sailing, biking, hiking. Home: Long Beach, Calif. Died Jan. 20, 2008.

GUNNISON, HUGH, counseling educator and hypnotherapist; b. Mt. Kisco, NY, Nov. 26, 1929; s. Hugh and Constance Hopkins (Frost) G.; m. Patricia Bushner, June 22, 1988; children: Jonathan, Stanley H. BA in English, St. Lawrence U., 1952, MEd in Counseling, 1959; EdD, Syracuse U., 1964. Diplomate Internat. Acad. Profl. Counselors and Psychotherapists. Asst. prof. psychology Onondoga Community Coll., Syracuse, 1962-64; lectr. Syracuse (N.Y.) U., 1964-65; prof. counseling St. Lawrence U., Canton, N.Y., 1965-78 and from 79, dir. London programme, 1991-92, prof. emeritus, 1992; prof. counseling George Peabody Coll.-Overseas Div. Vanderbilt U., Cambridge, Eng., 1978-79. Contbr. articles to profl. jours. With USCG, 1952-56. Fellow Nat. Bd. Cert. Clin. Hypnosis; mem. APA, AACD, Nat. Bd. Cert. Counselors (cert.), Cert. Clin. Mental Health Counelors (cert.). Avocations: reading, hiking, biking, sailing. Home: Canton, NY. Died Oct. 7, 2007.

GUNSALUS, IRWIN C., biochemistry educator, consultant; b. Sully County, SD, June 29, 1912; s. I. Clyde and Anna (Shea) G.; m. Dorothy Clark, Nov. 21, 1970 (dec. 1981); children: Gene (dec.), Glen, Ann, Robert, Richard, Tina, Kris. BS, Cornell U., 1935, MS, 1937, PhD, 1940; D.Sc. (hon.), Ind. U., 1984. Prof. bacteriology Cornell U., Ithaca, N.Y., 1940-47; prof. bacteriology Ind. U., Bloomington, 1947-50; prof. microbiology U. Ill., Urbana, 1950-55, head dept. biochemistry, 1955-66, prof. biochemistry, 1955-82, prof. emeritus, 1982—2008; sr. rsch. biochemist US Environ. Rsch. Lab., Gulf Breeze, Fla., 1993—2008. Asst. sec. gen. UN Indsl. Devel. Orgn., 1986; dir. Internat. Centre for Genetic Engring. and Biotech., 1986-89, sr. advisor; Fogarty scholar NIH, Bethesda, Md.; cons., scholar Salk Inst. Biol. and Indsl. Assocs., La Jolla, Calif. Co-recipient Mead Johnson award in biochemistry, 1946; Guggenheim fellow, 1949, 59, 68. Mem. Nat. Acad. Sciences (Selman A. Waksman award 1982), French Academie des Scis., AAAS, Am. Chem. Soc. (emeritus), Am. Soc. Biol. Chemists, Brit. Biochem. Soc. Am. Soc. Microbiology. Home: Champaign, Ill. Died Oct. 25, 2008.

GUPTA, ANSHOO SUDHIR, marketing professional; b. Kota, Rajasthan, India, Dec. 5, 1946; came to U.S., 1968; s. Dwarka Das and Vimla (Jain) G.; m. Jyotsna Anshoo Prasad, Dec. 24, 1973; children: Ankur Sudhir, Roli. BSEE with honors, Indian Inst. Tech., Kharagpur, 1968; MSEE, U. Rochester, 1969, MBA, 1971. V.p. fin. Systems Mktg. div. Xerox Corp., El Segundo, Calif., 1983-84, v.p. mktg. Bus. Systems Group, from 1985. Dir. Xerox Employees Fed. Credit Union, El Segundo, 1978-82. Home: Rncho Pls Vrd, Calif. Died Dec. 19, 2007.

GUTHRIE, EDGAR KING, artist; b. Chenoa, Ill., May 12, 1917; s. David McMurtrie and Emily Henrietta (Streid) G.; m. Eva Ross Harvey, Dec. 8, 1945 (dec. Jan. 1978); children: Melody Bliss Johnson, Mark King Guthrie (dec. Nov. 4, 2006). BEd, Ill. State U., 1939; MA, Am. U., 1958; graduate, Command and General Staff Coll., Ft. Leavenworth, Kan., 1967. Artist W.L. Stensgaard Co., Chgo., 1939-40, The Diamond Store, Phoenix, 1941-42; presentation artist CIA, Washington, 1955-72; instr. Columbia Tech. Inst., Arlington, Va., 1966-72; owner, later ptnr. Guthrie Art & Sign Co., Winchester, Va., from 1976; instr. U. Hawaii, Lihue, 1980-81; cartoonist The Kauai Times, Lihue, 1981-90; owner Alo-o-oha-ha-ha Caricatures, Lihue, Honolulu, from 1980. Cons., artist Shenandoah Apple Blossom Festival, Winchester, 1975-78; cartoonist Internat. Salon of Caricature, Montreal, Can., 1976-77; co-chmn. Kauai Soc. of Artists Art Show, Lihue, 1981. One man shows include 50 Yrs. of Painting-A Retrospective, Lihue, 1984; inventor Artists' Kit; Filmic Artist: (documentary film) The River Nile, 1960 (NBC Emmy Award). Bd. dirs. Civil Def., Virginia Hills, 1954; publicity com. Frederick County Taxpayers Assn., Winchester, 1973, Exch. Club, Winchester, 1977. Lt. col. U.S. Army, 1942-54. Decorated Purple Heart, Bronze Star with oak leaf cluster; recipient Spl. Merit award Boy Scouts Am. Aloha Coun., Lihue, 1982. Mem. Mus. of Cartoon Art, U.S. Naval Combat Artist, Daniel Morgan Mus. (contbr. 1976), Nat. Soc. Mural Painters (contbr. 1976), Allied Artists of Am. (contbr. 1977), Pastel Soc. Am. (contbr. 1977-78), Am. Watercolor Soc. (contbr. 1982—), Greek Expeditionary Forces (hon.). Mem. Ch. LDS. Avocations: animation, cinematography, hiking, swimming, genealogy. Died Sept. 13, 2007.

GUTHRIE, FRANK ALBERT, chemistry professor; b. Madison, Ind., Feb. 16, 1927; s. Ned and Gladys (Glick) G.; m. Marcella Glee Farrar, June 12, 1955; children: Mark Alan, Bruce Bradford, Kent Andrew, Lee Farrar. AB, Hanover Coll., 1950; MS, Purdue U., 1952; PhD, Ind. U., 1962. Mem. faculty Rose-Hulman Inst. Tech., Terre Haute, Ind., from 1952, assoc. prof., 1962-67, prof. chemistry, 1967-94, prof. emeritus, from 1994, chmn. dept., 1969-72, chief health professions adviser, 1975-94. Kettering vis. lectr. U. Ill., Urbana, 1961-62; vis. prof. chemistry U.S. Mil. Acad., West Point, N.Y., 1987-88, 93-94, admissions coord., 1989—; vis. prof. chemistry Butler U., spring 2000. Mem. exec. bd. Wabash Valley coun. Boy Scouts Am., 1971-87, scoutmaster, 1979-82, adv. bd., 1988—, v.p. for scouting, 1976; mem. selection chmn. Leadership Terre Haute, 1978-80. Served with AUS, 1945-46 Recipient Vigil Honor Order of Arrow, Boy Scouts Am., 1975, Wood badge, 1976, Dist. award of merit, 1976, Silver Beaver award, 1980. Fellow Ind. Acad. Sci. (treas. 1966-68, pres. 1970, chmn. acad. found. trustees 1986—); mem. Am. Chem. Soc. (sec. 1973-77, editor directory 1965-77, chmn. divsn. analytical chemistry 1979-80; local sect. activities com. 1982-86, nominations and elections com. 1988-94, sec. 1992-94, coun. policy com. 1995, constn. and bylaws com. 1996-2002, membership affairs com., 2003—, chmn. Wabash Valley sect. 1958, counselor 1980—, steering com. for joint ctrl.-Gt. Lakes regional meetings, Indpls., 1978, 91, vis. assoc. com. profl. tng. 1984—, chmn. analytical chemistry exam. inst. std. exam. 1994, Disting. Svc. award 2005), Coblentz Soc., Midwest Univs. Analytical Chemistry Conf., Hanover Coll. Alumni Assn. (pres. 1974, Alumni Achievement award 1977), Masons (32 deg.), Sigma Xi (treas. Wabash Valley chpt. 1994-98), Phi Lambda Upsilon, Phi Gamma Delta, Alpha Chi Sigma (E.E. Dunlap scholarship selection com. 1986—, chmn. 1990—, dir. expansion 1995-99, profl. rep. 1997-2000), Osher Lifelong Learning Inst. Ind. State U. (steering com. 2008-). Presbyterian. Home: Terre Haute, Ind. Died June 11, 2009.

GUTHRIE, JOHN REILEY, retired military officer; b. Phillipsburg, NJ, Dec. 20, 1921; s. John Milton, Jr. and Claire (Reiley) G.; m. Rebecca Jane Jeffers, June 18, 1947 (dec. April 11, 2005); children: Rebecca Claire, Michael Reiley, John Jeffers, Peter Blair, Margaret, Kevin McCammon. Grad., Blair Acad., 1938; AB with honors, Princeton, 1942; grad., Command and Gen. Staff Coll., 1944, Nat. War Coll., 1961. Commd. 2d lt. U.S. Army, 1942, advanced through grades to gen., 1977; served in Hawaii and Japan, World War II; asst. to mil. attache London, Eng., 1946-49; with 39th Field Arty. Bn. and 3d Inf. Div. Arty., U.S., Japan and Korea, 1949-51; comdr. 602d F.A. Bn., 1952-53; mem. staff and faculty F.A. Sch., 1953-56; staff officer Office Chief Research and Devel., Dept. Army, 1956-58, mil. asst., asst. exec. officer to sec. of army, 1958-60; staff CINCPAC, 1961-64; comdr. 25th Inf. Div. Arty; chief of staff, asst. div. comdr. 25th Inf. Div., 1964-65; mem. Org. of the Joint Chiefs of Staff, 1965-66; dir. devels. Dept. of Army, 1966-67; asst. div. comdr. 2d Inf. Div., 1967-68; dir. research, devel. and engring. US Army Materiel Command, Washington, 1969-71, dep. comdr. for materiel acquisition, 1971-73; dep. chief staff CINCPAC, 1973-75; comdr. US Army Japan & IX Corps, 1975-77, US Army Materiel Devel. & Readiness Command (DARCOM), 1977-81; ret., 1981; dir. Landpower Edn. Program, Assn. U.S. Army, 1982-86. Chmn. bd. Cardion Inc., Woodbury, N.Y., 1989-98, St. John's Cmty. Svcs. Found., Inc. Trustee Princeton U., 1981-85, St. John's Cmty. Svcs., Washington; bd. dirs. Army and Air Force Mut. Aid Assn., 1982-93. Decorated D.S.M. with 1 oak leaf cluster; Legion of Merit with 2 oak leaf clusters; Bronze Star medal with 2 oak leaf clusters; Joint Service Commendation medal; Army Commendation medal; recipient Disting. Service award Federally Employed Women, 1980; Eagle award Nat. Guard Bur., 1981 Mem. Assn. U.S. Army, Air Force Assn., Nat. Security Indsl. Assn. (hon.), Ret. Officers Assn., Am. Def. Preparedness Assn. (Gold medal 1981), Soc. Logistics Engrs., Soc. Mil. Engrs., Res. Officers Assn. (Minuteman Hall of Fame award 1981), Nat. Contract Mgmt. Assn. (bd. advisers 1982-93). Clubs: Princeton (N.Y., Washington); Nassau

(Princeton). Presbyterian. Army staff action officer for devel. and launching of 1st U.S. artificial earth satellite, Explorer I (Jupiter C29), 1958. Home: Springfield, Va. Died May 25, 2009.

GUYBERSON, RANDY ALAN, writer; b. South Bend, Ind., Mar. 9, 1950; s. William J. Guyberson, Sr. and Lucille M. Guyberson. Diploma, Inst. Children Lit., 1999; home study course, McCall's Cooking Sch., 1980. Chef several restaurants, South Bend; owner, painter, paper hanger Guyberson's Painting Co., South Bend; owner, oper. Granny's Spot Restaurant, Wyatt, Ind.; owner, operator Launderette, Denver; writer. Avocations: cooking, designing, writing, dogs. Home: South Bend, Ind. Died Aug. 6, 2008.

GWATHMEY, CHARLES, architect; b. Charlotte, NC, June 19, 1938; s. Robert and Rosalie Dean (Hook) G.; m. Emily Gwathmey (div.); 1 child Annie; m. Bette-Ann Damson, Dec. 15, 1974; 1 stepchild Eric Steel. Student, U. Pa., Phila., 1956-59; M.Arch., Yale U., New Haven, Conn., 1962. Ptnr. firm Gwathmey Siegel & Associates Architects, NYC, 1968—2009. Vis. prof. archtl. design Pratt Inst., Yale U., Princeton U., Harvard U., Columbia U., Cooper Union, UCLA; William A. Bernoudy resident architecture, Am. Acad., 2005. Pres. bd. trustees Inst. Architecture and Urban Studies, NYC, 1978. Recipient Arnold Brunner prize AAAL, 1970; William Wirt Winchester traveling fellow, 1962-63; Fulbright grantee France, 1962-63; recipient AIA Nat. Honor awards for Straus residence, Purchase, NY, 1968, Whig Hall, Princeton U., 1976, Dormitory, Dining and Student Union SUNY, Purchase 1976, Taft Residence, Cin., 1984, Westover Sch., Middlebury, Conn., 1988, Ctrl. Pk. South Appt.NYC, 2008, AIA NY awards for Sch. Agr. Cornell U., 1991, Guggenheim Mus., NYC, 1995, Yale Alumni Arts award for outstanding achievement, 1985, Lifetime Achievement medal in visual arts Guild Hall Acad., 1988, Lifetime Achievement award NY State Soc. Archs., 1990. Fellow AIA (firm award 1982, Medal of honor 1983); mem. Am. Acad. Arts and Letters. Died Aug. 3, 2009.

GYGI, KAREN MAURINE, music educator; b. Panguitch, Utah, Sept. 30, 1934; d. Reuben Albert Joseph and Maurine (Bullock) Sidwell; m. Leland Ross Gygi, July 2, 1954; children: Janet, Kenneth, Darrell, Paula, Carolyn. BA, U. Utah, 1968. Ind. music tchr., Roosevelt, Utah, 1959-60, Morgan, Utah, 1960-62, Ogden, Utah, from 1962. Adjudicator, lectr. Utah Music Tchrs. Assn., 1970—, Utah Music Fedn., 1972-73; panelist Music Tchrs. Nat. Assn. nat. conv., 1976. Music dir. (mus. plays) Because of Elizabeth, 1979, Music Man, 1983; music, drama dir. Fiddler On the Roof, 1985; orchestrator, composer for various mus. prodns. Utah, Idaho, Nev., Calif. Rep. precinct co-chmn., Ogden, 1964, 70, chmn., 1972; del. Weber County Rep. Conv., 1980; area worker cancer dr., Ogden, 1970; mem. Symphonic Choir, Salt Lake City, Community Choir, Ogden. Mem. Music Tchrs. Nat. Assn. (v.p. S.W. div. 1985-88, pres.-elect 1988, pres. 1990, nat. exec. bd. 1990-94), Sempre Mus. Soc., People to People, Inc., Nat. High Sch. Auditions Com. (cert.), Educators' Mission to Thailand, Mu Phi Epsilon (scholarship), Phi Kappa Phi, Phi Beta Kappa. Mem. Lds Ch. Avocations: travel, gardening. Died July 25, 2008.

HABER, FLORENCE, retired hospital administrator; b. NYC, Oct. 31, 1916; d. Albert and Dora (Bernstein) Novick; m. Harry Haber, Nov. 22, 1939 (dec. Feb. 1991); children: Carol Diamond, Helen Bilgoray. BS in Health Sci. cum laude, Hunter Coll., 1971. Cert. registered record adminstr. Am. Med. Record Assn. Sec., attendance supr. Hicksville Pub. Schs., LI, NY; sec., prin. Temple Sinai Religious Sch., Roslyn, NY; dir. med. records Sydenham Hosp.-Health and Hosp. Corp., NYC, 1971-73; dir. psychiat. records Met. Hosp., NYC, 1973-78; discharge planning coord. Metropolitan Hosp., NYC, 1979-85. Pres. Sisterhood Temple Beth-El, North Bellmore, N.Y., 1954-55; bd. dirs. Temple Beth-El, North Bellmore, 1956-57. Recipient Svc. Achievement award Temple Beth-El, 1962; named Prime Time Vol. Area Agy. on Aging, Palm Beach, Fla., 1995. Mem. Jewish Fedn. South Palm Beach County (mem. Jewish edn. com. 1995—, chair elder hostel com. 1994—, sec. acad. Jewish studies com. 1992—, Vol. of Yr. 1996). Avocations: writing, bridge, travel. Home: Delray Beach, Fla. Died Dec. 3, 2007.

HABERMAN, CHARLES MORRIS, mechanical engineer, educator; b. Bakersfield, Calif., Dec. 10, 1927; s. Carl Morris and Rose Marie (Braun) H. BS, UCLA, 1951; MS in Mech. Engring., U. So. Calif., 1954, MS in Aeronautical Engring., 1960. Lead, sr. and group engr. Northrop Aircraft, Hawthorne, Calif., 1951-59, cons., 1959-61; asst. prof. to prof. mech. engring. Calif. State U., LA, 1959-91. Cons. Royal McBee Corp., 1960-61. Author: Engineering Systems Analysis, 1965, Use of Computers for Engineering Applications, 1966, Vibration Analysis, 1968, Basic Aerodynamics, 1971. Served with AUS, 1946-47. Mem. Am. Soc. Engring. Edn. Democrat. Roman Catholic. Home: Thousand Oaks, Calif. Died Sept. 13, 2008.

HACKLER, RHODA E. A., retired historian; b. NYC, Nov. 7, 1923; d. William Campbell and Rhoda Elizabeth Armstrong; m. Windsor Gregory Hackler, Mar. 31, 1951; 1 child, Jeffrey Madison. BA, U. Hawaii, 1970, MA, 1972, PhD, 1978. Adminstrv. asst. US Embassy Japanese Lang. Sch., Tokyo, 1955—56; with J.F. Begg Real Estate, 1962—65; lectr. history U. Hawaii, Honolulu, 1972—91; project dir. Hawaiian Hist. Soc., 1978—79; rsch. assoc. territory Hawaii history project San Jose State U., Calif., 1980—82; ret., 1982. Lectr. in field. Contbr. articles to profl. jours.; editor: (newsletter) Friends of East-West Center Newsletter, 1973—77, Friends of Iolani Palace Newsletter, 1976—88. Vol. Motor Corps., DC, 1941—42, Lennox Hill Hosp., NYC, 1946—47; chmn. historic rsch. on Iolani Palace Jr. League Honolulu, 1965—68; mem. restoration com. Friends of Iolani Palace, 1969—77, ops. & interpretation com., 1978—96, edn., publs. com., 1978—96, com. mem. Palace Shop, 1978—96; mem. Bishop Mus. Assn. Coun., 1982—86; mem. Liberal Arts Adv. Coun. Hawaii Pacific U., from 1988; mem. Bishop Mus. Assn. Coun., 1993—96; dir. Hawaii Opera Theatre & Edn., 1980—2006; mem. vestry Ch. Holy Nativity, Honolulu, 1987—89, from 1993, chair outreach com., 1992—93, chair United Thank Offering, Women Outreach, 1993—94; mem. Diocese Coun. Diocese Hawaii, 1989—92, mem. Campus Min., 1989—93, mem. Commn. Ministry, 1992—96, mem. Standing Com., 1997—2000, chair Nurture & Edn. Com., from 2003, diocesan coun., from 2003; bd. dirs. Friends of Iolani Palace, Honolulu, from 1968. Sgt. US Army, 1943—45, lt. USAR, 1949—57, 2d lt. USAR, 1951—54. Mem.: Caledonia Soc. Hawaii (sec. 2003—05), Hawaii Army Mus. Soc. (trustee from 2001), Soc. Asian Arts Hawaii (v.p. 1998—99, pres. 1999—2001), Kahala Cmty. Assn. (dir. 1995—96), Assn. Hawaiian Archivists, Hawaii Mus. Assn., Hawaiian Hist. Soc. (life; pres. 1977—79). Home: Honolulu, Hawaii. Died July 7, 2008.

HADDOCK, FREDERICK THEODORE, JR., retired astronomer; b. Independence, Mo., May 31, 1919; s. Fred Theodore Sr. and Helen (Sea) H.; m. Margaret Pratt, June 24, 1941 (div. Sept. 1976); children: Thomas Frederick, Richard Marshall; m. Deborah J. Fredericks, Dec. 7, 2003. SB, MIT, Cambridge, 1941; MS, U. Md., 1950; DSc (hon.), Rhodes Coll., Memphis, 1965, Ripon Coll., Wis., 1966. Physicist U.S. Naval Rsch. Lab., Washington, 1941-56; assoc. prof. elec. engring. and astronomy U. Mich., Ann Arbor, 1956-59, prof. elec. engring., 1959-67, prof. astronomy, 1959-88, prof. emeritus, 1988—2009. Lectr. radio astronomy Jodrell Bank U. Manchester, Eng., 1962; vis. assoc. radio astronomy Calif. Inst. Tech., 1966; vis. lectr. Raman Inst., Bangalore, India, 1978; sr. cons. Nat. Radio Astron. Obs., W.Va., 1960-61; founder, dir. U. Mich. Radio Astron. Obs., 1961-84. Contbr. chpts. to books, articles to profl. jours. and publs. Mem. Union Radio Sci. Internat., nat. chmn. commn. on radio astronomy, 1954-57; trustee Associated Univs., Inc., 1964-68; prin. investigator, five Orbiting Geophys. Observatories, 1960-74, and Interplanetary Probe 9, 1964-77; co-investigator on Voyager planetary probes, 1970-86, NASA, Washington; mem. astronomy adv. panel NSF, Washington, 1957-60, 63-66. With USN, 1944-45. Fellow IEEE (life), Am. Astron. Soc. (v.p. 1961-63); mem. Internat. Astron. Union (commn. on radio astronomy 1948-2009), NAS (adv. panel astronomy facilities 1962-64), AIA (hon. mem. Huron Valley chpt. 1980-2009), Sigma Xi (past pres. U. Mich. chpt. 1956-2009). Achievements include design and development of first submarine periscope radar antenna, 1943-44; early discoveries in microwave astronomy, gaseous nebulae in 1953 and early space detection of kilometer waves from galaxy and the sun, 1962. Home: Ann Arbor, Mich. Died Feb. 20, 2009.

HADLEY, LEILA ELIOTT-BURTON (MRS. HENRY LUCE III), writer; b. NYC, Sept. 22, 1925; d. Frank Vincent and Beatrice Boswell Eliott Burton; m. Arthur T. Hadley, II, Mar. 2, 1944 (div. Aug. 1946); 1 child, Arthur T. III; m. Yvor H. Smitter, Jan. 24, 1953 (div. Oct. 1969); children: Victoria C. Van D. Smitter Barlow, Matthew Smitter Burton Eliott, Caroline Allison F.S. Nicholson; m. William C. Musham, May 1976 (div. July 1979); m. Henry Luce III, Jan. 1990 (dec. Sept. 8, 2005). MD, St. Timothy's Sch., 1943; LLD (hon.), Mount St. Mary's Coll., Newburgh, NY, 2006. Author: Give Me the World, 1958, reprinted, 1999, Give Me the World, 2003, How to Travel with Children in Europe, 1963, Manners for Children, 1967, Fielding's Guide to Traveling with Children in Europe, 1972, rev., 1974, 1984, Traveling with Children in the U.S.A., 1974, Tibet-20 Years After the Chinese Takeover, 1979; author: (with Theodore B. Van Itallie) The Best Spas: Where to Go for Weight Loss, Fitness Programs and Pure Pleasure in the U.S. and Around the World, 1988, rev., 1989; author: A Journey with Elsa Cloud, 1997, paperback edit. with afterword, 2003, Give Me the World, 1999, A Garden by the Sea, 2005; assoc. editor Diplomat mag., N.Y.C., 1964—65, Saturday Evening Post, 1965—67, contbg. editor ICON: World Monuments Mag.; contbg. editor: Tricycle, the Buddhist Rev., from 1991; editl. cons. TWYCH, N.Y.C., 1985—87, book reviewer Palm Beach Life, Fla., 1967—72, consulting editor Tricyle, The Buddhist Rev., from 1991, garden columnist Fishers Island Gazette; contbr. articles to various newspapers, mags. Bd. dirs. Wings World Quest, Inc., 1992, Tibet House, 1995, Fishers Island Conservancy, 1995, Donald & Shelley Rubin Cultural Trust, 2001. Recipient Norman Vincent Peale award, 2002. Fellow Royal Can. Geog. Soc. (hon.); mem. Acad. Am. Poets, Soc. Woman Geographers, Authors Guild, Nat. Writers Union, Nat. Press Club, PEN, Explorers Club, Central Park Conservancy, Ocean Conservancy, N.Y. Acad. Medicine (guest bd.), The Kitchen Ctr. Haleakala, Inc., Nat. Arts Club, Lansdowne Club (Eng.). Home: New York, NY. Died Feb. 10, 2009.

HAENICKE, DIETHER HANS, retired academic administrator; b. Hagen, Germany, May 19, 1935; came to U.S., 1963, naturalized, 1972; s. Erwin Otto and Helene (Wildfang) H.; m. Carol Ann Colditz, Sept. 29, 1962; children: Jennifer Ruth, Kurt Robert. Student, U. Gottingen, 1955-56, U. Marburg, 1957-59; PhD magna cum laude in German Lit. and Philology, U. Munich, 1962; DHL (hon.), Cen. Mich. U., 1986; DHL, We. Mich. U., 1998. Asst. prof. Wayne State U., Detroit, 1963-68, assoc. prof., 1968-72, prof. German, 1972-78, resident dir. Jr. Year in Freiburg (Ger.), 1965-66, 69-70, dir. Jr. Year Abroad programs, 1970-75, chmn. dept. Romance and Germanic langs. and lits., 1971-72, assoc. dean Coll. Liberal Arts, 1972-75, provost, 1975-77, v.p., provost, 1977-78; dean Coll. Humanities Ohio State U., 1978-82, v.p. acad. affairs, provost, 1982-85; pres. Western Mich. U., Kalamazoo, 1985-98, interim pres., 2006—07. Asst. prof. Colby Coll. Summer Sch. of Langs., 1964-65; lectr. Internationale Ferienkurse, U. Freiburg, summers 1961, 66, 67 Author: (with Horst S. Daemmrich) The Challenge of German Literature, 1971, Untersuchungen zum Versepos des 20. Jahrhunderts, 1962; editor: Liebesgeschichte der schonen Magelone, 1969, Der blonde Eckbert und andere Novellen, 1969, Franz Sternbalds Wanderungen, 1970, Wednesdays with Diether, 2003, University Governance and Humanistic Scholarship (Festschrift), 2002; contbr. articles to acad. and lit. jours. Mem. Mich. State Atty. Discipline Bd. Fulbright scholar, 1963-65 Mem. MLA, AAUP, Am. Assn. Tchrs. of German, Mich. Acad. Arts and Scis., Mich. Coun. for Arts and Cultural Affairs, Phi Beta Kappa. Home: Kalamazoo, Mich. Died Feb. 15, 2009.

HAERTEL, CHARLES WAYNE, minister; b. Stevens Point, Wis., May 20, 1937; s. George Henry and Eva Georgia (Kingsland) H. BA, St. Olaf Coll., 1960; BD, Luther Theol. Sem., 1965; STM, Wartburg Sem., 1977; D Ministry, McCormick Sem., 1988; postgrad., Luth. Sch. Theology, 1994-95, cert. multicultural ministry, 1995; cert. in Islamic Studies, Luther Sch. Theology, 1999. Ordained to min. Evang. Luth. Ch. Am., 1965. Pastor Our Saviour's Luth. Ch., Almira, Wash., 1965-68, St. Jacob's Luth. Ch., Jackson Center, Ohio, 1968-72, Immanual Luth. Ch., Salem, Ohio, 1972-76, Zion Luth. Ch., Bridgewater, S.D., 1976-85, Cedar Valley-Looney Valley Luth. Parish, Houston, Minn., 1985-93, East Chain Luth. Ch., Blue Earth, Minn., from 1993; emeu Mideast Tour, 1996. Rep. nat. Am. Luth. Ch. Conv., Sioux Falls (S.D.) Conf., 1984-85; host refugee families Luth. Social Svcs., Sioux Falls, 1984; ELCA Mission tchr. Oshigambo H.S., Namibia, 1995-96. Mem. Peace and Justice Ctr., 1977-83; bd. dirs. Wellspring Wholistic Care Ctr., Freeman, S.D., 1980-85, M-2 State Penitentiary Visitation Program, 1980-85; Clin. Pastoral Edn. extended chaplain Hennepin County Med. Ctr., 1997-98; mem. Alban Inst., Rochester (Minn.) Symphony Choral; bd. dirs. Houston County Minn. Child Abuse Prevention Program, 1989-92, Luth. Campus Ministry, Winona State U., 1986-93; camping staff Holden Village, Wash., 1993; Laubach reading tchr., Fairmont, Minn., 1993—; sec. Improved Muslim/Christian Rels. Chgo., 1994—; choral dir.; mem. Christian fellowship, St. Paul, Minn., 1998-99. Scouting scholar Luth. Brotherhood, St. Olaf Coll., 1956, McCormick scholar, 1982; grantee Shaloam Continuing Edn. Program, 1980-82. Mem. NAACP, McCook County (S.D.) Clergy (pres. 1982-83), So. Ea. Minn. Mission Ptnrs. (mem. com., Synod conf. vice dean 1994), Amnesty Internat., Sierra Club, Nat. Geog. Toastmasters (pres. LaCrosse area club 1989-90, local area and divsn. gov. 1990—), Am. Philatelic Soc., Able Toastmaster (Bronze, Disting. Toastmaster award 1991), Kiwanis (pres. Jackson Center club 1969-70). Avocations: music, coin, stamp and rock collecting. Died Nov. 20, 2007.

HAFFORD, LEORA MARIE, music educator, keyboard artist; b. Hiteman, Iowa, Jan. 2, 1939; d. Howard Morgan and Armilda Caroline (Cox) Brock; m. Franklin Lee Hafford, Sept. 3, 1962; children: Wendy Lee Stevens, Bethany Ann Woodard, Nanette Kehrberg, Noelle. Diploma, Alton Meml. Sch. Nursing, Ill., 1962; BA in Sacred Music, Bible, Theology, Vennerd Coll. magna cum laude, Univ. Park, Iowa, 1990. RN Iowa; cert music tchr. Nat. and State Bd. Iowa. Dir. nursing Albia (Iowa) Manor, 1979-80; staff nurse Wayne County Hosp., Corydon, Iowa, 1980-83, VA Med. Ctr., Knoxville, Iowa, 1983; organist Christian Ch., Pleasantville, Iowa, 1989; minister of music Ch. of the Nazarene, Albia, Ottumwa, Fremont, Iowa, 1990-93; piano tchr. pvt. practice, Knoxville, Iowa, 1984-91, Ottumwa, Iowa, from 1991. Mem. Music Tchrs. Nat. Assn., Iowa Music Tchrs. Assn., S. Ctrl. Iowa Music Tchrs. Assn. Republican. Mem. Ch. Of The Nazarene. Avocations: music, reading, cats, needlecrafts. Died Feb. 9, 2008.

HAGAN, WESLEY DILLARD, minister; b. Tompkinsville, Ky., Jan. 16, 1924; s. Bascal and Effie (Carlock) H.; m. Maxine Britt, Mar. 15, 1951; children: Michael, David, Elizabeth Ann. Student, Clear Creek Bapt. Sch., Pine Valley, Ky., 1943-44, Campbellsville Coll., 1945-46, So. Bapt. Theol. Sem., 1956. Ordained to ministry So. Bapt. Conv., 1946. Pastor 1st Bapt. Ch., Friendsville, Tenn., 1946-51, Tenn. Ave. Bapt. Ch., Knoxville, 1951-55, McPheeters Bend Bapt. Ch., Church Hill, Tenn., 1965-67, 1st Bapt. Ch., Kuttawa, Ky., 1967-68, Beaumont Ave. Bapt. Ch., Knoxville, 1968-71, 1st Bapt. Ch, Philadelphia, Tenn., 1970-73, Bufflo Trail Bapt. Ch., Morristown, Tenn., 1971-73, North Athens (Tenn.) Bapt. ch., 1973-75, Forest Hill Bapt. Ch., Maryville, Tenn., 1973-76, White Plains Bapt. Ch., Scottsville, Ky., 1975-78, Indian Creek Bapt. Ch., Flippin, Ky., 1979-87, Rogers Creek Bapt. Ch., Athens, Tenn., from 1987. Moderator Chillihowee Bapt. Assn., Maryville, 1975-76, Loudon County Bapt. Assn., Philadelphia, 1977-78, Allen Bapt. Assn., Scottsville, 1981-82, Monroe Bapt.

Assn., Flippin, 1983-84. Author: Philadelphia History, 1822-1973, 1978, The Joy of Being His, 1980, Looking Upward, 1982, Lord, Teach Me to Pray, 1984. Died Mar. 25, 2008.

HAICH, GEORGE DONALD, English educator; b. Evanston, Ill., Feb. 27, 1928; s. Peter John and Ida (Campbell) H.; m. Gloria Deloris Lunick, Aug. 27, 1950; children: Pamela, Tanya, Christopher. AB, U. Rochester, 1952; MA, U. Nebr., 1966; PhD, U. Fla., 1970. Asst. prof. Concordia Coll., Seward, Nebr., 1961-67; interim instr. U. Fla., Gainesville, 1967-68; asst. prof. Ga. State U., Atlanta, 1970-78, assoc. prof., from 1978. Dir. lower level English Ga. State U., 1970-82, co-dir. summer writing workshop, 1978-88; reviewer, cons. to major textbook pubs., 1972-89; bus. writing cons. to corps. and assns., Atlanta, 1985-88. Contbr. articles to profl. jours. With U.S. Army, 1946-48. Mem. Nat. Coun. Tchrs. English, South Atlanta MLA, Ga. Coun. Tchrs. English, Assn. for Bus. Communication. Avocations: reading, travel, music, camping, swimming. Home: Suwanee, Ga. Died Nov. 9, 2007.

HAINES, THOMAS DAVID, JR., lawyer; b. Dallas, Oct. 30, 1956; s. Thomas David Sr. and Carol V. (Mullins) H.; m. Nanette Cluck, Mar. 1, 1986; children: Bennett Ann, Maison Cluck. BS in Polit. Sci., Okla. State U., 1979; JD, U. Okla., Norman, 1982. Bar: Okla. 1982, N.Mex. 1983, US Ct. Appeals (10th cir.) 1983, US Dist. Ct. N.Mex. 1983. Assoc. Hinkle, Cox, Eaton, Coffield & Hensley, Roswell, N.Mex., 1982-87, ptnr., from 1988. Contbg. editor N.Mex. Tort and Worker's Compensation Reporter, 1987-90, Employment Law Deskbook for New Mexico Employers, 1997, 99. Coach Roswell Youth Soccer Assn., 1995—98, 2001; youth sponsor First United Meth. Ch., Roswell, 1986—88, chmn. stewardship com., 1990—91, chmn. adminstrv. coun., 1998—99, trustee, 1996—98. Mem. State Bar Assn. N.Mex. (com. on continuing legal edn., young lawyers divsn. 1989-2002, mem. med.-legal rev. commn. 1988-2004, sec. 2003, treas. 2004, membership benefits com. 2006—), Chaves County Bar Assn.(pres., 2006-07), N.Mex. Def. Lawyer's Assn., N.Mex. Trial Lawyer's Assn., Kiwanis (Roswell Club, Outstanding Club Sec. award 1993-95, pres. 1998-99), named one Outstanding Young Men in Am. 1990, George L. Reese Am. Inn of Ct. (barrister), Phi Delta Phi, Phi Kappa Phi. Republican. Avocations: golf, basketball, music, politics. Home: Roswell, N.Mex. Died Jan. 8, 2008.

HALASZ, STEPHEN JOSEPH, retired electro-optical systems engineer; b. Eger-Csehi, Hungary; s. Sandor and Ilona (Huszák) H.; children: Stephen S., Christopher L. Jacqueline R. BS, Columbia U., 1955. Project engr. GE Co., Utica, NY, 1956—58; sr. physicist Avion divsn. ACF Industries, Paramus, NJ, 1958—65; head IR and Display Lab. Aerojet Gen., 1965—72; sr. specialist Xerox Electro-Optical, Pasadena, Calif., 1972—75, Ford Aeronutronic, Newport Beach, Calif., 1975—83; chief scientist Hughes Aircraft, El Segundo, Calif., 1983—92. Contbg. author: (handbook) IR Handbook, 1969. With U.S. Army, 1945. Achievements include numerous designs and research projects including optical guidance for satellite interception; IR moving target tracker; handheld thermal imager; scanned matrix for IR pattern recognition; high speed target acquisition with fused sensors; others; patentee in field. Home: San Francisco, Calif. Deceased.

HALBERG, CHARLES JOHN AUGUST, JR., mathematics professor; b. Pasadena, Calif., Sept. 24, 1921; s. Charles John August and Anne Louise (Hansen) Halberg; m. Ariel Arfon Oliver, Nov. 1, 1941 (div. July 1969); children: Ariel Walters, Charles Thomas, Niels Frederick; m. Barbro Linnea Samuelsson, Aug. 18, 1970 (dec. Jan. 1978); 1 stepchild, Ulf Erik Hjelm; m. Betty Reese Zimprich, July 27, 1985. BA summa cum laude, Pomona Coll., Claremont, Calif., 1949; MA (William Lincoln Honnold fellow), UCLA, 1953, PhD, 1955. Instr. math. Pomona Coll., Claremont, Calif., 1949-50; assoc. math. UCLA, 1954-55; instr. math. U. Calif.-Riverside, 1955-56, asst. prof. math., 1956-61, assoc. prof. math., 1961-68, prof. math., from 1968, vice chancellor student affairs, 1964-65. Dir. Scandinavian Study Ctr. Lund U., Sweden, 1976—78; docent U. Goteborg, Sweden, 1969—70; bd. dirs. Fulbright Commn. Ednl. Exch. between U.S. and Sweden, 1976—79. Author (with John F. Devlin): Elementary Functions, 1967; author: (with Angus E. Taylor) Calculus with Analytic Geometry, 1969; author: Aftermath, 1996. With USAAF, 1945—46. NSF fellow, U. Copenhagen, 1961—62. Mem.: Swedish Math. Soc., Am. Math. Soc., Math. Assn. Am. (chmn. So. Calif. sect. 1964—65, gov. 1968), Phi Beta Kappa, Sigma Xi. Home: Carlsbad, Calif. Died June 1, 2009.

HALE, DONALD RAY, society administrator; b. Leeds, Mo., Dec. 23, 1930; s. Lester Leonard Hale and Dorothy Helen Stuteville; m. Merline Cole, 1953 (div. 1971); 1 child, Raymond Lester; m. Phyllis Jane Savage, July 16, 1978. Grad. h.s., Kansas City, Mo., 1949. With Hallmark Cards, Kansas City, Mo., 1954-90. Author: They Called Him Bloody Bill, 1975, We Rode With Quantrill, 1975, Branded as Rebels, 1993. With U.S. Army, 1951-54. Mem. Kans. State Hist. Soc., Mo. State Hist. Soc., Jackson County Hist. Soc., William Clarke Quantrill Soc. (pres. 1997—), Lee's Summit Hist. Soc. (pres. 1995—). Avocations: studying Mo., Kans., and WWII history. Home: Lees Summit, Mo. Died Feb. 24, 2008.

HALE, MONTE, actor; b. San Angelo, Tex., June 8, 1919; s. H.M. and Louella Ely; m. Joanne Dorothy Hale, Nov. 22, 1977. Actor: (films) The Big Bonanza, 1944, The Topeka Terror, 1945, Steppin' in Society, 1945, Oregon Trail, 1945, The Purple Monster Strikes, 1945, Bandits of the Badlands, 1945, Rough Riders of Cheyenne, 1945, Colorado Pioneers, 1945, The Phantom Rider, 1946, California Gold Rush, 1946, Home on the Range, 1946, Sun Valley Cyclone, 1946, Man From Rainbow Valley, 1946, Out California Way, 1946, Last Frontier Uprising, 1947, Along the Oregon Trail, 1947, Under Colorado Skies, 1947, California Firebrand, 1948, Timber Trail, 1948, Son of Gods Country, 1948, Prince of the Plains, 1949, Law of the Golden West, 1949, Outcasts of the Trail, 1949, South of Rio, 1949, San Antone Ambush, 1949, Ranger of Cherokee Strip, 1949, Pioneer Marshall, 1949, The Vanishing Westerner, 1950, The Old Frontier, 1950, The Missourians, 1950, Yukon Vengeane, 1954, Giant, 1956, Gunsmoke (2 episodes), 1959-68, The Chase, 1966; (TV appearances) Adventures of Wild Bill Hickok, 1958, Tales of Wells Fargo, 1958, The Texan, 1959, Honey West, 1966, America 2-Night, 1978 V.p., bd. dirs. Gene Autry Western Heritage Mus., L.A. Mem. SAG, ASCAP. Died Mar. 29, 2009.

HALEY, CHARLOTTE, retired elementary educator; b. Benton Harbor, Mich., July 22, 1911; d. John Charles and Elizabeth Ann (Halfert) H. Cert. in teaching, Cass County Normal Sch., Mich., 1930; BS, Western Mich. U, 1942; MA, U. Mich., 1950. Cert. in teaching. Tchr. rural schs., Cass County, 1930-40, pub. schs., Ionia, Mich., 1942-45; tchr. physically and otherwise impaired students Bay City (Mich.) Pub. Schs., 1945-76; ret. pub. schs., Bay City, Mich., 1976. Mem. State Orthopedic Dept. com. and com. on reading, Lansing, Mich., 1950's, Governing Bd. Edn. Exceptional Children, Lansing, 1960's. Com. mem. Child and Family Svc., Bay City, 1976-79; mem. YWCA, Bay City, 1950—, mem. planning com., 1981-84; vol., mem. Bay County Hist. Soc., 1970—; vol. Saginaw Valley Blood Ctr., Bay City, 1976—. Mem. NEA (life), AAUW, Am. Assn. Ret. Persons, Mich. Soc. Ret. Sch. Pers. (life), Bus. and Profl. Women's Assn., Bay Area Assn. Ret. Sch. Pers., Delta Kappa Gamma. Presbyterian. Avocations: reading, hiking, fishing, bird watching. Home: Dowagiac, Mich. Died Jan. 31, 2008.

HALEY, ROBERT LEWIS, mechanical engineer, consultant; b. Winnebago, Ill., Sept. 29, 1919; s. Lew J. and Lottie (Smith) H.; m. Gretchen F. Skinner, Sept. 18, 1943; children: Pamela Joan, Mathew Leiws, Timothy Robert. BSME, Northwestern U., 1941, MBA, 1948. Registered profl. engr., Tenn. With Internat. Harvester Co., 1941-82, plant mgr. Memphis, 1974-82, ret., 1982; mgmt. engring. cons. Internat. Exec. Svc. Corps., Memphis, from 1982. Asst. prof. mech. engring. Miss. U., Oxford, 1955-57; chmn. bd. Synthesis, Inc., Dallas. Patentee in field. Mem. exec. bd. Chickasaw coun. Boy Scouts Am., Memphis, 1975-90; mem. pres.'s coun. Rhodes Coll., Memphis, 1980—; bd. dirs., past chmn. Agricenter Internat., Memphis, 1980—; mem. Memphis Civil Svc. Commn., 1983—; bd. dirs. Tenn. Waste Water Bd., Nashville, 1987—. Recipient Engr. of Yr. award Engring. Club Memphis, 1957. Mem. ASME (life, chmn. Memphis chpt. 1972-73), NRA (life), Park Ave. Commandery #31 Knights Templar, Big Creek Golf Club, Summit Club, Future Memphis. Presbyterian. Avocations: golf, hunting. Home: Memphis, Tenn. Died Nov. 19, 2007.

HALKIAS, DEMETRIOS GEORGE, retired microbiologist, pathologist, educator; b. Kosma, Arcadia, Greece, Aug. 6, 1932; came to U.S. 1951; s. George Chris and Kalliope (Golegos) H.; m. Evangeline Chris Paraskevas, June 10, 1962; children: George Kalliope, Chris, Evangelos. BS, U. Ill., 1957; MS, Loyola U., Chgo., 1957, PhD, 1964. Diplomate Am. Bd. Med. Microbiology. Instr. Creighton U., Omaha, 1963-66, asst. prof., 1966-69, assoc. prof., 1969-72, U. S. Fla., Tampa, 1972-78, prof. microbiology and pathology, from 1978; chief microbiologist J.A. Haley Vets Hosp., Tampa, from 1972. Lectr. U. Miami Sch. Medicine, 1984—; cons. St. Joseph Hosp., Tampa, 1976—. Contbr. articles to profl. jours., chpts. to books. Pres. St. John Greek Orthodox Ch., Tampa, 1980-83, 91—; v.p. Panarcadian Soc., Tampa, 1990—; treas. Am. Found. Greek Lang. and Culture, 1992—. Std. Oil Co. fellow, 1958, 59, Royal E. Cabell fellow, 1961. Mem. Am. Soc. Microbiology, Assn. Kosmiton, Hellenic Profl. and Cultural Soc., Tampa Bay Microbiology Group, Ahepa. Greek Orthodox Ch. Avocations: fishing, writing, church music and chanting. Home: Tampa, Fla. Died Apr. 19, 2008.

HALL, EDWARD TWITCHELL, retired anthropologist; b. Webster Groves, Mo., May 16, 1914; s. Edward Twichell and Jessie J. Gilroy (Warneke) H.; m. Mildred Ellis Reed, Dec. 16, 1946 (dec. Feb. 1994); children: Ellen McCoy, Eric Reed; m. Karin Bergh Hall, 2004 Student, Pomona Coll., 1929-30; AB, U. Denver, 1936; MA, U. Ariz., 1938; PhD, Columbia U., 1942; Dr. honoris causa, U. Louvain, Belgium, 1987. Asst. staff archeologist Lab. Anthropology, Santa Fe, 1937; staff dendroconologist Peabody Mus. Awatovi expdn., 1937-39; dir. Columbia U. Governador expdn., 1941; field work in Micronesia, 1946, Southwestern U.S., 1933-43, Europe, from 1952; econ. and cultural survey Micronesia, 1946; assoc. prof. anthropology, chmn. dept. U. Denver, 1946-48; faculty Bennington (Vt.) Coll., U.S. State Dept., 1948-51; dir. Point IV tng. program Prof. Fgn. Svc. Inst., 1950-55; dir. research and dep. dir. (Washington office, Human Relations Area Files), 1955-57; pres. Overseas Tng. and Research, Inc., 1955-60; dir. communications research project Washington Sch. Psychiatry, 1959-63; mem. exec. com., council fellows; prof. anthropology Ill. Inst. Tech., 1963-67; prof. anthropology Northwestern Univ., 1967-77; partner Edward T. Hall Assos., 1960-94. Cons. intercultural relations internat. bus. and govt.; Leatherbee lectr. Harvard Bus. Sch., 1962; dir. Ansul Corp., Marinette, Wis., 1968-79; mem. small grants com. NIMH, 1962-65; mem. bldg. research adv. bd. NRC, 1964-68 Author: Early Stockaded Settlements in Governador, N.M., 1942, The Silent Language, 1959, The Hidden Dimension, 1966, Handbook for Proxemic Research, 1975, (with Mildred Reed Hall) The Fourth Dimension in Architecture, 1975, Beyond Culture, 1976, The Dance of Life: The Other Dimension of Time, 1983, An Anthropology of Everyday Life, 1992, West of the Thirties, 1994; (with M.R. Hall) Hidden Differences: Doing Business with the Japanese, 1987, Understanding Cultural Differences: Germans, French and Americans, 1990. Trustee Brookfield Zoo; bd. dirs. Mus. Bldg. Arts; founding dir. Nat. Bldg. Mus. Capt. C.E. AUS, 1942-46, ETO, PTO. Fellow Am. Anthrop. Assn.; mem. Soc. Applied Anthropology, Am. Ethnol. Assn., Anthrop. Film Rsch. Inst. (pres. 1987-91). Home: Santa Fe, N.Mex. Died July 20, 2009.

HALL, FREDDIE LEE, JR., army chaplain; b. Richmond, Va., May 26, 1943; s. Freddie Lee and Thelma Lorrain (Henry) H.; m. Abna Reid Hall, Oct. 30, 1980; children: Michael Anthony, Derrick LaMont. BTh., Washington Bapt. Sem., 1972; BS, Luther Rice Coll., 1976; MDiv., Howard U., 1981; grad., Combined Arms Svc. Sch., Ft. Leavenworth, Kans., 1986, CGSC, Ft. Leavenworth, 1987. Commd. 2d lt. U.S. Army, 1976, advanced through grades to maj., 1989, chaplain 3/68th ADA Bn. Ft. Bragg, N.C., 1981-83, chaplain 530th S&S Bn., 1983-84, asst. DISCOM chaplain 2nd Inf. Div. SUP COM Camp Casey, Korea, 1984-85, group chaplain 46th Support Group Ft. Bragg, 1985-86, INSTL troops support chaplain, 1986-88, dep. COSCOM chaplain Ft. Bragg, 1988-89; with Command and Gen. Staff Coll., Ft. Leavenworth, from 1987; chaplain 160th Signal Brigade, Germany, 1989-91; dep. post chaplain Presidio, San Francisco, Calif., from 1992. Voting mem. Funds Coun., Ft. Bragg, 1986-89, Presidio, San Francisco, 1992—. Decorated Meritorious Svc. medal, Army Commendation medal with two oak leaf clusters. Mem. Assn. U.S., Am. Legion, Am. Mgmt. Assn., Assn. of U.S. Army and Mil. Chaplains Assocs. Democrat. Disciple of Christ. Avocations: bowling, gardening. Died Nov. 9, 2007.

HALL, HOUGHTON ALEXANDER, electrical engineer, municipal official; b. Kingston, Jamaica, W.I., Aug. 17, 1936; arrived in U.S., 1985; s. James Alexander and Clarice Viola Hall; m. Grace Yvonne Anglin, Feb. 22, 1964; children: Andrew Geoffery, Christine Elizabeth. BS, U. W.I., Kingston, 1958, diploma in chem. tech., 1959, diploma in mgmt., 1977. Registered profl. engr., Fla.; chartered engr. Great Britain. Elec. engr. Jamaica Pub. Svc. Co., Kingston, 1960—84; dir. R&D Ministry of Sci., Tech. and the Environ., Kingston, 1984—85; elec. engr. electric dept. City of Tallahassee, 1985—90, mgr. substation engring. electric dept., from 1990. Fellow Fla. Engring. Soc.; mem. IEEE (sr.), NSPE, Inst. Elec. Engrs., Tallahassee Sci. Soc. (charter pres. 1989-97, pres. 2000—04), Fla. Acad. Scis. (chmn. engring. sect. 1994-97, 2000—, pres. 1997-99). Baptist. Avocations: electronics, scientific pursuits. Home: Tallahassee, Fla. Deceased.

HALL, LYNNELLE MARIE MILLARD, artist, florist; b. Wichita, Kans., Dec. 12, 1946; d. Arthur Martin and Oleta Marie (Horton) Millard; divorced; 1 child, Christina Marie. BS in Elem. Edn., Wichita State U., 1968. Tchr. art, other subjects Springdale (Ark.) Pub. Schs. Floral designer Floral Magic, Flowers By Bebe, Livig Expressions of Natural Beauty, Wichita, 1990. Mem. DAR, Wichita Art Assn. Roman Catholic. Avocation: sculpture. Home: Andover, Kans. Died Aug. 20, 2008.

HALL, MARCEL SCOTT, nurse; b. Big Spring, Tex., Mar. 12, 1926; d. Nathan Graves and Nora Essie (Long) Scott; m. James W. Hall, Oct. 11, 1945 (div.); children: Deborah, Beviely, Rebekah. AS, Galveston Coll., Tex., 1981. Cert. Luback tchg. instr., Luboack Literacy; cert. poll mgr., cert. adminstr. CPR, cert. adminstr. first aid., Charleston County Election Commn. Nurse asst. Tex. Woman's Hosp., Houston, 1979; hosp. tech. asst. John Sealy Hosp., Galveston, Tex., 1979-81; nurse St. Francis Xavier Hosp., Charleston, S.C., from 1981. Mem. Neighborhood Safety, Charleston, 1981—. Mem. ANA, Nurses Svc. Orgn., S.C. Nurses Assn., Phi Sigma Alpha. Republican. Mem. Ch. of Christ. Avocations: sewing, bicycling, camping, walking. Home: Charleston, SC. Died Aug. 8, 2008.

HALL, MICHAEL, disability processing specialist; b. NYC, Sept. 20, 1947; s. Mark and Eva Hall; m. Karen Jane Klein; children: Ian D., Mitchell L. BA, CCNY, 1968; MA in Fgn. Affairs, U. Va., 1970; JD, Fordham U., 1975. Bar: N.Y. 1976, D.C. 1980. Disability processing specialist Social Security, Jamaica, NY. Home: Commack, NY. Died Oct. 10, 2007.

HALL, RICHARD HARRIS, writer, editor, consultant; b. Hartford, Conn., Dec. 25, 1930; s. James Augustus and Rachel Ernestine (Rudd) H. Diploma, The Gilbert Sch., Winsted, Conn., 1948; BA in Philosophy, Tulane U., New Orleans, 1958. Asst. dir. Nat. Investigations Com. on Aerial Phenomena, Washington, 1958-67; sci. writer United Fresh Fruit & Vegetable Assn., Washington, 1967-68; abstracts editor Am. Psychol. Assn., Washington, 1970-76; tech. editor John F. Holman & Co., Washington, 1977-79; abstracts editor Norman Hodges & Assocs., Rockville, Md., 1979; abstractor, indexer Congl. Info. Svc., Bethesda, Md., 1980-92. Chmn. Fund for UFO Rsch., Mount Rainier, Md.,

1993-97 Contbg. author: Encyclopedia of UFO's, 1980; author: Uninvited Guests, 1988, Patriots in Disguise, 1993, The UFO Evidence: Vol. II, 1998; contbr. articles to profl. jours. Mem. Author's Guild. Democrat. Avocations: gardening, horse race handicapping, baseball spectator, civil war research. Home: Brentwood, Md. Died July 17, 2009.

HALL, ROBERT KELLER, molecular biologist, researcher; b. Charleston, W.Va., Feb. 16, 1958; s. Harry Thomas and Evelyn Hall; m. Christia Lynn Watts, Oct. 30, 1980; children: Justin, Jared. BS, Clemson U., 1980, MS, 1982; PhD, Vanderbilt U., 1987. Postdoctoral fellow Vanderbilt U., Nashville, 1987-90, instr., 1990-94, rsch. asst. prof., from 1994. Dir. molecular biology resource facility Vanderbilt U., 1995—. Grad. tchg. assistantship NIH, 1980-82, 82-87, biochemistry traineeship, 1987-90. Home: Antioch, Tenn. Died Aug. 25, 2008.

HALLER, JORDAN D., cardiovascular surgeon, b. Pitts., Sept. 5, 1932; s. Max Leopold and Pearl H.; m. Carna Shrager, Dec. 28, 1996; children: Matthew, Nina, Andrew. BS, U. Pitts., 1953; MD, Ind. U., Indpls., 1957. Diplomate Am. Bd. Surgery, Am. Bd. Thoracic and Cardiovascular Surgery, Am. Bd. of Thoracic Sugery. Intern Ind. U. Med. Ctr., Indpls., 1957-58; resident Bronx Mcpl. Hosp. Ctr., NY, 1958-63; fellow in cardiovascular surgery St. Luke's Hosp., Tex. Children's Hosp., 1970; clin. investigator in cardiopulmonary surgery VA Hosp., Pitts., 1963-66; dir. thoracic and cardiovascular surgery Maimonides Med. Ctr., Bklyn., 1966-71; pvt. practice cardiovascular-thoracic surgery LA, 1972-84; founder, dir. Laser Inst. Shadyside Hosp., Pitts., 1984-85; med. dir. C.R. Bard, Inc., Billerica, Mass., 1985—91; lectr. biomedical tech. Columbia U., NYC, 1992—2000; v.p. med. and regulatory affairs, for excimer laser photorefractive keratectomy and LASIK Visx Inc., Sunnyvale, Calif., 1994—96; founder, pres., CEO Lajor BioMedical Tech. Inc., Pitts., from 1999. Asst. instr. surgery, Albert Einstein Coll. Medicine, 1962-63; instr. surgery, U. Pitts., 1963-66; dir. dept. thoracic and cardiovascular surg., residency tng. program, Maimonides Med. Ctr., 1966-71; asst. prof. cardiovascular-thoracic surgery, SUNY, Bklyn., 1966-71; guest prof. cardiovascular-thoracic surgery, Italian Hosp. Buenos Aires, 1977-81; sr. instr. advanced trauma course, Northridge Found. Hosp., 1979-83; sr. lectr. in engring., Carnegie-Mellon U., Pitts., 1985-86; sr. instr. advanced trauma course Am. Coll. of Surgeons; cons. cardiovascular thoracic medicine and surgery, 1991-; vol. faculty, med. ethics, U. Pitts. Sch. Medicine, 2003. Patentee, heart valves, vascular clamps, chest drainage devices, bioactive peptides; contbr. articles to med. publs. Fellow ACS, Am. Soc. Laser Medicine and Surgery; mem. Denton Cooley Cardiovascular Soc., N.Y. Soc. Thoracic Surgery, Soc. Clin. Vascular Surgery, Soc. Thoracic Surgeons, Western Thoracic Surg. Assn., AAAS, Am. Heart Assn., Am. Soc. Artificial Internal Organs, Assn. for Advancement of Med. Instrumentation, Internat. Soc. Artificial Organs, N.Y. Acad. Scis., Laser Inst. of Am. Avocations: music, theater, literature. Home: Mc Murray, Pa. Died June 9, 2009.

HALPERN, LEON (HAL PERRIN), composer; b. Bklyn., May 15, 1908; s. Jacab and Vera (Greenberg) H.; m. Fleurette Segalle, Dec. 6, 1936; 1 child, Tamara Ann. Student, Inst. of Musical Art, NYC, 1924-32. Accompanist Isadora Duncans Group, NYC, 1936-37, various dance groups, NYC, 1935-37. Composer numerous ballets, piano music. Scholar Inst. Musical Art, 1925. Mem. ASCAP. Home: Los Angeles, Calif. Died Nov. 9, 2007.

HALPINE, SUSANA MARIA (ANASUS H.), artist, biochemist; b. New Milford, Conn., Dec. 3, 1956; d. Stuart Francis and Miriam (Burns) H. Student, Boston U., 1975-78; BS in Biology, Worcester State Coll., 1979; MS in Nutrition, Columbia U., 1987. Staff rsch. assoc. Howard Hughes Med. Inst. at Columbia U., NYC, 1985-88; Mellon fellow Nat. Gallery of Art, Washington, 1988-90, biochemist, from 1990. Curator, mem. Grove St. Gallery, Worcester, Mass., 1980-83. Solo exhibits include Ligoa Duncan Gallery, N.Y.C., 1978, Grove St. Gallery, 1982, Burnham Libr., Bridgewater, Conn., 1988, Richard Dempsey Meml. Gallery, Tacoma Park, Md., 1991, Montpelier Cultural Arts Ctr., Laurel, Md., 1992, Mansion Art Gallery, Rockville, Md., 1993; group shows include Grove St. Gallery, 1981, 82, 83, 90, Gallery 12, N.Y.C., 1984, 85, Kraine Club Gallery, N.Y.C., 1985, Erector Sq. Gallery, New Haven, 1989 (Best of Show), Nat. Gallery of Art, 1989, 91, Md. Fedn. Art, 1991, 93, Greater Reston Art Ctr., 1991, Arts 901 Gallery, Washington, 1991, Arlington (Va.) Arts Ctr., 1991, Rockville (Md.) Arts Place, 1992, Strathmore Hall, Rockville, 1992, 93, Gallery 10 Ltd., Washington, 1992, many others; contbr. articles to jours., books. Residency grantee Millay Colony for the Arts, Austerlitz, N.Y., 1983. Mem. Arlington Arts Ctr., Washington Project for the Arts, Nat. Mus. of Women in the Arts, Guild of Nat. Sci. Illustrators, Soc. Children's Book Writers and Illustrators, Am. Chem. Soc., Elec. Vehicle Assn. Mem. Shakers. Avocations: swimming, computer graphics. Home: Takoma Park, Md. Died Nov. 6, 2007.

HALPRIN, HENRY S., lawyer, educator; b. NYC, May 5, 1924; s. Abraham J. and Julia Steiner Halprin; children from previous marriage: Karen K. Sims, Bruce S. LLD, U. Va., 1949, JD, 1970. Bar: N.Y. 1949, U.S. Dist. Ct. (ea. and so. dists.) N.Y. 1950, U.S. Supreme Ct. 1961, U.S. Dist. Ct. Conn. 1963, Conn. 1967. Asst. dir. spl. programs US Housing and Home Fin. Agy., NYC, 1955-61; sr. assoc. Demov & Morris, 1961-62, ptnr., 1962-64, Halprin & Goler, NYC, 1968—92; pvt. practice NYC, 1964—92. Adj. asst. prof. real estate NYU, NYC, from 1979; lectr. Baruch Coll., 1981—99. Trustee Westport (Conn.) Libr., 1987—91. Home: Southport, Conn. Died Nov. 29, 2007.

HALPRIN, LAWRENCE, landscape architect, urban planner; b. Bklyn., July 1, 1916; s. Samuel W. and Rose (Luria) H.; m. Ann Schuman, Sept. 19, 1940; children: Daria, Rana. BS in Plant Scis, Cornell U., 1939; MS in Plant Scis, U. Wis., 1941; B.Landscape Architecture, Harvard U., 1942. Sr. assoc. Thomas D. Church & Assos., San Francisco, 1946-49; prin. Lawrence Halprin & Assos., San Francisco, 1949-76; co-founder Round House, San Francisco, 1976-78; founder Lawrence Halprin Studios, 1978—2009; lectr. U. Calif.-Berkeley, 1960-65, Regents prof., 1982-83. Dir., Halprin Summer Workshop, 1966, 1968; prin. works include Ghirardelli Sq., San Francisco, Sea Ranch, Calif., Nicolett Mall, Mpls., Old Orchard Shopping Center, Skokie, Ill., Lovejoy Fountain, Pettigrove Park, Forecourt Fountain, Portland, Oreg., Market St. reconstrn, San Francisco, Seattle Freeway Park, Rochester Manhattan Park, Franklin Delano Roosevelt Meml, Washington, Levi Park and Plaza, San Francisco, Haas Promenade, Jerusalem, Bunker Hill Stairs, Central Library, Hope St. and Olympic Park, Los Angeles; author: Cities, 1963; rev. edit., 1972, Freeways, 1966, New York, New York, 1968, The RSVP Cycles, 1970, Lawrence Halprin Notebooks, 1959-71, 1972; co-author: The Freeway in the City, 1968, Taking Part: A Workshop Approach to Collective Creativity, 1974, The Sketch Books of Lawrence Halprin, 1981; filmmaker: Le Pink Grapefruit, Franklin Delano Roosevelt Memorial, How Sweet It Is!, Designing Environments for Everyone. Panelist White House Conf. Natural Beauty, 1965; mem. bd. urban cons. Bur. Pub. Roads, 1966-67; design cons. Calif. Div. Hwys., 1963-65; landscape architect, urban cons. San Francisco Bay Area Rapid Transit Dist., 1963-66; mem. Gov.'s Conf. Calif. Beauty, 1966, Nat. Council Arts, 1966—2009, Adv. Council, Historic Preservation, 1967—2009; bd. dirs., San Francisco Dancers Workshop Co., 1950—2009. Served to lt. (j.g.) USN, 1943-46. Named One of Leaders of Tomorrow, TIME mag. 1953, recipient awards including Allied Professions Gold medal AIA 1964, Thomas Jefferson award in architecture 1979, Richard J. Neutra award for Excellence, 1986, National Medal of Arts, 2002, Friedrich Ludwig von Sckell Golden Ring, 2002, Michaelangelo award, 2005; honored Changing Places Exhbn., San Francisco Mus. Modern Art, 1986. Fellow Am. Soc. Landscape Architects (Design medal 2003); mem. Am. Acad. Arts and Scis., Sierra Club. Democrat. Jewish. Died Oct. 25, 2009.

HALTIWANGER, ROBERT SIDNEY, JR., book publishing executive; b. Winston-Salem, NC, Mar. 15, 1923; s. Robert Sidney and Janie Love (Couch) H.; m. Marguarite C. LaBelle, Aug. 23, 1994. AB, Harvard U., 1947. Coll. field rep. Prentice-Hall Inc., Atlanta, 1947—56, Southeast regional mgr., 1956-65, dir. Two Year div. Englewood Cliffs, NJ, 1965-71; v.p. sales Prentice-Hall Inc, Englewood Cliffs, NJ, 1971-80, exec. v.p. coll. div., 1980-85, pres. sales and mktg. coll. div., from 1985. Cons. Simon & Shuster, 1988-89. Served to 1st lt. USAF, 1943-46, PTO. Recipient Chmn. award Gulf and Western, 1985, Frank Enenbach award Prentice-Hall Coll. Div., 1987. Mem. Am. Assn. Pubs. (liason com. 1975-82), Harvard Club (N.Y.C. chpt.), Knickerbocker Club. Democrat. Presbyterian. Home: Fort Lee, NJ. Died Nov. 17, 2008.

HAM, JOHN WILFRED, retail executive; b. Hendersonville, NC, Oct. 28, 1931; s. Edward W. and Harrett (Hosmer) H.; m. Mildred Tobey, June 5, 1955; children: Mark, Russell, Susan. BS in Mktg., U. Md., 1957. Trainee J.C. Penney, Silver Spring, Md., 1957-58, gen. mgr. Troy, Mich., 1980-92. Mem. exec. com. Better Bus. Bur. Ea. Mich., Southfield, 1989-92; chmn. bd. Mich. Mchts. Coun., Lansing, 1990-92, chrmn. pres. Adv. Counc., Walsh Coll., Troy, Mich., 1992—. Chmn. adminstrv. coun. Clarkston (Mich.) Meth. Ch., 1988-90. With USN, 1951-55, Korea. Avocations: travel, skiing, hiking. Home: Clarkston, Mich. Died Mar. 20, 2008.

HAMILTON, HARLAN BERNHARDT, humanities educator; b. Medford, Mass., Nov. 29, 1927; s. Harlan Lombard and Jean Isabel (Bernardt) H. BA, U. Colo., 1955; MA, Columbia U., 1966; EdD, Boston U., 1974. Prof. English Jersey City State Coll., from 1966. Mem. adv. bd. N.Y.C. Coun. Tchrs. English, 1983-94. Author: Lights and Legends, 1987, Hamilton Family of South Berwick, Maine, Part II, 1989; editor Hugenot Soc., 1993—. With USN, 1946-51. Fellow Phi Delta Kappa, Kappa Delta Pi; mem. Huguenot Soc. Am. (historian 1988—), Am. Topical Assn. (pres. N.Y. chpt. 1987—), Soc. of War of 1812, New Eng. Soc., Custer Battlefield Hist. and Mus. Assn., Maine Hist. Soc., Indoor Gardening Soc. Am., Am. Philatelic Soc., U.S. Lighthouse Soc., U.S. Naval Sailing Assn., Soc. Colonial Wars, SAR, Order of Founders and Patriots, Columbia U. Faculty Club, Coasters Harbor Navy Yacht Club, Regency Whist Club. Republican. Episcopalian. Avocations: stamp collecting/philately, photography, travel, sailing, indoor gardening. Home: New York, NY. Died Mar. 23, 2008.

HAMILTON, JAY MARTIN, genealogist, author; b. Salt Lake City, Oct. 29, 1921; s. Ernest Jacob and Pearl Edna Bernstrom (Norvald) H.; m. Ingeborg Marianne Haase, Aug. 9, 1947 (dec. Mar. 1976); children: Stephen Ernest Robert, Catherine Ann, Margaret Mary Elizabeth, Mark Antony Thomas; stepchildren: Barbara Josephine Prack Benson, Anton Otto Prack; m. Edith Barbara Vogt, Feb. 18, 1977. Student, Utah State Agrl. Coll., 1940-43; BA Sociology, So. Oreg. State Coll., 1968. Commd. 2nd lt. U.S. Army, 1944, advanced through grades to lt. col., 1963, ret., 1963; exec. dir. Winema Girl Scout Coun., Medford, Oreg., 1964-67; owner/operator Tree of Love Christian Bookstore, Medford, Grants Pass, Oreg., 1977-89. Author: Korean-English Language Collection of Grammatical Patterns, 1959, Hamilton Family History, 1983, Etymology of the Hamilton Name, 1984, Jay M. Hamilton Autobiography, 1985, The Hambleton-Reed Hamilton History, 1988, The Bernstrom-Helgeson Family History, 1996, Chronology of the 76th Infantry Division U.S. Army, 1988. Chmn. emergency med. com. Dist. 8 Comprehensive Health Coun. Jackson-Josephine County, Medford, 1973-76. Recipient Cert. of Svcs. Dist. 8 Comprehensive Health Coun., 1976. Mem. DAV (comdr., numerous awards), Ret. Officers assn. (life), Nat. Assn. for Uniformed Svc., 76th Inf. Divsn. Assn. Republican. Roman Catholic. Avocations: genealogy, history, writing. Home: Medford, Oreg. Died Apr. 17, 2008.

HAMLIN, CARY LEE, psychiatry educator, psychopharmacologist, medical informatician; b. Port Allegany, Pa., Oct. 15, 1949; s. Leon Cary and Dorothy Jane (Doll) H.; m. Elizabeth Carr, July 3, 1977; children: Karin, Jane Kiley, Adam. BS in Chemistry, U. Pitts., 1971, MD, 1975; diploma in Psychiatry, Dartmouth U., 1978. Diplomate Am. Bd. Psychiatry and Neurology. Postdoctoral fellow neurosci. and behavior Princeton U., N.J., 1978-79; resident in internal medicine Robert Wood Johnson Med. Sch., Piscataway, N.J., 1979-80; asst. clin. prof. Psychiatry U. N.J., Piscataway, 1980-86; pvt. practice Chester, N.J., from 1986; mem. Psychiatry staff Morristown (N.J.) Meml. Hosp., from 1983; asst. clin. prof. Columbia U., NYC, from 1986. Dir. anxiety clinic Fair Oaks Hosp., Summit, N.J., 1982-86, assoc. dir. outpatient rsch., 1983-86, dir. med. informatics Health Informatics, Inc., 1995—. Sr. author (book chpt.) Anxiolytics—Response Predictions, 1984; contbr. articles to profl. jours. Mem. AAAS, Am. Psychiat. Assn., Am. Med. Informatics Assn. Avocations: psychiatric informatics, landscape horticulture, skiing, european history. Home: Long Valley, NJ. Died Sept. 2, 2007.

HAMMACK, PHILLIP LARRY, surgeon; b. Norwood, Mo., Mar. 31, 1942; s. Sherman R. and Zelma O. (Worsham) H.; m. Catherine Linarelli, Dec. 26, 1964; children: Sherman John, Josephine M., Catherine Nicole, Phillip L. Jr. BS, Drury Coll., 1965; MD, U. Pitts., 1969. Fellow cardiovascular surgery U. Fla., Gainesville, 1974-75; staff surgeon Alexandria (Va.) Hosp., 1977—2009; staff surgeron Mt. Vernon Hosp., Alexandria, 1977—2009; co-med. dir. Vascular Imaging Ltd., Arlington, Va., 1989—2009. Lt. comdr. USN, 1975-77. Fellow ASC; mem. Alexandria Med. Soc., So. Surg. Soc., Soc. Laparoscopic Surgeons. Avocation: golf. Home: Alexandria, Va. Died Aug. 11, 2009.

HAMMERSCHLAG, MARIANNE, proofreader; b. Munich, Aug. 19, 1932; d. Willy and Anne (Cahen) Loewenstein; widowed; children: Robert, Alice, Lori. BA cum laude, Hunters Coll., 1954; postgrad., NYU, 1956. Cert. secondary tchr., N.Y. English tchr. Valley Stream North High Sch., Franklin Square, N.Y., 1956-59; with Wasko Gold Products, NYC, 1977-79; with sales Marsh's Men's Store, Huntington, N.Y., 1980; with Stepping Stones, Huntington, 1980; bus. communications tchr. proprietary sch. Katherine Gells, 1981-90; proofreader Voll Informal Scis., from 1990. Mem. Nat. English Honor Assn., Nat. English Honor Fraternity. Died July 1, 2008.

HAMMERSLEY, FREDERICK HAROLD, artist; b. Salt Lake City, Jan. 5, 1919; s. Harold Frederick and Anna Maria (Westberg) H. Student, U. Idaho, 1936-38, Chouinard Art Sch., 1940-42, 46-47, Ecole des Beaux Arts, Paris, France, 1945, Jepson Art Sch., 1947-50. Tchr. Jepson Art Sch., LA, 1948-51, Pomona Coll., Claremont, Calif., 1953-62, Pasadena (Calif.) Art Mus., 1956-61, Chouinard Art Sch., LA, 1964-68, U. N.Mex., Albuquerque, 1968-71. Guest artist Tamarind Inst., Albuquerque, 1973, 88, 91. On-man shows include Owings-Dewey Fine Arts, Santa Fe, 1992, Richard Levy Gallery, Albuquerque, 1993, Mulvane Art Mus., Washburn U., Topeka, 1993, Corcoran Gallery, 1994, Modernism, San Francisco, 1995, others; works shown in gruop exhibits at M. Knoedler Gallery, Smithsonian Inst., Corcoran Gallery of Art, Albright-Knox Mus. Art, Butler Inst. Am. Art, others; represented in permanent collections Corcoran Gallery Art, San Francisco Mus. Modern Art, LA County Mus. Art, others. Sgt. U.S. Signal Corps and Infantry, 1942-46. John Simon Guggenheim fellow in painting, 1973; grantee Nat. Endowment for the Arts, 1975-77; recipient numerous purchase awards. Avocations: photography, gardening. Died May 31, 2009.

HAMNER, JEAN, bioenergetic healing educator; b. Austin, Tex., Dec. 24, 1947; d. Robert and Emma Ruth (Randerson) H. Diploma nursing, Johns Sch. Nursing, Taylor, Tex., 1968; BS in Psychology, Southwestern U., Georgetown, Tex., 1973; MS in Psychophysiology, Maharishi Internat. U., Fairfield, Iowa, 1975; PhD in Comparative Religion, Sacred Coll., Reno, 1980; grad., Morris Pratt Inst., 1995. Cert. massage therapist. Bioenergetic bodywork, Austin, from 1989. Home: Lockhart, Tex. Died Apr. 19, 2007.

HAMPTON, JOE FRANKLIN, postal worker; b. Oak Grove, La., May 30, 1953; s. Joe Franklin and Rose Marie (Smith) H.; m. Mary Anthony, Aug. 29, 1954; children: Jeremy Slade, Patches Michelle, Anthony Trippe. BA in Acctg., Northeast La. U., 1986. Metal building contrn. Ruffin Pre-Fab., Oak Grove, Ill., 1972; plumber's helper Crosby Plumbing Co., Oak Grove, 1972-73; serviceman

Anderson Butane Co., Lake Providence, La., 1973; machine operator Wells Lamont Corp., Oak Grove, 1973-75; carpenter's helper Red-Rock Constrn. Co., West Monroe, La., 1976-78; freelance house remodeler Oak Grove, 1978-79; city letter carrier U.S. Postal Service, Monroe, La., from 1979, acting supr. delivery and collection, 1984-87, supr. delivery and collection, from 1987, mem. employee involvement com.; mgr. stas./brs. (B) U.S. Postal Svc., Monroe, La., from 1989. Dir. tng. union Victory Bapt. Ch., Monroe, 1982, dir. Sunday sch., 1983-84. Named one of Outstanding Young Men of Am., 1986. Fellow Am. Soc. Notaries. Democrat. Baptist. Avocations: fishing, woodworking, golf. Home: Monroe, La. Died Mar. 2, 2008.

HAMPTON, PHYLLIS ANN, lawyer; b. Logan, W.Va., July 16, 1940; d. Harold William and Dolly Melissa (Beaver) Fleming. BAE, U. Fla., 1962; JD, Fla. State U., 1984. Bar: Fla. 1984. Staff atty. Fla. Senate Jud. Civil Com., Tallahassee, 1985-86; sr. atty. div. elections Fla. Dept. State, Tallahassee, 1986-90, gen. counsel, 1990-95; asst. gen. counsel Gov.'s Legal Office, Tallahassee, 1995-99, Fla. Elections Commn., Tallahassee, 1999-2000, gen. counsel, from 2000. Home: Crawfordville, Fla. Died May 30, 2008.

HANCHETT, EFFIE SHERMAN, nurse educator; b. Syracuse, NY, Apr. 11, 1936; d. Arnold Churchill and Marion (Barlow) H. BS in Nursing, Nazareth Coll., 1958; AM, NYU, 1964, PhD, 1974. Assoc. prof. U. Toronto, Ontario, Canada, 1977-79, Wayne State U., Detroit, from 1979. Author: Community Health Assessment, 1979, Nursing Frameworks and Community as Client, 1989; contbr. articles to profl. jours. Home: Ann Arbor, Mich. Died Apr. 8, 2008.

HANEY, JUDITH LOUISE, printing and marketing company executive; b. Allentown, Pa., Aug. 26, 1946; d. Willard Lester and Madeline Adele (Ranck) Brobst; m. Robert Hoffman Benfer, Jr., Feb. 9, 1968 (div. 1974); 1 child, Michele Lee; m. Todd Henry Haney, Feb. 5, 1977. BS in Elem. Edn., Kutztown U., Pa., 1974. Tchr. Allentown Sch. Dist., 1974-79; mem. support staff Mchts. Bank N.A. div. 1st Fidelity N.J., Allentown, 1979-90; retail loan officer, mgr. customer svcs. CC Direct Mktg. Svcs., A Christmas Club Co., Easton, Pa., from 1990. Mem. support staff Walkathon, Allentown, 1986-90, Allentown Literacy Coun., 1987-90. Republican. Lutheran. Home: Allentown, Pa. Died June 19, 2008.

HANEY, LINDA ANN, social services administrator; b. Pontiac, Mich., Jan. 24, 1951; d. Sirrill Joseph La Barge and Marie Louie Theriault; m. Dan Wesley Haney, Jan. 29, 1966 (div. Aug. 1973); children: Michael Clifton, Danette Ann, Beth Marie, Blake Anthony. Student, U. Mich. Lic. adult foster care. Owner, operator Linda's Salon, Flint, Mich., 1975-77; factory worker Buick, Flint, 1977-88; owner, operator Recovery Unlimited, Otter Lake, Mich., 1988-91; pres., CEO Catlin's Angels Ltd., Lapeer, Mich., from 1994. Probation counselor Citizen's Probation Counsel, Laspeer, 1991—. Mem. Mich. Assisted Living Assn., Brain Injury Assn. Republican. Baptist. Avocations: painting, crocheting, gardening, photography. Home: Otter Lake, Mich. Died Oct. 16, 2007.

HANNA, MICHAEL STEPHEN, communications educator, consultant; b. Kansas City, Mo., Sept. 30, 1939; s. Russell Talbot and Marguerite Marie (Esser) H.; m. Judith Lee Walker, Aug. 17, 1963 (div. Sept. 1979); children: Paul Russell, Peter Manning, Ellen Marguerite; m. Nancy Hadden Sanders, Mar. 9, 1980; stepchildren: Shawn David Hall, Laura Nicole Hall. AB in Speech and Art, Cen. Mo. State Coll., 1962, MA, 1963; PhD, U. Mo., 1971. Asst. prof. speech communication So. Colo. State Coll., 1965-68; instr. in English and speech Kemper Mil. Sch. and Coll., 1968-69; asst. prof. speech communication No. Ill. U., 1971-78; assoc. prof. communication U. of the South Ala., Mobile, 1978-81, prof. communication, from 1981. Past dir. basic speech communication course No. Ill., U., 1971-76, asst. chmn. speech-communication dept., 1972-73, past dir. dept. speech-communication Office for the Study of Orgnl. Communication, 1977-78; spl. asst. to dean U. of South Ala. Coll. Arts and Scis. for Community Liaison, 1981, past dir. Inst. for Communication Svcs. and Rsch., 1978-83, chmn. dept. communication arts, 1978-83; mem. faculty Grad. Sch. Banking of the South, 1987—; cons. in field. Author: (with others) Audience Analysis: A Programmed Approach to Receiver Behavior, 1976, Communication in Business and Professional Settings, 1984, 88, 91, Groups in Context, 1986, 90, 93, Interpersonal Growth Through Communication, 1985, 89, 92, 95, Public Speaking for Personal Success, 1987, 89, 92, 95, Intro. to Human Communication, 1992. Mem. So. States Comm. Assn., Assn. for Bus. Comm. Avocations: painting, carpentry, fishing. Home: Theodore, Ala. Died May 18, 2008.

HANRAHAN, JOHN JOSEPH, scientist; b. New London, Conn., Mar. 19, 1932; s. John James and Celia (Cunningham) H.; m. Mary Ellen Ruddy, Aug. 24, 1957; children: Margaret, Maureen, Brian, Mary Kathryn. BA in Math. with honors, U. Conn., 1954, MS in Physics, 1962; diploma with distinction, Naval War Coll., 1987. Computer analyst Electric Boad div. Gen. Dynamics Corp., Groton, Conn., 1960-62; supr. ops. rsch. and analysis Naval Underwater Systems Ctr., New London, Conn., 1962-87; sr. scientist Bolt Beranek & Newman, Inc., New London, from 1987. Author: Predicting Convergence Zone Formation in the Deep Ocean. Proceedings of Internat. Congress on Underwater Acoustics, 1987; co-author Bottom-Interacting Ocean Acoustics, 1980. Capt. USAF, 1955-57. Fellow Acoustical Soc. Am.; mem. Assn. Hibernians, Sigma Pi Sigma. Roman Catholic. Avocations: photography, golf, music. Home: Waterford, Conn. Died Feb. 10, 2008.

HANSEN, CLIFFORD PETER, rancher, former Governor of Wyoming; b. Zenith, Wyo., Oct. 16, 1912; s. Peter Christoffersen and Sylvia Irene (Wood) H.; m. Martha Elizabeth Close, Sept. 24, 1934; children: Mary Elizabeth (dec. 1996), Peter Arthur. BS in Animal Sci., U. Wyo., 1934, LLD (hon.), 1965. Chmn. Teton County Bd. of Commissioners, Jackson, Wyo., 1943-51; pres. U. Wyo. Bd. of Trustees, Laramie, Wyo., 1955-63; commissioner Snake River, Idaho, Wyo., Columbia Interstate, 1943-50; pres. Wyo. Stock Growers Assn., Cheyenne, Wyo., 1953-55; chmn. Sec. of Agr. Adv. com., Washington, 1956-62; v.p. Jackson State Bank, Jackson, 1953-69; gov. State of Wyo., Cheyenne, 1963-66; US Senator from Wyo. Washington, 1967-78; owner Hansen Ranch, Jackson Hole. Mem. Com. on Federalism Washington 1981; bd. dirs. Pacific Power & Light Portland, 1979-83, 1st Wyo. Bank Corp. Cheyenne 1979-83. Trustee, U. Wyo., 1946-63; mem. U. Wyo. Found.; bd. dirs. emeritus Mountain States Legal Found., Gottsche Found. Rehab. Ctr.; trustee emeritus Buffalo Bill Hist. Assn., Polit. Economy Rsch. Ctr.; chmn. steering com. Jefferson Energy Found. Recipient Medallion Svc. award U. Wyo., Disting. Alumnus award Coll. Agr. U. Wyo., 1994; named to Hall of Great Westerners Nat. Cowboy Hall of Fame, 1995, Citizen of the West Nat. Western Stock Show and Rodeo, 1996, Stock Grower of the Century Stock Growers Assn., Cheyenne, 1972. Mem. Masons (33 degree). Republican. Episcopalean. Avocation: riding. Died Oct. 20, 2009.

HANSEN, DEBORAH ANN, corrections official; b. East Brunswick, NJ, July 25, 1950; d. Oscar and Julia (Keleman) H. Student, Worcester Coll., Eng., 1971-72; BA in Psychology, Trenton State Coll., NJ, 1972; MA in Criminal Justice, Rutgers U., 1980. Parole officer N.J. Dept. Corrections, Trenton, 1972-77, sr. parole officer, 1977-79, chief bur. interstate svcs., 1980-84, dep. compact administr., from 1984. Cons. D.C., 1986, Maine Dept. Corrections, 1983, also trainer; trainer affirmative action N.J. Dept. Corrections, Trenton, 1985-86; trainer basic course N.J. Police Tng. Commn., 1989-93; coord., project mgr. Nat. Commn. to Restructure the Interstate Compact for Parolees and Probations, 1985-89; project mgr. tng. task force Interstate Parole and Probation Initiatives, 1989-93. Contbr. articles to profl. jours. Twp. coord. Jim Courtier for Congress, East Brunswick, N.J. 1984; campaign writer, advisor Flemming/Bowen for State Assembly, East Brunswick, 1983; mem. Middlesex County (N.J.) Rep. Orgn. Recipient Proclamation N.J. Legis., 1987, Gov.'s award Outstanding Women in State Govt., 1988, Frederick's award Parole and Probation Compact Adminstrs. Assn., 1987. Fellow Coun. State Govts. (com. on suggested state legislation 1987-90); mem. Am. Parole and Probation Assn. (nat. program com. 1985-88), Interstate Compact Assn. Info. Network (chair subcom. on nat. law enforcement networking 1989-91), Parole and Probation Compact Adminstrs. Assn. (pres. 1986-87), Am. Probation and Parole Assn. (affiliate rep. 1991-92), Psi Chi. Roman Catholic. Avocations: pente, phys. workouts, creative cooking, interior design, modern art 1820-1950, textile/rug hooking. Home: East Brunswick, NJ. Died May 1, 2008.

HANSEN, EDWARD ALVIN CHARLES, feature animation executive; b. Berkeley, Calif., Sept. 7, 1925; s. Einar Aage Christian and Agnes (Beck) H.; m. Lorna Ida Tierney, Apr. 24, 1958; children: Candice Annette, Robert Paul, Janice Marie. Student, Miami U., Oxford, Ohio, 1944; AA, Hartnel Coll., 1950; student, UCLA, 1972, Los Angeles Valley Coll., 1979. Animation artist Walt Disney Prodns., Burbank, Calif., 1952-54, asst. dir., 1955-71, mgr., 1972-79, dir., 1980-83; v.p. feature animation, adminstrn. and prodn. Walt Disney Pictures, Burbank, 1984-87, prodn. cons., 1988-89. Curator Disney Traveling Mus. Show, 1988; nat. judge Nissan Focus Awards, N.Y., 1982—; lectr. Royal Viking Line, San Francisco, 1987—; creator Seemore the C'ni Bee, Nat. Inst. for the Blind, Vancouver, B.C., Nisse Mand, logo Solvang annual Danish Days; Welcome Home Logo, USS Enterprise, CVN 65, 1996. Asst. dir. 7 feature films, 1955-71; prodn. mgr. (feature film) The Fox and the Hound, 1981; prodn. exec.: (feature films) The Black Cauldron, 1985, The Great Mouse Detective, 1986; artist, craftsman Solvang Diorama, Elverhøj Mus. Bd. dirs. Solvang Heritage Assocs. Elverhoj Mus.; com. Solvang Danish Days Found., Elverhoy Mus. com., 1989—. Served with USN, 1943-46, PTO, 1950-51, Korea. Mem. Motion Picture Acad. Arts and Scis., Danish Brotherhood in Am. (past pres.), Rebild Soc., Am. Legion (past comdr. Santa Ynez Valley), Alisal Golf. Clubs: Alisal Golf. Avocations: art, golf. Home: Solvang, Calif. Died Dec. 11, 2007.

HANSEN, GENEVIEVE EVANS, financial planning executive; b. Valparaiso, Ind., May 12, 1931; d. Selwyn John and Henrietta (Kitchell) Horan; m. Carl L. Evans, Dec. 30, 1963 (div. June 1982); children: Steven, Jennifer, Michael; m. Keith L. Hansen, Aug. 6, 1983. Student, Stetson U., 1955. Investment broker Hamilton Funds, Denver, 1955-62, FSC Securities-WestAm. Fin., Deltona, Fla., from 1962. Mem. Internat. Assn. Fin. Planners, Deltona C. of C. (bd. dirs. 1986-90, v.p. 1988—), Univ. Women's Club. Baptist. Home: Deland, Fla. Died Apr. 11, 2008.

HANSEN, LEONARD JOSEPH, writer, journalist, editor, communications executive; b. Aug. 4, 1932; s. Elnar L. and Margie A. (Wilder) Hansen; m. Marcia Ann Rasmussen, Mar. 18, 1966 (div.); children: Barron Richard, Trevor Wilder. AB in Radio-TV Prodn. and Mgmt., San Francisco State U., 1956, postgrad., 1956—57; cert., IBM Mgmt. Sch., 1967. Jr. writer Sta. KCBS, San Francisco, 1952—54; assoc. prodr., dir. Ford Found. TV Rsch. Project San Francisco State U., 1955—57; crew chief live and remote broadcasts Sta. KPIX-TV, San Francisco, 1957—59, dir. air promotion, writer, 1959—60; pub. rels. mgr. Sta. KNTV-TV, San Jose, Calif., 1961; mgr. radio and TV promotion Seattle World's Fair, 1962; mgr. pub. rels. and promotion Seattle Ctr., Seattle, 1963—64; dir. pub. rels. Dan Evans for Gov. Com., Seattle, 1964; propr., mgr. Leonard J. Hansen Pub. Rels., Seattle, 1965—67; campaign mgr. Walter J. Hickel for Gov. Com., Anchorage, 1966; exec. cons. Gov. Alaska, Juneau, 1967; gen. mgr. No. TV Inc., Anchorage, 1967—69; v.p. mktg. Sea World, Inc., San Diego, 1969—71; editor, pub. Sr. World Publs., inc., San Diego, 1973—84; chmn. Sr. Pubs. Group, 1977—89; pres., editor-in-chief WriteRight, Inc., 1999—2008. Panelist pub. affairs radio programs, 1971—92; lectr. journalism San Diego State U., 1975—76; spkr., mktg. cons. to sr. citizens, 1984—92; chmn. Mature Market Seminars, 1987—90; pres., pub. Mature Market Editl. Svcs., 1991—98. Columnist: Mainly for Srs., 1984—99, Travel for Mature Adults, 1984—99, writer, journalist: Mature Market; contbg. editor: Mature Life Features, 1987—90; author: Life Begins at 50 - The Handbook for Creative Retirement Planning, 1989. Del. White House Conf. Aging, 1981; mem. Mayor's Ad Hoc Adv. Com. Aging, San Diego, 1976—79; founding mem. Housing Elderly and Low Income Persons, San Diego, 1977—78; vice chmn. Housing Task Force, San Diego, 1977—78; bd. dirs. Crime Control Commn., San Diego, 1980. With US Army, 1953—55. Recipient numerous svc. and citizen awards, Long Term Achievement in Nat. Media award, Am. Soc. Aging, 1999; fellow, Alicia Patterson Found., 1999; Nat. Press Found. fellow, 1994, 1997, 1998. Mem.: Am. Soc. Aging, Nat. Soc. Newspaper Columnists, Am. Soc. Journalists and Authors, Nat. Press Club, San Diego Press Club (Best Newswriting award 1976—77, Headliner of the Yr. award 1980), Soc. Profl. Journalists (Best Investigative Reporting award 1979). Died Dec. 15, 2008.

HANSEN, RUTH LUCILLE HOFER, business owner, consultant; b. Wellman, Iowa, Feb. 8, 1916; d. Harve Hiram and Frances Ada (Fitzsimmons) Hofer; m. Donald Edward Hansen, June 26, 1937 (dec. Feb. 1996); children: James Edward, Sandra Kaye. Student, Upper Iowa U., 1958, U. Northern Iowa, 1959. Co-founder, v.p. H & H Distbg. Co., West Union, Iowa, 1946-59, cons.; v.p., gen. ptnr., sec., treas. Don E. Hansen Family Partnership Ltd. Pres. United Presbyn. Women of Bethel Presbyn. Ch., West Union, Iowa, 1967—, mem. comty. planning and devel. commn.; pres. Lakes & Prairies Presbyterial, Cedar Rapids, Iowa, 1972-75; elder Bethel Presbyn. Ch., West Union, 1960-63; v.p., program chmn., camp dir., leader Camp Wyo. Ch. Camp; dist. Wapsipinicon coun. Girl Scouts, 1972-75; tchr. Vacation Bible Sch., Ch. Sch. for Adults, 1970; rep. John Knox Presbytery. Mem. Bus. and Profl. Women (pres.). Avocations: community plays, sewing, dance, golf, bridge. Died May 17, 2008.

HANSSON, RICHARD JOHN, lawyer; b. Jersey City, Apr. 20, 1952; s. Robert Wesley and Roberta Loretta (O'Brien) H.; m. Jacqueline Jean Brookes, Sept. 27 1990; children: Heather Brookes, Timothy Richard. BS in Acctg., St. Peter's Coll., 1975; JD, Seton Hall U., 1987. Bar: N.J. 1988. Acct., mgr. The Quaker Oats Co., Elizabeth, N.J., 1975-81; paramedic University Emergency Med. Svcs., Newark, N.J., from 1983; sole practice law Roselle, N.J., from 1987; chief exec. officer EMS Theory and Practice, Roselle, from 1989. Expert witness emergency med. svc. theory and practice, Roselle, 1990—. Co-founder, pres. Union Twp. Vols., 1979; treas., v.p. Roselle Vol. Ambulance, 1972-79. Mem. Nat. Assn. EMTs, N.J. Bar Assn., N.J. Trauma Awareness Found. (bd. dirs. 1989—). Died June 20, 2008.

HARBERT, GUY MORLEY, JR., retired obstetrician, gynecologist; b. Frederickburg, Va., Dec. 19, 1929; s. Guy Morley and Hannah (Turman) H.; m. Peggy Ann Simpson, Sept. 8, 1951; children— Lucille Hannah, Guy Morley, III, Michael Simpson. BA, U. Va., 1952, MD, 1956. Diplomate: Am. Bd. Ob-Gyn (maternal-fetal medicine). Intern Barnes Hosp., St. Louis, 1956-57; resident in ob-gyn U. Va. Hosp., 1959-63; med. faculty U. Va. Med. Sch., from 1963, prof. ob-gyn, 1976-95, prof. emeritus, 1995. Mem. human embryology and devel. study sect. NIH, 1975-79 Author articles in profl. jours., chpts. in books. Served as officer M.C. USAF, 1957-59. Mem. Soc. Gynecol. Investigation (exec. council 1973-76), Perinatal Research Soc. (exec. council 1977-79), So. Perinatal Assn. (exec. council 1974-77), Am. Gynecol. Soc., Am. Assn. Obstetricians and Gynecologists, N.Y. Acad. Scis., Am. Coll. Obstetricians and Gynecologists, Assn. Profs. Ob-Gyn, S. Atlantic Assn. Obstetricians and Gynecologists, Sigma Xi. Presbyterian. Home: Charlottesville, Va. Deceased.

HARDING, GLORIA MAE, lay worker, special education educator; b. Jeanerette, La., Dec. 20, 1940; d. Nathan and Lucinda (James) Gabriel; m. William Harding, Dec. 23, 1962. BS, Grambling Coll., 1962; MA, So. U., 1966. Cert. spl. edn., elem. tchr., La. Tchr. Iberia Parish Sch. Bd., Jeanerette, from 1963; tchr. Sunday Sch. First Ch. of God in

Christ, Jeanerette, 1977, dir. children's div., from 1978, dir. children's div., pres. dist. missions Franklin dist. Trustee, sec. 1st jurisdiction dept. missions First Ch. of God in Christ, Jeanerette, 1986—. Past sec. King Joseph Park Bd., Jeanerette, 1973-86; chairperson Parental Involvement Group, Jeanerette Elem. Sch., 1990-91. Mem. NEA, La. Assn. Edn., Iberia Assn. Edn. Democrat. Home: Jeanerette, La. Died May 2, 2008.

HARDING, RICHARD EVANS, pastor; b. Moberly, Mo., Dec. 17, 1937; s. Charles L. and Lois E. (Evans) H.; m. Susan Patterson; children: Nancy Harding Harris, John Charles. BA, U. Calif., Riverside, 1961; MDiv, Am. Bapt. Sem. of the West, Covina, Calif., 1969. Ordained to ministry Bapt. Ch., 1969. Tchr. Pasadena City Schs., Calif., 1961-62, Jurupa Unified Sch. Dist., Riverside, Calif., 1962-65; pastor First Bapt. Ch.-Rubidoux, Riverside, Calif., 1966-75; pastor, missionary Cordova Cmty. Bapt. Ch., Alaska, from 1975. Cons. Am. Bapt. Ch. and Inst., Alaska, 1990-96. Columnist Cordova Times, 1995—. Mem. Chem. People, Cordova. Recipient Vol. award Gov. of Alaska, 1990. Mem. Alaska Assn. Bapt. Chs. and Instns. (past pres. 1992-94). Avocations: photography, building and construction, computers. Home: Cordova, Alaska. Died July 28, 2008.

HARING, EUGENE MILLER, lawyer; b. Washington, May 16, 1927; s. Horace E. and Edith (Miller) H.; m. Janet K. Marshall, Apr. 10, 1971. AB summa cum laude, Princeton U., NJ, 1949, AM, 1951; LLB, Harvard U., Cambridge, Mass., 1955. Bar: N.J. 1955, U.S. Dist. Ct. N.J. 1955, U.S. Ct. Appeals (3d cir.) 1962, U.S. Supreme Ct. 1969, N.Y. 1983, U.S. Dist. Ct. (so. and ea. dists.) N.Y. 1992. Asst. in instrn. Princeton U., 1950-52; assoc. McCarter & English, Newark, 1955-61, ptnr., 1961-97, chmm. exec. com., 1982-97, of counsel, from 1997. Cert. mediator US Dist. Ct., from 1994; mediator CPR Inst. for Dispute Resolution, NJ Panel, 1994—2007; mem. roster of mediators Judiciary of State of N.J; mem. civil justice reform act adv. com. US Dist. Ct. NJ, 1997—2000. Contbr. articles to profl. jours. Chmn. Princeton Twp. Zoning Bd. Adjustment, 1979-80, mem. bd., 1975-79; vestryman Trinity Episc. Ch., Princeton, 1975-79, 97-2000, warden, 1980-84; mem. com. on constn. and canons Episc. Diocese of N.J., 1980-87, chancellor, 1983-94, 99—2006, hon. canon (life), 2001—; trustee Gen. Theol. Sem., N.Y., 1987-90; mem. vis. com. Rutgers U. Law Sch., 1994-2000; trustee N.J. Jersey Shore Found., 1988-92. Served with USNR, 1945-46. Woodrow Wilson fellow, Princeton U., 1949—50. Fellow Am. Bar Found. (life), Lawyers Adv. Com. (U.S. Ct. Appeals 3d cir. 1990-93, U.S. Dist. Ct. N.J. 1997—); mem. ABA, N.J. State Bar Assn. (emeritus), N.J. State Bar Found. (trustee 1986-87, v.p. 1987-88, chmn. 1988-90), Essex County Bar Assn. (Spl. Merit award 1998), Mercer County Bar Assn., Am. Law Inst. (life), Harvard Law Sch. Assn. N.J. (pres. 1971-72, nat. v.p. 1972-73), Hist. Soc. U.S. Dist. Ct. for Dist. N.J. (trustee 1987-90, 97—), Hist. Soc. 3d Cir. Ct. Appeals (bd., dirs. 1993-2000), Nassau Club, Princeton, Springdale Golf Club, Princeton, Monmouth Hunt Club, Phi Beta Kappa. Avocation: golf. Home: Princeton, NJ. Deceased.

HARKINS, KENNETH RICHARD, federal judge; b. Cadiz, Ohio, Sept. 1, 1921; m. Helen Mae Dozer, Dec. 26, 1942; children— M. Elaine, Richard A. BA in Econs., Ohio State U., 1943, LLB, 1948, JD, 1967. Bar: Ohio 1949. Atty. US Housing & Home Fin. Agy., 1949-51; trial atty. antitrust divsn. US Dept. Justice, Washington, 1951-55; co-counsel Antitrust Subcom. US House Judiciary Com., Washington, 1955-60, chief counsel, 1964-71; gen. counsel Stromberg Carlson div. and electronics div. Gen. Dynamics Corp., 1960-64; commr. US Ct. Federal Claims, Washington, 1971-82, judge, 1982—2000, sr. judge, 2000—09. Served to 1st lt. U.S. Army, 1943-46 Died Oct. 8, 2009.

HARKNESS, SAMUEL DACKE, III, materials scientist; b. Oct. 28, 1940; s. Samuel Dacke Jr. and Jane Margaret (Morin) H.; m. Christine Lee Hotchkiss, Dec. 28, 1963; children: Samuel, Laura, Matthew. B in Metall. Engring., Cornell U., 1963; PhD in Materials Sci., U. Fla., 1967; MBA, U. Pitts., 1983. Rsch. engr. dept. space power Atomics Internat., Canoga Park, Calif., 1963-64; mgr. radiation effects Argonne (Ill.) Nat. Lab., 1967-73, assoc. dir. fusion, 1976-79; mgr. materials tech. sect. Combustion Engring., East Windsor, Conn., 1973-76; mgr. materials tech. div. Bettis Atomic Power Lab., West Mifflin, Pa., 1979-90; gen. mgr. systems, processes and techs. div. Westinghouse Sci. & Tech. Ctr., Pitts., from 1990. Editor: Radiation Effects, 1975; contbr. 75 articles to profl. jours. Coach Youth Soccer, Peters Twp., Pa., 1982-85; mem. Sch. Bd., Peters Twp., 1983-86. Alfred P. Sloan scholar Cornell U., 1958-63; Engring. fellow U. Fla., 1964-67. Fellow Am. Soc. Metals, Am. Nuclear Soc. (materials sci. adv. bd. 1974-77); mem. AIME (Metall. Soc. awards com. 1970-73, Robert Lansing Hardy Gold Medal award 1969). Achievements include patent for advanced fusion reactor blanket concept; research on understanding void swelling in support of fast breeder reactor development. Home: McMurray, Pa. Died Dec. 13, 2007.

HARMON, GEORGE MARION, academic administrator; b. Memphis, Aug. 12, 1934; s. George Marion and Madie P. (Foster) H.; m. Bessie W. Porter, Dec. 27, 1958; children: Nancy R., Mary K., Elizabeth T., George Marion III. BA, Rhodes Coll., 1956; MBA, Emory U., 1957; DBA, Harvard U., 1963. Market rsch. analyst Continental Oil Co., Houston, 1957; rsch. assoc. Harvard U., 1960-63; asst. prof. Coll. Bus. Adminstrn., dir. Salzberg Meml. Transp. Program Syracuse U., NY, 1963-66; sr. assoc. sys. econs. divsn. Planning Rsch. Corp., Washington, 1966-67; prof., chmn. dept econs. and bus. adminstrn., dir. continuing edn. program in econs. and bus. adminstrn. Rhodes Coll. (formerly Southwestern at Memphis), Memphis, 1967-74; prof., dean divsn. bus. and mgmt. W.Va. Coll. Grad. Studies, Charleston, 1974-75; prof., dean Sch. Bus. and Mgmt. Saginaw Valley State Coll., University Center, Mich., 1975-78; pres. Millsaps Coll., Jackson, Miss., 1978-2000, pres. emeritus, sr. counsel spl. projects, 2000—05; mem. faculty fin. Sch. Banking of the South, La. State U., 1968-72; dir. Audio Visual Sys., Inc., Tenn., 1970-72; v.p., treas. Allen Industries, Inc., Tenn., 1970-72; co-founder, v.p. Computer Survey Sys., Inc., Tenn., 1972-73. Bd. dirs., chmn. exec. compensation com. MacCarty Farms, Inc., Magee, Miss., 1982-95; bd. dirs. Entex, Inc., Houston, 1981-99; mem. So. Regional Edn. Bd., Atlanta, 1994-98; bd. dirs. Regions Bank of Miss. Contbr. articles on bus. adminstrn. to profl. jours. Bd. dirs. Fayetteville-Manlius (N.Y.) Ctrl. Sch. Dist., 1961—63, John Houston Wear Found., Jackson, 1979—2000, Eudora Welty Found., 1999—2003, Jackson Symphony Orch. Assn., 1981—85, Miss. Opera Assn., 1981—86, Governance Coun., Cath. Charities of Miss., from 2002, Madison County Libr. Found., 2002—04, St. Catherine's Village Retirement Ctr. Found., 2002—07; trustee, chmn. pers. and labor rels. com. Saginaw Osteo. Hosp., 1977—78; chmn. So. Colls. and Univs. Union, 1983—86, Miss. Found. Ind. Colls., 1982; com. and sec. Jackson Internat. Airport Authority, 1991—97; chmn., bd. dirs. Jackson Med. Edn. Dist., 1998—2000; bd. dirs. Jackson Acad., 2005—07, St. Joseph HS, from 2008; dir. St. Dominic Health Svcs. Found., from 2007; univ. senate United Meth. Ch., 1990—2000; bd. dirs., mem. exec. com. Cath. Found., Diocese of Miss., from 2005. Decorated Knights of Columbia Equestrian Order Holy Sepulchre Jerusalem. Mem. NCAA (coun. 1986-92), KC, Jackson C. of C. (bd. dirs. 1981-84), Newcomen Soc. Miss. (pres. 2001-, chmn. 2001-), Soc. Internat. Bus. Fellows, Jackson Country Club, Univ. Club, Capitol City Club, Harvard Club (NYC), Rotary, Phi Beta Kappa, Beta Gamma Sigma, Omicron Delta Kappa, Kappa Sigma (Pres.'s Commn. 2000—). Roman Catholic. Died Dec. 17, 2008.

HARMON, MERLE REID, SR., retired sportscaster; b. Orchardville, Ill., June 21, 1927; s. Herschel and Oda Ethel (Holler) H.; m. Jeanette Kinner, Dec. 31, 1947; children: Reid, Keith, Kyle, Bruce, Kara. AA, Graceland Coll., 1947; BA, U. Denver, 1949. Pres. Merle Harmon Enterprises, Inc., Milw., from 1967; chmn. Fan Fair Corp., Milw., from 1977. Sportscaster, Topeka, Kans., 1949-52, Kansas. U. Network, Lawrence, 1952-54, baseball announcer, Kansas City A's, 1955-61, Milw. Braves, 1964-65, Minn. Twins, 1967-69, Milw. Brewers, 1970-79, sportscaster, ABC-TV, 1961-73, N.Y. Jets announcer, WABC Radio, N.Y., 1964-72, co-host, World Univ. Games from, Moscow, TVS Network, 1973, Big Ten Basketball, 1974-80, sportscaster, NBC Sports, N.Y.C., 1979-82, Tex. Rangers, 1982—89. Chmn. Easter Seal Campaign, Milwaukee County, Wis., 1981; bd. dirs. Easter Seal Soc.; trustee Park Coll., Parkville, Mo. Served with USN, 1944-46. Recipient Outstanding Alumnus award Nat. Assn. Intercollegiate Athletics, 1972, Disting. Svc. award Graceland Coll., 1978; named one of Top 50 Sportscasters Am. Sportscasters Assn., 2009. Mem. Nat. Assn. Sports Broadcasters, Brookfield Wis. C. of C., Wauwatosa Wis. C. of C. Mem. Reorganized Ch. of Jesus Christ of Latter-day Saints. Home: Arlington, Tex. Died Apr. 15, 2009.

HARMS, DAVID KENT, investment analyst; b. Dixon, Ill., Feb. 15, 1955; s. Byron G. and Gloria (Eckerd) H. Student, U. Ill., 1973-79. Gen. mgr. Rock River Valley Ent., Dixon, Ill., 1984-92; pres. Palmyra Capital Corp., Dixon, from 1993. Bd. dirs. B&H Assocs., Ltd. Trustee The Greater Need Trust, 1992—, The R.D.B. Fin. Trust, 1993—. Home: Dixon, Ill. Died May 31, 2008.

HARPHAM, VIRGINIA RUTH, retired violinist; b. Huntington, Ind., Dec. 10, 1917; d. Pyrl John and Nellie Grace (Whitaker) Harpham; m. Dale Lamar Harpham, Dec. 25, 1938 (div.); children: Evelyn, George. AB, Morehead State U., 1939. Violinist Nat. Symphony Orch., Washington, 1955-90, prin. of second violin sect., 1964-90; mem. Lywen String Quartet, 1960-69, Nat. Symphony String Quartet, 1973-82. Recipient Maud Powell Soc. award, 2008; named to Hall of Fame, Morehead State U., 2003. Episcopalian. Home: Washington, DC. Died Apr. 13, 2009.

HARREL, LEON JOHN, JR., lawyer, accountant; b. New Orleans, Dec. 15, 1955; s. Leon John Harrel Sr. and Ida Mae (Wilson) Harrel Green. BS in Acctg., So. La. U., 1976, JD, 1984; cert., Am. Sch. Realtors, 1979. Bar: U.S. Dist. Ct. (mid. dist.) La. 1984, U.S. Supreme Ct., 1984. Acct. grants and contracts So. U. Comptroller Office, Baton Rouge, 1977-81; legal asst. La. Atty. Gen., Baton Rouge, 1983-84; atty. La. Dept. Revenue & Taxation, Baton Rouge, from 1985. Named one of Outstanding Young Men Am., 1984, Hon. Sec. of State La., 1986. Mem. ABA, La. Bar Assn., La. Trial Lawyers Assn., Assn. Trial Lawyers Am., Phi Alpha Delta. Democrat. Baptist. Home: Baton Rouge, La. Died Nov. 16, 2007.

HARRIMAN, JOHN HOWLAND, retired lawyer; b. Buffalo, Apr. 14, 1920; s. Lewis Gildersleeve and Grace (Bastine) H.; m. Barbara Ann Brunmark, June 12, 1943; children— Walter Brunmark, Constance Bastine, John Howland. AB summa cum laude, Dartmouth, 1942; JD, Stanford U., 1949. Bar: Calif. 1949. Assoc. firm Lawler, Felix & Hall, LA, 1949-55; asst. v.p., then v.p. Security Pacific Nat. Bank, LA, 1955-72, sr. v.p., 1972-85; ret., 1985. Sec. Security Pacific Corp., 1971-85; dir. Master Metal Works; mem. nat. adv. coun. The Pub. Svc., 1992-93. Mem. L.A. adv. coun. Episcopal Ch. Found., 1977-79; mem. Republican Assocs., 1951-72, trustee, 1962-72; mem. Calif. Rep. Central Com., 1956-69, 81—, exec. com., 1960-62, 81-84; mem. L.A. County Rep. Central Com., 1958-70, exec. com., 1960-62, vice chmn., 1962; chmn. Calif. 15th Congl. Dist. Rep. Central Com., 1960-62, Calif. 30th Congl. Dist. Rep. Central Com., 1962; treas. United Rep. Fin. Com. L.A. County, 1969-70; chmn. L.A. County Reagan-Bush campaign, 1980, co-chmn., 1984; exec. dir. Calif. Rep. Party, 1985-86. With USAAF, 1943-46. Mem. Am. Bar Assn., State Bar Calif., Phi Beta Kappa, Theta Delta Chi, Phi Alpha Delta. Clubs: California (Los Angeles); Lincoln, Breakfast Panel (pres. 1970-71). Home: Los Gatos, Calif. Died July 7, 2008.

HARRINGTON, MARGARET BRANCHE, dietitian, researcher in human development; b. Watertown, NY, May 8, 1918; d. Amie Simeon and Alma Mary (Ransiear) Branche; m. Robert Maurice Harrington, Oct. 15, 1940; children: Mary Ann Coleman, James Maurice. AAS in Home Econs., Coll. Tech., Canton, NY, 1938; Dietitian, Buffalo Deaconess Hosp., 1939; student, Syracuse U., 1994. Cert. dietitian. Dietitian Sisters Hosp., Buffalo, 1939-40, Ellis Hosp., Schenectady, N.Y., 1939-41; food demonstrator Frozen Food Locker Plant, Towanda, Pa., 1941-45; seminars in librs., Ruskin, Fla., 1995-96; 1st person presentations of Susan B. Anthony, from 1996. Author: Freeze It, 1942; writer jour. for 4 Rivers Hist. Soc. Valleys on Susan B. Anthony. Active Coop. Extension, Meals on Wheels, Children's Ctrs. Recipient Outstanding Alumni award Syracuse U., 1999. Mem. Univ. Women's Club (Sun City Center, Fla.). Republican. Roman Catholic. Home: Sun City Ctr, Fla. Died Aug. 24, 2008.

HARRIS, E. LYNN, writer; b. Flint, Mich., June 20, 1955; Degree in Journalism, U. Ark., 1977. Salesman IBM Corp., 1977-88; writer, 1988—2009. Vis. prof. English U. Ark. Author: Invisible Life, 1991 (Essence mag. Best 10 Novels of 1991), Just As I Am, 1995 (Blackboard Novel of Yr.), And This Too Shall Pass, 1997, If This World Were Mine, 1998 (James Baldwin award for Lit. Excellence), Abide With Me, 2000, Not A Day Goes By, 2000, Any Way the Wind Blows, 2002 (Blackboard Novel of Yr.), A Love Of My Own, 2003 (Blackboard Novel of Yr.), What Becomes Of The Brokenhearted — A Memoir, 2004, I Say a Little Prayer, 2006, Just Too Good To Be True, 2008, Basketball Jones, 2009 (Publishers Weekly bestseller). Bd. dirs. Hurston/Wright Found., Evidence Dance Co. Recipient Distinguished Alumni award, U. Ark., 1999, Sprague Todes Lit. award, Harvey Milk Hon. Diploma; named one of 100 Leaders and Heroes in Black America, Savoy mag.; named to Ark. Black Hall of Fame, 2000, Most Intriguing Blacks list, Ebony mag., Out 100 list, Out Mag., Gay Power 101 list, NY Mag. Died July 24, 2009.

HARRIS, ROBERT ALTER, radiologist; b. Canton, Ohio, Sept. 24, 1955; s. Albert Harrold and Martha Ann (Alter) H.; m. Kathryn Galpin, Nov. 3, 1990. BA in Chemistry, Miami U., 1978; D.O., Ohio Univ., 1982. Diplomate Am. Bd. Radiology. Radiologist T.C. Hobbs & Assocs., Columbus, Ohio, from 1987. Mem. Am. Osteopathic Coll. Radiology, Radiol. Soc. North Am., Am. Inst. Ultrasound in Medicine, Am. Osteopathic Assn., Cen. Ohio Radiol. Soc. Avocations: golf, raquetball, travel, photography. Home: Columbus, Ohio. Died June 3, 2008.

HARRIS, ROBERT GEORGE, illustrator; b. Kansas City, Mo., Sept. 9, 1911; s. Harry George and Lena Mary (Stevens) H.; m. Marjorie Elnora King, Dec. 26, 1935; children: Craig, Marcia. Student, Kansas City Art Inst., 1928-30, Art Students League, NYC, 1931-32, Grand Cen. Art Sch., 1931-32. Illustrator Sat. Evening Post, Ladies Home Jour., McCall's, Cosmopolitan, RedBook, Good Housekeeping, 1939-65; portrait painter Justice Dept., Washington, Union Pacific R.R., N.Y.C., Ariz. State U., Beta Sigma Phi Hdqrs., Seabury Western Theol. Sem., many corp. and family portraits, 1965—. Mem. Soc. Illustrators (life). Avocations: flying, photography, vintage autos. Home: Carefree, Ariz. Died Dec. 23, 2007.

HARRIS, ROBERT LAIRD, minister, theology educator emeritus; b. Brownsburg, Pa., Mar. 10, 1911; s. Walter William and Ella Pearl (Graves) H.; m. Elizabeth Krugar Nelson, Sept. 11, 1937 (dec. 1980); children: Grace Sears, Allegra Smick, Robert Laird; m. Anne Paxson Krauss, Aug. 1, 1981. BSChemE, U. Del., Newark, 1931; postgrad, Washington U., 1931-32; ThB, Westminster Theol. Sem., 1935, ThM, 1937; MA in Oriental Studies, U. Pa., 1941; PhD, Dropsie Coll., 1947. Ordained to ministry Presbyn. Ch. Am., 1936; instr. Faith Theol. Sem., Phila., 1937-43, asst. prof. Bibl. Exegesis, 1943-47, prof. Bibl. Exegesis, 1947-56; prof. Covenant Theol. Sem., St. Louis, 1956-81, dean, 1964-71, prof. emeritus, from 1981; prof. Winona Lake Summer Sch. of Theology, 1964, 66-67, Near East Sch. Archaeology and Bible, Jerusalem, 1962; vis. prof. China Grad. Sch. Theology, Hong Kong, 1981, Freie Theologische Akademie, Giessen, Fed. Republic Germany, 1982-85, Tyndale Theol. Sem., Amsterdam, The Netherlands, 1986-2000, Bibl. Theol. Sem., Hatfield, Pa., 1992, J. Manoel Conceicao Presbyn. Sem., Sao Paulo, Brazil, 1995. Vis. lectr. Wheaton Coll., Ill., 1957-61; lectr. Japan, Korea, 1965, India, 1981, Australia, 1989; moderator Presbyn. Ch. in Am., 1982. Author: Introductory Hebrew Grammar, 1950, Inspiration and Canonicity of the Bible, 1957, 2d edit., 1995, Man-God's Eternal Creation, 1971, You and Your Bible, 1990; editor: Theological Wordbook of the Old Testament, 2 vols., 1981, Leviticus in Expositor's Bible Commentary, Vol. 2, 1990; mem. editorial bd. New Internat. Version of Bible, 1965-2000, chmn., 1970-74; contbg. author various books. Trustee Bibl. Theol. Sem., Hatfield, Pa., 1985-2000. DuPont fellow U. Del., 1930-31; recipient first prize Zondervan Textbook Contest, 1955; Foxwell Lecture lectureship Tokyo Christian Theol. Sem., 1981. Mem. Evang. Theol. Soc. (pres. 1961), Tau Beta Pi, Phi Kappa Phi Republican. Died Apr. 25, 2008.

HARRIS, SHERWOOD, editor; b. NYC, Nov. 26, 1932; s. Sterling G. and Edna M. (Sell) H.; m. Lorna Briggs Harris, Sept. 11, 1953 (dec. Sept. 1993); children: Michael, Suzanne Wilkinson, Catherine, Margaret Ware (dec. 2004) BA, Princeton U., 1954. Editl. asst. The Saturday Evening Post, Washington, 1957-60; freelance writer Washington, 1960-64; dep. editor Am. Illustrated USIA, Washington, 1964-68; sr. staff editor Reader's Digest Books, Pleasantville, N.Y., 1968-85; pres. Harris Editl. Assocs., Katonah, N.Y., 1985-94; editor pub. affairs staff Washington Nat. Cathedral, Washington, 1994-97. Author: The First to Fly: Aviation Pioneer Days, 1970, Great Flying ADventures, 1973, N.Y. Public Library Book of How and Where to Look It Up, 1991; co-author: (with Lorna B. Harris, book series) The Teacher's Almanac, 1988-90, (with Henry Sollan) Mastering Instrument Flying, 1989, (with Phil Dixon) Mastering GPS Flying, 2005 Comdr. USNR, 1954-71. Democrat. Episcopalian. Avocation: flying. Died Sept. 7, 2009.

HARRISON, FRANK GIRARD, former United States Representative from Pennsylvania; b. Washington, Feb. 2, 1940; s. Frank Gerard and Lillian Clarke Harrison. Lectr. Govt. & Politics, King's Coll., 1969—83, 1985—87; of counsel Rosenn, Jenkins & Greenwald, Wilkes-Barre, Pa., 1972—83, pvt. practice, from 1985; mem. bd. dir. Cmty. Econ. Opportunity Luzerne County, 1973—83; chmn. Luzerne County Bicentennial Com., 1975—76, Downtown Develop. Authority, Wilkes-Barre, 1978—83; mem. US Congress from 11th Pa. Dist., 1983—85; city atty. Wilkes-Barre, 1985—87; vis. scholar rsch., 1988; chmn. Nat. Debate Tournament Com., 1993—95; dir. forensics Trinity U., 1988—94, from 1994, asst. prof. speech, 1988—94, 1994—2009. Recipient Disting. Svc. award, Greater Wilkes-Barre Jaycees, 1976, John Jacobsohn award, U. West Va., 2001, Lucy M. Keele award, Svc. Debate, Nat. Debate Tournament, 2003. Mem.: Am. Debate Assn., Osterhout Free Lib. (bd. dirs. 1976—85, former pres.). Democrat. Roman Catholic. Died June 4, 2009.

HARRISON, JAMES BUTLER, lawyer; b. St. Louis, Oct. 11, 1930; s. Charles R. and Helen M. (Butler) H.; m. Ruth P. Ruble, Sept. 11, 1965. JD, St. Louis U., 1953. Claims adjuster Transport Ins. Co., St. Louis, 1957-59; pvt. practice Sullivan, Mo., from 1959. Served to comdr. USNR, 1953-86. Mem. ABA, Mo. Bar. Home: Sullivan, Mo. Died Apr. 29, 2008.

HARRISON, LINDA SUE, mortgage company executive; b. Ft. Worth, June 27, 1944; d. Paul Martin and Cora Edna (Daniel) Montgomery; m. Millard Dee Harrison, Jan. 2, 1964; children: Jessie Douglas, Paul David, Ronald Dale. Grad., Nat. Inst. Fin. Edn. Teller First Na. Bank, Plano, Tex., 1973-79; computer interface Edn. Service Ctr., Richardson, Tex., 1979-82; mortgage dept. mgr. Majestic Savs. Assn., McKinney, Tex., 1982-86; v.p. mortgage lending Multibanc Savs. Assn., Dallas, from 1986. Mem. Nat. Assn. Female Execs., Mortgage Bankers Assn., Tex. Mortgage Bankers Assn., Dallas Assn. Profl. Mortgage Women. Mem. Ch. of Christ. Home: Fort Worth, Tex. Died Nov. 10, 2007.

HARRISON, PATRICIA ANN, nurse, small business owner; b. Blue Hill, Nebr., Sept. 9, 1932; d. Edgar and Eva Teresa (Conniff) McBride; m. Frank Bernard Harrison, July 9, 1955; children: Patricia, Lisa, Mary, Thomas, Aimeé, Denise, Barbara, Gerard. RN, Creighton U. Sch. Nursing, 1954; cert. program in geriatrics and gerontology, U. Nebr., 1976; student, St. Leo's Coll. RNC. Dir. nursing Mt. Carmel Nursing Home, Kearney, Nebr., 1974-77; geriatric nursing cons. extended care facility Ft. Walton Beach (Fla.) Hosp., 1977-79; dir. nursing Westwood Retirement Ctr., Ft. Walton Beach, 1980-82, adminstrv. asst., 1983; adminstrv. cons. Lely Palms Retirement Ctr., Naples, Fla., 1983-84; owner Profl. Edn. Service, Ft. Walton Beach, from 1985; coordinator support services Air Force Enlisted Mens' Widow's Found., Ft. Walton Beach, from 1986; adminstr. Village at Sandestin SNF & ACLF, Destin, Fla. Named Nurse of Quarter, Am. Retailers. Assn. Retirement Living Ctrs. Div., 1982. Mem. Fla. Nurses Assn (mem. edn. com. 1986—). Republican. Roman Catholic. Avocations: stitchery, crafts, painting, plants. Home: Fort Walton Beach, Fla. Died May 15, 2008.

HARTER, ROGER KARR, retired telecommunications executive; b. Normal, Ill., Dec. 12, 1923; s. Omar Newton and Helena (Karr) H.; m. Claire Phylis Caverly, Dec. 23, 1944; children: Deborah, Duncan, Malcolm, Penelope. BA, Swarthmore Coll., 1942; MA, Harvard U., 1948; postgrad., U. Mich., 1949-51. Staff asst. New Eng. Telegraph & Telephone, Boston, 1948-49; gen. staff asst. Mich. Bell Telephone, Detroit, 1949-51; gen. staff supr. AT&T, NYC, 1951-58, Mich. Bell Telephone Co., Detroit, 1958-80. Chmn. bd. dirs. South Oakland Symphony Soc., Oak Park, Mich., 1960-62; pres. Southfield (Mich.) Symphony Soc.; state and regional pres. Navy League. of U.S., Mich., 1975-80, nat. dir., 1975—; nat. dir. U.S. Naval Sea Cadet Corps, Washington, 1989-92. Col. USMC, 1942-75. Mem. VFW, Nat. Assn. Parliamentarians (registered parliamentarian, nat. dir. 1989-93), Am. Legion, Mich. State Assn. Parliamentarians (pres. 1994-96), Res. Officers Assn. (state pres. 1976, nat. parliamentarian, nat. exec. com., 1990-92, 2004-), M.C. Res. Officers Assn. (chpt. pres.), Birmingham Power Squadron (charter), Mil. Inst. Windsor (charter), Marine Corps Assn., Fleet Res. Assn., Naval War Coll. Found., Naval Inst., Naval Order of U.S., Sovereign Mil. Order of Temple of Jerusalem. Republican. Presbyterian. Avocations: sailing, travel. Home: Birmingham, Mich. Died Sept. 19, 2007.

HARTIGAN, GRACE, artist; b. Newark, Mar. 28, 1922; d. Matthew A. and Grace (Orvis) H.; m. Robert L. Jachens, May 1941 (div. 1948); 1 son, Jeffrey A. (dec. 2006); m. Robert Keene, Dec. 14, 1959 (div. 1960); m. Winston H. Price, Dec. 24, 1960 (dec. 1981). Student pvt. art classes. Dir. Md. Inst. Grad. Sch. Painting, from 1965. One-woman shows Tibor de Nagy Gallery, N.Y.C., 1951-55, 57-59, Vassar Coll. Art Gallery, 1954, Martha Jackson Gallery, N.Y.C., 1962, 64, 67, 70, U. Chgo., 1967, Gertrude Kasle Gallery, Detroit, 1968, 70, 72, 74, Robert Keene Gallery, Southampton, N.Y., 1957-59, Gres Gallery, Washington, 1960, U. Minn., 1963, William Zierler Gallery, N.Y.C., C. Grimaldis Gallery, Balt., 1979, 81, 82, 84, 86, 87, 89, 90, 93, 95, 97, Hamilton Gallery, N.Y.C., 1981, Gruenebaum Gallery, N.Y.C., 1984, 86, 88, Kouros Gallery, N.Y.C., 1989, ACA Gallery, N.Y.C., 1991, 92, 94, 97, ACA Munich, 1996; exhibited in numerous group shows including Modern Art in U.S., 1955-56, 3d Internat. Contemporary Art Exhbn., 1957, 4th Internat. Art Exhbn., Japan, 1957, IV Biennial, Sao Paulo, 1957, New Am. Painting Show, Europe, 1958-59, World's Fair, Brussels, 1958, The Figure Since Picasso, Mus. Ghent, Belgium, Moca in Moca Chicago, Hand Painted Pop Moca L.A., Whitney Mus. Am. Art, N.Y.C., 1992-93, 99; represented in permanent collections Mus. Modern Art, Walker Art Center, Whitney Mus. Am. Art, Art Inst. Chgo., Met. Mus. Art, Raleigh Mus., Providence Mus., Bklyn. Mus., Mpls. Mus., Albright-Knox Gallery, Buffalo, numerous others. Recipient Merit award for art Mademoiselle Mag., 1957, Nat. Inst. Arts and Letters purchase award, 1974 Died Nov. 15, 2008.

HARTMAN, GUY LESLIE, pediatrician; b. Big Flats, NY, Sept. 11, 1922; s. Fred Charles and Ruth Agnes (Andrews) H.; m. Shirley Fenn Baldwin, Dec. 28, 1943; children: Eric Vreeland, Fenn Elizabeth, Christina Louise, Peter Bain, Juliana Middaugh. BA in Zoology, Alfred U., 1943; MD, U. Buffalo, 1946. Diplomate Am. Bd. Pediatrics. Commd. med. officer USAF, 1943, advanced through grades to maj., 1950, ret., 1952; intern Med. Ctr., Jersey City, 1946-47; pediatrics resident Children's Hosp., LA, 1957-59; pediatrician So. Calif. Permanente Med. Group, Fontana, 1952-87; med. cons. regional offices Diamond Bar, San Bernardino, from 1990. Chmn. Cen. Valley Child Abuse Team, Fontana, 1975-87, San Bernardino County Child Abuse Council, 1986-87; bd. dirs., v.p. Calif. Consortium Child Abuse, 1981-86; pres. Southwestern Pediatric Soc. Los Angeles, 1984-85. Contbr. articles to profl. jours. and mags. Speaker civic orgns. nationally, and internationally. Recipient Citation Domestic Violence Task Force San Bernardino, 1984, Martha Lou Berkey award Inland Empire Child Abuse Task Force, 1985. Fellow Am. Acad. Pediatrics; mem. Southwestern Pediatric Soc. (chmn. 1984-85), Los Angeles Pediatric Soc., Hinterland Pediatric Soc., Internat. Soc. Prevention of Child Abuse and Neglect, Def. of Children, Collegium Aesculapium (bd. dirs., assoc. editor jour.). Republican. Mem. Lds Ch. Avocations: music, poisonous plants. Home: Salt Lake City, Utah. Died Aug. 20, 2008.

HARTMAN, MARILYN D., English and art educator; b. Denver, May 2, 1927; d. Leland DeForest Henshaw and Evelyn Wyman Henshaw; m. James Hartman, Oct. 7, 1949 (dec. Dec. 1989); children: Charles, Alice, Mary Hale. Student, U. Denver, 1947; BA, U. Colo., 1958; MA, UCLA, 1965, EdD in English Edn., 1972. Calif. life std. tchg. credential English and art, Colo. secondary English and art. Tchr. Denver Pub. Schs., 1959—65; asst. prof. San Fernando Valley State U., Northridge, Calif., 1970—72, San Diego State U. Mem., presenter Am. Ednl. Rsch. Assn., L.A., 1965-72; mem. Nat. Coun. Tchrs. English, L.A., 1965-72; officer Pi Lambda Theta-Alpha Delta chpt., L.A., 1970-72; with Ctr. for the Study Dem. Instns., L.A., 1970-72; tchg. asst., 1964, discussion leader linguistics; tchr. evaluator UCLA, 1970-72, Iliff Sch. Theology, Denver U.; cons. Dept Edn., Riley, 1992-2000, State Dept., 1992-2000, to Pres. Clinton, 1992-2000. Author: Linguistic Approach to Teaching English, 1965, Two Letters and Some Thoughts, 1968, Sound and Meaning of BE Speech, 1969, Teaching a Dialect, 1970, Contrastive Analysis: BE and SE Teaching, 1972, Touch the Windy Finger, 1980, Under the Hand of God, 2000; author: (with Bill Kirton) (short stories) O God, 1970, On Her Own: To Know and Not Know, 2002; author: The Luckiest People, 2002. Chmn. Denver Metro Area Food Drive, 1985, Interfaith Alliance; mem. Dem. Nat. Com., 1992—2002. Mem.: VFW, NOW, AAUW, Women in the Arts, Interfaith Alliance, Nat. Philatelic Soc., Am. Philatelic Assn., Common Cause, Sierra Club, Franciscan Missions, Natural Resources Def. Coun., Kempe Children's Found., Colo. Fedn. Dem. Women's Clubs, Inc. (officer 2001). Avocations: singing, painting, writing, teaching, counseling. Home: Denver, Colo. Died June 24, 2008.

HARTMAN, MATTHEW ALOYSIUS, real estate administrator; b. NYC, July 18, 1922; s. Matthew Aloysius and Mary Agnes (Linskey) H.; m. Lillian Marie Broderick, Apr. 17, 1948 (div. 1958); children: Nancy Marie, Susan Marie; m. Margaret Gail Obert, Nov. 8, 1974; stepchildren: Kenneth Mark Wooden, Lorelei Jean Kaczmarski. LLB, St. John's U., Bklyn., 1945. Bar: N.Y. 1946. Law clk., atty. Burlington, Veeder, Clark & Hupper, NYC, 1945-46; mng. atty. Michelsen & Elliot, NYC, 1946-48; pvt. practice Huntington, N.Y., 1948-57; examiner Lane Title & Trust Co., Phoenix, 1958-60; sr. title examiner Ariz. State Hwy. Dept., Phoenix, 1961-71; real estate adminstr. Maricopa Co. Hwy. Dept., Phoenix, from 1972. Mem. Rep. Nat. Com., 1978— Mem. Internat. Right Way Assn., Maricopa Assn. Govts., Scottsdale Yacht Club (commodore 1977). Roman Catholic. Avocations: swimming, sailing, dance, coin collecting/numismatics. Home: Scottsdale, Ariz. Died Apr. 6, 2008.

HARTRIDGE, JUDI ANN, medical, surgical, geriatrics nurse; b. Scranton, Pa., Feb. 11, 1962; d. Peter M. and Peggy (LaBelle) Perry; m. John J. Hartridge, Sept. 19, 1987. BSN, Coll. Misericordia, Dallas, Pa., 1984. Staff nurse Moses Taylor Hosp., Scranton, Pa., 1984-85; charge nurse Scranton State Gen. Hosp., 1985-88; asst. dir. nurses Green Ridge Nursing Ctr., Scranton, 1988-90; DON Green Ridge Nursing Home, Scranton, 1990-99, Balanced Care, Kingston, Pa., from 1999. Mem. Pa. Assn. Dir. Nurses. Home: Scranton, Pa. Died Dec. 14, 2007.

HARTSTONE, ROGER D., publishing executive; b. Boston, June 11, 1950; s. Leon C. and Marcia R. Hartstone; children: Joseph, Laura. BA, U. Calif., Berkeley, 1972; JD, Southwestern U., 1982. V.p. Integrity Entertainment Corp., Gardena, Calif., 1973-77; mktg. cons. Expressive Ventures Corp., Encino, Calif., 1977-79; paralegal various law firms, LA, 1979-81; pres. Escalating Expectations Corp., Flagstaff, Ariz., 1984-95; CEO Next Generation, Inc., from 1995. Coord. No. Ariz. Earth Day Coalition, Flagstaff, 1989-91; coach AYSO Soccer, Flagstaff, 1986-88. Avocations: tennis, bike riding, reading. Died Mar. 27, 2008.

HARTSWICK, DONALD EDWARD, association executive; b. Baden, Pa., Oct. 31, 1935; m. Elaine Dorothy Stanier, Aug. 24, 1957; children: Timothy, Donel. BS in Edn., Slippery Rock U., 1957; MEd, U. Pitts., 1961, EdD, 1974. Cert. tchr., prin., supt., Pa. Tchr. Bethel Park (Pa.) Schs., 1957-61; supr. Armstrong Sch. Dist., Kittanning, Pa., 1961-64; prin. Oakmont (Pa.) Sch. Dist., 1964-65; asst. supt. North Allegheny Sch. Dist., Pitts., 1965-81; supt. Trinity Area Sch. Dist., Washington, Pa., 1981-88, Washington Sch. Dist., Warrendale, Pa., 1988-89; dir. edn. svcs. The Hosp. Coun. of WPA, Warrendale, from 1989. Home: Pittsburgh, Pa. Died Jan. 4, 2008.

HARTZELL, JOHN MASON, poet, service technician; b. Hardtner, Kans., Jan. 23, 1945; s. Kenneth and Freda Irene (Hamilton) H. AA in Nursing, Pratt County Jr. Coll., 1965; BA in Sociology, Southwestern Coll., 1973. Svc. technician Automacic Coin Machine Corp., Winfield, Kans., from 1975. Contbr. poetry to anthologies and profl. publs. Recipient numerous awards for poetry, including Nat. Libr. Poetry, Internat. Soc. Poets, Kans. Author's Club. Mem. VFW, Am. Legion. Presbyterian. Avocations: collecting records, horseshoes, poetry. Home: Winfield, Kans. Died Feb. 8, 2008.

HARTZELL, KARL DREW, retired dean, historian; b. Chgo., Jan. 17, 1906; s. Morton C. and Bertha V. (Drew) Hartzell; m. Anne Lomas, Sept. 7, 1935; children: Karl Drew, Richard Lomas, Julian Crane; m. Elizabeth Farnum Guibord, Oct. 2, 1993. PhB cum laude, Wesleyan U., 1927; AM, Harvard U., 1928, PhD, 1934. Mem. faculty European history and Western civilization Carleton Coll., 1930-31; mem. faculty European history and western civilization dept. Ga. Sch. Tech., 1935-40; with SUNY, Geneseo, 1940-47, exec dean SUNY Ctrl. Adminstrn., acting chief adminstrv. officer Stony Brook, 1962-65, adminstrv. officer, 1965-71, dean arts and sci.; archivist, historian N.Y. State War Coun., 1945-46; adminstrv. officer Brookhaven Nat. lab., 1947-52; dean Cornell Coll., Iowa, 1952-56, Bucknell U., 1956-62; libr. Inst. Advanced Studies World Religions, cons.; ret., 1972. Author: The Empire State at War: World War II, 1949, Opportunities in Atomic Energy, 1950, A Philosophy for Science Teaching, 1957, The Laws of the Living: American Values in Action, 2005; editor: The Upperclass Student and His Curriculum, 1955; co-editor: The Study of Religion on the Campus of Today, 1967. Wilbur Fisk scholar, Wesleyan U. Fellow: Soc. Values Higher Edn. (sr.); mem.: Soc. Christian Ethics, Phi Beta Kappa. Republican. Home: Ponte Vedra Beach, Fla. Died Dec. 6, 2008.

HARVEY, LYNNE COOPER, broadcast executive, civic worker; b. near St. Louis; d. William A. and Mattie (Kehr) Cooper; m. Paul Harvey, June 4, 1940; 1 child, Paul Harvey Aurandt. DHL (hon.), Rosary Coll., 1996; D (hon.), Washington U., 1988. Broadcaster ednl. program KXOX, St. Louis, 1940; broadcaster-writer women's news WAC Variety Show, Ft. Custer, Mich., 1941-43; gen. mgr. Paul Harvey News ABC, 1944—. Pres. Paulynne Prodn., Ltd., Chgo., 1968—, exec. prodr. Paul Harvey Comments, 1968—; pres. Trots Corp., 1989—; editor, compiler The Rest of the Story. Pres. women's bd. Mental Health Assn. Greater Chgo., 1967-71, v.p. bd. dirs., 1966—; pres. woman's aux. Infant Welfare Soc. Chgo., 1969-71, bd. dirs., 1969—, benefits hon. chmn., 1994, 96; mem. Salvation

Army Woman's Adv. Bd., 1967; reception chmn. Cmty. Lectures; women's com. Chgo. Symphony, 1972—; pres. Mothers Coun., River Forest, 1961-62; charter bd. mem. Gottlieb Meml. Hosp., Melrose Park, Ill.; mem. adv. bd. Nat. Christian Heritage Found., 1964—; mem. USO woman's bd., 1983, woman's bd. Ravinia Festival, 1972—; trustee John Brown U., 1980—; bd. dirs. Mus. Broadcast Comms., 1987—; adv. coun. Charitable Trusts, 1989—; mem. Joffrey Ballet Com.; chmn. Brookfield Zoo Whirl, 2000. Recipient Heritage of Am. award, 1974, Little City Spirit of Love award, 1987, Salvation Army Others award, 1989, disting. friend award, NCPCA, disting. alumni award, Washington U., Friske Meml. award, USO, 2000, Lynne Harvey scholarship named in her honor, Musicians Club of Women; named to, Mus. Broadcast Comm.-Radio Hall of Fame. Home: River Forest, Ill. Died May 2008.

HARVEY, PAUL, commentator, writer, columnist; b. Tulsa, Sept. 4, 1918; s. Harry Harrison and Anna Dagmar (Christensen) Aurandt; m. Lynne Cooper, June 4, 1940 (dec. May 3, 2008); 1 child, Paul Harvey. LittD (hon.), Culver-Stockton Coll., 1952, St. Bonaventure U., 1953; LLD, John Brown U., Ark., 1959, Mont. Sch. Mines, 1961, Trinity Coll. Fla., 1963, Parsons Coll., 1968; HHD, Wayland Bapt. Coll., 1960, Union Coll., 1962, Samford U., 1970, Howard Payne U., Tex., 1978, Sterling Coll., 1982; Degree (hon.), Rosary Coll., 1996; LHD (hon.), Hillsdale Coll., Mich., 2000. Announcer radio sta. KVOO, Tulsa; sta. mgr. Salina, Kans.; spl. events dir. radio sta. KXOK, St. Louis; program dir. radio sta. WKZO, Kalamazoo, 1941-43; dir. news and information OWI, Mich., Ind., 1941-43; news commentator, analyst ABC, from 1944; syndicated columnist Los Angeles Times Syndicate (formerly Gen. Features Corp.), from 1954; TV commentator, 1968. Author: Remember These Things, 1952, Autumn of Liberty, 1954, The Rest of the Story, 1956, You Said It, Paul Harvey, 1969, Our Lives, Our Fortunes, Our Sacred Honor, 1975, Paul Harvey's The Rest of the Story, 1977, More of Paul Harvey's The Rest of the Story, 1980, Paul Harvey's For What It's Worth, 1991; Album rec. Yesterday's Voices, 1959, Testing Time, 1960, Uncommon Man, 1962. Bd. dirs. John D. and Catherine T. MacArthur Found.; mem. bd. govs. Orchestral Assn. Chgo. Symphony Orch. Recipient citation DAV, 1949, 11 Freedoms Found. awards, 1952-76, radio award Am. Legion, 1952, citation of merit, 1955, 57, Cert. of merit VFW, 1953, Bronze Christopher's award, 1953, award of honor Sumter Guards, 1955, nat. pub. welfare services trophy Colo. Am. Legion, 1957,Great Am. KSEL award, 1962, Spl. ABC award, 1973, Ill. Broadcaster award, 1974, John Peter Zenger Freedom award Eagles, 1975, Am. of Year award Lions Internat., 1975, Outstanding Broadcast Journalism award, 1980, Gen. Omar N. Bradley Spirit of Independence trophy, 1980, Man of Yr. award Chgo. Broadcast Advt. Club, 1981, Golden Radio award Nat. Radio Broadcasters Assn., 1982, Best Speaking Voice award Am. Speech, Lang. and Hearing Assn., 1982, Horatio Alger award, 1983, Outstanding Broadcast Personality award Advt. Club Balt., 1984, Meritorius Svc. award Am. Acad. Family Physicians, 1984, Cert. of Appreciation Humane Soc. of U.S., 1985, Genesis award The Fund for Animals, 1986, Okla. Assn. Broadcasters award, 1987, Henry G. Bennett Disting. Svc. award Okla. State U., 1987, James Herriot award Humane Soc. U.S., 1987, Lowell Thomas award, 1989, Gold medal Internat. Radio & TV Soc., 1989, Others award Salvation Army, 1989, Journalism award Internat. Radio Festival, 1989, 5 Marconi awards Network Personality of Yr., 1989, 91, 96, 98, 2002, Dante award, 1990, William Booth award Salvation Army, 1990, Journalism award Chgo. Hall of Fame, 1990, Bd. of Dirs. award Nat. Religious Broadcasters, 1991, Great Am. Race Legend's award Interstate, 1991, Good Guy award Am. Legion, 1992, Outstanding Pub. Spkr. award Toastmasters Internat., 1992, Paul White award Radio T.V. News Dirs., 1992, Peabody award 1993, 94, Spirit of Broadcasting award NAB, 1994, Silver award Am. Advertising Fedn., 1994, Hall of Fame award Broadcasting & Cable Mag., 1995, Am. Spirit award USAF, 1996, Lifetime Achievement award Radio Mercury, 1997, Lifetime Achievement award Gold Angel, 1998, Lifetime Achievement award Radio Mercury, 1997, Tex McCrary award Journalism from Congl. Medal Honor Soc., 2000, Lifetime Achievement A.I.R. award Radio Broadcasters Chgo., 2001, R&R News/Talk Radio Lifetime Achievement award, 2003, NY Festivals World Gold Medal award best personality network/syndicated, 2004; Presdl. Medal of Freedom, The White House, 2005; elected to Okla. Hall of Fame, 1955, Nat. Assn. Broadcasters Hall of Fame, 1979; named Top Commentator of Yr. Radio-TV Daily, 1962, Father of Yr. Father's Day Coun., 1980, Laureate Lincoln Acad. of Ill., 1987 (Ill. highest honor); to Emerson Radio Hall of Fame, 1990; one of The Men of the Century Broadcast and Cable Mag., 1999; among 20th Century's Most Significant Americans George Mag., 1998. Mem. Washington Radio and Television Corrs. Assn., Aircraft Owners and Pilots Assn. Clubs: Chicago Press. Achievements include having broadcasts and columns reprinted in Congressional Record 102 times. Died Feb. 28, 2009.

HARVEY, VIRGINIA PEASELEY, organization consultant; b. Richmond, Va.; d. Gabriel B. and Florence V. (White) Peaseley; B.S., in Chemistry, U. Md., 1929; M.S. in Phy. Edn., U. Wis., 1932; Ed.D. in Ednl. Psychology, Western Res. U., 1963; postgrad. Temple U., 1966-67; m. E. W. Harvey, Apr. 8, 1939 (div. 1958); 1 dau., Virginia Lynn Harvey Schmitt. Instr. U. Mich., 1932-38; asst. prof. Kent (Ohio) State U., 1938-42, 44-46-54, assoc. prof., 1954-64, prof., 1964-76, prof. emeritus, 1976—, faculty senate vice chairperson, 1973-74. Vis. prof. group dynamics Temple U., summer 1967; mem. Nat. Tng. Lab. Inst. Applied Behavioral Sci.; pres. V. Harvey & Assocs. Recipient Disting. Tchr. award Kent State U., 1971, Service award Phi Delta Kappa, 1972. Amy Morris Homans fellow, 1962-63; licensed psychologist, Ohio. Past pres. Kent Dist. Sch. Bd. Mem. Orgn. Devel. Network, Kappa Kappa Gamma, Alpha Psi Omega, Delta Psi Kappa, Phi Delta Kappa, Omicron Delta Kappa. Died Nov. 7, 1995.

HARVEY, WILLIAM GIPSON, JR., physician; b. Tulsa, June 10, 1925; s. William Gipson and Bernice Cole (Johnson) H.; m. Willie Maude Weeks, Aug. 22, 1949; children: Gayle Allison, John Robert, Jan Elizabeth, Paul William. BS, Okla. Bapt. U., Shawnee, 1949; MD, U. Okla., 1953. Intern U. Okla. Hosps., Oklahoma City, 1953-54, resident, 1954-55; pvt. practice Beaver, Okla., 1961-90; physician Med Plus, Oklahoma City, from 1990. With USN, 1943-46. Republican. Baptist. Home: Oklahoma City, Okla. Died Aug. 22, 2008.

HARWICH, DAVID CURTIS, video design and production specialist; b. Hollywood, Calif., Sept. 1, 1955; Student, Chaffey Coll., Rancho Cucomonga, Calif. Various positions The Photographer, Upland, Calif., 1969-90, dir. videography, 1982-91; with Video Design & Prodn., Upland, Calif., from 1991. Dir.: (video) What is the Carden Method?, 1990, This Old House Restored, 1991; cinematographer: (motion pictures) True Dedication, 1988, Erosion, 1987, The Making of 17th, 1981; photographer: Family Life in Mexico, 1985 (Bronze medal 1986). Home: Upland, Calif. Died Feb. 17, 2008.

HASKIN, MARVIN EDWARD, radiologist, educator; b. Ardmore, Pa., May 28, 1930; m. Myra Singer; 1 child, Kenneth; m. Pamela Herr, 1973 BA, Temple U., Phila., 1951, MD, 1955. Diplomate: Am. Bd. Radiology. Intern Phila. Gen. Hosp., 1955-56, resident, 1956-57, 59-61; instr. radiology Temple U., 1961-63; chief diagnostic radiology Phila. Gen. Hosp., 1961-63; assoc. radiologist Hahnemann Hosp., Phila., 1964-66, clin. asst. prof., 1967-70, research asst. prof., 1969; prof. radiology, chmn. dept. Hahnemann U., Phila., 1970—91. Secretariat-chmn. Ansi N-44, N.Y.C.; rep. Ansi PH-2, N.Y.C.; cons. Internat. Electrotechnical Commn. Author: Roentgenologic Diagnosis, 1979, Surgical Radiology, 1981; editor: The Radiologic Clinics of North America, 1972, 83. Mem. Gov.'s Task Force on Nutrition, Chgo., 1974. Served with USAF, 1957-59. Fellow Am. Coll. Radiology, ACP, Phila. Coll. Physicians, Soc. Advanced Med. Systems; mem. Phila. Roentgen Ray Soc. (sec. 1974-77 Blue Ribbon), Radiol. Soc. N.Am. Home: Bryn Mawr, Pa. Died Mar. 1, 2009.

HASS, HERBERT EDWARD, lawyer, automotive products consultant; b. Chgo., July 21, 1919; s. Herman Reynold and Jeanette (Butler) H.; m. Marian Frances Bagg, Apr. 2, 1942; children: David Herbert, Jody Lynn. BA with honors, Andrews U., 1948; BTh, Seventh Day Adventist Sem., 1953; MA in Speech, Temple U., 1961; JD, U. Notre Dame, 1973. Bar: Mich. 1973, Pa. 1974, U.S. Dist. Ct. (we. dist.) Mich. 1976; ordained to ministry Lake Union Conf. Seventh Day Adventist, 1953. Dir. pub. relations Seventh Day Adventist State Confs., Ind., Ill., Pa., 1948-59, Faith for Today Internat. TV, LI, N.Y., 1959-63; assoc. dir. devel. Loma Linda (Calif.) U., 1963-67; dir. pub. relations N.Y. Ctr., NYC, 1967-70; found. dir., pub. relations dir. Southwestern Mich. Collge, Dowagiac, 1070-73; sole practice Berrian Springs, Mich., from 1973. Gen. counsel Gen. Motors Consumers, Chgo., 1982—, cons. in area of defective automotive products; pres., cons. A-1 Adminstrs., Berrien Springs, 1979—; cons. Concerned Car Owners, Lansing, Mich., 1984—, Gen. Motor Products Groups, Chgo., 1983—, Phillipine Med. Sch. for entry into U.S. med. internships; pres. Comp In, Berrien Springs, 1977—; bd. dirs. Adventist Radio and TV, Ltd., London, Ont., Can. and U.S., 1985—. Author: (manuscript) Life and Work of Stephen Tyng, 1962 (citation 1962); contbr. ency. Hist. of N.Y. Ctr., 1966; editor TV program Telenotes, 1959-63. Bd. dirs. Pioneer Meml. Univ. Ch., Berrien Springs, 1965—. Served to tech. sgt. U.S. Army, 1942-45. Mem. ABA (various coms. 1974—), Mich. Bar. Assn. (various coms. 1973—), Pa. Bar Assn. (various coms. 1974—), Nat. Assn. Coll. and Univs. Attys., Am. Inst. for Prevention of Addition, Inc. (sec.-treas. 1987), Audubon Soc. Republican (mem. Washington club). Lodge: Optimists (Berrien Springs). Avocations: tennis, jogging, stamp collecting/philately, woodworking. Home: Berrien Springs, Mich. Died Feb. 27, 2008.

HATHAWAY, JOAN BOYETTE, elementary/middle school administrator; b. Wilson, NC, Aug. 11, 1935; d. John Bunyon and Ruth (Fleming) B.; m. Richard Edward Hathaway, Sept. 1, 1956; children: Donna, Richard Edward. BA, Atlantic Christian Coll., Wilson, 1955-57; MEd., U. S.C., Columbia, 1977-78. Copy writer Sta. WGTM, Wilson, N.C., 1955-56; tchr. Jackson Sch., Newport News, Va., 1957-59; dir. First Presbyn. Ch. Sch., Lumberton, N.C., 1963-66; tchr. Kindergarten Pub. Sch., Milw.; tchr. Albermarle Acad., Elizabeth City, N.C., 1968-69; tutor, supr. Columbia (S.C.) Reading Found., 1972-75; tchr. Hammond Acad., Columbia, 1969-75; dir. Sandhills Acad., Columbia, from 1975. Cons., Thomas Hart Acad., Hartsville, S.C., 1986-88, Heritage Hall Acad., Norway, S.C., 1987-89, Richland Sch. Dist., Columbia, S.C., 1988; evaluator, Sandhills Acad., Columbia, 1979—; pres. ACLD, S.C., 1979. Author/presenter S.C. Coun. Exceptional Children, 1985, Orton Dyslexia Soc., 1988-93. Bd. mem. S.C. Literacy Assn., Columbia, 1982-88, Midlands Human Resources Devel. Commn.,Columbia, 1983-87; exec. com. S.C. Ind. Sch. Assn., Columbia, 1984-85; curriculum tech. adv. panel Gov.'s Initiative for Workforce Excellence, Columbia, 1988-. Rep. Presbyterian Avocations: boating, dance, shopping. Home: Columbia, SC. Died Oct. 14, 2007.

HAUPTFUHRER, BARBARA BARNES, retired corporate director; b. Greensboro, N.C., Oct. 11, 1928; d. J. Foster and Myrtle (Preyer) Barnes; BA cum laude, Wellesley Coll, 1949; m. George J. Hauptfuhrer, Jr., Sept. 9, 1950; children: George J. III, W. Barnes. Dir., Vanguard Group Investment Cos., Valley Forge, Pa., Great Atlantic and Pacific Tea Co., Inc., Montvale, N.J., Gen. Public Utilities Corp., Parsippany, N.J., 1976-79, Phila. Saving Fund Soc., J. Walter Thompson Co., Inc., N.Y.C., 1977-87, Knight-Ridder Newspapers, Inc., Miami, Fla., Mass. Mut. Life Ins. Co., Springfield, JWT Group, Inc., N.Y.C., 1980-87, Owens-Ill., Inc., Toledo, 1981-87; bd. dirs. Raytheon Co., Lexington, Mass., ALCO Standard Corp., Valley Forge, Pa.; public mem. regional adv. com. on banking policies and practices 3d Nat. Bank Region, 1976-77; adv. bd. Phila. Fin. Assn., Trustee Wellesley (Mass.) Coll., 1970-85, emeritus, 1985-2009, com. for Econ. Devel., 1979-88; bd. dirs. John and Mary R. Markle Found., 1976-86, Greater Phila. Partnership, 1975-85; bd. dirs. World Affairs Council Phila., 1977-87, vice chmn., 1978-80; bd. dirs. Phila. United Fund, 1960-65, United Way Southeastern Pa., 1979-87; trustee Salem Acad. and Coll., 1967-70, Eisenhower Exchange Fellowships, 1986—; mem. Harvard Vis. com. for Harvard and Radcliffe, 1972-78; mem. Presser Found., 1970-85; pres. Jr. League Phila., 1958-60, Meadowbrook Sch., 1962-63; mem. Phila. Orch. Council, 1979-88; mem. Mayor's Commn. for Women, Phila., 1981-83; mem. U.S. Sr. Women's Golf Assn. Recipient Disting. Alumna award Salem Acad., 1985. Mem. Wellesley Coll. Alumnae Assn. (pres. 1970-73). Lutheran. Home: Huntingdon Valley, Pa. Died Apr. 7, 2009.

HAVENS, CAROLYN CLARICE, librarian; b. Nashville, Sept. 11, 1953; d. Charles Buford and Iris Mae (Anderson) H.; m. Hilton Harris Huey, June 9, 1990; children: Heather Louise, Quentin Harris. AA, Sue Bennett Coll., 1973; BA in English, U. West Fla., 1974; MLS, U. Ky., 1981. Tchr. Escambia High Sch., Pensacola, Fla., 1974-75; salesperson Univ. Mall, Pensacola, 1975-77; libr. tech. U. Ky., Lexington, 1978-82; libr. Auburn (Ala.) U., from 1982. Contbr. articles to profl. jours. and newspapers; editorial bd.: A Dynamic Tradition, 1991. Bd. dirs. Nat. Kidney Found. Ala., Opelika, 1986-89; active Conscientious Alliance for Peace, Auburn, 1989—. Clergy and Laity Concerned, Atlanta, 1991—. Mem. ALA, Southeastern Libr. Assn., Ala. Libr. Assn., North Am. Serials Interest Group, Ala. Assn. Coll. and Rsch. Librs., Studio 218. Democrat. Methodist. Avocations: painting, writing, photography. Died Dec. 13, 2007.

HAWK, CLARK WILLIAMS, mechanical and aerospace engineering educator; b. Berea, Ohio, Sept. 16, 1936; s. Harry Lyle and Catherine (Williams) H.; m. Julia Ann Milthaler, Nov. 7, 1959; children: Sandra Lynn Smith, Brian Clark. BSME, Pa. State U., 1958; MSME, Purdue U., 1968, PhD, 1970. Registered mech. engr., Calif., Ala. Project engr. Propulsion Lab., Wright-Patterson AFB, Ohio, 1958-59, Rocket Propulsion Lab., Edwards AFB, Calif., 1959-67, sect. chief, researcher, 1969-71, br., sect. chief, 1971-81; div. dir. Astronautics Lab., Edwards AFB, Calif., 1983-91; lectr. U. So. Calif., LA, 1971; prof. mech. & aerospace engring., dir. Propulsion Rsch. Ctr. U. Ala., Huntsville, from 1991. Mem. NRC Earth To Orbit Propulsion Options, Washington, 1991-92; mem. NRC Com. on Advanced Space Techs., Washington, 1992-98. Contbr. articles to profl. jours. Recipient Gilbert award Antelope Valley YMCA, 1982, Meritorious Svc. award L.A. County Bd. Edn., 1985, Cert. of Merit, L.A. Sch. Trustees Assn., 1985, Excellence award Air Force Space Div., 1986. Fellow AIAA (assoc. editor Jour. Propulsion and Power 1986-90); mem. NSPE, Pi Tau Sigma. Achievements include conceiving and creating LPIAG and SPIAG which brought together U.S. liquid rocket engine and solid rocket motor manufacturers to solve problems of mutual concern; creation of JANNAF Rocket Nozzle Tech. Com. to establish a community of interest in carbon-carbon nozzle technology area. Home: Madison, Ala. Died Feb. 26, 2008.

HAWKINS, JO ANNE WALKER, library administrator; b. El Paso, Tex., Nov. 28, 1938; d. Alfred Hewlett and Jonell J. (Seargeant) Walker; m. Daniel Fleming Hawkins, Apr. 2, 1961; children: Laura, Frederick, Wendy. BS in Art, U. Tex., 1960, MLS cum laude, 1966, MPA, 1987. Graphic designer univ. publs. U. Tex., Austin, 1962-64, reference libr., 1967-69, head libr. inter-libr. borrowing, 1969-73, head libr. inter-libr. svc., 1973-75, head libr. circulation svcs. dept., 1975-86, head libr. Perry-Castaneda Libr., 1986-87, asst. dir. for pub. svcs. gen. librs., 1986-93, assoc. dir. for pub. svcs. gen. librs., from 1993. Recipient Libr. Excellence award gen. librs. U. Tex., 1983, Disting. Grad. award Grad. Sch. Libr. and Info. Sci., 1983. Mem. ALA, Tex. Libr. Assn. (chmn. publs. com. 1985-86, dist. III 1988-89, coll. and univ. librs. div. 1989-90), Tex. Assn. Coll. Tchrs. (pres. U. Tex. chpt. 1981-82, state sec.-treas. 1981-85), St. Vincent de Paul Soc. Avocations: painting, reading, gardening, travel. Home: Austin, Tex. Died Feb. 11, 2008.

HAWLEY, AMOS HENRY, sociologist, educator; b. St. Louis, Dec. 5, 1910; s. Amos Henry and Margaret Belle (Heltzclaw) H.; m. Gretchen Haller, Sept. 5, 1937; children— Steven Amos, Margie Lynn, Susan Esther, Patrice Ann. A.B., U. Cin., 1936; M.A., U. Mich., 1938, Ph.D.,

1941; D.Litt. (hon.), U. Cin., 1978. From instr. to prof. U. Mich., 1941-66; prof. sociology U. N.C., Chapel Hill, 1966-76, Kenan prof., 1971-76, prof. emeritus, 1976—2009; adviser in field. Author: Human Ecology, 1950; Urban Society, 1971; contbr. articles to profl. jours. and chpts. to books. Fellow Am. Acad. Arts and Scis., AAAS; mem. Am. Sociology Assn. (pres. 1978), Population Assn. Am. (pres. 1971), Delta Kappa Epsilon. Club: Chapel Hill Country. Home: Chapel Hill, NC. Died Aug. 31, 2009.

HAWS, HALE LOUIS, medical association administrator, consultant; b. Anaheim, Calif., June 15, 1923; s. Lloyd Albert and Nancy Jean (Hale) H.; m. JoAn Penn Haws; children: Kathleen Seghieri, Jay B., Jerald L. BA, Pepperdine Coll., 1947; MD, UCLA, 1958. Diplomate Med. Bd. Calif., Am. Bd. Preventive Medicine, Bd. Life Ins. Medicine. Intern Gorgas Hosp., Canal Zone, 1958-59; pvt. practice L.A., 1959-60; plant med. dir. Chrysler Corp., Commerce, Calif., 1960-71; physician, surgeon Narcotic Control, Dept. Corrections, LA, 1961-75; v.p. med. svcs. Pacific Mut. Life Ins. Co., Newport Beach, Calif., 1962-81; consulting med. dir. Calif., from 1981. Dir. Best Life Assurance Co. of Calif., Irvine, 1981-97; med. adv. bd. Equifax Svcs., Inc., Atlanta, 1977-81; spkr. in field. Mem. Church of Christ. Recipient Cert. of Appreciation, Selective Svc. Sys., 1975; scholar Kaiser Family Found., 1957. Fellow Am. Coll. Preventive Medicine, Am. Coll. Angiology, Am. Coll. Occupl. and Environ. Medicine, Am. Geriatrics Soc.; mem. Am. Acad. Ins. Medicine, Am. Coun. Life Ins., Calif. Scholastic Soc. (life), Pepperdine Alumni Assn. (dir. 1968-70). Avocations: art collecting, classic/antique autos, continuing medical education, reading, gardening. Home: Paradise, Calif. Died May 1, 2008.

HAYCOCK, CHRISTINE ELIZABETH, retired medical educator; b. Mt. Vernon, NY, Jan. 7, 1924; d. John B. and Madeline (Sears) H.; m. Sam Moskowitz, July 6, 1958 (dec. Apr. 1997). SB, U. Chgo., 1948; MD, SUNY, Bklyn., 1952; MA in Polit. Sci., Rutgers U., 1981. RN, N.J.; diplomate Am. Bd. Surgery. Intern Walter Reed Army Med. Ctr., Washington, 1952-53; resident in surgery St. Barnabas Med. Ctr., Newark, 1954-58, St. John's Episcopal Hosp., Bklyn., 1958-59; pvt. practice Newark, 1959-68; asst. prof. surgery, N.J. Med. Sch. U. Med. and Dentistry N.J.-N.J. Med. Sch., Newark, 1968-75; assoc. prof. surgery, N.J. Med. Sch. UMDNJ, Newark, 1975-89, prof. clin. surgery, 1989-92; prof. emeritus, from 1992. Chief GYN Svc., VA Hosp., East Orange, NJ Trauma Soc.; pres. Med. Amature Radio Coun., 1981, bd. dirs. (Coun. award 1978); adv. com. NJ Phys. Conditioning of the Police Tng. Commn., 1984-96. Editor: Trauma and Pregnancy, 1985, Sports Medicine for the Athletic Female, 1980; mem. editl. bd. Jour. NJ Med. Soc., 1979-95, The Physician and Sports Medicine, 1975-98, The Main Event, 1987; contbr. articles to profl. jours. Chmn. bd. Essex County chpt. Am. Cancer Soc., West Orange, N.J., 1978-79, bd. mgrs., Livingston, N.J., 1962—, hon. life mem., 1992. With U.S. Army, 1947-86, col. Res. ret. Recipient Outstanding Alumnae award Bloomfield Coll., 1971, Res. Forces Achievement award, 1974, Distinguished Lecturer award Downstate Med. Ctr., 1976, Dr. Frank L. Babbott Meml. award SUNY Alumni Assn., 1982, Pres. Honor citation, N.J. Assn. Phys. Edn. and Health Tchrs., 1982, Commendation medal, 1982, Meritorious Svc. medal, 1986, Presdl. Citation, N.J. Assn. for Health, Phys. Edn. and Recreation, 1984, Med. Bd. Svc. award Newark City Hosp., 1986, Bertha Van Hoosen award Am. Med. Women's Assn., 1997, Alma Dea Morani MD Renaissance Women of Yr. award Found. for History of Women in Medicine, 2004; named to Nutley Hall of Fame, 2005; grantee Abbott Labs, 1981-82. Fellow ACS (hon., life, N.J. com. on trauma 1970-91), Am. Coll. Sports Medicine (trustee 1978-80), Photog. Soc. Am. (chmn. video/motion picture divsn. 1993-95; Silver medal jour. award 2000, 02); mem. AMA, Am. Med. Women's Assn. (bd. dirs. 1976-86, pres. 1980, hosp. assn. com. 1985—, Silver Medallion award 1980), Zonta Internat., Assn. Women Surgeons (treas. 1989-91, chair found. com. 1991-95, sec. 1995-99, Disting. Surgeon award 1990), N.J. Women's Assn. (pres. 1976, treas. 1989-92, Woman of Yr. 1987), Amateur Radio Relay League. Avocations: photography, dog training and showing, sports, collecting elephants, amateur radio. Died Jan. 23, 2008.

HAYES, DIANE ELIZABETH, principal; b. East Liverpool, Ohio, Oct. 16, 1943; d. Daniel Paulovich and Elizabeth (Lozzi) Paulovich; m. H. Stuart Hayes, Mar. 24, 1963; children: Stuart, Darin, Elizabeth, Alyson. BA in English, Geneva Coll., 1973; MA in Edn. magna cum laude, Regent U., 1988. Tchr. English, substitute tchr. Western Beaver, Industry, Pa., 1967-74; prin., tchr. biblical studies Rhema Christian Sch., Coraopolis, Pa., from 1986. Tng. dir. SASCO, Dallas, 1983-85, conf. speaker. Feature editor Western Advertiser, Beaver Falls, Pa., 1972-80. Mem. ASCD, His Schs. Assn. (speaker edn. conf. 1988-92), Lambda Iota Tau. Lit. Honors Soc. Republican. Home: Murrysville, Pa. Died Apr. 18, 2008.

HAYES, ELIZABETH ROTHS, retired dance educator; b. Ithaca, NY, July 3, 1911; d. Leslie David and Emilie Christine (Roths) H AB, W.Va. U., 1932; MS, U. Wis., 1935; EdD, Stanford U., 1949. Instr. various colls., W.Va. and Ill., 1936—40; asst. prof. U. Wis., 1945; asst. prof. dept. modern dance U. Utah, Salt Lake City, 1941—44, 1946—49, assoc. prof., 1950—54, prof., 1955—88, prof. emerita, from 1988. Tchrs. summers Chico (Calif.) Tchrs. Coll., 1951, W.Va. U., 1952, U. Mich., 1957, U. Iowa, 1965; founder Modern Dance Maj. Program, U. Utah; spkr. in field; cons. univs Dancer, choreographer over 40 dances; dir. over 35 dance concerts and prodns.; contbg. editor Design for Arts In Edn., 1980-85; conbtr. numerous articles to profl. publs.; author: Introduction to the Teaching of Dance, 1964, Dance Composition and Production, 2d edit., 1993, The Evolution of Visual, Literary and Performing Arts: From Tribal Cultures to the Middle Ages, 2004 Fellow Utah Acad. Sci., Arts, & Letters, 2002; recipient Hon. Disting. Alumnus award, U. Utah, 1993, Sch. Edn. Alumni Achievement award, U. Wis., 1993; univ. faculty rsch. grantee U. Utah, 1986-87 Mem. Nat. Dance Assn. (various coms., chair 1969-71, Dance Heritage award 1977, Honor award 1981), Am. Dance Guild, Am. Acad. Phys. Edn., Nat. Dance Edn. Orgn. (founder, Lifetime Achievement award 2002), Coun. Dance Adminstrs. (founder, recipient Alma Hawkins Award for Excellence in Adminstr. Leadership, 2003), Phi Beta Kappa Home: Salt Lake City, Utah. Died Sept. 7, 2007.

HAYES, GEORGE OLIVER, clergyman; b. Coon Rapids, Iowa, May 20, 1924; s. Leonard Leroy and Violet Daisy (Wright) H.; m. Ruth Viola Rayl, May 12, 1945; children: Ellen Hayes Kunkle, Lois Hayes Stoltenberg, Mark Alvin. Degree, Capital City Comml. Coll., Des Moines, 1942; student, Kletzing Coll., 1943-45, Cascade Coll., 1947; Western Evang. Sem., 1949-52, Loma Linda U., 1959. Ordained to ministry Evang. Ch. N.Am., 1954. Min. Evang. United Brethren chs., Iowa, Oreg., Wash., 1945-68, Evang. Ch. N.Am., from 1968. Dir. pub. rels. Peniel Missions, Sacramento, 1963-66, gen. supt., 1966-71, 72-74; exec. dir. Fairhaven Home for Unwed Mothers, Sacramento, 1969-75; regional dir. World Gospel Mission, Portland, Oreg., 1976-84. Home: Oregon City, Oreg. Died Dec. 4, 2007.

HAYES, HAROLD O., JR., manufacturing executive; b. Evanston, Ill., Dec. 29, 1929; s. Harold O. and Frances E. (Henderson) H.; m. JoAnn Elaine Funkhouser, Dec. 24, 1951; children: Kenneth, Christopher, Jeffrey, Julie. BBA, Miami U., Oxford, Ohio, 1951; MBA, Northwestern U., 1955. Plant controller Walker Mfg., Lake Mills, Iowa, 1960-62, plant mgr., 1963-66; production mgr. HON Industries, Muscatine, Iowa, 1966-69; dir. mfg. Faultless div. Axia, Evansville, Ind., 1969-77, pres. and gen. mgr. Nestaway div. Cleve., from 1978. Served to lt. (j.g.) USCGR, 1951-53. Methodist. Avocations: golf, reading, photography, woodworking. Home: Liberty Lake, Wash. Died Feb. 12, 2008.

HAYES, VERNON HOLGATE, retired design engineer; b. Preston, Lancashire, Eng., Oct. 8, 1915; came to U.S., 1923; s. Henry and Veronika Annie (Hauser) H.; m. Bernice Elizabeth Kalmen, Oct. 15, 1948; children: Roger Martin, Kenneth Alan. Student, Wayne U., 1938-46, U. Minn., 1951-58. Mechanic Becker Motor Co., Springerville, Ariz., 1949; bldg. designer Hitchcock & Estabrook, Mpls., 1949; machine designer Continental Machines, Inc., Savage, Minn., 1950-54; topographic draftsman Cardarelle & Assocs., Eden Prairie, Minn., 1954; machine designer Bemis Rsch. Lab., Mpls., 1954-56; devel. engr. Univac/Sperry Rand Corp., Hopkins, 1956-62; project engr. Honeywell Corp., Hopkins, Minn., 1962-64, G.T. Schjeldahl Co., Northfield, Minn., 1964-65; design engr. Thermo King corp., Bloomington, Minn., 1965-66; rsch. engr. Pako Corp., Golden Valley, Minn., 1966-71; engring. tech. writer MTS Systems Corp., Hopkins, Minn., 1971-73, ret., 1974. Author: Say-Write English Alphabet Improved 20,000 Percent Over A-B-C English, 1989, TOPON Optimum Thought Code Improved 9,000,000 Percent Over A-B-C English, 1993; contbr. articles to profl. jours.; inventor in field. Mem. hist. commn. Val Verde County, Tex., 1978—. Cpl. U.S. Coast Artillery, 1940-43. Mem. ASME, Honewywell Engrs. Club (sr.), Standards Engrs. Soc. Avocations: astronomy, family history, nature, writing, tropical gardening. Home: Del Rio, Tex. Died Mar. 5, 2008.

HAYNES, DONALD KENNETH, education educator, researcher; b. Norwich, NY, Jan. 27, 1934; s. Raymond Louis and Gladys Abigail (Simmons) H.; m. Janet Ruth Shultz, Aug. 30, 1958; children: Bradley Richard, Linda Ruth Haynes Slowik. BS, SUNY, Cortland, 1960; MS in Pub. Health, U. N.C., 1961; PhD, SUNY, Albany, 1980. Health educator Ohio Dept. Health, Zanesville, 1961-63; sr. pub. health educator N.Y. State Dept. Health, Syracuse, 1963-68; dir. pub. edn. N.Y. State Dept. Mental Hygiene, Albany, 1968-75; asst. prof. SUNY, Brockport, 1975-82; assoc. prof. community health edn. U. Minn., Duluth, from 1983, coach women's varsity tennis, 1988-90. Contbr. articles to profl. jours. Chmn. heart at work Am. Heart Assn., Duluth, 1984, 86. With U.S. Army, 1954-56. Methodist. Avocation: tennis. Home: Duluth, Minn. Died July 16, 2008.

HAYS, ROGER LEE, rehabilitation executive, counselor; b. Omaha, Sept. 13, 1954; s. James F. and Patricia (Rogers) H.; m. Cristina Maria Bianchi, Mar. 18, 1978; 1 child, Melissa Cristina. BA in Sociology and Psychology, U. Iowa, 1980, MA in Edn., 1982. Job placement specialist Nebr. Dept. of Edn., Omaha, 1983; employment specialist Career Design, Inc., Omaha, 1983-85, program coord., 1985-86, v.p., from 1986. Dir. Worknet Project with Industry, Omaha; tech. expert Office of Spl. Edn. and Rehab./U.S. Dept. Edn., Washington, 1988—. Mem. exec. com. Omaha Transp. Coalition, 1987—. Mem. Nat. Rehab. Assn., Adminstrv. Mgmt. Soc., Rehab Assn. Nebr. (pres. 1990—, editor Job Placement Digest 1989—, bd. dirs. job placement div. 1989—). Avocations: boating, golf, travel. Home: Omaha, Nebr. Died Dec. 11, 2007.

HEAD, JAMES R., patent lawyer; b. Springfield, Ill., Oct. 16, 1928; s. James Earl and Clara E. (Mengerhausen) H.; m. Ruth Ann Schult, Jan. 1, 1952; children: James Stephen, John Richard, Jane Elizabeth, Justin Randolph, Teresa Juanita. BSME, Okla. State U., 1951; JD, U. Tulsa, 1957. Engr. Exline Engring., Tulsa, 1951-52; from engr. trainee to patent trainee Stanolind Oil & Gas Co., Tulsa, Russell, Kans., 1952-58; patent atty. Head, Johnson & Kachigian, Tulsa, from 1958. 2d lt. U.S. Corps Engrs. Mem. Okla. Bar Assn., Intellectual Property Law Assn. Home: Grove, Okla. Died June 7, 2008.

HEADLEE, RAYMOND, retired psychotherapist; b. Shelby County, Ind., July 27, 1917; s. Ortis Verl and Mary Mae (Wright) H.; m. Eleanor Case Benton, Aug. 24, 1941; children: Sue, Mark, Ann. AB in Psychology, Ind. U., 1939, A.M. in Exptl. Psychology, 1941, MD, 1944; grad., Chgo. Inst. Psychoanalysis, 1959. Diplomate: Am. Bd. Psychiatry and Neurology (examiner 1964—). Intern St. Elizabeth's Hosp., Washington, 1944-45, resident in psychiatry, 1945-46, Milw. Psychiat. Hosp., 1947-48, pres. staff, 1965-70; practice medicine specializing in psychiatry and psychoanalysis Elm Grove, Wis., from 1949; clin. asst. prof. psychiatry Med. Coll. Wis., 1958-59, clin. asso. prof., 1959-62, clin. prof., 1962-2000, chmn. dept. psychiatry, 1963-70; prof. psychology Marquette U., 1966-76; Bd. dirs. Elm Brook (Wis.) Meml. Hosp., 1969-71; ret., 2000. Author: (with Bonnie Corey) Psychiatry in Nursing, 1949, I Think, Therefore I Know, 1996; contbr. numerous articles to profl. jours. 1st lt. Ft. Knox Armored Med. Rsch. Lab., AUS, 1945, to col. USPHS. Fellow Am. Psychiat. Assn. (life), Am. Coll. Psychiatry (emeritus); mem. State Med. Soc. Wis. (editorial dir. 1971-77), Wis. Psychiat. Assn. (pres. 1971-72), Milw. Club. Home: Milwaukee, Wis. Died June 6, 2007.

HEALY, MARTIN JOHN, academic administrator; b. NYC, Apr. 5, 1939; s. John and Kathleen Ann (Hanley) H.; m. Ann Marie Brennan, Aug. 15, 1964; children: Lisa Ann, John Paul. BA, St. John's U., Jamaica, NY, 1964, MS, 1969. Writer Sta. WNEW, NYC, 1958-60; writer, producer Sta. WCBS, NYC, 1960-67; v.p. communications and pub. affairs St. John's U., from 1968. Mem. Internat. Radio and TV Soc. Roman Catholic. Home: Roslyn Heights, NY. Died June 30, 2008.

HEARD, ALEXANDER, retired academic administrator; b. Savannah, Ga., Mar. 14, 1917; s. Richard Willis and Virginia Lord (Nisbet) H.; m. Laura Jean Keller, June 17, 1949; children: Stephen Keller, Christopher Cadek, Francis Muir, Cornelia Lord. AB, U. N.C., 1938, LL.D., 1968; MA, Columbia U., 1948, PhD, 1951, LL.D., 1965; 25 other hon. degrees. U.S. Govt. service in depts. Interior, War and State, 1939-43; research assoc. bur. pub. adminstrn. U. Ala., 1946-49; research assoc. Inst. Research in Social Sci., U. N.C., 1950-51, research prof., 1952-58; asso. prof. polit. sci. U. N.C., 1950-51, prof. polit. sci., 1952-63, dean Grad. Sch., 1958-63; prof. polit. sci. Vanderbilt U., 1963-85, chancellor, 1963-82. Author: (asst. to V.O. Key, Jr.) Southern Politics in State and Nation, 1949, (with Donald S. Strong) Southern Primaries and Elections, 1950, A Two-Party South?, 1952, The Costs of Democracy, 1960, rev. edit., 1962, The Lost Years in Graduate Education, 1963, Made in America: Improving the Nomination and Election of Presidents, 1991, Speaking of the University: Two Decades at Vanderbilt, 1995; editor and contbr.: State Legislatures in American Politics, 1966; editor, contbr. (with Michael Nelson) Presidential Selection, 1987. Chmn. Pres.'s Commn. on Campaign Costs, 1961-62; spl. adviser to Pres. U.S. on campus affairs, The White House, 1970; Dir. Citizens' Research Found., 1958-71, pres., 1968-71; mem. U.S. Adv. Commn. Intergovtl. Relations, 1967-69, Trustee Ford Found., 1967-87, chmn., 1972-87; trustee Robert A. Taft Inst. Govt., 1973-76, Ctr. for Study of Presidency, 1988-91; chmn. Task Force on So. Rural Devel., 1974-77; public trustee Nutrition Found., 1976-82; mem. council Rockefeller U., 1977-82; mem. Commn. on U.S. Policy Toward So. Africa, Fgn. Policy Study Found., 1979-85. Lt. USNR, 1943-46. Mem. Internat. Polit. Sci. Assn., Am. Polit. Sci. Assn. (v.p. 1962-63), So. Polit. Sci. Assn. (pres. 1961-62), Assn. Am. Univs. (dir. council fed. relations 1969-70, v.p. 1973-74, pres. 1974-75), Council on Fgn. Rels., Belle Meade Country Club (Nashville), (N.Y.C.), Sigma Alpha Epsilon. Episcopalian. Home: Nashville, Tenn. Died July 24, 2009.

HEARNES, WARREN EASTMAN, lawyer, Former Governor of Missouri; b. Moline, Ill., July 23, 1923; s. Earle B. and Edna May (Eastman) H.; m. Betty Sue Cooper, July 2, 1948; children: Lynn, Leigh, Julia B. BS, US Mil. Acad., 1946; AB, LLB, U. Mo., 1952; LHD (hon.), Coll. Osteopathy & Surgery, Kirksville, Mo.; LLD (hon.), Culver-Stockton Coll., Canton, Mo., Univ Mo., Cent Methodist Coll., Fayette, Mo.; PhD (hon.), Rockhurst Coll. Bar: Mo. 1952. Mem. Mo. Ho. of Reps. from Mississippi County, 1951-61, majority floor leader, 1957, 59; sec. of state State of Mo., 1961-65, gov., 1965-73; exec. dir. South Mo. Legal Svcs., Inc., Charleston, 1981—97; judge 33rd Jud. Cir., 1980—81; atty.-at-law. Chmn. Nat. Gov. Conf.; pres. Coun. State Govt.; mem. Adv. Com. Intergovernmental Rels.; del. Dem. Nat. Conv. Served to 1st lt. US Army, 1946-49. Recipient Edwin P. Hubble Medal, 2005. Mem. Am., Mo. bar assns., VFW, Am. Legion, Masons, Shriners, Phi Delta Theta, Phi Delta Phi. Democrat. Baptist. Home: Charleston, Mo. Died Aug. 16, 2009.

HEBERT, JOEL JOSEPH, mechanical engineer; b. Melville, La., June 23, 1939; s. Octa Joseph and Winnie (Landry) H.; m. Beverly Anne Hebert, Apr. 20, 1968; children: Joseph Layne, Genevieve Marie. BSME, La. Tech. U., 1961; MSME, Ohio State U., 1962; PhDME, So. Meth. U., 1970. Registered profl. engr., Tex., La. Asst. prof. Rice U., Houston, 1969-74; sr. project engr. Fluor Corp., Houston, 1974-76; sect. mgr. Pace Engrs., Houston, 1976-77; sr. engr. Western Geophys., Houston, 1977-80; sect. mgr. Schlumberger, Houston, 1980-86; sr. engr. Triodyne, Inc., Niles, Ill., 1987-90; engring. mgr. CH&A Corp., Houston, 1991-96; sr. mgr. engr. Failure Analysis Assocs., Houston, from 1996. Home: Sugar Land, Tex. Died Feb. 11, 2008.

HEBERT, LESLIE ANN MARIE, nurse; b. Thibodaux, La., Aug. 15, 1970; d. Lester Joseph and Thelma Marie Hebert. Diploma in practical nursing, West Jefferson Tech. Inst., 1991. LPN, La. Pediatric nurse intern Children's Hosp., New Orleans, 1991, practical nurse, from 1992. Vol. Tulane Med. Ctr., New Orleans, 1984-88. Recipient St. Louise de Merillac medal for Outstanding Community Svc., Cath. Arthdiocese, 1988. Avocations: reading, cross-stitch. Home: Marrero, La. Died Apr. 21, 2008.

HEBERT, LYNN DAVID, science and computer educator, writer; b. Rutland, Vt., Aug. 6, 1940; s. Lynn Robert Hebert and Helen Elizabeth Jasmin. AB in Philosophy and Classics, St. Michael's Coll., Winooski, Vt., 1963; EdM in Sci. Edn., SUNY, Buffalo, 1976, EdD in Sci. Edn., 1986. Cert. secondary tchr. sci. and computers Vt. Adj. prof. biol. and phys. sci. Coll. St. Joseph, Rutland, Vt., from 1993; adj. prof. computer programming Castleton (Vt.) State Coll., from 1999; adj. prof. sci. and computers C.C. Vt., Rutland, from 1993; sci. and computer tchr. and coord. Fair Haven (Vt.) Union H.S., 1983—93; sci. tchr., dept. head Park Sch. Buffalo, Amherst, NY, 1969—80. Author: (novel) Bigfoot Autumn, 2001; contbr. poetry and stories to anthologies. With USNR, 1964—66. Avocations: hiking, camping. Home: Wallingford, Vt. Died Dec. 26, 2007.

HECHT, HAROLD ARTHUR, orchidologist, chiropractor; b. St. Louis, Mo., Apr. 30, 1921; s. William Frederick and Myrtle Regina (Hugo) H.; m. Barbara Evelyne Ross, Nov. 19, 1942. D Chiropractic Medicine, Logan Coll. Sole practice, St. Louis, 1942-95; orchidologist, from 1950. Judge Orchid Digest Corp., 1959; internat. lectr., photographer in field radiotelephone engr., 1942. Contbr. articles to profl. jours. Mem. World Orchid Cong. (founding com. 1954), Mid-Am. Orchid Cong. (founder, pres. 1959, judge 1968), Am. Orchid Soc. (grand jurist, judge 1968), Mark Twain Orchid Soc. (pres. 1966, 90), Mo. Orchid Soc. (pres. 1959), European Orchid Congress (USA com. 1967). Republican. Avocations: philatelist, numismatist, amateur radio operator, antiquary, linguist. Home: Saint Louis, Mo. Died Apr. 23, 2008.

HECK, GRACE FERN, retired lawyer; b. Tremont City, Ohio, Nov. 13, 1905; d. Thomas J. and Mary Etta (Maxson) H.; m. Leo H. Faust, May 25, 1977. BA cum laude, Ohio State U., 1928, JD summa cum laude, 1930. Bar: Ohio 1930, U.S. Dist. Ct. (so. dist.) Ohio 1932, U.S. Supreme Ct. 1960. Researcher, Nat. Commn. Law Observance and Enforcement U.S. Dist. Ct. (so. dist.) Ohio, 1930—31; researcher Ohio Judicial Council and Law Inst. Johns Hopkins U., 1931—32; prosecuting atty. Champaign County, Urbana, Ohio, 1933—37; sole practice Urbana, Ohio, 1937—43, 1973—93; Springfield, Ohio, 1947—73; ret., 1993; assoc. Corry, Durfey & Martin, Springfield, Ohio, 1943—47; mcpl. judge Champaign County, 1954—58. Exec. sec. War Price and Rationing Bd., Urbana, 1941-43; bd. trustees Spring Grove Cemetery Assn., 1954—; sec. bd. trustees Magnetic Springs Found., Ohio, 1957-62; pres. Ohio State U., Coll. Law Alumni Assn., Columbus, 1971-72; charter mem. Friends of Libraries Ohio State U., Friends of Hist. Costume and Textile Collection; mem. Nat. Council Coll. Law, Ohio State U. Columbus, 1971—; mem. Springfield Art Assn.; trustee Champaign County Arts Council, 1987-1994. Recipient Disting. Service award Ohio State U. 1971, Disting. Alumna award Ohio State U., 1990. Mem. Ohio State Bar Assn. (com. mem., 60 Yrs. Svc. to Pub. award 1991), Champaign County Bar and Law Library Assn. (pres. 1965), Springfield Bar and Law library Assn. (sec. 1946-59, pres. 1963), ABA, Ohio State U. Alumni Assn. (2d v.p. 1956-58, adv. bd. 1962-73, Alumni Centennial award 1970), Order of Coif, Phi Beta Kappa, Zeta Tau Alpha, Kappa Beta Pi, Delta Theta Tau (nat. v.p. 1938-40, nat. pres. 1941-42, bd. trustees 1942-45). Clubs: Springfield Country (Ohio); Troy Country (Ohio); Altrusa. Lodge: Order of Eastern Star. Democrat. Methodist. First female law school graduate from Ohio State U. and first female prosecutor in Ohio. Home: Troy, Ohio. Died 1994.

HEDGES, GEORGE REYNOLDS, lawyer, archaeologist; b. Phila., Feb. 26, 1952; s. Thomas Reed and Ann Hedges; m. Christy Susan Shonnard; children: George Shonnard, Duncan Fox. BA, U. Pa., Phila., MA, 1975; JD, U. So. Calif., LA, 1978. Bar: Calif. 1979. Founding ptnr. Hedges & Caldwell, 1988—98; ptnr. Quinn Emanuel Urquhart Oliver & Hedges, L.A., 1998—2009. Pres. The Archaeology Fund, LA, 1995—2009. Trustee Claremont Grad. U., Calif., 2006. Recipient Commendation award, LA County Bd. Suprs., 1992; named one of 100 Power Lawyers, Hollywood Reporter, 2007. Mem.: Penn Club NY, Athenaeum, Calif. Inst. Tech. (assoc.). Achievements include discovery of ancient incense roads in Southern Arabia. Died Mar. 10, 2009.

HEER, WILLIAM CHARLES, graphics company executive; b. Columbus, Ohio, Apr. 20, 1921; s. William Charles Heer Sr. and Hilda (Kemery) Herbst; m. Barbara Anna Mitcheltree, Oct. 8, 1958; children: Betsy, William C. III. BS in Printing Mgmt., Carnegie Tech. Inst., 1943. V.p., treas. F.J. Heer Printing Co., Columbus, 1943-68; v.p. Nat. Graphics Corp., Columbus, from 1968. Bd. dirs., treas. Scioto Downs Inc., Columbus. Mem.: Columbus Country. Democrat. Congregationalist. Avocations: golf, travel. Home: Columbus, Ohio. Died Jan. 27, 2008.

HEFFNER, PATRICIA TOBIN, sales executive; b. Milw., June 7, 1931; d. Emmett A. and Audrey P. (Haseley) Tobin; widowed; children: Audrey H., Carrie E. AA, Rider Coll., 1952. Sales cons. Schrock Realty, Morton, Ill., 1961-68; owner Peachtree Arts and Crafts, Naperville, Ill., 1968-76; v.p. U.S. Home-Lakewood, Naples, Fla., 1977-80; sales mgr. Arvida Realty Sales, Coral Gables, Fla., 1980-82; v.p. Lyle Fain Co., Providence, 1982-84, Arthur Rutenberg-Go, Collier County, Fla., 1984-88; dir. mktg. Century 21 Advisor, Naples and Bonita Springs, Fla., 1988-89; v.p. Heffner Group, Naples, 1989-91; dir. sales Bonita Bay Properties, Bonita Springs, 1991-93; dir. sales & mktg. JRB Devel. Group, Ltd., Bonita Springs, from 1993. Author: Home Design Window Concepts, 1989. Trustee Regional Sch. Bd., DuPage County, Ill., 1974-76. Mem. Fla. Assn. Realtors, Women's Coun. Realtors, Sales Mgrs. Roundtable (bd. dirs.), Collier County and Lee County Sales & Mktg. Coun., Nat. Home Builders Assn. (chmn. cert. sales profl. course 1993, 94, instr. cert. sales profl. course 1993, 94, Pinnacle award, Sales Mgr. of Yr. 1992), Bonita Springs Bd. Realtors. Republican. Episcopalian. Avocations: golf, travel, crafts. Home: Naples, Fla. Died July 4, 2008.

HEFNER, BILL (WILLIAM GATHREL HEFNER), former United States Representative from North Carolina; b. Elora, Tenn., Apr. 11, 1930; s. Emory James and Icie Jewel (Holderfield) H.; m. Nancy Louise Hill, Mar. 23, 1952; children: Stacye, Shelly. Grad. high sch. Mem. US Congress from 8th N.C. dist., Washington, 1975—99. Former owner Sta. WRKB radio, Kannapolis, N.C. Former profl. entertainer with Harvesters Quartet; former performer weekly gospel show, Sta. WXII-TV, Winston-Salem, N.C.; also appeared on Sta. WBTV, Charlotte, N.C., Sta. WRAL-TV, Raleigh, N.C., Sta. WGHP-TV, High Point, N.C., Sta. WBTW-TV, Florence, S.C. Mem. bd. visitors U.S. Mil. Acad., 1982—; mem. Dem. Congl. campaign com. Democrat. Died Sept. 2, 2009.

HEGSTED, DAVID MARK, nutritionist, educator; b. Rexburg, Idaho, Mar. 25, 1914; married; 2 children. AM, Harvard U., 1962; DSc, U. Idaho, 1986. Asst. biochemist U. Wis., 1936-41; rsch. chemist Abbott Labs, 1941-41; instr. to prof. nutrition Harvard U. Sch. Pub. Health, 1942-78; administr. Human Nutrition Rsch. USDA, 1978-82; emeritus prof. nutrition New England Regional Primate Rsch. Ctr., 1982—2009. Cons. Columbian Govt., Bogota, 1946-47, Inst. Inter-Am. Affairs, Lima, Peru, 1950-52; chmn. food and nutrition bd. Nat. Acad. Sci., Nat. Rsch. Coun.; mem. various exptl. coms. WHO, UN. Editor Nutritional Review, 1968-78. Recipient Eleanor Naylor Dana award Am. Health Found., Bristol-Myers Squibb award. Mem. NAS, AAAS, Am. Dietetic Assn. (hon. mem.), Am. Chemical Soc., Am. Inst. Nutrition (pres. 1972-73, Osborne-Mendel award 1965, Conrad Elvejhem award 1979) Home: Westwood, Mass. Died June 16, 2009.

HEIDERSBACH, JOHN AUSTIN, marketing executive; b. Elmhurst, Ill., Nov. 6, 1942; s. Robert Henry and Dorothy (Duntemann) H.; m. Patricia Louise Yax, July 26, 1967 (div. Aug. 1974); children: Amy L., Ann. M.; m. Ellen Kay Bakken, June 10, 1983; stepchildren: Kristofer K. Moffit, Matthew R. Moffit. BBA, U. Denver, 1970. Copywriter Valentine-Radford, Inc., Kansas City, Mo., 1972-73; account exec. Christenson, Barclay, Shaw, Kansas City, 1973-75; ptnr. Hedlund & Assocs., Mission, Kans., 1975-80; copy chief Gloria Aleff & Assocs., Waverly, Iowa, 1980-83; creative dir. Warren Anderson Advt., Davenport, Iowa, 1983-84; mktg. dir. Oster Communications, Cedar Falls, Iowa, from 1984. Stamp illustrator, Iowa Duck Stamp Design, Iowa Habitat Stamp Design, 1987, Pa. Duck Stamp Design, 1988. Vol. dir. Greater Kansas City March of Dimes, 1979-80, Cedar Valley chpt. March of Dimes, Waterloo, Iowa, 1981-83; bd. dirs. Cedar Valley Wetlands Found., Cedar Falls, Iowa, 1987—. Served as sgt. U.S. Army, 1962-65. Mem. N.E. Iowa Mktg./Advt. Club. Avocations: wildlife and western art, writing. Home: Cedar Falls, Iowa. Died Oct. 28, 2007.

HEIL, MARY RUTH, retired counselor; b. Westerville, Ohio, June 8, 1921; d. George Walter and Bertha Ellen (Shrodes) H. BS in Edn., Ohio State U., 1944; MEd, Wayne State U., 1956; cert. advanced study, Western Carolina U., 1987; cert. theol. edn., U. South, 1987. Cert. counselor, tchr. Ohio, Ky., Mich., N.C. Tchr. 7th grade Obuchite Bela, Ohio, 1942-43; tchr. biology, English Ohio Soldiers' and Sailors' Orphans' Home, Xenia, 1943-47; tchr. 7th grade Lakeview High Schs., Winter Garden, Fla., 1947-48; tchr. English, journalism Pine Mountain Settlement Sch., Ky., 1948-49; field and established camp dir. Columbus and Franklin County Girl Scouts, Ohio, 1949-50; tchr. Mary Lyon Jr. HS, Royal Oak, Mich., 1950-56, 57-62, Custon Secondary Modern Girls' Sch., Greenford, Middlesex, England, 1956-57; tchr. English West Henderson HS, Hendersonville, NC, 1962-65, guidance counselor, 1965-86. Chmn. Mayor's Com. Employment of Handicapped, Hendersonville, 1972-74; v.p. Mountain Ramparts Health Planning

Bd., Asheville, NC, 1972-76, Western Carolina Health Systems Agy. Bd., Morganton, NC, 1976-82; bd. dirs., sec., com. chmn., Henderson County Dispute Settlement Bd., 1989-95; exec. com., bd. dirs. Western Carolina Presbyn. Retirement Com., 1987-94; active Henderson County Coun. Women, Hendersonville, 1994-96, treas.; mem.-at-large Pisgah coun. Girl Scouts U.S., 1994-98, chair fund devel. com., 1995-98, exec. com., 1997-98; bd. dirs. Henderson County Coun. on Aging, 1998-2001, chair nominating com., 1999. Recipient award, Galludent U., Washington, 1986, Thanks Badge, Pisgah Coun., Girl Scouts U.S., 1998, state degree of Style, Dignity, Title and Honor of Dame, Baron of Shalford, Eng., 2000, cert., Rt. Hon. Thomas de Shalford, 2000; named Woman of Achievement, Hendersonville Bus. and Profl. Women's Club, 1978, Civitan Citizen of Yr., Civitan Club, Hendersonville, 1986; named to Order Ky. Cols., 1988. Mem. NEA, ACA, Royal Oak Edn. Assn. (pres. 1954-56), NC Assn. Educators (pres. dist 1970-72), Henderson County Mental Health Assn. (bd. dirs. 1965-74), Alpha Delta Kappa (NC 1st v.p. 1978-80, state pres. 1980-82, S.E. region grand v.p. 1987-89), Kappa Delta Pi. Democrat. Episcopalian. Avocations: golf, bowling, classical music. Home: Hendersonville, NC. Died June 18, 2008.

HEILPRIN, MARY ANN HARDY, television executive; b. Dyersburg, Tenn., July 13, 1948; d. John McLean and Betty (Brown) Hardy; m. Lawrence J. Heilprin, June 25, 1983; 1 child, Amanda Ruth Hardy. Student, U. North Iowa, 1966-69, Coe Coll., 1970-72. Mktg. dir. Gen. Growth Mgmt., Cedar Rapids, Iowa, 1972-73, Melvin Simon Mgmt., Anderson, S.C., Hurst, Tex., 1972-74, lease analyst Indpls., Ind., 1974-76; acct. exec. Sta. WTSO-WZEE Radio, Madison, Wis., In Bus. Mag., Madison, 1983-84; advt. mgr. Jel Ace Hardware, Wis., 1984-85, Petrie Sports, Madison, 1985-87; retail devel. Sta. WISC-TV, Madison, from 1987. Speaker's bur., Madison Advt. Fedn., 1986—; mem. TVB Retail Mktg. Bd., 1989—. Speaker Madison Bus. and Edn. Coord. Coun.,1985-87, Women in Bus. Conf., Madison, 1987—. Mem. Retail Advt. Conf. Avocations: cruises, photography. Home: Big Bear Lake, Calif. Died Dec. 15, 2007.

HEINIG, NORMAN THOMAS, consulting company executive; b. Chgo., Feb. 20, 1928; s. Oscar William and Agnes Kerchville (Lamar) Heinig; children: Norman, William, Mary, Barbara, Tanya, Randy. BS, Northwestern U., 1955; MS, San Francisco U., 1982. Apprentice Sanger Plumbing, 1945—50; engr., project mgr. Commonwealth Plumbing Co., Chgo., 1957—65; cons. engr. Architects Mech. Design Svc. Corp., Chgo., 1965—73; owner Heinig Cons. Plumbing Engring. Co., Mission Viejo, Calif., from 1974. Pres. PTA, 1967; leader Boy Scouts Am., 1955—65; bd. dirs. Chgo. Boys Club, 1961. Mem.: Am. Soc. Plumbing Engrs., Royal League, Chgo. Athletic, Elks. Republican. Roman Cath. Home: Lake Forest, Calif. Deceased.

HEINZE, RUTH-INGE, consciousness studies educator, researcher, writer; b. Berlin, Nov. 4, 1919; came to U.S., 1955; d. Otto and Louise (Preschel) H. Gr. Latinum, Interpreter Coll., Berlin, 1967; BA, U. Calif., Berkeley, 1969, MA, 1971, PhD, 1974. Producer, writer Ednl. Broadcast, Berlin, 1963-73; lectr. U. of Chiang Mai, Thailand, 1971-72; staff rsch. asst. human devel. dept. U. Calif., San Francisco, 1974, rsch. assoc. Ctr. for S.E. Asian Studies, from 1974. Lectr. Mills Coll., Oakland, Calif., 1974; adj. faculty Saybrook Inst., San Francisco, 1984—, Calif. Inst. for Integral Studies, 1984-93, Author: The Role of the Sangha in Modern Thailand, 1977, Tham Khwan - How to Contain the Essence of Life, 1982, Trance and Healing in Southeast Asia Today, 1988, Shamans of the 20th Century, 1991, The Search for Visions, 1994, The Nature and Function of Rituals: Far From Heaven, 2000. Prodr. Universal Dialogue Series, Berkeley, 1979—; nat. dir. Ind. Scholars of Asia, 1981—; bd. dirs. Oakland Asian Cultural Ctr., 1987-93. Recipient grant Am. Inst. for Indian Studies, 1975,78, Fulbright-Hays Rsch. grant, 1978-79. Mem. Internat. Assn. for Study of Traditional Asian Medicine, Internat. Soc. for Shamanic Rsch., Parapsychology Rsch. Group, Spiritual Emergency Network, Nat. Pictographic Soc., Ind. Scholars of Asia, Assn. for Asian Studies, Inst. Noetic Scis. Avocations: exploring, healing. Died July 20, 2007.

HEISEY, LOWELL VERNON, retired chemistry educator; b. Shou Yang Hsien, China, Oct. 1, 1919; s. Walter J. and Sue (Rinehart) H.; m. Hazel Snavely, July 1, 1945; children: Galen, Maylee Heisey Samuels, Loren, Curtis. AB, Manchester Coll., 1941; MS, Purdue U., 1945, PhD, 1947. Assoc. prof. chemistry McPherson (Kans.) Coll., 1947-50; prof., head dept. chemistry Bridgewater (Va.) Coll., 1950-77; ret., 1988. Editor rsch. publs. on cancer drugs. Pres. Bridgewater Ruritan Club, 1957. Fulbright lectr. in chemistry Am. Coun. Scholars, Liberia, 1986-87; named Alumnus of Yr. Manchester Coll., 1989. Mem. Am. Chem. Soc. (v.p. assn. 1971, Outstanding Chemist 1972). Avocations: stamp collecting/philately, photography, music. Home: Bridgewater, Va. Died Oct. 7, 2007.

HELD, EDWIN WALTER, JR., lawyer; b. Jacksonville, Fla., Feb. 14, 1947; m. Leslie Edwards, Aug. 18, 1974; children: Kimberly M., Eric E. BSBA, U. Fla., 1970; JD, Stetson U., 1973. Bar: Fla. 1973, U.S. Dist. Ct. (mid. dist.) Fla. 1973, U.S. Ct. Appeals (11th cir.) 1973. Assoc. Fischette, Parrish & Owen, Jacksonville, 1973-75; mem. Fischette, Parrish, Owen & Held, Jacksonville, 1975-90, Fischette, Owen & Held, Jacksonville, 1990-97, Fischette, Owen, Held & McBurney, Jacksonville, 1997—2004. Founding dir., bd. dirs. Jewish Cmty. Alliance, Jacksonville,

1990. Mem. Comml. Law League Am. (exec. con. bankruptcy and insolvency sect. 1990—, chmn. sect. 1997-98). Democrat. Avocations: boating, skiing, tennis, fishing, golf. Home: Jacksonville, Fla. Died Jan. 18, 2008.

HELDRETH, KIRK DARCE, dairyman; b. Rural Retreat, Va., Aug. 24, 1962; s. Don Main and Janet (Sult) H. Assoc. (hon.), Ferrum U., 1983; BS, Va. Poly. Inst. and State U., 1985. Herdsman, mgr. Heldreth Dairy Farms, Rural Retreat, from 1985. Bd. dirs. Wythe County Farm Bur., Wytheville, Va., 1987-89. Contbr. articles to local newspaper. V.P. Boosters, Rural Retreat, 1987—. Recipient Outstanding Transfer scholarship Va. Poly. Inst. and State U., 1983, SE Young Dairymen's award, SW Young Farmers award Va. Farm Bur. Mem. Jaycees, Rural Retreat Fair Assn., Holstein Assn., Am Jersey Cattle Club, Mountain Emphire Holstein Club, Wythe-Bland Dairy Herd Imporvement Assn. (v.p. 1987—). Republican. Lutheran. Died Aug. 4, 2008.

HELFFERICH, FRIEDRICH G., chemical engineer, educator; b. Berlin, Aug. 1, 1922; s. Karl and Anna Clara Johanna (von Siemens) H.; m. Barbara Schlubach, July, 1947; children: Christiane, Cornelia.; m. Hana M. Konecna, Feb., 1961; 1 child, Stefanie. BS, U. Hamburg, 1949, MS, 1952; PhD, U. Goettingen, 1955. Rsch. asst. Max Planck Inst., 1951-56, MIT, 1954, Calif. Inst. Tech., 1956-58; vis. scientist Max-Planck Inst., 1958; sr. rsch. assoc. Shell Devel. Co., 1958-79; lectr. U. Calif., Berkeley, 1962-63; vis. prof., lectr. U. Houston, Rice U., U. Tex., 1980, East China U. Chem. Tech., Shanghai, 1987; prof. chem. engring. Pa. State U., 1980-90, prof. emeritus, from 1990. Chmn. Gordon Rsch. Confs. on Ion Exch., 1967, on Separation and Purification, 1994; co-dir. NATO Sch. on Migration and Fate of Pollutants, 1992; cons. in field. Author: Ion Exchange, 1962, Multicomponent Chromatography, 1970, Kinetics of Homogeneous Multistep Reactions, 2001, Kinetics of Multistep Reactions, 2004; editor: Fire and Movement mag., 1978-84, Reactive Polymers, 1981-91; contbr. articles to profl. jours. Recipient award Am. Soc. Engring. Edn., 1985, Am. Chem. Soc., 1987, AIChE, 1989, Gold and Silver medals in race walking state and internat. Sr. Games, 1993-97; Fulbright scholar, 1954. Fellow AIChE, Am. Inst. Chemists (emeritus). Died Sept. 11, 2005.

HELLER, DOROTHY, artist; b. NYC, June 15, 1926; d. Samuel and Rebecca (Cohn) H. Studied with, Hans Hofman, NYC, 1942. One-woman shows include Tibor de Nagy Gallery, N.Y.C., 1953, Galerie Facchetti, Paris, 1955, Pondexter Gallery, N.Y.C., 1956, 57, East Hampton Gallery, N.Y.C., 1963, Betty Parsons Gallery, N.Y.C., 1972, 76, 78, U. Pa., 1976, Cathedral St. John the Divine, N.Y.C., 1976; exhibited in group shows Denver Art Mus., 1953, Whitney Mus. Ann., 1957, Mus. Modern Art Traveling Show, 1963, Betty Parsons Gallery, 1972-81, U. Calif. Art Mus., 1974, Met. Mus. Art, N.Y.C., 1979, Otis Art Inst., 1979, Bklyn. Coll. Art Gallery, 1990; represented in permanent collections Met. Mus. Art, N.Y.C., U. Calif. Art Mus., Berkeley, Cornell U., Johnson Mus., Ithaca, N.Y., Wadsworth Atheneum, Hartford, Conn., Smithsonian Instn. Archives, Washington, Zimmerli Mus., New Brunswick, N.J., Alexandria (La.) Mus., Auburn (Ala.) U., Whitney Comm., N.Y.C., Chase Manhattan Bank, N.Y.C., numerous others. Recipient Internat. Woman of Yr. award, 1976. Deceased.

HELLIE, RICHARD, historian, educator; b. Waterloo, Iowa, May 8, 1937; s. Ole Ingeman and Mary Elizabeth (Larsen) H.; children: Benjamin, Michael; m. Shujie Yu, Feb. 26, 1998. BA, U. Chgo., 1958, MA, 1960, PhD, 1965; postgrad., Ind. U., Bloomington, 1963, U. Moscow, 1963—64. Vis. asst. prof. Rutgers U., 1965—66; asst. prof. Russian history U. Chgo., 1966—71, assoc. prof., 1971—80, prof., 1980—2001, Thomas E. Donnelley prof., 2001—09. Presenter in field; chmn. coll. Russian Civilization course U. Chgo., from 1967, chmn. undergrad. studies in Russian Civilization, from 1970, chmn. Ea. European NDEA Title VI Area Com., 1974—78, coord. Coll. History, 1971—73, mem. Coun. U. Senate, 1976—79, mem. coll. com. academic standing, 1984—87, co-coord. Moscow exchange program, 1990—96, co-coord. Russian and Soviet studies workshop, sole coord. Russian and Soviet studies workshop, 1993—94, dir. Nat. Resource Ctr. Slavic, East European/Russian and Eurasian studies, 1997—2004, mem. faculty oversight com. on computing, 1999—2002, dir. Ctr. for East European, Russian and Eurasian studies, 1997—2004. Author: Muscovite Society, 1967, 1970, Enserfment and Military Change in Muscovy, 1971 (Am. Hist. Assn. Adams prize 1972), Slavery in Russia 1450-1725, 1982 (Laing prize U. Chgo. Press 1985, Russian translation with new post-Soviet foreword Kholopstvo v Rossii, 1450-1725, 1998), 1982, The Russian Law Code (Ulozhenie) of 1649, 1988, The Economy and Material Culture of Russia 1600-1725, 1999; editor: The Plow, the Hammer and the Knout: An Economic History of Eighteenth Century Russia, 1985, Ivan the Terrible: A Quarcentenary Celebration of His Death, 1987, The Frontier in Russian History, 1995, The Economy and Material Culture of Russia, 1999, The Soviet Global Impact 1945-1991, 2002; editor quar. jour. Russian History, 1988; translation editor: Kholopstvo v Rossii 1450-1725, 1998; contbr. numerous articles to profl. jours, presenter in field. Fgn. area tng. fellow Ford Found., 1962-65, Inter-Univ. Com. on Travel Grants award, 1963-64, Quantrell grant for Improvement of Tchg., 1969, Social Sci. Divsional Rsch. grants U. Chgo., 1970-88, 1991-94, 1996-97, 1998-99, Guggenheim fellow, 1973-74, fellow NEH, 1978-79; grantee NEH, 1982-83, summer, 1988, NSF, 1988-90, Bradley Found., 1988-91. Mem. PEN, Nat. Hist. Soc. (founding mem., bd. govs.), Am. Soc. Legal History (program com. ann. meetings 1976), Am. Assn. Advancement Slavic Studies (editl. bd. Slavic Rev. 1979-81), Econ. History Assn., Assn. Comparative Econ. Studies, Nat. Assn. Scholars, Jean Bodin Soc. Comparative Instl. History, Chgo. Consortium Slavic and East European Studies (pres. 1990-92), Nat. Hist. Soc. (founder, bd. govs. 1999-2002), Chgo. Com. Chgo. Coun. on Fgn. Rels. Home: Chicago, Ill. Died Apr. 24, 2009.

HELMAN, ALFRED BLAIR, retired academic administrator, educational consultant; b. Windber, Pa., Dec. 25, 1920; s. Henry E. and Luie (Pritt) H.; m. Patricia Ann Kennedy, June 22, 1947; children: Harriet Ann Helman Hill, Patricia Dawn Helman Magaro. AB magna cum laude, McPherson Coll., 1946, DD, 1956; MA, U. Kans., 1947, postgrad., 1948-51; LLD, Juniata Coll., 1976; LHD, Bridgewater Coll., 1977, Ind. U., 1981, Manchester Coll., 1986. Ordained to ministry Ch. of Brethren, 1942; pastor Newton, Kans., 1944-46, Ottawa, Kans., 1946-54, First Ch. of Brethren, Wichita, Kans., 1954-56; faculty Ottawa U., 1947- 48, 51-54, chmn. div. social scis., 1952-54; faculty U. Kans., 1951-54, Friends U., 1955-56; pres. Manchester (Ind.) Coll., 1956-86, pres. emeritus, 1986—2009. Chmn. com. on higher edn. Ch. of Brethren, 1965-67, 76-78, nat. moderator, 1975-76, mem. rev. and evaluation com., 1983-85, mem. denominational structure rev. com., 1989-91, mem. pension bd. restructure com., 1986-87; trustee McPherson Coll., 1951-56, chmn., 1955-56; trustee Kans. Found. Pvt. Colls. and Univs., 1955-56; pres. Ind. Conf. Higher Edn., 1960-61; mem. policy bd. dept. higher edn. Nat. Coun. Chs. of Christ Am., 1960-71; mem. pres.'s adv. com. Nat. Assn. Intercollegiate Athletics, 1966-70; mem. exec. com. Ind. Coun. Chs., 1960-62, bd. dirs., 1992-94; bd. dirs. Independent Colls. and Univs. of Ind., 1977-83, 84-86, chmn., 1978-79, 85-86; chmn., interim pres. Coun. Protestant Colls. and Univs., 1967, bd. dirs., 1961-69; bd. dirs. Ctrl. States Coll. Assn., 1965-77, chmn., 1968; pres. Assoc. Colls. of Ind., 1970-72, bd. dirs., 1956-86; mem. commn. on religion in higher edn. Assn. Am. Colls., 1968-71; bd. dirs. CTB, Inc., 1977-92. Author articles on religion and higher edn. Mem. IAUP-UN Commn. on Arms Control Edn., 1991—2002. Named Sagamore of Wabash, Gov. of Ind., 1980, Ky. Col., Gov. of Ky., 1964; recipient Outstanding Local Citizen award, 1972, Sparks-Jones award Associated Colls. Ind., 1977, Legion of Honor award Kiwanis Club North Manchester, 1976, Alumni Honor award, Manchester Coll., 1981, Citation of Merit, McPherson Coll., 2001, Citation for Responsible Philanthropy, Manchester Coll., 2003; elected to Ind. Acad., 1987. Mem. Soc. Historians of Am. Fgn. Rels., Internat. Assn. Univ. Presidents (mem. steering com. N.Am. coun. 1982-84), Ind. Assn. Ch.-Related and Ind. Colls. (pres. 1966-67), Am. Assn. Higher Edn., Am. Acad. Polit. and Social Sci., Nat. Assn. Ind. Colls. and Univs. (bd. dirs. 1983-84), Ind. Acad. Social Scis., Ind. Hist. Assn., Ft. Wayne Rotary (Paul Harris fellow), Quest Club (mem. bd. govs. 1988-90, 92-94, 97-99), Phi Beta Kappa, Phi Alpha Theta, Pi Sigma Alpha, Pi Kappa Delta, Tau Kappa Alpha (hon.). Home: North Manchester, Ind. Died Mar. 22, 2009.

HELTON, MAX EDWARD, minister, consultant, religious organization executive; b. Conasauga, Tenn., Nov. 24, 1940; s. Herman Marshall and Nellie Gladys (Haddock) H.; m. Jean Bateman, June 8, 1962; children: Elaine, Melanie, Crista, Becky. BA, Tenn. Temple U., 1963; DD (hon.), Hyles-Anderson Coll., 1973. Ordained minister Bapt. Ch., 1963. Sr. pastor Koolau Bapt. Ch., Kaneohe, Hawaii, 1964-71; exec. v.p. Hyles-Anderson Coll., Crown Point, Ind., 1971-77; sr. pastor Grace Bible Ch., White Plains, NY, 1977-83, West Park Bapt. Ch., Bakersfield, Calif., 1983-86; pastor outreach program Grace Bapt. Ch., Glendora, Calif., 1986—88. Founder, pres. Motor Racing Outreach, Harrisburg, N.C., 1988-2002; founder, CEO WorldSpan Ministries, 2002--. Author: Thirty Qualities of Leadership, 1975, Beyond the Checkered Flag, 1996; co-author: From the Heart of Racing, 2001; contbr. articles to profl. jours.; keynote speaker Commonwealth Youth Day, Cayman Brac, B.W.I., 1964. Dep. sheriff Lake County (Ind.) Sheriff Dept., Crown Point, 1974-77; mem. adv. bd. legis. N.Y., Albany, 1980-82, sch. bd. Bakersfield Christian Sch. Dist., 1985-86; bd. dirs. N.C. Racing Hall of Fame Mus., Sports Outreach Am. Recipient Bill France Excellence award, 1992, Mike Rich award, 1993. Mem. Internat. Sports Coalition, Conservative Bapt. Assn. (cons. 1983—, chmn. fellowship com. 1985-87), Nat. Assn. for Stock Car Auto Racing, Championship Auto Racing Teams. Republican. Avocations: motor sports, basketball. Home: Huntersville, NC. Died Mar. 30, 2008.

HEMPHILL, PAUL JAMES, writer; b. Birmingham, Ala., Feb. 18, 1936; s. Paul James Hemphill and Velma Rebecca Nelson; m. Susan Olive, Sept. 1961 (div. Oct. 1975); children: Lisa, David, Molly; m. Susan Farran Percy, Nov. 6, 1976; 1 child, Martha. BA, Auburn U., 1959. Sports writer News, Birmingham, Ala., 1959-61; sports info. dir. Fla. State U., Tallahassee, 1962; sports editor Chronicle, Augusta, Ga., 1963, Times, Tampa, Fla., 1964; gen. columnist Atlanta Journal, 1965-69; editor Atlanta Magazine, 1981; writer-in-residence Brenau Coll., Gainesville, Ga., 1986-92; faculty Emory U., Atlanta, 2000—09. Author: The Nashville Sound: Bright Lights and Country Music, 1970, Mayor: Notes on the Sixties, 1972, (with Ivan Allen Jr.), The Good Old Boys, 1974, Long Gone, 1979, Too Old to Cry, 1981, The Sixkiller Chronicles, 1985, Me and the Boy, 1986, King of the Road, 1989, Leaving Birmingham: Notes of a Native Son, 1993, The Heart of the Game, 1996, Wheels: A Season on Nascar's Winston Cup Circuit, 1997, The Ballad of Little River, 2000, Nobody's Hero, 2002, Lovesick Blues: The Life of Hank Williams, 2005, A Tiger Walk Through History: The Complete Story of Auburn Football from 1892 to the Tuberville Era, 2008 With USAF, 1959-62. Nieman fellow Harvard U., 1969. Avocations: camping, hiking, fishing. Died July 11, 2009.

HENAGER, CHARLES HENRY, civil engineer; b. Spokane, Wash., July 11, 1927; s. William Franklin and Mary Agnes (Henry) H.; m. Dorothy Ruth Parker, May 6, 1950; children: Charles Henry, Jr., Donald E., Roberta R. BSCE, Wash. State U., 1950. Registered profl. engr., Wash. Instrumentman Wash. State Dept. Hwys., Yakima, 1950—52; engr. GE, Richland, Wash., 1952—62, shift supr., reactor, 1962—63, sr. engr., 1963—65; sr. devel. engr. Battelle Pacific N.W. Labs., Richland, 1965—68, sr. rsch. engr., 1968—90, ret., 1990. Contbr. articles to profl. jours.; patentee in field. Mem. Village at Canyon Lakes Assn., bd. dirs., mem. archtl. control, 1996—98, v.p., 1998, 2000—03. With USN, 1945—46. Fellow: Am. Concrete Inst. (tech. activities com. 1987—89, Del Bloem award 1986); mem.: ASTM (subcom. 1980—92), ASCE (pres. Columbia sect. 1961—62), Kennewick Swim Club (pres. 1962—63), Phi Kappa Phi, Tau Beta Pi, Sigma Tau. Republican. Methodist. Avocations: calligraphy, genealogy. Home: Kennewick, Wash. Died May 29, 2008.

HENDERSON, GLADYS EDITH, retired social welfare examiner; b. Black River, NY, Jan. 17, 1928; d. Lynn Bruce and Ina Marion (Carey) Scott; m. Vern V. Leeder, May 4, 1947 (dec. Oct. 1950); children: Linda Leeder McCarthy, Thomas Leon. AS in Criminal Justice, Jefferson C.C., 1977; BA in Pub. Justice, SUNY, Oswego, 1979. Sec.-receptionist Delavan Warehouse, Syracuse, N.Y., 1968-69; self employed cosmetologist Black River, 1970-74; receptionist N.Y. State DEC, Watertown, 1979-80; social welfare examiner Jefferson County Dept. Social Svcs., Watertown, 1980-90, ret., 1990. Author of poetry. Mem. Civil Svc. Employees Assn., Watertown, from 1980, sec., 1986—89; treas. ladies' group Watertown Bapt. Temple, 1993—97. Recipient Pres.' award for lit. excellence Nat. Authors Registry, 1996, 98, 2000; inductee Internat. Poetry Hall of Fame, www.poetry-.com. Mem.: Black River Valley's Writers Club. Republican. Avocations: antiques and collectibles, crochet, embroidery, writing. Home: Watertown, NY. Died June 24, 2008.

HENDERSON, JAMES ROBERT, account supervisor; b. Phila., Jan. 22, 1947; s. George Hudson H.; m. Theresa Macri Henderson, Aug. 18, 1987; children: Dawn, Jennifer. BS in Journalism, U. Fla., 1969. Sports writer Tampa (Fla.) Tribune, 1969-83; v.p. pub. rels. Team Am. Soccer, Washington, 1983; pub. rels. dir. N.Am. Soccer League, NYC, 1984, U.S. Soccer Fedn., NYC, 1985; sr. account exec. Bozell, Jacobs, Kenyon & Eckhardt, NYC, 1985-86, Buzell, Jacobs, Kenyon & Eckhardt, Atlanta, 1986; v.p. pub. rels. Camp-Byers Pub. Rels., Atlanta, 1986-87; sr. account exec. Benito Pub. Rels., Tampa, 1987-88, account supr., from 1989. Mem. Exch. Club. Avocations: freelance broadcaster, sports. Home: Tampa, Fla. Died Feb. 14, 2008.

HENDERSON, MEREDITH TARVER, school principal; b. Greenwood, Miss., Apr. 23, 1940; d. Loyd Estes and Meredith (Mounger) Tarver; m. John Hughes Henderson Jr., Aug. 17, 1966 (div. 1988); children: John H., Loyd T. BS, Peabody Coll. of Vanderbilt U., 1962, MS, 1980. Cert. elem. tchr., elem. prin., Tenn. Tchr. 2d grade Natchez-Adams County Schs., Natchez, Miss., 1962-63, Williamson County Pub. Schs., Franklin, Tenn., 1963-64, Overseas Dependent Schs., Germany and Eng., 1964-66; tchr. 3d-6th grades Franklin Spl. Sch. Dist., 1975-88, asst. prin., 1988-91, prin., from 1991. Tchr. participant CRADLE, Wake Forest U., Winston-Salem, N.C., 19856. Mem. vestry St. Paul's Espiscopal Ch., Franklin, 1978-80, Sunday sch. supt., 1990-93; trustee Williamson County Pub. Libr., 1993-96. Mem. NAESP, ASCD, NEA, Nat. Coun. Social Studies, Tenn. Coun. Social Studies, Tenn. Edn. Assn., Franklin Spl. Sch. Dist. Edn. Assn., Tenn. Assn. Elem. Sch. Prins. (pres.-elect Mid. Tenn. 1993-94, pres. 1994-95). Avocations: reading, gardening. Home: Franklin, Tenn. Died Mar. 5, 2008.

HENDLER, EDWIN, aerospace physiologist; b. Phila., Aug. 29, 1922; s. David and Elene (Kalman) H.; m. May Snyder, May 13, 1945; children: Lynn Karen Slotkin, Sandra Dee. BS, Pa. State U., 1943; MS, U. Pa., 1956, PhD, 1959. Physiologist Naval Air Material Ctr., Phila., 1946-52, head acceleration br., 1952-55; mgr. life scis. rsch. group Naval Air Engring. Ctr., Phila., 1956-74; head life scis. div. Naval Air Devel. Ctr., Warminster, Pa., 1975-81; cons. in field Cherry Hill, N.J., 1981-91. Mem. NAS-NRC Com. on Hearing, Bioacoustics and Biomechanics, Washington, 1964-81; project officer, advisor Air Standardization Coord. Com. Working Party 61-Aerospace Med. and Life Support Systems, Washington, 1965-80. Co-author: Unusual Environments and Human Behavior, 1963; contbr. chpts. to Physiological Problems in Space Exploration, 1964, Thermal Problems in Aerospace Medicine, 1968. Comdr. USNR, ret. Recipient Paul Bert award Aerospace Physiol. Soc., 1973, Profl. Excellence award Life Scis. and Biomed. Engring. Br., 1988. Fellow Aerospace Med. Assn.; mem. Am. Physiol. Soc., Biophys. Soc., Sigma Xi. Achievements include patent for aviator protective helmet; research on physiological responses to acceleration, altitude, thermal extremes, decompression, and prolonged exposure to artificial gaseous environments. Died Mar. 30, 2008.

HENDRICKS, JACK E., publishing executive; b. Holland, Mich., July 31, 1948; s. Elmo S. and Jennie (Koopman) H.; m. Nancy Alice Bogue, Mar. 27, 1970; children: Amy, Beth. BA, Hope Coll., 1971. With Flashes Pubs., Allegan, Mich., from 1971, sales mgr., 1984-86, market dir., 1986-87, gen. mgr., 1987-88, pub., from 1989; sr. v.p., pub. Info Am. Phone Books, Inc., from 1996. Supt. Sunday sch., 1st Baptist Ch. Allegan, 1973-83; mem. adv. bd. Christian Sch. Bd., Otsego Bapt. Acad., 1980-85. Mem. Am. Mgmt. Assn., Am. Mktg. Assn. (bd. dirs.), Ind. Free Papers Am., Assn. Free Community Papers, Assn. N.Am. Directory Pubs. (program com.), Community Papers Mich. (pres.), Assn. Free Community Papers (bd. mem.), Assn. Directory Pubs. (bd. mem.). Republican. Avocations: cross country skiing, trap shooting, rhododendrons. Home: Holland, Mich. Died Apr. 10, 2008.

HENDRICKS, JAMES PATRICK, lawyer, estate planner; b. Chgo., Oct. 11, 1939; s. Edwin Leroy and Kathleen (Enright) H.; m. Susan A. Leshin, Fegb. 21, 1967. BA in Philosophy, U. Santa Clara, 1963; JD, U. Ariz., 1968; cert. in sports law, Sports Law Inst./U. Wis. Bar: Ariz. 1969. Trial and appeals atty. NLRB, Washington, Ft. Worth, 1969-72; prin. Jacobowitz & Hendricks, P.C., Phoenix, 1972-90, James P. Hendricks, P.C., Phoenix, from 1990. Co-author: Your Personnel Manager, 1988. Mem. ABA (com. labor law sect. 1973-90, forum on entertainment and sports industries 1988-90), Ariz. Bar Assn. (chmn. labor law sect.), Lions (pres. Phoenix Downtown). Avocations: professional basketball, magic. Home: Phoenix, Ariz. Died Sept. 23, 2007.

HENKELS, PAUL MACALLISTER, engineering and construction company executive; b. Phila., Oct. 7, 1924; s. John Bernard Jr. and Anne (McCloskey) H.; m. Barbara Brass, Jan. 4, 1958; children: Marin, Paul M. Jr., Christopher B., Andrew M., T. Roderick, Amy, Timothy W., Angela, Carol, Barbara. BA in Engring, Haverford Coll., Pa., 1947. V.p., then exec. v.p. Henkels & McCoy, Blue Bell, Pa., 1958-72, pres., CEO, 1972-87, chmn., CEO, 1987-91, chmn., 1991—2009. Bd. mgrs. Beneficial Mut. Savs. Bank; Mem. adv. council Coll. Arts and Letters, U. Notre Dame, chmn., 1968-70 Chmn. Montgomery County United Way, 1977, The REACH Alliance, 1993—; vice chmn. Cath. Charities Appeal, Archdiocese of Phila., 1980-84; trustee Temple U., Phila., 1968-72, 79-83, exec. com., 1969-72; bd. govs. Temple U. Hosp., vice chmn., 1975-79; trustee Ind. Colls. Pa., exec. com., chmn. bd., 1980-83; trustee Chestnut Hill Coll., 1978-84, St. Joseph's U., vice chmn., 1987-90, chmn. exec. com., trustee Found. for Ind. Higher Edn., treas. Recipient Man of Yr. award Notre Dame Club, Phila., 1980 Mem. Legatus Nat. Orgn. (bd. dirs.), Am. Nat. Standards Inst., Nat. Elec. Contractors Assn. (gov. 1963-67, Coggeshall award 1971), Atlantic Contractors Assn. (1st pres. 1965), Greater Phila. Utility Contractors Assn. (1st pres. 1972-74), Soc. Gas Lighters, Acad. Applied Elec. Sci. (dir., exec. com.), Knights of Malta, Knights of the Holy Sepulchre, Pine Valley Golf Club, Phila. Cricket Club. Republican. Roman Catholic. Home: Plymouth Meeting, Pa. Died Jan. 8, 2009.

HENKEN, BERNARD SAMUEL, clinical psychologist, speech pathologist; b. Everett, Mass., May 30, 1919; s. Issac Edward and Sarah B. (Shatzman) H.; m. Charlotte Popovsky, Dec. 20, 1953; children: Karen Beth, Donna Michele. Student, Boston Coll., 1938-41; BS, Harvard U., 1947; MS, Purdue U., 1950; DSc in Psychology, Calvin Coolidge Coll., 1955. Lic. psychologist, rehab. counselor; cert. sch. psychologist, cert. speech and language pathologist, Mass.; diplomate Am. Assn. Clin. Counselors; nat. cert. in speech lang. pathology. Psychologist Carney Hosp., Boston, 1950-51; dir. speech pathology, psychologist Audiology Ctr., Lynn, Mass., 1951-56; psychologist, chief clin. counseling svcs. Brusch Med. Ctr., Cambridge, Mass., 1956-80; speech pathologist Mass. Gen. Hosp., Boston, 1951-52; speech pathologist, sch. psychologist Everett Pub. Schs., 1955-85; psychologist Rescue Inc., 1959-71, v.p., 1972-74; psychologist, clin. counselor North Shore Children's Hosp., Salem, Mass., 1966-74; psychologist Medford (Mass.) Pediatric Assocs., 1974-94. Prof. psychology Calvin Coolidge Coll., Boston, 1958-69; lectr. psychology Lawrence Meml. Hosp., Medford, Mass., 1975-77, univ. extension courses Harvard U., 1960-68; psychologist Alfano Med. Inst., Melrose, Mass., 1956-64; guest lectr. Duke U. Med. Ctr., 1965, 72; co-chair symposium on clin. counseling and medicine Tufts U., 1974. Contbr. articles to profl. jours.; creator Henken Operator Safety Evaluation Technique; editor Clin. Counseling Bulletin, 1970-84. Cpl. M.C., U.S. Army, 1942-45, PTO. Recipient Lifetime Achievement award Mass. Sch. Psychology, 2001, Marie Curie medal of honor, Cambridge, Eng., 2006. Mem. APA (charter mem. divsn. psychotherapy), Am. Coll. Counselors (cert. forensic psychology), Am. Coll. Counselors, Mass. Speech and Hearing Assn. (treas. 1957-59), Am. Assn. Clin. Counselors (pres. 1959-63), Mass. Sch. Psychologists Assn. (pres. 1972-74). Republican. Jewish. Avocations: sports, music. Died Feb. 11, 2008.

HENNING, JOHN FRANCIS, retired labor union administrator; b. San Francisco, Nov. 22, 1915; s. William Henry and Lulu Frances (McLane) Henning; m. Margueritte M. Morand, Nov. 25, 1939 (dec. 1994); children: John F., Brian H., Patrick W., Nancy R., Daniel M., Thomas R., Mary T. AB, St. Mary's Coll., 1938, LLD, 1976, St. Anselm's Coll., 1965; DCS, St. Bonaventure U., 1966. Rsch. dir., adminstrv. asst. to exec. officer Calif. State Fedn. Labor, San Francisco, 1949—58; dir. Calif. Dept. Indsl. Rels., San Francisco, 1959—62; under sec. US Dept. Labor, Washington, 1962—67; US amb. to New Zealand US Dept. State, 1967—69; exec. sec.-treas. Calif. Labor Fedn. AFL-CIO, San Francisco, 1970—96. Bd. Permit Appeals, 1953—56, pres., 1955—56; mem. Pub. Welfare Commn., 1950—53, Equal Employment Opportunities Commn, all San Francisco, 1956—59; mem. bd. regents U. Calif., 1989—97. Recipient Ellis I. Medal of Honor, 1986. Died June 4, 2009.

HENRICH, WILLIAM JOSEPH, JR., lawyer; b. Phila., Jan. 13, 1929; s. William J. and Helen (Moylan) H.; m. Dorothy Kolsun, 1953; children: William III, Michael, David, Richard. BA in Econs., LaSalle U., 1950; JD, Temple U., 1956. Bar: Pa. 1957, Ct. Common Pleas 1957, U.S. Dist. Ct. (ea. dist.) Pa. 1957. Assoc. Dilworth, Paxson, Kalish & Kauffman, Phila., 1957-65, ptnr., 1965-84, sr. ptnr., 1988—2003; pres., gen. counsel Triangle Pub. Inc., Radnor, Pa., 1985-88. Bd. mgrs. Beneficial Bank, Phila. Bd. dirs. LaSalle U., Phila., Pa., 1985-2009; trustee The Annenburg Sch. Comm., U. Pa., 1985-2009, The Annenburg Sch. Comm., U. So. Calif., L.A., 1985-2009 Mem. ABA. Home: Lafayette Hl, Pa. Died Oct. 24, 2009.

HENRY, VERNON G., consulting company executive; b. Houston, Dec. 18, 1934; s. Vernon Polk and Gladys Mae (Douglas) H.; student Tex. A&M U., 1953-56; B.S. and B.Arch., U. Houston, 1958; m. Mary Lou, Sept. 9, 1967; 1 son, Paul Alex. Sr. planner, chief advance planning div. City of Houston, 1959-64; ptnr. planning divsn. Neuhaus & Taylor (now 3-D Internat.); pres. Vernon Henry & Associates, Inc., planning cons. and landscape architects, Houston, 1968—2009; vis. lectr. Tex. A&M U., Rice U. Pres., Zool. Soc. Houston, 1975-80; co-chmn. Houston Green Ribbon Com., 1980-82; founding dir. Houston Urban Bunch; pres. Houston Balloon Pilots Assn., Blvd. Oaks Civic Assn., 1984-85, pres., 1985—2009. North Edgemont Civic Club; mem. People to People tour People's Republic of China, 1981; v.p. The Park People, 1984-85. Served to capt. USAR, 1960-63. Recipient Meritorious Service award City of Houston, 1981. Mem. Am. Planning Assn. (merit award for planning design 1979), Am. Inst. Cert. Planners (pres. Tex.-La. chpt.), C. of C. (chmn. Houston flood control com. 1976-78), Urban Land Inst. (sustaining mem.). Home: Houston, Tex. Died Apr. 19, 2009.

HENRY, WALTER LESTER, JR., physician, educator; b. Philadelphia, Pa., Nov. 19, 1915; s. Walter Lester and Vera (Robinson) H.; m. Ada Clarice Palmer, Sept. 7, 1942. AB, Temple U., 1936; MD, Howard U., 1941; student, U. Pa. Grad. Sch. Medicine, 1948-49. Diplomate Am. Bd. Internal Medicine (bd. govs. 1970-77, mem. residency rev. com. 1970-77). Intern Freedmen's Hosp., Washington, 1941-42, resident, 1949-51; fellow endocrinology Michael Reese Hosp., Chgo., 1951-53; mem. faculty Howard U., 1953—2009, prof. medicine, 1963—90, chmn. dept., 1962-73, William B. Allen prof. medicine, 1972-73, John B. Johnson prof. medicine, 1973-90, prof. emeritus, 1990—2009. Mem. Washington Med. Care and Hosp. Com. Faculty trustee Howard U., 1970-75. Served to maj. M.C. AUS, 1942-46, Italy. Decorated Bronze Star with cluster; Markle scholar med. scis., 1953-58, alumni award Howard U., 1994. Mem. AMA, ACP (regent 1974-80, master 1987-2003, laureate 1994), Nat. Med. Assn., Am. Fedn. Clin. Rsch., NAACP, D.C. Med. Soc. (1st v.p.), Alpha Phi Alpha. Presbyn. (elder). Home: Washington, DC. Died Apr. 21, 2009.

HEPLER, KENNETH RUSSEL, manufacturing executive; b. Canton, Ohio, Mar. 31, 1926; s. Clifton R. and Mary A. (Sample) H.; m. Beverly Best, June 9, 1945; 1 child, Bradford R. Student, Cleve. Art Inst., 1946-47, Case Western Res. U., 1948-50. V.p., adminstr. A. Carlisle and Co., San Francisco, 1954-67; pres. K.R. Hepler and Co., Menlo Park, Calif., 1968-73, Paramount Press., Jacksonville, Fla., 1974-75; pvt. practice printing broker, 1976-80; chmn. Hickey and Hepler Graphics Inc., San Francisco, from 1981. Instr. printing prodn., San Francisco City Coll. With USAAC, 1943-45. Mem. San Francisco Litho Club (pres. 1972), Phila. Litho Club (sec. 1975-76), Newtown Exchange Club (pres. 1976), Elks. Republican. Presbyterian. Died June 19, 2008.

HEPPA, DOUGLAS VAN, computer specialist; b. Bklyn., May 26, 1945; s. Joseph Charles and Antoinette Palmer (Vanasco) H.; m. Barbara Zanlunghi. BS in Social Sci., Poly. Inst. N.Y., 1968, BS in Math., 1971, MS Insl. & Applied Math., 1973, postgrad., from 1983. Assoc. engr. Raytheon Co., Portsmouth, RI, 1968-70; systems engr. PRD Electronics, Syosset, NY, 1970-71; mathematician USN, New London, Conn., 1971; asst. computer engr. George Sharp, NYC, 1972-73; programmer N.Y.C. Dept. Social Svcs., 1975; quantitative analyst N.Y.C. Fire Dept., 1976-80, assoc. staff analyst, 1980-81, computer specialist, 1991—99; with Algorithm Devel. Co., Maspeth, NY, from 1999. Pres. Algorithm Devel. Co., Queens, NY, from 1985. Mem. Math. Assn. Am., Am. Mgmt. Assn., Soc. for Indsl. & Applied Math., Assn. for Computing Machinery, IEEE, Am. Math. Soc. Avocations: fishing, swimming, boating, amateur radio, astronomy. Home: Maspeth, NY. Died Dec. 5, 2007.

HERGESHEIMER, JOHN HOWARD, social studies educator; b. Hollywood, Calif., Oct. 22, 1932; s. Rees and Olive Eleanor (Hogle) H.; m. Elizabeth Ann Gordon, June 5, 1954; children: Mark Rees, Peter David, Ruth Ellen Hergesheimer Northrop. BA, Whittier Coll., Calif., 1954; MA, Long Beach U., Calif., 1961. Lic. tchr., Calif. Tchr. social studies Norwalk-LaMirada Unified Sch. Dist., 1957-93; chair dept. social sci. Norwalk H.S., 1963-73, 79-93; social studies tchr. Norwalk La Marada Adult Sch., from 1993. Mentor tchr. Norwalk-LaMirada Unified Sch. Dist., 1985-92. Editor: (curriculum booklets) The California Concepts Collection, 1990, 2d edit., 1999, Geography in the Framework, 1988; contbr. articles to profl. jours. Trustee South Whittier Sch. Dist., 1973-85, pres. sch. bd., 1974-76, 82-84. Recipient Outstanding Svc. award Whittier Area Sch. Adminstrs., 1987; JISEA fellow Keizai Koho Ctr., Japan, 1983, 95. Mem. NEA, Calif. Tchrs. Assn., Calif. Coun. for the Social Studies (pres. 1986-87, editor of newsletter 1988—, Ruth Delzell Svc. award 1992), Tchrs. Assn. of the Norwalk-La Mirada Area (pres. 1970-71), Los Coyotes Coun. for the Social Studies (bd. dirs. 1982—), Nat. Coun. for the Social Studies, Calif. Tchrs. Assn. (We Honor Ours award 1972). Methodist. Avocations: musical composition, genealogy, reading, painting, concert-going. Home: Whittier, Calif. Died Jan. 24, 2008.

HERING, HELEN DORA, controller; b. Birnamwood, Wis., Mar. 19, 1921; d. August Ferdinand Grosinske and Bertha Wilhelmina Kraege; m. Edwin R. Baeseman (dec. Sept. 18, 1962); 1 child, Randall Layne Baeseman; m. Alfons Frank Hering, Sept. 10, 1972 (dec. Aug. 1991); m. Claude E. Venne, 1964 (dec. 1970). Tchrs. diploma, Marathon County Normal Sch., Wausau, Wis., 1940. Grade sch. tchr. Marathon County Schs., Wausau, 1940—45; mem. statis. dept. Employers Mut. Ins. Co., Wausau, 1946—48; cashier, bookkeeper Employers Mut. Credit Union, Wausau, 1948—53; ptnr., bookkeeper Baeseman's Shoe & Clothing, Wausau, 1953—79; antiques dealer Hering House Antiques, Wausau, 1972—99; English editor Gwiazda Polarna (Polish lang. weekly newspaper), Stevens Point, Wis., 1993—95. Pub.: So, You Wanted America, 1996, author poetry. Recipient Valley Forge Honor cert., Freedoms Found., Milw., 1978, monetary prize, World of Poetry, Anaheim, Calif., 1988, World of Poetry, Las Vegas, 1990. Republican. Lutheran. Avocations: poetry, entering contests. Home: Wausau, Wis. Died Oct. 14, 2007.

HERKNER-BALLANCE, MILDRED LUELLA, psychiatry consultant; b. Traverse City, Mich., June 21, 1915; d. Oswald and Elsie (Rickerd) Herkner; m. L. Charles Ballance, June 19, 1940; children: Lee Charles, Stephen James, Ann Elizabeth, Robert Alan. BS, U. Mich., 1937, MD, 1940. Intern Cleve. (Ohio) City Hosp., 1940-41; pediatric resident Children's Hosp. Mich., Detroit, 1941-42, Herman Kiefer sr. resident in contagious diseases, 1942-43; clin. instr. pediatrics Bob Roberts Hosp., U. Chgo., 1943-44; pvt. practice pediatrics, Park Ridge, Ill., 1944-50, Traverse City, 1951-66; resident in adult psychiatry Traverse City Regional Psychiat. Ctr., 1966-68; resident in child psychiatry Hawthorn Ctr., Northville, Mich., 1968-70, sr. staff psychiatrist, 1973-81; clin. dir. Arnell Engstrom Children's Ctr., Traverse City, 1970-73; cons. in psychiatry Maple Clinic, Traverse City, from 1985. Psychiat. cons. Walled Lake (Mich.) Schs., 1974-83, Sarah Fisher Home, Detroit, 1973-83; clin. instr. U. Mich. Med. Sch., Ann Arbor, 1975-81. Pres. organizing com. YMCA, Traverse City, 1963, pres., 1967-68; regional speaker for drug edn. Probate Ct., No. Mich., 1974; spokesperson for com. to save Traverse City Regional Psychiat. Hosp., 1988. Fellow Am. Acad. Child Psychiatry (councillor Mich. regional chpt. 1983-87); mem. Mich. Med. Soc., Mich. Psychiat. Soc. Republican. Avocations: crafts, gardening. Home: Lake Leelanau, Mich. Deceased.

HERREN, LINDA ELIZABETH, emergency nurse; b. Natick, Mass., Dec. 16, 1950; d. Richard Wendell and Mary Ellen (Rogers) Howard; m. Billy Alvin Herren, June 26, 1971; children: Amy Bilinda Herren, Brian Howard Herren. Diploma, Faulkner Hosp. Sch. Nursing, Jamaica Plain, Mass., 1971; student, U. No. Iowa, 1987; AA with honors in Communications Media, Kirkwood Community Coll., 1989; BA in Journalism and Mass Comm. with honors, U. Iowa, 1990, postgrad., from 1992. Med.-surg. nurse Mary Greeley Hosp., Ames, Iowa, 1971; surg. nurse/supply technician Stange Meml. Clinic, Sch. Vet. Medicine, Iowa State U., Ames, 1971-74; staff nurse nursing home Lexington, Mass., 1974; operating rm. nurse Choate Meml. Hosp., Woburn, Mass., 1974-75; emergency dept. nurse St. Luke's Hosp., Cedar Rapids, Iowa, from 1975. Instr. RN refresher and update course Kirkwood C.C., Iowa, 1991, 92; Schwartz meml. lectr. and scholar St. Luke's Health Care Found., 1993. Co-editor: Whittier Home and Garden Club Cookbook, 1987. BCLS instr., trainer Am. Heart Assn.; vol. nurse health svcs. com. ARC; organizer, leader Whittier ladies aerobics; publicity coord. spl. events St. Michael's Episcopal Ch., chmn. 35th anniversary pictoral directory, 1988. Mark Westerbeck Meml. scholar, 1991. Mem. Pub. Rels. Students Soc. Am., Vis. Nurses Assn. (home health care nurse summer 1991, spring 1992), Springville Band Parents Assn., Springville PTA, Whittier Ladies Aid, Phi Theta Kappa. Home: Springville, Iowa. Died Jan. 3, 2008.

HERRERIAS, CARLA TREVETTE, epidemiologist, health science association administrator; b. Chgo., Apr. 8, 1964; d. Ludvik Frank and Carlotta Trevette (Walker) Koci; m. Jesus Herrerias, Feb. 25, 1989; children: Elena Mikele, Coco Trevette. BS in Med.Tech., Ea. Mich. U., 1987; MPH in Molecular and Hosp. Epidemiology, U. Mich., 1991. Med. clk. hydramatic divsn. GM, Ypsilanti, Mich., 1983-86; rschr., support staff dept. human genetics U. Mich., Ann Arbor, 1987-91; program mgr. Am. Acad. Pediat., Elk Grove Village, Ill., 1991-99, sr. health policy analyst, 1999—2003; clin. rsch. analyst Am. Coll. Chest Physicians, Northbrook, Ill., from 2003. Project mgr., contbr.: Clinical

Practice Guideline: Otitis Media with Effusion in Young Children, 1994. Mem. APHA, Ill. Pub. Health Assn., Acad. Health Svcs. Rsch. and Health Policy, Guidelines Internat. Network, U. Mich. Alumni Soc., U. Mich. Club Chgo. Avocations: reading, biking, needlecrafts, horseback riding. Home: Chicago, Ill. Died Dec. 12, 2007.

HERRIGEL, HOWARD RALPH, engineering company executive, chemical engineer; b. Seattle, Sept. 27, 1924; s. Walter Arthur and Violet Cleo (Keirman) H.; m. Judith Esther Robbins, Oct. 23, 1964; children: David Robbins, Nancy Ruth. BSChemE, U. Wash, 1952, postgrad., 1953-58, U. Pitts., 1979. Research engr. The Boeing Co., Seattle, 1958-71, Resources Conservation Co., Seattle, 1971-73, chief chemist, 1973-74, process engring. mgr. Bellevue, Wash., 1974-80, v.p., chief scientist, 1980-84, v.p. sci. and tech., 1984-87, sr. cons., from 1987. Patentee in field. Recipient Outstanding Contbrn. award AIAA, 1978. Mem. Am. Chem. Soc., AIChE, Nat. Assn. Corrosion Engrs., AAAS, Seattle Yacht Club, Sigma Xi, Phi Lambda Upsilon. Clubs: Seattle Yacht. Avocations: sailing, skiing, scuba diving, music, theater. Home: Seattle, Wash. Died Aug. 3, 2008.

HERRING, (WILLIAM) CONYERS, retired physicist, educator; b. Scotia, NY, Nov. 15, 1914; s. William Conyers and Mary (Joy) H.; m. Louise C. Preusch, Nov. 30, 1946; children— Lois Mary, Alan John, Brian Charles, Gordon Robert. AB, U. Kans., 1933; PhD, Princeton, 1937. NRC fellow Mass. Inst. Tech., 1937-39; instr. Princeton, 1939-40, U. Mo., 1940-41; mem. sci. staff Div. War Research, Columbia, 1941-45; prof. applied math. U. Tex., 1946; research physicist Bell Telephone Labs., Murray Hill, NJ, 1946-78; prof. applied physics Stanford (Calif.) U., 1978-81, prof. emeritus, from 1981. Mem. Inst. Advanced Study, 1952-53 Recipient Army-Navy Cert. of Appreciation, 1947; Distinguished Service citation U. Kans., 1973; J. Murray Luck award for excellence in sci. reviewing Nat. Acad. Scis., 1980; von Hippel award Materials Rsch. Soc., 1980, Wolf prize in physics, Wolf Found., Israel, 1985. Fellow Am. Phys. Soc. (Oliver E. Buckley solid state physics prize 1959), Am. Acad. Arts and Scis.; mem. AAAS, NAS, Am. Soc. Info. Scis. Home: Palo Alto, Calif. Died July 23, 2009.

HERRON, ROLLAND EDWARD, osteopath; b. Salem, Ohio, Feb. 27, 1934; s. James William and Nora Evelyn (Dunn) H.; m. Joanne Hicks, Aug. 7, 1965; 1 child, Pamela Kay Binns. BS, Ohio State U., 1955; DO, Kirksville Coll. Osteo. Medicine, 1962. Pvt. practice osteopathic internal medicine, Salem, Ohio, from 1967. Developer MediScript computer systems. Med. dir. Columbiana County Bd. of Health, 1985-86. Served with U.S. Army, 1955-56. Mem. Am. Osteo. Assn., Ohio State Med. Soc., Columbiana County Med. Soc. (past pres.) Republican. Lutheran. Avocations: computers; pvt. pilot, instrument rated. Died Apr. 11, 2008.

HERSCHEDE, JOAN ROTH, holding company executive; b. Portsmouth, Ohio, Jan. 14, 1940; d. Albert Joseph Roth and Leona Agnes Simon; m. Mark Paul Herschede, June 22, 1970 (dec. May 1991); children: Donald Lee Huffman II, Deborah Leona Huffman. Exec. Frank Herschede Co., Cin. Bd. dirs. Fifth Third Bank, Cin. Trustee U. Cin.; chmn. WCET-TV, Cin.; bd. dirs. United Way, Cin.; pres. Am. Classical Music Hall of Fame and Mus. Mem. Golden Key Nat. Honor Soc. Home: Cincinnati, Ohio. Died Dec. 1, 2007.

HERTL, WILLIAM, chemist; b. Phila., July 2, 1932; m. Pamela Rider, Sept. 19, 1964; children: Julia, David. BS, U. Pa., 1954; PhD, Cambridge U., 1962. Shift analyst Atlantic Refining Co., Phila., 1958; postdoctoral fellow CIBA, A/G, Basel, Switzerland, 1962-63; sr. rsch. assoc. Corning (N.Y.), Inc., from 1963. Prof. chemistry U. Andes, Merida, Venezuela, 1970-72; vis. scientist Cornell U., Ithaca, N.Y., 1987. Contbr. numerous articles to profl. jours.; patentee in field. Lt. (j.g.) USN, 1954-57. Mem. Am. Chem. Soc., Royal Soc. Chemistry, Am. Phys. Soc., Materials Rsch. Soc., Soc. for Applied Spectroscopy, Bohmische Phys. Soc. Home: Corning, NY. Died Sept. 17, 2007.

HESTON, NANCY BAUER, interior designer; b. Feb. 8, 1948; m. James R. Heston; children: Karen, Colin. BS in Art Edn. & Design, Butler U., 1974. Interior designer Kittle's, Indpls., 1970-74; dir. mktg. & promotions World Team Tennis, Indpls., 1975; sr. designer Marshall Field & Co., Oak Brook, Ill., 1975-78; interior designer Nancy Heston Interiors, Great Falls, Va., from 1978. Mem. Am. Soc. Interior Designers (profl. mem.), Nat. Hist. Soc., Nat. Mus. Women in Arts, Jr. League Washington. Republican. Avocations: tennis, cooking. Died Dec. 21, 2007.

HETRICK, MARY JO, fragrance company executive; b. Noblesville, Ind., Nov. 12, 1954; d. Joseph R. and Mary P. (Clark) Couden; m. Chet Hetrick, Dec. 11, 1976; 1 child, Joel. Founder, pres., CEO Good Scents Ltd., Princeton, Ill., from 1989. Cons. in field. Recipient Recognition award Ind. 4-H Alumni, 1981. Mem. Princeton Alliance Lady Mgr. (founder, chair 1991—), Princeton Mcht. Assn. (founding mem., sec. 1992-93, pres. 1993-94), Bus. and Profl. Women (networking specialist, membership com. 1988, Outstanding Working Woman award 1989). Home: Princeton, Ill. Died Sept. 27, 2007.

HETZLER, PATRICIA ANN, elementary school educator; b. New Wilmington, Pa., Mar. 16, 1947; d. Melvin Arthur and Ettamae (Konvolinka) H. BS in Elem. Edn., Youngstown State U., 1968; MS in Guidance and Counseling, Westminster Coll., 1970. Cert. elem. tchr., Ohio. Tchr. McDonald (Ohio) Bd. Edn., from 1968. Mem. Trumbull Reading Coun., Warren, Ohio, 1968—; chairperson bldg. level intervention and assistance team for psychol. testing and placement, McDonald Schs., 1984—. Sr. worker Contact Trumbull, Warner, 1969—; mentor McDonald, Roosevelt Bldg. Leadership Team; patron Fine Arts Coun. Trumbull County; mem. Animal Welfare League Trumbull County. Mem. NEA, Ohio Edn. Assn., Northeastern Ohio Edn., McDonald Edn. Assn. (pres. 1972-76), Delta Kappa Gamma (v.p. 1988). Republican. Methodist. Home: Warren, Ohio. Died June 4, 2008.

HEWITT, DON, retired television producer; b. NYC, Dec. 14, 1922; s. Ely S. and Frieda (Pike) H.; children: Jeffrey, Steven, Jill, Lisa; m. Marilyn Berger, Apr. 14, 1979. Student, NYU, 1941; degree (hon.), Brandeis U., 1990; DFA (hon.), Am. Film Inst., 1993. War corr., World War II; prodr. 1st Kennedy-Nixon TV debate, 1960; exec. prodr. CBS Evening News with Walter Cronkite, 1960-65, 60 Minutes, 1968—2004. Delivered 1st ann. William S. Paley lectr. Mus. of TV and Radio, 1993; author: Tell Me a Story: Fifty Years and 60 Minutes in Television, 2001 Recipient Paul White award Radio and TV News Dirs. Assn., 1987; Gold medal Internat. Radio and TV Soc., 1987, Broadcaster of Yr. award, 1980; Gold Baton award Columbia DuPont, 1988, Peabody award, 1989, Lowell Thomas Centennial award, 1992, 1st ann. Goldsmith award for Investigative Reporting, John F. Kennedy Sch. Govt. Harvard U., 1992, Lifetime award Prodrs. Guild Am., 1993, Founders award Internat. Coun. of TV Acad. Arts & Sciences, 1995, Com. to Protect Journalists 9th Ann. Burton Benjamin Meml. award Internat. Press Freedom, 1999, Edward R. Murrow award for Lifetime Achievement in Broadcast Journalism, Washington State U., 2008; named to Hall of Fame, NATAS, 1990. Home: New York, NY. Died Aug. 19, 2009.

HEWITT, RICHARD GILBERT, lawyer; b. Boston, Jan. 1, 1927; s. Ely Shepard and Frieda (Pike) H.; m. Shirley Adele Keddy, Mar. 18, 1950 (dec. Dec. 1986); children: Carolyn Spiegel, William; m. Genevieve Madeleine Fisch, Aug. 3, 1989. BA, Williams Coll., 1948; LLB, Columbia U., 1951. Bar: N.Y. 1951, U.S. Dist. Ct. (so., ea. and we. dists.) N.Y. 1954. Atty. Port of N.Y. Authority, NYC, 1950-53; assoc. Myles, Wormser & Koch, NYC, 1953-56; ptnr. Wormser, Kiely, Galef & Jacobs and predecessor firms, NYC, from 1957. Trustee Hale Matthews Found., N.Y.C., 1980—, Am. Contract Bridge League Charity Found., Memphis, 1983-91, Nat. Com. for Prevention of Child Abuse, Chgo., 1988-92; trustee Rsch. to Prevent Blindness, N.Y.C., 1993—, Scoville Found., N.Y.C., 1992—. Avocations: duplicate bridge, golf. Home: New York, NY. Died Aug. 2, 2008.

HEXTER, ALFRED CHARLES, epidemiologist; b. Portland, Oreg., Dec. 24, 1925; s. Edgar Carl and Bessie (Rogoway) H.; m. Stella Stender, Oct. 1, 1953; children: Barbara, Theodore. BS, U. Calif.-San Francisco, 1948; MA, U. Calif.-Berkeley, 1958, PhD, 1977. Researcher Calif. Dept. Health, Berkeley, 1961-73, U. Calif., Berkeley, 1973-79; epidemiologist Birth Defects Monitoring Program Calif. Dept. Health Svcs., Berkeley, 1980-89. Mem. Am. Pharm. Assn., Am. Statis. Assn., Royal Statis. Soc., Inst. Math. Stats., Biometric Soc. Home: Kensington, Calif. Died Nov. 16, 2007.

HEYMAN, SAMUEL J., chemical manufacturing company executive; b. NYC, Mar. 1, 1939; s. Lazarus S. and Annette (Silverman) Heyman; m. Ronnie Feuerstein, Nov. 1970; children: Lazarus, Eleanor, Jennifer, Elizabeth BS magna cum laude, Yale Coll., 1960; LLB, Harvard U., 1963. Bar: Conn. 1963. Atty. US Dept. Justice, Washington, 1963-64; asst. US atty. Dist. Conn., New Haven, 1964-67, chief asst. US atty., 1967-68; CEO Heyman Properties, Westport, Conn., 1968—2009; chmn. G-I Holdings Inc. (formerly GAF Corp.), Wayne, NJ, 1983—2009, Internat. Specialty Products Inc., Wayne, NJ, 1991—2009, CEO, 1991—99. Hon. dir. Benjamin N. Cardozo Sch. Law Yeshiva U., established The Samuel & Ronnie Heyman Ctr. on Corp. Governanance; bd. visitors Terry Sanford Inst. Pub. Policy Duke U., established The Samuel and Ronnie Heyman Ctr. for Ethics, Pub. Policy and the Professions; dean's adv. bd. Harvard Law; established The Heyman Chair in Legal Ethics Yale Law Sch.; founder & chmn. Partnership for Pub. Svc., Washington, 2001—09. Named one of Top 200 Collectors, ARTnews mag., 2000—08. Avocation: Collector modern and contemporary art, especially Miró, Léger, Gorky, Giacometti, and Dubuffet. Died Nov. 8, 2009.

HICKEY, DANIEL PAUL, aerospace engineer; b. Palo Alto, Calif., Nov. 18, 1932; s. Daniel Kilburn and Novia Maybelle (Rodgers) H.; m. Catherine May Grimson, Oct. 2, 1965; children: Daniel George, Elizabeth Anne. BS in Aero. Engring., Calif. Poly., 1954; MS in Aerospace Engring., U. So. Calif., 1965; MS in Mgmt. Sci., West Coast U., 1973. Registered aero. engr. Aero. rsch. engr. NASA, Moffett Field, Calif., 1954-57; engr. Douglas Aircraft Co., Santa Monica, Calif., 1957-75; staff mem. Thermeon Corp., Tustin, Calif., 1975-76; engr. Brunswick Corp., Costa Mesa, Calif., 1976-77; engr. specialist Boeing Mil. Airplane Co., Seattle, 1977-83, Northrop Grumman Corp., Newbury Park, Calif., 1983-95. Recipient Scholastic Achievement, Inst. of the Aero. Scis., San Luis Obispo, Calif., 1954. Mem. AIAA. Republican. Avocations: bowling, ballroom dancing. Home: Newbury Park, Calif. Died June 6, 2008.

HICKEY, THOMAS M., stockbroker; b. Joliet, Ill., July 26, 1954; BS, U. Ill., 1976; MS, Ga. Inst. Tech., 1977. Stockbroker Merrill Lynch, Chgo., from 1978. Mem. Union League Club Chgo. Avocations: martial arts, swimming. Home: Western Sprgs, Ill. Died June 6, 2008.

HICKMAN, FRANK ROBERT, lawyer; b. Tulsa, July 5, 1923; s. Frank N. and Ruth L. H.; m. June M. Hickman, Apr. 15, 1952; children: William, Steven, Scott. Grad., U.S. Merchant Marine Acad., 1945; LLB, Tulsa U., 1949. Bar: Okla. 1949, U.S. Dist. Ct. (no. dist.) Okla. With Hickman & Hickman, Tulsa, 1949-59, ptnr., from 1983. Pub. defender Tulsa County, 1950-52; past pres. Tulsa County Jr. Bar. Lt.j.g. USNR. Died Aug. 16, 2007.

HIEATT, ALLEN KENT, retired language educator; b. Indpls., Jan. 21, 1921; emigrated to Can., 1968, returned to U.S., 1986. s. Allen Andrew and Violet Rose (Kent) H.; m. Constance Bartlett, Oct. 25, 1958; children by previous marriage: Alice Coulombe, Katherine Hieatt. AB, U. Louisville, 1943; PhD, Columbia U., 1954. Lectr. Columbia U., NYC, 1944-45, instr., 1945-55, asst. prof., 1956-59, assoc. prof., 1960-69; prof. English U. Western Ont., London, 1969-86, emeritus and from 1987; sr. founding editor Spenser Newsletter, London, Ont., 1970-75; ret., 1987. Mem. editorial bd. Duquesne Studies, Pitts., 1976—, Spenser Studies, 1979—; editorial cons. Spenser Ency., 1990; co-editor: College Anthology of British and American Verse, 1964, Poetry in English: An Anthology, 1987; author: Short Time's Endless Monument, 1960, (with C. Hieatt) The Canterbury Tales of Geoffrey Chaucer, 1964, rev. edit., 1981, Spenser: Selected Poetry, 1970, Chaucer, Spenser, Milton, 1975; translator: (with M. Lorch) Lorenzo Valla, On Pleasure, 1977; co-author: (with C. Hieatt) (children's book) The Canterbury Tales of Geoffrey Chaucer, 1961. Cutting fellow, 1946-47; leave grantee Can. Council, Oxford, Eng., 1977-78; rsch. fellow Social Sci. and Humanities Rsch. Coun. Can., 1981-82 Fellow Royal Soc. Can.; mem. MLA (chmn. div. English lit. Renaissance 1978-79, William Riley Parker Prize, 1984), Spenser Soc. (pres.), Renaissance Soc. Am. (chmn. north central div. 1973-79) Deceased.

HIGBEE, ROBERT WILLIAM, executive recruiter; b. Lake Forest, Ill., Apr. 23, 1933; s. A. Kenneth and Burnette V. (Vanderkloot) H.; m. Ellen Ward, June 15, 1979. BA, Dartmouth Coll., 1954, MBA, 1955. Regional mgr. Armstrong Cork, Lancaster, Pa., 1958-70; nat. sales mgr. Knomark, Queens, N.Y., 1970-72; pres. Benmont, Bennington, Vt., 1972-74, Higbee Assocs., Inc., Rowayton, Conn., from 1975. Bd. dirs. Harbor Beach Assn., Norwalk, Conn., 1979. Served to capt. USAF, 1954-57. Mem.: Shore and Country (Norwalk). Republican. Avocations: sailing, tennis, skiing. Home: Norwalk, Conn. Died Feb. 7, 2008.

HIGHLAND, MARTHA (MARTIE), retired education educator, consultant; b. Lexington, Ky., June 3, 1934; d. William Thomas and Lyda Bruce (Wilson) H.; foster children: Barbara O. Noe, Teresa O. McKenzie, Debby O. Hodges, Joseph Owens, Kathy S. Coddington. AA, Cumberland Jr. Coll., 1955; BA in Edn., U. Ky., 1958; MA in Edn., U. Louisville, 1981. Cert. tchr., Ky. Tchr. Jefferson County Bd. Edn., Louisville, 1958-59, Ft. Knox (Ky.) Dependent Schs., 1959-65, Louisville City Schs., 1965-66, reading specialist, 1966-75, Jefferson County Sch. System, Louisville, 1975-89, remedial specialist in reading and math., 1989-91; ret., 1991. Substitute tchr., vol. Jefferson County Bd. Edn., Louisville, 1991—; faculty rep. Jefferson County Tchrs. Assn., 1981-91. Nominated Disney Tchr. of Yr., 1989. Mem. ASCD, Am. Bus. Women's Assn. (sec. 1989-92, v.p. 1988-89, 92-93, Woman of Yr. 1990). Avocations: academic coaching, reading, gardening. Home: Louisville, Ky. Deceased.

HIGHSMITH, WANDA LAW, retired medical association administrator; b. Cleveland, Mo., Oct. 25, 1928; d. Lloyd B. and Nan (Sisk) Law; m. Shelby Highsmith (div.); 1 child, Holly. Student, U. Mo., 1954-56. Various staff positions Am. Coll. Osteopathic Surgeons, 1960-72, asst. exec. dir., conv. mgr. Alexandria, Va., 1974-94; ret., 1994. Mem.: Profl. Conv. Mgmt. Assn. (emeritus). Methodist. Home: Arlington, Va. Died June 3, 2009.

HIGHTOWER, HELEN AUDE, science educator; b. Miami, Fla., Oct. 1, 1927; d. Carl E. and Doris (Willmore) Aude; m. Percy Alex Hightower, June 21, 1947; children: Doris Hightower Walker, Jane Hightwoer Roddy, A. Dirk, Peter, Carol. BA in Chemistry, U. Rochester, 1947, MA in Edn., 1974; postgrad., SUNY, Stony Brook, summers 1985-87. Cert. chemistry and gen. sci. tchr., N.Y. Tchr. sci. Rochester (N.Y.) City Schs., 1969-89; sch. trustee Wayne Ctrl. Sch., Ontario Center, N.Y., from 1995. Girl scout leader, adult trainer Girl Scouts USA, Seven Lakes Coun., 1960-80. Recipient H.S. Chemistry Tchr. of Yr. award Am. Chem. Soc., 1989. Mem. AAWU, Wayne County Master Gardeners, Ontario Garden Club (conservation chair 1995-97). Avocations: travel, gardening, writing. Home: Ontario, NY. Died July 31, 2008.

HILBERT, ROBERT S(AUL), optical engineer; b. Washington, Apr. 29, 1941; s. Philip G. and Bessie (Friend) H.; m. Angela Cinel Ferreira, June 19, 1966; children: David M., Daniel S. BS in Optics, U. Rochester, 1962, MS in Optics, 1964. Optical design engr. Itek Corp., Lexington, Mass., 1963-65, supr. lens design sect., 1965-67, asst. mgr. optical engr. dept., 1967-69, mgr. optical engring. dept., 1969-74, dir. optics, 1974-75; v.p. engring. Optical Rsch. Assocs., Pasadena, Calif., 1975-84, sr. v.p., 1985-91, pres.,

COO, from 1991, pres., CEO, from 2000, chmn. bd., from 2008. Lectr. Northeastern U., Burlington, Mass., 1967-69; mem. trustees vis. com. Sch. Engring. and Applied Sci., U. Rochester, 1995-97. Mem. devel. bd. Coll. Optical Sci., U. Ariz., from 2007. Recipient Future Scientist of Am. award, 1957; Am. Optical Co. fellow U. Rochester, 1962. Fellow Soc. Photo-Optical Instrumentation Engrs. (chmn. fellows com. 1998); mem. Optical Soc. Am. (engring. coun. 1990-92, mem. Fraunhofer award com. 1997-98), Lens Design Tech. Group (chmn. 1975-77). Jewish. Achievements include 6 patents in lens systems. Avocations: reading, movies. Home: Arcadia, Calif. Died 2009.

HILL, DOUGLAS, systems engineer; b. NYC, Aug. 2, 1925; s. Jack Douglas and Pearl Ruth (Doran) H.; m. Ruth Arlene Blake, Aug. 21, 1948; children: Jeffrey D., Gordon S., Heather. BAE, Rensselaer Poly. U., 1950; MS, Columbia U., 1958, EngScD, 1977. Lic. profl. engr., N.Y. Engr. Grumman Aircraft Engring., Bethpage, N.Y., 1949-57; mgr. econ. analysis Grumman Aerospace Corp., Bethpage, 1958-69; dir. environ. programs Grumman Ecosys. Corp., Bethpage, 1970-76; from engr. to project head Brookhaven Nat. Lab., Upton, N.Y., 1977-89; pres. Douglas Hill, P.E., P.C., Huntington, N.Y., from 1989. Adj. lectr. SUNY, Stony Brook, 1994—. Editor: The Baked Apple? Metropolitan New York in the Greenhouse, 1996, The East River Tidal Barrage, 1994; contbr. articles to profl. jours. Lt. USNR, 1943-46. Mem. Am. Soc. Civil Engrs., N.Y. Acad. Scis., Inst. Ops. Rsch. & Mgmt. Scis., Internat. Assn. Energy Econs. Avocations: sailing, discussing great books. Died Apr. 4, 2008.

HILL, EUGENE DUBOSE, JR., consulting engineer; b. Louisville, Aug. 22, 1926; s. Eugene DuBose and Lila Perrin (Robinson) H.; m. Margaret Preston Hodges, Feb. 18, 1950; children: Eugene DuBose III, Margaret Hill Hilton, Virginia Hill Martinson. BS in Engring., Princeton U., 1948. Asst. chemist Devoe & Raynolds Co., Louisville, 1948-50; rschr., salesman, asst. sec. Louisville Cement Co., 1950-59; sales rep., spl. masonry rep., asst. v.p. sales tech. svcs., dir. product quality and devel. Ideal Cement Co. (later divsn. of Ideal Basic Industries), 1959-85; assoc. Openaka Corp., Inc., Denver, from 1985. Lt. (j.g.) USNR, 1944-46. Fellow Am. Concrete Inst. (bd. dirs. 1981-84, tech. activities com. 1987-93); mem. ASTM. Episcopalian. Avocations: photography, tennis, skiing. Died Feb. 24, 2008.

HILL, LEWIS REUBEN, horticulturist, nursery owner, writer; b. Greensboro, Vt., July 1, 1924; s. Alvah Aaron and Grace Gibson (Towle) H.; m. Nancy May Davis, May 4, 1969. High sch. grad., Greensboro, Vt. Owner, mgr. Hillcrest Nursery, Greensboro, 1947-82, Vermont Daylilies, Greensboro, 1982-93, Berryhill Nursery, Greensboro, from 1993. Author: Fruits and Berries for the Home Garden, 1977, Pruning Simplified, 1979, Cold Climate Gardening, 1981, Secrets of Plant Propagation, 1985, Yankee Summer, 2000; co-author (with Nancy Hill): Country Living, 1987, Successful Perennial Gardening, 1988, Christmas Trees, 1989, Fetched Up Yankee, 1990, Daylilies, The Perfect Perennial, 1991, Bulbs-Four Seasons of Beautiful Blooms, 1994, Pruning Made Easy, 1997, Lawns, Grasses & Groundcovers, 1995, The Lawn and Garden Owners Manual, 2000, The Flower Gardener's Bible, 2003; (with others) Berries, 1991, Vines, 1992, Wise Garden Encyclopedia, 1997, 1990 edit., Vermont Voices, 1991, others; contbr. articles to popular mags. Del. State Rep. Conv. twice; various town offices and coms. Recipient Disting. Svc. award Vt. Edn. Assn., 1967, Gov's Commn. on Children and Youth, Montpelier, Vt., 1970; 4-H citation Nat. Extension Svc., Washington, 1974; cert. of appreciation Ea. Nurserymen's Assn., Montpelier, 1982; Lit. Excellence award Greensboro Libr., 1990, Vt. Horticulture Achievement award Vt. Profl. Horticulturists, 1993, Quill and Trowel award Garden Writers of Am., 1995. Mem. League Vt. Writers, Vt. Profl. Horticulturists (bd. dirs., pres.), Internat. Ribes Assn. Mem. United Ch. Avocations: photography, skiing, motorcycling, nature. Died Aug. 12, 2008.

HILL, MARTHA NELL, education educator; b. Clarksdale, Miss., Sept. 11, 1946; d. Edgar Hall and Virgia (Hill) McNeal. BS, LeMoyne Coll., Memphis, 1968; MEd, Trevecca Nazarene Coll., Nashville, 1987, postgrad., 1988-89. Cert. tchr. and adminstr., Tenn. Tchr., social studies dept. chmn. Memphis Bd. Edn., 1968-92; payroll clk. C.H. Hill & Son, Memphis, 1968-91; instr. LeMoyne-Owen Coll., Memphis, 1991-92. Tchr., sponsor The Close Up Found., Washington, 1981-86; mem. Prin.'s Adv. Com., Memphis, 1988-90; sponsor Whitehaven's Black History Program, Memphis, 1985-90; mem. Study Coun. for Better Schs. Program, Gov. Lamar Alexander Tenn.; mem. textbook adoption com. Memphis City Sch. System. Sponsor essay contests Whitehaven High Sch., VFW, sr. class advisor Whitehaven High Sch., 1984-90; mem. Memphis Regional Sickle Cell Coun., 1979, Facing History, 1987-89; writer curriculum on the bill of rights Memphis City Schs., 1990; mem. Career Ladder Program. Stratford scholar, 1984. Mem. NAACP, NAFE, NEA, ASCD (Leadership award 1985-90), Greenpeace, Nat. Coun. Social Studies (Tchr. of the Yr. 1984), West Tenn. Edn. Assn., Memphis Edn. Assn., Soc. of Preservation of Constn., Smithsonian Inst., Inner Circle, Black Issues in Higher Edn., Pi Lambda Theta, Pi Beta. Democrat. Baptist. Avocations: travel, reading, cooking, poetry, music. Died Jan. 4, 2008.

HILL, PATTI L., dietitian, health facility administrator; b. Conway, Ark., Mar. 13, 1951; d. Henry Wesley and Flossie Ilene (Rhoades) H.; 1 child, Amber Dawn. Student, U. Fla., 1975, Rice Belt Vocat.-Tech., Dewitt, Ark., 1979. Cert. dietician. Dietary mgr. St. Andrews Place, Conway, Ark., from 1974. Author: poems. Mem. Faulkner Cunty Humane Soc., 1995—; historian Poets Roundtable of Ark., 1992—; bd. dirs. Faulkner County Arts, 1992—; mem. Northside Ch. of Christ. Recipient Dir.'s Poetry award Ark. Writers Conf., 1991, Marion Michell Poetry award Ark. Writers Conf., 1994, Poetry Day Eve award, 2nd Place, Counselors Poetry Day Eve award, 2nd Place Poets Roundtable of Ark., 1997. Mem. Dietary Mgrs. Assn. Republican. Home: Conway, Ark. Died Dec. 29, 2007.

HILSENRATH, LEE BETTY, retired mathematics educator; b. Bklyn., Dec. 6, 1934; d. Samuel and Gussie (Gelfand) Batch; m. Daniel Wallace Hilsenrath, Dec. 24, 1961; children: Joel Alan, Mark Harris. BA, Bklyn., 1956, MA, 1959. Cert. tchr. Math. tchr. John D. Wells Jr. High Sch., Bklyn., 1956, New Utrecht High Sch., Bklyn., from 1956, ret., 1991. Dean of girls New Utrecht High Sch., 1972-85; student activities advisor New Utrecht High Sch., 1959-62; spl. edn. math. cons. New Utrecht High Sch. 1986-88. Mem. exec. bd., pres. Coney Island chpt. Am. Parkinson's Disease Assn.; mem. Midwood Civic Action Coun., Bklyn., from 1978, treas., from 2000; mem. Inst. for Retirees in Pursuit of Edn., Bklyn. Coll., from 1996, instr., from 1997, v.p., from 2001; pres. Inst. Retirees Pursuit Edn., from 2004; vol. math. tutor Dynamite Youth Ctr.; bd. dirs. Midwood Devel. Corp., from 2003. Recipient Outstanding Profl. Svc. Tchr. award Bklyn. High Sch. div. Bd. Edn. N.Y.C., 1988, Bklyn. High Sch. Recognition Day award New Utrecht High Sch., 1989. Democrat. Jewish. Avocations: photography, reading, sewing, bridge. Home: Brooklyn, NY. Died May 5, 2008.

HILTZ, ARNOLD AUBREY, retired chemist; b. Can., July 31, 1924; arrived in U.S., 1953; s. Aubrey Claremont and Fannie Mae (Bryanton) H.; m. Margery Jane (Beer), July 17, 1946; children: Sharon Lynne, Deborah Jane. BS in Chemistry, Acadia U., Wolfville, NS, Can., 1947; PhD in Phys. Chemistry, McGill U., Montreal, Que., Can., 1952; LLD (hon.), U. Prince Edward Island, 2004. Ordained deacon and priest Episc. Ch., 1976. Rsch. sci. officer Def. Rsch. Bd. Can., Quebec City, 1951—53; rsch. chemist Am. Viscose Corp., Phila., 1953—59, group leader, 1959—60, Avisun Corp., Phila., 1960—65; rsch. chemist Borden Chem. Co., Phila., 1965—66; sr. scientist GE, Phila., 1966—79, mgr. materials applications, 1979—91. Tutor math. and sci. Rose Tree Media, Pa. Sch. Dist., 1958-74. Contbr. articles to profl. journals; patentee in field. Docent Phila. Mus. Art, 1988—2003; sch. dir. Rose Tree Media Pa. Sch. Dist., 1969—74, tutor math. and sci. Rose Tree Media, 1958—74; bd. dirs., treas. Middletown Free Libr., Pa., 1964—69; vol. gallery guide Art Gallery N.S., 2004—06; treas. Halifax County Condo. Corp., 2004—06; hon. asst. to dean All Saints Cathedral, Halifax, 2003—07; bd. dirs. Sheepscot Island Co., MacMahan Island, Maine, 1983—85. Recipient Silver medal Gov. Gen. Can. 1942, Can. Def. medal, Can. Vol. Svc. medal, Claspto CVSM, War medal 1939-45, Gen. Svc. badge, Can. Overseas medal 1945, Frank J. Sensebrenner fellow McGill U., 1949-51. Mem.: Am. Chem. Soc. (chem. abstractor 1958—79, sci. lectr. 1958—2003), Halifax County Condominium Assn. (treas. 2004—06), Hebrides Home Owners Assn. (pres., bd. dir. 1999—2001, treas. 2002—05). Republican. Episcopalian. Avocations: art, music, reading, gardening, golf. Home: Swarthmore, Pa. Died Aug. 31, 2009.

HIMES, ROSE KENDRICK, elementary school educator; b. Okolona, Miss., Jan. 13, 1942; d. John Thomas and Annie Mae (Grisby) Kendrick; m. Joseph Lex Stone, Aug. 15, 1965 (div. Sept., 1972); m. Albert Himes, Sept. 20, 1980. AA, Okolona Coll., 1962; BEd, Rust Coll., 1964; MEd, Miss. Univ. for Women, 1971. Tchr. first grade Vine Elem. Sch., Aberdeen, Miss.; tchr. fourth grade Fairview Elem. Sch., Columbus, Miss., 1971-75, Calerman Elem., Columbus, 1975-79; tchr. Franklin Acad. Elem., Columbus, from 1979. Trustee United Meth. Ch., Columbus, Miss., 1989-94; cert. lay speaker United Meth. Ch., Miss., 1992-94. Mem. Columbus Classroom Tchrs. Assn., Columbus Reading Coun. Democrat. Avocations: reading, collecting pottery, horticulture, singing, lay speaking. Home: Columbus, Miss. Died Sept. 2, 2007.

HINCHEY, JAMES PATRICK, public relations consultant, advertising consultant; b. Berlin, NH, July 24, 1926; s. Patrick James and Albertine (Gonya) H.; m. Claire Elizabeth Morancy, Apr. 7, 1947; children: Paul Matthew, Stephen Henry. BA in Pub. Rels./Comm., Boston U., 1950. Pub. rels. mgr. Brown Company, Berlin, N.H., 1950-55; editor The Berlin Reporter, 1955-58; gen. mgr. WGUY, Bangor, Maine, 1959-65; account exec. WLBZ-TV, Bangor, 1959-65; sta. mgr. Sta. WHEB-Radio, Portsmouth, N.H., 1965-68; CEO, mng. dir. Portsmouth C. of C., 1968-72; pres. Employment & Career Opportunities, Portsmouth, 1973-84; owner, pres. TVUE Mag., North Conway, N.H., 1985 93; program mgr. Sta. WBUR. V.p. N.H. Broadcasters, Berlin, 1958; part-time instr. N.H. Coll., Portsmouth, 1969-71. Editor Brown Bull., 1950-55. With USN, 1944-46, PTO. Recipient Freedoms Found. award, 1950-51, 53. Mem. Am. Assn. Indsl. Editors (nat. dir.), Jaycees (pres. Gorham, N.H. 1952-53), Berlin C. of C. (bd. dirs. 1953-54). Avocation: skiing. Died June 20, 2008.

HINGLE, PAT, actor; b. Miami, Fla., July 19, 1924; s. Clarence M. and Marvin (Patterson) H.; m. Julia Wright, Oct. 25, 1979; children: Jody, Billy, Molly. BFA, U. Tex., Austin, 1949; PhD (hon.), Otterbein Coll., Westerville, Ohio, 1974. Actor: (films) On the Waterfront, 1953, The Strange One, 1957, No Down Payment, 1957, Splendor in the Grass, 1961, The Ugly American, 1963, Blues for Mr. Charlie, 1964, A Girl Could Get Lucky, 1964, Invitation to a Gunfighter, 1964, The Glass Menagerie, 1965, The Odd Couple, 1966, Nevada Smith, 1966, Johnny No-Trump, 1967, Sol Madrid, 1968, Jigsaw, 1968, Hang 'Em High, 1968, The Price, 1968, Bloody Mama, 1969, Child's Play, 1970, Norwood, 1970, WUSA, 1970, The Selling of the President, 1972, The Carey Treatment, 1972, Nightmare Honeymoon, 1973, One Little Indian, 1973, Happy as the Grass Was Green, 1973, The Super Cops, 1973, Super Cops, 1973, Running Wild, 1973, Independence, 1976, The Gauntlet, 1977, Norma Rae, 1979, When You Comin' Back, Red Ryder, 1979, Running Scared, 1980, Going Berserk, 1983, Running Brave, 1983, Sudden Impact, 1983, The Act, 1984, The Falcon and the Snowman, 1984, Brewster's Millions, 1985, Maximum Overdrive, 1986, In 'n Out, 1986, Baby Boom, 1987, The Land Before Time (voice only, 1988, Batman, 1989, The Grifters, 1990, Batman Returns, 1992, Lightnin' Jack, 1994, The Quick and the Dead, 1994, Batman Forever, 1995, Larger Than Life, 1996, Horror Story, 1997, Bastard Out of Carolina, 1996, A Thousand Acres, 1996, Batman and Robin, 1997, The Shining, 1997, Hunter's Moon, 1999, Muppets from Space, 1999, Morning, 2000, Shaft, 2000, The Greatest Adventure of My Life, 2001, Road to Redemption, 2000, Two Tickets to Paradise, 2006, The List, 2005, Talladega Nights: The Ballad of Ricky Bobby, 2006, Waltzing Anna, 2006, Undoing Time, 2008; actor, exec. prodr.: The Angel Doll, 2002; actor: (TV appearances) Suspense, 1954, Appointment with Adventure, 1955, Goodyear Television Playhouse, 1955, The Phil Silvers Show (2 episodes), 1955, Justice, 1955, The Philco Television Playhouse (3 episodes), 1955-56, The Alcoa Hour, 1956, Kraft Television Theatre, 1957, Studio One (3 episodes), 1954-57, Suspicion, 1957, Alfred Hitchcock Presents, 1957, Rendezvous, 1958, The United States Steel Hour, (2 episodes), 1957-59, Play of the Week, 1961, Cain's Hundred, 1961, The Eleventh Hour, 1962, The Untouchables (2 episodes) 1962-63, The Twilight Zone, 1963, Dr. Kildare (2 episodes), 1962-63, Route 66 (2 episodes), 1963, Kraft Suspense Theatre, 1963, Rawhide, 1965, Daniel Boone, 1965, The Fugitive (2 episodes), 1964-65, The Defenders, 1965, The Trials of O'Brien, 1966, The Andy Griffith Show, 1966, The Loner (2 episodes), 1966, A Man Called Shenandoah, 1966, Mission: Impossible, 1967, Bob Hope Presents the Chrysler Theatre, 1967, Judd for the Defense, 1967, Cimarron Strip, 1967, Run for Your Life, 1967, Gentle Ben, 1967, The Invaders, 1967, Felony Squad, 1967, The High Chaparral, 1968, Bonanza, 1969, Lancer, 1969, The Young Lawyers, 1971, NET Playhouse, 1971, Gunsmoke (6 episodes), 1971, The Bold Ones: The New Doctors (2 episodes), 1969-71, Ironside, 1972, The Bold Ones: The Lawyers (2 episodes), 1972, Owen Marshall: Counselor at Law, 1972, Kung-Fu, 1973, Hec Ramsey, 1973, The Rookies, 1973, The F.B.I., 1973, The Six Million Dollar Man, 1974, Medical Center (3 episodes), 1970-74, Lucas Tanner, 1974, McCloud, 1975, Barbary Coast, 1975, The Streets of San Francisco, 1979, Hawaii Five-0 (3 episodes), 1975-77, Nashville 99, 1977, Barnaby Jones (3 episodes), 1976-79, Vega$, 1979, M*A*S*H*, 1980, Trapper John, M.D. (2 episodes), 1981-85, Hart to Hart, 1982, St. Elsewhere, 1983, Simon & Simon, 1983, The Yellow Rose, 1984, Magnum, P.I., 1984, Hail to the Chief (3 episodes), 1985, Amazing Stories, 1985, Matlock, 1986, The Equalizer, 1989, Life Goes On, 1990, Murder, She Wrote (3 episodes), 1986-91, The American Experience, 1993, Cheers, 1993, In the Heat of the Night, (2 episodes), 1993-94, Wings, 1996, American Gothic, 1996, Homicide: Life on the Streets, 1998, Touched by an Angel, 1999, Dawson's Creek, 2001; (TV movies) Carol for Another Christmas, 1964, The Glass Menagerie, 1966, Certain Honorable Men, 1968, The Ballad of Andy Crocker, 1969, A Clear and Present Danger, 1970, The City, 1971, Sweet, Sweet Rachel, 1971, All the Way Home, 1971, If Tomorrow Comes, 1971, Trouble Comes to Town, 1973, Twigs, 1975, The Secret Life of John Chapman, 1976, Escape from Bogen County, 1977, Sunshine Christmas, 1977, Tarantualas: The Deadly Cargo, 1977, Stone, 1979, Elvis, 1979, When Hell Was in Session, 1979, Disaster on the Coastliner, 1979, Off the Minnesota Strip, 1980, The Private History of a Campaign That Failed, 1981, Of Mice and Men, 1981, Washington Mistress, 1982, Bus Stop, 1982, The Fighter, 1983, Noon Wine, 1985, The Lady from Yesterday, 1985, The Rape of Richard Beck, 1985, Casebusters, 1986, Manhunt for Claude Dallas, 1986, LBJ: The Early Years, 1987, Kojak: The Price of Justice, 1987, Stranger on My Land, 1988, The Town Bully, 1988, Everybody's Baby: The Rescue of Jessica McClure, 1989, Beanpole, 1990, Not of This World, 1991, Gunsmoke: To the Last Man, 1992, Citizen Cohn, 1992, The Habitations of Dragons, 1992, Against Her Will: The Carrie Buck Story, 1994, One Christmas, 1994, Truman, 1995, The Member of the Wedding, 1997, THe Runaway, 2000; (TV series) Blue Skies, 1988, the Court, 2002; (TV mini-series) Wild Times, 1980, War and Remembrance, 1988-89, The Kennedys of Massachusetts, 1989, The Shining, 1997. Served with USNR, 1942-46, 51-52. Home: Carolina Beach, NC. Died Jan. 3, 2009.

HINTERBUCHNER, L. P., neurologist; b. Zlatá Baña, Slovak Republic, Dec. 10, 1922; arrived in U.S., 1951; s. Frantisek and Margita Hinterbuchner; m. Catherine Nicolaides, Dec. 10, 1955. MD, Komensky U., Bratislava, Slovak Republic, 1947; postgrad., N.Y. Postgrad. Med. Sch., NYC, 1952—53. Instr. neurology Health Sci. Ctr., SUNY, Bklyn., 1956—61, clin. asst. prof. neurology, 1961—67, clin. prof. neurology, 1967—95, clin. prof. neurology emeritus, from 1995; vis. prof. neurology N.Y.

Coll. Osteo. Medicine, Westbury, NY, 1977—84; adj. prof. N.Y. Med. Coll., Valhalla, 1983—97. Dir. dept. psychiatry and neurology Kingsbrook Jewish Med. Ctr., Bklyn., 1961—66; chmn. dept. neurology Bklyn. Hosp. Med. Ctr., 1971—85, cons. in neurology, 1991—96. V.p. Slovak World Congress, Pasadena, Calif., 1996—2001; 1st v.p. Slovak League Am., Passaic, NJ, from 2006. Recipient Ellis Island Medal of Honor, Nat. Ethnic Coalition, N.Y.C., 2000. Fellow: N.Y. Acad. Sci.; mem.: AMA (life), Med. Soc. County of Kings (pres. 1994, chmn. bd. trustees), Am. Acad. Neurology (sr.). Died May 1, 2009.

HIPP, ARTHUR WILLIAM, surveyor, association administrator; b. Penfield Center, NY, Oct. 19, 1925; s. David William and Viola Pearl (Scofield) H.; m. Catherine Ann McGill, Feb. 12, 1944; children: James, Susan, Charles. BA in Geography, Hastings Coll., 1949; Master in Pub. Adminstrn., U. Colo., 1979. Registered land surveyor Alaska, Colo., Ga., Nebr., Wyo. Geologist, engr. Climax (Colo.) Molybdenum Co., 1950-56; surveyor U.S. Forest Service, Denver, 1957-86; sec./treas., exec. dir. Profl. Land Surveyors of Colo. Inc., Arvada, from 1986. Editor jour. Profl. Land Surveyors of Colo. Side Shots, 1975-86. Served with USMC 1942-45. Recipient Citizen Surveyor of Yr. award Profl. Land Surveyors of Colo., 1983. Fellow Nat. Soc. Profl. Surveyors of Am. Congress on Surveying and Mapping (Excellence in Profl. Journalism award 1983), VFW, DAV. Democrat. Roman Catholic. Died Sept. 19, 2007.

HIPPLE, SAUNDRA JEANNE, newspaper publisher; b. Balt., Nov. 12, 1942; d. Lester Elliott and Julia Olive (Redd) Lumpkin; m. Robert Bruce Hipple, Dec. 31, 1960; children: Robert, Donna, Lori, Michael, Richard. Circulation Balt. Observer, 1974-77; assembly worker Dupree, El Monte, Calif., 1978-81; from bookkeeper to owner Voice of the Valley, Maple Valley, Wash., from 1981. Bd. dirs. Cmty. Ctr., Maple Valley, Wash., 1981-86. Home: Maple Valley, Wash. Died June 19, 2008.

HIRATA, JOSEPH MASAO, manufacturing company executive, computer engineer; b. Fuknoka, Japan, June 1, 1922; came to U.S., 1953; s. Masaichi and Setsuyo (Hirata) H.; m. Yoshie C. Hirata, June 18, 1956. BS, Mil. Acad. Japan, Tokyo, 1943; BS in Physics, Georgetown U., 1957; student, Am. U., 1952-68. Product engr. Sprague Electric Co., Rockville, Md., 1959-67; project leader Lockheed Electronic Co., Greenbelt, Md., 1967-69; aerospace technologist NASA, Goddard, SFC, 1969-72; project engr. DEA, Justice Dept., Washington, 1972-83; gen. mgr., v.p. MTI Engring. Corp., City of Industry, Calif., from 1983. V.p., bd. dirs. Micro Encoder, Inc., Seattle, 1986—. Mem. IEEE. Home: La Puente, Calif. Died Nov. 9, 2007.

HIRES, WILLIAM LELAND, psychologist, consultant; b. South Orange, NJ, July 5, 1918; s. Harrison Streeter and Christine B. (Leland) H.; m. Karen Reynolds Perrott, July 12, 1975; 1 child, Jennifer Leland. BS, Haverford Coll., 1949; PhD, U. Pa., 1972. Asst. to dean of admissions, asst. dir of scholarships U. Pa., 1952-55; supr. psychol. svcs., spl. classes, asst. supt. Office Supt. Chester County (Pa.) Schs., 1956-59; assoc. prof. West Chester Coll., 1960-61; adminstrv. asst. Office of Pres., asst. to sec. U. Pa., 1961-64; assoc. Edward N. Hay & Assocs., 1964-65; asst. supt. pub. schs. Chester County, 1966-68, pvt. cons., 1968-75; dir. diagnostic and consultative svc. Chester County Intermediate Unit, 1975-76, pvt. practice psychology, 1976-78; dir. pupil svcs. Upper Darby (Pa.) Sch. Dist., 1978-81; dean acad. studies Curtis Inst. Music, Phila., 1981-86; ptnr. Hires Assocs., Phila., from 1987. With USMC, 1942—46, with US Army, 1941—42, with US Army, 1950—52, lt. col. AUS, from 1978, col. hon. Pa. Army N.G. ret. Mem. AAAS, APA, Soc. of Cin., Welcome Soc., Hist. Soc. Pa., 1st Troop Phila. City Cavalry (hon.), Soc. Colonial Wars Pa. (hon. gov.), Phila. Club, Franklin Inn Club, Merion Cricket Club, Harvard-Radcliffe Club of Phila., The Rabbit, Aztec Club of 1847. Home: Haverford, Pa. Died Feb. 14, 2009.

HIRSCH, WERNER ZVI, retired economist, educator; b. Linz, Germany, June 10, 1920; arrived in US, 1946, naturalized, 1955; s. Waldemar and Toni (Morgenstern) H.; m. Hilde E. Zwirn, Oct. 30, 1945; children: Daniel, Joel, Ilona. BS with highest honors, U. Calif., Berkeley, 1947, PhD, 1949. Instr. econs. U. Calif., 1949-51; econ. affairs officer UN, 1951-52; economist Brookings Instn., Washington, 1952-53; asst. rsch. dir. St. Louis Met. Survey, 1956-57; prof. econs. Washington U., St. Louis, 1953-63, dir. Inst. of Urban and Regional Studies; economist Resources for Future, Inc., Washington, 1958-59; dir. Inst. Govt. and Pub. Affairs UCLA, 1963-73, prof. economics, 1963—90, prof. emeritus, 1991—2009; mem. senate acad. coun. U. Calif., 1985-87, 89-91. Cons. Rand Corp., 1958—98, US Senate Pub. Works Com., 1972, Calif. Senate Select Com. Structure and Adminstrn. Pub. Edn., 1973, Joint Econ. Com. Congress, 1975—76, OECD, 1977—80; com. to improve productivity Govt. Com. Econ. Devel., 1975—76; scholar in residence Rockefeller Study Ctr., 1978, pre-retirement rels. com.; chmn. LA City Productivity Adv. Com., 1982—85; acad. senate faculty welfare com. U. Calif., 1984—96; chair u. faculty welfare com. UCLA, 1985—87, 1989—91, mem. restructure task force, 1993—95, long-range planning com., 1995—98, exec. bd. acad. senate, 1996—99, emeritus, 2005—09; tansit rsch. panel NRC, 1993—96; mem. Glion Colloquium on Challenges Facing Higher Edn., 1997—2009, Internat. Steering Com. Author: Introduction to Modern Statistics, 1957, Analysis of the Rising Costs of Education, 1959, Urban Life and Form, 1963, Elements of Regional Accounts, 1964, Program Budgeting, 1965, Regional Accounts for Public Decisions, 1966, Inventing Education for the Future, 1967, The Economics of State and Local Government, 1970, Regional Information for Government Planning, 1971, Fiscal Crisis of America's Central Cities, 1971, Program Budgeting for Primary and Secondary Public Education, 1972, Governing Urban America in the 1970s, 1973, Urban Economic Analysis, 1973, Local Government Program Budgeting: Theory and Practice, 1974, Recent Experiences with National Planning in the United Kingdom, 1977, Law and Economics: An Introductory Analysis, 1979, 2d rev. edit., 1988, 3d rev. edit., 1999, Higher Education of Women: Essays in Honor of Rosemary Park, 1978, Social Experimentation and Economic Policy, 1981, The Economics of Municipal Labor Markets, 1983, Urban Economics, 1984, Economist's Role in Government at Risk, 1989, Public Finance and Expenditures Under Federalism, 1990, Privatizing Government Services, 1991, Challenges Facing Higher Education at the Millennium, 1999, Renting, 2000, University High Tech Alliances in California: Gaines and Losses, 2000, Governance in Higher Education, 2001, As the Walls of Academia are Tumbling Down, 2002, Reinventing the Research University, 2004, Spillovers of University-High Tech Industry Alliances, 2005; mem. editl. bd.: Jour. Am. Statis. Assn., 1958—60; mem. editl. bd. Pakistani Jour. Applied Econs., from 1980, Internat. Rev. Law and Econs., 1985—88, Urban Affairs Quar., 1991—94; author: California Policy Options, 2006, 2008—09. Pres. Am. Friends of Wilton Pk., 1983—85, 2001—06, 2008—09, 2009; trustee U. Art Mus., Berkeley, 1991—2003; bd. dirs. Friends of Graphic Arts, 1974—79, Midwest Rsch. Inst., 1961—63, Calif. Coun. Environ./Econ. Balance, 1974—2009, Calif. Found. on Economy, 1979—89, U. Calif. Retirement Sys., 1986—94, Assoc. Students UCLA, 2000—06, Bel Air Assn., 2005—09, UCLA Faculty Assn., from 2006, Wilstein Inst., exec. com., 1993—99; exec. com. regional bd. Anti-Defamation League, 1986—2009; bd. govs. Edmund G. Brown Inst., 1981—86; gov. U. Calif. Faculty Ctr., 1992—94. Mem. Am. Econ. Assn., Am. Farm Econs. Assn., Internat. Biograph. Ctr. (mem. adv. coun. 1997—), Western Regional Sci. Assn. (bd. dirs., pres. 1978-80), Law and Econs. Assn., Soc. for Advancement of Socio-Econs., Town Hall West (pres. 1978-79), L.A. World Affairs Coun., Phi Beta Kappa, Sigma Xi., Oral History CLA Library Web. Home: Los Angeles, Calif. Died July 10, 2009.

HIRSCHMANN, RALPH FRANZ, chemist; b. Fuerth, Bavaria, Germany, May 6, 1922; came to U.S., 1937; s. Carl and Alice (Buchenbacher) H.; m. Lucy Marguerite Aliminosa, Mar. 9, 1951; children— Ralph F., Carla M. Hirschmann Hummel AB, Oberlin Coll., 1943, D.Sc. (hon.), 1969; MA, U. Wis., 1948, PhD, 1950, DSc (hon.), 1996. Asst. dir. Merck Sharp & Dohme Research Labs., Rahway, N.J., 1964-68, dir., 1968-71, sr. dir. West Point, Pa., 1972-74, exec. dir., 1974-76, v.p. Rahway, 1976-78, sr. v.p., 1978-87; rsch. prof. chemistry U. Pa., Phila, 1987—2006, Makineni prof. bioorganic chemistry Phila., 1994—2006, emeritus prof., 2006—09; prof. biomed. research Med. U. S.C., Charleston, 1987-97. Mem. N.J. Gov.'s Commn. on Sci. and Tech., 1984; mem. adv. com. NSF, 1985; mem. com. to survey opportunities in chem. scis. NRC, 1982; Romanes lectr. U. Edinburgh, Eng., 1985; Charles D. Hurd lectr. Northwestern U., 1985; Shell Disting. lectr., 1994, Monsanto lectr. Purdue U., 1996; mem. com. on chem. and pub. affairs Am. Chem. Soc. Contbr. numerous articles to profl. jours.; patentee in field Trustee Oberline Coll., 1986-93. Served with U.S. Army, 1943-46, PTO. Recipient Nichols medal, 1988, Chem. Pioneer award Am. Inst. Chemists, 1992, Gold medal Max Bergman Kreis, 1993, Alfred Burger award Am. Chem. Soc., 1994, Padmavathy and Noth Guthikonda Meml. award, 1996, Dr. Josef Rudinger award European Peptide Soc., 1996, Rsch. Achievement award in medicinal and natural products chemistry Am. Assn. Pharm. Scientists, 1996, Nat'l Acad. Sci. award for Industrial Application of Science, 1999, Arthur C. Cope Medal, 1999, Ed Smissman Bristol-Meyers Squibb award, 1999, Nat. Medal of Science, 2000, Williard Gibbs Medal, 2002. Fellow AAAS, ACS (Medicinal Chemistry award 1986, Carothers award Del. sect. 1994); mem. Am. Acad. Arts and Scis., Am. Soc. Biol. Chemists, NAS; sr. fellow, Institutes of Medicine. Home: Lansdale, Pa. Died June 20, 2009.

HIRZEL, CHARLES K., retired architect; b. Phila., Oct. 14, 1906; s. Carl Henry and Clara (Koch) H.; m. Helen E. Vogt, Dec. 5, 1936. BArch, U. Pa., 1927, MArch, 1930. Registered profl. arch., N.Y., N.J. Draftsman, renderer George E. Crane, 1926; draftsman Cherry and Matz, 1927-28; draftsman, designer, renderer, constrn. inspector Vahan Hagopian, NYC, 1929, 31-33, 46-56; draftsman Georgina Pope Yeatman, 1929-30, Austin Co., NYC, 1930, 1940; draftsman, designer R.H. Macy & Co., NYC, 1930-31; comml. artist Senff and Lang, 1932-33; draftsman M.V. Liddell, 1934-35; draftsman, designer L.I. Lighting Co., Mineola, N.Y., 1940-45; draftsman, designer, constrn. inspector Francis Keally FAIA, NYC, 1940, 1957—70, 1976—77; draftsman Spence and Rigolo, 1945-46, Myron R. Dassett, 1950-68; cons. architect Luth. Ch. Am., 1957, 1960—74; mng. assoc. Morris Ketchum, Jr., FAIA & Assoc., 1970; draftsman Meier-Marus, LI, 1977, 1979, 1981, George A. Bielich, 1971; designer, draftsman Giorgio Cavaglieri, FAIA, NYC, 1978-79; draftsman, designer P.H. Tuan, NYC, 1980, 82. Prin. works include modernization Christian Sci. Reading Rm. and Office, N.Y.C., addition St. James Episcopal Ch., Fordham, N.Y., alterations Collegiate Sch., N.Y.C., site plan and 1st unit St. John Greek Orthodox Ch., Tenafly, N.J.; contbr. articles to profl. jours. Bd. dirs. Luth. Social Svcs., N.Y.C.; bd. dirs. Covenant Luth. Ch., Ridgewood, N.Y., organist, choir dir., 1936-42; mem., sec. commn. on ch. architecture Luth. Ch. in Am.; mem. fin. and pers. com. Luth. Com. Svcs. and antecedents. Mem. AIA (chmn. com. N.Y. chpt.), NY Soc. Architects (profl. practices-ethics com., bldg. code com.), Nat. Trust Hist. Preservation. Avocations: gardening, church choir, travel. Home: Clearwater, Fla. Died Apr. 26, 2008.

HISCOCK, WILLIAM A., physicist, educator; m. Barbara Hiscock; children: John, Dale. BS in Physics, Calif. Inst. Tech., 1973; MS in Physics, U. Md., 1975, PhD in Physics, 1979. Prof. theoretical physics Mont. State U., Bozeman, 1993—2009, head physics dept., 2003—08; dir. Mont. Space Grant Consortium, 1991—2009, Mont. NASA EPS-CoR Program, 1994—2009. Mem. mission definition team for LISA NASA. Mem. editl. bd.: Jour. Air Transp.; contbr. articles to profl. jours. Achievements include research in quantum theory of gravity, space-based gravitational wave detection, relativistic fluid dynamics, and application of elementary particle physics to relativistic astrophysics and cosmology. Died Apr. 21, 2009.

HISER, PAULA J., medical/surgical nurse; b. Marietta, Ohio, Oct. 9, 1953; d. Larry Richard and Beverly Jane (Wintersteen) Bartmess; m. Gary W. Hiser, June 29, 1973; children, Jeremy Wayne, Joshua Ryan. Diploma, Lakeview Med. Ctr., Danville, Ill., 1984. Med.-surg. nurse United Samaritans Med. Ctr., Danville, Ill., 1989, recovery rm. nurse, from 2001. Home: Bismarck, Ill. Died Sept. 5, 2007.

HITE, CATHARINE LEAVEY, orchestra manager; b. Boston, Oct. 1, 1924; d. Edmond Harrison and Ruth Farrington Leavey; m. Robert Atkinson Hite, Aug. 28, 1948; children: Charles Harrison, Patricia Hite Barton, Catharine Hite Dunn. BA, Coll. William and Mary, 1945. Restoration guide Williamsburg Restoration, 1944-45; asst. edn. dept. Honolulu Acad. Arts, 1945-46; sec., tour guide edn. dept. office chief curator Nat. Gallery Art, 1946-48; opera liason/coord. Honolulu Symphony, 1972-73, asst. to gen. mgr., 1973-75, community devel. dir./opera coord., 1975-77, dir. ops./opera prodn. coord., 1977-79, orch. mgr., 1979-84, mem. exec. com., 1965-69, pres. women's assn., 1965-66; com. chmn., opera assn. chmn. Hawaii Opera Theatre, 1966-69. Mem. W. R. Farrington Scholarship Com., 1977—, chmn., 1982-94; mem. community arts panel State Found. Culture and the Arts, 1982, State Found. Music and Opera, 1984; docent Iolani Palace, 1990—; docent Honolulu Acad. Arts, 1996—. Mem. Jr. League, Alliance Française, Hawaii Watercolor Soc. Mem. Phi Beta Kappa. Episcopalian. Home: Honolulu, Hawaii. Deceased.

HITE, ROBERT WESLEY, wastewater reclamation executive; b. Ft. Scott, Kans., Mar. 18, 1936; s. Woodward Vannoy and Corinne Winifred (Wright) H.; m. Sarah Catherine Hoper, Aug. 20, 1960; children: Katherine, John, Laura, Martha, Amy. Student, Netherlands Coll., Breukelen, The Netherlands, 1956-57; BA, Colo. Coll., 1958; JD, NYU, 1961. Bar: Colo. 1961, U.S. Dist. Ct. Colo. 1961, U.S. Ct. Mil. Appeals 1965, U.S. Supreme Ct. 1965, U.S. Ct. Appeals (10th cir.) 1973. Judge advocate USN, Newport, R.I., 1962-65; sole practice Denver, 1965-69; sr. v.p., gen. counsel Mr. Steak Inc., Denver, 1969-88; mgr. Met. Denver Wastewater Reclamation Dist., from 1988, also bd. dirs. Pres. 7th Ave. Homeowners Assn., Denver, 1975—. Mem. ABA, Colo. Bar Assn., Denver Bar Assn., Colo. Assn. Corp. Counsel (pres. 1974-76), Colo. Wyoming Restaurant Assn. (bd. dirs. 1987-88), Assn. Met. Sewerage Agys. (bd. dirs. 1992—), Colo. Coll. Alumni Assn. (bd. dirs. 1984-88). Clubs: Law. Lodges: Rotary. Republican. Presbyterian. Home: Denver, Colo. Died Dec. 4, 2007.

HOAGLAND, MAHLON, biochemist, educator; b. Boston, Oct. 5, 1921; s. Hudson and Anna (Plummer) H.; m. Olley Virginia Jones, Jan. 10, 1961; children from previous marriage: Judith, Mahlon, Robin. Student, Williams Coll., 1940—41, Harvard U., 1941—43, MD, 1948; ScD (hon.), Worcester Poly. Inst., 1973, U. Mass., 1984. From rsch. fellow to asst. prof. medicine Med. Sch. Harvard U. at Mass. Gen. Hosp., 1948-60; assoc. prof. bacteriology and immunology Med. Sch. Harvard U., 1960-67; prof. biochemistry, chmn. dept. Med. Sch. Dartmouth, 1967-70; pres., sci. dir. Worcester Found. for Biomed. Rsch., Shrewsbury, Mass., 1970-85, pres. emeritus, 1985—2009. Rsch. assoc. Carlsberg Labs., Copenhagen, 1951-52, Cavendish Labs., Cambridge, Eng., 1957-58; cancer rsch. scholar Am. Cancer Soc., 1953-58; founder, spokesman Del. for Basic Biomed. Rsch., 1978-85. Author: 6 Books; contbr. over 68 articles to profl. jours. Recipient Franklin medal, 1976; 2 book awards Am. Med. Writers Assn., 1982, 96. Fellow Am. Acad. Arts and Scis.; mem. NAS. Achievements include discovery of mechanism of amino acid activation and (with P.C. Zamecnik) transfer ribonucleic acid. Home: Thetford, Vt. Died Sept. 25, 2009.

HOBART, EVERETT WINSLOW, JR., chemist, consultant; b. Cin., Dec. 15, 1931; s. Everett W. and Louise (Durst) H.; m. Marianne Swisher; children: Michael, Barbara, Elizabeth, Paul, John. BS, MIT, 1953. Jr. chemist Am. Cyanamid, Stamford, Conn., 1953-55; asst. project engr. Pratt & Whitney Aircraft, Middletown, Conn., 1956-65; asst. rsch. dir., lab. dir. Ledoux & Co., Teaneck, N.J., 1965-76, 80-92; tech. dir. Spectro Chem. Lab., Franklin Lakes, N.J., 1976-80; cons. Sabin Metal Corp., Scottsville, N.Y., from 1992. Contbr. articles to profl. jours. Mem. ASTM, Internat. Precious Metals Inst., Am. Chem. Soc. Avocation: reading spanish literature. Home: Spencerport, NY. Died Feb. 20, 2008.

HOCHSTADT, HARRY, mathematician, educator; b. Vienna, Sept. 7, 1925; s. Samuel and Amalie (Dorn) H.; m. Pearl Schwartzberg, Mar. 29, 1953; children— Julia Phyllis, Jesse Frederick. B.Chem. Engring., Cooper Union, 1949; MS, N.Y. U., 1950, PhD, 1956. Rsch. engr. W. L. Maxson Corp., NYC, 1951-57; mem. faculty Poly. U., from 1957; prof. math. Poly. Inst. Bklyn., 1961-92, head dept., 1963-90, dean arts and scis., 1974-76, dir. inst. rels., 1976-80, prof. emeritus, from 1992. Author: Special Functions of Mathematical Physics, 1961, Differential Equations, A Modern Approach, 1964, The Functions of Mathematical Physics, 1971, Integral Equations, 1973; Translation editor: Linear Equations of Mathematical Physics (Mikhlin), 1967; adv. editor: Wiley-Intersci. Series on Pure and Applied Mathematics. Served with inf. AUS, 1943-45. Decorated Bronze Star, Combat Inf. badge. Mem. Am. Math. Soc., Math. Assn. Am., Soc. Indsl. and Applied Math., Sigma Xi, Tau Beta Pi. Died May 4, 2009.

HODES, LOUIS, mathematician; b. Bklyn., June 19, 1934; s. Morris and Anna (Magid) H.; m. Susan Barbara Levine, Nov. 23, 1967. BEE, Bklyn. Polytechnical Inst., 1956, MS in Applied Math., 1958; PhD, MIT, 1962. Mathematician IBM Rsch. Ctr., Yorktown Heights, N.Y., 1961-65; vis. fellow NYU CourantInst., NYC, 1965-66; rsch. math. NIH Computer Divsn., Bethesda, Md., 1966-74, NIH Nat. Cancer Inst., Bethesda, from 1974. Contbg. author: Comprehensive Medicinal Chemistry, 1990; contbr. articles to profl. jours.; patentee Radiation Treatment Planning Program, 1976. Mem. IEEE, Am. Chem. Soc., Assn. Computing Machinery, Soc. Indsl. and Applied Math. Home: Rockville, Md. Died June 30, 2008.

HODES, ROBERT BERNARD, lawyer; b. Bklyn., Aug. 25, 1925; s. James and Florence (Cohen) H.; m. Florence R. Rosenberg, Dec. 22, 1946 (div. Nov. 1984); 1 child, Paul; m. Cecilia Mendez, Dec. 18, 1984; children: James, Maria Paz. AB, Dartmouth Coll., 1946; LLB, Harvard U., 1949. Bar: N.Y. Supreme Ct. 1950, U.S. Dist. Ct. (so. dist.) N.Y. 1951, U.S. Tax Ct. 1955, U.S. Claims Ct. 1957, U.S. Ct. Appeals (2d cir.) 1959. Assoc. Willkie Farr & Gallagher, NYC, 1949-56, ptnr., 1956-95, co-chmn., 1982-95, counsel, 1995—2005. Active Nat. Philanthropic Trust. Home: New York, NY. Died Jan. 15, 2009.

HODGE, GAMEEL BYRON, retired surgeon; b. Spartanburg, SC, Sept. 16, 1917; s. Charles B. and Mary (Bargoot) Hodge; m. Katie Adams Hodge, Sept. 22, 1943; children: Susan, Byron, John Adams. BS, Wofford Coll., 1938, DSc (hon.), 2003; MD, Vanderbilt U., 1942; PhD in Pub. Svc. (hon.), U. SC, 1982. Diplomate Am. Bd. Surgery. With M.C. USAR, 1942—53; intern Duke U. Med. Sch. and Hosp., Durham, NC, 1942—43, asst. resident, 1943—47, chief resident surgeon, 1947—48; attending surgeon Spartanburg Gen. Hosp.; cons. surgeon St. Luke's Hosp., Tryon, NC, 1948—58, Cherokee County Meml. Hosp., SC, 1948—74; thoracic surgeon Spartanburg County Tb Hosp., 1948—69; chief surgery Mary Black Meml. Hosp., 1969—72; assoc. clin. prof. surgery Med. U. SC, Spartanburg, 1970—2003, ret., 2003. Author: Reflections on Building an Institution, 2006; contbr. articles to profl. jours. Trustee Spartanburg Day Sch., 1958—2009; chmn. Spartanburg County Commn. Higher Edn., 1967—2009. Recipient Disting. Svc. award, U. SC Ednl. Found., 1991. Fellow: Indsl. Medicine Assn., Am. Fedn. Clin. Rsch., Internat. Acad. Proctology, NY Acad. Sci., Am. Coll. Chest Physicians; mem.: AMA, Spartanburg Area C. of C. (past pres., Neville Holcombe Disting. Svc. award 1988), Duke U. Med. Alumni Assn. (past pres.), Deryl Hart Surg. Soc., Am. Geriat. Soc., Spartanburg Med. Soc., SC Vascular Surg. Soc., SC Surg. Soc., SC Med. Assn., Am. Heart Assn., Carolina Country Club, Piedmont Club, Kiwanis (Citizenship of Yr. award 1969), Phi Beta Pi, Phi Beta Kappa, Order of Palmetto, Omicron Delta Kappa. Episcopalian. Home: Spartanburg, SC. Died Feb. 23, 2009.

HODGES, EDWIN CLAIR, company executive; b. Montgomery, Kans., July 9, 1940; s. Charles E. and Mary R. (Marvel) H.; m. Rebecca Carlisle; children: Mark E., Elaine L., Kelly M., Cheri E. Greer, William H. Edelen III. BA, U. Kans., 1964. Commd. 2nd lt. U.S. Army, 1964, advanced through grades to maj., 1974; with Adv. Team 33, Republic Vietnam, 1968; ret. U.S. Army, 1985; founder Q-Sys. Internat., Inc. (formerly Genesis Con., Ltd. Inc.), Arlington, Tex., 1985-88, pres., chmn. bd., CEO, from 1988. Chief force devel., test and evaluation, U.S. Army, Ft. Knox, Ky., 1974, chief operational test and evaluation, 1976, exec. office dir. chief Requirements team for Armored Gun System, 1980-83; security asst. officer, Ankara, Turkey, 1983-85. Contbr. articles and reports profl. jours. Mem. Masons (32), Knights of Malta. Republican. Died Nov. 1, 2007.

HODGSON, JOHN FREDERICK, II, information systems specialist, photographer; b. Chgo., Sept. 22, 1917; s. John Frederick Hodgson and Lucille Amelia (Blanchard) Horn; m. Connie (Macias) Davis, May 30, 1979 (div. Apr., 1984). AB, U. Chgo., 1956. Computer programmer Northrup Corp., Hawthorne, Calif., 1966-68; systems programmer N. Am. Rockwell, Downey, Calif., 1968-69, Ctrl. Data Corp., LA, 1969-70, Fed. Elec. Co., Vandenburg, Calif., 1970-72, Informatics, LA, 1972-74; sr. systems analyst Blue Cross of Calif., Woodland Hills, Calif., 1974-84; photographic artist Escondido, Calif, from 1984. Systems programmer System Devel. Corp., Santa Monica, Calif., 1959-66. With USNR, 1941-45, Alaska. Mem. North County Artists Coop. (bd. dirs. 1993-94). Avocations: photography, tennis. Home: Escondido, Calif. Died Feb. 6, 2008.

HODSON, NANCY PERRY, real estate agent; b. Kansas City, Mo., Nov. 19, 1932; d. Ralph Edward Perry and Juanita (Youmans) Jackman; m. William K. Hodson, Oct. 4, 1974 (div. Jan. 1985); children: Frank Tyler, Lisa Thompson, Suzanne Desforges, Robert Hodson. Student, Pine Manor Jr. Coll., 1950-51, Finch Coll., 1951-53. Cert. real estate agt., Calif.; cert. interior designer. Owner Nancy Perry Hodson Interior Design, L.A. and Newport Beach, Calif., 1974-82; agt. Grubb and Ellis, Newport Beach, 1990, Turner Assocs., Laguna Beach, Calif., 1990-92. Founder U. of Calif. Arboretum, Irvine, 1987, Opera Pacific, Costa Mesa, Calif., 1987; mem. U. of Calif. Rsch. Assocs., Irvine, 1986; pres. Big Canyon Philharm., Newport Beach, 1990; bd. dirs. Jr. Philharm., L.A., 1975-78. Mem. Big Canyon Country Club, L.A. Blue Ribbon 400 (1975-78), Jr. League Garden Club (pres. 1990-91), Big Canyon Garden Club (pres. 1989-91), Inst. of Logopedics (chmn. 30th Anniversary 1965), Guilds of Performing Arts Ctr. Presbyterian. Avocations: art, music, gardening. Died June 6, 2008.

HOFFBERG, JUDITH ANN, editor, publisher, consultant; b. Hartford, Conn., May 19, 1934; d. George and Miriam (Goldenberg) Hoffberg. BA cum laude, UCLA, 1956, MA, 1960, MLS, 1964. Cataloger Johns Hopkins U., Bologna Ctr., Italy, 1964—65; intern Libr. Congress, Washington, 1965—67; fine art libr. U. Pa., Phila., 1967—69; bibliographer art lit. and langs. U. Calif., San Diego, 1969—71; brand art ctr. Glendale Pub. Libr., Calif., 1971—73; exec. sec. Art Librs. Soc., N.Mex., 1973—78; editor Umbrella, 1978—2009; pvt. practice Pasadena, Calif., 1978—2009. Grant, Italian Govt., 1960—61, Kress Found., Eng., 1972, Nat. Endowment Arts, 1979—80, Fulbright grant, NZ, 1984. Mem.: ALA, Internat. Assn. Art Critics (Am. sect.), Coll. Art Assn. (bd. dirs. 1975—79), Soc. Arch. Historians (dir. 1977—80), Art Libr. Soc. North America (life; chmn., exec. sec.). Died Jan. 16, 2009.

HOFFMAN, BORIS AARON, electrical engineer, writer; b. Kharkov, Ukraine, USSR, Dec. 5, 1925; came to U.S. 1977. s. Aaron Victor and Clara Zinovy H.; m. Inna Vasily, Sept. 6, 1972; 1 child, Marie Boris. Diploma, Moscow Elctronic Inst., 1954. Sr. engr. Moscow Elec. Corp., 1954-76; engr. Am. Sci. Engring, Cambridge, Mass., 1978-81; electro-mech. designer Merrimack Labs, Hudson, Mass., 1981-85, Allied Analytical, Waltham, Mass., 1985-86; technician CMC, Wellesley, Mass., 1987-90; RE agent Castle Unltd., Newton, Mass., 1991-92. Tennis tchr., writer, Waltham, 1987—. Author: (plays) In The Mountains, A Week In August, 1991, Dedicated to Margarita, 1997, (essay) The Genetic Code of the Poet Mandelshtam, 1996; contbr. articles to profl. jours. Mem. Jewish Liberation Movement, Moscow, 1968-74. Home: Wellesley, Mass. Died Nov. 8, 2007.

HOFFMAN, NELSON MILES, JR., retired academic administrator, consultant; b. Phila., June 10, 1920; s. Nelson Miles and Sara (Suiter) H.; m. Marjorie Anne Mendenhall, Dec. 3, 1942; children: Nelson III, Michael, Elizabeth, George, Joseph. BA, Asbury Coll., 1942; MA, U. Kans., 1947, PhD, 1964. Ednl. missionary Meth. Ch., India, 1947-57, pastor Williamsburg, Kans., 1958-60; prof. history Emory-at-Oxford, Ga., 1960-63; dean acad. affairs Fla. So. Coll., Lakeland, 1963-68; v.p. acad. affairs W.Va. Wesleyan Coll., Buckhannon, 1969-70; headmaster Pennington (N.J.) Sch., 1970-78; pres. Midway (Ky.) Coll., 1978-85; v.p. Capital Formation Counselors, Belleair Bluffs, Fla., from 1988. Chmn. edn. com. N.J. Meth. Conf., Pennington, 1972-78; pres. Ky. Ind. Coll. Assn., Midway, 1982-84. Author: American Indian Policy of the Continental Congress, 1947, Godfrey Barnsley, 1805-1873, British Cotton Factor in the South, 1964. Lt. USN, 1942-46, ETO. Recipient Alumni "A" award Asbury Coll., Wilmore, Ky., 1992. Mem. Lions Club, Kiwanis, Rotary. Republican. Methodist. Avocations: sports, stamp collecting/philately, photography, gardening. Home: Versailles, Ky. Died Aug. 1, 2008.

HOFFMAN, PHILIP GUTHRIE, retired academic administrator; b. Kobe, Japan, Aug. 6, 1915; s. Benjamin Philip and Florence (Guthrie) H. (Am. citizens); m. Mary Elizabeth Harding, Aug. 31, 1939; children: Philip Guthrie (dec. 1987), Mary Victoria Hoffman Cobb, Ruth Ann Hoffman Cabler, Jeanne Hoffman Camp. Student, George Washington U., 1936-37; AB, Pacific Union Coll., 1938; MA, U. So. Calif., 1942; PhD, Ohio State U., 1948; H.H.D. (hon.), Jacksonville U.; LL.D. (hon.), U. Americas, U. Akron; L.H.D. (hon.), Pikeville Coll., Marshall U., U. Houston, 1987; D.L. (hon.), Kyung Hee U., Korea; D.H.C. (hon.), Autonomous U., Guadalajara (Mex.); Litt.D. (hon.), U. St. Thomas, 1979. Credit mgr. Harding Sanitarium, Worthington, Ohio, 1938-40, instr. history Ohio State U. Columbus, 1946-49; asst. prof. history U. Ala., Tuscaloosa, 1949-51, assoc. prof., 1951-53, dir. arts and scis. extension services, 1949-53; dean, assoc. prof. history gen. extension div. Oreg. System Higher Edn., Portland, 1953-55; prof. history Portland State Coll., Oreg., 1955-57, dean faculty Oreg., 1955-57; v.p., dean faculties, prof. history U. Houston, 1957-61, pres., 1961-79, pres. emeritus, 1979—2008. Cons. Mitchell Energy and Devel. Corp., Houston, 1980-81; pres. Tex. Med. Ctr. Inc., Houston, 1981-85; dir. Fed. Res. Bank Dallas Mem. Nat. Commn. on Accrediting; mem. Am. Council on Edn., Coll. Entrance Exam. Bd. Lt. (j.g.) USNR, 1943-45. Recipient Centennial Achievement award Ohio State U., 1970, Merit award U. So. Calif., 1975. Mem. Tex. Hist. Assn., Gulf Hist. Assn., Am. Hist. Assn., Assn. Tex. Coll. and Univs. (pres.), Assn. Urban Univs. (pres. 1965-66), Nat. Assn. State Univs. and Land-Grant Colls. (dir. 1971-75), So. Univ. Conf. (pres. 1976-77), Phi Kappa Phi, Phi Alpha Theta (nat. pres. 1952-54), Omicron Delta Kappa Clubs: Petroleum (Houston), Torch (Houston); Houston; River Oaks (Houston). Lodges: Rotary. Home: Houston, Tex. Died Oct. 29, 2008.

HOFFMAN, WALTER WILLIAM, retired investment company executive; b. Oxnard, Calif., Aug. 17, 1922; s. Walter Henry Jr. and Edith May (Hobson) H.; m. Sheila Louise Bergin, Oct. 25, 1945 (dec. 2006); children: Katherine Hoffman Russell, Carol Hoffman Hambleton. Student, U. So. Calif., 1941-44. Asst. mgr. Casitas Ranch Co., Ventura, Calif., 1946-55, mgr., 1955—98; ptnr. Hoffman, Vance and Worthington, Ventura, 1956—98. Bd. dirs. Bank of A. Levy, Oxnard, Automobile Club of So. Calif., Los Angeles, Ventura County Lemon Coop., St. John's Sem. Coll., Camarillo, Calif. Trustee Livingston Meml. Found., Oxnard; bd. dirs. Ventura County Taxpayers Assn.; Served to lt. USNR, 1941-46, PTO. Decorated Knight Comdr. Order of St. Gregory, Pope John XXIII, Rome, 1960. Mem. Am. Soc. Farm Mgrs. and Rural Appraisers, Am. Right of Way Assn. (sr. mem.), U.S. Naval Acad. (Fales com.). Clubs: Calif. (Los Angeles); Newport Harbor Yacht; Cruising Am. (N.Y.C.) (dir. 1980-84), Transpacific Yacht (dir. 1976-84); St. Francis Yacht (San Francisco); Ventura Yacht. Republican. Roman Catholic. Avocations: flying, amateur radio. Home: Camarillo, Calif. Died Nov. 13, 2008.

HOFFMAN, WILLIAM LARSEN, political scientist; b. Texarkana, Ark., Aug. 4, 1945; s. Dalton Paul and Ruth Elise (Larsen) H. BA, U. Tex., 1967; MDiv, Duke U., 1971. Fellow Office of U.S. Senator Mike Gravel, Washington, 1970-71, legis. aide, 1971-73, legis. asst., 1973-75, legis. dir., 1975-78, chief of staff, 1978-81; founder, prin. Gryphon Internat., Washington, from 1981. Died July 29, 2008.

HOFMAN, ELIZABETH ELVERETTA, retired mathematics educator, guidance counselor, dean; b. South Bend, Ind., Feb. 27, 1917; d. Curtis Hamilton and Ossie Marie (Meissner) Vernon; m. Raphael B. Hofman, June 10, 1942 (dec.). Diploma, Mich. County Normal Tng. Sch., Alpena, 1936—37; attended, Huntington Coll., Ind., 1941—42; BS, Western Res. U., Cleve., 1947, MA in Edn., 1948. Cert. HS math. tchr. Western Res. U., 1947, in pupil personnel svcs. Western Res. U., 1964. Tchr. grades K-8 Alpena County Schs., 1937—41; math. tchr. grades 4-8 Warrensville Heights Jr. HS, Ohio, 1945—63, math. tchr. jr. and sr. HS, advisor math., 1963—72, part time guidance counselor, 1960—64, 1963—72, tchr. math. grades 11 and 12, 1960—64, dean of girls, 1968—72, ret., 1972. Mem.: NEA, Ohio Ret. Tchrs. Assn., Nat. Ret. Tchrs. Assn. Home: Muskegon, Mich. Deceased.

HOHL, MARY CABRINI, chemistry educator; b. NY, July 4, 1923; d. George Charles and Letitia Josephine (Huttinger) H. BA, Marygrove Coll., 1945; MS, U. Detroit, 1958; PhD, Wayne State U., 1965. Tchr. St. Mary Acad., Monroe, Mich., 1950-58; prof., chair chemistry dept. Marygrove Coll., Detroit, 1959-73; prof. chemistry Madonna Coll., Livonia, Mich., 1973-85. Cons. IHM Congregation, Monroe, Mich., computer programming and use. Designer Semimicro Chem. Lab. Kit. Recipient Sci. Tchr. award NSF. Mem. Am. Chem. Soc. Roman Catholic. Home: Monroe, Mich. Died Sept. 22, 2007.

HOLLAND, ROBERT THURL, university dean, educator; b. Parkersburg, W.Va., Oct. 30, 1923; s. Thurl Otto and Alma Pearl (Boice) H.; m. Lois Jane Paloski. BSBA, Marietta Coll., 1948; MA in Econs., W.Va. U., 1952; PhD in Econs., U. So. Calif., 1963; DCS, London Inst. Econ. Rsch., 1978; EdD, Pacific So. U., 1987. Comml. rep. Gen. Telephone of Calif., Downey, 1954-55, valuation engr. Santa Monica, 1955-62; instr. U. So. Calif. and Occidental Coll., LA, 1962-63; burden budget analyst N.Am. Rockwell, Downey, 1963-67; chief economist Ralph M. Parsons Corp., LA, 1967-70; instr. Inst. Aerospace Safety and Mgmt. U. So. Calif., LA, 1970-72; prof. econs. Woodbury U., LA, 1972-89, prof. emeritus, from 1979; dean bus. adminstrn. Newport U., Newport Beach, Calif., from 1983. Vol. L.A. Pub. Libr., 1990—. Mem. Mensa, Order of Artus, Alpha Sigma Lambda, Alpha Kappa Psi, Omicron Delta Epsilon. Republican. Baptist. Avocation: photography. Died Jan. 17, 2008.

HOLLEB, MARSHALL MAYNARD, lawyer; b. Chgo., Dec. 25, 1916; s. A. Paul and Sara (Zaretsky) H.; m. Doris Bernstein, Oct. 15, 1944; children: Alan R., Gordon P., Paul D. BA, U. Wis., 1937; MBA, Harvard U., 1939; IA, 1941, JD, 1942. Bar: Ill. 1947, U.S. Supreme Ct. 1960. Assoc. Levenson, Becker & Peebles, Chgo., 1947-51; ptnr. Yates & Holleb, Chgo., 1952-59, Holleb, Gerstein & Glass, Chgo., 1960-81; sr. ptnr. Holleb & Coff, Chgo., 1982-2000; sr. counsel Wildman, Harrold, Allen & Dixon, 2000—07. Chmn. bd. dirs. Urban Assocs. Chgo., Inc. Contbr. articles to profl. jours.; profiled on PBS-TV program Chicago Stories, 2001. Trustee Acorn Fund, 1971-95; life trustee Hull House Assn., pres., 1980-82; trustee emeritus nat. Bldg. Mus., Chgo. Inst. Psychoanalysis; overseer Harvard Bus. Sch. Club Chgo.; founder, life trustee, gen. legal counsel Mus. Contemporary Art Chgo.; mem. adv. bd. Landmarks Preservation Coun., Fair Housing Ctr. Home Investments Fund, Citizens Sch. Com.; mem. vis. coms. Oriental Inst. and Visual Arts U. Chgo.; bd. dirs. Intenat.

Visitors Ctr., Mostly Music, Inc., Chgo. Fund. on Aging and Disability; mem. Ill. Internat. Trade and Port Promotion Adv. Com., 1982, Chgo.'s Future Project Com. of Trust, Inc., 1982, Pacific Basing Inst.; mem. nat. adv. bd. on internat. edn. programs U.S. Dept. Edn., 1981, City Chgo. Local Cultural Devel. Commn.; Mayor Daley's prin. for a day Chgo. Public Schs.; pres. Chgo. Theater Preservation Group Ltd., sec., bd. dirs. Arts Club Chgo.; bd. dirs. Chgo. Maritime Soc.; me. industry sector adv. com. on svcs. for trade policy matters U.S. Dept. Commerce, 1995-98; mem. nat. adv. com. and del. White House Conf. on Aging, 1971, 81; mem. Ill. Coun. Aging, 1961-81, chmn., 1973-81; panel mem. Ill. Statewide Comprehensive Outdoor Recreation Plan; mem. weatherization adv. com. Ill. Dept. Bus. and Econ. Devel., 1975—; mem. Ill. appeal bd. SSS, 1966-73; cons. Vt. rsch. project HUD. 1st lt. U.S. Army, Philippines and Japan, 1943-46. Recipient Humanitarian of Yr. Henry Booth House award Hull House Assn., 1979; Am. Heritage award Am. Jewish Com., 1986, Arts award Mostly Music Inc., 1986, City Brightener award Bright New City Chgo., 1987, Holleb Cmty. Svc. award, Lambda Alpha Internat., 2004. Mem. ABA, Ill. Bar Assn., Chgo. Bar Assn., Fed. Bar Assn., Am. Soc. Internat. Law, Am. Arbitration Assn. (nat. panel), Am. Inst. Planners, Nat. Assn. Housign and Redevel. Ofcls., Urban Land Inst., Harvard Law Soc. Ill. (bd. dirs.), Arts Club, Univ. Club, Bryn Mawr Country Club, Execs. Club (Chgo.), Lambda Alpha. Democrat. Home: Chicago, Ill. Died Dec. 7, 2008.

HOLLERAN, SHEILA, development officer; b. Irvington, NJ, May 1, 1939; d. Thomas Jerome and Loretta Dorothea (Griffin) Holleran. BA, Dunbarton Coll. Holy Cross, Washington, 1961; MA, Jersey City State Coll., 1969. Joined Sisters of Charity of St. Elizabeth, 1961; cert. sch. adminstr., N.J. Tchr. Sisters of Charity of St. Elizabeth, Convent Station, N.J., 1963-68, Ridgewood, N.J., 1968-70, elem. sch. prin. Tenafly, N.J., 1970-78, Montclair, N.J., 1978-86, grant dir. for aged Convent Station, N.J., from 1986, spl. events dir. for maj. fund raisers, from 1986, dir. direct mail program, from 1990. Mem. Nat. Cath. Devel. Conf., N.J. Soc. Fund Raising Execs. Avocations: writing, reading. Home: Morristown, NJ. Died June 7, 2007.

HOLLICH, STEPHEN EUGENE, aerospace engineer; b. NYC, July 11, 1932; s. Steve and Carrie (Bartoli) H.; m. Gail Litt, Oct. 24, 1953 (div. Apr. 1978); children: Stephen III, Paul John, Cara Ann; m. Stacey Lea Hollich, Sept. 7, 1984; children: Kitrik Lee, Kaitlin Carrie, Stephanie Jana. Diploma in Electronics, RCA Insts., NYC, 1952; BS in Elec. Engring., Ind. Inst. Tech., 1957; MBA, Ala. A&M U., 1974; D in Mgmt., Southeastern Inst. Tech., 1992. Supr. dragon and tow prodn. acceptance testing New Tech. Inc., Huntsville, Ala., 1974-75; dean edn. Alverson-Draughton, Huntsville, 1975-76; rsch. asst., cons. Northrup Svcs. Inc., Huntsville, 1976-78; proposal and systems cons. Mgmt. Svcs. Inc., Huntsville, 1978-80; sr. project engr. Titan systems SCI Systems Inc., Huntsville, 1980-81; aerospace engr., sr. system safety office George C. Marshall Space Flight Ctr., Huntsville, 1981-85, aerospace engr. sr. space sta. safety, 1985-88, aerospace engr. sr. tech. test group, 1988, aerospace engr. sr. materials control office, 1988-90, chief contamination control lab., from 1990. Chmn. stewardship and fin. Epworth Meth. Ch., Orlando, Fla., 1961, 62. With U.S. Army, 1953-54, Korea. Assoc. fellow AIAA (dir. pub. policy com. 1989-90, vice-chmn., program chmn. 1990-91, chmn. 1991-92, tech. com. on safety and system effectiveness 1990—, pub. policy award internat. 1990); mem. Huntsville Area Tech. Socs. (forum chmn., membership chmn.) Avocations: hiking, camping, hunting, music, travel. Home: Huntsville, Ala. Died July 12, 2008.

HOLLIS, MARY DEAN, business officer; b. Chalybeate, Miss., May 10, 1928; d. Diaz Taylor and Amy Earl (Jones) H. BA, Blue Mountain Coll., 1950. Sec. to pres. Blue Mountain (Miss.) Coll., 1950-63; sec. to edn. dir. First Bapt. Ch., Memphis, 1963-64; sec. to dean Sch. Basic Med. Scis. and Grad. Sch. U. Tenn., Memphis, 1964-65; with bus. office Blue Mountain Coll., from 1965, dir. bus. and fin. office, from 1977. Mem. AAUW, So. Assn. Coll. and Univ. Bus. Officers, Blue Mountain Coll. Nat. Alumnae Assn. (exec. bd. dirs. 1964-66, 71—, officer local alumnae club 1950—), Federated Women's Club. Baptist. Avocations: gardening, reading, sewing. Home: Walnut, Miss. Died Feb. 28, 2008.

HOLLIS, WILLIAM LEMUEL, olericulture food scientist, consultant; b. Richmond Hills, NY, May 26, 1921; s. Joseph Lemuel and Margaret (Seegar) H.; m. Barbara Thayer, Feb. 27, 1993. BS in Agrl. Edn., U. Del., 1953; PhD, U. Md., 1957. Assoc. prof. U. Md., College Park, 1957-66; assoc. dir. agr. div. Nat. Canners Assn., Washington, 1966-71; dir. sci. affairs Nat. Agr. Chem. Assn., Washington, 1975-85, dir. internat. affairs, 1985-87; agronomist Pesticide Assessment Lab., Agrl. Rsch. Svc., USDA, Beltsville, Md., from 1989, mem. nat. task force on faculty devel., 1983-87. Mem. adv. bd. Rutgers U. R & D Ctr., New Brunswick, N.J., 1967-71; mem. exec. bd. Agrl. Rsch. Inst., NAS, Washington, 1975-77, 81-83; numerous presentations on food crop prodn., 1967-87; chmn. tech. sales seminars on agrl. chemistry U.S. Dept. Commerce, Ea. Europe, 1975, 77, 79, 81. Contbr. numerous articles to profl. jours. Bd. dirs. U.S. Com. for UN Environment Program, Washington, 1985—, Friends Agrl. Rsch.-Beltsville, 1989—. Capt. USMCR, 1942-47, PTO, lt. col. Res. ret. Mem. AAAS, Am. Soc. Hort. Sci., Weed Sci. Soc. Am., VFW, Sigma Xi, Phi Kappa Phi, Alpha Zeta. Republican. Methodist. Home: Beltsville, Md. Died Oct. 3, 2007.

HOLLOWAY, DONALD PHILLIP, lawyer; b. Akron, Ohio, Feb. 18, 1928; s. Harold Shane and Dorothy Gayle (Ryder) Holloway. BS in Commerce, Ohio U., Athens, 1950; JD, U. Akron, 1955; MA, Kent State U., 1962. Bar: Ohio 1955. Title examiner Bankers Guarantee Title & Trust Co., Akron, 1950-54; acct. Robinson Clay Product Co., Akron, 1955-60; libr. Akron-Summit Pub. Libr., 1962-69, head fine arts and music divsn., 1969-71, sr. libr., 1972-82; pvt. practice Akron, from 1982. Payroll treas. Akron Symphony Orch., 1957-61; treas. Friends Libr. Akron and Summit County, 1970-72. Mem. ABA, ALA, Ohio Bar Assn., Akron Bar Assn., Ohio Libr. Assn., Nat. Trust Hist. Preservation, Music Libr. Assn., Soc. Archtl. Historians, Coll. Art Assn., Art Librs. N.Am. Republican. Episcopalian. Avocations: art, music, travel, architecture. Home: Akron, Ohio. Deceased.

HOLLY, JUNE SIEGERT, fundraising executive; b. Houston, Nov. 27, 1920; d. Francis Harrison and Mabel Helen (Verlander) Siegert; m. Austin J. Holly, Nov., 1942 (div. 1971); children: Mary Melissa Holly Cadenhead, Douglas Rhodes, James Barbour. B.A., Rice U., 1942; M.A. in Sociology, U. Houston, 1974, D. Edn. (teaching fellow 1976-79), 1980. Dir. parish edn. St. Mark's Episcopal Ch., Houston, 1964-69; coordinator tng., vols. Houston Met. Ministries, 1969-71; acting exec. dir, 1971-72; cons. edn., bus., med., religious instns., 1972-77; exec. dir. Houston Ctr. Humanities, 1977-84; dir community relations Dexion Programs in Mental Health; dir. devel. Harris County Heritage Soc.; adj. instr. behavioral, social scis., spl. edn. U. Houston. Mem. Houston Mayor's Task Force Arts, 1982-83; mem. steering com., Leadership Houston, 1981-87, program chmn., 1981-84; bd. dirs. Nat. Assn. Community Leadership Orgns., 1983-85; chmn. adult edn. St. Mark's Episcopal Ch., Houston, 1982-83; trustee St. James Episcopal Sch., Houston, 1980-84; pres. Coalition Non-profit Orgns., 1984-85. Grantee Houston Ctr. Humanities, NEH, 1979-83, Tex. Com. for Ctr., 1977-84; mem. pub. relations com. Houston Archeol. Commn. Mem. Am. Anthropol. Assn. (sec. treas. council anthropology, edn. 1980-83), World Future Soc., Cultural Arts Council Houston, Consortium Urban Edn. Houston, Houston Mus. Fine Arts, Tex. Assn. Museums (program com.), Nat. Soc. Fundraising Execs. Clubs: Houston Jr. Forum (pres. 1947-48), Bradford Townhome Assn. (pres. 1983-84, bd. dirs.). Home: Houston, Tex. Died Oct. 5, 2009.

HOLMER, RONALD JOSEPH, insurance company executive; b. Edwardsville, Ill., Sept. 23, 1936; s. Sylvester and Mary (Clarke) H.; m. Carole Marti, Jan. 2, 1960; children: Catherine, David, Christine, Steve, Lauron. BS, St. Louis U., 1959. Pres. Mid Am. Ins. Co., Kansas City, Mo., 1963-78; v.p. Union Fidelity Life Ins. Co., Phila., 1978-83; pres. United Gen. Life Ins. Co., St. Petersburg, Fla., from 1983. Mem. Nat. Assn. Life Underwriters, Nat. Assn. Health Underwriters, St. Petersburg Assn. Life Underwriters (bd. dirs. 1986—), Gulfcoast Assn. Heatlh Underwriters (bd. dirs. 1985—). Clubs: Feather Sound Country. Avocations: golf, reading, travel. Home: Wayne, Pa. Died Jan. 19, 2008.

HOLMES, ANN HITCHCOCK, journalist; b. El Paso, Apr. 25, 1922; d. Frederick E. and Joy (Crutchfield) H. Student, Whitworth Coll., 1940, So. Coll. Fine Arts, 1944. With Houston Chronicle, from 1942, fine arts editor, 1948-89, critic-at-large, 1989-98. Author: Presence, The Transco Tower, 1985, Joy Unconfined—Robert Joy in Houston: A Portrait of Fifty Years, 1986, Alley Theater: Four Decades in Three Stages, 1986. Mem. Houston Mcpl. Art Commn., 1965-74; mem. fine arts adv. coun. U. Tex., Austin, 1967—; bd. dirs. Rice Design Alliance, Houston, 1988-91, Alliance Francaise, Houston, 1989-93, Bus. Arts Fund, Houston, 1993-96. Recipient Ogden Reid Found. award for study of arts in Europe, 1953; Guggenheim fellow, 1960-61; recipient Ford Found. award, 1965, John G. Flowers award archtl. writing Tex. Soc. Architects, 1972, 74, 77, 80 Mem.: Am. Theater Critics Assn. (founding mem. 1974, exec. com. from 1975, co-chmn. 1987—88). Deceased.

HOLMES, ODETTA, singer; b. Birmingham, Ala., Dec. 31, 1930; d. Reuben and Flora (Sanders) Holmes; m. Don Gordon (div. 1959); m. Gary Shead, 1960 (div.); m. Iversen Minter, 1977. Degree in Classical Music/Musical Comedy, L.A. City Coll. Singer Turnabout Theater, Hollywood, Calif. Singer: (albums) Odetta Live at Blue Angel, 1953, The Tin Angel, 1954, Odetta Sings Ballads and Blues, 1956, Live at Gate of Horn, 1957, My Eyes Have Seen, 1959, Ballad for Americans and Other American Ballads, 1960, Odetta at Carnegie Hall, 1960, Odetta Sings Christmas Spirituals, 1960, Odetta and The Blues, 1962, Sometimes I Feel Like Crying, 1962, Odetta at Town Hall, 1962, One Grain of Sand, 1963, Odetta Sings Folk Songs, 1963, It's A Mighty World, 1964, Odetta Sings of Many Things, 1964, Odetta Sings Dylan, 1965, Odetta in Japan, 1966, The Best of Odetta, 1967, Odetta Sings the Blues, 1968, Odetta Sings, 1970, The Essential Odetta, 1973, Odetta, Verve/Folkways, Odetta, Archive of Folk and Jazz, 1974, Odetta at the Best of Harlem, 1976, (ballets) Movin' It On, 1987, (albums) The Best of Odetta: Ballads and Blues, 1994, Christmas Special, 1998, Blues Everywhere I Go, 1999, The Best of the Vanguard Years, 1999, To Ella, 1998, Livin' with the Blues, 2000, Looking for a Home (Thanks to Leadbelly), 2001, Gonna Let it Shine, 2005; performer: (films) Sanctuary, 1961, (TV films) The Autobiography of Miss Jane Pittman, 1974, The Fire Next Time, 1993; actor: (TV appearances) Have Gun, Will Travel, 1961; appeared in (documentaries) The Ballad of Ramblin' Jack, 2000, No Direction Home: Bob Dylan, 2005. Recipient Sylvania Award for Excellence, 1959, Key to the City of Birmingham, Ala., 1965, Nat. Medal of Arts, Nat. Endowment for the Arts, 1999, Duke Ellington Fellowship Award, Yale U., Lifetime Achievement award, Internat. Folk Alliance. Died Dec. 2, 2008.

HOLMES, SUSAN ANNETTE, accounting professional; b. Cin., Feb. 18, 1957; d. Herman Joseph and Patricia Ruth (Foster) Tallarigo; m. David R. Holmes, July 2, 1988; stepchild, Chad Jeffrey. Office mgr. The Brace Shop, Inc., Cin., 1978-86; accounts receivable supr. Profl. Mgmt. Svc., Cin., from 1986. Voting mem. Updowntowners, Cin., 1991—. Mem. Cin. Hist. Soc., Cin. Art Mus., Cin. Natural History Mus., Cin. Zool. Soc. Roman Catholic. Avocations: memorabilia collecting, volunteer work, reading, photography. Home: Cincinnati, Ohio. Died Feb. 7, 2008.

HOLSINGER, VIRGINIA HARRIS, chemist; b. Washington, Mar. 13, 1936; d. Raymond Wilson and Elizabeth Blackstone (Riley) H. BS, Coll. of William and Mary, Williamsburg, Va., 1958; PhD, Ohio State U., 1980. Rsch. chemist Agrl. Rsch. Svc., Ea. Regional Rsch. Ctr., USDA, Washington, 1958-74; rsch. chemist Agrl. Rsch. Svc., ERRC, USDA, Wyndmoor, Pa., 1974—99. Contbg. author publs. in field; contbr. articles to profl. jours. Recipient Col. Rohland Isker award R&D Assocs., Inc., San Antonio, 1983, award Fed. Lab. Consortium, 1986, Women in Sci. & Engring. Lifetime Achievement award, 1997 Mem. Am. Chem. Soc. (Disting. Svc. award 1986), Inst. of Food Techs. (chmn. dairy sect. 1990-91), Internat. Dairy Fedn., Am. Dairy Sci. Assn., Am. Cheese Soc., others. Episcopalian. Avocations: singing, gardening. Home: Philadelphia, Pa. Died Sept. 4, 2009.

HOLT, MAURICE, aerospace engineer, consultant; b. Wildboarclough, Cheshire, England, May 16, 1918; came to U.S., 1956; s. Percy Grimshaw and Elizabeth (Higgins) H.; m. Eileen Campbell, June 20, 1942; children: Nicholas Campbell, Christopher, Valerie, Helen, Caroline. BS, U. Manchester, England, 1940, MS, 1944, PhD, 1948. Trainee Metro-Vick Electric Co., Manchester, England, 1940; aeronautical engr. Blackburn Aircraft Co., Brough, England, 1940-45; lectr. math. Derby Tech. Coll., England, 1945-46; asst. lectr. math. U. Liverpool, England, 1948-49; lectr. math. U. Sheffield, England, 1949-51; prin. sci. officer Min. Supply for Halsted, England, 1952-55; vis. lectr. math. Harvard U., Cambridge, Mass., 1955; assoc. prof. applied math. Brown U., Providence, 1956-60; prof. aeronautical sci. U. Calif., Berkeley, 1960-97, prof. grad. sch., 1997—2008. Cons. for NASA and other aerospace cos., 1956-98. Author: Numerical Method in Fluid Dynamics, 1977, 2000; contbr. articles to profl. jours. Fellow AIAA, ASME, Am. Phys. Soc. Home: Berkeley, Calif. Died Nov. 7, 2008.

HOLT, ROBERT BLAINE, lawyer; b. Ft. Wayne, Ind., Dec. 26, 1956; s. Robert Elijah and Rowena (Stewart) H. BA, U. Denver, 1979; JD, Temple U., 1982; postgrad., U. Denver, 1988. Bar: Tex. 1982, U.S. Dist. Ct. (no. dist.) Tex. 1982, U.S. Ct. Appeals (5th cir.) 1982, Colo. 1988, U.S. Dist. Ct. Colo., 1988, U.S. Ct. Appeals (10th cir.) 1988. Briefing atty. Tex. Ct. Criminal Appeals, Austin, 1982-83; sr. staff atty. 5th Supreme Jud. Ct. Appeals, Dallas, 1983-85; sole practice Dallas, 1985-88; assoc. Russell & Wright P.C., Gunnnison, Colo., from 1988. Teaching asst. U. Denver, 1988; lectr. on AIDS various schs. and orgns. Mem. Lambda Legal Def. Fund, N.Y.C.; dir. bd. of advs. Nat. Lawyers Guild AIDS Network, San Francisco, 1985—, AIDS Resource Ctr., Dallas, 1985—; mem. N.Y. AIDS Task Force. Mem. ABA, Tex. Bar Assn., Dallas Young Lawyers Assn., Am. Judicature Soc., Temple U. Alumni Assn., U. Denver Alumni Assn., Phi Alpha Delta, Alpha Kappa Delta. Lodges: Masons. Republican. Methodist. Died Dec. 16, 2007.

HOLZER, HANS, author, paranormal investigator; b. Vienna, Jan. 26, 1920; s. Leo and Marta (Stransky) H.; m. Catherine Countess Buxhoeveden, Sept. 29, 1962 (div. June 1986); children: Nadine, Alexandra. Student, U. Vienna, Columbia U.; Ph.D in Parapsychology, London Coll. Applied Sciences. Formerly prof. parapsychology N.Y. Inst. Tech.; pres. Aspera Ad Astra, Inc. (film prodn. co.), NYC; own radio program Sta. WMCA, 1974. Research dir. N.Y. Com. for Investigation Paranormal Occurrences; lectr. Writer-prodr. documentaries on psychic subjects; writer-prodr. In Search Of, NBC, 1976-77; author of 124 books, including Ghost Hunter, 1963, Ghosts I've Met, 1965, Yankee Ghosts, 1966, Beyond Medicine, 1973, The Great British Ghost Hunt, 1975, Murder in Amityville, 1979, Inside Witchcraft, 1980, Love Beyond the Grave, 1992, Hans Holzer's Travel Guide to Haunted Houses, 1998; (novels) The Amityville Curse, 1981, The Secret of Amityville, 1985; contbr. mags. and newspapers. Mem. AAAS, ASCAP, AFTRA, SAG, Writers Guild of Am., East Inc., N.Y. Acad. Scis., Archaeol. Inst. Am., N.Y. Hist. Soc. Died Apr. 26, 2009.

HOMAN, JAMES D., engineering systems administrator; b. Le Mars, Iowa, June 15, 1963; AS, Western Iowa Tech., Sioux City, 1989. Design engr. Gomaco Corp., Ida Grove, Iowa, 1989-91, project mgr., 1991-94, engring. systems administrator, from 1994. Vol. leader Boy Scouts Am., Ida Grove, 1992—. Avocation: woodworking. Died Apr. 28, 2008.

HOMANS, PETER, retired psychology and religious studies educator; b. NYC, June 24, 1930; s. Howard Parmalee and Dora (Parker) H.; m. Celia Ann Edwards, Feb., 1958; children: Jennifer, Patricia, Elizabeth. Lectr. Trinity Coll., U. Toronto, Ont., Can., 1962-64; asst. prof. Hartford (Conn.) Sem. Found., 1964-65; asst. prof. psychology and religious studies U. Chgo., 1965-68, assoc. prof., 1968-78, prof., 1978-97, prof. emeritus, 1997—2009, vis. prof., 1997—2009. Mem. tchg. faculty Chgo. Ctr. for Psychoanalysis. Author: Theology After Freud, 1970, Jung in Context, 1979, 2d edit., 1995 (translated into Italian and Japanese), The Ability to Mourn: Dissillusionment and the Social Origins of Psychoanalysis, 1989; editor: The Dialogue Between Theology and Psychology, 1968, Childhood and Selfhood: Essays on Erik Eriksons Psychology, 1978; editor, contbr.: Morning, Monuments, and the Experience of Loss: Essays on Coming to Terms with the Past at Century's End, 1999. Soc. for Values in Higher Edn. grantee, 1973-74, Am. Theol. Soc. grantee 1978, Nat. Inst. Humanities summer seminar grantee, 1982, rsch. and travel grantee Am. Coun. Learned Socs., 1983. Mem. APA, Am. Acad. Religion, Am. Hist. Assn., Am. Acad. Psychoanalysis (sci. assoc.). Home: Chicago, Ill. Died May 30, 2009.

HOOPINGARNER, DOYLE ANSON, physician; b. Jackson, Mich., May 9, 1930; s. George Anson and Ethyl DeEtta (Harley) H.; m. Ruth Ann Bennett, Mar. 9, 1985; children: Lisa, Kirk, Polly, Pamella, Deanna, Darci, Seth. BS, Albion Coll., 1952; DO, Chgo. Coll. Osteopathic Med., 1956. Intern Met. Hosp., Grand Rapids, Mich., 1956-57; pvt. practice Belding, Mich., 1957-59, Ironwood, Mich., 1959-75; emergency medicine Met. Hosp., Grand Rapids, Mich., 1975-89; family practice Georgetown Med. Clinic, Jenison, Mich., from 1989; retired, 1995. Athletic team physician Ironwood (Mich.) High Sch., 1959-75; ski patrol physician Gogeric Ski Patrol, Ironwood, 1965-75. Assoc. pastor Meth. Ch., West Mich. Conf., 1978-80; youth leader, lay leader, tchr., choir dir. Ironwood (Mich.) Meth. Ch., 1960-75; bd. dirs. Ironwood C. of C., 1963-72, pres. 1967; bd. dirs. Youth for Christ, Ironwood, 1970-73; county chmn. Easter Seal, Ironwood; choir dir. Rockford (Mich.) Reform Ch., 1971-74, Kent City (Mich.) Meth. Ch., 1971-74; orch. dir. Fairhaven Reform Ch., Jenison, 1989-90; mem. Barbershop Chorus, Ironwood, 1959-75, dir. 1962-70; dir. Sweet Adelines, and others. Mem. Grandville Rotary (pres. 1991), Rotary Club (Ironwood pres. 1967), Rockford Rotary Club (past pres.), Rotary Internat. Dist. 6290 (dist. gov. 1994-95, permanent fund chmn., meritorious svc. award 1997), Great Lakes Barbershop Chorus. Republican. Avocations: fishing, gardening, travel, tennis, windsurfing. Home: Jenison, Mich. Died July 5, 2008.

HOPE, AMMIE DELORIS, computer programmer, systems analyst; b. Washington, Nov. 28, 1946; d. Amos Alexander and Amanda Irene (Moore) H. BA cum laude, Howard U., 1976; postgrad., Am. U., 1976-84. Police officer Met. Police Dept., Washington, 1972-73, officer, 1972; tchr. St. Benedict the Moor Cath. Sch., Washington, 1979; adminstrv. asst. Coun. of D.C., Washington, 1979-81; computer programmer, systems analyst IRS, Washington, 1984-96, comm. specialist, from 1996. Honoree Civic Assn.; Trustees scholar; Pub. Svc. fellow. Mem. Alpha Kappa Delta Honor Soc. Achievements include research on administration of justice, computer applications and systems development. Home: Arlington, Va. Died Sept. 21, 2007.

HOPKINS, HENRY TYLER, museum director, art educator; b. Idaho Falls, Idaho, Aug. 14, 1928; s. Talcott Thompson and Zoe (Erbe) Hopkins; children: Victoria Anne, John Thomas, Christopher Tyler. BA, Sch. of Art Inst., Chgo., 1952, MA, 1955; postgrad., UCLA, 1957—60; PhD (hon.), Calif. Coll. Arts and Crafts, 1984, San Francisco Art Inst., 1986. Curator exhbns., publs. LA County Mus. of Art, 1960-68; lectr. art history UCLA Ext., 1960—68; dir. Ft. Worth Art Mus., 1968-74, San Francisco Mus. of Modern Art, 1974-86; chmn. art dept. UCLA, 1991-94, dir. F.S. Wight Gallery, 1991-95, dir. Armand Hammer Mus. Art and Cultural Ctr., 1994-99, prof. art, 1999—2002, prof. emeritus, 2002—09. Instr. Tex. Christian U., Ft. Worth, 1968—74; dir. U.S. representation Venice Bienniel, Italy, 1970; dir. art presentation Festival of Two Worlds, Spoleto, Italy, 1970; co-commr. U.S. representation XVI Sao Paulo Biennale, Brazil, 1981; cons. NEA, mem. mus. panel, 1979—84, chmn., 1981; cons., mem. mus. panel NEH, 1976; archivist pers. archives Getty Rsch. Ctr., LA, 2005. Contbr. numerous articles to profl. jours. and mus. publs. With AUS, 1952—54. Decorated knight Order Leopold II, Belgium; recipient Spl. Internat. award, Art LA, 1992. Mem.: We. Assn. Art Museums (pres. 1977—78), Am. Assn. Museums, Coll. Art Assn., Assn. Art Mus. Dirs. (pres. 1985—86). Died Sept. 27, 2009.

HOPKINS, HOMER THAWLEY, chemist, researcher, retired chemist; b. Frederica, Del., July 27, 1913; s. Homer Thawley and Lillian Alexander Hopkins, Sr.; m. Victoria Lafferty, Oct. 26, 1940; 1 child, Rebecca. BS, U. Del., 1935; MS, Cornell U., 1939; PhD, U. Md., 1951. Asst. state chemist Bd. Agr., Dover, Del., 1935—37; soil scientist USDA, Washington, 1939—41, Beltsville, Md., 1941—52; chemist FDA, Washington, 1952—76; food scientist NAS, Washington, 1976—77; ret., 1977. Cons. in field; organizer, oper. office fgn. affairs Inst. Applied Agr., U. Md., 1977—82. Contbr. articles to profl. jours. Lt. USN, 1939—42. Republican. Methodist. Avocations: fishing, gardening, reading. Home: Sandy Hook, Conn. Died Aug. 18, 2008.

HOPKINS, SAMUEL, retired investment banker; b. Highland, Md., Oct. 18, 1913; s. Samuel Harold and Roberta (Smith) H.; m. Winifred Holt Bloodgood, Oct. 15, 1938 (dec. Oct. 1954); children: Samuel, Henry; m. Anne E. Dankmeyer, Oct. 20, 1955; children: Robert, Frederick. BS, Johns Hopkins U., 1934; LL.B., U. Md., 1938. With Fidelity & Deposit Co. of Md., 1934-69, asst. to treas., 1934-50, asst. treas., 1950-54, sec., 1954-67, v.p., sec., dir., 1967-69; dir., mem. trust com. Equitable Trust Co., Balt., 1954-81; sec., dir. Md. Life Ins. Co., 1963-69; gen. partner Alex, Brown & Sons (investment bankers), Balt., 1970-75, ltd. partner, 1976-87. Bd. dirs. Am. Maritime Cases, Inc. Mem. adv. com. housing for elderly U.S. Housing and Fin. Agy., 1956-60; mem. Balt. Bd. Recreation and Parks, 1965-77, pres., 1965-67, 74-77, v.p., 1968-74; Rep. candidate for Congress, 1952; mem. Md. Ho. of Dels., 1950-54; Rep. candidate for mayor, Balt., 1955; del. Rep. Nat. Conv., 1976; trustee Balt. Mus. Art, Peale Mus., Sheppard and Enoch Pratt Hosp., 1972-89; trustee, v.p. State Colls. Md., 1963-70; mem. Balt. City Planning Commn., 1985-95. Lt. USNR, 1942-45. Mem.: ABA, Chartered Security Analysts, Balt. Security Analysts Soc., Md. Hist. Soc. (treas. 1956—69, pres. 1970—75, chmn. bd. trustees 1988—90). Episcopalian. Home: Baltimore, Md. Died Nov. 5, 2008.

HORINE, MERRILL CACERES, retired food company executive; b. S.I., NY, Apr. 29, 1925; s. Merrill Castleberry and Grace (Caceres) H.; m. Grace Moerlius, 1948; 1 child, Richard Merrill. BS, Wagner Coll., 1949; postgrad. in personnel adminstrn., NYU, 1951-55. Asst. mgr. adminstrn., plans and compensation div. Exxon Co.-USA, NYC, 1948-62; pension and ins. supr. Ford Instrument Co. div. Sperry Rand Corp., NYC, 1962-66; mgr. employee benefits Amerada Hess Corp., NYC, 1966-77; dir. benefit planning and med. cost mgmt. Hershey (Pa.) Foods Corp., 1979-90; sec.-treas. ValuCare, Inc., New Cumberland, Pa., from 1991. Chmn. corp. bd. Internat. Found. Employee Benefits, 1987-88; lay mem. Pa. Blue Shield, 1987—; vice chmn. Pa. Statewide Health Coord. Coun. Mem. editorial adv. bd. Pension World, 1982-90. Dist. rep. S.I. Rep. Com., 1958-62; pres. Gt. Kills Little League, S.I., 1962-64; bd. dirs., exec. com. Health Care Alliance, Harrisburg, Pa., 1984-90. With inf. AUS, 1943-45, ETO. Mem. Council on Employee Benefits, NAM (employee benefits com.). Clubs: Hershey Country. Republican. Avocations: golf, chess, walking, opera, ballet. Home: Lancaster, Pa. Died May 12, 2008.

HORWIN, GARY STEVEN, chiropractor, accountant; b. Jersey City, Apr. 26, 1951; s. Lawrence James Horwin and Marguerite Ann (Adnerson) Bell. BS in Acctg., Fairleigh Dickinson U., 1973; D of Chiropractic, Sherman Coll., 1978. Diplomate of Nat. Bd. of Chiropractic, Colo. Asst. comptroller Vikoa Industries, NYC, 1973-75; owner Horwin Family Chiropractic Ctr., Lansdale, Pa., from 1979. Tchr. Pa. Coll. of Straight Chiropractic, Levittown, Pa., 1982-86, 92-96. Bd. regents Sherman Coll., 1981—. Recipient Disting. Alumni award Sherman Coll., 1983, Disting. Service award, 1985. Mem. Chiropractic Fellowship of Pa. (treas. 1981-85, pres. 1999—), Fedn. of Straight Chiropractic Orgns. (bd. dirs. 1983-87, treas. 1998—), Acad. of Straight Chiropractic (treas. 1980—), Sherman Coll. Alumni Assn. (bd. regents 1981—), Am. Acad. of Clin. Applied Spinal Biomechanical Engring. Republican. Home: Hatfield, Pa. Died Oct. 31, 2006.

HOSANG, ROBERT MICHAEL, research scientist; s. Bernard Otto Hosang and Patricia Anne Hawco. Student, Boston State Coll., 1970—73. Ind. rschr., from 1973. Author: The Relationship Between Matter and Energy, 1999, Gravity, 2001, The Frequency of Gravity, 2003, The Full Cycle, 2003, Beyond the Light Cycle, 2003. Mem.: Broadcast Music Inc. Died July 16, 2008.

HOSKINS, CHARLES ROY, III, numismatist; b. Athens, Ohio, Oct. 18, 1936; s. Charles Roy and Virginia Eubank (Segar) Hoskins; m. Sylvia Louise Harvey, 1961 (div. 1981); children: Christine, Bradford Hunter; m. Ann Joan Tiskus, May 7, 1983; 1 child, Anthony Roy. BFA, Ohio U., 1958. Account exec. Sta. WTAP-TV, Parkersburg, W.Va., 1960-61; asst. dir. Nat. Bank Detroit Money Mus., 1961-66, dir., 1966-70; pub. info. officer, head numismatic svcs. divsn. U.S. Mint, Phila., 1970-72; dir. Am. Numismatic Assn. Certification Svc., Washington, 1972-76, Internat. Numismatic Soc. Authentcation Bur., Aston, Pa., 1976-96. Cons. Dir. Mint, Washington, 1967-69. Author: The Story of the Dollar, 1970. V.p. Friends Free Libr., Phila., 1994-95; pres. Detroit Coin Club, 1969; chmn. bd. Grosse Pointe (Mich.) Numismatic Soc., 1970. Fellow Am. Numismatic Assn. (Merit medal 1967). Presbyterian. Avocations: chess, computers, gardening. Home: Lynchburg, Va. Died Mar. 21, 2008.

HOSKINS, JOHN HOWARD, retired urologist, educator; b. Breckenridge, Minn., Mar. 18, 1934; s. James H. and Ruth (Johanson) H.; m. Nancy Weih, Aug. 3, 1957; children: William, James, Laura, Sara. BA in History, U. Iowa, 1956; BS in Medicine, U. S.D., 1959; MD, Temple U., 1961. Diplomate Am. Bd. Urology. Practice medicine specializing in urology, Sioux Falls, SD, 1966-96; head sect. urology U. S.D. Sch. Medicine, Vermillion, 1977-93; ret., 1997. Maj. M.C. U.S. Army, 1967-69, Vietnam. Fellow: ACS; mem.: Am. Urol. Assn., Augustana Fellows, Rotary, Shriners, Masons. Republican. Methodist. Deceased.

HOUCK, LAURIE GERALD, agricultural researcher; b. Tucson, Aug. 13, 1928; s. Gerald Wesley and Laura Lee (Baker) H.; m. Marlene Moore, Sept. 20, 1958 (dec. Apr. 1970); children: Lorna Jeanne, Marlys Lee; m. Margaret Victoria Evers, July 28, 1978. BS, U. Ariz., 1952, MS, 1954; PhD, Oreg. State U., 1962. Research plant physiologist USDA, Phoenix, 1954-56, research plant pathologist Pomona, Calif., 1962-73, Riverside, Calif., 1973-77, Fresno, from 1977; asst. horticulturist U. Ariz., Mesa, 1956-58; research asst. Oreg. State U., Corvallis, 1958-62. Lectr. Calif. State Poly. U., Pomona, 1963, 64, 66. Contbr. numerous articles to profl. jours. and publs. Served with U.S. Army, 1946-48. S.C. Johnson Wax fellow U. Ariz., 1953-54. Mem. Am. Phytopath. Soc., Am. Soc. Hort. Scis., Fla. State Hort. Soc., Coun. Agrl. Sci. Tech., Toastmasters (all club offices Fresno chpt.), Sigma Xi. Unitarian Universalist. Avocations: hiking, gardening, travel. Home: Fresno, Calif. Died Feb. 5, 2008.

HOUGH, BRUCE HAROLD, minister; b. Centralia, Ill., Aug. 8, 1944; s. Shirley Harold and Bess Fern (Wilson) H.; m. Jean Elizabeth Baylor, Aug. 8, 1965; children: Cheryl Lynn, Kimberly Ann, Rebecka Sue. AS, Centralia Jr. Coll., 1964; BA in Ministry, Lincoln Christian Coll., Ill., 1968; BA in Christian Edn., Lincoln Christian Coll., 1968. Ordained to ministry Christian Ch. Min. Bethany Chapel Christian Ch., Fowler, Ind., 1967-69, Alma (Ill.) Christian Ch., 1969-72, Falmouth Christian Ch., Newton, Ill., 1972-75, Boyd Christian Ch., Dix, Ill., from 1975. Bd. dirs. Oil Belt Christian Svc. Camp, Flora, Ill., 1970—, So. Ill. Christian Counseling Ctr., Mt. Vernon, Ill., 1988—. Died June 4, 2008.

HOULIHAN, WILLIAM JOSEPH, chemist; b. South Amboy, NJ, July 24, 1930; s. William John H. and Ann Elizabeth (Howley) Martin; m. Piroska Maria Bizony, June 13, 1959; children: Peter William, Michael Joseph, Anna Maria. BS, Seton Hall U., 1951; PhD, Rutgers U., 1955. Asst. prof. St. John's U., Jamaica, N.Y., 1956-57, Seton Hall U., South Orange, N.J., 1957-59; project leader Universal Oil Products, East Rutherford, N.J., 1959-62; group leader Sandoz Rsch. Inst., East Hanover, N.J., 1962-68, sect. head, 1968-75, sect. dir., 1975-89, dir. medicinal chemistry, 1989-92; rsch. fellow emeritus C.A. Dana Rsch. Inst. Drew U., Madison, N.J., from 1993. Founder, co-chmn. Residential Sch. on Medicinal Chemistry, Madison N.J., 1987—; U.S. del. Internat. Union of Pure and Applied Chemistry, medicinal chemistry, 1982. Author, editor: Aldol Condensation, 1968, Platelet Activating Factor, 1990; editor: Indoles Vols. I-III, 1972, 79; patentee in field. Mem. Am. Chem. Soc. (chmn. North Jersey chpt. 1976). Roman Catholic. Avocation: stamp collecting/philately. Home: Hillsborough, NJ. Died Aug. 9, 2008.

HOUPIS, HARRY LOUIS FRANCIS, research physicist; b. Johnson City, NY, Jan. 18, 1954; s. Louis Harry and Annamarie Houpis.; m. Carole Lynn Turner, Jan. 28, 1984; children: Demetrius Vesalius, Carissa Selena. BS in Math., MIT, 1976, BS in Physics, 1976; MS in Physics, U. Calif. San Diego, La Jolla, 1978, PhD in Physics, 1981. Asst. rsch. physicist U. Calif. San Diego, La Jolla, 1981-87; vis. rsch. physicist Max Planck Inst. for Aeronomie, Katlenburg-Lindau, Fed. Republic Germany, 1985, Cen. Rsch. Inst. for Physics, Budapest, Hungary, 1986, Supercomputer Computations Rsch. Inst. Fla. State U., Tallahassee, 1986-87; vis. and assoc. rsch. physicist Space Physics Rsch. Lab. U Mich., Ann Arbor, 1987-88; tech. staff Mission Rsch. Corp., Monterey, Calif., 1988-90; dir. we. region Ctr. for Remote Sensing, Missoula, Mont., 1990-94; pres. EnviroSens, Inc., Missoula, Mont., from 1995. Lectr. in physics Hartnell C.C., Salinas, Calif., 1989-90; proposal refree NASA, NSF, Washington, 1985—; manuscript referee Jour. Geophys. Rsch. and Icarus, 1981-92. Author: The Physics of Comets; contbr. numerous articles to profl. jours. Pub. lectr. San Diego Speakers Bur., 1979-86. Fulbright sr. scholarship Coun. for Internat. Exch. of Scholars, 1985-86; Max Planck Soc. fellowship, Max Planck Inst., 1983, 85. Mem. Am. Geophys. Union, Am. Phys. Soc. Avocations: bicycling, family outings, ballroom dancing. Died Aug. 20, 2008.

HOUSNER, GEORGE WILLIAM, retired civil engineering educator, consultant; b. Saginaw, Mich., Dec. 9, 1910; s. Charles and Sophie Ida (Schust) Housner. BSCE, U. Mich., 1933; MS, Calif. Inst. Tech., 1934, PhD, 1941. Registered Calif. Engr. U.S. Corps Engrs., LA, 1941—42; ops. analyst 15th Air Force, Libya, 1943—45, Italy, 1943—45; Braun prof. engring. Calif. Inst. Tech., Pasadena, 1945—81, Braun prof. emeritus earthquake engring., 1981—2008; earthquake engring. cons. Pasadena, 1945—81. Mem. Gov.'s Earthquake Coun., 1971—76, L.A. County Earthquake Commn., 1971—72; chmn. com. on earthquake engring. NRC, 1983—92, com. on internat. decade natural hazard reduction, 1986—88; chmn. seismic adv. bd. CALTRANS, 1990—94. Author (3 textbooks); contbr. articles to profl. jours. Recipient Disting. Civilian Svc. award, U.S. War Dept., 1945, Bendix Rsch. award, Am. Soc. Engring. Edn., 1967, Nat. Medal Sci., The White House, 1988, The Washington award, Western Soc. Engrs., 1995; named a Disting. Alumnus, Calif. Inst. Tech., 2006. Mem.: ASCE (von Karman medal 1972, Newmark medal 1981), NAS (adv. panel on earthquake hazard 1981—83), NAE (Founders award 1991), Am. Acad. Arts & Sciences, Japan Acad., Earthquake Engring. Rsch. Inst. (pres. 1954—65, founding mem.), Internat. Assn. Earthquake Engring (pres. 1969—73), Seismol. Soc. Am. (pres. 1977—78, Harry Fielding Reid medal 1981). Home: Pasadena, Calif. Died Nov. 10, 2008.

HOUSTON, JAMES DUDLEY, writer; b. San Francisco, Nov. 10, 1933; s. Albert Dudley and Alice Loretta (Wilson) H.; m. Jeanne Wakatsuki, Mar. 27, 1957; children: Corinne, Joshua, Gabrielle. BA in Drama, San Jose State U., Calif., 1956; MA in Lit., Stanford U., 1962. Lectr. in writing Stanford U., 1968-69, U. Calif., Santa Cruz, 1969-83, vis. prof., 1987-93; disting. vis. writer U. Hawaii, Honolulu, 1983-84; Allen T. Gilliland prof. telecom. San Jose State U., 1985-86; vis. writer U. Mich., Ann Arbor, fall 1985, U. Oreg., Eugene, 1994, George Mason U., Fairfax, Va., 1999, 2007; disting. vis. prof. creative writing, Lurie chair San Jose State U., 2006. Mem. bd. dir. Squaw Valley Cmty. of Writers, Calif., 1990-2009, bd. dirs., 2001, Tandy Beal Dance Co., Santa Cruz, 1985-2009; adv. coun. Kiriyama Pacific Rim Book Prize, 2001; Lurie chair, disting. vis. prof. creative writing San Jose State U., 2006. Author: (novels) Between Battles, 1968, Gig, 1969 (Joseph Henry Jackson award 1967), A Native Son of the Golden West, 1971, Continental Drift, 1978, Love Life, 1985, The Last Paradise, 1998 (Am. Book award 1999), Snow Mountain Passage, 2001, Bird of Another Heaven, 2007; (non-fiction) Californians: Searching for the Golden State, 1982 (Am. Book award 1983), The Men in My Life, 1987, In the Ring of Fire: A Pacific Basin Journey, 1997, Hawaiian Son: The Life and Music of Eddie Kamae, 2004 (award of excellence in non-fiction Hawaii Book Pubs. Assn., 2005), Where Light Takes Its Color From the Sea: A California Notebook, 2008; co-author: (with Jeanne Wakatsuki Houston) Farewell to Manzanar, 1973, (with John R. Brodie) Open Field, 1975; films include Li'a, The Legacy of a Hawaiian Man, 1988, Listen to the Forest, 1991, The Hawaiian Way: The Art and Family Tradition of Slack Key, 1993, Words, Earth and Aloha: The Sources of Hawaiian Music, 1995 (Silver Maile award 1995), Luther Kahekili Makekau: A One Kine Hawaiian Man, 1997, The Sons of Hawaii: A Sound, A Band, A Legend, 2000; (with Jeanne Wakatsuki Houston and John Korty) Farewell to Manzanar, 1976 (NBC World Premiere movie 1976, Humanitas prize 1976); contbr. numerous articles to popular jours. Mem. Calif. Coun. for Humanities, San Francisco, 1983-87, cons., 1988-2009; mem. steering com. Pacific Rim Film Festival, Santa Cruz, 1988-2009. Wallace Stegner Writing fellow Stanford U., 1966-67, rsch. fellow East-West Ctr., Honolulu, 1984, Resident fellow Rockefeller Found., Bellagio, Italy, 1995; fiction grantee Nat. Endowment for the Arts, 1976. Mem. PEN West, Western Am. Lit. Assn. (Disting. Achievement award 1999), Calif. Studies Assn. (Carey McWilliams award 2000). Avocations: bluegrass music, ragtime piano, hatha yoga. Died Apr. 16, 2009.

HOVDE, CARL FREDERICK, language professional, educator; b. Meadville, Pa., Oct. 11, 1926; s. Bryn J. and Theresse (Arneson) H.; m. Jane Hale Norris, Aug. 27, 1960 (div.); children: Katherine Hale, Sarah Theresse, Peter Bryn; m. Bertha Rittenhouse Betts, 2000. BA, Columbia, 1950; MA, Princeton, 1954; PhD, 1956. Instr. English Ohio State U., 1955-58; vis. lectr. U. Muenster, W. Germany, 1958-60; mem. faculty Columbia U., NYC, 1960—2009, assoc. prof. English, 1964-69, prof. English, 1969—95, prof. emeritus, 1995—2009, dean Columbia Coll., 1968-72; chmn. Lionel Trilling Seminars. Vis. prof. U. Guanabara, Brazil, 1964, Umea, Sweden, 1989. Served with AUS, 1944-46. Fellow Villa Serbelloni, 1994. Home: New Canaan, Conn. Died Sept. 5, 2009.

HOVNANIAN, KEVORK S., real estate developer; b. 1923; s. Stepan K. Hovnanian; m. Sirwart Hovnanian; children: Ara, Sossie, Esto, Lucy, Nadia Founder Hovnanian Enterprises, Inc., Red Bank, NJ, 1959, CEO, 1967—97, chmn., 1967—2009. Co-chair. Fund for Armenian Relief. Recipient Nat. Quality Housing award, Nat. Assn. Homebuilders, Harvard Dively Award for Leadership in Corp. Pub. Initiatives, 1992, Ellis Island Medal of Honor, 1993, President's Medal, NJ Inst. Tech., 1996; named Man of the Yr., NJ Coun. for Christians & Jews. Died Sept. 24, 2009.

HOWARD, JOHN R., banker; b. Stamford, Conn., Dec. 23, 1940; s. Harold and Mildred Howard; c. Jessie Howard Brine, Nathaniel Paul Howard and Samuel Patrick Howard Grad., Middlebury Coll. Sr. v.p. Bankers Trust Co., NYC. Lt. USCG. Died Feb. 10, 2007.

HOWARD, WILLIE ABBAY, planter, former state official; b. Tunica, Miss., June 5, 1891; d. William G. and George Anne Elizabeth (Irwin) Abbay; student U. Miss., summer 1933; m. Thomas Percy Howard, Oct. 12, 1920 (dec.); children— Thomas Percy (dec.), George Anne Irwin (Mrs. Robert Peel Sayle), Elizabeth Irwin (Mrs. Cooper Yerger Robinson). Commr. Yazoo-Miss. Delta Levee Bd., 1955-75; welfare dir. DeSoto County, Miss., 1932-36, DeSoto and Tate counties, 1933-34; organizer, instr. Gulf div. ARC, 1917-18; co-organizer, trustee DeSoto County Library Bd., 1946—, chmn. bd. trustees, 1970-75; co-organizer Citizens Library Movement, DeSoto County, Miss., 1947, first Regional Library Miss., 1950, trustee, 1950-63; pres. Miss. Citizen's Library Movement, 1950-52; del. nat. conv. Nat. Rivers and Harbors Congress, Washington, 1964. Trustee Northwest Jr. Coll., Senatobia, Miss., 1943-77. Ptnr. Howard Plantation, Lake Cormorant, Miss., 1922—55, owner, operator, from 1955. Editor: DeSoto County C.L.M. Handbook, 1946. Recipient citation for flood control work Miss. River Commn., 1974, Outstanding Civilian Service medal, 1976; Meritorious Service award Yazoo-Miss. Delta Levee Bd., 1975; Spl. Alumni Assn. award, 1979; honored by naming of Willie Abbay Howard Coliseum, N.W. Jr. Coll., 1979. Mem. Miss. Fedn. Women's Clubs (state rec. sec. 1920-22), English-Speaking Union, Memphis Execs., Lower Miss. Valley Flood Control Assn. (v.p. 1961, 71), DAR, Colonial Dames 17th Century (Woman of Yr. Miss. 1977. Clubs: Memphis Country, Memphis Woman's (pres. 1968-69), Tunica County Woman's (founder 1914, pres. 1916, 1921, 28-29, trustee 1915—). Presbyterian. Died Sept. 4, 1988.

HOWE, DRAYTON FORD, JR., lawyer; b. Seattle, Nov. 17, 1931; s. Drayton Ford and Virginia (Wester) H.; m. Joyce Arnold, June 21, 1952; 1 son, James Drayton. AB, U. Calif., Berkeley, 1953; LLB, U. Calif., San Francisco, 1957. Bar: Calif. 1958. CPA Calif. Atty. IRS, 1958-61; tax dept. supr. Ernst & Ernst, San Francisco, 1962-67; ptnr. Bishop, Barry, Howe, Haney & Ryder, San Francisco, from 1968. Lectr. on tax matters U. Calif. extension, 1966-76. Mem. Calif. Bar Assn., San Francisco Bar Assn. (chmn. client relations com. 1977), Calif. Soc. CPA's. Died June 7, 2008.

HOWELL, CHARLES MAITLAND, dermatologist; b. Thomasville, NC, Apr. 14, 1914; s. Cyrus Maitl and Lilly Mae (Ammons) H.; m. Betty Jane Myers, Feb. 12, 1949; children: Elizabeth Myers, Pamela Jane. BS, Wake Forest U., Winston-Salem, NC, 1935; MD, U. Pa., Phila., 1937. Intern Charity Hosp., New Orleans, 1937—38; resident in medicine Burlington County Hosp., Mt. Holley, NJ, 1938—39; sch. physician Lawrenceville Sch., NJ, 1939—42; resident in pathology N.C. Baptist Hosp., Winston-Salem, 1947—48; resident in dermatology Columbia-Presbyn. Med. Ctr., NYC, 1948—50; resident in allergy Roosevelt Hosp., NYC, 1950—51; practice medicine specializing in dermatology Winston-Salem, from 1951. Mem. staff NC Bapt., Forsyth Meml. hosps.; mem. faculty Bowman Gray Sch. Medicine, Wake Forest U., 1951-86, head. sect., 1984-86, prof. dermatology, 1967-84, prof. emeritus, 1984, head sect., 1961-86, acting head sect., 1984-86. Served as officer M.C. AUS, 1942-46. Fellow Am. Acad. Dermatology, Am. Acad. Allergy; mem. N.Am. Clin. Dermatol. Soc., NY Acad. Scis., Old Town Club (Winston-Salem). Home: Winston Salem, NC. Died Nov. 9, 2008.

HOWELL, EVERETTE IRL, physicist, researcher; b. Shelby, Miss., Jan. 4, 1914; s. Thomas Daniel and Helen Lundy (Eason) H.; m. Beverly Ione McLaurin, June 12, 1943; children: Everette Irl, Marcia Marie, Beverly Jeannine. BA, Miss. Coll., 1936; MS, Vanderbilt U., 1937; PhD, U. N.C., 1940. Prof. phys. sci. Belhaven Coll., 1940-48; head dept. physics Miss. State U., 1948-79, prof., 1948-79, prof. emeritus, 1979—2009. Summer teaching physics dept. Vanderbilt U., 1946, U. Fla., 1947; summer research participant Oak Ridge Nat. Lab., 1950, 51 Contbr. articles to sci. publs. Mem. Am. Inst. Physics, Am. Phys. Soc., Am. Assn. Physics Tchrs., Miss. Acad. Scis., Sigma Xi, Phi Kappa Phi. Presbyn. (elder). Home: Pensacola, Fla. Died Sept. 13, 2009.

HOWELL, LEON, editor; b. Copperhill, Tenn. s. Francis Leon Sr. and Mary Lee (Haney) H.; m. Barbara Smith, June 26, 1965; children: Leah Ruth, Marya Lee. BA, Davidson Coll., 1957; MDiv, Union Theol. Sem., NYC, 1962. Communications sec. Univ. Christian Movement Nat. Coun. Chs., NYC, 1965-69, United Ministries in Higher Edn., NYC, 1969-70; editor Christianity and Crisis, NYC, 1985-90. Communications cons. World Coun. Chs., Geneva, 1977-85; ruling elder Chevy Chase Presbyn. Ch., Washington; bd. dirs. Associated Church Press, Nat.; mem. communication com. Presbyn. Ch. (USA), Louisville Author: Freedom City: The Substance of Things Hoped For, 1968, People Are the Subject, 1980, Acting in Faith, 1982; co-author: Asia, Oil Politics and the Energy Crisis, 1974, Southeast Asians Speak Out: Between Hope and Despair, 1975; editor: Ethics in the Presence Tense, 1991. Mem. Bi-Nat. Servants, Nat., Parent's Coun. Davidson (N.C.) Coll., 1988-91. 1st lt. U.S. Army, 1958-60, Korea. Recipient Best News Story award, Associated Church Press, 1983, Best Editorial award, 1988. Democrat. Home: Silver Spring, Md. Died Feb. 26, 2009.

HOYER, JOHN RICHARD, pediatrician; b. Mpls., May 13, 1938; s. Ludolf Julius and Inez (Fuglesteen) H.; m. Carol E. Anderson, Aug. 20, 1983; children: Rolf William, John Steen. BA, Grinnell Coll., Iowa, 1960; MD, Harvard U., 1964. Diplomate Am. Bd. Pediatrics. Intern in pediatrics U. Minn. Hosps., Mpls., 1964-65, resident in pediatrics, 1965-67, fellow in pediatric nephrology, 1970-73; med. researcher Phila.; asst. prof. pediatrics U. Minn., Mpls., 1973-74, Cornell Med. Coll., NYC, 1974-76, Harvard Med. Sch., Boston, 1976-79; prof. pediatrics UCLA, 1979-83, U. Pa. Sch. Medicine, Phila., from 1983. Vis. lectr. biol. chemistry Harvard Med. Coll., 1973-74; assoc. prof. medicine U. Pa., 1983-88, prof. medicine, 1988—; vis. scientist Dept. Medicine, U. Cambridge, 1989-90; established investigator Am. Heart Assn., 1974-79. Maj. U.S. Army, 1967-69. Mem. Phi Beta Kappa. Home: Wynnewood, Pa. Died Dec. 30, 2007.

HOYT, MARY G(ENEVIEVE), artist, educator; b. Oct. 7, 1929; d. Alvin Chase and Genevive Therese (Cahill) H.; children: John Frederick, Mary Elizabeth, Diane Marie, Jill Marie, Patricia Anne. BA in Art, Coll. St. Francis, 1950. Art instr. Malta Pub. High Sch., Dekalb, Ill., 1958; tchr. Lock Port (Ill.) Pub. Grade Sch., 1959; art tchr. Yauapai Coll., Prescott, Ariz., 1974-77, Allan Hancock Coll., Santa Maria, Calif., 1977-95. Lectr. in field; rschr., tchr. metaphysics and spirit, 1983-95. Author: the Spirit Masters' Guide Book to Enlightenment, 1995. Avocations: camping, fishing, reading, travel. Home: Salmon, Idaho. Died July 4, 2008.

HRISAK, DANIEL MICHAEL, public relations executive, marketing communication consultant, educator, financial writer; b. Pitts., Feb. 11, 1945; s. John and Mary Lucille (Hartman) H.; m. Mary-Ellen French, June 30, 1968; 1 child, Kerry. BA, Point Park Coll., 1968; MA, Fairfield U., 1983. Editor Nat. CSS, Norwalk, Conn., 1970-72; mgr. Data Processing Suppliers Assn., Stamford, Conn., 1972-74; pub. rels. mgr. Fin. Acct. Standards Bd., Stamford, Conn., 1974-78; editor Jour. of Accountacy, NYC, 1978-80; comm. mgr. The Singer Co., Conn., 1980-82; sr. acct. exec. Grey Advt., NYC, 1982-83; sr. technical mktg. writer Gen. Electric Co., Fairfield, Conn., 1983-85; pub. rels. dir. Inst. of Mgmt. Accts., Montvale, N.J., 1985-90. Writing cons. Fairfield U., 1980-85, instr. U. Bridgeport, 1982-84, Fairfield U., 1983-85; pres. Communication Resources, Marietta, Ga., 1983—. Editor: Jour. of Accountacy, 1979, Management Accounting, 1985-96, Controllers Update, 1989-97, Association Leader, 1990, The Small Business Controller, 1991-96, Corporate Controller, 1997, Chartered Accountants Jour. of New Zealand, 1993-97; editor: Controllers Update, 1996-97, Cost Management Update, 1996-97. V.p., Conn. Rep. State Nat. Coun., 1979. Mem. Pub. Rels. Soc. Am., Inst. Mgmt. Acc., Nat. Writers Union, Soc. Technical Comm. Avocations: info. technology. Died Oct. 15, 2007.

HSIUNG, CHUAN CHIH, mathematician; b. Shin-Gien, Jiangsi, People's Republic of China, Feb. 15, 1916; came to U.S., 1946; naturalized U.S. citizen, 1955; s. Mu Hun and Shih (Tu) H.; m. Wen Chin Yu, July 10, 1942; 1 child, Nancy. BS, Nat. Chekiang U., 1936; PhD, Mich. State U., 1948. Instr. U. Wis., Madison, 1948-50; lectr. Northwestern U., Evanston, 1950; asst. prof. Lehigh U., Bethlehem, Pa., 1952-55, assoc. prof., 1955-60, prof., 1960-84. Vis. assoc. prof. Math. Rsch. Ctr. U.S. Army, U. Wis., 1959-60; vis. specialist U. Calif., Berkeley, 1962; founder, editor-in-chief Jour. Differential Geometry, 1967—. Author: A First Course in Differential Geometry, 1981, John Wiley, 1997, Almost Complex and Complex Structures, 1995; contbr. over 100 articles to various internat. leading math. and scientific jours. Rsch. fellow Harvard U., 1951-52; C.C. Hsiung Fund for the Advancement of Math. named in his honor Lehigh U., 1989. Mem. Am. Math. Soc., Math. Assn. Am. Achievements include research in mathematics. Home: Weston, Mass. Died May 6, 2009.

HSU, TSONG HAN, chemist, researcher; b. Linhai, Zheqiang, China, Oct. 10, 1922; arrived in U.S., 1962; s. pao sun Hsu and Fon wha Ho; m. Qi Wen Zhang Hsu, May 18, 1995; 1 adopted child, Wu Jun; m. Mayaung Tai Hsu, Nov. 6, 1950 (dec. Feb. 11, 1987). BS, Amoy U., China, 1947; MS, Auburn U., Ala., 1964, PhD, 1968. Sr. scientist U.S. Plywood-Champion Papers, Brewster, NY, 1968—72; sr. rsch. and devel. chemist RSA Corp., Ardsley, NY, 1972—75; project dir. UN Internat. Devel. Orgn., Langoon, Myanmar, 1976—79; rsch. assoc. Jim Walter Rsch. Corp., St. Petersburg, Fla., 1980—82; sr. resin chemist Hillyard Chem. Co., St. Joseph, Mo., 1982—87. Fellow: Am. Inst. of Chemists. Achievements include patents for adhesives; paints; coatings. Home: Saint Petersburg, Fla. Died Jan. 29, 2008.

HUBBARD, FREDERICK DEWAYNE, trumpeter; b. Indpls., Apr. 7, 1938; Player trumpet, fluegelhorn, piano; with Montgomery Bros., Indpls., then with Sonny Rollins, Slide Hampton, J.J. Johnson, Quincy Jones, mem., Art Blakey's Jazz Messengers, 1961 touring Europe, Japan, Austria; appeared at Berlin Jazz Festival, 1965; played with Quincy Jones in soundtrack for film The Pawnbroker, 1964; rec. for Atlantic Records, 1966-70, Columbia Records, from 1974, Blue Note Records; recorded soundtracks for motion pictures The Bus Is Coming, 1971, Shaft's Big Score, 1972, Blowup, A Little Night Music, 1984, Sweet Return, 1984; (with Blakey) recs. include River, (with Coleman) Ah, (with Dolphy, Henderson) Blue Note; (albums) Hub-Tones, 1962, Breakin' Point, 1964, Backlash, 1966, Here to Stay, 1985, Double take, 1987, Life-Flight, 1987, Blue Spirits, 1987, Open Sesame, 1989, The Best of Freddie Hubbard, 1990, Windjammer, Bolivia, 1991, At Jazz Jamboree Warszawa, 1991, Topsy, 1991, A Tribute to Miles, 1995, The Artistry of Freddie Hubbard, 1996, Droppin' Things, Four X Four, V.S.O.P., The Quintet, Ascension, Caravan, Out to Lunch, Olé, Free Jazz, Takin' Off. Recipient Down Beat New Star award for trumpet 1961; Grammy award Best Jazz Group Performance 1972; Down Beat award for best trumpet 1973-76, Nat. Endowment for the Arts Jazz Masters award, 2006; winner Playboy Allstar Jazz Poll 1974-75. Mem. All Stars V.S.O.P. Died Dec. 29, 2008.

HUBER, DENNIS, educator; b. Washington, Jan. 18, 1942; s. Robert and Clara Francis (Fouche) H.; m. Cathrine Marie Benedict, Dec. 4, 1983; children: Erica, Stacy. AAS, SUNY, Buffalo, 1963; BFA, La. Coll., 1969; MA, Northwestern State U., Natchitoches, La., 1971; postgrad., U. So. Fla., 1974. Graphic artist Kenmore Color Plate, Buffalo, N.Y., 1964, Parker Pen Corp., Ft. Lauderdale, Fla., 1969, Groff Graphics, Tampa, Fla., 1973-74, Photo-engraving, Inc., Tampa, Fla., 1972-73; asst. instr. Northwestern State U., Natchitoches, 1971; instr. Hillsborough Community Coll., Tampa, Fla., 1971-74; program coordinator, instr. Trident Tech. Coll., Charleston, S.C., from 1974. Edn. cons. Beauford (S.C.) County Schs., 1975-76; graphics cons. Cameron Barkley, Inc., North Charleston, S.C., 1976-77; art and audio visual cons. to various cos., 1974—; lectr. Tri-County Sch. Dist., Charleston, 1974—. Mem. adv. bd. Cooper River Occupational Ctr., North Charleston, Orangeburg Vocat. Tech. High Sch., Orangeburg, 1977-82; mem. Southeastern

Graphics Council, Southeastern Coll. Art Conf. Served with USMC, 1965-68. Mem. Printing in the Carolinas (adv. bd.), Greater Charleston Printing Assn. (adv. bd.), Coll. Art Assn. Am., S.C. Tchr. Edn. Assn., S.C. Graphics Communication Instr. Assn. Avocation: rebuilding antique autos. Home: Summerville, SC. Died Mar. 3, 2008.

HUCKABEE, HARLOW MAXWELL, lawyer, writer; b. Wichita Falls, Tex., Jan. 22, 1918; s. Edwin Cleveland and Gladys Idella (Bonney) H.; m. Gloria Charlotte Comstock, Jan. 10, 1942; children: Bonney M., David C., Stephen M. BA, Harvard U., 1948; JD, Georgetown U., 1951. Bar: U.S. Dist. Ct. D.C. 1952, U.S. Ct. Appeals (D.C. cir.) 1952. Lawyer Fed. Housing Adminstrn., Washington, 1955-56, IRS, Washington, 1963-67; trial lawyer criminal sect., tax divsn. US Justice Dept., Washington, 1956-63, 1968-80, trial lawyer organized crime and racketeering sect., 1967-68. Author: Lawyers, Psychiatrists and Criminal Law, 1980, Mental Disability Issues in the Criminal Justice System: What They Are, Who Evaluates Them, How and When, 2000; contbr. articles to profl. jours. and legal publs. including Diminished Capacity Dilemma in the Federal System, 1991. Maj. U.S. Army, 1940-45, 48-55, ETO, Korea; lt. col. USAR, 1961. Methodist. Died Dec. 15, 2008.

HUDSON, FRANK PARKER, retired company executive; b. Americus, Ga., Dec. 12, 1918; s. Percy Wilbur and Janie Inez (Martin) H.; m. Elizabeth Lee Podlich, June 3, 1944; children: Frank Parker, Stephen Edward, James Burnett. BSChemE, Ga. Inst. Tech., 1941. Ptnr. Spotswood Parker & Co., Atlanta, 1946-65, pres., 1965-87; chmn. bd., chief exec. officer SyncroFlo, Inc., Atlanta, 1974-87. Gen. ptnr. Miami Circle Assocs., Ltd., Atlanta, 1984—; mgr. Causeway Properties, Atlanta, 1974—. Author: An 1800 Census for Lincoln County, Ga., 1977, A 1790 Census for Wilkes County, Ga., 1988, Wilkes County Georgia Tax Records 1785-1805, 1996; contbr. articles to profl. jours.; patentee in field. Trustee The R.J. Taylor, Jr. Found., Atlanta, 1987-89. Maj. U.S. Army, 1941-45. Mem Buckhead Club. Episcopalian. Avocation: history. Home: Atlanta, Ga. Died Jan. 8, 2008.

HUFFEY, VINTON EARL, clergyman; b. Luana, Iowa, July 7, 1915; s. Walter Angus and Tilda Boleta (Olson) H.; m. Lillian Bertha Crouse, June 22, 1942; children: Naomi, Rhoda, Stephen, Deborah. Student, Ctrl. Bible Coll., Springfield, Mo., 1936-38, North Ctrl. Bible Coll., Mpls., 1938-40. Ordained to ministry Assemblies of God, 1942. Pastor Assemblies of God, Oelwein, Iowa, 1940-43, LeMars, Iowa, 1943-47, evangelist Iowa and Mo., 1947-48, pres. youth Iowa and North Mo., 1948-52, editor News of West Ctrl., 1948-52, pastor Ames, Iowa, 1952-58, Monrovia, Calif., 1958-78, crusader inner-city evangelism, 1978-93, pastor South Pasadena, Calif., 1993-96. Motivation lectr. Assemblies of God, 1980-92; originator inner-city revolving loan fund, mem. urban task force So. Calif. Dist. Assemblies of God, Irvine, Calif., Springfield, Mo., Gen, Counsel of the Assemblies of God, 1982. Author: (pamphlet) The Church and America's Inner-cities, 1981; author of poems. Mem. Think Am. Com. City Coun., Duarte, Calif., 1962, lit. rev. com., 1965; chmn. What About Duarte? L.A. County Dept. Human Rels. City of Hope, Duarte, 1963. Recipient Decade of Harvest award So. Calif. Dist. Coun. Assemblies of God, Irvine, Calif., 1994. Republican. Avocations: travel, deep sea fishing. Died Feb. 25, 2008.

HUFFMAN, ROBERT MERLE, insurance company executive; b. Libertyville, Iowa, Nov. 8, 1931; s. Hollis Hiram and Jessie Ila (Harrison) H.; m. Carolyn A. Stowell, Dec. 10, 1955; children: Cheryl E. Hawkins, John D., Debra L. Otte. Student, Drake U., 1967. Various positions Grinnell (Iowa) Mut. Reins. Co., 1955-71; sec.-treas., CEO Clark Mut. Ins. Co., Kahoka, Mo., from 1971. Treas., mgr. Kahoka Housing Corp. (retirement facility), 1973-82; pres. Kahoka C. of C., 1973-74. Mem. Nat. Assn. Mut. Ins. Cos. (bd. dirs. Merit Soc. 1990-93, Svc. award 1993), Mo. Assn. Mut. Ins. Cos. (chmn. bd. 1989-90, bd. dirs. 1983-86, past vice-chmn., past chmn.-elect, chmn. 1989-90, former mem. legis. com.), Kiwanis (v.p.). Baptist. Home: Kahoka, Mo. Died July 9, 2008.

HUFFMAN, WILLIAM EUGENE, engineering professional; b. Birmingham, Ala., Sept. 15, 1943; s. Dempsey Eugene and Mary Elizabeth (Davis) H.; m. Nancy Anne Carlton, Nov. 26, 1966; children: Eugenia Anne, Carlton Eugene. BS in Chem. Engring., Auburn U., 1965. cert. hazards control mgr. Engr. U.S. Steel, Birmingham, 1965-66; maintenance supr. Allied Chem., Fairfield, Ala., 1966-68; engr. Monsanto Chem., Pensacola, Fla., 1968-72, mgr. Miamisburg, Ohio, 1972-87; specialist, engr. EG&G Mound Applied Techs., Miamisburg, Ohio, 1987-90; prin. Huffman Consulting, Birmingham, 1990-92; mgr. Ariz. Chem., Gulfport, Miss., from 1992. Chair OSHA com., Dayton, Ohio, 1977-79. Mem. AIChE (vice chair 1971, local chmn. 1972), Internat. Hazard Control Bd., Miss. Gulfcoast Manuf. Assn. (dir. 1994). Methodist. Home: Auburn, Ala. Died Oct. 31, 2007.

HUGHES, DOROTHY ZULA DILLARD, genealogy researcher, retired educator; b. Altus, Okla., July 21, 1909; d. James Melton and Wilma Katherine (Pelley) Dillard; m. Robert Claire Hughes, Aug. 19, 1934 (dec. Jan. 1968); children: Thomas James, Dorothy Barbara Hughes Buzzell. BA, U. N.Mex., 1929; MA, N.Mex. Highlands U., 1934. Cert. tchr., N.Mex., Tex. Tchr. grades 1 and 2 Eddy County, Cottonwood, N.Mex., 1927-28, tchr. grades 1, 2, 3 Loving, N.Mex., summer 1929; tchr. grade 2 Edison Sch., Carlsbad, N.Mex., 1929-33; tchr. grades 1-5 Eddy County, Otis, N.Mex., summer 1930; tchr. English, Carlsbad H.S., 1933-35; tchr. Coyote Canyon Day Sch., U.S. Indian Svc., Tohatchi, N.Mex., 1935-36; tchr. grade 1 West Sch., Carlsbad, 1937-38; tchr. English, Ysleta (Tex.) H.S., 1947-55, head dept. English, 1953-55; tchr. social studies and history O.L. Staton Jr. H.S., Lubbock, Tex., 1955; tchr. English, Lubbock H.S., 1955-72. Author, pub.: Nancy Anderson Chapter NSDAR, 1983, 84; author, compiler: Our Hughes Ancestors, 1990, Dillard in Culpeper County, Virginia, 1996; author: Teacher of the Navajo 1935-1936, 1985. Vol. geneal. aide Mahon Libr., Lubbock, 1974-2000; tchr. genealogy L.E.A.R.N., Tex. Tech U., Lubbock, 1980-82; lectr. on genealogy to various clubs, Lubbock, 1975-98; compiler Dillard Database, Dillard Family Assn., Dillard, Ga., 1994—. Fellow Tex. State Geneal. Soc. (2d v.p. 1985-87, 1st Place Manuscript award 1985, 96, 98, 2d Place 1993); mem. Nat. Geneal. Soc., Nat. Soc. DAR (regent Nancy Anderson chpt. 1982-86), Nat. Ret. Tchrs. Assn., Tex. Ret. Tchrs. Assn., Lubbock Ret. Tchrs. Assn., So. Plains Geneal. Soc. (Vol. award, pres. 1979-80), Soc. Genealogists London. Republican. Avocations: reading, writing, travel, gardening, research. Home: Houston, Tex. Died Jan. 19, 2008.

HUGHES, JOHN, film producer, director, screenwriter; b. Lansing, Mich., Feb. 18, 1950; m. Nancy Ludwig, 1970; children: John III, James. With Needham Harper & Steers, Chgo.; copywriter, creative dir. Leo Burnett Co.; editor National Lampoon; founder, pres. Hughes Entertainment, from 1985. Screenwriter: (films) National Lampoon's Class Reunion, 1982, National Lampoon's Vacation, 1983, Mr. Mom, 1983, Nate and Hayes, 1983, National Lampoon's European Vacation, 1985, 101 Dalmations, 1996, Maid in Manhattan, 2002, Just Visiting, 2001, Drillbit Taylor, 2008; screenwriter, prodr.: Pretty in Pink, 1986, Some Kind of Wonderful, 1987, The Great Outdoors, 1988, National Lampoon's Christmas Vacation, 1989, Home Alone, 1990, Career Opportunities, 1990, Dutch, 1991, Home Alone 2: Lost in New York, 1992, Dennis the Menace, 1993, Baby's Day Out, 1994, Miracle on 34th Street, 1994, 101 Dalmations, 1996, Flubber, 1997, Home Alone 3, 1997, Reach the Rock, 1998; screenwriter, dir.: Sixteen Candles, 1984, Weird Science, 1985; screenwriter, dir., prodr.: The Breakfast Club, 1985, Ferris Bueller's Day Off, 1986, Planes, Trains and Automobiles, 1987, She's Having a Baby, 1988, Uncle Buck, 1989, Curly Sue, 1991; prodr.: Only the Lonely, 1991, New Port South, 2001 Recipient Commitment to Chgo. award, 1990; named NATO/ShoWest Prodr. of Yr., 1990. Died Aug. 6, 2009.

HUGHES, LOIS JUNE HULME, home economics educator; b. Grand Island, Nebr., June 15, 1941; d. Orville George and Erna Lena-Marie (Kruse) Hulme; m. Harlan Gene Hughes, Aug. 23, 1961; children: Pamola Sue Hughes Gale, Patricia Ann Hughes Lewis. BS, U. Nebr., 1961; MEd, U. Mo., 1968, PhD, 1970. Cert. home economist. Tchr. home econs., sci. Ceresco (Nebr.) Pub. Sch., 1961-62, Nehawka (Nebr.) Consol. Schs., 1962-64, Centerville (Ohio) Pub. Schs., 1966-67; cons. Wis., 1972-73; asst. prof. continuing, vocat. edn. U. Wis., Madison, 1973-78; prof., head dept. div. home econs. U. Wyo., Laramie, 1978-81, prof., specialist State 4-H Office, 1981-83, instr. extended studies, 1982-85; cons. Dept. Edn. State of Wyo., Cheyenne, 1981-85; assoc. prof. Mankato (Minn.) State U., from 1985. Mem. Am. Vocat. Assn. (life), Am. Home Econs. Assn., Home Econs. Edn. Assn., Bus. and Profl. Women's Club, Zonta Club, Pi Lamba Theta, Phi Upsilon Omicron (dist. councilor 1978-84), Phi Delta Kappa (editor newsletter 1989—). Avocations: camping, downhill skiing, waterskiing. Home: Laramie, Wyo. Died Apr. 9, 2008.

HUGHES, ROBERT HARRISON, former agricultural products executive; b. Puunene, Hawaii, Mar. 23, 1917; s. Robert Edwin and Alice Thayer (Walker) H.; m. Nadine Jeannette Hegler, Aug. 24, 1940 (div. 1983); children: Robert Lawrence, Linton Alice, Carole Nadine.; m. Judith R. Gething, Jan. 28, 1983. B.Sc. in Sugar Tech, U. Hawaii, 1938. With Hawaiian Comml. & Sugar Co., 1939—62, sugar mill supt., 1962—65; prodn. mgr., v.p. tech. services C. Brewer & Co., Ltd., Honolulu, 1965-69, sr. v.p. Hawaiian ops., 1969-77, exec. v.p., 1977-80, dir. subs., 1966-80; pres. Hawaiian Sugar Planters Assn., Aiea, 1981—86; dir. Mauna Loa Resources Inc., 1986-95. Mem. bd. regents U. Hawaii, 1961-66; trustee Hawaii Conf. Found., 1966-85, Hawaii Loa Coll., 1980-89, Moloka'i Mus. and Cultural Ctr., 1984-91, Hawaiian Hist. Soc., 1990-94, U. Hawaii Found., 1963-65, 73-78, pres., 1967-68; bd. dirs. Hawaii Multi-Cultural Ctr., 1979-81, Samaritan Counseling Ctr. Hawaii, 1985-91; chmn. adv. bd. Cancer Rsch. Ctr., Hawaii, 1979-81; pres. Hawaii conf. United Ch. of Christ, 1962-63. Mem. Hawaiian Sugar Planters Assn. (dir. 1972-80), Hawaiian Hist. Soc, Home: Honolulu, Hawaii. Died Oct. 2, 2008.

HUGHES, THOMAS JOSEPH, retired military officer; b. Bklyn., Oct. 14, 1926; s. Thomas Joseph and Margaret (Dennigan) H.; m. Hazel Martha Koblitz, Feb. 18, 1948 (dec. Jan. 1993); children: Thomas, Alexander, Kevin, Theresa, Kathleen, Patricia, Mark, Michael; m. Nancy Rucker Vesper, July 1, 1995; 1 stepchild, Lisa BS, Harvard U., 1946; MS in Operational Analysis, US Naval Postgrad. Sch., 1962. Commd. ensign USN, 1946, advanced through grades to vice admiral, 1983, ret., 1987, engineer officer USS Massey, 1950—51, nuclear supr. Armed Forces Spl. Weapons Project, 1952—55, comdr. USS Chikaskia, 1967—69, head program devel & analysis section, 1969—71, comdr. Destroyer Squadron 36, 1971-72, staff mem. Naval Recruits Command Hdqs., 1972—74, asst. chief naval pers. for financial mgmt. & mgmt. info., 1974—76, comdr. Service Group 2, 1976-78, dep. dir. budget & reports, dep. dir. fiscal mgmt. divsn., Office Chief Naval Ops., 1978—80, dir. fiscal mgmt. divsn., 1980—81, asst. dep. chief naval ops. for manpower, pers. & training, 1981—83, dep. chief naval ops. for logistics, 1983—87; chmn. Navy Fed. Credit Union, 1975-76, pres., CEO, 1987—96; Conrad chair financial mgmt. US Naval Postgraduate Sch., 2002—07. Bd. dirs. Balt. br. Fed. Res Bank; mem. Thrift Inst. adv. coun. to Fed. Res. Bd., 1991-93; mem. Filene Rsch. Coun., Filene Rsch. Inst., 1990-94; bd. dirs. Visa-USA. Decorated D.S.M., Legion of Merit (5), Bronze Star, Joint Commendation medal (2); Cross of Gallantry (with gold star Vietnam); recipient USN Disting. Pub. Svc. award, 1996, Disting. Alumnus award, Naval Postgraduate Sch., 2007 Mem. Sigma Xi. Clubs: Lions. Roman Catholic. Home: Monterey, Calif. Died Jan. 13, 2009.

HUGHES-TEBO, JACQUELINE EMMA, regional coordinator; b. Baltimore, Md., Feb. 10, 1968; d. Hugh Price Hughes Jr. and Reta Theresa Hughes; m. Donald W. Tebo, Jr. BA in Psychology, Coll. Notre Dame Md., Balt., 1990; MBA, U. Phoenix, Columbia, Md., 2001; doctoral canidate, Capella U., from 2005. CPR, First Aid, and AED Instructor ARC, 2002. Armorer USMC Reserves, Savannah, Ga., 1988—99; counselor Mgmt. Tng. Corp., Washington, 1992—99; counseling mgr. Adams and Assocs., Laurel, Md., 1995—96; regional coord., info. systems specialist TCU Manpower Tng. Dept., Rockville, Md., from 1999. Innovation com. mem. Mgmt. Tng. Corp., Randallstown, Md., 1993; cultural diversity coord. Adams and Assocs., Laure, Md., 1995—96. Author: (poetry) Look, 1999. Chair, Relay for Life Am. Cancer Soc., 2002—03. Mem.: AAUW, NAFE. Avocations: travel, volunteer work. Home: Halethorpe, Md. Died Sept. 29, 2009.

HUKARI, ROBERT WILLIAM, fruit grower; b. Hood River, Oreg., July 4, 1922; s. William T. and Esther (Lingren) H.; m. Helen M. Gordon, Nov. 24, 1950; children: Amanda, Martta, Althea, Lori. Student, Oreg. State Coll., 1940-42, Okla. U., 1942-43, N.C. State Coll., 1943; BS, Oreg. State U., 1947. Ptnr. Indian Creek Orchards, Hood River, 1947-49; mgr. Hukari Bros., Hood River, 1949-52; ptnr. Hukari Orchards, Hood River, 1952-58; pres. Hukari Orchards Inc., Hood River, from 1959. V.p. Nat. Council Agrl. Employers, Washington, 1976-80. Bd. dirs. NW Farm Bur. Ins. Co., Salem, 1976-84, pres. 1984—; bd. dirs. (life) Western Farm Ins. Co., Denver, 1980-87. Lt. U.S. Navy, 1942-46, PTO. Mem. Hood River Grower/Shippers (pres. 1960-64), Oreg. Farm Bur. (v.p. 1976-83, pres. 1984-88), Mt. Rescue Orgn., Am. Mt. Rescue Assn., Hood River Crag Rats (pres. 1949-50), Elks, Am. Legion. Republican. Avocations: mountain climbing, skiing, swimming, boating. Home: Hood River, Oreg. Died July 8, 2008.

HULLEY, CHEYLA ANNE, physician assistant; b. Grafton, W.Va., Mar. 28, 1952; d. James DeWayne and Pauline (Jones) H. BS, Alderson-Broaddus Coll., 1974. Cert. physicians asst., W.Va. Physicians asst. Grafton City Hosp., 1974-75, VA Med. Ctr., Clarksburg, W.Va., from 1975. Assoc. prof. med. sci. Alderson-Broaddus Coll., Philippi, W.Va., 1974—. Active Bethel Temple, Bridgeport, W.Va. Mem. W.Va. Physicians Assts., VA Physicians Assts., Nat. Cert. Commn. Physician Assts., Nat. Psychiat. Physician Asst. Assn. Democrat. Avocations: piano, church ministry, crafts, gardening. Home: Grafton, W.Va. Died Aug. 21, 2008.

HULTMARK, GORDON ALAN, civil engineer; b. Chgo., Apr. 14, 1944; s. John Harold and Carolyn Bernice (Nelson) H.; m. Sarah Delle Carsey, Mar. 29, 1969; chidlren: Rifka, Menachem. BS in Civil Engring., U. Ill., 1967. Structural engr. Wilson, Andros, Roberts & Noll, Chgo., 1967-68; sales trainee Ceco Corp., Chgo., 1968-69; design engr. Mobile Homes Mfg. Assn., Chgo., 1969-70; plant engr. Union Tank Car Co., Chgo., 1970-77; project engr. Menasha Corp., Otsego, Mich., 1977-78; corp. project engr. Plainwell (Mich.) Paper Co., from 1978. Speaker in field. Chair Plainwell Constrn. Rev. Bd., 1985—; treas. Right to Life of Van Buren County, Bangor, Mich., 1987-89; del. Mich. Rep. Conv., 1988. Mem. ASCE, Audubon Soc. Republican. Jewish. Home: Grand Junction, Mich. Died Dec. 16, 2007.

HUMPHREYS, CAROL LEE, nursing educator; b. New Rochelle, NY, July 10, 1954; d. Joseph Warren and Edith (Cobelli) H. BSN, Keuka Coll., 1977; MS cum laude, Coll. New Rochelle, 1988. RN, Conn., NY; cert. childbirth educator; BLS (instr.). Charge nurse labor, delivery St. John's Riverside Hosp., Yonkers, NY, 1977-80, surg. charge nurse, 1980-81, nursing supr., 1981-88; asst. nursing instr. Cochran Sch. Nursing, Yonkers, 1987-88, nursing instr., 1988—95, adminstrv. coord., 1995—2003; charge nurse, relief nursing supr. Sarah Newman Nursing Home, Mamaroneck, NY, 1982-83; staff nurse, relief nursing supr. United Hosp., Port Chester, NY, 1985-89; instr. Dorthea Hopfer Sch. Nursing, Mt. Vernon, NY, 2003—04; dir. nursing, educator Michael Malotz Skilled Nursing Pavilion, from 2004. Adj. clin. instr. Westchester CC, Valhalla, NY, 1985-88, 2005-06, Coll. New Rochelle, NY, 1988, 90, 94-95, Pace U., 2004; child abuse instr., 1991-; AED instr., 1999-; faculty liason collaborative tchg. Mercy Coll., 1999-2001. Mem. nurse adv. bd. March of Dimes, 1990; mem. exec. com. Am. Cancer Soc., 1993-2003; support group facilitator St. John's Riverside Hosp., 1996-2003. Keuka Coll. scholar, 1975-76, 76-77; Keuka Coll. Nursing Student grantee,

1976-77, Lower Hudson Valley Bridges to Baccalaureate Program grantee, Mercy, Coll. Sch. Nursing. Mem. NY State Nurses Assn., Sigma Theta Tau. Home: Mamaroneck, NY. Died Oct. 25, 2007.

HUNGERLAND, JACKLYN ERLIN, psychologist; b. San Francisco, Nov. 9, 1930; d. Richard Lambert and Margaret Erlin; m. Thomas B. Boyd (div. 1961); children: Thomas deRussy Boyd, Margaret Boyd Andrews. BA, U. Calif., Santa Cruz, 1972; MA, Chapman U., 1978; PhD, U.S. Internat. U., 1980. Lic. clin. psychologist, Calif. Rsch. scientist Human Resources Rsch. Orgn., Alexandria, Va., 1961-78; pvt. practice clin. psychology Monterey, Calif., from 1984. Adj. prof. Golden Gate U., San Francisco, 1982—; cons. Vis. Nurse Assn., Monterey, 1984—. Contbr. articles to profl. publs. Bd. dirs. Vols. in Action, Monterey, 1982-84, Quota Club, Carmel, Calif., 1984. Capt. U.S. Army, 1979-82. Mem. APA (assoc.), Western Psychol. Assn., Monterey Bay Psychol. Assn. (bd. dirs. 1983-85), Del Monte Kennel Club (del. 1976—, pres. 1981-85, bd. dirs.), Poodle Club Am. (pres. 1990—), Am. Kennel Club, Inc. (bd. dirs. 1985—). Avocations: judging international dog shows, golf, swimming. Died Jan. 23, 2008.

HUNT, GUY (HAROLD GUY HUNT), former Governor of Alabama; b. Holly Pond, Ala., June 17, 1933; s. William Otto and Frances (Orene) Holcombe; m. Helen Chambers, Feb. 25, 1951; children: Pam, Sherrie Hunt Williams, Keith, Lynn Gaddis Brock. LLD (hon.), U. North Ala., 1987, Troy State U., 1987, Ala. A&M U., 1987, Mobile Coll., 1988; PhD (hon.), Jacksonville State U., 1991. Probate judge Cullman County, Ala., 1964-76; state chmn. for Ronald Reagan, Cullman, 1975-80; state exec. dir. agrl. stabilization & conservation svc. USDA, Montgomery, Ala., 1981-85; gov. State of Ala., 1987—93. State senatorial candidate, 1962; v.p. Ala. Reps., 1974-75; chmn. del. Rep. Nat. Conv., Kansas City, 1976; candidate for gov. of Ala., 1978; mem., chmn. Cullman County Lurleen Wallace cancer drive to raise funds for Birmingham Cancer Hosp.; chmn. fund drive United Fund; treas. ARC; officer, bd. dirs. Mental Health and Retarded Childen Assn. Served in US Army, Korean War. Decorated D.S.M. Mem. Probate Judges Assn., Juvenile Ct. Judges Assn. Lodges: Lions (charter mem. Holly Pond). Republican. Baptist. Avocations: softball, preaching, farming, biking. Home: Holly Pond, Ala. Died Jan. 30, 2009.

HUNT, JANE HELFRICH, volunteer; b. Buffalo, Jan. 3, 1925; d. Henry Jacob Helfrich and Julia Christina Swanson; m. Charles Stuart Hunt, Dec. 27, 1946; children: Stephen, John(dec.), Peter, Kathleen. BS Nursing, Skidmore Coll., Saratoga Springs, NY, 1945. RN NY State. RN Children's Hosp., Buffalo, 1946—48; lic. real estate agt. Hunt Real Estate Corp., Buffalo, 1963, lic. gen. ins. agt., 1966. Cons. Hunt Vanner Ins., Buffalo, from 1991; bd. dirs. Hunt Real Estate Corp., H.R.E. Comml. Corp. Mem. Ctrl. Pk. Meth. Ch., from 1948, choir; bd. dirs. Longview Niagara DayCare, Buffalo, Goodwill Industries, Buffalo. Recipient Dewitt Clinton Masonic award, Vol. Svc. to Cmty., 1998. Mem.: P.E.O. Sisterhood, Twentieth Century Club. Republican. Methodist. Avocations: golf, singing, bridge, painting, gardening. Home: Buffalo, NY. Died June 5, 2008.

HUNTER, HASSELL EUGENE, petroleum engineer, consultant; b. Haskell, Tex., May 18, 1923; s. Eugene Clark and Audrey Willis (Key) H.; m. Thelma Lucille Williams, Feb. 24, 1950 (dec. Sept. 1990); children: Karen Jane, Russell Eugene. BBA, Tex. A & I U., 1948; postgrad., Hardin-Simmons U., 1949, McMurry Coll., 1955, Tex. U., 1956. Registered profl. engr., D.C. Asst. mgr. F. M. Robertson Oil Co., Abilene, Tex., 1948-51; drilling engr. Rhodes Drilling Co., Abilene, 1951-64; chief drilling engr. U.S. Atomic Energy Commn., Las Vegas, Nev., 1964-73; sr. staff engr. Conoco, Inc., Houston, 1973-85; pres., chief engr. Hassell E. Hunter, Inc., Houston, from 1985. Bd. dirs. Inst. Shaft Drilling Tech., Seattle; designated rep. U.S. Nat. Com. on Tunneling Tech., Washington, 1983-86. Contbr. articles to profl. jours. Recipient cert. merit U.S. Army Air Forces, Sioux Falls, S.D., 1943, cert. appreciation Atomic Energy Commn., Las Vegas, 1970, spl. achievement award, 1971. Mem. AIME (Soc. Petroleum Engrs.), Inst. Shaft Drilling Tech. (dir. 1980-90, program dir. 1980-86, Disting. Svc. award 1986). Avocations: building furniture, skiing, swimming, gardening, photography. Died Dec. 31, 2007.

HUNTER, HOWARD J., JR, state legislator; b. Washington, Dec. 16, 1946; s. Howard and Madge Watford Hunter; m. Vivian Fluthe, 1986; children: Howard Hunter III, Chyla Toye. Former chmn. Youth & Families Com.; former mem. select com. Health Care Delivery & Tobacco Settlement; former v.p. & funeral dir. Hunter's Funeral Home Inc.; commr. Hertford County, NC, 1978—88; state rep. Dist. 5 NC, 1988—2007; chmn. children com.; mem. Alcoholic Beverage Control; mem. aging com.; mem. appropriations com.; mem. Econ Growth & Cmty. Devel. Com., Local Govt II & Travel & Tourism Com., Appropriations Subcom. Natural & Econ Resources; house rep. NC. Democrat. Baptist. Died Jan. 7, 2007.

HUNTER, KENNETH M., business information systems educator; b. Muskgeon, Mich., Jan. 11, 1943; s. Merlin Arthur and Dorothy Elaine Hunter. PhD, U. Wis., 1968. Asst. prof. math. La. State U., Baton Rouge, 1968—71; prof. William James Coll., Allendale, Mich., 1971—78; assoc. prof. Sangamon State U., Springfeld, Ill., 1978—79; sys. analyst Baxter Travenol Labs., Chgo., 1979—80; assoc. prof. U. Pacific, Stockton, Calif., 1980—83; asst. prof. San Francisco State U., 1983—84, prof. bus. info. sys., from 1988; assoc. prof. Aquinas Coll., Grand Rapids, Mich., 1984—85; sys. analyst W.W. Engring. and Sci., Grand Rapids, Mich., 1985—88. Democrat. Achievements include patents for search engines, fuzzy finite state nondeterministic automata. Home: San Francisco, Calif. Died Aug. 4, 2008.

HUNTER, KRISTIN EGGLESTON (MRS. JOHN I. LATTANY), writer, educator; b. Phila., Sept. 12, 1931; d. George Lorenzo and Mabel Lucretia (Monigault) Eggleston; m. Joseph E. Hunter, Feb. 29, 1952 (div. Jan. 1962); m. John I. Lattany, June 22, 1968; stepchildren: Leigh L. Norman, John I. Jr., Ramona, Andrew. BS, U. Pa., 1951. Sr. lectr. in English U. Pa., 1972—95. Writer in residence Emory U., 1979; lectr. U. Iowa, Haverford Coll., U. Ky., LaSalle Coll., Lincoln U., Nat. Coun. Tchrs. English, Libr. Assns. Conn., Mid-Atlantic States, No. Calif. and S.C., Alpha Kappa Alpha Sorority N.E. Regional Conv., and others. Author: God Bless The Child, 1964, The Landlord, 1966, The Soul Brothers and Sister Lou, 1968, Boss Cat, 1971, Guests in the Promised Land, 1973, The Survivors, 1975, The Lakestown Rebellion, 1978, Lou in the Limelight, 1981; contbr. short stories, poems, revs. and articles to jours. Recipient Univ. Wis. Children's Book Conf. Cheshire Cat Seal, 1970, Silver Slate-Pencil and Dolle Mina awards, The Netherlands, 1973, Chgo. Tribune Book World prize, 1973, Christopher award, 1974, Nat. Book award nomination, 1974, Drexel Univ. Children's Lit. award, 1981, N.J. State Coun. on the Arts Prose fellowship, 1981-82. Mem. PEN, Nat. Coun. Tchrs. English, Alpha Kappa Alpha. Home: Magnolia, NJ. Died Nov. 14, 2008.

HUNTINGTON, SAMUEL PHILLIPS, political science professor; b. NYC, Apr. 18, 1927; s. Richard T. and Dorothy S. (Phillips) H.; m. Nancy Alice Arkelyan, Sept. 8, 1957; children: Timothy Mayo, Nicholas Phillips. BA, Yale U., 1946; MA, U. Chgo., 1948; PhD, Harvard U., 1951. Instr. govt. Harvard U., Cambridge, Mass., 1950-53, asst. prof. govt., 1953-58, prof., from 1962, Thomson prof. govt., 1967-81, Clarence Dillon prof. internat. affairs, 1981-82, Eaton prof. sci. of govt., 1982, chmn. dept., 1982-95, Albert J. Weatherhead III Univ. prof., 1995—2008. Research assoc. def. policy Brookings Instn., Washington, 1952-53; faculty research fellow Social Sci. Research Council, NYC, 1954-57; asst. dir. Inst. War and Peace Studies, Columbia U., 1958-59, research assoc., 1958-63, assoc. dir., 1959-62, assoc. prof. govt., 1959-62, Ford research prof., 1960-61; research assoc. Ctr. for Internat. Affairs, Harvard U., 1963-64, mem. faculty, 1964-2008, exec. com., 1966-2008, assoc. dir., 1973-78, acting dir., 1975-76, dir., 1978-89; founder, dir. John M. Olin Inst. for Strategic Studies, 1989-2000; vis. fellow All Souls Coll., Oxford (Eng.) U., 1973; coordinator security planning Nat. Security Council, 1977-78; trustee Inst. Def. Analysis, 1985-98; cons. numerous govt. agys.; chmn. Harvard Acad. Internat. & Area Studies, 1996-2008 Author: The Soldier and the State, 1957, The Common Defense, 1961, Political Order in Changing Societies, 1968, American Politics: The Promise of Disharmony, 1981, The Third Wave: Democratization in the Late Twentieth Century, 1991, The Clash of Civilizations and the Remaking of the World Order, 1996, Who Are We: The Challenges to America's National Identity, 2004; co-author: Political Power: USA-USSR, 1964, The Crisis of Democracy, 1975, No Easy Choice: Political Participation in Developing Countries, 1976; editor: Changing Patterns of Military Politics, 1962, The Strategic Imperative, 1982; co-editor: Foreign Policy (quar.), 1970-77, Authoritarian Politics in Modern Society, The Dynamics of Established One-Party Systems, 1970, Global Dilemmas, 1985, Reorganizing America's Defense, 1985, Understanding Political Development, 1986, Culture Matters: How Values Shape Human Progress, 2000; also articles. Chmn. coun. on Vietnamese studies S.E. Asia Devel. Adv. Group, 1966-69; mem. Presdl. Task Force on Internat. Devel., 1969-70, Commn. on U.S.-Latin Am. Rels., 1974-76, Commn. on Integrated Long-Term Strategy, 1986-88, Commn. on Protecting and Reducing Govt. Secrecy, 1995-97; trustee Internat. Devel. Found., 1969-76. Served with AUS, 1946-47. Recipient Silver Pen award Jour. Fund, 1960, Grawemayer World Order award, 1992; fellow Ctr. for Advanced Study in Behavioral Scis., Stanford, 1969-70. Fellow Am. Acad. Arts and Scis.; mem. Internat. Polit. Sci. Assn. (coun. 1973-75), Coun. on Fgn. Rels., Internat. Inst. Strategic Studies, Am. Polit. Sci. Assn. (coun. 1969-71, v.p. 1984-85, pres.-elect 1985-86, pres. 1986-87). Democrat. Died Dec. 24, 2008.

HURD, LYDIA M., health facility administrator; b. Kearney, Nebr., June 12, 1928; d. John B. and Henrietta (Profaizer) Bertoldi; m. Lawrence L. Hurd, Feb. 3, 1951. Diploma in nursing, St. Mary's Hosp., Rochester, Minn., 1949. RN, Minn. Clin. dir. United Hosp., St. Paul, critical care and spl. care nurse, sr. clin. dir. Mem. Minn. Assn. Adminstrv. Nursing Suprs. (sec.). Home: Saint Paul, Minn. Died Nov. 25, 2007.

HURLEY, HARRY JAMES, JR., dermatologist, educator; b. Phila., Oct. 10, 1926; s. Harry James and Margaret (McHenry) Hurley; m. Jeanne Florence Geiger, July 15, 1950 (dec. 1996); children: Susan, Harry James III, Jeffrey, Marilyn, Nancy. Student, St. Joseph's Coll., Phila., 1943—45; MD, Jefferson Med. Coll., Phila., 1949; DSc in Medicine, U. Pa., 1958. Cert. Am. Bd. Dermatology. Rotating intern Fitzgerald-Mercy Hosp., Darby, Pa., 1949—50, resident in ob-gyn., 1950—51; resident in dermatology and syphilogy U. Pa. Hosp., 1951—53; rsch. fellow USPHS, 1955—56; mem. faculty U. Pa. Sch. Medicine, 1956—59, assoc. prof. dept. dermatology, 1962—68, prof. clin. dermatology, 1978—2009; prof. dermatology, chief sect., chief dermatol. sect. coll. hosp. Hahnemann Med. Coll., Phila., 1959—62; chief dermatology Phila. Gen. Hosp., 1962—73; asst. exec. dir. Am. Bd. Dermatology, 1985—92, exec. dir., 1993—2000. Attending dermatologist Fitzgerald-Mercy Hosp., 1956—80, Bryn Mawr Hosp., 1956—75, Am. Oncologic Hosp., Phila., 1960—62, U. Pa. Hosp., 1962—80; chmn. adv. bd. Nat. Program Dermatology, 1974—75; pres. Dermatology Found., 1975—76; cons., advisor in field. Bd. editors Modern Dermatology, 1968—2009, Dermatology Forum, 1984—2009, editl. Annals Internal Medicine, 1982—84; editor: Jour. Geriatric Dermatology, 1993—2009; contbr. numerous articles to profl jours. Capt. M.C. USAR, 1953—55. Recipient Rsch. Recognition award, Phila. chpt. Nat. Cystic Fibrosis Found., 1959, Clarence E. Shaffrey medal and award, St. Joseph's U., 1980, Finnerud award, Dermatol. Found., 1991. Fellow: ACP (chmn. self-assessment program sect. dermatology 1976); mem.: Phila. Dermatol. Soc. (editor proc. 1968—69, pres. 1970—71), Coll. Physicians Phila., Delaware County Med. Soc., Pa. Med. Soc., Pa. Acad. Dermatology (pres. 1969—70, Disting. Svc. commendation 1973), Soc. Investigative Dermatology, Am. Dermatol. Assn. (bd. dirs. 1977—82, pres. 1983—84), AMA (chmn. residency rev. com. 1979—82), Am. Acad. Dermatology (bd. dirs. 1972—75, chmn. coun. govtl. liaison 1974—75, mem. nominating com. 1977—80, chmn. nominating com. 1987, chmn. audit com. 1988—89, hon. mem., Liverpool lectr., Everett Fox lectr. and award 1994, award 2001), Am. Bd. Dermatology (examiner 1974—83, exec. com. 1978—79, chmn. edn. com. 1979—84, v.p. 1982—83, pres. 1983—84, exec. dir. 1993, exec. cons. from 2001, bd. dirs., Disting. Svc. award 1984), Overbrook Golf Golf Club (bd. dirs. from 1988, v.p. 1993), Alpha Epsilon Delta. Home: West Chester, Pa. Died July 26, 2009.

HURLEY, WILSON PATRICK, artist; b. Tulsa, Apr. 11, 1924; s. Patrick Jay and Ruth Wilson Hurley; m. Norma Frost, May 26, 1952 (div. Dec. 1964); children: Patrick Jay II, Norman Frost, Wilson Chapman, Mary DeMova, Robert Burke; m. Rosalyn Marie Roembke, May 22, 1969. BS in Mil. Engring., U.S. Mil. Acad., 1945; LLB, George Washington U., 1952; LHD (hon.), U. New Eng., 1991, Oklahoma City U., 1996. Pilot U.S. Army A.C. 13th AF, South Pacific, 1945-49; atty. Modrall, Seymour Sperling Roehl & Harris, Albuquerque, 1953-57; pvt. practice as atty. Albuquerque, 1961-65; chmn. of bd. Citizens Bank, Albuquerque, 1961-65; pilot N.Mex. Air N.G., Albuquerque, 1953-69, USAF 504 GP 21st TASS, Vietnam, 1968-69. Exhibited in solo shows at Nat. Cowboy Hall of Fame, Oklahoma city, 1977, Utah Mus. Fine Art, Salt Lake City, 1981, Gilcrease Mus., Tulsa, 1983, Whitney Mus., Cody, Wyo., 1985, Rockwell Mus., Corning, N.Y., 1986, Eiteljorg Mus., Indpls., 1991, others; represented in collections at Nat. Cowboy Hall of Fame, Gene Autry Western Heritage Mus., L.A., Colorado Springs Fine Art Ctr., Mus. Art and History, also pvt. collections. Lt. col. USAF. Murals exhibited at Noble Ctr., Cowboy Hall of Fame, Oklahoma City, 1996. Mem. Nat. Acad. Western Art (adv. bd. 1973-84, Prix de West 1984). Republican. Avocations: writing, radio controlled aircraft design. Home: Albuquerque, N.Mex. Died Aug. 29, 2008.

HURTIG, ANITA LANDAU, retired psychology professor; b. Chgo., Mar. 16, 1932; d. Isidore and Rose (Levinsky) Landau; m. Martin Russell Hurtig, Oct. 4, 1953; children: Janise, Anthony, Elliott. BA, Northwestern U., 1953, MS, 1971; PhD, U. Ill., Chgo., 1981. Lic. clin. psychologist, Ill. Tchr. learning disabilities Dist. 73 1/2, Skokie, Ill., 1971-75; cons. Michael Reese Health Plan, Michael Reese Hosp., Chgo., 1979-80; assoc. prof. pediatric psychology U. Ill., 1980—2008; cons. dept. psychology Michael Reese Hosp., Chgo., 1989—2008. Author: Psychosocial Issues in Sickle Cell Disease, 1983; also articles. Chmn. human rels. com. Dewey Community Conf., Evanston, Ill., 1972. Fellow NIMH, 1976-77. Mem. APA, Am. Orthopsychiat. Assn., Soc. for Pediatric Psychology, Ill. Psychol. Assn., Chgo. Assn. for Psychoanalytic Psycholoyg, Family Inst. (sec. alumni bd.), Phi Beta Kappa. Avocations: tennis, theater. Home: Evanston, Ill. Died Aug. 6, 2009.

HUTCHINS, CARLEEN MALEY, acoustical engineer, consultant; b. Springfield, Mass., May 24, 1911; d. Thomas W. and Grace (Fletcher) Maley; m. Morton A. Hutchins, June 6, 1943 (dec. 2004); children: William Aldrich, Caroline. AB, Cornell U., 1933; MA, NYU, 1942; DEng (hon.), Stevens Inst. Tech., 1977; DFA (hon.), Hamilton Coll., 1984; DSc (hon.), St. Andrews Presbyn. Coll., 1988; LLD (hon.), Concordia U., Montreal, Que., Can., 1992. Tchr. sci. Woodward Sch., Bklyn., 1934—38, Brearley Sch., NYC, 1938—49; asst. dir., asst. prin. All Day Neighborhood Schs., NYC, 1943—45. Sci. cons. Coward McCann, Inc., 1956-65, Girl Scouts America, 1967-65, Nat. Recreation Assn., 1957-65; permanent sec. Catgut Acoustical Soc., Montclair, NJ, 1962-2000; exec. dir. New Violin Family Assn. Inc., 2000-09; hon. cons. Catgut Acoustical Soc., Inc., 2000-04; maker violins. Author: Life's Key, DNA, 1961, Moon Moth, 1965, Who Will Drown the Sound, 1972; author (with others): Science Through Recreation, 1964; contbr. violin acoustics sect. Grove's Dictionary of Music and Musicians, 1964, 96; editor: (2 vols.) Musical Acoustics, Part I, Violin Family Components, 1975, Musical Acoustics, Part II, Violin Family Functions, 1976, The Physics of Music, 1978, Research Papers in Violin Acoustics, 1973-94, 96; contbr. articles to profl. jours. in Sci. Am. Jour. Acoustical Soc. Am., Jour. Audio Engring. Soc., Physics Today, Am. Viola Soc., Catgut

Acoustical Soc. Martha Baird Rockefeller Fund for Music grantee, 1966, 68, 74, NSF grantee, 1971, 74; Guggenheim fellow, 1959, 61; recipient spl. citations in music, Carleen Maley Hutchins medal (1st recipient) Catgut Acoustical Soc., Hon. Fellowship award Acoustical Soc. Am., 1998. Fellow AAAS (electorate nominating com. 1974-76, Outstanding Performance in the Scis. award 1994), Audio Engring. Soc. (life), Acoustical Soc. Am. (emeritus, membership com. 1980-86, exec. coun. 1984-87, medal and awards com. 1987-89, nominating com. 1987-88, Silver Acoustics Medal 1981, tech. com. music acoustics 1964-2009, chmn. pres.'s ad hoc com. 1987-88, archives com. 1988—, mem. com. on women 1989-97); mem. So. Calif. Violin Makers Assn. (hon.), Viola da Gambda Soc. Am. (hon.), Scandinavian Violin Makers Assn. (hon.), NY Viola Soc., Guild Am. Luthiers, Am. Viola Soc., Violoncello Soc., Amateur Chamber Music Players Assn., Am. Philos. Soc. (award violin acoustics 1968, 81), Mich. Violin Makers Assn., New Violin Family Assn. Inc. (exec. dir. 1999-2009), Materials Rsch. Soc., Three O'Clock Club, Dot and Circle, others, Sigma Xi, Pi Lambda Theta, Alpha Xi Delta. Died Aug. 7, 2009.

HUTCHINSON, MARJORIE, small business owner and operator; b. Nashville, Ga., Mar. 19, 1922; d. Johnie and Fanie (Harrell) Kent; m. Carlos Hutchinson, July 4, 1942; children: Hilda Ann Howington, Linda Kay Slade. Student, Bainbridge Jr. Coll., U. Ga. Dir., owner Children's World at Hutchinson's Day Care Ctr., Bainbridge, Ga., from 1966. Baptist. Died Aug. 8, 2008.

HUTH, JOHN HARVEY, electronics executive; b. Bakersfield, Calif., Nov. 12, 1922; s. Harvey Frederick and Mabel Lucinda (Belcher) H.; m. Marietta Brown, Dec. 21, 1950 (dec. 1975); m. Doris Moss Bitz, Oct. 9, 1976; 1 stepchild, Debbie Leigh Bitz. BS, U. Calif., Berkeley, 1943; MS, Stanford U., 1947, PhD, 1950. Registered profl. engr. Ops. analyst Rand Corp., Santa Monica, Calif., 1950-64; with sr. exec. svc. Dept. of the Navy, Washington, 1964-86; sr. analyst VSE Corp., Indian Head, Md., 1986-88; sr. exec. PRC, Inc., Indian Head, from 1988. Adj. prof. Cen. Mich. U., Washington, 1989—. Contbr. numerous articles to profl. jours. Lt. USN, 1945-46. Mem. U.S. Hovercraft Soc., Army-Navy Country Club. Avocations: photography, antique automobiles. Home: Arlington, Va. Died Apr. 26, 2008.

HUTH, THOMAS JOSEPH, retired surgeon; b. Cin., Mar. 15, 1921; s. Edwin C. Huth and Clara Beal; m. Margie Marie Heringer, Aug. 5, 1950; children: Margaret, Regina, Timothy, Daniel. MD, U. Cin., 1948. Diplomate Am. Bd. Surgery. Intern Cin. Gen. Hosp., 1948-49; resident in gen. practice St. Elizabeth Hosp., Covington, Ky., 1949-50; resident in pathology Good Samaritan/U. Hosp., Cin., 1954, U. Hosp., Cin., 1954—55; fellow surgery Louisville VA Hosp., 1955-59; surgeon St. Elizabeth Hosp., Covington; ret. Mem. ACS (emeritus), Am. Coll. Chest Physicians, Am. Thoracic Soc. Home: Fort Mitchell, Ky. Died Dec. 7, 2008.

HUTNER, HERBERT L., financial consultant, lawyer; b. NYC; s. Nathan M. and Ethel (Helhor) Hutner; m. Juli Reding, Nov. 28, 1969; children from previous marriage: Jeffrey J., Lynn M. Colwell 1 stepchild, Christopher D. Taylor. BA, Columbia U., 1928, JD, 1931. Bar: N.Y. 1932. Ptnr. Osterman & Hutner; mem. N.Y. Stock Exch., NYC, 1945—57; successively pres. N.E. Life Ins. Co., NYC; chmn. bd. Sleight & Hellmuth Inc., NYC, Pressed Metals of Am., Port Huron, Mich., Struthers Wells Corp., Warren, Pa., Plateau Mining Co. Inc., Oak Ridge, Tenn.; investor, cons. LA, from 1963; dir. United Artists Comm., Inc., 1965—87, Todd AO-Glen Glen, from 1987. Bd. dirs. L.A. Rams, 1972—75, mem. adv. bd.; chmn. bd. Cellvent, Inc. Composer: The Super Bowl Song, Go Rams Go, others. Chmn. Pres.'s Adv. Com. on Arts Kennedy Ctr., 1982—90; founder L.A. Music Ctr.; chmn. profl. sports com. United Way; corporator Schepens Eye Rsch. Inst., Boston; mem. internat. adv. com. Up With People. Decorated title DATO Sultan of Johore, Malaysia, Highest Order of the Crown. Mem.: ASCAP, Deepdale Golf Club (Manhasset, N.Y.). Died Dec. 7, 2008.

HUTSON, HARRY MARSHALL, history educator; b. Cumberland, Md., Dec. 14, 1920; s. Harry Myers Hutson and Myrtle Rita (Lemon) Heinrich; m. Betty Jane Rose, Oct. 24, 1945; children: Harry M. Jr., Sally J., Peter C., Andrew R. BA, U. Md., 1942; MA, U. Iowa, 1948, PhD, 1952. Instr. social studies Riverside Mil. Acad., Gainesville, Ga., 1943-44; asst. prof. history Linfield Coll., McMinnville, Oreg., 1952-55; prof. history Towson (Md.) State Coll., 1955-67; dean U. Wis., Menasha, 1967-69; prof. history U. Tenn., Martin, 1969-89, also chmn. dept., 1969-82, prof. emeritus, from 1990. Contbr. articles to profl. jours. Chmn. bd. dirs. Interfaith Ctr., U. Tenn., Martin, 1986-89; mem. Amnesty Internat., 1980—. 2nd lt. U.S. Army, 1944-47. Recipient fellowship, Danforth Found., 1961, Alumni Disting. Svc. professorship U. Tenn., 1972-89, Fellowship for Tchrs., NEH, 1981. Mem. So. Hist. Assn. (chmn. John Snell Meml. Prize com. 1989-91), Common Cause, Rotary, Phi Kappa Phi (pres. local chpt. 1984-85), Phi Eta Sigma. Democrat. Methodist. Avocations: photography, swimming, travel. Home: Durham, NC. Died Apr. 14, 2008.

HUXFORD, JOHN CALVITT, musician, educator; b. Homerville, Ga., Feb. 3, 1931; s. Folks and Orie Lois (Kirkland) H.; m. Ann Pearl McHugh, Dec. 19, 1954; children: John Clifford, Folks McHugh, Calvitt Johnson. AB, Bob Jones U., 1951; BS in Edn., Ga. So. Coll., 1955; MusM, Fla. State U., 1960, PhD, 1968. Instr. music, dir. Ga. Pub. Schs., 1953-54, 55-60; instr. Ga. So. Coll., Statesboro, 1954-55; asst. prof., asst. to dean of music U. of the Pacific, Stockton, Calif., 1961-66; from assoc. prof. to prof. music Valdosta (Ga.) State Coll., 1966-87, dir. div. fine arts, 1970-73, chmn. dept. art, 1971-72, chmn. dept. music, 1972-73, 80-85, prof. emeritus, from 1987. Pianist, condr. numerous concerts, U.S. and Europe, 1947—; v.p. S. Ga. Travel, Inc., 1988—. Composer numerous chamber, piano and orchestral pieces, 1956—. Served as cpl. U.S. Army, 1951-53. Mem. South Ga. Music Tchrs. Assn. (founder), Music Tchrs. Nat. Assn., Ga. Music Tchrs. Assn., Music Educators Nat. Conf., Am. Liszt Soc., Phi Mu Alpha, Pi Kappa Lambda. Clubs: Valdosta Country. Lodges: Elks. Democrat. Methodist. Avocations: collecting out-of-print music, records, cartography, gourmet cooking, sports. Home: Valdosta, Ga. Died Aug. 1, 2008.

HYAMS, JOSEPH, writer; b. Cambridge, Mass., June 6, 1923; s. Joseph Irving and Charlotte (Strauss) H.; m. Elke Sommer, Nov. 18, 1964 (div. 1993); children: Jay, Chris, Beverly, Dianne; m. Melissa Hyams, 1994 BS, NYU, 1948, MA, 1949. Editor Reporter Publs., 1947-50; columnist N.Y. Herald Tribune, 1950-64. Instr. U. Calif., L.A., 1963-64. Author: (with Walter Wanger) My Life with Cleopatra, 1964, (with Major Riddle) Weekend Gamblers Handbook, 1964, (with Peter Sellers) Sellers Market, 1965, (with Edith Head) How to Dress for Success, 1966, Bogie, 1966, A Field of Buttercups, 1968, (with Thomas Murton) Accomplices to the Crime: The Arkansas Prison Scandal, 1969, (with Tony Trabert) Winning Tactics for Weekend Tennis, 1972, Mislaid in Hollywood, 1973, (with Pancho Gonzales) Winning Tactics for Singles, 1973, Bogart and Bacall: A Love Story, 1976, The Pool, 1978, Zen in the Martial Arts, 1979, Playboy's Book of Practical Self-Defense, 1980, The Last Award, 1981, Murder at the Academy Awards, 1983, (with Chuck Norris) Secrets of Inner Strength, 1987, (with Michael Reagan) Michael Reagan: On the Outside Looking In, 1987, The Flight of the Avenger: George Bush at War, 1990, (with Jay Hyams) Little Boy Lost: A Biography of James Dean, 1992; editor: Billie Jean King's Secret of Winning Tennis, 1974; contbr. to periodicals including McCall's, Ladies' Home Journal, Cosmopolitan, Redbook, Reader's Digest, Playboy. Died Nov. 8, 2008.

ICHELSON, DAVID LEON, physician; b. San Francisco, Oct. 12, 1921; s. Maury Moses and Selene Diane (Jones) I.; m. Jean Pearch, June 14, 1946 (div.); m. Patricia Badali, Sept. 26, 1958 (div.); children: Suzanne, Kathryn, David Jr., Nancy, Mary Jane, Beth Ann; m. Katherine E. Shippey, Dec. 26, 1981 (div.). AB, Stanford U., 1943; MD, Bowman Gray U., 1950. Intern L.A. County Hosp., 1950-51; resident Tulare County Hosp., 1951-53; pvt. practice Calif., 1953-86, Sacramento, 1986-97. Chmn. gen. practice dept. Stanford Hosp., Palo Alto, Calif., 1976, Sequoia Hosp., Redwood City, Calif., 1979; chief staff Corning (Calif.) Meml. Hosp., 1987. Patent on athletic bra and hair clip for repairing scalp lacerations. Inf. U.S. Army, 1944-46. Mem. Am. Acad. Family Practice. Avocations: making muzzle loading guns, hiking. Home: San Francisco, Calif. Died Mar. 13, 2008.

IGOU, RAYMOND ALVIN, JR., orthopedic surgeon; b. Esterville, Iowa, Dec. 2, 1933; s. Raymond Alvin Sr. and Pearl Mildred (Christiansen) I.; m. Barbara Igou, Jan. 17, 1958 (div. June 10, 1980), Jane Ann Leboda, Jan 4, 1991 (div. Aug. 2003); children: Raymond Alvin III, Yvette Sharon. BS, N.Mex. State U., 1955; MD, Boston U., 1965. Diplomate Am. Bd. Orthopedic Surgery; lic. mortgage broker, Fla. Surg. internship Univ. Hosp., Boston, 1965-66; orthopedic resident Boston U. Sch. of Medicine, 1971-75; owner, operator Grant Buie Med. Ctr., Hillsboro, Tex., 1966-71; assoc. dir. dept. orthop. surgery, chief scoliosis clinic Boston City Hosp., from 1975, dir. rehab. svcs. City of Boston dept. health and hosps., 1975-80; asst. prof. ortho surg. Boston U. Sch. Medicine, 1979; med. dir. dept. rehab. svcs. New Eng. Meml. Hosp., Stoneham, Mass., 1979-95, chief orthopedic surgery, trustee, from 1987, chief of staff, 1989-90; orthopedic surgeon in pvt. practice, Stoneham, from 1975; chmn. dept. surgery Boston Regional Med. Ctr. (formerly New Eng. Meml. Hosp.), Stoneham, 1995. Sr. staff mem. Boston City Hosp., Univ. Hosp.; gen. ptnr. New Eng. MRI, L.P., 1989—; pres. Med Ptnrs. Ltd., 1988—; mem. Coun.-Boston Regional Med. Ctr., 1987, Gov.'s Adv. Coun. Indsl. Accidents, 1995; mng. gen. ptnr. WCPR Hartford Data Dispatch Ptnrs. Host talk show WALE, Providence, 1995-96; contbr. articles to profl. jours. Mem. Zoning and Planning Commn., Hillsboro, Tex., 1969-71; city councilman, Hillsboro, 1967-71; mem. Indsl. Found., Hillsboro, 1969-71. Capt. U.S. Army, 1955-60. Fellow Am. Acad. Orthopedic Surgeons; mem. Mass. Med. Soc., Boston Orthopedic Club, Freemasons, York Rites, Scottish Rites, Shriners. Republican. Avocations: flying, coin collecting/numismatics. Home: Stoneham, Mass. Deceased.

IIDA, JOHN, church administrator; b. Inglewood, Calif., Aug. 7, 1962; s. Harry Tatsuo and Florance Kimiyo (Wada) I. BBA, Linfield Coll., 1984; MBA, Oral Roberts U., 1986. Grad. asst. Oral Roberts U., Tulsa, 1984-85, grad. fellow Sch. Bus., 1985-86; adminstr. Harvest Fellowship Inst., Tustin, Calif., from 1989; office mgr. U.S. Lifestyles, Orange, Calif., 1990. Mem. Christian Ministries Assn. Home: Broken Arrow, Okla. Died Jan. 9, 2008.

IKE, REVEREND See EIKERENKOETTER, FREDERICK II

IMPREVEDUTO, ANTHONY NEIL, former state legislator; b. Jersey City, Apr. 11, 1948; s. Rocco and Ann (Ferrone) I.; m. Susan Jane Zaluski, 1971; children: Loren Ann, Jamie Lee. BS, Rider Coll., 1971; MA, Seton Hall U., 1975. Assemblyman Dist. 32 NJ State Assembly, 1988—2004. Committeman Secaucus Municipality, N.J., 1979-80, coun., 1981-2004; pres. RVG Corp., Secaucus, 1973-80; ptnr. Impreveduto Family Partnership, 1983-2004, Secaucus 83 Assn., Newark, 1983-2004; pres. Secaucus 84 Orgn., 1984-89. Bus. dept. supervisor Secaucus Bd. Edn., 1971-2004; founder New Dem. Orgn.; past pres Holy Name Soc. Immaculate Conception Ch. Mem. Nat. Assn. Secondary Sch. Prins. & Supervisors, Am. Legis. Exch. Coun., N.J. Prins. & Supervisors Assn., Rotary. Died Aug. 6, 2009.

INABA, YOSHIO, civil engineer, consultant; b. Holualoa, Hawaii, Jan. 1, 1911; s. Zentaro and Hatsuyo (Miyamoto) I.; m. Nora Yikeda, May 31, 1949; children: Eileen H., Alan I., Gordon Y., Melvin K., Barbara S. BSCE, U. Hawaii, 1935. Registered profl. civil engr., structural engr., land surveyor, Hawaii. Head bur. plans & survey County of Hawaii Dept. Pub. Works, Hilo, 2d asst. engr., chief engr., 1953-63; pres. Inaba Engring., Inc., Hilo, from 1964. Mem. Am. Consulting Engrs. Coun. Home: Hilo, Hawaii. Died Apr. 17, 2008.

INMAN, BEVERLY JEANNE, German and cultural history educator; b. Cedar Rapids, Iowa, June 17, 1944; d. Gorden Loren and Elva Gail (Spence) I. BA in German and History cum laude, Coe Coll., 1966; postgrad., U. Wash., 1966-67; MA in German-European History, U. Iowa, 1969, PhD in German Lang. and Lit., 1984, EdS in Higher Edn. Adminstrn., 1988. Cert. cmty. coll. tchr., Iowa. Grad. asst. German and lang. media U. Iowa, Iowa City, 1971-77; instr. German Quincy (Ill.) Coll., 1975-76; vis. instr. German Iowa State U., Ames, 1986; asst. prof. German Winona (Minn.) State U., 1984-85; instr. German U. Memphis, 1989-93; instr. German and humanities Talladega (Ala.) Coll., 1993-95; instr. German, history and humanities Kirkwood C.C., Cedar Rapids, Iowa, 1982-83 and from 96. English tchr. Geschwister-Scholl-Schule, Hannover, Germany, 1973-74. Assoc. editor U. Iowa, 1978-83. Scholar Fulbright Found., 1976, European Acad. for Urban Affairs, 1994; fellow German Acad. Exch. Svc., Cornell, U., Ithaca, N.Y., 1991. Mem. Fulbright Assn Home: Iowa City, Iowa. Died Aug. 25, 2007.

INMAN, BRYCE DAVID, electronics engineer; b. Marshalltown, Iowa, Nov. 29, 1921; s. David Rufo and Helen (Hyatt) I.; m. Pauline Constance Kattau, Oct. 23, 1943 (dec. 1972); children: Patrica Jane, David Rufo II; m. Suzanne Cole Green, Mar. 23, 1974. BSChemE, Ohio State U., 1943; BSEE, U.S. Navy Postgrad. Sch., 1951, MSEE, 1952. Commd. ensign USN, 1943, advanced through grades to capt., 1962, ret., 1970; radar br. head USN Bur. of Ships, Washington, 1964-67; commanding officer Navy Underwater Sound Lab./Naval Underwater Systems Ctr., New London, Conn., 1968-70; engring. mgr. RCA, Missile & Surface Radar Div., Moorestown, N.J., 1970-84, program dir., 1984-86. Decorated Navy Commendation medal, USN, 1965, 68, Meritorious Svc. medal, 1970. Mem. IEEE (sr.), Am. Soc. Naval Engrs. (life, Gold Medal award, 1982), U.S. Naval Inst. Achievements include co-development of combat systems for the USS Ticonderoga cruiser class and USS Arleigh Burke destroyer class. Home: Medford, NJ. Died Aug. 8, 2007.

IPES, THOMAS PETER JR., marriage and family therapist; b. Paterson, NJ, Feb. 25, 1948; s. Thomas Peter Sr. and Ruth Lydia (Kroncke) Ipes; m. Mary Anne Simmons, Aug. 16, 1970; children: Christine Marie, Melinda Joy, Thomas Peter IV. BA, Columbia Union Coll., 1970; MDiv., Andrews U., 1973; DMin., Lancaster Theol. Sem., 1982. Cert. sex therapist, sex educator, marriage and family therapist, clin. supr. Chaplain Wash. Adventist Hosp., Takoma Park, Md.; pastor The Christian Ch., Colorado Springs, Colo.; clin. dir. The Christian Counseling Ctr., Newburgh, Ind. Adj. faculty Western Ky. U., Bowling Green; speaker, host two weekly radio programs. Author newpaper column; contbr. articles to profl. jours. Recipient Disting. Hoosier award Gov. of Ind., 1985, Outstanding Man award, 1985, Disting. Community Svc. award, 1986. Fellow Nat. Acad. of Counselors and Family Therapists (supr., clin. mem.); Am. Assn. for Marriage and Family Therapy, Am. Assn. of Sex Educators, Counselors and Therapists, Am. Orthopsychiat. Assn., Christian Assn. for Psychol. Studies, Am. Enrichment, Nat. Coun. on Family Rels., Christian Med. Soc. Died Jan. 6, 2008.

IRELAND, DAVID KENNETH, artist; b. Bellingham, Wash., Aug. 25, 1930; Student, Western Wash. State U., Bellingham, 1948—50; BAA, Calif. Coll. Arts and Crafts, Oakland, 1953; postgrad., Laney Coll., Oakland, 1972—74; MFA, San Francisco Art Inst., 1974. One-man shows include Arts Club Chgo., 1996, Ctr. Arts Yerba Buena Gardens, San Francisco, 1996, Gallery Am. Acad., Rome, 1997, Gallery Paule Anglim, San Francisco, 1998, one-man shows include, 2001, 2006, Freedman Gallery, Reading, Pa., 2000, Jack Shainman Gallery, NYC, 2000, Christopher Grimes Gallery, Santa Monica, Calif., 2001, Oakland Mus. Calif., 2003—04, Addison Gallery Am. Art, Phillips Acad., Andover, Mass., 2003—04, Sheldon Meml. Art Gallery and Sculpture Garden, U. Nebr., Lincoln, 2003—04, Santa Barbara Mus. Art, Calif., 2003—04, numerous others. Died May 17, 2009.

IRELAND, ROBERT ABNER, JR., education consultant; b. Winterville, Miss., Nov. 13, 1918; s. Robert A. Sr. and Clara Lee (Johnson) I.; children: Robert A. III (dec.), Daniel G., Merry L., Kathleen, Joseph K., John E., Christopher M. BA, U. Va., 1941; MS, Columbia U., 1947; MA, Pepperdine U., 1974. Cert. counselor, Calif., career counselor. Commd. 2nd lt. U.S. Army, 1941, advanced through grades to lt. col., 1961, ret., 1972, edn. svcs. officer, counselor ednl.-vocat., 1976-80; cons. edn. U.S. Navy, LA, 1981-93; ind. cons. career devel. LA, 1988-93. Mem. AACD, APA, Academic and Profl. Soc. in Counseling, Am. Ednl. Rsch. Assn., Nat. Coun. on Measurement in Edn., Nat. Soc. for the Study of Edn., Mil. Testing Assn., Phi Delta Kappa, Chi Sigma Iota, Kappa Delta Pi. Died Nov. 1, 2007.

IRONS, SPENCER ERNEST, lawyer; b. Chgo., Sept. 15, 1917; s. Ernest Edward and Gertrude Bertwhistle (Thompson) I.; m. Betty M. Chesnut, Jan. 16, 1954; children: Janet L., Nancy G., Edward S. AB, U. Chgo., 1938; JD, U. Mich., 1941. Bar: Ill. 1941, U.S. Dist. Ct. (no. dist.) Ill. 1953, U.S. Supreme Ct. 1962. Assoc. Holmes, Dixon, Knouff & Potter, Chgo., 1946-50, McKinney, Carlson, Leaton & Smalley, Chgo., 1950-54, ptnr., 1955-58; sr. atty. Brunswick Corp., Skokie, Ill., 1959-82; pvt. practice Flossmoor, Ill., 1983-92; ret., 1992. Mem. bd. editors U. Mich. Law Rev., 1939-41. Mem. bd. trustees Flossmoor Pub. Library, 1959-61; mem. Chgo. Crime Commn., 1954-82. Lt. col. U.S. Army, 1941-46, 61-62. Mem. ABA, Ill. Bar Assn., Chgo. Bar Assn. (bd. of mgrs. 1954-56), Law Club. Republican. Unitarian Universalist. Home: Northbrook, Ill. Died Apr. 16, 2008.

IVES, EDWARD DAWSON, folklore educator; b. White Plains, NY, Sept. 4, 1925; s. Warren Livingston and Millicent Clarissa (Dawson) I.; m. Barbara Ann Herrel, Sept. 8, 1951; children— Stephen John, Nathaniel Edward, Sarah Ruth AB, Hamilton Coll., 1948; MA, Columbia U., 1950; PhD, Ind. U., 1962; LLD, U. P.E.I., 1986; DLitt, Meml. U., Newfoundland, 1996. Instr. English Ill. Coll., Jacksonville, 1950-53; lectr. CCNY, 1953-54; instr. English U. Maine, Orono, 1955-62, asst. prof., 1962-64, assoc. prof., 1964-69, prof. folklore, 1969-99, chmn. anthropology dept., 1983-89; dir. Northeast Archives Folklore and Oral History, 1971-99, Maine Folklife Ctr., 1992-99, emeritus, 1999—2009. Author: Larry Gorman: The Man Who Made the Songs, 1964, reprinted 1993, Lawrence Doyle: The Farmer-Poet of Prince Edward Island, 1971, Joe Scott: The Woodsman-Songmaker, 1978, The Tape Recorded Interview, 1980, reprinted 1995, George Magoon and the Down East Game War, 1988, reprinted 1993, Folksongs of New Brunswick, 1989; (with Bruce Jackson) The World Observed, 1996, The Bonny Earl of Murray: The Man, the Murder, the Ballad, 1997, Drive Dull Care Away: Folksongs from Prince Edward Island, 1999. Served with USMC, 1943-46 Guggenheim fellow, 1965—66. Fellow Am. Folklore Soc.; mem. Oral History Assn. Home: Orono, Maine. Died Aug. 1, 2009.

JACKSON, BERYL B., nursing educator, psychiatric-mental health nurse; b. Cambride, Jamaica, Oct. 2, 1923; d. Edward E. and Elsie M. (Miles) Haughton; m. McIver Jackson, Nov. 18, 1961; children: McIver Jr., Lenora Jackson West, Jacqueline A. Jackson Brooks. Diploma, Hackney Hosp. Sch. Nursing, London, 1954; BSN, Duquesne U., 1970; M in Nursing, U. Pitts., 1972, PhD, 1982. RN, Pa. Staff nurse Montefiore Hosp., Pitts.; clin. specialist Western Psychiat. Inst. and Clinic, Pitts.; asst. prof. U. Pitts. Sch. Nursing, assoc. prof. Contbr. articles to profl. jours. Recipient Hon. Recognition award Pa. Nurses Assn., 1991; Univ. scholar, 1980; grantee Nat. Inst. on Aging, 1987-89. Mem. ANA, Assn. Black Nursing Faculty in Higher Edn., Sigma Theta Tau. Home: Pittsburgh, Pa. Died Sept. 2, 2007.

JACKSON, DELLA M., critical care nurse; b. Idabel, Okla., Mar. 5, 1929; d. Johnny Sr. and Della (Wright) Shelton; m. David Jackson, Apr. 14, 1964; children: Carl, Carolyn, McKinley, Anthony. LPN, Oklahoma City Vocat. Coll., 1966; AD, Okla. State U., Oklahoma City, 1973; BS in Edn., Cen. State U., Edmond, Okla., 1977, MEd, 1983; BSN, Langston U., 1986. RN, Okla.; cert. HIV antibody testing counselor. Staff nurse Mercy Health Ctr., Oklahoma City, charge nurse post coronary care unit. Vol. ARC, Buddy Support Group for AIDS of The Cath. Charities of Okla. Mem. Nat. Black Nurse's Assn., Okla. Black Nurse's Assn., Okla. Lupus Assn. Home: Oklahoma City, Okla. Died Oct. 18, 2007.

JACKSON, GENE FRANKLIN, marketing company executive; b. Carlos, Ind., Apr. 18, 1929; s. Irvin and Lillie (Strahan) J.; m. Sharon L. Allison, July 15, 1970; children: Marta, Laura, Bruce, Rhonda, Tom, Gina. BSEE, Wichita State U., 1957; postgrad., Tex. Christian U., 1961. Sr. aerosystem engr. Gen. Dynamics, Ft. Worth, 1960-66; internat. marketing rep. Magnavox Corp., Ft. Wayne, Ind., 1966-68; mktg. mgr. ITT, Ft. Wayne, 1968-71; pres. Franklin Mktg. Group, Ft. Wayne, 1971-79; pres., chief exec. officer Franklin Mktg. Inc., Largo, Fla., from 1979, Govt. Purchasing Digest, Largo, Fla., from 1989, Govt. Purchasing Data Link, Largo, from 1989. Capt. USAF, 1950-59. Mem. Masons. Avocation: flying. Home: Seminole, Fla. Died June 15, 2008.

JACKSON, HELENE, social worker, educator; d. Jacob and Jennie Cooper; m. Abraham W. Berger, Oct. 9, 1982; children: David, Jonathan. BA, Simmons Coll., 1973; MSW, Boston U., 1975; PhD, Smith Coll., 1982. Clin. social worker VA, Boston, 1975—79, dir. rsch. and tng., 1979—82; dir. field instrn. Boston Coll. Sch. Social Work, Chestnut Hill, Mass., 1984—92; assoc. prof., dir. of continuing edn. Columbia U. Sch. Social Work, NYC, from 1992. Pvt. practice, from 1975. Editor: Using Self Psychology in Psychotherapy, 1991; author: Childhood Abuse: Effects on Clinicians' Personal and Professional Lives, 1997; contbr. articles to profl. jours.; cons. mem. editl. bd. Health and Social Wk. Jour., 1997—2001, editl. adv. bd. Sage Series on Counseling Women, 1994—99, Sage Violence and Rsch. Abstracts, 1994. Mem. adv. coun. Commonwealth Mass. Office for Children State Wide, 1991—93. Recipient Clin. Faculty Scholar award, NIH, 1987-1990; named Disting. scholar, Nat. Acad. of Practice, Edgewood, Md., 2001. Fellow: N.Y. Acad. Sci.; mem.: NASW (faculty liaison 1992—96), Coun. on Social Work Edn., Am. Profl. Soc. on the Abuse of Children (charter mem., mem. at large 1993). Died Apr. 21, 2008.

JACKSON, JAMES FRASER, physician; b. Coulsden, Surrey, Eng., Apr. 27, 1919; came to U.S., 1919; s. James Henry and Sara (McConnache) J.; m. Irene Sjoblom, Oct. 20, 1948; children: David, Anne, Robert. BA, U. Mich., 1941; MD, U. Pitts., 1944. Diplomate Am. Bd. Family Practice. Intern Allegheny Gen. Hosp., Pitts., 1944-45; resident internal medicine West Penn Hosp., Pitts., 1947-50; pvt. practice East Liverpool, Ohio, from 1950. Chmn. bd. Ctrl. Fed. Savs. and Loan. Capt., M.C. U.S. Army, 1945-47. Named 1st Doctor of Yr. Home Health Svc., East Liverpool, Ohio, 1989; named Outstanding East Liverpool High Sch. Grad., 1992. Mem. Lions. Republican. Presbyterian. Home: East Liverpool, Ohio. Died Oct. 17, 2007.

JACKSON, MICHAEL JOSEPH, singer; b. Gary, Ind., Aug. 29, 1958; s. Joseph Walter and Katherine Esther (Scruse) Jackson; m. Lisa Marie Presley, May 18, 1994 (div. Jan. 18, 1996); m. Debbie Jeanne Rowe, Nov. 15, 1996 (div. Oct. 8, 1999); children: Michael Joseph Jr., Paris Michael Katherine; 1 child, Prince Michael II. Student pvt. sch.; LHD (hon.), Fisk U., 1988. Singer The Jackson Five, 1966—84; solo artist, 1972—2009. Singer: (albums with The Jackson-Five) Diana Ross Presents the Jackson Five, 1969, ABC, 1970, Third Album, 1970, The Jackson Five Christmas Album, 1970, Maybe Tomorrow, 1971, Goin' Back to Indiana, 1971, Greatest Hits, 1971, Looking Through the Windows, 1972, Skywriter, 1973, The Jackson 5 in Japan, 1973, G.I.T.: Get It Together, 1973, Dancing Machine, 1974, Moving Violation, 1975, Joyful Jukebox Music, 1976, The Jacksons, 1976, Anthology, 1976, Goin' Places, 1977, Destiny, 1978, Boogie, 1979, Triumph, 1980, The Jacksons Live!, 1981, Victory, 1984, Soulsation!, 1995, Jackson 5: The Ultimate Collection, 1995, The Essential Jacksons, 2004, The Very Best of The Jacksons, 2004, (solo albums) Got To Be There, 1972, Ben, 1972, Music and Me, 1973, Forever, Michael, 1975, Off the Wall, 1979, Thriller, 1982 (Grammy Award for Best Male Pop Vocal Performance, 1983, Grammy Award for Album of the Yr., 1983, Grammy Award for Best Video Album, 1984), Bad, 1987, Dangerous, 1991, HIStory: Past, Present and Future, Book 1, 1995, Blood on the Dance Floor/History in the Mix, 1997, Invincible, 2001; actor: (TV series) The Jacksons, 1976—77; (films) The Wiz, 1978, Men in Black II, 2002, Miss Cast Away, 2004, (short films) Captain EO, 1986, Dangerous, 1993; performer: (TV specials) Michael Jackson: 30th Anniversary TV Special, 2001, (films) This Is It, 2009; author: (autobiography) Moonwalk, 1988, Dancing the Dream Poems and Reflections, 1992. Founder Heal the World Found., 1992—2002. Recipient Grammy Award for Best R&B Vocal Performance (Don't Stop 'til You Get Enough), 1979, Grammy Award for Best Recording for Children (E.T. The Extra-Terrestrial), 1983, Grammy Award for Best Rhythm & Blues Song (Billie Jean), 1983, Grammy Award for Best Male R&B Vocal Performance (Billie Jean), 1983, Grammy Award for Best Male Rock Vocal Performance (Beat It), 1983, Grammy Award for Record of the Yr. (Beat It), 1983, Grammy Award for Best Music Video (Leave Me Alone), 1989, Star on Hollywood Walk of Fame, 1984, MTV Vangaurd Award, 1988, Lifetime Achievement award, Guiness Book of World Records, 1993, MTV Movie Award for Best Movie Song (Will You Be There), 1994, Bob Fosse award, 1997, Best Selling Male Pop Artist of the Millennium award, World Music Awards, 2000; co-recipient w/ Quincy Jones, Grammy Award for Producer of the Yr. (Non-Classical), 1983, w/ Lionel Richie, Grammy Award for Song of the Yr. (We Are The World), 1985, w/ Janet Jackson, Grammy Award for Best Music Video (Scream), 1995, w/ Janet Jackson, MTV Video Music Award for Best Dance Video (Scream), 1995, w/ Janet Jackson, MTV Video Music Award for Best Art Direction (Scream), 1995, w/ Janet Jackson, MTV Video Music Award for Best Choreography (Scream), 1995; named to The Rock & Roll Hall of Fame, (as a mem. of The Jackson-Five), 1997, (as a solo artist), 2001, Songwriters Hall of Fame, 2002. Achievements include holding the record for most Grammys won in one year with 8 in 1983; record for best selling album of all-time (Thriller); record for the three best selling albums of all-time, (Thriller, Dangerous, Bad). Died June 25, 2009.

JACKSON, PATRICK JOSEPH, real estate company officer; b. Minn., Mar. 31, 1942; s. Paul Arthur and Lucille Margaret (Cummings) J.; m. Barbara Ann Simpson, July 19, 1964 (div. Apr. 1980); children: Laura Kathleen, Katherine Lucille; m. Shirley Ann Wellman, Sept. 12, 1982 (div. Oct. 1998); m. Kath Jo Holm, Sept. 9, 2001; 1 child, Liza Ann Holm. BS, Portland State U., 1968. Bank loan officer First Nat. Bank of Oreg., Portland, 1964-68; credit mgr. Meier & Frank Corp., Portland, 1968-70; agt., mgr. Aetna Life, San Jose, Calif., 1970-75; dist. mgr. Calif. Casualty, San Jose, 1975-78; gen. agt. Great So. Life, San Jose, 1978-82; account agt., agy. owner Allstate Ins., San Jose, 1982—2001; assoc. broker Home Realty, from 2001; pres. Delta Direct Enterprises, Sequim, Wash., from 2001. Instr. Santa Clara (Calif.) U., 1974-76. Author: (monograph) The Affairs of, 1978; newspaper columnist, 1978-04. Mem. ins. subcom. Calif. State Senate, 1978; officer Los Gatos (Calif.) Police Res., 1970-78, treas., 1974-78; mem. Sch. Site Coun., Saratoga, Calif., 1978-80; mem. City Coun., Discovery Bay, Calif., 1991-95, mayor, 1993-94; mem. port commn. Port Angeles, Wash., 2002-04. Named Man of Yr., Los Gatos Youth Unltd., 1978. Mem. San Jose Life Underwriters (bd. dirs. 1974-76), No. Calif. Tollycraft Assn. (sec. 1995-97), Sequim Bay Yacht Club, Puget Sound Anglers, Jefferson County Sportsman Club. Republican. Lutheran. Avocations: boating, fishing, shooting, reading. Home: Sequim, Wash. Died June 23, 2008.

JACKSON, ROBERT EVANS, construction company executive, consultant; b. Los Angeles, Aug. 29, 1928; s. Curtis and Genevee (Evans) J.; m. Jacqueline Kuemmel, June 18, 1950; children: Karen, Susanne. BSE, U. So. Calif., 1953. V.p. engrng. and mfg. Challenge Cook Bros., Industry, Calif., 1968-74, sr. v.p. engrng., 1974-80, v.p. internat. engrng., 1980-84; cons. in field Santa Ana, Calif., from 1985. Patentee in field. Served with USN, 1946-48. Mem. ASME. Clubs: Balboa Bay (Newport, Calif.). Republican. Presbyterian. Avocations: gardening, tennis, skiing. Home: Bend, Oreg. Died Nov. 30, 2007.

JACOB, LOUISE HELEN, secondary school educator; b. Cameron, Wis., May 19, 1924; d. Howard Walter and Agnes Augusta Elizabeth (Berger) Melbye; m. Wayne Thompson Jacob, July 21, 1956; children: Robert Douglas, Steven Allan. BS, Wis. State Coll., River Falls, 1946; MS, U. Wis., 1952; postgrad., Columbia U., NYC, summer 1955. Cert. tchr., Minn., Wis. English tchr. Barron (Wis.) Pub. Schs., 1946-48, Watertown (Wis.) Pub. Schs., 1948—51; dormitory counselor U. Wis., Madison, 1951—52; English tchr. Madison Pub. Schs., 1952—56, Robbinsdale (Minn.) Area Schs., 1956—59, 1966—91; chmn. English dept. Sandburg Jr. High Sch., Robbinsdale, 1968—72, 1978—88; retired. Condr. seminars on gifted edn. Minn. Dept. Edn., 1969-75, on women's rights, 1970-80. Del., precinct chairwoman, state edn. platform com. Rep. Party, Robbinsdale, 1964-74; mem. Robbinsdale Human Rights Commn., 1967. Mem. Robbinsdale Fedn. Tchrs. (legis. chmn. 1970-73, chmn. women's rights 1974-76), LWV (bd. dirs., chmn. pub. rels., v.p. Robbinsdale chpt. 1957-70), AAUW (bd. dirs. Mpls. chpt.) Lutheran. Avocations: travel, theater, reading, sewing. Home: Robbinsdale, Minn. Died Aug. 29, 2007.

JACOBI, LOU, actor; b. Toronto, Ont., Can., Dec. 28, 1913; s. Joseph and Fay J.; m. Ruth Ludwin, July 15, 1957 (dec. 2004) Student, Jarvis Collegiate Sch., Toronto. Drama dir. Toronto YMHA, 1940. Theatrical appearances include The Rabbi and the Priest, 1924, Spring Thaw, 1949, Remains to be Seen, 1952, Pal Joey, 1954, The World of Sholem Aleichem, 1955, Into Thin Air, 1955, The Diary of Anne Frank, 1955, The Tenth Man, 1959, Come Blow Your Horn, 1961, Fade In-Fade Out, 1964, Don't Drink the Water, 1966, A Way of Life, 1969, Norman Is that You?, 1971, Epstein, 1971, Eli the Fanatic, 1971, Milliken Breakfast Show, 1972, The Sunshine Boys, 1974, Cheaters, 1978; (films) Is Your Honeymoon Really Necesary?, 1953, The Good Beginning, 1953, A Kid for 2 Farthings, 1956, Charley Moon, 1956, The Diary of Anne Frank, 1959, Song Without End, 1960, Irma La Douce, 1963, The Last of the Secret Agents, 1966, Penelope, 1966, Cotton Comes to Harlem, 1970, Little Murders, 1971, Everything You Always Wanted to Know About Sex But Were Afraid to Ask, 1971, Next Stop, Greenwich Village, 1976, Roseland, 1977, The Magician of Lublin, 1979, The Lucky Star, 1980, Arthur, 1981, Chu Chu and the Philly Flash, 1981, My Favorite Year, 1982, Isaac Littlefeathers, 1984, Amazon Women on the Moon, 1987, Avalon, 1990, I Don't Buy Kisses Anymore, 1992, IQ, 1994; (TV movies) Kibbee Hates Fitch, 1965, Allan, 1971, Decisions! Decisions!, 1972, The Judge and Jake Wyler, 1972, Coffee, Tea or Me?, 1973, Ivan the Terrible, 1976, Rear Guard, 1976, Somerset, 1976, Better Late Then Never, 1979, Off Your Rocker, 1982, Joanna, 1985, If It's Tuesday, It Still Must Be Belgium, 1987, Takes from the Hollywood Hills: The Old Reliable, 1988, Deep Dish TV, 1992; (TV appearances) Douglas Fairbanks, Jr., Presents (2 episodes), 1953-54, The Texan, 1959, Playhouse 90, 1959, Play of the Week, 1960, The Defenders, 1962, Sam Benedict, 1963, The Alfred Hitchcock Hour (2 episodes), 1963-64, The Dick Van Dyke Show, 1965, The Trials of O'Brien, 1965, The Man From U.N.C.L.E., 1966, ABC Stage 67, 1966, That Girl (2 episodes), 1969, Love, American Style (5 episodes), 1969-73, Make Room for Granddaddy, 1971, The Courtship of Eddie's Father, 1971, Barney Miller, 1975, Sanford and Son, 1975, King of Kensington, 1979, Tales of the Unexpected, 1982, Too Close for Comfort (2 episodes), 1983-84, Tales from the Darkside, 1984, Cagney & Lacey, 1985, St. Elsewhere, 1985, Comedy Factory, 1986, Melba (6 episodes), 1986, ABC Weekend Specials, 1986, L.A. Law, 1989 Died Oct. 23, 2009.

JACOBS, MERLE EMMOR, zoology educator, researcher; b. Nov. 30, 1918; s. Paul Anthony and Trello Elizabeth (Risch) J.; m. Elizabeth Beyeler, June 6, 1959. BA, Goshen Coll., 1948; PhD, Ind. U., 1953. Assoc. prof. Duke U., Durham, N.C., 1953-57; prof. Bethany (W.Va.) Coll., 1957-61, Ea. Mennonite Coll., Harrisonburg, Va.,

1961-64; rsch. prof. Goshen (Ind.) Coll., 1964-86. Contbr. articles to profl. jours. Recipient Eigenmann award Ind. U., 1950. Home: Smithville, Ohio. Died Apr. 9, 2008.

JACOBS, RICHARD E. (DICK JACOBS), real estate company executive, former professional sports team executive; b. Akron, Ohio, June 16, 1925; children: Jeffrey, Nancy, Marilyn. BbA, Ind. U., 1949. Ptnr. Jacobs, Visconsi & Jacobs; chmn., CEO Cleve. Indians, 1986—2001. Served in US Army. Died June 5, 2009.

JACOBS, ROBERT NEIL, meat industry executive; b. LA, Jan. 27, 1938; s. Donald Henry and Bertha Amanda (Reeves) J.; m. Patricia Ann Dickinson, June 23, 1955 (div. May 28, 1983); children: Mary Patricia, Debra Elaine, Robert Neil Jr., Jeffrey David, George William, John Harold, Michael James, Michelle Elizabeth; m. Geraldine Yoko Pennell, Oct. 8, 1983. Salesperson H. Shenson, Inc., San Francisco, 1958-70; gen. mgr. Wing-Lee Valley Meat Co., Sacramento, 1970-78; owner Horatio's Restaurant, Sacramento, 1979-82; sales mgr. Luce & Co., Inc., San Francisco, 1983-84; dir. meat ops. Bi-Rite Food Svc., San Francisco, 1988-90; gen. sales mgr. Facciola Meat Co., Palo Alto, Calif., 1984-88, 90-93; pres. RNJ Assocs., San Francisco, from 1991; dir. sales No. Calif. Durham Meat Co., San Jose, Calif., from 1994. Pres. Little League, Sacramento, 1969-71. Mem. Pacific Coast Chefs Assn. (assoc.). Republican. Baptist. Avocations: gardening, travel, cooking. Home: San Francisco, Calif. Died May 12, 2008.

JACOBS, WILLIAM RUSSELL, II, lawyer; b. Chgo., Oct. 26, 1927; s. William Russell and Doris B. (Desmond) J.; m. Shirley M. Spiegler, Mar. 21, 1950; children: William R. III, Richard W., Bruce Allen. BS, Northwestern U., 1950, JD, 1953. Bar: Ill. 1953, U.S. Dist. Ct. (no. dist.) Ill. 1958, U.S. Ct. Appeals (7th cir.) 1958, U.S. Supreme Ct., 1962. Atty. Continental Casualty Co., Chgo., 1955-58; assoc. Horwitz and Anesi, Chgo., 1958-62; prin. William R. Jacobs and Assocs., Chgo., from 1962. Adj. prof. Lewis Coll. Law, Glen Ellyn, Ill., 1975-76; dir., tchr. Ct. Practice Inst., Chgo., 1974—; lectr. Ill. Inst. Continuing Legal Edn., Chgo., 1967—. Elected alderman Des Plaines (Ill.) City Coun., 1953-54; mem. Ill. Bar Assembly, 1973—. 1st lt. inf. U.S. Army, 1946-48. Mem. Ill. State Bar Assn., Am. Acad. Matrimonial Lawyers. Congregationalist. Died Sept. 6, 2007.

JACOBUS, MARY, publishing executive; b. 1957; m. Dean Jacobus; children: Kelly, Kimberly, Bill. BA in English, Le Moyne Coll., Syracuse, NY, 1979. With Buffalo News, NY, Buffalo Courier Express, NY, Long Beach Press-Telegram, NY, 1981—89; dir. sales & mktg. Escondido Times Adv., Calif., 1989—95; v.p. sales & mktg. Colorado Springs Gazette, 1995—98; pres., pub. News Tribune, Duluth, Minn., 1998—2001; pub. News-Sentinel, Ft. Wayne, Ind., 2001—05; CEO Ft. Wayne Newspapers, Inc., Ft. Wayne, Ind., 2001—05; pres., gen. mgr. Boston Globe, 2006; pres., COO Regional Media Group NY Times Co., 2006—09. Bd. dirs. AP, 2007—09. Died Feb. 20, 2009.

JAFFE, STEVEN, librarian; b. NYC, Sept. 7, 1928; s. Aaron and Rose (Levine) J.; m. Louise M. Jaffe, Aug. 26, 1962 (div. Dec. 1974); 1 child, Aaron L.; m. Rae R. Jaffe, Dec. 26, 1976; stepchildren: Claudia L. Finneran, Lauren A. Finneran. BA, Yeshiva Coll., 1952; MA in History, Columbia U., 1953, MLS, 1958. Reference librarian Pollack Library Yeshiva U., NYC, 1958-60; librarian U.S. Naval Applied Sci. Lab., Bklyn., 1960-70; corp. librarian Consol. Edison Co., NYC, from 1970. Mem. Spl. Libraries Assn. (pres. N.Y. chapter 1974-75), U.S. Naval Inst., Navy League, Civil War Round Table of N.Y. Clubs: Edison Camera (pres. 1974-76). Avocations: photography, travel, walking. Home: Forest Hills, NY. Died Apr. 19, 2008.

JAMES, WAYNE EDWARD, electronic engineer; b. Racine, Wis., Apr. 2, 1950; s. Ronald Dean James and Arlene Joyce (Mickelsen) Dawson; m. Edith Yvonne Cone, Apr. 6, 1997; children: Terry Scott, Kevin Arthur. BS in Electronic Engring. Tech., U. So. Colo., 1976; MS in Computer Sci., Colo. U., 1996. Electronic technician Lawrence Livermore (Calif.) Nat. Lab., 1976-80, Inmos Corp., Colorado Springs, Colo., 1980-86, CAD engr., 1986-87, United Techs. Microelectronics Ctr., Colorado Springs, 1988-97, ASIC engr., from 1997. Sec.-treas. Stratmoor Hills Vol. Fire Dept., Colorado Springs, 1983, 84, lt., 1985, capt., 1986. Served with USN, 1968-72. Named Fireman of Yr., Stratmoor Hills Vol. Fire Dept., 1983. Lutheran. Home: Hemet, Calif. Died Apr. 4, 2008.

JAMISON, JOHN, mortgage banker, author; b. Asheville, NC, Sept. 19, 1938; s. John R. and Alice (Wild) J.; m. Laura Rayburn, Nov. 26, 1983. BA, Vanderbilt U., 1960; ThM, So. Seminary, Louisville, 1965. Chaplain U. Md., College Park, 1965-69; gen. mgr. Flintridge Corp., Phoenix, 1969-71; asst. v.p. Kissell Co., Phoenix, 1971-77; v.p. United Mortgage Co., Denver, 1977-78, Rainier Mortgage Co., Seattle, 1978-82; pres. Comml. Mortgage of Santa Barbara, Calif., 1983-87; v.p. City Commerce Bank, Santa Barbara, 1987-91; pres. Loan Svc. Assocs., San Francisco, from 1991. Contbr. articles to various profl. jours. Pres. Washington Coalition for Affordable Housing, Seattle, 1980-81; bd. dirs. Tri-County Red Cross, Santa Barbara, 1990-91. Capt. USAR, 1960-68. Mem. Coun. for Innovative Housing Solutions (pres. 1991—), Flat Earth Soc. (sec. 1987-91), Phi Beta Kappa. Avocations: glider pilot, scuba diving, writing. Home: San Francisco, Calif. Died Apr. 21, 2008.

JANITSCHEK, HANS, journalist; b. Vienna, Nov. 6, 1934; s. Norbert J and Grete Helene Janitschek; m. Elfriede Gerda Ruisinger Janitschek, Aug. 6, 1959; children: Stefan Patrick, Angela Judith. BA, Haverford coll., Haverford, PA, 1953—54; MA, U. of Vienna, Vienna, Austria, 1955—57. Staff corr. United Press, Vienna, 1955—57, Reuter's, Vienna, 1958—59; fgn. editor Express Newspaper, Vienna, 1960—62; vice consul Austrian Govt., New York, NY, 1963—64; sec. gen. Socialist Internat., London, 1965—76. Chmn./pres. Earth Soc. Found., New York, NY, 1992; pres. Un Soc. Of Writers &Art, New York, NY, 1988; US corres. Kronenzeitung newspaper, Vienna, 1994; v.p. World Security Network Found., NYC, 2004. Author: (book) Mario Soares, Portrait, Oscar Arias, Pursuit Of Peace, Hans Dichand, Biography. Mem. Dutch Treat Club, New York, NY, 1979, Met. Club, New York, NY, 1979. Roman Catholic. Died Feb. 21, 2008.

JANSEN, LAMBERTUS, retired state agency administrator, judge, criminal justice educator; b. Salt Lake City, Oct. 27, 1934; s. Lambertus Christianus and Cobi Maria (van Ekelenburg) J.; m. Rosemary Van Dyke, Aug. 22, 1958 (div. 1969); children: Jackie Lyn, David Scott; m. LaNita Joyce Lindley, Sept. 10, 1982. AA, Westminster Coll., Salt Lake City, 1954, BS, 1959; JD, U. Utah, 1968. Bar: Utah 1968, NY 1983. Tchr. English Jordan Sch. Dist., Sandy, Utah, 1959-62; fraud investigator Utah Job Svc., Salt Lake City, 1962-65; instr. U. Utah, Salt Lake City, 1965-68; lawyer Jansen Law Office, Salt Lake City, 1968-83, Hyatt Legal Svc., Syracuse, NY, 1983-87, Shanley Law Office, Oswego, NY, 1987-92; city ct. judge Oswego, 1992-2000; hearing officer Utah Dept. Health, Salt Lake City, 2000—05; ret. Adj. prof. criminal justice Salt Lake C.C. Dir. Utah Housing Devel. Agy., Salt Lake City, 1969-71; mem. steering com. Oswego County Anti-Drug Program, 1996-97; mem. Oswego County Drug Ct. Program, 1996-97. Mem. Am. Judges Assn., NY State City Ct. Judges Assn., Am. Trial Lawyers Assn., Utah State Bar, Utah Bar Assn., Salt Lake County Bar. Roman Catholic. Avocations: skiing, hiking, golf, camping. Home: Tooele, Utah. Died Sept. 4, 2008.

JANSON, RICHARD WILFORD, manufacturing executive; b. Canton, Ohio, Mar. 4, 1926; s. Wilford Sherwood and Mary Rebecca (Elliott) J.; m. Nancy Louise Davies, Oct. 31, 1955; children: Hollis L., Daniel W., Raymond E., Eric H. BA, Denison U., 1949; MA, Kent State U., 1982, PhD, 1986. Ptnr. Janson Industries, Canton, from 1949. Ptnr. Sta. WJAN TV 17 Canton, 1967-77; bd. dirs. Molecular Tech., Canton, 1987-88; treas., bd. dirs. J.C. Tech., Inc., Canton, 1986—; chmn. Edison Bd., Columbus, Ohio, 1983-93; adj. prof. Kent (Ohio) State U., 1987—; charter mem. Thomas Edison Program, 1982—, chmn., 1983-93. Author: Model of Spatial Revitalization, 1986; inventor stage hardware, 1980-90; contbr. articles to profl. jours. Trustee The Wilderness Ctr., Wilmot, Ohio, 1967-88; chmn. W. Va. Seating Co., Huntington, 1975-78. With USN, 1945-47. Mem. Am. Geog. Soc. (councilor), Ohio Acad. Sci. (past pres.). Democrat. Presbyterian. Achievements include 10 patents for aluminum extrusions, structural applications, and track systems; development of methodology for interregional simultaneous determination of output, real income, and commodity flows for n commodities and k regions. Home: Canton, Ohio. Died Apr. 6, 2008.

JANSSON, JOHN PHILLIP, architect, consultant; b. Phila., Nov. 27, 1918; s. John A. and Isabelle (Ericson) Jansson; m. Ann C. Winter, Apr. 8, 1944 (div. Oct. 1970); children: Linda Ann, Lora Jean; m. Elizabeth Clow Peer, Jan. 21, 1978 (dec. May 1984). BArch, Pratt Inst., 1947; postgrad., SUNY, 1949. Registered arch., N.Y., lic. Nat. Coun. Archtl. Registration Bd.s. Architect various firms, 1949—54; pvt. practice NYC, from 1949; cons. mktg. products, materials and svcs. to bldg. and constrn. industry, from 1949; exec. v.p. Archtl. Aluminum Mfrs. Assn., NYC, 1954—58; mgr. market devel. Olin-Metals Div., NYC, 1958—62; dir. Pope, Evans & Robbins, cons. engrs., 1970—82; ptnr. Morris Ketchum, Jr. and Assocs., Archs., 1964—68; exec. dir. N.Y. State Coun. Architecture, 1968—73; dir. Gruzen & Ptnrs., 1972—74; pres. Bldg. Constrn. Tech., 1975—78; v.p. Ehrenkrantz Group, 1974—82. Cons. N.Y. State Pure Waters Authority, 1968—69; chmn. N.Y. State Architecture-Constrn. Interagency Com., 1968—74; sec. N.Y. State Gov.'s Adv. Com. State Constrn. Programs, 1970—71; dir. U.S. trade mission leader to Nigeria Dept. of Commerce, 1981. Mem. N.Y. State Citizens Com. Pub. Schs., 1952—55; v.p. citizens adv. com. Housing Authority, Town of Oyster Bay, NY, 1966—68; bd. dirs. Bldg. Industry Data Adv. Coun., 1976—78, Park Ten Coop., 1981—82; instr. Outward Bound, Hurrican Island, Rockland, Maine, from 1982; media specialist Image Ctr. Am.'s Cup, 1987. Served to capt. USMCR, 1943—46. Mem.: AIA (mem. archs. govt. com. 1971—77), Soc. Mil. Engrs. Soc. N.Y.C., Am. Mgmt. Assn., Associated Coun. Arts, Nat. Trust Historic Preservation, Soc. Archtl. Historians, N.Y. State Assn. Archs. (dir.), N.Y. Bldg. Congress, Archtl. League N.Y., Nat. Inst. Bldg. Scis., BRAB Bldg. Rsch. Inst., Nat. Inst. Archtl. Edn., Constrn. Specialist Inst., Am. Arbitration Assn., Fleety Res. Assn., Victorian Soc. Am., Mus. Modern Art, U.S. Naval Acad. Officers and Faculty Club, Md. Capital Yacht Club (bd. dirs. 1993—94). Deceased.

JANUS, CHRISTOPHER GEORGE, writer; b. Charleston, W.Va., Mar. 25, 1911; s. George and Olympia (Xenopoulos) J.; m. Beatrice Short, May 30, 1940 (dec. 1989); children: Andronike, Christopher Jr., Lincoln. BS in Philosophy, Harvard U., 1936; postgrad., Oxford U., Eng., 1937. Registered rep. Prudential Bache, Chgo., 1955-80; cons. Standard Oil of Ind. (now Amoco), Chgo., 1978-82. Prin. Eximport Assocs., Chgo., 1947-67. Author: Miss 4th of July, Goodbye, 1986, What They Always Wanted, 1989; (short stories) The George Quartette, 1983; co-author: The Search for Peking Man, 1976; pub.: Only for Your Eyes, 1955; Greek Heritage Quar., 1963-65. Econ. asst. U.S. Dept. State, Washington, 1943-44; chief Greek desk, chief Balkan intelligence UNRRA, Cairo, Egypt and Athens, Greece, 1944-45; alt. del. UNRRA Conf., Atlantic City, 1944; del. Time-Life Internat. Indsl. Devel. Cons., San Francisco, 1957, Fgn. Aid and Point Four Seminar, Washington, 1958, First Cultural Delegation from U.S. to People's Republic of China, 1972; trustee Poetry Mag., 1950-82, Athens Coll., 1951-52; mem. com. Mayor's Office for Sr. Citizens and Handicapped, 1981-84, Friends of Chgo. Pub. Library, 1978; chmn. All Am. Com. United Rep. Fund of Ill. for Pres. Eisenhower Dinner, 1957-58. Served to lt. USNR, 1953-55. Recipient Services award Mus. Natural History, Beijing, 1979, Adelphi Achievement award Sta. WTTW, Washington, 1957, Spl. Commendation, Govt. of Greece, 1945, Friends of Lit. award for Best Novel, 1986. Mem. Nat. Probation and Parole Assn., Greek War Relief Assn. (chmn. Chgo. chpt. 1941-45). Clubs: Harvard, Overseas Press, Explorer's (New York); Harvard (pres. 1966-68), Caxton, Oxford-Cambridge, Tavern, Arts, Attic (Chgo.). Home: Wilmette, Ill. Died Feb. 19, 2009.

JAROS, ROBERT JAMES, information technology executive; b. Port Reading, NJ, June 30, 1939; s. Michael and Marian (Kurta) J.; children: Marian Reilly, Jennifer, Christina Student, Rutgers U., 1957-65. With Prudential Ins. Co., Newark, 1957-77; sr. sys. analyst, project leader Ins. Svcs. Office, NYC, 1977-81; project mgr. Shearson Lehman Bros. Inc., NYC, 1981-88; cons. G & J Assocs., Cliffwood, NJ, from 1988; commn. Middletown Housing Authority, 1995—2005. Trustee, v.p. Lin-Mid Corp., 1997—2005. Mem. Middletown Twp. Transp. Com., 1988-2005; mem., past pres. Rolling Knolls Civic Assn.; mem. U.S. Power Squadron, Watchung Power Squadron; Rep. County committeeman, Monmouth County, 1989-2001. With USAR, 1962-68. Fellow Life Mgmt Inst. Soc. of Greater N.Y.; mem. Am. Soc. CLU's, Am. Legion. Roman Catholic. Died Sept. 16, 2007.

JARRE, MAURICE ALEXIS, composer; b. Lyons, France, Sept. 13, 1924; s. André and Gabrielle (Boullu) J.; m. Dany Saval, Jan. 30, 1965 (div.); children: Stephanie, Jean-Michel; m. Laura Devon, Dec. 30, 1967 (div. March 14, 1984); m. Khong Fui Fong, Dec. 6, 1984. Composer: (film scores) Hotel des Invalides, 1952, Toute la memoire du monde, 1956, Le Theatre national populaire, 1956, Sur le pont d/Avignon, 1956, Le Bel indifferent, 1957, Vel' d'Hiv, 1959, Head Against the Wall, 1959, The Chasers, 1959, Danger in the Middle East, 1959, Les Etoilles de midi, 1959, Vous n'avez rien a declarer, 1959, Eyes Without A Face, 1960, The Itchy Palm, 1960, Lovers on a Tightrope, 1960, Crack in the Mirrror, 1960, Recourse in Grace, 1960, Le Temps du ghetto, 1961, The President, 1961, Spotlight on a Murdere, 1961, The Big Gamble, 1961, Three Faces of Sin, 1961, Famous Love Affairs, 1961, Les Travestis du diable, 1962, Sun in Your Eyes, 1962, Dragon Sky, 1962, Your Shadow Is Mine, 1962, The Olive Trees of Justice, 1962, Therese, 1962, The Longest Day, 1962, Sundays and Cybele, 1962, Lawrence of Arabia (Acad. award for Best Musical Score, 1963), 1962, The Animals, 1963, Pour l'Espagne, 1963, To Die in Madrid, 1963, A King Without Distraction, 1963, Judex, 1963, Behold a Pale Horse, 1964, The Train, 1964, Weekend at Dunkirk, 1964, Le dernier matin de Guy de Maupassant, 1965, The Collector, 1965, Dr. Zhivago (Acad. award for Best Score, 1966), 1965, Is Paris Burning?, 1966, The Professionals, 1966, Gambit, 1966, Grand Prix, 1966, The Night of the Generals, 1967, The Twenty, 1967, Villa Rides, 1968, 5 Card Stud, 1968, The Fixer, 1968, Isadora, 1968, The Extraordinary Seaman, 1969, The Damned, 1969, Topaz, 1969, A Season in Hell, 1970, The Only Game in Town, 1970, El Condor, 1970, Ryan's Daughter, 1970, Plaza Suite, 1971, Red Sun, 1971, Jean Vilar, une belle vie, 1972, Pope Joan, 1972, The Life and Times of Judge Roy Bean, 1972, The Effect of Gamma Rays on Man-in-the-Moon Marigolds, 1972, The MacKintosh Man, 1973, Ash Wednesday, 1973, Grandeur nature, 1974, The Island at the Top of the World, 1974, Mandingo, 1975, Posse, 1975, Mr. Sycamore, 1975, The Man Who Would Be King, 1975, The Message, 1976, Al-Risalah, 1976, Shout at the Devil, 1976, The Last Tycoon 1976, Crossed Swords, 1977, March or Die, 1977, La Tortue sur le dos, 1978, Two Solitudes, 1978, Die Biechtrommel, 1979, Winter Kills, 1979, The Magician of Lublin, 1979, The Black Marble, 1980, The American Success Company, 1980, The Last Flight of Noah's Ark, 1980, Resurrection, 1980, Lion of the Desert, 1981, Die Falschung, 1981, Taps, 1981, Firefox, 1982, Young Doctors in Love, 1982, Don't Cry, It's Only Thunder, 1982, The Year of Living Dangerously, 1983, Au now de tous les miens, 1983, Dreamscape, 1984, A Passage to India (Acad. award for Best Score, 1985), 1984, Top Secret!, 1984, Witness (British Acad. award for Best Score, 1986), 1985, Mad Max Beyond Thunderdome, 1985, The Bride, 1985, Enemy Mine, 1985, Tai-Pan, 1986, The Mosquito Coast, 1986, Solarbabies, 1986, Le Palanquin des larmes, 1987, Shuto Shoshitsu, 1987, No Way Out, 1987, Fatal Attraction, 1987, Julia & Julia, 1987, Gaby: A True Story, 1987, Wildfire, 1988, Moon Over Parador, 1988, Gorillas in the Mist (Gloden Globe award for Best Score, 1989), 1988, Distant Thunder, 1988, Chances Are, 1989, Dead Poets Society (British Acad. award for Best Score, 1990), 1989, Prancer, 1989, Enemies: A Love Story, 1989, Ghost, 1990, Solar Crisis, 1990,

Almost An Angel, 1990, After Dark, My Sweet, 1990, Jacob's Ladder, 1990, Only the Lonely, 1991, Fires Within, 1991, School Ties, 1992, Rakuyo, 1992, Shadow of the Wolf, 1992, Mr. Jones, 1993, Fearless, 1993, Walk in the Clouds, 1995 (Golden Globe award for Best Score, 1995) The Sunchaser, 1996, Sonnenschein, 1999, I Dreamed of Africa, 2000; (TV movies) De fil en aiguille, 1960, Othello, 1962, Les Rustres, 1963, Great Expectations, 1974, The Silence, 1975, The Users, 1978, Ishi: The Last of His Tribe, 1978, Shogun, 1980, Enola Gay: The Men, the Mission, the Atomic Bomb, 1980, Vendredi ou la vie sauvage, 1981, Coming Out of the Ice, 1982, The Sky's No Limit, 1984, Samson and Delilah, 1984, Apology, 1986, The Murder of Mary Phagan, 1988, Uprising, 2001; (TV mini-series) Jesus of Nazareth, 1977, Mourning Becomes Electra, 1978, Au nom de tous les miens, 1985; (TV episodes) Cimarron Strip, 1967, ABC Afterschool Special, 1978. Legion of Honor (France), comdr. of Arts and Letters (France). Died Mar. 29, 2009.

JASIORKOWSKI, ROBERT LEE, real estate broker, computer consultant; b. Milw., Nov. 17, 1954; s. Thomas Joseph and Alice Rosemary (Lee) J. BA, U. Wis., Milw., 1987. Dir. info. tech., real estate broker, property mgr. Nat. Realty Mgmt., Inc., Milw., from 1990. Real estate broker ERA Worth Realty, Inc., Glendale, Wis., 1991-94; computer cons. Hometrak Realty, Milw., 1986-90. Mem. Nat. Assn. Realtors, Nat. Assn. Real Estate Appraisers (cert.), U. Wis.-Milw. Alumni Assn. (life). Republican. Avocations: photography, astronomy. Died Aug. 24, 2007.

JASSMAN, OPAL BERYL, retired medical/surgical nurse; b. Gentry, Ark., Dec. 11, 1915; d. James Thomas and Ida E. (Garnett) Lawlis; m. Harold Jassman, July 20, 1953. Diploma, St. Catherine's Hosp., Garden City, Kans., 1941; cert., Children Hosp. Mich., Detroit, 1944. Staff nurse state sanatorium, Norton, Kans.; gen. duty nurse St. Anthony Hosp., Garden City; rotating nurse Casper (Wyo.) Med. Ctr. Died Nov. 22, 2007.

JAY, JERRY LEON, SR., retired publishing executive; b. Jenkins, Mo., Mar. 22, 1951; s. George Henry and Mary Louisa J.; children: Jerry L. Jr., Drake Allen. Journeyman Seneca Controls, Fraser, Mich., 1978-81; maintenance mgr. Kent-Moore Corp., Detroit, 1981, S.R. of Tenn., Riply, 1982-85; ret. Jerry L. Jay Publ., Verona, Mo., 1985. Author: Patent Applications Simplified, 1996; patentee pneumatic desedimentiation machine improvement, process and apparatus for separating plastics from contaminants, pneumatic desedimentation machine. Home: Aurora, Mo. Died Nov. 11, 2007.

JAY, SARA D'ORSEY, arbitrator, lawyer; b. Washington, June 1, 1951; d. John Elliott and Martha (Lowsley) J.; 3 children. BA with highest honors, U. Minn., 1977, JD cum laude, 1980. Bar: Minn. 1980, U.S. Dist. Ct. Minn. 1981. From law clk. to staff atty. Mpls. Star and Tribune Co., Minn., 1978-82; assoc. law offices Michael Colloton, Mpls., 1983-87; gen. counsel Maxims Beauty Salons, Mpls., 1987-89; administrv. law judge Minn. Office of Administrv. Hearings, Mpls., 1990—2002, from 2004; pvt. practice Mpls., from 1991. Mem. Iowa Pub. Rels. Bd. Mem. ABA (labor law sect.), Fed. Mediation and Conciliation Svcs., Nat. Acad. Arbitrators, Wis. Employee Rels. Commn., Minn. Bur. Mediation Svcs., Minn. State Bar Assn., Hennepin County Bar Assn., Am. Arbitration Assn. Died Mar. 28, 2008.

JECKELL, WILLIAM WILSON, retired financial executive and journalist; b. Youngstown, Ohio, Nov. 7, 1912; s. Charles and Grace Bell (Patterson) J.; m. Betty Virginia Smith, July 1, 1935; children: Judy, Jeana. BS in Journalism, Ohio State U., 1934. Adjuster Comml. Credit Co., Youngstown, 1934-36, unit mgr., office mgr. Pitts., 1936-44, office mgr. Columbus, Ohio, 1946-55, asst. divsn. mgr. Cin., 1955-57, divsn. v.p., 1957-73; pres., bd. dirs. Greenhills (Ohio) Jour., 1973-93; ret., 1993. Columnist, reporter Greenhills Jour., 1959—. Precinct exec. Rep. Party, Greenhills. Lt. USN, 1944-46. Mem. Am. Legion, Athletic Committeemen Ohio State, Elks, Chi Phi (nat. pres. 1969-73), Sigma Delta Chi. Episcopalian. Avocations: Ohio State U. football, travel, golf, civic activities. Home: Cincinnati, Ohio. Died Nov. 19, 2007.

JEFFERSON, BLANCHE WAUGAMAN, art educator, writer; b. McKeesport, Pa., Apr. 30, 1909; d. George Timothy and Anna Mary (Scott) Waugaman; m. William Lynn Jefferson, June 16, 1954 (dec. June 1980); 1 child, Patricia. Student, Pa. State U., 1932, U. Colo., 1941; BS in Art Edn., Ind. U., Pa., 1945; MA, Columbia U., 1948, EdD, 1954. Cert. sch. administr., Pa. From elem. tchr. to art supr. Vandergrift Pa. Pub. Sch. Dist., 1929-49; assoc. prof. art edn. Ind. U., 1949-54; prof., head dept. art edn. U. Pitts., 1954-67; ret., 1967. Lectr., demonstrator art edn. various sch. dists., Puerto Rico, 1965; state evaluator for pub. sch. and univ. art edn. programs State of Pa., 1948-67; com. on art edn. Mus. Modern Art, N.Y.C., 1952-66; workshop leader Nev. Art Tchrs. Legis., Las Vegas, 1960; sec. Westmoreland Coord. Com. for Pa. Tchrs., 1947-49; adminstrv. coun. U. Pitts., 1957-66; advisor Pitts. Head Start Program; participant Internat. Panel Educators, 1956. Author: Teaching Art to Children, 1957 (Internat Biennial award Delta Kappa Gamma 1958), My World of Art, 1960, So. Strong This Bond, 1995; prin. works include Ind. U. Mus. Sec. Internat. Soc. for Edn. Through Art, 1946-52; lectr., rschr. Ea. Arts Assn., 1945-66, Nat. Art Edn. Assn., Washington, 1945-66; Western Pa. com. sec. State of Pa., 1945-49. Mem. Nat. Art Edn. Assn., Naples Art Assn. Democrat. Avocations: beach walking, travel, playing piano, reading. Home: Naples, Fla. Deceased.

JEFFERSON, LETITIA GIBSON, rehabilitation counselor; b. Providence, Dec. 5, 1937; d. Walter J. Vreeland (stepfather) Jr. and Mary Ledore Halton; m. Carl F. Jefferson, Jr., Sept. 13, 1961 (div. 1968); children: Halton Matthew, Nancy, Robert. BA, Wells Coll., 1959; postgrad., Syracuse U., NY, 1966. Sr. employment counselor N.Y. State Dept. Labor, Albany, 1963-67; labor specialist Suffolk County Dept. Labor, Hauppauge, NY, 1967—99, asst. dir.; ret., 1999. Mem. St. Marks Choir, Hampton Coun. of Chs. Ecumenical Choir, Westhampton Beach, N.Y., mem. prayer group, St. Phillip Ch., Brevard, NC; lay leader, chalice adminstr., eucharistic min. St. Marks Ch.,; performer Hampton Theatre Co., Quogue, N.Y.; co-founder Eleventh Step Meditation Workshop, St. Marks Ch. Mem. Nat. Rehab. Assn. (co-founder Suffolk chpt.), Suffolk County Rehab. Coun. (past pres.), Southampton Town Rep. Club. Republican. Episcopalian. Avocations: sailing, poetry, theater, art, singing. Home: Hendersonville, NC. Died Oct. 6.

JEFFREY, MARY KATHLEEN, nurse, administrator; b. Freeport, Ill., Apr. 24, 1922; d. Louis J. and Kathleen P. (O'Connor) Balles; m. William L. Jeffrey, June 30, 1951; children: David J., Susan Jeffrey Kaney, Barbara Jeffrey Hoffberg, JoAnne. BS, St. Xavier Coll., Chgo., 1944; cert. in pub. health nursing, Loyola U., Chgo., 1947. Staff nurse, asst. head nurse U. Chgo. Hosp.; commd. ensign USN Nurse Corps; staff nurse U. Mich. Hosp., Ann Arbor; dir. sch. nurses Sch. Dist. 145, Freeport; dir. nursing Vis. Nurse Assn./Amity Soc., Freeport, 1973-92. Home: Freeport, Ill. Died Apr. 17, 2008.

JELENIC, ROBERT M., retired newspaper publishing executive; b. Canada, 1951; s. Tom and Dana Jelenic; m. Joy Jelenic; 1 child, Laine. BA, Laurentian U. Chartered acct., Can. With Arthur Andersen, Toronto, Toronto Sun Pub. Cho., 1976—88, Jour. Register Co., Trenton, NJ, 1988—90, pres., CEO, 1990—2000, chmn., pres., CEO, 1997—2007. Mem. Newspaper Assn. Am. (dir.). Avocation: golf. Died Dec. 3, 2008.

JENKINS, GEORGE POLLOCK, retired insurance company executive; b. Clarksburg, W.Va., Feb. 24, 1915; s. Roy N. and Gertrude S. (Pollock) J.; A.B., Princeton U., 1936; M.B.A., Harvard U., 1938; m. Marian E. O'Brien, Apr. 10, 1945; children— James P., Robert N., Richard G. With Met. Life Ins. Co., N.Y.C., 1938-80, v.p., 1956-62, fin. v.p., 1962-65, chmn. fin. com., 1965-80, vice chmn., 1969-73, chmn. bd., 1973-80, ret., 1980; dir. W.R. Grace & Co., Bethlehem Steel Corp., Chgo. Pacific Corp., Capital Cities/ABC Inc., Trammell Crow, Real Estate Investors. Trustee Blair Acad., Blairstown, N.J. Served to capt. AUS, 1942-46. Mem. Phi Beta Kappa. Clubs: Links (N.Y.C.); Baltusrol Golf (Springfield, N.J.). Died Oct. 14, 2009.

JENKINS, WARDELL LEWIS, telecommunications administrator; b. Washington, Dec. 18, 1940; s. James Lewis and Leitha Beatrice (Gamble) J.; m. Johnella Tolliver, Nov. 24, 1962; children: Antoine Lewis, Shawn Kimberly. Grad., Cardoza High Sch., Washington, 1955-58; postgrad., Washington Tech. Inst., 1974-77, Fed. City Coll., Washington, 1980-82. Telecommunications operator U.S. Dept. State, Washington, 1963-85, communication mgr., from 1985, also chief systems & network control, from 1989. Participant Strategic Arms Limitation talks, Helsinki, 1970, Presdl. Econ. Conf., Ottawa, Can., 1981. Mem. Fairfield Knolls Civic Assn., District Heights, Md. Sgt. USAF, 1958-62. Mem. Am. Legion, Non-Commd. Officers Assn., Am. Assn. Retired Persons, Armed Forces Communications & Electronic Assn., Parents of Alumni-Marquette U. Roman Catholic. Avocations: basketball, football, golf, tennis, swimming. Home: Capital Hts, Md. Died July 12, 2007.

JENNINGS, DONNA, school psychologist, consultant; b. Colby, Kans., Mar. 8, 1948; d. Herman Joseph and Lorreta Schippers; m. David L. Jennings, Nov. 28, 1968; children: Jeff, Gina, Josh. BA, Ft. Hays State U., Hays, Kans., 1970, MS, 1991, EdS, 1994. Sch. psychologist No. Kans. Ednl. Svc. Ctr., Oakley, from 1989. Mem. ASCD, AAUW, Nat. Assn. Sch. Psychologist, Kans. Assn. Sch. Psychologists, Phi Delta Kappa (treas.). Home: Colby, Kans. Died June 30, 2008.

JERMAN, ALBERT CHARLES, historian, dentist; b. Bristol, Conn., Nov. 12, 1935; s. Frank M. and Estelle W. J.; m. Grace J., Jan. 25, 1963 (div. Dec. 1978); children: Rachel E., Eric A.; m. Beverly S., June 19, 1982. BA, Yale U., 1957; DDS, U. Nebr., 1961. Commd. 1st lt. USAF, 1961, advanced through grades to col., 1982, dental officer various locations, 1961-82; historian Robert Todd Lincoln's Hildene, Manchester, Vt., from 1989. Rsch. tchr. USAF, San Antonio, 1967. Contbr. articles to profl. jours. County chmn. Rep. party Bennington County, Vt., 1988-94; mem. state com. Vt., 1988-96. Fellow Am. Coll. Dentists; mem. Lincoln Forum (adv. com., lectr.). Avocations: crossword puzzles, reading, singing. Home: Arlington, Vt. Died Oct. 4, 2007.

JERMYN, JOHN WILLIAM, III, physician; b. Balt., Feb. 14, 1951; s. John William II and Patricia J.; m. Deborah Anne DeCoursey, Aug. 17, 1983. BS in Chemistry, Tex. A&M U., 1973; DO, Tex. Coll. Osteo. Medicine, 1980. Diplomate Am. Bd. Emergency Medicine. Intern. Normandy Hosp., St. Louis, 1980-81, staff physician, 1981-86; dir. emergency svcs. Community Hosp., Grand Junction, Colo., 1986-87, Moberly Regional Med. Ctr., Mo., 1987-90; asst. prof., dept. surgery Univ. Mo., Columbia, 1990-98; clin. instr. St. Louis Univ. Hosp., Mo., 1990-93; physician Emergency Physicians Mid-Mo., from 1998. Dir. emergency med. svc. Randolph County Ambulance Dist., Moberly, 1987-97; site reviewer Commn. Accreditation Ambulance Svcs. Fellow Am. Coll. Emergency Physicians (nat. sec. rural emergency med. sect., EMA para-hosp. and disaster preparedness sects.); mem. AMA, Am. Osteo Assn., Mo. Coll. Emergency Physicians (chmn. emergency med. svcs. com., pres. 2000—), State Coun. on Emergency Med. Svcs. Republican. Episcopalian. Avocations: antiques, house and auto restoration, woodworking. Home: Moberly, Mo. Died May 15, 2008.

JESWALD, JOSEPH, artist; b. Leetonia, Ohio, May 17, 1927; s. Philip and Susan Jeswald; m. Hester Parker Jeswald; children: Peter, Paul, Melissa. Founder, first pres. Montserrat Coll. Art, Beverly, Mass. Represented in permanent collections Hirschorn Mus., Wash. DC, Addison Gallery of Am. Art, Andover, Mass., Rockefeller Found., NYC, Simmons Coll., Boston, Cape Ann Hist. Assn., Gloucester, Ma., Roy M. Neuberger Mus., Purchase, NY. Sgt. US Air Corps, 1945—46, ETO. Recipient 1st prize, Northeast Regional Invitational Exhbn., 1962. Home: Sarasota, Fla. Died Mar. 21, 2009.

JOBELMANN, HERMAN FREDERICK, musician, music union administrator; b. Portland, Oreg., May 20, 1913; s. Fred William Jobelmann and Matilda Miriam (Singer) Chapman; m. India Mabel Keplinger, Apr. 20, 1984. Grad., Lincoln High Sch., Portland, 1934. Pit musician various theatres, Portland, 1933-38; prin. bass Portland, Oreg. Symphony, 1934-83, Metro. Opera Nat., NYC, 1965-67; libr., bass Sarah Caldwell's Boston Opera, 1968-70; prin. bass Roger Wagner Chorale, 1970-71, Clebanoff Strings, 1972; double bass Hollywood (Calif.) Studios, 1971-73; pres. local 99 Am. Fedn. Musicians, Portland, from 1986. Adj. prof. Lewis and Clark Coll., Portland, Marylhurst Coll., Portland, Reed Coll., Portland. Mem. Portland Oreg. Visitor's Assn., Portland C. of C. Mem. Masons, Shriners. Democrat. Presbyterian. Home: Tigard, Oreg. Died Jan. 13, 2008.

JOHNS, WILLIAM HOWARD, psychiatrist, neurologist; b. Hamilton, Ohio, Apr. 18, 1941; s. Howard William and Martha (Sleigh) J.; m. Catherine Marie O'Keefe, May 30, 1982; children: Howard William II, Stephanie Marie. AB, Princeton U., 1963; MS in Anatomy, U. Cin., 1968; DO, Kirksville Coll. Osteo. Medicine, 1973; student spl. student program, Topeka Inst. Psychoanalysis, 1984—90. Instr. anatomy Kirksville Coll. Osteo. Medicine, Mo., 1967—73; intern Grandview Hosp., Dayton, 1973—74; resident neurology Cleve. Clinic Hosp., 1974—77; asst. prof. neurology Ohio U. Coll. Osteo. Medicine, Athens, 1977—78; pvt. practice neurology Dayton, Ohio, 1978—82; resident psychiatry Menninger Found., Topeka, 1982—86, psychiatrist, staff psychiatrist, 1985—96, asst. team leader, 1985—89, comprehensive out-patient evaluations, 1985—89; faculty mem. Karl Menninger Sch. Psychiatry, Topeka, 1990—95; pvt. practice psychiatry, from 1995. Dir. Psychotic Disorders Study Program, 1993-95, neuropsychiatry consultations, 1992-95; clin. asst. prof. neurology Wright State U. Sch. Medicine, Dayton, 1979-82, Ohio U. Coll. Osteo. Medicine, Athens, 1979-82, W.Va. Sch. Osteo. Medicine, Lewisburg, 1979-82; staff psychiatrist St. Francis Hosp. and Med. Ctr., Topeka, 1995—; staff psychiatrist Storment-Vail Hosp., Topeka, 1999—, pvt. practice psychiatry, 1996—, staff psychiatrist Kanza Menal Health Ctr., Hiawatha, Kans., 2003—, med. dir. adult unit Parkview Hosp., Topeka, 1996, v.p. med. staff, 1996, pres., 1997-98. Recipient Outstanding Clin. Faculty award Dayton region Ohio U. Coll. Osteo. Medicine, 1982, Sydney M. Kanev Meml. award Am. Coll. Neuropsychiatrists, 1985, Outstanding Clun. Faculty award Dayton region Ohio Coll. Osteo. Medicine. Avocations: reading, sports, travel. Home: Topeka, Kans. Died May 19, 2008.

JOHNSON, ADAIR ARCHIBALD, middle school educator; b. Norfolk, Va., Oct. 31, 1950; d. William Louis and Pauline Elizabeth (Buchanan) Archibald; m. Lee Virgil Johnson, June 14, 1974. BS, James Madison U., 1973. Cert. tchr., Miss. Art tchr. Hayden Jr. High Sch., Franklin, Va., 1973-74, Nichols Jr. High Sch., Biloxi, Miss., 1975-79, Fernwood Jr. High Sch., Biloxi, Miss., 1979-82, Biloxi High Sch., 1982-84, Fernwood Middle Sch., Biloxi, from 1984. Named Tchr. of the Month, Fernwood Middle Sch., 1992. Avocations: needlecrafts, travel, sewing, walking. Home: Ocean Springs, Miss. Died May 30, 2008.

JOHNSON, BRIAN KEITH, electrical engineering educator; b. Madison, Wis., Mar. 11, 1965; s. Alton Cornelius and Virginia Rae (Korener) Johnson; m. Elizabeth M. Williams, Jan. 3, 1998; children: Erica Pearl, Mark Macrae, Cora Marie, Heidi Rose. BS, U. Wis., 1987, MS, 1989, PhD, 1992. Registered profl. engr., Wis., Idaho. Teaching asst. U. Wis., Madison, 1988, rsch. asst., 1988-92; engr. Lawrence Livermore Nat. Labs., Livermore, Calif., 1989; asst. prof. U. Idaho, Moscow, 1992-97, assoc. prof., 1997—2004, prof., from 2004, chair dept., from 2006. Instr. Coll. Engring. Tchg. Asst. Tng., U. Wis., Madison, 1988, Engring. profl. devel., 1992-98; co-advisor Iron Cross Leadership Soc., Madison, 1988-92, U. Idaho IEEE Student Chpt., 1995—; dir. Western Virtual Engring., 1996-99. Lodge chief Order of the Arrow, Boy Scouts Am., 1982-84, dir. Brownsea

Double 2Course, Madison, 1987, advisor, 1990-92. Recipient Vigil Hon. Membership, Order of the Arrow, Boy Scouts Am., 1988, Leadership award, Exploring Boy Scouts Am., 1986, Outstanding Young Faculty award U. Idaho Coll. Engring., 1995. Mem. IEEE (chair working group on utility applications of supercondrs. 1999—, sec. working group on modeling and simulation of distributed resources, 2001—, mem. AdCom intelligent transp. systems coun., ITS coun.), Am. Soc. Engring. Edn., Internat. Coun. on Large Electric Sys. Roman Catholic. Avocations: cross country skiing, bicycling, backpacking. Home: Moscow, Idaho. Died Dec. 9, 2007.

JOHNSON, BRUCE DICKIE, social science research director; b. Feb. 22, 1943; BS, U. Wis., 1965; PhD, Columbia U., 1971. Asst. prof. Manhattanville Coll., Purchase, N.Y., 1972-74; asst. prof. Rutgers U., New Brunswick, N.J., 1974-75; sr. rsch. assoc. N.Y. State Divsn. Substance Abuse, NYC, 1976-89; dir. ISPR Nat. Devel. & Rsch. Insts., NYC, from 1989. Home: New York, NY. Died Feb. 21, 2009; unknown.

JOHNSON, BRUCE KING, internist; b. Harriman, Tenn., Oct. 24, 1918; s. Samuel King and Laura Monro (Jones) J.; m. Leila N. Wright Johnson, Apr. 3, 1942 (dec. Nov. 1957); m. Iris Dudley Thomas, May 14, 1959 (dec. Nov. 1991); m. Patricia Jean Miller, Aug. 13, 1994. BS, Birmingham So. Coll., 1940; MD, U. Tenn. Health Scis., Memphis, 1944. Diplomate Am. Bd. Internal Medicine; recert. Gen. practice medicine, Flat Creek, Ala., 1945-49; resident N.C. Bapt. Hosp., Winston-Salem, N.C., 1949-51; sr. resident U. Ala. Hosp., Birmingham, 1951-52; pvt. practice internal medicine Birmingham, 1952-59; med. dir. Birmingham Med. Group, 1959-68; practice medicine Simon Williamson Clinib, 1968-87; physician advisor staff clin. quality mgmt. Bapt. Med. Ctr.-Princeton Unit, Birmingham, from 1987. Mem. adminstrv. bd. First Meth. Ch., Birmingham, 1965-95. Recipient Physicians Recognition award AMA, 1972, 79, 84, 87, 91, 94. Fellow ACP (life); mem. Med. Assn. Ala. (50 yr. award 1995), Alpha Omega Alpha. Avocations: photography, travel. Home: Birmingham, Ala. Died Feb. 10, 2008.

JOHNSON, CRAIG W., lawyer; b. Pasadena, Calif., Dec. 28, 1946; m. Rose-Ann Rotandaro, Aug. 15, 2009. BA magna cum laude, Yale U., 1968; JD, Stanford U., 1974. Bar: Calif. 1974. Computer programmer Burroughs Corp., Pasadena; atty. Wilson, Sonsini, Goodrich & Rosati, Palo Alto, Calif., 1974—93; founder Venture Law Group, 1993—2009; co-founder Virtual Law Partners LLP, 2008—09. Bd. visitors Stanford U. Law Sch., 1974-77. Mem. State Bar Calif. Died Sept. 29, 2009.

JOHNSON, DOUGLAS WAYNE, secondary school educator; b. Rochester, Pa., July 26, 1952; s. Fred P. and Jean O. (Henry) J.; children: Megan, Matthew, Marcie. Student, U. Valencia, Spain, 1973; BS, Slippery Rock U., 1974; elem. edn. cert., Geneva Coll., Beaver Falls, Pa., 1978. Cert. instrnl. II, Pa. Spanish tchr. Ingomar Mid. Sch. North Allegheny Schs., Pitts., from 1985; part-time driver edn. coord. C.C. Allegheny County-North Campus, Pitts., from 1984; part-time dir. edn. Ingomar United Meth. Ch., Pitts., 1983-93. Mem. Carson Total Quality Team, Pitts., 1995-97; rep. North Allegheny profl. devel. com., Pitts., 1993—. Treas. QUALITY, Pitts., 1988-90; pres., v.p. Monaca (Pa.) Borough Coun., 1975-79; mem. Monaca Vol. Firemen, 1974-79; pres. Ingomar Elem. PTA, 1995-97; student council advisor Ingomar Mid. Sch., 1997-2004; mem. Pa. Dist. # 3 Student Coun. Bd.; mem. North Allegheny Dist. Band Patrons, 2d v.p., 2002-03, sec., 2005-06, exec. v.p., 2006-07, pres., 2007-. Mem. Assn. for Supervision and Curriculum Devel., Pa. State Modern Lang. Assn., North Allegheny Fedn. Tchrs. (state rep. 1994, 96, exec. coun. mem. 1993-97, bldg. rep. 1993-97), Slippery Rock Alumni Assn. (homecoming rep. 1974—), Leotha Hawthorne Reading Coun. Republican. Methodist. Home: Ingomar, Pa. Died Apr. 9, 2008.

JOHNSON, ELMER CARL, geneticist; b. Bend, Oreg., Oct. 28, 1920; s. Charles E. and Ebba Marie (Lindquist) J.; m. Dorma Lee Rees, Dec. 21, 1947; children: Kristine Kay, Eric Scott. BS, Oreg. State, 1947; PhD, U. Minn., 1958. Certification specialist Oreg. State U., Corvallis, 1947-55; grad. student U. Minn., St. Paul, 1955-58; plant breeder and geneticist The Rockefeller Found., Mexico City, 1958-81, Internat. Plant Rsch. Inst., San Carlos, Calif., 1981-88, Escagenetics Corp., San Carlos, from 1988, Sogetal, Hayward, Calif., 1983-91. Vis. scientist Chinese Acad. Agriculture and Forestry, Beijing, China, 1977; cons. in field. Contbr. articles to profl. jours. Team mgr. Little League Baseball, Mexico City, 1964-68. 1st Lt. Infantry, 1943-47. Recipient Silver Star U.S. Army, 1945, Honor of Merits, 1982. Mem. Am. Soc. Agronomy, Sociedad Latinoamericano del maiz, Am. Genetic Assn. Achievements include development of short statured tropical maize varieties and specialty starch corn hybrids; initiation of drought tolerance selection in corn; establishment of basic maize breeding populations. Home: Belmont, Calif. Died Oct. 23, 2007.

JOHNSON, FRANCIS SEVERIN, physicist; b. Omak, Wash., July 20, 1918; s. Ralston Severin and Elizabeth (Gruenes) J.; m. Maurine Marie Green, Sept. 12, 1943; 1 dau., Sharan Kaye. B.Sc. with honors in Physics, U. Alta., Can., 1940; MA in Physics and Meteorology, UCLA, 1942, PhD in Meteorology, 1958. Head, high atmosphere research sect. U.S. Naval Research Lab., Washington, 1946-55; mgr. space physics research Lockheed Missiles & Space Co., 1955-62; head, atmospheric and space scis. div. S.W. Center Advanced Studies, Dallas, 1962-64, dir. earth and planetary scis. lab., 1964-69; acting pres. U. Tex., Dallas, 1969-71; dir. Center for Advanced Studies, 1971-74, Cecil H. and Ida M. Green honors prof. natural sci., 1974-89, prof. emeritus, 1989—2003, exec. dean grad. studies and research, 1976-79; asst. dir. astron., atmospheric, earth and ocean scis. NSF, Washington, 1979-83. Cons. ionospheric physics subcom., space scis. steering com. NASA, 1960-62, mem. planetary atmospheres subcom., space scis. steering com., 1962-67, chmn. lunar atmospheric measurements team, Apollo sci. planning teams, 1964-67, mem. adv. bd. Mars space missions, 1964-67, mem. lunar and planetary missions bd., 1967-71; mem. adv. panel atmospheric scis. NSF, 1962-67; mem. working group IV COSPAR, 1965-80, v.p., 1975-80; mem. Nat. Acad. Scis. panel adv. to central radio propagation lab. Nat. Bur. Standards, 1962-65, mem. panel weather and climate modification Nat. Acad. Scis., 1964-70, mem. space sci. bd., 1969-81, mem. geophysics research bd., 1971-77, mem. bd. on atmospheric scis. and climate, 1984-87, mem. Nat. Acad. Scis. com. adv. to NOAA, 1966-71, mem. climate research bd., 1977-79; mem. adv. com. research to coordinating bd. Tex. Coll. and Univ. System, 1966-67; mem. sci. advisory bd. USAF, 1968-79; mem. nat. adv. com. Oceans and Atmosphere, 1971-73; pres. Spl. Com. on Solar Terrestrial Physics, 1974-77; mem. Aerocibo adv. bd. and vis. com. Nat. Astronomy and Ionsphere Ctr. Cornell U., 1985-88. Author: Satellite Environment Handbook, 1965; also numerous articles. Served with USAAF, 1942-46. Decorated Bronze Star medal; recipient Henryk Arctowski award NAS, 1972, Exceptional Sci. Achievement medal NASA, 1973, Meritorious Civilian Service award USAF, 1979, Disting. Tex. Sci. award Tex. Acad. Scis., 1984, Disting. Alumni award U. Alta., 2001. Fellow Am. Geophys. Union (vice chmn. sect. geomagnetism and aeronomy 1964-68, pres. sect. solar planetary relationships 1970-72, John Adam Fleming award 1977), AAAS (council mem. 1968-72), Am. Meteorol. Soc. (councilor 1976-78), IEEE, AIAA (chmn. tech. com. space and atmospheric physics 1961-64, Space Sci. award 1966); mem. Internat. Assn. Geomagnetism and Aeronomy (exec. com. 1967-71), Internat. Union Radio Sci. (chmn. U.S. Commn. IV 1964-67, sec. U.S. nat. com. 1967-70, vice chmn. 1970-73, chmn. 1973-76), Internat. Union Geodesy and Geophysics (U.S. nat. com. 1973-76). Home: Dallas, Tex. Died Sept. 17, 2009.

JOHNSON, FRANKLIN MCBEE, wholesale distribution executive; b. Seattle, Feb. 26, 1927; s. Leonard Franklin and Hazel Elisabeth (McBee) H.; m. Colleen Margaret Seiling, Sept. 10, 1956; children: Cappi Willey, Kerri McCaul. Student, U. Wash., 1945-57, 79. Owner retail grocery store, Seattle, 1947-62; v.p. sales Secoma Distbg. Co., Seattle, 1962-71; gen. mgr. gen. mdse. Assoc. Grocers Inc., Seattle, 1971-76, v.p. mktg., 1976-87, sr. v.p. mktg., from 1987. Bd. dirs. Wash. State Food Distbrs. Assn., Seattle, 1987-93; pres. Gen. Merchandisers Assn., Seattle, 1975; frequent speaker in field. Contbr. articles to trade publs. Bd. dirs. Edmonds (Wash.) Community Coll., 1989-92; mem. Edmonds City Planning Group, 1975; bd. dirs. Husky Fever Com., Seattle, 1985—. Mem. We. Assn. Food Chains, N.W. Planning Group, Food Mfrs. Inst., Masons. Republican. Methodist. Avocations: motor home travel, furniture making, gardening, camping. Home: Edmonds, Wash. Died July 29, 2008.

JOHNSON, HENRY FRED, clergy; b. Colorado Springs, Aug. 23, 1948; s. Nathan Eugene Johnson Sr. and Jessie Bell (Stovall) Crowder; m. Christine Johnson, May 20, 1967; children: Diedre M., Tina D., Tevin AA in Social Work, Pikes Peak C.C., Colorado Springs, 1990; B in Biblical Studies, Nazarene Bible Coll., Colorado Springs, 1993, B in Christian Edn., 1995; M in Bibl. Studies, Andersonville Bapt. Sem., 1998, PhD in Bibl. Studies, 2000. Ordained Baptist Min. Personnel sr. sgt. U.S. Army, 1967-87; program coord. Martin Luther Home, Colorado Springs, 1988—2000; youth pastor Friendship Missionary Bapt. Ch., Colorado Springs, 1991-99; co-pastor Chapel Pueblo (Colo.) Minimum Ctr., 1993—2001; writer Henry Johnson Min., Colorado Springs, from 1995; instr. Nat. Bapt. Youth Convention, New Orleans, 1995—2000; cmty. coord. Resource Exch., Colorado Springs, from 2000; interim pastor Friendship Missionary Bapt. Ch., 2001—04. Dir. Christian edn. Gen. Missionary Bapt. Conv. of Colo., 1999-2002, dean of congress, 2002-05, dir. congress, 2005; assoc. editor, adv. Praisenet.org, 2002—; 2d vice moderator Pikes Peak Bapt. Dist., 2004—. Author: Challenge of the Teens in the 90's and Beyond, 1995, Book of James, 1998, Arise and Rebuild, 1997, Book of Revelation, 2000. Baptist. Home: Colorado Springs, Colo. Died July 9, 2008.

JOHNSON, JAMES ROBERT, physicist, consultant; b. Dallas, Apr. 9, 1951; s. Samuel Robert Johnson and Shirley Lee Melton; m. Anita Miller, June 8, 1948; m. Cynthia Mary Morita, Sept. 22, 1976 (div.); children: Elizabeth Mary, Robert Joseph. PhD, Tex. A&M U., 1979. Rsch. assoc. U. Ariz., Lunar and Planetary Lab., Tucson, 1979—84; sr. engr. E-Systems Sci. and Tech., Garland, Tex., 1984—86, mgr. infrared exploitation group, 1986—96; dir. Sci. and Tech. Raytheon, 1996—99; chief scientist Raytheon Intelligence and Info. Systems, 1999—2003; pres., chief scientist ADB Consulting, Santa Fe, from 2003; advisor to Collin coun. dir. homeland security Collin County Homeland Security, McKinney, Tex., from 2003. Mem. U. Tex., Grad. Rsch. Adv. Com., Richardson, from 2001; advisor dir. Smithsonian, Washington, 2002—02; advisor to dir. Measurements and Signatures Analysis, Arlington, Va., 2000—02. Mem. Planning Bd., McKinney, Tex., 1984—87, City Coun., Murphy, 1985—87. Recipient Departmental Physics award, Navarro Jr. Coll., 1971, Departmental French award, 1971. Achievements include discovery of Methane atmosphere on Pluto (1980); patents for Estimation of surface temperatures using mutli-angle satellite infrared imagery; Estimation of surface temperatures using multi-spectral satellite imagery; research in Raytheon Highest Achievment Award (1996); Research Project of the Year Award from Raytheon (1995); Publish first infrared spectrum of a comet (1982); Generated first absolutely calibrated spectrum of a comet from 0.1 to 5.5 microns wavelength, used to select filters for International Halley Watch; discovery of Water in clay material on Asteroid Ceres (1982); development of first all hazards homeland security intelligence capability at a local level in the United States. Avocations: computers, tennis, travel, investment. Home: Santa Fe, N.Mex. Died June 8, 2008.

JOHNSON, JAY WITHINGTON, former United States Representative from Wisconsin; b. Bessemer, Mich., Sept. 30, 1943; s. Ruben W. and Catherine W. (Withington) J.; m. Jane Sholtz (div.); m. Jo Lee Works, June 26, 1982; stepchildren: Christopher, Joanna AA, Gogebic Community Coll., 1963; BA, No. Mich. U., 1965; MA, Mich. State U., 1970. Disk jockey Sta. WFMK, Lansing, Mich., 1968-69; news anchorman Sta. WILX-TV, Lansing, 1969-70; radio news reporter Sta. WOWO, Ft. Wayne, Ind., 1970-73; news anchorman Sta. WPTV-TV, West Palm Beach, Fla., 1973-76; radio news reporter Sta. WVCG/WLVE-FM, Miami, Fla., 1976; TV producer Sta. WPLG-TV, Miami, 1976; news anchorman, mng. editor Sta. WPEC-TV, West Palm Beach, 1977-80; news anchorman Sta. WOTV-TV, Grand Rapids, Mich., 1980-81, Sta. WFRV-TV, Green Bay, Wis., 1981-87, Sta. WLUK-TV, Green Bay, 1987-96; mem. US Congress from 8th Wis dist., 1997—99; acting dep. asst. sec. for congressional rels. USDA, 1999-2000; dir. US Mint, Washington, 2000-2001; founder Jay Johnson Coins & Consulting, 2002—09. Vol. Big Bros./Big Sisters, Green Bay, 1982-87 (Vol. of Yr. 1985); pres., bd. dirs. Family Violence Ctr., Green Bay, 1982-87; v.p. communications United Way, Green Bay; adv. bd. Libertas Alcohol Treatment Ctr.; With U.S. Army, 1966-68. Recipient Gov's award Gov. Tommy Thompson, 1988, American Numismatic Assn. Pesdl. award, 2001; named Citizen of Yr. Masons, 1987. Democrat. Died Oct. 17, 2009.

JOHNSON, JOHN EDLIN, JR., neuroscientist; b. Ft. Worth, Aug. 21, 1945; s. John E. and Mary (Thompson) J.; m. Susan Edwards, June 15, 1968; 1 child, Cynthia Brooke. BS in Psychology, Zoology, U. Wash., 1968; MS in Psychology, Tulane U., 1970, PhD in Neurosci., 1973. Fellow NASA, Mt. View, Calif., 1973-76; staff fellow NIH, Balt., 1976-80; asst. prof. neurology Johns Hopkins Med. Sch., Balt., 1979-89; vis. scholar U. Calif., Berkeley, 1990-91; pres. Sci. Design & Info., Redwood City, Calif., from 1991. Editor-in-chief Microscopy Rsch. and Technique, 1983—, SYNAPSE, 1987—. Editor 6 textbooks on microscopy and pathology. 1st lt. USAF, 1973-80. Avocations: photography, music, writing. Home: Redwood City, Calif. Died Sept. 8, 2007.

JOHNSON, JOHN LOWELL, research physicist; b. Butte, Mont., Mar. 18, 1926; s. Lowell Wallace and Esther (Thornwall) J.; m. Barbara Marion Hynds, June 30, 1951; children: Lowell John, Lesley Jean Johnson Gelb, Jennifer Ruth Johnson Goodall. BS, Mont. State U., 1949; MS, Yale U., 1950, PhD, 1954. Rsch. asst. Yale U., New Haven, 1949-54; sr. scientist comml. atomic power dept. Westinghouse, Pitts., 1954-64; fellow engr. Westinghouse Rsch. Labs., Pitts., 1964-68, adv. scientist, 1968-79; cons. scientist Westinghouse R & D Ctr., Pitts., 1979-85; mem. vis. rsch. staff Princeton (N.J.) U., 1955-68, vis. rsch. physicist, 1968-71, vis. prin. rsch. physicist, 1971-85, prin. rsch. physicist, from 1985. Vis. scientist Culham (Eng.) Lab., Los Alamos (N.Mex.) Sci. Lab., Max Planck Inst. for Plasma Physics, Garching, Germany, Australian Nat. U., plasma physics lab. Kyoto U.; vis. prof. Nagoya (Japan) U., 1987; logistics supr. 9th Internat. Atomic Energy Agy. Internat. Conf. on Plasma Physics and Controlled Nuclear Fusion Rsch., 1982, 13th, 1990; conf. presenter in field. Contbr. over 100 articles to physics jours. Scoutmaster troop 88 George Washington coun. Boy Scouts Am., 1971-87; mem. Princeton Com. on Alcohol and Drug Abuse, 1985-86. With USN, 1944-46. Recipient Silver Beaver award Boy Scouts Am., 1978. Fellow Am. Phys. Soc. (sec.-treas. div. plasma physics 1974-78, organizer meetings and Sherwood confs.); mem. Sigma Xi (sec., treas., v.p., pres. Princeton chpt. 1981-88). Methodist. Home: Princeton, NJ. Died Nov. 16, 2007.

JOHNSON, LARRY WAYNE, investment officer, consultant; b. Nottingham, Eng., Sept. 6, 1952; came to U.S., 1968; s. Tommy Lee and Inez Ruth (Fields) J. BBA, Tex. A&M, 1973. Sales assoc. Sears, Washington, 1977-79; mgmt. trainee Fields Food, Inc., Washington, 1979-81; cons. Nat. Food Assn., Washington, 1981-85; chief exec. officer LWJ Internat. Investment, Ft. Worth, from 1985. Chmn. bd. dirs. Stien Designs, Ft. Worth, Rynie Rynee Hair Salon Inc. Active Big Bros., Ft. Worth, 1985-91. Capt. USMC, 1973-77, VietNam. Fellow Century II Club; mem. Twelfth Man Squad Tex. A&M, Tex., A&M Century Club. Avocations: sky diving, scuba diving. Home: Fort Worth, Tex. Died Aug. 25, 2007.

JOHNSON, LEWIS THOMAS, leasing company executive; b. Ga., Oct. 26, 1928; s. Curtis Henry and Clara (Blount) J.; m. Nita Peterson, 1950. BBA, U. Ga., 1954. V.p.

Berman Leasing, Inc., Atlanta, 1956-64; v.p., gen. mgr. Coile Leasing Corp., Atlanta, 1964-67; v.p. Rollins Leasing Co., Atlanta, 1967-79; v.p., gen. mgr. Interstate Truck Leasing, Albany, Ga., from 1979. Pres. Catrala, Ga., 1969; bd. dirs. GMTA, Ga., v.p., 1984—. Served to 1st lt. USAF, 1946-49. Home: Hernando Bch, Fla. Died May 21, 2008.

JOHNSON, LINDA THELMA, information specialist; b. New Britain, Conn., May 18, 1954; d. Oren and Lois Elizabeth (Armstrong) J.; 1 child, Portia Lauren. BS in Econs., Va. State U., 1978; cert. in computer programming, Morse Sch. Bus., 1978; cert. in legal assisting, Morse Sch. Bus., Hartford, Conn., 1994. Programmer analyst Vitro Automation Industries, Silver Spring, Md., 1980-83; sr. analyst Sci. Mgmt. Corp., Lanham, Md., 1984-86; sr. programmer analyst Applied Mgmt. Scis. Inc., Silver Spring, 1986; programmer analyst Computer Data Systems Inc., Rockville, Md., 1986-88; project leader systems cert. dept. Arbitron Co., Laurel, Md., 1988-90; systems analyst Engring. and Econ. Rsch., Inc., Vienna, Va., 1990; computer cons. Comsys Tech. Svcs. Inc., Rockville, 1990, CPU Inc., Fairfax, Va., 1991; quality assurance cons. Cigna Corp., Bloomfield, Conn., 1992; info. systems specialist The Travelers Ins. Group, Hartford, Conn., 1994-96. Mem. rsch. bd. advisors The Am. Biographical Inst., Inc. Mem. NAFE, NAACP, Am. Bus. Women's Assn. Democrat. Baptist. Avocations: crossword puzzles, horseback riding. Home: Hartford, Conn. Died Feb. 16, 2008.

JOHNSON, MARGARET HELLER, artist, educator; d. Henry and Elsie Heller; children: Kimberly Lauder, Adrienne. BA in Edn., U. Del., Newark, 1965. Cert. tchr. Del. Tchr. Wesley Presch., Dover, Del., 1979—85; art educator Capital Sch. Dist., Dover, from 1985. Contbr. art to profl. publs.; exhibitions include Del. Mus. Contemporary Art, Briggs Mus. Am. Art, Rehobeth Art League, Del. Women's Conf. Handmade paper demonstrator Winterthur Mus., Wilmington, Del., 2005, mem. tchr.'s adv. bd., from 1997; handmade paper demonstrator Lewes Hist. Soc., Del.; pres. Littleton Hosp. Aux., NH, 1974—76; mem. Del. Art Mus., Dover, 1991—2006. Excellence In Edn. grantee, MBNA, 2003. Mem.: Capital Educators Assn. (mem. exec. bd. from 2001). Home: Dover, Del. Died Mar. 13, 2008.

JOHNSON, MICHAEL ALMER, educator, lawyer, consultant; b. St. Paul, Minn., Apr. 17, 1944; s. Almer M. and Marvel C. (Heinen) J.; m. Carol J. Neumann, Nov. 5, 1966; children: Michael K., Jill L. BA in Counseling Psychology, U. Minn., 1966; JD, William Mitchell Coll. Law, 1974. Bar: Minn. 1975. Dir. mgmt. devel. Minn. Transp. Dept., St. Paul, 1968-74; sole practice St. Paul, from 1975; co-owner, sr. v.p. Performax Systems, Mpls., 1976-84; owner, pres. M. Johnson & Assocs., St. Paul, from 1984; prof. organizational mgmt. U. Minn. Sch. Dentistry, Mpls., from 1975. Dental contract and bus. cons. to various U.S. dental orgns. and clinics; mgmt. devel. and profl. tng. cons. IBM, Apple Computer, Citicorp, other orgns. Author: (with Randall Berning) Personalized Guide to Dental Legal Issues, 1985. Grantee Am. Dental Assn., Chgo., 1985-86; recipient cert. of appreciation for valuable sci. contbn. Minn. Dental Assn., 1986 Mem. ABA, Minn. Bar Assn., Oreg. Soc. Dentistry for Children (hon.). Roman Catholic. Avocations: golf, tennis. Home: Saint Paul, Minn. Died July 17, 2008.

JOHNSON, PETER FORBES, transportation executive, business owner; b. Salem, Mass., May 7, 1934; s. William Bennett and Sarah Loraine (Nee) J.; m. Mikell Kraus, Oct. 11, 1958; children: Krista, Todd, Karyn, Jennifer. BS, U.S. Mcht. Marine Acad., 1957. Deck officer Texaco, Port Arthur, Tex., 1958-63; from deck officer to master Reynolds Metals Co., Corpus Christi, Tex., 1963-65, port capt., 1965-68, operating mgr., 1968-71; internat. marine mgr. Gulf Miss. Marine Corp., New Orleans, 1971-72; cons. Peter F. Johnson & Assocs., New Orleans, 1972-73; exec. v.p. Pyramid Marine, Inc., New Orleans, 1973-76; owner, chmn. bd., pres. Pacific-Gulf Marine, Inc., New Orleans, 1976—2006, owner, chmn. bd., from 2007. Trustee U.S. Mcht. Marine Acad., Kings Point, NY. Lt. (j.g.) USNR, 1959-63. Mem. Coun. Am. Master Mariners, Soc. Naval Architects and Marine Engrs., Propeller Club U.S. (Maritime Man of Yr. 1986), U.S. Navy League, English Turn Country Club. Republican. Roman Catholic. Avocations: fly fishing, golf, hunting, sailing. Died Dec. 8.

JOHNSON, RAYMOND ALFRED, marketing executive; b. Chgo., Oct. 7, 1922; s. Alfred J. and Agda (Johanson) J.; m. Ellen Mae Clauson, May 25, 1946; children: Ronald Alan, Nancy Rae Johnson Marks, Diane Mae Johnson Hynes. Student, Rutgers U., 1974-75. With AT&T, Chgo., 1940-55, account mgr. Milw., 1955-66, industry mgr. NYC, 1966-79, staff mgr. anti-trust dept. Orlando, Fla., 1979-81, staff mgr. strategic planning, 1982, ret., 1982; dir. mktg. Anderson Assocs. Internat., Tenants Harbor, Maine, from 1983. Cons. Passamaquaddy Indian Tribe, Perry, Maine, 1983—; internat. trade rep. Svc. Corps Ret. Execs., Augusta, Maine, 1987—. Author: Communications for the Trucking Industry, 1967. Served with Signal Corps. U.S. Army, 1941-45, ETO. Mem. AIA (assoc.), Soc. Am. Mil. Engrs., Telephone Pioneers Engrs., Telephone Pioneers Am. (pres. Maine 1985), Kiwanis (bd. dirs. Rockland and Maine club 1983—). Republican. Congregationalist. Died Apr. 23, 2008.

JOHNSON, RICHARD GREENE, physician, psychiatrist, psychoanalyst; b. Louisville, June 3, 1921; s. Greene Johnson and Anne Wood Stout; m. Agnes Campbell Johnson, Nov. 2, 1945; children: Carole, Richard Jr., Craig, Holly. Student, Centre Coll. Ky.; BA, U. Louisville, 1943, MD, 1946; PhD, So. Calif. Psychoanalytic Inst., 1956. Diplomate Am. Bd. Psychiatry and Neurology. Rotating internship Met. Hosp. N.Y.C. Dept. Hosp., 1946-47; residency Emory U./Walter Reed Army Hosp.; pvt. practice, from 1955. Clin. faculty dept. psychiatry UCLA, 1954—; asst. clin. prof. dept. psychiatry UCLA; cons. dept. dermatology UCLA; organizer, med. dir., chmn. bd. dirs. Westwood Psychiatric Hosp., 1959-70; organizer Mental Health Clinic Westwood Cmty. Meth. Ch., 1955; cons. LA County Dept. Mental Health, 1968-73, LA Protestant Cmty. Svcs., 1957-73; area chmn. Acad. of Religion and Mental Health; mem. rsch. com. Nat. Assn. Psychiatric Hosps., 1964. Capt. U.S. Army, 1948-54. Mem. L.A. County Med. Assn. (pres. sect. on psychiatry com. on mental health and clergy), So. Calif. Psychiat. Soc. (pres. 1980, Disting. Svc. award 1990), Calif. Psychiat. Assn., Am. Group Psychotherapy Assn., Am. Psychiat. Assn., Am. Psychoanalytic Assn. Republican. Avocations: golf, tennis, hiking. Died Jan. 17, 2008.

JOHNSON, RICHARD MILTON, finance executive; b. Denver, Nov. 29, 1940; s. Carl Milton and Alice Adeline (Sunblade) J.; m. Norma Sue Shelton, Sept. 1978. BS, Ariz. State U., 1968, MBA, 1970. Govt. programs adminstr. Blue Cross/Blue Shield Ariz., Phoenix, 1969-73; fiscal services dir. Walter O. Boswell Meml. Hosp., Sun City, Ariz., 1973-78; exec. v.p. Flagstaff (Ariz.) Health Mgmt. Corp., from 1978-. Bd. dirs. Ariz. Voluntary Hosp. Fedn., Ariz. Dept. Health Services. Fellow Healthcare Fin. Mgmt. Assn. (pres. 1986-87), Sigma Iota Epsilon. Republican. Lutheran. Avocations: golf, hiking, cross country skiing, reading. Home: Tubac, Ariz. Died May 2, 2008.

JOHNSON, ROBERT E., marketing professional, educator; b. NYC, Aug. 20, 1942; BA, Alfred U., 1964; MA, U. Mass., Boston, 1968, PhD, 1973. Assoc. prof. polit. sci. Mercy Coll., Detroit, 1973-78, assoc. acad. dean, 1978-81, assoc. v.p. acad. affairs, 1981-84, v.p. mktg. and advancement, 1984-90; dir. mktg. and pub. affairs U. Detroit Mercy, from 1990. Cons. Coun. Ind. Colls., Washington, 1980—; mem. adv. bd. Symposium for Mktg. of Higher Edn., 1989, 91. Mem. editorial bd. Jour. Mktg. for Higher Edn., 1988—. Exec. bd. N.W. Instl. Leadership Action Coun., Detroit, 1985—. Capt. U.S. Army, 1968-70. Mem. Am. Mktg. Assn., Direct Mktg. Assn. Home: Bloomfield Hills, Mich. Died Apr. 11, 2008.

JOHNSON, ROSEMARY WRUCKE, personnel management specialist; b. Leith, ND, Sept. 21, 1924; d. Rudolph Aaron and Metta Tomina (Andersen) Wrucke; m. Robert Johnson Jr., Sept. 28, 1945 (div. 1964). Student, George Washington U., 1944-45, 47, Nat. Art Sch., Washington, 1943-45. Supr. Displaced Persons Commn., Frankfurt, Germany, 1950-52, FBI, Washington, 1942—49, 1952—81; cons. position mgmt. orgn. design Arlington, Va., from 1981. Mem. NAFE, Classification and Compensation Soc., Soc. FBI Alumni (membership chmn. 1985-91), Internat. Platform Assn. Lutheran. Avocations: painting, sketching. Died Feb. 28, 2008.

JOHNSON, STANLEY OWEN, engineering consultant; b. Bismarck, ND, Dec. 28, 1930; s. Clifford and Olga May (Steen) J.; m. Janet Ayers Chord, Aug. 3, 1957 (div. Dec. 1982); children: Kristin Marie, Eric Robert. BSEE, U. Colo., 1953; postgrad., U. Pitts., 1954-56. Registered profl. engr., Idaho. Engr. Westinghouse Electric Corp., Pitts., 1953-56, supr., 1956-61; sect. head Phillips Petroleum Co., Idaho Falls, Idaho, 1961-68, br. mgr., 1968-71, Idaho Nuclear Corp., Idaho Falls, 1971-73; pres. Intermountain Technologies, Inc., Idaho Falls, 1973-86; engring. cons. Idaho Falls, from 1986. V.p., bd. dirs. Aspen Security Advisors, Idaho Falls, 1985—, The Rockwood Growth Fund, Idaho Falls, 1985—. Contbr. articles to profl. jours.; inventor. Fellow Am. Nuclear Soc. (Exceptional Service award 1980); mem. NSPE, Idaho Soc. Profl. Engrs., Idaho Falls C. of C. Presbyterian. Avocations: flying, skiing. Home: Idaho Falls, Idaho. Died May 31, 2008.

JOHNSON, VAN, actor; b. Newport, RI, Aug. 25, 1916; s. Charles and Loretta J.; m. Eve Abbott Wynn, Jan. 25, 1947 (div.); 1 dau., Schuyler Van. Grad. high sch. Began as worker in father's plumbing office, 1936. 1st stage appearance in chorus of musical New Faces, 1937; later toured as singer with vaudeville act; appeared in stage prodns. Eight Men of Manhattan, Too Many Girls, 1940, Pal Joey, 1941, La Cage aux Folles 1985; film debut Murder in the Big House, 1941; other films include Remains to Be Seen, Easy to Love, The Caine Mutiny, The End of the Affair, Mating Game, Thirty Seconds Over Tokyo, Ziegfield Follies, It's a Big Country, Brigadoon, Miracle in the Rain, Enemy General, Wives and Lovers, Where Angels Go...Trouble Follows, Eagles Over London, The Purple Rose of Cairo; TV appearances include Rich Man, Poor Man, Kennedy Ctr. Honors, 1982, Murder She Wrote, numerous others; toured in: musicals Damn Yankees, summer 1963. Died Dec. 12, 2008.

JOHNSON, VINCENT ARNOLD, biologist, educator; b. York, Nebr., Jan. 5, 1928; s. Alfred Johannes and Frances Kathryn (Murphy) J.; m. Lucille Margaret (Strohm, May 31, 1953; children: Krista Ellen, Cydna Rhee, Curtis John. BS, U. Nebr., 1952, MSC, 1955, PhD, 1964. Sci. tchr. Scotia (Nebr.) Consol. Schs., 1955-57; spl. instr. U. Tex., Austin, 1957-61; asst. prof. Augustana Coll., Rock Island, Ill., 1964-67, St. Cloud (Minn.) State U., 1967-69, assoc. prof., 1969-72, prof., from 1972. With USN, 1945-46. Mem. Am. Soc. Zoologists, Human Anatomy and Physiology Soc., Minn. Hort. Soc., St. Cloud Garden Club, Sigma Xi (pres. local chpt.). Republican. Lutheran. Home: Saint Cloud, Minn. Died Apr. 25, 2008.

JOHNSON, WILLIAM CLARKE, research and development engineer; b. Jamestown, NY, Aug. 20, 1927; s. Arvid Wilhelm and Alice (Clarke) J.; m. Lois May Stephens, Aug. 19, 1955; children: Karen, Stephen, Gail. BSChemE, U. Wis., 1951, MSChemE, 1953, PhD, 1960. Instr. U. Wis., Madison, 1953-58; sr. engr. 3M Co., St. Paul, 1958-62, research specialist, 1962-73, sr. engring. specialist, from 1973. Adj. prof. U. Minn., Mpls., 1978—. With U.S. Army, 1945-46. Mem. Am. Inst. Chem. Engrs. (continuing edn. com. 1986—), Am. Sch. Soc., East Parks Lions. Republican. Mem. United Church of Christ. Avocations: music, band, orchestra. Home: Saint Paul, Minn. Died Feb. 27, 2008.

JOHNSON, WILLIAM DAVID, retired academic administrator; b. Bloomington, Ind., Aug. 9, 1924; s, Ben and Ida Grace (Garlock) J.; m. Audrey Aelise Thurston; 1 child, Sheryn Aelise Johnson Peters BS, Ind. U., 1946. Asst. bursar U. Va., Charlottesville, 1947-54; comptroller George Washington U., 1954 69, dir. planning and budgeting, 1969-82, assoc. provost, 1982-84, provost, 1984-89. Served to 1st lt. U.S. Army, 1943-46; ETO Mem. Fin. Exec. Inst. (chpt. pres. 1969-70), Eastern Assn. Coll. and Univ. Bus. Officers, Nat. Assn. Coll. and Univ. Bus. Officers, Omicron Delta Kappa, Delta Chi Republican. Presbyterian. Avocations: woodworking, golf, skeet shooting. Home: Falls Church, Va. Died Apr. 19, 2009.

JOHNSON, WILLIAM LLOYD, training specialist, retired; b. Chgo., Mar. 28, 1925; s. William and Fannie Helen (Booth) J.; m. Lucille Althea Fulton, Mar. 8, 1959; 1 child, Melrose. BS, Chgo. State U., 1985, MS, 1986. Photographer, Chgo., 1945-50; photostat operator U.S. Arsenal, Joliet, Ill., 1950-51; postal worker U.S. Postal Svc., Chgo., 1951-79; shift mgr. Salvation Army T.C., Chgo., 1986-89; tng. specialist City Coll. Chgo., 1989-92. With U.S. Army, 1943-45, ETO. Mem. Acad. Criminal Justice Scis., Midwest Criminal Justice Assn., Nat. Geneal. Soc., Afro-Am. Geneal. and Hist. Soc. Chgo., Alpha Phi Sigma. Democrat. Avocations: civil war enthusiast, walking. Home: Chicago, Ill. Died July 13, 2008.

JOHNSON, WILLIAM R., retired state supreme court justice; b. Oct. 21, 1930; married; 2 children. Student, Dartmouth Coll., Harvard U. Pvt. practice law, Hanover; state senator N.H. Gen. Assembly, Concord, state rep.; judge N.H. Superior Ct., Concord, 1969-85; assoc. judge N.H. Supreme Ct., Concord, 1985—2000. Instr. law Dartmouth Coll., Hanover. Died May 30, 2009.

JOHNSTON, CHARLES THEODORE, automotive executive; b. NYC, Mar. 11, 1947; s. Charles Thomas and Roberta (Morning Star) J.; m. Dorothy Mary Muskopf, Sept. 21, 1968 (div. Oct. 11, 1994); children: Charles Thomas, Collin Timothy; m. Denise Aldine Leibmann, July 25, 1996. Student, Pace Coll., 1966-67. Notary Pub., N.Y., Fla.; paralegal, Fla. Mgr. Queens Auto Wrecking, Flushing, N.Y., 1964-68; gen. mgr. Companies Salvage Bur., Flushing, N.Y., 1968-73, pres., 1973-74, True Trading Corp., Ft. Lauderdale, Fla., 1978-83, Average Auto Rental, Ft. Lauderdale, Fla., 1975-83, Surfside Trading Co., Ft. Lauderdale, Fla., 1983-86; buyer Family Auto Brokers, Ft. Lauderdale, Fla., 1976-86, Thomas A Brokers, Miami, Fla., 1986-93; pres. Am. Eco-Traders Corp., from 1993. Auto salvage cons. various ins. cos., N.Y., Fla., 1975—; phys. damage cons. auto, various attys., N.Y., Fla., 1975—; environ. Equip Cons. Electrox Corp., San Mateo Calif., 1995—; proposal writer World 200, Mar Inc., Ft. Lauderdale, 1993—. Co-author: (manual) N.Y. State Drivers Manual, 1969. Mem. Hon. Order of Ky. Cols., Bardstown, 1975—; mem. Golden Eagle, NRA, Washington, 1987—. Mem. Fla. Ind. Auto Dealers Assn., Notary Pub. Assn., Scuba Divers Assn., N.Am. Fishing Assn., Tower Club, Navy League. Republican. Episcopalian. Avocations: saltwater, sport fishing, scuba diving, golf, photography, poetry. Home: Tamarac, Fla. Died Mar. 5, 2008.

JOHNSTON, DUART JENNETTE, operating room nurse; b. Washington, Oct. 11, 1936; d. Alexander T. and Mary Virginia (MacLean) Jennette; m. Donald C. Johnston, Dec. 21, 1956; children: Donald C. Jr., Alexander J., William M., George N., Franklin P., Edward A. BSN, George Mason U., 1987; student, Salem Coll., 1954-56. Cert. oper. nurse. Staff nurse Fairfax Hosp., Falls Church, Va., Reston Hosp. Ctr., Va.; staff nurse oper. rm. Pitt County Meml. Hosp., Greenville, N.C. Mem. Assn. Operating Rm. Nurses. Home: Washington, NC. Died Aug. 23, 2008.

JOHNSTON, GORDON ROBERT, chemist, educator, consultant; b. Portland, Oreg., July 13, 1928; s. Earl Gordon and Catherine Cecilia (Bieker) J.; m. Elizabeth Mary Ann Lane, Aug. 6, 1960; children: Catherine, Therese, William, Dennis. BS, U. Portland, 1950, MS, 1952; PhD, U. Ill., 1956. Rsch. chemist Dow Chem. Co., Midland, Mich., 1956-58; rsch. assoc. U. Oreg. Med. Sch., Portland, 1958-60; rsch. chemist Crown Zellerbach Corp., Camas, Wash., 1960-62, Aerojet-Gen. Corp., Azusa, Calif., 1962-63; postdoctoral fellow Calif. Inst. Tech., Pasadena, 1963-64; prof. San Diego Coll. for Women, 1964-66, Pa. State U., Monaca, 1966-91; ret., 1991. Cons. Pa. Right to Know Law, Beaver, 1986—. Active sch. bd. Beaver, 1971-76, 1985-89; candidate U.S. Ho. of Reps., Pa., 1988, 90, 92. Mem. Am. Chem. Soc., Sigma Xi. Republican. Roman Catholic. Home: Pittsburgh, Pa. Died Nov. 20, 2007.

JOHNSTONE, JOHN ALBERT, healthcare facility executive; b. Lynn, Mass., Dec. 10, 1927; s. Donald Albert and Marjorie Lydia (Hills) J.; m. Dorothy Wentworth, Sept. 11, 1949; children: Cheryl Ann Sweet, Karen Lynn Best, Debra Sue Frazier, Charles Albert, John Wentworth. BSBA, Boston U., 1952. Bus. mgr. Stars & Stripes European Edit., Frankfurt, Germany, 1946-48; gen. mgr., fin. mgr. GE Co., Schenectady, N.Y., 1950-68; cons., dir. Celanese Corp., Transamerica, NYC, San Francisco, 1969-71; pres. Ops. Rsch., Inc., Mpls., Albuquerque, 1972-88, N.Mex. Fin. Svcs., Alburquerque, 1984-94, Ledgewood Manor Inc., Lenoir, N.C., from 1994. Pres. Kachina Constrn. Co., Albuquerque, 1986-92, Candlelight Devel. Co., Albuquerque, 1986-92, The Tax Club, Albuquerque, 1986-92; treas. bd. dirs. Netcomm, Inc., Hickory, N.C., 1995-96. Author: Auditing With Your Computer, 1969. Mem., chair Minn. Loaned Exec. Action Program, St. Paul, 1971-72; chair, founder The Patterson Sch. Found., Lenoir, 1993-96, pres., incorporator, 1993-96. Maj. U.S. Army/USAF, ETO. Named outstanding citizen Govt. Minn., 1973, disting. citizen Commonwealth of Mas., 1962. Mem. VFW, Am. Legion, Masons. Republican. Episcopal. Avocations: volunteering, church activities, educational support groups, healthcare. Home: Lenoir, NC. Died Mar. 28, 2008.

JOINER, LORELL HOWARD, real estate development and investment executive; b. Temple, Tex., Nov. 27, 1945; s. Burt Lawrence and Geneva Evelyn (Howard) J.; m. Cynthia Ann Morin, Mar. 30, 1968. BEcons., Trinity U., San Antonio, 1967; MArch, U. Tex., 1977. Retired architect, Tex. Exec. v.p. Tex. Diversified Properties, San Antonio, 1964-68, Gen. Properties Devel., San Antonio, 1970-76, pres., chief exec. officer, from 1976, Gen. Properties Investment Inc., San Antonio, from 1979. Bd. dirs. Internat. Modelbau GMBH, Geneva, 1986—. Author: Reliable Trackwork Construction, 1986; contbr. articles to profl. publs.; author script, narrator TV programs, Computer Show, 1987, Real Time Interface, 1987. Bd. dirs. San Antonio Community Theater, 1986-89, Tex. Transp. Mus., San Antonio, 1978—; vol. San Antonio Big Bros./Big Sisters, 1986—; mem. com. Muscular Dystrophy Assn. 1st lt. U.S. Army, 1968-70. Named Master Archtl. Model Builder, Nat. Model Bldg. Assn., 1976. Fellow Internat. Modelbau (bd. dirs. 1986—); mem. AIA (assoc., 1st place award for design 1980), Rolls Royce Owner's Club. Avocations: collecting rolls royces, chinese porcelain, books and wine, rail transportation. Home: San Antonio, Tex. Died Dec. 8, 2007.

JOINER, RONALD LUTHER, toxicologist; b. Ponchatoula, La., Mar. 19, 1945; s. Luther Lawrence and Rosalie Lillian (Lavigne) J.; m. Michelle Elizabeth Baham, Jan. 21, 1967; children: Randall Lee, Corey Alexander, Kyle McCahill. BS, Southeastern La. U., 1966; MS, La. State U., 1968; PhD, Miss. State U., 1971. Rsch. asst. La. State U., Baton Rouge, 1966-68; rsch. assoc. biochemist Miss. State U., State College, 1968-71; postdoctoral fellow Tex. A&M U., College Station, 1971-73; supr. toxicology Stauffer Chem. Co., Richmond, Calif., 1973-76; dir. COESH SRI Internat., Rosslyn, Va., 1976-80; v.p. health Battelle Meml. Inst., Columbus, Ohio, 1980—90; gen. mgr. TSI Redfield (Ark.) Labs., 1991-92; pres. Joiner Assocs., Inc., Sherwood, Ark., 1992-94; dir. health and environ. sci. Golder Assocs. Inc., Atlanta, 1994-97; mgr. global toxicology GE Co., from 1997. Bd. dirs. N.C. State U./Battelle Meml. Inst., Raleigh, 1989-91; mem. instnl. rev. bd. Riverside Meth. Hosp., Columbus, 1989-90; mem. biotech. adv. bd. Nat. Ctr. for Toxicol. Rsch., Jefferson, Ark., 1991-94; presenter in field. Contbr. more than 60 articles to profl. jours., 2 chpts. to books. V.p. Homeowner's Assn., Springfield, Va., 1978-80, pres., Dublin, Ohio, 1986-91; campaign co-mgr. Shadid Election Group, Sherwood, Ark., 1993. Robert A. Welch Found. fellow, 1971-73. Mem. AAAS, Am. Chem. Soc., Soc. Toxicology, Soc. Risk Assessment (membership com. 1994-97). Democrat. Roman Catholic. Avocations: golf, coin collecting/numismatics, dance, sports. Home: Pittsfield, Mass. Died May 11, 2008.

JOLLY, WILLIAM THOMAS, language educator; b. Helena, Ark., Apr. 8, 1929; s. Sidney Eugene and Eva (Jones) J. BA, Southwestern at Memphis, 1952; MA, U. Miss., 1958; PhD, Tulane U., 1968. Assoc. ancient langs., chmn. dept. Millsaps Coll., Jackson, Miss., 1959-65; assoc. prof. Greek and Latin Rhodes Coll., Memphis, 1965-75, prof., 1975-94, chmn. dept. fgn. langs., 1975-79, prof. emeritus, from 1994. With USN, 1953-55. Recipient Clarence Day award Day Found., 1991. Mem. Am. Philol. Assn/, Linquistic Soc. Am., Archaeol. Inst. Am., Classical Assn. Mid. West & South, Tenn. Classical Assn., Tenn. Philol. Assn., Am. Classical Legue. Democrat. Methodist. Home: Memphis, Tenn. Died Nov. 4, 2007.

JONES, CHARLES M., economics educator, investment banking consultant; b. NYC, July 6, 1966; m. Daphne Dwyer, July 1, 1989; 1 child, Caroline. BS in Math., MIT, 1987; PhD in Fin., U. Mich., 1994. Fin. analyst Merrill Lynch, NYC, 1987-89; asst. prof. econs. Princeton (N.J.) U., from 1994, asst. dir. Ctr. for Econ. Policy Studies, from 1994, acting dir. Fin. Rsch. Ctr., from 1995. Contbr. articles to profl. jours. Mem. Am. Fin. Assn., Am. Econ. Assn., Econometric Soc. Home: Princeton, NJ. Died Sept. 27, 2007.

JONES, DORIS MORELAND, minister, author; b. Mt. Vernon, Ill., Mar. 25, 1927; d. Gail O. Rutherford and Theo Mareta (Eater) Moreland; m. Harry Wilmont Jones, Mar. 22, 1945 (widowed Sept., 1991); children: Margaret M.J. Hostetter, James Michael. BA, Ky. Wesleyan Col., 1966; MDivinity, Methodist Theological Sch., Delaware, Ohio, 1969; M in Sacred Theology, Christian Theological Seminary, 1971; DDiv (honorary), Ky. Wesleyan Col., 1981. Diplomate Am. Assn. Pastoral Counselors. Pastor various U. Methodist chs. in Ky. and Ohio, 1961-69; dir. Buchanan Counseling Ctr. Methodist Hosp., Indpls., 1969-76; dir. Ordained Ministry U. Methodist Bd. Higher Edn., Nashville, Tenn., 1976-80; dir. counseling ctr. Methodist Evangelist Hosp., Louisville, Ky., 1980-92, Middletown (Ky.) U. Methodist Ch., from 1992. Bd. govs. Am. Assn. Pastoral Counselors, Washington; Nat. Bd. Col. Chaplains, Schomburg, Ill., 1975; adj. faculty Garrett Evangelical Theological Seminary, Evanston, Ill., 1981-91, Louisville (Ky.) Presbyn. Seminary. Author: And Not One Bird Stopped Singing, 1997, (with others) New Witnesses: United Clergywomen, 1980, Clergy Women: Problems and Satisfactions, 1984, God's Gift of Anger, 2005; editor: (book) Guidebook: Interviewing Pastoral Evaluation, 1979. Fellow Coll. Chaplains; mem. Am. Assn. Marriage and Family Therapy, Assn. Clin. Pastoral Edn., Theta Phi Beta. Avocations: walking, gourmet cooking, reading, writing. Home: Louisville, Ky. Deceased.

JONES, DOUGLAS S., geologist, educator, museum director; b. Morristown, NJ, June 6, 1952; BA in Geology with high honors, Rutgers U., 1974; MA in Geol. and Geophys. Scis., Princeton U., 1976, PhD in Geol. and Geophys. Scis., 1980. From asst. prof. to assoc. prof. U. Fla., 1979-84, assoc. curator, assoc. prof. Fla. Mus. Natural History, 1985-89, curator, prof. Fla. Mus. Natural History, from 1989, chair dept. natural scis. Fla. Mus. Natural History, 1994-96, interim dir. Fla. Mus. Natural History, 1996-97, dir. Fla. Mus. Natural History, from 1997. Series editor: (with N. H. Landman) Topics in Geobiology; contbr. articles to profl. jours. Grantee NSF, 1977-79, 82-83, 87-89, 87-90, 94-97, 95-99, 96, 97-98, U. Fla., 1979-80, 80, 80-81, 81, 82-83, 83, 84, 85, 86, 92, 95-96, NIH, 1980-81, 82-83, U. R.I., 1984, 84-85, 86-87. Fellow Geol. Soc. Am.; mem. Paleontol. Soc., Am. Geophys. Union, Paleontol. Rsch. Instn., Nat. Shellfisheries Assn., Soc. Sedimentary Geology, Am. Assn. Mus., Southeastern Geol. Soc. (pres. 1986-87), Fla. Acad. Sci., Fla., Paleontol. Soc., Phi Beta Kappa, Sigma Xi. Died Nov. 18, 2006.

JONES, ELIZABETH ANNE, mental health nurse; b. Success, Ark., Apr. 15, 1934; d. Albert and Velma (Sharpe) Jackson; m. Rex R. Jones, Sept. 7, 1980; children: Randall Sparkman, Kendall Sparkman. BSE magna cum laude, S.E. Mo. State U., Cape Girardeau, 1958; BSN magna cum laude, Abilene Christian U., Tex., 1986. RN; cert. tchr., Mo., Tex. Exec. sec. Western Mktg., Abilene; office mgr. Girardeau Park Family Medicine, Cape Girardeau; tchr. various locations, Mo., Ky.; intermittent evening charge nurse Waco (Tex.) VA Med. Ctr. Mem. Am. Bus. Women's Assn., Sigma Delta Tau. Home: Jackson, Mo. Died May 10, 2008.

JONES, GEORGE HILTON, retired history educator, writer; b. Baton Rouge, Jan. 11, 1924; s. William Carruth and Elizabeth Fly (Kirkpatrick) J. BA, La. State U., 1947; DPhil, Oxford U., Eng., 1950. Instr. Hofstra Coll., Hempstead, N.Y., 1950-51; asst. prof. Ind. U., Bloomington, 1951-52; asst. editor Am. Book Co., NYC, 1953-54; asst. prof. Washington Coll., Chestertown, Md., 1954-56, Tex. Technol. Coll., Lubbock, 1958-61, Kans. State U., Manhattan, 1961-64; assoc. prof. Olivet (Mich.) Coll., 1964-66; from assoc. to full prof. Ea. Ill. U., Charleston, 1966-89, prof. emeritus, from 1989. Ednl. advisor R.J. Best, Inc., San Francisco, 2001—. Author: The Main Stream of Jacobitism, 1955, Charles Middleton, The Life and Times of a Restoration Politician, 1968, Convergent Forces, Immediate Causes of the Revolution of 1688 in England, 1991, Great Britain and the Tuscan Succession Question, 1999; co-author: Southern Regional Education Board, 1960; maj. contbr. Huguenot Soldiering Project, 2002—. Cpl. U.S. Army, 1943-45. Rhodes scholar, Oxford, 1947-50; fellow Newberry Libr., Chgo., summer 1959, Guggenheim Found., London, 1960-61. Fellow Royal Hist. Soc.; mem. AAUP, N.Am. Conf. on Brit. Studies, United Oxford and Cambridge Univ. Club. Democrat. Avocation: writing light verse. Home: Charleston, Ill. Died Apr. 28, 2008.

JONES, GEORGE YOVICIC, civil engineer; b. Belgrade, Yugoslavia, June 2, 1927; m. Sofia Jones, 1960; 1 child, Steven. BSCE, Northwestern U., 1951, MSCE, 1956, PhD Bus. Adminstrn., 1958; PhD (hon.), Hamilton State U., U. Fla., 1972. Registered profl. engr. Wis. Civil engr. Hollabird & Root, Chgo., 1956—57; profl. engr., gen. mgr. Arcadia Engring. Internat., Inc., 1956—70, chmn. bd., from 1970. Civil engr. U.S. Civil Engrs., 1951—54; prof. structural engring. Northwestern U., Evanston, Ill., chmn. dept. econs. U. Ill., Chgo.; legis. asst. Gen. Assembly, Ill.; pres. Tetrakear & Assocs., Inc.; bd. dirs. 1st Nat. Bank Chgo., Skokie Cmty. Hosp., Ill. Author: The Pneumatic Tube Goes Modern, 1958, Opportunities in Construction, 1960, Management and Labor, 1962; contbr. articles to profl. jours. Bd. chmn. Oakton Coll.; pres. Hamilton State U. Maj. US Army. Mem.: NSPE, ASCE, US Army Vet. Avocations: swimming, tennis. Died July 16, 2008.

JONES, HARRIETT GUNN, pediatrics nurse; b. Atlanta, Dec. 3, 1937; d. Harold Webster and Coralee (Lunsford) Gunn; m. Bobby E. Jones, July 18, 1964; children: Nancy Gail, Robert Eugene. Diploma, The Johns Hopkins Hosp., 1959; student, McCoy Coll., 1960-61, Ga. State U., 1963. Head nurse pediatric surgery Johns Hopkins Hosp., Balt., 1961-62; head nurse Grady Meml. Hosp., 1962; field nurse Fulton Country Health Dept., 1963-64; supr. Ga. Regional Hosp., Atlanta; part time staff nurse Clayton Gen. Hosp., Riverdale, Ga.; staff nurse, field nurse Lee County Health Dept., Ft. Myers, Fla.; part time staff nurse Lee Meml. Hosp., Ft. Myers. Died Sept. 27, 2007.

JONES, JAMES EDWARD, minister; b. Birmingham, Ala., Dec. 2, 1934; s. Fred S. and Annie (Dews) J.; m. Martha Elizabeth Bell, Feb. 4, 1956; children: Angela, Darlene, Byron. BA, Samford U., 1957; BD, So. Bapt. Theol. Seminary, Louisville, 1961, D of Ministry, 1982. Various pastoral positions to Valley View Bapt., Louisville, 1964-73; pastor Eastern Hills Bapt., Montgomery, Ala., 1973-81, Campbellsville (Ky.) Bapt. Ch., from 1981. Pres. Ky. Bapt. Conv., 1989-90; exec. com. So. Bapt. Conv., Nashville, 1983-91, chmn. budget com., 1990-91. Author: The Implementation of a Perennial Program of Evangelism, 1982. Chaplain Rescue Squad, Campbellsville/Taylor, Ky., 1982—. Named Man of Yr., C. of C., Campbellesville, 1986. Mem. Kiwanis (bd. dirs. 1986), Mason. Home: Campbellsville, Ky. Died Dec. 11, 2007.

JONES, JENIVER JAMES, lawyer; b. Sutton, W.Va., Sept. 24, 1915; s. Lee Jackson J. and Mary Ida (Lewis) J.; m. Maxine Hickman, Oct. 3, 1939 (dec. Dec. 1993); children: Gary Keith, Glendon Kent, Ronnie Dale; m. Mary Frame, July 30, 1994; stepchildren: Debra Frame Brady, Joseph Frame. Student, Glenville Coll., W.Va., 1938; JD, W. Va. U., 1947. Bar: W. Va. 1947. Tchr. Braxton County Bd. Edn., Sutton, W. Va., 1936-43, attendance dir., 1947-48; aircraft inspector Glen L. Martin, Middle River, Md., 1943-45; pvt. practice Sutton, 1948-91, Gassaway, from 1991. W. Va. Rep. Supreme Ct. nominee, 1988. Mem. Lions Club Internat. (dist. gov. 1963-64, Sutton, W.Va.). Methodist. Avocations: reading, tennis, baseball, golf. Died Feb. 14, 2008.

JONES, JIM WAYNE, editor; b. Bowie, Tex., May 20, 1935; s. John Roy and Nancy Vera (Kilcreaste) J.; m. Audrey Lee Johnson, June 5, 1987. BA, U. N. Tex., 1957; MA, Tex. Christian U., 1967. Reporter Ft. Worth Star-Telegram, 1957, metro editor, 1963-76, religion editor, from 1979. Mem. adv. bd. Robert Wood Johnson Found., 1993-95. Served with USAF Res. Fellow Rockefeller Found, 1982; recipient Tex. Bapt. Press award Bapt. Gen. Conv. Tex., Dallas, 1963. Mem. Ft. Worth Soc. Profl. Journalists (pres. 1980-81), Religion News Writers Assn. U.S. and Can. (pres. 1992-93). Avocations: tennis, travel, genealogy. Died Dec. 19, 2007.

JONES, LEE A., school system administrator, consultant, small business owner; b. Seneca, Ill., Mar. 23, 1948; s. Chester N. and Ruth A. (Laymon) J.; m. Adrian Farris Jones, Mar. 9, 1969; children: Laura A., Trent L. BS, U. Ill., 1972, MEd, 1973; MS, Ea. Ill. U., 1987; PhD, Ind. State U., 1988. Tchr. Wheaton (Ill.) Sch. Dist. 200, 1977-83, Hutsonville (Ill.) Sch. Dist. 2, 1983-87; prin. Gibault Sch., Terre Haute, Ind., from 1987. Owner Country Woods Cabinets, Ill., 1973-88. Mem. Acad. & Athletic Booster Club, Casey, 1985-90; leader Boy Scouts Am., Casey, 1989-90. With USMC, 1966-70. Home: Seneca, Ill. Died Feb. 29, 2008.

JONES, MARY CUNNINGHAM, music educator; d. Jesse Clark Cunningham and Mary Lillian Puckett; m. James Sherman Jones, Dec. 25, 1980. BA, Asbury Coll., 1944; Counterpoint with Lewis Henry Horton, U. Ky., 1945, MA in Piano Pedagogy, Music Edn., 1949, Master Classes with John Jacob Niles, 1946—50; Master Classes with Guy Maier, Santa Monica, Calif., 1953; Master Classes with John Crown, Modesto, Calif., 1965; Master Classes with June Weybright, Oakland, Calif., 1969; Master Classes with Istvan Nadas, San Francisco, 1969—71, Master Classes with William Gillock, 1971. Cert. piano tchr. Am. Coll. of Musicians, 1997. Choir dir. Cavalier H.S., ND, 1945—46; elem. music supr. Baker City Schs., Baker City, Oreg., 1947—50; music tchr. Modesto City Schs., Calif., 1951—53, Ripon Christian Sch., Calif., 1954—61; pvt. piano tchr. Modesto, Calif., from 1954; adjudicator Nat. Guild of Piano Tchrs., Austin, from 1960; arts critic The Modesto Bee, Calif., 1970—71. Chmn. Modesto area Berkeley Jr. Bach Festival, Calif., 1961—64. Bd. mem, /asst. to dean, dir. of childrens'activities Calif. Redwood Christian Pk. Assn., Boulder Creek, 1959—74; lay mem. Calif./Nev. Ann. Conf., United Meth. Ch., Ceres, Calif., 1960—64; mem., dir. of publicity Modesto Cmty. Concerts Assn., Calif., 1967—71. Recipient Profl. Alumna of Yr. award, Asbury Coll. Alumni Assn., 1971. Mem.: Maier Mus. Assn., Music Tchrs.' Assn. Calif. (numerous positions 1959—71, Citation for 50 Yrs. of Meritorious Svc. 2004, State Public Relations trophy 1971), Nat. Guild of Piano Tchrs. (life; founder, chmn. Modesto Ch. 1959—00, Stanislaus County Br., Nat. Honor Roll, Hall of Fame). Methodist. Avocations: crocheting, attending concerts, attending dramatic performances. Home: Modesto, Calif. Died Oct. 25, 2009.

JONES, MASON, retired musician; b. Hamilton, NY, June 16, 1919; s. Frederick Mason and Elizabeth (Piotrow) J.; m. Eve Furlong, July 20, 1941 (dec. 1999); children: Frederick Mason III, Saralinda (Mrs. John H. Orr). Student, Curtis Inst. Music, 1936-38; MusD (hon.), Colgate U., 1970. Tchr. horn, woodwind and brass ensemble Curtis Inst. Music, 1946-95; faculty Temple U. Coll. Music, 1976-83. Condr. Episcopal Acad. Orch., 1958-60; condr. sch. concerts Phila.

Orch., 1972-82; founder, mem. Phila. Woodwind Quintet, 1950-80; co-founder Phila. Brass Ensemble, 1957-77; asst. condr. Phila. Chamber Orch., 1961-64. Mem. Phila. Orch., 1938-78, first hornist, 1940-78, personnel mgr., 1963-86; editor: Solos for the Horn Player, 1962, 20th Century Orch. Studies, 1971. Served with USMC, 1942-46. Recipient C. Hartman Kuhn award for service to Phila. Orch., 1953, 56, 68. Mem. Internat. Horn Soc. (pres. 1986-87), Musical Fund Soc. Clubs: Union League (Phila.); Merion (Pa.) Golf; Cripple Creek (Del.) Golf. Episcopalian. Home: Gladwyne, Pa. Died Feb. 18, 2009.

JONES, PIRKLE, photographer, educator; b. Shreveport, La., Jan. 2, 1914; s. Alfred Charles and Wilie (Tilton) J.; m. Ruth-Marion Baruch, Jan. 15, 1949 (dec. Oct. 1997). Grad., Calif. Sch. Fine Arts, 1949; PhD in Fine Arts (hon.), San Francisco Art Inst, 2003. Profl. free-lance photographer, 1949—2009; asst. to Ansel Adams, 1949—53; faculty Calif. Sch. Fine Arts, 1953-58, San Francisco Art Inst., 1971-97. Tchr. Ansel Adams Workshops, Yosemite.; Mem. Archtl. Adv. Com., Mill Valley, Calif., 1963-67 Exhibited in leading art mus.; photographic archive established Spl. Collections Libr., U. Calif., Santa Cruz; author: Portfolio One, 1955, (with Dorothea Lange) Death of a Valley, 1960, Portfolio Two, 1968; (with Ruth-Marion Baruch) Black Panthers, 1968, 2002, The Vanguard, A Photographic Essay on the Black Panthers, 1970; author: Berryessa Valley, The Last Year, 1994, Pirkle Jones California Photographs, 2001. Nat. Endowment for Arts photography fellow, 1977; recipient award of honor for exceptional achievement in field of photography Arts Commn. of City and County of San Francisco, 1983 Home: Mill Valley, Calif. Died Mar. 15, 2009.

JONES, REGINALD LORRIN, clinical psychologist, consultant; b. St. Petersburg, Fla., Dec. 12, 1951; s. Daniel George Jones and Susie Beatrice (Lewis) W.; divorced; children: Tammy LeVette Jenkins, Myla Carmel, Regina Yvonne, Deneale Elizabeth Luckie. BA, Clark Coll., 1973; MA, U. Cin., 1977, PhD, 1980. Lic. psychologist, Ohio. Statistician Atlanta Pub. Schs., 1973-74; psychology trainee U. Cin., 1974-80; team leader, supr. Social Skills Program, Cin., 1980-81; psychologist, unit dir. Day-Mont West, C.M.H.C., Dayton, Ohio, 1981-83; field psychologist advisor Ohio Indsl. Commn., Dayton, 1983-87. Pvt. practice psychology, Dayton, 1983—; clin. asst. prof. Wright State U., Dayton, 1981—; cons. Adapt Inc., Springfield, Ohio, 1986-94; cons. Sickle Cell Awarness Group, Cin., 1986-90, v.p., 1981. Mem. adv. bd. Drew Sickle Cell Ctr., 1989-92; trustee Family Svc. Assn. Dayton, 1989-92. Named One of Outstanding Young Men of Am., 1984. Mem. Nat. Assn. Black Psychologists, Dayton Assn. Black Psychologists (pres. 1983-84, Svc. award 1986). Democrat. Avocations: african history and culture, gardening, basketball, gourmet cooking, travel. Home: Dayton, Ohio. Died Sept. 19, 2007.

JONES, RICHARD GRAY, JR., advertising executive; b. Cleve., Oct. 7, 1932; s. Richard Gray and Lida Margaret (Creese) J.; m. Virginia Louise Smith, Dec. 1, 1962; children: Marjorie Louise, Richard G. III. BA, Princeton U., 1954; MBA, Harvard U., 1958. Research trainee Young & Rubicam Inc., NYC, 1958-59, research account exec., 1959-63, account exec., 1963-73, account supr., 1973-87, mgmt. supr., 1987-97; retired. Adj. prof. Pace U., Pleasantville, N.Y., 1984-88. Served to 1st lt. U.S. Army, 1954-56. Mem.: Birchwood Swim & Tennis. Republican. Presbyterian. Avocations: tennis, skiing. Home: Chappaqua, NY. Died Nov. 15, 2007.

JONES, WILLIAM HENRY, retired military officer; b. Black Diamond, Wash., Apr. 1, 1924; s. Stanley Ernest Jones and Lena Ellenor Nott; m. Barbara Ann Liestman, May 17, 1960; 1 child, Denise; m. Shirley Ann Williams, Jan. 27, 1946 (div. May 12, 1960); 1 child, Robert. Grad. summa cum laude, Naval Sch. Hosp. Adminstrn., 1950; AA, San Diego City Coll., 1963; BA, San Diego State Coll., 1964; grad., Fed. Health Care Execs. Inst., Chgo., 1972. Apprentice seaman USN, 1942, advanced through grades to capt., combat hosp. corpsman various WWII battles, 1942—45, various enlisted assignments, 1945—50, commissioned ensign med. svc. corps, 1950, asst. fin. officer Naval Hosp. Mare Island Vallejo, Calif., 1950—54, adminstrv. officer med. dept. USS Hancock, 1954—56, asst. adminstrv. officer Naval Hosp. Bethesda, Md., 1956—58, adminstrv. officer Naval Hosp. Corps Sch. San Diego, 1958—60, dir. Amphibious Med. Indoctrination Coronado, Calif., 1960—64, chief patient affairs Naval Hosp. Oakland, Calif., 1964—66, med. adminstrn. officer Hosp. Ship USS Repose - Vietnam War, 1966—67, adminstrv. officer Naval Hosp. St. Albans, NY, 1967—69, Yokosuka, Japan, 1969—71, dir. Health Care Adminstrn. Naval Regional Med. Ctr. Long Beach, Calif., 1971—73, exec. officer Nat. Naval Med. Ctr. Bethesda, Md., 1973—74, commanding officer Field Med. Svc. Sch. Camp Pendleton, Calif., 1974—79, officers selection bd., 1974—79, ret., 1979. Decorated Meritorious Svc. medal (2), Navy Commendation medal, Legion of Merit; recipient Poet of the Year, Famous Poet Soc., 2003. Mem.: Fleet Res. Assn., Fed. Health Care Execs., Am. Coll. Hosp. Adminstrs., Internat. Poetry Hall of Fame, Internat. Poets Soc. (disting.). Avocations: reading, walking, writing. Home: San Marcos, Calif. Died May 27, 2008.

JORDAN, JOHN JOSEPH, lawyer; b. Scranton, Pa., Jan. 30, 1965; s. John Joseph and Anne Marie Jordan; m. Lorena M. Alvarez, Dec. 26, 1993; 1 child, Maximiliano José. BS in Agr., U. Ariz., 1989; JD, St. Mary's U., 1996. Bar: Tex. 1996, U.S. Dist. Ct. (so. dist.) Tex. 1997, U.S. Ct. Appeals (5th cir.) 1997. Briefing atty. U.S. Dist. Ct. (so. dist.) Tex., Brownsville, 1996-97; atty. Roerig Oliveira & Fisher, Brownsville, from 1997. Home: Brownsville, Tex. Died Aug. 8, 2008.

JORDEN, WILLIAM JOHN, writer, retired ambassador; b. Bridger, Mont., May 3, 1923; s. Hugh G. and Jane Ann (Temple) J.; m. Eleanor Harz, 1944 (div.); children: William Temple, Eleanor Harz, Marion Telva; m. V. Mildred Xiarhos, 1972. BA with honors, Yale, 1947; MS, Columbia, 1948. Instr. Japanese Yale U., 1945—46; reporter Vineyard Gazette, Edgartown, Mass., 1947; radio news writer NY Herald Tribune, 1948; fgn. corr. A.P., Japan and Korea, 1948—52, NY Times, Japan and Korea, 1952—55, chief of bur. Moscow, 1956—58; diplomatic corr. NY Times (Washington bur.), 1958-61; mem. Policy Planning Coun., US Dept. State, 1961-62, spl. asst. to under sec. for polit. affairs, 1962-65, dep. asst. sec. for pub. affairs, 1965-66; sr. mem. staff NSC, 1966-68, 72-74; mem., spokesman Am. del. Vietnam Peace Talks, Paris, 1968-69; asst. to Pres. Lyndon B. Johnson The White House, 1969-72; US amb. to Panama US Dept. State, Panama City, 1974-78. Scholar-in-residence LBJ Libr.; adj. prof. LBJ Sch. Pub. Affairs, U. Tex., 1978-80, U.S. chmn. U.S.-Panama Consultative com., 1992-95. Author: Panama Odyssey, 1984; co-author: Japan Between East and West. Served with AUS, 1943-45. Shared Pulitzer prize for internat. corr., 1958; Recipient Disting. Honor award Dept. State, 1978; Pulitzer traveling fellow, 1948-49; Council Fgn. Relations fellow, 1955-56; Decorated order of Vasco Nunez de Balboa (Republic of Panama) Mem. Coun. Fgn. Rels., Acad. Polit. Sci., Author's Guild. Clubs: Yale of Washington, Fgn. Corrs. Japan (pres. 1952-53). Home: N Dartmouth, Mass. Died Feb. 20, 2009.

JORGENSEN, LORI SUSAN, physical education educator; b. S.I., NY, Sept. 8, 1961; d. George and Tanya Marilyn (Stanlecker) J.; m. Joachim O. Gensecke, Aug. 26, 1988. BS in Athletic Adminstrn., St. John's U., 1984; JD with honors, Fla. State U., 1993, MS in Phys. Edn., 1995. Corrections officer Pinellas City Sheriff's Office, Largo, Fla., 1989-90; law clk. Fed. Bur. of Prisons Dept. Justice, Washington, summer 1992; grad. teaching asst. Fla. State U., Tallahassee, from 1992. Capt. U.S. Army, 1984-88. Mem. AAHPERD, Fla. Assn. for Health, Phys. Edn., Recreation, Dance and Driver's Edn. Avocations: tennis, swimming, running, racquetball, reading. Home: Hudson, Fla. Died Dec. 8, 2007.

JOSEY, ELONNIE JUNIUS (E.J. JOSEY), librarian, retired state agency administrator; b. Norfolk, Va., Jan. 20, 1924; s. Willie and Frances (Bailey) J.; m. Dorothy Johnson, Sept. 11, 1954 (div. Dec. 1961); 1 dau., Elaine Jacqueline. AB, Howard U., 1949; MA, Columbia U., 1950; MLS, SUNY, Albany, 1953; LHD, Shaw U., 1973; DPS, U. Wis., Milw., 1987; HHD, N.C. Cen. U., 1989; LittD, Clark Atlanta U., 1995; LHD (hon.), Clarion Univ. of Pa., 2001. Desk asst. Columbia U. Libraries, 1950-52; libr. tech. asst. central br. N.Y. Pub. Libr., NYC, 1952; libr. I Free Libr., Phila., 1953-54; instr. social scis. Savannah State Coll., 1954-55, libr., assoc. prof., 1959-66; libr., asst. prof. Del. State Coll., 1955-59; assoc. divsn. libr. devel. N.Y. State Edn. Dept., Albany, 1966-68; chief Bur. Acad. and Rsch. Libraries, 1968-76, Bur. Specialist Libr. Svcs., 1976-86; prof. U. Pitts. Sch. Libr. and Info. Scis., 1986-95, prof. emeritus, 1995—2009. Mem. bd. advisors Children's Book Rev. Service, Bklyn. Editor, contbg. author: The Black Librarian in America, 1970, What Black Librarians Are Saying, 1972, New Dimensions for Academic Library Service, 1975; co-compiler, co-editor: Handbook of Black Librarianship, 1977; co-editor: A Century of Service: Librarianship in the United States and Canada, 1976, Opportunities for Minorities in Librarianship, 1977, The Information Society: Issues and Answers, 1978, Libraries in the Political Process, 1980, Ethnic Collections in Libraries, 1983, Libraries, Coalitions, And the Public Good, 1987, Politics and the Support of Libraries, 1990, Festchaift E.J. Josey: an Activist Librarian, 1992, The Black Librarian in America Revisited, 1994, Handbook of Black Librarianship, 2001; mem. editl. bd. Dictionary of Am. Library History, 1974—; mem. editl. adv. bd. ALA Yearbook, 1975-83; spl. advisor: World Ency. Black People, 1974-80; contbr. numerous articles to profl. jours. Mem. Albany Interracial Coun., 1972—86; state youth advisor Ga. Conf., 1962—66, 1st v.p., 1981—82, pres., 1982—86, life mem., from 1971, chmn. program, 1972—76, trustee; mem. tech. task force Econ. Opportunity Authority of Savannah, 1964—66; mem. adv. coun. Sch. Libr. Sci. N.C. Ctrl. U.; mem. adv. coun. Sch. Libr. and Info. Sci. SUNY, Albany, Sch. Libr. and Info. Sci. Queen's Coll. CUNY; mem. exec. bd. Savannah (Ga.) br. NAACP, 1960—66; mem. exec. bd. Albany br. Ga. Conf., 1970—72; mem. exec. bd. Albany Opportunity Authority; bd. dirs. Freedom to Read Found., 1987—91. With AUS, 1943—46. Recipient cert. of Appreciation Savannah br. NAACP, 1963, NAACP award Savannah State Coll. chpt., 1964, Merit award for work on econ. opportunity task force Savannah Chatham County, 1966, award for disting. service to librarianship Savannah State Coll. Library, 1967, Jour. Library History award, 1970, N.Y. Black Librarians Inc. award, 1979, N.J. Black Librarians Network award, 1984, Joseph W. Lippincott award, 1980, Disting. Alumnus of Yr. award SUNY Albany Sch. Library and Info. Sci. and Policy, 1981, 89, Disting. Service award Library Assn. of CUNY, 1982, Martin Luther King Jr. award for disting. community leadership SUNY, Albany, 1984, award for contbns. to librarianship D.C. Assn. Sch. Librarians, 1984, award Kenyan Library Assn., 1984, Disting. Service award Afro-Caribbean Library Assn., Eng., 1984; ALA Hon. Mem. Award, 2002. Mem.: ACLU, AAUP, ALA (hon.; founder, chmn. Black Caucus 1970—71, mem. coun. 1970—2009, mem. exec. bd. 1979—86, v.p./pres.-elect 1983—84, pres. 1984—85, John Cotton Dana award 1962, 1964, Black Caucus award 1979, ALA Equality award 1991, Black Caucus Demco award for disting. svc. to librarianship 1994, Wash. office award from 1996, Humphrey/OCLC/Forest Press award for contbns. to internat. librarianship 1998), Am. Soc. Info. Scis., Internat. Platform Assn., N.Y. Libr. Assn. (Disting. Svc. award 1985), Am. Acad. Polit. and Social Sci., Assn. Study Afro-Am. Life and History, Pa. Libr. Assn. (Disting. Svc. award 1996), N.Y. Libr. Club, Kappa Phi Kappa, Alpha Phi Omega. Democrat. Died July 3, 2009.

JOSHI, VIJAY S., physics and mathematics educator; b. Pune, India, May 25, 1939; came to U.S. 1970; s. Sitaram and Kamala (Ghatpande) J.; m. Rohinikumari Purohit, May 15, 1962; children: Swati, Madhavi. BS in Math., Gujarat U., Ahmedabad, India, 1959; MS in Physics, Gujarat U., 1962, PhD in Physics, 1969. Math. tchr. J. Kenan High Sch., Warsaw, N.C., 1971-73; physics instr. Fayetteville (N.C.) Tech. C.C., 1973-81; prog. dir. microelectronics tech. Durham (N.C.) Tech. C.C., from 1981. Mem. Nat. Coun. Tchrs. Math., Math. Assn. Am., Am. Assn. Physics Tchrs. Hindu. Avocations: computers, recreational math. Home: Bristol, Va. Died Dec. 10, 2007.

JULLE, KEITH LEROY, oil executive; b. Lagrand, Oreg., May 13, 1939; s. William Leroy and Eleta Catherine (Spangler) J.; m. Marilyn Jean Biekofsky, Aug. 14, 1965; children: Pamela J., Kevin L. BS, S.W. Mo. State U., 1966; MBA, Pepperdine U., 1979. With sales dept. Shell Oil Co., St. Louis, 1966-72, with sales and mgmt. dept. Chgo., 1972-73, LA, 1973-77, with mgmt. Houston, 1977-79; pres. Mohave Oil Co., Kingman, Ariz., from 1979. Mem. adv. bd. Valley Nat. Bank, Kingman, 1986—. Pres. 2005 Indsl. Devel., Kingman, 1986, Kingsmen Promotional Group, Kingman, 1986. With USN, 1960-64. Mem. Kingman Area C. of C. (bd. dirs. 1982-88, pres. 1986-87), Rotary, Elks (all chairs exalted ruler 1987-88). Republican. Lutheran. Avocations: racquetball, fishing, boating. Home: Kingman, Ariz. Died Feb. 20, 2008.

JUSTICE, WILLIAM WAYNE, federal judge; b. Athens, Tex., Feb. 25, 1920; s. William Davis and Jackie May (Hanson) Justice; m. Sue Tom Ellen Rowan, Mar. 16, 1947; 1 child, Ellen Rowan. LLB, U. Tex., 1942; LLD (hon.), So. Meth. U., 2001. Bar: Tex. 1942. Ptnr. Justice & Justice, Athens, 1946-61; part-time atty. City of Athens, 1948-50, 52-58; US atty. (ea. dist.) Tex. US Dept. Justice, Tyler, 1961-68; judge US Dist. Ct. (ea. dist.) Tex., Tyler, 1968-80, chief judge, 1980-90, sr. judge, 1998—2009. Subject William Wayne Justice, Judicial Biography (Frank R. Kemerer), 1991. Adv. coun. Dem. Nat. Com., 1954; alt. del. Dem. Nat. Conv., 1956, presdl. elector, 1960; v.p. Young Dems. Tex., 1948. 1st lt. US Army, 1942—46, CBI. Recipient Nat. Outstanding Fed. Judge award, ATLA, 1982, Outstanding Civil Libertarian award, Tex. Civil Liberties Union, 1986, Lifetime Achievement award, NACDL, 1996, Thurgood Marshall award, ABA, 2001, Morris Dees Justice award, U. Ala. Sch. Law & Skadden, 2006; named William Wayne Justice Fund for Pub. Svc. in his honor, U. Tex. Sch. Law, 2004. Episcopalian. Home: Austin, Tex. Died Oct. 13, 2009.

KADNER, CARL GEORGE, retired biology educator; b. Oakland, Calif., May 23, 1911; s. Adolph L. and Otilia (Pecht) K.; m. Mary Elizabeth Moran, June 24, 1939; children: Robert, Grace Wickersham, Carl L. BS, U. San Francisco, 1933; MS, U. Calif., Berkeley, 1936, PhD, 1941. Prof. biology Loyola Marymount U., Los Angeles, 1936-78, prof. emeritus, from 1978. Trustee Loyola U., Los Angeles, 1970-73. Served to maj. U.S. Army, 1943-46. Mem. Entomol. Soc. Am. (emeritus), Sigma Xi, Alpha Sigma Nu. Republican. Roman Catholic. Avocation: photography. Home: Los Angeles, Calif. Died Feb. 5, 2008.

KAERCHER, MARILYN ANITA, nurse; b. Blooming Prairie, Minn., Mar. 26, 1924; d. Konard D. and Signe (Peterson) Wold; m. Donald G. Kaercher, Nov. 9, 1947; children: Anita Dorsch, Mark D., Heidi Ott, Todd E. Diploma, Fairview Hosp. Sch. Nursing, 1945; postgrad., Pitts. CCNC, 1970-73. RN, Minn. Oper. rm. nurse Fairview Hosp., Mpls., 1945-47, oper. rm. supr., 1947-49. Sec. bd. aux. N.H. Passavant Hosp., 1973; pres. Richland Aux., N.H. Passavant Hosp., Pitts., 1973, 87-89; pres. bd. dirs. St. John Luth. Care Ctr., Pa., 1974-91; sec. Luth. Affiliated Svcs., Pa., 1989-92; vol. hospice Allegheny Gen. Hosp., 1985-87; mem. coun. Trinity Luth. Ch., 1974-77, pres., 1977; bd. dirs. Mars Housing Inc., 1988-92; sec. Fairview Alumna, Mpla., 1947. Named Trustee of Yr., Am. Assn. Homes for Aging. Republican. Avocation: volunteer work. Home: Gibsonia, Pa. Died June 22, 2008.

KAFFER, ROGER LOUIS, bishop emeritus; b. Joliet, Ill., Aug. 14, 1927; s. Earl Louis and Helen Ruth (McManus) Kaffer. BA, St. Mary of the Lake, Mundelein, Ill., 1950, STB, 1952, MA, 1953, licentiate in Sacred Theology, 1954; licentiate of Canon Law, Pontifical Gregorian U., Rome, 1958; D in Pastoral Ministry, St. Mary of the Lake, Mundelein, Ill., 1983; MEd, DePaul U., 1965; LHD (hon.), Felician Coll., 1986; DHL (hon.), Coll. St. Francis, 1990; doctorate (hon.), Lewis U., 1990. Ordained priest Diocese of Joliet, Ill., 1954, Eccles. notary, 1954—56, asst. chancellor, 1958—65; rector St. Charles Borromeo Sem., Lockport, Ill., 1965—70; prin. Providence HS, New Lenox, Ill., 1970—85; rector Cathedral of St. Raymond, Joliet, 1985;

vicar gen., vicar for clergy Diocese of Joliet, 1985—2004; ordained bishop, 1985; aux. bishop Diocese of Joliet, 1985—2002, aux. bishop emeritus, 2002—09. Past. mem. Marriage Tribunal, Diocesan Sem. Bd., Diocesan Bd. Religious Edn. Recipient DeLa Salle medallion, Lewis U., 1984, Lifetime Achievement award, Joliet C. of C., 1999, award, Paluch Family Found., 2002; named Cleric of Yr., KC, 1973, Citizen of Yr., New Lenox Assn. Commerce, 1976, Man of Yr., Joliet Cath. High Alumni Assn., 1978, Citizen of Yr., UNICO, Joliet, 1996. Mem.: Nat. Conf. Cath. Bishops Conf. Ill., KC (Ill. state chaplain 1993). Roman Catholic. Died May 28, 2009.

KAHMANN, ANTHONY ROBERT, mechanical engineer; b. Washington, Mo., June 26, 1921; s. Anthony Alexander and Louise Gertrude (Stauder) K.; m. Marguerite Mae Brubeck, Mar. 2, 1946; children: Barbara, Deborah, Anthony R. Jr., Thomas. BSME, U. Mo., 1948. Registered profl. engr., Okla. Vacuum specialist Tenn. Eastman Corp., Oak Ridge, Tenn., 1944-46; mem. mech. engring. staff Phillips Petroleum Corp., Bartlesville, Okla., 1948-51; chief engr. Chandler Engring., Tulsa, 1951-81; dir. engring. EG&G Chandler Engring., Tulsa, 1981-90, cons., from 1990. Author curriculum materials, instr. Internat. Sch. Hydrocarbon Measurement, Norman, Okla., 1951-90, Appalachian Gas Measurement Inst., Corapolis, Pa., 1955-90. Patentee in field. Sgt. U.S. Army, 1943-46. Mem. ASME (life, chmn. Mid-continent sect. 1969-70), Nat. Soc. Profl. Engrs. Republican. Roman Catholic. Avocation: golf. Home: Tulsa, Okla. Died May 9, 2008.

KAHN, ALFRED JOSEPH, social services researcher, educator; b. NYC, Feb. 8, 1919; s. Meyer and Sophie (Levine) K.; m. Miriam Kadin, Sept. 3, 1949 (div. 1980); 1 child, Nancy Valerie. B in Social Sci., CCNY, 1939; B in Hebrew Lit., Sem. Coll. Jewish Studies, NYC, 1940; MS, Columbia U., 1946, D in Social Welfare, 1952; DHL (hon.), Adelphi U., 1984; DSc (hon.), U Md., 1989; Dr. (hon.), York U., Eng., 1998. Psychiat. social worker Jewish Bd. Guardians, NYC, 1946-47; mem. faculty Sch. Social Work Columbia U., 1947-89, prof. Sch. Social Work, 1954-89, prof. emeritus, 1989—2009; co-dir. Cross Nat. Studies Rsch. Program, 1973—2005; Disting. vis. prof. Grad. Sch. Social Svc., Fordham U., 1990-2001. Staff cons. Citizens Com. for Children, N.Y.C., 1948-72; mem. summer faculty Smith Coll. Sch. Social Work, 1949-54; cons. govts., founds., vol. agys., 1949-2004; mem. numerous adv. coms.; mem. adv. com. child devel. NRC-Nat. Acad. Scis., 1971-76, mem. com. child devel. rsch. and pub. policy, Acad. Scis., 1977-83, chmn., 1980-83; mem. adv. bd. Inst. Rsch. Poverty, U. Wis., 1967-2002. Author: A Court for Children, 1953, Planning Community Services for Children in Trouble, 1963, Neighborhood Information Centers, 1966, (with Anna Mayer) Day Care as a Social Instrument, 1966, Theory and Practice of Social Planning, 1969, Studies in Social Policy and Planning, 1969, Social Policy and Social Services, 1973; co-author: Not for the Poor Alone, 1975, Social Service in the U.S., 1976, Social Services in International Perspective, 1977, Child Care, Family Benefits and Working Parents, 1981, Helping America's Families, 1982, Maternity Policies and Working Women, 1983, Income Transfers for Families With Children, 1983, Child Care: Facing the Hard Choices, 1987, The Responsive Workplace, 1987, Mothers Alone, 1988, Social Services for Children, Youth and Families in the United States, 1989, Social Services for Children, Youth and Families: The New York City Study, 1990, A Welcome for Every Child, 1994, Social Policy and the Under 3s, 1994, Starting Right, 1995, Big Cities in the Welfare Transition, 1998, Contracting for Child and Family Services, 2000; contbr. monographs, articles to profl. jours., chpts. to books; editor: Issues in American Social Work, 1959, Shaping The New Social Work, 1973; co-editor: Family Policy: Government and Famlies in Fourteen Countries, 1978, Child Support, From Debt Collection to Social Policy, 1988, Privatization and the Welfare State, 1989, Child Care, Parental Leaves and The Under 3s: Policy Innovation in Europe, 1991, Children and Their Families in Big Cities, 1996, Family Change and Family Policies in Great Britain, Canada, New Zealand, and the United States, 1997, Beyond Child Poverty: The Social Exclusion of Children, 2002. With USAAF, 1942-46. Mem. AAUP, Nat. Assn. Social Workers (chmn. div. practice and knowledge 1963-66, bd. dirs. 1967-70), Council Social Work Edn., Assn. for Policy Analysis and Mgmt. Died Feb. 13, 2009.

KAHN, EDWIN LEONARD, retired lawyer; b. NYC, Aug. 1, 1918; s. Max L. and Julia (Rich) K.; m. Myra J. Green, Oct. 20, 1946 (dec. 1994); children: Martha L., Deborah K. Spiliotopoulos. AB, U. N.C., 1937; LLB cum laude, Harvard U., 1940. Bar: N.C. 1940, D.C. 1949. Atty., asst. head legislation and regulations div. Office Chief Counsel IRS, 1940-52, dir. tech. planning div., 1952-55; ptnr. Arent, Fox, Kintner, Plotkin & Kahn (now Arent Fox PLLC), Washington, 1955—86, of counsel, 1987—2009; ret., 1987. Lectr. NYU Tax Inst., mem. adv. bd., 1959-70; lectr. tax insts. Coll. William and Mary, U. Chgo., U. Tex. Editor: Harvard Law Rev, 1939-40; mem. editl. adv. bd. Tax Advisor of Am. Inst. CPA's, 1974-86. Bd. dirs. Jewish Community Ctr. Greater Washington, 1972-78; trustee Cosmos Club Found., 1989-93, chmn., 1989-91. With U.S. Army, 1943-46, ETO. Decorated Bronze Star. Fellow Am. Bar Found. (life); mem. ABA (coun. 1963-66, vice chmn. sect. taxation 1965-66), Fed. Bar Assn. (chmn. taxation com. 1967-68), D.C. Bar Assn., Nat. Tax Assn.-Tax Inst. Am. (adv. coun. 1967-69, bd. dirs. 1969-73), Am. Law Inst. (life), Am. Coll. Tax Counsel, J. Edgar Murdock Am. Inn Ct. (master bencher 1988-91), Phi Beta Kappa (life mem. fellows). Jewish. Home: Arlington, Va. Died Aug. 18, 2009.

KAIGE, ALICE TUBB, retired librarian; b. Obion, Tenn., Jan. 27, 1922; d. George Easley and Lucile (Merryman) Tubb; m. Richard H. Kaige, Aug. 1952; children: Robert H., Richard C. (dec.), John S. (dec.) BA, Vanderbilt U., 1944; BS in Libr. Sci., Geo. Peabody Coll., 1947. Libr. Martin HS, Tenn., 1946-47, Demonstration Sch. Geo. Peabody Coll. Joint U. Librs., Nashville, 1947-52; acquisitions libr. Lincoln Libr., Springfield, Ill., 1967-70; office coord. Springfield chpt. ACLU, 1974; staff rep. Am. Fed. State, County & Mcpl. Employees, Springfield, 1975; libr. Ill. Dept. Commerce and Cmty. Affairs, Springfield, 1976-89. Vice chmn. Women's Internat. League for Peace and Freedom, 1969-70, various coms., 1970—; treas. Cen. Ill. Women's Lobby, 1971-72; com. on local govt. League of Women Voters, 1973-76; career day com. Urban League Guild, 1970-71; co-founder West Side Neighborhood Assn., Springfield, 1977. Recipient Elizabeth Cady Stanton award, Springfield Women's Political Caucus, 1982. Mem. Sangamon County Hist. Soc., Women's Internat. League for Peace and Freedom, War Resisters League, Ill. Audubon Soc., Ill. State Hist. Soc., World Affairs Coun. Ctrl. Ill. Avocations: reading, walking. Home: Springfield, Ill. Died Oct. 5, 2007.

KAKALEC, JOSEPH MICHAEL, priest; b. McAdoo, Pa., Feb. 23, 1930; s. Peter and Mary (Pensock) Kakalec. BS in Fgn. Svc., Georgetown U., 1953; PhL, MA in Polit. Sci., St. Louis U., 1962; MDiv, Woodstock Coll., 1968; postgrad., U. Pa., 1968-70. ordained priest, Roman Catholic ch., 1967. Founder, counselor North Cen. Community Orgn., Phila., 1970-74; exec. dir. Phila. Coun. Neighborhoods, 1974-82; tchr. West Catholic High Sch. Girls, Phila., 1974-82; exec. dir. Regional Coun. Neighborhood Orgns., Phila., from 1982; instr. politics St. Joseph's U., Phila., from 1989. Cons., organizer Met. Christian Coun. Phila.; instr. polit sci. and regionalism, Temple U., Phila., 1988—. Contbr. articles on urban problems to numerous publs. Past bd. dirs. Cedar Park Neighbors, Women in Transition, Phila. Coun. Neighborhood Edn., Phila. Century Four Celebration Com., Phila. City-Wide Devel. Corp., others; mem. Cardinal's Urban Affairs Commn. on Human Rels., Phila., Urban Affairs Partnership, For the People, Inc., Chester, Pa. Mem. Soc. of Jesus. Died Aug. 26, 2007.

KALTER, THOMAS RAYMOND, personnel director; b. Chgo., Dec. 15, 1947; s. Clarence Raymond and Elsie Marie (von Oepen) K.; m. Cheryl Ann Johnson, June 1966 (div. July 1969); children: Michael Thomas, Jean Marie; m. Rose Marie Sundler, Oct. 11, 1969; children: Ronald James, Jonathan Randolph. Assoc. degree, El Paso Community Coll., 1978; BS, Regis Coll., 1989. Mil. personnel officer Personnel Directorate, Washington, 1969-72; mgmt. intern Office Chief of Staff, U.S. Army, Washington, 1972; personnel intern Army Personnel Office, Washington, 1973, compensation specialist, 1974, recruiting specialist, 1975; compensation specialist Civilian Personnel Office, Ft. Carson, Colo., 1975-76, chief compensation div., 1976-85, asst. personnel officer, 1985-88; dir. Directorate of Civilian Personnel, Ft. Carson, from 1988. Mem. Fed. Personnel Coun., Denver, 1988—. Mem. Classification and Compensation, Denver, 1976-85; sec. Ridgewood Water Co., Woodland Park, Colo., 1989; mem.-at-large Ridgewood Homeowners Assn., Woodland Park, 1989, 90, v.p., 1988. With U.S. Army, 1966-69. Mem. Assn. of U.S. Army, Pikes Peak Fencing Club. Avocations: fencing, tennis, cross country skiing, hiking, cooking. Home: Woodland Park, Colo. Died Aug. 14, 2008.

KAMINSKY, STUART M., screenwriter, writer; b. Chgo., Sept. 29, 1934; s. Leo and Dorothy Zelac K.; m. Merle Gordon, Aug. 11, 1959 (div. Sept. 1986); children: Peter, Toby, Lucy; m. Enid Lisa Perll, Jan. 7, 1987; 1 child, Natasha. BS in Journalism and Comm., U. Ill., 1957, MA in English Lit. with honors, 1960; PhD in Speech, Film-TV, Theatre Arts, Northwestern U., Evanston, Ill., 1972. Telephoto operator UP, Chgo., 1959; reporter Hollister Press, Willmette, Ill., 1960; sci. writer U. Ill., Chgo., 1962-64; editor news svc. U. Mich., Ann Arbor, 1965-66; dir. pub. rels., asst. to v.p. pub. affairs U. Chgo., 1966-69; faculty Dept. Radio-TV-Film Northwestern U., Evanston, 1972-89, chmn. dept. Radio-TV-Film, 1987-89, dir. grad. studies in film, 1980-87; dir. Fla. State U. Conservatory of Motion Picture, TV and Recording Arts, Sarasota, 1989-94, prof., 1989—94; ret., 1994. Prof. in residence U. N.C., 1982, Oldfields Sch., 1993; lectr. in field. Author: (non-fiction) Don Siegel: Director, 1973, Clint Eastwood, 1974, American Film Genres: Approaches to a Critical Theory of Popular Film, 1974, Ingmar Bergman: Essays in Criticism, 1975, John Huston: Maker of Magic, 1978, Coop: The Life and Legend of Gary Cooper, 1980, Basic Filmmaking, 1981, American Television Genres, 1984, Writing for Television, 1988; (fiction) Bullet for a Star, 1977, Murder on the Yellow Brick Road, 1977, Death of a Dissident, 1981, When the Dark Man Calls, 1983, Black Knight in Red Square, 1984, A Cold Red Sunrise, 1988 (Edgar Allen Poe award 1989, Prix du Roman D'Aventure award 1990), Exercise in Terror, 1985, Lieberman's Folly, 1991, THe Melting Clock, 1991, Poor Butterfly, 1991, Lieberman's Choice, 1993, The Green Bottle, 1996, Devil on My Doorstep, 1997, Hidden and Other Stories, 1999, Vengeance, 1999, Murder on the Trans-Siberian Express, 2001, To Catch a Spy, 2002, Not Quite Kosher, 2002, Retribution, 2002, Mildred Pierced, 2003, Now You See It, 2004, The Last Dark Place, 2004, Denial, 2005, Always Say Goodbye, 2006, Terror Town, 2006, The Dead Don't Lie, 2007, People Who Walk in Darkness, 2008, Bright Futures, 2009; (short films) More Pampered Than Pets (screenplay), 1965, Last Minute Marriage (co-screenplay, co-dir.), A Black and White Film in Sound and Color (dir. screenplay); feature length films Once Upon a Time in America (dialogue writer) 1983, Shepard's Tower (screenplay), 1985, A Woman in the Wind, 1987, Enemy Territory (story and co-screenplay), 1987, Frequence Meurtre (story), 1988, Ain't Got No Tears Left (screenplay), 1989, Growing Up Rich, 1989, Get Serious, 1990, Hidden Fears, 1991, (story) When a Dark Man Calls, 1995; television series cons. Falcon Crest V. Yellow Rose; plays Here Comes the Interesting Part, 1967, You Can Run But You Can't Hide, 1997; contbr. short stories, articles, book chpts. to profl. pubs. Program chmn., co-artistic dir., bd. mem. Sarasota French Film Festival; chair Festival of Jewish Films, Sarasota, Fla., 1998—; past bd. mem. Chgo. Film Festival Bd., Ill. Arts Coun., Nat. Endowment Humanities, coun. for Internat. Exchange of Scholars, Fla. Media Arts Coun., Enzian Theater. With U.S. Army, 1957-59, France, Germany. Named Grand Master, Mystery Writers of America, 2006. Mem. Soc. for Cinema Studies, Univ. Film and Video Assn., Mystery Writers Am. (pres. 1998), Internat. Assn. Crime Writers (U.S. del. Internat. bd. mtg. in Moscow, 1991), Crime Writers Assn. of Europe, Private Eye Writers of Am., Popular Culture/Am. Culture Assn., Writers Guild of Am. Jewish. Avocation: coaching childrens soccer and basketball. Home: Sarasota, Fla. Died Oct. 9, 2009.

KAN, HENRY, state agency administrator; b. Kwangtung, Republic of China, Oct. 10, 1921; came to U.S., 1969; s. Sing-Yeuk and Wai-Sing Kan; m. Linda Kan, May 5, 1951; children: Grace, John. BS, Nat. Sun Yat-Sen U., Republic of China, 1945; MS, CUNY, 1967; MBA, Golden Gate U., 1976. Registered profl. engr., Calif. Agt. life and disability, fire and casualty Calif. Dept. Ins., from 1987; engr., mgr. Taiwan Sugar Corp., 1946-67; engring. supr. Bechtel, San Francisco, 1969-85. Pres. Kans Enterprise, Danville, Calif., 1988—; agt. Prudential Ins. Co., San Francisco, 1987-88. Contbg. editor: Taiwan Sugar Handbook, 1952. Elder Golden Gate Christian Reformed Ch., San Francisco, 1970; trustee Rep. Presdl. Task Force, Washington, 1989. Recipient Ministry Econ. Affairs citation Republic of China, 1956. Mem. ASME. Avocations: gardening, travel, swimming, boating, tennis. Home: Brentwood, Calif. Died Jan. 4, 2008.

KANE, CHERYL MARIE, educational association administrator; b. Great Barrington, Mass., Dec. 26, 1947; d. Alexander and Mildred (Tatsapaugh) Shmulsky. BA, U. Mass., 1969; MA, U. Colo., 1979; PhD, Fla. State U., 1988. Project dir. Colo. State Dept. Edn., Denver, 1977-79; rsch. assoc. Nat. Inst. Edn., Washington, 1979-81; pvt. practice cons. Washington, 1981-88; assoc. exec. dir. Nat. Found. for the Improvement of Edn., Washington, 1988-92; dir. rsch. Nat. Edn. Commn. on Time and Learning, Washington, 1992-94; dir. strategy New Am. Schs. Devel. Corp., Arlington, Va., 1994-99; sr. assoc. office ednl. rsch./improvement U.S. Dept. Edn., 1999-2000, exec. dir. nat. commn. on H.S. sr. yr., 2000—01, sr. rsch. assoc., from 2001. Cons. U.S. Dept. Edn., Washington, World Bank, Washington, Acad. for Edn. Devel., Washington, 1981—88. Author: Prisoners of Time: What We Know and What We Need to Know, 1994; contbr. chpts. in books. Sec. Logan Circle Cmty. Assn., Washington, 1993. Mem.: Am. Edn. Rsch. Assn., Phi Delta Kappa. Avocations: sailing, gardening, photography, travel. Home: Canaan, Conn. Died Mar. 5, 2008.

KANEFIELD, MARVIN, psychiatrist; b. Phila., Nov. 18, 1935; s. Albert and Lillian (Bass) K.; m. Isabel Sultan, June 15, 1958; children: Jeffrey, Susan, Karen. BS, Villanova U., 1957; DO, Phila. Coll. Osteopathic Med., 1961. Pres. Psychiatric Cons., Inc., Phila., from 1993. Home: Blue Bell, Pa. Died Nov. 5, 2007.

KANOVITZ, HOWARD EARL, artist, educator; b. Fall River, Mass., Feb. 9, 1929; s. Meyer Julius and Dora (Rems) K. m. Mary Rattray (div.); m. Carolyn Oldenbusch BS, Providence Coll., 1949; postgrad., R.I. Sch. Design, 1949-51, NYU, 1959-61. Instr. Bklyn. Coll., 1962-64, Pratt Inst., 1964-66; prof. Southhampton Coll., 1977-78, Sch. Visual Arts, NYC, 1981-85. Artist, painter exhibited Tibor de Nagy Gallery, 1956, Stable Gallery, 1962, Jewish Mus., 1966, Waddell Gallery, 1969; one-man shows include U.S. and Europe, Stefanotty Gallery, N.Y.C., 1975, Galerie Jöllenbeck, Cologne, 1977, Benson Gallery, Bridgehampton, L.I., N.Y., 1977, Akademie der Kunste, Berlin, 1979, Kestner Gesellschaft, Hannover, 1979, Alex Rosenberg Gallery, 1982, Inge Baecker Gallery, 1987, 88, 91, Cologne, 1987, Marlborough Gallery, 1988, 90, Hokin-Kaufman Gallery, Chgo., 1989, Gana Art Gallery, Seoul, 1990, Ulrich Gering Gallery, Frankfurt, 1997, Nabi Gallery, Sag Harbor, L.I., 1998; group exhibits include Whitney Mus., N.Y.C., 1972, Dokumenta 5, Kassel, 1972, Berlin Nat. Gallery, 1976, Guild Hall, East Hampton, L.I., 1976, Dokumenta 6, Kassel, 1977, Alex Rosenberg Gallery, 1978, Louise Himmelfarb Gallery, Watermill, L.I., 1979, L.A. Mus. Contemporary Art, 1984, Indpls. Mus. Art, 1985, Ludwig Mus., Cologne, 1988, Parrish Art Mus., Southampton, L.I., 1988, Fla. Internat. U., Miami, 1989, Met. Mus., N.Y.C., 1991, Weatherspoon Art Gallery, Greensboro, N.C., 1991; represented in permanent collections Met. Mus., N.Y., Whitney Mus. Am. Art, N.Y., Hirshhorn Mus. and Sculpture Garden, Washington, L.A. County Mus. Modern Art, Guild Hall Mus., East Hampton, N.Y, Folkwang Mus., Essen, Germany. Died Feb. 2, 2009.

KANTROWITZ, ADRIAN, surgeon, educator; b. NYC, Oct. 4, 1918; s. Bernard Abraham and Rose (Esserman) K.; m. Jean Rosensaft, Nov. 25, 1948; children: Niki, Lisa, Allen. AB, NYU, 1940; MD, L.I. Coll. Medicine, 1943; postgrad. physiology, Western Res. U., 1950. Diplomate: Am. Bd. Surgery, Am. Bd. Thoracic Surgery. Gen. rotating intern Jewish Hosp. Bklyn., 1944; asst. resident, then resident surgery Mt. Sinai Hosp., NYC, 1947; asst. resident Montefiore Hosp., NYC, 1948, asst. resident pathology, 1949, fellow cardiovascular rsch. group, 1949, chief resident surgery, 1950, adj. surg. svc., 1951-55; USPHS fellow cardiovascular rsch., dept. physiology Western Res. U., 1951-52; asst. prof. surgery SUNY Coll. Medicine, 1955-56, assoc. prof. surgery, 1957-64, prof., 1964-70; dir. cardiovascular surgery Maimonides Med. Ctr., Bklyn., 1955-64, dir. surgery, 1964-70; chmn. dept. surgery Sinai Hosp. Detroit, 1970-75, chmn. dept. cardiovascular surgery, 1975-85; prof. surgery Wayne State U. Sch. Medicine, 1970; owner LVAD Tech., 1983. Contbr. articles profl. jours. 1st lt. to major M.C. AUS, 1944—46. Recipient H.L. Moses prize to Montefiore Alumnus for outstanding rsch. accomplishment, 1949; 1st prize sci. exhibit Conv. N.Y. State Med. Soc., 1952; Gold Plate award Am. Acad. Achievement, 1966; Max Berg award for outstanding achievement in prolonging human life, 1966; Theodore and Susan B. Cummings humanitarian award Am. Coll. Cardiology, 1967 Fellow ACS, N.Y. Acad. Sci.; mem. Internat. Soc. Angiology, Am. Soc. Artificial Internal Organs (pres. 1968-69, Barney Clark award 1993, Lifetime Achievement award, 2001)), N.Y. County Med. Soc., Harvey Soc., N.Y. Soc. Thoracic Surgery, N.Y. Soc. Cardiovascular Surgery, Am. Heart Assn., Am. Physiol. Soc., Am. Coll. Cardiology, Am. Coll. Chest Physicians, Bklyn. Thoracic Surgery Soc. (pres. 1967-68), Pan Am. Med. Assn., Soaring Soc. Am., Am. Ski Assn. Achievements include being pub. pioneer motion pictures taken inside living heart, 1950; contbr. to devel. pump-oxygenators for human heart surgey; pioneer devel. mech., artificial hearts; performed 1st permanent partial mech. heart surgery in humans, 1966; 1st use phase-shift intra-aortic balloon pump in patient in cardiogenic shock; 1st human heart transplant in U.S., Dec. 1967. Died Nov. 14, 2008.

KANTROWITZ, ARTHUR ROBERT, physicist, researcher, educator; b. NYC, Oct. 20, 1913; s. Bernard A. and Rose (Esserman) K.; m. Rosalind Joseph, Sept. 12, 1943 (div.); children: Barbara, Lore, Andrea; m. Lee Stuart, Dec. 25, 1980. BS, Columbia U., 1934, MA, 1936, PhD, 1947; DEng (hon.), Mont. Coll. Mineral Sci. and Tech., 1975; D.Sc. (hon.), N.J. Inst. Tech., 1981. Physicist NACA, 1935-46; prof. aero. engring. and engring. physics Cornell U., 1946-56; founder, dir., chmn., chief exec. officer Avco-Everett Research Lab., Everett, Mass., 1955-78; sr. v.p., dir. Avco Corp., 1956-79; prof. Thayer Sch. Engring., Dartmouth Coll., from 1978. Vis. lectr. Harvard U., 1952; Fulbright and Guggenheim fellow Cambridge and Manchester univs., 1954; fellow Sch. Advanced Study, MIT, 1957, vis. inst. prof., 1957—; Joseph Wunsch lectr. Technion, Haifa, Israel, 1968; mem., fellow lectr. Am. Inst. Chemists, 1977; Messenger lectr. Cornell U., 1978; 1st Hastings lectr. NIH, 1977; hon. prof. Huazhong Inst. Tech., Wuhan, China, 1980; mem. Presdl. Adv. Group on Anticipated Advances in Sci. and Tech., head task force on sci. ct., 1975-76; mem. tech. adv. bd. U.S. Dept. Commerce, 1974-77; mem. adv. panel NOVA, Sta. WGBH-TV, 1975—; bd. overseers Center for Naval Analyses, 1973-83; mem. adv. council Israel-U.S. Binational Indsl. Research and Devel. Found., 1978-81; bd. govs. The Technion (hon. life); mem. adv. council NASA, 1979, 80; life trustee U. Rochester; past mem. sci. and engring. adv. com. U. Rochester, Princeton U., Stanford U. and Rensselaer Poly Inst.; vis. prof. U. Calif., Berkeley, 1983. Contbr. articles to profl. jours.; patentee in field. Bd. dirs. Hertz Found., 1972—. Recipient award Am. Acad. Achievement, 1966, Theodore Roosevelt medal, 1967, Kayan medal Columbia U., 1973, MHD Faraday Meml. medal UNESCO, 1983, Beamed Energy Propulsion award First Internat. Symposium, 2002-. Fellow AAAS, AIAA (1st Von Kármán lectr. 1964, Fluid and Plasmadynamics medal 1981, Aerospace Contbn. to Soc. award 1990, hon. fellow 1998), Am. Acad. Arts and Scis., Am. Phys. Soc., Am. Astronautical Soc., Am. Inst. for Med. and Biol. Engring.; mem. NAS, NAE, Internat. Acad. Astronautics, Am. Inst. Physics, Sigma Xi. Achievements include lead developer of intra-aortic balloon pump and inventor of principle; scientific collaboration on MHD energy conversion; high-energy lasers, interplanetary shock waves; solved missile nose cone heating problem during re-entry from space; early work in fusion, supersonic source for molecular beams and the total energy variometer noteable. Home: Hanover, NH. Died Nov. 29, 2008.

KAPILEVICH, MENDEL BERKOVICH, mathematician; b. Ukraine, USSR, Mar. 1, 1923; came to U.S., 1988; s. Berka Mendelevich and Alexandra Leibovna (Khazanova) K.; m. Khana Leibovna Kaplan, Jan. 29, 1961; children: Boris Mendelevich, Liliya Mendelevna. Student, U. Moscow, 1945-49, PhD, 1957; degree in mech. engring., MAI, Moscow, 1948. Rsch. assoc. Cen. Aero-Hydrodynamical Inst., Moscow, 1948-53; sr. lectr. in math., chmn., head math. dept. Moscow Evening Metall. Inst., 1953-87, ret. Author: (in Russian) Linear Differential Equations of Mathematical Physics, 1964, Eng. edit., 1967, German edit., 1967; contbr. numerous articles to profl. publs. Recipient medal Pres. of Supreme Soviet, 1984, Vet. of Labor, USSR. Mem. Am. Math. Soc., Soc. for Indsl. and Applied Math. (orthogonal polynomials and spl. functions activity group). Home: Brighton, Mass. Died Aug. 28, 2007.

KAPLAN, MARTIN NATHAN, electrical and electronic engineer; b. Beloit, Wis., Nov. 14, 1916; s. Abraham Louis and Eva (Schomer) K.; m. Florence Helen Grumet (div. 1956); 1 child, Kathy Sue; m. Sylvia Greif, Dec. 7, 1963. BSEE, U. Wis., 1942. Sr. electronics engr. Convair, San Diego, 1951-56; rsch. engr. AMF/Sunstrand, Pacoima, Calif., 1956-59; sr. rsch. engr. Ryan Electronics, San Diego, 1959-63; sr. design engr. N.Am. Aviation, Downey, Calif., 1963-66; rsch. specialist Lockheed, Burbank, Calif., 1966-70; mem. tech. staff Aerospace Corp., El Segundo, Calif., 1980-82; rsch. scientist Motorotor, North Hollywood, Calif., from 1983. Lt. (j.g.) USNR, 1943-46. Mem. IEEE (life), Am. Phys. Soc. (life). Achievements include patents for Statorless Homopolar Motor, and Electromagnetic Transmission for Control of Rotary Power in Vehicles; established presence of quantized ether using Lorentz forces; now developing force field propulsion for spacecraft. Died Feb. 13, 2008.

KAPLAN, STANLEY HENRY, retired educational center administrator; b. NYC, May 24, 1919; s. Julius and Ericka (Herson) K.; m. Rita Gwirtzman, Jan. 25, 1949; children: Paul (dec. 1991), Susan, Nancy BS, CCNY, 1939, MS, 1941. Founder, pres. Stanley H. Kaplan Ednl. Center, NYC, 1938—92; sec. bd. dirs. Council Non-Collegiate Edn., Richmond, Va., from 1979; editor Barron's How to Prepare for College Entrance Examinations, 1953; editor, author Barron's How to Win a Scholarship, 1957, Barron's Regents Exams Series, 1945-70. Co-author (with Anne Farris): Test Pilot: How I Broke Testing Barriers for Millions of Students and Caused a Sonic Boom in the Business of Education, 2001. Pres. bd. dirs. Bklyn. Philharm. Symphony Orch., 1977—; pres. bd. dirs. City Coll. Fund, Manhattan, 1986—; bd. dirs. United Jewish Appeal, N.Y.C., 1984—, Rita and Stanley H. Kaplan Cancer Center, NYU Med. Ctr., 1982—, Sutton Place Synagogue, 1982— Mem. Gallatin Soc. NYU (life), Phi Beta Kappa Clubs: 100 (bd. dirs. 1983-85) (N.Y.C.). Lodges: B'nai B'rith, Am. Jewish Congress. Home: New York, NY. Died Aug. 23, 2009.

KAPRAL, CHARLES ANTHONY, systems analyst; b. Luzerne, Pa., Nov. 3, 1944; s. Samuel Kapral and Hermina (Jenny) Britz; m. Marie Andrea Lazar, Jan. 9, 1971. Tech. cert., RCA Inst., 1970. Engring. assoc. Western Elec., 1970-75; systems analyst Fedders Corp., 1976-83, Culbro Corp., 1983-86; sr. project analyst Wakefern Food Corp., 1986-92; MIS supr. HIP/Rutgers, from 1993. Sgt. USAF, 1963-67. Recipient Cert. Honor Am. Lunar Soc., 1991. Mem. Am. Lunar Soc., Assn. of Luner and Planet Obs., Am. Astron. Assn. Avocations: astronomy, photography. Home: Edison, NJ. Died May 27, 2008.

KAREL, FRANK, III, retired foundation administrator; b. Orlando, Fla., Aug. 30, 1935; s. Frank and Helen (P'Pool) K.; m. Graciela Guerrero, Aug. 17, 1957; children: Elizabeth Ann, Barbara Ann. BS in Journalism, U. Fla., 1961; M.P.A., NYU, 1983. Sci. writer Miami Herald, (Fla.), 1961-64; assoc. dir. pub. relations Johns Hopkins Med. Instns., Balt., 1964-67; pub. info. officer div. regional med. programs HEW, Bethesda, Md., 1967; exec. assoc. The Commonwealth Fund, NYC, 1968-70; dir. planning Nat. Jewish Hosp. and Research Ctr., Denver, 1970-72; assoc. dir. Nat. Cancer Inst., HEW, Bethesda, 1972-74; v.p. communications Robert Wood Johnson Found., Princeton, NJ, 1974—87, 1993—2001, The Rockefeller Found., NYC, 1987-93. Past bd. dirs. Coun. on Founds.; bd. dirs. Am. Hosp. Pub. Inc.; v.p. comm. The Robert Woods Johnson Found., Princeton, N.J., 1993—. Mem. Pub. Rels. Soc. Am. (past chmn. health sect.), Pub. Awareness Assn. of Consultative Group on Internat. Agr. Rsch. (chmn.), Nat. Assn. Sci. Writers, AAAS, Comms. Network in Philanthropy (founding chmn.). Home: Lawrenceville, NJ. Died Sept. 19, 2009.

KARLINSKY, SIMON, language educator, writer; b. Harbin, Manchuria, Sept. 22, 1924; arrived in U.S., 1938, naturalized, 1944; s. Aron and Sophie (Levitin) Karlinsky; m. Peter Carleton, Oct. 2008. BA, U. Calif., Berkeley, 1960, PhD, 1964; MA, Harvard U., 1961. Conf. interpreter, music student Europe, 1947-57; tchg. fellow Harvard U., Cambridge, Mass., 1960-61; asst. prof. Slavic langs. and lits. U. Calif., Berkeley, 1963-65, prof., 1967-91, prof. emeritus, 1991—2009, chmn. dept., 1967-69. Vis. assoc. prof. Harvard U., 1966. Author: Marina Cvetaeva: Her Life and Her Art, 1966, The Sexual Labyrinth of Nikolai Gogol, 1976, 2d edit., 1992, Russian Drama from Its Beginnings to the Age of Pushkin, 1985, Marina Tsvetaeva: The Woman, Her World and Her Poetry, 1986, 2d edit., 1988, 2009, Italian edit., 1989, Spanish edit., 1990, Japanese edit., 1991; editor: The Bitter Air of Exile, 1977; editor, annotator: Anton Chekhov's Life and Thought: Selected Letters and Commentary, 1974, 2d edit., 1997, The Nabokov-Wilson Letters, 1979, 2d edit., 2001, French edit., 1988, German edit., 1995, Japanese edit., 2002; co-editor: Language, Literature, Linguistics, 1987, O RUS! Studia literaria slavica in honorem Hugh McLean, 1995; contbr. articles to profl. jours. Guggenheim fellow, 1969—70, 1977—78. Mem.: Phi Beta Kappa. Home: Kensington, Calif. Died July 5, 2009.

KARP, STANLEY ROBERT, lawyer, corporate executive; b. Narilsk, Russia, Mar. 19, 1953; came to U.S., 1961; s. Henry and Liona (Prohorov) K.; m. Lynne D. Gienau, Sept. 16, 1984; children: Katie, Colin, Lauren. BA, SUNY, Binghamton, 1975; diploma in internat. law, Inst. Internat. Droits Homme, Strasbourg, France, 1979; JD, NYU, 1983. Bar: N.Y., 1984. Law clerk Continental Ins., NYC, 1982-83; assoc. Sidman-Eritoff, Morrision, Warren & Ecker, NYC, 1983-87; asst. gen. counsel The CIT Group, Inc., NYC, from 1987. Mem. Assn. Coml. Fin. Attys. Home: East Northport, NY. Died Nov. 15, 2007.

KARSTEN, KENNETH STEPHEN, retired chemist, real estate salesman; b. Holland, Mich., July 24, 1913; s. Stephen and Lena Anna (Bolhuis) K.; m. Julia Bouws, Nov. 22, 1939 (dec.); children: Jayne Lynn, Kalmia Stephanie, Mary Sue, Kenneth Stephen Jr.; m. Bouneva Farlow, May 19, 1985. BS, Hope Coll., 1935; MS, U. Nev., 1937; PhD, U. Wis., 1939. Chemist/analyst Sullivan Mining Co., Kellogg, Idaho, 1937; tchr. Bklyn. Coll., 1939-41; organic chemist FMC Corp., Middleport, N.Y., 1941-45; formulation chemist Rohm & Haas Co., Bristol, Pa., 1945-47; chemist R.T. Vanderibilt Co., Inc., Norwalk, Conn., 1947-50, sales mgr., 1951-70; v.p. dir. rsch. R.T. Vanderbilt Co., Inc., Norwalk, Conn., 1971-78; realtor assoc. ERA Pearson Realty, Spring Hill, Fla., 1987-92; staff corr. Hernando Today News, Brooksville, Fla., 1991-92. Cons. R.T. Vanderbilt Co., Inc., Norwalk, 1978-84. Author: Science of Electronic Flash Photography, 1968, Abstract Photography Techniques, 1970; patentee in field. Mem. Am. Chem. Soc. Avocations: photography, computers, aviculture. Home: Spring Hill, Fla. Died Dec. 19, 2007.

KASTER, SUSAN GRIER, social worker; b. Marion, Ind., Mar. 25, 1944; d. Harold Addison and Leah Mary (Stump) Grier; m. William Raymond Kaster, Sept. 6, 1964; children: Mary, Michael, Peter, Rebecca. BSW, Valparaiso U., Ind., 1978, MAABS, 1988. Instr. in home start Porter County Assn. for Retarded Citizens, Valparaiso, 1978-79; sch. social worker Portage (Ind.) Twp. Schs., 1979-98; social worker Rise, Inc./ARC, from 1998. Presenter in field. Mem. NASW (rep.), N.W. Ind. Assn. Attendance Officers and Social Workers (treas.). Methodist. Avocations: swimming, camping, music, reading, boating. Home: Plymouth, Ind. Died Sept. 22, 2007.

KATSENELINBOIGEN, ARON JOSEF, economist; b. Isaslavl, Ukraine, Sept. 2, 1927; arrived in US, 1973, naturalized, 1980; s. Josef Jacob and Ida Gersh (Feldman) Katsenelinboigen; m. Gena L. Gabin, Jan. 31, 1954; children: Gregory, Alexander. C.A., Moscow State Econ. Inst., 1946; PhD, Inst. Econs. USSR Acad. Scis., 1957; D in Econ. Scis., Inst. Nat. Economy, 1966. Head, dept. complex sys. Ctrl. Econ. Math. Inst. USSR Acad. Scis., 1966—73; prof., economics Moscow State U., 1970—73; vis. lectr., economics U. Pa., 1974—78, prof., social sys. scis., 1978—87, prof., decision scis., from 1988, chmn., social sys. scis., 1984—86. Contbr. chapters to books. Bd. dirs. Hebrew Immigrants Aid Soc., 1980—83. Grantee, Ford Found., 1975—77, Am. Coun. Learned Socs., 1978, Nat. Coun. Soviet Studies, 1980—82. Mem.: Soc. Gen. Sys. Rsch. Died July 30, 2005.

KATZ, ADRIAN IZHACK, physician, educator; b. Bucharest, Romania, Aug. 3, 1932; came to U.S., 1965, naturalized, 1976; s. Ferdinand and Helen (Lustig) K.; m. Miriam Lesser, Mar. 31, 1965; children— Ron, Iris. MD, Hebrew U., 1961. Research fellow Yale U., 1965-67, Harvard U., 1967-68; intern Belinson Med. Center, Israel, 1961, resident, 1962-65; practice medicine specializing in internal medicine and nephrology New Haven, 1966-67, Boston, 1967-68, Chgo., from 1968; attending physician U. Chgo. Hosps., 1968—2002, head nephrology sect., 1973-82; asst. prof. medicine U. Chgo., 1968-71, assoc. prof., 1971-74, prof., 1975—2002, prof. emeritus, 2002—09. Fogarty sr. internat. fellow, vis. scientist Lab Cell Physiology, Coll. de France, Paris, 1977-78; vis. prof. cellular and molecular physiology Yale U., 1988; vis. scientist dept. molecular medicine Karolinska Inst., Stockholm, 1994-2009. Co-author: Kidney Function and Disease in Pregnancy; contbr. chpts. to books, articles to profl. jours. Fellow A.C.P.; mem. Am. Physiol. Soc., Am. Soc. Clin. Investigation, Assn. Am. Physicians, Am. Soc. Nephrology, Internat. Soc. Nephrology, Central Soc. Clin. Research, N.Y. Acad. Scis. Home: Chicago, Ill. Died Aug. 17, 2009.

KATZ, DAVID, retired anesthesiologist; b. St. Paul, Nov. 5, 1923; MD, U. Health Scis./Chgo. Med Sch., 1950. Diplomate Am. Bd. Anesthesiology. Intern Mt. Sinai Hosp., Chgo., 1950-51; resident in anesthesiology VA Hosp., Hines, Ill., 1951-53; mem. staff Desert Hosp., Palm Springs, Calif.; ret., 1992. Fellow Am. Coll. Anesthesiology, Internat. Coll. Surgeons; mem. Internat. Anesthesiology Rsch. Soc. Home: Marina Dl Rey, Calif. Died Sept. 3, 2007.

KATZ, JAY, retired psychiatry and law educator; b. Zwickau, Federal Republic of Germany, Oct. 20, 1922; came to U.S., 1940, naturalized, 1945; s. Paul and Dora (Ungar) K.; m. Marilyn B. Arthur, June 18, 1989; children from previous marriage: Sally Jean, Daniel Franklin, Amy Susan. BA, U. Vt., 1944, DS (hon.), 1995; MD, Harvard U., 1949; DS (hon.), Northeastern Ohio U., 1994. Intern Mt. Sinai Hosp., NYC, 1949-50; resident Northport (N.Y.) VA Hosp., 1950-51, Yale U., 1953-55, instr. psychiatry New Haven, 1955-57, asst. prof., 1957-58, asst. prof. psychiatry and law, 1958-60, asso. prof. law, asso. clin. prof. psychiatry, 1960-67, adj. prof. law and psychiatry, 1967-79, prof., 1979-81, John A. Garver prof. law and psychoanalysis, 1981-90, Elizabeth K. Dollard prof. law, medicine and psychiatry, 1990-93, Elizabeth K. Dollard prof. law, medicine and psychiatry emeritus, Harvey L. Karp Profl. lectr. in law and psychoanalysis, 1993—2008. Tng. and supervising psychiatrist Western New Eng. Inst. for Psychoanalysis; cons. to asst. sec. for health & sci. affairs US Dept. Health Edn. & Welfare, 1972-73, mem. artificial heart assessment panel, 1972-73; active Presdl. Adv. Com. on Ho. Radiation Experiments, 1994-95. Author: (with Joseph Goldstein) The Family and the Law, 1964, (with Joseph Goldstein and Alan M. Dershowitz) Psychoanalysis, Psychiatry and Law, 1967, Experimentation with Human Beings, 1972, (with Alexander M. Capron) Catastrophic Diseases— Who Decides What?, 1975; The Silent World of Doctor and Patient, 1984 Bd. dirs. Family Service of New Haven. Served to capt. M.C. USAF, 1951-53. Recipient Henry K. Beecher award Hastings Ctr. for Ethics and Life Scis., 1993; John Simon Guggenheim Meml. Found. fellow, 1981. Fellow ACP (William C. Menninger award 1983), Am. Psychiat. Assn. (Isaac Ray award 1975), Am. Orthopsychiat. Assn., Am. Coll. Psychiatry, Center for Advanced Psychoanalytic Studies; mem. Inst. Medicine, Nat. Acad. of Scis., Group for Advancement of Psychiatry, Am. Psychoanalytic Assn. Jewish. Home: New Haven, Conn. Died Nov. 17, 2008.

KATZEN, RAPHAEL, consulting chemical engineer; b. Balt., July 28, 1915; s. Isidor and Esther (Stein) K.; m. Selma M. Siegel, June 19, 1938; 1 child, Nancy Katzen Riedel. B.Chem. Engring., Poly. U. Bklyn., 1936, M.Chem. Engring., 1938, D.Chem. Engring., 1942. Registered profl. engr. in 13 states. Tech. dir. Northwood Chem. Co., Phelps, Wis., 1938-42; project mgr. Diamond Alkali Co., Painesville, Ohio, 1942-44; mgr. engring. divsn. Vulcan, Cin., 1944-53; mng. partner Raphael Katzen Assos., Cin., 1953-80; chmn. Raphael Katzen Assos. Internat., Inc., 1956—97. Contbr. articles to profl. jours; patentee in field. Mem. Cin. Air Pollution Bd., 1972-75. Recipient Disting. Alumnus award Poly. Inst. Bklyn., 1970, Dedicated Alumnus award, 1977; Disting. cons. award Ohio Assn. Cons. Engrs., 1978; Profl. Accomplishment, Disting. Engr. award Tech. and Sci. Socs. Coun., 1978, 79, Personal Achievement in Chem. Engring. award Chem. Engring., McGraw Hill, 1988, Renewable Fuels Assn. Lifetime Achievement award, 1999, 16th Ann. Fuel Ethanol Workshop award of excellence, 2000, others; Poly. U. fellow, 1981. Fellow AIChE (Chem. Engring. Practice award 1986, Robert L. Jacks Meml. award 1990, Founders award 2001), Nat. Renewable Energy Lab., Dept. Energy (Raphael Katzen award 2008), Am. Inst. Chemists; mem. NAE (elected 1996), TAPPI, PAPTAC, Am. Chem. Soc. (Spl. Lifetime Achievement award 2000), Sigma Xi, Tau Beta Pi, Phi Lambda Upsilon. Home: Bonita Springs, Fla. Died July 12, 2009.

KAUFMAN, SEYMOUR, biochemist; b. Bklyn., Mar. 13, 1924; s. Charles and Anna Kaufman; m. Elaine Elkins, Feb. 6, 1948; children: Allan, Emily, Leslie. BS, U. Ill., 1945, MS, 1946; PhD, Duke U., 1949. Fellow Dept. Pharmacology, NYU Med. Sch., 1949-50, instr., 1950-53, asst. prof., 1953-54; biochemist Lab. Cellular Pharmacology NIMH, Bethesda, Md., 1954-56, chief sect. on cellular regulatory mechanisms Lab. of Gen. and Comparative Biochemistry, 1956-68, acting chief Lab. Neurochemistry, 1968-71, chief Lab. Neurochemistry, 1971-99. Contbr. articles to profl. jours.; author: Overcoming a Bad Gene, 2004 U.S. Pub. Health fellow Duke U., 1949; recipient Disting. Svc. award, US Dept. Health, Edn. & Welfare (HEW), 1980, Mem. Am. Soc. Biol. Chemists, Am. Chem. Soc. (Hillebrand prize, 1991), Am. Acad. Arts & Sciences, Internat. Soc. for Neurochemistry, Am. Soc. for Neurochemistry, Nat. Acad. Sci. Home: Bethesda, Md. Died June 23, 2009.

KAUL, ARTHUR JESSE, journalism educator; b. St. Louis, Dec. 4, 1945; s. Arthur Oscar and Beulah Bernice (Solberger) K.; m. Nancy Jo Deneke, Jan. 19, 1968; 1 child, Stephen Todd. BA in Psychology and English, Ctrl. Meth. Coll., Fayette, Mo., 1968; MS in Journalism, So. Ill. U., Carbondale, 1971, PhD in Journalism, 1982; MA in Humanities, Western Ky. U., 1978. Reporter, copy editor Messenger-Inquirer, Owensboro, Ky., 1972-78; grad. tchg. asst. So. Ill. U., 1978-81, vis. instr., 1981-82; higher edn. writer Columbia (Mo.) Daily Tribune, 1981; asst. prof. Western Ky. U., Bowling Green, 1982-84; asst. prof. journalism U. So. Miss., Hattiesburg, 1984-87, assoc. prof., from 1987, chmn. dept., from 1989. Mem. editl. adv. bd. Jour. Mass Media Ethics, 1985—, Jour. Monographs, 1985-88. Contbr. articles to profl. jours. Recipient Excellence in Tchg. award U. So. Miss., 1989; nat. tchg. fellow Poynter Inst. for Media Studies, St. Petersburg, Fla., 1987. Mem. Assn. for Edn. in Journalism and Mass Comm. (chmn. ethics com. 1986-88, James E. Murphy rschl award), Am. Journalism Historians Assn. Lutheran. Avocations: reading, collecting old and rare books, gardening. Home: Hattiesburg, Miss. Died Apr. 29, 2008.

KAUPELIS, ROBERT JOHN, artist, retired educator; b. Amsterdam, NY, Feb. 23, 1928; s. Benjamin and Clara Irene (Weidemann) K.; m. Norma Jean Peckham, Nov. 17, 1951 (dec.); children: Khym Robert, Khy Jean. BS, Buffalo State Coll., 1951; cert., Albright Art Sch., Buffalo, 1951; MA, Columbia U., 1955, EdD, 1959. Tchr. art pub. schs., N.Y., 1951-55; instr. art New Paltz (N.Y.) State Coll., 1953-55; instr. Tchrs. Coll., Columbia U., NYC, 1955-56; prof. art NYU, NYC, 1956-85, ret., from 1985. Author: Learning to Draw, 1966, Experimental Drawing, 1980; exhibited in 60 one-man shows, 1953—, latest being Bertha Schaefer Gallery, 1969, 70, 72, 74, Image South Gallery, 1976, 78, 79, 82, U. Alaska, 1986, Jack Gallery, Soho, N.Y., 1987, 88, Walton St. Gallery, Chgo., 1989, Gallery Camino Real, Boca Raton, Fla., 1989, Walton St. Gallery, Chgo., 1989, Circle Gallery, Cherry Creek, Denver, 1989, Circle Gallery, Toronto, Ont., Can., 1990, Alan Brown Gallery, Hartsdale, N.Y., 1990, Westchester Community Coll., 1991, Reece Gallery, N.Y.C., 1994, Silvermine Guild Artists, 1998, St. Bonaventure U., 1998, The Studio, N.Y., 2001; exhibited in numerous group shows, 1951—, latest being Katonah (N.Y.) Gallery, 1988, 2003 Silvermine (Conn.) Guild, 1991, Zenith Gallery, Washington, 1992; represented in numerous permanent collections including NYU, Potsdam U., Housatonic Mus. Art, Montclair State Coll., U. Mass., Duke U., Albright Coll., Oneonta U., Atlanta Art Inst. With U.S. Army, 1946-47. Mem. Silvermine Guild Artists (trustee 1987), Inst. for Study Art in Edn. Home: Yorktown Heights, NY. Died June 12, 2009.

KAUSLER, DONALD HARVEY, retired psychology professor; b. St. Louis, July 16, 1927; s Charles Richard and Pauline Ann (Svejkovsky) K.; m. Martha Blanche Roeper, Oct. 25, 1952; children— Renee, Donald Harvey, Jr., Jill, Barry. AB, Washington U., St. Louis, 1947, PhD, 1951. Rsch. psychologist USAF, Mather AFB, Calif., 1951—55; asst. prof., assoc. prof. U. Ark., 1955—60; assoc. prof., prof. St. Louis U., 1960—71, chmn. dept. psychology, 1963—71; prof. psychology U. Mo.-Columbia, 1971—89, Curator's prof., 1989—92; Curator's prof. emeritus, from 1992. Author: Psychology of Verbal Learning and Memory, 1974, Experimental Psychology and Human Aging, 1982, Experimental Psychology, Cognition and Human Aging, 1991, Learning and Memory in Normal Aging, 1994, The Graying of America: An Encyclopedia of Aging, Health, Mind, and Behavior, 1996, 2001, The Essential Guide to Aging in the 21st Century, 2007; editor: Readings in Verbal Learning, Contemporary Theory and Research, 1966—; columnist Scripps Howard News Svc., 2001-05; contbr. articles to profl. jours. 2d. to 1st lt. USAF, 1953—55. Mem. APA, Gerontological Soc. Am., Assn. for Pschol. Sci., Phi Beta Kappa, Sigma Xi. Home: Columbia, Mo. Deceased.

KAUZMANN, WALTER JOSEPH, retired chemistry professor; b. Mt. Vernon, NY, Aug. 18, 1916; s. Albert and Julia Maria (Kahle) K.; m. Elizabeth Alice Flagler, Apr. 1, 1951; children: Charles Peter, Eric Flagler, Katherine Elizabeth Julia Kauzmann Pacala. BA, Cornell U., 1937; PhD, Princeton U., 1940; PhD (hon.), U. Stockholm, 1992. Westinghouse research fellow Westinghouse Mfg. Co., E. Pittsburgh, Pa., 1940-42; mem. staff Explosives Research Lab., Bruceton, Pa., 1942-44, Los Alamos Lab., 1944-46; asst. prof. Princeton U., 1946-51, assoc. prof., 1951-60, prof. chemistry, 1960-82, chmn. dept., 1964-68, David B. Jones prof. chemistry, 1963-82, chmn. biochem. sci. dept., 1980-81; vis. scientist Atlantic Research Lab., NRC Can., 1983. Vis. lectr. Kyoto U., 1974; vis. prof. U. Ibadan, 1975 Author: Quantum Chemistry, 1957, Kinetic Theory of Gases, 1966, Thermal Properties of Matter, 1967, (with D. Eisenberg) Structure and Properties of Water, 1969. Recipient Linderstrom-Lang medal, 1966, Stein and Moore award, 1993; Jr. fellow Soc. Fellows, Harvard U., 1942. Fellow: AAAS, Am. Phys. Soc., Am. Acad. Arts and Scis.; mem.: NAS, Royal Astron. Soc. Can., Fedn. Am. Scientists, Am. Chem. Soc., Am. Geophys. Union, Protein Soc., Am. Soc. Biochemistry and Molecular Biology, Sigma Xi. Died Jan. 27, 2009.

KAY, ALBERT JOSEPH, textile executive; b. Cleve., June 3, 1920; s. Simon and Eszter (Rosenzweig) K.; m. Irene Pramisloff, June 11, 1944; children: Leslie Andrzejewski, Stephen, Adrienne Gallagher. Student, Cuyahoga Community Coll., 1961. Sales rep. The Carnegie Textile Co., Cleve., 1938-68, v.p., gen. mgr., 1968-94, pres., from 1994. Mem. citizens adv. com. Centerior Energy, 1991-97; adv. bd. ARC, 1988-93. Pres. Mayfield H.S. PTA, 1968-69, Friends Mayfield Regional Libr., 1998-99; former pres. Mayfield Boys Baseball League; past. sect. chmn. United Way; founder Mayfield Heights Bicentennial Com., Mayfield Area Recreation Coun.; mem. Citizens Com. for Edn., 1968; chmn. Citizens for Honest Govt., 1965; past pres. Friends of Hillcrest Libr.; coun. mem. City Mayfield Heights, 1969-97, coun. pres., 1981-85, 1996-97; campaign co-chmn. Aveni for State Rep., Ohio, 1975; chmn. levy renewal com. Cuyahoga County Pub. Libr., 1989; past. mem. exec. com. Hillcrest Dem. Caucus, Mayfield Schs. Acad. Booster's Club; former chmn. planning and zoning commn. City Mayfield Heights; trustee Schnurmann House, 1970-2001, Assn. Retarded Citizens, 1992-94; cmty. coord. Clinton-Gore campaign, 1992; mem., founder Edn.-Bus. Cmty. Alliance, Mayfield City Schs., 1994—; former pres. Hillcrest Coun. of Couns., 1977; mem. Cuyahoga County Dem. Exec. Com.; mem. Mayfield Heights Planning Commn., 1998—; founder, chmn. Mayfield Dist. Millenium Celebration, 2000; gov. Cuyahoga County Bd. Mental Health, 2001-2004. With U.S. Army, 1943. Recipient Cmty. Svcs. award Hillcrest Cleve. Exch., 1977, Civic Svcs. award Citizens League of Cleve., 1996, Cmty. Svc. award Nat. Exch. Club, 1984, Outstanding Svc. award Mayfield Heights C. of C., 1979, Citizenship award VFW, 1976, Disting. Svc. award Assn. for Retarded Citizens, 1991, Citizen of Yr. award (with wife) Mayfield City Schs., 1995, Award for Disting. Svc., Citizens League of Cleve., 1996, Cert. of Appreciation for Pub. Svc., Gov. Ohio, 1997, Cuyahoga County Commrs., 1997, Ohio Ho. of Reps., 1997, Ohio State Senate, 1997; commendation Ohio State Sen. for Disting. Cmty. Svc., 1997; named Mayfield Schs. Citizen of Yr., 1995—. Mem. Mayfield Heights Planning Commn., 1998, Friends of Mayfield Regional Libr. (pres. 1998-2000), Internat. Assn. Wiping Cloth Mfrs. (bd.dirs. 1981-85, 89-93, Outstanding and Dedicated Svc. award 1985), Am. Assn. Ret. Persons (bd. dirs. East Suburban Cuyahoga County chpt. 371 1993-95), Secondary/Materials and Recycled Textiles, Jewish Vets Cleve. (comdr. 1946-48), East Cleve. Bus. Alliance (pres.), Masons. Democrat. Jewish. Avocations: politics, piano. Died Mar. 24, 2008.

KAYE, EDWARD T., developmental kinesiologist; b. Chgo., Sept. 6, 1937; s. Edward Chester and Evelyn Victoria (Szymanski) Kwiatkowski; m. Mary Lou Struzynski, Sept. 29, 1962 (div. July 28, 1994); 1 child, Kenneth Steven Dan. BS in Phys. Edn., U. Ill., 1961; MS in Edn., No. Ill. U., 1963. Phys. edn. tchr. Bd. Edn. Dist 103, Lyons, Ill., 1962-94; dir. Devel. Ctr., Palos Heights, Ill., from 1967. Author: Developmental Center Handbook, 1967, rev., 1989, Teaching Elementary Physical Education, 1991. Mem. AAHPERD, AARP, U. Ill. Athletic Alumni, Moose. Roman Catholic. Died Sept. 18, 2007.

KAYS, SISTER ELOISE CLAIRE, school directress; b. Phillipsburg, NJ; d. Ponsford David and Claire Louise (Tirrell) K. BA, Georgian Ct. Coll., 1967; MA, Rider Coll., 1969. Tchr. Red Bank Cath. HS, NJ, 1952-58, Notre Dame HS, Lawrenceville, NJ, 1958-67, assoc. prin., 1967-69; co-founder, assoc. prin. St. Pius X Regional HS, Piscataway, NJ, 1969-84; directress Mt. St. Mary Acad., Watchung, NJ, 1974—75, 1984—2000. Acting supt. schs. Metuchen Diocese, 1981. Recipient Carl B. Zoerner award for excellence Rider Coll., 1967, Outstanding Educator award Diocese of Metuchen, 1991, St. Joseph medal for outstanding contbn. to St. Joseph Sem., Princeton, N.J., 1992; Mich. State U. Bus. Edn. grantee, 1964. Mem. Nat. Cath. Edn. Assn. (Outstanding Educator award 1992), Nat. Ind. Sch. Assn., N.J. Ind. Sch. Assn., N.J. Prins. Assn., Mid. States Assn., Assn. Secondary Schs. Curriculum. Died May 28, 2009.

KEADLE, HOMER LEE, lumber manufacturing company executive; b. Forsyth, Ga., Nov. 4, 1924; s. Homer Lee and Neva Ruth (Haygood) K.; m. Marjorie Jacqueline Clements, May 2, 1948; children: Steve Clements, John Keith. Diploma, Gordon Mil. Coll., 1942; student mech. engring., The Citadel, 1943-44. Owner, mgr., pres. Keadle Lumber Enterprises, Inc., Thomaston, Ga., from 1947. Trustee SLMA-Self Inf. Fund, Jonesboro, Ga., 1970—; mem. exec. com. Export-Wood Fiber Mktg. Corp., Savannah, Ga., 1977-81. Mem. Nat. Forest Products Assn., Nat. Hardwood Lumber Assn., Southeastern Lumber Mfrs. Assn. (treas. 1988-89, v.p. 1989-90), So. Hardwood Lumber Mfg. Assn. (bd. dirs. 1980—), Nat. C. of C., Bus. Coun. Ga. Home: Forsyth, Ga. Died Oct. 9, 2007.

KEARNEY, IRENE SPRUILL, elementary school educator; b. Warrenton, NC, May 17, 1937; d. Hughley and Janet (Alston) Spruill; m. Raymond Kearney, Sr.; children: Alfreda, Raymond Jr. BS, Elizabeth City State U., 1959; MEd, N.C. Cen. U., 1976; EdD, Nova U., 1987; PhD, Am. Theol. Sem., 1988. Cert. early childhood edn., supervision, adminstrn., middle sch., pastoral counseling. Camp dir. N.C. Cen. U. PTA, Durham; pvt. prac. Warrenton, N.C.; cons., tchr. Warren County Schs., Warrenton. Author: Sparking Divergent Thinking, 1985. Mem. NEA, Warren County Assn. Educators (pres.) Franklinton Assn. Univ. Women (V.p.), Alpha Kappa Alpha, Phi Delta Kappa. Home: Warrenton, NC. Died Nov. 8, 2007.

KEARNS, FRANCIS XAVIER, health care executive; b. Montclair, NJ, Nov. 23, 1943; s. Vincent Francis and Dorothy Elenor (McDonald) K.; m. Patricia Anne Leuf, Feb. 9, 1964; children: Theresa Lynn, Denise Michelle, Cheryl Melissa. BA, Calif. State U., Northridge, 1970; MS in Med. Tech., Calif. State U., Dominguez Hills, 1975; cert. in mgmt., Claremont Grad. U., Calif., 1978; MBA, Westminster Coll., Salt Lake City, 1988. Cert. med. tech., clin. bioanalyst. Rsch. asst. Holy Cross Hosp., San Fernando, Calif., 1968-70, clin. lab technologist, 1970-72; tech. dir. Smith Kline Clin. Lab., LA, 1972-75, v.p., gen. mgr. Burbank, Calif., 1975-80; v.p. svc. group BSL Tech., Salt Lake City, 1980-82; prin. cons. Diversified Health Assocs., Salt Lake City, 1982-84; v.p. bus. devel. ARUP Inc. Med. Labs., Salt Lake City, 1984-85, exec. v.p., 1985-90. Pres., chief exec. officer Biotrace Labs., Salt Lake City, 1990—; asst. clin. prof. U. Utah Sch. Medicine Pathology, Salt Lake City, 1986—; instr. med. tech. U. Utah Coll. Pharmacy, 1985-86. Trustee Childrens Mus. Utah, Salt Lake City, 1987—; mem. health care task force Utah Coalition 2000, Salt Lake City, 1989—. Recipient Speaker award AT&T, 1988, Flying Col. award Delta Airlines, 1989. Roman Catholic. Avocations: fishing, golf. Died Dec. 1, 2007.

KEATON, LAWRENCE CLUER, safety engineer, consultant; b. Gainesville, Tex., Nov. 24, 1924; s. William Lenard and Lettie (Phipps) K.; m. Emalee Prichard, Feb. 22, 1947; children: Lawrel Larsen, L.C. Jr., T.E. BSME, U. Okla., 1945; MS in Safety Mgmt. (hon.), Western States U., 1989, PhD in Bus. Adminstrn. (hon.), 1989. Registered profl. engr., Tex.; cert. lightning protection inspector; diplomate Coun. of Engring. Specialty Bds. In various engring. positions Phillips Petroleum Co., Borger, Tex., 1946-65, project devel. engr. NYC, 1964-65; mng. dir. Nordisk Philback AB, Malmo, Sweden, 1965-73; dir. carbon black ops. Europe and Africa Phillips Petroleum Co., 1973-74, world-wide dir. carbon black ops., 1974-76; mng. dir. Sevalco Ltd., Bristol, Eng., 1976-81; ind. cons., 1981-85; mng. ptnr. System Engring. and Labs. Northwest Tex., Amarillo, from 1985. 5 patents in petrochem. processes. Lt. (j.g.) USN, 1943-45, PTO. Mem. ASME, Am. Soc. Safety Engrs., Lightning Protection Inst., Nat. Assn. Corrosion Engrs., Nat. Acad. Forensic Engrs., Nat. Assn. Fire Investigators, Nat. Assn. Profl. Accident Reconstruction Specialists, Nat. Soc. Profl. Engrs., Soc. Am. Mil. Engrs., Tex. Soc. Profl. Engrs., Amarillo Rotary, Shriners, Masons, Amarillo Club, Am. Legion, Tenn. Squires. Methodist. Avocations: gourmet cooking, gardening. Home: Amarillo, Tex. Died Jan. 19, 2008.

KEENAN, TERRANCE, retired foundation administrator; b. Phila., Feb. 1, 1924; s. Peter Joseph and Marie (Sloupova) K.; m. Joette Kathryn Lehan, Oct. 20, 1979. AB, Yale U., 1950; JD (hon.), Alderson-Broaddus Coll., Philippi, W.Va., 1973. Asst. headmaster Thomas Jefferson Sch., St. Louis, 1950-55; writer Merrill Lynch & Co. Inc., NYC, 1955-56; asst. editor office reports Ford Found., NYC, 1956-65; sr. exec. asso. Commonwealth Fund, NYC, 1965-72; v.p. Robert Wood Johnson Found., Princeton, NJ. Bd. dirs. Grantmakers in Health, Washington. With USNR, 1943-63. Mem. Pub. Relations Soc. Am., Phi Beta Kappa. Clubs: Yale (N.Y.C.); Nassau (Princeton). Republican. Roman Catholic. Home: Newtown, Pa. Died Feb. 25, 2009.

KEITH, CARL DONALD, retired chemist; b. Stewart Creek, W.Va., May 29, 1920; s. Howard and Mary (Rawson) Keith; m. Edith E. Birmingham (dec. 2000); children: Judith, Carla. Student, Salem Coll., 1943; MS in Chemistry, Ind. U., 1945; Ph.D, DePaul U., 1947. Chemist Sinclair Oil, 1943; with Engelhard Industries divsn. Engelhard Corp., 1957—85, pres., 1976—81; chmn. Engelhard Corp., 1981—85. Recipient Indsl. award of Decade, UN and U.S. Office Pres., Coun. Enviorn. Quality, 1982, Disting. Achievement award, Internat. Precious Metals Inst., 1983, Midgley award, Am. Chem. Soc., 1985, Clena Air award, Mfrs. Emissions Controls Assn., 1995, Arthur Dehon Little Innovation award, AIChE, 1999, Walter Ahistrom prize, Finnish Acad. Sci., 2001, Nat. Medal of Tech., US Dept. Commerce, 2002. Achievements include being the co-inventor of the automotive catalytic converter which drastically reduced tailpipe emissions, 1973. Home: Marco Island, Fla. Died Nov. 9, 2008.

KEITHLEY, DAVID ARVIN, JR., small business owner, insurance agent; b. Ft. Worth, June 11, 1954; s. David Arvin and Xezvus (Cockerham) K.; m. Mary Kathleen Pickle, Aug. 6, 1977 (div. Mar. 1988); children: David Arvin III, John William II; m. Sheri D'Lynn Pool, Mar. 17, 1990; 1 child, Alexander Patrick. BA in Drama, U. Tex., 1976. Mgr. Keithley and Co., Littlefield, Tex., from 1977; owner, pres. Keithley Ins. Agy., Littlefield, from 1985. Author: (novel) The Black Magus, 1987; playwright (play) The Tragedy of Abram Jules, 1972 (Berthrong Drama award 1972), and others. Founding pres. Littlefield Cmty. Theatre, 1977—; founding chmn. Lamb County Crime Stoppers, Inc., Littlefield, 1984—; state del. Dem. Party of Tex., Littlefield, 1980—, Lamb County chmn., 1993—. Mem. Rotary (sec. Littlefield chpt. 1985-92), K.C. Roman Catholic. Avocations: ancient coin collector, political memorabilia collector. Died Dec. 6, 2007.

KELIIAA, PAUL BERTRAND, artist; b. Washington, Mar. 21, 1954; s. John Bertrand and Leenora Keliiaa; children: Kris, Sara, Jason. Student, Inst. Am. Indian Arts, 1985—88. Democrat. Avocation: photography. Home: Makawao, Hawaii. Died Jan. 26, 2008.

KELLAR, MARY L., educator; b. Jacksonville, Tex., May 30, 1920; d. Charles Wilkie and Charlie (Cunningham) Nunn; m. Gerald D. Kellar, June 19, 1938; children: Jerrie Clea, Mark Kellar, Joseph, Sandra (dec.), Mary Ann (dec.). AA, Jacksonville Coll., Tex., 1938; BS, Stephen F. Austin U., Nacogdoches, Tex., 1952; MA, Stephen F. Austin U., 1959. Tchr. Jacksonville (Tex.) Coll., 1955-67; prof. Cen. Bapt. Coll., Conway, Ark., 1967-70; tchr. Parkwood High Sch., Joplin, Mo., 1970-83; prof. Southneastern Bapt. Coll., Laurel, Miss., from 1983. Author: Whether Thou Goest, 1988; contbr. articles to mags.; contbr. articles to profl. jours. Died Apr. 28, 2008.

KELLEHER, WILLIAM JOSEPH, pharmaceutical consultant; b. Hartford, Conn., July 18, 1929; s. Richard Francis and Julia Veronica (Bogash) K. BS in Pharmacy, U. Conn., 1951, MS in Pharmacy, 1953; PhD in Biochemistry, U. Wis., 1960. Registered pharmacist, Conn. Asst. prof. pharmacognosy U. Conn., Storrs, 1960-67, assoc. prof., 1967-70, prof., 1970-88, dept. chmn., 1971-76, asst. dean, 1976-81, interim dean, 1981; cons. Kelleher Cons. Svc., Storrs, from 1988. Contbr. chpts. to books; assoc. editor Jour. Natural Products, 1971-76. 1st lt. USMC, 1953-55, Korea. Grantee NIH, 1960-65, Nat. Cancer Inst., 1985-88. Mem. Am. Chem. Soc., Biochem. Soc., Am. Soc. Pharmacognosy (pres. 1973-74), Sigma Xi. Achievements include patents on pharmaceutical compositions and on sustained-release drug-delivery systems. Home: Storrs Manfld, Conn. Died Nov. 10, 2007.

KELLER, BEN ROBERT, JR., gynecologist; b. Big Spring, Tex., July 9, 1936; s. Ben Robert and Rowena Ward (Gibson) Keller; m. Anne Ivey Keller; children: Gwenyth Sue Keller Wood, Jennifer Lynn, Amy Jo Keller McGinnis, Ben Robert III, Destry S. L.(dec.). BA, U. Tex., 1959; MD, U. Tex., Dallas, 1961. Diplomate Am. Bd. Obstetrics and Gynecology. Intern Hermann Hosp., Houston, 1961-62, ob-gyn resident, 1962-65; pvt. practice Arlington, Tex., 1967-79 and from 87, Glenwood Springs, Colo., 1979-87, Arlington, from 1987. Clin. instr. U. Tex., Dallas, 1975—79; assoc. clin. prof. U. Colo., Denver, 1983—86; mem. active staff Arlington Meml. Hosp., from 1989; courtesy staff S. Arlington Med. Ctr., from 1990. Author: The Hormone Way to Health and Happiness. Chmn. spkrs. bur. Am. Cancer Soc., Arlington, 1968—73; mem. Arlington Drug Abuse Com., 1969—72, Glenwood Springs Coun. on Drug Abuse, Colo., 1984—87; chmn. Texpac com. Tarrant County, Ft. Worth, 1972—75; chmn. bd. elders 1st Christian Ch., Arlington, 1975—76; bd. dirs. Planned Parenthood N. Tex., 1990—98. Capt. M.C. USAF, 1965—67. Mem.: Tarrant County Med. Soc., Tex. Med. Assn. (del. 1972—79, treas. 1974—79), Sunlight Ski Club (chmn. bd. dirs. 1985—86), Rotary Internat. Republican. Mem. Christian Ch. (Disciples Of Christ). Avocations: creative writing, music, golf, tennis, hunting. Died July 18, 2008.

KELLER, GERALD DOUGLAS, lawyer; b. NYC, Oct. 24, 1943; s. Robert Irwin and Ann (Mund) K.; m. Judith Ann Singer, Mar. 22, 1964; children: Kevin Geoffrey, Rhondi Beth. BS in Psychology, Eastern Mich. U., 1967; JD, Detroit Coll. Law, 1972. Bar: Mich. 1972, U.S. Dist Ct. (ea. dist.) Mich. 1972, D.C. 1981. Spl. investigator Mich. Dept. Social Services, Detroit, 1968-72; assoc. Kozlow, Jasmer & Woll P.C., Southfield, Mich., 1972-74; ptnr. Levant, Keller & Grossman, Southfield, 1974-76, Keller & Katkowsky P.C., Southfield, from 1976. Counsel, bd. dirs. Entertainment Resources Internat., Inc., Royal Oak, Mich., 1976—, Raymarco, Ltd., Plymouth, Mich., 1980—, Lit-Pac, Inc., Detroit, 1980—. Mem. Mich. Bar Assn., Southfield Bar Assn., D.C. Bar Assn., Assn. Trial Lawyers Am., Mich. Trial Lawyers Assn. Republican. Jewish. Home: Southfield, Mich. Died Dec. 23, 2007.

KELLEY, MAURICE LESLIE, JR., gastroenterologist, educator; b. Indpls., June 29, 1924; s. Maurice Leslie and Martha (Daniel) K.; m. Carol J. Povec, Feb. 11, 1967; children: Elizabeth Ann, Mary Sarah. Student, U. Vt., Va. Poly. Inst., Princeton U., 1943-45; MD, U. Rochester, 1949. Intern, resident Strong Meml. Hosp., Rochester, NY, 1949-51, Bixby fellow in medicine, 1953-56; fellow in gastroenterology Mayo Clinic, Rochester, Minn., 1957-59; asst. prof. medicine U. Rochester, 1959-64, assoc. prof., 1964-67; practice medicine specializing in gastroenterology Rochester, NY, 1959-67; assoc. prof. clin. medicine Dartmouth Med. Sch., 1967-74, prof. clin. medicine, 1974-88; chmn. sect. internal medicine Hitchcock Clinic, 1972-74, chmn. sect. gastroenterology, 1974, 88; prof. medicine emeritus Dartmouth Med. Sch., from 1988; mem. staff Strong Meml. Hosp., Hitchcock Clinic, Mary Hitchcock Meml. Hosp. Cons. Canandaigua VA, Rochester Gen., Genesee hosps., VA. Med. Ctr., White River Junction. Contbr. articles to profl. jours., chpts. to books. Served with AUS, 1942-45; M.C. USAF, 1951-53. Fellow ACP (gov. for N.H. 1974-78, Laureate award 1993), Am. Gastroenterol. Assn.; mem. Am. Soc. Gastrointestinal Endoscopy, AMA (chmn. sect. gastroenterology 1970-71), Am. Physiol. Soc., Alpha Omega Alpha. Avocations: sports cars, cinema. Home: Hanover, NH. Died Oct. 19, 2008.

KELLOGG, ANN MARIE, retired publishing executive, consultant; b. Pitts., Oct. 2, 1939; m. Eugene Krasnoff (div.); children: Peter Lawrence, Stephanie Ann; m. Jack L. Kellogg, Nov. 10, 1979. BS, U. Wis., 1961. Prodn. and bus. mgr. Collective Advt., Inc., Princeton, N.J., 1973-83; dir. publs. Community Pride, Inc., Princeton, 1983-87, Exclusive Publs., Ltd./Relocation Guides, Boca Raton, Fla., 1987-94. Chair Abortion Law Reform Com. of N.J., Princeton, 1967-71. Mem. Soroptimist Internat. (pres. Pompano Beach chpt. 1991-92). Home: Williamsburg, Va. Died Dec. 24, 2007.

KELLY, CHRISTINE MARIE, director, adult education educator; b. Chgo., Sept. 22, 1941; d. Stanley Anthony and Irene Marie (Kantorowski) Wasielewski; m. Bernard James Kelly, Aug. 21, 1965; children: Robert James, Margaret Ann, Timothy James. BA in Math., De Paul U., Chgo., 1963; MEd, Nat. Coll. Edn., 1980; EdD, Nat. Louis U., 1993. Tchr. math. Resurrection H.S., Chgo., 1963-67, 80-94; substitute tchr. H.S. Dist. 214, Arlington Heights, Ill., 1970-80; coord. ACT rev. series High Sch. Dist. 214, Arlington Heights, Ill., 1985-93; cons. study skills Elk Grove High Sch., Elk Grove Village, Ill., 1991; curriculum dir. Resurrection High Sch., 1994—98; dir. adminstrv. leadership program Dominican U., River Forest, Ill., 1998, assoc. prof., from 1998. Tchr. religion St. Zachary Ch., Des Plaines, Ill., 1984, 93, dir. youth ministry, 1972-80, adult religious edn., 1993—; vol. elem. sch. Mem. ASCD, Ill. ASCD, Nat. Coun. Profs. Ednl. Adminstrn., Nat. Cath. Edn. Assn., Nat. Coun. Tchrs. Math., Ill. Coun. Tchrs. Math., Kappa Delta Pi. Roman Catholic. Avocations: crafts, baking, sewing, travel, hosting foreign exchange students. Home: Inverness, Ill. Died Mar. 12, 2008.

KELLY, DIANE LONGMAID, retired elementary school educator; b. Phila., Jan. 25, 1935; d. Sydney Esterbrook and Mary (Stokes) Longmaid; m. Joseph M. Kelly, May 4, 1964 (div. July 1978); children: Nina Kelly Pack, Kendal Stokes; m. Michael F. Bayer, July 30, 2005. Student, Colby-Sawyer Coll., New London, NH, 1953—55; BA in Elem. Edn. and Music, Concordia Coll., 1981; student, Norwalk CC, Conn., 1998—2000. Substitute tchr. Westport (Conn.) Pub. Schs., Greenwich (Conn.) Pub. Schs., Norwalk (Conn.) Pub. Schs., ret., 2003. Elem. piano tchr. freelance, from 1991. Vol., docent deYoung Mus., San Francisco, 1964—66, Portland (Oreg.) Art Mus., 1966—67; vol. Neighbor to Neighbor, Young Reps., Ardmore, Pa., 1962—63. Recipient 2d place for drawing, Rowayton Art Ctr., 1996. Mem.: Embroiderers Guild. Republican. Congregationalist. Avocations: reading, playing piano, singing, drawing, cross stitch. Home: Norwalk, Conn. Died June 18, 2008.

KELLY, SISTER DOROTHY ANN, retired academic administrator; b. Bronx, NY, July 26, 1929; d. Walter David and Sarah (McCauley) K. BA in History, Coll. New Rochelle, 1951; MA in Am. Ch. History, Cath. U., Washington, 1958; PhD in Am. Intellectual History, U. Notre Dame, 1970; LittD (hon.), Mercy Coll., Dobbs Ferry, NY, 1976; LLD (hon.), Nazareth Coll. of Rochester, NYC, 1979; DHL (hon.), Coll. St. Rose, 1981, Manhattan Coll., 1979, LeMoyne Coll., 1990, St. Thomas Aquinas Coll., 1990, St. Joseph Coll., Conn., 1996, Iona Coll., 1997. Joined Order of St. Ursula, Roman Cath. Ch., 1952. Assoc. prof. history Coll. New Rochelle, NY, 1957—2001, chmn. dept. history NY, 1965-67, acad. dean NY, 1967-72, acting pres. NY, 1970-71, pres. NY, 1972-97, chancellor NY, 1997—2001; superior Ea. Province of the Ursulines, New Rochelle, NY, 2001—03, provincial superior, 2003—09. Mem. Interreligious Coun. New Rochelle, exec. com., 1974-79, v.p., 1980-84, pres., 1984-88, mem. Commn. Ind. Colls. and Univs. State of N.Y., 1976-78, chmn. bd. trustees, 1978-80, mem. govt. rels. com., 1980-81; chmn. Com. Higher Edn. Opportunity, 1976-78; mem. commr. of edn. Adv. Coun. on Higher Edn. for N.Y. State, 1975-77, subcom. on postsecondary occupational edn., 1975-77; exec. com. Empire State Found. Ind. Liberal Arts Colls., vice chmn., 1977-81; trustee, mem. exec. com. Assn. Colls. and Univs. State of N.Y., 1976-80; mem. com. on purpose and identity Assn. Cath. Colls. and Univs., 1975-80; mem. steering com. Neylan Conf., 1978-81, mem. bishops and pres. com., 1979-84; mem. adv. coun. on fin. aid to students Office Edn., HEW, 1978-86; chmn. Women's Coll. Coalition, 1981-83; chmn. govt. rels. adv. com. Nat. Assn. Ind. Colls. and Univs., 1981-82, chair, 1987-88. Chair City-wide Conferences, New Rochelle, 1977-79; bd. dirs. United Way Westchester, 1977-84, mem. planning, allocations, evaluation com., 1977-80, nominating and campaign coms.; bd. dirs. Westchester County Assn., 1980-90, New Rochelle Community Action Program, 1982-83, New Rochelle Cmty. Fund, 1989-91; mem. steering com. Westchester County Women's Hall of Fame, 1984-85; bd. dirs. Vis. Nurse Svcs. in Westchester, Inc., 1983-86, chair nominating com., 1985-86; trustee LeMoyne Coll., 1982-88, vice chairperson, 1984-87; mem. bd. govs. New Rochelle Hosp. Med. Ctr.; trustee United Student Aid Funds, 1980-90, Ursuline Sch., New Rochelle, Cath. U. Am., Am. Coun. on Edn., Ind. Coll. Fund Am., 1982-85; mem. ofcl. U.S. del. to UN 4th World Conf. on Women in Beijing, 1995; mem. nat. adv. bd. Nat. Mus. Women in the Arts Recipient Medallion award Westchester C.C., 1978, Leadership award Am. Soc. Pub. Adminstrn., 1986, Sch. Svc. award Thornton-Donovan Sch., 1977, Henry D. Paley award, 1994, Father Theodore M. Hesburgh award, 1998, N.Y. State Gov.'s award for excellence, 1997; inducted into Westchester County/Avon Women's Hall of Fame, 1989; Paul Harris fellow, 1997. Mem. AAUP, AAUW, NCCJ (trustee), Am. Hist. Assn., Nat. Fedn. Bus. and Profl. Women, Am. Assn. Higher Edn., Nat. Assembly Women Religious, Am. Coun. Edn. (bd. dirs. 1990), Assn. Am. Colls. (bd. dirs. 1983-86), Tchrs. Ins. and Annuity Assn. Am. (trustee, fin. com. 1987-88, exec. com., audit com., products and svcs. com. 1990-91, nominating and pers. com. 1991), Assn. Colls. Mid-Hudson Area (pres. 1979-81, exec. com.). Home: New Rochelle, NY. Died Mar. 27, 2009.

KELLY, KEVIN GERARD, financial analyst; b. Libertyville, Ill., Jan. 31, 1956; s. Edwin J. and Jane C. (Larsen) K.; m. Susan Lee, Aug. 4, 1984. BSBA, Roosevelt U., 1984; MBA, Rollins Coll., 1986. Fin. analyst Star Enterprise, Maitland, Fla., from 1988. Com. mem. Seminole County fire and safety impact fee com., 1991. Mem. Soc. Competitive Intelligence Profls., Phi Theta Kappa. Avocations: investment science, computing. Home: Palo Alto, Calif. Died Oct. 1, 2007.

KELLY, MICHAEL JOHN, lawyer; b. NYC, Aug. 9, 1943; s. John E. and Vivian (McNamara) K.; m. JoAnn L. Villamizar, Feb. 2, 1987; 1 child, Shannon. BS in chemistry, Farleigh Dickinson Univ., 1969; JD, Seton Hall Univ., 1976. Bar: N.J. 1976, Conn. 1988, U.S. Ct. Appeals (fed. cir.) 1988, U.S. Supreme Ct. 1992. Rsch. chemist Lever Bros. Co., Edgewater, N.J., 1965-72, patent coord., 1972-76, sr. staff atty., 1976-80; asst. patent counsel Internat Playtex, Stamford, Conn., 1980-81; divsn. patent counsel Am. Cyanamid Co., Stamford, Conn., 1981-92; chief patent counsel Cytec Industries Inc., Stamford, Conn., from 1992, v.p., from 1998. Mem. N.Y. Intellectual Property Law Assn. (membership chair, 1991-94, dir. 1995-97). Home: West Redding, Conn. Died Feb. 7, 2008.

KELLY, R(ICHARD) DENNIS, software engineer; b. Pitts., July 7, 1945; s. Richard Elliot and Anna Elizabeth (Finsinger) K.; m. Nicole J. Cook Oct. 31, 1966 (div. Dec. 1980); children: Erin M., Morgen A. R.; m. Lili J. Byrer, Oct. 14, 1984; 1 child, Richard Ian. BA, Carnegie Tech. Inst., 1967. Safety and software engr. Westinghouse Electric, Pitts., from 1966. Avocations: travel, outdoors, woodworking. Home: Gibsonia, Pa. Died May 25, 2008.

KELLY, SANDRA A., health facility administrator; b. Winston-Salem, NC, Feb. 11, 1947; Assoc. in Nursing, SUNY, Farmingdale, 1967; BSN, SUNY, Stony Brook, 1969. RN, N.Y., N.C. Staff nurse Massapequa Gen. Hosp., Seaford, N.Y.; clin. instr. Forsyth Tech. Coll., Winston-Salem; dir. nursing Med. Pers. Pool, Winston-Salem; dir. nursing, med./surg. Lexington (N.C.) Meml. Hosp. Mem. ANA, N.C. Nurses Assn., NCONE. Died Mar. 24, 2008.

KELTON, ELMER STEPHEN, novelist; b. Andrews County, Tex., Apr. 29, 1926; s. Robert William and Neta Beatrice (Parker) K.; m. Anna Lipp, July 3, 1947; children: Gary, Stephen Lee, Kathryn Ann. BA in Journalism, U. Tex., 1948. Agrl. editor San Angelo (Tex.) Standard-Times, 1948-63; editor Sheep and Goat Raiser Mag., San Angelo, 1963-68; assoc. editor Livestock Weekly, San Angelo,

1968-90; ret., 1990. Author: (novels) Hot Iron, 1955, Buffalo Wagons, 1956, Barbed Wire, 1957, Shadow of a Star, 1959, The Texas Rifles, 1960, Donovan, 1961, Bitter Trail, 1962, Horsehead Crossing, 1963, Massacre at Goliad, 1965, Llano River, 1966, After the Bugles, 1967, Captain's Rangers, 1968, Hanging Judge, 1969, Shotgun Settlement, 1969, Bowie's Mine, 1971, The Day the Cowboys Quit, 1971, Wagontongue, 1972, The Time it Never Rained, 1973, Manhunters, 1974, Joe Pepper, 1975, Long Way to Texas, 1976, The Good Old Boys, 1978, The Wolf and the Buffalo, 1980, Eyes of the Hawk, 1981, Stand Proud, 1984, Dark Thicket, 1985, The Man Who Rode Midnight, 1987, Sons of Texas, Book One, 1989, Sons of Texas, Book Two, 1989, Sons of Texas, Book Three, 1990, Honor at Daybreak, 1991, Slaughter, 1992, The Far Canyon, 1994, The Pumpkin Rollers, 1996, Cloudy in the West, 1997, Bitter Trail, 1999, Way of the Coyote, 2001, Ranger's Trail, 2002, Lone Star Rising, 2003, Jericho's Road, 2004 Texas Vendetta, 2004, Sons of Texas, 2005, Six Bits a Day, 2005, Brush Country: Two Texas Novels, 2006, Sandhills Boy, 2007, Hard Trail to Follow, 2008, Many a River, 2008, Other Men's Horses, 2009; (non-fiction) Looking Back West, 1972, Frank C. McCarthy: The Old West, 1981, Permian, A Continuing Saga, 1986, Living and Writing in West Texas, 1988, The Art of Howard Terpning, 1992, The Art of Frank McCarthy, 1992, The Art of James Bama, 1993, The Indian in Frontier News, 1993, My Kind of Heroes, 1995 (rev. ed. 2004), Christmas at the Ranch, 2003, Tom Lovell, Storyteller with a Brush, 2005, Six Bits a Day, 2005. Bd. dirs., exec. com. West Tex. Boys Ranch, San Angelo. With U.S. Army, 1944-46. Recipient Western Heritage awards (4); Spur award (7); Nat. Cowboy Hall of Fame, Career award Western Lit. Assn., 1990. Mem. Western Writers Am. (7 Spur awards, pres. 1963-64), Tex. Inst. Letters (Tinkle-McCombs award for excellence 1985), Tex. Folklore Soc., West Tex. Hist. Soc. (pres. 1990-91), German Assn. Study of Western (hon.). Methodist. Avocations: reading, classic films. Home: San Angelo, Tex. Died Aug. 22, 2009.

KEMP, JACK FRENCH, former United States Representative from New York, former United States Secretary of Housing and Urban Development; b. L.A., July 13, 1935; m. Joanne Main, July 19, 1958; children: Jeffrey, Jennifer, Judith, James. BA in Physical Edn., Occidental Coll., 1957; postgrad., Long Beach State U., Calif. Western U. Quarterback Pitts. Steelers, 1957, San Diego Chargers (formerly L.A. Chargers), 1960—62, Buffalo Bills, 1963—69; spl. asst. to Gov. State of Calif., 1967; spl. asst. to chmn. Republican Nat. Com., 1969; mem. US Congress from 39th NY Dist., 1971—73, US Congress from 38st NY Dist., 1973—83, US Congress from 31st NY Dist., 1983—89; sec. US Dept. Housing & Urban Devel., Washington, 1989-92; co-dir. Empower America, Washington, 1993—2005; vis. fellow Hoover Inst.; co-dir. Empower America, 1993—2004; weekly columnist Copley News Service, 2000—09; founder Found. for the Defense of Democracies, 2001; chmn. Kemp Partners, from 2002; co-chmn. FreedomWorks Empower America, 2004—05. Chmn., US House Republican Conf., 1981-87; pub. relations officer Marine Midland Bank, Buffalo; candidate for Rep. Presdl. nomination, 1987-88; Rep. nominee for v.p., 1996; co-founder, NFL Players Assn.; bd. dirs. Oracle Corp., 1995-96, 1996-2009, Hawk Corp., IDT Corp., CNL Hotels & Resorts Inc., Six Flags Inc., 2005-09, InPhonic Inc., Mem. Pres.'s Council on Phys. Fitness & Sports; mem. exec. com. player pension bd. NFL; mem. advisory bd. Toyota's Diversity Initiative, Thomas Weisel Partners, Thayer Capital Named to Am. Football League Pro Bowl Team, 1961-66, 1969; Recipient Am. Football League MVP award, 1965, Am. Football Championship Game MVP, 1965; Disting. Service award N.Y. State Jaycees, Outstanding Citizen award Buffalo Evening News, 1965, 74, Warner award, 2004, Presdl. Medal of Freedom, The White House (awarded posthumously), 2009; named one of The Top 50 Quarterbacks of All Time, The Sporting News, 2005 Mem. Nat. Assn. Broadcasters, Engrs. and Technicians, Buffalo Area C. of C., Sierra Club, Am. Football League Players Assn. (co-founder, pres. 1965-70) Republican. Died May 2, 2009.

KENDALL, CHARLES TERRY, librarian; b. Chambersburg, Pa., Aug. 13, 1949; s. Guy William and Virginia Mae (Naugle) K.; m. Alice Marie Bienz, Aug. 21, 1971; children: Terri, Anita, Kendra. BA, Huntington Coll., Ind., 1971; MLS, George Peabody Coll., 1972; postgrad., Asbury Theol. Sem., 1982-83; MA in Religion, Anderson U., Ind., 1990. Head libr. Plymouth Pub. Libr., Ind., 1972—73; cataloger Mohave County Libr., Kingman, Ariz., 1975—78; resources libr. Starved Rock Libr. Sys., Ottawa, Ill., 1978—81; dir. Mifflin County Libr., Lewistown, Pa., 1981—82; cataloger Asbury Coll., 1982—83; dir. Byrd Meml. Libr. Anderson Sch. Theology, Anderson U., 1983-89; theol. studies libr. Anderson U. Libr., 1989-98, archivist, 1992-98; dir. Mabee Libr. Sterling Coll., Kans., 1998—2002; head circulation and tech. svcs. Alexandrian Public Library, Mt. Vernon, Ind., 2003—05, head collection svcs., from 2005. Mem. ALA, Public Library Assn. Deceased.

KENEDY, EUGENE THOMAS, JR., retail sales executive; b. Bay Shore, NY, Aug. 8, 1946; s. Eugene Thomas Kenedy and Joan Elizabeth McAvoy; m. Olga Josephine Silva, July 1, 1982; children: David, Katherine, Christopher, Kelly-Anne. Student, Columbia U., 1964-66; BA in English and Am. Lit. cum laude, SUNY, Stony Brook, 1970; M Religious Edn. cum laude, UTS Theol. Seminary, Barrytown, NY, 1981. Staff photographer New Future Films, Tarrytown, N.Y., 1976; features writer The News World, NYC, 1976, entertainment ad mgr., 1976-79; exec. dir. Collegiate Assn. for Rsch. of Prins., Miami, 1981-82; reporter-Metro N.Y. Tribune, NYC, 1982-83; system adminstr. C.A.U.S.A., Washington, 1983-85; asst. mgr. Sivel Sales, Washington, 1982; sales acct. exec. The Washington Times, from 1985. Photographer/contbr. Toward Our Third Century. Fundraiser HSA-UWC Ch., N.Y., D.C. Recipient 1st place display free colo photographer, Md.-Del. D.C. Press Assn., 1986, 2nd place, 1986. Mem. The Dir.'s Club (charter). Republican. Avocations: computers, desktop pub., ad layout design. Home: Alexandria, Va. Died Apr. 30, 2008.

KENLEY, JOHN, theatrical producer; b. Denver, Feb. 20, 1906; s. Anna Kremchek Machuga. Dancer Greenwich Village Follies, 1923-24, Artists and Models, NYC, 1925-26, Hit the Deck, NYC, 1927; mimic, performer Vaudeville, 1928-29; play reader Shubert Theater, asst. to Lee Shubert, 1930-40; with U.S. Mcht. Marines, 1941-47; producer summer theater Kenley Players, Pa., Ohio, 1940-95. Mem. Assn. Theatrical Pres Agts. and Mgrs. Home: Brecksville, Ohio. Died Oct. 23, 2009.

KENNEDY, BOB, retired sports association executive; m. Claire Kennedy; children: Robert, Terry, Coleen, Christine, Kathleen Profl. baseball player Chgo. White Sox, Cleve. Indians, Balt. Orioles, Detroit Tigers, Bklyn. Dodgers, 1939-57; asst. farm dir. Cleve. Indians, 1959-61; mgr. Chgo. Cubs, 1963-65, gen. mgr., 1977-81; mgr. Oakland A's, 1968; dir. player pers. St. Louis Cardinals, 1969-76; spl. asst. Houston Astros, 1981, v.p. baseball ops., 1982—85, San Francisco Giants, 1986—92; ret., 1992. Died 2005; Mesa, Ariz.

KENNEDY, DAVID LAURENCE, deacon; b. Racine, Wis., Jan. 17, 1936; s. Laurence Frank and Margaret Cecelia (Degrand) K. BS in Indsl. Tech., U. Wis.-Stout, Menomonie, 1965. Ordained deacon Roman Cath. Ch., 1975. Permanent deacon Sts. Edward and Rose Cath. Chs., Racine, Wis., 1975-91. Sr. tech. writer Eaton Corp., Kenosha, Wis., 1966—. Scoutmaster Boy Scouts Am., Racine, 1965-74. With USNR, 1954-62. Mem. Deacon Senate Assn. Home: Adams, Wis. Died Dec. 30, 2007.

KENNEDY, JOHN ELMO, JR., organic chemist; b. Louisville, June 21, 1932; s. John Elmo and Anna Louise (Smith) K.; m. Carolyn M. Kaleher, Sept. 11, 1954 (div. 1976); children: Kevin P., Eric B., John Elmo III, Brian B. BS in Chemistry, U. Louisville, 1959, PhD, 1963. Lab. technician Shenley Distillers, Louisville, 1955-56; asst. rsch. chemist Ky. Color & Chem. Co., Louisville, 1956-59; rsch. chemist Dept. Exptl. Medicine, U. Louisville, 1959-61; sr. rsch. chemist Brown & Williamson Tobacco Corp., 1963-64, group leader, 1964-70, rsch. area supr., 1970-76; instr. chemistry U. Louisville, 1976-77; pvt. cons. in organic chemistry Lexington, Ky., from 1977. Tutor organic chemistry, pharmacology, toxicology, U. Louisville, U. Ky., 1978—. Patentee in field; contbr. articles to profl. jours. Dist. exec. com. Boy Scouts Am., Louisville, 1969, scoutmaster, 1969-73. With U.S. Army, 1953-55. NIH predoctoral fellow, 1960-63. Mem. Am. Chem. Soc. (sect. chmn. 1975-76), Smithsonian Instn., N.Y. Acad. Sci., Sigma Xi, Phi Lambda Upsilon. Democrat. Avocations: music, canoeing, camping, shooting, photography. Died Jan. 8, 2008.

KENNEDY, JOHN MATTHEW, insurance company executive; b. Shelby, Ohio, Sept. 4, 1944; s. John M. and Dorothy (Watters) K.; m. Christine R. Roslund; children: Andrew J., Sally E. BA, Ohio State U., 1967. Spl. rep. Shelby Mut. Ins. Co., Dayton, Ohio, 1970-75, resident sec. Winter Park, Fla., 1975-83; v.p. mktg. Shelby (Ohio) Life Ins. Co., from 1983. With U.S. Army, 1968-70. Named Ohio Mktg. Rep. of Yr. Profl. Ins. Agts., 1975. Mem. CLU Soc. (pres. Mansfield chpt. 1988), CPCU Soc. (pres. Orlando chpt. 1983). Republican. Roman Catholic. Avocations: reading, golf, travel, snorkeling. Died Nov. 10, 2007.

KENNEDY, NANCY LOUISE, retired draftsman; b. Mar. 14, 1925; d. William Richardson and Mary Enroughty (Youmans) Humphrey; m. William Dwyer Kennedy, Sept. 3, 1952 (dec. May 1953); 1 child, Kathleen Dwyer. Student, Gulf Park Coll., 1943; B of Interior Design, Washington U., 1948. Land draftsman Carter Oil Co., Ft. Smith, Ark., 1954-60, Sinclair Oil and Gas, Oklahoma City, 1960-69, Atlantic Richfield Oil and Gas Co., Tulsa, 1969-82. Mem. Altar guild Trinity Episcopal Ch., Tulsa. Mem. Kappa Alpha Theta. Republican. Home: Tulsa, Okla. Died Oct. 26, 2007.

KENNEDY, TED (EDWARD MOORE KENNEDY), United States Senator from Massachusetts; b. Boston, Feb. 22, 1932; s. Joseph Patrick and Rose (Fitzgerald) K.; m. Joan Bennett Kennedy, Nov. 30, 1958 (div. Dec. 6, 1982); children: Kara Anne, Edward Moore Jr., Patrick Joseph; m. Victoria Anne Reggie, July 3, 1992; 2 stepchildren: Curran, Caroline AB in Govt., Harvard U., Cambridge, Mass., 1956; postgrad., Internat. Law Sch., The Hague, Netherlands, 1958; LLB, U. Va., Charlottesville, 1959; LLD (hon.), Harvard U., 2008. Bar: Mass. 1959, US Supreme Ct. 1963. Asst. dist. atty., Suffolk County, Mass., 1961-62; US Senator from Mass., 1962—2009; majority whip, 1969—71; chmn. US Senate Judiciary Com., 1979—81, US Senate Labor & Human Resources Com., 1987—95, US Senate Health, Edn., Labor & Pensions Com., 2001, 2001—03, 2007—09; mem. US Senate Armed Svcs. Com., Joint Econ. Com., Dem. Steering & Outreach Com., Nat. Security Working Group. Hon. chmn. Democratic Nat. Convention, 2004. Author: Decisions for a Decade: Policies and Programs for the 1970's, 1968, In Critical Condition: The Crisis in America's Health Care, 1972, A People of Compassion: The Concerns of Edward M. Kennedy, 1972, Words Jack Loved, 1977, Our Day and Generation: The Words of Edward M. Kennedy, 1979, American Back on Track, 2006, My Senator and Me: A Dog's Eye View of Washington, 2006, True Compass: A Memoir, 2009; co-author: (with Mark O. Hatfield) Freeze!: How You Can Help Prevent Nuclear War, 1979; appeared in: (documentaries) Teddy: In His Own Words, 2009 Pres., Joseph P. Kennedy Jr. Found.; bd. trustees John F. Kennedy Ctr. for Performing Arts; bd. dirs. Children's Hosp. Med. Ctr., John F. Kennedy Library, Mus. of Sci., Robert F. Kennedy Meml. Found. Served in US Army, 1951—53. Recipient Excellence in Pub. Svc. award, American Acad. Pediatrics, 1993, MLA award for Disting. Pub. Svc., Medical Library Assn., 1994, Pub. Svc. award, American Assn. Pub. Health Dentistry, 1998, Pub. Leadership in the Arts award, Americans for the Arts-US Conf. Mayors, 1999, Bipartisan Hero award, Nat. Assn. Pediatric Nurse Associates & Practitioners, 2001, Lifetime Achievement award, Nat. Assn. Ind. Colleges & Universities, 2001, George Bush award for Excellence in Pub. Svc., Bush Presdl. Library Found., 2003, Nat. Pub. Svc. award, American Heart Assn., 2003, Oates Shrum Leadership award, Gay & Lesbian Victory Fund & Leadership Inst., 2004, Hubert H. Humphrey award, Leadership Conf. on Civil Rights, 2005, John Adams Pub. Svc. award, Quincy, Mass. Partnership, 2005, Lincoln award, Ill. Coun. Against Handgun Violence, 2005, Champion award, Campaign for Tobacco Free Kids, 2005, Song of the Whale Found., Internat. Fund for Animal Welfare, 2005, USWA Wellstone award, United Steelworkers of America, 2006, Scopus award for Outstanding Pub. Svc., American Friends of Hebrew U., Solidarity award, Nat. Conf. on Soviet Jewry, John F. Kennedy Profile in Courage award, John F. Kennedy Library Found., 2009, Presdl. Medal of Freedom, The White House, 2009; named a Knight Comdr. of the British Empire (KBE), Her Majesty Queen Elizabeth II, 2009; named one of The 10 Outstanding Young Men, US Jaycees, 1967, America's 10 Best Senators, TIME mag., 2006, The World's Most Influential People, 2009. Fellow Am. Acad. Arts and Sci. Democrat. Roman Catholic. Home: Hyannis Port, Mass. Died Aug. 25, 2009.

KENNEY, JAMES DUNCAN, physician, university dean; b. Waterbury, Conn., July 27, 1929; s. Francis Joseph and Mary Clare (Duncan) K.; m. Elise Marie Karas, July 20, 1963; children: Christopher, Duncan, Anne Elizabeth. BA, Yale U., 1952; MD, Boston U., 1956. Diplomate in internal medicine and rheumatology Am. Bd. Internal Medicine. Rsch. assoc. Galton Lab., Univ. Coll., London, 1963-65; clin. prof. medicine Yale U. Sch. Medicine, New Haven, from 1966, assoc. dean for postgrad. and continuing edn., 1977—2001. Editor, author Med. Letter/Yale Sch. Medicine CME Program, 1978—; mem. editl. adv. bd. The Med. Letter on Drugs and Therapeutics, New Rochelle, NY, 1978-05. Lt. M.C., USN, 1958-60. Named Laureate, ACP, 1989. Fellow Am. Coll. Rheumatology; mem. AMA. Home: North Haven, Conn. Died Nov. 29, 2007.

KEREKES, JOSEPH JOHN, evangelist; b. Toledo, Oct. 28, 1949; s. Joseph John and Zelpha Fay (Hayes) K.; m. Sarah Helene Marantha, May 15, 1970; children: Jennifer, Constance, Melanie. Ordained to ministry Pentecostal Ch., 1980; cert. home health technologist. Pastor Ministry of Life Pentecostal Ch., Toledo, 1975-82; founder, sr. elder Shepherd of the Dove Ministries, Toledo, from 1983. Home health technologist, Dove Health Care, Toledo, 1987—. Usher Ministry of Life Pentecostal Ch., 1970-72, elder 1972-75. With USAF, 1969-70. Recipient Christian Patriot Leadership award Am. Christian Leadership Coun., 1989-90. Died July 11, 2008.

KERN, MARK SHERWOOD, chiropractor; b. Dover, Del., Dec. 17, 1959; s. Charles Edward Kern and Dauna Dale (Baker) Josephson. Student, Memphis State U., 1979; D Chiropractic, Life Chiropractic Coll., Marietta, Ga., 1983. Diploma Nat. Bd. Chiropractic Examiners. Pvt. practice, Ft. Myers, Fla., from 1984. Writer, announcer Active Life Tip, Sta. WBBH-TV, NBC, 1989—, on injury mgmt. Sta. WEVU-TV, 1987-88; dir. sports medicine Ft. Myers Jr. Football Assn., 1984-88; ringside physician Fla. Athletic Commn., 1987—; co-founder, co-dir. Sports Chiropractic Coun., Ft. Myers, 1986—; mem. med. adv. bd. Universal Boxing Assn., Lexington, Ky., 1987—; med. advisor S.W. Fla. Bicycle Racing Assn.; Lee County coord. Nat. Assn. for Seat Belt Safety Awareness. Organizer fun ride March of Dimes, Ft. Myers, l987; dir. City of Palms Century Ride, Ft. Myers, l986, 87; team physician Bishop Verot High Sch., Ft. Myers, l986, 87; co-organizer Home-Aid '90. Recipient awards Practice Mgmt. Assocs., l985, 86. Mem. Am. Coll. Sports Medicine, Am. Chiropractic Assn. (coun. on sports medicine), Internat. Chiropractic Assn. (coun. on sports medicine), Fla. Chiropractic Assn., Fla. Chiropractic Soc., Miami Ski Club. Republican. Avocations: golf, bicycling, running, alpine skiing, guitar. Died Jan. 1, 2008.

KERNAN, JEROME BERNARD, retired marketing educator, researcher; b. Cin., Nov. 22, 1932; s. E. B. and Alice (Gerver) Kernan; children: Kathleen Kernan Bedree, Brian Michael. BA, U. Cin., 1957; MS, U. Ill., 1959, PhD, 1962; post-doctoral studies in computer simulation, Carnegie Mellon U., Pitts., 1962; post-doctoral studies in math., U. Kans., 1963. Prof. emeritus George Mason U. Consumer rsch. cons., from 1965. Co-author: (book) Perspectives on Marketing Theory, 1968, Comparative Marketing Systems,

1968, Explorations in Consumer Behavior, 1968, Promotion: An Introductory Analysis, 1970, Managerial Analysis in Marketing, 1970, Perspectives in Marketing Management, 1971; contbr. over 120 articles to profl. jours. Pres. Sacred Heart Sch. Bd., Austin, Tex., 1964—67. With USAF, 1951—53. Co-recipient Ferber award, Jour. Consumer Rsch., 1992, Best Article award, Am. Acad. Advt., 1993. Mem.: Soc. for Consumer Psychology, Assn. for Consumer Rsch. (pres. 1978). Avocations: motorsport, golf. Home: Cincinnati, Ohio. Died Nov. 22, 2007.

KERR, JAMES WILSON, engineer; b. Balt., May 21, 1921; s. James W. and Laura Virginia (Wright) Kerr; m. Mary Thomas Montgomery, Feb. 25, 1945 (div.); children: April Kerr Miller, Catherine Kerr Wood(dec.), Wilson(dec.), Andrew; m. June Walker, Dec. 27, 1977 (div.); m. Janice White Bain, Jan. 19, 1985. BS with honors, Davidson Coll., 1942; MS, NYU, 1948; postgrad., Freiburg U., 1957—60, Brookings Inst., 1970, postgrad., 1975; PhD, Kennedy Western U., 1989. Registered profl. engr., Calif. Commd. 2d lt. U.S. Army, 1942, advanced through grades to lt. col., 1964, with inf., World War II, Korea, electronics staff Ft. Bragg, NC, 1948-51, weapons rsch. N.Mex., 1953-57, adviser French Army, 1957-60, staff electronics Ft. Monroe, Va., 1960-62, rsch. mgr., divsn. dir. CD Pentagon, 1962-64, as civilian, 1964-81; asst. assoc. dir. Fed. Emergency Mgmt. Agy. for Rsch., 1981-85; sr. staff, cons. Michael Rogers, Inc., Winter Park, Fla., 1986—2005. V.p. Latherow & Co., Arlington, Va., 1965—86; dr. Mt. St. Helen's Tech. Office, 1980; radiol. officer Talbot County, Md., from 1997. Author: Korean-English Phrase Book, 1951, 19th Century Korea Postal Handbook, 1965, 2d edit., 1990; editor: Korean Philately mag., 1971—80, 1985—95; contbr. articles to profl. jours. Active Boy Scouts Am., from 1933; vol. fireman NY, 1946—48; chmn. libr. bd. Orangeburg, NY, 1946—48; advanced English instr. French Army, 1957—60; cons. Am. Nat. Red Cross Mus., 1968—85, Smithsonian Instn. Dept. Postal History, 1966—85, NSF, 1976—85; vol. fireman, fire commr. Fairfax County, 1975—81, chmn., 1977—81, Orange County, Fla., from 1986, pres., 1987—90, Pike County, Ala., 1994—98, Talbot County, Md., from 1997. Decorated Bronze Star with three oak leaf clusters, Purple Heart; recipient Silver Beaver award, Boy Scouts Am., 1956, James E. West award, 1994; Fulbright fellow, Japan, 1986. Fellow: AAAS (life), Explorers Club (emeritus); mem.: SAR (Fire Safety medal 1995), NAS (mem. various coms. 1962—87), NSPE, IEEE (sr.), Presdl. Nat. Def. Execs., Nat. Fire Protection Assn. (chmn. hosp. disaster com. 1973—86), Fed. Fire Coun., Internat. Assn. Fire Chiefs (chmn. rsch. com. 1969—88, chief sci. adviser 1982—86), Korean War Vets. Assn. (nat. bd. dirs. 1999), Black Forest Mardi Gras (Germany), Univ. Club Fla., Nat. Comm. Club, Pentagon Officers Athletic Club, Elks, Phi Beta Kappa, Delta Phi Alpha, Gamma Sigma Epsilon. Presbyterian. Home: Winchester, Va. Died Mar. 18, 2008.

KERR, JUDITH P., lay professional ministry; b. Milroy, Pa., July 5, 1939; d. Ralph Lee Sr. and Mettie Pauline (Gardiner) K.; m. Walter Scott Sizer, July 9, 1977. BA, Western Md. Coll., 1961; B in Sacred Theology, Boston U., 1966. Cert. deaconess/diaconal min. United Meth. Ch. Dir. Christian edn. United Meth. Ch., Cochituate, Mass., 1963-68; social worker N.H. Dept. Welfare, Berlin, 1968-70; outreach worker Social Svc. Ctr., Springfield, Mass., 1970-72; dir. nutrition program for the elderly Home Care Corp., Springfield, 1972-77; part-time campus min. Wesley Found.-So. Ill. U., Carbondale, 1978-80; social planner Planning Divsn.-City Hall, Carbondale, 1978-80; program coord. Faith United Meth. Ch., Fargo, N.D., 1980-84; retreat leader Koinonia Ecumenical Spirituality Ctr., Grand Forks, N.D., 1989-91; rsch., editor Charis Ecumenical Ctr., Moorhead, Minn., 1994-96. Spiritual retreat leader various orgns., 1986-96. Rschr., author: Comprehensive Human Service Plan for Carbondale Illinois, 1979; rschr., co-author: Ecumenical Shared Ministry and The United Methodist Church, 1995. Active Bread for the World, 1974—, NOW, 1977—, LWV, 1977-80, Amnesty Internat., 1980-84. Mem. Nat. Assn. Deaconesses and Missionaries (regional pres. 1976-77). Democrat. Avocations: travel, hiking, reading. Home: Moorhead, Minn. Died Mar. 20, 2008.

KERSHAW, JOHN WILLIAM, minister; b. Salt Lake City, Sept. 4, 1943; s. Douglas H. and Joan E. (Weenig) K.; m. Jacqueline Elaine Holdsworth, May 23, 1983; children: John M., Paul, Joel. BA, U. Denver, 1965; MDiv, St. Paul Sch. Theology, 1969. Ordained deacon United Meth. Ch., 1966, elder, 1970. Pastor Riverbank United Meth. Ch., Wyandotte, Mich., 1969-70; pastor Elmwood-Aldersgate United Meth. Chs., Pontiac, Mich., 1970-75, First United Meth. Ch., Marine City, Mich., 1975-79, Berkley, Mich., 1979-89, Wayne, Mich., from 1989. Chairperson Mich. Area Sem. Grant Fund, 1972-80; sec. Detroit Conf. Standing Roles, 1980-88; chairperson Detroit Conf. Vols. in Mission, 1989—; bd. dirs. Intersharing, 1989—, Eastside Ministry of Social Svc., 1985—. Mem. Detroit Annual Conf. United Meth. Ch. Home: Monroe, Mich. Died Aug. 4, 2008.

KESSLER, RALPH, composer, conductor, educator; b. NYC, Aug. 1, 1919; s. Abraham Julius Kessler and Lillian Eisner; children: Ronny Hormung, Robert Kessler, Rory Bakke. BA, Juilliard Sch., 1948, MA, 1950. Arranger Columbia Broadcast Sys., NYC, 1952-58; creative dir. Music Matters, NYC, 1959-67; prin., owner R.K. Prodns., NYC, L.A., 1967-85, retired, 1985. Conductor Pacific Composers Forum, L.A., 1994-98, San Fernando Valley Symphony, L.A., 1996-98. Composer commercials including Yuban Coffee, Sanka, 1968-70 (Clio awards 1968-70), Gershwin Medley-Rodgers Medley, 1997-98, El Alfarero, 1997. Cpl. U.S. Army, 1941-45. Decorated Two Bronze Stars. Mem. Am. Soc. Music Arrangers Composers (bd. mem. 1984-95, v.p. 1996-97), Toastmasters (pres. 1998—), Nature Conservatory, World Wildlife Fedn., Sierra Club. Democrat. Avocations: squash racquets, bridge, swimming. Home: Walnut Creek, Calif. Died Oct. 5, 2007.

KETCHAM, RAY WINFRED, JR., art dealer; b. Hartford, Ala., Dec. 4, 1922; s. Ray Winfred and Flora Dell (White) K.; m. Thelma Catherine Taylor, Dec. 19, 1947; children: Victoria Suzanne, Peter Daughtry. Student, Ringling Sch. Art, Sarasota, Fla., 1946-48. Freelance advt. artist/designer to Coca-Cola Co., Atlanta, 1949-67; owner, dir., art gallery curator and conservator Ray Ketcham Gallery, Atlanta, 1966-83, pvt. dealer, from 1983. Lectr. in field. Designer, prodr. Coca-Cola Home Calendar, 1955-67; designer graphic wall mural Delta Airlines, Chgo., 1967. With U.S. Army, 1943-46, PTO. Named Freelance Artist of the Yr., Profl. Artists Assn. Atlanta, 1965. Republican. Avocations: collecting old music, records. Died Mar. 21, 2009.

KETTERMAN, ROBERT CHARLES, musician; b. Chgo., Sept. 28, 1957; s. Robert and Mildred Mary (Pesek) K. Student, Chgo. State U. Studio musician on keyboards various rec. studios, Chgo., 1975-87; pres., chief engr. Launching Pad Studio, Chgo., from 1988. Pres., rec. engr. Half Moon Enterprises Ltd., Villalba, Puerto Rico, 1980; arranger, vocalist, keyboardist with various bands, Chgo., 1982-85. Records include This Town/Espionage, 1982, Sky Blue/Trident Square, 1977, The Thirteenth Floor, 1988, Burn!!, 1990. Mem. Mid-Western Songwriter's Assn. Avocations: photography, travel, bicycling, hiking. Home: Chicago, Ill. Died Feb. 22, 2008.

KEUCHER, WILLIAM FREDERICK, minister; b. Atlantic City, June 6, 1918; s. Otto Ernest Rudolph and Margaret (Wilson) K.; m. Edith Warnick Kimber, Nov. 28, 1940; children: Margaret Valerie, Louise Sherilyn. AB, ThB, Eastern Coll., 1942; BD, Eastern Bapt. Theol. Sem., 1946, DD, 1971, Ottawa U., 1953, Kalamazoo Coll., 1971; HHD, Alderson Broadds Coll., 1980. Pastor Allegheny Ave. Bapt. Ch., Phila., 1942-48, 1st Bapt. Ch., El Dorado, Kans., 1948-52; exec. minister Kans. Bapt. Convention, Topeka, 1953-70; sr. minister Covenant Bapt. Ch., Detroit, 1971-81, pastor emeritus, from 1982; prof. pastoral theology Cen. Bapt. Theol. Sem., Kansas City, Kansas, 1982-87, pres., 1983-87, pres. emeritus, from 1987. Pres. Am. Bapt. Chs. USA, 1980-81, gen. bd., 1972-83, mem. exec. com., 1978-83; pres. Bd. Internat. Ministries, 1971, mem. exec. com., 1972-79, chmn. budget com., 1976-79, ministers and missionaries benefit bd., 1975-79; trustee Kalamazoo Coll., 1979-82, Ottawa U. (life); nat. chmn. Bd. Nat. Ministries Bicentennial Fund, 1982-83; vice chmn. Bapt. Joint Com. Pub. Affairs, Washington, 1974, mem. exec. com., 1974-82, chmn. pers. rels. 1978-82; bd. govs. Nat. Coun. Chs., 1976-81; adj. staff Ohio Bapt. Conv., 1989-91; interim minister First Bapt. Ch., Dayton, 1990-91; bd. dirs. Bapt. Peace Fellowship N.Am., 1990—; mem. Religious Liberty Coun., Washington, 1990—; pres. Kans. Bapt. Conv., 1952; chair nat. program com. Am. Bapt. Chs. in U.S.A., 1953, 63, pres. exec. mins.' coun., 1956, ann. preacher, 1973; pres. Am. Bapt. Fgn. Mission Soc., 1971. Author: An Exodus for the Church, 1973, Main Street and the Mind of God, 1974, Good News People in Action, 1975; contbr. articles to profl. jours. Sec. Detroit Christian Communication Council, 1977-78, chmn. div. fin. & bus., 1978-79; pres. Detroit Urban League, 1976-78, adv. bd. 1979-82; profl. div. group chmn. United Found. Torch Drive, 1976-77, clergy rep. 1976-82; bd. dirs. Met. Fund Detroit, 1976-82; clergy mem. Econ. Club Detroit, 1977-82; citizen's adv. council united Community Services, 1978-82. Recipient Award of Merit Am. Bapt. Chs. USA, 1960, Resolution of Merit Mich. Ho. and Senate, 1981. Past mem. Am. Acad. Religion, Acad. Polit. Sci., Menninger Found., Internat. Platform Assn., Wranglers Club, Rotary. Avocations: gardening, poetry. Died Oct. 15, 2007.

KIDD, VALLEE MELVINA, charitable foundation manager; b. Zora, Mo., Jan. 5, 1918; d. Alva Joseph and Pauline Louise (Nolte) Lefever; m. Vernon Noble Kidd, Nov. 5, 1937 (dec. Dec. 1970); children: Elaine Louise Green, Vernon N. Jr., Margaret Ruth Keener. Exec. asst. Grimes Gasoline Co. and related ops., Tulsa, 1977-86; mng. trustee Otha H. Grimes Found., Tulsa, from 1986. Pres. Gilcrease Mus. Service Orgn. (Gillies), Tulsa, 1973-74; bd. dirs. Thomas Gilcrease Mus. Assn., Tulsa, 1976-81. Mem. Tuesday Book Club (pres. 1974-75). Republican. Presbyterian. Home: Stillwater, Okla. Died July 27, 2008.

KIDDA, MICHAEL LAMONT, JR., psychologist, educator; b. Jackson, Miss., May 24, 1945; s. Michael Lamont and Annie Laurie (McKeithen) K.; m. Ellen Gordon, Aug. 23, 1977 (div. 2005); children: Patrick Gordon, John McKeithen. BA in English, Centenary Coll. La., Shreveport, 1969; MDiv, U. South, Sewanee, Tenn., 1972; MS in Social Psychology, U. Ga., Athens, 1984, PhD in Social Psychology, 1987. Youth cons. Cathedral St. Philip, Atlanta, 1974—76; counselor All Saints' Sch., Vicksburg, Miss., 1977—79; coord. assessment J.C. Smith U., Charlotte, NC, 1989—94, assoc. prof. psychology, from 1985, dept. head, 1987—89, 1999—2002. Coord. Grad. Student Conf./Personality and Social Psychology, Athens, 1981; bd. trustees NE Ga. Area Cmty. Resource Coun., Athens, 1980—83, v.p., 1982, tech. adminstrn., 84; data analysis cons., Athens, 1980—83; corp. sec. Kidda Enterprises, 1999—2004, pres., 2005; corp. sec. Carolina Cupboard, 2002—04; pres. Higher Edn. Evaluation and Devel., from 2002; evaluation cons. NSF-REU grant to UNC, Charlotte; presenter in field. Contbr. articles to profl. jours. and to On-line and CD-Rom data bases; author newsletter ETS Higher Edn. Assessment, 1993. Com. mem. cub scouts pack 19 Boy Scouts Am., Huntersville, NC, 1994—97; mem. Lions Club, Huntersville, 1996—99, Davidson, 1999—2001, membership com., 2000—01, dir. Hickory Grove, 2003—06, Tail Twister, 2006; bd. dirs. Metrolina Assn. for the Blind, 2006—07; mem. adv. bd. Washington Heights Project Nat. Children's Def. Fund, Charlotte, 1994; chair evaluation com. Fighting Back Against Drugs, Charlotte, 1992—94; bd. dirs. Lions Svcs. for the Blind, Charlotte, 1999—2005, pers. com. vice chair, 2002—05. Recipient Nat. Retention Excellence award Noel-Levitz Ctrs., Cross of Nails award St. Michael's Cathedral, Coventry, Eng., cert. of appreciation Washington Hts. Youth Svcs. Acad., 1997; Retention and Performance grantee Pew Charitable Trusts, 1994, Equipment grantee AT&T Found., 1991, grantee APA, 1996, United Negro Coll. Fund, 1996; fellow Inst. Non-Traditional Ministries, 1994-99. Mem. Am. Statis. Assn., Soc. Southeastern Social Psychologists, Lions, Sigma Xi (site coord. celebration of undergrad. rsch. 1999), Sigma Tau Delta, Psi Chi (chpt. adviser 2001—). Achievements include empirical demonstration of superiority of college-level inquiry curriculum over remediation in post-secondary education; research on causes of behavioral control on prosocial behavior; causal attribution on evaluation of people with disabilities; effects of accepting non-reciprocal aid; development of relationship mapping as a curriculum assessment tool. Home: Charlotte, NC. Died 2008.

KIEBART, JOHN S., JR., protective services official; b. Catskill, NY, May 26, 1944; s. John S. Sr. and Emma (Lynch) K.; m. June L. Celli, May 24, 1969; 1 child, Jeannine E. Grad. H.S., Catskill. Police officer Police Dept. Saugerties, N.Y., 1965-66; trooper zone sgt. N.Y. State Police, Albany, 1966-91; sheriff Greene County Sheriff's Office, Catskill, from 1992. Cpl. U.S. Army, 1963-65. Democrat. Roman Catholic. Avocations: scuba diving, hunting, fishing, outdoorsman. Home: Catskill, NY. Died May 8, 2008.

KIEPPER, ALAN FREDERICK, retired transportation executive, former city official; b. Syracuse, NY, July 3, 1928; s. John Carl and Sarah Esther (McFadden) K.; m. Edith Harper, June 28, 1953 (div. 1984); children: Patricia Ellen Kiepper Ferebee, Jane Elizabeth Kiepper Rosser, Paul Frederick; m. Suzan Donna Russell, Jan. 31, 1987. BA, U. N.H., 1950; MPA, Wayne State U., 1960. Budget and mgmt. officer City of Richmond, Va., 1953-59; asst. to county mgr. Montgomery County, Rockville, Md., 1959-63; county mgr. Fulton County, Atlanta, 1963-67; city mgr. City of Richmond, 1967-72; gen. mgr. Met. Atlanta Rapid Transit Authority, 1972-82, Met. Transit Authority of Harris County, Houston, 1982-89; pres. N.Y.C. Transit Authority, 1990—96. Assoc. prof. pub. adminstrn. and mgmt. Rice U., Houston, 1982-89. Author: (with Robert T. Golembiewski) High Performance and Human Costs—A Public Sector Model of Organization Development, 1988; also articles. Vestryman Christ Ch. Episcopal Cathedral, Houston, 1986-89, sr. warden, 1989. 1st lt. U.S. Army, 1951-53. Fellow Nat. Acad. Pub. Adminstrn. (Nat. Pub. Svc. award 1986), Chartered Inst. Transport; mem. Am. Pub. Transit Assn. (vice chmn. 1989-90, chmn., 1990-91, Jesse Hugh award as Transit Man of Yr. 1985), Internat. Union Pub. Transport (bd. dirs. 1982-89, v.p. 1986-89), Am. Soc. Pub. Adminstrn. (pres. Va. chpt. 1969-70, Nat. Pub. Svc. award 1986). Home: New York, NY. Died Aug. 26, 2009.

KILBOY, TWYLA D., nurse educator; b. Atlanta, Tex., Apr. 20, 1964; d. Robert Lynn Sr. and Oleda Darlene Jones; m. Timothy J. Kilboy, Dec. 8, 1985; children: David, Steven. AS, Texarkana Community Coll., Tex., 1985. Cert. BCLS instr.; RN, Tex. Pediatric nurse St. Michael Hosp., Texarkana, Wadley Regional Med. Ctr., Texarkana; dir. of nursing Oak Manor Nursing Home, Texarkana; program coord. Career Acad., Texarkana. Mentor asst. B. State Women's Ctr. Mem. Tex. Nursing Student Assn. (pres.), Beta Simga Phi (v.p.). Home: Jackson, Tenn. Died Jan. 28, 2008.

KIM, KI HANG, mathematician; b. Moon Duck, Pyongnam, Korea, Aug. 5, 1936; arrived in U.S., 1953; s. Jin Gyong Kim and Mee Lan Hong; m. Myong Ja Kim, Aug. 1, 1963; children: John Churl, Linda Youngmee. BS in Math., U. So. Miss., 1960, MS in Math., 1961; PhD in Math., George Washington U., 1971. Instr. math. U. Hartford, 1961—66; lectr. math. George Washington U., Washington, 1970—72; assoc. prof. math. St. Mary's Coll. Md., St. Mary's City, Md., 1970—72, U. N.C., Pembroke, 1972—74; prof. math. Ala. State U., Montgomery, from 1974, disting. prof. math., from 1983. Vis. prof. U. Lisbon, 1974, Stuttgart (Germany) U., 1978, Chinese Acad. Scis., Beijing, 1983. Editor-in-chief: Math. Social Scis., 1981—94; editor: Jour. Pure and Applied Math., from 1987, Future Generations Computer Sys., from 1983; contbr. articles to profl. jours. Specialist US Army, 1955—57. Grantee, NSF, 1971—2003. Fellow: Korean Acad. Sci. and Tech. Died Jan. 15, 2009.

KIMELMAN, HENRY LEE, former ambassador; b. NYC, Jan. 21, 1921; s. Sigmund A. and Caroline (Hanenson) K.; m. Charlotte R. Kessler, Sept. 26, 1943; children:

Donald Bruce, Susan Kimelman Edwards, John David. BS, NYU, 1943; postgrad., Harvard U. Grad. Sch. Bus. Adminstrn., 1944; LHD (hon.), Dakota Wesleyan U., 2004. Vice pres. Ozark Mountain Distilling Co., Joplin, Mo., 1945-48, pres., 1949-50; pres., treas. V.I. Hotel and V.I. Realty, St. Thomas, 1950-61; commr. commerce V.I., 1961-64; chmn. bd. Island Block Corp. & Henry Elliot, Ltd., St. Thomas, 1964-67; asst. to sec. US Dept. Interior, Washington, 1967-69; pres., chmn. bd. West Indies Corp., St. Thomas, 1969-80; US amb. to Haiti US Dept. State, Port-au-Prince, 1980-81. Dir. W.I. Bank & Trust Co., Am. Hotel Assn., Diners Club, Inc., Leeward Islands Transport, Antigua, W.I. Chmn. Econ. Devel. Bd. of V.I., 1961-64, V.I. Rum Council, 1961-64; V.I. adminstr. for U.S. Area Redevel. Adminstrn., Washington, 1961-64; dir. U.S. Nat. Parks Found., 1968-72; mem. adv. com. on arts J.F. Kennedy Ctr. Performing Arts, 1979-82; chmn. McGovern for Pres. Com., 1971-72; dep. chmn., finance chmn. Church for Pres., 1976; bd. dirs. Psychiat. Inst. Found., 1974-80, Council Am. Ambassadors, 1985—; chmn. child devel. adv. bd. Child Devel. Assoc. Consortium; chmn. V.I. fund drive Boy Scouts Am., 1978-79. Served to lt. (j.g.), Supply Corps USNR, 1942-46. Recipient Distinguished Service award State of Israel Bonds, 1959, also Interfaith Movement award, 1961; Disting. Beverage Alcohol Wholesaler award Time mag., 1980; Grand Cross of Nat. Order of Honor and Merit Republic of Haiti, 1983 Mem. Young Pres.'s Orgn. (pres. Caribbean chpt. 1964-66), World Bus. Council, Chief Execs. Forum. Clubs: Mason. Home: Charlotte Amalie. Died Nov. 9, 2009.

KING, BRUCE, former Governor of New Mexico; b. Stanley, N.Mex., Apr. 6, 1924; s. William and Molly (Schooler) K.; m. Alice Marie Martin, June 1, 1947 (dec. Dec. 7, 2008); children: Bill, Gary. Student, U. N.Mex., 1943-44. Rancher, farmer, Stanley; mem. Santa Fe County Commn., 1955-58, chmn., 1957-58; mem. N.Mex. House of Reps., 1959-68, speaker, 1963-68; pres. N.Mex. Constl. Conv., 1969; gov. State of N.Mex., 1971—75, 1979—83, 1991—95. Co-owner King's Butane Co., Stanley. Mem. Gov.'s Task Force on Edn., 1968; mem. v.p. N.Mex. Soil and Water Conservation Commn.; mem. steering com. Edn. Commn. States, 1971; chmn. Four Corners Regional Commn., 1972, Nat. Oil and Gas Compact Commn., 1973; vice chmn. Western Gov.'s Conf., 1973, chmn., 1974; mem. nat. adv. com. Dem. Party; chmn. N.Mex. Dems., 1966; bd. dirs. Edgewood Soil Conversation Commn. With F.A., AUS, 1944-46, PTO. Mem.: Northern N.Mex. Fair Assn., Cattle Growers Assn., Farm & Livestock Bur. Democrat. Home: Stanley, N.Mex. Died Nov. 13, 2009.

KING, D. KENT, state official, school system administrator; b. Preston, Mo., 1943; m. Sandy King; 3 children. BA, Ctrl. Mo. State U., 1964; MA, Drury Coll., Springfield, 1967; PhD in Ednl. Adminstrn., Okla. State U., 1972. From tchr. to prin. Houston Sch. Dist., Tex. County, Mo., 1964—70; supt. Licking Sch. Dist., Mo., 1971—77, Rolla Sch. Dist., Mo., 1977—96; dir. Mo. Sch. Improvement Program, 1996—99; dep. commr. Mo. Dept. Edn., Jefferson City, Mo., 1999—2000, commr., 2000—09. Died Jan. 7, 2009.

KING, DAVID SJODAHL, Former United States Representative from Utah; b. Salt Lake City, June 20, 1917; m. Rosalie Lehner, 1948; 8 children Grad., U. Utah, 1937; JD, Georgetown U. Sch. Law, 1942. Law clk. to Hon. Harold Stephens, US Ct. Appeals (Dc cir.), 1943, counsel, US Tax Commn., 1944-46, prof. comml. law, Henager Bus. Coll., 1946-58, mem., US Congress, Utah, 1959-63 & 65-67; US amb. to Malagasy Republic, Madagascar, 1967-69, Mauritius, 1968-69. Member, bd. dirs., World Bank, 1979-81, Interfaith Conf. Washington DC Greater Area; pres., Mormon Mission, Haiti, 1986-89, Washington Mormon Temple, 1991-93. Author: Come to the House of the Lord, 2000. Democrat. Mem Lds Church. Died May 5, 2009.

KING, DONALD NEAL, psychologist; b. Puxico, Mo., Jan. 20, 1925; s. Dolph A. King and Thelma (Stanley) Voelker; m. Mabel E. Williamson, Dec. 30, 1955; children: Janice, Clare, Douglas, Candi. BSEd, Southeast Mo. State U., 1958; MSEd, U. Mo., 1961; EdD, Okla. State U., 1970. Lic. psychologist, S.D., sch. psychologist, S.D.; cert. counselor, S.D. Elem. tchr. Fagin Sch. Dist., Puxico, 1949-50; elem. tchr., prin. Oran (Mo.) Schs., 1955-57; tchr. high sch., counselor Perryville (Mo.) Schs., 1958-62; prof. psychology No. State U., Aberdeen, S.D., 1962-89; pvt. practice Aberdeen, from 1962; sch. psychologist Spl. Edn. Coop., Pierre, S.D., 1989-91. Cons. Luth. Social Svcs., Aberdeen, 1989—, Cath. Social Svcs., Aberdeen, 1987—, others. Author: King Pre-Retirement Checklist, 1984. Recipient award Nat. Def. Edn. Act Inst., 1962, 65, 67-68. Mem. Am. Assn. Counseling and Devel., Adult and Aging Devel. Assn., S.D. Counseling Devel. Soc., North Cen. Assn., S.D. Adult and Aging Assn., Am. Legion. Methodist. Avocations: reading, guitar repair, walking. Home: Leola, SD. Died Sept. 25, 2007.

KING, JAMES E., state legislator; b. Bklyn., Oct. 30, 1939; s. James King and Esther Emma (Williams); m. Linda Braddock; children: Monta Michelle, Laurie Anne. AA, St. Petersburg Jr. Coll., Fla., 1959; BA, BS, Fla. State U., 1961, MBA, 1962. Exec. v.p. Norrell-Southeastern Corp., 1966—70; owner King Temporary Staffing, Inc., Southeastern Resources, Inc., King Leasing Corp., Jim King Co.; real estate mgr., owner; mem. Dist. 17 Fla. House of Reps., Tallahassee, 1986—99; mem. Dist. 8 Fla. State Senate, Tallahassee, 1999—2009, majority leader, 2000—02, senate pres., 2002—04. Named Outstanding Bd. Mem. Fla. State U. Seminole Boosters, Inc., 1981, Most Outstanding Duval Legislator Jacksonville Jewish Fedn., Most Outstanding Caucus Mem. 1992; recipient Outstanding Bus. & Industry Legislature award, 1988, Outstanding Legislator award Fla. Bd. Realtors, Guardian of Bus. award Nat. Assn. Ind. Bus., Hospice Hall of Fame award, D.I. Rainey Legislature award Fla. Chiropractic Assn., Outstanding Leadership award Fraternal Order Police. Mem. Jacksonville C. of C. (task force chmn.), Multiple Sclerosis Soc. (mem. Fla. adv. bd.), Jacksonville Kingfish Assn. (mem. exec. bd.), Gator Bowl Assn. (mem. exec. bd., 1990), Fla. State U. Boosters (bd. dirs.), Univ. Club Jacksonville (bd. gov.), Jacksonville Marine Inst. (bd. dirs.). Republican. Episcopalian. Died July 26, 2009.

KING, LOWELL RESTELL, pediatric urologist; b. Salem, Ohio, Feb. 28, 1932; s. Lowell Waldo and Vesta Ethylwin (Snyder) K.; m. Mary Elizabeth Hill, July 9, 1960; children: Andrew Restell, Erika Lillie. BA, Johns Hopkins U., 1953, MD, 1956. Intern Johns Hopkins Hosp., Balt., 1956-57, resident in urology, 1957-62; asst. prof. urology Johns Hopkins U., 1962-63, Northwestern U., 1963-67, assoc. prof., 1967-70, prof., 1970-81, prof. urology and surgery, 1974-81; prof. urology and pediatrics Duke U., Durham, NC, 1981-97, prof. emeritus, 1997; prof. surgery/urology U. N.Mex., Albuquerque, from 1997. Prof., chmn. dept. urology Presbyn.-St. Luke's Hosp., 1968-70; surgeon-in-chief Children's Meml. Hosp., Chgo., 1974-80; examiner Am. Bd. Urology, 1968-94, trustee, 1975-81. Author: (with P.P. Kelalis) Clinical Pediatric Urology, 1976, (with A.B. Belman) 5th edit., 2007, Bladder Replacement and Continent Urology Diversion, 1986, 2d edit., 1991, Urologic Surgery in the Neonate and Young Infant, 1992, Reconstructive Urology, 1992, Urologic Surgery in Infants and Children, 1997, Office Guide to Pediatric Urology, 2002; cons. editor Urology; editor profl. jours.; contbr. articles to profl. jours. Vestryman, sr. warden Ch. of Our Savior, 1974-80; bd. dirs. Gads Hill Settlement House, 1969-73. Recipient Gold medal All India Urologic Congress, 1996, Gold medal Mex. Coll. Urology, 1991, Valentine medal N.Y. Acad. Medicine, 2002, Kretchmer medal Chgo. Urol. Soc. Mem. AMA, Am. Urol. Assn. (hon., career achievement award 1996, Merit award 2005), Am. Acad. Pediats. (chmn. sect. urology 1969-72, sec. 1975-76, pres. 1977-78, Urology medal 1992), Soc. Pediat. Urology (pres. 1983), Soc. Univ. Urologists, Am. Assn. Genitourinary Surgeons, Clin. Soc. Genitourinary Surgeons (pres. 1996). Episcopalian. Home: Albuquerque, N.Mex. Died Oct. 26, 2008.

KING, MARY LOU, artist, tchnologist; b. Vernon, Tex., Apr. 11, 1927; d. H. Raymond and Alma Vivian (Davenport) Hudson; m. Jack E. King, June 3, 1948 (dec. May 2002); children: Paul Hudson, Karen Anne, Julie Louise; m. Bert B. Thompson, July 11, 2003(dec. June 24, 2006) BS in Biology and Med. Tech., N. Tex. State U., 1948; AS in Art, Midland Coll., Tex., 1987. Bd. cert. med. technologist Am. Soc. Clin. Pathologists. Dept. head Santa Rosa Hosp., San Antonio, 1948-49; lab. dir. Drs. Offices, San Antonio, 1949-50; artist pvt. practice, Midland, 1986—98. One-woman shows include Silvers Gallery, Midland, Tex. State Capital Bldg., Austin, Gallery of the Woman's Club, Midland, Gallery Theatre Ctr., Midland; invitational shows in China, Norway and Japan; 20 commns.; featured in publs. including Artists of Texas, vol. II & IV, American Artists, Illustrated Survey of Leading Contemporary Watercolorists, Splash IV, The Splendor of Light, Contemporary Watercolorists, Keys to Painting Light and Shadow, 1999, Texas Watercolor Society: Fifty Years of Excellence, 1999, Watercolor (mag.), 1999, The Artist Sketch Book, 2001, Capturing Texture in Watercolors, 2002, Textuur Annbrengen, 2003. Bd. dirs. First United Meth. Ch., Midland, 1963-85, adult class leader and lay speaker, 1970—; Troop leader Girl Scouts U.S.A., Midland, 1958-75, officer, dir. coun., trainer, coord., 1968-80. Recipient Thanks award, Girl Scouts Am., 1975, Life Membership award, 1990, Woman of Distinction award, 2000. Mem. Tex. Water Color Soc. (signature mem. 1987, regional del. 1988-89, mem. Purple Sage Soc. 1995), West Tex. Watercolor Soc. (signature mem. 1995), So. Watercolor Soc. (signature mem. 1993, regional del. 1995—), Midland Arts Assn. (bd. dirs., officer 1983—), Arts Assembly of Midland (chmn. visual arts, mem. planning coun. 1983-86, Outstanding Svc. award 1985), Watercolor USA Hon. Soc. Avocations: travel, dance, poetry. Home: Midland, Tex. Died Oct. 6, 2007.

KING, RANDOLPH DAVID, publishing executive; b. Oak Park, Ill., Apr. 19, 1954; s. Perry Benjamin and Elaine Agnes (McManus) K.; m. Carrie Dawn Millar, Oct. 19, 1981; children: Kyle Randolph, Ryan David, Sean Charles. BS, S. Ill. U., 1976; MBA, Marshall U., 1977. Sales service mgr. Crain Communications, Chgo., 1977-78; mgr. new bus. Laven, Fuller & Perkins, Chgo., 1978-79; media dir., acct. supr. Fensholt, Chgo., 1979-81; mgr. midwest regional sales Cahners Publ., Des Plaines, Ill., from 1981, pub. Electronic Packaging & Production Mag.; pres. Marshall, Southern & York, Inc., Chgo., from 1985. Mem. Theta Zeta Alumni Assn. (pres. 1982-83). Avocations: Karate, target pistol. Home: Elmhurst, Ill. Died Feb. 5, 2008.

KING, THOMAS M., theology studies educator, priest; b. Pitts. s. William Martin and Catherine (Mulvihil) K. BA in Economics & Speech, U. Pitts., 1951; MA, Fordham U., 1959; Doctorat es Sci. Religeuse, U. Strasbourg, 1968. Joined Jesuits, 1951, ordained priest Roman Cath. Ch., 1964. Prof. Theology Georgetown U., Washington, 1968—2009. Author: Sartre and the Sacred, 1974, Teilhard's Mysticism of Knowing, 1981, Teilhard de Chardin, 1988, Enchantments, 1989, Merton: Mystic at the Center of America, 1992; editor: Teilhard and the Unity of Knowledge, 1983, Letters of Teilhard and Lucile Swan, 1993, Jung's Four and Some Philosophers, 1999, Teilhard's Mass, 2005. Co-founder, bd. dirs. Cosmos & Creation, Loyola Coll., Balt., 1982-2009, Univ. Faculty for Life, Washington, 1989-2009. Roman Catholic. Home: Washington, DC. Died June 23, 2009.

KINSBRUNER, JAY, history educator; b. NYC, Jan. 10, 1939; s. Mac and Florence (Reitman) K.; m. Karen Hillman, Mar. 14, 1972; children: Jennifer, Mieca. BA, Syracuse U., 1960; PhD, N.Y.U., 1964. Instr. Nassau County Coll., Garden City, N.Y., 1964-65; asst. to prof. Queens Coll. CUNY, Flushing, from 1965. Vis. scholar Inst. Caribbean Studies, Rio Piedras, P.R., 1984; mem. nat. screening com. for Fulbright Program, 1999—; vis. prof. history U. Miami, spring 2000. Author: Independence in Spanish America, 1994, 2d edit., 2000, Not of Pure Blood, 1996. Fulbright lectr. Fulbright Commn., Venezuela, 1967. Mem. Am. Hist. Assn., Conf. on Latin Am. History, L.Am. Studies Assn. Home: Miami Beach, Fla. Died Oct. 6, 2007.

KIRALY, BÈLA KÀLMÀN, retired history professor; b. Kaposvar, Hungary, Apr. 12, 1912; came to U.S., 1956; s. József and Lutz Etelka Kiraly; m. Sarolta Gömbös, Dec. 6, 1947 (div. Aug. 1955); adopted children: Ference, Miklos, Sarolta Szendrey. BA, Ludovika Mil. Acad., Budapest, Hungary, 1935; MA, Gen. Staff Acad., Budapest, 1942, Columbia U., 1958, PhD, 1962; D in Mil. Sci. (hon.), Zrinyi Miklo's Mil. Acad., Budapest, 1994; LHD (hon.), Bklyn. Coll., 1994. With Hungarian Army, 1930-56, advanced through grades to col. gen., 1948-51; imprisoned by communists, Budapest, 1951-56; mem.-in-exile Hungarian Com., NYC, 1957-66; from instr. to prof. history Bklyn. Coll., CUNY, 1962-82, prof. emeritus, 1982—2009; pres. Atlantic Rsch. & Publications Inc., Highland Lakes, NJ; col. gen. Hungarian Army, Budapest, from 1992; mem. Hungarian Parliament, Budapest, 1990-94. Author: Hungary in the Late 18th Century: The Decline of Enlightened Despotism, 1969, Ferenc Deak, 1975, The First War Between Socialist States, 1981, Basic History of Modern Hungary, 2001; editor-in-chief: Atlantic Studies on Society in Change, 105 books, Named Ky. col. State of Ky., 1960, Tchr. of Yr., Bklyn. Coll., 1964; recipient award of merit U.S. Mil. Acad., 1982, Righteous Among Nations award Yad Vashem, Jerusalem, 1993; fellow Columbia U. faculty seminar, 1975. Mem. Am. Hist. Assn., World Fedn. Hungarian Historians (co-pres. 1992). Democrat. Roman Catholic. Avocation: pigeon breeding. Died July 4, 2009.

KIRCHNER, LEON, composer, pianist, conductor; b. Bklyn., Jan. 24, 1919; s. Samuel and Pauline K.; m. Gertrude Schoenberg, July 8, 1949; children: Paul, Lisa. AB, U. Calif., Los Angeles and Berkeley, 1939-40; studies with Arnold Schoenberg, Ernest Bloch, Roger Sessions, Arnold Schoenberg. Mem. faculty San Francisco Conservatory, 1946-48, U. So. Calif., 1950-54; faculty, Luther B. Marchant prof. music Mills Coll., Oakland, Calif., 1954-61; Slee prof. U. Buffalo, 1958-59; prof. music Harvard U., 1961-66, Walter B. Rosen prof. music, from 1966. Vis. prof. UCLA, 1970-71; condr. Harvard Chamber Orch. and Friends, Phila. Symphony, St. Paul Chamber Orch., Buffalo Philharm., San Francisco Symphony, NY Philharm., Boston Symphony; participant, pianist, condr., composer Lincoln Ctr. Chamber Players, Marlboro Mus. Festival, Charleston and Spoleto Festivals, Santa Fe, Aspen, Tanglewood, Blue Hill, others; piano soloist Boston Symphony, NY Philharm., Sudwestfunk, Baden-Baden, Tonhalle, Switzerland. Composer Duo for violin and piano, 1947, Piano Sonata, 1948, Piano Suite 49, 1949, String Quartet No. 1 (NY Critics Circle award), Sinfonia, 1951, Sonata Concertante, 1952, Concerto No. 1 for piano and orch., 1953 (Naumberg award), Trio for Piano, Violin and Cello, 1954, Toccata for Strings, Solo Winds and Percussion, 1955, String Quartet 2, 1958 (NY Critics Circle award), Concerto for Violin, Cello, 10 Winds and Percussion, 1960, Concerto No. 2 for piano and orch., 1963, Fanfare for Brass Trio, 1965, Words from Wordsworth for chorus, 1966, String Quartet No. 3, 1966 (Pulitzer prize 1967), Music for Orch, 1969, Flutings for Paula, 1973, (opera) Lily, 1977, Music for Flute and Orch., 1978, (song cycle) The Twilight Stood, 1982, Music for Twelve, 1985, Music for Violin Solo, 1985, Fanfare II, 1985, For Cello Solo, 1986, Illuminations, 1986, 5 Pieces for Solo Piano, 1987, For Solo Violin, 1987, Two Duos for Violin and Cello, 1988, For Solo Violin II, 1988, Triptych for cello and violin, 1988, Interlude, 1989, Music for Orch. II, 1990, Music for cello and orch., 1992 (Pulitzer prize nominee, Friedheim award), Trio II for violin, cello and piano, For the Left Hand, 1995, Of Things Exactly As They Are, 1997, Duo No. 2 for violin and piano, 2002, Interlude II for piano, 2003, Piano Sonata No. 2, 2003, String Quartet No. 4, 2006; also recs. Recipient Prix de Paris, 1942, NY Music Critics award, 1950, 60, Naumburg award, Libr. of Congress, 1954, Nat Music award, 1976; Guggenheim fellow, 1948-50, Ctr. for the Advanced Studies in the Behavioral Scis. fellow, Stanford U., 1974-75, Am. Acad. in Rome resident fellow; commd. by Libr. of Congress, Paul Fromm Found., NY State Opera, Nat. Endowment for the Arts, others. Mem. ASCAP, AAAL (Gold Medal for Music, 2009), Internat. Soc. Contemporary Music, League Am. Composers, Nat. Inst. Arts and Letters, Am. Acad. Arts and Scis., AAUP. Home: Cambridge, Mass. Died Sept. 17, 2009; NYC.

KIRKE, JAMES DAVID, law educator, researcher; b. Ft. Wayne, Ind., Oct. 2, 1948; s. James Hayes and Betty Joan (Cowan) K.; children: David, Melissa, Nicole, Heather. BS, Ind. U., Bloomington, 1970; JD, Ind. U., Indpls., 1973. Bar: Ind. 1974, U.S. Dist. Ct. (no. and so. dists.) Ind. 1974. Assoc. Higgins & Swift, Ft. Wayne, 1974-75; ptnr. Grimm & Kirke, Ft. Wayne, 1980-82, Payne & Kirke, Ft. Wayne, 1982-84; assoc. instr. paralegal studies program Ivy Tech. State Coll., Ft. Wayne, 1995-97; assoc. prof. paralegal studies program El Centro Coll., Dallas, from 1997. Student govt. advisor Ind.-Purdue U., Ft. Wayne, 1978-80; hearing officer Ft. Wayne Met. Human Rels. Commn., 1978-80. Democrat. Lutheran. Avocations: water-skiing, sailing, scuba diving, photography. Home: Dallas, Tex. Died Feb. 4, 2008.

KIRKPATRICK, JAMES JOSEPH, psychologist; b. Washington, Aug. 3, 1922; s. Luther James and Helen Jordan Kirkpatrick; m. Shirley Ann Mathews, Dec. 31, 1965; children: Martha M., Alan, Lori, James. AB in Psychology, U. Tenn., 1948, MA in Psychology, 1949; PhD in Psychology, Syracuse U., 1953. Diplomate Indsl. Psychology, Am. Bd. Examiners in Profl. Psychology. Project dir. Am. Inst. Rsch., Pitts., 1952—54; v.p. Harless & Kirkpatrick, Assocs., Tampa, Fla., 1954—65; assoc. prof. NYU, NYC, 1965—67; prof. Calif. State U., Long Beach, 1967—87, prof. emeritus from 1987. Expert witness on equal employment opportunity issues, 1967—2001; cons. U. Chgo. IRC, 1975—81. Contbg. author: Readings Psych Tests and Measures, 1964, sr. author: Testing and Fair Employment, 1968, contbg. author: Comparative Studies of Blacks and Whites, 1973. Pilot USAF, WW II. Named Boss of Yr., Am. Bus. Women's Assn., 1962. Fellow: APA (chair ethics); mem.: Fla. Psychology Assn. (pres. elect 1965), Kiwanis. Democrat. Baptist. Avocations: photography, tennis. Home: Los Alamitos, Calif. Died Jan. 19, 2008.

KIRSCHSTEIN, RUTH LILLIAN, federal agency administrator, retired physician; b. Bklyn., Oct. 12, 1926; d. Julius and Elizabeth (Berm) Kirschstein; m. Alan S. Rabson, June 11, 1950; 1 child, Arnold. BA magna cum laude, LI U., 1947; MD, Tulane U. Sch. Medicine, New Orleans, 1951; PhD, LLD, Tulane U., 1997; DSc (hon.), Mt. Sinai Sch. Medicine, 1984; LLD (hon.), Atlanta U., 1985; DSc (hon.), Med. Coll. Ohio, 1986; LHD (hon.), LI U., 1991; PhD (hon.), U. Rochester Sch. Medicine, 1998, Brown U., 1999; DSc (hon.), Spelman Coll., 2001, Georgetown U., 2001. Cert. Anatomic Pathology & Clinical Pathology. Intern Kings County Hosp., Bklyn., 1951-52; resident pathology VA Hosp., Atlanta, 1952, Providence Hosp., Detroit, 1952—54, NIH Clin. Ctr., Bethesda, Md., 1956; experimental pathology rschr., divsn. biologics standards NIH, 1957—72, chief Lab. Pathology, 1961—74, asst. dir., divsn. biologics standards, 1972, dep. dir. FDA bur., 1972—74, dir. Nat. Inst. Gen. Med. Scis., 1974-93, acting assoc. dir., Office Rsch. on Women's Health, acting dir. NIH, 1993, 2000—02, dep. dir., 1993—99, sr. advisor to dir., 2003—06, acting dir. Nat. Ctr. Complementary & Alternative Medicine (NCCAM), 2007—09. Fellow Nat. Heart Inst., Tulane U., 1953—54; mem. Inst. Medicine NAS, from 1982; mem. rsch. adv. com. Office Tech. Assessment, from 1989; co-chair PHS Coordinating Com. on Women's Health Issues, from 1990. Recipient Superior Svc. award, HEW, 1971, USPHS, 1978, Presdl. Meritorious Exec. Rank award, 1980, Spl. Recognition award, 1985, Presdl. Disting. Exec. Rank award, 1985, Pub. Svc. award, Fedn. Am. Soc. Exptl. Biology, 1993, Nat. Pub. Svc. award, Am. Pub. Adminstrn./Nat. Acad. Pub. Adminstrn., 1994, Roger W. Jones award for exec. leadership, Am. U., 1994, Georgeanna Seegar Jones Women's Health Lifetime Achievement award, 1995, Albert Sabin Hero of Sci. award, 2000, Women Achievement award, Jewish Anti-Defamation League, 2001, J. Richard Nesson award, Harvard Med. Sch., 2002, Pub. Svc. award, Am. Soc. Biochemistry & Molecular Biology, 2003. Fellow: Am. Acad. Arts & Scis.; mem.: AMA (Dr. Nathan Davis award 1990), Am. Acad. Microbiology, Am. Assn. Pathologists, Am. Assn. Immunologists. Achievements include appointment as 1st woman director of an NIH institute-the National Institute of General Medical Sciences in 1974. Home: Bethesda, Md. Died Oct. 6, 2009.

KIRWAN, KATHARYN GRACE (MRS. GERALD BOURKE KIRWAN JR.), retired small business owner; b. Monroe, Wash., Dec. 1, 1913; d. Walter Samuel and Bertha Ella (Shrum) Camp; m. Gerald Bourke Kirwan Jr., Jan. 13, 1945. Student, U. Puget Sound, 1933—34; BA, BS, Tex. Woman's U., 1937; postgrad., U. Wash., 1941. Libr. Brady (Tex.) Sr. High Sch., 1937-38, McCamey (Tex.) Sr. High Sch., 1938-43; mgr. Milady's Frock Shop, Monroe, 1946-62, owner, mgr., 1962-93. Mem. Monroe Breast Cancer Screening Project cmty. planning group Fred Hutchinson Cancer Rsch. Ctrs., 1991-93; meml. chmn. Monroe chpt. Am. Cancer Soc., 1961-93; co-chair hon. com. YMCA Pool program, 2005-; mcm. Snohomish County Police Svcs. Action Coun., 1971; mem. Monroe Pub. Libr. Bd., 1950-65, pres. bd., 1964-65; mem. Monroe City Coun., 1969-73; mayor City of Monroe, 1974-81; commr. Snohomish County Hosp. dist. 1, 1970-90, chmn. bd. commrs., 1980-90; mem. East Snohomish County Health Planning Com., 1979-81; mem. Snohomish County Law and Justice Planning Com., 1974-78, Snohomish County Econ. Devel. Coun., 1975-81, Snohomish County Pub. Utility Dist. Citizens Adv. Task Force, 1983; sr. warden Ch. of Our Saviour, Monroe, 1976-77, 89, sr. warden, 1976-77, 89-90; co-chair hon. com. pool program YMCA, 2005. With USNR, 1943-46. Recipient Malstrom award for Hist.

Homes and Bldgs. of Monroe, 2000, award of project excellence Washington Mus. Assn., 2000, Pres.'s Call to Svc. award, 2006, Pres.'s Coun. on Svc. and Civic Participation award, 2006, U.S. Pres.'s Vol. Svc. award, 2006. Mem. AAUW, U.S. Naval Inst., Ret. Officers Assn., Naval Res. Assn., Bus. and Profl. Women's Club (2d v.p. 1980-82, pres. 1983-84), Washington Gens., Snohomish County Pharm. Aux., C. of C. (pres. 1972), Valley Gen. Hosp. Guild (pres. 1994, 95, 96), Valley Gen. Hosp. Found. (sec. 1993-97). Episcopalian. Home: Sultan, Wash. Died July 16, 2008.

KISSINGER, WARREN STAUFFER, minister; b. Akron, Pa., Sept. 8, 1922; s. Howard Elmer and Anna Adams (Stauffer) K.; m. Jean Thelma Young, Sept. 1, 1951; children: John Howard (dec. 2008), David Charles, Ann Constance, Adele Marya. AB, Elizabethtown Coll., 1950; BD, Yale Divinity Sch., 1953; MST, Luth. Theol. Sem., Gettysburg, Pa., 1964; MLS, Drexel U., 1968. Ordained, Ch. of the Brethren, 1947. Pastor Windber Ch. of Brethren, Pa., 1953-57, Carlisle Ch. of Brethren, Pa., 1957-60; asst. prof. religion, philosophy Juniata Coll., Huntingdon, Pa., 1960-64, Drexel Hill Ch. of Brethren, 1964-70; subject cataloger religion Libr. Congress, Washington, 1968—93. Author: The Sermon the Mount, 1975, the Parables of Jesus, 1979, The Buggies Still Run, 1983, The Lives of Jesus, 1985; editor: Brethren Life and Thought, 1981-90. Mem. Am. Theol. Libr. Assn. Democrat. Home: Hyattsville, Md. Died Dec. 14, 2008.

KISTLER, HERBERT DONALD, lawyer; b. Butte, Mont., Mar. 15, 1908; s. Herbert Daniel and Katherine Celeste (Helferstine) K.; m. Margaret Phyllis Belangie, June 6, 1935 (dec. 1952); children: Margaret Frances, Herbert Daniel; m. Melva Florence Ruehlmann, Oct. 30, 1965. BA, Princeton U., NJ, 1930; LLB, Stanford U., Calif., 1934. Assoc. Law Offices J. Bruce Kremer, Washington, 1934-40, Kremer & Bingham, Washington, 1940-46; ptnr. Bingham, Collins, Porter & Kistler, Washington, 1946-60, Collins, Robb, Porter & Kistler, Washington, 1960-64, Robb, Porter, Kistler & Parkinson, Washington, 1964-69, Jackson, Gray & Laskey, Washington, 1969-76; assoc. Jackson, Campbell & Parkinson, Washington, 1976-80, of counsel, 1980-83, Jackson & Campbell, P.C., Washington, 1983-90, ret., 1990. Mem. bd. mgrs. Chevy Chase (Md.) Village, 1958-72, chmn. bd. mgrs., 1969-72. Fellow Am. Coll. Trust and Estate Counsel; mem. ABA, Calif. Bar Assn., D.C. Bar Assn., Barristers (pres. Washington chpt. 1953-54), Bar Supreme Ct. U.S., Met. Washington Bd. Trade (chmn. law and legis. com. Washington chpt. 1957-60), Lawyers Club of Washington (bd. govs. 1972-74), Univ. Club, Chevy Chase Club, Rotary (bd. dirs. Washington chpt. 1971-74), Delta Theta Phi. FEllow Am. Coll. Probate Counsel; mem. ABA, Calif. Bar Assn., D.C. Bar Assn., Barristers (pres. Washington chpt. 1953-54), Bar Supreme Ct. U.S., Met. Washington Bd. Trade (chmn. law and legis. com. Washington chpt. 1957-60), Lawyers Club Washington (bd. of govs. Washington chpt. 1972-74), Univ., Chevy Chase, Rotary (bd. dirs. Washington chpt. 1971-74), Delta Theta Phi. Republican. Episcopalian. Home: Bethesda, Md. Died Dec. 29, 2008.

KITT, EARTHA MAE, actress, singer; b. St. Matthews, SC, Jan. 17, 1927; d. John and Anna K.; m. William McDonald, June 1960 (div. 1965); 1 child, Kitt Shapiro. Grad. high sch. Soloist with Katherine Dunham Dance Group, 1948; night club singer, 1949—, appearing in France, Turkey, Greece, Egypt, N.Y.C., Hollywood, Las Vegas, London, Stockholm; actress: (plays) Dr. Faustus, Paris, 1951, New Faces of 1952, N.Y.C., Mrs. Patterson, N.Y.C., 1954, Shinbone Alley, N.Y.C., 1957, Timbuktu, 1978, Blues in the Night, 1985, Mimi Le Duck, 2006; (films) New Faces, 1953, Accused, 1957, Anna Lucasta, 1958, Mark of the Hawk, 1958, St. Louis Blues, 1957, Saint of Devil's Island, 1961, Synanon, 1965, Up The Chastity Belt, 1971, Dragonard, Ernest Scared Stupid, 1991, Boomerang, 1992, Fatal Instinct, 1993, Harriet the Spy, 1996, Ill Gotten Gains (voice), 1997, (TV movies) The Wild Thornberrys (voice), 1998, The Emperor's New Grove (voice), 2000, Feast of All Saints, 2001, Santa Baby!, 2001, Standard Time, 2002, Holes, 2003; (TV series) Batman, 1967-68; (broadway shows) The Wizard of Oz, 1998, The Wild Party, 2000 (Tony nominee), Rodgers & Hammerstein's Cinderella, 2001; (documentary appearances) All By Myself, 1982; albums include That Bad Eartha, 1953, Down to Eartha, 1955, Thursday's Child, 1956, St. Louis Blues, 1958, The Fabulous Eartha Kitt, Eartha Kitt Revisited, 1960, Bad But Beautiful, 1962, My Way: A Musical Tribute to Rev. Dr. Martin Luther King Jr., 1987, Best of Eartha Kitt, 1983, Thinking Jazz, 1991, Miss Kitt, To You, 1992, Back in Business, 1994, Sentimental Eartha, 1995, Standard/Live, 1998, The Best of Eartha Kitt: Where Is My Man, 1998, Lovin' Spree, 2005, She's So Good, 2006; author: Thursday's Child, 1956, A Tart Is Not a Sweet, Alone With Me, 1976, I'm Still Here: Confessions of a Sex Kitten, 1991; co-author: Down to Eartha, 2000, How to Rejuvenate: It's Not Too Late, 2000 Recipient Nightlife Legend award, 2006; named Woman of Yr. Nat. Assn. Negro Musicians, 1968; nominated 2 Grammys, 2 Tony awards, 1 Emmy. Died Dec. 25, 2008.

KITT, EUGENE CLARK, organization administrator, poet, songwriter; b. NYC, Aug. 11, 1950; s. William and Jessie (Felder) K. BS in Edn., CCNY, 1975; MS in Urban Edn., Fordham U., 1977; MS in Non-Profit Mgmt., New Sch. Social Rsch., 1991; LHD, Ea. North Theol. Inst., 1997. Guidance counselor Madison Sq. Boys & Girls Club,

1973-78; exec. dir. Co-op City's Youth Activities Com., 1978-80; assoc. dir. Upward, Inc., NYC, 1980-87, exec. dir., from 1987, cons., from 1996; sr. program mgr. NYC Housing Authority. Author: Profiles of Excellence - Achieving Excellence in the Non-Profit Sector, 1991, Poetry to Live By, 1999. Named Community Leader of Yr. Salem Bapt. Ch., 1990, Proclamation N.Y. State Senate, 1996; named to Internat. Poetry Hall of Fame, 1998; holder Guinness World Record for most songs written in a year, 2001. Mem. Am. Mgmt. Assn. Democrat. Baptist. Avocations: fishing, photography, songwriting. Home: Elmont, NY. Died July 8, 2008.

KLAGES, JOHN WILLIAM, automotive parts company executive; b. Columbus, Ohio, July 11, 1922; s. Reynold E. and Corinne M. (Krag) Klages; m. Helen Virginia Booze, Feb. 14, 1948 (dec. 1993); children: Ellen J., Mary K., Sarah M. AB, Harvard U.; MBA, Capital U. Mgmt. trainee The Columbus (Ohio) Auto Parts Co., 1948-53, asst. plant supt., 1953-62, exec. v.p., 1962-71, pres., CEO, 1971-87, ret., 1987. Author: History of Zanesfield Rod and Gun Club, 1989, The Covered Bridges of Fairfield County, Ohio, 1996. Bd. dirs., treas. United Way of Franklin Co., Columbus, 1976-82, Vols. of Am., Inc., New Orleans, 1984-97; bd. dirs., chmn. Vols. of Am. So. Ohio, 1958—; bd. dirs. Crittenton Family Svcs., Columbus, 1965-72, 84-91, emeritus bd. mem., 1991—. With U.S. Army, 1942-45. Named Boss of Yr. Worthington Jaycees, 1973, Exec. of Yr. Nat. Secs. Assn., 1977; recipient Award for Vol. Svcs. Mayor's Office, 1978, George Meany award AFL-CIO, 1986. Mem. Columbus Country Club, Zanesfield Rod and Gun Club (treas., pres., trustee). Avocations: watercolor painting, fishing, travel. Home: Columbus, Ohio. Died Apr. 8, 2008.

KLAYMAN, JOSEPH JASON, electrical engineer; b. Boston, July 11, 1925; s. Louis and Sarah (Broder) K.; m. Dina Souchot, Mar. 2, 1952; children: Valerie Sharon, Karen Lee. BSEE, Northeastern U., 1946. Engr. Research Assocs. Inc., Woodland Hills, Calif. Mem. IEEE. Clubs: Dorchester-Roxbury Mattapan, (Los Angeles) (treas. 1981—). Republican. Jewish. Home: Woodland Hls, Calif. Died July 5, 2008.

KLEIN, DALE MATHEW, civil engineer; b. Alton, Iowa, Oct. 12, 1934; s. Mathew Frank and Margaret (Streff) K.; m. Joan Carolyn Graves, Oct. 28, 1956; children: Kathryn, Mathew, Valerie, Michael. AA, Mesa Coll., 1954; BSCE, Colo. State U., 1956; MSE, U. Mich., 1966. Commd. ensign USN, 1956, advance through grades to comdr., 1969, ret., 1979; phys. plant dir. Claremont (Calif.) Colls., from 1979. Arbitrator Am. Arbitration Assn., 1987—; cons. in field, 1987—; dir. San Antonio Gardens, Claremont, 1991—. Mem. Am. Energy Engrs., Assn. Profl. Engrs., Am. Soc. Plant Engrs., Pacific Coast Assn. Phys. Plant Adminstrs. (pres. 1990-91), Assn. Phys. Plant Adminstrs. (pres. 1991—), Rotary (dir. 1988-91). Republican. Roman Catholic. Home: Laguna Beach, Calif. Died Sept. 15, 2007.

KLEIN, HEINZ KARL, information systems researcher; b. Germany, Nov. 25, 1939; arrived in U.S., 1984; s. Karl K. and Waltraud Franzl; m. Nora E., 1972 (div. 1986); children: Charlotte, Thomas, Ellen; m. Linda F., 2002. Dipl.-Kfm., U. Munich, Germany, 1965, Dr.rer.publ., 1969; Dr.h.c., Oulu U., Finland, 1998. Rsch. assoc. Econ. Rsch. Inst., Munich, Germany, 1965-66; faculty asst. U. Regensburg, Germany, 1967-69; asst. rschr. U. Mannheim, Germany, 1969-70, rsch. assoc., 1970-77; asst. prof. mgmt. sci. McMaster U., Hamilton, Ont., Can., 1978-83; assoc. prof. SUNY, Binghamtom, 1984-2000, Temple U., Phila., from 2001. Vis. assoc. prof. SUNY, Buffalo, 1972-73, McMaster U., 1973-74; prof. invité U. Nautes, 2003. Author: Heuristic Decision Models, 1971, Business Logistics Systems, 1973, Information Systems Development for Human Progress, 1989, Information Systems Research: Contemporary Approaches and Emergent Traditions, 1991, Information Systems Development and Data Modeling: Conceptual and Philosophical Foundations, 1995, Signs of Work, Semiosis and Information Processing Organisations, 1996; contbr. articles to scholarly jours. (MISQ Best Paper award 1999). Vis. scholar, London Sch. Econs., 1982, U. Jyäskylä, 1985, 1989, U. Aalborg, 1990, Auckland U., 1994, U. Pretoria, 1995, 2002. Avocations: sailing, skiing, tennis, travel. Home: Binghamton, NY. Died June 18, 2008.

KLEIN, HERBERT GEORGE, newspaper editor; b. LA, Apr. 1, 1918; s. George and Amy (Cordes) K.; m. Marjorie Galbraith, Nov. 1, 1941 (dec. 2008); children: Joanne L. (Mrs. Robert Mayne) (dec. 2008), Patricia A. (Mrs. John Root). AB, U. So. Calif., 1940; PhD (hon.), U. San Diego, 1989, U. So. Calif., 2006. Reporter Alhambra (Calif.) Post-Advocate, 1940-42, news editor, 1946-50; spl. corr. Copley Newspapers, 1946-50, Washington corr., 1950; with San Diego Union, 1950-68, editl. writer, 1950-52, editl. page editor, 1952-56, assoc. editor, 1956-57, exec. editor, 1957-58, editor, 1959-68; mgr. comm. Nixon for Pres. Campaign, 1968-69; dir. comm. The White House, 1969-73; v.p. corp. rels. Metromedia, Inc., 1973-77; media cons., 1977-80; editor-in-chief, v.p. Copley Newspapers, Inc., San Diego, 1980—2003; nat. fellow Am. Enterprise Inst., 2004—09; cons. Copley Newspapers, Inc., San Diego, 2004—09. Publicity dir. Eisenhower-Nixon campaign in Calif., 1952; asst. press. sec. V.P. Nixon campaign, 1956; press sec. Nixon campaign, 1958; spl. asst., press sec. to Nixon, 1959-61; press sec. Nixon Gov. campaign, 1962; dir. comm. Nixon presdl. campaign, 1968; mem. Advt. Coun., N.Y. Author: Making It Perfectly Clear: An INside Account of Nixon's Love Hate Relationship With the Media, 1980.

Trustee U. So. Calif.; past chmn. Holiday Bowl; bd. dirs. Greater San Diego Internat. Sports Coun.; mem. com. Super Bowls XXII, XXIII, and XXXVII; active Olympic Tng. Site Com.; trustee U. So. Calif.; trustee U. Calif. San Diego Found; bd. dirs. San Diego Econ. Devel. Com. With USNR, 1942-46; comdr. Res. Recipient Fourth Estate award U. So. Calif., 1947, Alumnus of Yr. award U. So. Calif., 1971, Gen. Alumni Merit award, 1977, Spl. Svc. to Journalism award, 1969, Headliner of Yr. award L.A. Press Club, 1971, San Diego State U. First Fourth Estate award, 1986, Golden Man award Boys and Girls Club, 1994, Newspaper Exec. of Yr. award Calif. Press Assn., 1994; named Cmty. Champion, Hall of Champions, 1993, Mr. San Diego, 2001. Fellow Am. Enterprise Inst.; mem. Am. Soc. Newspaper Editors (past dir.), Calif. Press Assn., Pub. Rels. Seminar, Gen. Alumni U. So. Calif. (past pres.), Alhambra Jr. C. of C. (past pres.), Greater San Diego C. of C. (mem. exec. com.), Kiwanis, Rotary (hon.), Sigma Delta Chi (chmn. nat. com., chmn. gen. activities nat. conv. 1958), Scripps Inst. (dir.'s cabinet Oceanography), Delta Chi. Presbyterian. Home: San Diego, Calif. Died July 2, 2009.

KLEIN, MARTIN JESSE, physicist, science historian, educator; b. NYC, June 25, 1924; s. Adolph and Mary (Neuman) K.; m. Miriam June Levin, Oct. 28, 1945 (div. 1973); children: Rona F., Sarah M. Klein Zaino, Nancy R. Klein; m. Linda L. Booz, Oct. 8, 1980 (div. 2005); 1 child, Abigail M.; m. Joan Warnow-Blewett, July 9, 2005 (dec. 2006). AB, Columbia U., 1942, MA, 1944; PhD, MIT, 1948. With OSRD for USN, 1944-45; research assoc. in physics MIT, Cambridge, 1946-49; instr. physics Case Inst. Tech., Cleve., 1949-51, asst. prof., 1951-55, assoc. prof., 1955-60, prof., 1960-67, acting dept. head, 1966-67; prof. history physics Yale U., New Haven, 1967-74, Eugene Higgins prof. history physics and prof. physics, 1974-91, 95-99, Bass prof. history sci., prof. physics, 1991-95, chmn. dept. history sci., 1971-74, William Clyde De Vane prof., 1978-81, prof. emeritus, 1999—2009. Van der Waals guest prof. U. Amsterdam, 1974, Pieter Zeeman guest prof., 1993; vis. prof. Harvard U., 1989-90, Rockefeller U., 1975, adj. prof. 1976-79. Author: Paul Ehrenfest, Vol. I: The Making of a Theoretical Physicist, 1970; editor: Collected Scientific Papers of Paul Ehrenfest, 1959; sr. editor The Collected Papers of Albert Einstein, 1988-97; editorial adviser Ency. Brit, 1956-76; translator: Letters on Wave Mechanics, 1967; contbr. articles to profl. jours. NRC fellow Dublin (Ireland) Inst. Advanced Studies, 1952-53; Guggenheim fellow Leyden, Netherlands, 1958-59; Guggenheim fellow Yale, 1967-68; recipient Abraham Pais Prize, 2005 Fellow Am. Acad. Arts and Scis., Am. Phys. Soc.; mem. NAS, AAUP, History of Sci. Soc., Am. Assn. Physics Tchrs., Internat. Acad. History of Sci., Phi Beta Kappa, Sigma Xi. Home: Chapel Hill, NC. Died Mar. 28, 2009.

KLEIN, REGI See CHARVAT, REGINA

KLEIN, SOPHIA H., entrepreneur; b. Dayton, Ohio, Aug. 17, 1915; d. Felix Frank Borkowski, Helen Marie Sichujainska; children: Helen Marie, Betty Jean. Owner Oak Hill Optical, Dayton, Town & Country Water Softener, Dayton, Klein Enterprises, Dayton, Country Squire Supper Club, Dayton, Bagel Connection, Dayton, Exquisitely Yours Jewelers, Dayton. Initiator rosary ministry various chs. worldwide; program creator Radio Rosary Hour Sta. WGXM-FM; promoter Pope John Paul II Cultural Ctr., Washington, 2000. Mem.: Dayton Cath. Bus. Women's Club (pres., Dayton Woman of Yr. 1988), Holy Seplecher (Lady of the Cross from 1987, U.S. Rep. Millennium visit to Vatican 2000). Democrat. Roman Catholic. Avocation: golf. Home: Cincinnati, Ohio. Deceased.

KLEINER, HENRY EDWARD, JR., printing and publishing company executive; b. Ashland, Ky., Jan. 15, 1928; s. Henry Edward and Alyce Marguerite (Wilson) K.; m. Virginia May Rosenbaum, July, 3, 1954; children: Kendra Lee Kleiner McKee, Lisa Kay. Student, U. Louisville, 1945-47; Columbia Tech. Sch., 1949-50. Assoc. art dir. Mechanization, Inc., Washington, 1954-63; prodn. mgr. AIA, Washington, 1963-65, bus. mgr. jour., 1965-70; v.p. Bus. Pubs, Silver Spring, Md., 1970-80, also bd. dirs.; pres. Newsletter Press, Inc., Silver Spring, from 1980, also bd. dirs.; ptnr. Tri-State Leasing Assn., Silver Spring, from 1978. Pub. Government Training News and Consumer Credit Letter. Vestryman St. John's Episcopal Ch., McLean, Va., 1981-84. Served to 1st lt. Mil. Police, U.S. Army, 1950-52. Mem. Nat. Assn. Quick Printers, Nat. Newsletter Assn., Am. Legion (vice comdr. 1975-76), Lions (bd. dirs. 1987—). Republican. Avocation: coin collecting/numismatics. Home: Vienna, Va. Died Feb. 3, 2008.

KLEIS, JOHN DIEFFENBACH, physics consultant; b. Hamburg, NY, Feb. 1, 1912; s. Herbert and May Genevieve (Dieffenbach) K.; m. Marie Elizabeth Dahl, May 30, 1939; children: Lynne Marie, Cheryl Ann, John Dieffenbach. BA in Physics, U. Buffalo, 1932, MA in Physics, 1933; PhD in Physics, Yale U., 1936; Cert., Harvard U., 1957. Physicist Fan Steel Met. Corp., North Chgo., 1936-42, asst. dir. rsch., 1942-46, dir. rsch., 1946-52, v.p. rsch., 1952-58, v.p. mfg., 1958-69, dir., 1964-69; pres., v.p. Stern Metals, Mt. Vernon, N.Y., 1969-79, dir. rsch., 1979-82; cons. J.D. Kleis Assoc., Inc., Greenwich, Conn., from 1982. Pres. John D. Kleis & Assocs., Inc., 1983—. Patentee in field. Recipient Ralph Armington Achievement award IEEE, 1991. Mem. IEEE (life, steering com. 1982-93). Republican. Avocations: golf, tennis, cards. Home: Bunnell, Fla. Died Oct. 26, 2007.

KLEMA, ERNEST DONALD, nuclear physicist, educator; b. Wilson, Kan., Oct. 4, 1920; s. William W. and Mary Bess (Vopat) K.; m. Virginia Clyde Carlock, May 23, 1953; children: Donald David, Catherine Marion. AB in Chemistry, U. Kans., 1941, MA in Physics, 1942; postgrad., Princeton U., 1942, U. Ill., 1946-49; PhD in Physics, Rice U., 1951. Staff scientist Los Alamos Sci. Lab., 1943-46; sr. physicist Oak Ridge Nat. Lab., 1950-56, prin. physicist, 1958; assoc. prof. nuclear engring. U. Mich., 1956-58; prof. nuclear engring. Northwestern U., 1959-68, chmn. dept. engring. scis., 1960-66; prof. engring. sci. Tufts U., 1968-86, dean Coll. Engring., 1968-73, adj. prof. internat. politics Fletcher Sch. Law and Diplomacy, 1973-83, dean emeritus, prof. emeritus Coll. of Engring., from 1987. Vis. scholar physics Harvard U., 1985-86; chmn. subcom. on neutron standards and measurements NRC, 1958-62; del. Internat. Atomic Energy Agy. symposium neutron detection, dosimetry and standardiazation, Harwell, Eng., 1962; cons. Oak Ridge Nat. Lab., Argonne Nat. Lab. Author articles fission cross-sects., gamma-gamma angular correlations, empirical nuclear models, thermal neutron measurements, semiconductor radiation detectors.;patentee purification hydrogen-argon mixtures. Fellow Am. Phys. Soc., Am Nuclear Soc.; mem. IEEE (sr.), Phi Beta Kappa, Sigma Xi, Pi Mu Epsilon, Alpha Chi Sigma. Clubs: Harbor (Seal Harbor, Me.). Home: Bar Harbor, Maine. Died Oct. 14, 2008.

KLENICKI, LEON, rabbi; b. Buenos Aires, Sept. 7, 1930; came to U.S., 1959; s. Isaias and Inda (Kuzewika) K.; m. Ana Raquel Klenicki, Aug. 1959 (div. 1983); m. Myra Cohen, Nov. 30, 1985; children: Ruth Sharon, Daniel Raphael. BA in Philosophy, U. Cin., 1963; BA in Rabbinics, Hebrew Union Coll., Cin., 1964; MA in Hebrew Letters, Hebrew Union Coll., 1967. Ordained rabbi, 1967. Dir. World Union for Progressive Judaism, Argentina, 1968-73; dir. Jewish-Catholic affairs Anti-Defamation League of B'nai B'rith, NYC, 1973—84, dir. interfaith affairs, 1984—2001. Prof. Jewish theology, Immaculate Conception Sem., Seton Hall U., N.J.; v.p. Stimulus Found., 1985. Author: Passover Celebration; editor: In Our Time: The Flowering of Jewish-Catholic Dialogue, A Dictionary of the Jewish-Christian Dialogue; contbr. to religious publs. Named a Papal Knight of the Order of St. Gregory the Great, The Vatican, 2007. Home: New York, NY. Died Jan. 25, 2009.

KLEVIT, ALAN BARRE, art director, publishing executive, foundation administrator; b. Balt., June 25, 1935; s. Robert and Minnie (Goodman) K.; m. Marilyn Rosenthal, Nov. 26, 1955; children: Mindy Faith, Lawrence Michael, Richard Steven. BS in Econs., Georgetown U., 1956, MA in Econs., 1960; MA in Pub. Adminstrn. and Urban Affairs, Am. U., 1970. Asst. mgr. AS Beck Shoe Co., Washington, 1956-57; stat., economist Commerce Dept., Washington, 1957-60; securities analyst, rsch. dir. T.J. McDonald & Co., Washington, 1960-62; mgmt. analyst, div. chief Fed. Aviation Adminstrn., Washington, 1962-73; CEO Art Fair, Inc., Silver Spring, Md., 1974-90; founder, dir. Klevit Fine Art, Internat., Silver Spring and Malibu, Calif., from 1987; founder, exec. officer Robert Klevit Found. for Humanitarianism, Silver Spring and Malibu, Calif., from 1987; dir. Stardust Pub., Malibu, from 1990; co-founder, dir. Charity Editions, Silver Spring and Malibu, 1987. Mem. faculty Mgmt. by Objectives Fed. Exec. Sch., Charlottesville, Va., 1969-71; motivational speaker, Malibu, 1988—; guest spkr. on fine art, 1996—. Author: Three Days in Sedona, 1990, How to Make Your Dreams Come True, 1991, Follow the Rainbow, 1991, (book and audiocassette) Pass the Pickles, Please and Other Stories, 1995, The Art Beat, 2003; (video) Journey Within, 1993; host radio show: Today's Art World with Alan Klevit, 1983-84, (TV show) Off the Beaten Path with Alan Klevit, 1992-2000, (TV show) The Art Beat, 1998-2002; syndicated columnnist The Art Beat, 1996—; contbr. articles to mags. and newspapers including regular contbns. to Malibu Mag.; writer, prodr., featured performer tv commls., 1994—. Bd. dirs. Summer Opera, Washington, 1987—, Marine & Mountain Wildlife Rescue, Malibu, 1991—; mem. Hammer Mus., LA County Mus. Mem. Inst. for Econometric Rsch., World Wildlife Fedn., Inst. for Noetic Scis., Planetary Soc., Malibu C. of C., Masons. Avocations: charity art auctioneer, theater, classical music, travel, gourmet cooking. Home: Thorndale, Pa. Died July 7, 2007.

KLICKA, MARY V., dietitian, consultant; b. Winnepeg, Manitoba, Canada, Apr. 30, 1921; Came to the U.S., 1923; d. William Henry and Clara Myrtle (Ferguson) Richardson; m. William John Klicka, Sept. 20, 1946 (div. Oct. 1953); 1 child, William John Klicka. Intern Michael Reese Hosp., Chgo., 1945; dietitian Rsch. & Ednl. Hosp. U. Ill., Chgo., 1945-47; dietitian Quality Control Group Western Electric Co., Cicero, 1947-51; cons. dietitian Shriners Children's Hosp., Chgo., 1950-51; nutritionist Quartermaster Food & Container Inst., Chgo., 1951-63, U.S. Army Rsch., Devel. & Engring. Ctr., Natick, Mass., 1963-75, chief ration design & evaluation branch, 1975-86; sr. scientist Geo-Centers, Inc., Newton Centre, Mass., 1990-94; retired. Panelist biomass processing tech. panel Am. Inst. Biol. Scis., Washington, D.C., 1987-88; cons. dietitian Compu-Cad, Inc., Taunton, Mass., 1988-89; NSCORT site visit team panel mem. Am. Inst. Biol. Scis., Washington, D.C., 1995. Contbr. articles to profl. jours. Mem. Inst. Food Technologists. Died Aug. 26, 2007.

KLIETZ, SHELDON HENRY, minister; b. Chgo., Feb. 26, 1935; s. George Henry and Edna Bertha (Neumann) K.; m. JoAnne Marie Thomas, June 7, 1959; children: Mark Thomas, Beth Jeannine, Todd Stephen. AA, Concordia Coll., 1954; BA, Concordia Theol. Sem., St. Louis, 1960. Ordained to ministry Luth. Ch.-Mo. Synod, 1960. Pastor St. Paul's Luth Chs., Campbell-Nashua, Minn., 1960-65, Grace Evang. Luth. Ch., Hazel Crest, Ill., 1965-74, Trinity Evang. Luth. Ch., Marseilles, Ill., 1974-83, Faith Evang. Luth. Ch., Oak Lawn, Ill., 1983-91, Grace Luth. Ch. and Sch., El Centro, Calif., from 1991. Part-time chaplain Tinley Park (Ill.) Mental Health Ctr., 1965-88, Howe Developmental Ctr., Tinley Pk., Ill., 1974-91; dist. bd. dirs. Standing Com. for the Retarded, Hillside, Ill., 1978-88; contact campus pastor Morraine Valley Community Coll., Palos Hills, Ill., 1983-88; bd. dirs. Marseilles Nursing Svc., 1975-78, 82-83. Mem. Marseilles Ministerial Assn. (sec. 1978-82). Home: El Centro, Calif. Died Oct. 16, 2007.

KLINGBERG, FRANK LEROY, educator; b. Elmo, Kans., July 23, 1908; s. William August and Viola May (Garver) K.; m. Leota Lorraine Wagner, Sept. 1, 1936; 1 child, Caryl Ann Lyons. BA, U. Kans., 1928, MA, 1936; PhD, U. Chgo., 1939. Tchr. Eudora (Kans.) High Sch., 1928-35; asst. assoc. prof. James Millikin U., Decatur, Ill., 1939-43; assoc. prof. Knox Coll., Galesburg, Ill., 1943-46; assoc. prof., prof. Southern Ill. U., Carbondale, Ill., 1946-76, emeritus prof., from 1976; visiting prof. Northwestern U., Ill., 1947, U. Ill., Urbana, 1955. Expert cons. Dept. War, Washington D.C. 1945. Author: Cyclical Trends in America Foreign Policy Moods, 1983. Exec. sec. pres. bd. mem. S. Ill. chpt. United Nations Assn., Carbondale 1951--, pres. Youth World. Mem. Midwest Political Sci. Assn., Am. Political Sci. Assn., Internat. Studies Assn., Midwest Internat. Studies Assn., Am. Soc. Internat. Law, Acad. Political Sci., Rotary Internat. (pres. 1957-58). United Presbyterian. Home: Carbondale, Ill. Died Apr. 11, 2008.

KLOTZ, LOUIS HERMAN, structural engineer, educator, engineering executive, consultant; b. Elizabeth, NJ, May 21, 1928; s. Herman Martin and Edna Theresa (Kloepfer) K.; m. Virginia Helen Roll, Apr. 3, 1966 (dec. Oct. 1995), m. Kathy Lublfsor, Dec. 31, 2007 (dec. Apr. 3, 2008); Emily Louise, Jennifer-Claire Virginia. BSCE, Pa. State U., 1951; MCE, N.Y.U., 1956; PhD, Rutgers U., 1967. Registered profl. engr., N.J., N.H. Structural engr. various firms, NY, NJ metro area, 1951-65; asst. prof. civil engring. U. N.H., Durham, 1965-69, assoc. prof. civil engring., 1969-86, chmn. dept. civil engring., 1971-74; spl. projects dir. ASCE, NYC, 1986-87; cons. Klotz Assocs., Inc., New Castle, N.H., 1987-88; project mgr. Universal Engring. Corp., Boston, 1988-91; exec. dir. New Eng. States Earthquake Consortium, 1991-94; pres. Klotz Consultants Group, Inc., New Castle, N.H., from 1994; reservist FEMA, 1999—2002. Cons., evaluator Office of Energy Related Inventions, Gaithersburg, Md., 1978—; mem. energy policy adv. group N.H. Ho. of Reps., Concord, 1979-82; founding mem. N.H. Legis. Acad. Sci. & Tech., Concord, 1980-83. Editor: Energy Sources, The Promises and Problems, 1980; author: Users Manual Small Hydroelectric Financial/Economic Analysis, 1983; (monograph) Water Power, Its Promises and Problems; contbr. articles to Procs. of 1st Internat. Conf. on Computing in Civil Engring., Hydro Rev. Advisor Environ. Protection div. N.H. State Atty. Gen.'s Office, Concord, 1972-76; mem. New Castle (N.H.) Budget Com., 1977-79; tech. reviewer N.E. Appropriate Tech. Small Grants program Dept. Energy, Boston, 1979-80; bd. dirs. Family Svcs. Assn. Portsmouth, 1995-98, Seacoast Hospice, 1996-98. Ford Found fellow, 1962-65, Ford Found. grant, 1968, Systems Design fellow, NASA, Assn. for Engring. Edn., Houston, 1975; named Gen. Acctg. Office Faculty Fellow, U.S. Gen. Acctg. Office, Washington, 1975-76. Mem. AAAS, ASCE (com. on coordination outside ASCE 1978-86), Am. Assn. Engring. Edn., N.Y. Acad. Scis. Republican. Episcopalian. Home: Merrimack, NH. Died Apr. 3, 2008.

KNAPP, VIRGINIA ESTELLA, retired secondary education educator; b. Washington, May 11, 1919; d. Bradford and Stella (White) Knapp. BA, Tex. Tech. U., 1940; MA, U. Tex., 1988; postgrad., Sul Ross Coll., 1950, Stephen F. Austin U., 1964—68. Tchr. journalism HS, Silverton, Tex., 1940—41, Electra, Tex., 1941—42, Joinerville, Tex., 1942—60, Carthage, Tex., 1961—69; tchr. history and journalism Longview (Tex.) HS, 1969—80; instr. Trinity U., San Antonio, summer, 1972; fellowship tchr. Wall St. Jour., Tex. A&M U., Coll. Sta., 1964—67. Chmn. Rusk County (Tex.) Hist. Commn., 1980—2002; pres. Rusk County Hist. Found., Henderson Main St. Bd. Contbr. hist. papers. Recipient Wall St. Jour. award, Outstanding Journalism Tchrs. of Yr., 1965—66, Trail Blazer award, Tex. HS Press Assn., 1980, Woman of Yr. award, 1983. Mem.: Gaston Mus. (bd. mem., finance chmn.), Tex. Press Women, Women Comm. (pres. Longview chpt. 1972—74, Svc. award 1975), Rusk County Hist. Commn., Rusk County Heritage Assn., Tex. Assn. Jour. Dirs., Classroom Tchrs. Assn., Tex. State Tchrs. Assn. Episcopalian. Home: Henderson, Tex. Died May 13, 2009.

KNEE, RUTH IRELAN, social worker, health care consultant; b. Sapulpa, Okla., Mar. 21, 1920; d. Oren M. and Daisy (Daubin) Irelan; m. Junior K. Knee, May 29, 1943 (dec. Oct. 1981). BA, U. Okla., Norman, 1941, cert. social work, 1942; MA in Social Svcs. Adminstrn., U. Chgo., 1945. Psychiat. social worker, asst. supr. Ill. Psychiat. Inst., U. Ill., Chgo., 1943-44; psychiat. social worker USPHS Employee Health Unite, Washington, 1944—49; social work assoc. Army Med. Ctr., Walter Reed Army Hosp.,

Washington, 1949-54; psychiat. social work cons. HEW, Region III, Washington, 1955-56; with NIMH, Chevy Chase, Md., 1956-72; chief mental health care adminstrn. br. Health Svcs. and Mental Health Adminstrn., USPHS assoc. dep. adminstr., 1972-73; dep. dir. Office of Nursing Home Affairs, 1973-74; long-term mental health care cons.; mem. com. on mental health and illness of elderly HEW, 1976-77; mem. panel on legal and ethical issues Pres.'s Commn. on Mental Health, 1977-78; liaison mem. Nat. Adv. Mental Health Coun., 1977-81. Mem. editl. bd. Health and Social Work, 1979-81. Bd. dirs. Hillhaven Found., 1975-86, governing bd. Cathedral Coll. of the Laity, Washington Nat. Cathedral, 1988-94, Cathedral Fund Com., 1997—,bd. of visitors sch. of social work, Univ. of Okla., 2000— Recipient Edith Abbott award, U. Chgo. Sch. Social Svc. Adminstrn., 2001, Disting. Alumna award, U. Okla. Coll. Arts and Scis., 1999. Fellow APHA (sec. mental health sect. 1968-70, chmn. 1971-72), Am. Orthopsychiat. Assn. (life), Gerontol. Soc. Am., Am. Assn. Psychiat. Social Workers (pres. 1951-53); mem. Nat. Conf. Social Welfare (nat. bd. 1968-71, 2d v.p. 1973-74), Inst. Medicine/NAS (com. study future of pub. health 1986-87), Coun. on Social Work Edn., Nat. Assn. Social Workers (sec. 1955-56, nat. dir. 1956-57, 84-86, chmn. competence study com., practice and knowledge com. 1963-71, presdl. award for exemplary svc. 1999), Acad. Cert. Social Workers (NASW Found. co-chair social work pioneers 1993—), Am. Pub. Welfare Assn., DAR, U. Okla. Assocs., Woman's Nat. Dem. Club (mem. gov. bd. 1992-95, ednl. found. bd. 1992-2000), Cosmos Club (Washington, chair program com. 1998-2001), Phi Beta Kappa (fellow), Psi Chi. Home: Edmond, Okla. Died Oct. 8, 2008.

KNELLER, JOHN WILLIAM, academic administrator, retired literature and language educator; b. Oldham, Eng., Oct. 15, 1916; s. John William and Margaret Ann (Truslove) K.; m. Alice Bowerman Hart, Apr. 30, 1943; 1 dau., Linda Hart. AB, Clark U., 1938, LittD, 1970; AM, Yale U., 1948, PhD, 1950; French Govt. and Fulbright fellow, U. Paris, France, 1949-50. Asst. in instrn. Yale U., 1947-49; instr. French Oberlin Coll., 1950-52, asst. prof., 1952-55, assoc. prof., 1955-59, prof. French, 1959-65, chmn. dept. Romance langs., 1958-65, dean Coll. Arts & Sciences, 1967-68, provost, 1965-69; pres. Bklyn. Coll., CUNY, 1969-79, pres. emeritus, 1979—2009. Univ. prof. humanities & arts Hunter Coll. and Grad. Ctr., CUNY, 1979-95, prof. emeritus, 1995-2009; mng. editor French Rev., 1962-65, editor-in-chief, 1965-68; co-chair bd. dirs. Henri Peyre Inst. for the Humanities, 1980-2001; cons. NEH; chmn. subcom. on enrollment goals and projections N.Y. State Edn.; Commr.'s Adv. Coun. on Higher Edn., Adv. Coun. on Higher Edn. Co-author: Initiation au francais, 1963, Introduction a la poesie francaise, 1962; assoc. editor Yale French Studies, 1948-50, gen. editor, Henri Peyre: His Life in Letters, 2005; contbr. articles to jours. in field. Bd. dirs. Independence Savs. Bank, 1973-93. Sgt. AUS, 1942-46. Decorated comdr. Ordre des Palmes Académiques (France). Mem. Am. Assn. Tchrs. French (exec. council 1962-68), Modern Lang. Assn. (exec. council 1965-69), Yale Grad. Sch. Assn. (exec. com. 1967, 71), Bklyn. C. of C. (dir.), Kappa Delta Pi (hon.), Alpha Sigma Lambda (hon.) Clubs: Century (N.Y.C.), Yale (N.Y.C.), Southport Racquet. Home: Westport, Conn. Died July 2, 2009.

KNERR, GEORGE FRANCIS, retired academic administrator; b. NYC, Dec. 27, 1921; s. George Frank and Irene (Collins) K; m. Agnes Marie Doyle, Feb. 2, 1944; children: Kathleen, Maureen, Eileen, Joan, Paul, Rita, Francis, Bernadette, Marybeth. BA, St. John's U., Bklyn., 1948, MA, 1949; PhD, NYU, 1957. Tchr. Xavier High Sch., NYC, 1948-49; asst. prof. St. John's U., Bklyn., 1949-56; assoc. prof. Pace U., NYC, from 1952, dir., acting dean grad. div., 1958-63, dean admissions, 1959-61, dean student pers., 1961-65, asst. to pres., 1965-67, v.p., 1967-92; ret., 1992. Cons. Peirce Jr. Coll., Phila., World U., N.Y. Inst. Credit, N.Y.C., San Juan (P.R.) Bautista Med. Sch.; pres., permanent sect. Mid Atlantic Assn. Colls. Bus. Adminstrn., 1979, 72-90. Trustee Maryknoll (N.Y.) Sch. Theology, 1983—. With U.S. Army, 1942-45, ETO. Avocation: photography. Home: New City, NY. Died Oct. 24, 2007.

KNIGHT, ALLAN RUNYON, minister; b. Plainfield, NJ, July 28, 1912; s. John Marcus and Edith Maria (Leonard) K.; m. Pearl Prescott, Sept. 18, 1937; children: Phyllis Marie Rinehart, Douglas A., Rolf T., Karl W. Diploma, Practical Bible Tng. Sch., Bible School Park, NY, 1932; BA, Wheaton Coll., Ill., 1935; ThM, So. Bapt. Theol. Sem., Louisville, 1937; ThD, Eastern Bapt. Theol. Sem., Phila., 1946. Ordained to ministry Am. Bapt. Chs. in U.S.A., 1938. Pastor Mansfield Bapt. Ch., Port Murray, N.J., 1937-41, Meml. Bapt. Ch. and Summer Hill Bapt. Ch., Cortland, N.Y., 1941-48, Moulton Meml. Bapt. Ch., Newburgh, N.Y., 1948-53, First Bapt. Ch., Council Bluffs, Iowa, 1953-65; exec. minister Am. Bapt. Chs. Nebr., Omaha, 1965-77. Mem. Gen. Coun., Am. Bapt. Ch. in U.S.A., Valley Forge, Pa., 1956-62, 65-77; pres. Am. Bapt. Chs. N.Y. State, Syracuse, 1952-53, Iowa Bapt. Conv., Des Moines, 1960-61. Co-author: New Life, 1947; editor Nebr. Bapt Messenger, 1965-77. Chairperson Mayor's Com. on Human Rels., Council Bluffs, 1959-65; co-chmn. Billy Graham Greater Omaha-Council Bluffs Crusade, 1964; bd. dirs. Omaha Opportunities Industrialization Ctr., Omaha, 1968-77; chairperson Bentonville (Ark.) Ednl. Enrichment Program Adv. Coun., 1982-88. Recipient Effective City Ch. Citation, Am. Bapt. Home Mission Soc., Valley Forge, 1957, Medal of Merit, Relief Project Bentonville-Bella Vista Rotary Club, 1981-82; named Alumnus of Yr., So. Bapt. Theol. Sem., Louisville, 1975, Pastor Emeritus South Broadway Bapt. Ch., Pittsburg, Kans., 1987. Mem. Soc. Bibl. Lit., Mins. Coun. Am. Bapt. Chs. U.S.A. (life), Coun. Retired Execs. Am. Bapt. Chs. in U.S.A. (coord. 1981-91, editor Esprit de C.O.R.E. 1981-91), Rotary. Home: Bella Vista, Ark. Died Nov. 30, 2007.

KNIGHT, H. STUART, law enforcement official, consultant; b. Sault St. Marie, Ont., Can., Jan. 6, 1921; s. Alexander G. and Muriel C. (Breathwaite) K.; m. Betty Cooley, June 29, 1946 (dec. 2001); children: Suzanne Cawley, Bill, Bob, John, Barbara Powell. BS, Mich. State U., 1948; postgrad., Princeton U., 1965-66. Police officer, Berkeley, Calif., 1949; with US Secret Svc., US Dept. Treasury, 1950-82, dir., 1973-82. Vice chmn. Guardsmark Inc., Memphis, 1984-2009; v.p. Interpol, Paris, 1974-81; disting. faculty fellow Fed. Execs. Inst., Charlottesville, Va., 1981; mem. adv. bd. Am. Products Devel. Co.; mem. steering com. Ctr. for Strategic and Internat. Studies. Bd. dirs. Falls Church (Va.) Homeowners Assn., 1982-84; bd. dirs., pres. INKODE Govt. Sys.; mem. lottery bd. State of Va. Staff sgt. U.S. Army, 1942-46, PTO. Decorated Silver Star, Bronze Star, Purple Heart; recipient Mr. Sam award, Touchdown Club, Washington, 1979; named original mem. Gallery of Fame, Mich. State U., to Wall of Fame, 2001, Fed. Exec. of Yr., 1982. Mem. Internat. Assn. Chiefs of Police (life, mem. bd. officers 1974-81), Nat. Sheriffs Assn. (life), Civitan. Avocations: bicycling, golf, puzzles. Died Sept. 7, 2009.

KNIGHT, JOHN ALLAN, minister, theology studies educator; b. Mineral Wells, Tex., Nov. 8, 1931; s. John Lee and Beulah Mae (Bounds) K.; m. Justine Anne Rushing, Aug. 22, 1958; children— John Allan, James Alden, Judith Anne. BA, Bethany Nazarene Coll., 1952; MA, Okla. U., 1954; B.D., Vanderbilt U., 1957, PhD, 1966. Ordained to ministry Ch. of Nazarene, 1954; pastor Tenn. Dist. Ch. of Nazarene, 1953-61, 71-72; prof., chmn. dept. philosophy and religion Trevecca Nazarene Coll., Nashville, 1957-69; chmn. dept. philosophy and religion Mt. Vernon (Ohio) Nazarene Coll., 1969-71, pres., 1972-75; pastor Grace Nazarene Ch., Nashville, 1971-72; pres. Bethany (Okla.) Nazarene Coll., 1976-85; gen. supt. Internat. Ch. of the Nazarene, 1985—2001, vice chair Bd. Gen. Supts., 1990-92, chair Bd. Gen. Supts., 1992-94; ret., 2001. Coordinator U.S. Govt. Project Studying Possible Coop. Ventures for Tenn. Colls. and Univs., 1969; mem. gen. bd. Internat. Ch. of Nazarene, 1980-85 Author: Commentary on Philippians, 1968, The Holiness Pilgrimage, 1971, In His Likeness, 1976, Beacon Bible Expositions, Vol. 9, 1985, What the Bible Says About Tongues - Speaking, 1988; co-author: Sanctify Them -- That the World May Know, 1987; co-author: Go -- Preach, The Preaching Event in the 90s; author: All Loves Excelling, 1995, Bridge to Our Tomorrows, 2000; editor-in-chief: Herald of Holiness, Kansas City, Mo., 1975-76. Pres. bd. govs. Okla. Ind. Coll. Found., 1979-81; trustee So. Nazarene U., Okla. Recipient Lily Found. Theology award Vanderbilt U., 1958-59; Carré fellow Vanderbilt U., 1960-62 Mem. Soc. Sci. Study Religion, Am. Acad. Religion, Wesley Theol. Soc. (pres. 1979), Evang. Theol. Assn. Clubs: Kiwanis Internat. Mem. Ch. Of Nazarene. Died Feb. 1, 2009.

KNOLL, CATHERINE BAKER, lieutenant governor; b. Pitts., Sept. 3, 1930; d. Nicholas James and Theresa Mary (May) Baker; m. Charles A. Knoll Sr. (dec. 1987); children: Charles A. Jr., Mina B., Albert B., Kim Eric. BS in Edn., Duquesne U., 1952, MS in Edn., 1973. Dir. western Pa. region Safety Adminstrn. Dept. Transp., Pitts., 1971-79; exec. dir. community svc. Dept. of Adminstrn., Allegheny County, Pa., 1980-88; treas. State of Pa., Harrisburg, 1988—2003, lt. gov, 2003—08. Owner, operator pvt. bus. firm, Pitts., 1952-70. Mem. Pa. Dem. State Com., Pa. Fedn. Dem. Women, YMCA Bd., Pitts., Harrisburg, Duquesne U. Alumni Bd., Mom's House, Zontas Inc. Bd. Mem. Nat. Assn. State Treas., Women Execs. in State Gov., Coun. State Gov. (exec. com. ea. region). Democrat. Roman Catholic. Achievements include being the first woman elected lieutenant governor of the Pennsylvania, 2002. Died Nov. 12, 2008.

KNOLL, PEM CARLTON, real estate development executive; b. Columbus, Ohio, Aug. 31, 1954; s. Milton and Nora Jean (Marvin) K. BS in Acctg., La. State U., 1977; MBA, U. Tex., 1980. CPA, La. Acct. L. A. Champagne & Co., Baton Rouge, 1978, Touche Ross & Co., New Orleans, 1978-79; v.p. The Knoll Group, Newark, Ohio, 1980-83; pres. Carolina Summit Properties, Inc., Hilton Head, S.C., 1983-87, P. Carlton Knoll Interests, Inc., Hilton Head, from 1987. Instr. U. S.C., 1985—. Mem. La. Bd. CPA's, Hilton Head Homebuilders Assn. (exec. officer award), Hilton Head C. of C. Republican. Presbyterian. Avocations: reading, bridge, racquetball. Home: Hilton Head, SC. Died Feb. 8, 2008.

KNOLL, RAYMOND L., physician, surgeon, consultant; b. Newkirk, Okla., May 11, 1907; s. Daniel L. and Delia Elizabeth (DeMott) K.; m. Victoria A. Tetz, Aug. 8, 1932 (dec. Feb. 1963); children: M. Dean, R. Manley, Vance L.; m. Marie M. Sommers, July 29, 1964. BA, Union Coll., 1929; MD, Loma Linda Sch. Medicine, Loma Linda, Calif., 1944. Pvt. practice, Lodi, Calif., 1947-64; cons. Pollock Pines, Calif., from 1964. Author, pub.: How to Live to Be 101 and Be Able to Enjoy It, 1998. Home: Pollock Pines, Calif. Died Nov. 20, 2007.

KNOPF, ALFRED, JR., retired publisher; b. White Plains, NY, June 17, 1918; s. Alfred A. and Blanche (Wolf) K.; m. Alice Laine, July 27, 1952; children: Alison, Susan, David. Grad., Phillips Exeter Acad., 1937; AB, Union Coll., Schenectady, 1942. With Atheneum Pubs., NYC, 1959-88, chmn. bd., 1964-88. Vis. chmn. Scribner Book Cos.; sr. v.p. MacMillan Pub. Co. (ret.). Capt. USAAF, 1941-45. Decorated Disting. Flying Cross. Mem. Delta Upsilon. Clubs: Dutch Treat (N.Y.C.); Tavern (Chgo.). Home: New York, NY. Died Feb. 14, 2009.

KNOWLES, BARBARA WAGONER, publisher; b. Greensboro, NC, May 29, 1928; d. Vaden W. and Florence Edna (Dumas) Wagoner; children: Carolyn A., Robert Vaden, William David. BA, Woman's Coll U. N.C., 1950. Changes not made are inappropriate to house style. Art tchr. Arlington County, Va., 1950-51; cartographic tech. U.S. Geol. Survey, Washington, 1951-53, 55-58; chief cartographer, plant mgr. Marshall Penn-York, Inc., Syracuse, N.Y., 1973-79; map pub. Candlewood Publs., Fayetteville, N.Y., 1979-96. Literacy tutor R.E.A.C.H., Syracuse, 1995-96; staff Camillus Erie Canal Restoration, 1980-96; vol. Citizens Advocacy, Syracuse, 1994-96. Mem. Am. Congress on Surveying & Mapping, Am. Cartographic Assn., Manlius C. of C. Avocations: sailing, gardening. Home: Fayetteville, NY. Died Dec. 12, 2007.

KNOX, JON BRUCE, cultural organization administrator; b. New London, Conn., Jan. 23, 1939; s. Frank Judd and Anna (Ware) K.; m. Susan Jean Busse, June 1961; children: Sharon, Barbara, Susan. Community program dir. Pasadena (Calif.) YMCA, 1961-65; community program and camp dir. Tacoma YMCA, 1965-69; exec. Puyallup Valley Br., Tacoma, 1969-72; program dir. Joliet (Ill.) YMCA, 1972-76, met. program dir., 1976-81; dir. Briggs Family Ctr., Joliet, 1979-81; assoc. gen. dir. Joliet YMCA, 1980-81; bus. mgr. program resources YMCA of USA, 1981-84; exec. dir. Internat. Mgmt. Coun. of YMCA, Des Plaines, Ill., 1984-88; dir. internat. office for Europe YMCA of USA, Cleve., from 1988. Mem. nat. exec. com. Y-Indian Guide Program, 1975-76; mem. Nat. Y-Indian Guide Conv. Com., 1976-78; trainer YMCA Positive Parenting; trainer/mgr. YMCA Career Devel. Program. Field mgr. Youth for Understanding, Washington, 1979-80; nat. bd. dirs. United Cerebral Palsy, 1985-88, Will County, Ill., 1978-88, pres., 1983-85; organizer, bd. dirs. Friends United Cerebral Palsy, Joliet, 1982-88. Mem. Inst. Cert. Profl. Mgrs. (regent 1984-88), Assn. Profl. YMCA Dirs. (cert.). Republican. Mem. United Ch. of Christ. Avocations: camping, travel, history. Home: Lockport, Ill. Died Jan. 14, 2008.

KNOX, YOLANDA YVETTE BRECKENRIDGE, legal/enforcement processor; b. Oakland, Calif., July 23, 1962; d. Orlandis Whitley and Ray Jean (Smith) Breckenridge; m. David Anthony Knox, June 24, 1989; 1 child, Alaina Nicole. BS in Criminal Justice Adminstrn., Calif. State U., Hayward, 1984; MS in Justice and Pub. Safety, Auburn U., 1992. Salesperson Montgomery Ward, Richmond, Calif., 1979-85; dep. sheriff I Alameda County Sheriff's Dept., Oakland, Calif., 1985; salesperson Macy's Calif., Richmond, 1985-89; police clk., criminal records officer El Cerrito (Calif.) Police Dept., 1986-87; fed. investigator U.S. Office Pers. Mgmt., San Francisco, 1987-88; sr. clk. undergrad. office asst. dept. English U. Calif., Berkeley, 1988-89; intern Lee County Sheriff's Dept., Opelika, Ala., 1991; sec., office mgr. ext. horticulture dept. Auburn (Ala.) U., 1989-92; legal/enforcement processor Stanislaus County Dist. Atty. Family Support Divsn., Modesto, Calif., from 1992. Link Program vol. Friends Outside, 1993-94. Recipient Spirit of Excellence award Auburn U., 1991. Mem. Lambda Alpha Epsilon, Alpha Phi Sigma. Avocations: reading, writing, research, piano, rollerskating. Home: San Diego, Calif. Died Apr. 10, 2008.

KNUDSON, PATRICIA ANNE, music educator; b. Melrose Park, Ill., Sept. 14, 1941; BA in Piano and Music Edn., Chgo. Conservatory of Musci. Home: Phoenix, Ariz. Died June 29, 2008.

KOBRICK, JOHN LEO, research psychologist, educator; b. Hazleton, Pa., Sept. 11, 1925; s. John and Theresa (Demcik) K.; m. Alice Charlotte Lindsay, Aug. 28, 1954; children: John Douglas, Christopher Stuart. BS, Pa. State U., 1948, MS, 1950, PhD, 1953. Lic. psychologist, Mass. Grad. asst. dept. psycyhology Pa. State U., State College, 1948-53; rsch. psychologist U.S. Army Q.M. Climatic Rsch. Lab., Lawrence, Mass., 1953, U.S. Army R & D Command, Natick, Mass., 1953-64, U.S. Army Rsch. Inst. Environ. Medicine, Natick, from 1964, acting dir. Behavioral Scis. Lab., 1971-72, acting dir. health and performance div., 1981-83. Sr. lectr. Northeastern U. Univ. Coll., Boston, 1962—; U.S. Army rep. com. on vision NAS-NRC, bioeffects adv. group U.S. Army Med. R & D Command; mem. Tri-Svc. Joint Working Group for Assessment Drug-Dependent Degradation Mil. Performance; mem. Nat. Rsch. Coun. Com. on Toxicology, 1986; presenter to numerous confs. and profl. meetings. Contbr. over 75 articles to profl. jours., chpts. to books. Fellow APA, Am. Psychol. Soc.; mem. Psychonomic Soc., Human Factors Soc. (v.p., treas. New Eng. chpt. 1962-64), Aerospace Med. Assn., N.Y. Acad. Scis., Ea. Psychol. Assn., New Eng. Psychol. Assn., Mass. Psychol. Assn., Nat. Rsch. Coun. (com. on toxicology), Sigma Xi (pres.-elect Natick chpt. 1989-90). Home: Holliston, Mass. Died Mar. 19, 2008.

KOCH, GLENN A., minister; b. Eustis, Nebr., May 5, 1929; s. Arthur Otto Henry and Viola Belle (Lehmann) K.; m. Martina Marie Hanson, June 7, 1953; children: Vickie, Sandra, Donna, David, Ruth. BA, Christ Christian Coll., 1963; MA, U. No. Colo., 1974; MDiv, Concordia Sem., 1975; PhD, Christ Evang. Coll., 1975. Ordained to ministry Luth. Ch., 1962. Pastor, counselor Zion Luth. Ch., Burley, Idaho, 1962-68; chaplain USAF, Richards Gebarur, Mo., 1968-70, Bein Hoa, Vietnam, 1970-71, Davis Monthan, Ariz., 1971-75, Elmendorf, Alaska, 1976-79, Hill, Utah, 1979-83, Minot, N.D., 1983-85, Kaiserslautern, Germany, 1985-88, Layton, Utah, from 1989. Pres. Cassia County Mental Health Group, Burley, 1963-67; pastoral advisor in field. Author (poetry): Tribut to Rain, 1957, The Counselor, 1960, The Losing Battle, The Aging Snowman, Speed, 1969, Thank You, 1975, Answer to a Mystery, 1976, Life's Changing Scenes, 1976, The Freeway, 1974. Dir. Subs for Santa, Hill AFB, Utah, 1982, Baskets for the Needy, Minot AFB, 1984. Cpl. USMC, 1946-53. Recipient Victor Medal, 1946-48, Bronze Star, 1971, Outstanding Svc. Medal, 1975, Meritorious Svc. Medal, 1979, 83, 85. Mem. Am. Bd. Christian Psychology (clin.). Died June 30, 2008.

KOCHER, MARGARET, technical writer; b. Salem, Mass., Feb. 6, 1921; d. J. Willard and Margaret (Mason) Helburn; m. Eric Kocher, Apr. 26, 1947; children: Eric Glenn, Terry, Christopher, Debra Margaret Mildred. BA cum laude, Harvard U., 1941; MA, Am. U., 1969. Lic. comml. pilot, instrument and instr. rating, FAA. Casting aide, stage mgr. The Theatre Guild, NYC, 1941-42; sales pilot Republic Aviation, Farmingdale, N.Y., 1945; analyst, writer, crash injury rsch. Cornell Med. Ctr., NYC, 1946-47; tech. and chief editor Vitro Engring., Washington, 1956-59; rschr., writer Ctr. for Applied LInguistics, Washington, 1967-69; instr. linguistics Queens Coll., NYC, 1970-72, Adelphi U., Garden City, N.Y., 1970-72; exec. sec. project 208 N.Y.C. Dept. Environ. Protection, 1976-80; writer N.Y. Inst. Tech., Old Westbury, 1981-82; pub. participation specialist Helen Neuhaus Assocs., NYC, 1980-83; prin. Kocher Assocs., NYC, from 1982. Author: Guide to Koala Lumpur, 1955, Energy Information Guidance Manual, 1982, The World of Waste, 1988; co-author: Human Resources Directory, 1981. Chair bldg. and grounds com. Alley Pond Environ. Ctr., 1993-95; mem. nominating com. Citywide Recycling Adv. Bd., N.Y.C., 1991-93; bd. dirs. Alley Pond Environ. Ctr., N.Y., 1991-2001. Pilot, USAF, 1943-44. Recipient Cert. of Appreciation U.S. EPA, 1979, Earthling award for Lifetime Achievement, The City Club of N.Y., 1993. Mem. LWV (chair environ. com. N.Y.C. chpt. 1982-93, bd. dirs. Tri-State met. region 1986-98), Transp. Alternatives, Environ. Def. Fund, Nat. Resources Def. Coun., Nat. Wildlife Fedn., Nature Conservancy, Sierra Club. Avocations: bicycling, hiking, swimming, knitting, crossword puzzles. Home: Atlanta, Ga. Died Apr. 4, 2008.

KODNER, MARTIN, art dealer, consultant; b. St. Louis, Nov. 25, 1934; s. Charles and Sofia K.; m. Penny Ann Worth. BS, St. Louis Coll. Pharmacy, 1956. Pres., dir. Kodner Gallery, St. Louis, from 1974. Bd. dirs. Centerre Bank Ladue, St. Louis; mem. adv. bd. Boatmans Bank, Ladue, Mo.; expert cons. on Am. artists Oscar E. Berninghaus, Charles (Carl) Wimar. Contbr. articles to profl. jours. Mem. Jefferson Soc., Mo. Hist. Soc., St. Louis City Art Mus., Appraiser's Assn. Am., St. Louis Club, Lotos Club (N.Y.). Died 2008; unknown.

KOEHLER, MYRON, retired secondary school educator; b. Kirby, Tex., Oct. 28, 1927; s. Otto Albert and Annie (Biesenbach) Koehler; m. Marie Sherwood, May 14, 1954; children: Carol Ann, Sharon Marie, Carrie Lynn, Rene Lee. BS, SW Tex. State U., San Marcos, 1950, MEd, 1955; EdD, Tex. A&M U., College Station, 1972. Jr. HS tchr. San Antonio Sch. Dist., 1950—53; HS tchr. NE Sch. Dist., San Antonio, 1954—62, 1967—68, HS vice prin., 1962—67; rschr., prof. Tex. A&M U., 1968—79; HS prin. Somerset Sch. Dist., Tex., 1979—81; HS tchr. Bryan Sch. Dist., Tex., 1982—86; ret., 1986. Driver edn. cons. SW Tex. State U., San Marcos, 1976, Prairie View A&M U., 1977, USAF, 1978. Contbr. rsch. reports, article to profl. publs. Mem. Coulter Airfield adv. com. City of Bryan, Tex., 1997—2004; coordinator Habitat for Humanity, Bryan, 2002, 2008; asst. scoutmaster Boy Scouts Am., Bryan, 1997—2008, mem. Order of Arrow Vigil, 1997—2008; mem. Brotherhood of St. Andrews, Episc. Ch., Bryan, 2002—08. With USAAC, 1946—47, sgt. USAFR, 1951—53, lt. col. USAFR, 1958—87. Recipient Silver Beaver award, Boy Scouts Am., Houston, 1977, Meritorious Svc. medal, Nat. Security Agy., Ft. Meade, Md., 1980; named Disting. Commr., Boy Scouts Am., Houston, 1987; James West fellow, Boy Scouts Am., Irving, Tex., 1999. Mem.: Tex. Ret. Tchrs. Assn. (life; pres. 2000—02), VFW, Am. Legion (life), Lions Club (pres. Bryan Breakfast club 1989—90, 1995—96, co-chmn. dist. convention 1998, co-chmn. state convention 1999, pres. Lions Dist. Gov. 2003—04, Tex. Lions Found. 2005, Lion of Yr. Bryan Breakfast Club 1970, 1991, Pres.' Silver award 1989, Melvin Jones fellow 1992—2004, Jack Wiech fellow Tex. Lions Camp, Kerrville 2002, Pres.s award 2002). Republican. Episcopalian. Achievements include invention of carrier lock automatic mechanism for plegias. Avocations: hunting, fishing, camping, travel, stamp collecting/philately. Home: Bryan, Tex. Died Apr. 5, 2009.

KOEPKE, DON LORENZ, manufacturing executive; b. Rice Lake, Wis., Apr. 27, 1938; s. Lawrence Herman and Genevieve Marie (Kavanaugh) K.; m. Marion Ruth Zordel, Nov. 21, 1959; children: Julie Ann, Susan Lee, Douglas Lorenz. Student, Monmouth Coll., Ill., 1958. V.p. Koepke Sand and Gravel Co., Appleton, Wis., 1954-60; pres. Concrete Pipe Corp., Appleton, 1960-82, Visions Unlimited of Am., Inc., Appleton, from 1983. Bd. dirs. Valley Nat. Bank, Appleton. Mem. Mayor's Citizens Adv. Commn., Appleton; telethon chmn. Rawhide Boy's Ranch, New London, Wis.; bd. dirs. United Cerebral Palsy, Oshkosh, Wis. Served to 2d lt. U.S. Army. Mem. Concrete Pipe Assn. Wis. (pres. 1972), Wis. Assn. Tng. and Devel., Wis. Profl. Speakers Assn. Lodges: Rotary, Elks. Avocations: restoring old cars, fishing, hunting, trap shooting, pub. speaking. Died Sept. 25, 2007.

KOFF, FRED WILLIAM, retired research chemist; b. Haapsalu, Estonia, July 21, 1922; s. Fritz and Matilde (Lindström) K.; m. Annemarie Fehmel, June 13, 1947 (div. Apr. 1989). Degree in marine navigation, Merchant Marine Acad., Tallinn, Estonia, 1944. Rsch. chemist Chem. Rsch. Ctr. Allied Chem. Corp., Morristown, NJ, 1959-84. Contbr. articles to profl. jours. including Hydromctallurgy, Jour. Am. Chem. Soc.; patentee in field. Freedom fighter against Russian encroachment into the affairs of the Baltic States, Ctrl. and East European Coalition in U.S., N.Y.C., 1994—. Lutheran. Avocations: sailing, classical music. Died Feb. 13, 2008.

KOHN, HENRY, lawyer, director; b. St. Louis, May 2, 1917; s. Henry and Hannah (Lederer) K.; m. Anne Frankenthaler, Sept. 23, 1945; children: Margaret, Barbara, Alice. BA, Yale U., 1939, LL.B., 1942. Bar: Mo. 1942, N.Y. 1946. With Bd. Econ. Warfare, 1942; practice with George Frankenthaler, NYC, 1946-48; pvt. practice NYC, 1949-56; sr. ptnr. Frankenthaler, Kohn, Schneider & Katz, NYC, from 1957. Former pres., dir. Fiduciary Mut. Investing Co., Mercer Fund Inc.; bd. dirs. Meta Health Tech., Inc. Chmn. bd., founder Am. Jewish Soc. for Service; former treas. and bd. dirs. Nat. Jewish Welfare Bd.; bd. dirs. Lavanburg Corner House Found.; pres. Ed. Lee and Jean Campe Found., Sam and Louise Campe Found.; dir., past pres. and chmn. bd. dirs. 92d St. YM-YWHA; former dir. Edison Bros. Stores Inc., Graphic Sci. Inc. Served to capt. AUS, 1942-46. Mem. ABA, N.Y. County Lawyers Assn., Assn. Bar City N.Y., Order of Coif, Phi Beta Kappa. Clubs: New York Lawn Bowling, Harmonie, The India House (N.Y.C.). Jewish. Died Sept. 2008.

KOHNSTAMM, LEE W., corporate executive; b. NYC, Apr. 3, 1936; s. Edgar J. and Therese (Werner) K. BS in Econs., U. Pa., 1958. V.p. internat. V & E Kohnstamm Inc., Bklyn. Died Dec. 13, 2007.

KOLAKOWSKI, MARILYN, computer graphics specialist; b. Alliance, Ohio, Sept. 18, 1953; d. Eugene Dominic and Mary Stephanie (Galanzosky) K. Student, No. Mich. U., Marquette, 1971-73, El Centro Coll., Dallas, 1980-81, City Coll., San Francisco, 1989-90. Graphics specialist Bevilacqua-Knight Inc., Oakland, Calif., 1985-88; cons. Levi Strauss & Co., San Francisco, from 1988. Avocations: martial arts, music. Home: Oakland, Calif. Died Mar. 29, 2008.

KOLANKO, JOHN RAYMOND, priest; b. Milw., Apr. 8, 1913; s. John and Victoria (Dentkosz) K. BA, St. Francis Sem. Ordained priest, 1940. Priest St. Joseph Ch., West Allis, SS Cyril & Methodius Ch., Milw., Blessed Sacrament Ch., Milw., Holy Family & St. Columbkille, Reeseville, St. James Ch., Franklin, Wis., 1959-80, Our Lady of Good Hope Ch., Milw., from 1980. Avocation: lapidary work track-5 mile. Home: Milwaukee, Wis. Died Nov. 22, 2007.

KOLASA, PATRICIA ANN, education educator; b. Beloit, Kans., Nov. 14, 1940; d. Virgil Richard and Doris Moeta (Pratt) Studt; m. Bernard Kolasa, June 1, 1973; 1 child, Andrea. BS, Ft. Hays Kans. State Coll., 1963, MS, 1967; PhD, U. Kans., 1973. Tchr. Gunnison (Colo.) Sch. Dist., Randall (Kans.) Elem. Sch.; teaching asst. U. Kans., Lawrence; assoc. prof. U. Nebr., Omaha, from 1990. Mem. ASCD, APA, AAUP, Am. Ednl. Rsch. Assn. Home: Omaha, Nebr. Died Aug. 1, 2008.

KOLBE, KARL WILLIAM, JR., lawyer; b. Passaic, NJ, Sept. 29, 1926; s. Karl William Sr. and Edna Ernestine (Rumsey) K.; m. Barbara Louise Bogart, Jan. 28, 1950 (dec. Aug. 1992); children: Kim E., William B., Katherine B.; m. Patricia L. Coward, Apr. 30, 1994. BA, Princeton U., 1949; JD, U. Va., 1952. Bars: N.Y. 1952, D.C. 1976, U.S. Supreme Ct. 1966. Ptnr. Thelen, Reid & Priest, NYC, 1966-92, of counsel, from 1993. Dir. Bessemer Trust Co. (N.A.), N.Y.C.,1977-97, Carolinas Cement Co., 1994-98, World Trade Corp., 1987-2002; vice-chmn. The Friends of Thirteen Inc. Bd. dirs. N.J. Ballet Co., West Orange, 1970-98, Ocean Liner Mus., 1992-2003. With USN, 1944-46. Mem. ABA (chmn. pub. utility law sect. 1984-85). Clubs: Univ. (N.Y.C.); Metro. (Washington). Home: Essex Fells, NJ. Died Oct. 2006.

KOLFF, WILLEM JOHAN, retired internist, medical educator; b. Leiden, Holland, Feb. 14, 1911; arrived in U.S., 1950, naturalized, 1956; s. Jacob and Adriana (de Jonge) Kolff; m. Janke C. Huidekoper, Sept. 4, 1937 (div. 2000); children: Jacob, Adriana P., Albert C., Cornelis A., Gualtherus C.M. Student, U. Leiden Med. Sch., 1930—38; MD summa cum laude, U. Groningen, 1946; MD (hon.), U. Turin, Italy, 1969, Rostock U., Germany, 1975, U. Bologna, Italy, 1983; DSc (hon.), Allegheny Coll., Meadville, Pa., 1960, Tulane U., 1975, CUNY, 1982, Temple U., 1983, U. Utah, 1983; D. of Tech. Scis. (hon.), Tech. U. Twente, Enschede, The Netherlands, 1986; DSc (hon.), U. Athens, 1988, Aix-Marseille II, 1993. Internist, head med. dept. Mcpl. Hosp., Kampen, Holland; dir. divsn. artificial organs Cleve. Clinic Found., 1950—67; privaat docent, dept. medicine U. Leiden, 1950—67; prof. surgery U. Utah Coll. Medicine, Salt Lake City, 1967—86, Disting. prof. medicine & surgery, 1979—86, prof. internal medicine, 1981—86, dir. Kolff's Lab., 1986—2009, dir. Inst. Biomed. Engring., dir. divsn. artificial organs, 1967—86, prof. emeritus, 1986—2009. Decorated Commandeur Order Van Oranje Netherlands, Orden de Mayo al Merito en el Grade de Gran Official Argentina; recipient Landsteiner medal for establishing blood banks during German occupation in Holland, Netherlands Red Cross, 1942, Cameron prize, U. Edinburgh, Scotland, 1964, Gairdner prize, Gairdner Found., 1966, Valentine award, N.Y. Acad. Medicine, 1969, 1st Gold medal, Netherlands Surg. Soc., 1970, Leo Harvey prize, Technion, Israel, 1972, Sr. U.S. Scientist award, Alexander Von Humboldt Found., 1978, Austrian Gewerbeverein's Wilhelm-Exner award, 1980, John Scott medal, City of Phila., 1984, Japan prize, Japan Found. Sci. and Tech., 1986, Rsch. prize, Netherlands Royal Inst. Engrs., 1986, 1st Jean Hamburger award, Internat. Soc. Nephrology, 1987, 1st Edwin Cohn-De Laval award, World Apheresis Assn., 1990, Fed. prize, Fedn. Sci. Med. Assn., 1990, Father of Artificial Organs award and medal, Internat. Soc. Artificial Organs, 1992, Christopher Columbus Discovery award in biomed. rsch., NIH, 1992, Legacy of Life award, LDS Deseret Found., 1995, Lifetime Achievement award, Ahmedabad, India, 1996, Russ prize, Ohio U. and Nat. Acad.of Engring., 2003, Albert Lasker award for Clinical Medical Rsch., 2002; named one of The 100 Most Important Americans in the 20th Century, Life mag., 1990, Utah's Most Disting. Achievers, 1996; named to The Nat. Inventors Hall of Fame, 1985, On the Shoulders of Giants Hall of Fame, Cleve., 1989. Mem.: ACP, NAE (City of Medicine award 1989), AAUP, AAAS, AMA (Sci. Achievement award 1982), European Dialysis and Transplant Assn., Nat. Kidney Found., Am. Soc. Artificial Internal Organs, N.Y. Acad. Scis., Soc. Exptl. Biology and Medicine, Am. Physiol. Soc., Academia Nacional de Medicine (hon.; Colombia), Austrian Soc. Nephrology (hon.), Rotary. Achievements include patents for ventricular assist device and method of manufacturing; collapsible artificial ventricle and pumping shell; ventricular assist device with volumne displacement chamber; electrohydraulic heart with septum mounted pump; muscle and air powered left ventricular assist device; development of artificial kidney for clinical use, 1943; heart-lung machine, 1949; first membrane oxygenator, 1955; disposable twin-coil kidney, 1956; balloon pump, 1962; wearable artificial kidney (WAK), 1981; artificial heart, 1958; human implantation, Dr. Barney Clark, 1982. Home: Newtown Square, Pa. Died Feb. 11, 2009.

KOLTRACHT, ISRAEL, mathematics educator; b. Chernovitz, USSR, Jan. 22, 1949; came to U.S., 1983; s. Michael and Chana (Lokay) K.; m. Marina Stolyarov, Apr. 5, 1987; children: Jane Michelle, Michael Rolen. PhD, Weizmann Inst., Rehovot, Israel, 1983. Rsch. asst. Stanford U., Calif., 1983-84, U. Calgary, Can., 1984-87; asst. to assoc. prof. U. Conn., Storrs, from 1987. Contbr. articles to profl. jours. Recipient Rsch. grants NSF, Washington, 1988-96. Home: Storrs Mansfield, Conn. Died Feb. 17, 2008.

KOOMANOFF, FREDERICK ALAN, systems management engineer, researcher; b. NYC, Sept. 2, 1926; s. Alexander Theodore and Margaret Theresa (McKendry) K.; m. Lora Gahimer, May 27, 1955; children: Vivre, Heather, Elena. BS in Indusl. Engring., NYU, 1952, MS in Indusl Engring., 1953. Dir. system scis. Battelle Meml. Inst., Columbus, Ohio, 1958-67; sr. assoc. Planning Rsch., Inc., Washington, 1967-70; dir. diversification Ea. Airlines, Washington, 1970-72; pres. Stentran Systems, Inc., Vienna, Va., 1972-76; dir. SPS program Dept. of Energy, Office Basic Energy Scis., Washington, 1978-81, dir. CO2 program, 1981-89, sci. facility mgr., 1989-95; prin. assoc. Space Solar Power Agy., Arlington, Va., from 1995. Bd. dirs. Sunsat Energy Coun.; cons. Com. on Mgmt. Improvement in Govt., Washington, 1970-72; mem. at large R&D Aerospace Policy IEEE, Washington, 1989—. Author: Cybernetics on the Railways, 1962, Energy The Enabler and CO2, 1989, Solar Power Via Satellite, 1993; also pubs. on environ. concerns, transp. and comm. systems. Cadet USAF, 1944-45. Recipient Calling of an Engr. award, Engring. Soc. Can., 1957. Mem. Sigma Xi. Home: Garrett Park, Md. Died May 13, 2008.

KORENMAN, GARY, neurologist; b. NYC, Sept. 29, 1937; s. Irving and Minnie (Klein) K.; m. Ella Mary Kopelman, June 4, 1961; children: Eric, Jeffrey. AB, Dartmouth Coll., 1959, 2-yr. diploma in medicine, 1960; MD, Cornell U., 1962. Intern St. Luke's Hosp., NYC, 1962-63; resident in neurology Mt. Sinai Hosp., NYC, 1965-68; staff neurologist St. Luke's-Roosevelt Hosp., NYC, from 1968; staff, neurology Mt. Sinai Hosp., NYC, from 1968; cons. in neurology Isabella Geriatric Ctr., NYC, from 1968; pvt. practice, NYC, from 1968. Chmn. ann. fund alumni coun. Dartmouth Med. Sch., 1993-95, pres., 1995—). Capt. M.C., U.S. Army, 1963-65. Mem. Am. Acad. Neurology, Marshall Chess Club, Alpha Omega Alpha. Republican. Jewish. Home: New York, NY. Died Sept. 14, 2007.

KORITANSKY, GREGORY EMIL, lay church worker; b. Cleve., June 30, 1949; s. Emil Jerry and Anna Lorraine (Prentis) K.; m. Gloria Ann Paschali, Dec. 5, 1970; children: Michael, Lorrie, Daniel. AAS in Electronics, Lakeland Community Coll., Mentor, Ohio, 1969. Deacon Hambden

Congl. Ch., Chardon, Ohio, 1984-87 and from 90, trustee, 1988-89. Electronic technician ARGO-TECH, Cleve., 1979—. Staff sgt. USAF, 1970-77. Home: Chardon, Ohio. Died Feb. 26, 2008.

KORKEGI, ROBERT HANI, aerospace engineer; b. Milan, Dec. 3, 1925; came to U.S. 1941; s. Hani Jacob and Ethel Maud Essery (Pound) K.; m. Michele C. Caratini, Apr. 9, 1946; children: Paulette, Danielle. BSME, Lehigh U., 1949; MS in Aerospace Engring., Calif. Inst. Tech., 1950, PhD, 1954. Rsch. assoc. U. So. Calif., LA, 1954-57; tech. dir. von Karman Inst., Brussels, 1957-64; dir. Hypersonic Rsch. Lab., ARL, Dayton, Ohio, 1964-75, NATO Adv. Group for Aero R&D, Paris, 1976-79; vis. prof. George Washington U., Washington, 1979-81; dir. Aero & Space Bd., NRC, Washington, 1981-90. Vis. prof. U. Md., College Park, 1990—; bd. dirs. von Karman Inst., Brussels, 1976-79; active various coms. NRC, NATO, NASA, others. Editor: Viscous Interaction Phenomena at High Speed, 1969; contbr. numerous articles to profl. jours. With U.S. Army, 1944-46; ETO. Recipient Pub. Svc. award NASA, 1988, Group Recognition award, NRC, 1985, Sci. Achievement award, USAF, 1972. Fellow AIAA; mem. AAAS (chmn. vol. orgn. Sr. Scientists and Engrs. 1995), Kenwood Golf and Country Club. Achievements include development of simple criterion for flow separation at supersonic and hypersonic speeds, of device to measure accurately static and total pressures from transonic and supersonic aircraft. Died June 11, 2008.

KORN, CLAIRE VEDENSKY, secondary school educator, writer; b. Berkeley, Calif., Aug. 12, 1933; d. Dmitri Nicholas and Helen Ingalls (Montmorency) Vedensky; m. Harold A. Korn, July 26, 1958 (dec. Feb. 1990); 1 child, Alexander David. Student, U. Calif., Berkeley, 1951; BA, Stanford U., 1955, PhD, 1969; MA, U. Minn., 1958. Instr. U. Minn. Sch. Medicine, Mpls., 1957-58; rsch. assoc. Dept. Psychology Stanford U., Calif., 1958-60; with Cons. Psychologists Assn., Palo Alto, Calif., 1959-69; guidance counselor Palo Alto Unified Sch. Dist., 1968-69; asst. prof. Fla. State U., Tallahassee, 1970-71; founder, dir. Natural Bridge Sch., Tallahassee, 1974-80; open sch. coord. Ann Arbor Pub. Schs., 1985-86; free-lance writer, from 1984. Co-author: Furee Sukuru: Sono Genjtan to Yume, 1984; Author: Michigan State Parks: Yesterday Through Tomorrow, 1989, Alternative American Schools, 1991, Flashes and Lies, 2002; contbr. articles to profl. jours. Mem. Detroit Women Writers (v.p. 1991—), Am. Psychol. Assn., Soc. Childrens Bookwriters. Home: Berkeley, Calif. Died Nov. 5, 2007.

KORNEGAY, HORACE ROBINSON, trade association administrator, former United States Representative from North Carolina; b. Asheville, NC, Mar. 12, 1924; s. Marvin Earl and Blanche Person (Robinson) K.; m. Annie Ben Beale, Mar. 25, 1950; children: Horace Robinson, Kathryn Elder Kornegay Cozort, Martha Beale Kornegay Howard. BS, Wake Forest U., Winston-Salem, NC, 1947, JD, 1949. Bar: NC 1949, U.S. Supreme Ct. 1959, DC 1979. Practice in, Greensboro, NC; asst. solicitor Superior Ct. Guilford County, 1951-53; dist. solicitor 12th Solicitorial Dist., 1955-60; mem. US Congress from 6th NC Dist., NC, 1961—69; v.p., counsel The Tobacco Inst., Washington, 1969-70, pres., exec. dir., 1970-81, chmn., 1981-86; counsel Adams Kleemeier Hagan Hannah & Fouts, Greensboro, NC, 1987-2000; ret., 2000. Bd. dirs. Greensboro Mcht. Assn. Pres. Guilford Young Dem. Club, 1952, N.C. Young Dem. Clubs, 1953-54; chmn. bd. visitors Sch. Law, Wake Forest U., 1979-93; past chmn. adminstrv. bd. Concord-St. Andrew's United Meth. Ch., Bethesda, Md.; mem. adminstrv. bd. West Market St. United Meth. Ch., Greensboro. With AUS, 1943-46. Decorated Purple Heart, Bronze Star, Combat Inf. badge, Expert Infantryman's badge; recipient Americanism award Anti-Defamation League, B'nai B'rith, Washington, 1985. Mem. ABA, Fed. Bar Assn., NC Bar Assn. (chmn. dispute resolution com. 1989-92), Greensboro Bar Assn. (pres. 1992-93), DC Bar Assn., Am. Judicature Soc., Wake Forest Univ. Lawyers Alumni Assn. (past pres.), SAR (trustee), Alpha Sigma Phi Edn. Found. (trustee), Am. Legion, VFW, Royal Brit. Legion (hon.), Congl. Country Club, Greensboro Country Club, Masons, Shriners, Rotary, Phi Delta Phi, Alpha Sigma Phi. Democrat. Home: Greensboro, NC. Died Jan. 21, 2009.

KOSA, ALEX STEPHEN, lawyer; b. South River, NJ, Oct. 19, 1931; s. Stephen and Amelia (Toth) K.; m. Edry Loretta Seals, Oct. 24, 1955; 1 child, Stephen Alexander. BA, Norwich U., 1953; LLB, U. Wis., 1961. Bar: Wis. 1961, U.S. Dist. Ct. (we. and ea. dists.) Wis. 1981, U.S. Supreme Ct. 1981. Assoc. Gwin & Fetzner, Hudson, Wis., 1961-63; pvt. practice Hudson, Wis., from 1963. Ct. commr. St. Croix County, Wis., 1967-95. 1st Lt. U.S. Army 1953-58. Mem. Am. Trial Lawyers Assn., Wis. State Bar, St. Croix Valley Bar Assn., Masonic Lodge (lodge master 1973). Avocations: fishing, rod crafting, hunting, landscaping, real estate development. Home: Saint Petersburg, Fla. Died Aug. 13, 2008.

KOSS, ROSABEL STEINHAUER, retired health and physical education educator; b. Phila., Sept. 3, 1913; d. Arthur H. and Agnes (Temple) Steinhauer; m. Franklyn C. Koss, July 6, 1947 (dec. 1987); children: C. Lynn Knauff, Susan Kreiner, Carolyn Ruef, Rosalind Diehl. BS, Coll. of N.J., 1935; MA, Columbia U., NYC, 1942; DEd, Columbia U., 1964; diploma, Hasmors Gym Leaders Inst., Lilsved, Sweden, 1970, Pensioner's Program, Lilsved, 1972. Cert. health edn. specialist, 1989. Supr. health and phys. edn. Flemington Pub. Schs., NJ, 1935-37; tchr. health and phys. edn. Ridgewood HS, 1937-40, Passaic Valley Regional High Sch., Little Falls, 1940-48; asst. prof. Montclair State Coll., Upper Montclair, 1958-61, Upsala Coll., East Orange, 1964—71; assoc. to full prof. Ramapo Coll NJ, Mahwah, 1971-84, dir. tchr. edn., 1974-79, prof. emeritus, 1985; adj. prof. Richard Stockton Coll. NJ, Pomona, 1985-95. Asst. sport attachee Royal Swedish Embassy, N.Y.C., 1964-74. Author: (with others) Dance for Older Adults, 1988, Mature Stuff. Physical Activity for Older Adults, 1989, Exercise for the Older Adult, 1998; contbr. articles profl. jours. Mem. Little Falls (N.J.) Bd. Edn., 1954-63; trustee, treas. Bergen County (N.J.) Ret. Sr. Vol. Program, 1979-84; mem. recreation adv. com. Stone Harbor Bd. Health, v.p., 1995; mem. Cape May County Freeholders Adv. Commn. on Women, 1986—, Cape May County Human Svcs. Adv. Coun., 1989—; vestrywoman St. Mary's Episcopal Ch., Stone Harbor; mem. N.J. Commn. on Aging, 1992-98, chmn., 1996-98; mem. Health Promotion and Planning Lab, State of N.J., 1998; del. White House Conf. on Aging, 1995; mem. adv. com. Cape May Human Svcs. Recipient Athletic Alumni Women's award, Coll. N.J., 1976, citation, State of N.J. Senate and Gen. Assembly, 1994, Cape Women's Resource Honor award, 1994, Alice Stokes Paul award, Cape May County Adv. Commn. on Status Women, 2003; named Gerontologist of Yr., Soc. on Aging N.J., 1993; named to Athletic Hall of Fame, Coll. N.J., 1980, Trenton State Coll. Alumni Athletic Hall of Fame, 1987, Nat. Women's Wall of Fame, 1994, Athletic Hall of Fame Ramapo Coll. N.J., 2003; grantee, The Royal Swedish Consulate, N.Y.C., 1968, 1970, 1972. Fellow: Assn. for Gerontology in Higher Edn.; mem.: AAUW, AAHPERD (life; coun. on aging and adult devel., profl. achievement award, N.J. 1973, honor award fellow 1979, merit award Ea. Dist. 1980, disting. leadership award 1996, Rosabel Koss award named in her honor), Vols. in Medicine, Internat. Soc. Comparative Phys. Edn. and Sport, Nat. Coun. on Aging, N.J. AHPERD (Disting. Leadership award), Gerontol. Soc. N.J. (parliamentarian 1988—89), Wetlands Inst. (docent), Cape May County LWV, Stone Harbor Women's Civic Club, Garden Club. Avocations: travel, gardening, salt marsh ecology, swimming. Home: Stone Harbor, NJ. Died Dec. 2, 2007.

KOSTENBAUER, JOHN HARRY, personnel director; b. Sheridan, Wyo., June 15, 1946; s. John and Jean (Babcock) K.; divorced; children: Brian John, Stacy Annette. BS, U. Md., 1970; MS, U. Oreg., 1984. Community dir. U.S. Army Health Svc., 1970-75; supr. pub. health State of Wyo., Cheyenne, 1975-77; mgr. preventive health County of Lane, Eugene, Oreg., 1977-80, pers. analyst, chmn. compensation/classification com., 1981-83, dir. health and human svcs., 1984-87; pers. mgr. Atlas Cylinder div. Parker Hannifin Corp., Eugene, from 1987. Mem. Springfield (Oreg.) Budget Com., 1987-88, City of Eugene Parks and Recreation Bd., 1981-87, Applied Tech. Adv. Bd., Eugene, 1988—; active Human Svcs. Planning Project, Eugene, 1985-87; pres. Springfield Booster Club, 1986-88; commr. Am. Youth Soccer, 1983-85; referee U.S. Soccer Fedn., 1980—. Capt. U.S. Army, 1970-75. Mem. Pers. Mgmt. Assn., Am. Soc. for Pers. Adminstrn., Oreg. Nurses Assn. Avocations: tennis, soccer. Home: Eugene, Oreg. Died Mar. 3, 2008.

KOURY, THOMAS LEO, plastic and reconstructive surgeon, educator; b. Upland, Pa., Nov. 15, 1923; m. Elizabeth Koury; children: Carol Anne, Thomas Edwin, Virginia Lee, Jennifer Elaine. Student, Swarthmore Coll.; DDS magna cum laude, Temple U., 1948, MD, 1952. Diplomate Am. Bd. Plastic Surgery. Intern Temple U. Hosp., Phila., 1952-53; gen. surg. resident Vets. Hosp., Phila., 1953-54, Kansas U. Med. Ctr., Kansas City, 1956-57, plastic surg. resident, 1957-59; pvt. practice plastic and reconstructive surgery Silver Spring, Md., 1959-97; chief attending plastic surgeon D.C. Maternal Health-Children With Special Needs, Washington, 1963-94; asst. prof. plastic surgery Georgetown U., Washington, from 1963. Pres. I Care-Children of The Andes Found., Silver Spring, 1990—; chief plastic surgery Holy Cross Hosp., Silver Spring, 1990-94; lectr. cleft lip and palate and orthognathic surgery Howard U. Orthodontic Sch., Washington, 1982—; lectr. surg. procedures dept. plastic surgery Georgetown U. Med. Sch., Washington, 1963—; surgery tchr., contbr. Naval Hosp. and Hosp. del Ninos, Lima, Peru, 1989—, Hosp. Militar # 3 Cuenca, Ecuador, 1994—. Mem. Woodside Pk. Civic Assn., Silver Spring, 1991. Lt., M.C., USN, 1954-56. Mem. Am. Soc. Plastic and Reconstructive Surgeons, Am. Soc. Maxillo-Facial Surgeons, Am. Cleft Palate-Cranofacial Assn. Avocations: woodcrafting, boating, fishing, travel. Died Oct. 5, 2007.

KOVACS, ANDREW CHARLES, marketing executive, consultant; b. Szekesfehervar, Hungary, June 10, 1954; came to U.S., 1958; s. Lajos Karoly and Emilia (Godor) K.; m. Lisa Hedge, July 26, 1975 (div. Apr. 1988); children: Stephen, Angelica. BBA, Western Conn. State U., Danbury, 1980; postgrad., Washington U., St. Louis. Account exec. C.A. Roberts Co., Indpls., 1976-80; nat. mktg. dir. McDonald & Co., Indpls., 1980-83; pres., CEO Ind. Power Sources, Inc., Indpls., 1983-87, Universal Mktg. Group, Inc., Indpls., 1987-88, MeadowTech, Inc., Indpls., also Vienna, from 1989, Cen. European Mktg. Group, Indpls., also Vienna, from 1991. Cons. Alaska Diesel Electric, Seattle, 1987, U.S. Dept. Justice, Indpls. and Washington, 1987-90, Cummins Engine Co., Columbus, Ind., 1987, Quantum-Fulcrum Group, Budapest, Hungary, 1989-90. Author: (novel) Slangtight, 1989, (short story) They Got It Made, 1991. Mem. Hungarian Polit. Forum, Budapest, 1990, Hungarian Boy Scouts Internat., Toronto, 1990. Recipient St. Stephen award Hungarian Scouting, 1991, Letter of Commendation, U.S. Dept. Justice, 1990, Tom Stasko award Lakewood (Ohio) Civic Forum, 1989, Julian Atherby award Astor Found., 1988. Mem. Am. Inst. Exporters, Am.-Hungarian C. of C., Elec. Systems Mktg. Assn., Am. Soc. Mktg. Profls. (Kaise award 1992). Avocations: painting, musical composition. Died June 19, 2008.

KOVALCHUK, FEODOR SAWA, priest; b. Wakaw, Sask., Can., Mar. 5, 1924; came to U.S., 1926; s. Sawa John and Rose M. (Boryk) K.; m. Anna Ivanovna Korewik, May 23, 1948; children: Sergius, Basilissa, Natalia (dec.). AB, Columbia U., 1945; diploma, St. Vladimir's Sem., 1946; MA, Western Res. U., 1967, postgrad., from 1970. Ordained deacon, priest Russian Orthodox Cath. Ch., 1948, mitered archpriest. Asst. pastor St. Nicholas Cathedral, NYC, 1948; pastor St. George Serbian Ch., Pitts., 1948-49, Holy Trinity Ch., Balt., 1949-52, Nativity of Christ, Youngstown, Ohio, from 1952; pastor of missions St. Seraphim's Ch., Cambridge, Mass., 1949, St. Mary's Ch., Holdinsford, Minn., 1949. Dean Cen. States Deanery Russian Orthodox Cath. Ch., Youngstown, Ohio, 1983—, exec. sec. patriarchal parishes, 1971—. Translator, compiler: Abridged Typicon, 1974; editor, compiler: Holy Liturgy and Other Prayers, 1965, 7th edit., 1990, Wonder-Working Icons of Theotokos, 1985; editor One Church, 1977—; author pamphlets, booklets. Mem. Eastern Orthodox Clergy Assn. Home: Canfield, Ohio. Died Apr. 22, 2008.

KOYAMA, KOSUKE, theologian; b. Tokyo, Dec. 10, 1929; s. Zentaro and Tama (Uma) K.; m. Lois Eleanor Koyama, 1958; children: James, Elizabeth, Mark. BDiv, Drew U., 1954; MTh, Princeton U. Theol. Sem., 1955, PhDTh, 1959. Lectr. in theology Thailand Theol. Sem., Chiengmai, Thailand, 1960-68; dean S.E. Asia Grad. Sch. of Theol., Singapore, 1968-74; sr. lectr. U. Otago, Dunedin, New Zealand, 1974-80; prof. Union Theol. Sem., NYC, 1980-82, prof. John D. Rockefeller Jr., 1982—96. Author: Waterbuffalo Theology, 1974, No Handle on The Cross, 1977, Three Mile An Hour God, 1979, Mount Fuji and Mount Sinai: A Pilgrimage in Theology, 1984. Fellow The Soc. for Arts, Religion and Contemporary Culture; mem. Am. Acad. Religion, Am. Theol. Soc. Home: New York, NY. Died Mar. 25, 2009.

KOZAK, NANCY, community health, psychiatric-mental health nurse; b. Balt., Sept. 9, 1946; d. Joseph Kozieracki and Helen (Sopirak) Matlak; children: Lew McCutcheon, Ron McCutcheon. AS in Nursing, Community Coll. Beaver County, Monaca, Pa., 1981. RN, Pa. Charge nurse adolescent unit Mayview State Hosp., Bridgeville, Pa., 1981-83, 89-93, charge nurse forensic unit, 1983-85, charge nurse children's unit, 1987-89; home health nurse St. John's Hosp., Pitts., Pa., 1989-90; community health nurse Corrections Health, from 1993. Mem. Am. Nurses Assn. (cert. psychiat.-mental health nurse), Pa. Nurses Assn. Home: Beaver, Pa. Died Oct. 16, 2007.

KOZLOW, RICHARD, artist; Author, illustrator book Of Man's Inhumanity to Man, 1964. Represented in permanent collections Chrysler Corp., William Kessler Assocs., Archs., Mich. Nat. Bank Corp. hdqs., Weight Watchers Internat., others, Detroit Inst. Arts, Smithsonian Nat. Mus. Am. Art, Washington, State of Mich. Libr. Mus., Lansing, others, Wayne State U., one-man shows include Detroit Artists Market, 1950, Instituto Allende, Mex., 1960—61, Raymond Burr Gallery, L.A., Calif., 1963, Arwin Galleries, Detroit, 1963, Rehn Galleries, N.Y.C., 1958, 1967, Foster Harmon Gallery of Am. Art, Sarasota, Fla., 1983, Arwin Gallery, 1973, Shweyer-Galdo Galleries, Birmingham, Mich., 1983, Malton Gallery, Cin., 1985, Rubiner Gallery, West Bloomfield, Mich., 1990, Posner Gallery, Farmington Hills, Mich., 1983, 1984, Birmingham, 1999, Mex. Nat. Inst. de Bellas Artes, 1994, U. Mich. Holocaust Series, 1998, exhibited in group shows at Butler Art Inst., Youngstown, Ohio, 1950, 1952, Detroit Scarab Club, 1952, 1953, Provincetown (Maine) Arts Festival, 1958, Hudsons Salutes to the Detroit Artists Market, 1963, Mus. of Art of Ogunquit Maine, 1964, Am. Embassy, London, 1966, Lithografias de la Collecion Mourlot, P.R., 1971, Birmingham Temple, West Bloomfield, 1988, featured in publs. With USN, 1944—46. Recipient Socrates award for outstanding advt., Detroit Art Dirs. Awards, Nat. Outdoor Advt. 1st award for best painted billboard, Mich. Founders award, Detroit Inst. Arts, 10-Yr. Retrospective award, Lois and Alvin Spector Found. for Arts award for outstanding achievement. Died July 29, 2008.

KRABACHER, WILLIAM EDWARD, aerospace engineer; b. Cin., Nov. 6, 1948; BA in Math., Physics and Philosophy, Wilmington Coll., 1972; MA in Relativity Theory & Math. Analysis, Ind. State U., 1975. Aerospace engr. Wright Lab. Landing Gear Devel. Facility, from 1978. Mem. design loads for future aircraft working group NATO Adv. Group for Aerospace R & D, 1997—; mem. Dark Star Unmanned Air Vehicle Ind. Rev. Team, 1996. Contbr. articles to profl. jours. Mem. Soc. Automotive Engrs., Sigma Xi, Pi Mu Epsilon, Sigma Pi Sigma, Sigma Zeta. Achievements include research in the field of aircraft landing gear dynamics and vibration. Died Jan. 4, 2008.

KRACKOV, LAWRENCE MARTIN, financial executive, recording industry executive; b. Newark, Sept. 2, 1943; s. Nathan and Betty Ruth (Kulis) K.; m. Susan Leslie Hammett, Nov. 20, 1976; children: Robin Renee, Rebecca Wendalyn Deborah. BA cum laude, Cornell U., 1965; JD cum laude, Columbia U., 1968, MBA, 1969. With Armour Foods, Dobbs Houses, Pepsico, 1969-76; dir. fin. planning and control Monstano Co., St. Louis, 1976-78; asst. to chmn. Coca-Cola N.Y., Hackensack, 1978-79; dir. acquisitions, asst. treas. CBS Inc., NYC, 1979-87; v.p., treas. Sony Music Entertainment Inc., NYC, from 1987. Instr. Memphis State U., 1971-73; from asst. prof. to prof. fin. Pace U., N.Y.C., 1982—. Co-author: The Practical Financial Manager, 1988, Multinational Financial Management, 1989. Dir., treas. Ins. TJ Martell Found., N.Y.C., 1987—; mem. dinner com. Nat. Conf. Christians & Jews Ins. Sect., N.Y., 1990. Mem. N.Y. Treas. Group (treas. 1990—), Fin. Execs. Inst., Nat. Assn. Corp. Treas., Soc. Internat. Treas. Avocations: poetry writing, history and religion studies. Home: Tempe, Ariz. Died May 3, 2008.

KRAEHE, ENNO EDWARD, history professor; b. St. Louis, Dec. 9, 1921; s. Enno and Amelia Roth (Henckler) K.; m. Mary Alice Eggleston, May 25, 1946; children: Laurence Adams, Claudia. BA, U. Mo., 1943, MA, 1944; PhD, U. Minn., 1948. Instr. history U. Del., 1946-48; asst. prof. history U. Ky., 1948-50, asso. prof., 1950-63, prof., 1963-64, U. N.C., 1964-68, U. Va., 1968-71, Commonwealth prof., 1971-77, William W. Corcoran prof., 1977-91, William W. Corcoran prof. emeritus, from 1991. Vis. prof. U. Mo., 1946, U. Va., 1955, U. Tex., 1955, U. Minn., 1963; U.S. Dept. State Specialist in, Germany, 1953; mem. regional selection com. Woodrow Wilson fellowship Found., 1959-60; mem. Sr. Fulbright-Hayes History Screening Com., 1970-73 Author: Metternich's German Policy Volume I: The Contest with Napoleon 1799-1814, 1963; author: Volume II: The Congress of Vienna, 1814-1815, 1983; editor: The Metternich Controversy, 1971; mem. editl. bd. Ctrl. European History, 1967-72, Austrian History Yearbook, 1969-74; contbr. entries and articles to encys. and hist. jours., U.S. and Europe. Active Charlottesville Com. on Fgn. Rels.; mem. Nat. Coordinating Com. for Promotion of History, mem. policy bd., 1985-88; mem. Met. Opera Guild, Friends of Ky. Ctr. Recipient Best Book award Phi Alpha Theta; Fulbright scholar Austria, 1952-53; Guggenheim fellow, 1960-61, Am. Coun. Learned Socs. fellow, 1969, 73, resident fellow Rockefeller Ctr. in Bellagio, 1983; grantee NEH, 1973, 80, 83, NEH Libr. Preservation Screening Com., 1988 Mem. Am. Hist. Assn., Conf. Group for Ctrl. European History (mem. exec. bd. 1966-68), German Studies Assn. (mem. exec. coun. 1985—), So. Hist. Assn. (chmn. European sect. 1974, 75, Disting. Svc. award European sect.), Charlottesville Com. on Fgn. Rels., Colonnade Club, Blue Ridge Swimming Club, Phi Beta Kappa. Episcopalian. Home: Charlottesville, Va. Deceased.

KRALICK, RICHARD LOUIS, lawyer; b. Youngstown, Ohio, Dec. 7, 1933; s. Joseph Martin and Dorothy Louise (Canada) K.; m. Roselle A. Richmond, Sept. 10, 1955; children: Kris Ann, Richard II, Kolleen, Kathleen, Michael. BA, Mich. State U., 1955; JD, U. Mich., 1959. Assoc. Baker, Hammond and Baker, Adrian, Mich., 1960-62; ptnr. Hammond Baker and Kralick, Adrian, from 1963. Chmn. Mich. Girls Tng. Sch., Adrian, 1966-67; bd. dirs. Lenawee County Human Svcs. Coun., 1991-95, Lenawee United Way, 1991—; pres. Lenawee Family Coun. and Children's Svcs., Adrian, 1970-71; bd. dirs. Adrian YMCA, 1969-72, Lenawee Ams. with Disabilities Act Coun., 1993-95; v.p. Goodwill Industries, Adrian, 1972-73; bd. dirs. (LEAH) Lenawee Emergency Affordable Housing. Named Mich. Vol. of Yr. Mich. Family Coun. and Children's Svcs., 1971; recipient Good Willie award Goodwill Industries, Adrian, 1972, Disting. Svc. award Lenawee Cancer Soc., 1973, Crisis Hot Line, Adrian, 1992. Mem. ABA, Lenawee County Bar Assn. (pres. 1968-69), Mich. Trial Lawyers Assn., Mich. Def. Trial Lawyers, Mich. Bar Assn. Home: Manitou Beach, Mich. Died Nov. 14, 2007.

KRAMER, CAROLE REE, retired special education educator; d. Peter and Luetta Marie (Wallace) Mihay; m. Donald Louis Kramer, Nov. 23, 1979; 1 child, Jenée Marie. BA in Elem. Edn., Mich. State U., 1964; M in Spl. Edn., Oakland U., 1981. Elem. tchr. Waverly (Mich.) Sch. Dist., 1964—65, Hayward (Calif.) Unified Sch. Dist., 1965—71, Waterford (Mich.) Sch. Dist., 1971—81, spl. edn. tchr., 1982—95; ret., 1995. Exhibitions include, Raleigh, N.C., 2003. Mem.: Morganton New Comers Club (pres. 1999—2002). Home: Morganton, NC. Died June 30, 2008.

KRAMER, JANICE LYNN, banker; b. Queens, NY, Oct. 24, 1962; d. Jerold and Rosalind (Mann) K. AAS, Suffolk Community Coll., 1982, AA, 1983; BBA in Mgmt., Hofstra U., 1985, postgrad., 1986-89. Mgmt. trainee Chase Manhattan Bank, New Hyde Park, N.Y., 1985-86, mktg. officer NYC, 1986-88, asst. treas., 1987-88; product mgr., asst. v.p. Republic Nat. Bank N.Y., NYC, from 1988. Notary pub., Suffolk County, 1982. Mem. NAFE, Soc. Advancement of Mgmt., MBA Assn., Nassau County Reps., Personal Dynamics Network. Avocations: bowling, softball, travel. Home: Mineola, NY. Died Jan. 16, 2008.

KRATKA-SCHNEIDER, DOROTHY MARYJOHANNA, psychotherapist; b. New Britain, Conn., Apr. 29, 1934; d. Josef Matthew and Mari Catherine (Stifil) Kratka; m. Warren Andrew Schneider, Apr. 26, 1975 BSN, Columbia U., 1960; MSW, Fordham U., 1969; EdD Counseling Psychology, U. San Francisco, 1983. RN, Conn. Instr. pub. health nursing U. Conn., Storrs, 1963—64; participant Voter Registration Dr., Greenwood, Miss., 1965; pub. health nurse Jesuit Med. Mission Bd., Tanzania, Tanzania, 1965—67; chief psychiat. social worker Knickerbocker Hosp., NYC, 1969—74; coord. social svcs. Rockefeller U. Hosp., NYC, 1974—77; asst., assoc. prof. Calif. State U., Sacramento, 1985—88; counseling psychologist VA, San Francisco, 1987—89; psychologist, social worker Dept. Transp., 1989—93; pvt. practice Contracts in Crisis Counseling, Novato, Calif., from 1993. Mem. Cath. Charities Bd. for Aging, San Francisco, 1985, bd. dirs., 1983—85; apptd. to Marin County Mental Health Bd., Calif., 1998—2002, Marin County Grand Jury, Superior Ct., 1999—2000; bd. dirs. Health Sys. Adv. Com., San Francisco, 1978. Grantee, NIMH, 1967—69. Mem. APA, NASW (diplomate clin. social work, bd. dirs. Referral Svc. San Francisco 1984-86), Internat. Assn. Profl. Counselors and Psychotherapists (diplomate psychotherapy), Register Clin. Social Workers, Amnesty Internat., Kappa Delta Pi Democrat. Roman Catholic. Avocations: hiking, painting, flying, swimming. Home: Novato, Calif. Died Apr. 2008.

KRAUS, HENRY EMERY, rabbi; b. Papa, Hungary, Aug. 27, 1914; came to U.S., 1957; s. Emil and Janka (Revesz) K.; m. Clara Pasternak, Sept. 17, 1946; 1 child, Marianne Janoff. PhD, Budapest U., Hungary, 1938. Ordained rabbi, 1940. Rabbi Jewish Community, Siklos, Hungary, 1939-44, Kaposuar, Hungary, 1946-56, Temple Beth Torah, Gardena, Calif., 1957-69, Tempel Beth Ami, West Covina, Calif., 1969-85; chaplain City of Hope, Duarte, Calif., from 1985. Chaplain sheriff dept. L.A. County, L.A., 1982—, Police Dept. L.A., 1987—, UCLA Med. Ctr., 1989—. Mem. Rabbinical Assembly Am. Home: Los Angeles, Calif. Died May 4, 2008.

KRAUS, JENNIFER ELAINE, microbiologist, musician; b. Saginaw, Mich., Sept. 20, 1955; d. Kenneth George and Ruth Gwendolyn (Hodder) Kraus; m. Paul David Scheerer (div. Nov. 1991); children: Stephanie Ruth Kraus-Scheerer, Phoebe Laurel Kraus-Scheerer. BS in Biology, Mich. State U., 1978, BS in Botany and Plant Pathology, 1981; PhD in Genetics and Cell Biology, Wash. State U., Pullman, 1987. Tech. asst. dept. botany and plant pathology Mich. State U., East Lansing, 1975-78; rsch. technician Dept. Energy Plant Rsch. Lab., East Lansing, 1979-81; rsch. assoc. program in genetics and cell biology Wash. State U., Pullman, 1981-88; plant pathologist Hort. Crops Rsch. Lab., ARS, USDA, Corvallis, Oreg., 1988-89; faculty rsch. assoc. dept. botany and plant pathology Oreg. State U., Corvallis, 1989-95, faculty rsch. assoc. dept. microbiology, from 1995. Contbr. chpts. to books, articles to profl. jours. Pres. Palouse Folklore Soc., Moscow, Idaho, 1985-86. NSF grad. fellow, 1982-85. Democrat. Avocations: playing/studying guitar music from brazil, playing/singing jazz and swing, teaching music, whitewater rafting, gardening. Home: Corvallis, Oreg. Died Feb. 16, 2008.

KRAUSE, DALE CURTISS, marine scientist, researcher; b. Wichita, Kans., Dec. 27, 1929; s. Peter and Susie B. (Unruh) K.; divorced; children: Tara, Daniel. BS in Geology, Calif. Inst. Tech., 1952; MS in Oceanography, UCLA, 1957; PhD in Oceanography (Marine Geology), U. Calif., San Diego, 1961. Mining geologist Cerro de Pasco Corp., Yauricocha, Peru, 1952-54; surveyor U.S. Army, U.S., Panama, Chile, 1954-56; grad. asst. U. Calif. San Diego, La Jolla, 1956-61; NSF postdoctoral fellow New Zealand Oceanographic Inst., Wellington, 1961-62; prof. oceanography U. R.I., Kingston, 1962-72; rsch. oceanographer NOAA, Miami, Fla., 1972-73; dir. divsn. marine scis. UNESCO, Paris, 1973-89; cons. Paris, 1990-91; sr. rsch. oceanographer U. Calif., Santa Barbara, from 1992. Contbr. numerous articles to profl. jours. With C.E., U.S. Army, 1954-56. Recipient numerous rsch. grants; U.S. Nat. Acad. Sci./USSR Acad. Scis. exch. fellow, 1967-68. Fellow Geol. Soc. Am.; mem. Am. Geophys. Union. Achievements nclude 37 oceanographic cruises in Pacific and Atlantic Oceans as chief scientist and researcher; discovery and scientific understanding of many ocean floor features and areas. Home: Buena Park, Calif. Died Aug. 17, 2007.

KRAUSE, DENNIS ROGER, mechanical engineer; b. Lincoln, Nebr., Mar. 25, 1936; s. Herbert E. and Myrtle I. (Zuver) K. BS, U. Nebr., 1960, MS, 1964. Engr. John Deere, East Moline, Ill., 1960-61, Dempster Mill Mfg., Beatrice, Nebr., 1961-64, McDonnell Douglas Astrophysics, Santa Monica, Calif., 1964-81; sr. scientist Spectron Devel. Labs., Costa Mesa, Calif., 1981-88; program mgr. PDA Engring., Costa Mesa, 1988-92, L'Garde, Tustin, Calif., 1992-98. Contbr. articles to profl. jours. Recipient Cert. of Recognition, NASA. Mem. ASME, Sigma Xi, Sigma Tau, Pi Mu Epsilon. Home: Adams, Nebr. Died July 10, 2008.

KRAUSS, HERBERT MAX, retirement village administrator; b. Chgo., Mar. 28, 1915; s. Willy Arno and Elizabeth Minna (Winkler) K.; m. Ethelyn Mary Rasmussen, July 5, 1948; children: Stephen Herbert, Kirsten Elizabeth, Keary Richard, Herbert Andrew. BA with honors, Beloit Coll., 1937; MA, Oberlin Coll., 1941; MBA, U. Chgo., 1948. Adminstr. Burlington (Iowa) Hosp., 1948-54, Latrobe (Pa.) Hosp., 1954-63; assoc. dir. Genesee Hosp., Rochester, N.Y., 1963-67, dir., 1967-72; exec. dir. The Presbyn. Home, Evanston, Ill., 1973-82; ret., 1982. Contbr. articles to profl. jours. Bd. dirs. Genesee Valley Planning Coun., 1971-73. With U.S. Army, 1942-46. Decorated Silver Star, Purple Heart. Fellow Am. Coll. Hosp. Adminstrs.; mem. Am. Hosp. Assn., U. Chgo. Hosp. Adminstrs. Alumni Assn. (pres. 1960-61). Home: Penfield, NY. Died Oct. 14, 2007.

KRAUT, HARRY JOHN, music producer, consultant; b. Bklyn., Apr. 11, 1933; s. Harry and Margaret Grace (Pflaum) K. AB, Harvard U., 1954, postgrad., 1954-56. Asst. to mgr. Boston Symphony Orch., 1958-68, assoc. mgr., 1968-71; adminstr. Tanglewood Music Ctr., Lenox, Mass., 1962-71; exec. v.p. Amberson, Inc., NYC, from 1971; pres. Arts Planning and Design, Inc., Key West, Fla., from 1988, Pacific Music Festival Found., NYC, from 1991; executor Estate of Leonard Bernstein, NYC, from 1990; advisor Schleswig-Holstein Musik Festival, 1985-90, Pacific Music Festival (Sapporo), from 1990, Festival Bourgogne, from 2000; dir. Performing Arts Ctrs., Key West, Fla., from 2002. Mem. adv. bd. London Symphony Orch., 1995—, N.Y. Festival of Song, N.Y.C., 1992-, EOS Orch., N.Y.C., 1998—; trustee Peabody Conservatory, BAlt., 1983-87; pres. Harvard Glee Club Found., Cambridge, Mass., 1958-69. Exec. prodr. some 150 classic music films and videos, 1961—. Served with U.S. Army, 1956-58. Mem. Acad. TV Arts and Scis. (Emmy award 1978, 88), Harvard Musical Assn., Tennessee Williams Soc. (sec. 2003—). Democrat. Home: Key West, Fla. Died Dec. 11, 2007.

KRAXBERGER, CLETUS FRANCIS, banker; b. Stover, Mo., Jan. 3, 1927; s. Francis Joseph and Luenda Meta (Hagadorn) K.; m. Helen Joetta Sharp, Feb. 24, 1952; children: Steve Alan, Kenneth Lynn. Grad high sch., Stover. With Fidelity State Bank and Trust Co., Dodge City, Kans., from 1948, teller supr., 1960-68, security guard, bank card officer, 1968-88; retired, 1988. Active Stana Fe Trail council Boy Scouts Am.; mem. landscape commn., Dodge City. With U.S. Army, 1945-48. Mem. United Security Profl. Assn., Am. Legion, VFW, St Bernard 222, Shriners, Masons, Jaycees (chartered treas.). Democrat. Avocations: hunting, fishing, golf. Died Feb. 25, 2008.

KREMER, ALVIN WEBSTER, JR., (WEBB KREMER), military officer; b. Washington, Nov. 30, 1939; s. Alvin Webster and Ann (Foy) K.; m. Judith Heatwole, Aug. 9, 1961; children: Stephen Todd, Brooke Ann. BS in Engring., U.S. Mil. Acad., 1961; BS, MS in Mech. Engring., Ga. Tech. U., 1969; MA in Internal. Transactions, George Mason U., 1992; postgrad., USN War Coll., 1980-81. Commd. 2d lt. U.S. Army, 1961, advanced through grades to col., 1983, various positions, 1961-76, with ODCSOPS Washington, 1977-78, bn. comdr. 1st brigade Ft. Knox, Ky., 1978-80, brigade comdr., 1980, with force structure policy/strategy dept. joint chiefs Washington, 1982-83, comdr. armor brigade 1st armor div. Germany, 1983-85, chief of staff 7th army tng. command, 1985-87; dept. dir. U.S. Army Armor Sch., Ft. Knox, 1989-90. Owner internal. bus. in Soviet Union and eastern Europe. Decorated Legion of Merit with 2 oak leaf clusters, Bronze stars, Air medals. Mem. U.S. Army Armor Assn., Assn. U.S. Army, Assn. Grads. U.S. Mil. Acad. Lutheran. Avocations: skiing, golf, racquet sports, travel, military history. Home: Annandale, Va. Died Sept. 14, 2007.

KRIMS, MARVIN BENNETT, psychiatrist; b. Jan. 23, 1928; BS in Biochemistry, Tufts Coll., 1947; MD cum laude, Boston U., 1951. Diplomate Am. Bd. Psychiatry and Neurology, Am. Bd. of Psychiatry and Neurology in Child Psychiatry. Intern Boston City Hosp., 1951-52; resident Boston State Hosp., 1952-53, 55; staff psychiatrist R.I. div. of Alcoholism, 1955-58, Children's Hosp. Med. Ctr., 1957-67; supr. psychotheraphy study unit Mass. Mental Health Ctr., 1968-69; assoc. clin. prof. psychiatry Tufts Med. Sch., from 1985; lectr. in psychiatry Harvard Med. Sch., from 1992. Psychiat. cons. Boston Com. on Alcoholism, 1956-58, Youth Svc. Bd., 1957-58, Jewish Family and Children's Svc., 1957-89, Walker Home for Children, 1965-66, Children's Mission to Children, 1965-66; asst. in psychiatry Harvard Med. Sch., 1957-67; assoc. vis. physician child psychiatry dept. Boston City Hosp., 1967-72; asst. clin. prof. Boston U. Sch. of Medicine, 1967-75, chief investigator rsch. project, 1980—, mem. faculty psychoanalytic lit. criticism Boston Psychoanalytic Soc., 1970—; cons. Mass. Dept. Pub. Health, 1974-75 Contbr. articles to profl. publs. With USN, 1953-55. Fellow Am. Psychiat. Assn.; mem. Boston Psychoanalytic Soc., New Eng. Psychiat. Assn. (chmn. childhood and adolescence com. 1966-71), Mass. Med. Soc., New Eng. Coun. Child Psychiatry (pres. 1973-75, chmn. program com. 1973-74, chmn. continuing edn. program 1974-83, chair psychoanalytic lit. criticism colloquium 1988—). Home: Newton, Mass. Died Oct. 1, 2007.

KRISTOL, IRVING, social sciences educator, editor; b. Bklyn., Jan. 22, 1920; s. Joseph and Bessie (Mailman) K.; m. Gertrude Himmelfarb, Jan. 18, 1942; children: William, Elizabeth. BA, CCNY, 1940; LittD, Franklin and Marshall Coll., 1972; LLD, U. Dallas, 1974, Kenyon Coll., 1977. Mng. editor Commentary mag., 1947-52; co-founder, co-editor Encounter mag., 1953-58; editor The Reporter mag., 1959-60; exec. v.p. Basic Books Inc., NYC, 1961-69; co-founder, co-editor The Pub. Interest mag., 1965—2002; mem. faculty NYU, 1969-88; assoc. fellow Am. Enterprise Inst., 1972—77, sr. fellow, 1977—88, John M. Olin disting. fellow, 1988—99, fellow emeritus, 1999—2009; John M. Olin prof. social thought Grad. Sch. Bus. Adminstrn. NYU, 1979-88. Mem. Pres.'s Commn. on White House Fellowships, 1981—84, Nat. Coun. on the Humanities, 1972—77, Coun. Fgn. Rels. Author: On the Democratic Idea in America, 1972, Two Cheeers for Capitalism, 1978, Reflections of a Neoconservative, 1983, Neoconservatism: The Autobiography of an Idea, 1995; editor: (with Stephen Spender and Melvin Lasky) Encounters, 1963, (with Daniel Bell) Confrontation: The Student Rebellion and the University, 1969, Capitalism Today, 1971, The Crisis of Economic Theory, 1981, (with Nathan Glazer) The American Commonwealth, 1976, (with Paul Weaver) The Americans, 1976, (with Moran, Barnes, Mertes and Oduber) Third

World Instability, 1985; contbr. numerous articles. Served with US Army, 1944—46. Recipient Presdl. Medal of Freedom, The White House, 2002. Fellow: Am. Acad. Arts and Scis.; mem.: Century Assn. Republican. Died Sept. 18, 2009.

KRISTY, JAMES E., financial consultant; b. Kenosha, Wis., Sept. 3, 1929; s. Eugene H. and Ann T. Kristy; m. Edith L. Reid, Feb. 19, 1955; children: James R., Ann E., Robert E. BS in Econs., U. Wis., 1951; MBA in Fin., U. So. Calif., 1964; postgrad., Claremont Grad. Sch., Calif.; PhD in Mgmt. and Edn., Columbia-Pacific U., 1981. V.p. Lloyds Bank Calif., LA, 1969-71; chief treasury officer Computer Machinery Corp., LA, 1971-75; sr. v.p., CFO Century Bank, LA, 1979; vis. prof. Chapman U., from 1995. Cons., writer and lectr. in field; seminar leader Frost & Sullivan, London, CEL Ltd., Hong Kong, U. Calif., U. Hawaii, U. Colo., Temple U., Rutgers U., Tulane U. Author: Analyzing Financial Statements: Quick and Clean, 6th edit., 2003, Handbook of Budgeting, 1992; (with others) Finance Without Fear, 1983, Commercial Credit Matrix Software, 2002. 1st. lt. U.S. Army, 1951-53, Korea. Recipient Pub. Svc. award SBA, 1971. Died Nov. 24, 2007.

KRIZ, MARJORIE MINSK, writer; b. Evanston, Ill., May 2, 1920; d. Louis David and Helen (Tavenner) Minsk; m. Jack Jerome Kriz, children: Helen Marshall, John Jerome III. BS, Northwestern U., 1942, MA, 1943; postgrad., Oxford Christ Ch. Coll., 1985, U. Wis., 1986. From prodn. asst. to pub. rels. dir. Northwestern U. Theatre, Evanston, 1940-43; writer Am. Theatre Wing, NYC, 1943; reporter, editor City News Bur., Chgo., 1944-54, aviation editor, 1967-71; asst. pub. affairs officer Great Lakes region FAA, 1971-88. Author: Soaring Above Setbacks, 1996, Paperback, 1997; contbr. articles to profl. jours. Bd. dirs. Milw.'s Mitchell Gallery Flight Mus. Mem. Aviation Space Writers Assn., Chgo. Newspaper Reporters Assn., Chgo. Press Vets. Assn. (bd. dirs.), Soc. Midland Authors, Zeta Phi Eta. Home: Evanston, Ill. Died Sept. 18, 2007.

KRONICK, JANE COLLIER, political science professor; b. Hudson, NY, May 1, 1932; d. Charles Armstrong and Marion Jane (Lasher) Collier; m. Paul Leonard Kronick, July 21, 1957; children: Rani, Oren Collier, Charles Ivar. AB, Columbia U., 1953; MS, Yale U., 1956, PhD, 1960. Tchg. asst. Yale Univ., New Haven, 1956-57; instr. Univ. Del., Newark, 1958-59, Bryn Mawr Coll., Pa., 1959-61, asst. prof. to prof. Pa., 1961—95; dir. rsch. Coll. of Social Work, Univ. Tenn., Knoxville, Tenn., 1990-92, acting assoc. dean, 1990-92, emeritus prof., 1995—2009. Vis. prof. Univ. Canterbury, Christchurch, New Zealand, 1974-75. Contbr. chpt. to books and articles to profl. jour. Bd. mem. Haverford (Pa.) Friends Sch., 1980-90, clk. Haverford (Pa.) Soc. Friends, 1986-89. Recipient Fulbright fellowship Fulbright Commn. to New Zealand, 1954, Nat. Sci. grants NSF, Washington, 1976-84, Legion of Honor award for outstanding cmty. svc., Phila., 1980, Lindback award for disting. tchg. Lindback Found., 1988. Mem. AAUP, Am. Sociol. Assn., Friends in Higher Edn. Home: Kennett Square, Pa. Died Mar. 19, 2009.

KRUEGER, JAMES ELWOOD, pharmaceutical executive; b. Marinette, Wis., Apr. 2, 1926; s. Jesse and Beulah (Elwood) K.; m. Claire Pickener, June 20, 1953 (dec. 1966); children: David, Jonathan, Thomas; m. Virginia Cochrane Webb, Aug. 16, 1969; children: Virginia, Cynthia, Gregory. BS, U. Wis., 1949; PhD, MIT, 1954. Cert. quality auditor. Rsch. fellow Harvard Med. Sch., Brookline, Mass., 1953-55; rsch. chemist Dow Chem. Co., Midland, Mich., 1955-61; group leader Am. Cyanamid Co., Pearl River, N.Y., 1961-69, sr. rsch. chemist, 1969-79, sr. quality auditor, 1979-90; v.p. quality assurance I.N.D. Mgmt., Upper Saddle River, N.J., from 1990. Author: NMR Spectra Vol. I, 1965, Vol. II, 1966, ISO 9000: Guidelines For Use by the Chemical and Process Industries, 1992, Pharmaceutical Process Validation, 2nd edit., 1993; patentee in field. Bd. dirs. Hudson River Counseling Svc., Mt. Kisco, N.Y., 1973-79. With U.S. Army, 1945-46. Mem. Am. Soc. Quality Control (sr., chair Tappan Zee sect. 1991—). Home: Rochester, NY. Died Aug. 15, 2008.

KRUG, JUDITH FINGERET, school librarian; b. Pitts., Mar. 15, 1940; d. David and Florence (Leiber) Fingeret; m. E. Herbert Krug, Oct. 12, 1963; children: Steven, Michelle. BA in Polit. Theory, U. Pitts., 1961; MA, U. Chgo., 1964; LLD, U. Ill., 2005. Reference librarian John Crerar Library, Chgo., 1962-63; cataloguer dental sch. libr. Northwestern U., Chgo., 1963-65; rsch. analyst ALA, Chgo., 1965-67, dir. Office Intellectual Freedom, 1967—2009; exec. dir. Freedom to Read Found., Chgo., 1969—2009. Mem. com. on pub. understanding about the law ABA, Chgo. 1985-91; founder, Banned Books Week, 1982-2009 Editor Newsletter on Intellectual Freedom, Freedom to Read Found. News; exec. producer (film) The Speaker, 1977 (Silver Cindy award 1978, Silver Screen award 1979). Bd. dirs. Chgo. chpt. Am. Jewish Commn., Coun. Lit. Mags. and Presses; chair Media Coalition Recipient Irita Van Doren Book award Am. Bookselllers Assn., 1976, Harry Kalven Freedom of Expression award ACLU, 1976, Robert B. Downs award U. Ill., Champign-Urbana, 1978, Carl Sandburg Freedom to Read award Friends Chgo. Pub. Libr., 1983, Open Book award Am. Soc. Journalists and Authors, 1984, Pres.'s award MCLU, 1985, Intellectual Freedom award Ill. Libr. Assn. 1990, Ohio Ednl. Libr. Media Assn. Intellectual Freedom award, 1994, Freedom to Read Found. Roll of Honor award, 1995, Joseph W. Lippincott award, 1998, William J. Brennan award Thomas Jefferson Ctr. for the Protection of Free Expression, 2009 Mem. ALA, Phi Beta Kappa (assoc., exec. commn. Chgo. area, pres. 1991-94) Home: Evanston, Ill. Died Apr. 11, 2009.

KRUGGEL, REUBEN AUGUST, pastor; b. Lake Mills, Iowa, June 15, 1926; s. August and Elizabeth (Glietz) K. BA magna cum laude, St. Olaf Coll., 1947; BD, MDiv, Northwestern Luth. Sem., 1950; STM, Concordia Sem., 1951; postgrad., No. Ill. U., 1963-65; LittD (hon.), London Inst., 1980. Ordained minister Am. Luth. Ch., 1955. Tchr. Concordia Coll., Moorhead, Minn., 1952-53; assoc. in ministry First Luth. Ch., Decorah, Iowa, 1953-54, pastor Lee, Ill., 1955-62, supply pastor, from 1962; product contr., then asceptic product mixer Del Monte, Rochelle, Ill., 1962-88. Active Luth. Social Svcs. Ill., 1994—. Mem. Moose. Avocations: railroad, travel. Home: Rochelle, Ill. Died Aug. 2, 2008.

KRULAK, VICTOR HAROLD, retired military officer; b. Denver, Jan. 7, 1913; s. Morris and Besse M. (Ball) K.; m. Amy Chandler, June 1, 1936 (dec. 2001); children: Victor Harold Jr., William Morris, Charles Chandler. BS, U.S. Naval Acad., 1934; LL.D., U. San Diego. Commd. 2d lt. USMC, 1934; advanced through grades to lt. gen.; service in China, at sea, with USMC (Fleet Marine Forces), 1935-39; staff officer, also bn. regimental and divsn. comdr. World War II, World War II; chief staff (1st Marine Div. Korea); formerly comdg. gen. (Marine Corps Recruit Depot), San Diego; formerly spl asst. to dir., joint staff counterinsurgency and spl. activities (Office Joint Chiefs Staff); comdg. gen. Fleet Marine Force Pacific, Pacific, 1964-68; ret., 1968; v.p. Copley Newspaper Corp., 1968-79; pres. Words Ltd. Corp., San Diego. Author: First to Fight, 1984. Trustee Zool. Soc. San Diego. Decorated D.S.M., Navy Cross, Legion of Merit with 3 oak leaf clusters, Bronze Star, Air medal, Purple Heart (2) U.S.; Cross of Gallantry; Medal of Merit Vietnam; Distinguished Service medal (Korea), Order of Cloud and Banner, Republic of China. Mem. U.S. Naval Inst., U.S. Marine Corps Assn., Am. Soc. Newspaper Editors, InterAm. Press Assn., U.S. Strategic Inst. (chmn.). Home: San Diego, Calif. Died Dec. 29, 2008.

KRUSE, MARIE MAXINE, retail executive, councilman; b. Bedford, Ind., Oct. 6, 1928; d. Ted Roosevelt and Bertha (Baker) Crane; m. Samuel William Kruse, July 4, 1953; children: Samuel William Jr., Lynn Renee Kruse McCreary, Doran Spencer, Jan Merle, Lea Anne. Grad. high sch., Bedford. Advt. and display mgr. J.C. Penney and Co., Bedford, 1947-61, W.T. Grant Co., Bedford, 1965-70; office mgr. Gene B. Glick Co., Bedford and Washington, Ind., 1976-78; mgr., promotion dir. Stone City Mall (Nooney Co.), Bedford, from 1979. Contbr. numerous articles to profl. jours. Pres. Lawrence County Library Bd., Bedford, 1981—; pres. Legion Aux. Post 33, Bedford, 1985-87; mem. Lawrence County City Coun., Bedford, 1988—; tourism chmn. Lawrence County, Bedford, 1985—; mem. adv. com. Vocat. Sch., Bedford, 1979—; mem. Green Hill Cemetery Bd., Bedford, 1980—; state vocat. ednl. team, Bedford, 1980—. Mem. Bedford Area C. of C. (treas., tourism chmn. 1984—, Community Svcs. award 1986, Pres.'s award 1986), DAR (regent 1980-82), Lawrence County Hist. Soc. Republican. Methodist. Home: Bedford, Ind. Died July 11, 2008.

KRYJAK, MICHAEL ANTHONY, counselor; b. Shenandoah, Pa., Feb. 7, 1955; s. Paul Frank and Sylvia Theresa K. BA with honors in Sociology, Schiller U., Heidelberg, West Germany, 1976; postgrad., Harvard U., 1988; cert. clin. inverview in psychiatry, Yale U., 1989; cert. fundamental econs., Henry George Inst., NYC; postgrad., Audio Digest Found., from 1988. Security aide Bloomsburg (Pa.) U., 1974-75; libr. staff Schiller U., Heidelberg, Germany, 1975-76; ind. ednl. cons. Shenandoah, Pa., 1978-81; sec.-treas. Shenandoah Mchts. Assn., 1979-81; com. mem. Shenandoah Downtown Task Force, 1979-81; rsch. asst., lectr. Pa. State U., Hazleton, 1981-83; residential advisor Keystone Job Corps Ctr., Drums, Pa., 1985-86; sr. counselor Schuylkill County Prison, Pottsville, Pa., from 1986; psychiat. caseworker St. Joseph's Med. Ctr., Reading, Pa., from 1995; facilitator/lead facilitator dept. gen. edn. faculty Rosemont (Pa.) Coll., from 1995. Mem. adj. faculty Reading (Pa.) Area C.C., 1988—; mental health counselor Brandywine Hosp. and Trauma Ctr., Coatsville, Pa., 1988; guest lectr. King's Coll., Wilkes-Barre, Pa., 1981, Kutztown (Pa.) State Coll., 1982, Pa. State U., 1982; guest lectr. Pa. State U., Bloomsburg (Pa.) State Coll., Pa. State U., Hazleton, 1982, 83; co-dir. support group Family Svc. Agy., Pottsville, Pa., 1989—; presenter in field. Rsch. asst.: The Disaster is Above Ground, 1990. Mem. Am. Sociol. Assn., Am. Orchid Soc., Colonial Williamsburg Found., The Cymbidium Soc. Am., British Broadcasting Corp. World Svc. Radio Club, Health Systems Agy. Northeastern Pa. Home: Shenandoah, Pa. Died Oct. 18, 2007.

KUEBLER, DAVID WAYNE, insurance company executive, private investigator; b. New Orleans, Apr. 18, 1947; s. Royce Matthew and Rosemary (West) K.; children: Kira Louise, Krystal Lynn. B. in Bus. Mgmt., Loyola U., New Orleans, 1969. Lic. ins. broker, investment mgr.; lic. investigator, La. Asst. mgr. Winn-Dixie, Inc., New Orleans, 1962-69; account exec. Travelers Ins. Co., St. Louis, 1969-74; sr. account exec. Gen. Am. Life., St. Louis, 1974-76; dist. mgr. Guardian Life Ins., New Orleans, 1976-81; pres. Profl. Planners, Inc., Kenner, La., from 1981, Louisianadetectives.com, 2001, Pro-Care, Inc., from 1983. Asst. chief of staff civil mil. ops. 377 Taacom, New Orleans, 1987. Coach girls athletics, Metairie, La., 1987. Col. USAR. Mem.: John E. Reid Inst., Bus. Espionage Controls and Countermeasures Assn., Met Plus Group Millionaires. Democrat. Avocation: coaching girls softball and basketball. Home: Kenner, La. Died Oct. 15, 2007.

KUEHLER, JACK DWYER, engineering consultant; b. Grand Island, NB, Aug. 29, 1932; m. Carmen Kuehler; children: Cindy, Daniel, Christy, Michael, David BS, Santa Clara U., 1954, MS, 1974; DSc, Clarkson U., 1989. Assoc. engr. San Jose rsch. lab IBM Corp., 1958-67, dir. Raleigh (N.C.) comm. lab, 1967-70, dir. San Jose and Menlo Park devel. labs, 1970-72, v.p. gen. prodn. divsn., 1972-74, v.p. devel., 1974-77, pres. system prodn. divsn., 1978—80, v.p., pres. gen. tech. divsn., 1980-81, sr. v.p., 1982, group exec., tech. group, 1982-88, vice-chmn., 1988-89, pres., 1989-93; ret., 1993; ind. cons., 1993—2008. Asst. group exec. systems devel. Data Processing Prodn. Group, 1977-78, info. systems and tech. group exec., 1981, mem. corp. mgmt. bd., 1985, exec. v.p., 1987 Fellow IEEE, Am. Acad. Arts and Sci.; mem. NAE. Died Dec. 20, 2008.

KUHN, ROBERT FREDERICK (BOB KUHN), artist, illustrator; b. Buffalo, Jan. 28, 1920; s. Edward George and Marie W. (Trapp) K.; m. Elizabeth Jane Casey, July 26, 1941; children: Robert Casey, Karen Elizabeth, Julie Ann. Student, Pratt Inst., 1937-40. Writer, illustrator: The Animal Art of Bob Kuhn, 1973; represented in permanent collections Gilcrease Mus., Tulsa, Nat. Cowboy Hall of Fame, Oklahoma City, Genesee County Mus., Rochester, N.Y., Nat. Mus. Wildlife Art, Jackson, Wyo. With USMS, 1943-45. Recipient numerous awards including Prix de West, 1991, Gold medal (2), Silver medal, Award of Merit (5) Soc. Animal Artists, Rungius medal Nat. Mus. Wildlife Art, 1989, Disting. Wildlife Artist award Leigh Yawkey Woodson Art Mus., Wausau, Wis., 1990. Died Oct. 1, 2007.

KULL, FRANCIS RAYMOND, manufacturing company executive, consultant; b. Phila., Sept. 26, 1921; s. John Hans and Hattie (Nickles) K.; m. Pauline Elizabeth Brown; children: Francis Jr., Richard, Patricia, James. BSME, Drexel U., 1953, MS in Engring Mgmt., 1973. Registered profl. engr., Pa. Sr. machine designer STD Pressed Steel Co., Jenkintown, Pa., 1940-50, project engr., 1950-60; mgr. product devel. SPS Techs., Jenkintown, 1960-70, mgr. rsch. svcs. and contract rsch., 1970-87; pres. FRK Cons., Warminster, Pa., from 1987. Mgr. contract referrals Govt. Contracts Prin. Investigator; lectr. in field. Contbr. articles to profl. jours.; inventor of fasteners, fastener tools, mfg. equipment and tools. Mem. ASME, Soc. Automotive Engrs. Republican. Avocations: flying, skiing, boating, golf, bowling. Home: Warminster, Pa. Died July 15, 2008.

KUNZEL, ERICH, JR., conductor, arranger, educator; b. NYC, Mar. 21, 1935; s. Erich and Elisabeth (Enz) Kunzel; m. Brunhilde Gertrud Strodl, Sept. 5, 1965. AB in Music, Dartmouth Coll., 1957; postgrad., Harvard U., 1957—58; AM, Brown U., 1960; LittD, No. Ky. State U., 1973; D of Arts, Coll. Mt. St. Joseph, 1996; D in Musical Arts, U. Cin., 2000. Condr. Sante Fe Opera, 1957, Santa Fe Opera, 1964, 1965; music faculty Brown U., 1958—65; asst. condr. R.I. Philharmonic, 1963—65; resident condr. Cin. Symphony Orch., 1965—77; condr. Cin. Summer Opera, 1966, 1973, Cin. Ballet Co., 1966—68; assoc. prof. U. Cin. Coll.-Conservatory Music, 1965—71, chmn. opera dept., 1968—70; music dir. Philharmonia Orch., 1967—71, New Haven (Conn.) Symphony Orch., 1974—77, San Francisco Art Commn. Pops, 1981—83; condr. Cin. Pops Orch., 1977—2009; prin. pops condr. Naples Philharm. Orch., 1993—2009. Guest condr. Boston Symphony, Cleve. Orch., Boston Pops, Phila. Orch., San Francisco Symphony, Buffalo Philharm., Rochester Philharm., Pitts. Symphony, Atlanta Symphony, Chgo. Symphony Orch., Interlochen Arts Festival, Dallas Symphony, Detroit Symphony, Toronto Symphony, Montreal Symphony, St. Louis Symphony, Nat. Symphony, London Symphony, China Nat. Symphony, Can. Opera Co., San Francisco Opera, others. Editor, arranger choral works, recs. for Decca Gold Label, Atlantic Records, Telarc Internat., Vox Records, Caedmon Records, Pro Arte Records, Fanfare, MMG, MCA Classics Gold. V.p. Pierre Monteux Meml. Found., Met. Opera Guild; chmn. Greater Cin. Arts and Edn. Ctr., from 1998. Recipient Grand Prix du Disque, 1989, Sony Tiffany award, 1989, Classical Record of Yr. award, Japan, 1989, Grammy nomination, 1989, 1991, 1993, 1995, Ohioana Pegasus award, 2000, Nat. Medal Arts, Nat. Endowment Arts, 2006; named Billboard Crossover Artist of Yr., 1988, 1989, 1990, 1991; named to Hon. Order Ky. Cols. Mem.: Am. Symphony Orch. League, Delta Omicron, Phi Mu Alpha Sinfonia, Phi Delta Theta (Disting. Alumnus award 1996). Home: Swans Island, Maine. Died Sept. 1, 2009.

KURLOWICZ, LENORE H., geropsychiatric nurse specialist; b. Shenandoah, Pa., Mar. 12, 1953; d. Leonard Stanley and Marie Ann (Siedlarz) K. Diploma in nursing, Sacred Heart Hosp., Allentown, Pa., 1973; BSN, U. Pa., 1980, MSN, 1983, PhD in Nursing, 1995. Staff nurse step down surgery, cardiac ICU Hosp. of U. Pa., Phila., 1973-75, staff nurse post anesthesia recovery rm., 1975-80, staff nurse psychiatry, 1980-83, psychiat. consultation-liaison nurse, from 1983. Contbr. articles to profl. jours. Recipient Writer's award Jour. Med.-Surg. Nursing, 1994. Mem. ANA (cert. specialist/adult psychiat. mental health nurse), Gerontol. Soc. Am., Internat. Soc. Psychiat. Consultation Liaison Nurses (founding mem.), Sigma Theta Tau (Xi chpt.). Home: Philadelphia, Pa. Died Sept. 21, 2007.

KURNIT, DAVID MARTIN, pediatrician, educator; b. Bklyn., Dec. 24, 1947; s. Victor and Helen (Oxhandler) K.; m. Kristine Kurnit, May 1, 1993; children: Katherine, Jennifer. BA, CUNY, 1968; PhD, Albert Einstein Coll. Medicine, 1974, MD, 1975. Diplomate Am. Bd. Pediatrics, Am. Bd. Medical Genetics. Intern Childrens Hosp., Pitts., Pa., 1975-76, resident, 1976-77; fellow med. genetics U. Washington, Seattle, 1977-79; asst. prof. pediatrics Harvard Med. Sch., Boston, 1979-84, assoc. prof., 1985-86; investigator Howard Hughes Med. Inst., Ann Arbor, from 1986; prof. pediatrics and human genetics U. Mich. Med. Ctr., Ann Arbor, from 1986. Contbr. articles to Procs. NAS, Am. Jour. Human Genetics, Nature Genetics. Bd. dirs. Ann Arbor Ctr. for Ind. Living, 1992; chmn. adv. com. Ann Arbor Transp. Authority, 1992. Grantee NIH-SUPHS, 1968-75, NIH, 1977-79, 1982—. Mem. Am. Soc. Human Genetics, Phi Beta Kappa. Achievements include development of recombination-based assay to isolate genes; elaboration of stochastic mechanism that underlies phenotypic defects in a plurality of subjects. Home: Ann Arbor, Mich. Died Jan. 30, 2008.

KUSKIN, KARLA, writer, illustrator; b. NYC, July 17, 1932; d. Sidney T. and Mitzi (Salzman) Seidman; m. Charles Kuskin, Dec. 4, 1955 (div. August 1987); children: Nicholas, Julia; m. William L. Bell Jr., July, 1989 (dec. 2006). Student, Antioch Coll., 1950-53; BFA, Yale U., 1955. Tchr., cons. schs. at elem. and univ. levels. Illustrator: (books) Xingu, 1959, Sing for Joy, 1961, Credos & Quips, 1964, Look at Me, 1967, Big Enough, 1970, Stone Soup, 1984; author, illustrator: (books) Roar and More, 1956 (Am. Inst. Graphic Arts Book Show awards 1955-57), 2d edit., 1990, James and the Rain, 1957, 2d edit., 1995, The Animals and the Ark, 1958, In the Middle of the Trees, 1958 (Am. Inst. Graphic Arts Book Show award 1958), Just Like Everybody Else, 1959, Which Horse is William?, 1959, Square as a House, 1960 (Am. Inst. Graphic Arts Book Show awards 1958-60), The Bear Who Saw the Spring, 1961, All Sizes of Noises, 1962, Alexander Soames: His Poems, 1962, (as Nicholas J. Charles) How Do You Get from Here to There?, 1962, ABCDEFGHIJKLMNOPQRSTUVWXYZ, 1963, The Rose on My Cake, 1964, Sand and Snow, 1965, (as Nicholas J. Charles) Jane Anne June Spoon and Her Very Adventurous Search for the Moon, 1966, The Walk the Mouse Girls Took, 1967, Watson, the Smartest Dog in the U.S.A., 1968, In the Flaky Frosty Morning, 1969, Any Me I Want to Be: Poems, 1972, What Did You Bring Me?, 1973, Near the Window Tree: Poems and Notes, 1975 (Children's Book award Internat. Reading Assn. 1976), A Boy Had a Mother Who Bought Him a Hat, 1976, Herbert Hated Being Small, 1979, Dogs & Dragons, Trees & Dreams: A Collection of Poems, 1980 (ALA award 1980), Night Again, 1981, Something Sleeping in the Hall, 1985, Soap Soup, 1992, A Great Miracle Happened Here: A Chanukah Story, 1993, Patchwork Island, 1994, City Dog, 1994 (Best Picture N.Y. Times 1995), City Noise, 1994; author: (books) A Space Story, 1978 (Children's Sci. Book award N.Y. Acad. Scis. 1980), The Philharmonic Gets Dressed, 1982 (ALA award 1982, Nat. Book award nomination 1983), The Dallas Titans Get Ready for Bed, 1986, Jerusalem, Shining Still, 1987, (with paintings by Milton Avery) Paul, 1994, The Upstairs Cat, 1997, Moon, Have You Met Your Mother? The Collected Poems of Karla Kuskin, 2003; contbg. editor: Saturday Review, 1973; book reviewer: Record-Poetry Parade; contbr. articles to publs. including, New York mag., House and Garden, N.Y. Times, Wilson Library Bull., Horizon mag. Recipient Nat. Coun. Tchrs. English award, 1979, John S. Burroughs Sci. award 1995; named Outstanding Bklyn. Author, 1981, award N.Y. Acad. Scis., 1979. Jewish. Died Aug. 20, 2009.

KUTSCHINSKI, DOROTHY IRENE, elementary school educator; b. Denison, Iowa, Feb. 19, 1922; d. Gustave Waldemar and Wilhelmina Louisa (Stahl) Wiese; m. Alvin Otto Kutschinski; children: Karen E. Kutschinski Christensen, Linda K. Kutschinski Nepper. BA, Morningside Coll., 1965, MA in Teaching, 1970. Tchr. Crawford County (Iowa) Rural Schs., 1940-53, Charter Oak (Iowa) Community Schs., 1953-90; substitute tchr., from 1990. Apptd. to Crawford County Coun. Local Govt. for Hist. Preservation, 1992—, chair 1996—; tchr. Bible class St. John Luth. Ch., Charter Oak, Iowa, 1956—; sec. Crawford County Rep. Ctrl. Com., 1980-91, 98—; pres. Crawford County Rep. Women, 1978-86 trustee Iowa N.W. Regional Libr., 1991-2001; co-founder, sec., charter Oak-Ute Cmty. Sch. Edn. Found., 1994—, apptd. to adv. com., sec., 1993-2001. Recipient Tchr. of Yr. award, Denison Newspapers, 1985, Women of Excellence award, Women Aware, Inc., 2001; named Outstanding Elem. Tchr. of Am., 1973. Mem. AAUW (treas. 1985-90, pres. 1991-93), Iowa State Hist. Soc., Crawford County Hist. Soc. (life), The Smithsonian Assocs., The Audubon Soc., Living History Farms, Iowa Natural Heritage, Crawford County Arts Assn. (pres. 1986-88, bd. dirs. 1972—, sec. 1996—), Delta Kappa Gamma, Alpha Delta (sec. 1984—). Avocations: reading, sewing, bird watching, walking, writing. Home: Charter Oak, Iowa. Died June 24, 2008.

KUZMA, GEORGE MARTIN, retired bishop; b. Windber, Pa., July 24, 1925; s. Ambrose and Anne (Marton) Kuzma. Attended, Benedictine Coll., Lisle, Ill.; BA, postgrad., Duquesne U., U. Mich.; grad., SS Cyril and Methodius Byzantine Cath. Sem. Ordained priest, 1955; asst. pastor SS Peter and Paul Ch., Braddock, Pa., 1955—57; pastor Holy Ghost Ch., Charleroi, Pa., 1957—65, St. Michael Ch., Flint, Mich., 1965—70, St. Eugene Ch., Bedford, Ohio, 1970—72, Annunciation Ch., Anaheim, Calif., 1970—86; rev. monsignor Byzantine Cath. Ch., 1984, titular bishop, 1986; aux. bishop Eparchy of Passaic of the Ruthenians, NJ, 1986—90; ordained bishop, 1987; bishop Eparchy of Van Nuys for the Ruthenians, Calif., 1991—2000, bishop emeritus, 2000—08. Judge matrimonial tribunal, mem. religious edn. commn., mem. commn. orthodox rels. Diocese of Pitts., 1955—69; judge matrimonial tribunal, vicar for religious Diocese of Parma, 1969—82; treas., bd. dirs., chmn. liturgical commn., mem. clergy & seminarian rev. bd., liaison to ea. Cath. dirs. religious edn., bd. dirs. Diocese of Van Nuys, 1982—86, diocesan credit un, chmn. diocesan heritage bd., chmn. diocesan ecumenical commn., 1982—86; vicar gen. Diocese of Passaic; Episcopal vicar for Ea. Pa.; chmn. Diocesan Retirement Plan Bd.; pres. Father Walter Cizsek Prayer League; chaplain Byzantine Carmelite Monastery, Sugarloaf, Pa. Assoc. editor: Byzantine Cath. World; editor: The Apostle. With USN, 1943—46, PTO. Roman Catholic. Died Dec. 7, 2008.

KUZNESOF, PAUL MARTIN, food chemist; b. NYC, Aug. 13, 1941; s. Benjamin Kuznesof and Betty (Gordon) Fox; m. Elizabeth Anne Parks, Apr. 19, 1969 (div. 1976); 1 child, Adam Aeschylus; m. Laura Marie McDonald, Sept. 18, 1982 (div. 1991). ScB in Chemistry, Brown U., 1963; PhD in Chemistry, Northwestern U., 1967. Postdoc. fellow U. Calif., Lawrence Berkeley Lab., Berkeley, 1967-69; asst. prof. San Francisco State U., 1969-70; assoc. prof. Universidade Estadual de Campinas (Brazil), 1970-75; lectr. U. Mich., Ann Arbor, 1975-76; visiting assoc. prof. Trinity Coll., Hartford, Conn., 1976-78; postdoc. fellow USN Rsch. Lab., Washington, 1978-79; assoc. prof. Agnes Scott Coll., Decatur, Ga., 1979-83; rev. chemist FDA, Washington, 1984-87; supervisory chemist Food and Color Additives Rev. Sect., Washington, 1987—2009. Contbr. articles to profl. jours. Troop com. Boys Scouts Am., Decatur, Ga., 1980-82; commr. Decatur-DeKalb YMCA soccer, 1981-82. Grantee Found. for Rsch. Support in the State of Sao Paulo, Brazil, 1971, Rsch. Corp. Cottrell Sci. Grant, Trinity Coll., 1977, NSF, Agnes Scott Coll., Ga., 1981; recipient Career Svc. award, FDA, 2007 Mem. Am. Chem. Soc. (trea. Ga. chpt. 1982-83), AAAS, Chem. Soc. Washington, Sigma Xi. Democrat. Home: Silver Spring, Md. Died Oct. 2, 2009.

KWART, ARNOLD MARTIN, urologic surgeon; b. NYC, May 29, 1942; s. Sam and Esther Molly (Goldberg) K.; m. Cathryn Kahn, May 13, 1984. BS cum laude, U. Fla, 1964; MD, Duke U., 1968. Diplomate Am. Bd. Urology. Intern/resident physician NYU, NYC, 1968-70; resident physician urology Johns Hopkins Hosp., Balt., 1970-74; urologic surgeon U.S. Army, Seoul, Korea, 1974-77; asst. prof. urology George Washington U., Washington, 1977-80, assoc. clin. prof. urology, 1980-87, clin. prof. urology, 1988—97; ptnr. Urologic Surgeons Washington, D.C., 1980-97; assoc. clin. prof. urology and urologic oncology Georgetown U. Hosp., 1996—2008; chair dept. urology Washington Hosp. Ctr., Washington, 1997—2006, med. staff bd., 1997—2008, chair anesthesiology com., 2001, bd. dirs., 2003—08. Pres. Attending Physicians Assn., George Washington U. Hosp., 1985-86; mem. various coms. George Washington U. including cost containment com., 1980, joint conf. com., 1983-86, 86-89, working group GWU/AMI study, 1984, exec. com. faculty senate, 1985-86, chmn. com. on pub. rels., 1986-88, search com., v.p. med. affairs, 1988, physicians adv. coun., 1989-2008, med. ctr. devel. com., 1989, chmn. ad hoc med. staff com., 1989-90, chmn. oper. rm. com., 1990-96, chmn. urologic com., 1996-2008; mem. tumor bd. Sibley Meml. Hosp., 1980-2008, tumor bd. com., 1981, continuing med. edn., 1981-83, tranfusion com., 1988-2008, organized prostate cancer awareness week, 1990-2008; presenter in field. Contbr. articles to profl. jours. Lectr. Fed. Res. Sys., 1985, Multiple Sclerosis Soc., 1985; vol. Am. Cancer Soc., 1977-2008; adv. bd. Md. Ostomy Assn., 1989-2008; vol. physician Jewish Social Svcs. Agy., 1991-2008. Maj. U.S. Army, 1974-77. Recipient Johns Hopkins Med. and Surg. Assn. Best Presentation award The Brady Urologic Inst., 1981, First Pl. Sci. Exhibit, Percutaneous Removal of Kidney Stones, D.C. Med. Soc., 1983; recognized as one of the best urologists in Washington, D.C. area by Washingtonian Mag., 1986, 91, 93, 97, 2002. Fellow ACS; mem. AMA, Am. Urol. Assn. (alt. to socioeconomics com. 1989, mem. mid-Atlantic sect. 1977-2008, membership com. 1987-90, chmn. membership com. 1990, credentials com. 1987-88), D.C. Med. Soc. (cancer com. 1980-85, grievance com. 1988-90, long-range planning com. 1989, nominating com. 1989, vice chmn. utilization and peer rev. com. 1990, chmn. utilization and peer rev. com. 1993, chmn. sci. program com. 1996-2008), Washington Urologic Soc. (membership chmn. 1989, treas. 1990, sec. 1991, v.p. 1992, pres. 1993), Soc. Univ. Urologists, Jacobi Med. Soc., Am. Cancer Soc., Endourological Soc., Phi Beta Kappa, Phi Kappa Phi, Phi Eta Sigma, Alpha Epsilon Delta. Jewish. Achievements include inventor of Kwart Retroinject Stent-Cook Urol. Mfr., Endosnare-Cook Urol. Mfr. Home: Chevy Chase, Md. Died Nov. 4, 2008.

KYTE, LYDIANE, retired botanist; b. LA, Jan. 6, 1919; d. Aurele and Helen Scott (Douglas) Vermeulen; m. Robert McClung Kyte, June 2, 1939; children: Katherine Liu, Bobbin Cave, William Robert Kyte. BS, U. Wash., 1964. Supt. Weyerhaeuser Co., Rochester, Wash., 1972-77; lab mgr. Briggs Nursery, Olympia, Wash., 1977-80; co-owner Cedar Valley Nursery, Centralia, Wash., from 1980. Cons. Internat. Exec. Service Corps, Brazil, 1987, Egypt, 1990. Author: Plants From Test Tubes: An Introduction to Micropropagation, 1983, 2d rev. edit., 1988, 3d edit., 1996. Mem. Port Townsend Marine Sci. Ctr. Mem. AAUW, Internat. Assn. Plant Tissue Culture. Avocation: gardening. Home: Centralia, Wash. Died Aug. 4, 2008.

LACHMAN, MORTON, writer, theatrical director and producer; b. Seattle, Mar. 20, 1918; s. Sol and Rose (Bloom) L.; m. Elaine Lachman, June 23, 1940; children: Joanne, Dianne, Robert; m. Natalie Gittelson; stepchildren: Celia, Eve, Tony BA, U. Wash., Seattle, 1939. Exec. producer: (TV series) Kraft Music Hall Presents: The Des O'Connor Show, 1970, All in the Family (Emmy award for Outstanding Comedy Series, 1978), 1976-79, In the Beginning, 1978, Archie Bunker's Place, 1979, Sanford, 1980, No Soap, Radio, 1982, Spencer, 1984, Kate & Allie, 1984-88, Gimme A Break, 1985, The Stiller & Meara Show, 1986, Baghdad Cafe, 1990; prodr.: (TV movies) Not in Front of the Kids, 1984, The Mating Call, 1984; (TV specials) The Bob Hope Vietnam Christmas Show, 1971; head writer, prodr., dir. The Bob Hope Show, 1947-1975; head writer 11 Acad. Award shows; co-writer: (films) Mixed Company, 1974, Yours, Mine & Ours, 2005; dir. (TV episodes) That's My Mama (2 episodes), 1975, ABC Afternoon Playbreak: The Girl Who Couldn't Lose, (Emmy award for Outstanding Individual Director for a Daytime Special Program), 1975. With AUS, 1942-45. Mem.: El Caballero, Queens, Tamerisk, Rangoon Racquet. Died Mar. 17, 2009.

LAFRANKIE, JAMES V., retired water utility holding company executive; b. Elizabeth, Pa., Mar. 26, 1927; s. John Lewis and Susan Marie (Heidrick) L.; m. Nancy Louise Wiegel, June 12, 1954; children: Terence, James Jr., Jane, Donna, Kenneth, Mark, William BS in Mgmt., Georgetown U., 1964. With Am. Water Works Co. Inc., Elizabeth, 1948—84, pres., 1984—91. Dir., exec. com. Am. Water Works Co. Inc., Voorhees, N.J. Served in US Army, 1945—47. Mem. Am. Water Works Assn. (Fuller award, hon. mem.), Nat. Assn. Water Cos. (past chmn. bd.) Republican. Roman Catholic. Home: Williamsburg, Va. Died Oct. 8, 2009.

LAGRANGE, MARILYN ANN, marketing financial management and planning specialist; b. Morganfield, Ky., Jan. 8, 1949; d. Lewis George and Wilma Grace (Shoulders) Martin; m. David Gabriel LaGrange, Oct. 3, 1975 (div. May 1989); children: D. Gabriel II, Kathryn Lew. BS, Western Ky. U., 1972. Auditor State of Ky., Frankfort, 1972-74, Riney McKee & Co. CPAs, Owensboro, Ky., 1975; dir. fin. analysis-glass Ball Corp., Muncie, Ind., 1975-81, dir. strategic planning-plastics, 1981—86, sr. fin. analyst glass, 1989-91, dir. pricing adminstrn.-glass, 1989-92, dir. process re-engring., 1993-94; dir. sales adminstrn. Ball Corp. (now St.-Gobain Containers, Inc), Muncie, Ind., from 1994. Mem. vestry Grace Episcopal Ch., Muncie. Home: Muncie, Ind. Died Feb. 4, 2008.

LAI, HIM MARK, history professor, writer; b. San Francisco, Nov. 1, 1925; s. Mark Bing and Hing Mui (Dong) L.; m. Laura Jung, June 12, 1953. AA, San Francisco Jr. Coll., 1945; BS in Engring., U. Calif., Berkeley, 1947. Mech. engr. Utilities Engring. Bur., San Francisco, 1948-51, Bechtel Corp., San Francisco, 1953-84; lectr. Chinese Am. history San Francisco State U., 1969, 72-75, U. Calif., Berkeley, 1978-79, 84. Dir. Chinese of Am. 1785-1980 Exhbn. Chinese Cultural Found. San Francisco, 1979-80; coord. Chinese Am. in Search of Roots Program; cons. Asian Am. Studies Program Chinese Materials Rsch. Collection U. Calif., Berkeley, 1986-88, nat. edn. program Ams. All, 1992-96; adj. prof. Asian Am. studies dept. San Francisco State U.; coord. Chinese Cmty. Hour Cantonese radio program, 1971-84. Co-author: Chinese of America, 1785-1980: Exhibition Catalog, 1980, Island: Poetry and History of Chinese Immigrants on Angel Island, 1910-1940, 1980; author: A History Reclaimed: An Annotated Bibliography and Guide of Chinese Language Materials on the Chinese of America, 1986, From Overseas Chinese to Chinese American: History of Development of Chinese American Society During the Twentieth Century, 1992; assoc. editor: A History of the Chinese in California, A Syllabus, 1969; co-editor: Collected Works of Gilbert Woo, 1991; mem. editl. bd. Amerasia Journal, Chinese America: History and Perspectives; contbr. articles to profl. jours. Mem. Chinese Hist. Soc. Am. (pres. 1971, 76, 77, bd. dirs. 1972-81, 84, 85-91, 93-98, 2000), Chinese Culture Found. San Francisco (bd. dirs. 1975-85, 87-94, 96—, pres. 1982, chmn. bd. 1983, 84, 85, 89). Home: San Francisco, Calif. Died May 21, 2009.

LAMARCHINA, MARILYNNE MAY, elementary school educator; b. Tustin, Calif., Oct. 11, 1932; d. William Stimson and Elizabeth Myrtle (McCarter) Hatch; m. Robert Antonio LaMarchina (dec.); children: Lisa, Vita, Floria, Adriana. AA, Fullerton Jr. Coll., 1950—52; BA, San Jose State Coll., 1952—54; studied with Philip Zimbardo, Stanford U., Calif., 1984. Elem. tchr. Newport Mesa Dist., Newport Beach, Calif., 1954—67, Dept. Edn., Honolulu, 1968—95, sub. tchr., 1995—2005. Mem. Women's Support Group, Honolulu, 1984—2000. Bd. dirs. Hawaii Philharmonic, Honolulu, 1984. Mem.: Am. Business Women's Assn., Outrigger Canoe Club. Democrat. Avocations: writing, gardening. Home: Kaneohe, Hawaii. Died June 12, 2008.

LAMBORN, MARILYN LOIS, nurse, educator; b. Long Beach, Calif., Sept. 3, 1946; d. George Harry and Alberta Thomas (Reeves) L. Diploma, Ga. Bapt. Hosp., 1967; BSN, Med. Coll. Ga., 1974, MSN, 1975; PhD, U. Tex., Austin, 1986. RN, Tex., Ga. Head nurse, clin. supr. med. nursing units Ga. Bapt. Hosp., Atlanta; chmn. med.-surg. nursing Piedmont Hosp. Sch. Nursing, Atlanta; acad. asst. to dean Sch. Nursing U. Tex., Austin; asst. prof. U. Tex. Health Sci. Ctr., San Antonio. Contbr. to profl. publs. Mem. ANA, Nat. League Nursing, Sigma Xi, Sigma Theta Tau, Phi Kappa Phi. Home: Pensacola, Fla. Died Dec. 12, 2007.

LAMONDS, HAROLD AUGUSTUS, energy company executive; b. Greensboro, NC, Aug. 22, 1924; s. Alexander and Lurah Victoria (Bonkemeyer) L.; m. Dorothy Veronica Richards, Mar, 17, 1945 (div. Feb. 1969); children: Lori Michelle La Borde, Mark Christopher; m. Dorothy Ileana Bough, May 15, 1976. BS, N.C. State U., 1953, MS, 1954, PhD, 1958. Dept. head N.C. State U., Raleigh, 1960-63; prin. engr., dept. head Aerojet Gen. Corp., Azusa, Calif., 1963-64; program mgr. EG&G, Inc., Santa Barbara, Calif., 1964-74; pres. Orion Scientific Corp., San Diego, 1974-76; prin. scientist IRT Corp., San Diego, 1976-77; v.p. EG&G Energy Measurements, Inc., Las Vegas, Nev., from 1977. Author: Nuclear Reactor Laboratory Manual, 1961; contbr. articles to profl. jours. With USAF, 1943-45. Mem. Am. Legion, Rotary Club, Phi Kappa Phi. Lodges: Elks. Republican. Avocations: golf, sailing. Home: Las Vegas, Nev. Died July 2, 2008.

LAMPL, PEGGY ANN, retired public information officer; b. NYC, Dec. 12, 1930; d. Joseph and Alice L. BA, Bennington Coll., 1952. Dir. program devel. dept. mental health AMA, Chgo., 1962-66; spl. asst. NIMH, HEW, Washington, 1967-69; public relations dir. League Women Voters, Washington, 1969—73, exec. dir., 1973—78; dep. asst. sec. for congressional relations US Dept. State, Washington, 1978-81; dep. dir. Iris Systems Devel., 1982-83; exec. dir. Children's Def. Fund, Washington, 1984-89, League Women Voters, Washington, 1989—90; project mgr. Crimes of War, W.W. Norton, 1999; bd. dirs. Crimes of War Project, Washington, 1998—2009. Home: Washington, DC. Died July 24, 2009.

LANCASTER, LINDA RAE, insurance agent; b. Elkhart, Ind., Oct. 7, 1949; d. Victor Gordon and Eulia Mae (Douglas) L. BA, Western Mich. U., Kalamazoo, 1970. CLU, Chartered fin. cons. Tchr. jr. high Duval County Schs., Jacksonville, Fla., 1971-77; ins. agt. Conn. Mut. Life Ins. Co., Jacksonville, 1977-83; equity sales coord. and ins. salesman Mass. Mut. Life Ins. Co., Jacksonville, 1983-88; bus. owner Pearce-Lancaster & Co., Jacksonville, from 1988. Mem. Nat. Assn. Life Underwriters (nat. quality award, nat. health ins. award, nat. sales achievement award 1979—), CLUs (bd. mem. 1987), Jacksonville Life Underwriters (bd. mem. 1987-89), Jacksonville C. of C. (bd. mem. 1985-86), Mandarin Bus. Assn., Women Bus. Owners, North Fla. Estate Planning Coun., MIllion Dollar Round Table, Jacksonvill Ski Club. Republican. Methodist. Avocations: boating, skiing, reading. Died Dec. 21, 2007.

LAND, ROBERT DONALD, business consultant; b. Niagara Falls, Ont., Can., Feb. 16, 1926; came to the U.S., 1953; s. Allan Reginald and Beatrice Beryl (Boyle) L.; m. Beverly Grace Hook, July 23, 1955 (div. Nov. 1977); children: Brian, Diane, Susan. BA, U. Toronto, Ont., Can., 1948. Assoc. Life Office Mgmt. Assn. Inst.; cert. profl. bus. cons., Inst. Profl. Bus. Cons. Investment analyst Toronto Gen. Trusts, 1948-50; actuarial acct. Crown Life Ins. Co., Toronto, 1950-53; pres. PM Detroit, Inc., Southfield, Mich., 1953-87, PM Group-Don Land & Assocs., Southfield, from 1988. Pres., dir. Practice Mgmt. Assocs., Toronto, 1969—. Mem., vol. Jaycees, Detroit, 1954-56; coach Royal Oak (Mich.) Hockey Assn., 1974-76. Seaman Royal Can. Navy, 1944-46. Mem. Nat. Assn. Accts., Nat. Assn. Healthcare Cons., Nat. Assn. Tax Profls., Inst. Cert. Bus. Cons. (trustee 1975-76), Nautical Rsch. Guild, U.S. Naval Inst., Soc. Nautical Rsch., Ind. Accts. Mich. Republican. Episcopalian. Avocations: nautical research, photography, boating. Died Oct. 12, 2007.

LANDREAU, ANTHONY NORMAN (TONY LANDREAU), anthropologist, museologist; b. Washington, Apr. 2, 1930; s. Norman Bayly and Caroline (Griffin) L.; m. Anita Jester, Oct. 15 (div. 1985); children: John Celestin, Christopher Anselm, Geoffrey Olson. BA, Black Mountain Coll., NC, 1954; MA in Anthropology, Temple U., Phila., 1993, PhD in Anthrpology, 1996. Faculty mem. Black Mountain Coll., 1954-56; owner arts and crafts studio, Washington, 1959-67; curator Textile Mus., Washington, 1967-71, dir., 1971-75; curator Carnegie Mus., Pitts., 1975-81; pres. Internat. Collections, Inc., Pitts., 1981-87; dir. Island Heritage Trust, Deer Isle, Maine, 1988-90; rsch. assoc. anthropology Temple U., Phila., 1995—2009; vis. faculty mem. Yakima Valley C.C., 1998—2009. Bd. dirs. Am.-Turkish Assn., Washington, 1972-75, Iran-Am. Soc., Washington, 1973-75; pres. Collaborative for Arts in Pitts. Edn., 1977-79. Author: From the Bosporus to Samarkand; Flat-Woven Rugs, 1969, American Underfoot, 1976, Flying Carpets, Earthbound Women, 1999. Trustee Kindler Found., Washington, 1972-75. Seaman USN, 1948-50. Grantee Near East Rsch. Ctr., Washington, 1973, 75, 81, Nat. Endowment Art, Washington, 1973, 75, NEH, Washington, 1983. Mem. Am. Anthrop. Assn., Am. Ethnol. Assn., Assn. Third World Studies, Assn. Feminist Anthropology. Avocations: art, photography. Home: Yakima, Wash. Died May 30, 2009.

LANDY, DAVID, anthropologist, educator; b. Savannah, Ga., June 4, 1917; s, Charles Edwin and Matilda (Rabinowitz) L.; m. Louise Fleming, Mar. 18, 1949 (dec. 1988); children: Laura Louise, Lisa Ann, Jonathan Fleming; m. Margaret Randall Holt Parish, Jan. 1, 1991. AA, Armstrong State Coll., 1948; BA in psychology, sociology, U. N.C., 1949, MA in anthropology, 1950; PhD in anthropology, Harvard U., 1956. Lectr., sch. social work Boston (Mass.) U., 1953-56; prin. investigator Harvard U., Boston, 1955-60, rsch. assoc. med. sch., 1955-60; prof. and assoc. prof. pub. health U. Pitts., 1960-70, prof. and chair anthropology, 1963-70, U. Mass., Boston, 1970-75, prof. emeritus, from 1985; adj. prof. anthropology U. N.C., Wilmington, from 1992. Author: Tropical Childhood, 1959, 1965; co-author: Halfway House, 1969, editor, co-author: Culture, Disease Healing, 1977; assoc. editor: Ethnology, 1963-70, Behavioral Science, 1965-70; contbr. articles to profl. jours. Treas. 1st Parish Ch., Scituate, Mass., 1987-90; trustee Unitarian Universalist Fellowship, Wilmington, 1991-93; pres. Soc. Med. Anthropology, Washington, 1980-82, mem. exec. com., 1978-80, 91-93. With U.S. Army, 1944-46, ETO. Recipient numerous grants. Fellow Am. Anthrop. Assn.; mem. Soc. Med. Anthropology (past pres., exec. com.), Soc. for Ethnohistory, So. Anthrop. Soc., Am. Assn. for the History of Medicine, Soc. for the Social History of Medicine, Assn. N.C. Anthropologists, Am. Ethnol. Soc., Soc. Psychol. Anthropology. Avocations: reading, music, travel, tennis, swimming. Home: Wilmington, NC. Died Nov. 6, 2007.

LANE, ARDYTHE, infection control specialist; b. Sewickley, Pa., Nov. 30, 1931; d. Adolph and Mary (Knott) Rotondo; m. John E. Lane, Feb. 6, 1954; children: Kevin, Barbara, Thomas, John. Diploma, Providence Hosp. Sch. Nursing, 1953; BS in Health Care Adminstrn., St. Joseph's Coll., Wyndam, Maine, 1985. RN, Pa. Staff nurse Med. Ctr., Beaver, Pa., infection control specialist. Mem. Assn. Practitioners Infection Control. Home: Surfside Bch, SC. Died Dec. 18, 2007.

LANE, RUSSELL WATSON, retired water treatment consultant; b. Morrison, Ill., June 18, 1911; s. Ralph T. and Elizabeth (Alldritt) L.; m. Ione Leola Sundberg, June 16, 1934; children: Joan K. Korbas, Patricia D. Hogeland. BS, Knox Coll., 1933; MS, Ill. Inst. Tech., 1945. Registered profl. engr. Ill., Calif.; cert. corrosion specialist NACE. Chemist Libby McNeil & Libby, Morrison, Ill., 1933-41; rsch. chemist Nalco Chem. Co., Naperville, Ill., 1941-49; head chemistry sect. Ill. State Water Survey, Champaign, Ill., 1949-81; water treatment cons. Champaign, Ill., from 1970. Initiator Electric Utility Chemistry Workshop, U. Ill., Urbana-Champaign. Author: (book) Control of Scale and Corroision in Building Water Systems, 1993; contbr. more than 50 articles on water treatment to profl. and popular publications. Recipient Max Hecht award ASTM, 1975, award of merit, 1985, citation of recognition Nat. Corrosion Engrs. Internat., 1981. Mem. Lions Club, Elks Club. Achievements include seven patents on water treatment methods and methods of analysis. Died Dec. 5, 2007.

LANG, PEARL, dancer, choreographer; b. Chgo., 1921; d. Jacob and Frieda (Feder) Lack; m. Joseph Wiseman, Nov. 22, 1963. Student, Wright Jr. Coll., U. Chgo.; DFA (hon.), Juilliard Sch. Music, 1995; PhD (hon.), Juilliard Sch., 1995, DFA, 1995. Formed own co., 1953; faculty Yale, 1954-68; tchr., lectr. Juilliard, 1953-69, Jacobs Pillow, Conn. Coll., Neighborhood Playhouse, 1963-68, Israel, Sweden, Netherlands. Founder Pearl Lang Dance Found.; mem. Boston Symphony, Tanglewood Fest. Soloist, Martha Graham Dance Co., 1944-54; featured roles on Broadway include Carousel, 1945-47, Finian's Rainbow, 1947-48, Danced Martha Graham's roles in Appalachian Spring, 1974-76, El Pentitente, 1954, Primitive Mysteries, 1978-79, Diversion of Angels, 1948-70, Herodiade, 1977-79; role of Solvieg opposite John Garfield Broadway include, ANTA Peer Gynt; choreographer: TV shows CBC Folio; co-dir. T.S. Eliot's Murder in the Cathedral, Stratford, Conn., Direction, 1964-66, 67, Lamp Unto Your Feet, 158, Look Up and Live TV, 1957; co-dir., choreographer: full length prodn. Dybbuk for CBC; dir. numerous Israel Bond programs; assumed roles Emily Dickinson: Letter to the World, 1970; Clytemnestra, 1973; Jocasta in: Night Journey, 1974, for Martha Graham Dance Co.; choreographer: dance works Song of Deborah, 1952, Moonsung and Windsung, 1952, Legend, 1953, Rites, 1953, And Joy Is My Witness, 1954, Nightflight, 1954, Sky Chant, 1957, Persephone, 1958, Black Marigolds, 1959, Shirah, 1960, Apasionada, 1961, Broken Dialogues, 1962, Shore Bourne, 1964, Dismembered Fable, 1965, Pray for Dark Birds, 1966, Tongues of Fire, 1967, Piece for Brass, 1969, Moonways and Dark Tides, 1970, Sharjuhm, 1971, At That Point in Place and Time, 1973, The Possessed, 1975, Prairie Steps, 1975, Bach Rondelays, 1977, I Never Saw Another Butterfly, 1977, A Seder Night, 1977, Kaddish, 1977, Icarus, 1978, Cantigas Ladino, (10 sephardic songs), 1978, Notturno, 1980, Gypsy Ballad, 1981, Hanele The Orphan, 1981, The Tailor's Megilleh, 1981, Bridal Veil, 1982, Stravinsky's opera Oedipus Rex, 1982, Song of Songs, 1983, Shiru L'adonay, 1983, Tehillim, 1983, Sephardic Romance and Tfila, 1989, Koros, 1990, Eyn Keloheynu, 1991, Schubert Quartetsatz No. 12, 1993, Schubert Quartet 15 1st Mov., 1994, And Again a Begining, 1994, Dream Voyages, 1996, Memories and Dreams of Isaac the Blind, 1997, A Bouquet of Love Song Waltzes, 1998, Song of Azerbaijan, 1999, Icarus, 1999, The Time Is Out of Joint, 2000, Dance Panel #7, 2000, Cityscape, 2000. Recipient 2 Guggenheim fellowships; recipient Goldfadden award Congress for Jewish Culture, Achievement award Artists and Writers for Peace in the Middle East, Cultural award Workmen's Circle, Queens Coll. award, 1991, Jewish Cultural achievement award Nat. Found. for Jewish Culture, 1992; named to Hall of Fame, Internat. Com. for the Dance Libr. of Israel, 1997. Mem. Am. Guild Mus. Artists. Died Feb. 24, 2009.

LANGFORD, GERALD TALMADGE, oil company executive; b. Kilgore, Tex., Jan. 13, 1935; s. DeWitt Talmadge and Lillian (Easterling) L.; m. Ora Kay Hess; children: Cheryl Kay, Randall DeWitt, Robin Leigh, David Larkin, Matthew Talmadge, Mary Camille. Student, Southwestern U., Georgetown, Tex., 1952-53; BS in Geology, U. Tex., 1957. Pres. Tex-L Exploration Corp., Longview, Tex., 1958-63, Cal-L Exploration Corp., Santa Barbara, Calif., 1964-69, Sabre Exploration Corp., Dallas, 1969-80, Condor Energy Corp., Dallas, 1981-82, DH&L Exploration Corp., Houston, 1982-83; cons. Sunbelt Energy Co., Dallas, from 1983, also bd. dirs. Cons. various other cos., Dallas; bd. dirs. Solar Corp., Norco, La. Contbr. articles to profl. jours. Avocations: skiing, competitive shooting, flying, racquetball, tennis. Died Feb. 20, 2008.

LANGFORD, THOMAS A., elder; b. Alice, Tex., Oct. 20, 1930; s. Homer Thomas and Nettie Beatrice (Clemons) L.; m. Nellie Jo Cunningham, Aug. 23, 1953; children: David Ross, Curtis Paul. BA in English, U. Calif., 1956; MA in English, Tex. Tech. U., 1963; PhD in English, Tex. Christian U., 1967. Ordained to ministry Chs. of Christ, 1950. Elder Quaker Ave Ch. of Christ, Lubbock, Tex., from 1976. Assoc. dean Tec. Tech. U., Lubbock, 1970—, prof. English dept., 1976—; lectr. chs. in various states, 1970—; leader seminars various chs., 1975—; chmn. vis. com. Abilene (Tex.) Christian U., 1983-87, Lubbock Christian U., 1988-90; bd. dirs. Smithlawn Maternity Home, Lubbock, 1988—, Misson Jour., Chapel Hill, N.C., 1975-85. Author numerous articles in religious/profl. jours., 1950—; editor proceedings Annual Conf. of So. Grad. Schs., 1986-91. Cabinet mem. United Way, Lubbock, 1978. Recipient Univ. fellowship Tex. Christian U., Ft. Worth, 1965, fellowship U.S. Office Edn., Washington, 1967, NEH, 1985. Mem. Assn. Tex. Grad. Schs. (pres. 1989-90), Modern Lang. Assn., Browning Inst., Tennyson Soc., Phi Kappa Phi (pres. 1989-90). Home: Lubbock, Tex. Died May 2, 2008.

LANNING, HOWARD HUGH, astronomer; b. El Centro, Calif., May 26, 1946; s. James Clyde and Ethel Mary (Malan) L.; m. Sheryl Marie Falgout, Aug. 20, 1983. AA in Astronomy, Imperial Valley Jr. Coll., Imperial, Calif., 1966; BS in Astronomy, San Diego State U., 1969, MS in Astronomy, 1974. Life community coll. instr. credential, Calif. Rsch. asst., observer Hale Obs., Pasadena, Calif., 1970-72; grad. teaching asst. astronomy dept. San Diego State U., 1972-73, rsch. asst. NASA Ames Rsch. Ctr., 1973-74; night asst., observer Mt. Wilson (Calif.) Obs., 1974-85; sci. ops. specialist Space Telescope Sci. Inst., Computer Scis. Corp., Balt., 1985-90, ops. astronomer, from 1990, GHRS instrument scientist, 1995-97, STIS instrument scientist, from 1997. Sci. writer Calipatria (Calif.) Herald, 1979-83. Contbr. articles to astron. jours. Recipient 1st ann. achievement award Space Telescope Sci. Inst., 1989. Fellow Royal Astron. Soc.; mem. Am. Astron. Soc., Astron. Soc. Pacific, Internat. Astron. Union. Achievements include discovery of several binary star systems, including white dwarfs, red dwarfs, cataclysmic variables. Died Dec. 20, 2007.

LA PAGLIA, UMBERTO, retired secondary education educator; b. Phila., Feb. 1, 1927; s. Ignazio and Concetta La P. BSEd, Temple U., 1952, MA in History, 1956. High sch. tchr. Sch. Dist. of Phila., 1952-90. Exch. tchr. Fitzmaurice Grammar Sch., Bradford-on-Avon, Eng., 1961-62. Author: Exploring World Cultures, 1974. With U.S. Army, 1946-47, Korea. Mem. Orgn. Am. History. Avocation: travel. Home: Cherry Hill, NJ. Died Nov. 2, 2007.

LARGE, DEWEY EDMUND, JR., computer scientist; b. Princeton, W.Va., Aug. 6, 1949; s. Dewey Edmund Sr. and Jettie Mae (Swimm) L.; m. Jacqueline Marie Moyer, June 6, 1975; children: Steven Dale, Jessica Elaine Thayer. Student, Prince George's Community Coll., Largo, Md., 1969-71, Johnson Bible Coll., 1975-78. Asst. mgr. F.W. Woolworth, Oak Ridge, Tenn., 1978-81; various positions AVCO Electronics Div., Huntsville, Ala., 1981-85; ops. mgr., co-owner Automated Design Systems, Huntsville, 1985; sr. data base adminstr., CAD system supr. Sci. Atlanta, Atlanta, from 1985. Avocations: organist, water-skiing, camping, rafting. Home: Buford, Ga. Died Mar. 20, 2008.

LARGESS, GEORGE JOSEPH, retired educator, naval officer; b. Malden, Mass., Oct. 20, 1917; s. James Edmund and Ellen (Hyland) L.; m. Zoe McCombs, Feb. 2, 1942; children: George Joseph, Robert P., Dennis N., Mary Jude, William M. BS, U.S. Naval Acad., 1939; postgrad. U.S. Naval Postgrad. Sch., 1945; MST, Am. U., 1972. Commd. ensign USN, 1939, advanced through grades to comdr., 1949; comdr. U.S.S. Altair, 1952-53, U.S.S. Keppler, 1957-58; ret., 1961; project engr. Booz-Allen Applied Research, Inc., 1961-68; instr. math. St. Cecilia's Acad., Washington, 1968-69, Bullis Sch., Silver Spring, Md., 1969-70, Md. and D.C. Public Schs., 1970-80; mem. adv. group on electronic warfare U.S. Dept. Def., 1959-61. Pres., Crestwood Citizens Assn., 1960-61, del. D.C. Fedn., 1961-62; pres. Holy Name Soc., 1962-64, treas., 1974-75, del. Archdiocesan Union, 1961-68; pres. Cath. Youth Org., 1958-61; leader Capital council Boy Scouts Am., 1953-56; sec. Archdiocesan Union Holy Name Socs., 1968-71; mem. St. Matthew's Cathedral Council, 1968-85, pres., 1984-85; mem. Calvert Sch. Bd., 1968-70. Recipient Holy Name Soc. Appreciation award,

1964, Georgetown U.-D.C. Schs. award, 1980. Mem. Nat. Council Cath. Men, IEEE, Mil. Order World Wars, Washington Ops. Research Council, Math. Assn. Am., Nat. Council Tchrs. Math., Am. Math. Soc., Am. Security Council, John Carroll Soc., Thomas More Soc., Phi Delta Kappa. Club: Serra of Washington (pres., dist. trustee 1981-84, del. Rome conv. 1983, dist. gov. 1988-89, vice chmn. Serra Internat. cov. com. 1991). Home: Washington, DC. Died Dec. 11, 2008.

LARKIN, JON ANDREW, lawyer, consultant; b. Pitts., Jan. 27, 1946; s. Peter and Helen (Francko) L.; m. Gail Graber, June 22, 1968 (div. Nov. 1983); 1 child, Theodore. BA, Pa. State U., 1967, M in Pub. Adminstrn., 1975; Masters, Duquesne U., 1970; JD, Delaware U., 1983. Bar: Pa. 1984, U.S. Dist. Ct. (ea. dist.) Pa. Tchr. various schs., 1968-73; cons. Dauphin County, Harrisburg, Pa., 1974-75; dir. dept. labor State of Del., Wilmington, 1975-76; exec. dir. Wilmington Sr. Ctr., 1976-84; sole practice law Chadds-ford, Pa., from 1985. Elected del. White House Conf. Aging, Wilmington, 1980-81; committeeman Democratic Party, New Castle County, Del., 1973-74. Recipient Outstanding Service award Wilmington City Council, 1980, Mayor of Wilmington, 1979, United Way, Wilmington, 1981. Mem. ABA, Am. Trail Lawyers Assn., Pi Alpha Alpha. Clubs: University Whist (Wilmington). Democrat. Home: Mendenhall, Pa. Died Sept. 3, 2007.

LARSON, JANE WARREN, ceramist; b. San Francisco, June 2, 1922; d. Stafford Leak and Viola (Lockhart) Warren; m. Clarence Ernest Larson, Apr. 21, 1957; children: Lawrence Ernest, Lance Stafford, Robert Edward. Student, Swarthmore Coll., 1939—41; BA with honors, U. Rochester, 1943; MFA in Ceramics, Antioch Coll., 1972. Sci. reporter, tech. editor Tenn. Eastman Corp., Oak Ridge, 1943-46; chief Tech. Info. Ctr. Carbide & Carbon Chem. Corp., Oak Ridge, 1946-51; tech. editor physics div. Rand Corp., Santa Monica, Calif., 1954-55, tech. libr. Washington, 1955-57; ceramist Janeware, Santa Monica, 1953-55; pres., bldg. founder Oak Ridge Cmty. Art Ctr., 1963-66, ceramic tchr., 1965-69; ceramic tchr. Inst. Learning in Retirement Am. U., Washington, 1985-88, 94. One-person shows at AAAS, Washington, 1990, Studio Gallery, Washington, 1992, 95, Cosmos Club, Washington, 1998, others 1973—, Creative Ptnrs. Gallery, Bethesda, Md., 1996; group shows at Bader Gallery and others, 1971—, Internat. Sculpture Conf., Washington, 1990, U. Md. Sculpture Show, 1994-95; vanishing diversity murals with water Guest Quarters Hotel gardens, Bethesda, Md., 1987, Oak Ridge Com. Art Ctr. garden, energy and life murals, 1992, Fed. City Shelter, Washington, 1988, U. Md. Chemistry Bldg., 1997; columns: Johns Hopkins Ctr. Internat. Studies, Washington, 1990, NAE, Beckman Ctr., Irvine, Calif., 1990, Asia Nora Restaurant, Washington, 1994; permanent collections include U. Md., College Park, (sculpture) AAAS, Am. Ctr. Physics, College Park, Renwick Gallery Nat. Mus. Am. Art; commns. include 4 murals 20 vases Germaines Restaurant, Washington, 1978, East Wind Restaurant, Alexandria, Va., 1980; lobby murals Nat. Milk Producers Assn., Rosslyn, Va., 1983, U. Md. Chem. Bldg., 10 Molecules that Shaped the World, 1997, 10 Molecules that Matter to Medicine, 1998, NIH Libr. Medicine, The Arrow of Time, 1999, Arlington County Libr., Ubby Blake H.S., 2000, ORNL Reborn, 2003-04; contbr. articles to profl. jours. including Cosmos 2000, It Is Time for Durable Records. Commr. Cable TV Commn., Montgomery County, Rockville, Md., 1989-90. Recipient Tile Heritage award, Tile Heritage Found., 2001, Pin with Diamond prize, ORNL, 2003. Mem. Ind. Agy. Women (pres. 1964-65), Kiln Club Washington (1st prize ann. show 1993), Achievement Rewards Coll. Sci., Inc. (v.p. 1980-81), Artists Equity, Internat. Sculpture Ctr., Bethesda Ceramic Guild (1st prize ann. show 1994, 95), Cosmos Club Washington, Phi Beta Kappa. Avocation: poetry. Died Aug. 11, 2008.

LARSON, LORELL VINCENT, aviation consultant; b. Mpls., Oct. 24, 1918; s. Carl Adolph and Josephine (Olstad) L. BS in Aerodyn. Engring., U. Minn., 1940. Chief analysis and integration CAM-87 Engring. Aero Systems Div., Dayton, Ohio, 1958-61; chief analysis and integration Aero. Systems div. F-111 Engring., Dayton, 1961-63; sr. analyst Ltd. War Office, Dayton, 1963-69; chief engr. Pave Tack Program Aero Systems Div., Dayton, Ohio, 1969-75; aviation cons. Destin, Fla., from 1975. Chmn., mem. Delivery Accuracy Group Joint Tech. Coordinating Group for Munitions Effectiveness, Washington, 1964-67. Mem. Am. Def. Preparedness Assn., USN Inst. (assoc.). Avocation: photography. Home: Destin, Fla. Died July 20, 2008.

LASKOWSKI, LEONARD FRANCIS, JR., microbiologist; b. Milw., Nov. 16, 1919; s. Leonard Francis and Frances (Cyborowski) L.; m. Frances Bielinski, June 1, 1946; children— Leonard Francis III, James, Thomas. BS, Marquette U., 1941, MS, 1948; PhD, St. Louis U., 1951. Diplomate: Am. Bd. Microbiology. Instr. bacteriology Marquette U., 1946-48; mem. faculty St. Louis U., from 1951, prof. pathology and internal medicine, Div. Infectious Diseases, 1969-90, prof. emeritus, from 1990, assoc. prof. internal medicine, 1977-90—. Dir. clin. microbiology sect. St. Louis U. Hosps. Labs., 1965—; cons. clin microbiology Firmin Desloge Hosp., St. Louis U. Group Hosps., St. Marys Group Hosps.; cons. bacteriology VA Hosp.; asst. dept. chief Pub. Health Lab., St. Louis Civil Def., 1958—; cons. St. Elizabeths Hosp., St. Louis County Hosp., St. Francis Hosp., Alexian Bros. Hosp., St. Clements Hosp., St. Mary's Hosp., East St. Louis. Contbr. articles to profl. jours. Health and tech. tng. coordinator for Latin Am. projects Peace Corps, 1962-66. Served with M.C. AUS, 1942-46. Fellow Am. Acad. Microbiology; mem. Soc. Am. Bacteriologists, N.Y. Acad. Scis., Am., Mo. pub. health assns., AAUP, Med. Mycol. Soc. Am., Alpha Omega Alpha. Home: Villa Ridge, Mo. Deceased.

LAUB-NOVAK, KAREN, artist, sculptor; b. Mpls., Aug. 25, 1937; m. Michael Novak; 3 children. BA, Carleton Coll., 1959; MFA, U. Iowa, 1961; studied with Oskar Kokoschka, studied with Mauricio Lasansky. Free-lance artist, sculptor, painter, lithographer, 1963—2009; instr. Carleton Coll., Northfield, Minn., 1961-62, Stanford U., Palo Alto, Calif., 1965-68, SUNY, Old Westbury, 1970, Syracuse (N.Y.) U., 1976-78, Mt. Vernon Coll., Washington, 1979, Georgetown U., Washington, 1980-81. One-man and group shows include Union Court Gallery, San Francisco, Los Robles Gallery, Palo Alto, Calif., Harvard U., Cambridge, Mass., Yale U., New Haven Conn., Rochester Art Ctr., Des Moines Art Mus., Fox Hall Gallery, Washington, Union Station, Washington, St. Petersburgh, Russia, 2003, others; sculptures commd. for Empower Am., Becket Fund, Am. Enterprise Inst., Youth for the Third Millennium, Manhattan Inst., others; represented in pvt. collections St. Vincent's Arch-Abbey, Amb. M. Brement, Amb. Jeane Kirkpatrick, Philip Merrill. Died Aug. 12, 2009.

LAUER, JAMES LOTHAR, physicist, researcher; b. Vienna, Aug. 2, 1920; came to U.S., 1938, naturalized, 1943; s. Max and Friederike (Rapaport) L.; m. Stefanie Dorothea Blank, Sept. 4, 1955; children: Michael, Ruth. AB, Temple U., 1942, MA, 1944; PhD, U. Pa., 1948; postgrad., U. Calif., San Diego, 1964-65. Scientist Sun Oil Co., Marcus Hook, Pa., 1944-52, spectroscopist, 1952-64, sr. scientist, 1965-77; asst. prof. U. Pa., 1952-55; lectr. U. Del., 1952-58; rsch. fellow mech. engring. U. Calif., San Diego, 1964-65; rsch. prof. mech. engring. Rensselaer Poly. Inst., Troy, NY, 1978-85, prof. mech. engring., 1985-93, prof. mech. engring. emeritus, from 1993; rsch. sci. Ctr. Magnetic Recording Rsch. U. Calif., San Diego, 1993-95, vis. scholar applied mechanics and engring. sci., 1995—2008. Sr. faculty summer rsch. fellow NASA-Lewis Rsch. Ctr., 1986-87; vis. prof. Ctr. for Magnetic Rec. Rsch., U. Calif., San Diego, 1991; cons. Digital Equipment Corp., 1992-94, NASA-Lewis Rsch. Ctr., 1993-95. Author: Infrared Fourier Spectroscopy--Chemical Applications, 1978; co-author: Handbook of Raman Spectroscopy, 2001; mem. editl. bd. Tribology Letters, 1995—; contbr. articles to profl. jours. Active Penn Wynne Civic Assn., 1959—77, Country Knolls Civic Assn., 1978—93. Sun Oil Co. fellow, 1964-65, Air Force Office Sci. Rsch. grantee, 1974-86, NASA Lewis Rsch. Ctr. grantee, 1974-86, Office Naval Rsch. grantee, 1979-82, Army Rsch. Office grantee, 1985-89, NSF grantee, 1987-95, Innovative Rsch. award Soc. Mech. Engrs., 1991, Discovery awards NASA, 1993, 96. Fellow: Inst. Physics (U.K.); mem.: AAAS (life), Optical Soc. Am. (emeritus), Soc. Applied Spectroscopy, Am. Phys. Soc. (emeritus), Am. Chem. Soc. (emeritus), Materials Rsch. Soc., Sigma Chi. Jewish. Achievements include patents in field. Home: San Diego, Calif. Died Nov. 16.

LAURSEN, GLADYS MARIE, retired elementary school educator; b. Wiota, Iowa, Dec. 6, 1914; d. Jens and Marie (Nielsen) L. BA, Wayne State U., 1954. Educator Monona County Rural Sch., Turin, Iowa, 1939-43, Ute (Iowa) Pub. Sch., 1943-46, Onawa Pub. Sch., 1946-57, Lansing (Ill.) Pub. Sch., 1957-76. Recipient Honors award Lansing (Ill.) Edn. Assn., 1978. Home: Sioux Falls, SD. Died July 19, 2008.

LAVENDA, NATHAN, physiology educator; b. NYC, Dec. 10, 1918; s. Zukin and Etie Feige (Weinstein) L.; m. Selma Lavenda, Aug. 24, 1943 (div. June 1961); children: Bernard, Ronald; m. Harriet Rebecca Lavenda, June 24, 1961; children: Elaine, David. MS, NYU, 1947, PhD, 1952. Aquatic biologist U.S. Fish and Wildlife Svc., NYC, 1944-47; biologist USPHS, SI, N.Y., 1947-50; instr. physiology Howard U. Med. Sch., Washington, 1952-56; chmn. dept. biology North Adams (Mass.) State Coll., 1961-67; chmn. dept. physiology Ill. Coll. Podiatric Medicine, Chgo., 1967-69; rsch. assoc. Michael Reese Hosp., Chgo., 1970-82, U. Ill., Chgo., from 1983. Chmn. physiology Nat. Bd. Podiatric Examiners, Chgo., 1967-69. Contbr. articles to profl. jours. With USAF, 1941-44. Recipient grant U.S. Atomic Energy Commn., 1953. Mem. Am. Soc. Zoologists, Soc. for Study Reproduction. Achievements include discovery of sex reversal in Atlantic Sea Bass, staining reaction in cancer cells, cytochemical demonstration of viruses. Home: Skokie, Ill. Died Feb. 16, 2008.

LAVERY, WILLIAM EDWARD, retired academic administrator; b. Geneseo, NY, Nov. 20, 1930; s. John Raymond and Mary Irene (O'Brien) L.; m. Peggy J. Johnson, Apr. 7, 1956; children— Debra, Kevin, Lori, Mary. BS, Mich. State U., 1953; MA, George Washington U., 1959; PhD, U. Wis., 1962. Tchr. Clarence Ctrl. HS, NY, 1953-54; asst. to adminstr. Fed. Extension Service Dept. Agr., Washington, 1956-66; dir. adminstrn.-extension div. Va. Polytech. Inst. and State U., Blacksburg, 1966-68, v.p. finance, 1968-73, exec. v.p., 1973-75, pres., 1975-87. Cons. to El Salvador, US Agy. for Internat. Devel. (USAID) 1969; Dir. Dominion Bankshores Corp. Mem. United Fund-Community Fedn., 1968-72; Bd. dirs. Montgomery County Hosp. Served with AUS, 1954-56. Kellogg Found. fellow, 1960-62 Mem. Omicron Delta Kappa, Epsilon Sigma Phi, Phi Kappa Phi, Phi Delta Kappa. Clubs: Rotary (Blacksburg). Died Feb. 16, 2009.

LAW, FLORA ELIZABETH (LIBBY LAW), retired community health and pediatrics nurse; b. Biddeford, Maine, Sept. 11, 1935; d. Arthur Parker and Flora Alma (Knutti) Butt; m. Robert F. Law, 1961; children: Susan E., Sarah F., Christian A., Martha F.; m. John F. Brown, Jr., 1982. BA, Davis and Elkins Coll., W.Va., 1957; postgrad., Cornell U.-N.Y. Hosp., NYC, 1960; BSN, U. Nev., Las Vegas, 1976, MS in Counseling Edn., 1981. RN, Nev.; cert. sch. nurse. Staff nurse So. Nev. Community Hosp. (now Univ. Med. Ctr.), Las Vegas, 1975-76; relief charge nurse Valley Psychiat. Inst., Las Vegas, 1976; pub. health nurse Clark County Dist. Health Dept., Las Vegas, 1977-78; sch. nurse Clark County Sch. Dist., Las Vegas, 1978-94; ret., 1994. Chair task force on sch. nursing Nev.'s Commn. for Profl. Standards in Edn.; mem. nurse practice act revision com. Nev. State Bd. Nursing. Mem. Nat. Assn. Sch. Nurses (past state dir., sch. nurse liaison Clark County Tchrs. Assn.), Clark County Assn. Sch. Nurses (past pres.), Sigma Theta Tau. Home: Las Vegas, Nev. Died Apr. 28, 2008.

LAWHORN, VIRGINIA DUZAN, geriatric services coordinator; b. Belton, Tex., Oct. 12, 1934; d. Arthur Alonzo and Lockie (Morrison) Duzan; m. Ronald E. Lawhorn, Dec. 29, 1955; children: Cynthia, Terri, Ronald II, Bruce. Diploma, Scott & White Hosp., Temple, Tex., 1955; BS, U. Md., 1982, MS, 1986. Cert. community health nurse. Head nurse Spring Grove Hosp. Ctr., Catonsville, Md.; staff nurse community health Balt. County Dept. Health, Towson, Md., field nursing supr.; coord. geriatric svcs. Balt. County Dept. Aging, Towson. Mem. Md. Nurses Assn., Md. Pub. Health Assn., Md. Gerontol. Assn. Home: Ellicott City, Md. Died Oct. 2, 2007.

LAWRENCE, JACK, composer, lyricist, theatre executive; b. N.Y.C., Apr. 7, 1912; s. Barnet Mordecai and Fanny Shana (Goldman) Schwartz; 1 adopted child, Richard Debnam. Dr. Podiatry, L.I. U., 1930. Employed with numerous motion picture studios including Walt Disney, Metro-Goldwyn-Mayer, RKO and Republic, 1938-55; producer, owner Jack Lawrence Theatre and Audrey Wood Theatre, N.Y.C., 1983-88. Prodr.: Lena Horne The Lady and Her Music, 1980-82, Come Back to the Five and Dime, Jimmy Dean, 1983, KUNI LEML (winner Outer Critics Circle award for best musical of 1985); author, composer Broadway shows Courtin' Time, 1953, I Had a Ball starring Richard Kiley and Buddy Hackett, 1965; writer numerous musical works including Tenderly, All or Nothing At All, Beyond the Sea, If I Didn't Care, Sleepy Lagoon, Ciribiribin, Sunrise Serenade. Served to lt. USN, 1942-45. Mem. ASCAP, Am. Guild Authors and Composers, Motion Picture Acad. Arts and Scis., Dramatists Guild. Democrat. Jewish. Avocation: swimming. Home: New York, NY. Died Mar. 16, 2009.

LAWRENCE, JOYCE WAGNER, health facility administrator, educator; b. NYC, Apr. 3, 1942; d. Edward William and Bertha Beatrice (Merz) Wagner; m. William Robert Lawrence, Feb. 9, 1969; 1 child, Rebecca Suzanne. Diploma, Washington Hosp. Ctr., 1963; BS, St. Joseph's Coll., Windham, Maine, 1990. Cert. health care mgr., Va. Supr. Profl. Support Svcs., Virginia Beach, Va.; supr., asst. dir. nursing Med. Staff Svcs., Virginia Beach; supr. Health Care Resources, Inc., Norfolk, Va.; corp. dir., instr., coord. med./cna programs Tidewater Tech, Virginia Beach, Va. Instr. nurse aide program LTH, Norfolk. Lt. (j.g.) USNR, 1968-70. Recipient South Hampton Rds. Women-In-Transition award YWCA, 1991. Mem. Oncology Nurses Assn. (chmn., sec. local chpt.), Hampton Roads Home Health Assn. (chmn. com.), Southeastern Va. Am. Soc. Tng. and Devel., ABWA. Home: Leesburg, Va. Died May 12, 2008.

LAWS, RICHARD DWIGHT, university administrator; b. Moab, Utah, Nov. 26, 1939; s. Julian Asa and Marie (Black) L.; m. Linda Lorraine Heurkens, July 13, 1962; children: Jodi, David, Roger, Richard, Ryan, Juli, Reed, Dru, DuVall. BA in Mgmt., U. Utah, Salt Lake City, 1974; PhD in Instructional Sci. and Tech., Brigham Young U., Provo, Utah, 1985. Traffic dir. KSL Radio and TV, Salt Lake City, 1962-67; reservation clk. Pan Am. World Airways, Denver, 1968-69; regional mgr. KLM Royal Dutch Airlines, Phoenix, 1970-74; adminstrv. asst. Utah Navajo Industries, Blanding, 1975-80; asst. city mgr. City of Blanding, 1981-83; assoc. dir. travel study Brigham Young U., Provo, 1984-87, dir. confs. and workshops, 1988-92, dir. Ind. study, from 1993. Cons. Utah State Sch. Bd. Edn., Salt Lake City, 1985—. Pres. sch. bd. San Juan Sch. Dist., Monticello, Utah, 1976-83. Mem. Phi Kappa Phi. Republican. Mem. Lds Ch. Home: Provo, Utah. Died Mar. 10, 2008.

LAWSON, MARGUERITE PAYNE, small business owner; b. Detroit, Apr. 30, 1935; d. LeRoy and Marguerite Lenore (Archambeau) Payne; m. William Allen Stanke, Sept. 4, 1954 (div. Sept. 1962); children: Elizabeth Susan Hankey, Elaine Kathryn Dinwiddie; m. Vernon Arthur Lawson, Aug. 15, 1975. BA in Social Sci., Mich. State U., E. Lansing, 1957. Lic. real estate assoc.; cert. tax preparer. Tchr. El Segundo Unified Sch. Dist., Calif., 1957-58, Las Virgenes Unified Sch. Dist., Calif., 1962-66, Timber Unified Sch. Dist., Thousand Oaks, Calif., 1966-72, Muroc Unified Sch. dist., Edwards, Calif., 1972-78; store owner Margie Lawson's Gourmet Ctr., Lancaster, Calif., from 1978. Tour leader Royal Cruise Line voyages, 1987-92; speaker various local clubs, TV sta., Lancaster and Palmdale, Calif., 1977—. Contbr. newspaper articles to Antelope Valley Press, 1975—, also photojournalist; pub. travel writer. Candidate Lancaster (Calif.) City Coun., 1977, Antelope

Valley Hosp. Bd., 1982; pres. College Terrace Park Condo Assn., 1987-92; founder, chmn., judge Curtain Call, 1989—; judge Gourmet Products Show, 1992—; patron to 4 local theatrical groups, 1986—. Mem. AAUW, Mensa, Intertel, Am. Booksellers Assn., Asst. League Antelope Valley, Desert Amigas-Domestic Violence (affiliate), Alpha Charter Guild. Republican. Avocations: cruising, world travel, photography, theater, tournament poker. Home: Lancaster, Calif. Died Feb. 21, 2008.

LEAF, HOWARD WESTLEY, retired military officer; b. Menominee, Mich., Sept. 22, 1923; s. Joseph Conrad and Hilda Eugene (Lavoy) L.; m. Madonna Anne; children: Mary Elizabeth, Timothy M., Barbara Anne, Anne Marie Moore, Thomas M., James D. BS, Colo. Sch. Mines, 1950; MS, St. Louis U., 1955; grad., Command and Staff Coll., 1961, Indsl. Coll. Armed Forces, 1969. Commd. 2d lt. USAF, 1951, advanced through grades to lt. gen., 1980, ret., 1985, staff officer Hdqrs., 1966-68, 69-71, insp. gen. Washington, 1980-83; aviation cadet, 1950-51; jet pilot Korea, 1952-53; test pilot, 1955-60; geophysicist, 1961-64; ops. officer 49th Tactical Fighter Wing, Europe, 1965; squadron comdr. S.E. Asia, 1966; wing comdr. 1st and 366th Tactical Fighter Wings, 1971-74; dep. chief staff for requirements Tactical Air Command, 1974-76; comdr. Air Force Test and Evaluation Ctr., Kirtland AFB, N.Mex., 1976-80; insp. gen. USAF, Washington, 1980—83, asst. vice chief of staff, 1983—85; 1985sr. v.p. BDM Internat. Corp., McLean, Va., 1985—91; dir. test and evaluation US Dept. Def., Washington, 1992—97. Mem. Air Force Sci. Adv. Bd. Decorated D.S.M., Silver Star with one oak leaf cluster, Legion of Merit, D.F.C.; recipient Eugene M. Zuckert Mgmt. Award, 1978, Disting. Achievement award Colo. Sch. Mines, 1982, Exceptional Svc. award USAF, 1997. Mem. Internat. Test and Evaluation Assn. (sr. adv. bd., Allen R. Mattews Award, 1994). Presbyterian. Home: Brandywine, Md. Died Apr. 25, 2009.

LEAMY, HARRY JOHN, metallurgical engineer; b. Alton, Ill., Nov. 15, 1940; s. Harry J. and Myrtle C. (Hogue) L.; m. Janet Rhea Leamy, May 29, 1965; children: Harry J., Jennifer R., Gillian D. BS in Metall. Engring., U. Mo., Rolla, 1963; PhD in Metallurgy, Iowa State U., 1967. Postdoctoral fellow Max Planck Inst. fur Metallurgy, Stuttgart, Germany, 1967-69; tech. staff materials physics rsch. dept. AT&T Bell Labs., Murray Hill, N.J., 1969-76, 77-79, tech. staff electronic materials rsch. dept., 1979-82, supr. projection display tech. group, 1982-84, supr. advanced VLSI packaging dept., 1984-86, head battery devel. dept., 1986-89; head energy sys. rsch., devel. and engring. dept. AT&T, Mesquite, Tex., 1989-92; vis. scientist N.V. Philips Rsch. Labs., Eindhoven, Netherlands, 1976-77; dir. CC Cameron Applied Rsch. Ctr. U. N.C., Charlotte, from 1992. Bd. dirs. Pielco Electronics, Inc., OxiDyn Inc. Prin. editor Jour. Materials Rsch.; contbr. over 100 articles to profl. jours. Mem. AAAS, Am. Assn. for Crystal growth, Am. Phys. Soc., Materials Rsch. Soc. (past pres.), Assn. of Univ. Tech. Mgrs., Am. Soc. for Engring. Edn., N.C. Electronics and Info. Tech. Assn. (bd. dirs.), Tau Beta Pi, Sigma Gamma Epsilon, Alpha Sigma Mu, Sigma Xi (past club pres.). Achievements include 11 patents. Home: Charlotte, NC. Died July 23, 2008.

LEBAN, WILLIAM VICTOR, JR., mechanical engineer; b. Chgo., Sept. 30, 1946; s. William Victor Sr. and Marie Ann (Bucar) L.; m. Donna Jean Niemiec, Oct. 24, 1970; children: Gregory, Todd. BS in Mech. Engring., U. Ill., 1969; MBA, Loyola U., Chgo., 1974; M in Project Mgmt., Keller Grad. Sch. Mgmt., 1994. Registered profl. engr., Ill.; cert. project mgmt. profl. Planning engr. Western Electric, Cicero, Ill., 1969-75; design engr. Natural Gas Pipeline, Lombard, Ill., 1975-96; program mgr. Keller Grad. Sch., from 1996. Pres. Sch. Dist. 92.5, Westchester, Ill., 1992-93, v.p., 1994; pres. WestchesterTennis Assn., 1991-92; treas. Westchester Baseball Inc., 1986-89. Named Man of Yr. Westchester Baseball, Inc., 1989; recipient George P. Doherty Leadership award, 1995. Mem. ASME, AACE, Project Mgmt. Inst. (v.p. programs Midwest chpt. 1996, v.p. prof. devel. 1997), Pipeliners, Toastmasters Club (pres. 1984). Home: Westchester, Ill. Died Apr. 15, 2008.

LEBARON, MELVIN JAY, consulting company executive; b. Barnwell, Alberta, Can., Nov. 14, 1930; s. Hower Neal and Luella (Wight) LeB.; m. Joan M. Mackay, July 16, 1953; children: Wendy Davison, Janeal, Brad, Graydon. BS, Brigham Young U., 1958; MSPA, U. So. Calif., LA, 1961, EdD, 1970. Prof., adminstr. U. So. Calif. Sch. Pub. Adminstrn., LA, 1959-77; pres. Humanistic Consulting, Inc., Brea, Calif., from 1977. Part time faculty various colls. and univs., 1970-80; chief of party U.S. State Dept., S.E. Asia, 1971-72. Contbr. articles to profl. jours. Mayor, councilman City of Brea, 1978-82. Recipient Adminstrv. medal Govt. So. Vietnam, Saigon, 1972. Mem. Lds Ch. Home: Canyon Lake, Calif. Died June 19, 2008.

LEBECK, CAROL E., artist, educator; b. Spokane, Wash., Sept. 8, 1931; d. Birger John and Cecile Lebeck. BA, MA, UCLA, 1958; postgrad., Swedish State Sch. DEsign, Stockholm, 1958—59. Tchg. asst. dept. art UCLA, 1956—57; art tchr. Grossmont H.S., San Diego, 1959—66; art instr. Grossmont Coll., El Cajon, Calif., 1962—85. Exhibitions include include Spectrum Gallery, San Diego, 1983, exhibitions include Gallery 8, LaJolla, 1980, Fine Arts Gallery, San Diego, 1979, Celebrations Gallery, 1979, San Diego Acad. Fine Art, 1978, Grossmont Coll. Gallery, El Cajon, Calif., 1978, Mus. Contemporary Crafts, N.Y.C., 1978, L.A. Inst. Contemporary Art, 1977, The Sculpture Gallery, San Diego, 1977, Wise and Wesler Gallery, Encino, Calif., 1977, Crocker Art Gallery, Sacramento, 1977, numerous others, one-woman shows include Spectrum Gallery, San Diego, 1981, Triad Gallery, 1976, 1975, Represented in permanent collections Ariz. State U. Fellow, Swedish Am. Soc. fellow, Stockholm, 1958—59. Died Feb. 11, 2008.

LEBLANC, ROBERT BRUCE, chemist; b. Alexandria, La., Jan. 28, 1925; s. Moreland Paul and Carmen Mary (Haydel) LeB.; divorced; children: Robert, Destin, Gregory, Carmen, David, Sophia, Ann; m. Donna Rita LeBlanc, June 22, 1996. BS, Loyola U., New Orleans, 1947; MS, Tulane U., PhD, 1950. Asst. prof. chem. Tex. A&M U., College Station, 1950-52; group leader Dow Chem. Co., Freeport, Tex., 1952-63, sect. head Midland, Mich., 1963-68; rsch. mgr. Nat. Cotton Coun., Memphis, Tenn., 1968-70; pres. LeBlanc Rsch. Corp., East Greenwich, R.I., 1970-86, Tallulah, La., from 1986. Contbr. 65 articles to profl. jours. and books. Lt. (j.g.) USNR, 1943-46, PTO. Mem. ASTM, Am. Chem. Soc., Am. Assn. Textile Chem. & Coll., Nat. Fire Protection Assn. Achievements include 17 patents in U.S. and fgn. countries. Home: Mandeville, La. Died May 6, 2008.

LEBOW, LEONARD STANLEY, musician; b. Chgo., Feb. 25, 1929; s. Philip and Rose (Wintergreen) L. B in Music, Roosevelt U., 1952; M in Music Composition, Chgo. Mus. Coll., 1959. Freelance trumpet player, Chgo., 1947-52; trumpet player, arranger Sahara Hotel Prodns., Las Vegas, Nev., 1952-54; tchr. Chgo. Pub. Schs., 1954-64, Los Angeles City and County, from 1964; freelance musician, composer, from 1954. Composer numerous works for brass ensembles and mus. prodns., 1956—. Mem. ASCAP. Avocations: video production and photography, media presentations. Died Dec. 22, 2007.

LECHOWICZ, THADDEUS STANLEY (TED LECHOWICZ), retired state senator; b. 1938; s. Frank and Rose Loboda Lechowicz; m. Suzanne H. Keiler, 1964; children: Edward John, Laura Ann. Former committeeman 30th Ward Regular Dem. Orgn.; former committeeman 30th Ward Regular Dem. Orgn.; former chmn. Exec. Appointments & Vet. Affairs, Adminstrn. Com.; former mem. Legislature Info Needs Com., Nat. Conf. State Legislators; state senate Adminstrn. Com., Ill.; mem. Elec. & Reapportionment Com., Econ. & Fiscal Commn.; House rep. Eex-officio all Com., Ill.; rep. 35th Ward Young Dem. Cook Co. & Ill., 1960—68; mem. Transp. & Exec. Com.; bd. dirs. 35th Ward Regular Dem. Orgn., Ill., 1960—69; W area chmn. Young Dem. Cook Co., 1962—63, chmn., 8th congl. Dist., 1966; regional dir. Cook Co. Young Dem. Ill, 1965—67, 2nd v.p., 1968; dir. data processing Toll Highway Commmn., Ill., 1965, asst. dir. fin., 1966—68; mem. Ill. House rep. Dist. 17, 1969—83; asst. majority leader, 1977—82; mem. Eex-officio all Com., 1977—82; state senate Dist. 6, 1983—91; mem. Appropriations I Com. Recipient Outstanding Young Dem., State Ill., 1969, Outstanding Svc. award, Young Dem. Ill., 1975, Best Legislature award, Polish America Polit. League, 1976, Man of Yr. award, Polish America Police Assn., 1977; named to Legislator Yr., 1972. Mem.: Chgo. Soc., Polish Nat. Alliance, Amvets, Holy Name Soc. Democrat. Catholic. Died Jan. 5, 2009.

LEDERMAN, ALVIN, management consultant; b. NYC, July 11, 1918; s. Isadore and Yetta Lederman; m. Celeste Lederman, June 28, 1976; children: Susan, Laurie, Stephanie, Scot. BA, CUNY, 1939; M in Pub. Adminstn., NYU, 1951; PhD in Mgmt., Am. Internat. U., 1980. Adminstr., dep. region dir. U.S. Dept. Def., NYC, 1942-70; tng. specialist N.Y. State Dept. Labor, NYC, 1970-72; prin. mgmt. analyst N.Y.C. Dept. Health, 1972-82; mgmt. cons. U.S. Office Personnel Mgmt., NYC, 1982-89. Instr. faculty Baruch Sch Pub. Adminstrn., N.Y.C., 1951, grad. sch. NYU, N.Y.C., 1952-60; pres. Personalized Seminar Assocs., N.Y.C., 1983—. Contbr. articles to mags. Served to capt. U.S. Army, 1944-46, ETO, with Res., 1948-60. Decorated Bronze Star with oak leaf cluster, Battle Stars (3), Combat Inf. Badge; recipient 40 awards from U.S. Def. Dept. Mem. Fed. Procurement Officer Assn. (pres. 1954-56). Died May 30, 2008.

LEDSKY, NELSON CHARLES, retired diplomat; b. Cleve., Sept. 30, 1929; s. Nathan and Bertha (Glattstein) L.; m. Cecile Helen Waechter, Aug. 26, 1951 (dec. 1998); children: Rebecca, Jonathan, Karen; m. Helen Coleman Ledsky BA, Case Western Res. U., 1951; MA, Columbia U., NYC, 1953. With US Dept. State, 1959—92, dept. asst. sec. for congressional rels. Washington, 1978-81, min. Berlin, 1981-85, prin. dep. dir. policy planning staff, 1985—87, spl. coord. to Cyprus, 1989—92; spl. asst. to Pres. for nat. security affairs, sr. dir. for European & Soviet affairs NSC, 1987—89. Cpl. U.S. Army, 1955-57. Mem. Am. Coun. to Germany, B'nai B'rith. Home: Washington, DC. Died June 19, 2009.

LEE, ALEXANDRA SAIMOVICI, civil engineer; b. Negrest, Vaslui, Romania, Nov. 6, 1932; came to U.S., 1969; d. Leonidas and Etlea (Schreibman) Saimovici; m. Jack Lee, July 14, 1972. Grad. in constrn. engring., Constrn. Inst., Bucharest, Romania, 1956. Registered profl. engr., S.C. Structural engr. Energo Constructia, Bucharest, 1956-61, Elcora Constrn. Metalicas, Buenos Aires, 1961-69, Walter Kidde, NYC, 1969-70, John Kassner, NYC, 1970-72; civil engr. I, City of Columbia, S.C., 1972-77, design engr. S.C., 1977-82, civil engr. II S.C., from 1982. Mem. NSPE, Am. Pub. Works Assn. Home: Brookline, Mass. Died Feb. 3, 2008.

LEE, CRISTI JAYNE, medical/surgical nurse; b. Charlottesville, Va., Aug. 1, 1957; d. Gordon Clyde and Vanna B. (Walsh) Stauffer; m. David Curtis Lee, Aug. 8, 1980. Student, Old Dominion U., 1975-77; AAS magna cum laude, Piedmont Va. Community Coll., Charlottesville, 1988. RN; cert. nurse clinician. Nurse Med. Coll. Va./Va. Commonwealth U., Richmond. Died Mar. 20, 2008.

LEE, DAVID HARMON, architect, consultant; b. Bklyn., Aug. 7, 1925; s. Emery Harmon Ivory and Adelia Gertrude (Baker) L.; m. Alice Rose Kippola (div. 1972); children: Kimball E., Russell K.; m. Nancy Carol Laing Craig, May 27, 1986. BARCh., U. Mich., 1950. Draftsman Karl Krusmark, Casper, Wyo., 1950-53; asst. project architect Smith, Hinchman & Grylls, Detroit, 1953-54; sr. architect Argonaut Realty div. G.M.C., Detroit, 1954-56; project architect Walter J. Rozycki & Assocs., Detroit, 1956-62; project mgr. Smith, Hinchman & Grylls, Detroit, 1962-66, assoc., 1967-74; dir. facilities mgmt. U. Louisville, from 1974. Served as lt. comdr. USNR, 1943-70. Mem. AIA (Cen. Ky. chpt.), Assn. Univ. Architects, Ky. Soc. Architects. Clubs: Louisville Boat. Lodges: Optimists (pres. Livonia chpt. 1962-63), Rotary. Democrat. Avocations: golf, tennis. Home: Louisville, Ky. Died Feb. 25, 2008.

LEE, ERNEST SALTMARSH, trade union consultant; b. Santo Dominigo, Dominican Republic, Apr. 12, 1923; s. Harry and Mercedes Henrietta (Saltmarsh) L.; m. Eileen Patricia Meany, May 13, 1957; children: Ernest P., Harry, Christopher Martin, Michael Meany. BS in Fgn. Svc., Georgetown U., 1955. Enlisted USMC, 1942; advanced through grades to maj. USMCR, 1955; ret., 1968; officer Prudential Savs. and Loan, Washington, 1954-58; internat. affairs ofcl. United Food and Comml. Workers, AFL-CIO, Washington, 1958-62; ofcl. AFL-CIO, Washington, 1962-83; owner, cons. Trade Union Cons., Rockville, Md., from 1983. Recipient Silver star USMC, 1952. Mem. Coun. on Fgn. Rels. Democrat. Roman Catholic. Avocations: computers, gardening, writing. Home: Rockville, Md. Died Apr. 4, 2008.

LEE, GENEVIEVE BRUGGEMAN, publishing company executive; b. Mahnomen, Minn., May 23, 1928; d. Joseph William and Mary Martha (Bastain) Bruggeman; m. Joel Kenneth Lee, Aug. 23, 1946; children: Rebecca Marie, Joel Gregory. Clk. Family Svc. Assn., NYC, 1946-47; counselor Cin. Employment Svc., 1968-70; exec. sec. Ch. Bulls. of Buffalo, Inc., 1970-73, v.p., from 1973. Bd. dirs. Woodgate Assn., East Amherst, N.Y.; mem. adv. bd. Schofield Residence, Buffalo, 1983-85, mem. exec. bd., sec., 1985-90, vice chmn./sec., 1991-94, chmn. bd. dirs., 1994-99, treas., 1999-2005 Mem. Ken-Ton C. of C., Zonta (pres. Kenmore 1984-86, bd. dirs. area 3, 1986-88, 2000-07, sec. dist. IV 1988-90), Kenmore C. of C., Printing and Imaging Assn. Western NY. Republican. Roman Catholic. Home: East Amherst, NY. Died June 6, 2008.

LEE, JACQUELINE IRIS, community development planner; b. Spokane, Wash., Nov. 18, 1952; d. Reverend Daniel and Ruth Thelma (Clark) L.; m. Reginald M. Burke, Sept. 15, 1973 (div. Dec. 1980). BA, St. Mary's U., San Antonio, 1975, MA, 1978; M of City and Regional Planning, U. Calif., Berkeley, 1982; student, Barbizon Sch. Modeling, 1983. Ct. reporter Dun & Bradstreet, San Antonio, 1972-73; research asst. St. Mary's U., 1973-75; manpower planner City of San Antonio, 1978; planner Spanish Speaking Unity Counil, Oakland, Calif., 1980-83; project adminstr. The John Stewart Co., Sausalito, Calif., 1983-84; housing asst. Jubilee West Inc., Oakland, 1985-86; cons. Naomi Gray and Assocs. and Apape Works, San Francisco, 1984-86; employment monitor County of Bexar, San Antonio, from 1986. Cons. Ctr. for Black Concern, Oakland, 1984—, Beckman Image Devel., Oakland, 1984—, Naomi Gray & Assocs., San Francisco, 1984—, East Oakland Youth Devel. Ctr., 1984-87. Mem., leader Topeka and San Antonio chpts. Girl Scouts U.S., 1958-71; coordinator Voter Registration and Awareness Project, San Antonio, 1978; activist S. African Apartheid, Black Student Union, 1970-73; mem. G. Givens Voices of Zion, San Antonio, 1986-87; mem. Allen Temple Bapt. Ch., Oakland, 1980-86, Second Bapt. Ch., 1986—. Mem. Nat. Assn. Planners. Baptist. Avocations: modeling, writing, needlepoint, lecturing, bible study. Home: San Antonio, Tex. Died Aug. 12, 2008.

LEE, JHONG SAM, electronics company executive; b. Kiljoo, Korea, Dec. 20, 1935; came to U.S., 1955; s. Dong Kyu and Boon Don (Chung) L.; m. Helen H. Chang; children: Mary, Grace, David. BSEE, U. Okla., 1959; MSEE, George Washington U., 1961, DSc, 1967. Sr. engr. FXR, Inc., Woodside, N.Y., 1960-64; asst. prof. elec. engring. George Washington U., Washington, 1965-68; expert cons. U.S. Naval Rsch. Lab., Washington, 1965-73; adv. engr. IBM Corp., Gaithersburg, Md., 1968-69; assoc. prof. elec. engring. Cath. U. America, Washington, 1969-73; assoc. dir. Magnavox Advanced Sys. Office, Silver Spring, Md., 1973-76; pres., CEO J.S. Lee Associates, Inc., Rockville, Md., 1976—2009, Dae Young Elec. Co. Ltd., Seoul, Korea, 1985-86. Cons. Radiation Sys., Inc., McLean, Va., 1968-72, Comsat Labs., Washington, 1965, 71, Dae Young Electronics Co. Ltd., Seoul, 1977-84. Contbr. articles to profl. jours. NASA doctoral fellow, 1964. Fellow IEEE; mem. Am. Def. Preparedness Assn. (life), Armed Forces Comm. and Electronics Assn. Home: Potomac, Md. Died June 5, 2009.

LEE, JOHN MARSHALL, JR., retired newspaper editor; b. Walterboro, SC, June 28, 1930; m. Rebecca Lee, 1956 (dec. 2003); children: Edward, John III. Grad., Duke U.; MA in Journalism. Bus. editor The News Leader, Richmond, Va., 1957—61; staff mem. The NY Times, NYC, 1961—76, asst. bus. editor, 1972—76, bus. editor, 1976—85, asst. mng. editor, dir. editl. devel. regional newspaper group, ret., 2001. Served in USAF. Died Jan. 6, 2009.

LEEWER, WILLIAM GEORGE, JR., education educator; b. Camden, NJ, Nov. 17, 1950; s. William George Leewer, Sr. BA in Lit., R. Stockton State Coll. NJ, Pomona, 1975; MEd in Curriculum and Instrn., U. So. Miss., Hattiesburg, 1987, PhD in Edn., 2000. Cert. English tchr. grades K-12 NJ, secondary lang. arts Colo., AAAA edn. lic. secondary edn. Miss., advanced ops. aerial NJ State Fire Coll. Sr. grad. rsch. asst. So. Edn. Consortium and State Sch. Ctr., Hattiesburg, 1997—99; faculty chair, head trainer Koch Crime Inst., St. Mary's, Kans., 1999—2001; lang. arts tchr. Adams City H.S., Denver, 2001—02; asst. vis. prof. edn. U. So. Miss., Hattiesburg, 2002—03, trainer,. F. Karnes Ctr. Gifted and Talented Edn., from 2002; asst. prof. edn. Miss. State U., Meridian, from 2003, grad. coord., from 2004. Participant NJ State- China Tchr. Exch. Program, 1988; cons., trainer, editor So. Edn. Consortium, Meridian, from 1997, U. Ctrl. Ark. Grad. Sch., Conway, from 2003; cons., trainer East Miss. Ctr. Edn. Devel., Meridian, from 2003; invitee Oxford Round Table on Poverty and Depravation, England, 2007, Oxford Round Table on Ch. and State, 2007. Editor: School Safety and Security Legal News, from 1999, Legal Update: Southern Education Consortium, from 2002, Legal Update for C.C., from 2003. Founding mem., mem. leadership coun. Wall of Tolerance, So. Poverty Law Ctr., 2002; mem. Commanders Club DAV, 2003; founding mem. Nat. WWII Meml., Washington, 2004; charter mem. Nat. WWII Mus., New Orleans, 2005; ptnr. Spl. Olympics, 2004—06. Recipient cert. appreciation, Easter Seals, 2005, 2006; named Bronze Leader, DAV, 2003, Good Samaritan of Yr., 2005, Silver Leader Comdr.'s Club, 2007, Miss. Donor of Yr., WWII Veterans Com., 2004, Disting. Donor, VFW, 2005, Miss. Donor of Yr., Help Hospitalized Veterans, 2005, Donor of Yr., 2007, Patriot of Yr., 2007; named one of Outstanding Young Men Am., 1975—76; named to The Wall Soc., Vietnam Veterans Meml., from 2007. Mem.: ACLU, So. Poverty Law Ctr., The Wall Soc. (disting. donor 2004), Kappa Delta Pi, Pi Delta Kappa (hon.). Avocations: fishing, stamp collecting/philately, etymology. Home: Marion, Miss. Died May 26, 2008.

LEFELHOCZ, IRENE HANZAK, nurse, business owner; b. Cleve., Nov. 10, 1926; d. Joseph J. and Gisella Elizabeth (Biro) Hanzak; m. Joseph R. Lefelhocz, Aug. 7, 1948; 1 child, Joseph R. III. RN, St. Luke's Hosp. Sch. Nursing, 1948; BSN, Case Western Res. U., 1963; MEd, John Carroll U., 1971; MSN, Case Western Reserve U., 1973. RN, Ohio, Ala. Adminstrv. cons. The Episcopal Kyle Home, Gadsen, Ala., 1986-88; pres., mgr. The Joseph House, Gadsen, 1989-97; nurse cons. Ala. Dept. Health, Montgomery, Ala., 1988-90; supr., evening and night nurse adminstr. Riverview Med. Ctr., Moragne Park, Gadsden; counselor Sch. Nursing Holy Name of Jesus Med. Ctr, 1990-92; psychology therapist, counselor to inpatient population Mountain View Hosp., Gadsden, 1994-97, mem. spkrs. bur. Mem. allocations com. United Way, Etowah County; active numerous other community orgns.; bd. dirs., vice chmn. Etowah County chpt. ARC. Mem. NEA, Ohio Edn. Assn., ARC (past pres.). Died Jan. 17, 2008.

LEFEVER, ERNEST WARREN, retired think-tank executive; b. York, Pa., Nov. 12, 1919; m. Margaret Louise Briggs, 1951; children: David, Bryce. AB, Elizabethtown Coll., 1942; BD in Christian ethics, Yale U., 1945, PhD, 1956. Field sec. World Alliance of YMCA's, U.K. and W. Ger., 1945-48; internat. affairs specialist Nat. Council Chs., NYC, 1952-54; mem. faculty dept. govt. U. Md., 1956-57; mem. research staff, acting head fgn. affairs div. Library of Congress, Washington, 1957-59; fgn. affairs staff Sen. Hubert Humphrey of Minn., 1959-60; research assoc. Washington Center Fgn. Policy Research, Johns Hopkins U., 1960-61; sr. staff Inst. Def. Analyses, Washington, 1961-64; sr. fellow fgn. policy studies Brookings Instn., 1964-76; founder, pres. Ethics and Public Policy Center, Washington, 1976-89, sr. fellow, 1989—2009. Professorial lectr. dept. govt. Georgetown U.; lectr. Nat. War Coll., Army, Navy and Air Force War colls., Japan Def. Coll., numerous univs.; cons. sec. Dept. State, 1981-83; mem. Internat. Inst. Strategic Studies, London, 1960-89; participant numerous internat. confs. Author: Ethics and U.S. Foreign Policy, 1957, (with others) Profile of American Politics, 1960, Crisis in the Congo, 1965, Uncertain Mandate: Politics of the U.N. Congo Operation, 1967, Spear and Scepter: Army, Police, and Politics in Tropical Africa, 1970, (with others) Ethics and World Politics, 1972, TV and National Defense, 1974, Amsterdam to Nairobi: The World Council of Churches and the Third World, 1979, Nuclear Arms in the Third World: U.S. Policy Dilemma, 1979, The CIA and the American Ethic, 1980, The Irony of Virtue: Ethics and American Power, 1998, America's Imperial Burden: Is the Past Prologue?, 1999, Liberating the Limerick, 2006; Editor: Arms and Arms Control, 1962, Will Capitalism Survive?, 1979; co-editor: The Apocalyptic Premise: Nuclear Arms Debated, 1982, Nairobi to Vancouver: The World Council of Churches and the World, 1975-87, 1987, Perestroika: How New Is Gorbachev's New Thinking?, 1989; mem. editorial bd. Policy Rev.; editorial adv. bd. The Washington Times; contbr. articles to profl. jours. and newspapers. Mem. Md. State Commn. Values in Edn., 1979-83. Mem. Washington Inst. Fgn. Affairs, Coun. Fgn. Rels., Johns Hopkins U. Soc. Scholars, Soc. Values in Higher Edn., Phila. Soc. (1st v.p. 1986-87), Cosmos Club (Washington, Yale Club (Washington and N.Y.C.). Home: Virginia Beach, Va. Died July 29, 2009.

LEFEVRE, THOMAS VERNON, retired utilities executive; b. Dallas, Dec. 5, 1918; s. Eugene H. and Callie E. (Powell) L.; m. Lillian Herndon Bourne, Oct. 12, 1946; children: Eugene B., Nicholas R., Sharon A., Margot P. BA, U. Fla., 1939, LLB, 1942; LLM, Harvard U., 1946. Bar: Fla. 1945, N.Y. 1947, D.C. 1951, Pa. 1955, U.S. Supreme Ct. 1953. Atty. IRS and various firms, NYC, Washington, and Phila., 1946-55; ptnr. Morgan, Lewis & Bockius, Phila., 1956-79; pres., CEO UGI Corp., Valley Forge, Pa., 1979-85, chmn., 1983-89. Chmn. G.P. Hospitality, Inc., 1981-2009; mem. Commr.'s Adv. Group IRS, 1976-77. Bd. dirs. Zool. Soc. Phila., 1982-91, WHYY Inc., 1982-96; chmn. U. Arts, 1986-89; trustee Franklin Inst., 1980-89, Fox Chase Cancer Ctr., 1979-88. With USMC, 1942-46. Fellow ABA (vice chmn. govt. rels. sect. of taxation 1976-79), Am. Bar Found.; mem. Pa. Bar Assn., Merion Cricket Club, Merion Golf Club, Sankaty Head Golf Club, Nantucket Yacht Club. Episcopalian. Home: Bryn Mawr, Pa. Died June 29, 2009.

LEGATZ, ALAN WAYNE, investment advisor, accountant; b. Bay City, Mich., June 13, 1945; s. Peter and Hilda Legatz; m. Heather Henry, June 25, 1967; 1 child, Sarah Heather. BA, Mich. State U., 1967; MBA, Ctrl. Mich. U., 1968. CFP, CPA, Mich., Fla.; registered investment advisor. Tax acct. Ernst & Ernst CPAs, 1975; instr. St. Clair C.C., 1976-79; tax acct. Edmond A. Swab, CPA, 1975-76; acct. Alan W. Legatz, CPA, from 1976; pres. Competent Profl. Advisors, from 1986; instr. AICPAs, from 1986; pres. Tax Free Exch. Svcs., Inc., from 1996, Alan Legatz Investment Adv. Co., Naples, Fla., from 1996. Instr. fed. tax workshops, 1986-92, Practitioners Pub. Co., 1986-92, Alliance for Tax, Legal & Acctg. Seminars, 1999; mem. adv. com. Registry of Fin. Planning Practitioners; advisor Delta Coll. PFP Program. Contbr. articles to jours. and newspapers. Mem. AICPA (tax force on personal fin. planning, exceptional faculty award 1987-88, 88-89, 89-90), Fla. Inst. CPAs (outstanding discussion leader award 1988), C. of C., Rotary. Home: Harbor Beach, Mich. Died June 9, 2008.

LEHMANN, ERICH LEO, statistics educator; b. Strasbourg, France, Nov. 20, 1917; came to U.S., 1940, naturalized, 1945; s. Julius and Alma Rosa (Schuster) L.; m. Juliet Popper Shaffer; children: Stephen, Barbara, Fia. MA, U. Calif., Berkeley, 1943, PhD, 1946; DSc (hon.), U. Leiden, 1985, U. Chgo., 1991. From asst. dept. math. to prof. U. Calif., Berkeley, 1942-55, prof. statistics, 1955—88, prof. emeritus, 1988—2009, chmn. dept. statistics, 1973-76. Vis. assoc. prof. Columbia, 1950-51, Stanford, 1951-52; vis. lectr. Princeton, 1951 Author: Testing Statistical Hypotheses, 1959, 3d edit. (with J. Romano), 2005; (with J.L. Hodges, Jr.) Basic Concepts of Probability and Statistics, 1964, 2d edit., 1970, Nonparametrics: Statistical Methods Based on Ranks, 1975, Theory of Point Estimation, 1983; (with Casella) 2d edit., 1998, Elements of Lange Sample Theory, 1998 Recipient Fisher award Coms. of Pres. Stats. Socs. in N.Am., 1988; Guggenheim fellow, 1955, 66, 79; Miller rsch. prof., 1962-63, 72-73; recipient Samuel S. Wilks Meml. medal Am. Statis. Assn., 1996, Gottfried Noether award Am. Statis. Assn., 2000. Fellow Inst. Math. Stats., Am. Statis. Assn., Royal Statis. Soc. (hon.); mem. Internat. Statis. Inst., Am. Acad. Arts and Scis., Nat. Acad. Scis. Died Sept. 12, 2009.

LEHR, LAURENCE JON, travel executive; b. Miami, Fla., May 30, 1943; s. Milton H. and Harriet (Smerling) L.; m. Bonnie June Murray; children: Benjamin, Jennifer. BFA, NYU, 1965. With CBS Internat. News Prodn., NYC, 1967-69; v.p. Internat. Video Prodns., Miami, 1970-81; pres. Am. Travel Club, Miami, 1982-87, Cinema Mgmt. Corp., 1976-81; v.p. Bob Kuechenberg and Assoc., Miami, 1988, Atlas Travel, Miami, from 1988. Bd. dirs. Jewish Community Ctr., Miami Beach, Fla., 1988—; mem. Rep. Nat. Com., 1983—, mil. affairs com. Homestead AFB, Fla. Mem. Rotary, Optimist. Republican. Home: Miami, Fla. Died June 28, 2008.

LEHRER, JULIUS MARSHALL, lawyer; b. Chgo., Feb. 7, 1921; s. Charles I. and Etta (Zuckerman) L.; m. Dorothy Levitan, Mar. 16, 1968. BA, U. Chgo., 1942, JD, 1948. Pvt. practice, Chgo., from 1948. Pres. Adolf Kraus B'nai B'rith, Chgo. With U.S. Army, 1943-47. Mem. Chgo. Bar Assn. (chmn. lawyer referral 1990), Am. Legion (sr. vice comdr. Highland Park, Ill. unit 1990-91). Home: Highland Park, Ill. Died Mar. 17, 2008.

LEIBEL, STEVEN ARNOLD, oncologist; Undergrad., Mich. State U. S, 1967, Mich. State U. Coll. Medicine, 1970; MD, U. Calif., San Francisco, 1972. Cert. Am. Bd. Radiology. Intern U. Calif., San Francisco, 1972—73, resident radiation oncology, 1973—76, asst. prof., 1980—82, assoc. prof. radiation oncology, 1982—88; radiation oncologist Nat. Naval Med. Ctr., Bethesda, Md., 1976—78, chmn. radiation oncology NYC, 1977—78; asst. prof. Johns Hopkins Hosp., 1978—80; vice chmn., clin. dir. dept. radiation oncology Meml. Sloan-Kettering Cancer Ctr., NYC, 1988—98; chmn. radiation oncology Meml. Sloan Kettering Cancer Ctr., NYC, 1998—2004; Ann and John Doerr Medical Dir. Stanford Cancer Ctr., 2004—08. Mem.: Am. Bd. Radiology (pres.). Died Feb. 7, 2008.

LEIBOVITZ, ALBERT, microbiologist, researcher; b. NYC, Nov. 30, 1915; s. Bernard and Rachel (Jacobson) L.; m. Bettie Cowles, Jan. 21, 1948 (dec.); m. Elsa Gordon, Dec. 18, 1983; children: Jeffrey, Robyn, Ethel. BS, U. Conn., 1938; MS, U. Minn., 1940. Microbiologist Southbury (Conn.) Tng. Sch., 1940-42; enlisted U.S. Army, 1942, advanced through grades to col., 1960; head microbiology sect. 5th Army Med. Lab., St. Louis, 1956-60; head microbiology div. 6th U.S. Army Med. Lab., Sausalito, Calif., 1960-70; ret. U.S. Army, 1970; chief microbiologist Scott and White Clinic, Temple, Tex., 1970-79; rsch. assoc. U. Ariz. Cancer Ctr., Tucson, 1979-92. Virology cons. USN, Berkeley, Calif., 1966-70, dermatology div. U. Calif. Sch. Medicine, San Francisco, 1966-70. Contbr. articles on microbiology, media, cell culture to Jour. Hygiene, Advances in Cell Culture, numerous others. Mem. Habbjach Dollars for Scholars, Tucson, 1984—; bd. dirs. Temple Emanuel, Tucson, 1989-91, 95-97, Jewish Family and Children's Svc., 1991-97. Decorated Legion of Merit; rsch. grantee U.S. Army, 1961-70, Nat. Cancer Inst., 1984-92. Mem. Am. Soc. Cancer Rsch., Am. Soc. Microbiology, Tissue Culture Assn., Sigma Xi. Achievements include development of tissue culture medium which permits growth of tissue cells in free exchange with the atmosphere; supervision and monitoring of field testing of adenovirus vaccines for Army recruits; establishment of over 300 human tumor cell lines. Home: Tucson, Ariz. Died Nov. 30, 2007.

LEIGHTON, RICHARD K., accounting company executive; b. Jasper, Ind., Aug. 18, 1945; s. Harold Robert and Catherine M. (Schuler) L.; m. Anne Margurite Feltman, Aug. 10, 1968; children: Michele, Christine, Jennifer. BS, Ind. U., 1967. Ptnr. Robert M. Finn & Co., Indpls., 1967-81, King Main Hurdman, Indpls., 1982-86; prin. Richard K. Leighton & Co., Carmel, Ind., from 1987. Author: (with others) Government Accounting and Auditing, 1987. Bd. dirs. Marquette Manor, Indpls., 1981-83, Voice of Good News, Inc., Indpls., 1982—, Ind. Justice Task Force, Indpls., 1984-86. Served with U.S. Army, 1967-73. Mem. Am. Inst. CPA's, Ind. CPA Soc. (bd. dirs. 1982-83). Clubs: Meridian Hills Country, Skyline (Indpls.). Lodges: Sertoma (pres. Carmel/Clay chpt. 1986-87). Republican. Roman Catholic. Avocations: reading, golf, tennis. Home: Carmel, Ind. Died Oct. 18, 2007.

LEITA, TONY SCOTT, anchorman, program director; b. Yakima, Wash., May 16, 1958; s. Louie J. and Marvelle E. (Ensinminger) L.; m. Rebecca A. Abbott, Nov. 8, 1984. Degree in polit. sci., U. Wash., 1980. Anchorman Sta. WSAZ-TV, Huntington, W.Va., 1981-1983; anchorman, host Sta. WTHI, Terre Haute, Ind., 1983-84; anchorman, program dir. Sta. KSNT-TV, Topeka, from 1984. Host United Way and Leukemia Found. talent shows, Kans., 1986, 87. Named highest rated weatherman Neilson Ratings, Topeka, 1986, 87; recipient Best Weather Show award Colorgraphics Inc., Madison, Wis., 1985. Mem. Nat. Assn. TV Programming Execs., Am. Meteorl. Soc. Republican. Roman Catholic. Avocations: camping, travel, raising labrador retrievers. Home: Topeka, Kans. Died Oct. 3, 2007.

LEMOINE, GANO D., JR., lawyer, pharmacist; b. Cottonport, La., Apr. 2, 1938; s. Gano D. and Therese D. Lemoine; m. Carolyn Y. Lemoine, July 13, 1963; children: Gano D. III, Jean Louis. BS in Pharmacy, U. Houston, 1960; LLB, JD, Tulane U., 1964. Bar: U.S. Dist. Ct. (mid. and ea. dists.) La. 1964, U.S. Dist. Ct. (we. dist.) La. 1988, U.S. Ct. Appeals (5th cir.) 1981, U.S. Supreme Ct. 1981; registered pharmacist, La. Sr. ptnr. Andrus, Boudreaux, Lemoine & Tonore, Lafayette, from 1987. Pres. Cottonport Bank, 1985, v.p., 1981-84, bd. dirs.; pres. Lemoine Contracting and Antique Co., 1979-81; mem. plaintiff's steering com. La. Breast Implant Litig., 1992—. Pres. St. Mary's Sch. Bd., 1979-81. Mem. ABA, La. Bar Assn., Avoyelles Parish Bar Assn. (past pres. 1972), Am. Soc. Pharm. Law, La. Pharm. Assn., Nat. Assn. Retail Druggists, Am. Pharm. Assn., Am. Bankers Assn., Am. Coll. Legal Medicine, ATLA (pharm. and toxic tort com.), La. Trial Lawyers Assn., Grand Lake Gun and Rod Club (pres. 1980-81), Cottonport Svc. Club, Sigma Alpha Epsilon. Democrat. Roman Catholic. Avocations: tennis, horseback riding, swimming, golf, hunting. Home: Cottonport, La. Died Dec. 29, 2007.

LEMPICKI, ALEXANDER, physicist, researcher; b. Warsaw, Jan. 26, 1922; came to U.S., 1955; s. Dominik and Janina (Czaplicki) L.; m. Antonina Hirschberg, Sept. 27, 1952; children: Maria, Veronica. PhD, Imperial Coll., London, 1960. Rsch. physicist EMI, Eng., 1949-55, Sylvania, N.Y., 1955-72, GTE Labs., Waltham, Mass., 1972-82, prof. physics and chemistry Boston U., from 1983. Cons. NASA, Washington, 1979, Baxter Troverwl, 1985, Corning Glassworks, 1983-87. 2nd lt. Inf. Fellow Am. Phys. Soc., Optical Soc. Am. Avocation: writing proposals. Died Dec. 23, 2007.

LENARD, LLOYD EDGAR, financial consultant; b. West Monroe, La., July 29, 1922; s. James Edward and Doshie (Boyette) L.; m. Betty-Jo Sawyer, Dec. 23, 1947; children: Carla Dawn, Brian Drury, Lloyd E. BA in Journalism, La. State U., 1943; MA in Advt. and Mktg., U. Mo., 1947. CLU, ChFC. News reporter Shreveport (La.) Times, 1946; exec. trainee Neiman-Marcus, Dallas, 1947-48; advt. mgr. Sta.

KNOE, Monroe, La., 1948-52; life ins. agt. Aetna Life, Monroe, 1952-53, asst. agy. mgr. Shreveport, 1953-56; agy. mgr., owner Pan Am. Life, Shreveport, 1956-80; freelance fin. cons. Shreveport, 1980-96; county commr. Caddo Parish Commn., Shreveport, 1983-94, pres., 1988-89, 89-90. Radio talk show host Sta. KWKH, Shreveport; TV talk show host Sta. KSLI, Shreveport. Author The Last Confederate Flag, 2000, Miracle on the 13th Hole, 2000, Papa Left Us...But Mama Pulled Us Through, 2000; contbr. articles to profl. jours. Chmn. Reps., Caddo Parish, La., 1975; chmn. Reps. five parish area; treas. La. Rep. Party; mem. Rep. State Ctrl. Com., Heart Assn. Named Young Man of Yr. Jr. Chamber, 1956, Gen. Agt. of Yr. Pan Am. Life, 1963; recipient various speech trophies. Mem. Nat. Assn. County Govts. (taxation and fin. steering com.), Kiwanis, Mid-City Kiwanis Club Sport (dist. lt. gov. 1978). Republican. Baptist. Avocations: writing, speaking, physical fitness, walking, golf. Died June 11, 2008.

LENZ, HENRY PAUL, management consultant; b. NYC, Nov. 24, 1925; s. Ernest and Margaret (Schick) L.; m. Norma M. Kull, Jan. 25, 1958; children: Susan, Scott, Theresa. AB, U. N.C., 1946; MBA, Coll. Ins., 1974. Underwriter U.S. Casualty Co., NYC, 1948-55; underwriting mgr. Mass. Bonding & Ins. Co., NYC, 1955-60; with Home Ins. Co., NYC, 1960-85, sr. v.p., 1972-75, exec. v.p., dir., 1975-85; chmn. bd. Lenz Enterprises Ltd., Chatham, NJ, from 1985. Former pres., dir. Home Indemnity Co.; pres., dir. Home Ins. Co. Ind., Home Ins. Co. Ill., City Ins. Co., Home Group Risk Mgmt.; chmn. bd. Home Reins. Co., Scott Wetzel Services Inc.; chmn., pres. Cityvest Reins. Ltd., City Ins. Co. (U.K.) Ltd.; trustee Am. Inst. Property and Liability Underwriters, Ins. Inst. Am. Served with USNR, 1944-47, 52-53. Decorated Army Commendation medal. Mem. Soc. CPCU's, Phi Beta Kappa, Sigma Nu. Home: Florham Park, NJ. Died Feb. 20, 2009.

LEONARD, JOHN DILLON, film and literature critic; b. Wash., DC, Feb. 25, 1939; m. Christiana Morison (div.); children: Andrew, Amy; m. Sue Leonard; 1 stepchild, Jen Nessel. Attended, Harvard U.; BA, U. Calif. Berkeley. Former writer Nat. Review Mag.; former dir. drama and lit. KPFA Radio; lit. critic New York Times Book Review, 1967—71, from 1975, exec. editor, 1971—75; co-editor, books section The Nation Mag., 1995—98. Contbr. articles to newspapers and mags. incl. The Nation, The New Republic, NY Times Review Books, Harper's, Atlantic Monthly, Playboy, Esquire, Harper's Bazaar, Vogue, Newsweek, The Village Voice, and Washington Post; author: (books) The Naked Martini, 1964, Wyke Regis, 1966, Crybaby of the Western World, 1969, Black Conceit, 1972, This Pen for Hire, 1973, Private Lives in the Imperial City, 1979, The Last Innocent White Man in America, 1994, Smoke and Mirrors: Violence, Television, and Other American Cultures, 1997, When the Kissing Had to Stop: Cult Studs, Khmer Newts, Langley Spooks, Techno-Geeks, Video Drones, Author Gods, Serial Killers, Vampire Media, Alien Sperm Suckers, Satanic Therapists and Those of Us Who Hold a Left-Wing Grudge in, 1999, Lonesome Rangers: Homeless Minds, Promised Lands, Fugitive Cultures, 2002. Recipient Ivan Sandrof Lifetime Achievement award, Nat. Book Critics Circle, 2007. Died Nov. 5, 2008.

LEONARD, RAYMOND W., historian, educator; b. Wichita, Kans., May 19, 1959; BA in History, Wichita State U., Kans., 1981, MA in History, 1985; MA in Soviet and East European Studies, U. Kans., Lawrence, 1987, PhD in History, 1997. Instr. dept. history and anthropology U. Ctrl. Mo., Warrensburg, Mo., 1998—2003, asst. prof. history dept. history and anthropology, from 2003. Actor: (game) Purged in Blood; contbr. numerous book reviews, articles to encyclopedias. Recipient Oswald P. Backus II Meml. award, U. Kans., 1998; fellow, Ky. U. Ctr. Russian and East European Studies, 1998, Nat. Holocaust Edn. Found., 2000. Home: Warrensburg, Mo. Died Apr. 15, 2008.

LEONETT, ANTHONY ARTHUR, banker; b. Summit, NJ, Jan. 4, 1929; s. Joseph J. and Margaret (DiGuglielmo) L.; m. Ann Marino, Oct. 6, 1974; 1 son by previous marriage, Anthony Arthur. BS, Seton Hall U., 1950; cert., Am. Inst. Banking, 1956; postgrad., U. Wis., 1962. Mgr. First Nat. Bank & Trust Co., Summit, 1950-56; sr. v.p., auditor Nat. State Bank, Elizabeth, NJ, 1956-91; ret., 1991. Instr. principles of auditing and bank ops. Am. Inst. Banking; mem. faculty N.J. Data Processing Sch., Princeton, Bank Adminstrn. Sch. of U. Wis. Bd. dirs. N.J. affiliate Am. Heart Assn. With U.S. Army, 1951-53. Recipient Irving Grabiel award for outstanding leadership in banking, 1979 Mem. Am. Inst. Banking (dir. chpt.), Bank Adminstrn. Inst. (N.J. state dir. 1977-79, pres. N.J. chpt., dist. dir. 1979-81) Clubs: K.C., Minisink (Chatham 2006-07). Republican. Roman Catholic. Home: Chatham, NJ. Died Jan. 25, 2009.

LESINSKI, JOHN ANTHONY, pharmacist; b. Wyandotte, Mich., Oct. 21, 1942; s. John Joseph and Antoinette (Berlinski) L.; m. Barbara Ann Reynolds, Aug. 23, 1963 (div. Mar. 1983); children: John Scott, Sandra Marie; m. Cynthia Ann Mongan, Apr. 2, 1983; children: Steven Anthony, Patricia Ann. BS in Pharmacy, Ferris State U., 1966; MBA, Nat. U., 1985. Bd. cert. psychiatric pharmacist. Dist. mgr. Cunningham Drugs, Detroit, 1966-74; pharmacy program coord. Riverside Osteo. Hosp., Trenton, Mich., 1974-77; dir. of pharmacy svcs. Mesa Vista Hosp., San Diego, from 1977. Guest lectr. Sandoz Pharms., Calif., 1983-90, Maric Coll. Nursing, San Diego, 1985-87. Contbr. articles to profl. jours. Fundraiser MDA, Chula Vista, Calif., 1989-93; fundraiser, pres., mgr. Vista La Mesa Little League, 1989-94. Grantee various pharms. cos., 1994—. Mem. San Diego Soc. Hosp. Pharmacists (bd. dirs. 1977—), San Diego County Pharmacists Assn., Calif. Soc. of Hosp. Pharmacists, Am. Soc. of Hosp. Pharmacists, Calif. Pharmacists Assn. (edn. com. 1977—), U.S. Pharmacists Panel on Pharm. Care. Avocations: movies, sports, theme parks. Home: La Mesa, Calif. Died Apr. 6, 2008.

LEVE, SHIRLEY BOOK, jewelry designer; b. NYC, July 21, 1917; d. Isidor and Malvina (Karp) Book; m. Samuel Leve, Sept. 26; 1 child, Teri. BA, Bklyn. Coll., 1938; postgrad., Hunter Coll., Columbia U., NYU, Syracuse U., U. Colo., 1961, U. R.I., 1962-63. Cert. secondary art tchr. Advt. artist Ben Lewis Studio, NYC, 1939-41; asst. art dir. Art News, Art Tech. mags., NYC, 1942-44; prodn. mgr. Mademoiselle mag., NYC, 1945; TV and theatre advertiser NYC, 1945-56; art tchr. James Kieran Jr. H.S., NYC, 1961, Inwood Jr. H.S., NYC, 1964, George Washington H.S., NYC, 1965, acting chmn. art dept., 1980-83; ret., 1983. Case worker in art therapy New Sch. Social Rsch., N.Y.C., 1965-70. Jewelry designer, 1985—. Mem. N.Y.C. Art Tchrs. Assn., Coun. of Suprs. and Adminstrs. Avocations: piano, dance, crafts, nutrition, swimming. Home: New York, NY. Died May 19, 2008.

LEVEL, DOROTHY MAE, petroleum engineer, oil and gas company executive, consultant; b. Columbia, Mo., Aug. 16, 1940; d. Russell Lloyd and Mildred Faye (Phillippe) L. BS in Petroleum Engring., U. S.W. La., 1976. Registered profl. engr., Tex. Asst. purchasing agt. Shell Oil Co., Midland, Tex., 1959; regional mapping staff U.S. Geol. Survey, Rolla, Mo., 1960-63; pipeline divsn. analyst FPC, Washington, 1964-66; dist. adminstrv. supr. and engr. Coastal States Gas Corp., Lafayette, La., Houston, 1968-77; cons. in tech. litigation support, engring., and contract compliance Dorothy Level & Assocs., Lafayette, La., Houston, from 1977; ops. mgr. Terry Petroleum Co., Houston, from 1993. Presenter, organizer of seminars in field. Active mem. Lupus Support Groups, Lafayette and Houston, 1988—; basketball team tutor, U. S.W. La., Lafayette, 1983-88; adult literacy tutor, Lafayette, 1984-86; Sunday Sch. tchr., United Meth. Ch., Lafayette, 1970-73; coach, mgr., umpire Little League Baseball and Softball, St. Elmo, Ill. (founder), Lafayette, and Timbergrove and Spring, Klein, Tex., 1967-81; founder, writer/prodr./actor St. Elmo's Women's Club, 1967-68. Mem. NSPE, Soc. Petroleum Engrs., Women Engrs. of Am. (founder U. S.W. La. chpt.), Tex. Soc. Profl. Engrs., Tau Beta Pi, Sigma Gamma Epsilon (W.A. Tarr award 1977). Republican. Methodist. Achievements: first woman to receive degree in petroleum engring. at U. S.W. La. Home: Columbia, Mo. Died Apr. 8, 2008.

LEVIN, FLORA JEAN, English and language arts educator; b. Atlanta, Apr. 5, 1942; d. Sol Harry and Sally (Monroe) L. BA cum laude, Ga. State U., 1976; MEd in English, West Ga. Coll., 1981. Cert. secondary tchr. Sec. Goodyear Tire and Rubber Co., Atlanta, 1966-68; dir., tchr., writer, actress Acad. Theatre, Atlanta, 1966-72, 78-80; instr. drama Callanwolde Fine Arts Ctr., Atlanta, 1978-80; tutor English Ga. State U., Atlanta, 1977-78; tchr. English Riverwood High Sch., Atlanta, 1980-92; tchr. Roswell (Ga.) High Sch., from 1992. Pub. rels. rep. Riverwoods High Sch., 1991-92, newsletter writer, 1991-92. Mem. PTSA, Riverwood High Sch., 1980-92. Named Star Tchr., Riverwood, 1991-92. Mem. Am. Film Inst., NEA, Ga. Assn. Educators. Jewish. Avocations: film, theater, arts, music, walking. Home: Atlanta, Ga. Died May 3, 2008.

LEVINE, BERNARD, inspector general; b. Cleve., Dec. 13, 1929; s. Aaron and Celia (Schneider) L.; m. Gail Rebecca Cohen, Aug. 10, 1958; children: James David, Jo Beth Zucker, Michael Alan. BA, Western Res. U., Cleve., 1953, LLB, 1956. Bar: Ohio, 1956. Field atty. region 8 NLRB, Cleve., 1959-63, supervisory atty., 1963-69, asst. regional atty., 1969-72, dep. asst. gen. counsel Washington, 1972, asst. gen. counsel, 1972-73, regional dir. region 8 Cleve., 1973-83, dep. asst. gen. counsel Washington, 1984-89, inspector gen., from 1989; assoc. Wickens, Herzer & Panza, Lorain, Ohio, 1983-84. Chmn. Cleve. State U. Indsl. Rels. Ctr., 1982. Pres. Adat Shalom, Montgomery County, Md., 1990; bd. mem. Park Synagogue, Cleve., 1979-84. Master sgt. U.S. Army, 1951-52. Mem. Indsl. Rels. and Rsch. Assn. (pres. N.E. Ohio chpt. 1979), Exec. Coun. on Integrity and Efficiency. Jewish. Avocations: gardening, tennis, racquetball. Home: Twinsburg, Ohio. Died Apr. 16, 2008.

LEVINE, IRVING R., commentator, dean, lecturer, writer, educator; b. Pawtucket, RI, Aug. 26, 1922; s. Joseph and Emma (Raskin) L.; m. Nancy Cartmell Jones, July 12, 1957; children: Jeffrey Claybourne Bond, Daniel Rome, Jennifer Jones. BS, Brown U., Providence, RI, 1944, LHD (hon.), 1969; MS, Columbia U., NYC, 1947; LHD (hon.), Bryant Coll., Smithfield, RI, 1974; D.Journalism (hon.), Roger Williams Coll., 1985; LLD (hon.), U. RI, Kingston, 1988; LHD (hon.), Lynn U., Boca Raton, Fla., 1992; LLD (hon.), Northeastern U., Boston, 1993; D.Journalism (hon.), RI Coll., Providence, 1996. Writer obits. Providence Jour., 1940-43; fgn. news editor Internat. News Service, 1947-48; chief Vienna (Austria) bur., 1948-50; with NBC, 1950-95, war corr. in Korea, 1950-52; radio anchor World News Roundup, NYC, 1953-54; chief corr. NBC, Moscow, 1955-59, Rome, 1959-71, London, 1967-68, chief economics corr. Washington, 1971-95; dean emeritus Coll. Internat. Communications, Lynn U., Boca Raton, Fla., 1995—2009. Commentator Consumer News and Bus. Channel Cable TV affiliate svc. NBC TV News, 1990-96; commentator Pub. Broadcasting Sys. TV, Nightly Bus. Report, 1997—; spl. writer London Times, 1955-59; covered assignments in Can., China, Czechoslovakia, Bulgaria, Poland, Japan, Vietnam, Formosa, Thailand, Eng., France, Germany, Switzerland, Algeria, Congo, Israel, Turkey, Tunisia, Greece, Yugoslavia, Union of South Africa, Denmark, Sweden, Ireland; press group with pres. Ford, Carter, Reagan, Bush, Clinton; attended G-7 Econ. Summits, 1975-95; world affairs lectr. Holland Am. Cruise Line. 1995-97, Cunard Cruise Line, 1998-2001, Radisson Seven Seas Cruise Line, 2000-04, Celebrity Cruise Lines, 2004-07; lectr. univs., bus. groups, cruise ships; writer Internet World Traveler Column, 1997-99; moderator Bus. Update TV Program, Fla. TV programs, 1998-99; nat. spokesperson First Penn-Pacific Life Ins. Co., 1997-99; anchor Bus. Trends TV program, 2000. Author: Main Street, USSR, 1959, Travel Guide to Russia, 1960, Main Street, Italy, 1963, The New Worker in Soviet Russia, 1973; contbr. articles to nat. mags.; guest on numerous TV shows including Johnny Carson, 1960, Murphy Brown, 1989, David Letterman Show, 1990, Jay Leno Show, 1990. 2d lt. Signal Corps, U.S. Army, 1943-46, Philippines, Japan. Recipient award for best radio-TV reporting from abroad Overseas Press Club, 1956, Award for Outstanding Radio Network Broadcasting Nat. Headliners Club, 1957, 50th Anniversary award Columbia Sch. Journalism, 1963, Emmy citation 1966, Martin R. Gainsbrugh award for best econ. reporting, 1978, William Rogers award Brown U., 1988, Silver Circle award Nat. Acad. TV Arts and Scis., 1990; named one of 10 Outstanding Young Men, U.S. Jaycees, 1956; named to R.I. Hall of Fame, 1972, Pawtucket Hall of Fame, 1986, Nat. Broadcasters Hall of Fame Lifetime Achievement award, 1995, TJFR and Master Card award as one of 100 top bus. news luminaries, 2000; named Among 100 Most Accomplished Graduates, 20th Century Brown Alumni mag., 2000; honoree Loyola Coll.'s Beta Gamma Sigma, 1994; fellow, Coun. Fgn. Rels., 1952-53. Mem. Cosmos, Phi Beta Kappa, Beta Gamma Sigma. Died Mar. 26, 2009.

LEVINE, NORMAN, publishing executive; b. Bklyn., Jan. 9, 1930; s. Charles and Nina (Knox) L. BA, Bklyn. Coll., 1956, MA, 1957. Cons. pvt. practice, NYC, Washington, 1960-81; pres. Plucked String, Inc., Kensington, Md., from 1982. Film prodr. short subjects, Danoral, Inc., N.Y.C., 1960-64; concert mgr., presenter, Norman Levine Presents, Kensington, 1994—; pub. Mandolin Quar. Mag., Kensington, 1995—; pres. Plucked String Found., Kensington, 1996—. Contbr. articles to mags. Cpl. U.S. Army, 1952-54. Mem. Fretted Instrument Guild Am., Am. Banjo Frat., Classical Mandolin Soc. Am. (founder, pres. 1986-89). Died Dec. 8, 2007.

LEVITE, ALLAN EUGENE, administrative assistant; b. Chgo., Oct. 29, 1947; s. Louis and Rose Levite. BSBA, Roosevelt U., 1970. Sales adminstr. Hammer Storage Solutions, Newark, Calif., 1992-97; adminstv. asst. Socket Comm., Newark, 1997-99; support analyst Superior Cons., San Francisco, 1999-2000. Author: Guilt, Blame and Politics, 1998; contbr. articles to profl. jours. Libertarian. Home: San Francisco, Calif. Died May 5, 2008.

LEVITT, MADELYN MAE, philanthropist, fund raiser; b. Des Moines, Nov. 23, 1924; d. Ellis I. and Nelle (Seff) L.; divorced; children: Linda Toohey, Jeffrey Glazer, Susan Burt, Ellen Ziegler. BS, Ohio State U., 1946; LHD (hon.), Drake U., 1993. Exec. com. United Way, Des Moines, 1968-95; bd. dirs. exec. com. Drake U., Des Moines; exec. com. Network of Women in Philanthropy, Madison, Wis., Des Moines Art Ctr.; mem. gov. bd. Blank Children's Hosp. Recipient Nat. award for philanthropy Nat. Soc. Fund Raising Execs., 1995. Home: Des Moines, Iowa. Died Nov. 7, 2007.

LEVITT, SERENA FARR, nursing administrator; b. Washington, June 10, 1938; d. James Franklin and Evelyn Estelle (Richards) Farr; m. Edward Isaac Levitt, Jan. 2, 1966; children: Daniel Clifford, Richard Curtis, Lynette Cecelia, David Samuel Charles. AAS in Nursing, N. Va. C.C., Annandale, Va., 1977. Registered nurse. Clk. typist U.S. Dept. of Agr., Washington, 1956-58; pubs. asst. Jansky & Bailey Atlantic Rsch., Springfield, Va., 1960-61; spl. asst. avionics pubs., prodn. supr. Howard Rsch., Arlington, Va., 1962-64; tech. writer Computer Usage, Washington, 1964-65; pubs. supr. Tracor, Rockville, Md., 1965; pubs. engr. Fairchild-Hiller, Bladensburg, Md., 1965-66; dir. documentation, program mgr. Krohn-Rhodes Rsch. Inst., Washington, 1966-67, Documentation Logistics Corp., Fairfax, Va., 1967-74; supr. Leewood Nursing Home, Annandale, Va., 1977-78; med. liaison Dept. Navy, Yokosuka, Japan, 1986-88; nursing supr., office mgr. Dr. Bruce E. Lessin, MD, McLean, Va., 1990-94. Recipient scholarship Zonta Club of Arlington, 1956. Mem. ANA, AAAS, IEEE, Am. Assn. Office Nurses, Nat. League Nursing, Soc. Tech. Writers and Pubs. Jewish. Avocations: jewelry design, painting, crafts, crochet, sewing. Home: Acworth, Ga. Died Apr. 4, 2008.

LEVREAULT, ROSEMARY BOWERS, retired school counselor; b. Beaucoup, Ill., Aug. 21, 1927; d. Raymond Ellsworth and Mary Bertha (Schwind) Bowers; m. Lionel Paul Levreault, June 22, 1957. BS, So. Ill. U., 1949; MA Ohio U. Resident counselor U. Ill., Urbana, 1953-57; social worker Charles V. Chapin Hosp., Providence, 1957-61; sch counselor Cumberland Valley Sch. Dist., Mechanicsburg Pa., 1962-65, West Shore Sch. Dist., Lemoyne, Pa., 1965-92; ret., 1992. Mem. DAR (seimes microfilm chair, regent Cumberland County chpt. 1989-92). Home: New Cumberland, Pa. Died Nov. 29, 2007.

LEVY, JEROME EDWARD, dean, consultant, engineering educator; b. NYC, June 2, 1918; s. Harry and Mollie (Raab) L.; m. Freda Levy, Aug. 1, 1947; children: Ellen, Richard. BS magna cum laude, CCNY, 1938; MA, NYU, 1940. Cert. gen. sci. tchr., N.Y. Instr. in math. and physics N.Y.C. Bd. Higher Edn., 1937-39, tchr. math. secondary sch., 1939-41; tng. specialist USN Bur. of Ordnance, Washington, 1946-51; founder, pres. Washington Engring. Svcs. Co., Kensington, Md., 1951-69; cons. Systems Cons., Magnolia, Mass., 1970-86; dean Gordon Inst., Wakefield, Mass., from 1987. Cons. Instrumentation Lab., MIT, Cambridge, 1957-65; cons. Analogic Corp., Peabody, Mass., 1969-85, Mass. Gen. Hosp., Siemens Corp. Mem., chair com. Peabody Edn. Coun., 1985-91. Lt. comdr. USNR, 1941-46, PTO. Decorated Legion of Merit; Charles Hayden Found. scholar, 1938; co-recipient Bernard M. Gordon prize, NAE, 2007. Mem. IEEE, Am. Soc. Engring. Edn., Assn. Computing Machinery, Phi Beta Kappa. Avocations: mathematical puzzles, computer design, golf. Home: Peabody, Mass. Died July 22, 2008.

LEVY, MORTON FRANK, organic chemist; b. NYC, May 31, 1925; s. Leo and Tillie (Pasternak) L.; divorced; children: Brooke Levy Greene, Drew Levy Irvin, Alisa. BS, Queens Coll., 1950; MA, Columbia U., 1951; PhD, Yale U., 1955. Organic chemist Argus Chem. Co., Bklyn., 1955-60, Wallace & Tiernan, Belleville, N.J., 1960-64; sr. chemistr IBM Corp., Endicott, N.Y., 1964-70, sr. chemist San Jose, Calif., from 1970. Editor and pub. Primary Lateral Sclerosis newsletter, also founder; contbr. articles to profl. jours.; patentee in field. With U.S. Army, 1943-46, ETO, ATO. Mem. AAAS, Am. Chem. Soc. Avocations: acting, directing, ceramics. Home: Los Gatos, Calif. Died Feb. 19, 2008.

LEWIN, RALPH ARNOLD, biologist; b. London, Apr. 30, 1921; arrived in US, 1947; s. Maurice and Ethel Lewin; m. Joyce Mary Chismore, June, 1950 (div. 1965); m. Cheng Lanna, June 3, 1969. BA, Cambridge U., Eng., 1942, MA, 1946; PhD, Yale U., 1950; ScD, Cambridge U., Eng., 1973. Instr. Yale U., New Haven, Conn., 1951-52; sci. officer Nat. Rsch. Coun., Halifax, N.S., Can., 1952-55; ind. investigator NIH, Woods Hole, Mass., 1956-59; from assoc. prof. to prof. U. Calif., La Jolla, from 1960. Editor: Physiology and Biochemistry of Algae, 1962, Genetics of Algae, 1976, Biology of Algae, 1979, Origins of Plastids, 1993, Internacia Vortaro de Mikroba Genetiko, 1994; co-editor: Prochloron, a microbial enigma, 1989; transl. Winnie-La-Pu (Esperanto), 1972, La Dektri Horlogoj, 1993, Merde, 1999, (poems) Biology of Women and Other Animals, 1981, Abacus & Swallows, 2000, Poems on Politics, Pollution and Religion, 2003, Blue Green, 2003. Served with British Army, 1943-46. Mem. Phycological Soc. Am. (pres. 1970-71, Darbaker prize 1963). Avocations: languages, recorder. Home: La Jolla, Calif. Died Nov. 30, 2008.

LEWIS, ALAN ERVIN, internist; b. Milw., Feb. 1, 1936; s. Morris and Mildred Lewis; m. Sandra Briskin, Aug. 17, 1961; children: Scott, Brandt. BA, U. Wis., 1957; MD, Marquette U. & Med. Coll. Wis., 1960. Diplomate Am. Bd. Internal Medicine. Asst. in medicine Tufts U., Boston, 1967-69; from instr. to assoc. prof. Hahnemann U., Phila., 1969-87; pvt. practice Mesa, Ariz., from 1987. V.p. West Pk. Hosp., Phila.; mem. medicine com., credentials com. Desers Samaritan Hosp., Mesa. Contbr. studies to profl. jours. Lt. USNR, 1961-63. Fellow ACP; mem. Am. Diabetes Assn. (affiliate assn. com., nat. bd. dirs., Ariz. affiliate, pres. chmn. bd. dirs. Phila. affiliate), Am. Assn. Clin. Rsch., Endocrine Soc., Pa. Med. Soc., Phila. County Med. Soc., Ariz. State Med. Soc., Maricopa Med. Soc. Home: Scottsdale, Ariz. Died May 21, 2008.

LEWIS, DONALD EVERETT, chemistry educator; b. Paducah, Tex., July 3, 1931; s. Byrd Ray and Edith Lucile (Walls) L.; m. Ina Marian Crowson, July 7, 1968; children: Donna Marie, Paul Anthony. BS, Abilene Christian U., 1952; MS, Fla. State U., 1954, PhD, 1957. Assoc. prof. chemistry Queens Coll., Charlotte, N.C., 1957-66; assoc. prof., prof. chemistry Abilene (Tex.) Christian U., from 1966. Vis. prof. U. Tex., Austin, 1980-81. Mem. Am. Chem. Soc. Mem. Ch. of Christ. Home: Abilene, Tex. Died Oct. 24, 2007.

LEWIS, GARY DIN AUMAN, obstetrician, gynecologist; b. Reading, Pa., Aug. 2, 1941; s. Howard Hill and Dorothy Mae Hatfield (Auman) L.; m. Carole Ann Furdyna, Dec. 30, 1965; children: Carla Lynn, Howard Hill II. BS, Albright Coll., 1963; DO, Phila. Coll. Osteo. Medicine, 1967. Diplomate Am. Bd. Ob-gyn. Intern Metro. Hosp., Grand Rapids, Mich., 1967-68, resident in ob-gyn., 1968, 1970-74; pvt. practice Harrisburg, Pa., from 1974. Capt. U.S. Army, 1968-70, Vietnam. Fellow ACOOG (trustee 1874-86, sec., treas. 1986-90, v.p. 1990-91, Disting. 1991); mem. Vietnam Vets. Am., Am. Legion. Republican. Lutheran. Avocation: computer science. Home: Hummelstown, Pa. Died June 12, 2008.

LEWIS, JACK (CECIL PAUL LEWIS), publishing executive, editor; b. North English, Iowa, Nov. 13, 1924; s. Cecil Howell and Winifred (Warner) L.; children: Dana Claudia, Brandon Paul, Scott Jay, Suzanne Marie Zachary. BA, State U. Iowa, 1949. Publicist savs. bonds U.S. Treasury Dept., Des Moines, 1948-49; reporter Santa Ana (Calif.) Register, 1949-50; motion picture writer Monogram Pictures, 1950; reporter Daily Pilot, Costa Mesa, Calif., 1956-57; editor Challenge Pub., North Hollywood, Calif., 1957-60; pres. Gallant/Charger Publs. Inc, Capistrano Beach, Calif., 1960-98; editor, pub. Gun World, 1960-97. Author: (autobiography) White Horse, Black Hat, 2002, 14 novels, 33 other books, 11 TV shows, 8 motion pictures; editor 27 books; contbr. articles to mags. Served to lt. col. USMCR, 1942-46, 50-56, 58, 70. Decorated Bronze Star, Air medal (4), Meritorious Service medal, Navy Commendation medal. Mem. Writers Guild Am., U.S. Marine Corps Combat Corrs. Assn. (pres. 1970-71, 73-74, 80-81, chmn. bd. 1972-78), Sigma Nu, Sigma Delta Chi. Republican. Home: Pahoa, Hawaii. Deceased.

LEWIS, RICHARD SCUDDER, public relations and advertising executive; b. Glen Cove, NY, Apr. 8, 1946; s. Ralph Scudder and Elizabeth (Carlisle) L.; m. Janet Marie Russo. BA in English, Colby Coll., 1968. Editor Oyster Bay (N.Y.) Guardian, 1968; asst. pub. relations mgr. Instrument Systems Corp., Jericho, N.Y., 1968-70, corp. mgr. pub. relations, 1970-72; prin. Richard Lewis Communications, Bayville, N.Y., 1972-77; exec. v.p. Cove, Cooper, Lewis, Inc., NYC, 1978-89; pres. Richard Lewis Communications, Inc., from 1989. Adj. assoc. prof. mktg. and communications St. John's U., Jamaica, N.Y., 1972-76. Died May 17, 2008.

LEWIS, ROBERT E., aerospace engineer; b. Geary, Okla., Oct. 26, 1932; s. Arthur Ready and Mary Kathryn (Hoffman) L.; m. Gayle Venice Saywer, Aug. 24, 1952 (div. Apr. 1968); children: Robert II, Lisa, Carol; m. Marian Louise Moore, Oct. 4, 1968 (div. Oct. 1993); children: Michael; m. Betty Jo Hall, Dec. 31, 1993; 1 stepson, Kevin S. Moody. BS Engring. Physics, U. Tulsa, 1954; JD, U. Houston, 1977. Bar: Tex. Rsch. engr. Stanolind Oil and Gas Rsch. Lab, Tulsa, 1953-54; project engr. aerospace electronics Tex. Instruments, Inc., Dallas, 1956-63; lunar module guidance navigation and control mgr. NASA JSC, Houston, 1963-69, shuttle avionics mgr., 1969-73, shuttle avionics integration mgr., 1973-89; space station verification mgr. NASA-Marshall Space Station, Huntsville, Ala., 1989-98; system integration mgr. NASA Hdqrs. Space Sta., Houston, from 1994. Atty. State Bar of Tex., Houston, 1977-99. Trail leader Sierra Club, Houston, 1977-86. Fellow AIAA (assoc.). Methodist. Avocations: nature conservancy, nature photography, hiking, opera, symphony. Died May 27, 2008.

LEWY, MICHAEL MORRIS, small business owner; b. NYC, July 19, 1943; s. Martin and Ellen (Newmark) L.; m. Xenia Adelina Bosch, July 13, 1973 (div. May, 1987). BA, U. Vermont, 1965; certificate, Free U. Berlin, 1966. Comml. pilot's lic. Rsch. product devel. staff Berkey Photo, NYC, 1967-72; owner B&B Equipment, Mayfield, N.Y., 1972-81; pres. Orthotronics, Inc., Gloversville, N.Y., from 1982. Cons. Schaber Foods, Inc. Gloversville, N.Y., 1984-86, Halo Optical, Gloversville, 1984—, Beebie Art Agy., Gloversville, 1986—, Vlock Labs., Gloversville, 1986—. Inventor: Orthodontic recycling technologies, 1982, oxidation reduction by electropolishing, 1988, stairwalker, 1989. Cochmn. Mayfield (N.Y.) Lake Assn., 1987—, chmn. (house) Jewish Community Ctr., Gloversville, 1987—, (avionics) Fulton County Pilots Assn., Johnstown, N.Y., 1989—. 1st Lt., U.S. Army, 1965-67. Recipient Conservation award, Sacandaga C. of C., Fulton County, N.Y. Jewish. Avocations: "tinkering", flying, sailing, cross country skiing, target shooting. Home: Gloversville, NY. Died July 16, 2008.

LEY, RALPH JOHN, German language educator; b. NYC, June 17, 1929; s. William and Katharine (Jaeger) L.; m. Teresa Ann Appezzato, Mar. 20, 1966; children: Mary V., John M. AB, St. Joseph's Sem., Yonkers, NY, 1951; AM, Rutgers U., 1958, PhD, 1963. Instr. German, Rutgers U., New Brunswick, N.J., 1959-63, asst. prof., 1963-68, assoc. prof., 1968-79, prof., 1979-95, chmn. dept., 1981-90, undergrad. dir. dept., 1993-95, prof. emeritus, from 1995. Co-author: Drama of German Expressionism, 1960, Teaching German through the Short Story, 1987; author: Brecht as Thinker, 1979; editor: Boell for Contemporaries, 1970; co-editor: Studies in Modern German Literature, 1978; co-translator, The Poetry of Heinrich Boell, 1976, Dawn of Humanity, 1994. With U.S. Army, 1953-55. Mem. AAUP, Am. Assn. Tchrs. German, German Studies Assn. Democrat. Roman Catholic. Home: Scotch Plains, NJ. Died Dec. 29, 2007.

LIDDY, JAMES DANIEL REEVES, English educator; b. Dublin, July 1, 1934; came to U.S., 1967; s. James and Clare (Reeves) L. MA, Univ. Coll., Dublin, 1954; barrister-at-law, Kings Inns, Dublin, 1958. Prof. english U. Wis., Milw., 1976—2009. Author: In a Blue Smoke, 1964, Blue Mountain, 1968, A Munster Song of Love and War, Corca Bascinn, Baudelaire's Bar Flowers, Collected Poems, Gold Set Dancing, I Only Know that I Love Strength in My Friends and Greatness, The Doctor's House: An Autobiography, 2004 Mem. Am. Conf. for Irish Studies, MLA. Home: Milwaukee, Wis. Died Nov. 4, 2008.

LIEBER, CHARLES SAUL, internist, educator; b. Antwerp, Belgium, Feb. 13, 1931; came to U.S., 1958, naturalized, 1966; s. Isaac and Lea (Maj) L.; m. M. A. Leo; children: Colette, Daniel, Leah, Samuel, Sarah. Candidate in natural and med. sci., U. Brussels, 1951; MD, 1955. Cert. Am. Bd. Clin. Nutrition, 1967. Intern, resident U. Hosp., Brugmann, Belgium, 1954—56; research fellow med. found. Queen Elizabeth, 1956-58; research fellow Thorndike Meml. Lab. Harvard Med. Sch., Boston, 1958—60, instr., 1961; assoc. Harvard U., 1962; assoc. prof. medicine Cornell U., 1963-68; dir. liver disease and nutrition unit Bellevue Hosp., NYC, 1963-68; chief sect. liver disease, nutrition and alcohol Tng. Program VA Hosp., Bronx, NY, 1968—97; prof. medicine Mt. Sinai Sch. Medicine, NYC, 1969—2009, prof. pathology, 1976—2009, dir. Alcohol Rsch. and Treatment Ctr., 1977—2009. Assoc. vis. physician Cornell Med. div. Bellevue, Meml., James Ewing hosps., 1964-69; Am. Coll. Gastroenterology disting. lectr., 1978, Henry Baker lectr., 1979. Recipient award of Belgian Govt. for rsch. on gastric secretion, 1956, Rsch. Career Devel. award NIH, USPHS, 1964-68, E.M. Jellinek Meml. award, 1976, A. Boudreau award Laval U., 1977, W.S. Middleton award highest honor for med. rsch. Dept. Vets. Affairs, 1977, Leahy Rsch. award highest honor for outstanding investigator, 1994, first Mark Keller award NIAAA-NIH, 1996, AMA Sci. Achievement award The Christopher D. Smithers Found., 1998, R. Brinkley Smithers award in rsch. and edn. in alcohol 2003. Master ACP; fellow AAAS, Am. Soc. Nutritional Sci., Am. Gastroent. Assn. (Disting. Achievement award 1973, Hugh R. Butt award for liver/nutrition 1992); mem. Assn. Am. Physicians, N.Y. Gastroent. Assn. (pres. 1974-75), Am. Soc. Biochemistry and Molecular Biology, Am. Soc. Addictive Medicine (pres. 1974-77, Sci. Achievement award 1989, Disting. Scientist award 1996), Assn. Clin. Biochemists (Kone award 1994), Am. Soc. Clin. Nutrition (McCollum award 1973, pres. 1975-76, Robert H. Herman Meml. award 1993), Am. Soc. Clin. Investigation, Am. Soc. Pharmacol. Exptl. Therapy, Rsch. Soc. on Alcoholism (pres. 1977-79, Sci. Excellence award 1980, Disting. Svc. award 1992), Am. Coll. Nutrition (Outstanding Achievement award 1990). Home: Englewood Cliffs, NJ. Died Mar. 1, 2009.

LIEBERKNECHT, GILBERT (GIL LIEBY), composer; b. Nov. 7, 1931; Composer over 50 copyrighted ragtime piano selections, including Trophy Rag, 1966, Goldenrod Rag, 1966, Raggin' Up Fremont Street, 1968, Li'l' White Fuzzy Rag, 1971, A Ragtime Oddity, 1971, Li'l' Ruthie Waltz, 1972, Anathema Blues, 1973, Moods in Heiding, 1997, Washboard Blues, 1998. Home: Omaha, Nebr. Died Apr. 27, 2008.

LIEBESKIND, DAVID, business management consultant, educator; b. Paterson, NJ, Nov. 30, 1931; s. Abraham Hyman and Jean (Elkin) L.; m. Judith Elinor Seibel, Feb. 9, 1957; children: Anne Michele, John Gary, Susan Amy. BS in Chemistry, Seton Hall U., 1954; MBA in Bus. Mgmt., Fairleigh Dickinson U., East Rutherford, NJ; PhD in Bus. Adminstrn., N.Y.U., 1972. Tech. field rep. The Dow Chem. Co., Midland, Mich. and NYC, 1956-61; asst. to pres. Chem. Insect Corp., Metuchen, N.J., 1962-63; various mktg. & sales positions Union Carbide Corp., NYC, 1963-73, mgr. strategic planning, 1973-76, internat. area mgr. far east, 1976-80, ops. mgr. Danbury, Conn., 1980-82, dir. mktg., 1982-83, dir. health & safety Spl. Chems. Divsn., 1983-94; prin. Bus. Improvement Assocs., Stamford, Conn., 1994-96; pres. High Ridge Assocs., Stamford, Conn., from 1996. Adj. prof. mgmt. N.Y.U., N.Y.C., 1994—; dir. Comml. Devel. Assn., Washington, 1977-79. Author: The Liebeskinds from My Perspective, 1994; contbr. articles to profl. jours. Bd. dirs. Stamford Jewish Cmty. Ctr., Jewish Cmth. Endowment Found. of Stamford, NYU Alumni Assn. Bd. Capt. U.S. Army. Mem. Am. Chem. Soc., N.Y.U. Stern Sch. Alumni Assn. (past pres., dir.), Clifton Masonic Lodge. Avocations: jogging, hiking, sailing. Home: Stamford, Conn. Died July 27, 2008.

LIEM, KAREL FREDERIK, biologist, educator; b. Jogya, Java, Indonesia, Nov. 24, 1935; came to U.S., 1964; s. Soen Ging and Maria Carolina (Bader) L.; m. Hetty Khouw, Sept. 4, 1965; children— Karel Frederik, Erika Elise. B.Sc., U. Indonesia, 1957, M.Sc. cum laude, 1958; PhD, U. Ill., 1961; A.M. (hon.), Harvard, 1972. Asst. prof. U. Leiden, Netherlands, 1962-64; asst. prof., then asso. prof. U. Ill., Urbana, 1964-72; asst. curator, then asso. curator of anatomy Field Museum Natural History, Chgo., 1966-72; Henry Bryant Bigelow prof. biology, curator ichthyology Harvard U., 1972—2009. Mem. vis. com. New Eng. Aquarium; trustee Cohasset (Mass.) Marine Biol. Lab.; mem. com. Latimeria, Nat. Acad. Scis. Editor: Copeia, 1974 Guggenheim fellow, 1970 Fellow Linnean Soc.; mem. Am. Soc. Ichthyologists and Herpetologists, Am. Soc. Zoologists, Zool. Soc. London (sci. fellow), Soc. Study Evolution. Home: Cambridge, Mass. Died Sept. 3, 2009.

LIN, HUNG CHANG, retired electrical engineer; b. Shanghai, Aug. 8, 1919; m. Anchen Lin; children: Robert, Daniel. BSEE, Chiao Tung U., 1941; MSE, U. Mich., 1948; D in Engring., Poly. Inst. Bklyn., 1956. Engr. Ctrl. Radio Works of China, 1941-44, Ctrl. Broadcasting Adminstrn. China, 1944-47; rsch. engr. RCA, 1948-56; mgr. appliance CBS Semiconductor Ops., 1956-59; lectr. U. Md., College Park, 1966-69, vis. prof. elec. engring., 1969-71, prof. elec. engring., 1971—90. Adv. engr. Rsch. Lab., Westinghouse Corp., Balt., 1959-63; adj. prof. U. Pitts., 1959-63; vis. lectr. U. Calif., Berkeley, 1965-66. Named to The Innovation Hall of Fame, U. Md. Clark Sch. Engring., 1990. Fellow IEEE (Ebers award Electron Device Soc. 1978), Sigma Xi. Avocations: tennis, dance. Died Mar. 5, 2009.

LINDBERG, JANICE BETHANY, nurse; b. Flint, Mich., Aug. 30, 1936; d. Lawrence J. and Florence B. (Cogan) Vanderberg; m. Edwin J. Lindberg, Aug. 18, 1962; 1 child, Karen E. BSN, U. Mich., 1958; MS, Columbia U., 1961; PhD, U. Mich., 1979. Instr. med.-surg. nursing specialities U. Mich. Sch. Nursing, Ann Arbor, 1961-63, instr., asst. prof., 1965-66, asst. prof., 1971-77, asst. prof., acting chmn. fundamentals, 1977-78, chmn. fundamentals area of instrn., 1978-82, assoc. prof., 1979, asst. dean student and alumni affairs, 1982-86, asst. dean student affairs, 1986-89, assoc. dean student affairs, from 1989, interim chmn. med.-surg.

nursing, 1988-91, interim dir. div. acute critical and long term care programs, 1991-92. Author: The Nurse Person, 1978, Introduction to Person Centered Nursing, 1983, Introduction to Nursing, 1990. Cons. Burns Park Sr. Citizen Ctr., Ann Arbor, 1976-83. U. Mich. Faculty grantee, 1975. Mem. ANA, Mich. Nurses Assn. (bd. dirs. 1986-87, program chmn.), Sigma Theta Tau (pres. 1978-81, 81-83, Excellence in Nursing award 1990). Home: Ann Arbor, Mich. Died Dec. 27, 2007.

LINDGREN, FRANK TYCKO, research biophysicist, lipoprotein methodologist; b. San Francisco, Apr. 14, 1924; s. Ty and Grace Orissa (Lund) L.; m. Helen Darrow, Aug. 8, 1953. BA in Physics, U. Calif., Berkeley, 1947, PhD in Biophysics, 1955. Asst. research biophysicist Donner Lab., U. Calif., Berkeley, 1955-56, research assoc., 1956-67, research biophysicist, 1967-78, sr. staff biophysicist, from 1978. Lipids cons. NIH, 1972-80, reviewer Jour. Lipid Research, 1960—, reviewer grants, 1970—. Assoc. editor Lipids, 1966-76; contbr. numerous articles to profl. jours. V.p. and treas. Berkeley Dem. Club, 1960-76. Served to 1st lt. U.S. Army, 1943-47. Fellow Council on Arteriosclerosis of Am. Heart Assn.; mem. AAAS, Am. Oil Chemist Soc., Sigma Xi, Phi Beta Kappa. Clubs: U. Calif. Faculty (Berkeley). Democrat. Avocations: hiking, classical piano playing. Home: Berkeley, Calif. Died Apr. 6, 2008.

LINDHOLM, BARBARA, human resources specialist, director; b. NY, Feb. 11, 1937; d. L. E. Lindholm and Anna Johnson; children: Andrew, David, Christine, Karen. BA with hons. in Sociology, Mercy Coll., 1974; student, Fordham U., 1954—55. Dir. human resources Nathan Kline Inst., Orangeburg, NY, 1977—85, NY State Psychiat. Inst., 1985—89, Manhattan Children's Psychiat. Ctr., 1989—95, Manhattan (N.Y.) Psychiat. Ctr., NYC, 1994; interpreter Hist. Hudson Valley, Tarrytown, NY, from 1999; dir. human resources Bronx Children's Psychiat. Ctr., 1995—97, Manhattan Psychiat. Ctr., 1997. Del. Dem. Nat. Convention, 1972; chmn. town Yorktown Dem. Party, 1975—76; mem. Westchester Dem. Com., 1975—76. Democrat. Roman Cath. Avocation: travel. Home: Mahopac, NY. Died May 13, 2008.

LINDSAY, CRAIG CURTIS, automobile company executive; b. Elyria, Ohio, Feb. 13, 1952; s. Walter Lowry and Wilma Evelyn (Harnack) L.; m. Cindy Lee Ritchie, Nov. 7, 1983; 1 child, David Christopher. BS, Ariz. State U., 1977, MBA, 1984. CPA, Ariz. Staff acct. Coopers and Lybrand, Phoenix, 1977-79; tax supr. J. McDonald and Co., Phoenix, 1979-84; tax mgr. Peat Marwick Mitchell, Phoenix, 1984-85; fin. cons. Phoenix, 1986-87; chief fin. officer The Ryerson Co., Phoenix, 1987-88, Scottsdale (Ariz.) Automotive Group, from 1988. Founder Mountaineers Inc., Phoenix. Contbr. articles to profl. jours. Vice-chmn. Citizen's Adv. Com. South Mountain Master Plan, Phoenix, 1987-88. Recipient Environ. Action award Valley Forward, Phoenix, 1987. Mem. AICPA, Ariz. Soc. CPAs. Republican. Avocations: micro computers, environmental issues, auto racing. Home: Paradise Vly, Ariz. Died June 26, 2008.

LINDSAY, REGINALD CARL, federal judge; b. Birmingham, Ala., Mar. 19, 1945; s. Richard and Louise L.; m. Cheryl E. Hartgrove, Aug. 15, 1970. Cert., U. Valencia, 1966; AB in Polit. Sci. cum laude, Morehouse Coll., 1967; JD, Harvard U., 1970; LLD (hon.), New Eng. Sch. Law, 2003. Bar: Mass. 1971, US Ct. Appeals (1st cir.) 1971. Assoc. Hill & Barlow, 1970-75, 78-79, ptnr., 1979-93; judge US Dist. Ct. Mass., Boston, 1994—2009. Arbitrator, mem. comml. arbitration panel Am. Arbitration Assn., 1994-2009; commr. Mass. Dept. Pub. Utilities, Boston, 1975-77; pres. adv. bd. Mus. of Nat. Center of Afro-Am. Artists, 1975-81, v.p., 1981—2009; trustee Thompson Islands Edn. Center, Boston, 1975-81; bd. dirs. United Way of Mass. Bay, 1981-84, Morgan Meml. Goodwill Industries, Boston, 1992-2009, Ptnrs. for Youth with Disabilities, Boston; mem. Nat. Consumer Law Ctr. (bd. dirs.), Mass. Commn. on Jud. Conduct, 1982-88; trustee Newton (Mass.)-Wellesley Hosp. Recipient Ruffin-Fenwick Trailblazer award Harvard Black Law Students Assn., 1994, Amanda V. Houston cmty. svc. award Boston Coll., 1998, Frederick E. Berry Expanding Ind. award Easter Seals, 1999, Heroes Among Us award Boston Celtics, 2001, Leadership award New Eng. Black Law Students Assn., 2001, N. Neal Pike prize N. Neal Pike Inst. Boston U. Sch. Law, 2005. Mem. ABA, Nat. Bar Found., Mass. Bar Assn., Boston Bar Assn. (coun. 1977-2009, citation jud. excellence 1999), Pi Sigma Alpha, Phi Beta Kappa. Died Mar. 12, 2009.

LINDSAY, VICTOR ERNEST JOHN, aerospace engineer; b. San Francisco, Apr. 1, 1944; s. Victor Frank and Alicia Maryann (Martorella) L.; m. Barbara Marie Cressey, Feb. 9, 1969; children: Alicia Marie, Rena Kay. BS in Engring., Santa Clara U., 1966. Structural engr. Boeing Aerospace, Seattle, 1966-70, tech. lead, from 1977; pres. V.E. Lindsay Co. Inc., Soquel, Calif., 1970-75; regional sales engr. Union Metal Mfg., Fremont, Calif., 1975-77. Ptnr. Lindsay & Assocs. polit. cons., Bellevue, Wash., 1982—. Rep. precinct committeeman, Bellevue, 1977—. Mem. Soc. Advancement Materials and Process Engring., AIAA. Clubs: Corvair Soc. (Tukwila, Wash.). Republican. Episcopalian. Avocations: vegetable gardens, auto restoration. Home: Carmel, Calif. Died Oct. 4, 2007.

LINDSEY, JAMES KENDALL, civil engineer; b. Poteau, Okla., Jan. 15, 1924; s. Ray Vernett and Mattie Frances (Kendall) L.; m. Loah Joyce Crowley, July 14, 1946 (dec. 1996); children: Marcia Gay Morgan, Mark Ray, James Neill, John Kendall; m. Mary L. Chambers, Jan. 16, 1998. AS, Clemson U., 1944; BCE, Okla. State U., 1948; MS in Pub. Health, U. Mich., 1950. Registered profl. engr., Okla.; registered land surveyor, Okla. Mobile labs. engr. Okla. State Dept. Health, Oklahoma City, 1947-49, dist. engr., 1949-53; cons. engr. USA Ops. Mission, Addis Ababa, Ethiopia, 1954-55, various water and pollution control facilities, Okla., from 1955. Mem. environ. health com. Okla. Health Planning Coun., Oklahoma City, 1968-75. With U.S. Army, 1943-46. Named Okla. Water Pioneer Gov. of Okla., 1994. Mem. NSPE, Am. Waterworks Assn. (Okla. trustee 1958), Water Environ. Fedn., Okla. Water and Pollution Control Assn. (sec. 1948-53, pres. 1957), Lions (pres. Tahlequah club 1964-65), Tahlequah (Okla.) C. of C. Avocation: ranching. Died May 19, 2008.

LINDSEY, JOHN HALL, JR., software company executive; b. Malvern, Ark., July 29, 1938; s. John Hall and Jeannette Francis (Stuart) L.; m. Renetta Louise Harms, July 14, 1962; children: Sabra, Lemecia, Lance. Student, Ark. Poly. U., 1956-58, Okla. State U., 1958-60; BS in Bus., U. Utah, 1964; MBA, U. So. Calif., 1968. Data base mgr. NCR corp., Rancho Bernardo, Calif., 1966-75; data base adminstr. Kal Kan Foods, Vernon, Calif., 1975-77; data base supr. Kaiser Steel, Fontana, Calif., 1977-79; mgr. data base and tech. support Western Gear, Lynwood, Calif., 1979-84; mgr., sr. cons. data base Citicorp/TTI, Santa Monica, Calif., 1984-86; prin. Lindsey & Assocs., Eureka, Calif., from 1986; ptnr. Lazio Family Products, 1990-94. Ptnr. Lindsey/Milligan Cos., Houston; mem. computer adv. com. Ontario/Montclare Schs., Calif. 1980-82; mem. industry advisor Cullinet Corp., Westwood, Mass., 1986-91; bd. dirs. IDMS User Assn., Westminster, chmn. large users adv. com., 1985-88; bd. dirs. S.W. User Assn., L.A.; guest lectr. U. So. Calif., 1975-76. Author: IDMS DB Design Review, 1982. Elder local Presbyn. Ch., 1980-82; vol. Culver City (Calif.) YMCA, 1986, Santa Monica (Calif.) Real Soccer Club, 1985-86; pres. Mt. Baldy Swim Team, Upland, Calif., 1975-80; bd. dirs. Ontario Community Credit Union, 1979-80; pres. Redwood Heritage Found, Inc., 1990—. Served with USNG, 1956-64. Mem. IDMS User Assn., SW Area IDMS User Assn. (chmn. 1982-84), Assn. System Mgmt. (v.p. 1966-68), Soc. for Mgmt. Info. (co-founder), Eureka C. of C., North Coast Fly Fishers, Trout Unltd., Rotary. Avocations: children's groups, personal computers, woodworking, writing, swimming. Died Dec. 21, 2007.

LINDSEY, W. H. (PAT LINDSEY), state legislator; b. Meridian, Miss., Mar. 17, 1936; children: Lori, Patrick. BS in Geology, U. Ala., 1958, JD, 1963. Mem. Ala. State Senate, Montgomery, 1967—74, Ala. State Senate from 22nd Dist., Montgomery, 1982—2009; chmn. econ. expansion and trade com. Ala. State Senate, Montgomery, vice chmn. rules com., bus. and labor com., confirmations, finance and taxation gen. fund com., judiciary com., conservation, environment and natural resources com., health com., tourism and mktg. com. Mem. ABA, Ala. Bar Assn., Choctaw County C. of C., U. Ala. Alumni Assn. Democrat. Methodist. Avocations: hunting, fishing, coaching youth sports. Home: Butler, Ala. Died Jan. 11, 2009.

LINT, LEWIS E., director of pastoral services; b. Van Meter, Iowa, July 7, 1926; s. Lewis and LaDeana Mae (Whitlow) L.; m. Edna Reimann, Apr. 19, 1943 (dec. Jan. 1946); children: Sharon, Cynthia, David, Victoria, Lewis; m. Elizabeth Nora Hooks. BA, Iowa Wesleyan Coll, 1965; MDiv, Boston U., 1968. Exec. sec. Iowa Tax Commn., Des Moines, 1956-61; pastor United Meth. Ch., Winterset & Libertyville, Iowa, 1961-65, Tewksbury, Mass., 1965-68, Fairfield & Redwood City, Calif., 1968-78, sabbatical Wilson, N.C., 1978-79; chaplain Duke U. Med. Ctr., Durham, N.C., 1979-81, Cape Fear Valley Hosp., Fayetteville, N.C., 1980-82; dir. pastoral svcs. Pitt County Meml. Hosp., Greenville, N.C., from 1983. Bd. dirs. Am. Cancer Soc. (chmn. Svc. & Rehab. Com. 1989—), N.C. Author: (pamphlet) God's Lent Child, 1984, (booklets) The Book of Prayers, 1984, Why Me?, 1984, Why Our Baby?, 1990; editor newsletter N.C. Chaplains Assn.; inventor Arrowhead, 1960. Active Housing Comm., Redwood City, Calif., 1976; chair Human Rels. Coun., Greenville, N.C., 1990—. Recipient Vol. of the Year award Am. Cancer Soc., 1986. Mem. Elks, Masons, Shriners (chaplain 1988—). Democrat. Avocations: motorhoming, woodworking, amateur radio, painting, perfumery. Home: Cape Coral, Fla. Died Nov. 7, 2007.

LIPIN, SEYMOUR BARRY, retired investor; b. Chgo., Oct. 7, 1920; s. Bernard and Mary (Schrier) Lipin; m. Priscilla Richter Lipin, Oct. 7, 1952; m. Rachel Kucheck Lipin, Nov. 21, 1976 (dec. Apr. 1992); m. Judith Marie Lund Wingader Lipin, Oct. 9, 2005. Student, Ill. Inst. Tech., 1939—41, DePaul U. Commerce, 1943—44, DePaul Coll. Law, 1944—45. Founder/owner New & Used Automobile Sales Co., Chgo., 1945—97, US Auto Lcasing Co., Chgo., 1954; chmn., CEO Lipin Enterprises Inc. (U.S. Auto Leasing Co., Lipin Rent-A-Car, Automobile Corp. N.Am., Rifco Auto Leasing Co., Modern Cars Inc.), Chgo., 1982—97, Presdl. Car Rental, Ltd. (and predecessors), Chgo., Presdl. Limousine Ltd.; pres., CEO Paul-Sey Investment Corp.; founder S. Barry Lipin LLC, Denver, 2004—09; mem. gov.'s adv. coun. Ill.; mem. allied industries coun. Hope. Bd. dirs. Am. Hearing Rsch. Found., Lipin Found., Michael Reese Hosp. Med. Rsch. Inst. COun., Jewish Vocat. Svc.; trustee internation hdqs. Inst. Crit. Care, Palm Springs, Calif., 1993. Recipient Bonds award, State of Israel, 1980, Spirit of Life award, City of Hope, 1983, Humanitarian award, Holocaust Meml. Found. Ill., 1987; named Man of Yr., Automotive Industry-Leasing Divsn. Mem.: Ill. C. of C., Chgo. Assn. Commerce and Industry, Automotive and Allied Industries Coun. (pres.), Am. Automotive Leasing Assn., Exe. Club, Variety Club, Canyon Country Club (Palm Springs, Calif.), Mid-America Club, Covenant Club, Phi Kappa Tau. Home: Lake Forest, Ill. Died Feb. 2, 2009.

LIPP, CARL FREDERICK, geological engineer; b. Gulfport, Miss., Dec. 31, 1924; s. Carl Frederick and Frances (Mullaney) L.; m. Marcella Elliott, June 14, 1951; children: Christine, Catherine, Carl III, Constance. BS in Geology, Colo. Coll., 1951; postgrad., U. Tex., 1952-53, U. Colo., 1953-55. Registered profl. engr.; cert. profl. geologist. Geologist N.J. Zinc Co., Grand Junction, Colo., 1956-63; geol. engr., cons. Grand Junction, 1963-67, 70-75; dist. geologist Cotter Corp., Grand Junction, 1967-70; mgr. ops. Minerals Recovery Corp., Denver, 1975-82; cons. geol. engr. Denver, from 1982. Moderator Dem. Conv., 1963. With USN, 1943-46, PTO. Mem. AIME, Am. Inst. Profl. Geologists. Episcopalian. Avocations: gardening, walking, hiking, bird watching. Home: Broomfield, Colo. Died Oct. 29, 2007.

LIPPOLD, ROLAND WILL, retired surgeon; b. Staunton, Ill., May 1, 1916; s. Frank Carl and Ella (Immenroth) L.; m. Margaret Cookson, June 1, 1947; children: Mary Ellen Lippold Elvick, Catherine Anne Lippold Rolf, Carol Sue Lippold Webber. BS, U. Ill., 1940, MD, 1941. Diplomate Am. Bd. Surgery. Intern Grant Hosp., Chgo., 1941-42, resident in surgery, 1942-43, 47-48, St. Francis Hosp., Evanston, Ill., 1946-47; fellow in pathology Cook County Hosp., Chgo., 1947-48, resident in surgery, 1949-50; practice medicine specializing in surgery Chgo., 1950-53; also asst. in anatomy U. Ill., Chgo., 1950-53; practice medicine specializing in surgery Sacramento, 1953-68; chief med. officer No. Reception Ctr.-Clinic, Calif. Youth Authority, Sacramento, 1954-68, chief med. services, 1968-79; ret. Cons. in med. care in correctional instns.; cons. Calif. State Personnel Bd. Contbr. articles to med. publs. Chmn. Calif. Expn. Hall of Health, 1971-72. Comdr. M.C., USNR, 1943-73, PTO. Mem. Sacramento Surg. Soc., Sacramento County Med. Soc., Calif. Med. Assn., AMA, Sacramento Hist. Soc. (life). Republican. Lutheran. Home: Sacramento, Calif. Deceased.

LIPSCOMB, LINDA ANN, critical care nurse; b. Etowah County, Ala., Sept. 27, 1944; d. William W. and Ethel N. Parker; m. Howard J.P. Lipscomb, Nov. 8, 1962; children: Kelly Marie, Michael Shawn. AS in Nursing cum laude, Gadsden State Jr. Coll., 1980; cert. in cosmetology, Keevil Curl Sch. Cosmetology, Gadsden, Ala., 1963. RN, Ala. Cert. advanced cardiac life support. Cosmetologist, owner Linda's Beauty Salon, Gadsden; staff nurse Holy Name Med. Ctr., Gadsden, 1980-85; staff nurse med./surg., ICU/CCU, 1985-92; staff nurse ICCU U. Ala. Med. Ctr., Birmingham, from 1992. Dir. women's missionary union James Meml. Bapt. Ch., 1993—, Sunday Sch. tchr.; pst pres. PTA. Home: Gadsden, Ala. Died Feb. 14, 2008.

LISONBEE, LORENZO KENNETH, retired science educator, consultant; b. Mesa, Ariz., Nov. 25, 1914; s. James Lorenzo L. and Eda Amelia Kohlhepp; m. Margaret Kleinman, Oct. 13, 1938 (div. 1980); children: James, LeeAnne, Robert, Margaret, Katherine, Russel, Tamara; m. Dorothy Brown, Apr. 17, 1980. BA, Ariz. State U., 1937, MA, 1940, EdD, 1963. Cert. secondary sch. tchr. Tchr. pub. elem. sch., Mesa, Ariz., 1937-40, high sch., Coolidge, Ariz., 1940-42, USAF Tech. Sch., Scottfield, Ill., 1942-44, pub. high sch., Phoenix, 1945-80; assoc. faculty State U., Tempe, Ariz., 1963-70. Chmn. bd. biology com. Coll. Entrance Exam., Princeton, Ill., 1955-65; cons. Am. Geol. Inst., Duluth, Minn., 1959. Author: (textbook) Your Biology, 1958; contbr. over 100 articles to profl. jours. Dist. committeeman Boy Scouts Am., Mesa, 1945-65. Radio officer USCG, 1944-45. Named Eminent Grad. Alumnus Ariz. State U., 1998, named to its Hall of Fame. Fellow AAAS; mem. Am. Assn. Ret. Persons (mem. econ. security com.), Nat. Sci. Tchrs. Assn. (life, Citation for Disting. Svc. to Sci. Edn. 1985). Democrat. Mem. Lds Ch. Achievements include pioneering work in development of text and lab materials for academic extremes. Home: Tempe, Ariz. Died July 29, 2008.

LISTER, JOHN JOSEPH, retired actuary; b. Phila., Sept. 2, 1927; s. George Aloysius and Elizabeth Marie (O'Hara) L.; m. Mary Agnes Jackson, Apr. 26, 1952 (dec. Nov. 1983); children: John, Gerald, Mary Ann, Kathleen, Colleen, Janine; m. Helen Fitzgerald Lister, 1988 BS, St. Joseph's U., 1951; JD, Villanova U., 1956. Bar: Pa. 1957. Enlisted USMC, 1945, advanced through grades to lt. col., 1966, ret., 1976; asst. v.p. Marsh & McLennan, Phila., 1970-84; cons. Wm. M. Mercer, Inc., Phila., 1970-84; pvt. practice retirement planning actuary Phila., 1984—2009. Fellow Life Office Mgmt. Inst., mem. Am. Acad. Actuaries, Am. Pension Conf. Roman Catholic. Avocation: sports official. Died Sept. 23, 2009.

LITTELL, FRANKLIN HAMLIN, theologian, educator; b. Syracuse, NY, June 20, 1917; s. Clair F. and Lena Augusta (Hamlin) L.; m. Harriet Davidson Lewis, June 15, 1939 (dec. 1978); children: Jennith, Karen, Miriam, Stephen; m. 2d Marcia S. Sachs, 1980; children: Jonathan, Robert, Jennifer. BA, Cornell Coll., 1937, DD, 1953; BD, Union Theol. Sem., 1940; PhD, Yale U., 1946; Dr. Theology (hon.), U. Marburg, 1957; ThD (hon.), Thiel Coll., 1968; other hon. degrees, Widener Coll., 1969, Hebrew Union Coll., 1975, Reconstructionist Rabbinical Coll., 1976, Gratz

Coll., 1977, St. Joseph's U., 1988, Stockton State Coll., 1991, U. Bridgeport, 1996, U. New England, 2001, Ohio Wesleyan U., 2004. Dir. Lane Hall, U. Mich., 1944-49; chief protestant adviser to U.S. High Commr., other service in Germany, 1949-51, 53-58; prof. Chgo. Theol. Sem., 1962-69; pres. Iowa Wesleyan Coll., 1966-69; prof. religion Temple U., 1969-86. Adj. prof. Inst. Comtemporary Jewry, Hebrew U., Israel, 1973-94; Ida E. King disting. prof. Holocaust studies Richard Stockton Coll., 1989-91, 96-98; disting. prof. Holocaust and Genocide Studies, 1998-2009; Robert Foster Cherry disting. vis. prof. Baylor U., 1993-94; guest prof. numerous univs. Author numerous books including The Anabaptist View of the Church: an Introduction to Sectarian Protestantism (Brewer award Am. Soc. Ch. History), 1952, rev. edit., 1958, 64, 99, From State Church to Pluralism, 1962, rev., 1970; (with Hubert Locke) The German Church Struggle and the Holocaust, 1974, 90; The Crucifixion of the Jews, 1975, 86, 96, The Macmillan Atlas History of Christianity, 1976, German edit., 1976, 89, (with Marcia Sachs Littell) A Pilgrim's Interfaith Guide to the Holy Land, 1981; A Half-Century of Religious Dialogue: Amsterdam 1939-1989, 1989, Historic Atlas of Christianity, 2001, Christian Response to Holocaust: Addresses and Papers 1952-2002, 2003; editor or assoc. editor numerous jours. including Jour. Ecumenical Studies, A Jour. of Ch. and State and Holocaust Genocide Studies; author weekly syndicated columns, also over 300 major articles or chpts. of books in field of modern religious history. Cons. NCCJ, 1958-83; mem. exec. com. Notre Dame Colloqium, 1961-68; vice chmn. Ctr. for Reformation Research, 1964-77; nat. chmn. Inst. for Am. Democracy, 1966-69, sr. scholar, 1969-76; co-founder, pres. Ann. Scholars' Conf. on Ch. Struggle and Holocaust, 1970-2009; pres. Christians Concerned for Israel, 1971-78, Nat. Christian Leadership Conf. for Israel, 1978-84, pres. emeritus 1985-2009; founder, chmn. ecumenical com. Deutscher Evangelischer Kirchentag, 1953-58; co-founder, cons. Assn. Coordination Univ. Religious Affairs, 1959-2009; mem. U.S. Holocaust Meml. Council, 1979-93; founder, pres. Nat. Inst. on Holocaust, Temple U., 1975-83, Anne Frank Inst., Phila., 1983-89; co-founder, pres. Phila. Ctr. on Holocaust, Genocide and Human Rights, 1989-2009; mem. exec. com. Remembering For The Future, Oxford and London, 1988, Berlin, 1994, hon. chmn. Oxford and London, 2000; named observer to Vatican II; mem. Internat. Bd. of Yad Vashem, Jerusalem, 1981-2009. Decorated Grosse Verdienstkreuz (Fed. Republic Germany); recipient Jabotinsky medal, Israel, Ladislaus Laszt Internat. Ecumenical award Ben Gurion U. of Negev, 1991, Buber Rosenzweig medal, Germany, 1996. Mem. European Assn. Evang. Acads. (co-founder 1965), Pen and Pencil Club, Phi Beta Kappa, Phi Beta Kappa Assocs. Home: Merion Station, Pa. Died May 23, 2009.

LITTLE, DAVID EATON, osteopath; b. Kirksville, Mo., Nov. 12, 1951; s. Walter George and Joan Mary (Olive) L.; m. Sarah Hope Smith, Nov. 3, 1984 (div. June 1991); stepchildren: Bryan, David, Chad. BS, Oral Roberts U., 1973; DO, Kirksville Coll. Osteo. Medicine, 1978. Diplomate Am. Bd. Family Practice, Am. Coll. Gen. Practitioners Osteo. Medicine. Intern Doctors' Hosp., Columbus, Ohio, 1978-79; gen. practice osteo. medicine Pickerington, Ohio, 1979-96; clin. asst. prof. Coll. Osteo. Medicine Ohio U., from 1988; founder OpHealth Internat., from 1996. Bd. dir. osteo. medicine service Doctor's Hosp., Columbus, Ohio, 1979-80. Mem. Am. Osteo. Assn., Am. Acad. Osteopathy, Ohio Osteo. Assn., Am. Coll. Gen. Practioners Osteo. Medicine, Pickerington Area C. of C. (bd. dirs. 1980-81). Republican. Avocations: science fiction books and films, travel, tennis, macintosh computers. Home: Pickerington, Ohio. Died Feb. 17, 2008.

LIVELY, JOHN K., public relations executive; b. Marshalltown, Iowa, June 11, 1933; s. Kenneth Verlou and Helen Irene (Ethington) L. AB, Cornell Coll., Mt. Vernon, Iowa, 1955; MS, Columbia U., 1956. Asst. news dir. Sta. KFJB, Marshalltown, 1958-63; night editor Sta. WHO-AM-FM TV, Des Moines, 1963-66; pub. relations counselor 3M Co., St. Paul, 1966-73, audio-visual communications mgr., 1973-78, mgr. Ea. pub. relations NYC, 1978-81, dir. pub. relations svcs. St. Paul, from 1981. Served with U.S. Army, 1956-58. Mem. Pub. Relations Soc. Am. (accredited). Methodist. Avocations: swimming, computers. Home: Minneapolis, Minn. Died Aug. 18, 2008.

LIVERIGHT, BETTY FOUCHE, actress, writer; b. La Grange, Ill., Oct. 20, 1913; d. Squire and Edna Amanda (Wright) Fouche; m. Herman Elsas Liveright, Feb. 1, 1936; children: Beth, Timothy. BA, Temple U., 1963. Actress L'Aiglon, NYC, 1934, White Plains (N.Y.) Comty. Theater, 1947-52; coord., actress TV Tulane U., New Orleans, 1953-56; actress TV Commercials, New Orleans, 1954-56; rschr. Friends Libr. Swarthmore (Pa.) Coll., 1956-69; pub. rels. agt. Highlander Rsch. and Edn. Ctr., Knoxville, Tenn., 1969-71; co-dir. Berkshire Forum, Stephentown, N.Y., 1972-90. Editor, co-coord.; (bulletin) This Just In : A Bulletin for News of Politcal Prisoners and POWs, 1991—. Pres. Yorkville Peace Coun., N.Y.C., 1940-42; bd. dirs. Women's Internat. League for Peace and Freedom, Phila., 1965-85. Died June 9, 2008.

LIVERMORE, ARTHUR HAMILTON, chemist; b. Aug. 14, 1915; s. Hamilton Arthur and Helena Victoria L.; m. Janet Elizabeth Hays, Sept. 15, 1 940 (div., 1964); children: Barbara, Arthur, Audrey, Lewis, David; m. Jane Easter Marye, June 12, 1964 (dec. 2006; 1 child, John. BA, Reed Coll., 1940; PhD, U. Rochester, 1945; postdoc. rschr., Cornell Med. Coll., 1944-48. Prof. chemistry Reed Coll., Portland, Oreg., 1948-65; dir. edn. AAAS, Washington, 1963-81; cons. Triangle Coalition Sci. & Tech. Edn., Washington. Cons. China Assn. Sci. & Tech., Bejing, China, 1980; USAID advisor Regional Ctr. Sci. & Math. Edn., Penang, Malaysia, 1971-72; TV host Secrets in Science, KGW-TV, Portland, Oreg., 1956-60. Recipient Guggenheim fellowship, Biochem. Labs., Cambridge (England) U., 1955-56. Fellow AAAS, ACS, Cosmos Club, Phi Beta Kappa, Sigma Xi. Episcopalian. Avocations: sailing, gardening. Home: Gloucester, Mass. Died Oct. 12, 2009.

LIVINGSTON, ALAN WENDELL, communications executive; b. McDonald, Pa., Oct. 15, 1917; s. Maurice H. and Rose L. (Wachtel) L.; m. Nancy Olson, Sept. 1, 1962; children: Peter, Laura, Christopher. BS, U. Pa., 1940. Exec. v.p. Capitol Records, Inc., Hollywood, Calif., 1946-55, pres., chmn., 1960-68; v.p. programming NBC, Burbank, Calif., 1955-60; pres. Mediarts, Inc., Los Angeles, 1968-76; exec. v.p., pres. entertainment group 20th Century Fox Film Corp., Beverly Hills, Calif., 1976-80; pres. Pacific Rim Entertainment, Los Angeles, 1980-95; novelist, cons. Access Fund and Atlanta Investment Fund, Inc., Beverley Hills, 1995—2009. Creator various children's books, records and Bozo the Clown, 1946-2009; author: Ronnie Finklehof, Superstar, 1988; writer, producer (animated film) Sparky's Magic Piano, 1988. Bd. dirs. Ctr. Theater Group, Los Angeles. Served to 2d lt. inf. U.S. Army, 1943-46. Mem. ASCAP, Nat. Acad. Rec. Arts and Scis., Acad. TV Arts and Scis., Acad. Motion Picture Arts and Scis. Home: Beverly Hills, Calif. Died Mar. 13, 2009.

LIVINGSTON, VICKI MAY, artist; b. Norfolk, Va., May 8, 1942; d. Willard Crandall and Pauline Mae (Cleveland) Rheubottom; m. Domingo Polimeni, Dec. 31, 1966 (div. Feb. 1974); m. Brian Alexander Livingston, Oct. 4, 1974. BFA, Va. Commonwealth U., 1963. Solo exhibitions include Zodiac Gallery, Richmond, Va., 1963, Va. Commonwealth U., 1963, Ruth Sherman Gallery, N.Y.C., 1965, Mondragon Corp. Offices, L.A., 1986, Orlando Gallery, L.A., 1988, 90, 93, Torrance (Calif.) Cultural Arts Ctr., Joslyn Gallery, 1992, Palos Verdes Art Ctr., Stewart Gallery, 1993; exhibited in group shows at Va. Mus. Fine Arts, 1963, Va. Union, U., 1962, Richmond Artists Assn., 1962, Carillon Gallery, 1963, Va. Commonwealth U. Gallery, 1962, 63, Twentieth Century Gallery, 1963, 62, Westhampton Coll., 1962, 63, U. Va., 1963, Va. Commonwealth U. Fine Art Dept. Travelling Exhbn., 1962, 63, Ruth Sherman Gallery, 1965 (Best in Show and Solo Exhibit 1965), Sarasota Art Assn. Gallery, 1979, 80, Burbank Fine Arts Fedn. Sixth Ann. Multimedia, 1981, Santa Paula 45th Ann. Juried Exhibit, 1981, Wing Gallery, L.A., 1982, Orange County Ctr. for Contemporary Art, 1982, LA Harbor Coll. Gallery, 1984, Laguna Beach Mus. Art, 1983, 84, Bowers Mus., 1985, Radius Gallery, 1984, 85, Carnegie Art Mus., 1986, Brea Civic-Cultural Ctr. Gallery, 1982, 84, 85, 86, Riverside Mus. of Art, 1987, Brand Art Libr. Gallery, 1987, Long Beach Arts, 1988, Palos Verdes Art Ctr., 1989, S.I.T.E., 1989, Finegood Art Gallery, 1990, Orlando Gallery, 1987, 88, 89, 90, 91, 92, Artspace, L.A. Mcpl. Satellite Gallery at Woodland Hills, 1991; work reviewed in various art mags. Recipient Best in Show and Solo Exhibit award Ruth Sherman Gallery, 1965, Merit award, Annual Juried Open, Sarasota, Fla., 1980, Second Place/First Painting award Bowers Mus., 1985, Hon. Mention Ann. Juried Exhbn., Palos Verdes, 1989, Merit award 84th Open Juried Exhbn., Long Beach, Calif., 1989, Bronze award Mixed Media and Silver award Contemporary Painting, Discovery 1993, Art of California Mag. Competition. Democrat. Avocations: reading, writing, home renovation. Home: Rancho Palos Verdes, Calif. Died Jan. 8, 2008.

LLOYD, PAUL MAX, Romance languages educator; b. Rochester, NY, Sept. 15, 1929; s. George Max and Ruth Pauline (Franklin) L.; m. Joan Parnall Archibald, Aug. 23, 1952; children: Virginia Grace, Robert Earl. BA, Oberlin Coll., 1952; AM, Brown U., 1954; PhD, U. Calif., Berkeley, 1960; AM (hon.), U. Pa., 1972. Teaching asst. Spanish Brown U., Providence, 1952-54, U. Calif., Berkeley, 1954-58; instr. Romance langs. Dartmouth Coll., Hanover, N.H., 1958-60; linguistic scientist Fgn. Svc. Inst., Dept. of State, Washington, 1960-61; asst. prof. of Romance langs. to prof. U. Pa., Phila., from 1961. Vis. prof. Temple U., Phila., 1975-76. Author: From Latin to Spanish, 1987 (John F. Lewis award 1988), Verb-Complement Compounds in Spanish, 1967. Com. mem. Dem. Com. of Upper Darby, Pa., 1970-88. With Signal Corps, U.S. Army, 1946-48. Mem. MLA, Linguistic Soc. of Am. Democrat. Unitarian Universalist. Avocations: photography, calligraphy. Home: Media, Pa. Died Dec. 6, 2007.

LLOYD-JONES, SIR HUGH, writer; b. St. Peter Port, Guernsey, Sept. 21, 1922; s. William and Norah Leila (Jefferd) Lloyd-J.; m. Frances E. Hedley, 1953 (div. 1981); children: Edmund Stephen, Ralph Alexander, Antonia; m. Mary R. Lefkowitz, 1982. MA, Oxford U., Eng., 1947, DHL (hon.), U. Chgo., 1970; PhD (hon.), U. Tel Aviv, 1984, Thessalonica U., 1999, U. Göttingen, 2002. Author: The Justice of Zeus, 1971, 2d edit., 1983, Blood for the Ghosts, 1982, Classical Survivals, 1982, (with P.J. Parsons) Supplementum Hellenisticum, 1983, (with N.G. Wilson) Sophoclis Fabulae, 1990, (with N.G. Wilson) Sophoclea, 1990, Academic Papers, 2 vols., 1990, 3 vols., 2005, Greek in a Cold Climate, 1991, Sophocles, 3 vols., 1994-96, (with N.G. Wilson) Sophocles: Second Thoughts, 1997, Supplementum Supplementi Hellenistici, 2005; others; translator Oresteia (Aeschylus), 1970. With Brit. Army, 1942—46. Fellow Jesus Coll., Cambridge (Eng.) U., 1948-54; fellow and E.P. Warren praelector in classics Corpus Christi Coll., Oxford, 1954-60; Regius prof. Greek, Oxford U., 1960-89; vis. prof. Yale U., 1964, 67, U. Chgo., 1972, Harvard U., 1976; Sather prof. U. Calif., Berkeley, 1969. Fellow: Acad. Athens, Brit. Acad.; mem.: Am. Philos. Soc., Bayerische Acad., Lettere e Belle Arti, Accademia di Archeologia Naples, Nordrhein-Westfälische Acad., Am. Acad. Arts and Scis. Died Oct. 5, 2009.

LOADER, JAY GORDON, retired utilities executive; b. Plainfield, NJ, Aug. 3, 1923; s. Carl and Madalyn (Wright) L.; m. Joan Merrell, Aug. 19, 1965; children: Michael Jay, Sandra Lee, Gigi Ann. BS, U. Ala., 1951. C.P.A., Ga. Auditor Arthur Andersen & Co., Atlanta, 1951-55; with Fla. Power Corp., St. Petersburg, Fla., 1955-82, asst. sec., asst. treas., 1960-67, sec.-treas., 1967-82, v.p., 1980-89; v.p., sec. Fla. Progress Corp., St. Petersburg, 1983-89; ret., 1989. Served with AUS, 1943-44. Mem. AICPA, Am. Soc. Corp. Secs., Fin. Analysts Soc. Ctrl. Fla., U. Ala. Alumni Assn., St. Petersburg Yacht Club, Phi Eta Sigma, Beta Gamma Sigma, Beta Alpha Psi. Died Aug. 31, 2005.

LOBELLO, PETER, artist; b. New Orleans, Nov. 18, 1933; Attended, Tulane U. Sch. Arch.; ind. study, Sicily, Tunisia, Libya, Egypt, and Iran; artist-in-residence, Rome, 1967—68. Prin. works include Grand Hyatt Hotel, NYC, 1978—80, New Istana Palace, Capital City Bandar Seri Begawan, Brunei (Borneo) Southeast Asia, 1984, Madison Equities and Grey Advt., NYC, 1985, Poydras Plz., New Orleans, 1986, Gates Commn., Seattle, 1994—97, Legier & Matherne, New Orleans, 1996—97, Connecticut Ballet, Stamford, 1998, Represented in permanent collections Aldrich Mus. Contemporary Art, Ridgefield, Connecticut, Geneva Mus. Art, Switzerland, New Mus., NYC, Miriam Walmsley Gallery, New Orleans, Sadruddin Aga Kahn, Collonge Bellerive, Geneva, Victor Emmanuel and Marina Savoia, Heckler Corp., NYC, Foster White Gallery, Seattle, Bumper Collection, Calgary, Alberta, Miller Orgn., NYC, U. Minn., BHF-Bank, NYC, Frankfurt, one-man shows include Hugo de Pagano Gallery, N.Y., 1998, exhibited in group shows at Sarah Y. Rentschler Gallery, N.Y.C., 1984, Galerie Les Hirondelles, Geneva, 1987, 1989. Home: New Orleans, La. Died Oct. 28, 2007.

LOCICERO, JOSEPH LAWRENCE, electrical engineer, educator; b. NYC, Sept. 18, 1947; s. Lawrence Augustus and Anne Marie (Cairo) LoC.; m. Sandra Sorin, Oct. 24, 1976; 1 child, Jennifer Suzane. BEE, CCNY, 1970, MEE, 1971; PhD in Elec. Engring., CUNY, 1976. Grad. rsch. assoc. elec. engring. dept. CCNY, 1975-76; asst. prof., assoc. prof. elec. engring. Ill. Inst. Tech., Chgo., 1976-87, prof., from 1987, asst. chmn. ECE dept., 1982-86, chmn. ECE dept., 1986-88, interim chmn. ECE dept., 1997-98. Lectr. CCNY Sch. Engring., 1972-75; cons. Western Electric Co., 1973, Cortron, 1977-78, IIT Rsch. Inst., 1981, AT&T Bell Labs., 1982-96, Kirkland & Ellis, 1992, 99, Lucent Tech., 1996-97, Charles Industries, Ltd., 1997—, Fish & Neave, 1998—. Editor: Tutorials in Modern Communication, 1983, Television Technology Today, 1985; editor-in-chief IEEE Trans. on Comm., 1992-95; bd. dirs. Comm. Soc. 1994-97; contbr. chpts. to books, more than 75 articles to profl. jours. Bd. dirs. Riverside Little League, 1991-95. Grantee NSF, Engring. Found., Rehab. Inst. VA, AT&T Bell Labs., Lucent Techs., Charles Industries, Ltd., 1976—; recipient IIT Excellence in Tchg. award, 1987. Mem. IEEE Comms. Soc. (sr.; comm. theory com., chmn. 1989-92, publs. editor Trans. on Comm. 1976-87, Donald W. McLellan Meritorious Svc. award 1993, Book Author award 1983), Am. Soc. Engring. Edn., Soc. Motion Picture and TV Engrs., Sigma Xi (grantee), Eta Kappa Nu, Tau Beta Pi. Achievements include patents for Economical High Definition TV; for Extended Aspect Ratio Picture; for Compatible High Definition TV; for Aspect Ratio Improvements; for Automatic Speech Recognition. Home: Riverside, Ill. Died July 19, 2008.

LOCKHART, JAMES BICKNELL, JR., retired manufacturing executive; b. Taunton, Mass., Mar. 27, 1918; s. James Bicknell and Charlotte Bradford (Babbitt) L.; m. Mary Ann Reigel, Oct. 2, 1943; children: Joan Riegel, James B. II, Ann Murchie, Brenda Margaret. BS, Yale U., 1940; MBA, Northwestern U., 1941; MS, USN Acad., 1945. Cost acct. GE, Lynn, Mass., 1941-42; mgmt. cons. MacDonald Bros., Boston, 1945-48; chief indsl. engr. Riegel Paper Corp., NYC, 1948, purchasing agt., 1948-50, asst. to v.p. prod., 1950-51, mill mgr., 1951-54, N.Y. mgr. indsl. and mcht. sales, 1954-57, corp. sec., 1955-63, dir., 1957-67, v.p., 1957-63, corp. controller, 1958-63; pres., CEO Conwed Corp., St. Paul, 1963-71, Lockhart & Co., St. Paul, 1971-74, Monier Co., Orange, Calif., 1974-78; with Isolite Corp., Hawthorne, Calif., 1978-85; pres., CEO Locknell Corp. Author: SMG: The Stock Market Game, 1987. Pres., dir. Riegelsville (Pa.) Cemetery; v.p., dir. Minn. Sci. Mus. (permanent exhibit named in honor 1974), Big Bros. of Am. (recipient Svc. award 1973, 77), mem. com. Nat. UN Day, 1978; founder, dir., Old Town Restorations, 1970. Lt. USNR, 1942-46, PTO. Recipient Honor award Wisdom Soc., 1975, Key to City San Bernadino (Calif.), 1977. Mem. Specialty Paper and Bd. Assn. (exec. com. N.Y. sect.), Acoustical Insulating Materials Assn. (pres., dir.), Mayflower Soc., Travelers Century Club, Circumnavigators Club. Republican. Episcopalian. Avocation: travel. Home: Orange, Calif. Died June 26, 2007.

LOCKWOOD, LAVON EILEEN, nursing educator; b. Ft. Belvoir, Va., Oct. 30, 1947; d. Edgar M. and Rose I. (Newport) Greene; m. Mark L. Lockwood, Feb. 17, 1968;

children: Joshua, Rebecca, Sarah. BSN, Trenton State Coll., 1977; MS in Nursing, U. Tex., San Antonio, 1982. Nurse Stars Float Pool Med. Ctr. Hosp., San Antonio; staff nurse Bexar County Hosp. Dist., San Antonio; asst. prof. San Antonio Coll. First Aid Trainer Girl Scouts U.S. mem. disaster health svcs ARC. Sgt. USAF, 1966-71. Home: San Antonio, Tex. Died Sept. 30, 2007.

LÖE, HARALD, retired dentist, educator, researcher; b. Steinkjer, Norway, July 19, 1926; s. Haakon and Anna (Bruem) Löe; m. Inga Johansen, July 3, 1948; children: Haakon, Marianne. DDS, U. Oslo, 1952; D in Odontology, 1961; degree (hon.), U. Gothenburg, 1973, Royal Dental Coll., Aarhus, 1980, U. Athens, 1980, Cath. U., Leuven, 1980, U. Lund, 1983, Georgetown U., 1983, U. Bergen, 1985, U. Md., 1986, Med. U. NJ, 1987, Royal Dental Coll., Copenhagen, 1988, U. Toronto, 1989, U. Detroit, 1990, SC Med. U., 1990, U. Helsinki, Finland, 1992, Pacific U., 1993, U. Milan, Italy, 1994. Instr. Sch. Dentistry, Oslo U., 1952-55; rsch. assoc. Norwegian Inst. Dental Rsch., 1956-62; Fulbright rsch. fellow, rsch. assoc. dept. oral pathology U. Ill., Chgo., 1957-58; Univ. rsch. fellow Oslo U., 1959-62, asso. prof. dept. periodontology, 1960-61; prof. dentistry, chmn. dept. periodontology Royal Dental Coll., Aarhus, Denmark, 1962-72, asso. dean, dean-elect, 1971-72; prof., dir. Dental Rsch. Inst., U. Mich., Ann Arbor, 1972-74; dir. Nat. Inst. Dental Rsch. Nat. Inst. Dental Rsch., Bethesda, Md., 1983-96; dean, prof. periodontology U. Conn. Health Ctr. Sch. Dental Medicine, Farmington, 1974-82, univ. prof., 1994-97; vis. prof. U. Bern, Switzerland, 1997—2006. Vis. prof. periodontics Hebrew U., Jerusalem, 1966—67; hon. prof. Med. Scis. U. Beijing, 1987; cons. FDA, WHO, NIH; lectr. in field. Contbr. over 350 articles to sci. publs. With Norwegian Army, 1944—48. Decorated knight of Danebrog, comdr. Royal Norwegian Order of Merit; recipient War medal, 1940—45, 75th Anniversary award, Norwegian Dental Assn., 1958, prize, Aalborg Dental Soc., 1965, William J. Gies Periodontology award, 1978, Alfred C. Fones medal, U.S. Surgeon Gen.'s medal and Exemplary award, 1988, Internat. award, Swedish Dental Assn., 1989, Harvard medal, 1992, Scandinavian Pub. Health award, 1994. Mem.: ADA (Gold medal 1994, Callahan medal 1995, Spenadel medal 1995, U. Conn. medal 2003, Pierre Fauchard medal 2003), AAAS, Mass. Dental Soc. (Internat. award), Am. Soc. Preventive Dentistry (Internat. award), Scandinavian Assn. Dental Rsch., Danish Dental Assn., Am. Acad. Periodontology, Am. Coll. Dentists, Inst. Medicine NAS, Internat. Assn. Dental Rsch. (pres. 1980, Basic Rsch. in Periodontology award 1969), Internat. Coll. Dentists, Am. Assn. Dental Rsch. (hon.). Home: Österaas, Norway. Died Aug. 9, 2008.

LOENGARD, RICHARD OTTO, JR., lawyer; b. NYC, Jan. 28, 1932; s. Richard Otto and Margery (Borg) L.; m. Janet Sara Senderowitz, Apr. 11, 1964; children: Maranda C., Philippa S.M. AB, Harvard U., 1953, LLB, 1956. Bar: N.Y. 1956, U.S. Dist. Ct. (so. dist.) N.Y. 1958. Assoc. Fried, Frank, Harris, Shriver & Jacobson, predecessor firms, NYC, 1956-64, ptnr., 1967-97; of counsel Fried, Frank, Harris, Shriver & Jacobson, NYC, from 1997; dep. tax legis. counsel, spl. asst. internat. tax affairs U.S. Dept. Treasury, Washington, 1964-67. Mem. Commerce Clearing House, Riverwoods, Ill. Editl. bd. Tax Transaction Libr., 1982-94; contbr. articles to profl. publs. Fellow Am. Coll. Tax Counsel; mem. ABA, N.Y. State Bar Assn. (exec. com. tax sect. 1984—, sec. 1994-95, vice chair 1995-97, chair 1997-98), Assn. Bar City N.Y. Home: Bernardsville, NJ. Deceased.

LOEWENSTEIN, GEORGE WOLFGANG, retired physician, UN consultant; b. Germany, Apr. 18, 1890; m. Johanna Sabath, Nov. 27, 1923; children: Peter F. Lansing (dec.) and Ruth Edith Gallagher (twins). Student, Royal William Coll., Germany, 1909, Friedrich William U., Germany, 1919, London Sch. Tropical Hygiene and Medicine, 1939. Dir. pub. health Neubabelsberg, 1920-24, Berlin, 1924-34; dir. pub. health and welfare City of Berlin, 1923-33; pvt. practice medicine, Chgo., 1940-46, Chebeague and Dark Harbor, Maine, 1947-58; instr. Berlin Acad. Prevention of Infant Mortality, Postgrad. Acad. Physicians; permanent cons., v.p., rep. Internat. Abolitionists Fedn. at ECOSOC, UN, 1947-90; med. cons. German Gen. Consulate, Atlanta, Miami, Fla., 1963; lectr. Morton Plant Hosp., Clearwater, Fla., also Clearwater campus St. Petersburg Jr. Coll.; guest prof. U. Bremen, Berlin, 1981-82. Author: Public Health Between the Time of Imperium and National Socialism, The Destruction of Public Health Reforms of the First German Republic, 1985, others; transl. from the Japanese Origin of Syphilis in the Far East, Static Atony, Sexual Pedagogic; contbr. 300 articles to med. jours. and revs. to books. Served with German Army, 1914-18. Decorated Cross Merit I Class (Germany), 1965; recipient Commendation awards Pres. of U.S., 1945, 70, 65 Year Gold Service Pin, AMA and ARC, 1985, Service to Mankind award Sertoma, 1972-73, Sport award Pres. Carter, 1977, Musicologist award Richey Symphony, 1979, Reconciliation award Germany-U.S.A., 1983, Friendship award Fed. Republic of Germany, USA, 1985, Teaching award Morton Plant Hosp., 1988, 70 Yrs. Svc. Red Cross, others. Fellow Am. Acad. Family Physicians (charter, life, 40-Yr. Svc. award 1986), AAAS, Am. Coll. Sport Medicine (emeritus, charter, life), Am. Pub. Health Assn. (life, 40-Yr. Svc. award 1984), Brit. Soc. (emeritus); mem. World Med. Assn. (life), German Assn. History of Medicine (life), Acad. Mental Retardation (charter, life), Am. Pub. Health Assn. (life, 40 Yr. Svc. award), Fla. Health Assn. (life), Brit. Pub. Health Assn. (life), AMA (hon.), Am. Assn. Mil. Surgeons (life), Acad. Preventive Medicine (life), Steuben Soc., Richey Symphony Soc. (charter, Musicologist 1979), World Peace Through World Law Ctr. Clubs: City (Chgo. chmn. hygiene sect. 1944-46). Lodges: Rotary (life, Harris fellow 1980), Masons (32 deg.), Shriners (comdr., life v.p.). Home: Pelham, Mass. Died May 27, 1998.

LOGAN, LEE ROBERT, orthodontist, department chairman; b. LA, June 24, 1932; s. Melvin Duncan and Margaret (Seltzer) L.; m. Maxine Nadler, June 20, 1975; children: Chad, Casey. BS, UCLA, 1952; DDS, Northwestern U., Evanston, Ill., 1956, MS, 1961. Diplomate Am. Bd. Orthodontics. Gen. practice dentistry, Reseda, Calif., 1958—59; pvt. practice Northridge, Calif., from 1961, from 2000; vice chair dental dept., from 2006; chief staff dental dept. Northridge Hosp., from 2008. Med. staff Northridge Hosp., 2000—, vice chair med. staff dental dept.; owner Maxine's Prodn. Co., Maxine's Talent Agy.; guest lectr. dept. orthodontics UCLA, U. So. Calif. Contbr. articles to profl. jours. Achievements include patent and licensing agreement with 3M for a device to attach braces, 2001, Can. patent, 2004, patents U.K., Germany, France, Japan. Served to lt. USNR, 1956-58. Recipient Nat. Philanthropy award, 1987, winner, Logan's Run, 2005—08, Founder's award, Autistic Assn., 2007; named 1st Pl. winner, Autistic Jogathon, 1981—2001, (with wife) Couple of Yr., Autistic Children Assn., 1986, in his honor Logan's Run, Walk for Autism; named to Best Dentist's in Am., 2004—07. Mem. ADA, San Fernando Valley Dental Assn. (pres. 1998), Am. Assn. Orthodontists, Pacific Coast Soc. Orthodontists (dir., pres. so. sect. 1974-75, chmn. membership 1981-83), Foudn. Orthodontic Rsch. (charter mem.), Calif. Soc. Orthodontists (chmn. peer rev. 1982-93), G.V. Black Soc. (charter) Angle Soc. Orthodontists (pres. 1981-82, bd. dirs. 1982—, nat. pres. 1985-87), U. S.C. Century Club Fraternity, Northridge Hosp. Med. Ctr. (chief staff), Xi Psi Phi, Chi Phi. Achievements include patents in field. Home: Encino, Calif. Died July 13, 2009.

LOGAN, STEPHEN BEAN, III, retired safety engineer; b. Lexington, Ky., Nov. 1, 1932; s. Stephen Bean II and Minnie Howell (Davies) L.; m. Rayma Jean Sharp; children: Leah, Lori, Lynda, Stephen IV, Jill; stepchildren: Joey, Barry. BSCE, U. Ky., 1959. Registered profl. engr., Calif. Estimator, sales engr. Ferry Bros. Constrn. Co., El Cajon, Calif., 1967-68; regional safety engring. mgr. Allstate Ins. Co., Santa Ana, Calif., 1968-70; resident loss control mgr. Kemper Ins. Group, Washington, 1970-74; mgr. loss control Levi Strauss Co., San Francisco, 1974-75; pvt. practice safety cons. Danville, Calif., 1975-76; corp. safety engr. Morrison-Knudsen Co., Boise, Idaho, 1976-77; pres. Logan & Assocs., Inc., Boise, 1977-80; indsl. safety and fire protection mgr. TVA, Decatur, Ala., 1980-88; corp. environ. and safety mgr. Crain Industries, Ft. Smith, Ark., 1988-90; dir. occupational health and safety Lexicon Inc., Little Rock, 1990-98; mgr. environ. safety health & seucirty Champion Internat., Camden, Tex., 1998-2000; ret., 2000. Cons. in field. Contbr. articles to profl. publs. With USAF, 1951-55. Mem. Am. Soc. Safety Engrs. (treas. 1968-70, v.p. Ark. chpt. 1993, pres. 1994), Constrn. Safety Assn. Am. (life, founder, pres. 1971-72, award 1972, 81, 91), Nat. Safety Mgmt. Assn., Nat. Fire Protection Assn., Am. Legion, Tex. Safety Assn. (bd. dirs.). Democrat. Baptist. Avocations: hunting, fishing, archery. Home: Casa, Ark. Died Sept. 2, 2007.

LOMBARD, JOHN CUTLER, retired lawyer; b. Berkeley, Calif., Oct. 9, 1918; s. Norman and Ellen (McKeighan) L.; m. Dorothy Brandt, July 9, 1946; children: Lawrence, John, David, Laurie. BA, Principia U., 1946; JD, Northwestern U., 1949. Assoc. Jones, Birdseye & Grey, Seattle, 1950-60; ptnr. Hamley & Lombard, Seattle, 1960-70, Day, Taylor, Lombard & Kiefer, Seattle, 1970-85; pvt. practice Seattle, from 1985. Mem. com. Jud. Counsel, 1980-84. Trustee King County Mcpl. League, 1980-84. With USAF, 1941-45. Decorated D.F.C., 5 Air medals, presdl. citation. Mem. Seattle King County Bar Assn. (chmn. probate com. 1975-76, chmn. lawyer referral com. 1989-90), Rainier Club. Avocations: golf, skiing, bridge, playing piano. Home: Seattle, Wash. Died Feb. 8, 2008.

LONDON, DAVID ALAN, communications educator, consultant; b. Sunbury, Pa., Oct. 30, 1950; s. William McMann and Betty June (Strouse) L.; 1 child, Patrick David. BS, Bloomsburg U., 1972, MA, 1988; postgrad., Pa. State U., from 1995. Assoc. prof. comm. Pa. Coll. Tech., Williamsport, from 1989. Cons. Comm. Workers of Am., 1988—. Mem., advisor Valley Players, Inc., Selinsgrove, Pa., 1973—. Mem. Speech Comm. Assn., Speech Comm. Assn. Pa. Avocations: opera, reading, theater. Home: Sunbury, Pa. Died May 3, 2008.

LONG, DALE GORDON, interior designer; b. Reading, Pa., Mar. 13, 1949; s. Gordon Wyndham and Evelyn Viola (Beaupre) L. BS in Psychology, Tulane U., 1971. Renovator Robert Hines Realty, New Orleans, 1974-76; chief asst. Harrison Cultra, Inc., NYC, 1976-84; pres. Long-Steever, Inc., NYC, from 1984. Designs featured in N.Y. Times mag., 1985, The Internat. Book of Lofts, 1986. Presbyterian. Avocation: Italian and La. cooking. Home: New York, NY. Died Apr. 11, 2008.

LONG, GARDA THERESA, lay worker; b. Cleve., Aug. 11, 1925; d. Francis Ralph and Suzanne Margaret (Smithson) Delaney; m. William Harley Long, Sept. 27, 1948; children: Margaret, Deborah, William P., Sharon. Prin. CCD, Andover, Ohio, 1970-89, coord. confirmation, 1968-89, coord. re-new program, 1987-89, tchr. 8th grad., from 1990. Sec. Altar Rosary Soc., Andover, 1989—; sec. Mission Soc., Andover, 1987—; spl. min., canton, Andover; chmn. Christian formation Parish Coun.; mem. Diocesan Pastoral Coun., 1987-91, mem. friendly visitors com., 1990, outreach com., 1980, co-chmn., coord. ann. dinner. Presiding judge Election Poll Booth, Andover. Mem. VFW Aux. Democrat. Home: Andover, Ohio. Died May 26, 2008.

LONG, JAMES E., state official; b. Burlington, NC, Mar. 19, 1940; s. George A. and Helen L. Long; m. Peg O'Connell; 2 children. AB, JD, N.C. State U. Pvt. practice law, from 1967; mem. N.C. Ho. Reps., 1970-75, legal counsel to speaker, 1980-84, chmn. N.C. commn. property tax, 1981-84; chief dep. commr. N.C. Dept. Ins., Raleigh, 1975-76; state commr. ins. State of NC, Raleigh, 1985—2009. Chmn. N.C. Manufactured Housing Authority, N.C. Arson Awareness Coun., Fire Commn. N.C., Firemen's Pension Fund Bd., N.C. and Capitol Planning Commn. Co-author: Douglas Legal Forms. Named Alumnus of Yr. N.C. State U. Mem. Nat. Assn. Ins. Commrs. (v.p. 1989-90, pres. 1990-91), Legion Honor, Internat. Order Demolay, Tau Kappa Epsilon Internat. Democrat. Episcopalian. Home: Raleigh, NC. Died Feb. 2, 2009.

LONG, JOHN JOSEPH, communications executive, insurance executive; b. Niagara Falls, NY, July 3, 1933; s. Harry C. and M. Fredericka (Potts) L.; children: John Jr., Joan, James, Jessica, Amy. BBA, Niagara U., 1956. Lic. ins. agt., broker. Pres. Woodward, Long and Rieger, Niagara Falls, from 1950, Outdoor World Prodns., Inc., Niagara Falls, from 1979; v.p. Nat. Conservation Corp., Elma, N.Y., from 1986. Editor, producer (TV series) Outdoor World, 1981. Del. Conservation Fund Adv. Council, Albany, N.Y., 1988—; chmn. N.Y. State Fish and Wildlife Mgmt. Bd. Region 9, 1973—; pres. Niagara County Fedn. Conservation Clubs, Lockport, N.Y., 1965. Served to lt. inf. U.S. Army, 1956-57. Recipient Oliver Jones Meml. award Niagara County Fedn. Conservation Clubs, 1966, Pres's. award Niagara River Anglers Assn., 1986. Mem. Outdoor Writers Assn. Am., N.Y. State Outdoor Writers Assn. (pres. 1983-85), N.Y. State Conservation Council (Conservationist of Yr. 1987), Nat. Assn. Ins. Agts., Am. Fisheries Soc. Clubs: Fin, Feather and Fur (Lewiston, N.Y.) (pres. 1960-61); Lasalle Sportsman (Niagara Falls). Democrat. Roman Catholic. Avocations: photography, hunting, fishing, snowmobiling, archery. Home: Niagara Falls, NY. Died Aug. 29, 2007.

LONG, MICHAEL ELDON, government and history educator; b. Charleston, W.Va., Aug. 15, 1950; s. Roy Eldon and Alice Mae (Leonard) Long; m. Marilyn Sue Branscome, May 25, 1970 (div. Sept. 1997); children: Lisa Michelle, Michael Brent. BA, U. Charleston, 1973; postgrad., George Washington U., 1974—75, U. Hawaii-Manoa, 1983; MS, Cen. Mich. U., 1985; postgrad., Marshall U., 1999, U. S. Fla., 2002. Enlisted U.S. Army, 1977, commd. officer, 1978—97; maj. (ret.) USAR, 1997; asst. prof. history and polit. sci. Pasco-Hernando C.C., from 2001. Adj. prof. govt. and history Southside Va. C.C., 1992—93, St. Petersburg Jr. Coll., Fla., 1999—2001, U. Charleston, W.Va., 1999, Pasco-Hernando C.C., Fla., 2000—01, Fla. Met. U., Tampa, 2000—01; cons. Discussant Southwestern Polit. Sci. Assn., 2001. Manuscript/book reviewer: Jour. Politics, White Ho. Studies, Fla. Hist. Qur., W.Va. History, Richmond Times-Dispatch, Mil. Rev. Dir. Ft. Scammon Hist. Assn., South Charleston, W.Va., 1964—65; seasonal ranger-historian Nat. Pk. Svc., Petersburg Nat. Battlefield, Va., 1972; curator divsn.hist. preservation Fairfax County Pk. Authority, Annandale, Va., 1973—75; participant Woodlawn Conf. Hist. Site Adminstrn., Mt. Vernon, Va., 1974; curator collection and exhibits Hist. Bethlehem, Inc., Pa., 1975—76; exec. dir. Parkersburg (W.Va.) Arts Ctr., 1976—77; bd. dirs. Meherrin River Arts Coun., Emporia, Va., 1990—91, South Charleston Mus. Found., 1998—99. Mem.: So. Polit. Sci. Assn. (panel chair 2001), Am. Polit. Sci. Assn., Acad. Polit. Sci., Am. Hist. Assn., Assn. U.S. Army Club (Suncoast chpt.), Am. Legion. Republican. Roman Catholic. Avocation: historic preservation. Home: Tarpon Springs, Fla. Deceased.

LONG, ROBERT LEROY, retired utilities executive, consultant; b. Renovo, Pa., Sept. 9, 1936; s. John Leroy and Mary Geraldine (Olmstead) L.; m. Ann Gullborg, Sept. 2, 1957; children: Beth, Jeff, Mark. BSEE, Bucknell U., 1958; MS in Engring., Purdue U., 1959, PhD in Nuclear Engring., 1962. Rsch. assoc. exp. reactor physics Argonne Nat. Lab., 1960-62; reactor specialist nuclear effects br. White Sands (N.Mex.) Missile Range, 1962-65; from asst. prof. to prof. nuclear engring. U. N.Mex., Albuquerque, 1965-78, asst. dean., 1972-74, chmn. chem. and nuc. engring. dept., 1974-78; with GPU Service Corp. (name now GPU Nuc. Corp.), Parsippany, NJ, 1978-96, mgr. generation productivity dept., 1978-79, dir. reliability engring. dept., 1979-80, dir. tng. and edn., 1980-82, v.p. nuclear assurance Parsippany, NJ, 1982-87, v.p. planning and nuclear safety, 1987-89; v.p. corp. svcs. GPU Nuc. Corp., Parsippany, 1989-93, v.p. svcs., 1993-95, v.p. nuclear svcs., 1995-96; recovery officer, v.p. human resources N.E. Nuc. Energy Co., from 1998. With rsch. partic. Sandia Corp., 1965-78; cons. White Sands Missile Range Fast Burst Reactor Facility, 1965-78, Sandia Lab., Albuquerque, 1965-70, Con Edison, N.Y.C., 1970-73, Electric Power Rsch. Inst., Palo Alto, Calif., 1976-78, NSF, U.S. Dept. Energy, others; rsch. assoc. nuc. rsch. divsn. Atomic Weapons Rsch. Estab., Eng., 1966-67; mem. Nuc. Stewardship, LLC. Contbr. articles to profl. jours. Served to capt. U.S. Army, 1962-64. AEC fellow, 1958-59; recipient Disting. Engring. Alumnus award Purdue U., 1993. Fellow Am. Nuc. Soc. (chmn. edn. divsn. 1974-

75, chmn. nuc. engring. dept. heads com. 1975-76, chmn. No. N.J. chpt. 1986-87, 88-89, v.p., pres.-elect 1990-91, pres. 1991-92, Pioneer in Nuc. Tng. award 1999); mem. Nuc. Energy Inst., Profl. Reactor Operators Soc. Presbyterian. Avocations: church school teaching, woodworking, reading, choir, model garden railroading. Home: Albuquerque, N.Mex. Died July 9, 2009.

LONG, SPEEDY O., Former United States Representative from Louisiana; b. Tullos, La., June 16, 1928; s. Felix F. and Verda Pendarvis Long; m. Florence Marie Theriot, 1955; children: Felix Paul, David Theriot. State sanator, La., 1956—64; state rep. La., 1965—73; atty. 28th jud. LaSalle Parrish, La., 1973—85; jud. temp., 1994; atty-at-law. Mem.: Shrine, Mason. Democrat. Baptist. Died Oct. 5, 2006.

LONG, WILLIAM ALLAN, retired forest products company executive; b. Columbus, Ohio, Aug. 25, 1928; s. Allan C. and Dorothy (Crates) L.; m. Ann Cors, Aug. 27, 1954; children: Leslie, David, Steven, Jeffrey. BA, Ohio Wesleyan U., 1951. Vice pres. Diamond Internat., NYC, 1951-70; exec. v.p. Overhead Door Corp., Dallas, 1970-75; v.p. St. Regis Paper Co., NYC, 1975-79; group v.p. Inland Container Corp., Indpls., 1979-93; ret., 1993. Sgt. U.S. Army, 1946-47. Republican. Presbyterian. Died Aug. 24, 2005.

LOOMAN, JAMES R., lawyer; b. Vallejo, Calif., June 5, 1952; s. Alfred R. and Jane M. (Halter) L.; m. Donna G. Craven, Dec. 18, 1976; children: Alison Marie, Mark Andrew, Zachary Michael. BA, Valparaiso U., Ind., 1974; JD, U. Chgo., 1978. Bar: Ill, 1978, U.S. Dist. Ct. (no dist.) Ill. 1978, U.S. Claims Ct. 1979. Assoc. Isham, Lincoln & Beale, Chgo., 1978—83, Sidley & Austin, Chgo., 1983—86; ptnr. Sidley Austin LLP, from 1986. Assoc. gen. counsel Comml. Fin. Assn., from 2002. Bd. dirs. Valparaiso U., Ind., from 2006. Fellow Am. Coll. Comml. Fin. Lawyers; mem. ABA, Chgo. Bar Assn. (chmn. comml. and fin. transactions com. 1996-97, 2002-03), Skokie Country Club, Univ. Club Chgo. Lutheran. Home: Glencoe, Ill. Died 2009.

LOOMANITZ, CLARA, early childhood education educator, consultant; b. NYC, Aug. 13, 1922; d. Benjamin and Anna (Kotick) L. BA, Hunter Coll., 1943; MA, NYU, 1950; EdD, Yeshiva U., 1964. Cert. in early childhood edn. and spl. edn., N.Y. Tchr. nursery schs., NYC, 1943-46; ednl. dir. Day Care Ctrs., NYC, 1946-50, dir., 1950-54, Parent Coop. Nursery Sch., NYC, 1954-58; prof., dir. Washburne Early Childhood Ctr. of Bklyn. Coll., NYC, 1958-91; cons. in child devel., early childhood edn., spl. edn. Bklyn., from 1990. Cons. Bd. Jewish Edn., N.Y.C., 1970-83, pub. schs., N.Y.C., 1970—, Project of Bruner Found., N.Y.C., 1991-93, parents and parent groups, N.Y.C., 1968—. Vol. The Lighthouse Inc., N.Y.C., 1994—; mem. Riverside Choral Soc. Mem. Internat. Assn. for Edn. of Pre-schoolers, Nat. Assn. for Edn. of Young Children, N.Y. Assn. for Edn. of Young Children. Avocation: pianist with chamber music groups. Home: New York, NY. Died July 1, 2008.

LOOMIS, HENRY, retired broadcast executive; b. Tuxedo Park, NY, Apr. 19, 1919; s. Alfred Lee and Ellen Holman (Farnsworth) L.; m. Mary Paul Macleod, May 18, 1946 (div. Jan. 1974); children: Henry, Mary, Lucy, Gordon; m. Jacqueline C. Williams, Jan. 19, 1974; stepchildren: Charles Judson Williams, John Chalmers Williams, David Finley Williams, Robert Wood Williams. AB, Harvard, 1941; student, U. Calif., 1946. With radiation lab. U. Calif., 1945-47; asst. to pres. MIT, 1947-50; asst. to chmn. rsch. & devel. bd. US Dept. Def., 1950- 51; cons. Psychol. Strategy Bd., Washington, 1951-52; staff Pres.'s Com. Internat. Info., 1953; chief Office Rsch. & Intelligence USIA, 1954-57, dir. broadcasting service Voice of Am., 1958-65; staff to spl. asst. to Pres. for sci. & tech. The White House, 1957-58; dep. commr. edn. US Dept. Health Edn. & Welfare, 1965-66; ptnr. St. Vincents Island Co., NYC, 1966-69; dep. dir. USIA, 1969-72; pres. Corp. for Pub. Broadcasting, Washington, 1972-78. Trustee, vice chmn. bd. dirs. Mitre Corp., 1967-69, 78-91. Vice chmn. bd. dirs. Nat. Mus. Natural History, Smithsonian Instn., 1991-92, trustee, 1992-95; trustee Mus. Sci. and History, Jacksonville, 1991-96; bd. dirs., hon. mem. Jacksonville Zool. Soc., 1991-96. Recipient Rockefeller Pub. Service award for fgn. affairs, 1963 Home: Jacksonville, Fla. Died Nov. 2, 2008.

LORD, CLAUDE FRANKLIN, JR., advertising and public relations consultant; b. Texarkana, Tex., Dec. 9, 1921; s. Claude Franklin and Viola Love (Shamburger) L.; m. Clara Eugenia Shipp (dec. Apr. 1989); children: Eva Cynthia Lord Cook, Samananthia Elaine Lord Spence; m. Norma Evelyn Stone, Jan. 13, 1990. BSBA, East Tex. Bapt. U., 1950. Advt. supr. R.G. LeTourneau, Inc., Longview, Tex., 1954-63; merchandising mgr. Tex. Instruments Inc., Dallas, 1963-83; advt. cons. C.F. Lord & Assocs., Richardson, Tex., 1983 89; advt. and pub. rels. cons., Mesquite, from 1989. Sgt. USAAF, 1942-46, CBI. Mem. Am. Legion, Masons. Presbyterian. Avocations: gardening, fishing, reading. Home: Mesquite, Tex. Died July 25, 2008.

LORELL, JACK, retired mathematician; b. Bklyn., Oct. 7, 1916; s. Jack and Frances (Goldstein) L.; m. Doris Venick, Jan. 4, 1942; children: Kenneth Roy, Mark Allen. AB, Bklyn. Coll., 1936, AM, 1938; postgrad., Brown U., 1938-40. Mathematician Aberdeen (Md.) Proving Ground, 1940-46; rsch. specialist Jet Propulsion Lab., Calif. Inst. Tech., Pasadena, 1946-56, 58-83; mathematician TRW, LA, 1956-58. Exec. editor jour. Celestial Mechanics, 1974-77; contbr. articles on selenodesy and gravity field analysis of the Moon and of Mars. Mem. Am. Math. Soc. Home: Pasadena, Calif. Died Mar. 13, 2008.

LORTIE, JOHN WILLIAM, solar research company executive; b. Chgo., July 11, 1920; s. William Arthur and Alice Marie (McNamee) L.; m. Mary Elaine Sullivan, Sept. 21, 1946; children: Colleen, Kevin, Timothy. Student, Ill. Inst. Tech., 1940-42, U. Ala., 1976. Radar technician Western Electric Co., Westchester, Ill., 1946-50; pres. William A. Lortie & Sons, Westchester, 1950-65, Monark Instant Homes, Ocean Springs, Miss., 1965-75; dir. rsch. Energy Rsch. Corp., Mobile, Ala., 1974-88; pres. Essential Solar Products, Mobile, from 1980. Pres. Energy Internat. Innovations, Mobile, Ala., 1981—; solar cons.; bd. dirs. Internat. Solar Acad., 1988—; head dept. solar tech. Carver State Tech. Coll., 1976-81; internat. rep. Barclay Group Fin. With U.S. Army, 1942-46. Mem. Ala. Acad. Scis., Ala. Solar Energy Assn. (state chmn.), Ala. Solar Industries Assn. (bd. dirs., pres.), Internat. Solar Energy Soc., Nat. Assn. Solar Contractors. Republican. Roman Catholic. Achievements include research subspecialties in combustion processes, fuels and sources, solar pond power generation, solar aeration fish ponds, solar desalination, super conductivity/solar cells, patent research, laser guidance systems, design of flexible amorphous silicon photovoltaic cloth, magnetic energy recovery from earth core, ultra high power projection through the atmosphere. Home: Mobile, Ala. Died Apr. 23, 2009.

LOVE, RICHARD HARVEY, lawyer; b. Washington, Aug. 31, 1915; s. Leo Young and Grace Marie (Jett) L.; m. Betty Zane Schofield, Nov. 14, 1942 (dec. Sept. 1967); children: Richard (dec. 2000), Robert, Edward, William, Elizabeth (dec. June 1996). AB, U. Md., 1936, LLB, 1938. Bar: Md., D.C. 1939. Law clk. U.S. Dist. Ct., Balt., Md., 1938-40; pvt. practice Washington, Md., 1940-41 and from 46. Counsel Bd. Zoning Appeals, Prince Georges County, Md., 1953-55 Editor Judge Adv. Jour., 1948-81. Served to maj. AUS, 1941-46; col. Judge Adv. Gen.'s Corps Res., 1946-75. Decorated Legion of Merit U.S. Army, 1972. Mem. ABA, Md. Bar Assn., Bar Assn. D.C., Prince Georges County Bar Assn., Judge Advocates Assn. (exec. sec. 1948-81, dir. emeritus 1981-2009), Res. Officers Assn., Mil. Order Fgn. Wars (past nat. comdr. gen.), Assn. U.S. Army, Army-Navy Club, Order of Colf, Phi Kappa Phi. Republican. Roman Catholic. Died Aug. 18, 2009.

LOVELACE, ELDRIDGE HIRST, retired landscape architect, city planner, civil engineer; b. Kansas City, Kans., Mar. 16, 1913; s. Charles Wilson and Eva (Hirst) L.; m. Marjorie Van Evera, May 15, 1937; children: Jean (Mrs. William C. Stinchcombe), Richard. B.F.A. in Landscape Architecture, U. Ill., 1935. Registered profl. engr., Mo. With Harland Bartholomew & Assocs., Inc., St. Louis, 1935—81, mem., 1943-79, chmn. bd., 1979— 81. V.p. Internat. Fedn. Landscape Architects, 1975-77, sec. gen., 1980—81. Author: Harland Bartholomew: His Contributions to American Urban Planning. Mem. bd. commrs. Tower Grove Park, 1971—, pres. 1986-94. Fellow Am. Soc. Landscape Architects (past sec.), ASCE; mem. Am. Inst. Cert. Planners. Achievements include development of comprehensive plans for 100 American cities; master plans for military bases in US, Pacific, Hawaii and P.I; final design plans for Jefferson National Expansion Memorial (The Arch), St. Louis. Home: Saint Louis, Mo. Deceased.

LOW, FRANK JAMES, physicist, researcher; b. Mobile, Nov. 23, 1933; s. Albert S. and Flora (Woodruff) L.; m. Edith Estella Morgan, Sep. 8, 1956; children: Valerie Ann, Beverly Ellen, Eric David. BS, Yale, 1955; MA, Rice U., 1957, PhD, 1959. Mem. tech. staff Tex. Instruments, Inc., Dallas, 1959-62; assoc. scientist Nat. Radio Astronomy Obs., Green Bank, W.Va., 1962-65; research prof. U. Ariz., Tucson, 1965—96, Regents prof., 1988—96; prof. space sci. Rice U., Houston, 1966-71, adj. prof., 1971-79; founder Infrared Laboratories, Inc., 1967—2007. Bd. dirs. Tucson East YMCA-YWCA, 1973-75. Recipient H.A. Wilson award Rice U., 1959, Spl. founders prize Tex. Instruments Found., 1976, Disting. Alumnus award Rice U., 1982, Creative Sci. award U. Ariz. Found., 1984, medal for exceptional sci. achievement NASA, 1984, Rumford Medal for discoveries in light and heat, Am. Acad. Arts and Scis., 1986. Mem. NAS, Am. Astron. Soc. (Helen B. Warner prize 1968), Am. Phys. Soc., Astron. Soc. of Pacific (Catherine Wolfe Bruce Gold medal 2006), Am. Acad. Arts and Scis., Sigma Xi. Home: Tucson, Ariz. Died June 11, 2009; Tucson, Ariz.

LOWE, CONNIE DELORES, nonprofit association administrator, accountant; b. Brown County, Ind., Aug. 7, 1941; d. Ira W. and Edna Pauline (Loy) Shafer; m. Walter C. Lowe, Oct. 28, 1960; children: Kirk D., Vicki D. Student, Milligan Coll., Tenn., 1959, U. Houston, 1960. Acct., contr. Chas. Heyne Co. Inc., Houston, 1973-88; owner K.V.'s Boogies, Willis, Tex., 1986-91; acct., contr. Walsh & Albert Co. Inc., Houston, from 1988; chair bd. dirs., exec. dir. Friends of a Peeper, Inc., Willis, from 1993. Owner Record Keeper's Grapevine. Author: (children's books) I Know, I Know, I Know, 1991, My Name Is, 1992, Safety on the Go, 1993; editor Travel Trivia. Vol. Tri County Mental Health Mental Retardation, Conroe, Tex., 1986-87. Home: Willis, Tex. Died Nov. 5, 2007.

LOWENSTEIN, LOUIS, law educator; b. NYC, June 13, 1925; s. Louis and Ralphina (Steinhardt) L.; m. Helen Libby Udell, Feb. 12, 1953; children: Roger Spector, Jane Ruth, Barbara Ann. BS in Bus., Columbia, 1947, LL.B., 1953; M.F.S., U. Md., 1951. Bar: N.Y. 1953. Pvt. practice law, NYC, 1954-78; law clk. to Assoc. Judge Stanley H. Fuld, N.Y. Ct. Appeals, 1953-54; assoc., then partner Hays, Sklar & Herzberg, 1954-68; ptnr. Nickerson, Kramer, Lowenstein, Nessen, Kamin & Soll, 1968-78; Simon H. Rifkind prof. emeritus law & fin. Columbia U. Law Sch., 1980—2009, project dir. Instl. Investor Project, 1988-94; pres. Supermarkets Gen. Corp., Woodbridge, NJ, 1978-79. Bd. dirs. Liz Claiborne, Inc. 1988-96; mem. pub. oversight bd. Panel on Audit Effectiveness, 1998-2000. Author: What's Wrong with Wall Street, 1988, Sense and Nonsense in Corporate Finance, 1991, The Investor's Dilemma: How Mutual Funds Are Betraying Your Trust and What to Do About It, 2008; contbr., co-editor: Knights, Raiders and Targets, 1988; editor in chief Columbia Law Rev., 1951-53. V.p., mem. exec. com. Fedn. Jewish Philanthropies N.Y.; pres. Jewish Bd. Family and Children's Svcs. N.Y., 1974—78; trustee Beth Israel Med. Ctr., NYC, 1975—81; dir. Goddard-Riverside Cmty. Ctr., 1996—2002; mem. Citizens Budget Commn., 2003—09, NY State Commn. Pub. Authority Reform, 2005—06; chmn. bd. dirs. Coalition for the Homeless, 1997—2004, chmn. emeritus, 2004—09. Mem.: ABA, Am. Law Inst., Assn. Bar City of NY. Home: Larchmont, NY. Died Apr. 18, 2009.

LOWRANCE, MURIEL EDWARDS, retired educational specialist; b. Ada, Okla., Dec. 28, 1922; d. Warren E. and Mayme E. (Barrick) Edwards; 1 child, Kathy Lynn Lowrance Gutierrez. BS in Edn., E. Ctrl. State U., Ada, 1954. Cert. profl. contract mgr. Nat. Contract Assn. Acct., adminstrv. asst. to bus. mgr. E. Ctrl. State U., 1950—68; grants and contracts specialist U. N.Mex. Sch. Medicine, Albuquerque, 1968—72, program specialist IV, dept. orthopaedics, 1975—86; asst. adminstrv. officer N.Mex. Regional Med. Program, 1972—75. Bd. dirs. Vocat. Rehab. Ctr., 1980—84. Mem.: AAUW, Amigos de las Americas (dir.), Am. Bus. Women's Assn. (past pres. El Segundo chpt., Woman of Yr. award 1974), Pilot (Albuquerque) (pres. 1979—80, dir. 1983—84, dist. treas. 1984—86, treas. S.W. dist. 1984—86, gov.-elect S.W. dist. 1986—87, gov. S.W. dist. 1987—88). Democrat. Methodist. Home: Gulf Breeze, Fla. Died Feb. 23, 2009.

LU, MATTHIAS, priest, educator; b. Presidio Lu Kia-tun, Pao-ting, Hebei, China, June 2, 1919; came to U.S.; naturalized; s. Paul and Rose (Yang) L. Student, St. Vincent's Maj. Sem., Peiping, China, 1937-38; PhB, Pontifical Urbaniana U., Rome, 1939, BTh., 1941, Licentiate in Philosophy, 1942, Licentiate in Sacred Theology, 1944, PhD, 1946; postgrad., U. Toronto, Can., 1948-56, Pontifical Inst. Mediaeval Studies, 1948-59, St. Francis Xavier U., Antigonish, Can., 1949-51; PhD (hon.), Scicluna Internat. U., 1987; ThD (hon.), Albert Einstein Internat. Acad. Found., Kansas City, Kans., 1993. Ordained priest Roman Cath. Ch., 1942. Lectr. in philosophy Fujen U., Peiping, China, 1946-48; asst. pastor, chmn. ednl. com. for parish co-ops Thorold, Ont., Canada, 1951-56; instr. U. Notre Dame, Ind., 1956-58; asst. prof. St. John's U., Collegeville, Minn., 1959-62, St. Mary's Coll., Moraga, Calif., 1962-72, scholar in residence, from 1973, dir. St. Thomas Aquinas Internat. Ctr. for Everyone, from 1974. Prof. U. Ottawa, Can., 1957-59; vis. lectr. St. Bonaventure U., N.Y., 1958-59, Cath. U. Paris, 1960; rsch. assoc. U. Calif., Berkeley, 1962—; chaplain Christian Bros. St. La Salle Schs., 1963—, local br. 11, Italian Cath. Fedn., Oakland, Calif., 1983—, Oakland coun. KC, 1978—; instr. Holy Names Coll., Calif., 1965-69; assoc. prof. John F. Kennedy U., Calif., 1966; vicar for Chinese and East Asian peoples Roman Cath. Ch., 1969-86; mem. Oakland Priests' Senate, 1972-75; vis. prof. Ignatius Inst., U. San Francisco, 1981-82; dir. Chinese transls. Lublin U. Internat. Transl. Ctr., 1984-86; cons. doctoral com. Union Inst. Grad. Coll., Cin., 1997—. Author, translator in field; also articles; producer program Stas. KUSF-FM, KSMC-FM, 1972—. Recipient Pro Ecclesia et Pontefice medal Pope Pius XII, 1939, Gold medal Pope John Paul II and Bishop of Oakland, 1985, Einstein medal Internat. Albert Einstein Acad. Found., 1988, Internat. Peace prize United Cultural Convention, 2003. Hon. mem. Mexican Cath. Philos. Soc.; mem. AAAS, UNESCO, Am. Philos. Assn., Am. Cath. Philos. Assn., Am. Oriental Soc., Am. Acad. Polit. and Social Sci., Cath. Theol. Soc. Am., Soc. Internat. pour l'Etude de la Philosophie Médiévale, Chinese Hist. Soc. Am., Internat. Soc. St. Thomas Aquinas, Internat. Jacques Maritain Soc., Internat. Soc. Metaphysics, Internat. Assn. Symbolic Logic, Internat. Soc. Chinese Philosophy, Internat. Assn. for Christian Thought, World Congregation of Bros. Christian Schs., (affiliated bro. 1988—), Internat. Assn. Educators for World Peace (vice chmn. spl. cons.), UN Econ. and Social Coun. in UN Assembly, UN Dept. Pub. Info., UN Conf. on Environment and Devel., 1998—. Died June 25, 2008.

LUBENSKY, EARL HENRY, diplomat, anthropologist; b. Marshall, Mo., Mar. 31, 1921; s. Henry Carl and Adele Gertrud (Biesemeyer) L.; m. Anita Ruth Price, June 27, 1942 (dec. July 1992); children: Tom, Gerald, John Christopher; m. Margot Truman Patterson, Mar. 26, 1994 (dec. Mar. 28, 2008), m. Marian L. Reed, Aug. 19, 2008. BA, Mo. Valley Coll., 1948, LLD (hon.), 1968; BS, Georgetown U., 1949; MS, George Washington U., 1967; diploma, Nat. War Coll., 1967; MA, U. Mo., 1983, PhD, 1991. Mgr. Tavern Supply Co., Marshall, Mo., 1938—42; real estate salesman Mitchell Quick Realtor, Silver Spring, Md., 1948; analyst rsch. Georgetown U., Washington, 1949; reference asst. Libr. Congress, Washington, 1949; fgn. svc. officer Dept. of State, Washington, 1949—79, inter-Am. reg. polit. affairs officer, 1956—61, served in Germany, Philippines, Spain, Ecuador, Colombia and El Salvador, 1950—78, officer-in-charge Antarctic affairs Washington, 1958—59. Diplomat-in-residence, Olivet, Albion and Adrian Colls., Mich., 1973-74; sr. staff mem. internat. affairs Coun. on Environ. Quality, Washington, 1974-76; spl. amb. to inauguration Pres. Romero, El Salvador, 1977; adj. rsch. assoc. anthropology U. Mo., 1992—. Author: The Westermans of Westphalia, Missouri, Their Ancestors and Descendants, 1989, The Ferdon Collections of Prehistoric Ceramic Vessels an Sherds from Esmeraldas Province, Ecuador, 1991, The Excavation of Structures P-12 and P-20 in Cihuatan, El Salvador, 2005; contbr. articles to profl. jours. Mem. bd. dirs. Columbia Entertainment Co., 1993-99; co-founder Heartland chpt. Global Action to Prevent War, Columbia, Mo., 2007; organizer, dir. archael. excavations in Ecuador, El Salvador and Mo. With Mo. N.G. 1937-40, 48, Mo. State Guard, 1940-42, US Army, 1942-45, lt. col. USAR, 1948-81. Eagle Scout Boy Scouts Am., 1939. Mem. Mo. Archaeol. Soc. (charter, treas. 1981-90, chmn. bd. trustees 2001-03, trustee 1991—, co-founder chpt. Boonslick Archaeol. Soc., 1985, Appreciation award 1991, 2002, disting. svc. award, 2003), Soc. for Am. Archaeology (Presdl. Recognition award 1991), Inst. Andean Studies, Fgn. Svc. Assn., Diplomatic and Consular Officrs Retired, Boone County Hist. Soc., The Theatre Soc. (treas. 1993-99), Nat. Eagle Scout Assn., Great Rivers Eagle Scout Assn. (organizer Boy Scout Lone Patrols, Marshall, Mo., 1933, Madrid, 1955, organizer, dir. Boy Scout Camp Peñalara, Spain, 1956). Democrat. Avocations: genealogy, gardening, music, amateur radio, stamp collecting/philately. Died May 1, 2009.

LUBIN, RUTH, art educator; b. St. Louis, May 22, 1911; d. Harry and Anne (Levinson) Shapiro; m. Alfred Lubin, June 29, 1930 (dec. 1985); children: Barbara Lubin Berger, Mardene Lubin Conrad. AA, Pasadena Jr. Coll., 1951; BA, UCLA, 1953; MFA, U. So. Calif., 1960. Tchr. art Monrovia (Calif.) High Sch., 1953-54, Downey (Calif.) High Sch., 1954-55, Arcadia (Calif.) High Sch., 1955-78; instr. art Pasadena (Calif.) City Coll., 1985—. Exhibited in group shows Art Inst. Chgo., 1943, 45, 46, Pasadena Art Inst., 1950, Los Angeles County Mus., 1951. Lectr. to womens clubs in San Gabriel Valley, 1970—; vol. U. So. Calif., 1990, 91. Art scholar UCLA, 1951-53; recipient trophy Eugene McCarthy, former U.S. Senator, 1992; named Ms. Calif. Senior, 1994. Mem. Opera Buffs, Andrus Assocs. Avocations: singing, poetry. Home: Palos Verdes Estates, Calif. Died Mar. 4, 2008.

LUBKER, ROBERT ALFRED, retired metal products company executive; b. Puyallup, Wash., May 19, 1920; s. Christen Pedersen and Ella (Lee Pla) L.; m. Virginia Cora Hartmann, June 16, 1945; children: Barbara Lubker Lunding, Beverly Lubker Fantini. BS in Metall. Engring., U. Wash., 1942; MS in Metall. Engring., Carnegie-Mellon U., 1946. Sect. engr. Westinghouse Electric Corp., East Pitts., 1942-46; mgr. metals rsch. dept. IIT Rsch. Inst., Chgo., 1946-58; v.p. Alan Wood Steel Co., Conshohocken, Pa., 1958-67; dir. R & D, CF&I Steel Corp., Denver, 1967-70, Gen. Cable Corp., Union, N.J., 1970-72; v.p. Assoc. Metals & Minerals Corp., NYC, 1972-74, Ava Steel Products Internat., Inc., NYC, 1974-80; pres. M&R Refractory Metals, Inc., Winslow, N.J., 1980-83, ret., 1983. Contbr. numerous articles to profl. jours. Mem. Sawgrass Country Club, Tau Beta Pi. Republican. Presbyterian. Home: Jacksonville, Fla. Died Apr. 22, 2008.

LUCAS, ROBERT FRANK, lawyer; b. Beacon Falls, Conn., Nov. 11, 1935; s. Otto F. and A. Helen (Schuster) L.; m. Regina Abbiati, July 16, 1960; children: Robert Frank Jr., David R., Jennifer J. AB, Bates Coll., Lewiston, Maine, 1956; JD, Boston U., 1959. Bar: Mass. 1960, US Dist. Ct. Mass. 1962, US Supreme Ct. 1973. Trial atty. Boston Legal Aid Soc., 1960-63; prin. Nigro, Pettepit & Lucas, Wakefield, Mass., from 1963. Mem. standing list of masters Mass. Superior Ct., Cambridge, from 1979. Chmn. bd. appeals City of Melrose, Mass., 1982—2003, city solicitor, 2003—05; trustee Melrose H.S. Permanent Scholarship Fund, from 1979; mem. Rep. City Com., Melrose, 1980—84; lay leader 1st United Meth. Ch., Melrose, 1979—82. With USAR, 1959—65. Mem.: ABA, 1st Dist. Ea. Middlesex Bar Assn. (pres. 1987—88), Middlesex County Bar Assn. (bd. dirs. 1986—99), Mass. Bar Assn. (bd. dels. 1980—83, chmn. fee arbitration bd. 1983—84, 20th Century Club 1985, exec. com. 1993, bd. dels. from 2004, treas. 2006—07, v.p. from 2007, Cert. of Appreciation 1988, Cmty. Svc. award 1989), Bellevue Golf Club, Masons (dist. dep. grand master 1982—83). Avocations: music, choral singing, youth sports. Home: Melrose, Mass. Died July 11, 2008.

LUCAS, SHIRLEY AGNES HOYT, management executive; b. Chicago, Aug. 21, 1921; d. Howard L. and Lucille P. (Von Krippenstapel) Hoyt; m. William H. Lucas, Feb. 2, 1952; 1 child, Lucille Shirley. Student, Northwestern U., 1941-42. V.p. Lucas Co., Chgo., from 1980. Mem. Ill. Hosp. Assn. (Leadership award 1975), Aux. Christ Hosp. and Med. Ctr. (life, past bd. dirs., cotillion chmn., housewalk chmn.). Republican. Lutheran. Avocations: tennis, horseback riding, golf, biking, needle point. Died Sept. 27, 2007.

LUCE, Mrs. HENRY See HADLEY, LEILA

LUDWIG, FREDERICK JOHN, SR., analytical chemist; b. St. Louis, June 20, 1928; s. Robert Julius and Angela Abigail (Chevraux) L.; m. Carole Louise Hoelzer, Oct. 13, 1956; children: F. John Jr., Lawrence Charles. AB, Washington U., St. Louis, 1950; PhD, St. Louis U., 1953. Rsch. chemist Mallinckrodt, St. Louis, 1955-59; chemist, group leader, rsch. specialist Petrolite, St. Louis, 1959-98; cons. Baker Hughes, 1998, ret., 1998. Contbr. articles to profl. jours. Mem. dads com. Boy Scouts Am., St. Louis, 1972-79. With U.S. Army, 1953-55. Mem. Am. Chem. Soc., Sigma Xi. Mem. Christian Ch. Achievements include patentee in field. Home: Saint Louis, Mo. Died Mar. 16, 2008.

LUESSENHOP, ALFRED JOHN, retired neurosurgeon; b. Chgo., Feb. 6, 1926; s. Alfred Lewis and Gertrude L.; m. Frances Matthews; children: Cynthia, Constance, John, Charles, Suzanne, Laura. BS, Yale U., 1949; MD, Harvard U., 1952. Intern U. Chgo. Hosps., 1952-53; resident in neurosurgery Mass. Gen. Hosp., Boston, 1953-59; research fellow in surgery Harvard U., Cambridge, Mass., 1959; vis. scientist NIH, Bethesda, Md., 1960; prof. surgery Georgetown U. Med. Sch., Washington, 1963—95, chief neurosurgery divsn., 1963—93, prof. emeritus, 1995—2009. Contbr. numerous articles to profl. jours. Served with AUS, 1943-46. Mem. Am. Assn. Neurol. Surgery, Congress Neurosurgery, Am. Acad. Neurosurgery, Soc. Neurosurgery Republican. Presbyterian. Died Feb. 21, 2009.

LUFF, GERALD MEREDITH, JR., sales and marketing executive; b. Vineland, NJ, Oct. 19, 1937; s. Gerald Meredith and Harriet Mary (Lippincott) L.; m. Kathryn Margaret Desmond, Dec. 12, 1964; children: Gerald M., Kelleen M., Jeffrey P., Jennifer D., Bradley S., Valerie A. B Chem. Engring., Rensselaer Poly. Inst., 1960. Various positions Linde Div. Praxair (formerly Union Carbide Indsl. Gases), various locations, from 1961; product mgr. Linde div. Union Carbide Corp., NY hdqrs., 1973-74, area bus. mgr., 1974-76, mktg. mgr. various locations, 1977-87; sales mgr. Linde div. Union Carbide Corp., Danbury, Conn., 1988-90, dir. sales and mktg., from 1990. Commr., Nottingham Civic Assn., Houston, 1972-73; dist. leader New Canaan (Conn.) Republicans, 1978—; commr. New Canaan Parks and Recreation, 1979-88, com. chmn., 1987. Mem. Am. Chem. Soc., Country Club of New Canaan. Roman Catholic. Avocations: golf, coin collecting/numismatics, gardening. Home: New Canaan, Conn. Died July 31, 2008.

LUGO, EMIL J., retired secondary school educator; b. NYC, Sept. 7, 1946; s. Abraham and Margaret Lugo; m. Yvette Corsino-Lugo, July 19, 1980; children: Karl P., Cynthia M. BA, St. John's U., NYC, 1968; MA, Fordham U., Bronx, 1976. Cert. tchr. secondary edn. N.Y. Tchr. social studies Automotive H.S., Bklyn., 1971—72, Washington Irving H.S., NYC, 1973—76; tchr. social studies and Japanese lang. Stuyvesant H.S., NYC, 1968—72, 1972—73, 1976—2000; ret., 2000. Del. United Fedn. Tchrs., NYC, 1973—75; N.C. English/Spanish interpreter, from 2004. Bd. dirs. Watauga, Avery, Mitchell, Yancey Counties Cmty. Action, Inc., 2005—07, vice-chmn., 2006—07. Recipient Tchr. Who Made a Difference award, N.Y. Times, 2001; Summer Study grantee, N.Y. State, 1969, Fulbright scholar, Fulbright/Japan Found., 1985. Mem.: High Country Amigos (English instr. 2000—06). Republican. Roman Catholic. Avocation: home repair, remodeling, and Japanese rock gardening. Home: New York, NY. Died May 16, 2008.

LUKENS, WALTER PATRICK, retired electronics executive; b. Merced, Calif., May 19, 1924; s. Walter R. and Alicia (McKeon) L.; m. Sylvia A. Canova, Nov. 6, 1948. BS, U.S. Mil. Acad., 1947; JD, Stanford U., 1955. Bar: Calif. 1955, U.S. Supreme Ct. 1963. Counsel, guidance and control div. Litton Industries, Woodland Hills, Calif., 1967-68, v.p., group counsel def. and space systems Beverly Hills, Calif., 1968-71, dir. Washington Office Washington, 1971-76, corp. v.p., 1976-91. Mem. policy com., past chmn. Council Def. and Space Industry Assns., Washington, 1971-85; appointed mem. industry sector adv. com. on Capital Goods for Trade Policy Matters. Mem. adv. bd. Litton Employees Polit. Assistance Com., 1975-91; mem. nat. adv. bd. Goodwill Industries. Served to lt. col. U.S. Army, 1947-67, C.Z., Korea, Ger. Decorated Legion of Merit; decorated Bronze Star (2), Combat Infantryman's Badge Mem. Nat. Security Indsl. Assn. (dir. chpt.), Nat. Machine Tool Builders Assn. (chmn. pub. affairs com. 1982-85), Washington Indsl. Round Table (treas.), Siasconset (Mass.) Casino Assn., Army-Navy Country Club (Arlington, Va.), Sankaty Head Golf and Beach Club (Nantucket Island, Mass.). Roman Catholic. Home: Alexandria, Va. Died Oct. 9, 2009.

LUND, HARRY AUSTIN, investment banking executive; b. Metuchen, NJ, Apr. 20, 1936; s. Harry Anthony and Theresa Marie (Hanley) L.; m. Elaine Barbara Foss, Oct. 7, 1961; children: Mark, Sharon. BA, Catholic U. Am., 1958; MBA, U. Va., 1960; JD, NYU, 1966. Fin. analyst E.I. DuPont de Nemours & Co., Wilmington, Del., 1960-62; strategic planner Esso Research & Engring. Co., Florham Park, N.J., 1962-66; capital mgmt. officer Am. Brand, Inc., NYC, 1966-67; investment banker Irving Trust Co., NYC, from 1967. Home: Flemington, NJ. Died Mar. 12, 2008.

LUNDBY, MARY ADELAIDE, state legislator; b. Carroll County, Feb. 2, 1948; d. Edward A. and Elizabeth Hoehl; m. Michael Lundby, 1971; 1 child, Daniel. BA in History, Upper Iowa U., 1971. Staff asst. to Senator Roger Jepsen US Senate; mem. Iowa Ho. Representatives from 47th dist., 1987—93, Iowa Ho. Representatives from 51st dist., 1993—95, spkr. pro tempore, 1993—95; mem. Iowa State Senate from 26th dist., Des Moines, 1995—2002, Iowa State Senate from 18th dist., Des Moines, 2003—09, minority leader, 2006—07, co-majority leader, 2006. Active Solid Waste Adv. Com. Named an Outstanding Young Women in America, Am. Assn. University Women, 1982. Republican. Home: Marion, Iowa. Died Jan. 17, 2009.

LUNDY, ROBERT DONALD, advertising executive; b. Kansas City, Mo., July 1, 1926; s. Garland Andrew and Dorothy Elizabeth (Colvin) L.; m. Miriam Collins, Aug. 20, 1947; children: Bruce G., Douglas R., Gordon C. BA in Math. and English, Columbia U., 1947, MA in English, 1948; PhD in English, U. Calif. Berkeley, 1956. Mem. faculty U. Calif., Berkeley, 1952-54, U. So. Calif., LA, 1954-56; faculty mem. U. Calif., Berkeley, 1958-60; prof. English lang. Luigi Bacconi U., Italy, 1960; mgr. proposal ops. TRW Systems Group, Redondo Beach, Calif., 1960-65, dir. mktg. svcs., 1965-70; dir. pub. affairs TRW Def. & Space Systems, Redondo Beach, 1970-72; v.p. pub. rels. and advt. TRW Inc., Cleve., from 1973. With USN, 1944-46. Mem. Western Res. Hist. Soc. (trustee), Cleve. Advt. Club (bd. dirs.). Home: Tigard, Oreg. Died Jan. 5, 2008.

LUPINSKIE, ROBERT EDWARD, government agency executive, school system administrator; b. NYC, Oct. 18, 1946; m. MaryAnn Generoso, Apr. 1, 1972; children: Lorraine, Stephanie. Program mgr. Social Security Adminstrn., Balt., 1985, project dir., 1985-86; process br. mgr. Northeastern Program Svc. Ctr., 1990-91; dir. Social Security Adminstrn., NYC, from 1983. Ctr. dir. Community Dispute Resolution Ctr., Glen Cove, N.Y., 1989—. Mem. bd. edn. Glen Cove City Sch. Dist., 1991—, pres. 1992-94; com. mem. Glen Cove Hall of Fame, 1991—; trustee Glen Cove Citizens Com. Against Substance Abuse, 1990—; com. mem. BOCES Budget Adv. Com., 1992—; coop. adv. com. York Coll., CUNY, 1988-90; coach commr., registrar, pres. Glen Cove Jr. Soccer League, 1979-92; recording sec., trustee Glen Cove High Sch. Booster Assn., 1986—. Recipient Commendation for Outstanding Svc., 1991, Vol. of the Yr. award L.I. Jr. Soccer League, 1992, Innovative Mgr. of Yr. award Social Security Adminstrn., 1990, Commr.'s Citation, 1988, Dep. Commr.'s citationn, 1994, Assoc. Commr.'s Citation, Social Security Adminstrn., 1982. Mem. Am. Arbitration Assn., Coun. Fed. Date Ctr. Dirs., Nat. Systems Programmers Assn., Info. Ctr. Mgrs. Assn. of N.Y., Info. Systems Security Assn., IEEE Computer Soc., N.Y. State Sch. Bds. Assn., Nassau-Suffolk Sch. Bds. Assn. (trustee 1994—), N.Y. State Assn. Sml. Cities Sch. Dists. (bd. dirs. 1994—), Nat. Sch. Bds. Assn. Roman Catholic. Avocations: golf, skiing, soccer, fishing. Home: Glen Cove, NY. Died Apr. 3, 2008.

LURKIS, ALEXANDER, electrical engineer, consultant; b. NYC, Oct. 1, 1908; s. Louis and Rebecca (Friedman) L.; m. Carin Tendler, Nov. 8, 1930; 1 child, Jeffry. BSEE, Cooper Union, NYC, 1930, NYU, 1934; postgrad., SUNY, NYC. Registered profl. engr., N.Y., Fla. Asst. engr. 8th & 9th Ave. Rwy. Co., NYC, 1925-28; elec. draftsman N.Y.C. Bd. Edn., 1928-30; from jr. engr. to sr. elec. engr. N.Y.C. Transit Authority, 1930-58; acting commr. Dept. Water Supply, Gas and Electricity, City of N.Y., 1961; chief engr. N.Y.C. Bur. Gas and Electricity, 1959-64; prin. ptnr. Alexander Lurkis Assocs., NYC, 1964-80; pres. Alexander Lurkis P.C., Cons. Engrs., NYC, 1971-90; prin. Alexander Lurkis, P.E., NYC, 1991-95. Author: The Power Brink, 1983, A Serpent at Her Breast, 1994; contbr. articles to profl. jours. Pres. Civil Svc. Tech. Guild Local 375 AFSCME-AFL/CIO, 1954-58, Dem. Club of Queens, 1955-58. Fellow Illuminating Engring. Soc. (chmn. energy mgmt. com. 1974-77), N.Y. Acad. Sci.; mem. IEEE (sr.), Cooper Union Alumni Assn. (bd. govs. 1960-66), Queens Mus., Hollis-wood Civic Assn. (v.p. 1974-76). Jewish. Achievements include patents for traffic light using one visual field for 3 colors, for art security system, for utility pole bolt system to anchor base; 8 U.S. and foreign patents for multiservice pole; organization of relighting of N.Y.C. from incandescent to mercury vapor, supervision of electrical code; consulting concerning facade and fountain lighting of Metropolitan Museum of Art, facade lighting of American Museum of Natural History, lighting of Central Park skating rink, 42d Street Library projects. Died June 16, 2008.

LUSSKY, WARREN ALFRED, librarian, educator, consultant; b. Chgo., Apr. 16, 1919; s. Arthur W. and Alma (Proegler) L.; m. Mildred Joann Island, June 12, 1948 Student, U. Ill., 1941-42; BA, U. Colo., 1946; MA, U Denver, 1948. Asst. libr. Pacific Luth. Coll., Parkland Wash., 1948-49; libr. Hopkins Transp. Libr., Stanford, 1950 Rocky Mountain Coll., Billings, Mont., 1950-55; head libr Nebr. Wesleyan U., Lincoln, 1955-56; dir. libr., assoc. prof Tex. Luth. Coll., Sequin, 1956-85. Libr. cons.; mem. accrediting team Tex. Edn. Agy., 1961, 84. Prin. contbr. to design new Tex. Luth. Coll. Libr.; rsch. and publs. on design and functions coll. libr. bldgs. Mem. Am. Libr. Assn., Tex. Libr Assn. (dist. vice chmn. 1965, chmn. 1966), S.W. Libr. Assn. Coun. Rsch. and Acad. Librs. (bd. dirs. 1968-85, pres 1976-78). Died Sept. 2, 2005.

LUTALI, AIFILI PAULO, former governor; b. Aunu'u American Samoa, Dec. 24, 1919; married. Gov. Am. Samoa 1985—89, 1993—97; spkr. of the House Senate, Am Samoa, 1956-57, pres., 1965-67, former v.p., mem. 1988—92. Chair Constnl. Conv., 1966. Mem. Am. Samoa Bar Assn. (founder 1972). Democrat. Roman Catholic. Died Aug. 1, 2002.

LUTTRELL, GEORGIA BENA, musician; b. Carbondale, Ill., Oct. 24, 1927; d. George Newton and Phyllis Bena (Gent) Gher; m. Claude Edward Luttrell, Mar. 25, 1964 (dec. Aug. 1987). BA, So. Ill. U., 1947; MusM, Northwestern U., Evanston, Ill., 1948; postgrad., various univs. Asst. prof. music Huntingdon Coll., Montgomery, Ala., 1948-50; music supr. Community Unit Dist. 2 Williamson County, Marion, Ill., 1950-53; music tchr. Dubois Grade Sch., Springfield, Ill., 1953-55; dir. choral music Feitshas High Sch., Springfield, 1955-67; chairperson music dept. Springfield S.E. High Sch., 1967-83; ind. music coord./pianist Springfield, from 1983. Accompanist various soloists and choirs, 1944—; accompanist Ill. Music Educators Assn., 1956-66; talent adjudicator Ill. High Sch. Assn., 1957-89, Ill. Elem. Sch. Assn., 1957-89. Pianist Springfield Symphony Orch., 1954-55; author (poet): American Poetry Anthology, 1988, Love's Greatest Treasures, 1989. Dir. choirs Douglas United Meth. Ch., Springfield, 1964-72; choir dir. Unity Ch., Springfield, 1981-85; vol. vocalist Ill. Symphony Chorus, formerly Springfield Symphony Chorus, 1986—. Grantee Carnegie Rsch. Found., 1949, State of Ill., Evanston Twp. High Sch., 1968. Mem. Internat. Platform Assn. (gov., music dir., pianist), Ill. Ret. Tchrs. Assn. Avocations: swimming, writing, sewing, dance, crafts, travel. Home: Springfield, Ill. Died Dec. 8, 2007.

LYLE, AARON KERR, III, financial analyst, consultant; b. Washington, Pa., Feb. 4, 1929; s. Aaron Kerr Jr. and Eunice Dowler (Husted) L.; m. Isabel Tryon, Dec. 29, 1951; children: Catherine Ann, Philip Tryon, William Aaron. AB, Colgate U., 1951; MBA, U. Minn., 1953. With GE, 1953-89, fin. analyst Roanoke, Va., 1970-80, cons. office automation, 1981-89, ret., 1989. Scoutmaster Boy Scouts Am., Roanoke, 1971-92, mem. woodbadge staff, 1983-92. Sgt. U.S. Army, 1953-55. Named Father of Yr., Mchts. Assn. Roanoke, 1977; recipient Silver Beaver award Boy Scouts Am., 1978, Scoutmaster award Nat. Eagle Scout Assn., 1980, Umpire of Yr. award Va. Tennis Assn., 1991. Mem. Edison Club (v.p., bd. dirs. 1958-60), Waynesboro Country Club (fin. com. 1964-66). Republican. Presbyterian. Avocations: backpacking, golf, tennis umpire and referee. Home: Sarasota, Fla. Died May 9, 2008.

LYMAN, DOROTHY GRACE, artist, writer, arts and crafts shop executive; d. William Amasa and Dorothy Harriet (Marsh) Lyman; m. Fay Rosklin Sutton, Aug. 14, 1939 (div. 1958); children: Steven, Sierra, Daniel, Paul, Michael(dec.); m. LaMar Bushman, Jan. 15, 1965 (div. 1972); m. Donald Rex Gardner, Sept. 7, 1974 (div. 1989). Student, Art Instrn., Inc., 1954—56, U. Utah, 1969—72, Ririe Sch. Music, 1973—74. Cert. clothier dir. Clk., Paris Co., 1941—42; welder Everett Pacific Shipyard, 1943—45; substitute tchr. Salt Lake City, 1954—57, 1969—72, Emery County, Utah, 1975—76, Carbon County (Utah) HS, 1977—87; pres., councillor drama and speech, music dir. Young Women's Mut. Improvement Assn., Salt Lake City, 1957—74, Lynndyl, Utah, 1974—78, Spring Glen, Utah, 1980—82. One-woman shows include Ricks Coll., Rexburg, Idaho, Springfield Mus. Art, Utah State Fair, 1967—68, others, exhibited in group shows at Utah State Capitol, Salt Lake City, 1969, also Salt Lake City pub. schs. and malls, others; newspaper corr.: Green Sheet, Sun Adv., Emery County Progress, Millard County Chronicle. Legis. reporter Utah State Women's Legis. Coun., 1974—76; counsellor ward status R.S. and YWMIA, 1957—74; GOP pres. legis. com. mem. at large; chmn. dist. Republican party, 1968—72; election judge, 1959—74; rep. Rep. Presdl. Task Force, 1984—88; pres. Ch. of Jesus Christ of Latter-day Saints Relief Soc., Eldredge Ward, 1964—68; tchr. Sunday Sch., 1957—83; temple worker Salt Lake LDS Temple, 1989—96, Jordan River Temple, 1989—96. Recipient Leadership awards, Ch. of Jesus Christ of Latter-day Saints, 1957—73, Golden Poet award, art awards, Utah State Fair, Salt Lake County Fair, Millard County Fair, Emery County Fair, Intermountain Soc. Artists, others, presdl. citation for outstanding commitment, Pres. Reagan, Pres. George H.W. Bush, Pres. George W. Bush. Mem.: Intermountain Soc. Artists, Sand and Sage Art Group (sec. 1972—74), U.S. Def. Com., Daus. Utah Pioneers (hist. editor 1965—74), Eagles Aux. (chaplain 1977—81). Died Sept. 7, 2008.

LYNCH, MARY PATRICIA, insurance sales executive; b. Chgo., Oct. 31, 1932; d. Thomas and Nora Marie (Cooney) Lavelle; m. Terrence Brons Lynch, Oct. 9, 1954 (div. 1985); children: Patrice M., Michael J., Thomas F., Teresa J. Student, Loyola U., Chgo., 1951-53, U. Calif., Sacramento, 1956, Rollins Coll., 1981, Valencia Community Coll., 1982; cert., Am. Coll., Bryn Mawr, Pa., 1980-86. CLU, chartered fin. cons. Office mgr. Guardian Life Ins. Co. Am., Orlando, Fla., 1971-80; ptnr. Macsay, Lynch & Assocs., Casselberry, Fla., 1980-85; owner, operator Mary "Pat" Lynch, CLU, Chartered Fin. Cons. & Assocs., Longwood, Fla., from 1985. Moderator Life Underwriter Tng. Course, Orlando, 1989-91. Vice pres. Govt. Point Homeowners Assn., 1990, pres., 1991. Mem. Ctrl. Fla. Soc. CLUs and ChFCs (chmn. Huebner Sch. 1983-84, Golden Key chair 1994-95, pub. rels. chair 1995-96), Ctrl. Fla. Women's Life Underwriters (bd. dirs. 1985-91), Women's Life Underwriters Confdn. (bd. dirs. 1985—). Democrat. Roman Catholic. Home: Longwood, Fla. Died Jan. 25, 2008.

LYNCH, MAUREEN, communications executive; b. Jersey City, May 28, 1938; d. Thomas Edward and Mary Margaret (Doust) L. AA with honors, Marymount U., 1957; BA with honors, Rosemont Coll., 1959. Beauty and fashion editor Ladies Home Jour. Mag., 1974-82; pres. Maureen Lynch & Co., Inc., from 1982. Dir. communications grad. sch. bus. adminstr. Fordham U., 1985—; bd. dirs. Blue Hill Troupe, Ltd., 410-57 Corp. Active Friends of Am. Ballet Theater. Recipient awards N.Y. Art Dirs. Club. Mem. Fashion Group Internat. (v.p. exec. com.), Cosmetic Exec. Women, Trends, West Side Tennis Club, Seabright Lawn Tennis and Cricket Club, NOW, Beta Gamma Sigma. Died Dec. 21, 2007.

LYNCH, VIRGINIA (LEE) M., art gallery director, owner; b. Greenville, Tex., May 27, 1915; d. Oscar Roscoe and Catherine Claudine (Cooper) McGaughey; m. Eric Noble Dennard, June 16, 1938 (div. 1960); children: Katherine Fryer, Eric Jr. (dec.); m. William Stang Lynch, May 7, 1962 (dec. 1977); stepchildren: F. Bradley, James B., Mrs. Edward T. Barrett. BA, Baylor U., 1937, MA, 1960; DFA (hon.), R.I. Sch. Design, 1997. Tchr. Tatum (Tex.) High Sch., 1937-38; part-time and substitute tchr. Waco (Tex.) Pub. Schs., Tyler (Tex.) Jr. Coll., 1950-60, Laselle Jr. Coll., Newton, Mass., 1959-60; dir. women Brandeis U., Waltham, Mass., 1960-62; owner Virginia Lynch Gallery, Tiverton, R.I., from 1983. Guest curator Newport Art Mus., 1992-95. Hon. life trustee R.I. Sch. Design, Providence, 1980—; trustee Newport (R.I.) Art Mus., 1987-92, hon. life trustee, 1993—; mem. R.I. State com. Nat. Gallery Women in Arts, 1987—; mem. Town Planning Bd., Little Compton, R.I., 1980-86, Village Improvement Soc., Little Compton, 1963—, Save the Lighthouse Com., Little Compton; deacon United Congl. Ch., Little Compton, 1980-82; bd. dirs. Little Compton Hist. Soc., v.p., 1980-84. Recipient Citizen of Yr. award R.I. Sch. Design, 1983, State of the Arts award R.I. State Coun. on the Arts, 1992, Best Gallery award R.I. Monthly, 1992-94. Mem. Little Compton Garden Club (pres. 1975-77), Sakonnet Golf Club, Brown U. Faculty Club. Avocations: gardening, hiking, visiting museums, studios, and galleries. Home: Little Compton, RI. Died Dec. 6, 2007.

LYNN, GORDON A., lawyer; b. Chatsworth, Calif., June 16, 1958; BA, U. Md., 1980; JD, Whittier Coll., 1985. Bar: Md., Washington. Assoc. Meyers, Young & Grove, P.A., Hagerstown, Md., 1989-90; ptnr. Metzner & Lynn, Hagerstown, 1990-94; pvt. practice Hagerstown, from 1994. Scout master Boy Scouts Am., Hagerstown, 1968—. Capt. U.S. Army, 1985-89. Mem. Nat. Assn. Criminal Def. Lawyers, Md. State Bar Assn., Washington county Criminal Def. Bar Assn. Republican. Methodist. Avocation: golf. Died Sept. 10, 2007.

LYONS, JOHN LEO, management educator, consultant; b. Hartford, Conn., Feb. 22, 1923; s. John and Sarah (Muldowney) L.; m. Nancy Kelly, Nov. 8, 1952; children: Margaret, Michael, Anne. BS, Yale U., 1944; MBA, Northwestern U., 1948; ABD, London U. Grad. Sch. Bus. Registered marine engr. Internat. mgmt. cons. Cresap, McCormick & Paget, NYC, 1948-54; mng. dir. PDI sub. Time Inc., London, 1954-68; pres., chief exec. officer PDI world wide sub. Time Inc., NYC, 1968-71; pvt. practice internat. mgmt. cons. London, 1972-77; prof. internat. mgmt. Pace U., Pleasantville, N.Y., 1978-86. Cons. mgmt. internat. projects, 1972-86. Served to lt. USNR, 1943-46, PTO. Mem. Acad. Internat. Bus. Clubs: Yale (N.Y.C.); Saville (London). Home: Greenwich, Conn. Died Apr. 16, 2008.

LYOU, KEITH WEEKS (KAY LYOU), editor; b. Los Angeles, Aug. 2, 1930; d. Howard Keith Weeks and Ruth Manson (Day) Wood; m. Joseph Lyou, Mar. 26, 1955 (div. 1972); children: Tracy Ann, Joseph Keith. BS, Lindenwood Coll., 1977, MA, 1979. Cert. cmty. coll. instr., Calif. Editl. asst. t. Annals of Biomed. Engring., Culver City, Calif., 1971-76; exec. asst. Biomed. Engring. Soc., Culver City, 1974-81; editor Inkslingers, Culver City, from 1974. Editor biotechnology lab. UCLA, 1974-81, campus advisor theses and dissertations, 1983-86; exec. asst. Biomed. Engring. Soc., Culver City, 1974-81; instr. adult sch. Culver City Unified Sch. Dist., 1979-81. Mng. editor Am. Intra-Ocular Implant Soc. Jour., Santa Monica, 1982-83. Trustee Culver City Bd. Edn., 1981-89, pres. bd., 1987; counselor Adv. Ctr. for Edn. and Career Counseling, Santa Monica, Calif., 1981-82; mem. project area com. Project and Redevel., Culver City, 1975—, vice chair 1975-77, 85, chair 1979-82; bd. dirs. Culver City Foster Children's Assn., 1981-90; mem. Culver City Coun. PTA (hon. svc. award 1988), sch. attendance rev. bd., Culver City/Beverly Hills Sch. Dists., 1989—, school-age parent and infant devel. adv. com., 1989—, strategic planning com, 1989—; mem. Culver City Youth Health Ctr. Adv. Com., 1986—, Pepperdine U. Cmty. Adv. Com. Tchr. Edn., 1989—; vice chair gen. adv. com. revision of Culver City gen. plan, 1991—; chair Culver City Redevel. and Preservation Com., 1997—. Recipient Citizen Recognition award Culver City C. of C., 1986, Cmty. Arch. (honorable Gwen Moore) 47th Dist. award, 1994, Women of Excellence award Culver City Youth Health Ctr., 1994, Woman of Yr. award Culver City Soroptimist Internat., 1994-95. Mem. LWV, Bus. and Profl. Women, Biomed. Engring. Soc., Calif. Elected Women's Assn. for Edn. and Rsch., UCLA Grad. Students Assn. (outstanding adminstrv. award 1970). Democrat. Avocations: gardening, writing. Home: Culver City, Calif. Died Nov. 6, 2007.

LYST, JOHN HENRY, retired editor; b. Princeton, Ind., Mar. 28, 1933; s. John Henry and Marguerite (McQuinn) L.; m. Sharon Long, Dec. 29, 1956; children: Shannon M., Bettina A., Audrey K., Ellen K. AB, Ind. U., 1955. Reporter Indpls. Star, 1956-67, bus. columnist, 1967—79, editor editl. page, 1979—2000. Corr. NY Times, 1964-2000 Served with AUS, 1956-59. Mem. Indpls. Press Club (pres. 1968, bd. dirs. 1969), Sigma Delta Chi. Home: Indianapolis, Ind. Died June 23, 2009.

MACDONALD, DAVID ROBERT, lawyer, former federal official; b. Chgo., Nov. 1, 1930; s. James Wear and Frances Esther (Wine) M.; m. Verna Joy Odell, Feb. 17, 1962; children: Martha, Emily, David, Rachel, Rebecca. BS, Cornell U., 1952; JD, U. Mich., 1955. Bar: Ill. 1955, Mich. 1955, D.C. 1983. Assoc. Kirkland, Ellis, Hodson, Chaffetz & Masters, Chgo., 1957-62, ptnr., 1962, Baker & McKenzie LLP, Chgo., 1962-74, 77-81; asst. sec. for enforcement, ops. & tariff affairs US Dept. Treasury, Washington, 1974-76; under sec. Dept. Navy, US Dept Def., 1976-77; dep. Trade Rep. Exec. Office of the Pres., 1981-83; ptnr. Baker & McKenzie LLP, Chgo., 1983-96. Bd. dirs. Mestek, Inc. (N.Y. Stock Exch.). Pres. David R. Macdonald Found., 1996-2008 Mem. ABA, D.C. Bar Assn., Chgo. Assn. Commerce and Industry (bd. dirs. 1977-81), Order of Coif, Econ. Club (Chgo.), Cosmos Club (Washington), Grolier Club (N.Y.C.). Home: Bethesda, Md. Died Nov. 28, 2008.

MACDONALD, WILLIAM EDGAR, JR., toxicologist, consultant; b. Columbus, Ohio, Nov. 21, 1916; s. William Edgar Sr. and Helen Enther (Acton) MacD.; m. Sarah Roberta Butler, July 28, 1940. AS, Emory Jr. Coll., 1937; BA, Emory U., 1939; MS, U. Fla., 1951; PhD, U. Miami, 1961. Diplomate Am. Bd. Indsl. Hygiene, Am. Bd. Toxicology. Instr. chemistry and physics Emory (Ga.) U., 1938-39; toxicologist Biscayne Chem. Labs., Miami, 1939-40, Fla. State Bd. Health, Jacksonville, 1941-55; instr. toxicology U. Miami Med. and Grad. Schs., Coral Gables, Fla., 1955-62; asst. prof. toxicology and pharmacology U. Miami, Coral Gables, Fla., 1962-75; toxicologist Tracor Jitco, Rockville, Md., 1975-83; toxicology cons. Jacksonville, from 1984. Contbr. articles to profl. jours. Lt. (j.g.) USNR, 1942-45. Scholar Emory U. Alumni Assn., 1935-37; grant-in-aid USPHS, 1949-50; tchg. fellow U. Miami, 1957-61. Mem. Sigma Xi (pres. Jacksonville br. 85 1985-86). Democrat. Baptist. Avocation: gardening. Died June 7, 2008.

MACE, VERA CHAPMAN, retired marriage counselor, writer, educator; b. Leeds, Eng., Jan. 24, 1902; d. George Henry and Caroline (Hodgson) Chapman; m. David Robert Mace, July 26, 1933; 2 children. Diploma in teaching, Bingley Coll., Eng., 1923; MA, Drew U., 1943; LHD (hon.), Alma Coll., 1977; D in Social Sci. (hon.), Brigham Young U., 1977. Exec. dir. Girls' League, Eng.; cons. marriage and family life World Council of Chs., worldwide; co-founder Assn. Couples in Marriage Enrichment, Winston-Salem, 1973. Author: (with David R. Mace) Marriage: East and West, 1960, The Soviet Family, 1963, Sex, Love and Marriage in the Caribbean, 1965, Sex, Marriage and the Family in the Pacific, 1969, We Can Have Better Marriages-If We Really Want Them, 1974, Men, Women and God, 1976, Marriage Enrichment in the Church, 1976, Toward Better Marriages, 1976, How to Have a Happy Marriage, 1977, What's Happening to Clergy Marriages?, 1980, Letters to a Retired Couple-Marriage in the Later Years, 1985, The Sacred Flame: Christian Marriage Through the Ages, 1986, When the Honeymoon's Over, 1988, (with others) 365 Meditations for Women, 1989, (with C. and D. Avp) Preparing the Family for Living in the Twenty-first Century, 1994. Recipient citation Merill-Palmer Inst. Human Devel. and Family Life, 1968, Disting. Contbn. award Am. Assn. Marriage and Family Counselors, 1975, Disting. Service to Families award Nat. Council on Family Relations, 1975, citation N.C. Family Life Council, 1975, Richard B. Boren Whole Person award State of N.C., 1981, 1st Ann. award Nat. Symposium on Family Strengths, 1983, Irvin V. Sperry award N.C. Family Life Council, 1983, Disting. Service award Christian Life Commn. Bapt. Gen. Conv. Tex., 1983, leadership award Am. Assn. for Marriage and Family Therapy, 1984; elected to Groves Acad. for Disting. Family Life Specialists, 1984; recipient Internat. Yr. of the Family award UN, 1994. Mem. Assn. Couples in Marriage Enrichment (Disting. Service award 1976). Methodist, mem. Soc. of Friends. Avocation: needlepoint. Home: Black Mountain, NC. Died July 22, 2008.

MAC FADDIN, JEAN FRANCES, microbiologist, writer; b. Dover, Del., Oct. 20, 1931; d. John Willis and Dorothy (Roe) Mac F. AA, Hartnell Jr. Coll., 1953; BA in Med. Tech., San Jose State U., 1967; MS in Microbiology, Incarnate Word Coll., 1970. Enlisted U.S. Army, 1955, advanced through grades to sgt. 1st class, 1968; med. lab. technologist U.S. Army Hosps., Ft. McClellan, Ala. and Landstuhl, Fed. Republic Germany, 1955-68; instr. microbiology Acad. Health Scis, U.S. Army, Ft. Sam Houston, Tex., 1968-75; ret. U.S. Army, 1975; free-lance scientific writer microbiology Salinas, Calif., from 1975. Author: Biochemical Tests for Identification of Medical Bacteria, 1975, 2d rev. edit., 1980, Media for Isolation-Cultivation Identification-Maintenance of Medical Bacteria, 1985. Mem. Registry of Med. Technologists Am. Soc. Clin. Pathologists (lic.), Nat. Registry Microbiologists Specialists Microbiologists (lic.), Clin. Lab. Technologists Calif. (lic.), Am. Soc. Microbiology. Republican. Lutheran. Home: Salinas, Calif. Died May 30, 2008.

MACFARLANE, MALCOLM HARRIS, physicist, educator; b. Brechin, Scotland, May 22, 1933; came to U.S., 1956; s. Malcolm P. and Mary (Harris) M.; m. Eleanor Carman, May 30, 1957; children: Douglas, Kenneth, Sheila, Christine. MA, U. Edinburgh, Scotland, 1955; PhD, U. Rochester, 1960. Research asso. Argonne (Ill.) Nat. Lab.,

1959-60; asst. prof. physics U. Rochester, 1960-61; asso. physicist Argonne Nat. Lab., 1961-68, sr. physicist, 1968-80; prof. physics U. Chgo., 1968-80, Ind. U., Bloomington, 1980—2003, prof. emeritus, 2003—08. Vis. fellow All Souls Coll., Oxford (Eng.) U., 1966-67; mem. nuclear scis. adv. com. Dept. Energy-NSF, 1983-87; cons. Ency. Brit. Contbr. articles of theoretical nuclear physics to profl. jours. Guggenheim fellow physics, 1966-67; Alexander von Humboldt Found. sr. scientist award, 1985. Fellow Am. Phys. Soc.; mem. Nuclear Physics sect. Am. Phys. Soc. (mem. exec. com. 1969-71) Home: Bloomington, Ind. Died Sept. 25, 2008.

MACHI, RITA MAE, retired obstetrical nurse; b. Riverside, Calif., May 7, 1927; d. Lambert Joseph Sr. and Helen Ann Ninteman; m. Rocco Alfred Machi (dec.); m. Salvatore Alfred Machi, Dec. 27, 1957 (dec.); children: Rosemary Machi Gunsett, Terrie Machi Faust, Judith Machi Daviau. Attended, Riverside Jr. Coll., Calif., 1944, attended, 1947, U. Calif., Berkeley, 1944—46; diploma in nursing, Mercy Coll. Nursing, San Diego, 1951; BA in Nursing Edn. and Adminstrn. summa cum laude, San Jose State Coll., Calif., 1955; postgrad., St. Anselm's Coll., Manchester, NH, 1958, U. Calif., San Diego, 1965—70, San Diego State U., 1968—70. RN Calif.; cert. tchr. Calif. Entomoloyg lab. asst. U. Calif., Riverside and Berkeley, 1944—46; charge nurse Golden Hill Convalescent Hosp., San Diego, 1955—56; clin. instr. Sacred Heart Hosp., Manchester, NH, 1956; staff nurse Elliott Hosp., Manchester, 1957—60; staff/charge nurse Dr.'s Hosp., San Diego, 1960—64; charge nurse Salvation Army Door of Hope, San Diego, 1964—70, asst. dir., 1970—75, dir. nursing, 1975—80; instr. childbirth preparation, child devel. CC Dist., San Diego, 1975—90; ret., 1990. Asst. editor: various sch. newspapers, newsletters; contbr. articles to profl. publs. Treas., reference dir. Parenthood Coun., San Diego, 1971—75; pres., sec., co-author bylaws Profl. Tchg. Prepared Childbirth, San Diego, 1970—80; mem., co-author bylaws Perinatal Coalition, San Diego, 1970—74; mem. Child Abuse Coun., San Diego, 1972—73; fundraiser Italian-Cath. Fedn., San Diego, 1970—80. Scholar, Panhellenic Soc., 1944—45. Roman Cath. Avocations: reading, history, science fiction, cooking, music. Home: San Diego, Calif. Died July 10, 2008.

MACHLUP, STEFAN, physics educator; b. Vienna, July 1, 1927; came to U.S., 1936; s. Fritz and Mitzi (Herzog) M.; m. Toni Berger, July 28, 1961 (div. 1966); children: Peter Ridwan, Eric Roland; m. Marilyn Ruth Hamre, Nov. 20, 1971. BA, Swathmore Coll., Pa., 1947; MS, Yale U., 1949, PhD, 1952. Asst. in instruction Yale U., New Haven, 1949-51; rsch. asst. Woods Hole (Mass.) Oceanographic Inst., 1950, 51; AEC fellow U. Cambridge, Eng., 1951-52; mem. tech. staff Bell Telephone Labs., Murray Hill, N.J., 1952-53; rsch. assoc. U. Ill., Urbana, 1953-55; sci. officer U. Amsterdam, Netherlands, 1955-56; from asst. to assoc. prof. Case Western Res. U., Cleve., from 1956. Cons. Ednl. Svcs., Inc.; mem. commn. of scholars Ill. Bd. of Higher Edn., 1978—; cons., evaluator North Cen. Assn., 1973—. Author: Physics, 1988; contbr. articles to profl. jours. Officer AAUP. With USNR, 1945-46. Fellow AAAS; mem. Am. Phys. Soc., Am. Assn. Physics Tchrs., Cleve. Chamber Music Soc., Sigma Xi. Home: Cleveland, Ohio. Died Aug. 16, 2008.

MACKALL, HENRY CLINTON, lawyer; b. Ft. Lauderdale, Fla., Apr. 6, 1927; s. Douglass Sorrel, Jr. and Mildred (Parker) M.; m. Mary Margaret Sullivan, June 21, 1952 (dec. Dec. 23, 2002); children: Caroline Clark, Nancy Sorrel, Lucy Parker BA, U. Va., 1950, LLB, 1952. Bar: Va. 1951. Ptnr. Mackall, Mackall & Gibb, P.C. and predecessors, Fairfax, Va., from 1952. Asst. commr. accounts Fairfax County (Va.), 1963-2006; spl. commr. in chancery for audit functions for Cir. Ct. Fairfax County, 1976-2006; substitute judge Fairfax County Ct., Juvenile and Domestic Rels. Ct. Fairfax County, 1964-69 Trustee Fairfax Hosp. Assn., 1966-75; with Va. State Bar Client Security Fund Bd., 1976-88, chmn., 1977-78; past bd. dirs. The McLean Bank, F&M Bank, No. Va.; dir. Chain Bridge Bank. Served with AUS, 1945-46 Fellow Am. Coll. Trusts & Estate Counsel, Am. Coll. Real Estate Lawyers, Va. Law Found.; mem. ABA, Va. Bar Assn. (regional v.p. 1963-64), Fairfax County Bar Assn. (pres. 1966-67), Hist. Soc. Fairfax County (pres. 1970-72), Jamestowne Soc. (gov. 1995-97), River Bend Golf and Country Club (Gt. Falls, Va., pres. 1967-68), Georgetown Assembly, Washington, Orgn. Vestry St. Francis Episcopal Ch. Great Falls, Va. Democrat. Episcopalian. Home: Mc Lean, Va. Died July 7, 2009.

MACKAY, NEIL DUNCAN, plastics company executive, consultant; b. Chelsea, Mass., Nov. 5, 1931; s. Allan Foster and Helen May (Smith) MacKay; m. Marcia Ann McCarthy, Aug. 22, 1953 (dec. 1979); children: Duncan, Jerry, Alan, Neil, Bonnie; m. Beverly J. Burke, May 31, 1991. BSBA, Northeastern U., Boston, 1954. Gen. mgr. Plastic Molding Corp., Newtown, Conn., 1954-67; market specialist Chem. div. Uniroyal, NYC, 1967-70; project mgr. Colt Ind. Korean Project, NYC, 1970-76; pres. Automatic Injection Molding Corp., Berkeley Heights, NJ, 1976-87, Diamond Mgmt. Cons., Inc., Winchester, NH, from 1988. Bd. dir. Frazier & Son, Inc., Lor-Tech Plastics, Inc. Author: Korean Plastics, 1973. Mem. Rep. Nat. Com., Washington, 1986—92. Recipient Outstanding Performance award, Ministry Nat. Def. Republic of Korea, 1974. Mem.: Plastic Pioneers Assn., Soc. Plastics Engrs. (sec. 1963—70, treas. 1983—86), Am. Profl. Capt.'s Assn., Scottish-Am. Cultural Soc., Am. Yacht Club, Stuyvesant Yacht Club, St. Andrews Soc. N.Y. Republican. Presbyterian. Avocation: sailing. Home: Winchester, NH. Died Apr. 13, 2008.

MACKENZIE, JOHN, retired oil industry executive; b. 1919; BS, N.Y. U., 1948. Accountant S.Am. Devel. Co., NYC, 1938-41; financial comptroller French Oil Ind. Agy.-Groupment D'Achat des Carburants, N.Y., 1946-53; v.p., treas. George Hall Corp., 1954-56; asst. treas. Am. Petrofina, Inc., 1956-61, sec., 1961-64, v.p., sec., 1964-68, sr. v.p., sec., 1968-84; pres. Am. Petrofina Holding Co., 1968—84; ret., 1984. Decorated comdr. Order of Crown (Belgium) Died Mar. 5, 2009.

MACKIE, JOHN C., b. Toronto, Canada, June 1, 1920; Highway dir., Mich., 1957—65; US rep. Mich., 1965—67; former pres. Mackie Eng Co. Recipient Man Yr. award, Engr. News Record, 1962, Am. Rd. Builders Assn., 1963, Disting. Svc. award, Mich. State. U., 1963, Man Yr. award, Nat. Limestone Inst., 1965. Mem.: SAE, America Rd. Builders Assn. (v.p. 1964), America Assn. Highway Ofcls (pres. 1963). Democrat. Episcopalian. Died Mar. 5, 2008.

MACLEAN, ALAN SCOTT, marketing executive; b. Providence, Mar. 29, 1940; s. Arthur and Hazel (Brown) MacL.; m. Brenda Burgess, June 23, 1962 (div. 1981); children: Michael Keith, Karen Lynne, Marilyn Ann. BA in Bus., U. Vt., 1962. Mgr. internat. sales dept. Eastman Kodak Co., Rochester, N.Y., mgr. advt. dept., 1966-81; mktg. dir. Bausch & Lomb, St. Petersburg, Fla., 1981-84; v.p. mktg. Alderman Co., St. Petersburg, 1984-88, CamGroup, St. Petersburg, from 1988. Author: God Please Help, 1988, Oh God What Next, 1990. 1st lt. USAF, 1962-66. Republican. Avocations: camping, tennis. Home: Seminole, Fla. Died May 22, 2008.

MACLEAN, HUGH CAMERON, bridge professional, international bridge master; b. Mpls., Feb. 24, 1938; s. Hugh Cameron and Clare Amelia (McClelland) MacL.; m. Mary Anne Nelson, May 22, 1991. Represented U.S. in Open Pair Olympiad, Las Palmas, 1974. Nat. awards include 2d pl. Advanced Sr. Masters, NAC, 1962, 1st pl. Life Master Mens Pairs, 1970, 1st pl. Men's Team, 1974, 2d pl. Open Pairs, 1974, 2d pl. Blue Ribbon Pairs, 1975, 2d pl. Vanderbilt, 1977, 1st pl. Golden Cup Masters Pairs, 1978; regional awards include Mid. Am.-Can. Teams, 1962, 64, 65, Mens, 1963, Mixed Pairs, 1965, Masters, 1966, Gopher Mens Pairs, 1966, 71, Gopher Knockouts, 1967, 71, Can. Prairie Masters, 1970, Champagne Mens Pairs, 1970, Pheasant Knockouts, 1970, 72, 75, Tri Unit Mixed Pairs, 1971, Can. Prairie Mens, 1972, Can. Prairie Knockouts, 1972, Iowa Knockouts, 1972, Gopher Master Pairs, 1973, Iowa Mens Pairs, 1973, Tri Unit Knockouts, 1974, Can. Prairie Knockouts, 1975, Can. Prairie Open, 1975, Can. Prairie Masters, 1975, Pheasant Mens Pairs, 1975, Iowa Masters, 1975, Summer Open Teams, 1975, Dist. 15 Open Teams, 1975, Mo. Valley Knockouts, 1975, Thunderbay Knockouts, 1975, Thunderbay Swiss Teams, 1975, Thunderbay Masters Pairs, 1975, Cambrian Shield Open Teams, 1976, Can. Prairie Knockouts, 1976, Can. Prairie Open Pairs, 1976, Can. Prairie Mens Swiss Teams, 1976, Pitts. Open Teams, 1976, Pitts. Knockouts, 1976, Great Lakes Masters, 1976, Motor City Masters, 1976, So. Calif. Knockouts, 1976, Gopher Swiss Teams, 1976, Iowa Open Teams, 1976, Dist. 8 Open Pairs, 1977, Dist. 8 Masters Pairs, 1977, Tri Unit Mens Swiss Teams, 1977, Intermountain Open Pairs, 1977, Pacific N.W. Knockouts, 1977, Polar Knockouts, 1977, Bellville Masters Pairs, 1977, Bellville Open Pairs, 1977, Puget Sound Knockouts, 1977, Dist. 20 Knockouts, 1977, Cambrian Shields Knockouts, 1977, 83, Ctrl. States Winter Open Teams, 1977, Ctrl. States Men's Swiss Teams, 1978, Mpls. Knockouts, 1978, Champagne Open Pairs, 1978, 79, Dist. 14 Knockouts, 1983, Cambrian Shield Open Teams, 1983, Madison Flight A Swiss Tams, 1983, Des Moines Knockouts, 1983, Canadian Prairie Open Pairs, 1984, Dist. Grand Nat. Teams, 1986, 87, 88, Canadian Prairie Men's, 1986, Ctrl. States Open Pairs, 1987, Gopher Masters Pairs, 1988, 89, Fargo Swiss Tams, 1990, Winnipeg Flighted Open, 1992, Winnipeg Flighted Team, 1992, Omaha Regional KO, 1993, Gopher Flighted KO, 1993, Green Bay Regional KO, 1993, Cedar Rapids Regional KO, 1994. Home: Gonzales, Tex. Died Apr. 17, 2008.

MADDALENA, ROSALIE ANNE, retired educator; b. Grove City, Pa., Sept. 15, 1946; d. Albert Michael Maddalena and Maria Sepe. BS, Grove City Coll., Pa., 1968; MS, Ea. Mich. U., 1972. Bus. edn. tchr. Riverside H.S., Dearborn Heights, Mich., 1968-85; office tech. tchr. Henry Ford C.C., Dearborn, 1972-84; bus., social studies tchr. Crestwood H.S., Dearborn Heights, 1985-98, ret., 1998. Instr. CPS exam reviewer Schoolcraft Coll., Livonia, Mich., 1982-87; bus., social studies dept. head Crestwood H.S., 1987-95, advisor nat. honor soc., 1985-92, curriculum coun., 1986-95, class sponsor, 1992-96. Co-author: (textbook/workbook) Microcomputer Applications, 1989. Recipient Spl. Tribute State of Mich. Legislature, 1998. Mem. Delta Pi Epsilon. Roman Catholic. Avocations: historic preservation, films, party planning. Home: Philipsburg, Pa. Died May 7, 2008.

MADDOX, JULIE, nursing administrator; b. Niles, Mich., May 11, 1957; d. John Fabian and Marie Lydia (Butler) M.; children: Ross, Ryen. ADN, Southwestern Mich. Coll., 1977; BSN, Ind. U., South Bend, 1982; MS in Nursing Adminstrn., La. State U., New Orleans, 1987. RN, Ind., La.; cert. CPR instr., ACLS instr. Staff nurse ICU, coronary care and open heart recovery Meml. Hosp., South Bend, 1978-81, instr. staff devel., 1981-83, asst. head nurse ICU, 1983, head nurse cardiac intermediate unit, 1983-85; head nurse surg. ICU, Pendleton Meml. Meth. Hosp., New Orleans, 1985-88; assoc. dir. nursing svc. Mercy Hosp., New Orleans, 1988, acting dir. nursing svc., 1988-89, asst. adminstr. nursing svc., from 1989. Named One of Great 100 Nurses, New Orleans Dist. Nurses Assn., 1987. Mem. New Orleans Assn. Nurse Execs., Sigma Theta Tau. Home: Richardson, Tex. Died Apr. 2, 2008.

MADDOX, MARTHA LACEY GARDNER, artist; b. Birmingham, Ala., Jan. 5, 1926; d. Searcy Preston and Willard Morris Gardner; m. Steve Wilson Maddox, Mar. 3, 1946; children: Steve Wilson Jr., James Wayne, David Worthington. B in Applied Art, Ala. Poly. Inst. (now Auburn U.), 1947. Cert. tchr. Ala., Fla. Art prof. U. Ala., Tuscaloosa, 1947, 1948; H.S. and elem. sch. tchr. Ala. Sch. Bd., Flomaton, 1949—51; tchr. Byrneville (Fla.) Elem., 1951—52. Exhibitions include Vincent Price Touring Exhbn., Golden Heritage Exhbn., Cheaha Exhbn., Old Mobile Exhbn., Dauphin Island Exhbn., Art for Art's Sake, Wiregrass Mus. Art, Outstanding Artists S.E., Met. Mus. Art, High Mus. Art, Fine Arts Mus. of the South, Birmingham Mus. Art, Ea. Shore Art Ctr., Alpha Omicron Pi scholar, 1947. Mem.: Exptl. Artists Ala., Pastel Soc. Am., United Pastelists Am., Oil Pastel Soc., Watercolor Soc. Ala., Ea. Shore Art Assn., Mobile Art Assn., Nat. Women in the Arts, Malone Painters, Panama Art Assn., Hoover Art Assn., Dothan-Wiregrass Art League. Methodist. Died Feb. 7, 2008.

MADL, ALFRED WILLIAM, industrial designer, lecturer, consultant, artist; b. Allhau, Burgenland, Austria, Apr. 17, 1923; came to U.S., 1931; s. Joseph and Theresa (Binder) M.; m. Dorothy Anne Kroening, June 19, 1954; children: Margot Anne and Marsha Lynne (twins), Michelle Jean. Student, Northwestern U., Chgo., 1941-43; diploma in indsl. design, Art Inst. Chgo., 1949. Indsl. design Hoosier-Cardinal Corp., Evansville, Ind., 1949-50; indsl. designer, engr. Nesco, Inc., Milw., 1950-52; dir. indsl. design Oster Corp., Milw., 1952-87; indsl. design cons. A. Madl-Design, Glendale, Wis., from 1987. Panel mem. industry round table Appliance Mfg. mag., 1970; mem. adv. coun. Appliance Exhibit and Conf., Chgo., 1970-71, mem. conf. adv. com., 1971-72 Contbr. articles to Appliance Mfr., Plastics Design Forum, Precision Metal, also others; products exhibited at major nat. art mus. Sgt. USAAF, 1943-45, ETO. Recipient gold medal for electric blender design Brno (Czechoslovakia) Trade Fair, 1974. Mem. Indsl. Designers Soc. Am., Oster Mgmt. Club (pres. 1983-84, plaque 1985). Lutheran. Achievements include over 90 patents in design and mechanical categories in U.S., Can., Mex., P.R., Brazil, Uruguay, Venezuela, Colombia, France, Portugal, Spain, Italy, Fed. Republic Germany, Switzerland, Austria, Norway, Sweden, Czechoslovakia, Gt. Britain, Australia. Died Sept. 1, 2007.

MADOW, LEO, psychiatrist, educator; b. Cleve., Oct. 18, 1915; s. Solomon Martin and Anna (Meyers) Madow; m. Jean Antoinette Weisman, Apr. 16, 1942 (dec.); children: Michael, Robert; m. Barbara N. Young, Dec. 26, 2000. AB, Western Res. U., 1937, MD, 1942; MA, Ohio State U., 1938. Diplomate Am. Bd. Psychiatry and Neurology. Intern Phila. Gen. Hosp., 1942-43; resident Phila. Gen. Hosp., Jefferson Hosp., Inst. Pa. Hosp., 1943-46; practice medicine specializing in psychiatry Phila., 1948—2009; prof., chmn. dept. neurology Med. Coll. Pa., Phila., 1958-65, prof., chmn. dept. psychiatry and neurology, 1965-70, prof., chmn. dept. psychiatry, 1970-81, clin. prof. psychiatry Hershey Med. Ctr., 1982—2009; sr. cons. psychiatry Inst. Pa. Hosp., Phila., 1975—2009. Tng. analyst, past pres. Phila. Psychoanalytic Inst.; past pres., mem. med. staff Inst. Pa. Hosp. Author: Anger, 1972, Love: How to Understand and Enjoy It, 1983, Guilt: How to Recognize and Enjoy It, 1989; editor: Dreams, 1970, Sensory Deprivation, 1970, Psychomimetic Drugs, 1971, Integration of Child Psychiatry with Basic Resident Program, 1975. Served to capt. US Army, 1944—46. Named Outstanding Educator, Am. Med. Coll. Pa., 1972. Fellow: ACP, Am. Coll. Psychoanalysts (pres. 1989—90, Laughlin award 1990), Am. Coll. Psychiatrists, Am. Psychiat. Assn. (life), Phila. Psychiat. Soc. (past pres., Lifetime Achievement award 1991); mem.: Phila. Psychoanalytic Soc. (past pres.), Am. Neurol. Assn., Am. Psychoanalytic Assn., Phi Soc., Alpha Omega Alpha. Died June 1, 2009.

MAHAFFEY, KATHRYN ROSE, risk management consultant, former federal agency administrator; b. Johnstown, Pa., Dec. 24, 1943; d. William T. and Harriet L. Mahaffey; m. Samuel Nelson Kramer, June 1977 (div. 1984); children: Harriet Mahaffey Kramer, Charles Herbert Kramer; m. David Ernst Jacobs, Oct. 13, 1996. BS in Nutritional Sci., Pa. State U., 1965; MA in Nutritional Sci., Rutgers U., 1966, PhD in Nutritional Sci., 1968. Sr. environ. scientist Nat. Inst. Environ. Health Sci., Research Triangle Park, NC, 1987-93; sr. environ. scientist Nat. Ctr. for Environ. Assessment EPA, Cin., 1993-99, br. chief, 1983-87, dir. divsn. exposure assessment Office of Prevention, Pesticides, Toxic Substances, Washington, 1999—2008. Asst. prof. dept. pathology U. N.C. Sch. Medicine, Chapel Hill, 1969-71. Editor: Dietary and Environmental Lead: Human Health Effects, 1985, (with others) Clinical Effects of Environmental Chemicals, 1989; contbg. author books and reports; author articles. Recipient Arnold J. Lehman award, Soc. Toxicology, 2006, Bronze medal for Commendable Svc.,

EPA, 2007. Mem. Am. Soc. for Nutritional Scis., Am. Soc. for Clin. Nutrition, Soc. for Internat. Nutrition Rsch. Home: Washington, DC. Died June 2, 2009.

MAHANES, MICHAEL WAYNE, organizational development executive; b. Fulton, Mo., Jan. 18, 1956; s. Paul W. and Betty Catherine (Kelsey) M.; m. Cynthia Anne Ward, June 13, 1981; children: Catherine Anne, Michael Wayne Jr., Ian Ward. BFA, Westminister Coll., 1977; MSc, Leicester U., 2002. Tchr. William Woods Coll., Fulton, 1978—79; dir. audio-visual studio Daniel/Flour Internat., Fulton, 1979—81; dir. audio-visual dept. and Lifelong Learning Ctr., tng. coord. MEMC Electronics Materials Co., Spartanburg, SC, 1981—98; corp. dir. orgnl. devel. Lockwood Greene, CH2M Hill, Spartanburg, from 1998. Mem. com. Malcolm Baldrige Nat. Quality Award; dir. Skills Enhancement Ctr., Next Step Program, Life-Long Learning Ctr.; master trainer Zenger Miller; team interventions, 1980—, team building, 1979—; cons. in field, 1982—. Writer, dir., cameraman (video) Collective Works of Michael Mahanes, 1979—; writer, editor over 500 videos; co-inventor electronic data gathering indsl. problem solving method, 1981. Pre-sch. tchr. Southside Bapt. Ch., Spartanburg, 1982—; pre-sch. tchr. Southside Bapt. Ch., Spartanburg, 1986—, deacon, chmn. broadcast sound; active ARC; mem. Edn. Consensus Project, 1992—; cubmaster Cub Scout Pack 3. Mem. Am. Soc. Tng. and Devel., Internat. TV Assn., Carolina Soc. Tng. and Devel. Republican. Avocation: old movies. Home: Moore, SC. Died May 24, 2008.

MAHER, BRENDAN ARNOLD, retired psychology educator, editor; b. Widnes, Eng., Oct. 31, 1924; came to US, 1955; s. Thomas F. and Agnes (Power) M.; m. Winifred Barbara Brown, Aug. 27, 1952; children: Rebecca, Thomas, Nicholas, Liam, Niall. BA with honours, U. Manchester, Eng., 1950; MA, Ohio State U., 1951, PhD, 1954; student, U. Ill. Med. Sch., 1952-53; AM (hon.), Harvard, 1972; DPhil (hon.), U. Copenhagen, 1998. Diplomate Am. Bd. Examiners in Profl. Psychology. Psychologist Her Majesty's Prison, Wakefield, England, 1954-55; instr. Ohio State U., Ohio, 1955-56; asst. prof. Northwestern U., 1956-58; asso. prof. La. State U., La., 1958-60; lectr. Harvard, 1960-64; chmn. Ctr. Rsch. Personality, 1962-64; prof. U. Wis., 1964-67, 71-72; vis. fellow U. Copenhagen, 1966-67, vis. fellow and rsch. scientist, 1979, 96-98; prof. psychology Brandeis U., 1967-72; dean Brandeis U. (Grad. Sch.), 1969-71, dean faculty, 1971-72; E. C. Henderson prof. psychology Harvard U., 1983-99, E.C. Henderson rsch. prof., 1999—2004, E.C. Henderson prof. emeritus, from 2004, prof., from 1972, chmn. dept. psychology and social relations, 1973-78, chmn. dept. psychology, 1987-89, dean Grad. Sch. Arts and Scis., 1989-92; assoc. psychologist McLean Hosp., Belmont, Mass., 1968-77, psychologist, 1977-84; prof. emeritus, from 2004. Cons. in medicine Peter Bent Brigham Hosp., Boston, 1977-85; cons. in psychology Mass. Gen. Hosp., 1977-2002. Author: Principles of Psychopathology, 1966, Introduction to Research in Psychopathology, 1970, A Passage to Sword Beach, 1996; co-editor: National Research Council: Rsch. Doctorate Programs in the United States, 1995; editor Progress in Exptl. Personality Rsch., 1964-87, Jour. Cons. and Clin. Psychology, 1972-78; cons. editor Rev. Personality and Social Psychology, Clin. Psychology Rev. Served with Brit. Royal Navy, 1943-47. Recipient Zubin award for rsch. in psychopathology, 1998. Fellow AAAS, Am. Psychol. Soc.; mem. Brit. Psychol. Assn. (chartered psychologist UK), Soc. Rsch. in Psychopathology (pres. 1985-87), Phi Beta Kappa. Home: Durham, NC. Died Mar. 17, 2009.

MAHMOUD, BEN, artist, art educator; b. Charleston, W.Va., Oct. 6, 1935; s. Ben Mahmoud and Ina (Lilly) Mahmoud-Waybright; m. Wendy Kravit, Aug. 1987; children: Jermy, Amanda, Kassandra. Cert., Columbus (Ohio) Art Sch., 1957; BFA, Ohio U., 1958, MFA, 1960. Instr. Columbus Coll. Art & Design, 1960-61; asst. prof. La. U. InterAm., San Germán, P.R., 1961-63, W.Va. State Coll., Institute, 1963-65; from asst. prof. to prof. No. Ill. U., DeKalb, 1965-88, pres., rsch. prof., 1988—92, Disting. rsch. prof., 1998, Disting. prof. emeritus, 1998—2009. One-man shows include Zaks Gallery; represented in permanent collections Art Inst. Chgo., Bklyn. Mus., Mus. Contemporary Art Chgo. Nat. Endowment for Arts fellow in painting, 1978. Home: New Prt Rchy, Fla. Died June 2, 2009.

MAHONEY, DOROTHY REED, photojournalist; b. Chgo., July 1, 1919; d. Earl Howell and Edith (Lobdell) Reed; m. Edward Ansel Mahoney, Aug. 13, 1960 (div. Nov., 1980). BA, Conn. Coll., 1941. Assoc. editor Esquire Magazine, Chgo., 1944-45; youth editor Woman's Home Companion, NYC, 1946; freelance writer, photojournalist Chgo., 1947-60; photojournalist Roanoke, Va.; developer First Roanoke (Va.) Crafts Festival, k, 1971; developer, dir. Va. Mountain Crafts Guild, Claytor Lake, Va., 1975-79; developer Va. Mountain Crafts Guild Fair, Claytor Lake, Va., 1979; cons. on crafts Roanoke, Va., from 1979-. Cons. Richmond Crafts Fair, 1978. Author: A Farm for Andy, 1951, Zippy's Birthday, 1954; writer, photographer, sound film, Barbara's Christmas, 1956. Democrat. Avocations: reading, hiking, photography. Home: Roanoke, Va. Died Sept. 20, 2007.

MAKEEVER, ANN MEYER, religious organization administrator; b. Fargo, ND, Aug. 20, 1916; d. Roe Eugene Remington and Jessie Marie Jepson; m. William Frederick Rosser, Dec. 24, 1936 (div. Dec. 18, 1964); children: Carlyn Wood Duffy, Barry Lowell Rosser, Roberta Jean Zito, Kathleen Ann Rosser; m. Peter Victor Meyer, 1964. BA in Music, Coker Coll., 1936; DDiv, Tchg. of the Inner Christ, San Diego, 1975. Opera singer Opera Cos., NYC, 1945—54; singer, actor Starlight Opera, San Diego, 1955—64; soloist, practitioner First Ch. of Religious Sci., San Diego, 1956—64; co-founder Soc. for the Tchg. of the Inner Christ, San Diego, 1965—77; founder, exec. dir. Tchg. of the Inner Christ, Inc., San Diego, 1977—2000; ret. Author: Ten Lessons in Woman Awareness, 1968; co-author: Being a Christ!, 1975; author: Self Mastery in the Christ Consciousness, 1989, (autobiography) Who Is With Me?, 2003. Home: Medford, Oreg. Died Sept. 4, 2007.

MAKI, KAZUMI, physicist, researcher; b. Takamatsu, Japan, Jan. 27, 1936; s. Toshio and Hideko M.; m. Masako Tanaka, Sept. 21, 1969. BS, Kyoto U., 1959, PhD, 1964. Research asso. Inst. for Math. Scis., Kyoto U., 1964; research asso. Fermi Inst., U. Chgo., 1964-65; asst. prof. physics U. Calif., San Diego, 1965-67; prof. Tohoku U., Sendai, Japan, 1967-74; vis. prof. Universite Paris-Sud, Orsay, France, 1969-70; prof. physics U. So. Calif., Los Angeles, from 1974. Vis. prof. Inst. Laue-Langevin, U. Paris-Sud, France, 1979-80, Max Planck Inst. fur Festkorper Forschung, Stuttgart, Germany, 1986-87, U. Paris-7, 1990, Hokkaido U., Sapporo, Japan, 1993, Centre de Recherche sur Tres Basses Temperatures, Grenoble, France, 1993-94, Instituto de Ciencia de Materiales, Madrid, Spain, 1994, Max Planck Inst. Phys. Complex Sys., Dresden, Germany, 2001-02. Assoc. editor Jour. Low Temperature Physics, 1969-91; contbr. articles to profl. jours. Guggenheim fellow, 1979-80, Japan Soc. Promotion of Sci. fellow, 1993; Fulbright scholar, 1964-65; recipient Nishina prize, 1972, Alexander von Humboldt award, 1986-87, John Bardeen prize, 2006. Fellow Japan Soc. Promotion of Sci., Am. Phys. Soc.; mem. AAAS, Phys. Soc. Japan. Home: Santa Monica, Calif. Died Sept. 10, 2008.

MALDEN, KARL (MLADEN SEKULOVICH), actor; b. Chgo., Mar. 22, 1912; s. Peter and Minnie (Sebera) Sekulovich; m. Mona Graham, Dec. 18, 1938; children: Mila, Carla. Student, Goodman Theatre, Chgo., 1935-38. Pres. Acad. of Motion Arts and Scis., 1989-92; mem. Citizens Stamp Com., U.S. Govt., Washington. Stage appearances include Golden Boy, 1938, Gentle People, 1939, Key Largo, 1940, Flight to the West, 1942, Uncle Harry, 1940, All My Sons, 1949, A Streetcar Named Desire, 1950, Desire Under the Elms, 1952, Desperate Hours, 1954; (films) They Knew What They Wanted, 1940, Winged Victory, 1944, 13 rue Madeleine, 1947, Boomerang, 1947, Kiss of Death, 1947, The Gunfighter, 1950, Where the Sidewalk Ends, 1950, Halls of Montezuma, 1950, A Streetcar Named Desire (Acad. award for Best Supporting Actor, 1952), 1951, The Sellout, 1952, Diplomatic Courier, 1952, Operation Secret, 1952, Ruby Gentry, 1952, I Confess, 1953, Take the High Ground!, 1953, Phantom of the Rue Morque, 1954, On the Waterfront, 1954, Baby Doll, 1956, Fear Strikes Out, 1957, Bombers B-52, 1957, The Hanging Tree, 1959, Pollyanna, 1960, The Great Imposter, 1961, One Eyed Jacks, 1961, Parrish, 1961, All Fall Down, 1961, Birdman of Alcatraz, 1962, How the West Was Won, 1962, Gypsy, 1962, Come Fly With Me, 1963, Dead Ringer, 1964, Cheyenne Autumn, 1964, The Cincinnati Kid, 1965, Nevada Smith, 1966, Murderers' Row, 1966, Hotel, 1967, The Adventures of Bullwhip Griffin, 1967, Billion Dollar Brain, 1967, Blue, 1968, Hot Millions, 1968, Patton, 1970, Cat o' Nine Tails, 1971, Wild Rovers, 1971, Summertime Killer, 1972, Beyond the Poseidon Affair, 1978, Meteor, 1979, The Sting II, 1982, Twilight Time, 1982, Billy Galvin, 1987, Nuts, 1987; dir., actor: (films) Time Limit, 1957; actor: (TV films) Captains Courageous, 1977, Word of Honor, 1981, Miracle on Ice, 1981, With Intent to Kill, 1983, Fatal Vision, 1984 (Emmy award for Supporting Actor, 1985), Alice in Wonderland, 1985, My Father My Son, 1988, The Hijacking of the Achille Lauro, 1989, Call Me Anna, 1990, Absolute Strangers, 1991, Back to the Streets of San Francisco, 1992, They've Taken Our Children: The Chowchilla Kidnapping, 1993; (TV series) Streets of San Francisco, 1972-77, Skag, 1980; (TV appearances) The Ford Theatre Hour, 1949, Armstrong Circle Theatre, 1950, Omnibus, 1955, The West Wing, 2000; co-author: (with Carla Malden) When Do I Start: A Memoir, 1988 Recipient Donaldson award, 1950, Critic's award, 1950, Lifetime Achievement Award, Screen Actors Guild, 2003; Barrington Station post office in L.A. renamed in his honor, 2005. Died July 1, 2009.

MALE, DONALD WARREN, minister; b. Niskayuna, NY, Apr. 12, 1922; s. Charles Thomas and Mildred (Schairer) M.; m. Shirley Rogers, May 28, 1944 (div. 1968); children: Sherry Ellen, Jennifer, Peggy Lou, Carl, Connie Sue; m. Sue Anderson, May 15, 1971. BS in Chemistry, Union Coll., 1943; MS in Physics, Case Sch. Applied Sci., 1950; MS in Mgmt., MIT, 1958; DMin, Vanderbilt U., 1976. Aerospace scientist USAF, 1954-74, advanced through grades, ret., 1974; min. Unitarian Ch., Tullahoma, Tenn. Sloan fellow, 1957-58. Fellow AIAA (assoc.); mem. Middle Tenn. Astro. Soc. (pres. 1965—), Unitarian Universalist Assn. (sec. 1983-87). Unitarian Universalist. Avocations: astronomy, canoeing. Died Aug. 14, 2008.

MALKIN, MICHAEL M., lawyer; b. New Haven, Nov. 1, 1944; s. Eli B. and Gladys (Pollak) M.; children: Andrea, Lisa, Daniel. BA, U. N.Mex., 1966; JD, NYU, 1969. Bar: N.Y. 1970, U.S. Dist. Ct. (so. dist.) N.Y. 1971, U.S. Dist. Ct. (ea. dist.) N.Y. 1971, U.S. Ct. Appeals (2d cir.) 1972, U.S. Supreme Ct. 1984. Assoc. Weil, Lee & Bergin, NYC, 1970-76, Weil, Guttman & Davis, NYC, 1976-77, ptnr., 1977-82, Weil, Guttman, Davis & Malkin, NYC, 1982-86, Weil, Guttman & Malkin, NYC, 1986-95, Weil, Guttman & Malkin, LLP, NYC, 1995—2001. Judge Giles Sutherland Rich Moot Ct. Competition, N.Y.C., 1982; arbitrator Civil Ct. of City N.Y., 1984-88. Mem. editl. bd. Trademark Reporter, 1973-75, 88-90, contbg. editor, 1974-75. Mem. N.Y. State Bar Assn., U.S. Trademark Assn., Phi Delta Phi, Alpha Epsilon Pi. Home: Scottsdale, Ariz. Died Dec. 19, 2008.

MALKIN, MOSES MONTEFIORE, retired employee benefits administration company, diversified financial services company executive; b. Revere, Mass., Sept. 18, 1919; s. Irving and Annie (Helfant) M.; m. Hannah Lacob, Oct. 11, 1941. AB, U. N.C., 1941; BSME, Columbia U., 1948. Enrolled actuary; CLU. Engr. GE, Schenectady, NY, 1948-50; engr. Gen. Bronze, Inc., Jersey City, 1950-51; v.p. Malkin Warehouse, Inc., New Haven, 1951-57; pvt. practice actuary and adminstr. New Haven, 1957—72; chmn., actuary Profl. Pensions, Inc., Middletown, Conn., 1973—93; ret., 1993. Presenter pension issues at numerous confs., 1970-80. Pres., founder Milford, Conn., 1962, Milford Child Guidance Clinic, 1966; pres. Clifford Beers Child Guidance, New Haven, 1971, Jewish Family Svc., New Haven, 1973. With U.S. Army, 1941-45, ETO. Mem. Am. Acad. Actuaries (ret. mem.), Am. Soc. Pension Actuaries (ret. mem., instr. 1984), Am. Soc. CLUs (ret. mem.), Phi Beta Kappa, Tau Beta Pi. Jewish. Died Dec. 11, 2007.

MALLOY, JAMES JOSEPH, real estate manager; b. Milw., Feb. 25, 1941; s. Joseph James Malloy and Olga Ida (Heuiter) Auerbach; m. Kathleen Mary Vanden Elsen, Oct. 5, 1974; children: Steven, Scott. BS, U. Wis., Stevens Point, 1965; MS, No. Ill. U., 1969; postgrad., U. Iowa, 1969-73. Dir. cartographic svcs. No. Ill. U., Dekalb, 1965-68, instr. geography, 1968-69; transp. planning coord. East Cen. Wis. Regional Planning Commn., Neenah, Wis., 1973-80; dir. sales and mktg. Wis. & So. RR Co., Horicon, 1980-82, asst. gen. mgr., 1982-85, gen. mgr., 1985-86, sr. v.p., gen. mgr., 1986-88; exec. v.p., COO Wis. & So. R.R. Co., Horicon, 1988-94; realtor Prudential Preferred Properties, Brookfield, Wis., from 1994. Bd. dirs. Midwest Adv. Bd., Homewood, Ill., 1985-94; prog. devel. coun. Operation Lifesaver, Inc., Alexandria, Va., 1987-90. Staff sgt. U.S. Army Nat. Guard, 1965-72. Mem. Midwest Adv. Bd. (pres. 1990-91, bd. dirs. 1985-94, Am. Shortline RR Assn. (regional v.p. 1990-94, bd. dirs. 1986-94), Am. Assn. RR Supts., Wis. Operation Lifesaver Com., Clearwater Lakes Condo Assn. (bd. dirs. 1994-96). Home: New Berlin, Wis. Died Dec. 23, 2007.

MALONE, VERNON, state legislator; b. Dec. 20, 1931; Commr. Wake County, NC, 1984—2002; state senate mem. Dist. 14 NC, 2003—09. Democrat. Baptist. Died Apr. 18, 2009.

MALOOF, SAM (SAMUEL SOLOMON MALOOF), woodworker; b. Chino, Calif., Jan. 24, 1916; m. Alfreda Ward, 1948 (dec. 1998); children: Samuel, Marilu; m. Beverly Wingate, 2001; 1 stepchild, Todd. With VORTOX, 1934—39, Harold Graham Industrial Designer, 1940—41; graphic artist Millard Sheets, 1946—48; design project in Iran and Lebanon US State Dept., 1959, design project in El Salvador, 1963. Former pres. So. Calif. Designer; former trustee Southeast Region Am. Craft Coun., former chmn. Acad. Fellows; former bd. dir. US sect. World Craft Congress. Exhibitions include Calif. Design I-XI, 1954—71, Smithsonian Inst., Washington, 1970, Renwick Gallery, Smithsonian Am. Art Mus., 1971, 1992, 2004, Mus. Contemporary Art, Chgo., 1976, Vatican Mus., Rome, 1978, Vice President's House, Washington, DC, 1980, J.M. Kohler Arts Ctr., Sheboygan, Wis., 1983, Barnsdell Art Ctr., LA, 1984, Anderson Ranch Arts Ctr., Aspen, Colo., 1984—85, Euphat Gallery, Cupertino, Calif., 1986, Joanne Lyon Gallery, Apsen, 1987, Laguna Beach Mus. Art, 1988, Dallas Mus. Art, 1989, University Art Gallery, Riverside, Calif., 1993, LA County Fair, 1993, Chgo. Internat. New Art Forms Exposition, Navy Pier Joanne Rapp Gallery, 1993, Wustum Mus. Fine Arts, 1993, Connell Gallery, Atlanta, Ga., 1996, Craft and Folk Art Mus., LA, 2003, Ruth Chandler Williamson Gallery at Scripps Coll., 2004, public collections, Minn. Art Mus., 1959, Oakland Art Mus., Calif., 1969, 1984, Fine Art Mus., Boston, 1976, The White House, 1981, St. Louis Art Mus., 1983, Carter Presdl. Library, 1985, Dallas Art Mus., 1986, Met. Mus. Art, NYC, 1988, Phila. Mus. Art, 1981, 1991, Renwick Gallery, 1992, Toledo Mus. Art, Ohio, 1992; author: Sam Maloof: Woodworker, 1983. Served with US Army, 1941—45. Died May 21, 2009.

MALTBY, FREDERICK LATHROP, retired engineering executive; b. Bradford, Pa., Dec. 14, 1917; s. Fred Lathrop and Nellie (Brown) M.; m. Mildred Maltby, May 6, 1944 (dec. 2006); children: Lewis, Laura. BS in Gen. Engring., Grove City Coll., 1940; postgrad., Cornell U., 1940-42; MA in Nuclear Physics, U. Buffalo, 1943. Asst. prof. U. Buffalo, N.Y., 1942-44; tech. dir. and chief project engr. Bristol Co., Waterbury, Conn., 1944-52; tech. dir. Fielden Div. Robert Shaw Controls, Phila., 1952-57; founder Drexelbrook Cons., Jenkintown, Pa., 1957-63; pres. Drexelbrook Engring., Horsham, Pa., 1963-91, chmn., CEO, 1991—99. Recipient Product Advancement award Pollution Engring., 1979, 5 Star award, 1980, Outstanding Technical Achievement award, Instrumentation, Systems, & Automation Soc., 2000 Fellow Instrument Soc. Am. (Standards and Practices Honors award 1971); mem. IEEE, Internat. Electrotech. Commn. (CT-31 adv. com.), Am. Phys. Soc., Am. Inst. Physics, Nat. Fire Protection Assn., Sigma Xi. Home: Jenkintown, Pa. Died July 11, 2009.

MANAHAN, ANNA, actress; b. Ireland, Oct. 18, 1924; m. Colm O'Kelly (dec.). Student, Gaiety Sch. Acting. Actress Edwards/MacLiammoir Co., Nat. Theatre, London, Walter Kerr Theatre, NYC. Appeared in numerous theatrical prodns., including The Rose Tattoo, Moon for the Misbegotten, Bloomsday, Entertaining Mr. Sloane, The Killing of Sister George, Cat on a Hot Tin Roof, the Gingerbread Lady, Lovers (Tony nomination), Live Like Pits, The Plough and the Stars (Oliver award nomination), The Leenana Trilogy, the Loves of Cass Maguire, I do Not Like Thee Dr. Fell, the Shaughraun, the Matchmaker, The Taylor, Ansty, Dr. Fell, The Beauty Queen of Leenane (Tony award 1998), The Matchmaker, 2002, Sive, 2002, Sisters, 2006 and numerous others; TV appearances include Me Mammy, The riordans, Leave it to Mrs. O'Brien, the Irish RM, (TV/films) the Bill, Lovejoy, 1986, Young Indiana Jones Chronicles, 1992, the Treaty, Blind Justice, Hear My Songs, 1991, Clash of the Titans, 1981, A Man of No Importance, 1994, Woman Found Dead in Elevator, 2000, On the Edge, 2000, Black Day at Black Rock, 2001, others. Recipient Tony award, Theatre World award, Freedom of City award, 2002. Died Mar. 8, 2009.

MANERI, JOSEPH GABRIEL, jazz composer; b. Bklyn. m. Sonja Holzwarth; children: Mat, Salvatore, Abraham, Nina, Gloria. With New England Conservatory, Boston; co-dir. NEC Enchanted Circle. Solo artist various instruments, repertoire includes jazz and ethnic music. Piano concerto includes Metanoia; co-author: (with Scott Van Duyne) Preliminary Studies in the Virtual Pitch Continuum, 1985; co-inventor microtonal keyboard. Mem. Boston Microtonal Soc. (founder, pres.), Pi Kappa Lambda (pres. NEC chpt.). Died Aug. 24, 2009.

MANISCALCO, JOSEPH, artist, educator; b. Tampa, Fla., Feb. 24, 1921; s. Michaelangelo and Rosa (Belluccia) M.; m. Ann Lynn Laurence Cadman, Sept. 24, 1954 (div. June 1962); children: Michael, James, Elizabeth, Robert; m. Barbara Ann Fisher Insley, Jan. 3, 1976. Student, Art Students League of N.Y., 1939-41, 46-49. Portrait artist, from 1941. Lectr. in field; judge exhbns. Represented in permanent collections including Mich. Supreme Ct., U.S. House of Reps., Nat. Archives, Washington. With U.S. Army, 1942-46, ETO and PTO. Recipient Fitch award Mich. Acad. Letters, Arts and Sci., Artistic Excellence and Cmty. Commitment award Wayne County Coun. of the Arts, 1992. Mem. Scarab Club (bd. dirs. 1967—, pres. 1972-73, 80-81, 4 gold medals, 1st prize Silver Medal Show), Prismatic Club of Detroit (pres. 2000), Grosse Point Theatre (scenic artist), Fine Art Soc. of Detroit (chmn. art com. 1975), Adcraft Club of Detroit. Avocations: acting and singing in community theater productions, church choral singing. Home: Novi, Mich. Died Oct. 31, 2007.

MANN, LESTER PERRY, mathematics educator; b. Milford, Mass., May 30, 1921; s. Lester P. and Viola E. (Tracy) M.; m. Dorothy M. Davis, Oct. 11, 1947; children: Kelly P., Leslie P. BS with high honors, U. Md., 1964; MEd, U. Alaska, Anchorage, 1974; EdD, Boston U., 1983. Cert. elem. tchr., reading specialist and supr., Mass.; cert. elem. tchr., reading specialist, Alaska. Commd. 2nd lt. USAAF, 1941; advanced through grades to maj. USAF, 1954, navigator, weather officer, 1941-64; ret., 1964; resident counselor OEO-Job Corps, 1965-66; flight navigator Südflug, Braniff, Capitol and Japan Air Lines, 1966-73; instr. math., adminstr., curriculum developer U. Alaska, 1974-86, adj. instr., 1987-99; instrnl. assoc. Mann Assocs., Applied Lifelong Learning, Anchorage, 1983-99. Instr. Anchorage Community Coll., 1974-86; asst. prof. Embry-Riddle Aero. U., Anchorage, 1987-98, acad. advisor, 1987-90; mem. for remedial reading Alaska Talent Bank; vis. adult educator German Adult Edn. Assn., 1984. Mem. Math. Assn. Am., Nat. Coun. Tchrs. Math., Internat. Reading Assn., Am. Assn. Adult and Continuing Edn. (profl., past mem. nomination and election com.), Am. Meteorol. Soc. (emeritus), Phi Alpha Theta, Phi Kappa Phi. Died May 3, 2008.

MANN, MAYBELLE, writer, educator; b. Joliet, Ill., May 27, 1915; d. Saul and Helen (Schoenbrun) Mittleburg; m. Samuel Kart (div. Sept. 1965); children: Merna, Laura; m. Alvin Lloyd Mann, Apr. 29, 1967. BA, Queens Coll., 1965; MA, NYU, 1968, PhD, 1972. Lectr. NYU, NYC, 1974, Orange County C.C., Middletown, N.Y., 1974-76, Palm Beach C.C., Palm Beach Gardens, Fla., 1974; art editor Herald-Record, Middletown, N.Y., 1974-78; art columnist Jewish World, Palm Beach County, Fla., 1978-81; lectr. New Dimensions, Palm Beach County, Fla., from 1981. Author: Francis William Edmonds: Mammon and Art, 1977, The American Art-Union, 1977, rev., 1987, Walter Launt Palmer: Poetic Reality, 1984; contbr. articles to books and jours. Lectr. Ret. Sr. Vol. Program, Palm Beach County, 1980—. Recipient Svc. award Ret. Sr. Vol. Program, 1992, 94, Svc. award New Dimensions, 1991. Mem. Nat. Coun. Jewish Women (bd. dirs. Palm Beach chpt.). Home: Tequesta, Fla. Died Oct. 31, 2007.

MANNING, WINTON HOWARD, psychologist, educational administrator; b. St. Louis, Feb. 9, 1930; s. Winton Harry and Jane (Swanson) M.; m. Nancy Mercedes Groves, Aug. 1, 1959; children: Cecelia Groves Tazelaar, Winton H. III. AB with honors, William Jewell Coll., 1951; PhD in Psychology, Washington U., St. Louis, 1959. Instr. psychology William Jewell Coll., Liberty, Mo., 1954-55, asst. prof., acting head dept. psychology, 1955-56; rsch. psychologist Washington U., St. Louis, 1956-58, rsch. assoc., 1958-59; from asst. prof. to prof. psychology Tex. Christian U., Ft. Worth, 1959-65, assoc. dir. univ. honors program, 1962-65; from assoc. dir. rsch. to exec. dir. R & D Coll. Entrance Examination Bd., NYC, 1965-69; from dir. devel. rsch. divsn. to sr. v.p. R & D Ednl. Testing Svc., Princeton, N.J., 1969-83, v.p., 1970-77, sr. v.p. devel. and rsch., 1977-83, sr. scholar, 1983-93; pres. Ednl. Devel. Svc., Princeton, 1993—2000. Vis. fellow Princeton U., 1982-83; cons. Gallup Internat. Inst., 1990—, Applied Ednl. Rsch., 1993-95; cons. Grad. Mgmt. Admissions Coun., 1992-95, Carnegie Found. for the Advancement of Tchg. 1993-95; vis. lectr. Washington U., St. Louis, summer, 1961. Author: The Pursuit of Fairness in Admissions to Higher Education, 1977; Student Manual for Essentials of Psychology, 1960. Contbr. articles on ednl. measurement and psychology of learning to profl. publs. Patentee in field U.S. and Europe. Trustee Assn. for Advancement of Mentally Handicapped, 1975-78, Nat. Chicano Coun. on Higher Edn., 1977-85, N.J. Arts Festival, 1980-85; vice-chmn. Found. for Books to China, 1980-98; chmn. bd. trustees Princeton Day Sch., 1981-93; trustee Princeton Area Found., 1991-94, Our House Found., 1991-92; bd. dirs. The Princeton Singers, 1992-99, Christian Renewal Effort in Emerging Democracies, 1992-94, George H. Gallup Internat. Inst., 1992-98; chmn., trustee Trinity-All Saints' Cemetery, 1993-98; chmn. Affordable Housing Bd. of Princeton Borough, 1987-89; chmn., commr. Princeton Pub. Housing Authority, 1995-99, 2000-03; sr. warden All Saints Episc. Ch., 1987-89; chmn. ins. com. Diocese N.J., 1993-95; coun. mem. Diocese of N.J., 1996-99, 2003—, mem. audit com., 1997-98, mem. standing com., 1998-2002, 03—, mem. fin. com., 2003—; adv. coun. U. Okla. Ctr. for Rsch. on Minority Edn., 1987-92, Ind. Sch. Chmn. Assn., 1987-92; trustee Friends of Princeton Open Space, 1995-98; trustee Russian Ministry Network, 1995-98; cons. Carnegie Found. for Advancement of Tchg., 1987-95; cons. The Coll. Bd., 1988-91; spl. cons. Commn. on Admission to Grad. Mgmt. Edn., 1987-89; chair Princeton Residents Traffic Safety Com., 1994—2002; mem. Princeton Borough Traffic and Transp. Com., 2003—. Recipient Alumni Achievement citation William Jewell Coll., 1970; named Gallup Scholar in Edn., 1995. Fellow Am. Psychol. Soc. (charter), Eastern Psychol. Assn., Psychometric Soc., Nat. Assn. Scholars, Am. Ednl. Rsch. Assn., Nat. Coun. on Measurement in Edn. (mem. com. on legal issues in measurement 1977-79), N.Y. Acad. Scis., Nassau Club, Pendragon Soc., Old Guard of Princeton, Oratory of Good Shepherd, Phi Beta Kappa, Sigma Xi, Order of St. John of Jerusalem (comdr.). Home: Princeton, NJ. Died May 29, 2004.

MANTOULIDES, CHRISTINA, advertising agency executive; b. NYC, Dec. 10, 1960; d. Jack and Popi Koutellou; m. Taso Mantoulides, Oct. 17, 1982. BA in Psychology, CUNY, 1982. Media buyer The Target Group, NYC, 1982-84; media buyer, supr. Levine, Huntley, Schmidt & Beaver, NYC, 1984-89; dir. local broadcast Levine, Huntley, Vicker & Beaver, NYC, 1989-91; v.p. dir. local broadcast Campbell, Mithun, Esty, NYC, 1991-93; v.p. mgr. local broadcast True North Comm., NYC, 1993-96; dir., sr. ptnr. Bozell, Jacobs, Kenyon & Eckhardt Advt., NYC, from 1996. Recipient Media All Star award for Local Spot Broadcast, Media Week/Ad Week Mags., 1993. Home: Palm Harbor, Fla. Died Aug. 18, 2008.

MARABLE, SIMEON-DAVID, artist; b. Phila., May 10, 1948; s. Daniel Berry and Marsima (Maddela) M.; m. Pamela Joyce Sorenson, June 1, 1969; children: Simeon-David dePaul (dec.), Daniel-Dale Christopher (dec.), Jason-Andrew Bartley, Jo Anna Lee, Benjamin Arthur Kurtis. BA in Art and English, Lea Coll., Minn., 1970; postgrad., Tyler Sch. Art, Phila. Art tchr. 7-8th grade Pennsbury Sch. Sys., Pa., 1970—88; Art tchr. 9-10th grade Charles H. Boehm H.S., Pennsbury, from 1988, Medill Bair H.S., Pennsbury, from 1990; Art tchr. 9-12th grade Pennsbury H.S. W, from 2002. Tchr. Neshaminy Adult Edn., 1972-82; resident artist Middletown Hist. Assn., 1976, Three Arches Corp., 1975, treas.; founder, creator Rivulet Art 2000. Permanent collections include Albert Lea (Minn.) Libr., chapel Ft. Dix, N.J., pencil/charcoal Am. Eagle superimposed over outline Levittown, Pa., James A. Michener Mus., 2003; portraits of Mr. Mike Schmidt, Mr. Lee Elia; creator Phila. City of Champs logo, 50th anniversary logo Fairless Hills, Pa. 1951-2001 Celebration; creator children's ednl. programs Falls Twp. 300th Pa. statehood; artwork represented in Middletown Twp. calendar, 1992, Falls Twp. calendar, 1992; creator Olde Phila. Ednl. Program and Pa. Statehood Program, Nat. Rep. Conv., Phila., 2000; creator scale model homes exhibit Pa. Hist. Mus., 2002; author: Levittown Pennsylvania 1952-2002 A Garden Community, 2002; sketch presented to Gov. of Pa. 2002, papers written of John S. Levitt, 2005, Raymond Fletcher Proffitt, profl. pilot and close friend of William J. Levitt, 2005; publisher and editor Levittownian Herald News, a Community News Letter Serving 17, 311 Gomes in Levittown, Pa., 2008, illustrator LANDIA, 2009; proprietor William J. Levitt and Family Hist. Mus. exhibit ctr., 2009. Vol. Rep. Nat. Conv., Phila., 2000; mgr. Boys Soccer League, Boys Little League, Middletown Twp.; sr. Babe Ruth coach, mgr. Langhome Athletic Assn., 1988-89; sr. coach Babe Ruth League, 1989; J.V. baseball coach, 1989; mem. Presdl. Task Force; elected to Nat. Trust for Hist. Preservation, 1995; involved with ednl. program Honoring the 200th Anniversary U.S. Constn. Commemorative Olde Phila. Constn. Atty.; curator Levittown Exhibit, Pa.; pres. Levittown Internationally Known Communities Inc., 2003—; program dir. Dream of America 1952 Photographs and Memorabilia of Levittown and Bucks County, Pa., Snowball Gate Dr. Levittown Exhibit Ctr., 2003. Served with USAR, 1970. Recipient Rep. Senatorial Am. Spirit medal, Rep. Party, US Senate, 2007; named Artist of Yr., Albert Lea Lions Club, 1970, Dir. Archtl. Planning and Cmty. Design, The Bucks Hub Conf. Mem. Buck County Art Educators (pres. 1973-74), Levittown Artists Assn., Nat. Soc. Arts and Lit., Internat. Platform Assn. Roman Catholic. Achievements include development of Levitt Mobile that houses memorabilia and photog. of the 1950's in Buck's Co., Pa. Died June 23, 2009.

MARBURY, VIRGINIA LOMAX, insurance and investment executive; b. Ruston, La., June 25, 1918; d. Dallas Daniel and Della (Southern) Lomax; m. William A. Marbury Jr., Sept. 5, 1943; children: Rebekah, Caroline. BA, La. Tech. U., 1936, LLD (hon.), 1987; MusB, La. State U., 1938. Exec. v.p. Marbury Corp., Ruston, La., from 1944; sec.-treas. Bankers Life La., Ruston, from 1959. 1st v.p., membership chmn. Lincoln Parish Mus. and Hist. Soc., Ruston, La., 1992—. Recipient Tower Medallion award La. Tech. U., 1991. Mem. Shreveport Symphony Soc. Republican. Episcopalian. Died Feb. 19, 2008.

MARCELLO, ANTHONY JAMES, systems engineer; b. Phila., Jan. 12, 1967; s. George and Loretta (Bartolomeo) M.; m. Jodi Lynn Dill, Feb. 14, 1992; 1 child, Holly Marie. BBA, Temple U., 1988. Pres., CEO Computerized Bus. Systems, Phila., 1987-88; systems engr. Electonic Data Systems, Fairborn, Ohio, from 1989, Electonic Data Systems LFI Intergrated Systems, Fairborn, from 1991. Asst. advisor Explorer Post Boy Scouts Am., 1992—; tchr. computers Girl Scouts U.S., Dayton, 1991. Avocations: scuba diving, underwater photographer, landscaping, cooking, building models. Home: Valrico, Fla. Died Nov. 18, 2007.

MARCHI, JOHN JOSEPH, retired state senator; b. SI, NY, May 20, 1921; s. Louis B. and Alina M. (Marchi-Giardello) M.; m. Maria Luisa Davini, Nov. 14, 1948; children: Joan, Aline. BA, Manhattan Coll., 1942, LLD (hon.); JD, St. John's U., 1950, LLD (hon.); JSD, Bklyn. Law Sch., 1953, LLD (hon.), Wagner Coll., 1985. Bar: N.Y. 1951, U.S. Dist. Ct. (ea. and so. dists.) N.Y., U.S. Supreme Ct. Mem. NY State Senate, 1957—2006. Of counsel Whitman, Breed, Abbott & Morgan, N.Y.C. Staten Island Del. N.Y. State Constl. Conv., 1967, chair Staten Island Charter Commn.; past chmn. Coun. State Govts. Lt. col. U.S. Army, ret. Decorated comdr. Order of Merit (Italy); recipient Charles Carroll award Guild Cath. Lawyers, 1991. Mem. VFW, Am. Legion, Urban League, B'nai B'rity, Holy Name Soc., KC. Republican. Roman Catholic. Home: Staten Island, NY. Died Apr. 25, 2009.

MARCK, WILLIAM JOHN, JR., travel company executive, educator; b. Balt., Aug. 23, 1924; BA, Johns Hopkins U., 1950, MEd, 1955, MA, 1960. Tchr., Md. Commd. U.S. Army, 1943, advanced through grades to capt.; tchr., dept. chmn. Balt. County, Towson, Md., 1950-80; prin. adult edn., Perry Hall, Md., 1970-81; travel agent, owner Marck Time Travel, Bel Air, Md., 1980-96; prof. Harford C.C., Bel Air, 1985-96, Villa Julie Coll., Stevenson, 1990-93. Editor C. of C. Harford County, Md., 1981-96, pres. 1993-94. Capt. U.S. Army Med. Corps., 1943-73. Coe fellow Stanford U., 1965; named Man of Yr. C. of C., Bel Air, Md., 1995; named to Hall of Fame C. of C., Harford, Md., 1996. Republican. Avocations: collecting records, photography, lacrosse, old movies. Home: Bel Air, Md. Died July 25, 2008.

MARGOLIS, BETTE SHULA, writer, educator; d. Daniel and Evelyn Margolis; children: Laurie Khan, Lisa Daugherty, Marcus Stern. BA in English and Journalism, Bklyn. Coll., 1972; MA in Art, NYU, 1974. Mktg. dir., art dir. Flexitoys, Berkeley, Calif., 1989—91, Harbor House Coffee Co., Novato, Calif., 1991—94; publisher, editor, dir. mktg. Bette's Books, Highlands Ranch, Colo., from 1995; dir. New Perspectives Workshop, Washingtonn, DC, from 2000; producer, writer, pres. Shakti Prodns., Colo., from 2003. Vis. lectr. DuCret Sch. of the Arts, Plainfield, NJ, The Dominican Coll., San Rafael, Calif., Contra Costa Coll., San Pablo, Calif., The Learning Annex, San Francisco, The Art League of Houston, Lee Coll., Baytown, Tex., First Class, Washington, Southwest Coll., Houston, U. Houston, Victoria, Front Range CC, Westminster, Colo., The Chatauqua, Boulder, Colo., Naropa U., Boulder, Colo. Author: A Heart Full of Love, 1999, Alive and Well: Into the New Millennium with Edgar Cayce's Health Care Wisdom, 2003; author: (illustrator) Saints' Craftbook, 1984, Salsa, 1998, Angora Kidd, 2003; illustrator Frogs, 1972, It's Great to Pray, 1973, Sister Death, 1974, I Can Hear the Cowbells Ring, 1994; prodr.: Women in the Arts, 1992; comml. advt. art & tech. illustrator Am. Mus. of Natural History, N.Y.C., 1971, freelance writer, illustrator Better Homes & Gardens, 1977, freelance writer Body Smart Mag., 1199, Venture Inward Mag., 2001, 2003. Mem.: Poetry Soc. Colo. Avocations: golf, bicycling. Home: Highlands Ranch, Colo. Died Feb. 19, 2008.

MARGOLIS, DAVID ISRAEL, industrial manufacturing executive; b. NYC, Jan. 24, 1930; s. Benjamin and Celia (Kosofsky) M.; m. Barbara Schneider, Sept. 7, 1958; children: Brian, Robert, Peter, Nancy. BA, CCNY, 1950, MBA, 1952; postgrad., NYU, 1952-55. Asst. treas. Raytheon Co., 1956-59; treas. IT&T, NYC, 1959-62; with Coltec Industries Inc., NYC, 1962-95, pres., 1968-91, CEO, 1984-95, chmn. bd. dirs., 1985-95, chmn. exec. com., 1995-99. Mem. bd. trustees NY Presbyn. Hosp.; bd. overseers NYU Stern Sch. Bus. Mem.: Coun. Fgn. Rels. Died Dec. 13, 2008.

MARGOLIS, HOWARD, public policy studies educator; b. Boston, Mar. 20, 1932; s. Abraham and Ann Margolis; m. Joan Olva Thuma, Jan. 17, 1962; children: Peter, Jenny, Sarah. BA, Harvard U., 1953; PhD, MIT, 1979. Speechwriter Sec. of Def., Washington, 1962-64; journalist Sci. Mag., Washington Post, Washington, 1960-62, 64-65; rsch. staff Inst. Def. Analyses, Arlington, Va., 1965-72; rsch. fellow MIT, Cambridge, 1972-81; vis. scholar Inst. Advanced Study & Russell Sage Found., NYC and Princeton, 1981-83; lectr. U. Calif., Irvine, 1983-85; prof. U. Chgo., 1985—2009. Author: Selfishness, Altruism and Rationality: A Theory of Social Change, 1982, Patterns, Thinking, and Cognition: A Theory of Judgment, 1987, Paradigms and Barriers: How Habits of Mind Govern Scientific Beliefs, 1993, Dealing with Risk: Why the Public and the Experts Disagree on Environmental Issues, 1996, It Started with Copernicus: How Turning the World Inside Out Led to the Scientific Revolution, 2002, Cognition and Extended Rational Choice, 2007 Avocations: skiing, hiking, windsurfing. Home: Chicago, Ill. Died Apr. 29, 2009.

MARGRABE, MARY VIRGINIA, retired secondary education educator, librarian; b. Brunswick, Md., May 21, 1923; d. John Anthony and Lula Brunswick (Darr) McMurry; m. Carl William Henry Margrabe Sr., Dec. 10, 1943 (dec. 1988); 1 child, Carl William Henry Jr. BA, Hood Coll., 1943; postgrad., Cath. U. Cert. tchr., Md. Tchr. Brunswick (Md.) H.S., 1943; libr. Linganore H.S., Frederick County, Md., Waverley Elem., Frederick County. Author: Now Library, 1973, Media Magic, 1979; co-author: Pre-1800 Houses of Frederick County, 1990; co-author, editor: Brunswick: 100 Years of Memories, 1990. Co-founder, charter mem. Brunswick Pub. Libr., 1962; co-founder Brunswick Railroad Mus., 1969, Brunswick Potomac Found., 1969, Brunswick Hist. Commn., 1976, pres., 1987-92. Mem. Hood Club of Frederick County. Libertarian. Episcopal. Avocations: writing, research. Home: Hagerstown, Md. Died July 27, 2008.

MARGULIS, MICHAEL HENRY, lawyer; b. NYC, Oct. 30, 1959; s. David H. and Eleanor Weinberg Margulis; m. Amy M. Sturmer, Mar. 19, 1989; children: Rebekah Geri, Daniel Aaron. AB, Princeton U., NJ, 1981; JD, Stanford U., 1984. Bar: N.Y. 1985. Assoc. Shea & Gould, NYC, 1984-93, ptnr., 1993-94, Duane Morris LLP, NYC, from 1994. Home: Towaco, NJ. Died Dec. 1, 2007.

MARK, ANDREW PEERY, producer; b. Phila., July 18, 1950; s. Louis B. and Vernon K. (Keys) M.; m. Cynthia Carpenter; children: Kimberly C., Christian A. AB in Langs., Lafayette Coll., 1972. Pres., exec. prodr. BRG Divsn. of Premiere Radio Networks, Wayne, Pa. Prodr. Pyramid Prodn. Music Libr. Contbr. articles to Advt. Age, Sound Mgmt.; composer numerous jingles. Bd. dirs. Radnor (Pa.) Twp. Sch. Dist., 1983-87; chmn. civil svc. commn. Radnor Twp. Mem. Broadcast Music Inc., Sons of the Revolution Pa. Soc. Republican. Avocations: music, travel. Home: Villanova, Pa. Died Feb. 24, 2009.

MARLENS, HANNA STEINER, psychologist; b. Vienna, Apr. 6, 1928; came to U.S., 1939; d. Bruno and Meta (Hoffman) Steiner; m. Alvin M. Marlens, Apr. 8, 1950; children: Steve, Neal. BA, Queens Coll., 1950; MA, CUNY, 1951; PhD, N.Y. U., 1959. Diplomate Am. Bd. Profl. Psychology; cert. sch. psychology, N.Y. Psychology intern Kings County Hosp., Bklyn., 1951-52; staff psychologist Dept. Pediatrics SUNY, Bklyn., 1952-54; rsch. psychologist Downstate Med. Schl., Bklyn., 1954-70; adj. prof. C.W. Post Coll., Brookville, N.Y., 1978-79; cons. psychologist Advanced Ctr. Psychotherapy, Hempstead, N.Y., 1972-75; rsch. cons. Ednl. Testing Svc. Inc., Princeton, N.J., 1970-77; sch. psychologist West Islip (N.Y.) PUbl. Schs., from 1963. Cons. Pub. Group, Allyn Bacon, 1979-89; lctr. 1963—. Author: (with others) Psychological Differentiation, 1962. Mem. APA, N.Y. Psychol. Assn., Sch. Psychologists N.Y., N.Y. Soc. Clin. Psychologists, Suffolk County Psychol. Assn. (bd. dirs., 1972-75), Nassau County Psychol. Assn. (bd. dirs. 1977-85). Avocations: travel, languages, books. Home: South Setauket, NY. Died Feb. 16, 2008.

MARSCHALL, ALBERT RHOADES, retired civil engineer; b. New Orleans, May 5, 1921; m. Maria Gamard; children: Thomas Rhoades, David Gamard, Laurel Marie, Pamela Joan, Albert Louis. BS, U.S. Naval Acad., 1944; BCE, MCE, Rensselaer Polytech. Inst., 1948. Chief of civil engineers USN, 1973-77; v.p. George Hyman Constrn. Co., Bethesda, 1977-79; commr. pub. bldg. Gen. Svc. Admin., 1979-81; cons., 1981—2008. Bd. dirs. Parsons Brinckerhoff Inc., Nat. Press Building Corp. Decorated Disting. Svc. medal, Meritorious Svc. medal, Legion of Merit. Mem. Nat. Acad. Engring., Am. Pub. Works Assn., Soc. Am. Mil. Engrs. (former pres.), Am. Inst. Arch. Home: Alexandria, Va. Died Nov. 18, 2008.

MARSH, PATRICIA GUYTON, humanities educator; b. Columbus, Miss., Mar. 17, 1947; d. Rickman Keith and Dora Hankins Guyton; m. Robert Tate Marsh, May 13, 1973; 1 child, Erin Tate. BA in Speech, Miss. State U., Starkville, 1968; MA in Theatre, U. Miss., Oxford, 1972, postgrad., 1972, postgrad., 2005, U. South Ala., Mobile, Miss. U. for Women, Columbus. Cert. English, speech and theatre tchr. Miss., Ala., Ga., Fla. Instr. Sidney Lanier Jr. HS for Boys, Macon, Ga., 1969, Warner Robins Sr. HS, 1969—71, U. Miss., Oxford, 1971—72, East Miss. Jr. Coll., Scooba, 1973, Pasco Comprehensive HS, Dade City, Fla., 1973—74, Pasco C.C., Dade City, Fla., 1974—75, Ala. Christian Coll., Mobile, 1975—76, St. Paul's Episcopal Sch., Mobile, 1976—2003, Columbus HS, 2003—04, East Miss. CC, Mayhew, from 2004. Adjudicator song writing divsn. Hank Williams Internat. Music Festival; adjudicator State 4H Oratorical Contest; guest lectr. Ala. Pub. Rels. Coun.; moderator Evenings with Ala. Writers series Spring Hill Coll.; actress Manhattan Theatre Co., NYC; actress, dir. Entertainer Dinner Theatre, Mobile, Ala.; dir. Granada Little Theatre, Miss., Warner Robins Little Theatre, Ga.; choreographer music and theatre depts. U. Miss.; dir. winning prodns. Southeastern Theatre Conf., Secondary Sch. Divsn., Crystal City, Va., Louisville. Dir., featured performer An Evening with Tennessee's Ladies Tennessee Williams Tribute, Columbus, 2005; mem. com. Roast and Boast, Columbus, 2005; dir. An Army of Stars benefit Salvation Army; site dir. Kaleidoscope benefit festival United Cerebral Palsy. Recipient Disting. Tchr. award, White House Commn. on Presdl. Scholars, Best Actress award, Southeastern Theatre Conf., Cmty. Theatre Divsn., Miss. State U., Joe Jefferson Playhouse, Mobile, Mobile Theatre Guild, Azalea City News and Review, Mobile; named Ala. Speech/Theatre Tchr. of Yr.; Pres. scholar, Miss. State U. Mem.: Ala. Speech Assn. (sec.), Ala. Theatre Assn. (sec.), Ala. Coun. Theatre/Speech, Southeastern Theatre Conf. Republican. Methodist. Avocations: travel, gardening, antiques, theater, football. Home: Columbus, Miss. Died July 22, 2008.

MARSHALL, FREDERICK JOSEPH, retired research chemist; b. Detroit, Aug. 14, 1920; s. Frederick Joseph and Nora Louise (Orleman) M.; m. Marcella Edith Campbell, Dec. 28, 1946; children: Mary Margaret, Suzanne, Frederick III, Rita, Jane, Timothy, Maureen. BS, U. Detroit, 1941, MS, 1943; PhD, Iowa State U., 1948. Sr. rsch. chemist Eli Lilly & Co., Indpls., 1948-75, rsch. scientist, 1976-83; ret., 1983. Author rsch. papers, jour. articles. Vice pres. Jesuit Alumni Assn., Indpls., 1964-66; treas. Indpls. Cath. Interracial Coun., 1968-74; Dem. precinct vice-committeeman, Indpls., 1975-79. Mem. Am. Chem. Soc., N.Y. Acad. Scis., Alpha Chi Sigma. Achievements include patent on marketed hypoglycemic agent, others. Home: Indianapolis, Ind. Died July 3, 2008.

MARSHALL, IRL HOUSTON, JR., franchise consultant; b. Evanston, Ill., Feb. 28, 1929; s. Irl H. and Marjorie (Greenleaf) M.; m. Barbara Favill, Nov. 5, 1949; children: Alice Marshall Vogler, Irl Houston III, Carol Marshall Allen. AB, Dartmouth Coll., 1949; MBA, U. Chgo., 1968; cert. franchise exec., La. State U., 1991. Gen. mgr. Duraclean Internat., Deerfield, Ill., 1949-61; mgr. Montgomery Ward, Chgo., 1961-77; pres., chief exec. officer Duraclean Internat., 1977-98; pres. Franchise Cons. Svcs., from 1998. Cons. Exec. Svc. Corps., 1999—. Inventor/patentee in field. Pres. Cliff Dwellers, Chgo., 1977; exec. com., treas., dir. Highland Park Hosp., 1971-80; bd. dirs. Better Bus. Bur. Chgo. & No. Ill., Chgo., 1988—. Named to Hall of Fame, Internat. Franchise Assn., 2002. Mem. Internat. Franchise Assn. (bd. dirs. 1981-90, pres. 1985, chmn. 1985-86, bd. dirs. Ednl. Found. 1984—, Hall of Fame 2002), Inst. Cert. Franchise Execs. (bd. govs. 1995—), Econ. Club Chgo., Exmoor Country Club, Univ. Club Chgo. Presbyterian. Home: Northbrook, Ill. Died Dec. 20, 2007.

MARSHALL, ROBERT JAMES, former head of religious order; b. Burlington, Iowa, Aug. 26, 1918; s. Robert McCray and Margaret Emma (Gysin) M.; m. Alice Johanna Hepner, Feb. 6, 1943 (dec. 1998); children: Robert Edward, Margaret Alice Niederer. AB, Wittenberg U., 1941; B.D., Chgo. Luth. Theol. Sem., 1944; postgrad., U. Chgo., 1949-52; D.D., Carthage Coll., 1961, Wittenberg U., 1963, Northwestern Luth. Sem., 1969, Waterloo U., 1970; L.H.D., Gettysburg Coll., 1965; LL.D., Augustana Coll., 1968, Wagner Coll., 1968, Muhlenberg Coll., 1969, Upsala Coll., 1969, Wittenberg U., 1969; S.T.D., Thiel Coll., 1971; J.C.D., Susquehanna U., 1969; Litt.D., Roanoke Coll., 1970; Lit.D., Newberry Coll., 1972; D. Theol., St. Olaf Coll., 1974. Ordained to ministry Lutheran Ch., 1944; pastor Grace Luth. Ch., Alhambra, Calif., 1944-47; instr. religion Muhlenberg (Pa.) Coll., 1947-49, head dept. religion, 1952-53; prof. O.T. interpretation Chgo. Luth. Theol. Sem., Maywood, Ill., 1953-62; pres. Ill. Synod Luth. Ch. in America, 1962-68, Luth. Ch. in America, NYC, 1968-78; dir. mission, service and devel. Luth. World Ministries, 1978-80; prof. O.T., Luth. Theol. So. Sem., Columbia, SC, 1981-93; adjunct prof. of Old Testament, sr. assoc. Ctr. for Global Mission Lutheran Sch. Theology, Chgo., from 1993; dir. Chgo. Ctr. for Global Ministries. Mem. exec. com. Luth. World Fedn., 1968-78; mem. central com., exec. com. World Council Chs., 1968-80, commn. on inter-ch. aid, refugees and world service, 1980—; mem. governing bd. Nat. Council Chs. of Christ in U.S.A., 1968-78, 85-87; mem. Commn. for a New Luth. Ch., 1982-86; mem. exec. com. Luth. Council in U.S.A., 1968-78; bd. dirs. Luth. World Relief, pres., mem. exec. council, 1964-68; chmn. on Evang. Luth. Ch. Am., 1963-64, mem. ch. council, standing com. on ecumenical affairs, 1987-93; mem. ch. world service com. Nat. Council Chs., chmn., 1985-87; mem. adv. com. vol. fgn. aid AID, vice chmn.; ann. prof. Am. Sch. Oriental Research, Jerusalem, 1958-59; exec. bd. Chgo. Conf. on Religion and Race, 1964-68 Author: The Mighty Acts of God. Bd. dirs. Grand View Coll., 1966-68, Augustana Coll., 1963-68, Luth. Sch. Theology, 1963-68, Augustana Hosp., Chgo., 1963-68, Luth. Hosp., Moline, Ill., 1963-68, Wheat Ridge Found. Mem. Chgo. Soc. Bibl. Research (sec. 1962-68), Nat. Assn. Profs. Hebrew, Soc. Bibl. Lit. and Exegesis, Am. Bible Soc. (bd. mgrs. 1968-80) Home: Columbia, SC. Died Dec. 22, 2008.

MARTIN, CLYDE VERNE, psychiatrist; b. Coffeyville, Kans., Apr. 7, 1933; s. Howard Verne and Elfrieda Louise (Moehn) Martin; m. Barbara Jean McNeilly, June 24, 1956; children: Kent Clyde, Kristin Claire, Kerry Constance, Kyle Curtis. Student, Coffeyville Coll., 1951—52; AB, U. Kans., Lawrence, 1955, MD, 1958; MA, Webster Coll., St. Louis, 1977; JD, Thomas Jefferson Coll. Law, LA, 1985. Diplomate Am. Bd. Psychiatry and Neurology. Intern Lewis Gale Hosp., Roanoke, Va., 1958—59; resident in psychiatry U. Kans. Med. Ctr., Kansas City, 1959—62, Fresno br. U. Calif.-San Francisco, 1978; staff psychiatrist Neurol. Hosp., Kansas City, 1962; practice medicine specializing in psychiatry Kansas City, Mo., 1964—84; founder, med. dir., pres. bd. dirs. Mid-Continent Psychiat. Hosp., Olathe, Kans., 1972—84; adj. prof. psychology Baker U., Baldwin City, Kans., 1969—84; staff psychiatrist Atascadero State Hosp., Calif., 1984—85; clin. prof. psychiatry U. Calif., San Francisco, from 1985; chief psychiatrist Calif. Med. Facility, Vacaville, 1985—87. Pres., editor Corrective and Social Psychiatry, Olathe, 1970—84, Atascadero, 1984—85, Fairfield, Calif., 1985—97; cons. psychiatrist Brit. Health Svc. Plymouth (Eng.) Trust, 1999—2001. Contbr. articles to profl. jours. Bd. dirs. Meth. Youthville, Newton, Kans., 1965—75, Spofford Home, Kansas City, 1974—78; del. Kans. East Conf. Meth. Ch., 1972—80, bd. global ministries, 1974—80. Served to capt. USAF, 1962—64, ret. col. USAF. Scholar Oxford Law and Soc., 1993. Fellow: Am. Orthopsychiat. Assn., World Assn. Social Psychiatry, Royal Soc. Health (London), Am. Assn. Mental Health Profls. in Corrections, Am. Psychiat. Assn.; mem.: AMA, Assn. Mental Health Adminstrs. (cert.), Am. Assn. Sex Educators, Counselors and Therapists (cert.), Assn. for Advancement Psychotherapy, St. James Club (London), Capitol Hill Club (Washington), Marines Meml. Club (San Francisco), Pi Kappa Alpha, Phi Beta Pi. Home: Fairfield, Calif. Died Feb. 16, 2009.

MARTIN, JAMES PATRICK, florist; b. Seattle, May 25, 1946; s. John Dennis and Catherine (Kirley) M.; m. Denise Marie Widen, Apr. 24, 1982; children: Michele, David, Nicholas, Patrick, Christopher. BA in Humanities, Gonzaga U., 1968, BS in Philosophy, 1968; MBA in Bus., U. Seoul, Seoul, Korea, 1969. Capt. U.S. Army 7th Infantry Div., Korea, 1968-70; retail sales mgr. Pacific Coast Comml., Los Angeles, 1970-71; v.p. Ballard Blossom Inc., Seattle, from 1971. Fin. com. mem. Florists Transworld Delivery, Southfield, Mich., 1983-86, Am. Floral Mktg. Coun., Washington, 1986-88. V.p. Seattle Allied Florists, Seattle, 1974-78; asst. soccer coach Seattle Pacific U., 1980—; bd. dirs. N.W. Soccer Found.; mem. selected pres.'s coun. Gonzaga U.; mayoral appointment to King County Bd. of Alcohol and Drug Abuse, 1991; appointed to FTD Pres.'s Coun. on Govt. Affairs, Washington, 1991—; chmn. sch. commn. Christ the King, 1991—. Named Bus. Person of the Yr. Seattle C. of C.; recipient Small Bus. award Washington Gov., 1985, Florists Transworld Delivery Top 100 award, 1977—; elected fellow Seattle Pacific U., 1986; Seattle Pacific U. Nat. Champions, 1978, 83, 85, 86. Mem. FTD, Seattle Allied Florists (v.p. 1974-78, com. on govt. affairs 1991), Am. Acad. Floraculture (elected). Republican. Roman Catholic. Died Dec. 21, 2007.

MARTIN, JOHN C., structural engineer, consultant; b. Tacoma, Wash., Apr. 6, 1926; s. Harry Little Martin and Gladys Gervais Doud; m. Ruth Watson Martin; children: Amanda W., William W. B in Mech. Engring., Yale U., 1948, M in Civil Engring., 1956. Registered profl. engr., Conn., N.Y., Mass., Colo. Engr. Weiskopf & Pickworth, NYC, 1955—60, The Martin Co., Littleton, Colo., 1960—63, Henry A. Plisterer, New Haven, 1963—65; prof. mechanical engring. and civil engring. U. New Haven, Conn., 1965—89; pvt. practice New Haven, 1965—82, from 1994; engr. Martin-Horton Assocs., New Haven, 1982—94. Prof. emeritus U. New Haven, from 1998. Capt. Corps Engrs. US Army, 1950—52. Mem.: New Haven Lawn Club (dir. from 1999). Home: New Haven, Conn. Died June 9, 2008.

MARTIN, NOEL, graphics designer, educator; b. Syracuse, Ohio, Apr. 19, 1922; s. Harry Ross and Lula (Van Meter) M.; m. Coletta Ruchty, Aug. 29, 1942; children—Dana, Reid Cert. in Fine Arts, Art Acad. Cin., Doctorate (hon.), 1994. Designer Cin. Art Mus., 1947-93, asst. to dir., 1947-55; freelance designer for various ednl., cultural and indsl. orgns., 1947—2009; instr. Art Acad. Cin., 1951-57, artist-in-residence, 1993—2009. Design cons. Champion Internat., 1959-82, Xomox Corp., 1961-2009, Federated Dept. Stores, 1962-83, Hebrew Union Coll., 1969-2009; designer-in-residence U. Cin., 1968-71, adj. prof., 1968-73; mem. adv. bd. Carnegie-Mellon U., R.I. Sch. Design, Cin. Symphony Orch., Am. Inst. Graphic Arts; lectr. Smithsonian Instn., Libr. of Congress, Am. Inst. Graphic Arts, Aspen Design Conf., various additional schs. and orgns. nationally. One man shows include Contemporary Arts Ctr., Cin., 1954, 71, Addison Gallery Am. Art, 1955, R.I. Sch. Design, 1955, Soc. Typographic Arts, Chgo., 1956, White Mus. of Cornell U., 1956, Cooper & Beatty, Toronto, Ont., Can., 1958, Am. Inst. Graphic Arts, 1958, Ind. U., 1958, Ohio State U., 1971; exhibited in group shows at Mus. Modern Art, N.Y.C., Library of Congress, Musee d'Art Moderne, Paris, Grafiska Inst., Stockholm, Carpenter Ctr., Cambridge, Gutenberg Mus., Mainz, U.S. info. exhbns. In Europe, South America and USSR; represented in permanent collections Mus. Modern Art, Stedelijk Mus., Amsterdam, Cin. Art Mus., Boston Mus. Fine Arts, Cin. Hist. Soc., Library of Congress; contbr. to various publs. Served to sgt. U.S. Air Force,

1942-45 Recipient Art Directors medal, Phila., 1957, Sachs award, Cin., 1973, Lifetime Achievement award Cin. Art Dirs., 1989. Died Feb. 23, 2009.

MARTIN, ROBERT ALAN, lawyer; b. LA, Feb. 26, 1940; s. Richard Carl and Cleo Fern (Bonnell) M.; m. Katarina Eva Maria Schlyter, May 20, 1970; children: Erik, Carl, Anna. BA, Stanford U., Palo Alto, Calif., 1961; JD, Hastings Sch. Law, San Francisco, 1964. Bar: Calif. 1965. Assoc. McDougall & Schulz, Palo Alto, 1964-66, Brobeck, Phleger & Harrison, San Francisco, 1966-68, Jacobs, Blanckenburg, May et al, San Francisco, Colvin, Martin & Links, San Francisco, 1968-84, Farella, Braun & Martel, San Francisco, 1984-91; pvt. practice Walnut Creek, Calif., from 1992. Mem. Estate Planning Coun. of Diablo Valley. Mem. ABA, State Bar of Calif., Bar Assn. of San Francisco, Contra Costa County Bar Assn., Order of the Coif, Thurston Soc. Avocations: travel, photography. Died Aug. 25, 2007.

MARTIN, ROBERT MICHAEL, JR., lawyer; b. Brownwood, Tex., Aug. 5, 1921; s. Robert Michael and Fannie Caroline (Wilkinson) M.; m. Joan Hull, 1956 (div. 1969); children: Martha, Robert Michael III; m. Kay A. King, 1984. BA, BBA, U. Tex., 1942, LLB, 1947; postgrad., So. Meth. U., 1950-53. Bar: Tex. 1947. Instr. acctg. and bus. law U. Tex., Austin, 1946-48; with law dept. So. Union Gas Co., 1948-53; ptnr. Storey, Armstrong, Steger & Martin, Dallas, 1953-97. Bd. dirs. Downtown YMCA, Dallas, 1960-63. With AUS, 1942-45, ETO, maj. gen. USAF Res. Decorated D.S.M. Fellow Am. Bar Found., Tex. Bar Found.; mem. ABA, State Bar Tex. (chmn. mil. law sect. 1972-73, bd. dirs. 1982-85), Dallas Bar Assn. (bd. dirs. 1962-64), Dallas C. of C., Phi Beta Kappa, Beta Gamma Sigma, Phi Eta Sigma, Phi Gamma Delta. Presbyterian. Home: Dallas, Tex. Died Dec. 8, 2007.

MARTIN, ROBERT WAYNE, communications educator, counselor; b. Battle Creek, Mich., Aug. 17, 1954; BA, U. Mich., 1977, MA, 1981; PhD, U. Iowa, 1989. Asst. prof. comm. U. Maine, Orono, 1985-86, Purdue U., Ft. Wayne, Ind., 1986-93, Ithace (N.Y.) Coll., from 1993. Faculty adv. student chpt. Internat. Assn. Bus. Comm., Ft. Wayne, 1989-93. Recipient Bronze Quill Merit award Internat. Assn. Bus. Comm., Ft. Wayne, 1992. Mem. Internat. Soc. for Study Pers. Relationships, Speech Comm. Assn., Cen. States Comm. Assn. Home: Ithaca, NY. Died Apr. 14, 2008.

MARTIN, THEODORE KRINN, former university administrator; b. Blue Mountain, Miss., Jan. 2, 1915; s. Thomas Theodore and Ivy (Manning) M.; m. Lorene Garrison, Sept. 6, 1947; children: Glenn Krinn, Mary Ann, Janet Kay. AB, Georgetown Coll., Ky., 1935; MA, La. State U., 1941; PhD, George Peabody Coll., 1949. Tchr. Consol. Sch., Dumas, Miss., 1935-36; prin. Mississippi Heights Acad., 1936-39; tchr. Murphy High Sch., Mobile, Ala., 1940-41; registrar Miss. State U., 1949-53, registrar, adminstrv. asst. to pres., 1953-56, dean Sch. Edn., 1956-61, exec. asst. to pres., 1961-66, v.p., 1966-85, dir. Summer Sch., 1956-70, ret., 1985. Served as capt. AUS, 1941-46. T.K. Martin Ctr. for Tech. and Disability on Miss. State U. Campus named in his honor. Mem. Masons, Kappa Alpha, Phi Kappa Phi, Omicron Delta Kappa, Kappa Delta Pi, Phi Delta Kappa. Home: Starkville, Miss. Died Sept. 26, 1994.

MARUMOTO, WILLIAM HIDEO, management consultant; b. LA, Dec. 16, 1934; s. Harry Y. and Midori Mary (Koyama) M.; m. Jean Masako Morishige, June 14, 1959; children: Wendy H. Vlahos, Todd M., Lani M. Moore, J. Tamiko Smith. BA, Whittier Coll., 1957; postgrad., U. Oreg., 1957-58. Dir. alumni rels. Whittier (Calif.) Coll., 1958-65; assoc. dir. alumni and devel. UCLA, 1965-68; v.p. planning and devel. Calif. Inst. of the Arts, LA, 1968-69; sr. cons. Peat, Marwick & Mitchell, LA, 1969; asst. to sec. US Dept. Health Edn. & Welfare, Washington, 1969; spl. asst. to Pres. The White House, Washington, 1970-73; pres. The Interface Group Ltd., Washington, 1973-89; chmn. The Interface Group Ltd./Boyden, Washington, 1989-92, mng. dir., ptnr., 1992-2000, chmn., CEO, 2000—08. Lectr. on career strategy, planning and diversity, 1973-2008; mem. White House Pers. Task Force, 1981-88, White House Conf. on Small Bus., 1986; pres. and CEO Asian Pacific Am. Inst. for Congl. Studies, 2005-08. Trustee Whittier Coll., 1978-2002, Japanese Am. Nat. Mus., 1989-2008, Mex. Am. Legal Def. and Ednl. Fund, 1989-93, Wolf Trap Found. for Performing Arts, 1995-2001, Coun. for Advancement and Support Edn., 1980-84; chmn. Nat. Japanese Am. Meml. Found., 1994-97, chmn., 1995-97; chmn. Leadership Edn. for Asian Pacifics, Inc., 1994-97; bd. dirs. Congl. Asian Am. Caucus Inst., 1997-2008, chmn. 2001—08, Nat. Asian Pacific Ctr. on Aging, 1999-2008; mem. assocs. coun. George Washington U. Sch. Bus. and Pub. Mgmt., 1997-2008; mem. Pres. Adv. Com. on Performing Arts John F. Kennedy Ctr. Performing Arts, 2003-08. Recipient Stanley Suyat Meml. Leadership award Asian Am. Govt. Exec. Network, 2002; named one of Am.'s Top 150 Exec. Recruiters, Harper & Rowe Pubs., 1992, 94, One of 500 Most Influential Asian Americans, Ave. Avenue Mag., 1996, Most Influential Asian Am. in Washington, Asian Week, 1997. Mem. Assn. Exec. Search Cons. (bd. dirs. 1994-97), U.S. Nat. Assn. Corp. and Profl. Recruiters, Congl. Country Club. Republican. Methodist. Home: Mc Lean, Va. Died Nov. 25, 2008.

MARVIN, DANIEL EZRA, JR., bank executive; b. East Stroudsburg, Pa., Apr. 25, 1938; s. Daniel E. Marvin Sr. and Hazel (Meitzler) Marvin Doll; m. Maxine James, June 15, 1958; children: Brian, Laurie, Amy. Student, Susquehanna U., 1956-58; BS in Edn., E. Stroudsburg State Coll., 1960; MS in Zoology, Ohio U., 1962; PhD in Physiology, Va. Poly. Inst., 1966; DLitt (hon.), Hanyang U., Seoul, Republic of Korea, 1981. Asst. prof. biology Radford (Va.) Coll., 1962-67, prof., dean div. natural scis., 1967-68, v.p. acad. affairs, 1968-70, acting pres., 1968-69; assoc. dir., then dir. Va. State Council on Higher Edn., Radford, 1970-77; pres. Eastern Ill. U., Charleston, 1977-83, First Nat. Bank, Mattoon, Ill., from 1983, First Mid-Ill. Bancshares, Inc., Mattoon, from 1983. Bd. dirs. Ill. Consol. Telephone Co., Appalachia Ednl. Lab., Cen. Va. Ednl. TV Corp., Nat. Ctr. Higher Edn. Mgmt. Systems, Resource Ctr. Planned Change at State Colls. and Univs.; chmn. State Policy Bd. Automated Data Processing in Higher Edn., Nat. Adv. Council on Extension and Continuing Edn.; past pres. Gateway Collegiate Athletic Conf.; mem. U.S. del. univ. pres. to Poland, 1980, 82. Mem. editorial bd. Community/Jr. Coll. Research Quar.; contbr. to profl. jours.; subject of mag. interviews. Mem. Gov.'s Manpower Planning Council, State of Va.; bd. dirs. Sarah Bush Lincoln Health Ctr.; pres. East Cen. Ill. Devel. Corp., 1985-88; bd. dirs. Lakeland Coll. Found. Recipient Strategic Planning of Higher Edn. award, Ministry Edn., Republic of China, 1976, 81; grantee NSF, Ford Found. Mem. Ill. Ednl. Consortium (bd. dirs.), Am. Council Edn., Am. Assn. State Colls. and Univs., Ill. Bankers Assn. (bd. dirs.), Am. Bankers Assn., Community Bankers Council and Adv. Bd., Sigma Xi. Republican. Presbyterian. Avocations: model railroading, reading, hunting. Home: Mattoon, Ill. Died Apr. 21, 2008.

MASAITIS, CESLOVAS, retired researcher; b. Kaunas, Lithuania, Mar. 2, 1912; came to U.S., 1949; s. Joseph and Jadvyga (Butkevicius) M.; widowed; 1 child, Nijole. Diploma, U. Kaunas, 1937; PhD, U. Tenn., 1956. Asst. U. Vytautas The Great, Kaunas, 1937-39; sr. asst. U. Vilnius, Lithuania, 1939-44; lectr. Nazareth Coll., Bardstwon, Ky., 1950-52, U. Ky., Lexington, 1952-53, U. Tenn., Knosville, 1953-56; mathematician Ballistic Rsch. Lab., Aberdeen, Md., 1956-63, supervisory rsch. math., 1963-80, cons., 1980-84, ret., 1984. Lectr. U. Del., Newark, 1957-69, U. Vytautat The Great, 1990; rsch. asst. prof. U. Md. Balt., 1963-76. Contbr. articles to profl. jours. Pres. Alumni of Lithuanian Cath. Orgn., Aux. of Immaculate Conception Convent, 1981—, Lithuanian Christian Dem. Union, Chgo., 1989—. Fellow Ballistic Rsch. Lab. Mem. Am. Math. Assn., Lithuanian Cath. Acad. Sci. (exec. pres. 1984—). Roman Catholic. Avocation: poetry. Home: Putnam, Conn. Died Sept. 7, 2007.

MASCHKA, DENNIS LEE, parks and recreation director; b. Wabasha, Minn., July 12, 1945; s. Leroy John and Margaret LaRue (McDonough) M.; m. Linda Ann Becchetti, Aug. 1, 1970; children: Brian Louis, Megan Anne. BS, Mankato State U., 1972, M, 1992. Dir. cmty. edn. Litchfield (Minn.) Pub. Schs., 1972-76; asst. dir. parks, recreation and forestry City of Austin, Minn., 1976-92, exec. dir. parks, recreation and forestry Minn., from 1992. Author: The Coaches Book, 1985. Bd. dirs. Austin Youth Football, 1980—, Spruce Up Austin Com., 1989—; pres. Austin Jaycees, 1980-82; commr. Dist. 1 Softball, So. Minn., 1985—; chairperson Convention Visitors Bur., Austin, 1990-94; chair Ctrl. Catholic Sch. Bd., 1982-84. Recipient Leadership award Blanden Found., 1993; named Ten Outstanding Young Minnesotans, 1982, Outstanding Young Men Am., 1983. Mem. Minn. Park and Recreation (con. com. 1991, pres. So. chpt. 1988-90), Nat. Parks and Recreation, Austin Sports Commn. (chairperson), Austin Youth Football, Rotary Internat. Republican. Roman Catholic. Avocations: walking, reading, hot tubbing, all sports, wood carving. Home: Austin, Minn. Died June 22, 2008.

MASCLEE, KENT IVAN, publishing executive; b. Rochester, NY, May 15, 1943; s. Ivan and Bertha E. (Aldridge) M.; m. Christine M. Foster, Sept. 12, 1970 (div. 1981); m. Deborah Anne Dean, Jan. 1, 1989; Joseph, Amy, Arthur. BS, St. Lawrence U., 1965. Regional sales mgr. Congoleum Industries, Kearney, N.J., 1971-72; mktg. svcs. mgr. Worcester Controls Corp., West Boylston, Mass., 1972-79; mktg. mgr. Cahners Pub. Co., Newton, Mass., 1980-88, dir. rsch., from 1988. Lt. USNR, 1966-71. Mem. Am. Mktg. Assn. (v.p. indsl. Boston chpt. 1984-85). Home: North Reading, Mass. Died Nov. 13, 2007.

MASON, EDWARD A., filmmaker, psychiatrist; b. Elmira, NY, Mar. 18, 1919; s. Allen and Mary Lewis (Bacon) M.; m. Jean Kaltwasser, Sept. 2, 1944; children: Jeffrey Allen, Julia Lesley, Andrea Lisa. Student, Williams Coll., 1937-39; BA, Washington U., St. Louis, 1941, MD, 1944. Cert. psychiatrist Am. Bd. of Psychology and Neurology. Intern in pediatrics New Haven Hosp., 1944-45; resident in psychiatry McLean Hosp., Waverley, Mass., 1945-46; commonwealth fellow Putnam Children's Ctr. and Judge Baker, Boston, 1949-51; asst. psychiatrist Children's Hosp. Med. Ctr., Boston, 1951-54; instr. mental health Sch. Pub. Health Harvard U., Boston, 1954-57, asst. prof., 1957-64; asst. prof. psychiatry Harvard U. Med. Sch., Boston, 1964-78; assoc. prof. Harvard U. Med. Sch. and Mass. Mental Health Ctr., Boston, 1978-94. Dir., producer Documentaries for Learning, Boston, 1963-94; trustee Wediko Children's Svcs., Boston, 1970-73, 78—; pres. New Eng. Coun. Child Psychiatry, Boston, 1971-73, Am. Film and Video Assn., N.Y.C., 1977-78. Dir., producer: (films) Boys in Conflict, 1969 (Blue ribbon 1970), Gee, Officer Krupke, 1975 (Blue ribbon 1976), (videotape) Can You Love Two Moms, 1987 (Bronze medal 1987); dir., co-producer Breaking the Silence, 1984, Where's Mummy? (Blue ribbon 1991). Mem. adv. bd. to Congress, Cambridge (Mass.) Pub. Access Corp., 1986-90; trustee Coun. for Nontheatrical Events, 1988. Recipient Silver Hugo award Chgo. Internat. Film Festival, 1975, First prize Muir Med. Film Festival, 1978, Bronze medal Internat. Film and TV Festival, 1981, Assn. Visual Communicators, 1986. Fellow Am. Psychiat. Assn. (program coms.), Am. Orthopsychiat. Assn. (program com., dir. 1961-72). Avocations: painting, photography, computer enhanced photography. Home: Cambridge, Mass. Died Dec. 26, 2007.

MASON, ELI, accountant; b. NYC, Nov. 16, 1920; m. Claire Mason; children: Judy, Nina. BBA, Baruch Coll., 1940; LhD (hon.), CUNY, 1978. CPA, N.Y. Acct. RCA, NYC, 1940-41, Klein, Hinds & Fink, NYC, 1941-43; controller Hydrawmatic Machine Corp., NYC, 1943-46; mng. ptnr. Mason & Co., NYC, 1946—2003. Contbr. articles to profl. jours. Bd. dirs., chmn. Baruch Coll., N.Y.C., 1981-82. Recipient Townsend Harris medal CUNY, 1975, Beta Gamma Sigma medal, N.Y.C., 1989. Mem. N.Y. State Soc. CPAs (pres. 1972-73, Disting. Svc. award 1983), N.Y. State Bd. Pub. Accountancy (chmn. 1972-82), AICPA (v.p. 1968-69), Nat. Conf. CPA Practitioners (chmn. 1985-86). Died Aug. 3, 2009.

MASON, FRANK HERBERT, artist, educator; b. Cleve., Feb. 20, 1921; s. Walter Harrison and Mildred Mary (Corbin) M.; m. Anne Cary Crosby, Mar. 12, 1966; 1 son, Arden Harriman. Student, Nat. Acad. Design, 1937-38, Art Students League, NYC, 1938-51. Instr. fine arts Art Students League, from 1951. Represented in permanent collections: Ch. of San Giovanni di Malta, Venice, Italy (Cross of Merit for eight canvas murals on life of St. Anthony of Padua Sovereign Mil. Order of Malta), Am. Embassy, London, Duke U., Butler Inst. Am. Art, Eureka Coll., Phoenix Mus. Fine Arts, Mus. City of NY, St. Patrick's Old Cathedral, NY, San Antonio Mus. Art; 3 murals on naval history of Saudi Arabia, King Faisal Naval Base, Jiddah; (mural) And the Gods Smiled on These, Houston. Served with AUS, 1945-46. Recipient North Am. Continent award Expn. Intercontinentale, Monaco, 1968, Purchase prize, Am. Acad. Arts and Letters, Arthus Ross award, Newington-Cropsey award for Excellence. Mem. NAD (past treas.), Nat. Mural Soc., Allied Artist Am., Auduson Artists, Hudson Valley Artist Assn., Royal Soc. Arts, Salamagundi Club. Died June 16, 2009.

MASSARSKY, STEVEN JAY, entertainment lawyer; b. Jersey City, Mar. 21, 1948; s. Ashur and Yetta M.; married. AB, Brown U., 1970; JD, Rutgers U., Newark, 1975. Bar: Calif. 1975, N.Y. 1976. Pres. Guiding Light Mgmt., Inc., NYC, 1975-81; pvt. practice entertainment law NYC, from 1981; exec. v.p. Voyager Communications, Inc., NYC, from 1989. Mem. N.Y. State Bar Assn., Calif. State Bar Assn. Avocation: sports memorabilia. Home: Cold Spring, NY. Died Oct. 5, 2007.

MASSE', DONALD DUANE, obstetrician, gynecologist, educator; b. Lafayette, Ind., Dec. 9, 1934; s. Otto A. and Frances Maxine (Johnson) M.; m. Mary Perkins, June 6, 1964; children: Stephanie Ann, Mark Christopher. BS, Purdue U., 1956; MD, Marquette U., 1964. Diplomate Am. Bd. Ob-Gyn. Resident in ob-gyn Wayne State U. Med. Sch., Detroit, 1964-69, clin. asst. prof. ob-gyn., from 1969; pvt. practice Detroit, 1969—99. With U.S. Army, 1957-60. Named to Jefferson H.S. Hall of Fame, Lafayette, Ind., 2003. Fellow Am. Coll. Ob-Gyn; mem. Nat. Med. Assn., Mich. Med. Soc., Wayne County Med. Soc., Detroit Med. Soc. (fin. sec. 1971-75), Alpha Phi Alpha. Avocations: golf, fishing. Died June 17, 2008.

MASTNY-FOX, CATHERINE LOUISE, administrator, consultant; b. New Rochelle, NY, June 4, 1939; d. Louis Francis and Catherine Marie (Haage) Kacmarynski; m. Vojtech Mastny, July 25, 1964 (div. Oct. 1987); m. Richard K. Fox, Oct. 10, 1993; children: Catherine Paula (dec.), John Adalbert (dec.), Elizabeth Louise. BA magna cum laude, Coll. New Rochelle, 1961; MA, Columbia U., 1963, PhD, 1968. Lectr. in history various colls., NY, 1968-71, Calif.; researcher, writer H. W. Wilson Co., NYC, 1971-81; contbg. editor Columbia U. Press, NYC, 1972-74; v.p., exec. dir. Internat. Mgmt. and Devel. Inst., Washington, 1978-84, exec. dir., spl. asst. to chmn., 1986-91; v.p. Meridian House Internat., Washington, 1984-85; dir. corp. devel. Washington Music Ensemble, from 1991, also bd. dirs. Cons. in field; panelist NEH, Washington, 1983; internat. advisor Global Nomads, Washington, 1990—. Contbg. author: The American Book of Days, 1978, World Authors, 1970-1971, 1980; contbg. editor: Columbia Ency., 3d edit., 1975. Fulbright Found. grantee, 1961-62; fellow Woodrow Wilson Found., 1962-63, Walter L. Dorn, 1963-64, Konrad Adenauer fellow, 1965-66. Democrat. Roman Catholic. Avocations: travel, classical music, hiking, art collecting, gardening. Home: Bethesda, Md. Died June 28, 2008.

MASTROIANNI, LUIGI, JR., endocrinologist; b. New Haven, Nov. 8, 1925; s. Marion (Dallas) Mastroianni; m. Elaine Catherine Pierson, Nov. 4, 1957; children: John James, Anna Catherine, Robert Luigi. AB, Yale U., 1946; MD, Boston U., 1950, DSc (hon.), 1973; MA (hon.), U. Pa., 1970, MS in Bioethics, 2008. Diplomate Am. Bd. Ob-Gyn. and Reproductive Endocrinology and Infertility. Intern, then resident ob.-gyn. Met. Hosp. N.Y., 1950—54; fellow rsch. Harvard Med. Sch. and Free Hosp. for Women, Boston, 1954—55; instr. dept. ob-gyn. Yale U. Sch. Medicine, New Haven, 1955—56; asst. prof. ob.-gyn. dept. Yale U., New Haven, 1956—61; prof. U. Calif., LA, 1961—65; chief ob-gyn Harbor Gen. Hosp., LA, 1961—65; William Goodell prof. ob.-gyn., chmn. dept. U. Pa. Sch. of Medicine, Phila., 1965—87, William Goodell prof. ob.-gyn. dept., dir. human reproduction div., 1987—96. Contbr. articles to profl. jours. Recipient Squibb prize, Pacific Coast Fertility Soc., 1965, Christian R. and Mary Lindback award, 1969, Gold medal, Barren Found., 1977, King Faisal prize in medicine, 1989, Pub. Recognition award, Assn. Profls. of Gynecology and Obstetrics, 1990, Disting. Svc. award, Soc. Study Reprodn., 1992, Rector's medal, U. Chile, 1993, Axel Munthe award, 1996, Resolve Svc. award, 1997, medal, Coll. Physicians of Phila., 1998. Mem.: Soc. for Study of Reprodn. (Disting. Svc. award 1992), Endocrine Soc., Soc. for Exptl. Biology and Medicine, Soc. Gynecology Investigation (Disting. Scientist award 2004), Inst. of Medicine of NAS, Am. Physiol. Soc., Am. Soc. for Reproductive Medicine, Am. Gynecol. Club, Am. Gynecol. and Obstet. Soc., ACOG, ACS, Chilean Soc. Ob-Gyn. (hon.), Uruguan Soc. Sterility and Fertility (hon.), Israel Soc. Ob-Gyn. (hon.), Soc. Espanola de Fertilidad (hon.), Peruvian Fertility Soc. (hon.), Argentina Fertility Soc. (hon.), Italian Soc. Ob-Gyns. (hon.), Brazilian Fertility Soc. (hon.), Assn. Profs. Ob-Gyn. (hon.), N.C. Gynecol. Soc. (hon.), Tex. Assn. Ob-Gyns. (hon.), Ctrl. Assn. Ob-Gyns. (hon.), Pacific Coast Fertility Soc. (hon.), Alpha Omega Alpha, Sigma Xi. Home: Haverford, Pa. Died Nov. 25, 2008.

MATHER, ANTHONY DEL, data processing executive; b. Flint, Mich., Oct. 28, 1942; s. James Ethraim and Natalie Jeanne (Cranston) M.; m. Josephine Astolia Castro, Feb. 17, 1973. Student, Foothill Coll., 1966-67; BS in Computer Sci., Columbia Pacific U., 1981, MS in Computer Sci., 1982, PhD in Electronic Engring., 1983. Mgr. sales and pub. relations Universal Transport, Mountain View, Calif., 1965-69; dir. ops. Hunter Aero. Spls., Ogden, Utah, 1969-74; pres., engr. Amsel Corp., Ogden, from 1975. Bd. dirs. Biotronics Energy Engring., Clearfield, Utah; v.p. Assoc. Research and Devel., Ogden, 1985—. Avocations: amateur radio, astronomy, family activities. Died Jan. 13, 2008.

MATHES, DAVID WAYNE, music company executive; b. Steubenville, Ohio, Apr. 23, 1933; s. Ralph W. and Orva (Pugh) M.; m. Pauline Sexton, Sept. 25, 1955 (div. Feb. 1978); children: Melody, Dwayne; m. DeAnna S. Newman, Sept. 9, 1978 Cert. in recording engring., Fla. Inst. Tech., 1960. Tech. writer H.L. Yoh Co., Dayton, Ohio, 1950-52; asst. mgr. Coca-Cola Bottling Co., Sanford, Fla., 1957-60; owner, tchr. Mathes Music Studio, Sanford, Fla., 1960-62; chief engr. Globe Recording Studio, Inc., Nashville, 1966-69; engr. Monument Studios, Inc., Nashville, 1969-72; producer, engr. Dave Mathes Prodns., Nashville, 1972-79; asst. to pres. I.B.C. Records, Inc., Nashville, 1980; owner, cons. The Mathes Co., Nashville, 1981-86; pres. Music Machine TV Corp., Nashville, from 1986; creator, host The Music Machine, from 1986. Creator, host The Sound Machine, 1980; founder, sr. adminstr. Inst. Rec. Arts and Scis.; writer I Am Country Music, 1987—. Producer (album) Eddie Albert-Americana, 1976. Pres. Hardeman County (Tenn.) Arts Coun., 1997-98; v.p. Hardeman County chpt. Assn. for the Preservation of Tenn. Antiquities, 1998-99; mem. grant com. Tenn. Arts Commn. Served with USAF, 1952-54. Named to Hon. Order Ky. Cols., 1966; named an hon. dep. sheriff Davidson County Sheriffs Dept., 1977; named an a.d.c. Gov. of Ala., 1987. Fellow Audio Engring. Soc.; mem. Am. Fedn. Musicians, Nat. Acad. Recording Arts and Scis., Broadcast Music, Inc., Country Music Assn., Nat. Entertainment Journalist Assn. (life), Nat. Fedn. for Decency (pres. Nashville chpt. 1985-86), Nashville Area C. of C. (com. 1985). Republican. Mem. Ch. of the Nazarene. Clubs: The Cola Clan (Atlanta); Bankers (Louisville). Avocations: collecting coca-cola memorabilia, prospecting for gold. Died Jan. 30, 2008.

MATHURIN MAIR, LUCILLE, diplomat; Degree in history, London U.; PhD in History, U. West Indies, D (hon.), U. Fla., Gainesville, U. Ulster, Ireland. Lectr. U. West Indies, first warden, women's hall of residence; advisor on women's affairs Govt. of Jamaica; head Jamaican Info. Svc., 1974; dep. head Jamaica's Permanent Mission to the UN, NYC, 1975; amb. to Cuba Ministry Fgn. Affairs, Jamaica; undersec. gen. UN, 1979; sec. gen. World Conf. on the UN Decade for Women, 1980, UN Conf. on Palestine; spl. advisor on women's devel. UNICEF; mem. Jamaican Senate; min. of state Ministry Fgn. Affairs, Jamaica; permanent rep., Jamaica UN, 1992. Bd. govs. Internat. Devel. Rsch. Coun., Canada, Population Coun., Internat. Conf. on Apartheid, Nigeria; regional coord., women and devel. studies unit U. West Indies. Decorated Comdr. the Order of Distinction Govt. Jamaica, Order of Jamaica; recipient Women of Distinction award, OAS, 1987, Triennial award, CARICOM, 1996. Died Jan. 27, 2009; Kingston, Jamaica.

MATTHEWS, EDGAR MORTON, retail executive; b. Atlanta, Mar. 7, 1922; s. Paul Bell and Leta Giselle (Puckett) M.; m. Anne Estelle Wetmore, Apr. 7, 1951; children: Charles Wetmore, Paul Edward. BA, U. Ga., 1949. Editor Piggly Wiggly Corp., Atlanta, 1949-50, asst. mgr. advt. Jacksonville, Fla., 1950-52, mgr. advt., 1953-55, dir. advt., 1956-71, dir. trade relations, 1972-76, v.p. trade relations, from 1976. Editor: Piggly Wiggly Weekly News Letter, 1982—. Mem., pres. Neptune Beach Adv. Planning Bd., Fla., 1956-74; mem. Neptune Beach City Council, 1974-75. Served as corp. U.S. Army, 1943-46. Democrat. Episcopalian. Home: Jacksonville, Fla. Died Jan. 12, 2008.

MATTHEWS, GENE LEROY, liaison engineer; b. Chenalis, Wash., June 17, 1945; s. Rolla Roy and Frances Alvina (Plog) M.; m. Jodelle Eileen Fischer, May 9, 1981 (div. Sept. 1994). BSME, U. Wash., 1968. Supt. of utilities City of Winlock, Wash., 1971-74; city engr. City of Castle Rock, Wash., 1974-75; asst. supt. water-sewer utilities City of Olympia, Wash., 1976; liaison engr. The Boeing Co., Seattle, 1968, 70 and from 78. Commr. Kittitas County Sewer Dist., Snoqualmie Pass, Wash., 1977-82; del. state conv. Dem. Party, Spokane, 1970, Olympia, 1988. Avocation: hang gliding. Home: Winlock, Wash. Died Aug. 20, 2008.

MATTOX, JAMES ALBON, lawyer, former congressman; b. Dallas, Aug. 29, 1943; s. Norman and Mary Kathryn (Harrison) Mattox; m. Marta Jan Karpan; children: James Sterling, Janet Mary Kathryn. BBA magna cum laude, Baylor U., 1965; JD, So. Meth. U., 1968. Bar: Tex. 1968. Dem. precinct chmn. Precinct 215, Dallas, 1965; campaign mgr. Judge Robert Hughes for 3rd Congl. Dist., 68, 1968; criminal prosecutor Dallas County, 1968—70; precinct chmn. Dem. Precinct 254, 1968—70; asst. dist. atty. Dallas County, 1968-70; ptnr. Crowder & Mattox, Dallas, 1970-83; mem. Tex. Ho. Reps. from 33d Dallas Dist., 1972-76, US Congress from 5th Tex. Dist., 1977-83; atty. gen. State of Tex., 1983—90; of counsel Kreisner & Gladney. Mem., program chmn. Southern Meth. U. Young Dem., 1965—67; del. Dallas County Conv., 1966, 68, Senate Dist. Dem. Conv., 1972, Tex. State Dem. Conv., 1972, Dem. Nat. Conv., 1984, 88. Named Outstanding Freshman Rep. Tex. Intercollegiate Students Assn., 1973; Legislator of Yr. Dallas County Women's Polit. Caucus; recipient Watchdog of Treasury award, Nat. Assn. Businessmen, 1980, Combined Law Enforcement Assns. of Tex. award, Nat. award for Consumer Handbook on Solar Energy, 1987, Outstanding Contbn. award & Mary Polk Statewide Leadership award, People Against Violent Crime, medal for Outstanding Leadership in Internat. Affairs, Nat. Congress Editors & Communicators of Mex., award for Outstanding Serv in Cause of Civil Rights & Equal Opportunity, San Antonio Black Lawyers Assn., Outstanding Achievement award for Civil Rights & Affirmative Action, NAACP, Good Guy award, Tex. Women's Polit. Caucus, Outstanding Individual Achievement, Nat. Child Support Enforcement Assn., 6th Ann. Peggy Seale Found. award for Child Support Enforcement, Sunny von Bulow Crime Victims' Rights Advocacy award, League United Latin Am. Citizens award for Outstanding Contributions to Hispanic Cmty. of Tex. Mem.: Travis County Bar Assn., Tex. State Bar Assn. Democrat. Baptist. Home: Austin, Tex. Died Nov. 19, 2008.

MAUCH, JEANNINE ANN, retired elementary school educator; b. Scribner, Nebr., Apr. 17, 1944; d. Oscar Herman Frederick and Viola Fredricka (Backhus) M. BS in Luth. Tchg., Concordia Coll., 1966, MEd, 1988. Cert. tchr. Nebr. Tchr. 1st, 2d, 3d and 4th grades St. Paul Luth. Ch., Perham, Minn., 1966—68; tchr. 3d and 4th grades, dir. choir Wheat Ridge Luth. Ch., Colo., 1968—70; tchr., prin. St. Mark Luth. Ch., Yonkers, NY, 1970—86; tchr. 3d, 4th and 5th grades Zion Luth. Ch., Plainview, Nebr., 1987—2002, prin., 1999—2002, ret., 2002. Recipient 25-Yr. Svc. plaque Zion Luth. Ch., Plainview, 1992, 30-Yr. Svc. plaque, 1997, 35-Yr. Svc. plaque, 2002. Mem.: Luth. Edn. Assn. Avocations: travel, craft shows, punch embroidery. Home: Norfolk, Nebr. Died July 27, 2008.

MAUKE, OTTO RUSSELL, retired college president; b. Webster, Mass., Jan. 26, 1924; s. Otto G. and Florence (Giroux) M.; m. Leah Louison, June 18, 1950. AB, Clark U., 1947, A.M., 1948; PhD (Kellogg fellow), U. Tex., 1965. Tchr. history, acad. dean Endicott Jr. Coll., Beverly, Mass., 1948-65; acad. dean Cumberland County Coll., Vineland, NJ, 1966-67; pres. Camden County Coll., Blackwood, NJ, 1967-87, pres. emeritus, 1987—2009. Served with U.S. Army, 1943-46, PTO. Mem.: Indian River County Literacy Tutoring Program. Home: Sebastian, Fla. Died Feb. 6, 2009.

MAUNE, JAMES J., lawyer; b. NYC, Dec. 10, 1942; s. John Lawrence Maune and Catherine Becker; m. Audrey L. De Nio, Sept. 6, 1965. BS in Physics, Manhattan Coll., 1964; MS in Electrophysics, Poly. Inst. Bklyn., 1968; JD cum laude, St. John's U., Jamaica, NY, 1976. Devel. engr. Wheeler Labs., Great Neck, NY, 1964—67; engr. Sadco Systems, Farmingdale, NY, 1968—70; sr. devel. engr. Hazeltine Corp., Green Lawn, NY, 1970—73, law clk., 1973—75; from law clk. to ptnr. Brumbaugh, Graves, Donohue & Raymond, NYC, 1975—97; ptnr. Baker Botts, LLP, NYC, 1997—97, ret., 2003. Lectr. Practicing Law Inst., NYC, 1990—2002, Am. Intellectual Property Law Assn., Washington, 1995—2003; spl. prof. patent law Hofstra Law Sch., Hempstead, NY, 1989—94. Patentee in field. Adv. Tribunal-Diocese of Rockville Centre, NY, from 1997. Mem.: K.C. (St. Pius X chpt., Grand Knight 1992—93, 2004—05, Knight of Yr. 2002). Republican. Roman Catholic. Avocations: fishing, skiing. Home: Plainview, NY. Died Oct. 18, 2007.

MAW, NICHOLAS (JOHN NICHOLAS MAW), composer, music educator; arrived in US, 1984; s. Clarence Frederick Maw and Hilda Helen Chambers; children: Natasha Helen, Adrian Lindsay. Attended, Royal Acad. Music, 1955—58. Composition tutor Royal Acad. Music, London, 1964—66, Milton Avery Grad. Sch. Arts, Bard Coll., 1990—99; fellow commoner in creative arts Trinity Coll., Cambridge U., England, 1966—70; vis. prof. composition Yale Sch. Music, New Haven, 1984, 1985, 1989, Boston U. Sch. Fine Arts, 1986; prof. composition Peabody Conservatory Music, Balt., from 1999. Music panel mem. Arts Coun. Gt. Britain; coun. mem. Performing Right Soc. Composer: Scenes & Arias, 1962, Violin Concerto, Dance Scenes, Shahnama, Little Concert, Hymnus, Life Studies, 1976, Sinfonia, Sonata For Strings and Two Horns, American Games, La Vita Nuova, The Voice of Love, String Quartet No. 1, 2, 3 & 4, Chamber Music for Wind and Piano, Piano Trio, Flute Quartet, Ghost Dances, Roman Canticle, Night Thoughts for a solo flute, Sonata for Solo Violin, One Foot in Eden Still I Stand, Sophies Choice, Concert Suite, Voices of Memory, Spring Music, Summer Dances, Sonata Notturna, 1985, Odyssey, 1987, The World in the Evening, 1988, (Operas) One Man Show, 1964, The Rising of the Moon, 1967, Sophie's Choice, 2002. Recipient Lili Boulanger prize, 1959, Midsummer City of London prize, 1980, Sudler Internat. Wind Band prize, 1991, Elise L. Stoeger prize, Chamber Music Soc. Lincoln Ctr., 1993. Fellow: Assn. Profl. Composers (founding mem., first chmn.), Royal Acad. Music. Home: Washington, DC. Died May 19, 2009.

MAX, CAROL ANN, oil company executive; b. Chicago Heights, Ill., Jan. 12, 1947; d. Martin H. and Lydia Fern (Moore) Graham; m. James L. Max (div. Mar. 1972); children: Martin L., Cynthia S., Christopher A. Fiscal officer State of Ind., Valparaiso, 1971-73; v.p. Steelco Indsl. Lubricants, Valparaiso, from 1973. Mem. NOW, Am. Bikers Aimed Toward Edn. of Ind., Valparaiso Bus. and Profl. Women, Eagles. Republican. Baptist. Avocation: photography. Home: Valparaiso, Ind. Died Nov. 4, 2007.

MAY, ERNEST RICHARD, history professor, retired dean; b. Ft. Worth, Tex., Nov. 19, 1928; s. Ernest and Rachel (Garza) M.; m. Nancy Caughey, Dec. 15, 1950 (div. Feb. 1982); children: John Ernest, Susan Rachel, Donna LaRee; m. Susan B. Wood, June 22, 1988. AB, UCLA, 1948, MA (Native Sons of Golden West fellow in history), 1949, PhD (Univ. fellow), 1951; MA (hon.), Harvard U., 1959. Lectr. history Los Angeles State Coll., 1950; mem. hist. sect. Joint Chiefs of Staff, 1952-54; instr. history Harvard U., 1954-56, asst. prof., 1956-59, assoc. prof., 1959-63, prof., 1963—2009, Charles Warren prof. history, 1981—2009, chair history dept., 1976—79, dir. Charles Warren Ctr. for Studies in Am. History, 1995—98, Allston Burr sr. tutor, 1960-66, dean Harvard Coll., 1969-71, assoc. dean faculty arts & sciences, 1970-71, dir. Inst. Politics, 1971-74. Mem. Coun. Fgn. Rels.; Alfred Vere Harmsworth prof., U. Oxford, 1997-98 Author: The World War and American Isolation, 1914-17, 1959, The Ultimate Decision, The President as Commander in Chief, 1960, Imperial Democracy, The Emergence of America as a Great Power, 1961, The American Image, 4 vols, 1963, (with John W. Caughey) A History of the United States, 1964, (with editors of Life) The Progressive Era, 1964, War, Boom and Bust, 1964, From Isolation to Imperialism, 1898-1919, 1964, (with John W. Caughey and John Hope Franklin) Land of the Free, 1966, American Imperialism; A Speculative Essay, 1968, Lessons of the Past: The Use and Misuse of History in American Foreign Policy, 1973, The Making of The Monroe Doctrine, 1975, (with Dorothy G. Blaney) Careers for Humanists, 1981; author: A Proud Nation, 1983, Knowing One's Enemies: Intelligence Assessment before the Two World Wars, 1984, (with Richard E. Neustadt) Thinking in Time; The Uses of History for Decision Making, 1986 (Gravemeyer prize 1987), American Cold War Strategy: Interpreting NSC 68, 1994, (with Philip D. Zelikow) The Kennedy Tapes: Inside the White House During the Cuban Missile Crisis, 1997, Strange Victory: Hitler's Conquest of France, 2000; author also numerous articles. Chmn. bd. control John Anson Kittredge Trust. Served as lt. (j.g.) USNR, 1951-54. Guggenheim fellow, 1958-59; faculty research fellow Social Sci. Research Council, 1959-61; fellow Center for Advanced Study Behavioral Scis., 1963-64; fellow Woodrow Wilson Internat. Center, 1983 Mem. Mass. Hist. Soc., Am. Hist. Assn., Soc. Historians Am. Fgn. Relations (pres. 1982-83), AAUP, Am. Acad. Arts and Scis. Clubs: Belmont Hill. Episcopalian. Died June 1, 2009.

MAY, LOUIS PHILIP, III, church organization official; b. Lawton, Okla., Apr. 5, 1958; s. Louis Philip Jr. and Erma Dean (Burkhead) M.; m. Adrienne Marie Direen, Dec. 15, 1990. BA, Miss. Coll., 1980; postgrad., Southwestern Bapt. Theol. Sem., Ft. Worth, 1980-81, 83-87. Video prodn. asst. Bapt. Sunday Sch. Bd., Nashville, 1983; staff writer Restoration mag. James Robison Evangelism Assocs., Ft. Worth, 1984-85; coord. worship media Southcliff Bapt. Ch., Ft. Worth, 1984-87; sound and lighting specialist So. Bapt. Sunday Sch. Bd., Glorieta, N.Mex., from 1987; deacon 1st Bapt. Ch. Santa Fe, from 1989, speech coach, from 1990. Media cons. May Prodns., Ft. Worth, 1984-87; dir. media libr. Santa Fe Bapt. Assn., 1987—, mem. exec. coun., 1987—, sound and lighting cons., 1988—. Contbr. articles to profl. jours. Republican. Home: Santa Fe, N.Mex. Died Oct. 30, 2007.

MAY, ROBERT L., broadcast executive; b. Kansas City, Mo., June 19, 1948; married; 1 child. Student, N.W. Mo. State U., 1966-68, 71-72, various sales courses and confs., 1983. Cert. radio mktg. cons. Sales mgr. Sta. KVOR, Colorado Springs, Colo., 1982-84; collection mgr. Stas. KVOR, KSPZ, Colorado Springs, 1983-84, salesperson, 1984-85, Sta. KWTO, Springfield, Mo., 1985-86; gen. mgr., owner Sta. KVIN, Vinita, Okla., from 1986. Speaker on broadcasting, mktg. and advt. various schs. and community colls., 1976-84; rep. for Sta. KSSS as Country Music Sta. of Yr., Nashville, 1980; master of ceremonies Annual Fan Fair, Nashville, 1980. Bd. dirs. El Paso County Heart Assn., Colorado Springs, 1976-83 (chmn. 1981-82), Grand Lake

Assn., 1987— (1st v.p. 1988—); mem. Colorado Springs Conv. and Visitors Membership com., 1982-84, Mktg. Council Great Lake area, 1986—, Okla. Navy, 1986—, Econ. Devel. Assn., Vinita, 1987—; mem. adult edn. adv. bd. N.E. Okla. A&M, 1987-88. Served to sgt. Signal Corps, U.S. Army, 1968-71, Vietnam. Decorated Bronze Star; recipient Pacemaker of Yr. award Colo. Heart Assn., 1980. Mem. South Grand Lake C. of C. (bd. dirs. 1987—), Alpha Epsilon Rho, Blue Key. Clubs: Pikes Peak Civitan (Colorado Springs) (pres. 1978-79, named Civitan of Yr. 1979). Lodges: Vinita Lions. Died Feb. 8, 2008.

MAY, RUPERT HANS, psychiatrist; b. Darmstadt, Fed. Republic Germany, Apr. 30, 1923; came to U.S., 1953; s. Johannes and Johanna (Mueller) M.; children: Jeannette, Christine, Ralph, Rupert Jr., Manfred. MD, U. Tuebingen, Fed. Rep. Germany, 1951, U. Heidelberg, 1951; MS, Ohio State U., 1955-57. Diplomate Am. Bd. Psychiatry and Neurology. Staff psychiatrist Cleve. Psychiat. Inst., 1957-62; practice psychiat. medicine Parma, Ohio, from 1958. Mem. Am. Acad. Neurology, Am. Psychiat. Assn. Home: Geneva, NY. Died Mar. 4, 2008.

MAYER, RENEE G., lawyer; b. Elizabeth, NJ, Apr. 17, 1933; d. Harry and Bertha Sheinblatt Miller; m. Joseph C. Mayer, June 19, 1955; children: Douglas, Julia, Amy, Andrew. BS, Cornell U., 1955; JD, Hofstra U., 1978. Bar: NY 1979, US Dist. Ct. (ea. dist.) NY 1979, US Ct. Appeals (2d cir., fed. cir.) 1983, US Supreme Ct. 1982. Assoc. atty. Meyer, English & Cianciulli, Mineola, NY, 1978-79, Mineola, 1979-89; ptnr. Riebesehl, Mayer, Keegan & Horowitz, Garden City, NY, 1989-97; pvt. practice law Mineola, 1997-2001, Port Washington, NY, from 2001. Mem. NY State Bar Assn., Nassau Lawyers Assn. Long Island, Inc. (pres. 1996-97, first vice chancellor conf. of continuing legal edn. 1999-2006), Nassau County Women's Bar Assn. (pres. 1985-86), Nassau County Bar Assn. (dir. 1984-87, asst. dean acad. law 1987-91), Cornell Club (bd. govs. 1980-90), Democratic Com. (zone leader, Port. Washington, NY, 1980-93). Avocations: reading, theater, travel. Died Mar. 7, 2008.

MAYER, ROBERT ANTHONY, retired college president; b. NYC, Oct. 30, 1933; s. Ernest John and Theresa Margaret (Mazura) M.; m. Laura Wiley Christ, Apr. 30, 1960. BA magna cum laude, Fairleigh Dickinson U., 1955; MA, NYU, 1967. With N.J. Bank and Trust Co., Paterson, 1955-61, mgr. advt. dept., 1959-61; program supr. advt. dept. Mobil Oil Co., NYC, 1961-62; asst. to dir. Latin Am. program Ford Found., NYC, 1963-65, asst. rep. Brazil, 1965-67; asst. to v.p. adminstrn., 1967-73; officer in charge logistical services Ford Found., 1968-73; asst. dir. programs N.Y. Community Trust, NYC, 1973-76; exec. dir. N.Y. State Council on the Arts, NYC, 1976-79; mgmt. cons. NYC, 1979-80; dir. Internat. Mus. Photography, George Eastman House, Rochester, NY, 1980-89, mgmt. cons., 1989-90; pres. Cleve. Inst. of Art, 1990-97; ret., 1997. Author: (plays) La Borgia, 1971, Alijandru, 1971, They'll Grow No Roses, 1975; mem. editl. adv. bd. Grants mag., 1978—80, exhibited profl. photography, from 1993. Mem. state program adv. panel NEA, 1977—80; mem. Mayor's Com. Cultural Policy, NYC, 1974—75; mem. pres.'s adv. com. Bklyn. campus L.I. U., 1978—79; bd. dirs. Fedn. Protestant Welfare Agys., NYC, 1977—79, Arts Greater Rochester, 1981—83, Garth Fagan's Dance Theatre, 1982—86; trustee Internat. Mus. Photography, 1981—89, Lacoste Sch. Arts, France, 1991—96, sec., 1994—96; mem. dean's adv. com. Grad. Sch. Social Welfare, Fordham U., 1976; mem. N.Y. State Motion Picture, TV Devel. Adv. Bd., 1984—87, N.Y. State Martin Luther King Jr. Commn., 1985—90, Cleve. Coun. Cultural Affairs, 1992—94; chmn. Greater Cleve. Regional Transit Authority Arts in Transit Com., 1992—95; bd. dirs. Friends Ariz. State U. Ctr. Latin Am. Studies, 1997—99, Villa Solana Townhouse Assn., 2001—06, pres., 2000; bd. dirs. Mesa Art Ctr. Found., 2004—06; mem. nat. armed svcs. com. YMCA, 1976. Recipient Nat. award on advocacy for girls Girls Clubs Am., 1976 Mem. Nat. Assembly State Art Agys. (bd. dirs. 1977-79, 1st vice chmn. 1978-79), Alliance Ind. Colls. Art (bd. dirs. 1983-91, vice chmn. 1986-87, sec. 1987-89), N.Y. State Assn. Museums (bd. councilors 1983-86, pres. 1986-89), Assn. Ind. Colls. Art and Design (bd. dirs. 1991-97, exec. com. 1991-93, 96-97). Home: Scottsdale, Ariz. Died Dec. 2, 2008.

MAYES, DAVID MARK, analytical chemist; b. Sacramento, Calif., Sept. 1, 1964; s. Donald Warren Mayes and Jo Elaine (Scott) Berry. BS in Chemistry, Eastern Oreg. State Coll., 1986, BS in Physics, 1986; PhD in Chemistry, U. Wash., 1990. Owner Mayes Enterprises, Haines, Oreg., from 1979; chemometric programmer U. Wash., Seattle, 1990-91; pres. D2 Devel., La Grande, Oreg., from 1991. Contbr. articles to profl. jours. Named Eagle Scout Boy Scouts of Am., 1979. Mem. Am. Chem. Soc., Soc. Applied Spectroscopy, Soc. Physics Students (pres. coll. chpt. 1985), Sigma Pi Sigma. Episcopalian. Died July 18, 2008.

MAYES, SHARON SUZETTE, sculptor, educator; b. Sparta, Ind., Apr. 18, 1948; d. Herbert Franklin and Alma Sue (Keller) M.; m. David Allenberg Katzenstein, Dec. 25, 1983; 1 child, Melissa Sanders-Self. BA, Mich. State U., 1969; MPh, Yale U., 1972, PhD, 1974; MA in Clin. Psychology, Wright Inst., Berkeley, Calif., 1982. Asst. prof. U. Md., College Park, 1974-80; assoc. prof. U. Calif., San Diego, 1981-82; writer, sculptor pvt. practice, Berkeley, Calif., 1982-84; assoc. prof. Macalester Coll., St. Paul, Minn., 1984-86; dir., curator Modern Africa Gallery, Menlo Park, Calif., from 1989. Author: Immune, 1988; contbr. numerous articles and short stories to various publs.; sculptor: works included in juried shows, 1994—. Phi Beta Kappa. Home: Menlo Park, Calif. Died Dec. 19, 2007.

MAYHEW, AUBREY, music industry executive; b. Washington, Oct. 2, 1927; s. Aubrey and Verna June (Hall) M.; m. Carol de Onis, May 10, 1962 (div. 1971); children: Lawrence Aubrey, Michael Aubrey, Parris Mitchell, Casey Aran. Student, Wilson Tchs. Coll., 1948. Dir. WWVA, Wheeling, W.Va., 1947-54, WCOP, Boston, 1954-56; asst. to pres. MGM Records, NYC, 1957-58; v.p. mktg. Capitol Records, LA, 1958-60; prodr., dir. KCAM-TV Prodns., Nashville, from 1981. Pres., founder John F. Kennedy Meml. Ctr., 1968; authority on John F. Kennedy life and memorabilia. Author: (books) Commandants Marine Corps, 1953, World Tribute to John F. Kennedy, 1965; composer (music) Touch My Heart, 1966 (Broadcast Music, Inc. award, 1967); record producer, artist mgmt., 1947—2009; music pub., 1954—2009; developed careers numerous entertainers including Johnny Paycheck, Jeannie C. Riley, Bobby Helms. Served to cpl. U.S. Army Signal Corps, 1945-48. Named Govs. Aide, Nashville, 1978. Mem. Country Music Assn., Broadcast Music Inc., Manuscript Soc., N.Y. Numismatic Soc., Gospel Music Assn. Republican. Episcopalian. Avocations: collector, historian, author. Home: Nashville, Tenn. Died Mar. 2009.

MAZER, NORMA FOX, writer; b. NYC, May 15, 1931; d. Michael and Jean (Garlen) Fox; m. Harry Mazer, Feb. 12, 1950; children: Anne e., Joseph D., Susan R. (dec. 2001), Gina B. Author: I Trissy, 1971, A Figure of Speech, 1973 (Nat. Book award nominee 1974), Saturday, The Twelfth of October, 1975 (Lewis Carroll Shelf award 1976), Dear Bill, Remember Me? and Other Stories, 1976 (N.Y. Times Notable Book 1976, ALA NOtable Book, 1976, Sch. Library Jour. Best Books of Yr. 1976, Christopher award 1976, Lewis Carroll Shelf award 1977), (with Harry Mazer) The Solid gold Kid, 1978 (ALA bEst Books for Young Adults 1978, Internat. Reading Assn. Childrne's Choice, 1979, ALA 100 Best of the Best award 1968-93), Up in Seth's Room, 1979 (ALA Best Books for Young Adults 1979, SLJ Best Books of Yr. 1979, ALA Best of the Best Books 1970-83), Mrs. Fish, Ape and Me, The Dump Queen, 1980 (German Children's Literature prize 1982, List of Honor Austrian Children's Books 1983), Taking Terri Mueller, 1981 (Edgar award 1982, Calif. Young Readers' Medal 1985), summer Girls, Love Boys and Other short Stories, 1982, When We First Met, 1982 (Iowa Teen award 1985), Someone to Love, 1983 (ALA Best Books for Young Adults 1983), Downtown, 1984 (ALA Best Books for Young Adults 1984, N.Y. Times Notable Book 1984), Three Sisters, 1986, A, My Name is Ami (Internat. Reading Assn. Children's Choice 1987), B, My Name is Bunny, 1987, After the Rain, 1987 (Newbery Honor Book, ALA Notable Book, Sch. Library Jour. Best books 1987, ALA Best books for Young Adults 1987, Canadian Children's Book Coun. Choice 1988, Assn. Booksellers for Children Choice 1988, Horn Book Fanfare Book 1988), Silver, 1988 (ALA Best Books for Young Adults 1988, Iowa Teen award 1990-91, ALA 100 Best of Best award 1980-93), (with Harry Mazer) Heartbeat, 1989 (Internat. Reading Assn. Children's Choice 1990, Literature prize ZDF Germany), C, My Name is Cal, 1990, Out of Control, 1994, When She Was Good, 2000, Good Night Maman, 1999, What I Believe, 2005; editor: Waltzing on Water, 1989, C, My Name is Cal, 1990, D, My Name is Danita, 1991, Babyface, 1991 (Am. Booksellers pick of list, 1991, Internat. Reading Assn. Tchr.'s Choice), E, My Name is Emily, 1991, (with Harry Mazer) Bright Days, Stupid Nights, 1992 (Am. Bookseller Pick of List 1992), Out of Control, 1993 (Am. Booksellers Pick of List, 1993, ALA Best Books for Young Adults 1994), Missing Pieces 1995 (Am. Booksellers Pick of List, 1995); contbr. short stories, essays and articles to numerous anthologies, collections and mags. including Redbook, Playgirl, Voice, Ingenue, English Jour., The Writer, Alan Review, Scope, Young Miss. Home: Montpelier, Vt. Died Oct. 17, 2009.

MAZERO, T. JEAN LOUISE, college official; b. Latrobe, Pa., Jan. 25, 1924; d. Dominick B. and Elsie (Fiorina) M.; RN, Latrobe Hosp., 1944; BS in Nursing Edn., U. Pitts., 1946, MEd, 1955, PhD, 1972. Nurse, tchr., adminstr. hosps. in Pa., 1946-64; dir. nursing Latrobe Area Hosp., 1964-69; chmn. div. nursing Edinboro (Pa.) State Coll., 1973-74; asst. to pres. Westmoreland County Community Coll., Youngwood, Pa., 1975-87, coord. rsch. and planning, 1987-90; adj. mem. faculty Skidmore Coll., 1980; mem. community coll. com. Pa. Dept. Edn., 1979-83; ret., 1990. Mem. Nat. League Nursing, Assn. Instl. Rsch., Am. Vocat. Edn. Assn., Southwestern Pa. Higher Edn. Assn., Delta Kappa Gamma. Home: Latrobe, Pa. Died Nov. 25, 2008.

MAZUR, MICHAEL, artist; b. NYC, Nov. 2, 1935; s. Burton Boris and Helen (Isaacs) M.; m. Gail Lewis Beckwith, Dec. 28, 1958; children: Daniel Isaac, Kathe Elizabeth. BA, Amherst Coll., 1958; BFA, Yale U., 1959, MFA, 1961; PhD in Fine Arts (hon.), Lesley Coll., Cambridge, Mass., 2002; DFA (hon.), Coll. Creative Studies, Detroit, 2006. Asst. prof. fine arts Brandeis U., Waltham, Mass., 1965-76; instr. RISD, 1962-65. Vis. prof. Yale U. Sch. Art and Arch., 1972, 81, Queens Coll., CUNY, 1973, U. Calif., Santa Barbara, 1974-75, Boston U., 1982, Mass. Coll. Art, 1994, 95; lectr. Mus. Fine Arts, Boston, Brown U., U. Calif., Berkeley, New Sch. for Social Rsch., Bennington Coll., U. Iowa, Boston U., 1994-95, Katonah Mus., NY Studio Sch., 1994; vis. lectr. Carpenter Ctr., Harvard U., 1976, 78, 89, 92, 94, 95, 97, others; illustrator Fleur du Mal, 1984, The Inferno of Dante, Farrar, Strans & Giroux, 1994, Genesis, 1996; co-chair bd. Fine Arts Work Ctr., Provincetown, Mass., 1996-2009. Exhibited in one-man shows at Kornblee Gallery, NYC, 1960, 63, 66, Boris Mirski, Boston, 1963, 65, Phila. Print Club, 1964, Silvermine Guild, 1964, Fla. State U., 1966, Shoemaker Gallery Juniata Coll., 1966, Alpha Gallery, Boston, 1967, 68, 74, OGL Gallery, LA, 1968, Rose Art Mus., Brandeis U., 1969, A.A.A. Gallery, 1969, Inst. Contemporary Art, Boston, 1970, Terry Dintenfass, NYC, 1974, 76, Picker Gallery, Colgate U., 1973, Trinity Coll., 1976, Ohio State U., 1975, Robert Miller Gallery, NYC, 1977, 80, Harkus-Krakow, Boston, 1977, 79-80, Pace Gallery, NYC, 1980, John Stoller, Mpls., 1981, 85, 88, 91, William and Mary Coll., 1981, Ronald Greenberg, St. Louis, 1981, Janus Gallery, LA, 1982, 84, 88, Barbara Mathes Gallery, NYC, 1984, 86, Barbara Krakow Gallery, Boston, 1984, 86, 89, 91, 93, 95, 97-98, 2000, Art Club Chgo., 1985, Beaver Coll., 1985, Joe Fawbush, NY, 1987-88, Jan Turner Gallery, LA, 1988, Butler Gallery, Houston, 1989, Mary Ryan Gallery, NYC, 1990, 94-2000, Mus. Fine Arts, Boston, 2000, Cantor Ctr.-Stanford U., 2000, Zimmerli Art Mus., New Brunswick, NJ, 2000, Mus. di Castelvecchio, Verona, Italy, 2000, Am. Acad. Rome, 2000-06, Flemming Gallery, Vt., 2006, Fisher Gallery U. So. Calif., LA, 2006; exhibited group shows at, Mus. Modern Art, 1964, 75, Bklyn. Mus., 1960, 62, 64, 66, 76, 80, 84, 86, Fogg Art Mus., 1966, 76, 94, Art. Inst. Chgo., 1964, Pa. Acad., 1966, 93, Phila. Mus., 1966, 88, Boston Mus. Fine Arts., 1967-68, 76-77, 80, 88, 90-92, DeCordova Mus., Lincoln, Mass., 1965-67, 75, 86, 87, Whitney Mus. Am. Art, 1965, 81, 90, 92, Nat. Inst. Arts and Letters, 1965, 74, 80, 86, Sivermine Guild, 1965, Print Biennial of Americas, Santiago, Chile, 1965, Paris Biennale, 1969, Venice Biennale, 1970, Finch Coll. Mus., 1971-72, 2d and 3d Biennial Graphic Art, Cali, Colombia, N.A.D. Ann., 1974, Butler Inst., Youngstown, Ohio, 1974, Ball State U., 1974, America-1976, Sense of Place, Met. Mus., NYC, 1979-80, Montreal Mus. Fine Arts, 1977, Palais Royale, Brussels, 1979, Claude Bernard, Paris, 1980, Alan Frumkin, NYC, 1981, 82, Madison Art Ctr., 1989, Nat. Gallery of Art, Washington, 1990, Pratt Mus., NYC, 1990, Nat. Mus. Am. Art, 1997; traveling exhbns. include, Bicentennial Exhbn., 1976, State Arts Councils, Iowa, Kans., Mo., Nebr., 1973, Am. Monotypes, Smithsonian Instn., 1977; represented in permanent collections, Met. Mus., NYC, Mus. Modern Art, Smith Coll. Art Mus., Library Congress, Fogg Art Mus., Art Inst. Chgo., Whitney Mus., LA County Art Mus., Mus. R.I. Sch. Design, Oreg. Art Mus., U. Maine, Mpls. Inst., Pa. State U., Toledo Art Mus., Phila. Art Mus., U. Ohio Westminster Found., Boston Mus. Fine Arts, Boston Pub. Library, Bklyn. Mus., Addison Gallery, Andover Acad., Yale Art Gallery, Montreal Mus. Fine Arts; commd. Fed. Res. Bank, Boston, 1998, USB-Warburg-Dillon, Stanford, Conn., 1999; (Recipient 2d prize Soc. Am. Graphic Artists 1963, Nat. Inst. Arts and Letters award 1965). Co-founder Artists Against Racism and the War, 1968; bd. dirs. Artists Found., co-chair, 1995—; bd. dirs. Fine Arts Work Ctr., Provincetown, Mass.; mem. Mass. Coun. on Arts and Humanities; mem. Pennell com. Libr. of Congress, 1983-93; founder, dir. Art for Nuc. Weapons Freeze, 1983-84, New Provincetown Print Project, 1990-95; chmn. bd. Provincetown Fine Arts Work Ctr.; overseer Mus. Fine Arts, Boston. Grantee Tiffany Found., 1964, Tamarind Lithography Workshop, 1968; Guggenheim Found. fellow, 1964-65; winner numerous purchase awards; recipient Disting. Svc. "Printworks Emeritus", So. Graphics Coun., 2005. Home: Cambridge, Mass. Died Aug. 18, 2009.

MC AFEE, MARGARET ANNE, retired art educator; b. Denver, May 14, 1929; d. Abe I. and Anne M. Blomquist; m. George Lafayette Finn McAfee, July 22, 1972. AA, UCLA, 1947, BA, 1951; MA in Edn., Calif. State Coll., 1967. Cert. tchr. Calif. State Bd. Of Edn., 1955. Tng. tchr. UCLA, USC & Mt. St. Mary's Coll., 1955—66; art tchr. and dept. chmn. Hamilton Sr. HS, LA, 1952—69; tchr. and prof. of art emeritus LA (Calif.) C.C. Dist., 1969—89; assoc. tchr. art Saddleback C.C., Mission Viejo, Calif., 1990—2003. Cons. in field. Dir.: (TV series) How to Design, Make and Use Mosaic Projects In and Around the Home, 1961—66; contbr. articles to newspapers. Troop leader Girl Scouts Am., LA, 1949—50. Mem.: AAUW, Assn. Ret. Tchrs., The Enamelist Soc., Am. Fedn. Tchrs. Emeritus, Nat. Art Edn. Assn., Calif. Art Edn. Assn., Calif. Tchr.'s Assn., Phi Kappa Phi (hon.), Pi Lambda Theta (hon.). Avocations: gardening, drawing, cooking, reading, travel. Home: Mission Viejo, Calif. Died Jan. 20, 2008.

MCAHREN, ROBERT WILLARD, history educator; b. Sioux City, Iowa, Dec. 3, 1935; s. Willard Calvin and Winifred Mae (Small) McA. BA, So. Meth. U., 1958; PhD, U. Tex.-Austin, 1967. Instr. history Washington & Lee U., Lexington, Va., 1966-67, asst. prof. history, 1967-70, assoc. prof. history, 1970-75, prof. history, 1975—2009, asst. dean coll., 1971-73, assoc. dean coll., 1973-77, head dept. history, 1988—98. Editor (with David D. Van Tassel) document collection with interpretive introduction; European Origins of American Thought, 1969. Mem. Phi Beta Kappa. Democrat. Avocations: orchid growing; model railroading. Home: Lexington, Va. Died Aug. 4, 2009.

MCARDLE, LOIS WOOD, artist, educator; b. Jamestown, NY, July 26, 1933; d. Charles Edward and Marguerite Regina (Murray) McArdle; m. James Lombard Pettee, Aug. 6, 1977; children: Jane Hasson, David, Jonathan, Marguerite McArdle-Pettee, Catherine McArdle-Pettee. BA, U. Kans., 1955; MFA, George Washington U., 1966. Lectr. Corcoran Sch. Art, Washington, 1966-68; asst. divsn. chair for art, assoc. prof. No. Va. C.C., Annandale,

1968-78; assoc. prof. Art Inst. Boston, 1979-86; chair visual arts The Madeira Sch., McLean, Va., 1988-98; adj. prof. No. Virginia C.C., from 1998. Vis. prof. Georgetown U., Washington, summer 1973; adj. prof. Mass. Coll. Art, Boston, 1978-80; advanced placement reader Coll. Bd., Princeton, N.J., 1994—; master tchr. The Madeira Sch., 1991-95; vis. artist No. Va. C.C., 1984; cons. Accrediting Commn. of Nat. Home Study Coun., 1972. Author: Portrait Drawing, 1984; editor: Hilda Thorpe, 1989; illustrator: Visual Aids, 1967; commd. by U.S. Army Divsn. of Mil. History; solo exhbn. include Franz Bader Gallery, Washington, No. Va. C.C., Anandale, Habitat, Boston, Georgetown U., Washington, Jane Haslem Gallery, Washington; Mahler Gallery, Washington; group exbhns. include Boca Raton (Fla.) Mus., Jane Haslem Gallery, Washington, DeCordova Mus., Lincoln, Mass., Clark Gallery, Lincoln, Mass., Alexandria (Va.) Athenaeum, Smithsonian Instn., Washington; permanent public collections include DeCordova Mus., Touche Ross, Inc., Coopers & Lybrand, Inc., George Washington U., No. Va. C.C., U.S. Army. Chmn. bd. Sign of Jonah, Washington, 1972-74. Mem. Delta Phi Delta, Phi Beta Kappa. Democrat. Home: Adamstown, Md. Died Apr. 27, 2008.

MCAULEY, MILTON KENNETH, author, book publisher; b. Dunsmuir, Calif., Apr. 23, 1919; s. William Clear and Grace (Frentress) McA.; m. Maxine E. Laurenson, Mar. 16, 1942; children: Patricia L., Barbara A., William K. BS, U. Ill., 1956; postgrad., Calif. State U., Northridge, Calif. Luth. U., 1970-71. Commd. USAF, 1941-61, advanced through grades to maj., ret., 1961; engr. Navigation & Control divsn. Bendix, LA, 1961-70; pub./editor Canyon Pub. Co., Canoga Park, Calif., 1980—2008. Author: Hiking Trails of the Santa Monica Mountains, 1980, Hiking Topanga State Park, 1981, Hiking trails Point Mugu State Park, 1982, Hiking Trails Malibu Creek State Park, 1982, Wildflowers of the Santa Monica Mountains, 1985, Wildflower Walks of the Santa Monica Mountains, 1987, Guide to the Backbone trail, 1990. Mem. Ventura County Archaeol. Soc., Santa Monical Mountains Trails Coun., Sierra Club (Environ. award on S.C. 100th birthday 1994). Avocations: silversmith, stone cutting, hiking. Died Dec. 10, 2008.

MCCABE, JAMES JOSEPH, III, marine engineer; b. Oceanside, NY, Apr. 20, 1945; s. James Joseph and Mary Reada (Wood) McC.; m. Evelyn Adeline Rega, Nov. 20, 1973; children: Jennifer Loisann, Shawn Christopher. BSME, U.S. Mcht. Marine Acad., 1967. Marine operating engr. various U.S. Flag Steam Ship Companies, 1967-69; sr. operating engr. SS Santa Maria Prudential Grace Lines, 1970-72; controls engr. Howard Kipp Inc., Bklyn., 1973-75; project engr. R&D group York Rsch. Corp., Stamford, Conn., 1975-77; guarantee engr. Sun Ship Bldg. and Drydock Co., Chester, Pa., 1977-81; port engr. BP Oil (Marine), Cleve., from 1986; asst. marine engr. supt. The Standard Oil Co. of Ohio (now BP Oil), Cleve., from 1986, marine supr., 1991. Engring mktg. cons. Inventory Locator Svc., 1987—. Inventor: hot air crayon sharpener. Head coach Bay Village Recreational Basketball Program, 1990-91. Mem. Soc. Naval Architects and Marine Engring., Soc. Port Engrs., U.S. Mcht. Marine Acad. Alumni Assn. Republican. Presbyterian. Avocations: inventor, woodworking, skiing, tennis, volleyball. Home: Cleveland, Ohio. Died Jan. 15, 2008.

MCCABE, MARY WILLIAMSON, computer systems analyst; b. Memphis, Aug. 8, 1934; d. Edwin Lacey and Mary Maxine (Maners) Williamson; m. Henry Arthur McCabe, Sept. 22, 1973; stepchildren: Patrick, Anne, Kevin, Cathleen, John. BA, Rhodes Coll., 1956. Math. tchr. Bolton (Tenn.) High Sch., 1956-57; programmer/analyst Mallory AF Sta., Memphis, 1957-61; sr. systems specialist computer dept. GE, Huntsville, Ala., 1961-66; sr. systems specialist Honeywell Info. Systems, Phoenix, 1966-78, Honeywell Bull, Mpls., 1979-88. Pres. McCabe & Assocs., Inc., Minnetonka, Minn., 1990-91, v.p. 1992. Vol. Am. Cancer Soc., Minnetonka, 1980—91; co-dir. altar guild Christ Ch. Ascension, from 2002. Mem. Paradise Rep. Women's Club (cmty affairs chair 2002, 2d v.p. 2004), Alpha Omicron Pi (v.p. Kappa Omicron chpt. 1955-56). Republican. Episcopalian. Avocations: reading, photography. Home: Scottsdale, Ariz. Died Nov. 4, 2007.

MCCAHON, CHERYL DIAB, geriatrics nursing educator; b. Toledo, Nov. 20, 1942; d. Paul and Janet Diab; m. David McCahon, Sept. 1965; children: Mary, Kris. Diploma, St. Vincents Hosp., 1963; BSN, U. Pitts., 1969; MS in Gerontol. Nursing, Case Western Res. U., 1980; doctoral candidate, Kent State U. RN, Ohio. Instr. Case Western Res. U., Cleve.; assoc. prof. Cleve. State U. Mem. Ohio Citizens League for Nursing (chair com. on aging 1985-91), Golden Key Nat. Honor Soc., Sigma Theta Tau. Home: Chagrin Falls, Ohio. Died Aug. 3, 2008.

MC CANN, CECILE NELKEN, writer, artist; b. New Orleans, July 13, 1917; d. Abraham and Leona Nelken; children: Dorothy Collins, Cecile Isaacs, Annette Arnold, Denise Bachman, Albert Hews III. Student, Vassar Coll., Tulane U.; BA, San Jose State Coll., 1963, MA, 1964; postgrad., U. Calif.-Berkeley, 1966-67; Ph.D (hon.), San Francisco Art Inst., 1989. Tool designer Convair Corp., New Orleans, 1942-45; archtl. draftsman, various companies New Orleans and Clinton, Iowa, 1945-47, 51-53; owner, operator ceramics studio Clinton, 1953-58; instr. San Jose State Coll., 1964-65, Calif. State U., Hayward, 1964-65, Chabot Coll., Hayward, 1966-69, Laney Coll., 1967-70, San Francisco State U., 1977-78; founder, editor, pub. Artweek mag., Oakland, Calif., 1970-89; freelance writer, art advisor Kensington, Calif., 1989—2009. Cons. Nat. Endowment Arts, 1974—78, fellow in art criticism, 1976; panelist numerous confs. and workshops. One-woman shows include Davenport Mus. Art, Robert North Galleries, Chgo., Crocker Art Mus., Sacramento, Calif. Coll. Arts and Crafts, Oakland, exhibited in group shows at DeYoung Mus., San Francisco, Everson Mus. Art, Syracuse, N.Y., Oakland Mus., Pasadena Mus., Los Angeles County Mus. Art, Represented in permanent collections San Jose State Coll., Mills Coll., Coll. Holy Names, City of San Francisco, State of Calif. Trustee emerita Rene and Veronica di Rosa Found.; mem. Pub. Art Adv. Com., Oakland. Recipient Vesta award, Woman's Bldg., 1988, Media award, Bay Area Visual Arts Coalition, 1989. Mem.: Internat. Assn. Art Critics, Art Table (Honor award 1988, Achievement award 1992). Died July 2, 2009.

MCCARTY, ROBERT CLARKE, mathematician; b. Mountain View, Calif., Apr. 29, 1922; s. John Emmet and Eldora Lydia (Freeman) McC.; m. Netta Cassen, July 29, 1945 (div. Oct. 1968) 1 child, Stephanie Ann; m. Rita Ransier, July 29, 1969; children: Michael Wayne, Teresa Kay, Kathleen Gail. BA in Math., San Jose Sate U., 1950; MS in Math. and Statistics, U. Wash., Seattle, 1957; PhD in Math., Pacific Western U., 1990. Staff mathematician Boeing Rsch. Labs., Seattle, 1952-59; rsch. mathematician Stanford Rsch. Inst., Menlo Park, Calif., 1959-70; pres., cons. McCarty and Assocs., Gilroy, Calif., from 1976; sr. staff scientist ESL-TRW Corp., Sunnyvale, Calif., 1984-87; prin. staff scientist ARGO Systems, Sunnyvale, 1987-93. Sci. advisor to Congresswoman Zoe Lofgren, sci. com. US Congress, 1994—; rsch. proxy for Prof. A.S. Paulraj, Dept. Elec. Engring., Info. Scis., Stanford U., 1993-95; sr. rsch. mathematician Ares Corp., Arlington, Va., 1994-96; cons. in field. Contbr. articles to profl. jours. Lt. USCGR, 1941—52, WWII, European and Pacific, ret. lt. USCGR, 1951—52, Korean War, Ctrl. and North Pacific. Mem. Sigma Xi. Avocations: amateur radio, rifle and pistol marksmanship, swimming. Died Nov. 2, 2007.

MCCAULEY, JANE REYNOLDS, journalist; b. Wilmington, Del., Oct. 22, 1947; d. John Thomas and Helen (Campbell) McC. BA, Guilford Coll., 1969. Editor, sr. writer Nat. Geographic Soc., Washington, 1970-90; freelance writer, editor, artist, 1990-96; exec. editor AM Quilter's Soc., 1996-97; freelance editor, writer, from 1997. Former owner Unique Native Crafts; tropical bird specialist. Author of 15 children's books; co-author award-winning travel books, art revs. Mem.: Children's Book Soc. Home: Charlottesville, Va. Died July 4, 2008.

MCCLEARY, HENRY GLEN, geophysicist; b. Casper, Wyo., June 4, 1922; s. Raymond and Wyoma N. (Posey) McCleary Grieve; m. Beryl Tenney Nowlin, May 28, 1950; children: Gail, Glenn, Neil, Paul., Henry Slen(dec. Nov. 29, 2008) Geol. Engr., Colo. Sch. Mines, 1948. From geophysicist to party chief seismic Amoco, various locations, 1948-53; exploration mgr. Woodson Oil Co., Fort Worth, 1953-60; resident mgr. NAMCO, Tripoli, Libya, 1961-62; chief geophysicist to staff geophys. assoc. Amoco Internat. Oil Co., 1963-86, Cairo, London and Buenos Aires, 1963-73, Chgo., 1973-84, Denver, 1983-84, Houston, 1984-86; internat. geophys. cons., from 1986. Served with USN, 1943-46. Named Hon. Admiral Tex. Navy, 1968. Mem. Soc. Exploration Geophysicists, Soc. Petroleum Engrs., AAAS, Houston Gem and Mineral Soc., Profl. Oil People, Sigma Alpha Epsilon, Theta Tau. Clubs: Adventurers, Meml. Forest (Houston). Republican. Lutheran. Home: Houston, Tex. Died Nov. 29, 2008.

MCCLELLAND, KATE, librarian; Asst. dir., dir. youth svcs. Perrot Meml. Libr., Old Greenwich, Conn., ret., 2007. Contbr. articles to profl. publs. Recipient NY Times Libr. award, 2006. Mem.: Assn. Libr. Svc. to Children (bd. dirs. from 2005, mem. Notable Books for Children (jointly with ALA)). Died Jan. 28, 2009.

MCCLENAHAN, JOHN LORIMER, retired radiologist; b. Assiut, Egypt, Apr. 25, 1915; arrived in U.S., 1927; s. Robert Stewart and Janet Wallace McClenahan; m. Mary Tyler Cheek (dec. Jan. 16, 2005); children: John Spencer, Susan Starrett Stockdale. BA, Yale U., 1937; MD, U. Pa., 1941. Diplomate Am. Bd. Radiology. Intern Pa. Hosp., Phila., 1941—42; ward officer Walter Reed Gen. Hosp., 1942—43; rschr. in physiology Trudeau Sanatorium, NY, 1946—47; ship surgeon The Grace Line, NY, 1947; residen in radiology N.Y. Hosp.-Cornell Med. Ctr., NYC, 1950—52; asst. attending radiologist N.Y. Hosp., NYC, 1952—55; asst. in radiology Presbyn. Hosp., Phila., 1956—57; vis. radiologist Hosp. of U. Pa., Phila., 1957—68; clin. assoc. prof. radiology Thomas Jefferson Hosp., 1968—79; ret., 1979. Author: Radiology As an Art, 1968, On Going a Journey, 2002. 1st lt. MC, AUS, 1942—45. Recipient Cert. of Merit, Am. Roentgen Ray Soc., 1955. Mem.: Med. Soc. Va., Coll. Physicians. Phila. (Disting. Svc. medal). Democrat. Episcopalian. Avocation: writing. Home: Richmond, Va. Died Jan. 1, 2008.

MCCLUNG, FRANK DIXON, counselor; b. Greensboro, Md., Dec. 11, 1946; s. Dana Dixon and Wilma Louise (Fisher) McC.; m. Cheryl Theresa Chatman, Oct. 6, 1973 (div. 1990). AAS, C.C. Air Force, Maxwell AFB, Ala., 1980; BS in Mgmt., Troy State U., 1979, MS in Mgmt., 1982; MEd in Counseling, Boston U., 1988. Enlisted USAF, 1964, advanced through ranks to sr. master sgt., 1982, resigned, 1985, technician, 1964-82, logistician, 1982-85; ret., 1985; small bus. cons., Concord, N.H., 1988-89; counselor, rschr., Jane Lew, W.Va., from 1989. Mem. AACD, Nat. Employment Counselors Assn., English Speaking Union. Republican. Methodist. Avocations: special olympics, boy scouts, coin collecting/numismatics, model rail roading. Died Dec. 7, 2007.

MCCLUSKEY, NEIL GERARD, gerontologist, educator, literary agent; b. Seattle, Dec. 15, 1920; s. Patrick John and Mary Genevieve (Casey) McC.; m. Elaine Lituchy, June 5, 1977. AB, Gonzaga U., 1944, MA, 1945; Lic. in Sacred Theology, Gen. Theol. Union, Berkeley, 1952; PhD, Columbia U., 1957. Assoc. editor Am. (Nat. Cath. Weekly), NYC, 1955-60; dean sch. edn. Gonzaga U., Spokane, 1960-62, dir. hons. program, 1963-65, v.p. acad., 1963-66; prof. U. Notre Dame, South Bend, Ind., 1966-71, dean, dir. Inst. Studies in Edn., 1968-71; prof., dean profl. studies Lehman Coll. CUNY, 1971-75; dir. Ctr. Gerontol. Studies CUNY Grad. Sch., 1975-81; exec. dir. BHRAGS Social Svcs. Ctr., Bklyn., 1981-84; sr. cons. Retirement Advisors, Inc., NYC, from 1985. Pres. Westchester Lit. Agy., 1991—. Author: Public Schools and Moral Education, 1958, Catholic Viewpoint on Education, 1959, Catholic Education Faces Its Future, 1969; author, editor: Aging and Society, 1980, Aging and Retirement, 1981. Bd. dirs. Cath. Big Bros. N.Y., 1985—. Home: Fort Lauderdale, Fla. Died May 27, 2008.

MCCOOK, JAMES MARSHALL, banking consultant; b. Jersey City, May 30, 1952; s. James Felix and Catherine Uriel (Rogall) McC.; m. Louise Ann Shesniak, June 30, 1973; children: Jason. Tory, Katelyn. Banker, ATM mgr. Perth Amboy (N.J.) Savings Inst., 1971-84, First Atlantic Savings, South Plainfield, N.J., 1984-91; cons. JMM Consulting, Neptune, N.J., from 1991. Pres. Treas. Users Group, New Brunswick, N.J., 1985-86, advisor, 1986-89; mem. bd. advisors NCR Tristate Users Group, Phila., 1989-90; advisor MAC Users Group, Phila., 1989-90. Buddy Hyacinth Found., New Brunswick, 1992; treas. Atonement Luth. Ch., Asbury Park, N.J., 1988-92, feed-the-hungry, 1990-91. Avocations: cars, computers, consumer activism, legal rsch. Died Mar. 14, 2008.

MCCORD, JAMES RICHARD, III, chemical engineer, mathematician; b. Norristown, Ga., Sept. 2, 1932; s. Zachariah Thigpen Houser Jr. and Neilie Mae (Sumner) McC.; m. Louise France Manning, Oct. 1956 (div. 1974); children: Neil Alexander, Stuart James, Valerie France, Kent Richard. Student, Abraham Baldwin Agrl. Coll., Tifton, Ga., 1949-50; BChE with honors, Ga. Inst. Tech., 1955; postgrad., U. Pitts., 1955-56, Carnegie Inst. Tech., 1956-57; MS, MIT, 1959, PhD in Math, 1961. Asst. chem. engr. TVA, Wilson Dam, Ala., 1951-54; assoc. engr. Westinghouse Electric Corp., Pitts., 1955-57; rsch. asst. ops. rsch. MIT, Cambridge, Mass., 1957-59, tchg. asst. dept. math., 1959-61, rsch. assoc. dept. math., 1961-62, asst. prof., postdoctoral fellow dept. chem. engring., 1962-64; sr. engr., project analyst Esso Research and Engring. Co., Florham Park, N.J., 1964-68; asst. prof. Emory U., Atlanta, 1968-71; pvt. practice math. cons. Atlanta, 1971-80; instr. in math. Ga. So. Coll., Statesboro, 1980-81; inventory control Lovett & Tharpe, Inc., Dublin, Ga., 1981-84; Norristown-Adrian; farmer, businessman, from 1984. Contbr. numerous articles to sci. and math. jours. WEBELOS den leader Boy Scouts Am., Dunwoody, Ga., 1969-70; mem., vol. worker Key Meml. Found., Adrian-Norristown, Ga., 1965—. Mem. AIChE, Ga. Tech. Alumni Assn., MIT Alumni Assn., Sigma Xi, Tau Beta Pi. Republican. Methodist. Avocations: music, fishing, gardening, mathematical puzzles. Died May 3, 2008.

MCCORMICK, EDGAR LINDSLEY, language educator, writer; b. Wadsworth, Ohio, Mar. 12, 1914; s. Thomas Edward McCormick and Carrie Belle Van Sickle; m. Cora Lee Morrow, Aug. 11, 1945; 1 child, Carol Helen. BA, Kent State U., 1936; MA, U. Mich., 1937, PhD, 1950. Tchg. fellow U. Mich., Ann Arbor, 1939—41, 1945—46; head dept. of English Florence State Coll., Ala., 1946—50, Bethany Coll., W.Va., 1950—54; chair freshman English Kent State U., Ohio, 1956—60, asst. dean and assoc. dean, Coll. Arts and Sci., 1964—70, coord. Am. studies, 1966—78, prof. emeritus English, from 1979. Editor English Assn. Ohio Bull., 1959—62; dir. curator Kelso Ho. Mus., Brimfield, 1963—96. Author: Brimfield and Its People...1816-1941, 1988, Determined Lives...(Family History), 1989, Yesterday's Scholars...1932-1979, 2001, They Also Served: Citizen Soldiers (WWII), 1993, Fond Recollection, Country Life, 1918-1941, 2003. Staff sgt. USAF, 1942—45, N. Africa. Recipient Outstanding Achievement award, Ohio Assn. Hist. Soc., 1996. Mem.: Modern Lang. Assn. Democrat. Meth. Achievements include first to provide a detailed account of the 1839-1855 Nantucket migration to Portage County, Ohio. Avocations: history, poetry, photography, travel. Home: Kent, Ohio. Died Feb. 26, 2008.

MCCOURT, FRANK (FRANCIS), writer; b. Bklyn., Aug. 19, 1931; s. Malachy and Angela McCourt; m. Ellen Frey, 1994; 1 child from previous marriage, Margaret. BA in English, NYU, 1957; MA in English, Brooklyn Coll., 1967; degree (hon.), U. Western Ont., 2002. Tchr. McKee Vocat. & Tech. Sch., NYC, Peter Stuyvesant HS, NYC. Author: Angela's Ashes, 1996 (Nat. Book Critics Circle award, 1996, Pulitzer Prize for Biography, 1997, Boeke prize, South Arfica, 1997, ABBY award, LA Times Book award), 'Tis, 1999, Through Irish Eyes: Visual Companion to Angela in Court's Ireland, 2001, Teacher Man, 2005, Angela and the Baby Jesus, 2007. Served with US Army,

Germany. Recipient Action Against Hunger Humanitarian award, 2002; named to Am. Acad. Achievement, Washington, 1999. Mem.: Am. Fedn. Teachers, Nat. Arts Club. Died July 19, 2009.

MCCOY, BERTIE ELIZABETH, pastor; b. Jones, Okla., Apr. 9, 1922; d. Bert Earl and Lizzie Nellie (Wood) DeGroot; m. Frank LCarence McCoy, Aug. 3, 1948. Student, Hills Bus. coll., 1941. Founder, pastor Assemblies of God, Luther, Okla., 1945-55, evangelist Jones, Okla., 1956-58, 62-65, founder, pastor Arvin, Calif., 1958-61, Echoes of Faithod, Las Vegas, from 1966; check writer Fed. Reserve Bank, Oklahoma City, Okla., 1941-46. Pres., Youth Rallies Okla. County, Jones, 1945-55. Founded, built 7 Assemblies of Gof Chs., Oklahome City area, 1945-58, 1 Ch., Arvin, Calif., Orgn. Chs. Echoes of Faith, Las. Vegas, 1962—, 3 Chs., Las Vegas, 1 Ch. Flint, Mich.; missionary worker, Israel, China. Republican. Home: Oklahoma City, Okla. Died Nov. 12, 2007.

MCCOY, MILDRED BROOKMAN, retired elementary education educator; b. Princeton, W.Va., Nov. 23, 1924; d. Ralph William and Nannie Mae (Tabor) Brookman; m. Julius Rossey McCoy, Apr. 12, 1945 (dec. 1980); children: Michael David, Alan Dale. BA, Shepherd Coll., 1976. Elem. tchr. Baltimore County Bd. Edn., Balt., 1957-67, Washington County Bd. Edn., Md., 1967-86, ret., 1986. Docent Washington County Hist. Soc., Hagerstown, Md., 1990—, Washington County Art Mus., 1997—. AAUW grantee, 1993. Mem. Md. Ret. Tchrs. Assn., Hagerstown Women's Club, PEO. Episcopalian. Avocations: antiquing, hiking, travel, reading. Home: Hagerstown, Md. Died May 30, 2008.

MCCOY, PRISCILLA GATES, retired elementary school educator; b. Rochester, Minn., Jan. 5, 1928; d. Vernon Elnathan Gates and Edith Madge Pollock; m. Paul Wilbur McCoy, Mar. 21, 1955; children: Laurie, Hugh(dec.), Daniel, Lise, Mary Ann. BA, Carleton Coll., 1949; postgrad., U. Minn., 1950. Tchr. elem. sch. San Diego City Schs., 1949—87. Real estate agt. San Diego-Coldwell Banker, 1988. Chair Membrocean Beach Planning Bd., 1984—91, 1995—2003; bd. dirs. Main St. Mcht. Orgn., San Diego, 1985—2005, Hist. Soc., Ocean Beach, 1994—2005. Died Feb. 22, 2008.

MCCULLOH, GERALD WILLIAM, theology studies educator, researcher; b. St. Paul, May 3, 1941; m. Karen Jane Smith, June 10, 1967; children: Gerald J., Heather E. BA magna cum laude, Vanderbilt U., Nashville, 1962; MDiv, Harvard U., Cambridge, Mass., 1965; MA, U. Chgo., 1968, PhD, 1973. Chaplain McKinley Park Ch., Alaska, 1964; proctor Andover Hall, Meth. vicar campus ministry Harvard U., 1964; instr. humanities Ctrl. YMCA Coll., Chgo., 1968; with Loyola U., Chgo., 1968—2005, humanities rsch. coord., 1979-80, assoc. univ. chaplain, 1974-90, instr. theology, 1968-73, asst. prof., 1973-80, assoc. prof., 1980—2005, assoc. dir. univ. rsch. svcs., 1990-96, acting dir. univ. rsch. svcs., 1994-95; sr. rsch. assoc. Karen McCullon & Assocs., Chgo., from 2005. Vis. scholar Cambridge U., 1970; NEH fellow, participant Inst. on Post-Bibl. Founds. of Western Civilization, 1978, 79; reviewer NEH, Prism, Macmillan Press, ST. Martin's Press; cons. Conf. on Religious Texts and Social Locations, Lilly Found., Princeton Theol. Sem., 1987, Nat. Coun. Univ. Rsch. Adminstrs., 1990-97, NIH, 1991. Author: Christ's Person and Life-work in the Theology of Albrecht Ritschl: with Special Attention to the Munus Triplex, 1973, A Bibliography of Dissertations in Nineteenth Century Theology: 1960-76, 1976, An Introduction to the Study of Religion: Supplementary Readings, 1982; contbr. articles to profl. jours. Mem. Rogers Park Community Coun., 1974-80, bd. dirs., 1975-77; mem. Kilmer Sch. Community Coun., 1974-80, pres., 1976-78, sec., 1979-80; bd. trustees United Ch. of Rogers Park, 1977-83, v.p., 1977-80, 81-82; active ARC Blood Program, Boy Scouts Am. Alfred P. Sloan fellow, 1958-62, English-Speaking Union fellow Cambridge U., 1970-71; recipient Scholarship Harvard U., 1963, rsch. grants Loyola U. Chgo., 1973, 77, 87, 97. Mem. AAUP, Am. Acad. Religion (19th Century Theology Group, Currents in Contemporary Christology Group, Roman Catholic Modernism Group, sect. chair theology/philosophy of religion Midwest region 1987-92, exec. com. 1987-92), Am. Acad. Polit. and Social Sci., Am. Soc. Ch. History, Nat. Coun. Univ. Rsch. Adminstrs., Soc. Sci. Study Religion, Soc. Rsch. Adminstrs, Assn. Univ. Tech. Mgrs., Phi Beta Kappa (chair Kappa chpt. 1999-00). Methodist. Home: Morton Grove, Ill. Died Feb. 23, 2008.

MCCULLOUGH, WILLARD G., retired biochemist; b. Brighton, Mich., Nov. 13, 1914; s. George W. and Florence Bird McCullough; m. Barbara Isabel McMullen, Sept. 23, 1944; children: Andrew Scott, Robin Nelson. BS in Chemistry, Mich. State U., 1941, MS in Bacteriology, 1942; PhD in BioChem., U. Wis., 1949. Instr. U. Mich., Ann Arbor, 1949—50; from asst. to assoc. prof. Wayne State U., Detroit, 1950—60; rsch. biochemist USDA ARS Nat. Animal Disease Ctr., Ames, Iowa, 1960—78. Contbr. scientific papers to profl. jours. Capt. chem. br. US Army, 1943—46. Fellow: AAAS; mem.: Am. Soc. for Microbiology, Am. Chem. Soc. Home: Sears, Mich. Died Feb. 9, 2008.

MCCUTCHEON, JOHN TINNEY, JR., retired journalist; b. Chgo., Nov. 8, 1917; s. John Tinney and Evelyn (Shaw) McC.; m. Susan Dart, Feb. 1, 1943; children: Anne McCutcheon Lewis, Mary, John Tinney III. BS, Harvard U., 1939. Reporter City News Bur., Chgo., 1939-40, Chgo. Tribune, 1940-51, editor column A Line O' Type or Two, 1951-57, editorial writer, 1957-71, editor editorial page, 1971-82, columnist, 1967-70. Pres. Lake Forest (Ill.) Libr., 1970—72. With USNR, 1941—46. Mem. Soc. Midland Authors, Am. Soc. Newspaper Editors, Nat. Conf. Editorial Writers, Geog. Soc. Chgo. (pres. 1955-57), Chgo. Zool. Soc. (hon. trustee), Chgo. Hist. Soc. (life trustee), Inter Am. Press Assn. (dir., freedom of press com. 1978-87), Wayfarers Club (Chgo.), Tryon (N.C.) Country Club, Sigma Delta Chi. Home: Washington, DC. Died Sept. 30, 2008.

MCDANIEL, ARLIE LEO, clergyman; b. Lonoke, Ark., Oct. 7, 1915; s. Maud L. and Louverna (Stringer) McD.; m. Ella Mae Owens, Dec. 25, 1939; children: Arlie Leo, Alana McDaniel Combs, Angela McDaniel Cyr, Alice Ruth, Adrian Owen, Arden Allen, Anson Mark. AB, Baylor U., 1942; postgrad., Golden Gate Bapt. Sem., 1955-57; DD (hon.), Calif. Bapt. Coll., 1969. Ordained to ministry Bapt. Ch. Pastor Harvard-Terrace Ch., Fresno, Calif., 1952-57, First Ch., Barstow, Calif., 1957-60; exec. sec.-treas. Calif. Bapt. Found., Fresno, 1960-62; pastor Bethel Ch., Escondido, Calif., 1962-67, 1st So. Bapt. Ch., Ventura, Calif., from 1967. Mem. exec. bd. Ark. Bapt. Conv., 1950-52; pres. So. Bapt. Gen. Conv. Calif., 1957-58, pres. bd. dirs. 1957-58; pres. bd. child care and family svcs. So. Bapts. Calif. 1967-68; pres. bd. dirs. Calif. Bapt. Found., 1958-60, bd. dirs., 1962—. With U.S. Army, 1931-34, 42-46. Mem. Masons, Kiwanis (bd. dirs.). Republican. Home: Ventura, Calif. Died July 22, 2008.

MCDERMOTT, WILLIAM THOMAS, accountant, lawyer; b. New Orleans, Jan. 3, 1945; s. William Thomas and Delia Ethel (Belden) McD.; m. Geraldine Dorothy Constantine, Nov. 20, 1965; children: Lisa Anne, Shannon Marie. BSBA, Am. U., 1969, MBA, 1971; JD (with hon.), George Washington U., 1974; grad. exec. mgmt. program, J.L. Kellogg Grad. Sch. CPA, Va.; cert. mgmt. acct.; fellow Life Mgmt. Inst. Ptnr. for tax Ernst & Young, Richmond, Va., from 1969. Co-chmn. U. Va. Fed. Tax Conf., Charlottesville, 1981—; apptd. by Gov. of Va. to Commn. on Competitive and Equitable Tax Policy, 1996. Contbr. articles to profl. jours. Past chmn. bd. dirs. Richmond br. Tuckahoe YMCA, 1984; mem. citizens promotion bd. Henrico County Police Dept., Richmond, 1985; bd. dirs. Greater Richmond YMCA, 1983-84, Theater Va., Richmond, 1982-97; treas., bd. dirs., mem. exec. com. Arts Coun. of Richmond, 1988-96, Children's Home Soc., Richmond, 1987-97/ Recipient Cert. Appreciation award Henrico County Police Dept., 1985, Karl B. Wagner Service award Tuckahoe YMCA, 1986. Mem. ABA, AICPA (individual tax com. 1990-93, chmn. interest expense task force 1993-96), Inst. Mgmt. Accts. (nat. v.p. 1991-92, nat. dir. 1987-89, 95-97, chmn. nat. ethics com., prin. Va. Coun. 1987-88), Va. Soc. CPAs, D.C. Inst. CPAs, Bull and Bear Club, Hermitage Country Club. Roman Catholic. Home: Richmond, Va. Died May 23, 2008.

MCDONALD, JAMES S., investment company executive; b. Titirangi, New Zealand, 1953; arrived in U.S., 1960; AB, Harvard Coll., 1974; JD, U. Va., 1977. With Choate, Hall & Stewart, 1977—86, Boston Harbor Trust Co., N.A. (now Pell Rudman), from 1988; pres. Boston Harbor Trust N.A. (formerly Pell Rudman Trust Co. N.A.), 1988; COO Pell Rudman Trust Co., N.A., 1993—98, CEO, 1998—2000, Rockefeller & Co., Inc., NYC, 2000—09. Bd. dirs. NY Stock Exch., NYC, 2003—06, NYSE Group, Inc., 2006—07, NYSE Euronext, NYC, 2007—09; mem. Coun. Fgn. Rels. Died Sept. 12, 2009.

MCDONALD, JOHN JOSEPH, electronics executive; b. NYC, Apr. 18, 1930; s. John J. and Margaret (Shanley) McD.; m. Tessa de R. Greenfield, Aug. 22, 1956; children: Kathryn, Elizabeth, Andrew. BA, Bklyn. Coll., 1951. With Sperry Rand Corp., Blue Bell, Pa., 1954-75, v.p., 1972-75; mng. dir. Casio Electronics Ltd., London, 1975-78, pres. Casio Europe, 1975-78; pres., CEO Casio, Inc., Dover, NJ, 1978-99, also bd. dirs.; chmn. Casio Can. Ltd., 1988—99; pres., CEO McDonald Assoc., Dover, NJ, 1999—2008, Electric Fuel Corp. (Instant Power subs.), 2002. Mem. exec. com. Electronic Ind. Found., from 1994. Chmn. Electronics Industries Found., 1997-98; trustee Bklyn. Coll., CUNY, 1997-2008. Served with US Army, 1952-54. Mem. Electronic Industries Assn. (bd. gov.), Electronic Industries Found. (trustee 1987-2008), Consumer Electronics Assn.(dir.). Died Dec. 4, 2008.

MCDONALD, ROY PHILLIP, securities executive, financial consultant; b. Detroit, Nov. 15, 1928; s. Chalres Phillip and Mary Catherine (McGrath) McD.; m. Beverly Joyce Juhl, Aug. 17, 1958; children: Roy Jr., Charles, Craig. BA, Wayne State U., 1989. Expediter U.S. Postal Svc., Detroit, 1948-78; fin. advisor McDonald Investment Co., Madison Heights, Mich., 1981-87; pres. Suburban Maintenance Co., Madison Heights, Mich., 1954-87; security mgr. Pinkerton's Inc., Detroit, from 1981. Bd. dirs. Realible Maintenance Co., Ferndale, Mich.; dir. Home Securities, Madison Heights, 1971—; cons. Maintenance Securities of Mich., 1980—. Inventor in field. Dir. City of Madison Heights Little League, 1958-59; Scout master Boy Scouts of Am., Mich., 1962-67; pres. delegate Dem. Party, Mich., 1967; coord. Mich. Heart Assn., 1973. Mem. Maintenance Inst. Okland County, Metro. Club Am., NAACP, Am. Legion. Democrat. Avocations: flying, amateur radio operator, jogging, golf. Home: West Bloomfield, Mich. Died Dec. 15, 2007.

MCDONALD, SUSAN ANN, performance consultant; b. Tulsa, Okla., Nov. 2, 1950; d. Marvin Neil and Rosemary (Ramsey) M.; m. Robert Wilson Brown, Aug. 17, 1974 (div. Sept. 1986); children: William Ramsey, David Wilson; m. Bill Cullen, June 22, 2002. BA in English, Wake Forest U., 1973; MEd in Counseling, U. N.C., 1978. Tchr. English, guidance counselor Forsyth Country Day Sch., Winston-Salem, N.C., 1973-76; case mgr. Richland County Dept. Social Svcs., Columbia, 1976-77; grad. asst. U. N.C., Charlotte, 1977-78; dir. placement Queens Coll., Charlotte, 1978-81; employment mgr., tng. mgr. Barclays American, Charlotte, 1981-83; sales trainer, tng. mgr., sales mgr., sr. cons. NCNB-NOW Bank Am., Charlotte, 1983-92; account mgr. Omega Performance, Charlotte, 1992-94, mgr. cons., 1994—98; sr. cons. Right Mgmt. Cons., from 1998. Mem. Charlotte (N.C.) Choral Soc. Democrat. Baptist. Avocations: music, reading, gardening, psychology. Home: Charlotte, NC. Died Feb. 2, 2008.

MCDONNELL, WILLIAM JOHN, lawyer; b. South Amboy, NJ, June 9, 1950; s. William Thomas and Joan Alyce (Donnelly) McD.; m. Bridget Griggs, May 26, 1950 (div. July 1982); children: Neal G., Amy C.; m. Sharon Larkin, Oct. 1, 1952. BA in History, Fairfield U., 1972; JD, St. Mary's U., 1976. Bar: N.J. 1976. Ptnr. Tabman, Downs, McDonnell, 1976-78, Alan J. Karcher, PA (name changed to Karcher, McDonnell), 1978-90, Karcher, McDonnell merger Donington, Karcher, 1990-91; pvt. practice Sayreville, N.J., 1991-95, South Amboy, N.J., from 1996. Legis. aide N.J. State Assemlby, Trenton, 1980-86. Mem. ATLA, ATLA of N.J., Elks (sec. # 2555 1994), S.A. Irish Am. Assn. (grand marshall). Democrat. Roman Catholic. Avocation: boating. Home: East Brunswick, NJ. Died June 28, 2008.

MCDOUGALL, JACQUELYN MARIE HORAN, therapist; b. Wenatchee, Wash., Sept. 24, 1924; d. John Rankin and Helen Frampton (Vandivort) Horan; m. Robert Duncan McDougall, Jan. 24, 1947 (div. July 1976); children: Douglas, Stuart, Scott. BA, Wash. State U., 1946. Lic. therapist, Wash.; cert. nat. addiction counselor II. Pres. oper. bd. Ctr. for Alcohol/Drug Treatment, Wenatchee, 1983-85; sec. Wash. State Coun. on Alcoholism, 1988-89, supr. outpatient svcs., 1989-90. Treas. Allied Arts, Wenatchee, 1984; pres. Rep. Women, Wash., 1969-70. Home: Wenatchee, Wash. Died July 20, 2008.

MCDOWELL, BARBARA, lawyer; b. Oakland, Calif., Apr. 5, 1952; d. James Martin and Joyce (Benson) McD.; m. Robert S. Peck, Dec. 19, 1976 (div.); m. Jerry Hartman BA, George Washington U., 1974; JD, Yale U., 1985. Bar: Pa. 1986, D.C. 1988. Law clk. US Dist. Ct. Conn., New Haven, 1985-86; law clk. to Hon. Ralph Winter U.S. Ct. Appeals (2d cir.), NYC, 1986-87; law clk. to Justice Byron R. White US Supreme Ct., Washington, 1987-88; assoc. Jones, Day, Reavis & Pogue, Washington, 1988—97; asst. to the solicitor gen. US Dept. Justice, Washington, 1997—2004; staff atty., appellate advocacy program Legal Aid Soc., Washington, 2004—08. Recipient Rex E. Lee Advocacy & Pub. Svc. award, 2009. Mem. ABA. Democrat. Congregationalist. Died Jan. 2, 2009.

MCENULTY, TIMOTHY EUGENE, business executive; b. Kansas City, Kans., Nov. 2, 1959; s. Bernard Eugene and Melva Joan (Moses) McE.; m. Kimberly Nell Evans, Sept. 15, 1990. BSEE, Kans. State U., 1981. Flight test engr. McDonnell Douglas, St. Louis, 1981-83; engring. mgr. Aydin Monitoring Systems, Ft. Washington, Pa., 1983-87; sr. design engr. IFR Systems, Wichita, Kans., 1988-89, mgr. digital design, 1989-92, govt. product specialist, from 1989, mgr. design engring., 1992-97, dir. govt. bus. devel., from 1997. Named State scholar, State of Kans., 1977. Mem. Delta Chi Frat. Democrat. Methodist. Avocations: fishing, hunting, outdoor activities, electronics. Home: Wichita, Kans. Died Nov. 5, 2007.

MCEVOY, FRANCES JANE COMAN, writer, editor; b. Phoenix, May 11, 1929; d. James Lindley Coman and Pearl Catherine Bruns; m. Joseph Francis McEvoy, Nov. 10, 1956 (dec. Oct. 1997); children: David L., Stephen C., Anne G. BA, Ariz. State U., 1951; postgrad., Boston U., 1959—60. Editor Helios Lit. Mag. Ariz. State U., Tempe, 1948—50; editor Am. Acad. Arts and Scis., Boston, 1951—52; reporter Waltham News Tribune Dailey, Mass., 1952—54, State House News Svc., Boston, 1952—55; press sec. Senator Leslie B. Cutler, Boston, 1954—55; asst. dir. publicity Boston U., 1955—56; writer features Boston Herald, 1975—80; writer, contbr. Dell Horoscope Astrologers Newsletter, 1980—98; editor Geocosmic Mag. Nat. Coun. Geocosmic Rsch., from 1984. Author: Power of Yod & Quincuux, 1998, Out of Bounds Moon and Planets, 2002; contbr. articles to jours.; portrait artist, 1970—2002. Mem. pub. rels. com. Greater Boston Com., 1954, Rep. State Com., Boston, 1955. Mem.: Women's Edn. and Ind. Union, De Cordova Mus. (Lincoln, Mass.), Boston Mus. Fine Arts, Bostonian Soc., DAR, Tenn. Hist. Soc., New Eng. Hist. and Geneal. Soc., Daus. Colonial Wars. Avocations: painting, writing, historic research. Died Dec. 10, 2007.

MCFADDEN, JAMES FREDERICK, JR., surgeon; b. St. Louis, Dec. 5, 1920; s. James Frederick and Olivia Genevieve (Imbs) McF.; m. Mary Cella Switzer, Sept. 15, 1956 (div. Sept. 1969); children: James Frederick, Kenneth Michael, John Switzer, Mary Cella, Joseph Robert; m. Deanne Nemec Puls, Apr. 29, 1989. AB, St. Louis U., 1941, MD, 1944. Intern Boston City Hosp., 1944-45; ward surgeon neorsurg. and orthopedics McGuire Gen. Hosp., Richmond, Va., 1945; ward surgeon in internal medicine Regional Hosp., Fort Knox, Ky., 1946; ward surgeon plastic surgery Valley Forge Gen. Hosp., Phoenixville, Pa., 1946-47; intern St. Louis City Hosp., 1947-48; resident in surgery VA Hosp., St. Louis, 1948-52; clin. instr. surgery St. Louis U., 1952-62; gen. practice medicine specializing in surgery St. Louis, from 1952; mem. staff St. Mary's Hosp., 1952-77, St. John's Mercy Hosp., 1952-74, St. Louis U. (Desloge) Hosp., 1952-62; Cardinal Glennon Children's Hosp., 1952-62; mem. staff Frisco RR Hosp., 1953-64, DePaul Hosp., from 1954, Christian Hosp., 1955-66, 83-91. Mem. St. Louis Ambassadors, 1979-81; officer St. Louis County Aux. Police, 1973-75. Served to capt. AUS, 1945-47. Recipient Eagle Scout award, Order of the Arrow Honor award Boy Scouts Am. Fellow ACS, Royal Soc. Medicine, Internat. Coll. Surgeons; mem. St. Louis Med. Soc., Am. Coll. Occupl. and Environ. Medicine, Am. Soc. Clin. Hypnosis, Internat. Soc. Hypnosis, Am. Assn. RR Surgeons, St. Louis U. Student Conclave, Alpha Sigma Nu, Phi Beta Pi. Roman Catholic. Avocations: hypnosis, photography. Died Oct. 27, 2007.

MCFARLAND, RICHARD MACKLIN, retired journalist; b. Blockton, Iowa, Mar. 27, 1922; s. William Harold McFarland and Elsie (Sisson) McFarland Chavannes; m. Jacquelyn Jean Folske, Mar. 22, 1955; children: Bethany Rose, Scott Macklin, Elizabeth Ann McFarland Heyda, Kathryn Belle. BA, U. Iowa, 1944. Newsman UPI, Des Moines, 1944, Chgo., 1945, 46-47, bur. mgr. Bismarck, ND, 1944-45, Herrin, Ill., 1945, Sioux Falls, SD, 1947-49, Milw., 1949-51, legis. reporter Des Moines, 1947, Pierre, SD, 1949, Iowa mgr. Des Moines, 1951-54, NW mgr. Mpls., 1954-55, Wis. mgr. Milw., 1956-57, regional exec. sales, 1958-59, bur. mgr. Chgo., 1960-61, Minn. mgr. Mpls., 1961-69, Mich. editor Detroit, 1969-71, Minn. editor Mpls., 1971-84, bur. mgr.-capitol reporter St. Paul, 1985-89; ret., 1989. Former deacon Advent Luth. Ch., Roseville, Minn.; coun. mem. Redeemer Luth. Ch., Bradenton, Fla., 1996—98, pres. coun., 1998—99, coun. mem., 2001—05. With USN, 1943—44. Avocations: reading, music, fishing, backpacking, golf. Home: Bradenton, Fla. Died 2008.

MCGEE, MICHAEL VANHOOK, writer, playwright; b. Ft. Smith, Ark., July 23, 1928; s. Lillard Harold Weatherman and Hila VanHook McGee; m. Evelyn Elizabeth Weber; children: Michael VanHook Jr.(dec.), Patricia Lynn Mc Gee Gunderson, Sarah Valerie McGee Cannon. AB polit. sci., Univ. of the South, 1950; LLB, Southern Law U., 1957; MFA, U. Alaska, Fairbanks, 1982. Clk. and announcer Radio Sta. WMPS, Memphis, 1948; bank clk. Union Planters Bank, Memphis, 1950—51, bank teller, 1953—56; real estate ins. sales Galbreath Co., Memphis, 1956—62; writer, from 1979. Contbr. articles publ. to profl. jour. 2nd lt. USAF, 1951—53, ret. as maj. USAF, 1962—79. Mem.: Fairbanks Arts Assn. (bd. dirs. 1981—94, pres. 1994), Shriners, Masons. Anglican. Avocations: fishing, camping, painting. Home: North Pole, Alaska. Died Apr. 6, 2008.

MC GILLICUDDY, JOHN FRANCIS, retired banker; b. Harrison, NY, Dec. 30, 1930; s. Michael J. and Anna (Munro) McG.; m. Constance Burtis, Sept. 9, 1954; children: Michael Sean, Faith Burtis Benoit, Constance Erin Mc Gillicuddy Mills, Brian Munro, John Walsh. AB, Princeton, 1952; LL.B., Harvard, 1955. With Manufacturers Hanover Trust Co. subs. Manufacturers Hanover Corp., NYC, 1958-91, v.p., 1962-66, sr. v.p., 1966-69, exec. v.p., asst. to chmn., 1969-70, vice chmn., dir., 1970, pres., 1971-79, chmn., CEO, 1979-91, Chem. Banking Corp., NYC, 1992-93, ret., 1994. Bd. dirs. Kelso, Inc. Bd. dirs. life trustee, chmn. emeritus NY Presbyn. Hosp.; trustee emeritus Princeton U.; pres. Boy Scouts Am., Greater N.Y. Couns. Lt. (j.g.) USNR, 1955—58. Mem. Westchester Country Club (Rye, NY), Blind Brook Club (Port Chester, NY), Princeton Club (NYC), Augusta Nat. Golf Club (Ga.), Pine Valley Golf Club (NJ), Laurel Valley Golf Club (Ligonier, Pa.), Seminole Golf Club (north Palm Beach, Fla.), Links Club (NYC). Roman Catholic. Home: Rye, NY. Died Jan. 4, 2009.

MCGINNIS, JAMES JOHN, talent booking agent; b. New Orleans, Mar. 6, 1948; s. James John and Dorothy (Carpenter) McG.; m. Pamela Ann Figallo, Aug. 23, 1975. Student, La. State U., New Orleans, 1968-71. Personal mgr. Image Inc., New Orleans, 1970-75; personal promoter Zebra Band, Inc., New Orleans, 1976-80 and from 84; concert promoter Rock Factory (S. and S.E. regions), from 1990. Cons. Tough Love, 1990, Lillian Axe, 1982—, Razor White, 1985—; talent judge New Orleans Showcase, 1989-90. Composer, All The King's Horses, 1975; producer, Heavy Metal Mania, 1987. Capt. Neighborhood Watch Assn., New Orleans, 1980-90. Recipient Top Concert Promoter award, Regional Metal Fellowship Assn., 1988. Republican. Roman Catholic. Avocations: travel, classic automobile restoration. Home: New Orleans, La. Died July 6, 2008.

MCGOOHAN, PATRICK JOSEPH, actor; b. Astoria L.I., NY, Mar. 19, 1928; s. Thomas and Rose McG.; m. Joan Drummond, May 19, 1951; children: Ann, Frances, Catherine. Worked with Sheffield (Eng.) Repertory Co., Bristol (Eng.) Old Vic. Co. Stage debut in London in The Brontes, St. James Theatre, 1948; appeared: stage prodns. Serious Charge, London, 1955, Moby Dick, London, 1955, Brand, 1959 (Brit. award for best stage actor of yr., 1959), Pack of Lies, 1985; actor (films) Passage Home, 1955, High Tide at Noon, 1956, Hell Drivers, 1957, The Quare Fellow, 1962, Life for Ruth, 1962, Ice Station Zebra, 1968, Mary Queen of Scots, 1972, The Genius, 1975, Silver Streak, 1976, Brass Target, 1978, Scanners, 1981, Baby...Secret of the Lost Legend, 1985, Braveheart, 1995, The Phantom, 1996, A Time to Kill, 1996, Hysteria, 1998, (voice) Treasure Planet, 2002, (TV series) Danger Man, 1961 (in U.S. as "Secret Agent" 1965-66), The Prisoner, 1968-69, Rafferty, 1977, (TV movies) The Man in the Iron Mask, 1978, Koroshi, 1978, 3 Sovereigns for Sarah, 1985, Jamaica Inn, 1985, Of Pure Blood, 1986, Columbo: Agenda for Murder, 1990, The Best of Friends, 1991, Columbo: Ashes to Ashes, 1998; wrote, directed and appeared in various episodes in Columbo series (Emmy award Nat. Acad. TV Arts and Scis., 1975, 1990). Recipient Best Actor award, Brit. Acad. Film and TV Arts, 1960. Died Jan. 13, 2009.

MCGRADY, JAY ROSS, accounting executive; b. Elkton, Md., Aug. 18, 1958; s. Glenn Jr. McGrady and Eleanor Marie (Jackson) Mueller; m. Susan Denise Cardosi, Sept. 9, 1984. AA, Cecil Community Coll., Northeast, Md., 1978; BS, So. Coll., 1980. CPA, R.I. Staff acct. Bryant & Magoon CPA's, Tullahoma, Tenn., 1980-82; controller Pawtucket (R.I.) Inst., from 1982; acctg. mgr. Fuller Meml. Hosp., Attleboro, Mass., from 1984. Fellow R.I. Soc. CPA's; mem. Am. Inst. CPA's. Republican. Adventist. Home: Sandy Spring, Md. Died Sept. 11, 2007.

MCGUCKIN, JOHN HUGH, JR., lawyer; b. Bryn Mawr, Pa., Nov. 8, 1946; AB magna cum laude, Harvard Coll., 1968, JD, 1971. Bar: Mass. 1971, Calif. 1973. Assoc. Orrick, Herrington, Rowley & Sutcliffe, 1972-79; sr. counsel legal divsn. Bank Am., 1979-81; exec. v.p., gen. counsel, corp. sec. UnionBanCal Corp./Union Bank Calif., N.A., San Francisco, from 1981. Adj. instr. Hastings Coll. Law U. Calif., 1980-82; judge pro tem San Francisco Superior Ct. Contbr. articles to profl. jours. Mem. ABA, State Bar Calif. (v.p., treas., bd. govs., chmn. subcom. duties and liabilities trustees probate and trust law sect. 1985-86, legal svcs. trust fund commn. 1989-90, minimum CLE com.), Assn. Corp. Coun. (chmn. 2003-04), Phi Beta Kappa. Home: San Francisco, Calif. Died Dec. 2008.

MCGUIRE, PATRICIA JEAN, retired journalist; b. Chgo., June 10, 1928; d. Van Mark and Mary Florence (MacDonald) Feltus; m. Roger J. McGuire, Aug. 28, 1948; children: Stephen Edward, Kevin Mark, John Michael, Kimberly Jean. Student, U. Mo., 1946-48. Women's editor, columnist The Park Forest (Ill.) Reporter, 1951-53; reporter, feature writer The Birmingham (Ala.) News, 1969-80, ret., 1981. Mem. editorial bd.: Asheville Downtown Assn., 1989-91. Mem. community adv. bd. Birmingham Jr. League, 1978-80; bd. dirs. Birmingham Art Assn., 1977-80; v.p., organizer WNC Sheep Producer's Assn., Asheville, N.C., 1983-85; chair Western N.C. Pub. Radio, Inc., Asheville, 1984-89; chair Streetscape Task Force Asheville, 1987—; mem. Asheville-Buncombe Libr. Trust Fund Bd., 1991—. Recipient 1st Pl. award Associated Press, 1970, 72, 73, 76, 77, 78, 1st Pl. award women's news Sigma Delta Chi, 1973, 1st Pl. award features Ala. Women's Press Assn., 1972. Mem. N.C. Humanities Coun., So. Profl. Journalists. Democrat. Unitarian Universalist. Avocations: raise registered columbia sheep, gardening, landscape and urban design. Home: Asheville, NC. Died Nov. 11, 2007.

MCINTOSH, RICHARD TURNER, construction consultant, wood worker; b. Salem, Mass., Mar. 20, 1926; s. Perley Turner and Frmcuca Edson (Manning) McI.; m. Oct. 10, 1952; children: Susan, Sandra, Stephen, Sally. BA in History, Salem Coll., Mass., 1999. Bldg. inspector; constrn. inspector; home inspector. Treas. Mass. Bldg. Commn. and Inspectors Assn., 1986-96, Manning Assn., North Billerica, Mass., from 1994, Kilwining Orgn. of Boston, Swampscott, Mass., from 1996. Mem. planning bd. Town of Swampscott, 1994—. Cpl. U.S. Army, 1944-46. Mem. Scotts Charitable Soc. Avocations: woodworking, reading biographies, swimming, education. Died Oct. 3, 2007.

MCINTYRE, MARY VALENTINE, nursing administrator; b. Nashville, NC, Jan. 18, 1937; d. Itimous Thaddeus and Hazel (Armstrong) Valentine; 1 child, David Lawrence. Diploma, Rex Hosp., 1960; BSN, ECU, 1982. Staff nurse Presbyn. Home, High Point, N.C., 1966-74; PHN II Guilford County Health Dept., High Point, 1975-78; tchr. High Point City Sch., 1978-79; PHN II Nash County Health Dept., 1979-80; staff nurse Nash Gen. Hosp., Rocky Mount, N.C., 1980-82; DON Westwood Manor Nursing Home, Wilson, N.C., 1982-84; nursing quality assurance coord. Nash Gen. Hosp., Rocky Mount, N.C., 1984-94, critical pathways coord., 1994-95, mgr. quality improvement, from 1995. Mem. Town Planning bd., Nashville, 1984—; chair Nursing Home Adv. Com., Nashville; vice chair bd. dirs. Nash County Cultural Ctr., Nashville, 1990—; chair nominating com. Bapt. Ch., Nashville, 1989-91. Mem. N.C. Assn. Health Care Quality (charter 1988—, pres.-elect 1991-92), N.C. Assn. for Health Care Quality (pres. 1992-93). Avocations: restoration old home, needle work. Home: Nashville, NC. Died Mar. 3, 2008.

MCKEE, MICHAEL STUART, journalist; b. Greenwich, Conn., Aug. 10, 1955; s. Richard P. and Virginia C. (Alicoate) McK.; m. Patricia L. Coggins, Aug. 23, 1980; children: Kaitlyn Colleen, Tyler Patrick. BS in Comm., Colo. State U., 1977. Reporter Sta. KOB, Albuquerque, 1970-75, Sta. KRQE, Albuquerque, 1976-77, Sta. WMBD-TV, Peoria, Ill., 1977-78, Newsweek mag., NYC, 1982-85; statehouse corr. Sta. KTHV-TV, Little Rock, 1978-79; reporter, anchor Sta. KVOA-TV, Tucson, 1980-82; congl. corr. Conus TV, Washington, 1985-86, White House corr., 1986-95, Bloomberg Bus. Nes, Washington, from 1995. Recipient Iris award Nat. Assn. TV Program Execs., 1980. Mem. White House Corr. Assn. (bd. dirs. 1992-95). Home: Arlington, Va. Died Jan. 8, 2008.

MCKELVEY, ANDREW J., retired advertising executive; b. Oct. 13, 1934; children from previous marriages, Geoffrey, Christine, Amanda; m. Dena McKelvey; 1 son, Stuart J. McKelvey. BA, Westminster Coll., New Wilmington, Pa. Chmn., CEO Monster Worldwide Inc. (formerly TMP Worldwide, Inc.), NYC, 1967—2006, chmn. emeritus, 2006. Co-founder, McKelvey Found.; bd. dirs. Yellow Pages Pubs., Served in US Army. Mem. Assn. Director Mktg. (bd. dirs. 1994-96). Home: New York, NY. Died Nov. 27, 2008.

MCKENNA, HILDRED MAYE TUKESBREY, psychiatric nurse; b. Waynesburg, Pa., Jan. 1, 1930; d. John and Mary Elizabeth (Turney) Tukesbrey; m. Charles Richard McKenna, July 22, 1952; children: Richard Patrick, Joseph Ryan. Diploma, Canonsburg (Pa.) Gen. Hosp. Sch. Nursing, 1951; student, U. Pitts., U. Fla., U. North Fla. Cert. nursing adminstr. Nursing supr. Mayview (Pa.) State Hosp., St. Vincent's Hosp., Jacksonville, Fla.; asst. DON N.E. Fla. State Hosp, MacClenny, nursing supr. Recipient Merit award HRS Dist. IV. Mem. Pa. Nurses Assn., Fla. Nurses Assn. Home: Jacksonville, Fla. Died Dec. 5, 2007.

MCKEY, ARTHUR DUNCAN, lawyer; b. Washington; s. Richard Kendall and Mary Deru McKey; m. Virginia Ruth Hubbell, Mar. 19, 1983; 1 child, Richard. BA, Boston Coll., 1970, MA, 1973, U. Md., 1975; JD, U. Idaho, 1978. Bar: Idaho 1978, D.C. 1979; U.S. Dist. Ct. Idaho 1978, U.S. Dist. Ct. (D.C.) 1979, U.S. Ct. Appeals (D.C. cir.) 1979, U.S. Supreme Ct. 1983, U.S. Dist. Ct. (we. dist.) Mich. 1985, U.S. Ct. Appeals (6th cir.) Mich. 1985. U.S. Dist. Ct. (no. dist.) Tex. 1992, U.S. Dist. Ct. (no. dist.) Calif. 1992. Assoc., ptnr. Hanson O'Brien Birney & Butler, Washington, 1978-90; sr. atty. Whitman & Ransom, Washington, 1991-93; spl. appointment, Antitrust Divsn. USDept. Justice, Washington, 1993-95; ptnr. Hanson & Molloy, Washington, 1995—2009. Adj. faculty Dept. of Mass Comm. Washington State U., Pullman, 1978; adv. bd., Media law reporter Bur. Nat. Affairs, Washington Contbr. articles to profl. jours.; patentee in field. Gen. counsel The Children's Inn at NIH, Bethesda; chmn., gen. counsel Creative Internet Applications Inc., Washington Mem. The Barristers, Gibson Island Club and Yacht Squadron, Army and Navy Club, U.S. Sailing Assn. (Rescue medal 1992). Died Sept. 3, 2009.

MCKINNEY, JOHN EDWARD, physicist, educator; b. Altoona, Pa., Apr. 6, 1925; s. Clayton A. and Katie Ellen (Kessler) McK.; m. Ursula Katherine Guttstadt, Aug. 16, 1958. BS, Pa. State U., 1950; postgrad., U. Md., 1952-58. Physicist Nat. Inst. Sci. and Tech. (formerly Nat. Bur. Standards), Gaithersburg, Md., 1949-89; ret., 1989. Guest scientist Nat. Phys. Lab., Teddington, Eng., 1964, Nat. Inst. Sci. and Tech., 1989-2009; cons. in electro-mech. materials testing systems. Author handbook: Density and Compressibility of Liquids, 1972; contbr. chpt. to book. Chmn. transp. com. East Bethesda (Md.) Citizens Com., 1975-79. With U.S. Army, 1943-45, ETO. Recipient Bronze medal US Dept. Commerce, 1983. Mem. Soc. Rheology, Internat. Assn. Dental Rsch. Home: Bethesda, Md. Died Jan. 15, 2009.

MCKINNEY, THURMAN RAY, JR., pharmacist; b. Somerset, Ky., Feb. 15, 1931; s. Thurman Ray and Emily Gertrude (Jones) McK.; m. Carol Ann (Huddleston) Hancock, July 11, 1954; children: Jerry Morgan, George Michael, Timothy Ray. BS in Pharmacy, U. Ky., 1953. Pharmacist CDS#1, Bowling Green, Ky., 1953-54; pharmacist, mgr. Adairville (Ky.) Drug Co., 1954-87, Riley-White Drug #3, Adairville, from 1987. Town bd. mem. City of Adairville, 1960-61, 63, mayor, 1962; lay leader, sunday sch. supr. Adairville United Methodist Ch., 1954—. Mem. Nat. Assn. Pharmacists, Ky. Pharm. Assn. (4th dist.), Adairville C. of C. (Citizen of Yr. 1962). Home: Adairville, Ky. Died Feb. 5, 2008.

MCKINNON, ARNOLD BORDEN, retired transportation company executive; b. Goldsboro, NC, Aug. 13, 1927; s. Henry Alexander and Margaret (Borden) McK.; m. Oriana McArthur, July 19, 1950; children: Arnold Borden Jr., Colin McArthur, Henry Alexander. AB, Duke U., 1950, LLB, 1951; grad. Advanced Mgmt. Program, Harvard U., 1972. Bar: D.C. 1951, N.C. 1966. With Norfolk So. Corp. (formerly So. Ry. Sys.), Va., 1951-2000, from v.p. law to chmn., 1971-92, chmn. exec. com., 1992-2000, ret., 2000. Bd. trustees Chrysler Mus. Art; active Mil. Civilian Liaison Group; bd. dirs. Norfolk Forum, Inc. With US Army, 1946—47. Mem.: ABA, Am. Soc. Corp. Execs., D.C. Bar Assn., N.C. Bar Assn., Rotary, Norfolk German Club, Bonita Bay Club, Met. Club, Chevy Chase Club, Norfolk Yacht and Country Club. Presbyterian. Home: Norfolk, Va. Died May 18, 2009.

MCKNIGHT, PATRICIA GAYLE, musician, artist, writer, educator; b. Rochester, Minn., Aug. 9, 1935; d. William Robert and Maxine Matilda (Hutchings) McK.; m. James Russell Grittner, Nov. 24, 1962; children: Leah Kristin, Rachel Anne. BS in Music, U. Wis., Superior, 1982, MA in Art, 1990, MA in Art History, 1993; postgrad. in Musicology, U. Iowa, Iowa City, 1982—83. Asst. MS editor Am. Acad. Ophthalmology and Otolaryngology, Rochester, Minn., 1958-63. Musician U. Iowa Symphony Orch., U. Iowa Opera Orch., U. Iowa Small Ensembles, U. Wis. Superior Symphony Orch., Rochester Symphony Orch.

Exhibited in group shows including Kruk Gallery, Rochester Art Ctr., Rochester Cmty. Coll., Duluth Art Inst. Biennial, 1988, 90, Port Wing Gallery, Tile Show, Wis., 2006; author: Zenith City Arts newspaper. Mem. Hist. Preservation Commn. City of Superior, 1996—2007. Avocations: playing cello, viola da gamba, piano, art. Home: Superior, Wis. Died July 23, 2008.

MCLAFFERTY, GEORGE HOAGLAND, aerospace engineer; b. Newport, RI, June 11, 1926; s. George Hoagland and Sadie (St. Clair) McL.; m. Marilyn S., Oct. 21, 1950 (dec. June 1991); children: Steven S., Susan W.; m. Eunice T., June 28, 1992. BS, Mass. Inst. Tech., 1947, MS, 1948. Sr. program mgr. United Tech. Rsch. Ctr., East Hartford, Conn., 1948-76, Pratt & Whitney, West Palm Beach, Fla., 1976-87; pres. McLafferty Cons. Inc., North Palm Beach, from 1987. Mem. AAAS, AIAA, Am. Nuclear Soc. Holder 27 patents in field. Home: No Palm Beach, Fla. Died Sept. 9, 2007.

MCLANE, MICHAEL NELSON, actor; b. Honolulu, Oct. 24, 1958; s. Alpine Will and Mary Jane (Benson) McLane. BA in English, Coll. William and Mary, Williamsburg, Va., 1980; MA in Mass Communications, U. Fla., 1987, MFA in Theatre, 1990. Mktg. dir. Hippodrome State Theatre, Gainesville, Fla., 1990-93; dir. mktg. and aud. vcs. Civic Theatre Ctrl. Fla., Orlando, from 1993. Publicity asst. Wolf Trap Farm Park for Performing Arts, Vienna, Va., 1980; publicity dir. dept. music U. Fla., Gainesville, 1983, prof. theatre, 1988-90. Actor plays: Hotel Paradiso, 1987, Curse of the Starving Class, 1988, A View From the Bridge, 1988, Harvey, 1989, Hay Fever, 1989, Best Little Whore House, 1989, One Flew Over Cuckoo's Nest, 1989, Portraits, 1990, 1776, 1990, The Heidi Chronicles, 1991, Rumors, 1991, Love! Valour! Compassion, 1996. Bd. dirs. Gainesville Community Playhouse, 1985-90. Named Fla. Player of Yr., Fla. Players, Gainesville, 1989. Mem. Actor's Equity Assn., Soc. Collegiate Journalists, Alpha Psi Omega, Phi Kappa Phi. Home: Orlando, Fla. Died July 25, 2008.

MCLAUGHLIN, MARCELLUS H. MARK, III, writer, historian, activist; b. Bryn Mawr, Pa., Aug. 4, 1951; s. Marcellus H. Jr. and Caroline (Rollins) McL. AA in History, Northeastern Christian Jr. Col, Villanova, Pa., 1974; BA in History, Ea. Coll., St. Davids, Pa., 1976; MA, Villanova U., 1978; MS, 1983. Appraiser Main Line Coin and Stamp, Ardmore, Pa., 1981; archivist Villanova U., 1981; researcher, interviewer Ch. of the Redeemer, Bryn Mawr, 1983; tour guide, lectr. Old Christ Ch., Phila., 1983-84; libr. shelver Lexington Pub. Libr., Bryn Mawr, 1985; journalist Daily Liberty Gazette, Drexel Hill, Pa., 1987; subst. tchr. Ocean City (N.J.) Bd. Edn., 1990-93; writer, activist Citizens Historic Preservation, Inc. (CHIPS), Ocean City, from 1998. Historian (picture history) Greetings from Ocean City, N.J., 1995, Ocean City in Postcards, 999. Mem. SAR, Pa. SAR. (bell com. 2002-), N.J. SAR, Soc. War of 1812 (asst. sec. color guard 1975—, sec. asst. 85-90), Scotch-Irish Soc. Democrat. Lutheran. Avocations: antiques, historical research, travel, photography, collecting newspaper mastheads. Home: Ocean City, NJ. Died Apr. 6, 2008.

MCLEAN, ROBERT, III, real estate company executive; b. Balt., May 23, 1928; s. Robert Jr. and Mary Somerville (Iglehart) McL.; m. Elizabeth Madison Lewis, May 21, 1960; children: Elizabeth, Alexander, Mary, John. BA, Yale U., 1950; MA, U. Pa., 1965. Mktg. exec. Owens-Ill., Toledo, 1957-65; mktg. cons. Old Phila. Devel. Corp., Phila., 1966-70; vice chmn. Cushman & Wakefield, NYC, 1970—2001; chmn. directorate Cambridge Inst. of Applied Rsch., McLean, Va., 2001—08. Mem. real estate investment com. Yale U., New Haven, Conn., 1982-90; mem. bd. Cushman & Wakefield, N.Y.C., 1986-2000. Author: Countdown to Renaissance II, The New Way Corporate America Builds, 1984. Chmn. Nat. Bldg. Mus., Washington, 1992-95; mem. bd. Washington Nat. Cathedral, 1980-88. S/Sgt. USMC, 1953-56. Mem. Rolling Rock Club, Metropolitan Club, Center Club, Gibson Island Club. Republican. Episcopalian. Avocations: tennis, golf, skiing. Home: Gibson Island, Md. Died Nov. 11, 2008.

MCLENDON, JESSE WILBORN, poet, writer; b. Phenix City, Ala., Mar. 11, 1950; s. Jesse W. Sr. and Katie (Bell) McL.; m. Lou Ellen Emerson, Dec. 10, 1982; 1 child, Jeremy Patrick; children by previous marriage: Beverly E. Brown, Cynthia J. Rogers. Student, Columbus Coll., Ga., 1978-82; diploma in radio and TV repair, Columbus Vocat. and Tech. Sch., 1982. Author poems including That's Me, 1968, Keepsake, 1989, Dear Poet, 1989, Winter, 1989, Heaven Sent, 1989, Time, 1989, R.S.V.P. to the Class of '68, 1989, First Beatitude, 1989, Eagle, 1989, Morning Song, 1989, Beginnings, 1989, The Master's Hand, 1989, It's Still Love, 1989, Strange, 1989, Images, 1990, Live !!!, 1991, The Wedding, 1991, The Battle Hymn, 1991, Goodbye, 1992, The Touch, 1992, Honor Born, 1992, Fame Game, 1992, Fame!!!, 1992, Song of Conceit, 1992. With U.S. Army, 1972-74. Named Golden Poet, World of Poetry, Sacramento, 1989, Silver Poet, 1990; recipient World of Poetry award of merit, 1989, 1991, Am. Poetry Assn. poet of merit, 1989. Mem. So. Poetry Assn. (blue ribbon 1992). Died Oct. 27, 2007.

MCLOUGHLIN, ROBERT EMMETT, sales and marketing executive; b. White Plains, NY, Dec. 17, 1947; s. Robert Emmett and Helen Marie (Cook) McL.; m. Pamela Anne Smith, Aug. 3, 1985; 1 child, Digger. BBA in Mktg., Iona Coll., 1974, MBA in Mktg., 1979. Lic. life and health agt.; cert. mgmt. engring. technician. Fin. mktg. analyst Mitchum-Thayer div. U.S.V. Pharm. Corp., Tuckahoe, N.Y., 1971-74; gen. adminstr. Printex Corp., Ossining, N.Y., 1974-77; dir. mktg. Simuflite, Inc., Dallas, 1977-81; exec. v.p. The Hudson Group, Ghent, N.Y., 1981-83; pres. REM Assocs., Leeds, N.Y., from 1981. Author: Solar Power, The Energy Alternative, 1981. Founder We Care, Washington, 1970; assoc. Greene County Ctr. for Disabled, Catskill, N.Y., 1987. Sgt. USAF, 1967-71. Mem. Am. Mktg. Assn., Am. Mgmt. Assn., Nat. Assn. for Self-Employed. Roman Catholic. Avocations: cross country skiing, working with youth and disabled, restoring classic cars, breeding persian cats. Died Jan. 5, 2008.

MCMAHON, ED (EDWARD PETER LEO MCMAHON JR.), television and radio personality; b. Detroit, Mar. 6, 1923; s. Edward Leon and Eleanor McMahon; m. Alyce Ferrill, July 5, 1949 (div. 1976); children: Claudia, Michael, Linda, Jeffrey; m. Victoria Valentine, Mar. 6, 1976 (div. 1989); 1 adopted child, Katherine Mary; m. Pam Hurn, Feb. 22, 1992; 1 stepchild, Alex. Student, Boston Coll.; BA, Cath. U. Am., 1949. Spokesman Pride Mobility. Author: For Laughing Out Loud: My Life and Good Times, 1998, Here's Johnny!: My Memories of Johnny Carson, The Tonight Show, and 46 Years of Friendship, 2005, When Television Was Young, 2007; co-author: (with David Fisher) Ed McMahon's Barside Companion, 1969, Here's Ed or How to Be a Second Banana, From Midway to Midnight, 1976; TV announcer: The Tonight Show, 1962-92; actor: (films) The Incident, 1967, Slaughter's Big Rip Off, 1973, Fun with Dick and Jane, 1975, Butterfly, 1982, Love Affair, 1994, For Which He Stands, 1996, Just Write, 1997, Mixed Blessings, 1998, The Vegas Connection, 1999, Jelly, 2009, (TV films) Swing Out, Sweet Land, 1970, Lucy Calls the President, 1977, Legends of the Superheroes, 1979, The Kid from Left Field, 1979, The Great American Traffic Jam, 1980, The Golden Moment, 1980, Gridlock, 1980, The Star Maker, 1981, Safety Patrol, 1998, Bewitched, 2005; host (TV series) The Kraft Music Hall, 1968, Whodunnit?, 1979, TV's Bloopers and Practical Jokes, Ed McMahon's Star Search, Alf's Hit Talk Show, 2004, (TV specials) Thanksgiving Day Parade, (radio) Lifestyles Live, USA Radio Network, Orlando, (co-host) Jerry Lewis Labor Day Telethon; numerous other TV appearances; appeared on Broadway in The Impossible Years. Active Muscular Dystrophy Assn.; mem. bd. dirs. Horatio Alger Assn. With USMC, PTO; col. res., ret. Died June 23, 2009.

MCMAHON, PAUL FRANCIS, finance company executive; b. Malone, NY, Apr. 28, 1945; s. Philip Francis and Shirley (Roy) M.; m. Sheila Ann Lester, Nov. 30, 1963; children: Michael, Marsha BS, Syracuse U., 1968. CPA, N.Y., Oreg.; cert. mgmt. acct., mgmt. cons. With Ernst & Young, Syracuse, NY, 1968—79, mgr., 1975-79, ptnr. in charge of mgmt. cons. in Europe Brussels, 1979-84, vice-chmn. Cleve., 1984-87; exec. ptnr. Ernst & Young Internat., NYC, 1987-93; chmn. Ernst & Young Ea. Europe, 1990-93; regional dir. Asia/Pacific Ernst & Young Internat., Singapore, 1994-96; contr. Coop. Mktg. Agy., Syracuse, 1973-75; COO Amrop Internat., Brussels, 1997-2001; ptnr. Network Journey, 2002—04. Treas. Chamber Music N.W.; chair lit. and hist. com. Arlington Club; bd. mem. Oreg. Coun. of Humanities; mem. adv. bd. Humaninet; treas. Health Bridges Internat.; mem. adv. bd. Humaninet. Mem.: AICPA, Nat. Acad. Scis., Coun. Consulting Orgns. (past chmn.), Assn. Mgmt. Consulting Firms (bd. dirs.), Inst. Mgmt. Acctg., N.Y. Soc. CPAs, Oreg. Soc. CPAs. Democrat. Roman Catholic. Avocations: sculpture, travel, gardening, biographies. Home: Portland, Oreg. Deceased.

MCMICKING, JAMES HARVEY, chemical engineering educator; b. Detroit, Aug. 5, 1929; s. Herbert Raymond and Muriel Algiva (Howey) McM.; m. Katherine Ann Hestwood, July 2, 1955; children: James Clinton, Jane Kirsten, John Howey, Joan Colleen. BSChemE, Wayne State U., 1953, MSChemE, 1955; PhDChemE, The Ohio State U., 1961. Asst. prof. chem. engring. Wayne State U., Detroit, 1958-62, assoc. prof., from 1962. Contbr. articles to profl. jours. Named outstanding chem. engring. tchr., 1991, 92, 94; recipient outstanding svc. award, 1991, 93, 94. Mem. AIChE, U.S. Power Squadron. Lutheran. Home: Troy, Mich. Died Aug. 9, 2008.

MCMILLAN, WENDELL MARLIN, retired economist; b. Dallastown, Pa., June 14, 1923; s. John Walter and Alice Mary (McCormick) McMillan; m. Eleanor Unser, July 14, 1946; children: Susan, Barbara, Douglas. Grad., York Jr. Coll., Pa., 1943; BS, Juniata Coll., 1948; MS, Pa. State U., 1950, PhD, 1954. Rsch. & extension asst. Pa. State U., 1950-54; agrl. economist, asst. dir. U.S. Dept. Agriculture, Washington, 1955-64; project mgr., mktg. advisor Food and Agriculture Orgn. of UN, Jordan, Saudi Arabia and Afghanistan, 1964-72; agrl. economist The World Bank, Caribbean, Sudan, 1972-76; agrl. and policy economist U.S. Dept. Agr./USAID, Syria, Indonesia, Lesotho, Liberia, 1977-80; agrl. economist Africa Bur. USAID, Washington, 1980-89, ret., 1989. Mem. mktg. subcom. Nat. Commn. Cooperative Devel., Washington, 1964; adj. prof. York (Pa.) Coll., 1990. Author: tech./policy publs. agr. Dist. chmn. Campfire Girls No. Va., 1959—61; chmn. bd. dirs. Am. Cmty. Sch., Amman, Jordan, 1966—67, UN Staff Assn., Kabul, Afghanistan, 1969—70; bd. dirs. Hist. York, Inc., 1987—97, pres., 1995—97; mem. Hist. Soc. York County, from 1987, mem. libr. com., from 1990; trustee York County Acad., from 1991. Recipient Merit cert., USDA, 1960, 1984, Hall of Fame award, William Penn Sr. HS, 1999; Fulbright grantee, U. Copenhagen, 1954—55. Mem.: Soc. Internat. Devel., Am. Agrl. Econs. Assn., Alumni Assn. Juniata Coll. (Nat. Alumni Achievement award 1984), Alumni Assn. York Coll. (bd. dirs. 1986—91, Svc. award 1991, Disting. Alumnus 1982, Dir. Emeritus award 1997), Pi Gamma Mu. Democrat. Avocations: stamp collecting/philately, nature study, opera. Home: York, Pa. Died Apr. 1, 2008.

MCNAIR, STEVE LATREAL, retired professional football player; b. Mount Olive, Miss., Feb. 14, 1973; s. Lucille and Selma McNair; m. Mechelle McNair, 1997; 4 children. BS in Biology, Alcorn State U., 1994. Quarterback Houston Oilers, 1995—96, Tenn. Oilers, 1997—98, Tenn. Titans, 1999—2006, Baltimore Ravens, 2006—08; ret., 2008. Recipient Walter Payton award, 1994, Ed Block Courage award, 1999, NFL MVP award, AP, 2003; named to Am. Football Conf. Pro-Bowl Team, 2000, 2003, 2005. Died July 4, 2009; Nashville, Tenn.

MCNAUGHTON, MARGARET J., pediatric nurse, family nurse practitioner; b. Kansas City, Mo., Sept. 26, 1949; BSN, U. Alaska, 1979, MSN, 1989. Cert. family nurse practitioner. Advanced nurse practitioner Pediatric Consultants of Alaska, Anchorage; faculty liaison U. Alaska Coll. Nursing, Anchorage. Mem. ANA, Alaska Nurses Assn. (conv. com.), Alaska Nurse Practitioner Assn., Sigma Theta Tau. Home: Snohomish, Wash. Died Feb. 7, 2008.

MCNICHOLS, JAMES ROBERT, insurance executive; b. Chgo., July 31, 1946; s. Robert J and Anna A. (Allegretti) McN.; m. Deborah J. Locke, Sept. 21, 1968. Degree in mktg. mgmt., Elgin Community Coll., 1968; AAS, DeVry Inst. Tech., 1969. Agt. Prudential Ins. Co., Elgin, Ill., from 1971. Served with USN, 1969-71, Vietnam. Mem. McHenry chpt. Life Underwriters, Million Dollar Round Table. Roman Catholic. Avocation: golf. Home: Elgin, Ill. Died July 15, 2008.

MCNULTY, JAMES FRANCIS, JR., Former United States Representative from Arizona; b. Boston, Mass., Oct. 18, 1925; m. Jacquie Boevers, 1945; children: Michael, Cynthia, Amy. LLB, U. Ariz., 1951. Atty. Bisbee, Tombstone & Huachuca City, Ariz.; chmn. Cochise County Democratic Com.; mem. Gentry & Gentry, 1951—83; delegate Democratic Nat. Conv., 1960; gen. counsel Ariz. Electric Power Corp., 1961; mem. Ariz. State Senate, 1969—75; coord. Carter & Mondale Presidential Campaign, Southern Arizona, 1976; state co-chmn Babbitt Gov. Campaign, Ariz., 1978; mem. Arizona Bd. Regents, 1980, US Congress from 5th Ariz. Dist., Ariz., 1983—85; counsel Brown & Biain, 1992—2000. Author: Running Uphill: Recollections of a Congressman from Arizona, 2003. Served in US Army, 1944—45. Eagleton Inst. fellowship, Rutgers U. Mem.: State Hosp Bd., State Legislature Salary Comn., Ariz. State Bd Edn., Ariz. State Bar. Democrat. Roman Catholic. Died June 30, 2009.

MC PHERSON, ROLF KENNEDY, clergyman, religious organization administrator; b. Providence, Mar. 23, 1913; s. Harold S. and Aimee (Semple) McP.; m. Lorna De Smith, July 21, 1931 (dec.); children: Marlene (dec.), Kay; m. Evangeline Carmichael, Jan. 31, 1997. Grad., So. Cal. Radio Inst., 1933; D.D. (hon.), L.I.F.E. Bible Coll., 1944; LLD (hon.), L.I.F.E. Bible Coll., Los Angeles, 1988. Ordained to ministry Internat. Ch. Foursquare Gospel, 1940. Pres. Internat. Ch. Foursquare Gospel, LA, 1944-88, pres. emeritus, 1988—2009, dir. LA, 1944-92; pres., dir. L.I.F.E. Bible Coll., Inc., LA, 1944-88. Mem. Echo Park Evangelistic Assn. (pres. 1944-2009). Mem. Internat. Ch. Foursquare Gospel. Died May 21, 2009.

MCQUAID, LUCILLE, brokerage firm account executive; b. Cleve., Sept. 24, 1928; d. Peter and Beatrice (Coughlin) McQuaid. BA, Case Western Reserve U., 1950; MBA, U. Calif., 1957. Personnel adminstr. Greyhound Corp., Cleve., 1950-55; acct. exec. Dean Witter Reynolds, San Francisco, from 1957. Sec.-treas. San Francisco Young Republicans, 1974-75. Mem. Bay Area Women in Finance (chmn. 1962-68, dir. 1968-75). Home: San Francisco, Calif. Died Nov. 21, 2007.

MCQUEEN, MICHAEL ANTHONY, journalist, communications educator; b. Jacksonville, Fla., Nov. 3, 1956; s. Otto John and Carolyn Irene (Cubanks) McQ.; m. Glenda Kay Wright; children: Michael Jr., Otto Sinclair. BA, Fla. State U., 1982; MA, Fla. Atlantic U. Reporter Tallahassee (Fla.) Democrat, 1977-79, Fla. Times-Union, Jacksonville, Fla., 1979-80; writer AP, Tallahassee, 1980-84; reporter, editor Miami (Fla.) Herald, 1984-94; reporter USA Today, Arlington, Va., 1989; instr. to chmn. and assoc. prof. dept. journalism and broadcasting Fla. Internat. U., Miami, 1995—2004; mng. editor Macon Telegraph, Ga., 2004—06; asst. bureau chief AP, New Orleans, 2006—09. Mem. South Fla. Vision 2020, Fort Lauderdale, Fla., 1994-95; workshop dir. Dow Jones Newspaper Fund, Princeton, N.J., 1996, 97. Author: (poetry) Apalachee Quar., 1977. Recipient Pulitzer prize (given to staff) Pulitzer Prize Bd., 1994. Nat. Assn. Black Journalists (bd. dirs. 1985-86, conv. chmn. 1986), Suth Fla. Black Journalist Assn., Soc. Profl. Journalists (bd. dirs. 1995), Assn. for Edn. in Journalism/Mass. Comm. (newsletter editor 1997). Roman Catholic. Died Oct. 25, 2009.

MC QUEENEY, EDNA FERINA KLAUS, retired emergency nurse; b. Alta., Can., May 8, 1922; d. Edward and Pauline (Niethal) Klaus; m. Andrew Joseph Mc Queeney, May 9, 1974. Diploma in nursing, Royal Alexandra Hosp., Edmonton, Alta., 1955. RN, Hawaii. Staff emergency nurse, asst. head nurse, relief head nurse Cottage Hosp., Santa Barbara, Calif., 1957-73; emergency nurse Kaiser Found., Honolulu, 1974-93, ret., 1993. Fellow Emergency Nursing Assn. (cert. emergency nurse); mem. Nat. Emergency Nurses Assn. (hon.). Avocations: tennis, exercise classes, volunteer activities. Died Jan. 17, 2008.

MEAD, BEVERLEY TUPPER, physician, educator; b. New Orleans, Jan. 22, 1923; s. Harold Tupper and Helen Edith (Hunt) M.; m. Thelma Ruth Cottingham, June 8, 1947. BS, U. S.C., 1943; MD, Med. Coll. S.C., 1947; MS, U. Utah, 1958. Intern Detroit Receiving Hosp., 1947-48, resident, 1948-51; asst. prof. U. Utah, 1954-61; assoc. prof. U. Ky., 1961-65; prof. psychiatry and behavioral sci. Creighton U. Sch. Medicine, Omaha, 1965—2002, emeritus prof., 2002—09, chmn. dept., 1965-77, assoc. dean for acad. and faculty affairs, 1980-88. Home: Omaha, Nebr. Died Mar. 13, 2009.

MEAGHER, ROBERT FRANCIS, international economic law consultant; b. Bklyn., May 13, 1927; s. Frances Xavier and Marie Janet (Tallent) M.; m. Donna Marie Dowsett, May 21, 1973 (div. Mar. 1974). B Social Sci., CCNY, 1949; JD, Yale U., 1952. Bar: N.Y. Assoc. Winthrop Stimson Putnam & Roberts, NYC, 1954-58; lawyer UN Relief & Works Agy., Beirut, 1958-60; vis. and adj. prof., assoc. dir. internat. legal rsch. Columbia U. Law Sch., NYC, 1961-73; internat. econ. law cons. Somerville, Mass., from 1964; CEO Robert F. Meagher Assocs., Somerville, Mass., from 1993. Adj. prof. law Columbia Law Sch., N.Y.C., 1964-71; prof. internat. law Fletcher Sch. Law and Diplomacy Tufts U., Medford, Mass., 1967-92, prof. emeritus, 1992—; prof. Tufts Inst. for Learning in Retirement, 2002; legal advisor India Interest Group, 1993—; vis. sr. fellow Overseas Devel. Coun., Washington, 1975-76; vis. prof. Law Harvard Law Sch., Cambridge, Mass., 1984, 89, Melbourne (Australia) U., Monash U., Australia, 1981, Indian Law Inst., New Delhi, 1987-88; lectr. on fgn. policy, fgn. aid, fgn. investment; mem. study groups Coun. Fgn. Rels.; coord. Peace Corps tng. program for lawyers going to Somalia, 1967; coord. workshops in field; lectr. on various fgn. policy issues Asia, Africa, Mid. East and U.S., 1952—. Editor, contbr. chpt. Law and Social Change, 1988; co-author: International Financial Aid: A Comparative Study of Policies, Institutions and Methods, 1966, monographs on Turkey, Kenya, Tanzania, Senegal, Thailand and India; author: An International Redistribution of Wealth and Power on Public International Development Firms: A Study of the Charter of Economic Rights and Duties of States, 1979, Proposed Options for the Future Activities of the U.S. Office of International Activities of of the Environmental Protection Agency, 1979; cons. Popular Participation and Development in the Least Developed Countries: Case Studies of Tanzania, Nepal and Bangladesh for UNCTAD, 1991; contbr. articles, revs. to profl. publs. Chmn. fgn. policy com. N.Y. Young Dems., N.Y.C., 1956-58; exec. dir. Citizens for Johnson & Humphrey, N.Y.C., 1964; fgn. policy cons. Michael Dukakis, Boston, 1988, bd. dirs. Ontime Travels, PVT., LTD., New Delhi, India, 2003-. With U.S. Army, 1945-46, ETO. Fulbright scholar Bombay (India) Sch. Econs., 1952, 67, Indian Law Inst., 1987-88; Ford Found. grantee, 1961, Rockefeller grantee, 1975. Mem. ABA (African law subcom., Mid. Eastern law subcom.), African Studies Assn., Am. Fgn. Law Assn., Am. Soc. Internat. Law (bd. rev. and devel. 1980-85, panel on pvt. investment in less developed countries), Asia Soc. (India coun., program com. 1967-69), Assn. Asian Studies, Assn. Bar City of N.Y. (fgn. law com. 1956-58, 65-68, internat. commn. jurist com. 1965-67, lawyers' role in search for peace com. 1976-78, 80-82), Inter-Am. Affairs (program com. 1977-79), Coun. African-Am. Inst., Coun. Fgn. Rels., Internat. Law Assn. (com. fgn. investment), Soc. Internat. Devel., Trade Policy Rsch. Ctr., UN Assn. (bd. dirs. greater Boston/Mass. 1978—), World Peace Through Law Ctr (com. fgn. investments 1967-74). Avocation: wine tasting. Died Dec. 31, 2007.

MEALEY, EDWARD HANLY, biochemist; b. Boston, July 28, 1925; s. John Francis and Elizabeth B. (Hanly) M.; widowed; children: Edward, Peter, Patricia. BS, Tufts, 1948; PhD, U. Kans., 1968. Chief LBBP div. of biologic standards NIH, Bethesda, Md., 1960-67; tech. dir. Hyland div. Baxter Labs., LA, 1967-70; sr. v.p. ICL Scientific, Fountain Valley, Calif., 1970-80; sr. v.p. tech. ops. Alpha Therapeutic Corp., LA, 1981-91, cons., from 1992. Lt. USNR, 1943-46, PTO. Mem. AAAS, N.Y. Acad. Sci., Am. Soc. Quality Control, Parenteral Drug Assn., Sigma Xi. Democrat. Roman Catholic. Home: Fountain Vly, Calif. Died Sept. 2, 2007.

MEAR, CHARLES EUGENE, geologist, consultant; b. Dec. 2, 1926; s. Charles Russell Mear and Alice Inez Porche; m. Tonie Margaret Kubesch, Sept. 1, 1951; children: Diane, Charles E. Jr., David R., John P., Mark E., Kathryn, Caroline, Steven. BA in Geology, U. Tex., 1951, MA in Geology, 1953. Cert. petroleum geologist, profl. geoscientist geology Tex., 2003. Petroleum exploration geologist numerous oil cos., Midland, Tex., 1952—67; geologist hard minerals La. Land Exploration Co., Midland, 1967—76, Denver, 1967—76; dist. geologist mgr. Southland Royalty Co., Midland, 1976—82, v.p. geology and geophysics Ft. Worth, 1982—86; v.p. exploration Cross Timbers Oil Co., Ft. Worth, 1986—93; rsch. fellow Tex. Archeol. Lab., Austin, Tex., 1993—96; cons. geologist Austin, 1996—2003. Editor: Petroleum Geology of Mississippian Carbonates in North Central Texas, 1989; contbr. articles to profl. jours. Paratrooper 11th airborne divsn. Pacific Theater US Army. Recipient Monroe G. Cheney Sci. award, W. Tex. Geol. Soc., 1991. Mem.: Soc. Sedimentary Geology (hon. life. mem. Permian Basin sect.), Am. Assn. Petroleum Geologists (sec. DPA 1997—99). Home: Austin, Tex. Died Sept. 18, 2007.

MEDAK, WALTER HANS, lawyer; b. Vienna, May 10, 1915; came to U.S., 1938; s. Hugo and Grete (Figdor) M.; m. Edith Rhodes, 1944 (div. 1957); 1 child, Ronald Harvard; m. Renée Rasens, 1996. Grad., Acad. of Commerce, Vienna, 1934, U. Vienna, 1938; postgrad., U. Ga., 1939-40; MA in Econs., U. Calif., Berkeley, 1949; JD, Harvard U., 1948. Prodn. mgr. Mabs, Inc., LA, 1942-43; prodn. engr. Kaiser Co., Richmond, Calif., 1943-45; atty. Belli & Medak, Walnut Creek, Calif., 1957-59; pvt. practice law Walnut Creek and Moraga, Calif., from 1950. Bd. dirs. Snyder/Newell, Inc., San Francisco; bd. dirs. Carnelian Woods, Carnelian Bay, Calif., pres., 1974-80. Mem. ABA, Calif. County Bar Assn., Assn. Trial Lawyers Am., Calif. Trial Lawyers Assn., Harvard Club (chmn. admissions and scholarship com. San Francisco chpt. 1973-74). Avocations: skiing, swimming, music, travel, French and German. Home: Walnut Creek, Calif. Died Feb. 19, 2008.

MEDICUS, HILDEGARD JULIE, retired dentist, orthodontist, educator; b. Frankfurt, Germany, July 25, 1928; came to U.S., 1961, naturalized, 1995; d. Gustav and Elizabeth Berta (Neunhoeffer) Schmelz; m. Heinrich Adolf Medicus, June 15, 1961. DMD, U. Marburg, W. Germany, 1953; orthodontics diploma, U. Düsseldorf, W. Germany, 1957. lic. dentist, N.Y. Postdoctoral fellow dental sch. U. Zürich, Switzerland, 1957; postdoctoral fellow U. Liège, Belgium, 1958, Forsyth Dental Ctr., Boston, 1959, orthodontic rsch. affiliate, 1963—74; sch. dentist Pub. Sch. Sys., Zürich, 1975—76; dental hygiene instr. Hudson Valley C.C., Troy, NY, 1976—77; pvt. practice Troy, NY, 1977—89; ret., 1989. Active Hudson Mohawk Swiss Soc. Mem. AAUW, ADA, European Orthodontic Soc., German Orthodontic Soc. Achievements include study of functional orthodontic appliances and growth and development. Home: Troy, NY. Died Aug. 20, 2008.

MEDIN, LOWELL ANSGARD, management executive; b. Shafer Twp., Minn., Aug. 28, 1932; s. Ansgaard Phillip Magnus and Adelaide Marie Christine (Grandstrand) M.; m. Frances Irene Knutson, Sept. 13, 1958; children: Kimberly June, James Lowell. AS in Liberal Arts, U. Minn., 1957, BBA, 1959. Dairy farmer Medin Farm, Franconia Twp., 1951-53; silo builder Lindstrom Silo, 1956-58; employment mgr. John Wood Co., St. Paul, 1959; salesperson Diversey Co., LaCrosse, Wis., 1959-60; rebuyer, inventory mgr. Montgomery Ward, St. Paul, 1960-67, rebuyer, rebuyer mgr. Chgo., 1967-85; with sales dept. J.T. Gen. Store, Palatine, Ill., 1986; rebuying mgr. Sportsmen's Guide, Golden Valley, Minn., 1987; inventory mgr. Donald Bruce and Co., Chgo., 1988-91; supr. Pinkerton Security Ops., 1992-96. Pics coord. Hickory Farms, Itasca, Ill., 1995-98. Author: (with others) Shafer Swamp to Village, 1978, The Pioneers of Chisago County 1838-1870, 1992, The Knutson/Stavenau Family Roots, 1994. Candidate for polit. office, Mpls., 1967; del. Minn. State Dem.-Farm Labor Conv., 1956, 58; chmn. cancer drive Village of Palatine, 1968, mem. dist. 6 adv. coun., 1989-97; mem. Homeowners Coun., Palatine, 1976-77; mem. coun. Christ Luth. Ch., Palatine, 1981-86; officer Chicago County DFL Party, 1956-60; del. Chicago County DFL Conv., 1956, 58; pres. Palonis Park Homeowners Assn., Palatine, 1976-82. Cpl. U.S. Army, 1953-55, ETO. Mem. No. Ill. Civil War Roundtable (chartered officer 1983-86, trustee, sec., 2d v.p.), VFW (life, post 981, Arlington Hts.), Am. Legion (life, post 690, Palatine), Alpha Phi Omega. Republican. Lutheran. Avocations: genealogy, gardening, American history, Civil War. Home: Palatine, Ill. Died Apr. 30, 2008.

MEHRING, MARGARET, filmmaker, retired educator; b. Milbank, SD, Sept. 3, 1925; d. Robert Dunbrack and Bernice (Case) Jones; m. William Samuel Mehring, June 21, 1947 (dec. June 1958); 1 child, William Dunbrack. BA, Lawrence Coll., 1947; MS in Edn., U. So. Calif., 1972, PhD in Cinema, 1978. Writer, dir., prodr. Mehring Prodns., LA, from 1953. Mem. faculty U. So. Calif. Sch. Cinema and TV, L.A., 1959-91, dir. filmic writing program, 1978-91, dir. emerita, 1991—; media edn. cons. Oglala Lakota Coll., Pine Ridge Indian Reservation, Kyle, S.D., 1996—. Author: The Screenplay, 1989; writer, dir., prodr. numerous ednl., documentary and indsl. tng. films for Employers Ins. Wausau, 1955, 57, 59-62, Golden State Ins. Co., 1964, Techno Electric Mfg. Co., 1965, Calif. Dept. Social Welfare, 1967, Andersen Windowall Corp., 1969, Golden State Mut. Life Ins. Co., 1983; writer, dir. ednl. films for MLA, U. So. Calif., 1959-60, John Tracy Clinic, 1961-62, Calif. Dept. Social Welfare, 1963-64, Am. Assn. Ret. Persons and Nat. Ret. Tchrs. Assn., 1965-67, Profl. Rsch., Inc., 1968, Acad. Comm. Facility, UCLA, 1969, ednl. sound film strips dept. daytime programs ans spl. projects UCLA Ext., 1971, San Diego County Dept. Edn., 1972, Iran film series Instrnl. Media Ctr., Mich. State U., 1975-77; writer films Who's Behind the Wheel, Part 1, 1966, Part II, 1967, Mayday, Mayday, 1970, The Man, Part I, 1972, Part II, 1973, How To Manage Your resources-Safety, Part I, 1973, Part II, 1974 (all for USAF), Immunity-The Power To Resist a Disease, 1970. Pres. El Moro Dem. Club, Los Osos, Calif., 1994-95; bd. dirs. Ctrl. Coast Women's Polit. Com., San Luis Obispo, Calif., 1995-96; vol. Global Vols.-Poland, 1995; Global Vols., China 1999; vol. instr. Oglala Lakota Coll., Pine Ridge Indian Reservation, Kyle, S.D., 1995, vol. cons., designer degree media program, 1998—; project dir. First Amendment/Blacklist Project. Mem. Univ. Film and Video Assn., Script Coalition for Industry, Profls. and Tchrs., Delta Kappa Alpha (assoc.). Died July 3, 2008.

MEHROTRA, SUBHASH CHANDRA, hydrologist, consultant; b. Barabanki, India, July 5, 1940; came to U.S., 1965; s. Keshav Chandra and Shanti (Tandon) M.; m. Anju Kapoor, Aug. 13, 1974; children: Anupum, Apurva. PhD, UCLA, 1973. Rsch. asst. U. Iowa, Iowa City, 1965-67; postgrad. rsch. engr. U. Calif., LA, 1968-73; sr. engr. Bechtel Corp., San Francisco, 1974-77, sr. engring. specialist Oak Ridge, Tenn., from 1979; assoc. prof. Howard U., Washington, 1977-79. Cons. O'Brien & Gere, Syracuse, N.Y., 1978-79, Waste Policy Inst., Blacksburg, Va., 1991—. Contbr. articles to profl. jours. Sec. Indian Student Assn., U. Iowa, 1966. Recipient Internat. scholarship U. Iowa, 1966-67, Deutsch Co. fellowship UCLA, 1969. Mem. Am. Geophys. Union, N.Y. Acad. Sci. Home: Oak Ridge, Tenn. Died Feb. 17, 2008.

MEINEL, MARJORIE PETTIT, optical engineer; b. Pasadena, Calif., May 13, 1922; d. Edison and Hannah (Steele) Pettit; m. Aden Baker Meinel, Sept. 5, 1944; children: Carolyn, Walter, Barbara, Elaine, Edward, Mary, David. BA, Pomona Coll., Claremont, Calif., 1943; MA, Claremont Coll., 1944. Rsch. assoc. Calif. Inst. Tech., Pasadena, 1944-45, U. Ariz., Tucson, 1974-85; mem. tech. staff Jet Propulsion Lab., Pasadena, from 1985. Vis. faculty Nat. Cen. U., Chung-Li, Taiwan, 1978-80; commr. Ariz. Solar Energy Commn., Phoenix, 1975-81; mem. office tech. assessment U.S. Congress, Washington, 1974-79. Author: Applied Solar Energy, 1977, Sunsets, Twilights and Evening Skies, 1983; patentee in field. Recipient Exceptional Svc. medal Nat. Aeronautics and Space Adminstrn., Kingslake medal. Fellow Internat. Soc. Optical Engring. (Gold medal). Lutheran. Avocations: playing organ for church, adult bible teacher. Home: Santa Barbara, Calif. Died June 24, 2008.

MEINERT, WALTER, retired chemical company executive, consultant; b. Walcott, Iowa, May 18, 1922; s. Minnie and Theodore F. Meinert; m. Delores C. Mengel, Oct. 24, 1946; children: Susan Diane, Lawrence David, Walter T. Meinert Jr. BS, St. Ambrose U., 1947; MS, Inst. of Textile Tech., 1949. V.p. Emery Industries, Cincinnati, Ohio, 1949—80. Mem. Hamilton County Hosp. Commn., 1982—85, Bd. Trustees St. Francis-St. George Hosp., 1980—85. Lt. U.S. Navy, 1942—46, Wwii. Mem.: The Hidden Valley Golf Club. Home: Cincinnati, Ohio. Died Oct. 21, 2007.

MEISEL, GEORGE VINCENT, lawyer; b. St. Louis, Sept. 24, 1933; s. Leo Otto and Margaret (Duggan) M.; m. Joy C. Cassin, May 18, 1963 BS summa cum laude, St. Louis U., 1956, JD cum laude, 1958. Bar: Mo. 1958. Assoc. Grand Peper & Martin, St. Louis, 1961-64, ptnr., 1965; jr. ptnr. Bryan Cave McPheeters & McRoberts, St. Louis, 1966-69; ptnr. Bryan Cave, LLP, St. Louis, 1970-2000, of counsel, from 2000. Served to 1st lt. USAF, 1958-61 Mem. ABA, Bar Assn. Met. St. Louis, Mo. Bar Assn. Clubs: Saint Louis, Mo. Athletic (St. Louis). Roman Catholic. Home: Saint Louis, Mo. Died Sept. 13, 2008.

MELANDER, A. HOWARD, accountant; b. Rural Wayside, Kans., Apr. 14, 1922; s. Alfred J. and Rose Eva (Bain) M.; m. Betty Anne Singleton, Sept. 7, 1947; children: David Lair, Nicholas Howard. BSBA, McPherson Coll., Kans., 1960; postgrad., Wichita State U., 1963-65; Graduate, Toledo U., 1966-67, Ball State U., 1980-85. Auditor, tax acct. Beech Aircraft Corp., Wichita, Kans., 1962-65; asst. controller Dura Corp., Toledo, 1965-67; comptroller Ind. Tel. Co., Seymour, 1967-70; corp. controller H.O. Canfield Co., Seymour, 1970-71; pvt. practice Indpls., 1971-73, 77; comptroller Oxide & Chem. Corp., Indpls., 1973-77, Cutting, Inc., Hartford City, Ind., 1978-84; pvt. practice Hartford City, from 1984. Dir. v.p., Nat. Assn. Accts., E. Cen. Ind., 1967—; sec., treas., Middletown Enterprises Inc, Hartford City, Ind., 1986—, also bd. dirs. U.S. Army 1942-46, CBI, 1950-52, Korea. Rotary fellow. Decorated U.S. Army Commendation medal. Mem. Nat. Assn. Accts. (pres. local chpt. 1989-90), Hartford City C. of C. (dir. 1980-84), Blackford Country Club. Democrat. Presbyterian. Avocations: golf, photography, music. Home: Hartford City, Ind. Died Apr. 15, 2008.

MELLOR, BARBARA LOUISE, educator, librarian, counselor consultant; b. Fall River, Mass., Jan. 27, 1945; d. Ernest and Dorothea Vera (Phelps) M.; m. Joseph John Cabaup, June 26, 1965 (div. 1986); children: Joseph Ernest, Jean Marie. AA, Sch. Lifelong Learning, Durham, NH, 1981, BGS in Libr./Media, 1983; MEd, Plymouth State Coll., 1988. Cert. media generalist, guidance counselor, N.H. Tchr., libr. Littleton (N.H.) Jr.-Sr. High Sch., from 1980. Author: (books and tchr. guide) Activities for the Occupational Outlook Handbook (3 grade levels), 1989. Mediator Youth and Family Mediation Program, Littleton, 1988—; bd. trustees Bethlehem (N.H.) Pub. Libr., 1977—. Mem. NEA, AACD (N.H. chpt.), N.H. Sch. Counselors Assn., N.H. Career Devel. Assn., N.H. Ednl. Media Assn., Phi Delta Kappa. Avocations: gourmet cooking, cross country skiing. Home: Bethlehem, NH. Died July 10, 2008.

MELNICK, DANIEL, film producer; b. NYC, Apr. 21, 1932; s. Benjamin and Celia Melnick; m. Linda Rogers, 1955 (div. 1971); children: Peter, Gabrielle Ptnr. Talent Associates; v.p., then sr. v.p. charge worldwide prodn. Metro Goldwyn Mayer, 1972-76; in charge worldwide prodn. Columbia Pictures Industries Inc., 1977-78, pres.

motion picture div., 1978; independent prodr. Indie Prodn. Co. Prodr.: (films): Original Cast Album-Company, 1970, Straw Dogs, 1971, That's Entertainment II, 1976, First Family, 1981, Making Love, 1982, Quicksilver, 1986, Roxanne, 1987, Punchline, 1988, Mountains of the Moon, 1990, Air America, 1990, L.A. Story, 1991, The Quick and the Dead, 1994; exec. prodr. films: That's Entertainment, 1974, All That Jazz, 1979, Altered States, 1980, Unfaithfully Yours, 1984, Footloose, 1984, Universal Soldier: The Return, 1999, Blue Streak, 1999; (TV movies) Get Smart, Again!, 1989; prodr.: (TV series) Mr. Broadway (12 episodes), 1964, Run Buddy Run (12 episodes), 1966, He & She (25 episodes), 1967-68, N.Y.P.D. (5 episodes), 1967-69 Recipient Nat. Acad. TV Arts and Scis. Emmy award for Death of a Salesman and The Ages of Man. Home: Los Angeles, Calif. Died Oct. 13, 2009.

MELTON, FRANK, Mayor, Jackson, Mississippi; b. 1950; m. Ellen Melton; children: Matthew, Lauren. CEO WLBT TV-3, Inc., 1984—2002; current chmn. & CEO TV-3 Found.; nat. bd. dirs. Broadcast Music Industry, chmn. Performing Rights Com.; mayor City of Jackson, 2005—09. Vol. instr. Sch. Bus. & Mass Comm. Dept. Jackson State U.; chmn. Miss. Dept. Youth Svcs.; bd. mem. Tex. Bd. Mental Health and Mental Retardation, Miss. Dept. Human Svcs., Miss. State Bd. Edn.; former dir. Miss. Bureau Narcotics; former bd. mem. Liberty Broadcasting, Cmty. Broadcast Group, NBC Affiliates. Vol. Parish St YMCA; former bd. mem. Metro Jackson C. of C., United Way. Recipient Disting. Leadership award, U. Miss., Disting. Alumnus award, Stephen F. Austin State U. Democrat. Died May 7, 2009.

MELTZER, ALICE, pianist, music educator; b. Bklyn., Apr. 13, 1926; d. Aaron and Ida Jennie (Goldberg) Galmitz; m. Robert Jason Meltzer, June 20, 1948 (div. Apr. 1966); children: Ellen Frances, Curtis Adam. BS in Elem. Edn., Brockport State U., 1977. Cert. elem. educator, N.Y. Substitute tchr. City of Rochester, N.Y. Pvt. piano tchr. Author poetry, Nat. Book of Poetry Anthology, 1996. Democrat. Jewish-Christian. Avocations: reading, writing, poetry, singing. Died Jan. 11, 2008.

MELTZER, MILTON, author; b. Worcester, Mass., May 8, 1915; s. Benjamin and Mary (Richter) M.; m. Hilda Balinky, June 22, 1941; children: Jane, Amy. Student, Columbia, 1932-36. Adj. prof. history U. Mass., Amherst, 1977-80. Author: Mark Twain Himself, 1960; author: (with Walter Harding) A Thoreau Profile, 1962; author: Langston Hughes: A Biography, 1968, Bread and Roses, 1967, Never to Forget: The Jews of the Holocaust, 1976, Dorothea Lange: A Photographer's Life, 1978; author: (with Langston Hughes, C. Eric Lincoln, Jon Michael Spencer) A Pictorial History of African-Americans, 1994; co-editor: Lydia Maria Child: Selected Letters, 1817-1880, 1982, The Black Americans, 1984, Mark Twain: A Writer's Life, 1985, George Washington and the Birth of Our Nation, 1986, The American Revolutionaries, 1987, Benjamin Franklin: The New American, 1988, Rescue: The Story of How Gentiles Saved Jews in the Holocaust, 1988, Starting From Home: A Writer's Beginnings, 1988, Voices From the Civil War, 1989, Columbus and the World Around Him, 1990, The Bill of Rights: How We Got It and What It Means, 1990, Thomas Jefferson: Revolutionary Aristocrat, 1991, The Amazing Potato, 1992, Slavery: A World History, 1993, Lincoln: In His Own Words, 1993, Andrew Jackson and His America, 1993, Gold, 1993, Cheap Raw Material: How Our Youngest Workers Are Exploited and Abused, 1994, Theodore Roosevelt, 1994, Weapons and Warfare, 1996, Tom Paine, 1996, The Many Lives of Andrew Carnegie, 1997, Ten Queens: Portraits of Women of Power, 1998, Food, 1998, Carl Sandburg, 1999, Witches and Witch Hunts, 1999, Driven from the Land, 2000, They Came in Chains, 2000, Ten Kings, 2001, Ain't Gonna Study War No More, 2002, The Day the Sky Fell, 2002, Great Inventions: The Cotton Gin, 2003, Great Inventions: The Printing Press, 2003, Herman Melville, 2003, Edgar Allan Poe, 2003, Hour of Freedom: American History in Poetry, 2003, Hear That Train Whistle Blow! How the Railroad Changed the World, 2004, Milton Meltzer: Writing Matters, 2005, Emily Dickinson, 2006, Henry David Thoreau, 2007, Not Having Hawthorne, 2007, Tough Tunes: A Novel, 2007, John Steinbeck, 2008, Willa Cather, 2008, Albert Einstein, 2008. Served with USAAF, 1942-46. Recipient Laura Ingalls Wilder award, Am. Libr. Assn., 2001, Regina medal, Cath. Libr. Assn., 2000. Mem. Orgn. Am. Historians, Authors Guild, P.E.N. Died Sept. 19, 2009.

MENDEZ, OLGA A., former state legislator; b. Mayaguez, PR, Feb. 5, 1925; BA, U. PR; MEd, Columbia U., 1960; PhD in Ednl. Psychology, Yeshiva U., NYC, 1975. Assoc. prof. SUNY-Stony Brook, research psychologist Albert Einstein Coll. Med., N.Y.C., dep. commr. N.Y.C. Agy. for Child Devel.; dep. commr. Agy. for Childhood Devel. NYC; mem. Dist. 30 NY State Senate, Albany, 1978—92, mem. Dist. 28, 1993—2004; chairwoman NY State Senate Labor Com., 2004—05. Del. Dem. Nat. Conv., 1980 Republican. Home: New York, NY. Died July 29, 2009.

MENES, PAULINE H., retired state legislator; b. NYC, July 16, 1924; d. Arthur B. and Hannah H. Herskowitz; m. Melvin Menes, Sept. 1, 1946 (dec. 2000); children: Sandra Jill Menes Ashe, Robin Joy Menes Elvord, Bambi Lynn Menes Gavin. BA in Bus. Econs. and Geography, Hunter Coll., NYC, 1945. Economist Quartermaster Gen. Office, Washington, 1945-47; geographer Army Map Svc., Washington, 1949-50; chief clk. Prince George's County Election Bd., Upper Marlboro, Md., 1963; substitute tchr. Prince George's County H.S., Md., 1965-66; mem. Md. House of Delegates, Annapolis, 1966—2007, mem. judiciary com., 1979—2007, parliamentarian, 1995—2007. Com. on rules and exec. nominations, Md. Ho. of Dels., Annapolis, 1979-94, 95—, chmn. spl. com. on drug and alcohol abuse, 1986-2007, chmn. Prince George's County del., 1993-95. Mem. Md. Arts Coun., Balt., 1968-95, Md. Commn. on Aging, Balt., 1975-95; bd. dirs. Prisoner's Aid Assn., Balt., 1971-94. Recipient Internat. Task Force award Women's Yr., 1977, Ann London Scott Meml. Excellence award NOW, 1976; named to Hall of Fame Hunter Coll. Alumni Assn., 1986, Women's Hall of Fame Prince George County, 1989, Md. Women's Hall of Fame, 2008 Mem. NOW, Nat. Conf. State Legislators (com. on drugs and alcohol 1987), Nat. Order Women Legislators (pres. 1979-80), Women's Polit. Caucus, Bus. and Profl. Women. Democrat. Avocations: theater, music, dance show attending, stamp collector. Home: Silver Spring, Md. Died May 16, 2009.

MENGEL, RONALD KEITH, industry affairs director; b. Springfield, Ill., May 3, 1934; s. John Ivan and Lela May (O'Neal) M.; m. Susan Jane Shoulty, Aug. 5, 1956; children: Deborah Sue, Lisa Ann. BEE, Purdue U., 1956. Mktg. engr. product line GE Co., Wayneboro, Va., 1959-61, sales engr. Chgo., 1961-67, regional process computer specialist, 1967-71; product mgr. Leeds & Northrup Corp., North Wales, Pa., 1971-75; v.p. sales, mktg. Esterline Angus Div., Esterline Corp., Indpls., 1975-80; mktg. mgr. Marposs Gauge Corp., Detroit, 1980-81; dir. internat. mktg. BRK Electronics Div., Pittway Corp., Aurora, Ill., 1981-89; dir. industry affairs Systems Tech. Group, Aurora, from 1989. Bd. dirs., chmn. Automatic Fire Alarm Assn., Barrington, Ill., 1990-92. Vol. Edward Hosp. Aux., Naperville, Ill., 1990—. Mem. Nat. Inst. Cert. Engring. Technologies, Nat. Fire Protection Assn. (tech. com. 1990—), Nat. Elec. Mfrs. Assn. (chmn. codes com. 1989—), Soc. Fire Protection Engrs. Republican. Presbyterian. Avocations: camping, computer technology, dog showing. Home: Naperville, Ill. Died Nov. 29, 2007.

MENKES, JOHN HANS, pediatric neurologist; b. Vienna, Dec. 20, 1928; came to U.S., 1940; s. Karl and Valerie (Tupler) M.; m. Miriam Trief, Apr. 14, 1957 (div. Feb. 1978); m. Joan Simon Feld, Sept. 28, 1980 (dec. Nov. 2000); children: Simon, Tamara, Rafael C.; m. Myrna Fox (July 1, 2004). AB, U. So. Calif., 1947, MS, 1951; MD, Johns Hopkins U., 1952. Diplomate Am. Bd. Pediat., Am. Bd. Psychiatry and Neurology. Intern, jr. asst. resident Children's Med. Ctr., Boston, 1952-54; asst. resident pediat. Bellevue Hosp., NYC, 1956-57; resident neurology, trainee pediatric neurology Columbia-Presbyn. Med. Ctr., Neurol. Inst. N.Y., NYC, 1957-60; asst. prof. pediat. Johns Hopkins U., Balt., 1960-63, assoc. prof., 1963-66, asst. prof. neurology, 1964-66, chief pediatric neurology divsn., 1964-66; prof. pediat. and neurology UCLA, 1966-74, chief pediatric neurology divsn., 1966-70, prof. psychiatry, 1970-74; chief Neurology-Neurochem. Lab. Brentwood (Calif.) VA Hosp., 1970-74; clin. prof. psychiatry, neurology and pediat. UCLA, 1974-77, clin. prof. pediat. and neurology, 1977-84, prof. pediat. and neurology, 1985-89, prof. emeritus pediat. and neurology, from 1989. Dir. pediatric neurology Cedars-Sinai Med. Ctr., 1997-99, dir. emeritus pediat. neurology, 1999-2008; mem. metabolism study sect. NIH, 1968-70, project com., 1969-70; mem. adv. com. Nat. Inst. Child Health and Human Devel., 1985-87; mem. Dept. Health Svcs., Calif., 1980-87; mem. vaccine safety commn. Nat. Inst. Medicine, 1995-2008; mem. Coun. Child Neurology Soc., Dysautonomia Found., med. adv. bd. Nat. Orgn. Rare Diseases, Nat. Wilson's Disease Found.; trustee Dystonia Med. Rsch. Found., Vancouver, Can., 1985-2008. Author: Textbook of Child Neurology, 6th edit., 2000; (play) The Last Inquisitor, 1985 (Drama-Logue Critics award 1985), The Salvation of Miguel Toruna, 1987; (screen play) Miguel, Open Ward, 1989, The Countess of Sligo, 1992, The White Darkness, 1996, Lady Macbeth Gets a Divorce, 2001, Native Born, 2003; (novels) The Secret Diary of Alice in Wonderland, 1998, The Angry Puppet Syndrome, 1999, After the Tempest, 2003, The Waiting Game, 2000, A View of Fuji, 2000; contbr. numerous articles to profl. jours. Served with USAF, 1954-56. Mem. Am. Acad. Neurology, Am. Acad. Pediatrics, Am. Chem. Soc., Soc. for Pediatric Rsch., Sociedad Peruana de Neuro-Psiquiatria (hon.), Am. Neurochem. Soc., Am. Neurol. Assn., Am. Pediatric Soc., Child Neurology Soc. (Hower award 1980), Dramatist Guild, PEN. Jewish. Home: Los Angeles, Calif. Died Nov. 22, 2008.

MENNIS, EDMUND ADDI, investment management consultant; b. Allentown, Pa., Aug. 12, 1919; s. William Henry and Grace (Addi) M.; m. Selma Adinoff, Sept. 25, 1945; children: Ardith Grace, Daniel Liam. BA, CCNY, 1941; MA, Columbia U., 1946; PhD, NYU, 1961. Security analyst Eastman, Dillon & Co., NYC, 1945-46; sr. rsch. asst. Am. Inst. Econ. Rsch., Great Barrington, Mass., 1946-50; security analyst Wellington Mgmt. Co., Phila., 1950-61, dir. rsch., 1958-61, v.p., mem. investment com., 1958-66, economist, 1953-66; sr. v.p., chmn. trust investment com. Republic Nat. Bank, Dallas, 1966-72; sr. v.p., chmn. investment policy com. Security Pacific Nat. Bank, LA, 1973-81; pres., dir. Bunker Hill Income Securities, Inc., 1973-81; chmn. bd. Security Pacific Investment Mgrs., Inc., 1977-81; ind. cons. to investment mgmt. orgns., from 1982. Tech. cons. Bus. Coun., Washington, 1962-66, 72-77, 79-81; econ. adviser sec. commerce, 1967-68; mem. investment adv. panel Pension Benefit Guaranty Corp., 1981-83. Author: How the Economy Works, 1991, 2d edit., 1999, Chinese edit., 2000; assoc. editor Fin. Analysts Jour., 1960-88; editor: C.F.A. Digest, 1971-86, Bus. Econs., 1985-99, editor emeritus, 2000—; editor: Banker's Econ. & Investment Alert, 1993—; author or editor books, chpts., numerous articles in field of econs. and investments. Trustee Fin. Analysts Rsch. Found., 1981-86. 1st lt. USAAF, 1942-45; capt. USAF, 1951-53. Fellow Nat. Assn. Bus. Economists (coun. 1967-69, David L. Williams Lifetime Achievement award 1996); mem. Fin. Analysts Fedn. (dir. 1970-72, Graham and Dodd award 1972, Molodovsky award 1972), Am. Econ. Assn., Am. Fin. Assn., LA Soc. Fin. Analysts, Conf. Bus. Econ. (vice chmn. 1977, chmn. 1978), Inst. CFAs (pres. 1970-72, trustee 1968-74, C. Stewart Sheppard award 1978). Home: Rancho Palos Verdes, Calif. Died Mar. 2009.

MENOYO, ERIC FELIX, lawyer; b. NYC, May 9, 1944; s. Enrique and Frances (Villela) M.; m. Deirdre Caitlin Ryan, Aug. 12, 1967; children: Eric Edward, Sarah Micela Holch. AB in English, Georgetown U., 1966, JD, 1969; LLM in Taxation, NYU, 1975. Bar: NY 1969, Mass. 1976, US Dist. Ct. (ea. dist.) Mass. 1976, US Ct. Appeals (1st cir.) 1976. Assoc. Barrett Smith Schapiro & Simon, NYC, 1969-76, Palmer & Dodge, Boston, 1976-77, ptnr., 1978—2005, Edwards Angell Palmer & Dodge LLP, Boston, 2005—09. Lectr. law Northeastern U., 1986-87, Mass. Continuing Legal Edn., Boston, 1978—09; trustee Cora du Bois Charitable Trust, 1995-09. Trustee Nashoba-Brooks Sch. Concord Inc., Mass., 1984-90, 1st Parish Sudbury, 1979-82, Sudbury Valley Trustees, Inc., 1991—, pres., 1994-96. Fellow Am. Coll. Trust and Estate Counsel; mem. ABA, Boston Bar Assn., Am. Law Inst., Larchmont Yacht Club. Unitarian Universalist. Avocations: sailing, hiking. Home: Sudbury, Mass. Died Mar. 15, 2009.

MENSHOV, ALEXANDER ALEXANDROVICH, hygiene; b. Astrahan, Astrahan, Russia, Sept. 30, 1925; arrived in Ukraine, 1944/; s. Alexander Dmitrievich and Nina Alexandrovna (Merquleva) M.; m. Agnessa Mihailovna Zadessenets, Nov. 23, 1957; 1 child, Igor. Physician, Grad. Med. Scu., U. Kiev, Ukraine, 1948; diploma of med. dr., Moscow, USSR, 1968, diploma of prof. Hygiene, 1971. Mem. staff Med. U. Kiev, 1948-51; younger sci. collaborator Inst. of Profl. Disease, Kiev, 1951-55; chief of lab., noise and vibration Inst. Occupl. Health of the Acad. Med. Scis., Ukraine, 1955-95. Author: Effect of Industrial Vibration and Noise on the Human Organism (Russia), 1977; co-author: Combined Effect of Industrial Noise and Vibration on the Organism (Russia), 1980; (textbook) Occupational Hygiene (Moscow), 1974, Occupational Hygiene in Agricultural Production (Russia), 1981; also brochures, abstracts, and articles (Russia, U.S. Japan, Ukraine, Germany, Hungary, Bulgaria, Sweden). Mem. N.Y. Acad. Scis., Acoustical Soc. Am., Inst. Noise Ctrl. Engring. Achievements include patents in device for determining human vibro-motor reaction; (with other) in sound absorbing screen, in a sound absorber, in shelving noise screening, in individual noise protection device. Died Mar. 3, 2008.

MERENSTEIN, GERALD BURTON, pediatrician, educator; b. Pitts., Feb. 14, 1941; s. Morris and Sarah (Shrinsky) M.; m. Barnetta Maryn, Aug. 21, 1960. BS, U. Pitts., 1962, MD, 1966. Diplomate Am. Bd. Pediatrics; lic. physician, Calif., Colo. Intern then resident Fitzsimons Gen. Hosp., Aurora, Colo., 1966-69; fellow Children's Hosp. San Francisco, 1969-71; program dir. neonatal-perinatal fellowship Fitzsimons Army Med. Ctr., Aurora, Colo., 1975-86, chmn. dept. pediatrics, 1979-86; dir. Lubchenco Perinatal Ctrs. U. Colo./Children's Hosp., Denver, from 1986, acting chmn. dept. pediatrics, 1988-90, dir. child health assoc. program, physician asst., from 1994, prof. of pediatrics, vice chmn. acad. affairs, 1990-97; sr. assoc. dean Edn. Sch. Medicine, from 1997. Mem. accreditation rev. com. Edn. Physician Assts., 1995—, vice chair, 1998—. Co-editor: Handbook of Neonatal Intensive Care, 1985, 2d edit., 1989, 3d edit., 1993, 4th edit. 1997, Handbook of Pediatrics, 16th edit., 1991, 17th edit., 1994, 18th edit. 1997. Bd. dirs. Nat. Cert. Corp., Chgo., 1988-96; mem. steering com., mem. com. on perinatal health March of Dimes, White Plains, N.Y., 1990-93. Col. U.S. Army, 1966-86. Named Outstanding Man of Yr., Denver Jaycees, 1974. Fellow Am. Acad. Pediatrics (chair com. fetus and newborn 1989-93, exec. com. sect. on prenatal pediatrics 1996—); mem. Am. Pediatric Soc., Assn. Pediatric Program Dirs. (exec. com., councilor), Alpha Omega Alpha. Democrat. Jewish. Avocations: travel, photography, skiing. Home: Denver, Colo. Died Dec. 14, 2007.

MERKEL, DONALD HENRY, marketing executive; b. Mineola, NY, Jan. 13, 1934; s. Otto Merkel and Angelina (DeMarino) Cavanagh; m. Lois Joanne Sessions, Oct. 21, 1935; children: Anthony, Todd, Gregory. BBA, U. Wash., Seattle, 1960; MBA, Seattle U., 1974. CPCU. Advt. rsch. mgr. The Seattle Times, 1960-66; mgr. rsch. and planning Unigard Ins., Seattle, 1966-75; product planner Seattle First Nat. Bank, 1975-76; rsch. mgr. Am. Strevell, Kent, Wash., 1976-78; v.p. rsch. Consumer Attitude Rsch., Renton, Wash., 1978-81; asst. v.p. mktg. rsch. United Ins. Co. Am., Chgo., from 1981. Mem. Mountlake Terr. Planning Commn., 1963-67, Seattle Area Indsl. Coun., 1963-68. With USAF, 1952-56. Mem. Am. Mktg. Assn. (chpt. pres. 1966-67), Soc. Ins. Rsch. (pres. 1975-76), LIMRA (rsch. com. 1989—). Republican. Roman Catholic. Home: Loveland, Colo. Died July 16, 2008.

MERLIN, SALLY BARBARA, communications executive; b. LA, Apr. 12, 1946; d. Merlin and Sally Barbara (Smitten) Merlin; m. Emanuel Aron, May 19, 1965 (div.

May 1966); m. Dennis Edmund Jones, Dec. 14, 1973 (div. Feb. 1991); 1 child, David. Grad., New England Conservatory, 1991, Howard U., 1995. Script doctor The Complete Screenplay and More, 1967—2002; freelance writer, 1967—2002; prodr. Prometheus Prodns., LA, 1985-92; East coast editor Script mag. Tchr. UCLA Ext., 1986, writers' consortium, 1986-2002. Editor Script mag., 1993—. Chairperson Diane Thomas award, L.A., 1988-91. Mem. Writers Guild Am. Democrat. Home: Kensington, Md. Died Sept. 16, 2007.

MERRICK, ROSWELL DAVENPORT, educational association administrator; b. Kings County, NY, July 20, 1922; s. George Roswell and Marguerite Regina M.; m. Gladys K. Kinley, June 26, 1948; children— Gregory, Susan, Peter. BS, Springfield Coll., 1944; MA, N.Y. U., 1947; Ed.D., Boston U., 1953. Assoc. prof., head basketball coach Ctl. Conn. U., New Britain, 1946-53; asst. dean (Coll. Edn.); dir. div. health, phys. edn., recreation and athletics So. Ill. U., Carbondale, 1953-58; exec. dir. Nat. Assn. Sport and Phys. Edn., Reston, Va., 1958-91, US Fitness and Sport Coun., from 1991. Contbr. articles to profl. jour. Mem. US Olympic Com. Served with USAAF, 1944-46. Mem. AAHPERD, Mt. Vernon Yacht Club. Methodist. Died Jan. 24, 2004.

MERRIM, LOUISE MEYEROWITZ, artist, actress; b. NYC; d. Leo and Jeanette (Harris) Meyerowitz; m. Lewis Jay Merrim, June 27, 1948; children: Stephanie, Andrea Merrim Goff (dec.). BFA, Pratt Inst., 1947; MFA, Columbia U., 1951; postgrad., Post Coll., 1971-72, New Sch., 1977-78. Art tchr. pub. schs., NYC, 1947-51, Port Washington, NY, 1970-83. One-woman shows include Plandome Gallery, L.I., Isis Gallery, N.Y., San Diego art Inst., Pan Pacific Hotel, San Diego; exhibited in group shows at Nassau County Fine Arts Mus. (Bronze award), Heckscher Mus. (Nora Mirmont award), Nat. Acad., Nat. Assn. Women Artists (Medal of Honor, Charlotte Whinston award), Audubon Artists (Stephen Hirsch Meml. award), Cork Gallery, Warner Comm. Gallery, L.I. Art Tchrs. (two awards of excellence), L.I. Art Tchrs. Award Winners Show, Pt. Washington Libr. Invitational, Glen Cove (2nd prize), Manhasset Art Assn. (best in show, five 1st prizes), San Diego Art Inst., San Diego Mus. Art (Gold award), Oceanside Mus. Art, Hank Baum Gallery, San Francisco, Tarbox Gallery, Clark Gallery, Knowles Gallery, San Diego, Golden Pacific Arts Gallery, San Diego, Henry Chastain Gallery, Scottsdale, Boehm Gallery/Palomar Coll., Hyde Gallery/Grossmont Coll., Timmons Gallery, Rancho Santa Fe, Calif.; included in permanent collection of San Diego Mus. Art; appeared in numerous theatrical prodns. including Fiddler on the Roof, Barefoot in the Park, N.Y., Anything Goes, The Musical Comedy Murders of 1940, Anastasia (Drama award), Fiddler on the Roof, The Music Man, What's Wrong With this Picture?, Marvin's Room, San Diego, The Foreigner; dir. Under Milkwood; dir., appeared in Spoon River Anthology. Mem.: Nat. Assn. Women Artists, NY Soc. of Women Artists, Contemporary Artists Guild of NY, Audubon Artist (NY), San Diego Art Inst., Artists Guild of San Diego Art Mus. (pres. 1993), Artists Equity, Actors Alliance. Avocations: tennis, poetry, travel. Home: La Jolla, Calif. Died May 6, 2007.

MERRITT, HENRY NEYRON, SR., psychotherapist; b. Darlington, SC, Nov. 9, 1919; s. Henry Orme and Lilllian (Parrott) M.; m. Bess Castles, Aug. 21, 1953; children: Henry Neyron Jr., JoAnn. BS, Clemson U., 1941; MD, Kans. City U., Mo., 1944; MEd, U. S.C.; PhD, Phiathea Coll., London, Ont., Can., 1969. Diplomate Am. Bd. Med. Psychotherapists, Fla. Psychol. Practitioners Assn. Physician Bloudias Clinic, Columbia, S.C., 1944-53; biologist Montgomery County Bd. Edn., Silver Spring, Md., 1953-64; adj. prof. U. Md., College Park, 1953-64; assoc. prof. Frostburg (Md.) State U., 1964-67, Va. Poly. Inst., Blacksburg, 1967-68; prof., chmn. dept. health U. Wis., LaCrosse, 1968-72; dir. drug ctr. U. S. Navy, Jacksonville, Fla., 1972-76; dir. Psychotherapy Ctr., Jacksonville, from 1976. Fellow Am. Orthopsychiat. Assn., Masons, Shriners. Republican. Mem. Unity Ch. Avocations: travel, reading, gardening. Home: Orange Park, Fla. Died June 4, 2008.

MERWIN, HARMON TURNER, retired regional planner; b. Middlefield, Ohio, July 10, 1920; s. Harry Elverton and Ora (Turner) M.; m. Eldred Louise Merwin, Apr. 10, 1954; children: Elaine, Brian, Kathryn (dec.). B in Landcape Architecture, Ohio State U., 1950. Planner, then dir. Franklin County Regional Planning Commn., Columbus, Ohio, 1951-69; dep. dir. Mid-Ohio Regional Planning Commn., Columbus, 1970-74, program mgr., 1975-80, spl. projects sr. cons., 1975-80, sr. cons., 1981-91; retired, 1991. Cons. in field. Bd. dirs., Columbus Met. Area Community Action Orgn., 1963-65; mem. facilities com., environ. health subcom., Mid-Ohio Health Planning Fedn., Columbus; pres. Ohio Planning Conf., 1963-65. Sgt. USAAF, 1942-46, ETO. Mem. Am. Inst. Cert. Planners (past pres. Ohio chpt.). Republican. Methodist. Avocations: photography, ping pong/table tennis, travel. Home: Stevensville, Mont. Died Feb. 1, 2008.

MERZ, PAUL LOUIS, organic polymer chemist; b. New Haven, June 1, 1918; s. Paul and Marie Louise (Schumacher) M.; m. Esther Jane Simson, Aug. 21, 1950; children: Charles, Brian, Bruce, Cheryl. BS in Chemistry, Union Coll., 1940; PhD in Organic Chemistry, Yale U., 1951. Research and devel. chemist Beech-Nut Packing Co., Canajoharie, N.Y., 1940-43, head polymer lab., 1945-47, cons., 1947-51; group leader, project dir. U.S. Rubber Co., Naugatuck, Conn., 1951-62; sr. plastics chemist Lawrence Livermore (Calif.) Lab., 1962-64; staff scientist, sr. engring. specialist Gen. Dynamics Convair, San Diego, 1964-82; cons. Merz Research, Ophir, Oreg., from 1982. Contbr. articles to profl. jours.; patentee in field. Scout master Boy Scouts Am., La Jolla, Calif., 1966-69; chmn. Commn. Christian Edn. Meth. Ch., La Jolla, 1971-72; elder Presbyn. Ch., Gold Beach, Calif., 1989. Served as cpl. U.S. Army, 1943-45, ETO. Mem. AAAS (emeritus), Am. Chem. Soc. (emeritus), Sigma Xi (emeritus). Republican. Presbyterian. Avocations: camping, swimming, diving. Home: San Diego, Calif. Died Jan. 11, 2008.

MESCHELOFF, MOSES, rabbi; b. NYC, June 12, 1909; s. Mayer and Bessie (Kroll) M.; m. Magda Schonfeld, Mar. 10, 1935; children: Renah Rahelle, Efraim Zev, David Joseph. BA, CCNY, 1932; DHL, Hebrew Theol. Coll., 1980. Ordained rabbi, 1932. Rabbi Congregation Machzike Hadas, Scranton, Pa., 1932-36, Congregation United Sons of Israel, North Adams, Mass., 1936-37, Congregation Beth Jacob, Miami Beach, Fla., 1937-55, Congregation K.I.N.S. of West Rogers Park, Chgo., from 1955. Author: In the Priest's Office, Covenant of Abraham, Right Before the King, The Parting of Ways. Mem. exec. com. Northtown Rogers Park Mental Health Coun., Coun. for Jewish Elderly; mem. Mayor's Commn. of Dept. Human Svcs., Chgo. Named to Hall of Fame, City of Chgo., 1986. Mem. Chgo. Bd. Rabbis (exec. com.), Chgo. Rabbinical Coun. (exec. com.), Chgo. Zionist Orgn. (exec. com.), North Town Community Coun. (exec. com.), Associated Talmud Torahs (bd. dirs.), Religious Zionist Coun. (bd. dirs.). Home: Chicago, Ill. Died May 9, 2008.

MESCHUTT, DAVID RANDOLPH, historian; b. NYC, May 29, 1955; s. Philip Frederick and Mary Evelyn (Mahanes) M.; m. Sarah Caroline Bevan, July 14, 1990. BA in Journalism, Washington and Lee U., 1977; MA in History Mus. Studies, SUNY, Cooperstown, 1988; postgrad., Attingham Summer Sch., Gt. Britain, 1988-98, postgrad., 2004, Royal Collection Studies Programme, 2000; PhD in Art History, U. Del., 2005. Rschr. Thomas Jefferson Meml. Found., Charlottesville, Va., 1977-78, Frick Art Reference Libr., NYC, 1980-86; curator art West Point (N.Y.) Mus./U.S. Mil. Acad., 1988-98; consulting curator N.Y. State Office of Pks., Recreation and Hist. Preservation, Waterford, NY, from 1999. Guest curator N.Y. State Hist. Assn., Cooperstown, 1986-87, Brandywine River Mus., Chadds Ford, Pa., 1992, Va. Hist. Soc., Richmond, 1999; curator (permanent installation) John Browere's life masks, Fenimore Art Mus. and writer of accompanying brochure; cons. Curatorial Office, U.S. Dept. Treasury, Washington, 1988, Albany (N.Y.) Inst. History and Art, 1988, NY State Office of Parks, Recreation, and Historic Preservation. Author: A Bold Experiment: John Henri Isaac Browere's Life Masks of Prominent Americans, 1988; co-author: The Portraits and History Paintings of Alonzo Chappel, 1992; assoc. editor Am. Nat. Biography, Oxford U. Press, 1994-99, contbr., 1994; contbr. Am. Art Jour.; contbr. articles to profl. jours. Bd. dirs. Friends of Stony Point Battlefield, NJ. Nourse Found. fellow, 1986-87, Nat. Endowment for Arts fellow, 1987, Soc. Colonial Wars fellow, 1988, Andrew W. Mellon fellow Va. Hist. Soc., 1992, Anne S.K. Brown fellow Brown U., 1993, Mayers fellow Huntington Libr. and Art Gallery, 1997. Mem.: Walpole Soc., N.Y. State Hist. Assn., Va. Hist. Soc., Ralph Vaughan Williams Soc., Herbert Howells Soc., Historians Brit. Art, Assn. Historians Am. Art. Methodist. Avocation: music. Died July 8, 2005.

MESERVE, BRUCE ELWYN, mathematics educator; b. Portland, Maine, Feb. 2, 1917; s. Walter Joseph and Bessie Adelia (Bailey) M.; m. Gertrude Morey Holland, June 7, 1941 (div. 1961); children: Arthur, Virginia, Donald; m. Dorothy Spencer Tucker, Aug. 5, 1961. AB, Bates Coll., Lewiston, Maine, 1938; MA, Duke U., 1941, PhD, 1947. Tchr. Moses Brown Sch., Providence, R.I., 1938-41; from instr. to asst. prof. U. Ill., Champaign, 1946-54; from assoc. prof. to prof., chmn. math. dept. Montclair State Coll., Upper Montclair, N.J., 1954-64; prof. U. Vt., Burlington, 1964-83, prof. emeritus, 1983—2008. Co-chmn. Internat. Study Group on Rels. Between History and Pedagogy of Math., 1980-84. Author: Fundamental Concepts of Algebra, 1951, Fundamental Concepts of Geometry, 1955, and others; contbr. articles to profl. jours.; editor several books. Moderator Town of Fairfax, Vt., 1976-84. Fellow AAAS; mem. Am. Math. Soc., Math. Assn. Am., Nat. Coun. Tchrs. Math. (pres. 1964-66, bd. dirs. 1958-67), Phi Beta Kappa, Sigma Pi Sigma. Died Nov. 14, 2008.

MESSICK, MYRTLE ELIZABETH, medical/surgical nurse; b. Keller, Va., Sept. 8, 1920; d. John Cornelius and Mary Evva (Kilmon) Drewer; m. Gerald Martin Messick, Oct. 19, 1942; 1 child, Neil Warren. Diploma, Peninsula Gen. Hosp. Sch. Nursing, 1941. RN, Md. Med.-surg. nurse Peninsula Gen. Hosp., Salisbury, Md., staff nurse; pvt. duty nurse, Bivalve, Md.; part-time nurse C.V. Surgs. & Assocs., Salisbury. Mem. ANA, Md. Nurses Assn., Peninsula Gen. Hosp. Sch. Nursing Alumni Assn. Home: Bivalve, Md. Died July 17, 2008.

MESSNER, HOWARD MYRON, retired professional association executive, former federal official; b. Newark, June 10, 1937; s. Elias and Freda (Trachtenberg) M.; m. Aletha Bragg, 1960 (div. 1980); children: Jennifer, Linda, David; m. Melba June Meador, June 22, 1986. BA in Polit. Sci., Antioch Coll., 1960; MA in Pub. Adminstrn., U. Mass., 1962. Mgmt. analyst, Office Gov. State of Mass., Boston, 1960-61; staff asst. to adminstr. NASA, Washington, 1962-65; mgmt. analyst Bur. Budget, Washington, 1965-71; dir. adminstrn. EPA, Washington, 1971-75, asst. adminstr. for adminstrn., 1983-87; asst. dir. Congl. Budget Office, Washington, 1975-77; asst. dir. for mgmt. programs Office Mgmt. & Budget, Exec. Office of the Pres., Washington, 1977-83; contr. US Dept. Energy, Washington, 1983; exec. v.p. Am. Cons. Engr. Coun., 1987—99, 2006—07; pres., CEO Nat. Acad. Pub. Adminstrn., Washington, 2004—07. Bd. dirs. Kelly, Anderson Inc., 2005—08. Recipient William A. Jump Meml. award, EPA, 1971, Chancellor's medal U. Mass., 1978, Exceptional Svc. award, Nat. Acad. Pub. Adminstrn., 1979, Presdl. Disting. Exec. award, 1986, Outstanding Pub. Service award Nat. Capital chpt. Am. Soc. Pub. Adminstrn., 1986 Mem. Nat. Acad. Pub. Adminstrn. (pres., 2003, '06), Cosmos Club. Democrat. Jewish. Home: Gambrills, Md. Died Dec. 4, 2008.

METCALF, ROBERT JOHN ELMER, industrial consultant; b. Glen Ellyn, Ill., June 27, 1919; s. Elmer Simpson and Vida Marie Metcalf; m. Rosemarie Rusch, Sept. 11, 1947; children: Kathleen, Karen, Patti, Pamela. BSME, U. Pitts., 1947. Asst. staff supr. Westinghouse Electric Co., Buffalo, 1949—52, assoc. engr., 1952—54; assoc. Gemar Assocs., Inc., Greenwich, Conn., 1954—66, v.p., 1966—83; cons., 1983—92. With US Army, 1943—46. Mem.: Inst. Mgmt. Cons. (founding). Roman Catholic. Died Oct. 20, 2007.

METTLER, DARLENE DEBAULT, English educator; b. Effingham, Ill., Dec. 3, 1942; d. Delmar D. and Eileen (Davis) D.; m. George B. Mettler; children: Jaime, Sean. BA, Milligan Coll., 1964; MA, U. South Fla., 1974; PhD, Ga. State U., 1986. Tchr. Roanoke (Va.) County Schs., 1963-65, Pinellas County Schs., St. Petersburg, Fla., 1965-71; instr. Macon (Ga.) Coll., 1974-85; asst. prof. Tift Coll., Forsyth, Ga., 1985-87; assoc. prof. Wesleyan Coll., Macon, from 1987; chair English dept., from 1992. Author: Musical Allusion and Imagery in the Novels of Iris Murdoch, 1991. Fulbright scholar, 1989. Mem. South Atlantic MLA, Iris Murdoch Soc., Southeastern Soc. for 18th Century Studies. Avocations: jogging, playing piano, travel. Home: Forsyth, Ga. Died Mar. 28, 2008.

METZ, JAMES WITTINGTON, lawyer; b. Amityville, NY, June 9, 1949; s. Dave Wittington and Mary A. (Bruckner) M.; m. Kathleen Danielle Rowley, Jan. 29, 1972; children: James W. II, Timothy J., Daniel J., Kathryn T., Julie A. BA in History and English, Boston Coll., 1971; JD, U. Detroit, 1973. Bar: Mich. 1974, N.Y. 1990, U.S. Dist. Ct. (ea. dist.) Mich. 1974, U.S. Ct. Appeals (9th cir.) 1974. Assoc. G.B. Bailey, Jr., Romeo, Mich., 1974-75; asst. pros. atty. IV Wayne County Pros., Detroit, from 1975. Mem. fin. com. Ojibwa dist. Boy Scouts Am., Pontiac, Mich., 1996-97. Mem. State Bar Assn. Mich. (rep. assembly 1982-88, juvenile law sect. coun. 1988-92). Republican. Roman Catholic. Home: Lexington, Mich. Died July 1, 2008.

MEYER, B. FRED, small business executive, builder, home and product designer; b. LI, NY, Jan. 6, 1918; s. Barthold Fred and Edna May (Clark) M.; m. Mary E. Carman, July 18, 1951; children: Patricia Meyer Sauer, Susan Meyer Sachs. Student, Pratt Inst., 1935-39, Johns Hopkins U., 1946-48, Wayne State U., 1954-55. Registered builder, Fla. Project engr. Lear, Inc., Grand Rapids, Mich., 1948-51; engring. exec. GM Corp., Warren, Mich., 1951-75; pres. BFM Assocs., Inc. (name Fred Meyer, Inc. 1990), Sarasota, Fla., from 1975. Capt. USAAF, 1942-46, ETO. Achievements include 23 patents including pendulum type seat belt retractor, automotive power window switches, automotive power window activator. Avocations: golf, computers, travel. Died Dec. 27, 2007.

MEYER, BARBARA ANN, tax specialist; b. Indpls., Mar. 20, 1924; d. Horace Wright and Sibyl Conklin (Lindley) Townsend; m. Robert James Scott, Dec. 15, 1941 (dec. 1949); children: Sue Meyer Suppiger, Randolph David, Steven James; m. Fred J. Meyer, Jan. 3, 1950; 1 child, Johanna Laura Meyer-Mitchell. Student, U. Md., 1958-60, Big Bend C.C., 1965-69. Cert. enrolled agent, U.S. Treasury, 1980. Owner, mgr. Meyer Tax. Svc., Coulee Dam, Wash., 1969-94, cons., from 1994; enrolled agent emeritus. Income tax tchr. Big Bend C.C., Coulee Dam, 1975-80. Contbr. articles to newspapers. Chair svc. to mil. families ARC, Ephrata, Wash., 1941—, Roosevelt History Month, Grand Coulee, 1995-96; bd. chmn. Pub. Hosp. Dist. #6, Grand Coulee, 1990-94. Mem. Nat. Assn. Enrolled Agents, Wash. State Soc. Enrolled Agents (v.p. 1984—, bd. dirs. 1985-88), Am. Cancer Soc. (bd. dirs. 1995—), Calif. Soc. Enrolled Agents (affiliate), Grand Coulee C. of C. (life, hon., pres. 1979-80), Grand Coulee Yacht Club (life, hon.), Grand Coulee Dam Rotary (pres. 1992-93). Democrat. Avocations: cooking, gardening, bird watching. Home: Moses Lake, Wash. Died June 14, 2008.

MEYER, BARRY JOEL, communications company executive; b. Columbia, SC, Aug. 6, 1942; s. Paul H. Meyer and Florence (Kline) Fox; m. Diane, Mar. 15, 1972; 1 child, Jason. BS in Indsl. Mgmt., Clemson U., 1966. Asst. personnel mgr. Shakespear Inc., Columbia, S.C., 1966-70; real estate sales Arthur Ravenel Jr. Co., Charleston, S.C., 1970-73; asst. project mgr. Med. Univ. of S.C., Charleston, 1973-78; owner Tidewater Hardware, Beaufort, S.C., 1978-84; mgr. Radio Comm. of Charleston/First Page, from 1984. Com. mem. United Way, Charleston, 1976-78, Water Festival, Beaufort, 1979-81; state bd. dirs. Ducks Unltd., S.C., 1973-84; coach Dixie Youth Baseball, Charleston, 1987—. Sgt. S.C. Air Nat. Guard, 1966-72. Recipient Disting. Svc. award Ducks Unltd., 1982, Conservation Svc. award, 1981.

Mem. Metro Exchange Club, Nat. Assn. Bus. & Ednl. Radio, Assn. Pvt. Carrier Paging. Republican. Jewish. Avocations: boating, fishing. Home: Charleston, SC. Died Feb. 23, 2008.

MEYER, RUDOLF X., retired space technology executive, engineering educator; b. Rapperswil, Switzerland, Jan. 13, 1922; came to U.S., 1947; s. Carl and Alice A. (Muller) M.; m. Jeanne A. Meyer, Feb. 8, 1947; children: Jacqueline C. Meyer-Donaher, Dorothy A. Works. Diploma Engr., Swiss Inst. Tech., Zurich, 1945; D of Engring, Johns Hopkins U., 1955. Engr. De Laval Steam Turbine Co., Trenton, N.J., 1947-48; asst. prof. aeronautics U.S. Naval Postgrad. Sch., Annapolis, Md., 1948-52; project mgr. The Hydrofoil Corp., Annapolis, 1952-55; dept. head The Ramo-Wooldridge Corp., LA, 1955-60; from assoc. dir. phys. rsch. lab. to gen. mgr./chief engr. The Aerospace Corp., LA, 1960-87; adj. prof. Sch. Engring. UCLA, from 1987. Mem. adv. bd. Dept. Def., Washington, 1980-81; invited lectr. MIT, Naval Postgrad. Sch., Naval. Acad., U. So.Calif. Assoc. editor AIAA, 1975-80; contbr. more than 70 articles to profl. jours.; patentee in field. Served with Swiss Army, 1942-45. Recipient Air Force Space div. Excellence awrd USAF, 1985; Regents lectr. U. Calif., 1987. Fellow AIAA. Republican. Roman Catholic. Avocations: history, art, languages, mathematics. Home: Pacific Palisades, Calif. Died Jan. 31, 2008.

MEYERHOFF, ALBERT HENRY, JR., lawyer; b. Stafford, Conn., Sept. 20, 1947; s. Albert and Ruth Meyerhoff; m. Marcia Brandwynne, July 7, 2007; 1 child, Leah. B, U. Conn., 1969; JD, Cornell U., NY, 1972. Bar: Calif. Atty. Calif. Rural, 1972—81; legal asst. Natural Resources Defense Council, Calif., 1981—98; ptnr. Lerach, Coughlin, Stoia & Geller, Beverly Hills, Calif., 1998—2008. Contbr. articles to newspapers and profl. jours.; invited guest (tv show) 60 Minutes. Recipient Lawyer of Yr. award, TCPJ, Lifetime Achievement award, ACLU, League Conservation Voters. Mem.: Sierra Club (bd. trustees). Democrat. Died Dec. 21, 2008.

MEYERSON, MARTIN, aerospace engineer; b. East Orange, NJ, Oct. 22, 1927; s. Max and Anna (Slobodin) M.; children: Mark Lawrence, Jann Lesley Sidorov, Jack David. BSEE, NJ Inst. Tech., 1948, MSEE, 1951. Asst. project engr. Kay Electric Co., Pinebrook, NJ, 1949-50; program mgr. U.S. Army Signal Engring. Labs., Ft. Monmouth, NJ, 1950-57; dir. advanced sys. Martin Marietta Corp., Orlando, Fla., 1957-79, dir. programs Balt., 1977-79; dep. program dir. Fairchild Rep. Co., Farmingdale, NY, 1979-87; dir. bus. analysis Allied Signal Aerospace Co., Arlington, Va., 1987-88; dir. bus. planning Ford Aerospace Corp., McLean, Va., 1988-90; asst. to pres., dir. bus. devel. Elec. Systems div. Grumman Corp., Great River, NY, 1990-94; v.p. bus. devel. and strategic planning, electronics and sys. integration divsn. Northrop Grumman, Bethpage, NY, 1994-95; cons. to aerospace industry, from 1995. Mem. faculty, lectr. Dept. Def. Weapon Systems Mgmt. Ctr., Dayton, Ohio, 1967-71; mem. study panel, cons. Congl. Commn. on Govt. Procurement, Washington, 1971-72; mem. seminar team on environ. quality U.S. Dept. Commerce, Prague, Czech Republic, 1972; chmn. environ. quality Md. Gov.'s Sci. Adv. Coun., Annapolis, 1957-77. Author articles, reports in field. Mem. by-laws com. Admiralty Bd. Dirs., Bay Shore, NY, 1983-85. Fellow AIAA (assoc.), IEEE (sr.). Democrat. Jewish. Avocations: golf, walking, reading. Home: Bethesda, Md. Died July 13, 2008.

MICHAELS, MARION CECELIA, newswriter, editor, news syndicate executive; b. Black River Falls, Wis. d. Leonard N. and Estelle O. (Payne) Doud; m. Charles Webb (div.); children: Charles, David, Robert; m. Mark J. Michaels (div.); 1 child, Merry A. BS in Bus. Edn., U. Wis., Eau Claire, 1978, MS in Spl. Edn., 1981. Mgr., instr. bus. program Blackwell Job Corps Ctr., 1987-89; mgr. Michaels Secretarial Sv., Black River Falls, Wis., 1979-83; columnist, editor Michaels News, Black River Falls, from 1983, pres., from 1989. Hon. appt. rsch. bd. advisors Am. Biog. Inst., 1996-2001. Author: The Little Cowboy: Pursuing Dana's Dream, 1998, September's Song from 2003, Dana's Dream, 2004, Loving Lisa, 2005; columnist Single Parenting, 1983—94, Parenting Plus, 1990—2004, editor, contbr. (column) Surviving Single, 1990—95, To Read or Not (Fiction), from 1985, To Read or Not (Non-Fiction), 1985—2004, Report From Planet Earth, from 1985, Travel Tidbits, 1991—95, Surviving Sane, 1995—98. Chmn. Brockway Cmty. Orgn., 1969-71; chair, counselor Brockway Youth Group, 1970-72; chmn. labor com. Dem. Platform Com., Wis., 1975-76; candidate State Assembly, 1978, 82; co-founder Franklin Delano Roosevelt Meml., 1997; mem. LWV. Named Patriot of the Yr., Held Hospitalized Vets., 2007; named to Internat. Poetry Hall of Fame, 1997. Mem.: Assn. Rsch. and Enlightenment, Physicians for Social Responsibility, Union Concerned Scientists, Internat. Soc. Poets (founding laureate mem. 2006, Internat. Poet of Merit award 1999, Outstanding achievement in poetry award 2005, 2006), Humane Soc. of US, Nat. Com. to Protect Soc. Security and Medicare, Peale Ctr. for Positive Living, Friends of the Earth, Nat. Trust for Pub. Edn., Smithsonian (assoc.), Pub. Citizen, Am. United, Nat. Parks, Clean Wis., So. Poverty Law Ctr., Natural Resources Def. Coun., Co-op Am., Amnesty Internat., Inst. for Noetic Sci., League of Conservation Voters, Wilson Ctr., Common Cause, Internat. Fund for Animals, Women's History Mus. (charter mem.), Phi Delta Kappa, Pi Omega Pi. Avocations: singing, dance, walking, swimming. Home: Chippewa Fls, Wis. Died Jan. 2009.

MICHAJLOW, EUSTACHY IOM, artist; b. Jeziory, Poland, Apr. 23, 1930; arrived in U.S., 1951; s. Victor Michajlow and Lidia Naumezyk; m. Dorina Boisjole Michajlow, Mar. 10, 1973; children: Vadim, Kora. Died May 18, 2008.

MICHENFELDER, ALBERT A., lawyer; b. St. Louis, July 21, 1926; s. Albert A. and Ruth Josephine (Donahue) M.; m. Lois Barbara Sullivan, Sept. 03, 1949 (div. May 2, 1967); children: Michael J., Ann C. Michenfelder Yancey, Elizabeth D. Michenfelder Brown; m. Ramona Jo Dysart, July 12, 1968 (dec. Jan. 2, 1998); 1 child, Julie D. Michenfelder Wolfe. B of Naval Sci., Marquette U., 1946; LLB, St. Louis U., 1950. Bar: Mo. 1950, U.S. Dist. Ct. (ea. dist.) Mo. 1950, U.S. Supreme Ct. 1975. Assoc. Flynn & Challis, St. Louis, 1950-54; pvt. practice St. Louis, 1954-55; of counsel Husch & Eppenberger LLC, St. Louis. Mem. 21st Cir. Jud. Commn., St. Louis, 1981-87. Contbr. articles to profl. jours. City atty. City of Webster Groves, Mo., 1966-79; mem. John Marshall Club, St. Louis. Lt. (j.g.) USNR, 1944-47. Mem. Mo. Bar Assn., Bar. Assn. Met. St. Louis, St. Louis County Bar Assn. (pres. 1966), Westborough Country Club. Republican. Avocations: golf, tennis. Home: Saint Louis, Mo. Died Sept. 26, 2009.

MIDDLETON, DAVID, physicist, educator; b. NYC, Apr. 19, 1920; s. Charles Davies and Lucile (Davidson) Middleton; m. Nadea Butler, May 26, 1945 (div. 1971); m. Joan Bartlett Reed, 1971; children: Susan Terry, Leslie Butler, David Scudder Blakeslee, George Davidson Powell, Christopher Hope, Andrew Bartlett, Henry H. Reed. Grad., Deerfield Acad., 1938; AB summa cum laude, Harvard U., 1942, AM, 1945, PhD in Physics, 1947. Tchg. fellow electronics Harvard U., Cambridge, Mass., 1942, spl. rsch. assoc. radio rsch. lab., 1942—45, NSF predoctoral fellow physics, 1945—47, rsch. fellow electronics, 1947—49, asst. prof. applied physics, 1949—54; cons. physicist Cambridge, 1954—2004, Concord, Mass., 1957—71, NYC from 2005; adj. prof. elec. engring. Columbia U., 1960—61; adj. prof. applied physics and comm. theory Rensselaer Poly. Inst., Hartford Grad. Ctr., 1961—70; adj. prof. communication theory U. R.I., from 1966; adj. prof. math. scis. Rice U., 1979—89. US del. Internat. Radio Union, Lima, Peru, 1975; lectr. NATO Advanced Study Inst., Grenoble, France, 1964, Copenhagen, 80, Luneburg, Germany, 84; invited lectr. Russia Acad. Sci. Acoustic Inst., 1973, 76, 79, 84; mem. Naval Rsch. Adv. Com., 1970—77; mem., cons. Inst. Def. Analyses; mem. sci. adv. bd. Supercomputing Rsch. Ctr., 1987—91; cons. physicist from 1946, Johns Hopkins U., SRI Internat., Rand Corp., USAF, Cambridge Rsch. Ctr., Comm. Satellite Corp., Lincoln Lab., NASA, Raytheon, Sylvania, Sperry-Rand, Office Naval Rsch., Applied Rsch. Labs., U. Tex., GE, Honeywell Transp. Sys. Ctr. Dept. Transp., Dept. Commerce Office Telecom., NOAA, Office Telecom. Policy Exec. Office Pres., Nat. Telecom. and Info. Adminstrn., Sci. Applications Inc., Naval Undersea Warfare Ctr., Lawrence Livermore Nat. Labs., Planning Rsch. Corp., Applied Physics Labs. U. Wash., from 1992, Kildare Corp., from 1995, Karmanos Cancer Inst., 1997—2001, Air Force Rsch. Lab, Hanscomb Air Force Base, from 2006, Gen. Dynamics Info. Tech. Inst., from 2006, others. Author: Introduction to Statistical Communication Theory, 1960, 3d edit., 1996, Russian edit. Soviet Radio Moscow, 2 vols., 1961, 1962, Topics in Communication Theory, 1965, 1987, Russian edit., 1966; sci. editor: English edit. Statistical Methods in Sonar (V. V. Ol'shevskii), 1978; mem. editl. bd. Info. and Control, Advanced Serials in Electronics and Cybernetics, 1972—82; contbr. articles to tech. jours. Recipient Prize paper award (with W.H. Huggins), Nat. Electronics Conf., 1956, First prize, 3d Internat. Symposium on Electromagnetic Compatibility Rotterdam, Holland, 1979, 2 Prize paper awards, US Dept. Commerce, 1978, Wisdom award of Honor, 1970, 1st prize, 3d Internat. Symposium Electromagnetic Compatibility, 1979, Prize Paper award, US Dept. Commerce, 1978; co-recipient, Nat. Electronics Conf., 1956. Fellow: NAE, AAAS, IEEE (life, Prize paper award 1977, 1979), Electromagnetics Acad. MIT, N.Y. Acad. Scis., Acoustical Soc. Am., Am. Phys. Soc.; mem.: Am. Math. Soc., Author's Guild Am., Dutch Treat (N.Y.C.), Explorers Club, Cosmos Club (Washington), Harvard Club (N.Y.C.), Sigma Xi, Phi Beta Kappa. Achievements include research in radar, telecommunications, underwater acoustics, oceanography, seismology, systems analysis, electromagnetic compatibility; a founder of Statistical Communication Theory. Died Nov. 16, 2008.

MIDDLETON, GEORGE, JR., clinical child psychologist; b. Houston, Feb. 26, 1923; s. George and Bettie (McCrary) M.; m. Margaret MacLean, Nov. 17, 1953. BA in Psychology, Birmingham-Southern Coll., 1948; MA in Psychology, U. Ala., Tuscaloosa, 1951; PhD in Clin. Psychology, Pa. State U., 1958. Lic. psychologist, La.; diplomate Am. Coll. Forensic Examiners, Am. Bd. Psychol. Specialities. Asst. clin. psychology Med. Coll. Ala., Birmingham, 1950-52; dir. dept. psychology Bryce Hosp., Tuscaloosa, 1952-54; instr. counseling Coll. Bus. Adminstrn. Pa. State U., 1956-58; asst. prof. spl. edn. McNeese State U., 1962-65, assoc. prof. spl. edn., 1962-65; dir. La. Gov.'s Program for Gifted Children, from 1963; prof. spl. edn. McNeese State U., 1965-73, prof. psychology, 1973-74; pvt. practice clin. psychology and neuropsychology, from 1974; cons. psychologist Calcasieu Parish Sch. Bd., from 1975. Vis. scholar U. Victoria, BC, Can., 1970-71. Mem. Am. Psychol. Assn., Nat. Acad. Neuropsychology, Internat. Neuropsychol. Soc., La. Psychol. Assn. (pres. 1973-74), La. Sch. Psychol. Assn., S.W. La. Psychol. Assn.

(pres. 1965, 73, 84), La. State Bd. Examiners Psychologists (chmn. 1977-78), Coun. for Exceptional Children, Am. Coll. Forensic Examiners, 1996. Assn. for the Gifted. Episcopalian. Died Apr. 27, 2008.

MIDGETT, ANN SPROULE, corporate librarian; b. Schenectady, NY, Feb. 16, 1947; d. Thomas and Elizabeth (Stephen) S.; m. Michael Earl Midgett, Dec. 28, 1974; 1 child, Matthew Thomas. BA, So. Meth. U., 1969; MLS, U. Tex., 1972. Librarian Dallas Pub. Library, Dallas, 1973-83; corp. librarian TU Electric Co. (formerly Tex. Power & Light Co.), Dallas, from 1983. Mem. Spl. Library Assn. Episcopalian. Home: Dallas, Tex. Died Jan. 31, 2008.

MIERSWA, RUTH MILDRED, counselor, writer; b. Rice Lake, Wis., Apr. 4, 1917; d. John Peter Stoik and Julia Margaret Hessel; m. Richard Darrel Mierswa, June 12, 1941; children: Daniel, Richard, Peter. BA, U. Wis., Whitwater, 1939. Tchr. H.S., Sheboygan Falls, Wis., 1939—41; metaphys./astroligical counselor, from 1973. Author: Ray Centered Astrology, 1986, Who You Are and Why You Are Here, 1998. Mem.: Am. Fedn. Astrology, Nat. Coun. Geomic Rsch. Achievements include development of a phase of astrology for finding one's life purpose and personality type. Avocations: gardening, hiking, reading. Home: Fairport, NY. Died Oct. 12, 2007.

MILAN, MARJORIE LUCILLE, primary school educator; b. Ludlow, Colo., June 24, 1926; d. John B. and Barbara (Zenonian) Pinamont; m. John Francis Milan, June 18, 1949; children: Barbara, J. Mark, Kevin. BA, U. Colo., 1947, MA, 1978; PhD, U. Denver, 1983. Cert. tchr., adminstr., supt., Colo. Tchr. Boulder (Colo.) Pub. Schs., 1947-49, Denver Pub. Schs., 1949-51 and from 67; adminstr. T. Tot Kindergarten, Denver, 1951-55; tchr. Colo. Women's Coll., Denver, 1956-57; adminstr. Associated Schs., Denver, 1956-67. Adv. bd. George Washington Carver Nursery, Denver, 1960-85. Mem. Assn. Childhood Edn. (state bd. 1960—, Hall of Excellence 1991), Rotary (pres. chpt. 1994-95), Philanthropic Ednl. Orgn., Phi Delta Kappa, Delta Kappa Gamma. Avocations: swimming, music. Home: Lakewood, Colo. Died Dec. 22, 2007.

MILLAR, JAMES ROBERT, economist, former dean; b. San Antonio, Tex., July 7, 1936; s. James G. and Virginia M. (Harrison) M.; m. Gera Ascher, July 4, 1965; children: Leo Schaeg (dec. 1988), Mira Gail. BA, U. Tex., 1958; PhD in Econs., Cornell U., 1965. Asst. prof. dept. econs. U. Ill., Urbana, 1965-70, assoc. prof., 1970-72, prof., 1973-89, assoc. vice chancellor for acad. affairs, 1984-89, dir. internat. programs and studies, 1984-89; prof. econs. and internat. affairs George Washington U., Washington, 1989—2004, prof. emeritus, 2004—08, dir. Inst. for European, Russian and Eurasian Studies, 1989-01, assoc. dean Elliott Sch. Internat. Affairs, 1989-95, acting dean, 1994. Mem. acad. coun. Kennan Inst. Advanced Russian Studies, 1975-84; young faculty exchanger Moscow State U., 1966; cons. to congressmen and various U.S. govt. depts., 1972-2008; dir. Soviet Interview Project, 1981-88; sec., bd. dirs. Midwest Univs. Consortium for Internat. Activities, 1984-88, chmn. bd., 1988-89; bd. dirs., chair fin. com. Internat. Rsch. and Exchs. Bd., 2002-06. Author: The ABCs of Soviet Socialism, 1981 (non-fiction award Soc. Midland Authors, 1981), The Soviet Economic Experiment, 1990; editor, contbr. The Soviet Rural Community, 1971; editor: Slavic Rev., Am. Quar. Soviet and East European Studies, 1975-80, Problems of Post-Communism, 1996-2003; editor, contbr. Politics, Work and Daily Life, A Survey of Former Soviet Citizens, 1987; editor, contbr. Cracks in the Monolith: Party Power in the Brezhnev Era, 1992, The Social Legacy of Communism, 1994; editor-in-chief: Encyclopedia of Russian History, 4 vols., 2004; contbr. articles on studies on Soviet/Russian economy and econ. history to scholarly jours. Served with Q.M-C. U.S. Army, 1960. Ford Found. fgn. area fellow, 1961-64; sr. scholar rsch. travel grantee to USSR, 1972; Internat. Rsch. and Exchs. Bd./USSR Acad. Scis. travel exchangee, 1979; fellow Woodrow Wilson Internat. Ctr. for Scholars, 1988-89, Guggenheim fellow, 1995-96; Internat. Rsch. and Exchs. Bd. advanced rsch. grantee, 1996. Mem. AAAS, Internat. Com. Ctrl. and East European Studies (bd. dirs., v.p. 2001—), Econ. History Assn., Am. Assn. Advancement Slavic Studies (del. Am. Coun. Learned Soc. 1992-98, bd. dirs. 1995-2001, v.p. 1998-99, pres. 1999-2000, chair coun. mem. insts. 1995-99, treas. 2004—, Disting. Contbn. Slavic Studies award, 2006), Am. Coun. Learned Soc. (treas., bd. dirs. 1996-2002, sec. 1994-96, mem. exec. com. del., chair 1992-95, mem. joint com. with Social Sci. Rsch. Coun. 1990-95), Nat. Coun. for Ea. Europe and Eurasia (bd. dirs. 2004-08, treas. 2007-08), N.Y. Acad. Sci., Phi Beta Kappa (pres. Alpha chpt. 1998-01). Home: Washington, DC. Died Nov. 30, 2008.

MILLEN, JOHN CLYDE, minister; b. Landour, U.P., India, Sept. 9, 1941; came to U.S., 1966; s. Theodore Wier and Charis (Murley) M.; m. Priscilla Anne Sherwin, June 8, 1967; children: Scot Andrew, Laura Anne, Chad William, Katharine Irene. AA, Monmouth Coll., 1963; BS, U.S. Naval Acad., 1967; MDiv, Va. Sem., 1974. Ordained to ministry Episcopal Ch. as priest, 1976. Asst. chaplain Episcopal High Sch., Alexandria, Va., 1974-78; assoc. rector St. John's Episcopal Ch., McLean, Va., 1978-80; rector St. Francis Episcopal Ch., Great Falls, Va., 1979-85, St. Mark's Episcopal Ch., Columbus, Ohio, 1985-89, Ch. of the Holy Nativity and Sch., Honolulu, from 1989. Sec. standing com. Diocese of Hawaii, 1990—; chair commn. on ministry Diocese of So. Ohio, 1987-89; dean region 5 No.

Fairfax County, Diocese of Va., 1981-85; pres. United Coll. Ministries in No. Va., 1981-83; mem. Commn. on Ministry, Hawaii, 1990—; mem. program com. Camp Mokuleia, Hawaii, 1990—; mem. Fuller Sem., Hawaii, 1989—. Bd. dirs. Community Mental Health, Alexandria, 1972-74; bd. dirs. PTA, Cooper Intermediate Sch., McLean, 1980-82. Capt. USMC, 1967-71. Mem. Hawaii Episcopal Clergy Assn., East Oahu Clergy Fellowship. Home: Honolulu, Hawaii. Died Dec. 20, 2007.

MILLER, ANNE C., nursing administrator; b. London, Nov. 27, 1937; d. D.W. M. Pierotti Obe and Fredina (Finney) Obe; m. Walter Miller, Aug. 20, 1970 (dec.); children: Walter Jr., Emily. RN, Chase Farm Hosp., Enfield, Eng., 1959; B.C.M., Marston Green Maternity Hosp., Marston Green, Eng., 1963; BS, Upsalla Coll. Asst. DON State of N.J., Greystone Park. Mem. Royal Coll. Nurses U.K., Royal Coll. Nurses Australia, Royal Coll. Midwives, C.W.A. (br. pres. local 1040). Home: Lincoln Park, NJ. Died Nov. 18, 2007.

MILLER, BARBARA JANE, judge; b. Milw., June 12, 1951; d. Lawrence Martin and Mary Magdalene (McGinley) Miller. B.A. in Communications, U. Ky., 1973; J.D., U. San Francisco, 1978. Bar: Calif. 1978. Paralegal Ga. Indigents Legal Services, Inc., Atlanta, 1973-74; juvenile counselor City and County of San Francisco, 1974-75; legal asst., clk. firm Hall, Henry, Oliver & McReavy, San Francisco, 1975-77; law clk. firm Walker, Schroeder, Davis & Brehmer, Monterey, Calif., 1977-78; assoc. firm Thelen, Marrin, Johnson & Bridges, San Francisco, 1978-84; assoc. firm Knox, Ricksen, Snook, Anthony & Robbins, Oakland, Calif. and San Francisco, 1984—87, commr., Alameda County Superior Ct., 1987-97, judge, 1996-2009, presiding judge, 2004-05; lectr., panelist on estate planning. Recipient commendation State Bar Calif., 1983. Mem. San Francisco Bar Assn. (vice chmn. estate planning com. 1979-80, chmn. 1980-82), Barristers (dir. 1982-83). Democrat. Home: Oakland, Calif. Died Nov. 6, 2009.

MILLER, DEAN JEFFREY, lawyer; b. Chgo., July 13, 1951; s. Phillip Albert and Reneé (Miller) Zaks; children: Kevin, Kristy, Jacob. BA, Am. U., 1973; JD, Pepperdine U., 1977. Bar: Calif. 1986, U.S. Dist. Ct. (ea., no. and cen. dists.) Calif. 1986, U.S. Dist Ct. Hawaii 1988, mem. bar U.S. Supreme Ct. Staff mem. U.S. Senator Edmund Muskie, Washington, 1969-70, U.S. Senator Adlai Stevenson III, Washington, 1970-71, U.S. Senator Frank Church, Washington, 1971-72; investigator Pub. Def. Svc., Washington, 1972-73; rep. Met. News, LA, 1974-75; atty. Law Office of George Boyle, Bakersfield, Calif., from 1986. Instr., program coord. paralegal program Career Com Coll. of Bus., Bakersfield, 1988-91; judge pro tem South Kern Jud. Dist., Lamont, Calif., 1988—. Mem. Assn. of Trial Lawyers Am., Calif. Trial Lawyers Assn., L.A. Trial Lawyers Assn., San Diego Trial Lawyers Assn., Kern County Trial Lawyers Assn. (bd. dirs. 1988—), Phi Alpha Delta, Natl. Assn. of Criminal Defense Attorneys. Democrat. Jewish. Avocations: scuba, travel, flying, sports. Home: Bakersfield, Calif. Died Dec. 6, 2007.

MILLER, DONALD KENNETH, engineering consultant; b. St. Louis, Oct. 18, 1925; s. Henry Edward and Ernestine Elizabeth (Schmeer) M.; m. Arline Louise Heckman, Feb. 27, 1953; children: Garry Edwin, Kristine Louise Miller Morris. BSChemE, Mo. U., 1950. Registered profl. engr., Pa. Application engr. York Corp., St. Louis, Houston, York, Pa., 1951—62; mgr. quality control York divsn. Borg Warner Corp., 1962-65, chief engr., 1965-85; refrigeration specialist York Internat. Corp., 1985-88; pres. MDK Engring. Corp., York, from 1988. Author: (with others) Plant Engineering Handbook, 1959, ASHRAE Handbook, 1981-94, Applied Thermal Design, 1989; contbr. articles to ASHRAE Jour. and IIR/IIF Internat. Congress Procs.; inventor desuperheater control in a refrigeration apparatus. With USNR, 1944—46. Mem. NSPE, AIChE, ASHRAE (life mem., cen. Pa. chpt., sec. 1972-73, treas. 1973-74, v.p. 1974-75, pres. 1975-76, Disting. Svc. award 1992), Svc. Corps Ret. Execs. (past bd. mem., sec.), Rotary. Avocations: sketching, computers. Home: York, Pa. Died May 18, 2009.

MILLER, GEORGE WELLS, transportation company executive; b. Troy, NY, Dec. 5, 1930; s. Ruth W. Wells. BSBA, Siena Coll., 1956; student, Albany Law Sch., 1956-57; MBA, Northwestern U., 1959. Acct. Arthur Anderson & Co., NYC, 1959-62; controller Fifth Ave. Coach Lines, NYC, 1962-64; asst. controller Trans World Airlines, NYC, 1964-70; v.p., controller Sea Land Svc. Inc., Newark, 1970-73, Pan Am. World Airways, NYC, 1973-74; v.p. fin., treas. Am. Satellite Corp., Washington, 1975-76, Marine Transport Lines, NYC, 1977-79; treas. Southeastern Pa. Transport Authority, Phila., 1980-84; exec. v.p. N.Y. Transit Authority, NYC, from 1984. Cons. pvt. practice, Peapack, N.J., 1975-80, N.Y.C., 1980—. With U.S. Army, 1951-53. Mem. Am. Pub. Transit Assn. (conf. bd. mem.) Avocations: geology, urban devel., photography, travel. Home: Silver Spring, Md. Died Aug. 9, 2007.

MILLER, JOHN R., construction company executive; b. Ft. Jennings, Apr. 6, 1943; s. Carolus J. and Mary M. (Fortman) M.; m. Margaret M. Kehres; children: Michelle, Scott. Grad. high sch., Ottoville, Ohio. Sales mgr. Kahle-Langhals Redi-Mix, Kalida, Ohio, from 1962. Trustee Jennings Twp., Ft. Jennings, Ohio, 1969—; mem. planning commn. Putnam County, Ottawa, Ohio, 1978—; bd. dirs. Emergency Med. Svc., 1973-93, Ft. Jennings Park; mem. Putnam Twp. Assn., 1969—; Ft. Jennings vol. fireman; ctrl. committeeman Putnam County Rep. Ctrl. Mem. Elks. Roman Catholic. Avocation: collecting antiques. Home: Fort Jennings, Ohio. Died Jan. 31, 2008.

MILLER, JORDAN YALE, humanities educator; b. Manhattan, Kans., Sept. 2, 1919; s. Edwin Cyrus and Della (Slye) M.; m. Elaine Elizabeth Graham, Dec. 31, 1945; children: Sherry Elaine, Adrienne Elizabeth. Student, Kans. State U., 1937-38; BA, Yale U., 1942, postgrad., 1946-47; PhD, Columbia U., 1957. Mem. faculty Kans. State U., Manhattan, 1950-69, prof., 1967-69; prof. English dept. U. R.I., Kingston, from 1969, chmn. dept., 1969-80, prof. emeritus, from 1985. Fulbright lectr. drama and theatre, Bombay, India, 1964-65; vis. exchange prof. Sch. English and Am. Studies, U. East Anglia, Norwich, Eng., 1977-78; cons. American Quar., Publ. Modern Lang. Assn., Nat. Endowment for Humanities. Author: American Dramatic Literature, 1961, Eugene O'Neill and the American Critic, 1962, 2d edit., 1973, Playwright's Progress: O'Neill and the Critics, 1965, 20th Century Interpretation of A Streetcar Named Desire, 1971, Heath Introduction to Drama, 1976, 4th edit., 1992; co-author: American Drama between the Wars, 1991; field editor: Twayne's Critical History of American Drama, Vol. 1: American Drama between the Wars, 1991. Served with AUS, 1942-45. Mem.: MLA. Unitarian-Universalist. Home: Essex, Conn. Died Sept. 23, 2008.

MILLER, JUDITH SCANNELLA, school placement administrator; b. Trenton, NJ, Sept. 10, 1952; d. Anthony Michael and Lucy Theresa (Di Paola) Scannella; m. Bruce Noble Miller, Aug. 5, 1978; 1 child, Amanda Kathryn. BA, Rider Coll., 1974. Food program specialist United Progress Inc., Trenton, N.J., 1975-77, dir. summer food program for children, 1975-77; investigator State of N.J., Office Pub. Advocate, Office Pub. Defender, Hackensack, 1977-79; customer svc./sales rep. Manpower Temp. Svcs., Paramus, N.J., 1981-82; customer svc. rep., office mgr. Western Temp. Svcs., Paramus, 1981-82; polit. cons. Bergan County Dem. Orgn., Hackensack, from 1979; regional pers. asst. Lane Bryant Inc., Secaucus, N.J., 1982-83; placement dir. Nat. Edn. Ctr. Radio Electronic TV Sch. Campus, Nutley, N.J., 1983-89, Phillips Bus. Sch., Paterson, N.J., from 1991. Author: Job Placement Handbook, 1989 (Honorable Mention award 1989). Mem. NOW, Hackensack, 1989, LWV, Glen Rock, N.J., 1990, N.J. Fedn. Dem. Women, Trenton, 1974. Mem. NAFE. Avocations: cooking, reading, music. Died Dec. 29, 2007.

MILLER, LARRY (LAWRENCE HORNE MILLER), professional sports team owner, auto dealer, broadcast executive; b. Salt Lake City, Apr. 26, 1944; s. Howard Hanley West and Mary Lorille (Horne); m. Karen Gail Saxon, Mar. 25, 1965; children: Gregory Scott, Roger Lawrence, Stephen Frank, Karen Rebecca, Bryan Joseph. LLD (hon.), U. Utah, 1991; degree (hon.), Utah Valley State Coll., Salt Lake Cmty. Coll., Weber State U., Ogden, Utah. With auto parts bus., Denver and Salt Lake City; owner auto dealerships, Salt Lake City, Albuquerque, Denver and Phoenix, 1979—2009; co-owner NBA Utah Jazz, Salt Lake City, 1985—86, owner, from 1986, Sta. KJZZ-TV, Salt Lake City, 1993—2009, Larry H. Miller Group, Salt Lake City, 1993—2009, CEO, 1993—2008, chmn. governing bd., 2008—09. Recipient award, Am. Import Auto Dealers Assn., Sports Illus.; named Utah Master Entrepreneur of Yr., 1997; named to Internat. Softball Congress Hall of Fame. Died Feb. 20, 2009.

MILLER, MARGARET JEAN, retired secondary school educator; b. Coffeyville, Kans., Jan. 5, 1919; d. Merritt Eugene and Florence May (Johnson) Thompson; m. Paul Alfred Miller, Sept. 7, 1941; children: Timothy, Michael, Gretchen, Jeffrey. BS, Pittsburg State U., Kans., 1940; MA, Wichita State U., 1964. Cert. tchr., Kans.; cert. Braille transcriber. Tchr. Wichita H.S. East, 1963-78, Wichita State U., 1960-63; exec. bd., PRO Miller Recycling Ctr., Clark, W.Va., from 2004. Editor: (newsletter) Recycling in Kans., from 1988. Mem. consumer info. bd. Kans. Corp. Commn., Topeka, 1980-85; co-chair Residential Utility Consumers' Office, Kans., 1982-89; founder Citizens for Recycling Coalition, Wichita; chair Waste Control and Recycling Coalition; mem. environ. awareness coun. Kans. Dept. Health and Environ. Waste Buddy; mem. Nev.'s Citizens Alert; vice chair City/County Solid Waste Mgmt. Com., 1993-2004 Recipient Environmentalist of Yr. award Kans. Natural Resource Coun., 1989, Nat. Conservation award DAR, 1990; Waste Reduction Recognition award State of Kans., 1997, 2005, Earth Stewardship award Great Plains Earth Inst., 2004; featured as one of five environmentalists for Earth Day, Nat. Geographic mag., Apr. 1995; named to Kans. Dept. of Health and Environ. Hall of Fame, 2005; named Pub. Libr. Vol. of Yr., Wichita Pub. Libr. Mem. Sierra Club (life, editor state newsletter 1977-83), Nature Conservancy (life), Environ. Def. Fund, Union of Concerned Scientists, Common Cause, OxFam, Amnesty Internat., Greenpeace, Audubon, Am. Assn. Ret. Persons (sec. state legis. com. 1986-90, Meritorious award for consumer legislation 1989). Achievements include active every year in Earth Day and Am. Recycles Day. Avocations: camping, walking and hiking, reading, travel, quilts. Home: Wichita, Kans. Died Dec. 23, 2007.

MILLER, MARJORIE CAVINS LEEPER (MIDGE MILLER), educator, former state legislator; b. Morgantown, W.Va., June 8, 1922; d. Lorimer V. and Neva (Adams) Cavins; student Spokane Jr. Coll., 1939-40, Morris Harvey Coll., 1940-41; B.A., U. Mich., 1944; M.S., U. Wis., 1962; m. Harry Dean Leeper, Nov. 5, 1944 (dec. 1954); children: Steven Lloyd, David Dean, Linda Jean, Kenneth Chandran; m. Edward Ernst Miller, May 12, 1963 (dec. 1995); step-children: Mark, Sterling, Jeffrey, Nancy, Randy. Teen-age program dir. Ann Arbor YWCA, 1944-45; married women's program dir. New Haven YWCA, 1945-46; teaching asst. U. Wis., Madison, 1957-60, asst. dean letters and sci., 1960-66, coordinator univ. religious activities, 1966-68; mem. Wis. State Assembly, 1970-84, chmn. commerce and consumer affairs, 1977-82, state affairs com., 1975-76, higher and vocat. edn., family and econ. assistance, 1983-84; co-chmn. law revision com., 1979-84; vice chmn. Dane County Democratic Com., 1967-68; mem. Dem. Nat. Com., 1975-84; mem. nat. adv. bd. Interchange Resource Center; founder Nat. Council Alternative Work Patterns; founder, chmn. The Madison Inst. Mem. Nat. Women's Polit. Caucus (nat. adv. com.). Methodist. Home: Madison, Wis. Died Apr. 17, 2009.

MILLER, MARY RITA, retired adult education educator; b. Williamsburg, Iowa, Mar. 4, 1920; d. James Carl and Bernadette (O'Meara) Rush; m. Clarence Glenn Miller, June 2, 1947 (dec. Aug. 1987); 1 child, Ronald Rush; m. William J. Gibbons, July 14, 1992 (dec. June 2001). BA, U. Iowa, 1941; MA, Denver U., 1959; PhD, Georgetown U., 1969. From instr. to asst. prof. Regis Coll., Denver, 1962-65; from asst. prof. to prof. U. Md., College Park, 1968-91, prof. emeritus, from 1991. Author: Children of the Salt River, 1977, Place—Names of the Northern Neck of Virginia, 1983; contbr. numerous articles and revs. Avocations: research, travel, reading, farming. Home: Washington, DC. Died Apr. 10, 2008.

MILLER, MELVIN ORVILLE, JR., artist; b. Balt., May 16, 1937; s. Melvin and Edith Amelia (Schmier) M. Diploma, Md. Inst. Art, 1959; BFA (hon.), Md. Inst. Coll. Art, 1996. Mem. Six Realists Gallery of Balt., 1962-63; participant Art in Embassies Program, Freetown, Sierra Leone, 1986-88. One man shows include I.F.A. Galleries, Washington, 1970, Center Club, Balt., 1980, 92, Nassau Gallery, Rehoboth Beach, Del., 2000; exhibited in numerous group shows Washington, Balt., Ohio, Mass., Va., N.Y.C., Conn., R.I., Calif., Fla., N.J., Wash.; exhibited in shows at Karachi, Pakistan, 1970s, Port-Au-Prince, Haiti, 1970s; invitational exhibits include Midwest Mus. Am. Art, Elkhart, Ind., 1997, Butler Inst. Am. Art, Youngstown, Ohio, 1998; invitational exhibits include Evergreen House, Johns Hopkins U., Balt., 1998, Washington County Mus. Fine Arts, Hagerstown, Md., 1998, Nassau Gallery, Rehoboth Beach, Del., 2000; represented in numerous pvt. collections in Eng., Germany, Greece, Brazil, other fgn. countries. With USAFR, 1959-65. John F. and Anna Lee Stacey scholar, 1965. Mem. Am. Soc. Marine Art (charter), Charcoal Club (Balt.), Oil Painters Am. (assoc.). Democrat. Home: Baltimore, Md. Died Nov. 26, 2007.

MILLER, MICHAEL REGIS, research programmer, educator; b. Pitts., Aug. 25, 1964; s. Regis Raymond and Bobbi Marie (Morrow) M.; m. Margaret Ellen Alberti, Oct. 17, 1992. BS in Math., BS in Computer Sci., Drexel U., 1987, MS in Math., MS in Computer Sci., 1996. Co-op engr. Gen. Instrument, Hatboro, Pa., 1983-84, 84-85; co-op software engr. RCA-Missile and Surface Radar, Moorestown, N.J., 1985-86, 86-87; sys. engr. Gen. Instrument, Hatboro, 1987-93, staff engr., 1994-97; sr. mem. engring. staff Martin Marietta-Advanced Tech. Labs., Moorestown, 1993-94; rsch. programmer Siemens Corp. Rsch., Princeton, N.J., from 1997. Adj. asst. prof. Drexel U., Phila., 1996—. Mem. Assn. for Computing Machinery, Math. Assn. Am., Pi Mu Epsilon, Upsilon Pi Epsilon. Achievements include three patents in cable television technology Functionally Modifiable Cable Television System, Apparatus for Selective Distribution of Messages Over a Communications Network, Method and Apparatus for Communicating Different Categories of Data in a Single Data Stream. Home: Mount Holly, NJ. Died May 18, 2008.

MILLER, NEIL ALLEN, police agent; b. Lincoln, Nebr., Dec. 5, 1952; s. Royce Jordan Miller and Norma Jean (Kahlbau) Poucher; m. C. Susan Wright; children: Sarah Louise, David Allen. AS, Pikes Peak C.C., 1979; BS in Criminology, Met. St. Coll., 1990. Security guard St. Francis Hosp., Colorado Springs, 1977-81; police officer U. Colo. Med. Ctr. Police Dept., Denver, 1981-83, Broomfield (Colo.) Police Dept., 1983-90; police agt. Lakewood (Colo.) Police Dept., from 1990; team watch mem. USN Res., Aurora, from 1991. Coach spl. olympics Fletcher-Miller Sch., Lakewood, 1991—. Sgt. USMC, 1971-78. Recipient Svc. to Handicap award Internat. Toastmasters Club, 1993, World Bench Press Record 198# USPF/World Police-Fire Athletic Assn., 1993, Nat. Bench Press Records 198# NASA Drug Free Assn., 1993, Colo. State Powerlifting Record 198# NASA and Colo. Police and Fire Athletic Assn., 1986-93, Colo. Police/Fire Athletic. Assn. 198#/220# title/record holder powerlifting, 1986-97, NASA Powerlifting Nat. and World Records, Masters, 220 lb., 1996, Colo. Police-Fire Assn. Masters 220 lb. Record Holder Powerlifting, 1996, NASA World Bench Press Record 227#, 1996, Colo. Police-Fire Assn. Record and Title Holder Powerlifting, 1996-97, Colo. ADFPA State Record, BP, Masters 220#, 1995-97. Mem. Vietnam Vets of Am., VFW, Am. Legion, Fraternal Order of Police, Am. Fedn. of Police, Lakewood Police Athletic League. Avocations: travel, historical locations, camping/hiking, competitive weightlifting, antiques. Home: Broomfield, Colo. Died Mar. 19, 2008.

MILLER, RAYMOND HERBERT, manufacturing executive; b. Chgo., Nov. 6, 1948; s. William H. and Adeline A. (Latko) M.; m. Jeanne Louise Halverson, Sept. 6, 1969 (div. Jan. 1987); children: David, Andrew, Jennifer, Steven, Thomas, Grant; m. Christina Ann Wood, Apr. 18, 1987. BA, North Pk. Coll., Chgo., 1969. Asst. mgr. sales Armstrong-Blum Mfg. Co., Chgo., 1976-84; nat. sales mgr. Kysor Machine Tool, Strongsville, Ohio, 1984-85; mgr. U.S. ops. H. Ruhl Machinery, Toronto, Ont., Can., 1985-86; nat. mktg. mgr. Startrite, Inc., Kalamazoo, 1986, v.p., 1986-87, pres., from 1987. Sgt. U.S. Army, 1970-73. Mem. Woodworking Machinery Importers Assn., Mfr.'s Agts. Nat. Assn., Antique Auto Club Am. (Hershey, Pa.), Horseless Carriage Club (L.A.). Republican. Roman Catholic. Avocations: fishing, photography, gardening, baseball, tennis. Died June 13, 2008.

MILLER, RICHARD BRUCE, electronics company executive; b. Bryn Mawr, Pa., Jan. 2, 1947; s. Robert and Kathryn (Marks) M; m. Nedra Lynn Herbert, Aug. 28, 1971; children: Sean Patrick and Ryan Cameron. BA in Polit. Sci., Shippensburg State U., 1969, MA in Polit. Sci., 1975. Asst. city mgr. City of Chambersburg, Pa., 1970-72; city mgr. City of New Cumberland, Pa., 1972-76, Montgomery Twp., N.J., 1976-78; from internal control mgr. to contr. Xerox Corp., Harrisburg, Pa., 1978-83, field adminstrn. ops. mgr. Stamford, Conn., 1983-85; ctr. mgr. N.Y., 1985-88; transition mgr. bus. ops. Stamford, Conn., 1988-89; mgr., ops. support Ea. region, 1989-90; mgr. quality/customer satisfaction Xerox Corp., Stamford, 1990-91, mgr. customer svc. ops., 1991-92, mgr. sys. products adminstrn. Rochester, N.Y., 1992-93, mgr. customized solutions adminstrn., 1993-94, market to collection, 1994-95; from infrastructure delivery mgr. to applications mgr. Office Document Products, 1995-97, applications mgr., 1997; applications framework mgr. Year 2000 Program Office Xerox Corp. Info. Mgmt., Rochester, 1997-2000; mgr. productivity office Xerox Corp., 2000-01, mgr. fin. outsourcing N.Am. info. mgmt., from 2001. Mem. All Star Club Xerox Corp., 1982-83, 85-86, 87-88, 89-90, grad. Astronaut VII, 1987, chief info. officer Leadership award, 1995. Bd. dirs. So. Conn. Child Guidance Ctr., 1988-90, Child Care Ctrs., Stamford, 1990-92; cubmaster Boy Scouts Am., Fairport, N.Y., 1994-95; youth sports coach Southeast YMCA, Pittsford, N.Y., 1993-96, Fairport Youth Lacrosse, 1994-2000; registrar Perinton Youth Hockey, 1998-2000. Republican. Roman Catholic. Avocations: tennis, boating, amateur radio, reading. Home: Fairport, NY. Died July 23, 2008.

MILLER, RICHARD I., lawyer, educator; b. NYC, May 28, 1929; s. Samuel M. Miller and Mathilda (Doushkess) Miller Cuneo; m. Carol Hope Kestenbaum; children: Tami L., Rima L., Ehren D. AA, U. Calif., Berkeley, 1948, BA, 1950; JD, Yale U., 1953; postgrad., Harvard U., 1956. Bar: N.Y. 1955, Mass. 1956, U.S. Supreme Ct. 1984. Assoc. Morrison, Mahoney & Miller, Boston, 1957-66; v.p. Harbridge House, Inc., Boston, 1966-81; ptnr. Perkins, Smith & Cohen, Boston, from 1982. Adj. prof. law Brandeis U., Waltham, Mass., 1981-87. Author: Legal Aspects of Technology Utilization, 1974, Law of War, 1975; contbr. articles to pofl. jours. Mem. Lexington (Mass.) Town Meeting, 1963-74; chmn. Dem. Com., Lexington, 1988-92. 1st lt. JAG, USAF, 1953-55, Korea. Justice fellow NEH, 1976; sr. faculty fellow Gordon Pub. Policy Ctr. Brandeis U., 1987. Mem. Boston Bar Assn. (chmn. com. sci. and tech.), ABA (com. chmn. sci. and tech.), Washington Cosmos. Home: Lexington, Mass. Died Oct. 1, 2007.

MILLER, ROBERT HASKINS, retired state supreme court chief justice; b. Columbus, Ohio, Mar. 3, 1919; s. George L. and Marian Alice (Haskins) M.; m. Audene Fausett, Mar. 14, 1943; children: Stephen F., Thomas G., David W., Stacey Ann (dec.). AB, Kans. U., 1940, LL.B., 1942; grad., Nat. Coll. State Trial Judges, Phila., 1967. Bar: Kans. 1943. Practice in Paola, 1946-60; judge 6th Jud. Dist. Kans., Paola, 1961-69; U.S. magistrate Kans. Dist., Kansas City, 1969-75; justice Kans. Supreme Ct., Topeka, 1975-88, chief justice, 1988-90, ret., 1990. Chmn. Kans. Jud. Coun., 1987-88. Contbg. author: Pattern (Civil Jury) Instructions for Kansas, 2d edit, 1969. Served with AUS, 1942-46. Mem. Kans. Bar Assn., Wyandotte County Bar Assn., Shawnee County Bar Assn., Am. Legion, Phi Gamma Delta, Phi Delta Phi. Presbyterian. Home: Topeka, Kans. Died Sept. 10, 2009.

MILLMAN, IRVING, microbiologist, educator, retired inventor; b. NYC, May 23, 1923; BS, City Coll. N.Y., 1948; MS, U. Ky., 1951; PhD, Northwestern U., 1954. Asst. prof. Northwestern U., 1954; formerly with Armour & Co., Pub. Health RSch. Inst. of N.Y.C., Merck Inst. Therapeutic Rsch.; adj. prof. Hahnemann U., Phila. Inducted Nat. Inventors Hall of Fame, 1993. Fellow Am. Acad. Microbiology; mem. N.Y. Acad. Scis., AAAS, Am. Soc. Microbiology. Achievements include development of test to identify Hepatitis B in blood samples. Died Aug. 3, 1999.

MILLS, AGNES EUNICE KARLIN, artist; b. NYC, Apr. 2, 1915; d. Herman Karlin and Celia (Ducoffe) Karlin; m. Saul Mills, May 10, 1938 (dec. Nov. 1993); children: Karen, Marghe. Grad., Cooper Union Art Sch., NYC, 1938; BFA, Pratt Inst., 1975; student, NYU. One-woman shows include Carus Gallery, N.Y.C., Unitarian Soc., Manhasset, N.Y., Harbor Gallery, Cold Spring Harbor, N.Y., North Truro Art Gallery, Cape Cod, Mass., Alfredo Valente Gallery, N.Y.C., Robbins Gallery, East Orange, N.J., Nuance Galleries, Tampa, Friends of Tampa Ballet, Graphic Eye Coop Gallery, Pt. Washington, N.Y., City Ctr. Gallery, N.Y.C., Lincoln Ctr. Art Gallery, N.Y.C., North Shore Cmty. Arts Ctr., Great Neck, N.Y., Delray Beach Works in Progress Gallery, Boca Raton Cmty. Ctr., Palm Beach Pub. Libr., Gramercy Park Armory, N.Y.C.; exhibited in group shows at Alfredo Valente Gallery, N.Y.C., Audubon Soc., N.Y.C., Bowdoin Coll. Mus. Art, Brunswick, Maine, Brandeis U., Waltham, Mass., Bklyn. Mus. Art, Brown U., Providence, Butler Inst. Am. Art, Youngstown, Ohio, Colgate U. Libr., Hamilton, N.Y., Cornell U., Ithaca, N.Y., East Hampton (N.Y.) Guild Artists, Gallery K, Woodstock, N.Y., Graphic Eye Coop Gallery, Port Washington, N.Y., Heckscher Mus., Huntington, N.Y., Hunterdon County Mus., Clinton, N.J., Joan Avnet Gallery, Great Neck, N.Y., Lincoln Ctr. Libr. Performing Arts, N.Y.C., Madison Gallery, N.Y.C., Boca Raton City Hall, Boca Raton Cmty. Ctr., Boca Raton Libr.; represented in permanent collections at Boca Raton Mus. Art, Nat. Women in the Arts Mus. Died Mar. 9, 2008.

MILLS, EDWARD WARREN, corporation executive; b. NYC, Apr. 7, 1941; m. Maria Parascandolo Mills, Sept. 19, 1971; children: Edward Warren, Foy Fitzhugh, Joseph V.O. BS, Wash. U., Lee U., 1962; MBA, Hofstra U., 1974; JD, NY Law Sch., 1977. Bar: NY 1977, DC 1978. Acct. Wasserman & Taten, NYC, 1962—69; exec. v.p. L.H. Keller Inc., Hugo P. Keller Inc., NYC, 1969—74; pres. Gen. Ruby & Sapphire Co., 1974—94, Qualistar Corp., 1974—94, EWM Gen. Corp., from 1993. Mem.: ABA, NY State Bar Assn., DC Bar Assn. Home: New Port Richey, Fla. Died Aug. 2008.

MILLS, FRANK CRAIGHILL, controller; b. Albany, Ga., Feb. 12, 1946; s. Luther Rice and Elizabeth Reece (Craighill) M.; m. Mary Anne Glenn, June 18, 1969. BBA in Mgmt., Augusta Coll., Ga., 1971, BBA in Acctg., 1975. Field office acct. So. Roadbuilder, Augusta, 1971-75; staff acct. Henderson-Shaw, CPA's, Macon, Ga., 1975-76; asst. div. controller Menaldi-Southern, Augusta, 1976-77; plant controller Polson Rubber Co., Warrenton, Ga., 1977-79, Muehller & Co., Clinton, S.C., 1979-80; corp. controller Warrenton Rubber Co., from 1980. Republican. Episcopalian. Home: Warrenton, Ga. Died Oct. 9, 2007.

MINARIK, STEPHEN JOSEPH, III, communications executive, former political organization administrator; b. Rochester, NY, Jan. 2, 1960; s. Stephen Joseph Jr. and Eleanor Emily (Synkowski) M.; m. Patricia Williams, 1987 (div. Aug. 1996); 1 child, Stephen J. IV.; m. Renee Forgensi; children: Stephanie, Kathleen, Christopher BA in Polit. Sci., U. Rochester, 1982. Asst. dep. clk. Monroe County Legis., Rochester, 1988-89, legis. dir., 1989-90; exec. dir. Monroe County Rep. Com., Rochester, 1990—2005, chmn., 1991—2005, 2006—08; ptnr. Impact Comm. LLC, Rochester, 1997—2009; chmn. NY Rep. State Com., Albany, 2005—06. Mgr. Rochester Youth Hockey, 1996-97; coach Webster (N.Y.) Soccer League, 1997. Republican. Roman Catholic. Avocations: golf, hockey, lacrosse. Home: Webster, NY. Died Apr. 12, 2009.

MINIER, LEE N., funeral director; b. Utica, NY, Feb. 17, 1950; s. Hugh B. and Ann D. Minier; m. Meredith L. Leigh, July 7, 1974; 1 child, Marissa. AB, Ill. Coll., Jacksonville, 1972; MS, SUNY, Brockport, NY, 1974; PhD, U. Colo., Denver, 1979. Lic. funeral dir. N.Y. Postdoctoral fellow Nat. Multiple Sclerosis Soc., Richmond, Va., 1979—81; rsch. assoc. U. Colo. Health Sci. Ctr., Denver, 1981—83; v.p., funeral dir. Christopher-Mitchell Funeral Homes, Inc., Albion, NY, from 1990. Contbr. articles to profl. jours. Pres., bd. dirs. Oak Orchard Cmty. Health Ctr., Albion, NY, 1990—92, Brockport, NY, 1990—92; bd. dirs. Ea. Orleans Red Cross, Albion, 1993; campaign chairperson United Way, Orleans County, NY, 2000, 2002. Mem.: Soc. for Vertebrate Paleontology, Nat. Ctr. for Sci. Edn. Avocations: weightlifting, canoeing, bicycling. Died Nov. 16, 2007.

MINTER, JERRY BURNETT, electronics executive; b. Ft. Worth, Oct. 31, 1913; s. Claude Joe and Roxie (Ayers) M.; m. Monica Rose Hanlon, Mar. 2, 1940; children: Claude, Mark (dec.), Byron, Claire, Maureen. BSEE, MIT, 1934. Engr. Boonton Radio Corp., NJ, 1935-36, Ferris Instruments Co., Boonton, 1936-39; v.p., chief engr. Measurements Corp., Boonton, 1939-53; pres. Components Corp., Denville, NJ, from 1946. Contbr. articles to tech. jours. Pilot CAP, Morristown, NJ, 1947-50. Fellow IEEE (life, past chmn. No. NJ sect.), Audio Engring. Soc. (past pres.), Radio Club Am. (life, pres. emeritus, past pres., Armstrong medal 1968); mem. AIAA, Am. Soc. Metals (life), NY Acad. Scis., Soc. Motion Picture and TV Engrs. (life), Internat. Soc. Photo-Optical Instrumentation Engrs., Quiet Birdmen. Achievements include 26 patents in field. Home: Morristown, NJ. Died May 2009.

MINTON, JOHN WILLIAM, management educator; b. Alexandria, Va, May 22, 1946; s. John William and Irma Christie (Hay) M.; m. Nancy Elizabeth Niles, Dec. 19, 1970. MA in Social Sci., U. No. Colo., 1975; MBA, MS in Mgmt., Memphis State U., 1983; PhD in Bus. Adminstrn., Duke U., 1988. Dir. cmty. devel. CIty of Asheboro, NC, 1973-77; circuit-riding mgr. Mid-East Commn., Washington, NC, 1977; exec. dir. office cmty. devel. County of Columbus, Chadbourn, NC, 1977-78; mgr. Town of Carolina Beach, NC, 1978-80; administr. City of Germantown, Tenn., 1980-81; asst. prof. dept. mgmt. Appalachian State U., Boone, NC, 1986-88, assoc. prof., 1993-97; Jefferson-Pilot prof. mgmt. Pfeiffer U., Charlotte, Misenheimer, NC, 1997—2000; pres. Havatar Assoc. Inc., from 1998; prof. of bus. Tusculum Coll., Greeneville, Tenn., from 2003, Knoxville, Tenn., from 2003. Vis. asst. prof. Duke U., 1988-93; profl. edn. rsch. fellow Nat. Inst. for Dispute Resolution, 1985-86. Author: (with others) Negotiation, multiple editons, Negotiation: Readings, Exercises and Cases, multiple edit., Orgnl. Justice: The Search for Fairness in the Workplace, 1992; contbr. articles to profl. jour.; ad hoc reviewer Mgmt. Sci., Orgn. Sci. Mem. ASTD, Acad. Mgmt. Democrat. Home: Maryville, Tenn. Died Sept. 20, 2007.

MINTON, SYLVIA C., information specialist; b. Statesville, NC, June 3, 1939; d. Vernon Spencer Sr. and Rachel (Nickles) Church. BS, ASU, 1961; MLS, U. South Fla., 1973; postgrad., Assumption U., 1983. Libr. Libr. of Congress, Washington, 1961-69, RL Sikes Libr., Crestview, Fla., 1974-78, Mitchell (S.D.) Libr., 1980-85; info. specialist Memory Bank, Statesville, N.C., from 1985. Cons. Genealogy Soc., Mitchell, 1980-85, Crestview, Fla., 1974-78. Cataloger RL Sikes Congressional Papers, Crestview, 1975; mem. Exec. Women, Statesville, 1990; coord. Govs. Vols., Statesville, 1991. Mem. AAUW, C. of C., Kiwanis (sec. 1991—). Episcopalian. Avocations: travel, reading. Died May 24, 2008.

MIRRAS, KATHERINE, educational consultant; b. Lowell, Mass., Apr. 4, 1955; d. Theodore and Vasilo Liacopoulos Mirras. BS, Framingham State Coll., 1973; MEd in Ednl. Tech., Fitchburg State Coll., 1990. Tchr. Billerica Pub. Schs., Mass., 1977—91; sr. cons. Info. Mapping Inc., Waltham, Mass., 1992—99; sr. project mgr. Fidelity Investments, Boston, from 1999. Designer (tech. tng.) GPS Training (Outstanding Instrnl. Product or Intervention, 1999). Mem.: Internat. Soc. for Performance Improvement (Mass. chpt. pres. 1995—96). Home: Lowell, Mass. Died Dec. 29, 2007.

MISKOFF, ALVIN RICHARD, physician; b. Bklyn., Jan. 7, 1942; s. Irving Louis Miskoff and Mollie Ethel (Nesenman) Epstein; m. Cheryl Ann Bachman, Aug. 25, 1965 (div. Jan. 1992); children: Barbara, Cary, Jeffrey; m. Barbara Jean Florentino, Sept. 19, 1992; 1 child, Kristy. AB, Rutgers U., 1963; DO, U. Health Scis., Kansas City, Mo., 1968. Diplomate Am. Bd. Internal Medicine; medical oncology, 1975; hematology, 1982. Intern Detroit Osteo. Hosp., 1968-69, resident, 1969-70, Brooke Army Med. Ctr., 1970-72; fellow Walter Reed Army Med. Ctr., 1972-74; pvt. practice in hematology, oncology Menlo Park Med. Group, Ediston, N.J., 1976-78, 1976-78, A. Richard Miskoff, DO PA, Ediston, N.J., from 1978. Bd. dirs. Woodbridge (N.J.) Dept. of Health, 1980-86. Author: Guide to Therapeutic Oncology, 1979. Maj. U.S. Army, 1970-76. Mem. ACP, Am. Osteo. Assn., Am. Soc. Clin. Oncology, Am. Soc. Hematology, Middlesex County Osteo. Assn. (pres. 1992—). Avocations: playing piano, reading. Home: Middletown, NJ. Died Mar. 5, 2008.

MITCHELL, CATHERINE SUE, retired principal, educational consultant; b. Memphis, Dec. 13, 1941; d. Robert Louis Sr. and Sarah Evelyn (Cole) Rawls; 1 child, Shawn Fitzgerald. BA, Lemoyne Coll., Memphis, 1967; cert., U. S.C., 1978; MEd, Memphis State U., 1978, postgrad., 1979-80. Cert. tchr., Tenn. Tchr. Memphis City Schs., 1967-80, asst. prin., 1980-84, prin., 1984—2006; ret., 2006. Owner C & S Enterprises, Memphis; assessor Profl. Assessment Devel. and Enhancement Ctr.; prin. mentor Memphis City Schs; offload mgr. FDX, 1998-2004; cons in field. Active State Career Ladder Sounding Bd., Leadership Memphis, 1992, 93; mem. Tenn. Tenn. 3d Grade Adv. Bd., 1990; mem. adv. bd. Chickasaw coun. Boy Scouts Am. Named Tenn. Exemplary Educator, Tenn. Dept. Edn.; fellow, GE Corp., 1978, Nat. Assn. Elem. Sch. Prins., 1986. Mem. Memphis Pub. Sch. Prin. Assn. (parliamentarian 1987-88, treas. 1988-90, pres. 1990—), Women in Edn. (sec. 1987—), Prin.'s Study Coun. (sec. 1987-90, del. 1987—, v.p. 1990—), Black Bus. Assn., Memphis Area C. of C. Democrat. Baptist. Avocations: reading, walking, bowling, bicycling, computers. Home: Memphis, Tenn. Died Mar. 12, 2008.

MITCHELL, CHARLES ELLIOTT, engineering executive, researcher, educator; b. Newark, Apr. 14, 1941; s. William Alexander and Ruth Chilla (Cobbey) M.; m. Beth Dunn, Apr. 10, 1970 (div.); m. Veta Jean Johnson, Sept. 14, 1973; children: Charles, Darla, Lynne. BS in Engring., Princeton U., NJ, 1963, MA, 1966, PhD, 1967. Rsch. asst. Princeton U., 1963-67; engr. Aerojet Gen. Corp., Sacramento, 1963; prof. Colo. State U., Ft. Collins, from 1967; pres. Combustion Systems Analysts of Colo., Ft. Collins, from 1986. Cons. RSSG Inc., Denver, 1986-87, Rockwell Internat., Canoga Park, Calif., 1986-87, SRS Tech., Huntsville, Ala., 1986-89, Aerojet TechSystems, Sacramento, 1989-91. Patentee in field; contbr. numerous articles to profl. jours. Volunteer track coach Colo. State U., Ft. Collins, 1972—; v.p. Red Mountain Rd. Assn., Livermore, Colo., 1981-91. Grantee NASA, NSF, Dept. of Edn., Dept. of Def. Dependents Sch. Mem. Combustion Inst. Avocations: running, hiking, skiing, mountain climbing. Home: Livermore, Colo. Died Mar. 8, 2008.

MITCHELL, EDITH (BERTSCHE), secondary school educator; b. NYC, Oct. 1, 1924; d. Carl Victor and Hertha (Woelfler) Bertsche; m. Lee Carlyle Mitchell, June 22, 1946 (dec. May 1995); children: Lee Clark, Alan Wallace, Curtis Carl, Linda Claire, Ronald Bruce, Janet Susan. BA with honors, Swarthmore Coll., 1945; MS, Hofstra U., 1962. Cert. permanent tchr., NY; cert. for pvt. schs. profl. staff, cert. edn. profl., Hawaii. Dir. Head Start, Bay Shore, NY, 1967-68; organizer, dir. Windward Tutoring Project, Waimanalo, Hawaii, 1970-72; tchr. Title I Hawaii State Dept.

Edn., 1975-78; tchr. Acad. of Pacific, Honolulu, 1979-87, 88-90, Fairhaven Sch., 1987-88, Hawaii State Dept. Edn., Kaneohe, 1990-96, Windward Sch. for Adults, Kailua, 1997—2003. Behavioral counselor Hawaii State Dept. Edn., Enchanted Lake, 1973-74; tchr. Assn. for Retarded Children, Bay Shore, N.Y., 1964-67. Sch. supt. United Meth. Ch., Bay Shore, 1953-55; co-founder United Meth. Action com., 1961; sch. supt. United Meth. Ch., Kailua, Hawaii, 1971-73, Stephen min., 1988-89; leader Cub Scout troop Boy Scouts Am., Bay Shore, 1956-58; leader Brownie troop Girl Scouts U.S., Bay Shore, 1959-61. Recipient tchr. of year, Windward Sch. for Adults, 2003. Mem. Religious Soc. of Friends. Avocations: swimming, reading, gardening, writing family memories, contacting friends and family. Died Aug. 10, 2008.

MITCHELL, JOHN FRANCIS, retired electronics company executive; b. Chgo., Jan. 1, 1928; s. William and Bridie (Keane) Mitchell; m. Margaret J. Gillis, Aug. 26, 1950; children: Catherine, John, Kevin. BEE, Ill. Inst. Tech., 1950. Exec. v.p. & asst. COO Motorola Inc., Schaumburg, Ill., 1953—80, pres., 1980—87, pres. & COO, 1987—95, vice chmn., 1995—98. Served to lt. (j.g.) USNR, 1950—53. Mem.: IEEE (sr.), Inverness Country Club (Ill.). Achievements include patents in field. Died June 11, 2009.

MITCHELL, JOHN JAMES, oil company executive; b. Manchester, Conn., July 13, 1934; s. Joseph James and Catherine Suzanne (Haberern) M.; m. Della Jeanne Taylor; children: John James Jr., Mark Francis, Matthew Dean, David Michael. AA, Hillyer Coll., Hartford, Conn., 1955. Prodn. dept. Pratt & Whitney Co., West Hartford, Conn., 1955-57; pres., owner Mitchell Fuel Co., Inc., South Windsor, Conn., from 1957. Chmn. South Windsor Charter Revision Commn.; councilman Town of South Windsor; mayor Town of South Windsor, 1983-87, elected treas., 1989; bd. dirs. South Windsor Ambulance Corps, 1983—. Mem. New Eng. Fuel Inst., Conn. Coal Dealers Assn. (v.p. 1982—), Ind. Conn. Petroleum Assn. (bd. dirs. 1982—, mem. Twenty-Five Yr. club), South Windsor C. of C. (pres.), Rotary (pres. South Windwor chpt. 1978-79). Republican. Avocations: gardening, travel. Home: South Windsor, Conn. Died June 28, 2008.

MITCHELL, LOUISE TYNDALL, special education educator; b. St. Louis, Oct. 25; d. Walter Eugene and Nellie May (Otey) Tyndall; m. Felix Mitchell Sr., Sept. 30, 1958; children: Felix Jr., Jeane Mitchell-Carr. AA, Stowe Tchrs. Coll., St. Louis, 1947; BA, Harris Tchrs. Coll., St. Louis, 1958; MA, St. Louis U., 1965. Cert. elem. tchr., secondary English and math., reading clinician. Tchr. math. Hadley High Sch., St. Louis, 1958-59; tchr. Emerson Elem. Sch., St. Louis, 1969-67; head dept. spl. edn. Laclede Elem. Sch., St. Louis, 1967-68, coord. curriculum, 1968-70; adminstrv. asst. Delmar High Sch., St. Louis, 1970-72; assoc. prof., reading clinician, mgr. apprentice tchrs. Harris Tchrs. Coll., 1972-78; chair dept. spl. edn. Cleveland High Sch., St. Louis, 1978-84, chmn. faculty, 1982-84; head dept. spl. edn. S.W. High Sch., St. Louis, 1984-87, tchr., mentor, from 1987. Mentor St. Louis Pub. Schs., 1988-89. Author: (handbook) Teachers Aide, 1987, curriculum guides, 1974, 78; co-author (curriculum guide) Fundamental Curriculum, 1990. Chair Rsch. and Status Black Women, St. Louis, 1974; charter mem. Triagle Club YWCA, 1970. Recipient Community Svc. award Top Ladies Distinction, St. Louis, 1981, 50 Yrs. Outstanding Svc. award A.M.E. Ch., St. Louis, 1987, Salute to Excellence in Edn. recognition St. Louis Am. Newspaper, 1991. Mem. NAACP, Am. Fedn. Tchrs., Nat. Coun. Negro Women, Colored Womens' Fed. Clubs, Women Achievement (coord. youth 1989), St. Louis U. Alumni Assn., (Svc. award 1986), Ch. Women United, Order Ea. Star (past Worthy Matron 1978), Sigma Gamma Rho (chaplain 1988-90), Phi Delta Kappa. Avocations: reading, writing, drama, singing, public speaking. Home: Saint Louis, Mo. Deceased.

MITCHELL, RUTH SHERWOOD, retired nurse; b. Buffalo, Nov. 11, 1929; d. Richard Hamilton and Ruth Amanda (Sykes) Sherwood; m. Ronald Alexander Mitchell Jr., Feb. 29, 1964. BSN, Columbia U., 1960; RN, Presbyn. Hosp. Sch. Nursing, 1952. Grad. head nurse Psycho-Surg. N.Y. State Psychiat Inst., NYC, 1952-53; grad. head nurse supr. oper. rm. Presbyn. Hosp., NYC, 1953-64; instr. Charles H. McCann Vocat. Sch., North Adams, Mass., 1981, staff coord., asst. supr., supr. med.-surg., 1964-93, charge nurse cen. svc., 1964-93. Bd. dirs. Ambulance Svc., Adams. Mem. Town Meeting, Adams. Mem. Mass. Nurses Assn. Avocations: photography, animals, antiquing. Home: Adams, Mass. Died July 1, 2008.

MITCHELL, TIMOTHY ANTHONY, retired philosophy educator, writer; b. NYC, Feb. 17, 1927; s. Timothy and Catherine (Lavery) M.; m. Julia Zuback. BA in Social Studies, St. Francis Coll., Bklyn., 1966; MA in Theology, St. John's U., 1967, MA in Philosophy, 1972, PhD, 1980. Tchr. Cathedra Prep., NYC, 1967-72; educator philosophy St. John's U., Queens, N.Y., 1980-81, St. Francis Coll., Bklyn., 1980-83, ret., 1983. Editor: Pro Ecclesia Found., N.Y.C., 1970—; publ. Pro Ecclesia mag., 1974—; contbr. articles to profl. jours. and pamphlets. Candidate for City coun., State Sen., and Congress, Conservative Party, N.Y. State, 1972—. Recipient awards Oriel Soc., League of Pope John Paul, Cath. War Vets., Christian Law Inst. Home: New York, NY. Died Sept. 18, 2007.

MITTERER, ADOLPH VICTOR, mining company executive; b. Denver, Aug. 24, 1927; s. Adolph Victor Sr. and Louise (Halverson) M.; m. Shirley Ann Brown, Aug. 25, 1951; children: Steven A., Thomas R. Engr. of mines, Colo. Sch. Mines, 1952; postgrad., MIT, 1974. Registered profl. engr., N.Mex., Colo., Utah, Wyo. Chief mining engr. Internat. Minerals and Chems., Carlsbad, N.Mex., 1954-68, Skokie, Ill.; mgr. mining and milling, minerals dept. Conoco, Inc., Denver, 1968-78; v.p. Rocky Mountain Energy, Broomfield, Colo., from 1978. Mem. Minerals Availability Com., Am. Mining Congress, Washington, 1985—. Uranium processing patentee; contbr. numerous articles on mining to profl. jours. Served to lt. C.E., U.S. Army, 1945-47, ETO. Named Met. Exec. of Yr., Nat. Secs. Assn., Denver, 1973. Mem. Soc. of Mining Engrs. of AIME, Colo. Mining Assn. (bd. dirs. 1982—), Can. Inst. Mining and Metallurgy, Mining Club of Southwest, Northwest Mining Assn., Nev. Mining Assn., Utah Mining Assn., Colo. Sch. Mines Research Inst., Colo. Sch. Mines Alumni Assn. (bd. dirs. 1985—). Clubs: Denver Athletic. Republican. Avocations: wine making, photography, home renovation. Home: Lakewood, Colo. Died Aug. 22, 2007.

MOBLEY, ROBERT DALE, nursing administrator; b. Mount Carmel, Ill., July 13, 1952; s. Nelson Harold and Revia Marie (Deischer) M. Cert. practical nursing, Wabash Valley Coll., 1971; AS in Nursing, Vincennes U., Ind., 1977. Cert. Addiction RN. Staff nurse Welborn Hosp., Evansville, Ind., 1977-79; asst. dir. nursing Deaconess Hosp., Evansville, 1979-85; asst. nurse mgr. St. Mary's Med. Ctr., Evansville, 1985-87, Welborn Hosp./Mulberry Ctr., Evansville, from 1992. Staff nurse emergency rm. Wabash Gen. Hosp., Mount Carmel, Ill., 1981-83; open heart recovery nurse Deaconess Hosp., Evansville, 1979-83. Mem. ANA (pres. 1994—), Nat. Nurses Soc. on Addiction (Sustained Contbr. to Peer Assistance award 1993), Ind. State Nurses Assn. (chairperson Peer Assistance Com. 1990—, pres. dist. 4 1994—, Pres. award 1993). Avocations: running, bike riding, swimming. Home: Fort Branch, Ind. Died Oct. 18, 2007.

MOCK, CONRAD DAVIS, SR., financial consultant; b. Pitts., Oct. 20, 1930; s. Edgar Davis and Marion Viola (Conrad) M.; m. Barbara Bell, Apr. 11, 1994. BS, Pa. State U., College Park, 1953; postgrad., Dale Carnegie Inst., 1958; G.R.I., Pa. State U., Phila., 1969. Sr. v.p. Ency. Britannica, Chgo., 1954-56, E. F. Hutton & Co., Phila., 1976-80, F. S. C. Securities, Atlanta, 1981-82; owner, founder Am. Sales Sch., NYC, 1957-69; pres., chmn. bd. dirs. Mutual Fund Mgmt., Jenkintown, Pa., 1970-75; founder, chmn. Money Mgmt. Advisors, Phila., from 1982. Hmn. bd. dirs. Money Mgmt. Adv., Feasterville, Pa., 1985-94; bd. dirs. Contact Internat., Newtown, Pa. Author: Survival, 1976, Why Buy Gold, 1980, Second To Die Insurance, 1989, C.D.A. Means Success, 1992, Victor or Victim, 1995. Fund raiser Boy Scouts Am., Doylestown, Pa., 1990-91, Jim Greenwood, Doylestown, 1992-93, Tom Ridge, Doylestown, 1994. Lt. USN, 1948-51. Mem. Internat. Assn. Fin. Planners (bd. dirs. 1991-93), Nat. Assn. Security Dealers (broker/dealer), Fellowship of Christian Fin. Advisors (founder), Am. Legion (bd. dirs. 1981-82), Masons, Shriners, Rotary (pres. 1992-93). Lutheran. Avocations: tennis, golf, travel. Home: Fstrvl Trvose, Pa. Died Jan. 14, 2008.

MOCK, HARMON ROY, transportation executive; b. Kansas City, Mo., Jan. 6, 1938; s. Harmon Paul and Martha DeLoris (Benson) M. BArch, U. Kans., Lawrence, 1963; postgrad., Morgan State U., 1974-77. Jr. planner City of Kansas City Planning Dept., Mo., 1962-67; planner II, jr. planner met. area planning commn. Wichita (Kans.)-Sedgwick County, 1967-72; planner II Mid-Ohio Regional Planning Commn., Columbus, Ohio, 1972-73; sr. planner Maryland-Nat. Capital Park and Planning Commn., Riverdale, 1973; transit analyst Mass. Transit Adminstrn., Balt., from 1977. Contbr. book: MTA State of the System, 1977, 78, 79. Named Eagle Scout Boy Scouts Am., 1952; recipient Letter of Commendation Gov. of Md., 1982. Mem. N.Am. Vexillogical Assn., Guild of Carillonneurs N.Am., U. Kans. Alumni Assn., Delta Sigma Phi, Alpha Phi Omega. Episcopalian. Home: Baltimore, Md. Died Feb. 28, 2008.

MOCK, ROBERT KERMIT, academic dean; b. Glens Falls, NY, Nov. 17, 1935; s. Kermit Loren and Jeanne Marie Mock; m. Gail Lynn Steger, Sept. 9, 1990. BSME, Ill. Inst. Tech., 1957; degree in meterology, U. Wis., 1959; MS in Sys. Mgmt., U. So. Calif., 1982. Commd. 2d lt. USAF, 1958, advanced through grades to col., 1977, ret., 1987, interceptor pilot Richards-Gebaur AFB, S.C., 1964-66, Naha AFB, Okinawa, 1966-69, test pilot Air Def. Weapons Ctr. Tyndell AFB, Fla., 1970-71, ops. officer 14th Tactical Reconassance Squadron Shaw AFB, S.C., 1973-75, comdr., 1975-77, dir. ops. 13th air force Clark Airbse, The Philippines, 1979-81; sec. Republic Philippines - U.S. Mut. Def. Bd., Manila, 1981-83; chmn. dept. aerospace studies U. Colo., Boulder, 1983-87; chmn. aerospace sci. dept. Met. State Coll., Denver, 1987-96, dean Sch. Profl. Studies, from 1996. Mem. Univ. Aviation Assn. (pres. 1991-92, Laursen award 1994, Wheatley award 1998), Coun. on Aviation Accreditation (trustee 1992-93), Order of Daedalians (flight capt. 1980-81). Home: Hghlnds Ranch, Colo. Died June 15, 2008.

MOEBUS, PATRICIA KATHLYNNE, nursing supervisor; b. Billoxi, Miss., Feb. 3, 1954; d. Ralph Wesley and Martha Alyce (Patrick) Clampitt; m. Jeffrey Glenn Moebus, Dec. 29, 1984. Diploma nursing, Newton Weslley Hosp., 1975. Cert. emergency care nurse. Staff nurse Humana Hosp., New Orleans, utilization review mgr., mgr. telemetry progressive care; nurse mgr. North Trident Regional Hosp., Charelston, S.C. Tutor Literacy Action. Capt. US Nat. Guard, 1985-92. Recipient New Orleans Great 100 Nurse award, 1995; decorated Army Achievement medal. Mem. Am. Holistic Nurse's Assn., Ala. Nat. Guard Officers Assn. (exec. com., v.p.), La. Assn. Post Anesthesia Nurses (edn. and mem. com.), Slidell Art League, Operation Smile Internat. Home: Anchorage, Alaska. Died Mar. 15, 2008.

MOEDDEL, CARL KEVIN, bishop emeritus; b. Cin., Dec. 28, 1937; s. Carl H. and Florence E. (Pohiking) Moeddel. AB, Athenaeum of Ohio; MA, MDiv., Mt. St. Mary's Sem. Ordained priest Archdiocese of Cin., 1962, asst. chancellor, 1963, asst. treas., 1963—71, vice chancellor, 1975—76, dir. fin., 1978—85, auxiliary bishop, 1993—2007, aux. bishop emeritus, 2007—09; asst. pastor St. Louis Ch., Cin., 1963; pastor St. Peter in Chains Cathedral, 1976—85, St. James of the Valley Parish, 1985; dean Cathedral Deanery, 1976—83; ordained bishop, 1993. Exec. sec. commn. ecumenical and interfaith relations Archdiocese of Cin., 1970—76, dir. continuing edn. of priests, 1971—76, vicar ecumenical and interfaith relations, 1973—78, chmn. Commn. Ecumenical and Interfaith Rels., 1973—76, vicar Fin., 1983—86, chmn. Fin. Coun., 1983—86; pres. Ohio Coun. Churches, 1973, chmn. fin. com., 1974—75, chmn. pub. policy com., 1976; pres. Met. Area Religious Coalition of Cin., 1976—77; Episcopal moderator Conf. Cath. Facility Mgmt. Chmn. governing bd. St. Rita Sch. for the Deaf. Roman Catholic. Died Aug. 25, 2009.

MOHR, CHRISTINA, retired economist; b. San Diego, Calif., June 1, 1949; d. Lloyd Crowell and Joan Watkins, Oliver Watkins (Stepfather); m. Peter Joseph Mohr, July 13, 1989; stepchildren: Robert, Tracie 1 child, Oliver Wise. BS in Polit. Sci, U. Pa., Phila., 1971; MA in Internat. Affairs, George Washington U., Washington, DC, 1979; PhD in Econs., U. Md., College Park, 1993. Cons. World Bank, Washington, 1982; analyst sci. resource Nat. Sci. Found., Washington, 1983—86, speech writer for dir., 1987—93; sci. diplomacy fellow US Agy. Internat. Devel., Washington, 1994—95; sr. analyst Nat. Sci. Found., Washington, 1996—2001; ret., 2001. Commr. People with Disabilities Commn., Montgomery County, Md., 1994—96. Home: Silver Spring, Md. Died July 24, 2008.

MOLENBEEK, ROBERT GERRIT, accountant, realtor; b. Grand Rapids, Mich., Feb. 7, 1944; s. Gerrit John and Jean (Wierenga) M.; m. Marsha Lee Rockel, Mar. 23, 1966; children: Rebecca, Tammy, Brian, Brent. AS in Bus. Adminstrn. with honors, Davenport Coll., 1964; BBA in Acctg. with honors, Ferris State U., 1966; MBA, Grand Valley State U., 1976. CPA, Mich.; cert. comml. investment mem.; cert. exch. consular; cert. buyer broker; cert. internat. property specialist; accredited land consular. Staff acct. various firms, Grand Rapids, 1969-72; staff acct., ptnr. Tuori Jacobson, CPA, Muskegon, Mich., 1972-73; sr. internal auditor Wolverine Worldwide, Rockford, Mich., 1973-75; pvt. practice acctg. Grand Rapids, from 1975; controller Sq. Real Estate, Grand Rapids, 1976-87, real estate salesman, from 1976. Cons. Property Corp. Am., 1976-94, S & S Supplies, Grand Rapids, 1986—, Ea. Gardens, Inc., 1987-89. Active West Mich. R.R. Hist. Soc., Grand Rapids, 1986—, Muskegon R.R. Hist. Soc., 1985—, Trade exch. Am., 1985—; active Realtors Land Inst., 1987—, dir., 1990, sec.-treas., 1990-91, v.p. 1992, pres., 1993, 95, nat. gov.-at-large, 1991—, nat. market session com. chmn. 1995, nat. v.p. fin. 1996, 97; gov. Comml. Indsl. Group Mich. Assn. of Realtors, 1993, chmn.-elect, 1995, chmn. 1996. Mem. AICPA, Mich. Assn. CPAs, Nat. Assn. Realtors (internat. sect.), Mich. Assn. Realtors, Grand Rapids Assn. Realtors (mem. comm./indsl. com. 1989-92), Grand Rapids Exchangers and Traders, Comml. Investment Real Estate Inst. (Multimillion Sales award 1976—, Ten Million Sales award 1980, Top Ten Sales award 1980), Internat. Real Estate Fedn., Mich. Bus. Brokers Assn., Mich. Assn. Real Estate Exchangers (assoc., sec. 1989, pres. 1990), Ind. Real Estate Exchangers (affiliate), Chgo. Area Real Estate Exchangers (affiliate). Avocations: railroads, hunting, railroad antiques dealer. Home: Grand Rapids, Mich. Died Apr. 2, 2008.

MOLINA, JUAN-CARLOS, lawyer; b. Buenos Aires, June 29, 1945; came to the U.S., 1963; s. Juan-Carlos and Juana (Cortes-March) M.; m. Margaret O'Brien, May 2, 1981; children: April, Andrew BS, U. Houston, 1972; JD, South Tex. Coll. Law, 1985. Clk. Chevron Oil Co., Houston, 1967-69; asst. engr. S.W. Rsch. Inst., Houston, 1969-72; engr. Turner, Collie & Braden, Houston, 1972-73; staff environ. engr. Diamond Shamrock Corp., Cleve., Houston, 1973-79, Crown Cen. Petroleum, Houston, 1979-80; prin. environ. engr. ARCO Chem. Co., Houston, 1980-86; pvt. practice Houston, 1986-87; atty. J. Michael Solar and Assocs., Houston, 1987-89; sr. environ. counsel Merichem Co., Houston, 1989—2009. Mem. Inst. Hispanic Culture (pres. 1991), Hispanic Bar Assn. (bd. dirs.), ABA (air quality com. 1992), Interam. C. of C. (bd. dirs. 1990), State Bar Tex. (fed. judiciary appointments com.). Avocations: dressage, skiing, power boating, fencing. Died Jan. 22, 2009.

MOLLOY, JOHN FITZGERALD, lawyer; b. LA, Aug. 18, 1917; s. Thomas D. and Anna Charlotte (Wadin) M.; m. Josephine Alexis, July 29, 1942 (div. 1984); children: John, Eva Jo, Marjorie, Karen, Thomas, Craig; m. Adela Allen, Nov. 27, 1985. BA, U. Ariz., 1939; LLB, U. Mo., 1944; JD,

U. Ariz., 1945, LLD (hon.), 1996. Bar: Mo. 1944, Ariz. 1946. Ptnr. Hall, Catlin & Molloy, Tucson, 1945-57; judge Superior Ct., State of Ariz., Tucson, 1957-64, Ct. of Appeals, State of Ariz., Tucson, 1964-69; ptnr. Molloy, Jones P.C., Tucson, 1969-71, Molloy, Jones, Donahue, P.C., Tucson, 1971-95; of counsel O'Connor, Cavanagh, Molloy, Jones, Tucson, from 1995. Contbr. articles to profl. jours. Pres. Marshall Found., Tucson, 1975-97, Metro. YMCA, Tucson, 1967-69; mem. Ariz. Bd. Tax Appeals, 1991; chmn. Pima County Dem. Party, Tucson, 1954. Diplomate Am. Bd. Trial Advocates; mem. Ariz. Judges Assn. (pres. 1965-66), Knight of Demolay, Rotary (bd. dirs. 1981). Home: Tucson, Ariz. Died July 12, 2008.

MONGELL, SUSAN JANE, economics educator; b. Connellsville, Pa., Jan. 29, 1958; d. Dominic and Teresa Ann (Rosendale) M. BA, Seton Hill Coll., 1980; MA, U. Pitts., 1984, PhD, 1988. Teaching asst. U. Pitts., 1980-83, teaching fellow, 1983-84; part-time instr. California U. at Pa., 1986-88; mem. adj. faculty Seton Hill Coll., Greensburg, Pa., 1988; part-time instr. U. Pitts., Greensburg, 1987-89; asst. prof. Calif. U. Pa., from 1989. Mem. Am. Econ. Assn., Ea. Econ. Assn., Econometric Soc., Pa. Econ. Assn. Home: Connellsville, Pa. Died Jan. 14, 2008.

MONROE, ROBERT B., psychologist; b. Worcester, Mass., Aug. 16, 1948; s. Robert M. and Rose M. (Trafecante) M.; m. Chris M. Peterson, Aug. 28, 1971; children: Lauren Marie, Lindsay Ann. AA, Worcester Jr. Coll., 1968; AB in Psychology, Clark U., 1970; MEd in Sch. Psychology, Fitchburg State Coll., 1974; CAGS, Anna Maria Coll., 1979. Lic. psychologist, Mass.; nat. cert. sch. psychologist; cert. sch. psychologist, guidance counselor, guidance dir., gen. supr., elem. edn., social studies, biology, health and music, Mass. Instr. sociology Quinsigamond C.C., 1969; sch. psychologist, guidance counselor, tchr. sci. West Boylston (Mass.) Pub. Schs., 1970-86; sch. psychologist Worcester (Mass.) Vocat. Schs., 1987-89, Athol-Royalston Regional Sch. Dist., from 1989. Adj. faculty in psychology Worcester State Coll., 1982-87; psychol. cons. Sports Edn. Found.; testing coord. MASS Basic Skills Testing. Mem. APA, NEA, Mass. Tchrs. Assn., Nat. Assn. Sch. Psychologists, Mass. Sch. Psychologists Assn., Internat. Coun. for Computers in Edn., Am. Fraternity of Musicians. Home: Millbury, Mass. Died Apr. 12, 2008.

MONT, HALLIE BUCHANAN, pediatrician; b. LA, May 9, 1922; d. Alfred Gordon and Edith Ellen (Hamilton) Buchanan; m. Charles Hansen Mont, June 26, 1944; children: Diane Patrice, Charmain Suzanne. BA, UCLA, 1944; MD, SUNY, 1947. Diplomate Am. Bd. Pediatrics. Intern Calif. Hosp., LA, 1947-48; resident in pediatrics L.A. Children's Hosp., LA, 1948-50; pvt. practice L.A. County, from 1950. Mem. staff L.A. Children's Hosp., St. Joseph Med. Ctr., Burbank, Calif.; courtesy staff Valley Pres Hosp., Van Nuys, Calif., Verdigo Hills Hosp., Glendale, Calif. Mem. L.A. County Med. Assn., Calif. Med. Assn., Southwestern Pediatric Soc., Am. Acad. Pediatrics. Home: Burbank, Calif. Died June 14, 2008.

MONTAGUE, MARY ELLEN, retired secondary school educator, small business owner; b. Georgetown, Ohio, Aug. 12, 1933; d. Carroll Russel and Martha Gail (Lucas) Martin; m. Patrick E. Montague, Feb. 14, 1958; children: Catherine, Michael. BS, Fla. State U., 1955; MS, West Ga. Coll., 1989. Cert. tchr., Ga., Fla., N.C. Tchr. Duval County Schs., Jacksonville, Fla., 1955-59, InterLangue, Paris, 1971-74, Jackson County Schs., Sylva, NC, 1976-79, Fulton County Schs., Atlanta, 1959-71, 80-95, Creekside H.S., Fairburn, Ga., until 1995; ret., 1995; writer, compiler family histories, short stories and poems; owner-operator The Freeze Ho. Bed & Breakfast, Sylva, NC, from 2003. Author various curriculum guides, 1964—. Hostess Tour of Homes, Fairburn, Ga., 1989, 90, 91; vestry person St. Andrews Ch., Peachtree City, Ga., 1989-92. Fellow Smithsonian Instn.; mem. Nat. Coun. Social Studies, Delta Kappa Gamma (1st v.p. 1990-91, pres. 1991-94, dist. treas. 1994—). Died Oct. 1, 2007.

MONTALBAN, RICARDO, actor; b. Mexico City, Nov. 25, 1920; s. Jenaro and Ricarda M.; m. Georgiana Young; children: Mark, Victor, Laura, Anita. Appeared in Mexican motion pictures, 1942-46; appeared in numerous films in U.S. including, Fiesta, 1947, Kissing Bandit, 1949, Neptune's Daughter, 1949, Battleground, 1950, Sombrero, 1953, Latin Lovers, 1954, Sayonara, 1957, Let No Man Write My Epitaph, 1960, Cheyenne Autumn, 1964, The Money Trap, 1965, Madame X, 1966, Sweet Charity, 1968, Escape From the Planet of the Apes, 1971, Conquest of the Planet of the Apes, 1972, The Train Robbers, 1972, Joe Panther, 1976, Won Ton Ton, The Dog Who Saved Hollywood, 1976, Star Trek II: The Wrath of Khan, 1982, Cannonball Run II, 1984, The Naked Gun, 1988; TV films include The Pigeon, 1969, The Aquarians, 1970, Fireball Forward, 1972, The Mark of Zorro, 1974, McNaughton's Daughter, 1976, Fantasy Island, Return to Fantasy Island, 1978; TV advertisements Chrysler, 1973—; TV appearances include Columbo, Star Trek, Return to Fantasy Island; starred in: ltd. series McNaughton's Daughter, 1976; TV series Fantasy Island, 1978-84 (Recipient Emmy award 1978), The Colbys, 1986-87, Heaven Help Us, 1994, (voice) Freakazoid, 1995. Mem. Acad. Motion Picture Arts and Scis. Died Jan. 14, 2009.

MONTAÑO, EDGAR J., language educator; b. Tumaco, Colombia, July 23, 1947; arrived in U.S., 1990; s. Manuel A. Montaño and Justa (Torres) de Montaño. BA in Modern Langs., U. De Tunja, Boyaca, Colombia, 1975; MEd in TESOL, Boston U., 1983; MA in Spanish and Lit., So. Ill. U., 1993. Asst. prof. modern langs. U. de Nariño, Pasto, Colombia, 1985—90; bilingual tchr. Migrant Bilingual Program, Cobden (Ill.) Unit Sch., 1991—93; assoc. prof. Spanish John A. Logan Coll., Carterville, Ill., from 1993. Mem.: NEA, TESOL, Ill. Coun. Tchrs. Fgn. Langs., Ill. Edn. Assn., Ill. Migrant Edn. Assn., Internat. Club John A. Logan Coll. Home: Carbondale, Ill. Died July 15, 2008.

MONTGOMERY, HENRY IRVING, financial planner; b. Dec. 18, 1924; s. Harry Biggs and Martha Grace (Wilkinson) Montgomery; m. Barbara Louise Hook, Aug. 14, 1948; children: Priscilla Ann, Barbara Ruth, Michael Henry, Kelly Anne, Andrew Stuart. Student, U. Iowa, 1942-43, 47-48; BBA, Tulane U., 1952; postgrad., U. Minn., 1976. CFP Colo. Field agt. OSS, SSU, CIG, CIA, Cen. Europe, 1945-47; pres. Nehi Bottling Co., Decorah, Iowa, 1952-64; prin. Montgomery Assocs., Mktg. Cons., Trieste, Italy and Iowa, 1965-72; pres. Planners Fin. Svcs., Inc., Mpls., 1972-95, chmn., 1992—2005. Prin. Montgomery Investment Mgmt., from 1992. Author: Race Toward Berlin, 1945. With US Army, 1943—46, ETO. Decorated Bronze Star; recipient P. Kemp Fain Profl. Svc. award, 1998, Lifetime Achievement award, Fin. Planning Assn., Minn., 2008. Mem.: VFW, DAV, Twin Cities Soc. CFPs, Twin City Fin. Planners (pres. 1975—78), Met. Tax Planning Group (pres. 1984—87), Mpls. Estate Planning Coun., Investment Co. Inst. (investment adviser com. 1982—2006), Internat. Assn. Fin. Planning (internat. dir. 1976—81, govt. rels. com. 1991—2005), Nat. Assn. Securities Dealers (dist. 8 com. 1988—91, vice-chmn. 1990), Inst. CFPs (bd. dirs. 1977—82, pres. 1980—81, chmn. 1981—82, chmn. fin. products stds. bd. 1984—88), Elks, Am. Legion, Beta Gamma Sigma. Avocation: languages (Italian, German). Home: Minneapolis, Minn. Died Sept. 28, 2008.

MOODY, RANDALL DOUGLAS, minister; b. Phoenix, Mar. 26, 1962; s. Don Arthur and Lora Faye (Cozort) M.; m. Lara Lee Williams, Dec. 13, 1986; children: Caleb Andrew, Cailee Jordan. BA in Communications, Abilene Christian U., 1985, BS in Ministry, 1985, MA in Communications, 1987. Ordained to ministry Chs. of Christ, 1978. Min. of youth Ch. of Christ, Farmington, N.Mex., 1987-89, involvement min. Pasadena, Tex., from 1989. Chmn. bd. Four Corners Youth Encampement, Farmington, 1988-89, bd. dirs. 87-88; bd. dirs. Houston Summer Youth Series, Pasadena, 1989—, Leadership Tng. for Christ, Dallas; speaker youth seminars. Author: One Another: The Allelon Deluge, 1991; contbr. articles to jours. in field. Mem. Pi Kappa Delta. Home: Houston, Tex. Died Sept. 1, 2007.

MOODY, ROBERT LEON, investments and futures trader; b. Stillwell, Okla., Aug. 30, 1944; s. Neal L. and Grace (Brown) M. BA in Physics, U. Tex., 1974; MA in Psychology, Tex. Women's U., 1977. Pub. Cycle Events Mag., Ft. Worth, 1970-73; elec. engr. Sterling Electronics, Dallas, 1977-79, Mostek Corp., Carrollton, Tex., 1979-80; pvt. practice psychotherapist Dallas, 1980-82; comml. real estate broker, appraiser Coldwell Banker and others, Dallas, 1982-86; pvt. practice investor and futures trader Dallas, from 1986. Author: White Cloud, 1990. Fund raiser Cath. Found., Dallas, 1989. Mem. Tex. Music Assn. Republican. Methodist. Avocations: song writing, music recording and prodn. Died Oct. 13, 2007.

MOODY, ROY ALLEYNE, mechanical engineer; b. Harvey, Ill., June 15, 1926; s. Roy and Gertrude Alena (Butterfield) M.; m. Roberta Jean Ware, July 18, 1953; 1 child, Diane Linda. BSME, Rose-Hulman Inst., 1952. Registered profl. engr., Ill. Research engr. Acme Steel Corp., Riverdale, Ill., 1952-59; v.p. corp. product devel. Panduit Corp., Tinley Park, Ill., from 1959. Patentee in field; contbr. articles to Model Airplane News, 1971-81. Mem.: Chgo. Radio Car (pres. 1976, 79), Radio Operated Auto Racing (Atlanta) (pres. 1972-76). Home: Flossmoor, Ill. Died Jan. 19, 2008.

MOODY, W. JARVIS (WHITSON JARVIS MOODY), retired bank executive; b. Mineola, NY, Apr. 23, 1928; m. Barbara Anderson; children: Debbie, Priscilla. BA, Harvard U., 1950; MBA, NYU, 1957. With Morgan Guaranty Trust, 1950—64; v.p. Am. Security Bank, 1964—68, sr. v.p., 1968—69, exec. v.p., 1969—73, pres., 1973—80, chmn., pres., CEO, 1980—85; chmn. Inst. for Def. Analyses, Alexandria, Va. Bd. mem. George Washington U. Served in USAR. Died Aug. 7, 2009.

MOONEY, DONALD JAMES, editor, publisher; b. Boston, Jan. 4, 1930; s. Albert Henry and Florence Rosilda (Hunt) M.; m. Phyllis Hilson; children: Donald, Marie-Elena, Julie-Anne, Christina. AB, Suffolk U., 1968. Profl. entertainer, 1950-60; with Boston Police Dept., 1960-75, served to sgt.; editor, pub. Boston Irish News, from 1976. Died Oct. 14, 2007.

MOORE, ALEDA MAJOR, insurance company executive, real estate executive; b. Greenville, SC, May 18, 1927; d. Carl Shaw and Amelia Marie (Kellett) Major; m. Curtis Odell Moore, Mar. 17, 1951; 1 child, Brian Stanley. Grad., Draughn's Bus. Coll., Greenville, 1950, Ins. Inst. Am., 1975, S.C. Assn. Realtors, 1980. Cert. pub. ins. woman. Sec. J.P. Stevens & Co., Greenville, 1945-55; legal sec. Bailey & Dority, Attys., Greenville, 1961-73; with ins. dept. Curtis Moore Co., Mauldin, S.C., from 1973, with real estate dept., from 1980. Mem. Nat. Assn. Realtors, Greenville Bd. Realtors, S.C. Assn. of Realtors, Nat. Assn. of Ins. Women, S.C. Ind. Ins. Agts., Greenville Assn. Ins. Women, Inc. Mem. Ch. of Christ. Avocations: swimming, tennis, travel. Home: Mauldin, SC. Died July 10, 2008.

MOORE, PATSY RUTH, retired nursing educator; b. Marlin, Tex., Sept. 9, 1936; d. Virgil and Janie Dee Needham; m. Jack Ray Moore, Feb. 4, 1957 (dec.); children: Randall Ray, Dawn Rachelle Moore Barrett. BSN, Boston U., 1961; MSN, Okla. U., 1976; MEd, Tex. Christian U., 1980. RN Bd. Nurse Examiners, 1961. Office nurse Dr. A.E. Caroe, Arlington, Tex., 1961—62; nursing instr. Meth. Hosp., Dallas, 1962—69, El Centro C.C., Dallas, 1969—71, Tex. Christian U., Ft. Worth, 1971—76, Dallas Bapt. U., 1976—80. Chair several coms. Northgate United Meth. Ch., Irving, Tex., from 1989. Mem.: Soc. Pediat. Nurses, Irving Evening Lions Club, Sigma Theta Tau. Methodist. Avocations: travel, camping, crossword puzzles, collecting accordian figurines. Home: Grand Prairie, Tex. Died July 13, 2008.

MOORE, RAYMOND ARTHUR, JR., manufacturing engineer; b. Lancaster, Pa., Mar. 8, 1943; s. Raymond Arthur and Dorothy May (Beck) M.; m. Elizabeth Sharon Ballagh, June 13, 1965; children: Diane Michelle, Linda Eileen. AA, San Jose City Coll., 1972; BS in Indsl. Tech., Calif. State U., San Jose, 1975. Cert. mfg. engr., Calif. Electronic technician Data Products Inc., Mountain View, Calif., 1966-68; assoc. electronic engr. Gen. Electric Co., San Jose, 1968-77; supr. United Techs., San Jose, 1977-81; sr. mfg. engr. Amdahl Corp., Sunnyvale, Calif., 1981-85, AMEX Systems Inc., Compton, Calif., from 1985. Chmn. bd. Christian edn. Apostles Luth. Ch. and Sch., San Jose, 1977-80, elder, 1981-84. Served with USAF, 1962-66. Mem. Soc. Mfg. Engrs. (sr., treas. chpt. 1985, 86, 3d vice chmn. 1984), Instrument Soc. Am. (sr., standards rev. bd.), Am. Mgmt. Assn. Republican. Avocations: playing french horn, fishing. Home: Anaheim, Calif. Died June 1, 2008.

MORAN, JAMES BYRON, federal judge; b. Evanston, Ill., June 20, 1930; s. James Edward and Kathryn (Horton) M.; m. Janet Remen; children: John, Jennifer, Sarah, Polly; stepchildren: Katie, Cynthia, Laura, Michael, Susan, Carol, Peggy, Tom, Lee. AB, U. Mich., 1952; LLB magna cum laude, Harvard U., 1957. Bar: Ill. 1958. Law clk. to Hon. J. Edward Lumbard US Ct. Appeals (2nd cir.), 1957-58; assoc. Bell, Boyd, Lloyd, Haddad & Burns, Chgo, 1958-66, ptnr., 1966-79; judge US Dist. Ct. (no. dist.) Ill., Chgo., 1979—95, chief judge, 1990—95, sr. judge, 1995—2009. Dir. Com. on Ill. Govt., 1960-78, chmn., 1968-70; vice chmn., sec. Ill. Narcotic Drug Adv. Coun., 1967-74; dir. Gateway Found., 1969—2009; mem. Ill. House of Reps., 1965-67; mem. Evanston City Council, 1971-75. Served with AUS, 1952-54. Mem. Chgo. Bar Assn., Chgo. Council Lawyers, Lawyers Club, Phi Beta Kappa. Home: Evanston, Ill. Died Apr. 21, 2009.

MORAN, MITCH, lawyer; b. Houston; BA, Northwestern U.; JD, Miss. Coll., 1996. Farmer, La.; atty. Tribal Chief Phillip Martin Miss. Band of Choctaw Indians, 1996; solo practice Moran Law Firm, Carthage, Miss., from 1998. Achievements include defense atty. for Edgar Ray Killen, convicted of the 1964 manslaughter of 3 civil rights workers, Andrew Goodman, James Chaney and Michael Schwerner in June 2005. Deceased.

MORGAN, ALICE RUTH, retired treasurer; b. Petersburg, Tex., Apr. 1, 1934; d. Cloyd D. and Lula Belle (Jay) Smith; m. Leroy Edward Miner, Aug. 6, 1955 (div. Dec. 1974); children: Steven Dale, Kevin Guy; m. Alfred Curtis Morgan, Apr. 29, 1978. BBA, U. N.Mex., 1956, MBA, 1969. With Sandia Nat. Labs., Albuquerque, 1963-73, mgr. acctg., 1973-84, asst. treas., 1984-93; ret., 1993. Bd. dirs. Family & Children Svcs., Albuquerque, 1974-88. Mem. Inst. Mgmt. Accts. (ret., bd. dirs. 1990-92). Republican. Episcopal. Home: Albuquerque, N.Mex. Died July 2, 2008.

MORGAN, BARBARA DOOLITTLE, law librarian; b. Welch, W.Va., Dec. 24, 1929; d. Claude M. Ellis and Elizabeth (Doolittle) Hamrick; divorced; children: Leslie, Matthew, Roger. Student, U. So. Calif., 1947-48, Columbia U., 1949-50, U. Cin., 1952-53; BS in Law, Northwestern Calif. U., 1985. Legal sec. various firms, Huntington, W.Va., 1963-84; law libr., mktg. adminstr., recruiting coord. Kay, Casto, Chaney, Love & Wise, Charleston, W.Va., from 1984. Author: Model Defense Interrogatories, 1987, Summary Proceedings and Structured Settlements, West Virginia Practice Handbook, 1991; contbr. articles to profl. jours. Home: Charleston, W.Va. Died Sept. 20, 2007.

MORGAN, MARY LOUISE FITZSIMMONS, fund raising executive, lobbyist; b. NYC, July 22, 1946; d. Robert John and Mary Louise (Gordon) Fitzsimmons; m. David William Morgan, Aug. 7, 1971; children: Mallory Siobhan, David William. BA, Marquette U., 1964; MA, Cath. U., 1966; postgrad., Columbia U., 2005. Asst. prof. Monmouth U., West Long Branch, NJ, 1966-69; campaign dir. United Way, NYC, 1969-80; pres. Morgan Communications, NYC, 1980-82; capital campaign dir. YMCA of Greater NY, 1982-85; dir. devel. NY Med. Coll., Valhalla, 1985-88; counsel Challenger Ctr., Va., 1988-89; v.p. Ctr. Molecular Medicine & Immunology, Newark, 1989-92, Garden State Cancer Ctr., Newark, 1989-92; chief devel. and pub. affairs officer Mental Health Assn., White Plains, NY, 1993-95; dir. external affairs St. Vincents Svcs., from 1996, mng. dir., from 2006. Adj. prof. Iona Coll., New Rochelle, NY, 1994-95; dir. Meth Ch. Home for Aged, Riverdale, NY, Casita Maria Inc., NYC, 1975-95; pres., founding dir.

Achievement Rewards for Coll. Scientists Inc., 1978-80. Sec. Darien (Conn.) Dem. Town Com., 1984—, vice chmn. Darien nominating com. 1986—. Recipient 50th Anniversary award Casita Maria Inc., N.Y.C., 1984, Iris award Bus. Communicators of Am., 1991, Nat. Depression Awareness Campaign award NMHA, 1994, Am. Graphic Design award, 2002. Mem. Nat. Soc. Fund Raising Execs., Nat. Soc. Hosp. Adminstrn., Spring Lake (NJ) Bath and Tennis Club. Democrat. Roman Catholic. Avocations: golf, gardening, tennis. Died June 5, 2007.

MORGAN, WALTER, retired poultry science educator; b. Ledyard, Conn., Dec. 22, 1921; s. Walter Clifford and Margaret (Allyn) M.; m. Marcella Hodge, Dec. 28, 1948 (div. 1960); children: Nancy, Peggy, Beth; m. Helen Naden, May 14, 1966. BSc, U. Conn., 1946; MSc, George Washington U., 1949, PhD, 1953. Animal husbandman Nat. Cancer Inst., NIH, Bethesda, Md., 1946-49; rsch. assoc. Nevis Rsch. Sta., Columbia U., Irvington-on-Hudson, N.Y., 1950-53; asst. prof. U. Tenn., Knoxville, 1953-54; assoc. prof., prof. S.D. State U., Brookings, 1954-85; ret., 1985; fgn. expert on English and genetics People's Republic China, 1991. Researcher biology div. Nuclear Energy Ctr., Mol, Belgium, 1968-69, genetics div. Commonwealth Sci. and Indsl. Rsch. Orgn., Sydney, Australia, 1975-76; cons., Kuala Lumpur, Malaysia, 1988, Europe, 1944, 69, 84, 95. Author: (poetry) Now and Then, 1982, Down Under, 1983, Hitchin' Around, 1985, Here and There, 1990, What's Good About China, 1992, In Europe 1944-1969-1994, 1995; contbr. over 100 articles to profl. jours. Former scoutmaster Boy Scouts Am., Brookings; pres. Men's Brotherhood, Brookings, 1974, U.S. Friends Fgn. Students, Brookings, 1986-97. Sgt. USAAF, 1942-45, ETO. Fellow AAAS; mem. Am. Genetics Assn., World Poultry Assn., N.Y. Acad. Scis., S.D. Acad. Sci. (pres.). Home: Sharon Springs, NY. Died Feb. 4, 2008.

MORGAN, WILLIAM DOUGLASS (BILL MORGAN), retired diplomat; b. Rochester, NY, Nov. 10, 1925; s. Richard Douglass and Jeanette (Harned) M.; m. Nancy Gardner, July 30, 1949 (dec. 1990); children: Patricia L., Thomas G. BA, U. Rochester, 1949; M.F.S., U. Paris, 1950. Second sec. U.S Delegation NATO, Paris, 1956-58; consul Birmingham, Eng., 1958-60; Russian lang. and area studies, 1960-62; second sec. US Embassy, Moscow, 1962-64, consul Beirut, 1968-73; insp. US Dept. State, Washington, 1974-76, dep. dir. visa office, 1976-78; consul gen. US Embassy, Paris, 1978-81, Montreal, 1981-85; dir. employee relations US Dept. State, 1985-87, ret. Co-author (with Charles Stuart Kennedy): The U.S. Consul at Work, 1991; co-editor: American Diplomats: The Foreign Service at Work, 2004. Served to pfc. U.S. Army, 1943-46, ETO. Mem. U.S. Fgn. Service Assn., Diplomatic & Consular Officers Ret. Home: Springfield, Va. Died Mar. 11, 2009.

MORIN, CHARLES RAYMOND, engineering executive, consultant, engineer; b. Burlington, Vt., Apr. 8, 1947; s. Charles Raymond Morin Sr. and Mary Louise (Sandusky) Hodges; m. Elizabeth Ann Worrel, Sept. 7, 1968; children: Amy, Jason, Karen, Kelly, Kevin. AAS in Metall. Engring. Tech., Columbus Inst. Tech., Ohio, 1968; B and MS in Metall. Engring., Ohio State U., 1972. Registered profl engr., Ill. Rsch. assoc. Ohio State U., Columbus, 1968-72; mem. tech. staff Packer Engring. Assocs. Inc., Naperville, Ill., 1972-85, pres., chief operating officer, 1985-87; chmn. bd. Engring. Systems, Inc., Aurora, Ill., from 1987. Prin. cons. Engring. Systems, Inc., Aurora, 1987—. Bd. dirs. H.W. Homeowners Assn., Naperville, 1986-88. Fellow Am. Soc. for Materials Internat. (chmn. 1988—); mem. ASTM, Nat. Assn. Corrosion Engrs., Nat. Soc. Profl. Engrs., Ill. Soc. Profl. Engrs., Tech. Assn. Pulp and Paper Industry. Avocation: blacksmith. Home: Naperville, Ill. Died Feb. 2, 2008.

MORING, JOHN FREDERICK, lawyer; b. Farmville, Va., Oct. 30, 1935; s. Scott O'Ferrall and Margaret Macon (Mitchell) M.; m. Margaret Ann Clarke, Mar. 30, 1959; children: Martha, Elizabeth, Scott, Lee. BS, Va. Poly. Inst., 1957; JD, George Washington U., 1961. Bar: Va. 1961, DC 1962, US Supreme Ct. 1964; cert. mediator civil disputes Supreme Ct. Va. 2004, US Dist. Ct. Va., 2004, US Cir. Ct., 2004. Assoc. Morgan, Lewis & Bockius, Washington, 1961-68, ptnr., 1969-78, Jones, Day, Reavis & Pogue, Washington, 1978-79; founding ptnr. Crowell & Moring, Washington, Irvine, NY, London, Brussels, 1979—2000. Sec. Associated Gas Distbrs., Inc., 1977-2000. Local gas utility columnist: Nat. Gas Jour., 1989—2000; mem. editl. bd. Natural Gas Contracts, 1994—2001. Mem. nat. panel neutrals Am. Arbitration Assn., 2003—09; chmn. bd. dirs. Washington Legal Counsel for Elderly, 2000—01; Rep. candidate 23d Dist./Va. Gen. Assembly, Alexandria, 1973; mem. bd. govs. St. Stephen's and St. Agnes Sch., Alexandria, 1989—95; pres. St. Stephen's Found., Inc., 1990—93; sr. warden Immanuel Ch. on the Hill, Alexandria, 1988, 1989; trustee Ch. Schs. of Diocese of Va., 1996—2008; mem. found. bd. Shrine Mont Conf. Ctr. Episc. Diocese Va., Orkney Springs, Va., from 2001; mem. bd. govs. St. Margaret's Sch., Tappahannock, Va., 2002—08. 2d lt. US Army, 1958. Mem.: ABA (natural resources law sect. 1982—86, coun.), Am. Arbitration Assn., Fed. Energy Bar Assn. (sec. 1963—66, pres. 1982—83), Indian Creek Yacht and Country Club (Kilmarnock, Va.). Episcopalian. Avocations: golf, fishing, canoeing. Home: White Stone, Va. Died May 12, 2009.

MORISON, JACK, international adventure travel company owner; b. Santa Monica, Calif., Dec. 17, 1954; s. James Sanford and Helene (Walker) M.; m. Julie Margaret Ogawa, Sept. 9, 1989; 1 child, Walker Martin. AA, Cabrillo Coll., 1978; student, Golden Gate U., 1986-87, Coll. of Marin, 1988. Mgr. and guide river trips in West and Southwest O.A.R.S. Inc., Angles Camp, Calif., 1971-85; mgr. internat. ops., participant expeditions 27 countries Sobek Expeditions, Angels Camp, Calif., 1979-84; coord. for internat. adventure travel trips, asst. Esprit De Corp, San Francisco, 1983-87; project coord. Project Russians and Ams. for Teamwork, from 1987; owner Adventure Travel Co. affiliate White Magic Unlimited, Mill Valley, Calif., from 1983. Cons. mktg. and sales Wilderness Travel, Berkeley, Calif., 1987; advisor ops. White Magic Nepal; leader first Albanian Black Drini Expedition, 1992. Producer film documentaries Bill Burrud Prodns., LA., 1979, Richard Kidd Prodns., Dallas, 1981, Wingstar Film Prodns., N.Y., 1982, Stan Boor Prodns., 1983, 2 films Pakistani TV, 1985, 86. Pres. Episcopal Youth Coun., 1972. Avocations: mountain biking, travel, philosophy, photography. Home: Mill Valley, Calif. Died Aug. 13, 2008.

MORLOK, EDWARD KARL, engineering educator, consultant; b. Phila., Nov. 3, 1940; s. Edward Karl and Anna Marie (Kurtz) M.; m. Ottilia Angela Husz, Dec. 14, 1968 (div. July 1983); 1 child, Jessica Angela; m. Patricia Campbell Conboy, Mar. 23, 1991. BE, Yale U., 1962; PhD, Northwestern U., 1967; MA (hon.), U. Pa., 1973. Civil engr., transp. US Dept. Commerce, Washington, 1966-67; from asst. prof. civil engring. to assoc. prof. Northwestern U., Evanston, Ill., 1967-73, asst. dir. rsch., transp. ctr., 1969-73; 1907 Found. assoc. prof. U. Pa., Phila., 1973-75, chmn., transp. grad. group, 1983-86, 91-95, UPS found. prof. transp., 1975—2009, prof. systems engring., 1986—2009, chair systems grad. program, 1988-91, prof. emeritus, 2004—09. Cons. nat. transp. policy study commn., Washington, 1978-79. Author: Analysis Transportation Technology and Network Structure, 1969, Introduction to Transportation Engineering and Planning, 1978; assoc. editor Transp. Rsch. Jour., 1975-2004; consulting editor series in transp. for McGraw-Hill Publ. Co., 1980-98; contbr. more than 80 articles to profl. jours. Mem. Nat. Assembly Engring. panel on innovation in transp., Washington, 1979-80, panel on hazardous material transp., Washington, 1980-81. Recipient U.S. Sr. Scientist award Alexander von Humboldt Found., 1980-81; Rsch. grantee Commonwealth of Pa., Consol. Rail Corp., K-Line Am., U.S. Dept. Transp., NASA, NSF. Mem. ASCE, Transp. Rsch. Forum (v.p. 1974-75, pres. 1975-76, bd. disting. mems. 1983-2009, Disting. Transp. Rsch. award 1998), Transp. Rsch. Bd. (rev. com. of coun. of univ. transp. ctrs. 1985-88, coun. mem. 1988-90, chair freight transp. planning and logistics com. 1994-99, chair com. on policy options for intermodal freight trans. 1996-98). Lutheran. Home: Swarthmore, Pa. Died Apr. 18, 2009.

MOROZ, CHESLEY ANN, marketing professional; b. Boulder, Colo., July 16, 1959; d. Chester Orville and Carla Bernadine (Caldwell) Harris; m. Francis Joseph Moroz, Oct. 9, 1982; 1 child, Katherine Elizabeth. BS, Bloomsburg U., 1981. Coord. product devel. and publs. Eastern Nat. Park and Monument Assn., Phila., 1981, merchandising mgr., v.p. mktg., from 1988. Speaker in field; cons. Nat. Trust for Historic Preservation. Mem. Nat. Assn. Interpreters, Mus. Store Assn., Am. Booksellers Assn., Am. Soc. Assn. Execs., Conf. Nat. Park Cooperating Assns. (bd. dirs. 1989—, v.p. 1993—, com. chair database survey 1990, 91, program com. San Antonio conv. 1992, com. chair bookstore planning and design 1992—, site com. chair Williamsburg, Va. conv. 1994). Home: Warminster, Pa. Died July 29, 2008.

MORRILL, DOROTHY S., lawyer; b. NYC, Dec. 30, 1944; d. Paul and Julia (Merlis) Solomon; m. William Morrill, May 29, 1965; children: Paul, Jonathan. BS, NYU, 1967; JD, Bklyn. Law Sch., 1981. Bar: N.Y., 1982, U.S. Dist. Ct. (ea. and so. dists.) N.Y. 1982, U.S. Supreme Ct. 1986. Dist. atty. Kings County Dist. Atty., Bklyn.; assoc. Fuchsberg & Fuchsberg, 1986-90, Sullivan & Lapakis, 1990-92, Queller & Fisher, NYC, from 1992. Lectr. in field. Mem. Breast Cancer Coalition Adv. Com., 1995—. Mem. ATLA, N.Y. State Trial Lawyers Assn. (mem. legis. com. 1994—), Bar Assn. of City of N.Y. (co-chair Tort Reform or Ins. Reform 1990, co-chair Senate task force on misconduct by therapeutic and healthcare profls. 1992). Avocations: tai chi, running, hiking. Died Jan. 23, 2008.

MORRIS, DOLEN RAY, agronomist, researcher; b. Poplar Bluff, Md., Dec. 2, 1948; s. Dolen and Nancy Jean (Maddox) M.; m. Prateung Pradapsuwan, Oct. 16, 1981; children: Deanne Renu, Deborah Rairi. MS, Cornell U., 1977; PhD, Tex. A&M U., 1985. Vol. U.S. Peace Corps, Bangkok, Thailand, 1977-79; rsch. assoc. Tex. A&M U., College Station, 1980-81, grad. rsch. asst., 1981-85; asst. prof. agronomy La. State U. Agrl. Ctr., Franklinton, 1985-90, asst. prof. agronomy and forage quality, from 1990; agronomist USDA, ARS, Beckley, WV, 1992-93. Agronomy cons. S.E. Rsch. Sta., Franklinton, 1985-92. Contbr. articles to profl. jours. With U.S. Army, 1969-72, Vietnam. Mem. Am. Soc. Agronomy, Soil Sci. Soc. Am., Am. Forage and Grassland Coun., Gamma Sigma Delta. Democrat. Achievements include discovery that fertilizer N may compliment the biologically fixed N in arrowleaf clover when grown in mixture with rygrass, that non-significant amounts of N are transferred from arrowleaf clover to ryegrass during the growing season, soybean rhizabia may survive saturated field soil conditions for several months, soybean growing in calcareus soils of Tex. are largely influenced by the highly reactive carbonate phase in the soil. Home: Ryl Palm Bch, Fla. Died Oct. 23, 2007.

MORRIS, JAMES LEO, financial software executive; b. Phila., Jan. 5, 1963; s. William Joseph and Frances Patricia (Cona) M. Student, U.S. Naval Acad., 1980-81; BS in Chem. Engring., U. Pa., 1984; MBA in Fin., Fordham U., 1989. Industry specialist Sel-Rex Plating Systems, Nutley, N.J., 1984-89; v.p. Internation Capital Markets Corp., NYC, from 1989. Republican. Roman Catholic. Home: New York, NY. Died Oct. 26, 2007.

MORRIS, LESLIE RONALD, retired librarian; b. Sewickley, Pa., Dec. 18, 1935; s. Harry and Elizabeth (Saperstein) M.; children: Hallie, Lee. BS, Geneva Coll., Beaver Falls, Pa., 1957; MS, Duquesne U., 1961; MLS, U. So. Miss., 1985. Cataloger St. Francis Coll., Loretto, Pa., 1961-63; head cataloger East Stroudsburg (Pa.) U., 1963-69; head tech. svc. SUNY, Fredonia, 1969-75; head libr. Xavier U., New Orleans, 1973-85; dir. libraries Niagara U., Niagara Falls, NY, 1985—2000. Editor: Choosing a Bibliographic Utility, 1988, Interlibrary Loan Policies Directory, 5th edit., 1994; editor Jour. Interlibrary Loan and Info. Supply, 1990. Fellow Molesworth Inst.; mem. ALA, Assn. Coll. and Rsch. Librs. Home: Buffalo, NY. Died Dec. 7, 2008.

MORRISON, H. ROBERT, small business owner, photographer, retired municipal official; b. Pitts., Apr. 7, 1938; s. Hugh and Gertrude Mary (Gehenio) Morrison; m. Meredith Wollenberg, Dec. 8, 1979; children: Justin William, Elizabeth Jeanne; 1 child from previous marriage, Hugh Robert Jr. BA in English, Howard U., 1969. Writer Nat. Geog. Soc., Washington, 1969-73, editor ednl. filmstrips, 1973-77, sr. writer, 1977-88, mng. editor nat. geography bee, 1988-89; elected treas. City of Falls Ch., Va., 1993—2006; ret., 2006. Exec. bd. dirs. Tapestry Theatre, Alexandria, Va.; bd. dirs. Falls Ch. Cable Access Corp., 1989—2008, pres., 1989—2008, Bonnie Briar Prodns., LLC, 2003—09; bd. dirs. TV & Internet Video Assn., 2002—08. Contbg. author: book As We Live and Breathe, 1971, The Ocean Realm, 1978, America's Majestic Canyons, 1979, Mysteries of the Ancient World, 1979, America's Magnificent Mountains, 1980, America's Hidden Corners, 1983, Exploring America's Valleys, 1984, America's Seashore Wonderlands, 1985; co-author: America's Atlantic Isles, 1981, prodr.; photographer Come What Way, National Catholic Pray Breakfast, The Seton Legacy, DC Divas, a Womens Full conta Football Team and DC Fringe Festible, Feeding the Soul of the City. Bd. dirs. TV Internat. Video Assn., 2002—08; vice chmn. Falls Church Dem. Com., 1988—89, 1998—99. With US Army, 1961—64. Named one of Vol. of Yr., DC Ctrl. Kitchen, 2005. Mem.: NAACP, Treas. Assn. Va. (bd. dirs. 1996—97), Clan Morrison N.Am. (life), St. Andrew's Soc. Washington. Avocations: reading, TV production, historic preservation. Died July 12, 2009.

MORRISON, SARAH LYDDON, author; b. Rochester, NY, May 19, 1939; d. Paul William and Winifred (Cowles) Lyddon. BA, U. Vt., 1961. Sec. asst. Glamour mag., NYC, 1961-63, Vogue mag., NYC, 1963-65; asst. editor Venture mag., NYC, 1966-71; dir. pub. rels. for tourism Commonwealth of P.R., NYC, 1971-75; asst. Am. Legion, Washington, 1988-98; owner Sarah Lyddon Morrison Pub. Rels., Washington, 1999—2003. Author: The Modern Witch's Spellbook, 1971, Book II, 1983, The Modern Witch's Dream Book, 1985, The Modern Witch's Book of Home Remedies, 1988, The Modern Witch's Book of Symbols, 1997, Modern Witch's Guide to Magic and Spells, 1998. Advisor to nat. security coord. John Kerry Presdl. Campaign, 2003—04. Mem. DAR (Emily Nelson chpt.), Women's Nat. Dem. Club, Colonial Dames XVII Century (nat. def. chmn.), Am. News Women's Club. Avocations: travel, reading, swimming, rock music, cooking. Home: Washington, DC. Died Nov. 15, 2007.

MORSE, WILLIAM CHARLES, psychology educator; b. Erie, Pa., Oct. 23, 1915; s. Melvin E. Morse and Ethel Dunbar; m. Bernice G. Szafran, Mar. 5, 1937; children: Susan, James. AB, U. Mich., 1935, MA, 1939, PhD, 1947. Lic. psychologist, Mich. Prof. emeritus psychology and ednl. psychology U. Mich.; rsch. prof. spl. edn. U. South Fla., from 1991. Cons. spl. edn. Ann Arbor pub. schs., Hawthorn Ctr. Editorial reviewer Jour. Behavioral Disorders, Jour. for Exceptional Children, Jour. of Emotional and Behavioral Problems; contbr. articles to profl. jours. Fellow Am. Orthpsychiat. Assn., Am. Psychol. Assn.; mem. Am. Ednl. Research Assn., Council for Exceptional Children, Council on Behavioral Disorders, Nat. Assn. of Sch. Psychologists, Mich. Assn. Emotionally Disturbed Children, Mich. Assn. Sch. Psychology, Mich. Psychol. Assn. Home: Ann Arbor, Mich. Died Jan. 25, 2008.

MOSCONA, ARON ARTHUR, biology educator, scientist; b. Israel, July 4, 1922; came to U.S., 1955, naturalized, 1965; s. David DeAbravanel and Lola (Krochmaal) M.; m. Malka Kempinsky, July 6, 1954; 1 child, Anne. M.Sc., Hebrew U., Jerusalem, 1947, PhD, 1950. Postgrad. fellow Strangeways Research Lab., Cambridge, Eng., 1950-52; vis. investigator Rockefeller Inst., NYC, 1955-57; prof. biology U. Chgo., 1958—92, Louis Block prof. biol. scis., 1972-92, Louis Block prof. emeritus, 1992—2009. Chmn. Com. on Devel. Biology, 1969-76; vis. prof. Stanford U., 1959, U. Montreal, 1960, U. Palermo, Italy, 1966, Hebrew U., Jerusalem, 1972, Tel-Aviv (Israel) U., 1977, 79, Kyoto U.,

Japan, 1980 Author: (with A. Monroy) Introductory Concepts in Developmental Biology, 1979; founder, editor: Current Topics in Developmental Biology, 1965; past mem. editorial bd. Jour. Molecular Neurosci., New Biologist, Mechanisms of Aging and Development, Cell Differentiation, Cancer Research, Devel. Neurosci, Experimental Cell Research; contbr. 260 articles to profl. jours. Recipient Claude Bernard medal in exptl. medicine, 1962, Alcon prize in visual sci., 1990, Gold medal Azabu Univ., Japan, 1991. Fellow AAAS, Am. Acad. Arts and Scis., Lombardo Inst. (Milan), N.Y. Acad. Scis.; mem. NAS, Internat. Soc. Devel. Biology (pres. 1977-81), Am. Soc. Devel. Biology, Internat. Soc. Cell Biology, Am. Soc. Zoology, Sigma Xi. Home: New York, NY. Died Jan. 14, 2009.

MOSER, M(ARTIN) PETER, lawyer; b. Balt., Jan. 16, 1928; s. Herman and Henrietta (Lehmayer) M.; m. Elizabeth Kohn, June 14, 1949; children— Mike, Moriah, Jeremy AB, The Citadel, Charleston, SC, 1947; LLB, Harvard U., 1950. Bar: Md. 1950, U.S. Supreme Ct., U.S. Ct. Appeals (4th cir.). Asst. states atty. City of Balt., 1951, 53-54; assoc. Blades Rosenfeld, Balt., 1950, 53-54; ptnr. Frank, Bernstein, Conaway & Goldman and predecessor firms, Balt., 1955-90, co-chmn. firm, 1983-86; counsel, 1991-92; of counsel DLA Piper US LLP, from 1992. Instr. U. Balt. Law Sch., 1954-56, 86, U. Md. Law Sch., 1986-87. Contbr. articles to profl. jours. Del., chmn. local govt. com. Md. Constl. Conv., 1967-68; mem. Balt. City Planning Commn., 1961-66, Balt. Regional Planning Council, 1963-66, Md. Commn. to Study Narcotics Laws, 1965-67, Mayor's Task Force on EEO, 1966-67, Met. Transit Authority Adv. Council, 1962, Com. to Revise Balt. City Planning Laws, 1962, Com. to Revise Balt. City Charter Provision on Conflicts of Interest, 1969-70; mem. Citizens Adv. Com. on Dist. Ct., chmn., 1971, Dist. Adv. Bd. for Pub. Defender System for Dist. 1, 1973-85; mem. Atty. Grievance Commn. of Md., 1975-78, chmn. 82-86; chmn. Md. State Ethics Commn., 1987-89; bd. dirs. Sinai Hosp., 1983-2004, 2007—, Lifebridge Health Sys., 1998—, Ct. of Appeals Comm. to Study the Model Rules, 1983-86, 2002-05; com. to review jud. conduct Md. Jud. Conf., 2007—. With JAGC, U.S. Army, 1951-53. Fellow: Balt. Bar Found., Md. Bar Found., Am. Bar Found. (pres. 2002—04); mem.: ABA (ho. of dels. 1978—2002, bd. govs. 1984—87, 1992—96, treas. 1993—96), Balt. Bar Assn. (pres. 1970—71), Md. State Bar Assn. (pres. 1979—80), Wednesday Law Club, Lawyers' Roundtable. Democrat. Jewish. Home: Baltimore, Md. Died Oct. 17, 2008.

MOSHER, SOL, lawyer; b. 1928; s. Jacob and Blanch Becker Mosher; m. Cora E. Walker, 1953; children: Janice May, Caryn Anne. Sports editor Mo. Daily News Digest, Springfield, 1954; news editor Sta. KICK, 1954—56, KYTV, 1956—58; civic affairs mgr. C. of C., 1958—60; adminstrn. asst.; congressman Durward G. Hall, 1961—69; spl. asst. to sec. for cong. rels. US Dept. Commerce, 1969—73; asst. sec. legis. affairs US Dept. Housing & Urban Devel., 1973—76; v.p. fed. affairs Crown-Zellerbach Corp., 1977—85; asst. US trade rep. cong. affairs US Dept. Housing & Urban Devel., 1985—89; sr. adv. internat. trade Preston Ellis Gates & Rouvelas Meeds, 1989—2008. Recipient Disting. Svc award, Springfield C. of C., award Excellence, US Dept. Housing & Urban Devel., 1976. Mem.: Missouri Soc. Washington, Bull Elephants. Republican. Died Dec. 30, 2008.

MOSIER, JERRY MICHAEL, advertising executive; b. Towanda, Pa., Jan. 4, 1955; s. James Malcolm and Janet Marie (Bates) M.; m. Roselee Blooston, Sept. 9, 1983; 1 child, Oliver Blooston. BA, SUNY, Oswego, 1976; postgrad., NYU, 1977-78. Copywriter Moss Advt., NYC, 1977-79, Marschalk Co., NYC, 1979-80; sr. copywriter D'Arcy MacManu Masius, NYC, 1980-82; pres. Cappadona, Mosier & Ptnrs., NYC, 1982-86, Advocacy Communication, Inc., NYC; exec. v.p., creative dir. Schoenfield Kahn, NYC, 1986-90; creative dir. Elliott Christie Mwien, NYC, 1990-95; exec. v.p., copy chief Keyes Martin, East Hanover, N.J., from 1995. Contbr. articles to profl. jours., periodicals. Bd. dirs. Afghanistan Relief Com., N.Y.C., 1986—, Northcote Parkinson Fund, N.Y.C., 1987—, U.S. English, 1992-96; active Com. For the Free World; coach Montclair Jr. Baseball, 1995—; active Ctrl. Presbyn. Ch., Montclair, N.J. Recipient ADDY award Advt. Women N.Y., 1987. Mem. Bus. Publ., Audit and Circulation, Inc. Republican. Avocations: writing, running, hiking, travel, kayaking. Home: Montclair, NJ. Died Jan. 28, 2008.

MOSLEY, WILBUR CLANTON, JR., materials scientist; b. Birmingham, Ala., Oct. 30, 1938; s. Wilbur Clanton and Clare Brokenshaw (Thomas) M.; m. Betty Earline LaFrange, Aug. 25, 1960; children: Benjamin Clanton, Mary Elizabeth. B in Engring. Physics, Auburn U., Ala., 1960, MS in Physics, 1962; PhD in Physics, U. Ala., 1965. Materials scientist Savannah River Tech. Ctr. Westinghouse Savannah River Co., Aiken, S.C., from 1965. Capt. USAR, 1960-70. Mem. ASM Internat., Microbeam Analysis Soc. Baptist. Avocation: music. Home: New Ellenton, SC. Died Dec. 1, 2007.

MOSS, JOHN FREDERICK, sales executive; b. Englewood, NJ, Aug. 7, 1943; m. Siri C, Dec. 31, 1967; 1 child Chris. BA, Parsons Coll. Steel supr. U.S. Steel Acctg. Dep., Gary, Ind., 1969-71; with Alexander Proudfoot Co., Chgo., 1971-72; sr. v.p. sales Scheduling Corp. of Am., Oak Brook, Ill., from 1972-. 1st lt. U.S. Army, 1966-68. Mem. Sales and Mktg. Execs., Nat. Speakers Assn. Republican. Avocations: sports, reading, sports cars, travel. Home: Frankfort, Ill. Died May 13, 2008.

MOTE, KARL WILLIAM, mining engineer; b. Plainview, Nebr., Mar. 27, 1927; s. Ross Allan and Louise (Ebinger) M.; m. Lois Jean Kirchoff, July 23, 1947 (div. Jan. 1974); children: Karen Quinn, Kristine Mote, Kathy Mote-lamp, Karl William, Kelly; m. Elva June Harlan Dike, June 20, 1981. MetE, Colo. Sch. Mines, 1949. Registered profl. engr., Utah. Various mgmt. positions U.S. Steel, various locations, 1949-70; gen. mgr. Vanguard Exploration, Spokane, 1970-73; asst. to mgr. exploration N/L Industries, Golden, Colo., 1973-74, St. Joseph Exploration, Toronto, 1975; exec. dir., v.p. Northwest Mining Assn., Spokane, from 1976. Mem. Fed. Emergency Mgmt.-Minerals, U.S. Dept. Interior, Washington, 1988—. Author book chpt. Died Apr. 4, 2008.

MOULDS, WILLIAM J., retired aeronautical engineer; b. Newton, Kans., Mar. 7, 1933; s. William J. and Edith M. (Cox) Moulds; m. Myra Teresa Cummins, Dec. 28, 1955; children: Michael J., Robert W., Barbara L., Anne T. Moulds-Laughlin, Patrick L., Margaret L. Moulds-Vittitow. BSME, U. N.Mex., 1957; MSME, N.Mex. State U., 1970. Registered profl. engr., N.Mex. Rsch. engr. rsch. lab. Allis-Chalmers, Cin., 1956—57; supr. aero. engr. Air Force Spl. Weapons Ctr., Albuquerque, 1958—63; sr. aero. rsch. engr. Air Force Weapons Lab., Albuquerque, 1963—72, theoretical rsch. engr., 1972—79, chief tech. svcs. divsn., staff rsch. engr. to comdr., 1979—89; ret., 1989. Contbr. articles to profl. jours.; patentee in field. Vol. Barrett House; founder, 1st pres. U. N.Mex. Sch. Engring Alumni Assn.; bd. dirs. N.Mex. State Bd. Registration for Profl. Engrs. and Land Surveyors, 1990—95, chmn. com. on rules, regulations and statues, 1992; com. mem. Barrett Found. Recipient Honor award, U. N.Mex. Sch. Engring., 2000; named to Sociedad de Ingenieros as Ingeniero Eminente, New Mex. State U., 1993. Republican. Roman Catholic. Home: Albuquerque, N.Mex. Died June 28, 2008.

MOUNTAIN, EVELYN MARIE, osteopathic physician; b. Brownsville, Pa., Dec. 4, 1917; d. Frank Lloyd Mountain and Katharyn Hensel. Postgrad., Allegheny Gen. Hosp., Pitts., 1938; BS, U. Pitts., 1950; DO, Des Moines Still Coll., 1955. Staff nurse Allegheny Gen. Hosp., 1939-44; head nurse, instr. medicine and urol. nursing Sch. Nursing Perry Twp., Fayette, Pa., 1944-51; intern Community Hosp. Lancaster, Pa., 1955-56, mem. staff, from 1956; pvt. practice Marietta, Pa., from 1956. Mem. Am. Osteo. Assn., Nat. Osteopathic Women Physicians Assn., Pa. Osteo. Med. Assn., Lancaster Soc. Osteo. Phys. Surgery, Psi Sigma Alpha. Republican. Avocations: golf, hunting. Home: Normalville, Pa. Died Mar. 20, 2008.

MUCKERMAN, NORMAN JAMES, priest, writer; b. Webster Groves, Mo., Feb. 1, 1917; s. Oliver Christopher and Edna Gertrude (Hartman) M. BA, Immaculate Conception Coll., 1940, M. in Religious Edn., 1942. Ordained priest Roman Catholic Ch., 1942. Missionary Redemptorist Missions, Amazonas, Para, Brazil, 1943-53, procurator missions St. Louis, 1953-58; pastor, adminstr. St. Alphonsus Ch., Chgo., 1958-67, St. Gerard, Kirkwood, Mo., 1967-71; mktg. mgr. circulation Liguori Pubs., Liguori, Mo., 1971-76; editor Liguorian Mag., Liguori, Mo., 1977-89. Author: How to Face Death Without Fear, 1976, Redemptorists on the Amazon, 1992, Preparation for Death, 1998, Into Your Hands, 2001, From the Heart of St. Alphonsus, 2002; contbg. editor: Liguorian, 1989—95; author: Ollie's Story: A Memoir of My Father, 2008. Recipient Nota Dez award Caixa Fed. Do Para, Brazil, 1958 Mem. Cath. Press Assn. (cons. 1971-95, bd. dirs. 1976-85, pres. 1981-84, St. Francis De Sales award 1985). Avocations: reading, writing. Home: Liguori, Mo. Deceased.

MULLER, DAVID EUGENE, retired mathematics professor, computer scientist, educator; b. Austin, Tex., Nov. 2, 1924; s. Hermann Joseph Muller and Jessie Marie Jacobs; m. Denise Josee Impens, Mar. 3, 1990; m. Alice Mimi Held (dec.); children: Kenneth, Chandra. BS, Caltech, Pasadena, 1947, PhD, 1951; PhD (hon.), U. Paris, 1989. Prof. U. Ill., Urbana, 1952—92, prof. emeritus, from 1992. Adj. prof. N.Mex. State U., N.Mex., from 1995. With USN, 1944—46. Fellow: AAAS. Died Apr. 27, 2008.

MULLIGAN, HUGH AUGUSTINE, retired journalist; b. NYC, Mar. 23, 1925; s. John Joseph and Jeanette (Wilton) M.; m. Brigid Mary Murphy, Jan. 14, 1948. BA summa cum laude, Marlboro Coll., 1948, LHD (hon.), 1973; MA in English Lit, Harvard U., 1951; MS in Journalism, Boston U., 1951. With AP, 1952—2000, feature writer NYC, 1956-65, fgn. corr. Vietnam, 1965-68, Biafra, Middle East, Paris Peace Talks, 1968-69, Cambodia, Laos, 1971, No. Ireland, Nigeria, Mid. East, China, Russia, Persian Gulf, Iceland, 1971-75, The Sahel, Angola, Ulster, Svalbard, Iran, 1975-77; as fgn. corr. covered wars in Vietnam, Middle East, Oman, Biafra-Nigeria, Cambodia, Upper Volta-Mali, No. Ireland; as spl corr. covered papal journeys (Pope John Paul II) Mex., Poland, Ireland, U.S., Africa, Cen. Am., Brit. Isles, Can., 1979—2000; columnist Mulligan's Stew, 1977-86. Author: The Torch is Passed, 1963, No Place to Die, The Agony of Vietnam, 1967, (with Sid Moody, John Barbour) Lightning Out of Israel, 1967, anthologies How I Got That Story, 1967, Reporting, Writing from Front Row Seats, 1971, Best Sports Stories, 1980, 82, The Family Book of Humor, The Best of Irish Wit an Wisdom, 1987, The Annotated Night Before Christmas, 1991, (with Sid Moody) The 50th Anniversary: Pearl Harbor, 1991; editor: anthologies The World in 1964, 1965; now A.P. sr. feature writer and roving reporter. Served with U.S. Army, 1944-46. Recipient Gold medal Am. Newspaper Pubs. Assn., 1951, award for feature writing Nat. Headliners, 1963, award for fgn. coverage, 1967, award for internat. reporting Overseas Press Club, 1967, award for fgn. corr. Sigma Delta Chi, 1970, Mng. Editor's award for top reportial performance AP, 1972, 78, Disting. Alumni award Boston U. Sch. Pub. Communication, 1983, Yankee Quill award Acad. New Eng. Journalists, 1993; Eugene Pulliam lectureship Ball State U., 1985. Mem. Overseas Press Club (bd. govs.), Silurians Club, Soc. 1st Divsn. 9th Air Force Assn., Nat. Soc. Newspaper Columnists. Roman Catholic. Home: Ridgefield, Conn. Died Nov. 26, 2008.

MULLIGAN, ROBERT, film director, producer; b. NYC, Aug. 23, 1925; s. Robert Edward and Elizabeth (Gingell) M.; m. Sandy Mulligan, 1961; children from previous marriage: Kevin, Beth, Christopher Grad., Fordham U. With editl. dept. NY Times; messenger boy CBS, prodn. asst. Dir.: (TV episodes) Goodyear TV Playhouse, 1951, Suspense (13 episodes), 1952-54, The Philco TV Playhouse (3 episodes), 1955, The Alcoa Hour (1 episode), 1955, Rendezvous, 1957, Playhouse 90, 1957, 1960, Studio One (3 episodes), 1957, The DuPont Show of the Month (6 episodes), 1958; dir.: (TV movies) The Moon and Sixpence, 1959 (Emmy award for Outstanding Directorial Achievement, 1960); (films) Fear Strikes Out, 1957, The Rat Race, 1960, The Great Impostor, 1961, Come September, 1961, The Spiral Road, 1962, To Kill a Mockingbird, 1962, Love with the Proper Stranger, 1963, Baby the Rain Must Fall, 1965, Inside Daisy Clover, 1965, Up the Down Staircase, 1967, The Stalking Moon, 1968, The Pursuit of Happiness, 1971, Summer of '42, 1971, Bloodbrothers, 1978, Same Time, Next Year, 1978, Clara's Heart, 1988, The Man in the Moon, 1991; dir., prodr.: (films) The Other, 1972, Nickel Ride, 1974, Kiss Me Goodbye, 1982. Served in USMC. Recipient Career Achievement award, LA Film Critics Assn., 2006. Died Dec. 20, 2008.

MULLINS, JEROME JOSEPH, real estate developer, civil engineer, consultant; b. Reedsville, Wis., June 3, 1925; s. James Raymond and Anna (Wilhelm) M.; m. Carol M. Fessler, Sept. 12, 1949; children: Maureen, Brian, Mallory, Bradley, Jerome J. Jr. BSCE, U. Wis., 1950. Registered profl. engr., land surveyor, Wis.; lic. real estate broker and appraiser, Wis. Engr. Gen. Engring. Co., Baraboo, Wis., 1950-51; engring. mgr. George Nelson & Sons, Inc., Madison, Wis., 1951-56, Weiler & Strang Architects/Engrs., Madison, 1956-64; pres. Sample-Mullins Architects/Engrs., Madison, 1964-69; chief exec. officer J.J. Mullins & Assocs., Inc., Madison, from 1969. Pres. Bayview Found., Madison, 1968-72, Greater Madison Conv. and Visitors Bur., 1976-78; bd. dirs. Downtown Madison, Inc., 1976—, Madison Conv. and Visitors Bur., 1986-90; mem. Madison Taxicab Com., 1977-78. Officer USN, 1943-46, PTO. Recipient award Capital Community Citizens, 1974, appreciation award Madison Conv. and Visitors Bur., 1976-79, 87-89, U. Wis. Athletics, 1983, Employer of Yr. award Goodwill Industries South Cen. Wis., 1981, award Downtown Madison, Inc., 1986, award for support Badger State Games, 1989. Mem. NSPE, AIA (assoc.), Nat. Bd. Realtors, Nat. Constrn. Specifications Instr., Wis. Soc. Profl. Engrs., Profl. Engrs. in Pvt. Practice, Wis. Soc. Registered Land Surveyors. Avocations: boating, hunting, reading. Home: Madison, Wis. Died May 25, 2008.

MULRYAN, LENORE HOAG, art curator, writer; b. Lompoc, Calif., Aug. 25, 1927; d. William Thomas and Lois Lorraine (Fratis) Hoag; m. Henry Trist Mulryan; children: Patricia Trist (dec.), James William, Carrie M. Neal. BA in Art History, UCLA, 1979, postgrad., 1979—81; Cert., Am. Inst. Fgn. Trade, Glendale, Ariz., 1949. Vis. art curator UCLA Fowler Mus. Cultural History, 1982—2004; art curator, editor, cons. Internat. Exec. Svc. Corps, 1998. Dir. fine art print calendars for Chapin Sch., Princeton, NJ, 1971-73; co-chair Fine Arts Tours, Princeton, 1973; cons. Internat. Exec. Svc. Corp., Zimbabwe, 1998, Romania, 1998. Author, art curator, editor: (books/exhbns.) Mexican Figural Ceramists and Their Works, 1982, UCLA Fowler Mus. Cultural History, Nagual in the Garden: Fantastic Animals in Mexican Ceramics, 1996, Ceramic Trees of Life: Popular Art from Mexico, 2003-04, UCLA Fowler Mus. Cultural History, 2003—, At the Crossroads of Tonala and Tlaquepaque: 1920-1945; curator Wilmot Collection of Mexican Art, 1982-1991. Mem. Eisenhauer Disting. Fgn. Leader Program U. So. Calif. Mem. Exec. Svc. Corps, Delphians (pres. 1963-64), Westwood Village Rotary Club (chair amb. scholarship selection com. 2000-05). Avocations: music, art, yoga, travel. Home: Pacific Palisades, Calif. Died Aug. 26, 2008.

MUNCY, ESTLE PERSHING, physician; b. Tazewell, Tenn., Apr. 9, 1918; s. William Loyd and Flora Media (Monday) M.; m. Dorothy Davis, Dec. 31, 1946 (div. Apr. 1980); children: Robert H., Teresa A., Dorothy J., Estle II,James; m. Jean Marie Hayter, Mar. 19, 1985. AB, Lincoln Meml. U., 1939; MD, U. Tenn., 1943. Resident Dallas Meth. Hosp., 1948; tchg. resident Tufts Med. Sch., Boston, 1949-50; physician Jefferson City, Tenn., 1950-96. Author: The Muncys in the New World, 1988, People and Places in Jefferson County, Tennessee, 1994. Alderman Jefferson City, 1974-77; chmn. Jefferson City Planning Commn., 1976-79. Capt. M.C., U.S. Army, 1944-46. Recipient Commendation for work on Tenn. history Gov. Don Sundquist,

Jefferson award Am. Inst. Pub. Svc., 1995, Covenant Health Platinum award, 2000; named to Lincoln Meml. U. Lit. and Profl. Halls of Fame, 1997. Mem. Tenn. Heart Assn. (pres. 1966-67), Hamblen County Med. Soc. (pres. 1960-61), Jefferson County Hist. Soc. (pres. 1993-94, historian 1995—). Republican. Baptist. Avocations: photography, gardening. Home: Jefferson City, Tenn. Died Dec. 20, 2007.

MUNOZ, ERIC, state legislator, surgeon; b. NYC, Oct. 14, 1947; s. William Munoz and Frances Turzanowsky; m. Nancy Foster, Jan. 21, 1984; children: William III, Eric Jr., Alexander, Elizabeth, Maximillian. BA, U. Va., 1969; MD, Albert Einstein Coll. Medicine, 1974; MBA, Columbia U., 1983. Diplomate Am. Bd. Surgery. Instr. Yale-New Haven Med. Ctr., 1978-79, NY Med. Coll., NYC, 1979-80, asst. prof., 1980-81; attending surgeon Lincoln Hosp. Ctr., NYC, 1981-83, Long Island Jewish Hosp., New Hyde Park, N.Y., 1983-88, Queens Hosp. Ctr., Jamaica, N.Y., 1983-88, physician-in-charge, 1983-85; mem. NJ State Assembly from Dist. 21, 2001—09, dep. conf. leader, 2006—09. Attending surgeon, med. dir., assoc. dean clin. affairs, prof., med. affairs liaison UMDNJ-NJ Med. Sch., Newark, 1988-2009; com. mem., NIH, 2002-09. Contbr. articles to profl. jours. Mem. City of Summit Common Coun., N.J., 1996-2001; chair, bd. dirs. Nat. P.R. Coalition, Washington, 1994-98, bd. dirs., 1998-2009; chair Med. Practitioner Rev. Panel, Trenton, N.J., 1990-2001; bd. dirs. N.J. Ballet, 1995-2009, Robert Treat Newark Boy Scouts, 1998-2009. Mem. Soc. Univ. Surgeons, Am. Surg. Assn. Republican. Avocations: antique cars, model steam engines, steamboats, reading, movies. Died Mar. 30, 2009.

MUNRO, MARTHA, opera company executive; b. Boston, Mar. 20, 1947; d. James C. and Kathryn (Walker) M. Student, Stephens Coll., Columbia, Mo., 1965-67. Artistic adminstr. Opera Co. Boston, 1967-73; dir. rehearsal dept. San Francisco Opera, 1970-72, founder, dir. Brown Bag opera, 1972-73, dir. publicity, 1973-74, dir. artistic devel., 1974-75; dir. mktg. and communications Houston Grand Opera, 1975-77; asst. artistic adminstr. Met. Opera, NYC, 1977-78; ptnr. Lombardo Munro Assocs., NYC, 1978-80; pres. Munro Artists Mgmt., NYC, from 1980. Mem. OperaAmerica. Democrat. Unitarian Universalist. Avocations: gardening, land conservation. Died Dec. 18, 2007.

MUNSON, NANCY K., lawyer; b. Huntington, NY, June 22, 1936; d. Howard H. and Edna M. (Keenan) Munson. Student, Hofstra U., 1959—62; JD, Bklyn. Law Sch., 1965. Bar: NY 1966, U.S. Dist. Ct. (ea. and so. dists.) NY 1968, U.S. Supreme Ct. 1970, U.S. Ct. Appeals (2d cir.) 1971. Law clk. to Hon. E. Merritt Weidner, Huntington, NY, 1959—66; pvt. practice, 1966. Legal adv. bd. Chgo. Title Ins. Co., Riverhead, NY, from 1981; bd. dirs., legal officer Thomas Munson Found. Trustee Huntington Fire Dept. Death Benefit Fund; pres., trustee, chmn. bd. dirs. Bklyn. Home Aged Men Found.; bd. dirs. Huntington Rural Cemetery Assn., Inc.; trustee Noyac Harbor Property Owners Assn. Mem.: DAR (trustee, treas. Ketewamoke chpt.), NRA, ABA, Federalist Soc. for Law and Pub. Policy Studies, Bklyn. Bar Assn., Suffolk County Bar Assn., N.Y. State Bar Assn., Soroptimists (past pres.). Republican. Christian Scientist. Died May 3, 2009.

MURCKO, DONALD LEROY, architect; b. Warren, Ohio, Jan. 24, 1953; s. Joseph Mathew and Sophie May (Hidukawich) M.; m. Marilyn A. Infante, Oct. 3, 1998. BArch, Kent State U., 1977. Registered architect, Ohio. Archtl. draftsman Angel Constrn. Co., Garrettsville, Ohio, 1977-80; apprentice architect E.S. Jakubick & Assoc.s, Warren, Ohio, 1980-82; assoc. architect Mosure & Assocs., Inc., Youngstown, Ohio, 1982-90; project architect MS Consultants, Inc., Youngstown, 1990-91, Buchanan Ricciuti Balog, Youngstown, Ohio, 1991-96, Ricciuti Balog and Ptnrs., Youngstown, from 1996. Cons. architect VA, Cleve., 1986—. Mem. Western Pa. Conservancy, Pitts., 1985—, Mahoning Valley Hist. Soc., Youngstown, 1989—, Butler Inst. Am. Art, Youngstown, 1991—. Recipient Cert. of Merit, Ohio Edison Co., 1976. Mem. AIA, Architects Soc. Ohio, Cath. Alumni Club Youngstown (past pres.). Democrat. Roman Catholic. Avocations: architecture, illustration, modelmaking, photography, travel. Died July 10, 2008.

MURDOCK, ROBERT MEAD, curator; b. NYC, Dec. 18, 1941; s. Robert Davidson and Elizabeth Brundage (Mead) M.; m. Ellen Rebecca Olson, Apr. 22, 1967 (div.); children: Alison Mead, Anne Davidson; m. Deborah C. Ryan, Apr. 28, 1995. BA, Trinity Coll., Conn., 1963; MA, Yale U., 1965; student, Mus. Mgmt. Inst., U. Calif., Berkeley, 1980. Ford Found. intern Walker Art Center, Mpls., 1965-67; curator Albright-Knox Art Gallery, Buffalo, 1967-70; curator contemporary art Dallas Mus. Fine Arts, 1970-78; dir. Grand Rapids (Mich.) Art Mus., 1978-83; chief curator Walker Art Ctr., Mpls., 1983-85; program dir. IBM Gallery of Sci. and Art, NYC, 1985-87, 90-93; dir. exhbns. Am. Fedn. Arts, NYC, 1987-[illegible]. Panelist, cons. Nat. Endowment for Arts, 1974-90. Author: (with others) Tyler Graphics: The Extended Image, 1987, A Gallery of Modern Art, 1994, Paris Modern, The Swedish Ballet 1920-1925, 1995, Works by Leland Bell, 1950's-1991, 2001, Constellation, Pavel Zoubok Gallery, NYC, 2006; contbr. articles on David Novros, William Conlon, 1985, Bill Freeland, 1989, Nassos Daphnis, 1990, Cai Guo-Qiang, 1998, John Evans, 2004; exhbn. catalogues Early 20th Century Art from Midwestern Museums, 1981, Berlin/Hanover: The 1920's, 1977, Richard Tuttle: Books and Prints, 1996, Lesley Dill, 1998, Jim Torok, 1999, Debra Bermingham, 2002. Nat. Endowment for Arts fellow, 1973 Died Oct. 9, 2009.

MURPHY, JUDITH L., nursing administrator, gerontology nurse; b. Cleve., June 11, 1945; d. Chester and Winona (Addis) Noel; children: Sean, Lisa. Diploma, Mercy Sch. Nursing, Toledo, 1966; student, Spokane Falls Community Coll., Graceland Coll., Lamoni, Iowa. RN, Ohio; cert. in gerontology. Home: Batavia, Ohio. Died Mar. 3, 2008.

MURPHY, KATHLEEN MARY, former law firm executive, alternative healing professional; b. Bklyn., Dec. 16, 1945; d. Raymond Joseph and Catherine Elizabeth (Kearney) Murphy. BA in Edn., Molloy Coll., Rockville Centre, NY, 1971; MS in Edn., Bklyn. Coll., 1975. Ordained minister Ch. of the Loving Servant; cert. hypnotherapist; cert. elem. sch. tchr., NY. Elem. sch. tchr. various parochial schs., LI, Bklyn., Queens, NY, 1969-80; from asst. prin. to prin. parochial sch. Queens, 1980-82; supr.-trainer Davis, Polk, Wardwell law firm, NYC, 1982-88; mgr. Schulte Roth & Zabel, NYC, 1988-95; Reiki master (alternative healing profl.), from 1996. Trainer program for new employees, 1984; speaker edn. topics, Bklyn., Queens, 1979-81. Mem.: NAFE, Reiki Alliance. Democrat. Roman Catholic. Avocations: psychic phenomenon, workings of mind, ancient histories, crossword puzzles, museums. Home: Brooklyn, NY. Died Oct. 20, 2008.

MURPHY, THOMAS E., III, telecommunications industry executive; m. Jennifer Murphy; 3 children. BA in History and Polit. Sci., U. Kans. With Jasculca Termin and Assocs., 1988; various acct. exec. pos. Bozell Inc. and Edelman Worldwide Pub. Rels.; acct. supr. Barkley Evergreen and Ptnrs. Pub. Rels.; dir. media rels. and fin. comm., PCS divsn. Sprint Corp., 1996—2000, v.p. comm. and pub. rels., PCS divsn., 2000—03, sr. v.p. corp. comm. and brand mgmt., 2003—05; v.p. corp. brand mktg. Sprint Nextel Corp., from 2005. Mem.: Cellular Telecomm. and Internet Assn. (bd. dirs. Wireless Found.). Died Aug. 16, 2009; Colorado.

MURRAY, BRUCE WELLINGTON, advertising executive; b. Buffalo, July 4, 1934; s. Roy Francis and Grace Emma (Philips) M.; m. Sandra Joyce Halley, Jan. 29, 1957 (dec. Nov. 1978); children: Heather, Dawn, Lisa; m. Charlotte Roberts Brown, Dec. 31, 1994. BS in Mktg., Lehigh U., 1956. Mgr. Market Research Assocs., Darien, Conn., 1956-57; research dir. Wilson Assocs., NYC, 1957-59; dir. mktg. O.E. McIntyre Metro Mail, NYC, 1960-64; exec. v.p. Chapman Direct Advt., NYC, 1964-90; pres. Murray Mktg. Assocs., Rockport, MA, from 1990. Author: Mailing Lists: A Practical Guide, 1984; columnist Direct Mag., 1990-93; contbr. articles to profl. mag. Bd. dirs. Wellspring House, Gloucester, Mass., 1993-97, Lighthouse Preservation Soc., Newburyport, Mass., 1992-97, chmn., 1996-97. Rcipient Silver EFFIE award Am. Mktg. Assn., 1985. Mem. Assn. Dir. Mktg. Agys., Direct Mktg. Assn. (ECHO awards 1979, 83), Dir. Mktg. Club N.Y. (bd. dirs. 1989, treas. 1989). Mem. Ch. of Christ. Club: Norwalk (Conn.) Yacht. Avocations: sailing, travel, reading, woodworking. Home: Rockport, Mass. Died Sept. 15, 2007.

MURRAY, CARL OTIS, JR., family practice physician, geriatrician; b. Crockett, Tex., Dec. 28, 1925; s. Carl Otis and Verna Emma (Harrison) M.; m. Roberta Evans, Oct. 2, 1976; children: Carla Elizabeth M. Shaver, William Hervey Wells. MD, Tulane U., 1948. Diplomate Am. Bd. Family Practice, Am. Bd. Geriat. Pvt. practice physician, Crockett, 1949-93; sch. physician Crockett State Sch., 1951-95; med. dir. Rural Primary Health Clinic, Crockett, from 1993. Episcopalian. Home: Crockett, Tex. Died Dec. 2, 2007.

MURRAY, EDWARD, retired state legislator; b. Decherd, Tenn., Aug. 16, 1928; s. Richard Oliver and Patty (Moffatt) M.; m. Sandra Gail Fields, 1969. Student, Univ. South, 1946-49; BS, Mid Tenn. State U., 1951; JD, YMCA Night Law Sch., 1965. Asst. dir. Tenn. Aeronaut Commn., 1965-67; mem. Tenn. House. Reps., 1971—90, speaker of house, 1987—90. With USN, 1951-53. Mem. Am. Legion, Quiet Birdmen, Franklin County C. of C. (past pres.). Died May 29, 2009.

MURRAY, ELEANOR F., educator, freelance writer; b. Omaha, Nov. 30, 1916; d. Fred Blatchford and Calista June (Reynolds) Greusel; m. Jack Earl Buckley, June 15, 1970 (dec. Nov. 1977); m. Hubert Larkin Murray; children: Thomas M. B. Hicks, Mary E. Sharp, Barbara R. Wilke. BS in Edn., U. Nebr., 1939. Cert. tchr. of English. Newswriter Etowah Observer, Alabama City, Ala., 1939-40; feature writer Stars 'n Stripes, Tokyo, 1947-51; columnist Japan Times, Tokyo, 1949-51; in pub. relations Am. Internat. Underwriters, Tokyo, 1948-51; writer news and features Paterson (N.J.) Evening News, 1952-54; tchr. Riverdale (N.J.) Sch., 1954-55, Panama Canal Zone Schs., 1955-60, Skokie (Ill.) Schs., 1961-66; freelance writer Sebring, Fla., from 1980. Author: (non-fiction) Bend Like the Bamboo, 1982, Growing Up In Aunt Molly's Omaha, 1990; (poetry) Cherokee County Summer, 1981, God's Green Valley, 1983; author articles. Democrat. Presbyterian. Avocations: reading, swimming. Died July 20, 2008.

MURRAY, JOHN EINAR, lawyer, retired military officer, federal official; b. Clifton, NJ, Nov. 22, 1918; s. Joseph Michael and Maru Elizabeth (Liljeros) M.; m. Elaine Claire Riehlmann (dec. 1970); 1 dau., Valerie Anne; m. Phyllis Irene Harris (div. 1989). Student, St. Johns U., 1938-41; LLB, N.Y. Law Sch., 1949, LLD, 1975; MA, George Washington U., 1961. lectr. U.S. Marine Corps Nat. Def. U.; mem. sci. panel of White House Agent Orange Working Group, Def. Intelligence Agy. Task Force on POWS and MIAS; participant Georgetown U. Panel on Crisis Mgmt. Drafted pvt. U.S. Army, 1941, advanced through grades to maj. gen., 1972; comdr. truck group Europe Mil. Ports, Vietnam and maj. logistic units, 1968; dir. Army Transp., 1969-70; chief logistics Pacific Command, 1970-72, Mil. Assistance Command, Vietnam, 1972-73; def. attache Vietnam, 1973-74; ret., 1974; v.p. Assn. Am. Railroads, Washington, 1974-84; spl. counsel Am. Internat. Underwriters, 1985; prin. dep. asst. sec. of def. for spl. ops. and low intensity conflict, 1988-89; with Am. Internat. Group Cos., Washington, 1989; spl. counsel Snavely, King & Assocs., Inc. (econ. cons.), Washington, from 1990. Adv. bd. U.S. Army Transp. Mus.; lectr. Nat. Def. U.; mem. sci. panel of White House Agent Orange Working Group, Def. Intelligence Agy. Task Force on POWs and MIAs; participant Georgetown U. Panel on Crisis Mgmt. Author: (with A.M. Chester) Orders and Directive, 1952, (with V.F. Caputo) Quick on the Vigor, 1966, The Myths of Business and the Business of Myths, 1975, The Third Curse of Moses, 1975, The Military Mind and the New Mindlessness, 1976, Lawyers, Computers and Power, 1977, Pothole Plague and Knothole Outlook, 1978, Railroads, Terrorism and the Pinkerton Legacy, 1978, Raising Corn and Beans and Hell, 1979, Remembering Who You Are, 1979, Running A Muck— The Folly of Coal Slurry, 1979, The Railroads and the Energy Crisis, 1980, U.S. Security Assistance— The Vietnam Experience, 1980, Hopeless Cause or Cause of Hope, 1980, War, Transport and Show Biz, 1981, Forget Everything You Ever Knew About the Japanese Railroads, 1981, Sweet Adversity: The U.S. Army-How It Motivates, 1982, Random Danger: The Railroad Response, 1983, Vietnam Logistics: An American Debacle, 1984, Dead Headheads and Warheads, 1987; Operation Desert Shield: The Smart Way to War, 1991; He Was There, 1992, The Logistics of Limited Wars, 1992, The United Nations: Sizing Up Consultant Prospects, 1992, How to Win a Lost War, 1997; contbr.: book revs. to Nat. Def. Transp. Mag., Time-Life books., Vietnam mag. Decorated D.S.M., Legion of Merit with 4 oak leaf clusters, Bronze Star medal, Joint Services Commendation medal with oak leaf cluster, Army Commendation medal with 2 oak leaf clusters, Sec. of Def. medal for Outstanding Pub. Svc., Italian Cross of War, Knight Order of Crown of Italy, Korean Chung Mu with gold star, Vietnamese Kim Khanh medal 1st class, Vietnamese Army Distinguished Service Order 1st class, Vietnamese Navy Distinguished Service Order 1st class, Vietnamese Air Force Distinguished Service Order 1st class, Vietnamese Gallantry Cross with palm, 1998, US Army Transportation Corps Hall of Fame. Mem. Spl. Forces Assn., Nat. Def. Transp. Assn., Army War Coll. Grad. Assn., Army and Navy Club, WWII Meml. Soc. (charter). Deceased.

MURRAY, PETER, retired metallurgist, manufacturing executive; b. Rotherham, Yorkshire, Eng., Mar. 13, 1920; came to U.S., 1967, naturalized, 1974; s. Michael and Ann (Hamstead) M.; m. Frances Josephine Glaisher, Sept. 8, 1947 (dec. 2007); children: Jane, Paul, Alexander. BSc in Chemistry with honors, Sheffield U., Eng., 1941, postgrad., 1946-49; PhD in Metallurgy, Brit. Iron and Steel Research Bursar, Sheffield, 1948. Research chemist Steetley Co., Ltd., Worksop, Notts, Eng., 1941-45; with Atomic Energy Research Establishment, Harwell, Eng., 1949-67, head div. metallurgy, 1960-64, asst. dir., 1964-67; tech. dir., mgr. fuels and materials, advanced reactors div. Westinghouse Electric Corp., Madison, Pa., 1967-74; dir. research Westinghouse Electric Europe (S.A.), Brussels, 1974-75; chief scientist advanced power systems divs. Westinghouse Electric Corp., Madison, Pa., 1975-81, dir. nuclear programs Washington, 1981-92; sr. cons. Nuc. Programs, 1992—2001. Mem. divisional rev. coms. Argonne Nat. Lab., 1968-73; Mellor Meml. lectr. Inst. Ceramics, 1963 Contbr. numerous articles to profl. jours.; editorial adv. bd.: Jour. Less Common Metals, 1968-2009 Recipient Holland Meml. Research prize, Sheffield U., 1949. Fellow Royal Inst. Chemistry (Newton Chambers Research prize 1954), Inst. Ceramics, Am. Nuclear Soc.; mem. Brit. Ceramics Soc. (pres. 1965), Am. Ceramic Soc., Nat. Acad. Engring. Roman Catholic. Home: Montgomery Village, Md. Died July 26, 2009.

MURRAY, RAYMOND LEE, retired clothing designer, writer; b. Decatur, Tenn., July 27, 1920; s. Floyd Lester and Ida Mae (McClure) M.; m. Melba Lee Murray, Dec. 21, 1947; 1 child, Alice Marie. Cert. indsl. engring., U. Tenn., 1946; cert. clothing designer, Am. Gentlemen Sch. Design, NYC, 1947. Foreman, designer Hardwick Clothes, Cleveland, Tenn., 1938-55; designer Sears Roebuck Plant, Rutherford, Tenn., 1956-59; designer, plant mgr. McGregor Sportswear, Corinth, Miss., 1960-67; plant mgr. Cable Industries, Tuskegee, Ala., 1968-69; gen. mgr. T&W Mfg. Co., Bremen, Ga., 1969; mem. R&D staff Hardwick Clothes, Cleveland, Tenn., 1970-86; pres. Murray-Wright Protection Clothing, Cleveland, Tenn., 1985-95. Cons. textiles and bullet-proof fabric Murray Textile Anaylsts, Cleveland, Tenn., 1985-95. Author: Grandpa Saw it Happen WWII Normandy Beach, To Elbe, 1993, How We Uprooted Our Roots and What We Found, 1996, Bradley Divided: During Civil War, 1992; contbr. articles to profl. jours. Bd. dirs. ARC, Cleveland chpt., 1980-83, Cleveland YMCA, 1950-54. With U.S. Army, ETO. Decorated 5 Bronze Stars. Mem. VFW, Internat. Assn. Clothing Designers (pres. 1977; pres. So. chpt. 1972), Am. Soc. Quality Control (chair Tenn. chpt. 1952), Am. Legion, Elks, Vets. Battle of the Bulge, Kiwanis. Presbyterian. Avocations: fishing, hunting. Home: Decatur, Ga. Died Nov. 20, 2007.

MURRAY, RUSSELL, II, aeronautical engineer, security consultant; b. Woodmere, NY, Dec. 5, 1925; s. Herman Stump and Susanne Elizabeth (Warren) M.; m. Sally Tingue Gardiner, May 22, 1954; children: Ann Tingue, Prudence Warren, Alexandria Gardiner. BS in Aero. Engring, MIT, 1949, MS, 1950. Guided missile flight test engr. Grumman Aircraft Engring. Corp., Bethpage, NY, 1950-53, asst. chief operations analysis, 1953-62; prin. dep. asst. sec. for systems analysis US Dept. Def., Washington, 1962-69; dir. long range planning Pfizer Internat., NYC, 1969-73; dir. review Ctr. for Naval Analyses, Arlington, Va., 1973-77; asst. sec. for program analysis and evaluation US Dept. Def., Washington, 1977-81; prin. Systems Research & Applications Corp., Arlington, Va., 1981-85; spl. counsellor Com. on Armed Services US Ho. Com. on Armed Services, 1985-89; cons. Ctr. for Naval Analyses, 1989—2004. Served with USAAF, 1944-45. Recipient Medal for Meritorious Civilian Svc., US Dept. Def., 1968, Disting. Public Service medal, 1981 Home: Alexandria, Va. Died Jan. 26, 2009.

MUSE, SCOTT THOMAS, JR., business owner; b. Oklahoma City, Sept. 6, 1930; s. Scott T. Sr. and Cathren (Fisher) M.; m. Lesta L. Muse, Aug. 6, 1950; children: Daniel, Pamela, Matthew, Mark. AA, Southwestern Coll., 1950, LittD, 1979. Owner Muse Investment Co., Rolla, Kans., 1954-70, Oklahoma City, 1970-76; pres. Southwestern Coll., Oklahoma City, 1976-80; owner Muse & Assocs., Oklahoma City, from 1980. Mem. Nat. Assn. Real Estate Appraisers, Southwestern Assn. Real Estate Appraisers. Avocations: skiing, raising orchids. Home: Stratford, Okla. Died Aug. 18, 2007.

MUSSER, THARON MYRENE, theatrical lighting designer, theatre consultant; b. Roanoke, Va., Jan. 8, 1925; d. George C. and Hazel (Riddle) M.; life ptnr., Marilyn Rennagel BA, Berea Coll., 1946; H.H.D., 1979; M.F.A., Yale U., 1950; H.H.D., Emerson Coll., 1980. Lighting designer over 100 Broadway prodns.; lighting designer for repertory theatre including, Jose Limon Dance Co., 1953-56, Group 20 Players of Mass., 1954-56, Phoenix Theatre Co., 1957-60, Am. Theatre Festival, Boston, 1961, Boston Arts Festival, 1962, Empire State Music Festival, 1959, Nat. Repertory Theatre Co., 1961-68, Am. Shakespeare Festival Theatre and Acad., 1963-68, Lincoln Center Repertory Theatre, 1968, Dallas Civic Opera, 1969-77, New Phoenix Repertory Co., 1972, Miami Opera Guild, 1975-78, Wolf Trap Found., Filene Center for Performing Arts, 1977; staff designer, Mark Taper Forum, Los Angeles Center Theatre Group, 1970-86; lighting designer internat. prodns. including, Jose Limon Dance Co. State Dept. Tour, S. Am., 1953; London prodns. Golden Boy, 1968, Mame, 1969, Applause, 1972, A Little Night Music, 1975, They're Playing Our Song, 1979, London Ballet Festival Romeo and Juliet, 1977; London prodn. Ziegfeld, 1988; internat. prodn. A Chorus Line, 1976; lighting designer and cons. internat. prodn., Ford's Theatre Restoration and TV prodn., Washington, 1968, Man and the Universe at, Hemisfair, San Antonio, 1968, Chgo. Auditorium, 1968, Los Angeles Shubert Theatre, 1971, Dallas Music Hall, Berea Coll. Dramatic Arts Center, 1976-80; London prodn. Children of a Lesser God, 1981, Cakewalk, 1996, 2 Pionas 4 Hands, 1997, 15 Neil Simon shows including, Broadway Bound, Rumors, The Goodbye Girl and Lost in Yonkers. Recipient Los Angeles Drama Critics' Circle award for Dream on Monkey Mountain, 1970, for Follies, 1972, for Pacific Overtures, a Chorus Line, 1976-77, for Terra Nova, 1979; Antoinette Perry award for Follies, 1971-72, for A Chorus Line, 1975-76, for Dreamgirls, 1981-82; Yale arts award, 1985; Theatre Hall of Fame award, 1985 Mem. United Scenic Artists, Soc. Brit. Theatrical Lighting Designers, U.S. Inst. Theatre Tech. Died Apr. 12, 2009.

MUSSLER, CAROLE A., medical/surgical nurse; b. St. Louis, Dec. 23, 1940; d. Herbert C. and Margaret A. (Winkelmann) M. Diploma, Luth. Med. Ctr., 1961; BS in Social Psychology, Park Coll., 1983; MS in Counseling, Ga. State U., 1988. RN, Mo., Ga., Va. Commd. 2d lt. U.S. Army, 1967, advanced through grades to maj.; asst. chief operating room DDE Army Med. Ctr., Ft. Gordon, Ga., Fitzsimmons Army Med. Ctr., Aurora, Colo.; chief operating room/CMS Martin Army Hosp., Columbus, Ga., staff nurse operating room, postanesthesia care unit; resigned U.S. Army, 1987. Decorated Bronze Star. Mem. Assn. Operating Room Nurses. Home: Radcliff, Ky. Died May 4, 2008.

MUTZEL, ROBERT ARTHUR, sociology and psychology educator, consultant; b. Lancaster, Pa., Jan. 31, 1948; s. Robert Louis and Esther M. (Miller) M.; m. Barbara Anne Karl, Aug. 25, 1990; children: Heather Erica, Sarah Ashley. BS, Elizabethtown Coll., 1974; MSS, Bryn Mawr Coll., 1976, postgrad., 1976-80. Adj. instr. sociology Del. Tech. and C.C., Wilmington, 1975-77, Del. County C.C., Media, Pa., 1977-87; mgmt. devel. instr., asst. dir. career svcs. York (Pa.) Tech. Inst., 1988-91; tech. prep. program coord., adj. instr. sociology, psychology Reading (Pa.) Area C.C., from 1991; adj. instr. mgmt. devel. Pace Inst., Reading, from 1995. Bd. dirs. Learning Quest Tng. and Devel., Sinking Spring, Pa., 1994—. Mem. ASTD, Reading Area Trainers Orgn. Avocations: tennis, reading, computers, personal fitness. Home: Ephrata, Pa. Died May 9, 2008.

MYERS, GERALD EUGENE, humanities educator; b. Central City, Nebr., June 19, 1923; s. Harold W. and Mary (Ferguson) M.; m. Martha Coleman, Aug. 7, 1948; 1 son, Curt. BA, Haverford Coll., 1947; MA, Brown U., 1949, PhD, 1954. Instr. Smith Coll., 1950-52; asst. prof. Williams

Coll., 1952-61; assoc. prof. Kenyon Coll., 1961-65; prof. C.W. Post Coll., L.I. U., 1965-67, Queens Coll. and Grad. Center, City U. N.Y., 1967—2009; dep. exec. officer Ph.D program Queens Coll. and Grad. Center, City U. N.Y. (Grad. Center); dir. intro. philosophy into N.Y.C. High Schs. project.; prof. emeritus CUNY. Dir. humanities-and-dance projects, philosopher-in-residence Am. Dance Festival, Durham, N.C., 1979; project dir. African-Am. Perspectives in Am. Modern Dance, Am. Dance Festival/NEH. Author: Self, Religion and Metaphysics, 1961, Self: An Introduction to Philosophical Psychology, 1969, The Spirit of American Philosophy, 1970, William James: His Life and Thought, 1986; editor: The Black Tradition in American Modern Dance, 1988, African American Genius in Modern Dance, 1992; co-editor: Emotion Philos. Studies, 1983, Echoes from the Holocaust, 1988, Who's Not Afraid of Marta Graham?, 2008; cons.: (documentaries) Free to Dance, 2001; contbr. articles to profl. jours. NEH fellow, 1981-82. Mem. Am. Philos. Assn. (past sec.-treas. Western div.), Metaphys. Soc. Am., Soc. Phenomenology and Existential Philosophy, Phi Beta Kappa. Home: New London, Conn. Died Feb. 11, 2009.

MYERS, GERALDINE RUTH, special education educator, consultant; b. Massillon, Ohio, Apr. 22, 1924; d. Clinton Alvin and Edna Frances (Piper) Koontz; m. Ralph Richards; children: Beth (Richards) Herthel, Robyn; m. Gerald Thomas Myers. BA, Heidelberg Coll., Tiffin, Ohio, 1946; MA, Wayne State U., Detroit, 1962. Tchr. South Rockwood H.S., Mich., 1946-48; secondary sch. tchr. Riverview Cmnty. Schs., Mich., 1953-59, secondary counselor Mich., 1959-63; social worker Washoe County Welfare Dept., Reno, 1963-64; tchr. Washoe County Sch. Dist., Reno, 1964-66, s.e. transitional counselor, 1966-90; ednl. cons., from 1990. Summer relief case worker Washoe County Welfare Dept., 1964-66; guest lectr. U. Nev., Reno, 1967-75, supr. student tchrs., 1990—; lectr. Truckee Meadows C.C., Reno, 1979-88. Editor: (newsletter sch. dist. s.e.) Of Special Note, 1969-90. Mem. Nev. Gov.'s Com. on Employment of Handicapped, 1990. Nev. winner for School-Work Experience Program, Nat. Sch. Adminstrs., 1989; inducted in Lake Hall of Fame, Hartville, Ohio, 1996. Mem. Coun. for Exceptional Children (pres. 1986-87, newsletter editor 1983-89, Frank South award 1987), Washoe County Tchrs. Assn. (disting. svc. award 1977), Phi Delta Kappa (educator of yr. 1984). Republican. Home: Reno, Nev. Died Oct. 10, 2007.

MYERS, LOUIS SAMUEL, obstetrician, gynecologist; b. Detroit, June 15, 1941; s. Cecil and Bessie Myers; m. Gloria A. Garber, Mar. 19, 1972; children: Stephanie, Robert. BA in Philosophy, Wayne State U., 1962, MD, 1966. Diplomate Am. Bd. Obstetrics and Gynecology. Rotating intern Wayne State U., Detroit, 1967; ob-gyn specialist tng. U. Chgo. Lying In Hosp., 1972; attending physician Prentice Hosp., Northwestern Meml. Hosp., Chgo., from 1972, Near North Adult Med. Ctr., Chgo., 1972-77; med. dir. Albany Med. Surgery Outpatient Ctr., Chgo., from 1974. From instr. to assoc. prof. dept. ob-gyn Northwestern U., 1972—. Mem. B'nai Brith. Served to capt. M.C., USAF, 1968-70. Mem. AMA, Ill. Med. Soc., Chgo. Med. Soc., Am. Coll. Ob-Gyn, Am. Fertility Soc., Assn. Profs. in Ob-Gyn, Assn. Gynecol. Laparoscopists, Assn. Planned Parenthood Profls., Pitts. Inst. Legal Medicine. Avocations: stamp collecting/philately, painting, swimming. Home: Northbrook, Ill. Died Feb. 8, 2008.

MYERS, LOWELL JACK, lawyer; b. LA, Jan. 26, 1930; s. Joseph and Annie (Shafer) M.; m. Sibyl Kagen, 1953 (dec. 1970); children: Lynda, Benjamin. BSc, Roosevelt U., 1951; MBA, U. Chgo., 1951; JD with honors, John Marshall Law Sch., 1956. Bar: Ill. 1956, U.S. Dist. Ct. (no. dist.) Ill. 1956, U.S. Ct. Appeals (7th cir.) 1958, U.S. Supreme Ct. 1960. Pvt. practice, Chgo., from 1956. Author: The Law and the Deaf, 1964, How to Handle Cases of Police Brutality, 1987. Named Disting. Alumnus, John Marshall Law Sch., 1979. Jewish. Died Nov. 7, 2006.

MYHRE, BYRON ARNOLD, pathologist, educator; b. Fargo, ND, Oct. 22, 1928; s. Ben Arnold and Amy Lillian (Gilbertson) M.; m. Eileen Marguerite Scherling, June 16, 1953; children: Patricia Ann, Bruce Allen. BS, U. Ill. Champaign/Urbana, 1950; MS, Northwestern U., Evanston, Ill., 1952, MD, 1953; PhD, U. Wis., Madison, 1962. Intern Evanston Hosp., Ill., 1953-54; resident Children's Meml. Hosp., Chgo., 1956-57, U. Wis. Hosp., Madison, 1957-60; assoc. med. dir. Milw. Blood Ctr., 1962-66; sci. dir. L.A. Red Cross Blood Ctr., 1966-72; dir. Blood Bank Harbor-UCLA Med. Ctr., Torrance, Calif., 1972-85, chief clin. pathology, 1985-2000; prof. pathology UCLA, 1972-2000, prof. emeritus from 2000. Author: Quality Control on Blood Banking, 1974; (with others) Textbook of Clinical Pathology, 1972, Paternity Testing, 1975; editor seminar procs.; contbr. articles to profl. jours., chpts. to books. With USAF, 1954—56. Mem.: AMA, Harbor-UCLA Faculty Soc. (past pres.), Wis. Blood Bank Assn. (past pres.), LA Acad. Medicine (past pres.), Calif. Blood Bank Sys. (past pres.), Calif. Med. Assn., Assn. Clin. Scientists (past pres.), Coll. Am. Pathologists (chmn. blood bank survey com.), Am. Assn. Blood Banks (pres. 1978—79), Am. Soc. Clin. Pathology (dep. commr. commn. on continuing edn.), Palos Verdes Breakfast Club (past pres.). Home: Palos Verdes Estates, Calif. Died Apr. 27, 2009.

NABHOLZ, JOSEPH VINCENT, biologist, ecologist; b. Memphis, Nov. 3, 1945; s. Martin Peter and Helen Kathleen (Garbacz) N.; m. Sue Ann Winterburn, Aug. 12, 1972;

children: Karen Stacey, Pamela Michelle. BS, Christian Bros. U., Memphis, 1968; MS, U. Ga., Athens, 1973, PhD, 1978. Sr. biologist EPA, Washington, from 1979. Reviewer NSF and profl. jours., 1973—, Standards Methods Com., Am. Water Works Assn., Denver 18th through 21st edits.; evaluator Office Exptl. Learning U. Md., College Park, Md., 1984-86. Author: Estimating Toxicity of Industrial Chemicals to Aquatic Organisms Using Structure Activity Relationships, 1988, 94; co-author: Methods of Ecological Toxicology, 1981, Testing for Effects of Chemicals on Ecosystems, 1981; contbr. articles to profl. jours. Bd. dirs. Comty. Assn. Rollingwood Village (4th sect.), Woodbridge, Va., 1981-90, v.p. 1981-82, pres. 1983-90, maintainence chmn. 1990—. Decorated Army Commendation medal with oak leaf cluster, US Army, Vietnam, 1969, '70. Mem. AAAS, Am. Inst. Biol. Scis. (life), Assn. Southeastern Biologists (life), Internat. Assn. Ecology, Ecol. Soc. Am. (life), Soc. Environ. Toxicology and Chemistry, Phi Kappa Phi (life). Roman Catholic. Achievements include pragmatic application of theory of chemical structure activity relationships for routine risk assessment of industrial chemicals for environmental toxicity. Home: Woodbridge, Va. Died Feb. 23, 2008.

NACOL, MAE, lawyer; b. Beaumont, Tex., June 15, 1944; d. William Samuel and Ethel (Bowman) N.; children: Shawn Alexander Nacol, Catherine Regina Nacol. BA, Rice U., Houston, 1965; postgrad., South Tex. Coll. Law, 1966. Bar: Tex. 1969, U.S. Dist. Ct. (so. dist.) Tex. 1969, U.S. Supreme Ct., U.S. Dist. Ct. (we. dist.), U.S. Ct. Appeals (5th cir.). Pvt. practice law, Houston, from 1969; escrow officer Land Am./Commonwealth Land Title Co., Houston; mem. bd. devel. Prosperity Bank, Houston. Author, editor ednl. materials on multiple sclerosis, 1981-85. Nat. dir. A.R.M.S of Am. Ltd., Houston, 1984-85. Recipient Mayor's Recognition award City of Houston, 1972. Mem. Fed. Bar Assn., Houston Bar Assn. (chmn. candidate com. 1970, membership com. 1971, chmn. lawyers referral com. 1972), Assn. Trial Lawyers Am., Tex. Trial Lawyers Assn., Am. Judicature Soc. (sustaining), Houston Fin. Coun. Women, Houston Trial Lawyers Assn. Presbyterian. Deceased.

NADEL, ANN HONIG, sculptor, educator; b. San Francisco, May 9, 1940; d. Louis and Miriam (Anixter) Honig; m. Joseph Nadel, June 10, 1962; children: Marcia, David. BA in Humanities, San Francisco State U., 1962, M in Edn., 1970; studied with Peter Voulkos, 1976. One woman shows include Judy Kay, Burlingame, 1978, Irene Drori Gallery, L.A., 1979, Bluxome Gallery, San Francisco, 1983, 85, Temple Emanu-El, San Francisco, 1988, Grad. Theol. Union, Berkeley, Calif., 1988, Earl McGrath Gallery, L.A., 1988, 90, 92, Jewish Mus., San Francisco, 1994, Bradford Smock Gallery, San Francisco, 1997; exhibited in group shows at Am. Crafts Coun., Kitchen Show, San Francisco, 1976, Gump's Gallery, San Francisco, 1981, No. Calif. Craft Exhbn., Mendocino (Calif.) Art Ctr., 1982, The San Francisco Arts Festival, 1983, San Francisco Internat. Airport Commn. Exhbn., 1985, Frederick Weisman Found. of Art, Cedars-Sinai Med. Ctr., L.A., 1986, Judah L. Magnes Mus., Berkeley, 1987, Jewish Mus., San Francisco, 1987, Bluxome Gallery, San Francisco, 1995, Earl McGrath Gallery, N.Y.C., 1992, Grad. Theol. Union, Berkeley, 1995, Bolinas (Calif.) Art Mus., 1995, Jewish Mus., San Francisco, 1993, Hebrew Union Coll., N.Y.C., 1997, L'Chaim Jewish Mus., San Francisco, 1998; represented in permanent collections at Residence of U.S. Vice Pres., Washington, Frederick Weisman Found. of Art, Advanced Micro Devices Corp., Hewlett-Packard Co., Fireman's Fund Ins., Koll Co., Steefel, Levitt & Weiss, Grad. Theol. Union, Berkeley, Calif., Cedars-Sinai Med. Ctr., L.A., Deloitte and Touche, San Francisco, Coudert Bros., Dr. Carl Djerassi, Palo Alto, Calif.; contbr. to various catalogs, revs., online, including Ceramic Monthly, Am. Craft, Libr. of Congress Catalog, Jewish Bull. of San Francisco. Avocations: swimming, water-skiing. Home: Mill Valley, Calif. Died Apr. 5, 2008.

NAEVE, MILO MERLE, retired curator, director; b. nr. Arnold, Kans., Oct. 9, 1931; s. Bernhardt and Fern (Yasmer) N.; m. Nancy Jammer, July 18, 1954. BFA, U. Colo., 1953; MA, U. Del., 1955. Curatorial asst. Henry Francis duPont Winterthur Mus., 1957, asst. curator, 1958, sec. of mus., 1959-63, registrar, 1963-65; editor Winterthur Portfolio, 1965-66; asst. dir. dept. collections Colonial Williamsburg, Va., 1967-69, curator, dir. dept. collections Va., 1970; dir. Colorado Springs (Colo.) Fine Arts Ctr., 1971-74; curator Am. arts Art Inst. Chgo., 1975-91; ret. Am. Arts, Art Inst. Chgo., 1991. Curator emeritus Field McCormick. Author: The Classical Presence in American Art, 1978, Identifying American Furniture: A Pictorial Guide to Styles and Terms, Colonial to Contemporary, 1981, 3rd edit., 1998, John Lewis Krimmel: An Artist in Federal America, 1987, 150 Years of Philadelphia Painters and Painting: Selections from the Sewell C. Biggs Museum of American Art, 1999; mem. editl. bd. Am. Art Jour.; contbr. articles to profl. jours. Trustee Skowhegan Sch. Painting and Sculpture, 1991-2005, Libr. Co. Phila., 1996-2008, Nat. Coun. the Fine Arts Mus. San Francisco, 1991-2005 Recipient Robert C. Smith award for most disting. article pub. in field in U.S., Decorative Arts Soc., 1996, Chmn. Smith award, 2003-. Fellow Royal Soc. Arts; mem. Coll. Art Assn. Am., Nat. Trust Hist. Preservation, Am. Assn. Museums, Museums Assn. (Eng.), Ill. Acad. Fine Arts (Lifetime Achievement award 1991), Century Assn., Grolier Club. Home: Kennett Square, Pa. Died Aug. 10, 2009.

NAGRIN, DANIEL, dancer, educator, choreographer, writer; b. NYC, May 22, 1917; s. Harry Samuel and Clara (Wexler) N.; m. Helen Tamiris, 1946 (dec. 1966); m. Phyllis A. Steele, Jan. 24, 1992. BS in Edn., CCNY, 1940; DFA, SUNY, Brockport, 1991; DHL, Ariz. State U., 1992; studied dance with Ray Moses, Martha Graham, Anna Sokolow, Helen Tamiris, Mme. Anderson-Ivantzova, Nenette Charisse and Edward Caton, 1936-56, studied acting with Miriam Goldina, Sanford Meisner and Stella Adler, 1936-56. Tchr. Silvermine Guild Art, New Canaan, Conn., 1957-66, SUNY, Brockport, 1967-71, U. Md., College Park, 1970, Davis Ctr. Performing Arts, CCNY, 1973-75, Nat. Theatre Inst., Eugene O'Neill Found., Waterford, Conn., 1974, Hartmann Theatre Conservatory, Stamford, Conn., 1975-77; long-term resident tchr., Nat. Endowment for Arts sponsorship U. Hawaii, 1978-80, tchr., 1981, Bill Evans Dance Workshop, Seattle, 1981; prof. dance dept. Ariz. State U., Tempe, 1982-92; tchr. grad. liberal studies program Wesleyan U., Middletown, Conn., 1984, Dance Workshop for Movement Rsch., NYC, 1984, Improvisation Workshop, Seattle, 1985, Improvisation, Choreography and Acting Technique for Dancers, Seattle, 1985, Dance Workshop, Glenwood Springs, Colo., 1990; prof. emeritus dance Ariz. State U., 1992. Tchr. summer sessions Conn. Coll., New London, 1959, 74; Am. Dance Festival at Conn. Coll., 1960, 77, Duke U., Durham, NC, 1978, 80, 82, 87-88, 92, Balasaraswati/Joy Ann Dewey Beinecke Chair Dising. Tchg., 1992; summer dance program Conn. Coll., 1979, E. La Tour Dance Workshop, Sedgewick, 1982, 83; dance workshop U. Minn. at Mpls., 1984, Stanford U., 1990; co-dir. Tamiris-Nagrin Summer Dance Workshop, Sedgewick, 1960-61, (with Tamiris) summer dance session C. W. Post Coll., Greenville, NY, 1962-63; dir. summer dance workshop Johnson (Vt.) State Coll., 1972-73, 75-76; lectr in field. Dancer (featured dance soloist on Broadway) Annie Get Your Gun, Lend an Ear, Touch and Go, Plain and Fancy (Billboard Donaldson award, 1954), (appearance in film) Just for You, (adapted and performed one-man theater piece) The Fall, from novel by Albert Camus, 1977—79, choreographer (solo works) Spanish Dance, 1948, Man of Action, 1948, Strange Hero, 1948, Indeterminate Figure, 1957, With My Eye and With My Hand, 1968, Jazz: Three Ways, 1958, 1966, Path-Silence, 1965, Not Me, But Him, 1965, The Peloponesian War, 1967—68, Untitled, 1974, Ruminations, 1976, Getting Well, 1978, Poems Off the Wall, 1981, Apartment 18C, 1993, Crosscurrents, 1997, Lost and Never Found, 1998, Someone for Theater X, Tokyo, Japan, What Did You Say?, 2001, others, (for groups) Faces from Walt Whitman, 1950, An American Journey, 1962, asst. choreographer (original Broadway prodns.) Up in Central Park, Stovepipe Hat, Show Boat, Annie Get Your Gun, By the Beautiful Sea, others; dir.: (off-Broadway) Volpone, 1957, The Firebugs, 1960, The Umbrella, 1961, Emperor Jones (Boston, 1963, others; (film choreography) His Majesty O'Keefe; actor: (video) The Art of Memory, 1985; (plays) Three Stories High, others; extensive touring U.S., Europe, The Pacific and Japan, 1957—84, conceived and directed (videos) Steps, 1972, The Edge is Also a Circle, 1973, Nagrin Videotape Library of Dances, 1985; author: How to Dance Forever: Surviving Against the Odds, 1988, Dance and the Specific Image: Improvisation, 1993, The Six Questions: Acting Technique for Dance Performance, 1997, Choreography and the Specific Image: Nineteen Essays and a Workbook, 2001. With spl. svcs. Army Airforce, 1942-43. Grantee Rebekah Harkness Found., 1962, Logan Found., 1965, NY State Coun. on Arts and Nat. Found. for Arts and Humanities, 1967-68, NY State Coun. on Arts, 1971-81, Anne S. Richardson Fund, 1971, 73-76, 78, Nat. Endowment for Arts, 1975, 79, 81, 83, Ariz. State U., 1983-86, 88; CAPS fellow NY State Coun. on Arts, 1977-78; fellow NEA, 1977-78, 80, 82-83, 90-91, Minn. McKnight Nat. fellow, 1996-97; commd. ballet Rebekah Harkness Ballet Found., 1986, honor Ctr. Nat. de Dausa, Pantir, France, 2007. Mem. Actors' Equity, Phi Kappa Phi (hon.). Avocation: reading. Died Dec. 29, 2008.

NAHIGIAN, RUSSELL ARA, retired mathematician; b. Brookline, Mass, Apr. 20, 1934; s. Moses Hovenes and Rose (Ashjian) Nahigian; m. Carol Jane Paboojian, July 16, 1960; children: Thomas, Susan, Laura. BA in Math. disting. mil. grad., Colby Coll., Waterville, Maine, 1956; postgrad., MIT, 1957; MS in Engrng. Mgmt., Northeastern U., Boston, 1971. Technician Minn-Honeywell, Brighton, Mass., 1960-61; analyst Edgerton, Germeshausen & Grier, Boston, 1961-65; sci. programmer Minn-Honeywell, Boston, 1965-67; sr. sci. programmer Svc. tech. Corp., Cambridge, Mass., 1970—85; mathematician U.S. Dept. Transp., Cambridge, 1985—96; currier Anacomp Inc., Medford, Mass., 1996—98; data entry staff Prostaff, Adecco, Waltham, Mass., 1996-99, Boston Co., Woburn, Mass., 1996-99; pricer MVP Sports, Wilmington, Mass., 1999—2001; ret., 2001. Contbr. articles to profl. jours. Deacon First Am. Ch., Belmont, Mass., 1994—96. 1st lt. USAF, 1956—60. Named Father of the Yr., First Armenian Ch., 1995. Republican. Home: Arlington, Mass. Died Jan. 31, 2008.

NALLS, ANNE LINDSAY, gifted and talented education educator; b. Macon, Ga., Oct. 20, 1936; d. Tom Wilson and Elizabeth Furman (Jones) N.; m. Henry Chovine Croom, Aug. 25, 1956 (div.); children: Meagan, Lindsay; m. Stephen Hill McCleary, June 18, 1989. AB, Wesleyan Coll., 1960; M in Counseling, Ariz. State U., 1979; EdD, U. Ga., 1986. English tchr. Willingham Boys' H.S., Macon, Ga., 1960-61; English and Modern Dance tchr. Wesleyan Coll., Macon, 1961-62; dir. religious edn. Unitarian-Universalist Ch., Phoenix, 1976; tchr. Banks County H.S., Homer, Ga., 1979-80; lead tchr. Elbert County Gifted Program, 1980-83; dir., tchr. Athens Middle Sch. for Arts and Scis., 1987-88; spl. edn. coord. N.E. Ga. Regional Ednl. Svc. Agy., 1988-89; coord. program for the gifted and talented Bowling Green (Ohio) City Schs., 1990-95; coord. Sandusky Co. Edn. Svc. Ctr., from 1996. Co-chair Ohio Assn. for Gifted Children State Conv., 1993; chair Ohio Future Problem Solving Bowl; adj. asst. prof. Bowling Green State Univ.; part-time assoc. prof. U. Ga., Athens. Bd. dirs. LWV, Bowling Green, 1992-3; vol. Habitat for Humanity, St. Paul's Homeless Shelter; bd. dirs. Unitarian-Universalist Ch., 1994, pres. 1993-94; area rep. Youth for Understanding, Athens, 1980-89, host parent for five exch. students, 1980-89, Ch. sch. tchr., Athens; bd. trustees Phoenix Elem. Sch. Dist. #1, pres. 1978-79, campfire leader, Phoenix; vol. probation officer Maricopa Youth Dept., Phoenix; pres., treas. Kenilworth Sch. PTO; vol. tutor Phoenix Elem. Sch. Torrance scholar Torrance Ctr. for Creative Studies, 1990. Mem. AAUW, Nat. Assn. for Gifted Children, Ohio Assn. of Gifted Children, N.W. Ohio Assn. of Coordinators of Gifted, Amnesty Internat., Greenpeace, Phi Delta Kappa, Delta Kappa Gamma. Avocations: scuba, tai chi, dance, backpack hiking. Home: Las Cruces, N.Mex. Died Mar. 28, 2008.

NASH, STANTON HARRIS, fundraiser, public relations consultant; b. New Roads, La., Feb. 6, 1915; s. Robert Meeker and Ethel Lee (Robbins) N.; m. Joy Annette Balyeat, Mar. 16, 1943; children: April Joy Nash Woods, Stanna Joy Nash Schreiber, Marel Joy Nash Buffington, Stanton Harris II. Student, LaSalle Extension U., 1936-38, Trinity U., 1939-40; B in Sacred Music, Southwestern Bapt. Theol. Sem., 1948. Cert. fund raising exec. Min. music edn. Indian Oaks Bapt. Ch., Ft. Worth, 1939, First Bapt. Ch., Waxahachie, Tex., 1939-40, Ranger, Tex., 1945-46, min. edn., ch. adminstrn. Oklahoma City, 1949-59, Atlanta, 1963-64; min. music edn. Coll. Ave. Bapt. Ch., Ft. Worth, 1946-48, Dauphin Way Bapt. Ch., Mobile, Ala., 1948-49; v.p. devel. Golden Gate Bapt. Theol. Sem., Mill Valley, Calif., 1965-81; dir. planned giving Southwestern Bapt. Theol. Sem., Ft. Worth, 1981-92; dir. Joseph Fund, Dallas Bapt. U., 1992-93; planned gifts rep. Annuity Bd., So. Bapt. Conv., Dallas, from 1993. Exec. sec., treas. Hawaii Bapt. Conv., Honolulu, 1959-63; pres. Stonehaven Pubs., Ft. Worth, 1989—. Author, editor: Adult Axioms, 1954, Training Manual, 1990. Chmn. Found. Arts, San Rafael, Calif., 1968-70. Maj. U.S. Army, 1941-45, ETO. Decorated Bronze Star, 1945; named Outstanding Educator, 1975. Mem. Coun. Advancement and Support of Edn., Nat. Soc. Fund Raising Execs. (v.p. 1972-74, cert. fund raising exec.), Tex. Bapt. Devel. Officers Assn., Bapt. Pub. Rels. Assn. (pres. 1976-77), Masons, Shriners. Republican. Avocations: golf, fishing, coin collecting/numismatics. Home: Fort Worth, Tex. Died Sept. 26, 2007.

NASON, RAYMOND WILLIAM, JR., financial executive; b. Pitts., Feb. 18, 1938; s. Raymond William and Helen (Tuckey) N.; m. Mary Louise Kovacs, Aug. 4, 1964; Natalie Ann, Raymond William III, Michaele Lynn. BS in Chem. Engring., Carnegie Mellon U., 1959; MBA, U. Pitts., 1965. Comptroller USS Agrichems. div. U.S. Steel, Atlanta, 1973-77, Universal Atlas div. U.S. Steel, Pitts., 1977-79; dir. planning and acctg., resource devel. group U.S. Steel, Pitts., 1979-80; v.p., controller Terra Chems. Internat., Inc., Sioux City, Iowa, 1980-84, v.p. fin., 1983-84; v.p. fin. and adminstrn. Savin Corp., Stamford, Conn., from 1984, also bd. dirs. various subs. Vice chmn. Siouxland Assn. Bus. and Industry, Sioux City, 1983-84; bd. dirs. Marian Regional Health Ctr., Sioux City, 1983-84, Boys Clubs Sioux City (sec. 1981-84). Served to 1st lt. C.E. U.S. Army, 1960-62. Mem. Fin. Exec. Inst. (chmn. long-range planning com., 1976-77), Fertilizer Inst. (chmn. fin. execs. com., 1976-77), Skywalk Assn. (pres., 1984). Republican. Roman Catholic. Avocations: investments, tennis. Home: Wilton, Conn. Died Apr. 1, 2008.

NATRELLA, VITO, economic consultant; b. Bklyn., Dec. 2, 1916; s. Michael and Mary (Orobello) N.; m. Elinor Entrekin, Jan. 14, 1950 (dec. 1992; children: Michael, Steven. B.A., Bklyn. Coll., 1937; M.A., Am. U., 1962. Fin. statistician SEC, Washington, 1939-60, asst. dir. trading divsn., 1960-64; dir. stats. divsn. IRS, Washington, 1964-80; econ. cons., Joel Popkin & Associates, Arlington, Va., 1980—2009. Author (with others) Volume and Composition of Individual Saving, 1954. Editor: The Flow of Funds Approach to Social Accounting, 1962. Contbr. articles to profl. jours. Fellow Am. Statis. Assn.; mem. Am. Econ. Assn., Nat. Economists Club. Club: Cosmos (Washington). Died Jan. 9, 2009.

NEAL, PHILIP MARK, retired manufacturing executive; b. San Diego, Aug. 28, 1940; s. Philip Mark and Florence Elizabeth (Anderson) N.; children: Brian, Kevin. BA, Pomona Coll., 1962; MBA, Stanford U., 1964. Mgr. financial planning and analysis CBS, Hollywood, 1964-66; cons. McKinsey & Co., LA, 1966-73; v.p., contr. Avery Internat. Corp. LA, 1974-78, sr. v.p. fin. Pasadena, Calif., 1979-88, group v.p. materials group N.Am., 1988-90, exec. v.p., 1990, pres., COO, 1990-98, pres., CEO, 1998-2000, chmn., CEO, 2000—05, chmn., 2005. Bd. dirs. Edwards Lifescis. Corp. Trustee Pomona Coll.; bd. govs. Town Hall of Calif.; bd. dirs. Pacific Basin Inst., Music Ctr. Los Angeles County. Mem.: Calif. Bus. Roundtable (bd. dirs.). Republican. Episcopalian. Died Oct. 29, 2008.

NEAL, SUSAN KAY, accountant; b. Inglewood, Calif., Nov. 4, 1958; d. James Hampton and Betty Kay (Frydenlund) Neally; m. Lawrence Patrick Neal, June 4, 1990; children: Kate Alexa, Megan Elizabeth. BS in Acctg., Loyola Marymount U., 1980; MS in Tax, Golden Gate U., 1994. CPA, Calif., Tex. V.p. Gumbiner, Savett, Finkel, FIngleson & Rose, Inc., Santa Monica, Calif., 1980-94; pvt. practice Round Rock, Tex., from 1994. Co-editor: Propsed Audit and Accounting Guide: Audits of Future Commission Merchants and Commodity Pool, 1986. Counselor Tax Counseling for Elderly, Round Rock, 1996. Mem. AICPA, Calif. Soc. CPAs, Tex. Soc. CPAs, Better Bus. Bur., Round Rock C. of C. Republican. Lutheran. Avocations: reading, golf, nutrition, volunteering. Died Jan. 8, 2008.

NEGAHBAN, EZATOLLAH, archaeologist; b. Ahwaz, Iran, Mar. 1, 1926; s. Abdol Amir and Roghieh (Dideban) N.; m. Miriam Lois Miller, May 1955; children: Ali, Bahman, Mehrdad, Babak, Daryus. BA, U. Tehran, Iran, 1948; MA, U. Chgo. Oriental Inst., 1954; Doctorate, Council of Edn., Tehran, Iran, 1956. Assoc. prof. U. Tehran, 1956-62, prof., 1962-78, dir. Inst. Archaeology, 1957-78, head dept. archaeology, 1968-75, dean faculty of letters, 1975-78; tech. dir. Iranian Archaeol. Service, Tehran, 1960-65; tech. advisor to Ministry of Culture, Tehran, 1965-79; dir. Iran Bastan Mus. 19, Tehran, 1966-68; vis. curator, vis. prof. U. Mus., U. Pa., 1980—2001. Sec. gen. Internat. Congress of Iranian Art and Archaeology and dir. 5th Congress, Tehran-Shiraz, 1968; dir. excavation of Mehranabad, 1961, Marlik, 1961-62, Haft Tepe, 1966-78, Qazin Plain Expdn. (Zaghe, Qabrestan, Sagzabad, 1970-78), Archaeol. Survey of N.E. Iran, 1965, Mazandaran highlands, 1975. Author: Buffware Sequence in Khuzistan, 1954, Preliminary Report on Marlik Excavation, 1964, Metal Vessels from Marlik, 1983, Excavation of Haft Tepe. Mem. Deutsches Archaeologische Inst., Internat. Congress of Pre and Protohistory. Muslim. Avocation: persian calligraphy. Home: Philadelphia, Pa. Died Feb. 2, 2009.

NEHRE, LAWRENCE EUGENE, human services administrator; b. Ottumwa, Iowa, Jan. 4, 1951; s. Raymond Eugene and Deloris Elayne (Freshour) N.; m. Carolyn Louise Brown, June 30, 1975 (div. Dec. 1988); 1 child, Jennifer Ann. Student, Cen. Coll., Pella, Iowa, 1969-72; cert. agrl. tech., floriculture, Kirkwood Community Coll., Cedar Rapids, Iowa, 1986. Social worker St. Francis Hosp., Waterloo, Iowa, 1971-75, Quakerdale Group Homes, New Providence, Iowa, 1975-81, Found. II Crisis Center, Cedar Rapids, 1981-84; info. specialist United Way Iowa, Cedar Rapids, 1984-85; mgr. Pierson's Florists, Cedar Rapids, 1985-89; program planner II Iowa State Foster Care, Cedar Rapids, from 1989. Chairperson Iowa Foster Care Rev. Bd., Cedar Rapids, 1984—; v.p. adv. bd. Iowa Council on Aging, 1984—; mem. Linn County Child Abuse Prevention Coalition, 1981—; pres. alumni assn., bd. dirs. Kirkwood Community Coll., 1988—; active ARC Disaster Services, United Way East Cen. Iowa. Mem. Am. Soc. Florists, Iowa Soc. Florists, Am. Horticulture Soc., Nat. Assn. of Social Workers. Presbyterian. Avocations: reading, music, tennis. Died Sept. 13, 2007.

NEILAND, BONITA JUNE, botanist, educator; b. Eugene, Oreg., June 5, 1928; d. Herbert Eugene and Ann Lavina (Thompson) Miller; m. Kenneth Alfred Neiland, Dec. 23, 1955. BS in Biology, U. Oreg., 1949; MA in Botany, Oreg. State Coll., 1951; diploma in rural sci., U. Coll. Wales, 1952; PhD of Botany, U. Wis., 1954. Instr. biology U. Oreg., Eugene, 1954-55; asst. prof. biology State Sys. Higher Edn. Gen. Ext. Divsn., Eugene, 1955-60; from asst. prof. to prof. Botany and Land Resources U. Alaska, Fairbanks, 1961-87; ret., 1987. Cons. plant ecology. Contbr. articles to profl. jours. Bd. dirs. Deschutes Soil and Water Conservation Dist., Bend, Oreg. Fulbright fellow, 1951-52; grantee NSF, 1955—, John Muir Inst., 1955. Mem. AAAS (fellow 1975), Brit. Ecol. Soc., Soil and Water Conservation Soc., Sigma Xi, Phi Beta Kappa, Phi Kappa Phi. Avocations: gardening, travel, bird watching, cat watching. Home: Redmond, Oreg. Died Dec. 25, 2007.

NELSON, CHRISTOPHER ARNOLD, computer sales support representative; b. Santa Monica, Calif., Aug. 16, 1952; s. Theodoret Arnold and Donna Mae (Norem) N.; m. Kathleen Mary Fields, Aug. 21, 1976; children: Heather Kristine, Steven Christopher Owen. BA in Biology, Calif. State U., 1975. Ops. foreman Disneyland, Anaheim, Calif., 1970-77; client rep. Sci. Dynamics Corp., Torrance, Calif., 1978-83, tng. mgr., sales adminstr., 1984-87; rep. sales support Shared Med. Systems, Long Beach, Calif., from 1987. Adminstr. of sales Sci. Dynamics Corp., Torrance, Calif., 1987-88; owner Can'd Software Consulting, Anaheim, Calif., 1986—. Republican. Lutheran. Avocations: woodworking, silversmithing, travel, skiing. Home: Anaheim, Calif. Died May 13, 2008.

NELSON, GAILON WALKER, minister; b. Andalusia, Ala., Jan. 20, 1931; s. James Monroe and Eunice (Walker) N.; m. Ruth Owens, Dec. 31, 1954; children: Ruth Maria Nelson Ulmer, Gailon Owens. Ordained to ministry So. Bapt. Conv., 1953. Enlisted U.S. Army, 1948; assigned to Fed. Republic Germany, Vietnam, Korea, Hawaii; ret., 1969; pastor New Chapel Bapt. Ch., 1974-81, Bethanyy So. Bapt. Ch., Kinston, Ala., from 1981. Mem. VFW, DAV (comdr. Andalusia), Am. Legion, Civitans. Democrat. Died May 29, 2008.

NELSON, H. H. RED, insurance company executive; b. Herman, Nebr., June 2, 1912; m. Ruth Hansen; children: John, Steve. BA, U. Nebr., 1934, JD, 1937. Bar: Iowa, Nebr. 1938; CLU, 1948. Asst. mgr. life accident group depts. Travelers Inc. Co., Omaha, 1939-44; chmn. bd. Redlands Ins. Co., Omaha, from 1945, Ins. Agts. Inc., Council Bluffs,

Iowa, from 1945, Am. Agrisurance Co., Council Bluffs, from 1969, Am. Growers Ins., Council Bluffs, from 1995, Acceptance Ins., Tex., Council Bluffs, from 1988; chmn. Silverstone Group, Council Bluffs, 1997-2001, chmn. emeritus, from 2001. Chmn. Redland Group Cos. Pres. United Fund, Western Iowa council Boy Scouts Am.; bd. dirs. Nat. Scout Council; pres. Christian Home Orphanage, Council Bluffs Indsl. Found. Named to, Iowa Ins. Hall of Fame, 1997. Home: Council Blfs, Iowa. Died Feb. 2007.

NELSON, JACK (JOHN HOWARD NELSON), journalist; b. Talladega, Ala., Oct. 11, 1929; s. Howard Alonzo and Barbara Lena (O'Donnell) N.; m. Virginia Dare Dickinson, Aug. 4, 1951 (div. Nov. 1974); children: Karen Dare, John Michael, Steven Howard; m. Barbara Joan Matusow, Dec. 7, 1974. Student, Ga. State Coll., 1953—57. Reporter Biloxi (Miss.) Daily Herald, 1947-51, Atlanta Constitution, 1952-65; so. bur. chief L.A. Times, Atlanta, 1965-70, with Washington bur., from 1970, Washington bur. chief, 1975-96, chief Washington corr., 1996—2002. Author: (with Gene Roberts, Jr.) The Censors and the Schools, 1963, (with Jack Bass) The Orangeburg Massacre, 1970, (with R.J. Ostrow) The FBI and the Berrigans, 1972, Captive Voices, Shocken Books, 1974, Terror in the Night, 1993. With AUS, 1951-52. Recipient Pulitzer prize for local reporting under deadline pressure, 1960; Drew Pearson award for gen. excellence in investigative reporting, 1974; Nieman fellow Harvard U., 1961-62, Shorenstein fellow Harvard U., 2002. Mem. The Gridiron Club. Home: Bethesda, Md. Died Oct. 21, 2009.

NELSON, KATHY MARTIN, mathematics educator; b. Cartersville, Ga., Mar. 26, 1951; d. H.E. and Evelyn Laura (Irwin) Martin; m. Robert Harold Nelson, June 18, 1972; children: Julie, Martin. BA in Early Childhood, West Ga. Coll., 1972, M Early Childhood, 1974; EdS, Troy State, 1990. Tchr. Headstart, Cartersville, Ga., summer 1972; elem. tchr. Cartersville City Sch. System, 1972-76; kindergarten tchr. Forrest Road Elem., Columbus, Ga., 1976-78; dir. presch. Striplin Terrace Meth. Ch., Columbus, 1979-80; presch. tchr. Morningside Bapt. Ch., Columbus, 1982-83, dir. presch., 1983-87; tchr. Blanchard Elem. Sch., Columbus, 1988-91, Fort Mid. Sch., Columbus, 1991-95, Blackmon Road Mid. Sch., Columbus, 1995-99, math. tournament dir., 1994-95, team leader, 7th grade math. coord., 1994-96, 7th grade level coord., from 1997, Bridges prep. coord., 1997-98. Mem. math. textbook and curriculum task force Muscogee County Sch. Dist., 1994-95; presenter League Profl. Schs., 1997; sponsor St. Jude Math-a-thon. Mem. Ga. PTA (hon. life), Ft. Mid. Sch., 1994—. Recipient Tchr. Ledger Enquirer award, 1994, 95. Mem. Nat. Coun. Tchrs. Math. (mem. hospitality at regional conf. 1992), Chattahoochee Coun. Math., Kappa Delta Pi, Delta Kappa Gamma. Home: Albany, Ga. Died Dec. 27, 2007.

NELSON, LARRY EUGENE, broadcasting executive; b. Kansas City, Mo., Sept. 8, 1942; s. Isadore and Edith Katherine (Risburd) N.; m. Diane Cooper, June 28, 1964 (div. 1974); children: Andrea, Richard; m. Bernetta Arlene Kochan, Oct. 6, 1974; children: Adam, Mark, Jodi, Heidi. BSEE, U. So. Calif., 1965. Chief elec. engr. Colortron, Burbank, Calif., 1966-69; nat. sales mgr. Strand Lighting, Rancho Domingoe, Calif., 1969-74, v.p. sales, 1974-76; v.p. TV sales Kliege Bros., NYC, 1971-74; pres. L E Nelson Corp., Las Vegas, Nev., from 1976. Mem. Illuminating Engr. Soc. Republican. Jewish. Avocation: photography. Died Aug. 12, 2008.

NELSON, MARCUS THOMAS, playwright, producer; b. Elizabeth, Miss., Oct. 29, 1919; s. Benjamin Marshall and Maude Elizabeth (Threlkeld) N.; m. Vivian O. Walker, Dec. 5, 1942 (div. Mar. 1950); m. Susan Hill, Oct. 22, 1960 (div. May 1963); m. Sally Lou Spurgat Nelson, April 25, 1973 (div. Febr. 1983). Leader Civilian Conservation Corps., Aledo, Ill., 1937-39; spice grinder LaSalle Mfg. Co., Chgo., 1939-43; machinist journeyman Pearl Harbor Navy Yard, Honolulu, Hawaii, 1943-49; streetcar motorman Chgo. Transit Authority, 1949-51; machinist, journeyman Kodiak (Alaska) Naval Air Base, 1951-52; photo-journalist The Good Publishing Co., Paris, 1953; bus operator Chgo. Transit Authority, 1954-65; cab driver The Yellow Cab Co., Chgo., 1965-66; theatre mgr. Hull House Parkway Cmty. Theatre, Chgo., 1966-68; short order cook USAR-McNair Barracks, Berlin, Germany, 1968-69; specialist in theatre U. Wis.-Downer Campus, Milw., 1970-71; playwright prodr. The Village Church, Milw., 1971-73, New Concept Theatre, Chgo., from 1973. Playwright/poet The Nat. Libr. of Poetry, Owings Mills, Md; mgr. The Modern Bookstore, Chgo., 1985-88. Adaptor: (plays) The Lord is Thy Passion, 1986, The Jogger Story, 1988, author over 42 plays including; listed playwright Black Playwrights, 1823-1977 Annotated Bibliography of Plays (James V. Hatch and Omanii Obdullah), 1977; contbg. poet: (anthologies) Beyond the Stars, 1995, 96, The Best Poems of the '90s, 1996, Take Us The Foxes II, 1998. Mem., resource person Chgo. Theatre Coalition, 1974; mem. Chgo. Alliance for the Performing Arts, 1975; co-founder, mem. Black Theatre Alliance, Chgo., 1975; mem. South Shore Cultural Coun., Chgo., 1977. Recipient Playwright grantee Wis. Arts Coun., NEA, 1972, Ill. Arts Coun., 1976, 80, 81, 91, Playwright/Producer grantee Mayor's Office of Tng. and Employment, 1975, Chgo. Office of Fine Arts, 1977, Robert R. McCormick Found., 1978, Continental Bank Found., 1980, Chgo. Coun. on Fine Arts, 1980, 81, Midwest Playwrights Program, East Mpls., 1982, Chgo. Dept. Cultural Affairs and Ill. Arts Coun. Access Program, 1991. Democrat. Mem. Ch. of God. Avocations: reading, yoga, exercise, walking, cooking. Home: Chicago, Ill. Died Apr. 11, 2008.

NELSON, MARY ANN, language professional, consultant; b. Tacoma, Aug. 7, 1938; d. Stanley Arthur and Marion (Stanley) N. BA, U. Puget Sound, 1960; MA, U. Washington, 1965. Tchr. Tacoma Pub. Schs., 1960-66, curriculum specialist, 1966-67; asst. prof. English Ea. Washington U., Cheney, 1967-72, assoc. prof., 1973-82, prof. English, from 1982. Cons. Area Sch. Dist., Washington, Idaho, 1975—; dir. Ea. Washington U. Young Writers Conf., Cheney, 1985—, Ea. Washington U. Ctr. for Excellence in Teaching English, Cheney, 1989—. Author: A Comparative Anthology of Children's Literature, 1972, How To Teach Students to Write Effectively, How To Teach Students to Speak Effectively; contbr.a rticles to profl. jours. Pres. Cheney (Wash.) Libr. Bd., 1977-80, Friends of the Cheney Libr., 1980-83. Recipient Citation of Achievement award Wash. Libr. Trustee Assn., 1982. Mem. Nat. Coun. Tchrs. English, AAUP, Wash. State Coun. Tchrs. of English, Children's Lit. Assembly. Avocations: reading, cooking, collecting oriental art. Home: Cheney, Wash. Died Sept. 26, 2007.

NELSON, MICHAEL UNDERHILL, educational association administrator; b. Balt., May 5, 1932; s. Cyril Arthur and Elise (Macy) N.; m. Barbara Gail Hutchins, June 25, 1960; children: Kevin Underhill, Bronwyn Hastings, Gayle Hutchins, Corey Williams. AB, Rutgers U., 1957, EdM, 1968. Salesman J & N Distbg. Co., New Brunswick, NJ, 1957-59; extension assoc. Univ. Coll., Rutgers U., New Brunswick, 1959-61; asst. dir. summer session Rutgers U., 1961-68; asst. dean sch. continuing edn., dir. summer sch. Washington U., St. Louis, 1969-81, dir. div. of profl. and community programs sch. continuing edn., 1975-78; exec. sec. N.Am. Assn. Summer Sessions, from 1979; account exec. Trio Printing Co., 1982-84; sr. procedures analyst McDonnell Douglas Corp, St. Louis, 1984-96. Bd. dirs. Adult Edn. Council of Greater St. Louis, 1975-78. Served with USMC, 1951-54. Mem. North Ctrl. Conf. Summer Schs. (pres. 1974-75), Am. Assn. Univ. Adminstrs., Assn. Univ. Summer Sessions, Am. Summer Sessions Senate, N.Am. Assm. Summer Sessions (pres. 1978), Alpha Sigma Lambda, Phi Delta Kappa. Episcopalian. Died Sept. 7, 2008.

NELSON, RALPH ALFRED, physician; b. Mpls., June 19, 1927; s. Alfred W. and Lydia (Johnson) N.; m. Rosemary Pokela, Aug. 7, 1954; children: Edward Ancher, Audrey Anne, Elizabeth Marie, Andrew William, Evan Robert. BA, U. Minn., 1949, MD, 1953, PhD, 1961. Diplomate Am. Bd. Internal Medicine. Intern Cook County (Ill.) Hosp., 1953-54; resident U. Minn. Hosps., Mpls., 1954-55, U. Minn., Mpls., 1955-56; fellow in physiology Mayo Grad. Sch., Rochester, Minn., 1957-60, resident in internal medicine, 1976-78; practice medicine specializing in internal medicine and clin. nutrition Sioux Falls, SD, 1978-79, Urbana, Ill., from 1979. Bd. dirs. Scott Research Lab., Fairview Park Hosp., Cleve., 1962-67; assoc. in physiology Western Res. U., Cleve., 1962-67; asst. prof. physiology Mayo Grad. Sch., 1967-73, Mayo Med. Sch., 1973, assoc. prof. nutrition, 1974; cons. in nutrition Mayo Clinic, 1967-76; assoc. prof. medicine U. S.D. Sch. Medicine, Sioux Falls, 1978-79; prof. nutrition U. Ill. Coll. Medicine, Urbana-Champaign, 1986—2002, chmn. dept. medicine prof. nutritional sci., physiology, biophysics dept. food sci. Sch. Agr., 1979-2002, also prof. medicine, exec. head dept. internal medicine, 1989-2002, exec. head four sites of Coll. Medicine, 2002, emeritus prof. internal medicine, emeritus prof. nutritional scis.; dir. med.research Carle Found. Hosp., Urbana, 1979—; cons. nutritional support service Danville (Ill.) VA Hosp., 1980—. Co-author: The Mayo Clinic Renal Diet Cookbook, 1974; contbr. articles on nutrition, physiology, and hibernation to sci. jours.; editor: Geriatrics, 1980—2002, The Physician and Sportsmedicine, 1980-88, Am. Jour. Clin. Nutrition, 1980-83. Cons. in nutrition Nat. Cancer Inst., 1976; cons. in nutrition HEW, 1976, 79, 89, Nat. Heart and Lung Inst., 1976. Served with USAF, 1945-47. Fulbright scholar, Morocco, 1988. Fellow ACP; mem. Am. Physiol. Soc., Am. Inst. Nutrition, Am. Soc. Clin. Nutrition, Central Soc. Clin. Research, Am. Gastroent. Assn. Lutheran. Home: Ames, Iowa. Died Feb. 7, 2009.

NELSON, RICHARD C., geriatrician; b. Orlando, Fla., Aug. 24, 1956; s. Robert C. and Joan M. (Kruse) N.; m. Pamela S., June 22, 1985; 1 child, Christopher. MD, U. South Fla., 1981; fellowship diploma, VA Hosp. Geriatric Rsch. Ctr., Gainesville, Fla., 1986. Diplomate Am. Bd. Internal Medicine. Resident internal medicine Orlando (Fla.) Regional Med. Ctr.; fellow geriatric medicine VA Hosp., Gainesville, Fla.; chief geriatric svc., asst. dir. internal medicine Orlando Regional Med. Ctr.; assoc. program dir. internal medicine Western Pa. Hosp., Pitts. Named to Phi Beta Kappa. Mem. Am. Geriatric Soc., Am. Coll. Physicians, Am. Acad. Home Care Physicians, Soc. Gen. Internal Medicine. Home: Titusville, Fla. Died May 11, 2008.

NELSON, ROBERT GEORGE, minister; b. Racine, Wis., Nov. 21, 1928; s. Harold George and Augusta Marie (Due) N.; m. Arlene Marie Sandberg, Dec. 30, 1951; children: Joel K., Karen L. Nelson Smith, Katherine L. Nelson Flahive, Roberta A. Nelson Bowie. BA, Cana Coll., 1952; BD, Trinity Theol. Sem., Blair, Nebr., 1955; MDiv, Wartburg Theol. Sem., 1977; D Ministry, San Francisco Theol. Sem., 1982. Ordained to ministry Evangelical Luth. Ch. Sr. pastor Our Savior's Luth. Ch., Lincoln, Nebr., 1961-66, Trinity Luth. Ch., Ft. Collins, Colo., 1966-77, Morningside Luth. Ch., Sioux City, Iowa, 1977-79, Peace Luth. Ch., Sterling, Colo., 1979-84, Our Savior's Luth. Ch., Colorado Springs, Colo., from 1984. Mem. nat. stewartship com. Am. Luth. Ch., Mpls., 1962-74, mem. com. Internat. Yr. Disables, 1981—; mem. congl. life bd. Evangelical Luth. Ch. Am., Chgo. and Denver, 1988—. Bd. dirs. Eben-Eber Luth. Care Ctr., Brish, Colo., 1979-84. Capt. USAF, 1955-61. Mem. Mil. Chaplain Assn., Kiwanis. Home: Red Feather Lakes, Colo. Died Oct. 7, 2007.

NELSON, ROSE ESTELLE, optician; b. El Paso, Tex., June 1, 1943; d. Walter G. and Frances (Vale) Million; m. Robert G. Nelson, Jan. 26, 1962; children: Patricia A., Joanna M., Jennifer L. Student, Draughon's Bus. Sch., San Antonio, 1961. Clk., typist CSC, Sacramento, 1961-62, supply clk. Orlando, Fla., 1962-63; optician Midland Optical, Biloxi, Miss., 1989-90; owner, optician The Op Shop, Biloxi, from 1990. Editor PTA Update, 1985; co-editor PTA Coun. Handbook, 1989. Leader, chmn. Girl Scouts U.S.A., Biloxi, 1978-87; pres. Girls' Softball League, Biloxi, 1986-88; sec. Biloxi First, 1989—. Mewm. Nat. Assn. Opticians, Miss. Assn. Dispensing Opticians. Home: Biloxi, Miss. Died May 7, 2008.

NEMZEK, THOMAS ALEXANDER, retired nuclear engineer; b. Fargo, ND, Mar. 22, 1926; s. Alexander Jerome and Anne Jane (Hagen) N.; m. Margaret Clare Peters; children: Paula, Alexandra, Thomas, Michael. BS, U.S. Naval Acad., 1949; MS in Nuclear Engring., N.C. State U., Raleigh, 1952. Mgr. tech. ops. Chgo. Ops. Office, U.S. AEC, Argonne, Ill., 1959-64; dept. mgr. San Francisco Ops. Office, U.S. AEC, Berkeley, 1964-69; mgr. Richland (Wash.) Ops. Office, U.S. AEC, 1969-73; div. dir. reactor devel. AEC/ERDA, Washington, 1973-76; pres. J.A. Jones Applied Rsch. Co., Charlotte, N.C., 1976-93; ret., 1993. Capt. USAF, 1949-57. Recipient Disting. Svc. award, U.S. AEC, 1971, Spl. Achievement award, U.S. ERDA, 1976. Mem. Am. Nuclear Soc., Tech. Transfer Soc., Rotary (pres. 1989). Home: Richland, Wash. Died Jan. 13, 2008.

NESLAGE, JOHN E., lawyer; b. Pampa, Tex., Aug. 13, 1946; AA cum laude, N.Mex. Milit. Inst., 1966; BBA magna cum laude, Tex. Tech. U., 1969; JD cum laude, U. Houston, 1972. Bar: Tex. 1972. Mem. Baker Botts L.L.P., Houston. 1st lt. US Army, 1969—73. Named one of Best Lawyers in Am., 1990—2005. Fellow Houston Bar Found.; mem. ABA, State Bar Tex., Houston Bar Assn., Phi Kappa Phi, Phi Alpha Delta, Order of the Barons, Houston and Am. Bar Assn., State Bar Tex. Died Apr. 13, 2009.

NESTER, WILLIAM RAYMOND, JR., (BILL NESTER), retired academic administrator; b. Cin., Feb. 19, 1928; s. William Raymond and Evelyn (Blettner) N.; m. Mary Jane (dec.); children: William Raymond, Mark Patrick, Brian Philip, Stephen Christopher. BS, U. Cin., 1950, EdM, 1953, PhD, 1965, DHL (hon.), 2005, No. Ky. U., 2001, U. Nebr., 2002, U. Cin., 2005. Dir. student union U. Cin., 1952-53, asst. dean of men, 1953-60, dean of men, 1960-67, assoc. prof. edn., 1965-70, dean of students, 1967-69, vice provost student and univ. affairs, 1969-76, prof. edn., 1970-78, assoc. sr. v.p., assoc. provost, 1976-78; v.p. student svcs. Ohio State U., Columbus, 1978-83, prof. edn., 1978-83; pres. Kearney State Coll., Nebr., 1983-91, prof. edn. Nebr., 1983-93; chancellor U. Nebr., Kearney, 1991-93, prof. emeritus, chancellor emeritus, 1993—2009; v.p. univ. rels. devel. No. Ky. U., 1996-99. Pres. emeritus Mus. Nebr. Art, 1991-2009; cons. on higher edn., 1993-2009 Pres. Metro-Six Athletic Conf., 1975-76. Mem. Am. Assn. State Colls. and Univs. (bd. dirs.), Ctrl. States Intercollegiate Conf. (pres. 1986-89), Nat. Assn. Student Pers. Adminstrs. (past regional v.p., mem. exec. com.), Am. Assn. Higher Edn., Ohio Assn. Student Pers. Adminstrs. (past pres.), Nat. Intrafrat. Conf. (pres. 1991-92), Frat. Scholarship Officers Assn. (past pres.), Mortar Bd., Pi Kappa Alpha (nat. pres. 1978-80, pres. nat. interfrat. conf. 1988-89, past pres. Pi Kappa Alpha Ednl. Found.), Omicron Delta Kappa, Phi Delta Kappa, Phi Alpha Theta, Phi Eta Sigma, Sigma Sigma. Episcopalian. Home: Bellevue, Ky. Died June 24, 2009.

NETTLER, GWYNNE, writer, retired educator; b. NYC, July 7, 1913; s. Harry Lester and Dorothy (Wald) N. AB, UCLA, 1934; MA, Claremont Coll., 1936; PhD, Stanford U., 1946. Dir. child rsch. project Community Coun., Houston, 1957-59; assoc. psychologist Dando, S.A., Mexico City, 1959-61; sr. clin. psychologist Nev. Dept. Health, Reno, 1961-63; prof. emeritus U. Alta., Edmonton, Can., 1963-85. Author: Explanations, 1970, Explaining Crime, 1974, 78, 84, Social Concerns, 1976, Criminal Careers, 1982, Criminology Lessons, 1989. Recipient Achievement award Govt. of Alta., 1982. Fellow Royal Soc. Can., Am. Soc. Criminology (E.H. Sutherland award 1982), Am. Sociol. Assn. Home: San Diego, Calif. Died Oct. 5, 2007.

NEU, WILLIAM CARL, insurance company executive; b. Springfield, Ill., June 11, 1911; s. William Florian and Wilhelmina (Schniepp) N.; m. Shirleen Stevenson, June 7, 1963; children: Larry William, Shelly Rae Ainsworth. BA, Ill. Coll., 1932. Asst. actuary H.N. Bruce, Peoria, Ill., 1932-39, Alliance Life Ins. Co., Peoria, 1932-39; field mgr. Order Ry. Conductors, Cedar Rapids, Iowa, 1939-43; v.p., sec. Security Life of Denver, 1946-76, v.p. spl. projects, from 1984; exec. v.p. Internat. Arabian Horse Assn., Burbank, Calif. now Denver, 1976-82. Mem. Lakewood (Colo.) Park Bd. Served with USN, 1943-46, 50-51. Recipient Dirs. award Internat. Arabian Horse Assn., 1977; named Colo.

Vocat. Man of Yr., Colo. Vocat. Edn. Assn., 1970. Mem. Adminstr. Mgmt. Soc. (pres., bd. dirs. 1951-70), Actuarial Club Pacific States. Republican. Methodist. Home: Beulah, Colo. Died Jan. 20, 2008.

NEUBECK, GERHARD, retired education educator; b. Dortmund, Germany, Feb. 28, 1918; arrived in US, 1940; s. Sigfried and Emmy Neubeck; m. Ruth Hess Neubeck, Jan. 18, 1941; children: Ralph, Eva, Peter. BS, NYU, 1943; MA, Northwestern U., Ill., 1946; EdD, Columbia U., NY, 1955. Prof. U. Minn.; ret. Author: numerous poems; contbr. articles to profl. jours. Pres. Nat. Coun. Family Rels., Am. Assn. Marriage Counselors. Mem.: APA. Home: Saint Paul, Minn. Died Jan. 28, 2008.

NEUHAUS, MAX HENRY, artist, composer; b. Beaumont, Tex., Aug. 9, 1939; s. Max Werner N. and Harriet Rachel Ocker.; m. Silvia Neuhaus B.Mus., Manhattan Sch. Music, 1961, M.Mus., 1962. Fellow DAAD Kunstler Program, W. Berlin, 1977; founder, 1974; since dir. HEAR Inc. (aural environ. as a resource), NYC; created sound events for nat. radio networks and telephone systems Radio Net, 1977; series permanent sound installations for specific urban sites Times Sq., 1977, also for; museums, Abby Aldrich Rockefeller Sculpture Garden, Mus. Modern Art, NYC, 1978; Mus. Contemporary Art, Chgo., 1979; Domaine de Kerguehennel, Bignan, France, 1986; Documenta IX, Kassel, Germany, 1992; CACP Museé D'Art Contemporain, Bordeaux, France, 1993. Percussion soloist, Karlheinz Stockhausen, others, 1963-64, solo recitalist, Carnegie Hall, N.Y.C., 1964-65, artist-in-residence U. Chgo., 1964-65, solo tour of Europe, 1965-66; one-person exhbns. Musee d'Art Moderne de la Ville de Paris, 1983, Kunsthalle Basel, 1983, Kunsthalle Bern, Switzerland, 1988, Dallas Mus. Art, 1990. Nat. Endowment Arts music fellow, 1973; NEA visual arts fellow, 1977, 81, 90. Introduced concept of sound installation, 1967. Died Feb. 3, 2009.

NEUHAUS, RICHARD JOHN, minister, religious organization administrator; b. Pembroke, Ont., Can., May 14, 1936; Came to U.S., 1950; s. Clemens Henry and Ella Carolina (Prange) N. MDiv, Concordia Sem., 1960; DD (hon.), Benedictine Coll., Atchison, Kans., 1985, Gonzaga U., Spokane, Wash., 1985, Valparaiso U., Ind., 1986, Nichols Coll., Dudley, Mass., 1986, Boston U., 1988. Ordained to ministry Luth. Ch., 1960; ordained priest Roman Cath. Ch., 1991. Pastor St. John The Evangelist, Bklyn., 1961-78; sr. editor Worldview Mag., NYC, 1972-82; dir. Rockford Inst. Ctr. on Religion and Soc., NYC, 1984-89, Inst. on Religion and Pub. Life, NYC, 1989—2009. Author: Freedom for Ministry, 1979, The Naked Public Square, 1984, The Catholic Moment: The Paradox of the Church in the Postmodern World, 1987, America Against Itself, 1992, Doing Well & Doing Good, 1992, Evangelicals and Catholics Together, 1995, The End of Democracy?, 1997, Appointment in Rome, 1998; The Eternal Pity, 2000, Death on a Friday Afternoon: Meditations on the Last Words of Jesus From the Cross, 2000; As I Lay Dying: Meditations Upon Returning, 2002; Catholic Matters: Confusion, Controversy, And the Splendor of Truth, 2006, American Babylon: Notes of a Christian Exile, 2009; editor-in-chief First Things Mag., N.Y.C., 1990-2009. Bd. dirs. U.S. Inst. Peace, 1986-91, Inst. on Religion and Democracy, 1981-2009, Ethics and Pub. Policy Ctr., 1982-2009. Named one of The 25 Most Influential Evangelists in America, TIME mag., 2005, New York's Influentials, NY Mag., 2006. Mem.: Becket Fund Adv. Bd. Died Jan. 8, 2008.

NEUMANN, ALFRED JOHN, music director; b. Bklyn., Dec. 15, 1928; s. Erich Paul and Elsa (Kleiber) N. BS, Davidson Coll., 1951; MMus, U. Mich., 1954. Asst. to music dir. Brevard (N.C.) Music Ctr., 1948-52; dir. of bands Furman U., Greenville, SC, 1951-52; asst. instr. in music U. Mich., Ann Arbor, 1952-54; music dir. Nat. Conv. of United Ch. of Christ, Washington, 1976, Christ Congregational Ch., Silver Spring, Md., 1958-94; accompanist Washington Performing Arts Soc. Concerts in Schs., Washington, 1972-97, Todd Duncan Voice Studio, Washington, 1992-98. Mem. adv. bd. to select the Bicentennial hymn, U.S. Army, Washington, 1976; student condr. U. Mich. Choirs, Ann Arbor, 1952-54; accompanist U. Mich. Opera Dept., Ann Arbor, 1952-54, The Mozart Trio, Washington, 1958-68. Composer: (church anthems) Truly, We Shall Be in Paradise, 1970, I Sing to Thee, 1983, (sacred opera) An Opera for Christmas, 1961, An Opera for Easter (both premeired on NBC-TV, Washington); contbr. articles to profl. jours. Organizer, dir. concerts to benefit AMA Colls., Washington, 1974, 75; music dir. Nat. Conv. of the United Ch. of Christ, Washington, 1976. Recipient Cert. commendation, Can. Internat. Exhbn., Montreal, Can., 1967, Performance award, WGMS Good Music Sta., Washington, 1980, 1981. Democrat. United Ch. of Christ. Home: Silver Spring, Md. Died Oct. 23, 2008.

NEUMANN, CHARLES AUGUST, regional drainage engineer; b. Walla Walla, Wash., Apr. 10, 1935; s. Elmer Henry Neumann and Thelma Viola (Ostrom) Burgess; m. Mary Martha Havens, June 4, 1960; children: Mary, Bob, Alan, Kelly, Chris, Thomas, Martha. BS in Agrl. Engring., Wash. State U., Pullman, 1957. Tool engr. Boeing Airplane Co., Seattle, 1957-58; hydraulic engr. Bur. of Reclamation, Ephrata, Wash., 1958-59, 60-70, Warden, Wash., 1959-60, chief drainage design br. Othello, Wash., 1970-77, 85-87, Ephrata, 1977-85, regional drainage engr., 1987-96; drainage cons. Neumann Drainage Cons. Svc., from 1996. Contbr. articles to profl. jours. Lt. U.S. Army, 1958. Mem. Am. Soc. Agrl. Engrs. (chmn. drainage of irrigated lands com. 1985-88), Res. Officers Assn. (chpt. sec. 1976-93, chpt. pres. 1994—). Free Methodist. Avocations: stamp collecting/philately, coin collecting/numismatics, camping, walking. Home: Moses Lake, Wash. Died Sept. 8, 2007.

NEUMANN, MAY ALTHEA, retired special education educator; b. Balt., Mar. 23, 1924; d. Henry Neumann and Dorothea Augusta Clas BS, Capital U., Columbus, 1946; MEd, U. Pitts., 1953. Elem. tchr., Geneva, Ohio, Bridgeport, Ohio, 1948-50; tchr. USAF Oversea Sch., Landsberg, Germany, 1950-51; spl. edn. tchr. Martins Ferry, Ohio, 1951-68, Middlesex Elem. Sch., Balt., 1968-89; ret., 1989. Pres. St. Luth. Ch., 1986-89, Women of Luth. Ch., 1986-95. Mem. NEA. Republican. Avocations: knitting, travel. Home: Edgewood, Md. Died May 29, 2008.

NEWELL, DONALD EDWARD, otolaryngologist; b. Portland, Oreg., Nov. 17, 1950; s. Merwyn Jackson and Katherine Ethyl (Kent) N.; m. Shanna Marie Page, June 13, 1981; 1 child, Christine Morgan. BS, Willamette U., Salem, Oreg., 1973; MD, U. Oreg., Portland, 1981. Product analyst ICN Pharm. Co., Portland, 1975-76; surg. resident UCLA Med. Ctr., Torrance, 1981-82; otolaryngology resident Navy Hosp. Bethesda (Md.), 1982-86; asst. dept. head otolaryngology Navy Hosp. Camp Lejeune, Jacksonville, N.C., from 1986. Diplomate Am. Bd. Otolaryngology. Served with USN, 1982—. Fellow Am. Acad. Otolaryngology; mem. AMA, ACS, Am. Acad. Facial Plastic Surgery. Republican. Avocations: skiing, camping, outdoor activities. Home: Jacksonville, NC. Died Feb. 29, 2008.

NEWELL, PETE (PETER FRANCIS NEWELL JR.), retired college basketball coach; b. Vancouver, BC, Can., Aug. 31, 1915; s. Peter Francis and Alice Newell; m. Florence Newell (dec. 1984). Head coach U. San Francisco, 1946-50, Mich. State U., 1950-54, U. Calif., Berkeley, 1954-60, athletic dir., 1960—68. Head coach US Olympic basketball team, 1960. Served in USN. Named Coach of Yr., 1960, Basketball Hall of Fame, 1978. Achievements coaching the University Cal Berkeley to a national championship in 1959 and the US Olympic basketball team to a Gold medal in 1960. Died Nov. 17, 2008.

NEWHOUSE, KEVIN THOMAS, small business owner; b. Fostoria, Ohio, Oct. 31, 1955; s. Vernon Lowell and Edith Mae (Peters) N.; m. Peggy Sue Bohlen, Nov. 14, 1986 (div. May 1987). Journeyman electrician. Owner, electrician Newhouse Electric of Fostoria, from 1987. Rep. candidate for Mayor of Fostoria. With USN, 1975. Home: Fostoria, Ohio. Died Apr. 30, 2008.

NICHOLS, CICELY, book editor, writer, business consultant; b. Seattle, Dec. 29, 1937; d. William Robert and Anna Cicely (Smith) Nichols; m. John Francis Speicher; children: Hilda, Jennifer and Christine Speicher. Freelance editor for book and periodical pubs., 1963—68, freelance, 1970—82, freelance editor, 1996—2002; sr. editor Grove Press, 1968-70; founder, pres. Knickerbocker Cove, Inc., NYC, 1977-88, editor, pub., direct-mail fundraiser, 1987-88; v.p. devel. and pub. affairs Metro Marine Express, Ltd., NYC, 1987—91; freelance writer, from 1971. Author: The Family Formula Book, 1978, In a Time of Fear: Sacco and Vanzetti, 1979, Bread and Roses: Mother Jones, 1980. Grantee Wis. Cmty. Fund, 1982-83, Ford Found., 1972-73. L.M. Rabinowitz Found., 1972-74, others. Mem. Editl. Freelancers Assn. (co-founder). Home: New York, NY. Died Apr. 2, 2008.

NICHOLS, WARREN WESLEY, toxicologist; b. Collingswood, NJ, May 16, 1929; s. David W. and Marie A. (Ringheiser) N.; m. June Helms, Aug. 28, 1953; children: Warren W. Jr., Sean H., Lisa Karin. BS, Rutgers U., 1950; MD, Jefferson Med. Coll., 1954; PhD, U. Lund, Sweden, 1966. Diplomate Am. Bd. Pediat. Intern Cooper Hosp., Camden, N.J., 1954-55; resident Children's Hosp., Phila., 1956-57; chief pediat. Lake Charles (La.) AFB, 1957-59; chief med. staff Camden (N.J.) Mcpl. Hosp., 1959-61; asst. dir. Inst. Med. Rsch., Camden, 1959-84, S. Emlen Stokes prof. genetics, 1975-84; sr. dir. genetic/cellular toxicology, dept. safety assess. Merck Sharp and Dohme Rsch. Labs., West Point, Pa., 1983-89, exec. dir. genetic and cellular toxicology, from 1989. Mem. U.S. Japan Coop. Med. Sci. Prog., DHEW, 1972-74; co-chmn. USA USSR Mammlian Genetics, Nat. Cancer Inst., 1976-80, sci. counselor divsn. cancer cause and prevention, 1979-82. Co-editor: Cellular Senescence and Somatic Cell Genetics, Vols. 1-5, 1977-79, Mycoplasma Infection of Cell Cultures, Vol. 3, 1978, Handbook of Mutagenicity Test Procedures, 1977, 2d edit., 1984, others; contbr. articles to profl. jours. Capt. USAF, 1957-59. Recipient Rsch. Career Devel. award NIH, 1963-72, Alumni Achievement award Jefferson Med. Coll., 1980. Mem. Am. Assn. Cancer Rsch., Am. Soc. Human Genetics, Environ. Mutagen Soc. (councillor 1970-77, sec. 1973-77). Achievements include research on virus chromosome relationships. Home: Green Lane, Pa. Died Nov. 19, 2007.

NICHOLSON, DUWAYNE ERVIN, protective service official; b. Carrington, ND, June 25, 1936; s. Ervin Dorn and Martha (Taverna) N.; m. Judith Karen Haugen, Jan. 1964; children: Dawn Michelle, Karen Michelle. Student, Jamestown Coll., 1955-56, Valley City Coll., ND, 1956-60. Cert. law enforcement officer, N.D. Policeman Valley City (N.D.) Police Dept., 1961-62, patrolman, 1962, sgt., from 1971, tng. officer, from 1974. Cert. instr. N.D. Atty. Gen. Office, Bismarck, N.D., 1983—. Contbr. articles to newspaper. Recipient Cert. Appreciation Kiwanis Club Valley City N.D., 1977-87; Ref. for Law award Frat. Order of Eagles Valley City N.D., 1972; 25th Yr. Svc. award Valley City Police Dept. N.D., 1987; 10 yr Participation award Amvets of N.D., 1987. Mem. N.D. Police Officers Assn., Barnes County Emergency Mgmt. Agy. (Instr. 1978—, Optimists (chancellor comdr. 1970-71), Masons, Elks, Eagles (law award Valley City club 1972), KP (grand outer guard and grand lodge rep. N.D. club 1988, prelate Valley City club 1988). Avocations: camping, travel, fishing, hunting, photography. Home: Valley City, ND. Died Dec. 30, 2007.

NIEMEIER, CYNTHIA LEE, critical care nurse; b. Phila., Feb. 13, 1952; d. David Baine and Norma June (Beucus) Johnston; divorced; 1 child, Seth Christian. ADN with honors, Sinclair C.C., 1981. Cert. provider BLS; cert. instr. BCLS, cert. provider ACLS, Am. Heart Assn. Staff nurse Miami Valley Hosp., Dayton, Ohio, 1982; staff nurse CCU St. Elizabeth Med. Ctr., Dayton, 1982-84; staff nurse med.-surg. ICU/CCU Humana Hosp., Lexington, Ky., 1984; staff nurse med. ICU VA Hosp., Lexington, 1984-85; staff nurse med.-surg. ICU Good Samaritan Hosp., Lexington, 1985-88; staff nurse PACU Swedish Hosp., Seattle, 1988-90, Polyclinic Surgery Ctr., Seattle, from 1990; staff nurse ICU, CCU CIC Providence Med. Ctr., Seattle, 1992, mem. polyclinic code team, from 1994. Instr. BCLS Am. Heart Assn., Ky., 1988-89, ARC, Dayton, 1983-84; ACLS provider Am. Heart Assn., Wash., 1990—. Mem. Caledonian and St. Andrews Soc., Phi Theta Kappa. Republican. Avocations: aerobics, music, travel. Home: Seattle, Wash. Died July 23, 2008.

NOBLE, MARY CATHERINE, physical therapist, nurse; b. Hamilton County, Kans., Mar. 20, 1920; d. Hartwell John and Margaret Katherine (Williamson) N. Diploma in Nursing, Paradise Valley Sch. Nursing, National City, Calif., 1945; BS in Nursing Edn., Pacific Union Coll., Angwin, Calif., 1950; student, Royal Coll. Nursing, London, 1953, Loma Linda U., 1955. Registered phys. therapist, Calif., Colo., Kans. Supr. nursing Paradise Valley Hosp., National City, 1946-49; sister tutor, matron Andrews Meml. Hosp., Kingston, Jamaica, 1950-51; clin. supr. Washington Adventist Hosp., Takoma Park, Md., 1954-59; asst. chief therapist Loma Linda (Calif.) San and Hosp., 1960-62; chief therapist Paradise Valley Hosp., 1962-64; clinic therapist Med.-Dental Clinic, Eugene, Oreg., 1964-68; pvt. practice Action Assocs., Eugene, 1968-72; chief therapist Atlanta West Hosp., 1972, Battle Creek (Mich.) Adventist Hosp., 1972-74, Madison (Tenn.) Hosp., 1974-81. Pvt. practice Action Assocs., Johnson, Kans., 1982—. Co-author: Hydrotherapy and Massage, 1964; co-editor: Stanton County History, 1987; columnist Life and Health, 15 yrs. Sec.-treas. Stanton County Hist. Soc., Johnson, Kans. Mem. Am. Phys. Therapy Assn. Republican. Seventh-day Adventist. Avocations: dogs, bird watching. Home: Johnson, Kans. Died Dec. 21, 2007.

NOEL, JAMES ALFRED, logistician, transportation executive; b. Vanderpool, Tex., Mar. 2, 1921; s. James Alfred and Martha Josephine (Webb) N.; m. Dorothy Jean Walker, Aug. 31, 1941 (dec. Nov. 1987); m. Rebekah Elizabeth Noel, Jan. 29 1994. BA in Math and Physics, S.W. Tex. State Tchrs. Coll., 1942. Adminstrv. asst. to shops supt. San Antonio Air Material Area, Kelly AFB, 1952-54, chief radar repair sect. to supt. electronics br., 1954-57, dep. chief tech. svc. divsn., 1957-59, dep. chief jet engine inventory mgmt. divsn., 1959-69; dep. chief aerospace ground equipment divsn. San Antonio Air Logistics Ctr., Kelly AFB, 1969-76, chief logistics mgmt. br., 1976-78, dep. chief, item mgmt. divsn., 1978-87; dir. TQM Sunset Resources, Inc., San Antonio, from 1987. With USN, 1944-46. Mem. Nat. Assn. of Watch. Clock Coll., Am. Radio Relay League, Soc. for Pres. Barbor Shop and Quartet Singing, Mensa, Masons. Baptist. Avocations: watch clock repair, antique auto restoration. Home: San Antonio, Tex. Died Jan. 30, 2008.

NOFFKE, FRANK EDWARD, educational planner, writer, educator; s. Harry John and Elsie Strack Noffke; m. Ruth Ann Thompson, July 23, 1943 (dec. June 20, 1978); children: James T., Cody. BA, Ind. U., Bloomington, 1938; EdM, Wash. State, Pullman, 1957. Math. instr. U.S. Mil. Acad., West Point, NY, 1945—46; asst. dean student union and activities Case Inst. of Tech., Cleve., 1946—49; planning dir. Compton student union and activities Wash. State, Pullman, 1949—59; v.p. Coll. Planning Assoc., Kalamazoo, 1959—61; planning dir. Coll. union, student activities and values rsch. Baldwin-Wallace Coll., Berea, Ohio, 1961—64; planning dir. student union (designated father of the union) Calif. State U., Long Beach, 1964—80; pres. Frank Noffke Assoc., Pentwater, Mich., from 1950; instr. grad. sch. edn. Calif. State U. at Long Beach, 1972—75. Cons. coll. union and long range planning for universities Frank Noffke Assoc., from 1950; counselor/dir. emeritus veterans affairs dept. Calif. State U., Long Beach, 1972—80, counselor Peace Edn. on campuses World U., Ojai, Calif., 1983—83; chair inter-assn. com. Assn. of Coll. Unions; chair Coun. of Nat. Student Pers. Assns.; mem. Calif. State Post-Secondary Evaluation Team for New Universities, 1984—86, 1995; cons. in field. Author: Planning for a Coll. Union, 1965, 2d edit., 1996; contbr. articles to profl. jours. Mem. UN Non-Governmental Com. on Disarmament, 1995—2000, from 2003; chair and peace adv. OPEN Peace Edn. Network of West Mich., Pentwater, Mich., from 1988; liaison rep. to Rep. Kucinich OPEN Peace Network of West Mich., Washington, from 2001. Maj. Signal Corps US Army, 1941—46. Recipient cert. of appreciation, U.S. Dept. Health, Edn. and Welfare, 1979,

Hon. Citizen of Tucson, Ariz., Edn. Com. Excellence award, Nat. Assn. of Veterans Program Adminstrs. Mem.: Pentwater Svc. Club, Phi Kappa Phi (life). Independent. Congregational U.C.C. Achievements include first to organize peace enclave in W. Mich; invention of regional Peacekeeper O.P.E.N. award. Avocations: tennis, reading, writing. Home: Pentwater, Mich. Died Feb. 4, 2008.

NOLAN, JOAN T., elementary school educator; b. Bklyn., Jan. 31, 1942; d. Thomas Louis and Vivian LaForte; m. Gerard Thomas Nolan, Nov. 19, 1996 (div. Oct. 1994); children: Kenneth, Andrew. BA, Bklyn. Coll., 1963; MS, Hunter Coll., 1968. Classrm. tchr. Bd. Edn., City of N.Y., Bklyn., 1963-68, Richardson (Tex.) Ind. Sch. Dist., from 1981. Cooperating tchr. for student tchrs. Forestridge Elem. Sch., Richardson, 1993, 97, sci. fair coord., 1995-99, initiator sci. club, 1999—. Mem. AAUW (cultural rep., Ednl. Found. Gift given in her name 1999), Assn. Tex. Profl. Educators, Sci. Tchrs. Assn. Tex., Sierra Club. Roman Catholic. Avocations: reading, needlecrafts, exercising, travel, cooking. Home: Richardson, Tex. Died Oct. 26, 2007.

NORRIS, JOHN STEVEN, healthcare company executive; b. Chgo., Apr. 25, 1943; s. Norris Dale and Olive (Grissinger) N.; m. Susan Jean Armstrong, May 3, 1975; children: Lindsey Jean, Whitney Ann, John Scott. BA, U. Ariz., Tucson, 1967, MPH, 1995; B in Fgn. Trade, Thunderbird Grad Sch. Internat. Mgmt., Glendale, Ariz., 1968. lic. nursing home adminstr., gen. contractor, real estate broker. Inspection officer Citicorp, Brazil, Colombia, Mex., Peru, Venezuela, 1968—73, asst. cashier NYC, 1973—74; pres., gen. mgr. Phoenix Athletic Club, 1974-76; bus. mgr. Phoenix Pub. Inc., 1976-77; project mgr. Environ. Constn. Co., Phoenix, 1977-79; pres. AGN Devel. Corp., Phoenix, from 1979, Valley View Realty, Inc., Phoenix, 1981-87; exec. v.p., sec., pres. RGW Constrn. Co., Inc.; pres. Norris/Roberts Group, Inc., Phoenix, 1987-90; CEO Christian Care Co., Inc., Phoenix, from 1990. Chmn. Covenant Health Network, 2001—; mem. CASP curriculum devel. expert panel U. North Tex. Ex officio bd. dirs. Christian Care Found.; chmn. bd. dirs. Dove's Transitional Housing, Inc.; bd. dirs., past chmn. region 1 Area Agy. Aging. Recipient award of honor Ariz. Assn. Homes and Svcs. for Aging, 1999, Time and Talent award Am. Assn. Homes and Svcs. for the Aging and U. North Tex., 2004. Fellow: Am. Coll. Healthcare Exec., Am. Assn. Home Svcs. Aging (retirement housing profl.), Am. Coll. Healthcare Adminstrs.; mem.: Rotary Internat. (treas., past pres. Phoenix club, Paul Harris fellow, Service Above Self award 2002), Phi Delta Theta. Republican. Avocations: skiing, racquetball, horsemanship. Home: Phoenix, Ariz. Died May 3, 2006.

NORRIS, WILLIAM RANDAL, psychologist; b. Lake City, Fla., Feb. 25, 1961; s. William Edgar and Katherine Irene (Brady) N.; m. Susan Ann Walter, Aug. 13, 1989; 1 child, William Christian. AA, Lake City Community Coll., Lake City, Fla., 1980; BS, U. Fla., 1984; MS, U. So. Miss., 1986, PhD, 1989. Lic. psychologist, Tex. Psychologist II Ellisville (Miss.) State Sch., 1988-90; clin. psychologist II Denton (Tex.) State Sch., from 1990, asst. chief psychologist, from 1990. Mem. adj. faculty North Ctrl. Tex. Coll. Contbr. articles to profl. jours. Active with Trinity United Meth. Ch., Denton. Recipient U. So. Miss. grad. assistantship, 1986-88. Mem. Tex. Assn. for Behavior Analysis, Assn. for Behavior Analysis Internat., Psi Chi, Phi Theta Kappa. Avocations: crossword puzzles, reading, animals and animal rights, ecology. Home: Wichita Falls, Tex. Died Apr. 24, 2008.

NORTON, DONALD ALAN, retired adult education educator; b. Mt. Kisco, NY, Mar. 15, 1920; s. Arthur Alonzo and Anne Bertha Norton; m. Jane Louise Lemke, 1948; children: Anne Louise, Janet Marie. BS, Harvard U., 1941; PhD, U. Wis., 1949. Maj. US Army, 1942—45. Home: Davis, Calif. Died July 7, 2008.

NOVAK, ROBERT DAVID SANDERS, syndicated columnist, commentator; b. Joliet, Ill., Feb. 26, 1931; s. Maurice Pall and Jane Anne (Sanders) Novak; m. Geraldine Williams, Nov. 10, 1962; children: Zelda, Alexander. AB, U. Ill., 1952; LLD (hon.), Kenyon Coll., 1987; LittD (hon.), U. Ill., 1998; DHL (hon.), U. St. Francis. Reporter Joliet Herald-News, 1947-51, Champaign-Urbana Courier, Ill., 1951-52, AP, Omaha, Lincoln, Nebr., Indpls. and Washington, 1954-58, The Wall St. Jour., Washington, 1958-63; syndicated columnist NY Herald-Tribune, Washington, 1963-66; commentator Corinthian Broadcasting, Washington, 1963-65, Metromedia, Washington, 1966-76, RKO-Features, Washington, 1976-78; syndicated columnist Chgo. Sun-Times, Washington, 1966—2009; commentator CNN, Washington, 1980—2005, Am. Voice, 1993—2002, Fox News, 2006—09. Pub. Evans-Novak Polit. Report, Washington, 1967—2001, Evans-Novak Tax Report, Washington, 1985—92, Evans-Novak Japan Report, Washington, 1989—92. Author: The Agony of the GOP, 1965, Lyndon B. Johnson: The Exercise of Power, 1967, Nixon In The White House, 1971, The Reagan Revolution, 1981, Completing the Revolution: A Vision for Victory, 2000, Prince of Darkness: 50 Years of Reporting in Washington, 2007. Trustee Bullis Sch., Potomac, Md., 1987—98, Phillips Found., 1991—2009, Children Charities Found., 1994—2009, Youth Leadership Found., 2003—09. 1st lt. US Army, 1952—54. Recipient Cable ACE award, 1990; named to Laureate Order of Lincoln, Lincoln Acad. Ill., 1999. Mem.: Soc. Profl. Journalists, Nat. Press Club (Fourth Estate award 2001), Army-Navy Club, Washington Gridiron Club. Home: Washington, DC. Died Aug. 18, 2009.

NOVICK, ANDREW CARL, urologist; b. Montreal, Apr. 5, 1948; came to U.S., 1974; s. David and Rose (Ortenberg) N.; m. Thelma Silver, June 29, 1969 (div. Dec. 1983); 1 child, Lorne J.; m. Linda Friedman, May 24, 1992; children: Rachel H., Eric D. BSc, McGill U., 1968, MD, CM, 1972. Diplomate Am. Bd. Urology. Resident in surgery Royal Victoria Hosp., Montreal, 1972—74; resident in urology Cleve. Clinic Found., 1974—77, staff dept. urology, from 1977, head sect. renal transplant, from 1977, chmn. Urol. Inst., from 1985, chmn. Organ Transplant Ctr., 1985—92. Trustee Am. Bd. Urology, 1995—2001, Urology Residence Rev. Com., 1997—2002. Editor: Vascular Problems in Urology, 1982, Stewart's Operative Urology, 1989, Renal Vascular Disease, 1995, Innovations in Urologic Surgery, 1997, Campbell's Urology, 2002, 2007, Operative Urology at the Cleveland Clinic, 2006; contbr. more than 500 articles to profl. jours. Fellow ACS, Med. Coun. Can.; mem. Am. Urol. Assn., Am. Assn. Genito-Urinary Surgeons, Clin. Soc. Genito-Urinary Surgeons. Home: Beachwood, Ohio. Died 2009.

NUGENT, MAYNARD CHARLES, construction executive; b. Cleve., May 9, 1934; s. Osborne Lionel and Gertrude (Lowenthal) N.; m. Ann Taber, Nov. 20, 1961; children: Brian Taber, Glenn Webber, Lisanne. BS in Engring., Davis & Elkins Coll., 1957; postgrad., U. Pa., 1960-62, Temple U., 1969-70. Registered profl. engr., N.J., Pa. Adminstrv. engr. City of Phila., 1965-68, chief bridge constrn. engr., 1968-73; dir. engr. Constrn. Industry Advancement Fund of N.J., Pennington, 1973-77; mng. dir. Constrn. Industry Advancement Program of N.J., Cranbury, from 1977. Contbr. articles to profl. jours. Mayor Twp. of Ewing (N.J.), 1980, mem. town coun., 1977-80, mem. econ. devel. commn., 1975-91. Recipient Town Coun. Svc. award Twp. Mayors Coun., 1987; named Employee of Yr. Bur. of Surveys and Design, Phila., 1970 Fellow ASCE (dir. Phila. chpt. 1972-73, com. contract adminstrn. 1970—, com. specifications 1977-82); mem. NSPE, Profl. Engrs. in Constrn. of N.J. (treas. 1986—). Unitarian Universalist. Avocations: swimming, motorcycling, pistol shooting, travel. Home: Trenton, NJ. Died Oct. 29, 2007.

NUSSBAUM, A(DOLF) EDWARD, mathematician, educator; b. Rheydt, Fed. Republic Germany, Germany, Jan. 10, 1925; came to U.S., 1947; s. Karl and Franziska (Scheye) N.; m. Anne Ebbin, Sept. 1, 1957; children: Karl, Franziska. MA, Columbia U., 1950, PhD, 1957. Mem. staff electronic computer project Inst. Advanced Study, Princeton, N.J., 1952-53, mem., 1962-63; instr. math U. Conn., Storrs, 1953-55; asst. prof. Rensselaer Poly. Inst., Troy, N.Y., 1956-58; vis. scholar Stanford U., Calif., 1967-68; asst. prof., then assoc. prof. Washington U., St. Louis, 1958-66, prof., 1966-95, prof. emeritus, 1995—2009. Contbr. articles to profl. jours. Grantee NSF, 1960-79 Mem. Am. Math. Soc. Died Oct. 31, 2009.

NYBAKKEN, JAMES WILLARD, marine biology educator; b. Warren, Minn., Sept. 16, 1936; s. Clarence G. and Effie Pearl (Knutson) N.; m. Bette Halvorsen, Aug. 20, 1960; children: Kent Edward, Scott Jordan. BA summa cum laude, St. Olaf Coll., Northfield, Minn., 1958; MS, U. Wis., 1961, PhD, 1965. Curator zool. museum U. Wis., 1961-62, 64-65; mem. faculty Calif. State U., Hayward, 1965—98, prof. marine ecology and invertebrate zoology, 1972—98; mem. staff Moss Landing Marine Lab., Calif., 1966—98; ret., 1998. Environ. cons., 1972— Author: Readings in Marine Ecology, 1971, 2d edit., 1986, Elements of Zoology, 4th edit, 1977, General Zoology, 6th edit, 1979, Guide to the Nudibranchs of California, 1980, Marine Biology: An Ecological Approach, 1982, 2d edit., 1987, 3d edit., 1992, 4th edit., 1996, 5th edit., 2001, 6th edit., 2005, Diversity of the Invertebrates: A Laboratory Manual, 1996; editor: Interdisciplinary Encyclopedia of Marine Science (3 vols.), 2003. Fellow Calif. Acad. Scis.; mem. AAAS, Am. Soc. Zoologists, Am. Malacological Union (pres. 1985-86), Ecol. Soc. Am., Malacological Soc. London, Western Soc. Malacologists (pres. 1974-75), Western Soc. Naturalists (pres.-elect 1985, pres. 1986, secretariat 1990-96), Sigma Xi. Home: Carmel Valley, Calif. Died June 20, 2009.

NYHUS, LLOYD MILTON, retired surgeon, educator; b. Mt. Vernon, Wash., June 24, 1923; s. Lewis Guttorm and Mary (Shervem) N.; m. Margaret Goldie Sheldon, Nov. 25, 1949 (dec. 2006); children: Sheila Margaret, Leif Torger. BS, Pacific Luth. Coll., 1945; MD, Med. Coll. Ala., 1947; Doctor honoris causa, Aristotelian U., Thessalonika, Greece, 1968, Uppsala U., Sweden, 1974, U. Chihuahua, Mex., 1975, Jagallonian U., Cracow, Poland, 1980, U. Gama Filho, Rio de Janeiro, 1983, U. Louis Pasteur, Strasbourg, France, 1984, U. Athens, 1989. Diplomate Am. Bd. Surgery (chmn. 1974-76). Intern King County Hosp., Seattle, 1947-48, resident in surgery, 1948-55; practice medicine specializing in surgery Seattle, 1956-67, Chgo., from 1967; instr. surgery U. Wash., Seattle, 1954-56, asst. prof., 1956-59, assoc. prof., 1959-64, prof., 1964-67; Warren H. Cole prof., head dept. surgery U. Ill. Coll. Medicine, 1967-89, prof. emeritus, 1989—2008, established Lloyd M. Nyhus, MD chair of gen. surgery, dept. surgery Chgo., 2007. Emeritus surgeon-in-chief U. Ill. Hosp.; sr. cons. surgeon Cook County, West Side VA, Hines VA hosps., Ill.; cons. to Surgeon Gen. NIH, 1965-69. Author: Surgery of the Stomach and Duodenum, 1962, 4th edit., 1986, named changed to Surgery of the Esophagus, Stomach and Small Intestine, 5th edit., 1995, Hernia, 1964, (book name change) Nyhus and Condon's Hernia, 5th edit., 2002, Chinese (Mandarin) edit., 2004, Abdominal Pain: A Guide to Rapid Diagnosis, 1969, 95, Spanish edit., 1996, Russian edit., 2001, Manual of Surgical Therapeutics, 1969, latest rev. edit., 1996, Mastery of Surgery, 1984, 3d edit., 1997, Spanish edit., 1999, Surgery Ann., 1970-95, Treatment of Shock, 1970, 2d rev. edit., 1986, Surgery of the Small Intestine, 1987; editor-in-chief Rev. of Surgery, 1967-77, Current Surgery, 1978-90, emeritus editor, 1991—; assoc. editor Quar. Rev. Surgery, 1958-61; editl. bd. Am. Jour. Digestive Diseases, 1961-67, Scandinavian Jour. Gastroenterology, 1966-97, Am. Surgeon, 1967-89, Jour. Surg. Oncology, 1969-99, Archives of Surgery, 1977-86, World Jour. Surgery, 1977-95; contbr. articles to profl. jours. Served to lt. M.C. USNR, 1943-46, 50-52. Decorated Order of Merit (Poland); postdoctoral fellow USPHS, 1952-53; recipient M. Shipley award So. Surg. Assn., 1967, Rovsing medal Danish Surg. Soc., 1973; Disting. Faculty award U. Ill Coll. Medicine, 1983, Disting. Alumnus award Med. Coll. Ala., 1984, Disting. Alumnus award U. Wash., 1993, 99; Guggenheim fellow, 1955-56. Fellow ACS (1st v.p. 1987-88), Assn. Surgeons Gt. Brit. and Ireland (hon.), Royal Coll. Surgeons Eng. (hon.), Royal Coll. Surgeons Ireland (hon.), Royal Coll. Surgeons Edinburgh (hon.), Royal Coll. Physicians and Surgeons Glasgow (hon.), Internat. Soc. Surgery Found. (hon., sec.-treas. 1992-2001); mem. Am. Gastroent. Assn., Am. Physiol. Soc., Pacific Coast Surg. Assn., Am. Surg. Assn. (recorder 1976-81, 1st v.p. 1989-90), Western Surg. Assn., Ctrl. Soc. Clin. Rsch., Chgo. Surg. Soc. (pres. 1974), Ctrl. Surg. Assn. (pres. 1984), Seattle Surg. Soc., St. Paul Surg. Soc. (hon.), Kansas City Surg. Soc. (hon.), Inst. Medicine Chgo., Internat. Soc. Surgery (hon. fellow 2001, pres. U.S. sect. 1986-88, pres. 34th World Congress 1991, internat. pres. 1991-93), Internat. Soc. for Digestive Surgery (pres. III world congress Chgo. 1974, internat. pres. 1978-84), Soc. for Surgery Alimentary Tract (sec. 1969-73, pres. 1974), Soc. Clin. Surgery, Soc. Surg. Chmn., Soc. U. Surgeons (pres. 1967), Duetschen Gesellschaft für Chirurgie (hon.), Polish Assn. Surgeons (hon.), L'Academie de Chirurgie (France) (corr.), Nat. Acad. of Medicine (France, Argentina and Brazil, hon.), Swiss Surg. Soc. (hon.), Brazilian Coll. Surgeons (hon.), Surg. Biology Club, Warren H. Cole Soc. (pres. 1981), Japan Surg. Soc. (hon.), Assn. Gen. Surgeons of Mex. (hon.), Columbian Surg. Soc. (hon.), Costa Rican Coll. Medicine & Surgery (hon.), Assn. Surgeons Costa Rica (hon.), Internat. Fedn. Surg. Colls. (hon. treas. 1992-99), Sigma Xi, Alpha Omega Alpha, Phi Beta Pi. Home: Chicago, Ill. Died Dec. 15, 2008.

OBERHELLMAN, THEODORE ARNOLD, JR., marketing executive, mechanical engineer; b. St. Louis, Nov. 22, 1934; s. Theodore Arnold Sr. and Emma Estelle (Vietmeier) O.; m. Benita Louise Nolan, June 8, 1957; children: Theodore Arnold III, Mark Joseph, Scott Thomas, Lynn Marie, John Robert. BSME, Washington U., St. Louis, 1957. With Allis-Chalmers Corp., 1964-88, gen. sales mgr. solids process group Aurora, Ill., 1977-80; v.p. mktg. Stephens Adamson Div. Allis-Chalmers Corp., Aurora, Ill., 1980-88, Stephens-Adamson Div. Boliden Allis Inc., Aurora, from 1988, v.p., acting gen. mgr., from 1989. 2d lt. U.S. Army, 1958. Mem. Nat. Stone Assn. (bd. dirs. mfrs. and svcs. div. Washington chpt. 1981, 83-85). Avocation: skiing. Home: Ocala, Fla. Died Jan. 17, 2008.

O'BRIEN, ANNA BELLE CLEMENT, retired state senator; b. Scottsville, May 6, 1923; d. Robert S. Clement; m. Charles H. O'Brien (dec. 2007); 3 stepchildren. Student, McMurry Coll., Abilene, Tex. Chief of staff to Gov., State Tenn., 1963—67; mem. Tenn. House Reps., 1975—77, Tenn. State Senate, 1977—91. Active mem. Am. Legion Aux., Cumberland County Mental Health Assn., DAR, Cumberland County Beautiful Assn., Hosp. Aux.; bd. dirs. Plateau Mental Health Ctr., Cookeville, Tenn., Wharton Nursing Home, Cumberland County, Crossville C. of C.; adv. coun. mem. Maccasin Bend Psychiat. Hosp., Chattanooga. Mem.: Bus. & Profl. Women's Club, Lake Tansi Village Women's Club, Marie Ervin Home Demonstration Club, Top Town Garden Club, Dem. Women's Club. Baptist. Home: Crossville, Tenn. Died Aug. 31, 2009.

O'BRIEN, JAMES HENRY, JR., former county assistant district attorney; b. White Plains, NY, Sept. 5, 1946; s. James Henry Sr. and Winona Melissa (Lombard); m. Patricia Lee Hill, June 24, 1972 (div. Sept. 1979); children: Christopher James, Craig Patrick; m. Deborah Ann Boldon, July 17, 1987 (dec. Mar. 1997); children: James Henry III, Timothy Malcolm. BA, Baldwin Wallace Coll., 1968; JD, Cleve. State U., 1973. Bar: N.Y. 1974, Conn. 1996, U.S. Dist. Ct. (so. and ea. dists.) N.Y. 1975, U.S. Ct. Appeals (2d cir.) 1975, U.S. Supreme Ct. 1982. Asst. dist. atty. Westchester County Dist. Atty.'s Office, White Plains, N.Y., 1973-94; pvt. practice Harrison, N.Y., from 1994. With USAF, 1969-70. Mem. Westchester County Bar Assn., White Plains Bar Assn., Am. Legion (post 135, White Plains), Phi Alpha Delta. Republican. Methodist. Avocations: sports, boating, children. Home: White Plains, NY. Died June 9, 2008.

O'BRIEN, JOHN M., savings and loan executive; b. Phila., Sept. 29, 1930; s. James W. and Julia A. (Doyle) O'B.; m. Mary Ellen Thompson, Oct. 8, 1955; children: James, Maureen, Michael, Denise, MaryEllen, Kevin. BS, Temple U., 1955. Corp. sec., mortgage officer North Phila. Savs. & Loan Assn., 1949-66; pres. Cen. Pa. Savs. Assn., Shamokin, from 1966, Cen. Pa. Fin. Corp., Shamokin, from 1986. Bd. dirs., past vice chmn. Fed. Home Loan Bank Pitts.; bd. dirs. Ctr. for Fin. Studies. Bd. dirs. Boy Scouts

Am.; active United Way. Recipient cert. of appreciation Pa. Savs. and Loan League, 1974-75, Laredo Achievement award 1972; named Man of Yr., Phila. Soc. Savs. and Loan Mortgage Officers, 1972. Mem. U.S. League Savs. Instns. (bd. dirs., pres. 1973-74), Nat. Coun. Savs. Instns. (bd. dirs.), Pa. Assn. Savs. Instns. (legis. chmn.), Shamokin C. of C., Indian Hills Golf and Tennis Club, Susquehanna Valley Country Club, Moose, Elks, Kiwanis (past lt. gov., Outstanding Leader award). Democrat. Roman Catholic. Avocations: golf, reading. Home: Shamokin, Pa. Died Jan. 27, 2008.

O'BRIEN, MICHAEL M., lawyer; b. Hancock, Mich., Mar. 16, 1957; s. Richrd and Barbara (Cannon) O'B.; m. Anne Marie O'Brien, Dec. 5, 1987; children: Katie, Patricia, Andrew, John Connor. BS, No. Mich. U., 1979; JD, Creighton U., 1983. Bar: Nebr. 1983. Ptnr. Cannon, Goodman, O'Brien & Grant, P.C., Omaha, 1983-96, Michael O'Brien P.C., Omaha, from 1996. Mem. ABA, Nebr. Bar Assn., Nebr. Trial Attys. Assn., Omaha Bar Assn. Republican. Roman Catholic. Died Dec. 2, 2007.

O'BRIENT, DAVID WARREN, sales executive, consultant; b. Toledo, Oct. 2, 1927; s. Earl James and Jessie Carlton (Edwards) O'B.; m. Enid Jo Wynne O'Brient, Feb. 21, 1962 (div. Apr. 1978); 1 child, David Warren Jr. BS in Archtl. Engring., U. Tex., 1949. Registered profl. engr., Tex. Sales engr. Smith Engring. Co., Houston, 1949-53; dist. sales mgr. Dunham-Bush, Inc., Hartford, Conn., 1953-60; sales mgr. W.L. Lashley & Assoc., Houston, 1960-67; pres., owner OJ & C. Co., Inc., Houston, 1967-78, exec. v.p., 1980-83; pres., owner O'Brient Engring. Co., Houston, 1983-89. Mem., phone solicitor Rep. Party, Houston, 1962—; mem. adminstrv. bd. First United Meth. Ch., Houston, 1969—. With USN, 1945-46, 50-52, PTO, Korea. Mem. ASHRAE, Phi Eta Sigma, Tau Sigma Delta, Tau Beta Pi. Avocations: sports, music. Died Dec. 5, 2007.

O'CONNELL, WALTER EDWARD, psychologist; b. Reading, Mass., Aug. 2, 1925; s. Walter Edward and Margaret Cecilia (Turner) O'C.; m. Gloria June Kane, Aug. 5, 1960. BA, U. Mass., 1950; MA, U. Tex., 1952, PhD, 1958. Diplomate Am. Bd. Profl. Psychology; licensed psychologist, Tex. Rsch. and clin. psychologist VA Med. Ctr., 1955-86; clin. assoc. prof. Baylor Coll. Medicine, Houston, 1967-92, U. Houston, 1967-86; dir. Natural High Ctr., Bastrop, Tex., from 1986. Adj. prof. U. St. Thomas, Houston, 1966-86, Baylor U., Waco, Tex., 1959-66, Union Inst., Cin., 1984—; pvt. practice in psychotherapy, Houston, 1973-86; cons. to hosps., univs., chs., schs., and bus., 1965-86. Author: Action Therapy and Adlerian Theory, 1975, 80; contbr. chpts. to books and 350 articles to Voices, The Art and Sci. of Psychotherapy, Individual Psychology, Adlerian Jour. Rsch., Theory and Practice; columnist: Bastrop Advertiser, 1991-94. Legislator dist. II Tex. Silver-Haired Legislature, Austin, 1992; officer, chairperson Bastrop County Retirement Orgns., 1987-94. With U.S. Army, 1943-45. Recipient award Roth Foun., 1977, Annual Nat. VA Profl. Svc. award for therapeutic svc. to vets., 1983. Fellow APA, Internat. Acad. Eclectic Psychotherapists, Acad. Clin. Psychology, Am. Assn. Applied Preventive Psychology; mem. N.Am. Soc. Adlerian Psychology (life, pres. 1972, bd. dirs. 1966-72, 74-77, Outstanding Performance awards 1977, 92), Am. Acad. Psychotherapists (life, mem. editl. bd. 1965-70, 76-83). Democrat. Achievements include research in natural high theory and practice, psychospiritual approach to wellness and interactive health, theory and practice of self-esteem, sense of humor, encouragement, community connectedness, didactic experiential methods. Died Oct. 25, 2007.

O'CONNOR, JAMES DRISCOLL, educational director, psychologist; b. Lawrence, Mass., May 26, 1949; s. John J. and Dorothy C. (Sullivan) O'C.; m. Linda M. Wolfenden, June 15, 1985; 1 child, Sarah Marie. BA, Villanova U., 1971, MA, 1972; Cert. Advanced Grad. Studies, Boston State Coll., 1980; EdD, U. Mass., 1990. Cert. adminstr. spl. edn., prin., counselor, tchr., psychologist. Guidance dir. Austin Prep. Sch., Reading, Mass., 1972-74; elem. tchr., elem. prin. Methuen (Mass.) Schs., 1974-80; coord., psychologist Salem (Mass.) Pub. Schs., 1980-81, asst. dir. spl. edn., 1981-89, dir. spl. edn., 1989-99, dir. pupil pers. svcs., from 1999. Assoc. prof. grad. sch. Salem State Coll., 1986—. Mem. NEA, Coun. Exceptional Children, Mass. Assn. Spl. Edn. Adminstrs. Home: Hampton, NH. Died Mar. 25, 2008.

O'CONNOR, JOHN JAY, III, retired lawyer; b. San Francisco, Jan. 10, 1930; s. John Jay and Sally (Flynn) O'C.; m. Sandra Day, Dec. 20, 1952; children: Scott, Brian, Jay. AB, Stanford U., 1951, LLB, 1953. Bar: Calif. 1953, Ariz. 1957, D.C. 1981. Mem. Fennemore, Craig, von Ammon & Udall, Phoenix, 1957-81, Miller & Chevalier, Washington, 1982-88; ptnr. Bryan Cave LLP, Washington and Phoenix, 1988-99, of counsel, 2000—09. Judge pro-tem Superior Ct. State of Ariz., 1979-81. Chmn. Ariz. Crippled Children's Svcs., 1968; Chmn. planning and zoning commn. Town of Paradise Valley, 1967; Chmn. Maricopa County Young Republicans, 1960, Ariz. Young Rep. League, 1962; bd. dirs. Ariz. Tax Rsch. Assn., 1966-81; chmn. bd. dirs. Maricopa County Gen. Hosp., 1967-70; exec. com. bd. visitors Stanford Law Sch., 1976-80; pres. Stanford Law Fund, 1980-82; mem. nat. coun. Salk Inst. Biol. Studies, San Diego, 1977-90; pres. Phoenix-Scottsdale United Way, 1977-79; bd. dirs. World Affairs Coun. of Phoenix, 1970-81, Legal Aid Soc. Phoenix, Maricopa County Mental Health Assn.; trustee Meridian House Internat., Washington, 1982-88; mem. policy devel. com. Phoenix Cmty. Svc. Fund, 1978; mem. exec. com. Valley Leadership, 1979-81; bd. dirs. Trusteeship for St. Luke's Hosp., 1979-81; mem. adv. com. Nat. Postal Mus., Washington, 1992-98. Served to 1st lt. AUS, 1954-57. Mem. ABA, Stanford Assocs., Paradise Valley Country Club, Ariz. Club (pres. 1979-81), Valley Field Riding and Polo Club, Stanford Club of Phoenix (pres.), Iron Springs Club (pres. 1974-76), Bohemian Club, Met. Club, Alfalfa Club, Alibi Club, Delta Upsilon, Phi Delta Phi. Died Nov. 11, 2009.

O'CONNOR, WILLIAM RIORDAN, lawyer, educator; b. Bronx, NY; s. Charles Samuel O'Connor and Elizabeth Mary Riordan; 1 child, Charles. BA, Fordham Coll., Bronx, 1973; MA, Fordham U., Bronx, 1977, PhD, 1982; JD, Cardozo Sch. Law, NYC. Asst. prof. philosophy Siena Coll., Londonville, NY, 1983—84; law clk. Weg and Myers, PC, NYC, 1987—90, assoc., 1990—91; pvt. practice Bronx, NY, from 1996. Adj. lectr. St. Peter's Coll., Jersey City, from 1991; assoc. Law Offices of Stephen K. Seung, NYC, from 1999; arbitrator small claims NYC Civil Cts., from 2004, guardian ad litem, from 2006. Mem.: Am. Philos. Assn., NY County Lawyers Assn., Assn. Bar NYC. Democrat. Roman Catholic. Home: Hopewell Junction, NY. Deceased.

O'DELL, ARVIN CARLON, chiropractor; b. Trenton, Mich., Jan. 20, 1954; s. Carson Sherman and Blanche Mae (Bauer) O'D.; m. Deborah Ann Mason, Sept. 10, 1955; children: Kristin Joy, Luke Daniel. AA, U. Cin., 1974; D. Chiropractic, Sherman Coll., 1977. Owner, chiropractor O'Dell Chiropractic Clinic, Ypsilanti, Mich., from 1978. Trustee Ypsilanti Bd. Edn., 1989—, v.p. sch. bd., 1992-93. Recipient Appreciation award Ypsilanti Pub. Schs., 1987, Huron Valley coun. Girl Scouts U.S., 1990, 91, 92. Mem. Mich. Union Chiropractors (sec. 1989-90), Optimists, Order Eastern Star (assoc. patron 1991-92, worthy patron elect 1992-93), Phoenix Lodge. Avocations: fishing, hunting, bicycling, baseball, reading. Died May 17, 2008.

ODEN, ROBERT RUDOLPH, surgeon; b. Chgo., Dec. 2, 1922; s. Rudolph J. E. and Olga H. (Wahlquist) Oden; m. Nancy Clow; children: Louise, Boyd, Beach, Lisbeth. BS, U. Ill., 1943; MD, Northwestern U., 1947, MS in Anatomy, 1947. Intern Augustana Hosp., Chgo., 1947-48, resident in surgery, 1948-49; resident in orthopaedics Hines Vets. Hosp., Chgo., 1949-51; resident in children's orthopaedics Shriner's Hosp., 1953-54; pvt. practice Chgo., 1954-57, Aspen, Colo., from 1957. Clin. assoc. prof. orthopedics U. Colo.; orthop. surgeon U.S. Olympic Com., 1960, 72, 76, 80; founder, trustee Pitkin County Bank, from 1983. Assoc. editor: Clin. Orthopedics and Related Rsch. Founder Aspen Inst. Theol. Futures, 1978, Gt. Tchrs. and Preachers Series Episc. Ch., 1989; trustee U.S. Ski Ednl. Found., 1967—82, Aspen Valley Hosp., 1978—86; founder Aspen Orthop. and Sports Medicine Pub. Found., 1985; mem. organizing com. Aspen World Cup, 1976—92; founder Aspen Pitken Employee Housing, 1975. Recipient Biegan award Most Outstanding Svc. to U.S. Skiing, 1985, Halsted award, U.S. Ski Assn., 1987; named to Colo. Ski Hall of Fame, 2002, U.S. Ski Hall of Fame, 2002. Mem.: SICOT, ACS, Internat. Knee Inst., Internat. Soc. Knee, ACL Study Group, Internat. Ski Safety Soc., Am. Orthop. Soc. Sports Medicine (Hall of Fame 2004), Can. Orthop. Assn., Rocky Mountain Traumatologic Soc., Am. Assn. Bone & Joint Surgeons, Western Orthop. Assn., Internat. Coll. Surgeons, Am. Acad. Orthop. Surgeons, Phi Beta Kappa. Home: Aspen, Colo. Died May 18, 2008.

ODEN, WILLIAM ARTHUR, minister, artist; b. Dallas, Mar. 27, 1920; s. William Arthur and Mattie Lee (Griffin) O.; m. Dorothy Lee Robinson, Nov. 21, 1941; children: Anna Lee, William Arthur III, Virginia Christina Oden Martin, Nicholas Robinson, Samuel Garner. BA, U. Tex., El Paso, 1953, MA, 1959; BFA, U. N.Mex., 1987. Ordained to ministry, Anglican Cath. Ch., 1991. Clerical N.Am. Aviation Co., Grand Prairie, Tex., 1941-42; examiner, auditor U.S. VA, Dallas, 1948-51; air traffic control specialist CAA and FAA, El Paso, Tex. and Albuquerque, 1951-77; artist Placitas, N.Mex., from 1977; min. Anglican Cath. Ch., Albuquerque, from 1991. Chmn. Air Traffic Control Assn., El Paso, 1959-61; catechist Anglican Cath. Ch., Albuquerque, 1987—. Pioneered air traffic control procedures USAF, 1942-46; supply priest Anglican Cath. Ch., 1993—; author, speaker Air Traffic Control Goes to Coll., 1959; author, editor Fisherman publ., 1990—. Bd. dirs. Ranchos De Placitas Water and Sanitation Dist., 1980-94. Sgt. USAF, 1942-46. Mem. Art in the Mountain, Sons of Am. Revolution, Md. Geneol. Soc., Sandoval County Hist. Soc., Vintage Thunderbird Club Internat. Democrat. Avocations: singing liturgical music, viticulture, horses, architecture, history research. Home: Placitas, N.Mex. Died Mar. 26, 2008.

ODHIAMBO, ATIENO E. S., history educator, researcher; b. Kisumu, Nyanza, Kenya, Sept. 11, 1946; came to U.S., 1988; s. Zablon and Rosbella (Akumu) Ogwamor; m. Jane Erose Audi, Mar. 15, 1968; children: Susan, Caroline, Michael, Samson. BA in History with first class honors, Makerere U., Kampala, Uganda, 1970; PhD in History, Nairobi U., Kenya, 1973. Spl. asst. dept. history Nairobi U., 1970-71, tutorial fellow dept. history, 1971-73, lectr. dept. history, 1973-78, sr. lectr. dept. history, 1978-87, assoc. prof. dept. history, 1987; prof. history Egerton U., Njoro, Kenya, 1988, Rice U., Houston, 1989—2009. Jr. rsch. assoc. St. Anthony's Coll., Oxford, England, 1971-72; vis. rsch. scholar Hoover Instn., Sanford, Calif., 1979-80; vis. lectr. dept. history Stanford U., 1980; rsch. scholar Cologne U., Germany, 1980; vis. prof. dept. history Johns Hopkins U., 1985, 86; vis. assoc. prof. dept. history Rice U., 1988-89; sr. rsch. fellow African Studies Ctr., U. Witwatersand, Johannesburg, South Africa, 1990; sr. fellow Harry S. Truman Inst. for Peace, Hebrew U. Jerusalem, 1990-91; vis. prof. dept. anthropology Witwatersand U., 1992. Author: The Paradox of Collaboration and Other Essays, 1974, A History of East Africa, 1977, Siasa: Politics and Nationalism in East Africa 1888-1939, 1982, (with Peter Wanyande) History and Government of Kenya, 1988, (with D. W. Cohen) Siaya: Historical Anthropology of an African Landscape, 1989, Burying S.M.: The Politics of Knowledge and the Sociology of Power in Africa, 1992; editor (with W. O. Oyugi et al) Democratic Theory and Practice in Africa, 1988; contbr. over 40 articles and book reviews to profl. jours. Grad. fellow Rockefeller Found., 1971-72; Fullbright scholar Syracuse U., 1978; grantee NEH, 1992. Died Feb. 25, 2009.

ODOM, SCOTT J., college administrator, educator; b. Oak Park, Ill., Sept. 10, 1958; s. Bruce Stuart and Patricia (Keleher) O.; m. Christine M. Callinan, Apr. 7, 1990; children: Zachary, Rachel, Georgia. BA, SUNY, Purchase, 1988; MA, Loyola Marymount U., LA, 1995. Fin. aid adminstr. Loyola Marymount U., LA, 1989-92, admissions and fin. aid adminstr., 1992-98, instr. English, from 1995. Author theatre criticism L.A. Theatres Mag., 1994-96; author cultural criticism Daily Web Mag., 1995-97; contbr. fiction and poetry to mags.; on-air personality, theater critic KXLU Radio, 1990-97. Democrat. Roman Catholic. Avocation: guitar. Home: Los Angeles, Calif. Died Nov. 30, 2007.

O'DONNELL, EDWARD JOSEPH, bishop emeritus, retired editor; b. St. Louis, July 4, 1931; s. Edward Joseph and Ruth Mary (Carr) O'Donnell. Student, Cardinal Glennon Coll., 1949-53; postgrad., Kenrick Sem., 1953-57. Ordained priest Archdiocese of St. Louis, 1957; assoc. pastor in 5 St. Louis parishes, 1957-77; pastor St. Peter's Ch., Kirkwood, Mo., 1977-81; assoc. dir. Archdiocesan Commn. on Human Rights, 1962-70; dir. Archdiocesan Radio-TV Office, 1966-68, Archdiocesan Vocation Council, 1965; editor St. Louis Rev., 1968-81; vicar-gen. Archdiocese of St. Louis, 1981-84, aux. bishop, 1984-94; ordained bishop, 1984; bishop Diocese of Lafayette, 1994—2002, bishop emeritus Lafayette, La., 2002—09. Bd dirs Nat Cath Conf Interracial Justice, 1980—85; chmn Interfaith Clergy Coun Greater St Louis, 1963—67; NAACP, 1964—66; bd dirs Urban League St Louis, 1962—68. Named to Golden Dozen, Int Soc Weekly Newspaper Eds, 1970, 1977. Mem.: Nat Asn TV Arts and Scis, Cath Press Asn. Roman Catholic. Home: Saint Louis, Mo. Died Feb. 1, 2009.

ODUM, MARIA ELIZABETH, infection control practitioner; b. Huntington, NY, Aug. 27, 1945; d. John and Angela (Guagliardi) Bagatta; m. William Odum, Nov. 18, 1972. BA, Coll. Mt. St. Vincent, Riverdale, NY, 1967; MA, Fordham U., Bronx, NY, 1969; BS in Nursing, U. Va., Charlottesville, 1980; AD in Fine Arts, Piedmont Va. C.C., Charlottesville, 1990. Cert. infection control practitioner; ordained to ministry Universal Life Ch. EMT shock-trauma technician, infection control officer Charlottesville-Albemarle Rescue Squad, from 1982; office nurse Peyton Taylor, MD, Charlottesville, 1982-83; insvc. dir., infection control nurse Eldercare Gardens Nursing Home, Charlottesville, 1983-88; cons. infection control Martha Jefferson Hosp., 1988-89; cons. in infection control, 1989-92; Reiki therapist Healing Hands Chiropractic and Holistic Health Ctr., Ivy, Va., 1992-94; Reiki master, Aura-Soma practitioner, ptnr., co-owner Light Ctr. for Healing Arts, Inc., Charlottesville, Va., from 1994. Mem. Sigma Theta Tau, Alpha Mu Gamma. Home: Stanardsville, Va. Died July 15, 2008.

OGIER, WALTER THOMAS, retired physics educator; b. Pasadena, Calif., June 18, 1925; s. Walter Williams and Aileen Vera (Polhamus) O.; m. Mayrene Miriam Gorton, June 27, 1954; children: Walter Charles, Margaret Miriam, Thomas Earl, Kathryn Aileen. BS, Calif. Inst. Tech., 1947, PhD in Physics, 1953. Research fellow Calif. Inst. Tech., 1953; instr. U. Calif. at Riverside, 1954-55, asst. prof. physics, 1955-60, Pomona Coll., Claremont, Calif., 1960-62, assoc. prof., 1962-67, prof. physics, 1967-89, prof. emeritus, from 1989, chmn. dept., 1972-89. Contbr. articles on metals, liquid helium, X-rays and proton produced X-rays to profl. jours. Served with USNR, 1944-46. NSF Sci. Faculty fellow, 1966-67 Mem. Am. Phys. Soc., Am. Assn. Physics Tchrs. (pres. So. Calif. sect. 1967-69), Tau Beta Pi. Home: Atascadero, Calif. Died May 5, 2009.

O'HAGAN, WILLIAM D., metal products manufacturing executive; Grad., Rutgers U., Harvard U. V.p., gen. mgr. NIBCO Inc.; with Cambridge-Lee Industries, Phelps Dodge Copper Products Co.; pres., COO Mueller Industries, Memphis, 1992—94, pres., CEO, 1994—2008. Died Oct. 27, 2008.

O'HALLORAN, WILLIAM JOHN, priest, university administrator; b. Springfield, Mass., Nov. 26, 1927; s. F. Thomas and Dorothy M. (Keegan) O'H. AB, Boston Coll., 1951, MA, 1952; PhL, Weston Coll., 1952; MA, Fordham U., 1955, PhD, 1964; STL, Facultés St. Louis, Chantilly, France, 1964. Tchr. Boston Coll. High Sch., 1952-54; prof. Coll. of the Holy Cross, Worcester, Mass., 1964-75; pres. LeMoyne Coll., Syracuse, N.Y., 1976-81; devel. officer Coll. of the Holy Cross, Worcester, 1981-84, v.p., from

1984. Bd. dirs. Jesuits of Holy Cross Coll., Inc., Worcester, 1989—, Unity Mutual Life Ins. Co., Syracuse, 1983—. Mem. Jesuits, APA, Eastern Psychol. Assn., Mass. Psychol. Assn., Sigma Xi, Alpha Sigma Nu. Home: Worcester, Mass. Died Feb. 26, 2008.

O'HARA, JOHN PATRICK, lawyer, consultant; b. NYC, Jan. 11, 1930; s. Thomas James and Anne (Henry) O'H.; m. Mary Ann Leavey, Oct. 15, 1955; children: Ann O'Hara Carroll, Kathleen O'Hara Geary, Maureen O'Hara-Padden. BBA in Acctg., St. John's U., NYC, 1952; JD, U. Balt., 1960. Bar: Md. 1960. Acct. Am. Cyanamid Corp., 1954—55; spl. agt. FBI, 1955-62; chief counsel, staff dir. emeritus subcommittee on investigations and oversight US House Com. on Pub. Works & Transp., Washington, 1962-86; dir. corp. security Flying Tiger Ln., LA, 1986-89; ptnr. Burgess & O'Hara, Upper Marlboro, Md., 1990-91; cons. Legal Svcs. Corp., Washington, 1990-91, pres., 1991-94; cons., 1994—2009. 1st lt. USMC, 1952-1960. Decorated Nat. Def. Svc. medal, UN medal, Korean Svc. medal. Mem. Md. Bar Assn., Bolling AFB Officers Club, Marines Meml. Assn., Am. Legion. Home: Alexandria, Va. Died Apr. 16, 2009.

O'HERN, DANIEL JOSEPH, retired state supreme court justice; b. Red Bank, NJ, May 23, 1930; s. J. Henry and Eugenia A. (Sansone) O'H.; m. Barbara Ronan, Aug. 8, 1959; children: Daniel J., Eileen, James, John, Molly. AB, Fordham Coll., 1951; LLB, Harvard U., 1957. Bar: N.J. 1958. Law clk. to Justice William J. Brennan Jr. US Supreme Ct., Washington, 1957-58; assoc. Abramoff, Apy & O'Hern, Red Bank, NJ, 1966-78; commr. NJ Dept. Environ. Protection, Trenton, 1978-79; counsel to Gov. State of NJ, Trenton, 1979—81; assoc. justice NJ Supreme Ct., Trenton, 1981—2000; counsel Gibbons, Del Deo, Dolan, Griffinger & Vecchione, Newark, 2000—09. Former mem. adv. com. profl. ethics N.J. Supreme Ct.; commr. Nat. Conf. Commrs. Uniform State Laws, 2001-09. Past trustee Legal Aid Soc. Monmouth County, (N.J.); mayor Borough of Red Bank, 1969-78, councilman, 1962-69. Served as lt. (j.g.) USNR, 1951-54. Fellow Am. Bar Found.; mem. ABA, N.J. Bar Assn., Monmouth County Bar Assn., Harvard Law Sch. Assn. N.J. (past pres.) Home: Little Silver, NJ. Died Apr. 1, 2009.

O'HERN, ELIZABETH MOOT, microbiologist, writer; b. Richmondville, NY, Sept. 1, 1913; d. Carl Melvin and Margaret Esther (Dibble) Moot; m. William J. O'Hern, Jan. 4, 1952. BA in Bacteriology, U. Calif., Berkeley, 1945, MA in Bacteriology, 1947; PhD in Microbiology (grad. fellow), U. Wash., 1956. Instr. SUNY, Bklyn., 1957-62; asst. prof., microbiology George Washington U., Washington, 1962-65; prin. investigator rsch. Bionetics Rsch. Lab., kensington, Md., 1965-67; adminstr. rsch. grants microbiology/genetics/anesthesiology NIH, Nat. Inst. Gen. Med. Scis., Bethesda, Md., 1968-75, spl. asst. to dir., 1975-77, adminstr. spl. programs, 1977-86, also programs adminstr. Mem. bd. examiners in basic scis. Commn. on Licensure to Practice Healing Arts in D.C., 1974-75; panel mem. Washington Area Office, U.S. Civil Svc. Commn., 1977-86; program cons. U. Calif., 1990; mem. People-to-People Microbiology Delegation to China, 1983. Author: Profiles of Pioneer Women Scientists, 1986; contbr. articles to profl. publs. Fellow AAAS, Am. Acad. Microbiology; mem. AAUW (pres. Washington br. 1967-69, trustee edn. found. 1976-81), Am. Inst. Biol. Sci., Am. Pub. Health Assn., Am. Soc. Cell Biology, Am. Soc. Microbiology (chmn. status of women in the profession 1975-78), Am. Soc. Cell Biology, Am. Soc. Tropical Medicine and Hygiene, Med. Mycology Soc. Am., Mycol. Soc. Am., N.Y. Acad. Sci. (honoree 1998), Wash. Acad. Sci., Assn. Women in Sci., Astron. Soc. Pacific, Planetary Soc., Sigma Delta Epsilon (Grad. Women in Sci.) (nat. sec. 1974-77, chpt. pres. 1979-80, historian 1994-97), Sigma Xi. Home: Fairport, NY. Died Feb. 19, 2003.

OHLKE, CLARENCE CARL, public affairs administrator; b. Kansas City, Mo., Feb. 16, 1916; s. William Erdman and Amanda (Rubin) O.; m. Frances Woodley Nicholson, Oct. 9, 1954; children: Daniel N., Carl E., Amanda A. AA, Kansas City Jr. Coll., 1935; BS, U. Mo., 1940. Personnel examiner, rsch. asst. to city mgr. Mcpl. Govt., city of Kansas City, 1940-41; personnel specialist WPB, Washington, 1942; dir. civilian personnel Chief Naval Operations, Washington, 1946-47; successively personnel specialist, asst. dir. community ops., dir. contracts br., prodn. div. AEC, Washington, 1947-58, spl. asst. to chmn. and commr., 1959-61, asst. dir. operations div. contracts, 1961, asst. to asst. gen. mgr. ops., 1962-63, dir. Office Econ. Impact and Conversion, 1964-66; spl. asst. to dir., head congl. and pub. affairs, govt. and pub. programs dir. NSF, Washington, 1966-73; cons., dir. Center Urban Research and Environ. Studies Drexel U., 1973-75; cons. pub. affairs, from 1976. Served to lt. USNR, 1942-46. Recipient Disting. Service award NSF, 1973; resolution of commendation Pres.' Nat. Sci. Bd., 1973. Mem.: AAAS (pub. understanding of sci. com. 1977—80). Died July 8, 2004.

OHM, DAVID LEE, school principal; b. Fremont, Nebr., Feb. 18, 1948; s. Harold Jason and Jayne Ann (Furstenau(O.; m. Anita Jane Shepp, Aug. 21, 1975; children: Jason Edward, Janine Lael. BS in Edn., Oreg. State U., 1970; MS in Counseling, Portland State U., Oreg., 1974, MS in Adminstrn., 1978. Cert. counselor. Various counseling, tchg. postitions, Oreg., 1970-85; asst. prin. Roseburg (Oreg.) H.S., 1985-92, co-prin., 1992-93; dir. secondary edn. Roseburg Sch. Dist., 1993-95; prin. East Sutherlin Sch., Sutherlin, Oreg., from 1995. Chair Gov.'s Coun. on Alcohol and Drug Abuse, Oreg., 1987-92; mem. Pub. Safety Coord. Coun., Douglas County, Oreg., 1995-98, mem. Juvenile Adv. Coun., 1987—, mem. County Commr.'s Adv. Bd., 1988. Recipient Youth Svcs. award Columbia Douglas Med. Ctr., Roseburg, 1988, Svc. award State of Oreg., 1991, Hon. Chpt. Farmer award FFA, Roseburg, 1987, 95. Mem. Nat. Elem. Prins. Assn., Oreg. Reading Assn., Conf. Oreg. Sch. Adminstrs. Avocations: reading, fishing, rodeo. Home: Sutherlin, Oreg. Died June 2, 2008.

OHM, JACK ELTON, mathematics educator; b. Milw., Sept. 23, 1932; s. Walter C. and Mabel S. (Elton) O. BS, U. Chgo., 1954; PhD, U. Calif., Berkeley, 1959. NSF postdoctoral fellow Johns Hopkins U., Balt., 1959-60; asst. prof. U. Wis., Madison, 1960-65; postdoctoral fellow U. Calif., Berkeley, 1964-65; assoc. prof. La. State U., Baton Rouge, 1965-69, prof. in math., 1969-83, prof. emeritus, from 1983. Vis. prof. Purdue U., West Lafayette, Ind., 1971-72, U. Wis., Milw., 1978-79. Mem. Am. Math. Soc. (speaker southeastern sect. meeting 1979), Math. Assn. Am. Home: Baton Rouge, La. Died May 24, 2008.

O'HORGAN, TOM (THOMAS FOSTER O'HORGAN), composer, director; b. Chgo., May 3, 1924; m. Julia O'Horgan. BA, MA, DePaul U. Chgo. Debut performance in Fallout; off-Broadway revue, 1959; directing debut with prodn. The Maids, 1964; dir.: Hair (Tony award nominee 1968), Lenny (Drama Desk award 1971), Jesus Christ Super Star, Inner City, Six from La Mama, The Hessian Corporal, Futz (Obie award 1967, Drama Desk award 1968), Tom Paine (Drama Desk award 1968), Massachusetts Trust, Dude, The Leaf People, Sergeant Pepper's Lonely Hearts Club Band on the Road, Capitol Cakewalk, 1990, The Architect and The Emperor of Abyssinia, The Other Side of Broadway, 2002; composer: music for numerous prodns. including Open Season at Second City Senator Joe (also dir.), 1989, The Body Builder's Book of Love, 1990; music for films including Futz, 1969, Alex in Wonderland, 1970, Rhinocerous, 1974; actor: (films) All Men Are Apes, 1965. Recipient Creative Arts award Brandeis U., 1968; named Theatrical Dir. of Yr., Newsweek, 1968 Died Jan. 11, 2009.

OKAMURA, ARTHUR SHINJI, artist, educator; b. Long Beach, Calif., Feb. 24, 1932; s. Frank Akira and Yuki O.; m. Elizabeth Tuomi, Aug. 7, 1953 (div.); children: Beth, Jonathan, Jane, Ethan; m. Kitty Wong, 1991. Student, Art Inst. Chgo., 1950-54, U. Chgo., 1951, 52, 57. Faculty Ctrl. YMCA Coll., Chgo., 1956, 57, Evanston (Ill.) Art Center, 1956-57, Art Inst. Chgo., North Shore Art League, Winnetka, Ill., Acad. Art, San Francisco, 1957, Calif. Sch. Fine Arts, 1958, Ox Bow Summer Art Sch., Saugatuck, Mich., 1963, Calif. Coll. Arts and Crafts, Oakland, 1958-59, prof. arts, 1966-97, prof. emeritus, from 1997. Instr. watercolor painting, 1987; dir. San Francisco Studio Art, 1958; tchr. watercolor workshops, Bali, Indonesia, 1989, 92; lectr. in field. Author (with Robert Creeley): 1, 2, 3, 4, 5, 6, 7, 8, 9, 0, 1971; author: (with Joel Weishaus) Ox-Herding, 1971; author: (with Robert Bly) Basho, 1972, Ten Poems by Issa, 1992; author: (with Steve Kowit) Passionate Journey, 1984; author: (with David Rosen and Joel Weishaus) The Healing Spirit of Haiku; author: Magic Rabbit, 1995, The Paper Propeller, 2000; one-man shows include Charles Feingarten Galleries, Chgo., 1956, 1958, 1959, San Francisco, 1957, Santa Barbara Mus. Art, 1958, Oakland Mus. Art, 1959, Legion Honor, San Francisco, 1961, Dallas, 1962, La Jolla (Calif.) Mus., 1963, U. Utah, 1964, San Francisco Mus. Art, 1968, Hanssen Gallery, 1968, 1971, Ruth Braunstein, San Francisco, 1981, 1982, 1984, 1986—88, 1990, 1994, 1997, 2000, 2003, 2006, Commonweal Gallery, Bolinas, Calif., 2001, Claudia Chapline Gallery, Stinson Beach, Calif., 2007, exhibited in group shows at Pa. Acad. Fine Art, U. Chgo., U. Wash., U. Ill., Art Inst. Chgo., L.A. County Mus., Am. Fedn. Art, Denver Mus., NAD, De Young Mus., San Francisco, Knoedler Gallery, N.Y.C., Feingarten Galleries, Whitney Mus. Art, others; retrospective at Bolinas Mus., 2002, Claudia Chapline Galleries, Stinson Beach, Calif., 1995; Represented in permanent collections Art Inst. Chgo., Borg-Warner Collections, Chgo., Whitney Mus. Art, Santa Barbara Mus. Art, San Francisco Mus. Art, Ill. State Normal, Corcoran Mus., Nat. Collection Fine Arts, Smithsonian Instn., many others. Served as pvt. AUS, 1955-56. Recipient 1st prize religious art U. Chgo., 1953; Ryerson travelling fellow, 1954; Martin Cahn award contemporary Am. paintings Art Inst. Chgo., 1957; purchase award U. Ill., 1959; purchase award Nat. Soc. Arts and Letters, N.Y.C., 1960; Neysa McMein purchase award Whitney Mus. Art, 1960; Schwabacher-Frey award 79th Ann. of San Francisco Mus. Art, 1960 Mem.: Commonweal (bd. dirs. 1993—2007). Home: Bolinas, Calif. Died July 10, 2009.

O'KEEFE, GERALD JAMES, plastics office accessories manufacturing company; b. Springfield, Mass., Dec. 11, 1937; s. Gerald Edward and Mildred Brown O'K; m. Susan M. Lyons, June 20, 1970; children: John Ryan, William Neil. Student, Bridgewater State Coll., 1955-57; BA, U. Mass., 1957-59. Sales rep. Calif. Chem. div. Standard Oil Calif., 1961-66; sales rep. Mercedes Benz Co., 1966-70; European del cons. Lowery Corp., Hartford, Conn., 1970-71; sales rep. Papermate div. Gillette Co., New Eng., NYC, 1971-75, Gates Paper div. SCM Corp., Marion, Ind., 1975-77; sales mgr. for east coast Eldon Office Products Co., Glastonbury, Conn., 1977-80; gen. mgr. Arlac Werk, Hamburg, Fed. Rep. Germany, Branford, Conn., 1980-82; pres. Alexander & O'Keefe, Inc., from 1982. Active Glastonbury Service Club. Mem. Nat. Office Products Assn. Home: Glastonbury, Conn. Died Sept. 25, 2007.

OKNER, SEYMOUR N., retired insurance company executive; b. Berwyn, 1927; m. Anne Matthew, 1949; children: Sam, Joel, Ellyn. Grad., Roosevelt U., 1949. With Montgomery Ward Life, pres., COO, 1985—89; pres. Signature Group, Schaumburg, Ill.; pres., sec. Marusa Marketing, Ltd., 1992—96; chmn. Market USA. Named Marketer of Yr., Direct Marketing Assn., 1985. Jewish. Died Nov. 7, 2008.

OLAR, TERRY THOMAS, health facilities administrator; b. Hammond, Ind., Mar. 1, 1947; s. Thomas and Gladys (Kaleta) O.; m. Sally Kaye Walker, Sept. 5, 1970 (div. 1983); 1 child, Kristin Rene; m. Cheryl Ann Renz, Feb. 10, 1990; children: Danielle Jade, Robert David, Brandon Michael. BS, Purdue U., 1973; MS, Wash. State U., 1975; PhD, Colo. State U., 1984. Tech. dir. Genetic Resources, San Marcos, Tex., 1984; lab. dir. High Plains Genetics, Rapid City, S.D., 1984-85, Swedish Med. Ctr., Denver, 1985-87; scientific dir. Fertility Inst. New Orleans, from 1987. Asst. prof. Dept. Obstetrics and Gynecology Tulane U. Sch. Medicine, New Orleans, 1990—; cons. Northwest Fla. Fertility Inst., Gulf Breeze, 1988—, St. Francis Med. Ctr., Monroe, La., 1988—, Humana Hosp., Brazos Valley, Tex., 1989, Humana Hosp., Lake Charles, La., 1990. Contbr. articles to profl. jours. Bd. dirs. La. Wildlife Fedn., v.p., 1994—. Sgt. USAF, 1965-69. Grantee Am. Kennel Club, 1982, 83, Humana Hosp. Inc., 1988-92. Mem. AAAS, Am. Fertility Soc., Soc. for Study of Reproduction, Am. Soc. Andrology, Am. Assn. Tissue Banks, N.Y. Acad. Scis., Am. Assn. Bioanalysts, Am. Legion, VFW, KC. Republican. Roman Catholic. Avocations: fishing, hunting, gourmet cooking, backpacking, camping. Home: Burlington, Ky. Died June 3, 2008.

OLDFIELD, FRANK EUGENE, retired aerospace engineering executive; b. Ft. Morgan, Colo., Apr. 20, 1931; s. Henry Johnstone and Florence Ona (King) O.; m. Mary Rose Barrett, Sept. 20, 1975; children: Vanessa L. Lawson, Perry D. BS in Electronics, San Diego State U., 1958. Aerospace engr. Teledyne Ryan Aero., San Diego, 1958-63, computer sys. mgr., 1963-68, advanced projects dir., 1968-88, v.p., chief engr., 1988-93, ret., from 1993. Aerospace cons. AAI Corp., Hunt Valley, Md., 1988-94. Author: (book) Mankind Metamorphosis, 1997. Mem., v.p., treas., pres. Smoketree Condo. Assn., 1988-98. Sgt. U.S. Army, 1955-58. Recipient Pioneer award Assn. for Unmanned Vehicle Sys., 1987; tribute to Frank Oldfield recorded in Congl. Records, Ho. of Reps., 1987. Mem. NRA, Early Am. Coppers. Republican. Home: La Mesa, Calif. Died Nov. 7, 2007.

OLDS, JAMES HOWARD, minister; b. Owen County, Ky., Sept. 4, 1945; s. James H. and Sadie Mae (Stewart) O.; m. Sandra Lewis, Sept. 19, 1964; children: Wesley Howard, Bradley Stewart. BA, Asbury Coll., 1966; MDiv, Asbury Theol. Sem., 1970; D in Ministry, Lexington Theol. Sem., 1977. Ordained to ministry Meth. Ch., 1970. Pastor Woodlawn-Beech Fork United Meth. Ch., Bardstown, Ky., 1966-70, Eminence (Ky.) United Meth. Ch., 1970-75, Crestwood (Ky.) United Meth. Ch., 1975-84, Trinity Hill United Meth. Ch., Lexington, Ky., 1984-91, St. Paul United Meth. Ch., Louisville, from 1991. Vice chairperson Ky. Conf. Coun. on Ministries, Lexington, 1988—; chairpersonKy. Conf. Vision 2000, Lexington, 1990—; pres. Ky. Conf. Retirement Home, inc., Lexington, 1989—; mem. Ky. State Wesley Found., Frankfort, 1982—, Southeastern Jurisdiction Communications, Atlanta, 1991—. Pres. Community Kitchen Bd. Dirs., Lexington, 1988—; mem. Mayors Task Force on Homelessness, Lexington, 1989-90; chmn. Gov.'s Commn. on Prison Chaplains, Crestwood, Ky., 1979. Named to Honorable Order of Ky. Colonels; recipient Harry Denman Evangelism award Ky. Conf. of United Meth. Ch., 1983. Mem. Rotary, Lions. Democrat. Home: Louisville, Ky. Died July 23, 2008.

O'LEARY, ARTHUR FRANCIS, architect, construction arbitrator, author; b. Omaha, Oct. 11, 1924; s. John J. and Helen C. (Redmond) O'L.; m. Eithenee J. Masterson, July 16, 1949 B.Arch., U. So. Calif., 1951; cert. in real estate, UCLA, 1971. Lic. architect, Calif., 12 other states. Ptnr. O'Leary Terasawa Ptnrs., LA, from 1949. Lectr. U. So. Calif., 1953-63; mem. curriculum com. L.A. Trade-Tech. Coll., 1965-86; mem. archtl. adv. com. Woodbury U., L.A., 1984-86. Author: Construction Administration in Architectural Practice, 1991; co-author: Architectonics, vols. I-IV, 1963; Businessman's Guide to Construction, 1980; Avoiding Liability in Architecture, Design and Construction, 1983; also articles in archtl., constrn. jours. Served as sgt. U.S. Army, 1946-49 Fellow AIA (bd. dirs. 1973-76); mem. Am. Arbitration Assn., Am. Coll. Constrn. Arbitrators (gov. 1982-85), Royal Inst. Architects of Ireland, London Ct. Internat. Arbitration, Chartered Inst. Arbitrators (Irish br.). Clubs: Serra (pres. local club 1970). Republican. Roman Catholic. Home: County Louth, Ireland. Died Mar. 28, 2009.

OLGEIRSON, ERIK ROBERT, ecologist, consultant; b. Bismarck, ND, Dec. 11, 1946; s. Robert Hagen and Evelyn (Nack) O.; m. Kathleen Leroux, June 4, 1966 (div. Apr. 1984); children: Christopher, Ian Joseph; m. Jane Vonderahe, Oct. 25, 1986. BA, U. Colo., 1969, PhD, 1972. Instr. Kent Country Day, Englewood, Colo., 1972-73; sr. ecologist Colo. Div. Hwys., Denver, 1973-74, Atlantic-Richfield Co.,

Denver, 1974-76, Shell Oil Co., Denver, 1976-77; pres. ERO Resources Corp., Golden, Colo., 1977-87; cons. ecologist Denver, from 1986. Mem. Colo. Water Congress, Denver, 1985—, Colo. Assn. Commerce, Denver, 1985—, Rocky Mountain Oil and Gas, Denver, 1973-75, Adv. Com. on Improved Plant Materials for Reveg. of High Altitiudes, Ft. Collins, Colo., 1927-73; adj. prof. grad. faculty U. Colo., Denver, 1986—. Contbr. tech. reports to profl. publs. Treas. Evergreen (Colo.) Soccer Assn., 1978-84; bd. dirs. Nat. Repertory Orch., Evergreen, 1985—. Mem. Brit. Ecol. Soc., Ecol. Soc. Am., Wildlife Soc., Soc. Range Mgmt., Calif. Bot. Soc., Assn. Wetland Mgrs. Avocations: skiing, water sports, interior design, cooking, woodworking. Died July 18, 2008.

OLIKER, STEPHEN LAWRENCE, advertising executive; b. Pitts., Dec. 4, 1935; s. Jerry and Madelene (Marlin) O.; m. Carol Joy Rubin, June 22, 1958; children: David Charles, Robert Jacob, Diane Lynn. BS, Syracuse U., 1957. Sr. copywriter Keller-Crescent, Evansville, Ind., 1969-75, assoc. creative dir., 1975-80, adminstrv. asst., 1980-82, creative dir. retail, creative bus. mgr., from 1982. Served with USAR. Home: Evansville, Ind. Died Jan. 31, 2008.

OLIVA, DEBORAH A., marketing executive, designer; b. Nov. 12, 1952; d. Robert A. and Kathleen (Rice) Lusardi. AAS in Mktg., Somerset County Coll., NJ, 1973; BS in Bus. Mgmt., Rutgers U., 1977. Programmer Bell Labs., Madison, N.J., 1970-73; asst. sales and mktg. mgr. AVCO, Rockaway, N.J., 1974-76; computer systems analyst Western Electric, Piscataway, N.J.; pres., chief exec. officer Cliché Cons., Edison, N.J., 1981-90; founder, pres. Creative Characters, Hackettstown, N.J., from 1990. Designer various characters with story lines; assistant developer workshops on coping with stress, time mgmt. and career planning; designer mktg. and nat. advt. campaigns, 1988. Author: (booklet) Making Money Doing Business, 1979, (creative character) Apple Fly, 1991. Asst. Dir. Ballot of Security-Ray Bateman, Somerset County, N.J., 1980; chmn. bd. Am. Cancer Soc., Somerset County, 1987-90, also crusade dir.; bd. dirs. John E. Toolan-Kiddie Keepwell Camp, 1988—; founder, spokesperson Clen Up Am. Recipient Up-FM-AM award Creativity 88, N.Y.C., 1988, Leadership award Somerset County chpt. Am. Cancer Soc., 1987, 88, 89, 90, also Community award, 1987; nominee for Woman of the Yr., 1988. Mem. N.J. Assn. Woman Bus. Owners (bd. dirs. 1980-85), Internat. Entrepreneurs Assn. Calif., Am. Soc. Advt. and Promotion, Kiwanis (sec., bd. dirs. 1989—, cert. adminstrv. excellence N.J. dist.). Avocations: travel, reading, painting, writing, designing artifacts and toys. Home: Hackettstown, NJ. Died Feb. 29, 2008.

OLIVER, MARY LOU, city official; b. Midland, Mich., Feb. 9, 1941; d. William Charles and I. Flora (Ahern) Goggin; m. Donald Bruce Oliver, Oct. 28, 1967; children: Stephen, Patricia. BA in Comml. Art, Marygrove Coll., Detroit, 1963; BA in Edn., U. Mich., 1964. Tchr. South Lyon (Mich.) Community Sch., 1964-69; mem. coun. City of San Ramon, Calif., from 1983, mayor Calif., 1985. Dir. Dougherty Regional Fire Authority; commr. San Ramon Redevel. Agy. Pres. Homeowners Assn. Twin Creek, San Ramon, 1979-81; founder San Ramon Incorporation Com., 1982. Named Woman of Distinction, Soroptomist Internat., San Ramon, 1985. Mem. AAUW (community area rep. 1985—). Republican. Avocations: sailboat racing, boating, skiing, horseback riding. Home: San Ramon, Calif. Died Apr. 26, 2008.

OLIVER, PHILIP MANUS, management consultant, president; b. Hartford, Conn., July 25, 1920; s. Bernard John and Elizabeth (Schtiff) O.; m. Elaine Frances Peterson, June 13, 1942 (div. Aug. 1972); children: Tracie Joy, Janice Eva; m. Jean Dorothy Bovard, Mar. 29, 1975; children: Sandra, Deborah, Guy. BA in Personnel & Bus. Mgmt., George Washington U., 1942. Personnel specialist Dept. Army, Chgo., 1940-43, personnel mgr. Washington, 1946-50; personnel officer U.S. High Commr. for Austria, Vienna, 1950-54; personnel mgr. Creole Petroleum, Caracas, Venezuela, 1954-56; mgr. compensation Tidewater Oil Co., San Francisco, 1956-58; personnel mgr. Lockheed Missiles and Space, Sunnyvale, Calif., 1959-64; personnel dir. Philco-Ford, Palo Alto, Calif., 1964-69; spl. asst., dir. mgmt. systems Dept. Labor, Washington, 1969-70, 72-80; dir. Job Evaluation and Pay Task Force, Washington, 1970-72; cons., pres. The Oliver System, Orrington, Maine, from 1980. Author: The Oliver System, a Job Evaluation and Pay Technology Widely Used in Federal and State Governments. Bd. dirs. Santa Clara United Fund., Sunnyvale, 1969, Hope for Retarded Children, San Jose, Calif., 1968. Recipient Disting. Career Svc. award Dept. of Labor, 1980. Mem. Bangor Art Soc. (treas. 1990—). Baptist. Avocations: reading, art, opera, golf. Died Aug. 24, 2008.

OLSON, GORDON BENNIE, retired academic administrator; b. Almont, ND, Oct. 19, 1924; s. Bernard T. and Huldah Mae (Monson) O.; m. Carley Yates, Jan. 20, 1945; children: Linda Olson Bittay, Corliss Olson Clark, Wendy Olson Sletto. BS, Dickinson Coll., 1948; MA, U. N.D., 1952, PhD, 1953. Supt. schs., Bucyrus, N.D., 1948-51; v.p. acad. affairs Dickinson State Coll., ND, 1953-67; pres. Minot State U., ND, 1967—92. Bd. dirs. Norwest Bank, Minot; mem. chancellor's cabinet N.D. U. System. Former bd. dirs. St. Joseph's Hosp., Minot, Salvation Army, Minot Luth. Ch.; bd. trustees N.D. Coun. Econ. Edn.; bd. dirs. Minot Area Devel. Corp. Served with AUS, 1943-46. Mem. Am. Assn. State Colls. and Univs. (nat. service com.), Am. Assn. Coll. Tchrs. Edn. (state liaison rep.), Minot C. of C. (bd. dirs.), Greater N.D. Assn., Lions, Elks. Home: Minot, ND. Died June 30, 2009.

O'MALLEY, THOMAS JOSEPH, retired engineering executive; b. Montclair, NJ, Oct. 8, 1915; s. Thomas and Alice Theresa (Martin) O'M.; m. Anne D. Arweth; children: Thomas, James, Kathleen. BS in Mech. Engring., Newark Coll. Engring., 1937. Divsn. mgr. exptl. testing. Wright Aero. Corp., Paterson, N.J., 1940-58; chief test conductor Convair Gen. Dynamics, Kennedy Space Ctr., Fla., 1958-67; v.p., gen. mgr. Rockwell Internat., Kennedy Space Ctr., 1967-82; ret., 1982. Bd. dirs. Brevard County (Fla.) United Way, 1970-80 (campaign chmn. 1971); mem. Cocoa (Fla.) C. of C., 1970-81; chmn. Canaveral Socs. Space Congress, 1972. Recipient Lifetime Achievement award Nat. Space Club, 1998, Silver Knight award Nat. Mgmt. Assn., 1981, NASA Disting. Svc. medal, 1981, NASA Snoopy award Kennedy Space Ctr., 1970; inducted into N.J. Aviation Hall of Fame by Astronaut Wally Schirra, 1996; presented Space Congress Achievement award for Outstanding Contributions and Dedicated Svc. to the Nation's Space Program by U.S. Sen. John Glenn, 1981. Home: Cocoa Beach, Fla. Died Nov. 6, 2009.

O'MALLEY, THOMAS PATRICK, retired academic administrator; b. Milton, Mass., Mar. 1, 1930; s. Austin and Ann Marie (Feeney) O'M. BA, Boston Coll., 1951; MA, Fordham U., 1953; STL, Coll. St.-Albert de Louvain, 1962; LittD, U. Nijmegen, 1967; LLD (hon.), John Carroll U., 1988, Sogang U., Seoul, Rep. of Korea, 1996. Entered Soc. of Jesus, 1952. Instr. classics Coll. of Holy Cross, Worcester, Mass., 1956-58; asst. prof., chmn. dept. classics Boston Coll., 1967-69, assoc. prof., chmn. dept. theology, 1969-73; dean Boston Coll. (Coll. Arts and Scis.), 1973-80; pres. John Carroll U., Cleve., 1980-88; vis. prof. Cath. Inst. W. Africa, 1988-89; assoc. editor AMERICA, NYC, 1989-90; rector Jesuit Com. Fairfield U., 1990-91; pres. Loyola Marymount U., L.A., 1991-99; adj. prof., arts, sci. honors program Boston Coll., 1999—2009. Author: Tertullian and the Bible, 1967. Trustee Boston Theol. Inst., 1969-73, Fairfield U., 1971-82, 89-91, John Carroll U., 1976-88, Xavier U., 1980-86, U. Detroit, 1982-88, Boston Coll. H.S., 1986-88, Boys Hope, 1986-88 Mem. AAUP, Soc. Bibl. Lit., N.Am. Patristic Soc. Died Nov. 4, 2009.

OMELENCHUK, JEANNE, mayor pro tem, owner; b. Detroit, Mar. 25, 1931; d. Harry Douglas and Blanche (George) Robinson; m. George Omelenchuk (dec.); 1 child, Kristin. BA in Fine Arts, Wayne State U., 1954, M in Art Edn., 1962, postgrad. Art tchr., English tchr. grades 1-9 Detroit Pub. Schs., 1955-74; mem. U.S. Olympic Team Speed Skating, Squaw Valley, Calif., 1960, Grenoble, France, 1968, Sapporo, Japan, 1972, World Championship Teams, Oostersund, Sweden, 1960, Edmonton, Can., 1963, West Allis, Wis., 1965, Flint, Mich., 1967, Helsinki, 1968, Grenoble, France, 1969, St. Paul, 1970, U.S. Team vs. Can., Saskatoon, Sask., Can., 1965, Edmonton, 1967, Winnipeg, Man., Can., 1969; owner Grandfather Clock Headquarters, 1976-91; mem. Warren City Coun., 1985-91, pres., mayor pro tem, 1991-95; owner Metro Bus, Inc., 1980-95; ret., 1995. Coach, sponsorship Macomb Bicycle Racing Club, 1965-86; sponsorship, meet dir. Detroit Speed Skating Clubs Ann. Gold & Silver Skates Meet, 1974-83; vol. instr., coach Mich. Spl. Olympics, Traverse City, 1986-93; founder Warren's Thanksgiving Day Parade, 1986; appointee Mcpl. Arts Commn., Ocala, Fla., 2000; mem. com. Tampa Olympics Bid 2012. Recipient Nat. Bicycle Racing Championship Titles, 1951, 55, 57-59, Nat. Championship Masters, 1978, 79, 80, 81, Nat. Speed Skating Championship Titles, St. Paul, 1954, 57-72, Nat. Champ Masters, 1987, 88, 89, 90, 91, Five N.Am. Championships 1957-59, 62-63, Nat. Bicycle Racing Championship, Antwerp, Belgium, 1957; named to Athletic Hall of Fame, Wayne State U., 1979, Amateur Skating U.S. Hall of Fame, 1979, Mich. Amateur Athletic Hall of Fame, 1981, U.S. Amateur Skating Union Hall of Fame, Chgo., 1984, Mich. Sports Hall of Fame, Cobo Hall, Detroit, 1984, Mich. Women's Hall of Fame, Lansing, Mich., 1994; recognized by YWCA for outstanding contbns. to world of sports on Nat. Women's Sports Day, 1996; recipient Internat. World Speedskating Championship, Master's Class record 33.3 for 300 meters, 1997, Pettit U.S. Olympic Tng. facility, 1997, others. Mem. Southern Mich. Athletic Assn. (founding mem., sponsor). Achievements include one mile national record; International Masters Championship, 2002—, West All's Wis. Petit U.S. Olympic Training Facility. Home: Capac, Mich. Died June 26, 2008.

O'NEIL, ROBERT JAMES, entomologist; b. Boston, July 14, 1955; s. Harold Francis and Margaret Mary (Ryan) O'Neil; m. Elizabeth Ann McDonough, May 11, 1978; children: Jennifer, Nate, Jon, Elspeth. BS, U. Mass., 1977; MS, Tex. A&M, 1980, PhD, U. Fla., 1984. Asst. prof. Purdue U., West Lafayette, Ind., 1984-90, assoc. prof., 1990-97. Adj. prof. Pan Am. Sch. of Agr., Tegucigalpa, Honduras, Central Amer., 1994-97; cons. Embrapa, Brazil, 1993-96, AID, Honduras 1984-97. Mem. Internat. Orgn. of Biol. Control (v.p. 1994-97). Avocations: fishing, travel, reading, baseball. Died Feb. 6, 2008.

O'QUINN, JOHN MAURICE, lawyer; b. Baton Rouge, La., Sept. 4, 1941; s. Leonard and Jean (Wilkes) O'Quinn. BS, U. Houston, 1965, JD magna cum laude, 1967. Bar: Tex. 1967, US Supreme Ct. 1972, US Ct. Appeals (5th cir.) 1984, US Dist. Ct. (so. and ea. dists. Tex.) 1986. Founding ptnr. O'Quinn, Kerensky, McAninch & Laminack, Houston, 1981—2009. Mem. adv. com. Tex. State Supreme Ct., 1984-94; trustee U. Houston Law Found., 1985—; adj prof. law, U. Houston, So. Tex. Coll. Law, Tex. So. Coll. Law. Regent U. Houston, 1993-99. Named one of The Top 10 Trial Lawyers in America, The Nat. Law Jour., 1993, 2004, The 100 Most Influential Lawyers in US, 1994, The 100 Legal Legends of Tex., Tex. Lawyer, The 5 Best Tex. Trial Lawyers of the Century, Houston Chronicle. Am. Trial Lawyers Assn., Tex. Trial Lawyers Assn. (dir.), Houston Trial Lawyers Assn. (dir.), Houston Bar Assn., State Bar Tex., U. Houston Law Alumni Assn. (pres. 1978). Democrat. Died Oct. 29, 2009.

ORAM, ROBERT W., library administrator; b. Warsaw, Ind., June 11, 1922; s. George Harry and Lottie Mae (Gresso) O.; m. Virginia White, June 16, 1949; 1 child, Richard W. BA, U. Toledo, 1949; MS in Library Adminstrn., U. Ill., 1950. Asst. to librarian U. Mo.-Columbia, 1950-56; circulation librarian U. Ill.-Urbana, 1956-67, dir. pub. service, 1968-71, assoc. univ. librarian, 1971-79, acting univ. librarian, 1975-76; dir. Central Univ. Libraries So. Meth. U., Dallas, 1979-89, dir. emeritus, 1989. Mem. adv. com. Ill. State Library, Springfield, 1975-79 Contbr. articles to profl. jours. Exec. sec. Friends of So. Meth. U. Librs., 1980-89; former mem. bd. dirs. Urbana Free Libr., Lincoln Trails Libr. Sys., Champaign, Ill.; trustee Friends Austin (Tex.) Pub. Libr., 1994-99. Mem. ALA (life, pub. com. 1975-79), Friends of Libraries U.S.A. (exec. bd. 1980-86), Ill. Library Assn. (treas. 1972-73), Democrat. Avocations: reading, music. Home: Austin, Tex. Died July 24, 2009.

ORLANS, HAROLD, writer and editor; b. NYC, July 29, 1921; married; 3 children. BS in Journalism, CCNY, 1941; PhD in Anthropology, Yale U., 1949; postdoctoral, London Sch. Econs., 1949-50. Reporter San Francisco Call-Bull., 1941-42; fellow Social Sci. Rsch. Coun., 1948-49; vis. lectr. anthropology U. Birmingham, Eng., 1950-51; sr. info. officer Social Survey, London, 1951-52; rsch. assoc. Inst. for Rsch. in Human Rels., Phila., 1952-54; analyst, sect. chief NSF, 1954-59; dir. studies White Ho. Conf. on Children and Youth, 1959-60; sr. fellow Brookings Instn., 1960-73; cons. com. on govt. ops. U.S. Ho. Reps., 1966-67; vis. assoc. program on tech. and society Harvard U., 1970-71; sr. rsch. assoc. Nat. Acad. Pub. Adminstrn., 1973-83; cons. Gallaudet Coll., 1983-84; spl. asst. U.S. Commn. on Civil Rights, 1984-86; freelance editor, from 1986. Editor Ind. Scholar, 1983-85; assoc. editor Minerva, 1986—; columnist, 1995—; author: Stevenage—A Sociological Study of a New Town, 1952 (London), 1953 (U.S.), (with A. Siegel and L. Greer) Puerto Ricans in Philadelphia, 1953, Effects of Federal Programs on Higher Education, 1962, Contracting for Atoms, 1967, The Nonprofit Research Institute, 1972, Contracting for Knowledge, 1973, Private Accreditation and Public Eligibility, 1975, GI Course Approvals (with others), 1979; editor: Federal Departmental Libraries, 1963, The Use of Social Research in Federal Domestic Programs, 4 vols., 1967, Science Policy and the University, 1968, Nonprofit Organizations, 1980, Human Services Coordination, 1982, Adjustment to Adult Hearing Loss, 1985, Affirmative Action Revisited (with June O'Neill), 1992, Lawrence of Arabia, Strange Man of Letters, 1993; contbr. articles to various publs. Fulbright scholar London Sch. Econs., 1949-50. Home: Bethesda, Md. Died Dec. 12, 2007.

ORN, MICHAEL KENT, safety engineer; b. Elkhart, Ind., May 19, 1942; s. C. Russell and Esther Minerva (Whittinghill) O.; m. Judith Louise Kelly, Jan. 20, 1968; children: Todd Michael, Dean Russell II, Catherine Mary-Elizabeth. BS, Purdue U., 1965. Cert. safety profl., Ill., N.D., Wash. Safety and radiation protection officer U.S. Army Depot, Savanna, Ill., 1966-68; safety officer U.S. Army Materiel Command Hdqrs., Washington, 1969-73; chief safety br. U.S. Army Safeguard Commn., Mickelson Safeguard Complex, N.D., 1973-76; exec. dir. Bd. Cert. Safety Profls., Savoy, Ill., from 1976. Author: Handbook of Engineering Control Methods for Occupational Radiation Protection; contbr. articles to profl. jours. Mem. SSS Appeals Bd., Champaign County, Ill., 1982—. Mem. System Safety Soc., Am. Soc. Assn Execs., Am. Soc. Safety Engrs. (chpt. pres. 1980-81, engring. div. adminstr. 1990-91). Methodist. Avocations: tennis, gardening. Home: Philo, Ill. Died Sept. 15, 2007.

ORR, VERNE (GEORGE VERNON ORR JR.), retired dean, former civilian military employee; b. Des Moines, Iowa, Nov. 12, 1916; s. George Vernon and Wilhelmina (Van Niewaal) Orr; m. Joan Peak, Mar. 31, 1941 (dec. 1988); children: Carolyn, Robert Vernon; m. Sarah Smith, 1989; stepchildren: Windsor, Geoffrey. BA, Pomona Coll., 1937, LLD (hon.), 1981; MBA, Stanford U., 1939; Ph.D, Claremont U., 2005. Salesman Verne Orr Motors, 1946—59; pres. Investors Savings & Loan Pasadena, 1963—66, dir. Dept. Motor Vehicles State of Calif., 1967—69, dir. fin., 1970—75; sr. adv. Ernst & Ernst, L.A., 1975—80; prof. govt. fin. U. So. Calif. Grad. Sch. Pub. Adminstrn., 1975—80; ptnr. Orr Enterprises, 1977—81; sec. Dept. Air Force, Us Dept. Def., 1981—85; dep. dir. Pres.-Elect Ronald Reagan's Transition team, 1980—81; dean U. La Verne's Sch. Bus. & Global Studies, 1999—2002, dean emeritus, 2002—08. Foreman L.A. County Grand Jury, 1962; mem. Pers. Devel. Agy. Com. State of Calif., 1968—70. Pres. United Way, L.A., 1963; pres. Family Svc. Pasadena, 1957; bd. regents U. Calif., 1976—81. Served in USN, 1941—45 USNR, 1945—51. Decorated Purple Heart, Order Nat. Security Merit; recipient Tong-Il medal, Republic of Korea, Brazilian Aero Merit award, Pasadena's Patriot award; named Pasadena's Man of Yr., 1970, Pasadena's Salvation Army Man of Yr. Mem.: Pasadena Mechanics Assn. (pres. 1948), Pasadena Chamber of Commerce, Kiwanis (pres. 1951), Masons, Alpha Delta Mu, Phi Betta Kappa. Republican. Died Nov. 27, 2008.

ORTMEYER, CARL EDWARD, retired demographer; b. Charles City, Iowa, Mar. 12, 1915; s. Arthur Herman and Sarah Emilie (Stoeber) O.; m. Anne Babuska O'Brien, Aug. 3, 1947 (dec. Dec. 15, 1995); 1 child, Kerry Michael; m. Ruth Forberg, Oct. 5, 1996. BA, U. Iowa, 1939; MS, Iowa State U., 1948, PhD in Rural Sociology, Demography, 1954. Rsch. assoc. bur. pub. health econs. Sch. Pub. Health U. Mich., Ann Arbor, 1954—56; sociologist Legis. Reference Svc., Libr. Congress, Washington, 1956—57; rsch. assoc. Social Security Adminstrn. U.S. Dept. HEW, 1957—58; rsch. assoc. Sch. Medicine Howard U., 1958—59; demographer Nat. Ctr. Health, Statistics Pub. Health Svc. U.S. Dept. HEW, 1959—68, demographer Nat. Inst. Occpl. Safety and Health CDC, 1968—80. Vol. caregiver Benedictine Nursing Ctr., Mt. Angel, Oreg., 1990-96, Wesley Homes Health Ctr., Des Moines, Wash., 1996—; mem. Wesley Found., Ams. for Democratic Action. Sgt. U.S. Army, 1941-45. Travel grantee London Sch. Econs. Rockefeller Found., 1969. Fellow APHA AAAS; mem. N.Y. Acad. Sci. Democrat. Mem. United Meth. Ch. Avocation: dance. Died May 19, 2008.

ORTON, WILLIAM H. (BILL ORTON), former United States Representative from Utah; b. North Ogden, Utah, Sept. 22, 1948; m. Jacquelyn Orton; children: Will, Wes. BS, Brigham Young U., 1973, JD, 1979. Adj. prof. Portland (Oreg.) State U./Portland C.C., 1974-76, Brigham Young. U., Provo, Utah, 1984-85; tax auditor IRS, 1966-77; owner/lectr. Tax Tng. Inst., Inc., 1978-90; lectr. continuing edn. seminars Real Estate Tax Inst., N.W. Ctr. Profl. Edn., and Tax Tng. Inst., various locations in U.S., 1978-90; corp. counsel WI Forest Products, Inc., Portland, Oreg., 1980-81; of counsel Merritt & Tenney, Atlanta, 1986-90; tax atty. pvt. practice, Utah, 1980-90, Washington, 1986-90; atty., 1980-90; mem. US Congress from 3rd Utah Dist., 1991—97; ptnr. Jones, Waldo, Holbrook & McDonough, Washington, 1997-99. Democrat. Mem. Lds Ch. Home: Paradise, Utah. Died Apr. 18, 2009.

OSBORN, WILLIAM GEORGE, savings and loan association executive; b. Alton, Ill., Dec. 9, 1925; s. Ralph A. and Pauline J. (Horn) O.; m. Hilda M. Alexander, Aug. 12, 1950 (dec.); children: Barbara K., David A., Robert W., James A. BS in Math., Shurtleff Coll., 1947; certificate, Grad. Sch. Savs. and Loan, Ind. U., 1946-48; A.M. in Econs., St. Louis U., 1962. With Germania Fed. Savs. and Loan Assn., Alton, 1946-90, exec. officer, 1955-86, pres., 1964-86, chmn., 1981-86, chmn. trust com., 1982-86; pres. Fin. Svc. Assocs., Ft. Lauderdale, Fla., 1986—2006. Pres. Germania Fin. Corp., 1970-86; owner Fin. Guidance, Alton, 1951-2006; mem. Opportunities Unltd., 1954-58; instr. Am. Savs. and Loan Inst.; bd. dirs. Nat. Coun. Savs. Instns., Washington, 1984-86. Author: Savings and Loan Operating Policies Manual, 1960, Economic Factors Influencing Savings and Loan Interest Rates, 1962. Pres. Alton Wood River Community Chest, 1959; bd. dirs. Piasa Bird coun. Boy Scouts Am., 1961-88, Mississippi Valley Jr. Achievement, Alton Area United Fund, 1961-63; founder, bd. dirs., treas. New Piasa Chautauqua Ch. Assembly, 1982-86; treas. Lewis and Clark Community Coll. Found., 1976-86; bd. dirs., sec. Riverbend Civic Progress, 1984-86; elder Presbyn. Ch. Served to lt. (j.g.) USNR, 1943-46, 50-52. Mem. Nat. Assn. Bus. Economists, Nat. Economists Club, St. Louis Economists Club, Am. Inst. Mgmt., Masons, Shriners, Chautauqua (Ill.) Yacht Club. Deceased.

OSBORNE, H. PAUL, priest; b. Garrison, Ky., Sept. 19, 1914; s. Lee and Virginia Elizabeth (Hickman) O.; married; children: Ann Harlan Mitchell Osborne, Thomas Lee, John Holland. AB cum laude, Ky. Wesleyan, 1938; MDiv, Lexington Theol. Sem., Ky., 1941; MA cum laude, Incarnate Word Coll., 1955. Ordained to ministry Episcopal Ch., 1945. Rector Epiphany Ch., Kingsville, Tex., 1945-48, St. Paul's Ch., San Antonio, 1948-55; v.p Well's Orgn., Chgo., 1955-58; regional mgr. Bond Div./U.S. Treasury, San Antonio, 1958-61; minister various churches, S.C., Kans., Mass., Ark., 1961-80; fund raising cons. Garrison, Ky., from 1980. Pres. Minister's Assn., San Antonio, 1953-54, Coun. of Churches, Great Bend, Kans., 1975-76, Kans. Ecumenical Body, 1978-80. Mem. housing commn. San Antonio Authority, 1952-54, Consortium on Seminaries, Boston, 1968-69. Mason. Democrat. Home: Cleveland, Ohio. Died Nov. 12, 2007.

OSHIRO, DOROTHY CLOYD, museum educator; b. La Habra, Calif., Nov. 30, 1929; d. Willard Wills and Ruth Frances (!Harris) Cloyd; m. Walter Noriyoshi Oshiro, Sept. 26, 1959; children: Willard, Courtney. AA, Fullerton CC, Calif., 1949; BA, U. Calif., Santa Barbara, 1951; MA, Columbia U., 1955; postgrad., Whittier Coll., 1952. Author: (guides) KaLima Hana, 1967, Hana No'eau, 1967, Studio 5, 1969, Printmaking: Its History and Techniques, 1973, Artists of Hawaii, 1985. Mem. NEA, Nat. Art Edn. Assn., Hawaii State Tchrs. Assn., Hawaii Art Edn. Assn. (past treas., newsletter chmn., sec., membership chmn.), Hawaii Mus. Assn. (nominating com. 1992-93), Dept. Edn. Art Tchrs. Assn. (past treas., newsletter chmn., sec., scholarship chmn.), Hawaii Alliance for Art Edn. (bd. dirs.), Delta Kappa Gamma (comm. chmn. 1988-90). Home: Honolulu, Hawaii. Died Feb. 19, 2008.

OSINSKI, MARGARET JEAN, occupational health nurse; b. Buffalo, June 20, 1939; d. Stanley Joseph and Rita (Milbrand) Sowa; m. Joseph George Osinski, Oct. 3, 1964; children: Joseph A. II, Susan M., Matthew S. Student, Canisius Coll., 1957-58; nursing diploma, Mercy Hosp. Sch. Nursing, Buffalo, 1960. RN; cert. occupational health nurse specialist. Staff nurse med. Kenmore Mercy Hosp., Kenmore, N.Y., 1960-61; staff nurse ob-gyn. Yonkers Gen. Hosp., Yonkers, N.Y., 1961; occupational health nurse Chevrolet div. Gen. Motors, Buffalo, 1961-66; staff nurse emergency Kenmore Mercy Hosp., 1974-80; occupational health nurse, safety coord. Nabisco Brands, Inc., Buffalo, 1980-87; occupational health nurse, employee assistance program coord Bell Aerospace Textron, Buffalo, 1987-91, safety rep., 1991-94. Mem. Western N.Y. Assn. Occupational Health Nurses (pres. 1987-89), Am. & N.Y. State Assns. Occupational Health Nurses, Am. Bd. Occupational Health Nurses, Am. Soc. Safety Engrs., Employee Assistance Profls. Assn., Grand Island (N.Y.) Jr. Football. Republican. Roman Catholic. Avocations: music, reading, buffalo bills football games. Home: Grand Island, NY. Died May 26, 2008.

O'SULLIVAN, BLYTHE ANN, marketing executive; b. Oak Lawn, Ill., Apr. 2, 1982; d. John Patrick and Joan Francis O'Sullivan. BS in mktg., Bradley U., 2004. Promotions intern Regent Broadcasting, Peoria, Ill., 2002—03; mktg. intern Marsh Affinity, Park Ridge, Ill., 2002—03, Soc. of Actuaries, Schaumburg, Ill., 2003—04; edn. and events coord. Denver Metro BOMA, Denver, 2004—05. Bus. mgr. Alpha Psi Omega, Peoria, Ill., 2003—04. Vol. usher Denver Civic Theatre, Denver, 2004—05. Recipient Student award for Mktg. Excellence, Bradley U., 2004. Mem.: Dog Owner Group, Beta Gamma Sigma, Phi Kappa Phi. Died Dec. 6, 2007.

OUTWATER, JOHN OGDEN, mechanical engineering educator; b. London, Jan. 2, 1923; came to U.S., 1924; s. John Ogden and Nenny (Boe) O.; m. Alice Hooker Davidson, Dec. 13, 1952; children— Anne Hooker, Catherine Boe (Mrs. Carl B. Colby), Alice Brookfield (Mrs. Robert B. Lang), John Ogden III. BS, Princeton U., 1943; MA, Cambridge U., Eng., 1948; PhD, MIT, Cambridge, MA, 1950, Cambridge, Eng., 1976. Registered profl. engr. Research engr. DuPont Co., 1950-52; project engr. Universal Moulded Products, 1952-53; indsl. liaison officer Mass. Inst. Tech., 1954-55; prof. mech. engring. U. Vt., Burlington, 1955—71, chmn., 1955-93, prof. emeritus, from 1993. Leader archaeol. expdns. Wenner-Gren Found., Central Mexico, 1954, Yucatan, 1955, Peru-Bolivia, 1957, Haiti, 1959; cons. non-metallic materials Naval Ordnance Lab., Nat. Acad. Scis., Monsanto Rsch. Corp., Smithsonian Instn., pres. Vt. Inst. Co., Inc. Author: (with others) Engineering Materials, 1959, Esplendor del Mexico Antigua; papers on metal cutting, plastics, archaeology, bones, ski safety, botany. Chmn. Vt. Instrument Co., Inc.; Mem. Vt. Conf. Econ. Growth; vestryman St. Paul's Cathedral, Burlington. Served as officer Brit. Army, 1943-47. Named Vt. Engr. of Year, 1970; grantee USPHS; Timken fellow MIT, 1950 Fellow ASME; mem. ASTM, Holland Soc., Vt. Soc. Engrs., Delta Psi, Tau Beta Pi. Achievements include patents for ski boot tension. Home: South Burlington, Vt. Died Aug. 12, 2009.

OWENS, LELAND L., insurance agent; b. Newton, Iowa, Feb. 20, 1925; s. George Alfred Owens and Rose Marie Vavra; m. Ruth Ann Danker, June 12, 1948; children: James George, Jay William. BS, Iowa State U., 1951. Pres. Profl. Ins. Agts., Des Moines, 1962-63; sec. Tama County Mut. Ins. Assn., Traer, Iowa, from 1964. Bd. dirs. Iowa Mut. Tornado Ins. Co., Des Moines, Mut. Ins. Assn. of Iowa, Des Moines. Comdr. Am. Legion, Traer, 1953. Served with USAF, 1943-45. Republican. Mem. United Ch. of Christ. Lodges: Lions (local pres. 1954), Masons (Master 1958). Avocation: golf. Home: Traer, Iowa. Died May 18, 2008.

OWINGS, RACHEL HARRIET (RAE OWINGS), graphic artist, illustrator, script writer; b. Bryn Mawr, Pa., July 8, 1926; d. Charles Croasdale and Rachel (Bulley) Trump; m. James Lee Owings, Nov. 1, 1947; children: Marjorie Lee, Charles Nathaniel, John Stanley. Student, Phila. U. Art, 1943-45. Children's tchr. art Phila. U. Art, 1944-46; designer custom needlepoint Sinkler Studio-Bryn Mawr Studio, Radnor and Bryn Mawr, 1948-52; illustrator, craft designer Jack and Jill mag., Phila., 1953-71; greeting card designer Abel Cards, Media, Pa., 1955-71; freelance TV illustrator and performer PBS TV, from 1955. Freelance illustrator to music with various symphony orchs., Phila., Washington, Balt., 1955—; freelance sch. assembly performer, Phila., N.Y.C., Mass., Washington, 1955—; book illustrator Clark Davis/Vantage Press, Darnestown, Md. and N.Y.C., 1988-90. Illustrator, co-dir. ednl. TV series Gather 'Round, 1978, Teletales, 1985 (Golden Eagle ward Coun. on Internat. Non-Theatrical Events 1985); illustrator: As A Pup Grows Up, 1988, The Tooth Fairy Is Broke, 1989. Leader, trainer Girl Scouts U.S.A., Gladwyne, Pa., 1959-66; leader, counselor Boy Scouts Am., Gladwyne, 1961-70; Sunday sch. tchr. Presbyn. and Congl. chs., Gladwyne and Worcester, Mass., 1970-74; bd. dirs. Fairfax County Coun. Arts, Annandale, Va., 1973-76. Recipient Ohio State award Inst. for Edn. by Radio-TV, 1975, 88, bronze medal V.I. Film Festival, 1976, medal for 25 yrs. appearances with children's concerts Phila. Orch., 1988. Mem. Childrens Book Guild Wash. (chmn. speakers bur. 1985—). Home: Vienna, Va. Died Nov. 11, 2007.

OWNBY, MIRIAM LEE, writer; b. Kingston, W.Va., May 27, 1920; d. Raymond Archer and Monad Atkinson (Bishop) Lee; m. Dillard Ralph Ownby, Apr. 19, 1946 (div. July 1974); children: Dennis R., Raymond L., Bruce C. AB, Concord Coll., 1942; MEd, Ohio U., 1968. Tchr. Rockbridge (Ohio) H.S., 1958-59; elem. tchr. Ohio Schs., 1959-66, U.S. Trust Territory of Pacific Islands/U.S. Dept. Interior, Colonia, Yap, 1966-69; patient accounts auditor Plantation (Fla.) Gen. Hosp., 1979-97; freelance writer Plantation, from 1985. Author: Explore the Everglades, 1992; contbr. articles to profl. jours; columnist Hollywood Sun Tattler, 1985-89. Treas. Broward County Sierra Club, Ft. Lauderdale, 1983-86, Environ. Coalition of Broward County, Ft. Lauderdale, 1985-87. Capt. WAAC, WAC with AAF, WWII, 1942-46. Mem. Fla. Freelance Writers Assn., Fla. Wildlife Fedn., South Fla. Book Group, Sierra Club (treas. Broward County chpt. 1987, Spl. Achievement award 1992). Home: Oakland Park, Fla. Died July 30, 2008.

PACK, HOWARD MEADE, retired transportation executive; b. NYC, Sept. 21, 1918; s. Benjamin and Ida Winograd Pack; m. Nancy Buckley (dec. 1959); children: Loren, Susan, Ellen, Warren, Daniel(dec.); m. Dorothy Culbertson, 1961. BS in Economics, Columbia U. Pres. Seatrain Lines, Inc., NYC, 1965—77, vice chmn., 1977—79, chmn., 1979—81. Served in USCG. Died Dec. 9, 2008.

PAGE, THOMAS CRAMER, management educator; b. Martinsville, Ohio, Mar. 28, 1920; s. Earl S. and Elizabeth Jane (Cramer) P.; m. Jessie Morris, Sept. 11, 1944; children: Patricia Page Sterrett, Thomas Morris, Susan. BBA, Miami U., Oxford, Ohio, 1942, DHL, 1986; MBA, Harvard U., 1947. Indsl. engr. Eastman Kodak Co., Rochester, N.Y., 1947-51; with mktg. planning, gen. mgmt. Ford Motor Co., Dearborn, Mich., 1952-69, group v.p., 1975-78, v.p. Ford Latin Am., 1978-79, v.p. diversified products ops., 1979-81, exec. v.p., bd. dirs., 1981-85, ret., 1985; prof. mgmt. Miami U., 1985-89. Bd. dirs. Firestone Tire & Rubber Co., Akron, Ohio, 1985-88; chmn. bd. Ford Aerospace and Communications Corp.; v.p. Ford Mktg. Corp., Dearborn, 1970-71; pres. Philco-Ford Corp., Dearborn, 1971-75. Vice chmn. Detroit United Fund, 1970-71. Maj. USAAF, 1943-46, USAF, 1950-52. Mem. Pres. Assn., Phila C. of C. (bd. dirs. 1972-73), Delta, Sigma Pi. Home: Farmingtn Hls, Mich. Died Dec. 29, 2007.

PAINTER, GAYLE STANFORD, research physicist, consultant; b. Columbia, SC, Feb. 27, 1941; s. Garland Lee and Pearl Elizabeth (Marler) P.; m. June Elaine Griffin, June 22, 1962; children: Angela, Jennifer. BS, U. S.C., 1963, PhD, 1967. Postdoctoral researcher Quantum Theory Project U. Fla., Gainesville, 1967-69; rsch. physicist Oak Ridge (Tenn.) Nat. Lab., 1969-74, sr. rsch. physicist, from 1975. Guest scientist H.H. Wills Physics Lab., U. Bristol, U.K., 1974, Inst. for Solid State Physics Kernforschungsanlage, Juelich, Germany, 1975; cons. Consultec, Inc., Knoxville, 1990—. Contbr. 60 articles to profl. jours. Leader youth mission 1st United Meth. Ch., Oak Ridge, 1990. Recipient Tech. Achievement award Martin Marietta Energy Systems, 1987, 89, Publ. award, 1988, 93; Woodrow Wilson fellow, 1963. Fellow Am. Phys. Soc.; mem. Phi Beta Kappa. Democrat. Avocations: woodworking, photography, watercolor, music, home repair. Home: Oak Ridge, Tenn. Died Mar. 26, 2008.

PAIVA, JOSEPH MOURA, biotechnology company executive; b. Rahway, NJ, Aug. 18, 1955; s. Joseph A. and Lucille S. (Moura) P.; m. Madeline A. Makoski, Sept. 9, 1978. BS in Acctg., Fairleigh Dickinson U., 1977; MBA, Rutgers U., 1982. CPA, N.J. Sr. acct. Peat, Marwick, Mitchell & Co., Hacksensack, N.J., 1977-80; contr. T.J. McGlone & Co., Inc., Edison, N.J., 1980-83; dir. fin., asst. sec. Cytogen Corp., Princeton, N.J., 1983-93; CFO, Cytorad Inc., Princeton, N.J., 1991-93; v.p., CFO Argus Pharm., Inc., The Woodlands, Tex., 1993-94; v.p. fin. Actimed Labs., Inc., Burlington, N.J., 1994-95; contr. Cephalon, Inc., West Chester, Pa., 1995-97; pres. Affinity Investment Advisors, Inc., Brick, N.J., from 1996; v.p., CFO, Orthovita, Inc., Malvern, Pa., from 1997. Bd. dirs., 1st v.p. So. N.J. Venture Capital Group, Mt. Holly, 1985-87; fin. cons., Howell, N.J., 1984-89; bd. dirs. Cephalon UK Ltd., Guilford, Eng. Mem. AICPA, N.J. Soc. CPAs, Assn. Biosci. Fin. Officers (pres. Phila.-Princeton chpt. 1992-93, 96-98, bd. dirs. 1994—, v.p. Houston chpt. 1993-94), Mensa, Phi Zeta Kappa, Phi Omega Epsilon. Roman Catholic. Avocations: volleyball, windsurfing, coin collecting/numismatics. Died Mar. 11, 2008.

PAJAK, JOHN J., retired federal judge; b. Buffalo, Aug. 24, 1932; s. John Keenan and Julia Josephine Pajak; m. Elizabeth Pierson Pajak, 1954 (div.); 1 child, Rebecca; m. Agnes Aranyi, 1997. BA magna cum laude, Syracuse U., 1954, JD, 1956. Bar: NY 1956, US Ct. Appeals (1st and 9th cirs.) 1958, US Ct. Appeals (4th cir.) 1959, US Supreme Ct. 1960, DC 1961, US Supreme Ct. 1961, US Tax Ct. 1965. Atty. US Dept. Justice, Washington, 1956—61, Office Alien Property, Litig. Sect., 1956—58; tax divsn. Appellate Sect., 1958—61; assoc. Hogan & Hartson LLP, Washington, 1961—66, Andrew F. Oehmann, Washington, 1966—69; ptnr. Oehmann & Pajak, Washington, 1970—72; resident counsel Nixon, Hargrave, Devans & Doyle, Rochester, NY, Washington, 1972—79; spl. trial judge US Tax Ct., Washington, 1979—2005, chief spl. trial judge, 1985—87. Mem.: ABA (tax sect.), Order of Coif, DC Bar Assn., Fed. Bar Assn., Phi Beta Kappa. Died Oct. 18, 2009.

PALM, BRUCE ARTHUR, retired advertising executive; b. Cleve., Jan. 13, 1932; s. Arthur C. and Eleanor Garnet (Berghoff) P.; m. Mary Anne Alexander, Apr. 25, 1983; children: T. Arthur, Scott, Susan, Linda. BA, Case Western Reserve U., 1953. Account exec. Palm & Patterson, Inc., Cleve., 1953-62, v.p., 1962-69, pres., 1969-79; sr. v.p. Bayless-Kerr, Inc., Cleve., 1979-83, McKinney Advt., Cleve., 1983-84, J.I. Scott Co., Grand Rapids, Mich., 1984-85; pres. Palm & Patterson, Inc., Science Park, 1985-94; ret., 1994. Mem. Bus. Profl. Advt. Assn., Indsl. Marketers Cleve., Cleve. Advt. Club, Soc. Explosive Engrs., Coun. Smaller Enterprises. Republican. Presbyterian. Home: Aurora, Ohio. Died June 8, 2008.

PALMER, JOHN ANTHONY, III, language professor, secondary school educator, music educator; b. Worcester, Mass., May 18, 1955; s. John Jr. and Barbara (Dufresne) P. BA in Spanish, Worcester State Coll., 1977, MEd in Ednl. Adminstrn., 1988. Cert. Spanish, French, German and music tchr., Mass. Tchr., head dept. fgn. langs. Mahar Regional Sch., Orange, Mass., 1979-88; tchr. French, Spanish and German Doherty Meml. HS, Worcester, 1992—99, Burncoat Sr. HS, from 1999. Adj. prof. Spanish, Worcester State Coll., 1988-90, Fla. Atlantic U., 1991-93, Quinsigamond CC, 1997—; instr. voice Worcester Poly. Inst., 1979-81; cantor Ch. of St. Peter, 1977-81, Worcester Eglise Notre Dame des Canadiens, Worcester, 1981-83; adjudicator vocal auditions All-State Music Educators Conf., 1988; dir. Mass. Tchrs. Assn., 2006-; bargaining chair 15 com. colls. of Mass. Tenor soloist Regis Coll., Boston, Worcester Poly. Inst., Worcester Chorus, Salisbury Singers, Simmons Coll., Boston, Ft. Lauderdale Opera Co., Opera Worcester, Smith Coll., North Hampton, Wells Coll., Aurore, N.Y. Mem. ASCD, Am. Coun. Tchrs. Fgn. Langs., Nat. Assn. Secondary Sch. Prins., Mass. Assn. Sch. Supts., Mass. Fgn. Lang. Assn., Mass. Tchrs. Assn. (dir.), Sigma Delta Pi. Democrat. Home: Worcester, Mass. Died Apr. 2009.

PALMER, ROBERT JOSEPH, advertising executive, winery owner; b. NYC, July 16, 1934; s. Patrick S. and Irene M. Palmer; m. Lorraine E. Wittmer; children: Linda, Katherine, Lori-Ann, Barbara. Media dir. Cunningham and Walsh Advt., NYC, 1950-67; pres. Kelly Nason, Inc., NYC, 1968-76, R.J. Palmer, Inc., NYC, 1977—2009; exec. v.p. Kornhauser and Calene, Inc., NYC, 1980-85; pres. Palmer Vineyards, Inc., NYC, 1983—2009. Chmn. R.J. Palmer Media Svc., 1985-09; pres. LI Wine Coun. 2005-09. Died Jan. 16, 2009; Huntington, NY.

PAMPLIN, ROBERT BOISSEAU, SR., retired textile manufacturing executive; b. Sutherland, Va., Nov. 25, 1911; s. John R. and Pauline P. (Beville); m. Mary K. Reese, June 15, 1940 (dec. 2008); 1 child, Robert Boisseau Jr. BBA, Va. Poly. Inst. & State U., 1933; postgrad., Northwestern U., 1933-34; LLD (hon.), U. Portland, Oreg., 1972; LHD (hon.), Warner Pacific Coll., 1976. With Ga.-Pacific Corp., Portland, 1934-76, adminstrv. v.p., 1952-55, exec. v.p., 1955-57, pres., 1957-67, chmn. bd., CEO, 1967—76; ret., 1976; chmn., CEO Mt. Vernon Mills Inc. (subs. R.B. Pamplin Corp.), Greenville, SC, retired, 1996. Bd. trustees Va. Polytechnic U., 1971—79. Recipient Merit award, Northwestern U., 1966, Disting. Svc. award, Va. Polytechnic Y. & State U., 1973; named Virginian of the Yr., Va. Press Assn., 1976. Died June 24, 2009.

PANCOAST, EDWIN C., retired senior foreign service officer, writer, researcher; b. Stratford, NJ, Aug. 20, 1925; m. Eunice Billings, June 12, 1948; children: Laurence E., Karen L., Joanne L. BA, Maryville Coll., 1949; MS in Internat. Affairs, George Washington U., 1971; grad., Nat. War Coll., Washington, 1971. Served U.S. Fgn. Svc., US Dept. State, 1949-53, USIA, 1953-86, sr. policy officer Washington, 1984-86; chief of policy Voice of America, 1975-79; ret., 1986. 1st lt. AUS, 1943-46, ETO. Died Mar. 13, 2009.

PANENKA, JAMES BRIAN JOSEPH, financial company executive; b. Milw., July 13, 1942; s. Alois J. and Jeanette (Buettner) P.; m. Kimberly A., Kerry A., Kristine A. BA, Marquette U., 1965. Sales rep. Pillsbury Corp., Milw., 1965-71; investment broker Marshall Co., Milw., 1971-72, E.F. Hutton, Milw., 1972-77; v.p. investments Dean Witter Inc., Milw., 1977-81; sr. v.p. investments First Union Securuties, Inc., Milw., from 1981. Mem. Pres.'s Coun., Kemper Securities Group, Inc., 1981—. Bd. dirs. Mental Health Assn. of Wis., Milw., 1981-91, Sherri Steinhauer LPGA Mental Health Golf Tournament, Madison, Wis., 1991—; life mem. Marquette U. Pres.'s Coun., Milw., 1985—. Mem. Western Racquet Club (Elm Grove, Wis.), Lac La Belle Golf Club, Milw. Yacht Club. Roman Catholic. Avocations: tennis, golf, yachting. Home: Elm Grove, Wis. Died July 1, 2008.

PAPADAKIS, CONSTANTINE N., academic administrator, civil engineer, educator; b. Athens, Greece, Feb. 2, 1946, came to U.S., 1969; s. Nicholas and Rita (Masciotti) P.; m. Eliana Apostolides, Aug. 28, 1971; 1 child, Maria. Diploma in Civil Engring., Nat. Tech. U. Athens, 1969; MS in Civil Engring., U. Cin., 1970; PhD in Civil Engring., U. Mich., 1973. Registered profl. engr., Ohio, Greece. Engring. specialist, geotechnical group Bechtel, Inc., Gaithersburg, Md., 1974-76, supr. and asst. chief engr. geotechnical group Ann Arbor, Mich., 1976-81; v.p., bd. dirs. water resources div. STS Cons. Ltd., Ann Arbor, 1981-84; v.p. water and environ. resources dept. Tetra Tech-Honeywell, Pasadena, Calif., 1984; head dept. civil engring. Colo. State U., Ft. Collins, 1984-86; dean Coll. Engring. U. Cin., 1986-95, dir. Groundwater Rsch. Ctr., 1986-95; dir. Ctr. Hill Solid and Hazardous Waste Rsch. Ctr. EPA, Cin., 1986-93; pres. Drexel U., Phila., 1995—2009. Adj. prof. civil engring. U. Mich., 1976-83; cons. Gaines & Stern Co., Cleve., 1983-84, Honeywell Europe, Maintal, Fed. Republic of Germany, 1984-85, Arthur D. Little, Boston, 1984-85, Camargo Assocs., Ltd., Cin., 1986, King Fahd U. Rsch. Inst., Dhahran, Saudi Arabia, 1987, King Abdulaziz City for Sci. and Tech., Riyadh, Saudi Arabia, 1991, Henderson & Bodwell Cons. Engrs. Inc., 1991, Cin. Met. Sewer Dist., 1992, Ohio River Valley Water Sanitation Commn., 1994; acting pres. Ohio Aerospace Inst., 1988-90; interim pres. Inst. Advanced Mfg. Scis. Ohio Edison Tech. Ctr., 1989-90; bd. govs. Edison Materials Tech. Ctr., 1988-95; adv. bd., founding mem. Hamilton County Bus. Incubator, 1988-95; bd. dirs. Nat. Commn. for Coop. Edn., Opera Co. of Phila., Hellenic Coll./Holy Cross Acad., Mace Security Internat., Inc., Met-Pro Corp., Aqua Am., Inc., Amkor Techs., Inc., CDI, Inc., Phila. Stock Exch. Author: Problems on Strength of Materials, 1968, Sewer Systems Design, 1969; editor: Fluid Transients and Acoustics, 1978, Pump-Turbine Schemes, 1979, Small Hydro Power Fluid Machinery, 1982; Megatrends in Hydraulics, 1987; contbr. more than 65 articles to profl. jours. Mem. Greater Cin. C. of C. Blue Chip Campaign for Econ. Devel. Task Force, 1988-93, bd. dirs. Bus. Assistance Ctr., 1989-95; mem. Ohio Coun. on Rsch. and Econ. Devel., 1988, Ohio Sci. and Tech. Commn. Adv. Group, 1989-90, 92-95; coun. mem. St. Nicholas Ch. Parish, Ann Arbor, 1981-84; mem. City of Ft. Collins Drainage Bd., 1984-86; bd. dirs. Dan Beard coun. Boy Scouts Am., 1995, Intelligent Vehicle Hwy. Soc. Ohio, 1994-95; bd. dirs. Liberty Bell Coun. of the Boy Scouts of Am., 1996—. Recipient Horace W. King scholarship civil engring. dept. U. Mich., 1971-73, 6 Bechtel Merit awards, 1974-79, Young Engr. of Yr. award Mich. Soc. Profl. Engrs., Ann Arbor, Mich., 1982, Disting. Engr. award Engrs. and Scientists Cin. Tech. Socs. Coun., 1989, Acad. of Achievement in Edn. award Am. Hellenic Ednl. Progressive Assn., 1995, Hellenic Univ. Club of Phila. Achievement award, 1996, Krikos Disting. Hellene Leader award, 1996, Svc. Learning award, Jr. Achievement Inc., 2001, Congl. medal of Ellis Island, 2001, Heart of Phila. award, Am. Heart Assn., 2001, Silver Beaver award, Boy Scouts Am., 2002, US Dept. Treasury medal of Merit, 2003, Disting. Hellene award, Hellenic Med. Soc. NY, 2003, End. award, Consular Corps Phila., 2003, Dennis Clark Immigrant Achievement award, 2004, Penn Club Ann. award, 2005, Amb. award, YMCA Phila., 2005, Interdependence Day Phila. award, 2006, Gold medal award Pub. Rels. Assn., 2006, Svc. to Humanity award March of Dimes, 2007, Global Citizen award Global Interdependence Ctr., 2007. Fellow ASCE (pres. Ann Arbor br. 1980-81, pres.-elect Mich. sect. 1983-84, hydraulics divsn. publ. com. 1980-83), ASME (chmn. fluid transients com. 1978-80, mem. fluids engring. divsn. awards com. 1981-84), Am. Soc. Engring. Edn.; mem. NSPE (legis. and govt. affairs com. 1994-95, chair profl. engrs. in edn. divsn. 1995), Order of the Engr., Internat. Assn. for Hydraulic Rsch., Ohio Engring. Dean's Coun. (chmn.-elect 1989-91), Rotary, Sigma Xi, Chi Epsilon, Tau Beta Pi. Greek Orthodox. Avocations: photography, classical music, travel, swimming, racquetball. Home: Wayne, Pa. Died Apr. 5, 2009.

PAPER, RENEE BETH, emergency department nurse; b. LA, Feb. 15, 1958; d. Harry W. and Fay A. (Armond) P. Diploma of Vocat. Nursing, Conejo Valley Vocat. Sch., Thousand Oaks, Calif., 1977; ADN, U. Nev., Las Vegas, 1980. CCRN. Staff nurse/team leader Westlake Community Hosp., Westlake Village, Calif., 1977-78; staff nurse ICU/CCU Valley Hosp., Las Vegas, Nev., 1978-79, Desert Springs Hosp., Las Vegas, Nev., 1979-80; staff nurse/relief charge PRN Nurses, Inc., Las Vegas, 1980-82; charge nurse emergency dept. St. Rose Dominican Hosp., Henderson, Nev., from 1982; program dir. Hemophilia Found. of Nev., Henderson, Nev., from 1992. Pres., founder Hemophilia Found. of Nev., 1990-92; founder, chmn. nurse practice com. St. Rose Dominican Hosp., Henderson, 1985-88; med./legal nurse cons. Mem. organizing com. Region IX Hemophilia program Maternal Child Health Bur. Named So. Nev. Emergency Nurse of the Yr. March of Dimes, Las Vegas, 1991. Mem. AACN, World Fedn. of Hemophilia, Emergency Nurses Assn. Avocation: Scrabble. Home: Henderson, Nev. Died Nov. 8, 2007.

PARAMEKANTHI, SRINIVASAN MANDAYAM, software services executive; b. Mysore City, India, July 1, 1940; arrived in U.S., 1970, naturalized, 1991; s. Appalacharya Paramekanthi and Singamma Budugan; m. Ranganayaki Srirangapatnam, June 18, 1967; children: Srikala, Srilatha, Sriharsha. BS, U. Mysore, 1959, BE in Mech. Engring., 1963; MS in Ops. Rsch., Poly. Inst. NY, 1974, MS in Computer sci., 1983. Costing engr. Heavy Engring. Corp., Ranchi Bihar, India, 1963—70; inventory analyst Ideal Corp., Bklyn., 1970—75; sys. analyst Electronic Calculus, Inc., NYC, 1975—76; cons. in software, project leader Computer Horizons Corp., NYC, 1976—85; pres. Compmusic, Bellerose, NY, from 1985. Tchr. classical Indian Karnatak music theory, acoustics and voice tng. Hindu Temple Soc., NYC; tchr., cons. in-house tng.; presenter seminars on classical Indian music theory. Founding mem. governing coun. Vishwa Hindu Parishad of USA, from 1973, pres. NY State chpt., 1977—86; chmn. Indian/South Asian Comty. Orgn. of Ea. Queens, NYC, 1996—98. Mem.: IEEE, Inst. Engrs. (India), Assn. for Computing Machinery. Democrat. Hindu. Home: Bellerose, NY. Died Nov. 7, 2008.

PARK, JAMES GRIMES, steel company executive, lawyer; b. Pitts., Nov. 24, 1930; s. Dale and Rebecca (Grimes) P.; m. Nancy J. Clarke, Aug. 15, 1953; children: Barbara J., Sally R., Marilyn A. AB, Dickinson Coll., 1952, JD, 1954. Bar: Pa. 1955, U.S. Dist. Ct. (we. dist.) Pa. 1955, U.S. Tax Ct. 1956, U.S. Ct. Appeals (3d, 4th, 5th and 11th cirs.), U.S. Supreme Ct. 1982, Fla. 1983. Assoc. Buchanan Ingersoll, Pitts., 1954-62, ptnr. then sr. ptnr., 1962-83; exec. v.p., gen. counsel Union Electric Steel Co., Pitts., 1983-84, pres., 1984-93, bd. dirs., from 1978. Bd. dirs. Bloom Engring. Co., Pitts., Lincoln Bank, Pitts., Std. Steel Specialty Corp., Union Electric Steel Co. Author: Coal Law, 1983. Pres., bd. dirs. Mt. Lebanon (Pa.) Sch. Bd., 1966-72; bd. dirs. Presby. Assn. on Aging, 1966—; chmn. Mt. Lebanon Rep. Com., 1970-74; mem. Electoral Coll., 1988. Served with USAR, 1953-55. Fellow Am. Bar Found.; mem. ABA, Pa. Bar Assn., Fla. Bar Assn., Allegheny Bar Assn. Clubs: Duquesne, St. Clair Country (Pitts.); Pinetree Country (DelRay Beach, Fla.). Lodges: Shriners. Republican. Presbyterian. Home: Pittsburgh, Pa. Died Aug. 17, 2008.

PARK, RICHARD JOHN, value engineer; b. Harrison, NJ, Mar. 23, 1922; s. Robert James and Marie Magdeline (Hassard) P.; m. Barbara Knoph, Nov. 28, 1948; children: Richard John, Jr., Barbara Christine Park O'Brien. B Mech. Engring., Clarkson U., 1946; M Mech. Engring., NYU, 1948. Cert. value specialist Soc. Am. Value Engrs. Piping engr. M.W. Kellogg, NYC, 1946-48; facilities engr. Propeller Divsn., Rocket Dept. Curtiss-Wright, Caldwell, N.J., 1948-49; rsch. devel. engr. Colgate Palmolive Co., Jersey City, 1949-51; acting divsn. head Arabian Am. Oil Co., NYC, 1951-60; purchasing cost engr. Bradford (Pa.) Dresser Mfg., 1960-63; chief of value engring. Continental Motors Corp., Detroit, 1963-67; mgr. value control Chrysler Corp., Highland Park, Mich., 1967-80; v.p. cons. divns. Pioneer Engring. and Mfg. Co., Warren, Mich., 1980-81; pres., value engr. cons. R.J. Park and Assoc., Inc., Birmingham, Mich., from 1981. Cons. value engring. Editor/author: (books) Function Analysis System Technique, 1975, Value Engineering, 1979, Park's Catalog of Functions, 1982, Orientation, Principles and Applications of Value Engineering, 1991, Value Engineering-A Plan for Invention, 1998; pub.: St. Lucie Press. Named Engr. of Distinction, Engr.'s Joint Coun., 1973. Fellow Soc. of Am. Value Engrs. (v.p. region 1973-76, v.p. profl. devel. and mem. certification bd. 1976-79, Value Engr. of Yr. 1972); mem. Save Internat. Engring. Soc. Detroit, Soc. Mfg. Engrs., VFW (life), Soc. N Scalers. Roman Catholic. Avocations: sailing, gardening, photography, travel, model railroading. Home: Birmingham, Mich. Died Feb. 8, 2008.

PARKE, M(ARGARET) JEAN, retired business owner, editor; b. Akron, Ohio, Aug. 23, 1920; d. Lawrence William and Rosella (Washburn) Beat; m. Harry Morris Parke, July 25, 1942; children: Richard Blake, Catherine Jean. BA magna cum laude, U. Toledo, 1942, MA, 1959. Adminstrv. asst. Dist. Office Price Adminstrn., Toledo, 1943-45; editing cons. Century Press, Inc., Toledo, 1955-72; cons. women's progs. U. Toledo, 1973-75; reports editor Price-Waterhouse & Co., Cleve., 1976-78; fin. officer, ptnr. Parke Supply Co., Avon Lake, Ohio, 1980-86; co-owner, sec. Woodlark Farms, Inc., Georgetown, Ky., 1978-94. Bd. trustees, past pres. Avon Lake Pub. Libr., 1981-90, Friends of the U. Toledo Libr., past pres. 1971-74; founding trustee Friends of Toledo-Lucas county Pub. Libr., 1970-73; trustee Avon Lake Pub. Libr. Found., Inc., 1991-97; organizer, past pres. Parkview Hosp. Evening Guild, Toledo, 1953; incorporator, sec. Ch. Women United of Toledo area, 1963-66; bd. dirs. LWV, Sylvania, Ohio, Avon Lake; mem. Friends of Avon Lak Libr. Jean Parke Conf. Rm. named in her honor Avon Lake Pub. Libr., 1981. Mem. AAUW (past pres., bd. dirs. Toledo br. 1981-90, Ednl. Found. Prog. honoree 1981), Avon on the Lake Garden Club, U. Toledo Alumni Assn. (trustee, officer Blue T award 1981), Chi Omega Alumnae Toledo (officer), Chi Omega Alumnae Ohio (state bd. dirs. 1983-85, Outstanding Ohio Chi Omega Alumna 1982). Republican. Episcopalian. Avocations: travel, great books, theater, college football, needlecrafts. Home: Avon Lake, Ohio. Died Jan. 15, 2008.

PARKER, DEREK, accountant; b. Key West, Fla., Sept. 8, 1960; BS in Acctg., Fin., Fla. State U., 1982. CPA, Fla. Acct. Kemp & Rosasco, CPA's, Key West, 1983-85; ptnr. Oropeza & Parker, CPA's, Key West, from 1985. Mem. Am. Inst. CPA's, Fla. Inst. CPA's (sec. 1983—). Home: Key West, Fla. Died Oct. 14, 2007.

PARKER, ROBERT CHAUNCEY HUMPHREY, clergyman, publishing executive; b. NYC, Apr. 6, 1941; s. Robert Humphrey and Edith Louise (Corya) P. Student, U. Va., Charlottesville, 1960—61, student, 1962—63; diploma, Inst. Psychorientology, Laredo, Tex., 1973. Ordained to ministry Ch. of Antioch-Malabar Rite, 1975. Law clk. Shearman & Sterling, NYC, 1961-62; owner Parker's Pronto Pups Inc., NYC, 1962-64; asst. to pres. UG Packaging, NYC, 1964-66; asst. nat. sales mgr. Elliott Svc. Co. Inc., Mt. Vernon, NY, 1966-67; pres., cons. Lenfield Assocs. & Cons., NYC and Washington, 1967-71; founder, pres. Occult Comm. Corp., NYC, Washington, and Danbury, Conn., 1971-76, New Awareness Corp., London and Mpls., 1973-81; dir., resident min. The Healing Ctr. at St. Patricia's, Inver Grove Heights, Minn., 1975; lectr., min. Ch. of Antioch-Malabar Rite, from 1975; editor New Awareness News, 1975—2006; founder, pres. Parker/Tofte Comm., Robert Parker Assocs., Minnetonka, Minn., 1977—2005; pres., CEO Am. Energy & Alcohol Corp., Mpls., 1981-84. Cons. Boat Owners Assn. US, Washington, 1967-70, Durance Co., 1994-95; rschr., cons. Am. Marine Corp., Marblehead, Mass.; pres. Field Harmonics Rsch. Group Inc., 1993-97, New Awareness Spkrs. and Pub. Group, Inc., 1997-2005; cons., spkr. in field. Author: Watergate Flight 553, 1974, Reabsorption Energy, 1975, Finding Your Own Four-Leaf Clover, 1993; author Telsa Newsletter, 1979; editor New Awareness Mag., 1973-75, (newsletter) Sunbeams; editor, pub. New Awareness News and Book News, 1977—2006, New Awareness Computer News, 1995—2006, psychic/parapscyhology internat. trade jours., 1971-75; designer, pub.: Henry's Hilarious One Liners, 1991, Henry's Just a Chuckle, 1992, Henry's Just a Laugh, 1992, Henry's Just a Witticism, 1992; contbr. articles to profl. jours.; featured on Dimension WCCO-TV, 1991, 93, Forbes Mag., 1996, Elizabeth Smart Recovery, Sta. WCCO-TV, 2003, Ruth Koscielak Show, Sta. KCCO-AM, 2003, Smart Predictions 100% Correct, 2003; host (cable) Astrology and Mind, Etc., 1994-96; syndicated columnist; ongoing guest WUO-AM, 2006. Bd. dirs. Toutorsky Ednl. Found., Washington, 1988—91. Mem. Nat. Press Club (Washington), Internat. Telsa Soc. Inc., Knickerbocker Greys Vet. Corps (NYC), Browning Sch. Alumni Assn. (NYC), Lenox (Mass.) Sch. Alumni Assn. Avocations: reading, travel. Died Dec. 21, 2007.

PARKHURST, VIOLET KINNEY, artist; b. Derby Line, Vt., Apr. 26, 1926; d. Edson Frank and Rosa (Beauchiene) Kinney; m. Donald Winters Parkhurst, Apr. 10, 1948. Student, Sch. Practical Arts, Boston, 1941—42, Baylor U., Waco, Tex., 1943, Calif. State U., LA, 1950—51. Contbr. articles to profl. mags.; exhibitions include galleries Ports of Call, San Pedro, Calif., Represented in permanent collections Stockholm Mus., Presidents Richard M. Nixon & others, one-man shows include Prominent Galleries; author: (book) How to Paint Books, 1966, Parkhurst on Seascapes, 1972, Paintings reproduced on covers South West Art, Hollywood Bowl Easter Sunrise Service program; numerous paintings. Mem. Ch. Religious Sci. Recipient 30 blue ribbons; fellow, Am. Inst. Fine Arts. Achievements include first artist in the world invited to present a painting to Pres. Jiang Zemin, Beisin, China, 2002 & the western artist to have a painting in China Nat. Mus. of Fine Arts & the Hall of the People. Home: Palos Verdes Estates, Calif. Died Jan. 12, 2008.

PARR, JOHN DAVID, not-for-profit executive; b. Lafayette, Ind., Feb. 7, 1948; s. Harlan and Dorothy (Widmer) P.; m. Robin Godfrey, May 1972 (div. Sept. 1976); m. Sandra Jean Widener, May 31, 1986; children: Chase Anna, Katherine Widener. BA in Polit. Sci., Purdue U., 1970; JD, U. Denver, 1976. Bar: Colo. 1977. Vol. coord., office mgr. Barnes for Congress, 1970; legis. coord., membership drive coord. Colo. Project/Common Cause, 1971, 73; coord. Campaign to Remove 1976 Winter Olympics from Colo. Citizens for Colorado's Future, 1971-72; dir. field orgn. Coloradans for Lamm, 1973-74; asst. to gov. Gov. Richard Lamm, 1974-77; campaign cons. Coloradans for Lamm, 1977; cons. ACTION, Washington, 1977-78; dir. Colo. Front Range Project Office of Gov., 1979-81; dir. Ctr. for Pub.-Pvt. Sector Coop. U. Colo., Denver, 1981-85; pres. Nat. Civic League, Denver, from 1985. Commr. Denver Urban Renewal Authority. Contbg. editor and author to profl. jours. Vol. Chinook Fund Fundraising Com., Denver Pub. Sch. Tutorial Program, U. Denver Fgn. Student Host Parent Program. Fellow Nat. Acad. for Pub. Adminstrn.; mem. Common Cause, Nature Conservancy, Vol. for Outdoor Colo., Friends of Denver Pub. Libr., Denver Natural History Mus., Nat. Pub. Radio Stas. KCFR and KUVO. Home: Denver, Colo. Died Dec. 22, 2007.

PARRY, LOIS IRENE, communications company executive; b. Indpls., Mar. 12, 1945; d. Hilbert Edward and Mary Olive (Lanman) Roth; m. Edward Hayden Parry, Nov. 5, 1966 (div. 1981); children: Jeffrey Alan, Matthew Edward, Jennifer Lynne. Student, Butler U., 1962-65, John Herron Art Ins., 1963-65, Ind. U., 1980-81. Dept. mgr. L.S. Ayres & Co., Indpls., 1980-81, asst. buyer, 1981-82, assoc. buyer, 1982; territory mgr. Charles of the Ritz Group, NYC, 1982-85; acct. exec. Lancome/Cosmair, NYC, 1985-88; advt./mktg. mgr. Cellular Systems, Inc., Carmel, Ind., from 1989. Pres. West Grove Elm. Sch. PTO, 1979; bd. dirs. White River Coalition, Greenwood, Ind., 1980-81; mem. membership com. Ind. Bus. Network, regional coordinating coun. Gov.'s Commn. Drug-Free Ind.; chpt. sec. Purdue U., Delta Tau Delta; mem. Parents Club, 1988; pres. Nu Tau chpt., Delta Theta Tau, 1980-82, nat. rep., 1976-79, treas., 1978-79. Republican. Avocations: reading, watercolors, fitness. Home: Indianapolis, Ind. Died June 22, 2008.

PASINSKI, EDMOND, programmer, analyst; b. Jersey City, Dec. 6, 1955; s. Chester and Ann (Sobolewski) P. BS in Acctg./Bus. Mgmt., St. Peter's Coll., 1978, MS in Sch. Supervision, 1989. Sr. programmer, analyst, coord. data processing Hudson County Vocat./Tech. Sch., North Bergen, N.J., from 1979. Democrat. Roman Catholic. Died Jan. 5, 2008.

PASTERNACK, HARVEY, consulting actuary, lawyer; b. Altoona, Pa., Nov. 6, 1945; s. Jack and Pauline (Swartzbart) P. BA, Pa. State U., 1967, MA, 1968; JD, St. John's U., Queens, NY, 1975. Bar: N.Y. 1982, U.S. Dist. Ct. (so. and ea. dists.) N.Y. 1986, U.S. Ct. Appeals (2d cir.) 1986, Pa. 1990. V.p. Seal and Lohse, Inc., Garden City, N.Y., 1979-82; prin., actuary Buck Cons., NYC, from 1986. Cons. Local 1 Distillery Workers Union, N.Y.C., 1980-82, actuarial advisor Social Security Fund hdqrs., Englewood, N.J., 1980-90; benefit cons. PaineWebber, N.Y.C., 1984—; mem. Multiemployer Task Force (U.S. gov. com.) 1985-86. Author: Qualified Plans Primer, 1978; contbr. articles to profl. jours. Bd. dirs., v.p. Little Neck Jewish Ctr., N.Y.C., 1984—; bd. dirs. Temple Torah, N.Y.C., 1985—. Recipient Am. Jurisprudence award St. John's U., Queens, 1977. Mem. AAAS, ABA, N.Y. State Bar Assn., Am. Acad. Actuaries, Am. Soc. Personnel Adminstrn., Soc. Human Resources Mgmt., Assn. Actuarielle Internationale. Republican. Avocations: pilot, legal history, mathematics, science. Home: State College, Pa. Died July 17, 2008.

PATEL, JAYANT A., pharmacologist, toxicologist; b. Indore, India, May 23, 1935; came to U.S., 1959; s. Ambalal J. and Hiraben A. P.; m. Kalawati J., May 28, 954; children: Vis BS in Chemistry, Saugar U., India, 1957, BS in Pharmacology, 1958; MS in Pharmacology, U. Mich., 1961, PhD, 1966. Pharmacist Univ. Hosp., Ann Arbor, Mich., 1961-84, toxicologist, from 1984. Cons. drug testing Consumers Energy, Jackson, Mich., 1990—, Diazem Corp., Midland, Mich. 1994—; crew chief drug testing NCAA, USOC, Kansas City, Kans., 1986—, IDTM, Indpls., 1994—. Grantee Roche Pharm. Co., N.Y., 1962; rsch. grantee, NCAA, Kansas City, Kans., 1992. Mem. Soc. of Forensic Toxicology, Am. Bonsai Soc. Avocations: photography, gardening. Home: Ann Arbor, Mich. Died Sept. 23, 2007.

PATEL, RUSI FRAMROZ, engineer; b. Bombay, July 14, 1948; came to U.S., 1971; s. Framroz Jamshedji and Dhun Framroz (Wadia) P.; m. Kashmira Rusi Majoo, Jan. 5, 1976; children: Karishma, Brianna. MS, Va. Inst. Tech., 1971; BS, I.I.T. Bombay, 1973. Registered profl. engr., Mass., N.Y., Va. Engr. Hinnant & Addison, Lynchburg, Va., 1973-75; energy engr. Hittmann Assoc., Columbia, Md., 1975-77; heating, ventilating, air-conditioning engr. Dale Engring., Utica, N.Y., 1977-78; sr. cons. Arthur D. Little, Inc., Cambridge, Mass., from 1978. Mem. ASHRAE, Assn. Energy Engrs. (charter). Parsi. Home: Concord, Mass. Died Jan. 22, 2008.

PATMAN, WILLIAM NEFF, former US Representative from Texas; b. Texarkana, Tex., Mar. 26, 1927; s. John William Wright and Merle (Connor) P.; m. Carrin Foreman Mauritz, Sept. 5, 1953; 1 child, Carrin Foreman. BBA, LL.B., U. Tex., Austin, 1953. Bar: Tex. bar 1953. Diplomatic courier US Fgn. Svc., 1949-50; legal examiner, oil and gas div. Tex. R.R. Commn., 1953-55; individual practice law, owner, operator farm and ranch Ganado, Tex., 1955—2008; city atty. City of Ganado, 1955-60; mem. Tex. State Senate, 1961-81, US Congress from 14th Tex. Dist., 1981—84. Pres. Jackson County (Tex.) United Fund, 1960; chmn. ofcl. bd. stewards First Methodist Ch., Ganado, 1960's. Served with USMC, 1945-46. Mem. Tex. Bar Assn., ABA, Ganado Jaycees (charter), Phi Alpha Delta, Delta Sigma Pi, Sigma Alpha Epsilon. Clubs: Am. Legion, Farm Bur. Lodges: Masons (past master). Democrat. Methodist. Home: Austin, Tex. Died Dec. 9, 2008.

PATTEN, WILLIAM THOMAS, priest, consultant; b. Chattanooga, Aug. 7, 1924; s. George Holmes and Margaret (Thomas) P.; m. Mary Lynn Chapin, June 16, 1948; children: Mary, George, Thomas, Anne Elizabeth, Dorris. BA, Princeton U., 1949; MDiv, U. South, 1971; postgrad., U. Tenn., 1993. Ordained priest Episcopal Ch., 1971. V.p. sales Chattem Drug, Chattanooga, 1950-58; pres. Patten Motor Co., Chattanooga, 1958-68; vicar, then rector Grace Ch., Paris, Tenn., 1971-74, Ch. of the Nativity, Ft. Oglethorpe, Ga., 1974-80, St. Alban's Ch., Chattanooga, 1980-83; various ch. assignments, 1984-90; exec. dir. DuBose Conf. Ctr., Monteagle, Tenn., 1990-92; cons. (pro bono) various non-profits, Sewanee, Tenn., from 1992. Bishop and coun. Diocese of Tenn., 1978-81; bd. dirs. Dandridge Trust, 1986-92; retreat leader and planner, 1972-91; treas. Cloud Forest Sch., Inc., Sewanee, Tenn., 1994—. Author: Episcopal Is Compelling, 1981, Fighting the Good Fight, 1992. Dist. chmn. Boy Scouts Am., Chattanooga, 1950s; campaign mgr. Hamilton County (Tenn.) Sheriff election, 1960s; treas. Friends of the South Cumberland State Park, Monteagle, Tenn., 1994—; sec.-treas. Ecol. Support, Inc., Sewanee, 1994—. With U.S. Army, 1943-46, Europe. Decorated Purple Heart, Combat Infantry Badge. Avocations: golf, fishing, family. Died Dec. 30, 2007.

PATTERSON, LUCILLE GREMILLION, foundation administrator, dietitian; b. New Orleans, Jan. 20, 1938; d. Seltz Gabriel and Elmira Cecile (Alexander) Gremillion; m. William Earl Patterson, Mar. 26, 1966 (div. Aug. 1984); 1 child, Ross Alexander. BS, La. State U., 1959; MS, Purdue U., 1972. Dietetic intern Vanderbilt U. Hosp., Nashville, 1961; clin. dietitian USAF Hosp., Maxwell AFB, Montgomery, Ala., 1961-62; chief dietitian, cons. to Tactical Air Command surgeon USAF Hosp., Langley AFB, Hampton, Va., 1962-64; dir. of dietetics, cons. to Pacific Air Command surgeon USAF Hosp., Tachikawa AB, Tachikawa, Japan, 1964-68; dir. of dietetics, cons. to Strategic Air Command surgeon USAF Hosp., Offutt AFB, Omaha, 1968-70; course supr. Dept. Biomed. Scis. USAF Sch. of Health Care Sci., Wichita Falls, Tex., 1972-77; dir. of dietetics, cons. to Pacific Air Command surgeon USAF Hosp., Clark AB, Philippines, 1977-79; dir. of dietetics, cons. to Air Tng. Command surgeon USAF Med. Ctr., Keesler AFB, Biloxi, Miss., 1979-84; pres. Wildwood Resources, Inc., Wildwood Child Care Food Program, Englewood, Colo., from 1984. Cons. in nutrition with USAF. Advisory bd. Big Bros./Big Sisters of YMCA, Colorado Springs, Colo., 1988-89. Mem. Am. Dietetic Assn., Colo. Dietetic Assn., Plaza Club (vice chair, soltero com. 1988-89), Going Concern (membership com., social com. 1988-89), Omicron Nu. Republican. Episcopalian. Avocations: skiing, travel, reading, cooking, dance, entertaining, music. Home: Larkspur, Colo. Died Nov. 12, 2007.

PATTERSON, SHIRLEY ABBOTT, artist, writer; b. Buffalo, Dec. 13, 1923; d. Walter DeForest and Eleanor Agnes (Flinn) Abbott; m. Ralph Gordon Patterson, Sept. 25, 1948; children: Lois Elaine (dec.), Brian Alan. Diploma, Albright Sch. Fine Art, Buffalo, 1944; BS, SUNY, Buffalo, 1945. Cert. tchr., N.Y. Tchr. art Griffith Inst. and Cen. Sch., Springville, N.Y., 1945-46; critic tchr. art Kenmore (N.Y.) Pub. Schs., 1946-49; pvt. practice art tchr. Wilmington, Del., 1958-70; founder, mgr. Today's Artists, Wilmington, 1974-77; freelance writer, artist Wilmington, from 1977. Advisor exhbn. U. Del., Newark, 1979, advisor books, 1981, lectr., 1983, 86; critic Studio Group, Inc., Wilmington, 1985-87; juror Del. Camera Club, 1986, 87, 88; radio art talks Sta. WXDR, 1986-89; moderator Writers' Workshop of Delaware Valley, 1986-89. Contbr. numerous stories to children's mags., 1955-67; contbr. book revs. to News Jour. Co., 1975-77; exhbns. include APRE Gallery, Wilmington, Del., 1976-90, South Windsor (Conn.) Pub. Libr., 1992, Edward Dean Gallery, South Windsor, 1990, 91, others; represented in numerous pub. and pvt. collections. Recipient Artist of Yr. award Wilmington Christmas Com., 1976. Mem. AAUW (group leader 1960-64), Nat. League Am. Pen Women (br. pres. 1978-80, 1st Prize Painting award 1977, 79, 81, 83, 85, 86, 1st Prize Short Story award 1981, Writer's scholarship 1983, moderator writer's workshop Delaware Valley chpt. 1987, 88, 89), Studio Group, Inc. (pres. 1978-80), Pa. Watercolor Soc. (signature, hon.), Ky. Watercolor Soc., Delta Zeta (chpt. pres. 1943-54, alumni chpt. pres. 1982-83). Republican. Avocations: reading, travel, photography. Died Aug. 15, 2008.

PATTERSON, VONCEILE BAXTER, accountant; b. Panama City, Fla., Apr. 6, 1926; d. Charles Kettler and Lillian (Bryan) Baxter; m. Albert R. Patterson Jr., Dec. 29, 1946; children: Reese, David, Charles, Paul. BS in Acctg., U. Ala., 1947. CPA, Ala., La., Tex. Chief acct. Kreeder Furniture, Tuscaloosa, Ala., 1950-52; acct. Chas. A. Senna CPA, Tuscaloosa, 1952-53; sr. acct. Jamison & Money CPA, Tuscaloosa, 1953-55; ptnr. Hawthorn, Waymouth & Carrol, Baton Rouge, 1956-72; prin. Vonceile B. Patterson CPA, Baton Rouge, from 1973. Mem. Am. Inst. CPA's, Soc. La. CPA's, Ala. Soc. CPA's, Am. Soc. Women Accts. (pres. 1973-74, charter pres.). Clubs: Quota (Baton Rouge) (pres. 1974-75, treas. 1985-86). Democrat. Methodist. Avocation: fishing. Home: Baton Rouge, La. Died Aug. 14, 2008.

PATTERSON, WILLIAM B., occupational and environmental medicine physician; b. Boston, Dec. 24, 1948; s. W. Bradford and Helen (Ross) P. BS, Harvard U., Boston, 1971; MD, U. Vt., 1976; MPH, Boston U., 1990. Diplomate Am. Bd. Internal Medicine, Am. Bd. Preventive Medicine with subspecialty in occupl. and environ. medicine; lic. physician, Mass. Asst. vis. physician Boston City Hosp., 1979-83, intern and resident, 1976-79; dir. employee and occupl. health dept. health and hosps. City of Boston, 1982-83; occupl. physician Med. Products Group, Hewlett Packard Corp., from 1983; med. dir. occupl. health svcs. Choate-Symmes Health Svcs., Inc., 1983-86, dir. occupl. health svcs., 1986-90; v.p. occupl. health svcs. Wellesley Med. Mgmt. Inc. d/b/a Health Stop, 1990-92; pres. New England Occupl. Health Svcs. dba New England Health Ctr., Wilmington, Mass., 1992-97; med. dir. M/A-COM, Inc., from 1994; Mass. med. dir., chair med. policy bd. Occupl. Health and Rehab., from 1997. Instr. medicine Boston U., 1979-81, asst. prof., 1981—, instr. socio-med. scis., 1979-82, adj. asst. prof. pub. health, 1982-85, asst. prof., 1985—; cons. physician Mass. Registry Motor Vehicles, Boston, 1994-96; cons. U.S. Army C.E., Waltham, Mass., 1992-97; cons. in field; mem. resident adv. com. occupl. medicine tng. program U. Boston U. Med. Ctr., 1988-93, Mass. Med. Ctr., 1991—; med. dir. occupl. health program Hale Hosp., Haverhill, Mass., 1992-96. Contbr. articles to profl. jours. Mem. worksite task force Mass. affiliate Am. Heart Assn., 1987-95, chmn. 1990-92, co-chmn. 1993-95. W.K. Kellogg Found. Nat. fellow, 1982-85 Fellow Am. Coll. Occupl. and Environ. Medicine; mem. ACP, APHA, Mass. Coalition for Occupl. Health and Safety, Am. Coll. Occupl. and Environ. Medicine, Assn. of Occupl. and Environ. Clinics, New England Coll. Occupl. and Environ. Medicine (bd. dirs. 1991—, program dir. 1992-93, v.p. 1993-94, pres. 1994-96), Roxbury Clin. Record Club, Mass. Med. Soc. (chair spl. com. on environtl. and occupl. health 1998—). Died Mar. 31, 2008.

PAUL, BESSIE MARGRETTE, retired weather forecaster; b. Absher, Mont., June 24, 1926; d. Fredrick Ernest Bergman and Margrette Marie Daly; m. Theodore Eugene Paul, Dec. 1, 1949 (dec. 1964); 1 child, Barbara Marie. AS, Eastern Montana Coll., 1988; BSBA in bus. adminstrn., Eastern Mont. Coll., 1992. Weather observer, map plotter US Weather Bur., Billings, Mont., 1944—53, map plotter San Francisco, 1955—56; forecaster Nat. Oceanic and Atmospheric Adminstrn., 1956—81; ret., 1981. Mem.: AAUW, Order of Eastern Star, Nat. Assn. Active and Ret. Fed. Employee. Avocations: cooking, baking, gardening, exercise, reading. Home: Billings, Mont. Died Oct. 23, 2007.

PAUL, LES, guitarist, inventor, entertainer; b. Waukesha, Wis., June 9, 1915; s. George and Evelyn (Stutz) Polfuss; m. Mary Ford, 1949 (div. 1964); children: Lester, Gene, Colleen, Robert, Mary. Student pub. schs., Waukesha. Appeared on numerous radio programs throughout Midwest in 1920's-30's; founder Les Paul Trio, 1936—37; appeared with Fred Waring NYC; appeared on first television broadcast with an orch. from NBC, 1939; music dir. WWJD and WIND, Chgo., 1941; appeared with Mary Ford on own TV show Mahwah, NJ, 1953—57; host Edison 100th Anniversary of invention of phonograph at Edison Home West Orange, NJ, 1977. Numerous TV, club appearances, NYC, recs. include How High The Moon, 1951 (Hall of Fame award 1979); musician: (albums) Hawaiian Paradise, 1949, The Hit Makers!, 1950, The New Sound, 1950, Les Paul's New Sound, 1951, Bye Bye Blues!, 1952, Les and Mary, 1955, Time to Dream, 1957, Lover's Luau, 1959, Bouquet of Roses, 1962, Warm and Wonderful, 1962, Swinging' South, 1963, Fabulous Les Paul & Mary Ford, 1965, Les Paul Now!, 1968, Guitar Tapestry, 1969, Lover, 1969, The Guitar Artistry of Les Paul, 1971, Chester & Lester, 1977 (Grammy award, Best Country Instrumental Performance, 1977), Guitar Monsters, 1978, Multi Trackin, 1979, California Melodies, 2003, Les Paul & Friends: American Made World Played, 2005 (Grammy awards for Best Rock Instrumental Performance and Best Pop Instrumental Performance, 2006). Served with Armed Forces Radio Service, World War II. Recipient Grammy Achievement award, 1983, Tech. Grammy award, 2001, Nat. Medal Arts, 2007; named to Grammy Hall of Fame (with Mary Ford), 1977, Rock 'N' Roll Hall of Fame, 1988, Wis. Performing Artists Hall of Fame, 1990, Nat. Inventors Hall of Fame, 2005. Mem.: SAG, ASCAP, AFTRA, Am. Fedn. Musicians, Audio Engring. Soc. Achievements include consultant, Gibson Guitar Corp., Nashville; invention of multi-track tape recorder; first 8-track tape recorder; sound-on-sound recording; design of Les Paul electric solid body guitars. Home: Mahwah, NJ. Died Aug. 13, 2009.

PAULEY, ROBERT REINHOLD, retired broadcast executive; b. New Canaan, Conn., Oct. 17, 1923; s. Edward Matthew and Grace Amanda (Smith) Pauley; m. Barbara Anne Cotton, June 22, 1946; children: Lucinda Teed, Nicholas Andrew, Robert Reinhold Jr., John Adams. Student, Harvard U., 1946, MBA, 1951; DSc (hon.), Curry Coll., 1966. With radio sta. WOR, 1951-52, NBC, 1953-56, CBS, 1956-57; account exec. ABC Radio Network, 1957—59; sales mgr. ABC, 1959-60, v.p. in charge, 1960-61, pres., 1961-67; CEO Mutual Broadcasting Sys., NYC, 1967—69; v.p. corp. fin. E.F. Hutton & Co., Inc., 1971-81; founder, chmn. TV News Inc., NYC; founder Nat. Black Network, NYC; founder, pres. Cablenet Internat. Corp. and Cablenet News, NYC. Disting. lectr. U. S.C., Spartanburg. Bd. dirs. Found. Improve TV; trustee Curry Coll. Mem.: SAR, Radio-TV Execs. Soc., Tryon Hounds Club, Myopia Hunt Club, Harvard Club (Boston, N.Y.C.), St. Nicholas Soc. Home: Madison, Conn. Died May 2, 2009.

PAULK, EARL PEARLY, pastor; b. Appling County, Ga., May 30, 1927; s. Earl Pearly and Addie Mae (Tomberlin) P.; m. Norma Lucille Davis, July 5, 1946; children: Rebecca Mae, Susan Joy, Roma Beth. BA, Furman U., 1947; BDiv, Candler Sch. Theology, 1951; MDiv, Emory U., 1972; DD, New Covenant Internat. Bible Coll., New Zealand, 1990; DD (hon.), Oral Roberts U., Tulsa, 1987. Ordained to ministry Ch. of God. Tchr. Lee Coll., Cleveland, Tenn., 1947-48; pastor Moultrie (Ga.) Ch. of God, 1948-49, Buford (Ga.) Ch. of God, 1949-50; youth dir. Dorabille (Ga.) Ch. of God, 1950-51; pastor Hemphill Ave Ch. of God (now Mt. Paran Ch. of God), Atlanta, 1951-60; sr. pastor Chapel Hill Harvester Ch. (Cathedral of the Holy Spirit), Decatur, Ga., 1960—2009. Presiding bishop Internat. Communion of Charismatic Chs., Atlanta; trustee Charismatic Bible Ministries, Tulsa; mem. steering com. Global Mission, L.A.; counselor, human svc. minister to chemically addicted, AIDS patients, single parents, sr. citizens. Author: Your Pentecostal Neighbor, Forward in Faith, The Divine Runner, Satan Unmasked, Subltle Doors to Satanism, The Wounded Body of Christ, Ultimate Kingdom, Sex Is God's Idea, Held in the Heavens Until, To Whom Is God Betrothed?, Thrust in the Sickle and Reap, That the World May Know, 101 Questions Your Pastor Hopes You Never Ask, The Church: Trampled or Triumphant?, The Local Church Says Hell No!. Trustee, regent Oral Rroberts U., Tulsa; mem. steering com. Community APPEAL to the Homeless, Atlanta; mem. adv. bd. Bd. Edn.-Ben Jones, Atlanta, 1990. Recipient Disting. Svc. award Empire Real Estate Bd., 1989. Mem. Network of Christian Ministries, Tikkun Ministries of Refernce (bd. dirs.), Rambo-McQuire, Found. for the Discovery America, Lord's Day Alliance Avocations: golf, tennis. Died Mar. 29, 2009.

PAULOS, JOHN ROBERT (BOB PAULOS), communications company executive; b. Wood River, Ill., Aug. 21, 1924; s. Peter John and Lola Myrtle (Springer) P.; m. Virginia Louraine Deeter, Sept. 13, 1945; 1 child, Patricia Ann. Mem. editorial staff Alton (Ill.) Evening Telegraph, 1940-43, 1945-48; gen. mgr. Sta. WOKZ, Alton, 1948; editor Wood River Jour., 1949; mem. editorial staff Idaho State Jour., Pocatello, 1950-53; editor Daily Inter Lake, Kalispell, Mont., 1953-58; pub. The Dalles Chronicle, The Dalles, Oreg., 1958-61, Enterprise-Courier, Oregon City, Oreg., 1961-63, Waikiki Beach Press, Honolulu, 1963-66; v.p. Hagadone Corp., Coeur d'Alene, Idaho, from 1966. Served to lt. USAF, 1943-45. Named Newspaper Man of Yr. Advt. Assn. of Hawaii, Honolulu, 1964, 65. Mem. Internat. Newspaper Promotion Assn. (bd. dirs. 1976, pres. western region, 1980, Silver Strand 1982), Honolulu Advt. Club (pres. 1965), Clubs: Hayden Lake (Idaho) Country. Lodges: Lions (dist. gov. 1956-57), Shriners. Republican. Avocation: golf. Home: Coeur D Alene, Idaho. Died July 29, 2008.

PAYNE, DEBORAH ANNE, retired medical company officer; b. Norristown, Pa., Sept. 22, 1952; d. Kenneth Nathan Moser and Joan (Reese) Dewhurst; m. Randall Barry Payne, Mar. 8, 1975 (div.). AA, Northeastern Christian Jr. Coll., 1972; B in Music Edn., Va. Commonwealth U., 1979. Driver, social asst. Children's Aid Soc., Norristown, Pa., 1972—73; mgr. Boddie-Noell Enterprises, Richmond, Va., 1974—79; retail food saleswoman Hardee's Food Systems, Inc., Phila., 1979—81; supr., with tech. tng. and testing depts. Cardiac Datacorp., Phila., 1981—95; tng. supr. Raytel Cardiac Svcs., Forest Hills, NY, 1995—98, supr. tech. support Haddonfield, NJ, 1998—2000; ret., 2000. Mem. NAFE, Delta Omicron (pres. Alpha Xi chpt. 1978-79, pres. Epsilon province 1980-85, chmn. Eastern Pa. alumni 1986-88, Star award 1979), Am. Soc. Profl. and Exec. Women. Democrat. Avocations: music, sports. Died Jan. 1, 2008.

PAYNE, FRED J., epidemiologist, educator; b. Grand Forks, ND, Oct. 14, 1922; s. Fred J. and Olive (Johnson) P.; m. Dorothy J. Peck, Dec. 20, 1948; children: Chris Ann Payne Graebner, Roy S. William F., Thomas A. BS, U. Pitts., 1948, MD, 1949; MPH, U. Calif., Berkeley, 1958. Diplomate Am. Bd. Preventive Medicine. Intern St. Joseph's Hosp., Pitts., 1949-50; resident Charity hosp., New Orleans, 1952-53; med. epidemiologist Ctr. Disease Control, Atlanta, 1953-60; prof. tropical medicine Med. Ctr. La. State U., New Orleans, 1961—66, dir. Internat. Ctr. for Med. Rsch. and Tng. Costa Rica, 1963—66; exec. sec. 3d Nat. Conf. on Pub. Health Tng., Washington, 1966-67; epidemiologist Nat. Nutrition Survey, Bethesda, Md., 1967-68; chief pub. health professions br. NIH, Bethesda, 1971-74; med. officer, sr. rsch. epidemiologist Nat. Inst. Allergy and Infectious Diseases, 1974-78; asst. health dir. Fairfax County (Va.) Health Dept., 1978-94; dir. HIV/AIDS case mgmt. program, 1988-94; cons. epidemiologist, from 1994; med. advisor Ams. for Sound AIDS Policy, from 1996, Childrens AIDS Fund, from 1997. Clin. prof. La. State U., 1966-76; cons. NIH, 1979-81; leader WHO diarrheal disease adv. team, 1960. Contbr. articles to profl. jours. Served with AUS, 1942-46, 49-52. Decorated Combat Medic Badge. Fellow Am. Coll. Preventive Medicine, Am. Coll. Epidemiology; mem. AAAS, AMA, Am. Soc. Microbiology, Internat. Epidemiology Assn., Soc. Epidemiol. Rsch., USPHS Commd. Officers Assn., Sigma Xi. Home: Shreveport, La. Died June 7, 2009.

PEACOCK, INEZ W., physical therapist; b. Kindersley, Sask., Can., Oct. 18, 1919; came to U.S., 1925; d. Milton and Muriel Inez (Carroll) Schroeder; m. Thomas Arthur Peacock, Sept. 11, 1942 (dec. June 1948); 1 child, Christine Carroll Peacock Powers. BS in Phys. Edn., Wash. State U., 1942; postgrad., U. Wash., 1943, secondary teaching cert., 1944; grad. cert. phys. therapy, Harvard U., 1944. Physical therapist Detroit Curative Workshop, 1945-46, Detroit Vis. Nurse Assn., 1946-48, Swedish Hosp., Seattle, Wash., 1949, Children's Orthopaedic Hosp., 1950-51, Dearborn Pub. Schs., 1952-82; Huntington's Disease phys. therapist, cons., from 1982. Contbr. articles to profl. jours. Founder Huntingtons Disease Camp, 1988, Huntingtons Disease Fun Olympics, 1995. Mem. Am. Phys. Therapy Assn. (life, past del., active pediatrics sect., licensure and regulation sect., geratrics sect., and neurology sect., Special Svc. award sect. on licensure and regulation 1978, Lucy Blair Svc. award 1978), Mich. chpt. Am. Phys. Therapy Assn. (active 1945-48, pres. 1953-55, archivist and historian 1990—, active ea. dist., Past Pres. award 1962, Outstanding Svc. award 1976), Am. Phys. Therapy Assn. Prime Timers (founder, chmn. 1987—), World Confdn. Phys. Therapy (speaker 1978, 87, 91, planner and chair program on internat. licensure and cert. Montreal 1974, chair special interest meeting 1995 Congress Washington, Appreciation award 10th Congress 1987), Huntingtons Disease Soc. Am. (cons. to S.E. Mich. chpt. 1983—, Svc. award 1987, Ruby and Joseph Horansky award for exemplary patient care 1993). Home: Dearborn, Mich. Died May 21, 2008.

PEACOCK, LAMAR BATTS, retired physician; b. Albany, Ga., Sept. 21, 1920; s. Herbert A. and Helen Marian (LeVan) P.; m. Jane Bonner, June 7, 1947; children: Helen Lee Wade, Linda Jane Gossage, Lamar Bonner BA, Emory U., 1941; MD, Med. Coll. Ga., 1946. Diplomate: Am. Bd. Internal Medicine. Intern U. Hosp., Augusta, 1946—47, resident, 1947—48, 1948—50; fellow internal medicine U. Va. Hosp., Charlottesville, 1948—49; practice medicine specializing in internal medicine and allergy Atlanta, 1950—91. Mem. staff St. Joseph's Hosp., Crawford Long Hosp., Piedmont Hosp., Grady Meml. Hosp., Hughes Spalding Pavilion, Northside Hosp., All Atlanta, Cobb Gen. Hosp., Austell, Ga., Douglasville (Ga.) Hosp.; instr. internal medicine Ga. Bapt. Hosp., Atlanta, 1950-58, chief medicine, 1958-72; mem. faculty Emory U. Sch. Medicine, Atlanta, 1950—, asst. clin. prof. medicine, 1962—; instr. internal medicine Sch. Dentistry, 1958— Chief med. br., health svcs. Atlanta Met. Area Civil Def., 1960-63, mem. Ga. Pub. Health Assn., 1967-69, Ga. Bd. Health, 1966-72, Ga. Vocat. Rehab. Coun., 1973—; pres. trustees Med. Coll. Ga. Found., 1963 Recipient Physicians Physician award, MCG, 1984. Fellow ACP, Am. Coll. Allergy, Asthma and Immunology (nat. pres. 1972-73), Am. Acad. Allergy, Asthma and Immunology; mem. AMA, Am. Heart Assn., Ga. Heart Assn., Am. Soc. Internal Medicine, Ga. Soc. Internal Medicine, 5th Dist. Med. Soc., Ga. Thoracic Soc., Med. Assn. Atlanta (prs. 1965), Med. Assn. Ga. (1st v.p. 1966-67), Southeastern Allergy Assn. (pres. 1963-64), So. Med. Assn., Cherokee Town and Country Club Episcopalian. Home: Evans, Ga. Died June 18, 2009.

PEADEN, RICHARD NELLO, plant breeding research agronomist; b. Salt Lake City, July 16, 1928; s. Charlie N. and Bertha Mae (Brock) P.; m. Joyce Bennion, Sept. 1, 1950; children: Calvin Richard, Brian J., Carolyn. BS, Utah State U., 1950, MS, 1957. With Vocat. Agr. Inst., Joliet (Mont.) Sch. Dist., 1950-51; rsch. agronomist USDA Agrl. Rsch. Svc., Reno, Nev., 1956-75, Prosser, Wash., from 1975. Contbr. articles to Crop Sci., Agronomy Jour., Phytopathology, Can. Jour. Plant Pathology, Plant Disease. With U.S. Army, 1951-53. Mem. Am. Soc. Agronomy, N.Am. Alfalfa Improvement Conf., Western Alfalfa Improvement Conf. (sec. 1967, vice chmn. 1969, chmn. 1971). Republican. Mem. Lds Ch. Achievements include release of alfalfa varieties Moapa 69, Washoe, Vernema. Home: Prosser, Wash. Died May 3, 2008.

PEARSALL, DAVID WILLIAM, educational specialist; b. East Orange, NJ, Oct. 15, 1943; s. Raymond Wesley and Anne (Simmons) P.; m. Deborah E. Betz, Nov. 27, 1970; 1 child, Pamela. BS, Seton Hall U., 1966, MA, 1968; PhD, Fordham U., 1976; diploma, U. East Asia, Macau, People's Republic China, 1985. Cert. English tchr., K-12 supr., prin., supt., N.J. Tchr. East Orange Bd. Edn., 1966-73, dist. dir. testing, 1973-79; supr. instrn. Bradley Beach (N.J.) Bd. Edn., 1979-81; spl. cons. in evaluation N.J. Dept. Edn., Trenton, 1981-82, sr. edn. specialist, from 1985; head dept. Hong Kong Internat. Sch., 1983-85. Author: (reference guide) Implementing School-based Collaborative Improvement Planning, 1995; contbr. to numerous state publs. in field. Commr. Manasquan (N.J.) Environ. Commn., 1976-77. Mem. ASCD, APA, Am. Ednl. Rsch. Assn., Hong Kong Soc. Tng. Profls. Republican. Home: Saint Augustine, Fla. Died Oct. 12, 2007.

PEARSON, JAMES BLACKWOOD, Former United States Senator from Kansas; b. Nashville, Tenn., May 7, 1920; children: James, William, Thomas, Laura. JD, U. Va., 1950. Asst. county atty. Johnson County, Kans., 1952—54; probate county judge, 1954—56; mem. Kans. State Senate, 1956—60; US Senator from Kans., 1962—78; dir. East-West Inst., 1983—91. Served in USN, 1943—46. Republican. Died Jan. 13, 2009.

PEASE, DORIS OWEN, magazine editor, artist; b. Eau Claire, Wis., Dec. 20, 1921; d. Lee F. and Irma Irmina (Ingram) Owen; m. Leon W. Pease, July 26, 1942; children: Terry, Steve, Gene, Mark, JoDee, LeAnn, Jon, Patti. Student, U. Minn., 1941-42, various art schs., Minn. Acct. Mpls. Star Jour. & Tribune, 1941-44; corr. West Cen. Daily Tribune, Willmar, Minn., 1952-57, New Ulm Daily Jour. and Redwood Falls Gazette, Minn., 1952-67; reporter, photographer, office mgr. Olivia (Minn.) Times Jour., 1967-70; asst. editor, advt. saleswoman Circulating Pines, Circle Pines, Minn., 1970-72; advt. sales cons. Osseo (Minn.) Press, 1972-74; owner, editor, pub. Dot Pub., Mpls., 1972-87; founder, editor Dancing USA Mag. and Entertainment Bits, Mpls., from 1972. Exec. sec. Minn. Ballroom Operators Assn., 1975-88, Nat. Ballroom and Entertainment Assn., 1985-88. Exhibited in numerous group exhbns., Minn., 1970—; editor Minn. Palette News, 1974-80. Founder, bd. dirs. Renville County Art Ctr., Olivia, 1965-72; founder Newcomer Welcome Svc., 1968, 75; former leader, trainer, camp dir. Girl Scouts U.S.A.; pres. Coon Rapids Fine Arts Commn., 1988, 92; bd. dirs. Banfill Locke Ctr. for Arts, 1980-82. Recipient Thanks Badge, Girl Scouts U.S.A., 1970, commendation Mayor of Coon Rapids, 1988. Mem. Artists del Norte (founder, pres. 1978-80, 84-85), Minn. Rural Artists Assn. (pres. 1981-84), North Star Watercolor Assn. Republican. Methodist. Avocations: ballroom dancing, photography, travel, outdoor activities. Home: Coon Rapids, Minn. Died Feb. 8, 2008.

PEEBLER, CHARLES DAVID, JR., venture capital executive; b. Waterloo, Iowa, June 8, 1936; s. Charles David and Mary E. (Barnett) P.; m. Susie Jacobs, June 5, 1958 (div. 1977); children: David Jacobs, Mark Walter; m. Tonita Worley, Nov. 12, 1979; 1 child, Todd Whitney. Student, Drake U., 1954-56. Asst. to exec. v.p. J.L. Brandeis & Sons, Omaha, 1956-58; with Bozell, Jacobs, Keyon & Eckhardt (formerly Bozell & Jacobs), 1958—97, v.p., mem. plans bd., 1960-65, pres. mid-continent ops. Omaha, 1965-67, pres., CEO, 1967-86, CEO, 1986-97; pres. True North Communications, Inc., NYC, 1997—99, chmn. emeritus, 1999—2009; chmn. bd., CEO True North Diversified Comapnies Group, 1999—2009. Bd. dirs. Valmont Industries, Veon, Dreamlife.com., youbet.com, Am. Tool Hotline, mPulse (chmn.), Corp. Fulfillment Inc., Presspoint. Hon. chmn. bd., dirs. Am. Craft Mus.; bd. dirs. Drake U., Juvenile Diabetes Found. Internat., NYC Partnership; mem. corp. com. Central Park Conservancy; mem. adv. bd. Naomi Berrie Diabetes Ctr. Columbia Presbyn. Med. Ctr. Named to The Advt. Hall of Fame, 2001. Died Apr. 18, 2009.

PEEBLES, ROBERT WHITNEY, retired school system administrator; b. Boston; m. Lois Querze (div.); children: James Q., Katherine N., Robert S.; m. Elizabeth Burr; stepchildren: Scott, Jon(dec.). Grad., Boston U., 1952; MA, Harvard U., 1953; EdD, NYU, 1967. High sch. tchr., Darien, Conn.; exec. dir. Edn. Collaborative for Greater Boston; supt. schools City of Stamford, City of Alexandria, Va., 1980—87. Founder Washington Area Sch. Study Coun. Author: School Desegregation: A Shattered Dream?, 2007. Served in USN. Avocation: jazz. Died June 30, 2009.

PEELE, LUTHER MARTIN, minister; b. Laurel Hill, NC, Jan. 20, 1929; s. Luther Martin and Mary Susanna (Falls) P.; m. Emma Lee Hayes; children: Luther Martin,

Raymond Hampton, Audrey Melinda. Student, N.C. State U., 1947-49; BA in Philosophy and Religion, U. N.C., Wilmington, 1974; MDiv, Duke U., 1979. Ordained to ministry Meth. Ch. Min. Wrightsboro Meth. Ch., Wilmington, N.C., 1972-81, Devon Park and Oleander Meth. Chs., Wilmington, N.C., 1981-85, Zion Meth. Ch., Leland, N.C., from 1985. Home: Leland, NC. Died Nov. 16, 2007.

PELCZAR, MICHAEL JOSEPH, JR., microbiologist, educator; b. Balt., Jan. 28, 1916; s. Michael Joseph and Josephine (Polek) P.; m. Merna M. Foss, Aug. 28, 1941 (dec. June 20, 2007); children: Ann Foss, Patricia Mary, Michael Rafferty, Rita Margaret, Josephine Merna, Julia Foss. BS, U. Md., 1936, MS, 1938; PhD, U. Iowa, 1941; DSc (hon.), Utah State U., 1986. Diplomate: Am. Bd. Microbiology. Instr. bacteriology U. Iowa, 1940-41; asst. prof., assoc. prof. bacteriology U. Md., College Park, 1946-50, prof. microbiology, 1950-78, prof. emeritus, 1978—2009, v.p. grad. studies and research, 1966-78, v.p. emeritus, 1978—2009; pres. Council Grad. Schs. in U.S., Washington, 1978-84, pres. emeritus, 1984—2009. Mem. microbiology adv. panel Office Naval Rsch., 1965-70; spl. cons. Random House Dictionary of English Lang., 1965; councilor Oak Ridge Asso. Univs., Inc., 1959-66; also bd. dirs.; mem. So. Regional Edn. Bd., Coun. Grad. Edn. in Agrl. Scis., 1967; mem. departmental com. on biol. scis. U.S. Dept. Agr. Grad. Sch., 1967-76; chmn. Spl. Meeting on Neisseria WHO, Geneva, Switzerland, 1964, mem. expert adv. panel on bacterial diseases, 1967-77; mem. Gov.'s Sci. Adv. Bd., 1967—, chmn., 1967-72; mem. organizing com. for XVII Gen. Assembly NRC, div. biology and agr. Internat. Union Biol. Scis., 1968; chmn. bd. on human resource data and analysis Commn. on Human Resources, NRC, 1975-79; mem. exec. com. Coun. Grad. Schs., 1976-78; mem. Nat. Sea Grant Rev. Panel, 1979-89; mem. adv. com. Nat. Rsch. Coun., 1987-90. Co-author: Microbiology, 5th edit, 1986, Elements of Microbiology, 1981, Microbiology: Concepts and Applications, 1993; editorial bd.: Jour. of Bacteriology, 1965-69; Contbr. sect. to: Ency. Brit, 1969, 94, 99; articles to profl. jours. Ency. Ednl. Research. Recipient Nat. Sea Grant Assn. award, 1991, ASM Disting. Svc. award, 1995. Fellow AAUP (past br. pres.). Nat. Adminstrn. Acad. Univ. Rsch. (founding mem. 1985); mem. AAAS, Am. Acad. Microbiology, Am. Inst. Biol. Scis. (bd. govs., past vis. lectr.), Am. Soc. Microbiology (bd. govs., past com. chmn., councilor, br. pres., hon. mem. 1986—), Internat. Assn. Microbiology, Washington Acad. Scis., Nat. Assn. State Univs. and Land-Grant Colls. (chmn. coun. for rsch. policy and adminstrn., cons. higher edn. rsch. adminstrn.), Cosmos Club, Phi Beta Kappa (assoc. 1989), Sigma Xi (ann. award sci. achievement 1968), Phi Kappa Phi, Sigma Alpha Omicron. Research microbial physiology. Home: Chester, Md. Died Oct. 13, 2009.

PELFREY, RONALD STEPHEN, mathematics coordinator; b. Lexington, Ky., Sept. 21, 1944; s. Roy Elwood and Agnes Marie (Daily) P.; m. Marta Wolderufael, Dec. 20, 1975; children: Mikael, Eric. BS, U. Ky., 1966, MA, 1972, EdD, 1982. Tchr. H.S. math. U.S. Peace Corps, Ethiopia, 1966-68; tchr. jr. high sch. math. Fayette County Pub. Schs., Lexington, Ky., 1970-75, math. coord., 1975-95; ednl. cons., from 1995. Instr. U. Ky., Lexington, 1981-88, 95—. Contbr. articles to profl. jours. With U.S. Army, 1968-70, Vietnam. Mem. Ky. Coun. Tchrs. Math. (pres. 1991, Outstanding Math. Educator award 1990), Ky. Assn. Sch. Adminstrs., Rotary (Outstanding Contbn. award 1993, 94), Phi Delta Kappa (v.p. 1982, pres. 1983, Svc. to Chpt. award 1984). Home: Lexington, Ky. Died July 27, 2008.

PELL, CLAIBORNE DEBORDA, former US Senator from Rhode Island; b. NYC, Nov. 22, 1918; s. Herbert Claiborne and Matilda (Bigelow) P.; m. Nuala O'Donnell, Dec. 1944; children: Herbert Claiborne III, Christopher T. Hartford, Nuala Dallas Yates, Julia L.W. Student, St. George's Sch., Newport, RI; AB cum laude, Princeton U., 1940; AM, Columbia U., 1946; 51 hon. degrees. Enlisted USCGR, 1941; served as seaman, ensign North Atlantic sea duty, Africa, Italy; hospitalized to, 1944; instr. Navy Sch. Mil. Govt., Princeton, 1944-45; capt. USCGR; ret.; on loan to State Dept. at San Francisco Conf., 1945, State Dept., 1945-46, US Embassy, Czech Republic, 1946-47; established consulate gen. Bratislava, 1947-48; vice consul US Embassy, Genoa, Italy, 1949; assigned US Dept. State, 1950-52; v.p., dir. Internat. Rescue Com.; US Senator from RI, 1961-96. Ranking minority mem. Fgn. Rels. Com., Labor and Human Resources Subcom. on Edn., Arts, and Humanities; mem. Rules and Adminstrn. Com., Joint Com. on Libr. and Congl. Intern Program, Senate Dem. Policy Com.; US del. Internat. Maritime Consultative Orgn., London, 1959, 25th Gen. Assembly, 1970; disting. vis. prof. Salve Regina U., Newport, RI, 1997. Author: Megalopolis Unbound, 1966, (with Harold L. Goodwin) Challenge of the Seven Seas, 1966, Power and Policy, 1972. Hon. bd. dirs. World Affairs Council RI; trustee St. George's Sch.; trustee emeritus Brown U.; Cons. Democratic Nat. Com., 1953-60; exec. asst. to chmn. RI State Dem. Com., 1952-54; chmn. RI Dem. Fund drive, 1952, Dem. nat. registration, chmn., 1956, co-chmn., 1962; chief delegation tally clk. Dem. Nat. Conv., 1956, 60, 64, 68. Decorated knight Crown of Italy, Grand Cross Order of Merit Italy, Red Cross of Merit Portugal, Legion of Honor France, comdr. Order of Phoenix Greece, Grand Cross Order of Merit Liechtenstein, Grand Cross Order of Christ Portugal, Order of Henry the Navigator, Portugal, Grand Cross Order of N. Star Sweden, Grand Cross of Merit Knights of Malta, Grand Officer of Merit Luxembourg, Grand Comdr. Lebanon; recipient Caritas Elizabeth medal Cardinal Franz Koenig, Grand decoration of honor in silver with sash Austria, Gold medal of St. Barnabas (Cyprus), recipient Pres.'s Fellow award RI Sch. Design, medal Nat. Order of Cedar, Hugo Grotius Commemorative medal The Netherlands, recipient Harold W. McGraw, Jr. Prize in Education, McGraw-Hill, 1988; named to Centennial Honor Roll, Am. Assn. Museums, 2006. Mem. Soc. Cin. Clubs: Hope (Providence); Knickerbocker (NYC), Racquet and Tennis (NYC), Brook (NYC); Metropolitan (Washington); Travellers (Paris); Reading Room (Newport); White's (London). Democrat. Episcopalian. Home: Newport, RI. Died Jan. 1, 2009.

PELLER, CHARLES HENRY, retired thoracic surgeon, educator; b. Albany, NY, May 8, 1930; s. Pincus and Tillie (Rockwitz) P.; m. Sherri Getz, Aug. 11, 1955; children: Howard D., Paul Ahron. BA in Chemistry, NYU, 1956, MD, 1960. Diplomate Am. Bd. Surgery, Am. Bd. Thoracic Surgery; lic. physician, N.Y., Ohio, Mich. Resident in gen. surgery U. Mich. Med. Ctr., Ann Arbor, 1960-65, resident in thoracic surgery, 1965-67, instr. surgery, 1963-67, asst. coord. for med. edn., 1964-65; pvt. practice thoracic surgery Aultman Hosp., Canton, Ohio, 1967-93; clin. assoc. prof. surgery Northeastern Ohio Univs. Coll. Medicine, Rootstown, from 1976. Cons. Peer Rev. of Ohio, Columbus, 1993-97; med. cons. Blue Cross Blue Shield Mich., 1997—. Author articles. Served with M.C., USN, 1950-54, Korea. Fellow ACS, Am. Coll. Chest Physicians; mem. AMA, Ohio State Med. Soc., John Alexander Thoracic Surg. Soc., Soc. Thoracic Surgery, Sierra Club (life). Avocations: classical music, violin playing, travel. Home: Ann Arbor, Mich. Died Nov. 30, 2007.

PELLEY, SHIRLEY NORENE, library director; b. Raymondville, Tex., Oct. 9, 1931; d. Llloyd Marshall and Lillian Norene (Southall) Ayres; m. May 14, 1954 (div.); children: Michael, Cynthia, Katheryne. BA in Music Edn., Bethany Nazarene Coll., 1954; MLS, U. Okla., 1966. Tchr. Hilldale Elem. Sch., Oklahoma City, 1954-56; music tchr. self-employed, Okla., Mo., 1956-64; circulation clk. Bethany (Okla.) Pub. Libr., 1964-65; libr. reference U. Okla. Libraries, Norman, 1966-83; dir. learning resource ctr. So. Nazarene U., Bethany, from 1983. Mem. ALA, Okla. Libr. Assn., Assn. Coll. and Rsch. Librs., Met. Librs. Network of Ctrl. Okla., Assn. Christian Librs. Republican. Nazarene. Avocations: reading, walking, travel. Home: Yukon, Okla. Died Feb. 23, 2008.

PELTZMAN, STEPHEN, municipal government official; b. Phila., Dec. 20, 1947; s. William and Norma (Miln) P.; m. Elaine Gloria Newhouse, Mar. 7, 1971; children: Suzanne Rebecca, Robert Michael. B in Engring., Manhattan Coll., 1971; MBA, Fairleigh Dickinson U., 1981. Cert. profl. pub. buyer. Project engr., cost engr. Exxon Rsch. and Engring., Florham Park, N.J., 1971-79; mgr. corp. purchasing Rhone-Poulenc Inc., Monmouth Junction, N.J., 1979-84; dir. materials mgmt. GAF Corp., Wayne, N.J., 1989; asst. commr., agy. chief contracting officer City of New York Dept. Sanitation, from 1990. Mem. Nat. Assn. Purchasing Mgmt., Nat. Inst. Govtl. Purchasing, IEEE, Delta Mu Delta, Eta Kappa Nu. Home: East Brunswick, NJ. Died Sept. 25, 2007.

PEMBERTON, JOHN DE JARNETTE, JR., retired legal association administrator; b. Rochester, Minn., Apr. 21, 1919; s. John de Jarnette and Anna Trego (Hogeland) P.; m. Frances E. Werner, July 23, 1973; children by previous marriage: Ann O., Sarah F., Caro G., Nancy S., James de Jarnette. BA, Swarthmore Coll., Pa., 1940; LL.B., Harvard U., 1947. Bar: N.C. 1949, Minn. 1950, N.Y. 1969, Calif. 1976. Acting asst. prof. Duke U. Law Sch., Durham, NC, 1947-50, assoc. prof.; ptnr. Pemberton, Michaels, Bishop & Seeger, Rochester, 1950-62; chmn. Minn. branch ACLU, 1955—58, nat. exec. dir., 1962-70; prof. U. San Francisco Law Sch., 1973-86; dep. gen. counsel, then acting gen. counsel EEOC, 1971-73, regional atty. dist. office San Francisco, 1986-94, ret., 1994. Adj. lectr. NYU Law Sch., 1968-70, U. San Francisco Law Sch., 1986-95; mem. legal com. No. Calif. chpt. ACLU, 1973-86. Assoc. editor and/or editor sects. in law jours. Chmn. Olmsted County (Minn.) Republican Party, 1958-61; commr. Minn. Fair Employment Practices Com., 1961-62; exec. com Leadership Conf. Civil Rights, 1967-68. Served with Am. Field Service, 1941-45. Mem. ABA, Calif. Bar Assn. Mem. Soc. Of Friends. Died Oct. 21, 2009.

PENN, IRVING, photographer; b. Plainfield, NJ, June 16, 1917; s. Harry and Sonia P.; m. Lisa Fonssagrives, 1950 (dec. 1992); 1 child, Tom. Attended, Phila. Mus. Sch. Industrial Art, 1934—38. Painter, 1941; first photographs pub. in Vogue, 1943; exhbns. include Mus. Modern Art, N.Y.C., 1984; rep. photographs in permanent collections Met. Mus. Art, Mus. Modern Art, N.Y.C.; author: Moments Preserved, collection of 300 photographs, 1960, Worlds in a Small Room, 1974, Inventive Paris Clothes 1909-1939, 1977, Flowers, 1980, Passage, 1991. Died Oct. 7, 2009.

PENNELL, VICKI L, art educator, artist; b. Kans. City, Kans., Sept. 28, 1949; d. Frank Charles Painter and Irene Winifred Billbe; children: Jeremy Allen, Hillary Dawn. BS in edn., Pitts. State U., 1971, MS in edn., 1973. Spl. edn. art tchr. Corpus Christi State Sch., 1971—72; art tchr. Northwest Jr. H.S., Kans. City, 1973—74, Odessa H.S., 1974—2001; lectr., adj. instr. Ctrl. Mo. State U., from 2002. Nelson Art Gallery, 1984. Mem.: Mo. Art Edn. Assn. (secondary art edn. chair 1986—90, Service award 1990—92, Art Tchr. of the Yr. 1985). Republican. Avocations: travel, gardening, music. Home: Warrensburg, Mo. Died July 27, 2008.

PERKINS, BENJAMIN PAUL, SR., mathematics educator, religious writer; b. Albany, Ga., Mar. 7, 1934; s. Eddie Paul and Estella (Flood) P.; m. Mary Louise Wilson, Dec. 24, 1960; children: Benjamin Paul II, Stella Marie. BS in Edn., Albany State Coll., 1958; MS in Edn., Ft. Valley State Coll., 1966; PhD in Philosophy, Northgate Grad. Sch., 1971; AA in Theology, Moody Bible Inst., 1983. Adv. mgr., reporter Southwest Georgian, Albany, Ga., 1948-60; printer, shop supr. Jour. Pub. Co., Albany, Ga., 1947-68; tchr. Dougherty County Schs., Albany, Ga., 1958-63; librarian Albany (Ga.) Pub. Schs., 1963-66; chmn. math dept. Dougherty County Schs., Albany, 1966-70, asst. prin., 1970-76; math.-sci. dept. Albany Pub. Schs., 1976-88; instr. Turner Job Corp., Albany, 1988-89; library asst. Dougherty Pub. Library, 5, from 1989. Tchr. Evang. Tchr. Training Assn.; various positions Dougherty County Assn. Edn., 1958-88. Author: Black Christians Tragedies, 1972, Church Without Change, 1975; contbg. editor TEMAC Study booklet, 1971; editor Sci. Interest booklet, 1966; contbr. over 200 articles to profl. mags. and newspapers. Reporter Albany-Dougherty Community Devel. com., 1980-91; program chmn. Albany-Dougherty Citizens Adv. com., 1980-91; regional reporter Accredited Press, Chgo., 1979-89; mem. Easter Seals Soc., Albany; elder C. K. Smith Presbyn. Ch. Recipient Honor award Quill & Scroll Internat. Soc., 1986; named Teacher of Yr., Region Nine Tchr. Assn., 1971, Outstanding Educator, Secondary Educators of Am., 1975, Outstanding Writer, Christian Writers Guild, 1986. Mem. NAACP (reporter 1980-91), Men's Senate, Young Men's Profl. Club. (sec.), Torch Club (v.p. 1980-91), Carver PTA. Avocations: photo-journalism, researching theology, teaching Sun. sch. Home: Albany, Ga. Died July 24, 2008.

PERKINS, FLOYD JERRY, retired theology educator; b. Bertha, Minn., May 9, 1924; s. Ray Lester and Nancy Emily (Kelley) P.; m. Mary Elizabeth Owen, Sept. 21, 1947 (dec. June 1982); children: Douglas Jerry, David Floyd, Sheryl Pauline; m. Phyllis Genevra Hartley, July 14, 1984. AB, BTh, N.W. Nazarene Coll., 1949; MA, U. Mo., 1952; MDiv, Nazarene Theol. Sem., 1952; ThM, Burton Sem., 1964; PhD, U. Witwatersrand, Johannesburg, South Africa, 1974; ThD, Internat. Sem., 1994. Ordained to Christian ministry, 1951. Pres. South African Nazarene Theol. Sem., Florida Transvaal, Africa, 1955-67, Nazarene Bible Sem., Lourenzo Marques, Mozambique, 1967-73, Campinas, Brazil, 1974-76; prof. missions N.W. Nazarene Coll., Nampa, Idaho, 1976; prof. theology Nazarene Bible Coll., Colorado Springs, Colo., 1976-97. Chmn., founder com. higher theol. edn. Ch. of Nazarene in Africa, 1967-74; sec. All African Nazarene Mission Exec., 1967-74; ofcl. Christian Council Mozambique, 1952-74. Author: A History of the Christian Church in Swaziland, 1974. Served with USN, 1944-46. Mem. Soc. Christian Philosophers, Evang. Theol. Soc., Am. Schs. Orientan Rsch., Am. Soc. Missiology, Assn. Evang. Missions Profs. Republican. Avocation: golf. Home: Nampa, Idaho. Deceased.

PERKINS, RITA WADE, historian, educator; b. Burlington, NJ, Aug. 11, 1948; d. Leo Thomas and Anna Dement Wade; m. James Perkins, Dec. 5, 1981; children: David Wesley, Jeffrey Wade, Elise Marie. BA, Rutgers U., Camden, NJ, 1970; MA, Rutgers U., 1979, Villanova U., Pa., 1972. Assoc. prof. Camden County Coll., Blackwood, NJ, from 1972. Lectr./presenter in field, from 2003. Photographer (photography exhibitions with lectures) Bridge of Tears (NJ. Coun. for Humanities Grants, 2003). Fellow, NEH, 1979. Mem.: Am. Conf. of Irish Studies. Achievements include research in Irish Famine Memorials. Home: Audubon, NJ. Died Mar. 29, 2009.

PERLE, GEORGE, composer; b. Bayonne, NJ, May 6, 1915; s. Joseph and Mary (Sanders) Perlman; m. Laura Slobe, 1940; m. Barbara Philips, Aug. 11, 1958 (dec.); children: Kathy, Annette; 1 stepchild, Max Massey; m. Shirley Gabis Daisy Rhoads, June 6, 1982; stepchildren: Paul Rhoads, Daisy Rhoads. MusB, DePaul U., 1938; MusM, Am. Conservatory of Music, 1942; PhD, NYU, 1956. Faculty U. Louisville, 1949-57, U. Calif., Davis, 1957-61, Juilliard Sch. Music, 1963, Yale U., 1965-66, U. So. Calif., summer 1965, Tanglewood, summers 1967, 80, 87; from asst. prof. to prof. CUNY, 1961-85, prof. emeritus, 1985—2009; composer-in-residence San Francisco Symphony, 1989-91. Vis. Birge-Cary prof. music SUNY, Buffalo, 1971-72; vis. prof. U. Pa., 1976, 80, Columbia U., 1979, 83; vis. Ernest Bloch prof. music U. Calif., Berkeley, 1989; vis. disting. prof. music NYU, N.Y.C., 1994. Author: Serial Composition and Atonality 1962, 6th edit., 1991, Twelve-Tone Tonality, 1977, 2d edit., 1996, The Operas of Alban Berg, vol. 1, 1980, vol. 2, 1985, The Listening Composer, 1990, The Right Notes, 1995, Style and Idea in the Lyric Suite of Alban Berg, 1995, 2d edit., 2001; contbr. articles in Am., fgn. mus. jours.; composer: Pantomime, Interlude and Fugue, 1937, Little Suite for Piano, 1939, Two Rilke Songs, 1941, Sonata for Solo Viola, 1942, Three Sonatas for Clarinet, 1943, Piano Piece, 1945, Hebrew Melodies for Cello, 1945, Lyric Piece for Cello and Piano, 1946, Six Preludes for Piano, 1946, Sonata for Solo Cello, 1947, Solemn Procession for Band, 1947, Sonata for Piano, 1950, Three Inventions for Piano, 1957, Quintet for Strings, 1958, Wind Quintet I, 1959, Sonata I for Solo Violin, 1959, Wind Quintet II, 1960, Fifth String Quartet, 1960-67, Three Movements for Orchestra, 1960, Monody I for flute, 1960, Music for The Birds of Aristophanes, 1961, Monody II for double bass 1962, Serenade I for Viola and Chamber Ensemble, 1962, Three Inventions for Bassoon, 1962, Sonata II for Solo Violin, 1963, Short Sonata for Piano, 1964, Solo Partita for Violin and Viola, 1965, Six Bagatelles for Orch., 1965, Concerto for Cello and Orch., 1966, Wind Quintet III, 1967, Serenade II for Chamber Ensemble, 1968, Toccata for Piano, 1969, Suite in C for Piano, 1970, Fantasy-Variations for Piano, 1971, Sonata Quasi una Fantasia for Clarinet and Piano, 1972, Seventh String Quartet, 1973, Songs of Praise and Lamentation for chorus and orch. 1974, Six Etudes for Piano, 1976, 13 Dickinson Songs, 1978, Concertino for Piano, Winds, and Timpani, 1979, A Short Symphony, 1980; Ballade for Piano, 1981, Sonata a quattro, 1982, Serenade III for Piano and Chamber Ensemble, 1983, Six New Etudes for Piano, 1984, Wind Quintet IV, 1984, Sonata for Cello and Piano, 1985, Sonatina for Piano, 1986, Sonata a cinque, 1986, Dance Fantasy for Orch., 1986, Lyric Intermezzo for fifteen players, 1987, Lyric Intermezzo for piano, 1987, New Fanfares for brass ensemble, 1987, Sinfonietta, 1987, Windows of Order for string quartet, 1988, Sextet for winds and piano, 1988, Concerto for Piano and Orch., 1990, Sinfonietta II, 1990, Concerto No. 2 for Piano and Orch., 1992, Adagio for Orch., 1992, Transcendental Modulations (commd. for 150 anniversary N.Y. Philharmonic), 1993, Phantasyplay for Piano, 1994, Duos for French horn and string quartet, 1995, Six Celebratory Inventions for Piano, 1995, Critical Moments for Six Players, 1996, Chansons Cachées for Piano, 1997, Musical Offerings for Piano (left hand alone), 1998, Brief Encounters for string quartet, 1998, Nine Bagatelles for Piano, 1999, Critical Moments (2) for Six Players, 2001, Triptych for Solo Violin and Piano, 2003, Bassoon Music for Solo Bassoon, 2004, Lyric Suite, Universal, 2005, The Operas of Alban Berg, 2005 (Otto Kinkeldey award); writer, editor: Preface of Berg's Lyric Suite, 2005. Served with AUS, 1943-46, ETO, PTO. Recipient award Nat. Inst. Arts and Letters, 1977, Pulitzer prize, 1986; Guggenheim fellow, 1966-67, 74-75, MacArthur fellow, 1986; grantee Am. Council Learned Socs., 1968-69, NEA, 1978-79, 85. Fellow Am. Acad. Arts and Scis.; mem. Am. Musicol. Soc., ASCAP (Deems Taylor award 1973, 78, 81), Am. Acad. Arts and Letters. Home: New York, NY. Died Jan. 23, 2009; NYC.

PERRIN, HAL See HALPERN, LEON

PERRY, RUTH, writer; b. Balt., Jan. 14, 1936; d. John Dean and Julia (Hicks) P.; 1 child. Student, Morgan State Coll., 1948—51, Cortez Peters Bus. Sch., 1951—52. Author: Behold: A Slave Child, Accent on Slavery, Aftermath Desires, Time Spent, I, Nebra; songwriter Give Me This Day, others; author numerous childrens stories; inventor (toy) Princess Sasha; lyricist 10 songs. Recipient poetry awards World of Poetry, Accomplishment of Merit award Creative Arts and Scis. Enterprises, 1992, 96. Mem. Poetry Soc. Am., Poetry Assn. Am., Nat. Libr. Poetry, Poetry Guild. Home: Baltimore, Md. Died Apr. 28, 2009; unknown.

PERRY, SAMUEL CASSIUS, retired animal science researcher; b. Aniwa, Wis., Sept. 25, 1937; s. Cassius R. and Elsie E. (Oesterreich) P.; m. Beverly J. Morrison, July 12, 1964; children: Pamela, Kimberly, Deborah, Stephen, Barbara, Michael. BS, U. Wis., River Falls, 1959; MS, S.D. State U., 1963; PhD, U. Tenn., 1967. Sr. rsch. bacteriologist Norwich (N.Y.) Pharmacal Co., 1967-70, sr. rsch. II nutritionist, 1970-72, rsch. leader, 1972-73, sect. chief, 1973-77; tech. svcs. nutritionist Hoffmann La-Roche Inc., Nutley, N.J., 1977-81, mktg. mgr., 1981-84, assoc. dir. poultry bus. unit, 1984-85, dir. mktg., 1985-87, dir. animal si. rsch., 1987-89, dir. animal sci. rsch., asst. v.p., 1989-93; sr. scientist Amoco Tech. Co., 1993-95. Mem. Am. Assn. Animal Sci., Poultry Sci., N.Y. Acad. Scis., Am. Rsch. Coun., Am. Dairy Sci. Assn. Republican. Lutheran. Avocations: reading, gardening, spectator sports. Home: Spearfish, SD. Died Oct. 26, 2007.

PESOLA, WILLIAM ERNEST, restaurant management executive; b. Marquette, Mich., Mar. 2, 1945; s. Ernest Ensio and Janice Mary (LeDuc) P.; m. Kathleen Mary Deschaine, July 9, 1966; children: Christie Lynn, Laurie Anne. BS, No. Mich. U., 1968, MS, 1971. Route driver Coca Cola Co., Marquette, 1963-68; tchr. Gwinn (Mich.) Schs., 1968-78, pub. Sch. News, 1969; pres. Pesola Mgmt., Marquette, from 1974, Humboldt Ridge, Marquette, from 1977; treas. Elite Bar, Inc., Marquette, from 1978; v.p., dir. Marquette Cablevison, 1981-85; pres. Upper Peninsula Big Boy, Marquette, from 1990. Cons. cable TV, 1985—, Bresnan Comm., 1984—. Pres. Gwinn Edn. Assn., 1975-77; regional pres. Upper Peninsula Edn. Assn., 1977-78; mem. Marquette City Commn., 1977-81. Mem. NEA, Marquette Econ. Club, Mich. Edn. Assn., Marquette C. of C. (Exemplary Citizen award 1990), Rotary. Roman Catholic. Home: Marquette, Mich. Deceased.

PESSEN, HELMUT, physical biochemist, researcher; b. Berlin, Sept. 6, 1921; came to U.S., 1940; s. Eugen and Charlotte (Bieber) P.; m. Norma Cooper Glasner, Mar. 12, 1966. BS in Chem. Engring., Drexel Inst. Tech., 1949; PhD, Temple U., 1961. Cert. agt. U.S. Patent Office. Control chemist Fred Whitaker Wool Co., Phila., 1943-46; rsch. assoc. Am. Viscose Corp., Marcus Hook, Pa., 1947-48; inspector FDA, Phila., 1950; rsch. chemist U.S. Army Q. M. Pioneering Rsch. Lab., Phila., 1950-57; free-lance tech. translator Phila., 1961-63; rsch. scientist, sr. scientist Eastern Regional Rsch. Ctr. USDA, Wyndmoor, Pa., from 1963. Author: Methods in Enzymology, 1973, 85, NMR Applications, 1990; co-editor: New Techniques and Applications of Physical Chemistry to Food Systems, 1991; contbr. numerous articles to profl. jours.; presenter at nat. and internat. confs. With U.S. Army, 1943-45, ETO. Mem. AAAS, Am. Chem. Soc., Am. Crystallographic Assn., Pa. Acad. Sci., Biophys. Soc., Phi Kappa Phi, Sigma Xi, Tau Beta Pi. Achievements include design and construction of novel state-of-the-art small-angle x-ray scattering instrument; development of theory and method of measurement by nuclear magnetic resonance (NMR) relaxation to determine protein hydration; elucidation of the structure of casein micelles, basic to cheese making, from combined resonance relaxation and x-ray scattering studies; comprehensive correlation of ultracentrifuge and x-ray scattering results to allow prediction of one type of data from another, obtained from a fundamentally different technique. Home: Elkins Park, Pa. Died June 1, 2008.

PETERS, JACQUELINE MARY, secondary school educator; b. Milw., Oct. 6, 1947; d. Arnold Martin and Rosalie Ellen (Mulherin) Fladoos; divorced; children: Casey Martin, Ann Marie. Student, Clarke Coll., Dubuque, Iowa, 1965-67; BA, Calif. State U., Long Beach, 1970; MA in History and Tchg., LaVerne Coll., Calif., 1973. Reading tchr. Chaffey H.S., Ontario, Calif., 1971-78, tchr. phys. edn., 1976-78, English tchr., 1978-90, tchr. history, from 1990. Mentor AAUW, cmty. schs., 1997-99. State rep. Trans Nat. Golf Assn., 1963-75; bd. dirs. Cmty. Challenge Grants, Ontario, 1996-00. Named to Sports Hall of Fame, Dubuque Sr. H.S., 1996; Med-Cal grantee, 1996, Project Yes grantee, 1997-99. Mem. AAUW (bd. dirs., br. pres. 1995-99, Edn. Foun. Gift Honoree 1998), Calif. Tchrs. Assn. Republican. Roman Catholic. Avocations: golf, fly fishing, pysanka, poetry, bridge. Died July 12, 2008.

PETERS, JUANITA TEAL, music educator; b. Dallas, Aug. 4, 1929; d. William Mosely and Vashti Elizabeth Teal; m. Dale Hugh Peters, June 4, 1960; children: Derek, Todd. MB, North Tex. State Coll., 1951; postgrad., U. Minn., 1952—53, Royal Acad. Music, London, 1956—57. Instr. Southeastern Okla. State U., Durant, 1967—79; lectr. U. North Tex., Denton, from 1974. Soloist: Dallas Symphony, Corpus Christi Symphony, Abilene Symphony, Wichita Falls Symphony, Ft. Worth Opera. Recipient G.B. Dealey award, Dallas Symphony, 1954, Wallace award, Wichita Falls Symphony, 1954, 1959. Home: Denton, Tex. Died Sept. 23, 2008.

PETERS, LEON, JR., retired engineering educator; b. Columbus, Ohio, May 28, 1923; s. Leon P. and Ethel (Howland) Pierce; m. Mabel Marie Johnson, June 6, 1953; children: Amy T. Peters Thomas, Melinda A. Peters Todaro, Maria C. Cohee, Patricia D., Lee A., Roberta J. Peters Cameruca, Karen E. Peters Ellingson. BSE.E., Ohio State U., 1950, MS, 1954, PhD, 1959. Asst. prof. elec. engring. Ohio State U., Columbus, 1959-63, assoc. prof., 1963-67, prof., 1967-93, prof. emeritus, from 1993, assoc. dept. chmn. for rsch. Columbus, 1990-92, dir. electro sci. lab., 1983-94. Contbr. articles to profl. jours. Served to 2d lt. U.S. Army, 1942-46, ETO. Fellow: IEEE. Home: Columbus, Ohio. Died Apr. 23, 2009.

PETERS, MICHAEL P., former mayor; m. Jeannette Peters; 3 children. Former firefighter City of Hartford; former owner small bus. Hartford; mayor City of Hartford, 1993—2001. Former chmn Hartford Civic Ctr. Commn., Hartford Redevel. Agy.; former mem. Bushnell Park Found.; founder Hartford Thomas Hooker Day Parade and Festival; mktg. com. Downtown Coun.; mem. Am. Leadership Forum, Dem. Town Com.; vol. neighborhood baseball and football teams; bd. dirs. Cedar Hill Cemetery. Democrat. Home: Hartford, Conn. Died Jan. 4, 2009.

PETERSEN, ROBERT C., retired psychopharmacologist; b. NYC, Mar. 2, 1931; s. Thorwald B. and Anna Bertha (Brenner) P.; m. Anne Oriel Petersen, Mar. 27, 1957 (div. 1981); children: David, Mark, Karen. BS, CUNY, 1953; PhD, U. Minn., 1961. Cert. clin. psychologist. Assoc. prof. Gallaudet Coll., Washington, 1962-66; chief ctr. for studies of narcotics and drug abuse NIMH, Rockville, Md., 1968-73; asst. dir. research Nat. Inst. on Drug Abuse, Rockville, 1973-81; sr. ptnr. Petersen & Cook Assocs., Silver Spring, Md., 1983—2002. Sci. adv. bd. Am. Council on Drug Edn., N.Y.C.; cons. to numerous orgns., including NIMH, Nat. Inst. Drug Abuse, Nat. Inst. Alcohol Abuse and Alcoholism, 1982-2002 Co-author: Addictions: Issues and Answers, 1980; Author, editor: Drug Abuse and Drug Abuse Research, 1987, 90; editor-in-chief for rsch. monograph series, 1973-80; contbr. numerous articles to profl. jours. Pres. Glenfield North Assn., Silver Spring, 1989. 1st lt. U.S. Army, 1953-55. Recipient J. Michael Morrison award Com. on Problems of Drug Dependency, 1982. Unitarian Universalist. Avocations: playing flute, photography. Died Dec. 12, 2008.

PETERSON, JAMES ALLAN, counselor educator, counseling psychologist; b. Redfield, SD, Oct. 11, 1932; s. Paul Waldemar Peterson and Ruby Viola (Collins) Bergman; m. Neysa Marion McCall, Mar. 23, 1957; children: Sheryl, Kathleen, Susan. BS, Dakota State Coll., 1958; MEd, S.D. State U., 1962; EdD, Boston U., 1968. Lic. psychologist, Vt. Music tchr. Arlington (S.D.) High Sch., 1958-62, counselor, 1960-62; instr., music Dakota State Coll., Madison, S.D., summer 1962; counseling supr. Boston U., 1962-66; prof. counselor edn. U. Vt., Burlington, from 1966. Vis. lectr. Fla. State U., Tallahassee, summer 1963, U. R.I., Kingston, summer 1965, 66. Author: Counseling and Values, 1970, 2d edit., 1990. With U.S. Navy, 1953-57. Home: Williston, Vt. Died Mar. 6, 2008.

PETERSON, JOHN IVAN, chemist; b. Syracuse, NY, Mar. 29, 1928; s. Ivan Nes and Katherine Phoebe (Anderson) P.; m. Lillian Taylor Waltman, 1950; children: C. Sue, Marsha, William, Jack, Thomas. BA, Syracuse U., NY, 1950, PhD, 1954. Chemist NIH, Bethesda, Md., from 1965. Contbr. articles to profl. jours. Mem. Am. Chem. Soc., Instrument Soc. Am. (pres. Washington sect. 1974, 75). Achievements include 12 patents in field; origination of fiber optic chemical sensors. Home: Falls Church, Va. Died Oct. 2, 2007.

PETERSON, MERRILL DANIEL, historian, educator; b. Manhattan, Kans., Mar. 31, 1921; s. William Oscar and Alice Dwinell (Merrill) P.; m. Jean Hymphrey, May 24, 1944 (dec. Nov. 1995); children: Jeffrey Ward, Kent Merrill. Student, Kans. State U., 1939-41; AB, U. Kans., 1943; PhD in History of Am. Civilization, Harvard U., 1950. Teaching fellow Harvard U., Cambridge, Mass., 1948-49; instr., then asst. prof. history Brandeis U., Waltham, Mass., 1949-55; asst. prof., bicentennial preceptor Princeton U., N.J., 1955-58; mem. faculty Brandeis U., Waltham, Mass., 1958-62, dean students, 1960-62; Thomas Jefferson Found. prof. U. Va., Charlottesville, 1962-87, prof. emeritus, 1987—2009, chmn. dept. history, 1966-72, dean faculty Arts and Scis., 1981-85; Mary Ball Washington prof. Am. History University Coll., Dublin, 1988-89; vol. Peace Corps, Armenia, 1997. Scholar in residence Bellagio Study Ctr., 1974; faculty Salzburg Seminar in Am. Studies, 1975; Lamar lectr. Mercer U., 1975; Fleming lectr. La. State U., 1980; lectr. at 20 European univs., 40 Am. colls. and univs. Author: The Jefferson Image in the American Mind, 1960 (Bancroft prize, Gold medal Thomas Jefferson Meml. Found.), Major Crises in American History, 2 vols., 1962, Democracy, Liberty and Property: The State Constitutional Convention Debates of the 1820s, 1966, Thomas Jefferson and the New Nation: A Biography, 1970, James Madison: A Biography in His Own Words, 1974, Adams and Jefferson: A Revolutionary Dialogue, 1976, Olive Branch and Sword: The Compromise of 1833, 1982, The Great Triumvirate: Webster, Clay and Calhoun, 1987; editor: Thomas Jefferson: A Historical Profile, 1996, The Portable Thomas Jefferson, 1975, Thomas Jefferson Writings, 1984, Thomas Jefferson: A Reference Biography, 1986, The Virginia Statute for Religious Freedom: Its Evolution and Consequences in American History, 1988, Visitors to Monticello, 1989, Lincoln in American Memory, 1994 (History finalist, Pulitzer prize, PBK Book award U. Va.), Coming of Age with the New Republic, 1938-1950, 1999, The John Brown Legend Revisited, 1859-2000, 2002, Starving Armenians: America and the Armenian Genocide. 1915-1930 and After, 2004, The President and His Biographer: Woodrow Wilson and Ray Stannard Baker, 2007. Bd. dirs. Thomas Jefferson Found.; chmn. Thomas Jefferson Commemoration Commn., 1993-94. Guggenheim fellow, 1962-63, Ctr. for Advanced Study in Behavioral Scis. fellow, 1968-69, NEH and Nat. Humanities Ctr. fellow, 1980-81; recipient 20th Anniversary award Va. Found. for Humanities, 1994, Nat. First Freedom award First Freedom Coun., 1997, Career Achievement award, 2005, Libr. Va. Fellow Am. Acad. Arts and Scis.; mem. Am. Hist. Assn., Am. Antiquarian Soc., Mass. Hist. Soc., Phi Beta Kappa. Died Sept. 23, 2009.

PETERSON, SUSAN HARNLY, artist, writer; b. McPherson, Kans., July 21, 1925; d. Paul Witmore and Iva Wilda (Curtis) Harnly; m. Jack L. Peterson, Oct. 8, 1949 (div. 1972); children: Jill Kristin, Jan Sigrid, Taäg Paul; life ptnr. Robert Schwarz Jr. AA, Monticello Coll., Alton, Ill., 1944; AB, Mills Coll., 1946; MFA in Ceramics, Alfred U., 1950. Cert. tchr. sec. schs. Head of ceramics Wichita Art Assn. Sch., 1947-49, Chouinard Art Inst., LA, 1951-55; prof. ceramics U. So. Calif., LA, 1955-72; head of ceramics Idyllwild (Calif.) Sch. of Music and Art, 1957-1987; prof. ceramics Hunter Coll. CUNY, 1972-1994. Author: Shoji Hamada, A Potter's Way and Work, 1974, The Living Tradition of Maria Martinez, 1978, Lucy M. Lewis, American Indian Potter, 1984, The Craft and Art of Clay, 1992, Working with Clay, 1998; 54 half-hour CBS TV shows, Wheels, Kilns and Clay, 1969-70. Recipient Binns award Alfred U. Ceramic Coll., 1998, Critics award Nat. Endowment for the Arts, Washington, 1985, Wrangler ward Nat. Cowboy Hall of Fame, 1978. Fellow Am. Craft Coun.; mem. World Craft Coun., Nat. Ceramic Educators Coun. Am. (Lifetime Achievement award 1997), Am. Ceramic Soc., PEO, Phi Beta Kappa. Home: Scottsdale, Ariz. Died Mar. 26, 2009.

PETERSON, WILLIAM JOSEPH, athletics coach; b. Dayton, Ohio, Apr. 26, 1957; s. William Joseph and Virginia (Williams) P. A, St. Petersburg Jr. Coll., Fla., 1977; BA, Eckerd Coll., 1980; MS, La. Tech. U., 1982. Asst. basketball coach La. Tech. U., Ruston, 1980-83; head basketball coach Union Coll., Barbourville, Ky., 1983-87, asst. basketball coach McNeese State U., Lake Charles, La., from 1987. Bd. dirs. Bill Peterson's Basketball Camp, Barbourville, 1983—. Head coach 1st U.S. team to travel to USSR, Athletes In Action, 1986. Mem. Nat. Assn. Basketball Coaches, Fellowship of Christian Athletes (Coach of Yr. 1984-85), Nat. Assn. Intercollegiate Athletic's Coaches. Republican. Roman Catholic. Avocations: tennis, waterskiing. Home: Lake Charles, La. Died Feb. 10, 2008.

PETRIE, BERNARD, lawyer; b. Detroit, Sept. 9, 1925; s. Milton and Yetta (Schwartz) P. Practice law, San Francisco. Home: San Francisco, Calif. Died Aug. 26, 2007.

PFISTER, GAIL WILLIAMS, economics educator, consultant; b. Seattle, May 6, 1936; d. Randall Smallwood Jr. and Jean (Miller) Williams; m. John S. Williams, Aug. 23, 1958 (div. 1979); children: Eric, Lori; m. Cloyd Harry Pfister, Apr. 24, 1982; stepchildren: Gaby, Cathy, Michael, Romi. AA, Marymount Coll., Rome, 1955; BA in Econs., Oberlin Coll., 1957; MA in History magna cum laude, Fairleigh Dickinson U., 1968; MA in Econs., NYU, 1976. Rsch. assoc., then lectr. Fairleigh Dickinson U., Teaneck, N.J., 1973-79; asst. prof. George Mason U., Fairfax, Va., 1979-82; lectr. U. Md., Heidelberg, Germany, 1982-84, U. Ariz., Tucson, 1984-86, U. South Fla., Tampa, 1986-89, Eckerd Coll., St. Petersburg, Fla., 1986-89; mem. faculty dept. bus. adminstrn. Marymount U., Arlington, Va., 1989-95; lectr. USDA Grad. Sch., 1991—95. Mem. rev. panels HHS, 1992—96. Author: Multinational Corporations: Problems and Prospects, 1975, Transborder Data Flows and Multinational Enterprise, 1988. Died Apr. 6, 2006.

PFLUG, EDUARD, contractor; b. Belgrade, Serbia, Apr. 25, 1938; came to U.S., 1961; s. Rudolf and Mary (Kovacevic) P.; m. Rose Marie Amato, Jan. 21, 1973. AAS, DeVry Inst., 1963; BA in Bus. Adminstrn. and Mgmt., Ind. Inst. Tech., 1992. Field tech. rep. East Coast and Midwest area Siemens Am., Inc., NYC, 1963-67; dist. svc. mgr. Midwest area Philips Electronic Instruments, 1967-88; regional svc. mgr. West Coast area Hitachi Instruments, Inc.; ind. contractor Pflug's Enterprises, from 1992. Mem. Assn. for Field Svc. Mgrs. Internat. (officer local chpt. 1982—), Nat. Orgn. for Self-Employed (enroller 1994—), Alpha Chi (Ind. Lambda chpt.). Republican. Seventh Day Adventist. Avocations: playing violin, swimming, travel, reading. Died Mar. 19, 2008.

PHILIPPI, ERVIN WILLIAM, mortician; b. Lodi, Calif., June 4, 1922; s. William and Rebecca (Steinert) P.; m. Emma Grace Mosely, May 8, 1958 (div. Mar. 1979); m. Helen Jo Hunt, June 3, 1979. Grad., Calif. Coll. Motuary Sci., 1948. Embalmer, mortician, mgr. Salas Bros. Chapel, Modesto, Calif., 1946-92; dep. coroner Stanislaus County, Calif., 1955-75. With U.S. Army, 1942-46. Avocations: old car restoration, travel. Home: Modesto, Calif. Died Oct. 2, 2007.

PHILLABAUM, LESLIE ERVIN, publisher; b. Cortland, NY, June 1, 1936; s. Vern Arthur and Beatrice Elizabeth (Butterfield) Phillabaum; m. Roberta Kimbrough Swarr, Mar. 17, 1962; children: Diane Melissa, Scott Christopher. BS, Pa. State U., 1958, MA, 1963. Editor Pa. State U. Press, 1961-63; editor-in-chief U. N.C. Press, 1963-70; assoc. dir., editor La. State U. Press, Baton Rouge, 1970-75, dir., 1975—2003, emeritus dir., from 2003. Served to 1st lt. US Army, 1959—61. Mem.: Assn. Am. Univ. Presses (dir. 1978—80, 1983—86, pres. 1984—85), Acacia, Alpha Kappa Psi, Omicron Delta Kappa. Democrat. Home: Baton Rouge, La. Died Jan. 14, 2009.

PHILLIPS, JAMES KENNETH, construction company executive; b. Tulsa, May 26, 1929; s. William Zachary and Sarah Edna (Roberts) P.; m. Constance Oberlander, Sept. 5, 1953; children: Wendy L. Phillips Rutland, Lori A., Vicki L. Phillips Katlin. BS, Tulsa U., 1957. Sec., treas. Phillips Construction Co. Inc., Kansas City, Kans., 1957-72, pres., from 1972. Bd. dirs. Merc. Bank of Kansas City. Mem. Code Appeals Bd., Overland Pk, Kans., 1976—; bd. dirs. Johnson County (Kans.) Community Coll. Found., 1985—. Served to sgt. USAF, 1950-53. Mem. Kansas City Builders Assn.(past pres. 1985), Phi Gamma Kappa. Clubs: Milburn Country (Overland Pk.), Hallbrook Country (Leawood, Kans.); Jesters;. Lodges: Optimists (lt. gov. 1963), Shriners. Republican. Avocations: golf, hunting, fishing. Home: Leawood, Kans. Died May 23, 2008.

PHILLIPS, OLIN RAY, state legislator; b. Gaffney, SC, Dec. 25, 1934; s. Cline G Phillips, Mae Annie Phillips; m. Barbara Ann Porter, 1957. Chmn. Cherokee County Dem. Com., SC; supr. election Sch. Dist. No 1; ex-officio dir. SC Transp. Policy & Research Coun., 1991; SC state rep. Dist. 29, 1979—92; SC state rep. Dist. 30, 1993—2008; mem. Oper. & Mgmt. Com., 1983—84; 2nd vice chmn. Edn. & Public Works Com., 1985—90; chmn. Aviation Subcom., Edn. Study Com.; mem. Labor, Commerce & Industry Com.; SC house rep.; pres. Joy Drive-Inst. Gaffney, SC, 1972—2008; mem.advisor.bd. Limestone Coll., 1982—84; vice chmn. Pyrotechnic Safety Bd., 1985; bd. trustees Univ. SC, 1991—92; vice chmn. Blue Ribbon Task Force Public Transp., 1991. Mem.: Aeronautics Com., Mason, WOW, Blacksburg Rotary, Gaffney Lions, Cherokee Co. & Union Co. Coun. Aging., Elm St PTA (pres.). Democrat. Baptist. Died Dec. 27, 2008.

PHILLIPS, VIRGINIA MCCLINTOCK, realtor; b. Dothan, Ala., Apr. 2, 1914; d. Herbert Richmond and Maude Susan (Howell) McClintock; m. Robert Lee Phillips; children: Virginia Lea Holloway, Barbara Lou. Student, Athens Coll., Ala., 1934; grad., Real Estate Inst. Cert. residential specialist. Sec. H. R. McClintock, Dothan, 1934-41; sec., classified advt. clk. The Dothan Eagle, 1941-42; sec., cashier Liberty Nat. Life Ins. Co., Dothan, 1942-46; co-owner W&M Optical and Jewelry, Talladega, Ala., 1946-47; sec. Dothan Pajama Mill, 1947; sec., bookkeeper Saad Jewelers Wholesale, Dothan, 1950, Sullivan Realty, Dothan, 1951-52; prin., homebuilder Phillips Realty, Dothan, from 1952, developer, from 1955. Organizing pres. Houston County Rep. Women's Club, 1985. Mem. Dothan Bd. Realtors (sec.-treas. 1968-75, charter), Dothan Women's Council Realtors (charter pres. 1975-76, bd. dirs.). Presbyterian. Avocations: tennis, golf, swimming. Died Oct. 6, 2007.

PHILLIPS, WILLIAM ALPHONZO, executive; b. Flushing, NY, Feb. 25, 1956; s. Marion Alphonzo Thomas and Doris Ernestine (Wade) P.; m. Sonya Faye Clack, Sept. 18, 1982; 1 child, William Alphonzo II. AS, Five Towns Coll., 1977; MusB, Howard U., 1981. Tchr. Amityville (N.Y.) Pub. Schs., 1981-82, Fulton County (Ga.) Sch. System, 1982-83; mgr. food svc. Appleby's Restaurant, Union City, Ga., 1983-84; tchr. Atlanta Pub. Schs., 1984-85; access coord. Prime Cable, Inc., Atlanta, 1985-86; studio mgr. People TV, Inc., Atlanta, from 1986. Teaching asst. DeKalb County Pub. Sch. System, 1987—. Bd. dir. TV ministry City of Hope Ministries, Atlanta, 1986-87; mem. NAACP. Named one of Outstanding Young Men Am., 1985. Mem. Atlanta Community TV Assn. (cons. media mgmt. 1986—). Lodges: Masons. Avocations: tennis, swimming. Died Dec. 25, 2007.

PHILLIPS, WILLIAM DAVID, history educator; b. Dallas, June 26, 1943; s. William David and Virginia (Mahan) P.; m. Carla Rahn, July 4, 1970. BA, U. Miss., 1964; MA, U. Tenn., 1966; PhD, NYU, 1971. Instr. R.I. Coll., Providence, 1969-70; asst. prof. history San Diego State U., 1970-75, assoc. prof., 1975-78, prof., 1978-88; prof. history U. Minn., Mpls., from 1988. Co-author: Spain's Golden Fleece, 1997 (Leo Gershoy award 1998), The Worlds of Christopher Columbus, 1992 (Spain in Am. second prize 1993); author: Slavery From Roman Times to the Early Transatlantic Trade, 1985, Enrique IV and the Crisis of Fifteenth-Century Castile, 1978; editor: Testimonies from the Columbian Lawsuits, 2000; sect. reviewer Archiv fur Reformationsgeschichte-Literaturbericht, Tübingen, Germany, 1985-94. Recipient Founders' Day award NYU, N.Y.C., 1972, grants U. Minn. and San Diego State U., grant-in-aid Am. Philos. Soc., Phila., 1980, fellowship NEH, Washington, 1988-89. Mem.: Forum on European Expansion and Global Interactions (founding mem.), Cnf. Latin Am. History (mem. Columbus quincentennial com. 1988—90), Soc. Spanish and Portuguese Hist. Studies (pres. 1994—96), Am. Hist. Assn. (sect. editor Recently Pub. Articles 1987—90, mem. Premio del Rey com. from 1998, chair 2000—01), Medieval Acad. Am. (life). Home: Minneapolis, Minn. Died Nov. 19, 2006.

PHO, LONG AMBROSE BA (PHO BA LONG), business educator, consultant; b. Hanoi, Vietnam, Apr. 25, 1922; arrived in U.S., 1975; s. Thuan Ba Pho and Ninh Thi Nguyen; m. Claire Trung-Nghia Dang, Oct. 15, 1940; children: Cyril Hong-Phong, Anne Le-Thu, Pacific Hong-Tam, Michael Hong-Quang, Helen Long-Chau, Edward Hong-Minh. Bachelor's degree 2e Partie, Lycee Albert Sarraut, Hanoi, 1944; Pharmacien d'Etat, U. Indochina, Hanoi, 1950; MBA, Harvard U., 1956. Advanced profl. cert. Program dir. Georgetown U., Washington, 1983-95; seminar escort interpreter US Dept. State, Washington. Bus. edn. cons. Vietnam Found., McLean, Va. Min. labor Govt. of Republic of Vietnam, Saigon, 1987-88. Capt., mil. pharmacist North Vietnamese mil., 1946-50. Recipient Congl. citation U.S. Senate, 1986. Mem. Vietnam Found. (hon. mem., founder, past pres. 1978-89). Home: Mc Lean, Va. Died Feb. 17, 2009.

PIAN, THEODORE HSUEH-HUANG, engineering educator, consultant; b. Shanghai, Jan. 18, 1919; came to U.S., 1943; s. Chao-Hsin Shu-Cheng and Chih-Chuan (Yen) P.; m. Rulan Chao, Oct. 3, 1945; 1 child, Canta Chao-Po. B in Engring., Tsing Hua U., Kunming, China, 1940; MS, MIT, 1944, DSc, 1948; DSc (hon.), Beijing U. Aeros. and Astronautics, 1990; PhD (hon.), Shanghai U., 1991. Engr. Cen. Aircraft Mfg. Co., Loiwing, China, 1940-42, Chengtu Glider Mfg. Factory, 1942-43; tchg. asst. MIT, Cambridge, 1946-47, rsch. assoc., 1947-52, asst. prof., 1952-59, assoc. prof., 1959-66, prof., 1966-89, prof. emeritus, 1989—2009. Vis. assoc. Calif. Inst. Tech., Pasadena, 1965-66; vis. prof. U. Tokyo, 1974, Tech. U., Berlin, 1975; vis. chair prof. Nat. Tsing Hua U., Hsin Chu, Taiwan, 1990, Nat. Ctrl. U., ChungLi, Taiwan, 1992; hon. prof. Beijing U. Aero. and Astronautics, Beijing Inst. Tech., Southwestern Jaiotong U., Dalian U. Tech., Huazhong U. Sci. and Tech., Changsha Rwy. U., Ctrl.-South U. Tech., Hohai U., Nanjing U. of Aero. and Astronautics, Dalian Rwy. U., Shashi U. of Sci. and Tech. of China. Recipient von Karman Meml. prize TRE Corp., Beverly Hills, Calif., 1974. Fellow AAAS, AIAA (assoc. editor jour. 1973-75, Structures, Structural Dynamics and Materials award 1975), U.S. Assn. Computational Mechanics (founding mem.); mem. ASME (hon.), NAE, Academia Sinica Taiwan, Am. Soc. Engring. Edn., Internat. Assn. for Computational Mechanics (hon. mem. gen. coun.). Died June 20, 2009.

PIATETSKI-SHAPIRO, ILYA, mathematics professor; b. Moscow, Mar. 30, 1929; arrived in Israel, 1976; s. Joseph and Sheina (Gurevitch) P.-S.; m. Edith Piatetski-Shapiro, 1978; children: Gregory, Nikki, Shlomit (Shelly). PhD, Moscow Pedagogical Inst., 1951; DSc, Steklov Inst., 1958. Prof. math. Moscow Inst. of Applied Mathematics, 1958—74, Moscow State U., 1964-72, Tel Aviv U., 1976, Yale U., New Haven, 1977, prof. emeritus. Recipient Moscow Math. Soc. prize for a Young Mathematician, 1952, Laureate of Israel prize in math., 1981, Wolf prize in math. Wolf Found., Israel, 1990. Mem.: Israel Acad. Sciences, Am. Math. Soc. Avocations: hiking, camping. Home: Tel Aviv, Israel. Died Feb. 21, 2009.

PIAZZA, DUANE EUGENE, biomedical researcher; b. San Jose, Calif., June 5, 1954; s. Salvador Richard and Mary Bernice (Mirassou) P.; m. Sandra Patrignani, Sept. 19, 1992. BS in Biology, U. San Francisco, 1976; MA in Biology, San Francisco State U., 1986. Staff rsch. assoc. I U. Calif., San Francisco, 1975—81; sr. rsch. technician XOMA Corp., San Francisco, 1981—82; biologist II Syntex USA Inc., Palo Alto, Calif., 1982—85; pres., cons. Ryte For You, Oakland, Calif., from 1985; rsch. assoc. I Cetus Corp., Emeryville, Calif., 1986—90; rsch. assoc. II John Muir Cancer and Aging Rsch. Inst., Walnut Creek, Calif., 1991—92; rsch. assoc. Pharmagenesis, Palo Alto, Calif., 1993—96; asst. lab. mgr. DeAnza C.C., Cupertino, Calif., 1996—99; lab. mgr. San Jose City Coll., 1999—2000; content scientist Ingenuity, Alviso, Calif., 2000—01; sr. biologist ALZA Corp., Mountain View, Calif., 2000—04, mem. emergency response team, from 2001; sr. biologist The Macroflux Internal Venture, Johnson and Johnson, from 2004. CPR & first aid instr. ARC, 1980-92, vol. 1st aid sta. instr., Santa Cruz, 1985-86, vol. 1st aid sta. disaster action team, Oakland, 1986-92, br. chmn. disaster action team, 1987-88; treas. Reganti Homeowner Assn., 1990-92. Mem. AAAS, Am. Assn. Lab. Animal Sci. Republican. Roman Catholic. Avocations: scuba diving, swimming, backpacking, photography, astronomy. Home: Sunnyvale, Calif. Died Sept. 10, 2007.

PICK, HEATHER, newscaster; b. Platteville, Wis., 1970; m. Joe Cygan; children: Julia, Jack. Reporter, anchor Sta. WREX-TV, Rockford, Ill.; anchor Sta. WBNS-TV, Columbus, Ohio, 2002—08. Died Nov. 7, 2008.

PIERCE, GORDON CARL, retired architect; b. Atlanta, Oct. 27, 1918; s. Carl Freeman and Leola May (Staebler) P. BArch, Carnegie Mellon U., 1941. Registered architect, Pa. Owner Gordon C. Pierce AIA, Greensburg, Pa., 1953-93; ret., 1993. Chmn. Greensburg City Planning commn., 1974-93. Mem. Greensburg City Redevel. Authority, 1975-90, G0-Greensburg C.D. Corp., 1970-90. Mem. AIA, Pa. Soc. Architects, Hist. Preservation Trust. Republican. Methodist. Avocations: art, gardening, poetry. Home: Scottdale, Pa. Died Jan. 18, 2008.

PIERCE, JOHN BURNHAM, JR., publisher; b. Boston, July 4, 1948; s. John B. Sr. and Helen C. (Merrill) P.; m. Sherin E. Costa, Aug. 23, 1993; children: Benjamin Z., Alexander J. Wight, Kristen K., Michael F. BA, Dartmouth Coll., 1971. V.p., group pub. Yankee Publishing Inc, Dublin, N.H., 1988-90, mng. editor, 1976-89, assoc. pub., 1988-90, pub., 1990-94, group pub., from 1994. Chmn. Conval Regional Sch. Bd., Peterborough, N.H., 1990-91. Avocations: hiking, gardening. Home: Dublin, NH. Died Apr. 10, 2008.

PIERCE, SHELBY CRAWFORD, oil industry executive, consultant; b. May 26, 1932; s. William Shelby and Iris Mae (Smith) Pierce; m. Marguerite Ann Grado, Apr. 2, 1954; children: Cynthia Dawn, Melissa Carol. BSEE, Lamar U., Beaumont, Tex., 1956; grad. program for sr. execs., MIT, 1980. With Amoco Oil Co., Texas City Refinery, from 1956, elec. engr., elec. foreman, area foreman, 1956—60, zone supr., gen. foreman, maintenance, 1961—67, oper. supt., 1967—69, coord. results mgmt., 1969—72; dir. results mgmt. Amoco Oil Co. Corp. Hdqs., Chgo., 1972-75; mgr. ops. Amoco Oil Co., Whiting (Ind.) Refinery, 1975—76, asst. refinery mgr., 1977-79; dir. crude replacement program Amoco Oil Co. Corp. Hdqs., Chgo., 1979-81, mgr. corp. refining and transp. engring., 1981—91, gen. mgr. engring. and constrn., 1992, v.p. internat. bus. devel., 1993-94, ret., 1994. Pres., dir. Amoco Eurasia Oil Co., Amoco Mex. Oil Co., Amoco India, Inc., Amoco Tech. Assistance Co., Trinidad; chmn., dir. Amoco Orient Oil Co.; v.p. Amoco Corp. Devel. Co., Latin Am., 1994; pres. Pierce Cons. Svc., from 1995; CEO, pres. Environ. Constrn. Co., 1996—98; mem. steering com. contractor safety U.S. Dept. Labor, 1989. Trustee Lamar U. Found., from 1994. Mem.: AIChE (mem. exec. bd. 1985—89, chmn. engring. constrn. contracting divsn. 1988, Divsn. Man of Yr. award 1995), N.W. Ind. Bus. Roundtable (organizer and user coun. chmn. 1986, chmn. exec. bd. 1986—87), The Bus. Roundtable (constrn. com., adv. bd., chmn. constrn. cost effectiveness task force 1992—94), Constrn. Industry Inst. (chmn. Bus. Roundtable coun., mem. strategic planning com. 1991—93), Flossmoor Country Club, Sigma Tau. Republican. Methodist. Died Nov. 2008.

PIERSOL, ALLAN GERALD, mechanical engineer; b. Pitts., June 2, 1930; s. Robert James and Irene Laticia (Dematty) Piersol; m. Gertrud Teresia Moller, June 8, 1958; children: Allan Gerald Jr., Marie Theresa, John Robert. BS in Engring. Physics, U. Ill., 1952; MS in Engring., U. Calif., 1961. Lic. profl. engr., Calif. Rsch. engr. Douglas Aircraft Co., Santa Monica, Calif., 1952-59; mem. tech. staff Ramo Wooldridge Corp., Canoga Park, Calif., 1959-63; v.p. Measurement Analysis Corp., Santa Monica, Calif., 1963-71; prin. scientist Bolt Beranek and Newman, Inc., Conoga Park, 1971-85; sr. scientist Astron Corp., Santa Monica, 1985-88; owner Piersol Engring., Woodland Hills, Calif., from 1988. Lectr. U. So. Calif., LA, 1965—95; adj. lectr. Loyola Marymount U., LA, from 2006. Co-author: (book) Measurement and Analysis of Random Data, 1966, Random Data: Analysis and Measurement Procedures, 1971, 2000, Engineering Application of Correletion and Spectral Analysis, 1980, 1993, Shock and Vibration Handbook, 2002. Mem.: ASME, Acoustical Soc. Am., Inst. Environ. Scis. and

Tech. (Irwin Vigness Meml. award 1991). Achievements include patents for method and apparatus for determining terrain surface profiles. Home: Woodland Hills, Calif. Died Mar. 1, 2009.

PINCUS, LIONEL I., venture capitalist; b. Phila., Mar. 2, 1931; s. Henry and Theresa Celia (Levit) P.; m. Suzanne Storrs Poulton, 1967 (dec. 1995); children: Henry, Matthew BA, U. Pa., 1953; MBA, Columbia U., 1956. Assoc. gen. ptnr. Ladenburg, Thalmann & Co., NYC, 1955-63; pres. Lionel I. Pincus & Co., Inc., NYC, 1964-66; pres., CEO E.M. Warburg & Co., Inc., NYC, 1966-70; chmn., CEO E.M. Warburg, Pincus & Co., LLC, 1970—2002, chmn. emeritus, 2003—09. Trustee NY Presbyn. Hosp.; trustee, chmn. emeritus Columbia U.; trustee German Marshall Fund USA, 1982-88; mem. bd. overseers Columbia Grad. Sch. Bus.; bd. dirs. Am. Mus. Natural History, Nat. Park Found., 1995-01; mem. Partnership for NYC; emeritus dir. Sch. Am. Ballet. Mem. Coun. Fgn. Rels., Nat. Venture Capital Assn. (Lifetime award), World Wildlife Fund (nat. coun.), Nat. Golf Links Am. Club, Meadow Club. Died Oct. 10, 2009.

PINKERSON, ALAN LEE, physician; b. Providence, Mar. 20, 1931; s. Harry and Fan Bass Pinkerson; m. Artemis Panageotis Simopoulos; children: Daphne, Lee, Alexandra. BA, Harvard Coll., 1952; MD, Boston U., 1956. Capt. US Army, 1960—64, Korea. Home: Washington, DC. Died July 19, 2007.

PINNIX, MARSHALL HENRY, insurance consultant, international correspondent; b. Oxford, NC, Jan. 12, 1927; s. Marshall Kerr and Katherine Jane (Page) P.; m. Sarah V. Costin, Oct. 13, 1957; children: Valerie Pinnix Spencer, Marshall Henry, Jr. BS, U. N.C., 1949. Security analyst Mercantile Trust Co., Balt., 1966-85; mgr. fin. analysis Alexander & Alexander, Inc., Owings Mills, Md., 1985-92; correspondent US, Lat. Am. Lloyd's of London Press, London, from 1992; pvt. practice Balt., from 1992. Mem. editl. adv. bd. Lloyd's of London Press, London, 1995—; spkr. in field. Author: Insurance in the United States: A Handbook for Professionals, 1993; co-author: Practical Security Analysis, 1989; contbr. articles to newsletters. Mem. Six Napoleons of Balt., Oxbridge Scholars. Avocations: languages, history, travel, opera, golf. Died Dec. 8, 2007.

PISCHKE, FRANK JOHN, retired otolaryngologist; b. Chgo., July 7, 1936; s. Frank Joseph Pischke and Edith Jeanette Godar; m. Elsa Mendez, Aug. 21, 1965; children: Andrew, Rebecca. BS in Biology, Rockhurst U., Kansas City, Mo., 1958; MD, Kans. U., Lawrence, 1962. Diplomate Am. Bd. Otolaryngology. Asst. prof. Kans. U. Med. Ctr., Kansas City, 1969—84, Mercer Med. Sch., Macon, Ga., 1985—2001; ret., 2001. Sr. surgeon USPHS, 1962—65. Recipient Eagle Scout, Boys Scout Am., 1953. Fellow: Am. Coll. Surgeons, Am. Acad. Otolaryn.; mem.: AMA, Am. Acad. Otolaryn. Allergy. Avocations: singing, bicycling, rowing, skiing, reading. Home: Holiday Island, Ark. Died Nov. 11, 2007.

PLACHER, WILLIAM CARL, philosophy and religion educator; b. Peoria, Ill., Apr. 28, 1948; s. Carl Henry and Louise Ellen (Swanson) P. AB, Wabash Coll., 1970; M. Philosophy, Yale U., 1974, PhD, 1975. Prof. philosophy and religion Wabash Coll., Crawfordsville, Ind., from 1974. Mem. Ctr. Theol. Inquiry, Princeton, 1987-88; vis. scholar dept. religious studies Stanford U., 1980-81. Author: A History of Christian Theology, 1983, Readings in the History of Christian Theology, 1988, Unapologetic Theology, 1989. Mem. com. to draft brief statement of faith Presbyn. Ch. USA, 1984—. Danforth fellow Danforth Found., 1970. Mem. Am. Acad. Religion (chair narrative group 1986-89). Home: Crawfordsville, Ind. Died Nov. 30, 2008; Indiana.

PLANK, (ETHEL) FAYE, editor, photographer, writer; b. St. Francisville, Ill., Oct. 15, 1912; d. Perry Austin and Nellie Sarah (Hardin) Winget; m. Edward Earl Plank, July 10, 1934 (dec. Mar. 1986); children: Earleen F., Eugene Earl, Richard J. Student, Tex. Wesleyan U., West Tex. State U., N.Mex. U., San Antonio Coll., U. So. Miss., Ea. N.Mex. U., U. N.Mex., Drake U., Rutgers U., Dartmouth U., U. Colo., Amarillo Coll., Frank Phillips Coll., Permaian Basin Jr. Coll. Pvt. tchr. art, Hereford, Tex., 1960-64; office mgr., bookkeeper West Tex. Devel. Co., Hereford, 1964-70; publicity writer Cowbelles, 1970-74; mng. editor Curry County Times, Clovis, N.Mex., 1974-77; writer advertising and news State Line Tribune, Farwell, Tex., 1977-82; corresp. Lubbock (Tex.) Avalanche Jour., 1977-82, Amarillo (Tex.) Globe News, 1977-86; owner, mgr. Ideas Unltd. (pub. rels. firm), 1977-82; owner, editor, pub. Your Paper, N.Mex., 1977-82; women's editor, photographer Dalhart (Tex.) Daily Texan, from 1983. Former writer advt. Spl. Roping and Rodeo, Clovis, Pioneer Days, Clovis, Curry County Fair, Clovis, mem. spl. commn. on publicity and promotion Mesa Redonda Cowboy Camp Mtg., N.Mex., 1980-82, with publicity Federated Rep. Women's Club, Clovis, 1976-82, Clovis Bus. and Profl. Women's Club, 1977-82; with publicity and promotion Miss Rodeo N.Mex. Pageant, 1977-82, Curry County Farm and Livestock Bur., 1977-82; spl. assignments, photographer N.Mex. Stockman, Albuquerque, N.Mex. Farm and Ranch Mag. Publicity chmn., bd. dirs. Keep Dalhart Beautiful; publicity chmn., v.p. Dalhart Ctrl. United Meth. Women; v.p., program chmn., pres. Dalhart Wesleyan Group, Ctrl. United Meth. Ch.; publicity chmn. Dalhart Youth Ctr. Bd.; bd. dirs., task force Dalhart Sr. Citizens; chmn. Dalhart Writer's Group; leader 4-H Club, Hereford, Camp Fire Club, Hereford; active sch. bd. Hereford Ind. Sch. Dist., 1960-62; active Methodist Women's Fellowship, Hereford Red Cross (Gray Lady, chmn.), Hereford Art Guild, Hereford Meth. Ch. Recipient 4-H Leaders award, 1952, Citizen of Yr. award Hereford Lions Club, 1960, appreciation award Am. Nat. Red Cross, 1965, N.Mex. Cowbelle of Yr. award, 1973, Community Leaders and Noteworthy Am. award, 1975-76, award of merit Miss Rodeo N.Mex. Pageant, appreciation award FFA, Pvt. Enterprise award Federated Club Women Am., 1978, Cert. Appreciation, Nat. Heart Edn. Assn., 1979, Golden Quill award N.Mex. Farm and Livestock Bur., 1981, Woman of Achievment award N. Mex. Press Women, 1981, Woman of Achievement award Nat. Fedn. Press Women, 1981, N.Mex. Friend of 4-H award Curry County, 1984, Dallam, Tex., County, 1984, Disting. Proud Ptnr. award Keep Tex. Beautiful, 1988, 89, Cert. merit, O. P. Schnabel Status Citizen, 1992, Outstanding Spl. Promotion award Am. Cancer Soc., ACE award 1990-91, 91-92, Recognition award 1991-92, Pace Setter award 1993, Edn. award 1993, Tex. Sch. Bell award Distinction, Tex. Retired Tchrs. Assn., 1991, Appreciation award Tex. Press Women, 1993, Merit award Kcet Tex. Beautiful Individual Leadership, 1994, Appreciation cert. Tex. Press Women, 1994-95, Merit award HOSTS, 1995; named Citizen of Yr., Dalhant (Tex.) Area C. of C., 1993. Mem. Nat. Fedn. Press Women (bd. dirs., regional chmn.-Tex., N.Mex., Colo., Okla., La.), Panhandle Press Assn., Tex. Press Assn., Soc. Profl. Journalists, N.Mex. Press Women (past pres.), Ea. N.Mex. Press Women (past pres.), N.Mex. Farm and Livestock Bur. (info. dir., former bd. dirs.), Am. Nat. Cowbelles (chmn. beef edn.), N.Mex. Cowbelles (state bd., legis. chmn., publicity, news media, TV dir.), Cattle Capital Cowbelles (local pres.), Bus. and Profl. Women's Club (v.p., pres.), Republican Women's Club (publicity chmn., Curry County Rep. Ctrl. com.), Pilot Club, PTA (pres.). Republican. Methodist. Avocations: reading, writing, travel, photography. Home: Dalhart, Tex. Died Oct. 9, 2007.

PNUELI, AMIR, computer science educator; b. Nahalal, Israel, Apr. 22, 1941; married; 3 children. BSc in Math., Technion U.; PhD in Applied Math., Weizmann Inst. Sci., 1967; doctorate (hon.), U. Uppsala, 1997, U. Joseph Fourier, 1998, Carl von Ossietzky U., 2000. Fellow Stanford U., Watson Rsch. Ctr., Yorktown; prof. computer sci. Weizmann Inst. Sci., Rehovot, Israel, sr. rschr., prof., 1981—99, head Minerva Ctr. Verification of Reactive Systems, 1998; prof. computer sci. NYU, 1999—2009. Co-founder Mini-Systems, 1971; founder, chmn. dept. computer sci. Tel-Aviv U., 1973; co-founder AdCad. Author (with Z. Manna): The Temporal Logic of Reactive and Concurrent Systems: Specification, 1991, Temporal Verification of Reactive Systems: Safety, 1995. Recipient A.M. Turing award,Assn. Computing Machinery, 1996, Israel Prize in Exact Sciences, 2000. Fellow: Assn. Computing Machinery; mem.: NAE, Israeli Acad. Arts and Scis. Achievements include seminal work introducing temporal logic into computing science; outstanding constributions to program and system verification. Died Nov. 2, 2009.

PODZIMEK, JOSEF, meteorology educator; b. Brandys, Prague, Czechoslovakia, Mar. 24, 1923; came to U.S., 1969; s. Josef and Ruzena (Podzimkova) P.; m. Miroslava Curinova, Dec. 12, 1950; children: Eva, Jana. MS in Applied Physics, Charles U., Prague, 1949, DNatural Sci. in Meteorology, 1952, PhD in Meteorology, 1959. Rsch. investigator Flight Rsch. Inst. Aerodynamics, Prague, 1949-53; dept. head, cloud physics Inst. Physics of Atmosphere, Prague, 1954-69, dir., 1962-69; lectr., assoc. prof. Charles U. Meteorology, Prague, 1960-69; prof. U. Mo., Rolla, from 1971; vis. prof. U. Vienna, 1993. Vis. scientist SUNY, Albany, 1969-71; vis. prof. J. Fourier U., Grenoble, France, 1986-88; prin. investigator U. Mo., Rolla, 1972-90; rsch. project dir. Inst. U. Navale, Naples, Italy, 1986-87. Author: Physics of Clouds and Precipitation, 1959; co-author: Elements of Aerodynamics and Mechanics of Flight, 1954; contbr. articles to profl. jours.; patentee in field. Recipient Achievement award, U. Mo., 1982. Mem. Am. Geophys. Soc., Am. Meteorol. Soc., Am. Assn. Aerosol Rsch., Gesellschaft fuer Aerosolforschung. Avocations: tennis, alpinist, swimming. Home: Groveland, Ill. Died Dec. 25, 2007.

POE, MARTIN, biophysicist; b. St. Louis, Sept. 26, 1942; s. Martin Turner and Rosemary (Raub) Poe; m. Joan Cathie Peterson, June 26, 1965; 1 child, Alison Crystal. BS in Physics, MIT, 1964; PhD in Biophysics, U. Pa., 1968. Postdoctoral fellow E.I. du Pont de Nemours & Co., Wilmington, Del., 1968-70; sr. rsch. biophysicist Merck & Co., Inc., Rahway, N.J., 1970-74, rsch. fellow, 1974-79, sr. rsch. fellow, 1979-84, sr. investigator, from 1984. Byron Reigel lectr. Northwestern U., Evanston, Ill., 1979. Contbr. articles to Proceeding NAS, Biochemistry, Jour. Biol. Chemistry. Mem. Am. Chem. Soc., Am. Soc. for Biochemistry and Molecular Biology, Biophys. Soc., N.Y. Acad. Sci. Achievements include patent on inhibitor of dihydrofolate reductase. Home: Scotch Plains, NJ. Died Aug. 14, 2008.

POHL, GUNTHER ERICH, retired library administrator; b. Berlin, July 22, 1925; came to US, 1927; s. Erich Ernst and Martha (Seidel) P.; m. Dorothy Edna Beck, Aug. 21, 1949; children: Christine, Louise, Elizabeth, Ronald BA, NYU, 1947, MA, 1950; MLS., Columbia U., 1951. Librarian local history and genealogy divsn. N.Y. Pub. Libr., NYC, 1948-69, chief local history and genealogy divsn., 1969-85, ret., 1985. Compiler: N.Y. State Biography and Portrait Index. Fellow N.Y. Geneal. and Biog. Soc.; mem. ALA (chmn. genealogy com. 1971-73, 76-78, History sect. award 1996), N.Y. Geneal. and Biog. Soc. (libr., trustee 1982-92), Sigma Phi Epsilon. Republican. Avocations: stamps, opera, collecting new yorkiana. Home: Wilmore, Ky. Died Feb. 20, 2009.

POHLAD, CARL RAY, professional sports team executive; b. West Des Moines, Iowa, Aug. 23, 1915; m. Eloise O'Rourke (dec. Nov. 20, 2003); children: Robert, William, James. Student, Gonzaga U. With MEI Diversified, Inc., Mpls., from 1959, chmn. bd., 1976—94; pres. Marquette Bank Mpls., N.A., pres., dir., Bank Shares, Inc.; owner Minn. Twins, 1985—2009. Bd. dirs. Meth. Hosp. Adminstrv. Group, T.G.I. Friday's, Tex. Air Corp., Ea. Airlines, Continental Airlines, Inc., Carlson Cos. Inc. Founder Mpls. Boys & Girls Clubs. Served in US Army. Recipient Purple Heart, Bronze Star; named one of Forbes' Richest Americans, 2006. Died Jan. 5, 2009.

POINDEXTER, WILLIAM MERSEREAU, retired lawyer; b. LA, June 16, 1925; s. Robert Wade and Irene M. Poindexter; m. Jani Jennifer Wohlgemuth, Feb. 14, 2000; children: James Wade, David Graham, Honour Hélené, Timothy John, Cory Todd, E. W. Greg. BA, Yale U., 1946; postgrad., U. Chgo., 1946-47; LL.B., U. Calif., Berkeley, 1949. Bar: Calif. 1952. Practiced in, San Francisco, 1952-54, Los Angeles, 1954—2009; mem. firm Poindexter & Doutre, Inc., 1964—2009. Pres. Consol. Brazing & Mfg. Co., Riverside, Calif., 1949—52. Pres. South Pasadena-San Marino YMCA, Calif., 1963; mem. San Marino Sch. Bd., 1965—69, pres., 1967, Conf. Ins. Counsel, 1975. With USMCR, 1943. Fellow: Am. Coll. Trust and Estate Counsel; mem.: ABA, State Bar Calif., Los Angeles County Bar Assn., Calif. Lincoln clubs (LA downtown chpt. chmn. 1997—2003), Yale Club (pres. So. Calif. chpt. 1961). Republican. Presbyterian. Home: Glendale, Calif. Died Feb. 20, 2009.

POINTER, MARSHA G., principal; b. St. Louis, Oct. 24, 1950; d. Robert Lee Gentry and Clarice Anita McClure; m. James Earl Pointer, Apr. 15, 1989; children: Tiffany, James Jr. BA, Albion Coll., 1973; MA, Mich. State U., 1977; prin. lic., U. Colo., Denver, 1995. Spl. edn. endorsement EBD (emotional and behavior disorder). Dean, tchr., coach Denver Pub. Schs., 1979—95, asst. prin., 1995—2001, H.S. prin., from 2001. Pres. Manual Leadership High Adv. Bd., Denver, 2001—03. Grantee, U.S. Dept. Edn., 1974, Bill and Melinda Gates Found., 2002. Mem.: Nat. Assn. Secondary Sch. Prins., Nat. Wildlife Assn. Jehovah'S Witness. Avocations: dance, gardening, reading. Died June 19, 2008.

POIRIER, RICHARD, literary critic, educator, editor; b. Gloucester, Mass., Sept. 9, 1925; s. Philip and Annie (Kiley) P. AB, Amherst Coll., 1949; MA, Yale U., 1951; PhD, Harvard U., 1959; student, U. Paris, France, 1944-45; H.H.D., Amherst Coll., 1978. Mem. faculty Williams Coll., 1950-52, Harvard U., 1953-63; Disting. prof. English Rutgers U., from 1963. Bd. dirs., co-founder, chmn. bd. Libr. of Am.; Beckman prof. U. Calif., Berkeley, 1973; chmn. adv. English com. Harvard U., 1988-91; delivered Gauss Seminars, Princeton U., 1990, T.S. Eliot lectures, U. Kent, 1991, Henry James lectures, NYU, 1992. Editor: Partisan Rev, 1963-73, O Henry Prize Stories, 1961-65; editor/founder Raritan Quar., 1981—; author: The Comic Sense of Henry James, 1960, In Defense of Reading, 1962, A World Elsewhere, 1966, The Performing Self, 1971, Norman Mailer, 1973, Robert Frost: The Work of Knowing, 1977, The Renewal of Literature, 1987, Poetry and Pragmatism, 1992, Trying It Out In America, 1999; founder, editor: Raritan Quar., 1981-2001; contbr. author numerous articles, revs. to profl. jours. Served with AUS, 1943-46. Recipient achievement award AAAL, 1978, Jay B. Hubbell award, 1988, Lit. Lion award N.Y. Pub. Libr., 1992; Fulbright scholar, Cambridge, Eng., 1952-53; Bollinger fellow, 1962-63, Guggenheim fellow, 1974-75, fellow NEH, 1978-79. Mem. Am. Acad. Arts and Scis., Am. Acad. Arts and Letters, P.E.N. (exec. bd. 1986), PMLA (editorial bd. 1977-79), nominating com. Nat. Medal for Lit., 1986, 87, Nat. Book Critics Cir., 1977-85, Century Club. Clubs: Century. Home: New York, NY. Died Aug. 15, 2009.

POLK, EMILY DESPAIN, conservationist, writer; b. Aberdeen, Wash., July 6, 1910; d. John Dove Isaacs and Constance Ashley (DeSpain) Van Norden; m. Benjamin Kauffman Polk, Aug. 23, 1946. Student, U. Oreg., 1928-29, Oreg. State U., 1929-31, Rudolph Shaefer Sch. of Art, San Francisco, 1931-32. Head display & design V.C. Morris, San Francisco, 1931-37; founder, CEO DeSpain Design, L.A. and NYC, 1937-44, 63-64; ornamental & interior design arch. Benjamin Polk Arch., Calcutta and New Delhi, 1952-63; owner Galeria de San Luis, San Luis Obispo, Calif., 1966-68; founder, CEO Small Wilderness Area Preservation, Los Osos, Calif., 1969-79. Author: Poems and Epigrams, 1959 (All India Book award 1959), Delhi Old and New, 1963, A Wild Part of California, 1991, Rockpool Trilogy, 1995, Shadows: A Giant Tree, Vols. I-II, 1995-96, A Pilgrimage through Time, 1996, A Moment in the Mind, 1997, Invisible Thresholds, 1997, Poems for Drums and Woodwinds, 1999, Praises-Hymns Without Music, 2000, From Stress to Serenity, 2001, The Rustle of Leaves-New Poems, 2001; co-author: (with B. Polk) India Notebook, 1987, (with others) Sri Lanka Buddhist Shrines, 1991; editor (poetry): Calcuttan Magazine, 1961-63; contbr. articles to jours.; designer interior and exhibits Internat. Wool Secretariat, World Trade Fair, New Delhi, 1955; hon. interior designer Pres. of India, New Delhi, 1955, Maharanee of Tripura, Calcutta, India, 1962-63, King of Nepal,

Kathmandu, 1962-63, Princess Pema Choki, Gantok, Sikkim, 1963; solo exhbns. paintings and montages India, 1963, U.S., 1963, 75, 89, 91, 98, 99, Eng., 1987, jewelry, U.S., 1948, fashion, India, 1955. Mem. coun. Nat. Mus. Women in the Arts, Washington, 1991-93; del., spkr. Pan Asian Cultural Conf., Calcutta, 1963, India House, N.Y., 1963, The Women's Club, 1964, AAUW, 1998. Recipient Kiwanis Citizenship Plaque Inscription, 1928, Golden Bear Conservation award Calif. Pks. and Recreation, Sacramento, 1972, Nat. Conservation award Am. Motors, 1972. Mem. Soc. Women Geographers (Calif. del., spkr. 50th Anniversary Celebrations 1972, Libr. of Congress Oral History Women of Achievement Program 1995), Small Wilderness Area Preservation, Calif. Hist. Soc., Calif. Oaks Found., Am. Women's Club (pres. 1962), Nat. Indian Assn. Women (pres.), English Speaking Union (bd. dirs.), Gyan Chakra Literary Gp. (founder). Home: Atascadero, Calif. Died Aug. 16, 2008.

POLK, LEWIS DAVID, retired public health service officer, pediatrician; b. Phila. s. Solomon and Jennie (Weisman) P.; m. Tobye Coleen Pellman, Apr. 7, 1963 (div. June 1977); m. Phyllis Rubin, Aug. 28, 1977. LHD, Pa. Coll. Podiatric Medicine, Phila., 1976; BA, U. Pa., 1949, MD, 1953; MPH, Johns Hopkins U., 1961. Diplomate Am. Bd. Pediatrics, Am. Bd. Preventive Medicine. Pvt. practice pediatrics, 1956-60; dep. health commr. Phila. Dept. Pub. Health, 1964-71, 81-86, health commr., 1972-81; coord. Americans with Disabilities Act, Bucks County, 1993—2003; dir. Bucks County Health Dept., Pa., 1985—2003. Pres. Phila. Bd. Health; adv. bd. Mental Health and Mental Retardation; sec. Phila. Gen. Hosp. Bd., Phila. Nursing Home Bd.; chmn. Health Dept.'s Instnl. Rev. Bd. on Protection of Human Subjects, others; hosp. staff positions include Hosp. of U. Pa., 1956-74, Albert Einstein Med. Ctr., 1957-67, Germantown Hosp., 1956-59, Phila. Gen. Hosp., 1956-77; faculty U. Pa., 1955-76, Temple U., 1965-73, Bryn Mawr (Pa.) Grad. Sch., 1968-72, Hahnemann U., 1967-82, Thomas Jefferson U., 1956-59, 67-69, others; presenter in field. Past editorial bd.: Clinical Pediatrics; contbr. articles to profl. jours. V.p. Bucks County Com. for AIDS Edn., Phila. Regional AIDS Commn.; exec. com. Delaware Valley Ctr. for Health Care Info., others. Fellow Am. Acad. Pediatrics, Am. Pub. Health Assn., Am. Coll. Preventive Medicine, Coll. Physicians of Phila.; mem. Am. Acad. Health Adminstrn. (pres.), U.S. Conf. City Health Officers (trustee), Bucks County Med. Soc. (liaison bd. dirs.), Coll. Physicians of Phila. (gov. coun.), Phila. Pediatric Soc. (bd. dirs.), Phila. County Med. Soc. (bd. dirs. and various coms.), others. Home: Philadelphia, Pa. Died Oct. 24, 2009.

POMEROY, CHARLES WILSON, SR., civil engineer, consultant; b. Front Royal, Va., Nov. 5, 1936; s. Woodrow Wilson and Eula (Henry) P.; m. Aug. 8, 1964 (div.); children: Charles Wilson Jr., Sean Frank; m. Frances Gail Clifton, Jan. 31, 1998. BS, Va. Poly. Inst., Blacksburg, 1959; MS, Tex. A&M U., College Station, 1966; MBA, Auburn U., Ala., 1972. Registered profl. engr., Ohio, Va., Fla. Commd. USAF, 1972, advanced through grades to col., 1981, dep. chief staff, engr. Hdqs. ECC Ramstein AFB, Germany, 1975-79, chief force mgmt. Hdqs. TAC Langley AFB, Hampton, Va., 1979-81, base engr. Griffiss AFB Rome, N.Y., 1981-83, dir. force devel. Hqrs TAC Hampton, 1983-87; project engr. Hampton Roads Sanitation, Virginia Beach, Va., 1987-88; project engr., mgr. City of Hampton, 1988-92; dir. pub. utilities Town of Front Royal, Va., 1992-2000; ret., 2000. Decorated Legion of Merit, Bronze Star. Mem. NSPE, ASCE, Am. Water Works Assn., Am. Pub. Works Assn., Ret. Officers Assn. (pres. 1999-2000). Republican. Baptist. Avocations: genealogy, woodworking, antiques. Died July 24, 2008.

PONSETI, IGNACIO VIVES, orthopaedic surgery educator; b. Cuidadela, Balearic Islands, Spain, June 3, 1914; s. Miguel and Margarita (Vives) P.; 1 child, William Edward; m. Helena Percas, 1961. BS, U. Barcelona, 1930, MD, 1936, D honoris causa, 1984; LHD (hon.), U. Iowa, 2007. Instr. dept. orthopaedic surgery U. Iowa, 1944-57, prof., 1957—2009. Author papers and a book on cogenital and developmental skeletal deformities. Capt. M.C. Spanish Army, 1936-39. Recipient Kappa Delta award for orthopaedic rsch., 1955. Mem. Assn. Bone and Joint Surgeons, Am. Acad. Cerebral Palsy, Soc. Exptl. Biology and Medicine, Internat. Coll. Surgeons, N.Y. Acad. Sci., AMA (Ketoen gold medal 1960), Am. Acad. Orthopedic Surgeons, ACS, Am. Orthopedic Assn., Pediatric Orthopaedic Soc. (hon.), Iowa Med. Soc., Orthopedic Rsch. Soc. (Shands award 1975), Sigma Xi, Asociacion Argentina de Cirugia (hon.), Asociacion Balear de Cirugia (hon.), Sociedad de Cirujanos de Chile (hon.), Sociedad Espanola de Cirugia Ortopedica (hon.), Sociedad Brasilera de Ortopedia e Traumatologia (hon.). Home: Iowa City, Iowa. Died Oct. 18, 2009.

POOLE, KATHLEEN ZADA, corporate writer; b. Cheverlly, Md., Oct. 18, 1953; d. Archie F. and Zada M. (Hung) P. BS, U. Fla., 1975. Various nursing positions, 1975-80; freelance copywriter, 1980-83; community rels. dir. West Lake Hosp., Longwood, Fla., 1983-85; freelance corp. writer and indexer, from 1985. Contbr. articles to profl. jours. and numerous mags. Mem. Editl. Freelancers Assn., Sierra Club, Sigma Theta Tau. Avocations: kayaking, photography, backpacking, travel. Died May 23, 2008.

POORMAN, LAWRENCE EUGENE, physics educator; b. Ft. Wayne, Ind., July 27, 1926; s. John Emery and Rosa Maud (Tharp) P.; m. Anita Jane Short, Aug. 26, 1951; children: Kevin Lynn, Kyle Barrett. BS in Math. & Physics, Ball State U., 1950; MEd, Ind. U., 1953; MS in Physics, Purdue U., 1965; EdD in Sci. Edn., Ind. U., 1967. Elem. tchr. Salem (Ind.) Pub. Sch., 1950-51; sci, math. tchr. Jamestown (Ind.) Jr. Sr. High Sch., 1951-52; sci. tchr. Edinburg (Ind.) Pub. Sch., 1952-54; physics tchr. Columbus (Ind.) High Sch., 1954-60; instr. physics Ind. U., Bloomington, 1960-66; rsch. assoc. Harvard U., Cambridge, Mass., 1966-67; prof. physics Ind. State U., Terre Haute, 1967-91. Coun. mem. State Sci. Adv. Coun., Indpls., 1967-85; dir. Ind. Jr. Acad. Sci., 1970-78. Contbr. articles to profl. jours. With U.S. Army, 1944-46. Mem. NEA, NSTA (OHaus Outstanding Coll. Sci. Tchr. 1974), Am. Assn. Physics Tchrs, Hoosier Assn. Sci. Tchrs., Sch. Sci. & Math. Assn., Ind. Acad. Sci. (fellow). Avocations: fishing, gardening, reading. Died Feb. 18, 2008.

POPE, ALEXANDER H., retired lawyer; b. NYC, June 4, 1929; s. Clifford H. and Sarah H. (Davis) P.; m. Katherine Mackinlay, Sept. 14, 1985; children by previous marriage: Stephen C., Virginia L., Daniel M. AB with honors, U. Chgo., 1948, JD, 1952. Bar: Ill. 1952, Republic of Korea 1953, Calif. 1955, U.S. Supreme Ct. 1970. Pvt. practice, L.A., 1955-77, 87-96; assoc. David Ziskind, L.A., 1955; ptnr. Shadle, Kennedy & Pope, L.A., 1956, Fine & Pope, L.A., 1957-59, 61-77; legis. sec. to Gov. State of Calif., Sacramento, 1959-61; county assessor L.A. County, L.A., 1978-86; ptnr. Mayer, Brown & Platt, L.A., 1987-88, Barash & Hill, L.A., 1989-92; of counsel Seyforth, Shaw, Fairweather & Geraldson, L.A., 1993-96; exec. dir. Calif. citizens budget commn. Ctr. Govtl. Studies, L.A., 1997-2000. Nat. bd. mem. Vols. for Stevenson, 1952; vice-chmn. L.A. County Dem. Cen. Com., 1958-59; pres. Westchester Mental Health Clinic, 1963; mem. Calif. Hwy. Commn., 1966-70; mem. L.A. Bd. Airport Commrs., 1973-77, v.p., 1973-75, pres., 1975-76; trustee, sec. L.A. Theatre Ctr., 1984-89; trustee Spring St. Found., 1990-2004. With US Army, 1952—54, Mo., Korea. Mem. ACLU, U. Chgo. Alumni Clubs Greater L.A. and San Francisco Bay area (pres. 1970-71), Population Connection, Ams. United for Seperation of Ch. and State, Sierra Club, Common Cause, Order of Coif, Phi Beta Kappa. Democrat. Unitarian. Home: Berkeley, Calif. Died July 21, 2009.

POPECKI, JOSEPH THOMAS, library director, consultant; b. Saginaw, Mich., Nov. 25, 1924; s. Joseph Sebastian and Anna Pearl (Schreiber) P.; m. Jeanne Marie Gillespie, Jan. 29, 1949; children: Judith Marie Holmgren, Matthew Joseph, Mark Andrew, John Michael. BA, Sacred Heart Sem., 1945; MLS, Cath. U. Am., 1949. Various positions Cath. U. Am. Librs., Washington, 1947-58, 50-67, acting dir., 1965-67, lectr. grad. edn., 1950-67; founder, pres. Mid-Atlantic Assoc., Inc., Washington, 1960-67; lectr. libr. sci. Grad. Sch. USDA, Washington, 1950-67; dir. libr. St. Michael's Coll., Colchester, Vt., 1967-90; dir. emeritus, archivist St. Michael's Coll. Libr., Colchester, Vt., from 1990; coord. Elderhostel program St. Michael's Coll., Colchester, Vt., from 1990. Commr., chair Chittenden County Transp. Authority, Burlington, Vt., 1973-83; mem. adv. coun. Vt. Local Rds. Program, Colchester, 1982—; mem., chair Vt. Adv. Coun. for Hist. Preservation, Montpelier, Vt., 1969-77; trustee, sec. Burlington Coll., 1980—. Author: Near-Print Duplication, 1954, Union List Serials, Washington, D.C., 1967, Institutional Self-Study of Saint Michael's College, 1990, The Parish of St. Mark, Burlington, Vermont 1941-91, 1991; editor: Thesaurus, Nursing, Biomedical Lit., 1967; contbr. numerous articles to profl. jours. Clk. ward 4 City of Burington, 1987—; chair St. Michael's Coll., United Way Campaign, Colchester, 1982-89; mem. adv. coun. RSVP, Burlington; commr. Fletcher Free Libr. Bd., Burlington. Mem. Vt. Archeol. Soc., Inc. (treas., past pres. 1968—), Vt. Libr. Assn., Vt. New Eng. Libr. Assn., Am. Mgmt. Assn., Vt. Hist. Soc., New Eng. Archivists, Northwestern Vt. Model Railroading Soc. (sec.). Democrat. Roman Catholic. Avocations: photography, graphic arts, model making, woodworking, gardening. Home: Burlington, Vt. Died Jan. 14, 2008.

POPLIN, JOHN SMITH, JR., production designer, producer; b. Los Angeles, Nov. 18, 1920; s. John S. Sr. and Margaret (Hifner) P.; m. Mary Margaret Daly, Jan. 30, 1965. Student, Art Ctr. Sch., summer 1934, Chouinard Art Inst., 1936-47. Interior designer various residential and comml. projects; illustrator, designer Ind. Films, 1948-51; designer props and make-up 20th-Century Fox, 1952-56, Warner Bros., ind., 1957-59 and from 65; art dir., assoc. producer Daystar Prodns., 1960-64. Art dir., prodn. designer: (feature films) God's Little Acre, City of Fear, Tall Story, Studs Lonigan, The Couch, The Slender Thread (Oscar award nomination), A Fine Madness, The Great Bank Robbery, Kotch, The Great Santini, 35 others, (TV pilots) Stoney Burke, The Outer Limits (Emmy award nomination), Mr. Kingston, John Stryker, McKeever and the Colonel, (commls.) Pittsburgh Paint, All-American Soup (Cannes award), Absent Minded Waiter (Cannes award), (set and prodn. designs) Gentle Ben series, Night of Courage, (pilots) Lassie: A New Beginning, Man From Atlantis, Command Five. Served with U.S. Army, ETO. Mem. Soc. Motion Picture and TV Art Dirs., Internat. Alliance Theatrical Stage Employees (pres. art dirs. unit), Acad. Motion Picture Arts and Scis. Died Oct. 15, 2007.

POPOV, EGOR PAUL, retired engineering educator; b. Kiev, Russia, Feb. 19, 1913; s. Paul T. and Zoe (Derabin) P.; m. Irene Zofia Jozefowski, Feb. 18, 1939; children: Katherine, Alexander. BS with honors, U. Calif., 1933; MS, MIT, 1934; PhD in Civil Engring./Applied Mechs., Stanford U., 1946. Registered civil, structural and mech. engr., Calif. Structural engr., bldg. designer, LA, 1935-39; asst. prodn. engr. Southwestern Portland Cement Co., LA, 1939-42; machine designer Goodyear Tire & Rubber Co., LA, 1942-43; design engr. Aerojet Corp., Calif., 1943-45; asst. prof. civil engring. U. Calif. at Berkeley, 1946-48, assoc. prof., 1948-53, prof., 1953-83, prof. emeritus, from 1983, chmn. structural engring. and structural mechanics div., dir. structural engring. lab., 1956-60. Miller rsch. prof. Miller Inst. Basic Rsch. in Sci., 1968-69. Author: Mechanics of Materials, 1952, 2d edit., 1976, Introduction to Mechanics of Solids, 1968, Engineering Mechanics of Solids, 1990, 2d edit., 1999; contbr. articles profl. jours. Recipient Disting. Tchr. award U. Calif.-Berkeley, 1976-77, Berkeley citation U. Calif.-Berkeley, 1983, Disting. Lectr. award Earthquake Engring. Rsch. Inst., 1993, George W. Housner medal Earthquake Engring. Rsch. Inst., 1999. Fellow AAAS (assoc.), Am. Concrete Inst.; mem. NAE, Am. Soc. Metals, Internat. Assn. Shell Structures (hon. mem.), ASCE (hon. mem., Ernest E. Howard award 1976, J. James R. Cross medal 1979, 82, Nathan M. Newmark medal 1981, Raymond C. Reese rsch. prize 1986, Norman medal 1987, von Karman medal 1989), Soc. Exptl. Stress Analysis (Hetenyi award 1967, William M. Murray medallion 1986), Am. Soc. Engring. Edn. (Western Electric Fund award 1976-77, Disting. Educator award 1979), Soc. Engring. Sci., Internat. Assn. Bridge and Structural Engring., Am. Inst. Steel Constrn. (adv. com. specifications, Lifetime Achievement award 1999), Ukrainian Acad. Constrn. (fgn. mem.), Sigma Xi, Chi Epsilon, Tau Beta Pi. Home: Medford, Oreg. Died Apr. 19, 2001.

POPPOFF, ILIA GEORGE, science writer, consultant; b. San Diego, Apr. 9, 1924; s. George Ilia and Stamatka P.; m. Betty Ann Sieh, Oct. 19, 1944; children: Mark David, Robin Marie, Christine Lea. Student, San Diego State U., 1942-43; BA, Whittier Coll., Calif., 1947; postgrad., U. Calif., Berkeley, 1947-48, Stanford U., 1954-55. Radiol. physicist U.S. Naval Radiol. Def. Lab., San Francisco, 1948-53; chmn. atmospheric scis., sr. physicist Stanford Rsch. Inst., Menlo Park, Calif., 1953-67; chief stratospheric projects NASA/Ames Rsch. Ctr., Mt. View, Calif., 1967-79; freelance sci. writer Carnelian Bay, 1980-90, Pebble Beach, Calif., from 1990. Organizer, editor of proceedings, chmn. Mountain Watershed Symposium, Crystal Bay, Nev., 1988. Co-author: (monograph) Physics of the Lower Ionosphere; (textbook) Fundamentals of Aeronomy; editor proceedings Internat. Mountain Watershed Symposium, 1990; contbr. articles to profl. jours. Commr. Tahoe Regional Planning Agy. Adv. Planning Commn., Zephyr Cove, Nev., 1983—; bd. mem. Calif. Regional Water Quality Control Bd., South Lake Tahoe, Calif., 1984-95; bd. dirs., pres. Tahoe Resource Conservation Dist., South Lake Tahoe, 1982-88. Mem. AAAS, Am. Geophys. Union, Am. Cetacean Soc. Home: Pebble Beach, Calif. Died June 9, 2008.

PORTER, DONALD EARL, real estate agency owner; b. Beloit, Wis., Oct. 16, 1929; s. William Earl and Thelma Faire (Ewald) P.; m. Carol Mae Shoemaker, Mar. 7, 1954; children: David Earl, Pamela June. BS, U. Kans., 1953. Lic. real estate agt., Kans.; cert. real estate appraiser, Kans. Owner Porter Hotel, Beloit, Kans., 1958; owner, mgr. Coffee House, Beloit, 1958-63, Porter Co., Beloit, from 1964, Mitchell County Real Estate, Beloit, from 1968, Porter Farms, Beloit, from 1972; pres. Waconda Travel, Beloit, from 1983. Author: (stage play) Brown vs. Quantrill, 1986. Commr. City of Beloit, 1980-88. Mem.: Elks, Masons, Shriners. Republican. Lutheran. Avocations: travel, stamp collecting/philately. Home: Beloit, Kans. Died Oct. 5, 2007.

PORTER, SHEILA J., community health nurse, educator; b. Worcester, Mass., Apr. 6, 1943; d. Norman E. and Alice G. (Horgan) Walker; m. John F. Porter, Apr. 28, 1962; children: John F. Jr., William, Kevin, Amy. ASN, Quinsigamond Community Coll., Worcester, 1969; MA in Health Adminstrn., Framingham State Coll., Mass., 1984, BSN, 1987; MS in Ambulatory Care Nursing, U. Mass., 1989. RN, Mass.; cert. adult nurse practitioner. Staff nurse Westborough Nursing Home, Westboro, Mass., 1975-78; health asst. instr. Blackstone Valley Regional Vocat. High Sch., Upton, Mass., from 1990; staff nurse Upton Health Svc., 1975-81; town nurse, adminstr. Goldberg Med. Assocs., 1981-90; nurse practitioner, from 1990. HIV/AIDS educator ARC/Mass. Dept. Pub. Health, 1988—. Chairperson profl. edn. com. Milford chpt. Am. Cancer Soc. Mem. Am. assn. Diabetes Educators, Mass. Pub. Health Assn. Home: West Upton, Mass. Died Sept. 17, 2007.

POST, NATALIE JENKINS, recreational vehicle executive; b. Youngstown, Ohio, Aug. 6, 1932; d. Stanley E. and Mabel V. (Anderson) Jenkins; m. Wayne M. Post, Sept. 3, 1955; 4 children. AA, Santa Rosa Jr. Coll., Calif., 1952, diploma in nursing, 1953. RN, Ohio. Staff nurse Sonoma County Hosp., Santa Rosa, 1953-56, Doctor's Hosp., Columbus, Ohio, 1957-61; v.p. Post Industries, Inc., Columbus, from 1966. Singer Columbus Symphony Chorus, 1973-75, Silver Tones, Welsh Soc. Ctrl. Ohio, McKendree United Meth. Ch. Mem. Ctrl. Ohio Recreational Vehicle Dealers Assn., Avion Travelcade Club, Westerville RN Club, Ohio Starcraft Camper Club. Home: Columbus, Ohio. Died Nov. 27, 2007.

POSTON, ERSA HINES, management consultant, former state official; b. Paducah, Ky., May 3, 1921; d. Robert S. and Adele (Johnson) Hines. AB, Ky. State Coll., 1942; MSW, Atlanta U., 1946; LLD, Union Coll., 1971, Fordham U., 1978; DHL, Mercy Coll., 1980. Cmty. orgn. sec. Hartford Tb and Health Assn., Conn., 1946—47; teen-age program dir. Westside Br. YWCA, NYC, 1947—48, adult dir., 1948—49; asst. dir. Clinton Cmty. Ctr., NYC, 1949—50, dir., 1950—53; field sec. NYC Welfare and Health Coun., 1953—55; field project supr. NYC Youth Bd., 1955, asst. dir. program rev., 1955—57; area dir. NY State Divsn. Youth, 1957—62, youth work coord., 1962—64; confidential asst. Gov. Rockefeller, 1964; dir. NY State Office Econ. Opportunity, 1964—67; pres. NY State Civil Svc. Commn., 1967—75, commr., 1975—79; vice-chmn. US Merit Sys. Protection Bd., 1979—83; pres. Poston Pub. Pers. Mgmt. Cons., Chevy Chase, Md., 1983—2009; mem. Commn. Study Fgn. Svc. Pers. Sys., 1988—89; former mem. Internat. CSC, Nat. Commn. Study Goals State Colls. and Univs.; mem. adv. coun. Federally Employed Women; chmn. Pres.'s Adv. Coun. Intergovtl. Pers. Policy; trustee Med. Coll. Pa.; bd. dirs. Pub. Pvt. Ventures; v.p. Nat. Urban League; US del. UN Gen. Assembly, 1976; vice presiding officer US Commn. Observance Internat. Woman's Yr. Bd. govs. Albany Med. Ctr. Hosp.; bd. dirs. Whitney M. Young Meml. Found. Recipient Achievement awards, Bklyn. Club Nat. Assn. Negro Bus. and Profl. Women's Clubs, Phi Delta Kappa, Dutchess of Paducah award, Dau. of Paducah plaque, Disting. Alumni award, Ky. State Coll., Disting. Svc. award, Greater NY Chpt. Links, Woman of Yr. award, Cen. Jersey Club Nat. Assn. Negro Bus. and Profl. Women's Clubs, Populus Dei award, Mercy Coll., Woman of Yr. award, Utility Club, Outstanding Woman of Yr. award, Iota Phi Lambda, Nat. Achievement award, Nat. Assn. Negro BPW Clubs, 1967, Outstanding Svc. award, 26th A.D. Rep. Orgn. Queens County, Trail Blazer award, Jamaica Club Nat. Assn. Negro BPW Clubs, Benjamin Potoker Brotherhood award, 1970, Equal Opportunity Day award, Nat. Urban League, 1976, Spl. award, Psi Nu Chpt. Omega Psi Phi, 1977, Disting. Pub. Servant award, Capital Press Club, 1978, IPMA Stockberger award, Ottawa, Can., 1987, Founders' Day award, Alpha Kappa Alpha, 1978, award, Nat. Black Pers. Assn., 1978; named Ky. Col., Woman of Yr., BPW Club Albany, 1970; named to Women's Hall of Fame, NY, 1980. Mem.: Nat. Coun. Negro Women, Links, Girlfriends Inc., Nat. Acad. Public Adminstrn., Internat. Pers. Mgmt. Assn. (life; hon. mem., Exec. Bd. award Nat. Capital area 1979, Walter Stockberger award 1987), Alpha Kappa Alpha (Outstanding awards Bklyn. Chpt. 1960, 1965), Lambda Kappa Mu (hon. Achievement award Nu Chpt.). Died Jan. 7, 2009.

POUR-EL, MARIAN BOYKAN, mathematician, educator; b. NYC; d. Joseph and Mattie (Caspe) Boykan; m. Akiva Pour-El; 1 child. AB, Hunter Coll.; A.M., Harvard U., 1951, PhD, 1958. Prof. math. U. Minn., Mpls., 1968—2000, prof. emeritus, 2000—09. Mem. Inst. Advanced Study, Princeton, N.J., 1962-64; mem. coun. Conf. Bd. Math. Scis., 1977-82, lectr. internat. congresses in math. logic and computer sci., Eng., 1971, Hungary, 1967, Czech Republic, 1973, 1998, Germany, 1983, 96-97, Japan, 1985, 88, China, 1987; lectr. Polish Acad. Sci., 1974; lectr. Fed. Republic of Germany, 1980, 1983, 87, 89, 91, 96 Japan, 1985, 87, 90, 93, China, 1987, Sweden, 1983, 94, Finland, 1991, Estonia, 1991, Moscow, 1992, Amsterdam, 1992; mem. Fulbright Com. on Maths., 1986-89; invited spkr. Internat. Congress on Computability and Complexity Theory, Kazan U., Russia, 1997, Workshop on Computability and Complexity in Analysis, held in conjunction with 23rd Internat. Symposium on Math. Founds. of Computer Sci. and Computer Sci. Logic, Brno, Czech Republic, 1998, IEEE Workshop on Real Number Computation, 1998 Author: (with I. Richards) Computability in Analysis and Physics, 1989; contbr. articles to profl. jours. Named to Hunter Coll. Hall of Fame, 1975; NAS grantee, 1966. Fellow AAAS, Japan Soc. for Promotion of Sci.; mem. Am. Math. Soc. (coun. 1980-88, numerous com., spkr., orgn. spl. sessions on math. logic), Assn. Symbolic Logic, Math. Assn. Am. (nat. panel vis. lectr.), Phi Beta Kappa, Sigma Xi, Pi Mu Epsilon (mathematics), Sigma Pi Sigma (physics). Achievements include research in mathematical logic (theoretical computer science) and in computability and noncomputability in physical theory—wave, heat, potential equations, eigenvalues, eigenvectors. Died June 10, 2009.

POWELL, BILLY (WILLIAM NORRIS POWELL), musician; b. Corpus Christi, Tex., June 3, 1952; s. Donald and Marie Powell. Roadie with Lynyrd Skynyrd, 1970—72, keyboardist, 1972—77, 1987—2009, Alias, 1979, The Rossington-Collins Band, 1980—82, Allen Collins Band, 1983—85, Vision, 1985—87. Musician: (albums with Lynyrd Skynyrd) Pronounced Leh-Nerd Skin-Nerd, 1973, Second Helping, 1974, Nuthin' Fancy, 1975, Gimme Back My Bullets, 1976, One More from the Road, 1976, Street Survivors, 1977, Skynyrd's First And...Last, 1978, Gold and Platinum, 1979, Best of the Rest, 1982, Legend, 1987, Southern by the Grace of God, 1988, Skynyrd's Innyrds, 1989, Lynyrd Skynyrd 1991, 1991, The Last Rebel, 1993, Endangered Species, 1994, Southern Nights, 1996, Boxed Set, 1997, Whats Your Name, 1997, Old Time Greats, 1997, Twenty, 1997, The Essential Lynyrd Skynyrd, 1998, Skynyrd's First: The Complete Muscle Shoals Album, 1998, Edge of Forever, 1999, A Retrospective, 1999, 20th Century Masters: The Millenium Collection: The Best of Lynyrd Skynyrd, 1999, Solo Flytes, 1999, All-Time Greatest Hits, 2000, Christmas Time Again, 2000, Then and Now, 2000, Vicious Cycle, 2003, 'Thyrty: The 30th Anniversary Collection, 2003, Lynyrd Skynyrd Live: The Vicious Cycle Tour, 2004, Then and Now, Vol. 2, 2005, Greatest Hits, 2005, Lyve from Steel Town, 2007, (albums) (albums with Alias) Contraband, 1979, (albums with The Rossington-Collins Band) Anytime, Anyplace, Anywhere, 1980, (albums) This is the Way, 1982, (albums with The Allen Collins Band) Here, There & Back, 1983, (soundtracks) Freebird: The Movie, 1996; appeared in (concert films) Lynyrd Skynyrd Tribute Tour, 1988, Freebird: The Movie, 1996, Lyve From Steel Town, 1998, The Vicious Cycle Tour, 2004, Lynyrd Skynyrd: Live from Austin, TX, 2007. Named to The Rock and Roll Hall of Fame (as a member of Lynyrd Skynyrd), 2006. Died Jan. 28, 2009.

POWELL, CAROLYN WILKERSON, retired music educator; b. Hamburg, Ark., Oct. 9, 1920; d. Claude Kelly and Mildred (Hall) Wilkerson; m. Charles Luke Powell, Dec. 12, 1923; children: Charles Luke Jr., James Davis, Mark Wilkerson, Robert Hall. AB, Ctrl. Meth. U., Fayette, Mo., 1942; MA in Tchg., U. NC, 1970. Life tchg. cert. Mo., cert. tchr. N.C. Choral dir. Maplewood-Richmond Heights Sch., St. Louis, 1943-45; pvt. piano tchr. Greensboro, NC, 1951-63; organist Presbyn. and Meth. chs., Greensboro, 1950-61; dir. ch. youth choirs, Greensboro, 1958-61; choral and humanities tchr. Page HS, Greensboro, 1963-67; choral dir. Githens Jr. HS, Durham, NC, 1967-80; ret., 1980. Chmn. Choral Festival N.C. Dist., 1968—78; accompanist, music dir. Altavista (Va.) Little Theatre, 1981—83. Den mother Boy Scouts Am., Greensboro, 1951—57; mem. Chapel Hill Preservation Soc., NC, from 1985; vol., chapel organist, pediat. tutor U. NC Hosps., Chapel Hill, 1984—89; mem. Chapel Hill Hist. Soc.; Sunday and vacation schs. tchr., organist Grace Meth. Ch., Greensboro; organist St. Peter's Episcopal Ch., Altavista, 1981—83; organist Episcopal ch. svc. Carol Woods Retirement Cmty., Chapel Hill, from 1999. Mem.: AAUW, NEA, Classroom Tchrs. Assn., Am. Organists Guild, Music Educators Nat. Conf., Ackland Art Mus. Assn., Carolina Club, Nat. Federated Music Club Euterpe, Chapel Hill Country Club, Univ. Woman's Club, Delta Kappa Gamma. Avocations: reading, golf, needlecrafts, gardening, travel. Home: Chapel Hill, NC. Died Oct. 6, 2007.

POWELL, ELIZABETH PEARCE, artist, illustrator; b. Boston, July 23, 1930; d. Ralph Dewey and Eugenia Whitehead (Norris) P.; m. Arthur Polier, Sept. 17, 1955 (dec. Nov. 1986); children: Nicole,David, Elizabeth (dec.), Alison (dec.), Stephen; m. Richard M. Ohmann, July 20, 1990. BA, Oberlin Coll., 1952; MFA, Sch. Visual Arts, NYC, 1988. Art critic Park East, NYC, 1961-73; instr, adult edn. Stamford (Conn.) Bd. Edn., 1973-76; instr. painting, dioramas Stamford Mus. and Nature Ctr., 1973-76; CEO, sculptor, instr. Greenwich (Conn.) Art Barn, 1976-80; high sch. tchr. N.Y.C. Bd. Edn., 1985-86; office asst. Sch. Visual Arts, NYC, 1987-88, office asst. pres., 1988-90; free lance illustrator Middletown, Conn., from 1990; art dir. Radical Tchr. Collective, from 1994. Instr. Wesleyan U. Grad. Liberal Studies Program, Middletown, 1992. Illustrator: (book) Citizenship, 1990. Chair marriage and divorce com. NOW, N.Y.C., 1971-73. Mem. Graphic Artists Guild. Democrat. Avocations: gardening, fine arts, water colors, wood sculpture, colored pencil. Died Sept. 15, 2007.

POWELL, JODY (JOSEPH LESTER POWELL JR.), public relations executive, former White House press secretary; b. Vienna, Ga., Sept. 30, 1943; s. Joseph Lester and June Marie (Williamson) P.; m. Nan Sue Jared, Apr. 23, 1966; 1 child, Emily Claire. Student, USAF Acad., 1961-64; BA in Polit. Sci., Ga. State U., 1966; post grad., Emory U., 1967-70. Press sec. Gov. Jimmy Carter, Atlanta, 1971-74, 75-76, Pres. Jimmy Carter, The White House, Washington, 1977-81; columnist Los Angeles Times Syndicate, 1982-87; news analyst ABC News, Washington, 1982-87; prof. Boston Coll., 1985-86; chmn., CEO Powell Adams & Rinehart, Washington, 1987-91, Powell Tate, Washington, 1991-99, Weber Shandwick Pub. Affairs, 1999—2009. Author: The Other Side of the Story, 1984; narrator: (documentaries) The Civil War, 1990, Baseball, 1994 Bd. advisors Spl. Ops. Warrior Found. Baptist. Avocations: golf, tennis, hunting, fishing, civil war history. Died Sept. 14, 2009.

POWELL, MARY FRANCES, media center coordinator; b. Shawnee, Okla., June 22, 1949; d. Archer I. and Mary Louise (Torian) Coppedge; m. Earl L. Powell, Dec. 30, 1971. BA, Okla. Bapt. U., 1971; M in Libr. Sci., U. Okla., 1973. Cert. tchr., Okla., libr. Okla. Libr. Norman (Okla.) Pub. Libr.; media ctr. coordinator Gordon Cooper Area Vocat. Sch., Shawnee, Okla., from 1975-. Bd. dirs. McLoud Friends of Libr., Pioneer Multi-County Libr. Treas., chair. Pott County Dem. Precinct, McLoud, Okla. Mem. Am. Vocat. Assn., U.S. Forum Com., Okla. Edn. Assn., Nat. Edn. Assn., Okla. Libr. Assn., Okla. Vocat. Assn. (pres. spl. needs personnel 1991, sec. 1989, treas. 1988), Delta Kappa Gamma (pres. Alpha Beta chpt.). Methodist. Avocations: travel, reading, camping. Home: Mcloud, Okla. Died May 13, 2008.

POWELL, WILLIAM ARNOLD, JR., retired bank executive; b. Verbena, Ala., July 7, 1929; s. William Arnold and Sarah Frances (Baxter) Powell; m. Barbara Ann O'Donnell, June 16, 1956; children: William Arnold III, Barbara Calhoun, Susan Thomas, Patricia Crain. BSBA, U. Ala., 1953; grad., La. State U. Sch. Banking of South, 1966. With Am. South Bank, N.A., Birmingham, Ala., 1953—93, asst. v.p., 1966, v.p., 1967, v.p., br. supr., 1968—72, sr. v.p., br. supr., 1972—73, exec. v.p., 1973—79, pres., 1979—83, vice chmn. bd., 1983—93; pres. AmSouth Bancorp., 1979—93; ret., 1993. Bd. dirs. AmSouth Bank, Fla. Bd. dirs. United Way Found.; past pres. United Way, campaign chmn., 1987; life mem. Birmingham Met. Devel. Bd.; bd. dirs. Warrior-Tombigbee Devel. Assn.; life trustee Ala. Ind. Colls.; pres.'s coun. U. Ala., Birmingham, life bd. visitors. Lt. US Army, 1954—56. Named William A. Powell, Jr. Endowed Professorship in his honor, U. Ala. Mem.: Met. Devel. Assn. (life; bd. dirs.), Birmingham Area C. of C. (life; bd. dirs.), Birmingham Country Club, The Club, Mountain Brook. Home: Birmingham, Ala. Died Aug. 22, 2009.

POWER, JUANA VICTORIA, social worker, psychotherapist; b. La Paz, Bolivia, Mar. 14, 1961; came to U.S., 1988; d. Salvador Elias and Marina Maria (Aburdene) Asbun; m. Michael Paul Power, Nov. 11, 1988; children: Jessica Valerie, Monica Priscilla Power-Asbun. BS in Clin. Psychology, Universidad Catolica, La Paz, Bolivia, 1988; MA in Marriage and Family Therapy, So. Conn. State U., 1997. Lic. marriage and family therapist, Conn. Clin. psychologist, La Paz, 1983-86; marriage and family therapist Cath. Family Svcs., New Haven, Conn., 1993-97, psychotherapist, from 1997. Bus. dir. Hi Andes, Clinton, Conn., 1997-99. Fellow Am. Assn. for Marriage and Family Therapy. Home: Clinton, Conn. Died Sept. 21, 2007.

POWER, JULES, television producer; b. Hammond, Ind., Oct. 19, 1921; s. Paul and Mary Pewowar; m. Dorothy Kutchinsky; children: Robert, Robin. Grad. with honors (Hardy scholar in speech and communications), Northwestern U., 1944. Chmn. Power-Rector Prodns., Inc.; pres. Jules Power Prodns. Sr. producer AM America, ABC-TV; prodr. (TV series) Watch Mr. Wizard, NBC-TV, 1951-61; exec. prodr.' TV show ABC-TV News and Pub. Affairs; creator, exec. producer TV prodn. Discovery, 1962-71; TV spl. How Life Begins, 1968, The Unseen World, 1970; producer ABC-TV series AM America, 1975; exec. producer TV series Over Easy, Pub. Broadcasting System, 1976-83; producer The Scheme of Things, Disney TV Channel, 1983, ednl. films for ABC-McGraw-Hill, Bits, Bytes and Buzzwords, PBS, 1983, State of the Lang., PBS, 1983; author: How Life Begins. Pub. info. advisor Buck Ctr. for Aging Rsch. Served with USAAF, World War II. Recipient 3 network Emmy awards, 11 Emmy nominations; Peabody award (2); Thomas Alva Edison award (3); Ohio State award (6); Am. Film Festival 1st place award (2), Internat. Film and TV Festival award (4); Hammond (Ind.) Ann. Achievement award, 1985. Mem. NATAS (past nat. vice-chmn., past pres. N.Y. chpt.), Writers Guild Am. East, Phi Beta Kappa. Home: Pikesville, Md. Died Oct. 9, 2009.

POWER, THOMAS EDWARD, insurance brokers, consultant; b. Barton, Vt., May 27, 1946; s. Richard Bertrand and Dorothy Hectorine (Currier) P.; m. Sheila Ann Pitt, Sept. 17, 1966; children: Thomas E., James R., Emily M. BS, U. Hartford, 1974. Analyst new. bus. Conn. Gen. Life, Bloomfield, 1967-71, underwriter group ins., 1971-77, sr. account exec. Springfield, N.J., 1977-84; v.p. sales CIGNA Employee Benefits, Atlanta, 1984-92; v.p. Willis Carroon, Dublin, Ohio, 1992-94; pres. T.E. Power and Co., Inc., Dublin, from 1995. Republican. Roman Catholic. Avocations: gardening, photography, woodshop, golf, personal computer. Died Jan. 5, 2008.

POZDRO, JOHN WALTER, retired music educator, composer; b. Chgo., Aug. 14, 1923; s. John and Rose Anna P.; m. Shirley Allison Winans, June 12, 1954; children— John Winans, Nancy Allison Thellman. Student, Am. Conservatory Music, Chgo., 1941-42; B.M. in Music, Northwestern U.-Evanston, Ill., 1948, M.M. in Music, 1949; PhD in Music, Eastman Sch. Music, 1958. Instr. Iowa State Tchrs. Coll., Cedar Falls, 1949-50; instr. to assoc. prof. U. Kans., Lawrence, 1950-64, prof. music, 1964-93, dir. theory and composition, 1961-88; ret., 1993; teaching fellow Eastman Sch. Music, Rochester, NY, 1956-57. Chmn. symposium com. U. Kans., Lawrence, 1958-69. Representative works include Third Symphony, 1960, Piano Sonata No. 4, 1976, Malooley & Fear Monster, 1977, Impressions, Winds, Piano, 1984, Tryptich for Carillon, 1996, the Spirit of Mt. Oread, 1989. Winds of Autumn, 1996. Served with U.S. Army, 1943-46. Recipient U. Calif. Berkeley medal for Disting. Svc., 1993; grantee Ford Found., 1960, Nat. Endowment Arts, 1976; nominated for Pulitzer prize in Music, 1960. Mem. ASCAP, Pi Kappa Lambda. Presbyterian. Avocations: golf, photography, writing. Home: Lawrence, Kans. Died Jan. 1, 2009.

PRAEUNER, HOWARD MYLAN, farmer; b. Battle Creek, Nebr., Oct. 23, 1932; s. John M. and Lydia M. (Hohenstein) P.; m. Phyllis J. Glandt, May 27, 1956; children: Wendy, Wade, Wanda. Student, Midland Coll., 1950-52. Bd. dirs. Battle Creek Coop., vice-chmn., 1984-87, chmn. bd., from 1987. Bd. dirs. Luth. Community Hosp., Norfolk, Nebr., 1985—, chmn. bd. 1989—, vice chmn. 1986-89. Recipient Farmland Ind. Dir. Leadership award, 1974. Republican. Avocations: golf, reading. Home: Battle Creek, Nebr. Died May 24, 2008.

PRASAD, SHARAD, engineering executive; b. New Delhi, Apr. 30, 1956; s. Gurdayal and Saroj (Gupta) P.; m. Elizabeth Jane Beek, Apr. 24, 1988; children: Tanya Vrinda, Krishna Niel. BSc, U. Bombay, India, 1976; Diploma in Engring., U. Erlangen/Nueremberg, Germany, 1982; PhD, U. Hannover, Germany, 1988. Rsch. asst. U. Hannover, 1985-89; supr. failure analysis LSI Logic Corp., Milpitas, Calif., 1989-92, staff engr. interconnect rsch., 1992-94, supr. tech. devel., 1994-95, mgr. R&D, from 1995. Editor: Microelectronics Manufacturing, 1996, Yield, Reliability and Failure Analysis, 1997. Mem. IEEE, SPIE (mem. tech. program com. microelectronic mfg. 1994-95, chmn. 1996—). Achievements include 2 patents. Died Nov. 1, 2007.

PRATT, ARTHUR D., printing company executive; b. Indpls., May 7, 1924; s. Arthur D. and Helen L. (Rikhoff) P.; m. Marjorie M. Zwally May 19, 1967 (div. Mar. 1974; m. Amal Marcos, Apr. 11, 1987; children: Margaret, Michael, Sarah, Andrew. Student, Sorbonne U., Paris, 1947. Pres. Found. Internat. Econ. Devel., 1949-56, Life Effectiveness Tng., Indpls., 1969-93, Pratt Printing Co., Indpls., 1972-93. Author: The Party's Over, 1976, Christ and America's Survival, 1977, The Great Idea of God, 1984, How to Help and Understand the Alcoholic, 1987, Christian Revolution, 1996, (poetry) (with Amal Pratt) The Meeting of East and West. Pres. Flynn Christian Fellowship Houses Inc., 1956-94, Cmty. Interfaith Housing Inc., 1966-73, Madras Coun., 1974-79. Mem. Athenaeum Club. Episcopalian. Home: Indianapolis, Ind. Died Jan. 23, 2008.

PRENZLOW, ELMER JOHN-CHARLES, JR., minister; b. Norfolk, Nebr., Apr. 4, 1929; s. Elmer Edward and Alvina C. (Henning) P.; m. Karen McHarg DeMoss, July 4, 1980; 1 child, Elmer Carl III. BA, Northwestern Coll., Watertown, Wis., 1950; BD in Theology, WELS Luth. Sem., Mequon, Wis., 1953; MA in English and Philosophy, U. Minn., 1961; MS in Edn. Psychology, U. Wis., 1969; PhD in Psychology and Criminal Justice, Walden U., 1975. Pastor St Paul's Lutheran Ch., Bloomer, Wis., 1953-62; chaplain, instr. U. Wis., Milw., 1962-79; dir. devel. and pub. relations Luth. Ch.-Mo. Synod, Southern Wis. Dist., Milw., 1979-82; major gifts counselor Luth. Ch.-Mo. Synod Internat. Hdqrs., St. Louis, 1982-88; dir. devel. and fin. resources Adult Christian Edn. Found. Bethel Series, Madison, Wis., 1988-89; world relief devel. counselor Luth. Ch.-Mo. Synod Internat. Hdqrs., St. Louis, 1989-94; v.p. major gifts Luth. Ch.-Mo. Synod Found., St. Louis, 1994-98; spl. asst. to pres. Luth. World Relief, NYC, from 1998. Vice chmn. Standing Com. Dept. Campus Ministry Luth. Coun. U.S.A., N.Y., 1964-83; chmn. Milw. Religious Counselors, 1965-72, dept. humanities Spencerian Bus. Coll., 1967-77; v.p. Patricia Stevens Career Coll., bd. dirs. 1978-91; spkr., lectr. in field. Contbr. articles to profl. jours. Mem. Wis. State Legis. Com for Kerner Report, Madison, 1968-69, Nat. Adv. Commn.U.S. Justice Dept. on Law Enforcement standards and goals, Washington, 1971-73, ad hoc com. for establishing U.S. Bur. Prisons Nat. Inst. for Corrections, Washington, 1973-75, 19th congr. dist. Wis. svc. acad. review bd., Milw., 1975-82; sub. pastor for vacations in North dist. of Lutheran Ch.-Mo. Synod, 1998-2004. Named Outstanding Prof. Spencerian Bus. Coll., Milw., 1972. Mem. Assn. of Luth. Devel. Execs., Optimists, Wis. Club, Lions Club. Republican. Avocations: travel, music, auto racing, golf, fishing. Deceased.

PRESTON, CHARLES MCDOWELL, III, telecommunication engineer; b. Atlanta, July 15, 1944; s. Charles McDowell Preston Jr. and Shirley S. Smith; 1 child, Kasandra. BS in Engring. Tech., DeVry Inst. Tech., 1976. Electric costume designer Hair, NYC, 1967-71; rec. engr. United Rec. Studios, NYC, 1968-70, Wally Heider Rec., San Francisco, 1970-73; crew lighting and sound engr. Grateful Dead-Rowan Bros., San Francisco, 1971-73; chief broadcast engr. Sta. WZGC-FM, Atlanta, 1976-78, Stas. WWGS and WCUP-FM, Tifton, Ga., 1979-80; chief contract engr. various AM radio stas., Atlanta, 1973-78; contract CATV engr. Cable Am., Atlanta, 1976-79; chief engr. TelePrompter CATV, Yucca Valley, Calif., 1980-81; sr. tech. engr. Valley Cable TV, Chatsworth, Calif., 1981-84, MediaOne, Atlanta, from 1986. Author: Amateur Radio Satellite Log Book, 1988; various inventions. With USN, 1962-65. Recipient Outstanding Work award AMSAT, 1989. Mem. Soc. Am. Magicians, Soc. Cable TV Engrs. (1st v.p. 1986—), Internat. Brotherhood Magicians, Internat. Magicians Soc., Ga. Magic Club (Blue Pen award 1995), Magic Castle (video com.) Avocations: woodworking, computers, amateur radio. Home: Lawrenceville, Ga. Died June 10, 2008.

PRESTON, PATRICIA ANN, language educator, researcher; b. Milw., Mar. 11, 1933; d. Charles Francis Preston, Dorothy Catherine Engman. BA in Spanish magna cum laude, Bryn Mawr Coll., 1955; MA in Spanish, Cath. U. Am., 1961, PhD in Spanish, 1964. Joined Sch. Sisters of Notre Dame. Prof. emerita Spanish and bilingual edn. Mt. Mary Coll., Milw., 1964—2005, acad. dean, 1971—76, 1984—92, dir. Ctr. for Assessment, 1998—2004. Founder, dir. Project Head Start Coun. for the Spanish Speaking, Milw., 1965—71, founder, dir. Guadalupe Ctr., 1966—71; cons., in-svc. trainer Milw. Pub. Schs. Bilingual Program & other local and regional schools and districts, Milw., Waukesha, Kenosha, Wis., from 1969; mem. corp. bd. Mt. Mary Coll., Milw., 1971—96; co-founder, bd. dirs. Milw. Spectrum Alternative H.S., 1972—95; cons., examiner North Ctrl. Assn. Colls., Chgo., 1974—77; co-rschr. Cath. Colls. Milw., 1981; vis. prof. English Notre Dame Women's Coll., Kyoto, 1990. Author: (Book) A Study of Significant Variants in the Poetry of Gabriela Mistral, 1964; contbr. Book Wagering on Transcendence, 1997. Active mem. Coun. on Urban Edn., Milw., 1965—68; apptd. mem. Wis. State Day Care Adv. Bd., Madison, 1967—70; chairperson, bd. dirs. Coun. for the Spanish Speaking, Milw., 1970—74; chairperson Project Head Start Coalition Bd., Milw., 1970—74; bd. dirs. Cath. Social Svcs., Milw., 1971—76; mem. edn. commn. Wis. Cath. Conf., Madison, 1975—79; apptd. mem. Wis. State Adv. Com. on Bilingual-Bicultural Edn., Madison, 1978—82. Recipient Edn.: A Family Affair award of excellence, U. Wis.-Milw., Milw. Pub. Schs., Wis. Dept. Pub. Edn., 1999, Profl. Excellence award, Wis. Assn. of Fgn. Lang. Tchrs., 2004; fellow, Woodrow Wilson Found., 1960—61, 1963—64, Fellow, Summer Seminar in Spain, Fulbright Found., 1966, Summer Seminar Fellow - Bilingualism, NEH, 1977, Summer Seminar Fellow - European Autobiography, 1993. Mem.: TESOL, Am. Nystagmus Network, Nat. Assn. for Bilingual Edn., Wis. Assn. Fgn. Lang. Tchrs., Am. Assn. for Tchrs. of Spanish and Portuguese. Avocation: active advocate for disabled, mentally ill, poor, under-educated persons, immigrants, children and youth. Died Jan. 12, 2008.

PRICE, CHRISTOPHER ELDREGE, aerospace engineer, consultant; b. Ottumwa, Iowa, Sept. 18, 1944; s. Warren Eldrege and Muriel Maxine (Jones) P.; m. Francis Paul, Nov. 15, 1970 (div. Mar. 1974); m. Gail Joyce Goodman, Aug. 4, 1984; 1 child, Gregory. BSEE, U. Neb., 1967; MS in Computer Sci., West Coast U., 1977. Engr., scientist McDonnell Douglas, Long Beach, Calif., 1967-73; tech. staff Rockwell Internat., Downey, Calif., from 1973. Bd. dirs. Bd. Realtors, Sacramento, 1981—. Mem. Mensa. Avocations: real estate, auto racing, sports cars. Home: Buena Park, Calif. Died Aug. 7, 2007.

PRICE, HARRY STEELE, III, corporate executive; b. Dayton, Ohio, Apr. 19, 1938; s. Harry Steele Jr. and Janet (Smith) P.; m. Valerie Knost, Aug. 29, 1961; children: Harry Steele IV, Paul Tobin. Student, Brown U., 1957-59; BSCE, U. Cin., 1966, MBA, 1967. Div. mgr. Price Bros. Co., Dayton, 1972-79; pres. EWP Corp., Wilmington, Ohio, 1979-81; exec. v.p. ACTS-BSC Inc., Plymouth, Mich., 1985-86, also bd. dirs.; pres. Flexiblast Co., Wilmington, from 1981, also bd. dirs. Inventor descaling machine, wire guide aparatus. Grad. Leadership Dayton, 1978; community adv. counsel Sycamore Hosp., Miamisburg, Ohio, former mem. Kettering Med. Assocs. Mem. Wire Assn. Internat. (continuing edn. com. 1986—), Wire Reinforcement Inst. (chmn. 1980-81). Clubs: Miami Valley Hunt (Spring Valley, Ohio), Camargo Hunt (Cinn.), Dayton Racquet. Lodges: Rotary (bd. dirs. Wilmington club 1981). Avocations: golf, skiing, sailing, foxhunting. Home: Scottsdale, Ariz. Died Jan. 9, 2008.

PRICE, JOHNNIE ULMER, retired music educator; b. North, SC, Jan. 8, 1929; d. John Shadrach and Mary Annie (Varn) Ulmer; m. Coker Nelson Price, Sr., June 21, 1951; children: Coker Nelson Jr., Joanne Price Glover, Donna Kay Price Peterson. BSc, Winthrop U., 1949; M in Music Edn., U. S.C., 1977. Ordained deacon First Baptist Ch., 1995; cert. elem. and secondary music tchr. SC. Music tchr. Whitmire (S.C.) Pub. Schs., 1949—51, Orangeburg (S.C.) Dist. 5 Schs., 1952—86; ret., 1986. Organist 1st Bapt. Ch., Orangeburg, 1955—57. Mem.: SC Music Educators Assn. (pres. choral divsn. 1980—82, mem. exec. bd. 1980—2005, v.p.choral divsn. 1982—84, editor state jour. 1986—97, ret. mems. chmn. 1997—2004, Hall of Fame 1998), Orangeburg Music Club (state bd. dirs. from 2000, pres. 2006), Delta Kappa Gamma (pres. 1980—82, com. chmn. music 2000—04). Avocations: gardening, travel, genealogy, reading. Home: Orangeburg, SC. Died Apr. 18, 2008.

PRICE, MARILYNN MATLOCK, retired elementary school educator; b. Spokane, Wash., Aug. 20, 1916; d. Jesse William and Mary Frances (Harlow) Matlock; m. Robert Edgar Price, July 17, 1938 (dec. May, 1979); children: Robert Dale, Charlotte Lee Price Wirfs, Carla Jean Price Perkins. Grad., Oreg. Normal Sch., 1936; BS, Oerg. Coll. Edn., 1971. Cert. tchr. Tchr. Tub Springs Sch., Oreg., 1937-38; tchr. grades 1-4 Peedee (Oreg.) Sch., 1942-43; phys. edn. tchr. Dallas (Oreg.) Jr. High Sch., 1943-45, 49-52; tchr. 5th grade Florence (Oreg.) Elem. Sch., 1953-56; tchr. 6th grade Bay City (Oreg.) Elem. Sch., 1958-60, East Sch., Tillamook, Oreg., 1962-82, 1982. Mem. AAUW, Tillamook Hist. Soc., Oreg., DAR (regent Tillamook chpt. 1989-93), Ret. Tchrs. Assn. (sec. 1982-91), Delta Kappa Gamma (pres. Alpha Gamma chpt. 1985-89). Avocations: knitting, crochet, reading, walking. Died Sept. 12, 2007.

PRIDDY, DOTTIE, state legislator; b. 1935; Former state rep. Dist. 45, Ky.; former chmn. Judiciary-Criminal Com.; house rep. Ky. Mem.: Fairdale Steering Com., Okolona Merchants and Businessmen's Assn., Okolona & Pleasure Ridge Women's Club, Ky. Businesswomen's Assn. Democrat. Baptist. Died June 30, 2008.

PRIMEAU, STEPHEN JOSEPH, nuclear engineer; b. Beeville, Tex., Oct. 7, 1959; s. Don Gene and Mary Jane (Coyne) P.; m. Eun Kyong Cho, Sept. 30, 1989. BS in Nuclear Engring., U. Va., 1981; MS in Nuclear Engring., MIT, 1983. Lic. profl. engr., Va. Mem. profl. staff Ctr. for Naval Analyses, Alexandria, Va., 1983-84; mem. tech. staff Eagle Rsch. Group, Inc., Arlington, Va., 1984-89, project leader Germantown, Md., 1989-94, mgr. Germantown ops., from 1994. Recipient Sherman R. Knapp fellowship in nuclear power engring. MIT, 1981. Mem. NSPE, Am. Nuclear Soc., Tau Beta Pi. Republican. Roman Catholic. Home: Springfield, Va. Died June 28, 2008.

PRINCE, SIDNEY, financial planning executive, broker; b. NYC, June 15, 1923; s. Marcus and Mollie (Bartel) P.; m. Adele Zweben, June 1, 1946; children: Richard Eric, Jeffrey Mark, Denise Robin. BS, L.I. U., 1943. Cert. investment specialist. Life underwriter Penn. Mut. Life Ins., Ridgewood, N.J., 1965-69, staff mgr. Orlando, Fla., 1969-70; pres., chief exec. officer Sid Prince & Assoc., Inc., Winter Park, Fla., from 1970. Pres. S.P. & Assocs, Inc. Fin. Services, Winter Park. Pres. Life Underwriter Tng. Council, Orlando, Fla., 1978-79. Fellow Nat. Assn. Life Underwriters; mem. Nat. Assn. Security Dealers, Fla. Assn. Life Underwriters, Internat. Assn. Registered Fin. Planners (treas. Orlando chpt. 1985—, designated RFP), Tuskawilla Country Club, Mercedes Benz Club (Orlando) (pres. 1985-86), Masons (32 degree) Shriners, Kiwanis (pres. Ctrl. Fla. chpt. 1980-81, Kiwanian of Yr. 1977). Avocations: fishing, gardening, orchid culture, travel, photography. Home: Winter Park, Fla. Died Dec. 4, 2007.

PRIOR, OLE, civil engineer; b. Aalborg, Denmark, Nov. 24, 1935; came to U.S., 1974; s. Helge and Mimi (Munck) P.; m. Margaret Bryant Hope, Dec. 14, 1967; 1 child, Ingrid Hope. MCE, The Tech. Univ. of Denmark, Copenhagen, 1960. Registered profl. engr., Denmark. Sales engr. F.L. Smidth & Co., Copenhagen, 1962-64, 66-67, Madrid, 1964-66, gen. mgr. Mexico City, 1970-74, export sales mgr. Creshill, N.J., 1974-77, sales dir., 1978-82, regional mgr. Atlanta, 1983-86; resident engr. Loma Negra, Buenos Aires, 1968-69; exec. v.p. Gunold & Stickma of Am., Marietta, Ga., 1986-89, pres., from 1989. Home: Fairhope, Ala. Died May 22, 2008.

PRITCHETT, ALLEN MONROE, III, healthcare administrator; b. St. Louis, June 29, 1949; s. Allen M. Jr. and Jane (Baird) P.; m. Linda Jasper (div. Apr. 1980); 1 child, Brett A. (dec.). AA, Meramec Coll., 1969; BS, U. Mo., 1971; MA, Webster U., 1978. Tchr. social studies Union (Mo.) High Sch., 1971-77; mgr. edn. and tng. Luth. Med. Ctr., St. Louis, 1977-78, asst. dir. human resources, 1978-81; dir. pers. Grandpa John's, Inc., Murphysboro, Ill., 1981-82; mgmt. instr. So. Ill. U., Carbondale, 1982-84; dir. human resources Meml. Hosp., Carbondale, 1984-93; v.p. So. Ill. Hosp. Svcs., Carbondale, 1993-95; pres. Pritchett/Baird Assocs., 1995-97; chief human resources officer Sparta (Ill.) Cmty. Hosp., from 1997. Mem. coun. on healthcare human resources Ill. Hosp. Assn., 1991-93; bd. dirs. So. Ill. Regional Social Svcs., Inc., 1994-97, sec./treas., 1996-97 Mem. bus. adv. com. Carbondale Cmty. H.S., 1984-95; mem. So. Ill. Bus./Employer Advisors, Carbondale, 1984-99; mem. Carbondale Postal Customer Adv. Coun., 1995-96; mem. human resources adv. bd. Commerce Clearing House, 1995-96. Mem. So. Ill. Healthcare Human Resources Assn. (pres. 1987-88, 90-91, exec. com. 1986—, sec. 1986-87), Am. Soc. Healthcare Human Resources Adminstrn. (pres. So. Ill. chpt. 1987-88, 90-91), Soc. for Human Resource Mgmt., Am. Coll. Healthcare Execs. (diplomate), Carbondale C. of C. (bd. dirs. 1995-96). Avocations: exercise, running, reading. Home: Du Quoin, Ill. Died Jan. 16, 2008.

PRIVITERA, JOHN NATHAN, corporate executive; b. Buffalo, July 27, 1944; s. James Francis and Marjorie Elaine (Sparks) P.; m. Lorraine Rheta Atherton, Dec. 30, 1977; children: Kristin, Noel. BS, LeMoyne Coll., Syracuse, NY, 1966; MS, Niagara U., NY, 1971; MBA, York Coll., U. Balt., 1981. Mgr. safety, sec. TRW, Jamestown, N.Y., 1966-67; plant personnel mgr. RJR Ind., Cambridge, Md., 1967-72; dist. personnel mgr. Sealtest div. Kraft, Balt., 1972-77; corp. labor rels. mgr. Dentsply Internat., York, Pa., 1977-79; mgr. employee rels. Continental Group, Greenwich, Conn., 1979-81; dir. indsl. rels. Clevepak Corp., White Plains, N.Y., 1981-85; v.p. human resources Union Corp., Pitts., 1985-86; sr. ptnr. J.T. Knowlton Assocs., Red Lion, Pa., from 1986. Instr. U. Balt., 1971-73; charter mem. Nat. Task Force for Protective Svcs., Wyncote, Pa., 1988—. Author: Productivity Improvement, 1991; columnist Security Mag., Bus. Mo. of Cen. Pa., 1987—. Bd. dirs. York Coll. Alumni Bd., 1988-89. Mem. ASTD, Indsl. Rels. Rsch. Assn., Soc. Human Resources Mgmt. (pres. 1971-72). Republican. Roman Catholic. Avocations: landscaping, cooking. Home: San Antonio, Tex. Died Dec. 11, 2007.

PROCUNIER, STELLA MARY STASIA, critical care nurse; b. Flint, Mich., Sept. 1, 1943; d. Chester J. and Helen Wanda (Kempisty) Bandurski; children: David, Mark. ADN, Flint Community Jr. Coll., 1970; BSN, U. Mich., 1980; MSN, U. Hawaii, 1990. RN, Mich., Hawaii, Nev., Fla., Wash., Calif. Staff-charge nurse ICU and adult psychiatry unit Hurley Med. Ctr., Flint, 1970-74, charge-staff nurse Franklin Wade regional burn unit, 1979-86, asst. dir. nursing, 1985-86; staff-charge nurse burn unit Straub Clinic and Hosp., Honolulu, 1986-91; critical care nurse, 1994-95; staff nurse cardiac progressive care Wm. Beaumont Hosp., Royal Oak, Mich., from 1995. Mem. AACN (treas. Hawaiian Islands chpt. 1990), Am. Burn Assn., Am. Trauma Soc., Sigma Theta Tau. Home: Auburn Hills, Mich. Died May 2, 2008.

PRODAN, JOHN, aviation executive; b. Orange, NJ, Nov. 17, 1924; s. Vasile and Cleda Blanche (Neville) P.; m. Ruth Jennie Larson, Dec. 29, 1945; children: Susan Ruth, Robert John, John Vernon, Donald Albert, Karen Ruth, Nancy Ann. BS in Aero. Engring., U. Ill., 1948; MS in Aero. Engring., MS in Instrumentation Engring., U. Mich., 1954; MBA, UCLA, 1980. Registered comml. pilot, cert. flight instr. Commd. 2d lt. USAF, 1943, advanced through grades to lt. col., 1966, squadron commdr. and asst. dep. wing commdr. Vietnam, 1971-72, asst. program dir. and mgr. shuttle program Los Angeles, 1972-74, ret., 1974; research pilot and engr. S.D. Sch. Mines and Tech., Rapid City, 1978-80; chief test pilot, sr. engr. Kohlman Systems Research, Lawrence, Kans., 1982-84; pres., chief engr. AV-CON, Rapid City, from 1980; sr. v.p. Highland Mfg. Inc., Rapid City, 1988-89. Vis. lectr. workshop on Meteorol. and Environ. Inputs to Aviation Systems, 1978-85; adj. prof. Embry-

Riddle Aeronautical U., Ellsworth AFB, S.D., 1988—. Contbr. articles and reports to profl. jours. Treas. First Bapt. Ch. Alamogordo, N.Mex., 1958-61, First So. Bapt. Ch., Canoga Park, Calif., 1974-78. Decorated D.F.C., Legion of Merit with one oak leaf cluster, Meritorious Service medal, Air medal with six oak leaf clusters; named Disting. Alumnus, U. Ill., 1980. Mem. Soc. Exptl. Test Pilots (chmn. weather subcom. 1980-84, sect. sec. 1984-85), AIAA, Soc. Automotive Engrs. (flight test com.), Tau Beta Pi, Sigma Tau. Republican. Baptist. Avocations: flying, swimming, golf, restoring old cars. Died May 10, 2008.

PROSKY, ROBERT (ROBERT JOSEPH PORZUCZEK), actor; b. Phila., Dec. 13, 1930; s. Joseph and Helen (Kuhn) Porzuczek; m. Ida Mae Hove, June 4, 1960, children: Stefan, John, Andrew Student, Temple U., Am. Theatre. Stage appearances include The Front Page, 1958, Death of a Salesman, Twelfth Night, Enemy of the People, Galileo; appeared on Broadway in Moonchildren, The Dybbuk, 1975, A View from the Bridge, 1983, Glengarry Glen Ross (Tony award nominee 1985), 1984, A Walk in the Woods, 1988 (Tony award nominee 1988, Best Actor award Outer Critics Circle, toured USSR and Lithuania 1989), Camping with Henry and Tom, 1997, The Golem, 2002, An American Daughter, 2002, Democracy, 2004, Awake and Sing!, 2004, The Price, 2008; (films) Thief, 1981, Monsignor, 1982, The Lords of Discipline, 1983, Christine, 1983, The Keep, 1983, The Natural, 1984, Big Shots, 1987, Broadcast News, 1987, Outrageous Fortune, 1987, The Great Outdoors, 1987, Things Change, 1988, Loose Cannons, 1990, Gremlins II: The New Batch, 1988, Funny About Love, 1990, Green Card, 1990, Life in the Food Chain, 1990, Age Isn't Everything, 1991, Far and Away, 1992, Hoffa, 1992, Life on the High Wire, 1992, Rudy, 1992, Last Action Hero, 1993, Mrs. Doubtfire, 1993, Miracle on 34th Street, 1994, The Scarlet Letter, 1995, Dead Man Walking, 1995, The Chamber, 1996, Mad City, 1997, The Lake, 1998, Dudley-Do-Right, 1998, Grandfather's Birthday, 2000, D-Tox, 2002, Death to Smoochy, 2002, Suits on the Loose, 2005, The Skeptic, 2008; (TV series) Hill Street Blues, 1984-87, Lifestories, 1990-91, Veronica's Closet, 1997-98; (TV movies) They Killed President Lincoln, 1971, Lincoln: Trial by Fire, 1974, Zalmen: or, The Madness of God, 1975, The Ordeal of Bill Carney, 1981, World War III, 1983, Into Thin Air, 1985, A Walk in the Woods, 1988, The Murder of Mary Phagan, 1988, Home Fires Burning, 1988, From the Dead of Night, 1989, The Heist, 1989, Dangerous Pursuit, 1990, Johnny Ryan, 1990, The Love She Sought, 1990, Double Edge, 1992, Teamster Boss: The Jackie Presser Story, 1992, Brother's Destiny, 1995, Swing Vote, 1999, The Valley of Light, 2007; (TV appearances) Appointment with Destiny, 1972, Beacon Hill, 1975, Lou Grant, 1981, Alfred Hitchcock Presents, 1986, Murder, She Wrote, 1987, Christine Cromwell, 1990, Coach, 1991, Brooklyn Bridge, 1992, Cheers, 1992, Frasier, 1996, LateLine, 1998, Touched by an Angel, 2000, Danny, 2001, The Practice, 1997, 1999, 2000, 2002, Danny, 2001, Once and Again, 2002, K Street, 2003, ER, 2007; mem. first Am. co. to tour Soviet Union, 1972., mem. Arena Stage Repertory Company. Joseph Jefferson award nominee, 1985; recipient Drama Desk award, 1985, Helen Hayes award, 1995, Am. Express Tribute to an Am. Actor, 1998. Home: Washington, DC. Died Dec. 8, 2008.

PRSHA, MARIE ALICE, administrator, educator; b. Pitts., Aug. 19, 1927; d. Joseph Albert and Sabina Elizabeth (Rauch) Yoest; m. William John Prsha, July 14, 1951 (wid. Oct. 1977); children: Jon Michael, Mark Steven, Jeffrey Alan, Jeanne-Marie. Grad., Queen of Angels Coll. Nursing, 1950; BS in Health Sci., Chapman U., 1984, MS in Health Adminstrn., 1989. RN, PHN, Calif. Clin. nurse, charge/obgyn. Queen of Angels Clinic, LA, 1950-52; staff nurse Huntington Meml. Hosp., Pasadena, Calif., 1993-94, St. Luke Hosp., Pasadena, 1955-56, La Vina Resp. Disease, Altadena, Calif., 1966; nurse nutritionist, high risk counselor ARC, San Diego, Calif., 1980-91, asst. dir. WIC svcs., 1991-93; nutrition edn. coord. dept. health svcs. County of San Diego WIC Program, 1993-96; asst. program dir. Women, Infants and Children Program San Diego State U., from 1996. Mem. adv. bd. Southeast Asian Devel. Disabilities Prevention Program, San Diego, 1993-95. Nurse educator Univ. Calif., San Diego, 1989-90. Recipient scholarship Immaculate Heart Coll., L.A., 1949; traineeship USPHS, San Diego, 1969. Mem. NLN, Am. Pub. Health Assn., Queen of Angels Alumni Assn., Chapman Univ. Alumni Assn. Republican. Roman Catholic. Avocations: reading, poetry, music, personal fitness, aviation. Home: San Diego, Calif. Died July 26, 2008.

PRUD'HOMME, ECK GABRIEL, JR., physician, consultant; b. Texarkana, Tex., Feb. 8, 1924; s. Eck Gabriel and Mary Anderson (Young) P.; m. Margaret Peavy Murray, Jan. 24, 1948; children: Ann Clark, Kay Eleanor. Student, Tex. A&M Coll., 1941-43, Rice U., 1947; BS in Meterology, U. Chgo., 1949; MD, U. Tex. Med. Br., Galveston, 1952. Cert. Am. Soc. Addiction Medicine. Intern Hermann Hosp., Houston, 1952-53; pvt. practice Winnie, Tex., 1953-57, Ft. Worth, 1957-77; CEO, med. dir. Schick Shadel Hosp., Ft. Worth, 1977-88; pvt. cons. Ft. Worth, from 1988. Contbr. articles to profl. jours. Pres., bd. dirs. Ft. Worth CLU, 1969-75 (Civil Libertarian of Yr. award 1973); founding dir., pres. Ballet Concerto, Ft. Worth, 1968-82, Ft. Worth City Ballet, 1975—; chmn. Tarrant County Task Force on Alcoholism, Ft. Worth, 1980-81; advisor Tex. Com. Alcohol and Drug Abuse, Austin, 1989 (William Heatly award 1990). Fellow Am. Acad. Family Physicians (charter); mem. AMA, Tex. Chem. Dependency Assn. (founding dir., pres. 1979—), Tarrant County Med. Soc., Better Influence Assn. (pres., bd. dirs. 1979), Kiwanis (pres. 1958). Roman Catholic. Avocations: travel, writing, improving, medical ethics, bridge. Died June 14, 2008.

PUCKETT, BARBARA CHANDLEY, freelance writer; b. Kansas City, Kans., Feb. 14, 1935; d. John Stothers and Edythe Raechel (Jones) Chandley; m. Robert Hugh Puckett, Dec. 23, 1964; 1 child, Sarah Anne. AA, Stephens Coll., 1955. Reporter Kansas City (Mo.) Star, 1956-58, asst. soc. editor, 1958-63, asst. women's page editor, 1963-64. Leader 4-H Club, Terre Haute, Ind., 1980—; mayoral appointee Bd. Assocs. to Archtl. Commn. Terre Haute Civic Improvement, 1974-76; bd. dirs. Terre Haute Woman's Symphony Assn.; bd. dirs., pres. Terre Haute YWCA, 1970-76; bd. dirs., pub. rels. chmn. Alternatives for Learning and Living Sch. Nursery Bd., 1984-90. Mem. Women in Communication, Inc., P.E.O., Columbia Club, MVP Club, Hyannis (Mass.) Yacht Club (assoc.). Avocations: quilting, genealogy. Home: Terre Haute, Ind. Died Oct. 19, 2007.

PUGH, MICHAEL A., mechanical engineering associate; b. Columbus, Ohio, Jan. 17, 1956; A in Mech. Engring., Columbus Tech. Inst., 1986. Design draftsman Wearever Proctor Sylex, Chilicothe, Ohio, 1983-85; supr. assembly/welding Nestle Dairy Systems, Columbus, Ohio, from 1985. Religious edn. tchr. St. Phillips Cath. Ch., Columbus, 1987-95. With USN, 1975-79. Republican. Roman Catholic. Avocation: basketball playing. Died Aug. 13, 2008.

PULLEN, JULIA M., psychiatrist; News corr. Orofino VFW Aux., 1994-97; news cor. Orofino Kiwanis Club, 1994—, neweletter editor, 1994—. Mem. Clearwater County adv. Com. for Commrs., 1965-66; active Clearwater County Dem. Party, 1994—, Twin Ridge Vol. Fire Dept.; mem. Clearwater Hosp. Aux. Mem. Am. Psychiat. Assn. (exec. sec. Western regional meeting 1962), Intermountain Psychiat. Assn. (exec. sec. 1962-66), Clearwater County Mental Health Assn., Idaho Mental Health Assn. (pres. 1963-64), Idaho Am. Assn. U. Women (social concerns com. chair 1963-70, del. biennial nat. conv. 1964, del. nat. ocnv. 1966), Idaho PTA (chair mental health com. 1960-69, sec. 1964, pres. Orofino 1957), Orofino Kiwanis, Clearwater Hist. Soc. (sec. 1997—), VFW Aux. (life). Home: Orofino, Idaho. Deceased.

PURDY, JAMES OTIS, writer; b. Fremont, Ohio, July 17, 1923; Attended, U. Puebla, Puebla, Mexico, U. Chgo., U. Madrid. Instr. Lawrence Coll., Appleton, Wis., 1949—53. Author: Don't Call Me by My Right Name, 1956, Dream Palace, 1956, Malcolm, 1959, The Nephew, 1961, Cabot Wright Begins, 1964, Eustace Chisholm and The Works, 1967, An Oyster is A Wealthy Beast, 1967, Mr. Evening, 1968, Jeremy's Version, 1970, On the Rebound, 1970, I Am Elijah Thrush, 1971, Sunshine is an Only Child, 1973, The House of the Solitary Maggot, 1974, In a Shallow Grave, 1976, Narrow Rooms, 1978, Sleep Tight, 1978, Mourners Below, 1981, On Glory's Course, 1984, Dawn, 1985, In the Hollow of His Hand, 1986, Are You in the Winter Tree?, 1987, Garments the Living Wear, 1989, Out With The Stars, 1992, Kitty Blue: A Fairy Tale, 1993, Island Avenue, 1997, Gertrude of Stony Island Avenue, 1998; (short stories) 63: Dream Palace, 1956, Color of Darkness, 1957, The Candles of Your Eyes, 1987, Moe's Villa and Other Stories, 2002; (plays) Children is All, 1962, A Day After the Fair, 1977, How I Became A Shadow, 1979, Proud Flesh, 1980, Scrap of Paper, 1981, The Berry Picker, 1981, A Room All to Itself, 1988, Enduring Zeal, Ruthanna Elder, 1989, Foment, 1998, In The Night of Time and Four Other Plays, 1992; (poetry) An Oyster Is A Wealthy Beast, 1968, Mr. Evening, 1968, On the Rebound, 1971, The Running Sun, 1971, Sunshine Is An Only Child, 1973, I Will Arrest the Bird that has No Light, 1978, Lessons and Complaints, 1978, Don't Let the Snow Fall, 1985, The Brooklyn Branding Parlors, 1986, Collected Poems, 1990, Recipient Morton Dauwen Zabel Fiction award Am. Acad. Arts & Letters, 1993, Oscar Williams & Gene Durwood award for Poetry & Art, 1995; subject of The Not-Right House, Essays on the Books of James Purdy (Bettina Schwarzschild), 1969-70. Died Mar. 13, 2009.

PURDY, TEDDY GEORGE, JR., programmer, analyst, researcher, consultant; b. Leadville, Colo., May 11, 1954; s. Teddy George and Geneva Ruth Purdy; m. Karen Ann Puleo, May 28, 1977 (div. Dec. 19, 1983); children: Christopher, Sarah. Student, Colo. U., 1972-75. Free-lance programmer/analyst, Boulder, Colo., 1975-84; pres., treas. IBEX Bus. Systems, Leadville, from 1984. Cons. Carlson Promotions, Mpls., 1987-91, Unidata, Inc., Denver, 1992, Household Fin., Chesapeake, Va., 1992—, Focus Tech., Dallas, 1992-98. Avocations: geology, biking, hiking, books, music. Died Jan. 9, 2008.

PURSELL, CARL DUANE, former United States Representative from Michigan; b. Imlay City, Mich., Dec. 19, 1932; s. Roy and Doris (Perkins) P.; m. Peggy Jean Brown, 1956; children: Philip, Mark, Kathleen. BA, Eastern Mich. U., 1957, MA, 1962; LLD (hon.), Madonna Coll., 1977, U. Mich., 1991. Former educator, small bus. owner; mem. Wayne County Bd. Commnrs., 1969-70; mem. 14th dist. Mich. State Senate, 1971-76; mem. US Congress from 2d Mich. Dist., 1977—93. Past mem. Mich. Crime Commn. Served in U.S. Army, 1957-59. Recipient award EPA, 1976 Republican. Died June 11, 2009.

PURTELL, MAUREEN GAIL, nursing administrator, mental health nurse; b. Lowell, Mass., Apr. 13, 1951; d. Frederick J. and Jennie H. (Jaskolka) Cody; m. Richard N. Purtell, Dec. 9, 1981; children: Keith, Kristin, Kyla, Melissa. BSN and BS in Psychology, Lowell State Coll., 1974; MS in Psychiat. and Mental Health Nursing, Boston Coll., Chestnut Hill, Mass., 1976. RN, Mass.; cert. adult psychiat. mental health nurse, advance RN practitioner/mental health. Nurse practitioner in mental health Edith Nourse Rogers Meml. VA Hosp., Bedford, Mass., 1975-89, coord. computer clin. applications, 1989-92, chief Vets. Community Care Ctr., from 1992; clin. nurse specialist N.E. Shelter Homeless Vets., Boston, from 1992; advance nurse practitioner/mental health Greater Lowell Psychiat Assocs., Chelmsford, Mass., 1998-2000, Boston Rd. Clinic, Worcester, Mass., from 2000. Mem. ANA (cert. adult psychiat.-mental health nurse), Nurses Orgn. VA, Sigma Theta Tau. Home: S Chelmsford, Mass. Died July 9, 2008.

PUSCAS, VASILE LOUIS, bishop emeritus; b. Aurora, Ill., Sept. 3, 1915; Attended, Quigley Preparatory Sem., Chgo., Oradea-Mare, Romania, Propaganda Fide Sem., Rome, Benedictine Coll., Lisle, Ill. Ordained priest, 1942; ordained bishop, 1983; vicar apostolic Eparchy of Saint George's in Canton (Romanian), 1983—87, bishop, 1987—93, bishop emeritus, 1993—2009. Roman Catholic. Died Oct. 3, 2009.

PUTNAM, GEORGE WASHINGTON, JR., retired army officer; b. Ft. Fairfield, Maine, May 5, 1920; s. George W. and Rae B. (Merrithew) P.; m. Elaine Anderson (dec. 1973); m. Claudine Mahin (div. 1995); m. Helen Guerin, 1995; children: James M. (dec. 2006), J. Glenn; stepchildren: Philip Mahin, Leslie Mahin. Enlisted man U.S. Army, 1941-42, commd. 2d lt., 1942, advanced through grades to maj. gen., 1970; comdg. gen. 1st Aviation Brigade, Vietnam, 1970, 1st Cav, Divsn., Vietnam, 1970-71; dir. Mil. Personnel Mgmt., Hdqrs. Dept. Army, Washington, 1971-75; comdg. gen. U.S. Army So. European Task Force, Vicenza, Italy, 1975-77, U.S. Army Phys. Disability Agy., Washington, 1977-81; ret. U.S. Army, 1981. Dir. Army Coun. Rev. Bds., 1977-81; pres. Nat. Capital Retiree Coun., 1982-85. Internat. judge 5th and 6th World Helicopter Championships, 1986, 89, 94, chief judge 7th World Championship, 1992; U.S. mem. Internat. Helicopter com. Fedn. Aeronautique Internationale, 1988-91, 93-95; bd. dirs. Army Aviation Mus. Found., 1987-2009, pres., 1993-96; chmn. bd. trustees Army Aviation Hall of Fame, 1996-2001. Recipient Elder Statesman of Aviation award, 1998; inducted Army Aviation Hall of Fame, 1980. Mem. Nat. Aero. Assn. (sr. v.p. 1991-98, Fedn. Aero. Internat. (v.p. 1995-98), Army Aviation Assn. Am. (sr. v.p., pres. 1983-87, pres. scholarship found. 1991-93), Helicopter Club Am. (pres. 1988-90). Home: Arlington, Va. Died Aug. 6, 2009.

PUTNEY, MARTHA SETTLE, writer, retired history professor; b. Norristown, Pa., Nov. 9, 1916; d. Oliver Benjamin and Ida (Bailey) Settle; 1 child, William Mathews. BA, Howard U., 1939, MA, 1940; PhD in European History, U. Pa., 1955; DHL (hon.), Bowie State U., 1999. Asst. prof. Morgan State Col., Balt., 1950-52; assoc. prof. Prairie View (Tex.) Agricultural and Mech. Col., 1954-55; prof. History Bowie (Md.) State Col., 1955-74; sr. lectr. Howard U., Wash., 1974-83. Presenter in field. Author: (books) Black Sailors, 1987, When the Nation Was in Need: Blacks in the Women's Army Corps during World War II, 1992, Blacks in the United States Army: Portraits Through History, 2003; contbr. articles to profl. jours. Vol. Smithsonian Inst., 1994-95. 1st lt. with Women's Army Corps, 1943-46. Recipient Danforth Found. fellowship, 1970-71, Cert. Appreciation, Myers Ctr. award Pres. of the U.S., World War II Commemoration Com., and Congressional Black Caucus, 1993, 95. Mem. Assn. for Study of Afro-Am. Life and History, Afro-Am. Hist. Genealogical Soc. Avocations: bridge, academic research. Home: Washington, DC. Died Dec. 11, 2008.

PYNCHON, JOSEPH HENRY, headmaster emeritus; b. Boston, Jan. 7, 1926; s. Joseph Henry and Susan Perry (Peckham) P.; m. Barbara Cheney, Aug. 4, 1954; children: David Lewis, Anne Pynchon Savage, Joseph Jr., William C. BA, Carroll Coll., 1950; EdM, Harvard U., 1954. Cert. tchr., Mass., tchr., adminstr., Hawaii. Elem. tchr. Angier Sch., Newton (Mass.) Pub. Schs., 1951-54; English tchr. North Shore Country Day Sch., Winnetka, Ill., 1954-61; chair English dept. Iolani Sch., Honolulu, 1961-63; headmaster La Pietra-Hawaii Sch. for Girls, Honolulu, 1963-91, headmaster emeritus, from 1991. Mem. accrediting commn. WASC Secondary Sch. Commn., Burlingame, Calif., 1975-28; bd. dirs. Nat. Assn. Ind. Schs., Boston and Washington, 1979-84. Trustee, chmn. Cen. Union Ch. Hon. Hawaii Bd., 1974-78. Vol. Am. Field Svc., U.S. Army, 1944-45. Mem. Hawaii Assn. Ind. Schs. (co-founder, trustee 1970-92), Country Day Schs. Assn., Rotary. Mem. United Ch. of Christ. Avocations: surfing, kayaking, travel, reading, home repair. Home: Boise, Idaho. Died Jan. 2, 2008.

PYNE, WILLIAM JOSEPH, chemist; b. Boston, Jan. 30, 1923; s. Thomas Francis and Mary (Reidy) P.; m. Martha Ellen Cannon, July 3, 1954 (dec. Oct. 1991); children: Thomas, James, Kevin, Colleen, Patricia, Brian. BS, Boston Coll., 1948, MS, 1950; postgrad., Western Res. U., Cleve., 1953-57, Ohio State U., 1970. Instr. King's Coll., Wilkes-Barre, Pa., 1950-51; rsch. chemist Diamond Shamrock Co., Painesville, Ohio, 1952-66, sr. rsch. chemist, 1966-77, rsch. assoc., 1977-82; sr. rsch. assoc. Quatum Technologies, Twinsburg, Ohio, 1984-85; corp. fellow in synthetic organic chemistry Rex Adv. Svcs., Painesville, from 1985. Lectr. in field. Contbr. articles to profl. jours.; patentee in field (20 U.S. and 36 fgn. patents). Mem Cmty. Devel. Com., Painesville, 1978. With U.S. Army, 1943-45. Recipient Squirrel award for patent Diamond Shamrock Co., 1982. Mem. Am. chem. Soc. (chpt. sec. 1976-77). Roman Catholic. Avocations: history, visiting civil war battle fields. Died Oct. 29, 2007.

QUESADA, FRANCINE BARBARA, social services administrator, therapist, educator; b. NYC, Nov. 21, 1942; d. Samuel David and Rose (Feiner) Weiss; m. Joseph R. Quesada, Nov. 25, 1979 (dec. Aug. 1988); children: Sherifa, Samora, stepdaughter Linda Lee. BS in Human Svcs., Empire State Coll., NYC, 1991; MS in Rehab. Counseling, U. Scranton, 1994. Cert. rehab. counselor, Pa.; nat. cert. counselor; masters addiction counselor; lic. profl. counselor; master practitioner neuro-linguistic programming. Office mgr. Dr. David Richter, NYC, 1973-91; exec. dir. Vision House, Inc., Scranton, Pa., 1992-96; intensive outpatient counselor, couples therapist A Better Today, Inc., Scranton, 1996; inpatient drug and alcohol counselor, lectr., therapist MARWORTH, Waverly, Pa., from 1996. Adj. prof. Marywood Coll., Scranton, 1994—; pvt. practice, Scranton, 2002-. Dist. leader Ind. Dem. Club, N.Y.C., 1987-87; sec. exec. bd. Village East Towers, Inc., N.Y.C., 1986-88; mem. Housing Coalition for Scranton Families, 1995—; sec., bd. dirs., Actor's Circle, Providence Playhouse, 2004-, actor in cmty. theatre. Avocations: opera, classical music, theater, cooking gourmet vegetarian meals for friends. Home: Scranton, Pa. Died Dec. 3, 2007.

QUIMBY, WALTER, recreational products executive; b. Balt., Apr. 9, 1946; s. Dudley Thomas and Joyce Sophie (Karlovich) Q.; m. Carole Ann Williams, Nov. 29, 1969 (div. 1989); children: Jonathan Kyle, Julie Elizabeth; m. Nancy Lee Sorrell, July 22, 1990. BS in Mktg., U. Md., 1972. V.p. Am. Original Foods, Bridgeville, Del., 1972-78, Jenkins Foods Corp., Milford, Del., 1978-81, Dover (Del.) Pool & Patio Ctr., Inc., 1981-85; pres. Water World, Inc., Easton, Md., from 1985. With USCG, 1968-72. Mem. NSPI (pres. Rehoboth, Del. chpt. 1988-89, pres., treas. Virginia Beach, Va. chpt. 1990-92). Democrat. Lutheran. Avocations: hunting, travel, golf, music, swimming. Home: Queenstown, Md. Died Dec. 5, 2007.

QUINN, JESSIE LAMBERT, retired medical/surgical nurse; b. Dayton, Ohio, May 6, 1922; d. Russell R. and Pearle Mae (Driskel) Lambert; m. Walter G. Quinn, Dec. 24, 1943 (dec.); children: Donald, Patricia, Judith, Michael. RN, Miami Valley Hosp., Dayton, Ohio, 1944; BA in Edn., Coll. of NJ, 1968. Staff nurse Millville (N.J.) Bd. Edn., 1957-68; sch. nurse Delsea Regional High Sch., Frankville, N.J., 1968-69, Deerfield Twp. Sch., Rosen Hayne, N.J., 1969-72; psychiat. nurse Cumberland County Guidance Ctr., Millville, 1970-74; sch. nurse Millville Sch. System, 1973-83; part-time staff nurse Millville Hosp., 1983-95, ret., 1995. Mem. Miami Valley Hosp. Alumnia Assn., N.J. Ednl. Assn. Home: Millville, NJ. Died May 28, 2008.

RADOSEVICH, SHARON KAY, critical care nurse; b. Pekin, Ill., Feb. 21, 1947; d. William E. and Lorraine A. Royse; m. David, 1999; children: Charles, David, Andrew. Student, U. Ill., 1965-67; RN Diploma, Michael Reese Hosp./Med. Ctr., Chgo., 1970; AA in Nursing, Golden West Coll., 1991; BSN, U. Phoenix, 1994. Asst. head nurse CCU Highland Pk. (Ill.) Hosp., 1970-73; staff nurse Carrier Psychiat. Clinic, Belle Mead, N.J., 1973-74; ICU charge nurse Herrin (Ill.) Hosp., 1980-82; patient care coord. Columbia Huntington Beach (Calif.) Hosp., 1982-91; night charge nurse Huntington Beach (Calif.) Med. Ctr., 1991-93, patient svcs. coord., from 1993, asst. dir. patient svcs., 1997-2000; dir. insvc. edn., from 2000. Speaker in field. Recipient Humana Nursing Excellence award for the Pacific Region, 1988, Columbia Caregiver award, 1996. Home: Prescott, Ariz. Died Nov. 27, 2007.

RAEL, JACK, talent manager; b. Milw., Nov. 21, 1919; s. Phillip and Millie Israel; m. Raquel Gordon, June 15, 1959 (div. 1976); children: Millicent Rael Brunk, Gordon Rael. BA, U. Wis., 1942. Mgr. of Patti Page, Los Angeles and NYC, from 1946, Everly Brothers, NYC, LA, 1960-75, Carmen McRae, Los Angeles and NYC, from 1970, Sue Raney, Los Angeles, from 1984, Bob Florence, Los Angeles, from 1984. Producer (record) Confess, 1947; record producer for Patti Dare, 1946-96. Served as sgt. U.S. Army, 1942-46. Democrat. Jewish. Home: Rancho Mirage, Calif. Died May 25, 2008.

RAFFENSPERGER, EDWARD C., physician; b. Dickinson, Pa., July 9, 1914; s. Edward Hubbard and Dora Cleveland (Snavely) R.; m. Mary Ames, Apr. 9, 1949 (dec). BS, Dickinson Coll., Carlisle, Pa., 1936; MD, U. Pa., 1940. Diplomate Am. Bd. Int. Med., Am. Bd. Gastroenterology. Prof. med. U. Pa., Phila., 1973—85, prof. emeritus, 1985—2009. Cons. Harrisburg Poly. Hosp., Children's Hosp., Phila., Lankeaso Hosp., Phila., 1965. Assoc. editor Gastroenterol. Abstracts, 1968. Trustee Dickinson Coll., 1956-97, emeritus trusteee, 1997-2009. Served to capt. U.S. Air Force, 1943-46, CBI. Named Physician of Yr. Coleostomy & Ileostomy Soc., Phila., 1981, Disting. Alumni award Dickinson Coll., 1988. Fellow ACP, Am. Gastroenterol. Assn., Am. Fed. Clin. Rsch.; mem. Alpha Omega Alpha (hon.). Democrat. Methodist. Avocations: squash, travel. Home: Philadelphia, Pa. Died Oct. 2, 2009.

RAFFENSPERGER, HELEN ELIZABETH, writer; b. Marion, Ind., Apr. 21, 1904; d. Oliver Wilbert and Isabelle M. (Pulaski) Gould; widowed; 1 child, John. Student, Purdue U., 1922-24. Libr. asst. Marion Pub. Libr., 1924-26, Elkhart (Ind.) Libr., 1926-28; libr. Henry (Ill.) Pub. Libr., 1943-71. V.p. Henry Hist. and Geneal. Soc., 1990—; columnist Henry News Rep., 1935—. Author: Henry, Best Town in Illinois by a Dam Site, 1976, Come to Our Fair, 1996; author, illustrator: Henry Homes in History, 1993; co-author Marshall County Census for 1860, 1870, 1880. Recipient Outstanding Svc. award Henry C. of C., 1931, 58; named Citizen of Yr., Rotary Club, 1987. Mem. Soc. Mayflower Descs., Ill. State Geneal. Soc., Purdue Alumni Assn. (life), Ill. State Hist. Soc., Presbyn. Women, Kappa Alpha Theta. Avocation: historical research. Home: Henry, Ill. Deceased.

RAGGIO, OLGA, museum curator, educator; b. Rome, Feb. 5, 1926; d. Enrico and Renee (Levine) R. Diploma, Internat. Library Sch., Vatican, 1947; PhD, U. Rome, 1949; student, NYU. With Met. Mus. Art, NYC, 1950—2008, assoc. rsch. curator, 1966-68, curator Western European arts, 1968-71, chmn. dept. European sculpture and decorative arts, 1971—2001, ret., 2008. Adj. assoc. prof. Inst. Fine Arts, NYU, 1964-68, adj. prof., 1968—2008 Author works in field. Am. Council Learned Socs. fellow, 1962-63, Metro. Mus. Art. Trustee fellow, 1969-70, Am. Acad. in Rome Resident in Art History, 1983-84. Mem. Coll. Art Assn. Am., Renaissance Soc. Am., Am. Assn. Museums, Internat. Com. Mus. Orgn. Roman Catholic. Died Jan. 24, 2009.

RAHRMAN, GLENN HENRY, computer company executive; b. St. Paul, Apr. 14, 1932; s. Harold Frederick and Eunice Marie (Baker) R.; m. Delores Zona Wynne, Dec. 29, 1956; 1 child, Mary Catherine. BA in Polit. Sci., Coll. St. Thomas, 1954; postgrad., U. Minn., 1954-56. Supr., mktg. engr., mfg. Honeywell, Hopkins, Minn., 1957-61; mgr. product control Sperry Univac, St. Paul, 1961-64; mgr. material Control Data Corp., Mpls., 1964-70, EM&M Corp., Hawthorne, Calif., 1970-72; mgr. subcontracts Litton, Van Nuys, Calif., 1972-78; group mgr. subcontracts Unisys (merger Sperry and Burroughs), St. Paul, from 1978. Cons. in field. Mem. CAble Adv. Bd., South St. Paul, 1982; commr. Police and Fire Commn., South St. Paul, 1984-87; chmn. airport adv. bd.; del. DFL, Dist. Conv., South St. Paul, 1984-88. Served with U.S. Army, 1956-57. Mem. Nat. Assn. Purchasing Mgmt., Nat. Contract Mgmt. Assn., Armed Forces Communications and Electronics Assn. (v.p. 1968-70). Clubs: S (South St. Paul) (sec., treas. 1960-70). Lodges: KC. Democrat. Roman Catholic. Avocations: reading, sports, home restorations. Home: Saint Paul, Minn. Died Mar. 30, 2008.

RAIKES, RONALD E., state legislator; b. Lincoln, Nebr., Mar. 11, 1943; m. Helen Holz Raikes, 1966; children: Heather, Abbie, Justin. Assoc prof. economics Iowa State U., Nebr.; mem. Dist. 25 Nebr. State Senate, Nebr., 1997—2008; chmn. Intergovt. Coop. Com.; vice chmn. Legislature Program Evaluation Com.; mem. Revenue & Edn. Com.; farmer; cattle feeder; soil conservation contractor. Mem.: Nebr. Land Improvement Contractors Assn., Nebr. Agr. Rels. Coun., Agr. Builders Nebr., Nebr. Farm Bus. Assn. Independent. Died Sept. 5, 2009.

RAINAL, ATTILIO JOSEPH, retired electronics engineer; b. Marion Heights, Pa., Feb. 14, 1930; m. Violet Dorothy Robel, June 29, 1957; children: Valery, Eric. BS in Engring. Sci., Pa. State U., University Park, 1956; MSEE, Drexel U., Phila., 1959; D of Elec. Engring., Johns Hopkins U., Balt., 1963. Engr. Applied Physics Lab. Johns Hopkins U., Silver Spring, Md., 1955; engr. Martin Co., Balt., 1956-59; mem. rsch. staff Carlyle Barton Lab. Johns Hopkins U., Balt., 1959-64; mem. tech. staff R & D AT&T Bell Labs., Whippany, Murray Hill, NJ, 1964-83, mem. disting. tech. staff R & D, 1983—2003; ret., 2003. Contbr. articles to profl. jours. With USAF, 1948—52. Mem.: IEEE (life), Info. Theory, Component, Hybrids and Mfg. Tech. Achievements include research in noise theory; signal detection and estimation; radiometry; radar; FM; first passage times of random processes; crosstalk; voltage breakdown; current carrying capacity of printed wires; performance limits of electrical interconnections; patents for balanced interconnections; laser intensity modulation; patents in field. Home: Morristown, NJ. Died Feb. 17, 2009.

RAINESS, ALAN EDWARD, psychiatrist, neurologist, educator; b. NYC, Sept. 24, 1935; s. George W. and Ida Rainess; m. Alice Maree Haber, June 5, 1968 (dec May 17, 2007); children: Alice Jeanne Rainess Jordan, James Alan (dec.). AB, Columbia Coll., 1957; MD, U. Paris, 1965. Diplomate Am. Bd. Psychiatry and Neurology. Intern Meadowbrook Hosp., East Meadow, L.I., 1965-66; resident in psychiatry NY VA Hosp., NYC, 1966-67; teaching fellow in psychiatry Harvard Med. Sch., Boston, 1967; chief resident in psychiatry Boston City Hosp., 1967; psychiatrist U.S. Army Hosp., Heidelberg, Germany, 1968—70; resident in psychiatry Walter Reed Med. Ctr., Washington, 1970-72; clin. dir. Noyes Divsn. St. Elizabeths Hosp., Washington, 1973-76; asst. chief psychiatry Andrews AFB Hosp., Camp Springs, Md., 1976-80, chief neurology, 1989-91; resident in neurology Wilford Hall USAF Med. Ctr., San Antonio, 1980-83; chief medicine and neuropsychiatry Air Univ. Hosp., Maxwell AFB, Ala., 1983-89, chief neurology, 1991-94; psychiatrist Manhattan Psychiat. Ctr., NYC, 1994—97, 1999—2002, clin. dir., 1997-99; psychiatrist Prison Health Svcs., Riker's Island, NYC, from 2002. Asst. clin. prof. psychiatry Georgetown U. Med. Sch., Washington, 1974-79, NYU Sch. Medicine, 1997-2002; assoc. prof. neurology and asst. prof. psychiatry Uniformed Svcs. U. Health Scis., Bethesda, Md., 1989-94. Maj. U.S. Army, 1968-73, col. USAF, 1976-94, ret. Fellow: Am. Psychiat. Assn. (disting. life); mem.: AMA, Am. Soc. Psychoanalytic Physicians (past pres. 1995—96), Uniformed Svcs. Soc. Neurologists (past pres. 1985—86), Med. Soc. State of NY, Harvard Club (N.Y.C.). Home: New York, NY. Died 2009.

RAINS, BAXTER SMITH, sculptor, consultant; b. Atlanta, July 2, 1938; s. Baxter, Jr. and Elinor (Nelson) Rains; m. Barbara Osmundsen, Sept. 20, 1986; children: Anne Douglass, David Sinclair, Elinor Houston, Holly Christine Delaney. Studied, Ga. Inst. Tech., Atlanta, 1964—65, Atlanta Coll. Art, 1966—68; B of Visual Arts, Ga. State U., Atlanta, 1968; MFA, U. Guanajuato, San Miguel de Allende, Mex., 1975. Tchr. The Westminster Schs., Atlanta, 1969—71; instr. Atlanta Coll. Art, 1969—71, U. Guanajuato, San Miguel de Allende, Mexico, 1972—75, Brevard Art Ctr. and Mus., Melbourne, Fla., 1992; prof. Ctr. for the Arts, Vero Beach, Fla., 2000—02; adj. prof. Indian River CC, Fort Pierce, Fla., 2000—02; adj. prof. art Brovard CC, Melbourne, Fla., from 2006. Dir., evening sch. Atlanta Coll. Art, 1970; founder, exec. dir. Sculptural Arts Mus., Atlanta, 1980—82; cons. U.S. Pres.'s Coun. on Handicapped, 1981—82, Brevard Cultural Alliance, Viera, Fla., 2003, Brevard Mus. Art and Sci., Melbourne, Fla., 2003—04; bd. dirs. Arts Festival of Atlanta, 1982—85; artist-in-charge Hope Dragon Found., Merritt Island, Fla., 1996. One-man shows include Ga. State U., Atlanta, 1967—68, The Westminster Schs., 1969, 1971, Galeria Roma, San Miguel de Allende, Mex., 1973—74, Pine Valley Ranch, Pine, Colo., 1977, El Rancho, Colo., 1977, Gallery Danielli, Toronto, 1979, Washington World Galleries, 1979, Southside Studio Sculpture Show, Richmond, Va., 1990—91, Fifth Ave. Art Gallery, Melbourne, Fla., 1992, Brevard Mus. Art & Sci., 2003, Indian River Sculpture Gallery, Vero Beach, Fla., 2004, Vero Beach (Fla.) Mus. Art, 2005, King Ctr. the Performing Arts, Melbourne, Fla., 2007, exhibitions include High Mus. Art, Atlanta, 1969, Mint Mus. Art, Charlotte, N.C., 1970, Galeria Del Conde, San Miguel de Allende, 1972—73, Fiesta de Santa Fe, 1977, Mus. of Touch, Atlanta, 1980, Christian-Brydon Gallery, Richmond, Va., 1989—91, Brigantine Gallery, Cocoa Beach, Fla., 1993, Raleigh Gallery, Design Ctr. of Ams., Dania, Fla., 1992—95, Gaier Contemp. Gallery, Orlando, Fla., 1994—96, Raleigh Gallery, Boca Raton, Fla., 1995—97, Vero Beach Mus. Art, 2000—03, Represented in permanent collections Brevard Mus. Art & Sci., Melbourne, Fla., Radford U. Sculpture Garden, Va., The Westminster Schs., Atlanta, Piedmont Hosp., Ga. State U. Mus., The Trane Corp., Our Lady of Perpetual Help Hosp., Bklyn., City of Atlanta, Office of the Mayor, First Presbyn. Ch., Atlanta, St. Francis Gardens, Albuquerque, Holy Name of Jesus Cath. Ch., Melbourne, Fla., commissioned, Parkway Indsl. Pk., Balt., 1987, Freedom 7 Cmty. Ctr., Cocoa Beach, Fla., 1992, Child Care Assn. of Brevard, Cocoa, Fla., 2004. Mem. Internat. Sculpture Ctr., Washington, 1988—94; bd. govs. Vector Arts Endowment, Indian Harbour Beach, Fla., from 1997; founder Barbara Osmundsen and Baxter Rains Found., from 2008. Avocations: archery, gardening. Died Feb. 12, 2009.

RAMES, DOUGLAS DWIGHT, civil engineer; b. Colorado Springs, Colo., Apr. 14, 1942; s. Dwight S. and Eleanor A. (Roach) R.; m. Audrey Joan Satter, Nov. 26, 1963; children: Steven D., Wendy M., Eydee J. BSCE, S.D. Sch. Mines & Tech., 1965; postgrad., Ind./Purdue U., 1989, Harvard U., 1995. Registered profl. engr., Colo. Project engr. Colo. Dept. of Hwys., Eagle, 1970-72, resident engr. Grand Junction, 1972-78, preconstrn. engr. Greeley, 1978-84, asst. dist. engr., 1984-88; region dir. Colo. Dept. Transp., Greeley, 1988-98, ret., 2005. Commr. urban renewal City of Greeley, 1993-98; mgr. transp. The Sear-Brown Group, 1998-2001, Kirkham Michael, 2001-2004. Avocations: genealogy, travel, fishing, old roadsters. Home: Greeley, Colo. Died Nov. 23, 2007.

RAMEY, CECIL EDWARD, JR., lawyer; b. Shreveport, La., Nov. 9, 1923; s. Cecil Edward and Blanche (Gwin) R.; m. Betty Loper, June 15, 1945; children— Martha L., L. Christine, Stephen E. BS summa cum laude, Centenary Coll., 1943; LLB, Yale U., 1949; postgrad., Tulane U., 1950-51. Bar: Wis. 1949, La. 1951. Assoc. Miller, Mack & Fairchild, Milw., 1949-50; mem. faculty Tulane U., 1950-54; assoc. Hargrove, Guyton, Van Hook and Hargrove, Shreveport, 1954-56, ptnr., 1956-63, Hargrove, Guyton, Van Hook and Ramey, Shreveport, 1963-73, Hargrove, Guyton, Ramey and Barlow, Shreveport, 1973-89, of counsel, 1989-94, Barlow and Hardtner, L.C., Shreveport, 1994-2001, Lemle Kelleher Barlow and Hardtner, Shreveport, 2001—03, Lemle & Kelleher LLP, Shreveport, 2003—05; ret., 2005. Adj. prof. Centenary Coll., 1992—98. Former chmn. Citizens Capital Improvements com. City of Shreveport; former mem. governing bd. Shreveport YMCA; former chmn. bd. trustees Broadmoor Meth. Ch., Shreveport, chmn. bd. stewards; former bd. dirs., former chmn. Shreveport-Bossier Found.; trustee Centenary Coll. With AC, U.S. Army, 1943-46. Named Shreveport's Outstanding Young Man of Yr., 1956, Mr. Shreveport, 1968; recipient Clyde E. Fant Meml. award community service United Way, 1979 Fellow Am. Coll. Trust and Estate Counsel; mem. ABA, La. Bar Assn., Shreveport Bar Assn. (pres. 1970), La. Law Inst., Shreveport C. of C. (pres. 1974), Centenary Coll. Alumni Assn. (past pres.), Shreveport Club, Order of Coif, Phi Delta Phi, Kappa Sigma. Clubs: Shreveport. Home: Shreveport, La. Died Apr. 8, 2009.

RAMIREZ, ARTHUR CHRISTOPHER, bank executive; b. Bklyn., Mar. 22, 1937; s. Arthur C. and Mary A. (Sierchio) R.; m. Frances Angela Laino, Feb. 9, 1958; children: Scott Arthur, Lois Ann Ramirez Carr. BS in Acctg., Rutgers U., 1968; cert. diploma, Stonier Grad. Sch. Banking, 1973. Loan interviewer Mfrs. Hanover Trust Co., NYC, 1956-62; mgr. consumer loan dept. Irvington (N.J.) State Bank, 1962-64; mgr. consumer lending Essex County State Bank, West Orange, N.J., 1964-65; sr. v.p. Hackensack (N.J.) Trust Co. (now Garden State Nat. Bank), 1965-80; 1st sr. v.p. Nat. Community Bank, Maywood, N.J., from 1980. Bd. mem. Hackensack (N.J.) Med. Ctr. Found., Tetecboro (N.J.) Aviation Mus. and Hall of Fame, Bergen County (N.J.) Girl Scouts Am., all present. 1st lt. USAR, 1955-63. Mem. Hudson County Bankers Assn. (past pres.). Avocations: piloting, aircraft owner. Home: North Haledon, NJ. Died June 24, 2008.

RAMO, VIRGINIA M. SMITH, civic worker; b. Yonkers, NY; d. Abraham Harold and Freda (Kasnetz) Smith; m. Simon Ramo; children: James Brian, Alan Martin. BS in Edn., U. So. Calif., DHL (hon.), 1978. Nat. co-chmn., ann. giving U. So. Calif., 1968-70, vice chmn., trustee, 1971—2009, co-chmn. bd. councilors Sch. Performing Arts, 1975-76, co-chmn. bd. councillors Schs. Med. and Engring. Vice-chmn. bd. overseers Hebrew Union Coll., 1972-75; bd. dirs. The Muses of Calif. Mus. Sci. and Industry, UCLA Affiliates, Estelle Doheny Eye Found., U. So. Calif. Sch. Medicine; mem. adv. coun. L.A. County Heart Assn., chmn. com. to endow Chair in cardiology at U. So. Calif.; vice chmn., bd. dirs. Friends of Libr. U. So. Calif.; bd. dirs., nat. pres. Achievement Rewards for Coll. Scientists Found., 1975-77; bd. dirs. Les Dames L.A., Cmty. TV So. Calif.; bd. dirs., v.p. Founders L.A. Music Ctr.; v.p. L.A. Music Ctr. Opera Assn.; v.p. corp. bd. United Way; v.p. Blue Ribbon-400 Performing Arts Coun.; chmn. com. to endow chair in gerontology U. So. Calif.; vice chmn. campaign Doheny Eye Inst,. 1986; co-chair, bd. overseers Keck Sch. Medicine U. So. Calif., 1999-2009 Recipient Svc. award Friends of Librs., 1974, Nat. Cmty. Svc. award Alpha Epsilon Phi, 1975, Disting. Svc. award Am. Heart Assn., 1978, Svc. award U. So. Calif., Spl. award U. So. Calif. Music Alumni Assn., 1979, Life Achievement award Mannequins of L.A. Assistance League, 1979, Woman of Yr. award Pan Hellenic Assn., 1981, Disting. Svc. award U. So. Calif. Sch. Medicine, 1981, U. So. Calif. Town and Gown Recognition award, 1986, Asa V. Call Achievement award U. So. Calif., 1986, Phi Kappa Phi scholarship award U. So. Calif., 1986, Vision award Luminaires of Doheny Eye Inst., 1994, Presdl. medallion U. So. Calif., 2002, USC Thornton Sch. of Music Founder's award, 2003. Mem. UCLA Med. Aux., U. So. Calif. Pres.'s Cir., Commerce Assocs. U. So. Calif., Cedars of Lebanon Hosp. Women's Guild (dir. 1967-68), Blue Key, Skull and Dagger. Died Aug. 19, 2009.

RAMPE, DAVID, editor; b. Cleve., 1948; BA in English, Miami U., Oxford, Ohio, 1970. Asst. fgn. editor, weekend The NY Times. Died Dec. 24, 2008.

RANDALL, JACK J., accountant; b. Rutherford, NC, July 1, 1940; s. Richard Kelly and Eunice Clair (Jones) R.; m. Agnes Ann Elliott, Mar. 25, 1943; children: Bethany Hope Randall Wasky, Vincent Scott, Wendy Ann. BS in Acctg., Va. Tech. U., 1962. CPA, Va. Staff acct. Haskins and Sells, CPAs, Charlotte, N.C., 1962-64, Leslie Heath, CPA, Charlotte, 1964-65, Berry, Dail and Co., CPAs, Salem, Va., 1965-68, ptnr., 1968-79; tax ptnr. Peat Marwick Mitchell and Co., Roanoke, Va., 1979-85; tax ptnr. in charge KPMG Peat Marwick, Roanoke, 1985-90, ptnr.-in-charge, from 1991. Sec. Salem Indsl. Revenue Authority, 1975-79; bd. dirs. Sherwood Meml. Park, Inc., Salem. Bd. dirs. Juvenile Diabetes Found., Roanoke, 1983, Salem Ednl. Found., 1984; adv. bd. planned giving Roanoke Coll., Salem, 1984. Mem. AICPA, Va. Soc. CPAs, Roanoke Valley Estate Planning Coun., Ferrum Coll. Estate Planning Coun. (chmn. 1988—), Rotary (Paul Harris fellow 1989), Va. Polytechnic U. Pres. Coun. (founder). Baptist. Avocations: physical fitness, reading, spectator sports. Home: Roanoke, Va. Died Dec. 27, 2007.

RANDALL, MALCOM, health care administrator; b. East St. Louis, Ill., Aug. 9, 1916; s. John Leeper and Merle Dorothy Randall; m. Christine Sheppard, Nov. 10, 1972 AB, McKendree Coll., 1939; M.H.A., St. Louis U., 1955; D of Pub. Svc. with honors, U. Fla., 1996. Chief br. office VA, St. Louis, 1946-49, asst. area dir. area office, 1949-53; spl. asst. to dir. VA Hosp., St. Louis, 1953-56, hosp. adminstr. Spokane, Wash., 1956-57, Chgo., 1957-58, Indpls., 1958-60, Wood, Wis., 1960-64, hosp. dir. Miles City, Mont., 1964-66; med. ctr. dir. and med. dist. dir. VA, Gainesville, Fla., from 1966, regional rep., from 1991; prof. health and hosp. adminstrn. U. Fla., Gainesville, from 1966. Pres. N. Cen. Fla. Health Planning Council; mem. Fla. State Health Planning Council; chmn. Gov.'s Commn. on Alzheimer's Disease; mem. Alachua County Emergency Med. Svcs. Coun.; bd. dirs. emeritus 1st Union Nat. Bank Fla., Regional Med. Programs; mem. editorial bd. Jour. Am. Coll. Health Care Execs.; cons. on health care Univ. Clin. Ctr., Ljubljana, Slovenia, 1982—, Ministry of Health, Hungary and Med. U. Debrecen, 1989—. Contbr. numerous articles to profl. jours. Bd. dirs. Civitan Regional Blood Ctr., Gainesville, 1970. Served to capt. USN, 1942-46 Recipient Presdl. Rank award Pres. U.S., 1983, Meritorious Svc. award U. Fla., 1984, Exceptional Svc. award, 1985, Exec. Performance award, 1986, all VA; named Citizen of Yr., Gainesville, 1977. Fellow Am. Coll. Health Care Execs. (council regents, VA liaison); mem. Inst. Medicine, Nat. Acad. Sci., Assn. Am. Med. Colls. (bd. dirs., council tchg. hosps.), Am. Health Planning Assn. (bd. dirs.), Am. Hosp. Assn. (governing council met. and fed. hosp. sect.). Clubs: Heritage. Lodges: Rotary. Home: Gainesville, Fla. Died Mar. 26, 2008.

RANDOLPH, CARL LOWELL, chemicals executive; b. Pasadena, Calif., May 30, 1922; s. Carl L. and Lulu (McBride) R.; m. Jane Taber, June 25, 1943; children: Margaret, Stephen. BA, Whittier Coll., 1943; MS, U. So. Calif., 1947, PhD, 1949; LLD, Whittier Coll., 1982; D in Pub. Svc. (hon.), U. Alaska, 1983. Prin. chemist Aerojet-Gen. Corp., 1949-57; v.p. U.S. Borax Rsch. Corp., Anaheim, Calif., 1957-63; asst. to pres. U.S. Borax & Chem. Corp., LA, 1963-66, v.p., 1966-68, exec. v.p., 1968-69, pres., 1969-86, vice chmn., 1983-87. Trustee, chmn. bd. Whittier Coll., emeritus, 1969—; bd. dirs., chmn. Ind. Colls. So. Calif., 1982—. Lt. (j.g.) USNR, 1944-46. Mem.: Phi Beta Kappa, Sigma Xi. Home: Anacortes, Wash. Died Jan. 3, 2009.

RAPOSA, PAMELA ADRIENNE, legal executive; b. Manchester, Conn., Sept. 13, 1946; d. Delphis and Minerva (Chappel) LaBonte; m. Gerald Silvio Brunette, Oct. 10, 1970 (div. Jan. 10, 1981); m. Richard Anthony Raposa, Mar. 8, 1991. AA, Greater Harford C.C., Conn., 1983; BA, U. Conn., West Hartford, Conn., 1986; JD, Western New Eng. Sch. Law, Springfield, Mass., 1990. Bar: Conn. 1990, Oreg. 1991, Am. Bar Assn., U.S. Ct. Appeals (9th cir.) Oreg. Exec. sec. Fairbanks Morse Divsn., St. Johnsbury, Vt., 1964-66, Colt Industries, Inc., West Hartford, Conn., 1966-70; contract adminstr. Dynamic Controls Corp., South Windsor, Conn., 1970-72; adminstrv. asst. Am. Postal Workers, East Hartford, Conn., 1972-91; asst. pub. defender Southwestern Oreg. Pub. Defenders, Coos Bay, Oreg., 1991-92, Multnomah Defenders, Inc., Portland, Oreg., 1992-93; chief, planning and rsch. unit State of Conn. Divsn. of Spl. Revenue, Newington, Conn., from 1993. Adjunct prof. Southwestern Oreg. C.C., North Bend, 1991-92, Lynnfield Coll., Portland, 1992-93. Officer, dir. Conn. Breast Cancer Found./Coalition, Thomaston, 1994—. Recipient Profl. Achievement award Conn./Mass. Postal Workers, 1986-88. Roman Catholic. Avocations: golf, reading, travel. Home: Citrus Spgs, Fla. Died May 18, 2008.

RAPP, ROBERT DAVID, lawyer; b. NYC, Mar. 19, 1950; s. Melville Benjamin and Rachel (Marx) R. BA in Econs., U. Tenn., 1973; JD, Antioch U., 1982. Bar: Tex. 1982, US Dist. Ct. (so. dist.) Tex. 1983, US Ct. Appeals (5th cir.) 1983, US Supreme Ct. 1985. Law clk. to presiding judge US Dist. Ct. (so. dist.) Tex., Houston, 1982-83; ptnr., dir., shareholder Mandell & Wright, P.C., Houston, 1983—97; pvt. practice Houston, from 1997. Instr. CLE Bates Coll. Law, U. Houston, 1986-87. Contbr. articles to law revs., profl. jours. and treatises. Mem. Fed. Bar Assn. (bd. dirs. Houston chpt. 1986-87, lectr. 1987), Houston Bar Assn. Home: Houston, Tex. Deceased.

RARICK, JOHN RICHARD, lawyer, former United States Representative from Louisiana; b. Waterford, Ind., Jan. 29, 1924; m. Marguerite Pierce, Dec. 27, 1945 (dec. 2003); children: John Richard II, Carolyn Cherie Rarick Brumfield, Laurie Lee Rarick Slattery; m. Frances Eldred Campbell, Jan. 21, 2004 Student, Ball State Tchrs. Coll., 1946; postgrad., La. State U., 1943-44; JD, Tulane U., 1949. Bar: La. 1949, U.S. Dist. Ct. (ea., mid. and we. dists.) La. 1949. Pvt. practice, St. Francisville, La., 1949-61; dist. judge 20th Jud. Dist. Ct., St. Francisville, La., 1961-66; mem. US Congress from 6th La. Dist., 1967—75; ptnr. Rarick and Brumfield, St. Francisville, 1974—2009. Recipient George Washington honor award Freedoms Found. Valley Forge, 1968, Watchdog of Treasury award Nat. Assn. Businessmen, 1968, 70, 72, 74, John Hampden Chalice SCV, 1968. Mem. DAV (life), Am. Ex-Prisoners War (life), VFW (life) NRA (life), Masons, Shriners. Democrat. Avocations: stamp and coin collecting, fishing. Home: Saint Francisville, La. Died Sept. 14, 2009.

RASCOE, STEPHEN THOMAS, artist, art educator; b. Uvalde, Tex., May 8, 1924; s. William Marion and Jane Grace (Johnston) Rascoe; m. Barbara Butler Rascoe, Dec. 1, 1951; children: Paul, Stephanie. BFA, Art Inst. Chgo., 1949, MFA, 1950. Draftsman/cartographer Texaco Shell, Houston, 1950—51; art prof. C.C. Jr. Coll., Corpus Christi, Tex., 1952—64, U. Tex., Arlington, 1964—92. One-man shows include Galerie Kornye West, Ft. Worth, Tex., 2004; contbr. articles to profl. jours. Cpl. USAF, 1942—45. Recipient Purchase award, Houston Mus. Fine Arts, 1956, First Prize, Dallas Mus. Fine Arts, 1957, DD Feldman Purchase award, Tex. Fine Arts Assn., 1959. Mem.: Tex. Fine Arts Assn., Dallas Art Assn., Arlington Art Assn. (pres. 1967—68), South Tex. Art League (pres. 1960—61). Home: Arlington, Tex. Died June 16, 2008.

RASMUSSEN, JO ANNE DICKENS, speech educator, theater director; b. Creston, Iowa, Feb. 24, 1928; d. Joseph Harrod and Therese Faye Partello Dickens; m. Richard Jens Rasmussen, June 7, 1953; children: Robin Joel, Lisa Anne. BFA, Drake U., Des Moines, 1945—49. Speech and drama dir. St. Patrick's H.S., Walla Walla, Wash., 1958—60, St. Paul's Sch. For Girls, Walla Walla, 1960—62; speech and acting instr. Whitman Coll., 1973—84; dir. of traveling theatre for children Walla Walla C.C., 1973—84, speech instr., 1973—84, dir. of drama and speech, 1984—2003. Profl. actress Dartmouth Theatre Co. at Dartmouth Coll., Hanover, NH, 1968. Actor: (plays) Mother Courage by Berthold Brect, Twelth Night by William Shakespeare, Antigone by Annilh; dir.: (outdoor amphitheatre productions) Various Broadway Musicals. Actress, dir. Walla Walla Little Theatre, 1953—83; dir. of living history theatre co. Walla Walla Hist. Soc., 1995—2000. Recipient Allied Arts award, Allied Arts Assn. of Wash., 1986, Exemplary Status, Wash. C.C. Humanities Assn., 1986, Honored for Tchg. Excellence, U. of Tex., 1989, Excellence in Tchg. Cert., Wash. Fedn. of Teachers, 1990, Spl. Recognition for Outstanding Direction, Am. Coll. Theatre Festival, 1992, Excellence in Acting, 1992, Excellence award, Walla Walla C.C. Found., 1994, Cmty. Svc. award, Walla Walla Valley C. of C., 1999, Recognition award, NW Drama Conf., 1998. Mem.: Am. Coll. Theatre Festival (assoc.), Walla Walla Little Theatre (life). Home: Walla Walla, Wash. Died Feb. 18, 2009.

RATHYEN, LUCILLE KLEIN, gifted and talented education educator; b. Passaic, NJ, Sept. 24, 1945; d. Frank Alexander and Rose Sophia (DeBuck) Klein; m. Ralph David Rathyen, Feb. 18, 1967; 1 child, Jill. BA in Elem. Edn., Paterson State Coll., 1967; MA in Elem. Math., William Paterson Coll., 1989. 5th grade tchr. Pequannock (N.J.) Twp. Bd. Edn., 1969-75; gifted/talented tchr. West Milford (N.J.) Twp. Bd. Edn., from 1981. State problem capt. Odyssey of the Mind Program, Glassboro, N.J., 1987-91. Author: Style in the B.M. Program, 1986. Chairperson Bergen/Passaic Convocation Ramapo Coll., Mahway, N.J., 1982—. Rockland Electric Energy grantee, 1987. Mem. N.J. Educators of the Gifted and Talented, N.J. Edn. Assn., N.J. Assn. for Gifted Children, NEA. Home: Oak Ridge, NJ. Died Mar. 9, 2008.

RAU, ROBERT NICHOLAS, pipe distribution executive; b. Phila., Oct. 14, 1927; s. Nicholas A. and Mary A. (McCandless) R.; m. Alice Marie Farrington, May 21, 1949; children: Robert N., Donna-Marie Murphy, Karen Gamble, Patricia A. Pinkston. Student, Drexel U., 1947-48. Clk. to inside sales Hajoca Corp., Phila., Lansdale, Pa., 1951-54; inside sales to v.p. Standard Pipe and Supply, Bala Cynwyd, Pa., 1954-71; pres. BBL Co., Kulpsville, Pa., 1971-94, CEO, 1994—2009. Contbr. articles to profl. jours. Coach Spl. Olympics; active Boy Scouts of America With USN, 1945-46, PTO. Named Vol. of Yr., Spl. Olympics, 1991, Knowles-Rubin Steine Award of Excellence, 1996. Mem. ASTM (sec.), Nat. Assn. Steel Pipe Distbrs. (bd. dirs., v.p. 1988-89, pres. 1989-92, Pres.' award 1992, award of Excellence 1996). Republican. Roman Catholic. Avocations: cross country skiing, spl. olympics, grandchildren, travel. Home: Lansdale, Pa. Died July 18, 2009.

RAUCH, JOHN KEISER, JR., architect; b. Phila., Oct. 23, 1930; s. John Keiser and Marjorie (Gretz) R.; m. Carol Pfaff, Mar. 11, 1953 (div. June 1978); children: John David, Charles Daniel, Kathryn Mari, Peter, Carol Anne; m. Carol A. McConochie, Jan. 10, 1981. Student, Wesleyan U., Middletown, Conn., 1948-51; BArch., U. Pa., 1957; grad. cert. program, Pa. Acad. Fine Arts, 2001. Draftsman Cope & Lippincott, Phila., 1957-60; architect Venturi and Short, Phila., 1960-64; partner Venturi and Rauch (Architects and Planners), Phila., 1964-79, Venturi, Rauch and Scott Brown, 1980-82, v.p., mng. prin., 1982-87, mgmt. cons., mediator, arbitrator, 1988-96; instr. U. Pa. Grad. Sch. Fine Arts, 1969-70, 89. Lectr. dept. architecture Princeton (N.J.) U., 1990-94. Trustee Found. for Architecture, 1977-84, mem. adv. com., 1994-2002; treas. Phila. Rehab., Inc., 1984-94; pres. Reading Terminal Market Pres. Fund, 1988-93, bd. dirs., 1994-2001; bd. dirs. United Cerebral Palsy Assn., 1988-91. Recipient Good Neighbor award Mellon/PSFS Bank, 1992. Fellow AIA (emeritus; Firm award 1983, John Harbeson Disting Svc. Phila. Chpt. award 1992); mem. Pa. Soc. Architects. Democrat. Home: Philadelphia, Pa. Died Apr. 9, 2006.

RAUTH, JOHN FRANCIS, construction executive; b. Farm-Wabash, Nebr., Jan. 15, 1921; s. Aaron Francis and Anna Theresa (Stander) R.; m. Elizabeth Bridget Cobb, Aug. 5, 1944; children: Joyce Ann Rauth Fears, Eileen Marie Strider, Mary Kay Farley, Patricia Hayes, Michael G., Jeanne F. sheehan, Reine Seiler. Student, St. Louis U., 1945-51, Mo. Western State Coll., 1986-91. Founder, owner John Rauth Constrn., St. Joseph, Mo., 1953-86, semi-retired, chmn. bd., from 1986. Founder, pres. St. Josephs Home Builders, 1957-61. 1st lt. U.S. Army Air Corps, 1940-45, ret. lt. col. USAF, 1969. Mem. KC, Soc. of Precious Blood. Independent. Roman Catholic. Avocations: yard work, gardening, travel. Home: Saint Joseph, Mo. Died Aug. 2, 2008.

RAWLINGS, GREGORY OWEN, science educator, consultant; b. Roswell, N.Mex., Jan. 29, 1951; s. Vernon Keith and Mildred Mary Rawlings; m. Virginia Lee Murphy, Oct. 26, 1985; 1 adopted child 1 child, Stephanie Janiece. BS, U. of Kans., 1973. Cert. adm. Kans. State Dept. of Edn. Intermediate sci. tchr. Unified Sch. Dist. #497, Lawrence, Kans., 1973—78, Unified Sch. Dist. #305, Salina, Kans., 1978—82; asst. mgr., cashier supr. Wal-Mart #558, Salina, 1983—84; account rep. Burroughs Computer Corp., Rochester, NY, 1984—85; tchr. 8th grade earth sci. and algebra Unified Sch. Dist. 469, Lansing, Kans., 1986—2008; prof. algebra studies, bus., med. ethics, and profl. devel. Brown Mackie Coll., Leneka, Kans., 2006—08. Resource person Harvard-Smithsonian Ctr. for Astrophysics - Project ES-TEEM. Mem. Dist. Site Coun., Lansing, 1995—2002, Dist. Steering Com., Lansing, 1986—94; mem. blue ribbon adv. bd. ShareNet Pan Ednl. Inst., Independence, Mo.,

1989—93. Named Outstanding Instr. of Yr., BrownMackie Coll., 2008. Mem.: NEA, Kans. Nat. Edn. Assn. (adminstrv. bd. dirs. 2003—04), Nat. Sci. Tchrs. Assn. Home: Lansing, Kans. Died Dec. 15, 2008.

RAWSON, JOHN ELTON, neonatologist, medical educator; b. Okolona, Miss., Jan. 31, 1938; s. Elton Phlemuel and Marjorie Morgan Jones Rawson; m. Mary Crouch Rawson, June 23, 1962; children: Katherine Asbury Rawson Kronzer, Edwin Lauderdale. BS in Chemisty, Millsaps Coll., 1960; MD, U. Miss., 1965. Diplomate Am. Bd. Pediat., Am. Bd. Neonatology and Perinatal Medicine; lic. physician, Miss. Clin. assoc. prof. pediat. U. Miss. Sch. Medicine, Jackson, from 1972; attending neonatologist, chief newborn medicine Ctrl. Miss. Med. Ctr., Jackson, from 1978; attending neonatologist Miss. Bapt. Med. Ctr., Jackson, from 1982. Chmn. bd. dirs. Health Choice of Miss., Jackson, 1991-98, Integrity Health Plan, Inc., Jackson, 1995-98, State Watch, Inc., Jackson, 1988-96; chief of staff Meth. Healthcare, Inc., Jackson, 1994-95. Editor: Newborn Ventilation, 1976. State chmn. March of Dimes, Jackson, 1972-82; mem. vestry St. James Episcopal Ch., Jackson, 1975-78; trustee St. Andrew's Day Sch., Madison, Miss., 1978-89, Meth. Lebouner Found., Memphis, 1991-2000. Capt. USAF, 1968-70. Mem. Rotary (Paul Harris fellow 1984). Home: Madison, Miss. Died Apr. 15, 2009.

RAY, JERRY W., golf professional; b. Boonville, Mo., June 30, 1944; s. William Earl and Effie Davis (Lloyd) R.; m. Donna Evelyn Mittlehauser, June 1, 1968; children: Shannon, Erin, Jeremy. BA in Polit. Sci. and Econs., Cen. Mo. State U., 1969. Cert. PGA of Am. Golf profl. L.F. Galbraith G.C., Oakland, Calif., 1971-73, Almaden Country Club, San Jose, Calif., 1973-75, Chillicothe (Mo.) Country Club, 1975-78, Paradise Valley Country Club, St. Louis County, Mo., 1978-84, owner, from 1984. Dir. PGA of Am., Palm Beach Gardens, Fla., 1991-94. With USN, 1963-66. Named Master Profl. PGA of Am., Palm Beach Gardens, 1987. Mem. Gateway PGA (sec. 1986-87, pres. 1987-88, Golf Pro of Yr. 1985). Republican. Mem. Christian Ch. (Disciples Of Christ). Avocations: golf, skiing, classic cars. Home: Ballwin, Mo. Died Oct. 7, 2007.

RAY, JOHN WALKER, otolaryngologist, educator, broadcast commentator; b. Columbus, Ohio, Jan. 12, 1936; s. Kenneth Clark and Hope (Walker) R.; m. Susanne Gettings, July 15, 1961; children: Nancy Ann, Susan Christy. AB magna cum laude, Marietta Coll., Ohio, 1956; MD cum laude, Ohio State U., 1960; postgrad., Temple U., Phila., 1964, Mt. Sinai Hosp., Columbia U., NYC, 1964-66, Northwestern U., Evanston, Ill., 1967-71, U. Ill., 1968, U. Ind., 1969, Tulane U., New Orleans, 1969. Diplomate Am. Bd. Otolaryngology. Intern Ohio State U. Hosps., Columbus, 1960-61, clin. rsch. trainee NIH, 1963-65, resident dept. otolaryngology, 1963-65, 66-67, resident dept. surgery, 1965-66, instr. dept. otolaryngology, 1966-67, 70-75, clin. asst. prof., 1975-82, clin. assoc. prof., 1982-92, clin. prof., 1992-2000, clin. prof. emeritus, from 2000; hon. staff, past chief of staff Good Samaritan Hosp., Zanesville, Ohio, from 1967, Bethesda Hosp., Zanesville, from 1967. Hon. active staff Meml. Hosp., Marietta, Ohio, from 1992; radio-TV health commentator, 1982—2006. Contbr. articles to profl. jours.; collaborator with surg. motion picture: Laryngectomy and Neck Dissection, 1964. Past pres. Muskingum chpt. Am. Cancer Soc. Capt. USAF, 1961-63. Recipient Barraquer Meml. award, 1965; named to Order of Ky. Col., 1966, Muskingum County Country Music Hall of Fame. Fellow ACS, Am. Soc. Otolaryn. Allergy, Am. Acad. Otolaryngology-Head and Neck Surgery (past gov.), Am. Acad. Facial Plastic and Reconstructive Surgery; mem. AMA, Nat. Assn. Physician Broadcasters, Muskingum County Acad. Medicine (past pres.), Ohio Med. Assn., Columbus Ophthalmol. and Otolaryn. Soc. (past pres.), Ohio Soc. Otolaryngology (past pres.), Am. Soc. Contemporary Medicine and Surgery, Acad. Radio and TV Health Commentators, Fraternal Order of Police Assocs., Internat. Bluegrass Music Assn., Phi Beta Kappa, Alpha Omega Alpha, Beta Beta Beta, Alpha Tau Omega, Alpha Kappa Kappa. Presbyterian. Home: Zanesville, Ohio. Deceased.

RAYMOND, SAMUEL, computer consultant, retired educator; b. Chester, Pa., Feb. 7, 1920; s. Samuel Murdock and Sara Taylor (Griffith) R.; m. Mary Vernon Hanson, Oct. 27, 1951; children: Elizabeth, Griffith. BA, Swarthmore Coll., 1941; MA, U. Pa., 1942, PhD, 1945; MD, Columbia U., 1957. Internship Grad. Hosp., Phila.; residency in pathology Hosp. U. of Pa., Phila., 1958-63; asst. prof. Columbia U., NYC, 1951-57; asst. to assoc. prof. U. Pa., Phila., 1958-91, prof. emeritus, from 1991. Inventor in field. Died Dec. 25, 2007.

RAYNOR, SHERRY DIANE, association administrator; b. Escanaba, Mich., Aug. 18, 1930; d. James Christopher and Ebba (Ebbesen) Nevans; married, 1949 (div. 1955); children: Robert Storrer, Christine Storrer, Sandra Storrer; married, 1959 (div. 1972); children: Ebba Raynor, Nels Raynor, Beatrice Raynor. BA, Mich. State U., 1965, MA, 1967. Cert. elem. tchr., edn. blind, spl. edn. Mich., Mass. Pres., founder, dir. Blind Children's Fund (formerly Internat. Inst. for Visually Impaired, 0-7, Inc.), East Lansing, Mich. and Auburndale, Mass., from 1978; supr., initiator Perkins Presch., Watertown, Mass., 1979-80; coordinator, initiator Perkins Infant/Toddler Program, Watertown, 1980-83; project dir. Project Outreach USA, Newton, Mass., 1983-84. Dir., founder Infant Program for Visually Impaired, IISD, Mason, Mich., 1972-79; chmn. ICEVH Subcom. Presch. Blind Children, 1987; pres. 1st Internat. Symposium on Infant and Presch. Visually Handicapped Infants and Young Children, Internat. Inst. for Visually Impaired, 0-7, Inc., Israel, 1981, 2d Internat. Symposium, Netherlands Antilles, 1983; mem. standing com. Annual Internat. Seminars on Presch. Blind. Author: (with others) (books for parents of blind children) Get a Wiggle On, 1975, Move It, 1977, (book for tchrs. of blind children) Mainstreaming Preschoolers: Children with Visual Handicaps, 1985. Mem. Assn. for Edn. and Rehab. of Blind and Visually Impaired (chmn. div. VIII Infants and Preschoolers 1984-86, Pauline M. Moor award 1986), Nat. Assn. Parents of Visually Impaired (award for exemplary practice 1986), Internat. Coun. for Exceptional Children, Internat. Coun. for Edn. of Visually Handicapped, World Blind Union, Am. Coun. for Blind, Assn. Childhood Edn. Internat., Nat. Fedn. Blind, Coun. Exceptional Children. Lodges: Zonta. Avocations: photography, sewing, writing, travel. Died Dec. 10, 2007.

RAZOR, MARY C., writer; b. Clinton, Iowa, Aug. 12, 1926; d. William Francis and Lillian Anne (Alvis) Curran; m. Al Razor, Jan. 8, 1973. BA magna cum laude, Drake U., 1985. Author: All Our Yesterdays, 1945, Hominy Ridge, 1981, Hello From Hominy Ridge, 1994. Founding mem. Seed Savers Exch.; mem. Iowa Woodland Owners Assn., Iowa Nut Growers Assn., Friends of Walnut Creek, Sea Shepherd, Earth First, Iowa Prairie Network, Beta Beta Beta, Sigma Tau Delta. Avocation: conservationist activities. Home: Iowa Falls, Iowa. Died Feb. 14, 2008.

READER, GEORGE G., retired internal-public health medicine educator; b. Bklyn., 1919; m. Helen Brown, May 23, 1942; 4 children. BA in Animal Biology, Cornell U., Ithaca, NY, 1940; MD, Cornell U., NYC, 1943; ScD (hon.), Drew U., 1988. Intern in medicine N.Y. Hosp., NYC, 1944-45, resident and fellow in medicine, 1946—50, resident in hematology, 1950—51; instr. medicine Cornell U. Med. Ctr., 1951—52, from asst. prof. to prof., 1952—89, emeritus prof. medicine, from 1989, Livingston Farrand prof. pub. health, from 1989. Former advisor Social Security Adminstrn.; former chmn. human ecology study sect. NIH; former chmn. tech. com. on tng. White House Conf. on Aging; former cons. OEO, Office Sec. of HEW, Health Svcs. and Mental Health Adminstrn.; head transition task force health adv. coun. N.Y. State Dept. Health, 1974—84; former chmn. N.Y. State Task Force on Health of Sch. Age Child and Health Manpower; rep. Cornell U. Med. Ctr. in Health Planning for N.Y.C.; mem. master plan com. N.Y.C. Hosp. Coun. Mem. N.Y.C. Mayor's Organized Task Force for Health Planning; mem. local planning bd. representing N.Y. Hosp., Health Sys. Agy., NYC. Scholar Regents scholar, Cornell U., 1940. Mem.: AOA, Inst. of Medicine (sr.), Skulls. Home: Florham Park, NJ. Died Oct. 13, 2005.

RECKER, THERESA LOUISE, medical educator; b. Chgo., Sept. 11, 1951; d. Joseph Walter and Marjorie Irene (Crowder) Lenahan; m. William Joseph Recker, Apr. 21, 1979. Student, Prairie State Coll., 1972; cert. in radiologic tech., Ravenswood Hosp. and Med. Ctr., 1974; student, Triton Coll., 1978, Coll. of DuPage, 1984. Cert. tchr., Ill.; cert. radiologic tech., Ill. Spl. procedures technologist Meml. Hosp. DuPage County, Elmhurst, Ill., 1974-79; radiologic technologist Sherman Hosp., Elgin, Ill., 1979-80; spl. procedures technologist Glendale Heights (Ill.) Hosp., 1980-82; instr. Nat. Edn. Corp., Chgo., 1982-88; instr. English illiteracy Coll. of DuPage, Glen Ellyn, Ill., from 1988. Contbr. articles to travel mags. and newspapers. Mem. Am. Society Radiologic Technologists. Republican. Roman Catholic. Avocations: downhill and cross-country skiing, bicycling, golf, travel. Died Oct. 6, 2007.

REDDING, ROBERT HULL, writer; b. Hilo, Hawaii, Dec. 3, 1919; s. Emily Hull; m. Grace Margaret Feeny, July 14, 1956. Freelance writer, Sequim, Wash., from 1977. Sgt. USAF, 1942-46. Avocations: swimming, hiking. Home: Sequim, Wash. Died Apr. 21, 2008.

REED, ALFRED, composer, conductor; b. NYC, Jan. 25, 1921; s. Carl Mark and Elizabeth (Strasser) Friedman; m. Marjorie Beth Deley, June 20, 1941; children: Michael Carlson, Richard Judson. Student, Juilliard Sch. Music, 1946—48; MusB, Baylor U., 1955, MusM, 1956; MusD, Internat. Conservatory of Music, Lima, Peru, 1968. Exec. editor Hansen Publs., NYC, 1955-66; prof. music U. Miami (Fla.) Sch. Music, 1966-93. Composer, arranger, N.Y.C., 1941-60; condr. Tri-State Music Festival, Okla., 1956-57, 60-66, 70, 73, Midwest Nat. Band Clinic, 1960-91, Bemidji (Minn.) Summer Music Camp, 1970-71, 75, Mid-East Instrumental Music Conf., Pitts., 1957-60, Can. Music Educators Assn., Edmonton, Alta., 1975; composer: Russian Christmas Music, 1944, Symphony for Brass and Percussion, 1952, Rhapsody for Viola and Orch, 1956, Choric Song, 1966, Titania's Nocturne, 1967, A Festival Prelude, 1962, Passacaglia, 1968, Music for Hamlet, 1973, Armenian Dances, 1974-75, Punchinello, Overture to a Romantic Comedy, 1974, Testament of an American, 1974, First Suite for Band, 1975, Othello, A Symphonic Portrait in Five Scenes, 1976, Prelude and Capriccio, 1977, Second Symphony, 1978, Siciliana Notturno, 1978, Second Suite for Band, 1978, The Enchanted Island, 1979, The Hounds of Spring, 1980, Third Suite for Band, 1981, Queenston Overture, 1982, Viva Musica!, 1983, A Little Concert Suite, 1983, El Camino Real, 1985, Centennial!, 1985, Three Revelations from the Lotus Sutra, 1985, Golden Jubilee, 1986, A Christmas Celebration, 1986, Praise Jerusalem!, 1987, Third Symphony, 1988, Eventide, 1988, Golden Eagle, 1989, Curtain Up!, 1990, A Springtime Celebration, Hymn Variants, 1991, With Trumpets and Drums, 1991, Concertino for Marimba and Winds, 1991, 4th Symphony, 1992, Fourth Suite for Band, 1993, Evolutions, A Concert Overture, 1993, 5th Symphony, 1994, Fifth Suite for Band, 1995, Two Bagatelles, 1997, Concerto for Trumpet and Winds, 1997, Divertimento for Flute and Winds, 1997, Sixth Suite for Band, 1998, Millenium III, 1999, Sumus Futuro, 1999, Carto e Camdombe, 1999, Jidai (Year of Years!), 1999, Acclamation!, 1999, Children's Suite, 2001, Five Cameos for Saxophone Ouartet, 2002, Joyeux Nöel, 2002, Music in the air, 2002, Seventh suite for Band, 2002, Fanfare and Processional, 2003, Rosalind in the Forest of Arden, 2003, Twelfth Night, 2003, others. With AUS, 1942-46. Mem. ASCAP, Am. Bandmasters Assn., Am. Fedn. Musicians, Nat. Band Assn., Music Educators Nat. Conv. Died Sept. 17, 2005.

REED, JACK WILSON, meteorologist, consultant; b. Corning, Iowa, Sept. 24, 1923; s. Charles Emory and VeraBelle (Wilson) R.; m. Lois Catherine Linville, Sept. 1, 1944; children: Rodger Lloyd (dec.), Margaret Louise. BS, U. N.Mex., 1948. Cert. cons. meteorologist. Meteorologist Sandia Nat. Lab., Albuquerque, 1948-89, JWR, Inc., Albuquerque, from 1989. Sci. adv. panel Atomic Energy Coun., Mercury, Nev., 1956-70, phys. effects NAS Sonic Boom com., Washington, 1962-70. Contbr. articles to profl. jours. Lt. col. USAF, Air Nat. Guard, 1943—, ret. Mem. AAAS, Am. Meteorol. Soc., Am. Geophys. Union, Acoustical Soc. Am. (chmn. shock and vibration standards com. 1976—), Am. Nuclear Soc., Air and Waste Mgmt. Soc., Internat. Standards Orgn. (chmn. tech. com. 108, 1993—). Democrat. Congregationalist. Achievements include development of methods for statis. winds predictions; methods for explosion and other shock wave propagation predictions in the atmosphere; methods for predicting airblast damage to windows; analyses of wind energy potentials. Home: Albuquerque, N.Mex. Died Nov. 30, 2007.

REED, VASTINA KATHRYN (TINA), child and adolescent psychotherapist; b. Chgo., Mar. 5, 1960; d. Alvin Hillard and Ruth Gwendolyn (Thomas) R.; 1 child, Alvin J. BA in Human Svcs. magna cum laude, Nat.-Louis U., Chgo., 1988; MA, Ill. Sch. Profl. Psychology, Chgo., 1991; tng. cert., Appelbaum Inst. Child Devel.; cert. family devel. specialist, U. Iowa, 2002; fashion cons. of Evangelist Audey Donson, Good Shepherd Grace Min., from 2002. Notary pub. Ill., lic. profl. counselor Ill., child and adolescent psychotherapist, nat. cert. counselor NBCC. Tchr. early childhood edn. Kendall Coll. Lab. Sch., Evanston, Ill., 1983-85, Rogers Park Children's Learning Ctr., Chgo., 1983-85; child life therapist Mt. Sinai Hosp., Chgo., 1988; child psychotherapist Nicholas Barnes Therapeutic Day Sch., Chgo., 1989-90; presch. instr. YMCA, 1999-2000; crisis line counselor Washington Security Corp., 2000—02; family support specialist Maywood (Ill.) Head Start, 2000—03; health care rep. Care Entrée, 2002—03; mental health svc. coord. Head Start Chgo. Dept. Children & Youth Svcs., from 2005. Den leader Boy Scouts Am., Chgo., 1989-92, scoutmaster, 1992-2000, merit badge counselor, 1999—, troop advisor for Order of the Arrow; vision ptnr., co-labourers Christ Ministry; editor, mem. praise and worship team Christ Outreach Deliverance Ctr. Ministry, 2001—; mem. Ill. Notary Public. Recipient Cub Scouter award Boy Scouts Am., 1990, Scoutmaster award of merit, 1993, 94, Scouters Vet. award, 1994, Scouters Tng. award, 1995, Scoutmasters Key award, 1996, Okpik Cold Weather Camping cert., 1994-95, Outstanding Women of 20th Century medal, 2000, Boy Scout Woodbadge Tng. award, 2001. Mem. APA, Nat. Orgn. for Human Svc. Edn., Order of the Arrow, Charles F. Menninger Soc. (patron), Phi Theta Kappa, Kappa Delta Pi. Democrat. Pentecostal. Avocations: camping, films, singing, music. Home: Chicago, Ill. Died Dec. 18, 2007.

REED, WALTER GEORGE, JR., retired osteopath; b. Ardmore, Okla., Sept. 10, 1928; s. Walter George and Lillian Dorene (Gee) Reed; children: Jay Walter, David George, Kimberly Sue. BA, Phillips U., 1955; DO, Kansas City U. Medicine and Bioscis., 1959. Intern Des Moines Gen. Hosp., 1959—60; pvt. practice Oklahoma City, 1960-63, Atoka, Okla., 1963-80; flight surgeon USAF, Omaha, 1980-84, Lubbock, Tex., 1984-86; chief med. officer Army Health Clinic, McAlester, Okla., 1986-96; ret. USAF, 1996. Mayor City of Atoka, 1967—72; v.p. Atoka Bd. Edn., 1974—79. Lt. col. USAF, 1980—96. Mem.: Assn. Mil. Surgeons U.S., Okla. Osteo. Assn. (life), Assn. Mil. Osteo. Physicians and Surgeons (life), Ret. Officers Assn. (life), Air Force Assn. (life), Masons (32d degree). Avocations: flying, hunting, computers, plate collecting. Home: Owasso, Okla. Died Apr. 2009.

REEDY, MARY CATHERINE, cell biologist; b. Chgo., Feb. 10, 1944; d. William C. and Alberta G. (Heintzberger) Hambley; m. Michael K. Reedy, Jan. 30, 1973; 1 child, M. Carter. BS, Rollins Coll., Winter Park, Fla., 1965; MS, Georgetown U., Washington, 1967. Rsch. asst. U. N.C., Chapel Hill, 1967-68; lab. mgr. Duke U. Med. Ctr., Durham, N.C., 1968-78, rsch. assoc., from 1978. Contbr. articles to profl. jours. Mem. Biophys. Soc. Episcopalian. Died Aug. 8, 2008.

REEVE, PAUL THOMAS, corporate communications specialist; b. Waterbury, Conn., May 2, 1950; s. Charles Thomas and Marjorie Mae (Wilkinson) R.; m. Nancy Jeanne Maynes, July 11, 1970; children: Thomas, Adam, Eric. BA in Econs., U. Conn., 1972; postgrad., Temple U., 1974. Asst. indsl. relations mgr. Uniroyal, Inc., Phila.,

1972-75; employee relations supr. Allied Chem. Corp., Phila., 1975-78; indsl. relations mgr. Philip Morris, Inc., Downingtown, Pa., 1978-79; corp. dir. tng., devel. Providence (R.I.) Jour. Co., from 1979. Mem. bus. labor adv. council Bryant Coll., Smithfield, R.I., 1986—. Mgr. Lower Lincoln (R.I.) Little League, 1981-83, Dept. Recreation Biddy Basketball Program, 1981—; deacon Sayles Meml. Ch., Lincoln, 1982-85; sec. Saylesville Highland Assn., 1981-82. Mem. Am. Mgmt. Assn., Am. Soc. Personnel Adminstrs., Am. Soc. Tng. and Devel., Am. Compensation Assn., Orgn. Devel. Network. Avocations: guitar playing, swimming, basketball, baseball. Home: North Scituate, RI. Died Jan. 1, 2008.

REH, SHEILA NATKINS, humanities educator; b. NY, Apr. 7, 1926; d. Benjamin F. Natkins and Bertha North; m. William S. Reh, Nov. 25, 1944 (dec. Dec. 21, 1969); 1 child, Virginia A. BA-English, NYU -Wash. Sq. Coll., New York, NY, 1942—45; MS-education, Wagner Coll., Staten Island, N Y, 1964—65. Tchr. Bd. of Ed., New York, NY, 1964—89. Actor: (acting) Emerson Little Theatre-Staten Island. Bd. of directors, exec. comm. Snug Harbor Cultural Ctr., Staten Island, NY, 1993—96, lead docent-dept. of ed., from 2005, co-chair b ook fair, 1996—98. Recipient, N ew York State Assembly, 1998, Vol. of the Yr., Snug Harbor Cultural Ctr., 2001, Vol. Of The Week, SI Advance, 2001 (Year of the Volunteer-UN). Avocations: tennis, drama. Home: Staten Island, NY. Deceased.

REHMUS, CHARLES MARTIN, arbitrator; b. Ann Arbor, Mich., June 27, 1926; s. Paul A. and Amy D. (Martin) R.; m. Carolyn Brown, Dec. 21, 1948 (div. July 1982); children— Paul, James, Jon, David; m. Laura Carlson, Sept. 4, 1982 AB, Kenyon Coll., 1947; MA, Stanford U., 1951, PhD, 1955. Commr. Fed. Mediation and Conciliation Service, San Francisco, 1952-58; staff dir. Presdl. R.R. Commn., Washington, 1959-61; prof. polit. sci. U. Mich., Ann Arbor, 1962-80, dir. Inst. Labor and Indsl. Relations, 1962-76; chmn. Mich. Employment Relations Commn., Detroit, 1976-80; dean N.Y. State Sch. Indsl. and Labor Relations, Cornell U., Ithaca, 1980-86; prof. law U. San Diego, 1988-97. Author: Final-Offer Arbitration, 1975, The Railway Labor Act at Fifty, 1977, Labor and American Politics, 1967, rev. edit., 1978, The National Mediation Board, 1984, Emergency Strikes Revisited, 1990. Chmn. 4 Presdl. emergency bds. at various times. Served to lt. USNR, 1943-45; PTO Mem. Internat. Inst. Labor Studies (bd. govs. 1984-92), Indsl. Rels. Rsch. Assn. (exec. bd. 1984-88), Nat. Acad. Arbitrators (hon. life mem. 2008). Home: San Diego, Calif. Deceased.

REICH, PAUL FRANK, retail specialist; b. Pitts., May 3, 1929; s. Samuel Joseph and Sara (Glick) R.; m. Jane Cansler, Feb. 23, 1946 (div. July 1986); children: Sara Andrea, Andrew Phillip, David Geoffrey. BS, U. Ariz., 1951. Sales rep. Revlon, Inc., Phoenix, 1952-59; buyer Diamonds Dept. Store, Phoenix, 1959-65, mdse. mgr., 1965-72, John A. Brown Co., Oklahoma City, 1972-80, Dayton Hudson Corp., Mpls., 1980-84, Dillard Dept. Stores, Ft. Worth, from 1984. Republican. Jewish. Avocations: stamp collector, travel. Died June 19, 2008.

REILEY, JOHN ECHOLS, writer; b. Hinton, W.Va., July 13, 1927; s. Earl Walton and Gladys Mary (Hansbarger) R.; m. Marjorie M. Martin (div. 1967); 1 child, Patricia Anne. BSEE, VPI, 1956. Rschr. electronic lab. GE, Salem, Va., 1957-67; owner Grandin Rd. T.V., Roanoke, Va., 1972-75; technician electronics Lee Hartman and Sons, Roanoke, from 1977. Mgr. Bonanza Restaurant, Roanoke, 1977, Loyal Order Moose, Roanoke, 1969-71; instr. VCR servicing Va. We. Coll., 1988, Augusta Correctional Ctr., Craigsville, Va., 1987. Author: Video Productions, 1987, Camcorder Operation, 1989, Death on Memphis Princess Mystery; poems read at Korean Vets. Reunion, Lincoln Terr. Grade Sch.; author (poem) Hopeful Peace (on Scroll in Libr. of Congress 1996). With U.S. Army, 1950-52, Korea. Mem. Internat. Soc. Poets (Bronze medal 1996), Roanoke Valley Writer's Club. Republican. Presbyterian. Home: Roanoke, Va. Died Jan. 28, 2008.

REINHARDT, DEBORAH ANN, music educator; d. James Willard Reinhardt and Wilma Ruth Gibler. MusB in Edn., Baldwin-Wallace Coll., Berea, Ohio, 1973; MusM, Ithaca Coll., NY, 1987; PhD in Music Edn., Case Western Res. U., Cleve., 1990. Music tchr. A.B. Hart Jr. High Cleve. Pub. Schs., 1973—77; music tchr. Kenston Pub. Schs., Chagrin Falls, Ohio, 1977—80, Busby Sch. of No. Cheyenne Tribe, Busby, Mont., 1980—82, Jonesport (Maine) Elem. Sch., 1982—85; asst. prof. music edn. U. Nebr., Lincoln, 1995—2000, Ball State U., Muncie, Ind., 1990—95; assoc. prof. music edn., dir. music edn. Calif. State U., Chico, from 2000. Author: (monograph) A Rich Tapestry: The Music Of Nebraska; contbr. articles to profl. jours. Coord. h.s. honor choir Calif. State U., Chico, 2002—05. Mem.: Calif. Coun. Music Tchr. Educators (chair from 2004), Am. Orff-Schulwerk Assn. (collegiate rep. 2003), Coll. Music Soc., Calif. Assn. Music Edn. (treas. no. sect. from 2003, coord. solo and ensemble festival, coord. large group choral festival 2002). Achievements include research in relationship between creative activities, music learning and curriculum. Avocations: folk dancing, swimming. Died Sept. 25, 2007.

REINHART, DIETRICH THOMAS, retired academic administrator, social studies educator; b. Mpls., May 17, 1949; s. Donald Irving and Eleanor Therese (Noonan) R. BA in History, St. John's U., Collegeville, Minn., 1971; AM in History, Brown U., 1976, PhD in History, 1984. Benedictine monk St. John's Abbey, 1971—2009; prof. history St. John's U., 1981—2008, dean of the coll., 1988-91, pres., 1991—2008, pres. emeritus, 2008—09. Dir. liturgy St. John's Abbey, 1983-88. Bd. dirs. Minn. Pvt. Coll. Coun., George A. MacPherson Fund, Hill Monastic Manuscript Library, Inst. for Ecumenical and Cultural Rsch., First Am. Nat. Bank St. Cloud.; bd. overseers St. John's Prep. Sch. Home: Collegeville, Minn. Died Dec. 29, 2008.

REINKE, FRANCES MARYLOU, science educator; b. Gary, Ind., June 10, 1941; d. Theodore George and Helen Stella (Zowal) Kasperek; m. Leonard J. Reinke, June 21, 1969 (dec. 1986). BS, Ind. U., 1963; MA, U. Mich., 1965; postgrad., Mont. State U., 1971; MS, Notre Dame U., 1972; postgrad., Concordia Coll., from 1988. Tchr. Detroit Redford High Sch., 1963-64, Gavit High Sch., Hammond, Ind., 1965-79, Clark High Sch., Hammond, from 1980, chmn. sci. dept., from 1987; instr. sci. Calumet (Ind.) Coll., Ind. U. Tutor Hammond Pub. Schs., 1965—; mem. Air. Force Acad. U.S. Space Found. Mem. Sch. Improvement Program, 1986—, Ind. Book Adoption Com., 1986-87, Hammond Drug and Alcohol Prevention Task Force, Snowflake and Snowball Drug and Alcohol Prevention Jr. and Sr. High Sch. Workshops, Parents Students Tchrs. Assn.; active middle sch. and high sch. sci. fairs; sci. olympiad coach; sponsor, mentor SADD; sponsor Nat. Geography Bee; acad. decathlon coach; active Hoosier Spell Bowl; pentathlon coach Hoosier Super Bowl. Recipient semi-finalist Presdl. award, 1987, PTSA Life award for Excellence in thcg., 2005; named Tchr. of Yr. Inland Steel, 1986; grantee, NSF, Nat. Inst. of Health, 1993, HHMI grant, 2004. Mem. NEA, Am. Fedn. Tchrs., Nat. Sci. Tchrs. Assn., Nat. Assn. Biology Tchrs., Ind. State Tchrs. Assn., Hammond Tchrs. Assn., Hammond Fedn. Tchrs., Calumet Assn. Sci. Tchrs., Nat. Honor Soc. (adv. bd.), Hoosier Assn. Sci. Tchrs. of Ind., Ogden Dunes Women's Club, Sierra Club, Sci. Club (sponsor), Chess Club (sponsor). Roman Catholic. Avocations: travel, painting, skiing, reading, outdoors. Home: Portage, Ind. Died July 6, 2008.

REISTER, RAYMOND ALEX, retired lawyer; b. Sioux City, Iowa, Dec. 22, 1929; s. Harold William and Anne (Eberhardt) R.; m. Ruth Elizabeth Alkema, Oct. 7, 1967 AB, Harvard U., 1952, LLB, 1955. Bar: N.Y. 1956, Minn. 1960. Assoc. Paul, Weiss, Rifkind, Wharton & Garrison, NYC, 1955-56; ptnr. Dorsey & Whitney LLP, Mpls., 1959-92; ret., 1993. Instr. U. Minn. Extension Divsn., 1964-66. Editor (with Larry W. Johnson): Minnesota Probate Administration, 1968. Trustee Mpls. Soc. Fine Arts, 1981-87; mem. exec. coun. Minn. Hist. Soc., 1984-2002; bd. dirs. Mpls. Athenaeum, 1992—, pres., 1998-2001; bd. dirs. Minn. Humanities Commn., 1997—. 1st lt. U.S. Army, 1956-59. Mem. Minn. Bar Assn., Hennepin County Bar Assn. Home: Minneapolis, Minn. Died Sept. 4, 2005.

REIT, SCOTT JOEL, lawyer; b. Kew Gardens, NY; m. Ann Marie Reit. BA, U. Mich., Ann Arbor, 1979; JD, George Washington U., DC, 1982; M in Taxation, U. Miami, Coral Gables, Fla., 1987. Bar: Fla. 1982, NY 1983, cert.: Fla. Bar Bd. Legal Specialization and Edn. (real estate atty.) 1993. Assoc. Fleming, O'Bryan & Fleming, PA, Fort Lauderdale, Fla., 1982—88, shareholder, 1989—99; assoc. Schroeder & Larche, PA, Boca Raton, Fla., 1998—99, Mombach, Boyle & Hardin, PA, Fort Lauderdale, from 1999. Sec. Broward County Real Estate Coun., Fort Lauderdale, from 2007. Vol. atty. Broward Lawyer's Care-Legal Aid Svc. Broward County, Inc., Fort Lauderale, from 1995. Mem.: Bankruptcy Bar Assn., Broward County Bar Assn. Avocations: sports, basketball. Deceased.

RENEHAN, CLAIRE, nursing education administrator; b. Providence, Oct. 20, 1928; d. Edmund James and Anna Mary Renehan. Diploma., R.I. Hosp., 1949; BSN, Salve Regina, 1981. RN, R.I., Va.; cert. nurse oper. rm. Educator oper. rm. Project Hope, Millwood, Va.; coord. insvc. edn. R.I. Hosp., Providence. Recipient award R.I. Hosp. Nurses Alumni, 1969. Mem. Assn. Oper. Rm. Nurses (congress del., bd. dirs.). Home: Providence, RI. Died May 29, 2008.

RENSE, WILLIAM ALPHONSUS, physicist, astrophysicist; b. Massillion, Ohio, Mar. 11, 1914; s. Joseph and Rose (Luther) R.; m. Wanda Evelyn Childs, May 5, 1942; children: William C., John A.L., Charles E.C. BS, Case Sch. Applied Sci., Cleve., 1935; MS, Ohio State U., 1937, PhD, 1939. Asst. prof. Rutgers U., New Brunswick, N.J., 1941-42, La. State U., Baton Rouge, 1943-47, assoc. prof., 1947-49; faculty U. Colo., Boulder, 1951-79, prof. physics, 1957-79; co-dir. Lab. for Atmospheric and Space Physics, Boulder, 1957-79. Author: (book) Physical Science, 1966; contbr. numerous articles to profl. jours., 1949-79. Bd. dirs., chmn., Ctr. For Sci., Tech. and Political Thought, Boulder, 1978-89. Mem. Am. Physical Soc., Am. Astron. Soc., Am. Geophysical Union, Rsch. Soc. Am., Explorers Club, Sigma Xi, Tau Beta Pi, Colo.-Wyo. Acad. Sci. (physics chmn.) Achievements include study and measurement of ultraviolet radiation from sun, rockets and satellites; discovery of solar hydrogen Lyman alpha line and solar lines in far ultraviolet; development of rocket and satellite optical instruments for solar ultraviolet measurements. Home: Allenspark, Colo. Died Mar. 28, 2008.

RETHY, ROBERT AARON, philosophy educator; b. NYC, Feb. 11, 1949; s. Richard Emmanuel and Florence (Gerstman) R.; m. Sonja Lorraine Thornberg, Aug. 22, 1979; children: Isaac Martin, Leah Britt, Alisa Rebecka. BA in English Lit. with honors, Trinity Coll., Hartford, Conn., 1969; MA in Philosophy, Pa. State U., 1975, PhD, 1980. Asst. prof. philosophy Pa. State U., University Park, 1980-81; reader U. Essex, Wivenhoe Pk., Eng., 1989-90; asst. prof. philosophy Xavier U., Cin., 1982-87, assoc. prof., 1990-95; prof., chair philosophy dept., from 1995. Referee Philosophy and Rhetoric, University Park, 1990—, Jour. of History Ideas, Altanta, 1991—; Xavier Rsch. sabbatical, 1992-93. Contbr. articles and revs. to profl. jours. and ency. Instr. adult edn. Temple Shalom, Cin., 1984, No. Hills Synagogue, Cin., 1991-92. Pa. State U. fellow, 1973-74; rsch. fellow Xavier U., summer 1984; recipient NEHsr. summer stipend. Mem. Ohio Coun. Humanities. Avocations: piano, squash, gardening, reading. Home: Cincinnati, Ohio. Died July 5, 2008.

RETTER, JAMES ROBERT, marketing educator, consultant; b. Pitts., Jan. 17, 1925; s. James Sigismund and Ida Teresa (Dietrich) R.; m. Florence McCarthy, July 3, 1948; children: James, Paul, Matthew, Patricia, Susan, Jane, Carol. BSChemE, U. Notre Dame, 1945; MBA, U. Conn., 1973; DProfl. Studies in Econs. and Fin., Pace U., 1984. Regional mgr. Union Carbide Corp., Charlotte, N.C., 1963-67, dir. distbn. NYC, 1967-70, dir. mktg. svcs., pricing adminstr., 1970-73, mgr. pricing svcs., 1973-76, product mgr., mem. hydrocarbons dept. mgmt. team, 1976-78; product mgr., regional sales mgr. Ga. Pacific Corp., Darien, Conn., 1978-82, mgr. N.W. region, mem. common chems. mgmt. team, 1982-85; adj. prof. econs. Sacred Heart U., Fairfield, Conn., 1985-87; mktg. dept. chair Western Conn. State U., Danbury, from 1987. V.p. Retcon Assocs., Stamford, Conn., 1987—. Author: Forecasting Demand for Selected Commodity Chemicals, 1984. Mem. Dem. Nat. Com., 1983—. Mem. Am. Chem. Assn., Am. Mgmt. Assn., Am. Mktg. Assn., Chem. Industry Assn., Chem. Mktg. and Econs. Group, N.E. Chem. Assn., Conn. Chem. Club. Roman Catholic. Avocations: golf, swimming, hiking, travel, chess. Home: Danbury, Conn. Died Apr. 20, 2008.

RETTERER, BERNARD LEE, electronic engineering consultant; b. Waldo, Ohio, Sept. 23, 1930; s. Calvin C. and Gertrude S. (Kries) R.; m. Mary Susan Gaster, Dec. 22, 1951; children: John, Jeffrey, Laura. BSEE, Ohio No. U., 1952; MS in System Mgmt., George Washington U., 1972. Registered profl. engr., Ohio. Program mgr. RCA, Cherry Hill, N.J., 1953-65; v.p. engring. ARINC Rsch., Annapolis, Md., 1965-90. Del. to Internat. Electrotechnical Commn., 1975-85; cons. Inst. for Def. Analyses, Alexandria, Va., 1990—. Contbr. 39 tech. articles on maintainability to profl. jours. Mem. adv. bd. Embry-Riddle U., Daytona Beach, Fla., 1988-90, Anne Arundel Coll., Arnold, Md., 1987-90. Mem. IEEE (v.p. tech-ops. 1982), Operation Rsch. Soc., Armed Forces Prep. Assn., Armed Forces Comms. Assn. Achievements include development (with others) of maintainability prediction technique for electronic equipment; research into the use of information content of failure symptoms as a predictor of diagnostic time. Home: Severna Park, Md. Died Jan. 12, 2008.

REY, NICHOLAS ANDREW, former ambassador; b. Warsaw, Jan. 23, 1938; m. Louisa Machado; 3 children. BA, Princeton U., 1960; MA, Johns Hopkins U., 1963. From economist to dir. exec. secretariat, staff asst. to sec. US Dept. Treasury, 1963-66; v.p. Drexel, Harriman, Ripley, Inc., 1968-70; staff mem. Pres.'s Commn. Internat. Trade and Investment Policy, 1970-71; mng. dir. Merrill Lynch Capital Markets, 1971-87, Bear, Stearns & Co., Inc., 1987-92; vice chair Polish-America Enterprise Fund, 1990-92; with Productivity Consulting Firm, 1992-93; US amb. to Poland US Dept. State, Warsaw, 1993—97. Bd. dirs. Resource Found.; chmn. adv. com. Internat. Capital Markets; mem. internat. com. Security Industry Assn., 1987-92; participant sem. on fin. markets Soviet-N.Y. Stock Exchange, Moscow, 1990; mem. econ. devel. com., transitional corp. and Third World devel. subcom., 1980; mem. Internat. Monetary Fund Study on Access to Capital Markets, Internat. Bank for Reconstrn. and Devel., 1978-79; mem. US Dept. Treasury Clinton-Gore Transition Team; mem. fgn. portfolio investment adv. com. US Dept. Treasury, 1979-80. Mem. Human Rights Commn., Larchmont, N.Y., 1984-92. With USAR, 1962-68. Died Jan. 14, 2009.

REYNIAK, J. VICTOR, gynecologist; b. Piekary Slaskie, Poland, Nov. 6, 1936; s. Wiktor W. and Wania Eleanor (Pokutynska) R.; m. Sibylle Maria Reyniak, Nov. 18, 1963; children: Andrew, Stefan. BS, Bielsko-Biala, 1953; MD, Med. Acad., 1960; MA, Jagiellonian U., 1962. Diplomate Am. Bd. Ob-Gyn., Am. Bd. Reproductive Endocrinology. Dir. divsn. reproductive-endorcinology N.Y. Med. Coll., 1967-78, Mount Sinai Med. Ctr., NYC, 1979-91, dir. reproductive surgery, from 1991. Editor: Principles of Microsurgical Techniques Infertility, 1982; contbr. numerous articles to profl. jours. Fellow ACS, Am. Coll. Ob-Gyn.; mem. N.Y. Obstet. Soc., N.Y. Gynecol. Soc. (pres. 1990-91). Republican. Roman Catholic. Avocations: skiing, hiking, classical music, opera, travel. Home: New York, NY. Died July 11, 2008.

REYNOLDS, CATHERINE E., medical/surgical nurse, educator; b. Phila., July 15, 1946; d. James W. and Catherine M. (DiCicco) Prentice; div.; children: Thomas J., Brian J. Diploma, Jefferson Hosp. Sch. Nursing, Phila., 1967; BSN magna cum laude, LaSalle U., 1985, postgrad. Cert. in nursing adminstrn.; BCLS instr. Nursing supr. Nazareth Hosp., Phila., clin. instr.; shift dir. Hosp. of Med. Coll. Pa., Phila., clin. instr. Mem. profl. edn. com. Am. Cancer Soc. Mem. LaSalle U. Grad. Nurse Orgn., Sigma Theta Tau. Home: Thorofare, NJ. Died Dec. 25, 2007.

REYNOLDS, CLARK WINTON, economist, educator; b. Chgo., Mar. 13, 1934; m. Nydia O'Connor Viales; children: Rebecca, C. Winton III, Matthew, Camila. AB, Claremont Coll., Calif., 1956; student, MIT, 1956—58, Harvard U. Div. Sch., 1957—58; MA, U. Calif., Berkeley, 1960, PhD in Econs., 1962. Asst. prof. Occidental Coll., LA, 1961-62; from asst. to assoc. prof. dept. edn. and econ. growth Yale U., New Haven, 1962-67; sr. fellow The Brookings Inst., Washington, 1975-76; prof. economics, prin. investigator, founding dir. Americas program Stanford U., Calif., prof. emeritus Calif., 1996—2009. Vis. prof. Nat. U. Mex., Chapingo, 1966, El Colegio de Mex., Mexico City, 1964, 65, 79, Hopkins-Nanjing Ctr. for Chinese and Am. Studies, Nanjing, China, 1999-2002, China Europe Internat. Bus. Sch., Shanghai, 2002, 03; vis. lectr. in econs. Stockholm U. Econs., 1968; fellow St. Antony's Coll., Oxford, 1975; vis. rsch. scholar Internat. Inst. for Applied Systems Analysis, Laxenburg, Austria, 1978; Fulbright chair in internat. econs. U. Viterbo, Italy, 2001; prof. Stanford Continuing Studies, 2007, 08. Author: The Mexican Economy, 1970, The New Regionalism: How Globalization Reorders the Three Worlds of Development, 2006; co-author: (with C. Tello) Essays on the Chilean Economy, 1965, (with Donald Nichols) Economic Principles, 1970, U.S.-Mexican Relations: Economic and Social Aspects, Las Relaciones Mexico Estados Unidos, 1983, Dynamics of North American Trade, 1991, North American Labor Market Interdependence, 1992, Open Regionalism in the Andes, 1996. Mem. Presdl. Commn. to Latin Am., Rockefeller Commn., 1969; founding dir. Monticello West Found., 1980-2003. Woodrow Wilson Found. fellow, 1956-57, Rockefeller Found. fellow, 1957-58, Doherty Found. fellow, 1960-61, Inst. Internat. Studies fellow Stanford U., 1990-2000; grantee Social Sci. Rsch. Coun., Ford Found., Hewlett Found., Rockefeller Found., Mellon Found., MacArthur Found., Tinker Found. Mem. Am. Econ. Assn. Avocations: travel, photography, journalism. Home: Palo Alto, Calif. Died Mar. 9, 2009.

RHEA, MILDRED LOUISE, writer, poet; b. Cleburne, Tex., Nov. 2, 1911; d. Henry Clay and Bettie (Miller) Bedinger; m. Roy H. Rhea, Nov. 2, 1929 (dec. 1956); children: Allure, Vivian, Marlene, Dale, Howard, Glenda, Karen, Henry. BEd, Humboldt State Coll., Arcata, Calif., 1960. Tchr. Shasta County (Calif.) pub. schs., 1949-53, Mendocino County Pub. Schs., 1953-54, Colusa County (Calif.) pub. schs., 1955-59, Contra Costa County (Calif.) pub. schs., 1959-68, Santa Cruz County (Calif.) pub. schs., 1968—77, ret. Author: Henry and Bettie, A Washington Bedinger Historical Family Story (trilogy), 1990, 91, Homestead on the Prairie, 1990, The War Years, 1993, Papa is Home, 1997, Billie and I and Some Other Guys, 2004, Pomp and Circumstantial Evidence (prose and poetry), 2005; poetry in anthologies: The Barn Loft, The Muse, A Fairy with a Dirty Face, Leo and the Pigs, Glenda, Picking Pie Cherries, Guinea Wink, The New Discovery, Hitch Hikers, Desert Storm Easter. Mem. Am. Assn. Retired Persons. Democrat. Methodist. Avocations: crocheting, painting, poetry, quilting. Home: Fallon, Nev. Died June 22, 2008.

RHOADS, DIANA AKERS, English literature educator; b. San Francisco, May 17, 1944; d. Charles O'Neal and Martha Rebecca Motte (Cabaniss) A.; m. Steven Eric Rhoads, June 3, 1967; children: Christopher Hamilton, Nicholas Akers, John Middleton. AB, Smith Coll., Northampton, Mass., 1967; AM, Boston U., 1969; PhD, U. Va., Charlottesville, 1979. Biology rsch. tech. Dr. Peter Marfey, Boston, 1967; biochemistry tech. Dr. Hans Muxfeldt, Ithaca, N.Y., 1967-68; instr. Marjorie Webster Jr. Coll., Washington, 1969-70, Bridgewater Coll., Bridgewater, Va., 1970-71; teaching asst. U. Va., Charlottesville, Va., 1974-76; lectr. Hampden-Sydney (Va.) Coll., 1981-82, 86-96. Author: Shakespeare's Defense of Poetry: A Midsummer Night's Dream and The Tempest, 1986; contbr. articles to profl. jours. Vol. lectr. and participant in pub. sch. activities Albemarle County Schs., Va., 1978-94; co-founder, chair Citizen's Support Group to Pub. Edn., 1980, 82-84. Recipient Wye fellow, Wye, Md., 1987. Mem. Shakespeare Assn. of AM., Modern Lang. Assn., South Atlantic Modern Lang. Assn. Avocations: tennis, squash, gardening. Home: Earlysville, Va. Died June 9, 2008.

RICCI, ROBERT RONALD, manufacturing executive; b. NYC, Jan. 11, 1945; s. George and Mary Pauline (Barbieri) R.; m. Sandra Piccione, Jan. 18, 1948; children: Jason, Sean. AAS, S.I. Community Coll., 1972; BBA, Bernard Baruch Coll., 1974, MBA, 1976. Sales mgr. G.A.F. Photo, Elizabeth, N.J., 1974-76; v.p. Photo Drive Thru, Pennsauken, N.J., 1976-80; head nat. accounts Berkey Photo, Phila., 1980-85; dir. nat. account sales Qualex, Inc., Durham, N.C., 1988-92, v.p. sales east, 1993-95; v.p. new acct. devel. sales National, 1995-99; sr. v.p. sales and mktg. Kodak Processing Labs, from 1999; ptnr., exec. v.p. AAA Imaging and Supplies, Inc., from 2002; pres. US and Can. San Marco Imaging, from 2004. Pres. Sanjasean, Inc., Marlton, N.J., 1978-86. Served with USN, 1966-70. Mem. Photo Mktg. Assn. Republican. Roman Catholic. Avocations: photography, carpentry, computers. Home: Laguna Niguel, Calif. Died Apr. 6, 2008.

RICE, MATTIE MAE, adult education educator, volunteer; b. Keo, Ark., Sept. 9, 1925; d. Lemuel Curtis and Bobbie (Baxley) Ball; m. William Alford Rice, Sept. 15, 1946; children: Mary Anita Rice Goodman, James Curtis. Student, Hendrix Coll., Little Rock, 1944-46; BA in Gen. Social Sci., U. Ark., 1975. Sec. Fed. Res. Bank, Little Rock, 1944-45; Asbury Meth. Ch., 1945-46; sec. St. Paul United Meth. Ch., Little Rock, dir. christian edn., 1955-66; sch. social worker Little Rock Pub. Schs., 1966-69; youth dir. Pulaski Heights United Meth. Ch., Little Rock, 1969-71; coord. pupil pers. Little Rock Pub. Schs., 1971-81; educator Planned Parenthood of Greater Little Rock, 1989-90. V.p. United Meth. Women, Little Rock, 1991-92; del. IFUW, Helsinki, Finland, 1989; coord. older adults Little Rock Conf., 1989, 92. Mem. Priorities Task Force, Little Rock, 1991-95; treas., founder, Ark. Coalition of Choice, 1989; v.p. Little Rock Conf. United Meth. Women, 1991-95; pres. Ark. Women's Com. for Pub. Affairs, 1991-95. Rockefeller Found. grantee, 1989-90. Mem. AAUW (treas. Little Rock br. 1991-92). Democrat. Avocations: knitting, crocheting, family, travel. Home: Little Rock, Ark. Died Mar. 4, 2008.

RICH, DOROTHY KOVITZ, educational association administrator, writer; b. Aug. 2, 1932; m. Spencer Rich; children: Jessica, Rebecca. BA in Journalism and Psychology, Wayne U.; MA, Columbia U.; EdD, Catholic U., 1976. Founder, pres. The Home and Sch. Inst., Inc., Washington, 1964—2009. Adv. coun. Nat. Health Edn. Consortium; adv. com. Ctr. for Workplace Prep. and Quality Edn., US C. of C.; mem. readiness to learn task force US Dept. Edn., urban edn. team Coun. Gt. City Schs.; legislative nat. initiatives including work on Family/Sch. Partnership Act, 1989, Improving America's Edn. Act, 1994; formulator New Partnerships for Student Achievement program, 1987; creator MegaSkills Edn. Ctr. The Home and Sch. Inst. Inc., 1990; designer MegaSkills Leader Tng. for Parent Workshops, 1988, MegaSkills Essentials for the Classroom, 1991, Learning and Working program for sch.-to-work initiatives, 1996, Career Megaskills, 1999, New MegaSkills Bond Tchr./Parent Partnership, 1994, Career MegaSkills materials and tng., 1998, Adult MegaSkills for Profl. Growth, 1999, MegaSkills Behavior Mgmt. Kit, 2002; developer NEA/MegaSkills nat. mentor tng. initiative, 2000-06, MegaSkills for the Job, 2002, Adult MegaSkills and MegaSkills for Teachers, 2002-06, MegaSkills for Teachers Video Programs, 2003, edn. columns McClatchy Ridder News Svc., 2004-07; bd. mem. Doubleday Children's Book of Month, 2007; guest columnist Education-News.org, 2006-07; selected commentary Edn. Wk., 2007. Author: MegaSkills in School in Life: The Best Gift You Can Give Your Child, 1988, rev. edit., 1992, What Do We Say? What Do We Do? Vital Solutions for Children's Educationsl Success, 1997, MegaSkills, 3d edit., 1997, 18 tng. books, MegaSkills: Building Children's Achievement for the Information Age, new and expanced edit., 1998, Improving Student Teaching through MegaSkills, All Around the House (early childhood literacy curriculum), 2005, The MegaSkills Way to Reading for Preschool, 2005, New MegaSkills Infancy/Toddler Curriculum, 2006, New MegaSkill Respect, 2006; TV appearances include The Learning Channel, NBC Today Show, Good Morning Am.; subject of videos nat. ednl. programs in Thailand, Singapore and China: Families and Schools: Teaming for Success, Survival Guide for Today's Parents. Recipient Am. Woman Leader award, Citation US Dept. Edn., Nat. Gov.'s Assn., Alumni Achievement award in edn. Cath. U., 1992, Golden Apple award for MegaSkills Tchrs. Coll., Columbia U., 1996; grantee John D. and Catherine T. MacArthur Found.; named Washingtonian of Yr., Adv. Bd. of McNeil-Lehrer NewsHour, 2004. Mem. Nat. Press Club. Home: Washington, DC. Died Oct. 25, 2009.

RICH, ROBERT PETER, retired mathematician; b. Lowville, NY, Aug. 28, 1919; s. Charles William and Agnes Catherine (Keegan) R.; widowed; children: Elaine Alice, David William. AB, Hamilton Coll., 1941; PhD in Math., Johns Hopkins U., 1950. Mathematician Applied Physics Lab. Johns Hopkins U., Laurel, Md., 1950-90. Author: Internal Sorting, 1972. Pres. Md. Acad. Scis., Balt., 1963-72. 1st sgt. AUS, 1941-45, ETO. Republican. Roman Catholic. Home: Austin, Tex. Died Sept. 11, 2007.

RICH, SUSAN JOLLIFFE, data processing executive; b. Oskaloosa, Iowa, Nov. 13, 1953; d. Robert Chester and Dorothy Mae (Clark) Jolliffe; m. Mar. 25, 1988; children: Paul Goodwin III, Christopher, Milton Rich Jr. Student bus. adminstrn., Coll. of St. Mary, Omaha, 1986. Sec. Physician's Mut. Ins. Co., Omaha, 1973-77, word processing specialist, 1977-80; lead wp specialist No. Natural Gas Co., Omaha, 1980-81; systems support technician No. Plains Natural Gas Co., Omaha, 1981-84, info. resource coord., 1984-86, systems support specialist, 1986-88, systems support mgr., from 1988. Democrat. Baptist. Home: Omaha, Nebr. Died Dec. 4, 2007.

RICHARD, MARK M., retired federal agency administrator, lawyer; b. NYC, Nov. 16, 1939; s. Louis and Rae (Karnefsky) R.; m. Sheila Levitan, Aug. 6, 1960; children: Cara, Alisa, Daniel. BA, Bklyn. Law Sch., 1961, JD, 1967. Bar: N.Y. 1968, D.C. Trial atty. fraud sect., criminal divsn. US Dept. Justice, Washington, 1967-75, exec. sec. Atty. Gen.'s White Collar Crime Com., 1975-76, chief fraud sect., criminal divsn., 1976-79, dept. asst. atty. gen. criminal divsn., 1979—99, rep. to European Union, 1999—2007. Mem. econ. crime com. ABA, Washington, 1977-79 Recipient Legal award Assn. Fed. Investigators, 1981, Meritorious Exec. award Pres. of U.S., 1980, Legal award Assn. Fed. Prosecutors, 1981, Presdl. Rank award, Atty. Gen. Exception al Svc. award (2), Director's award, CIA, Beatrice Rosenberg award for Excellence in Govt. Svc., DC Bar Assn.; fellow Harvard U., 1989. Mem. N.Y. State Bar Assn., D.C. Bar. Home: APO. Died May 23, 2009.

RICHARDS, FREDERIC MIDDLEBROOK, biochemist, educator; b. NYC, Aug. 19, 1925; s. George and Marianna Richards; m. Heidi Clarke, 1948 (div. 1955); children: Sarah, Ruth Gray; m. Sarah Wheatland, 1959; 1 child, George Huntington. BS, MIT, 1948; PhD, Harvard U., 1952; DSc (hon.), U. New Haven, 1982. Rsch. fellow in phys. chemistry Harvard Med. Sch., Cambridge, Mass., 1952-53; NRC postdoctoral fellow Carlsberg Lab., Denmark, 1954; NSF fellow Cambridge U., Eng., 1955; asst. prof. biochemistry Yale U., New Haven, 1955-59, assoc. prof., 1959-62, prof., 1963-89, Henry Ford II prof. molecular biophysics, 1967-89, Sterling prof. molecular biophysics, 1989-91, Sterling prof. emeritus, 1991—2009, chmn. dept. molecular biology and biophysics, 1963-67, chmn. dept. molecular biophysics and biochemistry, 1969-73. Dir. Jane Coffin Childs Meml. Fund Med. Rsch., 1976-91, bd. dirs., 1997-2009; mem. Nat. Adv. Rsch. & Resources Coun., 1983-87; mem. corp. Woods Hole Oceanographic Inst., 1977-83, 84-90; mem. bd. advisors Whitney Marine Lab., 1979-84, Purdue U. Magnetic Resonance Lab., 1980-84, Biology divsn. Argonne Nat. Lab., 1982-84, Brookhaven Nat. Lab., Nat. Synchrotron Light Source; mem. sci. adv. bd. structural biology Howard Hughes Med. Inst., 1988-89, adv. bd., 1989-92; mem. sci. adv. bd. Donaghue Found. Med. Rsch., 1991-92, external adv. bd. U. Ill. Beckman Inst., 1994-99. Mem. editorial bd. Jour. Biol. Chemistry, 1963-69, 82-84, Jour. Molecular Biology, 1973-75, Advances in Protein Chemistry, 1963-2009; contbr. articles on protein and enzyme chemistry. Sgt. U.S. Army, 1944-46. Recipient Pfizer-Paul Lewis award in enzyme chemistry, 1965, Kai Linderstrom-Lang prize in protein chemistry, 1978, Sci. medal State of Conn., 1995; Guggenheim fellow, 1967-68. Fellow AAAS, Am. Acad. Arts and Scis. (mem. coun. 1998-2009); mem. NAS, Am. Philos. Soc., Am. Soc. Biochemistry and Molecular Biology (Merck award 1988), Protein Soc. (Stein and Moore award 1988), Internat. Union Pure and Applied Biophysics (mem. coun. 1975-81), Am. Soc. Biol. Chemists (pres. 1979-80), Biophys. Soc. (pres. 1972-73), Am. Chem. Soc., Am. Crystallographic Assn., Conn. Acad. Sci. and Engring. Avocations: sailing, hiking trail maintenance. Died Jan. 11, 2009.

RICHARDS, FREDERICK, hematologist/oncologist; b. Aug. 28, 1938; m. Anne Irvine Walters, June 2, 1962; children: Frederick Jr., Laura Anne, Charles Patrick. BS, Davidson Coll., 1960; MD, Med. Coll. S.C., 1964. Diplomate Am. Bd. Internal Medicine, Am. Bd. Hematology, Am. Bd. Med. Oncology. From instr. medicine to assoc. prof. Bowman Gray Sch. Medicine, Winston-Salem, N.C., from 1971. Capt. USAF, 1966-68. Died Dec. 1, 2007.

RICHARDS, JESSIE POLLARD, postmaster; b. Montvale, Va., July 12, 1927; d. Jesse Witt and Julia Ethel (Smith) Pollard; m. Cecil Richards, Oct. 2, 1948; children: Cecilia, Jackolyn, Julia Ann, Ted. Student, Berea Coll., 1947-48. Tchr.'s aid Montvale Elem. Sch., 1944-45; clk. Bromena Grocery, Montvale, 1945-46; bookkeeper Walters Printing Co., Roanoke, Va., 1948-50; clk. U.S. Postal Svc., Montvale, 1961-68, postmaster, 1968-88. Bd. dirs., sec., treas., Montvale Water Co., Tchr. adult classes, Montvale Meth. Ch.; past bd. dirs., Montvale Library; driver, crew mem. Montvale Rescue Squad, 1970-90; past pres., Montvale PTA. Mem. Nat. League Postmasters (editor 1977-87, v.p. 1977, 88—). Democrat. Methodist. Avocations: sewing, reading, travel. Home: Montvale, Va. Died Jan. 24, 2008.

RICHARDS, PHYLLIS ANDERSON, nurse, health service executive; b. Stuart, Iowa, 1929; d. John Edward and Verna Mae (Hully) Anderson; m. Herbert Montaque Richards, Mar. 16, 1956; children: Pamela, Herbert III, Patricia, John. BS in Nursing, U. Wash., 1948—53. Surgery nurse Swedish Hosp., Seattle, 1953—56; delivery nurse Kapiolani, Honolulu, 1954; nurse Hawaii Prep. Acad., Kamuela, 1969—90, dir. health svcs., 1983—90; bd. dirs. Hawaii Island Hosp. Coun., 1960—70, Lucy Henriques Med. Ctr., Kamuela, 1981—96, North Hawaii Cmty. Hosp., from 1996. Bd. dirs. ARC, 1970—83, instr., 1970—88; bd. dirs. Girl Scouts Coun. Pacific Hawaii, from 1969. Recipient Alumni award, Hawaii Prep. Acad. Alumni, 1983, award, Girls Scouts USA. Mem.: Am. Nurses Assn., Hawaiian. Republican. Home: Kamuela, Hawaii. Deceased.

RICHARDSON, NATASHA, actress; b. London, May 11, 1963; d. Tony Richardson and Vanessa Redgrave; m. Robert Fox, Dec. 15, 1990 (div. June 30, 1993); m. Liam Neeson, July 3, 1994; children: Michael Richard Antonio, Daniel Jack. Trained, Ctrl. Sch. Speech and Drama. Acting debut on stage at Leeds (Eng.) Playhouse, 1983; stage appearances include A Midsummer's Night Dream, 1985, Hamlet, 1985, The Seagull, 1985, China, 1986, High Society, 1987, Anna Christie, 1993, (Tony award nominee 1993, Drama Desk award), Cabaret, 1998 (Tony award for Best Actress in a Musical, Drama Desk award, Outer Critics award), Closer, 1999, A Streetcar Named Desire, 2005; actress: (films) Every Picture Tells a Story, 1983, Gothic, 1987, A Month in the Country, 1987, Patty Hearst, 1988, Fat Man and Little Boy, 1989, The Handmaid's Tale, 1990, The Comfort of Strangers, 1991, Past Midnight, 1991, The Favor, The Watch and the Very Big Fish, 1992, Widow's Peak, 1994, (Best Actress Karlovy Vary), Nell, 1995, The Parent Trap, 1998, Blowdry, 2001, Wakin Up in Reno, 2001, Maid in Manhattan, 2002, The White Countess, 2005, Evening, 2007, Wild Child, 2008; (TV movies) In the Secret State, 1984, The Copper Beaches, 1984, Ghosts, 1986, Suddenly Last Summer, 1992, Hostages, 1993, Zelda, 1993, The Man Who Came to Dinner, 2000, Haven, 2001, The Mastersons of Manhattan, 2007; (TV miniseries) Ellis Island, 1984; (TV appearances) Oxbridge Blues, 1984, The Adventures of Sherlock Holmes, 1985, Worlds Beyond, 1987; actor, exec. prodr.: (films) Asylum, 2005 Recipient Most Promising Newcomer award Plays & Players, 1986; named Best Actress by London Theatre Critics, Plays & Players, 1990, Evening Standard Best Actress, 1990 Died Mar. 18, 2009.

RICHMAN, ALAN ELLIOTT, lawyer; b. Norwalk, Conn., Sept. 28, 1949; s. Daniel Powell and Louise (Woolf) R.; m. Kathryn Louise Hawks, July 15, 1978; children: Aaron Powell, Anne Ballinger. BA with distinction, U. Wis., 1971; JD, U. Denver, 1974. Bar: Colo. 1975, U.S. Dist. Ct. Colo. 1975, U.S. Ct. Appeals (10th cir.) 1982, U.S. Supreme Ct. 1985, Wyo. 1992. Assoc. Hoffman, McDermott & Hoffman, Denver, 1975-78; pvt. practice Denver, 1978-79; assoc. legal counsel Regional Transp. Dist., Denver, 1979-83; from assoc. to ptnr. Hansen & Breit P.C., Denver, 1983-84; ptnr. Breit, Best, Richman & Bosch P.C., Denver, 1985-95; ptnr., shareholder Richman & Hensen, P.C., Denver, from 1996. Lectr. and instr. in field. Mem. Colo. Bar Assn. (chmn. interprofl. com. 1985-87), Denver Bar Assn. (jud. adminstrn. com., professionalism com. 1996—). Home: Littleton, Colo. Died Feb. 5, 2008.

RICHMAN, ARTHUR SHERMAN, professional sports team executive; b. NYC, Mar. 21, 1926; s. Samuel Abraham and Clara (Ganbarg) R.; m. Martha Landgrebe, Nov. 9, 1979. Student, Bklyn. Coll., 1942-44. Baseball writer, columnist NY Mirror, NYC, 1943-63; acct. exec. Grey Pub. Rels., NYC, 1963-65; dir. promotions, pub. rels., traveling sec., spl. asst. to gen. mgr. NY Mets, Flushing, 1965-89; sr. v.p. NY Yankees, Bronx, 1989—2009. Contbr. articles to profl. and popular jours. Leader baseball groups USO/U.S. Dept. Def., Vietnam, Thailand, Japan, Korea, Philippines, Guam, Hawaii and Greenland, 1965-74 Recipient Ben Epstein Good Guy award N.Y. Baseball Writers, 1983, Long and Meritorious Svc. award Major League Baseball Scouts, 1984, Good Guy award N.Y. Press Photographers, 1988, George Sisler Long and Meritorious Svc. award St. Louis Browns Hist. Soc., 1996, Long Meritorious Svc. award N.Y. Baseball Writers Am., 1999; inductee Bklyn. Coll. Athletic Hall of Fame, 1984, St. Louis Browns Baseball Media Hall of Fame, 1986, Nat. Jewish Am. Sports Hall of Fame, 1996. Mem. Assn. Profl. Baseball Players Am. (v.p. 1986—). Jewish. Home: New York, NY. Died Mar. 25, 2009.

RICHMAN, HAROLD ALAN, social welfare policy educator; b. Chgo., May 15, 1937; s. Leon H. and Rebecca (Klieman) R.; m. Marlene M. Forland, Apr. 25, 1965; children: Andrew, Robert. AB, Harvard U., 1959; MA, U. Chgo., 1961, PhD, 1969. Asst. prof., dir. Ctr. for Study Welfare Policy, Sch. Social Svc., U. Chgo., 1967-69, dean, prof. social welfare policy, 1969-78, Hermon Dunlap Smith prof., 1978—2009, dir. of ctr., 1978-81, dir. Children's Policy Rsch. Project, 1978-84, dir. Chapin Hall Ctr. for Children, 1985—2002, faculty assoc. Chapin Hall Ctr. for Children, 2002—09, chmn. univ. com. on pub. policy studies, 1974-77. Chmn. Univ. Lab. Schs., 1985-88; cons. to gov. State of Ill., Edna McConnell Clark Found., 1984-95, Lilly Endowment, 1987-90, Ford Found., 1987-89; co-chair Aspen Roundtable on Cmty. Change, 1993—. Chmn. editl. bd. Social Svcs. Rev., 1970-79; contbr. articles to profl. jours. Bd. dirs. Chgo. Com. Fgn. and Domestic Policy, 1969-78, S.E. Chgo. Commn., 1970—, Jewish Fedn. Met. Chgo., 1970-75, Ill. Facilities Fund, 1989-94, Welfare Coun. Met. Chgo., 1970-72, Erikson Inst. Early Childhood Edn., 1972-79, Nat. Urban Coalition, 1975-86, Family Focus, 1980-89, Jewish Coun. Urban Affairs, 1982-87, Ctr. for Study Social Policy, 1983-92, chmn., 2003—; bd. dirs. Nat. Family Resource Coalition, 1990-93, Pub./Pvt. Ventures, 1992-98, Benton Found., 1994-2004; bd. dirs. Israel Ctr. on Children, chmn., 1995-04; bd. dirs. Info. and Rsch Ctr., Amman, Jordan, 2001-09, Michael Reese Health Trust, 2002-08, bd. dirs. U. Capetown Childen's Inst., dep. chair, 2002-09; mem. adv bd. John Gardner Ctr., Stanford U., 2003-08; bd. dirs. Brookdale Inst., Jerusalem, 2004-09, Interfaith Youth Core, 2005-09, SEED Found., 2005-09, Bull. Atomic Scientists, 2006-09. White House fellow, Washington, 1965-66; recipient Disting. Svc. citation U.S. Dept. Health, Edn. & Welfare, 1970, Quantrell award U. Chgo., 1990. Mem. White House Fellows Assn. (v.p. 1976-77), Am. Pub. Welfare Assn. (bd. dirs. 1989-92). Home: Chicago, Ill. Died July 30, 2009.

RICHMOND, ROBERT PAUL, chemical engineer, retired; b. Washington, Dec. 25, 1922; s. Paul and Helen Roberta (Moore) R.; m. Marian Alice Kraynak, Sept. 6, 1947; children: Barbara, Nancy. BSChE, MIT, 1943; JD, U. Balt., 1954. Registered profl. engr., La. Chem. engr. Exxon Co., Balt., 1943-58, Baton Rouge, 1958-88; ret., 1988. Mfg. mgr. Lube India Ltd., Bombay, 1968-69; supt. lubes process Esso Singapore Ltd., 1973-75. With USN, 1944-46. Mem. SAR (Baton Rouge chpt. pres., La. state treas., Patriot 1995). Democrat. Lutheran. Home: Phoenix, Ariz. Died Jan. 26, 2008.

RIDDLE, MICHAEL HOWE, retired military officer; b. Tulsa, Apr. 28, 1946; s. Jack Hall and Marjorie Faye (Moore) R.; m. Linda Ann Bates, Oct. 5, 1968; children: Jack Hall II, Steven Michael, Mark Scott. BA in History cum laude, U. Colo., Denver, 1976; AAS, Community Coll. of Air Force, Maxwell AFB, Ala., 1977; MA Social Sci., Pub. Adminstrn., U. No. Colo., 1979; JD with distinction, U. Nebr., 1991. Commd. 2d lt. USAF, 1977, advanced through grades to capt., 1981, telecommunications maintenance technician various locations, 1966-77, with profl. edn. Keesler AFB, Miss., 1977-78, chief maintenance Pease AFB, N.H., 1978-81, chief logistics Eielson AFB, Alaska, 1981-84, communication contr. and dep. missile combat crew comdr. SAC Offutt AFB, Nebr., 1984-86, very low frequency/low frequency systems integration mgr. SAC Hdqrs., 1986-88. Mem. City Coun., Papillion, Nebr. Decorated Air medal. Mem. Armed Forces Communications Electronics Assn., Air Force Assn. Methodist. Avocations: hiking, camping, personal computers, water sports. Home: Papillion, Nebr. Died Sept. 29, 2007.

RIDER, FAE B., freelance writer; b. Summit Point, Utah, Mar. 1, 1932; d. Lee Collingwood and Jessie (Hammond) Blackett; m. David N. Rider, Jan. 26, 1952; children: David Lee, Lawrence Eugene. BS, No. Ariz. U., 1971, MA, 1974; postgrad., U. Nev., Las Vegas, 1985-88. Lic. tchr. in elem., reading, spl. edn. Learning specialist, Las Vegas, summers 1974-76; tchr. kindergarten Indian Springs (Nev.) Pub. Schs., 1971-76, reading tchr. Las Vegas Pub. Schs., 1976-80; curriculum coord. Indian Springs Pub. Schs., 1980-91; tchr. 1st grade Las Vegas Pub. Schs., 1991-92, reading specialist, 1992-93; pvt. edn./reading cons. Las Vegas, from 1993. Author booklet: Door to Learning - A Non-Graded Approach, 1978. Bd. dirs. Jade Park, Las Vegas, 1988. Recipient Excellence in Edn. award, 1988, Outstanding Sch.and Cmty. Svc. award, 1990. Mem. Internat. Reading Assn., Ret. Tchrs. Assn., Am. Legion Aux., A.R.E study group, Delta Kappa Gamma (pres., Rose of Recognition), Kappa Delta Phi. Avocations: reading, writing, travel. Died Feb. 8, 2008.

RIDGEWAY, JOHANNA BOHACEK, retired language educator; d. Karel and Luise G. Bohacek; m. Don Ridgeway; children: Eva A. May, Paul C. BA in Russian, Vassar Coll., 1955; MA in History, NC State U., 1972. Cert. grad. tchr., supervisory cert. Part-time instr. U. Richmond, 1965—67; adminstr., tchr. ESL Wake County Pub. Schs., Raleigh, 1980—2004; ret., 2004. Mem. Raleigh Planning Commn., 1980—88. Mem.: UNA, League Women Voters, Phi Kappa Phi (award 1972), Phi Beta Kappa (award 1954). Democrat. Home: Raleigh, NC. Died Aug. 19, 2008.

RIDINGS, ANNE VERONICA, copywriter; b. Aldershot, Eng., Aug. 27, 1941; came to U.S., 1984; d. Richard Aloysius and Catherine Winifred (Glavin) Parker; m. Robert Lewis Ridings, Jan. 15, 1977. BA in Medieval and Modern History with honors, U. Nottingham, Eng., 1962. Jr. copywriter Glaxo Labs. Ltd., London, 1962-63, copy chief, 1970-72; copywriter Intercon Internat., London, 1963-64, Saward Baker, London, 1964-66, John Cresswell Assocs., London, 1966-69, Colman Prentis & Varley, London, 1969-70, 72-74; dir. advt. Avon Overseas Ltd., London, 1974-83; sr. copywriter Penny & Speier Inc., Houston, 1986-89; assoc. creative dir. LOIS/EJL, Houston, 1990-97. Mem. Tex. Com. of Conservatives Abroad, 1988-92. Recipient 10,000,000 Club award Reader's Digest, London, 1974, recognition certs. CLIO Awards, 1974. Mem. Houston Advt. Fedn., Women's Advt. Club London (assoc., treas. 1982-84), Daus. Brit. Empire (Tex. corr. sec. 1986-88). Roman Catholic. Home: Houston, Tex. Died Dec. 10, 2007.

RIDLEY, HARRISON, JR., history professor; b. Phila., Oct. 22, 1938; s. Harrison and Janet Collins Ridley; m. Jade Ridley, July 18, 1986. Cert. in Radio Tele-Type, U.S. Army, 1962. Instr. Temple U., Phila., 1975—2009. Host radio WRTI 90 FM Temple U., Phila., 1976—2009; master ceremonies African Am. Cultural Mus., Phila., 1990—2000; discographer Libr. Congress, Washington, 1992; spkr. in field; cons. in field. Specialist US Army, 1961—63. Recipient Master Tchr. award, Temple U., 1989, Preserving Jazz Heritage award, Vols. Am. Del. Valley, 1996, Jazz Studies citation, Commonwealth Pa. Ho. Reps., 1996, 20 Yrs. Broadcasting award, Temple U., 1996, Preservation African-Am. Music award, Nat. Assn. Negro Musicians, 1997, numerous others; named a Day in his hon., Mayor John F. Street, Phila., Pa., 2001; nominee Excellence in Jazz Broadcasting award, Jazz Journalists Assn., 2002. Mem.: Duke Ellington Soc., Clef Club (discographer 2000, historian, rschr. 1997—2002, 25 Yrs. Radio Broacasting award 2001). Avocations: basketball, collecting recordings, books. Home: Philadelphia, Pa. Died Feb. 19, 2009.

RIEFF, HARRIET LILLIAN, librarian; b. Bklyn., Feb. 15, 1923; d. Samuel and Eva (Raphael) Rosenbaum; m. Edward Rieff, Sept. 19, 1948; children: Samuel Evan, Raymond. BA, NYU, 1951, MA, 1959. English tchr. Great Neck (N.Y.) H.S., 1962-84; creator lasting literary Great Neck Libr., from 1985. Great books leader Great Neck Libr., 1985—; performer classical lit. librs., 1985—; ednl. TV & curriculum advisor Great Neck Sch. Dist., 1970-84; advisor to dir. Tilles Cultural Ctr., Greenvale, N.Y., 1992-94. With USN, 1943—48, WAVES. Mem. Am. Fedn. Tchrs., Great Books Assn., Nat. Coun. Arts, N.Y. State Tchrs. Assn., Vet. Adminstrn. Great Neck Tchrs. Assn., Actor's Guild. Avocations: theater, music, travel. Home: Great Neck, NY. Died Oct. 7, 2007.

RILEY, JOHN EDMUND, JR., human resources executive; b. Altoona, Pa., July 14, 1952; s. John Edmund Sr. and Dolores Ann (Copetta) R.; m. Cynthia Lou Schleich; children: Shannon, Courtney, Christopher. BA cum laude, Pa. State U., 1974. Dir. representation Pa. Labor Rels. Bd., Harrisburg, 1974-78; sr. cons. Modern Mgmt., Inc., Chgo., 1978-83; dir. employee rels. Manor Care, Inc., Silver Springs, Md., 1983-86, v.p. human resources, 1986-89; v.p. human resources and adminstrn. Royal Caribbean Cruises, Ltd., Miami, Fla., from 1989. Mem. Am. Mgmt. Assn., Am. Soc. Personnel Adminstrn. Roman Catholic. Avocations: swimming, reading, tennis. Home: Miami, Fla. Died Feb. 21, 2008.

RILEY, WILLIAM JOSEPH, manufacturing executive; b. Vincennes, Ind., Mar. 16, 1934; s. Joseph Victor and Estelle (Callis) R.; m. Patricia Updike, June 15, 1957; children: Cathleen J. Woods, Christopher J., Victoria Ellen, Kevin A. BA in Chemistry, Vanderbilt U., 1956. Sales trainee Kimble div. Owens-Ill., Houston, 1959, sales rep. Chgo., 1959-66; lab. mgr. eastern region Owens-Ill., Montclair, N.J., 1966-71; mgr. Kimble div. Owens-Ill., Toledo, 1971-74, v.p., gen. mgr., from 1980; pres., chief exec. officer Kimble-Terumo Owens-Ill., Elkton, Md., 1974-78. Bd. dirs. O-I Scott, Vineland, N.J., Enbosa, Monterrey, Mex., Buender Glas, Westfalen, W. Germany, Igar Jaya, Jakarta, Indonesia, Kimble Italiana, Pisa, Italy. Mem.: Inverness (Toledo). Roman Catholic. Avocations: golf, tennis. Home: Naples, Fla. Died Oct. 31, 2007.

RIMKUS, RONALD JOSEPH, company executive; b. June 29, 1938; CEO Amtec Products, Flossmoor, Ill., Ronacyn Investment Group, Flossmoor, Corp. Art Co., Chgo. Author: Celebrations of Life; patentee in field. Home: Tinley Park, Ill. Died June 9, 2008.

RINEHART, ARTHUR MIDDLETON, psychiatrist; b. Balt., Jan. 31, 1919; s. Thomas Warden and Janet (Grimes) R.; m. Louise Gail Schmeisser, Oct. 2, 1944; children: Gail W., William Warden. BS, Trinity Coll., 1940; MD, U. Md., 1943. Intern U. Hosp., Balt., 1944, resident, 1944; resident in psychiatry VA Hosp., Perry Point, Md., 1946-48; pvt. practice Balt., 1949-89. Capt. U.S. Army Med. Corps, 1944-46. Fellow Am. Psychiat. Assn.; mem. AMA, Am. Orthopsychiat. Assn., Am. Soc. for Adolescent Psychiatry, Md. Soc. for Adolescent Psychiatry, Md. Assn. Pvt. Practicing Psychiatrists (past. chmn.), Gibson Island Club. Avocations: sailing, riding, figure skating, home maintenance. Home: Cockeysville, Md. Died Jan. 27, 2008.

RINES, ROBERT HARVEY, lawyer, educator, physicist, composer; b. Boston, Aug. 30, 1922; s. David and Lucy (Sandberg) R.; m. Carol Williamson, Dec. 29, 1972 (dec. 1993); 1 son, Justice Christopher; children by previous marriage: Robert Louis, Suzi Kay Ann; m. Joanne Hayes, June 2, 1996; 1 stepchild, Laura Ellen Hayes-Heuer. BS in Physics, MIT, 1942; JD, Georgetown U., 1947; PhD, Nat. Chiao Tung U., Taiwan, 1972; DJ (hon.), New Eng. Coll. Law, 1974; DSc (hon.), Notre Dame Coll., 1994; LLD (hon.), Franklin Pierce Law Ctr., 2004. Bar: Mass. 1947, D.C. 1947, N.H. 1974, Va. 1983, U.S. Supreme Ct., FCC, Tax Ct., U.S. and Can. patent offices; Registered profl. engr., Mass. Asst. examiner U.S. Patent Office, 1946; partner Rines & Rines, Boston, NH, 1947—2009; pres., founder, chmn. emeritus, prof. Franklin Pierce Law Ctr., 1973-97. Pres. Jura Corp., 1996-; bd. dirs. Megapulse, Inc., Nat. Inventors Hall of Fame Found., 1997-99, New Eng. Fish Farming Enterprises-D.E. Salmon Inc., 1983-99, Acad. Applied Sci.-Project Orbis Bangladesh and Singapore Opthamology Programs and Loch Ness Rsch. Program, 1972—, Seagull Tech., Inc., 1994-98, New Eng. Aquarium, 1973-75, Albavision Ltd. U.K., Promotion of Am. Chinese Tech., Knox Mt. Licensors Inc., Ctr. Broadcasting Corp. of N.H., Accelerated Genomics Inc., 2001-04, Sotti Records; Gordon McKay lectr. patent law Harvard, 1956-58; lectr. inventions and innovation MIT, 1962-2008; commerce tech. adv. bd. Dept. Commerce, 1963-67, nat. inventors coun., 1963-67, 81—; mem. N.H. Gov.'s Crime Study Com., 1976-78; trustee Mass. Eye and Ear Infirmary, 2001. Author: A Study of Current World-Wide Sources of Electronic and Other Invention and Innovation; Computer Jurisprudence: Create or Perish--The Case for Patents and Inventions; patentee in field of radar and sonar, fish farming and plant nutrients; composer music for on and off broadway prodns. including Drums Under the Windows (S. O'Casey, P. Shyre), Different, Long Voyage Home (E. O'Neil, P. Shyre), Strindberg's Creditors, Whitman Portrait, Blasts and Bravos (H.L. Menken), Hizzoner the Mayor (Emmy winning tv prodn.), 1-800-Save Me and Friendly Acquaintances (Jack Betts), Bob's Dream Ballet, Lincoln Ctr., 1999, Life at MIT suite, (films) Search at Loch Ness, 2002, Irish Eyes, 2002-2004. Campaign chmn. United Fund, Belmont Mass., 1960; mem. adv. bd. Harvard-MIT Biomed. Engring. Ctr., 1976-80; bd. dirs. Allor Found. Capt. AUS, 1942-46, European and Pacific Theaters, WWII, Brevet Col., 1994, U.S. Army Signal Corps. Named to Nat. Inventors Hall of Fame, 1994, Wall of Fame U.S. Army Signal Corps, 1994; recipient Inventions citation Pres. Carter and U.S. Dept. Commerce, 1980, N.H. High Tech. Entrepreneur award, 1989, Beyond Peace award, 1989, Disting. Svc. award Bangladesh, 1990, 96, honors Town of Inverness, Scotland, 2003, Dinsdale award Soc. Sci. Exploration, 2004, Disting. Lifetime award Boston Patent Law Assn., 2004; Robert H. Rines Bldg. dedication at Franklin Pierce Law Ctr., 1993, Distance Learning Ctr. Bldg. dedication MIT, 2007. Fellow Internat. Soc. Cryptozoology; mem. IEEE (sr.), AAAS, ABA, Acad. Applied Sci. (pres., founder, Medal of Honor 1989), Am. Patent Law Assn. (Disting. Lifetime Achievement award Boston chpt. 2004), Sci. Rsch. Soc. Am., Aircraft Owners and Pilots Assn., NAE (patent com. 1969-80, cons. to exec. officer 1979-80), Explorers Club, Harvard Club, Chemists Club, MIT Faculty Club, Nat. Lawyers Club, Capitol Hill Club, Highland Club, Commonwealth Club, Sigma Xi. Unitarian Universalist. Achievements include inventing a prototype radar and sonar technology. Donated the radar patent to the US government and gave the imaging patent to be used by the world for free; used sonar and scanning inventions in attempts to prove the existence of the Loch Ness Monster, and claimed to have seen Nessie; patents in field. Died Nov. 1, 2009.

RIPLEY, JOHN WALTER, retired military officer, former academic administrator; b. Welch, W.Va., June 29, 1939; m. Molin B. Ripley, May 9, 1964; children: Stephen B., Mary D., Thomas H., John M. BSEE, U.S. Naval Acad., 1962; MS, Am. U., 1976. Commd. 2d lt. USMC, 1962, advanced through grades to col., 1984, ret., 1992, with 2nd Bn., 2nd Marines, 1966—67, sr. adv. to 3rd Vietnamese Marine Bn., 1971—72; asst. prof. history Oreg. State U., Corvallis, 1972-75; comdr. 1st Bn., 2nd Marines USMC, 1979—81; polit./mil. planner & branch chief, European Divsn., J-5 The Pentagon, Washington; dir. divsn. English and history US Naval Acad., Annapolis, Md., 1984-87; comdr. 2nd Marine Regiment USMC, Camp Lejeune, NC, 1988—90; commanding officer Naval ROTC unit Va. Mil. Inst., Lexington, 1990-92; pres. So. Va. Coll., Buena Vista, 1992-96, chancellor, 1996-97; pres. Hargrave Mil. Acad., Chatham, Va., 1997—99; dir. USMC Hist. & Museums Divsn., 1999. Lectr. in field. Decorated Navy Cross, Legion of Merit (2), Silver Star, Bronze Star (2), Purple Heart, Def. Meritorious Svc. medal, Meritoroius Svc. medal, Navy Commendation medal, Combar Action Ribbon, South Vietnamese Army Disting. Svc. Order, 2nd Class, South Vietnamese Cross of Gallantry with Gold Star; recipient Disting. Grad. award, US Naval Acad., 2002; named to The US Army Rangers Hall of Fame, 2008 Mem. Phi Alpha Theta. Died Nov. 2, 2008.

RISCH, PATRICIA ANN, critical care nurse, administrator; b. Cripple Creek, Colo., Mar. 17, 1942; d. Eno Leslie and Loretta Lorean (LaMontangue) DeWerff; divorced; children: Patricia L., James R., Peggy A., Robert M., Gregory W. AA, Otero Jr. Coll., 1965; BS in Allied Health, Colo. Women's Coll., 1974; diploma, Presbyn. Med. Ctr., 1969; MS in Mgmt., Fla. Inst. Tech., 1992. RN, La., Mo.; CCRN. Staff, charge nurse critical care Baton Rouge Gen.; asst. DON Biloxi (Miss.) Regional Med. Ctr.; DON West Feliciana Parish Hosp., St. Francisville, La.; clin. dir. critical care Slidell (La.) Meml. Hosp. & Med. Ctr.; clin. dir. emergency dept., ICU and critical care Thibodaux Hosp. and Health Care Ctr., from 1991; clin. nurse specialist Shaikh Khalifa Med. Ctr., Abu Dhabi, United Arab Emirates. Mem. AACN, ANA, Emergency Nursing Assn. (cert.). Home: Biloxi, Miss. Died July 17, 2008.

RITCHIE, GEORGE G., JR., retired psychiatrist; b. Richmond, Va., Sept. 25, 1923; s. George Gordon Ritchie and Katherine Elizabeth Dabney; m. Marguerite Shell Ritchie; children: Bonnie Louise Ritchie DeHaven, John Coleman. Grad., U. Richmond, 1943; MD, Med. Coll. Va., 1943. Intern Med. Coll. Va., 1950—51; pvt. family practice Richmond, 1951—64; resident psychiatry U. Va., 1964—67, instr. psychiatry, 1967—68; pvt. gen. psychiatry practice Charlottesville, Va., 1968—77; chief psychiatry Towers Hosp., Charlottesville, 1971—72; pvt. practice psychiatry White Stone, Va., 1977—80. Attending and cons. psychiatrist Martha Jefferson Hosp., 1968—77; med. exec. bd. Towers Hosp., 1971—72, chief psychiatry, 1971—72; chmn. bd. Arlington House Hosp., 1972—73; treas. Ctrl. Va. Psychiat. Assn., Inc., 1973—77; cons. psychiatrist Rappahanock Gen. Hosp., 1977—80, No. Neck Mental Health Clinic, 1978, Hopesville Boys Ranch, Dutton, Va., 1978—80, No. Neck Mental Health Clinic, 1979; med. exec. bd. NE Ala. Regional Med. Ctr. Hosp., 1980—82, chief psychiatry, 1980—82; cons. staff Stringfellow Hosp., Anniston, Ala., 1982, Johnston-Willis Hosp., Richmond, 1983—87; attending staff Westbrook Hosp., Richmond, 1983—87. Author: Return From Tomorrow, My LIfe After Dying; contbr. articles to profl. jours. Founder Offender Aid and Restoration, Charlottesville, Va.; founder, pres. Universal Youth Corps Inc. Va., 1957—83; elder East Hanover Presbytery, 1951—54; mem. adminstrv. bd. First United Meth. Ch., Charlottesville, Va., Centenary United Meth. Ch., Richmond, White Stone United Med. Ch., Va.; trustee, mem. commn. on edn. First United Meth. Ch., Anniston, Ala. With US Army, 1943—46, ETO. Recipient William James Rsch. award, U. Va. Dept. Psychiatry, 1967. Mem.: No. Neck Med. Assn., Neuropsychiatric Soc. Va., Va. Med. Soc. Home: Irvington, Va. Died Oct. 29, 2007.

RITCHIE, JAMES E., lawyer; b. Lordsburg, N.Mex., Sept. 16, 1936; m. Patricia Geis; children: Ian, Shana, Alexander. BA, Okla. State U., 1958; JD, U. Tulsa, 1960. Exec. v.p. corp. devel. Mirage Resorts Inc., Las Vegas; prin. Paragon Gaming, Las Vegas; ptnr. O'Connor & Hannan. Exec. dir. Presdl. Commn. on the Review of the Nat. Policy Toward Gaming. Served in US Army Judge Advocate Gen. Corps. Mem.: Bohemian Grove, Viaje de Portola of San Juan Capistrano, Ranchos Vistadores. Home: Las Vegas, Nev. Died Dec. 8, 2008.

RITCHIE, JERRY CARLYLE, ecologist; b. Richfield, N.C., Dec. 13, 1937; s. Clarence Lee and Bernice (Ballard) R.; m. Carole Jean Atanasoff, Sept. 17, 1966; children: Jarryl Brooke, Karen Lynn. A.B., Pfeiffer Coll., 1960; M.S., U. Tenn., 1962; Ph.D., U. Ga., 1967. Ecologist U. Ga., Tifton, 1967-68; botanist Agrl. Rsch. Svc., USDA, Oxford, Miss., 1968-78, staff scientist, Beltsville, Md., 1978-82, soil scientist hydrology lab., 1982—2009. Served with U.S. Army, 1962-64. Home: Laurel, Md. Died June 13, 2009.

RITCHIE, MARY PATTERSON, retired secondary school educator; b. Waverly, Tenn., May 11, 1906; d. William Valentine and Margaret (Lockett) Patterson; m. George Dewey Ritchie, Dec. 23, 1934 (dec. Dec. 1986); children: Roger Lowell (dec.), Martha Ruth Ritchie Klemm. AB, Western Ky. U., 1929; life cert., Concord Coll., 1940. Cert. secondary edn. tchr., Tenn., Ky., Miss., W.Va., Ind. Tchr. various schs., 1924-43; tchr. Vanderburgh County Bd. Edn., Evansville, Ind., 1962-70, ret., 1970. Pres. Trinity United Meth. Women, 1974-76. Recipient Svc. pin Trinity United Meth. Women, 1959. Mem. Evansville Ret. Tchr.'s Assn. (sec. 1977), Evansville Lapidary Soc. (sec. 1965-66, 66-67), AAUW (chmn. 1976-78), Order of Eastern Star (50 Yr. pin 1978). Avocations: quilting, gardening, reading, sewing, knitting. Died Sept. 21, 2007.

RITTER, HOPE THOMAS, JR., cell biologist, educator; b. Allentown, Pa., Sept. 24, 1919; s. Hope Thomas Martin and Sara Emma (Snyder) Ritter; m. Doris Applegate Ritter, Oct. 12, 1946 (div. May 1970); children: Hope III, Robin Rountree, Pamela Patton, Jennifer Laconis; m. Linda Jane Blissit, July 1, 1970; 1 child, Michael. AB, Cornell U., 1943; MS, Lehigh U., 1947, PhD, 1955. Asst. prof. Lehigh U., Bethlehem, Pa., 1955, Harvard U., Cambridge, Mass., 1955—62, SUNY, Buffalo, 1962—66; prof. U. Ga., Athens, 1966—87, cell biology rsch., from 1987. Author: Principles of Biology in the Laboratory, 1969; contbr. articles to profl. jours. Clk. session 1st Presbyn. Ch., Athens, 1991—93. With US Army, 1943—46. Grantee, NSF, 1963, 1974, 1983—85. Fellow: N.Y. Acad. Sci., Am. Soc. Cell Biology. Achievements include research in unidentified structure of the meiotic/central spindle detailed with polarized light and differential interference contrast light microscopic forms. Avocations: rowing, skiing, tennis. Died Dec. 7, 2007.

RIVERS, LAWRENCE ALAN, marketing professional; b. Sulphur, La., Mar. 26, 1956; s. Lawrence Harrison Jr. and Lois (Miller) R.; m. Roberta Choat, Oct. 7, 1978. B in Law Enforcement, La. State U., 1978; MS, Troy State U., 1982; JD, Tulane U., 1985. Bar: Colo. 1990, Calif. 1988, Tex. 1985, Ind. 1993. Assoc. Orgain, Bell & Tucker, Beaumont, Tex., 1985-87, Benton, Orr, Duval & Buckingham, Ventura, Calif., 1987-88; mktg. mgr. Santa Barbara Rsch. Ctr./Hughes Aircraft, Goleta, Calif., 1988-93; mgr. bus. devel. Delco Electronics Corp., from 1993. Instr. U. La-Verne, 1992-93. Mem. Gen. Plan Adv. Com., Lompoc, Calif., 1991-92, Cable TV Com., Lompoc, 1991-92. With U.S. Army, 1978-82; maj. USAR, 1982—. Named one of Outstanding Young Men of Am., 1987. Mem. Calif. State Bar, Tex. State Bar, Colo. State Bar, Ind. State Bar. Republican. Baptist. Avocations: scuba diving, skiing. Home: Carmel, Ind. Died June 19, 2008.

RIVETT, ROBERT WYMAN, retired pharmaceutical company executive; b. Omaha, Jan. 20, 1921; s. Paul S. and Frances E. (Wyman) R.; m. Myra Jean Bevins, Oct. 18, 1940; children: Suzanne, Teresa, Paul. BS, U. Nebr., 1942, MS, 1943; PhD, U. Wis., 1946. Rsch. microbiologist Abbott Labs., North Chicago, Ill., 1946-48, sect. head antibiotic devel., 1948-57, asst. dir. devel., 1958-59, dir. devel., 1960-64, dir. rsch. adminstrn., 1964-71, dir. corp. quality assurance, 1971-76, dir. quality assurance agr. vet. div., 1976-77, dir. quality assurance Abbott sci. products divsn. LA, 1977-78; v.p. quality assurance Alpha Therapeutic Corp., LA, 1978-81; cons. chem. and chem. engring. RWR Cons., San Gabriel, Calif., 1982-88. Mem. Waukegan (Ill.) Sch. Bd., 1955-60; former warden Ch. of Our Saviour, San Gabriel. Mem. Am. Chem. Soc., Elk. Republican. Avocations: golf, genealogy, bridge, recreational vehicle travel. Home: Green Valley, Ariz. Died Mar. 19, 2008.

RIZOR, NANCY LUCILE, retired bookkeeper, retired librarian, genealogist; b. Chapel Hill, Tenn., Jan. 2, 1904; d. Samuel Pitts and Gotha Pearl (Rone) Patterson; m. Webb Charles Rizor, Sept. 6, 1927; children: Webb, Hume, Lester, David. Bookkeeper ins. co., Nashville, 1922-30; office mgr. printing firm, Nashville, 1944-45, ice cream plant, Nashville, 1946-53; asst. libr. Disciple of Christ Hist. Soc., Nashville, 1976-93; ret., 1994. Registration staff Little Creek Cmty. House, 1947-50; pres. Civitan Aux., Nashville, 1954-56; tchr. Sunday sch., 1927-1954, Vacation Bible Sch., 10 yrs., Cumberland Presbyn.; deacons, elder Vine St. Christian Ch. Recipient Svc. pin Meth. Women's Misionary Soc., 1960. Mem. Woman's Club Nashville (life, leader dept. 1976). Avocations: reading, travel, quilting. Home: Nashville, Tenn. Died Mar. 10, 2008.

ROAF, ANDREE LAYTON, former state supreme court justice; b. Mar. 31, 1941; m. Clifton G. Roaf; 4 children. BS in Zoology, Mich. State U., 1962; JD with high honors, U. Ark., 1978; LLD (hon.), Mich. State U., 1996. Bar: Ark. 1978. Bacteriologist Mich. Dept. Health, Lansing, 1963—65; rsch. biologist FDA, Washington, 1965—69; staff asst. Pine Bluff (Ark.) Urban Renewal Agy., 1971—75; biologist Nat. Ctr. for Toxicological Rsch., Jefferson, Ark., 1978—79; assoc. Walker, Roaf, Campbell, Ivory & Dunklin, Little Rock, 1979—86, ptnr., 1986—95; assoc. justice Ark. Supreme Ct., Little Rock, 1995—96; appellate judge Ark. Ct. Appeals, Little Rock, 1997—2006. Editor: Ark. Law Rev. Mem. PTA bd. Forest Park Elem. Sch., 1972—74, 34th Ave. Sch., 1974—76, 1980—83, Southeast Jr. High, 1976—77; mem. ad hoc com. for voter registration Jefferson County, 1972—73; bd. trustees Southeast Ark. Arts and Scis. Ctr., 1972—75, sec., 1974—75, Pine Bluff OIC Bd., 1972—78, Pine Bluff Police-Cmty. Rels Task Force, 1973; mem. Jefferson County Com. on Black Adoptions, 1973—75, chmn., 1974—75; mem. Ark. Code of Ethics Commn., 1987, Friends of Sta. KRLE-FM, 1982—88, 1990—94, pres., 1985—86; trustee Winthrop Rockefeller Found., 1990—94; mem. Jefferson County Dem. Com., 1980—82; mem. vestry Grace Episcopal Ch., from 1995; bd. dirs. Ark. Coun. on Human Rels., 1972—73, Ark. for Arts, 1983, Ark. Student Loan Authority, 1977—81, Vocals, from 1989. Recipient disting. alumni award, Mich. State U., 1996; named Gayle Pettus Pontz outstanding Ark. woman lawyer, 1996; named to Ark. Black Hall of Fame, 1996. Mem.: ABA, W. Harold Flowers Law Soc., Jefferson County Bar Assn., Pulaski County Bar Assn. (chmn. hist. com. 1986—87), Ark. Bar Assn. (chmn. youth edn. com. 1979—80). Home: Pine Bluff, Ark. Died July 1, 2009.

ROBERTS, GEORGE EDWARD, retired systems engineer; b. Portsmouth, Hampshire, United Kingdom, Sept. 25, 1926; Author: (book) Table of Laplace Transforms. Home: Anacortes, Wash. Died Sept. 16, 2007.

ROBERTS, JAMES MILNOR, JR., retired military officer; b. Pitts., Sept. 16, 1918; s. James Milnor and Elizabeth (Bennett) R.; m. Virginia Lee Sykes, Mar. 15, 1947 (dec. Apr. 1995); children: James Milnor III, Mary Lee Roberts Newman, Deborah Lee Roberts Gillespie, Todd Osborn; m. Priscilla Bruce, Nov. 4, 1995. Student, Lehigh U., 1936-40, U.S. Army Command and Gen. Staff Coll., 1962, Nat. Def. U., 1963, Army War Coll., 1970. Commd. 2d lt. inf. U.S. Army, 1940, advanced through grades to maj., 1944, discharged, 1945; mem. U.S. Army Reserve, 1946-70; with 1st battle group U.S. Army Res. 314th Inf. Regt., Pitts., 1947-62; comdr. combat command sect. 79th Command Hdqrs., Pitts., 1962-64; with Office Chief Info., Dept. Army, Washington, 1964-67; comdr. 99th Army Res. Command, Pitts., 1967-70, promoted to maj. gen., 1971; dep. chief U.S. Army Res., Washington, 1970-71, chief, 1971-75; exec. dir. Res. Officers Assn. U.S., Washington, 1975-84; pub. The Officer mag., 1975-84. Pres. Nat. Intelligence Study Ctr.; sec., treas. High Frontier, Arlington, Va., 1996-2000 Chmn. Young Reps., Allegheny County, Pa., 1952-54; exec. v.p. Wind Symphony Orch., Pitts., 1961-62; bd. dirs. Pitts. Civic Light Opera, 1958-70; chmn. Com. for Free Afghanistan, 1983-93; pres. Nat. Hist. Intelligence Mus. Decorated D.S.M., Legion of Merit, Bronze Star; Croix de Guerre with silver star France; Mil. Cross Czechoslovakia; recipient USN Disting. Pub. Svc. award, USCG Disting. Pub. Svc. award, USAF Exceptional Svc. award; named Significant Sig Sigma Chi, 1973 Mem. Res. Officers Assn. (past chpt. officer), Am. Security Council, Assn. U.S. Army, Mil. Order World Wars, Ret. Officers Assn., The Dwight D. Eisenhower Soc. (chair 1992—), Soc. of Cin., SAR, VFW, Am. Legion, Army-Navy Club (Washington), Ft. Myer (Va.) Officers Club, Capital Hill Club, Masons. Home: Arlington, Va. Died Jan. 2, 2009.

ROBERTSON, ERNEST GARLAND, pastor; b. Richmond, Va., Nov. 26, 1931; s. William Thomas and Ruth Elanor (Reiben) R.; m. Patsy Ruth Day; children: Sharon, Gwen, Garland. BA, Bob Jones U., 1954; DST (hon.), Bapt. Christian Coll., Shreveport, La., 1975. Pastor Calvary Bapt. Ch., Landrum, S.C., 1954-57, Grace Bapt. Ch., Kinston, N.C., 1957-63, Faith Bapt. Ch., Easley, S.C., 1963-73, Connersville (Ind.) Bapt. Temple, 1973-77, New Testament Bapt. Ch., Hialeah, Fla., from 1977. Recipient Key to Miami, Mayor of Hialeah, 1986. Republican. Died Mar. 26, 2008.

ROBERTSON, LAWRENCE MARSHALL, JR., neurosurgeon; b. Denver, Feb. 4, 1932; s. Lawrence M. and Mildred Eleanor (Blackwood) R.; m. Joan T. White, May 13, 1958 (div. Oct. 1973); children: Colette M., Michele E., Laurienne J., Lawrence M. III; m. Lee Ann Crawford, Sept. 24, 1982; one child, William M. BA, U. Colo., 1954; MD, U. Colo., Denver, 1957; postgrad., U. Denver, 1981-85. Diplomate Am. Bd. Med.-Legal Analysis in Medicine and Surgery, Am. Bd. Clin. Neurol. Surgery, Am. Bd. Forensic Medicine. Intern Kings County Hosp., Bklyn., 1957-58; resident in gen. surgery St. Joseph Hosp., Denver, 1958-59; resident in neurology U. Colo., Denver, 1959-60; resident in neurosurgery Boston City Hosp., 1960-64; fellow in neurosurgery Lahey Clinic, Boston, 1963; practice medicine specializing in neurosurgery Denver, from 1964. Contbr. articles on malpractice to legal jours. Capt. USNR, 1979-83, 85. Recipient Continuing Edn. Cert., Am. Assn. Neurol. Surgeons and Cong. Neurol. Surgeons, 1976, 1980-83, Physicians Recognition award AMA 1976-79, 80-83, 84-87. Fellow Internat. Coll. Surgeons, Royal Coll. Surgeons; mem. AAAS, ACS, AMA, Colo. Neurosurg. Soc., N.Y. Acad. Scis., Naval Res. Assn., U.S. Naval Inst., Interurban Neurosurg. Soc., Rocky Mountain Traumatologic Soc., Phi Alpha Delta. Home: Aurora, Colo. Died June 24, 2008.

ROBERTSON, MELVINA, construction company executive; b. Guilford, Mo., June 3, 1934; d. Charlie Gale and Christina Gertrude (Nelson) Turner; m. Ponnie Leonard Robertson, June 3, 1955; children: Raymond Edward, Richard Leonard. Student, Cen. Mo. State Coll., 1966. Mgr. Knowles Restaurant, Kansas City, Mo., 1954-55; v.p. P.L. Robertson Concrete Found. Co., Inc., Ozark, Mo., 1972-90, pres., from 1990. Mem. Rose Soc. of Ozark, Nat. Audubon Soc. Mem. Reorganized Lds Ch. Avocation: reading. Died May 13, 2008.

ROBERTSON, NAN (NANCY ROBERTSON), retired journalist, correspondent; b. Chgo., July 11, 1926; d. Frank and Eva (Morrish) R.; m. Allyn Baum, Feb. 24, 1950 (div. 1961); m. Stanley Levey, Aug. 27, 1961 (dec. 1971); m. William Warfield Ross (dec. 2006); 5 stepchildren BS in

Journalism, Northwestern U., 1948. Spl. corr. Paris Herald Tribune, Paris, Berlin and London, 1948-55, Milw. Jour., Paris, Berlin and London, 1948-55, Stars and Stripes, Paris, Berlin and London, 1948-55, Am. Daily, Paris, Berlin and London, 1948-55; reporter, corr. The NY Times, NYC, Washington and Paris, 1955-83, reporter culture NYC, 1983—88. Author: Getting Better: Inside Alcoholics Anonymous, 1988, The Girls in the Balcony: Women, Men and The New York Times, 1992. Recipient Pulitzer prize for feature writing, 1983; recipient Page One award N.Y. Newspaper Guild, 1983, Front Page award N.Y. Newswomen's Club, 1961, 80, 82, N.Y. Press Club award, 1983; MacDowell Colony fellow, 1981, 83; Woodrow Wilson nat. fellow, 1983 Episcopalian. Died Oct. 13, 2009.

ROBERTSON, STERLING CLIFTON, musician, educator; b. Tientsin, Tiangjin, China, Jan. 22, 1928; arrived in U.S., 1932; s. Sterling Clifton and Mary Letitia (Grimes) Robertson. Student, Tex. Christian U., Ft. Worth, 1945—47, U. Tex., 1948—50, Julliard Sch. Music, NYC, 1952—53, Columbia U., 1952—53, Royaumont-12th Century Monastery-Libr. and Found. Artists; grad., Ft. Worth Conservatory Music, 1945. Tchr. piano, NYC, 1950—70, San Antonio, from 1970. Staff pianist Four Seasons Hotels, San Antonio, Hyatt Regency, San Antonio, Wyndham-St. Anthony, San Antonio; concert pianist Carnegie Hall, 1961, 63, Royal Danish Ballet, Royal Danish Ballet, Columbia Artist, 1961, Boston Music Ctr. (Music Circus), Ted Shawn's Jacob's Pillow. Grantee for piano study with George Copeland, Fairfield Found. and William Hale Harkness/Rebekah Harkness, 1952—53. Democrat. Avocations: theater, films, art. Died Aug. 12, 2008.

ROBINS, LEE NELKEN, medical educator; b. New Orleans, Aug. 29, 1922; d. Abe and Leona (Reiman) Nelken; m. Eli Robins, Feb. 22, 1946 (dec. Dec. 1994); children: Paul, James, Thomas, Nicholas; m. Hugh Chaplin, Aug. 5, 1998. Student, Newcomb Coll., 1938-40; BA, Radcliffe Coll., 1942, MA, 1943; PhD, Harvard U., Cambridge, Mass., 1951. Mem. faculty Washington U., St. Louis, from 1954, prof. sociology in psychiatry, 1968-91, prof. sociology, 1969-91, prof. social sci. & social sci. in psychiatry, 1991-2000, prof. emeritus, 2001—09. Past mem. Nat. Adv. Coun. on Drug Abuse; past mem. task panels Pres.'s Commn. on Mental Health; mem. expert adv. panel on mental health WHO; Salmon lectr. NY Acad. Medicine, 1983; Cutter lectr. Harvard U., 1997. Author: Deviant Children Grown Up, 1966; editor 11 books; mem. editl. bd. Psychol. Medicine, Jour. Studies on Alcohol, Social Psychiatry and Psychiatric Epidemiology, Epidemiol. e Psichiat. Sociale; contbr. articles to profl. jours. Recipient Rsch. Scientist award USPHS, 1970-90, Pacesetter Rsch. award Nat. Inst. Drug Abuse, 1978, Radcliffe Coll. Grad. Soc. medal, 1979, Sutherland award Am. Soc. Criminology, 1991, Nathan B. Eddy award Com. on Problems of Drug Dependence, 1993, Spl. Presdl. Commendation Am. Psychiat. Assn., 1999, Am. Acad. Arts and Scis., 1999, Commendation and Appreciation award Harvard Inst. Psychiat. Epidemiology and Genetics, 2000, Disting. Sci. Devel. award Soc. Rsch. in Child Devel., 2003, Peter Raven Lifetime award Acad. Sci. St. Louis, 2006; rsch. grantee NIMH, Nat. Inst. on Drug Abuse, Nat. Inst. on Alcohol Abuse and Alcoholism. Fellow Am. Coll. Epidemiology, Royal Coll. Psychiatrists (hon.), Am. Soc. Psychiatrists (hon.), Soc. Study of Addiction (hon.); mem. APHA (Rema Lapouse award 1979, Lifetime Achievement award sect. on alcohol and drug abuse 1994), Internat. Fedn. Psychiat. Epidemiology (com.1992-2002), World Psychiat. Assn. (sect. com. on epidemiology and cmty. psychiatry, 1985-2002, co-chmn. sect. on rsch. instruments in psychiatry), Soc. Life History Rsch. in Psychopathology, Am. Coll. Neuropsychopharmacology, Inst. Medicine, Am. Psychopath. Assn. (pres. 1987-88, Paul Hoch award 1978), World Innovation Found. (hon. mem. 2004). Home: Saint Louis, Mo. Died Sept. 25, 2009.

ROBINSON, ALLAN RICHARD, oceanography educator; b. Lynn, Mass., Oct. 17, 1932; married, 1955; 3 children. BA, Harvard U., 1954, MA, 1956, PhD in Physics, 1959; Dr. honoris causa, U. Liege, Belgium, 1988. NSF fellow in meteorology and oceanography Cambridge U., 1959-60; asst. prof. to assoc. prof. Harvard U., Cambridge, Mass., 1960-68, dir. Ctr. Earth and Planetary Physics, 1972-75, Gordon McKay prof. geophys. fluid dynamics, 1968—2009, chmn. com. oceanography, 1972-87. Co-chmn. Mid-Ocean Dynamics Expdn. I Sci. Coun. NSF, 1971-74; U.S. chmn. U.S.-USSR Polymode Expdn., 1973-81; co-chmn. Phys. Ocean East Mediterranean, Intergovernmental Oceanographic Commission-UNESCO, 1983-2009; guest investigator Woods Hole (Mass.) Oceanographic Inst., 1979-80; CNOC prof. Naval Postgrad. Sch., 1982; vis. scientist Applied Physics Lab. Johns Hopkins U., Laurel, Md., 1986-2009; Slichter vis. prof. UCLA, 1987; Franqui vis. prof. U. Liege, Belgium, 1988. Editor-in-chief: Dynamics of Atmospheres and Oceans, 1976-2009 Guggenheim fellow Cambridge (Eng.) U., 1972-73. Fellow AAAS, Am. Acad. Arts and Scis. Died Sept. 25, 2009.

ROBINSON, CLAUD ANDREW, insurance company manager; b. Birmingham, Ala., June 6, 1944; s. Claud Andrew Robinson and Grace Howard; children: C. Andrew III, M. Christopher, Shannon M.; m. Linda Gail Hornbuckle, Aug. 30, 1987. BA, Birmingham So. Coll., 1966. CLU, Chartered Fin. Cons. Agt. Protective Life Ins. Co., Birmingham, 1966-73; agy. mgr. and field underwriter Home Life Ins. Co., Birmingham, 1973-83; br. mgr. Mfrs. Fin. Group, Birmingham, from 1983. Bd. dirs. The Relay House, Birmingham, 1982—; chpt. mem., Jr. warden Cathedral Ch. of the Advent, Birmingham, 1985; adv. bd. to State Commr. of Ins., State of Ala., 1986; chmn. Episcopal Diocesan Major Gifts Com. Diocese of Ala., 1986, chmn. Episcopal Stewardship Com., 1987. Mem. Am. Soc. CLU's (pres.), Ala. Assn. Life Underwriters (2d v.p. 1985-86, pres. 1986-87), Nat. Assn. Life Underwriters, Birmingham Assn. Life Underwriters (pres.), Gold Key Soc. of Am. Soc. CLU, Million Dollar Round Table and Round Table Found., Chartered Fin. Cons. Clubs: Riverchase Country. Avocations: reading, ch. work. Home: Birmingham, Ala. Died Feb. 29, 2008.

ROBINSON, DONALD LOUIS, legislative educator; b. Ottawa, Ill., Dec. 8, 1936; s. Arthur and Louise Ethel (Freebury) R.; m. Sara Katharine Moore, Aug. 4, 1962; children: Marshall Jackson, Margaret Moore. BA, Northwestern U., 1958, MA, 1959; PhD, Am. U., 1963. Adminstrv. asst. to Congressman from Wis., Washington, 1963-73; exec. asst. to chmn. U.S. Ho. of Reps. Banking Com., Washington, 1973-75; dir. Washington Internship program Boston U., from 1976; pres. Robinson Assocs. Inc., Washington, from 1975. Founder, chmn. Congl. Internship Program, Washington, 1965-86; prof. polit. sci. George Washington U., Washington, 1965-80, Boston U., Washington, 1976—. Mem. agy. rev. com. United Way, Washington, 1980-85; treas. Met. Washington Arthritis Found., Washington, 1976—. Lt. (j.g.) USN, 1959-62. Mem. Alpha Tau Omega, Alpha Phi Omega, Phi Mu Alpha, Phi Alpha Theta, Pi Gamma Mu, Pi Sigma Alpha, Phi Kappa Phi, Phi Beta Delta. Democrat. Episcopalian. Home: Wellfleet, Mass. Died Apr. 29, 2008.

ROBINSON, FISHER JOSEPH, priest; b. Abbeville, La., Aug. 12, 1929; s. Fisher Joseph and Winnie (Smith) R. BA, Divine Word Coll., Epworth, Iowa, 1952; MA, Cath. U. Am., 1959. Joined Soc. of Divine Word, Roman Cath. Ch., 1950, ordained priest, 1958. Dir. formation St. Augustine Sem., Bay St. Louis, Miss., 1959-61; assoc. pastor Notre Dame Cath. Ch., St. Martinville, La., 1961-63; dir. formation Divine Word Sem., Riverside, Calif., 1963-66, instr., 1963-67; prin. Verbum Dei High Sch., LA, 1967-80; pastor St. Malachy's Ch., LA, 1980-89; vicar Black Caths., African-Am. Vicariate, LA, from 1986. Mem. Archdiocesan Coun. Priests, L.A., 1976-80; cons. Archdiocesan Bd. Consultors, L.A., 1979; bd. dirs. Ecumenical Ctr. Black Ch. Studies, L.A., 1980; chair L.A. Archdiocesan Team of Nat. Black Cath. Pastoral Plan on Evangelization L.A., 1987. Co-author: Pastoral of African-American Catholics in the Archdiocese of Los Angeles, 1987. Commr. L.A. County Probation Com., 1976; trustee St. Anne's Maternity Home, L.A., 1978; bd. dirs. Community Care and Devel., L.A., 1983; mem. task force Respect for Life, L.A. Archdiocese, 1987; sec., bd. dirs. St. John's Major Sem., L.A., 1988. Mem. Nat. Bd. Black Cath. Adminstrs. (bd. dirs., rep. western regional div. 1988). Home: Los Angeles, Calif. Died Oct. 18, 2007.

ROBINSON, MARY LU, retired accountant, artist; b. Bloomington, Ind., Nov. 11, 1919; d. Louis Cleveland and Ruby Olive (King) Welch; m. Robert Newlin Robinson, Sept. 27, 1948; children: Richard Louis, Rebecca Jane. Student, Ind. U., Bloomington, 1937-40, Ind. U., South Bend, 1954-55, Tex. Christian U., Ft. Worth, 1989, 90, 99. Ptnr. Robert N. Robinson, CPA, South Bend, 1950-82. Exhibited in group shows at Composers, Authors, Artists Am., N.Y.C., 1990, Soc. Watercolor Artists, Ft. Worth, 1989—, Internat. Soc. Exptl. Artists, 1992, Womans Club, Ft. Worth, 1989—, Women of Worth, Ft. Worth, Tex., 2005. Den mother Boy Scouts Am., South Bend, 1956-59; bd. dirs. Neoclassic group Nelson-Atkins Mus. Art, Kansas City, Mo. Mem. DAR, Nat. Assn. Pen Women, Inc. (chpt. pres. 1999—), Colonial Dames XVIIC (chpt. pres. 1995-97), Daus. Colonial Wars (state pres. 1992-95), Magna Charta Soc., Colonial Order of the Crown, Daus. Am. Colonists, Daus. of 1812, Washington Family Descs., Nat. Trust Historic Preservation, Order Eastern star (assoc. matron 1969-70), Johnson County Master Gardner Assn. Avocations: genealogy, travel, history, bridge, gardening. Home: Arlington, Tex. Died Feb. 28, 2008.

ROBINSON, ROSEMARY KATHLEEN, nutritionist, editor; b. Wheeling, W.Va., Mar. 26, 1947; d. Thomas Hugh and Kathleen Grace (Burke) Arbogast; m. Charles Joseph Robinson, June 21, 1969; children: Patrick, Kathleen, Elizabeth, Brian, Megan. BS, Spalding U., 1969; MS, Ohio State U., 1971; postgrad., U. Pitts., from 1992. Chief clin. nutritionist DePaul Cmty. Health Ctr., St. Louis, 1974-78; nutritionist Yale/New Haven Hosp., 1979-80; resident nutritionist Hines (Ill.) VA Hosp., 1987-90, nutritionist, 1990-92, U. Pitts., 1992-95; with U. Pitts., Women's Health Initiative, 1996, comm. specialist, from 1996. Cantor St. Edward Ch., Pa., 1992—, choir mem., 1992—; choir mem. Diocesan Choir, Pitts., 1993—. Mem. AAUW, Am. Dietitian Assn. (registered), Am. Assn. Am. Women. Home: Norfolk, NY. Died Aug. 19, 2008.

ROBY, CHARLES D., JR., funeral director; b. Belleville, Ill., Apr. 22, 1920; s. Charles D. Sr. and Sarah Helen (Rowley) R.; m. H. Bernice Kerwood, Sept. 6, 1942; children: Joyce Elaine and Judith Ann (twins), Gary L. Cert. embalmer and funeral dir., Worsham Coll., 1939. Owner Roby Funeral Chapel, Rushville, Ill., from 1958. Past bd. dirs. Community Chest, Am. Heart Assn., Am. Cancer Soc., Rushville; bd. dirs. Health Improvement and Blue Cross/Blue Shield, Rushville, 1958—. Served with USN, 1942-45. Mem. Nat. Funeral Dirs. Assn., Ill. Funeral Dirs. Assn., VFW, Am. Legion (past post commdr.). Lodges: Shriners, Masons. Republican. Methodist. Died Feb. 23, 2008.

ROCHELLE, WILLIAM CURSON, aerospace engineer, consultant; b. Houston, May 15, 1937; s. Wilbur Tillet and Lillian Verna (Curson) R.; m. Patricia Jane Perry, June 8, 1963; children: Jeremy Dee, William Shane, Derek Ernest. BS in Aerospace Engring., U. Tex., 1960, postgrad., 1961-63; MSME, Calif. Inst. Tech., 1961; grad., U.S. Army Guided Missile Sch., 1964. Registered profl. engr., Tex. Rsch. engr. Defense Rsch. Lab., Austin, Tex., 1961-63; mem. profl. staff TRW Systems, Houston, 1967-71; engr./scientist TRACOR, Inc., Austin, 1971-73; prin. engr. Lockheed Electronics Co., Houston, 1973-76; mem. tech. staff V Rockwell Internat., Houston, 1976-88; sr. advanced systems specialist Lockheed Engring. & Scis. Co., Houston, 1988-94, aerospace cons., 1994-96; group lead advanced sys. group Lockheed Martin, Houston, from 1996. Instr. solar energy Coll. of Mainland, Texas City, Tex., 1976; cons. TRACOR, Inc., Austin, 1975, Rockwell Internat., Houston, 1995; owner, operator William C. Rochelle Tax Svcs., 1993. Author: Entry Heating and Thermal Protection, 1980, Entry Vehicle Heating and Thermal Protection Systems, 1983; contbr. articles to profl. jours. Baseball coach NASA Area Little League and Pony League, Houston, 1970-79; football coach Tex. Jr. League, Houston, 1972-73; weightlifting instr. Clear Lake City Recreation Ctr., Houston, 1974-77; Sun. sch. tchr. Univ. Bapt. Ch., Houston, 1974-84. Capt. U.S. Army, 1964-67. Grad. fellow Tau Beta Pi, 1960; recipient Group Achievement awards NASA/Johnson Space Ctr., Houston, 1981, 82, Astronaut's Silver Snoopy award NASA, Houston, 1990, Artemis Common Lunar Landing award NASA/Johnson Space Ctr., 1993, Elite Team award NASA/Johnson Space Ctr., 1995, SPIFEX Group Achievement award NASA/Johnson Space Ctr., 1996; named Weightlifting Champion, Tex. and So. U.S., 1954-62. Mem. AIAA (assoc. fellow, mem. thermophysics tech. com. 1993, ground test chmn. 1987-89, Best Paper award 1984-87, reviewer tech. jours. 1971—), Nat. Mgmt. Assn. Republican. Baptist. Home: Houston, Tex. Died May 7, 2008.

ROCHLIN, PHILLIP, retired chemist, association executive, librarian; b. NYC, Mar. 24, 1923; s. Louis and Dora (Rubin) R.; m. Ruth Munt, Dec. 31, 1954 (div. 1987); children: Jennifer Louise, Kevin Louis. BS in Chemistry, CCNY, 1943; MS, NYU, 1949; MLS, Rutgers U., 1960. Chemist various cos., N.J., 1943-63; sci. analyst, engring. specialist Libr. of Congress, Washington, 1963; supervisory chemist, mgr. tech. libr. Naval Propellant Plant, Indian Head, Md., 1963-68; chief accessions and indexing br. Nat. Hwy. Safety Inst., Washington, 1968-69; supervisory chemist, dir. tech. info. div. Naval Ordnance Sta., Indian Head, 1969-78, chemist, tech. info. specialist, 1979-84. Adj. instr. Charles County (Md.) C.C., 1970-79. Editor Philatelic Lit. Rev., 1956-60; contbr. articles to profl. jours. Mem. Am. Chem. Soc., Assn. for Recorded Sound Collections (exec. dir. 1985—), Am. Philatelic Soc. Avocations: opera, collecting phonograph records. Home: Silver Spring, Md. Died July 22, 2008.

ROCKWOOD, FRANKLIN ALEXANDER, mechanical engineer; b. Elyria, Ohio, June 2, 1936; s. Frank and Thelma (Scott) R.; m. Barbara Anne Rockwood, June 7, 1958; children: Janet, Kimberely Rockwood Wannemacher, Karen Rockwood Ross. BS in Mech. Engring., Case Western Res. U., 1958; MBA, Ind. U., 1985. Registered profl. engr., Ohio. Mech. engr. E.W. Bliss Co., Canton, Ohio, 1958-60, Arthur G. McKee and Co., Cleve., 1960-61; mgr. engring. GM, Indpls., 1961-93; mgr. mfg. and quality engring. Allison Engine Co., Indpls., from 1993. Sec. Planning Commn., Zionsville, Ind., chmn. Bd. Zoning Appeals, 1980-83. Mem. ASME, Beta Gamma Sigma. Avocations: vocal, piano, organ, tennis, golf. Home: Zionsville, Ind. Died Nov. 2, 2007.

RODGERS, JOE M., former ambassador; b. Bay Minette, Ala., Nov. 12, 1933; m. Helen Martin, 1956; children: Jan, Mason BS in Civil Engring., U. Ala., 1956. Chief engr. Burgess, Inc., 1959-63; mgr. sales and prodn. Dixie Concrete Pipe Co., 1963-66; pres., chmn. bd. Rodgers Constrn. Internat., 1966-76; proprietor JMR Investments, Nashville, from 1976; chmn., pres. Am. Constructors, Inc., 1979-85; fin. chmn. Republican Nat. Com., 1979-81; chmn. bd. CRC Equities, Inc., 1980-85; commr. gen. U.S. sect. 1982 World's Fair, 1982; mem. Pres.'s Fgn. Intelligence Advisory Bd., 1981-85; fin. chmn. Reagan-Bush '84 Campaign Com., 1984, 50th Am. Presdl. Inauguration Com.; US amb. to France US Dept. State, Paris, 1985—89; Jennings A. Jones Chair of Excellence in Free Enterprise Middle Tenn. State U., Murfreesboro, 1989—99; acting, CEO, chmn. Berlitz Internat. Inc., Princeton, NJ, 1991. Bd. dirs. James S. Brady Presdl. Found., Fellowship of Christian Athletes, Randolph Macon Women's Coll. Served to lt. USCG & Geological Survey, 1956-58 Recipient Am. Enterprise award, Nat. Exchange Club; named a Grand Officier of the Legion of Honor, Govt. of France; named one of The Leaders of the Century, Associated Builders & Contractors, 2000. Mem. Ams. for Responsible Govt. Republican. Died Feb. 2, 2009.

ROESLER, ROSE PIEPER, retired geriatrics nurse; b. Chgo., May 27, 1923; d. Albert G. L. and Rose C. (Kenitz) Pieper; m. Gerald O. Roesler, Dec. 22, 1951; children: Jon E. Roesler, Julia R. Roesler Utroske. Diploma in nursing, Walther Meml. Hosp., Chgo., 1944; postgrad., Cook County

Hosp., Chgo., 1945. RN, Ind. Cert. to train nursing aides, Ind. U. Acting oper. rm. supr. Children's Meml. Hosp., Chgo., 1946-47; surg. nurse Hines VA Hosp., Maywood, Ill., 1947-49; staff nurse Luth. Home for the Aged, Arlington Heights, Ill., 1955-56; staff nurse labor and delivery, post partum Sherman Hosp., Elgin, Ill., 1956-58, 61-62; staff nurse post-partum, labor and delivery N.W. Community Hosp., Arlington Heights, Ill., 1962-66; float nurse Luth. Gen. Hosp., Park Ridge, Ill., 1966-70; med./surg. nurse N.W. Community Hosp., Arlington Heights, Ill., 1975; surg. nurse Sears, Roebuck and Co., Schaumburg, Ill., 1971-73; staff nurse the in-svc. dir. Willows Rehab. Ctr., Valparaiso, Ind., 1977-80, 82-84, program dir. nurse's aide tng., 1987-88; surg. asst. Valparaiso Eye Clinic, 1980. Instr. nursing aide classes Willows Rehab. Ctr., Valparaiso, 1989. Capt. ANC, 1945-46, 49-52. Home: Valparaiso, Ind. Died Mar. 4, 2008.

ROETHEL, DAVID ALBERT HILL, professional society administrator, consultant; b. Milw., Feb. 17, 1926; s. Albert John and Elsie Margaret (Hill) R.; children: Elizabeth Jane, Susan Margaret. BS, Marquette U., 1950, MS, 1952; cert., Oak Ridge Sch. Reactor Tech., 1953. Chem. engr. naval reactors br. AEC, Washington, 1952-57; mgr. profl. relations, asst. to exec. sec. Am. Chem. Soc., Washington, 1957-72; exec. dir. Nat. Registry in Clin. Chemistry, Washington, 1967-72, Am. Assn. Clin. Chemists, Washington, 1968-70, Am. Acad. Orthotists and Prosthetists, Am. Bd. Cert. in Orthotics and Prosthetics, 1973-76, Am. Orthotic and Prosthetic Assn., 1973-76, Am. Orthotic and Prosthetists Assn. Found., 1975—76; exec. dir., fellow Am. Inst. Chemists, Washington, 1977-90, bd. dirs., exec. com., 1981-90, exec. dir. Nat. Certification Commn. in Chemistry and Chem. Engring., 1977-90, exec. dir., trustee Am. Inst. Chemists Found., 1982-90, sec., 1990; pres. Peachtree Promotions, from 1991; dir. Chemical Heritage Found., 1992-98; v.p., treas. Cons. Consortium, 1994-98, pres., 1998-2000, bd. dirs., 1992—2003. Sec., vice chmn., then chmn. Intersoc. Com. on Health Lab. Svcs., 1966-72; v.p. Pensions for Profls., Inc., Washington, 1970-72; vice chmn., then chmn. Engrs. and Scientists Joint Commn. on Pensions, 1978-80, vice chmn., 1985-87, chmn., 1988-90, 94-95, sec., 1996-97; mem. Commn. Profls. in Sci. and Tech., 1978-96, sec.-treas., 1979-82, bd. dirs., 1989-96, v.p., 1990-91, exec. com., 1990-93, 95; sec. gen. 7th Internat. Congress in Orthotics and Prosthetics, 1975-76, 2d World Congress in Prosthetics and Orthotics, 1975-77; exec. dir. Am. Orthotic and Prosthetic Assn. Found., 1975-76; chmn. U.S. arrangements Can.-Am. Chem. Congress, 1982-84; bd. dirs. China-U.S. Sci. Exchanges, 1985-89. Editor: Almanac, 1973-76, Chemist, 1977-90. Mem. Md. Gov.'s Com. on Sci. Devel., 1969; bd. dirs. Episcopal Ctr. for Children, 1991-97, sec., 1992-93, pres., 1993-95; mem. Episcopal Sr. Ministries Coun., 2002—. Served with U.S. Army Air Corps, 1944-46, CBI. Recipient Outstanding Svc. award Intersoc. Com. on Health Lab. Svcs., 1972, Appreciation awards Nat. Reg. in Clin. Chemistry, 1972, Engrs. and Sci. Com. on Pensions, 1996, Stewart R. Macdonald award., Consultans Consortium, 2001. Mem.: Washington Soc. Assn. Execs. (bd. dirs. 1986—87, chair bylaws com. 1989—90, govt. affairs coun. from 1999, Md. com., Profl. Achievement award 1986), Washington Acad. Sci. (GMC rep. from 2000), Chem. Soc. Washington (bd. dirs. 2000—03, treas. 2004), Greater Washington Inst. Chemists (sec. 1992—94, bd. dirs. from 1992, pres.-elect 1995—97, pres. 1998—99, Honor Scroll award 1999), Am. Inst. Chemists, Coun. Engring. and Sci. Soc. Execs. (bd. dirs. 1983—86), Am. Chem. Soc. (dir. fed. credit union 1967—70, pres. 1968—70), Sports Car Club Am. (local officer 1960—74, bd. dirs. 1964—67, vice chmn., sec. 1967, 1975—76, bd. dirs. 1975—77, historian from 1989), Alpha Chi Sigma Washington Prof. Chpt. (pres. 1963—65, bd. dirs. from 1986, pres. 1995—98, newsletter editor 1998—2003, sec. 1998—2004, v.p. 2004—05), Pi Mu Epsilon, Sigma Gamma Chi, Alpha Chi Sigma (pres. 1963—64, nat. dist. counselor 1964—68, nat. profl. rep. Washington chpt. from 1986, pres. from 2005, disting. svc. award 2004). Died Sept. 9, 2005.

ROGALLO, FRANCIS MELVIN, mechanical, aeronautical engineer; b. Sanger, Calif., Jan. 27, 1912; s. Mathieu and Marie Rogallo; m. Gertrude Sugden, Sept. 14, 1939 (dec. 2008); children: Marie, Robert, Carol, Frances. Degree in Mech. and Aero. Engring., Stanford U., 1935. With Nat. Advisory Com. for Aeronautics (name changed to NASA), Hampton, Va., 1936-70; ret. Lectr. on high lift devices, lateral control, flexible wings and flow systems. Contbr. articles to profl. jours. Active Rogallo Found. Recipient NASA award, 1963, Nat. Air and Space Mus. trophy, Lifetime Achievement award Smithsonian Instn., 1992; named to N.C. Sports Hall of Fame, 1987. Mem. Am. Kite Assn., U.S. Hang Gliding Assn. Episcopalian. Achievements include patents for Flexible Wing, Corner Kite, others; research in aerodynamics, wind tunnels. Home: Kitty Hawk, NC. Died Sept. 1, 2009.

ROGERS, BERNARD WILLIAM, retired military officer; b. Fairview, Kans., July 16, 1921; s. William Henry and Lora (Haynes) R.; m. Ann Ellen Jones, Dec. 28, 1944; children: Michael W., Diane E., Susan A. Student, Kans. State Coll., 1939-40; BS, US Mil. Acad., 1943; BA (Rhodes scholar), Oxford U., Eng., 1950, MA, 1954, DCL (hon.), 1983; grad., Command and Gen. Staff Coll., 1954-55, Army War Coll., 1959-60; LLD, Akron U., 1978, Boston U., 1981. Commd. lt. US Army, 1943, advanced through grades to gen., 1974; aide to supt. US Mil. Acad., 1945-46, comdr. cadets, 1967-69; aide to high commr. Gen. Mark W. Clark US Army, Austria, 1946-47, bn. comdr. Republic of Korea, 1952; exec. to comdr.-in-chief Far East Command, 1953-54; mil. asst. to chief of staff US Army, 1956-59; exec. to chmn. Joint Chiefs of Staff US Dept. Def., 1962-66; asst. divsn. comdr. 1st Inf. Divsn., Vietnam, 1966-67; comdg. gen. 5th Inf. Divsn., Ft. Carson, Colo., 1969-70; chief legis. liaison US Army, 1971-72, dep. chief of staff for pers., 1972-74; comdg. gen. US Army Forces Command, 1974-76; chief of staff US Army, 1976-79; NATO supreme allied comdr., comdr. in chief US European Command (USEUCOM), 1979-87; ret. US Army, 1987. Former bd. dirs. Atlantic Coun. US, George C. Marshall Found., Gen. Dynamics Co., Kemper Nat. Ins. Co., Thomas Industries; former sr. cons. The Coca-Cola Co.; vol. chmn. USO World Bd. of Govs., 1988-94. Decorated DSC, Def. DSM with oak leaf cluster, DSM of Army, Navy and Air Force, Silver Star, Legion of Merit with 3 oak leaf clusters, D.F.C. with 2 oak leaf clusters, Bronze Star medal with V device; hon. fellow Univ. Coll., Oxford U.; recipient Disting. Svc. Citation U. Kans., 1984, Disting. Grad. award US Mil. Acad., 1995, Assn. US Army George C. Marshall medal, 1999. Mem.: VFW, Mil. Order of World Wars, Ret. Officers Assn., Assn. Am. Rhodes Scholars, Soc. 1st Inf. Divsn., Am. Soc. French Legion of Honor, Assn. US Army (bd. dirs.), Alibi, Alfalfa, Army and Navy Club, Army-Navy Country Club, Phi Delta Theta. Died Oct. 27, 2008.

ROGERS, ETHEL TENCH, piano instructor, composer; b. Newark, Feb. 21, 1914; d. Walter Jay and Herrine (Wagner) T.; m. Robert William Rogers, Sept. 1, 1934; children: Nancy Lynn, Philip. Studied privately. Composed over 200 anthems, cantatas, piano solos, organ, piano, and keyboard duos. Avocations: sewing, painting. Home: Fair Way, Kans. Died Jan. 25, 2008.

ROGERS, HOWARD SAMUEL, retired rental company executive; b. Milton, Pa., Mar. 26, 1921; s. Samuel Cyril and Harriet Rachel (Kelly) R.; m. Clara May Rouvellat, Apr. 8, 1947; children: Donna Dazio, Dianne Stoler, Debra Weber, Howard Samuel Jr. Student, Berry Coll., Rome, Ga., 1943; BS in Psychology, Pa. State U., 1948. Sales engr. Bonney Forge & Tool Wks., Allentown, Pa., 1948-52; owner Howard S. Rogers Co., Milton and Chalfont, Pa., 1952-70; pres., ptnr. Rogers & Greenberg, Abington, Pa., 1970-81; organizer, mgr. Slobird Rentals, Surprise, Ariz., 1987-92. Adv. bd. Borden Chem. Co., N.Y.C. and Columbus, Ohio, 1968-78, Triangle Corp., Alliance, Ohio and Orangeburg, S.C., Kal Equip. Co., Ostego, Mich., 1957-72; pres. Auto Boosters Internat., Phila., 1966-67. Creator auto. clinic for mass instrn. of mechanics, 1960-61. Active planning bd. NBT Twp., Bucks County, Pa., 1955, chmn. zoning bd., 1955, zoning officer, 1955-57. With USAAC, 1943-45. Mem. Am. Legion (life), Pa. State U. Club (pres. 1986-90), DAV, Masons, Lions (Lion of Yr. 1989, Leadership medal 1990), Daedalions. Republican. Mem. United Ch. of Christ. Avocations: organ, travel, bridge. Home: Sun City West, Ariz. Died Feb. 1, 2008.

ROGERS, JOHNNIE CALVIN, fraternal organization administrator; b. San Francisco, Aug. 22, 1948; s. Alfred Calvin and Evelyn Blanche (Crouse) R.; m. Gail Ann Rogers, Oct. 23, 1982; children: Dylan, Zachary, Chelsea. BS, Colo. Coll., 1974. CPA, Colo. Auditor May Zima & Co., West Palm Beach, Fla., 1974-76; sr. auditor Grant Thornton, Colorado Springs, 1976-78; city auditor City of Colorado Springs, 1978-86; dep. dir. Fire & Police Pension Assn., Englewood, Colo., 1986-87, exec. dir., from 1987. Served with U.S. Navy, 1967-71. Mem. AICPA, Am. Soc. Pub. Adminstrn., Govt. Fin. Officers, Assn. Institutional Investors. Democrat. Mem. Christian Ch. (Disciples Of Christ). Home: Colorado Springs, Colo. Died Jan. 12, 2008.

ROGERS, LORENE LANE, retired academic administrator; b. Prosper, Tex., Apr. 3, 1914; d. Mort M. and Jessie L. (Luster) Lane; m. Burl Gordon Rogers, Aug. 23, 1935 (dec. June 14, 1941). BA, N. Tex. State Coll., 1934; MA (Parke, Davis fellow), U. Tex., 1946, PhD, 1948; DSc (hon.), Oakland U., 1972; LLD, Austin Coll., 1977. Prof. chemistry Sam Houston State Coll., Huntsville, Tex., 1947-49; research scientist Clayton Found. Biochem. Inst. U. Tex., Austin, 1950-64, asst. dir., 1957-64, prof. nutrition, 1962-80, assoc. dean Grad. Sch., 1964-71, v.p. univ., 1971-74, pres., 1974-79, mem. exec com. African grad. fellowship program, 1966-71; research cons. Clayton Found. for Research, Houston, 1979-81. Vis. scientist, lectr., cons. NSF, 1959-62; cons. S.W. Research Inst., San Antonio, 1959-62; mem. Grad. Record Exams Bd., 1972-76, chmn., 1974-75; adv. com. ITT Internat. Fellowship, 1973-83; dir. Texaco, Inc., Gulf States Utilities, Republic Bank, Austin. Bd. dirs. Tex. Opera Theatre, Austin Lyric Opera; chmn. bd. trustees Texaco Philanthropic Found.; chmn. council of presidents Nat. Assn. State Univs. and Land-Grant Colls., 1976-77, mem. exec. com., 1976-79; mem. com. on identification of profl. women Am. Council on Edn., 1975-79, mem. com. on govt. relations, 1978-79; mem. target 2000 project com. Tex. A&M U. System; mem. ednl. adv. bd. John E. Gray Inst., Lamar U., Beaumont, Tex. Eli Lilly fellow, 1949-50; Recipient U. Tex. Students Assn. Teaching Excellence award, 1963; Disting. Alumnus award N. Tex. State U., 1972; Outstanding Woman of Austin award, 1950, 60, 71, 80; Disting. Alumnus award U. Tex., 1976; Honor Scroll award Tex. Inst. Chemists, 1980 Fellow Am. Inst. Chemists; mem. AAAS, Am. Chem. Soc. (sec. 1954-56), Am. Inst. Nutrition, Am. Soc. Human Genetics, Nat. Soc. Arts and Letters, Assn. Grad. Schs. (internat. edn. com. 1967-71), Sigma Xi, Phi Kappa Phi, Iota Sigma Pi, Omicron Delta Kappa. Achievements include research in hydantoin synthesis, intermediatry metabolism, biochem. nutritional aspects of alcoholism, mental retardation, congenital malformations. Home: Austin, Tex. Died Jan. 11, 2009; Dallas.

ROGERS, MARSHA SCOTT, retired secondary education educator, poet; b. Fresno, Calif., May 8, 1946; d. Thomas Henry and Elsie Mary (Myers) R. BA, Calif. State U., Fresno, 1968, tchg. credential, 1969. Tchr. Anderson Valley H.S., Boonville, Calif., 1971-73, Mineral County H.S., Hawthorne, Nev., 1978-99, retired, 1999; mem. staff CESA, Fennimore, Wis., from 1999. Mem. curriculum com. Dept. Edn. Nev., Carson City. Author of poetry. Mem. Nev. English/Lang. Arts Network (v.p. 1994-96, rural chair 1996-98). Died July 15, 2008.

ROGERS, THOMAS FRANCIS, foundation administrator; b. Providence, Aug. 11, 1923; s. Thomas Francis and H. Ann (Flaharty) R.; m. Estelle E. Hunt, July 6, 1946; children: Clare Hibschman, Judith Reynolds, Hope Grove. BS cum laude, Providence Coll., 1945; MA, Boston U., 1949. Rsch. assoc. Radio Rsch. Lab. Harvard U., Cambridge, Mass., 1944-45; TV engr. Bell and Howell Co., Chgo., 1945-46; electronics scientist AF Cambridge Rsch. Ctr., Cambridge, Mass., 1946-54; assoc. group leader MIT Lincoln Lab., Cambridge, 1951-53; lab. head AF Cambridge Rsch. Ctr., Bedford, Mass., 1954-59; div. head and steering com. mem. MIT Lincoln Lab., Bedford, 1959-64; asst. dir. def. rsch. & engring. US Dept. Def., Washington, 1964-65, dep. dir. def. rsch. & engring., 1965-67; dir. rsch. and tech. US Dept. Housing & Urban Devel., Washington, 1967-69; v.p. The Mitre Corp., Washington, Bedford, 1969-72; chmn. The Sophron Found., McLean, Va., from 1980; dir. US Congress Office Tech. Assessment Study on Civilian Space Staion and U.S. Future in Space, Washington, 1982-84; from pres. to chief scientist The Space Transp. Assn., Arlington, Va., 1992—2005. Founding chmn. bd. dirs. External Tanks Corp., Boulder, Colo.; bd. dirs. Internat. Radio Satellite Corp., Washington, Space Destinations Svcs., Inc., 1994-97; chmn. bd. dirs. Luna Corp., Great Falls, Va., 1991-95; dir. Share Space Found., 2000; chmn. POLARIS Command-Comm. Co., USN, 1960-64; mem. Satellite Comm. Panel, Pres.'s Sci. Adv. Com., 1961-63; mem. Dept. Def. NASA Satellite Comm. Com., 1961-64; U.S.A. del. UN Conf. on Applications of Sci. and Tech. by Lesser Developed Nations, Geneva, 1963; mem. Fed. Aeronautics and Astronautics Coordinating Bd., 1965-67; Fed. Coun. on Sci. and Tech., 1967-69; mem. Space Program Adv. Coun., NASA, 1971-73, chmn. applications com., 1972-73; mem. NAS com. on regional emergency med. comm. systems, 1976-78; mem. space applications bd. com. on NASA space comms. 1986-87; mem. com. on antenna, satellite broadcasting and emergency preparedness for Voice of Am., 1986-88; mem. adv. com. study space transp. U.S. Congrl. Office Tech. Assessment, 1994-95. Contbr. articles to jours., chpts. to books. Trustee X-Prize Found., 1995-2000. Recipient Outstanding Performance award CSC, 1957, cert. commendation Sec. Navy, 1961, Meritorious Civilian Svc. award and medal, Sec. Def., Constrn.'s Man of Yr. award Engring. News Record, 1969, Space Pioneer award Nat. Space Soc., 1988, Best Vision of the Future award Space Frontier Found., 1997, NASA Disting. Pub. Svc. award, 1999, Pioneer award Visionary Lifetime Achievement award Space Tourism Soc. Fellow IEEE (mem. transp. and aerospace policy com., chmn. 1991-95, Profl. Achievement award 1995, Citation of Honor 2005); mem. Internat. Acad. Astronautics (Paris), Cosmos Club (Washington). Died Feb. 13, 2009.

ROHRBACH, PETER ALPAUGH, lawyer; b. Hartford, Conn., Apr. 11, 1953; s. John Grandin and Caroline (Hanson) R.; m. Linda Alperin, Sept. 1, 1976; children: James, Andrew. BA, Yale U., 1975; JD, Stanford U., 1979. Bar: D.C. 1979. Ptnr. Hogan & Hartson LLP, Washington, 1979—2009, mem. exec. com., dir. comm. practice group. Sr. notes editor: Stanford U. Law Rev., 1978-79. Mem. Fed. Communications Bar Assn. Home: Mc Lean, Va. Died Oct. 25, 2009.

ROHRBAUGH, NOVA R., retired music educator; b. Brodbecks, Pa., Jan. 28, 1915; d. Adam Kaltreider and Florence Viola Grote; m. Norman S Rohrbaugh, Oct. 13, 1934; children: Machree M Baumgardner, Marlet R, Laura J Summers. BM, U. Ext. Conservatory, Chgo., 1961. Music tchr. Conewago Twp., Hanover, Pa., 1956—59; elem. tchr. Southwestern Sch. Dist., Hanover, 1959—69; music tchr. Conewago Valley Sch. Dist., Hanover, 1970—74, Spring Grove Sch. Dist., Pa., 1970—78. Pvt. music tchr., Pa., 1941—2000; church organist. Composer: (choral anthem) I Want to Live for the Master, The Lord is My Light, author several books of poetry including Words from the Heart: Heartstrings More Heartstrings, (childrens book) Chester the Nosy Pig, Daisy the Little Gosling, Benny the Little Goat, Mousey's Ride, Peppy and His Friends and Sonny the Bunny, Curious Molly, (autobiography) Life Line, 2004. Vol. Hanover Hall Nursing Home, Homewood Retirement Ctr., Pa., 1982—2001; organist Salem United Methodist Ch., Gettysburg, Pa. Mem.: AARP (sec. 1986—2000, outstanding svc. to cmty. 1992). Democrat-Npl. United Church Of Christ. Avocations: sewing, quilting, writing. Home: Hanover, Pa. Died Dec. 12, 2008.

ROLL, RENÉE F., retired psychologist, publishing executive; d. Leo and Helen Feldman; children: Stewart Daniel, Jeri Ann. BA, U. Calif., 1965, MS, 1967. Lic. psychologist Bd. Med. Examiners, Calif., 1973, marriage and family therapist Bd. Behavioral Scis. Calif., 1968, cert. diplomate psychologist Am. Psychotherapy Assn., 1998, therapist Nat.

Bd. Cognitive Behavioral Therapists, 1999. Tchr. Manesquan Sch. Dist., NJ, 1959—60, Montebello Unified Sch. Dist., Calif., 1961—70, psychologist, 1961—70; pvt. practice counselor Glendale, Calif., 1970—73; pvt. practice psychologist Chico, Calif., 1974; ret., 1974; cons. Dr. J.P. Haddock, Chico, 1975—82. Author: The Seeds of Growth, A History for the Future, 2002 (appears in the Libr. of Congress, DC), A Crooked Christmas Tree, 2004, A Tale of Two Boys and Wolf Pups, 2006. Vol. fireman Calif. Dept. Forestry, Butte Meadows, Calif., 1983. Recipient Outstanding Achievement award, Internat. Soc. Poets, 2003, Poet of Merit award, 2003, Outstanding Achievement in Poetry award, 2006. Mem.: AAUW, Nat. Assn. Female Execs., Natural Wildlife Assn., Writing Group Stockton, Purse Club. Avocations: piano, poetry, flowers, writing. Home: Stockton, Calif. Died Mar. 2, 2008.

ROMANO, EUGENE ANTHONY, lawyer; b. Bklyn., Oct. 29, 1953; s. Ernest Anthony and Gloria (Valentino) R.; m. Pamela DiBenedetto, Aug. 27, 1975; children: Eugene Joseph, Paul Anthony, Justin Robert, Kara Marie, Robert Andrew. BA, Bklyn. Coll., 1975; JD, Yeshiva U., 1979. Bar: N.Y. 1981, U.S. Dist. Ct. (ea. and so. dists.) N.Y. 1982. Assoc. Mariash, Levy & Super, Bklyn., 1979-81, Cullen & Oykman, Bklyn., 1981-84; pvt. practice Bklyn., from 1984. Chmn. real property divsn. Brooklun Bar Assn., 1987-88; tchr. Bay Ridge Real Estate Inst., Brooklyn, 1994. Recipient Appreciation award Visitation Acad., Brooklyn, 1994. Mem. Bay Ridge Real Estate Board Inc. (pres. 1995), Republican Club (asst. campaign chmn. 1994). Roman Catholic. Avocations: singing, guitar, coaching soccer. Home: Colts Neck, NJ. Died Mar. 13, 2008.

ROMO, JOSÉ LEÓN, library consultant; b. Roswell, N.Mex., July 16, 1930; s. Jose L. and Barbara (Romero) R. BA in Theology and Spanish, Coll. of Santa Fe, 1974; postgrad., Colegio Sant' Anselmo, Rome, 1975-76; MA in LS, U. Denver, 1980. Monk Order of St. Benedict, Pecos, N.Mex., 1970-75, 76-78, Rome, 1975-76; reference, libr. instrn. libr. Coll. St. Benedict, St. Joseph, Minn., 1980-84, St. John's U., Collegeville, Minn., 1980-84; reference libr., instr. Laredo (Tex.) Jr. Coll.-Laredo State U., 1984-87; libr. dir. St. Vincent de Paul Sem., Boynton Beach, Fla., 1988-96; libr. cons. Benedictine Order, Portales, N.Mex., from 1996. Latin Am. Affairs scholar, U. N.Mex., 1948-50; U. Denver. Libr. Sci. fellow, 1979-80. Mem. ALA, Am. Coll. and Rsch. Librarians, Am. Theol. Libr. Assn. Home: Portales, N.Mex. Died July 27, 2008.

RONDTHALER, EDWARD, graphic designer, lexicographer; b. Bethlehem, Pa., June 9, 1905; s. Howard Edward and Katharine (Boring) R.; m. Dorothy Reid; children: Edward, David Lee, Timothy. Student, Westminster Choir Coll., 1926-28; AB, U. N.C., 1929; DFA, Drake U., 1976. Asst. art dir. Montague Lee & Co., NYC, 1929-30; art dir. Lee & Phillips, Inc., NYC, 1930-33; inventor Rutherford Machinery Co., NYC, 1933-36; pres. Photo-Lettering, Inc., NYC, 1936-74, chmn. bd., 1974-86, cons. typography, 1980-87. Chmn. bd. Internat. Typeface Corp., N.Y.C., 1970-80; lectr. in field. Author: Life with Letters-As They Turned Photogenic, 1981; editor: Alphabet Thesaurus: A Treasury of Letter Designs, 1965, Fonetic Spelling Dictionary, 1986, Sound Speler Software 1990; mem. editorial bd. Simplified Spelling Jour. Chmn. Croton Free Library, Croton-on-Hudson, N.Y., 1964-66; bd. dirs. Am. Literacy Coun., N.Y.C. Mem. N.Y. Type Dirs. Club (v.p. 1960-62, medal 1975), Simplified Spelling Soc., Spelling Action Soc., Phi Beta Kappa. Mem. Moravian Ch. Home: Croton On Hudson, NY. Died Aug. 19, 2009.

RONNE, EDITH MASLIN, writer; b. Balt., Oct. 13, 1919; d. Charles Jackson and Elizabeth Viola (Parlett) Maslin; m. Finn Ronne (dec. 1980); 1 child, Karen Ronne Tupek. BA in History and English, George Washington U., 1940. With Nat. Geographic Soc., Washington, 1940-41; info. specialist US Dept. State, Washington, 1941-47; historian and corres. Antarctic Research Expedn. N. Am. Newspaper Alliance, 1947-48, corres., 1962, 71; writer, lectr. on Anarctic affairs Bethesda, Md., 1948—2009. Contbr. articles to profl. jours. Active Welcome to Washington, 1983, Salvation Army, Washington, 1976. Recipient medal for Antarctic Exploration, US Dept. Def., award US Bd. on Geographic Names, 1948, Spl. Achievement award George Washington U., 1989, Achievement awards for Coll. Scientists. Fellow Explorers Club; mem. Soc. Woman Geographers (pres. 1978-81, membership chmn. 1987-90), Nat. Soc. Arts and Letters (v.p. 1981-83). Columbian Women of George Washington U. Republican. Episcopalian. Achievements include being the first American woman to land in Antarctica, 1946. Avocations: swimming, skiing, tennis, reading. Died June 14, 2009.

ROONEY, JOHN MARTIN, chemical engineer; b. Dublin, Sept. 5, 1951; came to U.S., 1957; BSChemE, N.C. State U., 1973, PhD in Chem. Engring., 1975. Sr. chem. engr. Loctite (Ireland) Ltd., Tallaght, 1979-80, group leader process devel., 1980-82, mgr. product tech., 1982-86; assoc. dir. R & D Loctite Corp., Newington, Conn., 1986-88; asst. tech. dir. Sun Chem. Corp., Carlstadt, N.J., 1988-89, tech. dir., 1989-91, v.p. R & D, from 1991. Contbr. articles to profl. publs. Mem. Am. Chem. Soc., Tech. Assn. Graphic Arts. Achievements include 21 patents in polymer chemistry, organic synthesis, photochemistry and electronic materials. Home: Basking Ridge, NJ. Died June 11, 2008.

ROOSEVELT, JOSEPH WILLARD, composer, music educator; b. Madrid, Jan. 16, 1918; came to U.S., 1919. s. Kermit and Belle Wyatt (Willard) R.; m. Nancy Thayer Cummings, Dec. 1943 (div. Feb. 1954); children: Simon, Elizabeth; m. Carol Adele Russell, May 28, 1955; children: Dirck, Caleb, David. Student, Harvard Coll., 1936-38, Longy Sch. Mus., 1940-41; MusB, U. Hartford, 1959, MusM, 1960. Tchr. Turtle Bay Music Sch., NYC, 1940-50s; fellowship in teaching Hartford Coll. Music, Conn., 1959-60; lectr. Fairleigh Dickinson U., N.J., 1961-63, Columbia U., NYC, 1961-63; asst. prof. N.Y. Coll. Music, NYC, 1963-65. Appearances as pianist, accompanist, composer-pianist in concert halls includingMay Song It Flourish, 1961, Amistad, homenaje al Gran Morel-Dampos, 1966; commd. pieces including The Leaden Echo and Golden Acho, 1958, Our Dead Brothers Bid Us Think of Life, 1976; opera including And the Walls Came Tumbling Down, 1976. Mem. founding bd. dirs. Natural Resources Defense Council, N.Y.C., 1970. Mem. Am. Composers Alliance, Am. Music Ctr. Home: Orient, NY. Died May 18, 2008.

ROSATI, BETH ANN, systems engineer; b. New Brunswick, NJ, Mar. 28, 1964; d. Mark D. Rosati. BA, Alma Coll., 1986; student, L'Alliance Francais, Paris. Aem. inventory/traffic control staff Broder Bros., Oak Park, Mich., 1986-88; systems engr. EDS, Flint, Mich., 1988-95. Named Internat. Woman of Yr., 1991-92; recipient Silver Shield of Valor, 1992. Mem. NAFE, Smithsonian Inst., Nat. Audubon Soc., World Found. Successful Women, Nat. Trust for Hist. Preservation, Internat. Biog. Ctr. (adv. coun.), Am. Biog. Rsch. Assn. Home: Holly, Mich. Died Sept. 23, 2007.

ROSCOE, STANLEY NELSON, psychologist, aeronautical engineer; b. Eureka, Calif., Nov. 4, 1920; s. Stanley Boughton and Martha Emma (Beer) R.; m. Margaret Hazel Brookins, Dec. 21, 1948 (dec.); children: Lee Marin Roscoe Bragg, Jack; m. Elizabeth Frances Lage, Mar. 12, 1977 (dec.); 1 child, Catherine Marie; m. Gayle Buchanan Karshner, Mar. 15, 1990. AB in Speech and English, Humboldt State U., 1943; postgrad., U. Calif., Berkeley, 1942-46; MA in Psychology, U. Ill., 1947, PhD in Psychology, 1950. Cert. psychologist, Calif. Research asst. U. Ill., Urbana-Champaign, 1946-50, research assoc., 1950-51, asst. prof., 1951-52; assoc. dir. Inst. Aviation, head aviation rsch. lab., Savoy, 1969—75, prof. aviation, psychology, aero. and astronautical engring., 1969—79, prof. emeritus, from 1979; prof. psychology N.Mex. State U., Las Cruces, 1979-86, prof. emeritus, from 1986; with Hughes Aircraft Co., Culver City, Calif., 1952-69, 75-77, dept. mgr., 1962-69, sr. scientist, 1975-77; tech. adviser, cons. in field. Pres. Illiana Aviation Scis. Ltd., Las Cruces, N.Mex., 1976—; v.p. Aero Innovation, Inc., Montreal. Author: Aviation Psychology, 1980, Flightdeck Performance: The Human Factor, 1990, Heydays in Mattole, 1996, Predicting Human Performance, 1997, Keeping the Picture: The Measurement of Flow Control, 1999; editor: Aviation Research Monographs, 1971-72, Heydays in Humboldt, 1991, From Humboldt to Kodiak, 1992; assoc. cons. editor: Human Factors Jour., 1982—, Internat. Jour. Aviation Psychology, 1991—; contbr. more than 200 articles to profl. jours.; patentee, inventor in field. 1st lt. AC, U.S. Army, 1943-46. Fellow APA (divsn. of applied and engring. psychology, Franklin V. Taylor award 1976), Human Factors and Ergonomics Soc. (pres. 1960-61, Jerome H. Ely award 1968, 73, 89, 91, Alexander C. Williams award 1973, Paul M. Fitts award 1974, Pres.'s award 1990), Royal Aero Soc. (Eng.); mem. IEEE, AIAA, Inst. Navigation, Assn. Aviation Psychologists (ann. career award 1978), Aerospace Human Factors Assn. (Paul T. Hansen award 1994), Sigma Xi, Phi Kappa Phi, Phi Sigma, Chi Sigma Epsilon. Home: Mckinleyville, Calif. Deceased.

ROSE, JOY H., playwright, poet; b. Phila., May 24, 1927; d. Abraham Eliazer and Deborah (Feinberg) Hurshman; m. Bernard Rose, June 20, 1948; children: Joan Rose Easley, Linda Rose Hallowell. BA, Temple U., 1950, MFA, 1983. Co-owner, mgr. Roses' Newstand, Media, Pa., 1962-87; mng. dir. Rose and Swan Theater, Media, 1988-93. Author of 5 chap books of poetry; plays include This Is My Land, No Lovers To Scare, Sweet Vibella, Atlantis, In The Shadow of The Liberty Bell, Aunt Bessy and the Ghost of Tomasso, The Dowry, I am King Lear, A Dress For The Wedding, Do Randeer Really Fly? Tchr. Russel Sch. Broomall, Pa., 1992, home-schoolers, Delaware County, 1994; tchr./storyteller, Media Fellowship House, Media, 1995. Recipient prize for short story, Woman's Clubs of Delaware County, 1962, Cmty. Svc. award Media, 1989, Emma Lazarus award Shalom Aleichem Club, Phila., 1954; winner Twin City Sister award Pew Found., 1996; tied 1st place Pa. State Med. Sch., Hershey, 1994. Mem. Mad Poets' Soc., Phila. Dramatists Ctr. Jewish. Avocations: designing doll clothes, sketching, gardening, reading, knitting. Home: Media, Pa. Died Mar. 24, 2008.

ROSE, WALTER DEANE, retired engineering educator; b. Liberty, Ind., Jan. 10, 1920; s. Joseph Sims Rose., Sr and Dorothy Gray Rose; m. Edith Magdalena Dora Schroeder, May 11, 1959; m. Dorris Evelyn Dailey, Mar. 20, 1939 (dec. Feb. 2, 1945); m. Zoe Fern Wilcox, July 14, 1945 (div. Oct. 31, 1952); children: Dixie Rachel Rose-Phillips, Walter Deane Jr., John Gregory, Bonnie Zoe, Deane Michael, Edith Elisabeth. BS, U. of Chgo., 1944. Registered profl. engr., Colo. Rsch. chemist Affils. of Std. Oil of N.J., NYC, 1944—48; rsch. physicist Gulf R&D Co., Physics Divsn., Pitts. and Harmarville, Pa., 1948—50; lectr. in petroleum engring., asst. dir. Tex. petroleum rsch. com. U. Tex. and State of Tex. RR Commn., Austin, 1950—52; editor Gulf Coast dist. Oil and Gas Jour., Houston, 1952—53; group leader oil recovery processes Continental Oil Co. Rsch. Ctr., Ponca City, Okla., 1954—56; fossil energy recovery specialist Petroleum Rsch. Corp., Denver, 1954—55; prof. of petroleum engring. U. of Ill., Champaign, 1955—68; scholar French Petroleum Inst., Rueil Malmaison, France, 1962—63; Albert Albermann vis. prof. of civil engring. TECHNION, Israel Inst. of Tech., Haifa, 1968—69; vis. prof. of freshman engring. Purdue U., West Lafayette, Ind., 1970—71; dean of sci. and prof. of engring. Abadan (Iran) Inst. of Tech., 1971—72; editor, ghost writer Authors and Spkrs. Svcs., Chicago and Champaign, Ill., 1975—2001. Vis. prof. developing grad. student programs Mid. East Tech. U., Ankara, Turkey, 1969—70; rsch. lab. innovator Amdel Spl. Core Labs., Adelaide and Brisbane, Australia, 1991—92; tech. cons. Petronas Rsch. Inst., Kuala Lumpur, Malaysia, 1992—94; cons. on petroleum reservoir engring. matters Mex. Petroleum Inst., Mexico City, 2000—06; reservoir engring. cons. Woodside Peroleum, Perth, Australia, 2000; cons. Mex. Inst. of Petroleum, Mexico City, 2004—05, U. of NSW, Sydney, 1991, Chevron, Brisbane, Australia, 1991, Santos, Adelaide, Australia, 1991; vis. scientist Brit. Nat. Oil Co., London, 1976; vis. prof. U. Ibadan, Nigeria, 1971—74; dir. of rsch. and v.p. EG&G Continental Labs., Denver, 1984—86; vis. prof. UNESCO, Dacca, East Pakistan, 1970—71; vis. prof., head of dept. N.Mex. Inst. of Mining and Tech., Socorro, 1974—76; vis. prof., departmental head U. of Wyo., Laramie, 1976—77; vis. specialist on prodn. of coal bed methane Sci. Applications Internat. Assigned to DOE Funded Natural Gas Recovery Rsch. Projects, Morgantown, W.Va., 1978—79; assoc. dir. U.S. Dept. Fossil Energy Rsch. Projects Inst. of Gas Tech., Chgo., 1980—82; vis. sci. rsch. instigator Commonwealth Sci. Indsl. Rsch. Orgn., Canberra, Australia, 1987—89; vis. scientist Chinese Inst. of Porous Flow, Lang Feng, China, 1988. Contbr. articles to profl. jours. and books (travel and rsch. grants various insts. and univs.). Advocate 'natural law party concept. Recipient Cert. of Appreciation award, CEO of the Alta. Rsch. Coun. in Edmonton, 1998. Mem.: Soc. Petroleum Engring. (sr. Legion of Honor), Chgo. Press Club, Houston Press Club. Achievements include patents for Research Lab and Field Equipment Designs; Developing Mathematical Modeling Ideas; patents for dealing with design and utilization of laboratory and field equipment facilities, also mathematical modeling schemes; research in so-called APTPA applications (Additional Prospective Transport Process Algorithms). Home: Champaign, Ill. Died Jan. 19, 2009.

ROSEN, GERALD ROBERT, editor; b. NYC, Nov. 17, 1930; s. Sol and Essie (Shapiro) R.; m. Lois Lehrman, May 9, 1958 (dec. 1991); 1 son, Evan Mark. BS, Ind. U., 1951, MA, 1953. Intelligence analyst Dept. Def., NYC, 1955-58; assoc. editor Challenge: The Mag. of Econ. Affairs, NYC, 1959-61, mng. editor, 1961-64, 65-66; sr. editor Dun's Rev., NYC, 1964-65, nat. affairs editor, 1967—78; exec. editor Dun's Rev. (now Bus. Month), 1978-90; editor IMF survey Washington, 1990-93; mng. dir. Global Insights Svcs., Washington, 1993—2009. Fin. corr. Westinghouse Broadcasting Co. Served with CIC U.S. Army, 1953-55. Mem. Soc. Am. Bus. and Econ. Writers, N.Y. Fin. Writers Assn., White House Corrs. Assn. Clubs: Nat. Press. Home: Washington, DC. Died Aug. 28, 2009.

ROSEN, LOUIS, physicist; b. NYC, June 10, 1918; s. Jacob and Rose (Lipionski) R.; m. Mary Terry, Sept. 4, 1941 (dec. 2004); 1 son, Terry Leon. BA, U. Ala., 1939, MS, 1941; PhD, Pa. State U., 1944; DSc (hon.), U. N.Mex., 1979, U. Colo., 1987. Instr. physics U. Ala., 1940-41, Pa. State U., 1943-44; mem. staff Los Alamos Sci. Lab., 1944-90, group leader nuclear plate lab., 1949-65, alt. div. leader exptl. physics div., 1962-65, dir. meson physics facility, 1965-85, div. leader medium energy physics div., 1965-86, sr. lab. fellow, 1985-90, sr. fellow emeritus, 1990—2009; Sesquicentennial hon. prof. U. Ala., 1981. Panel on future of nuclear sci., chmn. subpanel on accelerators NRC of NAS, 1976, panel on instnl. arrangements for orbiting space telescope, 1976; mem. U.S.A.-USSR Coordinating Com. on Fundamental Properties of Matter, 1971-90 Mem. editl. bd. Applications of Nuclear Physics; co-editor Climate Change and Energy Policy, 1992; contbr. articles to profl. jours. Mem. Los Alamos Town Planning Bd., 1962-64; mem. Gov.'s Com. on Tech. Excellence in N.Mex.; mem. N.Mex. Cancer Control Bd., 1976-80, v.p., 1979-81; co-chmn. Los Alamos Vols. for Stevenson, 1956; Dem. candidate for county commr., 1962; bd. dirs. Los Alamos Med. Ctr., 1977-83, chmn., 1983; bd. govs. Tel Aviv U., 1986; bd. dirs. Sombillo Nursing and Rehab. Facility, 2004. Recipient E.O. Lawrence award AEC, 1963, Golden Plate award Am. Acad. Achievement, 1964, N.Mex. Disting. Pub. Svc. award, 1978; named Citizen of Yr., N.Mex. Realtors Assn., 1973; Guggenheim fellow, 1959-60; alumni fellow Pa. State U., 1978; Louis Rosen prize established in his honor by bd. dirs. Meson Facility Users Group, 1984; Louis Rosen Auditorium dedicated, 1995; recipient Los Alamos Nat. Lab. medal, 2002. Fellow AAAS (coun. 1989), Am. Phys. Soc. (coun. 1975-78, chmn. panel on pub. affairs 1980, div. nuclear physics 1985, mem. subcom. on internat. sci. affairs 1988). Achievements include research in nuc. sci. and applications of particle accelerators. Home: Los Alamos, N.Mex. Died Aug. 20, 2009.

ROSEN, MYOR, harpist, educator; b. NYC, May 28, 1917; s. Caesar and Rose (Seidenberg) R.; m. Esther Rosen, May 25, 1941; children: Linda, David. Diploma, Juilliard Sch. Music, 1940. Faculty Juilliard Sch. Music, 1947-69. Prin. harpist, Mexico Symphony Orch., 1941-42, Indpls.

Symphony Orch., 1941-42, Mpls. Symphony Orch., 1943-44, staff harpist, CBS, Columbia Records and free lanced, 1945-60, prin. harpist, N.Y. Philharm., 1960-87; Composer incidental music for; NBC series Arts and the Gods, 1946, CBS Camera Three, 1947, Solomon, The King, 1948. Served with U.S. Army, 1945. Mem. Am. Fedn. Musicians, Bohemians. Home: Pompano Beach, Fla. Died Mar. 13, 2009.

ROSEN, WILLIAM EDWARD, economics educator; b. Oceanside, NY, Jan. 24, 1951; s. Saul and Seena (Rudolph) R. BA, Boston U., 1973; MA, U. Calif., Davis, 1975, PhD, 1978. Lectr. U. Calif., Davis, 1978-79; prof. U. Nev., Reno, 1979-82, Colo. Coll. and U. Colo., Colorado Springs, 1982-85; field archaeologist Far Western Anthropology, Davis, 1985-87; prof. econs. Lake Tahoe Community Coll., South Lake Tahoe, Calif., from 1987. Cons. Sierra Stats., South Lake Tahoe, 1987—. Contbr. articles to profl. publs. Recipient Olinik award econs. dept. Colo. Coll., 1985. Mem. Am. Econ. Assn. Republican. Avocations: ice hockey, coaching basketball, writing fiction, guitar. Home: South Lake Tahoe, Calif. Died May 19, 2008.

ROSENAU, ANITA H., playwright; b. Phila., Aug. 25, 1923; d. Joseph S. and Anna (Altman) Halpern; m. Gary Rosenau, Apr. 24, 1945; children: Gail Rosenau Scott, Gareth W. BA, U. Pa., 1944; MA in Play Writing, Temple U., 1956. Works produced in staged readings including U. Denver/Aspen Playwrights Conf., 1980, Theatre Under the Jerome, 1984, 85, 86, No Smoking Theatre, N.Y.C., 1986, Aspen Art Mus., 1989, 90, Barbara Baracedess Theatre Lab., 1990, One, Two, Buckle My Shoe, 1991, 1991, Alive and Well, 1991, A Woman of Purpose (one woman play) Aspen Art Mus., 1994, (in collaboration with Edgar David Grana) Lancelot, Guinevere. Mem. Dramatists Guild, Poetry Soc. Am. Christian Scientist. Avocations: golf, skiing, travel, bridge. Died Apr. 20, 2008.

ROSENBERG, EDITH ESTHER, physiologist, educator; b. Berlin, Jan. 24, 1928; came to U.S., 1968; d. Theodor and Rela (Banet) R.; m. Leo Goldhammer, Jan. 9, 1968 (div. 1972). MA in Physiology, U. Toronto, Ont., Can., 1952; PhD in Physiology, U. Pa., 1959. Rsch. asst. Hosp. for Sick Children, Toronto, 1951-52; rsch. asst. in biophysics U. Western Ont., London, 1952-56; rsch. fellow in physiology U. Pa., Phila., 1979; asst. prof. dept. physiology Sch. Medicine, U. Montreal, Montreal, Can., 1959-62; asst. prof. dept. surgery, lectr. dept. physiology McGill U., Montreal, 1962-68; assoc. prof. physiology & biophysics Coll. Medicine, Howard U., Washington, 1968—97. Cons. to chief of surgery Royal Victoria Hosp., 1962. Contbr. articles to profl. jours., including Am. Jour. Physiology, Am. Jour. Applied Physiology, Respiration Physiology, Lung, Chest. Recipient Percy Hermant Gen. Proficiency scholarship, 1946-50, Alexander T. Fulton scholarship in sci., 1947, Daniel Wilson scholarship in physiology and biochemistry, 1949; grantee Nat. Rsch. Coun., Can., 1960-62, Med. Rsch. Coun. Can., 1963-68, Nat. Inst. Neurol. Diseases, 1972-75, Washington Heart Assn., 1970, 71. Mem. Am. Physiol. Soc. (sec. teaching of physiology sect. 1986-89), Biophys. Soc., Am. Thoracic Soc., Can. Physiol. Soc., N.Y. Acad. Scis., Sigma Xi. Jewish. Died Sept. 28, 2009.

ROSENBERG, HAROLD NMI, preventive medicine physician, consultant; b. NYC, Nov. 23, 1921; s. Jacob and Rose Rosenberg; m. Sharon Rosenberg, June 6, 1962; children: Marla Holben, Victor. BA, Drake U.; DO, Phila. Coll. Of Osteo. Medicine, 1951; MS, Columbia Coll. Physicians and Surgeons, 1999. Physician Health Awareness/lifesustainer, NYC, from 1999; cons./advisor LIFESUSTAINER, NYC, from 1999. Pres. Internat. Acad. Of Preventive Medicine, Houston. Author (sr. editor): Book Of Vitamin Therapy/web Site:lifesustainer. With US Army, 1944—46, ETO. Decorated Purple Heart, Bronze Star medal. Mem.: Internat. Acad. Preventive Medicine (pres. 1970—75), Mil. Order Of The Purple Heart (life; sr. vice comdr./N.Y. Dept. 2002—04). Independent-Republican. Hebrew. Avocations: swimming, hiking, painting landscape, portrates. Home: New York, NY. Died July 19, 2008.

ROSENBERG, MURRAY KENNETH, anesthesiologist; b. NYC, June 14, 1928; s. Jacob and Sarah (Kassouer) R.; m. Beverly Draznin, Aug. 28, 1988; children: Aaron Glen, Stuart Joel, David Arthur, Robert Loren. AB, NYU, 1947; MD, Chgo. Med. Sch., 1952. Diplomate Am. Bd. Anesthesiology, Am. Bd. Quality Assurance and Utilization Res. Chmn. dept. anesthesiology West Side VA Hosp., Chgo., 1955; attending anesthesiologist Michael Reese Hosp., Chgo., 1956-69; chmn. dept. anesthesiology N.W. Hosp., Chgo., 1969-83, Provident Hosp., Chgo., 1983-86, Meth. Hosp. Chgo., from 1986. Bd. dirs. Myer Kaplan Jewish Community Ctr., Skokie, Ill., 1955-65, Beth Emet Synagogue, Evanston, Ill., 1978-79, Skokie Valley Traditional Synagogue, 1986-89. Fellow Am. Coll. Anesthesiologists, Am. Coll. Chest Physicians; mem. Chgo. Soc. Anesthesiologists (pres. 1961-63, sec.-treas. 1963-65), B'nai B'rith. Home: Skokie, Ill. Died June 4, 2008.

ROSENBLATT, LOUIS, retired musician; b. Phila., Mar. 9, 1928; s. Paul and Celia (Seidman) R.; m. Renate Gisela Reiss, Aug. 2, 1953; children: William Reiss, Richard Henry. Diploma, Curtis Inst. Music, 1951. Mem. faculty Temple U. Coll. Music. Player oboe and solo English horn, Houston Symphony, 1954-55, New Orleans Philharmonic-Symphony, 1955-59, Phila. Orch., 1959—95. Served with AUS, 1951-54. Recipient C. Hartman Kuhn award, 1978 Mem. Am. Fedn. Musicians, Nat. Acad. Rec. Arts and Scis. Died Aug. 24, 2009.

ROSENBLUM, RICHARD SETH, insurance agent; b. Ft. Lee, Va., May 1, 1944; s. Leo and Marjorie (Lewitt) R.; Jayne Moorigian Mansfied, Oct. 1, 1966; 1 child, Leigh Kimberley (dec. 1966); m. m. Marilee Jane Erickson, Apr. 1, 1967; m. Barbara Jean Axelrod (div. Oct. 1982). BA, Upsala Coll., 1966; MAT, William Paterson Coll., 1973; MLS, Pratt Inst., 1974. Cert. fin. planner. Profl. athlete, 1966-69; tchr., libr. schs. and librs., N.J., 1966-81; ins. agt., registered rep. Mut. of Omaha Ins. Cos., Cherry Hill, N.J., 1982-90; ind. ins. agt. Marlton, N.J., from 1990. Mem. Inst. Cert. Fin. Planners, Princeton Area Soc. Cert. Fin. Planners, Pratt Inst. Alumni Assn., Montclair Acad. Alumni Assn. Avocations: chamber music, tennis, baseball. Home: Lakehurst, NJ. Died Mar. 8, 2008.

ROSENHEIM, MARGARET KEENEY, retired social welfare policy educator; b. Grand Rapids, Mich., Sept. 5, 1926; d. Morton and Nancy (Billings) Keeney; m. Edward W. Rosenheim, June 20, 1947 (dec. 2005); children: Daniel, James, Andrew. Student, Wellesley Coll., 1943-45; JD, U. Chgo., 1949. Bar: Ill. 1949. Mem. faculty Sch. Social Svc. Adminstrn. U. Chgo., Chgo., from 1950, assoc. prof., 1961—66, prof., 1966—96, Helen Ross prof. social welfare policy, 1975—96, dean, 1978—83, Helen Ross prof. emerita, 1996—2009; lectr. in law U. Chgo., 1980—97. Vis. prof. U. Wash., 1965, Duke U., 1984; acad. visitor London Sch. Econs., 1973; cons. Pres.'s Commn. Law Enforcement and Adminstrn. Justice, 1966-67, Nat. Adv. Commn. Criminal Justice Stds. and Goals, 1972; mem. Juvenile Justice Stds. Commn., 1973-78; trustee Carnegie Corp. N.Y., 1979-87; trustee Children's Home and Aid Soc. of Ill., chair, 1996-98; chair CHASI Sys. Inc., 1998-2001; dir. Nat. Inst. Dispute Resolution, 1981-89, Nuveen Bond Funds, 1982-97; mem. Chgo. Network Editor: Justice for the Child, 1962; contbr. 2d edit., 1977; editor: Pursuing Justice for the Child, 1976; editor: (with F.E. Zimring, D.S. Tanenhaus, B. Dohrn) A Century of Juvenile Justice, 2002; editor: (with Mark Testa) Early Parenthood and Coming of Age in the 1990s, 1992; contbr. articles to profl. jours. Recipient Norman Maclean Faculty award, U. Chgo., 1997. Home: San Francisco, Calif. Died Feb. 2, 2009.

ROSENTHAL, JOHN W., art slides producer; b. Munich, Mar. 25, 1928; s. Julius and Anny (Springer) R.; m. Patricia M. Murray, 1954; children: David, Judith, Sarah, John E. BA, U. Chgo., 1953. Profl. photographer Koopman-Neumer, Chgo., 1955-65; med. photographer St. Lukes Hosp., Chgo., 1950-55; pres. Rosenthal Art Slides, Inc., Chgo., 1965-95. Cons. photo Art Inst. Chgo., 1970-75, U. Ctrl. Fla., Orlando, 1989-91. Prin. works include slide sets of Master Paintings in the Art Inst. of Chgo., Chgo. Hist. Soc., World's Columbian Exposition, Mus. of Contemporary Art, Corcoran Gallery of Art, Washington, Nat. Mus. of Am. Art, Washington, Hirshhorn Mus., Washington, Pierpont Morgan Libr., N.Y.C., Simply Stunning in Cin. Art Mus., Textile Sets in Art Inst., Jewelry in Walters Art Gallery, Balt., Am. Glass in Toledo Mus. of Art and miscellaneous others. Author: The '90's Catalog, 1992; prin. works include slide sets of Master Paintings in the Art Inst. Chgo., Chgo. Hist. Soc., World's Columbian Expn., Mus. Contemporary Art, Corcoran Gallery Art, Washington, Nat. Mus. Am. Art, Washington, Hirshhorn Mus., Washington, Pierpont Morgan Libr., N.Y.C., Simply Stunning in Cin. Art Mus., Textile Sets in Art Inst., Jewelry in Walters Art Gallery, Balt., Am. Glass in Toledo Mus. Art, others. Avocations: skiing, sailing, raquetball. Home: Chicago, Ill. Died Jan. 21, 2008.

ROSENTHAL, TONY BERNARD, sculptor; b. Highland Park, Ill., Aug. 9, 1914; s. Nathan H. and Bessie (Baumgarden) R.; m. Halina Kotlowicz, Apr. 2, 1946 (dec. 1991); m. Cynthia Dillon, 1995. AB, U. Mich., 1936; student, Art Inst. Chgo., Cranbrook Acad. Arts; doctorate (hon.), Hofstra U., 1989. Exhbns. include Art Inst. Chgo., Met. Mus. Art, Mus. Modern Art, N.Y., Whitney Mus. Am. Art, N.Y.C., Pa. Acad. Fine Arts, Archtl. League, N.Y., Yale U., U. Ill., U. Nebr., 100 Biennale Exhbn., Sao Paulo, Brazil, Brussel's Fair, 1958, others; one man shows include San Francisco Mus, Western Mus. Assn. Travel Exhbn., Santa Barbara (Calif.) Mus., Long Beach (Calif.) Mus., Catherine Viviano Gallery N.Y., Kootz Gallery, N.Y.C., M. Knoedler & Co., Denise Rene Gallery, Paris, 1988, others; archtl. commn. include Temple Emanuel, Beverly Hills, Calif., 1955, IBM Bldg., 1958, Southland Ctr., Dallas, IBM Western Hdqrs., Los Angeles, Police Plaza, N.Y.C., Fullerton (Calif.) State Coll., Fin. Ctr. Pacific, Honolulu, Holocaust Meml., Buffalo, Metro-Rail Sta., Miami, S.E. Nat. Bank, Miami, Grove Isle, Miami, Met. Hosp., Phila., 1010 Lamar, Houston, Crantsrook Acad. Art, Bloomfield Hills, Mich., Steelpark, 400 E. 80th St, N.Y.C., Alamo, Astor Pl., N.Y.C., Rondo, 111 E. 59th St., N.Y.C., U. Ind., Hofstra U., N.Y., others; works in permanent collections Milw. Art Ctr., Ill. State U., Los Angeles County Mus., Long Beach, Lincoln (Mass.) Mus., Ariz. State Coll., Mus. Modern Art, Whitney Mus. Art, Albright Knox Art Gallery, Buffalo, U. Ill., NYU, Yale U., Middelheim Mus., Antwerp, Belgium, Guggenheim Mus., N.Y.C., Hofstra U. Fashion Inst. Art, N.Y.C., others; pvt. collections. Served with AUS, 1942-46. Recipient awards, prizes San Francisco Mus., 1950, Los Angeles City Exhbn., 1951, 52, Audubon Artists, N.Y., 1953, Pa. Acad. Fine Arts, 1953, Los Angeles County Mus., 1950, 57, Santa Barbara Mus. Art, 1959, Art in Steel award Iron and Steel Inst., 1974-75, Disting. Alumni award U. Mich., 1977, Sculpture award Inst. Arts and Letters, N.Y.C., 1985. Mem. NAD, (Academician) Home: Southampton, NY. Died July 28, 2009.

ROSENZWEIG, MARK RICHARD, psychologist, neuroscientist, educator; b. Rochester, NY, Sept. 12, 1922; s. Jacob and Pearl (Grossman) R.; m. Janine S.A. Chappat, Aug. 1, 1947 (dec. 2008); children: Anne Janine, Suzanne Jacqueline, Philip Mark. BA, U. Rochester, 1943, MA, 1944; PhD, Harvard U., 1949; doctorate (hon.), U. René Descartes, Sorbonne, 1980, U. Louis Pasteur, Strasbourg, France, 1998, U. Montreal, Can., 2006. Postdoctoral rsch. fellow Harvard U., 1949-51; asst. prof. U. Calif., Berkeley, 1951-56, assoc. prof., 1956-60, prof. psychology, 1960-91, assoc. rsch. prof., 1958-59, rsch. prof., 1965-66, prof. emeritus, 1991—2009, prof. grad. studies, 1994—2009. Vis. prof. biology U. Sorbonne, Paris, 1973-74; mem. U.S. nat. com. for Internat. Union Psychol. Sci., NRC and NAS, 1984-96. Author: Biologie de la Mémoire, 1976, (with A.L. Leiman) Physiological Psychology, 1982, 2nd edit., 1989, (with M.J. Renner) Enriched and Impoverished Environments: Effects on Brain and Behavior, 1987, (with D. Sinha) La Recherche en Psychologie Scientifique, 1988, (with W.H. Holtzman, M. Sabourin and D. Bélanger) History of the International Union of Psychological Science, 2000; editor: (with P. Mussen) Psychology: An Introduction, 1973, 2nd edit., 1977, International Psychological Science: Progress, Problems, and Prospects, 1992, (with A.L. Leiman and S.M. Breedlove) Biological Psychology, 1996, 3d edit., 2002, (with S.M. Breedlove and N.V. Watson) 5th edit., 2007; co-editor: (with E.L. Bennett) Neural Mechanisms of Learning and Memory, 1976, (with L. Porter) Ann. Rev. of Psychology, 1968-94, (with K. Pawlik) International Handbook of Psychology, 2000; contbr. articles to profl. jours. Served with USN, 1944-46. Recipient Disting. Alumnus award U. Rochester; Fulbright Rsch. fellow; faculty Rsch. fellow Social Sci. Rsch. Coun., 1960-61; Rsch. grant NSF, USPHS, Easter Seal Found., Nat. Inst. Drug Abuse. Fellow AAAS, APA (Disting. Sci. Contbn. award 1982, Disting. Contbn. award for Internat. Advancement of Psychology 1997), Am. Psychol. Soc.; mem. NAS, NAACP (life), Am. Physiol. Soc., Internat. Union Psychol. Sci. (hon. life, mem. exec. com. 1996-2009, v.p. 1980-84, pres. 1988-92, past pres. 1992-96), Internat. Brain Rsch. Orgn., Soc. Exptl. Psychologists, Soc. for Neurosci., Société Française de Psychologie, Sierra Club (life), Common Cause, Fulbright Assn. (life), Phi Beta Kappa, Sigma Xi. Home: Berkeley, Calif. Died July 20, 2009.

ROSENZWEIG, ROY ALAN, history educator; b. NYC, Aug. 6, 1950; s. Maxwell and Mae (Blatt) R.; m. Deborah E. Kaplan, Aug. 9, 1981. BA, Columbia U., 1971; postgrad., Cambridge U., Eng., 1971-73; PhD, Harvard U., 1978. Asst. prof. history Worcester (Mass.) Poly. Inst., 1978-80; Mellon fellow Wesleyan U., Middletown, Conn., 1980-81; asst. prof. George Mason U., Fairfax, Va., 1981-85, assoc. prof. history, dir. oral history program, 1985-92, prof. history, from 1992, dir. Ctr. for History and New Media, from 1995. Bd. dirs. Am. Social History project, N.Y.C., 1984—; mem. editorial bd. Radical History Rev., N.Y.C., 1973—. Author: Eight Hours for What We Will, 1983; co-author: The Park and the People, 1992, Who Built America? From the Centennial Celebration of 1876 to the Great War of 1914, 1993; editor: Presenting the Past, 1986, History Museums in the U.S., 1989. Guggenheim found. fellow, 1989-90, NEH fellow, 1984-85, Samuel Stouffer fellow Harvard-MIT Joint Ctr. Urban Studies, 1976-78, Kellet fellow Cambridge U., 1971-73. Mem. Orgn. Am. Historians, Am. Hist. Assn., Oral History Assn. Home: Arlington, Va. Died Oct. 11, 2007.

ROSS, BYRON WARREN, minister; b. LA, Apr. 22, 1920; s. Byron George and Ruth Nancy (Olson) R.; m. Letha Alice Ausherman, Apr. 13, 1941; children: Byron Leland, Myron Eldon, Nancy Lee Anne, Bryant Alan. AB, Master's Coll., 1943; postgrad., Nyack Missionary Coll., 1943-44; BD, L.A. Bapt. Theol. Sem., 1944; PhD, Temple Hall Coll., 1947. Ordained to ministry Christian and Missionary Alliance. Pastor Christian and Missionary Alliance Ch., Manhattan Beach, Calif., 1942-43, Faith Bible Ch., Ridgecrest, Calif., from 1988; missionary Christian and Missionary Alliance, 1948-63; pastor, prin. Christian Heritage Schs., various cities, Calif., 1966-76; prin. Valley Christian Sch., Ridgecrest, 1986-88, Immanuel Christian Sch., Ridgecrest, 1980-81. Dir. overseas lay-worker tng. Christian and Missionary Alliance, Lancaster, Calif., 1961-63; supr. King's Valley Christian Sch., Concord, Calif., 1976-79. Author: Expository Preaching, 1954, Sarangani Lay-Worker's Inst., 1958; pastnett Tape-Mate, 1963, Art-A-Graph, 1976. Republican. Home: Inyokern, Calif. Died June 28, 2008.

ROSS, JEANNE NMI, psychologist; b. Chgo., Jan. 10, 1923; d. Joseph Pacwa and (Prendota) Tillie; m. Milton Jaeger (dec.); m. Gunther Rothenberg (dec.). BA with hons., U. Ill., 1952, MA, 1954; EdD, U. N.Mex., 1969. Lic. adminstr. Calif., 1977, Ariz., 1977, cert. sch. psychologist Calif., 1977. Tchr. Alamogordo (N.Mex.) Pub. Schs., 1954—55, Rantoul Pub. Schs., Ill., 1954—59; instr. So. Ill. U., Carbondale, Ill., 1960—63; clin. dir. N.Mex. Girl's Sch., Albuquerque, 1968—69; sch. counselor Albuquerque (N.Mex.) Pub. Schs., 1969—71; dir. project, head title III Am. Indian program Sacaton (Ariz.) Sch. Dist., 1972—73; sch. psychologist Vista (Calif.) Unified Sch. Dist., 1977—87, ret., 1987. Contbr. articles to profl. jours. Pvt. women's corps. US Army, 1944—45. Recipient Chi Omega award, U. Ill., 1952, award, AAUW, 1967. Mem.: Calif. Ret.

Tchrs. Assn., Phi Kappa Phi (scholarship 1952), Alpha Lambda Delta (scholarship 1950). Independent. Avocations: photography, painting, travel, theater, opera, music. Died Jan. 10, 2008.

ROSS, SHIRLEY S., retired English educator; b. Hardy, Ky., Feb. 15, 1936; d. Thomas Jefferson and Margaret (Stiltner) Stacy; m. Clarence Edwin Ross, Aug. 17, 1957; children: Cheryl Ann, Elizabeth Kay, Naomi Ruth. BA, Milligan Coll., Tenn., 1958. 7th grade English tchr. Galion (Ohio) city schs. Part-time staff Lifeline Christian Mission, Haiti; lectr. in field. Mem. NEA, Nat. Coun. Tchrs. English, Ohio Edn. assn., Galion Edn. Assn., Order Ea. Star, Clan Ross Assn. U.S. (nat. sec., commr. of Ohio). Home: Galion, Ohio. Died Mar. 24, 2008.

ROSSAVIK, IVAR KRISTIAN, obstetrician, gynecologist; b. Stavanger, Rogaland, Norway, Nov. 3, 1936; came to U.S., 1982; s. Andreas and Bergit (Berge) R.; divorced; children: Line, Anne Britt, Kirsten, Solveig; m. Claudia Lagos, May 23, 1987; children: Claudia Kristina, Eevar Benjamin. MD, U. Oslo, 1962, PhD, 1982. Pvt. practice, medicine, Stavanger, 1974; asst. chief, acting chmn. U. Tromsoe, Norway, 1974-76; clin. fellow Nat. Hosp. of Norway, Oslo, 1976-81, Norwegian Radium Hosp./U. Oslo, 1981-82; pvt. practice Oslo, 1977-82; rsch. asst. prof. Baylor Coll. Medicine, Houston, 1983-86; assoc. prof. U. Okla., Oklahoma City, 1987-93, prof., 1993—2001; owner, cons. Clinica Guadalupana, from 2001. Inventor Rossavik Growth Equation, 1980; author: (textbook) Practical Obstetrical Ultrasound: With and Without A Computer, 1991 (Italian translation 1998). Lt. Royal Norwegian Navy, 1964-65. Lutheran. Avocation: computers. Home: Oklahoma City, Okla. Died Sept. 30, 2008.

ROSSI, ALICE S., sociology educator, writer; b. NYC, Sept. 24, 1922; d. William A. and Emma (Winkler) Schaerr; m. Max Kitt, Dec. 1941 (div. Sept. 1951); m. Peter H. Rossi, Sept. 29, 1951 (dec. 2006); children: Peter Eric, Kristin Alice, Nina Alexis. BA, Bklyn. Coll., 1947; PhD, Columbia U., 1957; 9 hon. degrees. Rsch. assoc. Cornell U., Ithaca, N.Y., 1951-52, Harvard U., Cambridge, Mass., 1952-55, U. Chgo., 1961-67, Johns Hopkins U., Balt., 1967-69; prof. sociology Goucher Coll., Balt., 1969-74, U. Mass., Amherst, 1974-91, prof. emerita, 1991—2009. Editor: Feminist Papers: From Adams to de Beavoir, 1973, Seasons of a Woman's Life: A Self Reflective Essay on Love and Work in Family, Profession and Politics, 1983, Gender and the Life Course, 1985, Of Human Bonding: Parent-Child Relations Across the Life Course, 1990, Sexuality Across the Life Course, 1996, Caring and Doing for Others: Social Responsibility in the Domains of Family, Work and Community, 2001; contbr. numerous articles to profl. jours. Founder, bd. mem. NOW, 1966-70; pres. Sociologists for Women in Soc., 1971-72. Career grantee NIMH, 1965-69, rsch. grantee Rockefeller Found., Ford Found., NIH, NSF, others; CommonWealth Disting. Scholarship award, 1988. Mem. Am. Sociol. Assn. (pres. 1983-84), Ea. Sociol. Soc. (pres. 1973-74). Avocations: design, sewing, gardening, creative writing. Home: Amherst, Mass. Died Nov. 3, 2009.

ROTH, AUDREY JOAN, English language educator, consultant in communications; b. Newark, Feb. 4, 1927; d. Eugene and Ida (Kaufman) Dynner; m. Raymond N. Roth, June 26, 1949; children: Sharon, David. BA, Ohio State U., 1946, MA, 1947; PhD, Union Inst., Cin., 1976. Freelance advt. dir., Youngstown, Ohio, 1951-55; instr. in communications Youngstown U., 1955-57; instr. humanities U. Miami, 1957-63; prof. English Miami-Dade Community Coll., 1963-96, prof. emerita, from 1996. Pres. Word Wise, Miami, 1974—. Author: The Research Paper, 7th edit., 1994, Elements of Basic Writing, 2d edit., 1995; co-author: Words People Use, 1972, Strategies for College Reading, 1989. Mem. Fla. Coll. English Assn. (pres. 1984-85), Fla. Coun. Tchrs. English (pres. 1979-80), Assembly on Computers in English (pres. 1984-85), Fla. Assn. Depts. English (exec. sec.-treas. 1989-92). Avocations: weaving, basketry, flying. Home: Hollywood, Fla. Died June 5, 2008.

ROTHAUSER, FLORENCE ARAX, artist; b. NYC, July 22, 1922; d. Harry Malcolm Raphaelian and Venus Aroosiag Kabakjian; 1 child, Diane Clark. Student, Pratt Inst., Bklyn., 1944. Asst. mural artist MmGreely Dept. Store, NYC, 1944—46; freelance mural painter, 1946—59. Color cons. NY Sch. Nursing, NYC, 1958. Avocation: cooking. Home: Norwood, Mass. Died Sept. 11, 2007.

ROTHKOPF, MICHAEL H., science educator, researcher; b. NYC, May 20, 1939; s. Abraham and Sadie (Meresman) R.; m. Laura Clar, June 12, 1960 (div.); children: Anne, Alan; m. Laura Valentine, Mar. 28, 1998. BA, Pomona Coll., 1960; MS, MIT, 1962, PhD, 1964. With math. dept. Shell Devel. Co., Emeryville, Calif., 1964-66, rsch. supr., 1966-71; div. head Shell Internat. Petroleum Co., London, 1971—73; rsch. scientist Xerox Palo Alto (Calif.) Rsch. Ctr., 1973-82; program leader, sr. scientist Lawrence Berkeley (Calif.) Lab., 1982-88; prof. Rutgers U., New Brunswick, N.J., from 1988. Part-time asst. prof. U. Calif., San Francisco, 1974-76; adj. assoc. prof. Stanford U., Palo Alto, 1980-81; lectr. U. Santa Clara, Calif., 1980, U. Calif., Berkeley, 1982-88. Mem. Inst. for Ops. Rsch. and the Mgmt. Scis. (pres. 2004), Internat. Assn. Energy Economists, Am. Economists Assn. Home: Piscataway, NJ. Died Feb. 18, 2008.

ROTHMAN, STEVEN J., materials scientist; b. Giessen, Germany, Dec. 18, 1927; came to U.S., 1938; s. Stephen and Irene E. (Mannheim) R.; m. Barbara A. Kirkpatrick, Oct. 14, 1951; children: Ann Rothman Fritcher, Nicholas. PhB, U. Chgo., 1947; BS, Stanford U., 1951, MS, 1953, PhD, 1955. Metallurgist Argonne (Ill.) Nat. Lab., 1954-93. Fulbright sr. lectr., 1973. Editor: Solid State: Nuclear Methods, 1983, Oxidation of Metals, 1987, Jour. Applied Physics, 1990—. Precinct committeeman Milton Twp. (Ill.) Dem. Orgn., 1960-94. Postdoctoral fellow NSF, 1962-63. Mem. Am. Phys. Soc., Metall. Soc., Materials Rsch. Soc. Home: Wheaton, Ill. Died May 31, 2008.

ROTTER, PAUL TALBOTT, retired insurance executive; b. Parsons, Kans., Feb. 21, 1918; s. J. and LaNora (Talbott) R.; m. Virginia Sutherlin Barksdale, July 17, 1943; children: Carolyn Sutherlin, Diane Talbott. BS summa cum laude, Harvard U., 1937. Asst. mathematician Prudential Ins. Co. of Am., Newark, 1938-46; with Mut. Benefit Life Ins. Co., Newark, from 1946, successively asst. mathematician, asso. mathematician, mathematician, 1946-59, from v.p. to exec. v.p., 1959-80, ret., 1980. Mem. Madison Bd. Edn., 1958-64, pres., 1959-64; Trustee, mem. budget com. United Campaign of Madison, 1951-55; mem. bd., chmn. advancement com. Robert Treat council Boy Scouts Am., 1959-64. Fellow Soc. Actuaries (bd. govs. 1965-68, gen. chmn. edn. and exam. com. 1963-66, chmn. adv. com. edn. and exam. 1969-72), Phi Beta Kappa Soc.; mem. Brit. Inst. Actuaries (assoc.), Am. Acad. Actuaries (v.p. 1968-70, bd. dirs., chmn. edn. and exam. com. 1965-66, chmn. rev. and evaluation com. 1968-74), Assn. Harvard Alumni (regional dir. 1965-69), Actuaries Club NY (pres. 1967-68), Harvard Alumni Assn. (v.p. 1964-66), Am. Lawn Bowls Assn. (pres. SW divsn.), Harvard Club NJ (pres. 1956-57); Harvard Club (NYC), Morris County Golf Club (Convent, NJ), Joslyn-Lake Hodges Lawn Bowling Club (pres. 1989-90). Home: San Diego, Calif. Died Feb. 24, 2009.

ROVELSTAD, GORDON HENRY, dentist, researcher; b. Elgin, Ill., May 19, 1921; s. Henry Randolph and Margot Helen (Greenhill) R.; m. Barbara Jean Johnson, Apr. 8, 1945 (dec. 2005); children: Craig Gordon, Martha Kay, Andrew Todd. Student, St. Olaf Coll., 1939-41; DDS, Northwestern U., Chgo., 1944, MSD, 1948, PhD, 1960; DSc (hon.), Georgetown U., 1970. Diplomate Am. Bd. Pediatric Dentistry. Asst. prof. pediatric dentistry Northwestern U., Chgo., 1946-53; head dental dept. Children's Meml. Hosp., Chgo., 1948-53; ensign USNR, 1943, advanced through grades to capt. Camp Peary, Va., 1945-46; with USNTC, Bainbridge, Md., 1954-59; dir. rsch. US Naval Dental Sch., Bethesda, Md., 1960-65; officer in charge US Naval Dental Rsch. Inst., Gt. Lakes, Ill., 1965-69; dir. rsch. USN Dental Corp., Washington, 1969-74; ret., 1974; asst. dean, prof. U. Miss. Sch. Dentist, Jackson, 1974-80; exec. dir. Am. Coll. Dentists, Gaithersburg, Md., 1981-94, exec. dir. emeritus, 1994—2009; pres. William J. Gies Found., 1982-98, pres. emeritus, 1998—2009. Hon. bd. dirs. William J. Gies Found. for Advancement of Dentistry, Am. Dental Edn. Assn., 2003—09. Contbr. articles to profl. jours. Fellow Am. Coll. Dentists (pres., v.p.), Internat. Coll. Dentists, N.Y. Acad. Sci., N.Y. Acad. Dentists; mem. ADA, Am. Acad. Pediatric Dentistry (pres., v.p.), Internat. Assn. Dental Rsch. (pres., v.p., sec.), Rotary Internat., Sigma Xi. Avocations: miniatures, music, golf, fishing. Died Apr. 13, 2009.

ROVIN, SHELDON, dentist, educator; b. Detroit, Dec. 6, 1932; s. Samuel H. and Fannie J. (Gooze) Rovin; m. Nancy May Gold, June 23, 1957; children: Lisa, Suzan, David. DDS, U. Mich., 1957, MS (USPHS trainee), 1960. Diplomate Am. Bd. Oral Pathology. Chmn. dept. oral pathology U. Ky., Lexington, 1962-70, dir. office devel. planning evaluation Sch. Dentistry, 1970-73, pres. Senate, 1971; dean Sch. Dentistry U. Wash., Seattle, 1973-77; VA adminstrv. scholar Washington, 1977-79; chmn. dept. dental care systems U. Pa., Phila., 1979—98, prof. health care systems Wharton Sch., 1980—98, prof. emeritus, 1998—2009. Assoc. dir. Leonard Davis Inst. Health Econs., 1980—98; dir. Johnson & Johnson-Wharton Mgmt. Program Nurse Execs., Smith Kline Beecham Leanord Davis Inst. Mgmt. Program Dirs. Hosp. Pharmacies, 1987—98; cons. to hosps. in planning and mgmt. Author: Oral Pathology, 1972, Managing Hospitals, 1991, Redisgn of U.S. Healthcare System, 1994, Medicine and Business: Bridging the Gap, 2001; co-author (with Russell Ackoff): Redisigning Society, 2003, Beating the System: Using Creativity to Outsmart Bureaucracies, 2005; contbr. articles to profl. jours. Served to capt. Dental Corps US Army, 1960—62. Recipient Preventive Dentistry award, ADA, 1974, Svc. award, Alpha Omega, 1974. Fellow: Am. Acad. Oral Pathology; mem.: Omicron Kappa Upsilon. Home: Wynnewood, Pa. Died July 11, 2009.

ROWLES, STACY AMANDA, musician; b. Hollywood, Calif., Sept. 11, 1955; d. James George and Dorothy Jewel (Paden) R. Grad. high sch., Burbank, Calif., 1973. Performer Monterey (Calif.) Jazz Festival, 1973; mem. Clark Terry All Star Band Wichita (Kans.) Jazz Festival, 1975; recording artist Concord (Calif.) Jazz Records Inc., 1984; performer Alive All Women's Quintet U.S. Tour, 1985, Charlie Hayden Liberation Orch., Los Angeles, 1986, Primavera Concert, Tucson, 1986; performer Woody Herman 50th Anniversary Tribute Concert Hollywood (Calif.) Bowl, 1986; band mem. Maiden Voyage All Female Jazz Orch.; recorded on Enja Records with Nels Cline, Orange/Blue with Ray Brown, Donald Bailey, Jimmy Rowles, Sweets Edison. Soloist: Looking Back with Father; appeared in Nice (France) Jazz Festival, 1989. Named Best Fluegelhorn Soloist Orange Coast Coll. Jazz Festival, Costa Mesa, Calif., 1973, 1974. Avocations: silversmithing, golf, softball, roller skating. Died Oct. 27, 2009.

ROWLEY, JAMES MAX, retail fuel oil and rental property company executive; b. Milton, Vt., Oct. 26, 1943; s. Raymond George and Hope Valerie (Garrand) R.; m. Leslie Joan Dwinell, Aug. 27, 1966; children: Christina, Jo-Ellen. BS, U. Vt., 1966. Mkgt. trainee Mobil Oil Corp., Rochester, N.Y., 1966-67; shift supr. Champlain Container Group, Shelburne, Vt., 1967-69; co-owner J & J Assocs., Milton, Vt., 1968-71, Milton Lumber Co., 1969-72. Pres. J.M. Rowley, Inc., Milton, 1970—, Rowley Fuels, Inc., Milton, 1980—; advisor Franklin-Lamoille Bank, Milton, 1989-94 Bd. dirs. Milton Community News, 1990—; mem. sch. bd. Milton Graded Sch. Dist., 1977-86; pres. Milton Dem. Com., 1978; coach Milton Girls' Softball League, 1979-84, 87-90. Mem. Milton Bus. Assn. (charter, pres. 1987-88), Fraternal Order of Eagles (charter, pres. 1990-91), Alpha Zeta. Avocations: skiing, golf. Died Mar. 17, 2008.

ROY, CHARLES EDWARD, retired religious studies professor; b. Birmingham, Ala., July 15, 1917; s. Moses Eugene and Bessie (Bennett) R.; m. Brona Nifong, Dec. 20, 1947; children: Rebecca Roy Benfield, AA, Young Harris Coll., 1938; AB cum laude, Piedmont Coll., 1940; MDiv, Candler Sch. Theology, 1944; MA, George Peabody Coll., 1949; DD (hon.), Greensboro Coll., 1980. Ordained elder United Methodist Ch. Chaplain, prof. religion, chmn. div. humanities Brevard Coll., N.C., 1944-84, emeritus, 1984-2008, acting pres., 1968-69. Pres. Transylvania County Youth Assn., 1965-68; bd. dirs. Transylvania-Henderson Counties Justice Alternatives; bd. mem. Community Relations Council, Schenck Job Corps, Brevard; chmn. Transylvania County Human Rels. Coun., Brevard, 1965-85; chmn. Transylvania County United Way, Brevard, 1971-72; mem. steering com. Transylvania Hospice Care, past. pres, bd. dirs. Recipient Gov.'s Vol. Service award, 1984, Outstanding Sr. Citizen's award Brevard Jaycees, 1985, Pres.'s Outstanding Citizen's award Brevard C. of C., 1987. Mem. Soc. Bibl. Lit., Am. Schs. Oriental Rsch., Transylvania County Ministerial Assn. Democrat. Lodge: Lions (pres. Brevard 1973-74). Avocations: travel, archeology, gardening, woodworking. Home: Brevard, NC. Died Nov. 1, 2008.

RUBY, CHARLES ANDREW, radio station executive; b. Elyria, Ohio, Apr. 23, 1951; s. Charles Andrew and Viola Mary (Raab) R.; m. Elizabeth Ann Ostanek, Oct. 27, 1984; 1 child, Nikolaus. BS in Speech, Kent State U., 1977. Announcer Sta. WKSU, Kent, Ohio, 1972; asst. news dir. Sta. WKSU-FM, Kent, 1973, producer, 1973-75, music dir., 1975-77, dir. ops., 1977-80; cultural affairs coord. Sta. WMFE-FM, Orlando, Fla., 1980-82, membership coord., 1982-83; mgr. Sta. WUCF-FM, Orlando, 1983-85, Sta. KRTU-FM, San Antonio, 1985-88; gen. mgr. Sta. WGTD-FM, Kenosha, Wis., from 1988. Engr., producer various folk music albums, 1978-82; performer Kent State U.'s Japanese Music Ensemble, 1976-79; host, producer (syndicated radio series) Cultural Perspectives, 1982-84. Eagle scout Order of the Arrow Boy Scouts Am., 1966, asst. scoutmaster, Orlando, 1983-85. Mem. Nat. Assn. Jazz Educators, San Antonio Radio Advt. and Broadcasting Execs., Racine Lions Club. Presbyterian. Avocations: history, swimming, snorkeling, canoeing, travel. Home: Kenosha, Wis. Died June 20, 2008.

RUDIS, VICTOR AUGUSTINE, research forester, ecologist; b. Boston, Aug. 27, 1950; s. Hans and Stella (Okuniewska) R.; m. Mary R. DeRonde, Aug. 14, 1976; children: Jeffrey, Jonathan. BS in Biology, Boston Coll., 1972; MS in Ecology, Rutgers U., 1975; MS in Forestry, U. Wis., 1978. Instr. Rutgers Prep. Sch., Somerset, N.J., 1972-73; tchg. asst. Rutgers U., New Brunswick, N.J., 1973-74, rsch. asst., 1974; grad. rsch. asst. dept. forestry U. Wis., Madison, 1976-78; planning asst. Wis. Dept. Natural Resources, Madison, 1979; rsch. forester forest inventory and analysis USDA Forest Svc., New Orleans, 1980-83, rsch. forester So. Rsch. Sta. Forest Inventory & Analysis Starkville, Miss., from 1983. Contbr. articles to profl. publs. V.p. Miss. State U. World Neighbors Assn., Mississippi State, 1990. Mem. Miss. Native Plant Soc. (bd. dirs. 1995-96, pres. 1992-94, editor 1990-91, sec.-treas. 1988-89), Soc. Am. Foresters, Ecol. Soc. Am., U.S. Internat. Assn. Landscape Ecologists, Starkville Swim Assn. (sec. 1996). Avocations: natural landscaping and restoration, native plants. Home: Knoxville, Tenn. Died Nov. 15, 2007.

RUNYON, PETER MARTIN, manufacturing company executive; b. Los Angeles, June 5, 1930; s. Fredrick G. and Sally (Jeffries) R. BA, Claremont McKenna Coll., 1956. Salesman Typecraft Inc., Pasadena, Calif., 1956-58, gen. mgr., 1959-61; pres. Housewarmer Inc., Pasadena, 1962-65, Victor Leather Goods, Los Angeles, from 1963. Sec. Ski Tip Lodge Inc., Los Angeles, Constrn. Vues Inc., Los Angeles, Wash. Ross Ins., Los Angeles. Pres. Claremont Young Reps., 1951; v.p. Pasadena Advt. Club, 1962; v.p. Pasadena Jr. C. of C., 1964-66; bd. dirs. Pasadena Boys Club, 1964-66. Recipient Man of Yr. award Pasadena Jr. C. of C., 1963. Mem. Western and English Mfg. Assn. (bd. dirs. 1977-80, treas. 1981, Outstanding Service award 1981). Clubs: University (Pasadena). Republican. Presbyterian. Avocations: skiing, gardening, sailing, flying. Died July 20, 2008.

RUSH, CECIL ARCHER, microchemist, consultant, researcher; b. Dillwyn, Va., Apr. 14, 1917; s. Archer Edward and Anne Elizabeth (Le Sueur) R.; m. Betty Anne Morgan;

1 child, Gordon David. BS, Coll. William and Mary, 1938; MS, U. Tex., 1940. Chief microanalytical rsch. lab. Aberdeen Proving Grounds, Edgewood, Md., 1940-70; microchemical cons., from 1971. Contbr. 40 articles to tech. jours. Recipient Sec. of Def. Outstanding Civilian Svc. award U.S. Dept. Def., 1950, First Peabody Sculpture award Md. Inst. Art, 1952. Mem. Am. Chem. Soc., Am. Crystallographic Soc., Rsch. Soc. Am. Avocations: sculpture, collecting european, indian, tibetan and african art, minerals, fossils, seashells. Home: Baltimore, Md. Died Mar. 7, 2008.

RUSH, KENNETH WAYNE, academic administrator; b. Phila., Sept. 12, 1939; s. M. LeRoy and Vera May (Johnson) R.; m. Ruth Miller, Apr. 6, 1963; children: Nancy Jeanne, Stephen Todd. ABA, U. Pa., 1970, BBA, 1980. Actuarial clk. Presbyn. Mins. Fund, Phila., 1958-62, asst. sec., 1968-75, corp. sec., 1975-77; mgr. actuarial dept. Reliance Standard Life, Phila., 1965-68; controller Columbia (S.C.) Bible Coll., 1977-79; bus. mgr. Westminster Theological Sem., Phila., 1979-92, v.p. bus. and fin., from 1993. Author: (with others) Human Resources Management in Religiously Affiliated Institutions, 1991. Treas. Phil. presbytery Presbyn. Ch. Am., 1986-94, modrator, 1994; pres. Montgomery north camp Gideons Internat., Montgomery County, Pa., 1991-93, sec. 1996; dir. Covenant Counseling Ctr., Lansdale, Pa., 1991—. With USN, 1962-64. Republican. Avocations: hunting, fishing. Home: Harleysville, Pa. Died Apr. 24, 2008.

RUSSELL, GEORGE ALLEN, composer, theoritician, author, conductor; b. Cin., June 23, 1923; s. Joseph and Bessie (Sledge) R.; 1 son, Jock Millgardh; m. Alice Norbury, Aug. 4, 1981. Student in Pupil Composition, Stephan Volpe, 1949. Apptd. mem. faculty New England Conservatory Music, 1969. Also tchr. in Sweden, Norway, Finland, U.K., Italy, Austria, Germany, France and Japan; mem. panel Nat. Endowment of Arts, 1975-76 Composer (with Dizzy Gillespie); 1st composition featuring jazz and Latin influences Cubana-Be, Cubana Bop; presented Carnegie Hall, 1947; performed John F. Kennedy's People to People Music Festival, Washington, 1962, Philharmonic Hall, Lincoln Center, 1963, tours of Europe with Newport Jazz Festival, 1964, jazz orchestras 1970-2009; performed original compostions with large and small European ensembles for radio, TV and new music socs., in Scandinavia, Italy, Sweden, W.Ger., also other parts Europe, 1964-70; Carnegie Hall performance, 1975; participant 1st White House Jazz Festival, 1978; recs. for RCA Records, Decca, Prestige, Capitol, Atlantic, Columbia, Contemporary, Blue Note, Soul Note, numerous others.; commd. composer maj. jazz work, Brandeis U., 1957, Norwegian TV; other commns. include original music for ballet Othello, 1967, Norwegian Cultural Fund, 1st choral work Listen to the Silence, 1971, Columbia Recs., Living Time for big band featuring Bill Evans, 1975, Swedish Radio for orch., 1977, 81, 83, Mass. Council on the Arts, 1983, Boston Musica Viva, 1987, work for orch. New Eng. Presentors, 1988, work for Relache New Music Ensemble, 1989; sponsor Am. Music Week, 1985, 86; artist-in-residence Glasgow Internat. Festival, 1990, Ezzthetics with Don Ellis, Dave Baker, et al, N.Y. Big Band, New York, N.Y., Electronic Sonata for Souls Loved By Nature, The Essence of George Russell; tours of U.K., Europe, Japan with George Russell Living Time Orch., 1986-2009; co-commn. Swedish Concert Inst. and Brit. Coun., 1995; recordings Label Bleu, 1989, 96; seminars: Paris Conservatoire Nat. Superier, Royal Coll. Music, Stockholm, Huddersfield Contemporary Music Festival, Guildhall, others, 1986-96; author: Lydian Chromatic Concept of Tonal Organization, 1953, 59, 98. Recipient Outstanding Composer award Metronome mag., 1958, New Star Composer award Downbeat mag., 1961, Nat. Endowment for the Arts award, 1969, 76, 80, 81, Jazz Masters fellow, 1989; recipient Nat. Music award Am. Music Conf., 1976, numerous awards for recs.; Guggenheim fellow, 1969, 72; Nat. Endowment for Arts grantee, 1979; MacArthur Found. fellow, 1989. Mem. Internat. Soc. Contemporary Music, Norwegian Soc. New Music, Am. Fedn. Musicians, Royal Coll. Music (fgn. mem.). Died July 27, 2009.

RUSSELL, JAMES BRIAN, broadcast executive, media consultant; b. Hartford, Conn., Jan. 30, 1946; s. Seymour and Marian (Kamins) R.; m. Kathleen Anne Schardt, Dec. 28, 1968; children: Theodore, Jennifer, Kimberly. BA in Journalism, Am. U., 1968; postgrad. Wharton Sch. Bus., U. Pa.; postgrad., Stanford U. Reporter, prodr. WAMU FM, Washington; news dir. Sta. WPIK-AM, Arlington, Va., 1965-66; editor, anchorman Sta. WAVA-AM/FM, Washington, 1966-68; editor, corr. UPI, Washington, Cambodia and, Vietnam, 1968-71; from reporter to exec. prodr. All Things Considered Nat. Pub. Radio, Washington, 1971-78; sta. dir., sr. v.p. programming Stas. KTCA/KTCI-TV, Mpls./St. Paul, 1978-88; v.p. nat. prodns., exec. prodr. Marketplace U. So. Calif., LA, 1988-97; v.p. USC Radio and GM Marketplace Prodns., LA, 1990—99; sr. v.p. Minn. Pub. Radio, Am. Pub. Media & GM Marketplace Prodns., LA, 2000—06; pres. Jim Russell Prodns., from 2006, The Program Dr. Program inventor/creator: Marketplace; Weekend America; The World; Newton's Apple. Mem. prison visitor program AMICUS, St. Paul, 1984-85. Postgrad. fellow in journalism U. Mich.; recipient Nat. Headliner award 1972, 74, Ohio State award, 1973, 75, duPont Columbia awards Columbia U., 1979, 81, 97, Peabody award 2001, Nat. TV Emmy award Acad. TV Arts and Scis., 1989, William Kling award for Innovation and Entrepreneurship, 1998, Mo. Honor medal for disting. svc. in journalism, 2000. Died Jan. 18, 2006.

RUSSELL, MAURICE LLOYD, judge; b. Caldwell, Idaho, Aug. 6, 1950; s. Maurice Lloyd and Betty M. (Pledger) R.; m. Hilary Higginson, May 19, 1984. BA, U. Calif., Santa Cruz, 1972; MA, U. Calif., Santa Barbara, 1975; JD, UCLA, 1978. Bar: Oreg. 1978, U.S. Dist. Ct. Oreg. 1980. Gen. counsel Mid-Columbia Cmty. Action Coun., The Dalles, Oreg., 1978-79; assoc. Stephen H. Miller, Atty., Reedsport, Oreg., 1979-80; city atty., planner, asst. city m gr. City of Independence, Oreg., 1980-82; assoc. Chester Scott, P.C., Independence, Oreg., 1982-83; pres. M.L. Russell, P.C., Independence, Oreg., 1983-85; v.p., gen. counsel Citizens Savings & Loan Assn., Salem, Oreg., 1985-88; assoc. Churchill, Leonard et al, Salem, Oreg., 1988-93, Tarlow, Jordan & Schrader, Beaverton, Oreg., 1993-94; adminstrv. law judge State of Oreg. Dept. Transp., Salem, from 1995. Screenwriter, dir. (continuing legal edn. videotapes) Limits of Zealous Representation, 1995 (Inns of Ct. award 1995), Oregon Jury System, 1996, DUI—Recent Cases, 1996. Chair budget com. Chemekata Cmty. Coll., Salem, 1996-97; pres., bd. dirs. Mid-Vlley Arts Coun., Salem, 1991-93, chmn. bd. dirs. Salem Pastoral Counselling Ctr., 1993-95. Mem. Oreg. State Bar Assn. (bd. mem. debtor-creditor sect. 1992-93, legis. subcom. 1990-92, 93-96), Masons (Master), Willamette Valley Am. Inns of Ct. Democrat. Episcopalian. Avocations: writing, flytying, fishing, blacksmithing, music. Home: Independence, Oreg. Died Apr. 27, 2008.

RUST, JOSEPH HENRY, speech communication educator; b. Cheyenne, Wyo., Jan. 6, 1952; s. James Henry and Mary Frances (Courtney) R. BA, U. Wyo., 1974; MA, NYU, 1978. Tchr. Rock Springs (Wyo.) H.S., 1974-77; instr. McCook (Nebr.) C.C., 1978-80, Rend Lake Coll., Ina, Ill., from 1980. Author: The Principles of Effective Speaking: A Student Objective Handbook, 1993. Mem. Ill. Speech and Theatre Assn. (pres. 1991-93), Speech Comm. Assn. (chair Cmty. Coll. sect. 1992, Outstanding Cmty. Coll. Educator award 1993). Home: Cheyenne, Wyo. Died Dec. 6, 2007.

RUTH, CRAIG (CLARENCE MILLER RUTH JR.), business executive; b. July 18, 1930; s. Clarence Miller and Kathryn Dorothy (Buch) R.; m. Marion Nelson, Apr. 19, 1958; children: Robert Nelson, Lee Kathryn, William Walter, Ann Alva. BA, Muskingum Coll., 1952; postgrad., Northwestern U., 1956. Tchr., coach, NYC and Chgo., 1955-66; dir. mktg. Great Lakes Carbon Co., Los Angeles, 1966-68; exec. v.p. Ketchum, Peck & Tooley, Los Angeles, 1968-75; pres. Tooley & Co., Los Angeles, 1984—98. Mgr. Two Rodeo Dr., Beverly Hills; bd. dirs. Los Angeles Internat. Bus. Ctr.; council mem. Urban Land Inst. Bd. dirs. Bldg. Owner & Mgrs. Assn.; chmn. Elgin Baylor & Jerry West Nights Los Angeles Lakers, Ed Sherman Night, Muskingum Coll., Los Angeles, Muskingum Coll. Reunion Com.; vice chmn. USMC Scholarship Ball. Capt. USMC, 1953-55. Named one of Outstanding Men of Am. C. of C., 1965; recipient Humanitarian award Nat. Conf. Christians and Jews, 1988. Mem. Internat. Assn. Corp. Real Estate Execs., Spinal Cord Soc., 3rd Marine Divsn. (life), Japan Am. Cultural Coun., Beverly Hills Econ. Devel. Coun., Bus. Devel. Coun. (beverly Hills chpt.), Big Ten Club. Republican. Presbyterian. Avocations: tennis, playing trumpet, skiing, flying, boating. Home: Rolling Hills Estates, Calif. Died June 19, 2009.

RUTTAN, VERNON WESLEY, agricultural economist, educator; b. Alden, Mich., Aug. 16, 1924; s. Ward W. and Marjorie Ann (Chaney) R.; m. Marilyn M. Barone, July 30, 1945; children: Lia Marie, Christopher, Alison Elaine, Lore Megan. BA, Yale U., 1948; MA, U. Chgo., 1950, PhD, 1952; LLD (hon.), Rutgers U., 1978; D Agrl. Sci. ((hon.), U. Kiel, Germany, 1986, Purdue U., 1991. Economist TVA, 1951-54; prof. agrl. econs. Purdue U., 1954-63; staff economist President's Council Econ. Advisers, 1961-63; economist Rockefeller Found., 1963-65; head dept. agrl. econs. U. Minn., St. Paul, 1965-70, Regent's prof., 1986-99, Regent's prof. emeritus, from 2000. Pres. Agrl. Devel. Council, N.Y.C., 1973-77 Author (with Y. Hayami): Agricultural Development: An International Perspective, 1971, 1985; author: U.S. Development Assistance Policy, 1996, Technology, Growth and Development, 2001, Social Science Knowledge and Economic Development, 2003, Is War Necessary for Economic Growth, 2006. Recipient Alexander von Humboldt award, 1985. Fellow AAAS, Am. Acad. Arts and Scis., Am. Agrl. Econs. Assn. (pres. 1971-72, Publ. award 1956, 57, 62, 66, 67, 71, 79, 85, 97); mem. NAS. Home: Saint Paul, Minn. Deceased.

RYMER, ILONA SUTO, artist, retired educator; b. NYC, Dec. 1, 1921; d. Alexander and Elizabeth (Komaromy) Suto; m. Robert Hamilton Rymer, Mar. 27, 1944 (dec. Dec. 1999); children: Thomas Parker, Shelley Ilona. BA, Long Beach State U., 1953, MA, 1954. Tchr., cons. Long Beach (Calif.) Sch. Dist., 1953-56; tchr. Orange (Calif.) Sch. Dist., 1956-58; tchr., cons. Brea (Calif.)-Olinda Sch. Dist., 1958-80; ind. artist, designer Graphic House Studio, Solvang, Calif., from 1980, Stampa-Barbara, Santa Barbara, Calif., from 1990. Lectr. folk art Brea Sch. Dist., 1975—80; co-founder and mem. Gallery Los Olivos, pres, from 1993. Author: (instrn. book) Folk Art U.S.A., 1975 (Proclamation City of Brea, 1975); art editor, feature writer, illustrator: Arabian Conneciton mag., 1985—86; needlepoint designer Backstictch Store, Solvang, Calif., 1982—83; one-woman shows include Liberty Bell Race Track, Pa., 1970, Gallery Los Olivos, Calif., 2004, exhibited in group shows, 2006, Dennas Mus. Ctr., Northwestern Mich. Coll., 2001, Nat. Exhbn. Am. Watercolor, 2002, Adirondack's Nat. Exhbn. of Am. Watercolors, Old Forge, N.Y., from 2002, commission, Pres. Reagan's portrait on his stallion, Reagan Libr., Simi Valley, Calif., Khemosabi and Ruth, 1995. Artist and donor City of Solvang, Calif., 2005. Recipient 1st pl. Seminar award, Rex Brandt, 1961, Affiliate award, Laguna Art Mus., 1967, Best of Watercolor award, Orange County Fair, 1969, Bicentennial trip to France, Air France, 1975, Proclamation for Tchg., City of Brea, 1980, Theme award, Santa Barbara County Fair, 1991. Mem.: Mendocina Art Assn., Collage Artists Am., Artist Guild Santa Ynez Valley, Ctrl. Coast Art Assn., Santa Barbara Art Assn., Calif. Gold Coast Watercolor Soc. (signature). Presbyterian. Home: Solvang, Calif. Died Dec. 2008.

SAAVEDRA, LOUIS E., former mayor; b. Tokay, N.Mex., Mar. 18, 1933; s. Jose Ignacio and Nepumucena (Gabaldon) S.; m. Gail Griffith, Dec. 26, 1958; children: Ralph, Laura, Barbara. BA, MA, Eastern N.Mex. U., 1960, LLD (hon.), 1989; LHD (hon.), Albuquerque Tech.-Vocat. Inst., 1989. Pres. Albuquerque Tech.-Vocat. Inst., 1964-89; mayor City of Albuquerque, N.Mex., 1989—93. Commr. City Commn., Albuquerque, 1967-74. With U.S. Army, 1954-56. Recipient N.Mex. Disting. Pub. Svc. award State of N.Mex., 1977. Mem. Rotary. Democrat. Died Aug. 7, 2009.

SABANAS-WELLS, ALVINA OLGA, orthopedic surgeon; b. Riga, Latvia, Lithuania, July 30, 1914; d. Adomas and Olga (Dagilyte) Pipyne; m. Juozas Sabanas, Aug. 20, 1939 (dec. Mar. 1968); 1 child, Algis (dec.); m. Alfonse F. Wells, Dec. 31, 1977 (dec. 1990). MD, U. Vytautas The Great, Kaunas, Lithuania, 1939; MS in Orthopaedic Surgery, U. Minn., 1955. Diplomate Am. Bd. Orthopaedic Surgery. Intern Univ. Clinics, Kaunas, 1939-40; resident orthopaedic surgery and trauma Red Cross Trauma Hosp., Kaunas, 1940-44; orthopaedic and trauma fellow Unfall Krankenhous, Vienna, Austria, 1943-44; intern Jackson Park Hosp., Chgo., 1947-48; fellow in orthopaedic surgery Mayo Clinic, Rochester, Minn., 1952-55; assoc. orthopaedic surgery Northwestern U., 1956-72; asst. prof. orthopaedic surgery Rush Med. Sch., 1973-76; pvt. practice orthopaedic surgery Sun City, Ariz., 1976-89. Pres. cattle ranch corp. Contbr. articles to profl. jours. Fellow ACS; mem. Am. Acad. Orthopaedic Surgery, Physicians Club Sun City, Mayo Alumni Assn. Mem. U. Minn. Alumni Assn., Ruth Jackson Orthopedic Soc. Republican. Mem. Evang. Reformed Ch. Avocations: art, antiques, environment. Home: Las Vegas, Nev. Died Jan. 12, 2008.

SABISTON, DAVID COSTON, JR., surgeon, educator; b. Onslow County, NC, Oct. 4, 1924; s. David Coston and Marie (Jackson) S.; m. Agnes Foy Barden, Sept. 24, 1955; children: Anne Sabiston Leggett, Agnes Sabiston Butler, Sarah Coston. BS, U. N.C., 1944; MD, Johns Hopkins U., 1947; DSc (hon.), U. Madrid. Successively intern, asst. resident, chief resident surgery Johns Hopkins Hosp., Balt., 1947—53; successively asst. prof., assoc. prof., prof. surgery Johns Hopkins U. Med. Sch., Balt., 1955—64; Howard Hughes investigator Johns Hopkins Med. Sch., Balt., 1955—61; Fulbright rsch. scholar U. Oxford, England, 1960; rsch. assoc. Hosp. Sick Children, U. London, 1961; James B. Duke prof. surgery, chmn. dept. Duke Med. Sch., Durham, NC, 1964—94, chmn. dept. thoracic surgery, 1964—94; chief of staff Duke U. Med. Ctr., Durham, 1994—96, dir. internat. programs, 1996—2009. Chmn. Accreditation Coun. for Grad. Med. Edn., 1985—86. Editor: Textbook of Surgery, Essentials of Surgery, Atlas of General Surgery, Atlas of Cardiothoracic Surgery, A Review of Surgery; co-editor: Gibbon's Surgery of the Chest, Companion Handbook to Textbook of Surgery; chmn. editl. bd.: Annals of Surgery, mem. editl. bd.: Annals Clin. Rsch., ISI Atlas of Sci.: The Classics of Surgery Libr., Surgery, Gynecology and Obsetrics, Jour. Applied Cardiology, Jour. Cardiac Surgery, World Jour. Surgery. Capt. M.C., AUS, 1953—55. Recipient Career Rsch. award, NIH, 1962—64, N.C. award in Sci., 1978, Disting. Achievement award, Am. Heart Assn. Sci. Coun., 1983, Michael E. DeBakey award for Outstanding Achievement, 1984, Significant Sigma Chi award, 1987, Coll. medalist, Am. Coll. Chest Physicians, 1987; named named Disting. Physician, U.S. Va., 1995. Mem.: ACS (chmn. bd. govs. 1974—75, regent 1975—82, chmn. bd. regents 1982—84, pres. 1985—86), James IV Assn. Surgeons (bd. dirs. U.S. chpt.), Soc. Internat. De Chirurgie, Soc. Thoracic Surgeons Gt. Britain and Ireland, Soc. Surg. Chairmen (pres. 1974—76), Johns Hopkins U. Soc. Scholars, Soc. Surgery Alimentary Tract, Soc. Thoracic Surgery, Surg. Biology Club II, Halsted Soc., Soc. Univ. Surgeons (pres. 1968—69), Soc. Vascular Surgery (v.p. 1967—68), Internat. Soc. Cardiovasc. Surgery, Soc. Clin. Surgery, Am. Assn. Thoracic Surgery (pres. 1984—85), So. Surg. Assn., Am. Surg. Assn. (pres. 1977—78, sec. 1969—73, pres. 1973—74), Inst. Medicine of NAS, Am. Bd. Surgery (chmn. 1971—72, diplomate), Philippine Coll. Surgeons (hon.), Surg. Congress Assn. Espanola de Cirujanos (hon.), French Surg. Assn. (hon.), Japanese Coll. Surgeons (hon.), Brazilian Coll. Surgeons (hon.), Colombian Surg. Soc. (hon.), German Surg. Soc. (hon.), Royal Australasian Coll. Surgeons (hon.), Royal Coll. Surgeons Ireland (hon.), Royal Coll. Physicians and Surgeons Can. (hon.), Asociación de Cirugía del Litoral (Argentina) (hon.), Royal Coll. Surgeons Eng. (hon.), Royal Coll. Surgeons Edinburgh (hon.; editl. bd. jour.), Phila. Acad. Surgery (hon.), Ill. Surg. Soc. (hon.), University Club, Cosmos Club (Washington), Alpha Omega Alpha (Disting. Tchr. award 1992), Phi Beta Kappa. Home: Chapel Hill, NC. Died Jan. 26, 2009.

SACHS, ALVA, psychologist; b. Detroit, June 11, 1933; d. I. Ernest and Ann Rae (Fogelson) S.; m. Robert Chilton Calfee, June 1960 (div. 1974); children: Robert William Calfee, Elise Rael. BS, U. Mich., 1953; MS, UCLA, 1962, PhD, 1965. Lic. psychologist, Calif., Hawaii, Mich.; cert. elem. tchr., community coll. instr., community coll. counselor. Asst. tchr. art U. Mich., Ann Arbor, 1953-54; tchr. Loring AFB (Maine) Sub-Primary Sch., 1954-55, Alameda Sch. Dist., Downey, Calif., 1955-56, Redondo Beach (Calif.) Unified Sch. Dist., 1956-57, Inglewood (Calif.) Sch. Dist., 1957-58; clin. intern dept. psychology UCLA, 1959-60; regional supr. marketing research firm, 1960-61; psychology trainee VA Hosp., Palo Alto, Calif., 1963-64; psychologist U. Wis. Med. Sch., 1965-69; supr. sch. psychologists Ramat Gan, Israel, 1969-70; pvt. practice psychology, from 1971; tchr. Coll. San Mateo, Calif., 1973-78; psychologist Ten Southfield (Mich.) Clinic, 1978-80, West Hawaii Mental Health Service, Kealakekua, from 1980. Founding mem. Nat. Register Health Service Providers in Psychology; lectr. in field. Mem. exec. bd. Hawaii Family Support Council. Mem. APA, NOW, LWV, Western Assn. Women in Psychology, Assn. Women in Psychology, Am. Assn. Women in Cmty. and Jr. Colls., Women's Studies Assn., Older Women's League. Avocation: scuba diving. Home: Kailua Kona, Hawaii. Died July 25, 2008.

SACKS, ROBERT D., educational administrator, fund raiser; b. NYC, Oct. 29, 1931; s. Robert and Hortense (Saperstein) S.; divorced; children: David Robert (dec.), Michael Alan. BA, Amherst Coll., 1953; MS, Juilliard Sch., 1956; postgrad., Columbia U., 1951-52, NYU, 1959-62, Paris U., 1962-63. Instr. SUNY, Buffalo, 1963-65; asst. prof. Antioch Coll., Yellow Springs, Ohio, 1965-69; assoc. prof. Temple U., Phila., 1969-73; dean of faculty Phila. Musical Acad., 1973-75; assoc. dir. Transactional Dynamics inst., Glenside, Pa., 1976-82; exec. dir. Keswick Theatre, Glenside, 1982-84, Delaware Valley Coun. of Am. Youth Hostels, Inc., Phila., 1993-99. Commn. on Higher Edn. of the Mid. States Assn. Colls. and Schs. rep. in evaluation of colls. for accreditation/renewal of accreditation, 1974-75. Vol. Hoeffel for Congress, Montgomery County, Pa., 1996, 98, 99—, U.S. Senator Harris Wofford for Re-election, 1995; chmn. Amherst Coll. Vols. for Stevenson, 1952. With U.S. Army, 1957-59. Fulbright scholar, 1962-63; grantee Danforth Found., 1966-67, Ford Found., 1966-67, N.Y. State Regents fellow, 1960-61, Millicent James scholar and Univ. fellow NYU, 1961-62. Mem. Nat. Trust for Hist. Preservation, Preservation Pa. Avocations: gardening, woodworking, water sports. Died Dec. 18, 2007.

SAFIRE, WILLIAM, journalist, foundation administrator; b. NYC, Dec. 17, 1929; s. Oliver C. and Ida (Panish) S.; m. Helene Belmar Julius, Dec. 16, 1962; children: Mark Lindsey, Annabel Victoria. Student, Syracuse U., 1947—49. Reporter NY Herald Tribune Syndicate, 1949-51; corr. WNBC-WNBT, Europe and Mid. East, 1951; radio-TV prodr. WNBC, NYC, 1954-55; v.p. pub. rels. Tex McCrary, Inc., 1955-60; pres. Safire Pub. Rels., Inc., 1960-68; sr. White House speechwriter Pres. Richard Nixon, Washington, 1969-73; polit. columnist NY Times, Washington, 1973—2005; columnist On Language, NY Times Mag., 1979—2008. Trustee Syracuse U., 2008-09; chmn. Dana Found. Author: The Relations Explosion, 1963, Plunging into Politics, 1964, Safire's Political Dictionary, 1968, rev. edit., 1972—78, Before the Fall, 1975, Full Disclosure, 1977, Safire's Washington, 1980, On Language, 1980, What's the Good Word?, 1982, I Stand Corrected, 1984, Take My Word for It, 1986, Freedom, 1987, You Could Look It Up, 1988, Language Maven Strikes Again, 1990, Fumblerules, 1990, Coming to Terms, 1991, The First Dissident, 1992, Lend Me Your Ears, 1992, 1998, 2004, Good Advice on Writing, 1992, Quoth the Maven, 1993, In Love with Norma Loquendi, 1994, Sleeper Spy, 1995, Watching My Language, 1997, Spread the Word, 1999, Scandalmonger, 2000, Let a Simile Be Your Umbrella, 2001, No Uncertain Terms, 2003, The Right Word, 2004; co-author (with Leonard Safir): Good Advice on Writing, 1982, Words of Wisdom, 1989, Leadership, 1990; author: Safire's Political Dictionary, 5th edit., 2008. Mem. Pulitzer Bd., 1995-2004. With AUS, 1952-54. Recipient Pulitzer prize for Disting. Commentary, 1978, Presdl. Medal of Freedom, 2006. Republican. Died Sept. 27, 2009.

SAIDI, PARVIN, hematologist, educator; b. Teheran, Iran, Mar. 21, 1932; came to U.S., 1946; d. Ahmad and Fatemeh (Ashouri) S.; m. Allahverdi Farmanfarmaian, May 27, 1958; children: Dellara Farmanfarmaian Terry, Kimya Farmanfarmaian Harris. BS, Smith Coll., Northampton, Mass., 1952; MD, Harvard U., 1956. Diplomate Am. Bd. Internal Medicine, subspecialty hematology and med. oncology. Intern medicine UCLA Med. Ctr., 1956-57; resident internal medicine U. Calif., San Francisco, 1957-59; NIH rsch. fellow hematology U. Calif. Hosps. and Children's Med. Ctr., San Francisco, 1959-61, 63-64; asst. prof. medicine U. Medicine & Dentistry N.J. Rutgers Med. Sch., New Brunswick, 1968-71, assoc. prof., 1971-74; prof. U. Medicine & Dentistry N.J.-Robert Wood Johnson Med. Sch., New Brunswick, from 1974, chief divsn. hematology and oncology, dept. medicine, from 1972, Robert Wood Johnson U. Hosp., New Brunswick, from 1981, Melvyn H. and AB Motolinsky chair hematology, from 2000. Cons. internist, hematologist, oncologist St. Peter's Med. Ctr., New Brunswick, Douglass Coll., Rutgers U., New Brunswick, VA Hosp., Lyons, NJ, Muhlenberg Hosp., Plainfield, NJ, Princeton Med. Ctr., NJ; dir. Melvyn H. Motolinsky Lab. Hematology Rsch., NJ Regional Comprehensive Hemophilia Care Program, chmn. adv. bd.; mem. Gov.'s Adv. Coun. on AIDS; chmn. HHS region II Comprehensive Hemophilia Diagnostic and Treatment Ctrs., 1984-85, 89-90, 94-95, 99-2000, 04-05; chmn. med. adv. bd. Hemophilia Found. NJ; mem. med. adv. exec. com. NJ Blood Svcs. Cons. editor Am. Jour. Medicine; contbr. articles to profl. jours. Recipient Disting. Svc. award for rsch. in leukemia Melvyn H. Motolinsky Rsch. Found., 1977, Humanitarian award Hemophilia Assn. No. NJ, 1978, Physician of Yr. award Nat. Hemophilia Found., 2006. Fellow ACP (mem. sci. program com. N.J. region), Acad. Medicine N.J.; mem. Am. Soc. Hematology (edn. com.), N.J. Hemophilia Assn. (chmn. med. adv. com., spl. award, Dr. L. Michael Kuhn Meml. award 1996), Coop. Oncology Group N.J. (exec. com., chairperson subcom. on lymphoma), Am. Heart Assn. (coun. on thrombosis), Am. Fedn. Clin. Rsch., Royal Soc. Medicine (affiliate), Am. Soc. Clin. Oncology, World Fedn. Hemophilia, Alpha Omega Alpha, Phi Beta Kappa, Sigma Xi. Died 2009.

ST. GERMAIN, SHARON MARIE, retired writer; b. Mpls., Nov. 14, 1938; d. John Benjamin and Esther Lenoria Vandermyde; m. Donald Joseph St. Germain, June 17, 1961; children: Kim, Michael, Beth. BE, Hamline Univ., St. Paul, Minn., 1960. Co-dir. Writers Unlimited, White Bear Lake, Minn., 1969—2008; writing tchr. Hamline Univ., St. Paul, 1978—84, Mpls. Cmy. and Tech. Coll., 1981—2008, Century Coll., White Bear Lake, Minn., 1994—2008, Cmty. Edn. programs, Mpls., St. Paul, Rochester Cmty. Edn., Minn., 1997—2008, St. Cloud Cmty. Edn., Minn., 1997—2008. Writer-in -the-sch. Mid. Sch., Mpls., St. Paul, 1980—85; faculty presenter Midwest Writers Conf., River Falls, Wis., 1979; guest spkr. pub. sch., libr. and writing organizations, Mpls., St. Paul, 1980—2008. Author: (childrens book) The Terrible Fight, 1990, several others; contbr. mag. story Boys' Life, 1975, sport series book Highlights for Children, 1975, articles to numerous profl. jours. Mem.: Soc. Children's Book Writers and Illustrators, Writers Unlimited, World Wildlife Fund, Minn. Sr. Fedn., Am. Assn. Ret. People. Avocations: reading, travel, bicycling, swimming. Home: Maplewood, Minn. Died June 22, 2008.

SALMON, MARSHA CLAIRE, school system administrator; b. Shreveport, La., Sept. 13, 1937; d. James Derald and Elsie Claire (Turner) Boyd; m. Clifton Wales Salmon (wid.); children: Clifton Wales, Jr., Elizabeth Claire, Karen Suzanne, Laura Lynn. BA Early Elem. Edn., La. Tech. U., 1973, MA Elem. Edn., 1975. Cert. elem. tchr., French lang., adminstr./supr. Tchr. Webster Parish Sch. Bd., Minden, La., 1973-80, tchr. support, 1980-84, coord. fed. programs, from 1984. Mem. ASCD, La. Assn. Sch. Execs., Nat. Coun. Tchrs. Math., Internat. Reading Assn., DAR (treas. 1989-91, regent Dorcheat Bistineau chpt. 1991-94), Delta Kappa Gamma, Kappa Kappa Iota. Democrat. Baptist. Avocations: reading, gardening, entertaining grandchildren. Home: Minden, La. Died Feb. 19, 2008.

SALPETER, EDWIN ERNEST, retired physical sciences educator; b. Vienna, Dec. 3, 1924; came to U.S., 1949, naturalized, 1953; s. Jakob L. and Frieder (Horn) S.; m. Miriam Mark, June 11, 1950 (dec. Oct. 2001); children: Judy Gail, Shelley Ruth; m. Antonia L. Shouse, 2004. MS, Sydney U., 1946; PhD, Birmingham U., Eng., 1948; DSc, U. Chgo., 1969, Case-Western Reserve U., 1970, U. Sydney, 1994, U. New South Wales, Sydney, 1996. Research fellow Birmingham U., 1948-49; faculty Cornell U., Ithaca, NY, 1949-97, J.G. White Disting. prof. physical sciences emeritus, 1997—2008. Mem. U.S. Nat. Sci. Bd., 1979-85 Author: Quantum Mechanics, 1957, 77; mem. editorial bd. Astrophys. Jour, 1966-69; assoc. editor Rev. Modern Physics, 1971-92; contbr. articles to profl. jours. Mem. AURA bd., 1970-72. Recipient Gold medal Royal Astron. Soc., 1973, J.R. Oppenheimer Meml. prize U. Miami, 1974, C. Bruce medal Astron. Soc. Pacific, 1987, A. Devaucouleurs medal, 1992, Dirac Meml. medal U. New South Wales, 1996, Crafoord laureate Royal Swedish Acad. Scis., 1997, H. A. Bethe Prize, Am. Phys. Soc., 1999. Mem. NAS, Am. Astron. Soc. (v.p. 1971-73), Am. Philos. Soc., Am. Acad. Arts and Scis., The Royal Soc. (fgn.), Australian Acad. Sci., Deutsche Akademie Leopoldina. Home: Ithaca, NY. Died Nov. 25, 2008.

SALTARELLI, MICHAEL ANGELO, bishop; b. Jersey City, Jan. 17, 1933; s. Angelo Michael and Caroline (Marzitello) Saltarelli. BA, Seton Hall U., 1956; MA, Manhattan Coll., 1975. Ordained to ministry Cath. Ch., 1960. Assoc. pastor Holy Family Ch., Nutley, NJ, 1960—77; pastor Our Lady of Assumption, Bayonne, 1977—82; exec. dir. Archdiocesan Pastoral Svcs., Newark, 1982—85; pastor St. Catherine Of Siena Ch., Cedar Grove, 1985—90; aux. bishop Archdiocese of Newark, 1990—96; bishop Diocese of Wilmington, Del., 1995—2008, bishop emeritus, 2008—09. Vicar for priests Archdiocese of Newark, 1987—96. Roman Catholic. Died Oct. 8, 2009.

SALTHOUSE, THOMAS NEWTON, cell biologist, biomaterial researcher; b. Fleetwood, U.K., Mar. 8, 1910, came. to U.S., 1960; s. William and Edith Alice (Croft) S.; m. Mary Reynolds, Apr. 30, 1942; children: Andrew John, Robert William. Diplomate Royal Microscopical Soc. Sr. technologist U. Coll. E. Africa, Uganda, 1947-56; rsch. assoc. Atomic Energy Can., 1957-60; asst. pathologist E.I. DuPont, 1960-62; sr. scientist E.R. Squibb & Sons, 1962-68; sect. mgr. Ethicon Rsch. Found., 1968-81; vis. prof. bioengineering Clemson U., 1982-88. Author: (with others) Enzyme Histochemistry in Fundamentals of Biocompatibility, 1981, Biocompatibility of Sutures in Biocompatibility in Clinical Practice, 1982, Implant Shape and Surface in Biomaterials in Reconstructive Surgery, 1983; co-editor Soft Tissue Histology in Handbook of Biomaterials, 1986, 2d edit., 1996; editl. bd. Jour. Biomed. Material Rsch., 1978-84; contbr. articles to profl. jours. Recipient Phillip B. Hoffman award, 1974. Fellow N.Y. Acad. Scis., Inst. Biomed. Sci. London, Royal Photographic Soc. London; mem. Soc. for Biomaterials (sec., treas. 1976-78, pres. 1980-81, Clemson award 1978), Inst. Biomed. Scis., Dist. Sci. Ethicon Divsn. of Johnson Johnson (ret.). Achievements include research on cellular mechanisms involved in tissue response to surgical implantion of various devices. Home: Ellicott City, Md. Died Apr. 17, 2008.

SALTUS, PHYLLIS BORZELLIERE, music educator; b. Rochester, NY, Jan. 17, 1931; d. Nicholas and Sadie Veronica (Leone) Borzelliere; m. William Thomas Saltus, Aug. 21, 1965 (div. Apr. 1991); children: Julie Marie Nicole, William Nicholas. AA, Burlington County Coll., Pemberton, NJ, 1987; MEd in Measurement and Guidance, U. Maine, Orono, 1963; BS in Music Edn., SUNY, 1953, MS, 1957. Cert. student personnel svcs., music and guidance, N.J., N.Y., Me. Music tchr., choral dir. Rochester Pub. Schs., 1953-56, 62-63, 1969-70, high sch. guidance counselor, 1963-65; asst. prof. music edn. SUNY, Geneseo and Fredonia, 1956-62; music tchr, choral dir. Concord (Mass.) Pub. Schs., 1965-66; owner, dir. Saltus Music Studio, Medford, NJ, 1982—91. Music tchr., choral dir. Delanco (N.J.) Pub. Schs., 1984-86; prof. voice N.J.Dept. Edn. Sch. Arts, Rowan Univ., Glassboro (N.J.) State Coll., 1987-89; sr. adj. prof. & coordn., piano lab Burlington County Coll., Pemberton, N.J. and Ft. Dix Mil. Post, Cmty. Coll. of the Air Force at McGuire AFB, 1989—, Interactive Classroom Program, 1995—, Power Package Accelerated Program, 1995—, Telecourse for Distance Learners Program WBZC, 1995—; music coord., dist. tchr. for gifted and talented program Mt. Laurel (N.J.) Pub. Schs., 1989-94; music dir., founding mem. Triple Threat Prodns., Cherry Hill, N.J., 1991—, Burlington County Cmty. Chorus, N.J., 1995—, Kosciusko Boys Choir, Rochester, 1959-60, Young Adults Cath. Youth Orgn. Choir, Dunkirk, N.Y., 1960-62; faculty adv. N.Y. Province of Newman Clubs Fedn. SUNY, 1957-62, lectr., researcher in field. Artist: The Fredonia Main Street Diner, 1952-53, Clarence Welcome Wagon Gourmet Cook Book, N.Y., 1973; contbr. poems to various publs.; soloist Rochester Philharm. Orch. Concert Series, Songsters, Inc., 1953-59. Choir dir., organist, soloist St. Philip Neri R.C. Ch., Rochester, 1949-65, St. Peter's Episc. Ch., Medford, 1989-90; choir dir., accompanist Thessalonia Baptist Ch. Sr. and Jr. Choirs, Willingboro, N.J., 1990-91; vocal dir., accompanist Pineland Players of South Jersey Community Theatre, Medford, 1987-89, Cherry Hill East High Sch., N.J., 1991—; team capt. United Way, Rochester, 1953-56; membership chair Rochester Community Theater, 1955-56; founding mem. Sta. WCVF, 1952-58; trip advisor Ski Club, Monroe HS, Rochester, 1963; bd. dirs., founding mem. Rochester Chamber Orch., 1964-65, Medford (N.J.) Newcomers Club, 1977—; vol. Cmty. Companions of Erie County Office of the Aging, N.Y., 1972-76, Medford PTO, 1976-85; judge preliminary Miss Am. contest Jr. C. of C., Jamestown, N.Y., 1962, vocal dir., accompanist Miss Dunkirk (N.Y.) pageant, 1962, vocal coach Miss Burlington County Pageant, Jr. C. of C., 1989,97-99; active Welcome Wagon, Inc., Clarence, N.Y., pres., 1974, historian, 1981; chair Medford (N.J.) Evening Book Review Group, 1978-80; mem. Medford Morning Book Review Group, 1980—; active Meml. Health Alliance, Burlington County Women's Health Network. NDEA grantee, 1964; EEOC scholar, 1986-87; recipient Jr. County Rifle Championship award Monroe County Dept. Health and Recreation, 1948, Womens Student Table Tennis Championship award SUNY, 1952, Outstanding Scholarship award Charlotte Putnam Landers Outstanding Scholarship award SUNY, 1953, Doubles Table Tennis Championship award Monroe HS, Rochester, 1964-65. Mem. AAUP (treas. 1960-62, state del. 1961), Music Educators Nat. Conf., Am. Personnel and Guidance Assn., South Jersey Music Tchrs. Assn., Meml. Health Alliance, Women's Health Network, AARP Medford chpt. of Deborah Heart & Lung Hosp. Found., Red Lion Wildlife Refuge, Cedar Run Wildlife Refuge, Order Sons of Italy in Am., Kappa Delta Pi (del. Barnard Coll., N.Y., 1952, state del., Atlantic City, N.J., 1953). Roman Catholic. Avocations: reading and research, creative writing, golf, painting, crossword puzzles, gourmet cooking. Home: Southampton, NJ. Died July 12, 2008.

SAMAD, JACK LEE, audio/videotape recording company executive; b. Cin., Dec. 24, 1952; s. Leo Sam and Frances Norma (Winascott) S.; m. Joanne Mink, Aug. 9, 1975; children: Jacob Glenn, Christy Laura. BA, Eastern Ky. U., Richmond, 1976. Owner, gen. mgr. Video Tape Prodns., Cin., 1976-81; nat. account mgr. Am. Coin Amusements, Cin., 1981-85; mgr. media group Union Cen. Life Ins. Co., Cin., 1985-87; mgr. video svc. Cin. Milacron, from 1987; founder Creative Media Group of Cin., from 1989. Cons. producer, dir. Manhattan Life Ins. Co., N.Y.C., 1986-89, Nat. Amusements Co., Boston, 1990—. Producer, editor video: A Picture of Success, 1988; producer, dir., editor video: Welcome to Cincinnati, 1989, Manufacture with Confidence, 1990; videographer, dir., editor video: Because of You it Works, 1990, A Gift for the Future, 1989. Mem. Internat. TV Assn., Ins. Communications Assn., Sigma Alpha Epsilon. Presbyterian. Avocations: local ch. govt., home remodeling. Home: Cincinnati, Ohio. Died May 22, 2008.

SAMPLE, WINONA ELLIOTT, educational consultant; b. Red Lake, Minn., Oct. 21, 1917; d. Louis Leo and Mary (Head) Elliott; m. Herbert Conway Sample, June 1936 (dec.

Oct. 1966); children: Herbert Conway Jr., James Elliott. BA, San Jose State U., 1970; PhD (hon.), Wheeloch Coll., Boston, 1999. Dir., state child care ctrs. Santa Clara Office of Edn., Calif., 1945—65; edn. specialist Nat. Head State Bur., San Jose, Calif., 1965—75; chief Calif. Indian Health Svcs., State Health Dept., Washington; cons. Calif. State Dept. Edn. Office, Sacramento, 1975—88; pvt. edn. cons. Santa Clara, Calif., from 1988. Staff mem. Banx St. Coll., NYC, 1980—84, Enisson Inst., Chgo., 1982—87. Mem. UNICEF, Washington, 1984—88; vice chair Internat. Yr. of the Child, Washington, 1986—88. Mem.: Nat. Indian Edn. Assn. Avocations: reading, art, crafts. Home: Folsom, Calif. Died July 9, 2008.

SAMPLES, IRIS LYNETTE, elementary school educator; b. Ravenna, Ohio, July 28, 1948; d. Enzo Joseph and Iris Lynette (Wiley) Lanari; m. Charles Victor Samples, Aug. 24, 1968. BS in Edn., Kent State U., 1973; postgrad. in Reading Instruction, U. Akron, 1977-79; student, Gesell Inst. Human Devel., 1989. Cert. tchr., Ohio. Tchr. first grade Highland Local Schs., Medina County, Ohio, 1968-72, Barberton (Ohio) City Schs., 1973-77, reading tchr., from 1977. Mem. faculty adv. com. Woodford Sch., 1982-89, Right to Read activities coord., 1983—, Buckeye Book activities coord., 1990—, young authors coord., 1991—, tchr. kindergarten pilot program chpt. one students, 1987-88; sch. levy com. Barberton City Schs., 1982, 93, mem. reading curriculum com., 1987-88, mem. Right to Read dist. com., 1987—, reading textbook selection com., 1987-89. Tchr. Bible Sch., Sunday Sch. 1st Luth. Ch., 1978-82, coord. Christmas program, 1979-80; active Woodford PTA, past program chair; vol. various health founds., 1975—. Recipient Woodford Tchr. of Yr., Woodford PTA, 1994; nominated Am. Tchr. award Internat. Reading Assn., Akron chpt.; Jennings scholar, 1984. Mem. Kappa Delta Pi. Lutheran. Avocations: seminars, gardening, exercise, golf. Home: Barberton, Ohio. Died June 29, 2008.

SAMUELS, LESLIE EUGENE, marketing professional, management consultant; b. St. Croix, V.I., Nov. 12, 1929; s. Henry Francis and Annamartha Venetia (Ford) S.; m. Reather James, Oct. 24, 1959; children: Leslie Jr., Venetia, Yvette, Philip. MusB, NYU, 1956; JD, Blackstone Sch. Law, 1975; MBA, Columbia Pacific U., 1984, PhD, 1985. Concert soloist Van Dyke Studios, NYC, 1956-65; dir. Housing, Preservation and Devel., NYC, from 1966; bandmaster N.Y. State Dept. Rehab. and Recreation, NYC, 1967-76; pres., CEO Samuels and Co., Inc., NYC, from 1986, Coll. Philosophy and Edn., from 1998; exec. dir., CEO Samuels Inst. Hist. Rsch. of Christian Prins., from 1991. Cons. in field., 1984—; mem. N.Y., N.J. Minority Bus. Purchasing Coun., Inc., Nat. Minority Bus. Coun., Inc., Internat. Trade divsn.; evangelist, lectr. Principles of the Christian Faith; adj. prof. St. Martin's Coll. and Sem., 1995; dir. pvt. sch. state edn. dept., 1996. TV apperances include: Bill Silbert's Rev., 1953, Ladies Day, 1953; Author: Redemption, 2000. Mem. chmn. congrl. coun. of the Virgin Island, 1960-64, Bronx County Com., 1969; dist. leader Bronx 86th Assembly Dist., 1969; advisor Astor Home for Children, Bronx, 1973, Bronxville C. of C., Bklyn., 1975; charter mem. Rep. Presdl. Task Force, 1989; exec. dir. Samuels Inst. Hist. Rsch. Christian Principles, 1991—; mem. Nat. Rep. Senatorial Com., 1992. With U.S. Army, 1951-53. Mem. Maison Internationale des Intellectuels, Am. Mgmt. Assn., Nat. Black MBA Assn., Harvard Bus. Rev., Sloan Mgmt. Rev., Calif. Mgmt. Rev., Columbia Pacific U. Alumni Assn., Internat. Platform Assn., Smithsonian Assocs., Ind. Citizen's Club (pres. Bronx 1967-77). Republican. Avocation: sports. Home: Bronx, NY. Died June 9, 2008.

SANDARS, LEIBERT JOVANOVICH, radiologist; b. Balt., Apr. 17, 1914; s. Michael and Katherine (Jovanovich) Skandarski; m. Annel Branch, 1947; children: Jill Bonifield, Judy Klaich. MD, U. Chgo., 1941. Diplomate Am. Bd. Radiology. Intern St. Lukes Hosp., San Francisco, 1941-42; resident in radiology U. Calif., San Francisco, 1949-52; dir., founder Dept. Radiology, Washoe Med. Ctr., Reno, Nev., 1952-88; dir., cons. radiologist VA Hosp., Reno, Nev., 1954-68; chmn. Reno Radiol. Assocs., 1958-88. Artist in watercolor and oils. Lt. (j.g.) USNR, 1941-43. Fellow Am. Coll. Radiology (Nev. councilor 1954-68); mem. No. Calif. Radiol. Soc. (pres. 1964), Washoe County Med. Soc. (pres. 1964), Prospectors Club. Republican. Avocations: art, golf. Home: Reno, Nev. Died July 26, 2008.

SANDERS, EVELYN BEATRICE, postmaster, business owner; b. Parkersburg, W.Va., Sept. 20, 1931; d. William Perley and Beatrice Elizabeth (Mahaffey) Huffman; m. Kenneth Everett Sanders, Aug. 7, 1950 (dec. Nov. 1981); children: Stephen Patrick, Michael Alan. Postmaster Village of Torch, Ohio, from 1971; owner Sanders Gen. Store, Torch, from 1981. Mem. Nat. Assn. Postmasters, League of Postmasters. Democrat. Methodist. Avocations: reading, psychology, writing, medicine, philosophy. Died June 11, 2008.

SANDSTEAD, AURIEL J., retired secondary school educator, historian, researcher; d. Charles Ford and E. Fae (Stanley) Oram; m. Willard W. Sandstead, Mar. 16, 1946; children: Vicki Jo, Margo Dale, Shauna Gae. BA, Colo. State Coll. (now U. Northern Colo.), 1957, MA, 1961. Emergency tchg. certificate WWII Colo. Tchr. Weld County Dist. #93, New Raymer, Colo., 1942—44; tchr. classroom/gymnasium Logan County Jr. HS, Sterling, Colo., 1956—60; instr. English & Sports Northeastern Jr. Coll., Sterling, 1960—68; social worker, family & children svcs. Logan County Social Svcs., Sterling, 1969—77; ret., 1977. Local historian Keota, Along the Burlington R.R. Sterling to Cheyenne, Homesteaders, Schs., etc., Mary Stanley (1869-1955), quilt collection embodying three generations. Author: (poem) Fifty-one Syllables of Spring, in Best Poems of the 90s, 1995, Boundless, in Best Poems of the 90s, 1996; publisher A Cartouche Collection, 2000, A Cartouche Collection, 6th edit., 2004. Charter mem. Nat. Mus. Women in the Arts, 1987; charter pres. Colo. Quilting Coun., 1979. Recipient Heritage award, Colo. Coun. on the Arts, Denver, 2000; named to Hall of Fame (1st inductee), Colo. Quilting Coun., 1988. Mem.: Am. Quilt Study Group, High Plains Heritage Quilters (life), Alpha Delta Kappa. Avocations: reading, writing, quilting. Home: Sterling, Colo. Died Nov. 25, 2007.

SAPINSLEY, ELBERT LEE, rabbi; b. NYC, Nov. 17, 1927; s. Robert Browning and Jessamine (Moayon) S.; m. Dorothy Kaufman, June 15, 1952 (div. July 1973); children: Jesamine Leah Sapinsley Schiltz, David Jay; m. Susan Melton Fowler, June 12, 1978; children: Mark Daniel Fowler, Dianna Fowler. BS, U. Louisville, 1949; B of Hebrew Letters, Hebrew Union Coll., 1952, M of Hebrew Letters with honors in History, 1954, DD, 1979. Ordained rabbi, 1954. Rabbi Temple Hesed Abraham, Jamestown, N.Y., 1956-58, Temple Beth Sholom, Topeka, Kans., 1958-68; Hillel counselor Kans. State U., Manhattan, 1968-70; history faculty Kan. State U., 1963-79; Hillel counselor No. Ill. U., DeKalb, Ill., 1970-73; rabbi Congregation Ahavath Sholom, Bluefield, W.Va., 1975-92; ret., 1992. Chaplain VA Hosp., Topeka, 1958-70, Menninger Psychiat. Hosp., Topeka, 1964-66; vis. asst. prof. Kans. Univ. Sch. of Religion, Lawrence, 1960-65; instr. Hebrew, No. Ill. U., DeKalb, 1970-73; pres. Mid-Atlantic Region/Cen. Conf. of Am. Rabbis, 1986-88, sec., 2d v.p, 1982-86; mem. internat. exec. bd. Cen. Conf. Am. Rabbis, 1986-88. Contbg. author: Rabbis in Uniform, 1962; contbr. articles to profl. jours. Founder, chmn. Topeka Interfaith Coun. for Racial Justice, 1961; bd. dirs. Kans. Vocat. Rehab. Policy Planning Bd., 1966-68, mem. exec. com., 1967-68; founding mem., area chmn. Assn. of Reform Zionists of Am., 1978; bd. dirs. Greater Bluefield United Way, 1985; Jewish chaplain to Women's Fed. Prison, Alderson, W.Va., 1980-89; tchr. Hebrew Sch., adult classes in Biblical Hebrew Temple Beth Or, Raleigh, N.C., 1993—; rels. spkr. Jewish Fedn. Cmty., Wake County, N.C. 1st lt. U.S. Army, 1954-56. Merrill grantee (twice), 1969. Mem. Bluefield Ministerial Assn. (pres. 1984-85), Greater Carolinas Assn. of Rabbis (sec. 1985-86), Rotary (bd. dirs. 1983-85), B'nai Brith, Phi Alpha Theta. Home: Longs, SC. Died Jan. 22, 2008.

SATAVA, DAVID RICHARD, accounting professor; b. San Francisco, May 1, 1951; s. Marvin Satava and Louise Gibbons; m. Susan E. Brown, Oct. 7, 1973; 1 child, Steven. BA, San Francisco State U., 1979, MBA, 1987; DBA, Miss. State U., 1994. CPA, Calif. Acct. Boydstun & Klingner, San Francisco, 1983-86; contr. Audubon Cellars, Berkeley, Calif., 1986-89; pvt. practice Oakland, Calif., 1985-96; asst. prof. acctg. Ga. So. U., Statesboro, 1994-95; assoc. prof. acctg. U. Houston, Victoria, Tex., 1995—2009. Contbr. articles to profl. jours. Advisor Gamma Beta Phi, Victoria, 1995—; pres. PTO, Victoria, 1996. Recipient Meritorious Svc. award Gamma Beta Phi, 1996; named Tchr. of Yr., U. Houston, Victoria, 1998. Mem. AICPA, Am. Acctg. Assn. Avocation: golf. Home: Victoria, Tex. Died Oct. 16, 2009.

SATHER, SYLVIA CAROLYN, science educator, consultant; b. Morris, Minn., Feb. 27, 1944; d. Ralph Jennings and Clara Randina (Morseth) S. BA, Augusburg Coll., Mpls., 1966; MS, U. No. Colo., Greeley, 1976. Cert. elem. edn., phys. edn., gifted and talented, sci. and health endorsements. 3rd grade tchr. Mpls. Pub. Schs., 1966-68; tchr. grades 1-6 gifted/talented Denver Pub. Schs., from 1968, tchr. mid. sch. sci., math., 1987-92, tchr. biology H.S., from 1992; tchr. Denver Sch. Arts, 1997—2000. Cons. Energy & Mans Environ., Salt Lake City, 1970-82; prof. Colo. Sch. Mines, Golden, 1975-90; grad. asst. U. Denver, 1980-81; adj. prof. Wartburg Coll., 2000—. Author: Best of Energy, 1977, Energy Man's Environment, 1971-76. Mem. Nat. Sci. Tchrs. Assn., Phi Delta Kappa. Democrat. Avocations: potter, furniture maker, naturalist, ornithologist, travel. Home: Denver, Colo. Died Feb. 19, 2008.

SAULSBURY, OLIN BAKER, banker; b. Pampa, Tex., July 4, 1934; s. Olin Don and Ruby Treva (Brown) S.; m. Sammie Fowler, May 24, 1958. BBA, Tex. Tech U., 1957. Mgmt. trainee Oilwell Supply-USS, Odessa, Tex., 1957-59; mgr. trainee CIT Credit Co., Odessa, 1959-62; field rep., regional rep., br. mgr. Ford Motor Credit Co., Lubbock, Tex., Louisville, Chgo., 1962-85; sr. v.p. Premier Bank, Monroe, La., from 1985. Bd. dirs. Beautification Bd. Monroe, 1986-89. Mem. Monroe C. of C., La. Automobile Dealers Assn. (affiliate), Little Theatre of Monroe, N.E. La. Arts Council, Big Timers Dance Club, Bayou DeSiard Country Club, Bayou DeSiard Men's Golf Assn., Rotary (pres. 1988, Paul Harris fellow 1989), Masons, Shriners. Avocations: golf, reading, lawn and yard work, all spectator sports. Home: Monroe, La. Died Mar. 3, 2008.

SAUNDERS, GEORGE WENDELL, management consultant, retired government official; b. Hubbard, Ohio, Oct. 17, 1917; s. Phillip and Mary (Shafer) S.; m. Audrey Edna Bogue (dec. Nov. 1979); children: Wayne George, Wendy Jean; m. Virginia Hutson Baker, June 25, 1987; stepchildren: John Milton Jr., Kathee Eloise. B in Acctg., Rider Coll., 1937; postgrad, Harvard U., 1943; grad., Indsl. Coll. Armed Forces, 1955, Fgn. Service Inst., Naval War Coll.; student, Grad. Sch. Dept. Agr., Dept. Def. Computer Inst. Auditor, acct. U.S. Rubber Co., NYC, 1937-39; acct., office mgr. S. King Fulton, Inc., Washington, 1939-40; with War Dept. and Civil Aero. Adminstrn., Washington, 1940-41; adminstrv. asst., sr. investigator Bur. Fed. Supply Treas. Dept., Washington, 1941-47; ops. planning analyst, orgn. and methods examiner, supply specialist Fed. Supply Services GSA, Washington, 1957-55, dep. dir. stores mgmt. div., 1955-61, dir. supply distbn. div., acting asst. dir. nat. buying div., 1956-61, dir. distbn. programs div., 1961-64, asst. commr. supply distbn., 1964-71, asst. commr. trans. and pub. utilities, 1971-73, dep. commr., 1973-75; v.p. Washington Mgmt. Group, Washington Mktg. Group, 1975-79; pvt. practice cons., from 1979. Mem. Fed. Safety Council, Fed. Fire Council and Nat. Def. Trans. Bd., 1970-75 Contbr. to govt. publs. Chmn. bd. dirs., past pres. North Chevy Chase Swimming Pool Assn., 1960; vestryman, treas. Episc. Ch., Silver Spring, Md., 1950. Served with USN World War II, PTO, ATO, comdr. Res. ret., 1975. Recipient Adminstrs. Exceptional Service award GSA, 1975. Mem. Ret. Officers Assn., Am. Legion (exec. bd. Thad Dulin chpt. 1986-87, adj. 1988, vice comdr. 1989-91, comdr. 1994-95), Leisure World Golf Club, Kenwood Country Club, Montgomery Village Golf Club, Lions (pres. Rossmoor Club Silver Spring, 1988-89), Fireside Forum (v.p., bd. dirs.), Leisure World. Republican. Avocations: golf, travel, aviation, swimming. Died Apr. 23, 2008.

SAUNTRY, SUSAN SCHAEFER, lawyer; b. Bangor, Mine, May 7, 1943; d. William Joseph and Emily Joan (Guenter) Schaefe; m. John Philip Sauntry, Aug. 18, 1968 (div. Jan. 1998); 1 child, Mary Katherine. BS in Fgn. Svc., Georgetown U., JD, 1975. Bar: DC 1975, US Dist. Ct. DC 1975, US Ct. Appeals (DC cir.) 1975, US Ct. Appeals (4th cir.) 1977, US Ct. Appeals (6th cir.) 1978, US Ct. Appeals (10th cir.) 1983, US Supreme Ct. 1983. Congl. relations asst. OEO, Washington, 1966—68; program analyst EEO Com., 1968—70, US Dept. Army, Okinawa, 1970—72; assoc. Morgan, Lewis & Bockius, Washington, 1975—83, ptnr., 1983—94; of counsel Howe, Anderson & Steyer, PC, Washington, 1994—2009. Author: Employee Dismissal Law: Forms and Procedures, 1986; contbr. articles to profl. jours. Mem.: AAUW, ABA, Nat. Assn. Women Bus. Owners, DC Women's Bar Assn., DC Bar Assn., Pi Sigma Alpha, Phi Beta Kappa. Democrat. Home: Rockville, Md. Died Aug. 6, 2009.

SAVAGE, CHARLES, physician; b. Berlin, Conn., Sept. 25, 1918; s. Willis Isaac and Louisa Close (Howard) S.; m. Ethel Maurine Truss, May 9, 1940 (dec. Nov. 1990); children: Elma Louise, Charles Wilfred III. BA, Yale U., 1939; MS, U. Chgo., 1943, MD, 1945. Diplomate Am. Bd. Psychiatry; cert. psychoanalysis. Resident in pyschiatry Yale U., New Haven, Conn., 1945-46, USNH, Bethesda, Md., 1947-49; rsch. psychiatrist NIMH, Bethesda, 1953-58; pvt. practice in psychiatry Palo Alto, Calif., 1958-65; dir. rsch. Spring Grove State Hosp., Balt., 1965-69; asst. dir. Md. Psychiatric Rsch., Balt., 1969-72; chief of psychiatry VA Med. Ctr., Balt., 1972-82; psychiatrist Dept. of Health, St. Thomas, V.I., 1987-92, Ea. Shore Hosp. Centre, Cambridge, Md., 1992-94. Physician-interpreter Iglesia Santa Ana, Chichicastenango, Guatemala, 1993-96; prof. psychiatry U. Md., Balt., 1965-82; asst. prof. psychiatry Johns Hopkins U., Balt., 1965-82, asst. prof. emeritus, 1982—. Editor: Drug Abuse Controversy, 1971; co-editor: Research in Psychotherapy, 1967; contbr. articles to profl. jours. Bd. dirs. Friends Med. Sci. Rsch. Ctr., Balt., 1965-96. Lt. med. corps USN, 1943-53. Fellow Ctr. for Advanced Study, Stanford, Calif., 1957-58; Wilson lectr. U. Va., Charlottesvilla, 1967. Fellow APA; mem. Am. Psychoanalytic Assn., Undersea and Hyperbaric Med. Soc., Am. EEG Soc., AAAS. Republican. Moravian. Avocations: sailing, diving. Home: Saint John. Died Dec. 12, 2007.

SAVAGE, JAMES AMOS, ophthalmologist; b. Joliet, Ill., July 4, 1949; s. Amos Lehle and Anna Elizabeth (Doxsee) S.; children: Anne Catherine, Abigail Elizabeth; m. Mary Catherine Beringer, Aug. 31, 1991. BA in Chemistry, Northwestern U., 1971; MD, U. Cin., 1975. Diplomate Am. Bd. Ophthalmology. Intern Baylor U. Med. Ctr., Dallas, 1975-76; resident in ophthalmology Ohio State U., Columbus, 1976-79, chief resident, 1978-79; ophthalmologist West Tex. Med. Assocs., San Angelo, 1979-82; fellow in glaucoma Mass. Eye & Ear Inf. Harvard U. Med. Sch., Boston, 1983-84; pvt. practice Columbus, 1984-85; assoc. clin. prof. ophthalmology U. Southwestern Tex., Dallas, from 1985; ophthalmologist Ophthalmology Assocs., Ft. Worth, from 1985. Attending ophthalmologist Focus Eye Hosp., Abak, Nigeria, 1979; cons. Med. Instrument Rsch. Assoc., Waltham, Mass., 1984—, Alcon Labs., Ft. Worth, 1985—; mem. clin. faculty Merck Sharp and Dohme, West Point, Pa., 1986—. Fellow Am. Acad. Ophthalmology, Am. Glaucoma Soc.; mem. AMA (physician recognition award 1986, 90), Pan-Am. Glaucoma Soc. (bd. dirs. 1988-89), Tex. Med. Assn., Tex. Ophthalmologic Soc., Chandler Grant Soc., Pan-Am. Ophthalmologic Assn., Am. Coll. Legal Medicine (assoc.), U.S. Golf Assn. (sectional affairs com. 1991—), Tex. Golf Assn. (bd. dirs. Austin, Tex. chpt. 1988—), So. Golf Assn. (assoc. bd. dirs. Birmingham, Ala. chpt. 1988—). Home: Fort Worth, Tex. Died Dec. 3, 2007.

SAWICKI, FLORENCE BERNIECE, education educator; b. Jersey City, Nov. 2, 1942; d. Adolph and Blanche (Wilk) S. BA, Jersey City Coll., 1964, MA, 1967; PhD, Ariz. State U., 1972. Elem. tchr. Bayonne (N.J.) Pub. Schs., 1964-67; reading cons. Midland Park (N.J.) Pub. Schs., 1967-76; grad. asst. Ariz. State U., Tempe, 1970-72; asst.

prof. St. Joseph's Coll., Rensselaer, Ind., 1972-75; assoc. prof. Ind. U. Northwest, Gary, from 1975, dir. reading and early childhood dept., from 1975. Cons. and speaker to various schs. and groups. Author: Key Words to Reading, 1979. Fundraiser Freedom Against Annexation, Ross Twp., Ind., 1989. Mem. Internat. Reading Assn., Nat. Assn. Edn. Young Children, Ind. Assn. Edn. Young Children (state conf. coordinator). Roman Catholic. Home: Gary, Ind. Died Dec. 26, 2007.

SAWYER, DAVID NEAL, petroleum industry executive; b. Paducah, Ky., Sept. 27, 1940; s. David A. and Lois (Neal) S.; children: Laura Kathleen, Allen Neal. BS, La. State U., 1964; PhD, U. Wis., 1969. Registered profl. engr., Tex. Process engr. Shell Chem. Co., Norco, La., 1964-65; instr. chem. engring. U. Wis., Madison, 1969-70; sr. rsch. engr. Atlantic Richfield Co., Plano, Tex., 1970-73; staff reservoir engr. Arco Oil and Gas Co., Dallas, 1973-84; pres. Plantation Petroleum Co., Houston, from 1984. Dir. Miss. CO2 Enhanced Oil Recovery Lab., 1990-95; cons. in field; presenter, Beijing; presenter seminar internat. mktg. petroleum products, Lagos, Nigeria, 1986, 91; presenter seminar enhanced oil recovery, Lagos, 1991. Author of seminars. Panel mem. Leadership Devel. Seminar, 1986. Recipient Warrior Basin study, U.S. Dept. Energy, 1990-92; NSF fellow, 1965-69. Mem. Geosci. Inst. Oil and Gas Rsch. (state rep., bd. dirs. 1989-94), Am. Soc. Engring. Edn. (presenter 1989), Soc. Petroleum Engrs. (bd. dirs.), AAAS, Tau Beta Pi, Sigma Xi. Avocations: coaching children's baseball, fishing. Home: Houston, Tex. Died July 28, 2008.

SAWYER, HOWARD JEROME, physician; s. Howard C. and Dorothy M. (Risley) S.; m. Janet Carol Hausen, July 24, 1954; children: Daniel William, Teresa Louise BA in Philosophy, Wayne State U., Detroit, 1952, MD, 1962, postdoctoral, 1969-72. Diplomate Am. Bd. Preventive Medicine in Occupational and Environ. Medicine. Intern William Beaumont Hosp., Royal Oak, Mich., 1962-63, resident in surgery, 1963-64; chief physician gen. parts div. Ford Motor Co., 1964-66; med. dir. metall. products dept. Gen. Electric Co., Detroit, 1966-73, chem. and metal div., 1972-73; staff physician Detroit Indsl. Clinic, Inc., 1973-74; pres., med. dir. OccuMed Assocs., Inc., Farmington Hills, Mich., 1974-84; dir. OccuMed div. Med. Service Corp. Am., Southfield, Mich., 1984-86; dir. occupational, environ. and preventive medicine Henry Ford Hosp., 1987-91; pres. Sawyer Med. Cons., P.C., from 1991. Adj. asst. prof. occupational and environ. health scis. Wayne State U., 1974—, lectr. occpl. and environ. medicine Sch. of Medicine, 1998—; lectr. Sch. Pub. Health, U. Mich., Ann Arbor, 1977-88; cons. med. dir. St. Joe Minerals Corp., 1976-87, Chesbrough Pond's Inc., 1979-83; cons. Anaconda, Bendix, Borg Warner Chems., Fed. Mogul, Gen. Electric, Gt. Lakes Chems., other corps. Contbr. articles to profl. jours., chpts. to textbooks. Fellow Am. Coll. Preventive Medicine, Am. Occupational and Environ. Med. Assn., Mich. Occupational and Environ. Med. Assn. (pres. 1986), Am. Acad. Occupational Medicine; mem. AMA, Detroit Occupational Physicians Assn. (pres. 1984), Mich. State Med. Soc., Oakland County Med. Soc., Am. Indsl. Hygiene Assn., Mich. Indsl. Hygiene Soc. Died Mar. 12, 2009.

SAZ, HOWARD JAY, biology educator; b. NYC, Sept. 29, 1923; s. Michael and Molly (Perlmutter) S.; m. Rosalyn Pollack, Apr. 7, 1946; children: Daniel, Marjory, Wendy. BS, CCNY, 1948; PhD, Western Res. U., 1952. Rsch. assoc. Western Res. U., Cleve., 1952-53; postdoctoral fellow Nat. Found. Infantile Paralysis, Sheffield, Eng., 1953-54; rsch. assoc. La. State U., New Orleans, 1954-55, asst. prof., 1955-58, assoc. prof., 1958-60, Johns Hopkins U., Balt., 1960-69; prof. biology U. Notre Dame, Ind., from 1969. Cons. Army Med. Rsch. and Devel. Group, Washington, 1973-77; mem., chmn. tropical medicine and parasitology NIH, Washington, 1965-69, 69-70, 91-95; mem. study sect. NSF, 1984-86, cons. WHO, Geneva, Switzerland, 1980. Contbr. articles on biochemistry to profl. jours. Sgt. U.S. Army, 1943-45, ETO. Recipient Bronze Star, P.O.W.; NSF postdoctoral fellow La. State U., 1955. Fellow AAAS; mem. Am. Soc. Microbiology, Am. Soc. Biol. Chemistry, Am. Soc. Parasitologists (Bueding & von Brand meml. award 1989), British Biochem. Soc. Home: South Bend, Ind. Died Dec. 14, 2007.

SCALISE, NICHOLAS PETER, artist; b. Meriden, Conn., June 4, 1932; s. Peter Rosario and Rosina (Maletta) S.; m. Henrietta Mary Tiezzi; children: Lisa Rosemary, Rosann. Student art, Horace C. Wilcox Tech. Sch., Meridan, 1952; grad. with honors, Paier Art Sch., New Haven, 1959. Comml. artist Meriden Gravure, 1952-53, Risdon Mfg. Co., Waterbury, Conn., 1953-54; tchr. art Famous Artist Schs., Westport, Conn., 1959-69. 23 one-man shows; exhibited in group shows NAD, Nat. Art League, Allied Artists, Am. Watercolor Soc., Nat. Soc. Painters in Casein (all N.Y.C.), Butler Inst. Am. Art, Wadsworth Atheneum, Holyoke Mus., De Cordova Mus., New Britain Mus.; represented in pub. and pvt. collections throughout U.S. and fgn. countries; work featured in various publs. With U.S. Army, 1954-56. Recipient more than 164 awards in nat. and regional exhbns. including Samuel Lietman Meml. award Am. Watercolor Soc., 1986, MCAA award (1st prize) Mt. Carmel Art Assn. 36th annual spring exhbn., 1991, 1st prize Rockport Art Assn., 1991, Swift Tweed award Nat. Soc. Painters in Casein Acrylic, 1991, Trails and Streams medal Adirondacks Nat. Exhbn. Am. Watercolors, 1991, cert. merit Nat. Acad. Design 167th annual exhbn., 1992. Mem. Acad. Artists Assn. (Grumbacher gold medal 1988), Knickerbocker Artists, Hudson Valley Artists, Conn. Watercolor Soc. (CWS award 1988), Rockport Art Assn. Roman Catholic. Home: Meriden, Conn. Died Feb. 22, 2009.

SCANLON, ROBERT GILBERT, former state official; b. North Braddock, Pa., Apr. 15, 1933; s. Eugene Francis and Catherin Ann (Klagus) Scanlon; m. Charlotte Makar Scanlon, 1954 (dec. 2000); children: Jim, Mark, Kevin, Karen, Robin; m. Charlotte Ann Nakar Scanlon, June 19, 1954; children: Karen, Robin, James, Mark, Kevin, Christine. BS in Elem. Edn., Duquesne U., 1954, MA in Adminstrn., 1956; EdD, U. Pitts., 1966. Tchr. Churchill Boro Elem. Sch., Pitts., 1954—59; elem. adminstr. Orchard Hill Elem. Sch., Leetonia, Ohio, 1959—62; dir. elem. edn. Middletown, NY, 1962—66; adminstr. Oakleaf Elem. Sch., Pitts., 1964—66; program dir. individualizing learning program Rsch. Better Schs. Inc., Phila., 1966—72, exec. dir., 1972—79; sec. edn. Commonwealth Pa., Harrisburg, 1979—83; asst. to pres. Temple U., 1983, v.p. planning & ops., 1986—86; pres. Data Access Inc., 1984—86; v.p. Salick Health Care, 1989—99; pres. Archway Programs Inc., 1999—2003; chmn. nat. adv. bd. Ctr. Study Evaluation. Mem. editl. adv. bd. Urban Edn. Forum, Adaptive Learning Environment. Mem.: Coun. Chief State Sch. Officers, Am. Fedn. Info. Processing Socs., Am. Mgmt. Assn., Soc. Applied Learning Tech., Assn. Ednl. Data Sys., Am. Assn. Sch. Adminstrs., Assn. Supervision & Curriculum Devel., Am. Ednl. Rsch. Assn., Duquesne Century. Died June 7, 2009.

SCHAFER, ALICE TURNER, retired mathematics professor; b. Richmond, Va., June 18, 1915; d. John H. and Cleon (Dermott) Turner; m. Richard Donald Schafer, Sept. 8, 1942; children: John Dickerson, Richard Stone. AB, U. Richmond, 1936, DSc, 1964; MS, U. Chgo., 1940, PhD (fellow), 1942. Tchr. Glen Allen (Va.) High Sch., 1936-39; instr. math. Conn. Coll., New London, 1942-44, asst. prof., 1954-57, asso. prof., 1957-61, prof., 1961-62; prof. math. Wellesley Coll., 1962-80, Helen Day Gould prof. math., 1969-80, Helen Day Gould prof. math. emerita, from 1980, affirmative action officer, 1980-82; prof. math. Marymount U., Arlington, Va., 1989-96; ret., 1996. Instr. U. Mich., Ann Arbor, 1945-46; lectr. Douglass Coll., New Brunswick, N.J., 1946-48; asst. prof. Swarthmore (Pa.) Coll., 1948-51, Drexel Inst. Tech., Phila., 1951-53; mathematician Johns Hopkins Applied Physics Lab., Silver Spring, Md., 1945; lectr. Simmons Coll., Boston, 1980-88, Radcliffe Coll. Seminars, Cambridge, Mass., 1980-85; U.S. chair postsecondary math. edn. U.S./China Joint Conf. on Edn., 1992, co-chair Citizen Amb. program People to People U.S. and China Joint Conf. on Women's Issues, 1995, session women in sci. and math. Contbr. articles on women in math. and other articles to math. jours. Recipient Disting. Alumna award Westhampton Coll., U. Richmond, 1977; NSF sci. faculty fellow Inst. for Advanced Study, Princeton, N.J., 1958-59. Fellow AAAS (math. sect. A nominating com. 1979-83, mem.-at-large 1983-86, chair-elect sect. A 1991, chair 1992, retiring chair 1993, Assn. for Women in Math. rep., 1993, pres.), AAUP (chmn. nat. com. W 1980-83, mem. nat. coun. 1984-87), Am. Math. Soc. (chmn. postdoctoral fellowship com. 1973-76, affirmative action procedures com. 1980-82, chair com. on Human Rights of Mathematicians 1988-94), Soc. Indsl. and Applied Math., Am. Statis. Assn., Inst. Math. Stats., Nat. Coun. Tchrs. of Math. (chair com. on women 1976-81), Math Assn. Am. (adv. com. for Women and Math. program 1987-89, dir. fund raising 1989-92, lectr. 1982—, chair devel. com. 1988-92, Yueh-Gin Gung and Charles Y. Hu disting. svc. to math. award 1988), Internat. Congress Mathematicians (mem. fund raising com. 1986), Assn. for Women in Math. (pres. 1973-75, Alice T. Schafer Prize established 1989, chair fund raising com. 1992-94, leader math. del. women mathematicians to China 1990, Disting. Svc. award 1996), Emily's List (mem. majority coun.), Cosmos Club, Phi Beta Kappa, Sigma Xi, Sigma Delta Epsilon. Achievements include first study of singularities of space curves in projective differential geometry; research on undulation point of a space curve. Died Sept. 27, 2009.

SCHAFER, DIANE E., nutritionist; b. New Rockford, ND, Dec. 10, 1962; d. Donald Matthew and Eleanor Louise (Clelland) S.; 1 child, Benjamin Joseph Baker. BS, N.D. State U., 1987. Reg., lic. dietitian, La. Renal nutritionist El Paso (Tex.) Dialysis Ctrs., 1987-89; critical care specialist Providence Meml. Hosp., El Paso, 1989-90; pub. health nutritionist Indian Health Svc., Kyle, S.D., 1990-91; clin. dietitian Lakeland Med. Ctr., New Orleans, 1993-96; diabetes educator Terrebone Gen. Med. Ctr., Houma, La., from 1996. Renal cons., trainer BMA Dialysis, El Paso, 1989; bd. dirs. Diabetes Adv. Bd., Houma, 1996—. Mem. Am. Dietetic Assn., La. Dietetic Assn., New Orleans Dietetic Assn., Am. Diabetes Assn. (Recognition award 1996-97), Phi Omicron Upsilon. Roman Catholic. Avocations: exercise, singing, reading, poetry, travel. Home: Houma, La. Died June 22, 2008.

SCHAFER, THOMAS ANTON, religion educator; b. East Liverpool, Ohio, July 22, 1918; s. Anton Edward and Ellen (Sleven) S.; m. Eudora Jones, Aug. 18, 1944; children: Michal Ann, Polly Ruth, David Anton, Daniel Evan. AB, Maryville Coll., 1940; BD, Louisville Presbyn. Sem., 1943; PhD, Duke U., 1951. Ordained to ministry Presbyn. Ch., 1943. Instr. Bible Duke U., Durham, N.C., 1946, asst. prof. hist. theol., 1950-57, assoc. prof., 1957-58; asst. prof. Bible Rhodes Coll., Memphis, 1946-50; assoc. prof. ch. history McCormick Theol. Sem., Chgo., 1958-62, prof., 1962-86, prof. emeritus, from 1986. Mem. Presbytery of Chgo., 1958—. Contbr. articles to publs. Guggenheim fellow, 1956-57. Fellow Phi Beta Kappa; mem. Am. Soc. Ch. History, Am. Hist. Assn., Presbyn. Hist. Soc. (bd. dirs. 1961-70). Democrat. Home: Chicago, Ill. Died Aug. 8, 2008.

SCHAFFHAUSEN, ROBERT JOSEPH, retired structural engineer; b. Kansas City, Mo., June 12, 1926; s. Joseph John and Lorna Louise (Hahn) S.; m. Bette Fern Truskett, Apr. 22, 1951; children: Carol Ann, Cynthia Jean Hastings. BSCE, U. Mo., 1949; MS in Engring., U. Ala., 1976. Registered profl. engr., Ala. Jr. engr. Butler Mfg. Co., Kansas City, Mo., 1943-45, engr. Galesburg, Ill., 1949-52, plant product engr. Birmingham, Ala., 1952-66; regional engr. Am. Inst. Steel Constrn., Birmingham, Ala., 1966-79; pvt. practice Birmingham, Ala., 1980-83; sr. engr. So. Bldg. Code Congress, Birmingham, Ala., 1983-91; ret., from 1991. Instr. U. Ala., Birmingham. Pres. Rotary, Hoover, Ala., 1984-85. With U.S. Army Air Corps, 1944-45. Named Ala. Vol. Yr. Prison Fellowship Ministries, 1989, Disting. Svc. award, 1996. Mem. ASCE, Ala. Soc. Profl. Engrs. United Methodist. Avocations: volunteering, swimming, photography, courier. Home: Hoover, Ala. Died Jan. 9, 2008.

SCHARFENBERG, DORIS ANN, retired film producer; b. Newark, Feb. 24, 1917; d. Edgar Andrew and Anne E. Scharfenberg. AB, Bucknell U., 1938; MA in Edn., N.Y.U., 1949; LLD (hon.), Muhlenberg U., 1962; HHD (hon.), Lafayette U., 1979. With NBC, NYC, 1944-80, mgr. religious programs, producer and exec. producer, 1951-80; instr. classes in TV, freelance TV producer. Producer programs including: art documentary The Prado, 1971; drama This Is My Son, 1977 (Emmy award); film/documentaries Continuing Creation, 1978 (2 Emmy awards), This Other Eden, 1979; (Recipient Emmy awards for Duty Bound 1973, A Determining Force 1976). Trustee Bucknell U. Recipient Ohio State U. awards; Christopher awards, 1958, 73; Gabriel awards, 1965, 66, 67, 68, 71; Freedom Found. awards, 1953, 56, 59, 60, 61, 62, 64, 67, 73; NCCJ awards, 1954, 56, 62; Gabriel Personal Achievement award, 1969; Abe Lincoln award, 1979 Died Jan. 4, 2009.

SCHARPF, FRANCIS ROBERT, corporate planner; b. Teaneck, NJ, Dec. 26, 1938; s. Joseph Theodore and Mary Elizabeth (Mahoney) S.; m. Elizabeth Ann Ryan, Oct. 5, 1963; children: Jeanne-Marie, Daniel, Matthew, Thomas. BS, U.S. Mil. Acad., 1962; MA in Geography, Syracuse U., 1973; MBA, Notre Dame U., 1990. Commd. 2d lt. U.S. Army, 1962, advanced through grades to lt. col., asst. prof. U.S. Mil. Acad. West Point, N.Y., 1970-73, system staff officer Tng. and Doctrine Command Ft. Monroe, Va., 1973-76, program mgr., chief T & E Bradley Fighting Vehicles Detroit, 1977-81, chief fgn. mil. sales U.S. Mission for Aid to Turkey Ankara, 1981-82, ret., 1982; mktg. mgr. AM Gen. Corp., Detroit, 1982-86, program mgr. South Bend, Ind., 1986-88, dir. bus. planning, from 1988. Bd. dirs. Assn. of U.S. Army, Detroit, 1983-86; div. chmn. United Way, South Bend, 1991, acct. exec., 1990, 92. Home: Granger, Ind. Died May 4, 2008.

SCHAUFELE, WILLIAM E., JR., retired ambassador; b. Lakewood, Ohio, Dec. 7, 1923; s. William Elias and Lillian (Bergen) S.; m. Heather Moon, Feb. 1, 1950; children: Steven W., Peter H. BA, Yale U., 1948; MIA, Columbia U., 1950. Resident officer Dept. of State, Pfaffenhofen, Ilm, Germany, 1950-52, Augsburg, Germany, 1952, vice consul Duesseldorf, Germany, 1952-53, Munich, Germany, 1953-55, various positions Washington, 1956-59, vice consul Casablanca, Morocco, 1959-63, consul Bukavu, Congo, 1963-64, Congo desk officer, 1964-65; alt. country dir. ctr. African affairs, 1965-67; country dir. ctr. African affairs, 1967-69; U.S. amb. Ouagadougou (Upper Volta), 1969-71; amb. dep. U.S. rep. UN Security Coun., 1971-75; insp. gen. U.S. Fgn. Svc., 1975; asst. sec. of state for African affairs Dept. of State, 1975-77; U.S. amb. Poland, Warsaw, 1978-80; pres. Fgn. Policy Assn., 1980-83; dir. Inst. of World Affairs, 1983-89; sr. dir. for Africa Cath. Relief Svcs., 1985-87; ind. cons. Salisbury, Conn., from 1987. Dir. Fgn. Policy Assn., N.Y.C., 1980-84, Helsinki Watch, N.Y.C., 1983—, Am. Forum for Global Edn., N.Y.C., 1983—. Author: Polish Paradox, 1981; contbr. articles to profl. jours. With AUS, 1943-46, ETO. Recipient Wilbur Carr award Dept. of State, 1980, Disting. Alumnus award Columbia U., 1981. Mem. Yale Club, Am. Acad. Diplomacy, Coun. on Fgn. Rels., Am. Fgn. Svc. Assn., Diplomatic and Consular Officers Ret. Democrat. Avocations: cabinet-making, tennis, golf, reading. Died Jan. 17, 2008.

SCHEIER, IVAN HENRY, volunteer, writer, retired cultural organization administrator; b. Plattsburgh, NY, Jan. 7, 1926; s. Joel Henry and Melba Gottlob S. BA in Philosophy, Union Coll., 1948; MA in Psychology, McGill U., Montreal, 1951, PhD in Psychology, 1953. Vol. coord., project dir. Boulder County Juvenile Ct., 1965-69; interim dir. Vol. and Info. Ctr. of Boulder County, 1968; exec. dir. Nat. Info. Ctr. on Volunteerism, 1967-76; pres. Assn. Voluntary Action Scholars, 1973-74; chair Alliance for Volunteerism, 1975-76; pres. Yellowfire Press, 1981-89; dir. Ctr. for Creative Cmty., 1986-95; dreamcatcher-in-residence Voluntas Retreat Ctr., 1991-95; coord. Stillpoint Self-Help Healing Ctr., 1996—2003; ret., 2003. Freelance writer; mem. faculty McGill U., 1950-51, U. Ill., 1953-58, Nat. Coll. Juvenile Justice, 1970, U. Colo. Vol. Mgmt. Cert. Program, 1973-87; mem. White House Conf. on Children and Youth, 1970, Nat. Adv. Commn. Criminal Justice Stds. and Goals, 1971, Nat. Forum Volunteerism, 1979-80; mem. adv. com. U. Colo. Vol. Mgmt. Cert. Program, 1973-87; sr. advisor Resource

Devel., Assn. for Vol. Adminstrn., 1979-80, Citizen Advocacy for Devel. Disabled, 1980-82, New Road Map Found., 1990—; mem. adv. bd. Madrid-Cerrillos Med. Clin., 1993-94; mem. youth vol. leadership tng. project Sister Cities Internat., 1979-81. Author: Exploring Volunteer Space: The Recruiting of a Nation, 1980, Making Dreams Come True Without Much Money: The Midwifery of Dreams, 2000, When Everyone's a Volunteer, 1992, Images of the Future, 1994; pub., editor On Background, 1979-81, The Dovia Exchange, 1984-98, The Restless News, 1986-89, Ex Libris, 1987-90, Madrid Muse, 1991-95; hon. editor (e-jour.) e-volunteerism, 2003--. Pres. emeritus Nat. Info. Ctr. on Volunteerism, 1979—; chair com. NAACP, Urbana, Ill., 1956-59; vol. various orgns., U.S., Can., 1963—; mem. Sierra Pride Com. Turning Point, Truth or Consequences, N.Mex., 1999-2002; mem. policy bd. Assn. Voluntary Action Scholars, 1971-74, Nat. Ctr. for Voluntary Action, 1971-76, Nat. Info. Ctr.on Volunteerism, 1971-79, Alliance for Volunteerism, 1974-77, Nat. Orgn. Victim Assistance, 1977-79, Partners, Inc., 1979-82; bd. dirs. Madrid, N.Mex. Landowners Assn., 1993-94. Recipient Nat. Meritorious Svc. award Nat. Coun. Juvenile Court Judges, 1971, Meritorious Svc. award Province of Ont., 1976, Leadership award Alliance for Volunteerism, Inc., 1976, Disting. Svc. award State of Miss., 1982, Nat. Cmty. Svc. award Nat. Assn. on Vols. in Criminal Justice, 1987, Lifetime Achievement award Denver Dirs. of Vols. in Agys., 1997, Shakespeare award for excellence Famous Poets Soc., 2004. Mem. Assn. Vol. Adminstrn. (life, Nat. Disting. Svc. award 1984, editor Volunteer Adminstrn. 1979-81), Phi Beta Kappa. Avocations: tai chi, dance, hiking, reading, gardening. Home: Truth Or Consequences, N.Mex. Died Oct. 6, 2008.

SCHELL, GEORGE AARON, lawyer; b. Waco, Tex., May 11, 1939; s. George Alvin and Jessie Lee S.; m. Anne, 1960 (div. 1973); 1 child, Michael. BA, Baylor U., 1961, MA, 1963; JD, Loyola U., 1977; MS, Calif. State U., 1990. Bar: Calif. Prof. speech, comm. & debate Loyola Marymount U., LA, 1963-77; pub. defender Plumas County, Quincy, Calif., 1978-80; deputy city atty. City of L.A., 1977-78 and from 81. Home: Austin, Tex. Died Oct. 12, 2007.

SCHERR, HARRY, III, small business owner; b. Norfolk, Va., Apr. 19, 1944; s. Harry Jr. and Marguerite (LeCron) S.; m. Barbara Nadle, June 25, 1967; children: Marguerite LeCron, Laura Susan, Caroline Mary. BS, U. N.C., 1967; MBA, Columbia U., 1973. Ptnr., treas. Newburgh (N.Y.) Superior Packing Co., 1969-71; dir. ops. Pathmark div. Supermarkets Gen. Corp., Woodbridge, N.Y., 1973-80; owner, pres. Hilton, Gibson, & Miller, Newburgh, from 1980. Pres., v.p., com. mem. Newburgh Enlarged City Sch., 1982-91; mem. ethics com. Town of Newburgh, 1989—; mem. Orange County Citizens Found., 1986—, bd. dirs., 1994—. Mem. N.Y. State Assn. Convenience Stores (charter mem., bd. dirs. 1982-88), Orange County C. of C. (v.p. indsl. devel. 1980—), N.Y./N.J. Food Merchant Assn. (bd. dirs. 1994—). Republican. Home: Newburgh, NY. Died Dec. 21, 2007.

SCHEVILL, JAMES ERWIN, poet, playwright; b. Berkeley, Calif., June 10, 1920; s. Rudolph and Margaret (Erwin) S.; m. Margot Helmuth Blum, Aug. 2, 1966; children (by previous marriage): Deborah, Susanna. BS, Harvard U., 1942; MA (ad eundem), Brown U.; LHD (hon.), R.I. Coll., 1986. Mem. faculty San Francisco State Coll., 1959-68, prof. English, 1968, dir. Poetry Center, 1961-68; prof. Brown U., 1969-85, prof. emeritus, 1985—2009. Reader various univs., insts., and orgns. Author: New and Selected Poems, 2000. Served to capt. AUS, 1942-46. Ford Found. grantee, 1954, 60-61, R.I. Com. on Humanities grantee, 1975; Fund Advancement Edn., 1953-54, Office for Advanced Drama Rsch. fellow, 1957, Rockefeller fellow, 1964, Guggenheim fellow, 1981, McKnight fellow, 1984; recipient Performance prize Nat. Theatre Competition, 1945, 2d prize Phelan Biography Competition, 1954, 2d prize Phelan Drama Competition, 1958, William Carlos Williams award, 1965, Roadsted Found. award, 1966, Gov.'s award R.I., 1975, Best Story of Yr. award Ariz. Quart., 1977; story selected for O. Henry Awards Prize Stories, 1978; award in lit. Am. Acad. Arts and Letters, 1991; work commd. by Nat. Coun. Chs., 1956-61, Fromm Found., 1959, Trinity Repertory Co., R.I. State Coun. on the Humanities, 1986, Providence Coll., 1986, Magdalena Group, 1992. Home: Berkeley, Calif. Died Jan. 30, 2009.

SCHICHTEL, PAUL VINCENT, systems analyst; b. Springville, NY, May 21, 1952; s. Edward Paul and Elizabeth (Sauerwein) S.; m. Diah Elizabeth Gardner, Mar. 3, 1977; children: Laura, Paul, Christine, John. BA in Mgmt., Golden Gate U., 1980; MBA in Fin., Nat. U., San Diego, 1982; BS in Computer Sci., U. No. Fla., 1996. Commd. USMC, advanced through grades to capt., adminstr., 1972-92; computer systems mgr. Foley & Lardner, Jacksonville, Fla., 1992-94; lead programmer Autel Info. Svcs., Jacksonville, 1994-97; systems analyst Nations Bank, Jacksonville, from 1997. Adj. instr. St. John's River C.C., Orange Park, Fla., 1992—. Vol. Habitat for Humanity, Jacksonville, 1996-98, United Way, Jacksonville, 1992—. Decorated Meritorious Svc. medal USN. Home: Middleburg, Fla. Died Jan. 29, 2008.

SCHICK, IRVIN HENRY, academic administrator, educator; b. Wilkes-Barre, Pa., Aug. 10, 1924; s. Irvin and Elizabeth (Valentine) S.; m. Marilyn Freeman, July 17, 1954 (dec. Aug. 1961); m. Marjorie Bletch Beach, Dec. 23, 1967; 1 child, Carolyn Patricia. Diploma, Bliss Elec. Sch., 1947; BEE with distinction, George Washington U., 1958; MSEE (NSF fellow), U. Md., 1961. Engring. asst. Jeddo-Highland Coal Co., Pa., 1942-43; instr. Bliss Elec. Sch., Washington, 1947-50; prof. math. and elec. engring., dept. head Montgomery Coll., Rockville, Md., 1950-65, dir. ext., 1965-67, dean adminstrn., 1967-75, adminstrv. v.p., 1975-78, prof. emeritus, adminstrv. v.p. emeritus, 1978—2009. Tchr., tutor, cons. indsl. cos. Served with USAAF, 1943-46. Recipient Outstanding Alumni Achievement award, Montgomery Coll., 2002. Mem. AAUP, IEEE, Am. assn. Sch. Adminstrs., Internat. Platform Assn., Md. State Tchrs. Assn., Montgomery County Edn. Assn., Bliss Elec. Soc. (bd. govs., past pres.), Tent Troupe Theatrical Orgn. (bd. govs.), Theta Tau, Sigma Tau (past pres.), Sigma Pi Sigma, Tau Beta Pi. Home: Silver Spring, Md. Died Sept. 4, 2009.

SCHIER, DONALD STEPHEN, language educator; b. Ft. Madison, Iowa, Sept. 10, 1914; s. Francis and Marcella (Kenny) S. BA, State U. Iowa, 1936; MA, Columbia U., 1937, PhD, 1941. Mem. faculty State Tchrs. Coll., Bemidji, Minn., 1939-41, 41-42, Ill. Inst. Tech., 1946; mem. faculty Carleton Coll., Northfield, Minn., 1946-80, prof. French, 1953-80. Vis. prof. U. Wis., 1964-65; Brown tutor in French U. of South, Sewanee, Tenn., 1980-81 Author: Louis-Bertrand Castel, 1942; editor: (with Scott Elledge) The Continental Model, 1960, 2d edit., 1970; (Bertrand de Fontenelle), Nouveaux Dialogues des morts, 1965, rev. edit., 1974; translator: Letter on Italian Music (Charles de Brosses), 1978. Mem. selection com. Young Scholar Program, Nat. Found. Arts and Humanities, 1966-67. Served to capt. AUS, 1942-46. Mem. MLA, Am. Assn. Tchrs. French, Am. Soc. Eighteenth-Century Studies Died Apr. 21, 2009.

SCHINDLER, DONALD WARREN, biopharmaceutical engineer, consultant; b. Westfield, NJ, Apr. 2, 1925; s. Wilbur Vincent and Francis Lillian (Hollberg) S.; m. Scot N. Stahl, Sept. 7, 1947 (div. Aug. 1971); children: Leslie, Mark, Wendy (dec. 1971); m. Gail Robertson Hoff, July 26, 1972 (div. Dec. 1975); m. Dorothy Jean Bélanger Martin, July 1, 1982; stepchildren: William, Bruce, Judy, Patricia, Donna, Holly, Larry. AB in Biol. Scis., Marietta Coll., Ohio; postgrad., Rutgers U. Ordained deacon 1st Presbyn. Ch., Myersville, N.J.; ordained minister Universal Life Ch., 1999. Dir. biol. mfg. Ortho Pharm. Corp. divsn. Johnson & Johnson, Raritan, N.J., 1951-59; mgr. biol. mfg. Warner-Lambert Pharm. Co., Morris Plains, N.J., 1959-74; gen. mgr. Fisher Sci. Diagnostics Div., Orangeburg, N.Y., 1978-82; pres. SRC Assocs., Park Ridge, N.J., 1974-94, Schindler Assocs., Montvale, N.J., from 1994. Mem. adv. bd. Okla. Immunological Labs., Oklahoma City, 1972-78; cons. Serono Labs., Inc., Boston, 1982-91, U. Minn., Mpls., 1984-91, Ares Applied Rsch. N.V. Gen., 1982-90. Pres. Passaic Twp. Sch. Bd., Stirling, N.J., 1968-70; trustee 1st Congl. Ch., Park Ridge, N.J., 1987-90, Lord Stirling Sch. for Autistic Children, Basking Ridge, N.J.; regional dir. tng. Boy Scouts Am. Watchung Area coun., Plainfield, N.J., 1968-71. With USNR, 1942-46, PTO. Mem. VFW, Am. Chem. Soc., Am. Inst. Chemists, Am. Legion, N.Y. Acad. Scis., Newcomen Soc., Parenteral Drug Assn., Internat. Soc. Pharm. Engrs., U.S. Equestrian Team, Am. Horse Shows Assn., U.S. Combined Tng. Assn., Pharms. Mfg. Assn., The Protein Found., Beta Beta Beta, Alpha Sigma Phi. Republican. Home: Montvale, NJ. Died Mar. 13, 2008.

SCHLESINGER, NORMA HONIG, art historian, writer; b. NYC, Mar. 29, 1931; d. Jack L. and Estelle (Wieder) Honig; m. Mathias Spiegel, Oct. 19, 1952 (div. 1965); children: Paul Spiegel, Andrew Spiegel; m. Elmer Schlesinger, Apr. 10, 1969 (dec.). BA, Vassar Coll., 1952; MA, NYU, 1969. Art cons., San Francisco, from 1970; asst. prof. Sonoma State U., Rohnert Park, Calif., 1972-78; art editor Rev. West, San Francisco, 1978-81; rsch. asst. Fine Arts Mus., San Francisco, 1981-89. Lectr. Acad. Art Coll., San Francisco, 1992-95. Journalist Nob Hill Gazzette, 1995—. Trustee San Francisco Art Inst., 1975-81, L.S.B. Leakey Found., San Francisco, 1978-94, Univ. Art Mus., Berkeley, 1982-95, Calif. Coll. Arts and Crafts, 1990—, Calif. Coll. Arts and Crafts, 1990—; advisor Am. Art Study Ctr., San Francisco, 1997—. Mem. AAUP, Met. Club, St. Francis Yacht Club. Avocations: ranching, gardening, travel. Home: San Francisco, Calif. Died May 25, 2008.

SCHLIEMAN, MABLE STORIE, community worker, religious educator; b. Gouverneur, NY, Dec. 12, 1932; d. Theron William and Edith May (Clark) Storie; m. Donald B. Miller, Apr. 6, 1956 (div. Apr. 1976); children: Alan D., Kenneth B.; m. Robert Francis Schlieman, Apr. 24, 1976. BS in Early Childhood Edn., State U. Tchrs. Coll., Potsdam, NY, 1954; MA in Teaching of Speech, Columbia U., 1955. Assoc. Christian educator Reformed Ch. in Am., 1981. Elem. tchr. Niskayuna Pub. Schs., Schenectady, N.Y., 1957-60, Ballston Spa (N.Y.) Pub. Schs., 1955-56; dir. religious edn. Niskayuna Reformed Ch., Schenectady, from 1974; Meals on Wheels driver and intake worker Cath. Family and Community Svcs., Schenectady, 1977-80, Meals on Wheels coordinator, from 1980. Program assoc. cons. Albany Synod Reformed Ch. in Am., Schenectady, 1976—, TV awareness trainer, 1978—, tchr. Friendship Program for retarded adults, 1984-86; Stephen ministry leader Niskayuna Reformed Ch., 1986—. Treas., Birchwood PTA, 1967. Mem. AAUW, Christian Educators of Reformed Ch. in Am., Nat. Assn. Meal Programs. Avocations: travel, theater, reading, camping. Home: Niskayuna, NY. Died Dec. 4, 2007.

SCHMETZER, WILLIAM MONTGOMERY, aeronautical engineer; b. Bronx, NY, Aug. 15, 1924; s. Richard Edward and Margaret Roy (Montgomery) S.; m. Emma Frances Myers, June 21, 1952 (div. 1972); children: Margaret, Karen, Charles, Ann. BS in Aero. Engring., Purdue U., 1952; postgrad., Va. Poly., 1960-61. Project engr. Douglas Aircraft Co., Santa Monica, Long Beach, Calif., 1952-66; v.p., asst. chief engr. Strato Engring. Cons., Burbank, Calif., 1966-69; S. Robbins assoc. Mech. & Engring. Cons., Van Nuys, Calif., 1969-73; unit project engr. Hughes Aircraft, Culver City, Calif., 1973-76; project engr. Marquardt Co., Van Nuys, Calif., 1976-78; sr. design specialist Lockheed Skunk Works, Burbank, 1978-82; sr. preliminary designer Northrop B-2 Div., Pico Rivera, Calif., 1982-92; ret., 1992. Mem. material rev. bd. Hughes & Marquardt Co., Culver City and Van Nuys, Calif., 1973-78. 1st sgt. U.S. Army, 1943-46, ETO. Mem. AIAA, Soc. Automotive Engrs. Republican. Presbyterian. Achievements include patent for thrust and lift airfoil currently being evaluated; development of flying prototype of my design of first short take-off commuter jet of 10 ton payload capacity. Died Apr. 1, 2008.

SCHMIDT, CHRISTINE ALICE, art gallery owner; b. St. Albans, NY, Sept. 1, 1932; d. Paul Joseph and Alice Patricia (McKane) Schmidt. BA magna cum laude, Adelphi U., 1964; MA, Pratt Inst., 1968. Cert. clothing design McDowell Art Sch., 1952, edn. NY, 1964. Asst. buyer May Co., NYC, 1952—54; asst. and designer Finger & Rabiner, Linker, Grioni, NYC, 1955—59; fashion illustrator, freelance clothing designer NYC, 1959—63; parochial sch. art tchr. St. Brigid's, St. Francis, St. Christopher, 1963—64; art tchr. Cold Spring Harbor (NY) HS, 1964—84; owner, operator Christine's Gallery, Southwest Harbor, Maine, from 1972, Lamoine, Maine, from 2000, Christine's Etchings and Prints, Lamoine, from 2003. Etchings and watercolor paintings in numerous collections in Europe and US, from 1972. Ambulance driver Am. Red Cross, Garden City, NY, 1950—65; bd. mem. Southwest Harbor C. of C., Southwest Harbor, Maine, 1994—99. Achievements include various coat and suit designs advertised on the covers and interior of Vogue, Harper's Bazaar, Mademoiselle. Avocations: sewing, photography, european travel. Died June 26, 2009.

SCHMIDT, CLAUDE HENRI, retired science administrator; b. Geneva, May 6, 1924; came to U.S., 1935; s. Roger Auguste Schmidt and Lucette (Henriette) Wuhrman; m. Melicent Esther Hane, June 25, 1953; children— Valerie Lynn, Jeffrey Allan AB, Stanford U., 1948, MA, 1950; PhD, Iowa State U., 1956. With Agrl. Rsch. Svc., USDA, 1956-88; rsch. entomologist Orlando, Fla., 1956-62; project leader Fargo, N.D., 1964-67; br. chief Beltsville, Md., 1967-72; area dir. N. Cen. region Fargo, 1972-82; lab. dir., 1982-88; acting dir. Red River Valley Agrl. Rsch. Ctr., 1988; collaborator, 1988-94; with Cass County Vector Control Dist., 1994—2003; ret. Entomologist IAEA, Vienna, Austria, 1962-64; sec. Nat. Mosquito Fish and Wildlife Commn., Washington, 1968-72 Editor Leafy Spurge News, 1994—2005; contbr. articles to profl. jours. Mem. state legis. com. AARP, N.D., 2000-03; mem. Fargo Sr. Commn., 2001-07, chmn., 2003-07; docent Plaines Art Mus., Fargo, 2005—. With AUS, Signal Corps 1942-46, to 1st lt. Med. Service Corps, 1950-53. Fellow Washington Acad. Sci., AAAS; mem. Am. Mosquito Control Assn. (pres. 1981-82), Am. Chem. Soc., Entomol. Soc. Am., Nat. Assn. Ret. Fed. Employees (pres. N.D. fedn., 1988-89). Republican. Home: Fargo, ND. Died Feb. 4, 2009.

SCHMIDT, GLORIA JEAN, elementary school educator; b. Phila., June 23, 1943; d. Adolph J. and Elizabeth M. (Sokolowski) R.; m. Arthur F. Schmidt, Oct. 11, 1969 (dec. 1992); 1 child, Christopher. BA, Immaculata U., 1964; MEd, Temple U., 1967. Tchr. grade 4 Springfield Schs., Pa., 1964—2004; ret., 2004. Republican. Roman Catholic. Home: Glen Mills, Pa. Died Aug. 10, 2008.

SCHNABEL, ROBERT VICTOR, retired academic administrator; b. Scarsdale, NY, Sept. 28, 1922; s. Frederick Victor and Louise Elizabeth (Frick) S.; m. Ellen Edyth Foelber, June 7, 1946; children: Mark F., Philip P. Student, Concordia Sem., St. Louis, 1943-45; AB, Bowdoin Coll., 1944; MS, Fordham U., 1951, PhD, 1955; LLD (hon.), Concordia Coll., 1988. Tchr. St. Paul's Sch., Ft. Wayne, Ind., 1945-49; prin. St. Matthew's Sch., NYC, 1949-52; assoc. supt. edn. Central Dist., Luth. Ch.-Mo. Synod, 1952-56; asst. prof. philosophy Concordia Sr. Coll., Ft. Wayne, 1956-60, assoc. prof., 1960-65, prof., acad. dean, 1966-71; pres. Concordia Coll., Bronxville, NY, 1971-76; acad. v.p., dean Wartburg Coll., Waverly, Iowa, 1976-78; pres. Valparaiso (Ind.) U., 1978-88. Cons. Luth. Edn. Conf. N.Am., 1977-88. Contbr. articles to profl. jours. Mem. AAUP, Luth. Acad. Scholarship, Assoc. Colls. Ind., Nat. Assn. Ind. Colls. and Univs., Rotary, Phi Delta Kappa. Home: Linton, Ind. Died Sept. 1, 2009.

SCHNEEBERG, NORMAN GRAHN, retired physician; b. Phila., Feb. 21, 1915; s. Charles and Rhoda (Grahn) S.; m. Helen Bassen, Nov. 4, 1940; children— Susan, Karen. B.S., Temple U., 1935, M.D., 1939. Diplomate Am. Bd. Internal Medicine. Intern Mt. Sinai Hosp., Phila., 1939-41, resident in pathology, 1941-42, resident in internal medicine, 1942-43; fellow in endocrinology Michael Reese Hosp., Chgo., 1946-47; chief endocrinology Phila. Gen. Hosp., 1956-77; chief endocrinology West Park Hosp., Phila., 1966—98; prof. medicine Hahnemann U. Med. Sch., Phila., 1962—98; Contbr. articles to profl. jours. Author:

Essentials of Clinical Endocrinology, 1970. Mem. adv. bd. Physicians for Social Responsibility, Phila.; Served to capt. AUS, 1943-46. Recipient Excellence award Phila. Med. Lab., 1975. Fellow ACP.; mem. Am. Soc. Clin. Research, Endocrine Soc., Phila. Endocrine Soc. (pres. 1956-58). Democrat. Jewish. Avocations: tennis; photography. Home: Philadelphia, Pa. Died Mar. 1, 2009.

SCHNEIDER, GLORIA JEAN, psychotherapist; b. Temple, Tex., Apr. 7, 1928; d. Herman Lee and Essie Lou (Worsham) Craft; m. Robert Louis Schneider, June 4, 1949; children: Mark Wesley, Pamela Jean, Karen Lee. BRE, Bayridge Christian Coll., Houston, 1991; MA, Houston Grad. Sch. Theology, 1991. Tchr. various pub. and pvt. schs., Houston, 1950-66, Adventureland, Houston, 1966-67; founder, dir. St. Matthew's Sch., Houston, 1967-72, Bellaire Christian Sch., Houston, 1972-80, Tchrs. Listening to Children, Houston, 1987-91; co-founder, pres. Lumine Inc., Houston, 1989; founder, dir. TLC Counseling & Tng. Ctr., Houston, from 1991; co-founder Houston Rock Ballet, 1998. Co-founder Houston Rock Ballet, 1998. Author: Esteem Enhancing Discipline, 1993, Friendly Discipline, 1997; contbr. articles to profl. jours.; presenter in field. Asst. Tex. Cities Action Plan To Prevent Crime, Houston, 1993; spkr. Houston Mayor's Anti-Gang Office, 1994, vol. psychotherapist, 1995; vol. psychotherapist cmty. outreach dept. Houston Police Dept., 1995-96; spkr. numerous chs., schs. and TV stas. in Houston area, 1991—, parenting seminars, 1995—, St. Thomas U., Houston, 1995, Houston Area Gang Prevention Conf., Houston, 1995; presenter "Stop the Violence Youth Movement", Mayor Brown's Peace Initiative, Houston, 1998. Grantee Amoco Found., Inc., 1994, Musicians Band Together To Unplug Violence Benefit Concert, 1995, Houston Endowment, 1995-97, Houston Mayor's Anti-Gang Office, 1996, Hevrdejs Found., 1996, Helping Children Choose Peace Benefit, 1997. Mem. ACA, Am. Mental Health Counselors Assn. Methodist. Avocations: reading, writing, dance, nature. Home: Sugar Land, Tex. Died Sept. 4, 2007.

SCHNEIDER, KIRK JAY, investment advisor; b. West Point, Nebr., Dec. 27, 1951; s. Earl Emerson and Geraldine C. Schneider; m. Janel Hasten; children: Jessica, Justin. BS in Acctg., Utah State U., 1974; MBA, No. Ariz. U., 1976. CFP. Acct. S.W. Forest Industry, Phoenix, 1974-76; auditor Auditor Gens. Office-State of Ariz., Phoenix, 1976-79; investment broker Dean Witter Reynolds, Phoenix, 1980-90; first v.p. Prudential Securities, Inc., Phoenix, from 1990. Bd. dirs. Christian Care, Inc., Phoenix, 1986—. Republican. Avocations: fly fishing, hiking, travel. Died Sept. 3, 2007.

SCHNEIDER, MARGARET PERRIN, scriptwriter; b. NYC, Dec. 31, 1923; d. Sam and Peggy (Flood) Perrin; m. Paul Schneider, Apr. 10, 1950; children: Peggy Lee, Peter-Lincoln, Ann Rose. BA in Psychology and Edn., UCLA, 1949. Gen. elem. tchg. credential, Calif. Tchr. L.A. City Schs., North Hollywood, 1944-55; script writer MGM Studios, 1957-75; staff writer Universal Studios, 1957-75; head writer CBS Studios, NYC, 1975-76. Participant Women in Film, L.A., 1975; chmn. Writers Craft Conf., Arrowhead, Calif., 1975. Mem. Writers Guild Am. (freelance writers com. 1985), Dems. for Action. Avocations: wild flower photography, birding, gardening, travel. Died June 20, 2008.

SCHOELKOPF, DEAN HAROLD, retired editor; b. St. Cloud, Minn., July 4, 1932; s. Harold L. and Anne S. BA magna cum laude, U. Minn., 1954, MA, 1959. City editor Mpls. Tribune, 1954-63; nat. and fgn. editor Chgo. Daily News, 1963-66; cons. Econ. Devel. Adminstrn., 1966; White House corr. USIA, 1967; editor The Paper, Oshkosh, Wis., 1968-70; editor-in-chief Ency. Brit. Book of Yr., Brit. Yearbook of Sci., Compton Yearbook, Chgo., 1970-72; asst. mng. editor Detroit Free Press, 1972; editor KNT News Wire; v.p. KNT News Services, Inc., Washington, 1972-87. Served to 1st lt. USAF, 1955-56. Decorated Air Force Commendation medal; recipient Page One award Twin Cities News Guild, 1957, 60, News award Ill. AP, News award UPI, 1963-64, Stick of Type award Chgo. News Guild, 1964; Seymour Berkson Fgn. Assignment grantee, 1961 Mem. Soc. Profl. Journalists (Public Service award 1963) Home: Miami, Fla. Died Aug. 4, 2009.

SCHOELKOPF, R. GERALD, archivist, librarian; b. Reading, Pa., July 6, 1945; s. Russel Albert Schoelkopf and Stella M. Zarychta. BA, Villanova U., 1967; MLS, McGill U., Montreal, 1969. Circulation / reference libr. West Chester U., Pa., 1969—76, rare books libr. & Univ. archivist, from 1976. Author: (index) Centennial History of West Chester State College, 1992. Catholic. Avocations: photography, travel, horseback riding, kayaking, book binding. Home: King Of Prussia, Pa. Died Apr. 24, 2008.

SCHOEN, REGINA NEIMAN, psychotherapist; b. Bronx, NY, Feb. 21, 1949; d. Louis and Bertha (Hoffman) Neiman; m. Dennis Leo Schoen, Dec. 2, 1979; 1 child, Leah F. B, Hunter Coll., NYC, 1969; M, Columbia U., NYC, 1971; M (social work), Hunter Coll., NYC, 1977. Cert. Psychoanalytic Psychotherapist, Wash. Square Inst. N.Y.C., 1983, Family Therapist, Postgrad. Ctr. for Mental Health N.Y.C., 1986. Tchr., advisor Brandeis High Sch., NYC, 1972-75; family service counselor N.Y. Assn. for New Am., NYC, 1978-82; psychiatric social worker Lutheran Med. Ctr., Bklyn., 1982-84; mental health practitioner Montefiore Med. Ctr., Riker's Island, N.Y., 1984-86. Moderator, spkr. Nat. Assn. Social Workers Alcoholism Inst. N.Y.C., 1989, 91; presenter YWCA, N.Y.C., 1987—; spkr. Greater N.Y. Hosp. Assn., 1983; commentator WNYC Radio Women and Rape N.Y.C., 1982; mem. faculty Postgrad. Ctr. Mental Health, 1990—; spkr. Empire Blue Cross/Blue Shield, N.Y., 1990-95, Fashion Inst. Employee Assistance Program, 1994—. Mem. Nat. Assn. Social Workers. Home: Fair Lawn, NJ. Died Aug. 23, 2007.

SCHOENFELD, GERALD, theater owner; b. NYC, Sept. 22, 1924; m. Pat Schoenfeld, 1950; 1 child, Carrie. BS, U. Ill.; LLB, NYU, 1949; postgraduate, MIT, Columbia U.; DHL (hon.), CUNY, 1999, Emerson Coll., 2001. Faculty Yale Drama Sch.; chmn. The Shubert Orgn., NYC, 1972—2008. Adj. prof. Sch. Arts, Columbia U.; chmn. League Am. Theatres & Producers, League NY Theatres & Producers. Bd. mem. N.Y. Conv. & Vis. Bureau; chmn. Mayor's Midtown Citizens Com., NYC & Co. Recipient Humanitarian award, N.Y. Soc. Assn. Executives. Fellow: Am. Acad. Arts & Sci. Died Nov. 25, 2008.

SCHONFELD, RUDOLF LEOPOLD, secondary school educator; b. La Paz, Bolivia, Feb. 2, 1942; came to U.S. 1958; s. Walter and Eva (Fuchs) S.; m. Sonia Nussbaum, July 7, 1963; children: Walter, Miriam Schonfeld Giotta. BA, Wilkes Coll., 1963; MA, Seton Hall U., 1972; PhD, Ludwig Maximillian U., Heidelberg, Ger., 1974. Tchr. Parsippany (N.J.) High Sch., 1963-69, tchr. Spanish and German, 1969-82; supr. world langs. Parsippany-Troy Hills Sch. Dist., from 1982; vice-prin. Brooklawn Mid. Sch., Parsippany, N.J. Author: Voces y Vistas, 1989, Pasos y Puentes, 1989, Arcos y Alamedas, 1989. Mem. Masons (master 1990). Avocations: soccer, reading, counseling, values clarification. Home: Drums, Pa. Died July 12, 2008.

SCHONFELD, WALTER TIBOR, retired jewelry importer, writer; b. Vienna, May 14, 1917; came to U.S., 1951; s. Ferdinand Schonfeld and Irma Pollatschek; m. Beth Bond Valentine, Sept. 22, 1990. Student, Charles U., Prague, Czechoslovakia, 1939. Prosecutor War Crimes Trials, Nuremberg, Germany, 1945-49; case editor War Crimes Case Trials, Nuremberg, Germany, 1949—51; importer Sterling, Sheffield, London, 1952-56; jewelry salesman Balt., 1957-75; freelance writer Onancock, Va., 1976-88; writer, author Onley, Va., from 1989. Author: Nazi Madness Highlighted in Nuremberg. Mem. Country Yacht Club. Republican. Presbyterian. Home: Onley, Va. Died Feb. 20, 2008.

SCHRAM, JOSEPH H., retired sales executive; b. NYC, Feb. 17, 1927; BBA, Iona Coll., 1950. V.p. sales John V. McCarthy & Assocs., Southfield, Mich., from 1955. With USN, 1945-46. Roman Catholic. Home: Farmingtn Hls, Mich. Died Jan. 7, 2008.

SCHREIBER, WILLIAM FRANCIS, retired electrical engineer; b. NYC, Sept. 18, 1925; m. Marian Connor; children: Robert, Peter, Tatiana. BS, Columbia U., 1945, MS, 1947; PhD, Harvard U., 1953. Jr. engr. Sylvania Elec. Products, Inc., 1947-49; rsch. assoc. Harvard U., Cambridge, Mass., 1953; rsch. physicist Technicolor Corp., 1953-59; prof. elec. engring. Mass. Inst. Tech., Cambridge, 1959-90, prof. emeritus, 1990—2009, dir. advanced tv rsch. program, 1983-89. Fellow IEEE; mem. Nat. Acad. Engring., Sigma Xi. Died Sept. 21, 2009.

SCHREMP, FREDERIC WILLIAM, JR., oil field corrosion consultant; b. Utica, NY, Aug. 14, 1916; s. Frederic William and Elizabeth Alice (Doyle) S.; m. Janet May Edwards, Apr. 14, 1948 (widowed Mar. 1957); children: Barbara Ann, Frederic William III; m. Florence Lucille Barmore, Nov. 1, 1958; children: Paula C., Ellen S. BS in Chemistry, Rensselaer Poly. Inst., 1942; PhD in Phys. Chemistry, U. Wis., 1950. Registered profl. engr., Calif. Research engr. Am. Steel & Wire, Worcester, Mass., 1942-44; sr. research assoc. Chevron Oil Field, LaHabra, Calif., 1950-81; pvt. practice cons. Fullerton, Calif., from 1981. Contbr. several papers on corrosion and corrosion control, 3 papers on rheology of high polymers; 4 patents in field. Served to lt. USN, 1944-46, PTO. Mem. Am. Chem. Soc., Nat. Assn. Corrosion Engrs. (chmn. various tech. coms.), Sigma Xi, Phi Lambda Upsilon. Methodist. Avocations: computer programming, amateur radio, golf, backpacking, fishing. Died Feb. 1, 2008.

SCHROLL, EDWIN JOHN, retired secondary school educator, stage director; b. Watertown, NY, Feb. 14, 1941; s. Clarence Edwin and Frances Lucille (Snyder) S. BS, Lyndon State Coll., 1966; MS, Oswego State U., 1971. Cert. tchr. N.Y. English tchr. jr. h.s. Watertown (N.Y.) Sch. System, 1966-67; English tchr. h.s. Belleville (N.Y.) Cen. Sch., 1967-71, Massena (N.Y.) Cen. Sch., 1971-96, drama and speech tchr., 1988-96, drama coach, 1975-96, forensics coach; ret., 1996. Engr., announcer, programmer Pathways to Peace program Sta. WNCQ, Watertown, 1967-92; dir. Family History Ctr., Watertown, N.Y. Cinematographer, writer, narrator, prodr. (documentaries) The United States A Bicentennial Tour, 1976, Europe on $100 a Day, 1986; cinematographer: (TV) Wish You Were Here in Cape Vincent, 2000, Partying, 1989; co-author: Standard Operations Procedures and Duties of a Desk Clerk, 1963, Wish You Were Here in Cape Vincent, 2000; prodn. supr. (hist. pageant) 1,000 Seasons, 2001; dir. various high sch. prodns.; actor various community prodns. Bd. dirs. Youth in Action, 1993-94; active Nat. Family Opinion, 1991—; state advocate Ednl. Theatre Assn., 1996; del. Citizens Ambassador Program of People to People Internat. Theatre Edn. Delegation to China, 1996; active Cape Vincent Arts Coun., 1997—, Gravelly Point Players, 1997—, Breakwater Art Gallery, 1997—, Cape Vincent Christmas Com., 2005—. Mem. Nat. Geog. Soc., Ednl. Theatre Assn., Archaeology Inst. Am., Am. Film Inst., Nat. Trust Hist. Preservation, Cinerama Preservation Soc. Republican. Mem. Lds Ch. Avocations: stamp and coin collecting, gardening, historical research, genealogy, travel. Home: Cape Vincent, NY. Died Sept. 4, 2008.

SCHROTH, THOMAS NOLAN, editor; b. Trenton, NJ, Dec. 21, 1920; s. Frank David and Loretta (Nolan) S.; m. Colette Streit, May 1, 1948 (div. 1958); 1 child, Valerie; m. Patricia Wiggins, Sept. 27, 1958; children: Jennifer, Amy, Anne. Student, Tuck Sch. Bus. Adminstrn., 1942; AB, Dartmouth Coll., 1943. Reporter Time, Washington, 1946-47, UPI, Boston, 1947-48; reporter, news editor Bklyn. Eagle, 1948-51, mng. editor, 1951-55; editorial adviser Magnum Photos, Inc., NYC, 1955; exec. editor, pub. Congl. Quar. Inc. and Editorial Research Reports, Washington, 1955-68; founder, editor Nat. Jour. Ctr. Polit. Rsch., Washington, 1969-70; communications adviser Pub. Broadcasting Environment Ctr., Washington, 1970-71; asst. dir. pub. affairs for communications EPA, Washington, 1970-71, cons., 1972; exec. editor The Ellsworth (Maine) American, 1972-77; co-pub.-editor (with Patricia Schroth) Maine Life Mag., Sedgwick, 1977-81; editorial cons. U. Maine, Bangor, 1976-90; mng. editor South-North News Svc., Hanover, N.H., 1987-91; co-pub. New Leaf Pubs., Sedgwick, Maine, from 1990. Mem. Am. Press Inst. Seminar for Mng. Editors, 1953, Regional Transp. Adv. Com., 1996-99. Editor: Congress and the Nation, 1946-64-A Review of Government and Politics in the Postwar Years; editor Improving the U. of Maine trustee's pamphlet. Elected selectman Town of Sedgwick, 1989-94, moderator 1995-2009; bd. dirs. Blue Hill (Maine) Meml. Hosp., 1978-93, Bangor Symphony Orch., 1981-87, Blue Hill Concert Assn., 1991-2003; bd. dirs., v.p. Island Nursing Home, Deer Isle, Maine, 1985-2007; mem. Maine State Dem. Com., Augusta, 1985-92, 97-2009; bd. dirs. Downeast Transp., Inc., 1993-2006; del. Maine Dem. Nat. Conv., 2000. 1st lt. Army Airways Comm. Sys., USAAF, WWII. Avocations: gardening, walking, music. Died July 23, 2009.

SCHUESSLER, RICHARD JAY, insurance broker; b. Bklyn., Dec. 18, 1938; s. Oscar Joseph and Doris Lesly (Altenbrand) S.; m. Sarah Alexander Foster, Feb. 11, 1961; children: Richard J. Jr., Kemp Foster. BS in Bus. Adminstrn., Stetson U., 1962. V.p. Davis, Dorland & Co., NYC, 1965-82, Jardine, Emett & Chandler, Parsippany, N.J., 1982-86; pres. CPI Brokerage, Inc., Morristown, N.J., from 1986. Bd. dirs. Ardmore Minerals Corp., Ardmore, Okla., N.J. Mktg. Assocs., Whippany, N.J. Mem. Morris County Golf Club. Republican. Presbyterian. Avocations: golf, skiing. Home: Naples, Fla. Died Oct. 8, 2007.

SCHULBERG, BUDD, scriptwriter; b. NYC, Mar. 27, 1914; s. Benjamin P. and Adeline (Jaffe) S.; m. Virginia Ray, July 23, 1936 (div. 1942); 1 dau., Victoria; m. Victoria Anderson, Feb. 17, 1943 (div. 1964); children: Stephen, David (dec. 2005); m. Geraldine Brooks, July 12, 1964 (dec. 1977); m. Betsy Anne Langman, June 9, 1979; children: Benn Stuart, Jessica A. Student, Deerfield Acad., 1931-32; AB cum laude, Dartmouth Coll., 1936, LLD, 1960; LittD, Long Island U., 1983; DHL, Hofstra U., 1987, Five Points Coll., 2001. Boxing editor Sports Illustrated; pres., prodr. Schulberg Prodns. Founder, dir. Watts Writers Workshop, L.A., 1965-2009; founder, chmn. Frederick Douglass Creative Arts Ctr., N.Y.C., 1971-2009. Screenwriter, Hollywood, 1936-39; writer "The Schulberg Report", Newsday Syndicate; author: What Makes Sammy Run?, 1941, The Harder They Fall, 1947, The Disenchanted, 1950, Some Faces in the Crowd, 1953, Waterfront, 1955 (Christopher award 1955), Sanctuary V, 1969, The Four Seasons of Success, 1972, Loser and Still Champion: Muhammad Ali, 1972, Swan Watch, 1975, Everything that Moves, 1980, Moving Pictures: Memories of a Hollywood Prince, 1981, Writers in America, 1990, Love, Action, Laughter and Other Sad Tales, 1990, Sparring with Hemingway: And Other Legends of the Fight Game, 1995, La Foret Interdite, including dialogue in Black and White with James Badwin, 1997; editor: From the Ashes: Voices of Watts, 1967; screenwriter: (films) (with Samuel Ornitz) Little Orphan Annie, 1938, (with F. Scott Fitzgerald) Winter Carnival, 1939, (with Dorothy Parker) Weekend for Three, 1941, (with Martin Berkeley) City without Men, 1943, (with Dudley Nichols) Government Girl, 1943, On the Waterfront, 1954 (Academy award best original story and screenplay 1954, N.Y. Critics award 1954, Fgn. Corrs. award 1954, Screen Writers Guild award 1954, Venice Festival award 1954), A Face in the Crowd, 1958 (German Film Critics award 1957), Wind Across the Everglades, 1958, (teleplays) The Pharmacist's Mate, 1951, Paso Doble, Memory in White, The Legend That Walks Like a man, A Question of Honor, A Table At Ciro's; playwright: The Disenchanted: A Play in Three Acts, 1958, What Make's Sammy Run?, 1959, (musical) Senor Discretion Himself, 1985, (play in 2 acts) The Disenchanted, 1999, On the Waterfront, 2001; contbr. to Sports Illustrated, Life, N.Y. Times Book Rev., Esquire, Newsday Syndicate, L.A. Times Book Rev., N.Y. Times Sunday Mag., Playboy, The New Yorker, Vanity Fair. Bd. dirs. Westminster Neighborhood Assn., L.A., 1965-68, Inner City Cultural Ctr., L.A., 1965-68; mem. nat. adv. commn. on black participation John F. Kennedy Ctr. for Performing Arts; trustee Humanitas Prize. Lt. (j.g.) USNR, 1943-46, assigned to OSS. Awarded Army Commendation Ribbon for gathering photog. evidence of war crimes for Nuremberg Trial, 1945-46; recipient Susie Humanitarian award B'nai B'rith, Image award NAACP,

Journalism award Dartmouth Coll., Merit award Lotos Club., L.A. Community Svc. award, 1966, B'hai Human Rights award, 1968, spl. award for Watts Writers Workshop, New Eng. Theater Conf., 1969, Heritage award Deerfield Acad., 1986, Amistad award, award for work with black writers Howard U., Prix Literaire, Deauville Festival 1989, 2005, Westhampton Writers Lifetime Achievement award, 1989, World Boxing Assn. Living Legend award, 1990, 97, Southampton Cultural Ctr. 1st Annual Literature award, 1992, Denver Film Festival Outstanding Achievement in Art of Film, 1997, Best Screenplay award, 1998, New Bounty Boxing Hall Fame, 2000, Internat. Boxing Hall Fame, 2001, LA Lifetime Achievement award, 2003, Lifetime Achievement award Guild Hall, 2003, Pres. award Sony Rockford Co., 2004, Culture Clash Golden Jalepeno award, 2005, Lifetime Achievement award L.A. (Calif.) H.S., 2005, Ann. Achievement award Congresswoman Maxine Waters, 2005, Suffolk Golden Age Jewish Boxing, 2006, Barrymore award, Fort Lee Film Commn., 2007; named to Internat. Boxing Hall of Fame, 2003. Mem. Dramatists Guild, ASCAP, Authors Guild N.Y.C. (mem. council), ACLU, Writers Guild East (mem. coun.), Boxing Writers Am. (A. J. Liebling award 1997), P.E.N., Sphinx (Dartmouth), The Players Club, Yale/Dartmouth Club, Phi Beta Kappa. Home: Westhampton Beach, NY. Died Aug. 5, 2009.

SCHULER, ROBERT LEO, state legislator; b. Cin., Ohio, June 15, 1943; s. Del D. Schuler and Virginia S. Heyl; m. Shelagh Moritz Schuler, 1962; children: Jefrey Sherry Jordon, Robert C. A.A.B in Real Estate, U. Cin. City councilman, Deer Pk., 1978—85; pres. OKI Regional Coun. Gov., 1979—92; mem. Hamilton County Regional Planning, 1986—87, Solid Waste Policy, 1990—92; trustee Sycamore Township, 1988—92; state rep. Dist. 36 Ohio, 1993—2001; state senator Dist. 7 Ohio, 2003—09; state senator owner Comprehensive Appraisal Svc., Ohio, 1977—2009. Recipient Watchdog of Treasury award, UCO, 1993—98, Legislator of Yr., Ohio America Vets., 1994, award, Ohio Assn. Mortgage Brokers, 1995, Legislature Merit award, Ohio Licensed Beverage Assn., 1995, award, Hamilton County Township Assn., 1997, Ohio Pks. & Recreation, 2000, Raymond Walters Distin. Alumni award, U. Cin., 2000, Pub. Official of Yr., 2000, Meritorious Award, Ohio Brain Injury Assn., from 2001. Mem.: Cin. Bd. Realtors. Republican. Roman Catholic. Died June 19, 2009.

SCHULMAN, IRVING, physician, educator; b. NYC, Feb. 17, 1922; s. Louis and Minnie (Lowen) S.; m. Naomi Zion, May 28, 1950; children: Margaret, John. BA, NYU, 1942, MD, 1945. Intern. Queens Gen. Hosp., NYC, 1945-46; resident Bellevue Hosp., NYC, 1948-50; practice medicine specializing in pediatrics; assoc. prof. pediatrics Cornell U., NYC, 1950-58; prof. Northwestern U., Chgo., 1958-61; prof., head dept. pediatrics U. Ill.- Chgo., 1961-72; chief pediatrics U. Ill. Hosp, 1961-72; prof., chmn. dept. pediatrics Stanford U., Calif., 1972-92; pediatrician-in-chief Stanford U. Hosp., 1972-92; chief of staff Children's Hosp. of Stanford, 1982-91. Mem. research com. Chgo. Heart Assn., 1961-72, Leukemia Research Soc.; mem. med. adv. bd. Nat. Hemophilia Found., 1963-78; cons. NIH, 1961-67 Contbr. articles to profl. jours.; editor-in-chief: Advances in Pediatrics, 1969-76. Served to capt. M.C. AUS, 1946-48. Recipient Mead-Johnson Am. Acad. Pediatrics, 1960 Mem. Am. Acad. Pediatrics, Am. Pediatric Soc., Soc. Pediatrics Research, Am. Soc. Clin. Investigation, Phi Beta Kappa Home: Palo Alto, Calif. Died June 11, 2009.

SCHULMAN, ROBERT, journalist; b. NYC, July 7, 1916; s. Samuel and Rebecca (Yuster) S.; m. Eleanor Langham, Feb. 17, 1943 (div. May 1974); 1 child, Rebecca Schulman McIntyre; m. Louise Tachau, Nov. 4, 1976. BS, NYU, 1936; MS in Journalism, Columbia U., 1937; Hon. Alumnus, U. Louisville, 1996. Reporter Post-Dispatch, St. Louis, 1937-38; program dir. Community Chest, St. Louis, 1938-40; features writer, columnist Star-Times, St. Louis, 1940-42, 46-51; staff corr. Time-Life Mags., Chgo., 1951-53; spl. features dir. King Broadcasting, Seattle, 1959-69; news bur. chief, Pacific N.W. Time-Life Mags., Seattle, 1953-59; mag. writer, commentator WHAS-TV and Radio, Louisville, 1968-74; press critic, columnist Courier-Journal and Times, Louisville, 1974-81; exec. dir. Ctr. for Humanities U. Louisville, from 1984. Exec. dir. Design for Washington, Seattle, 1967-68; bd. dirs. Soc. Profl. Journalists, Louisville, 1969—. Author: (biography) John Sherman Cooper: Global Kentuckian, 1976. Bd. dirs. Family and Children's Agy., Louisville, 1986-95;, nat. bd. dirs. Family Assn. of Am., Seattle, 1962-65. Capt. Air Transport Command, 1942-46. Mem. Sigma Delta Chi (Disting. Editl. award/TV 1972). Jewish. Avocations: swimming, exercising, reading, theater, movie and concert-going. Home: Louisville, Ky. Died Jan. 6, 2008.

SCHULTZ, ARTHUR LEROY, clergyman, educator; b. Johnstown, Pa., June 14, 1928; s. Elmer Albert Robert and Alice Lizetta (Flegal) S.; m. Mildred Louise Stouffer, Nov. 29, 1947; children: Thomas Arthur, Rebecca Louise. BA, Otterbein Coll., 1949; MDiv, United Theol. Sem., 1952; MEd, U. Pitts., 1955, PhD, 1963. Sr. min. Albright United Meth. Ch., Pitts., 1952-56; dir. pub. rels. Otterbein Coll., Westerville, Ohio, 1956-65, adj. prof. religion and philosophy, 1990-98; pres. Albright Coll., Reading, Pa., 1965-77, Ashland (Ohio) Coll., 1977-80; exec. dir. Cen. Ohio Radio Reading Svc., Columbus, 1980-84; parish min. Ch. Master United Meth., Westerville, 1984-89; min. of visitation Ch. Messiah United Meth., Westerville, 1991—2002. Pres. Pa. Assn. Colls. & Univs., Harrisburg, 1974-75. Trustee Reading Hosp., 1967-77, Wyoming Sem., Kingston, Pa., 1971-80; v.p. Found. for Ind. Colls. Pa., Harrisburg, 1972-73; pres. Pa. Coun. on Alcohol Problems, Harrisburg, 1968-76; pres. Westerville (Ohio) Hist. Soc., 1986-89, Westerville Area Ministerial Assn., 1992-93. Named Outstanding Young Man of the Year Jr. C. of C., Westerville, Ohio, 1960. Mem. Brookstone Cmty. Assn. (sec. bd. trustees 1994-99, v.p. 1999-2000), Rotary (charter pres. 1959, dist. gov. 1965-66, dist. sec.-treas. 1982-93), Masons, Shriners, Torch Club. Republican. Methodist. Avocations: collecting post cards, golf, tennis, travel. Home: Westerville, Ohio. Died May 6, 2009.

SCHULTZ, HYMAN, analytical chemist; b. Bklyn., July 11, 1931; s. Joseph Israel and Mary (Reifen) S.; m. Shirley Miriam Befferman, Aug. 10, 1957; children: Richard Hirsch, Daniel Brian. BS, Bklyn. Coll., 1956; PhD, Pa. State U., 1962. Sr. rsch. engr. N.Am. Aviation, LA, 1962-67; head gas analysis Teledyne, Isotopes, Inc., Westwood, N.J., 1967-70; sr. tech. advisor U.S. Dept. Energy, Pitts., from 1971. Speaker in field. Contbg. author: Trace Elements in Coal, 1975, Chemistry of Coal Utilization, 1981; contbr. articles to tech. publs. Mem. State College (Pa.) Theatre Group, 1958-63; chmn. Friends of Libr., Rivervale, N.J., 1969-70; violinist South Hills Symphony Orch., Mt. Lebanon, N.J., 1975-77. With U.S. Army, 1952-53, Korea. Mem. Soc. Analytical Chemists Pitts. (fin. affairs com. 1993-94), Am. Chem. Soc. (head libr. com. Pitts. sect. 1979—), Pitts. Conf. (registration chmn. 1994—). Achievements include patent for method of determining low levels of oxygen in carbonaceous materials. Died Mar. 20, 2008.

SCHULZE, ERIC WILLIAM, lawyer; b. Libertyville, Ill., July 8, 1952; s. Robert Carl and Barbara (Mayo) Schulze. BA, U. Tex., 1973, JD, 1977. Bar: Tex. 1977, US Dist. Ct. (we. dist.) Tex. 1987, US Ct. Appeals (5th cir.) 1987, US Dist. Ct. (ea. and so. dists.) Tex 1988, US Dist. Ct. (no. dist.) Tex. 1989, US Supreme Ct. 1989, bd. cert. civil appellate law: Tex. Bd. Legal Specialization 1990. Rsch. asst. U. Tex., Austin, 1978; legis. aide Tex. Ho. Reps., Austin, 1979—81; editor Tex. Sch. Law News, Austin, 1982—85; assoc. Hairston, Walsh & Anderson, Austin, 1986—87; ptnr. Walsh, Anderson, Brown, Schulze & Aldridge, Austin, from 1988. Mng. ptnr. Walsh, Anderson, Brown, Schulze & Aldridge, Austin, Tex., 1993—2004; co-pub. Tex. Sch. Adminstrs. Legal Digest, 1991—2005, mng. editor, 1992—2005; editl. adv. com. West's Edn. Law Reporter, 1996—2006. Editor: Tex. Edn. Code Annotated, 1982—85, Tex. Sch. Adminstrs. Legal Digest, 1986—92. Del. Tex. State Dem. Conv., 1982, Travis County Dem. Conv., 1982, 1984, 1986. Recipient Merit award, Internat. Assn. Bus. Communicators (Austin br.), 1983, Coll. State Bar Tex., 1992. Mem.: Tex. Coun. Sch. Attys., Nat. Coun. Sch. Attys., Bar Assn. of 5th Cir., Travis County Bar Assn., Tex. Bar Assn., Fed. Bar Assn., Edn. Law Assn., Def. Rsch. Inst., Toastmasters (pres. Capital City chpt. 1995). Home: Galveston, Tex. Died Aug. 28, 2008.

SCHUMACHER, THOMAS L., architect, educator; b. NYC, Nov. 7, 1941; s. Joseph Gerald and Marcia Friedman Schumacher; m. Patricia Ellen Sachs, Dec. 19, 1982. MArch, Cornell U., 1966. Registered arch., NJ, 1977. Assoc. prof. architecture U. Va., Charlottesville; prof. architecture U. Md., College Park, 1984—2009. Terragni's Danteum. Recipient Rome prize for Architecture, 1967. Avocations: golf, travel, cooking. Home: Washington, DC. Died July 15, 2009.

SCHUPP, SANDRA LYNN, oncology nurse; b. Madison, Wis., May 25, 1960; d. John S. and Alice I. (Reck) Jenkins; m. Robert C. Schupp Jr., Mar. 3, 1984; children: Bobby, Kristy. BSN, Alfred U., NY, 1982. RN, N.Y.; cert. oncology nurse. Staff nurse Albany (N.Y.) Med. Ctr. Hosp., 1982-84, Glens Falls (N.Y.) Hosp., from 1984. Home: Bolton Landing, NY. Died Aug. 12, 2008.

SCHUSTER, GEORGE F., small business owner; b. Avoca, Minn., Aug. 4, 1934; s Arthur George and Marie Margaret (Wiener) S.; m. Helen Joan Hellwinkel, Sept. 18, 1955 (dec. Dec. 1987); children: Lorie Jo, Mark Alan, Terry Dale, Daniel Lynn; m. Linda Marie Tieg Adams, Apr. 7, 1990; stepchildren: Lori Marie, Brett. Farmer, Fulda, Minn., 1953-56; with Worthington (Minn.) Hatchery, 1956-57; mgr. sales Titonka (Iowa) Turkey Hatchery, 1958-61; owner/operator mgr. Titonka Farm Store, from 1961. V.p. bd. dirs. Titonka Telephone Co., 1986—. Mem. Titonka City Coun., 1965-75. Lutheran. Avocations: fishing, collecting dolls, collecting belt buckles, golf, flowers and gardening. Home: Titonka, Iowa. Died Aug. 20, 2008.

SCHWALM, THOMAS HARDY, beverage industry executive; b. Oshkosh, Wis., Oct. 11, 1944; s. A. Thomas and Doris (Hardy) S.; m. JoAnn Forrest, Sept. 6, 1969; children: Matson Forrest, Dugan Hardy, James Bradford. BS in History, U. Wis., Madison, 1968. With Joseph Schlitz Brewing Co., Milw., 1968-82, dist. sales mgr. Wis. and La., 1970-74, asst. mgr. sales analysis, brand coordination and pricing, 1975, supr. brand projects, 1976, mgr. brand projects, 1976-78, assoc. brand dir., 1978-80, brand dir., 1980-82; group mktg. dir. The Stroh Brewery Co., Detroit, 1982-83, from 1983; v.p. sales and mktg. Dribeck Importers, Inc., Greenwich, Conn., 1960. Co-founder South Beach Beverage Co. (SOBE) (sold to Pepsi); bd. dirs. Drinks Americas Holdings Ltd, 2005—09. Owner Thousand Islands Country Club; bd. dirs. Antique Boat Mus., Clayton. Republican. Episcopalian. Avocation: boating. Home: Greenwich, Conn. Died July 30, 2009.

SCHWARTZ, ARTHUR, social worker; b. Brockton, Mass., July 10, 1927; s. Morris and Esther C. Schwartz; m. Ruth May Silverstein, Jan. 30, 1955; children: Elizabeth, David Morris. BA, Northeastern U., Boston, 1951; MS in Social Svc., Boston U., 1953; PhD, Columbia U., 1965. Case worker Jewish Bd. Guardians, Bklyn., 1953-55, CCNY, 1955-59; rsch. assoc. YM-YWHAs of Greater N.Y., 1960-63; asst. prof. Sch. Social Work, Rutgers U., New Brunswick, 1963-66; assoc. prof. U. Chgo., Chgo., 1966-82; prof. Sch. Social Work, U. Hawaii, Honolulu, 1982-83, U. Md., Balt., 1983-94; scholar-in-residence Widener U., Chester, Pa., 1994-99; lectr. U. Pa., 1997—2009. Author: Social Casework: A Behavioral Approach, 1975, The Behavior Therapies, 1982, Depression, Theories and Treatment: Psychological, Biological and Social Perspectives, 1993 Mem. NASW, AAUP. Democrat. Jewish. Home: Philadelphia, Pa. Died Apr. 17, 2009.

SCHWARTZ, FRANK EDWIN, ophthalmologist; b. Beaver, Pa., Mar. 26, 1919; s. Frank Rambo and Ella Leona (Mackall) Schwartz; m. Betty Jean Carney, July 28, 1944 (div. 1957); children: Michael, Laurie; m. Betty Margaret Melvin, May 20, 1957; children: Jo-Hanna, Heidi Lyn. BS, MD, U. Pitts., 1943. Diplomate Am. Bd. Ophthalmology. Ophthalmologist, Millbrae, Calif., 1954—57, Lancaster, Calif., 1958—77, Newport, Oreg., from 1978. Maj. US Army, 1950—53, Korea. Decorated Purple Heart, Bronze star. Fellow: Am. Acad. Ophthalmology, Am. Coll. Surgery; mem.: AMA, Oreg. Med. Assn. Republican. Presbyterian. Died Dec. 7, 2007.

SCHWARTZ, JACK JAMES, physician, consultant; b. Newark, Dec. 9, 1922; s. Walter Sidney and Julia (Bodnar) S.; m. Lillian Feldman Schwartz, Dec. 22, 1946; children: Jeffrey Hugh, Laurens Robert. BA, Cornell U., Ithaca, NY, 1943; MD, Med. Coll. of Va., Richmond, 1946. Diplomate in pediatrics Am. Bd. Pediatrics. Asst. in pediatrics Washington U. Sch. Medicine, St. Louis, 1951; med. dir. Shugard Nursery & Shelter, Newark, N.J., 1952-62; dir. Nephrology Program N.J. Children's Hosp., Newark, 1956-70; dir. J.D. Infant and Child Devel. Ctr., West Orange, N.J., 1980-89; assoc. chief of staff N.J. Children's Hosp., Newark, 1967-69; assoc. clin. prof. pediats. Newark campus U. Coll. Medicine and Dentistry N.J., from 1967; clin. chief of pediats. St. Barnabas Med. Ctr., Livingston, N.J., 1979-81; pvt. practice Schwartz and Boodish, P.A., Millburn, N.J., 1951-94. Contbr. articles to profl. jours. Founder Kidney Disease Clinic, N.J. Children's Hosp., 1956, Jeffrey Dworkin Infant & Child Devel. Ctr., West Orange, N.J., 1980; mem. Bd. Health, Watchung, N.J., 1995. Capt. U.S. Army Med. Corps., 1948-50. Postdoctoral fellowship Nat. Inst. Health, 1948. Fellow Am. Acad. Pediatrics, Am.Acad. Cerebral Palsy and Devel. Medicine. Jewish. Avocations: gardening, music, piano, chinese study, study of religion, theater. Home: Watchung, NJ. Died Mar. 14, 2008.

SCHWARTZ, MODEST EUPHEMIA, real estate company executive; b. Chgo., Dec. 14, 1915; d. Giles E. and Evelyn (Tomczak) Ratkowski; m. Edward Joseph Schwartz, Feb. 9, 1946 (dec. July 1979); children: Kathryn Ann, Edward Thomas. BA, UCLA, 1936, MA, 1938; libr. credential, Immaculate Heart Coll., LA, 1958. Cert. tchr., libr., Calif. Tchr. Alhambra City Schs., Calif., 1938-58, libr. Calif., 1958-72; v.p. Fremont Svc., Alhambra, 1959-83, pres., 1983-86; v.p. Moulding Supply Co., Alhambra, 1967-83, pres., 1983-85; v.p., bd. dirs. Sequoia Mgmt. Co., Alhambra, 1969-86; mng. ptnr. SRSH Realty Ptnrs., Alhambra, 1986-89. Bd. dirs. Found. for Cardiovasc. Rsch., Pasadena, Calif., 1973-85, Progressive Savs., Alhambra, 1979-85; mem. Ret. Sr. Vol. Program, Alhambra, 1979—; mem. Alhambra Hosps. Aux., 1987—, med. libr., 1990—; mem. Friends of Alhambra Pub. Libr., 1981—, treas., 1993—; pres. bd. trustees Alhambra Pub. Libr., 1981-83, 89-96, mem., 1976-83, 85-93; pres. Alhambra Pub. Libr. Found., 1990-96; mem. Los Angeles County Art Mus., Met. Mus., N.Y.C.; sec. Friends of the Santa Clarita Librs., 1997—. Mem. ALA, NEA, AAUW (life, Edn. Found. grant in her name 1988, br. treas. 1986-88, 89-91, corr. and rec. sec. 1992-93, co-chair ways-and means com. 1993—, auditor 1995-98), Calif. Ret. Tchrs. Assn. (co-chair hospitality 1991-93, membership chmn., 2d v.p. membership Pasadena-Foothill divsn. 1993-95, chmn. neighborhood group Pasadena-Foothill divsn. 1995-98), UCLA Alumni Assn. Avocations: reading, travel. Home: Saugus, Calif. Died Apr. 4, 2008.

SCHWARTZ, WILLIAM BENJAMIN, internist, educator; b. Montgomery, Ala., May 16, 1922; s. William Benjamin and Molly (Vendruff) S.; m. Tressa Ruslander Miller: children from previous marriage: Eric A., Kenneth B., Laurie A. MD, Duke U., 1945. Diplomate: Am. Bd. Internal Medicine (mem. test com. nephrology). Intern, then asst. resident medicine U. Chgo. Clinics, 1945-46; asst. medicine Peter Bent Brigham Hosp., Boston; also research fellow medicine Harvard Med. Sch., 1948-50; fellow medicine Children's Hosp., Boston, 1949-50; mem. faculty Tufts U. Sch. Medicine, 1950-96, prof. medicine, 1958-96, Endicott prof., 1975-76, Vannevar Bush Univ. prof., 1976-96, chmn. dept. medicine, 1971-76; mem. staff New Eng. Center Hospitals, 1950-59, sr. physician, chief renal service, 1959-71, physician-in-chief, 1971-76; prof. medicine U. So. Calif., LA, 1992—2006; Disting. physician US Dept. Veterans Affairs, 1994-97. Established investigator Am. Heart Assn., 1956-61; chmn. gen. medicine study sect. NIH, 1965-69; mem. sci. adv. bd. USAF, 1965-68, Nat. Kidney Found., chmn.; mem. tng. com. Nat. Heart Inst., 1969-70; prin. adviser health scis. program, Rand Corp., 1977-88.

Co-author: (with Henry J. Aaron) The Painful Prescription: Rationing Hospital Care, 1984 Markle scholar med. scis., 1950-55 Mem. Inst. Medicine NAS, Am. Soc. Nephrology (pres. 1974-75), Acad. Arts and Scis., ACP, Am. Fedn. Clin. Research, Am. Physiol. Soc., Am. Soc. Clin. Investigation, Assn. Am. Physicians, Phi Beta Kappa, Sigma Xi, Alpha Omega Alpha. Died Mar. 15, 2009.

SCLAROW, MARSHALL HILLEL, lawyer; b. Duluth, Minn., Mar. 15, 1930; s. Abe M. and Bessie (Levine) S.; m. Dov Baer, Dec. 27, 1959; children: Halden L., Kendra Moshe. Student, Iowa State U., 1948-50; BA, U. Iowa, 1953, JD, 1955. Bar: Colo. 1955. Pvt. practice, Denver, 1957; ins. agt. various ins. cos., Boulder, Colo., 1957-73; pvt. practice Boulder, 1973-86, 87-89; prin. Denver, from 1989. Owner, with Joy and Ease unlimited. Pres. Har Ha Shem Congregation, Boulder, 1971-72, 83, Boulder County Estate Planning Coun., 1983. Lt. col. USAF, 1955-57, USAFR, 1957-78. Avocations: skiing, tennis, travel. Home: Golden, Colo. Died Mar. 13, 2008.

SCOTT, BRUCE LEWIS, chemical company executive; b. San Diego, June 4, 1949; s. Reid Montague and Billie Jean (Lewis) S.; m. Mary Bennett Botkin, Nov. 20, 1974; 1 child, Bennett Lewis. BBS, Gonzaga U., 1972; MBA, Purdue U., 1977. Mgr. fin. analysis B.F. Goodrich Co., Akron, Ohio, 1979-81, product mgr., 1981-83, dir. mktg., 1983-85, dir. bus. devel., from 1986. Chmn. CAPI, 1984-85. Served with U.S. Army, 1972-76. Republican. Avocations: triathlons, golf, travel. Home: Akron, Ohio. Died Jan. 22, 2008.

SCOTT, CARL WERNER, psychologist, research consultant; b. Houston, Oct. 29, 1953; s. William Howard Jr. and Dora Mae (Hoeflich) S.; m. Pamela Aimee Pepperell, May 26, 1984; children: David Pepperell, Sarah Estelle Pepperell. BA, Loyola U., New Orleans, 1975; MA, U. Houston, 1981, PhD, 1987. Instr. San Jacinto Coll. North, Houston, 1983-89; asst. prof. U. St. Thomas, Houston, 1989-91, assoc. prof., from 1992, dept. chair, from 1994; rsch. assoc. Ctr. Advancement of Sci., Engring, Tech., Houston, 1990-92; rsch. con. U. Houston, from 1991. Rsch. cons. So. Pacific Transp., Houston, 1978-83, Tex. Rsch. Ins. Mental Scis., Houston, 1981-84, San Jacinto Coll., 1983-89; statis. cons. Gulf Oil Corp., Houston, 1983-84. Grad. Student Rsch. award Tex. Psychol. Assn., 1982; Undergrad. Lab. grantee NSF, 1991, 94. Mem. APA, S.W. Psychological Assn.; frgn. affiliate British Psychological Soc. Avocations: nutrition, education, social injustice, critical thinking. Home: Houston, Tex. Died Jan. 21, 2008.

SCOTT, DAVID WINFIELD, artist, museum administrator; b. Fall River, Mass., July 10, 1916; s. Benjamin David and Edith May (Romig) S.; m. Tirsa Lilia Saavedra, July 10, 1947 (dec. Jan. 1986); children: Tirsa Margaret, Edith Elizabeth; m. Doris Jean Fitch White, Aug. 19, 1988. AB, Harvard Coll., 1938; MA, Claremont Grad. Sch., 1940, MFA, 1951; PhD, U. Calif., Berkeley, 1960; DFA, Corcoran Sch. Art, 1991. Instr. art Riverside (Calif.) Jr. Coll., 1940-41; from lectr. to prof. Scripps Coll., Claremont, Calif., 1947-63; dir. Nat. Collection Fine Art, Washington, 1964-69; planning officer Nat. Gallery Art, Washington, 1969-84; acting dir. Corcoran Gallery Art, Washington, 1990; artist, cons. pvt. practice, Whitehaven, Md., 1991—2004. Cons. in field. Capt. USAF, 1945. Home: Austin, Tex. Died Mar. 30, 2009.

SCOTT, JOHN FRANCIS, III, water resources engineer; b. Winchester, Mass., Nov. 21, 1949; s. John Francis Jr. and Vivian Gene (Miller) S.; divorced; children: Lindsey Melissa, Julia Patricia. BS, U.S. Mil. Acad., 1971; MS, Colo. State U., 1979, PhD, 1983. Research assoc. Colo. State U., Ft. Collins, 1977-83; water resources engr. Western Area Power Adminstrn., Loveland, Colo., 1983-87, No. Colo. Water Conservancy Dist., Loveland, from 1987. Bd. dirs. Ft. Collins Water Bd., 1984—. Served with U.S. Army, 1971-76. Mem. ASCE, Am. Geophys. Union, Sigma Xi. Home: Marco Island, Fla. Died Mar. 16, 2008.

SCOTT, MARY LOUISE, educator, writer; b. Ft. Worth, Tex., Oct. 15, 1932; d. Edward Hughes and Gertrude Elizabeth (Wiltshire) S. AB, U. San Diego, 1955; MA, San Diego State U., 1961; JD, U. San Diego, 1970. Bar: Calif. Tchr. San Diego Unified Sch. Dist., 1955-89; rsch. assoc. San Diego Aerospace Mus., 1989-94, edn. specialist, 1994-96; freelance writer, from 1996. Curriculum writer San Diego City Schs., 1972, 73, 80-89. Author: San Diego: Air Capital of the West, 1991; co-author: Young Adults in the Marketplace (2 vols.), 1979; contbr. articles to profl. jours. Recipient Citation of Honor Diocese of San Diego, 1955, cert. of appreciation San Diego State U., 1985, recognition Calif. State Assembly, 1991; ednl. mentor Old Globe Theatre, San Diego, 1987, 88, 89. Mem. U.S. Naval Inst., Navy League U.S., Zool. Soc. San Diego, Amnesty Internat., Call to Action, Woman's Ordination Conf. Democrat. Roman Catholic. Avocations: Biblical study, classic movies. Home: San Diego, Calif. Died Sept. 28, 2007.

SCOTT, WILLARD WARREN, JR., retired military officer; b. Fort Monroe, Va., Feb. 18, 1926; s. Willard Warren and Bernice (Peck) S.; m. Justine Dorney, June 12, 1948; children: Mary Frances, Elizabeth Marie, Willard Warren III, Catherine Carroll, Susan Margaret, Margaret Ann, Ann Marie BS in Mil. Sci., U.S. Mil. Acad., 1948; MS in Mech. Engring., U. So. Calif., 1960; PhD (hon.), St. Thomas Aquinas Coll., 1985. Commd. 2d lt. US Army, 1948, advanced through grades to lt. gen., 1980; comdg. gen. V Corps Arty. US Army Europe, 1973-74; comdg. gen. Army Readiness Region VI, Fort Knox, Ky., 1974-76, 25th Inf. Divsn., Schofield Barracks, Hawaii, 1976-78; asst. dep. chief ops., plans & security US Army, Washington, 1978-80; comdg. gen. V Corps US Army Europe, Frankfort, Germany, 1980-81; supt. US Mil. Acad., West Point, 1981—86. Former mem. exec. com. Pacific council Boy Scouts America, Honolulu, Atlantic council, now mem. exec. com. Hudson-Del. council Decorated D.S.M., Legion of Merit with oak leaf cluster, Bronze Star with oak leaf cluster, Air medal, Army Commendation medal with oak leaf cluster Mem. Phi Kappa Phi Clubs: University (N.Y.C.). Lodges: Rotary. Avocation: handball. Died Jan. 1, 2009.

SCOTTEN, ANGELA, mental health nurse, administrator; b. Nevada, Mo., Mar. 27, 1957; d. William E. and Anna E. (Hillier) Bailey; children: Clayton, Brandon. ADN, Ft. Scott Community Coll., 1980; BSN, Pitts. State U., Kans., 1988. Cert. psychiat./mental health nurse, cert. in nursing adminstrn. Staff nurse Nevada State Hosp., 1980-85, Heartland Hosp., Nevada, nurse mgr., 1986-89, asst. DON, from 1989. Mem. ANA, Sigma Theta Tau. Home: Walker, Mo. Died Aug. 1, 2007.

SCOVIAC, NEVA VIRGINIA, pediatrics nurse; b. Fayette, Ohio, Mar. 10, 1923; d. Israel C. and Ella Elizabeth (Beatty) Ort; m. Earl Scoviac, Aug. 19, 1949; children: Karen Ella Scoviac Moore, Beverly Ann Scoviac Walters, Rebecca Kay. Diploma, Community Hosp., Battle Creek, Mich., 1944; postgrad., Childrens Hosp., Detroit. Cert. critical care nurse. Ob., med.-surg. staff nurse Bixby Hosp., Adrian, Mich., 1944-45; gyn., pediatrics nurse Percy Jones Mil. Hosp., Battle Creek, 1947; staff and relief charge nurse Blodgett Hosp., Grand Rapids, Mich., 1959-85; med.-surg., ob. nurse Bixby Hosp., Adrian, Mich.; staff nad relief charge nurse Sturgis (Mich.) Meml. Hosp.; staff nurse, charge nurse Herrick Meml. Hosp., Tecumseh, Mich.; pediatrics charge nurse Leila Hosp., Battle Creek; long term care charge nurse Harbor Beach (Mich.) Community Hosp. Lt. U.S. Army, 1945-46. Mem. ANA, ARC. Home: Hudson, Mich. Died Feb. 23, 2008.

SCRABECK, JON GILMEN, retired dental educator; b. Rochester, Minn., Dec. 6, 1938; s. Clarence and Nancy Alma (Brown) S.; m. DeAnn Louise Jacks, June 16, 1962; children: Joan Louise, Erik Jon. Student, Contra Costa Coll., San Pablo, Calif., 1964-66, U. Calif., Berkeley, 1966-67; DDS, UCLA, 1971; MA in Edn., U. Colo., 1985. Pvt. practice, Santa Rosa, Calif., 1971-78; sr. instr. U. Colo. Sch. Dentistry, Denver, 1978-79, asst. prof., 1980-86, dir. patient care, 1979-80, acting dir. clin. affairs, 1980-81, acting assoc. dean, acting div. chmn., 1984-85; dept. chmn. Marquette U. Sch. Dentistry, Milw., 1986-90, assoc. prof., 1986—2003, assoc. prof. tenure, 1989, curricular head, 1990—2003; ret., 2003. Cons. Dental Student mag.,1983-86, Colo. Bd. Dentistry, Denver, 1985-86, Dentist mag., 1986-90, VA, Milw., 1987-90. Editor Jour. Colo. Dental Assn., 1980-86; contbr. articles and abstracts to dental jours. Mem. vol. staff Morey Dental Clinic, Denver, 1982-85, Health Fair, Denver, 1983-85; ofcl. judge S.E. Wis. Sci. Fair, Milw., 1988—. Fellow Internat. Coll. Dentists, Acad. Dental Materials, Am. Coll. Dentists, Pierre Fauchard Acad.; mem. ADA (coun. on journalism 1984-86, coun. on dental rsch. 1986-88, manuscript reviewer 1988—), Acad. Operative Dentistry, Wis. Dental Assn. (assoc. editor Jour. 1987—), Omicron Kappa Upsilon, Alpha Gamma Sigma. Roman Catholic. Avocations: foreign and domestic travel, photography, boating, fishing, water-skiing. Home: Littleton, Colo. Died Sept. 24, 2009.

SCROGGIE, LUCY ETHELYN, analytical chemist; b. Knoxville, Tenn., May 29, 1935; d. Everett and Ethelyn (Powell) S. BS in Chemistry, U. Tenn., Knoxville, 1957, MS in Chemistry, 1959; PhD in Chemistry, U. Tex., 1961. Analytical chemist Oak Ridge (Tenn.) Nat. Lab., 1961-66, Union Carbide Corp., South Charleston, W.Va., 1966-69, U.S. TVA, Muscle Shoals, Ala., 1970-75, rsch. chemist Chattanooga, Tenn., 1975-80, mgmt. trainee Norris, Tenn., 1980-81, project mgr. Knoxville, from 1981. Contbr. articles to profl. jours. Mem. Am. Chem. Soc., Am. Conf. Govtl. Indsl. Hygienists, Pilot Club Internat., Phi Beta Kappa, Sigma Xi, Phi Kappa Phi. Methodist. Avocations: woodworking, needlecrafts, calligraphy, photography. Home: Knoxville, Tenn. Died Nov. 14, 2007.

SCUDERI, PETER B., federal judge; b. Phila., Apr. 12, 1928; m. Loretta Esposito (dec. 2005); children: Peter, Joseph. BS, Temple U., 1949; LLB, Duke U., 1952. Bar: Pa. 1952. Pvt. practice, Phila., 1952-74; judge US Magistrate Ct. (ea. dist.) Pa., Phila., 1974—2008. Hearing examiner Pa. Liquor Control Bd., 1963-71. Mem. Phila. Bar Assn. Republican. Died Nov. 13, 2008.

SCULLY, GERALD WILLIAM, economics professor; b. NYC, June 13, 1941; s. Francis Joseph Scully and Helen Zimmerman; divorced; children: Deirdre K., Audra L. BA, Fairleigh Dickinson U., Teaneck, NJ, 1962; MA, The New Sch., NYC, 1965; PhD, Rutgers U., 1968. Asst. prof. economics Ohio U., Athens, 1966-69; assoc. prof. So. Ill. U., Carbondale, 1969-72; prof. So. Meth. U., Dallas, 1972-85, U. Tex., Dallas, 1985—2009; dean Sch. Mgmt., U. Tex., Dallas, 1987-88. Vis. prof. Harvard Coll., Cambridge, Mass., 1975-76; sr. fellow Nat. Ctr. for Policy Analysis, Dallas, 1980-2009; cons. World Bank, Washington, 1985-2009. Author: Business of Major League Baseball, 1989; Constitutional Environments and Economic Growth, 1992; contbr. articles on econs. to profl. jours. NIH grantee Bethesda, Md., 1971-72; Earhart Found. fellow, Ann Arbor, Mich., 1989, 90; Bradley scholar Heritage Found., Washington, 1990-2009. Mem. Am. Econ. Assn., Pub. Choice Soc., Mont Pelerin Soc., Dallas C. of C. Avocation: sailing. Died May 4, 2009.

SEABROOK, JOHN MARTIN, retired food products executive, chemical engineer; b. Seabrook, NJ, Apr. 16, 1917; s. Charles Franklin and Norma Dale (Ivins) S.; m. Anne Schlaudecker, Apr. 5, 1939 (div. 1951); children: Carol Ormsby (Mrs. Jacques P. Boulanger), Elizabeth Anne; m. Elizabeth Ann Toomey, 1956 (dec. 2005); children: John Martin, Bruce Cameron, Aiken SC. BS in Chem. Engring, Princeton, 1939; LL.D. (hon.), Gettysburg Coll., 1974. Registered profl. engr., N.J., Del. Engr. Deerfield Packing Corp., 1939-41; v.p. Seabrook Farms Co., 1941-50, exec. v.p., 1950-54, dir., 1941-59, pres., 1954-59, CEO, 1955-59; dir. Pa. Reading & Seashore Line, 1950-63, N.Y. Ctrl. R.R., 1964-69, Penn Ctrl. R.R., 1968-71; cons. IU Internat. Corp., Wilmington, Del., 1959, v.p., 1960-65, dir., 1963-87, pres., 1965-73, 74-78, chief exec., 1967-80, chmn. bd., 1969-82, chmn. exec. com., 1982-87. Pres., bd. dirs. Cumberland Automobile & Truck Co., 1954-59, Cumberland Warehouse Corp., 1954-59, Salem Farms Corp, N.J., 1948-2009; chmn. bd. dirs. Frick Co., Waynesboro, Pa., 1959-68; chmn., bd. dirs. S.W. Fabricating & Welding Co., Inc., Houston, 1964-68; chmn. Divcon, Inc., Houston, 1967-69; pres. bd. dirs. Internat. Utilities Overseas Capital Corp., Wilmington, 1966-82, chmn., 1970-80; v.p. Gen. Waterworks Corp., Phila., 1959-66, pres., 1966-68, chmn., 1968-71; chmn. bd. dirs. GWC Inc., Phila., 1971-73; pres. Brown Bros. Contractors, Inc., Phila., 1960, chmn. bd. dirs., 1965-67; pres. Am. Portable Irrigation Co., Eugene, Oreg., 1961, chmn. bd. dirs., 1966-68; chmn. bd. dirs. Gotaas-Larsen Shipping Corp., 1963, chmn., 1979, pres., CEO, 1982-88; chmn. bd. dirs. Amvit Corp., Cleve., 1964-68; bd. dirs. Echo Bay Mines Ltd., South Jersey Gas Co., Folsom, N.J., South Jersey Industries, Inc., Folsom, Bell Atlantic Corp.; dir. emeritus Bell Atlantic-N.J., Inc. Mem. N.J. Migrant Labor Bd., 1945-67, chmn., 1955-67; mem. N.J. Bd. Higher Edn., 1967-70, Pres.' Air Quality Adv. Bd., 1968-70; bd. dirs. Brandywine Conservancy, Inc., 1972-95, pres., 1992-93, hon. dir., 1997-2009; trustee Eisenhower Exch. Fellowships, 1974-85; trustee Hitchcock Found., 1991-96, chmn., 1993-96. Mem.: Coaching Club (N.Y.C. and U.K.), Wilmington (Del.) Club, Phila. Club, Knickerbocker Club (N.Y.C.), Racquet and Tennis Club (N.Y.C.), Phi Beta Kappa. Home: Aiken, SC. Died Feb. 11, 2009.

SEALS, DAN WAYLAND, country music singer; b. McCarney, Tex., Feb. 8, 1948; With England Dan & John Ford Coley, 1969-80; recording artist A&M, 1971-80, EMI Records, 1985-86, Liberty Records, 1988-92, Warner Bros., 1992—2009. Albums: (with John Ford Coley) Nights are Forever Without You, 1976, Dowdy Ferry Road, 1977, Dr. Heckle & Mr. Jive, 1979; (solo albums) Stones, 1980, Harbinger, 1982, Rebel Heart, 1983, San Antone, 1984, Won't Be Blue Anymore, 1985, On the Front Line, 1986, The Best, 1988, Rage On, 1988, On Arrival, 1990, Greatest Hits, 1991, The Songwriter, 1992, Walking the Wire, 1992, The Best of Dan Seals, 1994, Fired Up, 1994, In a Quiet Room, 1995, In a Quiet Room, 1998, Certified Hits, 2001, Make It Home, 2002; singles: (with John Ford Coley) I'd Really Love To See You Tonight, 1976, Bop, 1985 (Single of the Year, Country Music Assn., 1986), (with Marie Osmond) Meet Me in Montana, 1985 Recipient Duet of Yr. award (with Marie Osmond) for Meet Me in Montana from Country Music Assn., 1985, Single of Yr. award for Bop from Country Music Assn., 1988. Died Mar. 25, 2009.

SEARLE, WILLARD FRANKLYN, JR., retired marine and salvage engineer; b. Columbus, Ohio, Jan. 17, 1924; m. Peggy Dubois (div.); children: Jane, Polly, Wendy; m. N. Jean Searle Searle (div.); stepchildren: Karen, Paula. BS, U.S. Naval Acad., 1948; MS, MIT, 1952. Engring. duty officer USN, 1947-56, head engring. rschr. Exploratory Diving Unit, 1956-64, supr. salvage, 1964-69, project mgr. shipping acquisition, 1969-70; instr. ocean engring. Marine Maritime Acad., 1971-84; sr. vis. lectr. MIT, Cambridge, Mass., 1971-90; pres. Searle & Associates Ltd., Alexandria, Va., 1993—2009. Mem. various studies, coms., panels Marine Bd., Nat. Rsch. Coun., 1970-84; various adv. panels NOAA, Ocean Thermal Energy Conversion, Dept. Energy, UN Environ. Program & UN Relief Operation, Banladesh; com. diving & salvage Marine Tech. Soc. & MacKinnon Searle Consortium Ltd. Contbr. more than 100 articles to tech. publs.; co-author: Undersea Valor Mem. Am. Soc. Naval Engrs. (Harold E. Saunders award 1985), Nat. Acad. Engring., Inst. Nautical Architects, Soc. Naval Architects & Marine Engrs., Royal Inst. Naval Engrs., Soc. Am. Mil. Engrs. Died Mar. 31, 2009.

SEARS, WILLIAM JOHN, physiologist; b. Oskaloosa, Iowa, Apr. 13, 1931; m. Orpha Mae Fisk, Sept. 9, 1953; children: Michael, Cheryl, John, Patricia. BS in Zoology, Iowa State U., 1957; MS in Physiology, U. So. Calif., 1966, PhD in Physiology, 1968. Commd. 2d lt. USAF, 1957, advanced through grades to col., 1981, physiol. tng. officer March AFB, Calif., 1958-61, chief physiol. tng. Carswell AFB, Tex., 1961-64; grad. instr. U. So. Calif., LA, 1964-68; chief test facilities br. USAF Sch. Aerospace Medicine, Brooks AFB, Tex., 1968-73, chief crew protection br., 1975-81; exch. officer in physiology Royal Airforce Inst. Aviation Medicine, Farnsborough, U.K., 1973-75; dir. bioenviron. engring. S.W. Rsch. Inst., San Antonio, 1981-82; sr. scientist Tech. Inc., San Antonio, 1982-83; pres.

Aerospace Assocs., Inc., San Antonio, from 1983. Cons., lectr., presenter in field; mil. cons. in aerospace physiology USAF Surgeon Gen.; sci. advisor in aerospace physiology resident postdoctoral program AFSC Nat. Coun. Contbr. articles, guest referee to profl. publs.; patentee in field. Decorated Legion of Merit. Fellow Aerospace Med. Assn. (Fred A. Hitchcock award for excellence in aerospace physiology); mem. Aerospace Physiologists Soc. of Aerospace Med. Assn., Sci. Rsch. Soc. N.Am., Human Factors Soc., Air Force Assn. (1st Place Sci. award), Ret. Officers Assn., Sigma Xi. Avocations: hunting, fishing, bridge. Home: San Antonio, Tex. Died Sept. 30, 2007.

SECOR, WILLIAM ROBERT, writer; b. Indpls., Nov. 8, 1937; m. Mary Lou Mohler, Apr. 5, 1980; children: Patricia A., Michael P. BA in History, Ind. U., 1978, MS in Edn., 1979. Tchr. Denver Pub. Schs. Author: Who Knows?, 1999, B.S. Stumbling Toward Valhalla, 2005; co-author: (with Mary L. Secor) Flight of the Spheroid, 2005. Home: Sun City West, Ariz. Died Feb. 15, 2008.

SEDGWICK, EVE KOSOFSKY, literature educator, writer; b. Dayton, Ohio, May 2, 1950; d. Leon and Rita Kosofsky; m. Hal Sedgwick, Aug. 24, 1969. BA, Cornell U., 1971; PhD, Yale U., 1975; LittD (hon.), Amherst Coll. Asst. prof. English Hamilton Coll., Clinton, NY, 1978—81, Boston U., 1981—83; assoc. prof. English Amherst (Mass.) Coll., 1984—88; Newman Ivey White prof. English Duke U., Durham, NC, 1988—97; disting. prof. English CUNY Grad. Ctr., NYC, 1998—2009. Exhibitions include Floating Columns, In the Bardo, Bodhisattva Fractal World; co-editor (with Adam Frank): Shame and Its Sisters: A Silvan Tomkins Reader; co-editor: (with Andrew Parker) Performativity and Performance; co-editor: (with Gary Fisher) Gary in Your Pocket: Stories and Notebooks of Gary Fisher, 1996; author: Between Men: English Literature and Male Homosocial Desire, 1985, The Coherence of Gothic Conventions, 1986, Epistemology of the Closet, 1990 (MLA James Russell Lowell Award, hon. mention, 1991), Tendencies, 1993, Fat Art, Thin Art, 1995; editor: Novel Gazing: Queer Readings in Fiction, 1997; author: A Dialogue on Love, 1999, Touching Feeling: Affect, Pedagogy, Performativity, 2003; series co-editor Series Q, 1992—2003; contbg. editor: MAMM: Women, Cancer, Community, 1998—2003. Patient adv. Calif. Breast Cancer Rsch. Program, San Francisco, 2002; exec. coun. MLA, NYC, 1996—99; mem. supervisory com., trustee English Inst., Cambridge, Mass., 1986—97. Recipient Morton Dauwen Zabel award, Am. Acad. Arts and Letters, 1995, Brudner award in Gay/Lesbian Studies, Yale U., 2002; named Mrs. William Beckman vis. prof., U. of Calif., Berkeley, 1987, David Kessler lectr., Ctr. for Lesbian and Gay Studies, CUNY, 1998; fellow, John Simon Guggenheim Meml. Found., 1987—88, Nat. Humanities Ctr., 1991—92, NEH, 1995—96; Mellon Postdoctoral fellow in humanities, Cornell U., 1976—78, faculty fellow, Mary Ingraham Bunting Inst., 1983—84. Buddhist. Home: New York, NY. Died Apr. 12, 2009.

SEE, RUTH DOUGLAS, religious studies educator, editor, researcher; b. Balt., Mar. 16, 1910; d. Robert Gamble and Louisa (Douglas) Spear S. BA, Mary Baldwin Coll., 1931; MRE, N.Y. Theol. Sem., 1934; PhD, NYU, 1953. Instr. Stillman Inst., Tuscaloosa, Ala., 1938-45; curriculum editor Presbyn. Bd. Edn., Richmond, Va., 1949-68; asst. prof. Va. Commonwealth U., Richmond, 1968-74; rsch. historian Hist. Found. Presbyn. Ch., Montreat, N.C., 1974-84; ret., 1984. Work in edn., Taipei, Taiwan, 1956-57. Author: Make the Bible Your Own, 1959, What Can We Do?, 1965, R. Gamble See: A Memoir, 1981. Mem. planning com. Nat. Coun. Chs., N.Y.C., 1949-60; elder Presbyn. Ch. Recipient Mary Baldwin Coll. Sesquicentennial medallion, 1992. Mem. Presbyn. Hist. Soc., LWV, Nature Conservancy, Amnesty Internat., Common Cause. Avocations: music, reading, writing. Home: Winchester, Va. Died Oct. 2, 2007.

SEEGER, MICHAEL, musician, singer, folklorist; b. NYC, Aug. 15, 1933; s. Charles Louis and Ruth Porter (Crawford) S.; m. Marjorie L. Ostrow, Dec. 20, 1960 (div. 1968); children: Kim, Arley, Jeremy; m. Alice L. Gerrard, Aug. 16, 1970 (div.); m. Alexia Smith, Aug. 27, 1995. Guest lectr. English dept. U. Calif., Fresno, 1974; mem. jazz/folk/ethnic music sect. Nat. Endowment for Arts, 1973-77; dir. Am. Old Time Music Festival, 1975-78, Rockbridge Mountain Music Conv., Buena Vista, Va., 1986-92. Performs Appalachian vocal and instrumental music in a variety of styles at concerts, folk festivals, on radio and TV in U.S. and abroad; also numerous record albums and documentary recordings from traditional folk musicians and dancers; founding mem. New Lost City Ramblers, 1958-2009, Strange Creek Singers, 1968-76, Bent Mountain Band, 1981. Trustee John Edwards Meml. Found., UCLA, 1962—2009; bd. dirs. Newport (R.I.) Folk Festival, 1963-71, Nat. Folk Festival, Washington, 1972-78, Smithsonian Am. Folklife Co., 1970-76. Recipient 1st prize banjo category Galax Va. Old Time Fiddlers conf., 1975, Ralph J. Gleason Meml. award Rex Found., 1994; award of merit Internat. Bluegrass Music Assn., 1995; Grammy nominee for best traditional folk album, 1986, 91, 94, 97, 98; Nat. Endowment Arts grantee, 1975, 82, 84, 87; vis. scholar Smithsonian Instn., 1983; Guggenheim fellow, 1984. Home: Lexington, Va. Died Aug. 7, 2009.

SEENO, MARGARET ESTHER, mental health nurse, educator; b. Grindstone, Pa., Apr. 11, 1931; d. John S. and Charlette Brooks; m. Robert Seeno, June 1952; children: Cheryl Ann, Nancy Jo. Diploma, Westmoreland Sch. Nursing, 1952; BSNE, U. Pitts., 1959, PhD, 1982; MSN, Case Western Res. U., 1976. RN, Ohio. Dir. nursing svc. Metro Gen. Hosp., Cleve., dir. Sch. Nursing; asst. prof. U. Akron (Ohio); clin. specialist Clev. VA Med. Ctr. Adj. asst. prof. Case Western Res. U., Kent State U. Named Most Disting. Alumna Westmoreland Nurses' Assn., 1987. Mem. ANA (cert. adminstr.), Ohio Nurses' Assn., Greater Cleve. Nurses' Assn., Alpha Mu Soc. Home: Aurora, Ohio. Died Apr. 5, 2008.

SEGAL, SHELDON JEROME, biologist, educator, foundation administrator; b. NYC, Mar. 15, 1926; s. Morris M. and Florence (Bogen) S.; m. Harriet Ellen Feinberg, May 22, 1961; children: Amy Robin, Jennifer Ann, Laura Jane. BA, Dartmouth Coll., 1947; postgrad., U. Geneva, 1947-48; MS, U. Iowa, 1951, PhD, 1952; MD (hon.), U. Tampere, Finland, 1984, U. Upssala, Sweden, 1985; LHD (hon.), Mercy Coll. Rsch. scientist William S. Merrill Co., Cin., 1952-53; rsch. assoc., asst. prof. U. Iowa, 1953-56; asst. med. dir. Population Coun., NYC, 1956-63, med. dir., 1963-78, v.p., 1969-76, sr. v.p., 1976-78; affiliate Rockefeller U., NYC, 1956-76, adj. prof., 1977-87; dir. population scis. Rockefeller Found., 1978-91; disting. scientist Population Coun., NYC, from 1991. Lectr. Columbia U., 1959-61; vis. prof. All-India Inst. Med. Scis., New Delhi, 1962-63, Amir Chand lectr., 1975; mem. Marine Biol. Lab, Woods Hole, Mass.; cons. World Bank, WHO, NIH, Ford Found., Indian Govt., UN Office Sci. and Tech., UN Fund Population Activities; mem. com. on contraceptive tech. NAS, 1977-80, com. on health effects of marijuana Inst. Medicine, 1981-82, NAS com. on demographic impact of contraceptive tech., 1988-89, nat. rsch. con., overview com. for Indo-U.S. sci. initiative, 1985-89; adv. com. on human reproduction FDA; cons. to dir. Nat. Inst. Child Health and Human Devel., 1978-80; plenary lectr. 3d World Congress Endocrinology, 1968, Upjohn lectr. Am. Fertility Soc., 1971, plenary lectr. World Fertility Congress, 1975, Sigma Xi lectr. U. Idaho, 1976, plenary lectr. World Congress on Ob-Gyn., 1976, lectr. Chinese Acad. Scis., 1977, Carl Gemzell lectr. U. Upssala, 1982, Pierre Soupart lectr. Axel Munthe Found., 1988, Alpha Omega Alpha lectr. U. Pa. Coll. Medicine, 1989, plenary lectr. World Congress on Human Reproduction, 1990, 2005; hon. prof. Peking Union Med. Coll., Beijing, 1987, Chinese Acad. Scis., 1988; trustee Marine Biol. Lab., 1985—, chmn. bd. trustees, 1991-2004; pres. 10th World Congress on Human Reproduction, 1999, 2004. Co-editor 8 books; co-author: (with Elsimor M. Coutilho) Is Menstruation Obsolete?, 1999, (with Luigi Mastroianni Jr.) Hormone Use in Menopause and Male Amdropause: A Choice for Women and Men, 2003, Under the Banyan Tree: A Population Scientist's Odyssey, 2003; contbr. 300 articles to profl. jours. Trustee Rye Country Day Sch., 1979-85, pres. bd. trustees, 1981-85; trustee Ctr. for Reproductive Law and Policy, 1992—. Lt. (j.g.) USNR, 1943-45. Decorated Order Comdr. of Lion (Finland); recipient Honor award Innsbruck U., Austria, hon. citation Pres. of India, 1978, Clarence J. Gamble award World Acad. Arts and Scis., 1980, Joseph C. Wilson award Rochester Assn. for UN, 1981, UN Population award, 1984, Axel Munthe award in medicine Axel Munthe Found., Italy, 1985, Sci. award Planned Parenthood Fedn. Am., 1990, Dmitirus N. Chorafas award in medicine Swiss Acad. Scis., 1995, Joseph Bolivar DeLee Humanitarian award, U. Chgo. Hosps., 2007. Fellow AAAS, Royal Coll. Obstetricians and Gynecologists (hon.); mem. Am. Reproductive Med. Soc. (hon. v.p. 1975-76, trustee found. 1975-77), Endocrine Soc., Internat. Soc. for Study Reprodn. (pres. 1968-72), Coun. Fgn. Rels., Internat. Acad. Human Reproduction (hon. pres. 2005), Mexican Acad. Medicine (hon.), Inst. Medicine, Dartmouth Club N.Y., Woods Hole Yacht Club. Home: New York, NY. Died Oct. 17, 2009.

SEIDELMAN, RAYMOND MICHAEL, political science educator; b. Redwood City, Calif., Aug. 6, 1951; s. Herbert Lester and Thelma Marie (Manning) S.; m. Fay Chazin, May 30, 1982; children: Eva, Rosa. BA in Politics, U. Calif., Santa Cruz, 1973; MA in Govt., Cornell U., 1976, PhD in Govt., 1979. Asst. prof. Hobart & William Smith Coll., Geneva, N.Y., 1978-79; asst. prof. polit. sci. SUNY/Albany, 1979-82, Sarah Lawrence Coll., Bronxville, N.Y., 1982-91, prof. polit. sci., from 1991; sr. fellow Rockefeller Inst., Albany, 1986-87; Fulbright scholar Hankuk U., Seoul, 1992-93. Vis. prof. Johns Hopkins U., Nanjing, China, 1987-88. Author: Disenchanted Realists; co-editor: Discipline and History, 1993, The Democratic Debate, 1995; contbr. articles to profl. jours. Mem. Am. Polit. Sci. Assn., Rainbow Coalition N.Y. (advt. com. 1984-85). Democrat. Avocations: cross country skiing, canoeing. Home: Ossining, NY. Died Oct. 30, 2007.

SEIDEMAN, WALTER ELMER, food scientist, executive; b. West Bend, Wis., Jan. 21, 1933; s. Raymund F. and Clara Selma (Gerner) S.; m. Cathy A. Carnito, Sept. 7, 1958 (div. Apr. 1976); children: Russell C., Keith R., Bonnie A.; m. Ruth E. Young, May 21, 1988. BS, U. Wis., 1959; MS, U. Mo., 1962, PhD, 1966. Instr. in agr. U. Mo., Columbia, 1963-65; food scientist Wilson & Co., Chgo., 1965-70; asst. to rsch., tech. divsn. mgr. Wilson-Sinclair Co., Chgo., 1970-71, mgr. rsch.-tech. divsn., 1971-72; divsn. mgr. rsch.-tech. Wilson Co., Okla. City, 1972-76; owner Walter E. Seideman & Assocs., Okla. City, from 1976; dir. OKLABS, Inc., Okla. City, from 1989. Sci. adv. com. Nat. Cheese Coun., Chgo., 1966-70, Poultry & Egg Inst., Chgo. 1966-72, Am. Meat Inst. of Am., Chgo., 1971-76, Rsch. and Devel. Assn. for Mil. Food and Packaging Systems, 1971-76. Contbr. articles to Poultry Jour., 1963-69. Sgt. USMC, 1951-54, Korea. Mem. AOAC Internat., Inst. of Food Technologists, Am. Meat Sci. Assn., Poultry Sci. Assn. Achievements include creation of innovative food processing procedures and products. Home: Oklahoma City, Okla. Died July 23, 2008.

SEIDL, HENRY WILLIAM, advertising executive, retired; b. Balt., Dec. 23, 1924; s. Henry William and Sarah Rebecca (Evans) S.; m. Amelia Alonzo, Nov. 27, 1954; children: Kimberly Melia, Julie Anne. BS in Mktg., St. Louis U., 1949. Mgr. sales promotions Foster & Kleiser, San Francisco, 1953-60, mgr. eastern sales promotions San Francisco, Detroit, 1960-62, supr. sales Los Angeles, 1962-65, dir. sales promotions, 1965-71, v.p. mktg. services, 1971-84, sr. v.p., 1984-87, mktg. advisor, cons., 1987-88; sr. v.p. mktg. Computer Image Systems, Torrance, Calif., 1988-90; cons. Metromedia Techs., 1990-91; ret., 1991. Mem. exec. com., bd. dirs. The Advt. Council. Bd. dirs. Greater Los Angeles Visitors and Conv. Bur., 1985—. Served with USAAC, 1943-46; served to 1st lt. USAF, 1950-53. Decorated D.F.C., Air Medal with oak leaf cluster. Mem. The Advt. Council (bd. dirs., exec. com. 1985—). Republican. Avocations: photography, jewelry designing, bonsai cultivation, geography. Home: Van Nuys, Calif. Died Apr. 4, 2008.

SEIDMAN, LEWIS WILLIAM (BILL SEIDMAN), television commentator, publisher; b. Grand Rapids, Mich., Apr. 29, 1921; s. Frank E. and Esther (Lubetsky) S.; m. Sarah Berry, Mar. 3, 1944; children: Thomas, Tracy, Sarah, Carrie, Meg, Robin. AB, Dartmouth Coll., 1943; LL.B., Harvard U., 1948; MBA, U. Mich., 1949. Bar: Mich. 1949, D.C. 1977. Spl. asst. fin. affairs to Gov. State of Mich., 1963-66; nat. mng. partner Seidman & Seidman C.P.A.s, NYC, 1969-74; asst. to Pres. for econ. affairs The White House, 1974-77; CFO Phelps Dodge Corp., NYC, 1977-82, vice chmn., 1980-82; dean Coll. Bus. Adminstrn. Ariz. State U., Tempe, 1982-85; chmn. FDIC, Washington, 1985—91; chief commentator Sta. CNBC-TV, 1991—2009; pub. Bank Dir. mag., 1992—2009; econ. cons. The Bankers Bank, 2007—09. Chmn. Detroit Fed. Res. Bank Chgo., 1970, Resolution Trust Corp. (RTC), 1989-91; co-chair White House Conf. on Productivity, 1983-84. Co-author (with Steven L. Shancke): Productivity: The American Advantage: How 50 U.S. Companies Are Regaining the Competitive Edge, 1989; author: Full Faith and Credit: The Great S&L Debacle and Other Washington Sagas, 2000. Lt. USNR, 1942-46. Decorated Bronze Star. Mem. D.C. Bar Assn., Chevy Chase Club (Md.), Univ. Club (N.Y.C.), Crystal Downs Club (Mich.), Nantucket Yacht Club (MA). Home: Bradenton, Fla. Died May 13, 2009.

SEKULOVICH, MLADEN See MALDEN, KARL

SELIGER, CHARLES, artist; b. NYC, June 3, 1926; s. George Zekowski and Hortense S.; m. Ruth Lewin, June 20, 1948 (dec. May 1975); children: Robert, Mark; m. Lenore Klebanow, 1975. Student in pvt. art instrn., WPA Sch., 1940. Robert H. and Clarice Smith Disting. vis. prof. George Washington U., Washington, 1990; lectr. Katonah Art Mus., 1990; panelist Terra Mus. Art, Chgo., 1990, Whitney Mus. Am. Art, N.Y.C., 1990, Michael Rosenfeld Gallery, N.Y.C., 1994. One man shows include Peggy Guggenheim Gallery, N.Y.C., 1945-46, Carlebach Gallery, 1948, DeYoung Meml. Mus., San Francisco, 1949, Whitney Mus. ann., 1949-57, Willard Gallery, N.Y.C., 1951, 53, 55, 57, 61, 62, 66, 68, Seligman Gallery, Seattle, 1955, 58, 65, Nassau Community Coll., N.Y.C., 1965, Wooster Community Art Center, Conn., 1969, Andrew Crispo Gallery, 1973, 75, 76, 78, 80, 81, 83, Mus. Modern Art, Hayden Calhoun Gallery, Dallas, Makler Gallery, Phila., 1979, Miami-Dade Community Coll., 1981, Jacksonville (Fla.) Art Mus., 1981, Gallery Schlesinger-Boisanté, 1985, 86, Guggenheim Mus., 1986, Galerie Lopes, Zurich, Switzerland, 1986, 89, 95, 97, 99, 2003, 2006, Greenville County Mus. Art, S.C., 2003, others; exhibited in Norlyst Gallery, N.Y.C., 1942, 67 Gallery, N.Y.C., 1943, David Porter Gallery, Washington, 1945, Four Arts Club, Palm Beach, Fla., 1946, Va. Mus. Fine Arts, 1946, U. Iowa, 1946, Salon des Realites Nouvelle, Paris, France, 1948, Bklyn. Mus., 1949, Cornell U., 1951, Art Inst. Chgo., 1961, 64, Syracuse Mus. Fine Arts, 1953, Nebr. Art Assn., 1953, Am. Acad. Arts & Letters, 1965, 67, 68, Smithsonian Inst., 1968, Taft Mus., Cin., 1981, Okla. Art Ctr., 1981, Saidenberg Gallery, N.Y.C., 1983, 89, Wight Art Gallery, UCLS, traveling to Nat. Gallery Modern Art, New Delhi, 1987, 88, Frances Wolfson Art Gallery, Miami, Fla., 1987, Guggenheim Mus., traveling to Venice, Italy, 1987, 88, Sid Deutsch Gallery, N.Y.C., 1989, 90, Weatherspoon Gallery, Greensboro, N.C., 1989, Nat. Acad. Mus., NYC, 2005, many others.; exhbn. Abstract Expressionism: Other Dimensions traveling to Lowe Art Mus., Coral Gables, Fla, Terra Art Mus., Chgo. (also panelist), Jane Voorhees Zimmerli Art Mus., Rutgers, New Brunswick, 1990, 92; works in permanent collections Herbert F. Johnson Mus., Cornell U., Ithaca, N.Y., Norton Mus. Art, West Palm Beach, Fla., Addison Gallery, Andover, Mass., Munson Williams Proctor Mus., Utica, N.Y., Guggenheim Mus., Miss. Mus. Art, Whitney Mus., High Mus., Atlanta, Terra Mus. Am. Art, Evanston, Ill., Mus. Modern Art, Chgo. Art Inst., Newark Mus. Art, Iowa State U., Municipal Art Mus., The Hague, Holland, Tel Aviv Mus., Balt. Mus. Art, Hirshhorn Mus. and Sculpture Garden, Met. Mus. Art, N.Y.C., Phillips Collection, Washington, Carnegie Inst., Pitts., Rutgers U., Jane Voorhees Zimmerli Art Mus., New Brunswick, N.J., Worcester (Mass.) Art Mus., Nat. Mus. Am. Art Smithsonian Inst., Washington, Met. Mus. Art, NYC, Peggy Guggenheim Collection,

Venice, Italy, others, also numerous pvt. collections; artist, 1960—. Recipient Pollock-Krasner Lifetime Achievement Award. Home: Mount Vernon, NY. Died Oct. 1, 2009.

SELIGMAN, DANIEL, editor; b. NYC, Sept. 25, 1924; s. Irving and Clare (O'Brien) S.; m. Mary Gale Sherburn, May 23, 1953; children: Nora, William Paul. Student, Rutgers U., 1941-42; AB, NYU, 1946. Editl. asst. New Leader, 1946; asst. editor Am. Mercury, 1946-50; assoc. editor Fortune mag., 1950-59, editl. bd., 1959-66, asst. mng. editor, 1966-69, exec. editor, 1970-77, assoc. mng. editor, 1977-87, contbg. editor, 1988-97, Forbes mag., 1997—2009. Sr. staff editor all Time, Inc. (publs.), 1969-70. Author: A Question of Intelligence: The IQ Debate in America, 1992. Served in US Army. Home: New York, NY. Died Jan. 31, 2009.

SELLERS, WAYNE CHADICK, retired publisher, retired editor; b. Brady, Tex., Mar. 10, 1916; s. Marcellus Stephenson Sellers and Martha Jane Chadick; m. Camilla Ann Browning, June 29, 1946 (dec. June 1996). BA, Tex. Tech U., 1938; postgrad., U. Tex., 1940-41. Statistician Ft. Worth Star-Telegram, 1943-50; prodn. mgr. San Francisco News, 1951-52; bus. mgr. Sherman (Tex.) Democrat, 1953-59; pub. Rock Hill (S.C.) Herald, 1959-66; editor, pub. Palestine (Tex.) Herald-Press, 1966-80. Mem. bd. mgrs. Tex. State R.R., 1969-73; mem. adv. coun. U. Tex. Coll. communication, Austin, 1979—. Chmn. Palestine United Way, 1968, Northeast Tex. Lib. Sys. Adv. Coun., Garland, 1986—, Palestine Pub. Libr. Bd., 1979—; vol. lobbyist Tex. Libr. Assn., 1983; chmn. Reporter Bd., United Meth. Ch., Dallas, 1980-82. Named to Hall of Fame Tex. Tech U. Sch. Mass Comm., Lubbock, 1979; named Trustee of Yr. Tex. Libr. Assn., Houston, 1981, Nat. Advocacy Honor Roll Mem., Am. Libr. Assn., chgo., 2000, Builder of Palestine, Palestine C. of c., 1982, Mr. Books, Tex. State Libr. and Archives Commn., Austin, 1983. Democrat. Methodist. Avocations: amateur radio, travel, collecting books. Home: Palestine, Tex. Died Nov. 25, 2007.

SENGSTACK, DAVID KELLS, publisher; b. Bklyn., June 22, 1922; s. John Fred and Edna Josephine (Maloney) S.; m. Anita Elizabeth Browne, Aug. 12, 1944 (div. 1975); children: Jeffrey Scott, Lynn Ann, Gregg Clift; m. Arlene M. Rambaum Dec. 30, 1978 (div. 1986); m. Alice H. Fleischman, Sept. 30, 1988; adopted children: Michele Amy, Elizabeth Anne. BSME, Rutgers U., 1944. Mktg. dir. Birch Tree Group Ltd., Princeton, N.J., 1947-57, pres., chmn., 1957-89; owner, pres. The Sengstack Group, Ltd., from 1989. Pres. Early Childhood Found.; trustee Bucknell U., Lewisburg, Pa., 1980-84, McCarter Ctr. for Performing Arts, Princeton, 1983-90, Carrier Clin. Devel. Fund, 1987-93; mem. vis. com. Eastman Sch. Music, Rochester, N.Y., 1984-93. Served with C.E., AUS, 1942-47, 50-52, Korea. Mem. Cliff Dwellers Club, Mid-Am. Club, Nassau Club, N.Y. Athletic Club. Avocations: reading, travel, museums. Died Dec. 18, 2007.

SENN, PETER RICHARD, economist, consultant; b. Milw., Nov. 22, 1923; s. Paul and Dorothie (Severens) S.; m. Mary Stone, Aug. 28, 1947; children: Martha, Paul. Student, Oreg. State Coll., 1941-43; cert. in elec. engring., Syracuse U., 1944; MA in Econs., U. Chgo., 1947; Docteur en droit with honors, U. Paris, 1951. Asst. prof. econs. Pa. State U., 1950-52; assoc. prof. econs. and social sci. Wright Jr. Coll., Chgo., 1953-64; prof. econs. and social sci. Chgo. City Coll., 1964-84; prof. emeritus City Colls. Chgo., from 1984. Vis. prof. Pub. Adminstrn. and Pub. Fin. U. Tartu, Estonia, 2000—; asst. dir. ethical and moral stds. project Nat. Inst. Labor Edn., 1960-62; TV coord. Chgo. Bd. Edn., 1962; bd. dirs. Law in Am. Soc. Found.; trustee Ill. Coun. Econ. Edn., 1984-87; bd. dirs. Pivan Engring. Co., 1955-75, Rentronics Corp., 1973-75; keynote spkr. state legis. conf. Ill. coun. NASW, 1974; cons. in field. Author: Social Science and Its Methods, 1971, (with others) The World of Economics, 1988; contbr. articles on history of econ. thought to profl. jours. Project dir. Chgo. Area Plan for Workers' Mental Health Roosevelt U., Chgo., 1963-64' co-dir. cooperative project for 2-yr. colls. NSF, 1971; active Nat. Task Force on Test of Econ. Literacy Joint Coun. Econ. Edn., 1976-79. Tech. sgt. U.S. Army, 1942-46. Decorated Philippine Liberation medal with bronze star. Mem. Am. Econs. Assn., Am. Ednl. Rsch. Assn., Am. Evaluation Assn., Apple, IBM, Microsoft Programmers and Developers Assn. (cert.), Ill. Consumer Edn. Assn. (founder, parliamentarian 1973-80), Social Sci. Edn. Consortium (founder), Social Sci. History Assn., Ill. Econs. Assn. (pres. 1975). Avocations: wilderness camping, fishing, canoeing. Home: Evanston, Ill. Died Dec. 11, 2007.

SENYSZYN, JAMES NICHOLAS, market scientist; b. NYC, Sept. 1, 1944; s. Nicholas and Mary Stella (Shidlauskas) S. BS, SUNY, Stony Brook, 1966; MS, U. Ill., 1967; MBA, NYU, 1978, MPhil, 1982. Programmer analyst Fed. Res. Bank of N.Y., NYC, 1972-75; systems programmer G.T.E. Info. Systems, NYC, 1975-77; systems analyst Chase Manhattan Bank, NYC, 1977-78; staff supr. ATT Long Distance, Bedminster, N.J., 1978-80; sr. tech. specialist Western Union, Mahwah, N.J., 1980-82, cons., system analyst Upper Saddle River, N.J., 1982-84, dir. product mktg. of long distance svc., 1984-85; prin. engr. Gen. DataComm, Middlebury, Conn., 1985-91; cons. Audicom, South Plainfield, N.J., 1993-95; Market scientist First Union Bank, Charlotte, N.C., from 1996. Peace activist N.J. SANE/Freeze, Ridgewood, 1978-85, Ctr. for Def. Info., Washington, 1982—, Conn. SANE/Freeze, Hartford, 1985-93, Peace Action, 1993—; atheist activist Conn. Chpt. Am. Atheists, Bloomfield, 1986-89, Am. Atheists, 1987—, N.E. Atheist Assn., Simsbury, 1989-93; AIDS activist AIDS Coalition to Unleash Power, New Haven, 1988-93, ACT UP/N.J., Highland Pk., 1994-95. Named Atheist of Yr., Conn. Chpt. Am. Atheists, 1989, Martin Luther King Freedom award Ctrl. Conn. Humanist Assn., 1989, Atheist Outreach award Am. Atheists, 1990. Mem. Am. Atheists. Avocations: writing letters to editors, reading, listening to music, polit. campaigning, policy issue rsch. Home: Peoria, Ill. Died Nov. 29, 2007.

SEOANE, EMILIO, accountant; b. Havana, Cuba, Oct. 13, 1944; came to U.S., 1960; s. Emilio M. and Carmen Seoane; m. Angeles Gonzalez, Sept. 13, 1988; children: Heidi, Ledu. Acct., Havana U., 1959. Acct. Seoane Bookkeeping Svc., Miami, Fla., 1964-66, LA, 1967-79, Empresa Svcs. Hispanos, Anaheim, Calif., 1980-88, Latinos Enterprise, Inc., Santa Ana, Calif., from 1988. Mem. Nat. Soc. Pub. Accts., Nat. Notary Assn., Am. Soc. Notaries, Nat. Assn. Tax Cons., Nat. Soc. Tax Profls. Republican. Roman Catholic. Avocation: philatelist. Died Mar. 15, 2008.

SEPESI, JOHN DAVID, artist; b. Monessen, Pa., Aug. 12, 1931; s. John Lloyd and Gizella Elizabeth (Gnip) S. AA, San Bernardino Valley Coll., 1957; BA, Mexico City Coll., 1958. Head cashier Club Cal-Neva Casino, Reno, 1983-90. One-man shows include Washoe County Libr., 1987, Reno City Hall Gallery, 1990, Town Ctr. Gallery, 1992; exhibited in group shows at Wilbur D. May Mus., Reno, 1986, Reno City Hall Gallery, 1987, 88, Shoppers Sq., Reno, 1990-91, Brewery Art Ctr., Carson City, 1991-93, Las Vegas Hist. Soc. Mus., 1990, El Wiegand Mus., Reno, 1990, Town Ctr. Gallery, 1992-93, Nev. State Fair, Reno, 1993-95, River Gallery, Reno, 1994-95, Glenn Duncan Sch., Reno, 1995; contbr. articles to profl. jours. Staff sgt. USAF, 1952-56. Mem. Nev. Artists Assn. (v.p. 1990—, exec. bd. 1991—), Sierra Watercolor Soc., Sierra Arts Found., Nev. Mus. Art, Nev. State Coun. on the Arts, Nev. Alliance for the Arts. Republican. Home: Reno, Nev. Died Jan. 4, 2008.

SETZLER, EDWARD ALLAN, lawyer; b. Kansas City, Mo., Nov. 3, 1933; s. Edward A. and Margaret (Parshall) S.; m. Helga E. Friedemann, May 20, 1972; children: Christina, Ingrid, Kirstin. BA, U. Kans., 1955; JD, U. Wis., 1962. Bar: Mo. 1962, US Tax Ct. 1962. Assoc. Spencer, Fane, Britt & Browne, Kansas City, 1962-67, ptnr., 1968-2000, mng. ptnr., 1974-77, 78-82, chmn. trust and estate sect., 1974-2000; ptnr. Husch & Eppenberger, LLC, 2000—06, Lathrop & Gage, from 2006. Co-author: Missouri Estate Administration, 1984, supplements, 1987—2008, Missouri Estate Planning, 1986, supplements, 1988—2008; contbg. editor: Understanding Living Trusts, 1990—2004, A Will is Not the Way--The Living Trust Alternative, 1988; bd. editors: Wis. Law Rev., 1961—62. Bd. govs., bd. dirs., chmn. found. com. Am. Royal, 1982—2006; mem. planning giving com. Nelson Atkins Mus. Art, 1984—95; mem. deferred giving com. Children's Mercy Hosp., from 1991; mem. Kansas City Estate Planning Symposium Com., 1984—92, chmn., 1991; mem. adv. com. Greater Kansas City Cmty. Found., from 2000; trustee Zoo Learning Fund, from 2002; mem. adv. bd. Children's Svc. League, 2003—06. Fellow: Am. Coll. Trust and Estate Counsel (state chmn. 1992—97, mem. state membership com. 1986—2001); mem.: Assn. Conflict Resolutions, Estate Planning Soc. Kansas City (co-founder 1965, pres. 1983—84, dir. 1984—85, mem. social com. from 1968), Kansas City Met. Bar Assn. (lectr., chmn. probate and trust 1979, 1992, vice chmn. 1983—85, 1991, legis. rev. com. 1991—95), Mo. Bar Assn. (lectr., vice chmn. probate and estate planning com. 1994—97), Sigma Xi, Order of the Coif, Phi Delta Phi. Home: Kansas City, Mo. Died Jan. 4, 2009.

SEWALL, JOHN LADD, retired aerospace engineer; b. Wakefield, Mass., Mar. 30, 1920; s. William and Sarah Elizabeth (Trask) S.; m. Nellie Bigham Grier, Oct. 8, 1949; children: William Grier, Martha Dudley Sewall Rees, Richard Warren, Jonathan Mark. AB, Dartmouth Coll., 1942, CE, 1943; M in Applied Mechanics, U. Va., 1957. Registered profl. engr., Va. Specification writer Lockheed Aircraft Corp., Burbank, Calif., 1943-44; civil, aero. and aerospace engr. nat. adv. com. aeronautics NASA, Hampton, Va., 1946-80. Contbr. articles to profl. jours. Pres., v.p. various PTAs, Newport News, Va., 1960's, 70's; active, chmn. adv. com. for People with Disabilities, Newport News, 1984-89. Sgt. U.S. Army, 1944-46, ETO. Mem. AIAA, Engrs. Club Va. Peninsula, Dartmouth Soc. Engrs. Presbyterian. Avocations: photography, swimming, singing in church choir, woodworking. Home: Newport News, Va. Died Jan. 30, 2007.

SEXTON, CHARLINE, secondary school educator; b. Kennett, Mo., Dec. 01; d. Charles Jerome and Dora Myrtle (Wilburn) Lemonds; m. Marcus L. Sexton, Mar. 3, 1939; children: Charolyn Linch, Dan Sexton, Marc Sexton, Elizabeth Morrison. BA with honors, U. Tex Arlington, 1969, MA, 1976. Tchr. English Ft. Worth I.S.D., 1969-89. Author (mag.) Arlington Review, 1966. Lectr. various churches, Tex., Ark., Tenn., 1963-98. Mem. Ex Libris Book Review Club. Avocation: reading. Home: Fort Worth, Tex. Died Jan. 14, 2009.

SEXTON, WENDELL PHILLIP JAMES, elementary school educator; b. Kansas City, Mo., Mar. 28, 1928; BA, Ctrl. State U., Wilberforce, Ohio, 1954; student, U. Chgo., 1962; postgrad., Ind. U., Gary, 1962, U. Mo., Kansas City, 1964. Cert. tchr. Colo, Tex. Substitute tchr. Gary (Ind.) Pub. Schs.; tchr. Warren Beatty Me. Hosp., Westfield, Ind., Chgo. Pub. Schs.; writer Gary (Ind.)Crusader; tchr. Denver Pub. Sch.; interviewer Tex. Employment Office, Houston. Writer-in-residence Tex. Commn. on Arts, Palestine, 1974—75; writer, mem. Tex. Commn. on the Arts, Austin, 1975—2001. Author: Why Should I Love the White Man, 1970, Poet's Corner, 1975, The Making of an Afro Indian 1835 to 2002, 2002. V. p. Turner Elementary Sch. Coun., Houston, 1991. Mem.: NAACP, Buffalo Soldiers, Kappa Alpha Psi. Avocations: boxing, dance, genealogy, mathematics. Died Aug. 11, 2008.

SHAEFFER, JOHN NEES, historian, educator; b. Wapato, Wash., Dec. 7, 1929; s. John Nees Shaeffer and Helen May Kerns. BA, Wash. State U., 1953; AM, Harvard U., 1957; PhD, U. Wis., 1968. Instr. history Columbia Basin Coll., Pasco, Wash., 1957—63; prof. history Calif. State U., Northridge, 1968—92, prof. emeritus, from 1992. Contbr. articles to profl. jours. 1st lt. USAF, 1953—57, Korea. Mem.: Orgn. Am. Historians (life), Am. Hist. Assn. (life), Phi Kappa Phi (life). Deceased.

SHAFER, DALLAS EUGENE, psychology gerontology educator, minister; b. Holyoke, Colo., Jan. 26, 1936; s. Howard C. and Mary M. (Legg) S.; m. Opal Iline Bruner, Aug. 22, 1954; children: Kim, Jana, Amy. BA, Nebr. Christian, 1958; postgrad., U. Colo., Colorado Springs, 1968-72, U. So. Calif., LA, 1973; PhD, Walden U., 1978. Cert. clin. pastoral counseling; ordained to ministry Christian Ch., 1958. Minister Christian Ch., Colorado Springs, 1960-62, Julesburg, Colo., 1962-67; instr. of honors program U. Colo., Colorado Springs, 1974, 75; instr. psychology-gerontology Coll. of St. Francis, Colorado Springs, 1982, 84, 93; adj. grad. prof. U. Colo., Colorado Springs, from 1992; sr. minister counseling Christian Ch., Security, Colo., 1967-93; pastor of counseling Woodman Valley Chapel, Colorado Springs, 1995; prof. psychology/gerontology Pikes Peak C.C., Colorado Springs, 1969-96, dept. chair psychology/gerontology, 1969-92, pres. faculty assn., 1992-94, 95-96. Vice chair devel. team Westley White Rehab. Ctr., Julesburg, 1966-67; trainer-cons. Pikes Peak Hospice, Colorado Springs, 1980-81; cons. St. Thomas Moore Hospice, Canon City, Colo., 1982, Sante Cristo Hospice, Pueblo, Colo., 1983-84; trainer for grief teams in U.S. mil. pers., Hawaii, Japan, 1994. Author: Approaches to Palliative Care, 1978, 92, Delphi-80-Study of Ministry, 1981; contbr. articles to Christian Standard. Bd. dirs. Colo. State Bd. Examiner for Nursing Home, Denver, 1977-83, chmn., 1981-83; moderator Conf. on Prevention of Violence-Sch. Dist. # 3, Security, 1992. Mem. Colo. Edn. Assn. (mem. higher edn. com. 1992-94). Avocations: cross country skiing, hi country 4 wheeling, antiques. Home: Colorado Springs, Colo. Died Aug. 15, 2008.

SHAFFER, CLIFTON EUGENE, JR., bank executive; b. Akron, Aug. 10, 1931; s. Clifton Eugene Sr. and Flossie Ruth (Whippo) S.; m. Karole Lee Shank, Feb. 22, 1985; children: Lisa Marie, Jennifer K., C. Andrew, Timothy E. BA in Music, U. Akron, 1954. Asst. v.p. Evans Savs. Assn., Akron, 1957-69; v.p. Centran Bank, Akron, 1969-86, Society Bank, Akron, 1986-87. Student adv., U. Akron, 1980—. Mem. Bldg. Owners and Mgrs. Assn. (bd. dirs. 1980—). Republican. Avocation: amateur radio. Home: Akron, Ohio. Died Aug. 16, 2008.

SHAFFER, HENRY CARTER, theater educator, director; b. Newton, Mass., July 10, 1952; s. Larry Ewing and Carolyn Carter Shaffer. BA, Georgetown U., Washington, DC, 1979; MFA, Carnegie-Mellon U., Pitts., 1982. Prof. theater Bridgewater State Coll., Mass., from 1996, chair dept. theater and dance, from 2005. Theater dir. Inly Sch., Scituate, Mass., from 2007, Ft. Peck Summer Theater, Ft. Peck, Mont., from 2004. Costume designer Peterborough Players (Best Costume Design Cherry Orchard, 2003), Mint Theater, Walters Gallery of Art. Judge Mass. HS Drama Guild, Boston, 2006—07. Grantee, Nat. Endowment Humanities, 2007; fellow, Am. Assn. State Coll. U. Sasakawa Found., 2006. Home: Bridgewater, Mass. Died Dec. 15, 2008.

SHAFFER, SHIRLEY POLLACK, secondary school educator, sales executive; b. Bklyn., Dec. 5, 1921; d. Harry Lionel and Sylvia Ruth (Smith) Pollack; m. Alfred Shaffer, Feb. 14, 1943 (dec. July 1995); children: Robert Stuart, Steven Michael. BA magna cum laude, Bklyn. Coll., 1955; MA, Calif. State U., LA, 1967. Life certificates in elem. and secondary edn., Calif. Sec. Am. Foreign Credit, NYC, 1939-41, Victor M. Calderon Co., NYC, 1941-43, sales, 1943-46; tchr. Bklyn. Pub. Sch., 1955-56, West Covina (Calif.) S.D., 1957-83; retired, 1983; mem. Calif. Sr. Legis. Assembly, 1985-95. Mem. NEA, Calif. Tchrs. Assn. (local sec. 1983), Calif. Retired Tchrs. Assn. (legis. chair), Brandeis U. Women's Aux. Com., Phi Beta Kappa, Kappa Delta Pi, Sigma Delta Pi. Avocations: writing, reading, poetry, lecturing, local civic participation. Home: San Dimas, Calif. Died Feb. 19, 2000.

SHANE, ROBERT SAMUEL, chemical engineer, consultant; b. Chgo., Dec. 8, 1910; s. Jacob and Selma (Shayne) S.; m. Jeanne Felice Lazarus, Aug. 21, 1936; children: Stephen H., Susan R., Jacqueline G. SB, U. Chgo., 1930, PhD, 1933. Plant supt. Amecco Chems., Rochester, N.Y., 1941-42; plant chemist Bausch & Lomb Optical Co., Rochester, 1942-46; project supr. Wyandotte (Mich.) Chems. Corp., 1952-54; assoc. dir. rsch. Davis & Geck div. Am. Cyanamid, Danbury, Conn., 1954-55; mgr. chem., ceramics, powder metals Westinghouse Atomic Power, Forest Hills, Pa., 1955-57; nucleonics specialist Bell Aircraft Co., Niagara Falls, N.Y.,

1958-59; mgr. parts, materials, process engring. GE, Valley Forge, Pa., 1959-69; staff cons. Nat. Materials Adv. Bd., Washington, 1969-80; prin. Shane Assocs., Stuart, Fla., 1980-96. Cons. in field; editor material engring. Marcel Dekker, Inc., N.Y.C., 1983—. Author, editor: Space Radiation Effects on Materials, 1962, Predictive Testing, 1972, Materials and Processes, 1985; author: Technology Transfer & Innovation, 1982; editor: Testing for Prediction of Material Performance, 1972; contbr. articles to profl. jours. Adult leader Boy Scouts Am.; organizer Literacy Coun., Ardmore, Pa., 1988. Recipient Joseph Stewart award Am. Chem. Soc., 1987, medal Swedish Royal Acad. Engring., 1972; named to space tech. hall of fame NASA, 1995. Fellow ASTM (award of merit 1973, F-15 com. on consumer product stds.), AIChE; mem. Am. Chem. Soc. (emeritus), Am. Soc. for Metals Internat. (life), Sigma Xi. Died May 29, 2008.

SHANNON, SISTER MARY AGNES, parochial school educator; b. Fall River, Mass., Aug. 22, 1929; d.d John and Orelina (Fletcher) S. AB, Regis Coll., Weston, Mass., 1963; MA in Math., Boston Coll., 1966; MA in Physics, U. Wis., Superior, 1974. Cert. elem., secondary, music tchr., Mass.; joined Order St. Catherine of Sienna, Roman Cath. Ch., 1948. Elem. and secondary tchr., chmn. dept. math. Dominican Acad., Fall River, 1966-71; tchr. math. and sci. Bishop Gerrard High Sch., Fall River, 1971-76; tchr. CES/Computech, Framingham, Mass.; tchr. computers parochial sch., Fall River, 1987-93, New Bedford, Mass. Grantee NSF, 1965-66, Academic Yr. Inst., 1968-72. Mem. ASCD, Nat. Guild Music Tchrs., Nat. Coun. Tchrs. Math., Sigma Pi Sigma. Home: Fall River, Mass. Died June 10, 2007.

SHAPAR, HOWARD KAMBER, lawyer; b. Boston, Nov. 6, 1923; m. Elizabeth Lucille Aske Shapar (div.); m. Henriette Albertine Emilie van Gerrevink, 1977; children: Kristina Mae, Stephen Oscar Truman, Pieter Nicholas Kamber (dec.). BA, Amherst Coll., 1947; JD, Yale U., 1950. Bar: N.Mex. 1951, D.C. 1981, U.S. Ct. Appeals D.C., U.S. Supreme Ct. Chief counsel U.S. Atomic Energy Commn. Idaho Ops. Office, 1956-62; asst. gen. counsel for licensing and regulation U.S. Atomic Energy Commn., 1962-76; exec. legal dir. U.S. Nuclear Regulatory Commn., 1976-82; dir. Gen. OECD Nuclear Energy Agy., Paris, 1982-88; atty. Shaw, Pittman, Potts and Trowbridge, Chevy Chase, Md., 1988-99, Egan, Fitzpatrick & Malsch, 2001—03. Recipient Presdl. Award of Meritoious Excellence 1981. Mem. N.Mex. State Bar Assn., D.C. Bar Assn. Home: Bethesda, Md. Died Mar. 15, 2009.

SHAPIRO, DANIEL, psychiatrist; b. Chgo., July 6, 1926; s. Isadore H. and Goldie (Rosenthal) S.; m. LaVerne Ann Bicek, May 9, 1930; 1 child, Joan Nancy. BS, U. Ill, 1949, MD, 1953. Diplomate Am. Bd. Psychiatry and Neurology, Am. Bd. Psychiatry. Resident in psychiatry Michael Reese Hosp., Chgo., 1955-58; practice medicine specializing in psychiatry Chgo., from 1958. Sr. attending physician Michael Reese Hosp., 1958—. Active troop 94 Girl Scouts Am., Evanston, Ill., 1972-79. Served with USAF, 1945. Fellow Am. Pyschiatry Assn.; mem. AMA, Ill. Psychiatry Soc., Chgo. Med. Soc. Democrat. Jewish. Avocation: skiing. Home: Chicago, Ill. Died Sept. 10, 2007.

SHAPIRO, DAVID ISRAEL, lawyer; b. Bklyn., June 17, 1928; s. Louis Raymond and Rae (Remin) S.; m. Carolyn M. Foy, Feb. 3, 1980; children by previous marriage: Steven, Claudia, Anthony, James, Miles. Student, U. Wis., 1944-45, Bklyn. Coll., 1946; LL.B., Bklyn. Law Sch., 1949. Bar: N.Y. State bar 1949, U.S. Supreme Ct. bar 1955, D.C. bar 1958. Founder, ptnr. Dickstein, Shapiro & Morin (and predecessor firms), Washington, 1953—73, sr. partner, 1973—96; legal arbitrator, cons. SJ Berwin LLP. Served with USNR, 1944-46. Mem. Am. Bar Assn., A.C.L.U. Democrat. Home: Washington, DC. Died Oct. 1, 2009.

SHAPIRO, NATHAN, acoustical engineer, retired; b. Worcester, Mass., Mar. 25, 1915; s. Menachem Mendel and Emma (Rudashevski) S.; m. Rose Edythe Turbow, Jan. 10, 1943 (dec.); children: Matthew, Joel, David, Lainie; m. Eve Berman, Feb. 21, 1996. AB, Clark U., 1939; MS, Cath. U. Am., 1947. Physicist Nat. Bur. Stds., Washington, 1941-46, David Taylor Model Basin, Carderock, Md., 1946-49, Naval Ordnance Lab., Silver Spring, Md., 1949-52, Armour Rsch. Found., Chgo., 1952-55; rsch. engr., group leader Lockheed-Calif. Co., Exterior Noise Group, Burbank, 1955-85. Fellow AIAA (assoc.), Acoustical Soc. Am.; mem. Aerospace Industries Assn. (airplane noise control com. 1972-85, chmn. 1980), Soc. Automotive Engrs. (aircraft noise com. 1964-85), Inst. Noise Control Engring. (cert.), Sigma Xi. Achievements include development of acoustical design of Lockheed L-1011 Tristar. Home: Pacific Palisades, Calif. Died June 10, 2008.

SHAPIRO, ROBERT, orthopedist; b. Boston, Mar. 2, 1913; s. Nathan and Rebecca (Korolick) S.; m. Sylvia C. Cohen, July 5, 1935 (dec. Jan. 1996); children: Roberta S., Richard. AB, Harvard U., 1933; MD, Tufts U., 1937. Diplomate Am. Bd. Orthop. Surgery. Intern in medicine Carney Hosp., Boston, 1937-38; intern in surgery Cambridge (Mass.) Hosp., 1939-40; resident in orthop. surgery Lakeville (Mass.) State Hosp., 1946-47, Hosp. for Joint Disease, NYC, 1947-50; pvt. practice Brookline, Mass., from 1950; asst. clin. prof. orthopedic surgery Tufts U. Med. Sch., from 1990; ret. Maj. U.S. Army, 1940-46. Fellow ACS. Jewish. Died Nov. 23, 2007.

SHAPIRO, SUMNER LEROY, psychoanalyst; b. Boston, May 15, 1926; s. Harry Alexander and Eva (Goldberg) S.; m. widowered; children: Paul Steven, Carolyne Amy, Leslie Susan. AB, Harvard U., 1946, MA, 1947; MD, Boston U., 1953. Intern New Eng. Ctr. Hosp., 1955-56; resident Worcester State Hosp., 1958-60, 63-65; with L.A. Psychoanalytic Inst., from 1965; psychoanalyst pvt. practice, LA, from 1967. Various teaching positions, UCLA. Author: Moment of Insight, 1969, Beyond Insight, 1973, Beyond Case Histories, 1984, Well-Kept Secrets, 1993, A Psychoanalytic Cookbook: Recipes to Season and Preserve Relationships, 1996. Avocation: home improvements. Died Dec. 29, 2007.

SHARP, PAUL FREDERICK, retired academic administrator, educational consultant; b. Kirksville, Mo., Jan. 19, 1918; s. Frederick J. and L. Blanche (Phares) S.; m. Rosella Ann Anderson, June 19, 1939; children: William, Kathryn, Paul Trevor. AB, Phillips U., 1939; PhD, U. Minn., 1947; LLD (hon.), Tex. Christian U., 1961, Austin Coll., 1978, Drake U., 1980; LHD (hon.), Buena Vista Coll., 1967, U. Nev., Towson State U., 1980, Oklahoma City U., 1996, U. Okla., 1997; LittD (hon.), Limestone Coll., 1971; HHD, Okla. Christian U. Sci. & Arts, 1992. Instr. U. Minn., 1942, 46-47, vis. lectr., 1948; assoc. prof. Am. history Iowa State U., 1947-54; prof. Am. history, chmn. Am. Instns. program U. Wis., 1954-57, vis. lectr., 1953, San Francisco State Coll., 1950, U. Oreg., 1955; Fulbright lectr. Am. Institutions Universities, Melbourne, Sydney, 1952; pres. Hiram Coll., 1957-64; chancellor U. N.C., Chapel Hill, 1964-66; pres. Drake U., Des Moines, 1966-71, U. Okla., Norman, 1971-78, pres. emeritus, 1978-88, Regents' prof., 1978—88, Regents' prof. emeritus, 1988—2009; Disting. prof. history U. Sci. & Arts, Okla., 1990—96. Dir. Am. Coun. on Edn. Insts. for Coll. & Univ. Presidents, 1977-79; vis. lectr. Harvard U. Bus. Sch. summer session, 1970-72. Author: Agrarian Revolt in Western Canada, 1948, Old Orchard Farm, Story of an Iowa Boyhood, 1952, Whoop-Up Country, Canadian American West, 1955; cons. author: Heritage of Midwest, 1958; editor: Documents of Freedom, 1957; contbr. articles to profl. jours. Pres. Norman Cmty. Found., 1995-97, Okla. State Coun. Aging, 1997-99. USN liaison officer His Majesty's Australian Ship, Hobart, 1943-46. With USNR, 1943-47. Recipient Iowa State U. Alumni Fund award, 1952, Award of Merit Am. Assn. State and Local History, 1955, Silver Spur award Western Writers America, 1955, Fulbright award to Australia, 1952; named to Okla. Higher Edn. Hall of Fame, 1995; Minn. Hist. Soc. grantee, 1947, 48, Social Sci. Rsch. Coun. grantee, 1949, 51; Ford Faculty fellow, 1954, Guggenheim fellow, 1957. Mem. Phi Beta Kappa, Phi Kappa Phi, Phi Delta Kappa, Pi Gamma Mu, Phi Alpha Theta. Mem. Christian Ch. (Disciples Of Christ). Home: Norman, Okla. Died Feb. 18, 2009.

SHARP, WILLOUGHBY, art dealer; b. NYC, Jan. 23, 1936; s. Willoughby and Murielle MacMahon Sharp. BA, Brown U., 1961; MA, Columbia U., 1968; PhD, Milton Coll., Wis., 1975. Pub. Avalanche Mag., NYC, 1968-76; founder, v.p. Ctr. for New Art Activities, Inc., NYC, 1973-82; exec. dir. The Franklin St. Arts Ctr., Inc., NYC, 1974-78; dir. Fine Arts Ctr. U. R.I., Kingston, 1988-90; owner The Willoughby Sharp Gallery, NYC, 1988—2008; CEO, owner sharpgallery.com, NYC, 1997—2008; pub. TSAR. Faculty design and tech. dept. The New Univ. Parsons Sch. of Design, NY, from 2002. Home: Brooklyn, NY. Died Dec. 17, 2008.

SHARPE, JEAN ANDERSON, retired mathematics educator; b. Washington, Jan. 29, 1927; '. Frederick B. and Caroline (Morton) Anderson; m. Ralph Edwin Sharpe (dec. 1992); children: Ralph E. Jr., Reginald Earl. BS, D.C. Tchr.'s Coll., 1968; postgrad., Trinity Coll., U. of D.C. Tchr. 4th grade Houston Elem., D.C., 1968-74; math. tchr. Turner Elem., D.C., 1974-84; math. resource computer coord. Leckie Elem., D.C., 1984-87, recert. math. resource tchr. D.C., 1985-90; tchr. math. resource and computer literacy Washington Highland, 1987-89, tchr. adult edn. and computer literacy, 1987-90; tchr. 1st grade Wilkerson Elem., 1990-92. Math. tchr. Chpt. One, Renewal, 1980 African Methodist Episcopalian. Avocations: painting, sewing, spending time with grandchildren and great-grandchildren. Home: Washington, DC. Died Dec. 21, 2007.

SHARPE, WILLIAM R., former state legislator; b. Clarksburg, W.Va., Oct. 28, 1028; s. William R. Sharpe & Helen (Whitwam) S.; m. Pauline Lester, 1953 (dec. 2005) Student, Bliss Engring. Sch., Salem Coll., W.Va. U. Registered profl. engr., W.Va. Mem. W.Va. State Senate from Dist. 13, Charleston, 1960—80, 1984—92, majority whip, 1972-80, pres. pro tem., 1990-94; mem. W.Va. State Senate from Dist. 12, Charleston, 1993—2008. Mem. banking and ins. com., energy com., industry and mining com., fin. com., health and human resources com., rules com., small bus. com. Mem. W.Va. Dem. Exec. Com. Mem. Internat. Brotherhood Elec. Workers, Fraternal Order Eagles, Masons, Shriners, Elks, Moose. Democrat. Methodist. Died Feb. 15, 2009.

SHASHOUA, VICTOR E., pharmaceutical company executive; b. Kermanshah, Persia, Nov. 15, 1929; s. Ezra S. and Violet S. (Mouallem) S.; m. Angela M. Saleh, June 9, 1955; children: Karen, Edward, Michael. BSc, London U., 1952; PhD, U. Del., 1956. Rsch. assoc. DuPont Exptl. Sta., Wilmington, Del., 1952-64, MIT, Cambridge, 1964-70; assoc. prof. neurosci. Harvard Med. Sch., Boston, 1970-92, lectr., from 1993; assoc. biochemist McLean Hosp., Belmont, Mass., 1970-92; chief scientific officer, chmn. Neuromedica Inc., Cambridge, from 1992. Adj. prof. pharmacology and exptl. therapeutics Tufts U. Sch. Medicine, Boston, 1993-95. Contbr. articles to profl. jours.; patentee in field; mem. editorial bd. Jour. Neurochem. Rsch., 1992-97. Recipient award McKnight Found., Grant Found., 1971-73. Mem. Soc. for Neurosci., Am. Soc. for Neurochemistry, Internat. Soc. for Neurochemistry, Am. Assn. for Sci. Avocations: skiing, fishing, music, tennis. Home: Brookline, Mass. Died Apr. 7, 2008.

SHAW, MARTHA LOUISE, physical therapist; b. Springfield, Mass., Sept. 11, 1959; d. Lewis Albert and Carol (Roper) S. BS, Springfield Coll., 1981; cert. in phys. therapy, Mayo Sch. Health Related Scis., Rochester, Minn., 1983; postgrad., Kaiser Permanente, 1991. Bd. cert. clin. specialist in orthopedic phys. therapy, Am. Bd. Phys. Therapy Specialties. Phys. therapy resident, advanced orthopedic manual therapy Kaiser Permanente Orthopedic Phys. Therapy Program, Hayward, Calif., from 1991; staff phys. therapist Manchester Phys. Therapy, Bedford, N.H., 1983-88; sr. staff phys. therapist, facility mgr. Affiliated Phys. Therapists, Ltd., Phoenix, 1988-90; clin. specialist Hayward Phys. Therapy and Kaiser Permanente, 1992, Kaiser Permanente Hosp., Oakland, from 1992, Berkeley Phys. Therapy, 1993-95. Mem. Am. Phys. Therapy Assn. (chairperson membership N.H. chpt. 1986-88, pub. rels., 1985-88, orthopedic sect. 1988—). Avocations: bicycling, photography, golf. Home: Oakland, Calif. Died Feb. 29, 2008.

SHAW, RAY, retired financial publishing company executive; b. 1934; m. Kathleen Whitney Shaw; children: Whitney, Beth Ed., Tex. Western U., U. Okla. With Dow Jones & Co. Inc., NYC, 1960—89; mng. editor AP-Dow Jones, Dow Jones & Co., 1966-71, asst. gen. mgr., 1971-72, dir. devel., 1972-73, v.p. devel., 1973-75, v.p. gen. mgr., 1975-77, exec. v.p., 1977-79, pres., COO, 1979-89; ret. Dow Jones & Co. Bd. dirs. O'Haway Newpapers Inc., Extel Corp., Far Eastern Econ. Rev., Hong Kong Died July 19, 2009.

SHAW, WILLIAM (BILL SHAW), mayor, retired state senator; b. Fulton, Ark., July 31, 1937; s. McKinley and Gertrude (Henderson) S.; m. Shirley Shaw, 1957; children: Gina, Victor, Shawn, 3 stepchildren. Grad. high sch. Adminstrv. asst. to Alderman Wilson Frost 34th Ward; precinct capt. 24th ward and inspector City of Chgo.; pres. 9th ward Regional Dem. Orgn.; mem. Ill. Ho. Reps. from Dist. 34, 1983—93, mem. appropriations com. labor and commerce com., exec. and vet. affairs com., registration com., vice chmn. fin. insts. com., chmn. ins. com.; mem. Ill. State Senate from Dist. 15, 1993—2002, asst. majority leader, 1995—2002; mayor Village of Dalton, 1997—2008. Mem. Masons, C. of C. Democrat. Home: Chicago, Ill. Died Nov. 26, 2008.

SHEAFFER, CAREY NELSON, human resource management executive; b. McAlisterville, Pa., Sept. 22, 1947; s. Herman Clarence and Gladys Elaine (Losch) S.; m. Carol Jean Reigle, Oct. 23, 1965; children: Christopher, Jeffery. AS, Susquehanna U., 1974. Cert. sr. profl. in human resources Human Resource Cert. Inst. Ops. supr. Tri-County Nat. Bank, Middleburg, Pa., 1969-75; v.p., dir. human resources First Nat. Trust Bank, Sunbury, Pa., from 1975. Sgt. U.S. Army, 1966-69. Mem. Soc. Human Resource Mgmt., Am. Bankers Assn., Pa. Bankers Assn., Bank Adminstrn. Inst., Am. Inst. Banking, Susquehanna Pers. Mgmt. Assn. (pres. 1987-88), Sunbury C. of C., Am. Legion, Moose, Rotary (bd. dirs. Sunbury 1987-88). Democrat. Avocations: travel, camping, cross country skiing. Home: Selinsgrove, Pa. Died Feb. 5, 2008.

SHEEHAN, CAROLINE GRIFFIN (CARRIE SHEEHAN), medical researcher, writer; b. La Grande, Oreg., Dec. 13, 1928; d. John Henry and Lillian Louise (O'Connell) Griffin; m. Tom Edward Sheehan, Sept. 10, 1949 (wid.); children: Christie, Thomas, Patrick, Molly (dec.), Timothy, Mary, Michael, Caroline. BA in Public Affairs and Political Science, Seattle U., 1974. Rsch. coord. S.W. SIDS Rsch. Inst., Lake Jackson, Tex., from 1992; interviewer, CHAD/Flash program U. Wash., Seattle, 1995-97. Trustee Nat. SIDS Found., 1980; pres. bd. dirs., trustee Jubilee Women's Ctr., Seattle, 1990—; charter mem. Citizens for Rational Handgun Control, Seattle. Contbr. articles to jours., chpts. to books. Planning commr. City of Seattle, 1970-78, mem. landmarks bd., 1975-78; mem. police and cmty. task force Ch. Coun. of Seattle, 1975-85; candidate Seattle City Coun., 1979. Mem. Holy Names Acad. Alumnae Assn. (trustee, bd. dirs. 1991-97, Disting. Alumna award 1996). Democrat. Roman Catholic. Avocations: reading, writing, poetry, travel. Home: Seattle, Wash. Died July 13, 2008.

SHEEHAN, JAMES JOSEPH, social studies educator; m. Olivia Sheehan; children: Ryan, Matthew. BBA, Ohio U., Athens, 1988; MA in Internat. Affairs, Ohio U., 1990, MEd, 1992, MA, 1996, PhD, 1998. Cert. tchr. social studies Ohio. Instr. Ohio U., Athens, 1993—97; asst. prof. U. N.D., Grand Forks, 1997—98, Cleve. State U., 1998—2003, Miami U., Oxford, Ohio, 2003—06, assoc. prof. social studies, from 2006. Author: Justice, Idealogy and Education, 2001, NCSS Presidential Addresses, 2002, 2003. Grantee Sr. Rsch. awardee, Fulbright Found./U.S. Dept. State, 2005—06. Mem.: Ohio Coun. for the Social Studies (exec. dir. from 2005, conf. dir. 2001—06), Nat. Coun. for the Social Studies (pubs. chair 2005—06). Home: Athens, Ohio. Died May 4, 2008.

SHEEHAN, WILLIAM FRANCIS, chemistry professor; b. Chgo., Oct. 19, 1926; s. William Francis and Catherine Henriette S. BS with Honors, Loyola U., 1948; PhD, Calif. Inst. Tech., 1952. Chemist Shell Devel. Co., Emeryville, Calif., 1952-55; prof. Santa Clara (Calif.) U., 1955-91, prof. emeritus, from 1991. Contbr. articles to profl. publs. Roman Catholic. Home: Santa Fe, N.Mex. Died Jan. 30, 2008.

SHELLEY, WALTER BROWN, dermatologist, educator; b. St. Paul, Feb. 6, 1917; s. Patrick K. and Alfaretta (Brown) S.; m. Marguerite H. Weber, 1942 (dec.); children: Peter B., Anne E. Kiselewich, Barbara A. (dec.); m. E. Dorinda Loeffel, 1980; children: Thomas R., Katharine D., William L. BS, U. Minn., 1940, PhD, 1941, MD, 1943; MA honoris causa, U. Pa., 1971; MD honoris causa, U. Uppsala, Sweden, 1977; DSc (hon.), Med. U. Ohio, 2006. Diplomate: Am. Bd. Dermatology (pres. 1968-69, dir. 1960-69). Instr. physiology U. Pa., Phila., 1946-47, asst. instr. dermatology and syphilology, 1947-49, asst. prof. dermatology, 1950-53, assoc. prof., 1953-57, prof., 1957-80, chmn. dept., 1965-80; prof. dermatology U. Ill. Peoria Sch. Medicine, 1980-83; prof. medicine (dermatology) Med. Coll. Ohio, 1983-97, emeritus prof. medicine, 1997—2009. Instr. dermatology Dartmouth Coll., 1949-50; Regional cons. dermatology VA, 1955-59; mem. com. on cutaneous system NRC, 1955-59, Commn. Cutaneous Diseases, Armed Forces Epidemiological Bd., 1958-61, dep. dir., 1959-61; cons. dermatology Surgeon Gen. USAF, 1958-61, U.S. Army, 1958-61; mem. NRC, 1961-64 Author (with Crissey): Classics in Clinical Dermatology, 1953, 2003; author: (with Pillsbury, Kligman) Dermatology, 1956; author: Cutaneous Medicine, 1961; author: (with Hurley) The Human Apocrine Sweat Gland in Health and Disease, 1960; author: (with Botelho and Brooks) The Endocrine Glands, 1969; author: Consultations in Dermatology with Walter B. Shelley, 1972, 2006, Consultations II, 1974; author: (with Shelley) Advanced Dermatologic Therapy, 1987; author: Advanced Dermatologic Diagnosis, 1992, A Century of International Dermatological Congresses, 1992, Advanced Dermatogical Therapy II, 2001, Shelley's 77 Skins, 2001, Consultations in Dermatology, 2006, The Skin Around Me: Adventures in Dermatology, 2007; mem. editl. bd. Jour. Investigative Dermatology, 1961—64, Archives of Dermatology, 1961—62, Skin and Allergy News, 1970—93, Excerpta Medica Dermatologica, from 1960, Cutis, from 1972, Jour. Geriatric Dermatol, 1993; assoc. editor: Jour. Cutaneous Pathology, 1972—81; editl. cons. Medcom, from 1972. Served as capt. M.C. AUS, 1944-46. Recipient Spl. award Soc. Cosmetic Chemists, 1955, Hellerstrom medal, 1971, Am. Med. Writers Assn. Best Med. Book award, 1973, Dohi medal, 1981, Rothman medal Soc. for Investigative Dermatology, 1987, Rose Hirschler award, 1990, Humane Dermatologist award, 2005. Master ACP; fellow Assn. Am. Physicians, St. John's Dermatol. Soc. London (hon.); mem. AMA (chmn. residency rev. com. for dermatology 1963-67, chmn. sect. dermatology 1969-71), Assn. Profs. Dermatology (pres. 1972-73), Pacific Dermatol. Assn. (hon.), Am. Dermatol. Assn. (hon., dir., pres. 1975-76), Soc. Investigative Dermatology (hon. pres. 1961-62), Am. Physiol. Soc., Phila. Physiol. Soc., Brit. Dermatol. Soc. (hon.), Phila. Dermatol. Soc. (pres. 1960-61), Mich. Dermatol. Soc., Ohio Dermatol. Soc. (hon.), Am. Acad. Dermatology (Gold medal 1992, hon. pres. 1971-72), Pa. Acad. Dermatology (pres. 1972-73), Am. Soc. Dermatologic Surgery, N.Am. Clin. Dermatol. Soc. (hon.), Noah Worcester Dermatol. Soc., Royal Soc. Medicine; corr. mem. Nederlandse Vereniging Van Dermatologen, Israeli Dermatol. Assn., Finnish Soc. Dermatology, Swedish Dermatol. Soc., French Dermatologic Soc.; fgn. hon. mem. Danish Dermatol. Assn., Japanese Dermatol. Assn., Dermatol. Soc. S.Africa, Austrian Dermatol. Soc. Home: Grand Rapids, Ohio. Died Jan. 30, 2009.

SHELOR, CLAUD SWANSON, JR., mechanical engineer; b. Bloom, Kans., Nov. 6, 1923; s. Claud Swanson Sr. and Nellie Anna (Winkelman) S.; m. Roberta Rosemary Royston, May 26, 1946; children: Jerry, Claudia, Thomas, Steven. BSME, Kans. State U., 1956. Registered profl. engr., Okla.; land. surveyor, Kans. State-wide coord. recycling and market devel. Dept. of Commerce, State of Kans., Topeka, from 1991. Pres. Kiwanis, Dodge City, Kans., 1965. Mem. ASCE, NSPE, Kans. Engring. Soc. (pres. Topeka chpt. 1990-91), Arab Temple Shrine (noble). Democrat. Methodist. Home: Topeka, Kans. Died Feb. 28, 2008.

SHEPHERD, CHARLES CLINTON, real estate executive; b. Westport, Conn., May 25, 1929; s. J. Clinton and Gail Fleming (English) S.; m. June Stalls, June 19, 1956; children: Gail Paige, Susan Arlen, Richard Clinton. B in Landscape Arch., U. Fla., 1954, M in City Planning, 1956. Lic. real estate broker. Pres. Kendree and Shepherd, Phila., 1958-72; regional pres. Robino-Ladd Co., Palm Beach, Fla., 1972-75; v.p. Hovnanian Co., Lake Worth, Fla., 1975-78; pres. Gamina Co., Lake Worth, 1978-92, Charles Shepherd, Ent., Palm Beach, from 1992. Chmn. Whitpain Planning Commn., Blue Bell, Pa., 1967-72; mem. land use adv. bd. Palm Beach County, 1989-91. Contbr. articles to profl. jours. Mem. Palm Beach County Task Force, 1984, Downtown Devel. Authority, Lake Worth, 1985-88, chmn., 1988. 1st lt. arty. U.S. Army, 1952-54. Mem. Am. Soc. Planners, Home Builders Assn. Home: Lake Worth, Fla. Died Feb. 2, 2008.

SHEPHERD, MARK, JR., retired electronics company executive; b. Dallas, Jan. 18, 1923; s. Mark and Louisa Florence (Daniell) S.; m. Mary Alice Murchland, Dec. 21, 1945; children: Debra Aline Shepherd Robinson, MaryKay Theresa, Marc Blaine. BSEE, So. Meth. U., 1942; MSEE, U. Ill., at Urbana, 1947. Registered profl. engr., Tex. With GE, 1942-43, Farnsworth TV and Radio Corp., 1947-48, Tex. Instruments Inc., Dallas, 1948-88, v.p., gen. mgr. semiconductor-components div., 1955—61; exec. v.p., COO Tex. Instruments Inc, 1961—66; pres., COO Tex. Instruments Inc., 1967—69, pres., CEO, 1969—76, chmn., CEO, 1976—84, chmn., chief corp. officer, 1984—85, chmn., 1985—88; ret., 1988. Bd. dirs. Tex. Instruments Inc., 1963—93. Hon. trustee Com. for Econ. Devel.; councillor conf. Bd.; mem. Bus. Coun. Lt. (j.g.) USNR, 1943-46. Fellow IEEE; mem. NAE, Sigma Xi, Eta Kappa Nu. Home: Quitman, Tex. Died Feb. 4, 2009.

SHERMAN, JOHN KINGSLEY, retired industrial sales executive; b. Jackson, Mich., Nov. 8, 1914; s. Hugh Kingsley and Hetty Myra (Brittingham) S.; m. Dorothea von der Halben (dec. 1998); 1 child, William Hugh. BS in Mech. Engring., U. Cin., 1938. Registered profl. engr., Ohio. Draftsman William Powell Co., Cin., 1933-37, Cin. Gas and Electric Co., 1937-41; sales engr. White Indsl. Sales and Equipment Co., Cin., 1943-64; pres., chmn. bd. dirs. Sherman & Schroder Equipment Co., Cin., 1964-84; ret., 1984. With USN, 1941-43. Mem. Ret. Engrs. and Scientists of Cin. (pres. 1993-94), Engrs. and Scientists of Cin. (bd. dirs.), Masons. Republican. Presbyterian. Avocations: stamps, naval history, railroads, ships. Home: Cincinnati, Ohio. Died Jan. 24, 2008.

SHERR, PAUL MARTIN, systems analyst; b. Kansas City, Mo., Mar. 20, 1944; s. Paul Martin and Pearl (Shiffman) S.; m. Claire McGee, June 1968 (div. June 1972); 1 child, Maya Holmes. BBS in Journalism, U. Tex., 1967. Systems analyst Tex. Employment Commn., Austin, from 1969. Pub. rels. dir. Meat Cutters Union Local 408, Houston, 1974-82, Austin Ctrl. Labor Coun., 1983-93; bd. dirs. Tex. State Employees Union/Comms. Workers Am. Local 6186, Austin, 1984—, Tex. Coalition for Human Needs, Austin, 1988-92; coord. Labor Party Advs., Tex., 1964-92. Active Dem. Party, Tex., 1964-92; coord. Labor Party Advs., Tex., 1964-92. Avocations: music, photography, writing. Home: Austin, Tex. Died Apr. 30, 2008.

SHERTZER, MARGARET DELANO, freelance editor; b. Burlington, Vt., Oct. 23, 1922; d. Arthur Brookins and Mabelle Elizabeth (George) Delano; m. George Edwin Shertzer, Oct. 6, 1957; children: John Delano, Anne Elizabeth. AB, U. Vt., 1944; MA, Fairfield U., 1977. Asst. editor Harper & Bros., NYC, 1951-59; freelance editor Norwalk, Conn., from 1959. Author: How to Be a Top Secretary, 1954, The Elements of Grammar, 1986; co-author: The Secretary's Handbook, 1969. Pres. Greater Norwalk (Conn.) Cmty. Coun., 1985-89; bd. pres. Broad River Homes, Norwalk, 1993—. Mem. Norwalk LWV (bull. editor 1984-94), Delta Delta Delta (pres. 1942-43). Democrat. Unitarian Universalist. Avocation: cmty. vol. Home: Stratford, Conn. Died May 5, 2008.

SHERWOOD, HAROLD DEWITT, oil industry executive, consultant; b. Hackensack, NJ, Feb. 24, 1921; s. Harold Homer and Sara Estabrook (Barnett) S.; m. Betty Doll, Dec. 30, 1945 (dec. Jan. 1978); children: Richard H., Pamela Ann; m. Marjorie Vivian Hoffmann, Feb. 17, 1979. BSChE, Lehigh U., 1944. Engr. Sherwood Refining Co., Englewood, N.J., 1946-52; processing engr. Mobil Oil Corp., NYC, 1952-68; mgr. petroleum processing CE-Lummus, Bloomfield, N.J., 1968-81; cons. Lakehurst, N.J., from 1981. Lt. (j.g.) USNR, 1944-46. Republican. Avocations: bowling, golf, boating. Home: Melbourne, Fla. Died June 16, 2008.

SHIH, PHILIP C., library administrator; b. July 6, 1943; BS, Tunghai U., Taiwan, 1965; MLS, Fla. State U., 1969. Dir. Logansport (Ind.) Pub. Libr., from 1973. Mem. ALA. Home: Logansport, Ind. Died Dec. 20, 2007.

SHILLE, VICTOR MICHAEL, journal editor, theriogenology educator; b. Belgrade, Yugoslavia, Feb. 8, 1933; came to U.S., 1950; s. Michael Ernest and Ellen (Waskresensky) S.; m. Patricia Ann Sokol, June 29, 1963; children: Michael Victor, Theodore Richard, Thomas Patrick. BS, U. Calif., Davis, 1956, DVM, 1958, PhD, 1979. Diplomate Am. Coll. Theriogenologists. Vet. West Fifth Vet. Hosp., Santa Ana, Calif., 1959-72; NIH postdoctoral fellow U. Calif. Sch. Vet. Medicine, Davis, 1972-75, lectr., 1975-77; rsch. assoc. Swedish U. Agrl. Sci., Uppsala, 1977-78; assoc. prof. U. Fla. Coll. Vet. Medicine, Gainesville, 1978-89, prof., 1990-93, prof. emeritus, from 1993. Dir. Fla. Assn. Kennel Clubs Lab. Canine Reproduction, 1982-93; cons. Nat. Zoo, Washington, 1991—; mem. sci. review bd. AVMA, Schaumburg, Ill., 1997—. Author: (chpt.) Veterinary Clinics of North America, 1982, Current Techniques in Small Animal Surgery, 1983, Current Veterinary Therapy, 1989; editor: Current Therapy in Theriogenology, 1980; editor Theriogenology jour., 1980—. Coach Youth Soccer Inc., Gainesville, 1979-84. Recipient Barlett award Am. Coll. Theriogenologists, 1992. Mem. Soc. for Study of Reproduction, Soc. Theriogenology, Coun. Biology Editors, Sigma Xi, Phi Zeta. Avocations: sailing, wildlife watching, playing autoharp, russian history, poetry. Home: Gainesville, Fla. Died Sept. 9, 2007.

SHILLINGBURG, CONSTANCE JOANNE, historian, retired history professor; b. Las Vegas, N. Mex., May 10, 1938; d. John Bird and Grace Louise (Guffey) Murphy; m. Herbert Thompson Shillingburg, June 11, 1960; children: Lisa Grace, Leslie Susan, Lara Stephanie. BA Cum Laude, U. N. Mex., Albuquerque, 1960; degree, U. Southern Calif., LA, 1961, Moorpark Coll., Calif., 1972; MEd Summa Cum Laude, U. Ctrl. Okla., Edmond, 1978. Cert. secondary schs. tchr. N. Mex. English, journalism tchr. Woodrow Wilson HS, Long Beach, Calif., 1960—61; english tchr. North HS, Torrance, Calif., 1961, Highland HS, Albuquerque, 1967—68; adj. prof. Okla. City Cmty. Coll., Okla. City, 1978—80; US history tchr. Hefner Jr. HS, Okla. City, 1980—93; US world history tchr. Edmond Meml. HS, Okla., 1993—2000. Hist. interpreter Her Royal Majesties Hist. Interpretations, Edmond, 2001—08. Prodr.(writer): (plays, one act play) When Queens Collide, 2005—06;, author monologues. Young democrats Edmond Meml. HS, 2007—08. Named one of Tchr. of Yr., Hefner Jr. HS, Okla., 1990; grant, Commn. Bicentennial US Constn., Okla., 1985, grant Kids, Putnam City found., Okla., 1989, 1992, grant, Edmond Edn. Com., Okla., 1993—94, grant Advanced Placement Tng., Tex. Christian U., Okla., 1995, U. Tex. Austin, Okla., 1996, grant, Coll. Bd. Advanced Placement Tng., Tulsa U., 1998, grant AP computer equipment, State Okla., 1999. Mem.: Okla. City Chpt. English Speaking Union, Amer Assn. U. Women, (Calif.) (Best Chpt.Publicity Nat. award 1970—71), Ladies Music Club, (Okla.), Delta Kappa Gamma, (Okla.), Phi Alpha Theta, (N. Mex.) (Best Chpt.Publicity Nat. award 1966—67), Phi Kappa Phi, Mortar Bd. Sr. Women's, (N. Mex.), Theta Sigma Phi, (N. Mex.). Avocations: reading, travel, gardening. Home: Edmond, Okla. Died June 28, 2008.

SHINEMAN, EDWARD WILLIAM, JR., retired pharmaceutical executive; b. Canajoharie, NY, Apr. 9, 1915; s. Edward W. and Bertelle H. (Shubert) S.; m. H. Doris Thompson, Apr. 15, 1939; children: Edward T., Alan B. AB, Cornell U., 1937. With apparatus dept., acctg. dept. Gen. Electric Co., 1938-46, line auditor, 1942-46; with Beech-Nut, Inc. and predecessor cos., 1946-68, asst. treas., 1948-63, contr., 1959-63, treas., 1963-68; asst. sec.-treas. Squibb Corp., 1968-81. Bd. dirs. emeritus Taconic Farms, Inc. Trustee Arkell Hall Found.; mem. emeritus coun. Cornell U. Mem. Fin. Execs. Inst., Inst. Mgmt. Accts. Republican. Home: New York, NY. Died Jan. 12, 2009.

SHIPP, WILLIAM WELDON, accountant; b. LA, June 8, 1927; s. Pat and Mae (Harris) S.; m. Dorothy Forse, Sept. 23, 1967; children: Karyn, William. BS, U. San Francisco, 1952; MBA, Golden Gate U., 1963. CPA, Calif. Staff auditor Price Waterhouse, San Francisco, 1952-56; acctg. supr. CC Moore & Co., San Francisco, 1956-63; chief acct. Westland Life Ins. Co., San Francisco, 1963-66; audit mgr. Soule Steel Co., San Francisco, 1966-67; sr. acct. Bechtel Power Corp., San Francisco, 1967-82; pvt. practice Oakland, Calif., from 1983. Sgt. U.S. Army, 1945-46. Republican. Home: Oakland, Calif. Died Feb. 26, 2008.

SHIRA, GERALD DEE, II, retired financial executive; b. Cortland, NY, Mar. 14, 1933; s. Gerald Dee and Ruth Irene (Lugar) S.; m. Coral Lynne Faulring, June 16, 1956; children: Donna Lee, Scott Dee. BS, Syracuse U., 1955. With Eastman Kodak Co., Rochester, N.Y., 1957-67; adminstrv. mgr. Kodak Venezuela S.A., Caracas, 1967-72, Kodak Argentina S.A.I.C., Buenos Aires, 1972-74; dir. fin. svcs. Latin Am. Eastman Kodak, Rochester, 1974-76; dir. fin. and adminstrn. Kodak Brasileira Ltda., Sao Paulo, 1976-84; dir. fin. svcs. Europe Eastman Kodak Co., London, 1984-87, dir. fin. planning Latin Am. Rochester, 1987-92. Bd. dirs. Colegio Internacional de Caracas, 1967-72. With Army, 1955-57. Mem. Brazil/Am. C. of C., Coun. of Ams., Am. Philatelic Soc., Nat. Audobon Soc., Hilton Head Island Jazz Soc., Caracas Sports Club, Caracas Theatre Club, Beta Alpha Psi. Republican. Avocations: fishing, biking, boating, model building, stamp collecting/philately. Home: Hilton Head Island, SC. Died Oct. 22, 2007.

SHNEIDMAN, EDWIN S., psychologist, thanatologist; b. York, Pa., May 13, 1918; s. Louis and Manya (Zukin) S.; m. Jeanne E. Keplinger, Oct. 1, 1944 (dec. 2001); children: David William, Jonathan Aaron, Paul Samuel, Robert James. AB, UCLA, 1938, MA, 1940; MS, U. So. Calif., 1947, PhD, 1948. Diplomate: Am. Bd. Examiners Profl. Psychology (past v.p.). Clin. psychologist VA Center, Los Angeles, 1947-50, chief research, 1950-53; co-dir. Central Research Unit for Study Unpredicted Deaths, 1953-58; co.-dir. Suicide Prevention Center, Los Angeles, 1958-66; chief Center Studies Suicide Prevention NIMH, Bethesda, Md., 1966-69; vis. prof. Harvard U., 1969; fellow Ctr. Advanced Study in Behavioral Scis., 1969-70; clin. assoc. Mass. Gen. Hosp., 1969, Karolinska Hosp., Stockholm, 1978; prof. med. psychology UCLA, 1970-75, prof. thanatology, 1975-88, prof. emeritus, 1988—2009. Vis. prof. Ben Gurion U. of Negev, Beersheva, 1983 Author: Deaths of Man, 1973, Voices of Death, 1980, Definition of Suicide, 1985, Suicide as Psychache, 1993, The Suicidal Mind, 1996, Comprehending Suicide, 2001, Autopsy of a Suicidal Mind, 2004, A Commonsense Book of Death: Reflections at Ninety of a Lifelong Thanatologist, 2008; editor: Thematic Test Analysis, 1951; editor: (with N.L. Farberow) Clues to Suicide, 1957, The Cry for Help, 1961, Essays in Self-Destruction, 1967, (with M. Ortega) Aspects of Depression, 1969, On the Nature of Suicide, 1969, (with N.L. Farberow, L.E. Litman) Psychology of Suicide, 1970, Death and the College Student, 1972, Death: Current Perspectives, 1976, 80, 84, Suicidology: Contemporary Developments, 1976, Endeavors in Psychology: Selections From The Personology of Henry A. Murray, 1981, Suicide Thoughts and Reflections, 1981 Served to capt. USAAF, 1942-45. Recipient Harold M. Hildreth award Psychologists in Pub. Service, 1966; Louis I. Dublin award Am. Assn. Suicidology, 1969. Mem. Am. Assn. Suicidology (founder, past pres.), Am.

Psychol. Assn. (past div. pres., Disting. Profl. Contbn. to Pub. Svc. award 1987, Henry A. Murray award 1997), Melville Soc. Died May 15, 2009.

SHOEMAKER, FRANK CRAWFORD, retired physicist; b. Ogden, Utah, Mar. 26, 1922; s. Roy Hopkins and Sarah Parker (Anderson) Shoemaker; m. Ruth Elizabeth Nelson, July 11, 1944; children: Barbara Elaine, Mary Frances. AB, Whitman Coll., 1943, DSc (hon.), 1978; PhD, U. Wis., 1949. Staff mem. Radiation Lab. MIT, 1943-45; instr. physics U. Wis., 1949-50; mem. faculty Princeton (N.J.) U., 1950-89, prof. physics, 1962—89, prof. emeritus, from 1989, dir. undergrad. physics dept., 1981—89; assoc. dir. Princeton U. Pa. Accelerator, 1962-66; ret., 1989. Vis. scientist Rutherford High Energy Lab., 1965—66; main accelerator sect. head Nat. Accelerator Lab., 1968—69; prin. investigator Dept. of Energy High Energy Physics Contract, 1972—85. Fellow: Am. Phys. Soc.; mem.: Sigma Xi, Phi Beta Kappa. Home: Hightstown, NJ. Died Feb. 11, 2009.

SHOFFNER, KENNETH CRAIG, data processing executive; b. Salina, Kans., Aug. 6, 1952; s. Kenneth Ned and Lila Mae (Dearing) S.; m. Deborah Ann Wilson, Sept. 2, 1972; children: Brian Logan, April Kristine. Student, Northwest Mo. State, 1970-71, Elec. Computer Prog. Inst., 1972, Maple Woods Community Coll., from 1984. Computer operator supr. documentation specialist release mgr Seaboard Allied Millig Corp., Kansas City, Mo., 1972-80; staff analyst Fed. Reserve Bank Kansas City, 1980-83; system mgr. Clay County Assessor's Office, Liberty, Mo., 1983-88; sr. programmer Electronics Bus. Equipment, Inc., Kansas City, 1988-89; sr. programmer systems analyst Osborn Labs, Inc., Shawnee Mission, Kans., from 1989. Cons. Clay County Computer Task Force, Liberty 1984-86. Cert. CPR instr. Am. Red Cross, Liberty 1987-88, Cert. leader Boy Scouts Am., Gladstone, 1987-91, city com. chmn. dir. Clay County Rotational Softball Assn., Gladstone 1987-88, league pres. 1988—. Mem. Data Processing Mgrs. Assn., Internat. Asn. Assessing Officers, Mo. Mappers Assn., Assn. Records Mgrs. Adminstrn. (v.p., dir. 1981-83). Roman Catholic. Avocations: photography, gardening, collecting baseball cards and player autographs. Home: Kansas City, Mo. Died Apr. 17, 2008.

SHOR, GEORGE G., JR., geophysicist, oceanographic administrator, engineer; b. NYC, June 8, 1923; s. George Gershon and Dorothy (Williston); m. Elizabeth Louise Noble, June 11, 1950; children: Alexander Noble, Carolyn Elizabeth, Donald Williston. BS, Calif. Inst. Tech., 1944, MS, 1948, PhD, 1954. Joined Seismic Explorations, Inc., Houston, 1948, party chief, 1949-50; asst. research geophysicist to research geophysicist Scripps Inst. Oceanography, La Jolla, Calif., 1953-69, prof. marine geophysics, 1969-90, prof. emeritus, 1990—2009, assoc. dir., 1968-91; mgr. Calif. Sea Grant program, 1969-73. Mem. NAS-NRC panel on Mohole site selection, 1959; com. on underwater telecommunications, 1968, USN Marine Geophys. Survey Liaison Council, 1965-67; spl. adv. to Com. for Coordination of Joint Prospecting for Mineral Resources in Asian Offshore Areas, 1976-91; chmn. ship scheduling panel Univ. Nat. Oceanographic Lab. Systems, 1987-89; sci. leader oceanographic expdns. to various parts of Pacific and Indian oceans, 1955-82. Served to lt. (j.g.) USNR, 1943-46; now comdr. USNR Ret. Fellow Geol. Soc. Am., Am. Geophys. Union, Am. Bamboo Soc. (pres. 1994-96); mem. Soc. Exploration Geophysicists, Scholia Club Home: La Jolla, Calif. Died July 3, 2009.

SHORTWAY, RICHARD ANTHONY, retired publishing executive; b. Fairlawn, NJ, Feb. 17, 1924; s. Anthony and Blanche (Wiley) S.; m. Dorothy McDonald, Oct. 6, 1945 (div. Apr. 1963); children: Catherine Carina, Mary Lida; m. Sue Ann Taylor, Aug. 6, 1963 (div. Dec. 1969); m. Gretchen Swartzwelder, Nov. 27, 1971 (div. Apr. 1977); 1 son, Richard Anthony; m. Kay R. Larson, May 1977. Student, Western Res. U., 1942-43. Advt. rep. Womens Wear Daily, NYC, 1946-50; advt. rep. Glamour mag., 1950-54, Eastern mgr., 1954-59, advt. mgr., 1959-63, Vogue mag., 1963-64, advt. dir., 1964—69, pub., 1969—87; pub. dir. British Vogue, 1987—92; v.p. Conde Nast Internat. Served to 1st lt. USAAF, 1944-45. Decorated D.F.C., Air medal with oak leaf clusters. Mem.: Westchester Country (Rye, N.Y.), Coveleigh (Rye, N.Y.). Died Nov. 10, 2008.

SHOTWELL, JANICE BOLTE, law librarian; b. Bklyn., Nov. 8, 1948; d. Henry Frederick and Anna Marie (Knickerbocker) B.; m. Richard Thomas Shotwell, May 23, 1975; 1 child, Andrew Henry. BA, Wilson Coll., Chambersburg, Pa., 1970; MS in Libr. Sci., U. N.C., 1972; paralegal cert., Roosevelt U., Chgo., 1984. Cataloger Towson State Coll., Balt., 1973-76; asst. libr. Florence (S.C.)-Darlington Tech. Coll., 1977; cataloger South Portland (Maine) Pub. Libr., 1977-78, br. libr., 1978-80; children's libr. Schlow Meml. Libr., State College, Pa., 1980-83; adult svcs. libr. C. Berger & Co., Wheaton, Ill., 1985-88; reference libr. Coll. of DuPage, Glen Ellyn, Ill., 1987-88; law libr. Berkshire Law Libr., Mass. Trial Ct., Pittsfield, Mass., from 1989. Editor: Living With the Law, 1992, supplement, 1994; co-author: How to Grow a Law Collection, 1994, How to Build a Law Collection, 1995. Mem. Am. Assn. Law Librs. (sec.-treas. legal info. svcs. to pub. sect. 1993-94, stds. com. state, ct. and county sect. 1993-94, co-recipient pub. rels. award 1995). Democrat. Episcopalian. Avocations: reading, baking, gardening. Home: Williamstown, Mass. Died Sept. 17, 2007.

SHRADER, LINDA MARIE, sales and management trainer; b. Birmingham, Ala., Aug. 21, 1959; d. Michael David and Winnie Frances (Bryant) S. Mktg. asst. Nat. Bank Commerce, Birmingham, 1981-83; bus. cons. Neill Corp., Hammond, La., 1983-85; dist. mgr. Aveda Corp., Mpls., 1985-87; mgr. Southeast region OGGI, Internat., Beverly Hills, Calif., 1987; prin. Shrader Sales and Mgmt. Tng., Atlanta, from 1987. Mem. Beauty and Barber Supply Inst., ASTD. Avocation: exercise. Died Feb. 29, 2008.

SHREFFLER, GENEVIEVE, author; b. Kansas City, Kans., July 27, 1925; g. Raymond S. Gripkey and Genevieve Ruth O'Brien; m. S. Gordon Shreffler, Apr. 9, 1971; children: Steven Paul, Deborah Lynn, Rebekah Helena. BS in Polit. Sci., U. Ctrl. Okla., now postgrad. Designer Braille dress patterns, Colorado Springs, Colo., 1966-69; pub. rels. dir. Okla. Women's Polit. Caucus, 1971-72; legis. intern Okla. State Legislature, 1976-77; ctrl. and ea. European specialist Internat. Trade Svcs., Oklahoma City, from 1993. Author: At the Edge, 1989; editor: Legends of Poland, 1990. Bd. dirs. Oklahoma City chpt. UN, 1988-89; founder, past pres. Polish-Am. Refugee Resettlement and Edn. Com., 1984—; active Freedoms Found. Valley Forge, Oklahoma City, 1990—; ex-officio mem. Ctrl. European Resettlement and Edn. Com., 1980-84, pres., 1984—; mem. Oklahoma City mayor's steering com. Internat. Sister City Program, 1993—; mem. internat. rels. commn. City of Scottsdale, Ariz., 1995—. Decorated Golden Cross of Merit (Poland), officer's cross Order of Poland Restituta; recipient Svc. award Rotary Internat. Club, 1984, Nat. Honor medal DAR, 1991. Mem. AAUW, Am. Bus. Women's Assn., Nat. Fedn. Press Women (Communicator of Achievement award Oklahoma City chpt.), European Acad. Arts, Scis. and Humanities (corr.), Alpha Chi. Home: Tucson, Ariz. Died May 1, 2008.

SHRIVER, EUNICE MARY KENNEDY (MRS. ROBERT SARGENT SHRIVER JR.), foundation administrator, volunteer, social worker; b. Brookline, Mass., July 10, 1921; d. Joseph P. and Rose (Fitzgerald) Kennedy; m. Robert Sargent Shriver, Jr., May 23, 1953; children: Robert Sargent III, Maria Owings Shriver Schwarzenegger, Timothy Perry, Mark Kennedy, Anthony Paul Kennedy. BS in Sociology, Stanford U., Palo Alto, Calif., 1943; student, Manhattanville Coll. of Sacred Heart, LHD (hon.), 1963, D'Youville Coll., 1962, Regis Coll., 1963, Newton Coll., 1973, Brescia Coll., 1974, Holy Cross Coll., 1979, Princeton U., 1979, Boston Coll., 1990; LittD (hon.), U. Santa Clara, 1962, Yale U., 1996, Cardinal Strich U., 2002. With spl. war problems div. US Dept. State, 1943—46; sec. Nat. Conf. on Prevention and Control juvenile Delinquency, Dept. of Justice, Washington, 1947-48; social worker Fed. Penitentiary for Women, Alderson, W.Va., 1950, House of Good Shepherd & Juvenile Court, Chgo., 1951-54; exec. v.p. Joseph P. Kennedy, Jr. Found., from 1956; regional chmn. women's div. Community Fund-Red Cross Joint Appeal, Chgo., 1958; founder, CEO Spl. Olympics, 1968—90, founder, hon. chmn., 1990—2009. Cons. to Pres. John F. Kennedy's Panel on Mental Retardation, 1961; founder Community & Caring, Inc., 1981; mem. Chgo. Commn. on Youth Welfare, 1959-62; mem. bd. Special Olympics Internat. Editor: A Community of Caring, 1982, 85, Growing Up Caring, 1990. Co-chmn. women's com. Dem. Nat. Conv., Chgo., 1956. Decorated Legion of Honor; recipient Albert Lasker Pub. Svc. award, Lasker Found., 1966, Philip Murray-William Green award (with Sargent Shriver), AFL-CIO, 1966, Humanitarian award A.A.M.D., 1973, Nat. Vol. Service award, 1973, Phila. Civic Ballet award, 1973, Prix de la Couronne Française, 1974, Presdl. Medal of Freedom, The White House, 1984, Freedom From Want medal, Roosevelt Inst., 1993, Jewish Sports Hall of Fame Humanitarium award, 2000, Champion of Children award, Phoenix Found. for Children, 2000, Aetna Voice of Conscience award, 2002, Juanita Kreps award, 2002, Life award, Noel Found., 2002, Theodore Roosevelt award, NCAA, 2002; inducted into Nat. Women's Hall of Fame, 2002; appeared on Special Olympics World Summer Games silver commemorative coin, 1995. Died Aug. 11, 2009.

SHUBERT, GUSTAVE HARRY, research executive, consultant, social scientist; b. Buffalo, Jan. 18, 1929; s. Gustave Henri and Ada Shubert (Smith) S.; m. Rhea Brickman, Mar. 29, 1952; children: Wendy J., David L. BA, Yale U., 1948; MA, NYU, 1951. Staff mem. Lincoln Lab., MIT, 1955-57; adminstr. sys. engring. Hycon Ea., Inc., Paris, 1957-59; with RAND Corp., Santa Monica, Calif., from 1959, corp. v.p. domestic programs, 1968-75, sr. corp. v.p. domestic programs, 1975-78, sr. corp. v.p., 1978-89, trustee, 1973-89, sr. fellow, corp. advisor and adv. trustee, 1989—2008; founding dir. Inst. Civil Justice, 1979-87; trustee mutual funds Neuberger Berman, NYC. Cons. Keene Corp., N.Y.C., 1990-92; pres. N.Y.C. Rand Inst., 1972-73, trustee, 1972-79; trustee Housing Allowance Offices Brown County, Wis. and South Bend, Ind., 1973-80; mem. adv. coun. Sch. Engring., Stanford U., 1976-79; mem. policy adv. com. clin. scholars program UCLA, 1975-88; mem. adv. group evaluation and methodology divsn. GAO, 1986-96; mem. adv. commn. on professionalism ABA, 1985-87; mem. Calif. jud. system com. Los Angeles County Bar Assn., 1984-85; mem. com. on evaluation of poverty rsch. NAS. Mem. Pacific Coun. of Fgn. Affairs, 1991; mem. U.S. adv. com. Internat. Inst. Applied Sys. Analysis, 1998—; mem. history dept. adv. bd. Carnegie Mellon U.; Served in USAF, 1951-55. Decorated Air medal with 3 oak leaf clusters, Commendation medal. Mem. AAAS, Am. Judicature Soc. (bd. dirs. 1987-90), Inst. Strategic Studies (London), Coun. of Fgn. Rels. Home: Pacific Palisades, Calif. Died Nov. 25, 2008.

SHULAW, RICHARD A., lawyer; b. Bowling Green, Ohio, Oct. 14, 1934; s. Francis Marion and Mary Frances (Morehead) S. AA, Ferris State Coll., 1958; LLB, Detroit Coll. of Law, 1963, JD, 1968. Bar: Mich., U.S. Dist. Ct. (ea. and we. dists.) Mich., U.S. Ct. Appeals (6th cir.), U.S. Supreme Ct. Sole practice, Owosso, Mich., from 1963. Chief asst. pros. atty. Shiwassee County, Mich., 1971, cir. ct. commr., 1965-67; neutral mediator Emmett, Charlevoix and Shiawassee Counties. With U.S. Army, 1954-55. Fellow Mich. State Bar Found.; mem. ABA, ATLA, Mich. Bar Assn. (ins. sect., negligence sect., law sect.), State Bar Mich. (sec., treas., v.p., mem. various coms., elected twice to rep. assembly), Shiawassee County Bar Assn. (v.p.), Mich. Trial Lawyers Assn., Mich. Def. Trial Counsel Inc., Owosso Country Club, Elks, KC (4th degree), Moose, Delta Theta Phi (past pres.). Republican. Roman Catholic. Avocation: golf. Home: Owosso, Mich. Died June 21, 2008.

SHULMAN, LAWRENCE EDWARD, biomedical researcher, rheumatologist; b. Boston, July 25, 1919; s. David Herman and Belle (Tishler) S.; m. Pauline K. Flint, July 19, 1946; m. Reni Trudinger, Mar. 20, 1959 (dec. 2000); children: Kathryn Verena, Barbara Corina. AB, Harvard U., 1941, postgrad., 1941-42; PhD, Yale U., 1945, MD, 1949. Diplomate Nat. Bd. Med. Examiners. Intern Johns Hopkins Hosp., 1949-50, resident and fellow in internal medicine, 1950-53; dir. connective tissue div. Johns Hopkins U., 1955-75, assoc. prof. medicine, from 1964; assoc. dir. div. arthritis, musculoskeletal and skin diseases NIH, Bethesda, Md., 1976-86, dir., 1982-86, dir. Nat. Inst. Arthritis, Musculoskeletal and Skin Diseases, 1986-94, dir. emeritus, 1994—2009, emissary for clin. rsch., 1995—2009. Chmn. med. adminstrn. com. Arthritis Found., Atlanta, 1974-75, exec. com., 1972-77; dir. Lupus Found. Am.; med. adv. bd. United. Scleroderma Found., Watsonville, Calif., 1977-88; chmn. sci. group rheumatic diseases WHO, 1989; W.R. Graham meml. lectr., 1973; Cochrane disting. lectr., 1993; vis. prof. Imperial Coll., London, 2002. Discoverer: Eosinophilic Fasciitis, 1974, new med. sign friction rubs in scleroderma, 1961. Recipient Sr. Investigator award Arthritis Found., 1957-62, Disting. Svc. award, 1979, Heberden medal for rsch., London, 1975, Superior Svc. award USPHS, 1985, master Am. Rheumatism Assn., 1986, Spl. Recognition award Nat. Osteoprosis Found., 1991, Spl. award Am. Acad. Orthop. Surgeons, 1992, Presdl. citation for leadership Am. Acad. Dermatology, 1993, Leadership award Lupus Found. Am., 1994, Career Achievement award Am. Coll. Rheumatology, 1994, Outstanding Support Rsch. award Am. Soc. Bone Mineral Rsch., 1994, Gold medal Am. Coll. Rheumatology, 1995, award of Merit, NASA, 1995, Dean's Spl. Recognition award Johns Hopkins Medicine, 2004. Fellow ACP, AAAS; mem. Am. Rheumatism Assn. (pres. 1974-75), Pan-Am. League Against Rheumatism (pres. 1982-86, Morino Gold medal award 2002), Soc. Investigative Dermatology, Am. Soc. Bone Mineral Rsch. Home: Washington, DC. Died Oct. 10, 2009.

SHUMAN, NICHOLAS ROMAN, retired journalist; b. Chgo., June 30, 1921; s. Roman William and Pauline (Stasevich) S.; m. Marilyn Elaine Johnson, Feb. 23, 1952; children: Kristin Mary, Elizabeth Carol, Mark Nicholas. BA, U. Ill., 1943. With Chgo. Jour. Commerce, 1938-46; mem. staff Herald-American, Chgo., 1946-51, asst. photo editor, 1947-51; mem. staff Chgo. Daily News, 1951-78, fin. editor, 1961-65, asst. mng. editor, 1965-69, nat. and fgn. editor, 1969-77, chief editorial writer, 1977-78; editorial writer Chgo. Sun-Times, 1978-84; prof. journalism Columbia Coll., Chgo., 1984-91, cons., 1992—2009; columnist Chgo. Reporter, 1985-90; sr. editor World Book Ency., 1965-66; profl. instr. Medill Sch. Journalism, Northwestern U., 1954-61. TV commentator, 1958-61 Founding pres. Arlington Heights (Ill.) Human Relations Com., 1965. Served to 1st lt. AUS, 1943-46, ETO. Recipient awards Ill. AP, UPI, John Howard Assn., Inland Press Assn., Chgo. Newspaper Guild; nominated for Pulitzer prize 3 times. Mem. Alpha Kappa Lambda, Sigma Delta Chi. Home: Arlington Heights, Ill. Died Mar. 17, 2009.

SIDDONS, JAMES KENNETH, fuel company executive, mechanical engineer; b. Milw., June 15, 1928; s. James Kenneth and Loretta (Bush) S.; m. Dolores Gardner, Sept. 9, 1950; children: Jeffrey, Sarah Siddons Bowers, Paul David. BSME, Marquette U., 1951. Project engr. Am. Airlines, Tulsa, 1966-80; exec. v.p. Nat. Chassis, Kansas City, Mo., 1981; pres. Tri-State Refueler Co., Kansas City, Kans., from 1981. Mem. Soc. Automotive Engrs. Democrat. Avocations: sculpture, gourmet cooking. Home: Warrensburg, Mo. Died Mar. 9, 2008.

SIEGEL, BART HOWARD, financial planner, auditor; b. Glen Ridge, NJ, June 27, 1958; s. Martin and Norma (Kesselman) S.; m. Lunelle Mizell, Oct. 20, 1991. BS in Fin., Fla. State U., 1981; MBA, Rutgers U., 1988. CFP. Intern Stephens, Inc., Little Rock, 1981-82; owner That Spl. Touch Cleaners, Cherry Hill, N.J., 1982-83; fin. cons. Shearson Lehman Bros., Bloomfield, N.J., 1983-86; field analyst GE Capital Ccorp., NYC, 1988-90; internal auditor Fla. Dept. State, Tallahassee, from 1990. Registered investment advisor, SEC, 1986; cons. Bart H. Siegel, CFP, MBA, 1988—. Contbr. articles to profl. publs. Mem. Nat. Assn.

Securities Dealers, Jacksonville Jaycees. Republican. Jewish. Avocations: economic analysis, political author and commentator, canine training. Home: Tampa, Fla. Died Aug. 7, 2008.

SIFTON, CHARLES PROCTOR, federal judge; b. NYC, Mar. 18, 1935; s. Paul F. and Claire G. S.; m. Susan Scott Rowland, May 20, 1986; children: Samuel, Tobias, John. AB, Harvard U., 1957; LL.B., Columbia U., 1961. Bar: N.Y. 1961. Assoc. Cadwalader, Wickersham & Taft, 1961-62, 64-66; staff atty. US Senate Fgn. Rels. Com., 1962-63; asst. U.S. atty. (so. dist.) NY US Dept. Justice, NYC, 1966-69, chief appellate atty, 1968—69; ptnr. LeBoeuf, Lamb, Leiby and MacRae, NYC, 1969-77; judge US Dist. Ct. (ea. dist.) N.Y., Bklyn., 1977—2000, chief judge, 1995-2000, sr. judge, 2000—09. Mem.: Bar Assn. City of NY. Died Nov. 9, 2009.

SIGEL, DIANE E., elementary school educator; b. Pitts., Mar. 13, 1942; d. Alfred I. and Ida S. (Darling) Steinman; m. Bernard Sigel, June 20, 1965; children: Ellen, Meridith. BS, Pa. State U., 1964. Tchr. Brick Twp. (N.J.) Bd. Edn., 1965-67, Hammonton (N.J.) Bd. Edn., 1967-69, Pleasantville (N.J.) Bd. Edn., 1964-65 and from 70. Sec. Hammonton Recreation Club, 1982—, Temple Beth El, Hammonton, 1982-90. Mem. NEA, N.J. Edn. Assn., Atlantic County Edn. Assn., Pleasantville Edn. Assn. Avocations: working with foreign exchange students, travel agency work, travel. Home: Hammonton, NJ. Died July 13, 2008.

SIGLER, CHARLOTTE LEE LLEWEL, English and reading specialist; b. Frostburg, Md., Jan. 29, 1926; d. Thomas Price and Buelah (Willison) Llewellyn; m. Charles Harry Sigler, Oct. 12, 1947; children: Larry Allan, Dennis Wayne. BS, Frostburg State U., 1961, MEd, 1967; postgrad., W.Va. U., 1978-81. Cert. English and reading tchr., Md. Tchr. English, math., social studies and typing Allegany County Bd. Edn., Flintstone, Md., 1961-80, tchr. Mt. Savage, Md., 1981-83, English and secondary reading supr. Cumberland, Md., from 1983; tchr. English Mt. Savage High Sch., 1970-80; univ. supr., grad. asst. W.Va. U., Morgantown, 1980-81. Supr. writing English curricula Allegany County Bd.Edn., Cumberland, 1983-88. Mem. Network Women in Ednl. Leadership for Md. State Dept. Edn.; mem. Md. Vocat. Equity Program Network. Mem. AAUW (pres. 1976-80, editor newsletter 1978-80), Nat. Coun. Tchrs. of English, Assn. for Supervision and Curriculum Devel., Federated Garden Club (pres. 1977-79), Youghiogheny Mountain Lake Club, Phi Delta Kappa, Delta Kappa Gamma (prfes. 1982-84), Kappa Pi (life, pres. 1960-61). Avocations: ceramics, photography, bridge, piano, U.S. and fgn. travel. Home: Frostburg, Md. Died Nov. 25, 2007.

SIKER, ESTELLE, pediatrician; b. Port Chester, NY, Dec. 24, 1918; d. Samuel S. and Adele (Weiser) S.; m. Henry O. Bernstein, June 28, 1953; children: Joel J., Jonathan A. BA, NYU, 1939; MD, Med. Coll. of Pa., 1943; MPH, Yale Sch. Medicine, 1964. Lic. MD, Conn., N.Y., Calif.; Diplomate Am. Bd. Pediatrics. Pediatrician pvt. practice, Port Chester, N.Y., 1946-49; med. dir. pediatrics unit Montefiore Med. Group, Bronx, N.Y., 1949-53; crippled children physician Conn. State Dept. Health, Hartford, 1954-63, chief maternal & child health sect., 1964-67, dir. community health div., 1967-87; cons. self-employed Hartford, from 1987. Contbr. numerous articles to profl. health jours. Recipient CEA Winslow award Conn. Pub. Health Assn. Fellow Am. Acad. Pediatrics; mem. AMA, Conn. State Med. Assn., Conn. Pub. Health Assn. (past pres., bd. dirs. 1989—). Avocations: reading, needlecrafts, grandchildren, gardening. Home: East Hartford, Conn. Died June 29, 2008.

SILVER, PAUL GORDON, geophysicist; b. L.A., Nov. 30, 1948; s. Theodore L. and Rose (Cohen) S.; m. Nathalie Valetie, June 21, 1980; children: Karen, Celine. BA in Psychology magna cum laude, UCLA, 1970; BA in Geology, U. Calif., Berkeley, 1976; PhD in Geophysics, U. Calif., San Diego, 1982. Sr. staff scientist Carnegie Inst. DTM, Washington, 1982—2009; rsch. assoc. prof. dept. earth and planetary scis. Johns Hopkins U., Balt., 1986—2009. Participant various sci. expdns.; rep. to Am. Geol. Inst., Seismol. Soc. Am., 1997-2009; mem. com. of charis Inc. Rsch. Instns. for Seismology, 1996-2009. Assoc. editor Jour. Geophys. Rsch., 1987-90; contbr. articles to profl. jours. Recipient Carl Eckart award Scripps Inst. Oceanography, 1982; UNESCO lectr., 1988. Fellow Geol. Soc. Am., Am. Geophys. Union (pres. seismology section, 2002-04), Am. Acad. Arts & Scis.; mem. AAAS, Seismol. Soc. Am., Phi Beta Kappa. Home: N Bethesda, Md. Died Aug. 7, 2009.

SILVER, RON (RONALD ARTHUR SILVER), actor; b. NYC, July 2, 1946; s. Irving Roy and May (Zimelman) S.; m. Lynne Miller, Dec. 24, 1975 (div. 1997); children: Adam, Alexandra BA in Spanish & Chinese, U. Buffalo, 1969; MA in Chinese History, St. John's U./Chinese Culture, Yangmingshan, Taiwan, 1970; student, Yale Law Sch., 1991. Stage appearances include Kaspar, Public Insult, 1971, El Grande de Coca-Cola, 1972, 75, Lotta, 1973, More Than You Deserve, 1973, Awake and Sing, 1976, Angel City, 1977, In the Boom Boom Room, 1979, Gorilla, 1983, Friends, 1983-84, Hurly Burly, 1984-85, Social Security, 1986, Hunting Cockroaches, 1987, Speed-the-Plow (Tony and Drama Desk awards, 1988), 1988, 92, Broken Glass, 1994; (films) Tunnelvision, 1976, Semi-Tough, 1977, The Entity, 1981, Silent Rage, 1982, Best Friends, 1982, Lovesick, 1982, Silkwood, 1983, The Goodbye People, 1984, Garbo Talks, 1984, Oh God! You Devil, 1984, Eat and Run, 1985, Enemies: A Love Story, 1989, Blue Steel, 1990, Reversal of Fortune, 1990, The Good Policeman, 1991, Married to It, 1992, Live Wire, 1992, Mr. Saturday Night, 1992, Time Cop, 1994, Deadly Outbreak, 1996 Girl 6, 1996, The Arrival, 1996, Danger Zone, 1996, Black and White, 1998, The White Raven, 1998, Exposure, 2000, Festival in Cannes, 2001, Ali, 2001, The Wisher, 2002, Red Mercury, 2005, Find Me Guilty, 2006, The Ten, 2007, Distance Runners, 2008; (TV movies) The Return of the World's Greatest Detective, 1976, Murder at the Mardi Gras, 1978, Betrayal, 1978, Dear Detective, 1979, Word of Honor, 1981, Trapped in Silence, 1986, The Billionaire Boys Club, 1987, Das Rattennest, 1988, Fellow Traveller, 1989, Forgotten Prisoners: From the Amnesty Files, 1991, Blind Side, 1992, A Woman of Independent Means, 1995, Almost Golden: The Jessica Savitch Story, 1995, Kissinger and Nixon, 1995, Shadow Zone: The Undead Express, 1996, The Beneficiary, 1997, Skeletons, 1997, Rhapsody in Bloom, 1998, Love Is Strange, 1999, In the Company of Spies, 1999, Switched at Birth, 1999, Ratz, 2000, Cutaway, 2000, American Tragedy, 2000, When Billie Beats Bobby, 2001, Master Spy: The Robert Hanssen Story, 2002, Jack, 2004, Xenophobia, 2008; (TV appearances) The Mac Davis Show, 1976, Big Eddie, 1975, Rhoda, 1975, McMillan & Wife, 1975, The Rockford Files, 1975, The Stockard Channing Show, Hill Street Blues, 1983, Trying Times, 1987, Wiseguy (4 episodes), 1988-89, Chicago Hope, 1996, The Practice, 2001, Skin (6 episodes), 2003-04, Law & Order (2 episodes), 2004-07, Law & Order: Trial by Jury, 2006, Crossing Jordan, 2007; (TV series) Baker's Dozen, 1982, Chicago Hope, 1996-97, Veronica's Closet, 1998-99, The West Wing, 2001-06; (mini-series) Kane & Abel, 1985, A Woman of Independent Means, 1995; actor, dir. (TV movies) Lifepod, 1993 Recipient Israel Cultural award. Mem. AFTRA, SAG, Actors' Equity Assn. (pres. 1991-2000), Actors Studio, Actors Fund (trustee), Acad. Motion Picture Arts and Scis., The Creative Coalition (founder, pres. 1989-93), Coun. Fgn. Rels., Coun. Woodrow Wilson Internat. Ctr. for Scholars, Nat. Acad. TV Arts and Scis. Independent. Died Mar. 15, 2009.

SILVERANDER, CAROL WEINSTOCK, manufacturing executive; b. San Francisco, July 19, 1946; d. Vernon A. and Kathleen (Taylor) Davison; m. D. Michael Romano, Apr. 4, 1971 (div. Mar. 1979); children: Michael G. Romano, Kimberly A. Romano; m. Ronald D. Weinstock, Jan. 12, 1984 (div.); m. Michael David Silverander, Dec. 28, 1995. BA in Edn., U. Ariz., 1964-70, grad. work, 1977-82; MS in Photography, Brooks Inst. Photography, 1982-84. Exhibits Shalom-Salaam Liese Communal Svcs. Bldg., Tucson, 1980; photographer Jews of Ethiopia, 1982, Nat. Jewish Cmty. Rels. Adv. Coun., 1983, Jews of Ireland, 1985-87, Bet Hatefutsot Mus. of Diaspora, Tel Aviv, 1987-88, Westside Jewish Cmty. Ctr., LA, 1989, Irish Jewish Mus., Dublin, Ireland, from 1992; pres. EthnoGraphics, Santa Barbara, Calif., from 1987. Pres., owner EthnoGraphics Greeting Cards, 1987—. Exec. bd., adv. com. Jewish Fedn. So. Ariz., 1979-82 chmn. Run for Soviet Jewry, 1983-84. Recipient Internat. Greeting Card awards, 1988, 91-2000, Cmty. Svc. award Jewish Fedn. So. Ariz., 1981, Simon Rockower award for excellence in Jewish journalism, Excellence in Photography mag. category, 1992. Mem. Am. Soc. Media Photographers, Greeting Card Assn. (bd. dirs. 1994—, exec. bd 1999-2000). Died June 27, 2008.

SILVESTRIS, ELAINE JOY, employee relations administrator, notary public; b. Worcester, Mass., Jan. 8, 1943; d. Roland Joseph and Margaret Ann (Arnieri) Gustafson; m. Maurice Richard Silvestris, Nov. 6, 1965. Cert. in Human Resources, Moravian Coll., Bethlehem, Pa., 1985; student, Allentown Coll. of St. Francis de Sales, Center Valley, Pa., from 1988. Legal sec. Mirick, O'Connell, DeMallie and Lougee, Worcester, 1961-65, Edward J. Brady, Camden, N.J., 1966-69; legal sec. to ptnr. Sigmon, Briody, Littner and Ross, Bethlehem, 1969-70; legal sec. to sr. ptnr. Weaver, Weaver and Weaver, Catasauqua, Pa., 1970-76; adminstrv. sec. to pres. and v.p. sales Lehigh Sales and Products, Allentown, Pa., 1976-78; sr. stenographer U.S. Postal Svc., Lehigh Valley, Pa., 1978-82, injury compensation supr., 1982-85, employee relations mgr., from 1985. Account rep. DialAmerica Mktg., Inc., 1988; notary pub., Lehigh County, Pa., 1974— Recipient Cert. Appreciation for Outstanding Efforts in Hiring Visually Disabled People, Commonwealth Pa., 1987. Mem. Nat. Assn. Profl. Saleswomen (Lehigh Valley chpt.), Pa. Assn. Notaries, Pa. Soc. Profl. Engrs. (aux. group chmn. 1983-84, sec. 1978-80, v.p. 1978-79, 2nd v.p. and Pa. del. 1976-77), Nat. Assn. for Female Execs. Inc. Republican. Methodist. Avocations: gardening, knitting, swimming, walking, reading. Home: Allentown, Pa. Died Apr. 28, 2008.

SILVIS, DONN EUGENE, communications educator, consultant; b. Greeley, Colo., May 6, 1942; s. William Arthur and Mildred Ruth (Lowe) S.; m. Sharon Cowles, Apr. 24, 1966; 1 child, Donn Bradley. AA, East L.A. Community Coll., 1962, BS in Journalism, Calif. State Poly Tech., San Luis Obispo, 1965; MA in Mass Communications, Calif. State U., Fullerton, 1988. Coord. employee communications Norris Industries, LA, 1965-76; asst. v.p. mktg. communications Avco Fin. Svcs., Newport Beach, Calif., 1976-85; lectr. Calif. State U., Fullerton, 1982-88, asst. prof. LA, 1989, prof. comm. Dominguez Hills, from 1990. Owner Silvis Communications, Cerritos, Calif., 1986—. Assoc. editor: Newport Beach '75; co-editor: Inside Organizational Communications, 1981; co-author: Public Relations Writing: Strategies and Skills, 1991. Advisor Juvenile Diversion Project, Cerritos, 1971-75; bd. dirs. South Orange County Vol. Ctr., Santa Ana, Calif., 1981-86; mem. press, pub. rels. and publications commn. 1984 Olympics, L.A., 1981-84. Capt. U.S. Army, 1965-68, Korea. Fellow Internat. Assn. Bus. Communicators (v.p. 1976-78); mem. Pub. Rels. Soc. Am. Avocations: photography, golf, fishing, travel. Home: Cerritos, Calif. Died May 31, 2008.

SIMCIC, KENNETH JOSEPH, career officer, endocrinologist; b. Pitts., Oct. 19, 1956; s. Nicholas Francis and Margaret (Krotec) S.; m. Mary Margaret Welsh, June 12, 1982; children: Natalie Marie, Jacqueline Marie, Lauren Elizabeth. BS in Biology, Duquesne U., 1977; MD, Temple U. Med. Sch., 1982. Cert. Am. Bd. Internal Medicine, 1985, Am. Bd. Endocrinology and Metabolism, 1989, Nat. Bd. Med. Examiners, 1983. Commd. 2d lt. U.S. Army, 1982, advanced through grades to lt. col., 1994; intern internal medicine Fitzsimmons Army Med. Ctr., Aurora, Colo., 1982-83, resident internal medicine, 1983-85. Asst. clin. prof. Tex. Tech. U. Sch. Medicine, El Paso, 1990-95, assoc. prof. medicine, 1995—; presenter in field. Contbr. articles to profl. jours. Active Focus on Family. Fitzsimmons Army Med. Ctr. Endocrinology fellow, 1987-89; recipient Intern' award for Best Attending Physician/Dept. Medicine William Beaumont Army Med. Ctr., 1990. Fellow ACP; mem. Endocrine Soc., Soc. Uniformed Endocrinologists, Omicron Delta Kappa, Phi Kappa Phi. Republican. Roman Catholic. Avocations: baseball coaching, writing, skating, special olympics, medical ethics. Home: San Antonio, Tex. Died Feb. 3, 2008.

SIMKIN, THOMAS EDWARD, geologist; b. Auburn, NY, Nov. 11, 1933; s. William Edward and Ruth Helen (Commons) S.; m. Sharon Marie Russell, July 3, 1965; children: Shona Kathleen, Adam Javier. BS, Swarthmore Coll., 1955; PhD, Princeton U., 1965. Instr. SUNY, Binghamton, 1964-65; postdoctoral fellow U. Chgo., 1965-67; supr. geology Smithsonian Oceanographic Sorting Ctr., Washington, 1967-71; sr. curator petrology and volcanology Nat. Mus. Natural History, Smithsonian Instn., Washington, 1972—2003, sr. geologist and volcanologist Divsn. Petrology and Volcanology, 2003—09. Sec. for the Americas (sci.) Charles Darwin Found. for Galapagos Isles, 1970-90. Co-author: Volcanoes of the World, 1993, This Dynamic Planet; editor: Catalog of Active Volcanoes of the World, Internat. Assn. Volcanology, 1980; contbr. articles to profl. jours. Mem. Arlington County Environ. Improvement Commn., 1981-91. With US Coast and Geodetic Survey, 1956-58. Recipient Krafft Medal for outstanding contributions to volcanology, Internat. Assn. of Volcanology and Chemistry of the Earth's Interior, 2004, Award for lifetime contributions to sci., Va. Mus. Natural History. Mem.: Arlington County Parks and Recreation Commn. (founding mem.), Geological Soc. of Washington (former pres.), Internat. Assn. Volcanology, Am. Geophys. Union. Died June 10, 2009.

SIMMONDS, RAE NICHOLS, musician, composer, educator; b. Lynn, Mass., Feb. 25, 1919; d. Raymond Edward and Abbie Iola (Spinney) Nichols; m. Carter Fillebrown, Jr., June 27, 1941 (div. May 15, 1971); children: Douglas C. (dec.), Richard A., Mary L., Donald E.; m. Ronald John Simmonds, Oct. 9, 1971 (dec. Nov. 1995). AA, Westbrook Coll., Portland, Maine, 1981; B in Music Performance summa cum laude, U. Maine, 1984; MS in Edn., U. So. Maine, 1989; PhD, Walden U., 1994. Founder, dir. Studio of Music/Children's Studio of Drama, Portsmouth, NH, 1964-71, Studio of Music, Bromley, England, 1971-73, Bromley Children's Theatre, 1971-73, Oughterard Children's Theatre, County Galway, Ireland, 1973-74, Studio of Music, Portland, Maine, 1977-96, West Baldwin, Maine, from 1997; resident playwright Children's Theatre of Maine, Portland, 1979-81; organist, choir dir. Stevens Ave. Congl. Ch., Portland, 1987-95; field faculty advisor Norwich U., Montpelier, Vt., 1995. Field advisor grad. program Vt. Coll., Norwich U., 1995; cons./educator mus. tng. for disabled vets. VA, Portsmouth, N.H., 1966-69; show pianist and organist, mainland U.S.A., 1939-59, Hawaii, 1959-62, Rae Nichols Trio, 1962—; mus. dir. Theatre By the Sea, Portsmouth, N.H., 1969-70. Author/composer children's musical: Shamrock Road, 1980 (Blue Stocking award 1980), Glooscap, 1980; author/composer original scripts and music: Cinderella, If I Were a Princess, Beauty and the Beast, Baba Yaga - A Russian Folk Tale, The Journey - Musical Bible Story, The Perfect Gift - A Christmas Legend; original stories set to music include: Heidi, A Little Princess, Tom Sawyer, Jungle Book, Treasure Island; compositions include: London Jazz Suite, Bitter Suite, Jazz Suite for Trio, Sea Dream, Easter (chorale), Rae Simmonds Jazz Trio Songbook Series, (CD) Fascinatin' Gershwin Rae Simmonds Jazz Trio, 2000; contbr. Maine Women Writers Collection. Recipient Am. Theatre Wing Svc. award, 1944, Pease AFB Svc. Club award, 1967, Bumpus award Westbrook Coll., 1980; Nat. Endowment for Arts grantee, 1969-70; Women's Lit. scholar, 1980, Westbrook scholar, 1980-81, Nason scholar, 1983; Kelaniya U. (Colombo, Sri Lanka) rsch. fellow, 1985-86. Mem. ASCAP, Internat. Soc. Poets, Internat. League Women Composers, Music Tchrs. of Maine, Am. Guild of Organists, Music Tchrs. Nat. Assn., Internat. Alliance for Women in Music, Doctorate Assn. N.Y. Educators, Inc., Delta Omicron, Phi Kappa Phi. Democrat. Episcopalian. Avocations: travel, stamp collecting/philately. Home: West Baldwin, Maine. Died Feb. 9, 2008.

SIMMONS, EDWARD CLAY, dentist; b. Ashland, Kans., July 19, 1925; s. Earl Clay and Leona Bessie (Hughes) S.; m. Joan Redding, Dec. 26 1946; children: Rick, Tanya, Randy. Student, Kans. Wesleyan U., 1947-49; DDS, U. Mo.,

Kansas City, 1953. Gen. practice dentistry, Salina, Kans., from 1953. Adj. prof. dental hygiene Wichita (Kans.) State U., 1981—; instr. Kans. Wesleyan U., Salina, 1957-59. Mem. insdl. com. Salina C. of C., 1957-65; trustee St. John's Mil. Sch., Salina, 1964-68; mem. cen. regional testing state bd. of dental examiners U. Mo., Kansas City, 1973-80. Served with U.S. Army, 1944-46, ETO. Mem. Kans. State Dental Assn. (pres. 1981-82, Man of Yr. 1993), Kans. Soc. Dentistry for Children (pres. 1972-74), Acad. Gen. Dentistry (pres. 1975-76, Man of Yr. award 1983), Am. Assn. Endodontics, Golden Belt Dist. Soc. (pres. 1957-58). Clubs: Salina Country (bd. dirs. 1973-76). Lodges: Rotary, Masons, Shriners. Republican. Episcopalian. Home: Salina, Kans. Died Mar. 8, 2008.

SIMON, MELVIN, real estate developer, professional sports team owner; b. Oct. 21, 1926; s. Max and Mae Simon; m. Bren Burns, Sept. 14, 1972; children: Deborah, Cynthia, Tamme, David, Max (dec. 1999). BS in Acctg., CCNY, 1949, MBA in Real Estate, 1983; PhD (hon.), Butler U., 1986, Ind. U., 1991. Leasing agt. Albert Frankel Co., Indpls., 1955-60; co-founder Melvin Simon & Assocs., Indpls., 1959—2009, pres., 1960-73, co-chmn. bd., 1973; co-owner NBA Ind. Pacers, Indpls., from 1983; went pub. becoming Simon Property Group, 1993; chmn. bd. Simon Property Group, Inc., Indpls., 1993—95, co-chmn. bd. dirs., 1995—2009; merged with DeBartolo Realty Corp. to become Simon DeBartolo Group, 1996; reverted to Simon Property Group, 1998. Adv. bd. Wharton's Real Estate, Phila., 1986-2009 Exec. prodr. (films) Dominique, 1978, The Manitou, 1978, Matilda, 1978, When You Comin' Back, Red Ryder?, 1979, Seven, 1979, When A Stranger Calls, 1979, Scavenger Hynt, 1979, Cloud Dancer, 1980, The Stuntman, 1980, My Bodyguard, 1980, The Man With Bogart's Face, 1980, Zorro, the Gay Blade, 1981, Chu Chu and the Philly Flash, 1981, Porky's, 1982, Porky's II: The Next Day, 1983, Porky's Revenge, 1985, UFOria, 1985. Adv. bd. dean's coun. Ind. U., Bloomington; bd. dirs. United Cerebral Palsy, Indpls., Muscular Dystrophy Assn., Indpls., Jewish Welfare Found., Indpls.; trustee Urban Land Inst., Internat. Coun. Shopping Ctrs. Served in US Army. Recipient Horatio Alger award Boy's Club Indpls., 1986; named Man of Yr., Jewish Welfare Found., 1980; named one of Forbes' Richest Ams., 1999-2009, World's Richest People, 2005-09. Democrat. Jewish. Died Sept. 16, 2009.

SIMONEAUX, SANDI SUE, veterinarian; b. New Orleans, Oct. 1, 1969; d. Clarence Gabriel and Sandra Claire (Faust) (dec.) S. DVM, La. State U., 1995. Assoc. veterinarian Metairie (La.) Small Animal Hosp., 1995-96, Crowder Animal Hosp., New Orleans, 1996-98, Primary Vet. Care, from 1998. Mem. AVMA, Am. Holistic Veterinary Med. Assn., Am. Animal Hosp. Assn., La. Vet. Med. Assn., S.E. La. Vet. Assn. (social chmn., bd. dirs. 1996-97). Roman Catholic. Avocations: horseback riding, reading, golf, needlepoint, computers, target practice. Home: New Orleans, La. Died Nov. 11, 2007.

SIMONS, RICHARD STUART, retailer, owner; b. Marion, Ind., July 26, 1920; s. Erwin Philip and Tillie Ethel (Bernstein) S.; m. Rosmarie Roeschli, Mar. 5, 1957; 1 child, Charlotte S. AB, Ind. U., 1942. Editor Winchester (Ind.) Jour.-Herald, 1942-44, Tipton (Ind.) Daily Tribune, 1944-48; feature writer Indpls. Star Sun. Mag., 1949-85; owner Richard Clothing Co., Marion Ind., 1954-87; ret., 1987. Lectr. journalism Ind. U., Bloomington, 1952; bd. dirs. Menswear Retailers of Am., Washington, 1983-87. Author: The Rivers of Indiana, 1985 (Gov.'s award 1985); co-author: Railroads of Indiana, 1997 (recipient George W. and Constance M. Hilton Book award 1998); contbg. editor: (book) Popular Mechanics' Picture History of American Transportation, 1952; contbr. articles to profl. jours. Bd. trustees Marion (Ind.) Gen. Hosp., 1955-64, pres., 1963-64; pres. bd. dirs. Mississinewa Arts Coun., Marion, 1971-72, Marion Philharmonic Orch., 1974-75; bd. trustees Marion (Ind.) Pub. Libr., 1976-80, pres., 1977; bd. dirs. New Harmony (Ind.) State Meml. Commn., 1978-83; v.p. Nat. Railway Hist. Soc., Phila., 1988-94; pres. Ind. Hist. Soc., Indpls., 1989-94; bd. dirs. Minnetrista Cultural Ctr., Muncie, Ind., 1988—, Soc. for Advanced Study, Ind. U., 1990-95; historian for Grant County, 1998—. Recipient Sagamore of the Wabash award Gov. Ind., 1995, Hoosier Historian award Ind. Hist. Soc., 1996, Disting. Alumnus award Ind. U., 1984, Award of Merit, Am. Assn. for State and Local History, 1972. Mem. Kiwanis, Elks. Avocations: travel, profl. writing, spectator baseball, railroad-related activities. Home: Marion, Ind. Died Feb. 12, 2008.

SIMS, KONSTANZE OLEVIA, social worker, case manager, career counselor; b. Dallas, Dec. 20, 1944; d. Kenneth Winn and Odie Lee (Wells) S. Student, U. Dallas, 1963-64; BA, U. Tex., Arlington, 1968; MEd, U. North Tex., 1972. Sec. Stillman Coll. Regional Campaign Fund, Dallas, 1969; employment interviewer Zale Corp., Dallas, 1969-71; sch. counselor Bishop Dunne High Sch, Dallas, 1973-78; dir. guidance Notre Dame High Sch., Wichita Falls, Tex., 1978-81; taxpayer svc. rep. IRS, Dallas, 1981-83, acct. analyst, 1983-88; freelance Dallas, 1989-90; social worker Tex. Dept. Human Svcs., Dallas, 1991-96, Tex. Workforce Commn., 199-97; career counselor Lockheed Martin IMS, from 1997. Reader, North Tex. Taping & Radio for the Blind, Dallas, 1991—;; mem. Whale Adoption Project; mem. Union Chorale, St. Peter the Apostle Cath. Ch. Mass Choir, United in Praise Choral Group, Line 22 Knights of Peter Claver, Auxiliary. Mem. AAUW, Am. Counseling Assn., Nat. Specialty Merchandising Assn., Am. Multicultural Counseling Assn., Am. Bible Tchrs. Assn., Tex. Counseling Assn., Tex. Multicultural Counseling Assn., Assn. for Spiritual, Ethical, and Religious Values in Counseling, U. Tex Arlington Alumni Assn., U. North Tex. Alumni Assn. Avocations: reading, crossword puzzles, singing. Home: Dallas, Tex. Died Aug. 11, 2008.

SIMSON, BEVLYN, artist; b. Columbus, Ohio, Sept. 9, 1917; d. Amon and Fannie Florence (Gilbert) Thall; m. Theodore Richard Simson, Mar. 25, 1938; children: Sherran Blair, Douglas A. BFA, Ohio State U., Columbus, 1969, MFA, 1972. Author: Prints and Poetry, 1969; one-woman shows include J.B. Speed Art Mus., Louisville, 1970, Huntington Gallery, Columbus, 1970, 1973, United Christian Ctr., 1970, Bodley Gallery, NY, 1971, 1974, Gilman Galleries, Chgo., 1971, Gallery 200, 1972, Hopkins Hall Gallery, Ohio State U., Columbus, 1972, Meth. Theol Sch., Deleware, Ohio, 1973, Columbus Public Lib., 1973, Garfinkels, Washington, DC, 1973, City Hall, Mayor's Office, Columbus, 1974, 1982, Capital U., Bexley, Ohio, 1977, Hillel Found., Ohio State U., 1978, Columbus Tech. Inst., 1979, Springfield Art Mus., Ohio, 1980, Peace Luth. Ch., Gahanna, Ohio, 1981, Franklin U. Gallery, Columbus, 1981, Columbus Mus. Art Collectors Gallery, 1983, Ohio State U., Dept. Art Biennial Alumni Exhbn., 2005, exhibited in juried and invitational shows, Columbus Mus. Art-Ohio Art League, 1968, 1970, 1971, 1973—75, 1977—80, 1986, Ohio Statehouse and State Office Tower, Columbus, 1968—78, Battelle Meml. Inst., 1969—73, 1975, 1978, 1981, Schumacher Gallery, Capital U., Bexley, Ohio, 1969—85, 1987—88, Salles d'Exposition, Paris, 1969, Am. Culture Ctr., Kyoto, Japan, J.B. Speed Art Mus. Collector's Gallery, Louisville, 1970—85, Studio San Guiseppe, Mt. St. Joseph Coll., Cin., 1971, Ohio State U. Coll. Arts, 2nd Biennial Alumni Exhbn., Hopkins Hall Gallery, 1972, 2nd Internat. Art Exhbn., Paramaribo, Surinam, 1974, Mansfield Art Ctr., Ohio, 1971, Collector's Showroom, Chgo., 1971—82, Gov.'s Mansion State of Ohio, 1972, 1974, Western. Ill. U., Macomb, 1972, Albatross Gallery, Rome, 1972, Palazzo Dell Exprizioni, 1972, Chautauqua Assn., NY, 1973, Butler Inst. Am. Art, Youngtown, Ohio, 1973, 1976, Huntington Gallery, Columbus, 1973—74, Gallery 200, 1972—76, Columbus C. of C., 1974—75, Zanesville Art Ctr., Ohio, 1976, Columbus Inst. Contemporary Art, 1978, Nationwide Plaza Gallery, Columbus, 1980, Art in Columbus, 50 Years, State Office Tower, 1980, Franklin U., Columbus, 1980, Ohio Art League, 1987, Ohio State U., 1993, Jeffrey Mansion, Bexley, Ohio, 1996, 10th Ann. Women Artists Expo Seal of Ohio Girl Scout Coun., Inc., Columbus, 1996, Financial Group Gallery, Worthington, Ohio, 1997, Ohio Art League, 1997, 4th Hall Gallery, Ohio State U., 1997, Concourse Gallery, Upper Arlington, Ohio, 1998, 13th Ann. Women Artists Expo Art in The Nation Wide Atrium, Columbus, 1999, Bexley Art League, Ohio, Jeffrey Mansion, 2000, State Office Towers Exhbn. Gallery, 2003, exhibitions include Art League Mem. Curated Exhbn., Structure/Consequences, 1997, Fourth Biennial Alumni Exhbn.:ReSiDivist, Hopkins Hall Gallery, Ohio State U., 1997, Concourse Gallery, Arlington, Ohio, 1998, Bexley Art League, Precision Concepts, Dublin, Ohio, 1999, Art in the Atrium, Columbus, 1999, Art on Main Street, Schumacher Gallery, 2002, Represented in permanent collections Columbus Mus. Arts, J.B. Speed Art Mus., Louisville, Capital U., Bexley, Fordham U., NYC, Kyoto City U. Fine Arts, Springfield Art Mus., Ohio, Tyler Mus. Art, Tex., Wichita Mus. Art, Kans., Zanesville Art Ctr., Ohio State U., Columbus, Meth. Theol. Sch., Delaware, Ohio, Yerke Mortgage Co., Columbus, Marcorp, NY, Kresge Co., Detroit, IBM, Columbus, Chase Manhattan Bank, NYC, Chase Bank Ohio, Am. Bancorp., Columbus, Ohio Nat. Bank Plaza, Pan Western Life Ins. Co., First Investment Co., Children's Hosp., Phila., Franklin County Crippled Children's Ctr., Columbus, Zenith East, NYC, First Cmty. Bank, Columbus, First City Bank, Ronald McDonald House, Columbia Gas of Ohio, Midland Title Security Co., Ohio State U. Student Union, Columbus, Huntington Nat. Bank Ctr., Lehman Bros., NYC, Columbus Sch. for Girls, Eye Ctr. Found., Columbus, Eye Ctr., Ohioana Libr. Assn., Grand Prix Assocs., Inc., Columbus, Grant Hosp. Med Ctr., Libr. and Rsch. Ctr. Nat. Mus. Women in Arts, DC, Ohio State U. Libr. Rare Books Room Collection, Laredo Pub. Libr., Tex., represented in private collections. Mem. Nat. League Am. Pen Women, Nat. Artists Equity Assn., Bexley Art League, Columbus Mus. Art, Ohio Art League (bd. dirs. 1965-96, treas., sec., pres. 1977), Ohio State U. Alumni Assn., Pres.'s Club (Ohio State U.), Phi Sigma Sigma. Died Sept. 16, 2008.

SINCLAIR, ROBERT JOHN, retired automotive executive; b. Phila., Mar. 17, 1933; m. Anne Sinclair; children: Gregory, Robert John, Stephen, Rebecca, Elizabeth, Jennifer. Attended, Lafayette Coll. Various positions Saab Motors, Inc., 1958—62, Volvo, 1962—79; pres. Saab-Scania of America Inc., Orange, Conn., 1979—91. Named Comdr. of the Polar Star, King Carl Gustav XVI. Died May 10, 2009.

SINGER, CARL NORMAN, management executive; b. Malden, Mass., Sept. 6, 1916; s. Philip Friar and Rose (Nayor) S.; m. Marion Heller, Feb. 21, 1939; children: David, Phyllis. Student, William & Mary, 1934-35, Suffolk U., 1937-38. Pres. several cos., Chgo., Atlanta, NYC, 1959-69; pres. Renfield Corp., NYC, 1968-73, Chinook Corp., Newport Beach, Calif., 1976-79; chmn. Taco Viva, Pompano, Fla., 1976-86, Equipment Co. Am., Haleah, Fla., 1978-88, Vt. Contract Furnishings Co., Rutland, from 1979, Can Rad Inc., Newark, 1984-88, Robeson Industries, Mineola, N.Y., from 1989, Microdyne Corp., Ocala, Fla., 1989-91, Fundamental Mgmt. Corp., Miami, Fla., from 1984. Bd. dirs. Cameron Assocs., N.Y.C., Easy Day Mfg. Co., Framington, Mass. Mem. exec. com. Rep. Party Ga., 1966, com. of 100, N.Y., 1970-71; bd. dirs. Emory U., Atlanta; trustee L.I. Hillside Hosp., 1969-76. Avocations: golf, swimming. Home: Hollywood, Fla. Died Aug. 7, 2008.

SINGER, CHARLES BLANTON, oil and gas company executive; b. Duncan, Okla., Dec. 21, 1927; s. Morris and Louise E. (Marshall) S.; m. Naomi L. Skalovsky, May 31, 1954; children: Gayle S., Marla K. Grad. high sch., Enid, Okla. Ptnr. Singer Steel Co., Enid, 1945-47; pres. Standard Steel Co., Oklahoma City, 1957-60; pres., owner Agnew Steel Co., Oklahoma City, 1960-82; owner Singer Oil Co., Oklahoma City, from 1982. Bd. dirs. Guaranty Bank & Trust, Oklahoma City, 1988—. With USN, 1945-46. Mem. Okla. Ind. Petroleum Assn., Oklahoma City C. of C., Jewish Fedn. Oklahoma City, B'nai B'rith. Republican. Avocations: hunting, fishing, water sports, reading. Home: Oklahoma City, Okla. Died Sept. 27, 2007.

SINGER, NANETTE, real estate agent; b. Orange, NJ, Jan. 19, 1951; d. Leslie Herbert and Margaret McKendry Willis; m. William Harry Singer, July 28, 1989. AB in English History, Wilson Coll., 1973; MEd in Adult Edn., Pa. State U., 1998. Cert. sr. real estate specialist, accredited buyers rep. English instr. Lower Dauphin Sch. Dist., Hummelstown, Pa., 1973—2004; real estate agt. Brownstone Real Estate Co., Hershey, Pa., from 2004. Reader Coll. Bd., Princeton, NJ, from 1973. Lay reader, mem. vestry, edn. instr. St. Michael and All Angels Episcopal Ch., Middletown, Pa., from 1977. Mem.: Nat. Assn. Realtors, Rotary Club. Home: Palmyra, Pa. Died Dec. 14, 2007.

SINGER, WILLIAM HARRY, retired artificial intelligence applications developer, research scientist; b. Lancaster, Pa., Jan. 25, 1947; s. Wilbur Weitzel and Mildred (Myers) S.; m. Nanette Platt Willis, July 28, 1984. BS, U. Pitts., 1973; MS, Drexel U., 1982; PhD, U. Basel, 1985. Rsch. asst. dept. molecular biology Ea. Pa. Psychiatric Inst., Phila., 1976-81; rsch. fellow dept. biophys. chemistry Biozentrum, Basel, Switzerland, 1981-83; ltd. ptnr. Tech. Systems Software, 1983-86; gen. ptnr. Singer and Singer Assocs., 1993—2004; ret., 2007. Vis. scientist, rsch. fellow, dept. biophysical chem. Biozentrum, Basel, Switzerland, 1981—83; co-founder, prin. ptnr. Singer Cons. Inc., Palmyra, Pa., 1983—2000; adj. lectr. Wilson Coll., Chambersburg, Pa., 1994—96; founder Blue Dragon Ceramic Studio, 2003; adj. lectr. Ctrl. Pa. Bus. Coll., Summerdale, 2005; lectr. in field; cons. in field. Contbr. articles to profl. jours.; co-author: Diabetic's Daily Diary, 1987; world wide web site designer; prodr. abstract nonfunctional ceramic art, 2000—, mentor to several ceramic artists at Blue Dragon Studio, Lifetime Friend and Supporter of the Art, Assn. Harrisburg, Pa. Served with USAF, 1966—69, Vietnam. Swiss Nat. Sci. Found. rsch. fellow, 1981-83. Mem. NRA, Okinawa Isshinryu Karate Assn. (life), Wasserfahrverein Horburg of Basel (Switzerland) (life mem.), Am. Potters Council, Am. Ceramics Soc., Southern Poverty Law Ctr. Democrat. Roman Catholic. Achievements include research in manufacturing processes and development of AI software to record, analyze and predict potential problems based on statistical pattern analysis in order to prevent less of product & materials through catastrophic process failures; statistical analysis and control of serum glucose levels in Type II diabetics; and design and creation of ceramic works of art. Died Dec. 14, 2007.

SINSTEAD, RONEL EDMUND, minister; b. Toronto, Ont., Can., Dec. 3, 1930; s. Albert and Kathleen (McInnis) S.; m. Cori Swarzentruber, May 25, 1957; children: Dale Andrew, Carmen Joy. D Metaphysics, Coll. Universal Truth, 1959. Ordained to ministry Unity Ch., 1979. Min. Unity Ch., Palm Springs, Calif., 1979-86, Muskegon, Mich., 1986-96. Author: Child's Guide, 1969; contbr. articles to World Wide Web. Died Aug. 23, 2007.

SIPES, DONALD, film company executive; Grad., Harvard U., 1951. Television exec., prodr., and writer; sr. v.p. television CBS; pres. Universal Television; pres. COO MGM Films; chmn. CEO United Artists Corp., NYC. Died Apr. 5, 2006.

SIQUEIRA, EDIR BARROS, neurosurgeon; b. Belo Horizonte, Brazil, Apr. 4, 1931; came to U.S., 1955; s. Elvindo Dutra and Maria (Barros) S.; m. Mary Christine Kunka, Aug. 18, 1962; children: Kevin, Thais, Paul. MD, U. Minas Gerais, Brazil, 1955; MS, Northwestern U., 1962, PhD, 1970. Intern St. Lukes Hosp., Chgo., 1956; resident Chgo. Wesley Meml. Hosp. (name changed to Northwestern Meml. Hosp.), 1957-62; attending physician Northwestern Meml. Hosp., Chgo., 1962-84; chmn. dept. neuroscis. King Faisal Hosp., Riyadh, Saudi Arabia, from 1984. Contbr. more than 100 articles to profl. jours. Mem. Am. Assn. Neurol. Surgeons, Am. Neurol. Assn., Congress Neurol. Surgeons. Avocation: piano playing. Home: Lake Forest, Ill. Died Oct. 11, 2007.

SISBARRO, THOMAS A., business executive; b. Newark, Oct. 11, 1946; BSME, Newark Coll. Engring., 1969. Corp. mfg. engr. White Consolidated Industry, Mansfield, Ohio, 1984-87; plant engr. GE Aircraft Engines, Cin., 1987-91; pres. Environ. Closure Systems, Inc., Reynoldsburg, Ohio, from 1991. Cons. Flexible Technologies, Inc., Reynoldsburg, 1987-91. Patent degreaser door system; contbr. articles to profl. jours. Avocations: hunting, fishing, outdoor activities, archery. Home: Reynoldsburg, Ohio. Died Nov. 6, 2007.

SITZMAN, JERRY CLAYTON, consulting electrical engineer; b. Sheboygan, Wis., July 16, 1936; s. John and Elizabeth Sitzman. BS, U. Wis., 1963, MS, 1969. Project asst. Elec. Stds. and Instrumentation Lab., Madison, Wis., 1965-67; project engr. Space Sci. & Engring. Ctr., U. Wis., Madison, 1967-78, chief engr., 1978-95; pres. Primetics, engring. cons., Madison, from 1995. Cons. JCS Cons. Co., Madison, 1976-88. Patentee in field. Mem. IEEE, U. Wis. Flying Club Inc. (pres. 1971-73), Eta Kappa Nu, Tau Beta Pi, Phi Kappa Phi. Avocations: music, travel, computer recreation. Home: Madison, Wis. Died Jan. 1, 2008.

SIZER, THEODORE RYLAND, educational association administrator; b. New Haven, June 23, 1932; m. Nancy Faust; 4 children. BA in English Lit., Yale U., 1953; MAT in Social Studies, Harvard U., 1957, Phd in Am. History and Edn., 1961; PedD (hon.), Lawrence U., 1969; LittD (hon.), Union Coll., 1972; LLD (hon.), Conn. Coll., 1984; LHD (hon.), Williams Coll., 1984; MA ad eundem, Brown U., 1985; LHD (hon.), U Mass., Lowell, 1985, Dartmouth Coll., 1985, Lafayette Coll., 1991, Webster U., 1992, Ind. U., 1993, Mt. Holyoke Coll., 1993, U. Maine, 1993, Iona Coll., 1995, L.I. U., 1996, Bridgewater State Coll., 1996. English and math. tchr. Roxbury Latin Sch., Boston, 1955-56; history and geography tchr. Melbourne (Australia) Grammar Sch., 1958; asst. prof. edn., dir. MA in tchrs. program Harvard U., Cambridge, Mass., 1961-64, dean grad. sch. edn., 1964-72; headmaster, instr. in history Phillips Acad., Andover, Mass., 1972-81; chmn. A Study of High Schs., 1981-84; prof. edn. Brown U., Providence, 1984-96, chmn. edn. dept., 1984-89, Walter H. Annenberg prof. edn., 1993-94, dir. Annenberg Inst. Sch. Reform, 1994-96, univ. prof. emeritus, 1997—2009. Chmn. Coalition of Essential Schs., 1984—97, chmn. emeritus, from 1997; vis. prof. U. Bristol, England, 1971, Brown U., Providence, 1983; vis. prof. edn. Brandeis U., from 2001. Author: Secondary Schools at the Turn of the Century, 1964, The Age of the Academies, 1964, Religion and Public Education, 1967; author: (with Nancy F. Sizer) Moral Education: Five Lectures, 1970; author: Places for Learning, Places for Joy: Speculations on American School Reform, 1972, Horace's Compromise: The Dilemma of the American High School, 1984, rev. edit., 2004, Horace's School: Redesigning the American High School, 1992, Horace's Hope: What Works for the American High School, 1996; author: (with Nancy Faust Sizer) The Students Are Watching: Schools and the Moral Contract, 1999; author: (with Deborah Meier & Nancy F. Sizer) Keeping School: Letters to Families from Principals of Two Small Schools, 2004; author: The Red Pencil: Convictions from Experience in Education, 2004. Capt. U.S. Army, 1953-55. Named Guggenheim fellow, 1971; recipient citations Am. Fedn. Tchrs., Nat. Assn. Secondary Sch. Prins., Phillips Exeter Acad., Boston C. of C., Andover C. of C., Lehigh U. Edn. Alumni, 1991, Nat. Assn. Coll. Admissions Counsellors, 1991, Anthony Wayne award Wayne State U., 1981, Gold medal for excellence in undergrad. teaching CASE, 1988, Tchrs. Coll. medal Tchrs. Coll., Columbia U., 1991, Harold W. McGraw prize in edn., 1991, James Bryant Conant award Edn. Commn. States, 1992, Disting. Svc. award Coun. Chief State Sch. Officers, 1992, Coun. Am. Private Edn., 1993, Nat. award of Distinction U. Pa., 1993, Alumni award Harvard Grad. Sch. Edn., 1994. Fellow Am. Acad. Arts and Scis., Am. Philos. Soc.; mem. Nat. Acad. Edn. Died Oct. 21, 2009.

SKAGGS, MERRILL MAGUIRE, retired humanities educator; b. Florala, Ala., Oct. 1, 1937; d. John Henry and Clyde Louise (Merrill) M.; m. Calvin Lee Skaggs, Aug. 19, 1960 (div. Feb. 1994); children: Sylvia Merrill, John Adam. BA, Stetson U., DeLand, Fla., 1958, LLD, 1988; MA, Duke U., 1960, PhD, 1965. Tutor Duke U., 1961-62; lectr. Bklyn. Coll., 1965; assoc. editor The MacMillan Co., NYC, 1966-67; adj. asst. prof. English Drew U., Madison, NJ, 1975-76, adj. assoc. prof., 1976-79, assoc. prof., 1979-85, prof., 1985-86, dean-elect, 1985-86, dean Grad. Sch., 1986-92, Baldwin prof. of humanities, 1992—2008. Author: The Folk of Southern Fiction, 1972 (Edd Winfield Parks award), After the World Broke in Two: The Later Novels of Willa Cather, 1990, Axes: Willa Cather and William Faulkner, 2007; co-author: The Mother Person, 1975; editor: Willa Cather's New York: New Essays on Cather in the City, 2000 (with Joseph R. Urgo) Violence, the Arts and Cather, 2007, (with John J. Murphy) Willa Cather: New Facts, New Glimpses, Revisions, 2008; gen. editor: Willa Cather Series. Bd. dirs. Willa Cather Found., Red Cloud, Nebr., 1991—, NJ Com. for the Humanities, New Brunswick, 1990-95; clk. Summit Monthly Meeting, 2003-05. Recipient Book of Yr. award, Am. Jour. Nursing., Presdl. award, Drew U., 2006, Lifetime Scholarly Achievement award, 2006. Mem. Soc. Values in Higher Edn. (bd. dir. 1988-94), Soc. Study of So. Lit. (bd. dir. 1982, 83-85, 87-89). Democrat. Mem. Soc. Of Friends. Home: Madison, NJ. Died Nov. 3, 2008.

SKIDMORE, MARGARET COOKE, not-for-profit fundraiser; b. NYC, Sept. 10, 1938; d. M. Bernard and Mary Frances (Adams) Cooke; m. Louis Hiram Skidmore Jr., Sept. 10, 1960; children: Christopher, Elizabeth, Heather. BA, Chatham Coll., 1960; cert. Mgmt. Program, Rice U., 1986. Devel. asst. Yale U., New Haven, 1960-62, sec. French dept., 1963; devel. asst. Chgo. Symphony, 1976; dir. devel. Children's Meml. Hosp., Chgo., 1976-77, Mus. Fine Arts, Houston, 1981—2005. Adv. bd. mem. Cultural Arts Coun., Houston, 1990-96. Named Outstanding Women Am., 1971. Fellow Am. Leadership Forum (Class XV 1998); mem. Assn. of Fundraising Profls. (nat. bd. dirs. 1981-85, chpt. pres. 1982-83, bd. dirs. 1979-85, 88-91, cert., Outstanding Fundraising award 1980, 81, 82, Outstanding Fundraising Exec. award 1985), Art Mus. Devel. Assn. (pres. 1983, 98). Episcopialian. Avocations: tennis, needlepoint. Home: Houston, Tex. Died Nov. 9, 2009.

SKIE, CHARLES MARTIN, transportation executive; b. Chgo., July 19, 1938; s. Carl Oliver and Edith (Otten) S.; m. Diane Chiappe, Sept. 1, 1962; children: Martin, Lisa, David, Jason. BBA, Roosevelt U., 1963; MBA, Xavier U., 1983. CPA, Ill. Budget dir. Gillette Corp., Chgo., 1963-74; regional dir. SCA Services, Chgo., 1974-78; dir. corp. devel. Midland Enterprises, Cin., 1978-83, v.p. transp., from 1983. Served with USN, 1956-59. Mem. Am. Inst. CPA's, Assn. Corp. Growth. Lodges: Rotary. Republican. Roman Catholic. Home: West Chester, Ohio. Died May 31, 2008.

SKROMME, ARNOLD BURTON, educational writer, engineering consultant; b. Zearing, Iowa, Apr. 1, 1917; s. Austin and Belle (Holmedal) S.; m. Lois Lucille Fausch, Sept. 14, 1940; children: Roger, Keith, Deborah, Erik. Agrl. Engr., Iowa State U., 1941. Engr. Firestone Tire & Rubber Co., Akron, Ohio, 1941-45, Auto Splty. Mfg., St. Joseph, Mich., 1945-46; rsch. engr. Pineapple Rsch. Inst., Honolulu, 1946-50; asst. chief engr. John Deere, Ottumwa, Iowa, 1950-55; chief engr. John Deer Spreader Works, East Moline, Ill., 1955-70; mgr. value engring. John Deere Harvester Works, East Moline, 1970-84; writer and cons. East Moline, 1984—2002. Cons. to corps., 1984—. Author The 7-Ability Plan, 1989; The Cause and Cure of Dropouts, 1998; holder 44 patents. Chmn. Citizens Adv. Com., Moline, 1964-66. Mem. Am. Soc. Agrl. Engrs. (v.p. 1965-68, Honor Roll 1997). Lutheran. Avocation: research on children's education. Home: Moline, Ill. Died Aug. 8, 2008.

SLACK, MARK ROBERT, lawyer; b. Amherst, Ohio, Aug. 17, 1957; s. Robert James and Lois Jean (Basl) S.; m. Diana Joan Thomas, Sept. 23, 1994 BA Pub. Adminstrn. & History, Ohio No. U., 1979, JD, 1982. Bar: Ohio 1983, U.S. Dist. Ct. (no. dist.) Ohio 1983, U.S. Tax Ct. 1984, U.S. Ct. Appeals (6th cir.) 1984, U.S. Supreme Ct. 1986; cert. nat. and state Better Bus. Bur. arbitrator; cert. basic fireman, Ohio. Insp. new constrn. Ohio Hwy. Dept., 1977—78; social worker Columbiana County Welfare Dept., Lisbon, Ohio, 1979—80; criminal intern Allen County Welfare Dept., Lima, Ohio, 1982; social security intern Blackhoff Area Legal Svcs., Lima, 1982; mem. staff for docket indexing sys. juvenile divsn. Columbiana County Common Pleas, 1983, guardian ad litem, arbitrator, 1983—98; asst. pub. defender Columbiana County Pub. Defender's Office, Lisbon, 1984; criminal idigency appointment panel Columbiana County, all county cts., 1985—98; pvt. practice law Salem, Ohio, from 1983. Regional counsel Northeast Ohio Legal Svcs., Lisbon, 1984-2000, Youngstown, Ohio, 1988-89, Warren, Ohio, 1988 Editor: Reynolds Family Assn., from 1993. Active Columbiana County Big Bros., 1985-86; chmn. profl. divsn. No. Columbiana County United Way, 1984-85; vol. fireman Franklin Twp., 1972-76; chmn. Slack Family Reunion, 1997—; precinct judge Columbiana County Bd. Elections, 2005—; elder Holy Trinity Ch., Salem, coord. ch. finances, 1986-89; legal advisor Emmanual Luth. Ch., Salem, 2002-; mem. fin. com. Salem Cmty. Banquet Table, 2006—. Recipient 1st pl. cooking award Salem News, 1986; named Outstanding Young Men Am., 1980-89, 92, 96 Mem. ABA, Ohio Bar Assn., Columbiana County Bar Assn. (grievence com. 1996-97, Recognition for Pro Bono Svc. 1995, 96, 97, 98, 99. 2000), Mahoning Valley Astron. Soc. (legal advisor 1985—), Canal Soc. Ohio (trustee 1996—), Salem Hist. Soc. (v.p., legal advisor 1985-87, trustee 1997-99, divsn. editor Salem Bicentennial History 2005-07), Youngstown Outspoken Wheelman (legal advisor 1985-93, chmn. presdl. sports award 1986-93, Outstanding Svc. award 1986-93), Mayflower Descs. Am., Descs. of Soldiers of Valley Forge, Descs. Ohio Civil War Soldiers, Mahoning Valley Civil War Round Table, Mahoning Valley WWII Round Table, Sandy and Beaver Canal Assn. (founder 1988), Antique Tractor Assn., Phi Alpha Delta Avocations: bicycling, astronomy, regional history, cooking, genealogy. Home: Salem, Ohio. Died Apr. 21, 2008.

SLATE, MARY ELIZABETH, real estate agent, medical/surgical nurse; b. Ashburn, Ga., Mar. 15, 1938; d. Jacob and Mary Elizabeth Hampton; m. Robert W. Slate; children: Robert W. Jr., Elizabeth A. Cook, G. Brian, Benjamin W,. RN St. Joseph's Hosp., Atlanta, 1961; cert. real estate agt. North Ga. Tech. Sch., 1986. Surg. nurse St. Joseph's Hosp., Atlanta, 1961—64, Stephens County Hosp., Toccoa, 1971—78; real estate agt. Prudential Key Realty, from 1986. Recipient Over One Million in Sales award, Prudential Key Realty, 2000—05. Roman Catholic. Died Dec. 16, 2005.

SLATER, DONALD J., restaurant executive; b. June 1948; m. Valerie Periolat Slater. BS in Hotel and Restaurant Mgmt., Fla. State U., 1973. With Steak & Ale Restaurant Corp., Dallas, from 1976, regional mgr. S.W. region, 1983-84, v.p., gen. mgr. divsn. Bennigan's, 1984-85, sr. v.p., gen. mgr. divsn. Bennigan's, 1985-87, pres., 1987-89, pres., CEO, from 1989. Died Jan. 20, 2009.

SLATER, THOMAS C., state legislator; b. Providence, May 21, 1941; m. Jody McKiernan Slater; children: Gary, Scott, Ellen. Mem. Dist. 17 RI House Reps., Providence, 1994—2002, mem. Dist. 10, 1994—2009; mem. Providence Dem. City Com., 1967—78, 1980—94, Providence 10th Ward Dem. Com., 1967—78, Providence 8th Ward Dem. Com.; sales engr. & mgr. Genalco Inc. Mem.: St. Matthews Sch. Bd., America Assn. Ret Persons, South Elmwood Neighborhood Assn., South Elmwood Crime Watch, Cranston Coun. KC. Democrat. Died Aug. 10, 2009.

SLATER, VALERIE PERIOLAT, volunteer; b. Michigan City, Ind., May 6, 1949; d. Emmett Gerard and Alma Rosalee (Keys) Wozniak; m. John Grey Periolat, Jan. 24, 1970 (div. Aug. 1975); 1 child, Jason; m. Donald Joseph Slater, Mar. 30, 1976; stepchildren: Meredith M., Julie. Cert. in French, L'Inst. De'Catholique, Paris, 1968; student, Western Mich. U., 1968-69, U. South Fla., 1973-75. Registrar Tampa (Fla.) Bus. Coll., 1971-75; adminstrv. asst. Crown Ins., Tampa, 1975-77; key employee S&A Restaurant Corp., Atlanta and Miami, Fla., 1977-82; realtor Century 21, Atlanta, 1982-84; owner Horizon Concepts, Plano, Tex., 1988-89. Co-owner Horizon Properties, Plano, 1979-89. Vol. HCA Med. Ctr., Plano, 1986-95; bd. dirs. Cystic Fibrosis Found., Dallas, 1988, 89, 2000. Republican. Roman Catholic. Died Jan. 20, 2009.

SLATTERY, KENNETH F., retired academic administrator, priest; b. Bklyn., June 12, 1921; s. James J. and Ethel (Kegelman) S. Student, St. Joseph's Coll., Princeton, NJ, 1935-41, St. Vincent's Sem., Phila., 1941-43, Mary Immaculate Sem., Northampton, Pa., 1943-48; MA, Cath U. Am., 1950, PhD, 1952; LL.D. (hon.), St. John's U., Jamaica, NY, 1969; H.H.D. (hon.), Cath. U., PR, 1977. Joined Congregation of the Mission Roman Catholic Ch., ordained priest, 1948; tchr. Greek and German St. Joseph's Coll., Princeton, 1948-49; tchr. philosophy Cath. U. Am., 1950-52, Niagara U., N.Y., 1952-54; dean studies Mary Immaculate Sem., Northampton, Pa., 1954-56; tchr. philosophy St. John's U., Jamaica, N.Y., 1956-61; dean Sch. Edn. Niagara U., 1961-65, superior of Vincentians, 1965-69, chmn. bd. trustees, pres., 1965-76; v.p. communications St. John's U., 1976-79, acad. v.p. S.I. campus, 1979-86, v.p. S.I. Campus, 1986-88; v.p., dean Notre Dame Coll., 1985-89; chmn. dept. philosophy St. John's U., Jamaica, NY, 1989-91. Trustee Molloy Coll., Rockville Center N.Y., 1981—2000, Cardinal Newman Coll., St. Louis, 1979-84; chaplain stable area Belmont Park, 1977—2009; instr. Neumann Residence & Hall, St. Joseph's Sem., Yonkers, NY, 1991-2009. Recipient Interfaith award B'nai B'rith, 1970 Mem. Am. Cath. Philos. Assn., Fellowship of Cath. Scholars., Staten Island C. of C. (bd. dirs. 1983-86, 88-90). Died Apr. 21, 2009.

SLETTO, VERONA GWENDOLYN, adult coordinator, educator; b. Slope County, ND, Sept. 4, 1909; d. Peter Wilhelm and Mabel Julia (Urevig) Strom; m. Kenneth Sletto, June 27, 1937 (dec. Mar. 1972); children: Linda Rae Porten, Donald Alfred Sletto. BS, Dickinson State U., ND, 1966. Tchr. grade sch. Rhame (N.D.) Dist., 1949-59; libr. Dickinson Sch. Dist., 1968-75, tchr. English, 1975-82, tchr. ESL, 1977-78; coord. literacy program dept. pub. instruction Literacy Vols. for Illiteracy, Bismarck, N.D., from 1986. Media specialist Dept. Pub. Instruction 3, Bismarck, 1969-75. Sec. citizens adv. bd. St. Joseph's Hosp., 1984-87. Mem. AAUW (sec.), Golden Grads. Dickinson State U. (pres. 1993), Alpha Omicron (parliamentarian 1984-86, 2d v.p. 1986-88). Avocations: reading, nature, anthropology, rock collecting, music. Died Sept. 29, 2007.

SLIWINSKI, ROBERT LEO, physician; b. Cleve., Apr. 11, 1935; s. Frank M. and Mae N. (Koscinski) S.; m. M. Elizabeth Tinsley, Sept. 24, 1960; children: Lisa, Jennifer, David. BA, Western Reserve U., 1956; DO, U. Health Scis., 1960. Intern to resident Doctors Hosp., Columbus, Ohio, 1960-61; pvt. practice Ashville (Ohio) Clinic, from 1977. Assoc. clin. prof. Ohio Univ. Coll. of Medicine, 1980—; med. staff Doctors North and West Hosp., Columbus, Ohio, 1966—, Berger Hosp., Circleville, Ohio, 1977—, St. Anthony Med. Ctr. and Mercy Hosp., Columbus, 1987—. Active Pickaway County Bd. Health, 1980—. Home: Ashville, Ohio. Died July 1, 2008.

SLOAN, IRVING JOSEPH, secondary school educator, writer; b. NYC, Nov. 14, 1924; s. Nathan and Ella (Klauka) Slomowitz; m. Esther R. Sloan, May 29, 1955; 1 child, Philip Samuel. BA, U. Wis., 1946; JD, Harvard U., 1949; MS, Yeshiva U., 1959. Cert. tchr., N.Y. Legal assoc. L.L. Poses Law Office, NYC, 1950-55; exec. v.p. Brit. Book Centre Ltd., NYC, 1955-58; jr. H.S. English tchr. N.Y.C. Pub. Schs., 1958-61; social studies jr. H.S. tchr. Scarsdale (N.Y.) Sch. Dist., from 1961. Legal editor Oceana Publs., Inc., Dobbs Ferry, 1965-90. Author: The Blacks in America 1492 to 1977: A Chronology and Fact Book, 4th rev. edit., 1977, The Jews in America 1621-1977, 1978, American Landmark Legislation: Primary Materials, 10 vols., 1979, American Landmark Legislation Labor Laws, 5 vols., 1984; editor: Franklin Pierce 1804-1869: Chronology, Documents, Bibliographical Aids, 1968, James Buchanan 1791-1868; Chronology, Documents, Bibliographical Aids, 1968, Martin Van Buren 1782-1862: Chronology, Documents, Bibliographical Aids, 1969, A Desk-Top Guide to the U.S. Constitution: Chronology, Facts Documents, 1987, Rape, 1991, Ronald W. Reagon 1911 Chronology, Documents, Bibliographical Aids, 1990, Legal Almanac Series 1951-1988, 1991. Historian Village of Scarsdale, 1990—; dist. leader Scarsdale Dem. Com., 1978-90; v.p., trustee Scarsdale Pub. Libr., 1987-93; pres. Westchester chpt. Am. Jewish Congress, 1988-90. Recipient Superlative Feature award Am. Edn. Press, 1971; grantee Claiborne-Ortenberg Found., 1994—, Irving Sloan Edn. trust, 1993—. Mem. Nat. Coun. Social Studies, Am. Polit. Sci. Assn., Town Village Civic Club (bd. govs., Scarsdale village historian 1992—). Avocations: bicycling, reading. Home: Scarsdale, NY. Died July 31, 2008.

SLOANE, PHYLLIS LESTER, artist; b. Worcester, Mass., Sept. 27, 1921; d. Nathan and Goldie (Pollock) Lester; m. David J. Sloane, Nov. 25, 1943 (div. July 1986); children: Ginna, Nathaniel, Lisa. BFA, Carnegie Mellon U., 1943. Freelance product designer, NYC, 1944-45; co-owner PDA Design Co., Cleve., 1946-48, Sloane O'Sickey Gallery, Cleve., 1970-72; gallery dir. New Orgn. for Visual Arts, Cleve., 1972-74; freelance artist Cleve., from 1974. One-woman shows include Gallery 200, Columbus, Ohio, 1974, 1978, Cleve. Play House Gallery, 1972, 1974, 1976, 1981, 1983, 1985, Mansfield (Ohio) Art Ctr., 1977, 1996, Wooster (Ohio) Coll. Art Mus., 1978, Massillon (Ohio) Mus., 1979, Janus Gallery, Santa Fe, 1981, Women's City Club, 1982, 1988, Florence O'Donnell Wasmer Gallery, Ursiline Coll., 1987, Frank Croft Fine Art, Santa Fe, 1987, 1988, 1996, William Engle Gallery, Indpls., 1987, 1988, Bonfoey Gallery, Cleve., 1990, 1992, 1994, 1996, Harris-Stanton Gallery, Akron, 2002, Las Vegas (Nev.) Art Mus., 2004, N.Mex. Printmakers Gallery, 2006, 3 Women Exhibit, Fyre Gallery, Braidwood, Australia, 2009, exhibited in group shows at Mansfield Art Ctr., 1984, 1993, Pratt Graphics Ctr., N.Y., 1986, Calif. Coll. Arts & Crafts, 1987, Oreg. Sch. Arts & Crafts, Portland, 1987, Hudson River Mus., Yonkers, N.Y., 1987, Cleve. Ctr. Contemporary Art, 1987, Sigma Gallery, N.Y., 1990, Harris-Stanton Gallery, Akron, 2000, Eldridge, McCarthy Gallery, Santa Fe, 2003, 2004, Represented in permanent collections Cleve. Mus. Art, Argos Gallery, Hunterdon Art Ctr., Clinton, N.J., Phila. Art Mus., Massillon (Ohio) Mus., Rutgers U. Archives, N.J., Cleve. Pub. Libr., N.Mex. Mus. Fine Arts, Santa Fe, U. N.Mex. Art Mus., Las Vegas (Nev.) Art Mus. Recipient Purchase award, Hunterdon Nat. Print Exhbn., 1977, Print Club Phila., 1977, Anderson Winter Show, 1985, N.C. Print and Drawing Assn., 1985, Graphics award, Cleve. Mus. Art, 1978, Visual Arts award, City of Cleve., 1982, 1st prize, Miami Internat. Print Biennial, 1984, Nationwide Ins. award, Ohio Watercolor Soc., 1984. Mem.: Santa Fe Printmakers Gallery, Artists Archives Western Res., Cleve. Soc. Contemporary Art, Boston Printmakers (Purchase award 1984), Santa Fe Etchers Club, Print Club Cleve. (trustee 1991—2000). Home: Santa Fe, N.Mex. Died May 26, 2009.

SLOBODKIN, LAWRENCE BASIL, ecologist, educator; b. NYC, June 22, 1928; s. Louis and Florence (Gersh) S.; m. Tamara Jonas, May 11, 1952; children: Nathan, David, Naomi. BS, Bethany Coll., W.Va., 1947; PhD, Yale U., 1951. Chief red tide studies U.S. Fish & Wildlife Svc., Sarasota, Fla., 1952-54; asst. prof. U. Mich., Ann Arbor, 1954-57, assoc. prof., 1957-62, prof. zoology, 1962-67; prof., dept. ecology & evolution SUNY, Stony Brook, 1967—2004, prof. emeritus, dept. ecology and evolution, 2004—09. Founding chmn. dept. ecology and evolution SUNY, 1967-74. Author: Growth and Regulation of Animal Polulation, 1961, Simplicity and Complexity, 1992, A Citizen's Guide to Ecology, 2003, (chpt.) Ecology and Classification of North America Fresh Water Invertebrates, 1991, Water Quality and Stress Indicators in Marine and Freshwater Systems, 1994; contbr. articles to Hydrobiologia, Evolutionary Ecology. Ecology Guggenheim Found. fellow, 1966, 74, Woodrow Wilson Found. Ctr. fellow, 1990; grantee NSF, Ford Found., Mellon Found. Fellow Am. Acad. Arts & Sciences, AAAS; mem. Am. Soc. Naturalists (pres. 1985-86), Soc. Gen. Systems Rsch. (pres. 1965-66), Ecol. Soc. Am. (Eminent Ecologist award, 2005). Jewish. Achievements include first demonstration of stabilization of species competition by predation; development of theory of water masses in red tides, theory of evolutionary strategy from standpoint of existential game, theory of prudent predation; research in ecological efficiency using calorimetry, ecology and evolution of hydra; research in the role of simplification in science. Home: Setauket, NY. Died Sept. 18, 2009.

SLOTKIN, ALMA ISOBEL, artist; b. Kellettville, Pa., Apr. 18, 1914; d. Otto and Bertha (Anderson) Rosenquist; m. Edgar Slotkin (dec.); children: Edgar, Ellen Slotkin Lauber. RN, Buffalo Gen. Hosp., 1936; student in Medicine, Montreal Neurol. Hosp., Can., 1938; studied with Robert Blair. Art chmn. Temple Br'th Zion, Buffalo, 1969—79; donor in rental gallery Albright Knox Gallery, Buffalo, from 1970. One-woman shows include Cole Gallery Medaile Coll. Art Dialogue, 1963, exhibited in group shows at Buffalo Soc. Arts, 1960—66, Albright Knox Gallery, Buffalo, Butler Inst. Am., Ohio, 1975—86, Springfield Art Gallery, Mo., 1964—65, Cole Gallery, Medaile Coll., 1970—98, Art Dialogue, 2002, Burchfield Penny Gallery, 2004, exhibitions include US Dept. State. Mem.: Western N.Y. Artist Group, Buffalo Soc. Artists (pres. 1960—2005), Buffalo Club. Avocations: gardening, golf, reading. Home: Buffalo, NY. Died Oct. 9, 2007.

SLOVER, CLAUD WESLEY, retired engineer; b. Tahoka, Tex., Aug. 20, 1924; s. John Wesley and Annie Elizabeth (Rector) S.; m. Sarah Ruth McDougald, Sept. 1, 1951 (dec. Oct. 1995); children: Betty Ann, Sarah Jane, James Wesley, George Ray; m. Eleanor Medley, Nov. 29, 1996. BSME, Tex. Tech U., 1950. Registered profl. engr., field safety engr., Tex. Sr. design engr. Gen. Dynamics, Ft. Worth and Waco, Tex., 1951-70; safety engr. Employers Ins. Tex., Midland, 1971-89, ret., 1989. Cpl. U.S. Army, 1943-46. Mem. Am. Soc. Safety Engrs. (chpt. v.p. 1974). Baptist. Home: Midland, Tex. Died Nov. 4, 2007.

SLUSSER, BRETT WILLIAM, vocational education educator; b. Topeka, Kans., Jan. 19, 1952; s. Robert Dean and Velda Marie (Beedy) S.; m. Dianah Sue Raliff, Oct. 21, 1972; children: Tonya Marie, Antia Louise. Grad. high sch., Nixa, Mo., 1970. Cert. vocat. tchr., Okla. Mech. maintenance Langston (Okla.) U., 1979-81; dir. transp. Rekkins-Tryon Sch., Perkins, Okla., 1981-85; technician Bridwell Equipment Co., Stillwater, Okla., 1985; repairman Okla. State U., Stillwater, 1985; installer Cimarron Glass Co., Cushing, Okla., 1985-86; svc. clk. tech. Dennis Equipment Co., Pawnee, Okla., 1986; technican Janzen Motor Co., Stillwater, Okla., 1986-91; instr. Kiamichi ARea Vo-Tech. Sch., Stigler, Okla., from 1991. Fire fighter County Fire Dept., Stigler, 1991, rescue dept., 1991, civil def. dept., 1991. With USCG, 1971. Mem. NRA, Am. Vocat. Assn., Okla. Vocat. Assn., Green Coutnry Pullers Assn., Nat. Vocat. Indsl. Clubs Am., Masons. Democrat. Baptist. Avocations: tractor pulling, fishing, boating, camping, horse riding. Home: Stillwater, Okla. Died June 11, 2008.

SLY, JOHN EUGENE, advertising and marketing consultant; b. NYC, Feb. 14, 1917; s. Frederick Sanford and Alberta Belle (Coy) S.; m. Ethel Elizabeth Weldon, May 22, 1943; children: John E. Jr., Warren F. AB in Econs., Cornell U., 1938; cert. in Engring., N.C. State U., 1943. Salesman Diamond Match Co., NYC, 1939-40; info. specialist Ea. State Farmers Exchange, West Springfield, Mass., 1940-41; asst. dir. info. svcs. So. States Coop., Richmond, Va., 1946; various positions to mktg. communications mgr. Du Pont Co., Wilmington, Del., 1946-81; pres. The John Sly Group, Inc., Wilmington, 1983-91; advt. and mktg. cons., Wilmington, 1983-91. Exec. dir. Del. Com. for Effective Justice, 1982; pres. Ea. Indsl. Advertisers, Phila., 1958-60; dir. Tech. and Mgmt. Svcs., U. Del., Newark, 1983-87. Dir. Arthritis Found. Del., Wilmington, 1986-92. Lt. comdr. USNR, 1941-45, ATO, 1950-52, Korea. Mem. Greenville Country Club (pres. 1968-69), Recess Club Wilmington. Republican. Presbyterian. Avocations: photography, reading, walking, fishing. Home: Wilmington, Del. Died Feb. 15, 2008.

SMEAD, BURTON ARMSTRONG, JR., retired lawyer; b. Denver, July 29, 1913; s. Burton Armstrong and Lola (Lewis) S.; m. Josephine McKittrick, Mar. 27, 1943 children: Amanda Armstrong, Sydney Hall. BA, U. Denver, 1934, JD, 1950; grad., Pacific Coast Bank Trust Sch., 1955. With Wells Fargo Denver (formerly Denver Nat. Bank), 1934-78, trust officer, 1955-70; v.p., trust officer Norwest Bank Denver (now Wells Fargo), 1970-78. Author: History of the Twelfth Field Artillery Battalion in the European Theater of Operations, 1944-45, Captain Smead's Letters to Home, 1944-45; editor: Colorado Wills and Estates, 1965. Pres., trustee Stebbins Orphans Home Assn., resigned, 1998; chmn. bd. dirs. Colo. divsn. Am. Cancer Soc., 1961-68. Maj. U.S. Army, 1941-45, ETO. Decorated Bronze Star; Croix de Guerre (France). Mem. Colo. Bar Assn. (treas. 1970-88, chmn. probate and trust law sect. 1967-68, exec. coun., bd. govs. 1970-88, coun. bd. govs. 1970-88, hon. 1989—, award of merit 1979), Denver Bar Assn., Denver Estate Planning Coun. (co-founder, pres. 1971-72), Univ. Club (Denver). Republican. Episcopalian. Died Jan. 13, 2008.

SMERUD, SAMUEL, nursing administrator; b. LaCrosse, Wis., Feb. 2, 1953; s. Alfred J. and Lorna L. (Darling) S.; m. Barbara; children: Stacey, Sam Jr., Jennifer. BSN, Viterbo Coll., 1976; cert. in completion patient care adminstrn., U. Minn., 1985. Cert. advanced cardiac life support, advanced cardiac life support instr. Nursing supr. Sacred Heart Hosp., Tomahawk, Wis., 1976-82; asst. dir. nursing Wautoma (Wis.) Community Meml. Hosp., 1982-83; dir. nursing, nursing svc. adminstr. Pembina County Mem. Hosp. and Nursing Home, Cavalier, N.D., 1983-86; dir. nursing Custer (S.D.) Community Hosp., 1986-87, Grand River Hosp. Dist., Rifle, Colo., 1987-88; nursing svc. adminstr. Platte County Meml. Hosp. and Nursing Home, Wheatland, Wyo., from 1988. Home: Fargo, ND. Died Dec. 29, 2007.

SMILEY, DONALD ELBERT, energy executive; b. Shreveport, La., Sept. 18, 1931; s. James E. and Dorris (Cross) S.; m. Edna Guillory, Dec. 19, 1953 (dec. Feb. 22, 1973); children: Edna, Ernest, Donald J. (dec.), Leigh; m. Rebecca Reid, July 7, 1984. JD, La. State U., 1955. Bar: La., D.C. Ptnr. Sartain, McCollister & Smiley, Baton Rouge, 1957-61; atty. Humble Oil & Refinery Co., New Orleans, 1961-66; mgr. Exxon Corp., Washington, 1966—78, v.p., 1978—96, ret., 1996. First Lt., U.S. Army, 1955-57. Mem. La. State Bar, D.C. Bar Assn., Nat. Assn. Mfrs. Avocations: golf, boating. Home: Irvington, Va. Died Feb. 23, 2008.

SMITH, ALEXANDER WYLY, JR., lawyer; b. Atlanta, June 9, 1923; s. Alexander Wyly and Laura (Payne) S.; m. Betty Rawson Haverty, Aug. 31, 1946; children: Elizabeth Smith Crew, Clarence Haverty, Laura Smith Brown, James Haverty, Edward Kendrick, Anthony Marion, William Rawson. Grad., Marist Sch., 1941; student, Holy Cross Coll., 1941-42; BBA, U. Ga., 1947, LL.B. cum laude, 1949. Bar: Ga. 1948. Practiced in, Atlanta, 1948-98; ret. ptnr. Smith, Gambrell & Russell and predecessor, from 1994. Bd. dirs. Our Lady of Perpetual Help Free Cancer Home; bd. dirs., planning and devel. coun. Cath. Archdiocese Atlanta, Marist Sch., Atlanta, John and Mary Franklin Found. Served with USAAF, 1943-46. Mem. Ga. Bar Assn., Atlanta Bar Assn., Phi Delta Phi, Chi Phi, Piedmont Driving Club Atlanta, Peachtree Golf Club Atlanta (pres. 1989-91). Home: Atlanta, Ga. Died Nov. 19, 2008.

SMITH, ALVIN CLARENCE, textiles executive; b. Pickens, SC, June 8, 1929; s. Ernest Benjamin and Loe (Pace) S.; m. Daisy Ruth Medlin, Aug. 5, 1951; children: Mike, Terry, Rick. BA, Furman U., 1950. Systems mgr. Bigelow Sanford, Greenville, S.C., 1965-80; mgr. data processing dept. World Carpet, Dalton, Ga., 1980-81; contingency coordinator J.P. Stevens & Co., Inc., Greenville, from 1981. 1st lt. U.S. Army, 1951-53, USAR, 1953-60. Mem. Assn. for Systems Mgmt. (pres. 1974-75, Outstanding Svc. award 1974, 75). Republican. Baptist. Avocations: golf, walking, personal computers. Home: Easley, SC. Died July 18, 2008.

SMITH, CRAIG ALAN, lawyer; b. Valparaiso, Fla., May 1, 1953; s. George A. and Sara M. (Knop) S.; 1 child, Sean A. BA, U. Mo., Columbia, 1975, JD, 1978. Bar: Mo. 1976, U.S. Dist. Ct. (ea. dist.) Mo. 1986, U.S. Dist. Ct. (so. dist.) Ill. 1986, U.S. Ct. Appeals (7th cir.) 1988. Ptnr. Hindman & Smith, Columbia, 1978-85; prin. Sueltaus & Walsh, P.C., St. Louis, from 1986. Mem. Mo. Law Rev., 1976. Anthony R. Rollins scholar, 1971-75. Mem. Ill. Bar Assn., Mo. Bar Assn., Mo. Bankers Assn., Ill. Bankers Assn., Phi Beta Kappa. Home: Saint Louis, Mo. Died Jan. 8, 2008.

SMITH, DAVID ALDEN, sociologist, educator; b. Lockport, NY, Oct. 20, 1956; s. Alden E. and Betty (Carl) S. BA, U. Rochester, 1978; MA, U. N.C, 1981, PhD, 1984. Vis. asst. prof. sociology U. S.C., Columbia, fall 1983, 84; asst. prof. U. Calif., Irvine, 1984-91, assoc. prof., from 1991. Author: Third World Cities in Global Perspective, 1996; co-editor: A New World Order? Global Transformations in the Late Twentieth Century, 1995; contbr. articles to profl. jours. Mem. Dem. Socialists of Am., N.Y.C., 1981—; co-chair social concerns commn. So. Calif. Conf., United Ch. of Christ, 1988-90; pres. University Hills Condominium Owners Assn. Fellow East-West Population Ctr., Honolulu, sumemr 1984; Inst. for Far Eastern Studies rsch. fellow, Seoul, 1988; NSF grantee, 1988-90; Pacific Rim Studies grantee U. Calif., 1991-93. Mem. Am. Sociol. Assn., Polit. Economy of the World Sys. (mem. sect. exec. coun. 1990-93), Internat. Studies Assn. (exec. council polit. economy sect.), Internat. Network for Social Network Analysis, So. Sociol. Soc. Mem. United Ch. Christ. Club: Crash and Burn Track (Irvine). Home: Irvine, Calif. Died May 6, 2008.

SMITH, DAVID ANTHONY, chemical engineer; b. San Diego, May 4, 1945; s. Milton Anthony and Dorothea Clark (Miller) S.; m. Sara Mary Enion, Sept. 14, 1969 (dec. Sept. 6, 1994); children: Tobin E., Taiya M., Corbin R.; rem. Cecilia Mann, Dec. 31, 1997; stepchildren: Julie, Paul and Daniel Knoepflmacher. Student, Cal Poly., San Luis Obispo, Calif., 1963-65; BSChemE, U. Calif., Berkeley, 1968; SM in Food Sci. and Tech., MIT, 1970. Registered profl. engr., N.J., Mass. Rsch. engr. Du Pont-Freon Products, Wilmington, Del., 1969-70; devel. engr., tech. asst. Merck & Co., Rahway, N.J., 1970-74; plant engr. Firmenich Inc., Plainsboro, N.J., 1974-78; sr. project engr. Metex Process Equipment Corp., Edison, N.J., 1978-81; sr. process, project engr. Jacobs Engring., Mountainside, N.J., 1981-88; process mgr., mgr. process engring. H.R. Internat., Edison, 1988-90; dir. process engring. Sverdrup Inc., Princeton, N.J., 1990-92; sr. process engr. The Sigel Group, Narbreth, Pa., 1992-93; process consulting engr. Rayetheon E & C., Phila., from 1993. Mem. AICE, Internat. Soc. Pharm. Engrs. (presenter 1992). Achievements include creative process design of specialty chemical, pharmaceutical chemical, pharamceutical fill/finish and food production facilities. Home: Lawrenceville, NJ. Died Aug. 7, 2008.

SMITH, DAVID J., real estate broker, executive; b. Wilkes-Barre, Pa., Aug. 22, 1942; s. David Joseph and Gertrude Elizabeth (Sullivan) S.; m. Grace A. Adams; children: Paul R., Mark C. Student, Wilkes Coll., Wilkes-Barre, Pa., King's Coll., U. Pa. Cert. real estate appraiser, cert. comml. real estate appraiser. Salesman Lewith & Freeman, Wilkes-Barre, 1969-72; dir. real estate Wilkes-Barre Redevel. Authority, 1972-74; pres. Theta Land Corp., 1974-83; gen. mgr. real estate Pa. Gas & Water Co., 1974-83; pvt. real estate cons., 1983-86; pres. Penn Laurel Real Estate Inc., from 1986. Chmn. Rice Twp. Planning Commn., 1975—, Rice Twp. Zoning Hearing Bd., 1978—; mem. Luzerne County Tourist Promotion Agy. Mem. Assn. of Pa. Forest Fire Wardens, Greater Wilkes-Barre Bd. Realtors, Pa. Bd. Realtors, Nat. Assn. Realtors, Nat. Assn. Housing and Redevel. Authority Ofcls., Wyo. Valley Real Estate Investors Assn. (pres.), Pa. Real Estate Owners Assn. (polit. action com. chmn. 1991), Pa. Assn. Real Estate Owners, Nat. Assn. Home Bldrs., Bldg. Industry Assn. N.E. Pa., Pa. Economy League, Greater Wilkes-Barre C. of C. Home: Mountain Top, Pa. Died May 1, 2008.

SMITH, DAVID MARTYN, retired forestry educator; b. Bryan, Tex., Mar. 10, 1921; s. John Blackmer and Doris (Clark) S.; m. Catherine Van Aken, June 16, 1951; children: Ellen, Nancy. BS, U. R.I., 1941; postgrad., NYU, 1942; MF, Yale U., 1946, PhD, 1950; DSc (hon.), Bates Coll., 1986, U. R.I., 1993. From instr. to prof. Sch. Forestry and Environ. Studies, Yale U., 1946-90, asst. dean, 1953-58; Morris K. Jesup prof. silviculture Yale U., 1967-90, ret., 1990, Morris K. Jesup prof. emeritus, from 1990. Vis. prof. U. Munich, 1981. Author: Practice of Silviculture, 1954, 4th edit., 1997. Capt. Weather Svc., USAAF, 1942-45. Fellow Soc. Am. Foresters (Disting. Svc. New Eng. sect. award 1969, 93); mem. Am. Forests (Disting. Svc. award 1990), Nat. Acad. Forest Scis. Mex. (corr.), Ecol. Soc. Am., Conn. Forest and Park Assn. (dir.), Sigma Xi, Phi Kappa Phi. Mem. United Ch. of Christ. Home: Hamden, Conn. Died Mar. 7, 2009.

SMITH, DEBORAH ANN KING, time clock and alarm company executive; b. Luling, Tex., Aug. 28, 1951; d. W.O. and Marguerite June (Howerts) King; m. Kinch Smith, Nov. 10, 1973 (dec. 1991); 1 child, Jared Kincheloe. AA,

McLennan Community Coll., 1982. Sales rep. L'Eggs Pantyhose, Waco, Tex., 1973-77, Procter and Gamble, Waco, 1977-82; pres. Kinch Smith Enterprises, Inc., Waco, from 1980; med. sales rep. Whitehall Labs., Waco, 1986-93. Com. chmn. Hewitt (Tex.) C. of C., 1984-86; chmn. PTA, Hewitt, 1985. Republican. Avocations: skiing, scuba diving, water sports, antiques, crafts. Home: Hewitt, Tex. Died Jan. 4, 2008.

SMITH, DENNIS MATTHEW, biology educator, researcher; b. Chgo., Mar. 18, 1952; s. Stanley L. and Elaine Florence (Burke) S.; m. Sally K. Sommers, Aug. 2, 1980; 1 child, Matthew. BS, Loyola U., 1974, PhD in Human Anatomy, 1979. Postdoctoral fellow Med. Sch. Tufts U., Boston, 1979-80; asst. prof. Mass. Wellesley Coll., 1980-86, chmn. dept. biol. scis., 1988-90, assoc. prof., 1986-93, prof., from 1993. Cons. Merix Corp., Needham, Mass., 1989-90. Contbr. numerous articles to profl. jours. Mem., chmn. Hist. Commn., Burlington, Mass., 1986-87; mem. Biotechnology Com., Burlington. Grantee Coun. for Tobacco Rsch., Rsch. Corp., NIH. Mem. AAAS, Am. Assn. Anatomists, Am. Soc. for Cell Biology, Sigma Xi. Achievements include research on lung injury following chronic administration of propranol. Home: Burlington, Mass. Died Oct. 25, 2007.

SMITH, DONALD NORAN, real estate broker, insurance salesman; b. Augusta, Ga., Dec. 28, 1949; s. Donald Macon and Nora (Davis) S.; m. Jacqueline Ann Denany, Nov. 7, 1968 (div. 1971); 1 child, Michelle Ann; m. Lois Medora Windley, Jan. 16, 1972; children: Regina Lee, Robert Ray. N.Y. Regents, N.Y.C., 1976; BS in Health Care Svcs., So. Ill. U., 1978; BS in Health Sci., George Washington U., 1979; MA in Bus. Adminstrn., Webster U., St. Louis, 1987. Owner Morton & Co., Jacksonville, N.C., from 1989. With USN, 1969-89, ret., 1989. Mem. N.C. Real Estate Assn., Nat. Assn. Real Estate Appraisers, Am. Legion, Civitan (pres. 1992). Republican. Baptist. Avocations: horseback riding, swimming, camping. Home: Jacksonville, NC. Died Apr. 16, 2008.

SMITH, DONALD WILLIAM, telecommunications executive; b. NYC, Dec. 1, 1934; s. William Peter and Theresa Marie (Cahill) S.; m. Patricia Marie Elfstrom, June 30, 1956 (div. Jan. 1990); children: Kevin, Timothy, William, Donna Marie.; m. Yolande Jaouen, Aug. 20, 1991. BS, Cornell U., 1957; MBA, NYU, 1963. Installation supr. Western Electric, NYC, 1957-66, labor rels. mgr. Omaha, Neb., 1967-68, mfg. mgr. Cicero, Ill., 1968-71, area staff mgr. Atlanta, 1971-76, mng. dir. Tehran, Iran, 1976-78, Riyadh, Saudi Arabia, 1979-80; dir. sales AT&T Internat., Basking Ridge, N.J., 1981-89, v.p. Latin Am. Coral Gables, Fla., 1990-91, v.p. comm. svcs., from 1991. Pres. AT&T Argentina, Buenos Aires, 1987—, AT&T C.Am., San Jose, Costa Ra, 1989—; CEO Jamaica Digiport, Montego Bay, 1990—; bd. dirs. Transport Digitales Internat., Caracas, Venezuela, Coun. Ams., Mexico-U.S. Bus. Coun; advisory bd. Carribean, Latin Am. Action, Fla. Internat. U. Died Aug. 17, 2008.

SMITH, E. BERRY, television and radio consultant; b. Daytona Beach, Fla., Feb. 21, 1926; s. Samuel Rogers and Rosemary (Berry) S.; m. Mary Terese Hoffman, Apr. 3, 1948 (dec.); children: Kevin B., Martin J. BS, Butler U., 1949. Account exec. Sta. WIRE Radio, Indpls., 1949-54; dir. advt. and pub. relations Franklin Fin. Co., Hartford City, Ind., 1954-56; account exec. CBS Radio Network, Detroit, 1956-57; v.p. Sta. WFIE-TV, Evansville, 1957-61, Sta. WFRV-TV, Green Bay, Wis., 1961-62; exec. v.p. Sta. WLKY-TV, Louisville, 1962-64; pres. Sta. WTVW-TV, Evansville, 1964-80, Sta. WSBT, South Bend, Ind., 1981-89; sr. v.p. Schurz Comm. Inc., South Bend, 1989-2001, cons., from 2001. Dir. adv. bd. CBS-TV Affiliates Assn., 1984-87, sec., treas., 1988-90, chmn., 1990-91. Dir. Goodwill Industries, South Bend, 1984-85, Jr. Achievement Michiana, South Bend, 1984-91. 1st lt. U.S. Army, 1944-46, PTO. Recipient Silver medal Am. Advt. Fedn., Evansville, Ind., 1973; named to Ind. Broadcasters Assn. Hall of Fame, 1989; appointed Sagamore of the Wabash, 1993. Mem. South Bend C. of C. (bd. dirs. 1988-92), Ind. Soc. Chgo., Nat. Press Club, MENSA, Notre Dame U. Club, Elks. Roman Catholic. Home: South Bend, Ind. Died July 29, 2008.

SMITH, ELINOR ELAINE, rancher; b. French Camp, Calif., Aug. 6, 1924; d. Joseph and Mary Theresa (Benedetto) Jacopetti; m. Roy Harding Smith, Aug. 8, 1942. H.s. diploma, Calif. Army air corp. welder Army Air Force, Sacramento, Calif., 1940-42; aide nurse home care Vets. Adminstrn., Mo., 1972-96; rancher Dunnegan, Mo., from 1974. Author: (poetry) Anthology Library of Congress, 1996-97. Mem. Disabled Am. Vets., Mo., 1970—. Named Disting. Poet Internat. Soc. Poets, Washington, 1996. Disabled Am. Vet. Commanders Club Bronze Leader, 1995; recipient Editor's Choice award Internat. Soc. Poets, Washington, 1996, 97. Mem. Mus. for the Arts. Home: Dunnegan, Mo. Died Aug. 1, 2008.

SMITH, ELOUISE BEARD, restaurant owner; b. Richmond, Tex., Jan. 8, 1920; d. Lee Roy and Ruby Myrtle (Foy) Beard; m. Omar Smith, Nov. 27, 1940 (dec. July 1981); children: Mary Jean Smith Cherry, Terry Omar, Don Alan. Student, Tex. Womens U., 1937-39. Sec. First Nat. Bank, Rosenberg, Tex., 1939-41; owner Smith Dairy Queen chains, Bryan, Tex., from 1947. Author: The Haunted House, 1986; editor The College Widow, 1986. Omar and Elouise Beard Smith chair named in her honor Tex. A&M U., College Station, 1983, Elouise Beard Smith Human Performance Labs. named in her honor Tex. A&M U., 1984, Elouise Beard Smith Girls H.S. Viking Girls Softball Field named in her honor, Bryan, Tex., 1989. Charter Mem. AAUW. Republican. Baptist. Avocations: genealogy, restoring old cemeteries, exploring England. Home: Bryan, Tex. Died Nov. 3, 2007.

SMITH, ELTON EDWARD, clergyman, religious studies educator; b. NYC, Nov. 9, 1915; s. Elton Herbert Sherow and Christine (Conway) S.; m. Esther Greenwell, Oct. 17, 1942; children: Elton Greenwell, Esther Smith Shaw, Stephen Lloyd. BS, NYU, 1939; BDiv, Andover Newton Theol. Sem., 1940; MST, Harvard U., 1940; PhD, Syracuse U., 1961; DD (hon.), Berkeley Div. & Linfield Coll., 1960. Ordained min. Am. Bapt. Conv., 1940. Pastor various chs. in Mass., N.Y., Oreg., 1940-61; prof. Brit. lit. and the Bible U. South Fla., Tampa, from 1961, Askounes-Ashford Disting. faculty scholar, 1988; Legis. Gt. Tchr. Bible U. South Fla., Tampa, 1990; disting. prof. British lit. U. South Fla., from 1994. Vis. lectr. U. Paris, 1982, U. London, 1983; sr. Fulbright lectr. U. Algiers, 1969-70, Mohammed Univ., Rabat, Morocco, 1974-75; outside reader, cons. MLA, CLIO, Victorian Studies, U. Fla. Press, Case Western Res. U. Press, Harcourt Brace Jovanovich; Bible lectr. to over 50 chs. and colls. Author: The Two Voices: A Tennyson Study, 1964, (with E.M.G. Smith) William Godwin, 1965, Louis MacNeice, 1970, The Angry Young Men of the Thirties: Day Lewis, MacNeice, Spender, Auden, 1975, Charles Reade, 1976, Tennyson's "Epic Drama", 1997; contbr. articles to profl. jours. Named Disting. Prof. U. South Fla., 1994. Mem. MLA, AAUP, South Atlantic MLA, Southeastern Nineteenth-Century Studies, Conf. on Christianity and Lit. Home: Lutz, Fla. Died July 2, 2008.

SMITH, EMIL L., biochemist, educator; b. NYC, July 5, 1911; s. Abraham and Esther (Lubart) S.; m. Esther Press, Mar. 29, 1934 (dec.); children: Joseph Donald, Jeffrey Bernard BS, Columbia U., 1931, PhD, 1936. Instr. biophysics Columbia U., NYC, 1936-38; John Simon Guggenheim fellow Cambridge U., Eng., 1938-39, Yale U., New Haven, 1939-40; fellow Rockefeller Inst., NYC, 1940-42; biophysicist, biochemist E. R. Squibb & Sons, New Brunswick, N.J., 1942-46; assoc. prof. to prof. biochemistry U. Utah, Salt Lake City, 1946-63; prof. biol. chemistry Sch. Medicine UCLA, 1963-79, prof. emeritus, 1979—2009. Cons. NIH, Am. Cancer Soc., Office Naval Research Author: (with others) Principles of Biochemistry, 7th edit., 1983; also numerous articles Recipient Stein-Moore award Protein Soc., 1987. Mem. NAS, Am. Acad. Arts and Scis., Am. Philos. Soc., Am. Soc. Biochemistry and Molecular Biology, Am. Chem. Soc., Acad. Scis. Russia (fgn.). Home: Los Angeles, Calif. Died May 31, 2009.

SMITH, EVELYN JOYCE, family nurse practitioner; b. Elkhart, Ind., Nov. 15, 1938; children: Rebecca J., Amelia D. Diploma, Union Hosp. Sch. Nursing, 1959; BSN, St. Mary of Plains Coll., 1979; cert., Wichita State U., 1976, M Nursing, 1982. RN, Kans.; cert. family nurse practitioner ANCC. Staff nurse Elkhart Gen. Hosp., 1959-61, Lawrence (Kans.) Meml. Hosp., 1961-72; interim program coord. nurse clinician program Wichita (Kans.) State U., 1976-84; nurse practitioner Platte Med. Clinic, Platte City, Mo., 1984-86; coord. adult medicine Prime Health, Kansas City, Mo., from 1986. Med. ctr. mgr. Humana Health Care Plans, Kansas City. Mem. editorial Bd. Nurse Practitioner Jour., 1984—; contbr. articles to profl. jours. Nominee for Syntex NP of the Year Award, 1988. Mem. ANA, Am. Acad. Nurse Practitioners. Home: Platte City, Mo. Died Aug. 1, 2008.

SMITH, FRANCES M., nursing administrator; b. Cambridge, Mass., Feb. 23, 1933; d. John F. and Mary Edna (Dingler) S. Staff nurse Mt. Auburn Hosp., Cambridge, 1953-55; from staff nurse to assoc. chief nursing edn. VA Hosps., Boston and West Roxbury, Mass., 1955-69; asst. dir. nursing Faulkiner Hosp., Jamaica Plain, Mass., 1969-71; nurse clinician, assoc. to v.p. nursing U. Hosps. of Cleve., 1971-80; clin. instr., asst. clin. prof. Frances Payne Bolton Sch. Nursing Case Western Res. U., 1971-87; dir. nursing St. Vincent Charity Hosp. and Health Ctr., 1984-87; head nurse Margaret Wagner House, Cleve., 1987-96. Adj. prof. Kent State U., 1982-96; preceptor Ashland Coll., 1986-87. Mem. ANA, Ohio Nurses' Assn., Nat. Leaguefor Nurses, Internat. Congress Nurses, Ohio Citizens League for Nursing, Am. Assn. Nurse Execs., Ohio Soc. Nurse Execs., Greater Cleve. Nurses' Assn., Sigma Theta Tau (Alpha Mu chpt.). Home: Cleveland, Ohio. Died July 26, 2008.

SMITH, GOFF, industrial equipment manufacturing executive; b. Jackson, Tenn., Oct. 7, 1916; s. Fred Thomas and Mabel (Goff) S.; m. Nancy Dall, Nov. 28, 1942 (dec. 1972); children: Goff Thomas, Susan Knight; m. Harriet Schneider Oliver, June 23, 1973 (dec. 1998). BSE, U. Mich., 1938, MBA, 1939; MS, MIT, 1953. Trainee Bucyrus Erie, South Milwaukee, Wis., 1939-40; mem. sales staff Amsted Industries, Chgo. and NYC, 1946-55, subsidiary pres. Chgo., 1955-60, v.p., 1960-69, pres., dir., 1969-74, pres., CEO, dir., 1974-80, chmn., 1980-82. Pres. Village of Winnetka, Ill., 1967—69; pres., bd. dirs. United Way Chgo., 1976—85; bd. dirs. Rehab. Inst., Chgo., 1979—99, Chgo. Theol. Sem., 1979—99, Presbyn. Home, Evanston, Ill., 1979—2005. Maj. US Army. Sloan Fellow MIT, 1952-53. Republican. Avocations: hunting, fishing, golf. Home: Chicago, Ill. Deceased.

SMITH, JACK LOUIS, nutritionist, educator, academic administrator; b. Huntington, W.Va., July 15, 1934; s. William Baughman Smith and Violet Ruby (Roberts) York; m. Carol L. Schroherloher, Jan. 7, 1961; children: Karen, Michael. BS in Pharmacy, U. Cinn., 1956, PhD in Biochemistry, 1961. Asst. prof. biochemistry Tulane U., New Orleans, 1965-71, assoc. prof., 1971-74; assoc. prof. biochem. U. Nebr. Med. Ctr., Omaha, 1974-83; assoc. prof. dept. human nutrition and food svc. mgmt. U. Nebr., Lincoln, 1975-84; clin. prof. preventive medicine and pub. health Creighton U., Omaha, 1976-84; Swanson prof. biochemistry U. Nebr. Med. Ctr., Omaha, 1983-84; exec. v.p. Strategic Mktg. Assn., Inc., Mt. Laurel, N.J., 1984-87; prof. and chair dept. nutrition and dietetics U. Del., Newark, from 1989. Dep. dir. Swansons Ctr. For Nutrition, Inc., Omaha, 1976-84; adj. prof. U. Nebr. Med. Ctr., 1984-85; pres. J. Smith and Assocs., Inc., Newark, 1981—; dir. Network Ctr. Contemporary Nutrition U. Del., Newark, 1988—. Bd. dirs. Internat. Dietary Info. Found., 1979-82, pres. bd. dirs., 1982-92. Fellow Am. Coll. Nutrition; mem. Am. Bd. Nutrition (cert. specialist human nutrition sci.), Am. Dietetic Assn., Am. Soc. Clin. Nutrition, Inc., N.Y. Acad. Sci., Nutrient Databank Assn., Sigma Xi. Died Oct. 11, 2007.

SMITH, JOE MAUK, chemical engineer, educator; b. Sterling, Colo., Feb. 14, 1916; s. Harold Rockwell and Mary Calista (Mauk) S.; m. Essie Johnstone McCutcheon, Dec. 23, 1943; children— Rebecca K., Marsha Mauk. BS, Calif. Inst. Tech., 1937; PhD, Mass. Inst. Tech., 1943. Chem. engr. Texas Co., Standard Oil Co. of Calif., 1937-41; instr. chem. engring. Mass. Inst. Tech., 1943; asst. prof. chem. engring. U. Md., 1945; prof. chem. engring. Purdue U., 1945-56; dean Coll. Tech., U. N.H., 1956-57; prof. chem. engring. Northwestern U., 1957-59, Walter P. Murphy prof. chem. engring., 1959-61; prof. engring. U. Calif., 1961—86, prof. emeritus, 1986—2009, chmn. dept. chem. engring., 1964-72; hon. prof. chem. engring. U. Buenos Aires, Argentina, from 1964. Fulbright lectr., Eng., Italy, Spain, 1965, Argentina, 1963, 65, Ecuador, 1970, Brazil 1990; Mudaliar Meml. lectr. U. Madras, India, 1967; UNESCO cons., Venezuela, 1972-82; spl. vis. professorship Yokohama Nat. U., Japan, 1991. Author: Introduction to Chemical Engineering Thermodynamics, 1949, 4th edit, 1986, Chemical Engineering Kinetics, 1956, 3d edit., 1981. Guggenheim research award for study in Holland; also Fulbright award, 1953-54 Mem. Am. Chem. Soc., Am. Inst. Chem. Engrs. (Walker award 1960, Wilhelm award 1977, Lewis award 1984), Nat. Acad. Engring., Sigma Xi, Tau Beta Pi. Home: Davis, Calif. Died June 7, 2009.

SMITH, JOHN ALLEN, English educator; b. Milw., Sept. 17, 1959; s. Wayne and Rose Marie (Mirenda) S.; m. Karen Ruth Rasmussen, Jan. 4, 1986. BA, U. Wis., Milw., 1982, MA, 1985. Cert. English tchr., Wis. Instr. English Stratton Coll., Milw., 1986-88, Milw. Area Tech. Coll., from 1988, instrnl. chair west campus, from 1998, honors coord., from 1998. Chmn. dept. English Milw. Area Tech. Coll., 1991-93. Mem. Nat. Coun. Tchrs. English, Conf. Coll. Composition and Comm., Two Yr. Coll. English Assn., Phi Beta Kappa, Sigma Tau Delta, BMW Car Club Am. Avocations: physical fitness, automotive recreation, writing, performing arts viewing, cooking. Home: New Berlin, Wis. Died Aug. 1, 2007.

SMITH, JOHN KERWIN, lawyer; b. Oct. 18, 1926; 1 child, Cynthia. BA, Stanford U.; LLB, Hastings Coll. Law. Ptnr. Haley, Purchio, Sakai & Smith, Hayward, Calif.; pres. Calhoun Heights LLC, Garin Vista LLC. Pres. bd. dirs. Rowell Ranch Rodeo, Hastings Coll. Lawpres. Gen. ptnr. Oak Hills Apts., City Ctr. Commercial, Creekwood I and II Apts.; Road Parks commn. 1957; city coun. 1959-66, mayor 1966-70; chmn. Alameda County Mayors conf. 1968, revenue taxation com. League Calif. Cities, 1968; former vice chmn. Oakland-Alameda County Coliseum; vol. Hastings 1066 Found. (pres., vol. svc. award 1990), chmn. Martin Kauffman 100 Club; bd. dirs. Hastings Coll. of Law, 1999—, pres. bd. dirs., 2004—. Named Alumnus of Yr., Hastings Coll. Law, 1989. Mem. ABA, Calif. Bar Assn., Alameda County Bar Assn., Am. Judicature Soc., Rotary, 100 Club (chmn. bd. dirs.) Died Aug. 2008.

SMITH, MARJORIE WATKINS, retail executive; b. Pittsfield, Mass., Mar. 4, 1921; d. Walter Loring and Martha Elmina (Fuller) Watkins; m. Nellis Thrall Smith, Aug. 24, 1943; children: Eleanor Jean Lienau, Ivan Thrall II, Walter Nellis. Student, Skidmore Coll., 1940-42; BA, SUNY, Binghamton, 1963. Cellist Mus. Arts Trio, Elmira, N.Y., 1950-58; prin. cellist Elmira Symphony Orch., 1948-58; cellist Tri-Cities Opera Workshop, Binghamton, 1959-63, Binghamton Symphony, 1958-64, Huntsville (Ala.) Symphony, 1964-76; 6th grade tchr. Huntsville City Schs., 1964-69; prin. cellist Huntsville Opera Theater, from 1982; owner Smith String Studio, Huntsville, from 1979. Bd. dirs. Huntsville Youth Orch., past pres.; string demonstrator Arts in Edn., Huntsville Arts Coun.; guest Grunches & Grins, Huntsville Pub TV. Mem. AAUW, Am. String Tchrs. Assn., Mayflower Soc., Music Tchrs. Nat. Assn., Music Educators Nat. Conf., Internat. Suzuki Assn. Suzuki Assn. Am. Methodist. Avocations: knitting, travel, reading, community involvement. Home: Huntsville, Ala. Died Jan. 25, 2008.

SMITH, MARK MCCONAHA, venture capital executive; b. Redwood City, Calif., Oct. 10, 1958; s. Robert Ralph and Margaret (Fish) S. BA in Bus., Portland State U., 1984; MSBA in Internat. Bus., San Francisco State U., 1986. Asst. v.p. Futuretek Communications Inc., San Mateo, Calif., 1984-85; pres. Fashion Records Inc., San Francisco, from 1985, Flame Music Inc., San Rafael, from 1987; pres., chief exec. officer Richland Internat., Inc., from 1987. Cons. for telcommunications and music industry, 1985. Contbr. articles to profl. jours. Avocation: weightlifting. Died Mar. 7, 2008.

SMITH, MICHAEL FRANCIS, mechanical engineer; b. Ennis, Ireland, Sept. 29, 1922; came to U.S., 1957; s. Michael F. and Mary Josephine Ciss (Bredin) S.; m. Ena Wood, June 12, 1953; children: M. Paul, David J., Christina Wood, Dianne E. B of Mech. and Elec. Engring., Nat. U., Dublin, 1945; MSME, U. Conn., 1966. Registered profl. engr. Mass., Conn. Design engr. Westinghouse, Meadville, Pa., 1957-58; instr. engring. Pa. State U., Wesleyville, 1958-61; rsch. engr. Kaman Aerospace, Bloomington, Conn., 1962-66, AVCO, Wilmington, Mass., 1963-69, Lockheed MSC, Sunnyvale, Calif., 1984-86, Salinas, Calif., from 1987. Contbr. articles to profl. jours. Capt. Brit. Army, 1951-52. Mem. Am. Math. Soc., NSPE. Democrat. Achievements include the identification of the impossible 3D algebra, causing the invention of quaternion-based vector analysis by Heaviside, U.K. and Gibbs, U.S. in 1877. Died Dec. 16, 2007.

SMITH, PATRICIA A., lawyer, author; b. Staten Island, NY, May 11, 1956; BA, Bklyn. Coll., 1978; JD, Bklyn. Law Sch., 1986. Bar: N.Y. 1987, U.S. Dist. Ct. (so. and ea. dists.) N.Y. 1988, U.S. Supreme Ct. 1991. Atty. City of N.Y., 1988-90; assoc. for an ins. def. firm, NYC, 1990-96; ptnr. Smith Abbot, L.L.P., NYC, from 1996. Co-author: The Preparation and Trial of Medical Malpractice Cases, 1990; contbr. articles to profl. jours. Mem. Women's Bar Assn. State N.Y. (pres. Staten Island chpt. 1989-90), N.Y. County Lawyers Assn. Democrat. Roman Catholic. Avocations: skiing, photography. Died July 4, 2008.

SMITH, PATRICIA HAWK, educational consultant, researcher; d. Alfred Roy Hawk and Lucille Vivian Tate; m. Robert Harrison Smith, Aug. 25, 1956; children: Robert Fulton, Mallory Leigh, Randall Sears. BSc in Edn., Ohio State U., Columbus, 1956, MA in Edn., 1973. Cert. secondary edn., speech, social studies, English Ohio, 1956. Secondary tchr. Zanesville Bd. Edn., Ohio, 1956—59, Belpre, Ohio, 1963—64; tchr. Wash. County Bd. Edn., Beverly, Ohio, 1964, Dublin Bd. Edn., Ohio, 1971—72; cultural arts coord. City of Columbus, 1984—87; exec. asst. for ednl. policy Ohio Office Budget and Mgmt., Columbus, 1996—99; project dir., state of ohio tech. evaluation Ohio Sch. Net Commn., Columbus, 1999—2001; cons. Capital Partners, Columbus, 2001—07. Mem., pres. Worthington Bd. Edn., Ohio, 1974—81, State Bd. Edn., Columbus, 1983—92; mem. Nat. Adv. Coun. on Adult Edn., Washington, 1984—86. Author: (government report) Illiteracy in America: Extent, Causes and Suggested Solutions, (presentation) The Board's Role in Textbook Selection. Mem., vice chair Def. Adv. Com. on Women in the Armed Forces, Washington, 1982—85; pres. Ohio Fedn. Rep. Women, Columbus, 1977—81; mem. Ohio Arts Coun., Columbus, 1978—83, Columbus Jazz Arts Group, Ohio, 1981—89; pres. Columbus Area Internat. Ctr. Bd., Ohio, 1992—98; mem. Ohio Alliance Arts in Edn., Columbus, 1984—90; mem., steering com. Getty Insts. the Arts, Ohio State U.; founder, pres. Pioneer Nursery Sch., Marietta, Ohio, 1963—68. Recipient Outstanding Citizen the Yr., PPG Industries, 1971, Outstanding Sch. Bd. Mem., Ohio Sch. Bds. Assn., 1979, Cmty. Leader the Yr., Worthington-Dublin Rotary Club, 1982, Outstanding Civic Leadership, Ohio Assn. Gifted Children, 1984, Outstanding Achievement in Pub. Edn., AAUW, Worthington Br., 1985. Mem.: Columbus Met. Avocations: reading, gardening, writing, piano, tutoring. Home: Worthington, Ohio. Died July 2, 2008.

SMITH, RICHARD CHARLES, not-for-profit administrator, educator, consultant, advocate; b. St. Paul, July 30, 1947; s. Arthur George Smith, Edna Alma Smith; m. Joan Rita Oxendine. BA, Calif. State U., San Bernardino, 1976; MBA, U. Calif., Riverside, 1981. Dir. mktg. SCW and Assoc., Riverside, Calif., 1981—84; dir. mktg. and ops. Thomas and Assoc., Riverside, 1984—85; v.p. br. adminstrn. First Fed. Savings and Loan, Ridgecrest, Calif., 1985—90; gen. mgr. KLOA Radio, Ridgecrest, 1990—92; dir. mktg. Ridgecrest Auto Ctr., Ridgecrest, 1992—94; exec. dir. Independent Living Partnership, Riverside, from 1994. Mem. Riverside County C.A.R.E. Team, from 2001; sr. advisor The Beverly Found., from 2004; mem. Am. Soc. on Aging, from 2005; founding mem. Nat. Supplemental Transp. Program Exch., 2007; cons., spkr. in field. Prodr.: (ednl. videos) Health Education Program Series, 2002; contbr. articles to profl. jours. E5 Army, 1966—69, Vietnam. Home: Beaumont, Calif. Died Nov. 22, 2007.

SMITH, ROBERT JOHN, retired educator, writer; b. Dickinson, Pa., Aug. 11, 1925; s. John Arthur and Nellie Elizabeth (Waidley) S.; m. Linda Mae Baty, Aug. 28, 1948; 1 child, Evelyn Jean Smith Giray. BS in Bus. Edn., Shippensburg State U., Pa., 1950, M of Elem. Edn., 1965. Entrepreneur in trucking and newspaper bus., Dickinson, 1950-59; tchr. Carlisle (Pa.) Sch. Dist., 1959-78; freelance writer Shippensburg, from 1978. Editor: The Diary of John Lefever 1799-1864, 1982-83, The Diary of John Myers 1860-1938, 1986-87; author: Penn Township: 125 Years, 1985, Crescent Pipeline: Its People and Places, 1987; contbr. articles to profl. jours. Charter mem., 1st sec. Penn Twp. Fine Co., 1953-54; treas. Penn Twp. Horse Show, 1954-56; auditor Penn Twp., Cumberland County, Pa., 1963-68, 1974-85. Mem. Nat. Retired Tchrs. Assn., Pa. Retired Tchrs. Assn., Cumberland County Retired Tchrs. Assn., Cumberland County Hist. Soc., Shippensburg Hist. Soc. Democrat. Avocations: antique automobile restoration, metal and woodworking. Home: Shippensburg, Pa. Died Nov. 16, 2007.

SMITH, RUSSELL JACK, diplomat, consultant; b. Jackson, Mich., July 4, 1913; s. Lee C. and Georgia L. (Weed) S.; m. Rosemary Thomson, Sept. 5, 1938 (dec. 2004); children: Stephen M., Scott T., Christopher G. AB, Miami U., Oxford, Ohio, 1937; PhD, Cornell U., 1941. Asst. instr. English Cornell U., 1937-41; instr. English Williams Coll., 1941-45; with OSS, 1945; asst. prof. English Wells Coll., 1946-47; with CIA, 1947-74, mem. bd. nat. estimates, 1957-62, dir. current intelligence, 1962-66, dep. dir. for intelligence, 1966-71; spl. asst. U.S. Embassy, New Delhi, 1971-74; rsch. cons., 1975—82. Assigned Nat. War Coll., 1951-52, U.S. rep. Brit. Joint Intelligence Com., Far East, Singapore, 1954-56. Author: John Dryden, A Study in Controversy, 1941, The Unknown CIA: My Three Decades with the Agency, 1989, The Little Red House that Jack Built, 2002, Rosemary: A Memoir, 2004, (novels) The Secret War, 1986, The Singapore Chance, 1991, Lodestone, 1993, Whirligig, 1994, Always Afternoon, 1997, Time's Prism, 2000, Downriver, 2001, The Listener, 2002, Lodestar, 2004, Winterset, 2005. Recipient Nat. Civil Svc. League award, 1971, Disting. Intelligence medal CIA, 1974. Mem. Phi Beta Kappa, Phi Delta Theta, Omicron Delta Kappa. Home: Mc Lean, Va. Died Apr. 27, 2009.

SMITH, SHIRLEY EILEEN, family nurse practitioner; b. Wenatchee, Wash., Apr. 14, 1935; d. Max and Helen H. (Lippert) S. BS, Seattle U., 1957; MS, U. Colo., 1966; cert. FNP, U. Calif., Davis, 1980. Prof. nursing Chico (Calif.) State U., 1966-87; pvt. practice family nurse practitioner Napa (Calif.) Sr. Day Svcs., 1987-94; retired, 1995. Mem. ANA, Calif. Nurses Assn., AAUW, Sigma Theta Tau, Kappa Gamma Phi. Home: Napa, Calif. Died June 3, 2008.

SMITH, STANLEY EDSON, financial analyst; b. Concord, Mass., Nov. 16, 1959; s. Peter Walker and Lucile Elizabeth (Edson) S. BA, Dartmouth Coll., 1981; MBA, Cornell U., 1986; exchange student, London Bus. Sch., Oct.-Dec. 1985. Customer service rep. Chrysler Credit Corp., Bedford, N.H., 1982-83; mcpl. adminstr. Town of Concord, 1983-84; staff services officer BayBank, Waltham, Mass., 1986-89; sr. fin. analyst Silver, Burdette & Ginn, Needham, Mass., from 1989. Co-author: (instr.'s manual to text) How America is Ruled, 1980; contbr. articles to newspapers and mags. Mem. Internat. Churchill Soc., Dartmouth Alumni Assn. Ea. Mass. Avocations: hist. writing, journalism, chess. Home: Littleton, Mass. Died Mar. 11, 2008.

SMITH, STEPHEN BRENT, surgeon; b. Madison, Wis., Nov. 29, 1950; s. Vearl Robert and Ramona Irene (Yearsley) S.; m. Jan Christiansen, Feb. 15, 1974; children: Elliot Christiansen, Alexander Judson, Audrey Elizabeth, Mitchell Stephen, Quentin Christiansen. BA, U. Utah, 1974; MD, George Washington U., 1978. Diplomate Am. Bd. Surgery, Am. Bd. Colon and Rectal Surgery. Commd. officer U.S. Army, 1978, advanced through grades to lt. col., 1989; rotating intern Fitzsimons Army Med. Ctr., Denver, 1978-79; resident in gen. surgery Tripler Army Med. Ctr., Honolulu, 1979-83; fellow in colon and rectal surgery U. Min., Mpls., 1985-86; intern Fitzsimons Army Med. Ctr., Denver, 1978-79; resident in gen. surgery Tripler Army Med. Ctr., Honolulu, 1979-83; fellow in colon and rectal surgery U. Minn., Mpls., 1985-86; surgeon U.S. Army M.C., 1978-90; resigned, 1990; pvt. practice, Salt Lake Clinic, Sandy, Utah, from 1990. Fellow ACS; mem. Am. Soc. Colon and Rectal Surgeons. Mem. Lds Ch. Home: Sandy, Utah. Died Apr. 28, 2008.

SMITH, TERRY GORDON, electronics production manager; b. Cin., Aug. 7, 1937; s. Clifford John and Vivian Aileen (Stone) S.; m. Sylvia Ann Gehl, Jan. 20, 1959 (dec. Dec. 1984); children: Donald Melvin, Terri Ann. Student, Arizona State U.; BA, U. Phoenix, MA in Mgmt., MBA. Mgr., owner Pharmacy, Phoenix, 1959-65; mgr. Super X Pharmacy, Scottsdale, Ariz., 1965-70; supr. Motorola, Inc., Phoenix, 1966-71, prodn. mgr., from 1971. Mgmt. lectr. U. Phoenix, 1984—. Author: Metal Finishing Safety Manual, 1975. Mem. World Electroless Nickel Soc., Am. Mgmt. Assn., Am. Electroplaters Soc., Am. Soc. for Metal, Assn. for Mfg. Excellence. Republican. Home: Phoenix, Ariz. Died Sept. 23, 2007.

SMITH, THEOREN P., physicist; b. Denver, Sept. 1, 1954; s. Theoren Perlee and Kitty Helen (Webster) S.; m. Kathleen Agnes Baker, July 16, 1977, children: Kristen, Julia, Kimberley, Theoren IV. BS in Physics, U.S. Naval Acad., 1976; MS in Physics, Brown U., 1983, PhD in Physics, 1985. Officer USN, 1976-81; resident vis. scientist AT&T Bell Labs., Murray Hill, N.J., 1984-85; from rsch. staff to chief tech. officer IBM, Armonk, N.Y., from 1985. Internat. adv. com. Internat. Conf. Solid State Devices & Materials, 1990—; external adv. com. MIT Materials Rsch. Lab., 1993-95; vice chmn. external adv. com. Nat. High Magnetic Field Lab., 1989-99. Elder Calvary Bible Ch., Yorktown, N.Y., 1988-96. Mem. IEEE (sr.), ITT, Am. Phys. Soc., AAAS, Inst. Phys. Scis. (bd. dirs. 1994—), Am. Inst. Physics (adv. com. 1992-96). Avocations: basketball, reading, writing. Home: Great Falls, Va. Died Sept. 27, 2007.

SMITH, VICKIE, nursing consultant; b. Columbia, Miss, Sept. 14, 1951; d. Doyle and Helen (Stringfellow) Williamson; m. Danny Smith, Dec. 31, 1971; children: Gabriel, Jeshua, Rebekah. AS, Perkinston Jr. Coll., 1971; ASN, Miss. Gulf Coast Jr. Coll., 1972. Gastro nurse Beauregard Mem. Hosp., DeRidder, La.; back care cons. Boise Cascade, DeRidder, La.; nursing supr. various hosp., Arcadia, La.; prin. wellness cons., DeRidder, La. Contbr. articles to profl. jours. Vol. Baptist Med. Mission in Honduras. Mem. Am. Assn. of Occupational Health Nurses, Nat. Wellness Assn. Home: Deridder, La. Died June 19, 2008.

SMITH, WILLIAM LEFORD, JR., insurance executive; b. Birmingham, Ala., Feb. 1, 1945; s. William Leford and Helen Louisa (Vance) S.; m. Sue Ellen Davis, July 25, 1970; children: Leah Heather, Anna Nicole. BS, U. Ala., 1972; CLU, Am. Coll., 1980; CFP, Coll. for Fin. Planning, 1985; cert. profl. mgr., Purdue Mgmt. Inst., 1986. Sales agt. Lincoln Nat. Life, Birmingham, 1972-81; v.p. Lincoln Nat. Sales Corp., Birmingham, 1977-81, West Palm Beach, Fla., 1981-86; exec. v.p. Lincoln Nat. Fin. Svcs., Boca Raton, Fla., from 1986, also bd. dirs. Bd. dirs. Lincoln Nat. Sales Corp., 1979-81, Am. Mgmt. Inst. Pres. Nelle Smith Residence for Girls, Inc., North Palm Beach, Fla., 1990-92, Saint Clare Sch. Bd., North Palm Beach. With USN, 1968-72, Viet Nam. Decorated Silver star, Purple Heart, Navy Combat Commendation, Presdl. Unit Citation; Paul Harris fellow Rotary, 1985. Mem. Am. Soc. Chartered Life Underwriters, Internat. Assn. Fin. Planners, Gen. Agts. and Mgrs. Assn., Am. Mgmt. Inst., Life Agy. Mgmt. Program, Rotary (pres. North Palm Beach chpt. 1992). Roman Catholic. Avocations: golf, bridge, fishing, travel. Home: No Palm Beach, Fla. Died Dec. 30, 2007.

SMITH, WILLIAM LESLIE, minister; b. Hot Springs, Ark., Oct. 31, 1931; s. Felix Leslie and Lottie Virginia (Mixon) S.; m. Betty Jean Fowler, July 25, 1951; children: Debra Jean Marty, Sharon Deane James. BA, Ouachita Bapt. U., Arkadelphia, Ark., 1954; MDiv, Southwestern Sem., Ft. Worth, 1957. Ordained to ministry So. Bapt. Conv., 1951. Pastor Archview Bapt. Ch., Little Rock, 1957-58, First Bapt. Ch., Altheimer, Ark., 1958-61, Rosedale Bapt. Ch., Little Rock, 1961-66, First Bapt. Ch., Pecos, Tex., 1966-78, Parkhills Bapt. Ch., San Antonio, from 1978. Moderator, editor Pecos Valley Bapt. Assn., 1969-71; pres. Ark. Bapt. State Conv. Pastor's Conf., 1966; trustee Howard Payne U., Brownwood, Tex., 1969-76, exec. bd. Bapt. Gen. Conv. Tex., Dallas, 1970-75. Author booklet: How To Study Your Bible, 1975. Home: Arlington, Tex. Died Sept. 20, 2007.

SMYK, STEPHEN DOUGLASS, lawyer; b. White Plains, NY, Mar. 8, 1944; s. Stephen and Lillian Mae (Faruolo) S.; m. Diane Elaine Dittman, Aug. 25, 1965; children: Stephen P., Rebecca A. BA, Syracuse U., 1967, JD, 1970. Bar: N.Y. 1971, U.S. Dist. Ct. (no. dist.) N.Y. 1971, U.S. Dist. Ct. (mid. dist.) Pa. 1977. Assoc. Waite, Berry & Reiter, Binghamton, N.Y., 1971, Stearns & Stearns, Binghamton, 1971-75; ptnr. Stearns & Smyk, Binghamton, 1975-77, Kramer, Wales & McAvoy, Binghamton, 1977-78, Smyk & Smyk, Binghamton, from 1978. Clk., vestry Trinity Episc. Ch., Binghamton, 1978-84; trustee Binghamton Gen. Hosp., 1976-80; bd. dirs. Vols. Am., Binghamton, 1977-79. Home: Binghamton, NY. Died Feb. 22, 2008.

SNELLER, ROBERT CALVIN, optometrist; b. Hastings, Nebr., Dec. 25, 1926; s. Floyd Calvin and Lydia Sourezny; m. Marjorie Jeann Kurfman, Feb. 17, 1951; children: Todd, Jeff, Peggy, Scott, Sally. OD, No. Ill. Coll. Optometry, 1950. Practice optometry, Hastings, Nebr. Pres. bd. examiners Nebr. Dept. Health, Lincoln, 1968-77. Author: Vision and Driving, 1962. Served to lt. comdr. USNR. Fellow Am. Acad. Optometry; mem. Am. Optometric Assn. (trustee St. Louis chpt. 1962-64), Nebr. Optometric Assn. (optometrist of yr. 1978), Heart of Am. Contact Lens Soc. (pres. 1976), Royal Soc. Health. Republican. Episcopalian. Avocations: hunting, fishing, sailing. Home: Hastings, Nebr. Died Dec. 14, 2007.

SNODGRASS, W. D. (WILLIAM DEWITT SNODGRASS), writer, educator; b. Wilkinsburg, Pa., Jan. 5, 1926; s. Bruce DeWitt and Jesse Helen (Murchie) S.; m. Lila Jean Hank, June 6, 1946 (div. 1953); 1 child, Cynthia Jean; m. Janice Marie Ferguson Wilson, Mar. 19, 1954 (div. Aug. 1966); children— Kathy Ann Wilson (stepdau.), Russell Bruce; m. Camille Rykowski, Sept. 13, 1967 (div. 1977); m. Kathleen Brown, June 20, 1985. Student, Geneva Coll., 1943-44, 46-47; BA, State U. Iowa, 1949, MA, 1951, MFA, 1953; doctorate (hon.), Allegheny Coll., 1991. Faculty English dept. Cornell U., Ithaca, N.Y., 1955-57; faculty English dept. U. Rochester, N.Y., 1957-58; prof. English Wayne State U., Detroit, until 1968; prof. English and speech Syracuse U., N.Y., 1968-76; Disting. prof. of creative writing and contemp. poetry U. Del., Newark, 1979-94, retired, 1994. Faculty Morehead Writers' Conf., Ky., summer 1955, Antioch Writers' Conf., Yellow Springs, Ohio, summer 1958, 59; disting. vis. prof. Old Dominion U., Norfolk, Va.; instr. Narrative Poetry Workshop SUNY, Binghamton, 1977, Cranbrook Writers' Conf., Birmingham, Mich., 1981. Author: (poems) Heart's Needle (Pulitzer prize 1960), 1959, After Experience, 1968, Remains (under pseudonym S.S. Gardons) 1970, The Fuhrer Bunker, 1977, If Birds Build With Your Hair, 1979, The Boy Made of Meat, 1982, Magda Goebbels (poems from The Fuhrer Bunker, 1983), Heinrich Himmler (poems from The Fuehrer Bunker) 1983, D.D. Byrde Calling Jennie Wrenne, 1984, A Colored Poem, 1986, The House the Poet Built, 1986, 1987, Selected Poems, 1957-87, W.D.'s Midnight Carnival: Poems by W.D. Snodgrass and Paintings by DeLoss McGraw, 1988, The Death of Cock Robin: Poems by W.D. Snodgrass and Paintings by DeLoss McGraw, 1989, Autumn Variations, 1990; translator: (with Lore Segal) Gallows' Songs of Christian Morgenstern, Six Troubadour Songs, 1977, Traditional Hungarian Songs, 1978, Six Minnesinger Songs, 1983, The Four Seasons (translations of Vivaldi's Sonnets) 1984, (essays) In Radical Pursuit, 1975, Star and Other Poems, 1990, Five Romanian Ballads, 1991, Snow Songs, 1992, Each in His Season, 1993, The Fuehrer Bunker: The Complete Cycle, 1995; contbr. essays, poems, translations to lit. mags. Recipient Ingram-Merrill award, 1958, Longview lit. award, 1959, spl. citation Poetry Soc. Am., 1960, Pulitzer prize for poetry, 1960, Guinness Poetry award, 1961, Miles Modern Poetry award, 1966; Hudson Rev. fellow in poetry, 1958-59; fellow Guggenheim Found., 1972-73, Acad. Am. Poets, 1973, Bi-Centennial Medal William and Mary Coll., 1976, Centennial Medal Govt. Romania, 1977; Ingram-Merrill fellow 1979; sabbatical grantee Nat. Council on Arts, 1966-67, Ctr. for Advanced Study U. Del. grantee, 1983-84. Mem. PEN, Nat. Inst. Arts and Letters (grantee 1960), Poetry Soc. Am. Died Jan. 13, 2009.

SNOW, DASH (DASHIELL A. SNOW), photographer; b. NYC, July 27, 1981; m. Agatha Aparru (div.); 1 child, Secret. Exhibited in group shows at Interstate, Nicole Klagsbrun Gallery, 2005, Whitney Biennial: Day before Night, Whitney Mus. Am. Art, 2006, exhibitions include Silence Is The Only True Friend That Shall Never Betray You, Rivington Arms Gallery, NYC, 2006. Died July 13, 2009.

SNOW, RONALD LOUIS, lawyer; b. Franklin, NH, Aug. 3, 1935; s. Louis and Evangeline (Pinard) S.; m. Mary Ellen Holopainen, July 8, 1961; children: Mark R., Lisa Snow Wade, Ronald L. Jr. BA, Dartmouth Coll., 1958; LLD, Yale U., 1961. Bar: N.H. 1961, U.S. Dist. Ct. N.H. 1961, U.S. Ct. Appeals (1st cir.) 1961, US Supreme Ct, 2005. Head litigation dept. Orr and Reno Profl. Assn., Concord, N.H., 1980-90, pres., 1990-94, sr. ptnr., litigation, from 1994. Fellow Am. Coll. Trial Lawyers; mem. Am. Bd. Trial Advs. Republican. Roman Catholic. Home: Concord, NH. Died Mar. 14, 2008.

SNYDER, BRUCE FLETCHER, former college football coach; b. Santa Monica, Calif., Mar. 14, 1940; m. Linda Risvold; children: Jennifer, Tracy, Paige. BA, Oreg. U., 1965. Coach football Sheldon H.S., Eugene, Oreg., 1963-64; coach running back/quarterback Oreg. U. Ducks, 1964-71, N.Mex. State U. Aggies, 1972, Utah State U. Aggies, Logan, 1973-74; coach running back, coord. offense U. So. Calif. Trojans, 1974-75; head coach football Utah State U. Aggies, Logan, 1976-82; coach running backs L.A. Rams, 1983-86; head coach football U. Calif. Golden Bears, 1987-91, Ariz. State U. Sun Devils, Tempe, 1992—2000. Recipient Paul "Bear" Bryant award, Nat. Sportscasters & Sportswriters Assn., 1996; named Walter Camp Coach of Yr., Walter Camp Football Found., 1996, Pac-10 Coach of the Yr., 1990, 1996; named to The Ariz. State U. Athletic Hall of Distinction, 2009. Died Apr. 13, 2009.

SNYDER, MARY-JANE RYAN, communications executive; b. Chgo., July 25, 1916; d. Edward Groves and Florence Margaret (James) R.; m. Clark Quin Snyder, May 29, 1939 (dec.); children: Lindsay Eleanor, Nadine Frances, Kevan Maureen, Courtnay Margaret. BS in Journalism, U. Ill., 1938. Writer Southtown Economist, Chgo., 1938-40, Writing for You, Chgo., 1940-59; dir. pub. rels. Planned Parenthood, Chgo., 1959-70, pres., CEO, 1973-77; pres. M-J Enterprises, Wilmette, Ill., from 1977. Chmn. bd. dirs. Population Inst., Washington, 1978-94, 91-97; cons. UN Population Fund, USAID, Ford Found., East West Ctr.; cons. dept. sociology U. Chgo., 1963-83, Ill. Commn. on Status of Women, 1964-70. Sr. author: Use of Media in Family Planning, 1978; designer (media campaigns) Goal Birth Control, 1980, "No" and Other Birth Control Methods, 1981, Who's in Charge of Your Body? 1993. Founder, bd. dirs. Population Comm. Internat., 1979-87, Ill. Caucus Teen Pregnancy, 1977, Adolescent Pregnancy Network, 1980. Paul Harris fellow Rotary Internat., 1995; recipient Human Rights award UN Assn., Washington, 1996. Mem. NOW (founding mem.), Women in Comms. (Headliner award 1979, Lifetime Achievement award 1995). Episcopalian. Died Oct. 27, 2007.

SOARE, THOMAS FULTON, drama educator, consultant; b. NYC, Nov. 22, 1936; s. William Fulton and Valdora Joyce (Seissinger) S.; m. Roberta Anne Carr, July 1966 (div. 1971); 1 child, Robert Randolph; m. Carole Yvonne Stanton, Nov. 21, 1989; stepchildren: Catherine, Denver, Tamara, Michael. Student, U. N.Mex., 1954-56; BA, U. Denver, 1958, MA, 1966; PhD, Fla. State U., 1974. Entertainment dir. U.S. Army Spl. Svcs., Giessen, Germany, 1963-65; dir. drama Ft. Bragg (N.C.) Playhouse, 1965-69; dir. Lakeland (Fla.) Little Theatre, 1969-71, prof. drama Sam Houston State U., Huntsville, Tex., from 1971. Dir., actor, designer Frankfurt (Germany) Playhouse, 1961-64, Hill Country Arts Found., Ingram, Tex., 1975, Hilton Dinner Theatre, Cisco, Tex., 1986, 88, 89, 91; dir., actor Tex. Renaissance Festival, Todd Mission, 1978-80, 84-86; tchr. Lee Coll./Tex. Dept. Corrections, Baytown, Tex., 1984—; critic, judge Tex. U. Interscholastic League, 1974—. Dir., actor,. designer numerous plays for Sam Houston State U., Huntsville Enrichment Activities, Hill Country Arts, others; narrator Ednl. Filmstrips/Ednl. Video Network, 1974—. With U.S. Army, 1960-63. Mem. Am. ednl. Theatre Assn., Southeastern Theatre Conf. (chmn. Army Theatre project 1969), Tex. ednl. Theatre Assn., Southwest Theatre Conf., Tex. Assn. Coll. Tchrs., Tex. Faculty Assn. Avocations: swimming, sailing, water-skiing, photography, music. Died Sept. 25, 2007.

SODUMS, DZINTARS, writer; b. Riga, Latvia, May 13, 1922; arrived in U.S., 1963; s. Andrejs and Ella Brastins Sodums; m. Skaidrite Kronbergs, Feb. 23, 1946 (dec. May 1999); children: Andris, Marcis. Student, Lynn C.C., 1975—80. Transl.: Ulysses, 1960, 93, Narziss und Goldmund, 1951, 2002, Waste Land, 1990, Four Quartets, 1999 Mem. Latvian Writers Assn. in Exil Democrat. Home: Williamsport, Pa. Died May 18, 2008.

SOHAN, JOHN PATRICK, therapist, consultant, lecturer; b. Louisville, Jan. 2, 1939; s. Richard Peter and Dorothy Helen (Strubel) S. BA, St. Meinrad Coll., Ind., 1961; MA, Spalding U., 1971. Priest Roman Cath. Ch., Louisville, 1965-75; pvt. practice family therapist Louisville, 1975-78 and from 81; asst. safety dir. City of Louisville, 1978-80, dir. rsch. Energy Office, 1980-81. Lectr. stress mgmt. First Nat. Bank, Louisville, 1981—; instr., lectr. Ky. Sch. for Drugs & Alcohol Studies, Frankfort, Ky., 1983—; instr. adult edn. Ind. U., New Albany, 1985—; cons. adult edn. Roman Cath. Ch., Louisville, 1987—. Vol. Spl. Olympics, Louisville, 1980—; bd. dirs. YWCA Rape Relief Ctr., Louisville, 1982-89, Community Employment, Crestwood, Ky., 1984—. Mem. Am. Assn. Marriage and Family Therapists (clin. bd. advisors 1983-84, supr. 1989), Am. Assn. for Counseling and Devel., Internat. Assn. Marriage and Family Counselors. Democrat. Avocations: hunting, golf, walking, volunteer work. Home: Louisville, Ky. Died Apr. 4, 2008.

SOHRWIDE, MARY JO, oncology nurse, health facility administrator; b. Okla., Sept. 27, 1955; d. Harold and Gladys (Davis) Dillon; m. Kerry Patrick Sohrwide, Dec. 30, 1978; children: Laura, Taylor. BSN, Baylor U., 1977. RN, Okla.; cert. oncology nurse. Asst. head nurse - SICU Presbyn. Hosp., Oklahoma City; nursing supr. Stillwater (Okla.) Med. Ctr., oncology coord. Facilitator I CAN COPE support group; leader Cancer Support Group. Mem. Oncology Nursing Soc. Home: Stillwater, Okla. Died July 8, 2008.

SOKOL, MAE SANDRA, psychiatrist, educator; b. NYC, Apr. 11, 1951; d. Bernard Sokol and Ruth (Sher) Levitt; 1 child. BS in Biology cum laude, Bklyn. Coll., 1972; MD, U. Louvain, Belgium, 1980. Diplomate in psychiatry and in child and adolescent psychiatry Am. Bd. Psychiatry. Resident physician L.I. Coll. Hosp., Bklyn., 1980-81; resident physician psychiatry NYU Med. Ctr., Bellevue Hosp., NYC, 1981-84, resident physician child psychiatry, 1984-86; asst. dir. child inpatient unit N.Y. Hosp. Westchester div., White Plains, 1986-93; with Georgetown Univ. Med. Ctr., Washington, 1993-94; dir. inpatient eating disorders program Western Psychiat. Inst. and Clinic, Pitts., 1994-96; staff psychiatrist Menninger Clinic, Topeka, 1996-98, dir. eating disorders program, from 1998. Teaching asst. NYU Med. Sch., 1982-84, clin. instr., 1984-86; instr. psychiatry Cornell U. Med. Coll., 1986-89, asst. prof., 1989-93. Contbr. articles to profl. jours. Mem. AMA, Am. Acad. Child and Adolescent Psychiatry, Am. Psychiat. Assn., Acad. for EAting Disorders, EAting Disorders Rsch. Soc. Died Nov. 17, 2007.

SOKOLOFF, NORMAN FRED, orthopedic surgeon; b. Phila., May 29, 1946; s. Harry and Evelyn (Feldbine) S.; m. Ilene Edyth Safra, June 25, 1967; children: Bret Robert, Cari Jaye. BS, Pa. State U., 1967; MD, Jefferson Med. Coll., 1969. Diplomate Am. Bd. Orthopedic Surgery. Surg. intern St. Vincent's Hosp. and Med. Ctr., NYC, 1969-70; orthopedic resident Albert Einstein Bronx Mcpl. Med. Ctr., Bronx, N.Y., 1970-71, U. Calif., San Diego, 1971-74; orthopedic surgeon, chmn. of bd., pres. Camelot Med. Group, Inc., Sunnyvale, Calif., from 1976. Dir., treas. El Camino IPA, Mountain View, Calif., 1995-96. Maj. U.S. Army, 1974-76. Fellow Am. Acad. Orthopedic Surgeons; mem. Western Occupl. amd Environ. Med. Assn., Calif. Med. Assn., Santa Clara County Med. Assn. Avocations: commercial, multi-engine and land instrument pilot, golf. Died Oct. 29, 2005.

SOLOMON, ADAM, venture capitalist; b. Mexico City, Sept. 13, 1952; came to U.S., 1961; s. Anthony Morton and Constance (Kaufman) S.; m. Eve Elizabeth Slater, May 2, 1981; children: Peter, James. BA in Politics and Econs., Oxford U., Eng., 1973; MS in Mgmt., MIT, 1978. V.p. Salomon Bros., NYC, 1978-82; assoc. v.p. E.M. Warburg, Pincus & Co., NYC, 1982-88, mng. dir., 1988-92; chmn. Signature Properties Internat., Roseland, N.J., from 1993, Shaker Investments, Inc., Roseland, N.J., 1994. Bd. dirs. Meta Solv Systems, Inc., Dallas, Global Telecom Systems, Inc., N.Y.C. Dir. Rabbi Marc H. Tancenbaum Found., N.Y.C., 1993. Avocations: reading, tennis, music. Home: New York, NY. Died Apr. 3, 2008.

SOLOMON, FREDERIC, lawyer; b. Fort Valley, Ga., Aug. 1, 1911; s. Aaron Moses and Mayme (Wice) S.; m. Anita Ostrin, July 4, 1954; children: Andrew Mark, Laurie Ann. BS in Physics summa cum laude, U. Ga., 1933, JD with honors, 1933. Bar: Ga. 1933, D.C. 1949, U.S. Supreme Ct. 1938. Assoc. Powell, Frazer, Goldstein & Murphy, Atlanta, 1933-34; with Fed. Res. Bd., Washington, 1934-76; spl. counsel Colton and Boykin, Washington, 1976—2009; cons. Bur. Budget, Washington, 1947 Contbr. chpts. to books, articles to profl. jours. Served to maj. USMC, 1942—45, col. USMCR. ABA (chmn. banking com., adminstrv. law sect. 1979-82, vice chmn. internat. and comparative adminstrv. law com. 1984-88), Fed. Bar Assn., Am. Econ. Assn., Phi Beta Kappa, Phi Kappa Phi. Club: Gridiron, Sphinx, Woodmont. Jewish. Home: Bethesda, Md. Died Apr. 27, 2009.

SOLOMON, GEORGE MARTIN, furniture company executive, health facility administrator; b. Bklyn., Feb. 16, 1946; s. Daniel Robert and Sunny (Brown) S.; m. Sally Offenberg (div. July 1987); children: Traci, Carey, Sunny. BA, Tulane U., 1969. Tchr. Jefferson Sch. System, Metaire, La., 1969-72; owner King Furniture, Metaire, 1972-78; sales mgr. Cort Furniture Rental, New Orleans, 1975-78, asst. dist. mgr., 1978-81, regional dir. mktg. and advt. Metaire, 1981-87; dir. med. ops. Brown Med. Clinic, Ursturge, La., from 1987; v.p. mktg. and sales New Orleans Line, 1987-89; nat. dir. advt. Leitig- Eagan Cos., New Orleans, from 1989. Project designer Salvation Army, Kenner, La. 1987; program dir. United Way, Metairie, 1983-87. Mem.: Synagogue Men's (Metaire); New Orleans Ad. Democrat. Jewish. Avocations: racquetball, football. Home: Metairie, La. Died May 14, 2008.

SOLOMON, JUDITH ANNE, music educator, pianist; b. Nutley, NJ, Apr. 25, 1943; d. Ernest and Rachael (Schecter) S. BA, Rutgers U., 1965; MMus, Yale U., 1968. Assoc. prof. music Tex. Christian U., Ft. Worth, from 1968. Contbr. articles to profl. jours. Instructional devel. grantee, Tex. Christian U., 1975, 87. Mem. Soc. Music Theory, Coll. Music Soc., AAUP, Ft. Worth Piano Tchrs. Forum, Pi Kappa Lambda. Home: Fort Worth, Tex. Died Dec. 22, 2007.

SOLOMON, ROBERT DOUGLAS, retired pathology educator; b. Delavan, Wis., Aug. 28, 1917; s. Lewis Jacob and Sara (Ludgin) S.; m. Helen Fisher, Apr. 4, 1943; children: Susan, Wendy, James, William. Student, MIT, 1934—36; BS in Biochemistry, U. Chgo., 1938; MD, Johns Hopkins U., 1942. Intern John's Hopkins Hosp., 1942-43; resident in pathology Michael Reese Hosp., 1947-49; lectr. U. Ill., Chgo., 1947-50, fellow NIH pathology, 1949-50; asst. prof. U. Md., Balt., 1955-60; assoc. prof. U. So. Calif., LA, 1960-70; chief of staff City of Hope Nat. Med. Ctr., 1966-67; prof. U. Mo., Kansas City, 1977-78, SUNY, Syracuse, 1968-78; chief of staff The Hosp., Sidney, NY, 1985-86; adj. prof. biology U. N.C., Wilmington, 1989—2005, ret., 2005. Cons. VA Hosp., Balt., 1955-60, Med. Svc. Lab., Wilmington, 1989-93; active in field of bariatrics, 1997—. Co-author: Progress in Gerontological Research, 1967; contbr. papers and profl. jours. and rsch. in biochemistry, revascular of heart, carcinogenesis, cancer chemotherapy, atherogenesis, discovery of reversibility of atherosclerosis, chemistry of urochrome pigments. V.p. Rotary, Duarte, Calif., 1967; v.p., pres. Force for a Responsible Electorate. Capt. M.C., AUS, 1943-46, PTO. Grantee NIH, Fleischmann Found., Am. Heart Assn., Nat. Cancer Inst., 1958-70. Fellow ACP (pres. Md. chpt.), Western Geriat. Soc. (founding); mem. Coll. Am. Pathologists (past pres. Md. chpt.), Am. Soc. Clin. Pathologists, Assn. Clin. Scientists, Am. Chem. Soc., Royal Soc. Medicine (London), Phi Beta Kappa, Sigma Xi. Achievements include development of fiber-optic arterial catheter for visualization and making movies of aortic endothelium in vivo; first one to report experimental reversibility of atherosclerosis. Home: Wilmington, NC. Died Mar. 25, 2008.

SOLTYS, FLORENCE GRAY, social worker; d. Olsie Glenn Gray and Addie Rebecca Hill; m. John Joseph Soltys; children: Jacqueline, Rebecca. BS, U. TN, 1958; RD, Mass. Gen. Hosp., 1959; MSW, U. NC, 1984. Clin. dietitian Mass. Gen. Hosp., Boston, 1960—63; dir. social work & bereavement Triangle Hospice, Chapel Hill, NC, 1985—87; assoc. clin. prof. U. NC Sch. Medicine, Chapel Hill, from 1998; assoc. clin. prof. and chair aging U. NC Sch. Social Work, Chapel Hill, from 1998; adj. assoc. prof. U. NC Sch. Nursing, Chapel Hill, from 1998. Chair Chapel Hill Parks and Recreation, 1981—87, Orange County Aging Bd., Chapel Hill, from 1992, Master Aging plan for Orange County, Chapel Hill, from 2000. Editor (author): American Society on Aging; author: (documentary) An Unlikely Friendship. Bd. Intervention Reminiscing Soc., Wis., 1995; leadership coun. Am. Soc. on Aging, San Francisco, 1993; bd. chair Dept. on Aging, Chapel Hill, 2000; vice chair Carol Woods Retirement, Chapel Hill. Recipient Disting. Tchg., U. NC at Chapel Hill, 2001, Trustee Yr., Non-Profit Homes State NC, 2001, Leadership in Aging, Duke U., 2002, Sharon W. Wilder award, Long Term Care Assistance Advocacy, 2003; named Trustee of Yr., Am. Assn. Homes and Svcs. to Aging, 2003. Fellow: N.C. Inst. Aging (assoc.); mem.: NASW (assoc.; bd. mem. 1986—91), N.C. Commn. on Aging, Am. Soc. Aging (assoc.; leadership coun. 1993—2003). Died Sept. 27, 2007.

SOMMER, ROBERT GEORGE, retired airline pilot, lawyer; b. NYC, July 4, 1928; s. Irvin Cecil and Rose June S.; m. Ann Penelope Goodwin, May 20, 1950 (div. Aug. 1963); children: Daniel M., Douglas J.; m. Mary Elizabeth Cheetham, June 24, 1971; children: Eric H., Jody Lee. LLB, U. Fla., 1950, JD, 1967; grad., U.S. Army Command Gen. Staff Coll., 1971, Indsl. Coll. of Armed Forces, 1978. Bar: Fla. 1950, U.S. Dist. Ct. (so. dist.) Fla. 1950, U.S. Ct. Claims 1963, U.S. Ct. Mil. Appeals 1963, U.S. Supreme Ct., 1963, U.S. Tax Ct. 1986; cert. circuit ct. mediator, Fla.; cert. flight instr. FAA. Real property officer Bur. Land Mgmt., Dept. Interior, Alaska, 1953-55; ptnr. Sommer, Frank & Weston, Miami, Fla., 1955-60; pvt. practice Miami and Ocala, Fla., from 1960. Capt. Delta Air Lines, Miami and Atlanta, 1960-88; owner Crescent-S Thoroughbred Farms.

Col. USAR, 1984. Mem. Soc. Am. Mil. Engrs., Exptl. Aircraft Assn., Airline Pilots Assn., Res. Officers Assn. U.S., Quiet Birdmen (bd. govs. 1988-2000), Elks, Masons, Shriners. Avocations: skiing, hunting, fishing. Home: Anthony, Fla. Died Aug. 25, 2007.

SONNABEND, ROGER PHILIP, hotel company executive; b. Boston, Sept. 17, 1925; s. Abraham M. and Esther (Lewitt) S.; m. Elsa Golub, July 17, 1949 (div.); children: Andrea, Stephanie, Jacqueline, Alan; m. Joan Snider, Feb. 18, 1971; stepchildren: Heidi Norton, Andrea Stoneman. BA, MIT, 1946; MBA, Harvard U., 1949; LL.D. (hon.), U. N.H., 1969. CEO Sonesta Internat. Hotel Corp., Boston, 1954—2003, exec. chmn., 2003—08. Contbr. chpts. to books and articles to profl. jours. Mem. exec. com. Nat. Alliance of Businessmen, 1968-69; bd. dirs. Bus. Execs. for Nat. Security, Inc., Washington, 1983-86; exec. com. Northeast NCCJ, 1957, regional co-chmn., nat. v.p., 1960-68; trustee Inst. Contemporary Art Mem. World Bus. Coun., Chief Execs. Orgn., Harvard Club (Boston). Home: Key Biscayne, Fla. Died Dec. 8, 2008.

SONNENFELDT, RICHARD WOLFGANG, management consultant; b. Berlin, July 23, 1923; s. Walter H. and Gertrude (Liebenthal) S.; m. Shirley C. Aronoff, Dec. 23, 1949; m. Barbara A. Hausman, Mar. 8, 1981; children: Ann Elizabeth, Lawrence Alan, Michael William. BSEE, Johns Hopkins U., 1949; postgrad., U. Pa., 1953-56. Mgr. engring. and prodn. RCA, 1949-62; gen. mgr. digital systems div. Foxboro Co., 1962-65; chief exec. officer, pres., dir. Digitronics Corp., 1965-70; v.p. RCA Corp., 1970-79; chmn. bd. dirs., CEO Electronic Indsl. Engring. Corp., 1972-75; exec. v.p. ops. NBC, NYC, 1979-82; dean Sch. Mgmt. Poly Inst. N.Y., Bklyn., 1982-84, prof. mgmt., 1982—2009; chmn., CEO NAPP Systems, Inc., 1987-90; CEO Solar Outdoor Lighting, 1997—2009. Lectr. Harvard U. Bus. Sch., Sloan Sch., MIT; cons. in field; bd. dirs. Tetktronix, Inc., Foxboro Co., Lee Enterprises, Decision Industries Corp., Compuflight Corp., Biospherics Inc., Deerpark Baking Co., Tridex Corp., Internat. Harvest Group, Comm. Satellite Network Corp., Medlife Software Inc., Solar Outdoor Lighting Inc. Contbr. articles to profl. jours.; patentee in field; author: Witness to Nuremberg, 2006 Fellow IEEE; mem. Am. Coun. Germany, Coun. Fgn. Rels., Tau Beta Pi, Omicron Delta Kappa. Died Oct. 9, 2009.

SONTAG, FREDERICK EARL, philosophy educator; b. Long Beach, Calif., Oct. 2, 1924; s. M. Burnett and Cornelia (Nicholson) S.; m. Carol Furth, June 10, 1950; children: Grant Furth, Anne Burnett Karch. BA with great distinction, Stanford U., Calif., 1949; MA, Yale U., New Haven, Conn., 1951, PhD, 1952; LLD (hon.), Coll. Idaho, 1971. Instr. Yale U., 1951-52; asst. prof. philosophy Pomona Coll., Claremont, Calif., 1952-55, assoc. prof., 1955-60, prof., 1970—2009, Robert C. Denison prof. philosophy, 1972—2009, chmn. dept. philosophy, 1960-67, 76-77, 1980-84; chmn. coord. com. in philosophy Clarement Grad. Sch. and Univ. Ctr., 1962-65. Vis. prof. Union Theol. Sem., NYC, 1959-60, Collegio de Sant' Anselmo, Rome, 1966-67, U. Copenhagen, 1972; theologian-in-residence Am. Ch. in Paris, 1973; fulbright regional vis. prof., India, East Asia, Pacific areas, 1977-78; nat. adv. coun. Kent Fellowship Program of Danforth Found., 1963-66. Author Divine Perfection, 1962, The Future of Theology, 1966, The Existentialist Prolegomena, 1969, The Crisis of Faith, 1969, The God of Evil, 1970, God, Why Did You Do That, 1970, Problems Metaphysics, 1970, How Philosophy Shapes Theology, 1971, and other numerous books, the most recent being; Love Beyond Pain: Mysticism Within Christianity, 1977, Sun Myung Moon and the Unification Church, 1977, also German, Japanese and Korean transl.; (with John K. Roth) God and America's Future, 1977, What Can God Do?, 1979, A Kierkegaard Handbook, 1979, The Elements of Philosophy, 1984, (with John K. Roth) The Questions of Philosophy, 1988, Emotion, 1989, The Return of the Gods, 1989, Willgenstein and the Mystical, 1995, Uncertain Truth, 1995, The Descent of Women, 1997, The Acts of the Trinity, 1997, Truth and Imagination, 1998, 2001: A Spiritual Odyssey, 2001, The Mysterious Presence, 2002, A Kierkegaard Handbook, 2003, American Life, 2006. Pres. bd. dirs. Claremont Family Svc., 1960-64; trustee The Coro Found., LA and San Francisco, 1967-71; bd. dirs., chmn. ways and means com. Pilgrim Place, Claremont, 1970-77. With AUS, 1943-46. Vis. scholar Ctr. for Study Japanese Religions, Kyoto, Japan, spring 1974; vis. fellow East-West Ctr., Honolulu, summer 1974; Wig Disting. prof. award, 1970, 76, Medal of Merit, Pomona Coll. Bd. Trustees, 2009 Mem.: Am. Philos. Assn., Metaphys. Soc. Am., Soc. on Religion in Higher Edn. (Kent fellow 1950—52), Am. Acad. Religion, Phi Beta Kappa. United Ch. Of Christ. Died June 14, 2009.

SOPANEN, JERI RAINER, photography director; b. Helsinki, Finland, Aug. 14, 1929; arrived in US, 1950; s. Rainer and Helvi Raakel (Salminen) S.; m. Carolyn Maier, 1952 (div. 1956); 1 child, Erik; m. Eileen A. Humeston, 1961 (div. 1980); ptnr. Christine Huneke, 1975 (separated 1991); children: Anya Maarit, Mark; m. Marja Roth, 2000. MusB, Lawrence Coll., 1952; BA, U. So. Calif., 1956. Ind. dir. photography Sopanen Films, Inc., NYC, from 1966. Dir. photography: (films) My Dinner With Andre, 1982, The Gig, 1986, The Luckiest Man in the World, 1989; (documentaries) The Brain, 1986, The Ring of Truth, 1987, The Mind (Emmy award 1989); dir. photography Nova programs, 1991—, Gardens of the World with Audrey Hepburn, 1993. With U.S. Army, 1952-54. Mem. Dirs. Guild Am., Internat. Assn. Theatrical Stage Employees. Democrat. Avocation: cross country skiing. Died Sept. 21, 2008.

SOPPELSA, ANTHONY JOSEPH, graphic designer; b. Campbell, Ohio, Nov. 16, 1919; s. Joseph and Domenica Rosa (Gaiarsa) S.; m. Elizabeth Ann McCarthy, Jan. 6, 1944; children: Donna, Robert, John, James, Jean, Brian. BA, Youngstown U., 1942; cert., U. Wash., 1944; student, Cleve. State U., 1966-67. Lettering artist Manning Studios, Cleve., 1946-47, graphic designer, 1948-64, art dir., 1965-81; lectr. comml. art Fenn Coll., Cleve., 1953-61; graphic designer Cleve., from 1981; design instr. Cuyahoga C.C., Parma, Ohio, 1981-82, Polaris Vocat. Sch., Middleburg Heights, Ohio, 1983; designer/cons. Parma Heights, Ohio, from 1996. Adv. bd. Polaris Vocat. Sch., 1985-90. Paintings exhibited in various Ohio galleries including Cleve. Mus. Art May shows, Canton Art Mus. fall shows, various local art shows; paintings in pvt. collections; constructed copy Stradivarius violin; violinist Parma Symphony Orch. (bd. dirs. 1987—). Tech. sgt. U.S. Army, 1942-45, PTO. Mem. Phi Kappa Phi. Avocation: violin making/playing. Died Jan. 5, 2008.

SORKIN, SAUL, lawyer; b. NYC, June 24, 1925; s. Samuel and Paulene Sorkin; m. Ellen Weinberg, June 24, 1956; children: David J., Richard E., John E. BA, Bklyn. Coll., 1948; JD, Harvard U., 1951. Bar: N.Y., U.S. Dist. Ct. (so. and ea. dists.) N.Y., U.S. Ct. Appeals (2d cir.), U.S. Supreme Ct. Spl. atty., atty. gen. N.Y. State Dept. Law, NYC, 1991-93; assoc. Newman, Aronsen & Newmann, NYC, 1993-94; pvt. practice NYC; ptnr. Kroll & Trouct, NYC; of counsel Furman & Del Corp., Great Neck, N.Y. Sgt. U.S. Army, 1993-96. Home: New York, NY. Died Jan. 13, 2008.

SOTO, NELL, state legislator; m. Philip Soto (dec.). City councilwoman Pomona, 1986—98; state assemblywoman Dist. 61 Calif., 1999—2001, Calif., 2006—08; mem. Aging & Long Term Care, Edn., Govt. Orgn. Local Govt. & Transp. Coms., Coms. Indian Gaming, Edn. Tech., Calif-Mex Affairs & Calif. Children Coms., 1999—2001; state assembly Calif.; mem. state senate Dist. 32 Calif., 2001—06; mem. Local Govt. Coms., Govt. Orgn.; chmn. Transp., Ins-PERS; com. chair Urban Econ. Devel. Coms.; pub. affairs rep. LA Co. Met. Transp. Authority; bd. mem. S Coast Air Quality Mgmt. Dist. Recipient Woman Achievement award, YWCA, Disting. Svc. award, San Gabriel Valley; named Legis. of Yr., Outstanding Citizen of Yr., NAACP, Dem. of Yr., LA County Cmty. Coll. Democrat. Roman Catholic. Home: Sacramento, Calif. Died Feb. 26, 2009.

SOUCY, GERALD PAUL, psychologist, mental health program developer; b. Emunston, NB, Can., July 29, 1949; came to U.S., 1949; s. Roger and Theresa (Lausier) S. BA with honors, Boston U., 1971; MA with distinction, DePaul U., 1979, PhD with distinction, 1982. Lic. psychologist, Ill. Psychologist Northwest Mental Health, Arlington Heights, Ill., 1982-85; dir. Horizons Psychotherapy, Chgo., 1982-83; support services dir. AIDS project Howard Brown Clinic, Chgo., 1983-85, cons. NIH project, from 1985; dir. Met. Psychotherapy, Chgo., from 1983. Cons. Chgo. Dept. Health, 1985—; chmn. Mental Health Group, AIDS Interdisciplinary adv. council State of Ill., 1985—. Author: Psychological Aspects of Asthma, 1983; contbr. articles to profl. jours. Schmitt fellow, 1977, 81. Mem. Am. Orthopsychiat. Assn., Am. Pub. Health Assn., Ill. Pub. Health Assn. Avocations: swimming, skiing, tennis. Home: Chicago, Ill. Died Feb. 20, 2008.

SOULÉ, BETTY ANN, community health nurse; b. Klamath Falls, Oreg., Nov. 26, 1933; d. Jesse Jackson and Lena Violet (McDow) Howerton; m. Milton Forest Soul_248, June 23, 1957; children: Robin Lynn, Terry Wayne, Kenneth Scott. BSN, Walla Walla Coll., 1957; MPH, Loma Linda U., 1980. Pub. health nurse Yakima (Wash.) Dist. Health, Southwest Dist. Health Dept., Caldwell, Idaho; instr. ADN program Treasure Valley Community Coll., Ontario, Oreg.; adminstr. health dept. Malheur County, Ontario. Mem. Conf. Local Health Ofcls.; chmn. prenatal for Malheur area; adj. faculty Oreg. Health Scis. U., Ea. Oreg. State Coll. Home: Payette, Idaho. Died Nov. 25, 2007.

SOUTHALL, IVAN FRANCIS, author; b. Melbourne, Victoria BNA, Australia, June 8, 1921; s. Francis Gordon and Rachel Elizabeth (Voutier) S.; m. Joy Blackburn, Sept. 8, 1945; children: Andrew John, Roberta Joy, Elizabeth Rose, Melissa Frances; m. Susan Helen Westerlund, Nov. 11, 1976. Ed., pub. schs., Victoria. Freelance writer, from 1947. Retrospective exhbn. State Libr. of Victoria, 1998; author: (non-fiction) They Shall Not Pass Unseen, 1956, Journeys into Mystery, 1961, Indonesia Face to Face, 1964, Lawrence Hargrave in the Six Great Australians, 1964, Rockets in the Desert: The Story of Woomera, 1965, The Challenge: Is the Church Obsolete?, 1966, Parsons on the Track, 1961, (novels) Meet Simon Black, 1950, Hills End, 1962, Ash Road, 1965 (Children's Book of Yr., Australian Children's Book Coun., 1966), Let the Balloon Go, 1968, To the Wild Sky, 1968 (Children's Book of Yr., Australian Children's Book Coun., 1968), Sly Old Wardrobe, 1969, Bread and Honey, 1970 (Children's Book of Yr., Australian Children's Book Coun., 1971), Josh, 1971 (Carnegie medal Great Britain Libr. Assn., 1971), Fly West, 1975 (Book of Yr., 1976), The Long Night Watch, 1983 (Nat. Children's Book award Australian Children's Book Coun., 1986, Phoenix award ALA, 2003), Blackbird, 1988, Ziggurat, 1997. Found. pres. Knoxbrooke Day Tng. Ctr. for Intellectually Handicapped, Victoria, 1967—69. Served as flight lt. Royal Australian Air Force, 1942—47, Europe. Decorated Order of Australia, D.F.C. RAAF; recipient Emeritus Fellowship award, Australian Coun., 1993, Book of Yr. award, Australian Children's Coun., 1970, Phoenix award, Children's Literature Assn., 2003, Dromkeen medal, 2003. Methodist. Home: Healesville, Australia. Died Nov. 15, 2008.

SOUTHERLAND, HENRY DELEON, JR., retired lawyer, civil engineer; b. Birmingham, Ala., Sept. 8, 1911; s. Henry DeLeon and Edwina (Williams) Southerland; m. Helen Ashe (div.); 1 child, Mary Neill 1 stepchild, Carolyn Wilson Long; m. Louise Harris Wilson, Jan. 22, 1955. Student, Ga. Tech. U., 1929—31; BS, U. Ga., 1934; MS, U. Tenn., 1941; JD, Columbia U., 1948; MA, Samford U., 1983. Registered profl. engr., Tenn., 1942; bar: Ala. 1949. Engring. aide to hydraulic engr. water control planning TVA, Knoxville, Tenn., 1934—48; tax acct. US Steel Corp., Fairfield, Ala., 1948—51, staff asst. land dept., 1951—56, asst. mgr. land dept., 1956—68, mgr. so. lands timber, 1968—71; comml. agt. Birmingham So. RR Co., Fairfield, 1956—71; ret., 1971. Co-author: The Federal Road through Georgia, the Creek Nation, and Alabama, 1806-1836, 1949 (Best non-fiction award Ala. Hist. Assn., Best non-fiction award Ala. Libr. Assn.). Mem. Mountain Brook City Coun., Ala., 1976—80, pres. pro tem, 1980; chmn. planning commn. City of Mountain Brook, 1957—76. Lt. col. US Army, 1946, col. US Army, 1954. Mem.: S.R. (gen. v.p. emeritus), Newcomen Soc., Soc. War of 1812 (past grand marshall), Soc. Colonial Wars (past dep. gov. gen.), St. Andrews Soc. Mid. South (co-founder), Soc. of Cin. Episcopalian. Avocations: genealogy, gardening, fishing, history. Died Apr. 26, 2009.

SOWERS, MIRIAM RUTH, painter; b. Bluffton, Ohio, Oct. 4, 1922; d. Paul S. and Edith E. (Triplehorn) Hochstetler; m. H. Frank Sowers, Apr. 15, 1944; children: Craig V., Keith A. BFA, Miami U., Oxford, Ohio, 1944; postgrad., Chgo. Art Inst., 1946, U. N.Mex., 1957. Draftsman Army Map Service, Chgo., 1945-46; owner studio Findlay, Ohio, 1949-53, Albuquerque, 1953-60; owner Old Town Gallery, Albuquerque, 1961-80; owner pvt. studio Albuquerque, from 1980. One-woman shows include Tex. Agrl. and Indsl. U., Kingville, Houston Bapt. Coll., Winblad Galleries, San Francisco, L'Atelier Gallery, Cedar Falls, Iowa, Southwestern Galleries, Dallas, Albuquerque Unitarian Ch., Am. Bible Soc., N.Y.C., Peacock Gallery, Corrales, N.Mex., 1984, U. N.Mex. Community Ctr. Arts, Las Cruces, 1985, Wharton's Gallery, Santa Fe, 1985, Aliso Gallery, Albuquerque, 1986, Statesman Club, Albuquerque, Arts Internat. Gallery, Findlay, Findlay Coll., Springfield (Ohio) Mus. Art, Provenance Gallery, Maui, Hawaii, 1988, Saint Johns Coll., Santa Fe, 1988, King Kamehameha Hotel, Kailua-Kona, Hawaii, 1989, Marine Gallery, Kona, 1990, Kona Surf Hotel, 1990, Luigi De Rossi Gallery, Kealakaua, Hawaii, Blankley Gallery, Albuquerque, Blankley Gallery, Albuquerque, 1992, Southwest Cornerhouse Gallery, 93, 94, 95, 96, 97, 98, Albuquerque, 1993; group and gallery exhibits include Dayton (Ohio) Art Inst., Butler (Ohio) Art Inst., Akron (Ohio) Art Inst., Massilon (Ohio) Art Inst., Toledo Mus. Art (prize), Sun Carnival, El Paso, Chelmont Nat., El Paso, Tucson Fiesta Show, Santa Fe Biennial, Corrales All State Show (prize), N.Mex. State Fair (prize), Ohio Tri-State Show, Ohio State Fair, I.P.A. Nat., Washington, Roswell (N.Mex.) Mus., All Albuquerque Show and Jonson Gallery (prize), Galeria de Artesanos, Albuquerque, 1985, Little Studio Gallery, N.Y.C., Ft. Smith (Ark.) Art Ctr., The Gallery, Roswell, Gallery D., Mesilla, N.Mex., Creative Endeavors, Taos, N.Mex., Smith LTD. Galleries, Ruidoso, N.Mex., Alice Moxey Gallery, Midland, Tex., Linda Lundeen Gallery, Las Cruces, Hand Made U.S.A., Albuquerque, Reynolds Gallery, Albuquerque, El Dor Gallery, Albuquerque, Weems Gallery, Albuquerque, My Place, Albuquerque, Casa Manana Gallery, Albuquerque, Preusser Gallery, Albuquerque, Argosy Arts & Artifacts Gallery, Albuquerque, Fuller Lodge, Los Alamos, Kona Arts & Crafts, Volcano House Gallery, Volcano Nat. Pk., Hawaii, Universal Ctr. for the Arts, Las Cruces, N.Mex., Milagro Gallery, Taos, N.Mex., Eloise Contemporary, Taos, Wakefield Gardens Gallery, Honaunau-Kona, Hawaii, 1992, Kona Arts & Crafts Gallery, Kailua-Kona, Hawaii, 1992, Crystal Star Gallery, Kealaka Kua, Hawaii, 1992, Ken Dewey Gallery, Albuquerque, 1994, New Mexico's Own, Bernallilo, 1994, Foxfire Gall., Albuquerque, Shephard of the Valley Church, 1988, others; works pub.: (mags.) Western Rev., 1967, N.Mex. Cultural News, 1968, Albuquerque Clubwoman, 1969, S.W. Art Mag., 1973, Art Voices South, 1980, (books) Parables from Paradise, 1975, The Suns of Man, 1981, (poetry quar.) Encore, 1979, (video) Layerist Artists, 1990; included in books Leap, Limited Edition Art Prints, 1979-80, American Artists, 1985, New York Artists, 1988, Artists of New Mexico vol. 3, 1989, Layerist Artists, 1991, Merto Plus, Albuquerque Jour., 1992. Home: Albuquerque, N.Mex. Died Mar. 15, 2008.

SPADEA, DOMINICK GEORGE, manufacturing executive; b. Camden, NJ, Dec. 13, 1945; s. Dominick and Mary (Ficchi) S.; m. Joan Poprycz, Aug. 6, 1966 (div. Nov. 1986); children: Dominick George Jr. (dec.), William, Thomas, John. Student, Temple U., 1963-71. Founder, chmn. Spadea Swiss Products Co., Westmont, N.J., from 1974, Hatton Industries, Westmont, from 1979; co-founder, chmn. Jersey Arms Works, Inc., Westmont, from 1980; founder, chmn. Spadea Mfg. Co., Dallas, from 1980, Avenger Systems Corp., Haddonfield, N.J., from 1985. Campaign coordinator for N.J. Gubernatorial Election Rep. Primary campaign state chmn. Conservative Caucus of N.J. Mem. Am. Def. Preparedness Assn., Nat. Screw Machine Products Assn. (bd. dirs. 1968-71), NRA. Republican. Roman Catholic. Avocation: reading. Home: Cherry Hill, NJ. Died June 10, 2009; Cherry Hill, NJ.

SPANDIKOW, BETTY VALIREE, retired health care professional; b. Chgo., Sept. 27, 1923; d. Francis Oliver Redmond and Valiree Pearl Jones; m. Robert A. Wagner, Oct. 27, 1942 (dec. June 1975); children: Gail Gralzianna Robert, A. Wagner, Mary Ruth Wright, Margaret Dowd, Dorothea Rasmussen, Helen Huntley; m. Paul W. Spandikow, Nov. 6, 1993. Grad. h.s., Chgo. Exec. dir. LaLeche League Internat., Franklin Park, Ill., 1972-91. Spkr. to parents, health profls., and physicians, U.S. and abroad. Co-author: The Womanly Art of Breastfeeding. Home: Springville, Tenn. Died Oct. 26, 2008.

SPANGLER, MILLER BRANT, science and technology analyst, planner, consultant; b. Stoyestown, Pa., Sept. 1, 1923; s. Elbert Bruce and Raye Isabel (Brant) S.; m. Claire Labin Kussart, Sept. 20, 1947; children: Daryl Claire, Philip Miller, Coreen Sue. BS with honors, Carnegie-Mellon U., 1950; MA, U. Chgo., 1953, PhD, 1956. Chem. engr. Gulf Rsch. Corp., Harmarville, Pa., 1950-51; assoc. engr. rsch. corp. IBM, Yorktown Heights, N.Y., 1956-60, mgr., market rsch. fed. systems div. Rockville, Md., 1960-63; program economist U.S. Agy. for Internat. Devel., Turkey, India, 1963-66; dir. ctr. for techno-econ. studies Nat. Planning Assn., Washington, 1966-72; chief, cost benefit analysis br. U.S. Atomic Energy Commn., Washington, 1972-75; spl. asst. policy devel. U.S. Nuclear Regulatory Commn., Washington, 1975-89; pres. Techno-Planning, Inc., Bethesda, Md., 1989-94; freelance author Bethesda, 1994—2008. Mem. adv. bd. NSF Sea Grant Program, Washington, 1969, Environ. Profl. Jour., L.A., 1981-88. Author: New Technology and the Supply of Petroleum, 1956, New Technology and Marine Resource Development, 1970, The Role of Research and Development in Water Resources Planning, 1972, U.S. Experience in Environmental Cost-Benefit Analysis, 1980; contbr. numerous articles and papers to profl. jours. Recipient Planning Rsch. award Program Edn. and Rsch. in Planning U. Chgo., 1953. Mem. N.Y. Acad. Scis., Am. Assn. for the Advancement Sci., Nat. Assn. Environ. Profls., Soc. for Risk Analysis, Internat. Assn. for Impact Assessment., Tau Beta Pi. Republican. Methodist. Avocations: oriental gardening, travel, photography. Home: Gaithersburg, Md. Died Dec. 21, 2008.

SPARKS, BENNETT SHER, military officer; b. Pitts., Oct. 10, 1925; s. Julius and Anna K. Sparks; m. Elizabeth Sparks, May 8, 1943 (dec. Nov. 2005); children: Bennett Sher Jr., James Robert, Richard T.(dec.), John N., Julieann, Donna Beth(dec.). Diploma, Naval War Coll., 1973, Armed Forces Staff Coll., 1978, Nat. War Coll., 1978, The Army War Coll., 1985, The Nat. Def. U., 1980, The Indsl. Coll. Armed Forces; PhD in Philosophy (hon.), Sampson U., Oxford, Eng., 1986. Lic. aircraft pilot. Enlisted USCG, 1942, commd. ensign, 1955, advanced through grades to rear admiral, 1985, dist. insp. 11th Coast Guard Dist., sr. res. officer Pacific Area San Francisco, sr. res. officer Atlantic Area NYC, comdr. Navy's No. Calif. Maritime Def. Zone San Francisco, comdr. Navy's Maritime Def. Zone Sector 6 Charleston, SC, ret., 1996. Aviator Coast and Geodetic Survey, Ala.; chief US Del. to Confedn. Res. Officers (CIOR), NATO Hdqrs., Belgium, 1985-86; internat. sec.-gen. Inter-Allied Confedn. Res. Officers, Brussels, 1992-94. Mem. Calif. Vets. Bd., from 1995, chmn., 1998—99; bd. dirs. Sonoma County Area Agy. of Aging, Calif., from 2002, mem. legis. com., from 2002; bd. dirs. North Bay chpt. Alzheimer's Assn. No. Calif. and Nev., from 2002; bd. dirs. Bank of Hollywood. Decorated Legion of Merit, Coast Guard Commendation medals (2), Coast Guard Achievement medal, The Humanitarian Svc. medal, Arctic Svc. medal, Coast Guard Combat Air Crew Wings with three stars, knight Sovereign Mil. Order Temple of Jerusalem, the NATO Grand Priory, 1983, knight comdr., 1987, Meritorious Svc. medal and the Coast Guard Commmand Ashore Device medal; recipient Navy Disting. Pub. Svc. medal Sec. of Navy, 1983, Coast Guard Disting. Pub. Svc. medal Comdt. of Coast Guard, 1983, 93 (only person in history of Coast Guard to receive 2 awards) and numerous other milt. decorations. Mem. DAV, VFW, Am. Legion, Sonoma County United Vets. Coun., Navy League, Naval Res. Assn., Res. Officers Assn. US (nat. pres. 1982-83, nat. dep. exec. dir., dir. adminstrn. and dir. fin. 1988-91, chmn. bd. trustees, bd. dirs.), Coast Guard Chief Petty Officers Assn, Coast Guard Combat Vets Assn. Home: Windsor, Calif. Died May 22, 2009.

SPECA, JOHN M., retired law educator; b. Kenosha, Wis., Apr. 11, 1917; s. Danie and Emily (Mazzel) S. PhB, Notre Dame U., 1941, JD, 1942; LLM, Duke U., 1952. Prof. law U. Mo., Kansas City, 1947-85, prof. emeritus, from 1985. Contbr. articles to profl. jours. Died Sept. 10, 2007.

SPECTOR, MELBOURNE LOUIS, retired diplomat; b. Pueblo, Colo., May 7, 1918; s. Joseph E. and Dora (Bernstein) S.; m. Louise Vincent, Nov. 23, 1948 (dec. 2004); 1 son, Stephen David. BA with honors, U. N.Mex., 1941. Intern U.S. Bur. Indian Affairs, 1941, Nat. Inst. Pub. Affairs, 1941; personnel asst. Office Emergency Mgmt., 1941-42; chief classification div. War Relocation Authority, 1942-43, Hdqrs. USAAF, 1943-45; employment officer UNRRA, 1945-46; pvt. employment, 1946-47; pers. officer US Dept. State, 1947-49; detail Econ. Coop. Adminstrn., 1948; dep. dir. personnel Econ. Coop. Adminstrn., Marshall Plan, Paris, 1949-51; dep. dir., acting dir. personnel Econ. Coop. Adminstrn., Mut. Security Adminstrn., FOA, 1951-54; asst., dep. dir. Mission to Mexico, ICA, 1954-57, acting dir., 1957-59; chief C. Am., Mex. and Caribbean div. ICA, 1959-61; dir. Office Personnel Mgmt., AID, 1961-62; exec. dir. Bur. Inter-Am. Affairs, US Dept. State, 1962-64; counselor for adminstrv. affairs US Embassy, New Delhi, 1964-66; seminarian Sr. Seminar Fgn. Policy, Dept. State, 1966-67; exec. dir. U.S.-Mex. Commn. for Border Devel. and Friendship, 1967-69, Am. Revolution Bicentennial Commn., 1969-71; mem. mgmt., policy and coordination staffs US Dept. State, 1971-73. Mem. Fgn. Svc. Grievance Bd., 1976-77; advisor Peace Corps Dir., 1979-80; exec. dir. Am. Consortium for Internat. Pub. Adminstrn., 1980-84, 93-94, dir. Marshall Plan Oral History Project, 1987-97. Mem. Cosmos Club, Am. Soc. Pub. Adminstrn., Pi Kappa Alpha, Phi Kappa Phi. Home: Washington, DC. Died Sept. 22, 2009.

SPENCER, ERIC WILLIAM, former safety professional, consultant; b. NYC, Apr. 1, 1930; s. Eric William and Bertha (Eyer) S.; m. Eleanor Bevilacqua, Mar. 2, 1957; children: Jo-Anne, John E., David, Gina M. BBA, Hofstra U., 1953; AM (hon.), Brown U., 1975. Supr. safety & tng. Am. Can Co., Bklyn., 1957-61; safety officer MIT Lincoln Lab., Lexington, Mass., 1961-65; dir. safety Brown U., Providence, R.I., 1965-77; safety cons. M&M Protection Cons., Boston, 1977-79; safety officer Woods Hole (Mass.) Oceanographic Inst., 1979-92, ret., 1992. Bd. dirs. Mass. Safety Coun., Boston, 1981—; past pres. R.I. Safety Assn., Providence, 1970, '74, '75. Author: (with others) Handbook of Lab Safety, College and University Business Administration. Mem. Seekonk (Mass) Sch. Com., Sch. Bldg. Com.; trustee Seekonk Pub. Libr.; pres. Seekonk Citizens Scholarship Found.; Seekonk rep. Tri-County Regional Tech. Vocat., Franklin, Mass. Lt. USN, 1953-57. Named Man of Yr. R.I. Soc. to Prevent Blindness, Providence, 1970. Mem. Am. Soc. Safety Engrs. (chmn. admissions com., profl. paper awards com., mem. ethics rev. com., editorial bd. Profl. Safety jour., Tech. Paper award 1963), Health Physics Com. Soc. (plenary mem.), Nat. Protection Assn., Campus Safety Assn. (pres. 1972-73). Avocations: golf, bowling. Home: Seekonk, Mass. Died June 27, 2008.

SPENCER, IOLANTHA ESTELLA, academic affairs administrator; b. Tuskegee Institute, Ala., Dec. 25, 1953; BS, Tuskegee Inst., 1975, MEd, 1980. Cert. fundraiser. Clk., typist Sch. Vet. Medicine Tuskegee U., Tuskegee Inst., 1975-81, grants specialist Office Devel., 1981-84, recruiter, coord. Sch. Nursing & Allied Health, 1984-87, instr., 1987-90, dir. learning ctr., 1987-90, asst. dir. provost office, 1990-93, instr. acad. affairs, from 1993, asst. Title III coord. acad. affairs provost office, from 1993. Exec. dir. Tuskegee U. Nat. Athletic Assn., 1987—; mem. adv. coun. Macon County Cmty. Decision Making Coun., Tuskegee Institute, 1995-96, leadership com. Tuskegee/Macon County Town & Gown, 1995—. Mem. Macon County Dem. Club, Tuskegee, 1994; steering com. Campaign to Build City Police Dept., Tuskegee, 1995, Campaign to Elect Sheriff, Tuskegee, 1994. Mem. AAUW, NAACP, Continental Socs. Inc. (v.p. 1993-95, pres. 1995—, nat. fin. sec., regional parliamentarian), Alpha Kappa Alpha (editor newsletter 1993-95, chair stds. 1995—, parliamentarian Beta Xi Omega chpt., Vol. Svc. award 1992, Outstanding Svc. award 1995). Baptist. Avocations: computers, photography, tennis, swimming, fishing. Home: Tuskegee Institute, Ala. Died Aug. 18, 2007.

SPENCER, KEITH G., construction executive; b. Albany, NY, Feb. 15, 1943; s. Fred Mathias and Joan Spencer; m. Patricia Ann Miller, June 15, 1968 (annulled Aug. 18, 1981); 1 child, Kevin Patrick. Degree in Med. Field Specialty Sch., U.S. Army, 1965; BS in Human Svcs., SUNY, Saratoga, 1993, MA in Labor Studies, 1996; fire adminstrn., Nat. Fire Acad., 1995; student, SUNY; MSW, Brighton U. Lic. real estate N.Y., fire adjuster N.Y. Clk. U.S. Post Office, Albany, NY, 1965—67; multi-line adjuster Hartford Ins. Co., Delmar, NY, 1967—73; gen. constrn. Spencer Constrn. Co., Latham, NY, 1973—87, Albany, 1989—95; boys prefect The LaSalle Sch., Albany, 1987—89; tchr./semi-ret. St. Sophia Sch., Albany, from 1998. Inspector Kaplan Realtors, Delmar, NY, 1977—78. Author: Dunouer Cottage, 2001, Air Force Family 1942-1964, 2001, My Child's Keeper, 2002, U.S. History of Memorabilia, 2003. Mgr., coach Little League, Pop Warner, Babe Ruth Latham Little League, 1978—82; vol. Priests for Life, 2001; mem. The Archbishop Sheen Found., Peoria, Ill., 2003, St. Jude Hosp. Fund, Memphis, The Am. Legion, 1984—86; asst. committeeman GOP, No. Colonie, NY, 1973—74; advanced cert. catechist Diocese of Albany, 1982—95. Sgt. USAR, 1964—70, sgt. USAR, 1987—90. Mem.: KC (vol. 1975—77), Franciscan Mission Assocs., Elks Club. Roman Catholic. Avocations: reading, writing, golf, bowling, model ship building. Home: Albany, NY. Died Feb. 29, 2008.

SPENCER, MARY MILLER, civic worker; b. Comanche, Tex., May 25, 1924; d. Aaron Gaynor and Alma (Grissom) Miller; 1 child, Mara Lynn. BS, U. North Tex., 1943. Cafeteria dir. Mercedes (Tex.) Pub. Schs., 1943-46; home economist coord. All-Orange Dessert Contest Fla. Citrus Commn., Lakeland, 1959-62, 64; tchr. purchasing sch. lunch dept. Fla. Dept. Edn., 1960. Clothing judge Polk County (Fla.) Youth Fair, 1951-68, Polk County Federated Women's Clubs, 1964-66; pres. Dixieland Elem. Sch. PTA, 1955-57, Polk County Coun. PTA's, 1958-60; chmn. pub. edn. com. Polk County unit Am. Cancer Soc., 1959-60, bd. dirs., 1962-70; charter mem., bd. dirs. Lakeland YMCA, 1962-72; sec. Greater Lakeland Cmty. Nursing Coun., 1965-72; trustee, vice-chmn. Polk County Eye Clinic, Inc., 1962-64, pres., 1964-82; bd. dirs. Polk County Scholarship and Loan Fund, 1962-70; mem. exec. com. West Polk County (Fla.) Cmty. Welfare Coun., 1960-62, 65-68; mem. budget and audit com. Greater Lakeland United Fund, 1960-62, bd. dirs., 1967-70, residential chmn. fund drive, 1968; mem. adv. bd. Polk County Juvenile and Domestic Rels. Ct., 1960-69; sec. bd. dirs. Fla. West Coast Ednl. TV, 1960-81; mem. Polk County Home Econs. Adv. Com., 1965-71; mem. exec. com. Suncoast Health Coun., 1968-71; worker children's svcs. divsn. family svcs. Dept. Health and Rehab. Svcs., State of Fla., 1969-70, social worker, 1970-72, 74-82, social worker Overpayment Fraud Recoupment unit, 1977-81, with other pers. svcs., 1981-82, supr. Overpayment Fraud Recoupment unit, 1982-83, pub. assistance specialist IV, 1984-89; bd. dirs. Lake Region United Way, Winter Haven, 1976-81; mem. Polk County Cmty. Svcs. Coun., 1978-88; with other pers. svcs. Emergency Fin. Assistance Housing Program, 1990-96. Mem. AAUW (pres. Lakeland br. 1960-61), Nat. Welfare Fraud Assn., Fla. Congress Parents and Tchrs. (hon. life, pres. dist. 7 1961-63, chmn. pub. rels. 1962-66), Fla. Health and Welfare Coun., Fla. Health and Social Svc. Coun., Polk County Mental Health Assn., U. North Tex. Alumni Assn., Order Ea. Star. Democrat. Methodist. Home: Lakeland, Fla. Died 2008.

SPERO, NANCY, artist; b. Cleve., Aug. 24, 1926; BFA, Sch. Art Inst. Chgo., 1949; student, Ecole des Beaux-Arts, Paris, 1950, Atelier Andre l'Hote, 1950. One-woman shows include Hewlett Gallery, Carnegie-Mellon U., Pitts., 1989, Rhona Hoffman Gallery, Chgo., 1986, 94, Inst. Contemporary Art, London, 1987, Everson Mus. Art, Syracuse, NY, 1987, Mus. Contemporary Art, LA, 1988, Smith Coll. Mus. Art, Northampton, Mass., 1990, Haus am Walsee, Berlin, Germany, 1990, Barbara Gross Galerie, Munich, 1991, 95, 97-98, Salzburger Kunstverein, Austria, 1991, Christine König Gallery, Vienna, Austria, 1992, Ulmer Mus., Ulm, Germany, 1992, Josh Baer Gallery, NYC, 1993, Nat. Gallery Can., Ottowa, 1993, Greenville (SC) County Mus. Art, 1993, Printworks, Chgo., 1994, Kunststichting Kanaal Art Found., Kortrijk, Belgium, 1994, Malmö (Sweden) Konsthall, 1994, Am. Ctr., Paris, MIT List Visual Arts Ctr., Cambridge, 1994, Arthur M. Sackler Mus., Harvard U., 1995, Fine Arts Gallery, U. Md. Baltimore County, 1995, NY Kunsthalle, 1996, Vancouver Art Gallery, 1996, Hiroshima City Mus. Contemporary Art, 1996, Jüdisches Mus. der Stadt Wien, 1996, Heeresspital, Innsbruck, Tyrol, 1996, Jack Tilton Gallery, NYC, 1996, PPOW Gallery, NYC, 1996, Galerie im Taxispalais, Innsbruck, 1996, Elaine C. Jacob Gallery, Wayne State U., Detroit, 1997, Documenta X, Kassel, Germany, 1997, Crown Gallery, Brussels, 1997-98, Ikon Gallery, Birmingham, Eng., 1997-98, Internat. Biennale of Cairo, 1998, Festpielhaus Hellerau, Dresden, 1998, Galerie Montenay-Giroux, Paris, 1998, Barbara Gross Galerie, Munich, 1998, Miami U., Oxford, Ohio, 2000, others; exhibited in group shows at The Biennial of Sydney, Australia, 1986, Mus. Modern Art, NYC, 1988, The Bertha and Karl Leubsdorf Art Gallery, Hunter Coll., NYC, 1988, Le Grande Halle de La Villette, Paris, 1989, Bullet Space, NYC, 1989, Ctr. Internat. d'Art Contemporain, Montreal, 1990, Dum Umeni Mesta Brna, Brünn, Czechoslowakia, 1991, Boston U. Art Gallery, 1991, Mus. der Stadtentwässerung, Zurich, 1994, Stichting Artimo, Beurs van Berlage, Amsterdam, 1994, Sch. Art Inst. Chgo., Betty Rymer Gallery, Chgo., 1994, MIT List Visual Arts Ctr., Cambridge, 1995, Southeastern Ctr. for Contemporary Art, Winston-Salem, NC, 1995, Ctr. Georges Pompidou, Paris, 1995, Uffizi Gallery, Florence, Italy, 1995, Mus. Modern Art, NYC, 1996, Whitney Museum Am. Art, NYC, 1999, Venice Biennale, 2007, numerous others; represented in permanent collections Art Inst. Chgo., Australian Nat. Gallery, Boston Museum of Fine Arts, Brooklyn Museum, NY, Centro Cultural, Mex. City, Frac Nord Pas de Calais, France, Harvard U. Art Museums, Hiroshima City Museum of Contemporary Art, MIT List Visual Arts Ctr., Madison Art Ctr., Musée des Beaux-Arts de Montreal, Nat. Gallery of Canada, Ottowa, Phila. Museum of Art, Museum of Modern Art, NYC, U. Art Museum, Berkeley, Calif., Vancouver Art Gallery, Whitney Museum Am. Art, NYC. Mem.: Am. Acad. Arts and Letters (acad. 2004). Died Oct. 19, 2009.

SPIEGEL, HERMAN D.J., architecture and structural engineering educator; b. Boston, Dec. 31, 1924; s. Harry and Annie (Gittleman) S.; m. Sally Peery, June 2, 1957; children: Robert Stewart, William Steven. BS in Arch., RISD, 1953; M Structural Engring., Yale U., 1955. Registered profl. engr., Calif., Mass., R.I., D.C., Ky., Md., Va., Conn. Dean Sch. Arch. Yale U., New Haven, 1971—76, from instr. archtl. engring. to prof. emeritus, 1955—93, prof. emeritus arch. engring., from 1992; founder, prin. Spiegel Zamecnik & Shah Cons. Structural Engrs., New Haven, from 1956, Washington, from 1971. Lectr. in field. With U.S. Army, 1943-46, WW II, ETO and PTO. Recipient Alumni Gold medal, RISD, 1972. Fellow ASCE, Yale Eng. and Sci. Soc., mem. AIA (hon.), ASTM, Amigos de Gaudi (hon.), Assn. Collegiate Schs. Arch., Am. Concrete Inst., Am. Inst. Steel Constrn., Conn. Soc. Architects (hon.), Conn. bldg. Congress, Yale Engring. Soc., Army and Navy Club of Washington, Mory's Assn. Inc., Yale Club of N.Y.C., Yale Club of New Haven. Home: Madison, Conn. Died Apr. 13, 2008.

SPIELMAN, JOHN PHILIP, JR., retired history professor; b. Anaconda, Mont., June 16, 1930; s. John Philip and Lewanna (Coleman) S.; m. Danila B. Cole, Sept. 14, 1955. BA, U. Mont., 1951; MA, U. Wis., 1953, PhD, 1957. Instr. U. Mich., Ann Arbor, 1957-59; asst. prof. history Haverford

(Pa.) Coll., 1959-65, assoc. prof., 1965-70, prof., 1970-85, Audrey Dusseau meml. prof. humanities, 1985-97, dean, 1966-68. Author: Leopold I of Austria, 1977, The City and the Crown: Vienna and the Imperial Court, 1600-1740, 1993; co-author 2 textbooks; translator: Simplicissimus (Grimmelshausen), 1981. Served with U.S. Army, 1953-55. Mem. Am. Hist. Assn., Soc. French Hist. Studies, Soc. Austrian and Hapsburg Historians. Home: New Hope, Pa. Died Apr. 25, 2009.

SPIELMAN, RICHARD SAUL, genetics educator; b. NYC, Feb. 25, 1946; s. Ralph and Beatrice C. (Kramer) S.; m. Vivian G. Cheung. AB, Harvard Coll., 1967; PhD, U. Mich., 1971. Rsch. assoc. U. Mich., Ann Arbor, 1971-74; from asst. prof. to prof. U. Pa., Phila., from 1974. Home: Narberth, Pa. Died Apr. 25, 2009.

SPIEWAK, MICHAEL ISAAC, manufacturing executive; b. NYC, Apr. 4, 1951; s. Gerald and Shirley (Bell) S.; m. Ilene Skaler, June 8, 1974; children: Jason, David. BA, Syracuse U., 1973. Mgmt. trainee I Spiewak & Sons, Inc., NYC, 1973-76, sales mgr., 1976-81, v.p. sales and mktg., 1981-88, exec. v.p., from 1988. V.p. Trade Show Enterprises, N.Y.C., 1982—; v.p., bd. dirs. Ruleville Mfg. Vice pres. Lindenhurst Homeowner's Assn., Yardley, 1987—; bd. dirs. Jaycees of Del. Valley, 1989—. Mem. Nat. Outerwear Assn. div. Am. Apparel Mfg. Assn. (v.p., bd. dirs. 1978—), Nat. Assn. Uniform Mfrs. and Distbrs. (chmn. pub. relations com., vice chmn. indsl. uniform com. 1984—). Home: Yardley, Pa. Died Oct. 4, 2007.

SPINDLER, JUDITH TARLETON, elementary school educator; b. Dayton, Tenn., Mar. 4, 1932; d. Frank Willson and Julia Elizabeth (Venable) S. BS in Edn., Longwood Coll., 1953; MA in Edn., Va. Commonwealth U., 1976. Tchr. Oceana, King's Grant Sch., Virginia Beach, Va., 1953-66, Ginter Park Elem. Sch., Richmond, Va., 1966-67, Bon Air Elem. Sch., Chesterfield County, Va., 1967-87; ret., 1987. Founder, Web of Hope, 2006, St. Mary's Knitters, 2006. Recipient 86 ribbons for 1st, 2nd and 3rd pl. awards various knitting competitions, 5 Best in Show awards rosette competition, including blue ribbons State Fair Va., 1998, 6 ribbons Best in Show rosette Chesterfield County Fair, 1998, 2 Best in Show Chesterfield County Fair, 1 Best in Show State Fair of Va., 3 Blue ribbons Chesterfield County Fair, 2000, 2 Red Ribbons, 1 White Ribbon Va. State Fair, 2000, 3 Blue ribbons Chesterfield County Fair, 2 Red ribbons, 1 White ribbon 1 Blue, 5 in Va. State Fair, 2002, 1 Blue ribbon, 1 Red Ribbon, 3 Blue ribbons State Fair Va., 2004, 2 blue ribbons, 2 red ribbons State Fair Va., 2006; Humanitarian award ARC. Mem. NEA, Va. Edn. Assn., Knitting Guild Am. (qualified tchr.), Knit Wit Guild (founding mem.), West End Web of Hope and St. Mary's Knitters. Avocations: knitting, reading, travel. Home: Richmond, Va. Died Feb. 10, 2008.

SPINDLER, PAUL, communications executive, consultant; b. Chgo., May 2, 1931; s. Isaac Edward and Sophie (Stein) Spindler; m. Gail Klynn; children from previous marriage: Kevin, Makayla, Sydney, Jeffrey. BA in Journalism, Temple U., 1952. Reporter Akron Beacon Jour., Akron, Ohio, 1955-58, San Francisco Examiner, 1958-59; editor Santa Clara (Calif.) Daily Jour., 1959-63; dir. pub. affairs Litton Industries, Inc., Beverly Hills, Calif., 1963-68; dir. pub. relations Internat. Industries, Beverly Hills, 1968-70; pres. Paul Spindler & Co., LA, 1970-75; exec. v.p. Manning Selvage & Lee, Inc., NYC, 1975-85; pres. The Spindler Co., LA, 1985-87; pres. Western div. GCI Group, LA, 1987-91; pres. GCI Spindler, LA, 1991-96; chmn. Bristol Retail Solutions, Inc., Newport Beach, Calif., 1996-98; pres. Paul Spindler Co., LA, from 1998. Bd. dirs. Phoenix House Calif.; bd. visitors, Temple U. Sch. Comm. and Theatre; co-pres., dir., The Partnership Scholars, 2004—. Bd. dirs. Bright Future Adoption Found. Cpl. US Army, 1952—54. Mem. Mountain Gate Country Club (L.A.). Democrat. Jewish. Home: Los Angeles, Calif. Died Nov. 9, 2008.

SPINRAD, ROBERT JOSEPH, computer scientist; b. NYC, Mar. 20, 1932; s. Sidney and Isabel (Reiff) S.; m. Verna Winderman, June 27, 1954; children: Susan Irene, Paul Reiff. BS, Columbia U., 1953, MS (Bridgham fellow), 1954; PhD (Whitney fellow), MIT, 1963. Registered profl. engr., N.Y. Project engr. Bulova Research & Devel. Lab., NYC, 1953-55; sr. scientist Brookhaven Nat. Lab., Upton, NY, 1955-68; v.p. Sci. Data Systems, Santa Monica, Calif., 1968-69; v.p. programming Xerox Corp., El Segundo, Calif., 1969-71, dir. info. scis., 1971-76, v.p. systems devel., 1976-78, v.p. research Palo Alto Rsch. Ctr., 1978-83, dir. systems tech., 1983-87, dir. corp. tech., 1987-92, v.p. tech. analysis and devel., 1992-94, v.p. technology strategy, 1994-98; ret.; cons. in field, Palo Alto, Calif., 1998—2009. Contbr. articles to profl. jours. Fellow Am. Acad. Arts & Scis.; mem. Nat. Acad. Engring., Calif. Coun. on Sci. and Tech., Sigma Xi, Tau Beta Pi. Achievements include patents in field. Home: Palo Alto, Calif. Died Sept. 2, 2009.

SPITSBERGEN, JAMES CLIFFORD, chemist, consultant; b. Washington, Sept. 1, 1926; s. Henry Essing and Edith Lillian (Richter) S.; m. Margaret Ann Ableman, May 1957 (div. 1972); children: Glenn, Diane; m. Adelaide Mary Alvarez, June 28, 1980. BS, George Washington U., 1949; MS, U. Del., 1959, PhD, 1962. Chemist U.S. Army Engr. Corp, Ft. Belvior, Va., 1951; sr. chemist Electric Hose & Rubber, Wilmington, Del., 1951-61, DuPont, Wilmington, Del., 1962-68; project leader Witco Chem., Oakland, N.J., 1968-83; cons. Unitrode Corp., Watertown, Mass., 1983-85; mgr. Epoxy Consulting, Inc., Franklin Lakes, N.J., from 1985. Contbr. articles to profl. jours.; patentee in field. With USN, 1944-46. Recipient Nat. Lead fellowship, 1961. Mem. IEEE, Soc. for Advancement of Material and Process Engring., Internat. Electronics Packaging Soc., Internat. Soc. Hybrid Mfrs., Am. Chem. Soc., Soc. Plastics Engrs. (bd. dirs. elec. and electronic div. 1990—), Surface Mount Tech. Assn. Republican. Avocation: piano. Home: Hurdle Mills, NC. Died Mar. 15, 2008.

SPIVAK, IRWIN HOWARD, advertising executive; b. NYC, Oct. 8, 1926; s. Martin and Shirley (Kramer) S.; m. Janice Spencer, June 30, 1949; children: Sarah, Jane, Melissa. BS, NYU, 1949; MS, Queen's Coll., 1960; post-grad. in electronics, MIT, 1976-78. Designer, writer Batten Burtin Durstein & Osborne Advt., NYC, 1949-51; photographer, writer PIX, NYC, 1951-59; pres. Spencer Assocs., NYC, from 1959. Exec. v.p. (hon.) McKinney Advt., Boston, 1979-80, Dickinson Mktg., Boston, 1980-82; creative art dir. (hon.) Tandy Corp., Ft. Worth, 1982-83; assoc. prof. Bentley Coll., 1987—; assoc. prof., mem. com. for grad. studies Clark U. Author: I Have Feelings, 1975, What's in it for Us, 1996; one-man phtog. shows in various galleries. Bd. dirs. Boys and Girls Club Cambridge. Named Indsl. Photographer of Yr. Eastman Kodak, 1973, Photographer of Yr. Profl. Photographers Am., 1975. Mem. Am. Soc. Mag. Photographers. Jewish. Avocations: jazz musician (leader popular dance band savoy swing), tennis, electronic projects, reading, sailing. Died Aug. 6, 2008.

SPRAGUE, DEBORAH CONSTANCE, critical care nurse; b. Wyandotte, Mich., Aug. 24, 1952; children: Jason, Lydia. Student, Cen. Mich. U., 1970-72; ADN, Mid-Mich. Community Coll., 1984. CEN; cert. ACLS, TNCC: cert. human sexuality educator; cert. train-the-trainer; cert. clin. skills examiner. Staff nurse emergency dept., med./surg. Clare (Mich.) Community Hosp., 1984-88; staff nurse emergency dept. Mid-Mich. Regional Med. Ctr., Midland, Mich., from 1988; sch. nurse Clare Pub. Schs., 1989-91; nursing assts. instr. Clare-Gladwin Intermediate Sch. Dist., from 1992. Program coord., primary instr. nursing asst. program Clare-Gladen Inter Sch. Dist., 1992—; clin. skills examiner State of Mich. Vol. disaster health svcs. ARC, 1995. Home: Bluff, Utah. Died June 24, 2008.

SPRENGNETHER, RONALD JOHN, civil engineer; b. St. Louis, July 28, 1944; s. William Francis Sprengnether and Roberta Harris. BSCE, St. Louis U., 1967; MSCE, U. Mo., Rolla, 1984. Registered profl. engr., Mo. Civil engr. Sverdrup Corp., Maryland Heights, 1972—99; self-employed, from 1999. Lt. (j.g.) USNR, 1968-71. Mem. NSPE, ASCE, Am. Water Works Assn., Engrs. Club St. Louis. Roman Catholic. Home: Saint Louis, Mo. Died May 23, 2008.

SPRINGER, MARY, humanities educator; b. Chgo., Dec. 18, 1918; d. Fredorick and Mary Meyers Doyle; m. Norman Springer, Feb. 14, 1946; children: Mark Daniel, Joshua Paul. BA, Holy Names Coll., 1963; MA, U. Calif., Berkeley, 1965, PhD, 1975. Prof. English St. Mary's Coll., Moraga, Calif., 1965—2003, prof. emerita, from 2003. Author: Forms of the Modern Novella, 1975, A Rhetoric of Literary Character: Some Women of Henry James, 1978. Mem.: AAUP. Green Party. Avocation: piano. Died June 21, 2008.

SPRINGER, MICHAEL RICHARD, information consultant; b. Evanston, Ill., Oct. 23, 1942; s. Joseph Gotthold and Kathryn Dorothy (Houston) S.; m. Patricia Ann Fazio, Sept. 3, 1977; children: Michelle Ann, Mary Patricia, Maria Rene. BS in Fin., De Paul U., 1969, MBA in Fin., 1973. Cert. Mgmt. Cons. Systems analyst Continental Bank, Chgo., 1969-71, mgr. micrographics, 1971-72, audit mgr., 1972-73, mgr. personal banking, 1973-76; pres. Cons. for Info. Resource Mgmt. Inc., Naperville, Ill., from 1976. Mem. systems rev. com. Tex. Instruments Corp., 1982-83, competitive issues com., 1983-84, Computer Rev. Com. City of Naperville, 1989; instr. Am. Mgmt. Assn., 1971-79, Elmhurst (Ill.) Coll., 1977-82. Copyright portfolio acctg. system. Bd. dirs. Chgo. Jaycees, 1974-76, Bloomingdale C. of C., 1983-86, Wayne (Ill.) Twp. Promising Children, 1982-84. Served as cpl. USMC, 1960-65. Recipient Wall Street Jour. Achievement award, 1969. Mem. Soc. Info. Mgmt. (bd. dirs. 1981), Inst. Mgmt. Cons. Republican. Roman Catholic. Died July 1, 2008.

SPRINKEL, BERYL WAYNE, economist; b. Richmond, Mo., Nov. 20, 1923; s. Clarence and Emma (Schooley) S.; m. Lory Kiefer, Aug. 29, 1993; children: Gary L., Kevin G.; stepchildren: Janet, David Student, N.W. Mo. State U., 1941-43, U. Oreg., 1943-44; BS, U. Mo., 1947; MBA, U. Chgo., 1948, PhD, 1952; LHD (hon.), DePaul U., 1975; LLD (hon.), St. Michael's Coll., 1981, U. Mo., 1985, U. Rochester, 1985, Govs. State U., 1988, U. Nebr., 1988; Doctor of Pub. Adminstrn., Marion Coll., 1988. Instr. econs. and fin. U. Mo., Columbia, 1948-49, U. Chgo., 1950-52; with Harris Trust & Savs. Bank, Chgo., 1952-81, v.p., economist, 1960-68, dir. rsch., 1963-69, sr. v.p., 1968-74, economist, 1968-81, exec. v.p., economist, 1974-81; under sec. for monetary affairs US Dept. Treasury, Washington, 1981-85; chmn. Coun. Econ. Advisers, Exec. Office of the Pres., Washington, 1985-89; pvt. cons. economist, 1989—2009. Cons. Fed. Res. Bd., 1955-59, Bur. of Census, 1962-70, Joint Econ. Com. U.S. Congress, 1958, 62, 67, 71, Ho. of Reps. Banking and Currency Com., 1963, Senate Banking Com., 1975; econ. adv. bd. to sec. commerce, 1967-69; bd. economists Time mag., 1968-80. Author: Money and Stock Prices, 1964, Money and Markets-A Monetarist View, 1971; co-author: Winning with Money, 1977 Pres. Homewood-Flossmoor (Ill.) Community High Sch., 1959-60. With AUS, 1943-45. Recipient Hamilton Bolton award Fin. Analysts Assn., 1968, Alexander Hamilton award U.S. Treasury, 1985, Disting. Alumnus award U. Chgo., 1986, Disting. Alumnus award U. Mo., 2000. Fellow Nat. Assn. Bus. Economists; mem. Nat. Assn. Bus. Economists, Beta Gamma Sigma. Died Aug. 22, 2009.

SPRIZZO, JOHN EMILIO, federal judge; b. Bklyn., Dec. 23, 1934; s. Vincent James and Esther Nancy S.; children: Ann Esther, Johna Emily, Matthew John. BA summa cum laude, St. John's U., Jamaica, NY, 1956; LLB summa cum laude, St. John's U., 1959. Bar: N.Y. 1960. Atty. organized crime section, criminal divsn. US Dept. Justice, 1959-63, asst. US atty. (so. dist.) NY NYC, 1963-68, chief appellate atty., 1965-66, asst. chief criminal divsn., 1966-68; assoc. prof. law Fordham U. Law Sch., NYC, 1968-72; ptnr. Curtis, Mallet-Prevost, NYC, 1972-81; judge US Dist. Ct. (so. dist.) NY, NY, 1981—2000, sr. judge NY, 2000—08. Cons. Nat. Com. for Reform of Criminal Laws, N.Y.C., 1971-72; mem. Knapp Commn., 1971-72; assoc. atty. Com. of Ct. on Judiciary, N.Y.C., 1971-72 Co-contbr. articles to profl. law revs. Mem. ABA, D.C. Bar Assn., Assn. of Bar of City of N.Y. Died Dec. 16, 2008.

SPYRISON, DON ERNEST, biomedical engineering company executive; b. Chgo., May 10, 1945; s. Ernest C. and Ruth (Gaiver) S.; m. Linda Carol Winkler, 1971 (div. 1978); children: Kara Laurin, Amanda Marie; m. Elizabeth Spyrison, May 1987. BS in Internat. Affairs, U. So. Calif., Los Angeles, 1967, MBA, 1968. Dir. product mgmt. Travenol Labs., Deerfield, Ill., 1969-74, v.p mktg., 1974-76; v.p. sales and mktg. Telemed Corp., Hoffman Estates, Ill., 1976-80, pres., 1981; pres., chief exec. officer Aegis Med. Systems, Marlton, N.J., 1981-85, Amnion, Inc. (formerly Cardiovascular Systems), The Woodlands, Tex., from 1985, also bd. dirs. Mem. Woodlands Research Adv. Council, 1986—, FDA adv. com. devices, Washington, 1974-76. Served with U.S. Army, 1968-70. Mem. U. So. Calif. Alumni (pres. 1975-77). Avocations: scuba diving, tennis, sailing. Home: Sarasota, Fla. Died Jan. 13, 2008.

STADTMAN, VERNE AUGUST, retired foundation administrator; b. Carrizoso, N.Mex., Dec. 5, 1926; s. Walter William and Minnie Ethel (Reece) S.; m. Jackolyn Carol Byl, Aug. 26, 1949; children: Kristen Karen, Rand Theodore, Judith Dayna, Todd Alan. AB, Calif.-Berkeley, 1950. AUS, 1945-47; mng. editor Calif. Monthly, Calif. Alumni Assn., Berkeley, 1950-64; centennial editor U. Calif., Berkeley, 1964-69; assoc. dir., editor Carnegie Commn. on Higher Edn., Berkeley, 1969-73, Carnegie Council on Policy Studies in Higher Edn. Berkeley, 1973-80; v.p. gen. services Carnegie Found. for Advancement Teaching, Princeton, N.J., 1980-89. Trustee Editorial Projects Edn., Inc., 1957-91, pres., 1962-63, chmn. bd., 1980-86; guest scholar Hiroshima U., Japan, 1978 Author: California Campus, 1960, University of California, 1868-1968, 1970, Academic Adaptations, 1980; editor: (with David Riesman) Academic Transformation: Seventeen Institutions Under Pressure, 1973 (Book of Yr. award Am. Council Edn.); compiler-editor: Centennial Record of the University of California, 1967. Served with AUS, 1945-47. Recipient Alumnus Service award Calif. Alumni Assn., 1970 Mem. Am. Alumni Council (pres. 1963-64). Home: Sonoma, Calif. Died Feb. 25, 2009.

STAFFORD, GILBERT WAYNE, religion educator; b. Portageville, Mo., Dec. 30, 1938; s. Dawsey Calvin and Orell Elvesta (Smith) S.; m. Darlene Dawn Covert, Dec. 30, 1962; children: Matthew, Heather, Anne, Joshua. AB, Anderson Coll., 1961; MDiv, Andover Newton Theol. Sch., 1964; ThD, Boston U., 1973. Ordained to ministry Ch. of God, 1965. Pastor Malden (Mass.) Ch. of God, 1962-66; dir. Christian edn. First Congregational Ch. of Hyde Park, Boston, 1968-69; pastor East Ashman Ch. of God, Midland, Mich., 1969-76; faculty Anderson (Ind.) U. Sch. Theology, from 1976, assoc. dean, 1980-89, dean of chapel, 1984-89; speaker Christian Brotherhood Hour-English, Anderson, from 1986. Chair commn. on Christian unity, Ch. of God, Anderson, 1985-90; commr. working group on faith and order NCCC in USA, N.Y.C., 1984—; mem. task force on governance and polity Ch. of God, Anderson, 1987— Author: The Life of Salvation, 1979, Beliefs that Guide Us, 1977, The People of God, 1977, The Person and Work of the Holy Spirit, 1977, The 7 Doctrinal Leaders of the Church of God, 1977, Living as Redeemed People, 1976; author: (with others) Educating for Service, 1984, A Contemporary Wesleyan Theology, 1983, An Inquiry into Soteriology, 1981. Recipient Bethany Heritage award Bethany Ch. of God, Detroit, 1982, Disting. Ministry award Anderson U., 1991. Mem. Wesleyan Theol. Soc., Am. Acad. Religion. Home: Anderson, Ind. Died Mar. 30, 2008.

STAFFORD, WILLIAM EDWARD, electronics design/manufacturing company executive; b. Bluefield, W.Va., Nov. 17, 1934; s. Don Edward and B. Elizabeth (Penn) S.; m. Norma Stafford, June 26, 1957 (div. 1981); children: Susan, Victoria, Catherine, William; m. Jean J. Edwards, May 10, 1986; 1 child, Keith. BSc, Ohio State U., 1957. Mgr. Tex. Instruments Inc., Dallas, 1958-73; v.p. Motorola, Inc., Schaumburg, Ill., 1973-87; pres. Display TEK, Inc., Elgin, Ill., 1987-89; pres., CEO Appliance Control Tech., Inc., Addison, Ill., from 1989. Mem. Meadow Club (Rolling Meadows, Ill.). Republican. Episcopalian. Died Apr. 29, 2008.

STAHL, EDWARD ALLEN, JR., physics educator; b. McKeesport, Pa., July 11, 1933; s. Edward Allen and Dorothy Julian (Schaut) S.; m. Joyce Cromer; 1 stepson: Franklin F. BS in Physics, Math., Phys. Sci., Shippensburg State U., 1961; MS in Physics, Va. Polytechnic Inst. State U., Blacksburg, 1966, postgrad., Pa. State U., 1972. Cert. tchr. Pa.; cert. CPR, first aid, ARC. Process clk. AMP, Inc., Carlisle, Pa., 1956-57; cost acct. G.R. Kinney Shoe Co., Carlisle, 1957-58; sci., math. tchr. East Pennsboro Joint Sch. System, Enola, Pa., 1962-65; physics prof. Bucknell U., Lewisburg, Pa., 1967-69; physics prof., deans rep. Coll. of Sci. Pa. State U., Mont Alto, Pa., 1969-95. Cons. Lanu Machine Co., Waynesboro, Pa., 1974. Author: (book) Physical Science for Everyone, 1977; contbr. articles to profl. jours. CPR and first aid instr. ARC, Chambersburg, Pa., 1987—; nuclear, biol., chem. instr. U.S. Army Res., Harrisburg, Pa., 1984-94. With U.S. Army, 1991; sgt. USMC, 1952-56. Mem. Am. Assn. Physics Tchrs., Sigma Xi, Sigma Pi Sigma. Home: Greencastle, Pa. Died Mar. 3, 2008.

STAINBROOK, MARGARET COLLINS, retired school system administrator; b. Zanesville, Ohio, Mar. 24, 1927; d. Cecil Nicholas Collins and Mary Jane Roberts; m. Alfred Richard Stainbrook (dec. July 27, 2000); children: Ginger Margaret, Jeffrey Richard. BEd, Ohio U., 1966, MA in Edn. Adminstrn., 1970. Elem. tchr. Zanesville (Ohio) City Schs., 1960—71, elem. prin., 1971—92; ret., 1992. Docent Pioneer Hist. Assn., Zanesville, Ohio, 1992—2003; vol. Genesis Hosp., Zanesville, Ohio, 1993—2003. Grantee Jennings Scholar, Jennings Found., Ohio U., 1970. Mem.: Soroptimist Internat. (pres. 1975—76), DAR, Ohio Assn. Elem. Prins., Nat. Assn. Elem. Prins., Phi Delta Kappa. Avocation: genealogy. Home: Zanesville, Ohio. Died Oct. 2, 2007.

STALL, WILLIAM READ, retired newswriter; b. Phila., Feb. 21, 1937; s. Sidney Joseph and Helen (Read) S.; m. Carolee Ramsey, July, 1961 (div. 1979); children: Tracy Stall Roll, Erica Stall Wiggins; m. Anne Elizabeth Baker, Dec. 8, 1979. BS, U. Wyo., 1959. Reporter Laramie (Wyo.) Boomerang, 1956-59, Associated Press, Cheyenne, Wyo., 1960-63, corres. Reno, 1963-66, bur. chief, polit. writer Sacramento, 1966-74; press sec. Edmund G. Brown Jr., Sacramento, 1975-76; staff writer, asst. met. editor, corres. L.A. Times, 1976-81, editorial writer, 1984-90, polit. writer, 1990-96, editl. writer, 1997—2006; bur. chief Hartford Courant, Washington, 1981-84; ret., 2006. Sr. lectr. journalism dept. U. So. Calif., 1985-94. With U.S. Air N.G., 1960-67. Recipient Pulitzer prize for editl. writing, 2004; named Disting. Alumni, U. Wyo., 2005. Mem. Am. Alpine Club (dir. 1992-98). Episcopalian. Avocations: rock climbing, mountain climbing, sailing. Home: Sacramento, Calif. Died Nov. 2, 2008.

STANCILL, JAMES MCNEILL, retired finance educator; b. Orange, NJ, July 30, 1932; s. James Sr. and Anne Jeanne (Sauter) S.; m. Catherine Jackson, Sept. 25, 1954; children: Martha A., Mary C., Christine E. AB, George Wash. U., Washington, DC, 1954, MBA, 1957; PhD in Fin. and Econs., U. Pa., Phila., 1965. Buyer Melpar Inc., Falls Church, Va., 1954-59; instr., adminstrv. officer U. Pa., Phila., 1959-64; prof. fin. U. So. Calif., LA, 1964—2007, prof. emeritus, 2007—09. Prin. Stancill & Assocs., Pasadena, Calif., 1964—2009, The McNeill Bush Co. Ltd.; chmn. S.W. Products Co., 1991—97. Author: Management of Working Capital, 1970, Entrepreneurial Finance: for New and Emerging Businesses, 2004; contbr. numerous articles to Harvard Bus. Rev., from 1977. Avocations: genealogy, sailing, travel. Home: Pasadena, Calif. Died June 17, 2009.

STANFORD, HENRY KING, retired academic administrator; b. Atlanta, Apr. 22, 1916; s. Henry King and Annie Belle (Callaway) S.; m. Laurie Ruth King, Sept. 19, 1936; children: Henry, Lowry, Rhoda, Peyton. AB, Emory U., 1936, MA, 1940, LLD, 1961; postgrad., U. Heidelberg, Germany, 1936—37; MS in Govt. Mgmt., U. Denver, 1943, LLD, 1962; PhD, NYU, 1949; DCL, Jacksonville U., Fla., 1963; LLD, Loyola U., New Orleans, 1968, U. Akron, Kyung Hee U., Seoul, Korea, 1968, Rollins Coll., 1977, Barry Coll., 1979; DHL, U. Tampa, 1969; DLitt, U. R.I., 1970, U. Chile, Santiago, 1980; D in Higher Edn., U. Miami, 1981; DHL, Birmingham-So. Coll., 1987. Instr. Emory U., 1937-40; asst. prof. Ga. Inst. Tech., 1940-41; instr. NYU, 1943-46; prof. pub. administrn., also dir. sch. pub. administrn. U. Denver, 1946-48; pres. Ga. Southwestern Coll., Americus, 1948-50; dir. U. Ctr. in Ga., 1950-52; asst. chancellor U. Sys. of Ga., 1952-53; pres. Ga. State Coll. for Women, Milledgeville, 1953-56; chief of party NYU-Internat. Cooperation Adminstrn. Contract, Ankara, Turkey, 1956-57; pres. Birmingham-So. Coll., 1957-62, U. Miami, Fla., 1962-81, pres. emeritus, 1981—2008; interim pres. U. Ga., 1986-87, pres. emeritus, 1987—2008. Rsch. asst. Tax Found., N.Y.C., 1943-44; staff N.A.M. com. exec., 1944-46; chmn. Fed. Res. Bank Atlanta, 1969, 72. Trustee Knight Found., 1982-97; vice chmn. Invest in Am., 1981-86, chmn. 1986-87; chmn. Dade County Cmty. Rels. Bd., 1969-71; bd. visitors Air U., Maxwell AFB, Ala., 1963-66; trustee Caribbean Resources Devel. Found., 1978-85, pres., 1978-83, chmn., 1983-84; chmn. Jimmy Carter Hist. Site Adv. Commn., 1990-2001. Decorated Star of Africa medal Liberia, 1971; officer Order of Merit Fed. Republic of Germany, 1972; recipient Eleanor Roosevelt-Israel Humanitarian award, 1965, Outstanding Civilian Svc. award U.S. Army, 1966, Silver Medallion Fla. Region NCCJ, 1968, Ga. Region, 1987, Disting. Svc. award Ga. Coll., 1979, hon. alumnus, 1996, C.H.I.E.F. award Ind. Colls. and Univs. Fla., 1983, Sibley award Ga. Mil. Coll., 1991, Emory medal, 1991, Adrian Dominican Ednl. Leadership award Barry U., 1991, Atlanta Boys' High Alumnus award, 1992, James Blair Humanitarian award Americus, 1993, Westmeyer award pub. svc. NYU, 1993. Mem. So. Assn. Colls. and Schs. (chmn. commn. colls. 1960-62, pres. 1972-73), Nat. Assn. Ind. Colls. and Univs. (dir. 1976-80), Assn. Caribbean Univs. and Rsch. Insts. (v.p. 1965-79), Golden Key Honor Soc. (bd. dirs. 1982-91), Internat. Assn. Univ. Pres. (exec. com. 1977-81), Delta Phi Alpha, Phi Beta Kappa, Omicron Delta Kappa, Phi Sigma Iota, Alpha Kappa Psi, Phi Mu Alpha, Phi Kappa Phi, Rotary Club (pres. Americus club 1984-85). Methodist. Home: Americus, Ga. Died Jan. 1, 2009.

STANG, JOHN MCNAUGHER, physician educator; b. Elwood City, Pa., Nov. 9, 1946; s. Oliver Riley and Mildred Eleanor (Ralston) S.; m. Janice Marie Neel, Apr. 9, 1971; children: Alyson Marie, John William. BS, Muskingum Coll., 1968; MD, Ohio State U., 1972. Internship New Eng. Med. Ctr., Boston, 1972-73, resident in medicine, 1973-74; fellow in cardiology Ohio State U., Columbus, 1974-77, chief med. resident, 1977-78, asst. prof. medicine, 1978-83, assoc. prof. medicine, from 1983. Lectr. in field. Contbr. articles, abstracts to profl. jours. and chpts. to books. Dir. EMS-CME, Div. of Fire, Columbus, 1979-80; med. dir. Div. of FIre-Emergency Med. Svc., Columbus, 1980-84. Recipient Outstanding Tchr. award Ohio State U., 1979-82, 84, 87-88, 89-90, 96-97, Prof. of Yr. award, 1985, Meritorious Citation Dept. Pub. Safety, 1976-77, 79-80, First Ann. John M. Stang MD. award for advancement of excellence, 1994, Fellowship in Med. Edn., 1992. Fellow ACP, Coun. on Clin. Cardiology. Democrat. Avocation: photography. Home: Dublin, Ohio. Died June 10, 2008.

STANLEY, PATRICIA MARY, microbiologist, researcher; b. Oneonta, NY, Mar. 28, 1948; BS, Cornell U., 1970; PhD, U. Wash., 1975. Mem. rsch. faculty U. Minn., Mpls., 1976-79; prin. microbiologist Ecolab, Inc., St. Paul, 1979-86, scientist, from 1986. Contbr. articles to sci. publs. Mem. Am. Soc. Microbiology, Soc. Indsl. Microbiology, Am. Soc. Testing and Materials, Assn. for Women in Sci., Grad. Women in Sci. Avocations: travel, skiing, canoeing, hiking. Home: Minneapolis, Minn. Died Oct. 31, 2007.

STANTON, BLAINE WENDELL, gemologist; b. St. Joseph, Mo., Dec. 11, 1948; s. William J. and Helen H. (Hitchcock) S.; m. Leslee Ann Taylor, Nov. 23, 1970. Mktg. student, Mo. Western Coll., 1968-73; cert. gemology, European Gemological Inst., Antwerp, Belgium, 1978. Pres. Stanton & Co. Jewelers & Gemologists, St. Joseph, from 1972, Stanton Cellular Communications, St. Joseph. Mem.: Lions (pres. St. Joseph East Hills club 1980-81). Died Oct. 9, 2007.

STANTON, JACK PERSHING, chemical engineer; b. Chgo., Nov. 2, 1919; s. Joseph Patrick Stanton and Henriette (Fourestie) Berry; m. Virginia Gail Dudek Myers, Mar. 27, 1947; children: D. Larry, J. Terry, Maureen Lee. Student, U. Ill., 1939-43, Ill. Inst. Tech., 1944; student chem. engring., Ctrl. YMCA Coll., 1938. Registered profl. engr. Chem. engr. The Pure Oil Co., Northfield, Ill., 1943-47, asst. supt. Van, Tex., 1947-48, resident chemist Worland, Wyo., 1948-50; mgr. oil testing, cons. Comml. Testing and Engring., Chgo., 1950-52; chem. engr., product mgr. to mgr. new products application Nalco Chem. Co., Chgo., 1952-57; product mgr. corrosion control Visco div. Nalco Chem. Co., Houston, 1957-60; regional mgr. So. S.Am. Internat. divsn., Nalco Chem. Co., Buenos Aires, 1960-62; v.p. Oilwell Rsch. Co., Dallas, 1962-63; tech. dir. Cochrane Chem. Co., Wewoka, Okla., 1963-64; pres., cons. Am. Coordinated Technologists Inc., Houston, 1964-73; real estate investor R-Innovators, Houston, 1973-78, residential builder, 1978-93. Author: They Never Rise Again, 1991-92; inventor chem. applications, yacht design, constrn. techniques; contbr. articles to profl. jours. Pub. address speaker Houston Bd. Edn., 1993, United We Stand Am., 1993; founder Peoples' Activist Leaders' Soc. and Voters Vanguard, 1993-94. Mem. ASTM (com. chmn. Indsl., nat. vice chmn.). Avocations: tennis, ping pong/table tennis, horseshoes, bridge. Died Mar. 20, 2008.

STANTON, VIVIAN BRENNAN (MRS. ERNEST STANTON), retired counseling administrator; b. Waterbury, Conn. d. Francis P. and Josephine (Ryan) Brennan; m. Ernest Stanton Stanton, May 31, 1947; children: Pamela L., Bonita F., Kim Ernest. BA, Albertus Magnus Coll.; MS, Southern Conn. State Coll., 1962, degree, 1965; postgrad., Columbia U. Tchr. English, history, govt. Milford HS, Conn., 1940—48; tchr. English, history, fgn. Born Night Sch., New Haven, 1948—54, Simon Lake Sch., Milford, 1960—62; guidance counselor, psychol. examiner Jonathan Law HS, Milford, 1962—73; adv. Nat. Honor Soc., 1966—73; mem. Curriculum Councils, Graduation Requirement Council, Gifted Child Com., others, 1940—48, 1960—73; guidance dir. Foran HS, Milford, 1973—79, career ctr. coord., 1976—79, ret., 1979. Active various cmty. drives; mem. exec. bd. Ridge Rd PTA, 1956—59; mem. parent-tchr. coun. Hopkins Grammer Sch., New Haven; mem. Human Rels. Coun., North Haven, 1967—69; vol., patient rep. surg. waiting rm. Fawcett Meml. Hosp., P.C., Sun City Ctr. Emergency Squad, Good Samaritans. Mem.: LWV, AAUW, Milford, Conn., Conn. Assn. Sch. Psychol. Pers., Conn. Sch. Counselors Assn., Conn. Pers. and Guidance Assn., Nat. Assn. Secondary Schs. and Colls., Sun City Ctr. Golf and Racquet Club, Charlotte Harbor Yacht Club, Univ. Club. Home: Houston, Tex. Deceased.

STARK, RICHARD See WESTLAKE, DONALD

STARNER, DON EDWARD, radiologist, educator; b. Zanesville, Ohio, June 28, 1959; s. Larry and Sara Ann Starner; 1 child, Ryan. BS, The Ohio State U., 1982. Cert. Radiographer Am. Registry of Radiologic Technologists, 1982, Quality Mgmt. Radiographer Am. Registry of Radiologic Technologists, 2002, lic. Radiologic Technologist Fla. Dept. Health, 1988. X-ray technologist The Ohio State U. Hospitals, Columbus, Ohio, 1982—88; from clin. instr. to program dir. West Boca Med. Ctr. Sch. of Radiography, Boca Raton, Fla., 1988—91, program dir., 1991—96; dir. of clin. radiography edn. Indian River CC, Ft. Pierce, Fla., from 1996. Contbr. chapters to books Web-Based Training, 2001; actor: (films) Brubaker, 1980. Mem.: AAUP, Fla. Assn. of C.C., Am. Soc. of Radiologic Technologists, Am. Registry of Radiologic Technologists. Home: Port Saint Lucie, Fla. Died Oct. 5, 2007.

STARR, TERRELL, retired state senator; b. Clayton County, Ga., June 5, 1926; m. Celeste McKinney; children: Terry, JoAnn Kennedy. Grad., Atlanta Law Sch. Real estate broker, ins. agent; mem. Ga. State Senate, Atlanta, 1968—2006, pres. pro tempore, 2002. Past mem. Clayton County Commn., Clayton County Libr. Bd., Clayton County Bd. Health, Atlanta Regional Met. Planning Commn.; past trustee Forest Park Sch. Dist. Youth Ctr.; deacon, former chmn. bd. of deacons First Baptist Ch., Forest Park. With USN, 1944-46. Recipient Ga. Legis. of Yr. award Ga. Sch. Counselors Assn., Nat. Legis. of Yr. award Am. Sch. Counselors Assn., Legis. of Yr. award Ga. Parks and Recreation Assn., Disting. Svc./Citizen of Yr. award C. of C.; honores received Ga. Mcpl. Assn., Ga. Assn. Children with Learning Disabilities, Ga. Moose Assn., Ga. Assn. Home Health Agys., Elem. Sch. Prins. Assn., Ga. Assn. Edn. Leaders, Gridiron Hon. Society, Am. Acad. Pediats., Nat. Assn. Home Health Care; park named in his honor City of Forest Park; Terrell Starr Human Svcs. Ctrl named in his honor Jonesboro. Mem. Peace Officers Assn. Ga. (hon., life), Jaycees (past pres., Disting. Svc. award), Rotary, Masons, Royal Arch, Tara Club, Kiwanis (past pres.), Yaareb Temple. Democrat. Died Apr. 19, 2009.

STAUFFER, LOUISE LEE, retired secondary school educator; b. Altoona, Pa., Mar. 31, 1915; d. William Thomas and Mary Hall (Schroyer) Lee; m. John Nissley Stauffer, Aug. 20, 1938 (dec. Sept. 1983); children: Thomas Michael, Nancy Kay, John Lee, Donald David. BA, Juniata Coll., 1936; postgrad., Columbia U., U. Pa., Pa. State U. Tchr. Latin, Middletown High Sch., Pa., 1936-41; tchr. English and Latin, Roosevelt Jr. High Sch., Springfield, Ohio, 1949-57; tchr. French, North High Sch., Springfield, 1957-63; ret., 1963. Mem. Moorings Property Owners Assn., Naples, Fla., 1983—; Emmanuel Luth. Ch., Naples, 1980—; bd. dirs., editor newsletter, membership chmn., rec. sec., corr. sec., parliamentarian Naples Cmty. Hosp. Aux., 1985-92; chmn. Patient Mail, 1992—. Mem. AAUW, Am. Assn. Ret. Persons, Women's League (Juniata Coll.), Founders Club (Juniata Coll.), Moorings Country Club. Lutheran. Avocations: golf, singing, reading, walking, volunteering. Home: Columbus, Ohio. Died Jan. 28, 2008.

STAYMATES, JAMES DUANE, financial planner; b. Wilkinsburg, Pa., May 27, 1950; s. Arthur Kissler and Maria (Hopf) S.; m. Saundra S. Stamboni, Aug. 13, 1978; children: Maria Danielle, James Bret. BSBA, Towson State U., 1973; cert., Coll. Fin. Planning, Denver, 1987. Purchasing agt. Fair Lanes Inc., Balt., 1973-76, dir. racquet sports Chgo., 1976-79; owner, mgr. Staymates Fin. Concepts, Balt., from 1979. Fin. advisor Tchrs. Assn. Baltimore County, 1981—; instr. Harford Community Coll., Bel Air, Md., 1979—, Towson State U., 1979—, Carroll County Bd. Edn., Westminster, Md., 1981—. Recipient Century Club award Oppenheimer Co., 1983, prodn. award for excellence Cardell & Assocs., 1983, Broker Dealer, 1984-86. Mem. Inst. Cert. Fin. Planners, Internat. Assn. Cert. Fin. Planners. Democrat. Avocations: golf, tennis, swimming. Died Jan. 4, 2008.

STEFFANY, ALO WILLIAM, territorial senator; b. Fagasa, Am. Samoa, Oct. 22, 1911; s. Josef and Pepe Alo (Taisi) S.; m. Fiti Kereti, July 14, 1950; 15 children. Supt. Matson Navigation Co., Pago Pago, Am. Samoa; harbor master Govt. of Am. Samoa, wharf supt.; lic. capt., engr. Steffany Shipping, Govt. of Am. Samoa; owner Steffany's Inter-Island Shipping, Pago Pago; senator Govt. of Am. Samoa, Pago Pago, 1974—91, chmn. power and energy com., mem. govt. ops. com., agr. com., transp. and communications com. Mem. London Missionary Soc. Died July 12, 1991.

STEFFEE, NINA DEAN, publisher; b. Mahopac, NY, Apr. 11, 1917; d. Henry Jackson and Eliza May (Willson) Dean; m. Clay Runels Steffee, June 21, 1942; children: Eliza May Steffee Karpook, Clay Jackson, Henry Morgan. Student, Cornell U., 1934-36. Sec., asst. editor Fla. Audubon Soc., Maitland, 1965-71; owner/mgr. Flying Carpet Tours, Orlando, Fla., 1971-80, Russ's Natural History Tours, Kissimmee, Fla., 1980-83, Lake Helen, Fla., 1983-94; pub., compiler Nina Steffee Pub., Lake Helen, from 1994. Compiler bird checklists; contbr. articles to profl. jours. Mem.: West Volusia Audubon (pres.), Kissimmee Valley Audibon (pres.). Avocation: birding. Home: Gainesville, Fla. Died Aug. 8, 2007.

STEGALL, WHITNEY, retired lawyer; b. Rockvale, Tenn., Feb. 17, 1916; s. Benjamine Duggin and Nannie May (Love) Stegall; m. Orene E. Cowen, Dec. 30, 1936; children: Whitney Jr., Amy. BS, Mid. Tenn. State U.; JD, Vanderbilt U. Tchr. chemistry and biology Rutherford County Schs.; ednl. advisor Civil Coll. Corp.; solo practice atty.; chancellor, judge 16th Jud. Dist., Rutherford County, Tenn. Maj. Signal Corps US Army, 1943—47, Pacific. Democrat. Mehodist. Home: Murfreesboro, Tenn. Died Sept. 21, 2007.

STEGER, RALPH JAMES, chemist; b. Meridian, Okla., Jan. 24, 1940; s. Daniel Bose and Opal Creola (Brothers) S. BS in Chemistry and Math., Langston U., 1962. Cartographer Aeronautical Chart and Info. Ctr. ACIC USAF, St. Louis, 1962-63; lab. technician Sigma Chem. Co., St. Louis, 1963; phys. scientist U.S. Army Chem. Corps, Edgewood Arsenal, Md., 1963-65; rsch. chemist Chem. Rsch., Devel. and Engring. Ctr. SMCCR Rsch. Lab., Analytical Div., Aberdeen Proving Ground, Md., 1965-86; chemist Chem. Rsch., Devel. and Engring. Ctr. SMCCR-Detection, Detection Technology, Aberdeen Proving Ground, 1986-97. Adv. com. Garrison Gents, Balt., 1980—; ACOR monitoring govt. contracts, Balt., 1987—. Contbr. articles to profl. jours. Mem. AAAS, N.Y. Acad. Sci., Okla. Hist. Soc. Home: Baltimore, Md. Died Mar. 21, 2008.

STEIL, GEORGE KENNETH, SR., lawyer; b. Darlington, Wis., Dec. 16, 1924; s. George John and Laura (Donahoe) S.; m. Mavis Elaine Andrews, May 24, 1947; children: George Kenneth, John R., MIchelle Steil Bryski, Marcelaine Steil-Zimmermann. Student, Platteville State Tchrs. Coll., 1942-43; JD, U. Wis., Madison, 1950. Bar: Wis. 1950, U.S. Tax Ct. 1971, U.S. Dist. Ct. (western dist.) Wis. 1950. Assoc. J. G. McWilliams, Janesville, 1950-53; ptnr. McWilliams and Steil, Janesville, 1954-60, Brennan, Steil, Basting & MacDougall, Janesville, 1960-72; pres. Brennan, Steil & Basting (S.C., and predecessor), Janesville, from 1972. Lectr. law U. Wis., 1974; bd. dirs. Acuity Ins. Co., Sheboygan, Wis.; mem. fin. coun. Roman Cath. Diocese of Madison; mem. Wis. Supreme Ct. Bd. Atty. Profl. Responsibility, 1982-87, chmn., 1984-87; chmn. gov.'s adv. coun. jud. selection State of Wis., 1987-92; chmn. Wis. Lottery Bd., 1987-90. Bd. dirs. St. Coletta Sch. for Exceptional Children, Jefferson, Wis., 1972-76, 78-84, 86-89, chmn., 1982-83; bd. regents U. Wis., 1990-97, pres., 1992-94; bd. dirs. U. Wis. Hosp. Authority, 1996—2004, chmn., 2002-04; bd. dirs., chair U. Wis. Med. Found., 1996-99. Recipient Disting. Svc. award U. Wis. Law Alumni, 1991, Cath. Leadership awrd Diocese of Madison, 1998; named Knight of St. Gregory, Pope John Paul II, 1997. Fellow Am. Bar Found. (life), Am. Coll. Trust and Estate Counsel; mem. ABA, Jamesville Area C. of C. (pres. 1970-71), State Bar Wis. (pres. 1977-78), Wis. Bar Found. (bd. dirs. 1976-2003, Charles L. Goldberg Disting. Svc. award 1990). Roman Catholic. Home: Janesville, Wis. Died Mar. 29, 2009.

STEIN, HERMAN DAVID, social studies educator, educator; b. NYC, Aug. 13, 1917; s. Charles and Emma (Rosenblum) S.; m. Charmion Kerr, Sept. 15, 1946; children: Karen Lou Gelender, Shoshi Stein Bennett, Naomi Elizabeth. BSS., CCNY, 1939; MS, Columbia U., 1941, D. Social Welfare, 1958; L.H.D., Hebrew Union Coll.-Jewish Inst. Religion, Cin, 1969; LLD, Jewish Theol. Sem., 1995. Family case worker, dir. pub. relations Jewish Family Service, NYC, 1941-45; mem. faculty Sch. Social Work, Columbia U., NYC, 1945-47, 50-64, prof. social scis., 1958-64, dir. rsch. ctr., 1959-62; dean Sch. Applied Social Scis. Case Western Res. U., Cleve., 1964-68, provost for social and behavioral scis., 1967-71, John Reynolds Harkness prof., social adminstr., 1972-89, univ. provost, v.p., 1969-72, 86-88, univ. prof., provost emeritus, 1990—2009, univ. prof., faculty Ctr. for Internat. Health, 1989—2009. Founder, dir. Global Currents Lectures, 1983-88; vis. prof. Sch. Social Work, U. Hawaii, Honolulu, winter 1971-72; fellow ctr. for Advanced Study in Behavior Scis., 1974-75, 78-79; Dep. dir. budget and rsch. dir. welfare dept. Am. Joint Distbn. Com. (European Hdqrs.), Paris, 1947-50; sr. adviser to exec. dir. UNICEF, 1974-83; cons. UNICEF, UN Social Devel. Div., 1960-83; adv. com. NIMH, 1959-71; mem. Bd. Human Resources, Nat. Acad. Scis., 1972-74; lectr. Sch. Social Work, Smith Coll., 1951-62, Harvard U. Sch. Pub. Health, 1971-85; cons. indsl. and nonprofit orgns. Author: The Curriculum Study of the Columbia U. Sch. of Social Work, 1960; co-author: The Characteristics of American Jews, 1965; Editor: (with Richard A. Cloward) Social Perspectives on Behavior, 1958, Planning for the Needs of Children in Developing Countries, 1965, Social Theory and Social Invention, 1968, The Crisis in Welfare in Cleveland, 1969, Organization and the Human Services, 1981; mem. editorial bd.: Adminstr. in Social work, 1976—; contbr. to profl. jours. Chmn. Mayor's Commn. on Crisis in Welfare in Cleve., 1968. Recipient Disting. Svc. award Coun. on Social Work Edn., 1970, René Sand award Internat. Coun. on Social Welfre, 1984, Univ. medal Case Western Res. U., 1994, Garrett award Smith Coll. Sch. Social Work Day, 1998, Frank and Dorothy Humel Hovorka prize Case Western Reserve U., 2002; named to Alumni Hall of Fame, Columbia U. Sch. Social Work, 1998, Golden Anniversary Honoree Columbia Sch. Social Work, 2001. Mem. NASW (chmn. commn. internat. social welfare 1964-65, Lifetime Achievement award 1996), Am. Sociol. Assn., Soc. Applied Anthropology, Coun. Social Work Edn. (pres. 1966-69, Significant Lifetime Achievement award 1996), Internat. Assn. Schs. Social Work (pres. 1968-76, Rene Sand award 1984, Katherine A. Kendall award 1996), Internat. Conf. Social Welfare (Disting. Svc. award 1970, exec. com. 1976-80, internat. adv. bd. 1986-2009, bd. dirs. coun. internat. programs 1965-92, Significant Lifetime Achievement award 1996), Club of Rome (assoc. 1988-2009), Phi Beta Kappa. Home: Cleveland, Ohio. Died Oct. 2, 2009.

STEINBERG, MICHAEL, music critic, educator; b. Breslau, Germany, Oct. 4, 1928; came to U.S., 1943, naturalized, 1950; s. Siegfried and Margarethe (Cohn) S.; m. Jane Bonacker, July 26, 1953 (div. 1983); children: Peter Sebastian, Adam Gregory; m. Jorja Fleezanis, July, 1983. AB, Princeton U., 1949, M.F.A., 1951; Mus. D. (hon.), New Eng. Conservatory Music, 1966. Free-lance writer, from 1952; head history dept. Manhattan Sch. Music, NYC, 1957-64; music critic Boston Globe, 1964-76; dir. publs. Boston Symphony Orch., 1976-79; artistic adviser San Francisco Symphony, 1979-89, program annotator, lectr., 1989-99; artistic adviser Minn. Orch., 1989-92; artistic dir. Minn. Sommerfest, 1990-92; program annotator, lectr. N.Y. Philharmonic, 1995-2000. Vis. mem. faculty Hunter Coll., 1954, U. Sask. (Can.), 1959, Smith Coll., 1964, Brandeis U., 1964-65; faculty New Eng. Conservatory Music, 1968-71, Wellesley Coll., 1971-72, Brandeis U., 1971-72, Mass. Inst. Tech., 1973; disting. vis. prof. McMaster U., Hamilton, Ont., 1982; U. Mo., 2006; cons. NEH, Nat. Endowment for Arts, Mass. Council of Arts and Humanities, Calif. Arts Council, Rockefeller Found.; free-lance writer, lectr. Author: The Symphony: A Listener's Guide, 1995, The Concerto: A Listener's Guide, 1998, Choral Masterworks: A Listener's Guide, 2005, (with Larry Rothe) For the Love of Music, 2006. Served with U.S. Army, 1955-57. Recipient Sang prize for criticism in arts, 1969; citation for Excellence in Criticism Am. Guild Organists, 1972 Mem. Am, Internat. musicological socs. Home: Minneapolis, Minn. Died July 26, 2009.

STEINER, JEFFREY JOSEF, manufacturing executive; b. Vienna, Apr. 3, 1937; came to U.S., 1958; s. Beno and Paula (Bornstein) S.; m. Claude Angel, Apr. 11, 1957 (div. 1972); children: Eric, Natalia, Thierry; m. Linda Schaller, Mar. 6, 1976 (div. June 1983); children: Benjamin, Alexandra. Student textile design, U. London, 1956; student textile mfg., Bradford Inst. Tech., London, 1957; HHD (hon.), Yeshiva U., 1996. Mgmt. trainee Metals and Controls div. Tex. Instruments, Attleborough, Mass., 1958-59, mgr. internat., 1959-60, pres. Argentina, Brazil, Mex., Switzerland, France, 1960-66, Burlington Tapis, Paris, 1967-72; chmn., pres. Cedec S.A. Engring. Co., Paris, 1973-84; chmn., CEO Fairchild Corp., NYC, 1985—2008, Banner Aerospace, 1993—2008. Bd. dirs. Copley Fund, Fall River, Mass. Trustee Montefiore Med. Ctr., NYC; bd. dirs. Israel Mus., Yeshiva U. Bus. Sch. Decorated Knight of Arts (France), knight Indsl. Merit of France, chevalier de L'Ordre des Arts et des Lettres, 1990, chevalier de l'Ordre National du Merite (France), commandatore de la Republica (Italy); recipient mayor's medal City of Paris, 1990; named one of Top 200 Collectors, ARTnews Mag., 2004-08. Mem. City Athletic Club, Racing Club, Polo Club. Jewish. Avocations: tennis, sailing, collector of Impressionism, modern & contemporary art. Died Nov. 1, 2008.

STEINER, JOHN VICTOR, veterinarian; b. Bronx, NY, Apr. 11, 1944; s. John and Ludmilla (Kodalitch) S.; m. Diana Elizabeth Krehbiel, Oct. 18, 1969 (div. 1984); children: Jennifer, Jeffrey; m. Geraldine Frances Ferara, Oct. 5, 1985. DVM, Cornell U., 1968. Veterinarian Newton (N.J.) Vet. Hosp., 1968-70; pvt. practice Mahopac, N.Y., 1970-89, Lexington, Ky., 1989-92, Hagyard Davidson McGee Assocs. P.S.C., Lexington, from 1992. Cons. on equine and llama reprodn; dir. Bluegrass Classic Llama Sale, Inc., Lexington. Contbr. articles to profl. jours. Mem. Am. Assn. Equine Practitioners (reproduction com. 1990), Soc. for Theriogenology, Ky. Vet. Med. Assn., Cen. Ky. Equine Practitioners Assn., Greater Appalachian Llama Assn., Internat. Embryo Transfer Soc., Ky. Thoroughbred Farm Mgrs. Club. Home: Lexington, Ky. Died May 26, 2008.

STEINER, ROBERTA DANCE, not-for-profit organization executive; b. NYC, Nov. 28, 1937; d. Robert Freeman and M. Barbara (Rose) Dance; m. Alfred L. Burke, Jr., June 21, 1958 (div. May 1976); 1 child, Pamela Rose; m. Gilbert Steiner, May 21, 1987. AB, Vassar Coll., 1959. Cert. prevention specialist, substance abuse supr., N.J. Exec. dir. COPE Ctr., Inc., Montclair, N.J., from 1976. Mem. N.J. Counselor Cert. Bd., 1981-88. Mem. various coms. Jr. League, N.Y.C. and Montclair, 1960—. Mem. Assoc. Dept. Providers (bd. dirs. N.J. 1977—), Montclair Golf Club, Vassar Club (past pres., various coms.). Episcopalian. Avocations: golf, swimming, hiking. Home: Montclair, NJ. Died Nov. 9, 2007.

STEINMETZ, JAMES WILLIAM, pharmacist; b. Ashland, Wis., May 18, 1949; s. Edward Thomas and Virginia Anne (Paiement) S.; m. Myra Larson, Feb. 18, 1974 (div. May 1976); m. Louise Ann Memmer, May 10, 1990. BS in Pharmacy, Ferris State U., 1972. Pharmacist Albany Med. Ctr., Albany, N.Y., 1972-73; pharmacist, mgr. Lane Drug Co. (Peoples), Flint, Mich., 1973-74, S.S. Kresge Co. (K-Mart), Pueblo, Colo., 1974-77; chief exec. officer K & S Constrn. Co., Inc., Glenwood Springs, Colo., 1978-85; pharmacist, mgr. Sundance Drug Co., Inc., Snowmass Village, Colo., 1985-87; pharmacist, owner Basalt Clinic Pharmacy, Basalt, Colo., from 1987; owner Jim's Pharmacy/El Jebel (Colo.) Profl. Ctr., from 1990. Cons. Family Physicians Clinic, Snowmass Village, 1985—. Inventor sure-rod blind tie. Fellow Colo. Phamacal Assn.; mem. Nat. Assn. Retail Druggist's, Assn. Independent Pharmacy. Avocations: skiing, racquetball, golf. Died Aug. 4, 2008.

STELZNER, PAUL BURKE, textile company executive; b. Iowa City, Iowa, Jan. 1, 1935; s. Glenn W. and Ruth (Schroder) S.; m. Martha Jane Schneeberger, Aug. 23, 1958; children: Martha Elizabeth Beuke and Barrie Jane Lubbering. BS, Muskingum Coll., 1960; postgrad., Akron U., 1961-65. Tech. dir. Buckeye Fabric Finishing Co., Coshocton, Ohio, 1963-74; sec., sales mgr. Excello Fabric Finishers Inc., Coshocton, 1966-74; gen. mgr. Mineral Fiber Mfg. Corp., Coshocton, 1974-76, dir., 1998—2007; v.p., gen. mgr. Kellwood Co. Recreation Group, 1976-85; v.p. Am. Recreation Products, Inc., New Haven, Mo., 1985-88; v.p., gen. mgr. John Boyle & Co., Statesville, NC, 1989-93, pres., CEO, 1993—2005, dir., 1999—2007. Bd. dirs. Indsl. Fabrics Found., 1998-2002. Served with USN, 1953-57. Mem. Indsl. Fabrics Assn. Internat. (dir. 1973-74, 82-88, 94-99). Presbyterian. Home: Washington, Mo. Died Feb. 9, 2009.

STENLAKE, RONALD PAUL, publishing, printing and entertainment executive; b. NYC, Mar. 18, 1941; AB, Lafayette Coll., 1963; JD, U. Va., 1966. Bar: Va., 1966. Asst. to pres. Lafayette Coll., Easton, Pa., 1968-72; dir. program devel. Scholastic Inc., NYC, 1972-78, mgr. sch. divsn., 1978-81, v.p. book mfg. and inventory mgmt., 1981-86; ops. mgr. Lyrick Corp., Allen, Tex., 1986-92, v.p. ops. and info. systems, from 1992. Vol. Peace Corps, Ethiopia, 1966-68. Mem. Nat. Assn. Purchasing Mgmt., Am. Prodn. and Inventory Control, Nat. Peace Corps Assn., Allen C. of C. (treas., divisional v.p., bd. dirs., chmn. bd. dirs.), Friends of Ethiopia, Phi Delta Phi. Home: Plano, Tex. Died May 17, 2008.

STEPHENS, JOSEPH, psychiatrist, researcher; b. Frederick, Md., Apr. 9, 1927; s. Joseph Snyder and Mazie Naomi Stephens. BA, Johns Hopkins U., 1948, MD, 1952, MusM, 1959. Assoc. prof. psychiatry Johns Hopkins U., 1967. Contbr. articles to profl. jours. Lt. USNR, 1954—56. Recipient Honorary Denison Strong Fellow, 1952. Fellow: Am. Psychiat. Assn. (life); mem.: Parlovian Soc., Am. Psychopathology Assn. Avocation: music. Home: Baltimore, Md. Died May 29, 2008.

STEPHENS, LARRY DEAN, engineer, consultant; b. Sterling, Colo., Sept. 1, 1937; s. John Robert and Shirley Berniece (Rudel) S.; m. Carol Ann Wertz, Sept. 1, 1957 (div. May 1975); children: Deborah Lynn, Janell Diane, Dana Larry(dec.), Hilary Elizabeth Melton; m. Neslihan Ozlen, Aug. 18, 2000. BS in Engring., Colo. State U., 1960; MBA, U. Colo., 1967. Registered profl. engr., Colo. Engr. Bur. Reclamation, Denver, 1960-90, cons., from 1991. Exec. v.p. U.S. Com. on Irrigation and Drainage, Denver, 1971—; exec. dir. U.S. Soc. on Dams, Denver, 1986—. V.p. Internat. Commn. on Irrigation and Drainage, 1989-92. With USNG, 1961-62. Mem. Am. Soc. Agrl. Engrs., Assn. State Dam Safety Ofcls., Colorado River Water Users Assn., Coun. on Engring. and Sci. Soc. Execs., Univ. Club Denver. Republican. Methodist. Home: Denver, Colo. Died Feb. 2009.

STEPHENSON, PAUL LAURENCE, educational administrator; b. Phila., Jan. 27, 1946; s. Robert and Annie (Stewart) S.; m. Wilma West, Oct. 19, 1969; children: Jennifer E., Ann Marie. BS, Cheyney U., 1968; MA, U. Pa., 1972; postgrad., Rutgers U., from 1986. Asst. prof. Antioch Grad. Sch. of Edn., Germantown, Pa., Phila., 1972-73; dir. extension edn. Coll. Agriculture, Pa. State U., U. Pk., 1973-84; exec. dir. Nat. Assn. Social Workers, Trenton, NJ, 1984-86; adminstrv. asst. Camden Bd. Edn., NJ. Child study specialist Mt. Holly (N.J.) Sch. Dist. Mem. Bd. Edn. Willingboro (N.J.) Sch. Dist., 1982-84; dep. mayor Willingboro, 1984-2009 Recipient Disting. Service award 4-H Clubs, Phila., 1984, Willingboro Bd. Edn., 1984. Democrat. Avocation: distance runner. Home: Willingboro, NJ. Died June 30, 2009.

STEPKOSKI, ROBERT JOHN, automobile dealership executive; b. Floral Park, NY, Mar. 15, 1933; s. John Vincent and Mary Victoria (Rudnicki) S.; m. Caryl Diane Henderson, June 20, 1953; 1 child, Caryl Dale Stepkoski Yarley. 1000 hour cert., L.I. Drafting Sch., Freeport, NY, 1952; cert. in forms design, NYU, 1957; AAS, C.W. Post Coll., 1961; continuing edn. certs., Clemson U., 1981-82. Distbn. mapper and planner L.I. Lighting Co., Roslyn and Hicksville, 1952-57, records analyst Hicksville, 1957-58, statis. analyst Mineola, 1958-65, mgr. budget divsn., 1965-70, econ. analyst, 1970-71; sec.-treas., bus. mgr. Hunter Chevrolet Co., Hendersonville, N.C., 1971-85; compt., asst. sec., asst. treas. Hughes Chem. Corp., Flectcher, N.C., 1985-86; contr. Raleigh (N.C.) Toyota, 1986-87; dir. ops. Boyd Pontiac-Cadillac-Buick, Inc., Hendersonville, 1988-95; fin. cons., from 1995. With U.S. Army, 1953-55. Mem. Hendersonville Country Club, Kiwanis (bd. dirs. Hendersonville 1976-79, fund raising treas. 1976-86, Outstanding Committeeman award 1976, Disting. Svc. award 1981, Outstanding Svc. award 1995, 97, 30 Yr. Legion of Honor award 2004). Avocations: golf, model trains. Died Jan. 4, 2008.

STERN, ARTHUR ALEXANDER, retired pediatrician; b. NYC, May 5, 1922; s. Max and Beatrice (Fleischer) S.; m. Muriel H. Schneider, Dec. 24, 1946; children: Ellen Hope, Teri Beth. BS, U. Chgo., 1945; BS in Medicine, U. Ill., Chgo., 1948. Intern Coney Island Hosp., Bklyn., 1948-49, asst. resident, 1949-50, Mamonides Hosp., Bklyn., 1950-51; asst. contagious diseases Kingston Hosp., Bklyn., 1951-52; attending pediatrics Good Samaritan Hosp., Suffern, N.Y.; sr. attending pediatrics Nyack (N.Y.) Hosp., 1965-80, chief pediatrics, 1972-78; ret., 1980. Cons. in field, organized pediatric ICU Nyack Hosp. Avocations: golf, photography, stamps. Home: Silver Spring, Md. Died Aug. 23, 2008.

STERN, ELLIOT MARK, lawyer; b. Bronx, NY, Sept. 2, 1947; s. Milton and Miriam (Hochberg) S. BA in English, U. N.C., 1970; JD cum laude, St. Johns U., 1975; LLM in Taxation, NYU, 1982. Bar: Fla. 1990, N.Y. 1976. Law asst. 2d dept. Appellate Term N.Y.S., Bklyn., 1975-80; assoc. Mudge, Rose, Guthrie, Alexander & Ferdon, NYC, 1980-85, Sherman & Howard, Denver, 1985-86; atty. advisor Office of Tax Legis. Counsel U.S. Treasury Dept., Washington, 1986-89; shareholder Ruden, McClosky, Smith, Shuster & Russell, P.A., Ft. Lauderdale, Fla., from 1989. Pres. Easycalc, Inc., Ft. Lauderdale, 1991—. Author: (software) Bond, 1991. Mem. ABA, Nat. Assn. Bond Lawyers. Home: Hollywood, Fla. Died Apr. 30, 2008.

STERN, MICHAEL, retired journalist; b. N.Y.C., Aug. 3, 1910; s. Barnet and Anna (Agulansky) S.; B.S., Syracuse U., 1932; m. Estelle Goldstein, Nov. 11, 1934 (dec. 1995); children: Michael, Margaret. Reporter, Syracuse Jour., 1929-32, N.Y. Jour., 1932-33, Middletown Times Herald (N.Y.); staff writer McFadden Publs., 1935-42; adviser John Harlan Amen investigation into alliance between crime and politics in Kings County, N.Y., 1939-42; U.S. war corr. Fawcett Publs., 1942-45; lectr. Newhouse Sch. of Communication, Syracuse U. Bd. advs. The Intrepid Sea Air Space Mus., N.Y.C., The "21" Heart Fund, N.Y.C. Clubs: Overseas Press (U.S.); Aquasanta Golf. Named Syracuse U. Man of the Yr., 1986. Author: The White Ticket, 1936; Flight from Terror (with Otto Strasser), 1941; Into the Jaws of Death, 1944; No Innocence Abroad, 1954; An American in Rome (autobiography), 1963; Farouk, 1966; contbr. mags. Editor, publisher La Scienza Illustrata, 1948-49, Fisher House mag. Assoc. producer The Rover film; exec. producer Satyricon, The Heroes, Love the Italian Way, Run For Your Life; host-narrator The City, CBS. Exec. v.p., COO Fisher Ctr. Alzheimer's Disease Rockefeller U.; trustee, Intrepid Sea-Air-Space Mus., Fisher House Found. Died Apr. 7, 2009.

STERN, RAUL ARISTIDE, physics educator, researcher; b. Bucarest, Romania, Dec. 26, 1928; came to U.S., 1950; s. Henry Herman and Anna (Schonbaum) S.; m. Ruth Nathan, Feb. 3, 1953; children: Gabriella C. A., Susanna V. BS, U. Wis., 1952, MS, 1953; PhD, U. Calif., Berkeley, 1959. Mem. tech. staff Bell Telephone Labs., Murray Hill, N.J., 1960-81; prof. U. Colo., Boulder, 1978—2002, prof. emeritus, from 2002. Vis. prof. and cons. in field. Assoc. editor: The Physics of Fluids, 1984-87; contbr. and reviewer to articles in sci. jours. Evinrude Found. fellow U. Wis., 1953; Sherman Fairchild Found. Disting. scholar Calif. Inst. Tech., 1986. Fellow Am. Phys. Soc. Achievements include research in physics and gaseous electronics. Home: Boulder, Colo. Died June 22, 2008.

STEURY-LATTZ, CYNTHIA ANN, health facility administrator, nursing educator; b. Vincennes, Ind., Dec. 5, 1953; d. Carl Eugene and Wanda Aileen (Welker) S. ADN, Prairie State Coll., Chgo. Heights, Ill., 1978; BSN, Oliviet Nazarene U., Kankakee, Ill., 1987; MSN, Lewis U., 1992. Staff nurse St. Anthony Meml. Hosp., Effingham, Ill.; IV therapist Mercy Hosp., Urbana, Ill.; charge nurse/trauma St. Mary's Hosp., Kankakee, Ill.; living unit adminstr. Shapiro Devel. Ctr., Kankakee, Ill.; nursing instr. Kankakee (Ill.) Community Coll., Olivet Nazarene U., Kankakee. Mem. Ill. Nurses Assn. (coun. nurse educators, pres. dist. 17), Sigma Theta Tau. Home: Kankakee, Ill. Died June 11, 2008.

STEVENS, AILEEN, retired secondary school educator; b. Delano, Calif., Oct. 9, 1915; d. Floyd Edward Buoy and Melvina Waits; m. James Malcolm Stevens, Nov. 15, 1941; children: Aileen Margaret, James Christopher, Terrance Duane, Eleanor Melaina, Wanda Floriene. AA, Stockton Jr. Coll., Calif., 1936; BA, Coll. Pacific, 1940; MS, U. Calif., Chico, 1968. Tchr. Humphrey's Bus. Coll., Stockton, 1934—40; social worker State Relief Agy., Stockton, 1940; tchr. Angel's Camp, Bret Hart HS, Calif., 1941; English tchr., head dept. Marysville (Calif.) HS, 1960—80. Grantee, Coll. of Pacific, 1939. Mem.: LWV, Literary Guild, Lioness Club. Episcopalian. Avocation: reading. Home: Browns Valley, Calif. Died May 3, 2008.

STEVENS, MARK GREGORY, immunologist; b. Rocky Ford, Colo., Dec. 7, 1955; s. Herbert Averal and Margie Burl (Harkness) S. BS, Kans. State U., 1978, DVM, 1982; PhD, Wash. State U., 1988. Diplomate Am. Coll. Veterinary Microbiologists. Postdoctoral fellow Wash., Oreg., Idaho Regional Program in Veterinary Medicine, Pullman, Wash., 1984-88; immunologist Nat. Animal Disease Ctr., USDA, Ames, Iowa, from 1988. Bd. scientific reviewers Am. Jour. Veterinary Rsch., Schaumburg, Ill., 1992—. Contbr. articles to profl. jours. Mem. Am. Assn. Veterinary Immunologists, Am. Veterinary Med. Assn. (Harwal award 1982), Sigma Xi, Phi Zeta. Achievements include development of colorimetric assay for quantituting Bovine Neutrophil Bactericidal activity, identifying Interleukin-4 producing T-cell in cattle, testing and developing vaccines to eradicate Brucella Abortus infections in cattle. Home: Ankeny, Iowa. Died Feb. 27, 2008.

STEVENS, ROBERT GENE, retired bank executive; b. Marion, Ill., Jan. 4, 1930; s. Robert Bryan and Mae S.; children: David R., Craig R., Brian R. BS, So. Ill. U., 1951; MS, U. Ill., 1954, PhD, 1958; LL.D. hon., Mt. St. Joseph Coll., 1974. C.P.A, Ill. Auditor Arthur Andersen & Co., St. Louis, 1954-55; instr. acctg. U. Ill., Champaign Urbana, 1953-58; ptnr. Touche Ross & Co., NYC, 1958-68; v.p. First Nat. City Bank, NYC, 1968-70; pres., dir. Old Stone Bank, Providence, 1970-76; mng. trustee Old Stone Mortgage & Realty Trust, Providence, 1971-76; chmn., pres., CEO BancOhio Corp., Columbus, 1976-81; chmn., CEO BancOhio Nat. Bank, Columbus, 1979-81; pres., CEO First Am. Bancshares, Inc., Washington, 1982—89. Served to 1st lt. USAF, 1951-53. Mem. Phi Kappa Phi Clubs: Metropolitan (Washington). Home: Annapolis, Md. Died Sept. 14, 2009.

STEVENSON, A. BROCKIE, retired artist; b. Montgomery County, Pa., Sept. 24, 1919; s. Alfred Brockie and Caroline Lansdale (Sill) Stevenson; m. Jane Merriman Mackenzie, Dec. 23, 1978. Student, Pa. Acad. Fine Arts, 1940-41, 46-50, Barnes Found., 1946-48, Skowhegan Sch., Maine, 1950. Instr. Sch. Fine Arts, Washington U., St. Louis, 1960-62; head dept. painting and drawing Corcoran Sch. Art, 1965-81, from assoc. prof. to prof. design, painting, drawing & watercolor, 1965-98; ret., 1998. One-man shows include War Paintings, London and Salisbury, Eng., 1944, Instituto Cultural Peruano-Norteamericano, Lima, Peru, 1953, Art Ctr., Miraflores, Peru, 1958, 1960, Assn. Cultural Peruano-Britanica, Lima, 1959, Mickelson Gallery, Washington, 1970, Pyramid Galleries Ltd., 1973, No. Va. C.C., 1974, Fendrick Gallery, Washington, 1978, 1984, 1988, exhibited in group shows at Nat. Gallery Art, London, 1944, Pa. Acad. Fine Arts, Phila., 1948—51, Sociedad Bellas Artes del Peru, Lima, 1953—56, SUNY, Potsdam and Albany, 1971, Columbia (S.C.) Mus. Art, 1971, EXPO '74, Spokane, Wash., 1974, Corcoran Gallery, Washington, 1980, retrospective, Villanova (Pa.) U., 2002, Strathmore Hall Arts Ctr., Bethesda, Md., 2004, Represented in permanent collections Corcoaran Gallery Art, Washington, Dept. Def., Nat. Mus. Am. Art, Phillips Collection, Fed. Res. Bank, Richmond, Va., Woodward Found., Washington, Ogunquit (Maine) Mus. Art, Brown U. Libr. Milit. Coll., Providence, one-man shows include Villanova U., 2002. With US Army, 1941—45, ETO. Home: Glen Echo, Md. Died Sept. 1, 2009.

STEWART, ALVA WARE, librarian, writer; b. Marshallville, Ga., June 13, 1931; s. Joseph Benjamin and Elizabeth Clyde (Ware) S.; m. Barbara Jean Johnson, Oct. 23, 1965 (div. 1982); 1 child, Susan Jean; m. Margaret R. Causey, Sept. 14, 1985. AB, U. N.C., 1953; MA, Duke U., 1955; MLS, U. N.C., 1960. Cert. libr. Head libr. Meth. Coll., Fayetteville, N.C., 1960-64; reference libr. U. N.C., Charlotte, 1965-68; head libr. N.C. Wesleyan Coll., Rocky Mount, 1968-71; assoc. libr. Coll. William and Mary, Williamsburg, Va., 1971-77; head reference dept. Memphis State U., 1977-80; reference libr. N.C. Agrl. and Technol. State U., Greensboro, 1981-93; ret., 1993. Cons. N.C. League of Municipalities, Raleigh, 1983. Editor N.C. Libr. Jour.; contbr. articles to profl. and popular publs. 1st lt. USAF, 1954-56. Recipient fellowship Coun. Libr. Resources, 1973. Mem. U. N.C. Gen. Alumni Assn., Am. Assn. Ret. Persons. Democrat. Baptist. Avocations: square dancing, bird watching. Home: Greensboro, NC. Died Sept. 20, 2007.

STEWART, PATRICIA RHODES, former clinical psychologist, researcher; b. Vallejo, Calif., Feb. 11, 1910; d. Butler Young Rhodes and Sarah Virginia (Ryan) Rhodes; m. John Kenneth Stewart (div.); children: John K., Nancy Rush. AB summa cum laude, Stanford U., 1930; MA, San Jose State U., 1959; PhD, U. London, 1963. Tchg. asst. San Jose State U., 1959—60; staff psychologist Napa State Hosp., 1964—77; pvt. practice in psychotherapy Berkeley, Calif., 1978—94; pvt. rsch. in adolescent deviance, 1979—85. Staff psychologist Westwood Mental Health Facility, Fremont, Calif., 1985-88. Author: Children in Distress: American and English Perspectives, 1976. Chair criminal justice com. No. Calif. region Am. Friends Svc. com., San Francisco, 1977-80, chair exec. com. 1970-74, 80-83, bd. dirs., 1980-83; bd. dirs. Friends Com. on Legis., Sacramento, 1985-88, No. Calif. Ecumenical Coun., Oakland, Calif., 1989-95. Mem. APA, AAAS, Phi Beta Kappa. Mem. Soc. Of Friends. Home: Berkeley, Calif. Died July 8, 2008.

STEWART, RICHARD JARRETT, entomologist, biologist; b. El Paso, Tex., Dec. 9, 1949; s. Joy Vergil and Wanda Lee (Jarrett) S.; m. Patricia Corrine Pippin, Dec. 1976 (div. 1982); m. Kathryn Lee Benske, June 11, 1983. AA, Coll. of Sequoias, Visalia, Calif., 1970; BA, Calif. State U.-Fresno, 1973. Rsch. assoc. U. Calif.-Berkeley, Fresno, 1977-85, U. Calif.-San Francisco, Fresno, from 1985. Contbr. articles to profl. jours. Tchr. Peoples Ch., Fresno, 1980—. Mem. Am. Mosquito Control Assn., Entomol. Soc. Am., Am. Burn Assn., Undersea and Hyperbaric Med. Soc. Home: Fresno, Calif. Died June 12, 2008.

STEWART, ROBERT GALIS, oil company executive; b. Long Beach, Calif., June 17, 1928; s. Guy Galis and Marguerite (Green) S.; m. Betty Marion Davis, Oct. 10, 1955; 1 child, Ian Galis. BSEE, U. Calif., 1952. Planning mgr. Caltex Oil South Africa, Cape Town, 1965-70; gen. mgr. Caltex Oil New Zealand, Wellington, 1970-73; regional coordinator Caltex Petroleum Corp., NYC, 1973-75, Dallas, from 1979; v.p. Caltex Philippines Inc., Manila, 1975-79. Home: Dallas, Tex. Died Aug. 4, 2008.

STEWART, SHAKIR, music company executive; b. Oakland, Calif., Apr. 1974; BA in Mktg., Morehouse U., 1996. Club promoter, Calif., 1989; co-founder Noontime Music; creative dir. Hitco Music Pub., sr. v.p., gen. mgr., 1999—2004; A&R cons. LaFace Records, 2000—04; v.p. A&R Def Jam Recordings, NYC, 2004—06, sr. v.p. A&R, 2006—08, exec. v.p., 2008. Died Nov. 1, 2008.

STILLMAN, AGNES CORARUTH, librarian, archivist; b. Pittsfield, Mass., Sept. 26, 1945; d. Frank Henry Stillman and Ruth Elizabeth Perkins. EdD, Tchrs. Coll., Columbia U., NYC, 1987. Phys. edn. tchr. Mt. Greylock Jr.-Sr. HS, Williamstown, Mass., 1967—70; asst., assoc. prof., phys. edn. Russell Sage Coll., Troy, NY, 1971—94; assoc. prof., reference libr., coll. archivist Sage Colls., Troy, from 1994, Albany, NY, from 1994. Lector, eucharistic min. Ch. St. Mary, Clinton Heights, East Greenbush, NY, 1989—2008; asst., religious svcs. St. Peter's Nursing and Rehab. Ctr., RSM Motherhouse Chapel, Albany, 2002; assoc. Mercy NE Religious Sisters of Mercy Americas, Albany, from 2002. Recipient Disting. Svc. award, NY State Assn. for Health, Phys. Edn. and Dance, 1986, Disting. Faculty Svc. award, Sage Colls., 1990, 2000. Roman Catholic. Avocations: reading, travel. Home: Rensselaer, NY. Died May 13, 2008.

STILLMAN, CHARLES J., elementary school educator; b. Emmetsburg, Iowa, Sept. 6, 1945; s. Charles J. and Maureen Murphy Stillman. MEd, Creighton U., 1976. Cert. elem. edn. tchr. Iowa, 1980. Elem. tchr. Diocese of Omaha, 1969—80; elem. & mid. sch. tchr. Bishop Garrigan Schs., Algona, Iowa, 1980. History day sponsor Bishop Garrigan Schs., Algona, 1983. Recipient Iowa History Day Tchr. of Yr. award, Iowa State Hist. Soc. & Iowa History Day, 2001. Mem.: Iowa Reading Assn. Avocations: travel, movies. Home: Algona, Iowa. Died 2008; unknown.

STINES, BETTY IRENE PARHAM, artist; b. Stinesville, Ind., May 3, 1918; d. Claude Everett Parham and Helen Bryan Acuff Parham; m. Willard Russell Elliott, Oct. 11, 1936 (dec. Aug. 1969); children: Jerry Lee Elliott, Gillespie-Kathy Lyn Elliott Holtsclaw, Willard Keith Elliott; m. Edmond Glen Stines, Feb. 19, 1972. Grad. high sch., Bloomington, Ind. Organizer, mem. Hoosier Hills Art Guild, Bloomington, Ind., 1963—80; organizer Hoosier Hills Art Guild Ann. Student Art Exhibit, 1963—73; floral designer Unique Florist Shoppe, Ellettsville, Ind., 1963—69; hon. dir. Internat. Biog. Ctr., Cambridge, England. Oil and water color paintings, 1950—2001, exhibited in group shows at Ind. U., Manchester Coll., Swope Art Gallery, Terre Haute, Ind., Hoosier Hills Art Gallery, Bloomington, Ind., Owen County Art Gallery, Spencer, Ind., Represented in permanent collections, exhibited in group shows at Ind. State House Art Salon. Chmn., co-chair art exhibits Monroe County Festival, Ellettsville, Ind., 1950—60; Sunday sch. tchr. Gave Chalk Talks Bapt. Ch., 1950; leader Brownie Scouts, 1943—47. Recipient numerous First, Best in Show and Champion Exhibitor awards. Mem.: Ind. Women in Arts, Nat. Mus. Women in Arts. Baptist. Avocations: genealogy, antiques. Home: Bloomington, Ind. Died Aug. 12, 2008.

STITT, MILAN WILLIAM, playwright, drama and English educator; b. Detroit, Feb. 9, 1941; s. Howard Milan Jr. and Audrien Emma (Prindle) S. Student, Albion Coll., 1960; BA, U. Mich., 1963; MFA, Yale U., 1966. Playwright, 1961—2009; assoc. prof. NYU, NYC, 1984-88. Adj. assoc. prof. U. Mich., Ann Arbor, 1982-87; artist-in-residence Cen. State U., Edmond, Okla., 1985; chmn. playwriting dept. Yale U., 1987-93; adj. prof. N.Y.U.; vis. prof. Princeton (N.J.) U., 1987; dramaturg Circle Repertory Co., 1978-81, bd. dirs. 1979-82, 93-96; founder and dir. Circle Repertory Sch., 1992-95, EXEC. DIR., 1994-96; lectr. numerous insts. including Cen. Washington State Coll., 1978, Nat. Brandeis Women's Orgn., Hempstead, N.Y., 1979, Northville (Mich.) Pub. Library, 1981, El Centro Cultural de Los Estados Unidos, Madrid, 1983, Hofstra U. Writing Conf., 1985, Playwrights Conf., U. Ark., 1986, U. Ill. at Urbana-Champaign, 1987, Wittenberg U., 1990; dir. New Am. Theater Sch. Women's Project; head dramatic writing Carnegie Mellon U., 1997-2009. Playwright: Towers of Achievement, 1961 (Minor Avery Hopwood Playwright award 1961), The First 'R', 1964 (Major Avery Hopwood Playwriting award), Take a Little Chance, 1964, In Pursuit, 1967, The Runner Stumbles, numerous prodns. 1971-87 (Best Broadway Play award Best Plays of 1975-76), Edie's Home, 1975, Back in the Race, 1979, I Won't Be Here Forever, 1982, Labor Day, 1987, Places We've Lived, 1992; screenplays and teleplays include Between the Lions, 1973-74, Ephraim McDowell's Kentucky Ride, 1981, The Gentleman Bandit, 1981, A Hazzard of New Fortunes, 1990, The Aspern Papers, 1991, Long Shadows, 1993 (nominated best film, Internat. Emmy); dir.: Three Steps Under the Rainbow, Attic Theatre, Detroit, 1985, The Runner Stumbles, Carpenter Square Theater, 1987; contbr. numerous articles to mags. and profl. jours. Recipient CAPS award N.Y. State Council on the Arts, 1978; grantee Nat. Endowment for the Arts, 1978, Mich. Council on the Arts, 1985. Mem. Dramatists Guild, Authors League Am., Circle Repertory Co., Writers Guild Am., PEN, Nat. Acad. TV Arts and Scis. Home: New York, NY. Died Mar. 12, 2009.

STITZEL, ROBERT ELI, health science educator; b. NYC, Feb. 22, 1937; s. Louis H. and Betty (Podell) S.; m. Judith Gold, June 4, 1961; 1 child, David L. BS, Columbia U., 1959, MS, 1961; PhD, U. Minn., 1964. Asst. prof. W.Va. U., Morgantown, 1965-69, assoc. prof., 1969-73, prof., from 1973, acting chmn., 1978, 85, 87, assoc. chmn. dept. pharmacology and toxicology, from 1979, spl. asst. to provost, dir. grad. studies, 1991-94, sec. faculty senate, from 1997, dir. univ. grad. studies, from 1998. Vis. prof. U. Adelaide, Australia, 1973, U. Innsbruck, Austria, 1977;

chmn. study sect. NIH, Bethesda, Md., 1983-84, 84-85. Editor: Modern Pharmacology, 5 edits., 1980—; editor-in-chief jour. Pharmacol. Revs., 1989-95; contbr. articles to profl. jours. Sr. rsch. fellow Swedish Med. Rsch. Coun., Goteborg, 1966-67, hon. rsch. fellow Univ. Coll. London, 1977; vis. rsch. scientist divsn. human nutrition CSIRO, Adelaide, 1987; recipient Rsch. Career Devel. award NIH, 1970-75. Mem. AAAS, Am. Soc. for Pharmacology and Exptl. Therapeutics (sec.-treas. 1993-96). Avocations: collecting baseball cards, jazz, classical music, reading. Home: Morgantown, W.Va. Died Sept. 1, 2007.

STOCKING, MARION KINGSTON, English language educator, editor; b. Bethlehem, Pa., June 4, 1922; d. William Frank and Louise Anne Kingston; m. David Mackenzie Stocking, Dec. 21, 1955 (dec. 1984); 1 stepchild: Frederick B. AB, Mt. Holyoke Coll., 1943; PhD, Duke U., 1952; LittD (hon.), U. Maine, 1992. Licensed bird bander U.S. Fish and Wildlife Svc., 1960-92. Instr. English U. Maine, Orono, 1946-48, U. Colo., Boulder, 1950-54; from asst. prof. to prof. emerita Beloit (Wis.) Coll., from 1954. Faculty assoc. Coll. of the Atlantic, Bar Harbor, Maine, 1985—; publ. The Latona Press, Ellsworth, Maine, 1978—; pres. The Beloit Poetry Jour. Found., 1988—; panelist Maine Community Found., Ellsworth, 1988-93; dir. Freshman English Beloit Coll., 1955-63, dir. Porter Scholars Hons. Program, 1967-69, dir. Underclass Common Course, 1967-70, chairperson Dept. English, 1978-83. Editor: Journals of Claire Clairmont, 1968, The Beloit Poetry Jour., 1955—, (contbg.) Shelley and His Circle, V, 1974, The Clairmont Correspondence, 1995; contbr. profl. publs. Commnr. Maine Arts Commn., Augusta, 1993—, lit. panel, 1984-88, chair, 1987-88; panelist Maine Expansion Arts Program, 1988-93; founder, dir. Wis.-Minn. Poetry Cir.; active Quoddy Regional Land Trust. NEH rsch. fellow, 1979; recipient Dangerfield award Intenat. Byron Soc., 1997; named Scholar of Yr., Keats-Shelley Assn., 1996. Mem. AAUW, MLA, Keats-Shelley Assn. Am., Byron Soc., Maine Writers and Publs. Alliance, Sorrento Scientific Soc., Phi Beta Kappa. Avocations: conservation, environmental activism, wilderness canoeing, poetry reading. Died May 12, 2009.

STOCKWELL, NICHOLAS J(OHN), marketing executive; b. London, Dec. 24, 1946; came to U.S., 1965; s. Ronald Reginald William and Beatrice Ellen (Fryer) S.; m. Katharine U., Apr. 24, 1968 (div. Nov. 1982); children: Bonnie Christine, Kelly Denise. BS, MIT, 1969; MBA, U. Chgo., 1971. Acct. exec. Darcy MacManus, St. Louis, 1971-72; product mgr. Ralston Purina, St. Louis, 1972-74, Pillsbury, Mpls., 1974-75, mktg. mgr., 1975-78; pres. Alpha Investments, Winona, Minn., 1978-88; v.p. operations The Kerr Org, Mpls., 1988-89; v.p. sales & mktg. Diamond Brands Inc., Mpls., from 1989. Dir. Minn. Beer Wholesaler Assn., Mpls., 1986-88. Recipient Proud Lion award Stroh Brewery Co., 1984. Mem. Sales & Mktg. Execs. of the Twin Cities. Republican. Episcopalian. Avocations: boating, bicycling, golf, skiing. Home: Excelsior, Minn. Died Mar. 23, 2008.

STODDARD, GEORGE EARL, retired investment company executive; b. Perry, Oreg., Jan. 7, 1917; s. G. Earl and Elthira (Thomas) S.; m. Elma Skelton, Feb. 4, 1942; children: Evan, Jean, Robert Earl, Patricia. AB, Brigham Young U., 1937; MBA, Harvard U., 1939; LL.B., Fordham U., 1954. Investment analyst Central Hanover Bank & Trust Co., NYC, 1939-42; v.p. investment ops. Equitable Life Assurance Soc. U.S., NYC, 1945-79; chmn. fin. com. W. P. Carey & Co., NYC, 1979—2005. Bd. dirs. United Fund of Bronxville-Eastchester, N.Y., 1960-61; pres. Home Sch. Assn., Eastchester, 1962. Served to lt. USNR, 1942-45. Mem.: Univ. Club (N.Y.C.), Harvard Bus. Sch. Club (N.Y.C.). Home: Eastchester, NY. Died Mar. 30, 2009.

STODDART, LENORE T., volunteer; b. Denver, Dec. 26, 1922; d. Charles Sewell and Marie Wade Thomas; m. John T. Stoddart Jr., Dec. 1, 1945; children: Anne Ellen, Jane Wade, John T. III. Student, U. Denver, 1940—44. Pres. Children's Hosp. Assn., Denver, 1968—70, Margery Reed Day Nursery Bd., Denver, 1968—70; vol. co-chmn. Children's Hosp. Shop "La Cache", Denver, from 1982; trustee, trustee emeritus Denver Mus. Nature and Sci., from 1983; v.p. Associated Alumnae of the Sacred Heart, 1981—83, pres., 1983—85. Named Sustainer of the Yr., Jr. League of Denver, 1988, Vol. of Yr., Children's Hosp., Denver, 1989. Died Apr. 23, 2008.

STOENNER, JESSAMINE, music educator; b. Dalton, Ga., Aug. 12, 1908; d. John Fletcher and Johnnie Jessamine (Richardson) Tarver; m. Walter George Stoenner, June 22, 1930 (dec. July 1987); children: Jessamine Marie, June Louise, Willa Jean, James Tarver. B in Music, Mo. Valley Coll., 1928, BA, 1930; cert. piano tchr., Music Tchrs. Nat. Assn., Warrensburg, Mo., 1977. Music tchr.; ch. oganist Presbyn. Ch., Richmond, Mo., 1945-95; dir. Girls Glee Club, Mo. Valley Coll., Marshall, Mo., 1929, tchr. asst. music dept., 1929-30. Pres. PTA, Richmond Schs., 1942; leader Girl Scouts Am., Richmond, 1942-51; literacy tchr., Richmond, 1994-97; contbr., adoptee Children's Internat., 1996-99; mem. Ray County Meml. Hosp. Aux., Richmond, 1989-99, Ray County Cmty. Arts Assn., Richmond, 1993-99, Ray County Hist. Soc. Recipient Christian Family award Richmond Presbyn. Ch., 1976, Dedicated Svc. award, 1999. Mem. AAUW, PEO, DAR (regent 1949-50, Am. Heritage Music award 1998), Music Tchrs. Nat. Assn., Mo. Music Tchrs. Assn., Warrensburg Area Music Tchrs. Assn. Republican. Presbyterian. Avocations: reading, flowers, travel, poetry, bridge. Home: Richmond, Mo. Died Dec. 29, 2007.

STOHL, ESTHER A., senior citizen advocate; b. Olympia, Wash., Apr. 13, 1919; d. James Vernon and Anna Marie (Rixe) Snodgrass; m. Edwin F. Crowell, Sept. 4, 1938 (div. Apr. 1958); children: John Steven Crowell, Charles Edwin Crowell; m. Donald L. Stohl, Oct. 16, 1960 (dec. 1983). Grad. high sch., Olympia. Asst. to sales mgr. Ga.-Pacific Plywood, Olympia, 1937-41, 46-54; adminstrv. asst. Wash. Fedn. State Employees, Olympia, 1954-79; senate health-care com. aide Wash. State Legislature, Olympia, 1980; office mgr. Sr. Citizens Lobby, Olympia, 1980-83, 84-89; office asst. Wash. State Ret. Tchrs. Assn., Olympia, 1989-95. Pres. Srs. Educating Srs., Olympia, 1984-96; chmn. Area Agy. on Aging Adv. Coun., 1991-92. Author, editor Srs. Educating Srs. jour., 1984-96. Consumer advocate Wash. State Long Term Care Commn., Olympia, 1989-90. Mem. AFSCME (life), Wash. Fedn. State Employees (life), Am. Assn. Ret. Persons (lobbyist 1988-94), Sr. Citizens Lobby Wash., Ret. Pub. Employees Wash. Democrat. Lutheran. Avocations: reading, cooking, gardening, visiting in nursing homes. Home: Olympia, Wash. Died Mar. 2, 2008.

STOIA, VIOREL G., life underwriter; b. Aberdeen, SD, Feb. 13, 1924; s. John and Seana (Biliboca) S.; m. Donna Marie Maurseth Stoia, Sept. 10, 1949; children: Marsha Jo, Nancy Kay, Gregory Allen, Thomas John, James Vincent. BBA, U. Minn., 1949; D in Pub. Svc. (hon.), No. State U., 2002. CLU, ChFC, Am. Coll. Sr. agt. Northwestern Mut. Life, Milw., 1950—95; with Stoia Kusler and Assoc., Aberdeen, SD, 1981—2007. Co-founder, chmn. bd. Student Loan Fin. Corp., 1978—2003; mng. ptnr. Aberdeen Real Estate Ptnrs., 1979—92; co-founder, mng. ptnr. Tel Serv, 1983—97; co-founder Northwest Regional Health and Fitness Ctr., from 1999. Co-founder, pres. Northeastern Mental Health Ctr., 1957-59, North Plains Hospice, 1980-84; sec. Edn. Asst. Corp., 1978-97; bd. dirs. SD Crippled Children's Hosp., Avera Health Sys., 1996-2003; trustee Aberdeen YMCA, 1969-73, St. Luke's Hosp., 1969-96; co-founder, trustee Northern State U. Found., 1972-99; co-founder Great Plains Edn. Found., 1999—, Aberdeen Downtown Assn., 1999, Blackstone Devel. Corp., 2000, N.E. Regional Health and Fitness Ctr., 1999—. USN, C.P.O., 1942-46. Named Outstanding Civic Leader of Am., 1967; recipient Jefferson award Nat. Inst. of Pub. Svc., Sioux Falls, 1980, George award Aberdeen C. of C., 1979, 94, Gov.'s award for excellence in econ. devel., 2000, Disting. Trustee award SD Assn. Healthcare Orgns., 2002. Mem. Aberdeen Devel. Corp. (pres. 1972-87), Aberdeen Jr. C. of C. (pres. 1956), S.D. Soc. CLU's (co-founder, pres. 1958-59), Nat. Assn. Life Underwriters, Aberdeen Dist. Life Underwriters (pres. 1953-54), S.D. Assn. Life Underwriters (pres. 1959-60), Million Dollar Round Table (life), Moccasin Creek Country Club (v.p. 1969-75). Republican. Roman Catholic. Avocations: jogging, hunting, reading. Home: Aberdeen, SD. Died Jan. 28, 2008.

STOKES, WILLIAM THOMAS, petroleum geologist; b. Corsicana, Tex., Apr. 15, 1920; s. William T. and Thelma (Ficklin) S.; m. Fiona Doreen Carnazza, Sept. 26, 1959; children: William T. III, P. Bradley. Student, Tex. Christian U., 1947-48; BS in Geology, U. Tex., 1950; postgrad., Cambridge U., Eng., 1993. Cert. profl. geologist. Geologist Pure Oil Co., Tyler and Midland, Tex., 1950-53; exploration geologist Sun Oil Co., San Antonio, 1953-55; regional mgr. west Tex.-N.Mex. Bright & Schiff, Midland, 1955-58; pvt. practice Dallas, 1958-61; pres. Oliver & West, Inc., Dallas, 1961-73; exec. v.p. R.L. Burns Corp., Redlands, Calif., 1973-79, also bd. dirs.; exec. v.p. King Ranch Oil & Gas Inc., Dallas, 1980-87; cons., 1987-95; pres. Stex Energy, from 1995. Chmn. geology found. U. Tex., 1995-97. With air force USN, 1943-46. Mem. Am. Assn. Petroleum Geologists (cert., vice chmn. trustee assocs., nat. sec. ho. of dels.), Am. Assn. Profl. Landmen (charter), Dallas Geol. Soc. (hon. life), Dallas Petroleum Club (sec. bd. dirs. 1987-88), Northwood Club, Horseshoe Bay Resort Club. Presbyterian. Home: Dallas, Tex. Died Feb. 25, 2008.

STOLLINGS, JAN GENE, pharmacist, dentist; b. Xenia, Ohio, Jan. 6, 1954; s. Roger Neil and Ingrid Gertrude (Odenthal) S.; m. Debra Lynn Schafer, July 16, 1977; children: Carissa, Ty Justin. BS in Pharmacy, Ohio No. U., 1977; DDS, Ohio State U., 1983. lectr. in field; provider mobile dental care for elderly and homebound. Pharmacist Kettering (Ohio) Med. Ctr., 1977-79; gen. practice dentistry Dayton, Ohio, from 1983. Cons. various nursing homes, Xenia, 1986—. Mem. ADA, Acad. Gen. Dentistry. Lodges: Rotary, Shriners, Masons (32d degree), Elks, Moose. Republican. Avocations: sports, reading, family. Home: Xenia, Ohio. Died Dec. 26, 2007.

STONE, ELIZABETH WALKER, language educator; b. Washington, Aug. 17, 1921; d. Micajah Theodore and Isabelle Morris (Grinnage) Walker; m. Frank Daniel Reeves (div.); children: Deborah E., Daniel R.; m. French Franklin Stone. BA in English, Howard U., 1940, MA in Am. Lit., 1942; MFA in Drama, Cath. U. Am., 1948; EdD in Speech and Drama, Columbia U., 1956. From instr. to asst. prof. liberal arts Howard U., Washington, 1944—55; supr. speech therapists D.C. Pub. Schs., Washington, 1955—58; assoc. prof. speech and drama D.C. Tchrs. Coll., Washington, 1958—62; edn. specialist ISIA, Washington, 1965—67; dep. dir. Internat. Agy. Com. on Mexican-Am. Affairs, Washington, 1967—69; dir. univs. and founds. divsn. U.S. Dept. of Commerce, Washington, 1969—71; dir. stds. for edn. instns. Social and Rehab./HEW, Washington, 1971—73, dir. tng., 1973—75; dir. comm. skills Howard U. Sch. Law, Washington, 1975—90; writer, 1990—2008. Editor: Higher Education Aid for Minority Business, 1970; author, dir. (TV documentary) High Expectations, 1988 (Gannett award 1989); contbr. articles to profl. jours. Writer seconding nomination speech J.F. Kennedy Campaign, L.A. Conv., 1960; spl. asst. White House Conf. on Civil Rights, Washington, 1966; writer, dir. TV campaign commls. Doug Wilder, State of Va., 1985; writer, cons. Project Vote, Washington, 1987; mem. bd. visitors Mount Vernon, Va., 1988-95. Recipient First Outstanding Alumna award Howard U. Sch. Comm., Washington. Mem. Federally Employed Women (adv. bd., bd. mem.), Black Women's Agenda (founding nat. pres., 1st pres., Outstanding Svc. award 1990), Nat. Smart Set (nat. pres., Spl. Svc. award 1991), Nat. Gallery Art (vice chair widening horizons program), Woman's Nat. Dem. Club (co-chair art in overseas embassies). Episcopalian. Avocation: creative writing. Died Sept. 7, 2008.

STONE, ETHON LEON, pediatrician; b. Detroit, May 20, 1916; s. Louis H. and Frances (Fisher) S.; m. Winifred M. Adamcheck, Dec. 25, 1941 (dec. 1994); children: Pamela, Keith, Anne. BS, Wayne State U., 1935; MD, U. Mich., 1939. Diplomate Am. Bd. Pediatrics. Rotating intern San Diego County Gen. Hosp., 1939-40; pediatric resident Children's Hosp., Columbus, Ohio, 1940-41, 45-46; pvt. practice pediatrics Stone Ped Clinic, P.C., Jackson, Mich., from 1946. Chief staff Mercy Hosp., 1973-74; active staff Foote Hosp., 1946—, chief pediatrics to 1985. Capt. M.C., U.S. Army, 1940-45; ETO. Fellow Am. Acad. Pediatrics; mem. Western Mich. Pediatrics Soc. (pres. 1971-72). Republican. Avocations: sailing, working, organ. Home: Jackson, Mich. Died May 27, 2008.

STONE, HARRY CLINTON, marine, mechanical and civil engineer; b. St. Augustine, Fla., Oct. 4, 1924; s. Harry McKinley and Greta (Reding) S.; m. Kathryn Elizabeth Foxworth, Aug. 12, 1950; children: Harry James, Lewis Wayne, Janice Elizabeth. BS in Marine Engring., U.S. Merchant Marine Acad., 1946; BME cum laude, Vanderbilt U., 1950; BSCE, U. Fla., 1971. Registered mech. and civil profl. engr., Fla., Ala. Design and devel. engr. K-25 gassius diffusion plant Union Carbide Corp., Oak Ridge, Tenn., 1954-58; chief of metal pants inspection Thiokol Chem. Corp., Huntsville, Ala., 1958-65, chief of metal parts inspection Brunswick, Ga., 1958-65; plant engr. Johns Manville Pipe Plant, Green Cove Springs, Fla., 1965-70; county engr. Clay County Bd. of County Commrs., Green Cove Springs, 1970-73; owner, cons. engr. H.C. Stone Engring., Orange Park, Fla., 1973-89; sr. engr., cons. Stone, Joch & Mahoney Consulting Engrs., Orange Park, Fla., 1989-91, ret., 1991. Drafting program advisor St. Augustine (Fla.) Tech. Ctr., 1966—; ex-officio bd. dirs. Clay County Fair Assn., Green Cover Springs, 1994—. Bd. dirs. Penney Retirement Cmty. Penney Farms, Fla., 1995—. Lt. USNR, 1951-53. Mem. ASME, ASCE, Gideons Internat., Masons, Rotary Club. Republican. Methodist. Achievements include patents on shaft sealing system, bidirectional viscosity seal; research on an energy salvage system with potential energy recovery equal to 1.0% of the nations electric power. Home: Penney Farms, Fla. Died Apr. 4, 2008.

STONE, JAMES JIM-SHOWN, biomedical and mechanical engineer, educator; m. Jei-Bin Wei, Dec. 7, 1984; children: Daniel, Andrew, MaryAnn. BS, Nat. Ctrl. U., Chung-Li, Taiwan, 1979; MS, Mich. State U., 1984; PhD, U. Wis., 1992. Rsch. asst. Nat. Taiwan U., Taipei, 1981—83; rsch. asst., tchg. asst. U. Wis., Madison, 1985—92; rsch. assoc., rsch. follow Mayo Clinic Coll. Medicine, Rochester, Minn., 1992—95; assoc. prof. ND State U., Fargo, from 1995. Contbr. scientific papers to profl. publs. Recipient Rschr. of the Yr. award, Coll. of Engring., ND State U., 1999; Spine Rsch. grantee, Orthopaedic Rsch. and Edn. Found., 1993—95, Biomedical Engring. Rsch. grantee, Whitaker Found., 1996—98, Maj. Rsch. and Edn. Equipment grantee, NSF, 2003, Novel Nanocomposites for Space Rsch. Program grantee, NASA, from 2004. Mem.: ASME. Achievements include patents pending for prosthetic hip implants. Home: Moorhead, Minn. Died Nov. 27, 2007.

STONE, LAWRENCE MAURICE, lawyer, educator; b. Malden, Mass., Mar. 25, 1931; s. Abraham Jacob and Pauline (Bernstein) S.; m. Anna Jane Clark, June 15, 1963; children: Abraham Dean, Ethan Goldthwaite, Katharine Elisheva. AB magna cum laude, Harvard U., 1953, JD magna cum laude, 1956. Bar: Mass. 1956, Calif. 1958. Rsch. asst. Am. Law Inst., Cambridge, Mass., 1956-57; assoc. Irell and Manella, LA, 1957-61, ptnr., 1963, 79-96, of counsel, from 1997; internat. tax coordinator U.S. Treasury Dept., Washington, 1961-62, tax. legis. counsel, 1964-66; prof. law U. Calif., Berkeley, 1966-78. Vis. prof. law Yale U., New Haven, 1969, Hebrew U. Jerusalem, 1973-74, U. So. Calif., L.A., 1984; mem. adv. group to commr. IRS, Washington, 1973-74; mem. President's Adv. Commn. on Tax Ct. Appointments, Washington, 1976-80; tax advisory bd. Little Brown Co., 1994-96. Author: (with Doernberg) Federal Income Taxation of Corporations and Partnerships, (with Klein, Bankman and Bittker) Federal Income Taxation; bd. editors Harvard Law Rev., 1955-56. Fellow Am. Coll. Tax Counsel; mem. ABA, Am. Law Inst., Internat. Fiscal Inst., Am. Arbitration Assn., L.A. County Bar Assn. (recipient Dana Latham award 1995), Phi Beta Kappa. Deceased.

STONE, MARTHA MUNFORD, retired foundation (not-for-profit) administrator; b. Kansas City, Mo., July 1, 1934; d. Clifton Wood and Ruth (Borman) Munford; m. Thomas Frederic Stone, June 1, 1956 (dec. 1977); children: Elizabeth Stone Miller, David Philip. BA in Dramatic Lit. magna cum laude, Rockford Coll., Ill., 1956; MEd in Student Pers. Svcs., Tex. Christian U., 1980. Tchr. Whig Hill Sch. Dist., Rockford, 1956-60, Rockford Coll. Reading Clinic, 1957-60; substitute tchr. Ft. Worth Ind. Sch. Dist., 1971-75; adminstrv. asst. to rep. Chris Miller Tex. Ho. of Reps., Ft. Worth, 1975-76; dir. vol. service Ft. Worth State Sch., 1976-80; dir. vol. leadership tng. ctr. United Way Met. Tarrant County, Ft. Worth, 1980-81, mgr. community services div., 1981-95. Mem. Tarrant County Hist. Survey Com., 1971-72; edn. com. Ft. Worth Human Relations Commn., 1974-76, human relations com. Ft. Worth Ind. Sch. Dist., 1975-78; health manpower task force Tex. Area 5 Health Systems Agy., Inc., 1977-78; Ft. Worth Bldg. Standards Com., 1986092. Mem. ASTD, LWV (host, producer Voters Digest weekly TV program Ft. Worth 1970-85), Forum Ft. Worth, Phi Beta Kappa. Home: Southlake, Tex. Died Jan. 9, 2008.

STONNINGTON, HENRY HERBERT, retired physician, association administrator, educator; b. Vienna, Feb. 12, 1927; arrived in U.S., 1969; m. Constance Mary Leigh Hamersley. MB, BS, Melbourne U., Victoria, Australia, 1950; MS, U. Minn., 1972. Diplomate Am. Bd. Phys. Medicine and Rehab., 1973. Pvt. practice, Sydney, N.S.W., Australia, 1955-65; clin. tchr. U. N.S.W., Sydney, 1965-69; resident in Phys. Medicine and Rehab. Mayo Clinic, Rochester, Minn., 1969-72, mem. staff, 1972-83; assoc. prof. Mayo Med. Sch., Rochester, 1975-83; chmn. dept rehab. medicine Med. Coll. Va., Va. Commonwealth U., Richmond, 1983-88, prof. rehab. medicine, 1983-89, dir. rsch. tng. ctr., 1988-89; v.p. med. svcs. Sheltering Arms Hosp., Richmond, 1985-92; prof. and chmn. dept. phys. medicine and rehab. U. Mo., Columbia, 1992-94; med. dir. Meml. Rehab. Ctr., Savannah, Ga., 1994-97; clin. prof. rehab. medicine Emory U., Atlanta, 1997—2000; clin. prof. medicine sect. phys. medicine and rehab. La. State U., 2001—05. Med. dir. rehab. svcs. Meml. Hosp., Gulfport, Miss., 1998—2005; clin. prof. phys. med. and rehab. La. State U. Med. Sch., from 2001. Editor: Brain Injury, 1987—2001, Pediatric Rehabilitation, 1997—2000; contbr. articles to profl. jours. Recipient award Rsch. Tng. Ctr. Model Sys., Nat. Inst. Disability and Rehab. Rsch., Washington, 1987, 88, Disting. Clinician award Am. Acad. Phys. Medicine and Rehab., 2002. Fellow Australian Coll. Rehab. Medicine, Australasian Faculty Rehab. Medicine, Royal Coll. Physicians Edinburgh (Scotland), Am. Acad. Phys. Medicine and Rehab. (named Disting. Physician 2002), Am. Coun. Rehab. Medicine, Am. Assn. Acad. Physiatrists; mem. Internat. Brain Injury Assn. (v.p. for sci. affairs 1998-2002, bd. govs., Founder's award 2004). Home: Wiggins, Miss. Died May 31, 2009.

STORER, PETER FRANCIS, retired broadcast executive; b. 1928; s. George Storer; 4 children. Chmn., CEO Storer Comm., Inc., Miami, Fla., 1975—86. Died Nov. 8, 2009.

STORY, ANNE WINTHROP, psychologist, engineer; b. Havenhill, Mass., Jan. 12, 1914; d. John Winthrop and Anna Louise (Fennelly) S. Diplôme supérieure, Sorbonne, Paris, 1933; AB, Smith Coll., Northampton, Mass., 1934; PhD, U. Calif., Berkeley, 1957. Registered profl. engr., Mass. Rsch. psychologist USAF Flight Safety, San Bernardino, Calif., 1950; instr. Pa. State U., 1947-50; assoc. prof. U. Mass., Boston, 1972-74; engring. psychologist USAF, Bedford, Mass., 1958-66, NASA, Cambridge, Mass., 1966-70, U.S. Dept. Transp., Cambridge, 1970-77; pvt. practice cons., from 1977. Inventor, patentee flight safety devices. Died May 21, 2008.

STOTLER, PATRICIA S., interior designer; b. Mt. Pleasant Mills, Pa., Sept. 28, 1941; d. Lester Melvin and Sarah Louise (Schaffer) Sierer. BS, West Chester U., Pa., 1963; MS, Syracuse U., 1968. Ptnr. Stotler, Smithem, Loebe Design Group, Inc., West Palm Beach, Fla. Died Aug. 2, 2008.

STOTT, JAMES CHARLES, chemical company executive; b. Portland, Oreg., Sept. 5, 1945; s. Walter Joseph and Rellalee (Gray) S.; m. Caroline Loveriane Barnes, Dec. 7, 1973; children: William Joseph, Maryann Lee. BBA, Portland State U., 1969. Ops. mgr. Pacific States Express, Inc., Portland, 1970-73; bus. mgr. Mogul Corp., Portland, 1974-80; v.p. Market Transport, Ltd., Portland, 1980-85; pres., founder, chmn. bd. dirs. Chem. Corp. Am., Portland, from 1985, also bd. dirs. Chmn. bd. dirs. Carolina Industries, Portland. Mem. TAPPI. Clubs: University (Portland). Republican. Roman Catholic. Avocations: golf, outdoors. Home: Wilsonville, Oreg. Died Feb. 8, 2008.

STOUT, PATRICIA JOAN, educational specialist, counselor; b. Neptune, NJ, May 26, 1932; d. John Francis O'Keefe and Lillian Veronica (Olsen) Murray; m. Robert Paul Stout; children: Michael, Robin (dec.), Wendy Matson. BA in Edn., Kean Coll., 1974, MA in Guidance, 1978; EdS, Rutgers U., 1987. Tchr. English Holy Cross Sch., Rumson, NJ, 1962-64, St. James Sch., Red Bank, NJ, 1965-73, Fair Haven Pub. Schs., NJ, 1974-84, guidance counselor, from 1985. Author poetry. Mem. Statewide Community Orgn. Project, Fair Haven, 1984, After-Sch. Program for Children, Fair Haven, 1985. Mem. Nat. Bd. Cert. Counselors, Nat. Mental Health Assn., NEA, Monmouth County Edn. Assn., Monmouth Ocean Guidance Counselors Assn., NAFE, Monmouth County Elem. Sch. Guidance Consortium. Democrat. Roman Catholic. Avocations: poetry writing, gardening, travel. Home: Little Silver, NJ. Died Oct. 5, 2007.

STOVER, JANE ADELE, community health nurse; b. Phila., Aug. 3, 1929; d. Aime J. and Rachel E. (Cournoyer) Prudhomme; m. Roy L. Stover, Aug. 21, 1959 (dec.); 1 child, Jean Marie. Diploma, St. Elizabeth's Sch. Nursing, Brighton, Mass., 1950; student, Tuft's U., Medford, Mass., 1963; AS, St. John's Coll., Collegeville, Minn., 1959. Cert. health officer, cert. lead paint inspector. Staff nurse John Adams-Quigley Meml., Chelsea, Mass., 1950-51; supr. pub. health Bd. Health, City of Medford, from 1961. Mem. Task Force on AIDS, LIc. Day Care Ctrs., Ednl. Programs in Parochial Schs. on Sex, Drugs, Communicable Disease and Epidemiology. Contbr. articles to profl. jours. Mem. Tri-City Action Program, ARC. 1st lt. USAF, 1957-60. Mem. Am. Pub. Health Assn., Am. Lung Assn. Home: Framingham, Mass. Died Nov. 9, 2007.

STRADER, PARK M. (PARKEY STRADER), state legislator; b. Knoxville, Tenn., Feb. 15, 1945; m. Glenda Strader; children: John, Paula. CPA 2004; cert. assessment evaluator Internat. Assn. of Assessment Office, lic. real estate brokers Tenn. Assessor Knox County, Tenn., 1972—2000; state rep. Dist. 14 Tenn. House Reps, Tenn., 2005—09. Mem.: Nat. Rifle Assn., Knoxville Rep. Exec. Com., Concord Rep. Club, West Knoxville Rep. Club. Republican. Baptist. Died Aug. 19, 2009.

STRAUB, HILARY G., adult health and psychiatric nurse; b. Selma, Ala., Apr. 11, 1947; BS, U. Fla., 1969; MS in Adult Edn., Ind. U., 1978; PhD, U. Tex., 1993. RN, Idaho; cert. in gen. mental health practice. Surg. staff nurse Shands U. Hosp., Gainesville, Fla., 1969, Madigan Army Hosp., Tacoma, Wash., 1969-70; maternity nurse U. Wash. Hosp., Seattle, 1970-71, acting head nurse, 1971-72, staff devel. instr., 1972-74, St. Lukes Regional Med. Ctr., Boise, Idaho, 1974-77, childbirth educator, 1977-81; clin. instr. U. No. Colo., Greely, Colo., 1981-84; asst. prof. Boise (Idaho) State U., from 1984. Co-author: Modular Learning Program, 1977. Mem. Am. Holistic Nurses Assn., Nurse Healer Profl. Assn., Idaho Nurses Assn., Sigma Theta Tau. Avocations: outdoor sports, gourmet cooking. Home: Boise, Idaho. Died Apr. 16, 2008.

STRAUMAN, BRUCE EDWIN, secondary school educator; b. Modesto, Calif., May 2, 1949; s. Edwin Walter and Marjore Marie (Gilbert) S.; m. Nalani Rose Hillar, Aug. 14, 1971; children: Kimberly, Jennifer. BS, U. Oreg., 1972; postgrad. Cert. K-12 health and physical edn.; cert. instr. first aid and CPr, ARC. Tchr. grades 6-8 health, sci., phys. edn., grs. 1-4 phys. edn. St. Alice Cath. Sch., 1972-77; tchr. grades 7, 9 health and phys. edn. Cal Young Jr. H.S., 1977-79; tchr. grades 8, 9 health John F. Kennedy Jr. H.S., 1979-80; tchr. grades 7, 8, 9 health Ashland (Oreg.) Jr. H.S., 1980-84; tchr. health Ashland H.S., from 1985. Co-leader, spkr., team leader Seaside Health Conf., 1982—; presenter in field; coach St. Alice Cath. Grade Sch., 1972-77, North Eugene H.S., 1972-74, Marist H.S., 1975-76, Cal Young Jr. H.S., 1977-79, Kennedy Jr. H.S., 1979-80, Ashland Jr. H.S., 1980-84, Ashland H.S., 1986—, YMCA, 1982-89; instr. standard 1st aid adult child baby CPR, ARC, 1990. Subject video, 1990. Eucharistic min. Our Lady of Mountain Cath. Ch., asst. youth min., 1982-85, mem. Mex. mission trip, 1991, 92, mem. youth edn. bd., 1987-90, mem. pastoral coun., 1988-90; dist. coord. Great Am. Smokeout, 1986-87; coord. with Ashland Cmty. Hosp. on project Health Quest Wellness Week, 1986-87; creator Ashland Sch. Dist. health booth for cmty. health fair, 1987. Named Health Tchr. of Yr. for Secondary Edn. by Oreg. Assn. Advancement of Health Edn., 1989; grantee Gibbs Found. Avocations: mountain biking, road touring, camping. Home: Ashland, Oreg. Died Mar. 12, 2008.

STRAUSS, STANLEY ROBERT, lawyer; b. NYC, June 3, 1915; s. Maurice M. and Blanche Anna (Danciger) S.; m. Margaret Inglis Forbes, Mar. 13, 1944 (div. 1950); m. Helen Anne Cummings, Dec. 31, 1975 (dec. 1980). BA cum laude, Williams Coll., 1936; LLB, Columbia U., 1940. Bar: N.Y. 1941, D.C. 1964, U.S. Ct. Appeals (1st cir.) 1977, U.S. Ct. Appeals (3d cir.) 1986, U.S. Ct. Appeals (4th cir.) 1974, U.S. Ct. Appeals (5th cir.) 1970, U.S. Ct. Appeals (6th cir.) 1977, U.S. Ct. Appeals (8th cirs.) 1975, U.S. Supreme Ct. 1965. Assoc. Howard Henig, NYC, 1940-41; atty. NLRB, Washington, 1946-52, supervising atty., 1953-59, chief counsel, 1959-63; assoc. Vedder, Price, Kaufman & Kammholz, Washington, 1963-65, ptnr., 1965-90; of counsel Ogletree, Deakins, Nash, Smoak & Stewart, Washington, 1990—2009. Co-author: Practice and Procedure Before the National Labor Relations Board, 3d edit., 1980, 4th edit., 1987, 5th edit., 1996. Officer US Army, 1941—45, PTO. Decorated Bronze Star; Horn scholar, Columbia U. Law Sch., 1937—40. Mem. ABA, Fed. Bar Assn., D.C. Bar Assn., Kenwood Country Club. Avocations: golf, tennis. Home: Bethesda, Md. Died Aug. 20, 2009.

STRAWDERMAN, VIRGINIA, education educator; b. Jacksonville, Fla., Sept. 6, 1949; d. William Richard and Gladys Virginia (Fritts) Wright. BS, U. Tenn., Chattanooga, 1972; MACT, Murray State U., 1975; PhD, Ga. State U., Atlanta, 1985. Tchr. Belen (N.Mex.) High Sch., 1972-73; teaching asst. Murray State U., 1973-75; instr. Chesterfield Marlboro Tech. Edn. Ctr., Cheraw, S.C., 1975-77; tchr. No. Fulton High Sch., Atlanta, 1978; rsch. asst. Ga. State U., 1979, instr. maths. dept. Atlanta, 1980-83, instr. Div. of Devel. Studies, 1983-85, asst. prof. Atlanta, 1986-88; math. instr. The Math Set, Atlanta, from 1988. Co-chmn. Ga. Coun. of Tchrs. of Math., 1987-88. Author: Mathematics for Every Young Child, 1989, A Description of Mathematics Anxiety Using an Integrative Model, 1985. Mem. Nat. Coun. of Tchrs. of Math., Ga. Coun. of Tchrs. of Math. Christian Fellowships. Home: Kennesaw, Ga. Died Mar. 28, 2008.

STREETT, BETTY EVANS, mental health services professional, writer; b. Nashville, Nov. 9, 1939; d. William Thomas and Ruth (Vietch) Evans; m. Thomas Gray Dunlap (div. Aug. 20, 1965); children: Debbie, Jo Dee; m. David C. Streett, June 28, 1975 (dec. Aug. 13, 2001); children: Lawlor, Corbin. BA, Augusta Coll., Ga., 1975; MSSW, U. Tenn., 1998. MSSW, NCAC. Dir. cmty. counseling Dept. of Army, Ft. Gordon, Ga., 1975—88; dir. chem. dependency programs Region I Mental Health, Clarksdale, Miss., from 1989. Founder Fairland Inst., Dublin, from 1999; mem. adv. bd. dept. social work Delta State U., Cleve., from 1999; mem. curriculum com. State Dept. Mental Health, Jackson, Miss., from 1999, mem. dual diagnosis task force, from 1999. Author: 12 Steps to Loving Yourself, 1991, Satan Stalking, 1993 (Polly Bono, 1994), Smoke and Mirrors, 1995 (Award of Merit Episcopal Communicators), The Magical World of Chemical Dependency, (workbook) Recovery from Compulsive Gambling, 2001; contbr. articles. Mem.: Nat. Assn. Alcohol and Drug Abuse Counselors, Nat. Assn. Social Workers. Democrat. Episcopalian. Avocations: travel, gardening, swimming, horses. Died Mar. 12, 2008.

STREICH, FRANK, film and television writer, director, producer; b. Stanislau, Poland, Nov. 11, 1922; came to U.S., 1923; s. Max and Clara (Krauser) S.; m. Corrine Rubin, Oct. 18, 1930; children: Nina Rachel and Lori Barbara. Cert., New Sch. for Social Research, 1951. Chmn./managing dir. Streich Perkins Ltd., London, 1963-75; pres. Old Mill Prodns., NYC, from 1977. Pres. Silvercup Studios, Inc., N.Y., 1981-84. Producer, writer, dir. TV series Olympic Viewers' Guide, 1984. Founding chmn. Assn. Brit. Comml. Film Producers, 1970-73, N.Y. Motion Picture and TV Trades Assn., 1983. Recipient numerous Lion awards Cannes Commercial Film Festival, 1967-75, numerous Clio awards N.Y. TV Commercial Festival, 1968-75, various internat. awards, 1967-80. Home: Baltimore, Md. Died Mar. 27, 2008.

STREISFELD, STEVEN DAVID, obstetrician, gynecologist; b. Bklyn., May 11, 1940; Grad., LaFayette Coll., 1962; MD, SUNY, Bklyn., 1966; BA in Biology. Diplomate Am. Bd. Ob-Gyn. Intern Maimonides Med. Ctr., NYC, 1966-67, resident in ob-gyn, 1967-71, fellow in high risk pregnancy, 1971; practice medicine specializing in ob-gyn Ft. Lauderdale, Fla., from 1974; attending physician, chmn. dept. ob-gyn Plantation (Fla.) Gen. Hosp., from 1974, Broward Gen. Hosp., Ft. Lauderdale, from 1974. Instr. SUNY, Bklyn., 1974. Served to capt. M.C., U.S. Army. Fellow AMA, Am. Coll. Ob-Gyn. Home: Delray Beach, Fla. Died July 28, 2008.

STRICKLAND, CHERYL ANN, small business owner; b. Elkhart, Ind., May 13, 1951; d. Charles Austin and Lois Jean (Kilmer) Wernicke; children: Tara, Shannon. Grad. high sch., Plantation, Fla. Pres. Drapery Arts Interiors, Swannanoa, NC, 1979—89, C. Strickland Enterprises, Swannanoa, from 1988, Profl. Drapery Seminars, Swannanoa, from 1988; owner Custom Home Furnishings Trade Sch., Custom Home Furnishings Edn. Conf. and Trade Show; pub. SewWHAT? Mag. Leader seminars in field. Author: Professional Drapery Seminars Handbook, 1988, rev. edit., 1990, A Practical Guide to Soft Window Coverings, 1992; feature writer for Draperies and Window Coverings. Home: Swannanoa, NC. Died Apr. 2, 2008.

STRINGER, CHARLES COLUMBUS, JR., minister, protective services official, writer; b. Clarksdale, Miss., Oct. 21, 1944; s. Charles Columbus, Sr. and Vivian Nelson Stringer; m. Helen Jean Perkins, Dec. 17, 1964; children: Charles Columbus III, Natalie Nicole. BA, Calif. State U., Seaside, 2002. Funeral dir. Stringer Funeral Home, Clarksdale, Miss., 1964—75; pvt. investigator N. Delta Security, Clarkesdale, Miss., 1965—75; law enforcement officer Clarksdale Police Dept., Miss., 1969—75; pvt. investigator Stringer & Assocs., Seaside, Calif., 1975—2003; min. various Baptist chs., Seaside, Calif., 1977—2003; investigator Pebble Beach Co., Calif., 1984—94; patrolman Federal Police Dept., Calif., from 1985. Adv. bd. mem. City of Seaside, Calif., from 1980; chmn., redress com. NAACP, Clarksdale, Miss., 1994—96; writer, asst. editor Seaside Post News Sentinel, Calif., from 2002. Author: Diary of a Dixie Cop, 1986. Candiddate for sheriff Coahoma County, Miss., 1975; candidate for mayor City of Clarksdale, Miss., 1996. SP/4 US Army, 1961—64, Ft. Hood, Tex. Mem.: Am. Legion, VFW. Democrat. Baptist. Avocations: hiking, weightlifting, training dogs, reading. Home: Marina, Calif. Died Jan. 10, 2008.

STRINGHAM, LUTHER WINTERS, retired economist, health facility administrator; b. Colorado Springs, Colo., Dec. 14, 1915; s. Luther Wilson and Fern (Van Duyn) S.; m. Margret Ann Pringle, Dec. 1, 1942 (dec. May 1998); 1 child, Susan Jean; m. Kathryn Cochran Baehr, June 19, 1999. BA summa cum laude, U. Colo., 1938, MA in Econs, 1939; Rockefeller fellow pub. adminstrn., U. Minn., 1939-40, Nat. Inst. Pub. Affairs, 1940-41. Economist Dept. Commerce, also OPA, 1941-43; intelligence officer Def. Dept., 1946-55; program analysis officer Office of the Sec. HEW, 1956-63, chmn. sec.'s com. mental retardation, 1961-63; exec. dir. Nat. Assn. for Retarded Children, 1963-68; intergovtl. relations officer HEW, 1968-77; planning dir. Central Va. Health Systems Agy., 1977-83. Dir. TV series Healthy Virginians, 1981-83. Mem. Pres.'s Com. Employment Handicapped, 1963-68; pres. Music for People, Inc., 1971-74; lectr. CUNY, 1971-76; mem. nat. coun. Boy Scouts Am., 1963-83; co-founder Older Virginians for Action, 1983-84; bd. dirs. Capital Area Agy. Aging, 1984-87; Midlothian Dist. rep. Keep Chesterfield Clean Corp. Capt. AUS, 1943-46; lt. col. USAFR, 1946-56. Mem. Greater Richmond C. of C. (mem. quality coun. 1993-94), Va. Hist. Soc., Phi Beta Kappa, Pi Gamma Mu, Delta Sigma Rho. Home: Midlothian, Va. Died Jan. 9, 2009.

STROBBE, MICHAEL EMIEL, service executive; b. Ghent, Belgium, Sept. 5, 1924; came to U.S., 1946; s. Oscar A. and Johanna F. (Pirijns) S.; m. Hedwig Anna Kunkel, Sept. 4, 1959. BSBA, Boston U., 1950. Cert. hotel adminstr. Various staff positions Hilton Internat., Montreal, Que., Can. and Amsterdam, The Netherlands, 1957-63; mgr. Schine Hotels, Massena, N.Y., 1965-68; area supr. Esso Motor Hotels Europe, London, 1968-72; dir. devel. Sheraton Internat., Brussels, 1973-74; project mgr. Can. Pacific Hotels, Frankfurt, Fed. Republic Germany, 1975-77; owner, operator Flanders Inn, Massena, 1979-85; pres. Hospitality Mgmt. Svcs., Alburg, Vt., 1985-89; owner HMS Fin. Svcs., from 1987. Died Oct. 23, 2007.

STRONG, BARBARA HILLMAN, art history and anthropology educator; b. Berkeley, Calif., Aug. 1, 1946; d. Ray S. and Elizabeth R. (Brown) S. BA, U. Calif., Santa Barbara, 1969, MA, 1973. Tchg. asst. U. Calif., Santa Barbara, 1970-72; art history and anthropology instr. Coll. of The Sequoias, Calif., from 1973. Divsn. chair Coll. of The Sequoias, 1991-92, art dept. chair, 1992—, v.p. acad. senate, 1990-93, chair equivalency com., 1990-93. Author: A Handbook of Precolumbian Art and Culture, 1994; author (software) Pentimento, An Art Hist. Game, 1995, Maya Resource Companion, 1994, Women in Art History. Recipient grants Coll. of The Sequoias, 1976, 93, 94. Mem. Coll. Art Assn. Democrat. Avocations: reading, computer authoring, hiking, tennis, travel. Home: Three Rivers, Calif. Died Jan. 9, 2008.

STROUSE, HARRY D., JR., retired justice, lawyer; b. Rochester, NY, Oct. 21, 1923; s. Harry Dunlap and Augusta Blanche (Hermann) Strouse; m. Elizabeth Semmes, Aug. 13, 1949; children: Carol, Harry, Carson, Kenneth, Karen. Student, Miami U., Oxford, Ohio, 1941—42, Miami U., 1946—47; JD, U. Mich., 1950. Bar: Ill. 1950, Ill. (US Dist. Ct. (no. dist.)) 1956, US Ct. Appeals (7th cir.) 1965. Assoc. Nelson, Boodel & Will, Chgo., 1950—56; asst. US Atty. Northern Dist. Ill., Chgo., 1956—58; ptnr. Kaufman, Strouse, Wasnewski & Yastrow, Waukegan, 1959—66; police magistrate 4th Jud. Cir., Lake County, Ill., 1960—63; assoc. judge 19th Jud. Cir., Waukegan, 1966—68, judge, 1966—84, chief judge, 1975—76; justice Appellate Ct. 2nd Dist., Elgin, Ill., 1984—86; mem. Arbitration Forums Inc., Chgo., from 1987, NASD, Chgo., from 1988. Mem. chief justice Earl Warren Conf. Advocacy, 1977; trial judge Law Sch. U. Ill., 1965—85; mem. faculty Ct. Practice Inst., 1970, Nat. Jud. Coll., Reno, 1981—83, Ill. Jud. Conf., 1968—86; mem. Project Search, San Francisco, 1974; chmn. Ill. Jud. Edn. Com., 1975—84. Scoutmaster NW Suburban Coun. Boy Scouts America, Barrington, Ill., 1950—58; pres. Scots Internat. Shrine Pipe Band Assn., 1972—74; bd. dirs. Lake County Mental Health Soc., 1966—69, S. Lake County Family Svc. Orgn., 1966—68; pipe major Medinah Highlanders, 1970—84; pres. Ill. DeMolay Found.; bd. dirs. Buehler YMCA, 1966—72; chmn. bd. dirs. Ill. Masonic Children's Home, LaGrange, Ill., 1983—89; mem. Medinah Temple. Served 1st lt. JAGC US Army, 1944—50. Mem.: St. John's Red Cross Constantine (past sovereign), Commandery, Augustus Gage Coun. (Evanston, Ill.), Moviter Lounsbury Lodge Palatine Chpt. (comdr.), Mich. Law Student Assn., Am. Numismatic Assn., Nat. Assn. Trial Lawyers, Lake County Bar Assn. (chmn. malpractice com. 1978—79), Ill. State Bar Assn. (editor criminal law newsletter 1952—56, mem. jud. selection com. 1975—83, chmn. traffic com. 1978—79), Lake Barrington Shores Golf Club, Kachina Club, Miami U. Glee Club, Masons (comdr.-in-chief valley Chgo. AASR 1988—90, 33rd degree mason 1990), Phi Alpha Delta, Sigma Nu. Republican. Episcopalian. Avocations: coin collecting/numismatics, stamp collecting/philately, bagpipes, ballooning. Home: Barrington, Ill. Died Mar. 6, 2008.

STROUSE, WILLIAM A., contract computer consultant, writer; b. Los Angeles, Apr. 22, 1945; s. Wilbert W. and Ruth Strouse. Diploma, Control Data Inst., San Jose, Calif., 1971. Systems designer, Klystrom dept. Stanford Linear Accelerator, Menlo Park, Calif., from 1984. Cons. Tech. Services Corp., Sunnyvale, Calif., 1984—; founder Wild Bill's Pub. Remote Access System, 1984. Mem. Micro Bull. Bd. Systems (on-line support provider 1984—), Pub. Domain Software and Info. Exchange, Trail Info. and Vol. Ctr. (on-line support provider), Bay Area Morrow Designs Users Assn. (asst. systems operator 1985), Pub. Remote Access Computer Standards Assn. (trustee San Josechpt.). Died July 28, 2008.

STUART, ALLAN REEVES, minister; b. Tampa, Fla., Jan. 24, 1929; s. Herbert John and Elizabeth Lucille (Reeves) S.; m. Rebecca Anne Hinton, Oct. 4, 1953; children: Rebecca Susan, John Russell. BA, U. Fla., 1950; BDiv, Emory U., Atlanta, 1953, MDiv, 1972; Dr.Laws, Sarasota U., Fla., 1987. Ordained to ministry. Pastor Meth. Ch., various locations, 1953-60, Alachua (Fla.) Meth. Ch., 1960-64; sr. pastor First United Meth. Ch., Stuart, Fla., 1964-72, Dunedin, Fla., 1972-82; founding pastor North Bay Community Ch., Clearwater, Fla., from 1982. Editor: Manual of Church Practices, 1989. Pastoral care bd. Morton Plant Hosp., Clearwater, Fla. Mem. Internat. Coun. Community Chs., Fla. Fellowship Community Chs., Acad. Parish Clergy, Fellowship of Merry Christians, Am. Assn. for Counseling and Devel., Coun. of Orgns. (pres. 1978), Kiwanis (pres. 1976-77). Democrat. Home: Oldsmar, Fla. Died May 3, 2008.

STUART, FRANCES DEADERICK, retired music educator; b. Ft. Worth, Tex., Nov. 8, 1911; d. Claude Taylor Deaderick and Nina Clara Staiti; m. John James Stuart (dec.); children: John James Jr., Betty Lynne. MusB, postgrad., So. Meth. U.; cert. tchr., NY Sch. Music Arts. Cert. tchr. piano/music. Tchr. piano theory and pedagogy, Dallas. Judge Nat. Guild Piano Tchrs.; pres. emeritus Van Katwijе Piano Club; patron chmn. Mu Phi Epsilon. Chmn. Sunday concert series J. Erik Jonsson Found., Dallas. Avocations: dance, interior decorating. Died Nov. 5, 2007.

STURTEVANT, FRANK MILTON, JR., pharmaceutical consultant, pharmacologist; b. Evanston, Ill., Mar. 8, 1927; s. Frank M. Sr. and Marguerite Marie (Walsh) S.; m. Ruthann Patterson, Mar. 18, 1950; children: Barbara (dec.), Jill Rovani, Jan Cassidy. BA cum laude, Lake Forest Coll., Ill., 1948; MS, Northwestern U., 1950, PhD, 1951. Sr. investigator G.D. Searle & Co., Skokie, Ill., 1951-58; sr. sci. advisor, 1972-90; sr. pharmacologist Smith, Kline & French Labs., Phila., 1958-60; dir. sci. and regulatory affairs Mead Johnson Rsch. Ctr., Evansville, Ind., 1960-72; pvt. practice pharm. cons. Sarasota, Fla., from 1990. Lectr. in genetics U. Evansville, 1972. Mem. editorial bd. Internat. Jour. of Fertility; mem. editorial adv. bd. Chronobiology Internat., 1984-86; contbr. over 120 articles to profl. jours. Class agt., bd. govs., chmn. sci. fund Lake Forest Coll., 1960-93. With U.S. Army, 1945-46, ETO. Recipient Mead Johnson President's award, 1967, Alumni Disting. Svc. citation Lake Forest Coll., 1988, Nutrasweet award, 1986. Fellow AAAS; mem. Am. Fertility Soc., Am. Soc. Pharmacology and Exptl. Therapeutics, Am. Coll. Toxicology (charter), Drug Info. Assn. (charter), Fallopius Internat. Soc. (former treas.), Internat. Soc. for Chronobiology, Internat. Soc. Reproductive Medicine, Internat. Union Pharmacology Sect. N Toxicology, Soc. for Advancement of Contraception, Soc. for Exptl. Biology and Medicine, U.S. Internat. Found. for Studies in Reprodn. (adv. bd.). Home: Sarasota, Fla. Died June 30, 2008.

SUDARSKY, JERRY M., industrialist; b. Russia, June 12, 1918; s. Selig and Sara (Ars) S.; m. Mildred Axelrod, Aug. 31, 1947; children: Deborah, Donna (dec.). Student, U. Iowa, 1936—39; BS in Chem. Engring., Poly. U. Bklyn., 1942; DSc (hon.), Poly. U. NY, 1976; PhD Hebrew U. Jerusalem (hon.), 2002. Founder, CEO Bioferm Corp., Wasco, Calif., 1946-66; cons. to Govt. of Israel, 1966—72; founder, chmn. Israel Chems., Ltd., Tel Aviv, 1967-72; chmn. I.C. Internat. Cons., Tel Aviv, 1971-73; vice chmn., bd. dirs. Daylin, Inc., LA, 1972-76; pres., chmn. J.M.S. Assocs., LA, from 1976; vice chmn. bd. dirs. Jacobs Engring. Group Inc., Pasadena, Calif., 1982-94; chmn., CEO Health Sci. Prop. Holding Corp., 1994-97; chmn. Alexandria Real Estate Equities, Pasadena, 1997—2007, chmn. emeritus, from 2007. Patentee in field of indsl. microbiology. Bd. govs. Hebrew U., Jerusalem; trustee Polytechnic U. NY, 1976—; bd. dirs. Mgmt. Edn. Assn., UCLA, 1990-99. Served with USNR, 1943-46. Recipient Richard J. Bolt award for supporting industries, Chem. Heritage Found., 2008. Mem. AAAS, Am. Chem. Soc., Brentwood Country Club, Sigma Xi. Died Apr. 4, 2009.

SUGAR, JACK, physicist; b. Balt., Dec. 22, 1929; s. Fredel and Bessie (Silverman) S.; m. Judith Blumberg, Aug. 12, 1956; children: Ross, Eve, Erica. BA, Johns Hopkins U., 1955, PhD, 1960. Physicist Nat. Inst. Standards & Tech., US Dept. Commerce, Gaithersburg, Md., 1960—2009. Book: Energy Levels of Iron-Period Elements, 1985; contbr. over 139 articles to profl. jours. Grantee Fulbright 1966, NATO 1990; recipient Silver medal US Dept. Commerce, 1971. Fellow Optical Soc. Am. (dir. 1976-78). Achievements include interpretation of X-ray absorption in rare earth thin films; interpretation of emission spectra of rare earth ions; research on spectra of highly ionized atoms, compilations of atomic energy levels and wavelengths. Home: Garrett Park, Md. Died Aug. 15, 2009.

SUHRKE, HENRY CARL, editor; b. Sheboygan, Wis., Oct. 23, 1924; s. Henry Carl and Anna L. Suhrke. BS in BA, Northwestern U., 1945; MBA, Harvard U., 1947. With Ea. Air Lines, Inc., 1947-53; dir. devel. Eisenhower Exch. Fellowships, Phila., 1955-59; prin. Henry C. Suhrke, Inc., NYC, 1959-68; editor, pub. The Philanthropy Monthly, NYC, from 1968. Pub. Survey of State Laws Regulating Charitable Solicitation, N.Y.C., 1977—; chmn., moderator Philanthropy Monthly's ann. policy conf., 1977—. Past bd. assoc. editors Jour. Vol. Action Rsch.; contbr. articles to profl. jours. Past mem. stds. adv. bd. The Philanthropic Adv. Svc., Coun. Better Bus. Burs., model law com. State Charitable Solicitation Law, steering com. for Establishment Nat. Ctr. Charitable Stats., The Schaumburg Task Force, Ind. Sector, Inc., U.S. rep. Internat. Standing Conf. on Philanthropy, Eng., exec. com., dir. United Way Conn. Lt. (j.g.) USNR, 1943. Mem. Nat. Soc. Fund Raising Execs. Inst. (past dir.). Home: Bridgewater, Conn. Died July 27, 2008.

SULLIVAN, GEORGE MURRAY, transportation executive, consultant, retired mayor; b. Portland, Oreg., Mar. 31, 1922; s. Harvey Patrick and Viola (Murray) S.; m. Margaret Eagan, Dec. 30, 1947; children: Timothy M., Harvey P. (dec. July 1996), Daniel A., Kevin Shane, Colleen Marie, George Murray, Michael J., Shannon Margaret, Casey Eagan. D.P.A. (hon.), U. Alaska, 1981. Line driver Alaska Freight Lines, Inc., Valdez-Fairbanks, 1942-44; US dep. marshal Alaska Dist., Nenana, 1946-52; mgr. Alaska Freight Lines, 1952-56; Alaska gen. mgr. Consol. Freightways Corp. of Del., Anchorage, 1956-67; mayor of Anchorage, 1967-82; exec. mgr. Alaska Bus. Council, 1968; sr. cons. to pres. Western Air Lines Inc., 1982-87; former legis. liaison for Gov. of Alaska; now cons. Past mem. Nat. Adv. Com. on Oceans and Atmosphere, Joint Fed.-State Land Use Planning Commn.; past chmn. 4-state region 10 adv. com. OEO; mem. Fairbanks City Council, 1955-59, Anchorage City Council, 1965-67, Greater Anchorage Borough Assembly, 1965-67, Alaska Ho. of Reps., 1964-65. Trustee U. Alaska Found.; chmn. Anchorage Conv. and Visitors Bur.; bd. dirs. Western council Boy Scouts Am., 1958-59. Served with U.S. Army, 1944-46. Mem. Nat. Def. Transp. Assn. (life mem., pres. 1962-63), Nat. League Cities (dir.), Pioneers of Alaska, Alaska Mcpl. League (past pres.), Anchorage C. of C. (exec. com. 1963-65, treas. 1965-66, dir.), Alaska Carriers Assn. (exec. com.), Alaska Transp. Conf. (chmn.), U.S. Conf. Mayors (exec. com.), VFW (comdr. Alaska 1952) Clubs: Elks. Home: Anchorage, Alaska. Died Sept. 23, 2009.

SULLIVAN, JANE ST. AMANT, editor, educator; d. Peter Telesphore and Zemly Independence (Singletary) St. Amant; m. Lewis Frederick Sullivan, May 31, 1953; children: Jacquelyn Ann Fordyce, Peter James, Lajuanda Christine Daigle, Lewis Frederick (Rick) Jr., Bret Ralph, Martha Mary Cleveland. BS, La. State U., 1973. Cert. tchr. La. Sec. Gen. Contract Corp., Baton Rouge, 1953; band dir. Lindale (La.) HS, 1955; tchr. Northwestern Mid. sch., Zachary, La., 1973—79, East Baton Rouge Parish Sch. Bd., 1973—79; literacy program mgr. VISTA, Clinton, La., 1992; team leader Delta Svc. Corps, Baton Rouge, 1992—95; pub. editor Quad Area Cmty. Action Agy., Hammond, La., from 1993, literacy supr., from 1995. Author: (children's book) The River Runs Deep; editor: (newsletter) Quad Quest, Faith in Action. Sec. PTA, Baton Rouge, 1961—62; team mem. Cheshier Missionary Evangelistic Team, Springfield, Mo., Kenya, East Africa, 1989—2003; organist, soloist, adminstr. Faith Assembly of God, Baton Rouge, 1956—98, Bible tchr., 1956—2003. Grantee, East Baton Rouge Parish Sch. Bd., 1979. Mem.: Sierra Club, Audubon Soc., Order of Ea. Star (organist 1985—2003), Kappa Delta Pi, Phi Kappa Phi. Democrat. Avocations: travel, gospel music, photography, evangelism. Home: Slaughter, La. Died Oct. 15, 2007.

SULLIVAN, JOHN FALLON, JR., government official; b. Washington, Sept. 6, 1935; s. John Fallon and Thelma (Simmons) S.; m. Eliza Johnstone Buchanan, Dec. 27, 1958; children: John Fallon III, James S. BSCE, Va. Mil. Inst., 1958. Registered profl. engr., Ala., Wis., Miss. Asst. area engr. Fed. Hwy. Adminstrn., Montgomery, Ala., 1961-62, area engr. Atlanta, 1963-67, hwy. engr. Washington, 1967-69, dist. engr. Madison, Wis., 1970-74, asst. div. adminstr. Tallahassee, 1974-78, div. adminstr. Dover, Del., 1978-80, Jackson, Miss., 1981-94; ret., 1994. Mem. Arbitration Bd., 1995—. 1st lt. U.S. Army, 1959. Mem. ASCE. Methodist. Home: Clinton, Miss. Died Mar. 20, 2008.

SULLIVAN, PATRICIA A., retired academic administrator; b. SI, NY; m. Charles Sullivan. AB cum laude, St. John's U., 1961; MS in Biology, NYU, 1964, PhD in Biology, 1967. Tchg. fellow, NIH pre-doctoral fellow NYU; post-doctoral fellow in cell biology Upstate Med. Ctr., Syracuse, NY; vis. fellow Cornell U., 1976; tchr. Wells Coll., NY; dir. biology honors program Tex. Woman's U., 1979-81; dean Salem Coll., Winston-Salem, 1981-87; v.p. acad. affairs Tex. Woman's U., 1987-94, interim pres., 1993-94; chancellor U. N.C., Greensboro, 1995—2008. Pres. Assn. Tex. Colls. and Univs. Acad. Affairs Officers, Assn. So. Colls. for Women, N.C. Assn. Chief Acad. Officers; active numerous coms. Tex. Higher Edn. Coordinating Bd.; lectr. in field. Contbr. articles to profl. jours. Died Aug. 20, 2009.

SUMMY, ANNE TUNIS, artist; b. Balt.; d. Archer Carlton and Ethel Cleveland (Farlow) Tunis; student Pa. Acad. Fine Arts, 1933-36, Edison Community Coll., 1975-78; further studies at Inst. Allende (Mex.), Millersville (Pa.) Coll., Franklin and Marshall Coll; m. C. Frank Summy, Jr., Jan. 21, 1939. One-woman shows include: York Mus., 1968, William Penn Mus., Harrisburg, Pa., 1970, Goethaen Gallery Art, Lancaster, Pa., 1970, Millersville State Coll., 1980, Bradley Gallery, Naples, Fla., 1982; group shows include Edison Community Coll., Ft. Myers, Fla., 1977; represented in permanent collections: William Penn Meml. Mus., Court Art Trust, Washington, Bloomsburg (Pa.) Coll., Franklin and Marshall Coll., Millersville Coll., Armstrong Cork Co., Rehoboth (Del.) Art League, Landscape Painters Pa.; pres. Art Encounter, Inc.; juried shows include: Pa. Acad. Fine Art, 1969-70, Balt. Mus. Art, 1969-74, Butler Inst. Am. Art, 1968, Soc. Four Arts, Palm Beach, Fla., 1975-78, Sarasota Arvida Show, 1979-82, Jacksonville Art Mus., 1976, Met. Mus. and Art Center, Miami, Fla., 1977. Recipient Neuman medal Nat. Soc. Painters in Casein, 1968; Lorne medal, 1969; 1st award Cape Coral Nat., 1974; 1st award Naples Art Assn., 1979; 1st award Fla. Artists Group Area VII, 1977; awards Bloomsburg Coll., 1970, Harmon Gallery Major Fla. Artists Show, 1976, 80-86, Hamel award Fla. Artists Group Statewide Show, 1980. Mem. Fla. Artist Group, Inc. (pres. area VII), Club: Naples Yacht. Home: Naples, Fla. Died 1986.

SUNDBERG, EDGAR LEONARD, land management executive, manufacturing executive; b. Boston, May 30, 1920; s. Mattias Algot and Ruth (Nystrom) S.; m. Ruth Olive Kinsman, Feb. 19, 1944; children: Richard Lee, Heidi Lynn. AA, New Eng. Sch. Art, 1946. Asst. chief clk. Singer Sewing Machine Co., Boston, 1939-41, 46; sales engr. Coast Pro-Seal & Mfg. Co., LA, 1947-52; founder, ptnr. Deccofelt Products Co., Glendora, Calif., 1952-63; pres., chief exec. officer, chmn. bd. dirs. Deccofelt Corp., Glendora, 1963-81; pres. Dazey Mfg. Corp., Glendora, 1963-75; pres., chief exec. officer Sundberg Mgmt. Corp., Seal Beach, Calif., from 1981; co-ptnr. Casa del Norte Apts., La Habra, Calif., from 1987; ltd. ptnr. Sun-State Corp., Burbank, Calif., from 1988. Cons. mfg. Deccofelt Corp., Glendora, 1982—. Founder Bob Hope Cultural Ctr. for the Arts, Palm Desert, Calif., 1987—; trustee Glendora Meth. Ch., 1970-73, Long Beach (Calif.) Meth. Ch., 1982-84; mem. Kona (Hawaii) Cen. Union Ch., Palm Desert Presbyn. Ch. Sgt. USMC, 1942-45, PTO. Mem. Marina del Ray C. of C. (dir. 1974), USN League (life), Am. Legion Desert Horizons Country Club (current bd. dirs.), Calif. Yacht Club (commodore 1973), Transpacific Yacht Club, So. Calif. Yacht Assn. (bd dirs. 1974), Huntington Harbour Yacht Club (bd. dirs. 1979-80), Assn. Santa Monica Bay Yacht Club (bd. dirs. 1975), Rotary (internat dir. 1980). Republican. Methodist. Avocations: sailing, jogging, art, tennis, golf. Home: Kailua Kona, Hawaii. Died Aug. 7, 2008.

SUNDE, TRUMAN ORDELL, small business owner; b. Minot, ND, July 9, 1939; s. Trygue and Thelma Georgia (Solverson) S.; m. Carole Marilyn Hodgson, June 16, 1962; children: Trent Alan, Timothy Daryn. BA in Sociology, Psychology, Concordia U., St. Paul, 1975. Sales and svc. rep. Singer Sewing Machine, Fargo, N.D., 1963-67; computer technician Sperry/Unisys, Mpls., 1967-89; ind. cons. St. Paul, 1989-90; owner, mgr. Truman's Serge & Sew, St. Paul, from 1990. Designer computer modifications improvements. Mem. Ind. Sewing Machine Dealers, Vacuum Dealers Trade Assn., Am. Sewing Guild, Toastmasters (pres. Legion Rostrum 1981, founder Sperry Speakers club 1984, Toastmaster of Yr. 1982, 83, 84, Able Toastmaster 1985). Lutheran. Avocations: camping, leather craft, travel. Home: Saint Paul, Minn. Died Dec. 5, 2007.

SUNDER, SHYAM, chemistry educator; b. India, Apr. 8, 1935; naturalized 1966. s. Thakar Dass and Lajwanti; 1 child, Namrata K. MS, Auburn U., Ala., 1968; MBA, Butler U., Indpls., 1980. Faculty Gover. Coll., Rupers., India, 1961-65; rsch. chemist Ciba Pharm. Co., N.J., 1968-69, Dow Chem. Co., Indpls., 1969-80; rsch. chemist III Marion Merrell Dow Rsch. Inst., Indpls., from 1980. Contbr. numerous articles to profl. jours. Mem. Am. Chem. Soc. Achievements include patents in field of chemistry. Died Aug. 27, 2007.

SUNLEY, ROBERT M., social worker; b. Detroit, Mar. 27, 1917; children: Madeline, Christina. BA, New Sch. for Social Rsch., 1951; MSW, Adelphi U., 1953. Editor Prentice-Hall, Inc.; therapist, supr., chief social worker various psychiat. clinics, NYC and L.I., 1953-64; freelance writer, editor, 1939-50; assoc. dir. Family Svc. Assn. Nassau County, N.Y., 1964-83; cons., writer, from 1985. Cons. to nat. and local community orgns.; pvt. practice psychotherapy, 1960-85; lectr., mem. adj. faculty several univs. Author: Advocating Today, 1984, Serving the Unemployed, 1987; also numerous articles, chpts. to books. Mem. numerous nat. and local bds. and coms. in social svc. field; pres. North Shore Unitarian Universalist Soc.; chmn. Veatch Bd. Govs.; del. to nat. and internat. orgns. With AUS, 1942-45. Home: Port Washington, NY. Died Jan. 3, 2008.

SUSSKIND, JACOB LOUIS, social studies educator; b. Newark, Sept. 24, 1933; s. Isadore and Frieda (Halpern) S.; m. Regina Von Allmen (dec. 1985); children: Lisa, Jeremy; m. Olivia Tucker Merrill, May 17, 1986. BA, Montclair State Coll., 1963; PhD, Vanderbilt U., 1969. Cert. tchr., N.J. Asst. prof. social sci. and edn. Pa. State U., Harrisburg, from 1969. Field liaison global edn. Pa. Dept. Edn., Harrisburg, 1980-81; rsch. assoc. Nat. Intercultural Edn. Leadership Inst. Editor Social Studies Jour., 1987-95; contbr. articles to profl. jours., chpts. to books. Mem. Middletown Sch. Bd., 1981-85. With USAF, 1952-56. NDEA fellow, 1966-67, NEH fellow, 1989, 94; attendee summer seminar Fulbright Commn., India and Israel, 1977, 82; Fulbright tchr. exch., Hungary, 1991-92. Mem. AAUP, Am. Hist. Assn., Nat. Coun. Social Studies (chair profl. ethics 1990-91), Pa. Coun. Social Studies (pres. 1983-84), Mid Coun. Social Studies (assoc. editor), Phi Delta Kappa. Home: Harrisburg, Pa. Died Jan. 9, 2008.

SUTER, SHERWOOD EUGENE, art educator; b. Bluffton, Ohio, Sept. 22, 1928; s. Homer Sherwood and Margaret Frances (Cherry) S.; m. Pattie Sue Andrews, Mar. 7, 1970; children: Dawn, Mark. BS, Western Mich. U., 1950; BFA, Columbia U., 1956. Art tchr., supr. Norman-Dixon Rural Consol. Agrl. Sch., Brethren, Mich., 1950-51, South Haven (Mich.) Pub. Schs., 1953-56; art prof. McMurry Coll., Abilene, Tex., from 1957. Art cons., workshop tchr., Cin. Pub. Schs., 1964-65. Exhibited in group shows at Abilene Fine Arts Mus., 1970, 71 (1st Place award), Women's Forum, Wichita Falls, Tex., Brownwood, Tex., Sweetwater, Tex. Art tchr., judge Abilene Fine Arts Mus., 1960's, YWCA, 1970's. Cpl. U.S. Army, 1951-53, Korea. Mem. Nat. Coun. Art Adminstrs. Republican. Methodist. Avocations: photography, piano. Home: Abilene, Tex. Died June 4, 2008.

SUTHERLAND, JAMES WILLIAM, urologist; b. Glasgow, Scotland, Mar. 27, 1922; s. James William and Jean Cummings (Johnston) Sutherland; m. Annie Stewart McPhie, Mar. 20, 1964; children: Malcolm(dec.), Anne, Charles, June, Craig, Ron, Patsy. MB ChB, U. Glasgow, Scotland, 1944; ChM hons., U. Glasgow, 1956. FRCS, Edinburgh, 1948, FRCS, England, 1950, cert. Brit. Assn. Urol. Surgeons, 1956. Urologist Brit. NITS, Glasgow, Scotland, 1956—66; urologist pvt. practice, Quincy, Ill. Contbr. articles to profl. jours. Fl/Lieut Brit. Royal Air Force, 1945—47. Mem.: AMA, Adams County Med. Soc., Brit. Assn. Urol. Surgeons, Ill. State Med. Soc. (del. 1971—91), Am. Urol. Soc., Spring Lake Country Club, Quincy. Presbyterian. Avocations: golf, travel. Home: Quincy, Ill. Died Apr. 24, 2008.

SUTTER, JOHN RICHARD, manufacturer, investor; b. St. Louis, Jan. 18, 1937; s. Richard Anthony and Elizabeth Ann (Henby) S.; m. Madeline Ann Traugott Stribling, June 5, 1984; 1 child: William Stribling. BA, Princeton U., 1958; MBA, Columbia U., 1964. CPA, N.Y., Mo. Mgr. Price Waterhouse, NYC, 1964-71; pres. John Sutter and Co., Inc., St. Louis, 1972-86, Handlan-Buck Co., St. Louis, 1975-88; investor, from 1988; pres. Pamlico Jack Group, Oriental, N.C., from 1989. Pres. Sutter Mgmt. Corp., St. Louis, 1972-79. Mem. Chpt. Christ Ch. Cathedral, 1987-88. Lt. (j.g.) USNR, 1959-63. Mem. AICPAs, Mo. Soc. CPAs, Neuse Sailing Assn., Sailing Club of Oriental. Clubs: Princeton, Oriental Dinghy. Episcopalian. Avocations: painting, sailboat racing, ocean cruising, ceramic arts. Died Aug. 31, 2003.

SUTTON, DOLORES, actress, writer; b. NYC, 1927; BA in Philosophy, NYU. Appeared in broadway plays including Man With the Golden Arm, 1956, Career, 1958, Machinal, 1960, Rhinoceros, Liliom, She Stoops to Conquer, Hedda Gabler, Anna Karenina, Eccentricities of a Nightingale, Brecht on Brecht, Young Gifted and Black, Luv, The Friends, The Web and the Rock, The Seagull, Saturday, Sunday, Monday, The Little Foxes, What's Wrong With This Picture, The Cocktail Hour, My Fair Lady (Broadway revival), 1994, My Fair Lady (nat. tour), 1993-94; films include The Trouble With Angels, Where Angels Go, Trouble Follows, Crossing Delancey, Crimes and Misdeameanors, Tales of the Darkside; TV appearances include Studio One, Hallmark Hall of Fame Prodn. AH, Wilderness, Theatre Guild of the Air: Danger, Suspense, Gunsmoke, Valiant Lady, General Hospital, From These Roots, As the World Turns, Edge of Night, F. Scott Fitzgerald in Hollywood, Patty Hearst Story, All in the Family, Bob Newhart Show, All My Children, others, (TV writer) Lady Somebody, 1999, The Secret Storm, Loving; playwright: Down at the Old Bull and Bush, The Web and the Rock; Born Yesterday, 1995, A Perfect Ganesh, 1995, Detail of a Larger Work, 1995, The Front Page, 1996, The Exact Center of the Universe, 1997, A Drop in the Bucket, 1997, Spring Storm (newly discovered Tennessee Williams play), 1997, Signs and Wonders, 1998, It Gives Me Great Pleasure, 2001, Company Comin', 2006, and others; prodns. Free Ascent, 2001, Burial Society, 2001, The Find, 2002, (narrator) What If?, LA Opera, 2007; Voices - Poems by Women from the 5th Century to the Present, 2008. Mem. Actors Studio, League of Profl. Theatre Women (bd. dirs.), Ensemble Studio Theatre (bd. dirs.). Home: New York, NY. Died May 11, 2009.

SUTTON, DONALD DUNSMORE, science educator, consultant; b. Oakland, Calif., June 8, 1927; s. Ben Bryan and Mabel Dunsmore Sutton; m. Treva Rose Sudhalter Sutton, Dec. 24, 1981; children: Alice K., Peggy A. Kluthe, Donald C. AB in Bacteriology, U. Calif., Berkeley, 1951; MA in Microbiology, U. Calif., Davis, 1954, PhD in Microbiology, 1957. Rsch. asst. U. Calif., Davis, 1953—55, NSF predoctoral fellow, 1955—57; microbiology educator asst. prof. Ind. U. Med. Ctr., Indpls., 1957—59; Merck-Waksman postdoctoral fellow Inst. Microbiology Rutgers U., New Brunswick, NJ, 1959—60; biology educator Calif. State U., Fullerton, Calif., 1965—70; appl. microbiology vis. educator Tokyo U., Tokyo, 1970—71; microbiology educator Calif. State U., Fullerton, 1960—2002, chmn. dept. biol. scis., 1965—70. Cons. Environ. Assocs., Encinitas, Calif., 1982—2002. Contbr. articles to profl. jours. Electronic technician USNR, 1945—46, PTO. Mem.: Audubon Soc., Am. Soc. for Microbiology, Mycol. Soc. Am. Achievements include research in Bacterial diseases of orchids; Taxonomy of Genus Erwinia; glucose metabolism by Erwinia; yeast glycolysis; localization of sucrose and maltose fermenting systems; effect of nystatin on cellular permeability in yeast. Home: Encinitas, Calif. Died Apr. 23, 2008.

SVEEN, MICHAEL MELVIN, radio station official; b. La Crosse, Wis., Mar. 22, 1957; s. Maynard Lavern and Rita Catherine (Schneider) S.; m. Julie Ann Wegscheid, June 7, 1991; children: Joleeta Ray, Katherina Ellen. Grad., Austin Vocat. Inst., 1976. Announcer, asst. music dir. Sta. KYSM, Mankato, Minn., 1976-80; announcer, music dir. Sta. KFIL, Preston, Minn., from 1981. Music cons. Jr. Achievement, Mankato, 1977-80; mem. Preston City Coun., 1991-94. Democrat. Mem. Lds Ch. Avocations: music appreciation, reading, history, playing cards. Home: Preston, Minn. Died Jan. 6, 2008.

SVETLOVA, MARINA, ballerina, retired choreographer; b. Paris, May 3, 1922; arrived in U.S., 1940; d. Max and Tamara (Andreieff) Hartman. Studied with Vera Trefilova, Paris, 1930-36, studied with L. Egorova and M. Kschessinska, 1936-39; studied with A. Vilzak, NYC, 1940-57; D (hon.), Fedn. Francaise de Danse, 1988. Ballet dir. So. Vt. Art Ctr., 1959-64; dir. Svetlova Dance Ctr., Dorset, Vt., 1965-95; prof. ballet dept. Ind. U., Bloomington, 1969-92, prof. emeritus, 1992—2009, chmn. dept., 1969-78. Choreographer Dallas Civic Opera, 1964—67, (ballets) Ft. Worth Opera, 1967—83, San Antonio Opera, 1983, Seattle Opera, Houston Opera, Kansas City Performing Arts Found., The Fairy Queen, 1966, L'Histoire du Soidat, 1968, ballerina Ballet Russe de Monte Carlo, 1939—41, guest ballerina Ballet Theatre, 1942, London's Festival Ballet, Teatro dell Opera, Rome, Nat. Opera Stockholm, Suomi Opera, Helsinki, Finland, Het Nederland Ballet, Holland, Cork Irish Ballet, Paris Opera Comique, London Palladium, Teatro Colon, Buenos Aires, others, prima ballerina Met. Opera, 1943—50, N.Y.C. Opera, 1950—52; performer: (ballets) Graduation Ball; contbr. articles to profl. jours. Mem.: Nat. Soc. Arts and Letters (nat. dance chmn.), Conf. Ballet in Higher Edn., Am. Guild Mus. Artists (bd. dirs.). Died Feb. 11, 2009.

SWANTON, VIRGINIA LEE, writer, publisher; b. Oak Park, Ill., Feb. 6, 1933; d. Milton Wesley and Eleanor Louise (Linnell) Swanton. BA, Lake Forest Coll., Ill., 1954; MA in English Lit., Northwestern U., 1955; cert. in acctg., Coll. of Lake County, Ill., 1984. Editorial asst. Publs. Office, Northwestern U., Evanston, Ill., 1955-58; reporter Lake Forester, Lake Forest, 1959; editor Scott, Foresman & Co., Glenview, Ill., 1959-84; copy editor, travel coord. McDougal Littell/Houghton Mifflin, Evanston, 1985-94; sr. bookseller B. Dalton Bookseller, Lake Forest, Ill., 1985—2004; author, pub. poetry books, reference works Gold Star Publ. Svcs., Lake Forest, from 1994. Contbr. articles to profl. jours. Former sec. bd. dirs., newsletter editor Career Resource Ctr., Inc., Lake Forest; vol. Lake Forest/Lake Bluff Sr. Ctr.; mem. bd. deacons First Presbyn. Ch. Lake Forest. Mem.: Lake Forest/Lake Bluff Hist. Soc. (vol.), Chgo. Women in Pub. Presbyterian. Avocation: gardening. Home: Lake Forest, Ill. Died Nov. 6, 2007.

SWARTZ, DONALD PERCY, physician; b. Preston, Ont., Can., Sept. 12, 1921; s. Simon Wingham and Lydia Ethel Swartz; m. Norma Mae Woolner, June 24, 1944 (dec. May 1980); children: Ian Donald, Rhonda Swartz Peterson; m. Isabelle Liz Dales, Apr. 21, 1984. BA, U. Western Ont., 1951, MD cum laude, 1951, MSc cum laude, 1953. Intern Victoria Hosp., London, Ont., 1951-52; asst. resident Westminster Hosp., London, 1953-54; resident Johns Hopkins U., Balt., 1954-58; asst. prof. ob-gyn. U. Western Ont., London, 1958-62; prof. Columbia U., NYC, 1962-72; dir. ob-gyn. Harlem Hosp.; prof. dept. ob-gyn. Albany (N.Y.) Med. Coll., 1972-99, prof. emeritus, from 2000, chmn., 1972-79, chief sect. gen. gynecology, 1982-88, head. div. gen. gynecology, 1988—99, acting chmn., 1992, hon. attending, from 2006. Vis. prof. dept. Ob-Gyn. U. Rochester, N.Y., 1981 Assoc. editor: Advances in Planned Parenthood. Vice pres., pres. Assn. Planned Parenthood Physicians, 1972-74. Served with RCAF, 1942-45. NRC Can. fellow, 1952-53; Am. Cancer Soc. fellow, 1956-57; Markle scholar, 1958-63 Fellow ACOG, Royal Coll. Surgeons Can., Am. Gynecologic Soc., Am. Gyn-Ob Soc., Am. Fertility Soc., Royal Soc. Health, Soc. Gynecologic Surgeons. Home: Delmar, NY. Died 2009.

SWAYZE, PATRICK, actor, dancer; b. Houston, Aug. 18, 1952; s. Jesse Wayne & Patsy Swayze; n. Lisa Niemi, June 12, 1975 Student, Harkness Sch., Joffrey Ballet Sch. Actor: (films) Skatetown, USA, 1979, The Outsiders, 1983, Staying Alive, 1983, Uncommon Valor, 1983, Red Dawn, 1984, Grandview, USA, 1984, Youngblood, 1986, Dirty Dancing, 1987, Steel Dawn, 1987, Tiger Warsaw, 1988, Road House, 1989, Next of Kin, 1989, Ghost, 1989, Point Break, 1991, City of Joy, 1992, Father Hood, 1993, Tall Tale, 1994, To Wong Foo, Thanks for Everything, Julie Newmar, 1995, Three Wishes, 1995, Letters From a Killer, 1997, Vanished, 1998, Black Dog, 1998, Without a Word, 1999, The Winddrinker, 2000, Wakin' Up In Reno, 2000, Forever Lulu, 2000, Green Dragon, 2001, Donnie Darko, 2001, One Last Dance, 2003, 11:14, 2003, George and the Dragon, 2004, Dirty Dancing: Havana Nights, 2004, Keeping Mum, 2005, Jump!, 2007, Christmas in Wonderland, 2007, Powder Blue, 2009; (TV movies) The Comeback Kid, 1980, Return of the Rebels, 1981, The Renegades, 1982, King Solomon's Mines, 2004, Icon, 2005; (TV mini-series) North and South, 1985, North and South: Book II, 1986; (TV series) Renegades, 1983, The Beast, 2009; (TV appearances) M*A*S*H, 1981, Amazing Stories, 1986, Whoopi, 2004; (Broadway plays) Grease, 1972, Goodtime Charley, 1975, Chicago, 2003; (off-Broadway) Guys and Dolls, 2006; co-author: (with Lisa Niemi) The Time of My Life, 2009 Recipient Aftonbladet TV prize for Best Fgn. TV Personality, 1988, Golden Apple award, Male Star of Yr., ShoWest award, 1992 Died Sept. 14, 2009.

SWEEDLER, BARRY MARTIN, retired federal agency administrator; b. Bklyn., Mar. 11, 1937; s. Louis and Sadie (Sweedler; m. Kathryn Grace Stewart, June 26, 1988; children by previous marriage: Ian, Elizabeth. BME, CCNY,

1960; MBA, CUNY, 1966. Registered profl. engr., N.Y. From asst. and jr. engr. to sr. gas engr. N.Y. State Pub. Svc. Commn., NYC, 1960-69; chief pipeline safety divsn. Nat. Transp. Safety Bd., Washington, 1969-74, dep. dir. bur. surface transp. safety, 1974-76, dep. dir., acting dir. Bur. plans and programs, 1976-79, dep. dir. bur. tech., 1979-82, dir. bur. safety programs, 1982-90, dir. office safety recommendations, 1990—2000; ptnr. Safety & Policy Analysis Internat., Lafayette, Calif., 2000—09. Guest lectr. Inst. Gas Tech., 1973, U. Md., 1974, U. Calif., San Diego, 1986, 88-89, U. N.Mex., 1987, U. Calgary, 1988; participant Internat. Workshop on High Alcohol Consumers and Traffic, Paris, 1988; presenter on alcohol and drug abuse in transp.; co-editor proc., chmn. alcohol, drugs and traffic safety program 35th Internat. Congress on Alcoholism and Drug Dependencies, Oslo, Norway, 1988, the Internat. Conf. on Alcohol, Drugs and Traffic Safety, Cologne, 1992, Internat. Inst. on Prevention and Treatment of Alcoholism, Stockholm, 1991, World Congress of Internat. Assn. Accident and Traffic Medicine, 1992, Internat. Conf. on Alcohol, Drugs and Traffic Safety, Adelaide, Australia, 1995, Annecy, France, 1997, Stockholm, 2000, Montreal, 2002. Author: (with others) Gas Engineers Handbook, 1985, Alcohol - Minimizing the Harm, 1997; contbr. articles on transp. safety to jours.; mem. editorial bd. Jour. Traffic Medicine, 1989-95, Injury Control and Safety Promotion, 1997-; TV and print media interviews. Bd. dirs. Great Falls (Va.) Citizens Assn., 1980-85, Tysons Manor Home Owners Assn., Vienna, Va., 1973-77; mem. Fairfax County (Va.) oversight com. on drinking and driving, 1984-2009, chmn., 1986-88; mem. bd. advisors So. Calif. Safety Inst., 2002-09, editor newsletter, SCSI Safety Monitor, 2002-09 Recipient Presdl. Rank of Meritorious Exec. award, 1987, Presdl. Rank of Disting. Sr. Exec. award, 2000. Mem. ASME, Transp. Rsch. Bd. NAS (chmn. com. on alcohol, other drugs and transp. 1991-97, com. on transp. of hazardous materials 1972-78, chmn. users and vehicle sect. 1998-2003, chmn. system users group, 2003-09) Internat. Coun. Alcohol and Addictions (co-chmn. sect. on traffic safety 1988-2009), Internat. Coun. Alcohol, Drugs and Traffic Safety (sec. 1992-97, pres. 2000-2003, co-editor coun. newsletter ICADTS Reporter 1990-2009), Am. Acad. Forensic Scis. (adv. mem. drugs and driving com. 1988-2009), Operation Lifesaver (program devel. coun. 1987-98), Nat. Safety Coun. (motor vehicle occupant protection com. 1983-2009), Am. Pub. Works Assn. (exec. com. utility location and coordination coun. 1980-87, hon. life mem.), Internat. Transp. Safety Assn. (founding editor assn. newsletter ITSA Report 1994-2000). Jewish. Avocations: travel, hiking, bicycling. Died Oct. 27, 2009.

SWEET, BERYLE GREGORY, manufacturing executive; b. Rome, NY, Feb. 24, 1928; s. Blaine Graden and Julia Cecilia (Esche) S.; m. Dorothy Anne Palmer, Apr. 26, 1952; children: Michael Joseph, David Richard, Nancy Eileen, Kathleen Anne High sch. grad., Rome, NY. Sales correspondent Revere Copper & Brass Inc., 1949-53; salesman Rome Iron Mills, NY, 1953-58, sales mgr. NY, 1958-73; v.p., gen. mgr. Central Fence, Syracuse, NY, 1973-75; mktg. mgr. Page Fence Div. Am. Chain & Cable, Monessen, Pa., 1976-79, gen. sales mgr., 1979-84; v.p., gen. mgr. Page Fence Div. Page-Wilson Corp., Monessen, 1984-87; pres. Page Aluminized Steel Corp., Monessen, 1987-89, chmn., chief exec. officer, from 1989. With USN, 1946-53. Mem. ASTM (mem. sec. 1986—, coms.), Chain Link Fence Mfrs. Inst. (bd. dirs. 1988-89, sec.-treas. 1989). Republican. Episcopalian. Home: Brooksville, Fla. Died Apr. 30, 2008.

SWEET, WILLIAM RUSSELL, painter, sculptor, art restorer; b. Coventry, RI, Nov. 18, 1860; s. Amos Reynolds and Sarah Anne (Coggshall) Sweet; m. May De Laigle Herndon, Dec. 1, 1890; children: Russell Herndon, Margaret Grace, Leila Augsta. BA in Fine Art, Univ. RI, Kingston, RI, 1880. Art restorer Hist. Soc. Newport, RI Mansions, Newport, 1880—1940; painter, sculptor Pettaquamscutt, Kingston, RI, 1896—1946. Sculptor A Tribute to Hiawatha hutch cabinet, 1896, Family Coat of Arms Wooden Chair. Achievements include design of a carved wood hutch cabinet themed for Longfellow's poem Song of Hiawatha; cabinet was the focus during the 50th anniversary of the Pettaquamscutt Historical Society in 2009. Avocations: farming, bonesetter. Died Oct. 15, 1946; Peace Dale, RI.

SWEPSTON, STEPHEN MCGEE, sales executive, sales engineer; b. Columbus, Ohio, Feb. 14, 1950; s. Dwight Carroll and Ruth (Lee) S.; m. Maryann Coffeen, Sept. 23, 1978; children: Todd Stephen, Andrew Dwight. BBA, Capital U., 1978, M in Sales Mgmt., 1980. Sales engr. F. F. Leonard Inc., Columbus, 1972-75, Atlas Butler Inc., Columbus, 1975-79, sales mgr., 1979-86; pres. Swepston Heating and Cooling, Chillicothe, Ohio, 1986-88; sales engr. Trane Co., Cin., 1988-90; propr. Fayette Heating, Ventilating and Air Conditioning, Washington, Ohio, from 1990. Treas. Columbus Met. Area Community Action Orgn., 1979-83. Commr. Boy Scouts Am., Columbus, 1977-83, troop scout master, 1980; treas. community camp, cen. Ohio, 1975-80. Served with U.S. Army, 1970-72. Named Eagle Scout Cen. Ohio council, Columbus, 1964, Spark Plug of Yr., Columbus Jaycees, 1978. Mem. Am. Soc. Heating, Refrigeration and Air Conditioning Engrs., Air Conditioning Contractors Am., Air Conditioning Contractors Cen. Ohio, Lions, Sertoma, Rotary. Republican. Avocations: aviation, farming, amateur radio, church. Home: Washington Ct, Ohio. Died May 9, 2008.

SWERDLIN, EDWARD MALCOLMN, mergers and acquisitions executive; b. Akron, Ohio, May 25, 1928; s. Jack and Sophia Vivian (Pressman) S.; m. Harriet Natalie Rosenstock, Sept. 12, 1948; children: Richard Phillip, Frada Debra. Student in bus. adminstrn., Emory U., 1946, U. Miami, 1947. Owner, mfr. Cement Block Industries, Miami, Fla., 1946-65; sales mgr. Lehigh Portland Cement Co., Allentown, Pa., 1965-70; prin. ptnr. Tobin Assocs., Coral Gables, Fla., 1970-75; prin. Swerdlin Assocs., South Miami, Fla., from 1975. Bd. dirs. Univ. Bank Builders Assn. Mem. So. Fla. Home Builders Assn. (Spike 1958—, membership chmn. 1961-62). Clubs: Kings Bay Yacht and Country (Miami), Coral Gables. Lodges: Masons, Rotary, Hibiscus. Democrat. Jewish. Home: Boca Raton, Fla. Died Jan. 10, 2008.

SWIDERSKI, JOZEF, forest industries consultant; b. Czortkow, Poland, Jan. 1, 1917; came to U.S., 1969; s. Alicja Krystyna Zych, July 14, 1931; 1 child, Yvonne Leutzinger. MS, Poly. U., Lvov, Poland, 1940; D of Tech. Scis., Poly. U., Gdansk, Poland, 1960. Mgr. various wood processing enterprises, Poland, 1946-52; prof. wood tech. and forest industries planning Poly U., Gdansk, 1950-60; head dept. tech. and devel. Ministry of Forest Industries, Warsaw, Poland, 1953-65; chief mech. wood products divsn. Food and Agr. Orgn. UN, Rome, 1966-79; cons. Internat. Forest Industries Consultants, Darien, Conn., from 1980. Gen. sec., organizer internat. symposia including World Consultation on Wood Based Panels, FAO, New Delhi, 1976, Internat. Symposium on Use of Wood in Housing, Vancouver, B.C., 1970; work on a variety of forest industries projects in over 40 countries in all major regions of the world. Author: Technology of Cooperage Production, 1963, rev. edit., 1966; contbr. articles to profl. jours. Mem. adv. bd. Wood Tech. Inst. Mich. Tech. U., Houghton, 1990—. Home: Skillman, NJ. Died Apr. 6, 2008.

SWIHART, FRED JACOB, lawyer; b. Park Rapids, Minn., Aug. 19, 1919; s. Fred and Elizabeth Pauline (Judnitsch) S.; m. Edna Lillian Jensen, Sept. 30, 1950; 1 child; Frederick Jay. BA, U. Nebr., 1949, JD, 1954; M in Russian Lang., Middlebury Coll., 1950; grad., U.S. Army Command and Staff Coll., 1965. Bar: Nebr. 1954, U.S. Dist. Ct. Nebr. 1954, U.S. Ct. Appeals (8th cir.) 1977, U.S. Supreme Ct. 1972. Claims atty. Chgo. & Eastern Ill. R.R., 1954-56; atty. Assn. Amer. R.R.s, Chgo., 1956-60; assoc. Wagener & Marx, Lincoln, Nebr., 1960-61; prosecutor City of Lincoln, 1961-68; sole practice Lincoln, from 1968. Editor Law for the Aviator, 1969-71. Served to lt. col. U.S. Army, 1943-46, ETO, Korea, ret. col., USAR, 1979. Fellow Nebr. State Bar Found.; mem. ABA, Nebr. Bar Assn., Fed. Bar Assn., Assn. Trial Lawyers Am., Am. Judicature Soc., Aircraft Owners and Pilots Assn. (legis. rep.), Nebr. Criminal Def. Attys. Assn., Nat. Assn. Criminal Def. Lawyers, Mercedes Benz Club Am., Nebr. Assn. Trial Attys., Nat. Assn. Uniformed Svcs., Res. Officers Assn., Nat. Assn. Legion of Honor, Internat. Footprint Assn., Am. Legion (adm. Nebr. Navy), Mason (knight comdr. of ct. of honor), Shriners, The Cabiri. Republican. Presbyterian. Avocations: collecting art, music, pistol competition. Died May 16, 2008.

SWOPE, FRANCES ALDERSON, retired librarian; b. Richmond, Va., Dec. 5, 1911; d. Joseph Newman and Frances (Richardson) Alderson; m. Kenneth Dabney Swope, Dec. 27, 1958; stepchildren: Jeanne Weikel, Lee Smith. BA, U. Ky., Lexington, 1933; BS in Libr. Sci., U. Ill., 1939; postgrad., U. Va., U. Mich., U. London. Tchr. Alderson (W.Va.) H.S., 1933-39; ext. libr. Circleville (Ohio) Pub. Libr., 1939-41, Kanawha County Pub. Libr., Charleston, W.Va., 1941-43; alt. custodian comdt.'s confidential and secret files 3rd Naval Dist. Hdqrs., NYC, 1943-45; cataloguer Yale U. Libr., New Haven, 1946-47; chief ext. libr. Kanawha County Pub. Libr., 1947-67; archivist Greenbrier Hist. Soc., Lewisburg, W.Va., 1969-97. Named W.Va. History Hero, 1997. Mem. Nat. Trust Historic Preservation, Nat. Soc. Colonial Dames in Am., W.Va. Libr. Assn. Lt. USNR, 1943-45. Democrat. Presbyterian. Avocation: walking. Home: Harrisonburg, Va. Died Feb. 28, 2008.

SZUJEWSKI, PHILLIP ANDREW, architect; b. Madison, Wis., Jan. 16, 1948; s. Henry A. Szujewski and Betty Jean (Smith) Traut. BArch in Design, U. Ill., Chgo., 1975; MArch in Urban Design, Harvard U., 1975. Lic. architect, Ill. Architect, designer Holabird and Root, Chgo., 1977; architect, urban designer Skidmore, Owings & Merrill, Chgo., 1978-81; v.p. planning and design City Devel. Corp., Chgo., 1981-83; v.p. bldgs. design group Reynolds, Smith & Hills, Jacksonville, Fla., 1983-87; v.p., gen. mgr. Perkins & Will, Washington, from 1987. Contbr. articles to profl. jours. Mem. Pres.'s Urban Com., Washington, 1988; bd. dirs., Get Ahead, Washington, 1988. Mem. Urban Land Inst., Nat. Assn. Corp. Real Estate Execs., AIA (nat. and regional awards), Assn. Progressive Architecture, Washington Bd. Trade, Congl. Club, The Westin Club. Avocations: sailing, jet boat racing, exploring. Home: Washington, DC. Died Oct. 30, 2007.

TABOR, ANNA TOI GUD, retired nursing administrator; b. Pahala, Hawaii, Jan. 26, 1932; d. Kong Chem and Lim Kee (Ho) Fong; m. Alexander Yukio Ikeda, Oct. 3, 1950 (div. Oct. 1973); children: Valerie Jane Young, Peggy Ann Walter, Stephen Curtis Ikeda, Alexander Ikeda Jr. (dec.); m. James Edward Tabor, Aug. 1, 1980; stepchildren: Lisa Gay Conner, Lori Elizabeth Adcock. AA, Coffeyville Coll., 1952; BSN, Washington U., St. Louis, 1956, MSN, 1959. Diplomate Am. Bd. Quality Assurance & Utilization Rev. From head nurse surg. to quality improvement asst. dir. Barnes Hosp., St. Louis, 1959-94, ret., 1994. Co-leader med. explorer post Barnes Hosp., St. Louis; established Anna Ikeda-Tabor Rsch. scholar by Barnes Hosp. Adminstrs., 1994—; lectr., cons. in field. Active Mo. Botanical Garden, St. Louis. Named Outstanding Womans Double Century Cyclist, Am. Youth Hostel, 1977. Mem. Albert Einstein Soc., St. Louis Transport Mus. Assn., St. Louis Zoo Friends Assn., United Way Alexis de Tocqueville Soc., Sigma Theta Tau. Avocations: travel, cooking, biking, reading, gardening. Home: High Ridge, Mo. Died Mar. 27, 2008.

TAFF, CLYDE L., health facility administrator, consultant; b. Seymour, Iowa, July 3, 1924; s. Charles Riley and Maude (Nimocks) T.; m. Mary Lewis, July 1, 1950; children: Toni, David, Patricia. BS, U. Mo., 1948; MA, U. Colo., 1965. Cert. tchr. (life); lic. health care facility adminstr. Tchr. Princeton (Mo.) High Sch., 1948-51; tchr., adult and secondary Leon (Iowa) Pub. Sch., 1952-65; exec. dir. South Cen. Iowa Community Action, Leon, from 1966-; bd. pres. Westview Acres Care Ctr., Leon, 1966-73; bd. pres., owner Eastview Manor Care Ctr., Trenton, Mo., from 1967-; bd. pres. Princeton Care Ctr., from 1977-. Bd. dirs. State Private Industry Coun., Des Moines, 1978-83, Area XIV Private Industry Coun., Creston, 1984--, Decatur County Hosp., Bd., Leon, 1960-75; chmn. Decatur County Cancer Crusade, 1967. Sgt. USN, 1944-45. Mem. Iowa Assn. of Community Action Dirs. (pres. 1969), Region VII Community Action Dirs. (pres. 1970), Nat. Assn. of Community Action (bd. dirs. 1971), Leon Golf and Country club, Mo. Health Care Assn., Masons, Am. Legion. Avocations: golf, boating, skiing, travel. Home: Leon, Iowa. Died Sept. 10, 2007.

TAIT, AVIS RODNESS, psychiatric social worker; b. Clarkfield, Minn., Dec. 20, 1934; d. Clarence Wilfred and Irene (Christensen) Rodness; m. Kevin Spottiswoode Tait; children: Christopher, Timothy, Andrew, Matthew. BA, Augustana Coll., 1956; special cert., U. Oslo, Norway, 1956; MA, U. Chgo., 1959. Social worker Family Svc. Assn., Boston, 1959-63; chief social worker Language & Cognitive Devel. Ctr., Boston, 1977-81; group leader Parents with Toddlers, Brookline, Mass., from 1982; social worker Community Therapeutic Day Sch., Brookline, from 1981; pvt. practice Lexington, Mass., from 1982. Chairperson Commn. Temp. Ret. Social Workers, Boston, 1963-65; pres. PTA, Hancock, Lexington, 1979-80, PTA Lexington High Sch., 1982; precinct rep. Coun. Citizens for Lexington Pub. Schs., 1982-85. Recipient scholarship Norwegian Shipbuilders Assn., Oslo, 1956. Mem. Nat. Assn. Social Workers, Acad. Clin. Social Workers. Avocations: tennis, amateur theater, music, literary club. Home: Lexington, Mass. Died May 11, 2008.

TAKAHASHI, YASUO, psychiatrist; b. Sydney, Oct. 8, 1925; came to U.S., 1953; s. Goro and Chiyoko (Takekawa) T.; children: Nancy, Ken, Suzanne, Denise, Joy. Diploma, Shizuoka U., Japan, 1948; MD, Chiba U. Sch. of Medicine, Japan, 1952; postgrad., U. Pa. Diplomate Am. Bd. Psychiatry and Neurology 1960. Chief resident Dept. Psychiatry Med. Coll. of Va., Richmond, 1956-57; sr. psychiatrist Springfield Hosp. Ctr., Sykesville, Md., 1957-63; dir. Bur. Mental Health Prince Georges County Health Dept., Cheverly, Md., 1963-70; asst. prof. psychiatry Johns Hopkins U., 1971-82; med. dir. Team C, Adult Mental Health Clinic Dept. Addictions, Mental Health Svcs., Montgomery County, Md., 1989-91; med. dir. Mental Health Clinic, Kent County, Md., 1991-96; pvt. practice psychiatry, 1964-91. Mem. AMA, Am. Psychiat. Assn., Am. Soc. Clin. Hyponosis. Home: Chestertown, Md. Died Jan. 27, 2009.

TAKASUGI, ROBERT MITSUHIRO, federal judge; b. Tacoma, Sept. 12, 1930; s. Hidesaburo and Kayo (Otsuki) T.; m. Dorothy O. Takasugi; children: Jon Robert, Lesli Mari. BS, UCLA, 1953; LLB, JD, U. So. Calif., 1959. Bar: Calif. bar 1960. Practiced law, Los Angeles, 1960-73; judge East Los Angeles Municipal Ct., 1973-75, adminstrv. judge, 1974, presiding judge, 1975; judge Superior Ct., County of Los Angeles, 1975-76, US Dist. Ct. (ctrl. dist.) Calif., 1976—96, sr. judge, 1996—2009. Nat. legal counsel Japanese Am. Citizens League; guest lectr. law seminars Harvard U. Law Sch. Careers Symposium; commencement spkr.; mem. Legion Lex U. So. Calif. Law Ctr.; mem. Civil Justice Reform Act and Alt. Dispute Resolution Com., mem. Adv. Com. on Codes of Conduct of the Jud. Conf. of the U.S., 1987-92, Code of Conduct of Judges. Mem. editorial bd. U. So. Calif. Law Rev., 1959; contbr. articles to profl. jours. Calif. adv. com. Western Regional Office, U.S. Commn. on Civil Rights, 1983-85; chmn. blue ribbon com. for selection of chancellor L.A. C.C. With U.S. Army, 1953-55. Harry J. Bauer scholar, 1959; recipient U.S. Mil. Man of Yr. award for Far East Theater U.S. Army, 1954, Jud. Excellence award Criminal Cts. Bar Assn., Disting. Svc. award Asian Pacific Ctr. and Pacific Clinics, 1994, Freedom award Sertoma, 1995, Pub. Svc. award Asian Pacific Am. Legal Ctr. So. Calif., 1995, cert. of merit Japanese-Am. Bar Assn., Lifetime Achievement award, 2000, Trailblazer award So. Calif. region NAPABA, 1995, Spl. award Mex.-Am. Bar Assn., 1996, Spirit of Excellence award ABA, 1998, Pub. Svc. award Japanese Am. Citizens League, 1999, lifetime achievement award Japanese-Am. Bar Assn., 2000, PACE-Setter award Pacific Asian Consort. in Employment, 2003, Individual Diversity award State Bar Calif., 2004; named Judge of Yr. Century City Bar Assn.,

1995. Mem. U. So. Calif. Law Alumni Assn. (dir.), Criminal Cts. Bar Assn. (Jud. Excellence award 2002, Jud. Courage award 2003). Died Aug. 4, 2009.

TALBOT, DOROTHY MCCOMB, public health nurse and consultant; b. Hurley, N.Mex., Aug. 18, 1918; d. Parker Deems and Mildred (Willcox) McComb; m. Raymond James Talbot, Aug. 1, 1940 (dec. Apr. 1991); children: Raymond James Jr., Patricia Martin, Betty Sue. BSN, Tex. Women's U., 1945; MA, Columbia U., 1958; MPH, Tulane U., 1964, PhD, 1970. RN, N.C. Sch. nurse Tex. Women's U., Denton, 1939-40; dir. nursing Ruston (La.) Hosp., 1946-50; pub. health nurse Lincoln County, Ruston, 1952-57; instr. La. State U., New Orleans, 1958-62; chair pub. health nursing Tulane U., New Orleans, 1962-74; chair pub. health U. N.C., Chapel Hill, 1974-84. Cons. throughout U.S.; leader overseas workshops Profl. Seminar Cons., U. N.Mex., 1982, 85, 88. Recipient Meritorious award La. Pub. Health Assn., 1973, So. Health Assn., 1978. Fellow APHA (Disting. Pub. Health Nurse award 1984), Am. Acad. Nursing; mem. ANA, Sigma Theta Tau. Democrat. Episcopalian. Avocations: camping, hiking, golf. Home: Surprise, Ariz. Died July 10, 2008.

TALLENT, JIMMY ARNOLD, insurance executive; b. Gladewater, Tex., Sept. 7, 1935; s. Arnold Roy and Edna Jewel (Snyder) T.; m. Rose Marie Erwin; children: Timothy A., James R., Deborah K. A, Kilgore Jr. Coll., 1956; BS, Stephen F. Austin Coll., 1960. CLU. Gen. agt. USLife Life Ins. Co., Tyler, Tex., from 1960. Mem. Million Dollar Round Table, Tex., 1970—, Tex. Leaders Round Table, 1970—. Pres. Smith County Cancer Soc., Tyler, 1977, Heart Assn., 1975; state dir. Life Underwriter Polit. Action, 1975-85, Tex. Assn. Life Underwriters, 1984-86. Mem. Tyler Assn. Life Underwriters, Tyler Met. YMCA (2d. v.p., 1987, mem. chmn. 1970-72), Tyler Area C. of C. (edn. chmn. 1980), Sales Mktg. Exec. (pres. 1978-80). Mem. First Christian Ch. Lodge: Sharon Temple. Home: Tyler, Tex. Died Jan. 7, 2008.

TALLEY, DORIS LANIER, instructional technology specialist; b. Asheboro, NC, Aug. 21, 1949; d. James Wayne and Edith (Dunning) L.; m. Wayne F. Talley, Nov. 15, 1970; children: A. Suzanne Talley Hawkins, Elizabeth Crystal Talley. BS in Elem. Edn., Appalachian State U., 1971; MLS, U. N.C., Greensboro, 1979. Cert. tchr., media specialist, N.C. Classroom tchr. Randolph County Schs., Asheboro, N.C., 1971-83, media coord., 1983-99, instrnl. tech. specialist, from 1999. In-service instr. for Asheboro City and Randolph County tchrs., 1990-95; instr. in computer operation, Randolph C.C., Asheboro, N.C., 1996-97. Story Teller Seagrove (N.C.) Country Days, 1996, Randolph County (N.C.) Pub. Libr., various civic events, Asheboro, 1995-96. Mem. N.C. Assn. for Ednl. Comms. and Tech. (conf. presenter 1995), N.C. Libr. Assn. (conf. presenter 1988, 98), Delta Kappa Gamma (Delta Nu chpt.). Democrat. Methodist. Avocations: reading, story telling, exercise and fitness, travel. Home: Asheboro, NC. Died Feb. 27, 2008.

TALLMAN, ROBERT HALL, investment company executive; b. Creston, Iowa, Aug. 10, 1915; s. Ralph H. and Hazel Verne (Hall) T.; m. Elizabeth Childs, Sept. 19, 1938; children: Susan, Mary, Timothy. BS, U. Nebr., 1937. Trainee to dist. mgr. Firestone Tire & Rubber Co., Akron, Ohio, 1937-50; pres. Tallman Oil Co., Fargo, ND, 1950-80; chmn. bd. State Bank of Hawley, Minn., 1966-70, 1st Nat. Bank of Barnesville, Minn., 1965-88; pres. Tallman Investment Ent., Fargo, from 1980; pres., dir. Dak Tech. Inc. Dir. Bell Farms. Past pres. Fargo Bd. Edn., N.D. Petroleum Coun.; past pres. St. Lukes Hosp. Assn.; past chmn. trustees 1st Congl. Ch. of Fargo; trustee U. Nebr. Found., 1987—. Mem. Fargo C. of C. (past pres.), Am. Assn. Ret. Persons, Nat. Rifle Assn., N.D. State U. Teammakers Club (past pres.), Fargo Country Club, Kiwanis (past pres.), Masons, Shriners, Elks. Republican. Congregationalist. Avocations: golf, hunting, fishing, travel, photography. Died Nov. 26, 2007.

TAMKIN, ARTHUR S., psychologist; b. Montgomery, Ala., July 13, 1928; s. Sheer Sam Tamkin and Bertha (Hirsch) Sofness; m. Ruth Helen Goldberg, Feb. 12, 1950; children: Laura, Andrea, Jill, Roy. AB, Harvard U., 1950; PhD, Duke U., 1954; post doctoral study, Augusta State U., from 1990. Cert. applied psychologist, Ga. Clin. psychologist VA Med. Ctr., Northampton, Mass., 1954-58; rsch. project dir. Dept. Mental Hygiene, Columbus, Ohio, 1958-59; chief psychologist VA Clinic, Hosp., Providence, R.I., 1960-73, Fuller Meml. Hosp., South Attleboro, Mass., 1973-79; psychologist Data Gen. Corp., Westboro, Mass., 1979-80; chief clin. psychologist VA Med. Ctr., Augusta, Ga., 1980-90; cons. Augusta Cor. Med. Inst., Grovetown, Ga., 1993; psychologist First Mental Health, Nashville, Tenn., from 1994. Clin. psychologist pvt practice, Providence, R.I., 1959-79. Contbr. articles to Jour. Clin. Psychol., Psychol. Reports, Mil. Medicine. Mem. Augusta Area Psychol. Assn. Avocations: tennis, badminton, marksmanship, gardening, bridge. Home: Augusta, Ga. Died Dec. 25, 2007.

TANAKA, TOGO WILLIAM, retired real estate and financial executive; b. Portland, Oreg., Jan. 7, 1916; s. Masaharu and Katsu (Iwatate) Tanaka; m. Jean Miho Wada, Nov. 14, 1940; children: Jeannie, Christine, Wesley. AB cum laude, UCLA, 1936. Chmn. Gramercy Enterprises, LA; dir. T.W. Tanaka Co. Inc., LA Wholesale Produce Market Devel. Corp., 1979—89, Fed. Res. Bank, San Francisco, 1979—89; editor Calif. Daily News, 1935—36, LA Japanese Daily News, 1936—42; documentary historian War Relocation Authority, Manzanar, Calif., 1942; staff mem. Am. Friends Svc. Com., Chgo., 1943—45; editor to head publs. divsn. Am. Tech. Soc., 1945—52; pub. Chgo. Pub. Corp., 1952—56, Sch. Indsl. Press Inc., LA, 1956—60; city commr. Cmty. Redevel. Agy., LA, 1973—74; mem. adv. bd. Calif. 1st Bank, LA, 1976—78; bd. dirs. Meth. Hosp., Calif., 1978—93. Co-author (with Frank K. Levin): English Composition and Rhetoric, 1948; co-author: (with Dr. Jean Bordeaux) How to Talk More Effectively, 1948; co-author: (with Alma Meland) Easy Pathways in English, 1949. Bd. dirs. Goodwill Industries Southern Calif.; active mem. Nat. Strategy Info. Ctr. NY, Nat. Wellness Cmty., Western Justice Ctr. Found.; chmn. LA Chpt. Nat. Safety Coun.; mem., citizens mgmt. rev. com. LA Unified Sch. Dist., 1976—77; trustee Whittier Coll., Wilshire United Meth. Ch., 1976—78, Calif. Acad. Decathlon, 1978—81; adv. bd. YMCA Met. LA, 1977—91, Boy Scouts Am. Coun., 1980—86, Visitors and Conv. Bur., 1984—88, Am. Heart Assn., 1984—88, New Bus. Achievement Inc.; adv. coun. to assessor, LA county, 1981—84; mem. adv. coun. Calif. World Trade Commn., 1986—87. Recipient Merit award, Soc. Advancement Mgmt., 1950, Mag. award, Inst. Graphic Arts, 1953, 1st award, Internat. Coun. Indsl. Editors, 1955, UNESCO Literacy award, 1954, LA Archbishop's Ecumenical award, 1986, Frances Larkin award, ARC, 1993, Spirit of Wellness award, 1995. Mem.: Japan-Am. Soc. Southern Calif. (coun. mem. 1960—78), LA Area C. of C. (dir. 1975—77), Rotary (dir., pres., LA club 1983—84, Svc. award 1995), Masons, Shriners, Lincoln Club, LA Athletic Club, Pi Gamma Mu, Pi Sigma Alpha, Phi Beta Kappa. Home: Los Angeles, Calif. Died May 21, 2009.

TANCK, JAMES ROBERT, public works executive, consultant; b. Merrill, Wis., Apr. 8, 1944; s. Alfred Emil and Margaret Irene (Gaedeke) T.; m. Judith Ann Nilson, Aug. 14, 1965 (div. June 1973); m. Glenda Sue Harris, Sept. 20, 1987; children: Adrianne, Allison. BA, Mich. State U., 1966, MA, 1968. Instr., dir. Office Student Affairs Mich. State U., East Lansing, 1966-69; spl. asst. to sec. U.S. Dept. Housing & Urban Devel., Washington, 1969-70; dir. spl. program OEO, Washington, 1970-71; exec. dir. rent stabilization Cost of Living Coun., Washington, 1971-73; pres. Nat. Apt. Assn., Washington, 1973-74; sr. assoc. Kappa Systems, Inc., Arlington, Va., 1974-75; dir. bldg. programs U.S. Dept. Energy, Washington, 1975-81; v.p. Perdido Bay Resort, Pensacola, Fla., 1982-83; pres. Fla. Community Svcs. Corp., from 1984. Cons. Fla. Community Svcs. Corp., Walton County, Santa Rosa Beach, Fla., 1985—; pres. South santa Rosa Utilities, Gulf Breeze, Fla., 1989—. Author: Volunteerism, Helping People Help Themselves, 1981. Vice pres. Fla.'s Jr. Miss, Pensacola, 1988; trustee State Hist. Preservation Bd., Tallahassee, 1988—; pres. Pensacola Heritage Found., 1988, Fiesta of Five Flags, Pensacola, 1990, 91. Mem. Blue Key Soc., Tiger Bay, Rotary. Republican. Presbyterian. Home: Pensacola, Fla. Died Dec. 15, 2007.

TANEN, NED STONE, former film company executive; b. L.A., Sept. 20, 1931; m. Max Tanen (div.); children: Sloane, Tracy; m. Kitty Hawks (div.); m. Nancy Graham. BA in Internat. Rels., UCLA, 1954. Agent MCA Inc., Universal City, 1954, v.p., 1967, MCATTV, 1964-67; founder UNI Records, later MCA Records, 1967; exec. v.p. Universal City Records, Calif., 1967-69; pres. Universal Theatrical Motion Pictures divsn., 1976, Universal Pictures, 1979-82; ind. prodr., 1982; pres. motion picture group Paramount Pictures, 1984—88, cons., 1988—92; prodr. Sony Pictures Entertainment, 1992. Exec. prodr.: (films) Sixteen Candles, 1984, St. Elmo's Fire, 1985; prodr.: The Breakfast Club, 1985, Guarding Tess, 1994, Cops and Robbersons, 1994, Mary Reilly, 1996. Served with USAF, 1950-52. Died Jan. 5, 2009.

TANENHAUS, ROBERT GARY, information systems executive; b. Longbranch, NJ, Mar. 15, 1946; s. Abraham M. and Hilda Tanenhaus. BA in Liberal Arts, Ohio State U., 1967; MS in Urban and Regional Planning, Pratt Inst., 1972; postgrad., George Washington U., 1983-85. Lic. profl. planner, N.J. Urban and regional planner Regional Planning Orgns., NYC, 1969-70; dir. various offices and tech. mgmt. program N.Y.C. Govt., 1971-78, spl. asst. 1st dep. mayor, 1977-78; prin. adminstr. Orgn. Econ. Coop. and Devel., Paris, 1978-80; v.p., cons. Gordian Assocs., Cons., Washington, 1980-85; adj. asst. prof. George Washington U., 1985-90; pres. Info. Mgmt. Internat. Inc., Washington, from 1985. Advisor Nat. Transp. Consortium of States, Birmingham, Ala., 1992-98, U.S. Congressman, Washington, 1995—; cons., advisor U.S. Dep. Transp., Washington, 1993-98, U.S. Dept. Health and Human Svcs., Washington, 1993-95. Contbr. articles to profl. jours. Mem. AFCEA. Achievements include development of co-generation, energy-from-waste and solar energy projects, national energy plans, policies and models, national economic models, and information technology plans, policies and systems, currently work with smart sensor systems, image management and a laser-generated x-ray system. Home: Washington, DC. Died Apr. 20, 2008.

TANNENBAUM, HARVEY, defense technology consultant; b. NYC, June 26, 1923; s. Alfred and Ida (Kolbe) T.; m. Mildred Cohen, July 4, 1946; children: David Bruce, Mark Scott, Lynne Ellen. BS, NYU, 1946; postgrad., George Washington U., 1963-64. Chemist U.S. Army Chem. R & D Ctr., Aberdeen Proving Ground, Md., 1949-62, chief remote sensing, 1962-79; prin. staff engr. Honeywell, Inc., Clearwater, Fla., 1979-84; cons. Reistertown, Md., 1984—85; sr. program dir. SRI, Internat., 1985—88. Cons. EPA, CIA, Arms Control and Disarmament Agy., USAF, 1962-79; group chmn. NATO panel of experts on laser monitoring of atmosphere, Norway, 1976. Contbr. articles to profl. jours.; patentee in field. Served to cpl. USAF, 1942-45, ETO. Mem. Optical Soc. Am., Internat. Soc. Optical Engring., Infrared Symposia, Sigma Xi. Jewish. Achievements include patents in field; specializing in detection of chem-bio warfare agents. Avocations: bridge, photography. Died 2009.

TASHER, JACOB, otolaryngologist; b. Jerusalem, May 1, 1945; came to U.S., 1974; s. Avraham and Sarah T.; m. Patricia Monica Osores, Feb. 20, 1980 (div. May 1990); children: Maya, Avi, Aryeh; m. Debra Rachel Mock, July 23, 1995; 1 child, Charles-Alec. MD, Sackler Sch. Medicine, Tel Aviv, Israel, 1972. Diplomate Am. Bd. Otolaryngology. Pvt. practice, Covington, La., 1978-87; chief ear, nose, throat dept. Gallup (N. Mex.) Indian Med. Ctr., 1988-90, Walson Army Cmty. Hosp., Fort Dix, N.J., 1991-92; pvt. practice Amsterdam, N.Y., from 1992. Major M.C., U.S. Army, 1990-91, Saudi Arabia (Desert Storm). Recipient Army Commendation medal U.S. Army, 1991. Fellow Am. Acad. Otolaryngology, Head & Neck Surgery; mem. AMA, Am. Rhinological Soc., Am. Acad. Otolaryngic Allergy, Med. Soc. State N.Y. Avocations: tennis, swimming, travel, concerts, operas. Home: Slingerlands, NY. Died Nov. 7, 2007.

TATUM, WILBERT ARNOLD, editor, publisher; b. Durham, NC, Jan. 23, 1933; s. Eugene Malcolm Tatum and Mittie Novesta (Spell) Tatum-Smith; m. Susan Kohn, June 17, 1966; 1 child, Elinor Ruth. BS, Lincoln U., 1972; MS, Occidental Coll., 1972; DHL (hon.), Coll. Human Svcs., NYC, 1988. Dep. pres. Borough of Manhattan, NYC, 1970-71; dir. planning & devel. NYC, 1971-77; sr. v.p. Health Ins. Plan of Greater N.Y., NYC, 1978-86; editor, pub., CEO NY Amsterdam News, NYC, 1983—98. Vice chmn. Inner City Broadcasting, N.Y.C., 1970-73; chmn. bd. Tatum-Kohn Assn., N.Y.C., Amnews Corp., NYC, Palisades Amsterdam Comm. Cpl. USMC, 1951-54, Far East. Fellow Nat. Urban Fellows, 1971-72; recipient Lifetime Achievement award for Print Journalism, NY Assn. Black Journalists, 2008 Mem. Nat. Newspaper Pubs. Assn. (bd. dirs.), N.Y. Urban League (Bldg. brick 1993), Wallenberg Com. of U.S. (v.p.). Democrat. Baptist. Home: New York, NY. Died Feb. 26, 2009.

TAYLOR, BLANCHE MURRAY, organist; b. Phila., Aug. 23, 1927; d. James Andrew and Anna Delores (Best) Murray; widowed; 1 child, Renee Phillips. Student, Settlement Music Sch., Phila., 1945-48, Zechwer Hahn's Conservatory, 1948-51. Cert. med. adminstr. Organist Reunion Choir of Phila., from 1989; ch. organist, dir. Oak Grove Bapt. Ch., Phila., 1990-95; ch. organist Trinity AME Ch., Phila., from 1995. Composer, arranger Spiritual Medley, 1996; singer Tomlin Accapella Choir, Phila., Famous Ward Singers, Phila., Willettes, Phila., 1945-49. Recipient citation City Coun. Phila., Presdl. acknowledgment for 50 yrs. as ch. organist, 1993. Mem. Nat. Assn. Negro Musicians. Mem. AME Ch. Avocation: window shopping. Home: Philadelphia, Pa. Died May 14, 2008.

TAYLOR, DAVID, banker; b. Derby, Iowa, July 10, 1928; s. Carl E. and Erma Zoe (McMains) T.; m. Ruth Grady, Aug. 5, 1956; children: Cynthia Taylor Benson, John D., Jeffrey W. BS, State U. Iowa, 1950. CPA, Iowa. Sr. acct. Ernst & Ernst, Des Moines, 1952-59; treas. Stephens Industries, Inc., Des Moines, 1959-63; pres. 1st Fed. State Bank, Des Moines, 1963-74, Hawkeye Bancorp Investment Mgmt., Inc., Des Moines, 1974-76, Iowa Trust and Savs. Bank, Centerville, from 1976. Bd. dirs., prs. Appanoose Profl. Mgmt., Inc., Centerville, 1989—. Bd. dirs., treas. Appanoose Indsl. Corp., Centerville, 1984—. Named Citizen of Yr., Ad-Express and Iowegian, Centerville, 1983. Republican. Methodist. Avocations: golf, reading, walking. Died Feb. 23, 2009.

TAYLOR, DAVID GEORGE, retired banker; b. Charlevoix, Mich., July 29, 1929; s. Frank Flagg and Bessie (Strayer) Taylor; m. Robyne T. McCarthy, July 28, 1990; children from previous marriage: David, Amy, Jeanine. BS, Denison U., 1951; MBA, Northwestern U., 1953. With Continental Ill. Nat. Bank and Trust Co. Chgo., 1958—86, asst. cashier, 1961—64, 2d v.p., 1964—66, v.p., 1966—72, sr. v.p., 1972—74, exec. v.p., 1974—80, exec. v.p., treas., 1980—83, vice chmn., 1983—84, chmn., CEO, 1984; vice chmn. Irving Trust Co., NYC, 1986—89; group exec. Chem. Bank, NYC, 1989—94; ret., 1994. Mem. Dealer Bank Assn. Com. on Glass-Steagall Reform, 1985—86; bd. dirs. CNA Income Shares. Author: Bajan's Tale, 2005. Bd. dirs. Evanston Hosp., Glenbrook Hosp.; trustee Art Inst. Chgo., 1981—86; advisor J.L. Kellogg Grad. Sch. Mgmt., Northwestern U., from 1984. Served to lt. USN, 1953—56. Mem.: Assn. Ret. City Bankers (asset/liability com., govt. rels. com. from 1983), Govt. and Fed. Agys. Securities Com. (chmn. bd. dirs. 1982—83), Pub. Securities Assn. (chmn. 1977, bd. dirs. 1977—78, treas. 1978). Republican. Presbyterian. Died Feb. 23, 2009.

TAYLOR, DAVID NEIL, minister; b. Tampa, Fla., Feb. 15, 1954; s. O.L. Zack and Bessie Nell (Miley) T.; m. Laura Nanette Thompson, Oct. 29, 1977; children: Jonathan, Stephen, Christina. Student, U. So. Miss., 1972-75. Ordained to ministry Bapt. Ch., 1973. Youth pastor Ridgecrest Bapt. Ch., Hattiesburg, Miss., 1969-70; assoc. minister Big Level Bapt. Ch., Wiggins, Miss., 1971-74, Glendale United Meth. Ch., Hattiesburg, 1975; sr. pastor New Christian

Fellowship, Port Gibson, Miss., 1976-83, Word of Life Ch., Auburn, 1983, The Storehouse Ch., Hattiesburg, 1984-94; founder, pres. David Taylor Ministries, from 1976. Founder Youth Leadership Camps, 1979—, Nat. Intercessors Congress, 1981; officer, mem. exec. coun. Internat. Congress Local Chs., Washington, 1988—; vice chmn. Azusa Fellowship of Chs. and Ministries, 1993-94, bd. dirs., 1995-96. Pastor's coun. Ams. for Robertson, Miss. Chpt., 1987-88; state rep. Christian Coalition, 1991. Named to Outstanding Young Men of Am., 1986, Key to the City Sulphur, La., 1997. Home: Coral Springs, Fla. Died July 13, 2008.

TAYLOR, HELEN BERNELL, professional society administrator; b. Stillwater, Okla., Sept. 23, 1921; d. Murry B. and Mamie E. (Fowler) Finch; m. John L. Duroy, Feb. 2, 1940 (div. Sept. 1959); 1 child, Johnita H. Duroy; m. Fritz J. Hoeflein Jr., Apr. 14, 1962 (dec. Nov. 1968); stepchildren: Fritz J. III, Charles Ray, Monty Aaron; m. Dan L. Taylor, June 18, 1971; stepchildren: Rheta Joiner, Dan L. Jr. Student, Okla. U., 1966, Cen. State U., Edmond, Okla., 1969-70. Co-owner Duroy Real Estate, Ponca City, Okla., 1947-59; real estate salesperson various firms, Midwest City, Okla., 1965-68; exec. v.p. Mid-Del Bd. Realtors, Inc., Midwest City, Okla., 1969-89; real estate broker Glenn E. Breeding Co., Midwest City, Okla., from 1989. Officer Mid-Del Community Housing and Resources Bd., 1975—; mem. Okla. Bd. Pvt. Schs., Oklahoma City, 1981—, Midwest City Econ. Devel. Commn., 1985-89. Mem. Mid-Del Bd. Realtors (Extra Mile award 1976, Realtor of Decade 1978), Midwest City C. of C. (bd. dirs. 1984—), Del City C. of C., Mid-Del 100 Club, Women's Coun. Realtors (various offices, Woman of Yr. 1982), Epsilon Sigma Alpha (v.p. Delta Chi chpt. 1989—, 35 yr. svc. award 1989), Pythian Sisters (grand chief 1947). Democrat. Mem. Christian Ch. (Disciples Of Christ). Avocations: music, travel, bowling. Home: Oklahoma City, Okla. Died Feb. 22, 2008.

TAYLOR, IRVING, mechanical engineer, consultant; b. Schenectady, NY, Oct. 25, 1912; s. John Bellamy and Marcia Estabrook (Jones) T.; m. Shirley Ann Milker, Dec. 22, 1943; children: Bronwen D., Marcia L., John I., Jerome E. BME, Cornell U., 1934. Registered profl. engr., N.Y., Mass., Calif. Test engr. Gen. Electric Co., Lynn, Mass., 1934-37; asst. mech. engr. M.W. Kellogg Co., NYC, 1937-39; sect. head engring. dept. The Lummus Co., NYC, 1939-57; research engr. Gilbert and Barker, West Springfield, Mass., 1957-58, Marquardt Corp., Ogden, Utah, 1958-60, Bechtel, Inc., San Francisco, 1960-77; cons. engr. Berkeley, Calif., 1977-91. Adj. prof. Columbia U., 1950-60, NYU, 1950-60. Contbr. articles to profl. jours. Fellow ASME (life, Henry R. worthington medal 1990); mem. Pacific Energy Assn., Soaring Soc. Am. (life), Sigma Xi (assoc.). Unitarian Universalist. Avocations: sailplane soaring, skiing, lawn bowling. Home: San Rafael, Calif. Died June 9, 2008.

TAYLOR, KOKO, singer; b. Memphis, Sept. 28, 1928; m. Robert "Pops" Taylor (dec.). Singer: (albums) I Got What It Takes, 1975, The Earthshaker, 1978, From the Heart of a Woman, 1981, Queen of the Blues, 1985, Live from Chgo.: An Audience with the Queen, 1987, Jump for Joy, 1990, Force of Nature, 1993, Royal Blue, 2000, Deluxe Edition, 2002, Old School, 2007. Recipient Legend of Yr., Clearly Canadian, 1993, Howlin' Wolf award, 1996, Outstanding Generosity award, Children's Brittle Bone Found., 1997, Pioneer award, Rhythm & Blues Found., 2003; named to Blues Hall of Fame, 1997; Nat. Heritage Fellowship, NEA, 2004. Achievements include 2 Grammy awards, 8 Grammy nominations; March 3, 1993 declared by mayor "Koko Taylor Day" in Chgo. Died June 3, 2009.

TAYLOR, LAYNE HAROLD, pharmacist; b. Lawton, Okla., Oct. 12, 1956; s. Clinton Harold and Doris Lee (Nance) T.; m. Birgit Jacobs; 1 child, Brandon Layne. BS in Pharmacy, Okla. U., 1980. Registered pharmacist, Tex.; cert. alcohol and drug counselor. Supr. Comanche County Meml. Hosp., Lawton, Okla., 1980-82; pharmacy dir. Elk City (Okla.) Hosp., 1982-83; owner Walters (Okla.) Pharmacy, 1984-87; rancher, v.p. Lawton L-P Gas Co., Walters, Okla., from 1987. Mem. Nat. Assn. Sml. Bus., N. Am. Limousine Found., Walters C. of C., Rotary. Methodist. Avocations: skiing, hunting, counseling. Home: Walters, Okla. Died July 26, 2008.

TAYLOR, LUIS EARL, musician; b. Louisville, June 19, 1929; s. Chester Eugene and Katie Mae (Fields) T.; divorced; children: Sharnese, Michael, Luis, Kimberly. Cert. mortician. Drummer with Lionel Hampton, Gene Ammons, Sonny Stitts, Johny Griffin, King Kolax, Chgo., Coleman Hawkins, Wild Bill Davis, Roy Eldrige, Grant Green, George Coleman, N.Y.C., Carl Ellis, Louisville, Johnny Lytel, 1952-70; house drummer Just Jazz Club, Louisville, 1987. Performer with various entertainers including Bobby Shew, James Williams, Harry Pickins, Atila Zalla, Eddie Vinson, Jimmy Rainey, Dan Bradon, Michell Hendricks, Cal Collins, 1989-90, Ann Chamberlin, Joshua Breakstone; performer Luis Taylor Jazz Ensemble, Lincoln Found. Jazz Festival; guest drummer U. Louisville Jazz Band. Mem. Elks, Masons. Democrat. Baptist. Avocations: aviation, swimming, chess. Died Sept. 24, 2007.

TAYLOR, LYNN RAMONA, communications executive; b. Buffalo, May 2, 1962; d. Raymond Jonathan and Marie (Melson) T. BA, SUNY, Buffalo, 1984, postgrad., from 1989. Editorial asst. Jour. Black Studies, 1984; customer service rep. Empire Am., 1985-87, product devel. asst., budget coord., 1987-88, adminstr. communications, from 1988. Mem. NAFE, Delta Sigma Theta. Avocations: computer programming, photography, writing plays and manuscripts. Died Sept. 4, 2007.

TAYLOR, ROBERT SAXTON, retired dean; b. Ithaca, NY, June 15, 1918; s. James Barnaby and Flora Estelle (Brown) Taylor; m. Leni Reichenberger (dec.); m. Fay Ann Golden, Aug. 22, 1998. BA, Cornell U., 1940; MS, Columbia U., 1950; MA, Lehigh U., 1954. Asst. libr., dir., info. scis. Lehigh U., Bethlehem, Pa., 1950—67; dir., libr. ctr. Hampshire Coll., Amherst, Mass., 1967—72; dean, prof. Syracuse U., Sch. of Info. Studies, Syracuse, NY, 1972—83; ret., 1983; Fulbright lectr. Delft Tekniske Hogeschole, Netherlands, 1956—57. Reviewer Nat. Sci. Found., 1965—77; com. mem. info. sci. Nat. Inst. of Heath, Bethesda, Md., 1965—76; reviewer US Office of Edn., 1970—76. Author: Making of a Library, 1972 (Am. Soc. for Info. Sci. Best Book, 1972), Value Added Processes in Information Systems, 1986. Co-founder, mem. governing com. Chamber Music Society, Bethlehem, Pa., 1952—67. With CIC US Army, 1942—47. Decorated Bronze star. Mem.: Am. Soc. for Info. Sci. (pres. 1968). Home: Syracuse, NY. Died Jan. 1, 2009.

TAYLOR, SANDRA S., critical care nurse; b. Norton, Va., Nov. 2, 1950; d. Carl Willard and Margaret Lee (Yeary) Sexton; m. Claude Wayne Taylor, Mar. 11, 1966; children: Christopher Wayne, James Byron, LisAnn Michelle. AAS, Mountain Empire Community Coll, 1983. RN, Va.; cert. critical care, instr. ACLS, BCLS. Charge nurse obstetrics, labor and delivery, nursery Lonesome Pine Hosp., Big Stone Gap, Va.; staff nurse ICU, charge nurse ICU, dir. ICU, CCU Norton (Va.) Community Hosp. Instr. EKG, Introduction to Critical Care, Hemodynamic Monitoring. Mem. Am. Assn. Critical Care Nurses (pres., bd. dirs. S.W. Va. chpt.), Am. Cancer Soc. Home: Wise, Va. Died Sept. 16, 2007.

TEAS, RICHARD HARPER, lawyer; b. Streator, Ill., Sept. 24, 1930; s. Bert H. and Audrey C. Teas; m. Janice K. Eikenmeyer, July 29, 1960 (dec.); children: Catherine L. Teas-Rogers, Amelia H. AB, U. Ill., 1957, LLB, 1960. Bar: Ill. 1960, U.S. Dist. Ct. (so. dist.) Ill. 1960. Probate adminstr. Continental Nat. Bank and Trust Co. of Chgo., 1960-66; ptnr. Tracy, Johnson, & Wilson Law Offices, Joliet, Ill., from 1966. Comdr. USNR, 1952-69. Mem. Ill. State Bar Assn. (trust and estates sect. coun., chair, 2002-03, standing com. on legislation, task force on unauthorized practice of law), Will County Bar Assn. (probate com.), Am. Coll. of Trust and Estate Counsel, Estate Planning Coun. of Greater Joliet (pres. 1976) Avocations: tennis, golf. Home: Joliet, Ill. Died Nov. 2008.

TEATOR, ROBERT HEMINGWAY, technology education educator; b. New Haven, Feb. 2, 1948; s. Harry Hemingway and Edna Madeline (Anderson) T.; m. Patricia Ann Maddaloni, June 21, 1972; children: Matthew H., Mark V., John P. BS, Cen. Conn. State U., 1969, MS, 1972. Tech. edn. educator B.F. Dodd Middle Sch., Cheshire, Conn., from 1969. Adj. mem. faculty tech. edn. Ctrl. Conn. State U., New Britain, 1973-92; mem. curriculum com. Cheshire Bd. of Edn., 1989-92; cooperating tchr. for tchr. tng. program, 1975—. Treas. com. Boy Scouts Am. Troop 92, 1987-96. Decorated Chevelier, Order of DeMolay; recipient Lord Baden Powell award Boy Scouts Am., 1990. Mem. NEA (life), Internat. Tech. Edn. Assn. (life), Conn. Tech. Assn. (life), Conn. Edn. Assn. (social chair summer workshops Hartford chpt. 1982-91), Edn. Assn. of Cheshire, New Eng. Tech. Tchr. Assn. (life), Conn. Ind. Arts Assn. (registration chair spring conv. Hartford chpt. 1970-72), New England Tech. Tchrs. Assn. (conf. registration chair 2001, v.p. from Conn.). Avocations: hunting, camping. Home: Cheshire, Conn. Died Feb. 10, 2008.

TEIGEN, JAMES ARTHUR, mechanical engineer, engineering company executive; b. Lafayette, Ind., Nov. 12, 1946; s. Harold Arthur and Patricia Jean (Magnus) T.; m. Barbara Ann Pendleton, Jan. 16, 1971; 1 child, James Michael. BSME, La. Tech. U., 1968. Registered profl. engr., Mo., Mich. Mech. engr. Black & Veatch Engrs./Architects, Kansas City, Mo., 1968-80, resident engr., 1971, project engr., 1980-82, ptnr., asst. mgr. indsl. div., project mgr., from 1982. Life-cycle cost specialist Black & Veatch, Kansas City, 1976—. Contbr. articles to Energy Conservation Waste Heat Recovery. Mem. ASME, Assn. Energy Engrs. (treas. 1982-83), Nat. Soc. Profl. Engrs., Toastmasters Internat. (adminstrv. v.p. 1982-85, 87-88), Pi Tau Sigma. Republican. Methodist. Avocations: power boating, swimming, computers, do-it-yourself projects. Home: Overland Park, Kans. Died Oct. 15, 2007.

TEILHET-FISK, JEHANNE HILDEGARDE, art historian, educator, researcher; b. Palo Alto, Calif., May 16, 1939; d. Darwin L'ora and Hildegarde Blanche (Tolman) Teilhet; m. Zachary Fisk, Apr. 22, 1979; 1 child, Samantha Jehanne Fisk. Student, U. Calif., Davis, 1957—59; BA, UCLA, 1960, MA, 1967, PhD, 1972. Curator, dept. antiquities, Jos, Nigeria, 1968; asst. prof., art history U. Calif., San Diego, 1968—80, assoc. prof., from 1980. Guest curator, mus. Gauguin's Polynesian Symbolism, Musee Gauguin, Tahiti, 1980. Author: Dimensions of Black, 1970, Dimensions of Polynesia, 1973, Interpretation of Gauguin's Polynesian Symbolism, 1983; contbr. articles to various publs. Grantee, Maytag Found., Rockefeller Found., Kress Found., Nat. Endowment for Arts, Ford Found.; Mandeville grantee, Danforth Found. and U. Calif. San Diego fellow, 1975. Democrat. Home: Tallahassee, Fla. Deceased.

TENENBAUM, JEFFREY MARK, retired school librarian; b. Phila., Apr. 10, 1945; s. Paul and Hansi (Barber) T. BA, Pa. State U., 1966; MLS, McGill U., 1968. Documents libr., then reference libr. U. Toronto Libr., Ont., Canada, 1968—72; reference libr. U. Mass. Libr., Amherst, 1973—2003; ret., 2003; reference libr. Amherst Coll. Libr., 2006—07. Vis. ref. libr. McGill U., Montreal, 1984, Nat. Libr. Can., Ottawa, Ont., 1999; mem. Info. Access Co. Acad. Libr. Product Adv. Bd., Foster City, Calif., 1992-94. Mem. Amherst Pub. Art Commn., 1994-2000; docent Nat. Yiddish Book Ctr., Amherst, 2006-. Mem. ALA, Assn. Can. Studies in U.S., Am. Coun. Que. Studies, Mid-Atlantic and New Eng. Conf. for Can. Studies (sec. 1992-96), Pioneer Valley Assn. Acad. Librs. (pres. 1989-90), Assn. Coll. and Rsch. Librs., Beta Phi Mu, Phi Alpha Theta, Pi Gamma Mu. Jewish. Home: Amherst, Mass. Died Dec. 9, 2008.

TERKEL, STUDS (LOUIS TERKEL), writer, journalist; b. NYC, May 16, 1912; s. Samuel and Anna (Finkel) T.; m. Ida Goldberg, July 2, 1939; 1 son, Dan. PhB, U. Chgo., 1932, JD, 1934; LLD (hon.), Colby Coll., 2004. Disting. Scholar in Residence, Chgo. Hist. Soc., from 1998. Stage appearances include Detective Story, 1950, A View From the Bridge, 1958, Light Up the Sky, 1959, The Cave Dwellers, 1960; moderator: (TV program) Studs Place, 1950-53, (radio programs) Wax Museum, 1945— (Ohio State Univ. award 1959, UNESCO Prix Italia award 1962), Studs Terkel Almanac, 1952—, Studs Terkel Show, Sta. WFMT-FM, Chgo.; actor: (films) Beginning to Date, 1953, Eight Men Out, 1988; (TV movies) The Dollmaker, 1984; master of ceremonies Newport Folk Festival, 1959, 60, Ravinia Music Festival, 1959, U. Chgo. Folk Festival, 1961; Author: Giants of Jazz, 1957, Division Street: America, 1967, Hard Times: An Oral History of the Great Depression, 1970, Working: People Talk about What They Do All Day and How They Feel about What They Do, 1974 (Nat. Book award nomination 1975), Talking to Myself: A Memoir of My Times, 1977, American Dreams: Lost and Found, 1980, The Good War: An Oral History of World War II (Pulitzer prize for Non-fiction, 1985), Chicago, 1986, The Great Divide: Second Thoughts On The American Dream, 1988, Race: How Blacks and Whites Think and Feel About the American Obsession, 1992, Coming of Age: The Story of Our Century by Those Who've Lived It, 1995, My American Century, 1997, The Spectator: Talk About Movies and Plays With Those Who Make Them, 1999, Will the Circle Be Unbroken: Reflections on Death, Rebirth and Hunger for a Faith, 2001, Hope Dies Last: Keeping the Faith in Difficult Times, 2003, And They All Sang: Adventures of an Electric Disc Jockey, 2005, The Studs Terkel Reader: My American Century, 2007, .S. Further Thoughts From a Lifetime of Listening, 2008; co-author: (with Sydney Lewis) Touch and Go: A Memoir, 2007; author: (plays) Amazing Grace, 1959 Named Communicator of Yr. U. Chgo. Alumni Assn., 1969; recipient Nat. Humanities Medal, 1997, George Polk Career award, 1999, Nat. Book Critics Circle Lifetime Achievement award, 2004, Elijah Paris Lovejoy award, 2004, Dayton Lit. Peace prize, 2006 Mem.: AAAL. Home: Chicago, Ill. Died Oct. 31, 2008.

TERRIS, ALBERT, metal sculptor; b. NYC, Nov. 10, 1916; s. Aaron and Fania Teraspulsky; children: Susan, Abby, David, Enoch. BSS, CCNY, 1939; postgrad., NYU Inst. Fine Arts, 1939-42. Lectr. Met. Mus. Art, 1941-42; tchr. fine arts N.Y.C. High Sch. System, 1947-54; prof. emeritus Bklyn. Coll., 1947-86. Steel sculptures include Non-Fixed Relationship, 1948, Homely Cosmology, 1948, Anti-Gravity, 1950, Giraffes, 1953, Short Art, 1953, Pro-Gravity Chains, 1956, Tools, 1956, Crushed Sculpture, 1956, Words, 1957, Discursive-Illegible-Boustrophedon, 1975, Plates of Charlemagne, 1975, Fireharps, 1975, Cycle of Life, 1977, Wipes, 1996, Quantum Photography, 1995, Meals, 1998, Visitors, 1998, Twigs Door Music, 2001; one-man shows: Saidenberg, 1955, Duveen-Graham, 1958, Carnegie Internats., 1958, 62, Bklyn. L.I. Artists Bklyn. Mus. (awarded first prize), 1960, Allan Stone, 1962, Critics Choice, 1972, Artists Space, 1975, Gloria Cortella, 1977, (retrospective) The Artist in the Civil Service Bklyn. Coll. Gallery, 1985, Queensborough C. C., 2005; exhibited in group shows at Tanager Gallery, 1952-61, Stable Anns., 1952-60, Mus. Modern Art, N.Y.C., 1962, others; represented in permanent collections: Stephen Paine, Boston, Arnold Maremont, Evanston, G. David Thompson Estate, NBC-TV, others Served with 1st Allied Airborne, 1942-45. Home: Red Bank, NJ. Died May 10, 2008.

TERZUOLI, ANDREW JOSEPH, mathematician, educator; b. Bklyn., Oct. 5, 1914; s. Joseph Nicholas and Vincenza (Poliseo) T.; m. Frances Ample, Oct. 25, 1942; children: Andrew Joseph Jr., Richard J., MaryAnn, Robert J. BS, Bklyn. Coll., 1936; MS, NYU, 1948. Instr. Poly. U., Bklyn., 1946-54, asst. prof., 1954-58, assoc. prof., 1958-64, prof., 1964-86, prof. emeritus, from 1986. Capt. USAF, 1942-46. Mem. Am. Math. Soc., Am. Meteorol. Soc., Math. Assn. Am., Inst. Math. Stats. Home: Brooklyn, NY. Died Jan. 23, 2008.

TEST, GEORGE AUSTIN, English language educator; b. Oneonta, NY, Mar. 14, 1921; s. George Wesley and Fannie (Easter) T.; m. Doris Lucille McConnell, Sept. 7, 1946; children: David Wesley, Rebecca Lynn. BA, Swarthmore Coll., 1949; MA in English, U. Pa., 1951, PhD in English, 1961. Instr. of English Allegheny Coll., 1953-60; assoc. prof. English SUNY, Oneonta, 1960-63, prof., 1963-89, chmn. English, 1970-77, prof. emeritus, from 1989. Fulbright lectr. Nat. U., Santiago, Chile, 1966-67. Founder, editor Satire Newsletter, 1963-73; editor Oneonta Retired

Faculty Newsletter, 1990—; assoc. editor Encyclopedia of American Humorists, 1988; author: Satire: Spirit and Ark, 1991; contbr. articles to profl. jours. With U.S. Army, 1943-46. Danforth summer grantee, 1963, SUNY summer rsch. grantee, 1961, 63, 77. Mem. MLA, James Fenimore Cooper Soc. (editor newsletter 1990-92). Democrat. Methodist. Home: Oneonta, NY. Died Apr. 22, 2008.

TESTA, JOSEPH B., loan officer; b. Buffalo, Dec. 8, 1954; s. Anthony Salvatore and May Louise (Tripi) T.; m. Kathleen Mary Jones, Feb. 28, 1981; 1 child, Joseph B. III. BS, SUNY, Buffalo, 1977; JD, Atlanta Law Sch., 1980; MBA, Mercer U., 1986; postgrad., Nova U., from 1987. Auditor M & T Bank, Buffalo, 1974-77, Nat. Bank of Ga., Atlanta, 1978-80; cons. Gov.'s Staff, Atlanta, 1980-83; examiner CIT Comml. Fin., Atlanta, 1983-84, BancBoston Fin., Atlanta, 1984-86, loan officer, 1986-87; ptnr. Beckett, Testa & Assocs., Norcross, Ga., from 1987. Precinct chmn. Rep. Party, Lilburn, Ga., 1986-88; mem. Civil Air Patrol, Lilburn, 1970—. Mem. Internat. Computer Assn., TI User's Group, Ga. Trial Lawyers Assn., Ga. Bar Assn., Assn. Computer Profls. Clubs: Ga. Tech. Lodges: KC (youth dir. 1984-86, Merit award 1986). Republican. Roman Catholic. Avocations: chess, computers, collect german belt buckles. Home: New Orleans, La. Died Mar. 21, 2008.

THAYER, GAYLORD BERTRAM, JR., retired electronics executive, private investor; b. Jamestown, NY, July 2, 1944; s. Gaylord Bertram and Marion Brown (Klock) T. BSME, U. Rochester, 1966; MBA, Harvard U., 1968. Asst. to contr. Teradyne, Inc., Boston, 1968-70, mgr. MIS, 1970-72, sales engr., 1972-76, product mgr., 1976-84, divsn. mgr., 1984-91, mktg. dir., 1991-98; pvt. investor, from 1998. Exec.-in-residence entrepreneurship program Babson Coll., 2003—; adv. bd. Lexent Techs., Lexington, Mass., 1999—, Simply Media Inc., Lincoln, Mass.; gubernatorial appt. to Mass. Pub. Health Coun. Policy Bd. State Dept. of Pub. Health, 2003. Bd. dirs. New Eng. divsn. Am. Cancer Soc., Boston; elected town meeting mem., 2003—; bd. trustees Boston Collegiate Charter Sch. Mem.: Nat. Assembly Am. Cancer Soc. Avocations: cooking, reading, travel, flying. Home: Wellesley, Mass. Died Feb. 27, 2008.

THEIS, PETER GEORGE, retired classicist; b. Milw., Dec. 18, 1930; s. Peter Joseph and Laura Gertrude (Kornely) T.; m. Jane Elizabeth Grattan, Aug. 12, 1961; children: Peter Leo, Paul Joseph, Mary Ellen Brune, Thomas George. BA magna cum laude, Marquette U., 1952; AM, U. Chgo., 1957. Part-time instr. U. Wis., Milw., 1956; instr. Rockhurst U., Kansas City, Mo., 1960-61; instr., then asst. prof. classics Marquette U., Milw., 1961-90; ret., 1990. Mem. edn. bd. Holy Family Cath. Ch., Whitefish Bay, Wis., 1974-75; troop fundraising chmn. Boy Scouts Am., Whitefish Bay, 1976-77; pres. Post-Polio Resource Group of Southeastern Wis., Wauwatosa, 1987, Milw. Area Latin Tchrs. Assn., 1963-64, Fox River Valley Classical Assn., Milw., 1970-71, Wis. Latin Tchrs. Assn., Milw., 1976-78. Cpl. U.S. Army, 1953-55. NEH grantee, 1973. Mem. AAUP, Am. Classical League, Am. Philological Assn., Classical Assn. of the Mid. West and South, Wis. Assn. Fgn. Lang. Tchrs. (pres. 1980-82, Recognition award 1989), Paralyzed Vets. Am. (life), Disabled Am. Vets. (life), Wis. Latin Tchrs. Assn., Marquette U. Retirees Assn. Avocations: reading, puzzles. Home: Milwaukee, Wis. Died Dec. 30, 2007.

THELEN, ROBERT FREDERICK, electrical engineer, researcher; b. Burlington, Iowa, Jan. 14, 1950; s. Arthur Francis and Carol Ann (Luling) T.; m. Laurie Jean Noble, Mar. 22, 1975; children: Jennifer Carol, Haley Marie. BS, U. Houston, 1972; BEE, U. Tex., 1979, MSE, 1997. Registered profl. engr., Tex. Plant elec. engr. Aluminum Co. of Am., Rockdale, Tex., 1979-84; rsch. engr. U. Tex. Ctr. for Electromechanics, Austin, Tex., from 1984. Patentee in field. Mem. Grace Covenant Ch., Austin. Mem. IEEE (contbr. to jour.). Home: Austin, Tex. Died Feb. 9, 2008.

THEROUX, DENNIS ROBERT, engineering executive; b. New Haven, Conn., Aug. 17, 1951; s. Theogene Charles and Theresa Cecile (La Croix) T. BA, U. Conn., 1973; MS, U. Hawaii, Mamoa, 1975; cert. in occupational, safety, health, U. New Haven, 1986-88; postgrad., Columbia Pacific U. Cert. indsl. hygienist, safety profl. Pres. Hamden (Conn.) Pest Control Co., 1975-85; pres. and chief exec. officer Theroux Engring., Hamden, from 1985. Regional producer Hartford Pub. Access TV Cable Ch. 5. Author (with others): Radon-The Invisible Threat, 1986. Sponsor St. Francis Home for Children, New Haven, 1986—; co-founder Profl. Coun. for Edn., Hadlyme, Conn., 1990. Mem. Am. Soc. Safety Engrs., Am. Industrial Hygiene Assn., Am. Mgmt. Assn. (pres. assoc. 1990—), Conn. Environ. Health Assn., Conn. Pest Control Assn. Roman Catholic. Avocations: collecting musical instruments, harley-davidson touring. Home: Hadlyme, Conn. Died Apr. 1, 2008.

THIELSCHER, KARL LEAVITT, JR., marketing director; b. Buffalo, Sept. 2, 1929; s. Karl L. and Adele (Duhrssen) T.; m. Antoinette Sandhofer, Mar. 17, 1955; 1 child, Jeffrey David. BS in Bus. Adminstrn., Dartmouth Coll., 1952. Unit mgr. Procter & Gamble, Cin., 1955-65; v.p. mktg./sales P. Ballantine & Sons, Newark, 1965-69; mgr. western div. Gallo Winery, Modesto, Calif., 1970-71; v.p. mktg./sales Lammt Winery, Bakersfield, Calif., 1971-77; dir. mktg./sales Wine Imports Am., Hawthorne, N.J., 1977-81, Giumarra Vineyards, Bakersfield, from 1981. Guest lectr. Calif. State U., Bakersfield, 1987-88. Served to lt. U.S. Army, 1953-55. Republican. Episcopalian. Avocations: sailing, tennis, skiing. Home: Bakersfield, Calif. Died Mar. 14, 2008.

THODE, SUSAN ANN, health facility manager; b. Milw., June 10, 1952; d. John William and Roberta Judith (Wright) T. Diploma, Columbia Hosp. Sch. Nursing, 1974; BS in profl. arts, Cardinal Stritch Coll., 1988. RN, Wis. Staff nurse surgery St. Mary's Hosp., Milw., edn. coord., neurosurgery-laser technician, dir. surg. svcs.; health facility staff devel. coord. Columbia Hosp., Milw. Researcher in med. lasers St. Mary's Hosp., Genesis Laser Lab. Mem. Assn. Oper. Rm. Nurses, Nat. Nursing Staff Devel. Orgn., Delta Epsilon Sigma. Home: Brown Deer, Wis. Died Oct. 5, 2007.

THOMAS, ANDREW ROBERT, urologist; b. Sharon, Pa., Dec. 31, 1940; s. Andrew Theodore and Marie Eva (Varraux) T.; m. Colleen Murray, June 9, 1962; children: David, Matthew, Cynthia, Benjamin. BS, Allegheny Coll., 1962; MD, U. Cin., 1966. Diplomate Am. Bd. Urology. Intern Hennepin County Gen. Hosp., Mpls., 1966-67; resident in urology U. Cin., 1967-71; practice medicine specializing in urology Mesa (Ariz.) Urologists P.C., from 1971; chief of staff Mesa Luth. Hosp., 1985. Fellow ACS; mem. Am. Urol. Assn., Phoenix Urol. Soc., Ariz. Urol. Soc., AMA, Assn. Clin. Urologists. Clubs: Mesa Country. Republican. Methodist. Avocations: golf, backpacking. fishing. Home: Mesa, Ariz. Died Sept. 27, 2007.

THOMAS, CHARLES ALLEN, JR., molecular biologist, educator; b. Dayton, Ohio, July 7, 1927; s. Charles Allen and Margaret Stoddard (Talbott) T.; m. Margaret M. Gay, July 7, 1951; children: Linda Carrick, Stephen Gay. AB, Princeton U., NJ, 1950; PhD, Harvard U., 1954. Rsch. scientist Eli Lilly Co., Indpls., 1954-55; NCR fellow U. Mich., Ann Arbor, 1955-57; prof. biophysics Johns Hopkins U., Balt., 1957-67; prof. biol. chemistry Med. Sch. Harvard U., Boston, 1967-78; chmn. dept. cellular biology Scripps Clinic & Rsch. Found., La Jolla, Calif., 1978-81; pres., dir. Helicon Found., San Diego, from 1981; founder, CEO The Syntro Corp., San Diego, 1981-82; founder, CEO, dir. of R & D Pantox Corp., San Diego, 1989—2002. Mem. genetics study sect. NIH, 1968-72; mem. rsch. grants com. Am. Cancer Soc., 1972-76, 79-85. Mem. editl. bd. Virology, 1967-73, Jour. Molecular Biology, 1968-72, BioPhysics Jour., 1965-68, Chromosoma, 1969-79, Analytic Biochemistry, 1970-79, Biochim Biophys. ACTA, 1973-79, Plasmid, 1977—. With USNR, 1945-46. NRC fellow, 1965-66. Mem. AAAS, Am. Acad. Arts and Scis., Am. Fedn. Biol. Chemists, Genetics Soc. Am., Am. Chem. Soc. Achievements include research in genetic and structural organization of chromosomes and development of a practical assessment of the antioxidant defense system by analytical biochemistry. Home: La Jolla, Calif. Died Mar. 10, 2009.

THOMAS, DAVID LEE, marketing professional; b. Birmingham, Ala., Jan. 21, 1962; s. Cecil David and Margaret J. (McGaughy) T. BA, U. Tenn., 1985; MBA, Mercer U., 1990. Dep. exec. dir. Southeastern Oil Marketers Assn., Atlanta, 1987-89; mktg. cons. Prudential, Atlanta, 1989-91; exec. v.p. mktg. Thomas Pub., Atlanta, from 1990. Exec. dir. Jenkins Found., Atlanta, 1989—. Author: Past to Remember, 1986 (Freedom Found. award 1986); editor Marketer mag., 1988 (Ga. Soc. Assn. Execs. 1989). Vol. ARC, Atlanta, 1986-91, instr. trainer, Knoxville, Tenn., 1985; vol. del. Dem. Nat. Conv., Atlanta, 1988; vol. Greenpeace, 1990. Recipient Freedoms Found. award, 1985. Mem. Ga. Soc. Assn. Execs. (mem. found.), Assn. MBA Execs., Soc. Descs. of George Washington's Army at Valley Forge, Sons of the Confederacy. Republican. Presbyterian. Avocations: swimming, diving, weight lifing. Died Feb. 22, 2008.

THOMAS, EDDIE, composer, recording industry executive, producer, promoter; b. Chgo., Nov. 5, 1931; s. Edward E. and Lucille Thomas; m. Verlene Lofton, Dec. 7, 1997; children: Alvin, Denise, Parrish, Robert; m. Audrey Ruth Jones, 1968 (dec. Oct. 29, 1996); 1 child, Robert. Founder, owner Dogs of War, Chgo.; founder, mgr. The Impressions, Chgo., from 1957; pres., CEO CurTom Records, Chgo., 1963—70; pres. Thomas Mktg. Pub. Co., Chgo., 1970, Thomas Assocs., Chgo., 1970—90, Thomas First Class Limo, Chgo., 1971—80; pres., CEO Thomas Prodns. LlC, Chgo., from 2000. Cons. Probation Challenge, Chgo., from 2003. Co-writer: songs Otis Redding Anthology Album "Cigarettes & Coffee", 1996, We're The New York Giants, 1987 (Gold Record, 1987), 1994 George Foster Peabody award (documentary), The Rise and Fall of Vee-Jay Records, 1979 Invited to The White House by Pres. Jimmy Carter. Recipient Membership award, Chgo. Tourism, 1970, Cert. award, Cook County Sheriff Dept., 1980, award, History Makers, Chgo., 2000, Black Music award, Nat. Newspapers Pubs. Assn., 2005, Hall of Fame Achievement award, Wendell Phillips Acad., Chgo., 2006. Achievements include producer and promoter of many hit records and artists including Ray Charles, Barry White, Qunicy Jones, The Stylistics and Johnny Talyor. Avocations: exercise, travel. Home: Chicago, Ill. Died May 31, 2008.

THOMAS, GAYLE ELAINE, trade company executive; b. Independence, Mo., Oct. 17, 1946; d. James Morris and Thelma (Juanita) T.; m. Gerald Ernest Bell (div. 1974); 1 child, Kenneth Bradley; m. Evan Edward Cochrane, Dec. 6, 1980. AA, Spokane CC, Wash., 1969; BA, Whitworth Coll., 1972. Agt., mgr. personal lines Nationwide Ins. Co., Columbus, Ohio, 1972-77, Rogers & Rogers, Inc., Spokane, 1977-81; treas. Cochrane & Co., Spokane, from 1980, also bd. dirs.; owner, broker Jones & Mitchell/Thomas Ins. Assn., Spokane, from 1981, also bd. dirs.; mgr. import/export, pres. Gayle's Ltd., Spokane, from 1986, also bd. dirs. Instr. Ind. Agts. Assn. Wash., Spokane, 1978-86. Mem. exec. com. Deaconess Hosp. Found., Spokane, 1981—; tchr. Franklin Dance Sch. for Children, Spokane, 1985—; ednl. reader Planned Parenthood of Spokane, 1983—; bd. dirs. Colonial Clinic Rehab. Ctr., Spokane, 1985—; trustee St. George's Prep. Sch., Spokane, 1985-88, chmn. devel., 1986-87, chmn. mktg., 1987-88. Recipient Leadership award, Spokane YWCA, 1983, 84. Fellow, mem. Bus. Ptnrs., Inc., Inland N.W. World Trade Council, Am. Bus. Women's Assn. (chmn. 1982—, 86, Fund Raising award 1984, 85), Action Women's Exchange (charter 1978, 85), Profl. Resource Options (bd. dirs., founder 1983, Founder award 1986). Clubs: Spokane Country, Spokane Racquet. Lodges: Order of Eastern Star. Republican. Avocations: golf, tennis, biking, dance, reading. Died Feb. 1, 2008.

THOMAS, JAMES PHILLIP, otolaryngologic surgeon; b. Columbus, Ohio, Sept. 23, 1959; s. Charles Edmond and Lillian Carmen (Christiensen) T.; m. Susan Elizabeth Sienko, Sept. 26, 1987. BS in Biology, Pa. State U., 1981; MD, Hershey Med. Sch., 1985. Resident in surgery So. Ill. U. Sch. Medicine, Springfield, Ill., 1985-87, resident in otolaryngology, 1987-91. Mem. Am. Acad. Otoloryngology Head and Neck Surgery, Exptl. Aviation Assn. Avocation: aviation. Home: Portland, Oreg. Died Dec. 23, 2007.

THOMAS, MARY BETH, nursing administrator, mental health nurse; b. Thomaston, Conn., Oct. 4, 1944; d. Edward G. and Mary V. (Mochak) Landers; m. Seth R. Thomas, 1963; children: Rebecca, Seth, Sara, Mike. ADN, Bristol Community Coll., Mass., 1977; BSN, Youngstown U., Ohio, 1982; MSN, Kent State U., Ohio, 1984. RN, Ohio. Staff nurse St. Joseph Riverside Hosp., Warren, Ohio; clin. instr. Youngstown State U., clin. specialist, supr. mental health unit; dir. behavioral health nursing Robinson Meml. Hosp., Ravenna, Ohio; regional mgr. mental health svcs. Kaiser Permanente Med. Ctr., Cleve. Mem. Ohio Soc. Nurse Execs., Ohio Psychiat. Nurse Adminstrs. (coord. Cleve. chpt. 1989), Sigma Theta Tau. Home: Gibsonia, Pa. Died Oct. 3, 2007.

THOMAS, ROBERT CHANLER BRYANT, real estate broker, executive; b. Stony Point, NY, Oct. 4, 1951; s. William Ruben Francis and Mildren Edna (Baptist) T., m. Judith Carol, July 15, 1978; children: Kristina Elizabeth, Kimberly Caitlin. AA, Rockland Community Coll., 1971; BS, SUNY, Cortland, 1973; MA, Fairfield U., 1978. Educator North Rockland Cen. Sch. Dist., Garnerville, N.Y., from 1974; broker/owner/pres. Hudson House Real Estate, Ltd., Stony Point, N.Y., from 1988. Profl. educator North Rockland Cen. Sch. Mem. Rockland Political Action Com.; warden Episc. Diocese of N.Y. Mem. Am. Fedn. Tchr., Nat. Assn. Realtors, Rockland County Tchrs. Assn., N.Y. State Congress Parents and Tchrs., N.Y. State United Tchrs. Del., North Rockland Tchrs. Assn., Rockland C.C. Alumni Assn. (bd. dirs. 1994—), Rockland County Assn., Rockland County Cen. Labor Coun. (del.). Home: Stony Point, NY. Died Sept. 2, 2007.

THOMAS, SADIE MAE, critical care nurse; b. Gadsden, Ala., Dec. 26, 1926; d. Earnest and Hester (Sandlin) T. BSN, U. Tex., 1975. RN, Mich., Tex. Dir. continuing edn. Denton (Tex.) Meml. Hosp.; insvc. instr. S.W. Hosp., Grand Praire, Tex.; afternoon asst. chief nursing VA Med. Ctr., Allen Park, Mich. Mem. ANA, AACN (North Cen. Tex. chpt.), Mich. Nurses Assn., Detroit Black Nurses Assn. (v.p. membership svcs., Membership award 1989), Nurses Orgn. VA-Nurses Orgn. Vet. Affairs (nat. membership sec., Most Outstanding Membership award 1989), Dallas Black Nurses Assn. (Nurse of Yr. 1987). Home: Detroit, Mich. Died June 7, 2008.

THOMAS, TERRA L., human services institute executive, psychologist; b. Easton, Md., Oct. 16, 1947; d. Clarence S. and Betty (Leatherberry) T.; children: Brooks, Rheaves and Nia (triplets). BS in Exptl. Psychology cum laude, Morgan State U., Balt., 1969; MA in Counselor Edn., NYU, 1971; MA in Clin. Psychology, Adelphi U., 1973, PhD in Clin. and Sch. Psychology, 1982; MBA, Northwestern U., 1991. Acting dean women Bloomingfield (N.J.) Coll., 1969-71; psychol. cons. Brownville Child Devel., Inc., Bklyn., 1972-74, Ebony Mgmt. Assocs., Bklyn., 1976-77; cons., program coord. children's div. Ada S. McKinley, Inc., Bklyn., 1976-78; with Human Resources Devel. Inst., Inc., Chgo., from 1978, v.p. Office Employee Devel., Assistance and Tng., 1987-88, sr. v.p. Office Clin. Profl. Svcs., 1988-89, sr. v.p. Office Program Ops., from 1989, sr. v.p. Office Community and Support Svcs., from 1990, exec. v.p. Tech. Resources and Tng. Ctr., Inc., from 1984. Assoc. mem. faculty Northwestern U. Med. Sch., Chgo., 1983 ; adj. prof. Lewis Nati Coll. Edn., Chgo., 1982-83; mental health specialist Bobby Wright Comprehensive Mental Health Ctr., Chgo., 1975-77; sr. cons. Bakeman and Assoc., Chgo., 1983-87; presenter in field; trainer V.I. Dept. Health, 1988, Nat. Forum for Black Pub. Adminstrs., Chgo., 1990; instr. Jackson (Miss.) State U., summer 1988—; cons. Midwest AIDS Tng. Ctr., U. Ill., Chgo., 1987—, Nat. Inst. on Drug Abuse, 1987—; also others. Bd. dirs.-at-large Nat. Black Alcoholism Coun., 1984—; mem. Ill. Gov.'s Task Force on Consolidation, 1983-84; bd. dirs. Ill. Cert. Bds., Inc., 1985—, AIDS Found. Chgo., 1986-89; co-chmn. internal AIDS adv. panel Chgo. Dept. Health, 1987-88; mem. prevention communication adv. com. Ill. Dept. Alcoholism and Drug Abuse, 1988-89; mem. instl. rev. bd. Addiction Rsch. Inst., 1988—; bd. dirs. Nat. AIDS Network, 1988-90; mem. Ill. AIDS Adv. Coun., 1988—; also others. Recipient mayor's cert. of merit City of Chgo., 1985, Outstanding Alumni award Nat. Assn. for Equal Opportunity in Higher Edn., 1988, recognition award AIDS Found. Chgo., 1989; named One of 10 Outstanding Young Citizens, Chgo. Jr. Assn. Commerce and Industry, 1986. Mem. Assn. Black Psychologists (pres. 1976), Ill. Alcoholism and Drug Dependence Assn. (Prevention Leadership award 1987), NAACP (bd. dirs., edn. com. Chgo. chpt. 1988—), Psi Chi, Alpha Kappa Alpha. Avocations: travel, horseback riding, snow and water skiing, camping, roller skating. Home: Chicago, Ill. Died Oct. 12, 2007.

THOMAS, WILLIAM HENRY, accountant; b. Independence, Mo., Feb. 19, 1934; s. John Henryand Violet May (Thorpe) T.; m. Margie Faye, May 12, 1960 (div. July 1969); children: Teresa, Christine, Thomas; m. Virginia Miller, July 15, 1977; children: John, Joseph, Jeannette Rainey. BS in Psychology, Old Dominion U., 1973; BS in Acctg., Fla. State U., 1975; MBA in Acctg., Old Dominion U., 1981. CPA, Va. Enlisted USN, 1952, acct., 1952-71, resigned, 1971; acct. Epicurean Assn. Tallahassee, Tallahassee, Fla., 1974-75; office mgr. Morris & Eckels Inc., Norfolk, Va., 1975-77; city internal auditor City of Chesapeake, Va, 1977-82, City of Virginia Beach, Va., 1983-88; mem. W.H. Thomas, CPA, Chesapeake, from 1975. Tfin. planner, microcomputer cons. W.H. Thomas, CPA, Chesapeake, 1988—. Contbr. articles to profl. jours. Mem. AICPA, Va. Soc. CPAs, Inst. Internal Auditors (Best Article award 1980), Toastmasters (pres. Virginia Beach chpt. 1987-88) Civitan (treas. Norfolk chpt. 1989—). Republican. Avocation: running. Home: Chesapeake, Va. Died Aug. 15, 2008.

THOMPSON, LOUIS MILTON, agronomy educator, researcher; b. Throckmorton, Tex., May 15, 1914; s. Aubrey Lafayette and Lola Terry (Frazier) T.; m. Margaret Stromberg, July 10, 1937 (dec. Nov. 1972); children: Louis Milton, Margaret Ann, Glenda Ray (dec.), Carolyn Terry, Jerome Lafayette; m. Ruth Hiatt Phipps, July 7, 1990. BS, Tex. A&M U., 1935; MS, Iowa State U., 1947, PhD, 1950. Soil surveyor, Tex., 1935-36, 39-40; instr. Tex. A&M U., 1936-39, 40-42; asst. prof. soils Iowa State U., Ames, 1947-50, prof. soils, head farm operation curriculum, 1950-58, assoc. dean agr. charge resident instrn., 1958-83, emeritus prof. agronomy, from 1983, assoc. dean emeritus, from 1984. Author: Soils and Soil Fertility, rev. edit., 1957; co-author: rev. edit., 1978, 1983; contbr. articles on weather-crop yield models and climate change to profl. jours. Elder Presbyn. Ch. With AUS, 1942-46; col. Res. (ret.). Recipient Henry A. Wallace award for Disting. Svc. to Agr., 1982, Faculty citation Iowa State U. Alumni Assn., 1990, Disting. Achievement citation, 1993, Alumni Recognition medal, 1996, Disting. Iowa Scientist award Iowa Acad. Sci., 1991, Agr. Innovator award Iowa State U. Agr. Alumni Soc., 1992, Friends of Agrl. award Iowa Dept. Agr. and Nat. Agrl. Mktg. Assn., 1993, Disting. Svc. to Iowa Agr. award Iowa Farm Bur., 1995, Disting. Svc. to Agr. award Iowa chpt. Am Soc. Farm Mgrs. and Rural Appraisers, 2000; named one of 150 Iowans Who Made a Difference, Iowa Farm Bur., 1996. Fellow AAAS, Am. Soc. Agronomy, Soil Sci. Soc. Am., Soil and Water Conservation Soc. (pres.'s citation); mem. Farm House (hon.), Rotary (past local pres., Paul Harris fellow), Sigma Xi, Alpha Zeta (Tall Corn award 1957), Gamma Sigma Delta (nat. pres. 1956-58), Phi Kappa Phi (chpt. pres. 1961, Centennial medal 1997). Home: Ames, Iowa. Died July 24, 2009.

THOMPSON, MORRIS MORDECAI, civil engineer, researcher, consultant; b. Jersey City, Feb. 6, 1912; s. Barney and Rachel (Golub) T.; m. Sophia Esther Shapiro, Feb. 29, 1936 (dec. 2004); 1 child, Robert David. BS in Engring., Princeton U., 1934, CE, 1935. Registered profl. engr., D.C. Topographic engr. U.S. Geol. Survey, Chattanooga, Washington, 1939-65, Atlantic region engr. Arlington, Va., 1966-68, chief rsch. and tech. standards Washington, 1968-76, cons. Reston, Va., 1976-95. Author: Maps for America, 1979, 3d edit., 1988; editor-in-chief: Manual of Photogrammetry, 2 vols., 3d edit., 1966; prodn. editor Manual of Remote Sensing, 2 vols., 2d edit., 1983; also numerous articles, chpt. to book. Active Boy Scouts Am., Binghamton, N.Y., Chattanooga, Arlington, 1937-53. Recipient Disting. Svc. award US Dept. Interior, 1967. Fellow ASCE (life, chmn. surveying and mapping div. 1973-75, Surveying and Mapping award 1977), Am. Congress on Surveying and Mapping (life, bd. dirs. 1958-60, Cartographic Honors award 1980), mem. Am. Soc. Photogrammetry and Remote Sensing (hon., cert. photogrammetrist, publs. cons. 1979-84, chmn. publs. com. 1980-84, Fairchild award 1966); chmn. Jewish Residents Coun., 2007-09 Democrat. Jewish. Home: Springfield, Va. Died Jan. 6, 2009.

THOMPSON, RICHARD ARLEN, education educator; b. Brazil, Ind., Oct. 6, 1930; s. Richard Arlen and Janet Marie (Warken) T.; children: George, Kim, David, Tim, Carol. BS, Ind. State U., 1957; MS, Butler U., 1960; EdD, Ball State U., 1968. Cert. tchr., Ind. Tchr. elem. schs. Met. Sch. Dist. Warren Twp., Indpls., 1957-66; asst. prof. edn. McNeese State U., Lake Charles, La., 1968-69; prof. edn. U. Cen. Fla., Orlando, from 1969. Reading cons. pub. and pvt. schs. Cen. Fla., 1969—. Author: Energizers for Reading Instruction, 1973, Treasury of Teaching Activities for Elementary Language Arts, 1975; co-author: Teacher's Galaxy of Reading Improvement Activities, 1979, The Reading Skills Inventory, 1980, Effective Reading Instruction, 1984, Classroom Reading Instruction, 1991. Pvt. U.S. Army, 1948-51. Mem. Orgn. Tchrs. in Reading Edn. (jour. editor 1984—), Internat. Reading Assn., Coll. Reading Assn., Am. Reading Forum, Adult Lit. League Orlando, The Quill. Democrat. Roman Catholic. Avocations: reading, travel, golf, tennis, walking. Home: Orlando, Fla. Died June 27, 2008.

THOMPSON, RICHARD ELLIS, secondary school educator; b. Gary, Ind., May 5, 1935; s. Elijah and Roberta (May) T. AA, Ind. U., 1956; BA, Roosevelt U., 1963, MA, 1966; EdM, De Paul U., 1973. Cert. tchr., adminstr., Ill., Ind. Psychiatric aide Beatty Meml. Hosp., Westville, Ind., 1955-58; counselor child care Lake County Children's Home, Gary, 1958-59, 62-63; tchr., counselor Harlan HS, Chgo., 1963-70; instr. City Colls. Chgo., 1966-70, registrar, adminstrv. asst., 1973-79; employment counselor Ill. Dept. Labor, Chgo., summers 1966, 67; asst. prin. Harlan Cmty. Acad., Chgo., 1970—97; cons. CPS, 1998—2003; ret. Contbr. articles to profl. jours. Sgt. US Army, 1959—62. Recipient Good Conduct medal, US Army, 1961, Cert. outstanding svc., Fort Leonard Wood, 1962; named Fort Leonard Wood Soldier of the Month, 1960; named to Hall of Fame, Harlan HS, 2003. Mem. Chgo. Asst. Prins. Assn. (trustee 1973—, Outstanding Secondary Educator of Am. 1975, Disting. Educator Achievement award 1990), Ill. Notaries Assn., De Paul U. Club, Roosevelt Club, Phi Delta Kappa, Kappa Delta Pi. Democrat. Avocations: silent movies, travel. Home: Chicago, Ill. Died Feb. 8, 2008.

THOMSON, BARBARA PARKER, accountant; b. Bklyn., Dec. 11, 1940; d. Sidney and Eve (Rabinowitz) Schiffman; m. Samuel Robert Parker, Sept. 10, 1960 (div. 1971); children: Jean, Steven, Arthur; m. Malcolm Thomson, June 24, 1979. BA, U. Denver, 1964; MBA, NYU, 1977. CPA, N.Y. Acctg. audit and tax compliance supr. Coopers & Lybrand, NYC, from 1977. Treas., bd. dirs. 120 Owners Corp., N.Y.C., 1985-87. Treas. Fund for the Translation of Jewish Lit., N.Y.C., 1986—. Mem. Am. Inst. CPA's, N.Y. State Soc. CPA's. Republican. Jewish. Home: New York, NY. Died Dec. 1, 2007.

THOMSON, JULIUS FAISON, JR., retired lawyer; b. Goldsboro, NC, Apr. 26, 1923; m. Nancy Jones, Aug. 4, 1956; children: Louise Marshall Thomson East, Laurie Thomson Moore. AB, U. N.C., Chapel Hill, 1947; LLB, Wake Forest U., NC, 1951. Bar: N.C. 1952. Pvt. practtivce; ret. Mem. Goldsboro. Home: Raleigh, NC. Died Dec. 20, 2007.

THOMSON, LOUIS MILLS, JR., arbitrator; b. Toledo, Mar. 8, 1927; s. Louis Mills Thomson Sr. and Frances Dorward Hay Smith; m. Rose Marie Reuss, June 26, 1953; children: Louis II, Kyle, Alison, Stuart, Amy. BS, U. Toledo, 1950, MS, 1952. Dir. City of Toledo, 1960-71, exec. dir., 1972-91. Master sgt. U.S. Army, 1945-47, PTO. Fellow Nat. Acad. Arbitrators. Lutheran. Avocation: golf. Home: Toledo, Ohio. Died Apr. 11, 2008.

THORPE, JAMES, retired researcher; b. Aiken, SC, Aug. 17, 1915; s. J. Ernest and Ruby (Holloway) T.; m. Elizabeth McLean Daniells, July 19, 1941; children: James III (dec.), John D., Sally Jans-Thorpe. AB, The Citadel, 1936, LL.D., 1971; MA, U. N.C., 1937; PhD, Harvard U., 1941; Litt.D., Occidental Coll., 1968; L.H.D., Claremont Grad. Sch., 1968; H.H.D., U. Toledo, 1977. Instr. to prof. English Princeton, 1946-66; dir. Huntington Libr., Art Gallery and Bot. Gardens, San Marino, Calif., 1966-83; sr. research assoc. Huntington Libr., San Marino, Calif., 1966-99; ret., 1999. Author: Bibliography of the Writings of George Lyman Kittredge, 1948, Milton Criticism, 1950, Rochester's Poems on Several Occasions, 1950, Poems of Sir George Etherege, 1963, Aims and Methods of Scholarship, 1963, 70, Literary Scholarship, 1964, Relations of Literary Study, 1967, Bunyan's Grace Abounding and Pilgrim's Progress, 1969, Principles of Textual Criticism, 1972, 2d edit., 1979, Use of Manuscripts in Literary Research, 1974, 2d edit., 1979, Gifts of Genius, 1980, A Word to the Wise, 1982, John Milton: The Inner Life, 1983, The Sense of Style: Reading English Prose, 1987, Henry Edwards Huntington: A Biography, 1994, H.E. Huntington: A Short Biography, 1996, A Pleasure of Proverbs, 1996, Proverbs for Friends, 1997, Proverbs for Thinkers, 1998, The Gutenberg Bible, 1999, Poems Written at the Huntington Library, 2000, Proverbs for Our Time, 2003, Proverbs for the Future, 2004. Served to col. USAAF, 1941-46. Decorated Bronze Star medal.; Guggenheim fellow, 1949-50, 65-66. Fellow Am. Acad. Arts and Scis., Am. Philos. Soc.; mem. MLA, Am. Antiquarian Soc., Soc. for Textual Scholarship. Democrat. Episcopalian. Home: Bloomfield, Conn. Died Jan. 4, 2009.

THUNE, GERALDINE B., music educator; b. Portland, Oreg., Nov. 29, 1914; d. Harvey Talbert and Evelyn (Giddings) Blakeslee; 4 children. Grad., Monmouth Coll.; student, Oreg. State U. Pvt. piano tchr., Portland. Profl. singer. Democrat. Presbyterian. Avocations: walking, exercise, dance. Home: University Place, Wash. Died Sept. 23, 2007.

THURSTON, MARLIN OAKES, educator, engineering consultant; b. Denver, Sept. 20, 1918; s. Harold Marlin and Sylva Eleanor (Howard) T.; m. Helen Marie Dunton, Mar. 15, 1942; children: Richard B., Kenneth P., Charles M. BA, U. Colo., 1940, MSc, 1946; PhD, Ohio State U., 1955. Profl. engr., Ohio. Instr. U. Colo., Boulder, 1942; assoc. prof. USAF Inst. Tech., Dayton, Ohio, 1946-51; rsch. assoc. Ohio State U., Columbus, 1952-55, assoc. prof., 1955-59, prof., 1959-82, Critchfield prof. elec. engring., 1974-82, chmn. elec. engring., 1965-77, prof. emeritus, from 1982; pres. Thurston-Bell Assocs., Inc., Columbus, 1982-92, Thurston, Bell & Olson, Columbus, from 1992. Cons. Westinghouse Advanced Tech. Lab., Balt., 1962-82, Rsch. Adv. Bd. U.S. Nuclear Def. Lab., 1968-69, Scientific Adv. Bd. USAF, Washington, 1973-74; chmn. Nat. Engring. Consortium, Inc., Chgo., 1978-79. Inventor 10 U.S., 1 Japanese patents; contbr. articles to profl. jours. Lt. col. USAFR, 1942-46. Recipient Tech. of Yr. award Cen. Ohio, 1991, Lamme Gold medal Ohio State U. Coll. Engring., 1991; finalist Inventor of Yr. Intellectual Property Owners Found., Washington, 1989. Fellow IEEE (chmn. Columbus sect. 1965-66). Avocations: computer programming, photography, private pilot. Home: Columbus, Ohio. Died Sept. 18, 2007.

TIELEBEIN, JOHN THEODORE, insurance company executive; b. Mitchell, SD, Dec. 22, 1927; s. Fred R. and Anna O. (Anderson) T.; m. Helen Baker, Sept. 2, 1951; children: Rebecca, Larry R., Van D. Grad. high sch. Agt. Blitz Basic Securities, 1985. Mem. pres.'s club Lutheran Mutual, Waverly, Iowa, 1966-83. Mem. Iowa Leaders Club (pres. 1975). Avocations: woodcarving, photography. Home: Algona, Iowa. Died Oct. 30, 2007.

TIERNEY, GORDON PAUL, real estate broker, genealogist; b. Ft. Wayne, Ind., Oct. 17, 1922; s. James Leonard and Ethele Lydia (Brown) T.; m. Carma Lillian Devine, Oct. 17, 1946; 1 child, Paul N Student, Ind. U., 1940—41, Cath. U. Am., 1941—42. Br. mgr. Bartlett-Collins Co., Chgo., 1956—84; prin., broker Kaiser-Tierney Real Estate, Inc., Palatine, Ill., 1984—89; pres. Tierney Real Estate, Newburgh, Ind. Author: Burgess/Bryan Connection, 1978; assoc. editor Colonial Genealogist Jour., 1976-85 With US Army, 1943—45, China. Named Ky. Col Fellow Am. Coll. Genealogists (pres. 1977-2000); mem. SAR (life, v.p. gen. 1984-85, genealogist gen. 1981-83, Silver and Bronze medals 1978-80, Patriot medal 1976, Meritorious Svc. award 1983, Minutemen award 1984), Huguenot Soc. Ill. (state pres. 1978-80), Huguenot Soc. S.C., Nat. Huguenot Soc., Huguenot Soc. Ind. (pres. 1993-95), Nat. Geneal. Soc., Ind. Hist. Soc., Soc. Ind. Pioneers, First Families Ohio, Ohio Geneal. Soc., Va. Geneal. Soc., Md. Geneal. Soc., Augustan Soc., Gen. Soc. War 1812 (state pres. 1985), Sons and Daus. Pilgrims, Descs. Old Plymouth Colony, Mil. Order Stars and Bars, Soc. Descs. Colonial Clergy, Sons Union Vets., Sons Confederate Vets., Pioneer Wis. Families, Welcome Soc. Pa., Pa. Geneal. Soc., Nat. Soc. Archivists, Soc. Colonial Wars in Ill. (life), Soc. Colonial Wars in Ind. (gov. 1992-94), Soc. Colonial Wars in Commonwealth Ky. (life), Sons Am. Colonists (nat. v.p. 1971-74), Mil. and Hospitalier Order St. Lazarus of Jerusalem, Clan Johnston/e in Am., Order Descs. Ancient Planters, Hump Pilots Assn., Nat. Bd. Realtors, Ill. Bd. Realtors, Sword Bunker Hill, Tri-State Geneal. Soc., Jamestowne Soc., Baronial Order Magna Charta, Royal Order Scotland, Masons, Shriners, Rolling Hill Country Club, Legion of Honor (comdr. 2001-02, decorated) Republican. Presbyterian. Died May 3, 2008.

TIGER, PHILLIP EDWARD, brokerage house executive; b. Bklyn., May 4, 1940; s. William and Belle (Sisserman) T.; m. Sylvia Bellerman, Oct. 7, 1967 (div. 198; 1 child, Jahn Stefan. BS in Mining and Geology, Colo. Sch. Mines, 1961. Cert. commodity trading advisor. Prodn. foreman Alpha Metals, Inc., Jersey City, N.J., 1961-68; sr. mfg. engr. Hamilton Standard div. United Techs., Windsor Locks, Conn., 1968-70, project engr. cities svc. div. Reston, Va., 1970-72; account exec. H.S. Kipnis & Co., Washington, 1972-73; v.p. Conti Commodity Svcs., Washington, 1973-83, Shearson, Lehman, Hutton, Washington, from 1983. Editor, CEO Tiger on Spreads, McLean, Va., 1981—; speaker in field. Co-author: Commodity Research Bureau Yearbook, 1987, Trading Strategies, 1987; editorial rev. bd.: Commodities mag., 1978; contbr. articles to profl. jour. Mem. Nat. Futures Assn. Avocations: classical music, oriental art, textiles. Home: Chicago, Ill. Died Jan. 2, 2008.

TIGGES, JOHN THOMAS, writer, musician, lecturer; b. Dubuque, Iowa, May 16, 1932; s. John George and Madonna Josephine (Heiberger) T.; m. Kathryn Elizabeth Johnson, Apr. 22, 1954; children: Juliana, John, Timothy, Teresa, Jay. Grad., Loras Coll., 1950-54, 57; student, U. Dubuque, 1960. Night club entertainer, 1950-52; clk. John Deere Tractor Works, Dubuque, 1957-61; agt. Penn Mut. Life Ins. co., Dubuque, 1961-97; bus. mgr., bd. dirs. Dubuque Symphony Orch., 1960—68, 1971—74; v.p., sec. Olson Toy and Hobby, Inc., 1964-66; pres. JKT, Inc., 1978-82; rsch. specialist Electronic Media Svcs. (Scripp-Howard), 1983-85; violinist, 1937—85. Tchr. continuing edn. creative writing N.E. Iowa C.C., 1975—98; tchr. writing U. Wis. Outreach Program's Ednl. Teleconf. Network; summer writing workshop U. Iowa, 1993—94, 1997—98; tchr. Rhinelander Sch. of the Arts, 1993—94, 1997—98, Second Saturday Seminar on Writing; mem. faculty S.W. Writers Workshop, 1998; co-founder Dubuque Symphony Orch., 1960; founder Julien Strings, 1972; founder, bus. mgr. Dubuque Pops Orch., 1957—58, Dubuque Sch. of Novel, 1978, N.E. Iowa Writers Workshop, 1981; co-host Big Broadcast Radio Program, WDBQ Radio, 1979—82; founder Sinipee Critique/Editl. Svcs., 1988, Dubuque (Iowa) Sch. of the Novel, 1980, Sinipee Writers Workshop, 1985. Author: (novels) The Legend of Jean Marie Cardinal, 1976, Garden of the Incubus, 1982, Unto the Altar, 1985, Kiss Not the Child, 1985, Evil Dreams, 1986, The Immortal, 1986, Hands of Lucifer, 1987, As Evil

Does, 1987, Pack, 1987, Venom, 1988, Vessel, 1988, Slime, 1988, Book of the Dead, 1989, From Below, 1989, Comes the Wraith, 1990, Breed, 1990, Mountain Massacre, 1990, Blood on the Rails, 1990, One Man Jury, 1991, The Curse, 1993, Monster, 1995, (book of short stories) Nightales, 1990, (plays) No More-No Less, 1982, We Who Are About to Die, 1983; contbg. author Murder for Father, 1994, The New Amazons, 1997; co-author: (radio plays) Valley of Deceit, 1978; author: Rockville Horror, 1979, The Timid, 1982, All Bets are Down, 1991, (TV drama) An Evening with George Wallace Jones, 1983, (biographies) George Wallace Jones, 1983, John Plumbe Jr., 1983; prodr.: (TV series) The Loneliest Job, 1989; co-author: (nonfiction) The Milwaukee Road Narrow Gauge: The Bellevue, Cascade & Western, Iowa's Slim Princess, 1985, They Came from Dubuque, 1983, Milwaukee Road Steam Power, 1994, (non-fiction) Remember When...?, 1997, (nonfiction) Dubuque in the 19th Century, 2000, Dubuque in the 20th Century, 2000, Dubuque-Then and Now, 2000, The Mississippi River: Father of the Waters, 2000, Nightfeeders, 2002, The Railroads of Dubuque, 2005, Iowa's Last Narrow Gauge Railroad, 2006; editl. asst.: Julien's Jour.; contbg. editor: Over 49 News and Views; co-author, editor: A Cup and a Half of Coffee, 1977;; interviewer, spl. reporter: Editl. Assocs., 1982—84; columnist Memory Lane, What's the Difference, Telegraph Herald, syndicated columnist Tough Trivia Tidbits, Remember When?, The 20th Century in Review; syndicated columnist: Nostalgia Column; contbr. more than 3100 articles to profl. jours. Founder Better Quality Writing Pubs., 1996. Recipient Nat. Quality award, 1966-70, Carnegie-Stout Libr. World of Lit. honors award, 1981; John Tigges Writing contest named in his honor, John T. and Kathryn E. Tigges endowment scholarship for Writing Majors named in their honor, Loras Coll., Dubuque. Fellow World Lit. Acad.; mem. Horror Writers Am., Western Writers Am., Iowa Authors, Internat. Platform Assn., Toy Train Collectors Club, Dubuque Rails Model Railroad (co-founder 1987). Roman Catholic. Home: Dubuque, Iowa. Died 2008.

TILDEN, WESLEY RODERICK, writer, retired application developer; b. Saint Joseph, Mo., Jan. 19, 1922; s. Harry William and Grace Alida (Kinnaman) T.; m. Lorraine Henrietta Frederick, June 20, 1948 (dec. Mar. 1999). Grad., Navy Supply Corps Sch., 1945; BS, UCLA, 1948; BA, Park Coll., Mo., 1990. Purchasing agent Vortox Co., Claremont, Calif., 1951-61; lang. lab. dir. Mount San Antonio Coll., Walnut, Calif., 1962-65; computer programmer, operator General Dynamics, Pomona, Calif., 1967-70; ret., 1970. Author: Scota, The Egyptian Princess, 1994, Merit-Sekhet: Foster Mother of Moses?, 1996; photographer, textbooks, mags., newspaper, catalogs. Historian Claremont Sister City Assn., 1963-66. Lt. USNR, 1942-46 PTO. Recipient with Lorraine Tilden People to People award Reader's Digest Found., 1963-65; named Hon. Citizen Guanajuato, Mexico, 1963. Mem. Soc. Mayflower Descendants, Scottish Clans, UCLA Alumni Assn., Park Coll. Alumni Assn., Univ. Club of Claremont, The Scituate Hist. Soc. (Mass.). Republican. Avocations: history, genealogy, photography, gardening. Home: Claremont, Calif. Deceased.

TIMA, MA'O, Senator, America Samoa Legislature; b. Tafuna, American Samoa, 1952; married; 4 children. Senator Manu'atele County Dist. 1; with America Samoa Legislature, 2003—06. Died June 26, 2006; Tafuna village.

TINGLEY, JAY ALLEN, graphic designer; b. Detroit, Apr. 29, 1956; s. Maurice Edgar and Alice Joyce (Saari) T.; m. Diane Marie Hansen, Sept. 13, 1996. BS, Ferris State Coll., 1977. Print and broadcast prodr. LS&A Internat., various locations, 1986-93; biomed. photographer North Oakland Med. Ctr., Pontiac, Mich., 1993-96; media coord. Oakwood Hosp., Dearborn, Mich., 1996-99; owner Medcom Graphics, Waterford, Mich., from 1996. 35mm slide designer. Avocations: computer art, photography. Died June 1, 2008.

TINSLEY, ELEANOR WHILDEN, former city councilwoman; b. Dallas, Oct. 31, 1926; d. W.C. and Georgiabel (Burleson) Whilden; m. James A. Tinsley, 1948 (dec. Apr. 24, 2007); children: Tom, Kathleen, Marilyn. BA, Baylor U., 1946. Pres., mem. Houston Sch. Bd., 1969-73; mem. Houston City Coun., 1979—95. Recipient Leadership award Park People, 1985, Best Pub. Ofcl. award Houston City Mag., 1985, Liberty Bell award Lawyers Assn., 1986, Mayor's Outstandign Proud Ptnr. award Houston Clean City Comm., 1992, Pi Beta Phi Carolyn Lichtenberg Crest award, 1993; named to Tex. Women's Hall of Fame, 1989; honored for exceptional work toward lung health Am. Lung Assn. Tex., 1994. Democrat. Baptist. Home: Houston, Tex. Died Feb. 10, 2009.

TISZA, LASZLO, physicist, researcher; b. Budapest, Hungary, July 7, 1907; came to U.S., 1941; s. Bela and Camilla (Herzog) T.; m. Veronica Benedek, Aug., 1938 (div. 1963); m. Magda Pollaczek Buka, 1973. Student, Göttingen U., Fed. Republic of Germany, 1928-30, Leipzig U., 1930; PhD, U. Budapest, Hungary, 1932. Rsch. assoc. Ukranian Phys. Tech. Inst., Kharkov, USSR, 1935-37, Coll. de France, Paris, 1937-40; from faculty mem. to prof. MIT, Cambridge, 1941-60, prof., 1960-73, prof. emeritus from 1973. Vis. prof. U. Paris, 1962-63. Author: Generalized Thermodynamics, 1966; contbr. articles to profl. jours. Named Rsch. Fellow Guggenheim Found., Paris, 1962-63. Fellow Am. Acad. Arts and Scis., Am. Phys. Soc.; mem. Am. Assn. Physics Tchrs., Sigma Xi. Achievements include analysis of fundamental concepts in thermodynamics and quantum mechanics; initiation of two-fluid hydrodynamics leading to temperatures waves (second sound) in liquid helium. Home: Chestnut Hill, Mass. Died Apr. 15, 2009.

TOBIN, WILLIAM JOSEPH, newspaper editor; b. Joplin, Mo., July 28, 1927; s. John J. and Lucy T. (Shoppach) Tobin; m. Marjorie Stuhldreher, Apr. 26, 1952; children: Michael Gerard, David Joseph, James Patrick. BS, Butler U., 1948; LLD (hon.), Gonzaga U., 2006. Staff writer AP, Indpls., 1947-52, news feature writer NYC, 1952-54, regional membership exec. Louisville, 1954-56, corr. Juneau, Alaska, 1956-60, asst. chief bur. Balt., 1960-61, chief bur. Helena, Mont., 1961-63; mng. editor Anchorage Times, 1963-73, assoc. editor, 1973-85, gen. mgr., 1974-85, v.p., editor-in-chief, 1985-89, editor editl. page, 1990, asst. pub., 1991; sr. editor Voice of the Times, 1991—2008. Mem. devel. com. Anchorage Winter Olympics, 1984-91, bd. dirs. Anchorage organizing com., 1985-91; bd. dirs. Alaska Coun. Econ. Edn., 1978-84, Boys Clubs Alaska, 1979-83, Anchorage Symphony Orch., 1986-87, Blue Cross Wash. and Alaska, 1987—, chmn., 1990-91; chmn. Premera Corp., 1994-99; mem. adv. bd. Providence Hosp., Anchorage, 1974-91, chmn., 1980-85. Sgt. U.S. Army, 1950-52. Mem. Alaska AP Mems. Assn. (pres. 1964), Anchorage C. of C. (bd. dirs. 1969-74, pres. 1972-73), Alaska World Affairs Coun. (pres. 1967-68), Alaska Press Club (pres. 1968-69), Commonwealth North Club (Anchorage). Home: Anchorage, Alaska. Died Apr. 5, 2009.

TODD, JOHN WILLIAM, tobacco company executive; b. Lawrenceburg, Ind., Apr. 24, 1949; s. John S. and Berneice (Riddell) T.; m. Cherie Clemons, Jan. 8, 1972; 1 child, John W. Jr. BS in Bus. Mgmt., Murray State U., 1971; MA in Human Resources Devel., Webster U., 1985. Counselor Housing Opportunity, Inc., Lexington, Ky., 1971-72; area sales rep. Xerox Corp., Lexington, 1972-73; maintenance cons. Honeywell, Inc., Louisville, 1973-76; pers. supr. Lorillard, Inc., Louisville, 1976-77, asst. mgr. pers., 1977-86, mgr. pers. and labor rels., 1986-88; dir. human resources Nat. Tobacco Co. Ltd. Partnership, Louisville, 1988-90, v.p. human resources, from 1990. Active Urban League, Louisville, Black Achievers, Louisville, Louisville Employee Benefits Coun. Mem. ASTD (Louisville chpt.), Soc. for Human Resources Mgmt. (dist. dir. 1989-90), Ky. Safety and Health Network, Louisville Pers. Assn. (v.p. 1987-88, pres. 1988-89). Democrat. Baptist. Avocations: tennis, racquetball, home improvement, lawn and garden care. Home: Louisville, Ky. Died Sept. 29, 2007.

TOLL, HENRY WOLCOTT, JR., pathologist; b. Denver, Dec. 20, 1923; s. Henry Wolcott Toll and Cyrena Van Syckel Martin; m. Lydia Brewster Toll, Sept. 17, 1948; children: H. Wolcott, William Brewster, Ellen Toll, Lois Toll, Edward Wolcott. BA, Williams Coll., Williamstown, Mass., 1945; MD, U. Colo., Denver, 1950; JD, U. Denver, 1956. Diplomate Am. Bd. Anatomic Pathology, Clinical Pathology, Forensic Pathology. Fellow internal medicine Lahey Clinic, Boston, 1952—53; assoc. pathologist Denver Gen. Hosp., 1953—59, 1969—79, Presbyn. Hosp., Denver, 1959—69; asst. clin. pathology U. Colo., 1959—95. Bd. dirs. Webb Waring Lung Inst., 1970—73, Bell Bonfils Blood Bank, 1975—92. Lt. USNR, 1943—46. Recipient Silver and Gold award, U. Colo. Med. Alumni Assn. Mem.: Denver Colo. Med. Soc. (pres. 1976), Denver Athletic Club, Cactus Club, Denver Country Club. Home: Denver, Colo. Died Oct. 15, 2008.

TOMFOHRDE, MITCHELL GERALD, management consultant, consultant; b. Marshfield, Wis., Mar. 1, 1962; s. Gilbert Gerald Jr. and Carol Joy (Lubeck) T. BS in Bus., U. Wis., Stevens Point, 1984, BS in Teaching, 1986; MS in Edn., No. Ill. U., 1988. Cert. tchr. Spl. needs asst. Milw. Area Tech. Coll., 1989; mktg. cons. Milw. Symphony Orch., 1989-90; pvt. practice bus. cons. Milw., from 1989; exec. v.p. Unlimited Innovations, Inc., Grafton, Wis., 1992; sr. assoc. World Mktg. Alliance, Brookfield, Wis. Prodn. mgr. Landmark Edn., 1994-96, introduction to the forum leader, 1995-97. Author: You're Not Alone, 1985 (Bus. Communicators award 1985); author numerous poems. Vol. money mgmt. program Family Svc., Milw., 1990-95; tchr. YMCA, Milw., 1991-92. Named to Badger Assn. of the Blind, 1989—. Mem. Toastmasters (ednl. v.p 1990-91, area gov. 1991-92, area speech contest award 1991), Alpha Mu Gamma (fgn. lang. honor soc. 1980-82). Avocations: writing, stamp and coin collecting, football, baseball. Home: Milwaukee, Wis. Died Nov. 23, 2007.

TOMLINSON, GERALDINE ANN, microbiologist, educator; b. Vancouver, BC, Canada, Feb. 5, 1931; came to U.S., 1957, naturalized, 1992; d. Robert Vincent and Elizabeth Grace (Gervan) Waters; m. Raymond Valentine Tomlinson, May 25, 1957. BSA, U. British Columbia, 1957, PhD, 1964; MA, U. Calif., Berkeley, 1960. Cert. med. lab. technol., Canada Med. lab. technol. Vancouver Gen. Hosp., 1951-55; biochem. rsch. asst. U. Calif., Berkeley, 1957-59; grad. asst., 1959-60; rsch. assoc. Kaiser Found. Biol. Lab., Richmond, Calif., 1960-61; grad. asst. U. B.C., 1961-64; rsch. assoc. dept. pediatrics Children's Hosp., Buffalo, 1964-65; asst. prof. dept. biology Rosary Hill Coll., Buffalo, 1965-66; rsch. assoc. Stauffer Chem. Co., Mountain View, Calif., 1966-67; from asst. to prof. microbiology Santa Clara (Calif.) U., from 1967. Vis. asst. prof. SUNY, Buffalo, 1966; rsch. assoc. Ames Rsch. Ctr., Moffatt Field, Calif., 1967-90. Mem. Am. Soc. Microbiology, Wildlife Rescue, Injured and Orphaned Wildlife (v.p 1990-91). Avocations: fishing, camping, bird watching. Home: Ventura, Calif. Died Oct. 28, 2007.

TOMLINSON-KEASEY, CAROL ANN, academic administrator; b. Washington, Oct. 15, 1942; d. Robert Bruce and Geraldine (Howe) Tomlinson; m. Charles Blake Keasey, June 13, 1964; children: Kai Linson, Amber Lynn. BS, Pa. State U., University Park, 1964; MS, Iowa State U., Ames, 1966; PhD, U. Calif., Berkeley, 1970. Lic. psychologist, Calif. Asst. prof. psychology Trenton (NJ) State Coll., 1969-70, Rutgers U., New Brunswick, NJ, 1970-72; prof. U. Nebr., Lincoln, 1972-77, U. Calif., Riverside, 1977-92, acting dean Coll. Humanities and Social Scis., 1986-88, chmn. dept. psychology, 1989-92, vice provost for acad. planning and pers. Davis, 1992-97, vice provost for acad. initiatives, 1997-99, chancellor, 1996—2006. Author: Child's Eye View, 1980, Child Development, 1985, numerous chpts. to books; contbr. articles to profl. jours. Recipient Disting. Tchr. award U. Calif., 1986. Mem. APA, Soc. Rsch. in Child Devel., Riverside Aquatics Assn. (pres.). Home: Decatur, Ga. Died Oct. 10, 2009.

TOMOV, GEORGE IVAN, artistic director, choreographer; b. Macedonia, Yugoslavia, Mar. 18, 1933; came to U.S., 1967; s. Ivan and Annette (Patarova) T. Diploma in art, Pedagogy Acad., Skopje, Yugoslavia, 1962. Lead dancer Tanec Macedonian Nat. Folk Ballet, Skopje, 1953-63, Lado Nat. Croatian Folk Ballet, Zagreb, Yugoslavia, 1963-67; artistic dir., choreographer Tomov Yugoslav Folk Dance Ensemble, Woodside, N.Y., from 1967. Vis. prof., lectr. in folklore and folk dance various univs. and mus., U.S.A., Can. and Yugoslavia; dir. Folk Dance Found., Woodside, N.Y. Bd. dirs. Folk Dance Ctr., N.Y.C., 1972-82. Macedonian Orthodox. Avocation: sculpture. Died Aug. 5, 2008.

TOMPKINS, ALAN, artist; b. New Rochelle, NY, Oct. 29, 1907; s. Edward DeVoe and Maud Lillian (Peck) T.; m. Florence Catherine Coy (dec.); children: Alan DeVoe (dec.), Catherine Peck Tompkins Sizer (dec.). BA, Columbia U., 1929; BFA, Yale U., 1933; DFA (hon.), U. Hartford, W. Hartford, Conn., 1987. Instr. John Herron Art Sch., Indpls., 1934-38; mural painter U.S. Treasury Dept., Ind., N.C., 1935-43; instr. Cooper Union, NYC, 1938-43; design supr. GE, Bridgeport, Conn., 1943-47; lectr. Columbia U., NYC, 1947-51; asst. dir. Hartford (Conn.) Art Sch., Hartford, 1951-57, dir., 1957-69; vice chancellor U. Hartford, 1958-69; active artist painter Bloomfield, Conn., from 1969. Art cons. Conn. Gen. Life Ins. Co., Bloomfield. Represented in four mural U.S. post offices, 1935-43, murals in GE Co., 1946, murals in Cen. Bapt. Ch., Hartford, 1953. Commr. Fine Arts Commn., Hartford, 1960-67. Painting awards Conn. Acad. Fine Arts, 1968-86, Canton Artist Guild, 1977-81. Mem. Conn. Acad. Fine Arts (v.p. 1960-66). Avocation: painting. Home: Bloomfield, Conn. Died Nov. 22, 2007.

TOON, MALCOLM, former ambassador; b. Troy, NY, July 4, 1916; s. George and Margaret Harcomb (Broadfoot) T.; m. Elizabeth Jane Taylor, Aug. 28, 1943 (dec.); children: Barbara, Alan, Nancy. AB, Tufts U., 1937, LL.D. (hon.), 1977; MA, Fletcher Sch. Law and Diplomacy, 1938; student, Middlebury Coll., 1950, Harvard U., 1950-51; LL.D. (hon.), Middlebury Coll., 1978, Drexel U., 1980, Am. Coll. Switzerland, 1985, Grove City Coll., 1990. Fgn. service officer, 1946-79; assigned successively Warsaw, Budapest, Moscow, Rome, Berlin, Washington, 1946-60; assigned Am. embassy, London, 1960-63, counselor political affairs Moscow, 1963-67; with Dept. of State, Washington, 1967-69; ambassador to Czechoslovakia, 1969-71; to Yugoslavia, 1971-75; to Israel, 1975-76; to USSR, 1976-79. Mem. U.S. del. Nuclear Test Conf., Geneva, 1958-59, Four Power Working Group, Washington, London, Paris, 1959, Fgn. Ministers Conf., Geneva, 1969, Ten Nation Disarmament Com., Geneva, 1960; mem. SALT II del., 1977-79, U.S.-Soviet Summit Conf., Vienna, 1979; Brennen prof. U. N.C., Asheville, 1981; Finch prof. Miami U., Oxford, Ohio, 1982; Allis-Chalmers chair Marquette U., Milw., 1982 Trustee emeritus Tufts U.; bd. overseers Fletcher Sch. Law and Diplomacy, 1992; former chmn. U.S. Delegation to Joint U.S. Russian Commn. on POW's, MIA's. Served from ensign to lt. comdr. USNR, 1942-46. Decorated Bronze Star with combat V; recipient Freedom Leadership award Hillsdale Coll., 1980, Valley Forge Freedom award, 1981, Disting. Honor award Dept. State, 1980, Wallace award, 1984, Gold medal Nat. Inst. of Social Scis., 1987, Degree of Prof., Acad. Natural Scis. of the Russian Fedn., 1996, Silver medal, 1996. Died Feb. 12, 2009.

TORCHINSKY, ABE, musician, music educator; b. Phila., Mar. 30, 1920; s. Benjamin and Celia (Targan) T.; m. Berta Brenner, Aug. 17, 1941 (dec. 2005); children: Barbara Torchinsky Volger, Ann Penny Torchinsky Clark, Beth Ellen. Student, Curtis Inst. Music, 1939-42. Prof. music U. Mich., Ann Arbor, 1972-89, emeritus prof., 1990—2009; former mem. faculties Temple U., Curtis Inst. Music, Phila. Mus. Acad., Catholic U., Washington; instr. tuba Aspen Music Festival, 1973—2009. Mem. Phila. Brass Ensemble; trustee Srs. Symphony, Mystic, Conn.; program adminstr. emeritus Internat. Conf. Symphony Orch. Musicians; bd. dirs., editor Phila. Orch. Retirees and Friends. Solo tubist Nat. Symphony Orch., 1942-43, Carousel, 1944-46, NBC Symphony, 1946-49, musician Phila. Orch., 1949-72; Author: 20th Century Orchestra Studies, 1969, Dance Suites for Tuba, 1975, Orchestra Repertoire for the Tuba, Vols. I-XVI, Ten Duets for Tuba. Adv. bd. Tubist Universal Brotherhood, Bloomington, Ind. Recipient Hartman Kuhn award as mem. of Phila. Brass Ensemble, Grammy award NARAS, 1969, Grand Prix du Disque as mem. of Brass Ensemble, 1969. Mem. Am. Fedn. Musicians, Kappa Kappa Psi. Avocations: art, fishing. Died Aug. 18, 2009.

TORGOW, EUGENE N., electrical engineer; b. Bronx, NY, Nov. 26, 1925; s. Frank and Blanche Anita (Revzin) T.; m. Cynthia Silver, Mar. 19, 1950; children: Joan, Martha, Ellen. BSEE, Cooper Union, 1946; MSEE, Poly. Inst. Bklyn., 1949; Engr. in E.E., Poly. Inst. N.Y., 1980; postgrad., UCLA, 1983. Rsch. assoc., sect. leader Microwave Rsch. Inst., Poly. Inst. Bklyn., 1947-51, 53-60, instr., 1954-59; mgr. microwave lab. A.B. Dumont Labs, East Patterson, NJ, 1951-53; chief engr., mgr. microwave products Dorne & Magolin, Inc., Westbury, L.I., NY, 1960-64; chief engr., dir. rsch., dir. mktg. Rantec divsn. Emerson Electric, Calabasas, Calif., 1964-68; with Missle Sys. Group, Hughes Aircraft Co., Canoga Park, Calif., 1968-85, assoc. labs. mgr., 1981-85. Cons. various electronics firms, N.Y.C., 1956-59; cons., 1986—; cons. Exec. Svc. Corps of So. Calif., 1996—; pres. Cons. Adv. Coun., 1999-2000; lectr. Calif. State U., Northridge, 1986-91. Contbr. articles to profl. jours.; patentee in field. Mem. Fair Housing Coun. San Fernando Valley, LA, from 1967, L.A. Co. Mus. Assn., 1976—2001. With USAAC, 1946—47. Recipient Engr. '85 Merit award San Fernando Valley Engrs. Coun., 1985. Fellow IEEE (life), Inst. Advancement of Engring.; mem. WINCON (bd. dirs. 1984-89, chmn. bd. dirs. 1988-89), Microwave Theory and Techniques Soc. of IEEE (pres. 1966, mem. adminstrn. com. 1962-72, Svc. award 1978), Accreditation Bd. Engring. and Tech. (mem. engring. accreditation com. 1994-99), Amiotropic Lateral Sclerosis Assn. (trustee greater L.A. chpt. 1999-2004, adv. trustee 2004-06), Hughes Mgmt. Club (edn. chmn. 1979-80), Sigma Xi. Democrat. Home: Northridge, Calif. Died Nov. 25, 2008.

TOSSETT, GLORIA VAY, educator, administrator; b. Hamar, ND, Jan. 31, 1926; d. Oscar and Lena Bernice (Ellingson) Tossett; m. Arthur Andrew Borstad, Dec. 29, 1946 (dec.); children: Stafne Tossett Borstad, Ivy Vay Borstad. BS in Edn. and Religion, Concordia Coll., Moorhead, Minn., 1968; MS in Ednl. Adminstrn., N.D. State U., Fargo, 1972; degree in bus. adminstrn., Jamestown Coll., ND, 1982. Sch. coord. Harding County Schs., Buffalo, S.D., 1972-73; pub. sch. supt. Balfour (N.D.) Sch., 1975-76, Flaxton (N.D.) Sch., 1978-79; pub. sch. supt., prin. and bus. tchr. Buchanan (N.D.) Pub. Sch., 1981-82; tchr., curriculum coord. Little Hoop C.C., Ft. Totten, N.D., 1983-84; bilingual curriculum coord., adminstr., inst. art and music Trenton, N.D., 1986-89. Mem. Spl. Edn. Bd., Burke County, N.D., 1978-79, Stutsman County, N.D., 1981-82. Author: (children's lit.) Angel Album, 1989, Twuddleville Mouse, 1989. Candidate for state supt. of pub. instrn., N.D., 1984. Mem. Am. Assn. Ret. Persons, Order Eastern Star (officer). Avocations: organ, stamp collecting/philately, piano, reading, collecting books. Died Oct. 5, 2007.

TOSTESON, DANIEL CHARLES, physiologist, dean emeritus; b. Milw., Feb. 5, 1925; s. Alexis H. and Dilys (Bodycombe) T.; m. Penelope Kinsley, Dec. 17, 1949 (div. 1969); children: Carrie Marias, Heather Tosteson, Tor, Zoe Losada; m. Magdalena Tieffenberg, July 8, 1969; children: Joshua, Ingrid. Student, Harvard U., 1942-44, MD, 1949, DSc (hon.), 2008; DSc (hon.), U. Copenhagen, 1979; Dr. hon. causa, U. Liege, 1983; DSc (hon.), Med. Coll. Wis., 1984, NYU, 1992; DHL (hon.), Johns Hopkins U., 1993; Dr. honoris causa, Cath. U. Louvain, 1996, Duke U., 1996, Emory U., 1996; DMed (hon.), Ludwig Maximilians U., 2002. Fellow physiology Harvard Med. Sch., 1947-48; intern, then asst. resident medicine Presbyn. Hosp., NYC, 1949-51; research fellow medicine Brookhaven Nat. Lab., 1951-53; lab. kidney and electrolyte metabolism Nat. Heart Inst., 1953-55, 57, research fellow biol. isotope research lab. Copenhagen, 1955-56; research fellow Physiol. Lab., Cambridge, Eng., 1956-57; assoc. prof. physiology Washington U. Sch. Medicine, St. Louis, 1958-61; prof., chmn. dept. physiology and pharmacology Duke U. Sch. Medicine, 1961-75, James B. Duke Distinguished prof., 1971-75; dean div. biol. scis., dean Pritzker Sch. Medicine U. Chgo., Lowell T. Coggleshall prof. med. scis., v.p. for Med. Center, 1975-77; dean, Caroline Shields Walker prof. cell biology Harvard Med. Sch., Boston, 1977-97, dean emeritus, Caroline Shields Walker prof., 1997—2009, pres. Med. Ctr., 1977-97. Mem. molecular biology panel NSF, 1959-62; cons. sci. rev. com. NIH, 1964-67, nat. adv. gen. med. scis. coun., 1982-86; mem. U.S. Office Tech. Assessment, 1976; ethics adv. bd. HEW, 1977-80; nat. adv. gen. med. scis. coun. NIH, 1982-2009; mem. governing bd. NRC, 1977; mem. sci. com. Found. pour l'Etude du Systeme Nerveux Central et Peripherique, 1982-2009; nat. adv. com. biomed. scis. PEW Scholars Program, 1984-87. Recipient Harvard medal, 2002. Mem. Inst. Medicine NAS (coun. 1975-78, adv. bd. PEW scholars program 1984-85), AAAS, Acad. Arts and Scis. (pres. 1997-00), Am. Physiol. Soc. (council 1967-75, pres. 1973-74), Soc. Gen. Physiologists (pres. 1968-69), Biophys. Soc. (council 1970-73), Assn. Am. Med. Colls. (chmn. coun. acad. socs. 1969-70, chmn. assembly 1973-74, chmn. physician supply task force 1988-90, Abraham Flexner award 1991), Assn. Am. Physicians, Am. Acad. Arts and Scis. (pres. 1997-2000), Red Cell Club, Soc. Health and Human Values, Danish Royal Soc. (fellow), Alpha Omega Alpha. Achievements include spl. research cellular transport processes, red cell membranes. Died May 27, 2009.

TOTTEN, GEORGE OAKLEY, III, political science professor; b. Washington, July 21, 1922; s. George Oakley Totten Jr. and Vicken (von Post) Börjesson Totten Barrois; m. Astrid Maria Anderson, June 26, 1948 (dec. Apr. 26, 1975); children: Vicken Yuriko, Linnea Catherine; m. Lilia Huiying Li, July 1, 1976 (dec. Nov. 7, 2004); 1 child, Blanche Maluk Lemes. Cert., U. Mich., 1943; AB, Columbia U., 1946, AM, 1949; MA, Yale U., 1950, PhD, 1954; docentur i japanologi, Stockholm U., 1977. Lectr. Columbia U., NYC, 1954-55; rsch. assoc. Fletcher Sch. Law and Diplomacy Harvard U. and Tufts U., Mass., 1956—58; asst. prof. MIT, Cambridge, 1958-59, Boston U., 1959-61; assoc. prof. U. R.I., Kingston, 1961-64, Mich. State U., 1964—65; assoc. prof. polit. sci. U. So. Calif., LA, 1965-68, prof., 1968-92, chmn. dept., 1980-86, prof. emeritus, 1992—96, disting. prof. emeritus, from 1996. Dir., founder Calif. Pvt. Univs. and Colls. Yr.-in-Japan program Weseda U., 1967-73; 1st dir. East Asian Studies Ctr., 1974-77; 1st nonlinguistics dir. USC-UCLA Joint East Asian Studies Ctr., 1976-77; sr. affiliated scholar Ctr. for Multiethnic and Transnat. Studies, 1993-98; chair USC Korea Project, 1998—; vis. prof. U. Stockholm, 1977-79, 1st dir. Ctr. Pacific Asia Studies, 1986-89, sr. counselor bd. dirs., 1989—; hon. pres. Huaxiu Pvt. Sch., Anyang City, Henan Province, China, 1999—; vis. prof. Ctr. for Japanese Studies, U. Hawaii, Manoa, 1992-93. Author: The Social Democratic Movement in Prewar Japan, 1966, Chinese edit., 1987, Korean edit., 1997, internet edit., 2005; co-author: Socialist Parties in Postwar Japan, 1966, Japan and the New Ocean Regime, 1984, Japan in the World, the World in Japan, Fifty Years of Japanese Studies at Michigan, 2001; editor: Democracy in Prewar Japan: Groundwork or Facade?, 1965, Helen Foster Snow's Song of Ariran, 1973, Korean edit., 1991, Korean 2d and 3d edits., 2005, Chinese edit., 1993, Kim Dae-jung's A New Beginning, 1996, Lee Hee-ho's (Mrs. KimDae-Jung's) Praying for Tomorrow: Letters to My Husband in Prison, 1999; author, co-editor: Developing Nations: Quest for a Model, 1970, Japanese edit., 1975, The Whaling Issue in U.S.-Japan Relations, 1978, China's Economic Reform: Administering the Introduction of the Market Mechanism, 1992, Community in Crisis: The Korean American Community After the Los Angeles Civil Unrest of April 1992, 1994, Korean edit., 2003, Mini Topical Chinese-English Dictionary, 2005, co-trans.: Ch'ien Mu's Traditional Government in Imperial China, 1982, 1st paperback edit., 2000; contbr. Sources of the Japanese Tradition, 1958, Aspects of Social Change in Modern Japan, 1967, Japan in Crisis: Essays on Taishō Democracy, 1974, The Politics of Divided Nations, 1991, Chinese edit., 1995, Japanese edit., 1997, mem. editl. bd. Acta Koreana, 1997—2003. Mem. coun. China Soc. for People's Friendship Studies, Beijing, from 1991; mem. nat. adv. com. Assn. Korean Polit. Studies in N.Am., from 1992, v.p., 1996—98; advisor Chinese Am. Alliance for China's Peaceful Reunification, from 2002; mem. nat. adv. com. Japan Am. Student Conf., 1984—2005; v.p. Lilia Li's China Seminar, 1985—2004; mem. U.S.-China People's Friendship Assn., Washington, from 1974, Com. on U.S.-China Rels., NYC, from 1975; chmn. L.A.-Pusan Sister City Assn., LA, 1976—77; founding mem. L.A.-Guangzhou Sister City Assn., 1981, bd. dirs., from 1990; mem. World Feds., 1982—2004, Citizens for Global Solutions, from 2004; bd. dirs. Assn. for Study of Korean Culture and Identity, 1999—2000. 1st lt. AUS, 1942—46, PTO. Recipient plaque for program on Korean studies, Consulate Gen. of Republic of Korea, 1974, Philippine Liberation medal, 1994; grantee Ford Found., 1955—58, NSF, 1979—81, Korea Found., 1993, Rebuild L.A., 1993; fellow Social Sci. Rch. Coun., 1952—53. Mem.: U. So. Calif. Faculty Ctr., European Assn. Japanese Studies, Japan-Am. Soc. Calif. (bd. dirs. 1990—94), Japanese Polit. Sci. Assn., Internat. Studies Assn., Internat. Polit. Sci. Assn., Asia Soc., Am. Polit. Sci. Assn., Assn. Asian Studies, Swedish Club of L.A., Phi Beta Delta (founding mem. Beta Kappa chpt. from 1993). Episcopalian. Deceased.

TOURIN, RICHARD H(AROLD), physicist, educator; b. NYC, Dec. 4, 1922; s. Joseph Meyer and Rebecca (Greenberger) T.; m. Barbara Cotins, Aug. 29, 1948; children: Deirdre Beth, Emily Jean. BS in Physics, CUNY, 1947; MS in Physics, NYU, 1952. Div. mgr. Warner & Swasey Co., NYC, 1948-71; mktg. dir. Klinger Sci. Corp., NYC, 1972; program dir. N.Y. State Energy Rsch. & Devel. Authority, NYC, 1973-77; mktg. mgr. Stone & Webster Engring., NYC, 1978-80; devel. dir. Syska & Hennessy Engrs., NYC, 1981-83; project mgr. Office of the Mayor City of N.Y., 1984-87; cons. Tourin Assocs., NYC, from 1988. U.S. del. Internat. Flame Rsch. Found., IJmuiden, Holland, 1966-67. Author: Spectroscopic Gas Temperature Measurement, 1966, (with others) Advances in Energy Technology, 1978; contbr. over 50 articles to profl. jours. Sgt. U.S. Army, 1943-46, PTO. Fellow Optical Soc. Am.; mem. N.Y. Acad. Scis. (chmn. engring. sect. 1987-88, 92-94, vice chair 1985-86, 89-91), Combustion Inst., Adirondack Mountain Club (gov. 1978-80, 86-88). Democrat. Achievements include patents for temperature-sensing and radiation measurement systems and instruments; development of award winning rapid scanning spectrometers. Died May 17, 2008.

TRACY, LOIS BARTLETT, painter; b. Jackson, Mich., Dec. 9, 1901; d. James Elwood and Nellie (Allen) Bartlett; m. Donald Lockwood Walker, Sept. 20, 1923 (div. Sept. 1931); 1 child, Donald Lockwood Walker; m. Harry Herbert Tracy, Sept. 21, 1931; 1 child, Nathan Bartlett. BA, Rollins Coll., 1929; MA, Mich. State, 1958. Head of art dept. Southeastern Community Coll. U. Ky., Edison Jr. Coll., Fla. One-woman shows include Studio Guild, N.Y.C., 1939-41, 41-43, Norlyst Gallery, N.Y.C., 1945-47, Charles E. Smith Gallery, Boston, 1949, Center St. Gallery, Boston, Burliuk Gallery, N.Y.C., 1952, Gallerie Internationale, N.Y.C., 1963, Fine Arts Mus., Greenville, S.C., Morse Mus. Art, Winter Park, Fla., Mus. Art, Clearwater, Fla., Wustun Mus., Racine, Wis., Fitchburg Art Mus., Mass., Gibbs Gallery, Charleston, S.C., Boise Art Mus., Idaho, Columbia Mus. Art, S.C., Worcester Art Ctr., Appleton, Wis., San Francisco Mus. Art, Syracuse Mus., Asheville Art Mus., N.C., Stork Gallery, Lynchburg, Va., Maryhill Mus. Fine Arts, Washington; represented in permanent collections Cornelle Mus. Art, Winter Park, Fla., 1994, Met. Mus. Art, N.Y.C., 1994, NAOAL Mus., Washington; represented in numerous pub. and pvt. collections; author: (books) Paintings, Principles and Practices, 1967, Portuguese edit., 1998, Adventuring in Art, 1989. State bd. mem LWV, Laconia, N.H.; active Dem. Nat. Com. Named Tchr. of Yr. Edison Coll., Ft. Myers, Fla.; recipient Award of Merit State of Fla, 1935, Most Creative Work of Art award Currier Mus., N.H., Gaisman Award Nat. Assn. Women Artists, Arvida award, Sarasota Art Assn., Watercolor prize Southeastern Annual High Mus., Atlanta, Norfolk Mus. Art., Pen & Brush, N.Y., Nat. Assn. Women Artists, Nat. Acad. Gallery, Sarasota Art Assn. Mem. LWV, Nat. Assn. Women Artists, Am. Assn. Univ. Women, Nat. League of Am. Pen Women, Fla. Artists Group, Artists Equity, Art Assn., Internat. Platform Assn., Magna Charta Dames and Barons. Democrat. Avocations: religious activities, peace group. Home: Englewood, Fla. Died Apr. 8, 2008.

TRAGER, D. DAVID, retired pharmacist, consultant; b. Napa, Calif., Oct. 4, 1931; s. Louis D. (dec.) and Frances Amanda (Brose) T. (dec.); m. Ruth (Pacovsky), June 15, 1952 (div. Sept. 1978); children: Louis, Solomon; m. Sarah Ann (Brancato), Dec. 28, 1983 (dec. May 2000); children: Daryl, Randy, Missi Hasnas; m. Phyllis Baldwin (Douglas), Oct. 7, 2001; 1 stepchild, Robert Gordon Douglas. BS in Pharm., U. Calif., San Francisco, 1953; post grad. in Clin. pharmacy, U. So. Calif., 1976, post grad. in Drug action, 1978. Registered pharmacist Calif. Pharmacist multiple locations, Calif., 1953-59; pharmacist, pharmacy mgr. Longs Drugs, West Covina, Calif., 1959-60; pharmacist Bay Pharmacy, Pacific Palisades, Calif., 1960-65; pharmacist, v.p. Palisades Drug Co., Pacific Palisades, 1965—67; pharmacist Bi Rite, Westwood and Santa Monica, Calif., 1967-68; pharmacist, owner Trager, Pacific Palisades, 1968—72; pharmacist Kaiser Found. Hosp. Pharmacy, Panorama City, Calif., 1973—90, Woodland Hills, Calif., 1990-98; ret., 1998. Propr. P-I-E Software, Calif., from 1995; mentor first yr. pharmacy students U. Pacific, Calif., 1998—2001, tech. lit. cons., Calif., from 2001; per diem overnight pharmacist Kaiser Permanente Pharmacy, Woodland Hills, Calif., 2001—03; gen. cons. Mem.: Am. Inst. History of Pharmacy, Calif. Employee Pharmacist Assn., Am. Pharm. Assn. (life; emeritus), Scottish Rite, Scottish Rite Rsch. Soc. (life), Royal Arch Mason, Masons (life), Shriners, Kappa Psi. Republican. Jewish. Avocations: computers, reading, Masonic research, philosophy. Home: Pacific Palisades, Calif. Died Dec. 20, 2007.

TRAHAN, JEROME FRANCIS, accountant; b. Detroit, Aug. 23, 1935; s. William I. and Wilhelmina (Deibol) T.; m. Josephine T. Herman, Feb. 8, 1964; children: Susan W., Daniel J. B in Accountancy, Walsh Coll., 1962. CPA, Mich. Auditor Hogan Jungel, Detroit, 1960-63, Canton Rosenbaum, Grand Rapids, Mich., 1963-65; sec., treas. Eisenhour Constrn., East Lansing, Mich., 1965-75; controller Snell Environ., Lansing, Mich., 1975-79; chief acctg. and funds mgmt. Mich. State Med. Soc., East Lansing, from 1979. Bd. dirs. GLRANETS. Served to sgt. U.S. Army, 1958-61. Republican. Roman Catholic. Home: Okemos, Mich. Died Jan. 6, 2008.

TRANSUE, WILLIAM REAGLE, retired mathematics educator; b. Pen Argyl, Pa., Nov. 30, 1914; s. Ray Frank and Emily Beck (Reagle) T.; m. Monique Serpette, May 27, 1936; children: William, Jacques, John. BS, Lafayette Coll., 1935; MA, Lehigh U., 1939, PhD, 1941; Sc.D. (hon.), Kenyon Coll., 1983. Prof. math. Kenyon Coll., Gambier, Ohio, 1945-66; prof. math. SUNY, Binghamton, 1966—83. Fellow NSF, Paris, 1960-61; mem. Inst. for Advanced Study, Princeton, N.J., 1943, 48-49. Contbr. articles to profl. jours. Fulbright scholar, Pavia, Italy, 1951-52. Mem. Am. Math. Soc., Math. Assn. America Democrat. Avocations: gardening, tennis, sailing. Died Feb. 3, 2009.

TRAVIS, DEMPSEY JEROME, real estate company executive; b. Chgo., Feb. 25, 1920; s. Louis and Mittie (Strickland) T.; m. Moselynne Hardwick, Sept. 17, 1949. BA, Roosevelt U., 1949; grad., Sch. Mortgage Banking, Northwestern U., 1969; D.Econs., Olive Harvey Coll., 1974; D.BA (hon.), Daniel Hale Williams U., Chgo., 1976; PhD (hon.), Kennedy-King Coll., 1982; DHL (hon.), Governor State U., 2001. Cert. property mgr.; cert. real estate counselor. Pres. Travis Realty Co., Chgo., 1949—2009, Urban Rsch. Press, 1969—2009. Author: Don't Stop Me Now, 1970, An Autobiography of Black Chicago, 1981, An Autobiography of Black Jazz, 1983, An Autobiography of Black Politics, 1987, Real Estate is the Gold in Your Future, 1988, Harold: The People's Mayor, 1989, Racism: American Style a Corporate Gift, 1990, I Refuse to Learn to Fail, 1992, Views From the Back of the Bus During World War II and Beyond, 1995, The Duke Ellington Primer, 1996, The Louis Armstrong Odessey: From Jazz Alley to America's Jazz Ambassador, 1997, Racism: Revolves Like a Merry Go 'Round: 'Round 'n 'Round It Goes, 1998, They Heard a Thousand Thunders, 1999, The Life and Times of Redd Foxx, 1999, The Victory Monument: The Beacon of Chicago's Bronzeville, 1999, J. Edgar Hoover's FBI Wired the Nation, 2000, The FBI Files on the Tainted and the Damned, 2001, An American Story: In Red, White and Blue, 2002, Norman Granz The White Moses of Black Jazz, 2003, Jimmie Lumceford: The King of Jazzmocracy, 2004. Trustee Northwestern Meml. Hosp., Chgo., Chgo. Hist.

Soc., Auditorium Theater, Chgo., Roosevelt U.; bd. dirs. Columbia Coll. With AUS, 1942-46. Recipient award Soc. Midland Authors, 1982, Chgo. Art Deco Soc., 1985, The Human Rights award The Gustavus Myers Ctr. for Study of Human Rights in N.Am., 1995, Humanitarian award Kennedy-King Coll., 1997, Art Deco award, 1983, Soc. Midland Authors award for nonfiction, 1981; named to Jr. Achievement Chgo. Bus. Hall of Fame, 1995; named embedded in sidewalk of Bronzeville Walk of Fame, Chgo; inductee Internat. Literary Hall of Fame, Chgo. State U., 2000. Mem. United Mortgage Bankers Assn. Am. (pres. 1961-74), Dearborn Real Estate Bd. (pres. 1957-59, 70-71), Nat. Assn. Real Estate Brokers (1st v.p. 1959-60), Inst. Real Estate Mgmt., Soc. Profl. Journalists, Soc. Midland Authors (pres. 1988-90), NAACP (pres. Chgo. 1959-60), Econs. Club, Forty Club Chgo., Assembly Club, Cliff Dwellers, The Caxtons Club. Home: Chicago, Ill. Died July 2, 2009.

TRAVIS, ROBERT FREDERICK, lawyer; b. Grand Rapids, Mich., Feb. 2, 1924; AB, Columbia U., 1948, MA, 1949; JD, U. Mich., 1972. Bar: Mich. 1973. Ptnr. Bauckham, Reed, Lang, Schaeffer & Travis, P.C., Kalamazoo, Mich., 1973-85; pvt. practice law Kalamazoo, 1985-96. Contbr. articles to profl. jours. Mem. Kalamazoo County Bar Assn., Mich. Bar Assn. Died Aug. 18, 2008.

TREADWELL, KAREN ANN, financial company executive; b. Pitts., Aug. 7, 1959; d. Kenneth M. and Sally (Skeel) T.; m. Alan H. Eugley, Sept. 7, 1985. BA in History, Colgate U., 1981. Asst. treas. Bankers Trust Co., NYC, 1981-85; asst. v.p. Paribas, NYC, 1985-86; dir. corp. fin. Rockefeller Group Inc., NYC, 1986-92, asst. treas., 1992-94, treas., from 1994. Bd. dirs. Mchts. House Mus., N.Y.C., 1987—. Mem. Fin. Execs. Inst., Nat. Assn. Corp. Treas. (bd. dirs.). Home: Westport, Conn. Died Nov. 11, 2007.

TREEN, DAVID CONNER, former Governor of Louisiana, former United States Representative from Louisiana; b. Baton Rouge, July 16, 1928; s. Joseph Paul and Elizabeth Speir Treen; m. Dolores Brisbi, 1951 (dec. 2005); children: Jennifer Anne (Mrs. Jack Neville), David Conner Jr., Cynthia Lynn (Mrs. Lloyd Lunceford). BA Polit. Sci., History, Tulane U., 1948, JD with honors, 1950. Of counsel Deutsch, Kerrigan & Stiles, New Orleans, 1984—2003, assoc. atty., 1950—51; vp, legal counsel Simplex Mfg. Corp., New Orleans, 1952—57; assoc. atty. then ptnr. Beard, Blue & Schmitt & Treen, New Orleans, 1957—72; mem. US Congress from 3rd La. Dist., Washington, 1973-80; gov. State of La., Baton Rouge, 1980-84; chmn. Garrison Diversion Unit Commn. US Dept. Interior, Washington, 1984; of counsel O'Connor and Hannan, Washington, 1984—2009. Mem., Jefferson Parish Republican Exec. Com., La., 1962-67, chmn., 1963-67; mem., La. State Republican Central Com., 1962-74; chmn. La. Young Republican Fedn., 1962-64; mem. exec comt, 1964-66, gen. counsel, 1966; Republican cand. for Congress, 2nd Dist., 62, 1964 & 1968; del., Republican Nat. Conv., 1964, 1968, 1972, 1976, 1980 & 1984; chmn. La. deleg., 1968 & 1972, mem., Platform Comt. & co-chmn. platform subcomt. on peace, security & foreign policy, 1976; Republican cand. for Gov., La., 1971, 1979 & 1983; Republican Nat. Committeeman, La., 1972-74 Entered as 1st Lt. USAF, 1950—52, Sheppard Air Force Base, Tex & Hq, Third Air Force, England. Named Outstanding Alumnus, Tulane U., 1980. Mem.: Order of the Coif, Omicron Delta Kappa, Phi Delta Phi. Republican. Avocation: golf. Home: Mandeville, La. Died Oct. 29, 2009.

TREJO, JOSÉ DIAZ, accountant, consultant, computer software specialist, financial planner; b. Carrizo Springs, Tex., Feb. 11, 1948; s. Elisandro Briones and Maria Trinidad (Diaz) T. AA, Coll. DuPage, 1969; BA in History, No. Ill. U., 1971. CPA, Ill; lic. ins. producer, Ill. Revenue acctg. and banking Spector Industries, Inc., Bensenville, Ill., 1977-81; revenue auditor State of Ill., Springfield, 1982-84; practice acctg. Trejo & Assocs., Itasca, Ill., from 1985. Cons. in taxes, personal and corp. fin. planning, bus. valuation audits, pensions, mergers and acquisitions, leverage buy-outs. Mem. AICPA (tax div. 1986-87, personal fin. planning div. 1986-87), Ill. CPA Soc. (rev. instr., faculty mem., personal fin. planning, banks and continuing profl. edn. coms., small bus. assistance com.). Roman Catholic. Avocations: reading, writing, outdoor activities, social activities, guitar playing, songwriting. Home: Itasca, Ill. Died Aug. 18, 2008.

TRICULES, HOMER GEORGE, minister, psychotherapist; b. Perth Amboy, NJ, Apr. 13, 1931; s. George and Eva (Vlahos) T.; m. Magdalene Sathmary, June 11, 1955; children: Evamarie, Nancy Susan, Lori. BS in Edn., Rutgers U., 1953; MDiv, New Brunswick Theol. Sem., 1958; MA, Fairleigh Dickinson U., 1975. Ordained to ministry Am. Bapt. Ch., 1958. Pastor Calvary Bapt. Ch., Carteret, N.J., 1956-61; tchr. Pt. Pleasant Beach (N.J.) High Sch., 1961-64; pastor First Bapt. Ch., Long Branch, N.J., 1962-73; missionary chaplain Race Track Chaplaincy of Am., N.J., 1973-82; pastor Scotch Plains (N.J.) Bapt. Ch., 1982-88; nat. exec. dir. Race Track Chaplaincy of Am., Long Branch, from 1988. Founder, cons. Community Christian Counseling Ctr., First Bapt. Ch., Red Bank, N.J., 1976—; pres. Am. Bapt. Chs. of N.J., 1985. Author: (devotional book) Daily Oats. Mem. Long Branch Bd. Edn., 1990—. 2nd lt. U.S. Army, 1954. Mem. Am. Bapt. Mins. Coun. Avocations: organ, piano, and vocal music. Home: Long Branch, NJ. Died Aug. 26, 2008.

TRIMBLE, STEPHEN ASBURY, lawyer; b. Washington, July 25, 1933; s. South, Jr. and Elaine (Lazaro) T.; m. Mary Ellen Lynagh, Aug. 8, 1964 (dec. 2008) AB in Polit. Sci., U. N.C., 1955; LLB, Georgetown U., 1961. Bar: D.C. 1961, U.S. Ct. Appeals (D.C. cir.) 1961, U.S. Supreme Ct. 1965, U.S. Ct. Claims 1979. Dep. clk. U.S. Dist. Ct. D.C., 1958-60, law clk., 1960-62; asst. corp. counsel D.C., 1962; assoc. Hamilton & Hamilton, Washington, 1962-64, ptnr., 1964—2009. Mem. Sentencing Guidelines Commn. D.C. Superior Ct., 1984-92; lectr. in field. Contbr. articles to profl. jours. Sec. John Carroll Soc., Washington, 1965-77, bd. govs., 1979-83; mem. adv. bd. Salvation Army, Washington, 1982-2004; trustee Maret Sch., Washington, 1976-84, v.p., 1981-84. 1st lt. USMC, 1955-58. Named one of Best Lawyers in Am., 1994—2006. Fellow Am. Coll. Trial Lawyers (D.C. chmn. 1981-82), Am. Bar Found. (grievance com. U.S. Dist. Ct. D.C. 1978-83, chmn. 1981-83, counseling panel U.S. Dist. Ct. D.C. 1990-94, 2002-04, chmn. 1990-94); mem. ABA (ho. of dels. 1975-77), Bar Assn. D.C. (pres. 1976-77, dir. 1971-73, sec. 1973-75), D.C. Bar (dir. 1978-81), Nat. Assn. R.R. Trial Counsel (pres. 1977-78, dir. 1970—, Disting. Svc. award 1995, Recognition of Excellence award 2003), Nat. Conf. Bar Pres., The Counsellors (Washington, pres. 1972-73), D.C. Def. Lawyers (v.p. 1974), The Barristers (sec. 1971, pres. 1981), Def. Rsch. Inst., Nat. Assn. Coll. and Univ. Attys., D.C. Coun. for Ct. Excellence (dir. 1983-92, exec. com. 1984-86), Jud. Conf. D.C. Cir., Jud. Conf. D.C. Cts., Chevy Chase Club (bd. govs. 1982-87, pres. 1986-87), Lawyers Club Washington (pres. 1991), Met. Club, Kiwanis (v.p. local chpt. 1985-86, pres. 1986-87). Roman Catholic. Died Aug. 5, 2009.

TRIPPE, ANTHONY PHILIP, business consultant, technology manager, electronics company executive; b. Buffalo, Aug. 30, 1943; s. Anthony John and Carolyn Agnes (Peschio) T.; m. Dorothy Ann Fazzina, June 26, 1965; children: Anthony Joseph, Michael Anthony, Madonna Marie. BS in Chemistry, Rochester Inst. Tech., 1966; MS in Math., Fairleigh Dickinson U., 1972; DBA, U.S. Internat. U., 1982. Registered profl. engr., N.Y., profl. chem. engr., Calif. Co-op student/analytical Eastman Kodak Co., Rochester, N.Y., 1963-66; organic chemist Smith, Kline & French, Phila., 1966-67; chem. engr. U.S. Army-Picatinny, Dover, N.J., 1967-72; sys. analyst Calspan Corp., Buffalo, 1972-77; program mgr. IRT Corp., San Diego, 1977-82, v.p. govt. programs, 1982-87; bus. devel. mgr. Maxwell Labs., San Diego, 1987-93, v.p. sales and mktg., 1993-95; bus. cons. Coastal Pacific Consulting, San Diego, from 1995. Contbr. numerous papers to conf. procs., articles to profl. jours. Corp. leader United Way of San Diego County, 1988, 89, 92; project bus. cons. Jr. Achievement, San Diego, 1986, 90. Mem. IEEE, Am. Chem. Soc., Am. Def. Preparedness Assn., Armed Forces Comm. and Electronics Assn., Nat. Assn. Radio and Telecomm. Engrs. (cert. electromagnetic compatibility engr.), Internat. Soc. Optical Engring., Soc. Automotive Engrs. (cert. of appreciation 1991, 92), Assn. Old Crows. Republican. Roman Catholic. Avocations: opera, collect autographs of composers and scientists. Died Nov. 24, 2007.

TROCK, WARREN LEIGH, agricultural and natural resource economics educator; b. Pratt, Kans., June 30, 1926; s. Elmer and Lottie Marie (Lemons) T.; m. Bette Jene Sloan, Aug. 15, 1949; children: Daniel Leigh, Rebecca Ann, David Alan. BS in Agrl. Adminstrn., Kans. State U., 1950, MS in Agrl. Econs., 1957, PhD in Agrl. Econs., 1965. Extension economist Mont. State U., Bozeman, 1957-64; from asst. prof. to prof. agrl. econs. Tex. A&M U., College Station, 1964-73; extension economist Colo. State U., Ft. Collins, 1973—95; ret., 1995. Contbr. articles to profl. jours. Served as cpl. U.S. Army, 1944-46, 50-51. Recipient Hildreth award for achievement in pub. policy edn., 2002. Democrat. Avocations: fishing, photography. Died July 15, 2008.

TROKA, LYNDA MARILYN, audio-visual specialist; b. Petersburg, Alaska, Nov. 23, 1960; d. Wilhelm and Marilyn Eleanor (Frink) Jordan; m. Benon Troka, May 27, 1987; 1 child, Scott Benon. Student, U. Mont., 1979-80, Wash. State U., 1980-81; BA in Journalism, U. Alaska, Fairbanks, 1984. TV news photographer Sta. KATN, Fairbanks, 1984-85; TV news photographer/prodr. Sta. KCFW, Kalispell, Mont., 1985-87; TV news photographer Sta. KTVB, Boise, Idaho, 1987-91; video prodr./dir. Wash. State U., Pullman, from 1991. Freelance sports videography, Sta. KTVB, Prime Sports NW, Wash. State U., 1991—; freelance videography Survivors of Shoal, 1996—. Prdr./dir. of numerous videos including Sprayer Prep (with John & Daryl), 1993, Wetlands Stewardship Training, 1996, River Salmon Tour, 1996, Community Pride Ride, 1996, Sound Farming: An Investment in Our Community, 1997. Recipient numerous awards including 1st pl. Feature News Story Profl. Journalists, Pacific Northwest chpt., 1991, 1st pl. News Series Inland Press Club, 1990, 1st pl. Breaking News Photography Nat. Fedn. of Press Women, Idaho chpt., 1990, 1st pl. Best Single Story Idaho Associated Press, 1990, 1st pl. TV documentary Nat. Fedn. Press Women, 1996, award of Distinction Communicator Awards, 1996. Mem. Internat. TV Assn. (pres., sec.-treas. 1995—), Nat. Press Photographers Assn., Agrl. Communicators & Educators, Nat. Fedn. Press Women (Dist. and Honorable Mention award for 1st place documentary 1996). Avocations: videography, computers. Home: Moscow, Idaho. Died Mar. 30, 2008.

TROMBLEY, WILLIAM HOLDEN, retired journalist; b. Buffalo, June 18, 1929; s. William Albert and Eva (Atkinson) T.; m. Audrey Louise Ramsdell, Mar. 21, 1954; children: Suzanne, Patricia BA, Johns Hopkins U., 1952;

MS in Journalism, Columbia U., 1953. Reporter Life Mag., NYC, Chgo. and San Francisco, 1953-61; writer, editor Saturday Evening Post, Phila., 1962-63; staff writer Los Angeles Times, 1965-92; sr. editor Calif. Higher Edn. Policy Ctr., 1993. Recipient numerous awards for pub. affairs and ednl. reporting AAUP, Los Angeles Press Club, Calif. Tchrs. Assn., others, 1969-77 Avocations: reading; sports. Home: Sacramento, Calif. Died Sept. 6, 2009.

TROTTER, JOHNNY RAY, physician; b. Detroit, Aug. 30, 1950; s. Robert Terris and Johnnie Mae (Ivory) T.; m. Nadine Frances Simpson, July 7, 1973; children: Johnny Ray II, Charissa Nadine, David Louis, Jason Aaron. BA, U. Mich., 1972, MD, 1976. Diplomate Am. Bd. Family Practice. Resident Bon Secours Hosp., Grosse Pointe, Mich., 1976-79; instr. in family medicine Wayne State U., Detroit, 1979-82; pres., dir., physician Grace Family Health Ctr., P.C., Detroit, from 1982. Bd. dirs. Physician Lab. Svcs., Inc., Southfield, Mich., 1987—; mem. adv. com. dept. family practice Grace Hosp.; physician cons. Nat. Cons. Panel, Boulder, Colo., 1988—; speaker in field. Nat. Med. fellow, 1972; recipient Semmes award Sisters of Bon Secours, 1979. Fellow Am. Acad. Family Physicians; mem. Mich. Acad. Family Physicians (chmn. minority affairs com. 1983-87); Detroit Med. Soc. Democrat. Avocations: golf, video camera recording, bowling, tennis, chess. Died Feb. 7, 2008.

TROVA, ERNEST TINO, artist, sculptor; b. St. Louis, Feb. 19, 1927; One-man exhbns. include: Pace Gallery, Boston and N.Y.C., 1963, 69, 70, 71, 73, 75, 82, Hanover Gallery, London, Eng., 1964, 68, 70, Harcus/Krakow Gallery, Boston, 1968, Dunkelman Gallery, Toronto, Ont., Can., 1969, Hanover-Gimpel, Zurich, Switzerland, 1970, Galerie Der Spiegel, Cologne, Germany, 1970, Block Gallery, St. Louis, 1970, Galerie Brusberg, Hanover, Germany, 1970, Venezuela, 1971, Israel, 1971, Makler Gallery, Phila., 1972, Phoenix Art Mus., 1974, Hokin Gallery, Palm Beach, Fla., 1975, 83, 84, 87, So. Ill. U. Mus., 1982, Greenberg Gallery, St. Louis, 1983, 84, Hokin Gallery, Miami, 1988-90, Mangel Gallery, Phila., 1989, The Exbn. Space at 112 Greene St, N.Y.C., 1989, Galeria Freites, Caracas, Venezuela, 1989-90, Philharmonic Ctr. for the Arts, Naples, Fla., 1991, Philip Samuels Fine Art, St. Louis, 1991, Arij Gasiunasen Fine Art, Palm Beach, Fla., 1993, Bruce R. Lewin Gallery, N.Y.C., 1993, others; numerous group exhbns. including: Chgo. Art Inst., 1964, Pasadena (Calif.) Art Mus., 1964, De Cordova Mus., Documenta IV, Kassel, Germany, 1968, Mus. Modern Art, 1968, Internat. Biennale, Warsaw, 1968, Whitney Mus. Modern Art, 1968, Cleve. Inst. Art, 1969, Jewish Mus., N.Y.C., 1969, Contemporary Arts Center, Cin., 1970, 72, Princeton, 1970, U. Wis.-Milw., 1973, Hirshorn Mus. and Sculpture Garden, 1974, The Anchorage Mus. History and Art, 1987, 88, The Anchorage Mus., Juneau, Alaska, 1988, U. Alaska Mus., Fairbanks, 1988, Hanson Galleries,, La Jolla, Calif., 1989, ACA Galleries, N.Y.C., 1990, Hokin Galleries, Miami, 1990, Galeria Freites, Caracas, Venezuela, 1990, Philharm. Ctr. for Arts, Naples, Fla., 1991, Art Chgo., 1991, 93, Art Miami, 1992, 93, 94, Art L.A., 1992, Isetan Mus. Art, Tokyo, 1992, Daimaru Mus., Umeda-Osaka, Japan, 1992, Hiroshima (Japan) Mus. Contemporary Art, 1992, Internat. Biennale, Monte Carlo, 1993, Asian Internat. Contemporary Art Fair, 1993, Art Basel, 1993, others; represented in permanent collections including Mus. Modern Art, Aldrich Mus. of Contemporary Art, Israel Mus.-Jerusalem, Met. Mus. of Art, Guggenheim Mus., Hirshorn Mus., Nat. Mus. of Am. Art, St. Louis Art Mus., Phoenix Art Mus., Atkins Mus. Fine Art, Laumeier Sculpture Garden, Springfield Art Mus.-Mo., Tate Gallery-London, Whitney Mus. of Am. Art, Nat. Mus. Am. Art, Smithsonian Instn., Washington, also pvt., Whitney Mus., and corporate collections. Home: Saint Louis, Mo. Died Mar. 9, 2009.

TROWBRIDGE, ELISABETH WARD, physician; b. Newark, Sept. 4, 1906; d. William Rankin and Jennie (Prentiss) Ward; m. Frederick L. Trowbridge, May 20, 1939; children: Joan Trowbridge Wayland, Frederick L., John F. AB, Mt. Holyoke Coll., 1928; MD, Med. Coll. Pa., 1932. Intern Newark City Hosp., 1933-35; pvt. practice Newark and East Orange, N.J., 1932-59; gynecologist Cleve. Clinic, 1959-62, resident, 1962-65; med. dir. St. Anthony Ctr., Houston, 1968-72; pvt. practice Houston, 1971-74; dir. Breast Cancer Detection Ctr., Mt. State Tumor Inst., Boise, Idaho, 1974-82; v.p. Klamath Speach & Hearing, Klamath Falls, Oreg., from 1989. Chmn. family and children's div. Welfare Fedn., Newark, 1953-57, trustee, 1955-59; trustee Planned Parenthood, Boise, 1982-85; vol. Klamath Hospice, Merle West Hosp. Cancer Treatment Ctr., Klamath Falls, 1989—. Recipient Achievement award Mt. Holyoke Coll. Alumnae Assn., 1989; named Woman of Yr. Women's Svc. Club of Essex County, N.J., 1957, Alumnae Assn. Vail Dean Sch., 1958. Mem. Am. Med. Women Assn., Am. Fertility Soc. Republican. Avocations: skiing, music. Died Aug. 13, 2008.

TRUEHILL, MARSHALL, JR., minister; b. New Orleans, Sept. 5, 1948; s. Marshall Truehill and Inez Gray Williams; adopted s. Elizabeth (May) T.; m. Mary Ola Williams, Dec. 20, 1969 (div. 1972); m. Valli Maria Dobard, July 22, 1972 (div. 1999); children: Briana Traci, Marshall III, Jessica, Quentin; m. Miranda Sally Farr, Dec. 28, 1999. B in Music Edn., Xavier U., 1973; BTh, Christian Bible Coll., 1979; MDiv, Orleans Bapt. Theol. Sem., 1986; D Ministry, New Orleans Bapt. Theol. Seminary, 1990; postgrad., U. New Orleans; ThD, A.P. Clay Christian Theol. Coll., 2004. Ordained to ministry Bapt. Ch., 1980; cert.

tchr., La. Tchr. Orleans Parish Sch. Bd., New Orleans, 1973-78, Delgado Community Coll., 1975-78; pastor Faith in Action Bapt. Ch., 1982—95; founder, pastor First United Bapt. Ch., 1995—2008. Founder, dir. Faith in Action Evangel. Team, New Orleans, 1977-2008; lectr. Nat. Bapt. Conv. on Congl. Evangelism, New Orleans, 1977-79; cons. So. Bapt. Conv. Home Mission Bd., La., 1986-1997; CEO TradeWins Ptnrs. LLC, 2001. Bd. dirs. Project New Orleans, 1983-99, New Orleans Jobs Initiatives, vice chmn., 1997-2002; apptd. by mayor to New Orleans City Planning Commn., 1998-2007. Democrat. Avocations: computers, aquariums, interior decorating, aerobics. Home: New Orleans, La. Died Dec. 25, 2008.

TRUSLOW, GODFREY GROSVENOR, banker; b. Boston, Aug. 15, 1934; s. James Linklater and Anna Leigh (Kendall) T.; m. Olivia Hoadley Van Norden, July 20, 1963; children: Peter Crane, Edward Duncan. BA, Harvard U., 1956. Officer Morgan Guaranty Trust Co., NYC, 1960-66; dep. fin. adminstr. City of N.Y., 1966-69; v.p. Morgan Guaranty Trust Co., 1969-74; dir. Morgan & Cie Internat., Paris, France, 1974-75; v.p. Morgan Guaranty Trust Co., NYC, 1975-83; sr. v.p., mgr. Arab Bank Ltd., NYC, 1983-86; dep. gen. mgr. Nippon Credit Bank Ltd., NYC, from 1986. Dir. Nippon Credit Trust Co., N.Y. 1990—. With USN, 1956-58, Pacific. Trustee, East Woods Sch., Oyster Bay, N.Y.; bd. dirs. Tarratine Club Dark Harbor, Cold Spring Harbor Beach Club. Republican. Episcopalian. Avocation: sailing. Home: Cold Spring Harbor, NY. Died Sept. 23, 2007.

TSCHOEPE, THOMAS AMBROSE, bishop emeritus; b. Pilot Point, Tex., Dec. 17, 1915; s. Louis and Catherine (Sloan) T. Student, St. Thomas Sch. Pilot Point, 1930, Pontifical Coll. Josephinum, Worthington, Ohio, 1943. Ordained priest Diocese of Dallas, 1943; asst. pastor Ft. Worth, 1943—46, Sherman, Tex., 1946—48, Dallas, 1948—53; adminstr. St. Patrick Ch., Dallas, 1953—56; pastor St. Augustine Ch., Dallas, 1956—62, Sacred Heart Cathedral, Dallas, 1962—65; ordained bishop, 1966; bishop Diocese of San Angelo, Tex., 1966—69, Diocese of Dallas, 1969—90, bishop emeritus, 1990—2009; asst. pastor St. Joseph Parish, Waxahachie, Tex., 1990—2009. Roman Catholic. Died Jan. 24, 2009.

TUCK, GERALD ARTHUR, assistant principal; s. Jane Kennedy Tuck. B, U. Fla., Gainesville, 1976; MEd, Nova Southeastern U., Ft. Lauderdale, Fla., 1994. Tchr., asst. prin. Hinesville Mid. Sch., Ga., 1976—2000; asst. prin. Snelson-Golden Mid. Sch., Hinesville, from 2000. Mem.: Masons. Home: Hinesville, Ga. Died Sept. 15, 2007.

TUCKER, JOHN AVERY, retired academic administrator, electrical engineer; b. Milton, Mass, Jan. 28, 1924; s. Seth Davenport and Ruth Lincoln (Avery) T. BSEE cum laude, Northeastern U., 1949; M. of Engring., Yale U., 1950. Registered profl. engr., Mass. Mem. tech. staff Bell Tel. Labs., Inc., NYC, 1950; engr. New Eng. Tel & Tel. Co., Boston, 1951-56; instr. elec. engring., Lincoln Inst. Northeastern U., Boston, 1955; with dept. elec. engring. and computer sci. MIT, Cambridge, Mass., 1956—2002, 1st adminstrv. officer, 1963, dir. VI-A internship program in elec. engring./computer sci., 1969-87, spl. asst. to dept. head, 1987-89, emeritus dir. VI-A program, lectr., 1989—2002; ret., 2002. Deacon emeritus Wellesley Hills Congl. Ch., mem., 1936—; bd. dirs. Wellesley chpt. ARC, 1978; chief of staff Wellesley Vets. Parade, 1996. Sgt. U.S. Army Signal Corps, 1943-46, PTO. Recipient Outstanding Alumnus in Edn. award Northeastern U., 1994, G. Y Billard award MIT, 1981. Mem.: AARP (bd. dir. MIT/Cambridge chpt. 1990—97), IEEE (life), IEEE (sr.), Am. Soc. Engring. Edn. (life), Wellesley Hist. Soc. (bd. dir. from 1993, 1st v.p. 1995—98, 2000), MIT Alumni Assoc. (hon.; Hon. mem. 1985), Appalachian Mountain Club, Tau Beta Pi Assn. (v.p. NU chpt. 1949, chief advisor from 1971, Nat. Outstanding Advisor award 1998), Eta Kappa Nu (founder Northeastern U. chpt. 1950, faculty advisor MIT 1956—74, nat. bd. dir. 1959—61, faculty advisor MIT from 1989, Outstanding Svc. award 2000, Disting. Svc. Award 2002). Avocation: photography. Home: Wellesley, Mass. Died Mar. 22, 2008.

TUESDAY, CHARLES SHEFFIELD, retired industrial research executive; b. Trenton, NJ, Sept. 7, 1927; s. Frank Sheffield and Madeline (Schwind) T.; m. Jean Faith Quallis, Aug. 23, 1952; children: David Sheffield, Lora Faith, Verna Jean. AB, Hamilton Coll., 1951; MA, PhD, Princeton U., 1955. Rsch. chemist Panelyte div. St. Regis Paper Co., Trenton, 1950-51; rsch. asst. Princeton (N.J.) U., 1951-55; rsch. chemist GM Rsch. Labs., Warren, Mich., 1955-64, supervising rsch. chemist, 1964-67, asst. head fuels and lubricants dept., 1967-70, head, 1970-72, head environ. sci. dept., 1972-74, tech. dir., 1974-88, exec. dir., 1988-92. Cons. various panels NRC, Washington, 1972-81; chmn. air pollution adv. com. Coordinating Rsch. Coun., Atlanta, 1978-80, bd. dirs., 1987-92; alt. rep. Indsl. Rsch. Inst., Washington, 1987-92. Editor: Chemical Reactions in Urban Atmospheres, 1971; contbr. articles to profl. jours. With U.S. Army, 1946-48. McCay fellow Princeton U., 1953-54. Mem. AAAS (chmn. indsl. sci. sect. 1990-91), Am. Chem. Soc. (com. on corp. assocs. 1985-92, mem. adv. bd. C&E News 1992—), Soc. Automotive Engrs., Phi Beta Kappa, Sigma Xi. Home: Eugene, Oreg. Died June 18, 2008.

TULIS, RONALD LEE, airport consultant; b. Bklyn., Jan. 19, 1946; s. Theodore Gabriel and Ella (Kornberg) T.; m. Susan D. Dulebohn, Oct. 29, 1966; children: Jason Michael, Corey Scott. BArch, U. Calif., Berkeley, 1968. Urban designer City of Mpls., 1968-72; urban planner Sedway Cooke, San Francisco, 1972-73, Livingston & Blaney, San Francisco, 1973-74, Livingston & Assocs., San Francisco, 1974-77; airport cons. KPMG Peat Marwick, San Francisco, 1977-93, Leigh Fisher Assocs., San Francisco, from 1993. Mem. steering com., environ. com. Airports Coun. Internat.-N.Am., Washington, 1992—. Recipient HUD Urban Design award Mpls. Downtown Assn., 1974, Am. Assn. Planners, 1978. Home: Danville, Calif. Died Feb. 18, 2008.

TUNISON, ELIZABETH LAMB, education educator; b. Portadown, Northern Ireland, Jan. 7, 1922; arrived in US, 1923; d. Richard Ernest and Ruby (Hill) Lamb; m. Ralph W. Tunison, Jan. 24, 1947 (dec. Apr. 1984); children: Eric Arthur, Christine Wait, Dana Paul. BA, Whittier Coll., 1943, MEd, 1963. Tchr. East Whittier (Calif.) Schs., 1943-59; tchr. T.V. TV Channels 13 and 28, So. Calif. Counties, 1960-75; dir. curriculum Bassett (Calif.) Schs., 1962-65; elem. sch. prin. Rowland Unified Schs., Rowland Heights, Calif., 1965-68; assoc. prof. edn. Calif. State Poly. U., Pomona, 1968-71; prof. Whittier Coll., 1968-88, prof. emerita, from 1988. Bd. dirs. Restless Legs Syndrome Found., mem. adv. coun.; facilitator So. Calif. Orgn. Bd. dirs. Presbyn. Intercmty. Hosp. Found.; founder Restless Legs Support Group (chmn. 1995-2003), Restless Leg Syndrome, nat. adv. com., 2003-. Recipient Whittier Coll. Alumni Achievement award 1975; Helen Hefernan scholar 1963. Mem. AAUP, Assn. Calif. Sch. Adminstrs. (state bd., chmn. higher edn. com. 1983-86, region pres. 1981-83, Wilson Grace award 1983), PEO (pres. 1990-92, pres. Mt. San Antonio Garden Group 2005-06), Assistance League of Whittier (v.p. 1994-96), Delta Kappa Gamma (v.p. 1996-97, Woman of Yr. 2001). Home: Pomona, Calif. Died Nov. 22, 2008.

TURKEL, SOLOMON HENRY, physicist; b. NYC, Sept. 8, 1911; s. Bernard and Rebecca (Kirschenbaum) T.; m. Mildred Cohen, May 7, 1941; children: Susan Turkel Reininger, Patricia Turkel Landsberg. BS, CCNY, 1932, MS, 1933. Instr. high sch., N.Y., 1941-42; physicist Argonne Nat. Lab., 1944-46, U. Chicago, 1944-46; prin. physicist dir. tech. info. Nuclear Engine Propulsion Aircraft, Oak Ridge, Tenn., 1946-49; mem. tech. staff Ops. Rsch. Office of Johns Hopkins U., Washington, 1948-56; systems analyst Northrop Corp., Hawthorne, Calif., 1956-59; sr. engr. GE Co., Phila., 1959-61; staff scientist Hughes Aircraft Co., Culver City, Calif., 1961-63, Aerospace Corp., San Bernardino, Calif., 1963-66, Rockwell Internat., Downey, Calif., 1966-76; ret. Contbr. articles to profl. jours. Bd. dirs. Nat. Conf. Christians and Jews, Orange County, Calif., 1976—, Anti-Defamation League of B'nai B'rith, 1976—; pres. So. Calif. Coun. B'nai B'rith, L.A., 1963-64. With U.S. Army, 1943-46. Recipient UN Medal, 1952. Fellow AAAS. Democrat. Jewish. Achievements include discovery and identification of many nuclear isotopes and radioactive elements. Home: Fountain Vly, Calif. Died Mar. 13, 2008.

TURLEY, HANS, English language educator; b. Parkersburg, W.Va., Apr. 29, 1956; s. Edwin William and Patricia Noonan Turley. BA in English, U. Wash., 1989, MA in English, 1992, PhD in English, 1994. Adminstrv. asst., asst. prodr. ABC News, NYC, 1980-87; acting instr. U. Wash., Seattle, 1995; asst. prof. Tex. Tech U., Lubbock, 1996-98, U. Conn., Storrs, from 1998. Author: Rum, Sodomy and the Lash, 1999; contbr. articles to scholarly and profl. jours. Fellow Mellon Found., 1994, Am. Soc. 18th Century Studies, 1995, 97, Dorothy Co lin Brown Fund, 1993. Mem. MLA, Am. Soc. 18th Century Studies (chair grad. student group 1993-94, LGBT caucus 1994-96). Home: Willimantic, Conn. Died June 13, 2008.

TURMAN, GEORGE F., former lieutenant governor; b. Missoula, Mont., June 25, 1928; s. George Fugett and Corinne (McDonald) T.; m. Kathleen Hager, Mar. 1951; children: Marcia, Linda, George Douglas, John, Laura. BA, U. Mont., 1951. Various positions Fed. Res. Bank of San Francisco, 1954-64; mayor City of Missoula, 1970-72; mem. Mont. Ho. of Reps. from Dist. 18, 1973-74; commr. Mont. Pub. Svc. from Dist. 5, 1975-80; lt. gov. State of Mont., 1981-88, resigned; mem. Pacific N.W. Electric Power Planning and Conservation Coun., 1988; pres. Nat. Ctr. for Appropriate Tech., Butte, Mont. Sr. advisor, adj. staff mem., dir. New Horizon Techs., Inc., 1995. Served in US Army, 1951-58. Decorated Combat Inf. badge. Democrat. Home: Missoula, Mont. Died Dec. 9, 2008.

TURNER, DAVID BERTRAM, minister; b. Corpus Christi, Tex., Oct. 13, 1939; s. Sylvan and Stella Buford (Newman) T.; m. Mary Elizabeth Cave, Aug. 6, 1965; children: Michelle, Bert. BA, Baylor U., 1963; MDiv, S.W. Bapt. Sem., 1965, postgrad., 1966-67, McCormick Sem., 1972-76. Assoc. minister First Bapt. Ch., Augusta, Ga., 1967-70, sr. minister Rockmart, Ga., 1970-76, Toccoa, Ga., 1976-80, Easley, S.C., from 1980. Exec. com. Ga. Bapt. Conv., Atlanta, 1974-76, S.C. Gen. Bd., Columbia, 1988-89; gen. bd. S.C. Bapt. Conv., Columbia, 1987-89; moderator Coop. Bapt. Fellowship S.C., Anderson, 1993-94. Columnist Rockmart Jour., 1974-76; contbr. articles, lessons to Christian publs. Chmn. Heart Assn. Stephens County, Toccoa, 1975; pres., founder Toccoa Road Runners, 1974-75; mem. Meals on Wheels Coun., Pickens County, S.C., 1990-93. Recipient Art award Pickens County Art Mus., 1988. Mem. Easley Rotary Club (com. chair 1980-94), Toccoa Rotary Club (com. chair 1976-80), Rockmart Rotary Club (pres. 1974-76), Easley Ministerial Assn. (treas. 1992-94). Avocations: pastelist, running, photography, creative writing-poetry. Home: Greenville, SC. Died July 10, 2008.

TURNER, HENRY ASHBY, JR., history educator; b. Atlanta, Apr. 4, 1932; s. Henry and Katherine (Bradley) Ashby; m. June 14, 1958; children: Bradley, Sarah, Mathew. BA, Washington & Lee U., 1954; MA, Princeton U., 1957, PhD, 1960; DLitt, Washington & Lee U., 1978. From instr. to prof. Yale U., New Haven, 1958—2008. Author: Stresemaun and the Politics of the Weimar Republic, 1963, Nazism and the Third Reich, 1972, Faschismus und Kapitalismus in Deutschland, 1972, German Big Business and the Rise of Hitler, 1985, The Two Germanies Since 1945, 1987 Geisel des Jahrhunderts, 1989, Germany from Partition to Reunification, 1992, Hitler's 30 Days to Power: January 1933, 1996, General Motors and the Nazis: The Struggle for Control of Opel, Europe's Biggest Carmaker, 2005; editor: Reappraisals of Fascism, 1975, Hitler: Memoirs of a Confidant, 1985 Recipient Commander Cross of the Order of Merit, Fed. Rep. of Germany, 1989. Died Dec. 17, 2008.

TURNER, JOHN B., retired dean, social worker, educator; b. Ft. Galley, Ga., Feb. 28, 1922; s. Brister William and Virginia H. (Brown) Turner; m. Marian Floredia Wilson; children: Marian Elizabeth, Charles Brister. BA, Morehouse Coll., 1946; MS in Social Adminstrn., Case Western Res. U., Cleve., 1948; D in Social Work, Case Western Res. U., 1959. Program sec. Butler Street YMCA, Atlanta, 1948—50; instr. Atlanta U., 1950—52; dir. Welfare Fedn. Field Svc., Cleve., 1959—61; dean Sch. Applied Social Sciences Case Western Res. U., 1968—73; William Rand Kenan Jr. prof. social work U. N. C., 1974—81, dean Sch. Social Work Chapel Hill, 1981—93. Cons. Nat. Urban League, 1966—71; cons. in internat. rsch. program US Dept. Health Edn. & Welfare, 1972—75; mem., Mayor's Commn. on Cmty. Resources City of Cleve., 1968—70; vis. prof., cons. U. Minia, Egypt, 1977; pres. Nat. Conf. Social Work, 1978. Editor: Encyclopedia of Social Work, 19th edit, 1995, (compendium) Publcations About Black Americans, 1995. Bd. trustees Cleve. Inst. Art, 1970—74. Served in Tuskegee Airmen USAF, 1943—45. Mem.: Internat. Assn. Applied Social Scientists. Died Jan. 30, 2009.

TURNER, JOHN JOSEPH, advertising executive; b. Oklahoma City, Oct. 12, 1943; s. John Joseph and Barbara Ann (Payne) T.; m. Susan Joyce Hodge, Dec. 27, 1966; children: Sean, Ryan, Kasey. BS, U. So. Calif., 1966. Acct. exec. McCann Erickson, LA, 1967-70; sr. v.p. Davis Elen Advtg., LA, from 1970. Lt. USNR, 1966-72. Mem. Los Angeles Yacht Club, Palos Verdes Tennis. Republican. Methodist. Avocations: supt. broadcast production, sailing, alpine skiing. Home: Palos Verdes Peninsula, Calif. Died May 2, 2008.

TURNER, LLOYD DANIEL, musician; b. Hollywood, Calif, May 11, 1951; s. Lloyd Gardner and Mary Lorrina Turner. Student, Golden West Coll., 1983—86. With Electronic Factory, Culver City, Calif., 1966; jazz musician, road Rodger Williams; jazz musician Dottie Town Pipers Tahoe, Las Vegas, Nev. Home: Reseda, Calif. Died Aug. 6, 2007.

TURNER, MILDRED EDITH, day care owner; b. Winnebago, Wis., Jan. 11, 1926; d. Jewett Candfield and Angeline Mary (Long) T. BS, State Tchrs. Coll., 1949; MS of Edn., U. Wis., Milw., 1962; postgrad., U. Wis., Oshkosh, 1965-70. Cert. tchr., Wis. Tchr. Winnebago County, Omro, Wis., 1945-47, Plymouth (Wis.) Pub. Schs., 1949-51, Ripon (Wis.) Pub. Schs., 1951-53, Omro Pub. Schs., 1953-88; instr. U. Wis., Oshkosh, 1971, supervising tchr. of student tchrs., 1970-91; owner, operator Wee Care Children's Ctr., Omro, from 1974. Contbr. articles to newspapers, children's books, including Little Hoo. Acolyte coord. Algoma Blvd. United Meth. Ch.; supt. Sunday sch., pianist, choir dir., ch. music dir. Eureka/Waukau United Meth. Ch.; sub-dist. children's dir. Watertown sub-dist. United Meth. Ch.; founder Nativity Mus., Oshkosh, 1997. Named to Omro Wall of Fame, 1999. Mem. Ret. Tchrs. Assn. Winnebago County, Ret. Tchrs. Assn. Omro, Fox Valley Assn. for Edn. of Young Children, Word and Pen Christian Writers (sec.-treas.), Alumni Assn. U. Wis. Oshkosh), Alumni Assn. Omro (treas.), Odd Fellows (past noble grand Rebekah lodge), Omro Study Club (past pres.). Avocation: collecting nativity sets. Died Dec. 7, 2007.

TWEET, ORLANDO A., retired industrial chemist; b. Eleva, Wis., Dec. 22, 1915; s. Andrew N. and Inga Tonetta (Thompson) T.; m. Marion Jeanette Holman, Aug. 9, 1952; children: Victoria Suzanne, Christine Claire, Jean Ellen. BA, St. Olaf Coll., 1939; MS, U. Wis., 1947. Quality control analytical chemist S.C. Johnson Wax Co., Racine, 1947, sr. rsch. chemist in thermal analysis and chromatography. Judge S.E. Wis. Sci. and Engring. Fair, Marquette U., Milw., 1972—. Contbr. articles to profl. jours. Life mem. NAACP, Racine, mem. gov. bd., 1970-80; founder US/USSR Friendship Soc., Racine, 1984—; mem. Am. Luth. Ch., Madison, 1982-88; mem. peace and justice bd. dirs. Evang. Luth. Ch., Milw., 1988—; pres. Luth. Human Rels. Assn. Wis., 1978-86, Milw., 1966—. 2d lt. U.S. Army, 1942-45. Recipient Peace Svc. award World Fedn. Assn., 1987, Honor award NAACP, 1979, Peace Pilgrim award Coun. for Internat. Friendship, 1994, UN Day award, 1997. Mem. Am. Chem. Soc., Wis. State Hist. Soc., Sons of Norway (Racine). Democrat. Avocations: hiking, gardening, bird watching, genealogy, family history research. Home: Racine, Wis. Died Apr. 3, 2008.

TWISS, JOHN RUSSELL, JR., retired federal agency administrator; b. NYC, Sept. 16, 1938; s. John R. and Edith Jordan (Liddell) T.; m. Mary Hawthorne Sheldon, Jan. 20,

1973; children: John Stewart, Alison McIntosh, Emily Ellsworth. BA, Yale U., 1961. Polar rschr. U.S. Govt., 1961-63; NSF rep. in charge U.S. Sci. Programs in Antarctica, 1964-65; mem. staff internat. divsn. Smith Kline & French Labs., 1966-67; v.p. EPC Labs., 1967-68; sci. leader So. Ocean expdn. NSF, 1968-69, spl. asst. to head Internat. Decade Ocean Exploration, 1970-74; exec. dir. Marine Mammal Commn., Washington, 1974—2000. Mem. STudent Conservation Assn., 1986-2009; mem. strategic adv. coun. Sch. Forestry and Environ. Studies Yale U., 1990-94, assoc. fellow Branford Coll.; mem. adminstrv. bd. Michael C. Rockefeller Meml. fellowship Harvard U., 1991-97; chmn. bd. dirs. Kokrobitey Sch., Ghana, 1992-95; bd. overseers Leadership Decisions Inst.; lectr., cons. in field; mem. numerous adv. coms. and U.S. dels. Mem. Met. Club Washington, Army and Navy Club, Squadron A Club, Ends of the Earth Club. Home: The Plains, Va. Died July 23, 2009.

TYLER, LOUIS I., JR., pediatrician; b. Baton Rouge, Apr. 5, 1920; s. Louis Ira and Katherine Easton (McDonald) T.; m. Anna Mae Hoffpauir, Feb. 6, 1946 (div. Aug. 1975); children: Louis III, Robyn Easton, Thomas Lindsey, Brooks Brent; m. Audrey Bernice Penalber, Aug. 15, 1975. Student, U. Heidelberg, Germany, 1938; BS, Tulane U., 1940, MD, 1943. Diplomate Am. Bd. Pediatrics; lic. physician, La., Miss., Ala. Intern, house officer So. Bapt. Hosp., 1943-44; fellow in gen. surgery Ochsner Clinic, New Orleans, 1948; resident in pediatrics Childrens Hosp., Columbus, Ohio, 1949-51; pvt. practice Baton Rouge, 1951-75; asst. dir. health svcs., staff physician Partlow State Sch. and Hosp., Tuscaloosa, Ala., 1975-81; dir. health svcs. Partlow Devel. Ctr., Tuscaloosa, Ala., from 1981. Courtesy staff Druid City Hosp., Tuscaloosa, radiology cons. Rehab. Pavilion; instr. gen. surgery Tulane U., 1946-47; clin. instr. pediatric Children's Hosp., Columbus, 1949-50. With M.C. USN, 1944-46, S.W. Pacific Theater. Fellow Am. Acad. Pediatrics; mem. Med. Assn. Ala., Tuscaloosa County Med. Soc., Ala. Acad. Pediatrics. Avocations: stamp collecting/philately, coin collecting/numismatics, antiques, travel, photography. Home: Tuscaloosa, Ala. Died Oct. 1, 2007.

TYRELL-SMITH, PATRICK CREAGH, information systems director; b. Oakland, Calif., Dec. 26, 1933; s. Herbert Creagh and Patricia (McHugh) T.-S.; m. Kathleen Elizabeth; children: Lisa Suzanne, Timothy Creagh, Terrence Patrick. BS in Polit. Sci., U. San Francisco, 1955. Systems analyst Am. Fore Ins. Group, San Francisco, 1958-59; data processing mgr. Lockheed Missiles and Space Co., Sunnyvale, Calif., 1959-69; sr. systems mgr., asst. v.p. Fireman's Fund Ins., San Rafael, Calif., 1969-84; bus. cons. Pat Tyrell-Smith & Assocs., San Rafael, 1984-87; dir. info. systems Coll. of Marin, Kentfield, Calif., from 1987. Bus. editor Classified Gazette, San Rafael, 1985—. 1st lt. U.S. Army, 1955-57. Pres. San Rafael C. of C., 1979-80, Marin Arts Coun., 1986-87; chair citizens adv. com. Dominican Coll., San Rafael, 1983-84; chair Mother Lode Musical Theatre, Kentfield, Calif., 1985—. Mem. Nat. Assn. Profl. Saleswomen (bd. dirs. 1989—), Marin Forum, Marvelous Marin Breakfast Club (pres. 1986-87). Avocations: writing, reading, racquetball. Home: Las Vegas, Nev. Died May 4, 2008.

TYSON, LUTHER EWING, finance executive; b. Temple, Tex., Oct. 19, 1922; s. Joe Mickel and Venevian Brack (Murphy) T.; m. Mary Louise Griffis, Oct. 10, 1942; children: Joanna Griffis, Jonathan Pope. AB, Bethany Coll., 1944; STB, Boston U., 1947, PhD, 1968; postgrad., Harvard Grad. Sch., 1958. Assoc. minister Congregational Ch., Needham, Mass., 1949-50; pastor St. Stephen's United Meth. Ch., Marblehead, Mass., 1950-54, Grace United Meth. Ch., Haverhill, Mass., 1954-58; exec. dir. Boston Area Com. on Indsl. Rels., Boston, 1958-66; dir. and assoc. gen. sec. Bd. of Ch. and Soc., United Meth. Ch., Washington, 1966-85; pres. Pax World Fund, Inc., Portsmouth, N.H., 1970-97. Adv. bd. Nat. Coun. of Chs., N.Y.C., 1956-85, Bd. of Ch. and Soc., Washington, 1956-66; adj. prof. Boston U., 1962, U. N.H., 1962-64. Author publs. in field. Fellow in econs. Swift and Co., Chgo., 1960, Ch. Ctr. for Pub. Policty, Washington, 1980. Mem. Am. Sociol. Assn., Am. Soc. Christian Ethics. Democrat. Methodist. Avocations: gardening, travel, reading. Home: Palm Coast, Fla. Died Apr. 22, 2008.

UHLENBURG, DONALD GEORGE, heat treating company executive; b. Perrysville, Pa., Oct. 16, 1934; s. Willard L. and Crissie (Snyder) U.; m. Marjory Spang, Apr. 21, 1934; children: Cindy Lou Maloney, Jeffrey D. BSMetE, Lehigh U., 1956. Product metallurgist U.S. Steel Corp., Homestead, Pa., 1957-63; asst. chief metallurgist Interlake Steel, Riverdale, Ill., 1963-64, chief metallurgist, 1964-66, dir. metallurgy Chgo., 1966-68; dir. tech. svcs. Alan Wood Steel, Conshohocken, Pa., 1968-71; pres. Donovan Heat Treating, Phila., 1972—2000. Session Paoli (Pa.) Presbyterian Ch., 1971-74 Mem. Metal Treating Inst. (trustee 1982-88, pres. 1986-87). Republican. Avocations: fishing, boating, tennis. Home: Malvern, Pa. Died June 1, 2009.

ULLMANN, LEONARD PAUL, psychologist, educator, author, artist; b. NYC, May 28, 1930; s. Siegfried and Irma (Lichtenstadter) U.; m. Rina Kalb, June 5, 1951 (div. Apr. 19, 1972); children: Michael, Nancy; m. Wendy S. Ullmann, May 17, 1978. AB, Lafayette U., 1951; AM, Stanford U., 1953, PhD, 1955. Coord. psychiatric evaluation VA Hosp., Palo Alto, Calif., 1956-63; prof. psychology U. Ill., Urbana, 1963-72, U. Hawaii, Honolulu, 1972-81, U. Houston, 1981-88. Author: Case Studies in Behavior Modification, 1965, A Psychological Approach to Abnormal Behavior, 1969, 75, Institution and Outcome, 1968, Behavior Influence and Personality, 1973. Home: Incline Village, Nev. Died May 28, 2008.

ULMER, RONALD JOSEPH, deacon; b. Beverly, NJ, July 14, 1929; s. Joseph James and Harriet (Schooley) U.; m. Alfreda Olga Fortini, Sept. 24, 1949; children: Joanne Carol, Alfred Joseph. AS, Burlington County Coll., 1978. Deacon St. Joseph's Ch., Beverly, N.J., from 1988; tech. assoc. David Sarnoff Rsch. Ctr., Princeton, N.J., from 1962. Officer, mem. Beverly Fire Co. #1, 1946—, Beverly Emergency Squad, 1947—, Beverly City Bd. Health, 1981-85. With USN, 1951-55, Korea. Recipient Eagle Scout award Boy Scouts Am., 1946; named Commdr. of the Yr., 1964-65. Democrat. Home: Beverly, NJ. Died Sept. 15, 2007.

UNDERWOOD, CECIL HARLAND, Former Governor, West Virginia; b. Josephs Mills, W.Va., Nov. 5, 1922; s. Silas and Della (Forrester) U.; m. Hovah Hall, July 25, 1948 (dec. 2004); children: Cecilia A., Craig Hall, Sharon. AB, Salem Coll., W.Va., 1943; AM, W.Va. U., 1952; rsch. fellow, Amelia Earhart Found., Ann Arbor, Mich., 1954-56; LLD (hon.), Marietta Coll., Ohio, 1957, Bethany Coll., 1957, W.Va. U., 1957, W.Va. Inst. Tech., 1957; doctorate of Humanics (hon.), Salem Coll., 1957; degree in pub. adminstrn. (hon.), W.Va. Wesleyan Coll., 1958; LLD (hon.), Concord Coll., 1960, W.Va. State Coll., 1961; LHD (hon.), Shepherd Coll., 1964; LittD (hon.), Western New Eng. Coll., 1969; LHD (hon.), Marshall U., 1997; degree in pub. svc. (hon.), Alderson Broaddus Coll., 1997; DSc (hon.), W. Va. Sch. Osteopathic Med., 1998; degree (hon.), Davis and Elkins Coll., 1998, Fairmont State Coll., 1999. Tchr. high sch., 1943-46; staff Marietta Coll., 1946-50; v.p. Salem Coll., 1950-56; gov. State of W.Va., 1957—61, 1997—2001; v.p. Island Creek Coal Co., 1961-64; dir. civic affairs Monsanto Co., 1965-67, v.p., 1967; pres. Cecil H. Underwood Assocs., 1965-80, Franswood Corp., 1968-75, Bethany (W.Va.) Coll., 1972-75, Princess Coals, Inc., Huntington, 1978-81, Morgantown (W.Va.) Indsl. Park, Inc., 1983-96, Software Valley, 1989-92, Mon View Heights of W.Va., 1993-96; field underwriter N.Y. Life Ins. Co., 1976-78; chmn. bd. Princess Coals, Inc., Huntington, 1981-83. Sec. bd. dirs. Huntington Fed. Savs. and Loan Assn., 1961-96; pres. Huntington Found. Mem. W.Va. Ho. Dels., 1944-56, minority floor leader, 1949, 51, 53, 55; Mem. exec. com. Gov.'s Conf., 1959; chmn. So. Regional Edn. Bd., 1959-60, 1999-2000; Pres. Young Republican League of W.Va., 1946-50; parliamentarian Young Rep. Nat. Conv., Boston, 1951; del.-at-large Rep. Nat. Conv., 1960, 64, 72, 76, 80, 84, 88, 2000, temporary chmn., 1960; Chmn. bd. dirs. W.Va. Found. Ind. Colls., Appalachian Regional Hosps.; chmn. bd. dirs. W.Va. div. Am. Cancer Soc., nat. bd. dirs., chmn. nat. crusade com., 1976-77, chmn. com. on legacies and planned giving, 1979; chmn. bd. dirs. Salem Coll., 1978-89, Salem Internat. U., 1989—; bd. dirs. Higher Edn. Loan Program of W.Va., 1980-94; chair W.Va. Coun. on Vocat. Edn., 1982-96, W.Va. State Coll. System, 1991, Nat. Edn. Goals Panel, 1998-99; regional vice chmn. Boy Scouts Am., 1961-67; dir. Fed. Home Loan Bank of Pitts. Mem. Nat. Assn. State Coun. Vocat. Edn. (pres. 1994-96), Masons, Shriners, Elks, Rotary, Sigma Phi Epsilon, Pi Kappa Delta. Republican. Methodist. Home: Charleston, W.Va. Died Nov. 24, 2008.

UNVERFERTH, HAROLD SOEHNER, religious studies educator; b. Dayton, Ohio, May 9, 1917; s. Gerard Ambrose and Eleonara Louise (Soehner) Unverferth; m. Doris Alice Doyle (dec.); children: Jerry, Nicholas, Ann. BS in bus. adminstrn., U. Dayton, 1939; B in musical studies, U. Montreal, Canada, 1948. Charter mem. Gregorian Inst. of Am., Pitts., from 1939. Organist, choirmaster St. Mary's Ch. North Side, Pitts., St. Mary's Ch., Sharpsburg, Pa., St. James Ch., Wilkinsburg, Pa.; organist Carnegie Hall. Tech. sgt. US Army, 1941—45. Mem.: Nat. Pastoral Musicians, Am. Guild of Organists. Democrat. Cath. Home: Allison Park, Pa. Died May 9, 2008.

UPDIKE, JOHN HOYER, writer; b. Shillington, Pa., Mar. 18, 1932; s. Wesley Russel and Linda Grace (Hoyer) U.; m. Mary Entwistle Pennington, June 26, 1953 (div. 1976); children: Elizabeth, David, Michael, Miranda; m. Martha Ruggles Bernhard, Sept. 30, 1977; stepchildren: John, Jason, Frederic AB, Harvard U., 1954; student, Ruskin Sch. Drawing and Fine Art, 1954-55. With New Yorker mag., NYC, 1955-57. Author: (novels) The Poorhouse Fair, 1959 (Richard and Hinda Rosenthal Found. award Am. Acad. and Nat. Inst. Arts and Letters 1960), The Same Door, 1959, Rabbit, Run, 1960, Pigeon Feathers, 1962, The Centaur, 1963 (Nat. Book award for fiction 1963, Prix Medicis Etranger 1966), Olinger Stories, 1964, Of the Farm, 1965, The Music School, 1966, Couples, 1968, Bech: A Book, 1970, Rabbit Redux, 1971, Museums and Women, 1972, Warm Wine, 1973, A Month of Sundays, 1975, Marry Me, 1976, Couples, 1976, The Coup, 1978, From the Journal of a Leper, 1978, Problems, 1979, Too Far to Go: The Maples Stories, 1979 (Am. Book award nomination 1980), Three Illuminations in the Life of an American Author, 1979, Your Lover Just Called: Stories of Joan and Richard Maple, 1980, The Chaste Planet, 1980, Rabbit Is Rich, 1981 (Pulitzer prize for fiction 1982, Nat. Book Critics Circle award 1982, Am. Book award 1982), Invasion of the Book Envelopes, 1981, Bech Is Back, 1982, The Beloved, 1982, The Witches of Eastwick, 1984, Confessions of a Wild Bore, 1984, Roger's Version, 1986 (Nat. Book Critics Circle award nomination 1986), Trust Me, 1987, More Stately Mansions, 1987, S., 1988, Rabbit at Rest, 1990 (Pulitzer prize for fiction 1991, Nat. Book Critics Circle award 1991), Memories of the Ford Administration, 1992, Brazil, 1994, The Afterlife, 1994, In the Beauty of the Lilies, 1996, Toward the End of Time, 1997, Bech at Bay, 1998, Gertrude and Claudius, 2000, Licks of Love: Short Stories and a Sequel, Rabbit Remembered, 2000, The Complete Henry Bech, 2001, Seek My Face, 2002, The Early Stories 1953-75, 2003 (PEN/Faulkner award 2004), Villages, 2004, Terrorist, 2006, The Widows of Eastwick, 2008, My Father's Tears and Other Stories, 2009; (non-fiction) Assorted Prose, 1965, On Meeting Authors, 1968, A Good Place, 1973, Picked-Up Pieces, 1975, Hub Fans Bid Kid Adieu, 1977, Talk from the Fifties, 1979, Ego and Art in Walt Whitman, 1980, Hawthorne's Creed, 1981, Hugging the Shore, 1983 (Nat. Book Critics Circle award 1984), Emersonianism, 1984, Just Looking, 1989, Self-Consciousness, 1989, Odd Jobs, 1991, Golf Dreams, 1996, More Matter, 1999, On Literary Biography, 1999, Still Looking: Essays on American Art, 2005, Due Considerations: Essays and Criticism, 2007; (poetry) The Carpentered Hen and Other Tame Creatures, 1958, Telephone Poles, 1963, A Child's Calendar, 1965, The Angels, 1968, Bath after Sailing, 1968, Midpoint, 1969, Seventy Poems, 1972, Six Poems, 1973, Tossing and Turning, 1977, Sixteen Sonnets, 1979, Five Poems, 1980, Spring Trio, 1982, Jester's Dozen, 1984, Facing Nature, 1985, Collected Poems 1953-1993, 1993, A Helpful Alphabet of Friendly Objects, 1995, In the Cemetery High Above Shillington, 1996, Radiators, 1998, Americana: and Other Poems, 2001, Not Cancelled Yet, 2003, Endpoint and Other Poems, 2009; adapter: (librettos) The Magic Flute, 1962, The Ring, 1964; (plays) Bottom's Dream, 1969, Three Texts from Early Ipswich, 1968, Buchanan Dying, 1974; author words and music: (with Gunther Schuller) The Fisherman and His Wife, 1970; editor: Pens and Needles, 1970, (with S. Ravenel) The Best American Short Stories 1984, 1984, A Century of Arts and Letters, 1998, (with K. Kenison) The Best Am. Short Stories of the Century, 1999, Karl Shapiro: Selected Poems, 2003. Recipient O. Henry First Short Story award, 1966, 91, MacDowell medal for literature, 1981, Medal of Honor for literature Nat. Arts Club, 1984, PEN/Malamud Meml. prize PEN/Faulker award Found., 1988, Nat. Medal of Arts, 1989, Harvard Arts medal, 1998, Nat. Book Found. award Lifetime Achievement, 1998, Nat. Humanities medal, 2003, Golden Plate award, Acad. Achievement, 2004, Rea award for the short story, 2006, Gold Medal Fiction, 2007; Guggenheim fellow, 1959. Mem. AAAL, Am. Acad. Arts. and Scis. Democrat. Episcopalian. Died Jan. 27, 2009.

URAM, LOUISE SUSAN, graphic designer, illustrator; b. Pitts., Nov. 18, 1961; d. Martin John and Marcella Louise (Devera) U. Student, Chatham Coll., 1981; BFA in Art Illustration, Carnegie Mellon U., 1985. Artist Custom Printed Graphics, Pitts., 1984; computer graphic designer, illustrator Montefiore Hosp., Pitts., 1987-88; graphic designer, illustrator Uram & Assocs., Pitts., from 1985; computer graphic designer, illustrator Price Waterhouse, Pitts., from 1988. Publ. mgr., communitcations specialist, Computing and Info. Systems, U. Pitts., 1989—; free lance illustrator, Pitts. Post Gazette, Pitts., 1989—, Visual arts support vol. Three Rivers Arts Festival, Pitts., 1984—; community vol. United Way Agy. Southwestern Pa., Pitts., 1984—; mem. promotions com. South Side Local Devel. Co., Pitts., 1987—, bd. dirs., 1989—. Mem. Am. Inst. Graphic Arts (sec. N.Y. chpt. 1988—), Graphic Artists Guild. Avocations: tennis, photography, gardening. Home: Pittsburgh, Pa. Died Sept. 14, 2007.

USHER, ELIZABETH REUTER (MRS. WILLIAM A. SCAR), retired librarian; b. Seward, Nebr. d. Paul and Elizabeth (Meyer) Reuter; m. Harry Thomas Usher, Feb. 25, 1950; m. William Arthur Scar, Mar. 28, 1992. BS in Edn., U. Nebr., 1942; BS in Libr. Sci., U. Ill., 1944; Litt.D. (hon.), Concordia U., Seward, 1981. Tchr. Zion Luth. Sch., Platte Center, Nebr. and; St. Paul's Luth. Sch., Paterson, N.J.; library asst. charge res. book reading room U. Nebr., 1942-43; asst. circulation librarian Mich. State U., 1944-45; librarian Cranbrook Acad. Art, Bloomfield Hills, Mich., 1945-48; catalog and reference librarian Met. Mus. Art, NYC, 1948-53, head cataloger and reference librarian, 1953-54, asst. librarian, 1954-61, chief of art reference library, 1961-68, chief librarian, Thomas J. Watson Library, 1968-80, chief librarian emeritus, from 1980, acting librarian, 1954-57. Contbr. articles to profl. periodicals, library publs. Trustee N.Y. Met. Reference and Research Library Agy., 1968-80, sec. to bd., 1971-77, v.p., 1977-80; 1st v.p. Heritage Village Library, 1982-88, 91-92, pres., 1988-91, 95-2000. Mem. AAUW, Spl. Libraries Assn. (pres. 1967-68, dir. 1960-63, 66-69, Hall of Fame 1980—), Coll. Art Assn. (chmn. libraries session 1972-73), NY Libr. Club, Archons of Colophon (convener 1980-82), Heritage Village Rep. Club (pres. 1992-95, 97-99), Philanthropic Ednl. Orgn. (v.p. chpt. Q 1994-97, pres. 1997-98). Lutheran. Home: Lees Summit, Mo. Died June 16, 2009.

USINGER, MARTHA PUTNAM, counselor, educator, dean; b. Pitts., Dec. 10, 1912; d. Milo Boone and Christiana (Haberstroh) Putnam; m. Robert Leslie Usinger, June 24, 1938 (dec Oct. 1968); children: Roberta Christine (dec.), Richard Putnam. AB cum laude, U. Calif., Berkeley, 1934, postgrad., 1935—36, Oreg. State U., 1935—37, U. Ghana, 1970, Coll. Nairobi, 1970. Tchr. Oakland (Calif.) Pub. Schs., 1936-38, Berkeley (Calif.) Pub. Schs., 1954-57, dean West Campus, counselor, 1957-78. Lectr., photographer in field. Author: Ration Books and Christmas Crackers, 1989, Threading My Way, 3 vols., 2003; contbg. author: Robert Leslie Usinger, Autobiography of an Entomologist, 1972.

Mem. DAR, Berkeley Ret. Tchrs., U. Calif. Emeriti Assn., U. Calif. Alumnae Assn., Prytanean Alumnae Assn. (alumnae pres. 1952-54), Berkeley Camera Club, Mortar Bd., Am. Friends of Puttenham, P.E.O., Delta Kappa Gamma. Avocations: photography, slide shows and lectures, ethnic textiles, travel, geneology. Home: Kensington, Calif. Died Dec. 4, 2007.

VAGNOZZI, ALDO, former state legislator; b. Roseto, Abruzzi, Italy, Oct. 4, 1925; came to U.S., 1933; s. Attilio and Maria Grazia (Sinibaldi) V.; m. Lois Margaret Carl, Jan. 22, 1949 (dec. Nov. 1999); children: Steve, Paul, Nancy, Barbara. BA, Wayne State U., 1948. Asst. editor Mich. CIO News, Detroit, 1948-61; editor Mich. AFL-CIO News, Detroit, 1961-79; editl. cons. Cy Aaron Publs., Detroit, 1979-91, Inland Press, Detroit, 1991-94; editor Detroit Labor News, 1980-98; mem. Dist. 37 Mich. House Reps., 2002—06. Mem. adv. bd. Internat. Visitors Bur., Detroit; mem. Farmington Sch. Bd., 1969-73; vice chmn., Oakland County Democratic Com., 1973-79 Mem. city coun. City of Farmington Hills, Mich., 1987-99, mayor, 1991, 95-99 Served in US Army, 1943—46. Democrat. Roman Catholic. Avocation: crossword puzzles. Home: Farmington Hills, Mich. Died Mar. 21, 2009.

VALLEY, JOHN RICHARD, educational consultant, researcher; b. Cleve., Mar. 24, 1919; s. John and Olga (Lilliankampf) V.; m. Joan Squier Valley, May 15, 1944 (dec. 1956); children: John R. Jr., Jennifer Joan; m. Helen Danielly Valley, July 6, 1962; stepchild, Helen Elizabeth Hahn. BA, Case Western Reserve U., 1941, MA, 1947. Counselor, acting head Veterans Guidance Ctr., Cleve., 1945-47; asst. dean students Case Inst. Tech., Cleve., 1947-54; area dir. Ednl. Testing Svc., Princeton, N.J., 1954-84; ednl. cons., from 1984. Bd. dirs. Hilton Head (S.C.) Coll. Ctr.; mem. Beaufort County (S.C.) Higher Edn. Commn., 1985-90; mem. acad. coun. Thomas Edison State Coll., Trenton, N.J., 1974-80. Author: Increasing the Options, 1972, Career Education for Adults, 1977, The SAT: Four Major Modifications of the 1970-85 Era, 1992; co-author: Adult Learning and Training in Industrialized Countries, 1982; cons. editor: Jour. Higher Edn., 1974-83. Capt. USA, 1941-45, PTO. Recipient Leadership award Coun. for Adult and Experiential Learning, Columbia, Md., 1984; mem. emeritus Coun. on the Continuing Edn. Unit, Washington, 1984. Presbyterian. Home: Hilton Head Island, SC. Died Mar. 25, 2008.

VAN BRUGGEN, COOSJE, artist, author; b. Groningen, The Netherlands, June 6, 1942; came to U.S., 1978, naturalized, 1993; d. J.A.R. van Bruggen and A.M. Andriessen; m. Claes Oldenburg, July 22, 1977. DRS in Art History, Rijks U. Groningen, 1967; DFA (hon.), Calif. Coll. Arts and Crafts, 1996, Nova Scotia Coll. Art and Design, Halifax, 2005, Coll. Creative Studies, Detroit, 2005; DLitt (hon.), U. Teesside, Middlesbrough, Eng., 1999. Asst. curator Stedelijk Mus., Amsterdam, The Netherlands, 1967-71; prof. Acad. Fine Arts, Enschede, The Netherlands, 1971-76; sr. critic landscape arch. Harvard U., Cambridge, Mass., 1993; sr. critic dept. sculpture Yale U., New Haven, 1996-97. Co-editor Catalogue Sonsbeek, 1971; mem. selection com. Documenta 7, Kassel, Germany, 1982; curator (with Dieter Koepplin) Bruce Nauman: Drawings, 1965-1986, Basel, Switzerland, 1986-88. Author: Bruce Nauman, 1989, John Baldessari, 1990, Hanne Darboven, Urzeit, Uhrzeit, 1990, Frank O. Gehry: Guggenheim Museum Bilbao, 1997; co-author (with Claes Oldenburg): Sketches and Blottings Toward the European Desk Top, 1990, Large-Scale Projects, 1994, Claes Oldenburg Coosje van Bruggen, 1999, Down Liquidambar Lane: Sculpture in the Park, 2001, Images à la Carte, 2004, Sculpture by the Way, 2006; co-author: (with Claes Oldenburg and Frank O. Gehry) Il Corso del Coltello, 1985; two-person shows (with Claes Oldenburg), Leo Castelli Gallery, NYC, 1980, 1986, 1990, Palacio de Cristal, Madrid, 1986, No. Ctr. Contemporary Art, Sunderland, 1988, Leeds City Art Gallery, 1988, Palais des Beaux-Arts, Brussels, 1988, IVAM Ctr. Julio González, Valencia, 1988, Mus. Contemporary Art, LA, 1988, Musée Nat. d'Art Moderne, Ctr Georges Pompidou, Paris, 1989, Galleria Christian Stein, Milan, 1990, Guggenheim Mus. SoHo, NYC, 1993, Pace Gallery, 1994, Nat. Gallery Art, Washington, 1995, Solomon R. Guggenheim Mus., NY, 1995, Mus. Contemporary Art, LA, 1995, Hayward Gallery, London, 1996, Museo Correr, Venice, 1999, Museu Serralves, Porto, 2001, Met. Mus. Art, NYC, 2002, PaceWildenstein, 2002, Frederik Meijer Gardens and Sculpture Park, Grand Rapids, Mich., 2002, Whitney Mus. Am. Art, NYC, 2002, Chinati Found., Marfa, Tex., 2003, Paula Cooper Gallery, 2004, Pace Wildenstein Gallery, 2005, Konrad Fischer Galerie, Düsseldorf, 2005, Castello di Rivoli Mus. Contemporary Art, Rivoli-Turin, 2006, Fundació Joan Miró, Barcelona, 2007, Waddington Gallery, London, 2007, group shows with Claes Oldenburg, La Grande Halle, La Villette, Paris, 1989, Guggenheim Mus., NYC, 1993, Venice Biennale, 1997, Guggenheim Mus., Bilbao, 1998, Nat. Gallery, London, 2000, Solomon R. Guggenheim Mus., NY, 2001, Whitney Mus. Am. Art, NYC, 2002, Castello di Rivoli Mus. Contemporary Art, Rivoli-Turin, 2007, others, numerous pub. sculptures including, Nollen Plz., Civic Ctr., Des Moines, Mpls. Sculpture Garden, Walker Art Ctr., Mpls., Parc de la Villette, Paris, Ctrl. Gardens, Middlesborough, Eng., Guggenheim Found., Neumarkt Galerie, Cologne, Cheonguyeon Stream, Seoul, Korea, and many others. Recipient Lifetime Achievement award, Internat. Sculpture Ctr., Washington, 1994, Nathaniel S. Saltonstall award, ICA, Boston, 1996, Ptnrs. in Edn. award, Guggenheim, N.Y., 2002, Nat. Medal award, Sch. Mus. Fine Arts, Boston, 2004; co-recipient (with Claes Oldenburg) Distinction in Sculpture, Sculpture Ctr., N.Y.C., 1984. Died Jan. 10, 2009.

VAN DALEN, GORDON JOHN, physicist, educator; b. Tokyo, Sept. 19, 1951; came to the U.S., 1952; s. John and Ruth Margaret (Payne) Van D.; m. Carolyn Margaret Boutin, Apr. 8, 1978; children: John Edward, Stephen Michael. BS, U. Calif., Riverside, 1973, MS, 1975, PhD, 1978. From rsch. asst. to assoc. prof. U. Calif., Riverside, 1975-89, prof., 1990—2003; ret., 2003. Assoc. dean U. Calif., Riverside, 1990-93, dept. chmn., 1994-95; rsch. prof. Embry-Riddle Aeronautical U., 2003—. Contbr. articles to profl. jours. Mem. AAAS, Phi Beta Kappa. Achievements include research in experimental particles. Home: Prescott, Ariz. Died Apr. 30, 2009.

VAN DEN BRANDE, RENE ALBERT, retired accountant; b. Antwerp, Belgium, Aug. 14, 1916; arrived in Can., 1925; s. Henry Van den Brande and Maria Josephine Christ; m. Lily Pearson, July 7, 1947 (dec.). Cert. in pub. adminstrn., Queen's U., Ont., Can., 1963. Chartered acct., Can. Instr. Leamington Bus. Coll., Ont., 1938—40; asst. dept. head Dept. Nat. Revenue, Toronto, 1948—51; pvt. practice acct. Oakville, Ont., 1951—54; office mgr. Erb Lumber Co., Royal Oak, Mich., 1954—57; mgr. Sullivan Homes Inc., Dunedin, Fla., 1957—60; county adminstr. County of Essex, Ont., 1960—81; cons. Fed. Bank Can., Windsor, Ont., 1981—83; town adminstr. Town of South Palm Beach, Fla., 1983—88; ret. Flying officer Royal Can. Air Force, 1940—45, Camp Borden. Avocations: woodworking, reading. Deceased.

VAN-DEN-NOORT, STANLEY, neurologist, educator; b. Lynn, Mass., Sept. 8, 1930; s. Judokus and Hazel G. (Van Blarcom) van den N.; m. June Le Clere, Apr. 17, 1954; children: Susanne, Eric, Peter, Katherine, Elizabeth. AB, Dartmouth, 1951; MD, Harvard, 1954. Intern then resident Boston City Hosp., 1954-56, resident neurology, 1958-60; rsch. fellow neurochemistry Harvard U., 1960—62; instr. medicine Case Western Res. U., Cleve., 1962-66, asst. prof., 1966-69, assoc. prof., 1969-70; prof. neurology U. Calif., Irvine, 1970—2009, chief dept. neurology, 1970—72, chair dept. neurology, 1986—98, assoc. dean Coll. Medicine, 1972-73, dean, 1973-85. Mem. cons. staff U. Calif., Irvine (Calif.) Med. Ctr., Long Beach (Calif.) VA Hosp.; mem. revision com. U.S. Pharmacopoeial Conv., 1990-95. Mem. med. adv. bds., Nat. Multiple Scierosis Soc./Myasthenia Gravis Edn., 1971-2009, Orange County chpt. Nat. Multiple Scierosis Soc., 1971-2009, Orange County Health Planning Coun., 1971-85, Nat. Com. Rsch. in Neurol. Disease, 1982-87. Lt. M.C. USNR, 1956-58. Fellow ACP, Am. Acad. Neurol.; mem. AMA, Am. Neurol. Assn., Nat. Multiple Sclerosis Soc. (chief med. officer 1997-2002), Orange County Med. Assn., Calif. Med. Assn. Died Sept. 16, 2009.

VANDERLIP, ELIN BREKKE, professional society administrator, volunteer; b. Oslo, June 7, 1919; came to the U.S., 1934; m. Kelvin Cox, Nov., 1946 (dec. 1956); children: Kelvin Jr., Narcissa, Henrik and Katrina (twins). With Norwegian Embassy, Washington, Norwegian Fgn. Ministry, London, 1941-44, Red Cross, Calcutta, India; pres. Friends of French Art, Portuguese Bend, Calif. Sponsor of charity art conservation fundraising events Friends of French Art; tour leader Ile de France, Anjou, Bordelais, Provence-Cote d'Azur, Alsace, Dordogne, Lyonnais-Isere, Brittany, Burgundy, Normandy, Languedoc, Loire, Gascony, Le Nord, Charente, Champagne, Eure et Loir, 1978-96, Route de Berry, Auvergne and Toulouse. Author: (book) Eccentric Obstinate & Fabulous. Decorated Comdr. Order of Arts and Letters (France) Chevalier of the Legion of Honor. Died July 20, 2009.

VANDER SCHALIE, PAUL HENDRICK, viticulturist and vintager; b. Patterson, NJ, Oct. 13, 1949; s. Harry Hans and Marion (Hunter) V.S.; m. Peyton Carol McMahon, Feb. 15, 1975 (div. Apr. 1982); 1 child, Summer Peyton. Student, Coll. of Marin, 1971-72, Santa Rosa Jr. Coll., 1975-77; BS in Plant Sci., U. Calif., Davis, 1980. Winery worker Korbel Champaign Cellars, Guerneville, Calif., 1976-78; vineyard mgr. P. Sledge Vineyards, Guerneville; vineyard supr. Beringer Winery, St. Helena, Calif., 1980-83, Charles Krug Winery, St. Helena, from 1983. Tchr. Santa Rosa (Calif.) Jr. Coll., 1981—; viticultural cons. Sugarloaf Farming Corp., Calistoga, Calif., 1982—. Mem. ligistics com. Napa Valley Wine Auction, St. Helena, 1985; exec. com., co-founder Sonoma County Vineyard Tech. Group, 1981—; mem. Napa Vineyard Tech. Group, 1980—. Mem. Am. Soc. Viticulture and Enology, Ducks Unltd. (St. Helena chpt. organizational com.). Avocations: tennis, jogging, skiing, jet skiing. Home: Saint Helena, Calif. Died July 3, 2008.

VANDIVER, RENEE LILLIAN AUBRY, interior designer, architectural preserver; b. New Iberia, La., Nov. 7, 1929; d. Harold George and Josephine Fortier (Brown) Aubry; m. Arthur Roderick Carmody, Jr., Jan. 1952 (div. 1979); children: Helen Bragg Carmody Stroud, Renee Josephine Carmody Mathews, Arthur Roderick III, Patrick Gerard, Timothy H.A., Mary Joellyn, Virginia Caroline, Joseph Barry; m. Frank Everson Vandiver, Mar. 21, 1980. BFA, Sophie Newcomb Coll. Tulane U., 1951; postgrad., U. Paris, 1951-52, Centinary Coll., 1966-68, La. State U., Shreveport, 1978. Designer, supt. art New Iberia Parish Elementary Schs., 1951; archtl. drafter and designer Perry L. Brown, Inc., Baton Rouge, 1950-52; tchr. art St. Joseph's Elem. Sch., Shreveport, 1960-69; designer, illustrator, saleswoman Stierwalt Interiors, Shreveport, 1974-78; design cons. for president's homes and gardens North Tex. State U., Tex. A&M U., Denton, College Station, 1980-88; design cons., planner, saleswoman, pres. Renee Aubry Vandiver Interiors, College Station, Tex., from 1980; design cons. Am. U. in Cairo, from 1997; proofreader, editor, rschr., asst. Office of Frank E. Vandiver, College Station, from 1998. Interior design and house constrn. cons. Heritage Antiques and Interiors, New Iberia, 1972—; interior design cons., Tenn., La., S.C., 1980—; invited student Middle Eastern master painter Sabri Raghab; involved with consultations and contruction large new campus, pres.'s home grounds Am. U., Cairo. Editl. and illustrations collaborator works on gen. mil. history with Frank E. Vandiver, 1990—; works include design constrn. of new Pres.'s Home on campus of Am. U. of Cairo, 2004. Mem. NAFE, DAR, Constrn. Specifications Inst., Dallas Market Ctr., Houston Market Ctcr., Jr. League, Textile Mus., Mus. Women in Arts, Tex. A&M U. Women's Club (hon. pres. 1981—), Fedn. Tex. A&M U. Mother's Club. Avocations: painting, playing piano, gardening, travel, reading. Died Jan. 7, 2008.

VANGATES, DESS, retired military officer; b. Monticello, Fla., June 1, 1942; s. Fred and Rachel Etta Vangates. Contbr. articles to profl. jours. Sgt. US Army, 1975—81, Korea. Mem.: Vet. Foreign Wars of U.S. (life). Democrat. Achievements include research in global warming; the cause and effect of hydrogen part five, nitrogen part one-Avian bird flu influenza; 1N1HiV fussion recognizing germ 1N1 as base germ. Avocations: poker, reading, singing. Home: Miami Gardens, Fla. Died Aug. 14, 2007.

VANHILST, LUCAS, retired business analyst; b. Amsterdam, The Netherlands, Aug. 6, 1920; came to U.S., 1954, naturalized, 1959; s. Lucas Johannes Arnoldus and Dina (Overtoom) vanH.; m. Ruth Bauersfeld, July 9, 1947 (div. May 1981); children: Anke, Michael; m. Tina M. Van-Piggelen, Aug., 1985. BS in Mechanical Engring., Coll. of Amsterdam, 1950; MBA, U. Minn., 1961. Inventory analyst Honeywell, Mpls., 1954-60; programming analyst Univac, St. Paul, 1960-61; mgr. prodn. control electronics div. Gen. Mills, Mpls., 1962; programming cons. Super Valu Stores, Mpls., 1963-65; prin. cons., analyst Control Data Corp., Mpls., 1966-85; ret., 1985. Lectr. on bus. practices German Assn. for Bus. Sci., Stuttgart, 1953, Am. Mgmt. Assn., N.Y.C., 1968-72, U. Wis., Madison, 1968, U. Klagenfurt, Austria, 1987-88, Austrian Mgmt. Acad., Vienna, 1988. Chmn. Restructure Sch. Dist. Legis. and Referendum Campaign, Mpls., 1959-60; bd. dirs. Citizens League Mpls.-St. Paul Met. Area, 1960-61; pres. Minn. Coun. for Gifted, 1963-64; bd. dirs. Verde Valley Concert Assn., 1989—; mem. profl. adv. coun. Marcus J. Lawrence Med. Ctr. Hospice, 1989—; v.p. pub. rels. Marcus J. Lawrence Med. Ctr. Found., 1990-92, treas., 1992-93. Recipient (with wife) Health award Verde Valley C. of C., 1992. Mem. Soc. Of Friends. Avocations: philosophy, sailing, cross country skiing. Home: Cottonwood, Ariz. Died Mar. 22, 2008.

VAN HORN, TRENDA R., retail marketing management executive, consultant; b. Chevy Chase, Md., Apr. 1, 1949; d. Trenton M. and Angela M. (Vandoren) Richards; m. Jon H. Clayton, May 25, 1968 (div. 1971); 1 child, Kimberly Anne; m. Michael Van Horn, Sept. 1976 (div. 1980). BBA in Mktg. and Comm., U. Calif., Berkeley, 1968. With retail sales/mgmt., Dallas, NYC, Mpls., 1971-82; pres., owner Van Horn Enterprises, Dallas, 1982-86; dir. retail RFD Inc. divsn. Designer Fragrances, Inc., Carrollton, Tex., 1986-87; exec. v.p., COO Designer Fragrances, Inc., Carrollton, 1987-88; mgr. ops., mktg. Gump's, the Galleria, Dallas, 1988-91; contract cons., v.p. Bolos' Associated Cos., Inc., Carrollton, 1991-93. Contract cons., 1991—. Democrat. Roman Catholic. Died Apr. 13, 2008.

VANLANINGHAM, TODD ALAN, minister; b. Winfield, Kans., July 9, 1956; s. E.L. and Lois (Zehnder) VanL. BA, Calif. State U., 1983; MDiv, Pacific Luth. Theol. Sem., 1986. Ordained minister in Luth. Ch. Intern pastor Prince of Peace Luth. Ch., Saratoga, Calif., 1984-85; pastor Luth. Ch. of Our Redeemer, Sacramento, from 1986. Luth. rep. No. Calif. Ecumenical Commn., Sacramento, 1986-90. Author: (with others) Protocol for Care of HIV-ARC-AIDS in Northern California, 1989. Mem. pub. affairs com. Planned Parenthood Fedn. of Sacramento Valley, Sacramento, 1987-89. Democrat. Home: Sacramento, Calif. Died Jan. 27, 2008.

VAN LEER, BETTY LEE, newspaper publisher; b. Louisville, Ky., June 28, 1930; d. Earl and Marene (Marriott) Templeman; m. Robert Roy Van Leer, Feb. 16, 1952; children: Sherry Christina, Amy Melinda, Molly Rebecca, Sally Amanda. AA, Stephens Coll., 1950; B in Journalism, U. Mo., 1952. Country corr., then sch. corr. Elizabethtown (Ky.) News, 1942-44, 45-48; reporter, campus editor Stephens Life, Columbia, Mo., 1949-50; country editor Sterling (Ill.) Gazette, 1952-55; pub. Curry County Reporter, Gold Beach, Oreg., from 1956. Bd. dirs. Curry Pub. Libr., Inc., Gold Beach, 1960-85. Mem. Gold Beach C. of C., Oreg. State Button Soc., Nat. Button Soc., DuBois Family Assn., Huguenot Hist. Soc., Soc. Maureen Duvall Descendents, Delta Kappa Gamma. Democrat. Avocations: collecting, reading, mushroom hunting, gardening. Home: Gold Beach, Oreg. Died Jan. 23, 2008.

VAN LEEUWEN, WILLIAM HAROLD, insurance executive; b. Paducah, Ky., July 4, 1923; s. William Harold and Virginia Marie (Charles) VanL.; m. Lois Bolle, Aug. 18, 1948; children: Barbara Mullaney, Thomas M. AB, U. Ill., 1947, LLB, 1948. CPCU, CLU. Resident v.p. Sentry Ins.,

1948-65; asst. v.p. Lumbermens Mut. Casualty Co. & Am. Motorists Ins. Co., Chgo., 1965-67, 2d v.p., 1967-71, v.p., 1971-73; chmn. bd. dirs., chief exec. officer Kemper Investors Life Ins., Los Angeles, 1972-76; pres., chief exec. officer Nat. Automobile and Casualty Ins. Co., Los Angeles and Pasadena, Calif., from 1972. Pres. Pacific Ins. and Surety Conf. Chmn. bd. dirs. Ins. Council of Calif. for City of Hope, Los Angeles, 1986. Served to 1st lt. U.S. Army, 1943-46. Named Co. Person of Yr., Profl. Ins. Agts. Calif. and Nev., 1985. Mem. Am. Soc. Property and Casualty Underwriters Inc., Am. Coll. Life Underwriters, Assn. Calif. Ins. Co. (bd. dirs. 1986), Pacific Ins. and Surety Conf. (v.p. 1986). Clubs: Jonathan (Los Angeles); Annandale Golf (Pasadena). Home: San Marino, Calif. Died Oct. 21, 2007.

VAN METER, CLIFFORD HOLLY, JR., surgeon; b. Mar. 22, 1955; s. Clifford and Patty Sue (Henry) Van M.; m. Marianne Joan Mattingly; children: Logan Jade, Clifford Chancellor, Merritt Grace. BS in Biology cum laude with honors, Tulane U., 1977, MD, 1981. Diplomate Am. Bd. Surgery, Am. Bd. Thoracic Surgery. Surg. intern U. Va. Med. Ctr., Charlottesville, 1981-82, resident in gen. surgery, 1982-85, chief resident, 1985-86; fellow dept. surgery div. cardiothoracic surgery Washington U. Med. Ctr., St. Louis, 1986-88; staff dept. surgery Ochsner Clinic, New Orleans, from 1988. Mem. transplant adv. bd. Ochsner Clinic, New Orleans, 1988—; clin. asst. prof. dept. surgery Tulane U. Med. Ctr., 1993; mem. utilization review subcom. Alton Ochsner Med. Found., New Orleans, 1989—, coronary care unit com., 1989—, intensive care unit com., 1989—, cardiac transplant com., 1989—; presenter in field. Contbr. articles to profl. jours. Bd. dirs. La. Organ Procurement Assn.; rep. to thoracic organ com. United Network for Organ Sharing. Mem. AMA. Alton Ochsner Surg. Soc., New Orleans Surg. Soc., Tulane Surg. Soc., Muller Soc., So. Med. Assn., Orleans Parish Med. Soc., Southeastern Surg. Congress, Internat. Soc. Heart and Lung Transplant Assn., Assn. Am. Indian Physicians, Soc. Thoracic Surgeons, So. Thoracic Surg. Assn., Soc. Transplant Surgeons, Pi Eta Sigma, Beta BEta Beta. Republican. Episcopalian. Home: Atlanta, Ga. Died May 28, 2008.

VAN SCHILFGAARDE, JAN, retired agricultural engineer, federal agency administrator; b. The Hague, Netherlands, Feb. 7, 1929; came to US, 1946, naturalized, 1957; married; 3 children. BS, Iowa State Coll., 1949, MS, 1950, PhD in Agrl. Engring. and Soil Physics, 1954. Instr., assoc. agrl. engr. Iowa State Coll., 1949-54; asst. prof. agrl. engring. NC State Coll., 1954-57, assoc. prof., 1957-62, prof., 1962-64; drainage engr. Agrl. Rsch. Svc. USDA, Raleigh, NC, 1954-64, from chief water mgmt. engr. soil/water conservation rsch. divsn. to dir. Beltsville, Md., 1964—72, dir. Salinity Lab. Riverside, Calif., 1972-84, dir. Mountain States Area Agrl. Rsch. Svc. Ft. Collins, Colo., 1984-86, assoc. dir. no. plains area Agrl. Rsch. Svc., 1986-91, assoc. dep. adminstr. for natural resources Agrl. Rsch. Svc. Beltsville, Md., 1991-96, dir. Pacific West area, 1996-97; ret., 1997. Vis. prof. Ohio State U., 1962 Mem. ASCE, NAE, Am. Soc. Agrl. Engrs., Soil Sci. Soc., Soil Conservation Soc. Am. Home: Fort Collins, Colo. Deceased.

VANTAGGI, ZOLA MURIEL, musician; b. Hesper, Iowa, July 8, 1925; d. Ralph Leslie and Otilla Theodora (Ramlo) Fawcett; m. Reno Vantaggi, June 18, 1960. BA, Luther Coll., Decorah, Iowa, 1947; cert. in teaching, Sherwood Mus. Sch., Chgo., 1953. Tchr. Pub. sch., Lakefield, Minn., 1947-51, Chatfield, Minn., 1951-55; mgr. music store DeBellis Co., Riverside, Calif., 1955-56; tchr. Pub. Sch., Bloomington, Minn., 1956-60, Rochester, Minn., 1960-64; organist Gloria Dei Luth. Ch., Rochester, Minn., 1961-97. Therapist State Hosp., Rochester, 1966-67; pres. Gloria Dei Welca, Rochester, 1968-69, 89-90. AAUW grantee, 1993. Mem. AAUW, Am. Guild Organists (mem.-at-large, bd. dirs. 1990-95), Symphony Guild (pres. 1972-73). Home: Byron, Minn. Died Feb. 19, 2008.

VAS, IRWIN EMMANUEL, airplane manufacturing company executive; b. Bombay, Apr. 16, 1931; came to U.S., 1948; s. Emmanuel Joseph Vas and Primrose Mary Johnson; m. Manya Mary Milun, Mar. 26, 1965; children: Catherine Mary, Joseph Irwin. BME, Cath. U. Am., 1952, B. in Aerospace Engring., 1953; MS in Engring., Princeton U., 1955; PhD, NYU, 1970. From rsch. asst. to sr. rsch. engr. Princeton (N.J.) U., 1955-77; program mgr. ERDA, NYC, 1977-78; program mgr. wind energy Solar Energy Rsch. Inst., Golden, Colo., 1978-80; dir. rsch. and engring. Flo Wind Corp., Pleasanton, Calif., 1981-82, v.p. rsch. and engring. Kent, Wash., 1982-85, v.p. internat. mktg., 1986-87; mgr. Boeing Mil. Airplanes, from 1987. Cons. Gen. Electric Corp., Boeing Aerospace Corp., Bell Helicopters. Editor: (proceedings) Fifth Biennial Wind Energy Conf., 1981, Sixth Biennial Wind Energy Conf., 1983; author of numerous tech. reports. Fellow AIAA (assoc.); mem. ASME, Sigma Xi. Home: Huntsville, Ala. Died Nov. 8, 2007.

VAUGHAN, JAMES JOSEPH MICHAEL, lawyer; b. Mar. 19, 1942; s. James M. and Elizabeth (McDonnell) Vaughan; m. Jeanette Rae Gerber, Aug. 5, 1967; children: Karen, Adrianne, Jennifer. BS, U. Scranton, 1963; JD, Cath. U., 1966. Bar: U.S. Dist. Ct. Md. 1979, U.S. Ct. Appeals (D.C. cir.) 1972, U.S. Ct. Claims 1973, U.S. Supreme Ct. 1977. Assoc. Dukes, Troese, et al, Chevy Chase, Md., 1969—72; atty. Assn. Am. Law Schs., Washington, 1972—76, from 2001; mem. firm Giordano, Villareale & Vaughan, Upper Marlboro, Md., 1976—2001; pvt. practice, from 2001. Mem.: Prince George's County Bar Assn., Md. Bar Assn., D.C. Bar Assn., Bar Assn. D.C., Assn. Trial Lawyers Am. Democrat. Roman Catholic. Home: Fort Washington, Md. Died Mar. 29, 2009.

VAUGHN, EULALIA COBB, retired science educator, mathematician; b. Smithville, Tenn., Aug. 1, 1926; d. Luther Leonidas Fuson and Allie Pearl Redmon; m. Lewis Latane Cobb, Aug. 14, 1944 (dec. 1980); children: Carl Cobb, Luther Fuson Cobb, Lewis Cobb Jr., James Cobb, David R. Cobb, John Winston Cobb; m. Floyce Vaughn, 1983. BS, Mid. Tenn. State U., 1946, MEd, 1980. Tchr. Secondary Sch., Tulahoma, Tenn., 1946, sci. and math. tchr. Ark., 1947, Springdale, Ark., 1948, Pine Bluff, Ark., 1959, Birmingham, Ala., 1965, Nashville, 1965—91; ret. Chair dept. various schs., Tenn., 1967—91; pres. Dekalb County Ret. Tchrs. Assn., 1992—98; tchr. mission sch., from 1996; sponsor Sci. Olympiad Glencliff H.S., Nashville (state winner). Author: Poetry Book, 2001; contbr. articles to Nashville Tennesean. Voter registration Dem. Party, Smithville, 1995—2001, mem. steering com.; women's leader United Meth. Women, Cookeville, Tenn., 1991—2001, sec. comm., dist. pres., from 1992. Mem.: Family Cmty. Edn. (pres.). Democrat. Methodist. Avocation: family. Home: Knoxville, Tenn. Died Jan. 20, 2008.

VAUGHN, WILLIAM WEAVER, retired lawyer; b. LA, Aug. 29, 1930; s. William Weaver and Josephine (Sweigert) V.; m. Claire Louise M'Closkey, June 2, 1962; children: Robert, Gregory, Elizabeth, Anthony, Christina, James. BA, Stanford U., 1952; LLB, UCLA, 1955. Bar: Calif. 1956. Assoc. O'Melveny & Myers, L.A., 1955—56, 1957—64, ptnr., 1964-96, head litigation dept., 1986—93, of counsel, 1996—2002; ret., 2002. Served in US Army, 1956-57. Recipient Learned Hand award Am. Jewish Com., 1991, Joseph A. Ball award for outstanding advocacy Brennan Ctr. for Justice, 1998. Fellow Am. Coll. Trial Lawyers (bd. regents 1992-95); mem. L.A. County Bar Assn. (trustee 1976-78, 80-82), L.A. County Bar Found. (bd. dirs. 1991-95), Assn. Bus. Trial Lawyers (bd. govs. 1980-82), Order of Coif, Calif. Club, Chancery Club I(pres. 1997-98). Home: Pacific Palisades, Calif. Died Jan. 3, 2009.

VAYDA, ROSE K., community volunteer; b. NYC, Apr. 17, 1912; d. Max and Clara Kerner; widowed; children: Clara Kerner, Max Kerner, Rose, Sam, Sol, Ruth, Seymour, Harry, Kerner. Student, Washington Irving H.S., NYC. Drama coach Clark Settlement House, NYC, 1929; costumes person, extra Yiddish Art Theatre, NYC, 1930. Appeared in various films, TV commls., plays. Vol. Friendly Visitors, Miami, Fla., 1960, Hialeah (Fla.) Hosp., 1964-82, Lighthouse for Blind, Miami, 1985; vol. reader for the blind Broward C.C., Hollywood, Fla., 1993; active cancer support group Hollywood Med. Hosp. Recipient Cert. of Appreciation Mayor of Miami, 1985. Mem. Famous Poets Soc. (award 1996). Avocations: repertory theater, poetry group, piano. Home: Pembroke Pines, Fla. Died May 8, 2008.

VECCHIO, ROBERT PETER, business management educator; b. Chgo., June 29, 1950; m. Betty Ann Vecchio, Aug. 21, 1974; children: Julie, Mark. BS summa cum laude, DePaul U., 1972; MA, U. Ill., 1974, PhD, 1976. Instr. U. Ill., Urbana, 1973-76; mem. faculty dept. mgmt. U. Notre Dame, from 1976, dept. chmn., 1983-90, Franklin D. Schurz Prof. Mgmt., from 1986. Editor: Jour. of Mgmt., 1995—2000. Fellow: APA, Am. Psychol. Soc., Soc. for Indsl. and Orgnl. Psychology; mem.: Midwest Psychol. Assn., Midwest Acad. Mgmt., Acad. of Mgmt., Phi Eta Sigma, Delta Epsilon Sigma, Phi Kappa Phi. Home: Granger, Ind. Died Feb. 9, 2009.

VEGA, ELI SAMUEL, nurse anesthetist; b. Guayama, PR, Oct. 26, 1945; came to U.S., 1979; m. Maria J. Ramos, Apr. 22, 1972; children: Marieely, Samarys. Diploma in Nursing, Bella Vista Sch. Nursing, Mayaguez, PR, 1971; cert. in Anesthesia, Damas Hosp., Ponce, PR, 1973; posgrad., U. West Fla., 1990-92. RN. Staff nurse Bella Vista Hosp., Mayaguez, P.R., 1974-79; commd. lt. (j.g.) USN, 1979, advanced through grades to comdr., 1993; staff nurse anesthetist U.S. Naval Hosp., San Diego, 1979-81, head anesthetiology dept. Twentynine Palms, Calif., 1981-84, staff nurse anesthetist Jacksonville, Fla., 1984-87, asst. anesthesia dept. head Rota, Spain, 1987-90, staff nurse anesthetist Pensacola, Fla., 1990-94; asst. anesthesia dept. head Naval Hosp. Keflavik, Iceland, 1994-95; sr. nurse anesthetist Naval Hosp., Pensacola, Fla., from 1995, from 1996. Developer, instr. intravenous therapy program U.S. Naval Hosp., Rota, Spain, 1989. Decorated two Navy commendation medals. Mem. Am. Assn. Nurse Anesthetists, Fla. Nurse Anesthetist Assn., P.R. Nurse Anesthetist Assn. (v.p. 1976-77). Home: Pensacola, Fla. Died Jan. 29, 2008.

VELTFORT, THEODORE ERNST, electrical engineer, physicist; b. Cambridge, Mass., Feb. 23, 1915; s. Theodore Ernst and Helen (Gaston) V.; m. Helene Rank, Oct. 27, 1941 (div. Jan. 1952); children: Ruhama Danielle, Susan Marlene; m. Leonore Valeton, Oct. 14, 1954; children: Anna Cornelia, Kevin Daniel. BA in Econ., Columbia U., 1940; MS in Physics, Stanford U., 1947. Registered profl. engr., Calif. Chief devel. engr. Shand and Jurs Co., Berkeley, Calif., 1955-58; sr. project engr. Lynch Comm. Systems, San Francisco, 1958-59; chief electronics engr. Shockley Unit Clevite Corp, Stanford, Calif., 1960-61; sr. cons. engr. Sierra Electronics Corp., Menlo Park, Calif., 1961; prof. physics, dir. dept. solid state physics U. Havana, Cuba, 1962-68; chief engr. Bioelectric Instruments, Inc., Yonkers, N.Y., 1968-70; electronics systems engr. Mt. Sinai Med. Ctr., NYC, 1970-80; cons. engr. Veltek, Oakland, Calif., from 1981. Adj. prof., course advisor CCNY, 1971-78. Ambulance driver Cuerpo Sanitario de la Republica Espanola, 1937-38. Sgt. Signal Corps U.S. Army, 1942-45. Mem. IEEE (life), AAAS, Vets. the Abraham Lincoln Brigade (exec. sec. San Francisco chpt. 1983-84, fgn. corres. sec. 1985—), Sigma Xi (assoc.). Avocations: computer programming, snorkling. Died Apr. 7, 2008.

VERBOV, LEV FALKOVICH, metallurgical engineer, freelance/self-employed translator, writer; b. Leningrad, Russia, Jan. 10, 1937; arrived in US, 1977; s. Falka Shevelevich and Elka Abramovna Verbova; m. Larisa Ivanovna Fedkushova, Nov. 26, 1990; 1 child, Kristina Kulbe. MS in Metall. Engring., State Polytechnic U., St. Petersburg, Russia, 1962. Sr. engr. All-Union Inst. Aluminum, Magnesium and Electrode Industry, St. Petersburg, 1962-77; engr.-scientist Aluminum Co. of Am., New Kensington, Pa., 1979-82; asst. editor Chem. Abstracts Svcs., Columbus, Ohio, 1985-87; cons. R&D scientist ECC Am., Inc., Sandersville, Ga., 1988-90; clk., team mem. Local Census Ctr., Bklyn., 1999-2000; freelance writer Bklyn., from 1966; freelance translator, from 1982. Author: (books) Commercial Star, 1999, Swan Song of Ugly Duckling, 2000; composer: Solemn Melody, 1999; patentee in field. Deceased.

VERBY, JOHN EDWARD, JR., physician, educator; b. St. Paul, May 24, 1923; s. John E. and Amy (Martin) V.; m. Jane Verby, June 15, 1946; children: John E. III, Steve, Ruth, Karl. BA, Carleton Coll., Northfield, Minn., 1944; BS, U. Minn., 1946, MB, 1947, MD, 1948. Diplomate Am. Bd. Family Practice. Intern Hennepin County Gen. Hosp., Mpls., 1947-49; pvt. family practice Litchfield, Minn., 1949-51, 53-54; ptnr. Olmsted Med.-Surg. Group, Rochester, Minn., 1954-69; assoc. prof. U. Minn., Mpls., 1969-73, acting head family practice/community medicine, asst. head, 1970-71, 71-72, mem. Grad. Sch. faculty, from 1971; dir. Rural Physician Assoc. Program, Mpls., from 1971; prof. Dept. Family Practice/Community Health, U. Minn., from 1973. Cons. and lectr. in field; vis. prof. Welsh Nat. Sch. Medicine, Cardiff, Wales, 1977-78, N.Y. State U., Syracuse, 1988-89; developer Rural Physician Assoc. Program W.Va. Med. Sch., 1989-90. Author: Medical Examination Book in Family Practice, 1972, 4th edit., 1983; co-author: How to Talk to Doctors, 1978; contbr. articles to profl. jours. Lay liturgist Hillcrest United Mth. Ch., 1980—. With USN, 1942-45; 1st lt. U.S.Army, 1951-53. Grantee U. Minn. Hosps. and Clinics, 1985-89, Minn. Med. Found., 1980, 84, Fed. Health Professions Project, 1972-76, others; recipient Cert. Appreciation U. Minn. Bd. Regents, 1992. Fellow Am. Acad. Family Physicians (charter, Thomas W. Johnson award 1991), Am. Geriatric Soc.; mem. AMA (Physicians Recognition award 1969-85), Am. Rural Health Assn. (award 1981), Minn. Acad. Family Physicians (Tchr. of Yr. award 1988, John E. Verby award 1987), Internat. Soc. Gen. Medicine (bd. dirs., assoc. mem.), Hennepin County Med. Soc. Home: Minneapolis, Minn. Died Oct. 23, 2007.

VERDI, GERALD DELANO, plastic surgeon, educator; b. NY, Mar. 8, 1936; s. James and Ann (Calise) V.; m. Charlene Anne Bedell, Dec. 16, 1967; children: Michael, Sean, Marc, Christopher. DDS, U. Pa., 1960; MD, Albany Med. Coll., 1965. Diplomate Am. Bd. Surgery, Am. Bd. Plastic Surgery. Oral surgery intern Bellevue Hosp., NYC, 1960-61; surg. intern Columbia Presbyn. Med. Ctr., NYC, 1965-66, resident in surgery, 1968-69; resident in oral surgery Nassau County Med. Ctr., 1961-62, resident in surgery, 1969-71, resident in plastic surgery, 1971-73; pvt. practice plastic surgery Louisville, from 1973. Clin. prof. plastic and reconstructive surgery U. Louisville, clin. prof. oral and maxillofacial surgery. Chmn. sch. bd. Anchorage Sch., 1984-86. Lt. USNR, 1966-68. Fellow ACS. Home: Louisville, Ky. Died Dec. 28, 2007.

VERLINSKY, YURY, geneticist; b. Ischim, Russia, Sept. 1, 1943; came to U.S., 1979; s. Simon and Dora (Bolotna) V.; m. Lubov Maron, Oct. 26, 1968; 1 child, Oleg. BS, MS, PhD, Kharkov U., Russia. From lab. technician to sr. rschr. Inst. Endocrinology, Kharkov, 1963-78; dir. cytogenetics Michael Reese Hosp., Chgo., 1979-88; co-dir. IVF Ill., Inc., Chgo., 1986—2009; dir. Reproductive Genetics Inst., Chgo., 1988—2009. Died July 16, 2009.

VERMEULE, CORNELIUS CLARKSON, III, museum curator; b. Orange, NJ, Aug. 10, 1925; s. Cornelius Clarkson, Jr. and Catherine Sayre (Comstock) V.; m. Emily Dickinson Townsend, Feb. 2, 1957 (dec. Feb. 6, 2001); children: Emily D. Blake, Cornelius Adrian Comstock. Grad., Pomfret Sch., 1943; AB, Harvard, 1949, MA, 1951; PhD, U. London, Eng., 1953; DHL (hon.), Boston Coll., 1995. Instr. fine arts, then asst. prof. U. Mich., 1953-55; asst. prof. classical archaeology Bryn Mawr (Pa.) Coll., 1955-57; curator classical art Mus. Fine Arts, Boston, 1956-96, curator emeritus, 1996—2008, acting dir., 1972-73, hon. visitor ancient art, 2002—08; assoc. curator coins Mass. Hist. Soc., 1965-71, curator, 1971—86. Lectr. fine arts Smith Coll., 1960-64, Boston U., Harvard, Wellesley Coll.; vis. prof. Yale, 1969-70, 72-73; Thomas Spencer Jerome lectr. U. Mich., 1975-76; vis. prof. Boston Coll., 1978-97; vis. prof. U. Aberdeen, Scotland, 1993; pres. Internat. Com. to Save Jewish Catacombs of Italy, 1980-84, chmn., 1984-98, dir. 1998-2000; cons. classical art Worcester Art Mus., 1998-2001. Author: (with N. Jacobs) Japanese Coinage, 1948, 2d edit., 1972, Bibliography of Applied Numismatics,

1956, The Goddess Roma, 1959, 2d edit., 1974, Dal Pozzo-Albani Drawings, 1960, European Art and the Classical Past, 1964, Drawings at Windsor Castle, 1966, Roman Imperial Art in Greece and Asia Minor, 1968, Polykleitos, 1969, Numismatic Art in America, 1971, 2d edit., 2007; (with M. Comstock) Greek Etruscan and Roman Bronzes, 1972; (with N. Neuerburg) Catalogue of the Ancient Art in the J. Paul Getty Museum, 1973, Greek and Roman Sculpture in Gold and Silver, 1974, Greek and Roman Cyprus, 1976, (with M. Comstock) Sculpture in Stone, 1976, Greek Sculpture and Roman Taste, 1977, Roman Art: Early Republic to Late Empire, 1978; (with A Herrmann) The Ernest Brummer Collections, Vol. II, 1979, Greek Art: Socrates to Sulla, 1980, The Jewish Experience in Roman Art, 1981, Masterpieces of Greek and Roman Sculpture in America, 1982, Greek Art: Prehistoric to Perikles, 1982, Numismatic Studies, 1983, Alexander the Great Conquers Rome, 1985, The Cult Images of Imperial Rome, 1986, Numismatic Art of the Greek Imperial World, 1987, Philatelic Art in America, 1987; (with M. Comstock) Sculpture in Stone and Bronze, 1988; (with A. Brauer) Stone Sculptures, The Greek, Roman and Etruscan Collections of the Harvard University Art Museums, 1990; (with others) Le Sport dans la Grèce Antique, 1992, Du Jeu à la Compétition, 1992, El Deporte en la Grecia Antigua, La génesis del olimpismo, 1992-93, Vase-Painting in Italy, 1993, (with others) Eye of the Beholder, Masterpieces from the Isabella Stewart Gardner Museum, 2003, Art and Archaeology of Antiquity, Vols. I-IV, 2001-04, (with others) J.D. Beazley, The Lewes House Gems, 2002-05; mem. editl. bd. Minerva, 2002-08. Trustee Cardinal Spellman Philatelic Mus., 1980-93. Served to 1st lt. AUS, 1943-47. Recipient Bicentennial medal Boston Coll., 1976; Fulbright fellow, 1951-53; Guggenheim fellow, 1968 Fellow AAAS, Am. Numis. Soc. (life), Royal Numis. Soc., Soc. Antiquaries; mem. Coll. Art Assn. (life), Archaeol. Inst. Am. (life) German Archaeol. Inst., Holland Soc. N.Y., Colonial Lords of Manors in Am., Mass. Hist. Soc. (hon. curator); Tavern Club (medalist 1986, Boston). Home: Cambridge, Mass. Died Nov. 27, 2008.

VERNER, JAMES MELTON, lawyer; b. Selma, Ala., Sept. 19, 1915; s. Singleton Foster and Jennie (Harris) V.; m. Gretchen Gores, Aug. 12, 1939 (dec. 2004); children: Ann Verner Picardo, James Singleton, William Melton (dec. 2004). Student, Biltmore Coll., 1932—34; AB, U. N.C., 1936, JD, 1938. Bar: NC 1938, Tenn. 1947, D.C. 1950, Va. 1986. Assoc. firm Gover & Covington, Charlotte, NC, 1938; law clk. atty. gen. NC, 1938-40; atty. CAB, Washington, 1940-43; asst. gen. counsel Chgo. & So. Airlines, Memphis, 1946-47; atty. Air Transport Assn. Am., Washington, 1947-49; hearing examiner CAB, 1949-50, exec. asst. to chmn., 1950, exec. dir., 1950-53; from atty. to ptnr. Turney & Turney, 1953—60; ptnr. firm Verner, Liipfert, Bernhard, McPherson & Hand, Chartered (and predecessor firms), 1960-88; hon. mem. bd. dirs., spl. coun. Piper Rudnick Gray Cary (merged with Verner, Liipfert, Bernhard, McPherson & Hand, Chartered), Washington. Assoc. editor N.C. Law Rev., 1937—38. Former mem., chmn. policy bd. Legal Counsel for Elderly, Washington. Lt. (j.g.) USNR, 1943-46; legal officer Naval Air Transport Svc., 1945-46. Mem.: ABA, Cosmos Club (Washington), Order of Golden Fleece. Home: Arlington, Va. Died Oct. 6, 2009.

VERPLANKE, ANNA LOUISE, nutritionist; b. Camden, Tenn., Mar. 22, 1935; d. Wiley Leonard and Rosa Belle (Clark) Noles; m. Edward Ely Verplanke, Jul. 19, 1953; children: Rose Anne & Mary Anne (twins), Julia Edwina. Student, U. Fla., 1976-77; B of Restaurant and Hotel Mgmt., Purdue U., 1983. Cert. Dietetic Food Service Mgmt. Chef., asst. mgr. Paducah (Ky.) Country Club, 1955-65, Drew (Miss.) Country Club, 1965-71; dir. food service Lexington House Inc., Crestwood, Ill., 1971-73; chef, asst. mgr. Burlington (Iowa) Country Club, 1973-76; dir. dietetics Rosewood Convalscent Ctr., Memphis, 1976-80; dir. food service Carolina Village Inc., Hendersonville, N.C., from 1980. Cons. Dearfield Episcopal Home, Asheville, N.C., 1981; mem. organizing com. Satellite Food Program Elderly, Memphis, 1978. Vol. NRC, Paducah, 1961-65; troop leader Girl Scouts Am., Drew, 1968-71. Mem. Nat. Dietary Mgrs. Assn. (pres. 1984-86), Nat. Assn. Female Execs., bus. and Profl. Women's Club (Woman Day 1985). Democrat. Baptist. Avocations: gardening, golf, dance, collecting recipes, refinishing antique furniture. Home: Hendersonville, NC. Died May 10, 2008.

VICKERS, CLINTON JOHN, headmaster; b. South Hempstead, NY, Aug. 12, 1941; s. Robert Paul and Harriette Veronica (Parsons) V.; m. Emily Catherine Pisani, Sept. 2, 1967; children: Emilia Francoise, Clinton Cuchulain, Ethan Absalom, Liam Dankano. AB, Georgetown U., 1964; MA, Hofstra U., 1969; MA with honors, U. Coll. Dublin, Ireland, 1972; PhD, U. Mass., 1974. Vol. Peace Corps, Kru Coast, Liberia, 1964-66; tchr. Fishers Island (N.Y.) Sch., 1967-68; instr. Norwich U., 1968-70; sr. lectr. Abdullahi Bayero Coll., Ahmadu, Kano, Nigeria, 1972-75, univ. mgmt. com., 1973-75; assoc. prof. L.I. U., Southampton, N.Y., 1975-76; prof. U. Mohammed V, Rabat, Morocco, 1976-77; headmaster Rabat Am. Sch., Morocco, 1977-80, Am. Sch. Aberdeen (Scotland), 1980-82, Adelphi Acad., Bklyn, 1983-90, Beaufort (S.C.) Acad., from 1990. Pres. Coll. Choice Counseling; ednl. cons. Ednl. columnist: Lowcountry Ledger; contbr. articles to profl. jours. Mem. Prin.'s Coun. Coalition Essential Schs. Brown U., Providence, R.I., 1984—; chmn. Coun. Ind. Colls. and Schs. L.I., Bklyn., 1987-90; mem. Bay Ridge Community Assn., 1984-90; chmn. Fishers Islanders for McCarthy, 1967-68; committeeman Southampton Dem. Cen. Com., 1968-69; evaluator European Coun. Ind. Schs., Zurich, Switzerland, N.Y. State Assn. Ind. Schs., New Eng. Assn. Ind. Schs., 1985, 86—. Named Man of Yr. Adelphi Acad., 1985, 90, Educator of Yr. Assn. Tchrs. N.Y., 1986. Mem. Nat. Assn. Secondary Sch. Prins., ASCD, Guild Ind. Schs. N.Y.C. (adminstrv. com. 1987-90), Coll. Eng. Assn., MLA, Rotary, Lions. Anglican Catholic. Avocations: reading, swimming, baseball, internat. edn. Died Dec. 6, 2007.

VICKMAN, PATRICIA ANN, preschool educator; b. Green Bay, Wis., Nov. 3, 1951; d. Orville A. and Hyacinth C. (Rueckl) Van Laanen; m. Patrick John Vickman, Oct. 20, 1972; children: Sarah Anne, John Edward. BS in Growth and Devel., U. Wis., Green Bay, 1972; postgrad., Minot State Coll., 1975-76. Cert pre-kindergarten and kindergarten tchr., Minn. Head start instr. Hazel Green (Wis.) Pub. Schs., 1973; head tchr. Noah's Ark, St. Paul, 1973-74, Golden Hours Day Care, Eagan, Minn., 1974; tchr. asst. Cathedral of the Sacred Heart, Winona, Minn., 1981-82, pre-sch. tchr., 1982-86, Winona Area Cath. Schs., from 1986. Leader River Trails coun. Girl Scouts U.S.A., Winona, 1985-89; mem. adult choir Cathedral of Sacred Heart, Winona, 1984—, eucharistic min., 1990; sec. St. Stan's Band Boosters, 1988-90. Mem. Assn. for Childhood Edn. Internat., Nat. Cath. Edn. Assn., River City Rascals Winona Clown Club. Roman Catholic. Avocations: clowning, reading for self and children, travel, music. Home: Winona, Minn. Died May 7, 2008.

VIDIC, JEFFREY JON, clinical psychologist, consultant; b. Pasadena, Calif., Feb. 22, 1957; s. John Rudolph and Rose Ann (Mezgec) V.; m. Lisa Michelle Davis, May 23, 1992. AA, Glendale Coll., 1978; BA, U. So. Calif., 1980; PhD, U. S.C., 1988. Lic. clin. psychologist. Psychologist S.C. Dept. Youth Svcs., Columbia, 1983-85, S.C. Dept. Mental Health, Columbia, 1985-88, Calif. Dept. Mental Health, LA, 1988-89; psychol. cons. S.C. Dept. Disability, Columbia, from 1989. Instr. U. S.C., Columbia, 1982—. Contbr. chpt. to book and articles to profl. jours. Mem. APA, S.C. Psychol. Assn., Nat. Rehab. Assn., Phi Kappa Phi, Phi Beta Kappa. Avocations: weightlifting, racquetball, waterskiing. Home: Columbia, SC. Died May 1, 2008.

VILENCHIK, MICHAEL MARC, radiobiologist, biophysicist, bio-oncologist; b. Brjansk, Russia, May 30, 1938; s. Marc and Grunja G. (Smoljakova) V.; m. Valentina I. Vasilieva, Jan. 12, 1964 (div. 1967); 1 child, Joan; m. Julia N. Runova, Mar. 6, 1968 (div. 1971); 1 child, Vera. MD, 1st Med. Inst., St. Petersburg, Russia, 1961; PhD, Inst. Virology, Moscow, 1967. Postgrad. rsch. Inst. Virology, Moscow, 1963-66; rsch. scientist, sr. biophysicist, sr. resident Inst. Biophysics, Pushchino, Moscow, 1966-90; vis. scientist Med. Rsch. Coun., Didcot, England, 1990—2008; rschr. Inst. for Environ. Rsch., Tel Aviv, 1991; rsch. scholar SUNY Health Sci. Ctr., Syracuse, 1991-93, Cornell U., Ithaca, 1993-94; rsch. scientist Longevity Achievement Found. and Sally Balin Med. Ctr., Media, Pa., 1994—2008. Author: Biological Fundamentals of Aging and Longevity, 1976, 87, 89, Radiobiological Effects and Environment, 1983, 91, The Rules of Molecular-Genetic Action of Chemical Carcinogens, 1977, Dynamic DNA Instability and the Late Radiobiological Effects, 1987, Modification of Carcinogenic and Antitumor Actions of Ionizing Radiation, 1985; contbr. articles to profl. jours., chpts. to books. Mem.: Am. Assn. for Cancer Rsch. Achievements include research in biophysics of aging and carcinogenesis; mechanisms of radiation effects and biophyisics of the genome. Home: Media, Pa. Died Sept. 24, 2008.

VIRTUE, RICHARD L., chemical dependency counselor, priest; b. Yale, Okla., Nov. 7, 1921; s. C.R. Sr. and Olive (Cowan) V.; m. Sue Starr; children: Richard L.C., Nancy Virtue Lewis, Rebecca Virtue Smith, David Andrew. BA, Rutgers U., 1945. Cons. to Sch. Social Work U. Okla., Oklahoma City, 1973-81; exec. dir., counselor, intervention specialist Norman (Okla.) Alcohol Info. Ctr., from 1972. Mem. Gov.'s Task Force on Alcohol and Drugs, Okla., 1982-86; mem. Nat. Episc. Coalition on Alcohol and Drugs, 1985—; mem. Alcohol and Drug Problems N.Am., Washington, 1981—. Mem. Cleveland County Dem. Cen. Com., 1980-90. Named to Hall of Fame on Alcohol and Drug Intervention; honored Dick Virtue at the State Capitol by the Ho. and Senate. Mem. Okla. Assn. Alcohol and Drug Counselors (chmn. legis. com. 1978-85). Episcopalian. Avocations: basketball, football, baseball. Died Apr. 6, 2008.

VITALE, MARION KERR, retired community health nurse; b. Marksboro, NJ, Oct. 14, 1917; d. Wilbur Lee and Gertrude Willard (Mead) Kerr; m. John Vitale, Apr. 21, 1962. RN, Paterson Gen. Sch. Nursing, 1939; cert. phys. therapy, Harvard U., 1942; BS, U. Pa., 1949; MA, Columbia U., 1960. Staff nurse Bklyn. Vis. Nurse Assn., Newark Vis. Nurse Assn., 1943-45; intern supervision Boston Vis. Nurse Assn., 1946; orthopedic supr. Bklyn. Vis. Nurse Assn., 1947-50; asst. prof. St. John's U., Bklyn., 1953-59; dir. div. pub. health nursing Sussex County Health Dept., Newton, N.J., 1960-64; retired, 1988. Registered phys. therapist; cons. Joint Orthopaedic Nursing Adv. Svc., 1950-52. Contbr. articles and book revs. to profl. jours. Recipient Scholarship, Nat. Found. Infantile Paralysis. Mem. ANA, Nat. League Nursing, Am. Phys. Therapy Assn. (life). Home: Newton, NJ. Died Dec. 19, 2007.

VITALIANO, DOROTHY BRAUNECK, geologist, technical translator; b. NYC, Feb. 10, 1916; d. William Daniel and Adele (Bernhard) Brauneck; m. Charles J. Vitaliano, Oct. 19, 1940; children: Judith E., Peter W. AB, Barnard Coll., 1936; AM, Columbia U., 1938, MPhil, 1973. Geologic field asst. U.S. Geol. Survey, Nev., 1942-43, geologist Bloomington, Ind., 1953-86; freelance geologist-translator Bloomington, from 1986. Adj. prof. Ind. U., Bloomington, 1983-86; nat. lectr. Soc. Sigma Xi, 1981-83. Author: Legends of the Earth, 1973; co-author: Atlantis: Fact or Fiction, 1978; contbr. articles to profl. jours. Fellow AAAS, Geol. Soc. Am.; mem. LWV, Phi Beta Kappa, Sigma Xi. Democrat. Unitarian Universalist. Avocations: gourmet cooking, travel, puzzles. Died June 26, 2008.

VITANZA, ROBERT DOMINIC, personnel consultant; b. Bronx, Dec. 20, 1955; s. Basilio and Joan (Gaul) V.; m. Anne Beaupre Dubuque, Jan. 30, 1982. BA, Niagara U., NY, 1978. Recruiter Hipp Waters, Inc., Greenwich, Conn., 1979-84; exec. recruiter, owner Licari & Vitanza Assoc., Inc., Rye, N.Y., from 1984. Guest speaker R.I. Personnel Assn. Conf., Providence, 1982. Mem. Nat. Assn. Personnel Cons. (guest speaker 1981). Republican. Roman Catholic. Home: West Redding, Conn. Died June 9, 2008.

VOKES, HOLLY HURTT, principal, social worker, consultant; b. Evanston, Ill., Sept. 7, 1940; d. Harold Cecil and Mary Alice (Leslie) Hurtt; m. Frank Kanter Girardin, Aug. 10, 1962 (div. 1972); children: Jennifer Jeanne, Frank Kanter; m. A. Richard Vokes, Sept. 28, 1991. AA, William Woods Coll., Fulton, Mo., 1960; BA in Spl. Edn., Mich. State U., 1962, MA in Edn., 1990; postgrad., Cen. Mich. U., 1981-82. Tchr. Jack & Jill Schs., Colorado Springs, Colo., 1962-64, Univ. Liggett Schs., Grosse Pointe, Mich., 1970-72; counselor Community Family & Children Svcs., Gaylord, Mich., 1977-87, reg. cons., 1987-90, resource devel. staff, 1989-90, prog. dir., 1989-91; prin. elem. sch. Littlefield Pub. Schs., Alanson, Mich., from 1991. Cons. in field. Bd. dirs. Women's Resource Ctr., Petoskey, Mich., 1986-90, Halfway House, 1978-80, Alternative Programs, Boyne City, Mich., 1980-83; vol. United Way, Petoskey, 1977-90; mem. Displaced Homemakers Network, Vocat. Edn. Equity Coun., Bridge Area Counseling. Recipient various grants, 1977-90. Avocations: skiing, swimming, boating, golf. Home: Harbor Springs, Mich. Died Sept. 5, 2007.

VOLZ, CHARLES HARVIE, JR., lawyer; b. Richmond, Va., Sept. 15, 1925; s. Charles Harvie and Mary V. (Mallory) V.; m. Constance A. Lewis, July 30, 1976; children: Charles Harvie III, Judith C. BS, U. Ala., 1950, JD, 1951. Bar: Ala. 1951, U.S. Dist. Ct. Ala., U.S. Ct. Appeals (5th cir.), U.S. Ct. Mil. Appeals, U.S. Ct. Appeals (11th cir.), U.S. Supreme Ct. 1962. Spl. agt. FBI, 1951; claim mgr. Allstate Ins. Co., 1952-54; claims atty. State Farm Ins. Co., 1954-57; ptnr. Roberts, Orme & Volz, Gadsen, Ala., 1957-59; sole practice Montgomery, 1961-63; asst. dir. Dept. Indsl. Rels., Ala., 1959-63; pntr. Volz, Capouano, Wampold & Prestwood, 1963-84, Volz & Volz, 1984-95, Volz, Prestwood & Hanan, 1995—2001; of counsel Prestwood and Assocs., from 2001. Note editor Ala. Law Rev., 1950-51. Campaign dir. March of Dimes, 1958, Am. Cancer Soc., 1967; exec. sec. Gov.'s Com. on Employment of Physically Handicapped, 1959-62; mem. Pres.'s Com. on Employment of Physically Handicapped, 1959-62; pres., bd. dirs. Montgomery chpt. Am. Cancer Soc. 2nd lt. USAAF, 1943-45. Recipient Outstanding Service award Am. Cancer Soc., 1967 Mem. ATLA (state committeeman 1973-75), Am. Arbitration Assn. (mem. nat. panel), ABA, Ala. Bar Assn., Ala. Trial Lawyers Assn., Farrah Law Soc., Montgomery Country Club, Masons, Kiwanis, Phi Alpha Delta. Methodist. Deceased.

VOSBURGH, KENNETH VERNON, print shop owner; b. Auburn, NY, Aug. 20, 1933; s. Stanley Alvin and Anne (Moravec) V.; m. Betty Ann Mueller, May 4, 1957; children: Kenneth Eric (dec.), Karen Helen, Kay Ellen. BA, St. Lawrence U., 1956. Telephone directory rep. L.M. Barry Co., Rochester, N.Y., 1956-57; wholesale foods rep. Brewster-Crittenden Co., Rochester, 1957-59; food svc. rep. Carnation Co., Syracuse, N.Y., 1959-64; territory candy rep. E.J. Brach & Sons, Buffalo, 1964-74; owner K-Vee Sales Co., Buffalo, 1974-82, Printin' By Ken, Buffalo, from 1982. Pres. Assn. for Rsch. Childhood Cancer, Buffalo, 1972, 78, newletter editor, 1973-89, treas., 1974-75; mem. program com. Am. Cancer Soc., L.A., 1985. Recipient IV award Assn. for Rsch. Childhood Cancer, 1980. Mem. Masons (deacon 1980). Republican. Lutheran. Avocations: bowling, gourmet cooking. Home: Buffalo, NY. Died Sept. 3, 2007.

VOTTELER, THEODORE PAUL, pediatric surgeon; b. Portland, Oreg., Aug. 2, 1927; m. Vermelle McCain, Sept. 4, 1958. BS, U. Tex., Austin, 1947; MD, Tulane U., 1951. Diplomate Am. Bd. Surgery, Am. Bd. Pediatric Surgery. Intern Parkland Meml. Hosp., Dallas, 1951-52, resident, 1952-57; pediat. surgery fellow Children's Hosp., Phila., 1956-57; pres. Pediat. Surg. Assocs., Dallas, from 1957. Author: Practical Pediatric Therapy, 1985, Current Therapy in Pediatrics, 2d edit., 1989, Pediatric Therapy, 3d edit., 1993; contbr. articles to profl. jours. With USNR, 1945-47. Recipient Disting. Svc. award Children's Med. Ctr., 1993. Mem. Tex. Pediatric Surg. Soc. (pres. 1975), Tex. Med. Assn. (chmn. surg. sect. 1975), Tex. Surg. Soc. (v.p. 1985), Dallas Soc. Gen. Surgeons (pres. 1984-85), Doctor's Club (pres. 1982-83). Home: Dallas, Tex. Died May 23, 2008.

WACHTEL, JOSEPH HEINDEL, sculptor; b. Gura-Putila, Ukraine, Apr. 12, 1914; came to U.S., 1962; s. Israel and Shendel W.; m. S. Pouse (dec. 1991); 1 child, Peter L. Student, Palm Beach CC, Fla., 1983, 1999. Mech. technician, Czernovitz, Ukraine, 1933—41; with Ukraine mil., 1941—62; pres. Salisbury Fashion, NYC, 1968-78; quality control Space Legs, NYC, 1979-88. Author: Escape from the Hounds of Hell, 1993. Sculptures on permanent display at Temple Beth Tikvah, Lake Worth, Fla., Yad Vashem, Jerusalem, Nat. Holocaust Mus., Washington, Mus. of Tolerance, L.A. Mem. B'nai B'rith, Holocaust Survivors Orgn. Democrat. Jewish. Avocations: fishing, walking, reading. Home: Lake Worth, Fla. Died June 7, 2008.

WADDELL, BONNIE CARLENE, business executive; b. Brownsville, Apr. 21, 1944; d. Hughie Earnest and Grace Lee (Kinser) G.; m. Eldon Priddy, Dec. 22, 1958 (div. Aug. 1987); children: Jeffery Priddy, Barry Priddy, Michael Priddy, Mitchell Priddy; m. Otto Waddell Jr., Oct. 23, 1987. Student, Jefferson Community Coll., Louisville, Ky., 1980-85. Supv. Met. Bd. Pks., Louisville, 1968-74; acct. controller Merrill Lynch, Louisville, 1975; dir. Ridgewood Child Devel. Ctr., Louisville, 1976-80, Beechland Child Devel. Ctr., Louisville, 1980-82; exec. dir., adminstrv. asst. Am. Beefalo World Registry, Louisville, from 1982. Home: Louisville, Ky. Died Sept. 5, 2007.

WADDELL, ROBERT EARNEST, label company executive; b. Greensburg, Pa., Apr. 11, 1938; s. Cliff and Scott Waddell; children: Edward, Jennifer; m. Ruby Cassel, July 3, 1983. Salesman Addressograph Multigraph, Shreveport, La., 1963-65; nat. sales mgr. Flexi-Pak, Inc., Bossier City, La., 1965-71; pres., owner Custom Labels, Inc., Bossier City, from 1971. Pres. owner Epic Packaging, Bossier City, 1971-91, Custom Labels Inc. Va., Woodstock, 1990—; lectr. La. Tech. Coll., Shreveport, La., 1989. Bd. dirs. Bossier Arts Coun., Greater Bossier Econ. Devel. Found.; corp. sponsor Independence Bowl, 1990. Sgt. USAF, 1955-63. Recipient award for Custom Labels, La. Gov. Buddy Roemer, 1991, awards Mayors Bossier and Shreveport, La., 1991, award Sheriff Larry Deen., 1991. Mem. Shreveport C of C. (Small Bus. Person award 1990, award 1991), Bossier C. of C. (award 1991), Eagles. Republican. Presbyterian. Avocations: golf, reading, snow and water skiing, deer hunting. Home: Bossier City, La. Died Apr. 25, 2008.

WADDELL, WILLIAM HENRY, mental health therapist; b. Belo-Horizonte, Brazil, Oct. 30, 1939; s. Richard Lord and Margaret G. Waddell; m. Mary Ingalls, Dec. 27, 1969. Student, U. Dubuque, from 1987; BA, Whitworth Coll., 1962; MSW, Ariz. State U., 1975; MDiv, U. of Dubuque, 1991. Social worker San Diego County, 1966-68, State of Nev., Fallon, 1970-73; mental health therapist Grant County Mental Health Ctr., Moses Lake, Wash., 1975-87; student pastor Salem Presbyn. Ch., Alton, Ill., from 1990. Del. Dem. County Conv., Grant County, 1986. Served with U.S. Army, 1962-65. NIMH fellow, 1974-75. Mem. Wash. Assn. County Designated Mental Health Profls., Nat. Assn. Social Workers (cert.). Presbyterian. Avocation: sailing. Home: Middleton, Wis. Died Dec. 14, 2007.

WAGNER, CHARLES RUSSELL, accountant, educator, consultant; b. Delong, Ind., Aug. 14, 1922; s. Jacob George Wagner and Iona Elizabeth (Long) Steeb; m. Rutheda Meyer, Aug. 17, 1947; children: Skip, Barbara, Mary, William, David. BS in Acctg., U. Notre Dame, 1949; MBA in Mgmt., Creighton U., 1967; PhD in Acctg., U. Nebr., 1976. Cert. data processor, internal auditor, mgmt. acct., CPA, Ind., Minn. Commd. 2d lt. USAF, 1944, advanced through grades to lt. col., 1966, ret., 1969; asst. prof. acctg. Creighton U., Omaha, 1969-76; assoc. prof. U. S.D., Vermillion, 1976-78, Gustavus Adolphus Coll., St. Peter, Minn., 1978-83, St. Cloud State U., Minn., 1983-84; prof. Mankato (Minn.) State U., 1984-88, emeritus prof., from 1988. Cons. in field, 1973-87. Author: CPA and Fraud, 1979; contbr. articles and case studies to profl. publs., 1970-93. Bd. dirs. Good Neighbor Found., 1991-93; vol. medicare counselor, 1991-93. Home: Frazee, Minn. Died Jan. 17, 2008.

WAGNER, RICHARD E., artist; b. Trotwood, Ohio; BFA, U. Colo., 1950, MFA, 1952. Instr. Mansfield Art Ctr., Steamboat Springs, Colo., Castle Hill Art Ctr., Ispwich, Mass., U. Colo., 1950-53, Dartmouth Coll., 1953-66. Gallery reps. El Prado Galleries, Sedona, Ariz., The Darvish Collection, Naples, Fla., Courtyard Gallery, New Buffalo, Mich., Elinoff-Cote Gallery, Telluride, Colo. One-man shows include Grand Central Galleries, N.Y.C., Shore Gallery, Boston, Dartmouth Coll., DeCordova Mus., Lincoln, Mass., Fairleigh Dickinson U., N.J., Middlebury Coll., Telluride Gallery Fine Art, Colo., El Prado Art Galleries, Santa Fe, Sedona, Ariz., Western Colo. Ctr. Arts, Invitational Colorado Springs Rotary Show, 1995, 96, numerous others; group shows at Mus. Modern Art, Pa. Acad. Fine Arts, Joslyn Art Mus., Libr. Congress, Madison Square Gardens, Butler Art Inst.; contbr. articles to profl. jours.; represented in private collections. Recipient Colo. Springs Fine Arts Guild Juror's award, 1989, Pinon Arts Show First Pl., 1992, Naples Fla. Art Assn. First Pl., and others. Home: Tillamook, Oreg. Died Feb. 13, 2009; unknown.

WAITZKIN, STELLA, artist; Student, Alfred U., NYU, Columbia U. Artist-in-residence Rutgers U., New Brunswick, N.J., 1998. One-woman shows at Iris Clert, Paris, 1973, Yale U. Art Gallery, New Haven, 1974, James Yu Gallery, N.Y., 1974, 75, 77, Lowenstein Libr., Fordham U., N.Y., 1975, Donnell Libr., N.Y., 1976, E.P. Gurewitsch, N.Y., 1977, Everson Mus. of Art, Syracuse, N.Y., 1983, Creiger Sesen Gallery, Boston, 1984, Galerie Caroline Corre, Paris, 1989, Gay Head Gallery, Martha's Vineyard, Mass., 1990; exhibited in numerous group shows, including Franklin Furnace, N.Y.C., 1981, La Bibliotheque Publique de Ctr. Nat. D'Art et Culture Georges Pompideau, Paris, 1982, N.Y. Pub. Libr., 1984, Cleve. Mus. Art, 1984, Mus. Nat. Modern Art, Paris, 1985, Robeson Ctr. Gallery, Rutgers U., Newark, 1985, 87, Met. Mus. Art, N.Y.C., 1985, Bibliotheque Discotheque Faidherde, Paris, 1985, Jewish Mus., N.Y.C., 1986, Caroline Corre Gallery, Paris, 1987, Anita Shapolsky Gallery, N.Y.C., 1987, 89, 90, 94, Witkin Gallery, N.Y.C., 1987, Sweetbriar (Va.) Coll., 1987, Queens Mus., N.Y.C., 1987, Patricia Carrega Gallery, Washington, 1988, Ft. Wayne (Ind.) Mus. Art, 1988, Fox, Ley, Leech, Carrega Gallery, Washington, 1989, Fonds Regional D'Art Contemporien Normandie, Rouen, France, 1989, N.J. State Mus., Trenton, 1989, 93, Bibliotheek de wolfenbuttel, Germany, 1989, Hotel del La Region, Roune, 1989, Mediatheque D'Elbeuf, France, 1989, Barbara Fendrick Gallery, N.Y., 1990, Peter M. David Gallery, Mpls., 1990, Book Arts Ctr., N.Y., 1990, Le Chateau de Vascoeuil, France, 1990, Ctr. Culturel "La Nacelle" a Auberginville, France, 1991, Bi-Nat. Ctr., Bogota, Colombia, 1992, numerous others; represented in permanent collection Butler Inst. Art, Concoran Gallery Art, Washington, Nat. Mus. Am. Art, Washington, Patrick Lanon Found. Mus., Jewish Mus., Va. Mus., Richmond, Newark Mus., John Cotton Dana Libr. Rutgers U., N.J., N.J. State Mus., N.Y. Pub. Libr., N.Y.C., Israel Mus., Everson Mus. Fine Art, Syracuse, N.Y., Queens Mus. Fine Art, NYU Mus., Pottsdam, Yale U., Calhoun Coll. Recipient lifetime achievement award Krasner-Pollack Found., 1995, 96. Home: New York, NY. Died 2004.

WALBRIDGE, STEPHEN EDWARD, banker; b. Rutland, Vt., Apr. 11, 1948; s. Richard P. and Ruth P. (Perry) W. BS, St. Joseph's Coll., Rutland, Vt., 1984. Mgr. South Sta., Rutland, 1980-83; chief info. officer Vescos, Rutland, 1983-87, Marble Bank, Rutland, from 1987. Commr. Rutland City Sch. Bd., 1990—; bd. dirs. Rutland County Ct. Diversion, 1988—; sec. Killington (Vt.) Businessman's Assn., 1973—. Mem. 34/400 User's Group, Boston Computer Soc., Elks, Moose, Disabled Am. Vets, Am. Legion, Killington Country Club. Avocations: golf, pistol shooting, reading, walking. Home: Rutland, Vt. Died May 14, 2008.

WALD, MARKUS STANLEY, utility company executive; b. Bismarck, ND, Jan. 2, 1950; s. Stanley Markus and Helen Elizabeth (Bosch) W.; m. Rebecca Ann Boehm, Oct. 14, 1977; children: Stanley Markus, Theodore James. AS, Nat. Coll. Bus., Rapid City, SD, 1969; AS in Bus. Adminstrn., Bismarck Jr. Coll., 1976; BS in Mgmt., N.D. State U., 1978. Dataprocessing mgr. Lystad's Inc., Grand Forks, N.D., 1972-74; asst. v.p. Patterson Land Co., Bismarck, N.D., 1974-75; coordinator data processing State N.D., Bismarck, 1975-80; coordinator bus. system Basin Electric Power Cooperative, Bismarck, from 1980. Served with U.S. Army, 1970-72. Mem. N.D. Auctioneer Assn. Clubs: Toastmasters (pres. 1985-86). Lodges: Elks. Republican. Roman Catholic. Avocations: auctioneering, hunting, fishing. Home: Mandan, ND. Died Apr. 24, 2008.

WALDIE, JEROME RUSSELL, former United States Representative from California; b. Antioch, Calif., Feb. 15, 1925; m. Joanne Waldie; children: Jeff, Jonathon, Jill. BA, U. Calif. Berkeley, 1950. Mem. Calif. State Assembly, 1958—66, majority leader, 1961—66; mem. US Congress from 14th Calif. Dist., 1966—75; chmn. Fed. Mine Safety & Health Review Commn., 1978—79. Exec. dir. The White House Conf. on Aging, 1980; mem. Calif. Agrl. Rels. Bd., 1981—85, Tahoe Regional Planning Agy., 1992—2008. Served in US Army, 1943—46. Democrat. Died Apr. 3, 2009.

WALKER, L. HARRALL, insurance brokerage executive; b. Spartanburg, SC, June 10, 1925; d. William Prentiss and Charlotte (Harrall) W.; m. Betty Stephen, Aug. 17, 1948; children: Lem, Charlotte, Mary Elizabeth, Bruce. AB in Edn., U. S.C., 1949. CLU. Agt. Penn Mut. Life Ins. Co., Phila., from 1951; owner, broker Walker & Walker Ins., Spartanburg, from 1972. Sgt. USAAF, 1943-45, MTO. Mem. Western Carolina Soc. CLU's, Spartanburg Estate Planning Coun. (pres. 1975), Spartanburg Life Underwriters Assn. (pres. 1955), Million Dollar Round Table (life), Sertoma (pres. Spartanburg 1955, Exemplary Sertoman award 1983). Republican. Episcopalian. Avocations: golf, tennis, gardening. Home: Spartanburg, SC. Died July 25, 2008.

WALL, JACQUELINE JARDINE, art educator; b. Calcutta, India, Apr. 21, 1926; came to U.S., 1939; d. Geoffrey Owen and Olga Patricia (Bradlaugh) Jardine; m. Joseph Barrye Wall Jr., Nov. 1, 1952 (dec. Mar. 1972); children: Barrye Langhorne, Marjorie Lancaster, Geoffrey Hanes, Angus Alexander. BA in Psychology, Westhampton Coll., 1952; MA in Art Edn., Va. Commonwealth U., 1979. Feature writer, reporter The Farmville (Va.) Herald, 1953-57; art dir. Lab. Sch. Longwood Coll., Farmville, 1974-83; supr. art edn. Longwood Coll., 1974-83, instr. art, 1984; art specialist Prince Edward County Pub. Schs., Farmville, 1984-89; freelance sculpture Farmville, from 1989. Adj. instr. art Longwood Coll., 1989—; dir. Va. Gov.'s Sch., Farmville, 1982, 83; co-dir. Regional Va. Gov.'s, Hampden-Sydney, 1986, 87; adjudicator Va. Gov.'s Sch., 1987-89, 93. Leader Girl Scouts Am., Farmville, 1960-72. Recipient prize for Innovative Programming Am. Assn. Summer Schs., 1978. Mem. Richmond Women's Caucus Art (past chair 1991-93, exhibit chair 1994—), Longwood Ctr. Visual Arts (edn. coord. 1992—), Mortar Board, Phi Beta Kappa. Avocations: tree-farming, golf, exercise, books, music. Home: Farmville, Va. Died Dec. 10, 2007.

WALLACE, IRVING, retired stockbroker; b. Boston, Jan. 21, 1914; s. Frank and Zina (Sharfman) Wallace; m. Lillian Kahn, Apr. 6, 1967 (dec. 1985); stepchildren: Larry, Elisabeth, Jim. BA, Harvard Coll., 1934; MBA, Harvard U., 1936. Investment analyst various cos., Boston, 1936—39; economist U.S. Govt., Des Moines, Boston, Wash., 1939—54; stockbroker Ferris, Baker, Watts, Wash., 1954—63, sr. v.p. emeritus, dir., 1964—2008. Mem.: Internat. Club Wash., Harvard Club, Harvard Bus. Sch. Club. Home: Washington, DC. Died Oct. 29, 2008.

WALLACE, JOHN RICHARD See WEZALIS, JOHN RICHARD

WALLACE, WILLIAM EDWARD, research physicist; b. Charleston, W.Va., Sept. 25, 1942; s. William Edward and Zoe Wallace; m. Elisabeth Ann Fehl, July 1, 1970; children: Sarah Hart, David Bransford. BS in Physics, W.Va. U., 1963, MS in Physics, 1967, PhD, 1969. Postdoctoral associateship NRC U.S. Bur. of Mines, Morgantown, W.Va., 1969-70, rsch. physicist, 1970-76; asst. ctr. dir. U.S. Dept. of Energy, Morgantown, W.Va., 1976-80; rsch. physicist div. respiratory disease studies, leader molecular biophysics team, div. health effects lab. Nat. Inst. for Occupational Safety and Health, Morgantown, W.Va., from 1980. Adj. prof. dept. chem. engring. W.Va. U., Morgantown, 1982—, Coll. Mineral and Energy Resources, W.Va. U., Morgantown, 1990-95, Genetics and Devel. Biology Program, 1994—; grad. faculty Coll. Engring., W.Va. U., Morgantown, 1988—; com. synthetic fuels facilities safety NRC, LaJolla and Washington, 1981-82; working group WHO, Internat. Agy. for Rsch. on Cancer, Lyon, France, 1983; chmn. radiation safety com. Appalachian Lab. for Occupl. Safety and Health, Nat. Inst. Occupl. Safety and Health, 1983—; postdoctoral rsch. adv. associateship program NRC, 1991—. Editor: Silica and Silica-Induced Lung Diseases, 1995; referee Jour. Magnetic Resonance, 1972, ACS Jour. Environ. Sci. and Tech., 1974, Jour. Toxicology and Environ. Health, 1990, 93, Annals Occupl. Hygiene, 1991, Applied Occupational and Environmental Hygiene, 1998, Clay and Clay Minerals, 1998; patentee in field; contbr. articles to profl. jours. Chmn. admissions and allocations United Way Monongalia and Preston Counties, W.Va., 1992, chmn. donor rels. com., 1993-95, chmn. vol. action com., 1996-99. Recipient Shepard Sci. award nominee U.S. Ctr. for Disease Control, 1988, 93, Leadership award United Way, 1993, Alice Hamilton award Nat. Inst. for Occupl. Safety and Health, 1998, 2000. Avocation: great books discussion group. Home: Morgantown, W.Va. Died July 20, 2008.

WALLHAUSEN, MILDRED CAROLYN, publisher; b. NYC, Apr. 3, 1914; d. James Meroe and Frances (Bronson) Savell; m. Arthur Louis Wallhausen Sr., Sept. 25, 1936 (dec. Nov. 1969); children: Art L. Jr., Elizabeth Gail. Grad., Brown Bus. Coll., 1932. Proofreader Daily Am. Rep., Poplar Bluff, 1933-36; co-owner Enterprise-Courier, Charleston, 1936-69, pub., from 1969, East Prairie (Mo.) Eagle, from 1969. Illustrator: (children's book) Bobby Butterfly, 1986; watercolor artist. Mem. Mo. Gov.'s Adv. Coun., Comprehensive Health Planning Coun., 1969-73; mem. Bootheel CHP Coun,. 1971-72, Charleston Park and Recreation Bd., 1972-77, Sr. Citizens Housing Project, 1973, Miss. County TB Assn., 1945-53, S.E. Mo. Regional Coun. Alcoholism and Drug Abuse, 1976-78, Miss. County Child Welfare Coun., 1974-77; bd. dirs. Miss. County Child Devel. Ctr., 1974-77; pres. Eugene Field Elem. Sch. PTA, 1948, Charleston H.S. PTA, 1935; chpt. mother FHA, 1955, 62; mem. Miss. County Cmty. Chs.; commr. East Prairie Housing Authority, 1992—; SEMO State U. Copper Dome Soc.(pres. coun.), mem. citizens adv. bd. S.E. U., Cape Girardeau KRCU-Public Radio, 1996-1999. Inducted Mo. Press Assn. Hall of Fame, 2000. Mem. NAACP, S.E. Mo. Press Assn (pres. 1981, historian 1982-), Miss. County Sheltered Workshops (bd. mem. 1985-), Am. Legion Aux, Citzens' Adv. Bd. 1997-99. Republican. Episcopalian. Achievements include Sun. Sch. tchr. 70 yrs. Home: East Prairie, Mo. Deceased.

WALLICK, CHARLES C., minister; b. Red Lion, Pa., Sept. 6, 1916; s. Charles C. and Minnie B. (Smith) W.; m. Elizabeth Griswold, Aug. 22, 1942 (div. Sept. 1954); m. Nancy Cole, Oct. 30, 1954; children: Stephen W., David M. BA, Ursinus Coll., 1938; MDiv, Yale U., 1941; PhD, U. Edinburgh, Scotland, 1950; postgrad., U. Pa., 1951-52. CLU. Chaplain USN, 1942-46; asst. prof. Ursinus Coll., Collegeville, Pa., 1946-49. Lectr. U. Conn., Storrs, 1955-56; bd. dirs. Rocky Mt. Conf., United Ch. Christ, Denver, 1989—; mem. Christian bd. RSVP, Garfield County, Glenwood, Colo., 1989—. Contbr. articles to newspaper. Lt. comdr. USN, 1942-46. Recipient 3d Life award Cleve. Life Underwriters, 1966. Mem. Am. Legion (chaplain 1989-90), Lions (chaplain 1975-76). Home: Molina, Colo. Died June 6, 2008.

WALLING, JOHN DANIEL, III, construction management company executive; b. Leesburg, Fla., Nov. 12, 1937; s. John D. Jr. and Glenn C. (Connell) W.; children: Mark Daniel, Scott Lepton, Christopher Leigh, John Daniel IV. B of Bldg. Constrn., U. Fla., 1961. Lic. contractor, Fla. Regional mgr. U.S. Shell Homes, Chesapeake, Ohio, 1961-62; asst. dir. bldg. and zoning City of Miami Springs, Fla., 1962-63; chief project mgr. Daniel Internat., Jacksonville, Fla., 1963-71; mgr. Tampa Bay Frank J. Rooney Inc., Tampa, Fla., 1971-73; pres. Bullard & Walling Inc., Clearwater, Fla., 1973-76, Walling Constrn. Co., Largo, Fla., 1976-84; v.p. ops. Enterprise Bldg. Corp., Clearwater,

1984-86; pres. Affordable Small Bus. Solutions, Largo, from 1989, Profl. Analysis Corp., Belleair, Fla., from 1989. Presenter seminar on constrn. control system U. Fla., 1990. Author: Does Your Company Have Essential Ingredients and Balances, 1988. Mem. Acoustical Ceiling & Drywall Orgn. (exec. dir. 1989—), Am. Subcontractors Assn. Died Sept. 26, 2007.

WALSH, MYLES ALEXANDER, educator; b. Santiago, Cuba, Mar. 13, 1944; s. Myles Alexander and Ruth Elizabeth (Berg) W.; m. Judith Holt Wiggins, June 21, 1965 (div. Apr. 1994); children: Myles Alexander, Sarah Gard. BA, Harvard Coll., 1963; MS, Caltech Univ., 1964, PhD, 1967; MBA, U. Conn., 1971. Registered profl. engr. Conn., Mass. Project engr. Pratt & Whitney Aircraft, Hartford, Conn., 1967-71; treasurer KOR, Inc., Cambridge, Mass., 1972-82; pres. Cape Cod Rsch., Falmouth, Mass., from 1982. Dir. E Paint Co., Bourne, Mass., 1990—, Tracer Tech., Sommerville, Mass., 1992—; prof. Mass. Maritime, Buzzards Bay, Mass., 1971—. Patentee in field. Avocation: bridge. Died Feb. 7, 2008.

WALSKE, MAX CARL, JR., physicist; b. Seattle, June 2, 1922; s. Max Carl and Margaret Ella (Fowler) W.; m. Elsa Marjorie Nelson, Dec. 28, 1946; children: C. Susan, Steven C., Carol A. (dec.). BS in Math. cum laude, U. Wash., 1944; PhD in Theoretical Physics, Cornell U., 1951. Staff, asst. theoretical divsn. leader Los Alamos Sci. Lab., 1951-56; dep. rsch. dir. Atomics Internat., Canoga Park, Calif., 1956-59; sci. rep. AEC in U.K., London, 1961-62; theoretical physicist RAND Corp., 1962-63; sci. attache U.S. Missions to NATO and OECD, Paris, 1963-65; staff mem. Los Alamos Sci. Lab., 1965-66; asst. to sec. for atomic energy US Dept. Def., 1966—73, chmn. military liaison com. to atomic energy commn.; pres., COO Atomic Indsl. Forum, Inc., Washington, 1973-87. Chmn. Upper Hood Canal Watershed Mgmt. Com., 1994-2000; budget steering com. Kitsap County, 1996, budget com., 1997-99, participant strategic planning, 1997, planning commn., 1998-2000. Lt. (j.g.) USNR, 1943-51. Recipient Disting. Civilian Svc. medal Dept. Def. Fellow Explorers Club, Am. Phys. Soc.; mem. Am. Nuc. Soc., Phi Beta Kappa, Sigma Xi. Home: Silverdale, Wash. Died May 30, 2009.

WALTERS, THOMAS JOSEPH, automotive company executive; b. New Brunswick, NJ, Mar. 12, 1930; s. Robert Leonard and Mary Theresa (Sehulster) W.; m. Estelle Dorothy Diorio, Feb. 14, 1953; children: Thomas J. Jr., Joseph J., Janet E., Michael J., James E. Comptroller City Garage Inc., North Brunswick, N.J., 1953-61, Mid State Oil Heating Corp., North Brunswick, 1961-70, Perrine's Pontiac, Jamesburg, N.J., 1970-73; instr. Wassel Automotive Sch., Livingston, N.J., 1973-75; comptroller DeAngelis Buick, New Brunswick, N.J., 1975-81, Volvo of Princeton (N.J.), from 1981. V.p. North Brusnwick C. of C., 1970; pres. Midd. County Fuel Dealers Assn., 1968; pres. Sacred Heart Holy Name Soc., New Brunswick, 1965. Mem. KC. Roman Catholic. Avocations: reading, swimming, dance, home repairs. Home: Naples, Fla. Died July 2, 2008.

WALTON, HARRY A., JR., retired dairy manager; b. Covington, Va., Sept. 24, 1918; s. Harry A. and Madeline Lillian (Gaylor) W.; m. Virginia Robinson, May 4, 1942; children: Harriet Ann, Jeannie Marie, Bonita Carol, Mary Allyn, Dawn Elizabeth. Student, U. Va., 1937, Columbia U., 1939; BS, Lynchburg Coll., Va., 1939. Analytical chemist Indsl. Rayon Corp., Covington, Va., 1940-42; mgr. White Oak Dairy, Covington, 1945-80. Author: (catalogs) Exhibits at Lynchburg Coll., Coll. of William and Mary, Trinity Coll., Norfolk Mus., 1968-93; compiler selective index documents of Allegheny County, 1822-90. Chmn., mem. 5th Planning Dist., Roanoke, Va., 1960—, Alleghany Bd. of Suprs., Alleghany County, Val, 1962-86, Alleghany Sch. Bd., 1948-62; founder, pres., mem. Alleghany Assn. Retarded Citizens, 1948-96; fellow Pierpont Morgan Libr., N.Y.C., 1968-86; charter mem. Boiling Spring Ruritan, 1950—. With USAF, 1942-45, ETO. Mem. Holstein-Friesian Assn., U. Va. Bibliographic Soc. Avocations: book collecting, photography, local history. Home: Covington, Va. Died Sept. 26, 2007.

WALTS, LOU EUGENE, retired business executive, management consultant; b. San Francisco, May 31, 1932; m. Diane Mann, Dec. 7, 1958; children: Elisabeth Louise, Jackie Lynne. BS, San Francisco State U., 1958. CPCU; assoc. risk mgmt. Various underwriting and sales positions Fireman's Fund Ins. Co., Novato, Calif., 1958-65, mgr., 1965-70, asst. v.p., 1970-78, v.p., 1978-85, v.p. systems, 1985-90. Dir. Diablo Scholarships Inc., Concord, Calif., 1968—, pres., 1985; mem. Sea Exploring Sea Exploring/Sea Scouts, Boy Scouts Am., 1988—, nat. chmn./commodore, 1990-93. With USN, 1956-58. Mem. Commonwealth Club. Republican. Espiscopalian. Avocations: woodworking, electronics, baseball fan. Home: Walnut Creek, Calif. Died July 19, 2008.

WANG, SHEN K., orthopedic surgeon; b. Nanjing, China, Sept. 5, 1922; s. Chun-Hwa Wang and Chih-Hwa Liu; m. Eleanor Chao-Chih Wang, Sept. 5, 1946; children: Cathy S., Colbert L. MD, Harvard U., Cambridge, Mass., 1953. Bd. cert. Am. Coll. Surgeons. Cons., resident Children's Med. Ctr. and Morse Gen. Hosp.; chief resident Children's Hosp. Med. Ctr.; pvt. practice Fairmont, Va. Leader Cub Scout, Barrackville, W.Va., 1957—59. Fellow: Am. Coll. Surgeons. Died June 11, 2008.

WARD, HILEY HENRY, journalist, educator; b. Lafayette, Ind., July 30, 1929; s. Hiley Lemen and Agnes (Fuller) W.; m. Charlotte Burns, May 28, 1951 (div. 1971); children: Dianne, Carolee, Marceline, Laurel; m. Joan Bastel, Aug. 20, 1977. BA, William Jewell Coll., 1951; MA, Berkeley Bapt. Div. Sch., 1953; MDiv, McCormick Theol. Sem., Chgo., 1955; student, Northwestern U., 1948, 54, 56-57; PhD, U. Minn., 1977. News asst. Christian Advocate, 1953-55; editor jr. publs. David C. Cook Pub. Co., 1956-59; editor Record, Buchanan, Mich., 1960; religion editor Detroit Free Press, 1960-73; asst. prof. journalism Mankato (Minn.) State U., 1974-76; assoc. prof. journalism Wichita (Kans.) State U., 1976; prof. journalism Temple U., Phila., 1977-96, prof. emeritus, 1997—2009, dir. news-editorial sequence, journalism dept., 1977-80, chmn. dept., 1978-80. Instr. journalism Oakland U., Rochester, Mich., evenings 1963-66. Author: Creative Giving, 1958, Space-age Sunday, 1960, Documents of Dialogue, 1966, God and Marx Today, 1968, Ecumania, 1968, Rock 2000, 1969, Prophet of the Black Nation, 1969, The Far-out Saints of the Jesus Communes, 1972, Religion 2101 A.D., 1975, Feeling Good About Myself, 1983, Professional Newswriting, 1985, My Friend's Beliefs: A Young Reader's Guide to World Religions, 1988, Reporting in Depth, 1991, Magazine and Feature Writing, 1993, Mainstreams of American Media History, 1997; editor: Media History Digest, 1979-94; exec. editor: Kidbits, 1981-82; book editor: Editor and Publisher, 1989-98, Peters Rock, 2005-09, Understanding Reality Religion, 2007-09,; contbr. articles to profl. jours., feature articles to newspapers and mags.; also short stories and poems. Religious Pub. Rels. Coun. fellow, 1970; recipient citation Religious Heritage Am., 1962, Leidt award Epsic. Ch., 1969, citation U.S. Am. Revolution Bicentennial Adminstrn., 1976, Text and Acad. Authors citation, 1997. Mem. Religion Newswriters Assn. (pres. 1970-72), Am. Soc. Journalists and Authors, Am. Journalism Historians Assn. (bd. dirs. 1994-96, Kobre lifetime achievement award 1999), Overseas Press Club. Home: Warrington, Pa. Died Oct. 1, 2009.

WARD, RICHARD IVAN, real estate developer, aviation consultant; b. Pitts., Sept. 14, 1927; s. Ivan Walter Ward and Mildred (Benninghoff) Brown; m. Donna Wilson; children: Dane Clark, Mark Craig, Gregory Scott. FAA cert., Pitts. Inst. Aero., 1948. Chief instr. Martinsburg (W.Va.) Aircraft Service, 1950-52; prin. Ward Aero, Inc., Three Rivers, Mich., 1952-77, Forward Horizons, Three Rivers, from 1977. Contbr. articles to profl. jours. Served with USN, 1945-47. Recipient Disting. Alumnus award Pitts. Inst. Aero., 1968, Bus. Aviation award Ziff Davis Pub., 1972, Govt. Industry Rels. award Aviation Distbrs. and Mfrs., 1977. Mem. Quiet Birdman (Key Man 1973), Svc. Corps. Ret. Execs., Antique Airplane Assn., Aircraft Owners and Pilots Assn., Rotary (pres. Three Rivers club 1965). Republican. Presbyterian. Avocations: flying, aircraft restoration. Died May 16, 2008.

WARD, ROBERT VINCENT, advertising and public relations executive; b. Kansas City, Mo., May 30, 1931; s. Robert Lynn and Mary Christina (Bock) W.; m. Mary Susan Shaffer, Dec. 12, 1953; children: Robert Joseph, Timothy David, Michelle Suzanne, Thomas Vincent. AB in Polit. Sci. cum laude, Benedictine Coll., Atchison, Kans., 1953; postgrad., U. Mo., 1958; MBA with honors, Rockhurst Coll., 1980. Sales promotion mgr. Western Auto Supply Co., Kansas City, 1955-67; dir. mktg. Burstein-Applebee, Inc., Kansas City, 1967-68; dir. circulation, mktg. Intertec Pub. Co., Kansas City, 1968-70; pub. relations, advt. dir. United Bus. Communications, Inc., Kansas City, 1970-73, United Telecommunications, Inc., Kansas City, 1973-88, dir. adminstrn., from 1988. Ptnr. Ward & Ward Mktg. Cons., Kansas City, 1962—; bd. dirs. Scott's Custom Frames; adj. faculty Sch. Mgmt. Rockhurst Coll., 1983—. Contbr. articles to profl. jours. Bd. dirs. Kansas City Ballet, 1980; mem. com. Kansas City Cultural Mall, 1980—. With U.S. Army, 1953-55. Named Hon. Fellow Truman Library, Independence, Mo., Nat. Direct Mktg. Writer of Yr., 1973, Pub. Relations Profl. of Yr., Kansas City, Mo., 1981. Mem. Am. Mgmt. Assn., Bus. and Profl. Advt. Assn. (internat. v.p. 1978), Kansas City Advt. Fedn., Accredited Pub. Relations Soc. Am. (pres. Kansas City chpt. 1978, Meeting Planners Internat., Kansas City Conv. and Visitors Bur., Greater Kansas City C. of C. (com. nat. affairs 1977-78, sub.-com. chmn. edn. 1975), KC. Roman Catholic. Avocations: classical music, flowers, model airplanes, woodworking. Home: Independence, Mo. Died July 8, 2008.

WARF, JAMES CURREN, retired chemistry professor; b. Nashville, Sept. 1, 1917; s. James Curren and Susie (McCord) W.; m. Kyoko Sato, Dec. 28, 1965; children: Sandra Louise, Curren Walter, Barnaby Louis. BS, U. Tulsa, 1939; PhD, Iowa State U., 1946. Group leader Manhattan Project Atomic Energy Program, Ames, Iowa, U. Chgo., Oak Ridge, 1942-47; Guggenheim fellow Berne, Switzerland, 1947-48; prof. chemistry, research chemist U. So. Calif., 1948—88. Vis. prof. U. Indonesia, Jakarta, 1957-59, Airlangga U., Indonesia, 1962-64, Nat. U. Malaysia, Kuala Lumpur, 1974-75, Nat. U. Malaysia (Sabah br.), 1976, 82-83; research prof. Tech. U. Vienna, Austria, 1969-70, Hasanuddin U., Andalas U., Indonesia, 1978-79 Author: Physical Chemistry for Medical Students, 1964, Reference Book of Inorganic Chemistry, 1975, Textbook of Inorganic Chemistry, 1976, Inorganic Chemistry, 1979, English-Indonesian Dictionary for Chemists, 1979, Analytical Chemistry, 1982, All Things Nuclear, 1989. Recipient Disting. Alumnus award U. Tulsa, 1991; Office Naval Research grantee, 1952; Office Ordnance Research grantee, 1955; Research Corp. grantee, 1953; Austrian Ministry Edn. stipend grantee, 1969; NSF grantee, 1970, 78 Mem. Fedn. Am. Scientists (chmn. Los Angeles chpt. 1967-69), Am. Chem. Soc., So. Calif. Fed. Sci. (chair 1990), Sigma Xi. Home: Los Angeles, Calif. Died Nov. 7, 2008.

WARFIELD, SANDRA, mezzo-soprano; b. Kansas City, Mo., June 8, 1921; m. James McCracken, 1954 (dec. 1988); 1 child, Ahna. Grad., Kansas City Conservatory Music. Appeared with maj. opera cos. including, Vienna Staatsoper, Met. Opera, Zurich (Switzerland) Opera, Geneva Opera, Berlin Staatsoper, San Francisco Opera, New Orleans Opera Co., Seattle Opera, N.J. State Opera; N.Y.C. recital debut at Alice Tully Hall, 1978, recitals throughout country; appeared with symphony orchs. including, Phila. Orch., Chgo. Orch., Atlanta Symphony, Erie Philharm., Indpls. Symphony Orch., L.I. Symphony, Bergen Philharm. Orch.; performed with James McCracken at The White House, also at Presdl. salute to 25th Anniversary of UN; leading roles in: Duets of Love and Passion, London Records., Samson and Dalila, Ballo in Maschera, Carmen, Aida, Cosi fan Tutte, Trovatore, Der RosenKavalier, Greek Passion, La Prophete, Ring Cycle, La Giocanda, 1971; author: (with James McCracken) A Star in the Family, 1971. Died June 29, 2009.

WARMAN, RICHARD STANLEY, retired statistician; b. Columbus, Ohio, Sept. 30, 1920; s. Aaron Stanley and Stella Esmeralda (Deupree) W.; m. Dolores Hummel, June 12, 1951 (dec. Apr. 1992); 1 child, Robert Frederick. AB, Kenyon Coll., 1941; BS in Edn., Ohio State U., 1951. Tchr. govt. and Am. history Lebanon (Oho) Sch. Dist., 1951-52; med. libr. White Cross Hosp., Columbus, 1952-54; cataloguer Engring. Libr. N.Am. Aviation, Columbus, 1955-56; statistician Ohio Bur. Employment Svcs., Columbus, 1956-79, chief labor force reports, 1979-87. Pres. Ohio Civil Svc. Employees Assn., 1972-74. Pres., Columbus Chap. Am. Statistical Assn., 1971. Sgt. Med. Dept., U.S. Army, 1942-46, PTO. Home: Columbus, Ohio. Died Feb. 20, 2008.

WARNER, HAROLD WALTON, JR., minister; b. Hatboro, Pa., Nov. 15, 1929; s. Harold Walton and Marian (Hollowell) W.; m. Eleanor Mae Washington, Nov. 19, 1949; children: Philip Harold, John Keith. Student, Phila. Sch. Bible, 1948, Ref. Episcopal Sem., Phila., 1949-51; DD, Trinity Coll., Dunedin, Fla., 1967. Ordained to ministry So. Bapt. Conv., 1950. Pastor chs., Wellsboro, Pa., 1952-55; evangelist N.Am., W.I., Eng., 1955-60, 65-70; pastor Palm Ave. Bapt. Ch., Tampa, Fla., 1960-65, West End Bapt. Ch, Mobile, Ala., 1970-75, 1st Bapt. Ch. Citrus Park, Tampa, from 1980. Assoc. dir. Bay Islands Bapt. Bible Inst., Honduras, 1982—. Author: When the World's on Fire, 1965, Dear Hunting, 1968, The American Home and Its Needs, 1968. Mem. exec. bd. Tyoga Youth Ranch, Wellsboro, Pa., 1968-75. Republican. Home: Murphy, NC. Died Dec. 6, 2007.

WARREN, ALBERT DAVID, biostratigrapher; b. New Orleans, Jan. 5, 1929; s. Albert David and Harriet Arabelle (Beall) W.; m. Gloria Dean Turner, Oct. 18, 1957; children: David Denham, Wendy Ann, Steven Perry. BS in Geology, La. State U., 1952, MS in Geology, 1954. Registered geologist, Calif. Jr. geologist to geologist Magnolia Petroleum Co., Lake Charles, La., 1954-60; sr. geologist Mobil Oil Corp., Houston, 1960-65, lab mgr. LA, 1965-71, Dallas, 1971-74; cons., v.p. Anderson, Warren & Assocs., San Diego, 1974-80; lab. mgr. Bio Stratigraphics, Inc. of McClelland Engrs., Inc., San Diego, 1980-83; sr. biostratigrapher assoc. Atlantic Richfield Co., Anchorage, Alaska, from 1983. Trustee Paleontol. Rsch. Instn., Ithaca, N.Y., 1985—. Contbr. articles to profl. jours. Pres. La. State U. Grad. Student Coun., 1953. With USMC, 1946-49. Magnolia Petroleum Co. fellow, 1952. Fellow Geol. Soc. Am.; mem. Am. Assn. Petroleum Geologists, Soc. Econ. Paleontologists and Mineralogists, Swiss Geol. Soc., Phi Kappa Phi, Omicron Delta Kappa, Mu Sigma Rho. Achievements include research on ecology of foraminifera, calcareous nannofossil biostratigraphy, plankton biostratigraphy of Refugian. Home: La Jolla, Calif. Died May 19, 2008.

WASSERMAN, DALE, playwright; b. Rhinelander, Wis., Nov. 2, 1914; s. Samuel and Hilda (Paykel) W.; m. Martha Nelly Garza, 1984 Degree (hon.), U. Wis., 1980. Founder, artistic dir. Midwest Profl. Playwrights Lab.; Trustee, founding mem. Eugene O'Neill Theatre Center. Author: (with Bruce Geller) musical Livin' the Life, 1957; stage plays The Pencil of God, 1961, 998, 1962, One Flew Over the Cuckoo's Nest, 1963, Man of La Mancha, 1965 (Tony award for best musical 1966, N.Y. Drama Critics' Circle award for best musical 1966, Outer Circle award 1966, Variety award 1966, Spanish Pavilion award 1966), Play with Fire, 1978, Great Big River, 1981, Shakespeare and The Indians, 1983; (screenplays) World of Strangers, 1955, The Vikings, 1958, Two Faces to Go, 1959, Aboard the Flying Swan, 1962, Jangadeiro, 1962, Cleopatra, 1963, Quick, Before It Melts, 1964; writer, co-prodr.: (films) Mister Buddwing, 1965, A Walk With Love and Death, 1969, Man of LaMancha, 1972; (TV plays) Elisha and the Long Knives, 1954 (Publishers Guild award 1954), The Fog, 1957 (Writers Guild of America award 1957), Eichmann, 1958, Engineer of Death, 1959, The Citadel, 1959 (Writers Guild of America award 1959), I, Don Quixote, 1959, (Writers Guild of America award 1960), The Power and the Glory, 1960, The Lincoln Murder Case, 1961 (Writers Guild of America award 1961), Stranger, 1962, Burden of Proof, 1976, Scheherazade, 1977, The Seventh Dimension, 1984, My Name Is Esther, 1985, The Whole Truth, 1987, Green, 1987, A Fine American Family, 1988,

Players in a Game, 1989, Murder Among the Saints, 1989, The Girl From Botany Bay, 1990, Western Star, 1992, Beggar's Holiday, 1994, (plays) An Enchanted Land, 1997, How I Saved the Whole Damn World, 1997; (films) The Game, 1997 Mem. ASCAP, ALA, Writers Guild Am. East (nat. coun. 1960-64), Writers Guild Am. West, Dramatists Guild, Am. Acad. Motion Picture Arts and Scis., French Soc. Authors and Composers, The Jaques Brel Found. (gov.), Players Club, Monte Cristo Soc. Home: Paradise Vly, Ariz. Died Dec. 21, 2008.

WASSERMAN, PAUL, library and information science professor; b. Newark, Jan. 8, 1924; s. Joseph and Sadie (Ringelescu) W.; m. Krystyna Ostrowska, 1973; children: Jacqueline R., Steven R. BBA, Coll. City N.Y., 1948; MS in L.S., Columbia, 1949, MS, 1950; PhD, U. Mich., 1960; postgrad., Western Res. U., 1963-64. Advt. mgr. Zuckerberg Co., NYC, 1946-48; asst. to bus. libr. Bklyn. Pub. Library, 1949-51, chief sci. and industry div., 1951-53; librarian, asst. prof. Grad. Sch. Bus. and Pub. Adminstrn., Cornell U., 1953-56, libr., assoc. prof., 1956-62, librarian, prof., 1962-65; dean U. Md. Coll. Library and Info. Scis., 1965-70, prof., 1970-97, prof. emeritus, 1997—2009. Vis. prof. U. Mich., summers 1960, 63, 64, Asian Inst. Tech., U. Hawaii, U. Hong Kong, summer 1988, Chulalongkorn U., Bangkok, 1990, U. Wash., summer 1991, U. Wis., summer 1992, C.W. Post Coll., L.I. U., 1993, Inst. Sci. and Tech. China, Beijing, 1996; Isabel Nichol lectr. Denver U. Libr. Sch., 1968; market rsch. cons. Laux Advt., Inc., 1955-59, Gale Rsch. Co., Detroit, 1959-60, 63-64; rsch. planning cons. Ind. U. Sch. Bus., 1961-62; cons. to USPHS as mem. manpower tng. rev. com. Nat. Libr. Medicine, 1966-69, Ohio Bd. Regents, 1969, Omngraphics Inc., 1988-91, VITA, summer 1987; dir. Documentation Abstracts, Inc., 1970-73, v.p., 1971-73; Fulbright prof. Warsaw U., 1993-94; rsch. project dir. Kellogg Study, 1996-98. Author: Information for Adminstrators, 1956, (with Fred Silander) Decision Making, 1958, Measurement and Evaluation of Organization Performance, 1959, Sources of Commodity Prices, 1960, 2d edit., 1974, Sources for Hospital Administrators, 1961, Decision Making: An Annotated Bibliography, supplement, 1958-63, 1964, Librarian and the Machine, 1965; Book rev. editor: Adminstrv. Sci. Quar, 1956-61; editor: Service to Business, 1952-53, Directory of University Research Bureaus and Institutes, 1960, Health Organizations of the U.S. and Canada, 1961, and 2d to 4th edit., 1977, Statistics Sources, 1962 and 4th to 8th edits., 1984, (with Bundy) Reader in Library Adminstration, 1968, Reader in Research Methods in Librarianship, 1969; mng. editor: Mgmt. Information Guide Series, 1963-83, Consultants and Consulting Organizations, 1966, 4th edit., 1979, 5th edit., 1982, Who's Who in Consulting, 1968, 2d edit., 1974, Awards, Honors and Prizes: A Sourcebook and Directory, 1969, 2d edit., 1972, 4th edit. Vol. 1, 1978, International and Foreign Awards, 1975, New Consultants, 1973-74, 76-77, 78-79, Readers in Librarianship and Information Science, 1968-78, Ency. Bus. Information Sources, 1971, 3d edit., 1976, 4th edit., 1980, 5th edit., 1983, Library and Information Services Today, 1971-75, Consumer Sourcebook, 1974, 2d edit., 1978, 3d edit., 1980, 4th edit., 1983; series editor: Contributions in Librarianship and Information Science, 1969-99; coordinating mgmt. editor: Information Guide Library, 1971-83, The New Librarianship-A Challenge for Change, 1972; mng. editor: Museum Media, 1973, Library Bibliographies and Indexes, 1975, Ethnic Groups in the United States, 1976, 2d edit., 1982, Training and Development Organizations, 1978, 2d edit., 1983, Speakers and Lecturers: How to Find Them, 1979, 2d edit., 1982, Learning Independently, 1979, 2d edit., 1983, Recreation and Outdoor Life Directory, 1979, Law and Legal Information Directory, 1980, 2d edit., 1982, Ency. Health Info. Sources, 1986, Ency. Sr. Citizen Info. Sources, 1987, Ency. Pub. Affairs Info. Sources, 1987, Ency. Legal Info. Sources, 1987; mem. editorial bd. Social Scis. Citation Index, Inst. Scientific Info., 1972-95, Jour. Library Adminstrn., 1979-89, Social Sci. Info. Studies, 1979—, 1991 Education for Info.: The Internat. Rev. of Education and Tng. in Library and Info. Sci., 1983-88, The Best of Times: A Personal and Occupational Odyssey, 2000, New York from A to Z, 2002, Washington DC from A to Z, 2003, Weasel Words, The Dictionary of American Doublespeak, 2005, From Agincourt to Zanzibar, 2008. Active U.S. Com. on Edn. and Tng. for Internat. Fedn. for Info. and Documentation, 1993-94. Served with U.S. Army, 1943-46. Decorated Purple Heart, Bronze Star; recipient ALA Ref. Svcs. Divsn./Gale Rsch. Bus. Libr. award, 1997; Fulbright scholar, Sri Lanka, 1986-87, Poland, 1995. Mem. AAUP, ALA, Am. Soc. Info. Sci., Spl. Librs. Assn. (editor, chmn. publ. project., Disting. Mem. award bus. divsn. 1996-2009). Home: Bethesda, Md. Died May 8, 2009.

WASSERSTEIN, BRUCE JAY, investment banker; b. Bklyn., Dec. 25, 1947; s. Morris and Lola (Schleifer) Wasserstein; m. Laura Wasserstein (div. 1974); m. Christine Parrott (div. 1992); children: Ben, Pam, Skip; m. Claude Becker, 1996 (div. 2008); children: Zack, Dash; m. Angela Chao, Jan. 2009. BA with honors, U. Mich., 1967; MBA with high distinction, Harvard U., 1971, JD cum laude, 1971; diploma in law, Cambridge U., 1972. Assoc. Cravath, Swaine & Moore, NYC, 1972-77; mng. dir. The First Boston Corp., NYC, 1977-88; pres. Wasserstein, Perella and Co., NYC, 1988—2000; exec. chmn. Dresdner Kleinwort Wasserstein, NYC, 2000—01; chmn., CEO Lazard Ltd., NYC, 2001—09; chmn. Am. Lawyer Media, 1997—2009; owner The Daily Deal, 1999—2009, NY Mag., 2003—09; chmn. Wasserstein & Co., 2001—09. Author: Corporatwe Finance Law: A Guide for the Executive, 1978, Big Deal: Mergers and Acquisitions in the Digital Age, 1988. Mem. SEC Adv. Comm. Tender Offers; mem. vis. com. Harvard Law Sch., Harvard Bus. Sch., U. Mich, Columbia Journalism Sch., Cambridge U. Bus. Sch. Mem.: Coun. Fgn. Rels. Democrat. Died Oct. 14, 2009.

WATERS, DORIS B., community health nurse, administrator; b. Pottstown, Pa., July 28, 1931; d. Forrest J. and Elizabeth H. (Heffentrager) Buck; m. Douglas G. Waters, 1953 (div. 1979); children: Douglas G., Beth Ann. Diploma, Bryn Mawr Hosp., Pa., 1952; student, No. Va. Community Coll., Woodbridge. Cert. nurse adminstr. Dir. oper. rm. Hotel Dieu Hosp., El Paso; dir. oper. rm. and recovery rm. Prince William Hosp., Manassas, Va., Potomac Hosp., Woodbridge, dir. home health. Trustee Potomac Hosp. Mem. Assn. Oper. Rm. Nurses (nat. legis. com. 1983-85, pres. No. Va. chpt. 1980), Am. Orgn. Nurse Execs. Home: Woodbridge, Va. Died Mar. 10, 2008.

WATERS, FRANCES ROFFEY, retired educator; b. Providence, July 18, 1914; d. Bertram Ralph and Rachel Ellen (Curtis) Roffey; m. Gene Waters, June 18, 1937; 1 child, Frances I. Gregos. BS in Edn., New Haven State Tchrs. Coll., 1953; MS in Libr. Sci., So. Conn. State Coll., 1962. Cert. tchr. grades 1-8, libr. tchr. grades kindergarten-12. Libr. asst. Stratford (Conn.) Pub. Libr., 1952-53; children's libr. Milford (Conn.) Pub. Libr., 1953-56; libr. tchr. Stratford (Conn.) High Sch., 1956-60, Bunnell High Sch., Stratford, 1960-66, Stony Brook and Franklin Elem. Schs., Stratford, 1966-76; asst. editor Beverly Hills (Fla.) Visitor, 1982-83. Cons. State Dept. Edn., Conn., 1960-62. Active publicity Beverly Hills Civic Assn., 1981-85, Hospice of Citrus County, Fla., 1983-93, Beverly Hills Cmty. Ch., 1985—; mem. adv. bd. Citrus County Spl. Libr., 1992—; mem. publicity and exec. bd. Friends of Central Ridge Libr., 1995—; past pres. Friends of Beverly Hills Pub. Libr. Mem. AAUW (co-founder Citrus County br.), NEA, CEA, Beverly Hills Homemakers, Order Ea. Star. Republican. Avocation: crafts. Home: Valrico, Fla. Died Sept. 22, 2007.

WATSON, ROBERT H., electrical engineer; b. Mar. 22, 1943; MSEE, Northeastern U., Boston, 1971; MPA, U. N. Colo., Greely, 1981. Program mgr. Analysis & Tech., Middletown, R.I.; br. head arch., engring. NUWC, Newport, R.I. Home: New Hampton, NH. Died Dec. 28, 2007.

WATSON, VIRGINIA DREW, anthropologist, researcher; b. Tomah, Wis., June 17, 1918; d. Francis Henry and Eunice (Williams) Drew; m. James Bennett Watson, Mar. 18, 1943; children: Anne Thaxter, James Bennett. PhB, U. Wis., 1940; AM, U. Chgo., 1943, PhD, 1965. Clk. Am. Consulate, Sao Paulo, Brazil, 1944-45; lectr. Washington U., St. Louis, 1948-53, Seattle U., Wash., 1957-63; affiliate curator Burke Mus. U. Wash., Seattle, from 1969. Author: Wulfing Plates, 1950, Prehistory of the Eastern Highlands of New Guinea, 1977; co-author 3 vols. Batainabura, 1972; contbr. numerous articles to profl. jours. Fellow Am. Anthropol. Assn., Royal Anthropol. Soc. of Great Britain; mem. AAAS, Soc. Am. Archaeology, Indo-Pacific Prehistory Assn. Home: West Palm Bch, Fla. Died Dec. 7, 2007.

WATT, DOUGLAS BENJAMIN (BENJAMIN WATT), writer, drama critic; b. NYC, Jan. 20, 1914; s. Benjamin Douglas and Agnes Rita (Neimann) W.; m. Ray Mantel, Nov. 5, 1937 (div.); children: Richard David, James Douglas; m. Ethel Madsen, Aug. 13, 1951; children: Patricia, Katherine. AB, Cornell U., 1934. Copy boy N.Y. News, 1936-37, radio columnist, 1937-40, drama reporter, 1940-71, sr. drama critic, 1971-87, critic-at-large, 1987-93; staff writer New Yorker mag., 1946-95; profl. song writer; columnist Small World, 1955-70. Nominating com. Tony Awards, Pulitzer Awards, Theater World Awards; co-founder Drama Desk; chmn. Astarre Awards. Pres. Hampton Animal Shelter, 1965-79. Served with USAAF, World War II. Mem. ASCAP, N.Y. Drama Critics Circle (pres. 1975-77) Clubs: Dutch Treat (N.Y.C.) (bd. govs.). Home: New York, NY. Died Sept. 29, 2009.

WATTERS, LORAS JOSEPH, bishop emeritus; b. Dubuque, Iowa, Oct. 15, 1915; s. Martin James and Carolyn R. (Sisler) W. BA, Loras Coll., Dubuque, 1937; STB, Gregorian U., Rome, Italy, 1940; STL, Cath. U. America, 1941, MA, 1947, PhD, 1954. Ordained priest Archdiocese of Dubuque, Iowa, 1941, aux. bishop Iowa, 1965-69, supt. schs., 1967-69; asst. pastor St. Martin's Ch., Cascade, Iowa, 1941-45; mem. faculty Loras Coll., 1945-56; prin. Loras Acad., Dubuque, 1947-52, head edn. dept., 1954-56; spiritual dir. N.Am. Coll., Rome, 1956-60; dir. Am. Martyrs Retreat House, Cedar Falls, Iowa, 1960-65; ordained bishop, 1965; pastor Ch. of Nativity, Dubuque, 1965-69; bishop Diocese of Winona, Minn., 1969—86, bishop emeritus, 1986—2009. Mem. bishops' com. on priestly formation Nat. Conf. Cath. Bishops, 1970-78, chmn., 1972-75 Roman Catholic. Died Mar. 30, 2009.

WATTERS, MARIANNE GIBSON, bank administrator; b. Gastonia, NC, Dec. 29, 1954; d. Marion Eugene and Mary Louise (McSwain) Gibson; m. Clyde Stewart Fentress, Dec. 15, 1979 (div. 1981); m. James Patrick Watters, Aug. 30, 1986. BA, Gardner Webb Coll., 1978; postgrad., Cape Fear Tech. Cert. respiratory therapist. Pvt. practice piano tchr., Wilmington, N.C., 1979-86; respiratory therapist New Hanover Meml. Hosp., Wilmington, 1980-85; paralegal Michael R. Mitwol Offices, Wilmington, 1985-87; adminstrv. asst. Community Bank of Forest, Va., from 1987. Mem. Am. Inst. Banking, Nat. Orgn. Exec. Women, Nat. Guild Piano Tchrs., Alpha Psi Omega, Lynchburg Advt. Club. Democrat. Avocations: musical compositions, tennis, crafts, collecting albums, menus. Home: Forest, Va. Died Apr. 12, 2008.

WEATHERBY, DONALD ALAN, telecommunications industry executive, writer; b. Columbus, Ohio, Dec. 11, 1954; s. Virgil Byron and Janet JoAnn Weatherby. Student, Columbus State C.C. Mainframe sys. adminstr. Contract to Bell Labs., Columbus, 1981—86; ops. mgr. AT&T Labs., Reynoldsburg, Ohio, from 1996. Sys. developer and implementation AT&T Labs., Reynoldsburg, 1996—2002. Author: (tech. mgmt.) Geekology 101: Managing the Aliens, Your Computer Support Staff, 1999, (novels) The Star Spangled Specter, 1995; composer: (jazz rock lit.fusion) Plush Hush CD - Generation Y, 2000. Recipient Vol. award, Ohio Legal Rights Svc. - State of Ohio, 1999. Mem.: MUFON (assoc.; data specialist 1999—2002, award for creation of MUFON Web database 2001). Unitarian Universalist. Avocations: writing macabre fiction, astronomy, UFO researcher, jazz-literary music. Home: South Charleston, Ohio. Died June 15, 2008.

WEAVER, JOHN CARL, chemist, educator; b. Gibson, Ohio, Aug. 5, 1908; s. William Edwin and Rena Belle (Emerson) W.; m. Marian Louise King, 1940; children: John K., Susan E. BS in Chemistry, Denison U., 1930; MA in Chemistry, U. Cin., 1933, PhD in Chemistry, 1935. Instr. chem. engring. U. Cin., 1935—36; chemist Sherwin Williams Co., Cleve., 1936—73, dir. rsch., 1968—73, cons., 1974—79; adj. prof. Case We. Res. U., Cleve., from 1980. Mem. utilization rsch. adv. com. USDA, 1962-69, founding mem. Western Reserve Frontiers of Chemistry adv. bd., 1941-74, coord., supr. Sherwin William catalyst lab. on Western Reserve campus. Developer dehydrated castor oil, 1938; editor Jour. of Coatings Tech., 1963-72. Fellow ASTM (hon., bd. dirs. 1977-80, tech. com. ops. 1976-77, chmn D-1 1984-89), Fedn. Socs. Coatings Tech. (Heckel award 1976), Am. Chem. Soc., Sigma Xi. Avocation: genealogy. Home: Cleveland, Ohio. Died Jan. 8, 2008.

WEBB, RODNEY SCOTT, federal judge; b. Cavalier, ND, June 21, 1935; s. Chester and Aylza (Martin) W.; m. Betty M. Lykken, Aug. 31, 1957; children: Sharon, Crystal, Todd, Wade, Susan. BS, U. N.D., 1957, JD, 1959. Bar: N.D. 1959, U.S. Dist. Ct. N.D. 1965, U.S. Ct. Appeals (8th cir.) 1981. Assoc. Ringsak, Webb, Rice & Metelman, Grafton, N.D., 1959-81; state's atty. Walsh County, Grafton, 1966-74; mcpl. judge City of Grafton, 1975-81; spl. asst. atty. gen. State of ND, 1970-81; US atty. Dist. ND US Dept. Justice, Fargo, 1981-87; judge US Dist. Ct. ND, Fargo, 1987—2001, chief judge, 1993—2001, sr. judge, 2001—09. Col. JAG, N.D. Army N.G., ret. Mem. N.D. State Attys. Assn. (past pres.). Lutheran. Home: Fargo, ND. Died Aug. 9, 2009.

WEBB, RONALD C., engineering manager; b. Fayette, Iowa, Apr. 19, 1943; Owner Mfrs. Rep., Mpls., 1985-89; gen. mgr. Solder Clade, Inc., Mpls., 1989; mgr. engring. Graphic Circuits Corp., Cedar Rapids, Iowa, from 1990. Avocation: photography. Died Feb. 2, 2008.

WEBER, CHARLES WILLIAM, chemist; b. Streator, Ill., Dec. 28, 1922; s. Diedrich William and Maude (Cass) W.; m. Phyllis Ruth Starkey, Sept. 5, 1948; children: Kathy Weber Haney, Paul Diedrich, Andrew Leon. BS, Northwestern U., 1949; PhD, Ind. U., 1953. Analytical chemist Union Carbide Co., Oak Ridge, Tenn., 1953-58, sect. head analytical devel., 1958-62, dept. head chem. analysis, 1962-77, environ. analysis 5 plant coord., 1977-84, Martin Marietta Energy Systems, Oak Ridge, Tenn., 1984-94. Contbr. numerous articles to profl. jours. Bd. dirs. So. Appalachian Sci. and Engring. Fair, Knoxville, 1974-94. With USN, 1943-47, PTO. Fellow Am. Inst. Chemists; mem. ASTM, Am. Chem. Soc., Sigma Xi (chpt. treas. 1970), Phi Lambda Upsilon. Achievements include pioneering development of analytical instruments for on-line monitoring of highly corrosive fluoride-bearing gas processes; patents for analytical devices. Home: Oak Ridge, Tenn. Died Apr. 17, 2008.

WEBER, STEPHEN ROSS, broadcast technician; b. Fresno, Calif., Dec. 12, 1922; s. Andrew Edward and Florence Lucretia (Ross) W.; m. Deane Laverne Davis, Feb. 16, 1942 (dec. Jan. 1997); children: June Marie Ward, Anita Ann Dodson, Stephen Ross Jr.; m. Charlene Sue Bartholomew, Dec. 12, 1997. Grad. H.S., Fresno, 1940; mgmt. tng. course, Purdue U., 1978-79; Dale Carnegie, 1970-78. Lic. radio telephone operator. Aircraft electronics technician U.S. Civil Svc., Sacramento, Fresno, 1942-45; chief engr. Radio Sta. KERO, Bakersfield, Calif., 1945-48; radio engr. Radio Sta. KFRE, Fresno, 1948-53; engring. supr. KFRE Radio & TV, Fresno, 1953-65; chief engr. KFRE/KFSN Radio & TV, Fresno, 1965-85; ret., 1985; TV consulting engr. various, 1985-88. Mem. Soc. Broadcast Engrs. (local pres. 1970—), Fresno Amateur Radio Club (pres. 1952). Republican. Avocations: flying, skiing, ham radio (w6qon), exercising. Home: Toledo, Wash. Died Mar. 12, 2008.

WEBSTER, KENNETH FEWINGS, painter, consultant; b. Buffalo, Dec. 27, 1923; s. Gilbert Arthur and Llorene Jeannette (Fewings) W.; m. E. Janis Kenline Christenson, Sept. 1951 (div. Apr. 1974); children: Ford, Michael, Kim; m. Cheryl Ivy Burnett, June 1975. Student, U. Buffalo, 1946-48; cert., Pratt Inst., 1952. Creative dir., founder Design Directions, Reno, 1965-73; mem. design team audio-visual USN F-14 Top Gun Program, Miramar, Calif., 1976-77; exec. dir. art N.W. Ayer, Inc., San Francisco,

1978-80; creative cons. Shaklee Corp., San Francisco, 1981-86; instr. dept. art Coll. of Redwoods, Eureka, Calif., 1987-89; represented by Christopher Bell Collection, Alvarado Mall, Monterey, Calif., from 1986. Illustrator USAF Art Program, 1970-84. Author, artist: Southeast Asia Sketchbook, 1982; exhibited at Bolling Air Base, Washington, 1970, 82, N.Y. Soc. Illustrators, 1985, USAF Collection, Wright-Patterson Air Base. Recipient San Francisco Soc. Communicating Art award, 1980, Best Work award San Francisco Art Dirs. Show, 1983, Cert. of Excellence, Calif. Design, 1985. Home: Mariposa, Calif. Died July 7, 2008.

WEEKS, WILLIAM RAWLE, JR., oil industry executive; b. Denver, Oct. 23, 1920; s. William Rawle Sr. and Besse Elizabeth (Griffith) W.; m. June Suzanne Stephens, Jan. 22, 1944 (div. 1980); children: Stephen R., Tacy A. Weeks Hahn. BA, Stanford U., 1943. With book prodn. divsn. Stanford U. Press, 1948-49; advt. exec. Palo Alto, Calif., 1949-50; with CIA, from 1951; gen. ptnr. Weeks, Brewer & Assocs., 1971; CEO Fort Collins Consol. Royalties, Inc., Cheyenne, Wyo., from 1983. Author: Knock and Wait Awhile, 1957 (Edgar Allan Poe award 1958, Commonwealth award 1958). Nat. press and media advance man Muskie Vice Presdl. Campaign, 1968. 2nd lt. U.S. Army, 1943-46. Mem. Nat. Press Club, Denver Petroleum Club. Avocations: flying, skiing, golf, hiking. Home: Denver, Colo. Died May 2009.

WEEMS, CLARA C., educator, counselor, consultant; b. NYC, June 15, 1933; d. Joseph and Itala (Nerone) Carbonara; m. Clarence Norwood Weems, Dec. 28, 1954; children: Nancy M., Clarence N. BA in Chemistry, Hunter Coll., 1954; postgrad. in law, NYU, 1954-55, Franklin Pierce Coll., 1969-72. Cert. med. lab. technologist. Instr. chemistry lab. Fairleigh Dickinson U., Rutherford, N.J., 1956-57; tchr. med. techniques Mandl Sch., NYC, 1962-64; chmn. sci. dept. Holy Trinity High Sch., Westfield, N.J., 1973-76; med. lab. tchr. Advanced Career Tng., NYC, 1976-78; med. lab. tchr., placement dir. Allen Sch. for Physicians Aides, Jamaica, N.Y., from 1978; dir. placement, cons. Dir., organizer Clara Barton Sch., Nutley, N.J., 1986-87. Mem. AAUW, Am. Assn. Med. Assts., Faculty Wives of Franklin Pierce Coll. (pres. 1970-72). Roman Catholic. Home: Nutley, NJ. Deceased.

WEIL, JACK BAUM, clothing manufacturing company executive; b. Denver, Nov. 13, 1928; s. Jack Arnold and Beatrice (Baum) W.; m. Elizabeth Fried, 1956 (div. 1969); children: Steven Eugene, Judith B. Weil Oksner; m. Candace Helene Taylor, 1973 (div. 1983). BA, Tulane U., 1952. V.p. Rockmount Ranch Wear Mfg. Co., Denver, from 1954, designer, sales mgr., from 1957. Designer western apparel. Head planning group Humboldt Island Hist. Dist., Denver; planning com. City of Denver Chessman Park, 1996-; chmn. Commty. Coll. Denver Found. bd. dirs.; committeeman Denver Rep. Party, 1974-; del. Rep. county, dist. and state convs., 1974—; sec. Rep. Party Com., 1st Congl. Dist. Colo., 1993-94, chmn. 1995-99; sec. Colo. Rep. State Ctrl. Com., 1999-, Colo. Rep. party; mem. Colo. State Rep. Exec. Com., 1996-; bd. dirs. 1st Universalist Ch., Denver, Majority Reps. for Choice; mem. admissions com. Tulane U., 1994-; del. Rep. Nat. Conv., 1992, 96, 2000, 04, credentials com.; pres. CC of Denver Found. Bd. 1st lt. U.S. Army, 1952-54. Mem. West Coast Western Mktg. Assn., Midwest Western Wear and Equipment Assn. (bd. dirs.), NW Western Wear & Equipment Travelers Assn. (pres. Mpls.), SE Western, English and Equine Assn. (bd. dirs. Altanta), Denver Western Wear and Equipment Assn., Hat Inst. Am. (del. 1974—), Denver Athletic Club, Town Club, Lincoln Club (bd. dirs. 1997—), Rump Club, Kappa Delta Phi. Avocations: painting, politics, physical fitness, travel. Home: Denver, Colo. Died Jan. 22, 2008.

WEILBAKER, CHARLES R., retired education educator, consultant; b. Indiana, Apr. 20, 1924; s. Francis Earl and Maude Lucile (Evard) Weilbaker; m. Jean Marie Larson; children: Sharon Lynn, Jon Charles. BA, Ball State U., Muncie, Ind., 1949, MA, 1952, PhD in Education, 1958. Cert. travel cons. 1990, destination specialist 1991. Upper elem. tchr. Wayne Twp. Sch., Ft. Wayne, India, 1949—51; tchr. Burris Mid. Sch., Muncie; grad. asst. Ind. U., Bloomington, 1955—56; prof. U. Cin., 1957—89, prof. emeritus, 1989. Cons., bd. mem. Urban League, Cin., 1970—77; invited evaluator, accreditor North Ctrl. Ursuline Acad., 1973; invited evaluator Nat. Coun. Accreditation Tchr. Edn., SUNY New Paltz, Drake U., Memphis State U., U. Scranton, Hofstra U., SUNY Buffalo; invited rschr. Earthwatch Sites, 1988—91. Editor and contbr. Dictionary of Education, 1973; author: Changing Issues of Desegregation and Curriculum Development, 1977. Organizer Repeal of Ohio Death Penalty Gov. Dis-allies, 1961—63; founding mem. Greater Cin. Meml. Soc., 1963; dir. R&D Cin. Liaison Sister City, 1989—95; bd. mem. Small Bus. Loans, 1990—95, Hist. Southwest Ohio, 1989—2007. Pvt. 1st class inf. US Army, 1943—45, South Pacific. Decorated Expert Marksman, Combat Infantryman's Badge, Bronze Star US Army, 2 Purple Hearts, 3 Unit Citations; recipient hon. citizen, Liuzhou Guangn govt., China, 2001, Exemplary Leadership, Hist. Southwest Ohio, 2002. Mem.: Nat. Edn. Assn. (life), Nat. Soc. Study Edn. (life), Phi Delta Kappa (life). Democrat. Unitarian. Avocations: travel, cooking, gardening, woodworking. Home: Cincinnati, Ohio. Died June 7, 2008.

WEINBERGER, JANE DALTON, writer; b. Maine, Mar. 29, 1919; m. Caspar Willard Weinberger, Aug. 16, 1942 (dec. March 28, 2006); children: Caspar Willard, Arlin Weinberger. Student, U. Maine, 1936-38, student, 1938-41; BSN, Somerville Hosp. Sch. Nursing, 1940; postgrad., Boston U., 1941. Reg. nurse Calif. Vol. St. Luke's Hosp., San Francisco, 1947-77; owner, editor, author Windswept House Pubs., Mt. Desert, Maine, from 1984; ret., from 1999. Author: (Children's Books) The Little Ones, Lemon Drop, Tabitha Jones, Wee Peter Puffin, Fanny and Sarah, Cory the Cormorant, That's What Counts, VIM: A Very Important Mouse, 1984, Mrs. Witherspoon's Eagles, As Ever: A Selection of Letters from the Voluminous Correspondence of Jane Weinberger, 1970-1990, 1991, Canned Plums and Other Vissitudes of Life, Experience the Journey, 2003 Bd. Trustees Nat. Symphony Assn., Capitol Children's Mus., 1970-85; bd. dirs. Folger Shakespeare Libr., chmn. 1981-86; founding mem. New Globe Theatre, London, 1999; bd. vols. D.C. Gen. Hosp., 1970-75, hon. bd. mem.; bd. dirs. Jackson Lab. (Cancer Rsch. Inst.), mem. Internat. Coun. Jackson Lab.; mem. women's com. Washington Performing Arts Soc.; sponsor The Internat. Hospitality Soc., Washington, 1970-85, other vol. orgns.; Rep. coms. campaign mgr., San Francisco, 1964-68. 2nd lt. U.S. Army Nurse Corps, 1942-43, PTO. Recipient Svc. to Humanity award, Alpha chpt. Chi Eta Phi, 1974, Deborah Morton award, Westbrook (Maine) Coll., 1992. Mem. Maine Media Women, Nat. News Women, Maine Writers and Pubs. Alliance, Jr. Army Navy Guild (hon.), Soc of Sponsors USN, The Century Club of Calif., Congressional Club (Washington), Pal's Club, (Sacramento,Calif.). Episcopalian. Avocations: cooking, gardening, swimming, boating, collecting glass paperweights, miniature porcelain boxes. Home: Mount Desert, Maine. Died July 12, 2009.

WEINER, JANET, writer, educator, literary consultant; b. NYC, Apr. 12, 1930; d. Morris and Bessie (Okin) Lipschitz; m. Jerald Weiner, Mar. 26, 1950; children: Meryl S. Weiner Fern, Alan S., Ian D. Student, Richland Coll., Dallas, 1975-78, Rice U., 1981. Editor Candlelight Rev. Pub., Harrisburg, Pa., 1966-69; lit. cons. Manuscriptor's Lit. Svc., Houston, from 1984, instr. writing, from 1987, Houston Community Coll., 1986-88; script writer Pen and Video Prodns., Houston, from 1986. Author: (fiction) Black Badges Are Bad Business, 1984, (nonfiction) Journey through Divorce, 1988; also over 350 articles and short stories to nag. mags.; script writer writing related videos, 1989; initiated the Morris-Faye Press for publishing biographies, non-fiction books, family and corporate histories. Lectr. writing Houston and Ft. Bend Librs., 1985, 91, writing confs. Golden Triangle Writers Build, U. Tex., Dallas, 1991, Lamar U., Millsaps Coll., Jackson, Miss., 1992, Soc. Southwestern Authors, Tucson, Frontiers in Writing Conf., Amarillo, Tex., 1992-94; sec. The Writers Devel. Ctr., Houston. Mem. Nat. Writers Guild (profl.), Manuscriptors Guild (founder, v.p. 1985-86, pres. 1986-88, pub. rels. and publicity com. 1985—, Gratitude award1987, 94). Avocations: music docent, tending to needs of 3 cats. Home: Houston, Tex. Died Sept. 27, 2007.

WEINSTEIN, I. BERNARD, oncologist, geneticist, director, educator; b. Madison, Wis., Sept. 9, 1930; married, 1952; 3 children. BS, U. Wis., 1952, MD, 1955, DSc (hon.), 1992. Nat. Cancer Inst. spl. rsch. fellow bacteriology/immunology Harvard Med. Sch./MIT, Boston, 1959-61; career scientist Health Rsch. Coun., City of N.Y., 1961-72; assoc. vis. physician Francis Delafield Hosp., 1961-66; from asst. attending physician to assoc. attending physician Presbyn. Hosp., 1967-81, attending physician, from 1981; from asst. to assoc. prof. medicine Columbia U. Coll. Phys. and Surg., NYC, 1978-90; prof. medicine Columbia U., NYC, 1973—2008, prof. pub. health, 1978—2008, prof. genetics & devel., 1990—2008, Frode Jensen prof. medicine, 1990—2008, dir. comprehensive cancer ctr., 1985-96. Advisor Lung Cancer Segment, Carcinogenesis Program, Nat. Cancer Inst., 1971-74, Chem. and Molecular Biol. Segment, 1973-76; mem. interdisciplinary comm. program Smithsonian Inst., 1971-74, Pharmacology B Study Sect., NIH, 1971-75, numerous sci. and adv. coms. Nat. Cancer Inst., Am. Cancer Soc., 1976-88; advisor Roswell Park Meml. Inst., Buffalo, Brookhaven Nat. Lab., Divsn. Cancer Cause and Prevention, Nat. Cancer Inst., Coun. on Analysis and Projects, Am. Cancer Soc., Internat. Agy. for Rsch. on Cancer, WHO, Lyon, France; Nakasone vis. prof., Tokyo, 1987; GM Cancer Rsch. Found. vis. prof. Internat. Agy. Rsch. Cancer, Lyon, 1988; mem. adv. coun. Nat. Inst. Environ. Health Scis., 1995-2008; chmn. Bristol-Myers Squibb Cancer Awards, 1993-96; mem. adv. coun., GM Cancer Rsch. Found. Assoc. editor Cancer Rsch., 1973-76, 86-95, Jour. Environ. Pathology and Toxicology, 1977-84, Jour. Cellular Physiology, 1982-89, Oncogene, 1989-99, Clin. Cancer Rsch., 1998-2008 Recipient Meltzer medal, 1964, Clowes award, Am. Assn. Cancer Rsch., 1987, Silvio O. Conte award, Environ. Health Inst., 1990, Nakahara award, 1996, Anthony Dipple Carcinogenesis award, 2000, Disting. Achievement award, Am. Soc. Preventive Oncology, 2001, Am. Assn. Cancer Rsch./Am. Cancer Soc. award, 2001, Charles Heidelberger award, 2004; named Louise Weissberger lectr., U. Rochester, 1981, Mary Ann Swetland lectr., Case Western Res. U., 1983, Daniel Laszlo Meml. lectr., Montefiore Med. Ctr., 1983, Samuel Kuna Disting. lectr., Rutgers U., 1985, Ester Langer lectr., U. Chgo., 1989, Harris Meml. lectr., MIT, 1989, Rufus Cole lectr., 1997, travel fellow, European Molecular Biology Orgn., 1970—71. Mem.: AAAS (coun. del. 1985—88), N.Y. Acad. Sci., Am. Soc. Clin. Investigation, Internat. Soc. Quantum Biology, Am. Soc. Microbiology, Am. Assn. Physicians, Am. Acad. Arts and Scis., Inst. Medicine/Nat. Acad. Sci., Am. Assn. Cancer Rsch. (pres. 1990—91). Achievements include research in cellular and molecular aspects of carcinogenesis, environmental carcinogenesis, molecular epidemiology, cancer prevention. Home: New York, NY. Died Nov. 3, 2008.

WEINSTEIN, PAUL PETER, parasitologist, researcher, educator; b. NYC, Dec. 9, 1919; s. Max and Frieda (Hellinson) W.; m. Rachel Hazan, Sept. 18, 1954; children: Amy R., Michael P. BA, Bklyn. Coll., 1941; ScD, Johns Hopkins U., 1949. Jr. parasitologist USPHS, Jacksonville, Fla., 1942-44, commd. 2d lt. Atlanta and, P.R., 1944-45, advanced thru grades to capt., 1949-68; scientist, dir. NIH, Bethesda, Md., 1949-68; prof. dept. biol. scis. U. Notre Dame, Ind., 1969-90, prof. emeritus dept. biol. scis. Ind., from 1990. Instr. Marine Biol. Lab., Woods Hole, Mass., 1959, 60; vis. scientist Nat. Inst. for Med. Rsch., Eng., 1962-63; cons. NIH, 1969-73, 78-81, Walter Reed Army Inst. of Rsch., Washington, 1977-79; mem. adv. sci. bd. Gorgas Meml. Inst. Tropical Medicine, Washington, 1972-88; vis. prof. Juntendo U. Sch. of Medicine, Tokyo, 1989. Contbr. numerous articles to profl. jours. Fellow AAAS; mem. Am. Soc. Parasitologists (pres. 1972-73), Am. Soc. Tropical Medicine and Hygiene (pres. 1985-86), Helminthological Soc. Washington (pres. 1953-54), Japanese Soc. Parasitologists (award 1989). Avocation: photography. Home: South Bend, Ind. Died Jan. 5, 2008.

WEINSTOCK, KENNETH MARTIN, judge; b. Chgo., Nov. 13, 1927; s. Alexander Simon and Gertrude Victoria Weinstock; m. Marilyn Joan Vogelsang, Sept. 11, 1955; children: Amy Victoria Lowry, Charles William. AB, U. Mo., 1952; JD, St. Louis U., 1956. Bar: Mo., 1956. Ins. adjuster Safeco, St. Louis, 1952-58; pvt. practice various law firms, St. Louis, 1958-60; assoc. Markus and Maue, St. Louis, 1960-61, Dagen, Dorsey and Gray, St. Louis, 1961-62; ptnr. Feigenbaum & Weinstock, St. Louis, 1962-65; assoc. James F. Koester, St. Louis, 1965-72; ptnr. Saitz and Weinstock, St. Louis, 1972-81, Kenneth Weinstock, St. Louis, 1982-84; judge St. Louis County Ct., Clayton, Mo., 1984-97; ret., 1997. Bd. dirs. Friendship Villages West and South, St. Louis County, 1980-84. With U.S. Army, 1946-47. Mem. Am. Judges Assn., Am. Judicature Soc., Mo. Bar Assn., Mo. Assn. Trial Lawyers, Lawyers Assn. St. Louis, St. Louis Met. Bar Assn., St. Louis County Bar Assn., Gideons Internat. (sec. St. Louis-Florissant chpt. 1995—). Baptist. Avocations: jogging, golf, reading, church. Home: Saint Louis, Mo. Died Dec. 19, 2007.

WEIR, CAROL HERRING, lawyer; b. Austin, Tex., Dec. 6, 1939; d. Charles F. and Doris M. (Wallace) Herring; m. Warren N. Weir, May 29, 1964; children: Charles, Bruce, Carren. BA, Trinity U., 1976, MA, 1978; JD, St. Marys U., 1983. Bar: Tex. 1983. Teaching asst. Trinity U., San Antonio, 1977-78; psychologist Goodwill, San Antonio, 1978-79; atty. Offices Peter Torres, San Antonio, 1984-85; pvt. practice San Antonio, from 1985. Juvenile referee/master, 1995—; mem. bd. disciplinary appeals Supreme Ct. Tex., 1995—. Chair planning subcom. Govs. Com. on People with Disabilities, Austin, 1993-95; active Long Term Care Task Force, Austin, 1994; ad litem coord. 289th Dist. Ct., San Antonio. Mem. San Antonio Bar Assn., Bexar County Women's Bar, Criminal Def. Lawyers. Roman Catholic. Died May 8, 2008.

WEISE, FRANK EARL, III, retired food products company executive; b. Williamsport, Pa., July 30, 1944; s. Frank E. and Marian (Hagerman) W.; m. Deborah Dunstan, 1965; children: Frank E. IV, Alison S. BA in Economics, Lehigh U., 1966, MS in Bus. Econs., 1967. Various fin. mgmt. Procter & Gamble Co., Cin., 1967-79, comptr., CFO health and personal care div., 1983-86, dir. pers. and fin., 1986-88, comptr., CFO food and beverages div., 1988-91; fin. dir., CFO Procter & Gamble Benelux, Brussels, 1979-83; sr. v.p. fin., CFO Campbell Soup Co., Camden, N.J., 1992-95, sr. v.p., pres. confectionary divsn., 1995—97; CEO Confab, 1997—2004; operating ptnr. J.W. Childs Associates, 2004—07. Bd. dirs. Children's Hosp. Phila., Riverside Theater, Vero Beach. Mem. Fin. Execs. Inst., Cin. Country Club, Merion Golf Club (Ardmore, Pa.). Presbyterian. Avocations: golf, tennis. Died Nov. 11, 2008.

WEISKOPF, KIM ROBERT, television producer, writer; b. NYC, Apr. 10, 1947; s. Robert Jerome and Eileen May (Ito) W.; m. Jo Ellen Erwin Legendre, May 17, 1980; 1 child, Kathleen. BA in English Lit., San Francisco State U., 1969. Story editor, writer TV show Good Times, Hollywood, Calif., 1977; exec. script cons., writer TV show Three's Company, LA, 1979-80; prodr., writer TV show 9 to 5, LA, 1981; exec. prodr., writer TV show What's Happening Now, Burbank, Calif., 1985-87; prodr., writer TV show Full House, Culver City, Calif., 1988-91; supervising prodr., writer TV show Rachel Gunn, R.N., Hollywood, 1992-93; supervising/co-exec. prodr., writer TV show Married...With Children, Columbia TV, Culver City and Hollywood, 1994-96; exec. prodr., writer TV show Malcolm & Eddie, Tri-Star TV, Culver City, from 1996; co-exec. prodr., writer TV show Sister, Sister Paramount, Hollywood, Calif., 1997; writer TV show Baywatch, 1998; writer TV show Pigs Next Door Saban, 1999; writer TV show Los Beltran Telemundo/Tristar TV, 1999. Home: Encino, Calif. Died Apr. 22, 2009.

WEISS, EMILIO, retired microbiologist; b. Pakrac, Yugoslavia, Oct. 4, 1918; came to U.S., 1939; s. Edoardo and Vanda (Schrenger) W.; m. Hilda Damick, June 23, 1943; children: Natalie Ann Holzwarth, Elizabeth Rae. Student, U.

Rome, Italy, 1936-38; AB in Zoology, U. Kans., 1941; MS in Bacteriology, U. Chgo., 1942, PhD in Bacteriology, 1948. Teaching asst. U. Chgo., 1942, 47-48; instr. Loyola U. Med. Sch., Chgo., 1947-48; rsch. assoc. instr. U. Chgo., 1948-50; asst. prof. Ind. U., Bloomington, 1950-53; br. chief Chem. Corps Biology Labs., Frederick, Md., 1953-54; from asst. head to dir. dept. microbiology Naval Med. Rsch. Inst., Bethesda, Md., 1954-79, chair of sci., 1979-86, sci. emeritus, from 1986. Rsch. prof. uniformed svcs. U. of the Health Scis., Bethesda, 1977-85; lectr. U. Md., College Park, 1982-85. Contbr. articles to profl. jours. and chpts. to ref. books. Capt. U.S. Army, 1943-46, ETO. Mem. Am. Soc. for Rickettsiology (pres. 1980-82), Am. Soc. for Microbiology (editorial bd. 1972-83, sect. chairperson 1976), Soc. Experimental Biol. Medicine (sect. chairperson 1976), Am. Soc. Immunology. Avocations: hiking, wood working, music. Home: Advance, NC. Died May 30, 2008.

WEISS, GEORGE ARTHUR, orthodontist; b. Bklyn., Feb. 1, 1921; s. Nathan L. and Ida (Rosenthal) W.; m. Jacqueline Hellermann, Jan. 28, 1945; children: Ellen Joy Weiss Finberg, Leslie Donna Weiss Schoenfeld. BA, Bklyn. Coll., 1941; DDS, Columbia U., 1944, cert. Orthodontics, 1954. Diplomate Am. Bd. of Orthodontics. Dir. dentistry Dental Clinic Southen Japan, Kobe, 1946; chief dentistry Olmstead AFB, Middleburg, Pa., 1947; pvt. practice Orthodontics Bayside, N.Y., from 1947; chief orthodontics Community Svc. Soc., NYC, 1954-57; dir. orthodontics Jamaica (N.Y.) Hosp., from 1977. Cons. State Aid Orthodontic Program for Handicapped Children, Suffolk County, N.Y., 1987—. Founder, Oakland Gardens Jewish Ctr., Bayside, N.Y., 1949; Bayside Oaks Jewish Ctr., Bayside, 1954. Major U.S. Army, 1944-48, Japan. Recipient Chemistry award, Am. Inst. Chem., N.Y.C., 1941. Fellow Am. Coll. Dentistry; mem. Am. Bd. Orthodontists, Am. Assn. Orthodontists, Northeastern Soc. Orthodontists, Dental Soc. State of N.Y. (bd. govs. 1976-86, mem. coun. on ins. 1965-75), Queens County Dental Soc. (trustee 1960—, chief adminstr. retirement fund, 1964-72, pres. 1975, Disting. Svc. award, 1988), Old Westbury Golf and Country Club, Alpha Omega Dental Soc. Avocations: golf, finance, insurance. Died Feb. 18, 2008.

WEISS, SANFORD RONALD, neurosurgeon; b. Cleve., Jan. 22, 1931; s. Morris Fenmore and Rose Mary (Tomsick) W.; m. Oct. 1962 (div. 1966); 1 child, Leah Beth. BA, Case Western Res. U., 1955, MD, 1958. Diplomate Am. Bd. Neurosurgery. Surg. internship Columbia-Presbyn. Med. Ctr., NYC, 1958-59, surg. residency, 1959-60, neurosurg. residency, 1960-64; neurosurgeon pvt. practice LI, N.Y., 1964-66; neurosurgeon Kaiser Hosp., Oakland, Calif., 1966-70; neurosurgeon pvt. practice San Leandro, Calif., 1970-81. Asst. prof. neurosurgery U. Calif., San Francisco, 1966-81; hon. staff mem. Eden Hosp., Castro Valley, 1981—, San Leandro (Calif.) Hosp., 1981—. Contbr. numerous articles to profl. jours. Fellow Am. Coll. Angiology, Am. Geriatric Soc., Am. Coll. Surgeons, Internat. Coll. Surgeons; mem. Calif. Med. Assn., Am. Assn. Neurol. Surgeons, Calif. Assn. Neurol. Surgeons, Congress Neurol. Surgeons, Pan Pacific Surg. Assn. Republican. Jewish. Avocations: swimming, biking, surfing, horses, scuba diving. Home: San Leandro, Calif. Died Mar. 7, 2008.

WELLING, JOE MURRAY, market research consultant; b. Tulsa, Aug. 4, 1940; s. Joe R. and Coreta (Richards) W.; m. Freda Frances Chandler, Dec. 27, 1958; children: Chad, Shawn, Kerry, Gianna. BS in Journalism, U. Tulsa, 1962. Project dir. Louis, Bowles & Grove, Inc., Dallas, 1963-65; v.p. Spears & Co., Tulsa, 1965-67; pres. Southwest Surveys and Research Co., Tulsa, 1967-69; v.p. Leslie Brooks & Assocs., Inc., Tulsa, 1969-71, Cougar Petroleum Co., Inc., Tulsa, 1977-83; pres. Welling, Minton & Vanderslice, Inc., Tulsa, 1971-83; v.p. Ackerman, Hood & McQueen, Inc., Tulsa, 1985-87; pres. Welling & Co., Tulsa, from 1983. Bd. dirs. Welling & Co., Ltd., London; guest lectr. numerous colls. and univs., 1964—; chmn. bd. dirs. First Artists Mgmt. Enterprises, Tulsa, 1981-85; adj. prof. Grad. Sch. Bus., Oral Roberts U., Tulsa, 1984-85. Contbr. articles to trade and profl. jours. Bd. dirs. Brush Creek Boys Ranch, Jay, Okla., 1977-85, Hillcrest Med. Ctr. Assocs., Tulsa, 1978-90, The Gospel in Concert, Tulsa, 1978-85, Young Life, Tulsa, 1978-90; mem. ofcl. bd. First United Meth. Ch., Tulsa, 1982-91; adviser, pollster polit. campaigns, 1965—. Mem. U. Tulsa Alumni Assn. (pres. 1980-81), Am. Mktg. Assn. (sec. Tulsa chpt. 1962—), Mkt. Research Assn., Pi Kappa Alpha (pres. Tulsa alumni assn. 1967-75). Republican. Avocations: music, travel, reading, golf. Home: Houston, Tex. Died Aug. 24, 2008.

WELLMAN, MARIAN C., social worker; d. Vivian Cole; m. William Wellman (div.). BA in Psychology, Calif. State U., LA, 1965; MSW, UCLA, 1971. LCSW. Social worker L.A. County, LA, 1965—71, adoptions worker and supr., 1971—90; therapeutic counselor and practitioner in pvt. practice LA, 1990—2003. Oral examiner Bd. Behavioral Sci. State of Calif., 1992—98. Author: New Shades of Poetry, 1984, Living With the "I" Word, 2002. Mem. Black Women's Forum, LA, from 1995; big sister Big Sister League, LA, 1996—97; pres. Sat. Morning Lit. Workshop, LA, from 1982; mem. St. Paul's Luth. Ch., LA. Recipient Fannie Lou Hamer award, Internat. Black Writers of Am., 1997. Avocations: travel, music, theater, walking, bicycling. Home: Los Angeles, Calif. Died May 19, 2008.

WELLMAN, RICHARD KENT (DICK WELLMAN), retired broadcast engineer; b. Quincy, Ill., Dec. 29, 1940; s. Kenneth Joseph and Virginia Jean Wellman; m. Sharon Lee Fix, Dec. 19, 1969; children: Linda Jean, Richard Jr. Maintenance and ops. various radio and TV stas., Las Vegas, Nev., Hollywood, Calif., Phoenix, 1960-66; videotape maintenance engr. ABC-TV, Hollywood, 1966-69; maintenance engr. Sta. KTLA, Hollywood, 1970-73; engr. in charge, supr. TV truck, editing Editel, Hollywood, 1973-78; TV operations, maintenance Columbia Pictures, Burbank, 1978-79; freelance video ops. engr., video editor, video maintenance Hollywood, 1978-79; chief engr. The Post Group, Hollywood, 1979-81, Wichita State U., Kans., 1982-86, Disney channel, Hollywood, 1986, Sta. KLBY, Colby, Kans., 1986-89, Sta. KKTO, Albuquerque, 1990-92, Sta. KSWT, Yuma, Ariz., 1992-93, Sta. KYMA, Yuma, 1993-94. Served with USAFR, 1962-68. Mem.: Radio (Colby). Republican. Lutheran. Avocations: flying, amateur radio. Home: Albuquerque, N.Mex. Died Apr. 19, 2008.

WELLS, MAC (JOHN MCNEILL WELLS), artist, educator; b. Cleve., Feb. 3, 1925; s. Guy McNeill and Lynn (Kramer) W; m. Eileen Gorman, July 18, 1953; 1 child, Neill McNeill. B.A., Oberlin Coll., 1948; postgrad. Cooper Union, 1948-49, Clk., sr. clk. N.Y. Public Library, N.Y.C., 1950-65; vis. artist Purdue U., West Lafayette, Ind., 1966; assoc. prof. Moore Coll. Art, Phila., 1966-72; adj. instr. Hunter Coll., CUNY, 1966-71, assoc. prof., 1972—. One man shows include John Heller Gallery, 1953, Aegis Gallery, N.Y.C., 1963, Am. Sachs Gallery, N.Y.C., 1965, 67, Purdue U., 1966, Max Hutchinson Gallery, 1970, 72, Susan Caldwell Gallery, N.Y.C., 1975, Landmark Gallery, N.Y.C., 1979, 55 Mercer Gallery, N.Y.C., 1981. Del. Fine Arts Fedn., 1975—. Recipient Commn. 3-D Card award Mus. Modern Art, N.Y.C., 1965; Yaddo fellow, 1964, 65. Mem. Am. Abstract, Artists, Artists Tenants Assn., AAUP. Democrat. Died June 24, 2009.

WELLS, MARGARET KETTEL, retired nurse anesthetist; b. Gibson, N.Mex., Sept. 27, 1918; d. Charles and Elizabeth Kettel; m. Charles K. Wells, May 12, 1959; children: Jane Ann Wells Shields, Charlotte Kay Wells Kirk. Diploma, Hotel Dieu Sch. Nursing, El Paso, Tex., 1940. RN, Ill., Ariz. Office nurse Dr. Charles K. Wells, Mt. Vernon, Ill., Dr. Fritz Katzensign, Salem, Ill.; surg. nurse Indian Health Svc., USPHS, Ft. Defiance, Ariz.; ret. Lst lt. Nurse Corps, U.S. Army, 1942-45. Home: Saint Charles, Mo. Died Dec. 2, 2007.

WELMAKER, FORREST NOLAN, lawyer; b. McKinney, Tex., Aug. 13, 1925; s. Felix E. and Forrest Love (Baker) W.; div.; children: Forrest Nolan Jr., Mary Elizabeth Welmaker Young, Byron Skillin. BBA, U. Tex., 1950, LLD, 1953. Bar: Tex. 1953, U.S. Dist. Ct. (so. and we. dists.) Tex. 1956, U.S. Ct. Appeals (5th cir.) 1956, U.S. Tax Ct. 1959, U.S. Supreme Ct. 1956. Pvt. practice, San Antonio, from 1953. Past bd. dirs., officer United Fund San Antonio, San Antonio chpt. ARC, Children Welfare Bur. San Antonio, San Antonio YMCA. Capt. USNR, 1943-46, PTO, 1950-52, Korea. Fellow Tex. Bar Found., San Antonio Bar Found.; mem. San Antonio Bar Assn. (past bd. dirs., v.p., pres.), Tex. Assn. Def. Counsel, San Antonio Res. Officer Assn., Tex. Bar Assn. (past bd. dirs.), San Antonio German Club. Episcopalian. Avocations: handball, boating. Died Nov. 5, 2007.

WELSCHER, GEORGE FRANK, psychiatrist; b. Bronx, NY, June 1, 1922; s. George F. Sr. and Georgette U. (Maurer) W.; m. Beatrice B. Janda, Mar. 27, 1944; children: Karen Welscher Enlow, Craig A., Mark J. Student, NYU, 1940-43; MD, U. Buffalo, 1946. Diplomate Am. Bd. Psychiatry and Neurology. Intern Jersey City Med. Ctr., 1946-47; resident in psychiatry Warren (Pa.) State Hosp., 1947-50, Butler Hosp., Providence, 1950-51; from asst. sect. chief to sect. chief Topeka State Hosp., 1953-60, clin. dir., 1960-65; mem. staff Topeka Psychoanalytic Inst./Menningers, 1955-64; asst. dir. P.B. Cmty. Adulty Psychiat. Clin., 1965-67, dir., 1967-70; dir. adult out-patient sect. 45th St Mental Health Ctr., 1970-72; pvt. practice, from 1972; chief med. staff Lake Hosp., 1983-84, cons. adolescent unit, 1985-87, Humana Hosp., Palm Beach, Fla.; with courtesy staff Columbia Hosp., from 1992; cons. St. Mary's Hosp., 1993-95, staff, from 1995. Mem. faculty Menninger Sch. Psychiatry, 1953-65. Capt. USAF, 1951-53. Fellow Am. Psychiat. Assn.; mem. Fla. Med. Soc., Fla. Psychiat. Soc., Palm Beach County Med. Soc., Palm Beach County Psychiat. Soc. Died Sept. 16, 2007.

WENCEL, EMIL EUGENE, business owner; b. Chgo., Dec. 30, 1919; s. Caroline (Mrozek) W.; m. Claire T. Wencel, May 28, 1944. B in Music Edn., Am. Conservatory, 1942; BA, Henderson State Tchr.'s Coll., 1954; grad. Mgmt. Inst., Mich. State U., 1984; grad. Real Estate Inst., Garland Community Coll., Ark., 1990; degree (hon.), Garland Community Coll., 1990. Pvt. practice real estate assoc., Ill., 1948-53 and from 50; mgr. Happy Hollow Motel, from 1953. Instr. Chgo. Tech. Coll., 1946-48. Music dir. Hull House, Chgo., 1942; mem. Oak Park (Ill.) Riverside Symphony, 1938-39, 43—. 2d lt. USAF, 1943-44. Named to Hon. Order of Ky. Cols.; recipient Disting. Alumnus award Henderson State U., 1991. Mem. Hot Springs (Ark.) Bd. Realtors (Appreciation award 1977, Pres.'s award 1982), Ark. Motel Assn. (pres. 1977-78), Garland County Hospitality Assn. (Golden Key award 1991), Ark. Innkeepers (pres. 1978-79), Ark. Hospitality Assn. (nominating com. 1987-88, exec. com. 1977—, Membership award 1977, Golden Key award 1978, Hall of Fame 1988), Am. Legion, VFW, Toastmasters (past pres.). Roman Catholic. Died May 2, 2008.

WENDELL, BARBARA TAYLOR, retired real estate agent; b. Ames, Iowa, Jan. 30, 1920; d. Harvey Nelson and Ruby (Britten) Taylor; m. Donald Thomas Davidson Sr., May 22, 1942 (dec. Oct. 1962); children: Donald Thomas Jr., John Taylor, Ann Elizabeth Davidson Costanzo; m. Connell S. Wendell, Oct. 10, 1992 (dec. Sept. 1995). BS in Home Econs. Sci., Iowa State U., 1943. Assoc. tchr. Ames (Iowa) Pub. Schs., 1970-73; retail mgr. Gen. Nutrition Ctr., Ames, 1974-77; sales assoc. Century 21 Real Estate, Ames, 1978-82, Friedrich Realty, Ames, 1982-89. Pres. Ames City PTA Coun., 1950; leader, advisor Boy Scouts Am., Ames, 1952-58; chmn. Campfire Leaders' Assn., Ames, 1959-61; sec. bd. dirs. Campfire Girls, Ames, 1964-66; property com. United Meth. Ch., Ames, 1964-67; vol. Para-Legal Svcs. for Elderly; active Octagon for the Arts, Brunier Gallery, Med. Ctr. Aux., Art Gallery Com.; vol. at Med. Ctr., 1962—. Mem. Nat. Home Econs. in Homemaking (chmn. fgn. student rels. com.), Internat. Orch. Assn., Iowa State U. Meml. Union (life), Iowa State U. Alumni Assn. (life), Ames Community Arts Coun. Republican. Avocations: floriculture, wildlife and forest conservation, indian culture, fitness and nutrition, gerontology. Died Jan. 25, 2008.

WENDTLAND, MONA BOHLMANN, dietitian, consultant; b. Schulenburg, Tex., Mar. 30, 1930; d. Willy Frank and Leona A. (Bruns) Bohlmann; m. Charles William Ewing, Mar. 8, 1953 (div. Sept. 1975); children: Charles William Jr., Deborah Susan Ewing Richmond; m. William Wolters Wendtland, Jan. 12, 1991 (dec.). BS in Home Econs., U. Tex., 1952, postgrad., 1952-57. Registered dietitian, Tex. Dietitian sch. lunch program Port Arthur (Tex.) Ind. Sch. Dist., 1952-53; elem. tchr. Portsmouth (Va.) Sch. Dist., 1953-54; dietitian, mgr. lunch room E.M. Scarbrough Dept. Store, Austin, Tex., 1955-57; asst. chief adminstrv. dietitian John Sealy Hosp., Galveston, Tex., 1957-59; chief therapeutic dietitian USPHS Hosp., Galveston, 1959-60, asst. chief dietitian, 1960-62; cons. dietitian Sinton (Tex.) Nursing Home, 1963-65; dietary cons. Deaton Hosp., Galena Park, Tex., 1966-68; dir. food svcs. Nat. Health Enterprises, Houston, 1975-76; dietary cons. to nursing homes and retirement ctrs. Drug Abuse Ctr., Houston, from 1976; pvt. cons. Del. Internat. Congress Arts & Comm., 1993; chmn. Econ. Devel.; chmn. Friends of Libr.; sec. La County Appraisal Dist. Mem. Am. Dietetic Assn. (registered, ret.), Tex. Dietetic Assn., South Tex. Dietetic Assn. (chmn. cons. interest group 1978-79), U. Tex. Home Econs. Assn., Dietitians in Bus. and Industry (nat. rep. to mgmt. practices group 1980-83, treas. Houston chpt. 1980-81, pres. 1981-82, advisor 1983-84), Tex. Gerontol Nutritionists (sec. 1994-95), Tex. Cons. Dietitians in Healthcare Facilities, Tex. Nutrition Coun., Dietary Mgrs. Assn. (advisor Houston dist. 1979-92). Republican. Methodist. Avocations: cooking, gardening, interior decorating, genealogy. Died July 27, 2008.

WENNERBERG, GUNNAR, electrical engineer; b. Stockholm, June 3, 1918; came to the U.S., 1946; s. Gustaf Alfred and Elin Ida Kristina (Wennerberg) Gustafson; m. Elsie Christina Forzelius, July 9, 1949 (dec. 1991); children: Leif, Kim, Ingrid, Steffan, Monica. MSEE, Royal Inst. Tech., 1942. Registered profl. engr., Calif. Engr. Internat. Telephone & Telegraph, Stockholm, 1942-46, Lear, Inc., Santa Monica, Calif., 1947-59; engring. mgr. Lockheed Electronics Co., LA, 1959-65, Lockheed Missiles & Space, Sunnyvale, Calif., 1965-69; sr. staff scientist Measurex Corp., Cupertino, Calif., 1970-92; cons. in field. Contbr. articles to profl. jours. Fellow Instrument Soc. Am. (life; pres. local sect. 1976); mem. IEEE (life), AAAS, SPIE. Democrat. Achievements include 14 patents, including caliper sensor for paper making machines, radio direction finder for aircraft. Home: San Jose, Calif. Died July 1, 2008.

WENTWORTH, LAVERNE WELLBORN, curriculum consultant; b. Bryan, Tex., July 26, 1929; d. Charles Floyd and Ethel Berneice (Swanzy) Wellborn; m. Thomas Richard Wentworth, 1951 (wid. 1986); children: Jason Charles, Rance Richard, Paige Lynn Wentworth Honkerkamp. BA, Baylor U., Waco, Tex., 1949, MA in Am. Civilization, 1954; postgrad., State Tchrs. U. N.J., Southwestern State Tchrs. U., San Marcus, Tex., U. Ky., Lexington. Sch. tchr. Tex. and NJ, 1949—58; mem. JFK White House Paper on Youth, 1963; comm. edn. instr. Georgetown Coll., Ky., 1988—90; coord. Elderhostel program U. Ky., Lexington, 1992—2001; Boyce Sch. instr. So. Bapt. Theol. Seminary, Lexington, 1990; pers. dept. Cardinel Hill Rehab. Hosp., Lexington, 1987-93. Tchg. cons. US Steel Co., Trenton, NJ, 1957; cons., instr. Interdenominational Young People Confs., Pocono Plateau, Pa., 1958-87; field supr. US Dept. Commerce, Bur. of Census, Washington, 1970-88; guest lectr. Georgetown (Ky.) Coll. Author: (books) Manifest Destiny in Walt Whitman's Prose, 1954, Tryst, 1959 Pres. Princeton Theol. Sem. Wives, 1956-57, Rotary Anne, W.Va., 1982-83; mem. Scott County Women's Club, Georgetown, 1987-93; mem. by-laws com. Ky. Bapt. Fellowship, 2004—10; resident counsel Windsor Gardens, Georgetown. Recipient Ship of State award W.Va. State of Sec., 1983. Mem. AAUW (pres. 1987-90), Scott County Hist. Soc., Georgetown Coll. Woman's Assn. (life), Faith Bapt. Ch. of Georgetown (tchr., chmn. by-laws 1998—2006). Home: Georgetown, Ky. Died Sept. 13, 2007.

WERTH, ANDREW MICHAEL, retired telecommunications industry executive; b. Saarbruck, Germany, Mar. 2, 1934; came to U.S., 1944; s. Steven S. and Margot Werth; m. Eileen B. Pighini, Jan. 30, 1954; children: Gregory, Jeffrey, Karen. BS, Columbia U., 1955, MS, 1961. Project engr. ITT Labs., Nutley, N.J., 1959-64; mem. tech. staff

Comsat Corp., Washington, 1964-68; br. mgr. Comsat Labs., Clarksburg, Md., 1968-72; pres. Hughes Network Systems Internat., Germantown, Md., 1972—2000; chmn. Global VSAT Forum. Patentee in field. Capt. USAF, 1955-57. Recipient Mentoring award, Soc. Satellite Professionals Internat. Fellow IEEE; mem. AIAA, Cosmos Club. Roman Catholic. Achievements include winning the USA Cycling Masters Track National Championship in 2000, 2003 & 2004. Home: Washington, DC. Died Jan. 28, 2009.

WESMAN, VERNE ALVIN, mechanical engineer, consultant; b. Ewen, Mich., Apr. 20, 1934; s. Victor John and Rose Helen (Nippa) W.; m. Jean Eleanor Everette, Apr. 10, 1953; children: Karen Lynn, Debra Alison. Grad. in engring., Ford Community Coll., 1960; grad. in salesmanship, Sales Tng. Inst., Detroit, 1968. Ptnr. Pyramid Engring., Detroit, 1965-70; design engr. RCA Corp., Plymouth, Mich., 1970-73; mgr. prodn. control Ingersoll Rand, Farmington Hills, Mich., 1973-76; sr. prodn. engr. Ford Motor Co., Livonia, Mich., 1976-79; dir. engring. Agnew Machine, Highland, Mich., 1979-81; owner, operator Automa-Ton Corp., Livonia, from 1981. Instr. indsl. drafting adult edn. Livonia Pub. Sch., 1983; cons. engr. Indsl. Tech. Inst., Ann Arbor, Mich., 1986—. Patentee in field. Served to sgt. U.S. Army, 1954-56. Recipient Hon. Mention award James Lincoln Arc Welding Found., Cleve., 1972. Mem. Soc. Mfg. Engrs. (cert. 1975), Robotics Internat., of Soc. Mfg. Engrs. (sr., cert. 1981). Lodges: Lions. Republican. Lutheran. Avocations: creative designing and bldg., reading, hunting, gardening, fishing. Died Aug. 12, 2008.

WESSON, GARY DWIGHT, instrumentation educator, minister; b. Bloomburg, Tex., Nov. 27, 1945; s. Jeston Calvin and Rheba Frances (Barrington) W.; m. Billie Elizabeth Posey, Nov. 26, 1965; children: Kimmerly Rachalle, Sara Beth. Student, N.W. La. Voc.-Tech., Minden, 1963-65; teaching cert., La. State U., 1972. Cert. tchr., La. Salesman West & Co., Springhill, La., 1959-62; sales mgr. Willie Mack Dept. Store, Springhill, 1963; electronics technician Wesson Radio/TV Service, Springhill, 1960-65; engring. instrumentation technician MonoChem, Inc., Geismar, La., 1965-66; instrumentation dept. head and instr. N.W. La. Tech. Inst., from 1966. Cons. several instrument indsl. plants, 1966—, curriculum cons. various depts. of edn., 1970—. Author: textbooks Pneumatic Instrumentation, 1978, Instrumentation, 1980; contbr. instrumentation curriculums to profl. jours. Served with USNG, 1965-71. Mem. Instrument Soc. of Am. (sr., faculty sponsor 1963—), La. Vocat. Assn. (trade and industry div.). Lodges: Masons (32 degree), Order of Eastern Star (patron). Democrat. Baptist. Avocations: guitar, amateur radio, photography. Home: Minden, La. Died Apr. 29, 2008.

WEST, DAVID LYN, retired non-commissioned officer, poet; b. Ozona, Tex., Nov. 18, 1959; s. William Thomas Jr. and Ella Fay West; m. Jodi Margaurite West, May 5, 1991 (div. May 1998); children: David Bryant, Nicole Ross. Joined U.S. Air Force, 1980; tech. sgt. 3 Combat Comm. Support Squadron, Tinker AFB, Okla., from 1980; ret., 2000. Author: (poems) The Music of Silence, 1999, Above the Clouds, 1999; patentee in field. Mem. Internat. Soc. Poets. Christian. Home: Bishop, Tex. Died Mar. 23, 2008.

WEST, E. JOSEPH, financial analyst, portfolio manager; b. Kingston, Pa., Nov. 24, 1940; s. David Dimon and Elizabeth Irene (Emery) W.; m. Darla Jean Payne, Oct. 13, 1962 (div. Aug. 1972); 1 child, Emery Joseph II; m. Karen Marie Rowlands, Jan. 1, 1981. Grad., Mercersburg Acad., 1959; cadet-student, U.S. Air Force Acad., 1959—62; cert., Northwestern U., Evanston, Ill., 1964, U. Windsor, Ont., 1972, 73, 79, Rockford Coll., Ill., 1982; cert. investment mgmt., Princeton U., 1984; MBA, Coll. William & Mary, 1990. Chartered fin. analyst. Jr. investment analyst Tech. Stock Rev., Inc., NYC, 1962-63; investment analyst, broker Grant, Jones & Co., Inc., Washington, 1963-64; sr. acct. exec. W.E. Hutton & Co., Washington, 1964-74; investment exec. E.F. Hutton & Co., Inc., Washington, 1974-78; 1st v.p. investments and portfolio mgr. Drexel Burnham Lambert, Inc., Washington, 1978-89; 1st v.p., portfolio mgr. Citi Smith Barney, Washington, from 1989. Bd. dirs. Russian Cultural Ctr., 1997—; trustee and chmn. investment com. Fairfax County Retirement System, 1985-89. Active Fairfax County (Va.) Rep. Com., 1983-2001, Fairfax County Econ. Adv. Commn., 1992—, Fairfax County Com. 100, 1984—; bd. dirs. Va. Coll. Bldg. Authority, 1999-2002. Recipient Award Appreciation County of Fairfax Retirement System, 1989. Fellow Fin. Analysts Fedn., CFA Inst., Internat. Soc. Fin. Analysts; mem. CFA Soc. Washington, Nat. Assn. for Bus. Econs., Nat. Economists Club, Washington Assn. Money Mgrs., Soc. Profl. Forecasters Fed. Res. Bank of Phila., Mercersburg Acad. Alumni Coun., Belle Haven Country Club, The Tower Club (gov. 1998-2003). Republican. Lutheran. Avocations: golf, crossword puzzles, backgammon, Russian lacquer art, stamp collecting/philately. Home: Falls Church, Va. Died Jan. 8, 2008.

WEST, WILLIAM BARTLEY, JR., retail executive; b. Haskell, Tex., Sept. 20, 1928; s. William B. Sr. and Edna G. (Anderson) W.; m. E. Faye Arnold, Mar. 14, 1931; children: Maurice (dec.), Pamela Kay, Riggs. Grad. high sch., Stamford, Tex., 1945. Asst. mgr. sales R.B. Spencer and Co., Stamford, 1945-50, mgr. Weinert, Tex., 1950-52, Hale Ctr., Tex., 1952-64, Nat. Bldg. Supply, Hale Ctr., 1964-65; ptnr., mgr. West Builders Supply, Hale Ctr., from 1965. Mem. Hale Ctr., Jaycees (sec., pres. 1962), Hale Ctr. C. of C. (bd. dirs. 1965—). Lodges: Lions (pres. 1958—, sec. 1975-78, zone chmn. dist. 2T2 1979). Baptist. Avocations: table games, residential drafting. Home: Hale Center, Tex. Died July 29, 2007.

WESTERHOLD, RUTH ELIZABETH, psychologist, educator; b. Youngstown, Ohio, Aug. 4, 1926; d. Samuel Gordon and Grace Elizabeth (Green) Meadows; m. Walter Charles Westerhold, June 1, 1949; children: Marsha L., Carl E. BS, Youngstown U., 1946; postgrad., Ohio U., 1947, U. Ill., 1947-49; PhD, So. Ill. U., 1978. Cert. sch. psychologist, Mo., Ill. Chief clin. psychologist Alton (Ill.) State Hosp., 1952-55; psychologist St. Louis County (Mo.) Spl. Sch. Dist., 1963-68; chief psychologist Kaskaskia Spl. Edn. Dist., Centralia, Ill., 1968-78; dir. learing comms. East Miss. Jr. Coll., Scooba, 1978-83, coord. instructional techniques, from 1987, coord. devel. edn., 1987-88. Cons. psychologist div. vocat. rehab. State of Ill., Alton, 1954-55. Counselor, lectr., writer ethics-morality, health and nutrition, body-mind relationships, child rearing, family, learning. USPHS fellow U. Ill., 1947-49. Mem. Soc. Sci. Exploration, Psi Chi. Home: Starkville, Miss. Died Apr. 15, 2008.

WESTERMAN, ALBERT BARRY, marine surveyor and consultant; b. Phila., July 8, 1941; s. William Edward and Alice Beverly (Martin) W.; m. Madeline Rose Laugginger, July 23, 1943 (div. July 1974); children: Debra Lee Westerman Bordelon, Allan Keith; m. Lynn Marie Nesser, May 31, 1947; children: David William, Dawn Marie. Student, U. Md., Augsburg, Germany, 1961, Bucks County Tech., 1966, Tulane U., 1970-71, La. State U., 1987. Journeyman machinist Honeywell Corp., Tampa, Fla., 1967-68; resident surveyor Owensby & Kritikos, Inc., Gretna, La., 1968-70; field constrn. supr. Ocean Drilling & Exploration Co., New Orleans, 1970-73; gen. mgr. Weldit Engring. Ltd., Scunthorpe, Eng., 1973; v.p. Ocean-Oil Internat. Engring. Corp., New Orleans, 1973-74; pres. Internat. Cons. & Brokers, Inc., Metairie, La., 1974-76; v.p. Am. Gulf Shipping, Inc., Metairie, 1982-88; pres., dir. Nat. Radiometric Agy., Inc., Metairie, from 1987; pres. Albert B. Westerman & Co., Inc., Metairie, from 1973. Author, editor: Procedure and Operations Manual, 1987. With U.S. Army, 1960-61. Mem. NRA, Nat. Assn. Marine Surveyors, Soc. Naval Archs. and Marine Engrs., Am. Boat and Yacht Coun., Propeller Club. Lutheran. Avocations: diving, hunting, fishing. Home: Lafayette, La. Died Dec. 13, 2007.

WESTLAKE, DONALD EDWIN (TUCKER COE, RICHARD STARK), writer; b. NYC, July 12, 1933; s. Albert Joseph and Lillian Marguerite (Bounds) W.; m. Nedra Henderson, Aug. 10, 1957 (div. 1966); m. Sandra Foley, Apr. 9, 1967 (div. 1975); m. Abigail Adams, May 18, 1979; children: Sean, Steven, Tod, Paul; stepchildren: Adrienne Adams, Patrick Adams, Katharine Adams. Student, SUNY, Plattsburgh and Binghamton. Author: The Mercenaries, 1960, Killing Time, 1962, Killy, 1963, Pity Him Afterwards, 1964, The Fugitive Pigeon, 1965, The Busy Body, 1966, The Spy in the Ointment, 1966, God Save the Mark, 1967 (Edgar Allen Poe award Mystery Writers Am. 1967), Philip, 1967, The Curious Facts Preceding My Execution, and Other Fictions, 1968, Who Stole Sassi Manoon, 1968?, Somebody Owes Me Money, 1969, Up Your Banners, 1969, The Hot Rock, 1970, Adios, Scheherezade, 1970, I Gave at The Office, 1971, Under An English Heaven, 1971, Bank Shot, 1972, Cops and Robbers, 1972, (with Brian Garfield) Gangway, 1972, Help I Am Being Held Prisoner, 1974, Jimmy The Kid, 1974, Two Much, 1975, A Travesty, 1975, Brothers Keepers, 1975, Dancing Aztecs, 1976, Enough!, 1977, Nobody's Perfect, 1977, Castle in the Air, 1980, Kahawa, 1982, Why Me?, 1983, Levine, 1984, A Likely Story, 1984, High Adventure, 1985, Good Behavior, 1986, (with Abby Westlake) High Jinx, 1987, (with A. Westlake) Transylvania Station, 1987, Trust Me On This, 1988, Sacred Monster, 1989, Tomorrow's Crimes, 1989, Drowned Hopes, 1990, Humans, 1992, Don't Ask, 1993, Baby, Would I Lie?, 1994, Smoke, 1995, The Ax, 1997, Put a Lid on It, 2003, Thieves Dozen, 2004, The Road to Ruin, 2004, Watch Your Back!, 2005, What's So Funny?, 2006; (as John B. Allan) Elizabeth Taylor: A Fascinating Story of America's Most Talented Actress and the World's Most Beautiful Woman, 1961; (as Tucker Coe) Kinds of Love, Kinds of Death, 1966, Murder among Children, 1968, Wax Apple, 1970, A Jade in Aries, 1971, Don't Lie to Me, 1972; (as Richard Stark) The Hunter, 1963 (pub. as Point Blank, 1973), The Man with the Getaway Face, 1963 (pub. as The Steel Hit, 1971), The Outfit, 1963, The Mourner, 1963, The Score, 1964, The Jugger, 1965, The Seventh, 1966, The Handle, 1966 (pub. as Run Lethal, 1966), The Damsel, 1967, The Dame, 1967, The Rare Coin Score, 1967, The Green Eagle Score, 1967, The Black Ice Score, 1968, The Sour Lemon Score, 1969, The Blackbird, 1969, Deadly Edge, 1971, Slayground, 1971, Lemons Never Lie, 1971, Plunder Squad, 1972, Butcher's Moon, 1974, Stark Mysteries, 1981, Ask the Parrot, The Scared Stiff, 2002, Get Real, 2009; screenwriter: (films) Cops and Robbers, 1973, (with Michael Kane) Hot Stuff, 1979, The Stepfather, 1986, Why Me?, 1990, The Grifters, 1990 (Academy award nomination best adapted screenplay 1990), (TV movies) Supertrain, 1979, Jimmy the Kid, 1985, Fatal Confession: A Father Dowling Mystery, 1987. Served with USAF, 1954-56. Recipient Edgar Allen Poe Grand Master award Mystery Writers America, 1992 Died Dec. 31, 2008.

WESTLAKE, JAMES ROGER, retired federal program manager; b. Kansas City, Mo., Feb. 11, 1928; s. Roger A. and Helen (Treadway) W.; m. Joyce Rosemary Covey, May 14, 1946; children: Joyce Ann Westlake Morgan, Beverly Jeanne Westlake Simpson, James R. Jr., Richard Christopher. Student, Mo. U., 1944-45; BBA, Ga. State U., 1958, MBA, 1960; MPA, U. Ga., 1974. Sales Wohl Shoe Co., Kansas City, 1946-47; sales mgr. Bankers Life & Casualty Co., Columbus, Ga., 1947-49; from ptnr. to pres. So. Agys., Inc., Atlanta, 1949-71; dep. adminstr. EPA, Atlanta, 1971-76; dep. sec. rep. U.S. Dept. of Commerce, Atlanta, 1976-81; from specialist to chief econ. adv. divsn. Econ. Devel. Adminstrn., Atlanta, 1981-95. Chmn. bd. Atlanta Sch. Bib. Studies, Decatur, Ga., 1975—. Author: The Republicans Are Coming, 1968; columnist Decatur-DeKalb News, 1965-71; contbr. articles to profl. jours. State legis. (Ga.) representing DeKalb County, 1965-71; chmn. 4th dist. Ga. Rep. Com., Decatur, 1966-68; mem. adv. bd. Nat. Independence Day Parade and Festival Com., 1990-92; ruling elder Trinity Presbyn. Ch. With USN, 1945-46. Mem. SAR (pres. gen. 1989-90, Minuteman award 1989), Soc. CPCUs (pres. Ga. chpt. 1961), Soc. CLUs, Am. Coll. Chartered Fin. Cons., Nat. Soc. Washington Family Descendants (pres. gen. 1988-90), Nat. Congress Patriotic Orgns. (pres. 1991-92), Ga. State U. Alumni Assn. (pres. 1961), Barons of Magna Carta, Nat. Gavel Soc. and Old Guard of Atlanta (commandant), Sons Am. Colonists, Order Founders and Patriots, Honey Creek Golf and Country Club, Omicron Delta Kappa, Phi Kappa Phi, Sigma Chi, Delta Sigma Pi, Beta Gamma Sigma. Avocations: stamp and coin collector, historian, golf. Home: Covington, Ga. Died Mar. 25, 2008.

WESTPHAL, HUGO LOUIS, III, gifted education educator; b. Hutchinson, Kans., July 26, 1953; s. Hugo Louis Jr. and Clara (Childers) W.; m. Dorothy Mae Ellison, June 10, 1978; 1 child, Christine. BA in History, U. State N.Y., Albany, 1984; MA in Humanities, Calif. State U.-Dominguez Hill, Carson, 1989; PhD in History, Greenwich U., Hilo, Hawaii, 1991. Lab. clinician Nat. Park Archaeol. Ctr., Lincoln, Nebr., 1987; writer hist. trivia cards Bee-Wise Industries, Hastings, Nebr., 1987; instr. S.E. Community Coll., 1988; paraeducator Lincoln Pub. Schs., 1989-90; writer humanities curriculum Greenwich U., Hilo, from 1992; tutor student athletes U. Nebr., Lincoln, from 1991; mentor gifted students Lincoln Pub. Schs., from 1991. Adj. faculty Greenwich U. Author: The Hellenes, 1992. Mem. worship team Gardenview Assembly of God Ch., 1990—, head Christian edn., 1992—. Republican. Avocations: reading, playing music, military, modeling. Home: Lincoln, Nebr. Died June 27, 2008.

WEXLER, ANNE, lobbyist; b. NYC, Feb. 10, 1930; d. Leon R. and Edith R. (Rau) Levy; m. Joseph Duffey, Sept. 17, 1974; children from previous marriage: David, Daniel. BA, Skidmore Coll., 1951, LLD (hon.), 1978; DSc in Bus. (hon.), Bryant Coll., 1978. Co-chairwoman Eugene McCarthy for Pres., Conn., 1967—68; chief cons. Commn. on Party Structure & Delegate Selection, Dem. Nat Com., 1969—72; assoc. pub. Rolling Stone mag., 1974-76; personnel adviser Carter-Mondale transition planning group, 1976-77; dep. under sec. for regional affairs US Dept. Commerce, 1977-78; asst. to Pres. The White House, Washington, 1978-81; founder, exec. chmn. Wexler & Walker Pub. Policy Associates (formerly The Wexler Group), Washington, 1981—2009; govt. relations & pub. affairs cons., chmn. Wexler, Reynolds, Harrison & Schule, Inc., Washington, 1981-90; vice chmn. Hill & Knowlton PA Worldwide, Washington, 1990—92. Bd. dirs. Methanex, Dreyfus Index Funds, Wilshire Mut. Funds, Dreyfus Family of Funds. Bd. dirs. Washington Econ. Club, WETA. Decorated Officer Order of Australia; recipient Bryce Harlow award, 1989; named Outstanding Alumna, Skidmore Coll., 1972. Mem.: Nat. Women's Forum, Coun. on Fgn. Rels. Jewish. Home: Washington, DC. Died Aug. 7, 2009.

WEYRAUCH, WALTER OTTO, law educator; b. Lindau, Germany, Aug. 27, 1919; came to US, 1952; s. Hans Ernst Winand and Meta Margarete (Lönholdt) W.; m. Jill Carolyn White, Mar. 17, 1973; children from previous marriages: Kurt Roman (dec.), Corinne Harriet Irene, Bettina Elaine (dec.). Student, U. Freiburg, 1937, U. Frankfurt Main, Germany, 1940-43, Dr. iur, 1951; LL.B., Georgetown U., 1955; LL.M., Harvard, 1956; J.S.D., Yale, 1962; Golden Dr. diploma (hon.), U. Frankfurt Main, 2001. Referendar, Frankfurt, Germany, 1943-48; atty. German cts. US Ct. Appeals, Allied High Commn., Frankfurt, 1949-52; expert on trade regulations, visit in U.S. under auspices Dept. State, 1950; Harvard U. Dumbarton Oaks Library and Collection, Washington, 1953-55; asst. in instrn. Law Sch., Yale, 1956-57; assoc. prof. law U. Fla., Gainesville, 1957-60, prof., 1960-89, Clarence J. TeSelle prof. law, 1989-94, Stephen C. O'Connell chair, from 1994, disting. prof. law, from 1998, hon. prof. law Johann Wolfgang Goethe U., Franfurt Main, from 1980. Vis. cons. U. Calif. Space Scis. Lab., Berkeley, 1965-66; vis. prof. law Rutgers U., 1968; vis. prof. polit. sci. U. Calif., Berkeley, 1968-69; vis. prof. law U. Frankfurt, 1975; cons. Commn. of Experts on Problems of Succession of the Hague Conf. on Pvt. Internat. Law, U.S. Dept. State, 1968-71; Rockefeller Found. fellow, Europe, 1958-59; Weyrauch disting. ann. lectr. in family law U. Fla., Gainesville, 2006—; lectr. in field. Author: The Personality of Lawyers, 1964, Zum Gesellschaftsbild des Juristen, 1970, Hierarchie der Ausbildungsstätten, Rechtsstudium und Recht in den Vereinigten Staaten, 1976, Gestapo V-Leute: Tatsachen und Theorie des Geheimdienstes, 1989, 2d edit., 1992; author: (with Sanford N. Katz) American Family Law in Transition, 1983; author: (with Katz and Frances E. Olsen) Cases and Materials on Family Law: Legal Concepts and Changing Human Relationships, 1994; author: Das Recht der Roma und Sinti: Ein Beispiel autonomer Rechtsschöpfung, 2002; author, editor: Gypsy

Law: Romani Legal Traditions and Culture, 2001; contbr. chapters to books. Mem. Law and Soc. Assn., Internat. Soc. on Family Law, Assn. Am. Law Schs. (chmn. com. studies beyond 1st degree in law 1965-67), Order of Coif. Home: Gainesville, Fla. Deceased.

WEYRICH, PAUL MICHAEL, think-tank executive; b. Racine, Wis., Oct. 7, 1942; s. Ignatius A. and Virginia M. (Wickstrom) W.; m. Joyce Anne Smigun, July 6, 1963; children: Dawn, Peter, Diana, Stephen, Andrew. AA, U. Wis., 1962. Ordained deacon Melkite Greek Eparchy, 1990. News dir., announcer, program dir. WLIP, WAXO-FM, Kenosha, Wis., 1960-63; reporter Milw. Sentinel, 1963-64; polit. reporter, newscaster CBS, Milw., 1964-65; news dir. Sta. KQXI, Denver, 1966; press sec. to Sen. Gordon Allott US Senate, Washington, 1967-73, spl. asst. to Sen. Carl T. Curtis, 1973-77; founder, pres. Heritage Found., 1973-74; nat. chmn. Free Congress PAC, Coalitions for Am., from 1987, BOD, Amtrak, 1987-93; pres. Free Congress Rsch. & Ednl. Found., 1977—2002, chmn., CEO, 2002—08; pres. Krieble Inst., 1989—96. Nat. editor Transport Central, 1968-71; treas. Coun. Nat. Policy, 1981-92, pres. America's Voice, 1991-97; bd. dirs. All News Radio WEEI, Boston, 1984-90, Krieble Inst. Russia; nat. chmn. Com. for Effective State Govt.; chmn. bd. Yorktownuniversity.com, 1999-2008 Author: The Role of Rails series, 1964; pub. Polit. Report, 1975-89, The New Electric Rwy. Jour., 1988-96, Spotlight on Congress, 1989-93; host (daily talk show) Direct Line, 1993-98; co-host The New Electric Rwy. Jour., 1994-96, Ways & Means, 1994—. Recipient Youth of Yr. award Racine Optimist Club, 1960, Excellence in Reporting citation Milw. Common Council, 1964, Documentary of Yr. award for Wis. TV, 1965, Crystal Ball award for predicting outcome 1996 presdl. election Washington Post, 1996, Thomas Jefferson award for servant leadership Coun. Nat. Policy, 1997, Clare Boothe Luce award, 2005, named one of 25 Most Influential Republicans Newsmax Mag. 2008. Mem. Ctrl. Electric Railroaders Assn., Internat. Policy Forum (chmn. 1983-84); former mem. HUD Adv. Commn. on Regulatory Barriers to Affordable Housing. Greek Catholic. Home: Fairfax, Va. Died Dec. 18, 2008.

WEZALIS, JOHN RICHARD (JOHN RICHARD WALLACE), musician, agent, producer; b. Grosse Pointe, Mich., Oct. 11, 1937; s. John R. and Essie Mae (Robinson) W.; m. Jean Wezalis, Sept. 19, 1959; children: Susan, Kathleen, Julie. Cert. Bus. Adminstrn. Mktg., U. Detroit, 1969. Band leader Johnny Wallace 5, Detroit, from 1956, Johnny Wallace Little Big Band, Detroit, from 1980; booking agt. Lorio-Ross Entertainment, Royal Oak, Mich., 1972-83; booking agt., producer Grenier and Moore Prodns., Madison Heights, Mich., from 1983. Pres. Johnny Wallace Enterprises, Inc. Served with U.S. Army, 1958-60. Mem.: Detroit Yacht. Avocations: tennis, boating, video. Home: Warren, Mich. Died Nov. 22, 2007.

WHALEY, DAWN ELLEN, musician, educator; b. Bethel, Conn., July 17, 1953; d. Robert Edwin and Mary Ellen (Manion) W. BA, Western Conn. State U., 1976; postgrad., Juilliard, 1978-79, Johannesen Internat. Sch. Arts, 1980-82; MusM, U. Victoria, 1984; cert., Tanglewood Inst., 1984. Instr. The Melrose Sch., Brewster, N.Y., 1980-82; clarinetist Danbury Symphony Orch., 1984-90, prin. clarinetist, from 1990; clarinetist Ivy Chamber Players, New Canaan, Conn., 1986-88; instr. New Fairfield Conn. High Sch., 1987-89, Conn. Conservatory Music and Dance, from 1987. Treas. Danbury Music Ctr. Inc., Conn., 1995—, also bd. dirs.; instr. Maimonides Acad., Danbury, 1986-87, New Fairfield (Conn.) Mid. Sch., 1987-89; conv. asst. Ridenour Woodwind Svcs., Apopka, Fla., 1986—; freelance music copyist, clarinet clinician; founding mem. Trio di Camerati; bd. dirs. Danbury Dialysis Fund Inc. Recitalist; specialist in electroacoustic music forclarinet; editor E flat Symphonia Concertante (Jos. Myslivecek), 1984; contbr. articles, reviews to music mags. Justice of the Peace, Bethel, Conn. Named one of Outstanding Young Women of Am., 1981; U. Victoria fellow, 1982-84; scholar Apple Hill Ctr. for Chamber Music, 1983, Boston U. Tanglewood Inst., 1984. Mem. Internat. Clarinet Soc., Internat. Congress of Women in Music, Am. Fedn. Music (local chpt.), Western Conn. State U. Alumni Assn. (mem. exec. bd. 1977-79). Home: Bethel, Conn. Died May 17, 2008.

WHEATLEY, ELAINE JOHNSON, hotel executive, architectural designer; b. Unity, Wis., Aug. 29, 1929; d. Salem John and Edythe Engblom Johnson; m. Charles Fellows Wheatley Jr., May 23, 1959; children: Charles III, Mark. BA in Archtl. Interior Design, Mount Vernon Coll., Washington, 1980. Interior designer Classique Interiors, Potomac, Md., 1980; owner restoration of old houses pvt. practice, Va., Md., 1980-85; owner, hostess Bed and breakfast, Grasonville, Md., from 1995. Modeling tchr. Patricia Stevens, Washington, 1957-60; air line stewardess United Air Lines, Washington, N.Y.C., Chgo., Salt Lake City, 1951-59; profl. model Chgo., 1948-51. Mem. Democratic Women Queen Anns County, 1993-97, UAL Clipped Wings, 1980-97. Named Dean's List Mt. Vernon Coll., 1979-80. Mem. C. of C., Queen Anns County Visitors Ctr., AAUW. Democrat. Episcolapian. Avocations: antiques, needlepoint, canoeing, bird watching, opera. Died Feb. 15, 2008.

WHEATLEY, MELVIN ERNEST, JR., retired bishop; b. Lewisville, Pa., May 7, 1915; s. Melvin Ernest and Gertrude Elizabeth (Mitchell) W.; m. Lucile Elizabeth Maris, June 15, 1939; children: Paul Melvin, James Maris, John Sherwood (dec.). AB magna cum laude, Am. U., 1936, DD, 1958; BD summa cum laude, Drew U., 1939; DD, U. of Pacific, 1948. Ordained to ministry Meth. Ch., 1939. Pastor area Meth. ch., Lincoln, Del., 1939-41; assoc. pastor First Meth. Ch., Fresno, Calif., 1941-43; pastor Centenary Meth. Ch., Modesto, Calif., 1943-46, Cen. Meth. Ch., Stockton, Calif., 1946-54, Westwood Meth. Ch., LA, 1954-72; bishop Denver Area, 1972-84; ret., 1984. Instr. philosophy Modesto Jr. Coll., 1944; summer session instr. Hebrew-Christian heritage U. of Pacific; instr. Homiletics U. So. Calif., So. Calif. Sch. Theology, Claremont; lectr. St. Luke's Lectures, Houston, 1966; mem. Bd. of Ch. and Soc., Commn. on Status and Role of Women, United Meth. Ch., 1976-84; condr. European Christian Heritage tour, 1961, Alaska and Hawaii Missions, 1952, 54, Israel in behalf of Stockton Jewish Congregation, 1951. Author: Going His Way, 1957, Our Man and the Church, 1968, The Power of Worship, 1970, Family Ministries Manual, 1970, Christmas Is for Celebrating, 1977; contbr. articles to profl. jours. Chmn. Community Rels. Conf. So. Calif., 1966-69; pres. So. Calif.-Ariz. Conf. Bd. Edn., 1960-68; hon. trustee Iliff Sch. Theology; hon. dir., active mem. Parents and Friends of Lesbians and Gays, 1980-2005. Recipient Disting. Alumnus award Am. U., 1979, Ball award Meth. Fedn. Social Action, 1984, Prophetic Leadership award The Consultation on Homosexuality, Tolerance and Roman Cath. Theology, 1985, Human Rights award Universal Fellowship of Met. Community Congregations, 1985, award for social justice Calif.-Pacific Meth. Fedn. for Social Action, 2000, Lifetime Achievement award Denver Parents, Families and Friends of Lesbians and Gays, 2000, Outstanding Svc. award Parents Reconciling Network, 2000, Hilton award Nat. Pa. Reconciling Network, 2004. Methodist. Home: Laguna Woods, Calif. Died Mar. 1, 0209.

WHEELER, EDWARD NORWOOD, chemical consultant; b. Yancey, Tex., Oct. 11, 1927; s. Wilber Basel and Clara Clementine (Stafford) W.; m. Luella Jean Brossette, Nov. 21, 1950; children: Gordon A., Sterling R., Darrell S., Charlotte, Murray H. BS, Tex. A&I U., 1947, BSChemE, 1949; MA, U. Tex., 1951, PhD, 1953. Rsch. chemist Celanese Chem. Co., Corpus Christi, 1953-55, group leader, 1955-62, section mgr., 1962-67, dir. rsch., 1967-72, dir. devel., 1972-74, planning dir. NYC, 1974-75, dir. rsch. devel. planning, 1975-76, v.p. rsch. devel. planning, 1976-79, v.p. rsch. & devel. Dallas, 1979-83; cons. and expert witness White and Case, Hong Kong and NYC, 1986-91. Contbr. articles to profl. jours. Treas. Dallas Bethlehem Ctr., 1985-89; hon. life mem., adv. coun. U. Tex. Coll. Natural Sci. Found.; bd. trustees Tex. A&M U.-Kingsville Found., 1994-98; pres. North Tex. Conf. Coun. on Fin. and Adminstrn., United Meth. Ch., 1992-96. Recipient Disting. Alumnus award Tex. A&I U., Kingsville, 1981. Mem. Am. Chem. Soc., Indsl. Rsch. Inst., Synthetic Organic Chem. Mfrs. Assn. (bd. govs. 1977-81), Littlefield Soc. U. Tex. Methodist. Achievements include patents in field. Avocations: gardening, genealogy, cooking. Died Oct. 9, 2007.

WHEELER, FRANK KNOWLES BLASDELL, retired naval officer, business consultant; b. Mpls., Oct. 29, 1912; s. Walter Hall and Eva Maude (Blasdell) W.; widowed, Oct. 1991; children: Mary Ann Wheeler Masher, Frances Blasdell Wheeler Kindle, Charles Knowles. BSME, U.S. Naval Acad., 1935, PhD (Equivalent) Electronics, 1944. Registered profl. engr., Calif. Commd. ensign USN, 1935, advanced through grades to capt., 1944; commdg. officer U.S.S. Kearney, 1944-46; mem. various fleets/electronics staffs USN, 1960, ret., 1960; mfg. mgr. Hewlett Packard Co., Palo Alto, Calif., 1960-70; co. mfg. mgr. Fairchild, Mountain View, Calif., 1970-72; pres., bus. cons. Wheeler & Assocs., Los Altos Hills, Calif., from 1972. Mem. IEEE. Republican. Presbyterian. Avocations: electronics, preparing historical video productions. Died Dec. 9, 2007.

WHEELER, JULIA M., counselor; b. Birmingham, Ala., June 22, 1932; d. John and Julia (Carson) Glenn; m. Dura Wheeler, Oct. 26, 1956; children: Eric, Brenda. BS, Tuskegee Inst., 1957; MA, Wayne State U., 1972. Cert. guidance counselor; registered profl. counselor. Tchr. Clay County Bd. Edn., Lineville, La., Sacred Heart Enrichment Sem., Grosse Pointe, Mich., Detroit (Mich.) Bd. Edn., counselor. Sr. class advisor, Horizon Upward Bound Program, Martin Luther King Jr., Rosa Parks and Cesar Chavez scholarship program. Recipient Disting. Svc. award. Mem. Mich. Guidance Assn., Assn. Sch. Counselors, Assn. Christian Counselors. Died Nov. 21, 2007.

WHINNERY, JOHN ROY, electrical engineer, educator; b. Read, Colo., July 26, 1916; s. Ralph V. and Edith Mable (Bent) Whinnery; m. Patricia Barry, Sept. 17, 1944; children: Carol Joanne, Catherine, Barbara. BS Elec. Engring., U. Calif., Berkeley, 1937, PhD, 1948. With GE, 1937—46; part-time lectr. Union Coll., Schenectady, 1945—46; assoc. prof. elec. engring. U. Calif., Berkeley, 1946—52, prof., vice chmn. div. elec. engring., 1952—56, chmn., 1956—59, dean Coll. Engring., 1959—63, prof. elec. engring., 1963—80, univ. prof. Coll. Engring., 1980, univ. prof. emeritus Coll. Engring. Rsch. sci. electron tubes Hughes Aircraft Co., Culver City, 1951—52; vis. mem. tech. staff Bell Tel. Labs., 1963—64; mem. sci. and tech. com. Manned Space Flight, NASA, 1963—69; chmn. Commn. Engring. Edn., 1966—68; standing com. controlled thermonuclear rsch. AEC, 1970—73; mem. Pres.'s Com. on Nat. Sci. Medal, 1970—73, 1979—80. Author (with Simon Ramo): Fields and Waves in Communication Electronics, 1944; author: (with Ramo and Van Duzor) Fields and Waves in Communication Electronics, 3rd edit., 1994; author: (with D.O. Pederson and J.J. Studer) Introduction to Electronic Systems, Circuits and Devices; contbr. tech. articles. Recipient Lamme medal, Am. Soc. Engring. Edn., 1975, Centennial medal, 1993, Engring. Alumni award, U. Calif.-Berkeley, 1980, Nat. Medal of Sci., NSF, 1992; named to Hall of Fame, Modesto (Calif.) H.S., 1983, ASEE Hall of Fame, 1993;, Guggenheim Fellow, 1959. Fellow: IRE (bd. dirs. 1956—59), IEEE (life; bd. dirs. 1969—71, sec. 1971, Edn. medal 1967, Centennial medal 1984, Medal of Honor 1985), Am. Acad. Arts and Scis., Optical Soc. Am.; mem.: IEEE Microwave Theory and Techniques Soc. (disting. lectr. 1989—92, Microwave Career award 1977, Okawa prize in info. and telecom. 1997), NAS, NAE (Founders award 1986), Eta Kappa Nu (eminent mem.), Tau Beta Pi, Sigma Xi, Phi Beta Kappa. Congregationalist. Home: Berkeley, Calif. Died Feb. 1, 2009.

WHIPPLE, WILLIAM, JR., government policy consultant, writer; b. Cinclare, La., Feb. 4, 1909; s. William and Genevieve (Randolph) W.; m. Dixie Ancrum, Mar. 30, 1935 (dec. Oct. 1955); children: Anne Calhoun, William III, Claire Randolph; m. Renée Pauline Exiga, July 21, 1956 (div. May 1974); 1 child, Philip; m. Frances Edith Cheek, June 1, 1974 (dec. July 1983); m. Alice Terry Goodloe, Dec. 1, 1984. BS, U.S. Mil. Acad., 1930; BA, Oxford U., Eng., 1933, MA, 1937; Civil Engr., Princeton U., 1936. Registered profl. engr., N.J. Commd. 2d lt. Corps Engrs., U.S. Army, 1930, advanced through grades to brig. gen., ret., 1960; chief engr. N.Y. World's Fair Corp., Flushing Meadow, N.Y., 1960-64; pvt. practice cons. engr. NYC, 1964-65; dir. Water Resources Rsch. Inst. Rutgers U., New Brunswick, N.J., 1965-79, rsch. prof. Coastal and Environ. Inst., 1979-81; asst. dir. divsn. water resources Dept. Environ. Protection, Trenton, N.J., 1981-89, coord. nonpoint cource control program divsn. water resource, 1989-90; prin. Greeley Polhemus Group, Chester, Pa., 1990-2000; pvt. practice cons. Princeton, N.J., from 1999. Author: New Perspectives on Water Supply, 1994, Comprehensive Water Planning and Regulation, 1996, Water Resource: A New Era for Coordination, 1998; contbr. articles to publs. on water resources. Chmn. Flood Control Com., Princeton, N.J., 1975-81; adv. coun., Revision of N.J.'s Water Supply Master Plan, 2001. Recipient Trustees award N.J. inst. Tech., 1985, govt. award Water Resource Assn. of Delaware River Basin, 1987, Toulmin award for best articles Mil. Engr., 1975, Formal Commendation from Pres. of U.S., 1971. Fellow AAAS, ASCE (life, chmn. urban water resources rsch. coun. 1973-75, Lifetime Achievement award Inst. Environment and Water Resources 2001), Soc. Am. Mil. Engrs. (life), Am. Water Resources Assn. (pres. 1993, Icko Iben award 1978, William Ackerman medal 1989, Boggess award; mem. Am. Acad. Environ. Engrs. (diplomate), Univs. Coun. on Water Resources (chmn. 1976-78), Sigma Xi. Avocation: history and biography. Died Aug. 23, 2007.

WHITAKER, ARTHUR LUTHER, retired minister, psychologist; b. Malden, Mass., July 23, 1921; s. Robert William and Elizabeth Arveen (Hinton) W.; m. Virginia Aileene Carter, June 6, 1948; children: Ronald, Paul, Mark, Keith. BA, Gordon Coll., 1949; BD, Harvard U., 1952; MST, Andover Newton Theol. Sem., 1954, D in Ministry, 1973. Ordained to ministry Baptist Ch., 1951; lic. counseling psychologist and health provider, Mass.; diplomate Internat. Acad. Behavioral Medicine, Am. Bd. Forensic Examiners and Medicine, Am. Coll. Forensic Examiners, Am. Bd. Psychol. Svcs. Pastor Calvary Bapt. Ch., Haverhill, Mass., 1950-55; field rep. Am. Bapt. Home Mission, NYC, 1955-56; pastor Mt. Olivet Bapt. Ch., Rochester, NY, 1956-66, Pilgrim Bapt. Ch., St. Paul, 1966-70; assoc. exec. min. Am. Bapt. Chs. Mass., Boston, 1970-78; exec. min. Am. Bapt. Chs. N.Y., Syracuse, 1978-83; Protestant chaplain VA Med. Ctr., Syracuse, 1984-86; ret. exec. min. Am. Bapt. Chs. USA-N.Y. State Region, from 1986; counselor, vis. lectr. Harvard U. Divinity Sch., Cambridge, Mass., 1990-2000, Interfaith Counseling Svcc. Inc., Newton, Mass., 1990-92. Lectr. social psychology U. Rochester, 1958-66; cons. U.S. Commn. Civil Rights, U.S. Govt., Rochester, 1964, Nat. Office NAACP, Rochester, 1964-65; vis. prof. Afro-Am. studies Gordon Coll., Wenham, Mass., 1972; trustee Colgate Rochester Divinity Sch., Gordon Coll., Keuka Coll. Contbr. articles and revs. to profl. jours. Active Mass. Dem. Party, Boston; hon. mem. nat. steering com. Gore 2000; contbg. mem. Dem. Nat. Com., 1995—; keynote spkr. 7th ann. Martin Luther King, Jr. Meml. Luncheon, North Shore Black Women's Assn., 2000; preacher Dr. Martin Luther King Jr. Chapel, Hanscom AFB, Mass., 2002, Historic First Bapt. Ch. of Boston, Mass.; sr. guest min. Friendship Bapt. Ch., Charlotte, NC, 2003. Tech. sgt. U.S. Army, 1943-46, ETO. Recipient Whitaker Hall named in honor, Mt. Olive Bapt. Ch., Rochester, N.Y, 1991, Arthur L. Whitaker award, Am. Bapt. Chs. Mass., 1992; named Alumnus of Yr., Gordon Coll. Alumni Assn., Wenham, 1972; named to World War II: War Meml., Washington, 2004. Mem. APA, Mass. Psychol. Assn., Harvard Divinity Sch. Alumni Assn. (sec. 1990-92, Outstanding Svc. award 1998, commemorative luncheon spkr. Dr. Martin Luther King Jr. celebration, miniature 1775 Minuteman statue recipient, African-Am. heritage com.), Andover Newton Theol. Sch. Alumni Assn. (pres. 1996-97). Avocations: music, spectator sports, drama, swimming, reading. Home: Randolph, Mass. Died Oct. 16, 2007.

WHITAKER, BRUCE EZELL, retired academic administrator; b. Cleveland County, NC, June 27, 1921; s. Oveda E. and Fay A. Whitaker; m. Esther Adams, Aug. 22, 1947; children: Barry Eugene, Garry Bruce. BA, Wake Forest U., 1944; BD, So. Bapt. Theol. Sem., 1947, ThM, 1948, PhD, 1950; postgrad., George Peabody Coll., 1952; DL, Wake

Forest U., 1987. Ordained to ministry Bapt. Ch., 1945; pastor Smithfield, Ky., 1945-49; instr. sociology and philosophy Ind. U., 1947-50; prof. religion Cumberland U., Lebanon, Tenn., 1950-51, Belmont Coll., Nashville, 1951-52; prof. sociology, asst. to pres. Shorter Coll., Rome, Ga., 1952-53; assoc. pastor, min. edn. Atlanta, 1953-54; state sec., student dept. Bapt. State Conv., NC, 1954-57; pres. Chowan Coll., Murfreesboro, NC, 1957-89, pres. emeritus, 1989—2009. Mem. adv. com. to Nd. Higher Edn., 1962-66; pres. NC Conf. Social Svc., 1965-67, Assn. Governing Bds., 1973-82, Assn. So. Baptist Colls. and Schs., 1967-68, Assn. Eastern NC Colls., 1968-69; bd. dirs. Regional Edn. Lab. for Carolinas and Va. Pres. bd. trustees NC Found. Church-Related Colls., 1970-74; bd. dirs., v.p. Nat. Coun. Ind. Jr. Colls., 1974-75, pres., 1975-76; mem. adv. coun. presidents Assn. Governing Bds., from 1973; mem. NC Bd. Mental Health, from 1966; bd. dirs. Am. Assn. Cmty. and Jr. Colls., 1976-82; pres. NC Assn. Colls. and Univs., 1977-78; chmn. NC Commn. Mental Health/Mental Retardation Sers., 1978-81; mem. NC Commn. on Mental Health, Developmental Disabilities, and Alcohol & Drug Svcs. Author: From Plough Boy to College President, 2008. V.p. Bapt. State Conv. NC, 1989-91. Named Tarheel of Week Raleigh News and Observer, 1962, Boss of Year NC Jaycees, 1972; named to Hall of Fame, Cmty. Action Assn., 2005; tribute paid in Congl. Record, 1962, 89, NC Com. Action Assn. Hall of Fame, 2005; Whitaker Libr. at Chowan Coll. named for him; Whitaker Sch. at Butner, NC named for him; selected one of nation's 18 most effective coll. pres. in 1985, funded study Exxon Found.; featured in We the People of North Carolina, 1989. Mem. NC Lit. and Hist. Assn. (pres. 1970-71), Am. Acad. Polit. and Social Scis., NEA, Am. Assn. Community and Jr. Colls. (dir. 1976-82, Leadership Recognition award 1989), Nat. Assn. Ind. Colls. and Univs. (dir. 1977-78, 81-85), Am. Assn. Higher Edn., Am. Coun. Edn. (bd. dirs. 1985-89), Internat. Platform Assn., Omicron Delta Kappa. Clubs: Capital City (Raleigh, NC), Rotary (chmn. dist. student exchange com. 1969-72, Paul Harris fellow); Optimist; Beechwood Country (Ahoskie, NC); Harbor (Norfolk, Va.). Died May 5, 2009.

WHITCOMB, RICHARD TRAVIS, aeronautical consultant; b. Evanston, Ill., Feb. 21, 1921; s. Kenneth Frederick and Gladys (Travis) Whitcomb. BS in Aero. Engring., Worcester Poly. Inst., 1943, DEng (hon.), 1956; DSc (hon.), Old Dominion U., 1985. Aero. rsch. scientist Langley Rsch. Ctr. NASA, Hampton, Va., 1943—58, head transonic aerodynamics br., 1958—80, disting. rsch. assoc., 1980—85; pvt. practice aero. cons. Hampton, 1980—90. Patentee aero. equipment. Recipient Collier Trophy, Nat. Aero. Assn., 1955, Wright Bros. trophy, 1974, Nat. Medal of Sci., The White House, 1973, Award in Aero. Engring., NAS, 2000; named to Nat. Inventors Hall of Fame, 2003. Fellow: AIAA (hon. Reed award 1969, Daniel Guggenheim medal 2002); mem.: NAE. Avocations: music, reading, exercise. Home: Fairfax, Va. Died Oct. 13, 2009.

WHITE, ALVIN MURRAY, retired mathematics professor, consultant; b. NYC, June 21, 1925; s. Max and Beatrice White; m. Myra Goldstein, Dec. 4, 1946; children: Louis, Michael. BA, Columbia U., 1949; MA, UCLA, 1951; PhD, Stanford U., 1961. Instr. Stanford U., Calif., 1950—54; asst. prof. U. Santa Clara, Calif., 1954—61; postdoctoral fellow U. Wis., Madison, 1961—62; prof. math. Harvey Mudd Coll., Claremont, Calif., 1962—97, emeritus prof. math., 1997—2009. Vis. scholar MIT, 1975; initiator-facilitator humanistic math. network of over 2000 mathematicians worldwide; cons. coop. learning tutorial program Claremont Unified Sch. Dist. Editor: Interdisciplinary Teaching, 1981; founder, pub., editor: Humanistic Mathematics Network Jour., Essays on Humanistic Math., Math. Assn. Am., 1993; contbr. articles to profl. jours. Served with USN, 1943-46, PTO; tutor, Calif. Institution for Men in Chino, El Roble Intermediate Sch.; read and recorded textbooks, Recording for the Blind (now Recording for the Blind & Dyslexic) Grantee Fund for Improvement of Post-secondary Edn., Exxon Found.; Danforth Fellow. Mem. Am. Math. Soc., Math. Assn. Am., Nat. Coun. Tchrs. Math., Profl. Organizational Developers Network, Fedn. Am. Scientists, AAUP, Sigma Xi. Died June 2, 2009.

WHITE, DAVID ALAN, JR., manufacturing executive; b. Chgo., Feb. 18, 1942; s. David Alan and Janet (Fate) W.; m. Catherine Elizabeth Harman, June 12, 1971; children: Christopher Alan, John Michael. BS, U.S. Mil. Acad., 1964; MBA, U. Pa., 1971. Planning analyst Cooper Industries, Houston, 1971-74; exec. asst. The Cooper Group, Raleigh, 1974-76; v.p. fin. and planning Cooper Energy Svcs. Group, Mt. Vernon, Ohio, 1976-80; v.p., gen. mgr. Cooper Power Tools, Columbia, S.C., 1980-88; v.p. corp. planning and devel. Cooper Industries, 1988-96, sr. v.p. strategic planning, 1996—99. Capt. U.S. Army, 1964-69. Decorated Army Commendation medal. Republican. Episcopalian. Avocations: golf, reading. Died Oct. 2, 2007.

WHITE, ELEANOR MARGARET, retired elementary school educator; b. Hutchinson, Kans., Nov. 5, 1918; d. Edward Jackson and Mary Margaret (Baker) Fraser; m. Floyd Milton White, July 16, 1944 (dec. 1966); 1 child, Floy Elaine White Ice. AA, Dodge City CC, Kans., 1938; BS in Elem. Edn., Phillips U., Enid, Okla., 1960; postgrad., Hays State U. Tchr. grades 1-8 Rural Sch. Dist. 54, Hodgeman County, Kans., 1938-40, Rural Sch. Dist. 14, Ford County, Kans., 1941-42, Rural Sch. Dist. 37, Hodgeman County, 1955; tchr. Sch. Dist. 443, Dodge City, Kans., 1955-84; ret. Mem. and cons. Leadership Team in Drug Abuse Edn., State of Kans., 1970-73. Pres. bd. Hot Line,

Inc., Dodge City, 1974-78; exec. bd. Area Drug Abuse Coun., Dodge City, 1974-76, New Chance Alcohol Rehab., Dodge City, 1979-85, Meals on Wheels, Dodge City, 1984-92. Named Woman of the Yr. Bus. and Profl. Women, 1975-76; named Kans. Master Tchr. Emporia State U., 1976. Mem. AAUW (pres. 1969-70), Ret. Tchrs. Assn. (pres. 1991—), White Shrine of Jerusalem (High Priestess 1988-91), Order Eastern Star (Worthy Matron 1961, Dist. dir. 1982), Delta Kappa Gamma (pres. 1979-80). Republican. Christian Ch. Avocations: reading, bowling, exercise, crossword puzzles. Died Dec. 7, 2007.

WHITE, FREDERICK ANDREW, retired physicist, professor; b. Detroit, Mar. 11, 1918; s. Andrew Bracken and Mildred (Witzel) W.; m. Dorothy Janet Sibley, Nov. 7, 1942 (dec.); children: Wendell William, Lawrence Sibley, Eric Sibley, Roger Randolph (dec.) BS, Wayne State U., Detroit, 1940; MS, U. Mich., Ann Arbor, 1941; postgrad., U. Rochester, NYC, 1943—46; PhD, U. Wis., Madison, 1959. Insp. U.S. Army Ordnance, Rochester, 1941—43; rsch. asst. Manhattan project U. Rochester, 1943—45, grad. instr. rsch. Manhattan project, 1946; rsch. asst., rsch. assoc., cons. physicist Knolls Atomic Power Lab. GE, Schenectady, NY, 1947—62; adj. prof. nuc. sci. Rensselaer Poly. Inst., Troy, NY, 1961—62; prof. nuc. engring. and environ. engring., indsl. liaison scientist, 1962—81, prof. emeritus, 1981—96; ret., 1996. Cons. NASA, 1965-80; organist and acoustic cons., 1952—2001; rsch. and liaison scientist Rochester Gas and Electric Co., 1978-96; adj. prof. physics SUNY Albany, 1986-88 Author: American Industrial Research Laboratories, 1961, Mass Spectrometry in Science and Technology, 1968, Our Acoustic Environment, 1975, Mass Spectrometry: Applications in Science and Engineering, 1986 Mem. AIAA, IEEE, Optical Soc. Am., Am. Guild Organists Achievements include developing mass spectrometric instrumentation and its uses in measurements relating to nuclear and atomic physics; co-discoverer last naturally-occurring stable isotope. Home: Niskayuna, NY. Died Oct. 13, 2008.

WHITE, JOSEPH CALVIN, petroleum engineer, consultant; b. Crane, Tex., July 5, 1930; s. Thomas Reese and Verda (Loveless) W.; m. Jan. 26, 1954 (widowed); children: Patrick, Pamela, Timothy. BS in Petroleum Engring., Tex. A&M U., 1952, BS in Geol. Engring., 1952. Cert. profl. engr., Tex., Colo. Engr. Texaco Inc., Tex., 1954-68, engr. Okla., 1954-68, mgr. NYC, 1968-72, Denver, 1972-80; cons. engr. S & W Petroleum Cons., Denver, 1980-85, J.C. White & Assocs., Inc., Denver, from 1985. 1st lt. U.S. Army, 1952-54. Mem. Soc. Petroleum Engrs. Died Dec. 12, 2007.

WHITE, ROBERT FRANKLIN, computer systems development analyst; b. Indpls., Aug. 18, 1928; s. Walter Otis and Golda Margaret (Ray) W.; m. Vernie Irene Bennett, Mar. 10, 1974; children: Dennis, Claudia, Richard, Steffani. BBA magna cum laude, Indpls. U., 1969; MBA, Butler U., 1972. Systems analyst Navistar, Indpls., 1959-75, supr. material scheduling, 1975-79, supr. systems div., from 1979. Served as cpl. U.S. Army, 1950-52, Korea. Recipient Wall St. Jour. Achievement award Dow Jones, 1969. Mem. Am. Legion, Alpha Sigma Lambda, Epsilon Sigma Alpha. Home: Greenwood, Ind. Died Feb. 23, 2008.

WHITE, RUTH MELLBY, musician, writer; b. Thief River Falls, Minn., Aug. 26, 1908; d. Oscar Frederick and Louise Therese (Grindeland) Mellby; m. Edward Banker White, Jan. 10, 1942 (dec. April 1983); children: Katherine Louise, Edward Banker Jr., Jean Marie. BA, St. Olaf Coll., Northfield, Minn., 1929; MA, Columbia, NYC, 1941. Lectr. in field. Soloist: St. Celia's Soc., Columbia U. Chorus, Women's Club, Ridgewood, N.J., S.D. Normal Sch.; pianist; choral dir.; lead part in musical comedy in Zeigfield's; contbr. poems to anthologies. Mem. Coll. Club, Harvard Womens Club (bd. dirs.), Scandinavian Forum, Browning Soc., Friends of Boston U. Libr., Sigma Alpha Iota (life). Lutheran. Avocations: beading clothes, walking, swimming, reading. Home: Boone, NC. Died Feb. 28, 2008.

WHITED, WILLIAM ALBERT, communications engineer; b. Nashville, Dec. 28, 1965; s. Burton Franklin and Sandra May (Williams) W. BS in Physics, Ga. Inst. Tech., 1989. Engr. BellSouth Telecomm., Atlanta, from 1989. Contbr. articles to profl. jours. Avocations: reading, music, travel, writing. Home: Atlanta, Ga. Died Dec. 12, 2007.

WHITEMAN, GEORGIA A., medical/surgical nurse; b. Clinton County, Ind., July 23, 1933; d. Martin L. and Ruth M. (Maish) Dunn; m. Max L. Whiteman, June 3, 1956; 1 child, Elaine A. Diploma in nursing, Indpls. Meth. Hosp., 1955. Charge nurse Meth. Hosp., Frankfort; nurse Dr. Fred Flora, Franklin, Ind.; surg. nurse Clinton County Hosp., Frankfort, Ind.; charge nurse Milner Health Care, Rossville, Ind. Named Hon. Woman of Yr., 1958, Employee of Month, 1988, Employee of Yr., 1989. Home: Michigantown, Ind. Died Dec. 1, 2007.

WHITLOCK, MCDONALD LEE, product development chemist; b. Balt., Dec. 7, 1943; s. McDonald and Nora Lee (Brown) W.; m. Linda Ruth Dettery, Sept. 6, 1968 (div. Feb. 1974). BS, Ursinus Coll., 1967; postgrad., Temple U., 1967-69. Chemist U.S. Customs House, Phila., 1967; devel. chemist Benjamin Foster Co., Phila., 1969-75, Foster div., H.B. Fuller Co., Phila., 1975-78, Chem. Sealing Corp., Kansas City, Mo., 1978-87; R & D group leader Chemseco div., Sika Corp., from 1987. Mem. AAAS, ASTM, Am. Chem. Soc. Achievements include development of sealant

for insulation system of the Alaskan pipeline, of wide curing range vacuum bag sealant for aerospace industry, of series of asphalt modifiers for roofing and paving asphalts. Home: Pleasant Hill, Mo. Died Mar. 14, 2008.

WHITMORE, JAMES ALLEN, actor; b. White Plains, NY, Oct. 1, 1921; s. James Allen and Florence Belle (Crane) W.; m. Nancy Mygatt, Mar. 24, 1978 (div.); m. Audra Lindley (div. 1979); children: James, Steven, Daniel; m. Noreen Nash, Aug. 7, 2001 BA, Yale U., 1942; postgrad., Am. Wing Theatre Sch. Performances include: (Broadway plays) debut in Command Decision, 1947 (Tony award for Best Actor, 1948), Elba, Manhattan Theatre Club, Winesburg, Ohio, 1956, Inquest, 1970, Will Rogers U.S.A., Give 'Em Hell Harry, 1974, The Magnificent Yankee, Washington, 1976, Bully, 1977, Handy Dandy, 1985, (films) Battleground, 1949, Next Voice You Hear, 1950, Asphalt Jungle, 1950, Mrs. O'Malley and Mr. Malone, 1950, Outsiders, 1950, Please Believe Me, 1950, Across de Vide Missouri, 1951, It's a Big Country, 1951, Because You're Mine, 1952, Above and Beyond, 1952, Girl Who Had Everything, 1953, All the Brothers Were Valiant, 1953, Kiss Me Kate, 1953, The Command, 1954, Them!, 1954, Oklahoma, 1955, Battle Cry, 1955, McConnell Story, 1955, Eddy Duchin Story, 1956, Face of Fire, 1959, Who Was That Lady?, 1960, Black Like Me, 1964, Chuka, 1967, Waterhole 3, 1967, Nobody's Perfect, 1968, Planet of the Apes, 1968, Madigan, 1968, The Split, 1968, Guns of the Magnificent Seven, 1969, Chato's Land, 1972, Where the Red Fern Grows, 1974, Give 'Em Hell Harry, 1974 (Acad. award nomination 1975), Bully, 1978, The Serpent's Egg, 1978, First Deadly Sin, 1980, Nuts, 1987, Old Explorers, 1990, The Shawshank Redemption, 1994, The Relic, 1997, numerous others, (TV appearances) including The Law and Mr. Jones, 1960-61, My Friend Tony, 1969, Temperature Rising, 1972-73, Will Rogers U.S.A., 1973, (TV miniseries) Celebrity, 1986, Favorite Son, 1988, (TV movies) Glory! Glory!, 1989, Sky High, 1990. Served with USMCR, 1942-46. Nominated Acad. award, 1949; recipient Antoinette Perry award, 1947, Comedy award Am. Acad. Humor, Ace award, 1989; named Most Promising Newcomer, 1947. Died Feb. 6, 2009.

WHITNEY, LESTER FRANK, retired agricultural sciences educator; b. New Bedford, Mass., Mar. 21, 1928; s. Walter Elisha and Orasie (Lapointe) W.; m. Phyllis Marian Burrill; children: Marcia, Mark, Scott, Dean, David, John, Steven. BS in Agrl. Engring., U. Maine, 1949; MS in Agrl. Engring., Mich. State U., 1951, PhD, 1964. Registered profl. engr., Mass. Cons. engr. Jack H. Kelly Onion Farms, Inc., Parma, Mich., 1950-51; design, proj. engr. Ariens Co., Brillion, Wis., 1951-53; agrl. engr. Maine Potato Growers, Inc., Presque Isle, Maine, 1953-54; plant engr., chief engr., plant supt. Wirthmore Feed Div., CPC Internat., Brattleboro, Vt., 1954-59; asst. prof. agrl. engring. dept. U. Mass., Amherst, 1959-63, assoc. prof. food and agrl. engring. dept., 1963-67, prof. food engring. dept., 1977-91. Consulting machine designer, Douglas G. Peterson Assocs., Greenfield, Mass., 1981—. Patentee in field; contbr. articles to profl. jours. Chmn. Amherst Planning Bd., 1965-71; mem. Amherst Sch. Bldg. Com., 1965-67, Lake Amherst Com., 1966-69; elected town meeting mem. Amherst, 1964-69. Recipient NSF sci. faculty fellowship, E. Lansing, Mich., 1963, Hood Found. award, NSF, East Lansing, 1962, Mass. Soc. of Agr. award, 1962. Mem. Am. Soc. Agrl. Engrs., Inst. Food Tech., Sigma Xi. Republican. Protestant. Home: Amherst, Mass. Died July 31, 2008.

WHITNEY, MARILYN LOUISE, elementary school educator; b. Leominster, Mass., Mar. 6, 1943; d. Pasquale Vincent and Mildred Louise (Maxim) Marino; m. Thomas Despo Whitney, Aug. 16, 1968; 1 child, Jon Robert. BS in Edn., Fitchburg State U., 1965; MS in Edn., Duquesne U., 1970. Elem. tchr. Town of Leominster, 1966-68, Fox Chapel (Pa.) Country Day Sch., 1968-70, Town of Ware, Mass., 1970—2002; ret., 2002. Mem. Ware Tchrs. Assn. (v.p.), Mass. Tchrs. Assn. (rep. to NEA Assembly), NEA, Leominster Tchrs. Assn. (rep. 1967), AAUW, AARP. Democrat. Episcopalian. Avocations: skiing, swimming, travel. Home: Amherst, Mass. Died Nov. 17, 2007.

WHITTAKER, DAVID MICHAEL, sales executive; b. Boise, Idaho, Nov. 13, 1959; s. Donald Lee and Virginia (Chapman) W.; m. Jean Marie Royston, May 3, 1982; children: Matthew, Jacob, Jenna Lyn. BS in Bus. Mgmt., Brigham Young U., 1984. Sales rep. TSI, Salt Lake City, 1984-85; account mgr. NCR Corp., Salt Lake City, 1985-87; sales rep. Harris/3M, Salt Lake City, 1987-88; systems specialist Superior Bus. Comms., Reno, 1988-92, v.p. sales, from 1992. Mem. exec. sec. LDS Ch., Sparks, Nev., 1991-93; mem. VDI Adv. Coun., 1990—. Mem. Mgmt. Soc. Marriot Sch. Mgmt. Republican. Home: Las Vegas, Nev. Died Mar. 6, 2008.

WICKHAM, WOODWARD A., JR., foundation administrator; b. Jackson, Mich., June 13, 1942; s. Woodward Adams and Virginia (Mc Laren) W. BA, Harvard U., 1964, MA in Teaching, 1969. Tchr. Latin and English Wooster Sch., Danbury, Conn., 1964-66, dir. project Upward Bound, 1966-68; sr. edn. analyst Abt Assocs., Inc., Cambridge, Mass., 1969-70; fellow Inst. of Current World Affairs, NYC, 1970-76; prof. chmn. dept. edn. Universidad de las Ams., Cholula, Puebla, Mex., 1977-78; exec. asst. to pres. Hampshire Coll., Amherst, Mass., 1978-81; dir. devel., 1982-85; sr. v.p. Jan Krukowski Assocs., Inc., NYC, 1985—90; v.p. MacArthur Found., 1990—2003; pres. Weil Found.,

2005—09. Contbr. articles to profl. jours. Bd. Sta. WFCR-FM, Amherst, 1979-83; bd. mem. Benton Found. Democrat. Avocation: flyfishing. Home: Chicago, Ill. Died Jan. 18, 2009.

WIDNER, NELLE OUSLEY, retired elementary education educator; b. Loyston, Tenn., May 20, 1924; d. Jacob Milas and Myrtle (Longmire) Ousley; m. John DeLozier Widner; children: Stephen John, Beth Widner Jackson, David Earl. BA, Maryville Coll., Tenn., 1946; postgrad., U. Tenn. Cert. profl. educator. 1st grade tchr. Alcoa (Tenn.) City Schs., 1946-50, 74-87, tchr. remedial reading, 1966-74. Mem. AAUW, Alpha Delta Kappa (publicity chmn. 1982-84, chaplain 1984-86, sec. 1994-96), Order Ea. Star (worthy matron local chpt. 1941), Chilhowee Club, Epsilon Sigma Omicron (chmn. 1991-92), Passion Play Guild. Democrat. Methodist. Avocations: reading, sports. Home: Alcoa, Tenn. Died Aug. 5, 2008.

WIDNER, WILLIAM RICHARD, biology educator, gardener; b. Baxter County, Ark., Apr. 24, 1920; s. Walter Elum and Rena Mae (Long) W.; m. Edna Holcombe Sorelle, Aug. 17, 1962 (div. Feb. 1985); m. Dorothy Anne de Geurin, March 9, 1985. BA, Eastern N.Mex. U., 1942; MS, U. N.Mex., 1948, PhD, 1952. Rsch. asst. biomed. rsch. AEC, Los Almos, N.Mex., 1948-50; teaching asst. U. N.Mex., Albuquerque, 1950-52; indsl. hygienist AEC, Albuquerque, 1952-55; high sch. tchr. Albuquerque Indian Sch., 1955-56; chmn. biology Howard Payne Coll., Brownwood, Tex., 1956-59; biology prof. Baylor U., Waco, Tex., 1959-89, emeritus prof., from 1989. Capt. USN, 1972, USNR, 1946-80. Mem. KYCH, Masons (master 1985-86, high priest 1989, dist. dep. grand master dist. 20 1992, order of Silver Trowel 1989, royal order Jesters 1993). Republican. Southern Baptist. Avocations: gardening, hunting, photography. Died Jan. 16, 2008.

WIGGANS, SAMUEL CLAUDE, retired horticulturist, agronomist, consultant; b. Lincoln, Nebr., Sept. 2, 1922; s. Cleo Claude and Martha (Chinn) W.; m. Ruth Evelyn Littlefield, Sept. 7, 1957; children: James Claude, Thomas Claude. BS, U. Nebr., 1947; MS, U. Wis., 1948, PhD, 1951. Asst. prof. agronomy and botany Iowa State U., Ames, 1951-58; assoc. prof. horticulture Okla. State U., Stillwater, 1958-63; prof., chair dept. hort. sci. U. Vt., Burlington, 1963-65, prof., chair dept. plant and soil sci., 1965-80; prin. horticulturist USDA/Coop. State Rsch. Svc., Washington, 1980-92. Contbr. over 95 articles to profl. jours. Deacon 1st Congl. Ch., Burlington, 1973-77; chmn. Boy Scouts Am., Shelburne, Vt., 1974-75. With U.S. Army, 1942-46, col. USAR, 1947-76. Mem. AAAS, Am. Soc. Hort. Sci. (pres. N.E. region, bd. dirs. 1973-75), Am. Hort. Therapy Assn. (bd. dirs., treas. 1984-86), Am. Soc. Agronomy (bd. dirs. 1975-76). Home: Newport News, Va. Died Dec. 2, 2008.

WIGSTON, DAVID LAWRENCE, biologist, dean; b. London, Dec. 12, 1943; came to U.S., 1993; s. Frederic Roland Wigston and Joan Mavin; m. Patricia Anne Werner, May 25, 1991; 1 child, Alexa Joan Dobinson. BSc with 1st class honors, U. Exeter, Eng., 1965; PhD in Forest Ecology, U. Exeter, 1972. Lectr. in biology Exeter Coll., 1967-69; sr. lectr. biology Coventry (Eng.) U., 1970-74; reader environ. sci. Plymouth (Eng.) U., 1974-82; prof., chair dept. forestry Papua New Guinea U. Tech., Lae, 1982-86; prof. environ. sci. No. Territory U., Darwin, Australia, 1986-93, dean faculty of sci., 1986-92; rsch. prof. U. Fla., Gainesville, 1993-96; rsch. assoc. dean U. Mich., Flint, from 1996. Vis. fellow St. Cross Coll. Oxford (Eng.) U., 1980; cons. Swedish Biomass Energy Program, 1981-82; chief wildlife scientist No. Territory (Australia) Govt., 1992-93. Narrator (symphonic works) Peter & The Wolf, Jungle Book, Hassan, 1961—. Cons. Internat. Convention Biodiversity, Australia, 1992-93; pres., bd. dirs. Gainesville Symphony Orch., 1994-96. Fellow Australian Inst. Biology (sec. No. Territory br. 1987-93); mem. Ecol. Soc. Am., Soc. Human Ecology, Soc. Econ. Botany. Avocations: music, theater, art, literature. Deceased.

WILCK, CARL THOMAS, public relations executive; b. Quantico, Va., May 26, 1933; s. Carl and Glennie Alma (Jones) W.; m. Tommie England, June 16, 1961 (dec. Sept. 1985); m. Nadine Bagley Henry, May 21, 1989; 1 child, Jacqueline Leigh Henry. AA, Santa Monica Coll., 1955; BA in Polit. Sci., UCLA, 1957. Pres. Thomas Wilck Assocs., LA, 1960-70, chmn., pres.; asst. adminstr. SBA, Washington, 1971; dep. chmn. Rep. Nat. Com., Washington, 1972-73; v.p. pub. affairs Irvine Co., Newport Beach, Calif., 1973-85; pres. Thomas Wilck Assocs., Orange County, 1985-95; ptnr. Nelson Comm. Group, Irvine, Calif., from 1995. Bd. chmn. Coro Found., L.A., 1982-83. Sgt. USMC, 1950-52, PTO. Mem. Fellow Pub. Rels. Soc. Am. (Silver Anvil award 1964, 77); mem. CORO Found. (bd. dirs.), Orange County C. of C., Chmn., 1993. Republican. Presbyterian. Avocations: tennis, writing. Home: Irvine, Calif. Died July 24, 2008.

WILD, JOHN JULIAN, surgeon, researcher, medical educator; b. Sydenham, Kent, Eng., Aug. 11, 1914; came to U.S., 1946; s. Ovid Frederick and Ellen Louise (Cuttance) W.; m. Nancy Wallace, Nov. 14, 1949 (div. 1966); children: John O., Douglas J.; m. Valerie Claudia Grosenick, Aug. 9, 1968; 1 child, Ellen Louise. BA, U. Cambridge, Eng., 1936, MA, 1940, MD, 1942, PhD, 1971. Intern, resident U. Coll. Hosp., London, 1938-42; intern U. College Hosp., London, 1938-42; staff surgeon Miller Gen., St. Charles and North Middlesex Hosps., London, 1942-44; venereologist Royal Army Med. Corps, 1944-45; rsch. fellow, instr. depts. surgery and elec. engring., prin. investigator U. Minn., Mpls., 1946-51; dir. rsch. Medico.-Technol. Rsch. Dept. St. Barnabas Hosp., Mpls., 1953-60; dir. Medico-Technol. Rsch. Unit Minn. Found., St. Paul, 1960-63; pvt. practice Mpls., 1966—90; dir. Medico-Technol. Rsch. Inst. Mpls., St. Louis Park, Minn., 1965—2006. Lectr. in field of medical instruments, ultrasound. Contbr. articles to profl. jours. Recipient Japan prize in Medical Imaging, Sci. and Tech. Found. Japan, 1991, 1st Frank Annunzio award Christopher Columbus Fellowship Found., 1998, lifetime achievement award U. Minn. Med. Sch., 2000, Ian Donald Tech. Achievement aard ISUOG, 2000. Fellow Am. Inst. Ultrasound in Medicine (Pioneer award 1978); mem. AMA, World Fedn. Ultrasound in Medicine and Biology, Minn. State Med. Assn., Hennepin County Med. Soc., N.Am. Alvis Owners Club; hon. mem. Brit. Inst. Radiology, Japan Soc. of Ultrasound in Medicine. Achievements include patents in field; origination of ultrasonic medical imaging instruments and diagnostic techniques; origination of the field of pulse-echo ultrasonic diagnostic medicine. Died Sept. 18, 2009.

WILK, WANDA HELEN, pianist, musicologist; b. Detroit, Jan. 13, 1921; d. Michael and Lottie (Wedrychowicz) Harasimowicz; m. Stefan P. Wilk, Sept. 4, 1952; 1 child, Diane Wilk-Shirvani. MusM in Mus. Edn., U. So. Calif., 1976. Dir. Polish Music Reference Ctr. U. So. Calif., LA, 1985—96. Music dir. Polish-Am. Cultural Exhibit, L.A., 1979-80. Editor: Polish Music History Series. Founder, pres. Friends of Polish Music, U. So. Calif. Recipient medal Polish Composers Union, 1988, cert. of appreciation Mayor of L.A., 1980, Perspectives award, Washington, 1983, Polonia award, L.A., 1988. Mem. Internat. Com. L.A. Philharm. Assn., Mu Phi Epsilon. Avocations: golf, bridge, lectr. Home: Studio City, Calif. Died Feb. 18, 2009.

WILKERSON, JAMES EDWARD, physician, consultant; b. Kingsville, Tex., Oct. 2, 1945; s. Wiley Edward and Martha Lenora (Vick) W.; m. Doris Faye Wittenburg, 1966 (div. 1985); 1 child, Michelle Kathryn Wilkerson Miller; m. Eileen Marie Leeds, May 18, 1985. BS, Rice U., 1967, MA, 1968, MS, 1969; PhD, U. Oreg., 1970; MD, U. Miami, 1987. Diplomate Nat. Bd. Med. Examiners. Asst. rsch. physiologist Inst. Environ. Stress, U. Calif., Santa Barbara, 1970-75; instr. environ. physiology U. Calif. Ext., Santa Barbara, 1974-75; asst. prof. phys. edn. Sch. Health, Phys. Edn. and Recreation, Ind. U., Bloomington, 1975-79, assoc. prof., 1979-85; specialist systems analysis and computer programming OAO Corp./USAF Sch. Aerospace Medicine, Brooks AFB, Tex., 1984-85; resident in internal medicine U. Miami (Fla.)/Jacksom Meml. Hosp., 1987-90, cardiology fellow, 1990-93; admitting physician emergency rm. VA Med. Ctr., Miami, 1989-93, Palm Beach Gardens (Fla.) Hosp., 1990-91. Invasive cardiologist Valley Diagnostic Clinic, Harlingen, Tex., 1993—; founder, co-owner Scuba Rsch. Inst., 1984; founder, pres. AmeriFit Corp., 1984; v.p. Rsch. Hydrotonics Therapy Corp., Inc., Miami, 1986; cons. phys. fitness testing and devel. USAF, 1982-83, Sports Medicine Clinic, Children's Hosp. Balt., 1983; mem. faculty human factors engring. USN Safety Engring. Sch., Bloomington, 1976-83; adj. asst. prof. dept. physiology Ind. U. Sch. Medicine, 1976-79; vis. prof. Helwan U. Coll. Phys. Edn. and Sch. of Medicine, Cairo, 1978. Contbr. numerous articles to profl. jours. Asst. vol. coach Bloomington High Sch. South, 1979-80, 81-82; chmn. sci. subcom. U.S. Olympic Track and Field Devel. Com., 1979-80; rep. delegation Amateur Athletic Union Nat. Conv., Las Vegas, Nev., 1979, First Athletics Congress Nat. Conv., Las Vegas, 1979; corr. sec., pres. Isla Vista (Calif.) Homeowners Assn., 1973-74; bd. dirs. Bloomington YMCa, 1975-78. NDEA fellow U. Oreg., 1967-70, Santa Barbara Heart Assn. fellow U. Calif., 1971-72; NIH grantee, 1970-71; world record holder 4x110m hurdle relay, 1985, Pa. Relays. Fellow Am. Coll. Sports Medicine; mem. AMA, AAAS, ACP (assoc.), AAHPERD, Aerospace Med. Assn., Am. Physiol. Soc., N.Y. Acad. Scis., Am. Coll. Cardiology, Ind. Track Club (bd. dirs. Bloomington chpt. 1976-80), Sigma Xi. Democrat. Methodist. Avocations: civil war history, travel, cryptology. Died Aug. 25, 2008.

WILKES, JOHN SOLOMON, III, land commissioner; b. Birmingham, Ala., Sept. 13, 1937; s. John Solomon Jr. and Lola Louise (Day) W. BS, U.S. Mil. Acad., 1960; M in Engring., Tex. A & M U., 1966. Commd. officer U.S. Army, 1960, advanced through grades to lt. col.; dep. dist. engr. St. Louis (Mo.) Dist. Corps of Engrs., 1977-80; ret. U.S. Army, 1980; mgr. Arch Mineral Corp., St. Louis, 1980-82; campaign staff Gov. Richard D. Lamm, Colo., 1982-83; facility engr., engring. mgr. FELEC Svcs., Inc., Clear, Alaska, 1983-85; mem. State Bd. Land Commrs., Denver, from 1985. Coun. mem. Colo. Natural Areas, Denver, 1985—; pres. Western States Land Commrs. Assn., Colo., 1989-90; com. mem. Colo. Geog. Names, Denver, 1993—. Precinct chair Rep. Party, Denver, 1985-90. Decorated Legion of Merit, Bronze Star medal with two oak leafs, Meritorious Svc. medal, Joint Svcs. Commendatin medal, Army Commendation medal. Mem. West Point Soc. Denver, Army Athletic Assn., Denver Coal Club, Soc. Am. Mil. Engrs., Assn. U.S. Army, West Point Alumni Assn., Engrs. Club St. Louis, U.S. Com. on Large Dams. Republican. Episcopalian. Avocation: golf. Home: Denver, Colo. Died Feb. 26, 2008.

WILKES, LOWELL LYNDON, JR., electronics executive, consultant; b. San Antonio, Mar. 21, 1919; s. Lowell Lyndon and Elinor Helen (Goldbeck) W.; m. Rosemary Jarvis; children: Lowell Lyndon III, Ray Jarvis, William Thomas, Barbara Anne. BA, U. Tex., 1941; BS, U.S. Mil. Acad., West Point, NY, 1943; MBA, Harvard U., 1951. Commd. 2d lt. U.S. Army, 1943, advanced through grades to lt. col., 1952; advanced through grades to col. USAR, 1966; ret. U.S. Army, 1979; treas., v.p. Cambridge (Mass.) Thermionic Corp., 1958-82; v.p., ops. mgr. Electronic Connector div. Midland-Ross Corp., Cambridge, 1982-85; cons. Stancil Blacklans Assocs., Amherst, N.H., from 1986. Mem. Colby Coll. Parents com., Waterville, Maine, 1981-85. Baker scholar Harvard U., 1951. Mem. Phi Beta Kappa. Republican. Avocation: stamp collecting/philately. Home: Amherst, NH. Died Nov. 7, 2007.

WILKINSON, RACHEL D., academic administrator, retired; b. Winston-Salem, NC, Mar. 30, 1913; d. James Thackeray and Mabel (Kennedy) Diggs; m. William Henry Heberton Wilkinson Sr., June 10, 1950 (dec.). BS, Winston-Salem State U., 1933; MA, Columbia U., 1937; postgrad., Radcliffe Coll., 1946; PhD, N.Y. U., 1952. Tchr. pub. schs., Winston-Salem, 1933-40; alumni exec. sec., dean of women Winston-Salem State U., 1940-53; instr. CUNY, 1953-59; asst. prof. Yeshiva U., NYC, 1959-62; assoc. prof., coord. coll. discovery, dir. fin. aid Bronx Community Coll., CUNY, 1962-66; assoc. prof., dir. student counseling ctr. CUNY, 1966-68, full prof., dir. community rels. seek program, 1968-70, coord. evaluation and rsch., 1970-72. Newspaper reporter Winston-Salem Jour. and Sentinel, 1939-49; guest prof. grad. sch. Fla. A&M U., 1954; lectr. Brooklyn Coll., 1955; supr. student tchrs. Mills Coll. Edn., 1958-59; vis. prof. grad. sch. edn. NYU, 1962, Yeshiva U., 1963. Editor: (magazine) National Alumni Association, 1945-55; contbr. articles to profl. jours. V.p. Soroptimist, Bronx, N.Y., 1966-68; mem. Common Cause, Washington, 1979-82, NAACP, Balt., 1950—, Planned Parenthood, Washington, 1980—; bd. mgrs. High Point I Condominium, Hartsdale, N.Y., 1989-92. Recipient scholarship Bennett Coll., 1929, Citation of Achievement Wilson Coll., 1969, Disting. Alumnus award Winston-Salem State U., 1985; fellow Radcliffe Coll., 1945-46, Nat. Coun. Episcopal Ch., 1946. Mem. AAUP, AAUW (grantee N.Y.C. br. 1969), Am. Assn. for Counseling and Devel., Virginia Gildersleeve Internat. Fund for Univ. Women. Democrat. Episcopalian. Avocations: travel, theater, gardening, reading, bridge. Home: Winston Salem, NC. Died Feb. 9, 2008.

WILLIAMS, CECELIA PEAY, retired psychologist; b. Boston, Sept. 29, 1924; d. Moses and Rosa Ophelia Peay; 1 child, Rosa. Grad., Boston Clerical Sch., 1944; BA, Calif. State U., LA, 1966, MS, 1970. Legal secretary private practice Attorney's Office, Boston, Ma, 1944—45; sec. Washington D.C. Vet's Adminstrn., John Hay Whitney Found., NYC, Crippled Children's Soc., LA; adminstrv. sec. Galton Inst., LA, 1965—68; bus. tchr. L.A. Unified Sch. Dist., 1969—72, sch. psychologist, 1973—98, adminstrv. cons., from 2000. Oral commr. Bd. Behavioral Sci. Mem. Baldwin Hills Neighborhood Assn., LA, from 1988. Mem.: L.A. Assn. Sch. Psychologists (pres. 1980—81), Delta Kappa Gamma Beta Xi (pres. 1993—94), Chi State Delta Kappa Gamma. Home: Los Angeles, Calif. Died June 18, 2008.

WILLIAMS, DELORES JEAN, critical care nurse; b. Smithville, Tex., Mar. 5, 1941; d. James Leon and Doris Evelyn (Wilkes) Clark; children: Christopher Joe, Valerie Ann. Cert. in practical nursing, Kiamichi Vo-Tech., Idabel, Okla., 1980; ADN, Carl Albert Jr. Coll., Poteau, Okla., 1986. Cert. ACLS. Asst. dir. nursing Meml. Heights Nursing Home, Idabel, 1981-84; staff practical nurse McCurtain Meml. Hosp., Idabel, 1980-86, charge nurse, 1986-91; critical care nurse Bapt. Med. Ctr., Oklahoma City, from 1991. Home: Yukon, Okla. Died Aug. 15, 2007.

WILLIAMS, EARL DUANE, accounting executive; b. Hiwasse, Ark., Mar. 2, 1929; s. James Martin and Goldie Faye (Reeves) W.; m. Dorothy Jean Rasner, May 3, 1952; children: Earl Duane, Ronald Lee. BS, San Jose State U.; LLB, U. Chgo.; MBA, PhD, U. Calif. Acctg. mgr. Philco Ford, Palo Alto, Calif., 1966-69; instr. acctg. Foothill and Deanza Coll., Cupertino, Calif., 1967-69; contr., treas. Bekins Maintenance, LA, 1969-70; chief acct. Title Ins. & Trust Co., LA, 1970-72; contr. Continental Devel. Co., El Segundo, Calif., 1972-76; v.p. fin. Computer Infomatrix, Inc., LA, from 1976; pres. Nationwide Acctg. Svc., West Hills, Calif., from 1977. Instr. acctg. Calif. Credential CPA's. Chmn. Liaison League Rehab. Group, 1973—; co-chmn. Re-election Sen. Ed Davis; mem. com. re-election of L.A. County Sheriff com. to elect Senator Pete Wilson to Gov. of Calif.; mem., bd. dirs. West Hills Property Owners Assn.; mem. L.A. Philanthropic Found. With USAF, 1951-55. Recipient Cert. of Appreciation, Vikings of Scandia, 1975, 76, 77, 78, 88, Boy Scouts Am., 1967; named to Hon. Order of Ky. Cols. Mem. VFW, Nat. Assn. Accts., Contrs. Assn., Internat. Footprint Assn., Internat. Chili Soc., Nat. Soc. Pub. Accts., Calif. Assn. Ind. Accts., Nat. Soc. Tax Profls., Nat. Tax Certification Bd., Navy League (life), Gold Pennant Gourmet (pres.), Woodland Hills C. of C., West Hills C. of C., Canoga Park C. of C., Masons (32d degree), Elks, Friars, L.A. Club, Hollywood Press Club, Greater L.A. Press Club, Vikings of Scandia Club (chief 1984), Silver Dollar Club, Masquers Club, Town Hall Club, Kentucky Colonel, Shriners, Am. Legion. Republican. Home: West Hills, Calif. Died Sept. 1, 2007.

WILLIAMS, GALE R., realtor; b. Ava, Ill., Aug. 3, 1922; s. Denton Hubert and Bertha Mae (Lively) W.; m. Helen R. Falkenheim, Dec. 9, 1947. Student, So. Ill. U., John Logan Jr. Coll. Elected Jackson County Coroner, Springfield, Ill.,

1956-60; state rep. State of Ill, Springfield, 1960-70; mobile home sales Springfield, from 1960. With USMC, 1945-46. Mem. Elks, Am. Legion, Masons, Mississippi Valley Consistory, Murphysboro C. of C. Republican. Baptist. Home: Murphysboro, Ill. Died Nov. 3, 2007.

WILLIAMS, J.(JOHN) RODMAN, theologian, educator, clergyman; b. Clyde, NC, Aug. 21, 1918; s. John Rodman and Odessa Lee (Medford) W.; m. Johanna SerVaas, Aug. 6, 1949; children: John, Lucinda Lee, David Bert. AB, Davidson Coll., 1939; BD, Union Theol. Sem., 1943, ThM, 1944; PhD, Columbia U., 1954. Ordained to ministry Presbyn. Ch., 1943. Chaplain USNR, 1944—46; chaplain, assoc. prof. philosophy Beloit Coll., 1949—52; pastor First Presbyn. Ch., Rockford, Ill., 1952—59; prof. systematic theology and philosophy of religion Austin Presbyn. Theol. Sem., 1959—72; prof. Christian doctrine, pres. Melodyland Sch. Theology, Anaheim, Calif., 1972—82; prof. systematic theology Regent U., Virginia Beach, Va., from 1982. Author: Contemporary Existentialism and Christian Faith, 1965, The Era of the Spirit, 1971, The Pentecostal Reality, 1972, Ten Teachings, 1974, The Gift of the Holy Spirit Today, 1980, Renewal Theology, Vol. 1, God, the World, and Redemption, Vol. 2, 1988, Salvation, the Holy Spirit and Christian Living, Vol. 3, 1990, The Church, the Kingdom, and Last Things, 1992, Renewal Theology, 3 vols. in one, 1996. Home: Virginia Beach, Va. Died Oct. 18, 2008.

WILLIAMS, JUNE M., nursing educator; b. Telfair County, Ga., Oct. 17, 1935; d. Thomas Leonard and Myrtle (Batchelor) Marchant; m. Gene Maurice Williams, June 18, 1954; children: Vicki W. Morgan, Cindy Greene, Gina L. Diploma in nursing with honors, Macon Hosp. Sch. Nursing, 1956; BSN, Med. Coll. Ga., 1976; MEd with honors, Ga. Southern U., 1984. RN, Ga.; cert. tchr., Ga. Practical nursing instr. Ben-Hill Irwin Tech. Inst., Fitzgerald, Ga.; DON Dodge County Hosp., Eastman, Ga.; health occupations instr. Dodge County Bd. of Edn., Eastman, Ga.; practical nursing instr. Heart of Ga. Tech. Inst., Dublin, Ga. Instr. CPR, ARC. Mem. Am. Vocational Assn. (Ga. chpt.), Trade and Industrial Educators, Health Occupations Educators. Home: Milan, Ga. Died June 10, 2008.

WILLIAMS, KENNETH A., food service executive; b. Coeur d'Alene, Idaho, July 16, 1936; s. Lyle Ernest Williams and Helen Violet DesChamp; (div.); children: Ronda, Kelly, Lisa, Scott. BA, Wash. State U., 1960. Asst. v.p., supr. Szabo Food Svc., Seattle, 1960-69; pres. Food Mgmt. Control, Seattle, 1969-95; CEO, chmn. Food Mgmt. Corp., Seattle, from 1995. Home: Seattle, Wash. Died Sept. 13, 2007.

WILLIAMS, MARY HELEN, elementary school educator; b. Lebanon, Tenn., Nov. 15, 1932; d. Magellan and Willie Neal (Douglass) White; m. Robert Lee Williams, May 16, 1954; children: Desireé Starr Williams Ehimen, Angela Deanetta. BA, Tenn. State U., 1954, MA, 1972, postgrad., 1973-75; grad., Inst. of Children's Lit., 1998. Tchr. Shelby County Sch., Memphis, 1954-55, Nashville Christian Inst., 1958-63, Metro Nashville Schs., 1964-93. Freelance writer, poet. Author: Spellbound, 2002, Spellbound Two, 2005. Recipient Editors Choice award Nat. Libr. Poetry, 1998, Five Yr. Pencil Ptnr. award 1999. Mem. NEA, Tenn. Edn. Assn., Metro Nashville Edn. Assn., Internat. Soc. Poets, Soc. Children's Book Writers, Theta Alpha Psi, Alpha Delta Omega chpt. of Alpha Kappa Alpha (leadership award, Name that Soror award), Phi Delta Kappa (family of educators award 1989, career ladder three assn. Tchr of Yr. award, 1987, Achievement award, Soror of Yr. award 2003), Tenn. State Alumni Assn. Democrat. Mem. Ch. of Christ. Avocations: reading, acting, dance, writing, storytelling. Home: Nashville, Tenn. Died Feb. 22, 2008.

WILLIAMS, RALPH WATSON, JR., retired security firm executive; b. Atlanta, July 2, 1933; s. Ralph Watson and Minnie Covington (Hicks) W.; m. Nancy Jo Morgan, Mar. 19, 1955 (dec. Dec. 1989); children: Ralph Watson III, Nancy Jane, John Martin Hicks; m. Almonese Brown Clifton, Nov. 24, 1990. Grad., Sewanee Mil. Acad., 1951; BBA, U. Ga., 1955. Trainee banking Trust Co. Ga., Atlanta, 1955; mcpl. sales staff Courts & Co., Atlanta, 1955-57; v.p., salesman securities First Southeastern Corp., Atlanta, 1957-60; br. mgr. Francis I. duPont & Co., 1960-69; spl. partner duPont Glore Forgan Inc., NYC, 1969-70, gen. partner, 1970, exec. v.p., from 1971, sr. v.p., bd. dirs., mem. exec. com., from 1972; sr. v.p., dir., mem. exec. com. duPont-Walston Inc., 1973-74; sr. v.p. E.F. Hutton & Co. Inc., 1974-81; exec. v.p., dir. E.F. Hutton & Co., Inc., 1981-88; exec. v.p. Shearson Lehman Hutton Inc., Atlanta, 1988-89; ret., 1989. Former bd. trustees, chmn. fin. com. St. Andrews Sewanee (Tenn.) Sch.; former exec. com. mem. U. Ga., Ga. Tech. Found. Mem. Nat. Assn. Security Dealers (chmn. dist. com. 7), Benedicts Atlanta, Phi Delta Theta. Clubs: Commerce (Atlanta), Capital City (Atlanta), Piedmont Driving (Atlanta). Presbyterian. Home: Atlanta, Ga. Died 0000.

WILLIAMS, ROBERT LEON, retired psychiatrist, neurologist, educator; b. Buffalo, July 22, 1922; s. Leon R. and L. Paulyne (Ingraham) W.; m. Shirley Glynn Miller, Feb. 5, 1949; Karen, Kevin BA, Alfred U., 1944; MD, Albany Med. Coll., Union U., 1946. Chief neurology and psychiatry Lackland AFB Hosp., USAF, San Antonio, 1952-55; cons. neurology and psychiatry to USAF Surgeon Gen., 1955-58; faculty Coll. Medicine, U. Fla., Gainesville, 1958-72, prof., chmn. dept. psychiatry, 1964-72; prof. psychiatry Baylor Coll. Medicine, Houston, 1972-92, chmn. dept., 1972-90, prof. neurology, 1976-92, acting chmn. dept., 1976-77, prof. emeritus psychiatry and neurology, from 1992; ret. Mem. faculty various univs., part time 1949-58 including Albany Med. Coll. at Union U., Columbia Coll. Physisicans and Surgeons, Boston U., U. Tex., Georgetown U. Author: (with W.B. Webb) Sleep Therapy: A. Bibliography and Commentary, 1966, (with others) EEG of Human Sleep: Clinical Applications, 1974; editor: (with Ismet Karacan and Carolyn J. Hursch) Psychopharmacology of Sleep, 1976, Sleep Disorders: Diagnosis and Treatment, 1978, 2d edit., 1988; (with others) Phenomenology and Treatment of Anxiety, 1979, of Alcoholism, 1980, of Psychophysiological Disorders, 1982, of Psychosexual Disorders, 1983, of Psychiatric Emergencies, 1984 Served from 1st lt. to lt. col. USAF, 1949-58; col. Res., ret. Recipient Cert. Profl. Achievement USAF Surgeon Gen., 1967 Mem. Am. Psychiat. Assn., Am. Electroencephalographic Soc., Am. Coll. Psychiatrists (pres. 1982-83), Am. Acad. Neurology, AMA, Group for Advancement of Psychiatry, Benjamin Rush Soc. (pres. 1986-88), Accreditation Coun. for grad. Med. Edn. (residency rev. com. for psychiatry 1985-93), Alpha Omega Alpha. Achievements include research in basic psychophysiology of human sleep. Died Nov. 16, 2008.

WILLIAMS, SAM BARLOW, engineering executive; b. Seattle, May 7, 1921; BS in Mechanical Engring., Purdue U., 1947. Chmn., CEO Williams Internat. Corp., 1954—2009. Recipient Collier trophy, 1979, Wright Bros. Meml. trophy, 1988, Nat. Medal of Technology, 1995; named to Nat. Aviation Hall of Fame, 1998. Mem.: NAE. Died June 22, 2009.

WILLIAMS, THOMAS MARK, sales executive; b. Duluth, Minn., Apr. 17, 1940; s. Warren Milton and Frances Josephine (Knaus) W.; m. Emily Lois Bissonett, July 17, 1961 (dec. 1970); children: Thomas Mark Jr., Robin Lynn, Robert Warren (dec. June 1987), Alexander, Christopher; m. Constance Merle Raggio, Sept. 29, 1979; 1 child, Marc james. Student, U. Minn., 1958-59. Player U.S. Olympic Ice Hockey Team, Squaw Valley, Calif., 1960, Nat. Hockey League, Boston, 1961-69, Mpls., 1969-71, Oakland, Calif., 1971-72, World Hockey Assn., Boston, 1972-74, Nat. Hockey League, Landover, Md., 1974-76; dist. sales mgr. Robintech Inc., Vestal, N.Y., 1977-78; territory mgr. Certainteed Corp., Valley Forge, Pa., 1978-86; regional sales mgr. Nat. Pipe Co., Vestal, from 1986. Pres. Tommy Williams Realty Trust, 1987—; conf. mem. Pres.'s Council: Fitness and Sports, Washington, 1970-76. Chmn., treas. Clear Water Action Com., Boston, 1982—. Recipient Gold Medal Ice Hockey, Olympic Fedn., Squaw Valley, 1960; inducted U.S. Hockey Hall of Fame, Eveleth, Minn., 1981, U.S. Olympic Hall of Fame, 1989. Mem. Am. Arbitration Assn. (panelist 1982—). Lodges: Elks. Roman Catholic. Avocations: golf, fishing, music. Died July 28, 2008.

WILLIAMS, WILLIAM JOSEPH, retired insurance company executive; b. Cin., Dec. 19, 1915; s. Charles Finn and Elizabeth (Ryan) W.; m. Helen DeCourcy, May 26, 1941; children: Mary Frances Williams Clauder, William Joseph, Richard Francis, Carol Ann Williams Jodar, Sharon Mary Williams Frisbie, Thomas Luke AB, Georgetown U., 1937; postgrad. in bus., Harvard U., 1938. With Western-So. Life Ins. Co., Cin., 1939-54, chmn. bd., 1979-84, pres., COO, 1984-88, pres., CEO, 1988-89, chmn., pres., CEO, 1989; pres. N.Am. Mgmt. & Devel. Co., Cin., 1954-84; chmn. Cin. Reds Baseball Club, 1966-85. Dir. Cin. Bengals, Columbus Life Ins., Ohio. Chmn. bd. Good Samaritan Hosp., Cin., 1984-86, Taft Mus., Cin., 1984-87; trustee, v.p. Cin. Art Mus.; trustee Cin. Inst. Fine Arts; bd. dirs. Georgetown U. Served to capt. U.S. Army, 1941-45 Decorated knight Order Knights of Malta, knight comdr. Holy Sepulchre; honored by NCCJ, 1979 Mem.: Queen City (pres. 1982-84), Commercial (pres. 1983), Cin. Country (Cin.); Camargo; Royal Poinciana Golf (Naples, Fla.). Roman Catholic. Home: Cincinnati, Ohio. Died Aug. 23, 2009.

WILLIAMSON, NEIL SEYMOUR, III, aircraft company executive, retired Army officer; b. Dumont, NJ, Jan. 5, 1935; s. Neil Seymour and Mary Louise (Bittenbender) W.; m. Sue Carrole Cooper, Dec. 15, 1985; children: Deborah D., Leisa L., Neil S. IV, Dirk A., Wendy L. BS, U.S. Mil. Acad., 1958; MSME, U. Mich., 1963. Commd. 2d lt. U.S. Army, 1958, advanced through grades to col., 1976; assoc. prof. dept. earth, space and graphic scis. U.S. Mil. Acad., West Point, N.Y., 1965-68; chief edn. sect. U.S. Army, Ft. McNair, D.C., 1970-71, analyst armor infantry systems group Pentagon Washington, 1972-73, systems analyst requirements office Pentagon, 1974-75, program analyst, 1975-76, chief advanced systems concept office Redstone Arsenal, Ala., 1976-77, comdr., dir. fire control & small caliber weapon systems lab. Dover, N.J., 1977-78; project mgr. Tube-Launched, Optically-Tracked, Wire-Command-Link, US Army, Redstone Arsenal, 1978-81; ret. U.S. Army, 1981; program mgr. Hughes Aircraft Co., El Segundo, Calif., from 1981. Decorated Bronze Star with bronze oak leaf cluster, Legion of Merit with bronze oak leaf cluster, Air medal with silver oak leaf cluster and two bronze oak leaf clusters, Purple Heart. Mem. DAV, Soc. Automotive Engrs., Am. Def. Preparedness Assn., Army Aviation Assn. (pres. Tenn. Valley chpt. 1980), Am. Helicopter Soc., U.S. Armor Assn. Home: Santa Barbara, Calif. Died Sept. 17, 2007.

WILLIAMSON, WILLIAM OWEN, geological and chemical educator, consultant; b. Luton County, Eng., Jan. 30, 1911; came to U.S., 1959; s. Owen and Susan Winifred (Pollock) W.; m. Olive Zoe Tucker, Aug. 5, 1958. BSc in Chemistry with honors, London U., 1931, BS in Geology with honors, 1932, PhD in Geology, 1934, DSc in Geology and Chemistry, 1958. Chief asst. in ceramics North Staffordshire Tech. Coll., Stoke-on-Trent, Eng., 1934-42; rsch. officer Ministry of Supply, Birmingham, Eng., 1942-45; profl. officer Govt. Metall. Lab., Johannesburg, South Africa, 1945-47; prin. rsch. officer Commonwealth Sci. and Indsl. Rsch. Orgn., Melbourne, Australia, 1947-59; prof. Pa. State U., University Park, 1959-76, emeritus prof., from 1976. Contbr. chpts. to books, numerous articles to profl. jours. Fellow Royal Chem. Soc., Am. Ceramic Soc.; mem. Mineral. Soc. (U.K.), Geologists Assn. (U.K.), Archaeol. Inst. Am. Avocations: egyptian, roman and greek culture and languages. Home: State College, Pa. Died Jan. 3, 2008.

WILLIS, SHIRLEY ANN, retired secondary school educator; b. Findlay, Ohio, July 20, 1938; d. Mark H. and Annabelle D. (Cunningham) Donaldson; m. Gilbert Wayne Willis, July 20, 1963. BE, Bowling Green State U., Ohio, 1961; MA, Xavier U., 1977. Tchr. Middletown City Schs., Ohio, 1961-90. Active Ohio Educators Polit. Action Com., Columbus, 1977-79; precinct chair Dem. Cen. Com., Trenton, Ohio, 1986; chair Educators Polit. Action Com., Middletown, 1962-90; candidate Ohio Ho. of Reps. Mem. NEA (steering com. women's caucus Washington 1987), Middletown Bus. and Profl. Women (pres. 1983-84, 92-94), AAUW (treas. Ohio chpt. 1989-91, program v.p. 1992-93), White Shrine of Jerusalem (worthy high priestess 1983), Middletown Tchrs. Assn. (pres. 1986-89), Ohio Edn. Assn. (bd. dirs. Columbus 1975-79). Methodist. Avocations: reading, golf. Home: Middletown, Ohio. Died July 2, 2008.

WILLS, CHARLES FRANCIS, retired religious organization administrator; b. Avalon, NJ, July 26, 1914; s. Charles H. and Anna Margaret (Diemand) W.; m. Charlotte Emily Robson, Aug. 22, 1936; children: C. Frederic, Emily, Sally and Larry (twins). BS, Wheaton Coll., Ill., 1935; B.D., Eastern Bapt. Theol. Sem., 1938, Th.M., 1941; grad., Air War Coll., 1961. Commd. 1st lt. U.S. Army, 1941; advanced through grades to col. U.S. Air Force, 1963; chaplain AUS, 1941-49, U.S. Air Force, 1949-67; ret., 1967; exec. dir. chaplaincy services Am. Bapt. Chs., Valley Forge, Pa., 1969-75, exec. dir. profl. services, 1975-78; assoc. sec. Bapt. World Alliance, Washington, 1978-80, treas., 1980-81. Mem. Commn. on Doctrine and Interchurch Cooperation, 1980-90. Decorated Legion of Merit, Bronze Star, Purple Heart. Mem. Mil. Chaplains Assn., Mil. Order of Purple Heart. Home: Shelton, Wash. Died Oct. 26, 2006.

WILOCH, THOMAS, poet, editor; b. Detroit, Feb. 3, 1953; s. Joseph and Jane W.; m. Denise Gottis, Oct. 10, 1981. BA, Wayne State U., Detroit, 1978. Rsch. asst. Wayne State U., Detroit, 1976; editl. asst. The Gale Group, Farmington Hills, Mich., 1977-78, asst. editor, 1978-81, sr. asst. editor, 1981-85, sr. writer, 1985-89, assoc. editor, 1989—2004; freelance writer, from 2004. Prose poem collections include: Stigmata Junction, 1985, 2d edit., 2005, Paper Mask, 1988, The Mannikin Cypher, 1989, Tales of Lord Shantih, 1989, Mr. Templeton's Toyshop, 1995, Screaming in Code, 2006; cut-up haiku: Night Rain, 1991, Decoded Factories of the Heart, 1991, Narcotic Signature, 1992, Lyrical Brandy, 1993, Neon Trance, 1997; editor (with Leonard Kniffel): Directory of Michigan Literary Publishers, 1982, Contemporary Authors, New Revisions Series (asst. editor) Vols. 1-5, 1982—85, (sr. asst. editor) Vols. 6-15, 1982—85, (sr. writer) Vols. 16-27, 1986—89, (assoc. editor) Vols. 28-117, 1989—2003; editor Grimoire mag., 1982—85; author: Crime: A Serious American Problem, 2004, National Security, 2004, Prisons & Jails, 2005; contbr. to over 200 periodicals, including Pub.'s Weekly, Bloomsbury Rev., Fiction Rev., Small Press Rev., Factsheet 5, Kayak, Asylum, Wormwood Rev., others. Mem.: Nat. Assn. for Self Employed, Assn. Literary Scholars and Critics. Home: Canton, Mich. Died Sept. 2008.

WILSON, ARMIN, retired chemist; b. Sapulpa, Okla., Dec. 13, 1916; s. Joseph Bartholomew and Amelia (Heller) W.; m. Evelyn Hodes, June 8, 1943; children: Jonathan, Robert. BA, Rice U., 1939, MA, 1941; AM, PhD, Harvard U., 1945. Sr. chemist Merck Labs., Rahway, N.J., 1945-53; dept. head Bristol Myers, Hillside, N.J., 1953-68; prof. Rutgers U., New Brunswick, N.J., 1968-78. Contbr. articles to profl. jours. Fellow N.Y. Acad. Scis.; mem. Phi Beta Kappa, Sigma Xi. Avocation: poetry. Home: Kennett Square, Pa. Died May 7, 2008.

WILSON, DONNA ELIZABETH, music educator; b. Springfield, Ohio, Oct. 30, 1917; d. Howard Earl Sise and Gertrude Wright (Gordon) Sise McCallister; m. William Richard Wilson, June 7, 1944 (dec. 1964); children: Judith Wilson Hubbard, Gordon Richard (dec.), Rodger Mark (dec.) Cert. in tchr. tng., Wittenberg Coll., 1937; BS in Edn., West Tex. State U., 1957, MEd, 1967. Elem. tchr. Springfield (Ohio) Pub. Schs., 1937-41; elem. tchr. music Norman (Okla.) Pub. Schs., 1956-58, Canyon (Tex.) Ind. Schs., 1958-82; tchr. Payap U., Chiang Mai, Thailand, 1982-86; ret., 1986. Choir dir. Presbyn. Ch., Canyon, 1949-77, ordained elder, 1980-82, mem. mission interpretation task group, Lubbock, Tex., 1989-91, mission itineration coord., 1989-91 Recipient Tex. Panhandle Disting. Women's Svc. award Women's Forum, 1987. Mem. AAUW (leadership growth team), Tex. Music Educators Assn. (chmn. state elem. div. 1977-79). Died Nov. 9, 2007.

WILSON, ESTHER ELINORE, technical college educator; b. Uehling, Nebr., Nov. 4, 1921; d. Lorenz John and Dorothea Emma Rosena (Schmidt) Paulsen; m. Billy LeRoy

Wilson, Nov. 14, 1919; 1 child, Frances Ann Wilson Dellar. BS, Morningside Coll., 1950; postgrad., U. Nebr., 1947-80, U. S.D., 1954-83; MS, U. Minn., 1963. Cert. postsecondary tchr., Iowa. Tchr. Irvington (Nebr.) Pub. Schs., 1942-44, Immanuel Luth. Schs., Wichita, Kans., 1944-45, Winnebago (Nebr.) Pub. Schs., 1946-50, Nat. Bus. Coll., Sioux City, Iowa, 1950-51; tchr., asst. prin. Liberty Consol. Sch., Merrill, Iowa, 1951-55; mktg. tchr. coord. South Sioux City (Nebr.) Community Schs., 1955-86; adj. faculty prof. adult basic edn. Western Iowa Tech. Coll., Sioux City, 1989-94; mgr. rental properties Sioux City, 1950-2000. Real estate assoc. State Nat., Dakota City, Nebr., 1988-92, Century 21 Marketplace, Sioux City, 1987-88; advt. sales mgr. Auto Hotline, South Sioux City, 1986-87. Author: I Said I Would, 1995; contbg. author: Siouxland Anthology, 1995, Capturing Our Heritage, 1996, The Lutheran Message, 1999. Vol. tchr. N.E. Nebr. C.C., South Sioux City, 1987-90; supt. St. Paul's Luth. Sunday Sch., Sioux City, 1972-76; treas. Hope Luth. Ch., 1989-95, historian 1995-97, nursing home lamplighter 1987-92, 1995-2000; co-pres. Friends of Libr., South Sioux City, 1986-88; fundraiser South Sioux City Pub. Libr., 1984-85; pres. Am. Cancer Soc., Dakota County, Nebr., 1979-88; sponsor South Sioux City Distributive Club of Am., 1956-86; state pres. Nebr. Bus. Edn. Assn., 1979, Distributive Edn. Tchrs. Assn., 1980; pres. Luth. Svc. Aux., 2000-2001. Recipient Outstanding Svc. to State Orgns., Nebr. Vocat. Edn. Assn., 1976, Woman of the Yr. Am. Bus. Women Assn., 1972. Mem. Nebr. State Edn. Assn. (sec., treas., v.p., pres., Dedicated Svc. award 1986, Women of Excellence awards 1997), South Sioux City Chamberettes (sec., v.p., pres. 1972-89, 1st v.p. 1996-97, pres. 1998-99), Am. Federated Women's Club (sec. 1998, v.p., pres.), Svc. Corps Ret. Execs. (historian 1995-2002, sec. 1997-98, sec.-treas. 1998-2000), Am. Bus. Women's Assn. (sec. 1999-2001, Sr. SOOS 1998-2002). Avocations: reading, political and economic studies, internet, gardening, evangelism. Home: S Sioux City, Nebr. Died Sept. 19, 2007.

WILSON, JEANNETTE SOLOMON, retired elementary education educator; b. Columbus, Ga., Sept. 5, 1915; d. John C. and Mary L. (Parham) Solomon (adoptive parents, aunt and uncle); m. Harvie L. Wilson, Aug. 9, 1952; 1 child, Katrina M. Deese Turner. BS, Ft. Valley Coll., Ga., 1947; MS, Tuskegee Inst., Ala., 1951; postgrad., Syracuse U., 1961, U. Alaska, 1967. cert. elem. tchr. Elem. tchr. Muscogee County Sch. Dist., Columbus, 1939-53, 1954-60, 1969-71, home/hosp. tchr., 1971-75; elem. tchr. Am. Dependent Schs., Heilbronn, Fed. Republic Germany, 1953-54; ret., 1975. Cons. in field. Active Girls Scouts Columbus chpt. Named one of Women of Achievement Girl Scouts, Inc., 1989; recipient Outstanding Svc. award Am. Cancer Soc., 1983-84. Mem. AAUW, The Links Club (one of the founders Columbus, Ga. chpt. 1964), Urban League, Nat. Coun. Negro Women, Tuskegee Alumni Assn., Mr. and Mrs. Club (sec. 1960-64), Matrons Club (Gracious Lady of Ga. 1988), Alpha Kappa Alpha. Avocations: reading, volunteer community work, gourmet cooking, volunteer church work. Died Aug. 21, 2007.

WILSON, LOIS FAIR, school system administrator, educator; b. Redlands, Calif., Mar. 17, 1924; d. James Albert and Emma (Lederer) Fair; m. Herbert Blair Wilson (dec. Nov. 1989). BA, U. Redlands, 1945; MEd, U. So. Calif., LA, 1954; EdD, U. Ariz., 1972. Elem. tchr. Long Beach (Calif.) City Schs., San Bernardino County, 1945-51; curriculum cons. Office of San Bernardino (Calif.) County Schs., 1951-61; asst. prof., coord. elem. edn. U. Redlands, Calif., 1961-64, supr. student tchrs. Calif., from 1985; program asst. to coord. for kindergartens Tucson Unified Sch. Dist., 1965-72, curriculum coord. to elem. prin., 1965—83; supr. student tchrs. Calif. State U., San Bernardino, 1985-88; travel escort Hillsen's Tours and Travels, Redlands, 1984-92, Laura's Travel Svc., Redlands, 1992—95; escort San Diego Opera Summer Music Festival, 1993, 94. Tchr. hard of hearing and deaf program fostering learning Easter Seal Pre-Sch., Tucson, 1964—65; summer faculty World Campus Afloat, Chapman Coll., 1974—75, No. Ariz. U., 1978, 80; mem. steering com. Ariz. Young Readers' Conf., U. Ariz., 1975—84; mem. kindergarten curriculum guide com. State of Ariz.; tchr. Summer Demonstration Sch., 1954—56, Stanford U., 1956—58, team staff curriculum workshop, 1959; mem. 1st Ariz. State Kindergarten Curriculum Guide Com.; cons. in field. Contbr. articles to profl. jours. Mem. pre-sch. com. Tucson, 1967-68; bd. dirs. Town and Gown U. Redlands, 1985-92, pres., 1991-92, membership, sec., historian, reunion com., 1984—, class rep.1984—, chair San Bernardino County Agrl. Stabilization and Conservation Svc. Com., 1986-1990; mem. Assocs. of the Redlands Bowl, Assistance League of Redlands, 1988—, heritage aux. 4th grade program, 3d grade drug awareness program, Kimberly Jrs. Reunion Com., 1991; bd. dirs. Redlands Hist. Mus., 2d v.p, 1999—; vol. trainer Head Start. Recipient Cert. of Appreciation Dept. Edn. State of Ariz., 1984, Disting. Svc. award 1993, Centennial award U. Redlands, 2006-07. Mem.: ASCD, PEO (chpt. II treas. 1994—95), AAUW (pres. Calif. So. sect. and Ariz. 1960, pres. Ariz. chpt. 1980), Calif. Ret. Tchrs. Assn. (v.p. Redlands-Yucaipa divsn. 1990—92), Ret. Edn. Mgrs. of Calif. (region 12), Calif. Women for Agr., Redlands Art Assn. (endowment com.), U. Redlands Ret. Faculty Assn., Redlands Hist. Glass Mus., Redlands Symphony Assn. and Guild (coord., Gala Fund Raising Com. from 1987, bd. dirs., 2d v.p. 1988—90, chmn. youth music com. 1988—91, adv. com. 1994—99, bd. dirs., 2d v.p. 2003—05), Inland Orange Conservancy, Redlands Conservancy, Friends A.K. Smiley Libr., Lincoln Shrine Assn., Redlands Sister City Assn., Redlands Area Hist. Soc., Kimberly-Shirk Assn., Prospect Pk. Assn., U. Redlands Pace Setters (chmn. com. from 1992, scholarship for student in tchr. edn. named in her honor), April Morning Club (membership com. 1988—89, publicity 1989—90, yearbook 1991—92, pres. 1994—95, publicity from 2008), Redlands Contemporary Club, Alpha Delta Kappa Fidelis Iota (sec. 2001—04, publicity chair, historian 2001—04). Republican. Presbyterian. Avocations: travel, reading, classical music, writing, theater. Died July 13, 2008.

WILSON, LOUISE ASTELL MORSE, home economics educator; b. Corning, NY, Oct. 26, 1937; d. James Leland and Hazel Irene (Bratt) Morse; m. Robert Louis Wilson, Dec. 26, 1965 (dec. June 1981); 1 child, Patricia Louise. BS, SUNY, Buffalo, 1960; MS, Elmira Coll., 1971. Cert. home economist, N.Y. Tchr. Corning City Sch. Dist., from 1960. Com. mem. Corning Sch. Dist., 1991—. Mem. Internat. Fed. Home Econs. (area rep. 1991—), Am. Home Econs. Assn., Am. Vocat. Assn., N.Y. Home Econs. Assn. (treas. 1989-91), N.Y. State Home Econs. Tchrs. Assn. (area coord. 1988-89, Tchr. of Yr. 1993-94), Am. Coun. consumer Interests, Corning Tchrs. Assn. (exec. coun. 1981-91, 93—), Order Ea. Star (past matron), Corning Country Club. Republican. Methodist. Avocations: photography, sports, needlecrafts, glassware, coins. Home: Coopers Plains, NY. Died May 4, 2008.

WILSON, MARGARET BUSH, lawyer; b. St. Louis, Jan. 30, 1919; married; 1 child, Robert Edmund. BA cum laude, Talladega Coll., 1940; LL.B., Lincoln U., 1943. Ptnr. Wilson & Wilson, St. Louis, 1947-65; now with firm Wilson & Associstes. Asst. dir. St. Louis Lawyers for Housing, 1969-72; asst. atty. gen. Mo., 1961-62; atty. Rural Electrification Adminstrn., Dept. Agr., St. Louis, 1943-45; instr. civil procedure St. Louis U. Sch. Law, 1971; chmn. St. Louis Land Reutilization Authority, 1975-76; mem. Mo. Coun. Criminal Justice, 1972-2009; chmn. Intergroup Corp., 1985-87; bd. dirs. Mut. of N.Y. Mem. gen. adv. com. ACDA, 1978-81; trustee emeritus Washington U., St. Louis; chmn. bd. trustees Talladega Coll., Ala., 1988-92; nat. bd. dirs. ARC, 1975-81, United Way, 1978-84, Police Found., 1976-93; treas. NAACP Nat. Housing Corp., 1971-84, chmn. nat. bd., 1975-84; dep. dir./acting dir. St. Louis Model City Agy., 1968-69; adminstr. Mo. Commn. Svc. and Continuing Edn., 1967-68. Recipient Bishop's award Episcopal Diocese Mo., 1962; Juliette Derricotte fellow, 1939-40, Disting. Lawyer award Bar Assn. Metro St. Louis, 1997; Margaret Bush Wilson Endowed Professorship in Arts and Scis. established at Washington U., St. Louis, 2004. Mem. ABA (chmn. youth edn. for citizenship 1991-94, chmn. Nat. Law Day 1998-2000), Nat. Bar Assn., Mo. Bar Assn., Mound City Bar Assn., St. Louis Bar Assn., Alpha Kappa Alpha. Home: Saint Louis, Mo. Died Aug. 11, 2009.

WILSON, NANCY CAROL, retired office systems educator; b. Brighton, Tenn., July 11, 1940; d. John C. and Lillie Mai (Coates) W. BBA, Memphis State U., 1963, MEd, 1968. Cert. sec. tchr. bus. edn. Tchr. bus. Grand Junction, Tenn. H.S., 1962-64; tchr. 6th grade Munford (Tenn.) Elem. Sch., 1964-65; tchr. jr. high math. Munford (Tenn.) Jr. High, 1965-66; tchr. bus., dept. head Munford (Tenn.) H.S., 1966-71; asst. prof., program coord. office adminstrn. Hopkinsville (Ky.) Cmty. Coll., 1971-81, prof. office adminstrn., 1981-96, prof. office systems, 1996-98. Mem. Nat. Bus. Edn. Assn. (Ky. mem. chmn. 1974-76, So. Bus. Edn. Assn. sec. 1979, mem. adminstrv. com. 1982, 85, vice chmn. basic bus. divsn. 1973, chmn. 1974, sec. 1982, chmn. secretarial divsn. 1975, chmn. cmty. and jr. coll. divsn. 1977), Ky. Bus. Edn. Assn. (pres.-elect 1973-74, pres. 74-75, past pres. 1975-76). Methodist. Avocations: travel, reading. Home: Hopkinsville, Ky. Died Oct. 5, 2007.

WILSON, NOLLIE ANDREW, cultural organization administrator; b. Big Spring, Tex., June 7, 1938; s. Silas Andrew and Vina Lee (Lloyd) W.; m. Wilma Ruth Williamson, Nov. 10, 1960; children: Valarie Ann Wilson Sullivan, Noel Andrew, Amanda Ruth. BA Biology, Tex. Lutheran Coll., 1972. From tng. specialist to dir. USAF Scouting Liaison, Dobbins AFB, Ga., 1956-82; sr. dist. exec. Bay Area Boy Scouts Am., Galveston, Tex., from 1982. Adv. bd. criminal justice dept. Alvin (Tex.) C.C. Decorated commendation medal USAF, 1972; recipient Mayor's Commendation Big Spring City, 1976. Mem. Toastmasters, Rotary. Baptist. Avocations: sailing, computers, coin collecting/numismatics, entomology. Home: Alvin, Tex. Died May 6, 2008.

WILSON, ROBERTA LOUISE, writer, editor, journalist, activist; b. Hollywood, Calif., June 2, 1954; d. Robert Louis and Noreen Irvine Wilson; life ptnr. Jeff Lynn Moore; stepchildren: Tyron, Dashal, Adrianne 1 child, Dova Lindsay Moore. BA in Psychology, Chapman U., 1976. Editor Career Publs., Orange, Calif., 1976—81; freelance journalist Agoura Valley News, Westlake Mag., Agoura Hills, Calif., 1977—79; tech. writer Ashton-Tate, Torrance, Calif., 1983—87; tech. writer/project lead Microsoft Corp., Redmond, Wash., 1988—2000; freelance tech. writer Aldus Corp., Seattle, 1989—91. Officer Washtech/CWA Local 37083, Seattle, from 2002. Performance art for anti-nuclear UNARM, Business as Usual; contbr. articles to mags., websites. Media/People Power coord. Gt. Peace Mar. for Global Nuc. Disarmament, LA, 1986—86; state coordinating com. Green Party of Wash. State, Seattle, 2001—02; co-organizer/writer bill of rights resolution Bill of Rights Def. Com., Bainbridge Island, Wash., 2003. Mem.: Green Party of Kitsap County (v.p. 2000—05), Winslow Cohousing Group (bd. trustees 1991—93). Mem. Religious Soc. Of Friends. Achievements include walked across the country with the Great Peace March for Global Nuclear Disarmament; co-founding member of first owner-developed cohousing community in the United States. Home: Bainbridge Island, Wash. Died Apr. 6, 2008.

WILSON, THOMAS BENNETT, III, lawyer, educator; b. Mpls., June 5, 1946; s. Thomas Bennett and Marjorie Lee (Williams) W.; m. Gayle Gaumer, Aug. 5, 1978; children: Thomas Bennett IV, Ryan Converse, Corinne Lee. BA, U. Miami, Coral Gables, Fla., 1969; JD, Hamline U., 1979. Bar: Minn. 1980, U.S. Dist. Ct. Minn. 1981, U.S. Ct. Appeals (8th cir.) 1985, U.S. Supreme Ct. 1987, U.S. Mil. Ct. Appeals, 1991. Pvt. practice law, Edina, Minn., from 1980. Adj. prof. Hamline U. Sch. of Law, 1983-85; adj. tchr. N. Hennepin Community Coll., 1988; mem. Hennepin County Bar Commitment Def. Panel, 1982—; lectr. in field. Bd. dirs. Mental Health Assn. Minn., 1982-85, exec. com. 1985; Hennepin County Bar Found. for Charitable Grants; bd. dirs. Edina Gymnastics Assn., 1988, pres. 1989—. Recipient Cert. of Commendaton Gov. Minn., Dwight V. Dixon award Mental Health Assn. Minn., Commendation for Outstanding Legal Adv. Svcs. Mental Health Assn. Minn. Mem. ABA, Minn. Bar Assn., Hennepin County Bar Assn., Assn. Trial Layers Am Minn Trial Lawyers Assn., Fed. Bar Assn. Home: Minneapolis, Minn. Died May 19, 2008.

WIMMER, GEORGE ALBERT, chiropractor, consultant; b. Ogden, Utah, Sept. 3, 1918; s. Charles Warren and Neta Hortense (Benson) W.; m. Fern Bernice Holley, Oct. 19, 1942; children: Holly Kay, Michael Warren, Connie Louise, Douglas Max, Debra. BS, Weber State Coll., 1980; D Chiropractic, Tex. Chiropractic Coll., 1948, Philosopher of Chiropractic cum laude, 1948. Cook Bob's Bar-b-que, Ogden, 1935-36; night watchman Hill AFB, Ogden, 1941; assoc. Turley Chiropractic Clinic, San Antonio, 1948-50, Wheeler Chiropractic Ctr., Ogden, 1952-59; chiropractor Ogden, 1959-86; sr. cons., assoc. mem. Wimmer Chiropractic Ctr., Ogden, from 1986. Contbr. articles to profl. jours. Pres. Five Pts. Lions Club, Ogden, 1956; v.p. Lake Bonneville Coun., Boy Scouts Am., Ogden, 1957; pres. Ogden (Utah) City Sch. Bd. With USAF, 1941-45. Named Father of Yr., Ogden (Utah) City Coun., 1964. Mem. Lewis Peak Lions Club (bd. dirs., pres. 1990, Pres.'s award 1990). Republican. Mem. Lds Ch. Avocations: woodworking, fishing, photography. Home: Ogden, Utah. Died Dec. 27, 2007.

WINANS, BARBARA ANN, media director; b. Moberly, Md., Oct. 15, 1939; d. Carl R. and Daisy (Blackwell) W. AA, Columbia Coll., 1959; BE, U. Mo., 1961; MEd, U. Mo., 1966. Cert. elem. tchr., Mo. History tchr. Fulton (Mo.) High Sch., 1961-64; libr. instr. U. Mo. Lab Sch., Columbia, 1965-67; libr. West Jr. High, Columbia, 1967-68; media specialist Hickman High Sch., Columbia, 1968-73; media dir. Rock Bridge High Sch., Columbia, from 1973. Adv. coun. Grad. Sch. Libr. Information Sci., U. Mo., Columbia, 1977—; group discussion leader Mo. White House Govs. Conf. on Librarians, 1990. Bd. dirs. Boone County Tchrs. Credit Union, Columbia, 1989—; v.p. FA Chpt. PEO, Columbia, 1990—; mem. Parent Club West Highlant White Terrier Club Am., 1981. Recipient Alumnae Cert. Merit Zeta Tau Alpha, 1975, Sch. Manpower Project award Am. Assn. Sch. Librarians. Mem. Columbia Community Tchrs. Assn. (pres. 1965-66), Mo. State Tchrs. Assn., Mo. Assn. Sch. Librs. (pres. 1969-70, Spl. Svc. award 1973, Sch. Manpower Project award, 1973), Phi Delta Kappa, Delta Kappa Gamma (pres. 1974), Pi Lambda Theta. Democrat. Baptist. Avocation: breeding and showing terriers. Home: Columbia, Mo. Died May 20, 2008.

WIND, BARRY, art history educator; b. NYC, May 29, 1942; s. Fred and Minnie (Unger) Wind; m. Geraldine Dunphy; children: James Gardner, Clifford Dunphy. BA, CCNY, 1962; MA, NYU, 1964, PhD, 1973. Instr. Rutgers U., New Brunswick, N.J., 1965-66; asst. prof. U. Ga., Athens, 1967-71; from asst. prof. to assoc. prof. U. Wis., Milw., 1971-87, prof., 1987—2004. Author: Velazquez's Bodegones: A Study in 17th Century Genre, 1987, Genre in the Age of the Baroque, 1991, A Foul and Pestilent Congregation: Images of Freaks in Baroque Art, 1997; contbr. articles and revs. to profl. jours. Inst. Fine Arts fellow, 1964-65, NEH fellow Brit. Arts Ctr., Yale U., 1984, Brown U., 1992; Cook Travel grantee Inst. Fine Arts, 1965. Home: Milwaukee, Wis. Died Apr. 10, 2008.

WINDELS, PAUL, JR., lawyer; b. Bklyn., Nov. 13, 1921; s. Paul and Louise E. (Gross) W.; m. Patricia Ripley, Sept. 10, 1955 (dec. 1995); children: Paul III, Mary H., James H.R., Patrick D. AB, Princeton U., NJ, 1943; LLB, Harvard U., Cambridge, Mass., 1948. Bar: NY 1949. Spl. asst. counsel NY State Crime Commn., 1951; asst. U.S. atty. Ea. Dist. NY, 1953—56; NY regional adminstr. SEC, 1956—61, also spl. asst, U.S. atty. for prosecution securities frauds, 1956-58; lectr. law Am. Inst. Banking, 1950-57; mem. Windels, Marx, Lane & Mittendorf and predecessor firms, 1961—98, of counsel, from 1998. Author: Our Securities Markets-Some SEC Problems and Techniques, 1962. Trustee Bklyn. Law Sch.; trustee Lexington Sch. for the Deaf, Gerta Charitable Trust; past pres. Fed. Bar Coun. Capt. F.A., AUS, 1943-46, ETO; maj. USAR, ret. Recipient Flemming award for fed. svc.; decorated chevalier Order French Acad. Palms; officer Nat. Order Merit France. Fellow Am. Bar Found.; mem. ABA, NY State Bar Assn., Assn. of Bar of City of NY Republican. Presbyterian. Home: Saint James, NY. Died Sept. 8, 2009.

WINDSOR, MARGARET EDEN, writer; b. Flemington, Mo., Aug. 10, 1917; d. John Denny and Rhoda Belle (Morgan) Head; m. Eugene B. Windsor, Jan. 10, 1987. Instr. hematology; med. technologist, 1958; ret. med. technologist, 1982. Author: Murder in St. James, 1990, The Outhouse, 1996, Far Cry, 2004, Bell's Out House, 2004; editor: From Pandora's Box, 1993. Cpl. USAF, 1944-45. Mem. Columbia Chpt. Mo. Writers Guild (v.p. 1989-90). Democrat. Roman Catholic. Avocations: music, theater, reading, television. Home: Columbia, Mo. Died Oct. 11, 2007.

WINIKOW, LINDA, electric and gas utility executive; b. Bklyn., May 9, 1940; d. Ben and Minna (Rosenberg) Bord; m. Arnold Winikow, Dec. 24, 1961; children: Jeffrey, Scott. BA cum laude, Hofstra U., 1962; MS in Social Studies Edn., Queens Coll., 1966; LLD (hon.), St. Thomas Aquinas Coll., Sparkill, NY, 1978; LHD (hon.), Mercy Coll., Westchester County, NY, 1978. Tchr. history; v.p. corp. communications and pub. affairs Orange and Rockland Utilities, Inc., Pearl River, N.Y., 1984-85, v.p. human resources and external affairs, 1985-88, v.p. corp. policy and external affairs, from 1988. Bd. dirs. Savs. Bank Rockland County, N.Y. State Facilities Devel. Corp.; mem. adv. com. N.Y. State Thruway Authority Transition; mem. small bus. initiatives task force N.J. Gov.'s Econ. Conf.; mem. blue-ribbon adv. panel NOAA. Mem. Ramapo (N.Y.) Zoning Bd. Appeals, 1968-71; mem. Ramapo Town Coun., 1971-73; mem. Ramapo Sanitation Commn.; bd. dirs. N.J. Alliance for Action; mem. regional subscriber adv. coun. Blue Cross/Blue Shield; mem. N.Y. State Senate, 1974-84; past sec. Senate Dem. Conf.; bd. dirs. Stern Coll. for Women, Yeshiva U.; mem. community adv. bd. PBS-TV; mem. Rockland adv. bd. Salvation Army; mem. citizens adv. coun. Rockland County Dept. Social Svcs. Recipient numerous awards including George M. Estabrook Disting. Svc. award Alumni Assn. Hofstra U., 1982, award N.Y. State chpt. NOW, 1986, Disting. Citizen award Ramapo Coll., 1990, Community Svc. award Yeshiva U., Disting. Svc. award Rockland coun. Boy Scouts Am. Jewish. Home: Longboat Key, Fla. Died Aug. 24, 2008.

WINSTEAD, NASH NICKS, academic administrator, plant pathologist; b. Durham County, NC, June 12, 1925; s. Nash L. and Lizzy (Featherston) W.; m. Geraldine Larkin Kelly, Sept. 17, 1949; 1 dau., Karen Jewell. BS, N.C. State U., 1948, MS, 1951; PhD, U. Wis., 1953. Asst. prof. plant pathology, Raleigh, 1953-58; assoc. prof. N.C. State U., Raleigh, 1958-61, prof., 1961-90, prof. emeritus, from 1991, dir. inst. biol. scis., 1965-67, asst. dir. agrl. exptl. sta., 1965-67, asst. provost, 1967-73, assoc. provost, 1973-74, provost and vice chancellor, 1974-90, acting chancellor, 1981-82. Phillip Found. intern acad. adminstrn. Ind. U., 1965-66; bd. trustees N.C. Sch. Sci. and Math., 1985-90. Author: Home grown and Homemade, 1997, Mama's Book, 1998, The Provost's Office N.C. State U., An Informal History, 1955-93, 1999, The Civil War Campaigns Involving Corporal James Fletcher Winstead, 1999, Featherston Memories, 2002, Start Where You Are and Use What You've Got, 2005, Nash and gerry Go Places, The Civil War Campaigns Involvoing Sergeant James Robert Aester; contbr. articles profl. jours. Mem. N.C. Council on Higher Edn. for Adults, 1967-75; inst. rep. So. Assn. for Colls. and Schs., 1967-74; mem. Cooperating Raleigh Colls., 1968-90, pres., 1971-73, 83-85; chmn. interaction between protoplasm and toxicants com. So. Regional Edn. Bd., 1964-65; Bd. dirs. N.C. State U. YMCA, 1963-65; trustee Meth. Home for Children, 1980-88, pres., 1983-84, N.C. Wesleyan Coll., 1987-97. Served with USAAF, 1943-46. Recipient Sigma Xi research award, 1960 Fellow AAAS; Mem. Am. Phytopath. Soc. (chmn. disease, pathogen physiology com.), Am. Inst. Biol. Scis., N.C. Assn. Colls. and Univs. (exec. com. 1974-80, pres. 1978-79), Nat. Assn. State Univs. and Land Grant Colls. (edn. telecommunications com. 1980-85, equal opportunity com. 1985-88), Acad. Deans for So. States, N.C. Assn. of Acad. Officers (exec. com. 1986-89, v.p., pres. 1987-88), Sigma Xi, Phi Kappa Phi, Omicron Delta Kappa. Clubs: Torch Internat. (sec.). Home: Raleigh, NC. Died Oct. 18, 2008.

WINTER, ELMER LOUIS, business executive; b. Milw., Mar. 6, 1912; s. Sigmund and May (Kraus) Winter; m. Nannette Rosenberg, 1936 (dec. Jan. 1990); m. Hope Melamed, 1992; children: Susan, Lynn, Martha. BA, U. Wis., 1933; LLB, U. Wis., Milw., 1935, LLD (hon.), 1970. Bar: Wis. 1935. Ptnr. Scheinfeld & Winter, Milw., 1936—48; co-founder, pres. Manpower, Inc., Milw., 1948—76; chmn. Operation 3000, Milw. Chmn. Econ. Growth of Israel, 1976. Author 13 books;. Chmn. met. Milw. divsn. Nat. Alliance of Businessmen, 1968—69; co-founder, chmn. Milw. Voluntary EEO Coun.; organizer Youthpower, Milw.; del. White House Conf. on YOuth, White House Econ. Summit, 1974; mem. exec. com. Nat. Alliance to Save Energy; hon. pres. Am. Jewish Com. Recipient Leadership award, Met. Milw. Assn. Commerce; named to Wis. Bus. Hall of Fame. Mem.: Internat. Soc. Advancement Mgmt. (past v.p., Human Rels. award), Internat. Franchise Assn. (past pres.), Milw. Bar Assn., Wis. Bar Assn. Home: Milwaukee, Wis. Died Oct. 22, 2009.

WINTER, RALPH D., religious organization administrator, academic administrator; b. South Pasadena, Calif., 1924; s. Hugo H. and Hazel Winter; m. Roberta Winter, 1951 (dec. 2001); children: Elizabeth, Rebecca, Linda, Patricia; m. Barbara Winter. BCE, Calif. Inst. tech., Pasadena; MA in ESL, Columbia U., NYC; BD, Princeton Theol. Sem., NJ; attended, Fuller Theol. Sem., Pasadena; PhD. in Structural Linguistics, Cornell U., Ithaca, NY. Student pastor Lamington Presbyn. Ch., 1953—56; rural devel. specialist Presbyn. Ch., Guatemala, 1956—66; founder, dir. indsl. tng. for Guatemalan Indian pastors Industrias Técnicas, 1958—66; founder, dir. adult edn. ext. program Union Abraham Lincoln, Guatemala, 1961—66; prof. anthropology Landivar U., Guatemala, 1961—66; exec. dir. Asociacion Latinoamericana de Escuelas Teológicas, Norte, 1965—66; prof. hist. devel. of the Christian movement Fuller Theol. Sem., 1966—76, disting. missiologist in residence, from 1998; co-founder, sec.-treas. Am. Soc. of Missiology, 1972—75, pres., 1979—80; founder, gen. dir. Frontier Mission Fellowship, from 1976; gen. dir. US Ctr. for World Mission, 1976—90, dir. inst. internat. studies, 1990—97; pres. William Carey Internat. U., Pasadena, 1977—80, 1990—97, 2000—04, chancellor, 1997—99, 2005—09; editor Mission Frontiers Bulletin, 1977—2009; v.p. Southwest Evang. Missiol. Soc., 1992—99. Founder Inst. the Study of the Origins of Disease, 1999, William Carey Libr., 1969, Presbyn. Frontier Fellowship, 1975, Internat. Soc. Frontier Missiology, 1985; co-founder Assoc. Ch. Mission Committees, 1975; founder Presbyterian Ctr. for Mission Studies, 1973. Named one of 25 Most Influential Evangelicals in America, Time Mag., 2005. Died May 20, 2009.

WIRTZ, DAVID REINER, enologist; b. Hillsboro, Oreg., May 22, 1952; s. Reiner Shogren and Mary Ellen (Greip) W.; m. Mary Lois Wirtz, Oct. 28, 1978; 1 child, Thatcher. BS, Portland State U., 1976. Cellar master Coury Vineyards, Forest Grove, Oreg., 1971-77; wine maker Rueter Hill Vineyards, Forest Grove, 1977-80; instr. Clackamas Coll., Oregon City, 1980-84; wine grower Writz Vineyards, Forest Grove, from 1966. Cons. Oreg. Wine Industry, 1980—; mem. adv. bd. Viticulture and Winemaking, Clackamas Coll., Oregon City, 1980-84. Author: Wheels of Time, 1992. Mem. Am. Soc. Enologists, Sons and Daus. of Oreg. Pioneers, Am. Truck Hist. Soc. (historian 1988-93), Pacific N.W. Truck Mus., Antique Truck Club of Am., N.W. Car Collectors, Oreg. Winegrowers Assn. Avocations: fly fishing, culinary arts, music. Home: Forest Grove, Oreg. Died Dec. 8, 2007.

WISEMAN, WILLIAM FENTON, museum administrator; b. Chgo., July 16, 1939; s. William Parr and Mary Louise (Fenton) W.; m. Linda Faitoute White, June 25, 1962; children: Claire, Christopher. BA, Cornell U., 1961; MBA, Babson Coll., Wellesley, Mass., 1977. Adminstrv. asst. Little, Brown & Co., Boston, 1964-72; chief fin. officer Godine Pubs., Boston, 1972-80; bus. mgr. The Children's Mus., Boston, from 1980. With U.S. Army, 1961-63. Mem. Union Boat Club. Republican. Episcopalian. Home: Needham, Mass. Died Apr. 8, 2008.

WISHNER, CLARA P., retired educator; b. NYC, Sept. 11, 1917; d. Maximilian Louis and Tillie (Mendelson) Perlman; m. Joseph L. Wishner, July 1, 1939 (dec. 1972); children: Martha Picra, Mickey Watner, Deborah, Susannah Jeffers. AB, Hunter Coll., 1939; MEd, U. Buffalo, 1959; ABD in Reading, SUNY, Buffalo, 1972. Cert. English tchr. 7-12, reading specialist, N.Y. Head English dept. Condra Sch., Cattaraugus, N.Y., 1961-67; asst. prof. English campus sch. SUNY, Buffalo, 1967-72; reading tchr. Niagara Falls (N.Y.) Bd. Edn., 1972-83. Cons. reading tchr. Nat. Coun. Tchrs. English, N.Y.C., 1977; lectr., cons. N.Y. State Reading Coun.; mem. rsch. consortium U.S. Office Edn., Niagara Falls, 1970. Mem. Industry Edn. Coun., Niagara Falls, 1975-77. Mem. Mensa. Avocations: freelance writing, sewing. Died Mar. 31, 2008.

WITT, JAMES H., state agency administrator; b. Knoxville, Tenn., Dec. 23, 1934; s. Carlos Raymond and Ruby Cladia (Palmer) W.; m. Ella Anne Griffith, Feb. 14, 1957; children: Vicki Leigh Williams, Jay Alan. Grad., Ctrl. H.S., Knoxville, 1954. Cert. fire inspector, Tenn. Sales agt. Ind. Life Ins. Co., Knoxville, 1956-61; painter G.A. Tillett Paint Co., Knoxville, 1961-64; fire fighter, fire marshall Knoxville Fire Dept., 1964-95; dir. arson investigation State of Tenn. Dept. Commerce and Ins., Nashville, from 1995. Precinct chmn. Rep. Party, Knoxville, 1987-95, treas., 1993-95. With U.S. Army, 1954-56. Mem. IAAI, Internat. Assn. Fire Chiefs, Tenn. Fire Inspectors, So. Bldg. Code Congress Internat. Baptist. Avocations: travel, sports, walking. Home: Rutledge, Tenn. Died Nov. 29, 2007.

WITTE, NANCY MARIE, special education educator, occupational therapist; b. Richardton, ND, Mar. 31, 1946; d. Victor Earl and Agnes Catherine (Koller) W. BA in Edn., We. Wash. State Coll., Bellingham, 1968; MS in Spl. Edn., U. Oreg., 1973; M in Occupational Therapy, Tex. Woman's U., 1983. Cert. tchr.; registered/lic. therapist. Tchr. Manson (Wash.) Pub. Schs., 1968-71; vol. tchr. Children's Hosp. Sch., Eugene, Wash., 1972-73; master tchr. Busy Bee Presch., Anchorage, 1973-74; program dir., itinerant spl. edn. tchr. State Operated Schs. of Anchorage, Ft. Yukon, Alaska, 1974-76; program devel. careers and continuing edn. U. Alaska, Faribanks, 1976-78; staff developer, ednl. mgr. A Sch. For Me, Inc., Tohatchi, N.Mex., 1978-81; spl. edn. tchr., therapist for severe-profoundly retarded Fairbanks Sch. Dist., 1983-90, occupational therapist, from 1990. Cons. to spl. edn. presch. programs, Ft. Yukon, Delta, and Dillingham, Alaska, 1974-76. Founding mem., v.p. Assn. for Children with Learning Disabilities, Fairbanks, 1975; mem. St. Raphael's Parish Coun., Fairbanks, 1984-90, also pres.; mem. Interior Alaska Peace with Justice Coun., Fairbanks, 1985-89. Named to Outstanding Young Women of Am., 1981. Mem. Am. Occupational Therapy Assn., Peace with Justice Orgn., N.W. Directory of Occupational Therapists for Rural Consultation. Avocations: kayaking, canoeing, photography, writing, backpacking, cross country skiing. Died Sept. 17, 2007.

WITTER, ROBERT JAMES, sculptor; b. Calumet City, Ill., Sept. 11, 1932; s. Cecil John and Emma Jane (Koehler) W.; m. Ann Shirley Kazlauskis, June 10, 1962; 1 child, David Anthony. BS in Edn., Ind. U., 1955; MFA, U. Miss., 1958. With City Colls. Chgo., 1962-93. With U.S. Army, 1958-60. Avocation: gardening. Home: Chicago, Ill. Died Dec. 19, 2007.

WOHAR, GEORGE, JR., editor, lawyer; b. Corning, NY, Apr. 18, 1924; s. George and Mary (Choma) W. BA, U. Wyo., 1949; JD, U. Colo., 1953. Bar: N.Y. 1963. Editor Prentice-Hall Inc., Englewood Cliffs, N.J., 1957-89, Maxwell-Macmillan, Inc., Englewood Cliffs, N.J., 1989-91, Rsch. Inst. Am., NYC, 1991-97. Editor: Guide to Sales and Use Taxes, 1995. Sgt. USAF, 1943-46, PTO. Mem. N.Y. State Bar Assn. Home: Hackensack, NJ. Died June 11, 2008.

WOLF, ARNOLD JACOB, rabbi, educator; b. Chgo., Mar. 19, 1924; s. Max A. and Nettie (Schanfarber) W.; m. Margery Steiner, Nov. 1, 1948 (div. Mar. 1960); children: Jonathan, Benjamin; m. Lois Blumberg, Dec. 26, 1963 (div.); stepchildren: Sara, Justine, Sarah-Anne, Dara; m. Grace Weiner AA, U. Chgo., 1942; BA, U. Cin., 1945; M of Hebrew Lit., Hebrew Union Coll., Cin., 1948; DD (hon.), Hebrew Union Coll., NYC, 1973. Rabbi Congregation Solel, Highland Park, Ill., 1957-72; chaplain, instr. Yale U., New Haven, 1972-80; rabbi KAM-Isaiah Israel, Chgo., 1980—2008. Chmn. Breira, N.Y.C., 1976-79; dir. Jewish Coun. Urban Affairs, Chgo.; lectr. U. Chgo. Author: Challenge to Confirmands, 1963, Unfinished Rabbi: Selected Writings of Arnold Jacob Wolf, 1998; editor: What is Man?, 1968; Rediscovering Judaism, 1965 Mem. ethics com. City of Chgo.; Jewish rep. World Coun. Chs., Nairobi, Kenya, 1985. Lt. (j.g.) USNR, 1951-53. Mem. Cen. Conf. Am. Rabbis. Home: Chicago, Ill. Died Dec. 23, 2008.

WOLF, ARTHUR, lawyer; b. Chgo., Feb. 21, 1900; s. Henry and Etta (Bernstein) W.; m. Ruth Oberndorfer, Oct. 1, 1928 (dec. Apr. 1961); children— Joan Wolf Grauer, Marjorie Wolf Greenberg; m. Edith Weiskopf, Oct. 26, 1962. Ph.B., U. Chgo., 1920, J.D., 1922. Bar: Ill. 1922, U.S. Supreme Ct. 1965. Sole practice, Chgo. Mem. ABA, Ill. Bar Assn., Chgo. Bar Assn. Clubs: Standard (Chgo.); Northmoor Country (Highland Park, Ill.). Home: Highland Park, Ill. Died Feb. 1987.

WOLFE, CHARLES MORGAN, electrical engineering educator; b. Morgantown, W.Va., Dec. 21, 1935; s. Slidell Brown and Mae Louise (Maness) W.; children— David Morgan, Diana Michele BSE.E., W.Va. U., Morgantown, 1961, MSE.E., 1962; PhD, U. Ill., 1965. Research assoc. U. Ill., Urbana, 1965; mem. staff MIT Lincoln Lab., Lexington, Mass., 1965-75; prof. elec. engring Washington U., St. Louis, 1975-97, Samuel C. Sachs prof., 1982-90, dir. semicondr. research lab., sr. prof., 1979-90. Cons. MIT Lincoln Lab., 1975-76, Fairchild Semicondr., Palo Alto, Calif., 1975-76, Air Force Avionics Lab., Dayton, Ohio, 1976-79, U. Ill., 1983-85 Author: Physical Properties of Semiconductors, 1989; editor: Gallium Arsenide and Related Compounds, 1979; contbr. articles to profl. jours., chpts. to books Served as sgt. USMC, 1955-58 Fellow: IEEE (field awards com. 1984—87, Jack A. Morton award 1990); mem.: NAE, Electrochem. Soc. (Electronics divsn. award 1978). Home: Ballwin, Mo. Died Oct. 18, 2008.

WOLFF, HERBERT ERIC, banker, former army officer; b. Cologne, Germany, May 24, 1925; s. Hugo and Juanna Anna (Van Dam) W.; m. Alice (Billy) Rafael, Nov. 13, 1946 (dec. July, 1987); children: Karen (dec. Jan., 1992), Herbert E., Allen R. BA, Rutgers U., 1953; BS, U. Md., 1957; MA, George Washington U., 1962; grad., US Army War Coll., 1962, Harvard U., 1979. Commd. 2nd lt. US Army, 1945, advanced through grades to maj. gen.; served in Fed. Republic of Germany, Greece, Iran, Republic of Korea, Australia, New Guinea, The Phillipines, Japan and Socialist Republic of Vietnam; dep. dir. ops. NSA and Chief CSS, Ft. Meade, Md., 1973—75; dep. corps. comdr. V. Corps US Army, Frankfurt, Germany, 1975-77, comdr. gen. US Army Western Command Hawaii, 1977-81; with First Hawaiian Bank, Honolulu, 1981-2000, sr. v.p., corp. sec., to 2000; hon. consul gen. (Dató) US Pacific region Govt. of Malaysia, Honolulu, from 1985. Author: The Man on Horseback, 1962, The Tenth Principle of War Public Support, 1964, The Military Instructor, 1968. Exec. bd. Aloha coun. Boy Scouts Am.; bd. dirs. USO, Girl Scouts of US, Hawaii, Found. Armed Forces Ctr. Security Studies; vice chmn. March of Dimes; v.p. Hawaiii Com. Fgn. Rels.; past pres. Pacific Asian Affairs Coun., Hawaii Army Mus. Soc. Decorated Bronze Star with V and 3 oak leaf clusters, Air medal (24) US Army, Purple Heart, Gallantry Cross with 2 palms, Gallantry Cross with palm and silver star Nat. Order 5th class South Vietnam, Order Nat. Security Merit Choen-Su S. Korea, D.S.M. with oak leaf clusters (2), Silver Star with oak leaf cluster US Army, Legion of Merit with 3 oak leaf clusters, D.F.C., Combat Infantry Badge with two stars, master parachutist, Army aviator; named Citizen of Yr. Fed. Exec. Bd., 1987. Mem. 1st Inf. Divsn. Assn., 1st Cav. Divsn. Assn., Plaza Club (pres., bd. dirs.), Waialae Country Club, Rotary, Phi Kappa Phi. Deceased.

WONG, DONNA LEE, nursing researcher, consultant; b. Passaic, NJ, Mar. 30, 1948; d. Rudolph Mitchko and Madeline DePietropaolo; m. Ting Kin Wong, Dec. 18, 1971; 1 child, Nina. BSN magna cum laude, Rutgers U., 1970; MN in Nursing magna cum laude, UCLA, 1971; student, Seton Hall U., 1974; postgrad., Okla. State U. RN, Okla.; cert. pediatric nurse practitioner; cert. Brazelton Neonatal Behavior Assessment Scale. Charge nurse pediatrics U. Calif. Med. Ctr., LA, 1970-72; clin. specialist pediatrics Roosevelt Hosp., NYC, 1972-73; asst. prof. nursing Seton Hall U., South Orange, N.J., 1973-77; pvt. pract. nurse counselor, from 1975; cons. pediatrics Muhlenberg Hosp., Plainfield, N.J., 1976-80, Somerset Med. Ctr., Somerville, N.J., 1977-80; cons. pediatrics, burn unit Hillcrest Med. Ctr., Tulsa, Okla., 1981-83; cons. nursing dept. Children's Ctr. St. Francis Hosp., Tulsa, Okla., from 1985; cons. nursing dept. Ark. Children's Hosp., Little Rock, 1987-90, Children's Med. Ctr. Dallas, 1990-93. Nursing cons. Children's Hosp. at St. Francis Home, Tulsa; adj. assoc. prof. Coll Med., U. Okla.; adj. assoc. prof., cons. Oral Roberts U. Sch. Nursing. Author: Whaley and Wong's Nursing Care of Infants and Children, 1995 (Am. Jour. Nursing Book of Yr. award 1991), Essentials of Pediatric Nursing, 1993 (Am. Jour. Nursing Book of Yr. award 1993), Clinical Manual of Pediatric Nursing, 1990, Pediatric Quick Reference; author: (with others) Mosby's Assesstest, 1984, Mosby's Comprehensive Review of Nursing, 1987, The Addison-Wesley Handbook of Nursing Practice, 1983, Nursing Assessment and Strategies for the Family at Risk, 1986, Comprehensive Child and Family Nursing Skills, 1991; contbr. articles to profl. jours. Recipient Outstanding Alumni Rutgers Coll. Nursing award, 1995, Excellence in Maternal and Child Health award ONA, 1994, Outstanding Svc. award Am. Cancer Soc., 1980, Burns Pioneer award Nat. Burn Victim Found., 1977, Outstanding Educator of Am. award, 1974-75. Fellow Am. Acad. Nurses; mem. ANA (coun. maternal-child nursing), Internat. Assn. Study Pain, Am. Nurses Found., Assn. Pediatric Oncology Nurses, Nat. Assn. Pediatric Nurse Assocs. Practitioners (Henry K. Silver award 1991, Outstanding Svc. award Okla. 1992), Assn. Care Children's Health, Nat. Coun. Family Rels., Nat. Assn. Sch. Nurses, Am. Pain Soc., Okla. Nurses Assn. (Hon. Recognition award 1987), Rutgers U. Coll. Nursing Alumni Assn., U. Calif. Sch. Nursing Alumni Assn., Candlelighters Found., Compassionate Friends, Sigma Theta Tau (Zeta Delta chpt., Excellence in Rsch. award 1988; first recipient Audrey Hepburn award; Mosby award of Excellence 1995). Home: Tulsa, Okla. Died May 4, 2008.

WONG, YANIC, accountant; b. Hong kong, Republic of China, Dec. 14, 1954; came to U.S, 1976; m. Maria See, Jan. 25, 1981; 1 child, Calvin. BS in Acctg., U. Ill., Chgo., 1980. CPA, Ill. Field acct. Turner Constrn., Chgo., 1980-84, acctg. supr., from 1984. Sen. On-leung Assn., Chgo., 1985. Mem. Am. Inst. CPA's, Ill. Soc. CPA's, Chinatown C. of C. (bd. dirs.) Home: Naperville, Ill. Died July 4, 2008.

WOOD, BENTON, retired editor, priest; b. Arlington, Mass., Aug. 14, 1927; s. Edward E. Wood, Jr. and Dorothy Benton Wood; m. Joan Spodnyak Wood, Sept. 4, 1954; 1 child, John Benton. BS, Northwestern U., Evanston, IL, 1951; MS, State U. NY, Albany, NY, 1952; Religious Edn. Degree, Geneva Theol. Coll., Byfield, MA, 1974, Dr. (hon.) Humane Letters, 1979. Ordained Anglican Priest Diocese Albany, NY, 1957. Counsellor Camp Pasquaney, E. Hebron, NH, 1944—64; chaplain Northwood Sch., Lake Placid, NY, 1954—57, history dept. head, 1954—57; chaplain Trinity-Pawling Sch., Pawling, NY, 1958—62; dir. of studies, summer sch. St. Andrew's Sch., Boca Raton, Fla., 1962—65; headmaster York Sch., Monterey, Calif., 1965—67; academic dean Trinity Prepatory Sch., Winter Park, Fla., 1967—74; rector Ch. Annunciation, Anna Maria Island, Fla., 1975—88. Dir. St. Alban's Stamp Mission, Parrish, Fla., 1974—2001; editor Northwestern U. Alumni newsletter, Sarasota, Fla., 1990—2001; chaplain Baker St. Irregulars, from 1980. Author: (reference) Philatelic & Numismatic Holmes. Chaplain Anna Maria Fire Dept., Anna Maria Island, Fla., 1978—88. Pvt. U.S. Army, 1945—46. Recipient Two Shilling award, Baker St. Irregulars, 1997. Fellow: Am. Geog. Soc. Avocations: philatelist, sherlockian. Home: Parrish, Fla. Died Dec. 8, 2007.

WOOD, EARL HOWARD, physiologist, educator; b. Mankato, Minn., Jan. 1, 1912; s. William Clark and Inez (Goff) W.; m. Ada C. Peterson, Dec. 20, 1936; children: Phoebe Busch, Mark Goff, Guy Harland, Earl Andrew. BA, Macalester Coll., 1934, D.Sc., 1950; BS, U. Minn., 1939, MS, M.B., PhD, 1941, MD, 1942. Teaching fellow physiology U. Minn., 1936-39, instr., 1940; NRC fellow med. scis., dept. pharmacology U. Pa., 1941; instr. pharmacology Harvard Med. Sch., 1942; research asst. acceleration lab. Mayo Aero Med. Unit, 1943; asst. prof. physiology Mayo Found., U. Minn. Grad. Sch., 1944, prof. physiology and medicine, 1951—82; staff mem. sect. physiology Mayo Clinic, 1947—82; chmn. biophys. scis. unit Mayo Med. Sch.; career investigator Am. Heart Assn., 1962—67. Sci. cons. air surgeon USAF Aero Med. Ctr., Heidelberg, Germany, 1946; vis. prof. U. Bern, 1965-66; vis. scientist dept. physiology Univ. Coll., London, 1972-73; rsch. cons. Canadian Air Force, DCIEM, Toronto, 1993-99. Contbr. articles to profl. jours., chpts. to books. Recipient Presdl. certificate of merit, Disting. Lectr. award Am. Coll. Chest Physicians, 1974, Sr. U.S. Scientist Humboldt award Kiel, Fed. Republic Germany, 1985, Phillips Meml. award ACP, 1983, Lucian award for research in cardiovascular diseases McGill U., 1985, Stewart Meml. lectr. Royal Aero. Soc., 1987, Outstanding Achievement award U. Minn., 1991. Fellow Aerospace Med. Assn. (Disting. Research award 1983); mem. Am. Physiol. Soc. (past chmn. circulation group, pres. 1980-81, Daggs award 1995), Am. Soc. Pharmacology and Exptl. Therapeutics, Am., Central socs. clin. investigation, Soc. Exptl. Biology and Medicine, Am. Heart Assn. (Research Achievement award 1973, past chmn. basic sci. sect.), AAAS, Nat. Acad. Medicine Mex., Nat. Acad. Arts and Scis. (Netherlands), Federated Am. Socs. Exptl. Biology (pres. 1981—), German Soc. for Heart and Circulation Rsch., Carl-Ludwig Ehrenmünze, Phi Beta Kappa, Sigma Xi, Alpha Omega Alpha (Outstanding Achievement award 1991). Achievements include research, numerous publs. on devel. instrumental techniques and procedures for study heart and circulation in health and disease; applications of these procedures to detection and quantitation of various types of acquired and congenital heart disease, study of effects and compensatory reaction of heart and circulation to various types of circulatory stress; essential member of the team that invented a revolutionary pressurized garment, the G-suit, that helps pilots avoid blacking out while in flight; patents in field. Died Mar. 18, 2009.

WOOD, GARY WALTER, investment manager; b. Redding, Calif., Mar. 16, 1939; s. Carl Leslie and Vivian Clarie (Looney) W.; m. Sandra Louise Anderson, Dec. 7, 1967 (div. Feb. 1980); children: Andrea Claire, Jansen Hasbrouck, Melissa Diedre. BS, San Jose State U., 1961; MBA, Harvard Bus. Sch., 1965. Indsl. engr. United Techs., Sunnyvale, Calif., 1961-63; instl. salesman Goldman Sachs & Co., LA, 1965-70, Morgan Stanley & Co., NYC, 1970-76; dep. mgr. Brown Brothem Harriman, NYC, 1976-82; exec. v.p. Estabrook Capital Mgmt., NYC, 1982-85; pres. Schaenen Wood & Assoc., NYC, from 1985, also bd. dirs., from 1985. Mem. N.Y. Soc. Security Analysts. Republican. Avocations: tennis, reading, boxing, cooking, travel. Home: Sarasota, Fla. Died Nov. 29, 2007.

WOOD, HARLINGTON, JR., federal judge; b. Springfield, Ill., Apr. 17, 1920; s. Harlington and Marie (Green) W.; m. Cathryn Reuwer, 1974; 1 child from previous marriage, Alexa AB, U. Ill., 1942, JD, 1948. Bar: Ill. 1948. Practiced in, Springfield, 1948-69; mem. firm Wood & Wood, 1948—58, ptnr., 1961—69; US atty. (so. dist.) Ill. US Dept. Justice, 1958-61, exec. head US attorneys Washington, 1969-70, assoc. dep. atty. gen., 1970-72, asst. atty. gen. civil divsn., 1972-73; judge US Dist. Ct (so. dist.) Ill., Springfield, Ill., 1973-76, US Ct. Appeals (7th Cir.), Springfield, Ill., 1976—92, sr. judge, 1992—2008. Adj. prof. Sch. Law, U. Ill., Champaign, 1993; disting. vis. prof. St. Louis U. Law Sch., 1996-2000. Chmn. Adminstrv. Office Oversight Com., 1988-90; mem. Long Range Planning Com., 1991-96. US Army, 1942—46. Recipient Profl. Lifetime Achievement award, Inns of Ct., 2002. As rep. of US govt., his refusal to authorize use of force at Wounded Knee in 1973 is credited with helping bring a nonviolent end to the conflict. Died Dec. 29, 2008.

WOOD, KENNETH ANDERSON, small business owner, display designer; b. Cleve., May 11, 1913; s. George Robert and Leonore (Anderson) Wood; m. Ruth Eleanor Diehm, Sept. 14, 1937 (dec. May 1999). Student, Fenn Coll., Cleve., 1932-34, Cleve. Inst. Art, 1935-45. Artist Patterson Displays, Cleve., 1934-35; art dir. Bailey Meter Co., Wickliffe, Ohio, 1936-71; owner Kenwood Designers and Assocs., Chesterland, Ohio, from 1971; designer of stained glass windows, from 1979. Pres. Artist and Craftsman Assocs., Cleve., 1940—44, Geauga Artists Assn., Geauga County, Ohio, 1950—53. Exhibitions include nat., regional and local, 1939—97, Represented in permanent collections Butler Mus. Am., Youngstown, Ohio, Inlander Collection of Gt. Lakes Regional Paintings, Cleve. Mus. Art, numerous pvt. collections; patents for product design. Mem.: Indsl. Designers Soc. Am. (life). Republican. Seventh Day Adventist. Avocation: travel. Home: Chesterland, Ohio. Died Aug. 24, 2008.

WOOD, ROGER HOLMES, financial planner, educator; b. Corning, NY, Apr. 26, 1920; s. James Orville and Helen Lucille (Winemiller) W.; m. Phyllis Elizabeth Anderson, Dec. 26, 1947; children: Stephen, David, Elizabeth. AB, U. Pitts., 1944; MS, Columbia U., 1945; MA, San Francisco State U., 1951; PhD, Internat. Coll., 1978. CLU, CFP, ChFC, accredited estate planner. Tchr. Oakdale (Calif.) High Sch., 1947-49, Galileo High Sch., San Francisco, 1949-54; instr. Coll. San Mateo, Calif., 1960-70; mem. nat. faculty Am. Coll., Bryn Mawr, Pa., 1960-70; lectr. Golden Gate U., San Francisco, 1983-84; agt. N.Y. Life Ins. Co., San Francisco, from 1954; tchr. Jefferson High Sch. Dist., Daly City, Calif., from 1965. Pres. Leading Life Ins. Producers, San Francisco, 1960-62. Author: When Tankers Collide, 2002, A Forgiving at Assisi, 2002, Life is a Four Letter Word, 2002; contbg. editor Western Underwriter, 1959-63. Mem. bd. dirs. San Francisco Coun. Chs., 1954-60. With U.S. Army, 1940-42. Mem. Internat. Assn. Fin. Planning, Internat. Soc. Descs. of Charlemagne, The Barronial Order of Magna Charta, Internat. Transactional Analysis Assn., Am. Risk and Ins. Assn., Soc. Fin. Svc. Profls., Nat. Soc. Descs. of Early Quakers, San Francisco Estate Planning Coun., San Francisco Life Underwriters Assn. (v.p. 1960-62), Peninsula Estate Planning Coun., Soc. Genealogists (London), Soc. of The War of 1812, Soc. Col. Wars, Hon. Order Ky. Cols., SAR, Phi Delta Kappa, Phi Gamma Delta. Republican. Presbyterian. Avocations: world travel, photography, genealogy. Home: South San Francisco, Calif. Died Aug. 5, 2008.

WOOD, SAMUEL EUGENE, academic administrator, psychology professor; b. Brotherton, Tenn., Aug. 16, 1934; s. Samuel Ernest and Daisy J. (Jernigan) W.; m. Helen J. Walker, June 2, 1956; children: Liane Wood Kelly, Susan Wood Benson, Alan Richard; m. Ellen Rosenthal Green, Sept. 8, 1977; stepchildren: Bart M. Green, Julie Alice Green. BS in English and Music, Tenn. Tech. U., 1961; M in Edn. Adminstrn., U. Fla., 1967, D in Edn., 1969. Asst. prof. edn. W.Va. U., 1968-70, U. Mo., St. Louis, 1970-75, mem. doctoral faculty, 1973-75; dir. rsch. Ednl. Devel. Ctr., Belleville, Ill., 1976-81; prof. psychology Meramec Coll., St. Louis, 1981-94; pres. Higher Edn. Ctr., St. Louis, from 1985; prof. psychology Lindenwood Coll., from 1995. Exec. dir. Edn. Opportunity Ctrs., St. Louis, 1985—, Project Talent Search, St. Louis, 1991—; bd. commrs. Pub. TV Com., St. Louis, 1985—; planning com. St. Louis Schs., 1985-90; adminstr. German-Am. student exch. program Internat. Bus. Students, 1985—; sponsor Higher Edn. Ctr. Internat. Edn. Coun., 1985—; co-founder, pres. Higher Edn. Cen. Cable TV Channel, Sta. HEC-TV, St. Louis, 1986; v.p. St. Louis County Cable TV Commn., 1991—. Musician, composer with USN Band, 1956-59; composer A Nautical Musical Comedy, A Child's Garden of Verses in Song, 1979; numerous poems set to music; co-author: (with Ellen Green Wood) (textbook) The World of Psychology, 1993, 4th edit., 2002, Can. edit., 1996, The Essential World of Psychology, 2000; contbr. articles to ednl. and sci. jours. Served with USN, 1955-59. US Office Edn. grantee 1976-81, 85—. Mem. Internat. Edn. Consortium (bd. dirs. 1985-91), Phi Kappa Phi. Democrat. Baptist. Avocations: writing, reading, music composition and performance. Home: Saint Louis, Mo. Died Apr. 30, 2008.

WOODBURY, JAMES ROBERTS, electronics consultant; b. Hollywood, Calif., May 24, 1931; s. Walter Edgar Woodbury and Gladys Rose Rockwell (Roberts) Woodbury Abberley; m. Joyce Elaine Albaugh, June 27, 1953; children: Jennifer Lynne, Neal Walter, Elaine Dorothy. BSc in Electronics and Aero. Engring., Brown U., 1953; MSEE, Stanford U., 1962, MS in Math., 1964. Mem. tech. staff Bell Telephone Labs., Whippany, N.J., 1953-56, TRW (formerly Ramo Wooldridge), LA, 1956-59; rsch. engr. SRI Internat., Menlo Park, Calif., 1959-76; mem. tech. staff Phillips (formerly Signetics), Mountain View, Calif., 1976-81, Fairchild Semi Conductor, Mountain View, 1981-84; sr. mem. tech. staff MTel (formerly M/A Com Linkabit), San Diego, 1984-87; sr. design engr. Hughes Network Systems, San Diego, 1987-93; cons. Woodbury Electronics Cons., San Diego, from 1993. Mem. IEEE, Tau Beta Pi. Baptist. Avocations: golf, tropical fish, hiking, gardening. Died June 12, 2008.

WOODBURY, ROBERT LOUIS, retired academic administrator; b. Dover, NJ, Apr. 6, 1938; s. Glen P. and Barbara Carr W.; m. Anne Pelletreau, Aug. 29, 1959; children: Richard G., Mark P., John M. BA, Amherst Coll., 1960; MA, Yale U., 1962, PhD in Am. Studies, 1966; DHL (hon.), Bowdoin Coll., 1988, Westfield State Coll., 1989; LLD (hon.), Amherst Coll., 1990. Instr. history Calif. Inst. Tech., Pasadena, 1964-66, asst. prof., 1966-68; assoc. prof. edn. U. Mass., Amherst, 1968-71, prof., 1971-79, assoc. dean of edn., 1969-71, assoc. provost, 1971-76, vice chancellor for student affairs, 1976-78; pres. U. So. Maine, Portland, 1979-86; chancellor U. Maine System, Bangor, 1986-93, interim chancellor, 1995. Chmn. bd. Coun. on Internat. Ednl. Exch., 1988-93, Maine Pub. Broadcasting, 1992-93; chmn. New Eng. Bd. Higher Edn., 1990-92; bd. dirs. Coll. Constrn. Loan Ins. Assn., Am. Assn. State Colls. and Univs., Am. Univ. Bulgaria; vis. scholar U. London, 1974-75. Bd. dirs. Bangor Edn. Found., 1987-93, East Maine Med. Ctr.; bd. dirs. Amherst Coll., 1980-86. Woodrow Wilson fellow, 1960-61; Danforth fellow, 1960-64 Home: Harpswell, Maine. Died Sept. 12, 2009.

WOODRING, CARL, English language educator; b. Terrell, Tex., Aug. 29, 1919; s. Felix Jessie and Naomi (Cole) W.; m. Mary Frances Ellis, Dec. 24, 1942 (dec. March 2, 2003). BA, Rice U., 1940, MA, 1942; AM, Harvard U., 1947, PhD, 1949. Instr. English U. Wis., 1948-51, asst. prof., 1951-54, assoc. prof., 1954-58, prof., 1958-61, Columbia U., NYC, from 1961, chmn. dept. English, 1968-71, George Edward Woodberry prof. lit., 1976-88, George Edward Woodberry prof. lit. emeritus, from 1988, chmn., co-chmn. Columbia Soc. Fellows in the Humanities, 1975-78. English dissertation selection com. Woodrow Wilson Nat. Fellowship Found., 1962-66; Phi Beta Kappa vis. scholar, 1974-75 Author: Victorian Samplers—William and Mary Howitt, 1952, Politics in the Poetry of Coleridge, 1961, Wordsworth, 1965, Virginia Woolf, 1966, Politics in English Romantic Poetry, 1970 (Van Am award, Christian Gauss prize 1971), Nature into Art: Cultural Transformations in Nineteenth-Century Britain, 1989, Literature: An Embattled Profession, 1999 (Violet Crown award); editor: Prose of the Romantic Period, 1961, Table Talk of Samuel Taylor Coleridge, 1990, The Columbia History of British Poetry, 1993; co-editor: The Columbia Anthology of British Poetry, 1995; mem. editl. bd. Studies in English Literature, 1961—; editl. adviser: Wordsworth Circle, 1970—, Essays in Literature, 1973—. With USNR, 1942-45. Fellow Fund Advancement Edn., 1955, Guggenheim Found., 1955, Am. Coun. Learned Socs., 1965, Nat. Humanities Ctr., 1987; Dexter scholar Harvard Coll., 1948; recipient Bowdoin prize, 1947, Disting. Alumnu award Rice U., 1986. Mem. MLA (mem. exec. coun. 1965-68), Internat. Assn. Univ. Profs. of English, Keats-Shelley Assn. Am. (bd. dirs.,

Disting. Scholar award 1982), Am. Acad. Arts and Scis., Acad. Lit. Studies, Assn. Depts. English (pres. 1971), Grolier Club. Home: Austin, Tex. Deceased.

WOODS, BOBBY JOE, transportation executive; b. Frederick, Okla., June 20, 1935; s. Vivin Richard and Mattie Marie (Malone); m. Sherry Summers; children: Donald B., Kathryn M., David R., Lynda J. Student, U. Calif., Berkeley, 1955-56; AA, Phoenix Coll., 1955; student, Glendale Coll., Ariz., 1968-75. Pres. Southwest Prorate Inc., Phoenix, 1967-95, TCAB Registration Cons., Inc., 1993-2000; dist. exec. Boy Scouts Am., Phoenix, 1968-76; pres. Facing E's Enterprises, Inc., Yarnell, Ariz., 1991-93. Mem. Profl. Trucking Svcs. Assn. (pres. 1989-90), Lions Club (dist. gov. 1992-93, zone chmn. 1983-84, dep. dist. gov. 1984-85, lt. gov. 1991-92, dist. sight and hearing chmn. 1985-91, Sight and Hearing Found. bd. mem. 1987—, state hearing chmn. 1985-89). Republican. Avocations: hiking, camping, stamp collecting/philately, computers, collecting 78 rpm records. Home: Goodyear, Ariz. Died Mar. 26, 2008.

WOODS, KENNETH REGINALD, architect; b. Chgo., Apr. 14, 1925; s. Otis Clifford and May (Leeds) W.; m. Betty Jane Seline, Sept. 20, 1946; children: Geoffrey Scott, Candace Lynn Friedmann. BS, Northwestern U., Evanston, Ill., 1948. Registered architect, Ill.; registered profl. engr., Ill.; registered land surveyor, Ill. Engr. Ingersoll Utility div. Borg Warner, Chgo., 1948-49, Underwriters' Labs., Inc., Chgo., 1949-52, Argonne (Ill.) Nat. Lab., 1952-55; ptnr. Thulin, Woods & Isensee, Chgo., 1953-60; pres. Woods and Assocs., Inc., Naperville, Ill., 1960-86, Energy-Environment, Inc., Naperville, from 1986. Patentee insulated shutters assemblage, 1982. Commr. of property Naperville City Coun., 1967-69, councilman, 1969-71; bd. dirs. Naperville YMCA, 1975-81. With USNR, 1943-47. Mem. AAAS, AIA, NSPE, Am. Congress Surveying and Mapping, Ill. Registered Land Surveyors Assn., Ill. Solar Energy Assn., Inc. (pres. 1989—), Fox Valley Electric Auto Assn., Inc. (v.p. 1989—), Lions (pres. Naperville chpt. 1979-80), Moose, Sigma Xi. Presbyterian. Home: Boulder City, Nev. Died Apr. 19, 2008.

WOODWARD, SUSAN GRIMM, health facility administrator; b. Corvallis, Oreg., May 23, 1931; d. Clarence Gordon and Emma (Sasek) Grimm; m. S. W. Woodward, Feb. 24, 1955; children: Stephen, Scott, Sanford. BS in Nursing Edn., U. Oreg., Portland, 1953; BS in Nursing, Oreg. State U., 1954. Adminstrv. supr. Kino Community Hosp., Tucson, infection control coord. Mem. Assn. Practitioners in Infection Control (pres. So. Ariz. chpt. 1988-89). Home: Tucson, Ariz. Died Feb. 14, 2008.

WOODY, VICTOR MORTON, III, safety, health and environment professional; b. Rocky Mount, Va., May 8, 1943; s. Victor Morton Jr. and Lorene (Powell) W.; m. Cleo Ferguson, Nov. 25, 1963; children: Bruce Allen, Dreama Renee. Grad., Ferrum Jr. Coll., Va. Supr. E.I. duPont de Nemours & Co., Martinsville, Va., 1963-78, Charleston, S.C., 1978-86; safety mgr. Standard Warehouse Co., Charleston, from 1987. Instr. first aid, CPR and back safety ARC, Charleston, 1989—. Mem. Am. Soc. Safety Engrs., Emergency Preparedness Assn. Republican. Baptist. Home: Summerville, SC. Died Feb. 28, 2008.

WOOLERY, MICHAEL FORREST, small business owner; b. Enid, Okla., Apr. 29, 1949; s. Forrest and Shirley Coleen (Kurz) W.; m. Sarah A. Williams, June 20, 1970 (div. Feb. 1978); m. Catherine Hastings, June 7, 1978; chidlren: Katie, Susan, Matthew, John. BBA, U. Alaska, 1975, MBA, 1976; PhD, Kennedy-Western U., 1988. Cert. tax cons. and agt. Dist. mgr. Safeway Stures, Seaford, Del., 1983-85; owner Guideline Bus. Svcs., Okalhoma City, from 1985. Author: Seize The Day!, 1991; (with others) Creative Communicators, 1990. Coach little league Putnam City Optimists, Okalhoma City, 1986—. Sgt. USAF, 1971-74. Mem. Nat. Assn. Tax Perparers. Avocations: reading, old movies, fishing. Home: Oklahoma City, Okla. Died May 8, 2007.

WOOTEN, ROBERT E., music educator; b. Chgo., Feb. 17, 1930; s. John and Flora (Waits) W.; m. Frances Louise Carter, Aug. 26, 1956; children: Robert Jr., Carol Lynne, John D. BMus, Chgo. Conservatory Music, 1956; M in Music Edn., Roosevelt U., 1968; D in Music Edn., Va. Seminary & Coll., 1983. Min. music Beth Eden Bapt. Ch., Chgo., from 1941; founder, dir. Wooten Choral Ensemble, from 1949; dir. music Greater Harvest Bapt. Ch., 1950-86. Music dept. chair Parker H.S., Chgo., 1957-62; staff asst., Chgo. Pub. Schs. 1962-75, dist. adminstr., 1976-95. Recipient Local award, Nat. Assn. Study and Performance African Am. Music, 2005; named Living Legend in Ch. Music, Hampton U. Ministers Conf. and Choir Dirs. Guild, 2005. Mem. Am. Choral Dirs., Music Educators Nat. Conf., Nat. Assn. Study Performances of African Am. Music Home: Chicago, Ill. Died Mar. 27, 2008.

WORLEY, VIRGINIA KING, microbiologist; b. Pitts., Apr. 15, 1925; d. Wilbert Frederick and Helena Anna (Blotter) King; m. Carl Milton Worley, Apr. 14, 1945 (div. Dec. 1963); children: Mark, Seth, Paul, Marianne. BS in Microbiology, U. Pitts., 1946; M in Music Edn., Duquesne U., 1991. Part-time organist, choir dir. various chs., Pitts., 1944-85; environ. health sanitarian Allegheny County Health Dept., Pitts., 1969-87; music min. St. Peter Roman Catholic Ch., Pitts., 1985-94; dir. therapeutic music programs various schs. and chs., Pitts., from 1990; gen. music. tchr., from 1990; music min. Good Shepherd Luth. Ch., Pitts., 1994-98, Allegheny United Meth. Ch., 1999—2001, St. Luke Luth. Ch., from 2001, Allegheny United Ch. Christ, from 2001. Pvt. tutor piano and pipe organ, 1955—. Bd. dirs. Freedom House Enterprises, 1979—; founder Greater Pitts. Women's Ctr. and Shelter, 1975, Greater Pitts. Cmty. Food Bank, 1980; mem. Ctrl. Northside Citizen's Coun., Pitts., 1993—, Manchester Citizens' Corp., Pitts., 1983—; bd. dirs. Phoenix Youth Orch. Grantee various founds., 1990—. Mem. AAUW, Am. Guild Organists (bd. dirs. 1994-95), Nat. Orgn. Parish Musicians, Nat. Mus. Women Arts, Pitts. Assn. Arts Edn. and Therapy, Nat. Assn. Edn. of Young Children, Young Men and Women's African Heritage Assn., Choristers Guild, Pi Kappa Lambda. Democrat. Avocations: camping, hiking, nature study. Home: Pittsburgh, Pa. Died Jan. 4, 2008.

WORZEL, JOHN LAMAR, retired geophysicist; b. West Brighton, S.I., NY, Feb. 21, 1919; s. Howard Henry and Marie Alma (Wilson) W.; m. Dorothy Crary, Nov. 22, 1941; children: Sandra, Howard, Richard, William P. BS in Engring. Physics, Lehigh U., 1940; MA in Geophysics, Columbia U., 1948, PhD, 1949. Research assoc. Woods Hole (Mass.) Oceanographic Inst., 1940-46; geodesist Columbia U., NYC, 1946-48, research assoc., 1948-49, instr. geology, 1949, asst. prof., 1950-52, assoc. prof., 1952-57, prof., 1957-72; asst. dir. Lamont Geol. Obs., Palisades, N.Y., 1951-64, acting dir., 1964-65, assoc. dir., 1965-72; prof., dep. dir. earth and planetary sciences divsn. Marine Biomed. Inst., U. Tex. Med. Br., Galveston, 1972-74; acting dir. geophys. lab. Marine Sci. Inst., 1974-75, dir. geophys. lab., 1975-79; prof. geology U. Tex., Austin, 1972-79; adj. prof. Rice U., 1974-78. Bd. dirs. Palisades Geophys. Inst., 1970—2002, treas., 1970-74, pres., 1974—2002. Bd. dirs. Rockland County council Boy Scouts Am., 1964-72. Recipient USN Meritorious Pub. Service citation Dept. of Navy, 1964; Guggenheim Found. fellow, 1963; Columbia U. grad. resident scholar, 1948. Fellow Internat. Assn. Geodesy, Am. Geophys. Union, Geol. Soc. Am.; mem. Soc. Exploration Geophysicists (chmn. com. 1974-76, v.p. 1978-79), Pi Mu Epsilon, Tau Beta Pi. Republican. Lutheran. Research on gravity and seismic refraction and reflection at sea, sound transmission of sea water. Home: Wilmington, NC. Died Dec. 26, 2008; Wilmington, NC.

WRAY, ROBERT THOMAS, lawyer; b. Chgo., Oct. 23, 1935; s. George and Ann (Moriarty) W.; m. Lila Keogh (dec.); children: Jennifer, Edward, Hillary. BS, Loyola U., 1957; JD, U. Mich., 1960. Bar: DC, Ill. 1960. Assoc. Hopkins & Sutter, Chgo., 1964—69; gen. counsel US Agy. for Internat. Devel. (USAID), 1969—71; sr. counsel TRW, Inc., 1972—73, Export-Import Bank of the U.S., 1974—79; prin. Robert Wray Assocs., 1979—86; internat. ptnr. Pierson, Ball & Dowd, 1986—87; prin. Robert Wray Associates, 1988—2009; spl. counsel Graham & James, 1988—97; ptnr. Holland & Knight, Washington, 1997—2003; mng. mem. Robert Wray PLLC, Washington, 2003—09. Recipient Superior Honor medal US Dept. State., 1971 Mem.: Chevy Chase Club, Annapolis Yacht Club, Talbot Country Club, Met. Club, Bretton Woods Com. Avocation: yachting. Died May 15, 2009.

WRIGHT, HARROLD EUGENE, petroleum engineer; b. Vernon, Tex., Aug. 28, 1924; s. Jess Newton and Bess Bailey (Burroughs) W.; m. Joyce Overbay (div. 1970); m. Joy Lavon Robinson, Dec. 13, 1970; children: Marianne Wright Arnold, Elizabeth, Arthur L., Amy Wright Rosche, Bradley. BEE, Tex. Tech. U., 1944. Registered profl. engr., Tex. Resident engr. Freese & Nichols, Consulting Engrs., San Augustine, Tex., 1946-48; petroleum engr. Hiawatha Oil & Gas Co., Midland, Tex., 1948-52, San Juan Oil Co., Dallas, 1952-55; v.p. Producing Properties, Inc., Dallas, 1956-63; pres. Swift Ops., Inc., Dallas, 1963-68; pres., chief exec. officer Gene Wright, Inc., Dallas, from 1968, San Juan Exploration Co., Dallas, 1973-81, pres., from 1988, Olde English Village, Inc., Tyler, Tex., from 1981. Mem. U.S. Dept. Commerce Industry Adv. Com., 1983-90, chmn. 1983; chmn. liaison com. Cooperating Oil and Gas Assns., 1982-83; chmn. Petroleum Industry Security Coun., 1981-84. Chmn. Dem. Com. for Responsible Govt., Dallas County, 1966; chmn., vice chmn. Polit. Action for Petroleum Industry, Tyler, 1978-85; bd. dirs. Drug Free Youth in Tex., 1989-90. Lt. (j.g.) USNR, 1944-46, PTO. Mem. Soc. Petroleum Engrs. (chmn. admissions com. 1961-63), Am. Assn. Petroleum Geologists, Natural Gas Supply Assn. (chmn. 1981-82), Ind. Petroleum Assn. Am. (chmn. natural gas com. 1978-81), Tex. Producers and Royalty Owners Assn. (pres., chmn. 1981-83), Dallas Petroleum Club, Southwest Energy and Commerce Coun. (chmn. 1988—), East Tex. Producers and Royalty Owners Assn. (v.p. 1988—), Tyler Area C. of C. (retail and svcs. com. chmn. 1989-90), East Tex. C. of C. (v.p. 1983-87). Home: Tyler, Tex. Died Aug. 18, 2008.

WRIGHT, LAWRENCE ALAN, psychiatrist; b. Pitts., Oct. 1, 1937; s. Lawrence Alan and Claire (Frick) W.; m. Jean Kettering, July 2, 1960; children: Bruce Alan, Beth Wright Davis. BA in History, U. Pitts., 1959, MD, 1963. Diplomate geriatric psychiatry Am. Bd. Psychiatry and Neurology. Intern W.Va. U., 1963-64, med. resident, 1966-67; psychiat. resident Western Psychiat. Inst. and Clinic, Pitts., 1967-70; dir. resocialization program Mayview State Hosp., Bridgeville, Pa., 1970-73; chief, psychiatric svcs. VA Med. Ctr., Pitts., 1973-82; mng. ptnr., pres. Clin. Psychiatry Assocs., P.C., Pitts., from 1982. Reviewer Physicians Rev. Corp. Inc., Pitts., 1987-90; cons. Pa. Blue Shield, Camp Hill, Pa., 1988—; com. mem., med. reviewer Keystone Peer Rev. Orgn., Camp Hill, 1985—; clin. asst. prof. U. Pitts. Sch. Medicine, 1973—; pres. Pa. Small Arms Co., Pitts., 1989-90; med. staff Western Psychiat. Inst. and Clinic; chmn. dept. psychiatry St. Clair Meml. Hosp. Pres. Joint Bd. Trustees-Smithfield United Ch., Pitts., 1987-89. Capt. U.S. Army, 1964-66. Fellow Am. Psychiatric Assn.; mem. AMA, Pitts. Psychiatric Soc. (pres. 1982-83), Psychiatric Physicians of Pa. (pres. 1989-90), Allegheny County Med. Soc., Pa. Med. Soc., Am. Psychiatric Assn., Pitts. Acad. Medicine, Assn. Gen. Hosp. Psychiatrists, Am. Assn. Geriatric Psychiatry, Am. Geriatric Soc., Carroll F. Reynolds History of Medicine Soc. Republican. Avocations: tennis, gardening, photography, reading, golf. Home: Pittsburgh, Pa. Died June 22, 2008.

WRIGHT, RICHARD JAY, lawyer; b. Ogdensburg, NY, Sept. 20, 1944; s. Leo and Gene Marion (Graham) W.; m. Laura Esther Snow, Aug. 5, 1978 (div.); 1 child, Richard Parker; m. Carol Lee Coburn, Apr. 19, 1986. BA, U. Vt., 1966; JD, Boston U., 1972. Bar: Vt. 1972, U.S. Dist. Ct. Vt. 1974, U.S. Ct. Appeals (2d cir.) 1976, U.S. Supreme Ct. 1979. Dep. state's atty. Rutland (Vt.) County, 1972-73; assoc. Law Office Joseph A. DeBonis, Poultney, Vt., 1973-76; ptnr. DeBonis, Wright & Winpenney P.C., Poultney, from 1976. Served to 1st lt. U.S. Army, 1966-68, Vietnam. Mem. ABA, Vt. Bar Assn., Rutland County Bar Assn., Assn. Trial Lawyers Am., Vt. Trial Lawyers Assn. Lodges: Rotary (pres. Poultney 1976-77, 1985-86). Avocations: photography, golf, skiing. Home: Wells, Vt. Died Nov. 25, 2007.

WRIGHT, SARAH ELIZABETH, writer, poet; b. Wetipquin, Md., Dec. 9, 1928; d. Willis Charles and Mary Amelia (Moore) Wright; m. Joseph Gilbert Kaye, June 17, 1960; children: Michael, Shelley. Student, Howard U., 1945—49, Pa. State Tchrs. Coll., 1950—52, New Sch. Social Rsch., L.I. U.; BS, SUNY, Albany. MacDowell Colony fellow MacDowell Colony, Peterborough, NH, 1973; writer-in-residence Finkelstein Meml. Libr., Spring Valley, NY, 1978, 1979, 1980. Pres. Pen & Brush, Inc., NYC, 1992—93, cons., prodr. Black History Month celebration and commemoration; cons. for creative artists pub. svc. program N.Y. State Coun. on the Arts. Co-author (with L. Smith): Give Me A Child, 1955; author: (novels) This Child's Gonna Live, 1969, A. Philip Randolph, 1990 (N.Y. Pub. Libr. award, 1990). Recipient Disting. Writer award, Middle Atlantic Writers Assn., 1988, The Sarah E. Wright Best Grad. Paper award, Salisburg State U., 1997, Outstanding Contbn. to Am. Lit. award, Zora Neale Hurston Assn., U. Md. Ea. Shore, Princess Anne, Md., 1999. Mem.: Pen Am. Ctr. (events com.), Authors Guild, Inc. (coun. mem. 1980—90), Harlem Writers Guild, Inc. (v.p., pres. 1958—65, award enduring commitment 1998), Nat. Assn. for Poetry Therapy (cert. poetry therapist). Home: New York, NY. Died Sept. 13, 2009.

WRIGHT, WILLIAM LELAND, chemicals executive; b. Darbyville, Ohio, Aug. 14, 1930; s. William David and Rose Irma (Fullen) W.; m. Anita June Wendt, Sept. 6, 1952; children: Kimberly D., Scott D., Wendy L. BS, Ohio U., 1953, MS, 1957; PhD, Purdue U., 1963. Plant physiologist Dow Chem. Co., Freeport, Tex., 1957-58; with Eli Lilly and Co., Greenfield, Ind., 1958-72, dir. agr. regulatory affairs, 1972-80, dir. Elanco (Wash.) Office, 1980-82, dir. plant sci. internat. rsch., 1982-84, dir. quality assurance R & D Indpls., 1987-89, ret., 1989; product plans advisor Elanco Products Co., Indpls., 1972-74. Co-author: (chpt.) Herbicide dev., 1975; contbr. numerous articles to profl. jours. Mem. Greenfield City Park Bd., 1977-79; mem. Rep. Senate Inner Circle, Washington, 1989; sustaining mem. Rep. Nat. Commn., Washington, 1991—. Capt. USAF, 1953-55, Korea. Mem. Am. Soc. Plant Physiology, Am. Soc. Horticulture, CAST, Weed Sci. Soc. Am. (chmn. EPA rels. com. 1958—), Sigma Xi. Methodist. Avocations: golf, writing, painting. Home: Fishers, Ind. Died Dec. 5, 2007.

WRIGHT, WILLIAM PARK, JR., real estate executive; b. Pine Bluff, Ark., Feb. 5, 1923; s. William Park Sr. and Mary Virginia (McGaughy) W.; m. Virginia Lee Gist, Aug. 21, 1948; 1 child, Virginia Lee Wright Currey. BS in Bus. Adminstrn., U. Ark., 1948. CPA, Ark., Tex. V.p. Comml. Credit Corp., Charlotte, N.C., 1948-63; real estate salesman Stanley Hickman Co., Dallas, 1963-67; owner, realtor Bill Wright Realty Co., Dallas, from 1967. Served to capt. USAFR, 1943-83. Mem. Dallas Bd. Realtors, Am. Inst. CPAs, Tex. Soc. CPAs, Sigma Chi. Clubs: Northwood Country (Dallas). Republican. Roman Catholic. Avocations: golf, fishing. Home: Dallas, Tex. Died May 26, 2008.

WUITHIRANYAGOOL, TAWEESAK NGOUNMANEE, entomologist; b. Roi-Et, Thailand, June 16, 1947; came to U.S., 1975; s. Somponse Ngounmanee and Toon (Khaunkan) W.; m. Sompong Prangkum, Aug. 17, 1975; 1 child, Rosrin. BS in Pub. Health, Mahidol U., Bangkok, 1970; MS in Environ. Health, Drexel U., Phila., 1981. Sr. sanitarian Dept. Health, Bangkok, 1970-72; chief mosquito control unit dept. Communicable Diseases Control Ministry Pub. Health, Bangkok, 1973-75; asst. foreman Midland Metal Product, Chgo., 1976-79; inspector Harris County Mosquito Control, Houston, 1982-84; entomologist Harris County Mosquitor Control, Houston, from 1984. Home: Stafford, Tex. Died Feb. 29, 2008.

WURPTS, JOHN ALBERT, farmer; b. Adrian, Minn., Oct. 1, 1942; s. Albert Wurpts; m. Rosalee Ann Nyhof, Dec. 30, 1966; children: Mishelle Renee, Malachi John. BA, Northwestern Coll., Orange City, Iowa, 1965; M in Christian Edn., Western Sem., Holland, Mich., 1967. Tchr., admisntr. So. Normal Sch., Brewton, Ala., 1967-70; high sch. tchr. Dallas Center (Iowa)-Grimes Schs., 1970-74; farm worker Rhinehart Farms, Dallas Center, 1974-75, Stine Seed Farms, Adell, Iowa, 1976-77; farm mgr. Bergstom Farms Inc., Ogden, Iowa, 1977-83; farm owner, mgr. John Wurpts Farms, Ogden, from 1983. Asst. dir. Soil Conservation Svc., Boone, Iowa, 1989-90; mem., chmn. salary negotiations com. Iowa State Edn. Assn., Dallas Ctr. Grimes chpt., 1970-74; chmn. Boone County Soil & Water Conservation Dist. Commnrs., 1991—. Mem. Supts. Adv. Com., Ogden, 1988-90; mem. Lutheran Lake Side Coop. Bd., 1994—. Recipient Faculty award So. Normal Sch., Brewton, Ala., 1969, Outstanding Young Educator award Dallas Center Jaycees,. 1970. Mem. Boone County Mktg. Club (treas. 1989-90), Lions, Christian Motorcyclist Orgn. Republican. Lutheran. Avocations: square dancing, motorcycling. Died Mar. 1, 2008.

WYATT, WENDELL, Former United States Representative from Oregon; b. Eugene, Oreg., June 15, 1917; m. Anne Elizabeth Buchanan (div.); m. Faye Hill, 1962; children: Ann, Jane, Wendell, Larry. Chmn. Oreg. State Rep. Ctrl. Com., 1955—57; state bar delegate Oregon State Bar delegate; ABA house delegate, 1960—66; mem. US Congress from 1st Oreg., 1964—75; ptnr. Schwabe, Williamson & Wyatt, 1975—2001; bd. dirs. Bohemia Inc., Benjamin Franklin Savings, Loan Assn.; bd. trustees Emanuel Hosp. Recipient Alumni of Yr. award, U. Oreg., 1975, Disting. Svc. award, 1975, Aubrey Watzek award, Lewis & Clark Coll., 1976. Republican. Died Jan. 28, 2009.

WYCZALKOWSKI, MARCIN ROMAN, retired economist; b. Pieskowa Skala, Poland, Apr. 20, 1910; came to U.S., 1946, naturalized, 1965; s. Josef J. and Zofia K. (Wyczalkowski) W.; m. Maria M. Anisko, July 15, 1938; children: Anna M. (Mrs. Richard Furnival), Andrew V., Carin T. (Mrs. Brian Carter). MA in Econs., Warsaw U., Poland, 1936, D. of Econs., 1938; postgrad., London Sch. Econs.-Polit. Sci., 1938-39. From asst. prof. to prof. econs. Warsaw Acad. Commerce, 1936-38, asst. prof., 1942-44, dep. prof., from 1945, dep. rector, 1946; sr. advisor IMF, Washington, 1946-75, ret. Dir. econ. rsch. dept. Nat. Bank Poland, 1945-46; govt. advisor Union of Burma, 1958-59; advisor Govt. of Cyprus, 1962-64, Ctrl. Bank; advisor East Carribean Monetary Authority, 1975-76. Author: (Polish) Money in Market and in Planned Economy, clandestine edit., 1944; Economic Organizations of the UN, 1946, The Good World Society, 2000, Economic System Transformation in Poland, Critical Remarks, 2002, Life of a Controversial Man, 2004; chief editor econ. monthly, Poland, 1945-46. Served with Polish Armed Forces, 1939, Polish Underground Army (Armia Krajowa), 1942-45. Mem. Polish-Am. Arts Assn., Polish Econ. Soc. (hon. mem.). Avocation: writing. Home: Sterling, Va. Died June 27, 2008.

WYDRA, FRANK THOMAS, healthcare executive; b. Republic, Pa., May 11, 1939; s. Frank T. and Anne M. (Kois) W.; m. Karen Branch, June 24, 1961; children: Denise Lee, Sheryl Lynn, Frank Thomas III. BS in Mgmt., U. Ill., 1961. V.p. Allied Supermarkets, Inc., Detroit, 1967-75; sr. v.p. HGH Health System, Detroit, 1975-85; pres. Radius Health Care Sysytems, Inc., Detroit, 1983-85; cons. Birmingham, Mich., 1985-88; exec. v.p. The Chi Group, Ann Arbor, Mich., 1988-91; mng. ptnr., CEO, owner IRI, Mgmt. Cons., Detroit, from 1991. Lectr. various profl. groups; bd. dirs. Mich. Health Systems Inc., Saber-Salisbury Assocs. Inc., Midwestern Health Ctr., MultiCare Med. Inc., RHS Inc. Author: Learner Controlled Instruction, 1980, (with others) Hospital Survival Guide, 1984, The Cure, 1992; creator 2 mgmt. games Performulations, 1978, The Dynamics of Power and Authority, 1981; contbr. articles to profl. jours. Personnel program advisor Mich. State U. Sch. Labor Relations, 1979-83; chmn. new programs Wayne County Community Coll., Detroit, 1979-80; bd. dirs. Detroit Metro Youth Found., 1980-83, State Mich. Health Occupations Council, Lansing, 1982-85. Capt. U.S. Army, 1961-63. Recipient numerous awards ASTD, Nat. Soc. Performance and Instrn., Mich. SOc. Instructional Tech., Supermarket Inst. Mem. Am. Hosp. Assn., Planning Soc. of Am. Hosp. Assn., Hosp. Personnel Adminstrs. Assn. (pres. 1981-82, numerous awards), Am. Mgmt. Assn., Am. Soc. Hosp. Pers.Adminstrs. (bd. dirs. 1981-83), Mich. Soc. Instrnl. Tech. (life, pres. 1973-74), Mich. Hosp. Assn., Employers Assn. Detroit (bd. dirs. 1982-85), Detroit Athletic Club. Avocations: writing, sailing. Home: Clarkston, Mich. Died Aug. 2, 2008.

WYETH, ANDREW NEWELL, painter; b. Chadds Ford, Pa., July 12, 1917; s. Newell Converse and Carolyn (Bockius) W.; m. Betsy Merle James, May 15, 1940; children: Nicholas, James Browning. Educated pvt. tutors; DFA (hon.), Colby Coll., Maine, 1954, Harvard U., 1955, Dickinson Coll., 1958, Swarthmore Coll., 1958, Nasson Coll., 1963, U. Md., U. Del., Northeastern U., Temple U., 1964; LHD (hon.), Tufts U., 1963; DFA (hon.), Princeton U., 1965; LHD (hon.), Franklin and Marshall Coll., 1965, Lincoln U., 1966, Amherst Coll., 1967; DFA (hon.), Bowdoin Coll., 1970; LHD (hon.), Ursinus Coll., 1971; DFA (hon.), U. Pa., 1972; LHD (hon.), West Chester U., 1984; DFA (hon.), Dartmouth Coll., 1984, Bates Coll., 1987; LHD (hon.), U. Vt., 1988. Artist, landscape painter, 1936—2009; first one-man show William Macbeth Gallery, N.Y.C., 1937, first solo exhbn. ever held in White House, 1970, first exhbn. by living Am. artist Royal Acad. Arts, London, 1980; exhibited Doll & Richards, Boston, 1938, 40, 42, 44, Cornell U., 1938, Macbeth Gallery, 1938, 41, first tempera show, 1943, 45, Currier Gallery, Manchester, N.H., 1939, room of watercolors, Art Inst. Chgo., 1941; room at Realist and Magic Realist show, Mus. Modern Art, N.Y.C., 1943; one-man exhbn., M. Knoedler & Co., N.Y.C., 1953, 58, Mass. Inst. Tech., Cambridge, 1960, Fogg Art Mus., William Farnsworth Library and Mus., 1963, Helga Pictures at numerous art museums, other univs. and museums; also exhbns. Arnot Mus., Elmira, N.Y., 1986, Seibu-Pisa, Tokyo, 1986, Kenesaw (Ga.) Mus. Art, 1986, Thomasville (Ga.) Art Ctr., 1987, Acad. of the Arts of USSR, Leningrad, 1987, Acad. of the Arts USSR, Moscow, 1987, Nat. Gallery of Art, Washington, 1987, Corcoran Gallery Art, Washington, 1987, An American Vision: Three Generations of Wyeth Art, various mus., 1987, Dallas Mus. Art, 1987, Mus. Fine Arts, Boston, 1988, Terra Mus. Am. Art, Chgo., 1988, Mus. Fine Arts, Houston, 1988, Setagaya Art Mus., Tokyo, 1988, L.A. County Mus. Art, L.A., 1988, Palazzo Reale, Milan, Italy, 1988, Fitzwilliam Mus., Cambridge, Eng., 1988, Fine Arts Mus. San Francisco, 1988, Brandywine River Mus., Chadds Ford, Pa., 1988, Detroit Inst. Arts, 1989, Sezon Mus. Art, Tokyo, 1991, Heckscher Mus., Huntington, N.Y., 1989, Gilcrease Mus., Tulsa, 1989, Portland (Maine) Mus. Art, 1989, Nukaga Gallery, Japan, 1990, Marcelle Fine Art Inc., N.Y.C., 1990, Takuji Kato Modern Art Mus., Tokyo, 1991, Takuji Kato Modern Art Mus., Chichibu City, Japan, 1991, Jacksonville (Fla.) Art Mus., 1992, Portland (Maine) Mus. Art, 1993, Farnsworth Art Mus., Rockland, Maine, 1994, 2005, San Francisco Mus. Modern Art, 1995, Charles and Emma Frye Art Mus., 1995, William King Regional Arts Center, Va., 1996, Butler Inst.Am.Art, Ohio, 1997, Whitney Mus. Am. Art, 1998, Self Family Art Center, Hilton Head Island, SC, 2000, Greenville County Mus. Art, 2001, Telfair Mus. Art, Savannah, Ga., 2001; Cin. Art Mus., 2002, 2007, Creekwood Mus. Art, Nashville, 2002, Frye Art Mus. Collection, Seattle, 2003, Addison Gallery Am. Art, Mass., 2004, High Mus. Am. Art, Atlanta, 2005, Phila. Mus. Art, 2006; represented in permanent collections Met. Mus. Art, Nat. Gallery Art. Awarded 1st prize, Wilmington Soc. Fine Arts, 1939, Obrig prize, Am. Watercolor Soc., 1945, award of Merit, Am. Acad. Arts and Letters and Nat. Inst. Arts and Letters, 1947, 1st prize in watercolor, Nat. Acad., 1946, Gold medal, Nat. Inst. Arts and Letters, 1965, George Walter Dawson Meml. medal, Phila. Watercolor Club, 1957, Mellon Gold medal of Achievement, Pa. Artists Exhibit, Ligonier Valley, Pa., 1958, Arts Festival award and Citation for bringing dignity to Am. art, Phila. Mus. Art, 1959, Percy M. Owens Meml. award, Fellowship of Pa. Acad. Fine Arts, Phila., 1960, Presdl. Medal of Freedom, 1963, citation, LaSalle Coll., Phila., 1965, Gold medal of honor, Pa. Acad. Fine Arts, 1966, Carnegie Inst. award, award for excellence, 1st award recognize outstanding performance in arts, Washington Coll., Chestertown, Md., 1976; Gold medal, Nat. Arts Club, 1978, first Am. artist awarded Presdl. award, Gold Congl. medal, 1988, Nat. Medal Arts, 2007. Mem. Am. Watercolor Soc. (certificate of merit 1962), Nat. Inst. Arts and Letters, Soviet Acad. Arts (hon.), Academie des Beaux-Arts, Chester County Art Assn. (dir.), Audubon Soc. (dir.), N.Y. Watercolor Soc., Wilmington Soc. Fine Arts, Phila. Watercolor Club (dir.), Washington Watercolor Club (dir.), Balt. Watercolor Club (dir.), AAAL, NAD (Academician elect May 1945, Gold medal preeminence in painting 1965), Am. Acad. Arts and Scis., Royal Soc. Painters and Watercolours (London). Died Jan. 16, 2009.

WYLIE, CHARLES MURRAY, internist, geriatrician, educator; b. Dunfermline, Fife, Scotland, Sept. 20, 1924; came to U.S., 1949; s. Thomas and Mary (Symon) W.; m. Dorothy Joan Marion Hennessy, Jan. 31, 1959; children: Christine, John Adrian, Sheila, Robin. MD, BChir, U. Glasgow, Scotland, 1947; MD, U. Glasgow, 1957; MPH, Johns Hopkins U., 1952, DPH, 1956; DTM, U. London, 1958. Diplomate Am. Bd. Preventive Medicine. Med. intern, resident various hosps., Scotland and Eng., 1947-49; resident in medicine Overlook Hosp., Summit, N.J., 1949-50; health dir. State Dept. Health, Richmond, Va., 1950-53; rsch. assoc. Nat. Commn. on Chronic Illness, Balt., 1953-55; lt. comdr. med. corps U.S.N., 1955-57; from asst. prof. to assoc. prof. Johns Hopkins U., Balt., 1958-67; prof. pub. health adminstrn. U. Mich., Ann Arbor, 1968-86; pvt. practice Ann Arbor, 1986—2009. Contbr. numerous articles to profl. jours., chpts. to books. Fellow Faculty Cmty. Medicine, Eng., Royal Soc. Medicine, London Home: Ann Arbor, Mich. Died Mar. 14, 2009.

WYNN, JOHN CHARLES, clergyman, retired theology studies educator; b. Akron, Ohio, Apr. 11, 1920; s. John Francis and Martha Esther (Griffith) W.; m. Rachel Linnell, Aug. 27, 1943; children: Mark Edward, Martha Lois Borland, Maryan Kay Ainsworth. BA, Coll. Wooster, 1941; BD, Yale U., 1944; MA, Columbia U., 1963, EdD, 1965; DD, Davis and Elkins Coll., 1958. Ordained to ministry Presbyn. Ch. (U.S.A.), 1944. Student asst. pastor Trinity Luth. Ch., New Haven, 1943-44; assoc. minister First Presbyn. Ch., Evanston, Ill., 1944-47; pastor Presbyn. Ch. El Dorado, Kans., 1947-50; dir. family edn. and research United Presbyn. Bd. Christian Edn., Phila., 1950-59; prof. Colgate Rochester/Bexley Hall/Crozer Divinity Sch., 1959-85; prof. emeritus Colgate Rochester/Bexley Hall/Crozer Theol. Sem., from 1985; pvt. practice family therapy; vis. prof. U. Rochester, San Francisco Theol. Sem., St. Bernard's Sem., Wesley Theol. Sem., Hartford Theol. Found.; postdoctoral fellow Cornell U., 1973-74, St. John's U., 1980. Mem. summer faculty Union Theol. Sem., N.Y.C., San Francisco Theol. Sem.; del. study conf. World Coun. Chs., 1953, 57, 64, 65, 67, 75, 80; lectr. 5 univs., Republic of South Africa, 1968; chmn. com. on sexuality in human cmty. U.P. Ch.; vol. mem. chaplaincy staff Charlestown Care Ctr., Balt. Author: How Christian Parents Face Family Problems, 1955, Pastoral Ministry to Families, 1957, Families in the Church, A Protestant Survey, 1961, Christian Education for Liberation and Other Upsetting Ideas, 1977, Family Therapy in Pastoral Ministry, 1982 (rev. and expanded as Family Therapy in Pastoral Ministry: Counseling for the Nineties, 1991), The Family Therapist, 1987; Editor: Sermons on Marriage and Family Life, 1956, Sex, Family and Society in Theological Focus, 1966, Sexual Ethics and Christian Responsibility, 1970; Contbr. articles to mags. and religious jours. Bd. dir. Presbyn. Life, Planned Parenthood League Rochester and Monroe County, Family Service Rochester, Samaritan Pastoral Counseling Ctr. Fellow Am. Assn. Marriage and Family Therapy (approved supr.); mem. Religious Edn. Assn., Nat. Coun. Chs. of Christ in U.S.A. (chmn. com. family life 1957-60), Nat. Coun. Family Rels., Family Svc. Assn. Am., Rochester Coun. Chs. (dir.) Died Mar. 31, 2009.

WYSOCKI, ROBERT ADAM, telecommunications company executive; b. Syracuse, NY, Apr. 29, 1945; s. Adam Joseph and June Pauline (Guenthner) W.; m. Mary Tapogna, Feb. 9, 1969; children: Christopher R., Lauren M. BS, U.S. Mil. Acad., 1967; MBA, Pace U., 1984. Mgr. treasury N.Y. Telephone, Albany, 1973-76, corp. cash mgr. NYC, 1977-80, mgr. pension fund, 1980-81, mgr. long-term fin., 1981-82; investment dir. pension fund NYNEX Corp., NYC, 1983-87, dir. investor rels., from 1988. Dir. West Point Soc. of N.Y., 1978. Capt. Signal Corps U.S. Army, 1967-71. Mem. Investor Rels. Inst., Fin. Analyst Fedn., N.Y. Soc. Security Analysts. Republican. Roman Catholic. Home: Bridgewater, Conn. Died Jan. 23, 2008.

WYSZYNSKI, JAMES EDWARD, JR., lawyer, state government; b. Elyria, Ohio, Nov. 16, 1950; s. James Edward and June Eleanor (Coe) W.; m. Kay Boston, Nov. 17, 1979; 1 child, James Edward III. A in Gen. Studies, Macomb Cmty. Coll., 1981; B of Accountancy, Walsh Coll., 1983; JD, Detroit Coll. of Law, 1989. Bar: Mich. 1989. Controller Metro-East Drug Treatment Corp., Detroit, 1984-87; chief acct. Cmty. Case Mgmt., Inc., Detroit, 1987-89; rsch. atty. Mich. Ct. of Appeals, Lansing, 1989-90; law clk. Appeals Judge Donald Holbrook, Lansing, 1990-91; commr. Workers Compensation Appellate Commn., Lansing, 1991-93 and from 95, chmn., 1993-95. Contbr. articles to profl. jours. Chmn. Eaton County Hist. Commn., Charlotte, Mich., 1993-94, Eaton County Rep. Party, 1995-96; trustee Greater Lansing Cath. Edn. Found., 1995—, Eaton Area Habitat for Humanity, 1995—. Recipient Employee of Yr. award Metro-East Drug Treatment Corp., 1985, Scroll of Appreciation, Macomb Cmty. Coll., 1986, Recognition certificate Detroit Coll. of Law Rev., 1989, Top Paper award 21st Ann. Internat. Workers Compensation Coll., 1994. Mem. ABA, State Bar of Mich., Advocates Polish Am. Bar Assn., Mich. Polit. History Soc., DCL Alumni Assn. (bd. dirs. 1994-97), KC. Republican. Roman Catholic. Avocations: collect polit. memorabilia, golf. Home: Eagle, Mich. Died Apr. 1, 2008.

YAJKO, MARK A., lawyer; b. Steubenville, Ohio, May 31, 1958; s. Steve M. and C. Lorraine (Compa) Y.; m. Doreen D. Ludwig, May 17, 1980 (div. 1984); m. Barbara E. Barnes, June 24, 1989; children: Mallory Alyssa, Alyson Lian. BA in Pub. Adminstrn., U. Findlay, 1980; JD, Duquesne U., 1983. Bar: Ohio 1983, U.S. Dist. Ct. (no. dist.) Ohio 1984. Laborer Crucible Steel Co., Midland, Pa., 1976-80; felony staff investigator D.C. Pub. Defender Svc., 1980; assoc. Aronson, Fineman & Davis, East Liverpool, Ohio, 1983-95; pvt. practice East Liverpool, 1995-97; owner, operater Lighthouse Mediation & Cons. Svc., East Liverpool. Acting judge East Liverpool Mcpl.Ct., 1990-95; acting domestic rels. referee/magistrate Columbiana County Common Pleas Ct., 1995; instr. Ohio Valley Bus. Coll., East Liverpool, 1987-91; legal advisor Beaver Local Alumni Assn., East Liverpool, 1990—; adv. mock trial competition, 1992—; speaker on domestic rels. law. Mem. bd. edn. Beaver Local Sch. Dist., Lisbon, Ohio, 1992-95. Named Citizen of Yr. Calcutta Area C. of C., 1995. Mem. Columbiana County Bar Assn. (continuing legal edn. and rules chair 1990—), Calcutta Area C. of C. (bd. dirs. 1996), Elks. Avocation: boating. Home: East Liverpool, Ohio. Died Aug. 23, 2008.

YAKAN, MOHAMAD ZUHDI, political science educator; b. Tripoli, Lebanon, Aug. 28, 1938; came to U.S., 1988; s. Zuhdi Rasheed and Habibah (Shaaban) Y.; m. Sibylle Nickle, Apr. 8, 1988. HS, Internat. Coll., Beirut, Lebanon, 1956; BA, Am. U. Beirut, 1959; MA, A.U.B., Beirut, 1961; PhD, U. Mich., 1965. Asst./acting mgr. Prodeco/Pub. Rels.-Mktg., Beirut, 1965-71; asst. prof. Beirut U. Coll., 1965-71; lectr. law faculty Lebanese U., Beirut, 1966-71; asst. prof., dir. devel. and rel. Beirut U. Coll., 1971-88; lectr. Wayne State U., Detroit, 1988-89, Henry Ford Coll., Dearborn, Mich., 1988-89; v.p., gen. mgr. internat. I.A.S. Group, San Diego, 1989-90; lectr. U. San Diego, 1990-91; adj. prof. U.S. Internat. U., San Diego, 1991-93, assoc. prof., from 1994. Author: Lebanon and Challenges of Future, 1978, Political Authority in Lebanon, 1979, Hijrah Calendar, 1981; editor: Lebanese Constitutional Issues, 1975, Roman Law and Muslin Shari'a, 1975, Diwan Al-Mu'atamid Bin Abbad, 1975, Diwan Al-Shafi'e, 1981, Diwan Al-Baghdadi, 1983, Constitutional Law and Political Systems, 1982; co-editor: documents on Lebanon's Political System, 1975; author more than 100 articles and papers. Founding mem. Salwa Nassar Found., Beirut, 1970, Lebanese Polit. Sci. Assn., Beirut, 1959, Lebanese Assn. for Human Rights, Beirut, 1985, Internat. Coun. for Muslim-Christian Dialogue, Beirut, 1985. Recipient H.B. Earhart Found. award, 1965. Mem. Am. Polit. Sci. Assn., Middle East Inst. (assoc. Middle East rsch. and info. project), Acad. Polit. Sci.,

Western Polit. Sci. Assn., Acad. Polit. and Social Sci., Middle East Studies Assn., Fgn. Policy Assn., UN Assn., Internat. Studies Assn., World Affairs Coun. San Diego. Avocations: research, reading. Home: San Diego, Calif. Died Feb. 12, 2008.

YAMASAKI, MAMORU, former state senator; b. 1916; s. Isuke and Sode Kawaoka Yamasaki. Mem. Dem. Ctrl. Com., Territory Hawaii, 1956—64, Hawaii State Dem. Ctr. Com., 1960—66; asst. clerk, senate Ways & Means Com.; 30th territorial legislature, 1959; state rep. Hawaii, 1959—67; state senator Dist. 4 Hawaii, 1968—92; membership svc. dir., Maui County Divsn. Internat. Longshoreman's & Warehouseman's Union. Mem.: Maui County Coun. Boys Scouts (former adv. bd.), Maui United Fund., Maui Econ. Opportunity & Lahaina Restoration Found., Maui Salvation Army, KRR Fed. Credit Union (former bd. dir.). Democrat. Buddhist. Died Aug. 17, 1999.

YANG, WILLIAM, pediatrician, researcher; b. Qingdao, Shandong, China, Mar. 13, 1948; came to U.S., 1962; s. Maurice and Xing-Qing (Wang) Y.; m. Susan Terozita Depoliti, May 5, 1985; children: William Simone Jr., Adrienne C., Stephen C. BA in Math., Chemistry, U. Calif., Irvine, 1969; PhD in Chemistry, U. Ill., Chgo., 1973; MD, U. Chgo., 1976. Diplomate Nat. Bd. Med. Examiners, Am. Bd. Pediatrics. Intern in pediatrics Children's Hosp., Phila., 1976-77, resident in pediatrics, 1977-78, fellow in pediatric endocrinology and metabolism, 1978-81; asst. prof. pediatrics U. Pa., Phila., 1981-82; assoc. dir. clin. investigations research and devel. div. Smith Kline & French, Phila., 1982-84, med. dir. Far East, China, 1985-87; clin. assoc. Childrens Hosp. of Phila., from 1982; assoc. med. dir. research and devel. div. Berlex Labs., Cedar Knolls, N.J., 1984-85; med. dir. Ams., Far East, South Africa internat. div. Smith, Kline & French Labs., Phila., 1988-89; area med. dir. Japan, East Asia Smith Kline Beecham Pharms., Phila., 1989-93; v.p. pharm. devel. Pharmagenesis, Palo Alto, Calif., from 1994. Bd. dirs. Suzhou (China) Pres. Pharmagenesis Pharm. Corp. Contbr. articles to profl. jours. Recipient Young Investigator award NIH, 1982. Mem. AMA, Am. Chem. Soc. Avocations: fencing, scuba diving, chinese history. Home: Bear Creek, Pa. Died July 25, 2008.

YANG, XIANGZHONG, research scientist, administrator, educator; b. Weixian, Hebei, China, July 31, 1959; came to U.S., 1983; s. Wukui Yang and Fengrong Zhang; m. Xiuchun Tian, Jan. 5, 1986; 1 child, Andrew Chun. BS in Animal Sci. with honors, Beijing Agrl. U., 1982; diploma, Nanjing Argl. U., China, 1982; MS in Reproductive Physiology, Cornell U., 1986, PhD in Reproductive Physiology, 1990. Rsch. asst. Cornell U., Ithaca, NY, 1983-89, lab. program coord., 1987-90, postdoctoral fellow, 1990-91, sr. rsch. assoc., dir. Embryo Engring. Program, 1992-96; assoc. prof., head Transgenic Animal Facility Biotech Ctr./Animal Sci., U. Conn., Storrs, 1996-2000, prof., 2000—09; dir. Ctr. Regenerative Biology U. Conn., 2001—09. Adj. prof. Beijing Agrl. U., 1992; adj. prof. Cornell U., 1996; hon. prof. Chinese Acad. Agrl. Scis., Beijing, 1991, Beijing Agrl. U., 1992, Xinjiang (China) Acad. Animal Scis., 1993; dir. China-Cornell Fellowship Programs, Ithaca, 1992-96; dir. China Bridges Internat., Storrs, 1996; chmn. local arrangement com. Reproduction in Farm Animals Symposium, Ithaca, 1992; mem. internat. program com. Ann. M.C. Chang Meml. Conf., 1992; cons. sci. dir. Baylor Ctr. Reproductive Health, Dallas, 1993-94; cons. Gencyme Transgenics, Inc., Framingham, Mass., 1993-2009, PPL Therapeutics, Blacksburg, Va.; invited spkr. in field. Author: Biotechnology of Preimplantational Embroys, 1993; editor-in-chief Agr. Scis. Overseas, 1990-94; contbr. numerous articles to sci. jours., abstracts, tech. papers to conf. procs.; media coverage on CNN Headline News, ABC, CBS, BBC News, NY Times, Washington Post, Wall Street Journal, US News and World Report. Grantee Conn. U. Biotech., 1993, EAIC Inc., 1993-96, USDA, 1991-94, 92-95, 96-98, 2001, Rockefeller Found., 1991-95, 92-97, 97, Lingnan Found., 1995-97, 97-99, Vet Sch., 1993-94, 94-96, NIH, 2001, Transpharm. Inc., 1994, Baylor U., 1994-96, Genzyme Transgenic Corp., 1996, Conn. Innovations Inc., Biotech. R & D Corp.; fellow China State Edn. Commn., 1983-85, Cornell U. Grad. Sch., 1985. Mem. Internat. Embryo Transfer Soc. (edn. com. mem. 1992-94), Soc. Study of Reproduction (com. chair 1991-93), NY State Acad. Scis., Chinese Agrl. Assn. Students and Scholars (founder, pres. 1988-89, conf. chair 1989), Am. Fertility Soc., Chinese Soc. and Tech. Assn., Sigma Xi. Produced first male clones from breeding bull in the world in Japan in 1998. These clones were selected by the Guinness World Records as the largest clones in the world (published as a cover paper in the Proceedings of the NAS, USA); Produced the first clone cow of an adult farm animal (known as Amy, the calf) in the US in June, 1999, which was called "cloning milestone"; First to report that cloned animals have normal telomere lengths and have normal genetic age (published in Nature Genetics); First to document that adult clones can reproduce normally; First to report abnormal expression of X-linked genes in cloned animals which may contribute to the neonatal death of clones (published in Nature Genetics); First to report clones of first and second generations appear healthy and have normal telomere lengths (published in Nature Biotechnology). Died Feb. 5, 2009.

YATES, WILLIAM ALBERT, physician, hospital administrator; b. Ottawa, Ont., Can., Nov. 16, 1929; came to U.S., 1954; s. John Frederick and Mary Edna Irene (Stedman) Y.; m. Patricia Eileen Ellis, Aug. 23, 1953; children: Jeffrey, Donald, Cynthia, Scott. MDCM, Queen's Coll., Kingston, Ont., 1954. Diplomate Am. Bd. Surgery. Internship Conemaugh Valley Meml. Hosp., Johnstown, Pa., 1954-55; residency in gen. surgery Mercy Hosp., Pitts., 1955-59; chmn. dept. surgery Lee Hosp., Johnstown, Pa., 1959-88, v.p. med. affairs, 1988-96, med. dir. occupational health, 1990-96; ret., 1996. Chmn. United Fund, Johnstown, 1976. Flight lt. RCAF, 1950-53. Fellow ACS. Republican. Avocations: hunting, fishing, golf. Home: Johnstown, Pa. Died Jan. 14, 2008.

YAVITZ, BORIS, retired dean, finance educator; b. Tbilisi, USSR, June 4, 1923; came to U.S., 1946, naturalized, 1950; s. Simon and Miriam (Mindlin) Y.; m. Irene Bernhard, July 17, 1949; children: Jessica Ann, Judith, Emily. MA, Cambridge U., Eng., 1943; MS, Columbia U., 1948, PhD, 1964. Economic cons. Jewish Agy. for Palestine, NYC, 1948-49; mgmt. cons. Werner Mgmt. Cons., Larchmont, N.Y., 1949-54; owner, mgr. Simbar Devel. Corp., NYC, 1954-61; faculty Columbia U., NYC, 1964-94, prof. mgmt., 1964-94; dean Columbia U. Grad. Sch. Bus., 1975-82, Paul Garrett prof. pub. policy & bus. responsibility, 1982-94; dep. chmn., dir. Fed. Res. Bank N.Y., 1976-82; dean emeritus, Paul Garrett prof. emeritus Columbia U., 1994—2009; prin. Lear, Yavitz & Assocs. L.L.C., 1995—2009. Bd. trustees Am. Assembly, N.Y.C., 1975-82; vice chmn. The Inst. for the Future; bd. govs. Media and Soc. Seminars, 1983-84; mem. nat. adv. coun. W. Averill Harriman Inst. Advanced Study of Soviet Union; chmn. Nat. Assn. Corp. Dirs. Blue Ribbon Commn. on Corp. Governance. Author books; contbr. articles in field to profl. jours. Served to lt. British Royal Navy, 1943-46. Mem. ASME, Inst. Mgmt. Sci. Died Feb. 14, 2009.

YEDLICKA, WILLIAM GEORGE, retired sales professional; b. Apollo, Pa., Dec. 25, 1922; s. Joseph Frank and Katie (Cadena) Y.; m. Theresa Rosamond Unger, July 17, 1970; 1 child, Monte. BS, U. Pitts., 1949, M Letters, 1957. Asst. sales mgr. Bowers Battery & Spark Plug Co. div. Gen. Battery Co., Reading, Pa., 1965-66; regional sales mgr. Gen. Battery Co., Atlanta, 1966-67; spl. products mgr. East Pa. Mfg. Co., Inc., Lyon Station, 1967-74, sales mgr. R.R. and mining, 1974-79, v.p. sales, indsl., R.R. and mining, 1979-88. Bd. dirs., Molds Corp., Kansas City, Mo. Author tech. papers, procedural manuals. Lt. col. USAF, 1942-46. Decorated, DFC, Air medal with 4 clusters. Mem. Material Handling Inst., Material Handling Equipment Dealers Assn., Nat. Elec. Mfrs. Assn., Ind. Battery Mfrs. Assn., Battery Coun. Internat. (chmn. indsl. battery com.), Indsl. Truck Assn., Indsl. Battery Soc., Shriners, Elks. Republican. Presbyterian. Avocations: golf, swimming, astronomy. Home: Sun City West, Ariz. Died June 22, 2008.

YEDLOSKY, ROBERT JOSEPH, geologist, geologic engineering consultant; b. Morgantown, W.Va., Feb. 5, 1932; s. Joseph Martin and Eloise A. (Perrine) Y.; m. Myrtle Joyce Crabtree; children: Pamela R., Joyce G., Walter J., Franklin S. BS, W.Va. U., 1958, MS, 1960. Geologist U.S. Bur. Pub. Rds., Morgantown, 1957-59, Pan Am. Petroleum, Oklahoma City, Okla., 1962-66, Ft. Worth, 1966-68, Consol. Gas Supply Corp., Clarksburg, W.Va., 1968-72; cons. geologist in pvt. practice, Morgantown, 1972-74, Fairmont, W.Va., 1974-79 and from 91; v.p. Mert Devel., Inc., Fairmont, 1979-91. Contbr. numerous articles to profl. jours.; presenter in field. Sgt. U.S. Army, 1952-55. Died Mar. 8, 2008.

YEH, EDWARD HSIN-YANG, physicist; b. Hsin-chu, Taiwan, Republic of China, Jan. 1, 1930; came to U.S., 1958; s. Sueng-teh and Siang-hua (Tsai) Y.; m. Gretchen Ching-Yuang Lo, June 17, 1968; children: Henry T., Daniel N. MS, Kyusha U., Fukuoka, Japan, 1957; PhD, U. N.C., 1960. Rsch. physicist nuclear data NAS Nat. Rsch. Coun., Washington, 1960-61; sr. scientist E.G. and G. Inc., Boston, 1961-63; vis. scholar Dublin (Ireland) Inst. for Advanced Studies, 1963-66; prof. physics and astronomy Moorhead (Minn.) State U., 1966-87; sr. physicist Naval Weapons Ctr., China Lake, Calif., from 1984. Reviewer books and jours. in physics and math.; contbr. over 30 articles on physics, math. and engring. to profl. jours. Mem. Am. Phys. Soc., Soc. Photo-Optical Instrumentation Engrs., Sigma Psi Sigma. Home: Huntington Beach, Calif. Died Feb. 8, 2008.

YOHE, RUTH MCCHESNEY, physician; b. Elgin, Ill., Apr. 19, 1926; d. Oswald Belmont and Emma Amelia (Halsey) McChesney; m. Robert B. Yohe, Sept. 8, 1956; children: Virginia, Cynthia, Steven, Catherine. BA, State U. Iowa, 1948; MD, Med. Coll. Pa., 1954. Diplomate Am. Bd. Pediatrics, Am. Bd. Allergy and Immunology. Intern Broadlawns Polk County Hosp., Des Moines, 1954-55; resident Raymond Blank Meml. Hosp. for Children, Des Moines, 1955-57; fellow in allergy and immunology Kans. U., U. Mo., Kansas City, 1970-72; practice medicine specializing in allergy and immunology Overland Park, Kans., from 1972. Asst. clin. prof. pediatrics Kans. U. Med. Ctr., Kansas City, 1958—, U. Mo., Kansas City, 1958—. Mem. Am. Acad. Allergy and Immunology, Greater Kansas City Allergy Soc. (sec., treas., v.p., pres. 1985-87). Republican. Lutheran. Died Sept. 3, 2007.

YONDA, ALFRED WILLIAM, mathematician; b. Cambridge, Mass., Aug. 10, 1919; s. Walter and Theophelia (Naruscewicz) Y.; m. Mary Jane McManus, Dec. 19, 1949 (dec.); children: Nancy, Kathryn, Elizabeth, John; m. Peggy A. Terrel, June 22, 1975. BS, U. Ala., 1952, MA in Math., 1954. Registered profl. engr. Mathematician rocket rsch. Redstone Arsenal, Huntsville, Ala., 1953, U.S. Army Ballistic Rsch. Labs., Aberdeen, Md., 1954-56; instr. math. U. Ala., Tuscaloosa, 1954, Temple U., Phila., 1956-57; assoc. scientist, rsch. & devel. divsn. Avco Corp., Wilmington, Mass., 1957-59; sr. mem. tech. staff RCA, Camden, NJ, 1959-66; mgr. computer analysis and programming dept. Raytheon Co. Space and Info. Systems Divsn., Sudbury, Mass., 1966-70, mgr. software systems lab., 1969-70, prin. engr. missiles systems divsn., 1970-73; mgr. sys. analysis & programming GTE Govt. Systems Corp., 1973-77, mgr. software engring. Atlantic ops., 1977-82, sr. mem. tech. staff Command Control & Comm. Sector, 1983-91; software systems engr. Yonda Software Systems Cons., from 1991. Contbr. articles to profl. jours. Pres. Milford Area Assn. Retarded Children, 1970-74, vice chmn. fin. com. Town of Medway, 1973; bd. dirs. Blackstone Valley Mental Health and Retardation Area, 1970-76; trustee Medway Librs., 1973-82, chmn., 1974-81. With USAAF, 1943-46. Hon. fellow Advanced Level Telecomm. Tng. Ctr., Ghaziabad, India, 1981. Mem. AAAS, IEEE, Math. Assn. Am., N.Y. Acad. Scis., Sigma Xi, Phi Eta Sigma, Pi Mu Epsilon (pres. Ala. chpt. 1953-54), Sigma Pi Sigma. Died Feb. 12, 2009.

YOON, POKSYN SONG, education administrator, biochemical researcher; b. Howell, Mich., June 25, 1948; d. Doo Sun and Kyung Shyn (Song) Y. BS in Zoology, U. Mich., 1973; PhD in Biochemistry, U. Wis., 1979; postgrad., Johnson & Wales U., from 1997. Rsch. asst. U. Wis., Madison, 1973-80, U. Mich., Ann Arbor, 1982-88; asst. prof. Tufts U., Boston; staff biochemist Boston VA Hosp., 1988-92; dir. edn. and tng. ARC/Job Learning Ctrs., Providence, 1992-97; dir. Roger Williams U., Providence, from 1997. Contbr. articles to profl. jours. including Clin. Rsch., Blood, Jour. Immunology, Biochemistry, among others. Bd. dirs. R.I. HIV Prevention Com. Planning, Providence; vol. tng. staff R.I. chpt. ARC., 1988—, dir. edn. and tng., 1993-97, vol. trainer Grand Traverse chpt., 1994—; mem. R.I. chpt. Am. Heart Assn., 1991—. Grantee United Way, 1997, ARC, 1995, 97, E. Harris Found., 1995, 97; Fulbright-Hays Commn. lectureship, 1982. Mem. Fedn. for Exptl. Biologists, Sigma Xi. Avocations: grant writing, educational research, home improvements, piano, pets. Home: Providence, RI. Died Jan. 5, 2008.

YORK, HERBERT FRANK, retired physics professor; b. Rochester, NY, Nov. 24, 1921; s. Herbert Frank and Nellie Elizabeth (Lang) Y.; m. Sybil Dunford, Sept. 28, 1947; children: David Winters, Rachel, Cynthia. AB, U. Rochester, 1942, MS, 1943; PhD, U. Calif., Berkeley, 1949; DSc (hon.), Case Inst. Tech., 1960; LL.D., U. San Diego, 1964, Claremont Grad. Sch., 1974. Physicist Radiation Lab., U. Calif., Berkeley, 1943-58, assoc. dir., 1954-58; asst. prof. physics dept. U. Calif., Berkeley, 1951-54, assoc. prof., 1954-59, prof., 1959-61; dir. Lawrence Radiation Lab., Livermore, 1952-58; chief Advanced Rsch. Project Agy. US Dept. Def., 1958, dir. advanced rsch. projects divsn. Inst. for Def. Analyses, 1958, dir. def. rsch. & engring., 1958-61; chancellor U. Calif.-San Diego, 1961—64, acting chancellor, 1970—72, prof. physics, 1964—88, prof. emeritus, 1988—2009, chmn. dept. physics, 1968-69, dean grad. studies, 1969-70, dir. program on sci., tech. and pub. affairs, 1972-88; dir. Inst. Global Conflict and Cooperation, 1983-88, dir. emeritus, 1988—2009. Amb. Comprehensive Test Ban Negotiations, 1979-81; trustee Aerospace Corp., Inglewood, Calif., 1961-87; mem. Pres.'s Sci. Adv. Com., 1957-58, 64-68, vice chmn., 1965-67; trustee Inst. def. Analysis, 1963-96; gen. adv. com. ACDA, 1962-69; mem. Def. Sci. Bd., 1977-81; spl. rep. of sec. def. at space arms control talks, 1978-79; mem. task force future nat. labs. Sec. Emergy, 1994-95; cons. Stockholm Internat. Peach Rsch. Inst.; rschr. in application atomic energy to nat. def. problems of arms control and disarmament, elem. particles. Author: Race to Oblivion: A Participant's View of the Arms Race, 1970, Arms Control, 1973, The Advisors, 1976, Making Weapons, Talking Peace: A Physicist's Journey From Hiroshima to Geneva, 1987, Does Strategic Defense Breed Offense?, 1987, (with Sanford Lakoff) A Shield in the Sky, 1989, Arms and the Physicist, 1994; also numerous articles on arms or disarmament; bd. dirs. Bull. Atomic Scientists. Trustee Bishop's Sch., La Jolla, Calif., 1963-65. Recipient E.O. Lawrence award AEC, 1962, Vannevan Bush award, 2000, Clark Kerr award, 2000, Enrico Fermi award, 2000; Guggenheim fellow, 1972. Fellow AAAS, Am. Phys. Soc. (forum on physics and soc. award 1976, Leo Szilard award 1994), Am. Acad. Arts and Sci.; mem. Fedn. Am. Scientists (chmn. 1970-71, exec. com. 1969-76, 95-2000, pub. svc. award 1992), Pugwash Movement 1969-2009, Phi Beta Kappa, Sigma Xi. Home: La Jolla, Calif. Died May 19, 2009.

YORKE, MARY FRANCES, mathematician, educator; b. Osborne, Kans., Nov. 22, 1933; d. Francis Lafayette and Goldie Mae (McIntire) Overfield; 1 child, Jennifer F. BEd, Kans. State Tchrs. Coll., 1955; MS, Kans. State U., 1957. Instr. Rutgers U., Camden, N.J., 1959-66; asst. prof. Coll. Guam, Agana, 1966-68; lectr. Claremont Coll., Perth, Australia, 1968; asst. prof. Lawrence Inst. Tech., Southfield, Mich., 1969-73; programmer-analyst U. Mich., Ann Arbor, 1979-82; asst. prof. Ea. Mich. U., Ypsilanti, 1982—2002. Textbook reviewer, 1990-2002. Friend and advocate Parents and Friends of Lesbians and Gays, Ann Arbor, 1997—; support group leader Alzheimer's Assn., 2000-04. Democrat. Avocations: equestrian, depression glass, pets. Home: South Lyon, Mich. Died July 6, 2008.

YOSHIDA, RAY KAKUO, painter, art educator; b. Kapaa, Hawaii, Oct. 3, 1930; BA, Art Inst. Chgo.; M.F.A., Syracuse U.; postgrad., U. Chgo., U. Hawaii and with A.D. Reinhardt. Frank Harrold Sellers prof. art Art Inst. Chgo., 1960—2000.

Exhbns include, Inst. Contemporary Art, U. Pa., 1969, exhbns. include, Art Inst. Chgo. exhbns., 1969, 71, 77, Indpls. Mus. Art, 1972-77, 12th Bienal de Sao Paulo, Brazil, 1973, Mus. Contemporary Art, Chgo., Bklyn. Mus., Art Inst. Chgo., 1981, 82, Ceolfrith Gallery, Sunderland Arts Ctr., Eng., 1981; represented permanent collections, Everson Mus., Syracuse, N.Y., Art Inst. Chgo., Mus. des 20, Jahrhunderts, Vienna, Austria, AT&T, N.Y.C., Ball State U., Muncie, Ind. Recipient Thomas C. Thompson Purchase prize Everson Mus., 1953; recipient Walter M. Campana prize Art Inst. Chgo., 1960, Frank G. Logan medal and prize Art Inst. Chgo., 1971, Virgine K. Headberg prize Art Inst. Chgo., 1977 Died Jan. 10, 2009.

YOTHER, ANTHONY WAYNE, critical care nurse; b. Anniston, Ala., Jan. 30, 1964; s. Johnny Wayne and Carol Sue (Bradshaw) Y. BSN, Jacksonville State U., 1987; MSN, U. Ala., Birmingham, 1992; MS in Health Care Policy and Adminstrn., Mercer U., 1994; postgrad. in chiropractic, Life U., Marietta, Ga., 1998. RN, Ga.; cert. nursing adminstrn. Mem. Laurleen B. Wallace Coll. Nursing Alumni Assn. (v.p. 1988-90, pres. 1990-92), U. Ala.-Birmingham Alumni Assn., Mercer U. Alumni Assn., Jacksonville State U. Alumni Assn., Sigma Theta Tau Internat. Home: Anniston, Ala. Died Feb. 28, 2008.

YOUNG, CHARLES L., SR, state legislator; b. Meridian, Miss., Aug. 27, 1931; s. E. F. and Velma Beal Young; children: Deidra, Charles L. Jr., Arthur, Veldora F. Former mem. Bd. Corrections R & D Coun. & Econ. Devel. Bd.; dist. chmn., 3rd congl. dist. dem. com.; house rep. Miss.; del., dem. nat. conv., 1968, 1972, 1976; state rep. Dist. 82 Miss., from 1980; chmn. U. & Coll. Com.; mem. Fees & Salaries Pub. Officers Com., Transp. Com., Banks & Banking Com., Ways & Means Com.; pres. E. F. Young Jr. Mfg. Co.; v.p. TV-3, Minn. Mem.: VFW, NAACP, Miss. Action for Progress (mem., bd. dir.), Nat. Bus. League, Meridian Bus. League, C. of C., Elks, Mason. Democrat. Methodist. Died Apr. 29, 2009.

YOUNG, ELEANOR LOUISE, retired senior staff nurse; b. Cambridge, Mass., Oct. 10, 1930; d. Allison Homer and Florence May (Sheppard) Jones; m. Joseph Moses, May 6, 1951; children: Catherine, Joseph, Terence, Nora. Student, Mass. Gen. Hosp., Boston, 1949-51; ADS, Massasoit C.C., Brockton, Mass., 1972. Registered nurse, Mass., 1972. RN CCU South Shore Hosp., Weymouth, Mass., 1972-80, sr. staff nurse CCU, 1980-95; retired, 1995. Pacemaker instr., 1985-89, quality mgmt. 1988-94, South Shore Hosp., Weymouth, Mass. Mem. Am. Heart Assn., South Shore RN Assn., Alpha Nu Omega. Avocations: travel, knitting, needlepoint. Home: Hanover, Mass. Died Feb. 24, 2008.

YOUNG, JAMES EARL, retired academic administrator, art educator; b. Chgo., Dec. 20, 1922; s. James Alexander and Ellen (Chedister) Y.; children: Hugh Parker, Katherine Sue. BS, U. Ill., 1948; PhD, State U. N.Y. Coll. Ceramics Alfred U., 1962. Ceramic engr. Republic Steel Co., Chgo., 1948-52; ceramic engr. Armour Research Found., Chgo., 1952-55; research supr. Structural Clay Research Found., Geneva, Ill., 1955-57; research fellow State U. N.Y. Coll. Ceramics at Alfred U., 1957-61, asst. prof., 1961-63, assoc. prof., 1963-67, prof., chmn. dept., 1967-70; dean Coll. Arts and Scis., Rutgers U., Camden, N.J., 1970-73; provost Rutgers U., Newark, 1973-82, prof., 1984-93, prof. emeritus, 1993—2009; exec. dir. Commn. on State Colls. of N.J., 1982-84. Contbr. articles to tech. jours. Served with AUS, 1943-46. Am. Council Edn. fellow acad. adminstrn., 1966-67 Mem. Am. Ceramic Soc. Home: Somerset, NJ. Died June 18, 2009.

YOUNG, KATHLEEN, clinical psychologist; b. Morristown, NJ, July 11, 1961; d. Lawrence Henry and Sue Ann Y. BA, Conn. Coll., 1983; D of Psychology, Ill. Sch. Profl. Psychology, 1990. Lic. psychologist, Ill., Ind. Head counseling svcs. Greentree Shelter, Bethesda, Md., 1984-85; mental health worker Northwestern Meml. Hosp. Emergency Housing Program, Chgo., 1986-88; extern Northwestern Meml. Hosp. Eating Disorders Program, Chgo., 1987-88; psychology intern U. Ariz. Health Scis. Ctr., Tuscon, 1988-89; therapist Madison Ctr., South Bend, Ind., 1989-90, staff psychologist, 1990-92; psychologist Lake-Cook Psychol. Counseling Assocs., Arlington Hts., Ill., from 1992; clin. psychologist pvt. practice, Chgo., from 1992. Affiliate med. staff St. Joseph Hosp., Mishawaka, Ind., 1991-92. Mem. Am. Psychol. Assn., NOW, Internat. Soc. for Study of Multiple Personality and Dissociation, Div. Psychology Women. Home: Chicago, Ill. Died June 25, 2008.

YOUNG, MAUREEN SUSAN, community health nurse; b. Weymouth, Mass., Sept. 17, 1947; BSN, Boston U., 1969; MS in Edn., Lesley Coll., 1976, MSN, 1978. RN, Mass. RN coord. BSN program U. Mass., Boston, staff assoc., lectr., asst. prof. Assumption Coll., Worcester, Mass.; pediatric AIDS clin. specialist Vis. Nurse Assn. of Boston. Margaret Anderson Meml. scholar. Mem. ANA, Mass. Nurse's Assn., Nat. League for Nursing, ADA, Mass. Pub. Health Assn., Nat. Women's Health Network, Sigma Theta Tau. Died Feb. 10, 2008.

YOUNG, PHILIP HOWARD, library director; b. Ithaca, NY, Oct. 7, 1953; s. Charles Robert and Betty Irene (Osborne) Young; m. Nancy Ann Stutsman, Aug. 18, 1979. BA, U. Va., 1975; PhD, U. Pa., 1980; MLS, Ind. U., 1983. Asst. prof. history Appalachian State U., Boone, NC, 1980-82; reference asst. Lilly Libr. Ind. U., Bloomington, 1982-83; adminstr., info. specialist Ind. Corp. Sci. & Tech., Indpls., 1983-85; dir. Krannert Meml. Libr. U. Indpls., from 1985. Mem.: Archeol. Inst. Am., Am. Libr. Assn., Phi Beta Kappa, Beta Phi Mu, Phi Alpha Theta. Democrat. Home: Greenwood, Ind. Died Jan. 7, 2009.

YOUNG, REBECCA MARY CONRAD, state legislator; b. Clairton, Pa., Feb. 28, 1934; d. Walter Emerson and Harriet Averill (Colcord) Conrad; m. Merwin Crawford Young, Aug. 17, 1957; children: Eve, Louise, Estelle, Emily. BA, U. Mich., 1955; MA in Teaching, Harvard U., 1963; JD, U. Wis., 1983. Bar: Wis. 1983. Commr. State Hwy. Commn., Madison, Wis., 1974-76; dep. sec. Wis. Dept. of Adminstrn., Madison, 1976-77; assoc. Wadsack, Julian & Lawton, Madison, 1983-84; elected rep. Wis. State Assembly, Madison, 1985-99. Translator: Katanga Secession, 1966. Supr. Dane County Bd., Madison, 1970-74; mem. Madison Sch. Bd., 1979-85. Recipient Wis. NOW Feminist of Yr. award, 1996, Eunice Zoghlin Edgar Lifetime Achievement award ACLU, 1997, Outstanding Legislator award Wis. Counties Assn., 1998, Voice for Choice award Planned Parenthood Wis., 1998, Luan Gilbert award for outstanding activities in domestic violence intervention and prevention Domestic Violence Intervention Svc., 1998, Clean Sixteen in Appreciation, 1998, Eleanor Roosevelt award, Democratic Party of Wis., 2005, Sister House Pioneer of Change award, 2008, Justice award, 2008, Wis. Assembly Democrats award, 2008, Disability Rights Wis. Lifetime Advocate award, 2008. Mem. LWV. Democrat. Avocations: board games, hiking. Home: Madison, Wis. Died Nov. 18, 2008.

YOUNG, VERNON LEWIS, retired lawyer; b. Seaman, Ohio, Oct. 13, 1919; s. Ezra S. and Anna (Bloom) Y.; m. Eileen Humble, 1941; children: Robert, Loretta, Bettie Jo, Jon W., Denise L. Student, Alfred Holbrook Coll., Manchester, Ohio, 1938—39; JD, Ohio No. U., Ada, 1942. Bar: Ohio 1942. Employee War Dept., 1942; sole practice West Union, Ohio, 1942-50, 78-81; ptnr. Young & Young, West Union, 1959—78, Young & Caldwell, 1978—81, 1995—2003, ret., 2003; ptnr. Young-Caldwell & BUBP, West Union, 1981-95; ret. Spl. counsel Office of Atty. Gen., State of Ohio, West Union, solicitor Cities of Jamestown, Seaman, Winchester, Manchester, Ohio; pros. atty. Adams County, Ohio, 1952-56, acting county judge, 1968-79. Mayor City of Seaman, 1944-46; mem. Adams County Health Bd., West Union, 1968-75; chmn. membership com. Eastern Shore Inst. Lifelong Learning, Fairhope, Ala., 1983-84; mem. Rep. Presdl. Task Force, 1980-94. Mem.: Adams County Bar Assn. (former pres.), Jr. Bar (pres. Ohio No. U. 1941—42), Ohio State Bar Assn., Ohio No. Univ., Lions (pres. 1950—51, dist. gov. 1951—52), Masons (32 degrees), Sigma Delta Kappa (chancellor 1940). Avocations: fishing, hunting, gardening. Home: Seaman, Ohio. Died Dec. 29, 2008.

YOUNG, WILLIAM WADE, JR., health care executive; b. Printess, Miss., June 17, 1937; s. William Wade and Charlotte (Beard) Young; m. Mary Lee Foote Young, Aug. 3, 1964; children: William, Julie. BSBA, Northwestern State U., La., 1962; MS in Health Care Adminstrn., Trinity U., San Antonio, 1970. Adminstrv. resident Baylor U. Med. Ctr., Dallas, 1969—70; adminstrv. officer Madigan Gen. Hosp., Tacoma, 1963—64; exec. officer US Army Hosp., Paris, 1964—67; pers. officer Brooke Army Med. Ctr., Fort Sam Houston, Tex., 1967—68; adminstr. Hoblitzelle Women's & Children's Hosp. & Johnson Med. & Surg. Hosp. Baylor U. Med. Ctr., Dallas, 1970—72; asst. dir. Ctrl. Maine Med. Ctr., Lewiston, 1972—73, assoc. dir., 1973—76, exec. dir., 1976—83, pres., from 1983; mem. exec. com. Med. Care Devel., Inc., from 1983, dir., from 1976, chair med. audit com., 1983, treas., 1983—85; founding mem., bd. dirs., sec.-tres. Tri-County Emergency Med. Svc., Inc.; mem. Gov.'s Coun. State Emergency Med. Svcs.; chair Tri-County Hosp. Regional Conf., from 1980; mem. State Hosp. Licensing Bd., 1979—81; preceptor residency program Trinity U. Program Health Care Adminstrn.; past dir. Blue Cross, Blue Shield Maine; chmn. bd. Patrons-Oxford Mut. Ins. Co., from 1977; corporator Ctrl. Maine Healthcare Corp.; chmn., mem. adv. bd. Key Bank Maine, from 1983. Founding mem., bd. dirs. Maine Hosp. Assn. Rsch. & Ednl. Trust; chmn. bd. trustees Ctrl. Maine Med. Ctr. Sch. Nursing; past bd. dirs. Northern New Eng. Hosp. Trust, Inc.; bd. dirs. Lewiston-Auburn United Way, Lewiston-Auburn Jr. Achievement; mem. Lewistown Downtown Revitalization Com.; bd. dirs. chpt. ARC, 1981—82. Recipient Leonard A. Duce award, Trinity U. Health Care Adminsrn., 1980. Mem.: Lost Valley Junior Racing Ski (founder), Auburn Ski Association (dir.; chmn. 1982—84, pres. 1982), Internat. Health Econs. & Mgmt. Inst., Maine Health Mgmt. Forum (founding mem., chmn. 1974—75), Maine Hosp. Assn. (dir. from 1974, sec. 1976—78, chmn. 1981—82, Disting. Svc. award 1983), Am. Hosp. Assn. (alt. del. 1983—84, del. 1984—87), Am. Coll. Healthcare Execs. Republican. Congregationalist. Home: Auburn, Maine. Died May 26, 2006.

YOUNGE, WYVETTER HOOVER, state legislator; b. St. Louis, Aug. 23, 1930; d. Ernest Jack and Annie (Jordan) H.; m. Richard G. Younge, 1958; children: Ruth F., Torque E., Margrett H. BS, Hampton Inst., 1951; JD, St. Louis U., 1955; LLM, Wash. U., 1972. Asst. circuit atty. City of St. Louis, 1955—57; exec. dir. Neighborhood Ctrs. War on Poverty, 1965-68; mem. Ill. Ho. Reps. from Dist 114, 1975—2008, labor and com., vice chmn. energy, environ. and natural resources com., aging, edn. appropriations, human svc., reappointment committees, chmn. higher edn. com.; East St. Louis adv. and devel. nonprofit housing corp., from 1968. Author: The Implementation of Old Man River, 1972. Recipient Humanity award Project Upgrade, 1969, Citizen of Yr. award Monitor Newspaper, Cert. of Recognition Black Heritage Com. Mem. Alpha Kappa Alpha. Democrat. Episcopalian. Died Dec. 26, 2008.

YOUNGQUIST, GERALD LEE, minister; b. Gowrie, Iowa, Aug. 29, 1930; s. G. Alvin and Ruby (Jacobson) Y.; m. Rozella June Youngquist, Apr. 22, 1953; children: Grant, Andrew, Karl. BA, Gustavus Adolphus Coll., 1958; MDiv, Augustan Theol. Sem., 1962; postgrad., Inst. Advanced Pastoral Study, Detroit, from 1983. Ordained to ministry Evang. Luth. Ch. in Am., 1962. Pastor lst Luth. Ch., Kirkland, Ill., 1962-71, sr. pastor Monmouth, Ill., from 1971. Del. Luth. Ch. in Am. Conv., Chgo., 1978, Toronto, Ont., Can., 1984. Bd. dirs. Augustana Coll., 1972-82. With U.S. Army, 1951-53. Mem. Rotary (pres.). Democrat. Home: Monmouth, Ill. Died Mar. 23, 2008.

YOUREE, WILLIAM FRANK, healthcare executive; b. Nashville, Sept. 4, 1947; s. Frek Doak and Katherine (Bell) Y.; m. Cynthia K. Catlett, Aug. 26, 1972; children: Gregory, Douglas. BS in Acctg. with honors, U. Tenn., 1975, postgrad., 1975, Tulane U., 1976-77. CPA, Tenn. Corp. acct. Hosp. Affiliates Internat., Nashville, 1975-77; asst. contr. Tulane U. Med. Ctr. Hosp. and Clinic, New Orleans, 1977-78; contr. Westbank Med. Ctr., Ltd., New Orleans, 1978-81; v.p. fin. Nat. Med. Enterprises, New Orleans, 1981-82; adminstr. F. Edward Hebert Hosp., New Orleans, 1983-85; exec. v.p. Rehab. Hosp. Svcs. Corp., Camp Hill, Pa., 1985-87; v.p. ops. Nat. Rehab. Ctrs., Inc., Brentwood, Tenn., 1987; exec. v.p. Rebound, Inc., Hendersonville, Tenn., 1987-88; pres., CEO Rehability Corp., Brentwood, from 1988. Mem. Fedn. Am. Hosps. (mem. bd. govs. 1984), Fedn. La. Hosps. (pres. 1985). Died Apr. 10, 2008.

YOW, KAY (SANDRA KAY YOW), women's college basketball coach; b. Gibsonville, NC, Mar. 14, 1942; BS in English, East Carolina Coll., Greenville, NC, 1964; MS in Physical Edn., U. NC, Greensboro, 1970. Head women's basketball coach Allen Jay HS, Gibsonville HS, Elon Coll., NC, 1971—75, NC State U., Raleigh, 1975—2009. Head coach USA Basketball Women's Team World Univ. Games, 1981; asst. coach US Women's Olympic Team, LA, 1984, head coach, Seoul, Republic of Korea, 88. Recipient Laurel Wreath award, State of NC, 2007, Naismith award, Outstanding Contbn. to Women's Basketball, 2007, Jimmy V ESPY award for Perseverance, 2007; co-recipient Bob Bradley Spirit & Courage award, 2007; named to Guilford County Sports Hall of Fame, Elon Coll. Hall of Fame, Women's Sports Hall of Fame, NC Sports Hall of Fame, Fellowship of Christian Athletes Hall of Fame, Women's Basketball Hall of Fame, 2000, Naismith Basketball Hall of Fame, 2002. Achievements include coaching her teams to five ACC (Atlantic Coast Conf.) Championships. Died Jan. 24, 2009.

YUZEITIS, JAMES RICHARD, information specialist; b. Chgo., Nov. 11, 1942; s. Stanley J. and Amy B. (English) Y.; m. Susan C. London, Oct. 7, 1967; children: Timothy, David, Amy. BA in Econs., Loyola U., Chgo., 1965, MS in Personnel Mgmt., 1968. Personnel adminstr. Chgo. Police Dept., 1965-67; personnel asst. McDonald's Corp., Chgo., 1967-69, ops. trainee Washington, 1969-70, personnel mgr. Detroit, 1970-72, licensing mgr. Columbus, Ohio, 1972-73, internat. personnel cons. Oakbrook, Ill., 1973-80, dir. of human resources, 1980-86, dir. human resources devel., 1986-91; pres. Quality Surveys, Inc., Big Timber, Mont., from 1991. Cons. Ronald McDonald Children's Charities, Chgo., 1986-88. Cons. and vol. Ronald McDonald Houses, Chgo., 1987; vol. Crazy Mont. Mus. Soc., Big Timber, 1991-92; bd. dirs. Pioneer Med. Ctr., Big Timber, 1993—. Recipient medal of Merit Cath. Youth Orgn., Chgo., 1960. Mem. Soc. for Human Resource Mgmt., Human Resource Planning Soc., Indsl. Rels. Rsch. Soc. Avocations: ranch mgmt., fishing, music. Home: Washington, Utah. Died July 7, 2008.

ZAAGE, HERMAN, printmaker, educator; b. Jersey City, Apr. 2, 1927; s. Henry and Anna Zaage; m. Sylvia Beal, Feb. 12, 1949; children: Valeda, Peter. Black and white finisher Walker Engraving Corp., N.Y.C., 1955—94; printmaking instr. The New Sch., N.Y.C., 1964—2007, The Art Lab, Staten Island, from 1974. Abraxas Multiple Modern Gods, 1964, Seasons of the Mind Unconscious Victories, 1969, Mezzotint Print, 1988. Print donation Protectors of Pine Oak Woods, Staten Island, 2001, The Art Lab, Staten Island, 2000. With US Army, 1948—50, Tex. Recipient Jo Miller award, Nat. Acad., 1989, Audubon Artists Gold medal, Audubon Artists, 1997, Commission, Print Club Albany, 1999. Mem.: Audubon Artists, Soc. Am. Graphic Artists. Avocations: hiking, classical music, jazz. Home: Staten Island, NY. Died Feb. 29, 2008.

ZACHRY, JUANITA DANIEL, writer; b. Horn, Tex., Apr. 6, 1917; d. Allen M. Daniel and Exa (Pruitt) Green; m. B.A. Zachry, Dec. 10, 1934 (dec. Apr. 1981); children: Barbara Ann, Madlyn Beth, Charles Ralph. Degree, Nat. Bus. Coll., Abilene, Tex., 1934; student, U. Okla., 1967. Dep. clk. Taylor County, Abilene, 1952-56, 60-64; bookkeeper C.B. Ray, Abilene, 1957-58, Williams & Williams, Abilene, 1974-75. Tchr. Abilene Fine Arts Program; leader workshops in field. Author: Potosi, The First One Hundred Years, 1967-73, A History of Rural Taylor County, 1980-96, Abilene, The Key City, 1986, Buffalo Gap Historic Village, 1992, A Living History, 1999; co-author: Brands of the

Southwest, 1988; contbr. articles to mags. and jours.; contbg. editor Nat. Doll. World; columnist Scenes Mag., 1985-86; feature writer Focus Mag., 1985-86. Mem., sec. Taylor County Commn., Abilene. Mem. Abilene Writer's Guild (founder, pres., tchr. arts program), Abilene Folklore, West Tex. Hist. Assn. Baptist. Avocation: gardening. Died July 29, 2008.

ZAGORIN, PEREZ, historian, educator; b. Chgo., May 29, 1920; s. Solomon Novitz and Mildred (Ginsburg) Z.; m. Honoré Desmond Sharrer, May 29, 1947 (dec. April 17, 2009); 1 son, Adam. AB, U. Chgo., 1941; A.M., Harvard U., 1947, PhD, 1952. Various positions OWI, U.S. Govt., U.P. Syndicate, CIO, 1942-46; instr. Amherst Coll., 1947-49; lectr. Vassar Coll., 1951-53; from asst. prof. to prof. history McGill U., 1955-65; prof. U. Rochester, from 1965, Joseph C. Wilson prof. history, 1982-90, Joseph C. Wilson prof. history emeritus, 1990—2009, chmn. dept., 1968-69, acting chmn. dept., 1988-89; vis. prof. Johns Hopkins, 1964-65; Amundsen vis. prof. U. Pitts., 1964; William Andrews Clark Meml. Library prof. UCLA, 1975-76. Thompson lectr. history Vassar Coll., 1987. Author: A History of Political Thought in the English Revolution, 1954, 2d edit., 2000, The Court and the Country: The Beginning of the English Revolution, 1969, Culture and Politics from Puritanism to the Enlightenment, 1980, Rebels and Rulers 1500-1660, 2 vols., 1982, 2d edit., 2003, Ways of Lying: Dissimulation, Persecution, and Conformity in Early Modern Europe, 1990, Milton Aristocrat and Rebel: The Poet and His Politics, 1992, Francis Bacon, 1998 (named one of Best Academic Books, Choice, 1998), The English Revolution: Politics, Events, Ideas, 1998, How the Idea of Religious Toleration Came to the West, 2003 (named one of Best Books, LA Times, 2003), Thycydides: An Introduction for the Common Reader, 2005, Hobbes and the Law of Nature, 2009; co-editor: Philosophy Science and Religion in England 1640-1700, 1991, Guide to Historical Literature, 1994, Hobbes and The Law of Natures, 2009; contbr. numerous articles to hist. jours.; mem. editl. bd. Jour. of the History of Ideas. Sheldon travel fellow Harvard U., 1949-50, Fulbright fellow 1949-50, faculty rsch. fellow Social Sci. Rsch. Coun., 1958-59, 61-62, sr. rsch. fellow Folger Shakespeare Libr., 1964-65, fellow Inst. Advanced Study, Princeton, N.J., 1972-73, sr. fellow Nat. Humanities Ctr., 1978-79, fellow Ctr. Advanced Study in Behavioral Scis., 1983-84, Guggenheim fellow, 1983-84, Edgar F. Shannon Ctr. for Advanced Studies fellow U. Va., 1994-2009 Fellow Royal Hist. Soc., Am. Acad. Arts and Scis.; mem. Am. Hist. Assn. (chmn. Gershoy and Schuyler prize com. 1982-84). Home: Washington, DC. Died Apr. 26, 2009.

ZAJONC, ROBERT BOLESLAW, psychology professor; b. Lodz, Poland, Nov. 23, 1923; came to U.S., 1949, naturalized, 1953; s. Mieczyslaw and Anna (Kwiatkowska) Z.; m. Donna Benson, June 20, 1953 (div. 1981); children: Peter Clifford, Michael Anton, Joseph Robert; m. Hazel Markus, May 25, 1982; 1 child, Krysia Courcelle Rose PhD, U. Mich., 1955; Dr. hon. causa, U. Louvain, 1984, U. Warsaw, 1989. Asst. prof. psychology U. Mich., 1955-60, assoc. prof., 1960-63, prof., 1963-94, Charles Horton Cooley Disting. prof. psychology, 1983-94, rsch. scientist Inst. for Social Rsch., 1960-83, dir., 1989-94; prof. psychology Stanford (Calif.) U., 1994—2008. Directeur d'études Maison des Sciences de L'Homme, Paris, 1985-86; vis. prof. U. Oxford, 1971-72. Author: Social Psychology: An Experimental Approach, 1965; editor: Animal Social Psychology, 1970, The Selected Works of R. B. Zajonc, 2004; assoc. editor: Jour. Personality and Social Psychology, 1960-66. Guggenheim fellow, 1978-79; Fulbright fellow, 1962-63; recipient Disting. Prof. award of social sci., 1983. Fellow AAAS (co-recipient Psychol. prize 1976), APA (Disting. Sci. Contbrn. award 1978), Japan Soc. Promotion of Sci., N.Y. Acad. Scis.; mem. Soc. for Exptl. Social Psychology (Disting. Scientist award 1986), Polish Acad. Scis. (fgn.). Home: Stanford, Calif. Died Dec. 3, 2008.

ZALDASTANI, GUIVY, business consultant; b. Tbilisi, Republic of Georgia, Nov. 1, 1919; arrived in Paris, 1925, came to U.S., 1948, naturalized 1953; s. Soliko and Mariam (Hirsely) Z.; m. Meredeth Fowler, May 1956 (div. Jan. 1982); children: Nicholas, Tamara, Nina; m. Micheline de Bievre, May 12, 1984; 1 child, Brian O'Connell. License en Droit, Sorbonne U., Paris, 1945, Diplome d'Etudes Superieures en Droit, 1946; MBA, Harvard U., 1951. Dept. mgr., buyer Federated Dept. Stores, Boston, 1957-62; founder, pres. Finishing Touch, Boston, 1962-80, Ryan & Elliott Internat. Real Estate, Boston, 1980-83; pres. Zaldastani Cons., Boston, from 1982. Vis. prof. Tbilisi Tech. U. Editor Voice of Free Georgia, 1951-65, Iveria, 1970-80, periodical in Georgian lang. Cons. Ho. of Reps. crimes of Krushchev, 1960; pres. Georgian Youth Assn., Paris, 1942-47; founder, pres. Ga. Coastal Devel. Found., Inc., 1998—; charter mem. Rep. Presdl. Task Force, Washington, 1980; co-chmn. Harvard Bus. Sch. Reunion, Cambridge, 1961, 76, 86, 96, 2001. Served to lt. French Marines, 1940-41. Named Hon. Citizen, Rep. Georgia, 1997. Mem. Am. Acad. (Tbilisi, founder 1999—, pres. 2000—), Georgian Assn. in U.S. (pres. 1966-74, bd. dirs. 1974-95), Harvard Club (Boston), Sommerset Club (Boston), Harvard Faculty Club (Boston), Cercle de l'Union Interalliée (Paris). Republican. Avocations: piano, reading, travel. Home: Berlin, Mass. Died Oct. 12, 2007.

ZAMECNIK, PAUL CHARLES, oncologist, medical researcher; b. Cleve., Nov. 22, 1912; married; 3 children. AB, Dartmouth Coll., 1933; MD, Harvard U., 1936; DSc (hon.), U. Utrecht, 1966, Columbia U., 1971, Harvard U., 1982, Roger Williams Coll., 1983, Dartmouth Coll., 1988, U. Mass., 1994. Resident Huntington Meml. Hosp. Harvard U., Boston, 1936—37; intern U. Hosps., Cleve., 1938—39; Moseley traveling fellow Carlsberg Labs. Harvard U., Copenhagen, 1939—40; Finney-Howell fellow Rockefeller Inst., 1941—42; instr., assoc. prof. medicine Harvard U., 1942—56, Collis P. Huntington prof. oncologic medicine, 1956—79; dir. J.C. Warren Labs., 1956—79; chmn. exec. com. Dept. Medicine Harvard U., 1956—61; emeritus prof. oncological medicine Sch. Medicine, 1979—2009; prin. sci. Worcester Found. Experimental Biology, 1979—97; physician Mass. Gen. Hosp., 1956—79, hon. physician, 1979—2009, sr. scientist, 1998—2009. Vis. fellow dept. chemistry Calif. Tech. U., 1952; vis. Commonwealth scholar in chemistry U. Cambridge, 1962. Recipient Warren Triennial prize, Mass. Gen. Hosp., 1946, 1950, 1999, James Ewing award, 1962, Borden award, 1965, Am. Cancer Soc. Nat. award, 1968, Passano award, 1970, Nat. medal of sci., NSF, 1991, Hudson Hoagland award, 1992, City of Medicine award, Durham, N.C., 1995, Enterprize 2000 award, City of Worcester, Mass., 1996, Lasker-Koshland Spl. Achievement award in Med. Sci., Lasker Found., 1996, Lifetime Achievement award, Inst. Human Virology, 2004, Gene Expression Systems Conf., 2009. Mem.: NAS, Nat. Acad. Medicine, Am. Philosophy Soc., Am. Soc. Biol. Chemists (Merck award 1997), Mass. Med. Soc. (Ann. Orator 1998), Nat. Acad. Scis., Assn. Am. Physicians, Am. Assn. Cancer Rsch. (pres. 1964—65), Am. Soc. Biol. Chemists, Am. Acad. Arts and Scis., Interurban Club. Home: Boston, Mass. Died Oct. 27, 2009.

ZARNOWITZ, VICTOR, economist, educator; b. Lancut, Poland, Nov. 3, 1919; came to U.S., 1952, naturalized, 1957; s. Leopold and Bertha (Blumenfeld) Z.; m. Lena Engelman, Jan. 12, 1946 (dec. 2000); children: Steven L., Arthur H. Student, U. Cracow, Poland, 1937—39; MA in Econs, U. Heidelberg, Germany, 1949, PhD summa cum laude, 1951. Tutor, instr. economics U. Heidelberg, also Grad. Sch. Bus., Mannheim, Germany, 1949-51; analyst Nat. Bur. Econ. Research, 1952-59, mem. sr. research staff, 1963-78, research assoc., 1979—2009; lectr., then vis. prof. Columbia U., 1956-59; mem. faculty Grad. Sch. Bus., U. Chgo., 1959—2009, prof. economics & fin., 1965-90, prof. emeritus, 1990—2009. Dir. study of bus. cycle indicators, cons. Bur. Econ. Analysis, U.S. Dept. Commerce, 1972-93; rsch. assoc. Ctr. for Internat. Bus. Cycle Rsch., Columbia U., co-dir. rsch., 1994-95; dir. rsch. Found. Internat. Bus. and Econ. Rsch., 1995-2000; sr. fellow, econ. counselor The Conf. Bd., 1999-2009. Author: Unfilled Orders, Price Changes and Business Fluctuations, 1962, An Appraisal of Short Term Economic Forecasts, 1967, The Business Cycle Today, 1972, Orders, Production and Investment, 1973, An Analysis of Forecasts of Aggregate Income, Output, and the Price Level, 1979, Business Cycles and Growth, 1981, On Functions, Quality, and Timeliness of Economic Information, 1982, The Accuracy of Individual and Group Forecasts from Business Outlook Surveys, 1984, Recent Work on Business Cycles in Historical Perspective, 1985, Rational Expectations and Macroeconomic Forecasts, 1985, What is a Business Cycle?, 1992, Has Macro-Forecasting Failed?, 1993, Cyclical Indicators and National Accounts, 1998, Has the Business Cycle Been Abolished?, 1998, Theory and History Behind Business Cycles: Are the 1990s the Onset of a Golden Age?, 1999, The Old and the New in the U.S. Economic Expansion, 2000, Fleeing the Nazis, Surviving the Gulag, and Arriving in the Free World, 2008; co-author:,(with C. Boschan) Cyclical Indicators: An Evaluation and New Leading Indexes, 1975, (with G.H. Moore) Sequential Signs of Recession and Recovery, 1982, (with G.H. Moore) Major Changes in Cyclical Behavior, 1986, (with L.A. Lambros) Consensus and Uncertainty in Economic Prediction; Business Cycles: Theory, History, Indicators and Forecasting, 1992,(with Phillip Braun) Twenty Two Years of the NBER- ASA Quarterly Economic Outlook Surveys, 1993, (with Alan. L. Montgomery and George Tiao) Forecasting the U.S. Unemployment Rate, 1998, More Timely and Useful Index of Leading Indicators, 2001, Time Series Decomposition and Measurement of Business Cycles, Trends and Growth Cycles, 2002; co-author, editor: The Business Cycle Today, 1972; contbr. to books. Recipient William F. Butler Meml. award, NY Assn. Bus. Economists, 2001. Fellow Nat. Assn. Bus. Economists, Am. Statis. Assn.; mem. Am. Econ. Assn., Ciret (hon.). Home: New York, NY. Died Feb. 21, 2009.

ZATZKIS, MARK ASHER, cardiologist; b. Newark, Jan. 9, 1954; s. Henry and Natalie (Serlin) Z.; m. Melissa Harris, Aug. 25, 1984; 1 child, Elliot David. AB, Harvard U., 1975; MD, Columbia U., 1979. Dimplomate Am. Bd. Internal Medicine, 1982, Am. Bd. Cardiology, 1985. Fellow in cardiology U. Calif., San Francisco, 1983-85; sr. fellow in angioplasty San Francisco Heart Inst., 1985-86; clin. faculty memb. cardiology UCLA Hosp., from 1986. Cons. in coronary angioplasty, Calif. Fellow Am. Coll. Cardiology; mem. Am. Heart Assn., Alpha Omega Alpha. Avocations: bicycling, music. Died Oct. 24, 2007.

ZBUZEK, VLASTA KMENTOVA, biologist; b. Velka Losenice, Czechoslovakia, Sept. 6, 1933; came to U.S., 1969; d. Karel Kment and Anezka (Novotna) Kmentova; m. Vratislav Zbuzek, Oct. 23, 1965. MS, Charles U., Prague, Czechoslovakia, 1963, PhD cum laude, Dr. Rerum Naturalis, 1969, Candidate of Sci., 1969. Rsch. fellow Population Coun. Rockefeller U., NYC, 1969-71; rsch. scientist NYU, 1971-78; rsch. physiologist VA Med. Ctr., NYC, 1978-79; asst. prof. U. Medicine and Dentistry-N.J. Med. Sch., Newark, 1979-85; assoc. prof. U. N.J. Med Sch., Newark, from 1985. Author: Gonado-Thyroidal Relationship in the Rat, 1969; author, co-author numerous scientific papers in field. Grantee NIH, Bethesda, Md., 1982-85, Smokeless Tobacco Rsch. Coun., N.Y.C., 1987-90. Mem. Endocrine Soc., Gerontol. Soc., N.Y. Acad. Scis., Internat. Soc. Neuroendocrinology. Home: Pompton Lakes, NJ. Died Nov. 22, 2007.

ZEHNER, CAROL RUTH, insurance agent; b. Paterson, NJ, Jan. 30, 1942; d. Andrew Everett and Ruth Elizabeth (Van Eeuwen) Van Antwerp; m. Donald Paul Zehner, Oct. 24, 1964 (div. Apr. 1991); 1 child, Jill Zehner Davis. BA, Drew U., 1963. Customer svc. rep. Donald P. Zehner Agy., Caldwell, N.J., 1983-90; mktg. rep. Schlott Ins., Clifton, N.J., 1990-91; account exec. Weichert Ins., Morris Plains, N.J., from 1991. Mem. Paper Mill Playhouse Guild, Millburn, N.J., 1989—, Adventure on a Shoestring. Mem. Nat. Assn. Ins. Women. Avocations: cooking, theater. Home: Verona, NJ. Died Sept. 13, 2007.

ZELASKO, NANCY FABER, research scientist educator; b. June 4, 1951; d. Elaine Faber; m. Franciszek Jozef Zelasko (dec. 2000). BS, Georgetown U., 1973, MS, 1975, PhD, 1992. Program specialist D.C. Pub. Schs., Washington, 1974-79, project dir., 1979-80; asst. dir. Georgetown U. Bilingual Edn. Ctr., Washington, 1980-89; dep. dir. Nat. Assn. Bilingual Edn., Washington, 1989-99; sr. rsch. scientist Grad. Sch. Edn. and Human Devel., George Washington U., Washington, 1999; dep. dir. Nat. Clearinghouse for English Language Acquisition & Language Instruction Ednl. Programs, 1999—2003, dir., 2003—07. Home: Alexandria, Va. Died Dec. 14, 2008.

ZELDIN, RICHARD PACKER, publisher; b. Worcester, Mass., Aug. 7, 1918; s. M. and Virginia (Gealt) Z.; m. Virginia Graves, Nov. 25, 1950; children— Elizabeth Ann, Richard Shepherd. BS, West Chester U., Pa., 1942; grad. exec. program bus. adminstrn., Columbia U., 1966. Gen. mgr. profl. and reference book div. McGraw-Hill Book Co., Inc., 1948-68; v.p., publishing dir. Litton Ednl. Pub. Co., Inc., 1968-70; pres. R.R. Bowker Co., 1970-76, Xerox Coll. Pub., Xerox Individualized Pub., 1970-76; pub. John Wiley & Sons, Inc., 1976-83; v.p. Moseley Assocs. Inc., NYC, from 1983. Sec.-treas. sci., tech. and med. book pubs. group Assn. Am. Pubs., 1966-70; mem. adv. com. comml. publs. AEC, 1966-70 Author: A Tennis Guide to the USA, 1980, Business Forms on File, 1984, Personal Forms on File, 1984; contbr. Scholarly Publishing, Books, Journals, Publishers and Libraries in the 20th Century, 2002. Served to lt. USNR, 1942-46. Recipient Disting. Alumni award West Chester U., 1974. Mem. Info. Industry Assn. (sec. 1973—), IEEE, Am. Soc. Info. Sci., Soc. for Scholarly Pub. Clubs: Dutch Treat (N.Y.C.), Pubs. Lunch (N.Y.C.). Home: Red Bank, NJ. Deceased.

ZELLER, ANCHARD FREDERIC, retired psychologist; b. Clayton, N.Mex., Jan. 7, 1918; s. Roland Emil Zeller and Mabel Claire Hefner; m. Elizabeth Jean Uehren, July 9, 1948; children: Elizabeth, Juliana, Carolyn. BS, U. N.Mex., 1941, MA, 1942; PhD, Johns Hopkins U., 1948. Instr. U. N.Mex., Albuquerque, 1944—45; tchg. asst. The Johns Hopkins U., Balt., 1946—47; assoc. prof. U. Tulsa, Okla., 1947—52; aviation psychologist Inspector Gen.'s Office USAF, San Bernardino, Calif., 1952—84, ret., 1984. Lectr. U. So. Calif., LA, 1953—85. Contbr. articles to profl. jours. Recipient Meritorious Civilian Svc. award, USAF, 1974, Exceptional Civilian Svc. award, 1984; named to Wall of Honor, Nat. Air and Space Mus., 2003. Fellow: Aerospace Med. Assn. (Raymond F. Longacre award 1965, Harry G. Moseley award 1979); mem.: APA, AIAA (sr.), Nat. Assn. Ret. Fed. Employees (pres. chpt. 1988—90). Home: Redlands, Calif. Died Aug. 20, 2008.

ZEMBAL, THEODORE, producer, director, priest; b. Aberdeen, Wash., Mar. 26, 1930; s. Carl Joseph and Anna (Julia) Z. BA, Gonzaga U., 1965, MA, 1967; MA of Div., Boston Coll., 1968. Priest Soc. Jesus, Portland, Oreg., from 1968; dir. ethics Providence Hosp., Anchorage, 1979-88, Providence Med Ctr, Seattle, from 1988. Dir. Omega Video Images, Anchorage, 1985—. Dir., producer: (videos) Images for Easter, 1984, Images for Reflection, 1985, Suffering to Love, 1985, Images for Meditation: Suffering and Love, 1988; producer (video) Wilderness Lodge, 1987. Bd. dirs. Ch. Council Anchorage, 1981-87, Interfaith Council Anchorage, 1987-88. Served with Signal Corps, 1952-54. Mem. Soc. Health and Human Values, Am. Soc. Law and Medicine, Soc. Medicine and Philosophy, Bioethics Consultation. Home: Seattle, Wash. Died Jan. 13, 2008.

ZERIN, STEVEN DAVID, lawyer; b. NYC, Oct. 1, 1953; s. Stanley Robert and Cecilie Paula (Goldberg) Z.; children: Alexander James, J. Oliver. BS, Syracuse U., 1974; JD, St. Johns U., 1977. Bar: N.Y. 1978, U.S. Dist. Ct. (so. dist.) N.Y. 1985, U.S. Supreme Ct. 1986. Of coun. Sperry, Weinberg, Wels, Waldman & Rubenstein, NYC, 1982-85; ptnr. Wels & Zerin, NYC, from 1985. Trustee, mem. bd. govs. Daytop Village. Mem. ABA (exec. mem. and lectr. family law sect.), N.Y. State Bar Assn. (exec. com. family law sect.), Assn. of Bar of City of N.Y. Democrat. Died Nov. 2008.

ZIEFF, HOWARD B., film director; b. Chgo., Oct. 21, 1927; s. Ted and Shirley (Sudnow) Zieff; m. Ronda Gomez-Quinones. Attended, L.A. City Coll., 1945—46, Art Ctr. Coll. Design, Pasadena, Calif. Photographer US Navy; advertising print photographer. Dir. various TV commercials, (films) Slither, 1973, Hearts of the West, 1975, House

Calls, 1978, Main Event, 1979, Private Benjamin, 1980, Unfaithfully Yours, 1984, Dream Team, 1989, My Girl, 1991, My Girl 2, 1994. Served in USN. Died Feb. 22, 2009.

ZIEGLER, ARNOLD GERARD, lawyer, former marine corps officer; b. Boston, Feb. 16, 1926; s. Arnold Ulerich and Mary Sylvia (Day) Ziegler; m. Mae Aline, Oct. 8, 1949; 1 child, Arnold Dennis. BBA, MBA, George Washington U., 1966; JD, U. Md., 1978. Bar: Md. 1978, Fla. 1978, DC 1978, US Dist. Ct. DC 1978, US Dist. Ct. Md. 1979, US Ct. Appeals (DC cir.) 1979, US Ct. Appeals (4th cir.) 1982. With US Marine Corps, 1943; advanced through grades to col.; sr. policy exec.; sr. adminstr. and comm. ops. exec. Pacific, Washington, Republic of Korea, Vietnam; prin. tech. adviser to comm. dir. UN Mediator Palestine 1st and 2nd Truce, 1948; ret., 1974; assoc. Jeremiah Courtney, Blooston and Mordkofsky Law Offices, Washington, 1978—79; ptnr. Ziegler and Burman, Odenton, Md., 1979—80, Katz and Ziegler, Laurel, Md., 1980—82; pvt. practice Riverdale, Md., 1982—83, Silver Spring, Md., from 1992; of counsel Lipshultz & Hone, Chartered, Silver Spring, 1983—92. Decorated Legion of Merit, Navy Commendation Medal, Meritorious Svc. Medal. Mem.: AAJ, ABA, Montgomery County Bar Assn., Md. Trial Lawyers Assn., Fed. Comm. Bar Assn., Md. Bar Assn., Alpha Sigma Lambda (charter pres. chpt.). Republican. Roman Catholic. Home: Silver Spring, Md. Died June 10, 2007.

ZIEGNER, MARTHA MCHATTON, writer; b. Indpls., Aug. 12, 1919; d. Robert Everson McHatton and Stella Margaret Crull; children: Jean(dec.), Martha. Student, Butler U., Indpls., 1942. Mgr., editor trade jour. Hoosier State Press, Indpls., 1939—42, columnist, 1942—50, editor, 1942—51; freelance writer Indpls. News, from 1959. Author: News From Press Shack, 1989, The Mother Daughter Cookbook, 1999. Vol. Serv icemen's Ctr., Indpls., 1942. Mem.: Delta Delta Delta, Sigma Delta Chi. Democrat. Christian Ch. Avocation: cooking. Died Jan. 15, 2008.

ZIEMANN, GEORGE PATRICK, bishop emeritus; b. Pasadena, Calif., Sept. 13, 1941; Attended, Our Lady of the Angels Sem., San Fernando, Calif., 1959—61; BA, MA, St. John's Sem., Camarillo, Calif.; MS in Edn., Mt. St. Mary's Coll., LA. Ordained priest Archdiocese of L.A., 1967; assoc. pastor St. Matthias Parish, Huntington Park, Calif., 1967—71; tchr. of religion Mater Dei HS, Santa Ana, Calif., 1971—74; vice rector, dean of studies Our Lady Queen of Angels Sem., Mission Hills, Calif., 1974—87; aux. bishop Archdiocese of L.A., 1986—92; ordained bishop, 1987; bishop Diocese of Santa Rosa, Calif., 1992—99, bishop emeritus, 1999—2009. Episcopal advisor Nat. Assn. Cath. Chaplains, Region XI, Nat. Assn. Diocesan Dirs. of Campus Ministry, Nat. Cath. Cemetery Conf., Nat. Conf. Catechetical Leadership. Roman Catholic. Died Oct. 22, 2009.

ZIEMKE, EARL FREDERICK, history professor, researcher; b. Milw., Dec. 16, 1922; s. Otto and Frieda Ziemke; m. Ida Mae Saltenberger; 1 child, Caroline Frieda. BS in Edn., Milw. State Tchrs. Coll., 1948; PhD, Univ. Wis., Madison, 1952. Rschr. Columbia Univ., Alexadria, Va., 1951—55; supr. historian Dept. Army, Washington, 1955—67; rsch. prof. Univ. Ga., Athens, 1967—93. Author: The German-Soviet War 1941-45, 1968, The Red Army 1918-1941, 2004, USArmy in Occupation of Germany, 1975. Cpl. USMC, 1943—46, PTO. Decorated Purple Heart. Home: Athens, Ga. Died Oct. 15, 2007.

ZIMMERMAN, ANNE E., public relations company executive; b. LA, Jan. 11, 1942; d. Arthur John and Fanchon Hunter (Roberts) Eggenberger; m. Kent Topping Zimmerman, Feb. 14, 1975. BA, Northwestern U., Evanston, Ill., 1963; MA, UCLA, 1975. Youth coord. Bullock's, LA,

1963-64; publicity dir. Rose Marie Reid Swimwear, LA, 1964-65; asst. editor L.A. Herald-Examiner, LA, 1965-68; fashion dir. Ohrbach's West Coast Stores, LA, 1968-71; instr. Fashion Inst. Design, LA, 1971-74; sr. v.p. The Pub. Rels. Bd., Chgo., 1975-84; asst. prof. Drake U., Des Moines, 1984-88; dir. comm. Office of Gov., Des Moines, 1988-91; pres. Anne Zimmerman/Pub. Rels., Des Moines, from 1991. Recipient several Golden Trumpet awards Publicity Club of Chgo. Mem. Pub. Rels. Soc. of Am. (Silver Anvil 1975), Women in Communications, The Fashion Group, Inc. Republican. Presbyterian. Home: Des Moines, Iowa. Died Sept. 3, 2007.

ZIMMERMAN, HOWARD IRWIN (HOWARD DANIELS), actor, radiologist; b. Bklyn., May 10, 1930; s. Samuel and Betty (Coffee) Z.; m. Jeanette Zimmerman; children: David, Daniel, Jonathan. BS, Syracuse U., 1952; MD, Downstate Med. Coll., Bklyn., 1959. Diplomate Am. Bd. Radiology. Assoc. radiologist Bronx (N.Y.) Vets. Hosp., 1963-65; radiologist Lynbrook (N.Y.) Med. Ctr., 1965-75, Merrick (N.Y.) Med. Arts, from 1973, Franklin Gen. Hosp., Valley Stream, N.Y., from 1978, Belvis Treatment Ctr., Bronx, from 1994. Actor: (films) The Brother From Another Planet, Falling in Love, Radio Days with Woody Allen, (TV shows) Ryan's Hope, As The World Turns, (TV film) Foxfire, (prin. radio role) Presenting Lil & Co., (prin. guest) Ray Heatherton Breakfast Club 90.3 FM, (local theater) Gilbert and Sullivan operas, Don't Drink the Water, You Can't Take It With You, The Plays the Thing, Social Security, God's Favorite, numerous commls. including Burger King. Mem. Mises Inst. at Auburn U., 1985. Mem. AFTRA, Screen Actors Guild. Avocations: golf, coin collecting/numismatics, astronomy. Home: Somers, NY. Died June 27, 2008.

ZINKHAN, GEORGE MARTIN, III, marketing educator; b. Balt., Feb. 17, 1952; s. George Martin Jr. and Mary Elizabeth (Stoner) Z.; m. Marie Bruce (dec. April 25, 2009); children: George M. IV, Lydia F., Sam S., M. Elizabeth S., L. James G. BA in English Lit., Swarthmore Coll., 1974; MBA in Ops. Rsch., U. Mich., 1979, PhD in Bus. Adminstrn., 1981. Stats. lab. counselor U. Mich., Ann Arbor, 1978-79, teaching fellow, 1979-81; asst. prof. U. Houston, 1981-86, Conn prof. mktg., 1989-93; Coca-Cola prof. mktg. U. Ga., Athens, 1994—2009, head mktg. & distribution dept., 1994—2001. Vis. assoc. prof. U. Pitts., 1987-88; mem. exec. com. Faculty Senate, U. Houston, 1991-92; cons. FTC, Washington, 1992-93, San Francisco, 1994-96. Co-author: Electronic Commerce: The Strategic Perspective, 2000, Consumers, 2002, 2004; editor: Enhancing Knowledge Developments in Marketing, 1995, Advertising Research: The Internet, Consumer Behavior, and Strategy, 2002; editor Jour. Acad. of Mktg. Science, 2003-09; editor Jour. Advt., Richmond, Va., 1991-95, (spl. issue) Jour. Bus. Rsch., 1994, 2d edit. 1999, book rev. editor, mem. rev. bd. Jour. of Mktg., College Station, Tex., 1991-2009; mem. rev. bd. Jour. Current Issues, 1991-2009, Jour. Bus. Rsch., 1994-2009, Jour. MacroMarketing, 1998-2009. Mem. Am. Mktg. Assn. (track chair 1991-96, v.p. for rsch. 1996-98, pres. advt. spl. interest group 1996-2003, acad. coun. 2005), Am. Acad. Advt. (named one of Top 12 Contbrs. to Advt. 1990, one of Top 10 Contbrs. to Svcs. Advt. 1997, one of top 5 Contbrs. to Advt. Lit., Jour. of Advt., 1998, co-chair Nat. Conf., 2001, one of Top Fin. Contbrs., 2008, named one of 4 Contbrs. Re-advertising Lit., 2008), Acad. Mktg. Sci. (track chair promotion mgmt. 1994, track chair electronic commerce 1998), Assn. Consumer Rsch. (session chair 1990, program com. 1996, 2000, Judge Peabody awards 1989). Democrat. United Ch. of Christ. Avocations: soccer, basketball, swimming, tennis, chess. Home: Bogart, Ga. Died May 2009.

ZOLTON, RONALD G., director; b. Saginaw, Mich., July 30, 1937; s. Joseph A. and Leona D. (Frazer) Z.; m. Lois Ann, July 20, 1961; children: Darrell, Mark, Jill. BA, CMU, Mt. Pleasant, Mich., 1961, MA, 1965. Cert. Sch. Adminstr., Mich. Tchr. Saginaw Pub. Schs., Mich., 1960-69; media cons. Saginaw ISD/REMC-9, Mich., 1969-73, dir. media services Mich., from 1973-. Guest lectr/instr. CMU, Mt. Pleasant Mich. 1965-69, SVSU U. Ctr. Mich., 1973-74. Author: journal Media Spectrum 1974--, Media Standards State Document 1975. As SFC, NG 1954-61, U.S.A. Recipient Pres. award Mich. Inst. Media Assn., Lansing 1976, Bd. mem. award NARMC Wash., 1986, Ruby Brown award Mame Lansing, 1987. Mem. Nat. Assn. Regional Media Ctrs., Mich. Inst. Media Assn., Mich. Assn. Inst. Sch. Adminstrn., Am. Assn. Sch. Adminstrn., Kiwanis Club (pres. 1981-82), F.O.E. club. Lutheran. Home: Saginaw, Mich. Died Apr. 4, 2008.

ZORITCH, GEORGE, dancer, educator, choreographer; b. Moscow, June 6, 1917; came to U.S., 1935; s. Serge and Helen (Grunke) Z. Diploma, Lady Deterding's Russian Sch., Paris, 1933. Mem. Ida Rubinstein Ballet Co., Paris, 1933-34, Pavlova's Co., Eng., W.I., Australia, India, Egypt, 1934-35, Col. W. de Basil's Balle Russe de Monte-Carlo, U.S., Europe, 1935-37; soloist Denham Ballet Russe de Monte-Carlo, U.S., Can., S.Am., Europe, 1938-42; actor, dancer in plays, musicals, concert tours, Broadway and across U.S., S.Am. and Europe, 1943-50; actor 17 movies in Hollywood and Rome; premier danseur noble Grand Ballet de Marquis de Cuevas, Europe, Africa, S.Am., 1951-57, Denham Ballet Russe de Monte Carlo, U.S.A., 1957-62; founder George Zoritch Sch. Classical Ballet, West Hollywood, Calif., 1963-73; prof. fine arts, mem. dance faculty com. fine arts U. Ariz., 1973-87. Panelist New Orleans Internat. Ballet Conf. A Ballets Russes Celebration, 2000; hon. guest IX Internat. Competition of Ballet Artists, June 2001, courtesy of Bolshoi Theatre, Moscow; adjudicator ballet competitions including Arabesque Perm, Russia, 1996, 2002; with Pezzon Dance Mag. Author: (memoir) Ballet Mystique, 2000, Russian translation, 2004, Perm, Russia Honorary Adjud cated, 2008; editor records: George Zoritch for Classical Ballet, 1962-65. Hon. guest Bolshoi Ballet, Moscow, 2001, 2005. Recipient Key to Jacksonville (Fla.), 1968, Bolshoi Theatre medallion of merit award IV Internat. Ballet Competition, 2008, Ariz. Dance Treasures award Ariz. Dance Arts Alliance and Ariz. State U. Dept. Dance, 1992, Merit award Acad. Choreographic Sch. A. Vaganova, 1993, Vaslav Nijinsky medallion of merit award Consulate Gen. of Poland, 1994, Diaghilev House Silver Medallion of Merit award 6th Dance Competition of Paris, 1994, U. Ariz. Spl. Tribute, 2001, Life Time Achievement award Western Mich. U., 2002; named Amb. San Antonio World Hemisphere, 1968. Mem. Ariz. Dance Arts Alliance (hon. life), Phoenix Ballet Gild (hon.), Nat. Soc. Arts and Letters (Medallion of Merit award Valley of Sun chpt. 1990). Died Nov. 1, 2009.

ZUNK, DOLORES, secretary; b. Hooker, Okla., Apr. 21, 1930; d. Allen Walker and Hazel Pearl (Rollins) Loughridge; m. Robert Arnold Zunk, Mar. 26, 1950 (dec. 1998); children: Vickie Sue, Kathy Lynn, Steven Wayne, Beckie Gayle. Attended, Salt City Bus. Coll., Hutchinson, Kans., 1948-49. Meat clk., bookkeeper Hooker (Okla.) Locker, 1970-78; bookkeeper, sec. Tumbleweed Lock & Key Trophy & Engraving, Hooker, 1978-98. Vol. Hooker C. of C., from 1998. Mem.: DAR (rec. sec. High Plains chpt. 1989—92, vice regent 1993—95, regent 1995—97, recording sec. 1998—2001, historian 2001—02), Soc. of Descendants of W.Va. Pioneers, First Families of Twin Territories, First Families of Brown County, Ohio. Democrat. Mem. Christian Ch. (Disciples Of Christ). Avocations: oil painting and pastels, ceramics, genealogy. Home: Hooker, Okla. Died Aug. 14, 2008.